USA

Jeff Campbell

Alexis Averbuck, Sandra Bao, Andy Bender, Glenda Bendure,
Tim Bewer, Alison Bing, Becca Blond, Dominique Channell, Jim DuFresne,
Lisa Dunford, Ned Friary, Beth Greenfield, Michael Grosberg, Adam Karlin,
Beth Kohn, Mariella Krause, Nick Marino, Emily Matchar, Becky Ohlsen,
Brendan Sainsbury, Andrea Schulte-Peevers, Karla Zimmerman

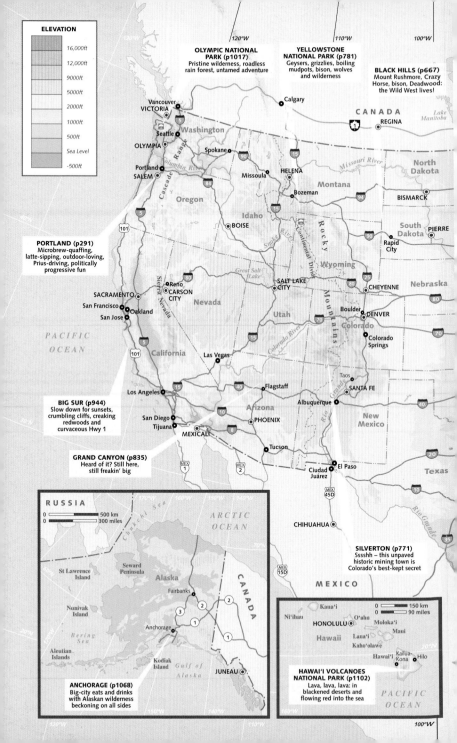

ELEVATION

16,000ft
12,000ft
9000ft
5000ft
2000ft
1000ft
500ft
Sea Level
-500ft

OLYMPIC NATIONAL PARK (p1017)
Pristine wilderness, roadless rain forest, untamed adventure

YELLOWSTONE NATIONAL PARK (p781)
Geysers, grizzlies, boiling mudpots, bison, wolves and wilderness

BLACK HILLS (p667)
Mount Rushmore, Crazy Horse, bison, Deadwood: the Wild West lives!

PORTLAND (p291)
Microbrew-quaffing, latte-sipping, outdoor-loving, Prius-driving, politically progressive fun

BIG SUR (p944)
Slow down for sunsets, crumbling cliffs, creaking redwoods and curvaceous Hwy 1

GRAND CANYON (p835)
Heard of it? Still here, still freakin' big

SILVERTON (p771)
Sssshh – this unpaved historic mining town is Colorado's best-kept secret

ANCHORAGE (p1068)
Big-city eats and drinks with Alaskan wilderness beckoning on all sides

HAWAI'I VOLCANOES NATIONAL PARK (p1102)
Lava, lava, lava: in blackened deserts and flowing red into the sea

CANADA

VICTORIA
Vancouver
Seattle
Washington
OLYMPIA
Spokane
Olympia
Portland
SALEM
Oregon
Missoula
HELENA
Montana
Bozeman
Calgary
REGINA
Lake Manitoba
North Dakota
BISMARCK
Missouri River

BOISE
Idaho
Snake River
Wyoming
South Dakota
PIERRE
Rapid City
CHEYENNE
Nebraska

SACRAMENTO
Reno
CARSON CITY
Nevada
Great Salt Lake
SALT LAKE CITY
Utah
Boulder
DENVER
Colorado
Colorado Springs

San Francisco
Oakland
San Jose
PACIFIC OCEAN

California
Las Vegas
Flagstaff
Taos
SANTA FE
Albuquerque
New Mexico

Los Angeles
Arizona
PHOENIX
San Diego
Tijuana
MEXICALI
Tucson
Ciudad Juárez
El Paso
Texas

MEX 1
MEX 2
MEX 45D
CHIHUAHUA
MEXICO

RUSSIA
Chukchi Sea
ARCTIC OCEAN
0   500 km
0   300 miles

St Lawrence Island
Seward Peninsula
Alaska
Fairbanks
CANADA
Nunivak Island
Bering Sea
Anchorage
Aleutian Islands
Kodiak Island
Gulf of Alaska
JUNEAU

Kaua'i
Ni'ihau
O'ahu
HONOLULU
Moloka'i
Lana'i
Maui
Kaho'olawe
Hawai'i
Kailua-Kona
Hilo
Hawaii
0   150 km
0   90 miles
PACIFIC OCEAN

120°W
110°W
100°W

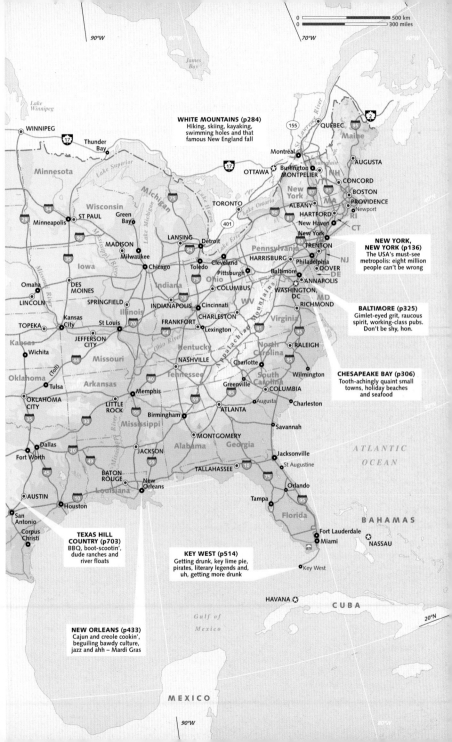

WHITE MOUNTAINS (p284)
Hiking, skiing, kayaking, swimming holes and that famous New England fall

NEW YORK, NEW YORK (p136)
The USA's must-see metropolis: eight million people can't be wrong

BALTIMORE (p325)
Gimlet-eyed grit, raucous spirit, working-class pubs. Don't be shy, hon.

CHESAPEAKE BAY (p306)
Tooth-achingly quaint small towns, holiday beaches and seafood

TEXAS HILL COUNTRY (p703)
BBQ, boot-scootin', dude ranches and river floats

KEY WEST (p514)
Getting drunk, key lime pie, pirates, literary legends and, uh, getting more drunk

NEW ORLEANS (p433)
Cajun and creole cookin', beguiling bawdy culture, jazz and ahh – Mardi Gras

0   500 km
0   300 miles

90°W   70°W

James Bay

Lake Winnipeg

WINNIPEG

Thunder Bay

Minnesota

Lake Superior

Wisconsin

ST PAUL   Green Bay

Minneapolis   MADISON   Milwaukee

Iowa   Chicago

Omaha   DES MOINES

LINCOLN   SPRINGFIELD   Illinois   INDIANAPOLIS

Kansas City   St Louis

TOPEKA   JEFFERSON CITY

Kansas   Missouri

Wichita

Oklahoma

Tulsa

OKLAHOMA CITY

Dallas   LITTLE ROCK

Fort Worth   Arkansas

Birmingham

AUSTIN   Mississippi   JACKSON   Alabama   MONTGOMERY

San Antonio   BATON ROUGE

Corpus Christi   Houston   New Orleans   Louisiana

Michigan   Lake Huron

LANSING   Detroit   Lake Ontario

Toledo   Cleveland   TORONTO   Lake Erie

Ohio   Pittsburgh   Pennsylvania

COLUMBUS   HARRISBURG   Philadelphia

Cincinnati   WV   Baltimore

Indiana   CHARLESTON   WASHINGTON, DC

FRANKFORT   Lexington   Virginia   RICHMOND

Kentucky   Appalachian Mountains

NASHVILLE   Charlotte   RALEIGH

Tennessee   Greenville   North Carolina

Memphis   South Carolina   Wilmington

ATLANTA   COLUMBIA   Charleston

Augusta   Savannah

Georgia

TALLAHASSEE   Jacksonville   St Augustine

Orlando   Florida

Tampa

Fort Lauderdale

Miami

Key West

HAVANA   CUBA

Gulf of Mexico

MEXICO

ATLANTIC OCEAN

BAHAMAS

NASSAU

20°N

QUEBEC   Maine

AUGUSTA

Montréal   CONCORD   BOSTON

Burlington   MONTPELIER   PROVIDENCE

OTTAWA   New York   Newport

ALBANY   HARTFORD

TORONTO   New Haven

New York   CT

TRENTON   NJ

DOVER   DE

ANNAPOLIS   MD

St Lawrence River

Lake Champlain

On the Road

ALEXIS AVERBUCK Being the dedicated researcher that I am, I dragged my weary self to the New Orleans Jazz & Heritage Festival (p440). Oh it was so hard. All those soft shell crabs. All that white chocolate bread pudding. The funky grooves of Jon Cleary and the Absolute Monster Gentlemen just swept me away.

SANDRA BAO Smith Rock is one of my favorite places in Oregon – for its glorious formations, scenic hiking and amazing rock climbing. I was here on my 40th birthday, leading my first outdoor 5.10B – scary but fun. This time I came to research and only had time for this photo…and some memories.

JEFF CAMPBELL
Coordinating Author
Hawai'i Volcanoes National Park (p1102) has the only trail signs I've seen warning of 'hot lava!' Truth is, stumbling over miles of blackened lava till I reached the molten rock entering the sea gave me 'chicken-skin.' Even long past dark, it was hard to leave.

TIM BEWER They can't match the majesty of mountains, but the wide open spaces of the plains (p637) provide their own sort of inspiration, especially when you get beyond the corn and wheat fields. The prairie has an undeniable beauty.

BECCA BLOND Duke (the dog) and I are watching Aaron fly-fishing on the river in Silverton (p771), Colorado here. It's gorgeous out, and I'm thinking how happy I am to be on the road with my future husband and my dog (who is now on his third Lonely Planet assignment, although his research mostly involves smells).

DOMINIQUE CHANNELL Drinking on the job – hmm, can I write this off? This out-of-the-way, small-production winery, where everything's done by hand in ancient-looking machines, was worth the long haul up the narrow bumpy road to the rough-redwood outdoor tasting 'room' – the fun-loving staff are still my friends.

BETH GREENFIELD My first day returning to my homeland – the Jersey Shore (p193) – was a chilly, wildly windy spring day. The huge sky was gray, and the sand was damp and sticking to my hair, and the cold ocean was frothy and tossing about from a crazy 'Nor'easter' storm that had hit the night before. These types of days on the NJ beaches are actually my favorite: unexpected and thrilling, and very alive.

LISA DUNFORD It was 95°F in April as I trudged through Terlingua's west Texas ghost town, where artists and free-thinkers inhabit abandoned miners' shacks. Several have sustainable gardens despite harsh conditions and no running water. I bought the general store's books on water collection, humanure; I thought, if they can make it work here…

ADAM KARLIN This is me, in front of the Lincoln Memorial, on the National Mall (p311), on July 4. The Mall was filled with every color and creed of American, and I was damn proud to be among them, celebrating the country, occasionally flawed but always home, that brings us all together.

MARIELLA KRAUSE At the Fountain of Youth (p523) in St Augustine, a nice couple offered to take my picture in front of this statue. An old man passing by said, 'Ponce de Leon never had it so good!' I told him that the fountain really worked and that I was 87 years old.

BETH KOHN The road from Lees Ferry to Monument Valley (p868) was so blindingly gorgeous, it was hard to imagine it could get any better. Rolling in just before dusk, the park was quiet and practically empty. The rock formations glowed a brilliant orange and the sunset seemed to last for hours.

NICK MARINO Breakfast at the Blue and White, a diner along Hwy 61 in the Mississippi Delta (p427). Look closely and you'll notice the essential travel accessories – car keys, camera bag, cell phone and sunglasses – resting on the counter next to an order of biscuits and gravy.

EMILY MATCHAR Standing on Pedro's foot at South of the Border (p398). When traveling down I-95, I can never avoid stopping at the kitsch carnival that is South of the Border and buying some neon taffy or giggling at the 'artifacts' in the Mexican souvenir shop.

NED FRIARY & GLENDA BENDURE Nantucket's just a two-hour ferry ride from bustling Hyannis Harbor (p248), and even though we've been there before, waiting for the boat to depart feels like an adventure. The harbor's abuzz with travelers hopping onto sightseeing boats, coming off the ferries and munching on fish and chips.

BRENDAN SAINSBURY Rain! Where else could I be? Standing on Ruby Beach on the windswept Washington coast, I was caught in one of the region's innumerable spring downpours. Poised on my arm, my son, Kieran, keeps an eye out for swooping eagles and foraging raccoons.

ANDREA SCHULTE-PEEVERS Yep, that's me – getting goosed by a bull elephant, notebook in hand, no less! I've met 'bulls' before, of course, in Spain's arenas, Germany's beer halls and LA's clubs. Few of them were as mannered as my friend here who only wanted to play. His name? Oh you know how it is, the day after…

KARLA ZIMMERMAN Ahh, Wrigley Field (p558) in Chicago. If the sun is shining and the breeze is blowing, there's nowhere in the country that beats an afternoon spent here. I'm particularly happy at this game since not only did the Cubs not get clobbered – they won.

See full author bios p1156

USA Highlights

When it comes to compiling a definitive list of a country's 'best' experiences, Americans are an opinionated bunch, and Lonely Planet staff and travelers are no exception. Here, we offer a random, personal, biased, nondefinitive, argument-starting compilation of what they consider the very best, most essential things to see and do in the good ole' US of A.

Have we missed your fave? Visit lonelyplanet.com/bluelist and recommend your own highlights.

TETRA IMAGES/ALAMY

1 NEW YORK CITY...'NUFF SAID

It's all right here. The world's best art, music, theater, food, festivals, shopping, clubbing, people-watching, urban park, urban legends and urban experiences. Of course there are the must-sees, such as the Statue of Liberty, Ellis Island, the Met, Central Park, Times Square, Grand Central, West Village cafés, East Village bars, SoHo shops, Brooklyn's everything... But amidst the exhilarating whirlwind experience of a day in NYC, the ultimate moment is a subtle one: when you come up from the subway and feel the city's frenetic energy course through your body – one of eight million bodies. No wonder they call it 'the city,' p136.

Emily K Wolman, Lonely Planet staff, Oakland

YOSEMITE NATIONAL PARK

Take the guided trolley tour through the valley floor, see breathtaking waterfalls, bears, huge cliff faces, and some totally mad rock climbers. More spectacular to look at than the Grand Canyon! Spend a few days camping beneath the towering pine trees, p989.

Mary Richmond, Bluelist contributor, Australia

THE NATIONAL MALL

The monuments and museums that pack 'America's front yard' – the Capitol, the Washington Monument, the Lincoln Memorial etc – are so heavily portrayed in popular media they risk becoming clichés of themselves. Well, guess what: the hype is justified. When you wander the buildings that house our nation's proudest achievements, such as the Constitution, the separated branches of government and the learning hubs of the Smithsonian, through the pathos of memorials to thousands of war dead, you really do come closer to both the ambiguity and appeal of the American experience, p311.

Adam Karlin, Lonely Planet author, Washington, DC

SAN FRANCISCO'S GOLDEN GATE PARK

This 48-block streak of wild idealism runs right through the heart of San Francisco. Everything the city holds dear is here: flower power, world-class art, baseball, pagan altars, free concerts, a bonsai forest, buffalo… if you could get a nice espresso and a decent burrito here, the locals would never leave, p961.

Alison Bing, Lonely Planet author, California

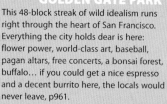

CANYON COUNTRY & MOAB, UTAH

Red-rock canyons, arches, the Colorado River, hiking, biking and an interesting town. The red desert literally beckons you to come out, play and get lost. Truly, as Edward Abbey (p865) put it, the most beautiful place in the world, p864.

Syed Faisal, traveler, Colorado

GARETH McCORMACK

5

YELLOWSTONE NATIONAL PARK

Cruise slowly through America's oldest national park, keeping an eye out for grizzlies and other mega-fauna, then stop at the historic lodge for a sundowner on the porch while Old Faithful puts on its almost hourly show, p781.

Becca Blond, Lonely Planet author, Colorado

BILL BACHMANN

6

HAWAIIAN ALOHA

Flying to Hawaii (p1085) feels more like you're leaving America than arriving. And exploring this paradise of white-sand beaches, coral reefs, rain forests and volcanoes (one of which spews hot lava) doesn't change that impression. Nor, for that matter, do the pidgin-speaking locals. Native Hawaiians boast a culture and welcoming hospitality you can't find anywhere else, period.

Jeff Campbell, Lonely Planet author, New Jersey

7

ADINA TOVY AMSE

MARDI GRAS IN NEW ORLEANS

How often do you get to mosey down a side-street and see the Pope, with a beer, greeting the devil? (p440)

Alexis Averbuck, Lonely Planet author, Louisiana

ALEXIS AVERBUCK

8

WILLIAM HARRIGA

9

SNORKELING THE KEYS

Clear, warm, blue water. White sands. A living barrier reef teeming with colorful fish. Wait a minute, we're not talking about the USA, are we? As a matter of fact, the world's third-largest coral barrier reef (after Australia and Belize) stretches over 200 miles just off the Florida Coast. Best for snorkelers? John Pennekamp Coral Reef State Park, where you can also watch the fish swim circles around an underwater statue of Christ, p510.

Mariella Krause, Lonely Planet author, California

NEIL SETCHFIELD

10 SOCO AND LIVE MUSIC IN AUSTIN

A perfect 24 hours in Austin looks something like this: awake in the Austin Motel, window-shop your way along South Congress to Guero's Taco Bar, settle onto the sunny porch, munch on tasty tortilla chips and salsa, swill Mexican beer, and watch the hipster cowgirls cower under the awning as the sky opens and dumps that hard, short but sweet summer rain. Sun's back! Two-step into cavernous Allen's Boots, grab a semi-swanky dinner at Vespaio, then scoot your new boots over to the Broken Spoke, the ultimate, authentic Texas dance hall, p695.

Emily K Wolman, Lonely Planet staff, Oakland

JOHN ELK III

11 CALIFORNIA'S COASTAL REDWOODS

Walk among the redwoods at Stout Grove, in northern California's Jedediah Smith Redwoods State Park, along the Smith River (just off US 199, northeast of Crescent City). I find this grove the most impressive of all those in Redwood National Park – certainly far better than that park's Ladybird Johnson Grove, where the tops have broken off most of the trees due to its hilltop location. For Stout Grove, picture a sheltered grove with the tops of the trees intact and a beautiful big river flowing by! (p981)

AnonnyMouse, traveler

OLYMPIC NATIONAL PARK

Where else can you go from snow-capped mountains to wide-open alpine meadows to dripping, mossy rain forest to rugged ocean beach in one day – and make it back to a fabulous foodie city (like Seattle) for dinner? Who cares? That's what Olympic National Park is for, p1017.

Emily K Wolman, Lonely Planet staff, Oakland

12

ANN CEC

ROAD-TRIPPING ALONG ROUTE 66

Kicks aside, it's the pickup you get from the Mother Road that makes the detour to Route 66 so compelling. You'll glimpse the parallel presence of the pre-war Chicago–LA highway while zooming down interstates through the glorious Southwest, a hiccup of buildings and ghostly towns across the sands. Detour at Amarillo, TX to tag sprouting tailfins at Cadillac Ranch; slop down green chili enchiladas in Gallup, NM; bunk in a (concrete) tepee in Holbrook, AZ before fast-tracking to Santa Monica, CA, where America's most famous highways ends where the sun meets the sea, p684.

Jay Cooke, Lonely Planet staff, Oakland

13

WITOLD SKRYPCZA

ANN CECIL

14 **SEDONA, ARIZONA**

It's a hot summer day in Arizona – need a place to cool off? Then head to Sedona; with its red rocks and cooler temperatures, Sedona is the perfect place to spend the day hiking, mountain biking or relaxing in one of the creeks outside of town, p833.

Laura Lorenz, Bluelist contributor, Arizona

AUTUMN IN CRESTED BUTTE, COLORADO

Aspens in shades of gold, orange and red, carpeting the mountainsides, set against a deep blue sky. What could be better? And a great little town to boot, p767.

Syed Faisal, traveler, Colorado

16

WITOLD SKRYPCZ

RICHARD CUMMINS

15

NASHVILLE, TENNESSEE

Maybe you're an aspiring country singer, arriving from North Dakota after days of hitchhiking, with nothing but your battered guitar on your back. Gaze up at the neon lights of Lower Broadway, take a deep breath of smoky, beer-perfumed air, feel the boot-stompin' rumble from deep inside the crowded honky-tonks, and say to yourself, 'I've made it.' Okay, maybe you're not an aspiring country singer – but you've still made it to Nashville! (p468)

Emily Matchar, Lonely Planet author, North Carolina

DAVID LYONS/ALA

17

HIT THE (MIAMI) BEACH

If you think all the beautiful people are luxuriating beside their hotel's infinity pool or secluding themselves at some private beach club, you'd be wrong. Pick your spot anywhere along this stunning stretch of sand and take in the Florida sun with beach-goers from all over the world, p494.

Julie O'Hara, Bluelist contributor, Florida

FAMILY DAY OUT AT OREGON'S CRATER LAKE

Crater Lake is a must-see. Created by a volcanic eruption, America's deepest lake is utterly beautiful. Much fun can be found in pretending to younger siblings you are going to push them over the edge, p1045.

Sarah Evans, Bluelist contributor, England

18

ROBERTO SONCIN GEROMETTA

GATES OF THE ARCTIC NATIONAL PARK, ALASKA

One of the last places in the United States that is largely untouched by civilization. Crossed by meandering rivers, thick with Arctic wildlife, ablaze with wildflowers in early summer. Bring lots of mosquito repellant, p1084.

Micah Reyner, Bluelist contributor, Minnesota

19

BRETT BAUNTON/ALAMY

GEORGIA'S GOLDEN ISLES

Wake up early, rent a bicycle and cruise all over trails on Jekyll Island. Hop off your bike to explore the historic district or sunbathe on the beach, just steps from the road. Head north to Savannah, south to isolated Cumberland Island, p419.

Jayme Amanda Rochester, Bluelist contributor, Alabama

20

LEE FOSTER

CHARLES BOWMAN/ALAM

21

MONUMENT VALLEY, ARIZONA/UTAH

Made famous by Hollywood movies, US 163 between Kayenta, Arizona, and Mexican Hat, Utah, splices right through Monument Valley. Detour to the Navajo Tribal Park, with its visitor center and scenic road, offering better views of the sandstone buttes. Best at sunrise or sunset, p843 and p868.

Jennifer Pringle, Bluelist contributor, Australia

JOHN ELK III

22 ## SEATTLE'S PARKS AND MARKETS

From Gas Works Park, get an awesome view of the Seattle skyline, fly a kite and picnic beside the picturesquely rusted-out skeletons of industry. And Pike Place Market – sure it's obvious, but it's still great – especially early in the morning, when real Seattleites do their shopping at the labyrinthine old market's fish and produce stands, p1003.

Becky Ohlsen, Lonely Planet author, Oregon

Contents

Regional Map Contents

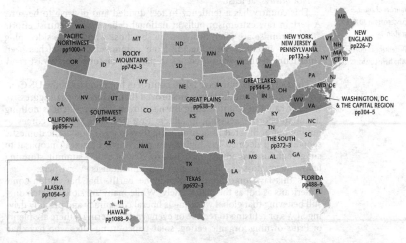

Destination USA

Paul Simon had such yearning in his voice when he sang, 'I've gone to look for America,' and anyone even vaguely familiar with this nostalgia-loving, future-obsessed, multiple-personality patchwork of a country can understand why.

This land is hard to pin down. Filled with so many different worlds and subcultures and belief systems, it's no wonder so many Americans experience an identity crisis at some point in their lives. Heading off into the sunset to drive these open roads, diving headlong into a thrumming big city or hiking into the gorgeous countryside for weeks at a time are the classic ways of figuring out what this American life is all about. That searching is an old, romantic notion, chronicled on the page by writers from Mark Twain to Jack Kerouac, and lived out, daily, among locals and visitors alike.

And this is certainly a wonderful place for a journey.

If you're looking for America, you might want to start somewhere in the middle – in the heartland's undulating fields of grain, among the soaring Rocky Mountains or under the endless sky of the Southwest desert, its vast expanse changing color with each subtle shift of the sun. Or you could go south, into the velvet heat of the Carolinas or Mississippi, toward the wondrous wetlands of the Florida Everglades or the dusty dream-catcher towns of New Mexico. And then there are the salty coasts. New Jersey, Maine or Oregon – lands of lighthouses and dune grass. And don't forget the cities. Brash New York, surreal Las Vegas, earthy San Francisco, indie-rock Austin, strong-willed New Orleans – each like a microcountry of its own.

But what might you find there, beyond the pulsing nightlife and awesome landscapes? That is a whole other story indeed – one with chapters on race, religion, class, sexuality and, of course, politics. It is the story of the USA experience, and it's never simple. Don't be frightened though; while CNN segments may paint Americans as a constantly bickering family of folks who love to hate each other, it's certainly not quite that bad.

Not *always*, at least.

This country has a tendency to feel divided and divisive to be sure. A certain raw extremism pulls at national debates, and centrist efforts at compromise are often drowned out by those who choose sides, plug their ears and start shouting. And our commander in chief has been chief flame fanner when it comes to partisan discord – on a vast array of topics.

The Democrats may have taken control of both houses of the US Congress as of 2007, but the legislators proved themselves less than aggressive when it came to counteracting Bush's moves. The president is nothing if not stubborn – refusing to adhere to a timetable when it comes to pulling out of ill-fated Iraq, promising to veto any Democratic domestic spending bill deemed too high, even rejecting a European proposal to cut greenhouse gas emissions in half by 2050 at a 2007 summit, stunning fellow negotiators and infuriating environmentalists everywhere.

It's this last topic, that of saving the Earth, that has gotten some Americans as hot as the planet lately. While many are slow to catch on – still believing that global warming is liberal conspiracy and proudly driving SUVs or refusing to recycle or even (*gasp!*) littering – there are plenty of Prius-owning, organic-eating, solar-panel–using folks who have had enough of the country's wasteful ways. That may be, of course, because it's trendy to be 'green' right now – witness the major boom in green building, worship of mega organic chain store Whole Foods and farmers markets, and locally-grown items on restaurant menus, at least in cities and towns deemed 'progressive.'

But whatever the reason behind the greening of America, at least something is beginning to shift. Many people credit former Vice President Al Gore with setting off the growing interest; his film *An Inconvenient Truth* stunned audiences and even snagged a couple of Academy Awards, and now everyone from Madonna (who headlined at the 2007 multi-city Live Earth benefit concert) to Leonardo DiCaprio (who has his very own 'Eco-Site,' complete with environmental mini-movies) are getting in on the action. And that can only be a hopeful thing in a country where so many folks are obsessed with monitoring – and trying to emulate – celebrities and their every little move.

The most prominent celebs lately have been the 2008 candidates for US president. The fuss started *way* in advance, with New York Senator Hillary Rodham Clinton announcing her run back in January 2007, followed by the long-anticipated declaration from Illinois Senator Barack Obama and the addition of former New York City Mayor Rudy Giuliani – an announcement that had New Yorkers thrilling over the possible public boxing match between two of their own. While much of the most obsessive interest lay in the battle between Clinton and Obama (the question of 'who will get elected first: a white woman or a black man?' has long intrigued Americans), curious eyes were also on Giuliani because of the Republican's early stance against outlawing abortion – a thorny, antiquated topic in this country that just won't go away.

The crux of that ongoing argument – when does life begin? – is generated by the same aspect that shapes many other conflicts in this country: religion. Generally, that means the belief system of the religious right, fueling its ever-growing hybrid of faith-based politics. It's displayed in a flagrant disregard for the 'separation of church and state' mandate (in the Constitution) when leaders invoke 'God,' 'the Bible' and other church-related topics often right on House or Senate floor.

Another issue that, like abortion, gets caught in this web is that of gay rights, specifically same-sex marriage. The notion has been played out in various states, and while a handful now permit civil unions for gay couples, many specifically ban it – just like the country does as a whole with its Defense of Marriage Act. Signed into law by President Bill Clinton back in 1996, it ensures that no gay marriage (legal only in the state of Massachusetts) will ever be honored on a federal level.

Of course the major source of consternation in recent years has been the war in Iraq, which began in spring 2003 as a centerpiece of President Bush's war on terrorism in the wake of September 11. Citing US intelligence that Iraq had assisted those terrorists and was in possession of 'weapons of mass destruction,' Bush launched a preemptive attack and took over the country. Neither of his charges turned out to be true, but some Americans still believe that doesn't matter, and relish the fact that a Middle East dictator has been toppled and replaced with a nascent, democratically elected Iraqi government. But criticism of how the Bush administration is conducting the war has risen as quickly as the number of US casualties.

At the time of writing, polls showed about 56% of Americans considered the war to be a mistake – and only 33%, not coincidentally, approved of Bush's job in office. Also at that time, the USA had spent $442 billion on the war and had around 160,000 troops stationed in Iraq, and the number of US deaths was over 3600. Iraqi civilian deaths were estimated at over 67,000, but most likely are much higher. As fighting continued, the Bush administration was trying to create a viable military exit strategy while avoiding putting a timetable on the process. Democrats and even some Republicans had begun to seriously challenge that stance in mid-2007, but it remained to be seen who would win in the end. But with just over a year left in office to clean up the mess, it certainly wouldn't be our Commander in Chief.

Bush really hasn't done much when it comes to breaking down the preconceived notions of Americans as greedy, myopic, pompous cretins. The president had never even been to Europe before taking office, his disregard for immigrants has been shocking and the lengths he's been willing to go for oil seem boundless. Still, it makes an odd sort of sense, and here's why: the United States of America is essentially a series of miraculous dichotomies, each helping its seeming opposite to thrive. It's a place where people embrace the technology of heart transplants with the same enthusiasm as yoga, a land where the nation's richest folks live among some of the poorest. Americans are diehard traditionalists – flocking to old-fashioned state fairs and barbecues and cotillions, and feeling in love with all forms of nostalgia – and yet they always keep an eye on the future and the cutting edge, glomming onto concepts like space travel and virtual reality and IVF babies with adventurous spirit. The people of this country can come across as America-centric, caring about nothing but their cars and clothes and images. But spend some time here as a foreigner who easily piques the interest of locals and you'll quickly see how curious, soulful and open-minded they can be.

The sum of this country's parts is indeed much greater than any politics or policies. And that's an important point to keep in mind when grappling with yet another political flashpoint in this country: immigration, especially the undocumented sort, which has been fueling what some see as a thinly veiled excuse for xenophobic, racist discussions. The Bush administration initially pledged to increase US-Mexican border security, but hasn't funded it, and has turned a blind eye to businesses that hire illegal immigrants. In mid-2007, the controversial Immigration Reform Bill – which aimed, among other goals, to allow undocumented residents to apply for citizenship – died in the Senate. It was a disappointing failure not only for Bush and for legislators, but for the millions of undocumented immigrants living in the USA, separated from families back home and working two, sometimes three, jobs to support them. Now a plan to build a reinforced fence all along the border has growing support among legislators, making it a shockingly real possibility.

It's all pretty ironic, considering this country's unwavering image as the great melting pot of the world. And while it would be too simple to dismiss the whole mess as just another dichotomy, it would not be so far from the truth. Because this is a country founded on the concept of immigration – of foreigners, with differences, coming together and living as a single nation. And despite all the bickering and hypocrisy and complex human emotions that drive both the good and the bad here, this is still a place that is incredibly diverse and desirable and passionate and gorgeous and, in endless cases, welcoming, in spite of itself. It's part of the great yin-yang that is the US of A. Come in, explore, see all sides for yourself. When it comes to presenting new perspectives, this country will not disappoint.

Getting Started

Got your map? Ready to plot your itinerary? Just remember: the USA covers a continent and more. Texas alone is twice the size of Germany, so you may need to adjust your sense of scale. It's easy to get overambitious, blow your budget and spend more time getting to sights than actually seeing them. That old chestnut about packing – lay out everything you need and put half back – applies here too: plan what you want to see in the time you have, then take out half the stops.

You'll also need to consider transportation options carefully, balancing cost, time and flexibility – and your carbon footprint. The 'best' mix varies by region and route. For more ecotravel advice, see 'Traveling Responsibly' (p27).

See Climate Charts (p1116) for more information.

WHEN TO GO

America's size plays to the traveler's advantage when it comes to weather: it's always perfect somewhere in the US and just shy of Hades somewhere else.

In other words, either your destination or your trip's timing may need tweaking depending on the season. For more specific regional info, see each chapter's 'Land & Climate' section. For current forecasts, visit www.weather.com.

The main holiday season is, naturally, summer, which typically begins on Memorial Day (the last Monday in May) and ends on Labor Day (the first Monday in September). But Americans take their holidays mainly in summer because schools are closed, not because the weather's uniformly ideal: yes, hit the beaches in August, because Manhattan is a shimmering sweat bath and the deserts are frying pans.

The seasons don't arrive uniformly either. Spring (typically March to May) and fall (usually September to November) are often the best travel times, but 'spring' in parts of the Rockies and Sierras may not come till June. By then it's only a sweet memory in Austin, while in Seattle, spring often means rain, rain, rain.

And winter? It's expensive high-season at ski resorts and in parts of the southern US (blame migrating snowbirds), but planned well, winter can mean you have the riches of America's landscape virtually all to yourself.

Whether you're planning to join them or avoid them, holidays (p1121) and festivals (p1119) are another thing to consider.

HOW MUCH?

Broadway show:
$100-250

Bottle of wine: $7-9

Gallon of milk: $3.50

Internet access per hour: $3-5

Pound of apples: $1.20

See also Lonely Planet Index, inside front cover.

COSTS & MONEY

An economical US trip is possible, but it is very, very easy to spend much more than you bargained for, no matter what your travel style. Mode of transportation is a big factor, as is destination: US cities don't chip away at budgets, they jackhammer them into pieces.

DON'T LEAVE HOME WITHOUT...

- Checking current US visa and passport requirements (p1127).
- Hotel reservations, particularly for your first night and near national parks (p1111).
- Your driver's license and adequate liability insurance (p1142). Not driving? Do it anyway – you might change your mind once you see how big this place is.
- A handful of credit cards – they're easier and safer than cash.
- An open mind. You'll find elites in the Ozarks and hicks in Manhattan, and everything in between.

To travel on the cheap, plan on camping or hosteling ($15 to $25 a night), cooking some of your own meals, and touring by bus.

Only the extremely thrifty will spend less than $100 a day. A comfortable midrange budget typically ranges from $175 to $225 a day; this usually gets you a car, gas, two meals, a good hotel and a museum admission or two. Spending over $300 a day isn't hard: just splash out a few times, drive a lot, and stay, eat and whoop it up in New York, Chicago, San Francisco etc.

In this guide, we define a 'midrange' hotel very broadly (as $80 to $200): in rural areas, $100 buys a princely night's sleep, but in some cities, clean places *start* at $200. The same math holds for meals.

To travel on the cheap, plan on camping or hosteling ($15 to $25 a night), cooking some of your own meals, and touring by bus. It's not hard, but it limits your flexibility and it's slower (which isn't so bad). Be wary of budget motel come-ons; the sign might flash $39, but it's probably for a single and won't include tax.

Traveling by car is often a necessity. A rental is a minimum of $40 a day (type of car, tax and level of insurance can push it higher), plus gas. Planning the great American road trip? Petrol could cost more than the car itself (say, another $20 to $40 per day).

Mainly, don't forget the second part of that travel chestnut: after you halve your clothes, double your estimated budget, and it'll work out fine.

TRAVEL LITERATURE

The American travelogue is its own literary genre. One could argue the first (and still the best) is *Democracy in America* (1835) by Alexis de Tocqueville, who wandered around talking to folks, then in pithy fashion distilled the philosophical underpinnings of the then-new American experiment.

America is often most vividly described by non-Americans: two Russian satirists, Ilya Ilf and Evgeny Petrov, road-tripped during the Great Depression searching for the 'real America' (doesn't everyone?), and their *Ilf and Petrov's American Road Trip* (1935 & 2007) is a comic masterpiece laced with pungent critiques.

Those who prefer their commentary, like their coffee, bitter and black should stuff *The Air-Conditioned Nightmare* (1945) by Henry Miller in their bag, written while the irascible Miller canvassed America during WWII.

Celebrated travel writer Jan Morris was clearly smitten with the country in *Coast to Coast* (1956); it's crisp, elegant and poignant, particularly her experience in the pre–Civil Rights South.

Two other famous, and not to be missed, American travelogues are Jack Kerouac's headlong *On the Road* (1957) and John Steinbeck's *Travels with Charley* (1962), about his trek across America with his poodle for company.

At a crossroad in life, William Least Heat-Moon's *Blue Highways* (1982) is a moving pastiche of 'average Americans' as it follows one man's attempt to find himself by losing himself.

Not strictly a travelogue, *On the Rez* (2000) by Ian Frazier provides a good taste of what it's like to be friends with an Oglala Sioux, and of contemporary Native American reservation life. It is a journey of history and heart that goes into America, rather than across it.

Some make a life of crossing America. In *American Nomads* (2003), Englishman Richard Grant meditates on all those mythic types (the Indians, cowboys, truckers and hobos) who, like him, can't seem to stop wandering the West. While family-man and cross-country warrior Robert Sullivan does much the same in *Cross Country* (2006), but with kids. Both make ideal companions.

See p65 for American literature.

TRAVELING RESPONSIBLY

Since our inception in 1973, Lonely Planet has encouraged our readers to tread lightly, travel responsibly and enjoy the serendipitous magic independent travel affords. International travel is growing at a jaw-dropping rate, and we still firmly believe in the benefits it can bring – but, as always, we encourage you to consider the impact your visit will have on both the global environment and the local economies, cultures and ecosystems.

In America, 'going green' has become seriously trendy, and businesses of all stripes now slap 'we're green!' stickers on their products and services (though many Americans would agree with *The Simpsons Movie* when it calls global warming 'an irritating truth'). For the traveler, determining how ecofriendly a business actually is can be difficult. Thankfully many resources are springing up, and we have tried to recommend ecofriendly businesses (and highlight local green initiatives) throughout this guide.

To Drive or Not to Drive

Where adequate public transportation exists, choosing it over renting a car will decrease your carbon footprint. But realistically, a car is often a necessity in the US – so, choose ecofriendly cars when available (ask the majors – they're getting them!). The auto association **Better World Club** (www .betterworldclub.com; p1141) supports environmental legislation and offers eco-friendly services.

Two US car rental companies specializing in hybrid and electric cars are **Bio-Beetle** (www .bio-beetle.com) and **EV Rental Cars** (www.evrental.com), though locations are currently limited (mainly Hawaii, California and Arizona).

To Buy or Not to Buy

State and regional tourism associations are springing up to certify ecofriendly businesses, hotels, services, tours and outfitters. Here is a list of some; review them before making reservations.

Alaska Wilderness Recreation and Tourism Association (www.awrta.org)

Chicago Sustainable Business Alliance (www.sustainablechicago.biz)

Go Nomad (www.gonomad.com) Ecotours worldwide.

Green Hotel Association (www.greenhotels.com) Ecofriendly hotels nationwide.

Greenopia (www.greenopia.com) San Francisco and Los Angeles ecoguides (eventually to a dozen cities).

Hawaii Ecotourism Association (www.hawaiiecotourism.org)

Travel Green Wisconsin (www.travelgreenwisconsin)

Vital Communities (www.vitalcommunities.org) Green restaurants and local farmers markets in Vermont and New Hampshire.

Sustainable Travel: The Bigger Picture

'Sustainable travel' is more than making 'green' choices; it's a way of interacting as you walk. It's practicing low-impact hiking and camping (p102). It's perhaps adding volunteering to a vacation (p1130). It's also simply learning about destinations and cultures and understanding the challenges they face. For national and regional issues, see the Environment chapter (p103) and check out these resources:

Climatecrisis.net (www.climatecrisis.net) Official website for the documentary *An Inconvenient Truth*; offers carbon offset programs, advice and information.

Hawaii 2050 (www.hawaii2050.org) State-sponsored initiative to create a sustainable Hawaiian economy.

National Geographic Center for Sustainable Destinations (www.nationalgeographic.com/travel /sustainable) Promotes 'geotourism' with its 'Geocharter maps'; currently three in the US: Arizona's Sonoran Desert, Vermont and Appalachia.

Sustainable Travel International (www.sustainabletravelinternational.org) Provides ecoguides, tour booking, a carbon-offset program and more.

TOP 10

Hawaii (USA)

UNITED STATES OF AMERICA Washington DC

PARTIES & PARADES

Americans will use any excuse to party. Seriously. There's a festival for *sock monkeys* (p574)! No slight to sock monkey fans, but here are 10 worth planning a trip around. For more, see the destination chapters, see p1119 and visit www.festivals.com.

1 Mummer's Parade, Philadelphia (Pennsylvania), New Year's Day (p206)

2 Mardi Gras, New Orleans (Louisiana), February or March (p440)

3 National Cherry Blossom Festival, Washington, DC, late March/April (p319)

4 Conch Republic Independence Celebration, Key West (Florida), April (p517)

5 Fiesta San Antonio (Texas), mid-April (p708)

6 Gullah Festival, Beaufort (South Carolina), late May (p399)

7 Red Earth Native American Cultural Festival, Oklahoma City (Oklahoma), early June (p683)

8 SF Gay Pride Month, San Francisco (California), June (p964)

9 Great American Beer Festival, Denver (Colorado), early September (p749)

10 American Royal Barbecue, Kansas City (Missouri), early October (p655)

GOOD BOOKS

A good book is as essential to a successful trip as gas in the car and money in your wallet. Here are our recommendations for 10 great recent novels that capture a kaleidoscope of American regional voices.

1 *Flight* (2007) by Sherman Alexie

2 *Later, at the Bar* (2007) by Rebecca Barry

3 *Talk Talk* (2007) by TC Boyle

4 *The Yiddish Policeman's Union* (2007) by Michael Chabonn

5 *I Love You, Beth Cooper* (2007) by Larry Doyle

6 *Wounded* (2005) by Percival Everett

7 *Returning to Earth* (2006) by Jim Harrison

8 *The Shape Shifter* (2006) by Tony Hillerman

9 *Sight Hound* (2005) by Pam Houston

10 *The Plot Against America* (2004) by Philip Roth

SCENIC DRIVES

A road trip is nothing without roads. Here are 10 doozies. Frankly, we had to arm-wrestle over favorites, so consider this list incomplete. See the Itineraries chapter (p30) for more, and for America's 'official' scenic roads, visit www.byways.org.

1 Hana Hwy (Hwy 360), Maui, Hawaii: 38 miles from Pauwela to Hana (p1106)

2 Turquoise Trail (Hwy 14), New Mexico: 45 miles from Albuquerque to Santa Fe (p875)

3 Columbia River Hwy (Hwy 30), Oregon: 74 miles from Troutdale to The Dalles (p1042)

4 Pig Trail Byway (Hwy 23), Arkansas: 80 miles from Ozark to Eureka Springs (p457)

5 Hwy 12, Utah: 107 miles from Torrey to Bryce Canyon NP (p868)

6 Overseas Hwy (Hwy 1), Florida: 160 miles from Miami to Key West (p510).

7 Delmarva Peninsula (Hwys 50 and 13): 210 miles from Annapolis, Maryland, to Virginia Beach, Virginia (p337 and p360)

8 Route 66 (initial section): 300 miles from Chicago, Illinois, to St Louis, Missouri (p576)

9 Pacific Coast Hwy (Hwy 1), California: 332 miles from San Francisco to Santa Barbara (p940).

10 Blue Ridge Parkway: 469 miles from Shenandoah NP, Virginia, to Great Smoky Mountains NP, North Carolina (p364)

INTERNET RESOURCES

Bathroom Diaries (www.thebathroomdiaries.com) A compilation of clean bathrooms worldwide (with awards!), including every state in the USA. Its bathroom stories are a hoot.

Johnny Jet (www.johnnyjet.com) Compiled by an inveterate traveler, this website links to perhaps all the travel information you'll ever need.

Lonely Planet (www.lonelyplanet.com) US travel news and summaries, the Thorn Tree bulletin board, and links to more web resources.

Roadside America (www.roadsideamerica.com) Sure, see the Statue of Liberty. But don't miss the 'Muffler Men'! For weird, wacky Americana, start here.

Roadtrip America (www.roadtripamerica.com) Planning the classic road trip? This site helps with nitty-gritty tips: routes, driving advice, fuel calculator, eating and much more.

USA.gov (www.usa.gov/Citizen/Topics/Travel.shtml) The closest thing to a national tourism information resource, on the US government's official website.

Itineraries
CLASSIC ROUTES

Why are easterners so cranky? Because East Coast highways couldn't be more congested. So why on earth do this road trip? Slow down, avoid rush hour, hit the beaches often, and for 1000 detour-laden miles it's one first-class metropolis after another.

CITIES BY THE SEA   10 Days to Three Weeks/Boston to Maryland

The nice thing about East Coast metropoli? They're near the beach! Balance culture, history and cuisine with coastal idylls and long naps in the sun.

Arrive in revolutionary **Bah-ston** (p229), then go to sandy **Cape Cahd** (p246), and keep going till you reach **Prah-vincetown** (p251), where the Pilgrims landed. Pretty, ain't it?

Scoot around on I-195 to Rhode Island's quaint **Newport** (p262); time your visit for a **music festival** (p264).

Now, tackle **New York City** (p136). Once you've had your fill of the bustling Big Apple, escape to **the Hamptons** (p179) on Long Island; what was the hurry, again?

In New Jersey, go 'down the shore' to **Long Beach Island** (p194), and if you're the gambling sort, **Atlantic City** (p195) and its boardwalk.

Then, make time for **Philadelphia** (p197), **Baltimore** (p325), and **Washington, DC** (p306). You did plan three weeks, right?

Finally, cross Chesapeake Bay and relax on **Maryland's Eastern Shore** (p337), and get your mellow back for good at **Assateague Island** (boxed text, p340).

THE LEFT COAST
Two to Three Weeks/Portland to Joshua Tree

Geographically and politically, the West Coast couldn't be further from Washington, DC. This is a trip for those who lean left, and who like their nature ancient and ornery. You won't need to shave but once or twice.

Pretty, affable **Portland** (p1028) is a great place to start. Then jump right into nature's bounty by driving east along the **Columbia River Gorge** (boxed text, p1042). At The Dalles, turn south and make for **Mount Hood** (p1043) for skiing or hiking (depending on the season). From **Bend** (p1044), enjoy more cascades adventures in the **Three Sisters Wilderness Area** (p1044) and **Crater Lake** (p1045).

Catch a Shakespearian play at **Ashland** (p1045), then trade the mountains for the coast: enter California via Hwy 199 and the magnificent **Redwood National Park** (p981).

Hug the coast through funky **North Coast towns** (p978), get lost on the **Lost Coast** (p980), catch Hwy 1 and buy art in **Mendocino** (p979). Make your way inland to **Napa Valley** (p974) for a wash-up and wine tasting, and thence to the hilly, defiantly strange burg of **San Francisco** (p950).

Return to scenic **Hwy 1** (p950) through **Santa Cruz** (p948), **Monterey** (p946) and most of all, **Big Sur** (p944), where you can get seriously scruffy again. By the time you reach **Hearst Castle** (p944) you can actually start swimming in the water.

Finally, **Los Angeles** (p900) – aka LA, la-la land, the city of angels. Go ahead, indulge your fantasies of **Hollywood** (p906), **Venice Beach** (p912) and **club culture** (p918). Then, creeped out by artifice perhaps, hop aboard a ferry for the wildlife-rich **Channel Islands** (p940) and make a desert pilgrimage to **Joshua Tree National Park** (p936). Aaah, that's better.

Let's see. In 1400 miles, is there eco-friendly outdoor adventure? Check. Microbrews and fine wines? Check. Heart-stopping ancient forests and mountains? Check. Legendary coastal drives? Check. Freaks, visionaries and radicals? Check. Surf beaches, gourmet cuisine, cutting-edge art, multicultural cities? Check, check, check. Why, it's the West Coast!

THE GREAT RIVER ROAD 10 Days to Two Weeks/Minneapolis to New Orleans

The Mississippi River marks a physical and psychological divide, and along this spine runs America's greatest music: blues, jazz, and rock and roll. Hwy 61 is the legendary route, though numerous other roads join up, run parallel and intersect with it.

Progressive, artistic, youthful **Minneapolis** (p623) is the easiest starting point, though some might want to start further north in **Hibbing** (p635), Bob Dylan's birthplace. Hwy 61 then winds scenically on either side of the Mississippi River to **Hannibal** (p650), Missouri, the birthplace of Mark Twain. Gateway to the West, **St Louis** (p643) also bills itself as the 'Home of the Blues,' though original rock-and-roller Chuck Berry still plays here, too.

The next major destination is **Memphis** (p460), where you can pay homage to Elvis Presley at Graceland and rock and roll at Sun Studio. To complete your musical pilgrimage, take a quick detour on I-40 to **Nashville** (p468), the home of country music. South of Memphis, Hwy 61 runs through the **Mississippi Delta** (p427), where the blues was born: **Clarksdale** (p427) is where Robert Johnson bargained with the devil. The town's still jumpin' with blues joints, while **Natchez** (p431) is full of antebellum homes.

South of Baton Rouge, a detour along Hwy 1 leads past the famous 19th-century **Mississippi River Plantations** (p449).

Then you arrive at **New Orleans** (p433), birthplace of jazz. The 'Big Easy,' despite its recent hard times (p432), is a place where lazy mornings blend into late nights, and you should leave plenty of time to go with the flow.

Just about all of the epic, legendary, even revolutionary history of American music can be experienced along this 1200-mile stretch of the Mississippi River. Throw in a 400-mile sidetrip to Nashville, and what you have is the musical journey of a lifetime.

GO EAST, YOUNG MAN   Three Weeks to One Month/San Francisco to Miami

For those contemplating the full monty, coast to coast, here's a suggestion: start in San Francisco and head into the rising sun. This route snags some seriously fun cities and some classic American scenery, but be warned: it'll be *hot* come July and August.

From anything-goes **San Francisco** (p950), head for **Yosemite** (p989) and **Sequoia National Parks** (p993) in the Sierra Nevada – now that's scenery! Skirt the **Mojave Desert** (p938) on I-15 and hit **Las Vegas** (p809) – now that's fun! Stop at the **Grand Canyon** (p835) for the obligatory photo-op, rattle around funky **Flagstaff** (p831) and **Sedona** (p833), and roll east on I-40.

In New Mexico, unlike Bugs Bunny, take that left at **Albuquerque** (p873) along the **Turquoise Trail** (p875) and detour to artsy, adobe **Santa Fe** (p879), just cause it's so cute.

Drop south on I-25 through scenic **southwestern New Mexico** (p890), pick up I-10 into Texas, and admire jaw-dropping **Big Bend National Park** (p734). Saunter through bucolic **Texas Hill Country** (p703) to **Austin** (p695), for good music and drinking. Pause for folk art in **Houston** (p710) then giddy-up for party-central, **New Orleans** (p433). Keep dancing and eatin' in **Cajun Country** (p450).

Depending on your time, explore fun-loving **Mobile** (p425) and the beaches of the **Florida Panhandle** (p538), but whatever you do, visit **Walt Disney World** (p535); like the Grand Canyon, it must be seen to be believed.

Now, along Florida's Gulf Coast, enjoy **St Petersburg** (p528), clown around in **Sarasota** (p530) and pick seashells at **Sanibel & Captiva Islands** (p531). Bisect the alligator-filled swamps of the tremendous **Everglades** (p506) and arrive in **Miami** (p492). Finally, with a beach, a mojito and some Cuban cuisine, you're ready to party till sunrise. Sweet!

This is the trip you have to do at least once – coast to coast, ocean to ocean, sunrise to sunset (or in this case, vice versa). It's 3500 miles, give or take. Some do it in days, others take months. There's no right or wrong, no rules, no 'best' route. Just go.

WESTERN MIGRATIONS
Two to Three Weeks/Chicago to Seattle

'The West' is not one thing. It's a panoply of landscapes and personalities that unfold as, like an eager pioneer, you journey from past to future. No single route could capture it all; this stretch of I-90 is book-ended by world-class cities and packed with heartbreakingly beautiful country.

From Midwest to Wild West to New West: this route is a 2700-mile meditation on America's evolving western frontier. Only by seeing the West's endless plains, eroded deserts, towering mountains and ragged coast can you begin to understand its inhabitants' singular multiple personalities.

Chicago (p547) – the Second City, the Windy City – is the Midwest's greatest city. Follow I-90 to youthful **Madison** (p617) and the quirk along **Hwy 12** (p619) to dispel any myths about Midwestern sobriety.

Detour north to arty **Minneapolis** (p623) for more Midwest liberalism. Return to I-90 and activate cruise control, admiring the corn (and the **Corn Palace**, p665) and the flat, flat South Dakota plains. See why Westerners are crazy?

Hit the brakes for the **Badlands** (p666) and plunge into the reckless Wild West. In the **Black Hills** (p667), contemplate competing monuments at **Mount Rushmore** (p670) and **Crazy Horse** (p670). Watch mythic gunfights in **Deadwood** (p669) and visit the sobering **Pine Ridge Reservation** (p666), site of the Wounded Knee massacre.

Halfway across Wyoming, take Hwy 14 to **Cody** (p779) for the rodeo. Save plenty of time for the wild majesty and wildlife of **Yellowstone** (p781) and **Grand Teton National Parks** (p785).

Through Montana, the newly hip ranching towns of **Bozeman** (p789) and **Missoula** (p792) make fun stops. For serious western adventure, detour to **Glacier National Park** (p795) and the **Bob Marshall Wilderness Complex** (p795).

Back on I-90 into Washington, stop in unassuming **Spokane** (p1024) and end in **Seattle** (p1003) – which embodies the high-tech, eco-conscious New West. Still got time? Take in **Mount Rainier** (p1025), **Olympic National Park** (p1017), and the **San Juan Islands** (p1021). See why everyone went west?

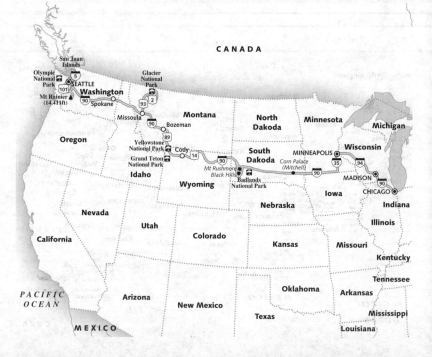

ROADS LESS TRAVELED

THE GRAND CIRCLE   Two to Four Weeks/Las Vegas to Las Vegas

In another era, the Grand Circle was a leisure-class journey to all the rugged, raw natural splendors of the New World. It took several months, and still can, but today you only need a few weeks to witness some of the most amazing geological spectacles Mother Nature has yet devised – as well as get acquainted with Southwest Native American cultures.

Nothing natural about **Las Vegas** (p809), but it's a great place to start. From here, take I-15 northeast to Utah's **Zion National Park** (p871). Catch Hwy 89 and then go east on **Hwy 12** (p868) – one of the most amazing drives in the world, containing as it does **Bryce Canyon National Park** (p870), the **Grand Staircase-Escalante National Monument** (p869) and **Capitol Reef National Park** (p868). You'll gain a new appreciation for rock.

Take Hwy 24 to I-70, head east, then catch Hwy 191 south to **Moab** (p865), **Arches National Park** (p866) and **Canyonlands National Park** (p867). Head southeast on Hwy 666 to **Mesa Verde National Park** (p776), then take your cultural wonder west on Hwy 160 to **Monument Valley** (p843) and the **Navajo National Monument** (p843). Double back to go south on Hwy 191 to catch **Canyon de Chelly National Monument** (p843), then west on Hwy 264 through the mesas of the **Hopi Indian Reservation** (p844).

Next, it's the granddaddy of river erosion, the **Grand Canyon** (p835). Go south and clean up in **Flagstaff** (p831), then return to Las Vegas by I-40 and Hwy 93, pausing to admire the concrete pile called **Hoover Dam** (p818).

Canyons a mile deep, deserts painted a rainbow, crumbling buttes, pueblo-topped mesas, ancient civilizations hidden in the cliffs – you can't make this stuff up. To see it all requires 1400 brutal miles of slow, sun-baked roads, and it's worth every saddle sore.

THE CONTINENTAL DIVIDE

**Two to Four Weeks/
Albuquerque to Glacier National Park**

On one side rivers run east, on the other, west. You'll trace the mountains in between, finding constant excuses to ditch the car and hike, climb, raft, bike, ski and get dirty. Just remember: the mountains only get prettier further north, so don't *forget* to drive.

Start in **Albuquerque** (p873) and take the **Turquoise Trail** (p875) to arty **Santa Fe** (p879). Between here and trippy **Taos** (p886), check out the **Pueblos** (p884), atomic **Los Alamos** (p885) and **Bandelier National Monument** (p885) for camping.

Follow Hwy 84 into Colorado. Enjoy bikes and brews in **Durango** (p770) and admire the ancient cliff-dwellings of **Mesa Verde** (p776). Ready for more scenery? Take the 'Million Dollar Hwy' (Hwy 550), stopping in **Silverton** (p771); for hot springs in **Ouray** (p772); and a quick detour to gorgeous **Telluride** (p773). Then go east on Hwy 50, through the **Black Canyon of the Gunnison** (p777), and north on Hwy 24 to ritzy **Vail** (p764).

Relax a spell in laid-back **Boulder** (p753) and **Rocky Mountain National Park** (p756). For time's sake, stay north on I-25, and in Wyoming, take I-80 west to Hwy 287: follow this to **Lander** (p780) for rock climbing. Now get thee to **Grand Teton** (p785) and **Yellowstone** (p781) National Parks.

In Montana, take Hwy 89 north and I-90 west to **Bozeman** (p789) and **Missoula** (p792), both enjoyable places to stock up before the final push. Serious wilderness calls in the **Bob Marshall Wilderness Complex** (p795) and **Glacier National Park** (p795).

And really, there's no reason not to keep following the Rockies into Canada; if anything, Banff and Jasper National Parks only get more dramatically beautiful. But that's a story for another book (namely, LP's *Canada*).

> Work hard, play hard – or at least, play hard. Name it, and you can probably do it in the Rocky Mountains. This 2000-mile route is built for those who don't want to just admire nature's munificence, but to roll around in it, then swap stories over a beer.

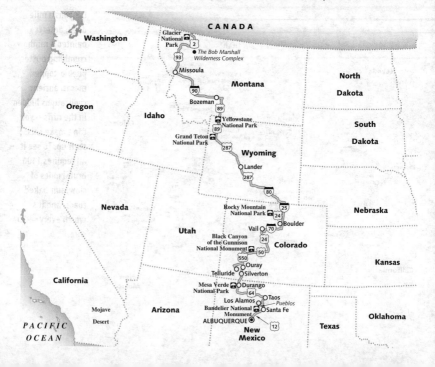

GENTLEMEN FARMERS & DAMN YANKEES   Ten Days to Three Weeks/ New York City to Acadia National Park

This is a good spring or summer trip, but in early fall – wow. Autumn dresses New England in auburn and scarlet, and the air is so crisp you can bite it. Stout personalities settled this region, which remains a mix of rugged wilderness, efficient towns and tidy farms.

Arrive in **New York City** (p136); soak up the excitement, the cacophony, the crowds. When you're full, rent a car and head north on I-87. Dip into the **Catskills** (p182) along Hwy 28 for a first taste of East Coast forests, then continue north for the real deal: the **Adirondacks** (p186). Settle in for a few days in **Lake Placid** (p186) and explore the wilderness.

Take the ferry across Lake Champlain to youthful, outdoorsy **Burlington** (p279), a great introduction to New England. A sidetrip to the **Lake Champlain Islands** (p279) is splendid, then take I-89 southeast, stopping at the ski-town of **Stowe** (p278). At **Montpelier** (p277), take Hwy 302 east to New Hampshire.

Hwy 302 turns into Hwy 112, the **Kancamagus Hwy** (p284), perhaps the prettiest drive in New England, through the magnificent **White Mountains** (p284): waterfalls, hikes and quaint villages abound. At Hwy 16, go south to historic, maritime **Portsmouth** (p281).

Now follow I-95 into Maine. Lively **Portland** (p291) has surprisingly good eats. From Hwy 1, meander the **Central Maine Coast** (p294): you're hunting clam chowder, fresh lobster and nautical ports to let loose your inner sailor. Visit **Bath** (p294), **Boothbay Harbor** (p294), and **Camden** (p296), for memorable **windjammer cruises** (p295).

Finally, book yourself an historic inn in **Bar Harbor** (p298) and dive into the unspoiled splendor of **Acadia National Park** (p297).

Never experienced fall in New England? Tired of hearing everyone blather on? Time this 1000-mile trip right, and you'll join the proselytizers. Heck, it's gorgeous any season, the chowder and lobster kill, the maritime air stirs your blood, and that damn Yankee ingenuity is a marvel.

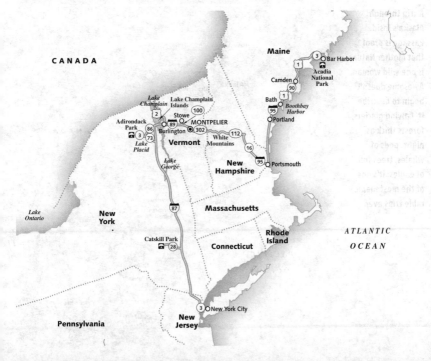

ALASKA'S INSIDE PASSAGE One to Three Weeks/Bellingham to Skagway

You can take a car, but if you are looking for an unforgettable journey that doesn't involve an automobile, consider cruising Alaska's Inside Passage.

In summer the Alaska Marine Hwy ferries stop at towns nearly every day, and with advance notice you can get on and off at every one, just as long as you keep traveling in the same direction. See p1059 for ferry information.

Fly into **Seattle** (p1003), Washington, and linger awhile or take a shuttle directly to **Bellingham** (p1021), where you catch the Alaska Marine Hwy ferry.

The first stop is **Ketchikan** (p1059), which still has a rugged Western feel. It might be worth renting a car once you land on **Prince of Wales Island** (p1060), which is the third-largest island in the USA.

Wrangell (p1060) was founded by Russians, while pretty **Petersburg** (p1061) has a Norwegian heritage. Rich with Native American culture and beautifully situated, **Sitka** (p1062) shouldn't be missed. Busy **Juneau** (p1063) is Alaska's capital, and from here it's easy to get close to magnificent **Mendenhall Glacier** (p1064).

Haines (p1065) is another sizable town, and **Skagway** (p1067) is the end of the line. It is a well-preserved, nonthreatening version of its once-lawless gold-rush self.

You can also fly into or out of Juneau, or make it a round-trip and take the ferry back to Bellingham.

A trip through Alaska's Inside Passage is proof that Mother Nature is one wild woman. Awesome doesn't begin to describe it. Calving glaciers, forests thick as night, pods of whales, trees full of eagles: it's one of the most memorable trips ever.

TAILORED TRIPS

DUDE, THAT'S WEIRD

Combine a fierce sense of independence with a vast landscape and what you get are crazies giving free rein to their obsessions. Call it 'Americana.' You've heard of the biggies (Mitchell's Corn Palace, Las Vegas). Here are some others you shouldn't miss.

First, what's up with Stonehenge? Modern, personal iterations include Nebraska's **Carhenge** (p674), Virginia's **Foamhenge** (p364), and Florida's **Coral Castle** (p509).

Looking for the world's largest…**catsup bottle** (p577)? **Chair** (p318)? Perhaps just a really **big chicken** (p412)? Americans know supersizing.

For sublime examples of 'outsider' or folk art, aim for **Lucas**, **Kansas** (p679); **Nitt Witt Ridge** (p950); the **Mystery Castle** (p825); **Dr Evermor's Sculpture Park** (p619); and Houston's **Beer Can House** (p713) and **Art Car Museum** (p713).

Sometimes Americans dress up madness by calling it a 'museum.' What do *you* make of the **Spam Museum** (p633), **Leila's Hair Museum** (p657), the **Bigfoot Discovery Museum** (p950), or – wait for it – the **American Sanitary Plumbing Museum** (p257)?

Americans celebrate strangely too! Join in the **Interstate Mullet Toss** (p541), the **Cow Chip Throw** (p619) and the **Sock Monkey Festival** (p574). Cheer on the inmates at the **Angola Prison Rodeo** (p450)!

Finally, if the folks on the ground aren't alien enough, look for the outer space kind at the **UFO Watchtower** (p769). Hey, get married while you wait!

BOTTOMS UP!

Americans like to drink. The US Constitution's 21st Amendment (which ended the 14-year dry spell called Prohibition) establishes that emphatically, even legally. And they're quite good at making the stuff, too.

These days, most states tout their 'wine countries,' and it ain't all plonk. California's **Napa** and **Sonoma Valleys** (p974) are justifiably famous, but don't neglect **Santa Barbara** (p940), which is so good it inspired a movie: *Sideways*. Other wine regions to tour include Washington's **Walla Walla** (p1027), New York's **Finger Lakes** (p183), Long Island's **North Fork** (p181), Virginia's **Charlottesville** (p361) and **Texas Hill Country** (p704). Cowboys knocking back merlot? Hell yeah.

Americans have been brewing beer from the start. Despite being the home of bland major-label beers (such as Pabst and Miller), **Milwaukee** (p614) remains a beer-lover's destination, as is **Chicago** (p547). The microbrewery renaissance began out west: notable cities include **Portland** (p1028), **Seattle** (p1003), **Boulder** (p753) and **Durango** (p770). In California, **Wine Country** (p950) and the **North Coast** (p950) are sprinkled with fine homemade suds.

Those who prefer the hard stuff should make time for Kentucky, whose **bourbon tour** (p484) makes for a genteel Southern experience.

ISLAND-HOPPING

Everybody wants to go across the USA, but traveling around it might make an even better trip. Start at Maine's **Acadia National Park** (p297) for a sunrise hike. Then go to historic **Martha's Vineyard** (p255), from where it's a quick tack to the USA's most famous island, **Manhattan** (p136). Off the Virginia coast is **Chincoteague Island** (p360), famous for its wild horses, and off North Carolina are the **Outer Banks** (p377) and **Cape Hatteras National Seashore** (p378), where the Wright brothers learned to fly, and you can too – by hang gliding.

Florida boasts **Amelia Island** (p525), the string-of-pearls **Florida Keys** (p510), the islands of **Dry Tortugas National Park** (p519) and shell collecting on **Sanibel** and **Captiva Islands** (p531).

Continuing along the Gulf of Mexico is Texas' resort town of **Galveston** (p718) and the gorgeously wild **Padre Island National Seashore** (p720) – not to be confused with **South Padre Island** (p721), where 'gorgeous and wild' describes the spring break party scene.

At this point, sail through the Panama Canal or go overland to California, where **Catalina Island** (p921) has great snorkeling and **Channel Islands National Park** (p940) is 'California's Galápagos.' Keep going to Washington's **San Juan Islands** (p1021) and thence to the islands of Alaska's **Inside Passage** (p1059). Finally, of course, don't forget **Hawaii** (p1085)!

WE'RE HERE, WE'RE QUEER

It's never been more fun to be gay in the USA. So long as you're not trying to get married, gay travelers will find numerous places where they can be themselves without thinking twice. Naturally, beaches and big cities tend to be the gayest destinations, and why not? They're the most fun!

Manhattan (p136) is too crowded and cosmopolitan to worry about who's holding hands, while **Fire Island** (p179) is the sandy gay mecca on Long Island. Other East Coast cities that flaunt it are **Boston** (p243), **Philadelphia** (p197), **Washington, DC** (p318) and **Provincetown** (p251), Massachusetts. Why even Maine brags a gay beach destination: **Ogunquit** (p289).

In the South, there's always steamy **'Hotlanta'** (p409) and Texas gets darn-right gay-friendly in **Austin** (p702) and parts of **Houston** (p716). In Florida, **Miami** (p492) and the 'Conch Republic' of **Key West** (p514) support thriving gay communities, though **Fort Lauderdale** (p504) attracts bronze boys too. Of course, everyone gets their freak on in **New Orleans** (p444).

In the Midwest, seek out **Chicago** (p564) and **Minneapolis** (p625). You will have heard of **San Francisco** (p950), the happiest gay city in America, and what can gays and lesbians do in **Los Angeles** (p900)? Hmmm, just about anything. In fact, when LA is too much, try **Palm Springs** (p934).

Lastly, for an island idyll, **Hawaii** (p1085) is gay-friendly generally, but particularly in **Waikiki** (p1097).

History

TURTLE ISLAND

Native peoples have always lived on the North American continent, which some called 'Turtle Island.' Or at least, that's what indigenous histories and myths say. By the time anyone came along to claim differently, two to 10 million people occupied every corner of the turtle's back and spoke over 300 languages.

The traditional Western explanation of the continent's peopling – that Asians migrated over a land bridge between Siberia and Alaska some 30,000 to 20,000 years ago – likely occurred but is considered insufficient to explain all the evidence. Also, by turning Native Americans into 'immigrants,' it's been criticized for becoming an occasional, strange justification for America's taking of the land.

The earliest identifiable Paleo-Indian cultures were the Clovis and Folsom, who lived throughout North America from about 10,000 to 8000 BC, or the end of the Ice Age. Since then, a vibrant mix of complex societies developed, some nomadic hunters and some settled farmers.

In the Ohio and Mississippi valleys, 'Mound Builders' dated from 3000 BC to AD 1300. In Illinois, Cahokia Mounds (p577) was once an urban metropolis of 20,000 people, the largest in pre-Columbian North America.

In the Southwest, Ancestral Puebloans occupied the Colorado Plateau until AD 1300; you can see their awe-inspiring cliff dwellings at Colorado's Mesa Verde (p776) and New Mexico's Chaco Culture National Historic Park (p889). Their descendents include the Hopi, whose 13th-century mesa-top pueblos (p844) are some of the continent's oldest, continuously inhabited settlements.

Northwest cultures are famous for their totem poles and canoes; the Makah Indian Reservation (p1020) contains an excavated 15th-century village.

However, Great Plains cultures came to epitomize 'Indians' in the American imagination, partly because they put up the best fight. Oklahoma offers several examples of pre-European life, at Anadarko (p685) and the Cherokee Heritage Center (p688).

EUROPEANS DISCOVER A NEW WORLD

When Europeans first sailed into the western hemisphere, they called the continents a 'New World.' The unexpected land was certainly startling, but the real new world was ocean-spanning seafaring: as it turned out, the sea wasn't earth's edge, but instead a cool new superhighway. This radically altered the political landscape of Europe and Asia and spurred modern capitalism, which of course affected the way Europeans reacted to the Americas.

A Nation Among Nations (2006) by Thomas Bender reframes US history within the context of world history. It's a compelling, illuminating and very lively antidote to parochial American 'exceptionalism.'

Focused on Southwest tribes, *The People* (1993) by Stephen Trimble is a beautiful account of Native American history and modern-day culture told largely by Native Americans themselves.

TIMELINE

8500–8000 BC	5500 BC–AD 100	1200–1300
Widespread extinction of Ice Age mammals like woolly mammoth, due partly to cooperative hunting by humans and partly to drying glacial climate. Hungry locals begin plant-gathering.	'Archaic period' marked by nomadic hunter-gatherer lifestyle. By period's end, corn, beans and squash (the agricultural 'three sisters') and permanent settlements are well-established.	In the Southwest, mysterious disappearance of Ancestral Puebloan peoples, who abandon cliff-dwellings. Concurrently, a rise in cities (especially in the Southwest and the Mississippi Valley) and development of irrigated agriculture.

In 1492, Italian explorer Christopher Columbus, backed by Spain, voyaged west – looking for the East Indies. He found the Bahamas. With visions of gold, more Spanish explorers quickly followed: Hernán Cortés conquered much of today's Mexico; Francisco Pizarro conquered Peru; Juan Ponce de León rattled around Florida looking for the fountain of youth. Not to be left out, the French explored Canada and the fur-rich Midwest, while the Dutch and the English cruised North America's eastern seaboard.

In their wake, European explorers left behind diseases to which Native peoples had no immunities. More than any other factor (the usuals: war, slavery, famine etc), disease epidemics decimated native populations by anywhere from 50% to 90%. By the 17th century, North American Indians numbered about a million, and many of the continent's once-thriving societies were in turmoil and transition.

In addition to seeking riches, European colonizers were driven by religious fervor: it seemed to them this underpopulated New World must have been reserved by god for Christians, and Spanish Catholic missionaries sought to convert the continent's indigenous cultures (eventually establishing strings of missions across the South and in California).

In 1607, English noblemen established North America's first permanent European settlement in Jamestown (p355). Earlier settlements had ended badly, and Jamestown almost did too: the English chose a swamp, planted their crops late and died in bunches from disease and starvation. Some despairing colonists ran off to live with the local Indian tribes, who provided the settlement with enough aid to eke out a meager survival existance.

For Jamestown and America, 1619 proved a pivotal year: the colony established the House of Burgesses, a representative assembly of citizens to decide local laws, and it received its first boatload of 20 African slaves. Having finally grown a successful export crop – tobacco – the English needed workers: they didn't have enough English servants (who, anyway, disdained field labor) and the Indians were difficult to convince or subdue. African slaves, by then well-established on Caribbean sugar plantations, fitted the bill.

The next year, 1620, was equally momentous, as a boatload of radically religious Puritans pulled ashore at what would become Plymouth, Massachusetts (p246). The Pilgrims were escaping religious persecution under the 'corrupt' Church of England, and in the New World they saw a divine opportunity to create a new society that would be a religious and moral beacon. The Pilgrims also signed a 'Mayflower Compact,' one of the seminal texts of American democracy, to govern themselves by consensus.

For decades, the Pilgrims and local Native tribes lived fairly cooperatively, but deadly conflict erupted in 1675. King Philips' War lasted 14 months and killed 5000 people (mostly Native Americans), with the remaining Indians being put on slave ships bound for the Caribbean.

In 1502, Italian explorer Amerigo Vespucci used the term 'Mundus Novus,' or New World, to describe his discoveries. His reward? In 1507, new maps labeled the western hemisphere 'America.'

Stiff-collared Pilgrims, generous Indians, Thanksgiving—*yawn!* *Mayflower* (2006) by Nathanial Philbrick breaks open the myth, vividly recreating the moment when extremist Puritans met natives embroiled in civil war.

1492	1607	1620
Columbus 'discovers' America, eventually making three voyages throughout the Caribbean. He mistakenly names the inhabitants 'Indians,' thinking he'd reached the Indies.	Within the first year of the Jamestown settlement, 80 out of 108 people die. The next year, called the 'starving time,' 440 of 500 settlers are buried. From 1619–22, 3000 of 3600 Jamestown settlers perish.	The *Mayflower* lands at Plymouth with 102 English Pilgrims. Sick and starving, they are saved by the Wampanoag tribe. Grateful Pilgrims throw a harvest festival, which today is celebrated annually as Thanksgiving.

And so, the 'American paradox' was born: white political and religious freedom would come to be founded on the enslavement of blacks and the elimination of Indians.

CAPITALISM & COLONIALISM

For the next two centuries, European powers – particularly England, France, Portugal and Spain – competed for position and territory in the New World, extending European politics into the Americas. As the British Royal Navy came to rule Atlantic seas, England increasingly profited from its colonies and eagerly consumed the fruits of their labors – sweet tobacco from Virginia, sugar and coffee from the Caribbean.

Anticipating the industrial revolution, these luxuries were profitable only when mass produced as export goods using cheap labor in rigidly organized plantations. In America, as the 17th century became the 18th century, slavery was slowly legalized into a formal institution to support this plantation economy, and as this happened, the colonies transitioned from a society with slaves to a slave-based society.

Overall, North America received only 6% of all slaves transported from Africa to the Americas, but slaves made up a large proportion of the American colonies: by the 1770s, one out of five persons was a slave.

Meanwhile, Britain mostly left the American colonists to govern themselves. Town meetings and representative assemblies became common, in which local citizens (that is, white men with property) debated community problems and voted on laws and taxes.

However, by the end of the Seven Years' War in 1763, Britain was feeling the strains of running an empire: they'd been fighting France for a century and had colonies scattered all over the world. It was time to clean up the bureaucracies and share the financial burden.

Britain stationed a permanent army in America. They passed laws forbidding settlement west of the Appalachian Mountains and north of the Ohio River (to avoid more wars), and they passed a series of taxes to raise funds for the Crown and its defense.

The colonists were not amused. Their arguments ran something like this:

Limit expansion? No way!
Pay taxes to fund Britain's military? Forget it!
Take orders from a monarch on a tiny island an ocean away? Nuts!

From 1763 onward, the colonies protested and boycotted English policies and engaged in a running public discussion of political theory that would culminate in the 1776 Declaration of Independence and the Federalist Papers. With these documents, the American colonists took many of the Enlightenment

If history is a partisan affair, Howard Zinn makes his allegiance clear in *A People's History of the United States* (1980 & 2003), which tells the often-overlooked tale of America's laborers, minorities, immigrants, women and radicals.

1756–63	1773	1775
In the Seven Years' War (or the 'French and Indian War'), France loses to England and gets kicked out of Canada. Britain now controls most of the territory east of the Mississippi River.	To protest the 1773 British Tea Tax, Bostonians crudely 'disguise' themselves as Mohawks, board East India Company ships and toss their tea overboard during the Boston Tea Party. Ever since, Americans prefer coffee.	On April 18, Paul Revere rides from Boston to warn colonial 'Minutemen' that the British are coming. The next day, 'the shot heard round the world' is fired at Lexington, starting the Revolutionary War.

1776 (2005) by David McCullough is a riveting war story, told from both sides, of the year when the American Revolution hung in the balance and fate could have swung either way.

ideas then circulating worldwide – of individualism, equality and freedom; of John Locke's 'natural rights' of life, liberty and property – and fashioned a new type of government to put them into practice.

In 1773, colonial and British frustrations came to a head with the Boston Tea Party, after which Britain clamped down hard, shutting Boston harbor, increasing its military presence and enforcing imperial authority.

In 1774, representatives from 12 colonies convened the First Continental Congress in Philadelphia's Independence Hall to air complaints and debate how to respond. Colonists, still identifying as aggrieved Englishmen, worked themselves up into a good lather, and both sides readied for a fight.

Then, in April 1775, British troops skirmished with armed colonists in Massachusetts, and the Revolutionary War began.

SO YOU SAY YOU WANT A REVOLUTION

Soon after shooting started, in May 1775, the Second Continental Congress met in Philadelphia and chose George Washington, a wealthy Virginia farmer, to lead the American army. Trouble was, Washington lacked gunpowder and money (the colonists resisted taxes even for their own military), and his troops were a motley collection of poorly armed farmers, hunters and merchants, who regularly quit and returned to their farms due to lack of pay.

The British 'Redcoats,' on the other hand, represented the most powerful military on earth. The inexperienced Washington had to improvise constantly, sometimes wisely retreating, sometimes engaging in ungentlemanly sneak attacks. During the winter of 1777 the American army nearly curled up in a ball and starved at Valley Forge (p212), Pennsylvania.

Want to read the Constitution, the Emancipation Proclamation and the Federalist Papers? Visit the National Archives website (www.archives .gov) and www.our documents.gov for these and much, much more.

Meanwhile, the Second Continental Congress was trying to articulate what exactly they were fighting for. In January 1776, Thomas Paine published the wildly popular *Common Sense,* which passionately argued for independence from England. Soon, independence seemed not just logical, but noble and necessary, and on July 4, 1776, a fortuitous collection of intellectuals finalized and signed the Declaration of Independence. Largely written by Thomas Jefferson, it elevated the 13 colonies' particular gripes against the monarchy into a universal declaration of individual rights and republican government. It was so moving it helped inspire revolutions elsewhere, and famously begins:

> We hold these truths to be self-evident: That all men are created equal; that they are endowed by their Creator with certain unalienable rights; that among these are life, liberty, and the pursuit of happiness. That to secure these rights, governments are instituted among men, deriving their just powers from the consent of the governed.

1776	1787	1791
On July 4, American colonies sign the Declaration of Independence. Significant Americans who created this document include John Hancock, Samuel Adams, John Adams, Benjamin Franklin and Thomas Jefferson.	Constitutional Convention in Philadelphia draws up the US Constitution; Alexander Hamilton and particularly James Madison play important roles. Federal power is balanced between the presidency, Congress and the judiciary.	Bill of Rights adopted as constitutional amendments articulating citizens' rights, including: freedom of speech, assembly, religion and the press; right to bear arms; and the right to due process of law and a speedy, fair trial by a jury of one's peers.

However, to succeed on the battlefield, General Washington needed help, not high sentiment; in 1778, Benjamin Franklin persuaded France (always eager to trouble England) to ally with the revolutionaries, and they provided the troops, material and sea power that won the war. The British surrendered at Yorktown, Virginia, in 1781, and two years later the Treaty of Paris formally recognized the 'United States of America.'

At first, the nation's loose confederation of states, squabbling and competing like hens at a grain bucket, were hardly 'united.' So the founders gathered again in Philadelphia, tinkered like mechanics, and in 1787 drafted a new-and-improved Constitution: the US government was given a stronger federal center, with checks and balances between its three major branches; and to guard against the abuse of centralized power, a citizen's Bill of Rights was approved in 1791.

With the Constitution, the scope of the American Revolution solidified: a radical change in government; and preservation of the economic and social status quos. Rich landholders kept their property, which included their slaves; Native Americans were excluded from the nation; and women were excluded from politics. These blatant discrepancies and injustices were widely noted (rather snidely by Europeans); they were the results of pragmatic compromise (such as to get slave-dependent Southern states to agree) and of the widespread belief in the essential rightness of arrangements.

As a result, from that moment till now, US history has pulsed with the ongoing struggle to define 'all' and 'equal' and 'liberty' – to take the universal language of America's founding and either rectify or justify the inevitable disparities that have bedeviled this democratic society.

WESTWARD, HO!

As the 19th century dawned, proof of the 'rightness' of the American experiment appeared everywhere, and self-satisfied optimism was the mood of the day. With the invention of the cotton gin (1793) – followed by threshers, reapers, mowers and later combines – agriculture was industrialized, and US commerce surged. The 1803 Louisiana Purchase doubled US territory, and expansion west of the Appalachians began in earnest.

Relations between the US and Britain – despite lively trade – remained tense. The British maintained forts in the Ohio Valley, and enjoyed inciting the Indians to harass American settlers, while Britain's navy harassed US ships. In 1812, the US declared war on England again, but the two-year conflict ended limply, without much gained by either side. The British abandoned their forts, and the US renewed its vow to avoid Europe's 'entangling alliances.' One result was the 1823 Monroe Doctrine, which declared that henceforth all of the Americas were closed to European colonialism. So there.

Undaunted Courage (1995) by Stephen Ambrose follows the Lewis and Clark expedition on its extraordinary journey west to the Pacific and back again. You can follow much of their route today.

Lincoln (1996) by David Herbert Donald is easily the best biography of perhaps the greatest American president. Humble yet driven, compassionate but fearless, Lincoln rose from nothing to save his nation.

1803	1803–6	1812
With the Louisiana Purchase, France's Napoleon (preparing for war with England) sells the Louisiana territory to the US for a measly $15 million, thereby extending US territory from the Mississippi River to the Rocky Mountains.	President Thomas Jefferson sends Meriwether Lewis and William Clark to kick the tires on the Louisiana Purchase. Their legendary expedition trailblazes from St Louis to the Pacific Ocean and back.	War of 1812 starts with battles against the British and Native Americans around the Great Lakes

In the 1830s and 1840s, eyes growing wider with nationalist fervor and dreams of continental expansion, many Americans came to believe it was 'Manifest Destiny' that some, no, *all* the land should be theirs. The 1830 Indian Removal Act aimed to clear one obstacle (see p49), while the building of the railroads cleared another, linking Midwest farmers with East Coast markets.

James McPherson is the Civil War's preeminent historian, and his *Battle Cry of Freedom* (1988) somehow gets the whole heartbreaking saga between two covers.

In 1836 a group of Texans fomented a revolution against Mexico (remember the Alamo? p707). Ten years later, the US annexed the Texas Republic, and when Mexico complained, the US simply waged war to take it – and while they were at it, they wanted California too. In 1848, Mexico was soundly defeated and ceded this territory to the US, adding just a bit more land with the 1853 Gadsden Purchase. This completed the USA's continental expansion. Except for those pesky Indians, Americans had it all, sea to shining sea.

By a remarkable coincidence, only days after the 1848 treaty with Mexico was signed, gold was discovered near Sacramento, California (p983). By 1849, surging rivers of wagon trains were creaking west filled with miners, pioneers, entrepreneurs, immigrants, outlaws and prostitutes, all seeking their fortune. This made for exciting, legendary times, but throughout loomed a troubling question that had simmered to the boiling point.

As new states were added to America, would they be slave states or free states? The nation's future depended on the answer.

A HOUSE DIVIDED

The US Constitution hadn't ended slavery, but it had given Congress the power to approve or disapprove slavery in new states. As a result, debates raged constantly over slavery's expansion, particularly since this shaped the unfolding balance of political power between the industrial North and the agrarian South, called the Slave Power.

Authoritative and sobering, *Bury My Heart at Wounded Knee* (1970) by Dee Brown tells the story of the late-19th-century Indian Wars from the perspective of the Native Americans.

Since the founding, Southern politicians had dominated government and rabidly defended slavery as 'natural and normal.' This enraged northern abolitionists (who also assisted the 'Underground Railroad,' a series of safe havens ferrying runaway slaves to the North). But most Northern politicians weren't so much anti-slavery as pro free labor. They feared ending slavery with a penstroke would be ruinous. Limit slavery, they reasoned, and in the competition with industry and free labor, slavery would wither without inciting a violent slave revolt – a constantly feared possibility. Indeed, in 1859, radical abolitionist John Brown tried (unsuccessfully) to spark just that by raiding the federal arsenal at Harpers Ferry, West Virginia (p367).

The economics of slavery were undeniable: in 1860, the market value of the South's human property was about $3 billion. Were plantation owners ever going to let that walk free? Also, the South exported three-quarters of the

1823	1841	1844
President James Monroe articulates the Monroe Doctrine, seeking to end European military interventions in the Americas. It is later extended (as by Teddy Roosevelt) to justify US interventions in Latin America and the western hemisphere.	First wagon trains follow new Oregon Trail to California. The route extends the older Santa Fe Trail, and by 1845, over 3000 pioneers a year are emigrating to the West.	Invented in 1838, the first telegraph line is inaugurated in 1844 with the phrase 'What hath God wrought.' In 1845, Congress approves plan for building the transcontinental railroad. Together, telegraph and train open the frontier.

world's cotton, which accounted for about half of US exports. The Southern economy supported the nation's economy, and it required slaves.

The 1860 presidential election became a referendum on this issue, and the election was won by a young politician who favored limiting slavery and the Slave Power: Abraham Lincoln.

For the South, even the threat of federal limits was too onerous to abide, and as Lincoln took office, 11 states (called the Confederacy) seceded from the union. Now, could Lincoln allow these states to walk free? If any unhappy state could leave the nation 'at pleasure,' wouldn't that destroy republican government itself? In 1865, in his second inaugural address, Lincoln eloquently expressed this dilemma: 'Both parties deprecated war; but one of them would make war rather than let the nation survive; and the other would accept war rather than let it perish. And the war came.'

In April 1861, the Confederacy attacked Fort Sumter in Charleston, South Carolina, and the Civil War came. Over the next four years the carnage was as gruesome as in any war to that point in history. By the end, 620,000 soldiers, nearly an entire generation of young men, were dead; southern plantations and cities (most notably Atlanta) lay sacked and burned. The course of the war, and all the ways it could have unfolded, remain the subject of impassioned debate. Both sides had their share of ineffectual and cunning leaders and used troops recklessly; both had moments of demoralization and determination. The North's industrial might provided an advantage, but its victory was not preordained; it unfolded battle by bloody battle.

As fighting progressed, Lincoln recognized that if the war didn't end slavery outright, victory would be pointless. In 1863, his Emancipation Proclamation expanded the war's aims and freed the South's four million slaves (an act officially accomplished by the Constitution's 13th Amendment in 1865). In April 1865, Confederate General Robert E Lee surrendered to Union General Ulysses S Grant in Appomattox, Virginia. Slavery was over, and the Union had been saved.

Beyond the Hundredth Meridian (1954), Wallace Stegner's biography of geologist John Wesley Powell, is essential reading – a wise, sharply written account of when America's Edenic continental visions first met the West's dry reality.

STIRRING THE POT: SEGREGATION & IMMIGRATION

Black Americans quickly learned that the Civil War ended an economic system of forced labor, but the society they entered remained largely, and often deeply, racist. During Reconstruction, from 1865–77, the civil rights of ex-slaves were protected by the federal government, which also extracted reparations from Southern states and generally lorded victory over the losers. Ill-will and bad feelings ran so deep that Civil War grudges are nursed to this day.

After Reconstruction, Southern states developed a system of 'sharecropping' that kept blacks indentured to the land for a measly share of crops, and they enacted endless laws aimed at keeping whites and blacks 'separate

Industrialization really did speed up American life. On farms, a bushel of wheat took three hours to produce in 1830, but only 10 minutes by 1900.

1849	1861–65	1882
After the discovery of gold near Sacramento in 1848, an epic gold rush sees 60,000 'forty-niners' flock to California's Mother Lode. San Francisco explodes from 800 to 25,000 folks, who mingle in a bawdy, lawless free-for-all.	American Civil War between the North and the South (delineated by southern Pennsylvania's Mason-Dixon line). The war's end on April 9, 1865, is marred by President Lincoln's assassination a week later.	Racist, anti-Chinese sentiment, particularly in California (where over 50,000 Chinese immigrants have arrived since 1848) leads to the 1882 Chinese Exclusion Act, the only immigration law to exclude a specific race.

In *The Colonial and Little Missie* (2005), Larry McMurtry amiably and wryly chronicles how Buffalo Bill Cody almost singlehandedly invented two essential American icons: the 'Wild West' and the superstar.

but equal.' Black men were given the vote in 1870, but the South's seg-regationist 'Jim Crow' laws (which remained until the 1960s Civil Rights movement) effectively disenfranchised and impoverished blacks in every meaningful sphere of daily life.

Meanwhile, free from war, the US could finally turn its full attention west: the telegraph and the transcontinental railroad (completed in 1869) shrank time and space; the interior West was systematically explored and mapped for the first time; and the continent's overflowing natural resources (its gold and silver, its coal and forests) fueled a galloping industrialization. Of course, to fully exploit the West, the US had to solve its lingering 'Indian problem' (opposite). Still, the US truly appeared to the world like a 'land of opportunity,' and immigrants flooded in from Europe and Asia (in total, about 25 million people arrived from 1880 to 1920). Poles, Germans, Irish, Italians, Russians, Jews, Chinese and more came to build the nation's railroads, smelt its steel, harvest its grain and slaughter its cattle.

This fed an urban migration that made the late 19th century the age of cities. In particular, New York, Chicago and Philadelphia swelled to rival London and Paris as global centers of industry and commerce. These crowded, buzzing multiethnic hives both spurred the xenophobic fears of whites and gave rise to the dream that America could become a unique 'melting pot' of the world's cultures.

ROBBER BARONS & PROGRESSIVE REFORMERS

For American business, laissez-faire economic policy, the industrial revolution and hordes of cheap labor equaled towering piles of cash. Industrialists like JP Morgan, Andrew Carnegy and John D Rockefeller became politically powerful 'robber barons' controlling vast monopolies (or trusts) in oil, banking, railroads and steel. These paragons of capitalism were America's version of royalty, to be crowned by Wall Street.

In *The Souls of Black Folk* (1903), W.E.B. Du Bois, one of America's most formidable intellects, poetically describes the racial dilemma facing 20th-century America. Sadly, it remains relevant for the 21st.

But as industrialism created wealth for the few, it consigned many to poverty and dangerous, even deadly work in choking factories and sweatshops; this was vividly depicted in *The Jungle* (1906), Upton Sinclair's muckraking exposé of Chicago's unsavory meatpacking industry. Mechanization and piecework might be godsends to farming, textiles and automobile manufacturing (Henry Ford started churning out economically-priced Model Ts in 1908), but unchecked they sowed pain and injustice. Increasing protests sparked new, heated arguments pitting the rights of private property against the rights of people. Put politically, wasn't it the federal government's duty to intervene when an unregulated free market was, in effect, abusing, impoverishing and killing its own citizens? Whose liberty, whose welfare, deserved society's protection: business or labor?

Well, Rockefeller wasn't running a charity. In the 1880s, the Populist movement (which sought to help farmers) was an early effort to transform

---

1896

In *Plessy v. Ferguson*, the supreme court rules (regarding segregated railroad cars) that 'separate but equal' public facilities for blacks and whites are legal, arguing that the Constitution addresses only political, not social, equality.

1898

US annexes Hawaii, and victory in the Spanish-American War gives US control of the Philippines, Puerto Rico, and Guam, and indirect control of Cuba. Ensuing, bloody Philippine war for independence convinces US colonialism isn't its cup of tea.

1908

The first Model T car is built; Ford is soon selling one million a year

America's emerging class anger into a political force. Populism eventually petered out, to be replaced by the urban and more radical socialist movement, whose militant fringe was occupied by the International Workers of the World (IWW or Wobblies). Labor unions blossomed and strikes were frequent and often violent.

THE LAST AMERICANS

One of America's formative paradoxes is that the continent's 'first peoples' were the last to become citizens. This occurred in 1924 (in part to honor Native American service in WWI), and it cemented the unresolved end to the 19th-century's brutal Indian Wars: Indian reservations would remain separate nations within the nation, with their own laws and sometimes unclear obligations on both sides.

This isn't what anyone wanted. From the start, the continent's immigrant and Native peoples had always agreed that the happiest arrangement was separation.

And yet, opinions always differed on who should get to live exactly where. Intending to end these conflicts forever, President Andrew Jackson enacted 'Indian Removal' in 1830. This designated land west of the Mississippi River as 'Indian territory.' Indians were meant to remove themselves there, thus clearing the fertile valleys west of the Appalachians for white settlement and marketplace capitalism.

Tribes resisted, but in typical fashion, the US cajoled, threatened and bribed Indians to sign treaties and cooperate; when that failed, they used guns. The worst incident was the 1838 Trail of Tears, a forced march that killed over 4000 Cherokee. By 1844, three-quarters of the 120,000 Indians who had once lived east of the Mississippi had been successfully 'removed.'

Then, after 1853, the US found itself holding nearly the entire continent, with Indian territory smack in the middle. Particularly after the Civil War, pioneers and miners flooded west, settling everywhere, regardless of treaty boundaries. The government shrugged: crazy pioneers – what're you gonna do?

By 1871, the US was making and breaking new treaties so fast that they simply quit writing them. Ultimately, the US broke over 470 treaties, every one meant to last 'as long as grass grows or water runs.' But the nation kept finding gold, or it wanted the real estate, and it tired of asking permission to take it.

Abandoning fairness, the US abandoned any pretense at peaceful coexistence. To aid direct war, the late-19th-century extermination of the buffalo was an explicit (and successful) military strategy to starve the 'wild' nomadic Plains tribes who resisted forced relocation to reservations.

When, in 1876, the Sioux won a shocking battle at Little Bighorn, the last vestiges of US restraint vanished. The military relentlessly hounded tribes until, with the end of the Apache Wars in 1886, no armed Indian resistance remained.

Sequestered on impoverished reservations, Indians needed US help to survive. What they got was the misguided 1887 Dawes Act, which aimed to 'assimilate' Indians into white society by forcing them to abandon their heritage and language. With insult now heaped upon misery, many Indians stubbornly refused.

So, 37 years later, unable to erase America's indigenous cultures, the US invited them into the nation, and they accepted, sort of.

1914	**1917–18**	**1919**
Panama Canal opens, linking Atlantic and Pacific Oceans. US wins right to build and run the canal by shrewdly inciting a Panamanian revolt from Colombia, and then sending forces to 'protect' Panama's freedom.	President Woodrow Wilson enters US into WWI, pledging 'to make the world safe for democracy.' US mobilizes over 4 million troops, which suffer around 100,000 of the war's 8.5 million deaths.	The temperance movement champions the 18th amendment, banning alcohol. Prohibition is wildly unsuccessful, leading to *increased* drinking, large-scale bootlegging, and a heyday for organized crime. In 1933, Prohibition is repealed.

John Steinbeck's *The Grapes of Wrath* (1940) is a saga of Okies trying to escape the Dust Bowl for the promised land of California during the Depression.

In the first decades of the 20th century, socialist movements developed worldwide; in the US, most citizens rejected actual socialism, but many embraced its ideas and ways of thinking. Still, the Socialist party was a real force, so much so that socialist candidate Eugene Debs won 6% of the vote in the 1912 presidential election.

In order to calm labor unrest and thwart socialism, Progressives pursued a slew of reforms: the trusts were busted up, and eventually regulations established a 40-hour work week, improved worker and food safety, and outlawed child labor, among others.

Meanwhile, the US was developing a novel approach to imperialism, which President Williiam Howard Taft dubbed 'dollar diplomacy.' To feed its overproductive economic engine, the US was desperate to gain access to new international markets. The 1898 Spanish-American War showed the way: rather than wage war for territory, the US would henceforth pursue an 'informal empire' using private commerce and banking. America would intervene militarily only as a paternal, well-meaning global 'policeman': not to impose its own colonial rule (so yucky and expensive), but instead to protect regional security, financial stability, private property and open markets.

President Woodrow Wilson also helped develop this approach, which still informs US foreign policy. By the start of WWI, the US had transitioned from a debtor to a creditor nation, and Wilson understood that, despite widespread parochial isolationism, the US needed to be engaged in the international community. Though Wilson's League of Nations failed, his idea of a cooperative 'concert of nations' would be realized after WWII.

As the Great War erupted in Europe in 1914, the US officially maintained neutrality, though it profitably sold armaments to the Allies. Germany responded by attacking US freighters, and in 1917 the US reluctantly entered the fight against the Central Powers. Wilson was hard pressed to sell the war at home, and suppression of anti-war dissent became standing policy.

Both biography and history, *No Ordinary Time* (1994) by Doris Kearns Goodwin illuminates the incomparable Franklin and Eleanor Roosevelt and how the US homefront reacted during WWII.

After the war, moralistic calls for social reform resumed: Prohibition (outlawing liquor) was inaugurated, and in 1920 the feminist movement won a major victory when the 19th amendment gave women the right to vote. However, a tide of good feeling drowned out further reformist voices. America had won the war, the economy was humming, capitalism's worst abuses were softened, wages were rising, unemployment was falling, and the Jazz Age burst into full swing. Middle-class Americans evolved into modern-day consumers, oohing and aahing over their new electric appliances, their clothes washers and refrigerators. For awhile, despite ongoing problems – ie poverty, crime, corruption – optimism ruled. Flappers danced the Charleston, radio and movies captivated millions, and stock prices kept going up, up, up, until…

1920s	1933–38	1941–45
Spurred by a massive African American migration to northern cities, the Harlem Renaissance inspires an intellectual flowering of literature, art, music and pride. Important figures are WEB Du Bois, Langston Hughes and Zora Neal Hurston.	Franklin D Roosevelt's New Deal establishes Social Security, the Fair Labor Standards Act, the Federal Deposit Insurance Corporation (protecting savings), Securities and Exchange Commission and the Federal Communications Commission.	US participation in WWII. America deploys over 16 million troops and suffers around 400,000 deaths. Overall, WWII civilian deaths outpace military deaths two to one, and total 60-70 million people from over 50 countries.

DEPRESSION, THE NEW DEAL, & WORLD WAR II

Whoops!

In October 1929, investors, worried over a gloomy global economy, started selling stocks, and seeing the selling, they panicked until they'd sold everything. The stock market crashed, and the US economy collapsed like a house of cards – revealing just how jerryrigged it actually was.

Thus began the Great Depression. Frightened banks called in their dodgy loans, people couldn't pay, and the banks folded. Millions lost their homes, farms, businesses and savings, and as much as 50% of the American workforce became unemployed. Scores hit the roads in search of work.

With despairing immediacy, Americans now understood that they didn't just need protection from industrialism's workplace sins, but society-wide insurance from market forces beyond their control. With belated embarrassment, the US moved to establish social programs that other industrialized nations had created decades earlier.

In 1932, Democrat Franklin D Roosevelt was elected president on the promise of a 'New Deal' to rescue the US from its crisis, and he would become a pivotal figure in US history. He significantly expanded the role of the federal government to protect citizens, such as with Social Security (insuring retirement savings), and he instituted government-funded employment programs and enormous public works (such as Hoover Dam, p818). In all, Roosevelt did much to ameliorate the pain of the Great Depression and of America's economic system; New Deal programs remain the foundation of US social policy.

When, once again, war broke out in Europe in 1939, the isolationist mood in America was as strong as ever. However, the extremely popular Roosevelt, elected to an unprecedented third term in 1940, understood that the US couldn't sit by and allow victory for the fascist, totalitarian regimes of Germany, Italy, Spain and Japan. Roosevelt did all he could to help Britain (such as providing military supplies with the Lend-Lease Act) and used his considerable persuasive powers to get a skittish Congress to go along.

Then, on December 7, 1941, Japan launched a surprise attack on Hawaii's Pearl Harbor (p1097), killing over 2000 Americans and sinking several battleships. As US isolationism transformed overnight into outrage, Roosevelt had the excuse he needed. Days later, Germany also declared war on the US, and America joined the Allied fight against Hitler and the Axis powers. From that moment, the US put almost its entire will and industrial prowess into the war effort.

Neither the Pacific nor the European theaters went well initially for the US. In the Pacific, fighting didn't turn around until the US unexpectedly routed the Japanese navy during a battle at Midway Island in June 1942. Afterward, the US drove Japan back with a series of brutal battles recapturing Pacific islands.

The Fifties (1993) by David Halberstam explores an almost schizophrenic era: television, Civil Rights, McCarthyism, Elvis Presley, suburbia and more coalesced into the decade that spawned modern America.

Civil Rights leader (and later Congressman) Andrew Young describes strategizing and marching with Martin Luther King in *An Easy Burden* (1996), a riveting, personal account from inside the Civil Rights movement.

1947–51	**1954**	**1963**
US Marshall Plan funnels $12 billion in material and financial aid to help Europe recover from WWII, and not coincidentally to help contain Soviet communist influence and to reignite the US economy.	In *Brown v. the Board of Education*, the Supreme Court rules that segregation in public schools is 'inherently unequal' and urges desegregation 'with all deliberate speed.' The fight to integrate schools spurs the Civil Rights movement.	President John F Kennedy assassinated by Lee Harvard Oswald on November 22nd while riding in a motorcade through Dealey Plaza, Dallas, Texas

The true story of a huge American business merger, *Barbarians at the Gate* (1993) oozes with the greed that was officially sanctioned during the Reagan 1980s.

In Europe, the US dealt the fatal blow to Germany with its massive D-Day invasion of France on June 6, 1944: unable to sustain a two-front war (the Soviet Union was savagely fighting on the eastern front), Germany surrendered in May 1945.

Nevertheless, Japan continued to battle. So newly elected President Harry Truman – worried that a US invasion of Japan would lead to unprecedented carnage – chose to drop experimental atomic bombs on Hiroshima and Nagasaki in August 1945. The products of a top-secret government program called the Manhattan Project, the bombs vaporized the cities and their inhabitants. Japan surrendered days later. The nuclear age was born.

SUBURBIA & THE SECOND AMERICAN REVOLUTION

Over the next three decades, the US enjoyed prosperity but little peace. World war was replaced with the Cold War, and America suffered a period of racial turmoil that was as violent as it was inevitable – the continuing steep price for the devil's bargain of the nation's founding.

Though wartime allies, the communist Soviet Union and the capitalist USA soon engaged in a running competition to dominate the globe. The two superpowers engaged in proxy wars (most notably the Korean War from 1950 to 1953 and the Vietnam War from 1959 to 1975), with only the mutual threat of nuclear annihilation keeping them from direct war. Founded in 1945, the United Nations couldn't overcome this worldwide ideological split and was largely ineffectual in preventing Cold War conflicts.

Its continent unscarred and its industry bulked up by the war, America entered an era of surreal affluence. In the 1950s, a mass migration left the cities for the suburbs, where affordable single-family homes sprung up like mushrooms after the rain. Americans drove cheap cars using cheap gas over brand-new interstate highways. They swam in the comforts of modern technology, swooned over television, and got busy, giving birth to a 'baby boom.'

No one captures Americans as well as Studs Terkel. In *Coming of Age* (1995) he asks septuagenarians what they think of America in the 20th century. They have, mmm, some sharp opinions.

Middle-class whites did, anyway. African Americans remained segregated, poor and unwelcome at the party. Echoing 19th-century abolitionist Frederick Douglass, the Southern Christian Leadership Coalition (SCLC), led by Martin Luther King Jr (p407), aimed to end segregation and 'save America's soul': to realize color-blind justice, universal equality and fairness in economic opportunity.

Beginning in the 1950s, King preached and organized nonviolent resistance in the form of bus boycotts, marches and sit-ins, mainly in the South. White authorities often met these protests with water hoses and batons, and demonstrations sometimes dissolved into riots, but with the 1964 Civil Rights Act, African Americans spurred a wave of Civil Rights legislation that swept away racist laws in what some called America's 'second revolution.' However, despite this, African Americans today still struggle to overcome persistent inequalities in education and employment.

1965–75	1969	1973
US military involvement in Vietnam War, in which it supports South Vietnam against communist North Vietnam. The war costs $150 billion and 58,000 American lives, compared to 4 million Vietnamese and 1.5 million Laotians and Cambodians.	American astronauts land on the moon, fulfilling President Kennedy's unlikely 1961 promise to accomplish this within a decade and culminating the 'space race' between the US and the USSR.	In *Roe v. Wade*, the Supreme Court legalizes abortion. Today, this victory for the women's liberation movement remains controversial and socially divisive, pitting 'right to choose' advocates against 'right to life' antiabortion foes.

Meanwhile, the 60s experienced further upheavals: rock 'n' roll spawned a youth rebellion, and drugs sent technicolor visions spinning in their heads. President John F Kennedy was assassinated in Dallas in 1963, followed by the assassinations in 1968 of his brother, Senator Robert Kennedy, and of Martin Luther King. Americans' faith in their leaders and government received further shocks: the bombings and brutalities of the Vietnam War, as seen on TV, led to horrified outrage and widespread student protests. Yet President Richard Nixon, elected in 1968 partly for promising an 'honorable end to the war,' only escalated US involvement and secretly bombed Laos and Cambodia. Then, in 1972, the Watergate scandal broke: a burglary at Democratic Party offices was, through dogged journalism, tied to President 'tricky Dick' Nixon, who became the first president to resign from office in 1974.

In addition, these decades saw the sexual revolution, women's liberation, the first struggles for gay rights and, with the 1962 publication of Rachel Carson's *Silent Spring,* the realization that the nation's vaunted industry had left a polluted, diseased environmental mess (p101).

Is it any wonder, then, that the 1970s became the solipsistic 'Me decade'? Cynical Americans, tired of fighting each other and being lied to by politicians, turned up the disco, popped birth-control pills and got their freak on. The US finally departed from Vietnam in 1975 (having failed to stop communism), and the economy hit the skids. The decade's popular music was so insipidly cheerful because in their hearts Americans couldn't have been more depressed.

A powerful, unmannered, nearly apolitical film, *United 93* (2007) recreates the September 11 attacks as they unfolded on the day terrorism shattered the USA's sense of safety and innocence.

PAX AMERICANA & THE WAR ON TERROR

In 1980, Republican California governor and former actor Ronald Reagan, correctly sensing the country's mood, campaigned for president by promising to make Americans feel good about America again. The affable Reagan won easily, and his election marked the start of a three-decade conservative shift in US politics and culture that continues to this day.

By 'feel good,' Reagan meant defeat communism, restore the economy, deregulate business and cut their taxes. To tackle the first two, he launched the biggest peacetime military build up in history, and dared the Soviets to keep up. They couldn't, and went broke trying, and the Soviet Union unexpectedly collapsed. Thus, the Cold War ended without a direct war between the superpowers.

What's the Matter with Kansas? (2004) by Thomas Frank is a hilarious, insightful, righteously indignant analysis of a state of mind – the right-wing conservative backlash – and where it came from.

However, military spending and tax cuts created enormous federal deficits, which hampered the presidency of Reagan's successor, George HW Bush. Despite winning a war – liberating Kuwait in 1991 after an Iraqi invasion – Bush was soundly defeated in the 1992 presidential election by a relatively unknown Democrat, Bill Clinton.

1980s	1989	1991
Over 500 New Deal–era financial institutions, deregulated under Reagan, play fast and loose with their customers' savings and fail, leaving the government on the hook for a $500 billion bailout. This cautionary tale goes unheeded.	In November, the Berlin Wall (built in 1961) is torn down, marking the official end of the Cold War between the US and the USSR (now Russia). The USA becomes the world's lone superpower.	The World Wide Web debuts on the internet. Over the next decade, Silicon Valley, CA, leads a high-tech revolution, remaking communications and media, and overvalued tech stocks drive the biggest boom and bust since the Great Depression.

Director Spike Lee's monumental documentary *When the Levees Broke* (2006) is an intimate, moving account of Hurricane Katrina's devastation of New Orleans and a shameful indictment of the government's response.

Clinton had the good fortune to catch the 1990s high-tech internet boom, which seemed to augur a 'new economy' based on white-collar telecommunications. The US economy erased its deficits and ran a surplus, and Clinton tried to pass universal health coverage (something left out of Roosevelt's New Deal). But conservatives blocked this expansion of the 'welfare state,' and then, when the promiscuous Clinton lied about an infidelity with a White House intern, Republicans came this close to impeaching him.

In 2000 (and again in 2004), George W Bush won the presidential elections so narrowly that the divided results seemed to epitomize an increasingly divided nation. The second Bush had the misfortune of presiding when the high-tech stock bubble burst in 2000, but he nevertheless enacted tax cuts (for the wealthy) that ensured federal deficits returned even greater than before.

Bush also championed the right-wing conservative 'backlash' that had been building since Reagan. This involved undoing environmental regulations, labor reforms and Civil Rights legislation, continuing Reagan's laissez-faire deregulation of industry, and fostering a moral, religious and cultural crusade espousing 'family values.'

Then, seemingly out of nowhere, on September 11, 2001 (now known as 9/11), Islamic terrorists flew hijacked planes into New York's World Trade Center and the Pentagon in Washington, DC. This catastrophic attack united Americans behind their president as he vowed revenge and declared a 'war on terror.' But the Al-Qaeda terrorists belonged to no nation, and it was quickly apparent this would mean a new kind of war.

Suspicious of political factoids? So are we – particularly during presidential elections. That's why we turn to Factcheck.org (www.factcheck.org) to help discern truth from 'truthiness'.

Bush passed the Patriot Act, which abridged citizen's civil rights in the effort to catch terrorists, and he revised long-standing US military policy to allow for 'preemptive attacks.' In October 2001 Bush attacked Afghanistan in an unsuccessful hunt for the Al-Qaeda terrorists, then he attacked Iraq in 2003 and toppled its anti-US dictator, Saddam Hussein. Since then, the president's justification for starting the Iraq War has been proven false, and Iraq has descended into a virtual civil war from which the US military can't seem to extract itself. Consequently, popular support for the war and for Bush have plummeted.

In 2005, the USA's most expensive natural disaster occurred when Hurricane Katrina devastated New Orleans and the Gulf Coast (p433 and p432). When federal relief efforts were slow to arrive and then inadequate, a sour mood reminiscent of the 1970s settled over the nation: government was untrustworthy, the economy was debt-ridden and troubled, the country was mired in an unwinnable war and morality-minded Americans were constantly bickering.

2001	**2003**	**2005**
On September 11, Al-Qaeda terrorists hijack four commercial airplanes, flying two into New York's World Trade Center towers (destroying them) and one into the Pentagon (the fourth plane crashes in Pennsylvania); 3000 people are killed.	On March 20, after citing dubious evidence Iraq possesses 'weapons of mass destruction,' Bush launches a preemptive war. Bush declares 'mission accomplished' on May 1, but guerrilla fighting and the Iraq War continues.	On August 29, Hurricane Katrina hits the Mississippi and Louisiana coasts, rupturing levees and flooding below-sea-level New Orleans. Over 1800 people die, and cost estimates range from $80 to $125 billion.

The Culture Karla Zimmerman

THE NATIONAL PSYCHE

To be honest, Americans are feeling a bit anxious. The country's superpowers are waning, and the nation – as well as most individuals – are living on borrowed money. The pesky war thing lingers, as do threats of terrorism. So when something like a sewer pipe breaks or a strange smell is sniffed on city streets, everyone gets jittery.

Meanwhile, more and more people keep immigrating to the USA, drawn to its wild and crazy image of success. Just look at that Bill Gates guy! He's raking in more than a billion bucks per year! But the country's rapidly changing ethnic makeup gives the old-timers pause. Who are these newcomers? Are they helping or hurting the country?

It's enough to make a nation stress eat – which may explain why it's gained a few pounds. By 2015, it's projected that 75% of Americans will be overweight and 41% obese, leading to epidemic proportions of diabetes, heart disease, strokes – OK, OK, enough already! Can someone please pass the fries? Or maybe turn on the TV? What would Oprah do?

For those who've been dwelling in caves, that's TV talk show host Oprah Winfrey, America's self-help queen. And she represents a big facet of American culture – the propensity to better oneself. Bookshelves, newspapers and television shows shout advice on how to tighten one's abs, cook healthier cupcakes, banish wrinkles, fall in love and most of all, become successful. According to the media, these things can be achieved through pilates, soy margarine and extreme wishing. Easy, huh? Plus self-help is classless. Everyone can improve their prospects in some capacity.

America's other great soothing and equalizing balm is pop culture. Without the connective tissue of Hollywood and rock 'n' roll, Homer Simpson and *American Idol*, it's possible the entire place would fall apart. For American society, pop culture's artistic faults become strengths – it's easy, fun, distracting, trendy, cheap and available to everyone. Americans will never all be the same, but through pop culture they have a public square and a common language. By the way, did you see what Angelina Jolie was wearing at her movie premiere? Shocking.

It should be noted that when we say Americans are 'not the same,' we mean it. The differences pile up so high it's a wonder the country doesn't blow its stack in chaos. There's rich and poor, red state and blue state (aka Republican conservative and Democratic liberal), white and ethnic, East Coast and West Coast. Americans use labels to try and make sense of it, ie NASCAR dad, soccer mom, Mexican American, Irish Catholic, Orthodox Jew. The labels never tell the whole story, though.

The United States remains an extraordinary study in contrasts. A place of incredible achievements and persistent inequalities, of perpetual optimism despite all evidence to the contrary. The latter is really the magic ingredient. Americans are living proof that a dream – and the freedom to pursue it – is the most transformative tool there is.

LIFESTYLE

What does the 'average' American family look like? It's hard to say. The nuclear family that defined the 1950s – with a stay-at-home mom, working dad and three kiddies – no longer fits. Well, it does for *The Simpsons*. But with nearly half of all marriages ending in divorce, and a quarter of children now living in single-parent homes, family life has changed.

Sure, it's strange the best film about American culture in recent years stars a sex-crazed, thong-wearing, chicken-toting foreigner, but see *Borat: Cultural Learnings of America for Make Benefit Glorious Nation of Kazakhstan* (2006) and believe it.

Lampooning a US high school civics textbook, complete with study guides and class exercises, Jon Stewart's *America: A Citizen's Guide to Democracy Inaction* (2004) was so subversive that Wal-Mart banned it.

It's trashy but captivating: TMZ (www.tmz.com) breaks entertainment's biggest stories, including celebrity arrests, breakups and who pigged out at dinner last night.

The median household income is $44,000. More often than not, if there are two parents in a household, both of them work. Eighty percent are high school graduates; 25% have graduated from college.

Americans are marrying later and having fewer children, though this applies mostly to US-born residents. Foreign-born immigrants tend to gather larger, multigenerational families under one roof. Over a quarter of immigrant households consist of five or more people, which is twice the national average.

Two-thirds of Americans own their own home, and be assured it's loaded up with a TV or four. The refrigerator likely is filled with junk food, which is why the nation is chubby and getting more so every year. The top five sources of calories in the typical diet are soda, pastries (mmm, doughnuts), hamburgers, pizza and potato chips. This explains why Americans, while fat, are also malnourished. Among preventable deaths, obesity-related problems remain the second-highest killer after tobacco.

It's not just the chips that are weighing on Americans – it's the lack of physical activity, too. Sitting around and watching the tube, surfing the internet, playing video games and driving everywhere does not make for a body beautiful. More than half of men and women only exercise a couple times per week; 25% don't exercise at all. That's nada, zilch. Not even a little walk.

Maybe it's because Americans are homebodies. When they travel, they like to stay local, heading to national parks and Disney World. Fewer than 27% have a passport, which means most people aren't leaving the country any time soon. Not that they'd have much time to go overseas: the average number of vacation days workers receive is a mere 12.4 annually – less than half that of Germany, France and most other European countries.

About 29% of Americans volunteer their time to help others or help a cause. This is truer in the Midwest, followed by the West, South and Northeast. And many Americans have decided to go green – sort of – as long as it doesn't inconvenience them too terribly. But certainly things like recycling and organic and local foods are on most people's radar screen.

Then there's health care, which has become a huge problem for most Americans. More than 15% of people are uninsured, and for those who are insured through their employers, out-of-pocket costs continue to climb to prohibitive amounts. A huge portion of the population can't access the care

---

58% of Americans age 18 to 25 think homosexuality is acceptable, compared to 50% of those age 26 and up, Pew Research shows.

One of America's favorite cultural symbols gets its close-up in Steven Ettlinger's *Twinkie, Deconstructed* (2007); learn what the snack cake's cream filling and rocket fuel have in common.

KNOW YOUR GENERATIONS

The American fondness for labels applies to age groups as well as everything else. Here's a quick rundown to help know your Generation X from Y, and then some.

- **Baby Boomers** – those born from 1946 to 1964. After American soldiers came home from WWII, they got busy with the ladies, and the birthrate exploded (hence the term 'baby boom'). This is the American-dream-grabbing generation: they worked hard, and financial rewards followed.

- **Generation X** – those born between 1961 and 1981, the angst-ridden group that doesn't buy into that American dream crap. Skepticism and alienation are its hallmarks.

- **Generation Y** – the group following Gen X, roughly those born from the early 1980s to early 1990s. Brash and self-confident, they came of age during the millennium and are the first to grow up with the internet.

- **Generation Next** – it overlaps with Gen Y, but basically applies to those born in the 1990s. Weaned on iPods, text messaging, instant messaging and MySpace, they are a work in progress. Stay tuned (and check their MySpace page for updates).

DOS & DON'TS

By and large, the American motto is to live and let live. But there are certain norms of behavior foreign visitors should be aware of.

- Do return friendly greetings. 'Hi. How are you?' is expected to receive a cheerful, 'Thanks, I'm fine,' not 'My boyfriend dumped me, my irritable bowel is acting up and my car got towed.' Actual complaints are frowned upon.
- Don't be overly physical when you greet someone. Some Americans will hug, but many more, especially men, will just shake hands. Borat-style lip kisses will likely get you slapped. Or arrested.
- Don't take your clothes off in public. Especially on beaches, don't disrobe or, for women, go topless, unless others are already showing skin.
- Don't expect Americans to know much about your country. Americans are usually excited to meet foreigners, but that doesn't mean they know where Germany is. And don't take it personally – only half of Americans can even find New York on a map.
- Do be on time. Americans consider it rude to be kept waiting.
- Don't smoke inside a building without asking first. Nonsmoking laws are increasingly common, and many people feel strongly against second-hand smoke in their homes.
- Do be respectful of police officers. Americans may be casual, but the police expect to be called 'Sir,' 'Ma'am' or simply 'Officer.' Note that Pig, Cop and Fuzz are *not* terms of endearment.

and medicine they need due to its cost. Meanwhile, America outspends other developed countries on health care by two to four times – to the tune of $1.7 trillion annually, or about $6000 per person. Still, covered or not, more and more Americans are just one serious health crisis away from poverty and bankruptcy.

ECONOMY

Ask an American like Bill Gates about the economy, and he'd reply, 'Rockin'!' Ask Joe Wal-Mart–Worker the same question, and he'd reply, 'Not so good.' That's because Bill makes $148,200 per hour, every hour of every day, or $1.3 billion per year. Meanwhile, Joe makes $8.25 an hour as a Wal-Mart associate (aka sales clerk), or $17,160 per year for his full-time, 40-hour-per-week gig. Intriguingly, the poverty level for a family of three is $17,170 per year. So it seems working full-time for the country's biggest private corporation leaves you destitute.

Of the 25 million kids in America between the ages of 9 and 14, 77% of them have a television in their bedroom.

The old adage of 'the rich get richer, while the poor get poorer' is becoming an American reality. Since 1975, almost all gains in household income have gone to the top 20% (the upper middle class and the millionaires), who also earn 55% of the nation's annual income and control 80% of its wealth. Meanwhile, the poverty rate has grown each year throughout the 21st century. At last count (in 2004), 12.7% of Americans were poor, or more than 36 million people. Minorities feel it most keenly – 24.7% of African Americans and 21.9% of Hispanics are poor, compared to 8.6% of whites and 9.8% of Asians.

Sicko (2007), a documentary by love him or hate him filmmaker Michael Moore, examines the crumbling US health care system and its impact on citizens.

Technology and the global marketplace have exerted major changes on the US economy. If other countries can do it cheaper, well, too bad for the American worker (especially a unionized one). That job gets 'outsourced' overseas. The USA's once-mighty manufacturing industry – whose factory workers made up much of the middle class – has been hardest hit. Take the state of Michigan, ground zero for auto-making. It has lost close to 370,000 jobs since 2000, as cars made more cheaply overseas capture the market. Bye-bye comfortable middle-class living for these folks, because even as

People tell true stories about developing superpowers, working in morgues and more on the radio show *This American Life* (www.thisamerican life.org); listen via the online archive.

unemployment remains officially low (4.8% in 2007), the jobs available to replace the lost ones don't buy an equal lifestyle. Many of them pay at or just above the federal minimum wage, which Congress finally agreed to raise after a 10-year lag. It will become $7.25 per hour by 2009. Note this is still less than Joe Wal-Mart–Worker's salary, and it makes for a pretty cut-rate American dream. It's one of several reasons why two working parents – once the exception in the idyllic 1950s family – is now the rule. It's also why there's a permanent underclass of people who feel the system is rigged against them, so they refuse to participate – preferring to drop out of school and the workforce rather than 'sell out.'

In short, America is a relentless and at times unforgiving meritocracy. The United States is practically alone among industrialized democracies in requiring citizens to survive solely on wages (and accumulated wealth), and this is a large reason why poverty and economic inequities remain so pervasive. Despite the occasional effort to nationalize a major public service – such as education, childcare or health care – the country resists because of its aversion to more taxes and federal intrusions into the private sphere. In the US, if you don't inherit it, you have to earn it, and what you earn often depends as much on where you start as on how hard you work.

The documentary *Maxed Out: Hard Times, Easy Credit and the Era of Predatory Lenders* (2006) tries to figure out why Americans keep spending money they don't have.

POPULATION

The total US population is around 300 million, making it the world's third-most populous country, but still well behind India and China, which both pack in over a billion people. Broken down by ethnicity, the USA is 67% white, 14.4% Hispanic, 12.8% African American, 4.3% Asian and 1% Native American.

Since the 2000 census, the US population has grown by roughly 6.4%, and ethnic populations are bulking up the fastest. While the number of whites grew by just 1%, all other major groups jumped between about 5% and 13%, with Hispanics leading the charge.

Immigration drives the story behind US population statistics, and accounts for well over half of the country's annual population growth. Immigrants tend to put down stakes in major metropolitan gateways, such as in California, Texas, New York, Florida and Illinois, which also happen to be the nation's five most populous states. Thus, immigrant settlement patterns mirror the country as a whole, which favors the coasts and big cities and leaves the middle of the country sparsely populated.

Which state is the healthiest? Smartest? Richest? Find out at the US Census Bureau (www .census.gov), where they've crunched the numbers.

So there's lots of room to roam out on the range. States like Wyoming, Montana and North Dakota each have less than 10 people per sq mile (psm). Alaska is the loneliest place of all, with a mere 1.2 psm (a number that pleases the local moose population greatly). Compare that to New Jersey, the most densely populated state, where people are practically living on top of each other at 1175 psm. Rhode Island could use a little elbow room, too, with 1030 psm. The USA as a whole has an average density of 84 psm, when stacked up next to Europe (134 psm) and Asia (203 psm).

Americans like all that company, though. Most are city folk, with 80% living in an urban environment. Rural dwellers are becoming few and far between.

One notable twist in America's population story is the decentralization of cities, which is happening faster than at any other time in history. Take Orlando, for example. In 30 years the city has grown fivefold in size, but the fastest growth has come at the city's margins where exurbs lure residents with larger houses and scads of new big-box retailers. It's a growing trend in metro areas.

AMERICA 2030: A NEW LOOK

For the next several decades, the face of America will develop two distinct profiles: one side will be older and predominantly white; the other side will be young and mostly ethnic.

The makeover is already in progress. In 2005, Whites' average age was 40.3 years, while Hispanics averaged 27.2 years. Of all ethnicities, Hispanics are the youngest; they currently account for more than 20% of America's preschoolers.

And their numbers are on the rise. By 2050, Hispanics are predicted to account for nearly 25% of the US population, African Americans 14.6% and Asians 8%. Whites will make up only 50% of the population – on the cusp of becoming the nation's largest minority. And an old one to boot.

As you may have heard, the baby-boomer generation (people born between 1946 and 1964) is nearing retirement. This population bubble will swell the ranks of seniors until, by 2030, one in five Americans will be over 65. The old-timers will concentrate in Florida, of course, the traditional land of golfing and early-bird suppers. It has the highest share of elderly residents at 16.8%. But New England is fast becoming the new Florida. Maine is the region's grayest state, with a median age of 41.1 years. By 2030, that's expected to rise to a rickety 47 years. No doubt Viagra and prune marketers will soon be making their way north.

MULTICULTURALISM

From the get-go, America was called a 'melting pot,' which presumed that newcomers came and blended into the existing American fabric. The country hasn't let go of that sentiment completely. On one hand, diversity is celebrated (Cinco de Mayo, Martin Luther King Day and Chinese New Year all get their due), but on the other hand, America likes its status quo.

In 2007 the nation's minority numbers topped 100 million people – a third of the total population – for the first time. And those numbers are expected to keep on rising (see box above), so within a quarter-century, America will be a nation of minorities, with no race in the majority. As the nation looks ahead to this momentous day, the dialogue over ethnicity is becoming far more complex than black and white.

Immigration is at the crux of the matter. It accounts for more than 40% of the USA's growth since 2000. About one million newcomers enter legally each year, with the majority from Mexico, then Asia and Europe. Estimates of illegal immigrants range from 7 million to 20 million currently in the country. And this is where Americans get edgy, especially as the issue gets politicized. 'Immigration reform' has become a Washington buzzword, as Congress tries to pass laws that make it tougher for immigrants to enter legally and harsher if they're caught here illegally. In response, immigrant communities – be they Mexican, Polish, Lao or Iraqi – have banded together to express their displeasure. May Day rallies in places like Chicago, Los Angeles and Dallas have drawn 300,000 to 500,000 people per event.

Meanwhile, America becomes a little less multi-culti tolerant, at least according to recent polls run by Pew research. Between 2000 and 2006, the percentage of people who felt immigrants are a burden because they take jobs and housing grew from 38% to 52%. More recently, those polled who say 'the growing number of newcomers threatens traditional American customs and values' grew from 40% to 48%. Such sentiments could be the product of a graying population. If we break the numbers up by age, more than half of 18 to 26 year olds believe immigration strengthens the nation, versus just a third of older folks.

Plus look at the evergrowing number of interethnic marriages and mixed-race children. Current projections are that by the year 2050, 45% of Hispanics, 35% of Asians and 20% of African Americans and whites will in fact be multiethnic or multiracial. By the 22nd century, those percentages will rise to 70%, 40% and 35%.

Author Joe Bageant takes readers on a wild tour through the taverns, churches and double-wide trailers of small-town, blue-collar Virginia in *Deer Hunting with Jesus: Dispatches from America's Class War* (2007).

Two-thirds of Americans age 18 to 24 can't find Iraq on a map, according to a *National Geographic* study. They can't find Louisiana or Ohio either (identified by only 33% and 43%, respectively).

However one characterizes America – as a melting pot, or a rainbow of not-yet-equal colors, or a mestizo nation – one thing is certain: something new is being created, and it will be here shortly.

RELIGION

When the Pilgrims came ashore, they unpacked their most cherished possession, the Protestant religion, and tilled its sensibilities into the USA's fertile soil. These funny-hat-wearing guys and gals valued the freedom to practice religion so highly they refused to make their faith official state policy. What's more, they forbade the government from doing anything that might sanction one religion or belief over another.

The irony is that, due to shifting religious preferences and recent immigration, Protestants no longer constitute the majority of Americans. Since 1993,

---

NATIVE AMERICA'S PEOPLE

Not that long ago they had the whole wide country to themselves. Today, Native Americans represent about 1% of the USA's total population.

Their 2.5 million people are spread out, though most live west of the Mississippi River (see p49 for the historical explanation why). Over half reside in 10 states: California and Oklahoma, which together contain 25% of the native population, followed by Arizona, Texas, New Mexico, New York, Washington, North Carolina, Michigan and Alaska. One-third of all Native Americans live on reservations. Many of the others have packed up to look for better opportunities in urban areas. Los Angeles and New York are the cities with the largest number of Native Americans. The award for largest percentage goes to Anchorage, where 7.3% of the city's population is Alaska Native (of which the primary group is Eskimo).

The Cherokee, Navajo, Choctaw, Sioux and Chippewa are the largest tribal groupings in the lower 48 (ie barring Alaska and Hawaii), with Cherokee leading the pack by far. The majority of groups speak English as their everyday language; the Navajo are the exception, where 43.6% speak their own language on a regular basis.

A host of social ills plague Native Americans. One in four lives in poverty, a rate that's twice that of the rest of the US population. Rates of alcoholism (550% higher), diabetes (200% higher), homicide (100% higher) and infant mortality are also disproportionate compared to other Americans. Are better times ahead? Tax-free gaming on reservations (in the form of casinos) has provided an influx of money for some groups. And a revitalization movement has emerged to encourage traditional song and dance, language programs, and healing and ritual ceremonies.

Powwows and festivals take place in spring and summer; Oklahoma's **Anadarko** (p685) and **Red Earth Native American Cultural Festival** (p683) are good places to take part in such activities. The Smithsonian's **National Museum of the American Indian** (p312) provides a high-level introduction to Native American culture, including languages, literature, arts, history and foods through its café.

Two authors offer excellent insight into contemporary Native American life. Sherman Alexie, a Spokane/Coeur d'Alene Native American, uses humor and wit to reshape Native American stereotypes. His book of stories *The Lone Ranger and Tonto Fistfight in Heaven* (1994) is a classic, following Thomas Builds-the-Fire, Victor and friends, and their exploits on the rez. Alexie published *Flight*, about a time-traveling half-Native America, half-Irish teen, in 2007. Louise Erdrich is a novelist and poet who draws on her Chippewa heritage to examine relationships among full and mixed-blood Native Americans and their questions of identity. *Love Medicine* (1984) tells the story of several disintegrating families on a North Dakota reservation; it won the National Book Critics Circle Award. In *The Painted Drum* (2005), the central character steals the title object in order to give it back to its rightful Native owners.

For further information, visit the **Native American Virtual Library** (www.hanksville.org/naresources), with links to activist, genealogy and media (*Chickasaw Times*) sites. The **Native Radio Network** (www.airos.org) has downloadable podcasts on Native issues.

Protestant numbers have declined steadily, from 63% to less than 50% currently, while other faiths have held their own or seen their numbers rise. Catholics represent about 25% of the country, with the denomination receiving a nice boost from the many Hispanics who immigrate here (although the recent priest sexual abuse scandals haven't helped recruitment efforts). Those practicing 'other religions' – Islam, Buddhism and Native American religions – have collectively risen from 3% to 7%. Judaism holds steady at 2%.

Interestingly, one of the fastest-growing categories is 'none.' The proportion of those who say they have 'no religion' has risen from 9% to 14% since 1993. Some in this catch-all category (perhaps as few as 5%) disavow religion altogether, but more nurse spiritual beliefs that simply fall outside the box. Age plays a role too – young people tend to be less religious than their elders. Twenty percent of 18 to 25 year olds say they practice no religion, according to a recent Pew survey.

All that said, America's biggest schism isn't between religions or even between faith and skepticism. It's between fundamentalist and progressive interpretations within each faith. So no one cares much if you're Catholic, Presbyterian, Buddhist or atheist. What they do care about are your views on abortion, contraception, gay rights, stem-cell research, teaching of evolution, school prayer and government displays of religious icons. America's Religious Right has pushed these issues onto center stage, and the group has been very effective at using politics to codify its conservative beliefs into law. This effort is unAmerican by constitution, and those Pilgrims we started with would be waving their hats in fury if they were around to see the separation of church and state they planted being uprooted.

It's one of America's biggest culture wars. And it's no coincidence it became inflamed when evangelical president George W Bush entered the White House.

MEDIA

Something has to fuel America's pop culture fixation, and the media is it. Once the domain of the daily newspaper and a handful of TV networks, American media has become much more over the past 15 years. And less – while the internet provides a dynamic free-for-all of expression, traditional media ownership consolidates at a worrisome pace.

Nearly every American home has a TV, and most homes have several. The official tally is 844 TVs per 1000 people. Pay the monthly fee, and a household can access hundreds of niche-focused cable channels. So if mom wants to see a cooking show on how to make crème brûlée (Food Network) or dad wants to rewatch the Bears tromp the Patriots in the 1986 Super Bowl (NFL Network), it's all at the tip of the remote control.

Three quarters of Americans log onto the internet regularly, and this is how many people get their news these days. Print media continues to struggle in the contest for American eyeballs, though plenty of newspapers, magazines and books still roll off the press. Radio stations crowd the dial, and new movies premiere weekly.

But aside from the internet, this great heaving beast of media is owned by a small handful of multinational conglomerates. Rupert Murdoch's News Corporation, Walt Disney Company, General Electric, Time Warner, Viacom, Sinclair and Clear Channel control most of the American market. Media domination is a newish state of affairs. It harkens back to 1996, when the Federal Communications Commission (FCC) deregulated media ownership. That meant a company like Clear Channel, which had been capped at owning 40 radio stations, could go on a spending spree and buy 1160 more (about half of all stations) – which is exactly what it did. It then came to own many

---

Sidebar notes:

Protestant numbers may be decreasing, but 'mega-churches' are growing: 1210 churches have weekly attendance of more than 2000 worshippers, a number that's doubled over the past five years.

Employees at the five major TV newsrooms (ABC, NBC, CBS, Fox and CNN) are over 90% white, over 85% male, and with one exception (CNN), over 75% Republican.

The Independent Media Institute runs www .alternet.org, a haven for independent, progressive journalism that includes current news, national columnists and individual blogs.

KIDS VERSUS PARENTS: THE TECHNOLOGY SMACKDOWN

It's being called the greatest generational divide since rock and roll. Kids fill their free time with YouTube, MySpace, instant messaging and text messaging, while their parents just shrug their shoulders in resignation. They don't understand it.

Literally – mom and dad can barely add a number into their cell phone; meanwhile, junior has his phone making short films that appear on the internet. Kids outpace their parents in technology to the extent that between 70% and 90% of families cede buying decisions to the younger generation, since the kids know more about computers, cell phones and related items. The situation is LOL, 4 sur.

major concert venues and ticketing agencies, and as a result, now wields a huge, homogenous influence over the music industry.

For more than a decade, this same story has played over and over. For companies, media concentration is great, as it lets them 'leverage' news, ideas and entertainment properties across the gamut of media outlets – to saturate markets, as they say. Consumers, however, are left with lots of channels, but few real choices. Good news coverage has been the prime casualty: mergers have led to staffing cuts, so that TV network foreign bureaus are half the size they once were, full-time radio news employees are down more than 40%, and newspapers continue to bleed journalists.

But then a funny thing started to happen. Rather than struggling in vain to make themselves heard through the mainstream media, Americans began using technology to go around it. People are now creating and sharing their own news, for free, person to person, via the internet. Blogs, websites and podcasts have achieved maximum cultural velocity. They're so mainstream at this point that 35% of internet users – or a total of 48 million Americans – have posted content to the web via a blog, web page or other method of electronic sharing. American cyberspace is chaotic, unwieldy, opinionated, obnoxious and passionate – it's basically democracy in action. With computers in hand, average citizens have changed the way the media game is played, and nothing could be more American than that.

'Bush Calls For Development of a National Air Conditioner' is but one of *The Onion*'s (www.the onion.com) outrageous, cheeky news stories.

SPORTS

Religion? Bah. Movies? Not so much. Family? Sorry. What really draws Americans together, sometimes slathered in blue body paint or with foam-rubber cheese wedges on their heads, is sports. It provides a social glue, so whether one is conservative or liberal, married or single, Mormon or pagan, come Monday at the office he or she is chatting about the weekend performance of their favorite team, along with everyone else.

Live out your (sports nerd) fantasies at www .fantasysports.yahoo .com, Yahoo's website for football, basketball and other fantasy league teams.

And Americans aren't just watching sports. They're also wagering on them. Football, in particular, brings out the wallet for the friendly bet. Fantasy Leagues do, too. It's estimated that 16 million adults, age 18 to 55, play fantasy sports in the USA, which entails not only minute statistical analysis of favorite players but also shelling out the cash to back up one's picks.

The fun and games go on all year long. In spring and summer there's baseball nearly every day. In fall and winter, a weekend or Monday night wouldn't feel right without a football game on, and through the long days and nights of winter there's plenty of basketball to keep the adrenaline going. Those are the big three sports. Car racing (see box opposite) has also revved up interest in recent years. Soccer limps along, basically attracting a following among immigrants who grew up with the sport in their country of origin. And poor ice hockey – no one cares except in northern climes (ie Minneapolis, Detroit, Buffalo).

You want to see American culture in all its glory? Head to the ballpark, football field or basketball court, and prepare for mania.

Baseball

C'mon, despite obnoxiously high salaries and its biggest stars being dogged by steroid rumors, baseball remains America's pastime. It may not command the same TV viewership (and subsequent advertising dollars) as football, but hey, baseball has 162 games over a season versus 16 for football.

Besides, baseball isn't about seeing it on TV – it's all about the live version. There's nothing better than being at the ballpark on a sunny day, sitting in the bleachers with a beer and hot dog, and indulging in the seventh-inning stretch, when the entire park erupts in a communal sing-along of 'Take Me Out to the Ballgame.' The play-offs, held every October, still deliver excitement and unexpected champions. The New York Yankees, Chicago Cubs and Boston Red Sox continue to be America's favorite teams, even when they suck. The most storied grounds are Chicago's Wrigley Field and Boston's Fenway, both beautiful in a historic kind of way and smack-dab in the middle of urban neighborhoods with bars on every corner. Newer stadiums attract crowds with gimmicks like an onsite swimming pool (Arizona's Chase Field), carousel and Ferris wheel rides (Detroit's Comerica Park) and sushi sold from the concession stands (Los Angeles' Dodger Stadium).

The website www.mlb.com is baseball's official home. Tickets are relatively inexpensive – bleacher seats average about $16 a seat at most stadiums – and easy to get for most games. Do it!

Don't know your on base percentage (OBP) from gross production average (GPA)? The Hardball Times (www.hardballtimes.com) can unleash your inner baseball stats-geek.

Football

Football has tackled the rest of American sports. It's big, it's physical, it's rolling in dough. With the shortest season and least number of games of any of the major sports, every match takes on the emotion of an epic battle, where the results matter and an unfortunate injury can be devastatingly lethal to the chances of an entire team.

Football's also the toughest because it's played in fall and winter in all manner of rain, sleet and snow. Some of history's most memorable matches have occurred at below-freezing temperatures. Green Bay Packers fans are in a class by themselves when it comes to severe weather. Their stadium in

In *Talladega Nights* (2006), funnyman Will Ferrell spoofs NASCAR. He plays dim-witted driver Ricky Bobby, racing's top star until pride brings him down. Can he regain his integrity (and wife, kids, money and car)?

START YOUR ENGINES

NASCAR – or more officially, the National Association for Stock Car Auto Racing – has played an unusual role in American culture. It flew under the radar for years, mostly thrilling fans in the Southeast, where it originated. Money started to flow in during the 1990s, and then it burst onto the national scene in a big way in 2002.

That's when the term 'NASCAR dad' entered the national lexicon, and came to define President George W Bush's support base – white, working class, conservative types who also happened to be fans of fast cars that drive around in circles. Much of the 2004 presidential campaign took place at racetracks, boosting the sport's reach even further. NASCAR races became the second-most-watched sport on TV, trailing only National Football League games. And more than one hundred Fortune 500 companies became involved via sponsorship. Dollar signs flashed.

Lately though, NASCAR is having an identity crisis. Its traditional fan base is irked that the sport tried to go upscale – merlot versus moonshine, as they say – and now NASCAR must woo them back.

Big names on the circuit include Jeff Gordon and Dale Earnhardt Jr. The Nextel Cup is the top-tier tour, with the Daytona 500 being the year's biggest race. Look for Republican candidates to be trackside.

Wisconsin, known as Lambeau Field, was the site of the infamous Ice Bowl, a 1967 championship game against the Dallas Cowboys where the temperature plummeted to 13°F below zero.

Different teams have dominated different decades: the Pittsburgh Steelers in the 1970s, the San Francisco 49ers in the 1980s, the Cowboys in the 1990s and the New England Patriots now. The league's official website, www.nfl.com, is packed with information. Tickets are expensive and hard to get (that's why many fans congregate in bars to watch instead).

This can even be true of college and high school football, which enjoy an intense amount of pomp and circumstance, with cheerleaders, marching bands, mascots, songs and mandatory pre- and post-game rituals, especially the tailgate – a full-blown beer and barbecue feast that takes place over portable grills in parking lots where games are played.

The rabidly popular Super Bowl is pro football's championship match, held in early February. The bowl games (ie Rose Bowl, Orange Bowl etc) are college football's title matches, held on New Year's Day and around.

The Super Bowl costs America $800 million dollars in lost workplace productivity as employees gossip about the game, make bets and shop for new TVs online

Basketball

Despite its prominence, professional basketball is starting to show signs of strain – mounting ticket prices prevent much of its traditional fan base from attending. At the same time, disadvantaged urban youth still play on street courts from coast to coast and cling to basketball as a way out. Increasing numbers of players are being recruited from Europe, South America and even China, giving the game an unexpectedly cosmopolitan flavor. The teams bringing in the most fans these days are the Chicago Bulls (thanks to the lingering Michael Jordan effect), Detroit Pistons (a rowdy crowd where riots have broken out), Cleveland Cavaliers (home of Lebron James, aka the new Michael Jordan) and San Antonio Spurs (recent winners of four championships). Small-market teams like Sacramento and Portland have some of the most true-blue fans, and such cities can be great places to take in a game. Check the National Basketball Association website (www.nba.com) for ticket information.

College level basketball also draws millions of fans, especially every spring when March Madness rolls around. This series of college play-off games culminates in the Final Four, when the four remaining teams compete for a spot in the championship game. The Cinderella stories and unexpected outcomes rival the pros for excitement. The games are widely televised – and bet upon. This is when Las Vegas bookies earn their keep.

Women play too, at both college and pro levels. It's not uncommon for certain college women's teams to outdraw the men's.

Arts

When searching for a metaphor that encapsulates America's arts, one is sorely tempted to use the Web (or, to be current, Web 2.0). Many of the characteristics of the internet revolution so perfectly match and amplify America's artistic persona that, if set free in a metaverse, the Web could be America's digital avatar.

Both are chaotic, democratic jumbles of high and low culture, in which the individual takes the reins of criticism and self-defined communities perform for themselves. Both are rebellious, obsessively personal, ahistorical (even antihistorical), deconstructive, collaborative and given to appropriation, if not outright theft. Both enjoy upsetting apple carts (anyone's, everyone's) and revel in the transformative dance of technology.

Historically, America's arts have shined brightest during modernism and postmodernism – and what's more postmodern than the internet? However, what the Web lacks is ethnicity and place, and no analogy for America will ever work without these. Geography and race together create the varied regionalism that is key to understanding America's arts. Further, despite Americans' affinity for technology, nature and wilderness inform the nation's soul and, consequently, much that its soul produces.

Discarding the Web as analogy and simply considering the fact of it, there is no question that digital technology is currently unmaking and remaking every single medium and influencing every aesthetic in the US. It's fun to guess but impossible to say exactly where this is going or how much, once the digits settle, will be different. What's exciting is that America (and the world) is in the middle of a real revolution, in which economics, production, distribution, tools, community, performance, expression and audience experience are all changing.

We can't wait to see what America 3.0 has in store.

LITERATURE

Not so long ago, the nation's imagination stirred whenever critics heralded the next 'Great American Novel.' Not *everyone* cared, but still, the novel was for over a century the vital engine of US culture and art. Now, who listens to critics, and have you seen what's on YouTube?

In today's glutted multimedia environment, US writers have to fight for wallets like everyone else, and the 'Great American Novel' is mere niche publishing. Yet reading survives. Americans spend over $25 billion a year on books, which is more than they spend on music and movie tickets combined. Bookstores are suffering due to web-retailers, but overall sales are growing.

Americans, it seems, are in no danger of losing their love of a well-told tale. Yes, taste has become personalized, ebooks and podcasts are changing storytelling, and the distinction between literature and genre fiction is playfully blurred. But each year reveals a pluralistic wealth of new and talented voices, all feverishly digesting what life in these United States is all about. In whatever form, great American writers still stir the pot.

Discovering America's Voice

America first articulated a vision of itself through its literature. Until the American Revolution, the continent's citizens identified largely with England, but after independence, an immediate call went out to develop a wholly American national voice. Despite much parochial hand-wringing, little

To read *Hip: The History* (2004) by John Leland is to watch an expert mechanic disassemble the racially charged, high-octane engine of American pop culture. It's so good it's bad.

Every American road trip needs some popcorn-salty satire: *Boomsday* (2007) by Christopher Buckley light-heartedly mocks the callous cynicism of US politics with a 'modest proposal' of Swiftian proportions.

In *The Fortress of Solitude* (2003), Jonathan Lethem evokes a block that contains a world: Brooklyn, the seventies, hip-hop, drugs and two boys – black and white – circling friendship.

progress was made until the 1820s, when writers took up the two aspects of American life that had no counterpart on the continent: wilderness and the frontier experience.

James Fenimore Cooper is credited with creating the first truly American literature with *The Pioneers* in 1823 (the first in his famous Leatherstocking adventures). Cooper portrayed the humble pioneer, gathering ethical and spiritual lessons through his contact with wilderness, as a more authentic, admirable figure than the refined European. In Cooper's crude humor and individualism, Americans first recognized themselves.

In his 1836 essay *Nature*, Ralph Waldo Emerson articulated similar ideas in intellectual terms. Emerson claimed that nature reflected God's instructions for humankind as plainly as the Bible did, and the individual could understand these through rational thought and self-reliance – in essence making a spiritual philosophy out of the Puritan religion. Emerson's writings became the core of the transcendentalist movement, which Henry David Thoreau championed in *Walden, Or, Life in the Woods* (1854).

Emerson's tragic opposite was Herman Melville, whose ambitious masterpiece *Moby Dick* (1851) was, in part, a cautionary tale of what happens when the individual accepts transcendentalist beliefs, and can thus distinguish good from evil with God-like clarity. Similarly, Nathaniel Hawthorne examined the dark side of conservative Puritan New England in *The Scarlet Letter* (1850).

Standing somewhat outside this dialogue, Edgar Allan Poe was the first American poet to achieve international acclaim. His gruesome stories (such as 'The Tell-Tale Heart,' 1843) helped popularize the short-story form, and he is credited with inventing the detective story, the horror story and science fiction, all extremely popular and enduring genres in America.

The celebration of the common man and nature reached its apotheosis in Walt Whitman, whose epic poem *Leaves of Grass* (1855) signaled the arrival of an American literary visionary. In Whitman's informal, intimate, rebellious free verse were songs of individualism, democracy, earthly spirituality, taboo-breaking sexuality and joyous optimism that encapsulated the heart of the new nation. Even today, Whitman remains a touchstone for American writers.

The Great American Novel

After the Civil War (1861–65), two lasting literary trends emerged: realism and regionalism. Exemplifying the first was Stephen Crane's *The Red Badge of Courage* (1895), depicting the horror of the Civil War, and Upton Sinclair's *The Jungle* (1906), a shocking exposé of Chicago's meatpacking industry. Regionalism was spurred by the rapid late-19th-century settlement of the West; two of the more popular 'local colorist' writers were Western humorist Bret Harte and novelist Jack London (*Call of the Wild*, 1903).

However, Samuel Clemens – better known as Mark Twain – would come to define American letters. Twain wrote in the vernacular, loved 'tall tales' and reveled in satirical humor and absurdity, while his folksy, 'anti-intellectual' stance endeared him to everyday readers. He then yoked these staples of American storytelling to a transcendent purpose in *Huckleberry Finn* (1884), which made explicit the quintessential American narrative: necessitated by a primal moment of rebellion against his father, Huck embarks on a search for authenticity through which he discovers himself. The image of Huck and Jim – a poor white teenager and a runaway black slave – standing outside society's norms and floating together toward an uncertain future down the Mississippi River challenges American society still.

American poets struggle for notice, but the US has an active scene: *Poetry* (www.poetryfoundation .org) has news, interviews, poems and podcasts.

Orion Horncrackle, Fiesta Punch, Budgel Wolfscale: these are just a few of the Wyoming denizens populating Annie Proulx's *Bad Dirt* (2005), a Twain-esque collection of tall tales, hard luck and barbed-wire wit.

Disillusionment & Diversity

With the horrors of WWI and a newly industrialized society for fodder, American literature came fully into its own in the early 20th century.

Dubbed the Lost Generation, a number of US writers became expatriates in Europe, most famously Ernest Hemingway. His novel *The Sun Also Rises* (1926) exemplified the era, and his spare, stylized realism has been often imitated, never bettered.

F Scott Fitzgerald (*The Great Gatsby*, 1925) eviscerated East Coast society life, while John Steinbeck (*The Grapes of Wrath*, 1939) became the great voice of the West's rural and working poor. William Faulkner (*The Sound and the Fury*, 1929) examined the South's social rifts in dense but mordantly funny prose.

In the 1930s, Poe's detective story got a good once-over by Dashiell Hammett (*The Maltese Falcon*, 1930) and Raymond Chandler (*The Big Sleep*, 1939), whose hard-boiled urban realism was so morally dark it was dubbed 'noir.'

Between the world wars, the Harlem Renaissance flourished, as African American intellectuals and artists sought to instill pride in their culture and to undermine racist stereotypes. Among the most well-known writers were poets Langston Hughes and Claude McKay and novelist Zora Neale Hurston (*Their Eyes Were Watching God*, 1937).

After WWII, American writers delineated ever-sharper regional and ethnic divides, pursued stylistic experimentation and often caustically repudiated middle-class society's values.

In particular, writers of the 1950s Beat Generation threw themselves like Molotov cocktails on the profusion of smug suburban lawns: Jack Kerouac (*On the Road*, 1957), poet Allen Ginsberg (*Howl*, 1956) and William S Burroughs (*Naked Lunch*, 1959) celebrated nonconformity and transgressive, stream-of-consciousness writing.

JD Salinger (*The Catcher in the Rye*, 1951) and John Updike (*Rabbit, Run*, 1960) used humor to capture the ironic disaffections of modern life, while Norman Mailer (*The Naked and the Dead*, 1948) and Nelson Algren (*The Man with the Golden Arm*, 1949) pursued a more brutal, unflinching realism.

The South, always ripe with paradox, inspired the masterful Flannery O'Connor (*Wise Blood*, 1952) and Eudora Welty (*The Optimist's Daughter*, 1972). The mythic rural West found its modern-day poet laureate in Larry McMurtry (*Lonesome Dove*, 1986).

African American writing became more complex and urgent at this time. Richard Wright (*Black Boy*, 1945) and Ralph Ellison (*Invisible Man*, 1952) wrote passionately about racism, while James Baldwin became both an acclaimed African American writer (*Go Tell It on the Mountain*, 1953) and America's first openly gay writer (*Giovanni's Room*, 1956). Starting in the 1980s, African American women writers also came to prominence – notably Toni Morrison (*Beloved*, 1987) and Alice Walker (*The Color Purple*, 1983) – along with an ever-more-diverse, multiethnic panoply of voices, reflecting the ever-more-diverse society they lived in.

The Emperor's Children (2006) by Claire Messud, seen as a 21st-century F Scott Fitzgerald, tenderly shatters the pretensions of East Coast elites, in which reside the nation's naive presumptions.

Pick up *The Namesake* (2003) for Jhumpa Lahiri's exquisite prose, which just happens to describe a moving intergenerational tale of an Indian family settling and assimilating in America.

Unknown authors languishing in dusty garrets pining for publication? No way – they're telling stories in serial podcasts! Visit Podiobooks (http://podiobooks.com); they're free, but donations are *greatly* appreciated.

MUSIC

American popular music is the nation's heartbeat. It's John Lee Hooker's thumping growl and John Coltrane's soulful cascades; it's Hank Williams' yodel and Elvis' pout. It's Beyoncé and Bob Dylan, Duke Ellington and Patti Smith. It's a feeling as much as a form – always a foot-stomping, defiant good time, whether folks are boot scooting to bluegrass or sweating to zydeco.

No other American art has been as influential. Blues, jazz, country, rock and roll, hip-hop: download them to your iPod and you've got the soundtrack for the 20th century. The rest of the world has long returned the love, and

American music today is a joyful, freewheeling multicultural feast, in which genres and styles are mixed, matched, blended and blurred.

Only the music industry is not dancing happy. The digital revolution hit music first, and the 'problems' digital life poses to business hit music hardest: the obsolescence of physical media; uncontrolled public access; lack of copyright protections. CD sales (still 85% of all sales) have been falling for seven years; digital sales are rising fast, but not enough to stop an overall decline. Music, a $14.5 billion industry in 1999, dropped to an $11.5 billion industry in 2006, with music retailers closing faster than independent bookstores.

Despite waves of lawsuits, the industry seems powerless to stop illegal downloading. Estimates are that a billion songs are traded illegally every month – a testament to both the power of music and the unintended consequences of new media.

Blues

The South is the mother of American music, most of which has roots in the combustive frisson and interplay of black–white racial relations, whose troubled course was first set by the 'peculiar institution' of slavery. The blues developed out of the work songs, or 'shouts,' of black slaves and out

---

THE END IS NIGH! Edward Nawotka

Maybe it's the creeping dread from the War on Terror or the hangover from the flooding of New Orleans after Hurricane Katrina, but American writers are feeling pessimistic. Not since the 1950s and '60s have they been so obsessed with the apocalypse. Cormac McCarthy's The Road, about a father and son trekking across an infertile, dust-covered land blasted by nuclear war, won the 2007 Pulitzer Prize. Matthew Sharpe's Jamestown recasts the story of America's first English colony in a baffling, post-apocalyptic near future where New York and Brooklyn are fighting a civil war and the Native Americans are red because of sunburn from the lack of an ozone layer.

Many are still trying to deal with September 11. Don DeLillo's Falling Man imagines the terrorist attacks from the perspective of the hijackers and their victims; John Updike's Terrorist conceives of a homegrown plot to bomb the Holland Tunnel between New York and New Jersey; while Jess Walter's The Zero depicts the life of a New York cop who works for the Office of Liberty and Recovery giving tours of Ground Zero. Ken Kalfus's A Disorder Peculiar to the Country portrays a bitter Brooklyn couple on the edge of divorce who, each believing the other has died in the terrorist attacks, are – perversely – overjoyed.

Still others, including Geraldine Brook's March, Charles Frazier's Thirteen Moons, and EL Doctorow's The March use the milieu of the Civil War as a way to comment on our own divisive Red State/Blue State politics. Perhaps the most entertaining are the satirists George Saunders and Kelly Link, whose surreal and fantastical short stories in the collections In Persuasion Nation and Magic for Beginners, respectively, offer a subtle, biting and entertaining critique of suburban consumer culture run amok.

Even For One More Day, the latest trite bestseller from feel-good guy Mitch Albom, is a bit of a downer, describing as it does how an alcoholic, after failing to commit suicide, is given one more day to spend with the ghost of his dead mother and seek reconciliation. Oh my!

In nonfiction, no book has been more influential than Thomas Friedman's The World is Flat, which posits that globalization may ultimately marginalize America. Still, memoirists offer the most direct route into the heart of American life. Among the best recent titles are Sean Wiley's Oh the Glory of It All, a hilarious portrait of his madcap youth in San Francisco with his butter-baron father and socialite mother; JR Moehringer's The Tender Bar, about Moehringer's education at the hands of a dozen drunken denizens of a Long Island tavern; and Jeannette Walls' The Glass Castle, a rags-to-riches story that tracks with Walls' itinerant, homeless childhood to the Park Avenue high life.

of black spiritual songs and their 'call-and-response' pattern, both of which were adaptations of African music.

After the Civil War, transformed by the crucible of African American life in white US society, slave work songs became the blues. Improvisational and intensely personal, the blues remain at heart an immediate expression of individual pain, suffering, hope, desire and pride. Nearly all subsequent American music has tapped this deep well.

At the same time, African American Christian choral music evolved into gospel, whose greatest singer, Mahalia Jackson, came to prominence in the 1920s.

At the turn of the 20th century, traveling blues musicians, and particularly female blues singers, gained fame and employment across the South. Early pioneers include Robert Johnson, WC Handy, Leadbelly and Bessie Smith, who is still considered the best blues singer who ever lived.

After WWII, the blues dispersed north, particularly to Chicago, in the hands of a new generation of musicians – such as Muddy Waters, Buddy Guy and John Lee Hooker. Today, the blues flame is tended, and updated, by musicians like Robert Cray and Keb' Mo'.

Martin Scorsese Presents the Blues (2003): Can you capture the blues in a book? The personal stories in this loving compilation come mighty close. Then watch Scorsese's concert film Lightning in a Bottle (2004).

Jazz

A sibling to the blues, jazz developed concurrently out of similar roots.

Congo Square in New Orleans (see p438) – where slaves gathered to sing and dance in the early 19th century – is considered the 'birthplace' of jazz. Here, ex-slaves adapted the reed, horn and string instruments used by the city's African American Creoles – who themselves preferred formal European music – to play their own 'primitive,' African-influenced music. This fertile cross-pollination produced a steady stream of innovative sound.

The first variation was ragtime, so-called because of its 'ragged,' syncopated African rhythms. Beginning in the 1890s, ragtime was popularized by Scott Joplin and Irving Berlin, and was made widely accessible through sheet music and player-piano rolls.

Two excellent jazz magazines are Down Beat (www.downbeat.com), with an online 'Jazz 101' history section, and Jazz Times (www.jazztimes .com), with an online festival guide.

Dixieland jazz, centered on New Orleans' infamous Storyville district, soon followed. Buddy Bolden is credited with being the first true jazz musician, although Jelly Roll Morton liked to boast that he was the one who created jazz.

In 1917 Storyville was shut down and New Orleans jazz musicians dispersed. In 1919, bandleader King Oliver moved to Chicago, and his star trumpet player, Louis Armstrong, soon followed. Armstrong's distinctive vocals and talented improvisations led to the solo becoming an integral part of jazz, and Armstrong remains one of jazz's most beloved figures.

The 1920s and '30s are known as the Jazz Age, but music was just part of the greater flowering of African American culture during New York's Harlem Renaissance. Swing – an urbane, big-band jazz style – swept the country, led by innovative bandleaders Duke Ellington and Count Basie. Jazz singers Ella Fitzgerald and Billie Holiday, as well as guitarist BB King, combined the blues with jazz.

Ornette Coleman won the 2007 Pulitzer Prize for Sound Grammar, a live 2005 concert that captures this jazz titan at his innovative, complex, frenetic best.

After WWII, 'bebop' or 'bop' arose as a reaction against the smooth melodies and confining rhythms of big-band swing. In this, saxophonist Lester Young influenced a new crop of musicians, including Charlie Parker, Dizzy Gillespie and Thelonious Monk. Critics at first derided such 1950s and '60s permutations as cool jazz, hard-bop, free or avant-garde jazz, and fusion (which combined jazz and Latin or rock music) – but there was no stopping the postmodernist tide deconstructing jazz. Pioneers of this era include Miles Davis, Charles Mingus, John Coltrane and Ornette Coleman.

Today, no particular style predominates. Ragtime, Dixieland and swing all enjoy revivals, while musicians like Wynton Marsalis and Joshua Redman keep expanding this ever malleable, resilient form.

Folk & Country

Early Scottish, Irish and English immigrants brought their own instruments and folk music to America, and what emerged over time in the secluded Appalachian Mountains was fiddle-and-banjo hillbilly, or 'country,' music; in the Southwest, 'western' music was distinguished by steel guitars and larger bands. In the 1920s, these styles merged into 'country-and-western' music and became centered on Nashville, Tennessee, particularly once the *Grand Ole Opry* (see p476) began its radio broadcasts in 1925.

Jimmie Rodgers and the Carter Family were some of the first country musicians to become widely popular. In Kentucky, Bill Monroe and his Blue Mountain Boys mixed country with jazz and blues to create 'bluegrass.' Other notable early country musicians include Hank Williams, Johnny Cash, Willie Nelson, Patsy Cline and Loretta Lynn.

The tradition of American folk music was crystallized in Woody Guthrie, who traveled the country during the Depression singing politically conscious songs. In the 1940s, Pete Seeger also emerged as a tireless preserver of America's folk heritage. Folk experienced a revival during the 1960s protest movements, but then-folkie Bob Dylan ended it almost single-handedly when he picked up an electric guitar to shouts of 'traitor!'.

Country music influenced rock and roll in the 1950s, while rock-flavored country was dubbed 'rockabilly' (and country + rap = 'hick-hop'). In the 1980s, country and western achieved new levels of popularity with stars like Garth Brooks. Today, traditional country musicians include Shania Twain, the Dixie Chicks, Dwight Yoakam and Alan Jackson. Occupying the eclectic 'alt country' category are Lucinda Williams, Lyle Lovett and Steve Earle. For the current Austin music scene, see p701.

Rock & Roll

Most say rock and roll was born in 1954 the day Elvis Presley walked into Sam Philips' Sun Studios and recorded 'That's All Right.' Initially, radio stations weren't sure why a white country boy was singing black music, or whether they should play him. It wasn't until 1956 that Presley scored his first big breakthrough with 'Heartbreak Hotel,' and in some ways, America never recovered.

Musically, rock and roll was a hybrid of guitar-driven blues, black rhythm and blues (R&B), and white country-and-western music. R & B evolved in the 1940s out of swing and the blues and was then known as 'race music.' With rock and roll, white musicians (and some African American musicians) transformed 'race music' into something that white youths could embrace freely – and boy, did they.

Rock and roll instantly abetted a social revolution even more significant than its musical one: openly sexual, celebrating youth and dancing freely across the US color line, rock honestly scared the nation. Authorities worked so diligently to control 'juvenile delinquents' and to sanitize and suppress rock and roll that it might have withered if not for the early 1960s 'British Invasion', whereby the Beatles and the Rolling Stones, emulating Buddy Holly, Little Richard and others, shocked American rock back to life.

The 1960s witnessed a full-blown youth rebellion, epitomized by the drug-inspired psychedelic sounds of the Grateful Dead and Jefferson Airplane, and the electric wails of Janis Joplin, Jimi Hendrix, Bob Dylan and Patti Smith. Ever since, rock has been about music *and* lifestyle,

Honky-tonk country star Alan Jackson becomes soulfully romantic on *Like Red on a Rose* (2006). His voice is so buttery warm you understand why women fall for cowboys.

The term 'rock and roll' was originally an African American euphemism for sex. It first appeared in blues singer Trixie Smith's 1922 song 'My Daddy Rocks Me (With One Steady Roll).'

For all the alt rock and garage bands (still playing garages!) that fly below the music industry's promotional juggernaut, plug into *Magnet* (www.magnet magazine.com).

alternately torn between hedonism and seriousness, commercialism and authenticity.

Punk arrived in the late 1970s, led by the Ramones and the Dead Kennedys, as did the working-class rock of Bruce Springsteen and Tom Petty. As the counterculture became the culture in the 1980s, critics pronounced 'rock is dead,' but they were a tad premature. Rock was saved, as it's always been: by Talking Heads, REM, Nirvana, Pearl Jam; by splintering and evolving, whether it's called new wave, no wave, heavy metal, speed metal, grunge, prog rock, world beat, skate punk, goth, electronica and on and on.

Despite hip-hop having become today's outlaw sound, rock remains relevent, and it's not going anywhere. Cue up the White Stripes, the Yeah Yeah Yeahs, My Chemical Romance, Beck or Modest Mouse to hear why.

> The album is dead! Long live the album! My Chemical Romance's *The Black Parade* (2006) is old-school, bombastic, self-conscious rock laden with sly winks, infectious hooks and emo-punk wails.

Hip-Hop TophOne

From the ocean of sounds coming out of the early 1970s – funk, soul, Latin, reggae and rock and roll – young DJs from New York's the Bronx began to spin a groundbreaking mixture of records together in an effort to drive their dancefloors wild. An emcee would man the microphone, calling out rhymes and urging the dancers, or b-boys, into a frenzy. Hip-hop was born. Groups like Grandmaster Flash & the Furious Five and Afrika Bambaataa's SoulSonic Force were soon taking the party from the streets to the trendy clubs of Manhattan and mingling with punk and new wave bands like the Clash and Blondie. Graffiti artists Futura 2000, Keith Haring and Jean-Michel

---

MUSIC IN THE HOT, HOT SUN

Americans love a grassy lawn and an outdoor stage, and the last five years have seen a renaissance in music festival extravaganzas. More than bandstands, these are some of the nation's top 'musical, cultural, community experiences,' to quote grandpappy Lollapalooza.

In general, single-day tickets run from $40 to $85 and multiday passes from $150 to over $300. Book early on festival websites, which often list hotel and transport options (and sometimes packages).

For more, see www.bluesfestivalguide.com, www.bluesrevue.com and www.dirtylinen.com.

South by Southwest (SXSW; www.sxsw.com); Austin, TX (p699). Gargantuan event with 1,500 bands, 240 films and a digital expo; 10 days in mid-March.

Coachella (www.coachella.com), Indio, CA. Rocking hard in the desert; three days in late April.

New Orleans Jazz Fest (www.nojazzfest.com), LA. Major jazz fest, from cajun to blues; two weekends in late April/early May.

Sasquatch! (www.sasquatchfestival.com), George, WA. Rock and roll on the gorgeous Columbia River; two days in late May.

Bill Monroe Memorial Bean Blossom Bluegrass Festival (www.beanblossom.com), Bean Blossom, IN. The USA's oldest bluegrass festival; eight days in mid-June.

Bonnaroo (www.bonnaroo.com), Manchester, TN. Big-name rock, plus a comedy tent; four days in mid-June.

Lollapalooza (www.lollapalooza.com), Chicago, IL. Overwhelming rock lineup; three dazed days in early August.

Newport Folk Festival (www.festivalproductions.net/newportfolk/index.php), Newport, RI. Dylan went electric at this, the nation's preeminent folk gathering; three days in early August.

Bumbershoot (www.bumbershoot.org), Seattle, WA. Not just rock but dance, theater and comedy too; three days in early September.

Austin City Limits (www.aclfestival.com), TX. The long-running TV show hosts this musical party; three days in mid-September.

San Francisco Jazz Festival (www.sfjazz.org), CA. Artistic director Joshua Redman ensures this is a don't-miss jazz celebration; three weeks beginning late October.

Basquiat moved from the subways to the galleries, and soon to the worlds of fashion and advertising. By the mid-'80s hip-hop touched everyone, young and old, black and white, and everywhere in between.

As groups like RunDMC and the Beastie Boys sold millions, the sounds and styles of the growing hip-hop culture rapidly diversified. The 'gangsta rap' sound of NWA came out of Los Angeles, as Japan's DJ Krush composed monumental soundscapes and MC Solaar rapped about Parisian housing projects. Throughout the 1990s kids from all corners of the globe were rapping, break dancing, and painting their names on walls in emulation of the artists they adored.

Come the turn of the millennium, what started as some raggedy gang kids playing their parents' funk records at illegal block parties had evolved into a multibillion-dollar business. Russell Simmons and P Diddy stood atop media empires, and stars Queen Latifah and Will Smith were Hollywood royalty. A white rapper from Detroit, Eminem, sold millions of records and hip-hop finally overtook country as America's second-most-popular music. At the same time, the underground essence of hip-hop still thrived. Pictures of fresh graffiti spread instantly over websites, and the development of cheaper and simpler music programs gave rise to thousands of bedroom producers. Regional styles such as the American South's 'krunk' and the Bay Area's 'hyphy movement' rose from the grassroots to gain major airplay.

Today, many view hip-hop as a vapid wasteland of commercial excess – glorifying consumerism, misogyny, homophobia, drug use and a host of other ills. But just as the hedonistic days of arena rock and roll gave birth to the rebel child of punk, the offspring of hip-hop and DJ culture are ubiquitous and ever-evolving, constantly breaking the rules to create something new and exciting. The dream of Afrika Bambaataa to unify the world through this music may not be too far from reality.

PAINTING & SCULPTURE   Karen Levine

An ocean away from Europe's aristocratic patrons, religious commissions and historic art academies, colonial America was not exactly fertile ground for the visual arts. Few settlers had the time or money to devote to fine art, and the modest portraits and prints of the time reflect their makers' Old World tastes. It is telling that the best-known American-born painter of the 18th century, Benjamin West, only made his name after going to Rome. When West first visited the Vatican and saw the Apollo Belvedere, he is said to have betrayed his Yankee roots by exclaiming, 'My God! How like it is to a young Mohawk warrior!'

Shaping a National Identity

Artists played a pivotal role in the USA's early-19th-century expansion, disseminating images of far-flung territories and reinforcing the call to Manifest Destiny. Thomas Cole and his colleagues in the Hudson River School – Albert Bierstadt, Frederic Edwin Church and John Frederick Kensett, among others – translated European romanticism to the luminous wild landscapes of upstate New York, while Frederic Remington offered idealized, often stereotypical portraits of the Western frontier. Other artists, such as George Caleb Bingham and William Sidney Mount, focused on genre paintings or scenes of everyday life and exalted the American virtues of hard work and democracy.

After the Civil War and its accompanying industrialization, realism became increasingly prominent. Augustus Saint-Gaudens and John Quincy Adams Ward produced masterful marbles and bronzes for a variety of national monuments. Eastman Johnson painted nostalgic scenes of rural

Your face hurts from smiling after listening to *St. Elsewhere* (2006) by Gnarls Barkley: this pop, rap, soul, retro, kooky hip-hop mashup is seriously silly and wickedly good.

North American Indian Art (2004) by David W Penney: a curator at the Detroit Institute of Arts offers a very accessible introduction to the artistic traditions of America's indigenous cultures.

life, as did Winslow Homer, who later become renowned for deft watercolor seascapes. Perhaps the most daring example of realism was Thomas Eakins' *The Gross Clinic* (1875), which scandalized Philadelphia with its graphic depiction of a surgical procedure. This once-reviled painting is now one of the city's most treasured artworks.

An American Avant-Garde

Polite society's objections to Eakins' painting had nothing on the near-riots inspired by New York's Armory Show of 1913 – this exhibition introduced the nation to European modernism and changed the face of American art. Impressionism, fauvism and cubism were showcased, including the notorious 1912 *Nude Descending a Staircase (No. 2)* by Marcel Duchamp, a French artist who later became an American citizen. In 1917 Duchamp shocked audiences again with *Fountain*. The sculpture – an upended porcelain urinal signed 'R. Mutt' that was Duchamp's first publicly exhibited 'readymade' – was rejected by exhibition organizers on the grounds it wasn't art, but Duchamp's gesture has inspired generations of American artist-provocateurs, from Robert Rauschenberg and Andy Warhol to Sherrie Levine and Bruce Nauman.

The Armory Show was merely the first in a series of exhibitions evangelizing the radical aesthetic shifts of European modernism, and it was inevitable that American artists would begin to grapple with what they had seen. Alexander Calder, Joseph Cornell and Isamu Noguchi produced sculptures inspired by surrealism and constructivism; the precisionist paintings of Charles Demuth, Georgia O'Keeffe and Charles Sheeler combined realism with a touch of cubist geometry.

A History of African-American Artists: From 1792 to the Present (1993) by Romare Bearden and Harry Henderson: this delightfully anecdotal survey was a labor of love for artist Bearden, a central figure of the Harlem Renaissance.

EARLY AMERICAN PHOTOGRAPHY *Karen Levine*

No discussion of American art is complete without mention of photography, a vast and important subject whose practice is central to American identity. Americans took up photography as soon as news of its invention crossed the Atlantic in 1839, and portrait studios – some on four wheels – began to crop up as entrepreneurs of all stripes (some former painters or miniaturists) exploited the commercial possibilities. Translated into engravings and published in journals such as *Harper's Weekly*, these photographs brought the visages of politicians and celebrities to a hungry and fast-growing American public. More accessible than painted portraits, photography also allowed people from all walks of life, in rural settlements and big cities alike, to commission keepsake images of relatives, friends and even recently deceased loved ones.

It was not long before intrepid photographers were lugging their heavy equipment into the American wilderness. Figures such as Timothy O'Sullivan and Carleton Watkins produced awe-inspiring views of the Rocky Mountains and Yosemite that helped to encourage westward expansion. Mathew Brady famously documented devastated Civil War battlefields, while Eadweard Muybridge experimented with panoramic views and stop-motion photography. Unlike paintings and sculptures, which could rarely be seen by large audiences, photographs were easily and inexpensively reproduced in books, magazines and as picture postcards. As it became a ubiquitous part of popular culture, photography contributed greatly to Americans' understanding of their shifting social and political landscape.

Ever since, American photographers have influenced historic events while advancing the medium as an art form. Lewis Hine and Jacob Riis' early-20th-century scenes of poverty and exploitation are crucial to our understanding of social injustices of the time, as are Walker Evans and Dorothea Lange's indelible documents of Depression-era poverty. Berenice Abbott, Charles Sheeler and Edward Weston framed iconic views of the Manhattan skyline, contributing to New York's reputation as the quintessential modern metropolis. More recent celebrated American photographers include Ansel Adams, Diane Arbus, William Eggleston, Robert Frank, Nan Goldin and William Klein.

Picasso and American Art (2006) describes how American artists reacted when Picasso's provocations landed on these shores.

Given the national aversion to public arts funding, it is ironic that government support did much to advance the American vanguard while stimulating art with a political bent. In the 1930s, the Works Progress Administration's (WPA) Federal Art Project, part of Franklin D Roosevelt's New Deal (p51), commissioned murals, paintings and sculptures for public buildings nationwide. Thomas Hart Benton, Ben Shahn and Grant Wood, among other WPA artists, borrowed from Soviet social realism and Mexican muralists to forge a socially engaged figurative style with regional flavor. African American and female artists also benefited from the nondiscriminatory policies of the WPA, which employed Romare Bearden, Stuart Davis, Aaron Douglas and other figures associated with the Harlem Renaissance as well as Lee Krasner, Alice Neel and Louise Nevelson.

Abstract Expressionism

In the wake of WWII, American art underwent a sea change at the hands of New York school painters such as Franz Kline, Jackson Pollock and Mark Rothko. Moved by surrealism's celebration of spontaneity and the unconscious, these artists explored abstraction and its psychological potency through imposing scale and the gestural handling of paint. The movement's 'action painter' camp went extreme; Pollock, for example, made his drip paintings by pouring and splattering pigments over large canvases. Barnett Newman and Rothko exercised more subdued brushwork, creating epic yet ethereal paintings dominated by carefully composed fields of color. In the early 1950s, some artists began rendering figural subjects using abstract expressionism's loose, spontaneous brushstrokes; at the forefront of California's Bay Area figurative school, Elmer Bischoff, Richard Diebenkorn and David Park forged a distinctive hybrid style with their vigorously painted interiors and landscapes.

Many museums offer free podcasts about current artworks. The best include SFMOMA (www.sfmoma.org), MoMA (http://moma.org), the Walker (www.walkerart.org) and the Met (www.metmuseum.org). Before you visit, load up your iPod!

Abstract expressionism is widely considered to be the first truly original school of American art. Intriguingly, art historians have argued that the US used it as a tool for Cold War propaganda. Evidence suggests that the CIA funded traveling exhibitions of abstract expressionist works in order to promote American individualism and democracy overseas. Abstraction, it was hoped, would serve as an instructive antidote to the realist styles favored by Soviet regimes.

Art + Commodity = Pop

Once established in America, abstract expressionism reigned supreme; indeed, one of its best-known practitioners, Philip Guston, was attacked by critics when he unveiled his first figurative paintings in 1970. However, stylistic revolts began much earlier, in the mid-1950s. Most notably, Jasper Johns came to prominence with thickly painted renditions of ubiquitous symbols, including targets and the American flag, while Robert Rauschenberg assembled artworks from comics, ads and even – à la Duchamp – found objects (a mattress, a boot, a stuffed goat). Both artists helped break down traditional boundaries between painting and sculpture, opening the field for pop art in the 1960s.

Looking for a carrot museum, a gallery of monster toys, or a survey of restroom hand dryers? Find these and more at the Museum of Online Museums (www.coudal.com/moom).

America's postwar economic boom also influenced pop. Not only did artists embrace representation, they drew inspiration from consumer images – billboards, product packaging and media icons. Employing mundane mass-production techniques to silkscreen paintings of movie stars and Coke bottles, Andy Warhol helped topple the myth of the solitary artist laboring heroically in the studio. Roy Lichtenstein combined newsprint's humble benday dot with the representational conventions of comics. Other prominent pop artists include James Rosenquist, Ed Ruscha and Wayne Thiebaud.

Minimalism & Beyond

What became known as minimalism shared pop's interest in mass production, but all similarities ended there. Like the abstract expressionists, artists such as Donald Judd, Agnes Martin, Robert Ryman and Tony Smith eschewed representational subject matter; their cool, reductive works of the 1960s and '70s were often arranged in gridded compositions and fabricated from industrial materials. Sol LeWitt, meanwhile, was busy theorizing the related strand of conceptualism, arguing that the idea behind an artwork was more important than the object itself. Robert Irwin and James Turrell explored the realm of perception through spare, dematerialized installations of light, while Eva Hesse, Robert Morris, Richard Serra and Richard Tuttle lent their sculptures a sense of impermanence through malleable materials such as latex, felt, molten lead and wire.

In many ways, minimalism aimed to critique the gallery context and undermine the status of art as commodity. This was perhaps most dramatically demonstrated by land artists Walter De Maria, Michael Heizer and Robert Smithson, who created immense earthworks in the American heartland that no one could buy or sell.

The Contemporary Scene

The past few decades have witnessed an explosion of artistic approaches on the American scene, not to mention considerable controversy. By the 1980s, civil rights, feminism and AIDS activism had made inroads in visual culture; artists not only voiced political dissent through their work but embraced a range of once-marginalized media, from textiles and graffiti to video, sound and performance. The decade also ushered in the so-called Culture Wars, which commenced with tumult over photographs by Robert Mapplethorpe and Andres Serrano and reached a bitter conclusion in 1998, when the Supreme Court ruled that the National Endowment for the Arts could withhold funding from artists violating 'standards of decency and respect for the beliefs and values of the American public.'

Throughout this firestorm and beyond, American artists have continued to innovate and inspire – and not just domestically. A sign of the times is the last Whitney Biennial, originally conceived as a show of Americans, for Americans. The curators in 2006 dispensed with any attempt to survey contemporary American art and instead mounted an international exhibition addressing the 'post-American' zeitgeist. Without a doubt, the best American artists working today are as well known abroad as they are on home soil. Several worthy of attention: painters John Currin, Jeff Koons and Barry McGee; sculptors Robert Gober and Kiki Smith; sculptor and filmmaker Matthew Barney; video artists Doug Aitken, Tony Oursler and Bill Viola; photographers Tina Barney and Cindy Sherman; and installation artists Felix Gonzalez-Torres, Ann Hamilton, Anthony McCall and Kara Walker.

Critic Tyler Green's blog Modern Art Notes (www .artsjournal.com/man) offers a smart, opinionated roundup of all the latest art-world news, from the happy to the scandalous.

Keep abreast of exhibitions and art-world happenings with the monthlies *ARTnews* (www.artnewsonline .com), *Artforum* (http:// artforum.com) and *Art in America* (www .artinamerica magazine.com).

FILM

How's this for a plot twist? No less an American icon as Hollywood, is increasingly the product of an internationalized cinema and film culture. While, true to their parochial hearts, American audiences remain steadfastly indifferent to foreign films, that hasn't stopped 'foreigners' from infiltrating Hollywood and – along with the dream factory's sexy A-list celebrities – creating the myths and amusements that so often embody America, to itself and the world.

This evolution is partly pure business: Hollywood studios are the gaudy baubles of multinational corporations, and funding flows to talent that brings the biggest grosses – measured globally, not nationally – regardless of nationality.

But this shift is also creative. It's Hollywood's recognition that if the studios don't incorporate the immense filmmaking talent emerging worldwide, they will be made irrelevant by it. Cooption is an old Hollywood strategy; most recently, it was used to subvert the challenge posed by the 1990s' independent film movement.

But finally, this is about murder (this *is* the movies, after all). Computers are killing celluloid; films can now be made and shown without using any film. Few mourn the victim, however, because with celluloid increasingly out of the picture, production and distribution – once so prohibitively expensive and complex they were easily controlled by a few raw-knuckled gatekeepers (ie, the studios) – have never been more accessible.

In these turbulent times, the only thing movie audiences can truly count on is a sequel.

The Magic of Moving Pictures

In the late 19th century, motion-picture cameras and projectors were developed simultaneously in France and the USA (though Thomas Edison was the first to use sprocketed celluloid film). For about five minutes folks puzzled over what to do with 'moving pictures,' then, d'oh: tell stories! The first movie house – called a nickelodeon because shows cost a nickel – opened in Pittsburgh in 1905.

The Great Train Robbery (1903) is famous because it was the first to be edited for dramatic effect: it cut to the chase. Emulating the stage, moviemakers enticed audiences by developing appealing stars and dependable genres. In the 1910s, Charlie Chaplin became the first movie star, and Mack Sennett's slapstick comedies – and his ever-bumbling Keystone cops – became cultural institutions.

DW Griffith was a pioneer of cinematic techniques. His landmark films *Birth of a Nation* (1915) and *Intolerance* (1916) introduced much of cinema's now-familiar language, such as the fade, the close-up and the flashback.

Meanwhile, competition fostered the studio system, which began in Manhattan, where Edison tried to create a monopoly with his patents. This drove many independents to move to a suburb of Los Angeles, where they could easily flee to Mexico in case of legal trouble – and thus, Hollywood was born.

In 1927, sound was first introduced in *The Jazz Singer,* and the 'talkies' ushered in the golden age of the movies, from the 1930s to the 1950s. Movie palaces and drive-in theaters sprung up everywhere, and glamorous stars such as Humphrey Bogart, Cary Grant, Katherine Hepburn enthralled the nation. Hollywood studios locked actors into exclusive contracts, ran production departments that handled every aspect of filmmaking and controlled distribution and exhibition in theaters. Bingo: the perfect racket.

Then, in the 1950s, TV arrived, and Americans discovered that laughing at Ralph Kramden in their living rooms was easier than driving to a show. Plus, the feds broke up Hollywood's monopoly. In the 1960s, struggling studios cut costs, ended actors' contracts, sold production departments and still sometimes went bankrupt.

In the 1970s, desperate studios took a risk on a generation of young, anti-establishment filmmakers who, reflecting the times, were interested in social realism, not musicals, romantic comedies or westerns. They included Martin Scorsese, Robert Altman and Francis Ford Coppola, whose provocative films remain high-water marks of excellence.

The '70s also spawned the blockbuster, courtesy of two innovators now synonymous with pop culture: Steven Spielberg and George Lucas.

For downloading independent movies and partaking in 'social cinema,' join up with GreenCine (www .greencine.com), Jaman (http://jaman .com) and IndieFlix (http://indieflix .com).

In the US, 2006 was a watershed year for digital projection: it jumped from 500 to 2,000+ movie screens, out of a total of 37,700 screens nationwide.

In 2000, 8% of US homes had DVD players; by 2007, 70% of homes did, making DVDs the fastest-adopted technology ever. Of course, experts now declare DVDs dead in 10, maybe 20 years.

Spielberg's *Jaws* (1975) and Lucas' *Star Wars* (1977) were such cultural phenomena – and their pleasures so visceral – that they provided a blueprint for the future: keep the heroes simple, the action fast, ladle on the special effects and open big. Lesson learned, the studios recovered and ever since have drawn record audiences with a steady diet of excess and event pictures.

In the 1990s, small, edgy, independently produced films (led by maverick Miramax) became the rage; they experimented with the new tools of digital filmmaking and rode the buzz generated in the USA's burgeoning film festival circuit. Today, all these influences continue, and almost anything goes: from the big screen to the computer screen, from environmental slideshows to $300-million comic book adaptations.

Indiewire (http://indiewire.com) is a great source of reviews, news and box office on the independent films that are actually, gasp!, *independent* of the studios.

Genre Expectations

Genres have defined American cinema since its birth. Here are some distinctly American ones.

CAMPFIRE TALES (ON STEROIDS) *Axel Alonso*

After *Spider-Man 3*, *Sin City* and *300* scorched the 2007 summer box office, and with *Heroes* lighting up the Nielson ratings, it's tempting to say that comic books have never been hotter. But the comic-book industry has been a vital landmark of the pop-culture landscape far longer than it's been filling multiplexes or selling toothpaste. Sure, the Pulitzer Prize–winning *Maus* long ago dispelled the notion that comics are just for kids, and *Manga*-reading Japanese commuters underscore a global industry, but the medium's enduring appeal can be found in the unique icon that drives it – the guy, or gal, in the cape and tights – and what it symbolizes for American culture.

The Sopranos inspired a decade of water cooler chats? Big deal. Spider-Man has been swinging strong for 40 years and counting. He's survived the Cold War, Vietnam, the Pet Rock, Disco, Reagan, *Seinfeld*, two Iraq Wars *and* Tony Soprano. And when September 11 tore out our collective heart, Spidey shed tears at Ground Zero with the rest of us. What other medium can boast a character that has been embraced by so many generations?

Why the love? Because comic books aren't really about superpowers; they're about individuals whose special abilities are always matched by problems that never, ever go away. The supervillains in their brightly colored tights are, just like Saddam Hussein or Paris Hilton, potholes in the road of life. If the superhero represents anything, it's the resilience of the human spirit. It's not about what he *can do*, but what he can endure.

Is there a more fertile ground for good storytelling? At the outset of the 21st century, comics are enjoying a creative renaissance, spurred on by an influx of talent from the broad spectrum of media. From award-winning authors like Stephen King and Jonathan Lethem, to pop-culture powerbrokers like Joss Whedon and Reginald Hudlin, artists are giving back to the medium that sparked their imaginations (and bringing their own fan bases with them). Conversely, comics icons like Stan Lee and Frank Miller have become familiar sights on Hollywood's red carpets. And while the two major companies – Marvel and DC – continue to slug it out for market share, alternative comics keep pressing the medium's boundaries. Take, for instance, Harvey Pekar's *American Splendor*, whose slice-of-life stories inspired one of 2003's most critically acclaimed films. Or Alison Bechdel's *Fun Home* – this graphic-novel memoir of family secrets and sexual politics makes *Desperate Housewives* look like *Leave it to Beaver*.

So don't be fooled. The latest crop of comic-book-inspired movies, toys and TV shows says more about the rest of pop culture than about the medium itself. Comic books have been a stray thread in the tapestry of American life for 70 years and counting because they provide something that can't be found anywhere else: serialized fiction that epitomizes the optimism at the core of the American spirit. Comics remind us that it's never, ever over.

THE WESTERN

In pop cinema terms, the mythic West *is* America: good guys versus bad guys, law versus lawlessness, all duking it out on the rugged frontier. The 1940s and '50s were the Western's heyday. For an unironic paragon of manhood, check out Gary Cooper in *High Noon* (1952). John Ford's influential *The Searchers* (1956) is pure Western poetry: John Wayne, Monument Valley and a deadly score to settle. Sam Peckinpah's ode to nihilistic violence, *The Wild Bunch* (1969), dragged the Western into the antiheroic modern day, as did Clint Eastwood's *Unforgiven* (1992) and *3:10 to Yuma* (2007) starring Russell Crowe.

Get the low-down on the profuse bounty of US film festivals, large and small, at www.filmfestivals.com.

THE MUSICAL

The golden age of Hollywood was defined by the musical, and *42nd Street* (1933) encapsulates the genre. Fred Astaire and Ginger Rogers were a match made in heaven; *Top Hat* (1935) adds a classic Irving Berlin score. The exuberant, impish Gene Kelly is showcased in *Singin' in the Rain* (1952), while no musical-fantasy is more parodied and exalted than *The Wizard of Oz* (1939). These days, musicals are only occasionally updated for modern tastes, as with the top-notch *Chicago* (2002) and *Dreamgirls* (2006).

GANGSTERS & CRIME

Admit it. You *want* Hollywood gossip with your film criticism. In *Easy Riders, Raging Bulls* (1998), Peter Biskind rips the lid off the 1970s 'auteur era' in this deliciously dishy tome.

The outsider status of the urban gangster is an often explicit metaphor for the immigrant experience, and the crime genre includes many of America's greatest films. The original tough guy was Edward G Robinson in *Little Caesar* (1930). The influential subgenre 'film noir' got the star treatment in John Huston's *The Maltese Falcon* (1941), Orson Welles' *Touch of Evil* (1958), Roman Polanski's *Chinatown* (1974) and Curtis Hanson's *LA Confidential* (1997). Francis Ford Coppola's *Godfather* trilogy (1971–90), which examines immigrants and American society through the prism of organized crime, is an almost unrivaled cinematic achievement. Martin Scorsese is the auteur of American mobsters: don't miss *Mean Streets* (1973), *GoodFellas* (1990) and *The Departed* (2006). For kinetic jolts of pop irony, try *Pulp Fiction* (1994) by Quentin Tarantino and *Fargo* (1996) by the Coen brothers. For an exposé of the US–Mexican drug trade, see Steven Soderbergh's *Traffic* (2000).

SCIENCE FICTION

The *Citizen Kane* of sublime vacuousness, pop-culture irony and irritating American optimism, *The Simpsons Movie* (2007) is the only cultural handbook foreign visitors will need.

Inherently cinematic and ever popular, sci-fi is often just the Wild West tricked out with lasers and spaceships, but at its best it's shot through with existential dread and postmodern fears of otherness and technology. For existentialism, see Stanley Kubrick's *2001: A Space Odyssey* (1968); for classic pulp, see the original *Star Wars* (1977), which burned a new mythology into America's cultural retina. Equally pulpy and jittery with techno-fears are *The Terminator* (1984) and *The Matrix* (1999). Terry Gilliam's *Brazil* (1985) is sublimely hilarious futureshock. Steven Spielberg remains a one-man sci-fi factory, from *Close Encounters* (1979) and *E.T.* (1982) to *War of the Worlds* (2005). Also see *Alien* (1979) and *Aliens* (1986), Ridley Scott's moody *Blade Runner* (1982), and *Children of Men* (2006).

TELEVISION

For the student of television, a koan: is TV still TV when it's the internet?

Until, oh, the last edition of this guide, it could be argued that TV was the defining medium of the modern age, but just like that, the internet swallowed TV whole, leaving an entire industry puzzling its very existence.

We exaggerate, of course. We kid because we care. On average, each American watches 31 hours of TV a week, an all-time high. By the age of two, 90% of US children watch 1.5 hours of TV a day. Americans *love* TV – which represents the doughy middle of US culture, as effortlessly addictive as a bag of potato chips – but they are watching differently: recording or downloading, viewing according to their schedules (not the networks') and *skipping the commercials*. As the internet messes with the economics of this corporate-owned, ad-driven entertainment, can you feel the executives shudder?

Television was developed in the USA and Britain in the 1920s and '30s, and the first commercial TV set was introduced at the 1939 New York World's Fair. After WWII, owning a set became a status symbol for America's blossoming middle class, and radio and movies instantly wilted under TV's cathode-tube glow. Cable arrived in the 1980s, expanding TV's handful of channels into dozens, and then hundreds.

Now, as the functional difference between TV and the internet dissolves, you can simply pluck what you like from the ether.

> From 1950 to 1960, the percentage of US homes with a TV shot from 10% to 87%, and today hovers at about 98% – or more than 101 million households. Talk about market saturation…

From Boob Tube to YouTube

Until the last decade fractured viewers into niches, TV programming strove constantly to attract the widest possible audience, invariably resembling a noisy vaudeville of trashy (if irresistible) amusements. For decades, critics sneered it was low-brow, and movie stars wouldn't be caught dead on it.

But high-quality, well-written, 'thought-provoking' TV has always existed. The original *I Love Lucy* show (1951–57) was groundbreaking: shot on film before a live audience and edited before airing, it pioneered syndication (or rebroadcast). It established the sitcom ('situation comedy') formula, and showcased a dynamic female comedian, Lucille Ball, in an interethnic marriage.

In the 1970s, *All in the Family* was nominally a comedy, but this made palatable its unflinching examination of prejudice – as embodied by Carol O'Connor's bigoted patriarch Archie Bunker. Similarly, the sketch-comedy show *Saturday Night Live*, which debuted in 1975, pushed social hot buttons with its subversive, politically charged humor.

In the 1980s, videos brought movies into the home. As this blurred the distinction between small screen and big screen, the stigma Hollywood attached to TV slowly faded. Another turning point in this decade was the success of *The Cosby Show*, starring comedian Bill Cosby. While not the first successful African American show, it became the nation's highest-rated program and spurred an increasingly multicultural small screen.

In the 1990s, TV audiences proved they could knock back straight shots of sitcom-free weirdness by embracing the cult show *Twin Peaks*, leading to a slew of provocative idiosyncrasies like *The X-Files*. By the 21st century, pay cable was targeting all manner of niche audiences (cooking channels, gay channels, baby channels) and producing sophisticated, complex dramas that surpassed most risk-averse Hollywood fare: *The Sopranos, Sex in the City, Deadwood, The Wire, The Shield, Rescue Me* and more.

Now, YouTube and its ilk (p80) are changing the rules again. Network TV has responded by creating more long-narrative serial dramas, like *Lost* and *24*, as well as favoring cheap-to-produce, 'unscripted' reality TV: what *Survivor* started in 2000, the contestants of *American Idol* and *Dancing with the Stars* keep alive. Americans, after all, still love a good pie in the face.

> Still don't believe the future of TV is on the internet? Start surfing: www.youtube.com, www.blip.tv, www.atomfilms.com, www.joost.com, http://network2.tv.

THEATER

American theater is a three-act play of sentimental entertainment, classic revivals and urgent social commentary. It truly opened in the 1920s – with the arrival of playwright Eugene O'Neill and New York's Little Theater movement, which emulated progressive European theater and developed into today's 'off-Broadway' scene.

From the beginning, Broadway musicals (www.livebroadway.com) have aspired to nothing more nor less than Don't-Miss-This-Show! tourist attractions. Considering that Broadway sells 12 million tickets a year, we have to agree: don't miss this show!

Always struggling and scraping, and mostly surviving, the country's 1500 nonprofit regional theaters are breeding grounds for new plays and foster new playwrights. Some also develop Broadway-bound productions, while some of the most popular are dedicated to the Bard himself, William Shakespeare (see Ashland, OR, p1045, and Cedar City, UT, p871).

Eugene O'Neill – the first major US playwright, and still widely considered the best – put American drama on the map with his magnificent trilogy *Mourning Becomes Electra* (1931), which sets a tragic Greek myth in post–Civil War New England. Other frequently revived works of his are

> If Shakespeare lived today, he couldn't write a better cops-and-robbers show than *The Wire*, an epic, morally ambiguous TV drama about those who profit from and prosecute Baltimore's drug trade.

LOVE IN A BINARY UNIVERSE

When new media come along, shaking up established players, a certain apocalyptic or revolutionary tone can creep in: after X, nothing will be the same.

X, in this case, is digital technology. And as one describes the radical changes transforming America's arts, it's easy to sound like just such a thundering, millennial prophet. That's when we try to take a deep breath and remember: love in the digital world is the same as on the page, the stage or the screen. Forms change; what moves us remains.

Still, what do you make of this?

In 2007, New York's Metropolitan Opera inaugurated a 'satellite season', in which it digitally simulcast six performances to 275 big-screen theaters. At a tough time for operas, every theater sold out. That's good!

But in 2003, Broadway musicians had to strike for four days to keep 'virtual orchestra' computer programs from replacing some musicians, though they couldn't keep computerized instruments out of touring Broadway orchestras. That's bad!

However, unknown composers can now 'record' realistic digital symphonies (using programs like the Fauxharmonic Orchestra) and create new music at a hundredth the cost of hiring live musicians. Um, good (mostly)!

Or, take authors: they post free serialized podcasts to generate audiences and book contracts, and then post videos on YouTube to promote their new books (such a 15th-century technology). Meanwhile, ebooks of copyright-free publications proliferate (www.gutenberg.org), and future ebooks will allow embedded video, voice, music and links. Whither the page-turner then?

With CDs, music went digital forever ago (okay, 20 years), but now internet downloading glorifies the single and renders the album archaic. In fact, miniaturization is a digital hallmark: newspapers become articles, movies become clips.

Did we say clips? *Have* you seen YouTube, Blip.tv, Atom Films? Sure, much of it is just tiny TV, self-conscious spoofs and plain ol' home movies. And yet these 'viral videos' and weblogs swirling through the media-sphere act like dirty thumbprints smudging the distinctions between art, life and commerce, while public/private spaces collapse into...

Paper bag! We're hyperventilating again.

Okay, what have we learned so far? The digital revolution is personalized, democratic, self-involved, self-produced, bite-size and inexpensive when it isn't free. It's watching what we want, where we want, when we want. It's making what we want in the way we want it.

And good or bad, it ain't over yet.

The Iceman Cometh (1946) and the autobiographical *Long Day's Journey into Night* (1956).

After WWII, American playwrights joined the nationwide artistic renaissance. Two of the most famous were Arthur Miller – who wrote *Death of a Salesmen* (1949) and *The Crucible* (1953) – and the prolific Southerner Tennessee Williams – who wrote *The Glass Menagerie* (1945), *A Streetcar Named Desire* (1947) and *Cat on a Hot Tin Roof* (1955). All these, and more, have been adapted into films.

As in Europe, American theater in the 1960s was marked by absurdism and the avant-garde. Few were more scathing than Edward Albee, who started provoking bourgeois sensibilities with *Who's Afraid of Virginia Woolf?* (1962) and continues to do so (see 2002's *The Goat* or, *Who Is Sylvia?*). Neil Simon arrived at around the same time; his ever-popular mainstream comedies (such as *The Odd Couple,* 1965) kept Broadway humming for 40 years.

Emerging in the 1970s, two other prominent, active American dramatists are David Mamet (*American Buffalo,* 1975) and Sam Shepard (*Buried Child,* 1978). August Wilson (*Fences,* 1985) created a monumental 10-play 'Pittsburgh Cycle' dissecting 20th-century African American life.

Today, American theater evolves in its effort to remain a relevant, even necessary, communal experience in an age of ever-isolating media. One-person shows, such as *Bridge & Tunnel* by Sarah Jones, are increasingly popular. 'Hip-hop theater' is a growing, if eclectic phenomena – bringing with it the casually diverse, multidisciplinary aesthetics of hip-hop. And new playwrights keep experimenting, like Suzan-Lori Parks (*Topdog/Underdog,* 2001), whose *365 Plays/365 Days* (2006) became a year-long play cycle unfolding over time and space across the country.

> For an excellent update on the US regional theater scene, check out *American Theatre* (www.tcg.org).

DANCE

America fully embraced dance in the 20th century, making modern ballet and modern dance what they are today. New York City has always been the epicenter for dance innovation and the home of most major companies, but every major city supports resident troupes, both ballet and modern.

> In the amusing, unexpected documentary *OT: Our Town* (2002), LA ghetto kids turn Thornton Wilder's hoary chestnut inside-out and learn that, sometimes, theater really can make a difference.

Ballet

Modern ballet is said to have begun with Russian-born choreographer George Balanchine's *Apollo* (1928) and *Prodigal Son* (1929). With these, Balanchine invented the 'plotless ballet' – in which he choreographed the inner structure of music, not a pantomimed story – and thereby created a new, modern vocabulary of ballet movement. In 1934, Balanchine founded the School of American Ballet; in 1948 he ran the New York City Ballet, turning it into one of the world's foremost ballet companies. Today, a number of cities have 'Balanchine companies' dedicated to preserving his legacy.

Jerome Robbins took over the New York City Ballet in 1983, after achieving fame on choreographing several of Broadway's biggest musicals, including *West Side Story* (1957). Broadway remains an important venue for dance. Companies such as San Francisco's Lines Ballet keep evolving contemporary ballet. *Dance* (www.dancemagazine.com) is an excellent modern ballet resource.

> The film *Ballet Russes* (2007) is a warm remembrance, told by the dancers, of this revolutionary troupe and how they changed ballet and then introduced it – and Balanchine – to America.

Modern Dance

The pioneer of modern dance, Isadora Duncan, didn't find success until she began performing in Europe at the turn of the 20th century. Basing her ideas on ancient Greek concepts of beauty, she challenged the strictures of classical ballet and sought to make dance an intense form of self-expression.

In the 1920s and '30s, New York–based Denishawn was the nation's leading modern-dance company, and its most famous and influential student was Martha Graham. She founded the Dance Repertory Theater in New York, and many of today's major American choreographers developed under her tutelage. In her long career she choreographed more than 140 dances and developed a new dance technique (Martha Graham technique), now taught worldwide, aimed at expressing inner emotion and dramatic narrative. Her two most famous works were *Appalachian Spring* (1944) and *Clytemnestra* (1957).

Carolyn Brown describes dancing with Merce Cunningham and rubbing elbows with John Cage and other artistic lions of the 1950s and '60s avant-garde in *Chance and Circumstance* (2007).

Merce Cunningham, Paul Taylor and Twyla Tharp succeeded Graham as the leading exponents of modern dance; all run active companies today. In the 1960s and '70s, Cunningham explored abstract expressionism in movement, collaborating famously with musician John Cage. Taylor and Tharp are known for plundering popular culture.

Another student of Martha Graham, Alvin Ailey, was part of the post-WWII flowering of African American culture. He made his name with *Blues Suite* (1958) and *Revelations* (1960), and in 1958 he founded the still-lauded Alvin Ailey American Dance Theater.

Other celebrated postmodern choreographers include Mark Morris and Bill T Jones. Beyond New York, San Francisco, Minneapolis, Chicago and Philadelphia are noteworthy for modern dance.

ARCHITECTURE

The 21st century is a good time to be an architect. Computer technology and innovations in materials and manufacturing now allow for curving, asymmetrical buildings once considered impossible, if not inconceivable. Further, architects are being challenged to 'go green', and the creativity this has unleashed is riveting. Who would have imagined eco-friendly skyscrapers? And yet up they fly, transforming skylines and changing the way Americans think about their environments. As for the public's architectural taste – well, it remains conservative, but never mind: international 'starchitects' are tarting up urban landscapes with radical visions that the nation will catch up with…one day.

The American Institute of Architects asked average Americans to name their 150 favorite buildings. Packed with nostalgia and tourist attractions, the list (www.aia150.org) sent modern architects into spasms of eye-rolling.

The Colonial Period

The only lasting indigenous influence on American architecture has been the adobe pueblo of the Southwest. Seventeenth- and 18th-century Spaniards incorporated elements of the pueblo, and this hybrid reappeared in 20th-century architecture as mission-revival style in Southern California and pueblo style in the Southwest.

Until the 20th century, Americans mainly adopted English and European styles and followed revivalist trends. For most early colonists, architecture served necessity rather than taste, while the would-be gentry aped grander English homes, a period well preserved in Williamsburg, Virginia.

After the Revolutionary War, the nation's leaders wanted a style befitting the new republic and adopted neoclassicism. The Virginia State Capitol (p349), designed by the multitalented Thomas Jefferson, was modeled on a Roman temple, and Jefferson's home, Monticello (p360), has a Romanesque rotunda.

Professional architect Charles Bulfinch helped develop the more monumental federal style, which paralleled the English Georgian style. The grandest example is the US Capitol in Washington. DC (p314), which became the model for state legislatures nationwide.

In the 19th century, mirroring English fashions, Americans preferred the heavier Greek-revival style and then the Gothic-revival style, seen today in many churches and college buildings.

The Frontier & the Suburbs

In the mid-19th century, small-scale building was revolutionized by 'balloon-frame' construction: a light frame of standard-milled timber joined with cheap nails. Easy and economical, balloon-frame stores and houses made possible the swift settlement of the expanding West and, later, the surreal proliferation of the suburbs. Though disposable and mass-produced, balloon-frame houses brought home-ownership within reach of average middle-class families, making real the enduring brass ring of the American Dream.

A notable variation was the more well-to-do 'Victorian,' which appeared in San Francisco and other cities. Larger and fancier, these homes added balconies, towers and ornate trim in an intricate mix of styles.

Beaux Arts

After the Civil War, influential architects studied at the École des Beaux-Arts in Paris, and American buildings showed increasing refinement and confidence. Major examples of beaux-arts style are Richard Morris Hunt's Biltmore Estate in North Carolina and San Francisco's City Hall.

In the 1850s, internal iron-frame buildings first appeared in Manhattan, and this freed up designs. After the 1880s invention of the Otis elevator, architects said, 'hey, we can make tall buildings!' The Chicago School added beaux-arts style and produced the skyscraper – considered the first 'modern' architecture and America's most prominent architectural contribution to the world. Interestingly, the first true skyscraper is in neither Chicago nor Manhattan but Buffalo, NY: the 13-story Guaranty Building, built by Louis Sullivan.

Frank Lloyd Wright

Initially an apprentice to Sullivan's firm, Frank Lloyd Wright created a unique architectural style and is one of the 20th century's great visionaries. Working mainly on private houses, Wright abandoned historical elements and references, making each building a unique sculptural form characterized by strong horizontal lines. Wright called them 'prairie houses,' though invariably they were built in the suburbs.

Interior spaces flowed openly rather than being divided into rooms, and the inside was connected to the outside rather than being separated by solid walls. Structural materials, not applied decoration, provided texture and color. Wright was innovative in his use of steel, glass and concrete, and he pioneered panel heating, indirect lighting, double glazing and air-conditioning.

As well as visiting the Guggenheim Museum in New York City (p155), head to southern Wisconsin (p619); eastern Pennsylvania (p222); and, of course, Chicago (p574).

Reaching for the Sky

Influenced by Wright and by art deco – which became instantly popular in the US after the 1925 Paris exposition – city high-rises soared, becoming fitting symbols of America's technical achievements, grand aspirations, commerce and affinity for modernism. Design emphasized the structural grid and surfaces of concrete, glass and steel. Notable examples are the 1930 Chrysler Building and the 1931 Empire State Building. Art deco also marked the 1932 Rockefeller Center and its Radio City Music Hall, and it appeared nationwide on movie houses, gas stations and resort hotels.

European architects absorbed Wright's ideas, and that influence bounced back when the Bauhaus school left Nazi Germany to set up in the USA. In America, Bauhaus became known as the International style, which favored

In the 1950s, sprawling middle-class suburbs appeared almost literally overnight. One major housing developer, Levitt and Sons, produced a new four-bedroom house every 16 minutes.

Idiosyncratic, sarcastic and opinionated, Narrow Larry (www.narrowlarry.com) plots cool modern architecture by US regions, including notable folk-art environments.

A landmark in the making, New York's World Trade Center Memorial Site (www.renewnyc.com) will include the Freedom Tower (a patriotic 1776ft) and a below-ground memorial called 'Reflecting Absence.'

glass 'curtain walls' over a steel frame. The best International-style buildings became abstract, sculptured shapes; a great example is New York's Seagram Building.

Then, rejecting these 'ugly boxes,' late-20th-century postmodernism reintroduced decoration, color, historical references and whimsy. In this, American architects like Michael Graves and Philip Johnson took the lead (see Johnson's AT&T Building in New York).

For a primer in cutting edge, CAD-CAM-enabled contemporary US architecture, turn to *All American* (2002) by Brian Carter and Annette Lecuyer.

Today, aided and abetted by digital tools, architectural design favors the bold and the unique. Leading this plunge into futurama has been Frank Gehry; his Walt Disney Concert Hall in Los Angeles (p904) is but one example. Other architects include Thom Mayne (LA's Caltrans District 7 Headquarters and San Francisco's Federal Building), Norman Foster (New York's Hearst Headquarters) and Daniel Libeskind (Denver Art Museum, p747). New museums (or additions) in Phoenix, San Diego, San Francisco, Boston, Kansas City and more bear witness to this innovative surge.

And the skyscraper? Chicago's Sears Tower (1730ft, p550) is currently the USA's tallest, but when completed in 2010, the Chicago Spire will rise 2000ft and twist like a drill bit into the bargain.

Food & Drink   John Mariani

Ever since the Wampanoag Indians helped the Pilgrims stave off starvation over the winter of 1620 and brought food to the first Thanksgiving in 1621, Americans have happily incorporated myriad food cultures to create their own, based on the rich bounty of the North American continent. From the very beginning Americans took pride in that bounty, drawing on the seafood of the North Atlantic, Gulf of Mexico, and Pacific Ocean; the fertility of Midwest farmlands; and technologies of animal husbandry and transport that made pork, beef and chicken everyday staples.

Massive waves of post–Civil War immigrants greatly enriched American gastronomy by adapting foreign ideas to US kitchens, from hamburgers, pizza and pastrami to borscht, huevos rancheros, and Irish corned beef and cabbage.

A vast market and transportation system made fresh, canned, boxed and frozen foods available to everyone – so much so that it can be argued Americans grew fat (and later, obese) on the abundance of fast food and junk food. It is not by accident that phrases like 'grab a sandwich,' 'get a bite,' and 'pick up some take-out' are quintessential American colloquialisms, along with 'road food,' 'prole food' and 'the munchies.' Such ideas had the effect of American food not being taken seriously by the rest of the world.

Not until the 1960s did food and wine become serious topics for newspapers, magazines and TV, led by a Californian named Julia Child who taught Americans how to cook French food in black-and-white on Boston's public television station. By the 1970s college-educated folks started turning their focus to issues of organic and natural foods and sustainable agriculture; and the term 'foodie revolution' encouraged entrepreneurs to open restaurants for well-traveled clientele featuring regional American cuisine, from Louisiana to the Pacific Northwest, that would rank with the best in France.

Most Americans still love their hamburgers and hot dogs, and some eat too many of them, yet they are also now more familiar with the world's food cultures than any population on earth.

Road Food, by intrepid noshers Jane and Michael Stern, is the result of 30 years of ferreting out the best local regional eateries, from Maine to Oregon, many dating back decades. They also maintain a website with heaps of free listings: www.roadfood.com.

STAPLES & SPECIALTIES

Americans have such easy access to regional foods that no section of the country can claim homogeneity. Indeed, once-unique specialties are now readily available everywhere: a Bostonian might just as easily have a taco for lunch as a Houstonian would eat Chesapeake Bay blue crabs for dinner.

Perhaps after a mid-morning coffee break, a worker's lunch hour affords a sandwich, quick burger or hearty salad. The 'business lunch' is more specific to big cities like New York, where food is not necessarily as important as the conversation, and many business dinners, especially among men, take place at steakhouses. Most folks take a mid-afternoon snack, like a candy bar, bag of chips or piece of fruit.

In the (usually early) evening, Americans settle in to a substantial dinner, which, given the workload of so many two-career families, might be take-out (eg, pizza or Chinese food) or prepackaged meals cooked in a microwave. Desserts tend toward ice cream, pies, and cakes – and, like most everything else, come in big servings. And while wine sales have soared in the last decade, less than 15% of Americans drink wine on even an occasional basis.

Big Night (1996) is a wonderful film about two Italian brothers who struggle to run an authentic, refined Italian restaurant in 1950s New Jersey, whose clients want basic Italian American food.

New York

Owing to its huge population and an influx of 35 million tourists annually, New York captures the title of America's greatest restaurant city, hands down. Its diverse neighborhoods serve up authentic Italian food and world-famous New York–style pizza, all manner of Asian food (both in and out of China-town), French *haute cuisine* and Jewish deli food, from bagels to pickles to piled-high pastrami on rye. Less common cuisines are found here as well, from Jamaican to Ukrainian. Breakfasts are casual and often on-the-go; lunch is at a fast-food spot or street vendor; and dinner is often eaten out either at favorite little bistros or among the torrent of new, exciting restaurants that open (and close) weekly in the city.

New England

New England's claim to have the nation's best seafood is quite accurate, for the North Atlantic offers up clams, mussels, oysters and huge lobsters, along with shad, bluefish and cod. New Englanders love a good chowder (seafood stew) and a good clambake, an almost ritual meal where the shellfish are buried in a pit fire with corn, chicken and sausages. Fried clam fritters and lobster rolls (lobster meat with mayonnaise served in a bread bun) are found throughout the region. There are excellent cheeses made in Vermont, cranberries (a Thanksgiving staple) harvested in Massachusetts and maple syrup from New England's forests. Maine's coast is lined with lobster shacks; baked beans and brown bread are Boston specialties; and Rhode Islanders pour coffee syrup over ice cream and embrace cornmeal johnnycakes as traditional favorites.

> Nathan's Famous International Hot Dog Eating Contest six-time champion ate 63 wieners at the 2007 race, only to be defeated by hungry Joey Chestnut, who stuffed down 66 dogs in 12 minutes.

Mid-Atlantic

From New York down through Maryland and Virginia, the Middle Atlantic states share a long coastline and a cornucopia of apple, pear and berry farms. New Jersey is famous for its tomatoes, New York's Long Island for its potatoes. Chesapeake Bay's blue crabs are the finest anywhere and Virginia salt-cured 'country-style' hams are served with biscuits. In Philadelphia, you must gorge on a 'Philly' cheesesteak, made with thin, sautéed beef and onions and melted cheese on a bun. And in the Pennsylvania-Dutch country, stop by a farm restaurant for chicken pot pie, noodles and the meatloaf-like scrapple. The wines of New York's Hudson Valley, Finger Lakes and Long Island are well worth sampling.

The South

No region is prouder of its food culture than the South, which has a long history of mingling Anglo, French, Italian, African, Spanish and Native American foods in dishes like slow-cooked barbecue, which has as many meaty and saucy variations as there are towns in the South. Southern fried chicken is crisp outside and moist inside; and in Florida dishes made with alligator, shrimp and conch incorporate hot chili peppers and tropical spices. Breakfasts are as big as can be, and treasured dessert recipes tend to produce big layer cakes or pies made with pecans, corn syrup, bananas, and citrus fruit. Light, fluffy hot biscuits are served well buttered and grits (ground corn cooked to a cereal-like consistency) are a passion among Southerners.

> *Arthur Schwartz's New York City Food*, by former food editor Arthur Schwartz, reveals where to find every New York specialty, from bagels and pizza to Gray's Papaya and street-vendor hot dogs.

LOUISIANA

Louisiana's cuisine, influenced by French Huguenots, Sicilians and Choctaw Indians, is legendary. Cajun food is found in the bayou country and marries native spices like sassafras and chili peppers to French home cooking. Creole food is more urban, centered in New Orleans, where dishes like shrimp remoulade, crabmeat ravigote, beignets and pain perdu are ubiquitous. The area's most famous dishes are gumbo, a stew of chicken and shellfish or sausage and often okra; jambalaya, a rice-based dish with tomatoes, sausage and shrimp; and blackened catfish. The coffee may be made from chicory and the classic po'boy sandwiches are slender loaves of French bread stuffed with everything from oysters to fried shrimp. Try local cocktails like the Ramos gin fizz and the Sazerac.

Midwest

You eat heartily all over the USA, but in the Midwest you eat big and with gusto. Portions are huge – this is still farm country, where people need a lot of sustenance to get their work done. So you might start off the day with eggs, bacon and toast; have a couple of hamburgers and potato salad for lunch; and swallow steak and baked potatoes for dinner – all washed down with a local beer like Budweiser or Miller. Barbecue is very popular here, especially in Kansas City and St Louis, where African Americans make the best 'que. Chicago is an ethnically diverse culinary center with some of the country's top restaurants. One of the best places to sample Midwestern foods is at a county fair, which offers everything from bratwurst to fried dough, and devil's food chocolate cake to soft ice cream.

Southwest

Southwest food culture is defined by two ethnic groups, the Spanish and Mexicans, who controlled territories from Texas to California until well into the 19th century. While there is little actual Spanish food today, the Spanish brought cattle to Mexico, which the Mexicans adapted to their own corn-and-chili–based gastronomy to make tacos, tortillas, enchiladas, burritos, chimichangas and other fancifully named dishes of corn or flour pancakes filled with everything from chopped meat and poultry to eggs. Steaks and barbecue are also much in evidence on Southwestern menus, and beer is the drink of choice with dinner and a night out. For a more up-and-coming foodie scene head to Las Vegas, where top chefs from New York and Los Angeles are sprouting satellite restaurants.

Alice Doesn't Live Here Anymore (1974) chronicles a woman who takes a job at Mel's Diner in Phoenix, Arizona, and must cope with his attitudes towards women and some hilarious co-workers.

California

Owing to its vastness and various climates, California is truly America's cornucopia for fruits and vegetables, and a gateway to myriad Asian ingredients that fill markets here. The influx of Asian immigrants, especially after the Vietnam War, enriched the state's urban food cultures with Chinatowns, Koreatowns, and Japantowns, along with huge enclaves of Mexican Americans who maintain their own culinary traditions across the state. In the 1980s California chefs like Alice Waters of Berkeley's Chez Panisse and Wolfgang Puck of Beverly Hills' Spago pioneered 'California cuisine' by incorporating only the best local ingredients into simple yet delectable preparations. The state's natural resources are overwhelming, with wild

WHAT DOES 'ORGANIC' REALLY MEAN?

The US Department of Agriculture defines *organic* and *natural* according to distinct standards. For crops, *organic* means they were grown without the use of conventional pesticides, artificial fertilizers, human waste or sewage sludge, and processed without being irradiated or with food additives. For animals, they must have been reared without routine use of antibiotics or growth hormones, and have not been genetically modified. *Natural* products are those that have been minimally processed and contain no artificial colorings or preservatives.

salmon, Dungeness crab, oysters and halibut; excellent produce year-round; and artisinal products like cheese, bread, olive oil and chocolate. And the fertile Napa, Sonoma, Mendocino, Santa Barbara and Alexander valleys produce some of the world's finest wines.

Pacific Northwest & Hawaii

The cuisine of the Pacific Northwest draws on the traditions of local Native Americans, whose diets center on game, seafood – especially salmon – and foraged mushrooms, fruits and berries. Seattle spawned the modern international coffeehouse craze with Starbucks; and the beers and wines of both Washington and Oregon have come up to international standards, especially Pinot Noirs and Rieslings. Faraway Hawaii has the additional benefit of a native food culture that takes full advantage of Pacific fish like mahimahi, wahoo and opakapaka, along with beach parties like luau, which include cooking kalua pig in a pit on hot stones under palm leaves. Hawaiian coffee and chocolate are first rate.

Anthony Dias Blue's Pocket Guide to Wine 2007, by Anthony Dias Blue, is the most comprehensive A-to-Z, country-by-country guide to thousands of international wines, but with particular emphasis on US wineries.

DRINKS

Americans are far from teetotalers, yet they're not big wine drinkers, despite increases in per capita consumption – about 12 bottles compared to 20 gallons of beer! Which is understandable: 19th-century German immigrants developed ways to make beer in vast quantities and to deliver it all over America. Today 80% of domestic beer comes from the Midwest. Beer is more than a thirst-quencher; it is a social beverage that's essential to a good picnic or a 'tailgate party' held outside a sports stadium before the game.

These days Americans are drinking more wine than ever and are on track to become to the world's largest consumers of wine overall, with about 25 percent of the market. But in per capita consumption the US is 33rd in the world, behind Canada and South Africa.

Liquor consumption and its abuses led to Prohibition – a ban on alcohol sales in America that lasted from 1920 to 1933 and held up the

---

AMERICAN WINES

From the moment Europeans arrived in the New World they made wine, first from the wild native grapes with names like Scuppernong, Catawba and Niagara, then from imported European varietals. Spanish missionaries brought vines to California in the 16th century, and by the 19th century there were flourishing vineyards there, as well as in New York, Ohio and Virginia. In fact, when the phylloxera bug devastated vineyards throughout Europe in the mid-19th century, phylloxera-resistant American vines were grafted onto European stocks to replenish the wine industries in France, Spain, Italy and Germany.

The onset of anti-alcohol Prohibition laws in the USA as of 1919 effectively put the American wine industry out of business until their repeal in 1932. Afterward, vineyards devoted themselves to producing mediocre wine in bulk, especially 'jug wines' in big bottles that held a liter or more. Only in the 1960s did California wineries begin to make wines that could compete with the best in Europe. Based on varietals like Cabernet Sauvignon, Chardonnay, Merlot, Pinot Noir and Riesling, American wines were often more intense in taste and higher in alcohol than their Old World counterparts. Zinfandel, which probably came from Croatia, has had wide plantings in the USA, making both a fruity red and a rose-colored 'white zinfandel.'

The success of California winemaking brought improvements in technology and viniculture that marked the production of wines elsewhere, so that the Finger Lakes region of New York now makes excellent Rieslings; Long Island, NY, makes very fine Merlots; and there are large numbers of good wineries opening in Virginia, Nebraska, Texas and New Mexico. And all are yours for the tasting!

development of a fine wine industry. Only in the 1960s did California winemakers, led by Robert Mondavi of Napa Valley, seek to compete with the best European wines. Today 90% of US wine comes from California; and Oregon, Washington and New York wines have achieved international status. Scores of varietal grapes are used to make wines, but the best regarded are Chardonnay, Sauvignon Blanc, Cabernet Sauvignon, Merlot, Pinot Noir and Zinfandel, all based on imported root stocks.

Rye, blended whiskey, gin and vodka are made in the USA, but bourbon, made from corn, is the only native spirit and by law made only in Kentucky (though Tennessee whiskey is very similar). From these, cocktails were created at bars in the early 19th century, including the long-standing classics: the martini, Manhattan, daiquiri and Bloody Mary (which originated in Harry's New York Bar in Paris). The tequila-based margarita came from Tijuana, Mexico. The current fashion is for cosmopolitans, vodka martinis and mojitos. Irish coffee is a San Francisco–born mix of hot coffee with Irish whiskey and whipped cream.

The water in the USA is always safe to drink. Most nonalcoholic drinks are quite sweet and served over ice, from Southern-style iced tea to the quintessential American beverage: Coca-Cola.

> Jack Daniels whiskey is distilled in Moore County, Tennessee, which has been a dry county since Prohibition days.

CELEBRATIONS

The late historian Arthur Schlesinger Jr noted that after just a single generation, American immigrants' children lost nearly all ties to their ethnicities except with regard to food. Indeed, Thanksgiving may be the only holiday (held the last Thursday in November) where most Americans would agree on the menu – roast turkey, stuffing, mashed potatoes, cranberry sauce, perhaps pumpkin pie – and even then the appetizers, side dishes, or desserts might be Latino, Swedish, German or African.

Americans celebrate their ethnic heritage on holidays in many ways. At Christmas, Italian Americans may, by tradition, serve fish the night before and a pasta dish on Christmas Day. At Easter many Americans will serve roast ham, while Greek Americans will serve lamb.

Other holidays may be observed only by certain groups of people. Jews celebrate Passover by eating matzoh ball soup and poultry, while at Hanukkah they indulge in fried foods like potato latkes. African Americans celebrate a December festival called Kwanzaa with foods of Africa, South America and the Caribbean. New Year's Day is a gourmet day for Chinese Americans (held weeks after the American New Year), while Italians hold street festivals serving fried seafood, pizza, sausage and fritters in honor of favorite saints. Oddly enough, on St Patrick's Day Americans traditionally serve corned beef and cabbage, which is practically unknown in Ireland.

> Chowhound (www.chow hound.com) is 'for those who live to eat.' Come here to ask locals about important issues – from the best all-beef hot dogs in Chicago to the tastiest beef-tongue tacos in Oakland, California.

Far less formalized are national holidays like the Fourth of July, Memorial Day and Labor Day, which symbolize the beginning and end of summer. Barbecues and beer predominate the festivities, with large gatherings in backyards or parks for meals of hamburgers, hot dogs, and ribs with corn on the cob, potato salad and fruit pies.

The biggest and by far the most expensive parties are wedding receptions, which in recent years have become extremely lavish, often held at a restaurant or banquet hall with copious amounts of food and drink – and, of course, the multi-tiered wedding cake. Traditionally, the bride and groom feed the first bite of cake to each other by hand.

On New Year's Eve Americans celebrate pretty much as people do all over the world: with a Champagne-filled evening replete with singing and kissing at midnight. The next day, good-luck dishes are served, like lentils by Italians, and black-eyed peas and rice by Southerners.

WHERE TO EAT & DRINK

Most Americans do not eat out often at expensive restaurants, and many consider one of the scores of chain restaurants with family-style fare – TGI Friday's, Denny's or Applebee's, for example – a reasonable alternative. Such places are dependable and consistent, the prices moderate and the setting casual, but the food rarely rises above the mediocre.

A much better idea: find the best individually owned, neighborhood restaurant around, maybe one that specializes in barbecue, fried seafood, roast beef, lobster or pancakes. These spots have an authentic, localized atmosphere, warmer hospitality and higher-quality food that give a truer sense of local color and culture than chain eateries ever could. Much of the USA is now blanketed with chain restaurants, so ask locals if there are any good privately owned places around. On the other hand, in the South the few remaining cafeteria chains like Piccadilly provide very good regional food at a very fair price and allow you to mix in with the locals.

The best breakfasts in America – often at amazingly good value – can be found at cafés and some family restaurants, including chains like IHOP and Denny's. The most expensive breakfasts are from hotel room service but they are rarely any good. Avoid them.

> Make advance dining reservations at OpenTable.com (www.opentable.com), which serves 20 major US cities and over 7000 restaurants.

A bar and grill may be little more than a bar or pub (as in a tavern) that serves modest food or, in an upscale version, a trendy restaurant with excellent American fare and a good wine list. Very often they have bars where solo diners can eat well and feel quite comfortable doing so. Coffee shops tend to open early and close late, which makes them good options for a light snack throughout the day.

For heartier appetites, the all-you-can-eat buffet is a stunning phenomenon: for a set price you can revisit the buffet as many times as you like, until you're completely stuffed or just plain embarrassed.

Some of the world's finest high-end restaurants are in the USA, and in bigger cities you'll find prix fixe menus and European-style service that lets you linger happily over your crème brûlée. But be prepared to pay for it. That said, these days the weak US dollar makes the occasional foray into a posh restaurant far less expensive than in cities like London, Paris and Tokyo. If you go for it, always call to make a reservation (or ask your hotel concierge to do so), ask if there are any dress guidelines and be prepared to accept a very early or quite late table at popular restaurants.

THE ZAGAT CAVEAT

The *Zagat Survey* series have become extremely popular little guides to restaurants all over the USA. Zagat calls its surveys 'a free market study of [the restaurant industry's] own customers' by asking diners to send in their comments and ratings on recently dined-in eateries. These are then cobbled together into a single review and rating for each establishment.

Yet some critics of Zagat guides argue that because the surveys are not administered by an independent, random poll, results are based on responses that may or may not really reflect what the average American's experience of a place might be. Also, the overwhelming majority of the ratings – from 0 ('poor to fair') to 30 ('extraordinary to perfection') points – are above 16 ('good to very good'), and most restaurants rate 20 points and above ('very good to excellent'), which makes one wonder if so many restaurants in any city could actually be of that quality. That said, there's no arguing that Zagat guides are handy, easy to use, and yet another source for opinionated assessments of a city's seemingly countless eating options.

DON'T FORGET TO TIP!

Service is almost never included on restaurant bills in the USA. A standard tip on the bill (before taxes are added) is 15% for good service, 20% for excellent service. A restaurant *may* add a service charge for parties of six or more or for banquets. If you do receive poor service, by all means bring it to the manager's attention and tip below 15%.

Quick Eats

There's so much more to fast food in America than American fast food. Eating from city street cars or roadside vendors carries a small risk that you might pick up some nasty bacteria, but generally American roadfood tends to be very safe and are usually supervised by the local health department. Don't miss a street-side Italian ice or, in New York, Sabrett's 'water dogs' (boiled hot dogs) that are as requisite as the big, soft pretzels sold at the same stand. At festivals and county fairs, take your pick from cotton candy, corn dogs, candy apples and local specialties like smoked turkey legs, fried funnel cakes and German sausages with onions. Farmers markets often have wholesome, affordable prepared foods.

VEGETARIANS & VEGANS

Vegetarianism and veganism once carried something of a cult-like onus in the USA, but those days are long gone. Indeed, one of the most highly regarded restaurants of any kind in the USA is Greens in San Francisco, run by the Buddhist Zen Center and beloved by vegetarians and carnivores alike. Today even a fast-food eatery probably carries vegetarian options, perhaps a hefty salad or grilled vegetables wrapped in a tortilla, and non–meat-eaters tend to do very well in Asian restaurants. Upscale restaurants have found that many of their guests avoid meat at lunchtime, so their daytime menus offer lighter soups, salads and pastas, and most will happily make a vegetarian dish if requested. Vegetarian restaurants now abound in major American cities, though not yet in smaller cities or towns.

If you do dine at a non-vegetarian restaurant that claims to serve vegetarian options, by all means ask if the food has been made with animal-based fats or broths. Do not assume that a naïve chef knows the variations.

Vegetarian and vegan eateries have been noted throughout this book. To find a vegetarian restaurant, visit www.vegdining.com.

EATING WITH KIDS

The US restaurant industry seems built on family-style service: children are not just accepted everywhere, but usually are encouraged through dedicated children's menus with smaller portions and prices. In some restaurants children under a certain age can even eat free. Other restaurants may engage the children with crayons and puzzles, even live performances by cartoon-like characters.

Restaurants without children's menus don't necessarily discourage kids, though higher-end restaurants might; always call ahead. Ask if the kitchen will make a small order of pasta with tomato sauce or butter and cheese (also ask how much it will cost), or if they will split a normal-size order among two plates for the kids. Chinese, Mexican and Italian restaurants seem to be the best bet for finicky young eaters. Restaurants usually provide high chairs and booster seats.

The Vegetarian Resource Group has found that less than 3% of Americans are completely vegetarian, but almost 60% of the population regularly chooses to eat meatless.

HABITS & CUSTOMS

Americans spend 13% of their budgets on food, but 40-50% of that money is spent in restaurants: about $1.3 billion per day.

Americans tend to eat early at restaurants and at home, so don't be surprised to find a restaurant half full at 11:45am or 5:30pm. Dinner parties for adults usually begin at 6:30 or 7pm with cocktails followed by a buffet or sit-down dinner. If invited to dinner, arrive within fifteen minutes of the designated time, and take a bottle of wine as a gift.

Americans are not so formal in their dining manners, though they wait until everyone is served before eating. They also eat with their fork in their right hand, after switching it from their left. Many foods are eaten with the fingers, and an entire piece of bread may be buttered and eaten all at once. Beer bottles are not uncommon on a dinner table and iced tea is more typical at lunch than beer or wine.

Don't worry, you're not expected to finish everything on your plate in the USA – portions tend to be so large that even a very refined French restaurant probably stocks 'doggie bags' in which to take home uneaten food to be consumed as leftovers the next day.

DUI (driving under the influence) is taken very seriously in the States. Designating a driver has become widespread practice among those who intend to drink alcohol at restaurants or parties.

COOKING COURSES

Approximately 62% of adult Americans (and 34% of children) are overweight. That's up from 47% in the late 1970s.

There has been a proliferation of cooking courses in the past decade as more Americans realize they want to cook better (or just plain cook). Cooking shows have become popular on TV, and cooking classes are now offered at some high-end cookware shops such as Williams-Sonoma (www.williams-sonoma.com) and Sur la Table (www.surlatable.com). Here is a sample of cooking schools that offer courses to amateur chefs on holiday:

DOS & DON'TS

Americans are more and more casual about even fine dining, but they do have their customs and rules.

- If invited to dinner, take flowers or a bottle of wine as a gift, though your host may not serve that wine that evening.

- Don't cut pizza with a knife and fork. Pick it up and fold it in half, as you'll see everyone else doing.

- Cell phones at the table are a big annoyance in restaurants, so excuse yourself and leave the dining room to make or take a call.

- Many cities and states outlaw smoking in restaurants and bars, so go outside to smoke unless there's an ashtray on your table.

- In nicer establishments, always make a reservation and do not be late! Most restaurants will not hold reservations more than 15 minutes. If you're running late, call to let them know.

- Expect restaurant wine prices to be marked up 100% to 300% above what you would pay in a wine shop.

- Always check your bill for questionable charges. Mistakes, intentional and otherwise, do occur.

- Ask for a 'doggie bag' to take leftovers home with you, even in a fancy *haute cuisine* restaurant. Americans hate to waste food and portions tend to be large.

- If you have your heart set on going to a very popular or trendy restaurant and can't get a table in mid-evening, consider a table at 6:30pm or 9:30pm, and you'll have a much better chance. Also, hotel concierges can work wonders in getting reservations on short notice.

Central Market Cooking School (www.centralmarket.com) In five major Texas cities.
Cookin' Cajun Cooking School (www.cookincajun.com) In New Orleans.
Cook's World (www.cooksworld.net) In Seattle.
French Culinary Institute (www.frenchculinary.com) In New York City (the Italian Culinary Academy is on the same premises).
Natural Gourmet Cookery School (www.naturalgourmetschool.com) In New York City, focusing on vegetarian and healthy cooking.
New School of Cooking (www.newschoolofcooking.com) In Culver City (outside Los Angeles).
Prairie Kitchens (www.prairiekitchens.com) In Chicago, Illinois.
Santa Fe School of Cooking (www.santafeschoolofcooking.com) In Santa Fe, New Mexico.
Tante Marie's Cooking School (www.tantemarie.com) In San Francisco.

Want to re-create your USA dining experience at home? Epicurious (www .epicurious.com) is a vast database of recipes from popular cooking magazines *Gourmet* and *Bon Appétit*.

FOOD GLOSSARY

angel's food cake – a light, tall puffy cake made with beaten egg whites.
bagel – a New York doughnut-like bread roll that is boiled then baked.
Bananas Foster – a New Orleans dessert of sliced bananas sautéed in butter, rum, and banana liqueur, then flamed and served with ice cream.
barbecue – a technique of slow-smoking spice-rubbed and basted meat over a grill.
beignet – a New Orleans fritter dusted with powdered sugar.
biscuit – a flaky non-yeast roll served in the South.
blintz – Jewish American pancake stuffed with various fillings like jam, cheese and potatoes.
blue plate – the special of the day in a diner or luncheonette.
Bloody Mary – a cocktail made with vodka, tomato juice, hot sauce and seasonings.
BLT – a bacon, lettuce and tomato sandwich.
Boston baked beans – beans cooked with molasses and bacon in a casserole.
brownie – a fudgy, cake-like bar cookie rich with chocolate and sometimes nuts.
Buffalo chicken wings – deep-fried chicken wings with spicy butter sauce, served with blue cheese dressing; a specialty of Buffalo, NY.
burrito – a Mexican American flour tortilla rolled around beans, meat, salsa and rice.
Caesar salad – romaine lettuce tossed with croutons and shaved Parmesan cheese in a dressing laced with raw egg.
California roll – a form of sushi first made in California, with avocado, crabmeat and cucumbers wrapped in vinegared rice.
chicken-fried steak – thin steak battered and fried like chicken.
chili – hearty meat stew spiced with ground chilies, vegetables and beans; also called chili con carne.
chimichanga – a deep-fried wheat tortilla stuffed with minced beef, potatoes and seasonings.
chips – thin, deep-fried potato slices; also crisp tortilla wedges.
chop suey – Chinese American dish of noodles, water chestnuts, bean sprouts and soy sauce.
clam chowder – potato-based soup full of clams, vegetables and sometimes bacon, thickened with milk.
club sandwich – a three-layered sandwich with chicken or turkey, bacon, lettuce and tomato.
Cobb salad – a California chopped salad of avocado, lettuce, celery, tomato, bacon, chicken, hard-boiled egg and Roquefort cheese.
cobbler – fruit dessert with a biscuit or pie-crust topping, baked and served with whipped cream or ice cream.
cold cut – thinly sliced meats and cheese served cold.
continental breakfast – coffee or tea, pastry and juice or fruit.
corned beef – salt-cured beef, traditionally served with cabbage on St. Patrick's Day (March 17).
crab cake – crab meat bound with breadcrumbs and eggs then fried.
cream cheese – soft cow's milk cheese that can be spread on bread or a bagel.
devil's food cake – layer cake made with dark chocolate and chocolate icing.
eggs Benedict – poached eggs, ham and hollandaise sauce on top of English muffins.
enchilada – baked tortillas stuffed with minced meats, cheese, sausage and chilies.
English muffin – round flat muffin made with flour, yeast and malted barley.

THE BAGEL PHENOMENON

Bagels are big in the USA, and if you buy one in an Iowa supermarket you may wonder why all the fuss about a bread roll with a hole in the middle. But if you get your hands on a New York–made bagel, you might just find out.

A true bagel, which really became a Jewish delicacy in this country, is made of just flour, water, salt – and malt for a little sweetness – and often is still rolled by hand. It is boiled, then baked, making it slightly crisp on the outside and deliciously dense and chewy inside. Traditional flavors include plain, poppy seed, sesame seed, onion, pumpernickel and egg, but modern-day bakeries have added things such as blueberries and sun-dried tomatoes. Bagels are sliced in half, then spread with cream cheese and often topped with lox (cold-smoked salmon).

If you're in New York City, find out why Americans love bagels at one of these more popular spots:

Absolute Bagels (☎ 212-932-2052, 2788 Broadway)
Ess-a-bagel (☎ 212-980-1010, 831 Third Ave; ☎ 212-260-2252, 359 First Ave)
H & H Bagels (☎ 212-595-8003, 2239 Broadway; ☎ 212-765-7200, 639 W 46th St)
Murray's Bagels (☎ 212-462-2830, 500 Sixth Ave; ☎ 646-638-1335, 242 Eighth Ave)

fajita – marinated skirt steak served in a wheat tortilla.
French toast – egg-dipped bread fried and served with maple syrup.
fries or French fries – deep-fried chipped potatoes.
fudge – semisoft, buttery candy, usually chocolate or vanilla, sometimes with walnuts.
granola – breakfast cereal of oats, honey and nuts.
grits – white cornmeal porridge for a Southern breakfast or side dish.
guacamole – mashed avocado dip with lime juice, tomatoes, onions, chilies and cilantro, served with tortilla chips.
hash browns – shredded fried potatoes.
huevos rancheros – Mexican breakfast of corn tortillas topped with fried eggs and chili sauce.
jambalaya – Louisiana stew of rice, ham, sausage, shrimp and seasonings.
jelly – fruit preserve; thinner than jam.
knish – Jewish American baked or fried pastry stuffed with potato, cheese, buckwheat or chopped liver.
lobster roll – lobster meat mixed with mayonnaise and seasonings, and served in a toasted frankfurter bun.
lox – Jewish American version of smoked salmon.
muffuletta – New Orleans sandwich made with a round Italian bread loaf, ham, salami, cheese and pickled olives.
nacho – Mexican American fried tortilla chip topped with cheese and jalapeño peppers or salsa.
pastrami – Jewish American brined beef that is smoked and steamed.
pickle – a pickled cucumber.
ranch dressing – salad dressing of mayonnaise, onion, garlic, buttermilk and seasonings.
refried beans – Mexican American side dish of fried, mashed pinto beans.
Reuben sandwich – sandwich of corned beef, Swiss cheese and sauerkraut on rye bread.
sloppy Joe – ground beef, onions, green peppers and ketchup cooked in a skillet.
smoothie – cold, thick drink made with pureed fruit, ice and sometimes yogurt.
stone crab – Caribbean crab whose claws are eaten with melted butter or mustard-mayonnaise sauce.
strawberry shortcake – biscuit pastry topped with whipped cream and strawberries.
submarine sandwich – a sandwich served on a thick roll slathered with mustard and mayonnaise, filled with thinly sliced deli meats and cheeses, as well as lettuce, onions, pickles and tomato; also called a hoagie, po'boy, hero or grinder.
surf 'n' turf – plate of both seafood (often lobster) and steak.
veal (or chicken) parmesan – Italian American dish of pounded veal cutlet baked with a topping of mozzarella cheese and tomato sauce.
wrap – a tortilla or pita bread stuffed with a wide variety of fillings.

Environment

Through luck, wars and purchase, the USA gathered to itself the entire lower half of the North American continent. Without this land, would the 'American experiment' in republican democracy have grown into the powerful nation it is today? Do bears frequent outhouses?

Decidedly not. In fact, the continent's immense riches fueled America's industrial might and inspired self-congratulatory dreams of Manifest Destiny, even as the continent's raw beauty wove itself into the nation's collective soul. Despite over 400 years of settlement and cities, of farming and mining, and sometimes raging conflicts over resources and environmental impacts, Americans regard the continent's unsurpassed natural wonders as a national treasure.

And in the last century and a half, Americans have tried to make concrete all that good feeling through the establishment of a wide array of parks, preserves and wildlife refuges. Exploring these is a highlight of any visit: for a colorful taste of the USA's national parks, see p105. But also, nature writing is one of the richest genres of American nonfiction, bringing to life America's distinctive spirit and its inextricable relationship to the land.

After all, without the wild frontier, where would American optimism have gone to bloom?

Normally, people change, nature abides. In *Chasing Spring* (2006), Bruce Stutz travels America and eloquently ponders the opposite: how a shifting climate is changing the world in our lifetime.

THE LAND

America is big, no question. Covering some 3,787,000 sq miles, it's the world's third-largest country by size, trailing only Russia and Canada, its friendly neighbor to the north. Continental USA is made up of 48 contiguous states ('the lower 48'), while Alaska, its largest state, is northwest of Canada, and the volcanic islands of Hawaii, the 50th state, are 2100 miles southwest in the Pacific Ocean.

It's more than just size, though. America feels big because of its incredibly diverse topography, which began to take shape around 50 to 60 million years ago.

In the conterminous US, the east is a land of temperate, deciduous forests that contains the ancient Appalachian Mountains, a low range that parallels the coast along the Atlantic Ocean. This coast is the country's most populated, urbanized region, particularly between Washington, DC, and Boston.

Just to the north are the Great Lakes, which the US shares with Canada. These five lakes, part of the Canadian Shield, are the greatest expanse of fresh water on planet earth, constituting about 18% of the world's supply.

Going south along the East Coast, things get wetter and warmer, till you reach the swamps of southern Florida and make the turn into the Gulf of Mexico, which provides the US with a southern coastline.

Geology is rarely a page-turner, but in *Annals of the Former World* (1998) John McPhee turns the history of North American plate tectonics into a thrilling, human spectacle of discovery.

West of the Appalachians are the vast interior plains, which lie flat as an *American Idol* contestant's high C all the way to the Rocky Mountains. The eastern plains are the nation's breadbasket, roughly divided into the northern 'corn belt' and the southern 'cotton belt.' The plains, an ancient sea bottom, are drained by the mighty Mississippi River, one of the world's great river systems. Going west, farmland slowly gives way to cowboys and ranches in the semiarid, big-sky Great Plains.

The young, jagged Rocky Mountains are a complex set of tall ranges that runs all the way from Mexico to Canada, providing excellent skiing.

West of these mountains is the Southwest desert, an extremely arid region that has been cut to dramatic effect by the Colorado River system. This land of

TERRY TEMPEST WILLIAMS: LOVE AND HUMILITY IN THE DESERT

A naturalist, teacher and writer, Terry Tempest Williams forms part of the West's long, distinguished heritage of conservationists and ecologists. Her latest book is *Mosaic: Finding Beauty in a Broken World*. We asked her to talk about the environmental state of the nation and what she loves about her home, the canyon country of southern Utah.

'One of the beautiful aspects of American democracy,' Williams said, 'is that we have given value to national parks and refuges. We have a Wilderness Act and an Endangered Species Act. To me this is a transformative, restorative justice. It's a movement born out of love and idealism. It's an expansive movement born out of expansive country. I love that.'

When asked about today's seemingly endless list of environmental threats – from global warming to national politics – Williams didn't hesitate: 'I refuse to engage in doomsday approaches. I don't think we can know what's ahead. The problem before us now is that we've failed to see the interconnectedness of things. To me the very heart of an environmental ethic is the notion of empathy based in community in the broadest sense. First and foremost, it's about good manners.

'I love thinking of those two words "climate change" literally – you know, a change of attitudes. And I do see a climate change in the American Southwest. The world is so beautiful, so fragile, particularly in desert landscapes, how can we not respond? It's important to look at global warming as local warming, which brings an immediacy to our own communities that we can no longer ignore.'

Nevertheless, she said, 'It's going to take us decades to undo what George Bush has set in motion environmentally. All one has to do is fly over southwest Colorado, the Colorado Plateau in Utah, western Wyoming, and your heart breaks.' More than rampant mining and drilling, 'public process has been abandoned. The Clean Air Act, the Clean Water Act, wetlands legislation – all

eroded canyons leads to the unforgiving Great Basin as you go across Nevada. Also an ancient sea bottom, the Great Basin is so unwanted it's where the military practices and where the US plans to bury its nuclear waste.

Then you reach America's third major mountain system: the southern, granite Sierra Nevada and the northern, volcanic Cascades, which both parallel the Pacific Coast. California's Central Valley is one of the most fertile places on earth, while the coastline from San Diego to Seattle is celebrated in song and legend – a stretch of sandy beaches, redwoods and old-growth forests.

But wait, there's more. Northwest of Canada, Alaska reaches the Arctic Ocean and contains tundra, glaciers, an interior rainforest and the lion's share of federally protected wilderness, while Hawaii to the southwest is a tropical string of Pacific island pearls.

Where the Bluebird Sings to the Lemonade Springs (1993) is an essential primer in Wallace Stegner and the misunderstood and mostly abused West. These essays are classics.

WILDLIFE

Standing in one of the carefully tended, surviving patches of original America, it's possible to imagine that long-ago continent: the great plains a rustling ocean of grass; the eastern seaboard a chattering blanket of forest; buffalo by the millions; wolves in every corner, howling. Occupying the same vast horizon, we easily see why the new nation believed its natural resources to be limitless.

They weren't, and America quickly proved it during its 19th-century westward expansion. By century's end, alarmed citizens and politicians suddenly realized that could actually use everything up.

In 1903, America began expressly preserving its wildlife when President Teddy Roosevelt set aside Florida's Pelican Island as the nation's first bird sanctuary, thereby creating the **National Wildlife Refuge System** (NWRS). Today, managed by the **US Fish & Wildlife Service** (FWS; www.fws.gov), the NWRS includes

these acts have been gravely undermined for short-term gain, and who's paying the price? Local communities in the interior West and ecological communities from pronghorns and sage to red rock and ravens.'

To counteract this, America's Red Rock Wilderness Act – which would preserve 9.4 million acres of Southwest desert – was submitted for congressional approval in 2007. Passing this act, Williams said, 'would be an extraordinary act of restraint, a bow toward beauty that says we can live with a sense of compassion toward other species.' In her writing, Williams often mentions restraint, but she also said, 'It's so important that we venture out into these vast wildlands because I think it reminds us what endures.

'What I love is, you know, talk to me about politics and greed in the middle of a flash flood. Just the other day I was out walking and I heard this dry rattle. I stopped and thought, *Where are you?* All of sudden just square in the wash was this rattlesnake. It's that kind of pause that makes me smile. There's no word for that kind of encounter.

'There's something so profoundly wonderful about the humility that one faces walking in a wild place. These rocks tell time differently, and they ask us to do the same. Perhaps therein lies our humility as a species.

'When people say "describe the American West" to me, I say take sage between your fingers, and roll it and smell. In that you can smell the aridity, you can smell the wisdom of the land, you can smell our history. What's been disturbed and what's been protected. There's something about sage that defines this region.

'I was born in the arid West. I am distrustful of trees. The stillness I have come to love and rely on in the desert is the stillness I recognize within my own heart.

'The red-rock desert of southern Utah is not just an acquired taste, it is a love affair.'

around 95 million acres, making it the world's largest system of preserves dedicated to protecting wildlife and habitat.

In 1964 the Wilderness Act was passed to preserve entire, self-regulating ecosystems. The US now has over 700 official wilderness areas totaling over 100 million acres; over half are in Alaska.

However, the most powerful and controversial environmental tool remains the 1973 Endangered Species Act (ESA). Currently, over 1280 plants and animals are listed in the US as either endangered or threatened. Some are mighty creatures like grizzly bears, but most are not so sexy (such as freshwater mussels, chubs and grasses). Since its inception, the ESA has been criticized for obstructing industry and commerce, but never more so than by the Bush administration, whose eight-year mission seems aimed at rendering the application and definitions of the law essentially meaningless.

Given all the stresses nature is enduring, what is most remarkable is how wild it can still seem. Hiking in a national park or wilderness area – spotting bears and wolves, elephant seals and condors, herds of bison and elk, old-growth redwoods and primordial swamps – is pure joy. These are just the tantalizing highlights.

The Wilderness Society (www.wilderness.org) is the USA's main advocacy organization for wilderness. Aldo Leopold, a founder and a former president, wrote the 1964 Wilderness Act.

Animals
LAND MAMMALS
Nineteenth-century Americans did not willingly suffer competing predators, and federal eradication programs nearly wiped out every single wolf and big cat and many of the bears in the continental US. Almost all share the same story of abundance, precipitous loss and, today, partial recovery.

Grizzly, or brown, bears are one of North America's largest land mammals. Male grizzlies can stand 7ft tall, weigh up to 600lb and consider 500 sq miles home. At one time, perhaps 100,000 roamed the West, but by 1975 fewer than 300 remained. Successful conservation efforts, particularly in the Greater Yellowstone Region, have increased the population in the lower 48 states to around 1200. By contrast, Alaska remains chock-full of grizzlies, with upwards of 30,000.

Despite declines, black bears still reside nearly everywhere. Smaller than grizzlies, these opportunistic, adaptable animals can survive in very small home ranges. Black bears enjoy an almost mythical status in America because of their intelligent, congenial personality. Indeed, they can become so comfortable with humans that national parks like Yosemite and Yellowstone have a constant problem with black bears poaching campsites and cars for food. Be mindful whenever you're in bear country.

Another extremely adaptable creature is the coyote, which looks similar to a wolf but is about half the size, ranging from 20lb to 50lb. An icon of the Southwest, coyotes are found all over, sometimes even in cities.

America has one primary big-cat species, which goes by several names: mountain lion, cougar, puma and panther. In the east, a remnant population of Florida panthers is nurtured in Everglades National Park. In the west, mountain lions are common enough that human encounters have begun occurring. These powerful cats are around 125lb of pure muscle, with short tawny fur, long tails and a secretive nature.

When it comes to wildlife slaughter, nothing can match what happened to the buffalo, or bison. No accurate count can ever be made, but they may have originally numbered as many as 65 million, in herds so thick they 'darkened the whole plains,' as Lewis and Clark wrote. They were killed for food, hides, sport, cash and to impoverish Native Americans, who depended on them. By the 20th century, a couple hundred remained. From these, new herds have been built up, so that one of America's quintessential animals can again be admired in its gruff majesty – among other places, in Yellowstone, Grand Teton and Badlands National Parks.

Defenders of Wildlife (www.defenders.org) is a major champion of endangered plants and animals, particularly wolves and predators. Its website has species fact sheets and status updates.

MARINE MAMMALS & FISH

Perhaps no native fish gets more attention than salmon, whose spawning runs up Pacific Coast rivers are famous spectacles. However, both Pacific and Atlantic salmon are considered endangered; hatcheries release millions of young every year, but there is debate whether this practice hurts or helps wild populations.

Due to melting glaciers, the newest endangered species may soon be the polar bear. In a first, the FWS is considering listing it because of climate change. For more, see p1061.

As for marine life, gray, humpback and blue whales migrate annually along the Pacific Coast, making whale-watching very popular. Alaska and Hawaii are important breeding grounds for whales and marine mammals, and the San Juan Islands in Washington are visited by orcas.

The Pacific Coast is also home to ponderous elephant seals, playful sea lions and endangered sea otters. In California, Channel Islands National Park and Monterey Bay preserve unique, highly diverse marine worlds.

For coral reefs and tropical fish, Hawaii and the Florida Keys are the prime destinations. The coast of Florida is also home to the unusual, gentle manatee, which moves between freshwater rivers and the ocean. Around 10ft long and weighing up to 1200lb, these agile, expressive creatures number around 3000, and may have once been mistaken for mermaids.

The Gulf of Mexico is another vital marine habitat, perhaps most famously for endangered sea turtles, which nest on south-coast beaches.

BIRDS

Bird-watching is the most popular wildlife activity in the US, and little wonder – all the hemisphere's migratory songbirds and shorebirds rest here at some point, and America consequently claims some 800 avian

---

RETURN OF THE WOLF

The wolf is a potent icon of America's wilderness. This smart, social predator is the largest species of canine – reaching 115lbs and 3ft at the shoulder – and an estimated 400,000 once roamed the continent from coast to coast, from Alaska to Mexico.

Unlike the domestic dog, wolves were not regarded warmly by the country's European settlers. The first wildlife legislation in the British colonies was a wolf bounty. As late-19th-century Americans tamed the West, they slaughtered the once-uncountable herds of bison, elk, deer and moose – replacing them with domestic cattle and sheep, which wolves found equally tasty.

To stop their intolerable poaching, the wolf's extermination soon became official government policy. For $20 to $50 an animal, wolves were shot, poisoned, trapped and dragged from dens until in the lower 48 states only a few hundred remained in northern Minnesota. Lacking wolves, bounty programs ended from 1935 to 1965.

In 1944, Aldo Leopold was the first to call for the return of the wolf. His argument was ecology, not nostalgia. His studies showed that wild ecosystems need their top predators to maintain a healthy biodiversity; in complex interdependence, all animals and plants suffered with the wolf gone. As Leopold cautioned, 'To keep every cog and wheel is the first precaution of intelligent tinkering.'

When the Endangered Species Act was enacted in 1973, gray and red wolves were among the first species listed. Despite dire predictions from ranchers and hunters, gray wolves were reintroduced to the Greater Yellowstone Region in 1995–96 and to Arizona in 1998. Problems since have been minor.

Protected and encouraged, wolf populations have recovered rapidly: in 2007, the western Great Lakes population of 4000 was considered self-sustaining and 'delisted.' The Yellowstone region had over 1200 and was proposed for delisting. Around 60 now live in Arizona–New Mexico, and about 100 reintroduced red wolves live in North Carolina; these populations remain protected.

---

species. If you need help finding and identifying them, the Sibley Field Guides are an indispensable resource, as is the **National Audubon Society** (www.audubon.org).

The bald eagle was adopted as the nation's symbol in 1782. It's the only eagle unique to North America, and half a million once ruled the continent's skies. By 1963, habitat destruction and, in particular, poisoning from DDT had caused the population to plummet to 417 breeding pairs in the lower 48. However, by 2007, bald eagles had recovered so well, increasing to around 9700 breeding pairs across the continent (plus about 50,000 in Alaska), that they've been removed from the endangered species list.

At Ebird (http://ebird .org), avid birders can put their efforts to good use by logging their counts and helping science.

Perhaps the only bird more impressive is the California condor, a prehistoric, carrion-eating bird that weighs 25lb and has a wingspan over 9ft. Condors were virtually extinct by the 1980s (reduced to six birds in captivity), but they have been successfully bred and reintroduced in California and northern Arizona, where they are sometimes spotted soaring above the Grand Canyon.

Plants

The eastern United States was originally one endless, complex deciduous forest that mixed with evergreens depending on altitude and latitude. Great Smoky Mountains National Park contains all five eastern forest types – spruce fir, hemlock, pine-oak, and northern and cove hardwood – which include over 130 species of trees. Spring wildflower and autumn hardwood color displays are a Northeast specialty.

In Florida, the Everglades is the last subtropical wilderness in the US. This vital, endangered habitat is a fresh- and salt-water world of marshes, sloughs and coastal prairies that support mangroves, cypresses, sea grasses, tropical plants, pines and hardwoods.

The grasslands of the interior plains are perhaps America's most abused ecosystem. The 19th-century 'sodbusters' converted them largely to agriculture, particularly the eastern tall-grass prairies, of which less than 4% remain. The semiarid short-grass prairies have survived somewhat better, but farmers have still cultivated them for monoculture row crops by tapping the underground aquifer. Theodore Roosevelt National Park is a good destination to see America's remaining grasslands.

The Southwest deserts are horizon-stretching expanses of sage, scrub and cacti that abut western mountain ranges, where abundant wildflowers in spring and electric-yellow quaking aspens in fall inspire pilgrimages.

West of the Cascades in wet, milder Washington and Oregon are the last primeval forests in America. These diverse, ancient evergreen stands, of which only 10% remain, contain hemlocks, cedars, spruces and, in particular, towering Douglas firs.

California, meanwhile, is famous for its two species of sequoias, or redwoods. The coast redwood is the world's tallest tree (with the very tallest in Redwood National Park; see p981), while the related giant sequoia is the world's biggest by volume. Sequoia National Park has the granddaddy of them all (p993).

> Aldo Leopold's *A Sand County Almanac* (1949) became a touchstone for American naturalists, and it remains a humble, unpretentious and powerfully moving testimony.

NATIONAL PARKS & FEDERAL LANDS

Over a quarter of the USA (or over 600 million acres) falls under some kind of federal protection or stewardship. That's a lot of public land, and nearly all of it can be visited. These diverse areas span the country, but they are most extensive in the scenic West and Alaska. Some have entrance fees and require permits (for instance, to camp or fish), and facilities range from nothing at all (in designated wilderness) to first-class hotels and gourmet restaurants (in top national parks).

These lands and historic sites have a bewildering array of designations (and regulations). They are managed mainly by four agencies: the **Bureau of Land Management** (BLM; www.blm.gov), the **US Forest Service** (USFS; www.fs.fed.us), the **US Fish and Wildlife Service** (FWS; www.fws.gov) and the **National Park Service** (NPS; www.nps.gov).

> *Nature Noir* (2005) by Jordan Fisher Smith is utterly unique and actually pulse-pounding: Smith's tales of being a state park ranger in the Sierra Nevada would make Raymond Chandler blanch.

US WORLD HERITAGE SITES

For more information on World Heritage Sites, visit Unesco's website: whc.unesco.org/en/list.

- Cahokia Mounds State Historic Site (p577)
- Carlsbad Caverns National Park (p894)
- Chaco Culture National Historic Park (p889)
- Everglades National Park (p507)
- Glacier Bay National Park & Preserve (p1065)
- Grand Canyon National Park (p835)
- Great Smoky Mountains National Park (p388)
- Hawai'i Volcanoes National Park (p1102)
- Independence Hall (p202)
- Mammoth Cave National Park (p485)
- Mesa Verde National Park (p776)

- Monticello (p360) and the University of Virginia (p360) in Charlottesville
- Olympic National Park (p1017)
- Redwood National Park (p981)
- Statue of Liberty (p140)
- Taos Pueblo (p887)
- Waterton-Glacier International Peace Park (p795)
- Wrangell–St Elias National Park (p1079)
- Yellowstone National Park (p781)
- Yosemite National Park (p989)

If you're looking for iconographic America – the Grand Canyon, perhaps? – chances are it's within the National Park Service (NPS). The NPS manages 391 parks, totaling 84 million acres. The jewels of the system are its 58 national parks, which by and large contain the best facilities and the most visitor services. For a complete introduction to the USA's national parks, see p105.

Most other federal lands, such as the BLM's 258 million acres and the USFS' 193 million acres, are managed under the concept of 'mixed use,' which means they must somehow balance recreation, resource extraction, grazing and preservation. Visitor facilities tend to be minimal, when they exist at all, but the scenery is often wonderful and less crowded than at higher-profile national parks.

A great place to start is by visiting www.recreation.gov, the government's main public-lands web portal. For more on fees, passes, permits, camping and so on, see 'National Parks: A User's Guide' (p113) and the Directory (p1111).

THE ENVIRONMENTAL MOVEMENT

America is well known for its political and social revolutions, but it also birthed environmentalism. The USA was the first nation to make significant efforts to preserve its wilderness and US environmentalists often push preservation efforts worldwide.

The nation did not start out this way. Indeed, America's Protestant settlers believed that civilization's Christian mandate was to bend nature to its will. Not only was wilderness deadly and difficult, but it was a potent symbol of humanity's godless impulses, and the Pilgrims set about subduing both with gusto.

Then, in the mid-19th-century, taking their cue from European Romantics, the USA's transcendentalists claimed that nature was not fallen, but holy – that it actually embodied God. In *Walden* (1854), iconoclast Henry David Thoreau described living for two years in the woods, blissfully free of civilization's comforts, and he persuasively argued that human society was harmfully distant from nature's essential truths. While largely anthropomorphic, this view marked a profound shift: God no longer spoke through the ax, but through the forest.

The continent's natural wonders – vividly captured by America's 19th-century landscape painters – also had a way of selling themselves, and rampant nationalism led to a desire to promote them. In 1864, a 10-sq-mile portion of Yosemite Valley was set aside as a state park; then in 1872, President Ulysses S Grant designated two million acres as Yellowstone National Park, the first such large-scale preserve in the world.

Yellowstone was established expressly to preserve its unique features for human enjoyment. But nature's greatest cheerleader, John Muir, soon emerged to champion wilderness for its own sake. Muir considered nature superior to civilization, and he spent much of his life wandering the Sierra Nevada and passionately advocating on behalf of the mountains and forests. Muir was the driving force behind the nation's emerging conservation movement, which had its first big victory in 1890 when Yosemite National Park was established expressly to preserve wilderness. Muir founded the Sierra Club in 1892.

By the end of the 19th century, the nation was also realizing the limits of its once boundless resources. In 1891 the Forest Reserve Act was passed to maintain and manage forests to ensure they'd keep fueling America's growth. This, then, epitomized the conservation movement's central conflict: whether to preserve nature for human use or for its own spiritual sanctity. These mutually exclusive aims underlie many conflicts today.

Famous cranky-puss Edward Abbey turned his job as an Arches National Park ranger into *Desert Solitaire* (1967), which swings from desert rhapsodies to prescient warnings about oncoming mass tourism.

To learn more about wilderness in America – its history, advocates, definitions, laws, current status and more – visit www.wilderness.net.

The Sierra Club (www .sierraclub.org) was the USA's first conservation group and it remains the nation's most active, with educational programs, organized trips and tons of information.

ARRIVE PREPARED, LEAVE NO TRACE

As you're out having an exciting adventure in America's wilderness, remember: one thought-less gesture – hiking off-trail through fragile soil or building an illegal fire – can take years for nature to repair. Many of America's most beloved landscapes are being loved to death. Each person makes a difference.

Most hiking and camping advice is common sense. First, know what you are getting into. Know what weather to expect and pack accordingly, even for just a few hours. Get trail maps and take five minutes to talk to a ranger before plunging ahead. Rangers can alert you to crowds, landmarks and trail conditions, and they can confirm that your abilities and equipment match your needs.

Once in the wild, do everything possible to minimize your impact. As they say, take only pictures, leave only footprints. Stick to established trails and campsites. Be particularly sensitive to riparian areas: don't wash yourself or your dishes in streams or rivers, and camp at least 200ft away from them. Use a stove for cooking and make fires only in established fire rings (using only downed wood). When you leave, take out everything you brought in and clean up every trace of your visit.

Conduct yourself as if you were a guest in someone's home – which you are. Observe wildlife, but don't approach or feed it. Leave cultural or historic artifacts as you find them. And finally, of course, be respectful of other hikers, both those around you and those to follow.

For further advice, contact the **Leave No Trace Center** (www.lnt.org).

In the early 20th century, the increasingly dark scars of industrial progress raised urgent new concerns. The 1916 National Park Service Act established a permanent federal mechanism for wilderness preservation (for more on national park history, see p116). But more importantly, the science of ecology emerged. Ecology proved yet another humbling of humankind – already knocked from the center of the universe, and arm in arm with monkeys – with its assertion that people were in fact interdependent with nature, not in charge of it. With ecology, America's 19th-century conservation movement became the modern environmental movement.

By turns self-effacing and earnest, Bill McKibben talks with Vermont farmers and friends about how to turn an ecological mind-set into a practical everyday reality in Wandering Home *(2005).*

Aldo Leopold was the first writer to popularize an ecological worldview with his idea of a 'land ethic,' which proposed that humans must act with respectful stewardship toward all of nature, rather than celebrating the parts they like and abusing the rest. The 1962 publication of *Silent Spring* by Rachel Carson provided the shocking proof: this exposé of how chemicals such as DDT were killing animals and poisoning the land horrified the nation and inspired an army of activists.

Over the next decade, the USA passed a series of landmark environmental and wildlife laws that have since resulted in significant improvements in the nation's water and air quality, and the partial recovery of many near-extinct plants and animals. The movement's focus also steadily broadened – to preserving entire ecosystems, not just establishing new parks – as it confronted the so-called 'five horsemen of the environmental apocalypse': disease, pollution, overkill of species, habitat destruction through human impact, and the introduction of alien or nonnative species.

Today, environmentalism is obviously a worldwide movement, one that understands that each nation's local problems also contribute to a global threat: climate change. In the USA, the dangers of global warming are inspiring an environmental awareness as widespread as at any time in US history. Whether or not average Americans still believe God speaks through nature, they're increasingly disturbed by the messages they are hearing.

ENVIRONMENTAL ISSUES

The USA seems to have reached a tipping point: the majority of citizens now accept the reality of global warming. National discussions have steadily shifted from whether climate change exists to what America should do about it. Even the Bush administration, which once shut its eyes tight against the possibility (and when that failed, manipulated scientific reports to discredit it), has conceded that, yes, perhaps the weather is changing after all.

To be sure, government and industry are dragging their feet, hard. They argue that global warming is a natural (not human-caused) cycle; that it won't be that bad; that there's nothing we can do about it; or that, most especially, making drastic changes to quickly combat global warming is too costly to the nation's economic health to consider.

Fierce battles over the environment have been a fixture of the American political landscape for over a century, and for business, this last argument has been a winner, whether the issue is pollution, dwindling resources or endangered species. This effectiveness rests, in part, on the dependable reluctance of US citizens to make sacrifices in their consumptive lifestyles.

Typically, Americans support regulations and alter their habits only when environmental problems become undeniable, quantifiable and urgent. With global warming, that moment seems to have arrived.

How to tell? Despite White House antagonism, state and local governments are passing environmental legislation and businesses are investing in alternative energy. For instance, 14 states have adopted stricter auto-emissions standards than the federal government's. When the **Environmental Protection Agency** (EPA; www.epa.gov) withheld permission to implement them, the states sued, and in 2007 the Supreme Court ruled that the EPA has both the authority and a 'duty' to regulate greenhouse gases under the Clean Air Act. Not coincidentally, Congress introduced a bill in 2007 to tighten federal auto-emissions standards for the first time in 20 years.

In 2007, 10 northeast states created the USA's first cap-and-trade program (modeled after the EU) to reduce power-plant emissions. Even average folks are responding: public-transit use has increased 30% since 1995 and is at its highest point in 50 years, and in 2006, voters passed 99 bond issues to protect land, willingly raising their taxes $5.73 billion.

Energy

The USA is the world's greatest consumer of energy (using more oil, electricity and natural gas per day than any other country) and hence its greatest polluter, accounting for a quarter of the world's greenhouse gases. Coal provides half of the nation's electricity, nuclear about 20% and renewable sources (mainly hydroelectric) almost 9%.

The USA contains a quarter of the world's coal reserves, and the Bush administration's current energy plan calls for building 150 new coal plants and pushing 'liquid' coal, even though these are among the dirtiest methods of generating electricity.

Increasing nuclear energy is another Bush goal. In early 2007, the Nuclear Regulatory Commission approved the first new nuclear plant site in 30 years, with more expected. Nuclear energy emits no greenhouse gases, but its waste poses other problems. In 2001, Nevada's Yucca Mountain was chosen as the nation's sole permanent nuclear-waste repository. However, the project has been plagued with controversy over the potential for leaks (see www.yuccamountain.org); it's currently due to open in 2017 (at a cost of $18.5 billion), unless state and Democratic politicians stop it altogether. What happens then to the high-level radioactive waste already stored at 126 sites nationwide remains an issue.

Need help conceptualizing the enormity of US consumption? Check out photographer Chris Jordan's exhibits *Running the Numbers* and *Intolerable Beauty* at www .chrisjordan.com.

Credit former vice president Al Gore. His documentary *An Inconvenient Truth* (2006) finally convinced Americans that global warming exists and that the US is throwing fuel on the fire.

Why is increasing domestic oil production such a big issue? The US imports over 60% of its oil, a percentage that has risen over 7% during Bush's presidency.

Meanwhile, interest in renewable technologies and fuels is exploding. One indication is that venture-capital investments in alternative fuels nearly quadrupled to $700 million in 2006. The US has recently led the world in installing wind turbines, which could provide 5% of US electricity by 2010. In 2007, Congress mandated that 4% of all motor fuels must come from renewable sources, increasing to around 7% by 2012; as a result, ethanol and biodiesel production have soared. Even Wal-Mart is putting solar panels on its buildings.

Hydrogen technology holds the most promise for zero-emission production, and in one of few instances of environmental leadership, President Bush has funded hydrogen research for several years. However, developing hydrogen into an affordable option could take decades.

Air Pollution

Concern for air pollution has lead to a society-wide discussion about greenhouse gases touching every aspect of modern life: from building design and light bulbs to auto emissions and planting trees. While states wrestle with the federal government over how much and how quickly to raise auto fuel-economy standards (currently averaging 21mpg), car-loving consumers are starting to vote with their pocketbooks: even as overall auto sales flatten, sales of hybrid cars climbed 28% in 2006 (still only 1.5% of all sales), while SUV sales plummeted.

The federal government's response has been mixed. On the one hand, the EPA passed significant new emissions restrictions for diesel engines and generators in 2004. Yet on the other, the Bush administration has sought to weaken Clean Air Act standards to (among other things) keep coal-burning power plants from having to adopt expensive 'near-zero emission' technology.

Water

The EPA estimates that 40% of US waters remain polluted, despite significant improvements in water quality since the Clean Water Act was enacted in 1972. One of the most widespread problems is the recent discovery of perchlorate, a chemical used in missile and rocket fuel, in the drinking water in 22 states. However, under pressure from the Bush administration, the EPA has set contamination standards so high that little cleanup is being required, even though these standards exceed by 2000% what the EPA had initially considered safe.

Water issues are particularly acute in the West: the region's underground aquifer is being drained at a phenomenal rate, and increasing water salinity is playing havoc with farming (see also p678). Also, the West has witnessed a surge in new oil and gas drilling, in part because of government-approved industry exemptions in 2005 to the Clean Water Act. An unlikely coalition of ranchers, hunters and conservationists is fighting this all-too-common sacrifice of health for cheap energy.

It takes a lot of energy to be an American: annually, each US citizen is responsible for emitting 21 tons of carbon dioxide. The global average: 4.5 tons per person.

The Union of Concerned Scientists (www.ucsusa .org) is a reliable source for independent updates on global warming, vehicle emissions, energy, nuclear technology and scientific integrity.

When Smoke Ran Like Water (2002) by Devra Davis traces how scientists painstakingly link pollution to disease and how easily politics and industry undermine their conclusions. A chilling tale.

USA's National Parks

SARA BENSON

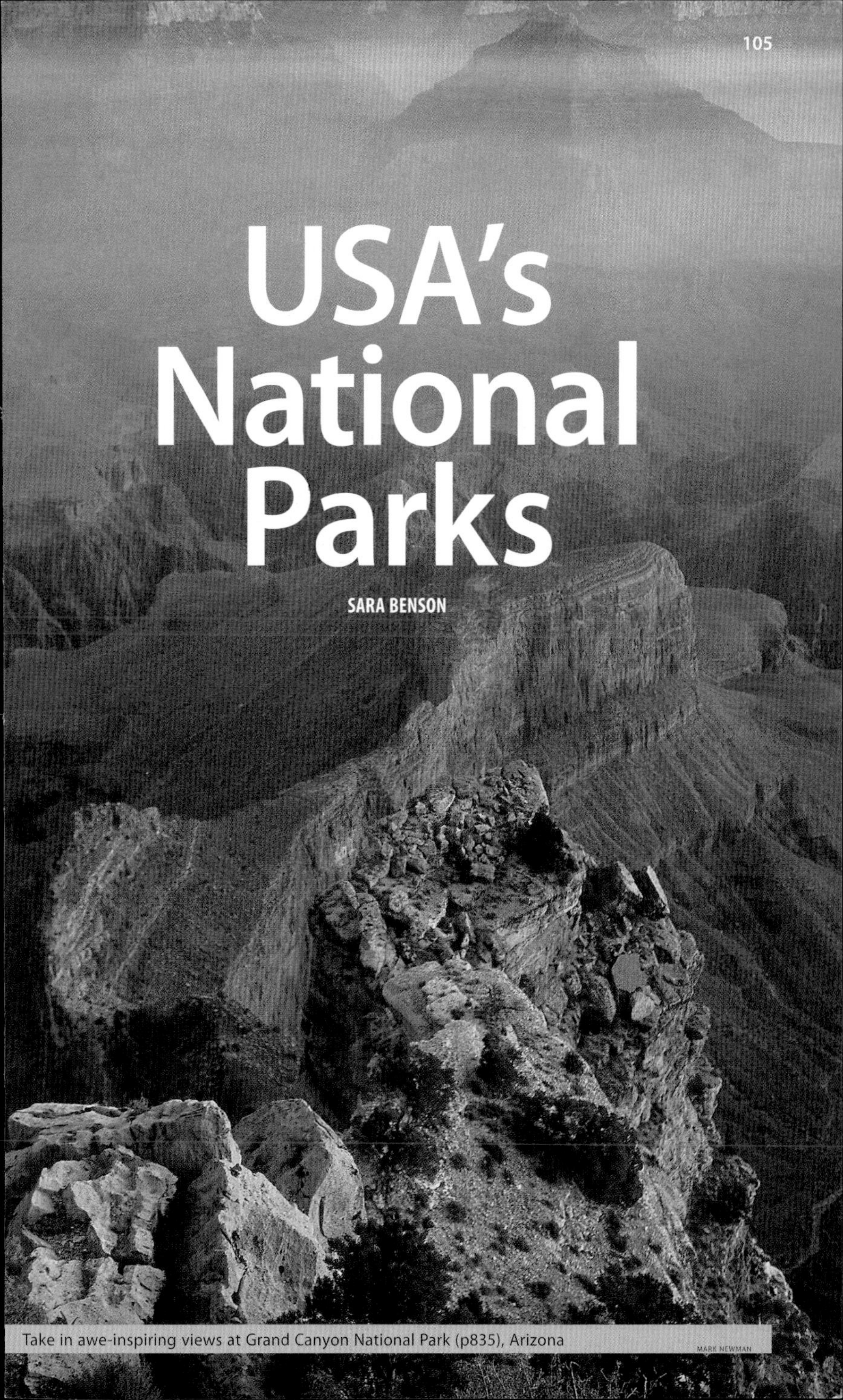

Take in awe-inspiring views at Grand Canyon National Park (p835), Arizona

MARK NEWMAN

Get the adrenaline pumping with some of the world's best rock climbing at Yosemite National Park (p989), California

National parks are Americans' big backyards. While many visitors' cross-country road trips connect the dots between the USA's big-shouldered cities, not everyone drives off the interstate to the rough-hewn doorsteps of the country's 58 national parks. If you do take that kind of detour – and rightly you should – you'll encounter truly wild territory.

Some parklands might look much the same as they did centuries ago, when this nation was just starting out. From craggy islands off the Atlantic Coast, to prairie grasslands and buffalo herds across the Great Plains, to the Rocky Mountains raising their jagged teeth along the Continental Divide, and onward to the tallest trees on earth – coast redwoods – standing sentinel on Pacific shores, you'll be amazed by the USA's natural bounty (for more, see the Environment chapter, p95). Luckily, much of it is protected by the National Park Service (NPS).

Historically speaking, the USA's voracious appetite for land and the material riches it promised drove not only the false doctrine of Manifest Destiny but also a bonanza of building pioneer homesteads, farms, barrier fences, great dams, concrete roadways and train tracks from sea to shining sea. Foreign to Native Americans, this infrastructure swallowed vast tracts of wilderness from the Appalachian Mountains, past the mighty Mississippi River and far into the West. That is, until the creation of a well-defended web of federal lands and national parks, where the express mission today is still to 'preserve unimpaired the natural and cultural resources…for the enjoyment, education, and inspiration of this and future generations.'

That means you, too. So pick a park, any park, and go play in the nation's backyard: 600 million acres of wilderness.

ADVENTURES

The USA's national parks are a living museum of natural history. They're also a gigantic outdoor playground designed for everyone to enjoy, from tots toddling down nature trails to grungy rock-climbing champions scaling high-flying domes.

Nothing is easier than just getting out of your vehicle and walking around. The parks enfold thousands of miles of hiking and backpacking trails. Take an easy walk through an alpine wildflower meadow or along a wild, natural beach. Long-distance footpaths include the famous 2175-mile Appalachian National Scenic Trail, which traces mountain ridges from Georgia up to Maine. Not feeling that hard-core? You need only a few days to backpack the Grand Canyon (p835) from rim to rim, just one night to sleep inside a technically still active volcano at Haleakala (p1107), and a few hours to hike across a steaming, living volcano at Hawai'i Volcanoes (p1102). Reserve your wilderness permits in advance for any popular backpacking route; see p114 for details on permits.

Mountaineering is a way to get even higher. Some hike the entire 211-mile John Muir Trail, connecting Yosemite (p989) to Sequoia & Kings Canyon (p993), just to climb Mt Whitney (14,495ft), continental USA's highest mountain. Peak bagging is a coast-to-coast pursuit, although keen climbers should look west of the Mississippi River to Rocky Mountain (p756), Grand Teton (p785), Mt Rainier (p1025), North Cascades (p1023) and Olympic (p1017) national parks, or almost anywhere in Alaska.

Glen Denny's photographic history *Yosemite: In the Sixties* may challenge you to go big-wall rock climbing yourself in Yosemite (p989), arrayed with granite domes. You can clamber up boulders in the wonderland of Joshua Tree (p936), which boasts over 8000 climbing routes. Experts belay the sea cliffs of Acadia (p297) and the Painted Wall deep in Black Canyon of the Gunnison (p777). Sounds like too much work? Go canyoneering, where you zoom down sheer walls instead of inching upward, in Zion (p871).

Horseback riding is a genteel way to survey the landscape. Trot along Cape Cod NS (p250) or Point Reyes NS (p972), or gallop along dizzying canyon rim trails all over the Southwest. You can take over mountain passes from the Appalachians to the Rockies on the back of a trusty steed or a humble mule. Private pack stations in dozens of national parks arrange stock rental and outfit rides, lasting from an hour to weeks. Their overnight trips usually require reservations.

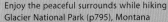

Enjoy the peaceful surrounds while hiking Glacier National Park (p795), Montana

JOHN ELK III

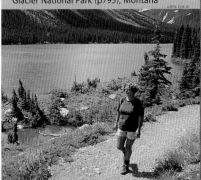

NATIONAL PARKLANDS ABBREVIATIONS

- NP: National Park
- NPres: National Preserve
- NM: National Monument
- NRA: National Recreation Area
- NS: National Seashore
- NHP: National Historic Park
- NHS: National Historic Site
- NMP: National Military Park

Novices and experts get their knees dirty while caving in lava tubes at Lava Beds NM (p986). Or you can get down at Carlsbad Caverns (p894), where subterranean adventures await in some of North America's largest limestone caves. Guided cave tours at Wind Cave (p671), Jewel Cave NM (p671), Mammoth Cave (p485), Sequoia (p993) and Great Basin (p822) let tourists snap photos of sci-fi–looking stalactites and stalagmites.

In the summertime, national parks are perfect places for getting your feet wet and cooling off, whether you're paddling in the perfect swimming hole in Yellowstone, sea kayaking in Alaska's Kenai Fjords (p1076) or California's Channel Islands (p940), launching a river-running raft in Arizona's Glen Canyon NRA (p842), snorkeling and scuba diving at Michigan's Isle Royale (p612) and Florida's Dry Tortugas (p519), canoeing in Minnesota's Voyageurs (p635), or boating in Florida's steamy Everglades (p507) or Alaska's icy Glacier Bay (p1065). Subject to local regulations and restrictions, fishing is also permitted in many national parks.

top five
PARKS FOR WILDLIFE

The USA's national parks are unmatched havens for viewing wildlife: from small, brightly colored tropical birds in Hawaii and Florida to majestic megafauna – bears, bison, wolves, elk, bighorn sheep, etc – in the American West. Here are a few of our favorite spots to go wild. See p128 for more tips on wildlife-watching opportunities, including in national parks.

- **Channel Islands** (p940), CA – the USA's answer to the Galapagos Islands.
- **Denali** (p1081), AK – domain of fierce grizzlies, caribou, moose and more.
- **Everglades** (p507), FL – orchid-laden haven for rare crocodiles, panthers and manatees.
- **Theodore Roosevelt** (p663), ND – where buffalo still roam (bighorn sheep and wild horses, too).
- **Yellowstone** (p781), ID, MT & WY – North America's largest intact ecosystem ('nuff said).

Without a doubt, summer is peak season at most parks, but winter sports such as snowshoeing, skiing, snowboarding and snowmobiling attract crowds, too. Expert downhill skiers won't find groomed black-diamond trails in national parks, but beginners can hit the slopes on skis or a snowboard in Yosemite, where cross-country routes lead to backcountry huts.

Watch wildlife in action at Yellowstone National Park (p781), Wyoming

MARK NEWMAN

Hardier heroes can go mountain skiing in Mount Rainier, sometimes even on July 4th. For guided snowmobile adventures, Yellowstone is unbeatable. Top spots for all kinds of winter sports include Montana's Glacier (p795), Grand Teton, Rocky Mountain and California's little-known Lassen Volcanic (p986). Anyone with a nuclear-powered inner body core can go snow camping at many parks. Brrr!

Live your life in Death Valley National Park (p939), California

ROBERTO SONCIN GEROMETTA

Almost all national parks prohibit mountain biking on trails, but bikers are usually allowed on designated dirt 4WD roads like in Utah's Capitol Reef (p868) and Joshua Tree. Cycling fans should look for recreational bike paths and scenic loop drives. Bicycles are also ideal for getting around congested park centers, like Grand Canyon Village and Yosemite Valley, and car-free zones, eg in Zion and Acadia. The rolling Blue Ridge National Parkway (p364 and p386) and the sheer Going-to-the-Sun Road (p796) in Glacier entice long-distance cyclists.

DO IT WITH A RANGER

No visit to a national park is complete without attending a ranger-led program.

Classic, heart-warming evening campfire sing-alongs and slide-show programs still happen at most parks. So do guided nature walks and hikes that explore miles of trails bursting with biodiversity while rangers teach you all about human and natural history, wildlife, ecology, geology and more.

Some national parks offer more extraordinary opportunities for outdoor adventures with the same friendly rangers as your guide. Expect that these special activities may happen only at certain times of year, cost a bit extra and require advance reservations, so plan ahead to avoid being disappointed.

Whatever outdoor activity you want to do, chances are a ranger can go with you (unless you don't want them to, of course). They snorkel in Biscayne (p510), accompany river-rafting trips at Glen Canyon (p842) and go boating in Everglades (p507). At Carlsbad Caverns (p894), you can literally follow in a ranger's footsteps on advanced caving tours involving free climbing, twisting through tight spaces and navigating slippery flowstone. In Hawaii, rangers will show you how to safely walk across lava fields. At Mount Rainier rangers will take you snowshoeing, and they'll go cycling around the National Mall & Memorial Parks in Washington, DC (p311).

After dark is an amazing time to explore a national park with a ranger. Guided moonlight hikes are popular all over the map, especially in the canyons of the Southwest. A few parks offer astronomy programs, ranging from telescopes set up atop the north rim of the Grand Canyon (p840) to the small observatory at Chaco Culture NHP (p889), which offers daytime solar viewing, too.

In ways that travelers do not often get to experience, national parks can provide authentic access to local culture and history. At Canyon de Chelly NM (p843), Navajo guides lead horseback and driving tours of ancient dwellings, while other Native American tribespeople lead artisan craft and cultural demonstrations, including at Yosemite (p989). Elsewhere, park rangers and an army of volunteers engage in living history programs and historical reenactments, especially in the eastern USA, like at Gettysburg NMP (p214), a Civil War–era battlefield. At **New Orleans Jazz NHP** (www.nps.gov/jazz) live concerts go on stage weekly, occasionally with music played by the rangers themselves.

Wired, tech-savvy national parks are now offering video podcasts to download from home before your visit. That way, you'll always have a ranger in your pocket as you keep exploring.

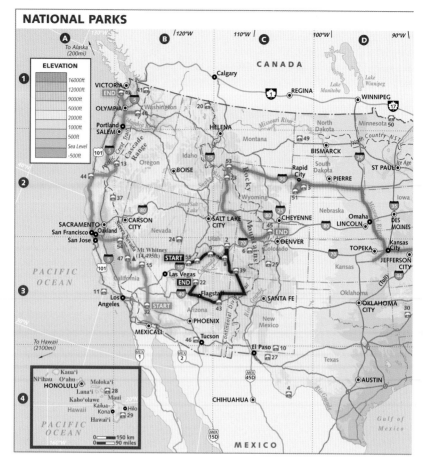

NATIONAL PARKS

ITINERARIES

Enthusiasts spend a lifetime checking off every NPS site on the master list, collecting park cancellation marks and special stamps along the way in their official gold-embossed, blue-covered national parks passports, which are sold at visitor centers and online at www .eparks.com/store.

But assuming you don't have all that much time on your hands, the following brief itineraries highlight the stars of the NPS system. These trips are meant to be inspirational, not prescriptive. Play around with our recommended routes, then design your own powerhouse parks trip. See the Itineraries chapter (p30) for more ideas.

Eastern USA

Two to Three Weeks / 2525 miles

Go stone-skipping down the Atlantic coast, from maritime **Acadia** (p297) to **Cape Cod NS** (p250). Head inland to gilded-age **Vanderbilt Mansion NHS** (p182) before braving NYC to visit iconic **Statue of Liberty NM** (p140). Learn of Civil War heart-break at **Gettysburg NMP** (p214).

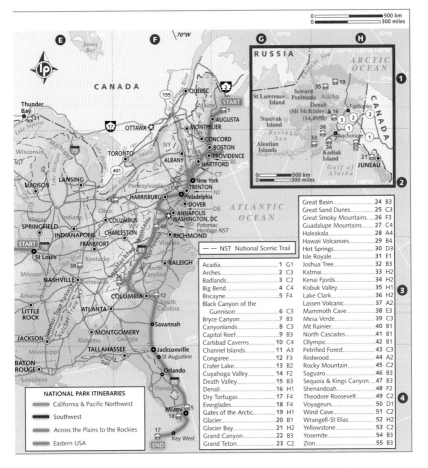

NATIONAL PARK ITINERARIES

████ California & Pacific Northwest

████ Southwest

████ Across the Plains to the Rockies

████ Eastern USA

Walk the nation's monumental corridors of power in **Washington, DC** (p311), then slow down for the Appalachians and cruise the **Blue Ridge National Parkway** (p364 and p386) from pastoral **Shenandoah** (p362) to **Great Smoky Mountains** (p388). Continuing south, paddle around **Congaree** (p400) before diving into **Biscayne** (p510) and lush **Everglades** (p507). Before heading home, board a ferry or seaplane to amazing snorkeling and diving into one of America's most remote national park, **Dry Tortugas** (p519).

Across the Plains to the Rockies
Two to Three Weeks / 2565 miles

Start your epic journey west inside St Louis' Gateway Arch at **Jefferson National Expansion Memorial NM** (p645). Drive into the USA's heartland to **Tallgrass Prairie NPres** (p680), the last vestige of a native ecosystem. Make the long haul north to the Dakotas, formerly frontier territory. Stop at the fossil-laden buttes of **Badlands** (p666) and tour a Cold War–era nuclear-weapons silo at **Minuteman Missile NHS** (p665). Gawk at the hubris of **Mount Rushmore NM** (p670), then detour to the **Crazy Horse Memorial** (p670). Clamber through honeycombed **Wind**

Cave (p671) or **Jewel Cave NM** (p671), the second-longest cave in the world. Tip your hat to **Devil's Tower NM** (p787), a sacred site for Native Americans, en route to **Yellowstone** (p781), the USA's most venerable national park, stuffed full of wildlife, geysers and hot springs. Next door are the peaks of **Grand Teton** (p785). Explore geology and paleontology at **Fossil Butte NM** (www.nps .gov/fobu) and **Dinosaur NM** (p864) before finishing at top-of-the-world **Rocky Mountain** (p756).

Southwest USA
Two Weeks / 1240 miles

Find the biblical promised land at **Zion** (p871), with its waterfalls flowing in the desert. Nearby **Bryce Canyon** (p870) shows off quirky hoodoo formations and horseshoe-shaped natural amphitheaters. Follow backroads and byways through **Grand Staircase-Escalante NM** (p869) and to **Capitol Reef** (p868), which sits atop a wrinkle in the earth's crust. Plumb the mazelike topography of **Canyonlands** (p867), then trek to eroded sandstone formations in **Arches** (p866). Wander through Native American lands, stopping at Ancestral Puebloan ruins in **Mesa Verde** (p776), **Chaco Culture NHP** (p889) and **Canyon de Chelly NM** (p843). Don't miss the Navajo rug room at **Hubbell Trading Post NHS** (p843). Cruise Route 66 through the painted desert of **Petrified Forest** (p844) to **Williams** (p833), where vintage steam trains depart for the south rim of **Grand Canyon** (p835).

California & Pacific Northwest
Two to Three Weeks / 2200 miles

Starting in Southern California deserts, the USA's outback, hop between boulders and palm oases in **Joshua Tree** (p936). Slide down sand dunes and stroll across salt flats at Badwater, the USA's lowest elevation, in **Death Valley** (p939). Then rise into the Sierra Nevada Mountains to wander giant forests in **Sequoia & Kings Canyon** (p993). Don't skip the glaciated valleys, alpine meadows and majestic waterfalls of **Yosemite** (p989). Head to San Francisco for a ferry ride to **Alcatraz Island** (p962), once an infamous prison, in Golden Gate NRA. Drive over the **Golden Gate Bridge** (p962) to the rocky headlands of **Point Reyes NS** (p972). Keep heading north to the towering trees of **Redwood** (p980). See the sky reflected in volcanic **Crater Lake** (p1045), meet a glacier-covered, rumbling giant in **Mount Rainier** (p1025) and, before trundling home, lose yourself in the rain forest, mountains and Pacific beaches of **Olympic** (p1017).

Trip out over surreal landscapes at Joshua Tree National Park (p936), California

Breathe in fresh mountain air at Great Basin National Park (p822), Nevada
ANDREW BAIN

top five

PARKS FOR ESCAPING THE CROWDS

Big Bend (p734), TX – find solitude in the desert and along the banks of the Rio Grande.

Black Canyon of the Gunnison (p777), CO – descend sheer cliffs into shadowy depths.

Great Basin (p822), NV – meditate alone among ancient bristlecone pines.

Lassen Volcanic (p987), CA – circumnavigate boiling mud pots and hissing fumaroles solo.

North Cascades (p1023), OR – climb icy glaciers and discover wild, lonely waterfalls.

NATIONAL PARKS: A USER'S GUIDE

Before you visit any national park, check out its comprehensive website first, using the navigation search tool on the www.nps .gov home page. You can find out so much online, from driving directions and printable maps, to operating hours and updates on road closures and trail conditions, to campground maps and lodging links. Dig deeper for information about outdoor activities, wilderness areas and ranger-led programs happening all over the park. Some NPS websites even have downloadable podcasts, PDF brochures, webcams and interactive activities for kids.

At the park's entrance station, get ready to fork over some cash (credit cards are often not accepted). Entrance fees vary, from nothing at all to $25 per vehicle for a seven-day pass. Due to federal budget shortfalls and chronic underfunding, parks fees regularly rise. That makes the 'America the Beautiful' annual pass ($80) a deal. It admits four adults and their children under 16 years old for free to all national parks and federal recreational lands for one year. For US citizens and permanent residents, those aged 62 years and older are eligible for a lifetime pass ($10), which is free for those with disabilities.

Bring extra cash to pay for campsites, wilderness permits (see p114), guided tours and other recreation. There aren't many ATMs inside the parks, and all apply a transactional surcharge. Credit cards are accepted at some park visitor centers (good for all of those books, maps and souvenirs you'll soon be buying) and private concessionaire businesses inside the parks (eg restaurants, lodges).

Soak in the pristine wilderness at Glacier National Park (p795), Montana.

ROB BLAKERS

If you don't have an accommodation reservation, that should be your first priority upon arrival. Park lodges are popular vacation destinations, so during peak seasons, reserve a room far in advance; to check on last-minute availability, call the lodge directly. Campsite reservations are also necessary during busy times, especially summer weekends from June through early September. **Recreation.gov** (☎ 518-885-3639, 877-444-6777; www.recreation.gov) reserves campsites at many federal recreational lands. Some parks have first-come, first-served campgrounds, in which case you should usually arrive between 10am and noon to secure a spot as other campers vacate sites.

For overnight camping in the backcountry (and sometimes for longer day hikes), you'll need a wilderness permit. Permit fees and advance-purchase procedures vary from park to park, so before your trip check out the park's website, or call its general information number and ask for the wilderness office. Walk-up permits may be available the day before or the morning of departure for less-popular wilderness backpacking routes.

When you're ready to get out and explore the park, stop by a visitor center. If the rangers are busy, browse the helpful signposted information while you wait. Want to know the weather forecast? Which trails are best for day hikes? If it's OK to build campfires? All of the answers are readily available, to help you make the most of your visit. You'll also be able to find schedules and information about park shuttles, so you can leave your car behind. Families should ask at visitor center desks about the junior ranger program. Children get an activity book to work on during their visit, after which they're awarded an official badge or collectible patch. Some parks have fully-loaded activity backpacks for families to freely borrow.

If you're camping or participating in outdoor activities (ie, anything more than just walking around), take along your own equipment. Stores in the parks may sell basic camping and outdoor supplies, but prices are inflated and they may be out of stock in the items you need (eg, different types of campstove fuel). Outdoor gear usually isn't rented in the parks, except for bear canisters when required for backcountry travel.

During your visit, please do your utmost to preserve the park's wild and beautiful natural environment. Review the principles of **Leave No Trace** (www.lnt.org) outdoor ethics, and see the advice in the boxed text 'Arrive Prepared, Leave No Trace' (p102). Follow all park policies and regulations, which are intended to keep you safe, as well as to protect the park's natural resources. Consider leaving Fido at home, because pets are not allowed outside of developed areas of the parks, where they must be kept on a leash and attended by their owner at all times – limiting the fun for all of you.

SO MUCH MORE THAN JUST NATIONAL PARKS...

Thanks to 20,000 employees and 145,000 volunteers, the giant National Park Service protects 319 different sites. That's much more than just 58 national parks, although that's what people usually think of first. Of course, the eastern USA's 'cannonball' historic parks can never compete with annual visitation at Yellowstone or Yosemite, but that doesn't mean you shouldn't check out NPS sites that aren't national parks. In fact, you can often avoid big crowds, engage in more recreational activities and see just as many amazing vistas and wildlife by visiting other types of NPS lands. The uniqueness of the site may be reason enough to make a special trip, or maybe it just happens to be on your way to somewhere else, so why not stop?

After national parks, the most popular places in the NPS system are National Preserves (NPres) and National Monuments (NM). The former are like national parks but with hunting and mining permitted, while the latter protect places of historical and scientific interest. The NPS offers a lot more for history buffs, from National Historic Sites (NHS) and Parks (NHP) to National Memorials (NMem) and National Battlefields (NB). If it's wild scenery and adventure you're after, head for a National Recreation Area (NRA), National Seashore (NS), National Lakeshore (NL) or National River (NR). Motorists cruise National Parkways (NPkwy) and National Historic Trails (NHT), while hikers follow National Scenic Trails (NST). Finally, there are also a dozen or so miscellaneous NPS parklands, including the National Mall in Washington, DC (p311).

Not only does it grant you access to *every* NPS site, but an 'America the Beautiful' pass (see p113) also throws open the doors to thousands of wild, natural areas managed by other federal recreational land agencies, including the **USDA Forest Service** (USFS; www.fs.fed.us), **US Fish & Wildlife Service** (USFWS; www.fws.gov) and **Bureau of Land Management** (BLM; www.blm.gov). Much like national parks, all of these federal lands have unique properties that justify putting them into a national treasure chest.

Because your time is limited, be aware that visiting these places is more of a do-it-yourself (DIY) experience than going to national parks. Yet the rewards can be huge. For example, free dispersed camping is allowed on many public lands (ie, you can camp almost anywhere you like; a campfire permit may be required), while the developed campgrounds, some of which can be booked and paid for in advance via **Recreation.gov** (☎ 518-885-3639, 877-444-6777; www.recreation.gov), may be less busy than in national parks. National forests provide plenty of solitude more easily accessed by car via scenic byways and 4WD roads, along with mountain biking trails, and sport fishing and hunting. For epic journeys, the USA's largest land manager, the BLM, has hidden nooks and crannies of wilderness still waiting to be discovered. The USFWS, which works to preserve threatened and endangered species, offers unparalleled opportunities for wildlife watching, especially birding in its protected wetlands. Some of its 548 National Wildlife Refuges (NWRs) are situated close to urban areas, if you want just a small taste of the great outdoors.

If you'd like to stay for a while longer, think about becoming a national park volunteer (click to www.nps.gov/volunteer for opportunities) or a seasonal ranger (check job vacancies and apply at www.sep.nps .gov and www.usajobs.gov) Students looking for summer internships and temporary employment can surf at www.nps.gov /youthprograms.

EVOLUTION OF THE PARKS

Although the National Park Service (NPS) didn't exist before 1916, the idea of national parks began even earlier during an era of helter-skelter nation building. Today the NPS protects over 391 parklands and 84 million acres of wilderness from coast to coast. For more on the USA's broader environmental movement, see 'The Environmental Movement,' p101.

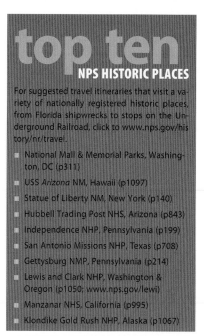

top ten
NPS HISTORIC PLACES

For suggested travel itineraries that visit a variety of nationally registered historic places, from Florida shipwrecks to stops on the Underground Railroad, click to www.nps.gov/his tory/nr/travel.

- National Mall & Memorial Parks, Washington, DC (p311)
- USS *Arizona* NM, Hawaii (p1097)
- Statue of Liberty NM, New York (p140)
- Hubbell Trading Post NHS, Arizona (p843)
- Independence NHP, Pennsylvania (p199)
- San Antonio Missions NHP, Texas (p708)
- Gettysburg NMP, Pennsylvania (p214)
- Lewis and Clark NHP, Washington & Oregon (p1050; www.nps.gov/lewi)
- Manzanar NHS, California (p995)
- Klondike Gold Rush NHP, Alaska (p1067)

Origins

During a trip to the Dakotas in 1831, artist George Caitlin had a dream. As he watched the USA's rapid westward expansion damage both the wilderness and Native American peoples, Caitlin penned a call to action, to create 'a nation's park, containing man and beast, in all the wild and freshness of their nature's beauty!' The next year, Congress established the USA's first national park, Hot Springs Reservation (p456) in Arkansas.

Be at one with nature while hiking through Sequoia National Park (p993), California

JOHN

Keep an eye out for 'gators while gliding through the Everglades National Park (p507), Florida

Forty years later, Congress designated Yellowstone National Park 'for the benefit and enjoyment of the people' and gave it to the Department of the Interior (DOI) to protect. The 1890s saw a rush of new national parks – Sequoia, Yosemite, Mount Rainier, Crater Lake and Glacier – as the idea of a national park system, as well as a nascent environmental movement, began to fire up the public's imagination. The Antiquities Act of 1906, signed by President Theodore Roosevelt, preserved a trove of archaeological and geological sites, especially from indigenous cultures, including Mesa Verde, Devils Tower, Petrified Forest and Chaco Canyon.

Back in the early days, tourism promotion, especially travel via railways and new-fangled automobiles, was a top priority for the parks, as was resource extraction, from timber logging to Yosemite's still-controversial Hetch Hetchy Dam. Because different governmental agencies managed those early national parks, notably African American army rangers who had served as 'buffalo soldiers' during the Civil War, there was no master plan for sustainable development.

Growing the Parks

When President Woodrow Wilson signed the Organic Act in 1916, nearly three dozen places were officially made part of the NPS. These were primarily located in the American West, but also in such far-flung territories as Alaska and Hawaii. The Organic Act, which came about in large part thanks to a public relations campaign funded by environmentally conscious private citizens, decreed that the primary mission of the NPS was conservation, a stance that sets it apart today from other federal land managers.

Over the next two decades, another 20 impressive parks were added to the NPS portfolio, including Denali (p1081), the Grand Canyon, Arches, Grand Teton and the Great Smoky Mountains. Then in the 1930s, President Franklin D Roosevelt changed the USA's national parks system forever. Not only did he authorize the transfer of 50 historic sites, memorials and military parks to the NPS, he also founded the **Civilian Conservation Corp** (CCC; www.cccalumni .org). For almost 10 years, two million Depression-era CCC workers built scenic byways, expanded infrastructure, opened up vast recreational opportunities and created an artisan legacy of rustic architecture in parks across the country.

Find some solitude at Death Valley (p939), California

WITOLD SKRYPCZAK

The advent of the American driving vacation during the post-WWII boom, when **Route 66** (www.nps.gov/history/rt66) really started to get its kicks, saw an explosion in national parks visitation. The parks quickly became overwhelmed. So, from 1956 until 1966, the NPS spent more than $1 billion on **Mission 66** (www.mission66.com/mission.html), a project that rebuilt the parks from the inside out and added a new archetypal feature: the modern visitor center. National parks also received increased legal protection with the poetic Wilderness Act of 1964, whereby it is now 'the policy of Congress to secure for the American people of present and future generations the benefits of an enduring resource of wilderness.'

The Parks Today

Into the 21st century, the NPS has kept expanding. Some of its growth has been controversial – for example, when local residents protested new restrictions on public land use in the Mojave NPres or when the NPS compromised indigenous community rights (for background reading, pick up Robert Keller and Michael Turek's *American Indians and National Parks*).

The NPS's biggest growth spurt happened in 1980, when the Alaska National Interest Lands Conservation Act turned over 47 million acres of wilderness to the NPS, more than

NATURAL HEROES

In a country founded on the constitutional philosophy that individuals matter, the solo voices of artists, explorers, environmentalists and US presidents have given shape to the USA's national parks as much as machinations of governmental bureaucrats.

In the late 19th century, the poet of the Sierra Nevada Mountains, John Muir (1838–1914), galvanized the public while campaigning for a national park system during his open-air lectures and writing about the spiritual value of wilderness beyond just its economic advantages. He inspired Teddy Roosevelt (1858–1919), a big-game hunter and US president, to establish wildlife preserves and national forests, as well as new national parks and monuments.

Women have been influential in national parks as well, as narrated in Polly Kaufman's *National Parks and the Woman's Voice: A History*. Western architect Mary Elizabeth Jane Colter (1869–1958), who built grand railway hotels for the Fred Harvey Company, devised the classic national-park architectural style seen in her masterwork, Grand Canyon Village.

First Lady during the 1960s, 'Lady Bird' Johnson (1912–2007) started by beautifying the nation's capital and its highways by planting wildflowers. Then she wrote a forward for the book *With Heritage So Rich*, which led to the National Historic Preservation Act of 1966. Her advocacy for national parks greatly influenced her husband, President Lyndon B Johnson, whose administration enacted more environmental-protection legislation than anyone since FDR. Lady Bird and her legacy of conservation are fittingly honored by a majestic memorial grove of trees in Redwood NP (p980).

LOCAL VOICE: NPS RANGER KEN HIRES

Why did you become a park ranger? When I was a child, I read a comic book with characters that traveled all over the American West. That's when I knew I wanted to work in the mountains someday. Since, I've worked at Yellowstone, Mt Saint Helens National Volcanic Monument and now Kings Canyon.

What kind of work do you do? I'm an interpretive ranger, which means I turn nature into English. I conduct evening programs, take visitors on guided walks, explain the various intricate workings of nature, give lots of directions and when anyone needs assistance, I help out.

What makes your job fun? I like working with kids and folks who really want to know things, the ones who ask me lots of questions about the natural environment.

How many visitors do you talk to a day? At least a hundred, sometimes many more.

What do visitors often forget to do in your park? They go for walks without taking any water.

What other parks do you like to visit? Point Reyes, the Mojave Desert, Grand Canyon, Zion and Bryce Canyon – the Western parks.

What's the oddest job you've done as a ranger? At Yellowstone, I went out and checked the temperatures of hot pools and geysers once a month with a thermometer and a fishing pole.

What do national parks need most right now? Maintenance funds to take care of the backlog of infrastructure repairs.

Do you think increased visitation has helped or hurt the parks? While more people have been coming to national parks, it represents a smaller percentage of the USA's total population. At the same time, more people are learning to appreciate parks, which is a good thing. In fact, 99.9% of the people I meet are very happy to be here.

Why is it important for visitors to follow the rules? The rules are in place to protect natural resources, like vegetation from being trampled by too many feet and wildlife from being pushed out of its habitat. Without rules, eventually the wilderness would not be itself. The very things that people come here to love would be destroyed by their love.

Any last words? When you visit a park, remember rangers are not there to hassle you; they're there to protect the park and help you enjoy it. Oh, and we don't feed the bears!

Hiking trails beckon at picturesque Mt Rainier National Park (p1025), Washington

RICHARD CUMMINS

doubling the agency's holdings. The newest NPS site is Colorado's **Sand Creek Massacre NHS** (www.nps.gov/sand). The **Martin Luther King Jr NM** (www.mlkmemorial.org) in Washington, DC, is just one of the proposed NPS lands still sitting on the Congressional docket.

Today the NPS system is again in crisis. Federal budget cuts and the enormous pressures of 272 million visitors every year together have taken huge tolls on park infrastructure. Much like 'Mission 66,' the ambitious new **National Parks Centennial Initiative** (www.nps.gov/2016) aims to fund major park improvements and repairs in time for the NPS's 100th anniversary.

Nonprofit partners like the **National Parks Conservation Association** (www.npca.org) and the **Western National Parks Association** (www.wnpa.org) help the parks thrive. These organizations raise money, staff visitor centers and interpretive programs, publish educational books and maps, promote conservation and do much more in the parks. A bigger media spotlight on national parks, including from environmental groups, has increased public awareness of the importance of the NPS, as will a new Ken Burns documentary (www.pbs.org/kenburns), *America's Best Idea: Our National Parks*, due out in 2009.

top five
PARKS FOR JAW-DROPPING SCENERY

Blue Ridge National Parkway, North Carolina (p386) & Virginia (p364) – Appalachian hills and horizons stretch along the rolling highway from **Shenandoah NP** (p362) all the way to **Great Smoky Mountains NP** (p388).

Glacier NP (p795), Montana – wildflower-strewn alpine meadows and lakes along the spine of the Continental Divide.

Grand Canyon NP (p835), Arizona – a millennia-old, kaleidoscopic chasm carved by the mighty Colorado.

Yosemite NP (p989), California – verdant valleys with hanging waterfalls and the Sierra Nevada sirens' call.

Zion NP (p871), Utah – monumental sandstone cliffs, gravity-defying canyons and lacy cascades.

Explore rock formations at Zion National Park (p871), Utah

CAROL POLICH

USA Outdoors Amy Marr

Admittedly, I've gotten around. But while I've kayaked the Abel Tasman, hiked in Pakistan's Swat Valley, skied the Alps, surfed in Mal Pais, cycled up Mt Ventoux, even skated my way through the Netherlands – all worthy, raffish adventures – my most impressive outdoor experiences have been smack in my backyard.

I started heading west when I was four. Come each summer, my family of six (plus Rufus the dog) piled into our red Ford van and drove from Boston through a night (or two) before arriving at some magical place: the Rockies, Lake Tahoe, Mesa Verde (p776).

While road-tripping, we often slept in our roomy tent and awoke in magnificent parks, gazing down at the Grand Canyon one day and craning our necks at Yosemite's Half Dome on another. We hiked to glacial lakes, splashed in streams, backpacked over mountain passes, galloped on horseback through Aspen thickets, and 'surfed' down sand dunes. Before my eyes, the country unfolded as one big outdoor playpen, full of accessible and diverse terrain – with plenty of ways to explore it.

Those influential road trips west, connecting the wilderness coast to coast, unveiled the country's true, untamed essence. So my advice: after reveling in the music, museums and mayhem of urban USA, take it outside. Steer in any direction into the country's wild soul, stretching your legs and your horizons. Hike along a ridgeline; learn to surf; mountain bike past redwoods; spot an eagle. Heck, go spelunking. Just get out there and dunk yourself, or at least your toes, in the invigorating, eye-popping natural splendors on offer in every state. Whatever lured you there first, the outdoor pleasures will likely become the memorable highlight.

For a wealth of resources on all of the activities described in this chapter, see p1113, and for even more suggestions of places to go and things to do, see p107.

Planning a road trip? www.randmcnally.com has useful tools that highlight interesting sites and activities, as well as maps with overnight suggestions.

With a database that's searchable by destination or activity, Away (www.away.com) lists thousands of active adventures and features content from *Outside* magazine.

SKIING & SNOWBOARDING

You can hit the slopes in 40 states, making for tremendous variety in terrain and ski-town vibe. Vermont's top-notch Stowe (p278) draws seasoned souls – freeze your tail off on the lifts, but thaw out nicely après ski in timbered bars

---

THE USA'S BEST CLASSROOM: OUTDOORS

Whether you're jonesing to catch a wave or dangle from a cliff, learn some new outdoor tricks in these high-thrill programs.

Club Ed Surf Camp (www.club-ed.com) Learn to ride the waves from Manresa Beach to Santa Cruz, with field trips to the surfing museum and surfboard companies.

Craftsbury Outdoor Center (www.craftsbury.com) Come here for sculling, skiing, biking and running – Vermont-style (crisp air and maple woods).

Joshua Tree Rock Climbing School (www.joshuatreerockclimbing.com) Local guides lead beginners to experts on 7000 different climbs.

Nantahala Outdoor Center (www.noc.com) Learn to paddle like a pro at this North Carolina school, which offers world-class instruction in canoeing and kayaking in the Great Smoky Mountains.

Otterbar Lodge Kayak School (www.otterbar.com) Top-notch kayaking instruction is complemented by saunas, hot tubs, salmon dinners and a woodsy lodge tucked away on California's north coast.

Steep and Deep Ski Camp (www.jacksonhole.com) Finesse skiing extreme terrain (and snagging first tracks) then wind down over dinner parties.

with local brews. Find more snow, altitude and attitude out West at Vail, CO (p764), Squaw Valley, CA (p987) and high-glitz Aspen, CO (p765). For an unfussy scene and steep vertical chutes, try Alta, UT (p860), Telluride, CO (p773), Jackson, WY (p786) and Taos, NM (p887). In Alaska, slopes slice through spectacular terrain outside Juneau, Anchorage and Fairbanks. Mt Aurora SkiLand has the most northerly chairlift in North America – and, spring to summer, the shimmering green-blue aurora borealis.

Thrill-seekers take note: Colorado's Steamboat Springs has five ski jumps and the largest natural ski-jump area in North America.

Here's a snow-stash secret: Hawai'i. Mauna Kea (p1101), the Big Island's 'white mountain' (actually a cone-shaped volcano) soars nearly 14,000ft and is often covered with snow, as is neighboring Mauna Loa. Don't expect lifts, grooming, or resorts; your rented 4WD does the hard work. Granted, it takes planning, but what a day! Skiing in the morning and snorkeling in the afternoon, powered by Kona coffee.

Wherever you ski, it won't come cheap. Find the best deals by purchasing multiday tickets, heading to lesser-known 'sibling' resorts (like Alpine Meadows near Lake Tahoe) or checking out mountains that cater to locals: Vermont's Mad River Glen (p277), Santa Fe Ski Area (p882) and Colorado's Wolf Grade come to mind.

On powdered slopes across the USA, snowboarding has become as popular as downhill skiing – all thanks to snow-surfing pioneer Jake Burton Carpenter, who set up a workshop in his Vermont garage and began to build snowboards in the mid-1970s. Vermont is still home central for snowboarders but airdogs also flock almost everywhere out west, including Sun Valley and Tahoe. For a fix during the summer months, head to Oregon's Mt Hood area (p1043), where several resorts offer snowboard camps.

Washington's Mt Baker, aka King of Snow, has the highest average accumulation (644in) of any lift-served ski resort in the world.

For a mellower schuss, find superb trail networks for Nordic skiers and snowshoers in New York's Lake Placid (p186); quaint Jackson, NH; California's Royal Gorge – North America's largest Nordic ski area – and Washington's sublime and crowd-free Methow Valley (p1023). Backcountry passionistas will be happily rewarded throughout the Sierra Nevada, with its many ski-in huts, and West Virginia's storm-pounded Dolly Sods Wilderness.

Novice dogsledders may not be ready for the Iditarod – Alaska's legendary, 1049-mile race from Anchorage to Nome, first forged by gold diggers – but how about a weekend on the trails of the gorgeous White Mountains National Recreation Area, 30 miles north of Fairbanks? Or, combine mushing and memorable dining with a twilight ride at Colorado's Krabloonik, North America's largest touring dogsled kennel.

For information on resources, see p1115.

CYCLING & MOUNTAIN BIKING

Thanks to the dynamic combo of Lance Armstrong's seven consecutive Tour de France wins and an escalating concern for the environment, cycling has hit a clamoring pace in the USA.

You can rent a road bike in any city, with bike-friendly all-stars including: Madison, WI, Boulder, CO, Austin, TX, Burlington, VT, and Portland, OR. Some of the country's best cycling is around San Francisco, where a pedal over the Golden Gate Bridge lands you in the gorgeous, hilly Marin Headlands. The toughest urban biking challenge in the States? Keeping upright when riding around the bridge's famous art-deco towers while battling gusty crosswinds off the Pacific.

The fact is, every state in the USA is proud of its cycling trails, and you'll find die-hard enthusiasts in every town. Numerous outfitters offer guided trips for all levels and durations. For the best advice on rides and rentals, stop by a local bike shop or Google the area you plan to visit.

Many states offer terrific, social multiday rides, such as Colorado's Ride the Rockies. For a modest fee, join the peloton on a scenic, well-supported route; your gear is ferried ahead to that night's camping spot (usually the football field in a scenic town). Other stand-out rides include: Arizona's Mt Lemmon, a thigh-zinging 28-mile climb from the Sonoran Desert floor to the 9157ft summit; Tennessee's Cherohala Skyway, 51 glorious miles of undulating road and Great Smoky Mountain views; and Missouri's Katy Trail (p650), a 200-mile crushed-limestone bike path through the heartland.

Mountain-biking enthusiasts will find trail nirvana in Boulder, CO (home of the Fat Tire Brewery; p753), Moab, UT; Bend, OR; Ketchum, ID; and Marin, CA, where Gary Fisher and Co bunny-hopped the sport forward by careening down the rocky flanks of Mt Tamalpais on home-rigged bikes. Premier long-distance trails abound, from North Dakota's Maah Daah Hey Trail, a 96-mile jaunt over rolling buttes along the Little Missouri River, to the Sun Top Loop, bouncing across the western slopes of Washington's Cascade Mountains. The 206-mile, hut-to-hut ride between Telluride, CO, and Moab, UT, is a sure thing; both towns are dazzling, and the scenery between them will make you feel like you've pedaled onto the set of a classic Western flick.

In pristine Alaska, even a ride on the highway feels like a wilderness encounter. Bike outfits with tours originating in Anchorage, Homer or Fairbanks will take you on your ideal ride – from an easy day trip to a nine-day expedition along mountain ranges and salmon-filled rivers. Then of course, there's the Iditarod Trail, which come summer morphs into the state's best mountain-biking adventure.

For more information on cycling and mountain biking, see p1114.

HIKING & BACKPACKING

Fitness-focused Americans take great pride in their formidable network of trails – literally tens of thousands of miles – and there's no better way (besides cycling!) to experience the countryside up close and at your own pace.

The wilderness is amazingly accessible, making for easy exploration. Within a few hours' drive from virtually any city, you'll find yourself engulfed by glorious scenery: jagged peaks, wildflower-dappled meadows, towering redwood forests, pristine seashore. For instance, a mere 30-mile drive north of San Francisco will land you in Point Reyes National Seashore (p972), where the trails reward with Pacific views and sand-soft camping spots – and, if you're lucky, a glimpse of the resident tule elk.

The real issue is deciding what kind of hike you're after. The national parks, for example, can be approached from three different perspectives. For the visitor on the go, there are short hikes – many less than a mile long – that showcase the natural highlights. In just a few hours, you can absorb the beauty of national parks like King's Canyon (p993), Glacier (p796) and Acadia (p297), to name a few. If you have more time to spare, ask a ranger (found at the visitor centers) to recommend a longer hike, from gentle ambles to sweaty slogs (the most popular of the these may well be Yosemite's Half Dome: a 12-hour trek tackled by dozens every day). And if you're hankering for nights in the wilderness in the company of Orion and Cassiopeia, plan on securing a backcountry permit in advance, especially in places like the Grand Canyon – spaces are limited, particularly during summer.

Beyond the parks, you'll find troves of trails in every state. There's no limit to the places you can explore: from the sun-blasted hoodoos and red spires in Arizona's Chiricahua Mountains to the dripping trees and mossy nooks in Washington's Hoh Rainforest (p1019); from the dogwood-choked Wild Azalea Trail in Louisiana to the tropical paradise of Kaua'i's Na Pali Coast

Recreation.gov is an online directory of recreational offerings on America's public land; search by activity or destination, and reserve a site at any of over 10,000 campgrounds listed.

The nonprofit Rails-to-Trails (www.railtrails.org) has created more than 13,500 miles of scenic trails nationwide from America's unused rail corridors.

Vermont's 270-mile Long Trail – America's oldest long-distance hiking path – follows the spine of the Green Mountains, spans the entire state and inspired the Appalachian Trail.

A Walk in the Woods: Rediscovering America on the Appalachian Trail is Bill Bryson's hilarious travelogue about tackling the venerable AT with a college buddy, both of them middle aged and out of shape.

(p1108). Almost anywhere you go, there's great hiking and backpacking within easy striking distance. All you need is a sturdy pair of shoes (preferably sneakers or hiking boots) and a water bottle.

Commitment-phobes should steer clear of the John Muir Trail in Yosemite (p991): 222 miles of scenic bliss, from Yosemite Valley up to Mt Whitney. The Appalachian Trail (AT) stretches north–south from Maine to Georgia, while the Colorado Trail spans almost 500 miles from Denver to Durango. And the Pacific Coast Trail (PCT) follows the spines of the Cascades and Sierra Nevada, traipsing the continent's edge from Canada to Mexico: that's 2650 miles, passing through six of North America's seven ecozones. About 300 hikers go for it every year; you'll make 301.

For information on these regional trails and other hiking resources, see p1114.

New Hampshire's 3165ft Mt Monadnock, America's most-climbed peak, has 40 miles of trails and a summit view of all six New England states.

ROCK CLIMBING

Scads of climbers flock to Joshua Tree National Park, an otherworldly shrine in southern California's sun-scorched desert. There, amidst craggy monoliths and the country's oldest trees, they pay pilgrimage on more than 8000 routes, tackling sheer vertical, sharp edges and bountiful cracks with aplomb. Or not. Fortunately, a top-notch climbing school offers classes for all levels.

TOP TRAILS IN THE USA

Ask 10 people for their top trail recommendations and no two answers will be alike. The country is so varied, and distances so enormous, there's little consensus. That said, you can't go wrong with the following all-star sampler. For more ideas, check out award-winning **Trails.com** (www.trails.com), with a database of 38,000 trails (and lots of topo maps so you won't get lost).

HIKING

Enchanted Valley, Olympic National Park, WA (p1018): Magnificent mountain views, roaming wildlife and lush rainforests – all on a 13-mile out-and-back trail.

Great Northern Traverse, Glacier National Park, MT (p795): A 58-mile haul that cuts through the heart of grizzly country and crosses the Continental Divide.

Kalalau Trail, Na Pali Coast, Kaua'i, HI (p1108): Wild Hawaii at its finest – 11 miles of lush waterfalls, hidden beaches, verdant valleys and crashing surf.

Mount Katahdin, Baxter State Park, ME (p301): A 9.5-mile hike over the 5268ft summit, with panoramic views of the park's 46 peaks.

South Kaibab/North Kaibab Trail, The Grand Canyon, AZ (p838): A multiday cross-canyon tramp down to the Colorado River and back up to the rim.

South Rim, Big Bend National Park, TX (p734): A 13-mile loop through the ruddy, 7000ft Chisos Mountains, with views into Mexico.

Tahoe Rim Trail, Lake Tahoe, CA (p987): This 165-mile all-purpose trail circumnavigates the lake from high above, affording glistening Sierra views.

MOUNTAIN BIKING

Downieville Downhill, Downieville, CA: Not for the faint of heart, this piney trail – located near this Sierra foothill town in Tahoe's National forest – skirts river-hugging cliffs, passes through old-growth forest and drops 4200ft in under 14 miles.

Finger Lakes Trail, Letchworth State Park, NY: A little-known treasure, 35 miles south of Rochester in upstate New York, featuring over 20 miles of singletrack along the rim of the 'Grand Canyon of the East'.

McKenzie River Trail, Wilamette National Forest, OR (p1042): Twenty-two miles of blissful singletrack winding through deep forests and volcanic formations.

Porcupine Rim, Moab, UT (p865): A 30-mile loop from town, this venerable high-desert romp features stunning views and hairy downhills.

Cool and piney by comparison, Yosemite National Park (p991), with its signature glacially polished domes, is climbing's most hallowed shrine – this is where American climbing first took hold in the 1930s. Surely anyone with a passion for rocks has seen gravity-defying pictures of climbers bivouacking on Half Dome, or Lynn Hill's legendary free ascent of the Nose. This venerable national park, protected by president Abraham Lincoln in 1890, offers superb climbing courses for first timers as well as for those craving a night in a hammock 1000ft above terra firma. South of the park and favored by many top climbers is Bishop (p995), a sleepy town in the Eastern Sierra, with fantastic boulders in the nearby Owens River Gorge and Buttermilk Hills.

Luckily, California didn't reap all the climbing spoils. A mere 10 miles west of Las Vegas is Red Rock Canyon (p818) and some of the world's finest sandstone climbing. In Wyoming's Grand Teton National Park, Exum Mountain Guides (p785) offers programs from basic climbing courses to two-day expeditions up to the top of Grand Teton itself: a 13,770ft peak with majestic views. Idaho's City of Rocks National Reserve has more than 500 routes up wind-scoured granite and pinnacles 60 stories tall. Located 70 miles west from Austin, TX, the Enchanted Rock State Natural Area, with its huge pink granite dome, has hundreds of routes and stellar views of the Texas Hill Country. And in Colorado, versatility's the word, from multipitch ascents in the Flatirons to alpine climbing in Rocky Mountain National Park, both close to Boulder.

Near Zion National Park, UT, multiday canyoneering classes teach the fine art of going *down*: rappelling off sheer sandstone cliffs into glorious, red-rock canyons filled with trees. Some of the sportier pitches are made in dry suits, down the flanks of roaring waterfalls into ice-cold pools.

East of the Mississippi, upstate New York's Shawangunk Ridge (p182) is located within a two-hour drive north of New York City. The ridge stretches some 50 miles, and the 'Gunks' are where many East Coast climbers tied their first billets.

For information on climbing and canyoneering resources, see p1115.

CANOEING, KAYAKING, RAFTING & SAILING

East of the Mississippi, West Virginia has an arsenal of legendary white water. First, there's the New River Gorge National River (p370), which, despite its misleading name, is one of the oldest rivers in the world. Slicing from North Carolina into West Virginia, it cuts a deep gorge, known as 'The Grand Canyon of the East,' producing frothy rapids in its wake. Then there's the Gauley, arguably among the world's finest white water. Revered for its ultrasteep and turbulent chutes, this venerable Appalachian river is a watery roller coaster, dropping more than 668ft and churning up 100-plus rapids in a mere 28 miles. Too gnarly? Six more rivers, all in the same neighborhood, offer training grounds for less-experienced river rats.

Out West there's no shortage of scenic and spectacular rafting, from Utah's Cataract Canyon, a thrilling romp through the red rocks of Canyonlands National Park, to the Rio Grande in Texas, a lazy run through limestone canyons. The Owyhee – whose popular north fork snakes from the high plateau of southwest Oregon to the rangelands of Idaho – features towering hoodoos. In California, both the Tuolumne and American Rivers surge with moderate to extreme rapids, while Idaho's Middle Fork of the Salmon River boasts it all: abundant wildlife, thrilling rapids, a rich homesteader history, waterfalls and hot springs. If you're organized enough to plan a few years in advance, snag a spot on the Colorado River, the

To be the first in the continental USA to see the sun pop over the horizon, park yourself atop Cadillac Mountain in Acadia National Park.

John Muir's spectacular *The Yosemite* features gorgeous photographs by Galen Rowell, who died when his plane crashed near his home in Bishop, CA.

Serious Sports (www .serioussports.com) is an award-winning online directory of outfitters, guides and schools for adventure-sports lovers.

quintessential river trip. And if you're not after white-knuckle rapids, fret not – many rivers have sections suitable for peaceful float trips or inner-tube drifts you can traverse with a cold beer in hand.

For exploring flatwater (no rapids or surf), opt for a kayak or canoe. While kayaks are seaworthy, they are not always suited for carrying bulky gear. So for big lakes and the seacoast, like the San Juan Islands, use a sea kayak. For month-long wilderness trips – say through the 12,000 miles of watery routes in Minnesota's Boundary Waters or Alabama's Bartram Canoe Trail, with 300,000 acres of marshy delta bayous, lakes and rivers – use a canoe.

You can kayak or canoe almost anywhere in the USA. Rentals and instruction are yours for the asking, from Wisconsin's Apostle Islands National Seashore and Utah's celebrated Green River (p864) to Hawaii's Na Pali Coast (p1108). Hire kayaks in Maine's Penobscot Bay to poke around the briny waters and spruce-fringed islets, or join a full-moon paddle in Sausalito's Richardson Bay, CA.

If you prefer your water vessel to be wind-propelled, sign up for a sailing charter. With the snow-capped Sierra as a backdrop, Lake Tahoe is ideal for an afternoon sail; on the East Coast, Chesapeake Bay is chock-full of schooners and racing catamarans, while Cape Cod and the islands harbor quiet coves and salty New Englanders.

For information on rafting resources, see p1115.

SURFING, WINDSURFING & KITESURFING

Some of the best surf in the continental USA breaks off the beaches of funky and low-key Santa Cruz, CA (p949). Bribe a local (a cold beer or two should do the trick) to share sweet spots, or plan to wait your turn at legendary sites like Pleasure Point, Sharks, and Steamer Lane, the fabled Westside surf break.

An hour north is Mavericks (p130), where the 30ft waves have been commanding surfers' respect since the 1970s. Supremely harsh and unpredictable, this offshore break draws the kings of big-wave riding to an (almost) annual winter competition: when Mavericks starts to go, the world's top 24 surfers get the call and have 24 hours to get there. Don't miss it if you're lucky enough to be in the area.

In San Francisco, urban swellers get their daily fix at Ocean Beach (a tough spot to learn!) or in Bolinas, 30 miles north, where locals routinely take down the town's sign to dissuade visitors. South, you'll find strong swells and Santa Ana winds in San Diego (p929), La Jolla, Malibu and Santa Barbara, all sporting warmer waters, fewer sharks of the great white variety, and a saucy SoCal beach scene; the best conditions are from September to November.

Other good surf spots include Seaside Beach, on Oregon's Pacific Coast (about 75 miles northwest of Portland), and North Carolina's Cape Hatteras (p378). During summer and fall, East Coasters rip it up at Ditch Plains, on Long Island, New Hampshire's Hampton Beach and Cape Cod's Nauset Beach.

But for the serious surfer looking for wave action between October and March, there's only one destination worth mentioning: Hawaii, the birthplace of surfing and the winter home of big waves, where the famed annual Pipe Masters competition draws the world's best surfers to O'ahu's North Shore (p1098).

Hawaii is also a great place for kitesurfing, also known as kiteboarding, the latest exhilarating water sport. The concept is simple: use an inflatable kite (from 15ft to nearly 50ft across) and a board like a surfboard, harness

For an international association representing travel outfitters, tour companies and outdoor educators (you can search by state or activity), check out www.americaoutdoors.org.

Stacy Peralta's ultra-engaging documentary film about the history of surfing, Riding Giants, has stellar clips from Hawaii and California circa the 1950s and '60s.

the power of the wind and ride the water surface at amazing speeds with acrobatic agility. Experienced kitesurfers take to the air, zipping off wave crests and flying above the whitecaps.

Kitesurfers can find the prerequisite warm water and consistent winds at Kanaha Beach in Maui (p1106) and scattered locations around O'ahu. Popular California haunts include Long Beach and, further north, San Francisco Bay, where the summer gusts provide thrilling rides off the Emeryville breakwater and novices can take lessons.

As kitesurfing and its cousin, windsurfing (which uses a sailboard, first developed by a 20-year-old sailor named Newman Darby in 1948), rely on similar conditions, you'll find that both sports sometimes share locales: places with good wind, ready access to the waves and reasonable proximity to a local watering hole. Texas' South Padre Island and Oregon's Columbia River Gorge, with wicked west gales and a frisky chop, both qualify.

SCUBA DIVING & SNORKELING

Let's be frank: the most exotic underwater destination in the USA is Hawaii. There, in shimmering aquamarine waters that stay warm year-round, you'll be treated to a psychedelic display of surreal colors and shapes. Swim alongside sea turtles, octopuses and fiesta-colored parrotfish – not to mention lava tubes and black coral. Back on shore, cap off the reverie with a Kona brew and *poke* made from just-caught 'ahi.

Despite the crowds, O'ahu's Hanauma Bay Nature Preserve (p1097) is still one of the world's great spots for snorkeling, with over 450 resident species of reef fish, some of which will swim right up to your mask. There's also fine snorkeling near Maui, favored by wild spinner dolphins, and on the Big Island in Kealakekua Bay (p1100), Captain Cook's old haunt. The best diving is off the coast or between the islands, so liveaboards are the way to go for scuba buffs. From the green turtles and WWII wrecks off the coast of O'ahu to the undersea lava sculptures near little Lana'i, the Aloha State offers endless underwater bliss – but plan ahead, as the dive sites change with the seasons.

Across that same ocean, California sports an underwater world that's enticing in a different way. Diving beneath Monterey Bay (p946), you'll feel like you landed in a dark forest, with shafts of sunlight casting eerie shadows as sea lions dart by. In all directions, 100ft-high kelp stalks sway toward the glittering surface while jumbo starfish float along the ocean's bottom.

Throughout the year, California's coastal waters host an impressive variety of life: colorful nudibranchs (fancy for sea slugs); wild dolphins; and gray whales on their annual migration between Mexico and Alaska. One of the most popular dive areas is the Point Lobos State Reserve (p946), part of the spectacular Monterey Bay (also home of the world's finest aquarium, p946, complete with resident great white sharks). The Channel Islands (p940), lying between Santa Barbara and Los Angeles, harbor spiny lobsters, angel sharks and numerous dive sites best accessed by liveaboard charter. In the chillier waters north of San Francisco, thick-skinned divers await April 1, the start of the season for north-coast red abalone, a local delicacy.

In the southeastern USA, there's terrific diving and snorkeling (and much warmer water) beyond the mangrove swamps of the Florida Keys, FL, boasting the world's third-largest coral system. Look for manatees off of Islamorada (p511) or take an expedition to Dry Tortugas (p519), where the expansive reef swarms with barracuda, sea turtles and a couple of hundred sunken ships.

The USA's most unexpected dive spot? Michigan's Lakes Superior and Huron, with thousands of shipwrecks lying strewn on the sandy bottoms...

Florida's long coastline boasts over 20 different areas offering undersea adventure, from Pensacola (p540) to Jacksonville (p524).

The USA's most unexpected dive spot? Michigan's Lakes Superior and Huron, with thousands of shipwrecks lying strewn on the sandy bottoms – just don't expect to see any angelfish!

WATCHING WILDLIFE

If your must-see list includes a bear, a moose or even a roseate spoonbill, you've come to the right country: there are loads of accessible spots for watching wildlife in its natural habitat. Of course, sightings are never guaranteed. Pick your season and time of day (hint: dawn and dusk), get yourself into the heart of the habitat (preferably by foot, bike or boat) and chances are good you'll be rewarded.

Start with the national parks, which represent a cross-section of natural habitats. (For the top national parks for wildlife, see p108.) Glacier (p795) is bear-country central, so be prepared for a personal encounter. Yellowstone (p781) is terrific for seeing elk (30,000 are in residence), gray wolves (recently reintroduced!), bison (North America's largest mammal) and deer, while the classic North Woods of Isle Royale (p612) showcase wolves and moose. Big Bend (p734) is tops for spotting birds and whitetail deer, while beavers and turtles haul out along the Rio Grande's big bend, for which the park is named. Spot cartoonish, colorful puffins in the waters surrounding Acadia (p297). For alligators, manatees, crocodiles and sea turtles, paddle the Everglades (p506), or hike Ding Darling National Preserve on Sanibel Island, FL, where the warm gulf waters draw frolicking dolphins. In Alaska, Denali's wide-open tundra makes for unobstructed viewing of Dall sheep, caribou, moose, grizzlies and wolves (p1081). Rocky Mountain National Park (p756) is home to mountain goats, elk, marmots and sure-footed bighorn sheep. And for that iconic image of buffalo roaming the Great Plains? Head to Theodore Roosevelt National Park (p663), Lewis and Clark territory, where wild horses and bison meander freely.

Boston's North Shore, particularly Plum Island, is one of the best places in the East to spot migrating birds (and sample outstanding lobster rolls). California's Monterey Bay teems with five species of seals and sea lions, cavorting in the kelp ribbons with otters, dolphins and porpoises. Ano Nuevo State Reserve, 55 miles south of San Francisco, hosts the world's largest mainland breeding colony for elephant seals; plan ahead to view the riveting (and loud!) spectacle of battling males and birthing females from December through March.

FISHING

No sport – except maybe baseball – is as central to the American mythos as fishing. From cruises in pursuit of deep-sea marlin off the Florida Keys and remote coastal fishing camps in salmon-rich Alaska to the many fly-fishing outfits in the Rockies, the entire USA is, in the eyes of many anglers, one big, glorious fishery.

Scores of websites and books provide advice and instruction on how to indulge in this ancient (but highly evolved) enterprise. Your best clues, however, will come from plying locals for secret spots. Five species of salmon spawn in Alaska, while Georgia produces the buttery Mississippi catfish (delicious pan-fried). Big-game fish, like tarpon and sailfish, leap above Florida's waters, and Minnesota offers the opportunity to reel in great northern pike. Deep-sea fishing is divine in Hawaii's Kona area, where you can tackle yellowfin and mahimahi for boat-side sushi. Beautiful Maine is where you'll go

Check out the world's best-preserved Permian-aged fossil reef at Carlsbad Caverns National Park in New Mexico.

to tangle – from shore – with striped bass, the quintessential sporting fish. And on Cape Cod and the islands, summer means surfcasting for bluefish, with a cooler of beer at sunset.

For sheer fishing delight, not to mention culinary enjoyment, think trout. Most anglers agree that fly-fishing is at its Zen best in the Colorado Rockies, Idaho, Washington's Methow Valley, and especially 'Big Sky' country: Montana. This is the state that spawned the filming of *A River Runs Through It*, and where one river alone – the Bighorn, beginning in Wyoming – is said to host over 6000 trout per mile. A guaranteed catch spot? Missouri's Bennett Spring, where the cool, clear waters are stocked with farm-fed trout every night.

Over the Edge: Death in Grand Canyon, by a river-guiding biologist and a wilderness doctor, is a terrifying chronicle of every ill-fated excursion in the Canyon; most adventurers could have avoided their unhappy endings.

HORSEBACK RIDING

Chances are you've seen a classic Western and could recognize a cowboy anywhere: a burly guy in chaps who boldly expunges evil from frontier towns, thunders across the sage-studded plains on horseback and gets the beautiful girl in the end.

Cowboy wannabes will be happy to learn that horseback riding of every style, from Western to bareback, is available across the USA. The best opportunities, through country that's still rugged and wild and, yes, resembles those old Westerns, are (of course!) in the West. We're talking everything from weeklong expeditions through the canyons of southern Utah and cattle wrangling in Wyoming to pony rides along the Oregon coast. Finding horses is easy; rental stables and riding schools are located around and in many of the national parks. Experienced equestrians can explore alone

---

WHALE-WATCHING

For a spectacular – if not terrifying – wildlife encounter, it's hard to beat seeing orcas breaching. Ten feet in front of you. From a kayak.

You can do this (I did and survived!) on Washington's Orcas Island, where pods of the island's namesake love to put on a show. For land-based viewing, opt for Lime Kiln Point State Park on neighboring San Juan Island (keep watch for bald eagles too).

Whether from a kayak, boat or bluff, there are plenty of opportunities to view whales in the USA. The key is learning where the pods swim during what time of year and knowing what to look for.

From spring through fall, humpbacks, blue whales, minkes, right whales and orcas swim south along the California coastline, seeking warmer waters. Prime viewing spots include Monterey Bay and SoCal's Channel Islands (also explore the spectacular tidepools), with plenty of options for whale-watching expeditions. In early January, close to 20,000 gray whales pass within a mile of Point Reyes National Seashore; from the bluffs, look for gray spouts out at sea.

The Atlantic waters surrounding Cape Cod offer spectacular whale-watching from spring through fall. Thanks to the Stellwagen Bank, a massive underwater plateau off the cape's northern point, minkes, pilots and northern rights (the rarest type of whale in the world) gather here to feast on a veritable buffet. Whale-watching cruises abound in Boston, Provincetown and numerous seaside communities along the Northeast Coast.

During the summer, Alaska's Glacier Bay plays host to humpbacks staying cool, which are best viewed by kayak. Some 5000 of these same savvy humpbacks winter in Hawaii's tropical waters, from October to May, swimming 3000 miles to get there. With the ultraclear waters providing exceptional visibility, sightings of Hawaii's state mammal are incredibly easy, especially along Maui's southern and western shores (p1104). Scan the surface for tail slapping, blows or other acrobatic maneuvers. A surefire way to see whales on Hawai'i, Kaua'i, Maui and O'ahu: volunteer for one of the ocean counts organized by the **Humpback Whale National Marine Sanctuary** (www.hawaiihumpbackwhale.noaa.gov).

TOP SPECTATOR ACTIVITIES

Insane or inspiring? Decide for yourself. These outdoor events – some quirky, others legendary – are fun to watch and grueling to do.

24 Hours of Moab (www.grannygear.com) Relay teams gather in the red-rock desert to ride a gnarly 15-mile loop under sun and stars.

American Birkebeiner Ski Race (www.birkie.com) Come February, 8000 cross-country skiers snow-sprint 30 tree-lined miles in Wisconsin's wilderness (in summer, swap skis for a mountain bike).

Boston Marathon (www.bostonmarathon.org) Held annually on the third Monday of April, the world's oldest marathon follows a historic, heart-pounding route.

Dipsea (www.thedipsea.org) For over 100 years, sure-footed souls have been tackling this supremely hilly 7.1-mile trail – to Stinson Beach, California – in America's oldest cross-country race. For sick kicks, there's a double and a quad, too.

Ironman (www.ironman.com) The big daddy of triathlons, held on Hawai'i's Kona coast every October, is known for killer head winds, ocean waves and black lava-covered terrain.

Mavericks (www.maverickssurf.com) Violent tides, sharky waters, hidden rocks, supersonic swells and the world's top big-wave riders guarantee a dazzling show just south of San Francisco. Mavericks goes off in winter, but the exact date is determined by Mother Nature and announced only a few days before the event.

Mt Washington Auto Road Bicycle Hillclimb (www.mountwashingtonautoroad.com) A 7.6-mile uphill race along grades of 12% to 22%, held each August, to the summit of New England's highest peak.

or in the company of guides familiar with local flora, fauna and history (much of which was made on horseback). Half- and full-day group trail rides, which usually include lunch in a wildflower-speckled meadow, are popular and plentiful.

California is terrific for riding, with fog-swept trails leading along the cliffs of Point Reyes National Seashore, longer excursions through the high-altitude lakes of the Ansel Adams Wilderness, and multiday pack trips in Yosemite. Utah's Capitol Reef (p868) and Canyonlands (p867) also provide spectacular four-hoofed outings, as can the mountains, arroyos and plains of Colorado, Arizona, New Mexico, Montana and Texas.

Dude ranches come in all varieties, from down-duvet luxurious to barn-duty authentic on working cattle ranches. Decide what kind of experience you want and do diligent research. They're found in most of the western states, and even some eastern ones (such as Tennessee and North Carolina). Real-life cowboys are included.

New York, New Jersey & Pennsylvania

These three states combined are only as big as Nevada, but what this trio lacks in size it makes up for with sheer diversity. It's a quality that's evident in both the region's natural offerings – the sweeping Jersey Shore, gently rolling Pocono Mountains, soaring Adirondack peaks and Long Island wine country – and also in its cultural bounty. This is, after all, where you'll find the larger-than-life NYC, home to Broadway theater, the New York City Ballet, pulsating nightclubs, architectural gems, fashion movers and shakers, and a dizzying array of global cuisine, courtesy of the immigrants who flock here from every corner of the world.

And the culture doesn't stop there. There are artists communities that brim with galleries throughout the Catskills region of Upstate New York, the Hamptons of Long Island and even Lancaster, Pennsylvania – a small city that's surrounded by the intriguing Amish country, where the 'plain people' are artisans who produce everything from quilts to homemade cheeses. Pittsburgh brims with top-notch theater and museums – as does Philadelphia, also now known for a gay-nightlife scene that thrives alongside historic attractions like the Liberty Bell and Independence Hall.

It's an eclectic threesome, to be sure, and a region with more riches than many folks initially expect. Get ready to find whichever ones you desire.

HIGHLIGHTS

- Traveling round the world in **New York City, NY** (p136), where the globe's cultures meet.
- Enjoying the kitsch and calm of the **Jersey Shore** (p193).
- Taking in arts and culture in surprising **Pittsburgh** (p215).
- Backpacking on the peaks of the **Adirondacks** (p186).
- People-watching at the world's gayest beach, **Fire Island** (p179).
- Soaking up the peace and beauty of **The Poconos** (p223).
- Wine tasting on **Long Island's North Fork** (p181).
- Strolling all the close-together neighborhoods of **Philadelphia** (p197).
- Driving the back roads of **Pennsylvania Dutch Country** (p213).
- Joining in the monthly First Friday gallery hops in **Lancaster** (p213).

NEW YORK, NEW JERSEY & PENNSYLVANIA

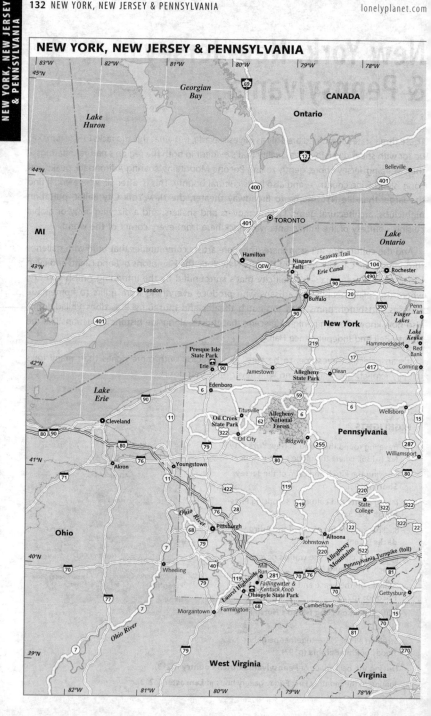

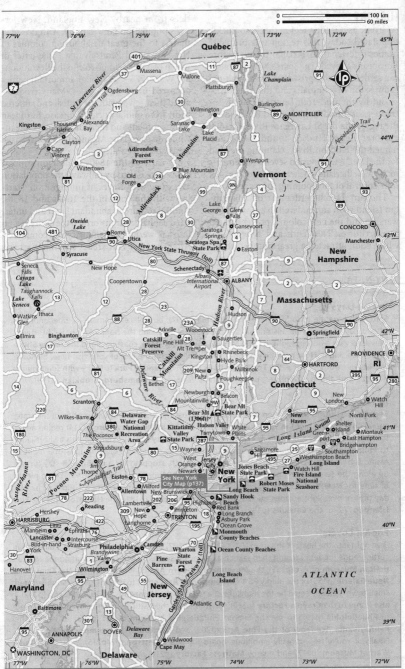

HISTORY

As ironic as it is for a region that is so thickly populated today, this region was probably home to fewer than 100,000 people before Europeans arrived. The sparse Native American settlements comprised two major cultural groups: the Algonquians and the Iroquois.

But by the mid-16th century, French fur trappers and traders had found their way to the region via the St Lawrence River. In 1609 explorer Henry Hudson found, sailed and named the Hudson River, claiming the land for the Dutch, who started several settlements in 'New Netherlands,' where the Iroquois took over control of the booming fur trade.

The tiny Dutch settlement on Manhattan Island soon surrendered to a Royal Navy warship and the new colonial power created two territories, 'New York' and 'New Jersey,' which soon attracted a great number of set-tlers from nearby New England. New Jersey's population grew rapidly, with no small thanks to the great neighboring colonies of New York and Pennsylvania – the latter of which played a leading role in the Revolutionary War (1775–83), though important battles occurred in all three states. Many Iroquois allied themselves with the British and suffered badly from military defeats, disease, European encroachment and reprisals. Farmers, meanwhile, displaced the Algonquians from coastal areas and river valleys.

As early as the 1840s the region's major cities were linked by railways; the population also grew with waves of immigration, starting with the Irish in the 1840s and 1850s. Natural resources, abundant labor and unfettered capitalism transformed the entire region into a powerhouse of industry and commerce. After the Civil War (1861–65), the West was

---

NY-NJ-PA...

In Five Days

Start with a gentle introduction in **Philadelphia** (p197), birthplace of American independence. After a day of touring the historic sites and a night of sampling the hoppin' nightlife, head into New Jersey for a bucolic night in **Cape May** (p196). On day three, coast up along the **Jersey Shore** (p193), landing in **New York City** (p136) by nightfall. Spend the rest of your visit here, blending touristy must-dos – such as the **Top of the Rock** (p153) or **Central Park** (p154) – with some quirky nightlife and dining adventures, perhaps in hipster haven **Williamsburg, Brooklyn** (p159).

In Two Weeks

Begin in **Pittsburgh** (p215), then take a road trip across the bucolic southern portion of the state, spending a second night in **Fallingwater** (p222), a third in the **Gettysburg** (p214) region and a fourth on a working Amish family farm in **Lancaster County** (p213). From here it's a short jaunt to **Philadelphia** (p197), which deserves at least a couple of nights. Follow it up with a night of casino fun in **Atlantic City** (p195) and then head north, stopping for a quaint B&B stay further up along the Jersey Shore, perhaps in **Spring Lake** (p194) or **Sandy Hook** (p193). Leave plenty of time for **New York City** (p136), and mix up the urban excitement with a couple of nearby day trips or overnight escapes, such as to the **Hudson Valley** (p181), the **Hamptons** (p179), **Fire Island** (p179) or the **Catskills** (p182).

For Art Lovers

Dive right into the heart of things in NYC's **Chelsea** (p147) district, scouring the many galleries for cutting-edge modern art, and then take in as many museums as you can – including the **Metropolitan Museum of Art** (p155), the **Museum of Modern Art** (p148) and perhaps the Klimt-filled **Neue Galerie** (p155) or the quirky **PS 1 Contemporary Art Center** (p161) in Queens. Sophisticated small-town galleries could be the highlight of a jaunt to the **Hamptons** (p179) or **Easton** (p212) – also home to the **Crayola Factory** (p212), for your inner-child artist – in Pennsylvania. Then head to **Philadelphia** (p197) to see the famous **Philadelphia Museum of Art** (p203), as well as the **Pennsylvania Academy of the Fine Arts** (p203) and **Institute of Contemporary Art** (p233). Finally, if you're feeling really ambitious, board a plane to **Pittsburgh** (p215), where the **Andy Warhol Museum** (p217) and nearby **Mattress Factory** (p218) await.

opened by steel railroad tracks made in Pittsburgh, the engines of growth using Pennsylvania coal and oil. All the region's cities were bursting with immigrants – blacks from the South, Chinese from California, and over 12 million Europeans who arrived at New York's Ellis Island. The constant flow of new people continues in the tri-state region to this day.

LOCAL CULTURE

Generally speaking, folks in these parts are in a bit of a hurry – and that goes for walking, driving or talking – although the pace of life tends to slow when you get away from cities and their suburbs and deep into the rural parts of the region. New York City's cultural hallmarks also tend to dominate, its tentacles spreading far throughout each state and thus informing people's tastes in fashion (trendy), food (global) and automobiles (SUVs, unfortunately). Jewish culture is deeply embedded in the food (bagels, anyone?) and language (*oy vey!*) of NYC, Long Island and New Jersey, but a bit less so in much of Pennsylvania, where the population is blonder and more Germanic. The city vibe in Philly is much less frenetic than that of nearby New York City, and the feel of Pittsburgh's urbania is actually closer to that of a college town, with a prominent, lasting blue-collar presence.

The trio of states comprises North America's densest population center. Because of that, there is a constant and palpable struggle between development and land protection – an interesting mix of appreciation for local farms (through green markets and restaurants that are beginning to tout local/sustainable menus) and their systematic destruction to make way for condo developments or strip malls.

Speaking of which, one thing that everyone has in common is the gift (or curse) of being excellent consumers. Malls are well loved throughout New York, NJ and PA – and all three rank in the country's top-10 list of states with the most square footage dedicated to shopping centers. Whoa.

LAND & CLIMATE

Most big cities are on one of the eastern coastal plain's main rivers – including the Hudson, Delaware, Susquehanna and Ohio Rivers. Low mountain ranges extend across the region's interior and are heavily forested with pine, red spruce, maple, oak, ash and birch trees.

All three states experience the full range of the four seasons. Temperatures are always a bit cooler to the north and warmer in the south, but generally, fall temperatures hover about the 40s to 50s Fahrenheit (4.4°C to 10°C), while winter can range from the teens to the high 30s (-10°C to 3°C). Expect temperatures from the 50s to the 70s (10°C to 22°C) in spring – plus some extra doses of rain – and summer temperatures from the high 60s to the mid-80s (15.5°C to 31°C).

PARKS

Parklands and recreation areas are in big supply here. In New York alone, you'll find 28 spots managed by the **National Parks Service** (www.nps.gov), many of them more of the historic-site than pure-green-space variety, and hundreds of leafy or beachy **state parks** (http://nysparks.state.ny.us).

New Jersey is home to 10 federally managed areas, including its southeastern **Pinelands National Reserve** (p194) and the **Delaware Water Gap National Recreation Area** (p192). Its many **state parks** (www.state.nj.us/dep/parksandforests) range from the beachy **Cape May Point State Park** (p196) to the mountainous, forested **Kittatinny Valley State Park** (p192) in the north.

Pennsylvania is home to 28 National Parks Service areas that range from historic sites to a significant portion of the Appalachian National Scenic Trail, a 2174-mile footpath that snakes its way from Maine to Georgia. Its **state parks** (www.dcnr.state.pa.us/stateparks) include a huge array of thick forests, rolling parklands and trails.

INFORMATION

For this vast and varied region, see individual states – New York on p178, New Jersey on p191 and Pennsylvania on p197.

GETTING THERE & AROUND

The big cities all have airports, but New York's John F Kennedy (JFK) is the region's major international gateway. Alternatives include Newark International Airport; La Guardia, in Queens, with mostly domestic flights; and the Long Island MacArthur Airport in Islip, also offering domestic travel (see p177). Philadelphia and Pittsburgh also have small international airports.

Greyhound buses serve main cities and towns, while **Peter Pan Trailways** (☎ 800-343-9999) and **Adirondack Trailways** (☎ 800-225-6815) are two regional bus lines. **Amtrak** (www.amtrak.com) provides rail services throughout the New York metropolitan area, linking New York with much of New Jersey, as well as to Philadelphia and Pittsburgh. Most popular day trips, at least when leaving from New York City, are easily accessible by one of the three commuter-rail lines (see p177). If you're driving, the main north–south highway is Interstate 95.

Regional driving distances:

Philadelphia to Pennsylvania Dutch Country: 60 miles
New York City to Philadelphia: 95 miles
New York City to Niagara Falls: 400 miles

NEW YORK CITY

Whatever you've heard about NYC, believe it – because this city is all that and more. It's loud and fast and pulsing with energy, but also peaceful and relaxing and generous. It's all about knowing where, and how, to look at its gifts. From the middle of Times Square to the most obscure corner of Central Park, you'll find extremes. From Brooklyn's Russian enclave in Brighton Beach to the mini South America in Queens, there are more – countries, in fact, and many more where they came from. You can experience a little bit of everything on a visit here, as long as you take care to travel with a loose itinerary and an open mind, letting the languages, foods, art, music, theater and fashion take the lead. It'll certainly be the ride of your life.

History

After Henry Hudson first claimed this land in 1609 for his Dutch East India Company sponsors, he reported it to be 'as beautiful a land as one can hope to tread upon.' Soon after it was named 'Manhattan,' derived from local Munsee Indian words and meaning 'Island of Hills.'

By 1625 a colony, soon called New Amsterdam, was established, and the island was bought from the Munsee Indians by Peter Minuit. George Washington was sworn in here as the republic's first president in 1789, and when the War of Secession broke out, New York, which supplied a significant contingent of volunteers to defend the Union, became an organizing center for the movement to emancipate slaves.

Throughout the 19th century successive waves of immigrants – Irish, German, English, Scandinavian, Slavic, Italian, Greek and central-European Jewish – led to a swift population increase, followed by the building of empires in industry and finance, and a golden age of skyscrapers.

After WWII New York City was the premier city in the world, but it suffered from a new phenomenon: 'white flight' to the suburbs. By the 1970s the graffiti-ridden subway system had become a symbol of New York's civic and economic decline. But NYC regained much of its swagger in the 1980s, led by colorful three-term mayor Ed Koch. The city elected its first African American mayor, David Dinkins, in 1989, ousting him after a single term in favor of liberal Republican Rudolph Giuliani (a 2008 primary candidate for US president at this writing). It was during his reign that catastrophe struck on September 11, 2001, when the 110-story twin towers of the World Trade Center became engulfed in balls of fire and then collapsed, killing 3000 people, the result of a now-infamous terrorist attack.

In 2001 New York elected its 108th mayor, Republican Michael Bloomberg, a wealthy philanthropist and president of his own financial empire; he was reelected for a second term in November 2005 and, for a short time in 2007, was even rumored to be preparing a run for US President (though he never threw his hat in the ring).

Orientation

New York City lies near the mouth of the Hudson River, which is linked to the Atlantic Ocean through the Verrazano Narrows. Its entire metropolitan area sprawls east into the neighboring state of Connecticut and is linked to urban areas of New Jersey, across the Hudson. That whole area, known as the 'tri-state area,' is home to more than 17 million people.

The City of New York proper comprises five boroughs: Manhattan (the densely packed heart of NYC and the epicenter of its attractions); Staten Island (a suburban appendage with an inferiority complex); Brooklyn (the place where most hipsters choose to live, after Manhattan); Queens (the largest borough, with endless foreign cultural perks and home to both of the city's

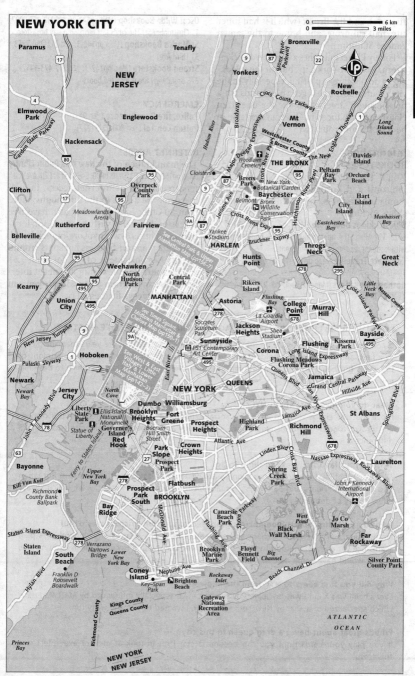

NEW YORK CITY

0 ——————— 6 km
0 ——————— 3 miles

Paramus

Tenafly

Bronxville

New Rochelle

NEW JERSEY

Yonkers

Mt Vernon

Boston Rd

Elmwood Park

Hackensack

Englewood

Westchester County

THE BRONX

Davids Island

Long Island Sound

Teaneck

Cloisters

Woodlawn Cemetery

Bronx Park

New York Botanical Garden

Pelham Bay Park

Orchard Beach

Hart Island

Clifton

Meadowlands Arena

Overpeck County Park

Baychester

Belmont

Bronx Wildlife Conservation Park

City Island

Rutherford

Fairview

Cross Bronx Expy

Eastchester Bay

Manhasset Bay

Belleville

HARLEM

Yankee Stadium

Bruckner Expwy

Throgs Neck

Great Neck

Weehawken

North Hudson Park

Hunts Point

Kearny

Central Park

MANHATTAN

Rikers Island

Flushing Bay

College Point

Murray Hill

Little Neck Bay

Nassau County

Union City

Astoria

La Guardia Airport

Bayside

Hoboken

Socrates Sculpture Park

Jackson Heights

Shea Stadium

Flushing

Kissena Park

Pulaski Skyway

Sunnyside

Corona

Flushing Meadows Corona Park

Newark

PS1 Contemporary Art Center

Jamaica

Jersey City

North Cove

QUEENS

NEW YORK

St Albans

Springfield Blvd

Bayonne

Liberty State Park

Ellis Island National Monument

Dumbo

Williamsburg

Highland Park

Richmond Hill

Statue of Liberty

Governers Island

Brooklyn Heights

Fort Greene

Prospect Heights

Laurelton

Red Hook

Boerum Hill Smith Street

Park Slope

Crown Heights

Atlantic Ave

Linden Blvd

Spring Creek Park

John F Kennedy International Airport

Richmond County Bank Ballpark

Upper New York Bay

Prospect Park

Flatbush

Prospect Park South

BROOKLYN

Bay Ridge

Canarsie Beach Park

West Pond

Black Wall Marsh

Jo Co Marsh

Far Rockaway

Staten Island

Verrazano Narrows Bridge

Lower New York Bay

Brooklyn Marine Park

Floyd Bennett Field

Big Channel

Silver Point County Park

South Beach

Franklin D Roosevelt Boardwalk

Coney Island

Neptune Ave

Key–Span Park

Brighton Beach

Rockaway Inlet

Beach Channel Dr

ATLANTIC OCEAN

Princes Bay

Kings County Queens County

Gateway National Recreation Area

NEW YORK NEW JERSEY

airports); and the Bronx (which is half inner city, half suburbia, and home to the famed Yankee Stadium).

Lonely Planet publishes a laminated pocket-size map of New York City, but for those looking to do obscure exploring, especially in the city's outer boroughs, get your hands on a five-borough street atlas, like the one from Hagstrom (produced in Queens) available in bookstores for around $15.

Information
BOOKSTORES

You'll trip over Barnes & Noble (www .bn.com) and Borders (www.bordersstores .com) superstores, but some great indie shops include:

Bluestockings Bookstore (Map pp142-3; ☎ 212-777-6028; 172 Allen St) A homegrown women's bookstore-café with frequent readings and other events.
Complete Traveller (Map pp150-1; ☎ 212-685-9007; 199 Madison Ave)
Gotham Book Mart (Map pp150-1; ☎ 212-719-4448; 41 W 47th St)

Oscar Wilde Bookshop (Map pp142-3; ☎ 212-255-8097; 15 Christopher St) The city's last remaining gay bookstore.
St Mark's Bookshop (Map pp142-3; ☎ 212-260-7853; 31 Third Ave)
Strand Bookstore (Map pp142-3; ☎ 212-473-1452; 828 Broadway) Great for used books.

EMERGENCY
Police, fire & ambulance (☎ 911)
Poison Control (☎ 800-222-1222)

INTERNET ACCESS

The main branch of the **New York Public Library** (Map pp150-1; ☎ 212-930-0800; E 42nd St at Fifth Ave) offers free half-hour internet access, though there may be a wait in the afternoons; more than 80 other local branches also have free access and usually with no wait; for locations, visit http://www.nypl.org/branch/local/. There are many wi-fi access hot spots around the city, see boxed text, p1121, for guide.

The hourly fee for surfing the net at internet cafés ranges from $1 to $12, or you can plug in to free wi-fi access. Try:

LOCAL VOICES: LINDA SIMPSON, DRAG PERFORMER & NIGHTLIFE HOSTESS

Ms Simpson has been a fixture on the downtown nightlife scene for more years than she'd care to admit, and can be found holding court at clubs below 14th St on just about any night of the week. But being around that long has given her plenty of experience on which to base her myriad opinions.

What do you love most about NYC?
I love that the city is such an incredible social experiment – so many different types of people thrown together who manage to live in harmony and respect and celebrate each other's differences.

What is your favorite weekend thing to do?
As far as nightlife, I prefer going out on weekdays to avoid the screeching masses. But when I do go out on Fridays and Saturdays, I usually hit the Cock (on 29 Second Ave), which always offers plenty of debauchery.

What do you think about Bloomberg's proposed congestion pricing? (see p140)
I'm not sure. I like New York's chaos and excitement, even the heavy traffic. Bloomberg's plan seems like yet another method to tame the city's wild ways. And if I wanted clean air in my life, I never would have come here in the first place.

Why did you first come to NYC from the Midwest?
Ever since I was a kid I was fascinated by the city. I was especially influenced by *MAD Magazine*, which specialized in a snappy New York sensibility. I wanted to join the witty fun.

What's great about being a drag queen in this city?
If you play your cards right you can become a star. I mean look at me, for example! I rule this town!

Easy Internet Cafe (Map pp150-1; ☎ 212-398-0724; 234 W 42nd St; ☼ 24hr) This is one of the cheapest ($2 per hour) and possibly the biggest place in town.

LGBT Community Center (Map pp142-3; ☎ 212-620-7310; 208 W 13th St; suggested donation $3) The cybercenter here has 15 computers, open to all.

Web2Zone (Map pp142-3; ☎ 212-614-7300; 54 Cooper Square btwn Astor Pl and 4th Ave; per hour $6; ☼ 9am-11pm Mon-Fri, 10am-11pm Sat, noon-10pm Sun) Also has extensive printing and design services, plus computer games.

MEDIA

For nonprint media, National Public Radio's local affiliate station is WNYC, either 820AM or 93.9FM. Bronx's Fordham University has the area's best alternative-music radio station (WFUV-90.7 FM). An excellent source of local news is NY1, the city's all-day news station on Time Warner cable's Channel 1.

Daily News (www.nydailynews.com) A daily tabloid with a heavy lean toward the sensational.

New York (www.newyorkmagazine.com) Features, listings and NYC-oriented gossip for the hip but established urbanite.

New York Post (www.nypost.com) Another daily tabloid covering media scandal and sports.

New York Times (www.nytimes.com) For thorough daily world and local news coverage.

Time Out New York (www.timeoutny.com) Comprehensive listings, including gay and lesbian events; every Tuesday with a website that's updated daily.

Village Voice (www.villagevoice.com) The troubled weekly tabloid is still well known for its listings of clubs and music venues, as well as real estate scoops.

MEDICAL SERVICES

24-hour Rite-Aid pharmacies (☎ 800-748-3243) A free locator service.

New York University Medical Center (Map pp150-1; ☎ 212-263-5550; 462 First Ave)

St Vincent's Medical Center (Map pp142-3; ☎ 212-576-6000; Sixth Ave at Greenwich St) In the Village.

Travel MD (☎ 212-737-1212; www.travelmd.com) A 24-hour visiting service for travelers and residents.

MONEY

Withdrawal fees average $3 at ATMs found in some of the most convenient places – nightclubs, supermarkets, delis, restaurants, you name it. Banks are normally open from 9am to 3:30pm weekdays, though the popular **Commerce Bank** (☎ 888-751-9000; www.commerceonline .com), with locations throughout Manhattan, is open seven days a week. Refer to the website for the 30 city locations.

POST

Find a local branch, with regular daytime hours, by checking www.ny/general/post offices.html. The city's main post office (p153) is an architectural sight worth seeing.

TELEPHONES

There are thousands of pay telephones lining the streets, but many of them are out of order; those maintained by Verizon are the most reliable. Manhattan's telephone area codes are ☎ 212 and ☎ 646; in the four other boroughs it's ☎ 718 and ☎ 347. You must always dial 1 + the area code, even if you are calling from a borough that uses the same one you're calling to.

The city's wonderful ☎ 311 service allows you to dial from anywhere within the city for info or help with any city agency, from the parking-ticket bureau to the noise complaint department.

TOILETS

Public toilets are hard to find, with the exception of those in train and bus stations, and those in commercial establishments are 'for customers only.' It's sometimes possible to slip into the bathroom of a busy bar or restaurant if you are discreet and well dressed, or if you ask nicely.

If you're in distress, head to a Starbucks (there's one on every other corner) and ask the indifferent counter person for the restroom key.

TOURIST INFORMATION

New York City & Company (Map pp150-1; ☎ 212-484-1222, 24hr toll-free ☎ 800-692-8474; www.nycvisit .com; 810 Seventh Ave at 53rd St; ☼ 8:30am-6pm Mon-Fri, 9am-5pm Sat & Sun) The official information service of the Convention & Visitors Bureau, it has helpful multilingual staff. The toll-free line provides information on special events and reservations. Other branches include Lower Manhattan (Map pp142-3; City Hall Park at Broadway); Harlem (Map pp156-7; 163 W 125th St at Adam Clayton Powell Blvd); Chinatown (Map pp142-3; Canal, Walker and Baxter Sts; ☼ 10am-6pm Mon-Fri, till 7pm Sat).

SIGHTS

While there's something to see on every block of every neighborhood, the most popular stops on the tourist circuit are clustered in or near Midtown. Others are way downtown, such as the Statue of Liberty and the New York Stock Exchange, or way uptown, like the Apollo Theater in Harlem.

Lower Manhattan & the Financial District

STATUE OF LIBERTY

This great statue, *Liberty Enlightening the World,* is an American icon and New York's best-known landmark. As early as 1865 French intellectual Edouard Laboulaye conceived a great monument to the republican ideal shared by France and the USA. French sculptor Frédéric-Auguste Bartholdi traveled to New York in 1871 to select the site then spent more than 10 years in Paris, designing and making the 151ft-tall figure. It was then shipped to New York, erected on a small island in the harbor and unveiled in 1886. Structurally, it consists of an iron skeleton (designed by Gustave Eiffel) with a copper skin attached to it by stiff but flexible metal bars.

Unfortunately, the **Statue of Liberty National Monument** (Map p137; ☎ 212-363-3200; www.nps.gov /stli; New York Harbor, Liberty Island; adult/child $11.50/4.50; ⏲ 8:30am-5:30pm) visitor experience has been significantly marred by post-September 11 security concerns. You can no longer go up to the crown or into the body of the statue – just glimpse it from the base, where a specially designed glass ceiling lets you look up into the striking interior. (Although a contingent of local politicians are spearheading an effort to get the lady's crown reopened by summer of 2008.) You can also enjoy the view from the 16-story observation deck or wander the grounds. The trip to its island, via ferry, is usually visited in conjunction with nearby Ellis Island. **Ferries** (Map pp142-3; ☎ 212-269-5755; ⏲ every 30 mins from 8:30am to 3:30pm, extended hours during summer) leave from Battery Park. South Ferry and Bowling Green are the closest subway stations.

ELLIS ISLAND

Ferries to the Statue of Liberty make a second stop at Ellis Island (Map p137), the country's main **immigration station** from 1892 to 1954, and the place where more than 12 million immigrants first set foot in their new world. The handsome main building has been restored as an **Immigration Museum** (☎ 212-363-3200; www.ellisisland.com; New York Harbor; adult/child $11.50/4.50, audio tours $6; ⏲ 9:30am-5pm), with fascinating exhibits and a film about immigrant experiences, the processing of immigrants and how the influx changed the USA. Special tip: to avoid the long lines to board the ferry, you might consider approaching from the New Jersey side of the harbor, from **Liberty State Park** (p191), accessible via PATH trains (see p177) from downtown or Penn Station.

GOVERNOR'S ISLAND

For decades New Yorkers have known this 172-acre swath of land only as an untouchable, mysterious patch of green in the harbor. But as of 2003 the 22-acre **Governor's Island National Monument** (Map p137; ☎ 212-514-8285; www .nps.gov/gois; admission free) administrators changed all that by offering a **ferry service** (☎ 212-514-8285; www.nps.gov/gois; ⏲ Wed-Sun, summer only) to the little gem, with optional guided **walking tours** (www.nps.gov/gois; ⏲ Wed-Fri 10am–1pm). Taking them up on their offer is quite a treat, especially on a balmy, sunny day, as highlights of the haven, just a five-minute boat ride from Manhattan, include two 19th-century fortifications – Fort Jay and the three-tiered, sandstone Castle Williams – plus open lawns, massive shade trees and unsurpassed city views. A master plan for the island's future has not yet been determined.

HOT TOPIC: CONGESTION FEES

Tensions between city-area folks who drive and those who don't have reached a boiling point, thanks to a seriously controversial proposal by Mayor Mike Bloomberg to charge an $8 congestion fee to people who choose to drive their automobiles into Manhattan, during business hours, south of 86th St. It was part of a package of sweeping changes the mayor put forth in honor of Earth Day 2007, and takes its cue from London, which has a similar, and quite successful, program. The proposal's aim is to reduce greenhouse gas emissions, but not everyone is feeling so groovy over it. Some politicians say it's a 'Manhattancentric' burden to the working poor who live far from subway lines; others counter that by saying that poor folks couldn't afford to drive anyway, since parking in Manhattan costs an average of $40 a day. Either way, the proposal, at research time, was stuck in its very own jam: that of the New York State Legislature. It's anyone's guess when it'll get moving, and in which direction.

BROOKLYN BRIDGE

This was the world's first **steel suspension bridge** (Map pp142–3), with an unprecedented span of 1596ft. It remains a compelling symbol of US achievement and a superbly graceful structure, despite the fact that its construction was plagued by budget overruns and the deaths of 20 workers. Among the casualties was designer John Roebling, who was knocked off a pier in 1869 while scouting a site for the western bridge tower and later died of tetanus poisoning. The bridge has been renovated several times, and the smooth pedestrian/bicyclist path, beginning just east of City Hall, affords wonderful views of Lower Manhattan and Brooklyn. Observation points under the two stone support towers have illustrations showing panoramas of the waterfront at various points in New York's history.

FINANCIAL DISTRICT

Wall Street, the metaphorical home of US commerce, was named for the wooden barrier built by Dutch settlers in 1653 to protect Nieuw Amsterdam from Native Americans and the British. To the east is **Federal Hall** (Map pp142–3; ☎ 212-825-6888; www.nps.gov/feha; 26 Wall St; admission free; ☽ 9am-5pm), New York City's 18th-century city hall, distinguished by a huge statue of George Washington on the steps and recently renovated. This is where the first US Congress convened and Washington was sworn in as the first president, though it is not the original building. Across the street, the **New York Stock Exchange** (Map pp142–3; ☎ 212-656-3000; www.nyse.com; 20 Broad St) has a facade like a Roman temple. The visitor center, unfortunately, is closed indefinitely due to security concerns. Feel free to gawk outside the exchange, though, where you'll see dozens of brokers dressed in color-coordinated trading jackets popping out for a quick cigarette or lunch from a vendor cart.

SOUTH STREET SEAPORT

This 11-block enclave is a pretty touristy alfresco mall of shops and historic sights. The **South Street Seaport Museum** (Map pp142–3; ☎ 212-748-8600; www.southstseaport.org; adult/child $8/4; ☽ 10am-5pm daily summer, 10am-5pm Fri-Sun winter) includes three galleries, a children's center and three historic ships to visit just south of the pier. You can also sail on the wonderful 1885 wooden schooner **Pioneer** (Map pp142–3; ☎ 212-748-8786; www.southstseaport.org; Pier 16; adult $25-30, child $15-20; ☽ sail times vary).

BOWLING GREEN PARK & AROUND

At **Bowling Green Park** (Map pp142–3; cnr State & Whitehall Sts), British residents relaxed with quiet games in the late 17th century. The large **bronze bull** (Map pp142–3) here is a tourist photo stop. **City Hall** (Map pp142–3; City Hall Park, Broadway), in the Civic Center precinct, has been home to New York City's government since 1812. The **National Museum of the American Indian** (Map pp142–3; ☎ 212-514-3700; www.nmai.si.edu; 1 Bowling Green; admission free; ☽ 10am-5pm), housed in the gorgeous and historic Alexander Hamilton US Customs House, has quite an extensive collection of Native American arts, crafts and exhibits, plus a library and a great gift shop. Just up Broadway from here is the **African Burial Ground** (Map pp142–3; ☎ 212-337-2001; 290 Broadway btwn Duane & Elk Sts; ☽ 9am-4pm Mon-Fri), discovered during preliminary construction of a downtown office building in 1991.

BATTERY PARK & AROUND

'New York, New York, it's a wonderful town. The Bronx is up and the Battery's down.' That's an *On the Town* reference, for all you non-fans of musicals, and it's talking about the southwestern tip of Manhattan Island, which has been extended with landfill over the years to form Battery Park, so-named for the gun batteries that used to be housed at the bulkheads. **Castle Clinton** (Map pp142–3), a fortification built in 1811 to protect Manhattan from the British, was originally 900ft offshore but is now at the edge of Battery Park, with only its walls remaining. Come summertime, it's transformed into a gorgeous outdoor concert arena.

West of the park, the **Museum of Jewish Heritage: A Living Memorial to the Holocaust** (Map pp142–3; ☎ 212-509-6130; www.mjhnyc.org; 18 1st Pl, Battery Park City; admission $10; ☽ 10am-5:45pm Sun-Wed, to 8pm Thu & 3pm Fri) depicts many aspects of New York Jewish history and culture, and includes a holocaust memorial. Also worth a look-see is the **Skyscraper Museum** (Map pp142–3; ☎ 212-968-1961; www.skyscraper.org; 39 Battery Pl; adult/senior & student $5/2.50; ☽ noon-6pm Wed-Sun), occupying the ground-floor space of the Ritz-Carlton Hotel and featuring rotating exhibits plus a permanent study of high-rise history.

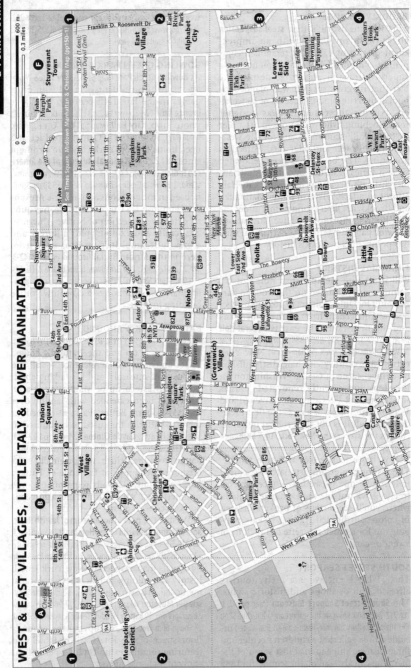

WEST & EAST VILLAGES, LITTLE ITALY & LOWER MANHATTAN

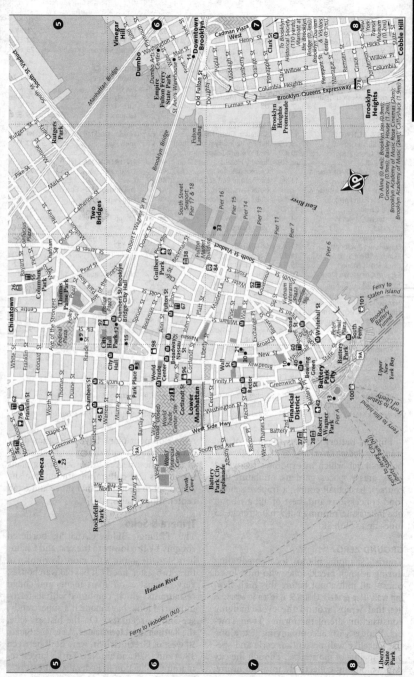

Finally, Battery Place is the start of the stunning **Hudson River Park** (☎ 212-627-2020; www.hudsonpark.org), which incorporates renovated piers, grassy spaces, gardens, miniature golf courses, basketball courts, a trapeze school, food concessions and, best of all, a ribbon of a bike/skate/running path that stretches 5 miles up to 59th St.

GROUND ZERO

Tourists snapping photos, locals meditating during a lunch break, folks who miss loved ones – all mill about before this high **viewing wall** (Map pp142-3; Church St at Fulton St; admission free) that wraps around the ever-changing construction site of the former Twin Towers. Photos with accompanying text along the fencelike wall present an eerie and specific timeline of the attacks. Though the city is now looking collectively into the future,

redevelopment plans have been incredibly delayed, fraught with drama and politicking of the highest degree. After scrapping plans for an arts and cultural institution, the site is now set to be just another office and retail center. Money talks.

Tribeca & Soho

The 'TRIangle BElow CAnal St,' bordered roughly by Broadway to the east and Chambers St to the south, is the more downtown of these two sister 'hoods. It has old warehouses, very expensive loft apart ments and chichi restaurants, which, combined with its retro-industrial look, have made it a supertrendy, see-and-be-seen area. On the historic side, the **Harrison Street townhouses** (Map pp142-3; Harrison St) west of Greenwich St, were built between 1804 and 1828 and are New York's largest remaining collection of Federal architecture.

Soho has nothing to do with its London counterpart, but instead, like Tribeca, takes its name from its geographical placement: SOuth of HOuston St. Soho is filled with block upon block of cast-iron industrial buildings that date to the period just after the Civil War, when this was the city's leading commercial district. It had a bohemian/artsy heyday that ended by the 1980s, and now this super-gentrified area is a major shopping destination, home to many chain stores and to hordes of consumers, especially on weekends.

Two small museums are worth taking a shopping break for: the **Museum of Comic and Cartoon Art** (Map pp142–3; ☎ 212-254-3511, www.moccany.org; 594 Broadway; adult/child $3/free; ✆ noon-5pm Fri-Mon, by appt Tue-Thu), recently relocated from its long-time home in Boca Raton, Florida, and helping everyone appreciate comic strips, cartoons, anime, animation, gag cartoons, political illustrations, caricature, graphic novels and more; and the **New York City Fire Museum** (Map pp142–3; ☎ 212-691-1303; www.nycfiremuseum.org; 278 Spring St; suggested donation $5; ✆ 10am-5pm Tue-Sat, to 4pm Sun) which is a grand old firehouse dating back to 1904.

Soho's hip cup overfloweth to the northern side of Houston St and east side of Lafayette St, where two small areas, **Noho** ('north of Houston') and **Nolita** ('north of Little Italy'), respectively, are known for excellent shopping and dining. Add them to Soho and Tribeca for a great experience of strolling, window shopping and café hopping, and you'll have quite a lovely afternoon.

Chinatown & Little Italy

More than 150,000 Chinese-speaking residents live in cramped tenements and crowded apartments in **Chinatown**, the largest Chinese community that exists outside of Asia (though there are two other major Chinatowns in the city – Sunset Park in Brooklyn and Flushing, in Queens). In the 1990s, the neighborhood also attracted a growing number of Vietnamese immigrants, who set up their own shops and opened inexpensive restaurants here; depending on what street you're on, you'll often notice more of a Vietnamese than Chinese presence.

While the best reason to visit Chinatown is to experience a feast for the senses – it's the only spot in the city where you can simultaneously see whole roasted pigs hanging in butcher-shop windows, get whiffs of fresh fish and ripe persimmons and hear the twangs of Cantonese and Vietnamese rise over the calls of knock-off-Prada-bag hawkers on Canal St. But there are sights, too. Start at the official **Explore Chinatown information kiosk** (Map pp142–3; ☎ 212-484-1216; www.explorechinatown.com; Canal St btwn Baxter & Walker Sts; ✆ 10am-6pm Mon-Sun, 10am-7pm Sat), where helpful, multilingual folks can guide you to specific spots. The **Museum of Chinese in the Americas** (Map pp142–3; ☎ 212-619-4785; www.moca-nyc.org; 70 Mulberry St at Bayard St; admission $2; ✆ noon-5pm Tue-Sun) has exhibits, and sponsors walking tours and workshops on Chinese crafts.

Once known as a truly authentic pocket of Italian people, culture and eateries, **Little Italy** (Map pp142–3) is a barely-there remnant that's constantly shrinking (a growing Chinatown keeps moving in). Still, loyal Italian Americans, mostly from the suburbs, flock here to gather around red-and-white checked tablecloths at one of a handful of long-time red-sauce restaurants. Join them for a stroll along **Mulberry Street**, and take a peek at the **Old St Patrick's Cathedral** (Map pp142–3; 263 Mulberry St), which became the city's first Roman Catholic cathedral in 1809 and remained so until 1878, when its more famous uptown successor was completed. The former **Ravenite Social Club** (Map pp142–3; 247 Mulberry St), now a gift shop, is a reminder of the not-so-long-ago days when mobsters ran the neighborhood. Originally known as the Alto Knights Social Club, where big hitters like Lucky Luciano spent time, the Ravenite was a favorite hangout of John Gotti (and the FBI) before his arrest and life sentencing in 1992.

Lower East Side

First came the Jews, then the Latinos, and now, of course, the hipsters. Today the place is either about being cool – by cramming into low-lit lounges and live-music clubs – or about being moneyed, by snagging a table at a pricey restaurant or a condo at one of many new luxury highrises. To keep the humble past in perspective, head to the **Lower East Side Tenement Museum** (Map pp142–3; ☎ 212-431-0233; www.tenement.org; 90 Orchard St at Broome St; $17; ✆ visitor center 11am-5:30pm), which puts the neighborhood's heartbreaking heritage on full display in several reconstructed tenements. Museum visits are available only as part of scheduled tours (the price of which is included in the admission), which typically operate every 40 or 50 minutes (but call ahead to check schedules).

The landmark **Eldridge Street Synagogue** (Map pp142–3; ☎ 212-219-0888; www.eldridgestreet.org; 12 Eldridge St btwn Canal & Division Sts), built in 1887, attracted as many as 1000 worshipers on the High Holidays at the turn of the 20th century. But membership dwindled in the 1920s with restricted immigration laws, and by the 1950s the temple closed altogether. The restorative Eldridge Street Project has been under way for years, and now the synagogue holds Friday evening and Saturday morning worship services, as well as **tours** (adult/senior & student $5/3; ☼ Sun 11am-4pm, Tue-Thu 11:30am-2:30pm or by appointment) of the building. Not far from here is the lively **Essex Street Market** (Map pp142–3; ☎ 212-312-3603; www.essexstreetmarket.com; 120 Essex St btwn Delancey & Rivington Sts; ☼ 8am-6pm Mon-Sat), a 65-year-old shopping destination with vendors hawking produce, seafood, Latino groceries, kosher wines and freshly baked bread.

East Village

Bordered roughly by 14th St, Lafayette St, E Houston St and the East River, the East Village has gentrified rapidly in the last decade, much to the horror of long-time tenants and punk-kid squatters, who have been floating around for decades. These days the real-estate developers seem to have the upper hand – although the 'hood has not yet shaken its image as an edgy, radical, be-yourself kind of place, which it still is, really. An afternoon stroll through its friendly streets is a treat.

TOMPKINS SQUARE PARK & AROUND

This **park** (Map pp142–3; btwn 7th & 10th Sts & Aves A & B) is an unofficial border between the East Village (to the west) and Alphabet City (to the east). Once an Eastern European immigrant area, you'll still see old Ukrainians and Poles in the park, but they'll be alongside punks, students, panhandlers and a slew of dog-walking yuppies. The historic **Russian & Turkish Baths** (Map pp142–3; ☎ 212-473-8806; www.russianturkishbaths.com; 268 E 10th St; admission $25; ☼ 11am-10pm Mon, Tue, Thu & Fri, from 7:30am Sat, to 2pm Sun) still offers a traditional massage followed by an ice-cold bath. It's ladies-only from 9am to 2pm Wednesday, men-only from 7:30am to 2pm Sunday and co-ed the rest of the time.

The recently expanded **Ukrainian Museum** (Map pp142–3; ☎ 212-228-0110; www.ukrainianmuseum .org; 222 E 6th St btwn Second & Third Aves; ☼ 11:30am-5pm Wed-Sun) is a testament to the fact that Ukrainians have a long history and still-strong presence here. Its collection of folk art includes ceramics and richly woven textiles.

ASTOR PLACE & AROUND

At the west end of St Mark's Place, **Astor Place** (Map pp142–3) was once an elite neighborhood and some of its impressive original Greek Revival residences remain. The large brownstone **Cooper Union** (Map pp142–3; www.cooper .edu; 51 Astor Pl) is a public college founded by glue millionaire Peter Cooper in 1859. Abraham Lincoln gave his 'Right Makes Might' speech condemning slavery before his election to the White House in the college's Great Hall.

West (Greenwich) Village

Once a symbol for all things artistic, outlandish and bohemian, this storied and popular neighborhood – known by most visitors as 'Greenwich Village,' although that term is not used by locals – can look downright somnolent these days, due to high-priced real-estate dwellers who demand a certain 'quality of life.' Still, this is the birthplace of the gay-rights movement, as well as the former home of beat poets and important artists, and that's a history hard to dismiss. (See more about this in the Village Radicals Walking Tour, p162).

NEW YORK UNIVERSITY

In 1831 Albert Gallatin, secretary of treasury under President Thomas Jefferson, founded an intimate center of higher learning, **NYU** (Map pp142–3; ☎ 212-998-4636; www.nyu.edu; Information Center at 50 W 4th St; ☼ 9am-5pm Mon-Fri), open to all students, regardless of race or class background. He'd scarcely recognize the place today, as it has swelled to a student population of 48,000, with high school grads attending 14 schools and colleges at six Manhattan locations.

WASHINGTON SQUARE PARK & AROUND

This **park** (Map pp142–3) began as a 'potter's field' – a burial ground for the penniless – and its status as a cemetery protected it from development. It is now an incredibly well-used park, especially on the weekend. Children use the playground, NYU students catch some rays and friends meet 'under the arch' – the recently renovated landmark on the park's northern edge, designed in 1889 by society architect Stanford White. A $16-million

REBIRTH OF THE HIGH LINE

The High Line itself is a 30ft-high abandoned stretch of elevated railroad track, which reaches from Gansevoort St in the Meatpacking District up to 34th St. Overgrown with thick weeds and not used since the 1960s, the blissfully empty space has inspired a group of activists to fight with the city for the right to turn it into a long ribbon of parkland – and, miracle of miracles, they won. The struggle for the site began nearly a decade ago, when a group of community activists, Friends of the High Line, lobbied to save the track from being demolished. Mayor Bloomberg supported the effort, both in spirit and finances. Construction began in 2006 (on time!), and the first portion of the public green space is on target to open in 2008. And coming along with the park with be high-end hotels, shops and a downtown outpost of the Whitney Museum of American Art (p155).

renovation plan will greatly rearrange the park's setup. The work is all just beginning, though, and is bound to go on for years.

CHRISTOPHER STREET PIER

Formerly the strict domain of young gay hustlers and sassy 'pier queens,' this completely renovated **concrete pier** (Map pp142-3; Christopher St at the Hudson River) is now a magnet for downtowners of all stripe, with a healthy dose of local yuppies and a sprinkling of young gay holdouts, most of whom travel from other boroughs and northern New Jersey to be a part of the scene. Part of the Hudson River Park Project, the developers paid special attention to this prime waterfront spot, adding a lawn and flower bed, wooden deck, tented shade shelters, benches and a grand stone fountain at its entrance.

SHERIDAN SQUARE & AROUND

The western edge of the Village is home to **Sheridan Square** (Stonewall Place; Map pp142-3), a small, triangular park where life-size white statues by George Segal honor the gay community and gay pride movement that began in the nearby **Stonewall Inn** (p162, recently renovated and still sitting just across the street from the square. A block further east, an appropriately bent street is officially named Gay St (prompting titillated queer folks to periodically swipe the street sign). Although gay social scenes have in many ways moved a bit further uptown to Chelsea, **Christopher Street** is still the center of gay life in the Village.

Meatpacking District

Nestled between the far West Village and the southern border of Chelsea is the recently gentrified **Meatpacking District** (Map pp142-3). Less than 10 years ago, the neighborhood – home to 250 slaughterhouses in 1900 but less than 35 wholesale meat companies today, as most have been squeezed out by high rents – was best known for its groups of tranny hookers, racy S/M sex clubs and, of course, its sides of beef. Though it's still active and odorous on weekday mornings, evenings and weekends draw the trendy set to high-ceilinged wine bars, Belgian and Cuban eateries, nightclubs, high-end 14th-St designer clothing stores and chic new hotels. The trendiness will only expand from here with the completion of the **High Line** (see above), which will have its southern terminus here.

Chelsea

This 'hood is popular for two main attractions: one, the parade of gorgeous gay men (known affectionately as 'Chelsea boys') who roam Eighth Ave, darting from gyms to trendy happy hours; and two, it's the hub of the city's art-gallery scene, which grows more expansive and popular by the year – it's currently home to nearly 200 modern-art art spaces, most of which are clustered west of Tenth Ave. Find specific galleries at www.westchelseaarts.com or pick up a copy of the monthly *Gallery Guide* (www.galleryguide.org), hard copies of which are available for free at most venues.

The **Chelsea Market** (Map pp150-1; www.chelseamarket.com; 75 Ninth Ave btwn 15th & 16th Sts) will thrill gourmet food fans with its 800ft-long shopping concourse, while **Chelsea Piers** (Map pp150-1; ☎ 212-336-6000; Hudson River at the end of 23rd St; www.chelseapiers.com) is a waterfront sports center that caters to the athlete in everyone. It's got a four-level driving range, indoor ice rink, jazzy bowling alley, Hoop City for basketball, a sailing school for kids, batting cages, a huge gym, indoor rock-climbing walls – the works.

Flatiron District

At the intersection of Broadway, Fifth Ave and 23rd St, the famous (and absolutely gorgeous) 1902 **Flatiron Building** (Map pp150–1) has a distinctive triangular shape to match its site. It was New York's first iron-frame high-rise, and the world's tallest building until 1909. Its surrounding district is a fashionable area of boutiques and loft apartments, and home to the peaceful **Madison Square Park** (www.madisonsquarepark.org) bordered by 23rd and 26th Sts, and Fifth and Madison Aves, where you'll find an active dog run, rotating outdoor sculptures, shaded park benches and a trendy burger joint. Flatiron is also where you'll find the **Museum of Sex** (Map pp150-1; ☎ 212-689-6337; www.museumofsex.org; 233 Fifth Ave at W 27th St; admission $14.50; ☺ 11am-6:30pm Mon-Fri, 10am-9pm Sat, to 6:30pm Sun), a surprisingly clean, but fascinating homage that intellectually traces the history of sex and the city.

Union Square

Today, **Union Square Park** (Map pp150-1; 14th St at Broadway) hops with activity; its southern end is the place for antiwar and other liberal-leaning demonstrators and, on most days, its north end hosts the colorful **Greenmarket Farmers' Market** (Map pp150-1; ☎ 212-477-3220; www .cenyc.org; 17th St btwn Broadway & Park Ave S; ☺ 8am-4pm Mon, Wed, Fri & Sat year-round), the most popular of the nearly 50 greenmarkets throughout the five boroughs, where even celebrity chefs come for just-picked rarities like fiddlehead ferns, heirloom tomatoes and fresh curry leaves.

Gramercy Park

This area, loosely comprising the 20s east of Madison Ave, is named after one of New York's loveliest parks; it's for residents only, though, and you need a key to get in! If you're strolling by, peer through the gates and get a good look at what you're missing. Nearby is **Theodore Roosevelt's Birthplace** (Map pp150-1; ☎ 212-260-1616; www.nps.gov/thrb; 28 E 20th St btwn Park Ave & Broadway; admission $3; ☺ Tue-Sat 9am-5pm), a National Historic Site – and a bit of a cheat, since the house where the 26th president was born was demolished in his lifetime. This building is simply a re-creation, albeit an interesting one, by his relatives.

Midtown

The classic NYC fantasy – shiny skyscrapers, teeming mobs of worker bees, Fifth Ave store windows, taxi traffic – lives here, in Midtown, home to many of the city's most popular attractions. While the hustle-bustle can be a bit intimidating at first, try to give yourself over to the excitement of it all. You're sure to become a quick convert.

EMPIRE STATE BUILDING

Catapulted to Hollywood stardom both as the planned meeting spot for Cary Grant and Deborah Kerr in *An Affair to Remember* and the vertical perch that helped to topple King Kong, the classic **Empire State Building** (Map pp150-1; ☎ 212-736-3100; www.esbnyc.org; 350 Fifth Ave at E 34th St; adult/child $20/18; ☺ 9:30am-midnight) is one of New York's most famous members of the skyline. It's a limestone classic built in just 410 days, or seven million man-hours, during the depths of the Depression at a cost of $41 million. On the site of the original Waldorf-Astoria Hotel, the 102-story, 1472ft (to the top of the antenna) Empire State Building opened in 1931 after the laying of 10 million bricks, installation of 6400 windows and setting of 328,000 sq ft of marble. Today you can ride the elevator to observatories on the 86th and 102nd floors, but be prepared for crowds; try to come very early or very late (and purchase your tickets ahead of time, online) for an optimal experience. A night trip to the top can be quite romantic – and don't miss the art-deco medallions around the lobby.

MUSEUM OF MODERN ART

Since its grand reopening in 2004 following the most extensive renovation project in its 75-year history, the **Museum of Modern Art** (MoMA; Map pp150-1; ☎ 212-708-9400; www.moma.org; 11 W 53rd St btwn Fifth & Sixth Aves; adult/senior/student/child $20/16/12/free, Fri 4-8pm free; ☺ 10:30am-5:30pm Sat-Mon, Wed-Thu, 10:30am-8pm Fri) has been both widely hailed and vilified for its physical design as well as the soul (or lack thereof) of its exhibits. The project added a sleek new design by architect Yoshio Taniguchi and doubled the museum's capacity to 630,000 sq ft on six floors, creating a veritable art universe of more than 100,000 pieces where you could easily hole up for a couple of days and still not properly see it all. Most of the big hitters – Matisse, Picasso, Cézanne, Rothko, Pollock and many others – are housed in the central five-story atrium.

Just prepare thyself for ridiculously long entrance lines and crushing crowds around the artwork.

TIMES SQUARE & THEATER DISTRICT
Several years into its major renaissance – or hellish 'Disneyfication,' depending on your point of view – **Times Square** (Map pp150–1) can once again trumpet its reputation as the 'Crossroads of the World.' Smack in the middle of Midtown Manhattan, this area around the intersection of Broadway and Seventh Ave has long been synonymous with gaudy billboards and glittery marquees. The square draws 27 million visitors annually, who spend something over $12 billion in Midtown. Massive chains like Sephora, Skechers and Cold Stone Creamery pull in folks who can find this stuff anywhere, and multiplex theatres draw crowds with large screens and stadium seating.

Times Square also continues to serve as New York's official **Theater District**, with dozens of Broadway and off-Broadway theaters located in an area that stretches from 41st to 54th Sts, between Sixth and Ninth Aves (see p174). The **Times Square Information Center** (☎ 212-869-5667; www.timessquarebid.org; 1560 Broadway btwn 46th & 47th Sts; ☒ 8am-8pm) sits smack in the middle of this famous crossroads, inside the beautifully restored landmark Embassy Theater.

COLUMBUS CIRCLE/TIME WARNER CENTER
The pair of sleek towers known as the **Time Warner Center** (Map pp156-7; ☎ 212-869-1890; www.shopsatcolumbuscircle.com; 1 Columbus Circle at 59th St; ☒ 9am-9pm), built for $1.8 billion and completed in early 2004 after much angst and anticipation, created a major buzz with their grand entrance, though much of that has faded. What remains here, in the spot that for years was home to the aging New York Coliseum, is a very tall mall. But the view of Central Park is quite special – as are the perfect chocolate sandwich cookies at Bouchon Bakery (p170) on the third floor.

GRAND CENTRAL TERMINAL
Built in 1913 as a prestigious terminal by New York Central and Hudson River Railroad, **Grand Central Station** (Map pp150-1; www.grandcentralterminal.com; 42nd St at Fifth Ave) is no longer a romantic place to begin a cross-country journey, as it's now the terminus for Metro North commuter trains to the northern suburbs and Connecticut. But even if you're not boarding a train to the 'burbs, it's worth exploring the grand, vaulted main concourse and gazing up at the restored ceiling, decorated with a star map that is actually a 'God's eye' image of the night sky. The bottom floor houses a truly excellent array of eateries, bringing the idea of 'food court' to grand new levels, while the balcony has a cozy and beautiful bar, Campbell Apartment.

CHRYSLER BUILDING
Just east of Grand Central Terminal, the **Chrysler Building** (Map pp150-1; 405 Lexington Ave), an art-deco masterpiece that's adorned with motorcar motifs, was designed by William Van Alen and completed in 1930 to be the headquarters for Walter P Chrysler and his automobile empire. Luckily, it's most magnificent when viewed from a distance, because visitors can't go up in the building (it's full of offices) and some details are barely visible from the ground. In the lobby, you can admire the African marble, onyx lights and other decorative elements. Nestled at the top, in the building's heyday, was the famed Cloud Club, a former speakeasy. For a long time, developers have been planning to convert part of the building into a hotel, but so far that remains only a pipe dream.

NEW YORK PUBLIC LIBRARY
The superb beaux-arts-style **New York Public Library** (Map pp150-1; ☎ 212-940-0830; Fifth Ave at 42nd St; www.nypl.org; ☒ 10am-6pm Tue-Sat) is a wonderful retreat from the Midtown bustle. The stately lion sculptures at the front entrance, elegant lobby, marble stairs and impressive halls lead to the brilliant 3rd-floor reading room with its natural light and magnificent ceiling. This, the main branch of the entire city library system, has galleries of manuscripts on display, as well as fascinating temporary exhibits.

ROCKEFELLER CENTER
It was built during the height of the Great Depression in the 1930s, and construction of the 22-acre **Rockefeller Center** (Map pp150–1) gave jobs to 70,000 workers over nine years and was the first project to combine retail, entertainment and office space in what is often referred to as a 'city within a city.' The biggest news here as of late has been the late-2005 reopening of the long-shuttered **Top of the Rock** (p153) observation deck, which

TIMES SQUARE, MIDTOWN MANHATTAN & CHELSEA

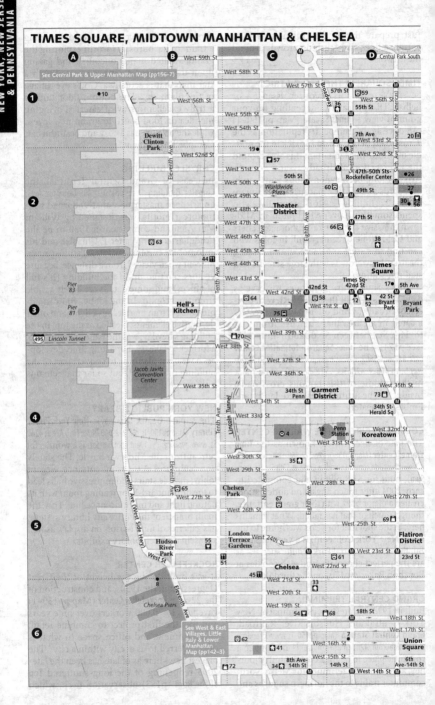

affords stunning views of the city. Architecture fans should look for the tilework above the Sixth Ave entrance to the GE Building; the entrance to the East River Savings Bank building at 41 Rockefeller Plaza; the triptych above the entrance to 30 Rockefeller Plaza; and the statues of Prometheus and Atlas. In winter the place is abuzz with ice skaters and Christmas-tree gawkers.

Within the complex is the 1932 **Radio City Music Hall** (Map pp150-1; ☎ 212-247-4777; www.radio city.com; 1260 Sixth Ave; tours $17; ☉ tours 11am-3pm Mon-Sun), a 6000-seat former movie palace and protected landmark that's been gorgeously restored in all its art-deco grandeur. To get an inside look at the place, join one of the frequent guided tours, which leave the lobby every half-hour.

NBC Studios (Map pp150-1; ☎ 212-664-3700; www.nbcstore.shopnbc.com; tours adult/child 6-16 & senior $18.50/15.50; ☉ tours 8.30am-5.30pm Mon-Sat, 9:30am-4:30pm Sun, extended hours during Nov-Dec holiday season) are here as part of the NBC television network, which has its headquarters in the 70-story GE Building. The Today Show broadcasts live 7am to 10am daily from a glass-enclosed street-level studio near the fountain, and tours of the NBC studios leave from the lobby of the GE Building every 15 minutes; note that children under six are not admitted on tours.

FIFTH AVENUE & AROUND

Immortalized in both film and song, Fifth Ave first developed its high-class reputation in the early 20th century, when it was considered desirable for its 'country' air and open spaces. The series of mansions called **Millionaire's Row** extended right up to 130th St, though most of the heirs to the millionaire mansions on Fifth Ave above 59th St sold them for demolition or converted them to the cultural institutions that now make up Museum Mile.

The avenue's Midtown stretch still boasts upscale shops and hotels, including the famous Trump Tower, where the Big D fires folks each week on *The Apprentice*. While a number of the more exclusive boutiques have migrated to Madison Ave – leaving outposts of Gap and H&M in their wake – several superstars still reign over Fifth Ave above 50th St, including **Henri Bendel** (p177) and the movie-famous **Tiffany & Co** (p177).

UNITED NATIONS

The **UN headquarters** (Map pp150-1; ☎ 212-963-8687; First Ave btwn 42nd & 48th Sts; tours $7.50; ☉ tours

---

ROCK OUT

Top of the Rock (Map pp150–1; ☎ 212-698-2000; www.topoftherocknyc.com; 30 Rockefeller Plaza; adult/senior/child $17.50/16/11.25 ; ☽ 8:30am-midnight) first wowed New Yorkers back in 1933, when John D. Rockefeller opened the open-air observation deck. But it became off limits for almost two decades starting in 1986, when renovation of the stunning Rainbow Room five floors below cut off access to the roof. The observation deck was reopened with much fanfare in November 2005, and, though it is no longer an alfresco perch, it's a sleekly remodeled haven that affords stunning, unobstructed, 360-degree views through panels of non-reflective safety glass.

9:15am-4:45pm Mon-Fri in winter) is technically on a section of international territory overlooking the East River. Take a guided tour of the facility and you'll get to see the General Assembly, where the annual fall convocation of member nations takes place; the Security Council Chamber, where crisis management continues year-round; and also the Economic & Social Council Chamber. There is a park to the south of the complex which is home to Henry Moore's *Reclining Figure* as well as several other sculptures with a peace theme. English-language tours of the UN complex depart every 30 minutes; limited tours in several other languages are also available.

HERALD SQUARE & AROUND

This crowded convergence of Broadway, Sixth Ave and 34th St is best known as the home of **Macy's** department store (see p176), where you can still ride some of the remaining original wooden elevators to floors ranging from home furnishings to lingerie. But the busy square gets its name from a long-defunct newspaper, the *Herald*, and the small, leafy park here bustles during business hours thanks to a recent and much-needed facelift. (Don't bother with the two indoor malls south of Macy's on Sixth Ave, where you'll find a boring array of suburban chain stores.)

West of Herald Sq, the **Garment District** has most of New York's fashion design offices, and while not much clothing is actually made here anymore, it is the place to shop for anyone into pawing through dreamy selection of fabrics, buttons, sequins, lace and zippers.

Nearby, sterile **Pennsylvania Station** (Penn Station; Map pp150–1; 33rd St btwn Seventh & Eighth Aves) is not the original, grand entrance to the city, though tens of thousands of commuters and travelers do pass through daily. **Madison Square Garden** (Map pp150–1; ☎ 212-465-5800; www.thegarden .com; Seventh Ave, btwn W 31st & W 33rd Sts), built over Penn Station, is a major sporting and enter-tainment venue. A block west, the 1913 **New York General Post Office** (Map pp150–1; www.ny.com /general/postoffices.html; 421 Eighth Ave at 33rd St; ☽ 24hr) is an imposing beaux-arts building that stands behind a long row of Corinthian columns. It's often obscured by scaffolding these days, though, as a project to move Penn Station into the GP has been proceeding (at a snail's pace) for years.

From 31st St to 36th St, between Broadway and Fifth Ave, **Koreatown** is a small but interesting and lively neighborhood that's really grown in the past few years. Look on 31st and 32nd Sts for a proliferation of Korean restaurants and authentic karaoke spots.

MIDTOWN MUSEUMS

Among the impressive lineup of art and culture museums in this area is the **Museum of Television & Radio** (Map pp150–1; ☎ 212-621-6600; www .mtr.org; 25 W 52nd St; admission $10, theater $6; ☽ noon-6pm Fri-Wed, to 8pm Thu), where more than 100,000 US TV and radio programs and advertisements are available at the click of a mouse. Here you can search the extensive catalogue on computer, and staff will find and play your classic TV or radio selection. A comfy theater shows some great specials on broadcasting history, and there are frequent special programming events.

Finally, the stunning **International Center of Photography** (Map pp150–1; ☎ 212-857-0000; www.icp .org; 1133 Sixth Ave at 43rd St; adult/senior & student $10/7, admission by 'voluntary contribution' Fri 5-8pm; ☽ 10am-6pm Tue-Thu, Sat & Sun, 10am-8pm Fri) is the city's most important showcase for major photographers, especially photojournalists. Its past exhibitions have included work by Henri Cartier-Bresson, Man Ray, Matthew Brady, Weegee and Robert Capa.

HELL'S KITCHEN (CLINTON)

For years, the far west side of Midtown was a working-class district of tenements and food warehouses known as Hell's Kitchen. A 1990s economic boom seriously altered the character and developers reverted to using the cleaned-up name Clinton, a moniker originating from the 1950s; locals are split on usage. New restaurants exploded along Ninth and Tenth Aves between about 37th and 55th Sts, and now it's a great place to grab a post-theater meal (if you can decide among the many options, that is). Antique lovers should note that the beloved Annex Antiques Fair & Flea Market (Chelsea Flea Market) has moved here, and that it's now the **Hell's Kitchen Flea Market** (Map pp150-1; ☎ 212-243-5343; www.hellskitchenfleamarket.com; 39th St btwn Ninth & Tenth Aves; ☽ 7am-5pm Sat-Sun), boasting 170 vendors of vintage clothing, antique jewelry, period furniture and many more treasures.

Central Park

This enormous gem of a **park** (Map pp156-7; ☎ 212-360-3444; www.centralparknyc.org; btwn 57th & 110th Sts & Fifth Ave & Central Park W) sits right in the middle of Manhattan, and is for many what makes NYC livable and lovable. The park's 843 acres were set aside in 1856 on the marshy northern fringe of the city. The landscaping (the first in a US public park), by Frederick Law Olmsted and Calvert Vaux, was innovative in its naturalistic style, with forested groves, meandering paths and informal ponds. Highlights include **Strawberry Fields** at 72nd St, dedicated to John Lennon, who lived at (and was murdered in front of) the **Dakota** apartment building across the street; the sparkling **Jacqueline Kennedy Onassis Reservoir**, encircled by joggers daily; the **zoo** (☎ 212-861-6030; www.wcs.org; 64th St at Fifth Ave; adult/child $8/3; ☽ 10am-5pm Mon-Fri, to 5:30pm Sat & Sun); and the formal, tree-lined promenade called the **Mall**, which culminates at the elegant **Bethesda Fountain**. A favorite tourist activity is to rent a **horse-drawn carriage** (Map pp156-7; 20-min tour $40 plus generous tip) at 59th St (Central Park South). For more information while you're strolling, visit the **Dairy Building visitor centre** (Map pp156-7; ☎ 212-794-6564; Central Park at 65th St; ☽ 10am-5pm Tue-Sat) in the middle of the park.

Upper West Side

Comprising the west side of Manhattan from Central Park to the Hudson River, and from Columbus Circle to 110th St, this is where you'll find massive, ornate apartments, a diverse mix of stable, upwardly mobile folks (with many actors and classical musicians

sprinkled throughout); and some lovely green spaces; **Riverside Park** stretches for 4 miles between W 72nd St and W 158th St along the Hudson River, and is a great place for strolling, running, biking or simply gazing at the sun as it sets over the Hudson River.

NEW-YORK HISTORICAL SOCIETY

The **New-York Historical Society** (Map pp156-7; ☎ 212-873-3400; www.nyhistory.org; 2 W 77th St; admission $10; ☽ 10am-6pm Tue-Sun), founded in 1804, is the city's oldest museum, featuring original watercolors from John James Audubon's *Birds of America* and a quirky permanent collection: only here can you see 17th-century cowbells and baby rattles, and the mounted wooden leg of Gouverneur Morris. The Henry Luce III Center for the Study of American Culture, which opened in 2000, is a 21,000-sq-ft showcase of more than 40,000 objects from the museum's permanent collection.

LINCOLN CENTER

A performance complex built in the 1960s, **Lincoln Center** (Map pp156-7; ☎ 212-875-5370; www.lincolncenter.org; cnr Columbus Ave & Broadway) has a dramatic courtyard with a massive fountain surrounded by various stunning venues. Fascinating **tours** (☎ 212-875-5350; admission $13.50) of the complex leave from the concourse level daily.

AMERICAN MUSEUM OF NATURAL HISTORY

Founded in 1869, this **museum** (Map pp156-7; ☎ 212-769-5000; www.amnh.org; Central Park West at 79th St; suggested admission adult/child $14/8, extra for space shows, IMAX shows & special exhibits; ☽ 10am-5:45pm) includes more than 30 million artifacts, interactive exhibits and loads of taxidermy. It's most famous for its three large dinosaur halls, an enormous (fake) blue whale that hangs from the ceiling above the Hall of Ocean Life and the elaborate **Rose Center for Earth & Space**. Just gazing at its facade – a massive glass box that contains a silver globe, home to space-show theatres and the planetarium – is mesmerizing, especially at night, when all of its otherworldly features are aglow. To get here take the subway to 81st St-Museum of Natural History.

Morningside Heights

The Upper West Side's northern neighbor, comprising the area of Broadway and west up to about 125th St, is anchored by the Ivy League **Columbia University** (Map pp156-7;

☎ 212-854-1754; www.columbia.edu; 116th St & Broadway). The highly rated, activist-filled college features a spacious, grassy central quadrangle that's dominated by the 1895 Low Library, one of several neoclassical campus buildings by McKim, Mead & White.

Two churches are big draws, too: the Episcopal **Cathedral of St John the Divine** (Map pp156-7; ☎ 212-316-7540; 1047 Amsterdam Ave at 112th St; ⏱ 8am-6pm) is the largest place of worship in the USA, and features High Mass, held at 11am Sunday, often with sermons by well-known intellectuals. West of here is the **Riverside Church** (Map pp156-7; ☎ 212-330-1234; www.theriversidechurchny.org; 490 Riverside Dr at 122nd St; ⏱ 7am-10pm), a 1930 Gothic-style marvel, famous for its 74 carillon bells that are rung every Sunday at noon and 3pm, as well as for its diverse and activist congregation.

Upper East Side

The Upper East Side (UES) is home to New York's greatest concentration of cultural centers, including the grand dame that is the Metropolitan Museum of Art (see below), and many refer to Fifth Ave above 57th St as Museum Mile. Beyond museums, you'll find intellectual draws which include the **92nd Street Y**, a cultural hub offering classes, performances and readings by folks from playwright Tony Kushner to novelist Joyce Carol Oates and chamber-music groups. The neighborhood, whose residents, by the way, are in a never-ending contest with those of the Upper West Side (UWS), just across the park, also includes many of the city's most exclusive hotels and residences.

METROPOLITAN MUSEUM OF ART

With more than five million visitors a year, the **Met** (Map pp156-7; ☎ 212-879-5500; www.metmuseum.org; 1000 Fifth Ave at 82nd St; suggested donation $20; ⏱ 9:30am-5:30pm Tue-Thu & Sun, to 9pm Fri & Sat) is New York's most popular single-site tourist attraction, with one of the richest coffers in the arts world. The Met is a self-contained cultural city-state, with two million individual objects in its collection and an annual budget of over $120 million. And since 2004 the Met has been eking out $155 million for a remodeling project that will put every inch of space to use; its 19th-century European paintings and sculpture galleries, for example, were to be greatly expanded and refurbished in the fall of 2007.

Highlights here include Egyptian Art, American Paintings and Sculpture, Arms and Armor, Modern Art, Greek and Roman Art, European Paintings and the gorgeous rooftop, which offers bar service and spectacular views throughout the summer. Note that the suggested donation (which is, truly, a *suggestion*) includes same-day admission to the Cloisters (see p158).

OTHER MUSEUMS

One of the northernmost museum attractions, the **Museum of the City of New York** (Map pp156-7; ☎ 212-534-1672; www.mcny.org; 1220 Fifth Ave at 123rd St; suggested admission adult/child/family $7/5/15; ⏱ 10am-5pm Tue-Sun) traces the city's history from beaver trading to futures trading with various cultural exhibitions. The opulent 1914 mansion housing the **Frick Collection** (Map pp156-7; ☎ 212-288-0700; www.frick.org; 1 E 70th St; admission $15; ⏱ 10am-6pm Tue-Sat, 11am-5pm Sun) tells a similar tale, but through its exquisite artwork by Holbein, Titian, Vermeer, Gainsborough and Constable.

One of the few museums that concentrates on American works of art is the **Whitney Museum of American Art** (Map pp156-7; ☎ 212-570-3676; www.whitney.org; 945 Madison Ave at 75th St; admission $15; ⏱ 11am-6pm Wed-Thu, Sat & Sun; 1-9pm Fri with pay-what-you-wish 6-9pm), specializing in 20th-century and contemporary art, with works by Hopper, Pollock and Rothko, as well as special shows, such as the much-ballyhooed Biennial. The Whitney will soon have a downtown outpost in the Meatpacking District, which is being built as part of the new Highline project, which will run from Gansevoort Street up to 34th Street

The inspired work of Frank Lloyd Wright, the **Solomon R Guggenheim Museum** (Map pp156-7; ☎ 212-423-3500; www.guggenheim.org; 1071 Fifth Ave; admission $18, donation 6-8pm Fri; ⏱ 10am-5:45pm Sat-Wed, to 8pm Fri) and its sweeping spiral of a staircase is a superb sculpture, holding 20th-century paintings by Picasso, Pollock, Chagall and Kandinsky. Unfortunately, the outside has been obscured by scaffolding since 2005 (and some inside galleries have been closed) due to an extensive renovation project that aims to fix the museum's many cracks; check the website for progress reports. One of the most pleasant museums in the 'hood is the focused and elegant **Neue Galerie** (Map pp156-7; ☎ 212-628-6200; www.neuegalerie.org; 1048 Fifth Ave at 86th St; adult/senior $10/7, children under 12 not admitted; ⏱ 11am-6pm

NEW YORK, NEW JERSEY & PENNSYLVANIA

CENTRAL PARK & UPPER MANHATTAN

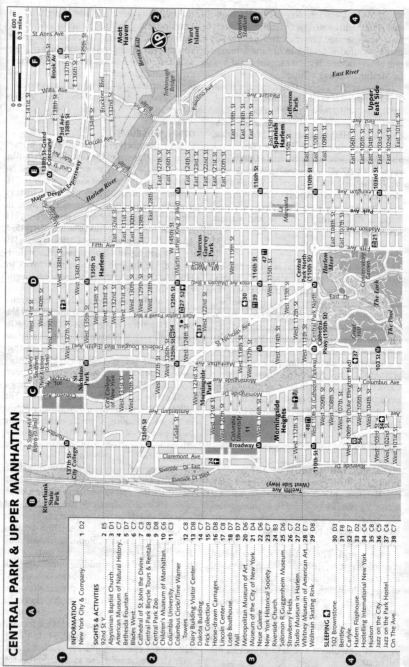

INFORMATION
New York City & Company........................ 1 D2

SIGHTS & ACTIVITIES
92nd St Y... 2 E5
Abyssinian Baptist Church...................... 3 D1
American Museum of Natural History.... 4 C7
Bethesda Fountain................................... 5 D7
Blades West.. 6 C7
Central Park Bicycle Tours & Rentals..... 7 C3
Cathedral of St John the Divine.............. 8 C8
Central Park Zoo...................................... 9 D8
Children's Museum of Manhattan.......... 10 C6
Columbia University................................ 11 C3
Columbus Circle/Time Warner
  Towers.. 12 C8
Dairy Building Visitor Center................. 13 D8
Dakota Building....................................... 14 C7
Frick Collection....................................... 15 D7
Horse-drawn Carriages........................... 16 D8
Lincoln Center... 17 C8
Loeb Boathouse...................................... 18 D7
Mall... 19 D7
Metropolitan Museum of Art.................. 20 D6
Museum of the City of New York........... 21 D4
Neue Galerie.. 22 D6
New York Historical Society.................... 23 C7
Riverside Church...................................... 24 B3
Solomon R Guggenheim Museum.......... 25 D6
Strawberry Fields..................................... 26 C7
Studio Museum in Harlem...................... 27 D3
Whitney Museum of American Art......... 28 E7
Wollman Skating Rink............................. 29 D8

SLEEPING
102 Brownstone....................................... 30 D3
Bentley.. 31 F8
Carlyle.. 32 E7
Harlem Flophouse.................................... 33 D2
Hostelling International New York.......... 34 C4
Hudson... 35 C8
Jazz on the City....................................... 36 C5
Jazz on the Park Hostel........................... 37 C4
On The Ave... 38 C7

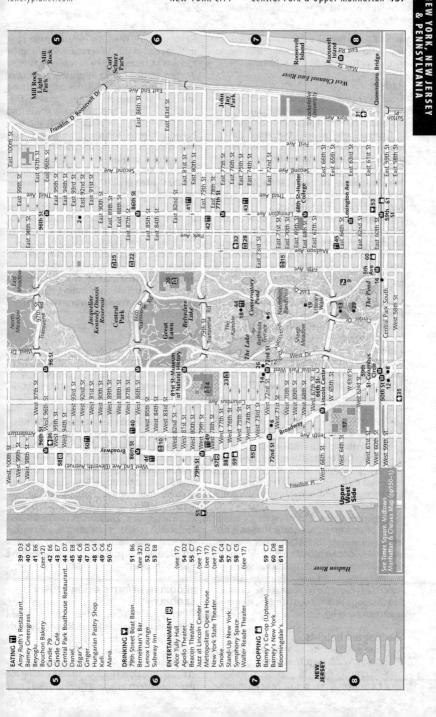

EATING 🍴	
Amy Ruth's Restaurant	39 D3
Barney Greengrass	40 C6
BeyoğIu	41 E6
Bouchon Bakery	(see 12)
Candle 79	42 E6
Candle Café	43 E7
Central Park Boathouse Restaurant	44 D7
Daniel	45 E8
Edgar's	46 C6
Ginger	47 D3
Hungarian Pastry Shop	48 C4
Kefi	49 C6
Mana	50 C5

DRINKING 🍷	
79th Street Boat Basin	51 B6
Bemelman's Bar	(see 32)
Lenox Lounge	52 D2
Subway Inn	53 E8

ENTERTAINMENT 🎭	
Alice Tully Hall	(see 17)
Apollo Theater	54 D2
Beacon Theater	55 C7
Jazz at Lincoln Center	(see 17)
Metropolitan Opera House	(see 17)
New York State Theater	(see 17)
Smoke	56 C4
Stand-Up New York	57 C7
Symphony Space	58 C5
Walter Reade Theater	(see 17)

SHOPPING 🛍	
Barney's Co-op (Uptown)	59 C7
Barney's New York	60 D8
Bloomingdale's	61 E8

See Times Square, Midtown Manhattan & Chelsea Map (pp150–1)

Sat, Sun & Mon; to 9pm Fri), a showcase for German and Austrian artists, with impressive works by Gustav Klimt and Egon Schiele.

Harlem

From its origins as a 1920s black enclave until now, the heart of African American culture has beat in Harlem. This neighborhood north of Central Park has been the setting for extraordinary accomplishments in art, music, dance, education and letters from the likes of Frederick Douglass, Paul Robeson, Thurgood Marshall, James Baldwin, Alvin Ailey, Billie Holiday, Jessie Jackson and many other African American luminaries.

Despite its past reputation as a crime-ridden no-man's-land, today Harlem – with the exception of some still-abandoned, eerily empty side streets – shouldn't cause you to exercise any more caution than you would anywhere else in New York.

For a traditional view of Harlem, visit on Sunday morning, when well-dressed locals flock to neighborhood churches. Just be respectful of the fact that this is a religious service, not a people-zoo. Unless you're invited by a member of a small congregation, stick to the bigger churches like the **Abyssinian Baptist Church** (Map pp156-7; ☎ 212-862-7474; www.abyssinian .org; 132 W 138th St). It's got a superb choir and a charismatic pastor, Calvin O Butts, who welcomes tourists and prays for them. Sunday services start at 9am and 11am – the later one is *very* well attended.

For straight-up entertainment, head to the historic **Apollo Theater** (Map pp156-7; ☎ 212-749-5838; www.apolloshowtime.com; 253 W 125th St), which still holds its famous (if very touristed) amateur night, 'where stars are born and legends are made.'

To glimpse the work of visual artists, meanwhile, be sure to visit the **Studio Museum in Harlem** (Map pp156-7; ☎ 212-864-4500; www.studiomuseum .org; 144 W 125th St; suggested donation $7; ✹ noon-6pm Wed-Fri & Sun, from 10am Sat), which has given exposure to the crafts and culture of African American people for 30 years. Look for excellent rotating exhibits from painters, sculptors, illustrators and other creators.

Washington Heights

Near the northern tip of Manhattan (above 155th St), Washington Heights takes its name from the first US president, who set up a Continental Army fort here during the Revolutionary War. An isolated rural spot until the end of the 19th century, Washington Heights attracted lots of new blood as New Yorkers sniffed out its affordable rents over the past several years. Still, this neighborhood manages to retain its Latino – mainly Dominican – flavor, and now what you'll find is an interesting mix of blocks that alternate between hipster former-downtowners and long-time residents who operate within a tight and warm community.

Most visitors to Washington Heights come to see the **Cloisters** (Map p137; ☎ 212-923-3700; www.met museum.org; Fort Tryon Park at 190th St; suggested admission $20; ✹ 9:30am-4:45pm Tue-Sun Nov-Feb, to 5:15pm Mar-Oct) in Fort Tryon Park, a branch of the Metropolitan Museum of Art. Constructed in the 1930s using stones and fragments from several French and Spanish medieval monasteries, the romantic, castle-like creation houses medieval frescoes, tapestries, courtyards, gardens and paintings, and has commanding views of the Hudson – not to mention a grassy park that's perfect for picnics.

Brooklyn

With 2.5 million people and growing, Brooklyn is the place where everyone wants to be these days. From well-to-do new parents seeking stately brownstones in Carroll Gardens to young band members wanting cheap rents near good gigs in Williamsburg, this outer borough has long succeeded Manhattan in cool factor in many people's minds. Its diversity of offerings has the small island beat; get ready for sandy beaches and breezy boardwalks at one end, of-the-moment foodie destinations at the other, with a massive range of ethnic enclaves, world-class entertainment, stately architecture and endless shopping strips in between. The **Brooklyn Tourism & Visitors Center** (Map pp142-3; ☎ 718-802-3846; www.brooklyn tourism.org; 209 Borough Hall, Joralemon St; ✹ 10am-6pm Mon-Fri), in Brooklyn Heights, is an informative place to begin.

BROOKLYN HEIGHTS & DOWNTOWN BROOKLYN

When Robert Fulton's steam ferries started regular service across the East River in the early 19th century, well-to-do Manhattanites began building stellar houses – Victorian Gothic, Romanesque, neo-Greco, Italianate and others – in Brooklyn Heights. Strolling along the tree-lined streets to gaze at them now is a lovely afternoon activity; don't miss the 1881 Queen Anne–style landmark building that houses the **Brooklyn Historical Society** (Map pp142-3; ☎ 718-222-4111; www.brooklynhistory.org; 128 Pierrepont St; admission $6; ✆ 10am–5pm Wed-Sun), which houses a library (with some 33,000 grainy digitized photos from decades past), auditorium and museum devoted to the borough. The society also leads several walking tours.

Montague St is the main avenue for cafés and bars; follow it down to the waterfront until you hit the **Brooklyn Heights Promenade**, which juts out over the Brooklyn–Queens Expressway to offer stunning views of Lower Manhattan.

The 1848 beaux-arts **Brooklyn Borough Hall** (209 Joralemon St) straddles both Brooklyn Heights and Downtown Brooklyn, characterized by its various courts, and busy street that feeds into the **Brooklyn Bridge** (see p141). Just south of here, the small but fascinating **New York Transit Museum** (☎ 718-694-1600; www.mta.info/mta/museum; Boerum Pl at Schermerhorn St; ✆ 10am-4pm Tue-Fri, noon-5pm Sat & Sun; adult/child $5/3) has an amazing collection of original subway cars and transit memorabilia dating back more than a century.

DUMBO

Dumbo's nickname is an acronym for its location: 'Down Under the Manhattan–Brooklyn Bridge Overpass,' and while this north Brooklyn slice of waterfront used to be strictly for industry, it's now the domain of artists and wannabes, who occupy huge loft spaces that are no longer real-estate bargains. **St Ann's Warehouse** (☎ 718-834-8794; www.stannswarehouse.org; 45 Main St) is a highly regarded artist-driven performance space; **Dumbo Arts Center** (☎ 718-694-0831; www.dumboartscenter.org; 30 Washington St) is one of the top galleries here, and host to the annual Dumbo Art Under the Bridge Festival, held each October.

BOERUM HILL, COBBLE HILL & CARROLL GARDENS (& RED HOOK)

A trio of *très*-hip 'hoods that's adopted a silly acronym as a moniker (BoCoCa), this is former-Manhattanite central. **Smith Street** is the main artery (and 'restaurant row') connecting to the most southerly area of the three, Carroll Gardens (which still maintains some of its old-school Italian charm through a few fresh-pasta groceries and red-sauce restaurants), to Boerum Hill. Even further west (and south) is **Red Hook**, a waterfront area whose fast-developing cobblestone streets and hulking industrial buildings are making it the latest hip place to be. Though it's a bit of a hike from the subway line, the formerly gritty area is now home to some cool bars and eateries, as well as a massive waterfront branch of Fairway, a beloved gourmet shop with main locations on the Upper West Side and in Harlem. Come check out the area before it's over.

PARK SLOPE & PROSPECT HEIGHTS

The **Park Slope** neighborhood is known for its classic brownstones, tons of great eateries and boutiques (especially along Fifth Ave, which is more cutting-edge than the other major strip, Seventh Ave), lesbian residents and stroller-pushing couples who resemble those on the Upper West Side (but have a backyard attached to their apartment). Beginning at its eastern border the 585-acre **Prospect Park** (☎ 718-965-8999; www.prospectpark.org), created in 1866, is considered the greatest achievement of landscape designers Olmsted and Vaux, who also designed Central Park. Next door is the excellent 52-acre **Brooklyn Botanic Garden** (☎ 718-622-4433; www.bbg.org; 1000 Washington Ave; admission $8, Tue free; ✆ 8am-6pm Tue-Fri, from 10am Sat & Sun), which features impressive cherry-tree blossoms in spring. And just beside that is the **Brooklyn Museum** (☎ 718-638-5000; www.brooklynmuseum.org; 200 Eastern Parkway; suggested admission $8, 11am-11pm 1st Sat of each month free; ✆ 10am-5pm Wed-Fri, 11am-6pm Sat & Sun), with comprehensive collections of African, Islamic and Asian art, plus the brand-new Elizabeth A Sackler Center for Feminist Art.

WILLIAMSBURG & GREENPOINT

Across the East River from the East Village, the enclave of hipsters continues – but even more so – in Williamsburg, full of slouchy young artsy types who sit in cafés, chain smoke, shop for skinny jeans, get tattoos, go to bars and basically look cool. The artery is **Bedford Ave** between N 10th St and Metropolitan Ave, where there are boutiques, cafés, bars and cheap eateries. But cool spots have also sprouted along N 6th St and Berry St, and even into the next neighborhood, **Greenpoint**, a traditionally Polish neighborhood that's lured those priced out of Billyburg with lower rents. Be sure to visit the excellent **Brooklyn Brewery** (☎ 718-486-7422; www.brooklynbrewery.com; 79 N 11th St; admission free; ✆ 6-11pm Fri, noon-5pm Sat), which hosts tours, special events and pub nights.

FORT GREENE

Spike Lee grew up here and Erykah Badu and Rosie Perez live here – and they are not alone. This residential neighborhood of late 19th-century brownstones and gospel churches is the hot new place to call home for a racially diverse group of young professionals. Its gem is the **Brooklyn Academy of Music** (Map pp142-3; ☎ 718-636-4100; www.bam.org; 30 Lafayette Ave), the oldest concert center in the country.

CONEY ISLAND & BRIGHTON BEACH

About 50 minutes by subway from Midtown, this popular pair of beach neighborhoods makes for a great day trip. **Coney Island** (Map p 137) is all about nostalgic charms, with its wide sandy beach, wood-plank boardwalk and famous 1927 Cyclone roller coaster; Astroland Park used to operate arcade games and a collection of carnival rides, but it was sold to make way for developers (who plan to transform the place into a sleek retail-residential city) and closed, to much outcry, after its 2007 summer season. Still intact, though, is **Sideshows by the Seashore** (☎ 718-372-5159; www .coneyisland.com; adult/child $6/4), a burlesque-type show with bearded ladies and tattooed men. The **Aquarium for Wildlife Conservation** (☎ 718-265-3400; Surf Ave btwn 5th & W 8th Sts; adult/child $11/7; ☽ 10am-4:30pm) is a big hit with kids, and **Key-Span Park** (Map p137; ☎ 718-449-8497) is the waterfront stadium for the minor-league Brooklyn Cyclones baseball team.

A five-minute stroll north along the boardwalk brings you to **Brighton Beach** ('Little Odessa'; Map p137), where folks enjoy pierogies and beer in the sun and then head into the heart of the 'hood, busy Brighton Beach Ave, to hit the many Russian shops, bakeries and restaurants.

THE BRONX

Brooklyn's fierce northern rival is this 42-square-mile borough, which has several claims to fame: the Yankees, fondly known as the Bronx Bombers, who can be seen in all their pinstriped glory at **Yankee Stadium** (Map p137; ☎ 718-293-6000; www.yankees.com; 161st St at River Ave) in the spring and summer; the 'real' Little Italy, or **Belmont** (Map p137; www.arthuravenuebronx .com), bustling stretches of Arthur and Belmont Aves that burst with Italian gourmet markets and eateries; and a super-sized attitude that's been mythologized in Hollywood movies from *The Godfather* to *Rumble in the Bronx*.

But it's also got some cool surprises up its sleeve: a quarter of the Bronx is parkland, including the city beach of Pelham Bay Park. It's home to the 250-acre **New York Botanical Garden** (Map p137; ☎ 718-817-8705; www .nybg.org; Bronx River Parkway at Fordham Rd; adult/child $135; ☽ 10am-6pm Tue-Sun), with nearly 3000 roses. The nearby **Bronx Wildlife Conservation Park** (Map p137; ☎ 718-367-1010; www.bronxzoo .com; Bronx River Parkway at Fordham Rd; adult/child $11/8; ☽ 10am-5pm Apr-Oct), otherwise known as the Bronx Zoo, is one of the biggest, best and most progressive zoos anywhere; and the famous, historic **Woodlawn Cemetery** (Map p137; ☎ 718-920-0500; www.thewoodlawncemetery.org; Webster Ave at 233rd St) is the fascinating, 400-acre burial ground of many notable Americans, including Irving Berlin and Herman Melville. Also up in these parts is the magically beachy City Island (see box, below).

The **Bronx Tourism Council** (☎ 718-590-3518; www .ilovethebronx.com) has visitor information, and the **Bronx County Historical Society** (☎ 718-881-8900; www.bronxhistoricalsociety.org) sponsors weekend walking tours.

Queens

Queens is the largest (282 sq miles), fastest-growing and most ethnically diverse borough in the city – about 150 nations are represented among its population of 2.2 million, and close to half its residents were born abroad. It's also home to two major airports, the Mets, a hip modern-art scene and a collection of truly fascinating, quietly fabulous communities. The **Queens Historical Society** (☎ 718-939-0647; www.queenshistoricalsociety.org) offers tours on many areas of the massive borough.

BEACHTOWN IN THE CITY

Only 15 miles from midtown but a complete world away is the surprising neighborhood of City Island (Map p137; www.cityislandcham ber.org), a 1.5-mile-long fishing community that's filled with boat slips, yacht clubs, waterfront seafood eateries and wind-swept little spits of sand. Victorian clapboard houses look more New England than the Bronx, and you can even go on a lobster dive, courtesy of **Captain Mike's Dive Shop** (☎ 718-885-1588; www.captainmikesdiving.com; 530 City Island Ave; $55-88). Talk about NYC having it all.

Astoria & Long Island City

Home to the largest Greek community outside of Greece, this is obviously the place to find amazing Greek bakeries, restaurants and gourmet shops, mainly along **Broadway**. But it's not as one-note as it used to be, as an influx of Eastern Europeans (such as Croatians and Romanians) and Middle Eastern folks have been pouring in, too. Then there are the hipsters, who have made this area Queens' answer to Williamsburg.

In recent years neighboring Long Island City has become quite the hub of art museums. **PS 1 Contemporary Art Center** (Map p137; ☎ 718-784-2084; www.ps1.org; 22-25 Jackson Ave at 46th Ave; suggested donation $5; ☯ noon-6pm Thu-Mon), run by MoMA, is dedicated solely to new, cutting-edge works.

If the weather is pleasant, don't miss the waterside **Socrates Sculpture Park** (☎ 718-956-1819; www.socratessculpturepark.org; Broadway at Vernon Blvd; admission free; ☯ 10am-dusk), an outdoor exhibit of massive, climbable sculptures by greats including Mark DiSuvero, who founded the space. Nearby is the peaceful **Isamu Noguchi Garden Museum** (☎ 718-204-7088; www.noguchi.org; 9-01 33rd Rd at Vernon Blvd; admission $10; ☯ 10am-5pm Wed-Fri, 11am-6pm Sat & Sun), with the sculptures of this Japanese artist. Nearby is a reminder that movie making started in Astoria in the 1920s: the **American Museum of the Moving Image** (☎ 718-784-0077; www.ammi.org; 35th Ave at 36th St; admission $10; ☯ noon-5pm Tue-Fri, 11am-6pm Sat & Sun), which exposes some of the mysteries of the craft with amazing exhibits and screenings.

Flushing & Corona

With many Asian immigrants, most recently from Korea and China, Flushing's **Main Street** is a bustling, diverse area known mainly for its cheap and delicious gastronomic wonders. **Flushing Meadows Corona Park**, meanwhile, is the home of **Shea Stadium** (Map p137), the **USTA National Tennis Center** and many lakes, ball fields, bike paths and grassy expanses; and was used for the 1939 and 1964 World's Fairs, of which there are quite a few faded leftovers – including Queens' most famous landmark, the stainless steel Unisphere, standing 120 feet high and weighing 380 tons. Also within this massive park is the **Queens Museum of Art** (☎ 718-592-9700; www.queensmuseum.org; New York City Bldg, Flushing Meadows Corona Park; suggested donation $5; ☯ 10am-5pm Wed-Fri, from noon Sat & Sun). In nearby Corona, the recently opened **Louis Armstrong House** (☎ 718-478-8274; 34-56 107th St; ☯ 10am-5pm

Tue-Fri, noon-5pm Sat & Sun; admission $8) is the home where the musical great lived during the peak of his career.

Jackson Heights

A fascinating mix of Indian (74th St) and South American (Roosevelt Ave) cultures, this is the place to purchase saris and 22-karat gold, dine on South Indian *masala dosas* – huge, paper-thin rice crepes folded around flavorful mixtures of masala potatoes, peas, cilantro and other earthy treats – and continue on with a plate of Colombian *arepas* (corn pancakes), a bite of Argentine empanadas and a cocktail at one of several Latin gay and lesbian bars, several of which line the main drag of Broadway. It's a crazy convergence that's not to be missed.

Staten Island

While many New Yorkers will say that Staten Island has more in common with its neighbor, New Jersey, because of its suburban house and car cultures, there are some undoubtedly compelling reasons to count this borough in your urban explorations. First and foremost is the free **Staten Island Ferry** (☎ 718-815-2628; www.siferry.com; ☯ 24hr), which shuttles blasé commuters to work while offering breathtaking views of the Statue of Liberty and the Manhattan skyline. Not far from the ferry station on the Staten Island side is the **Richmond County Bank Ballpark** (Map p137; ☎ 718-720-9200; www.siyanks.com; Richmond Terrace), home to the minor-league Staten Island Yankees, as well as the hipper than ever neighborhood of St. George.

ACTIVITIES
Biking & Inline Skating

Unless you're a bike messenger or otherwise experienced urban cyclist, pedaling through the streets can be a high-risk activity in Manhattan, as bike lanes are often blocked by trucks, taxis and double-parked cars. But **Central Park** has lovely bicycling paths, as does the **Hudson River Parkway** (see p154), which has a path shared by cyclists, runners, walkers and skaters; the auto-free road that runs round the perimeter of Brooklyn's **Prospect Park** (see p159); and the beautiful **Franklin D Roosevelt Boardwalk** (☎ 718-816-6804; cnr Father Capadanno Blvd & Sand Ln) along South Beach in Staten Island, hugging 4 miles of unspoiled beaches.

For bicycling tips and weekend trips, contact **Five Borough Bicycle Club** (☎ 212-932-2300). **Transportation Alternatives** (Map pp150-1; ☎ 212-

629-8080; www.transalt.org; 115 W 30th St), a nonprofit bicycle-lobbying group, is also a good source of information, as is **Bike Network Development (www.ci.nyc.ny.us/html/dcp/html/bike/home.html)**, which offers bicycling map downloads and more info on biking in the city. Gay bicycling enthusiasts should check the website of **Fast & Fabulous** (www.fastnfab.org), a gay bicycling club that organizes long weekend rides. For bike rentals, try **Loeb Boathouse** (Map pp156-7; ☎ 212-517-2233; Central Park btwn 74th and 75th Sts) or **Manhattan Bicycle** (Map pp150-1; ☎ 212-262-0111; 791 Ninth Ave btwn 52nd and 53rd Sts).

In-line skating is also popular in all of the above places – especially in Central Park, where a makeshift outdoor rink with DJs operates on summer weekends. For rentals, try **Blades West** (Map pp156-7; ☎ 212-787-3911; 120 W 72nd St), two blocks from Central Park.

Running

Central Park's (see p154) 6-mile roadway is closed to cars from 10am to 3pm weekdays and all weekend, and is perfect for running – as is its gleaming Jacqueline Kennedy Onassis Reservoir, encircled by a soft 1.5-mile path. Another good place to sprint is the **Hudson River Parkway** (see p144), which runs along Manhattan's western edge from Battery Park to 59th St, and north of there through the leafy **Riverside Park** (p154). The **New York Road Runner's Club** (☎ 212-860-4455; www .nyrrc.org) organizes weekend runs as well as the October **New York City Marathon**.

Watersports

With water, water all around, this city has plenty of opportunities for boating and kayaking. The **Downtown Boathouse** (Map pp142-3 ☎ 646-613-0740; www.downtownboathouse.org; Pier 40 near Houston St; free) is a public boathouse that offers 20-minute kayaking (including equipment) in the protected embayment of the Hudson River. You don't need a reservation, just head over on weekends between May 15 and October 15. Two other locations include **Clinton Cove** (Pier 96, west of 56th St) and at **Riverside Park** (W 72nd St). It even gives tips to first timers.

In Central Park, **Loeb Boathouse** (Map p156-7; ☎ 212-517-2233; Central Park btwn 74th & 75th Sts; $10 per hour; ☉ 10am-5:30pm Mar-Oct) rents row boats for romantic paddlings, and even fills Viennastyle gondolas in summer ($30 for 30 minutes). For a sailing adventure, hop aboard the *Schooner Adirondack* at **Chelsea Piers** (p147), or the *Pioneer* at **South Street Seaport** (p141).

If you'd rather get all wet, check out the cool new **Floating Pool Lady** (www.floatingpool.org), a 25-meter swimming pool on top of a massive barge that moves around the Hudson and docks in various city locations. Admission is free but limited to 175 people, so expect to wait on hot days. Its inaugural 2007 summer was spent in Brooklyn, but check the website to see where it is these days.

Surfers may be surprised to find a tight group of wave worshipers within city limits, at Queens' **Rockaway Beach** at 90th St, where you can hang ten after only a 45-minute ride on the A train from midtown.

WALKING TOUR: VILLAGE RADICALS

Manhattan's most unruly maze of streets can be found in Greenwich Village – and that's not only because it's the only corner not laid out in a neat grid. It's historically been a hotbed for upstarts by being home (and protest central) to radicals, bohemians, poets, folk singers, feminists, and freedom-seeking gays and lesbians.

To begin, disembark the subway at Christopher St and double back east one short block, where you'll find the last remaining LGBT bookstore in the city, the **Oscar Wilde Bookshop (1**; p138). A simple brick townhouse, it has bucked the mainstream by selling queer books and periodicals since 1967. Now go west to tiny **Christopher Park (2)**, where two white, life-size statues of same-sex couples (*Gay Liberation*, 1992) stand guard. On its north side is the legendary **Stonewall Inn (3)**, where a clutch of fed-up drag queens rioted for their civil rights in 1969, signalling the start of the gay revolution. Cross Seventh Ave South and continue west along Christopher St, still known as the pulse of gay life here. At Bedford St turn left and enjoy the quietude of the quaint block (if it's a weekday afternoon, that is); stop and peer into **Chumley's (4)**, the site of a prohibition-dodging socialist-run speakeasy that is marked by a simple air-conditioning unit over its wooden door.

WALK FACTS

Start Oscar Wilde Bookshop
Finish Oscar Wilde's home
Distance 2 miles
Duration two hours

Continue along Bedford St for several blocks, make a left on Downing St and cross Sixth Ave. To the south you'll see a plaque marking **'Little Red Square' (5)**, so-named not for communists but for the original site of the experimental Little Red Schoolhouse, founded by Elisabeth Irwin in 1921 and still thriving nearby. Continue east on the crooked Minetta St, home to the unremarkable Panchito's Mexican Restaurant. But above its red facade is the faded sign for the **Fat Black Pussycat (6)** – called The Commons in 1962 when a young Bob Dylan wrote and first performed 'Blowin' in the Wind' here.

Turn right on Minetta La and right on MacDougal St to find the historic **Minetta Tavern (7)**, a great place for a pit stop. The bar and restaurant, its walls now lined with photos of celebs who have visited, opened as a speakeasy in 1922. It was later frequented by one of the most famous local eccentrics, Joe Gould, who was immortalized through the writings of journalism great Joseph Mitchell (a friendship further depicted in the 2000 flick *Joe Gould's Secret*). Also on this block is the former site of the **Folklore Center (8)**, where Izzy Young established a hangout for folk artists including Dylan, who found his first audience at the music venue **Cafe Wha? (9)**.

Double back along MacDougal to another possible fuel stop, the cozy **Caffe Reggio (10)**, whose original 1927 owners claimed to be the first to bring cappuccino from Italy to the US. Just past here are two former hotspots:

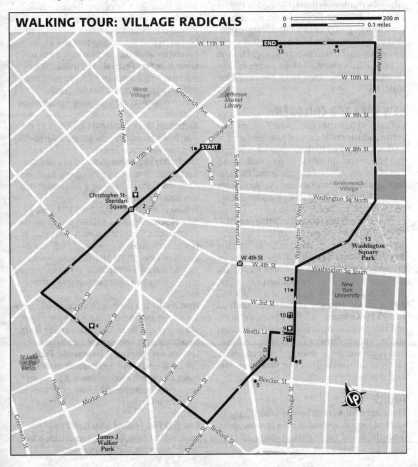

WALKING TOUR: VILLAGE RADICALS

the **Provincetown Playhouse (11)**, founded on a Provincetown, MA, wharf in 1915 as an experimental theatre, was moved to this converted stable and managed by a young Eugene O'Neill; and next door, the current Research Fellows & Scholars Office of the NYU School of Law is the former site of the **Liberal Club (12)**, 'a meeting place for those interested in new ideas' that was founded in 1913 by free thinkers including Jack London and Upton Sinclair.

Beyond here is the southwest entrance to **Washington Square Park (13**; p146), which has a long history as a magnet for radicals. Leave the park at the iconic arch and head up Fifth Ave. Make a left on W 11th St, where you'll wrap up the tour with two notable townhouses. First is the infamous **Weathermen House (14)**, used in 1970 as a hideout and bomb factory for the radical anti-government group until an accidental explosion killed three members and destroyed the house; it was rebuilt in its current angular form in 1978. Further west, the tour comes full circle with a former, albeit brief, home of **Oscar Wilde (15)**.

NEW YORK FOR CHILDREN

Contrary to popular belief, New York can be a pretty child-friendly city – it just takes a bit of guidance to find all the little creature comforts that you're accustomed to having back home. Fun playscape options include **Central Park's Safari Playground**, **Battery Park** and the **Glass Garden** (Map pp150-1; ☎ 212-263-6058; 400 E 34th St at First Ave; ❂ 8am-5:30pm Mon-Fri, 1-5:30pm Sat-Sun).

The **Children's Museum of Manhattan** (Map 156-7; ☎ 212-721-1234; www.cmom.org; 212 W 83rd St btwn Broadway and Amsterdam Ave; ❂ 10am-5pm Tue-Sun) and the **Brooklyn Children's Museum** (☎ 718-735-4400; www .brooklynkids.org; 145 Brooklyn Ave, Prospect Heights) are excellent respites, as are children's theaters, movie theaters, book and toy stores, aquariums and kid-friendly restaurants, such as **Bubby's Pie Company** (p168). For more hints and information on traveling with children, pick up Lonely Planet's *Travel With Children*. And when you get to town, get your hands on a copy of the weekly *Time Out Kids* magazine, available at newsstands.

TOURS

There are endless numbers of folks willing to lead lost tourists around to their favorite spots, from the usual top sights to more obscure curiosities. Here's just a sampling:

Big Onion Walking Tours (☎ 212-439-1090; www .bigonion.com; tours $15) Popular and quirky guided tours specializing in ethnic and neighborhood tours.

Municipal Art Society (☎ 212-935-3960; www.mas .org; 457 Madison Ave; tours adult $12) Various scheduled tours focusing on architecture and history.

On Location Tours (☎ 212-209-3370; www .screentours.com; $15-40) Helps you live out your fantasy of sitting on Carrie Bradshaw's stoop and checking out the restaurant from *Spiderman*.

A Slice of Brooklyn Pizza Tour (☎ 212-209-3370; www.bknypizza.com; adults/kids $65/55 incl pizza) This focused tour takes you on a gut-busting journey through pizza joints and their neighborhoods.

FESTIVALS & EVENTS

Festivities never cease in New York – even when there isn't anything special scheduled, which is rare. From cultural street fairs to foodie events and outdoor concerts, you are bound to find something that will excite you, no matter what time of year you are in town.

Lunar New Year Festival (☎ 212-966-0100) Chinatown's much-anticipated New Year celebration, held in late January or early February, features displays of fireworks and lavish parades in and around Chinatown.

Restaurant Week (☎ 212-484-1222; www.nycvisit .com) Dine at top restaurants for $20 and $30 deals – first in February and again in June.

The Armory Show (www.thearmoryshow.com) New York's biggest contemporary art fair sweeps the city in March, showcasing the new work of thousands of artists from around the world.

Tribeca Film Festival (☎ 212-941-3378; www .tribecafilmfestival.com) Robert DeNiro co-organizes this local downtown film fest in May, that's quickly rising in prestige on the circuit.

Bike New York (☎ 212-932-2453; www.bikemonthnyc .org) The main event of Bike Month, in May, has thousands of cyclers doing this 42-mile ride through each of the five boroughs.

Fleet Week (☎ 212-245-2533) It's the annual convocation of sailors and their naval ships and air rescue teams, who descend upon the city in their formal whites like the characters in *On the Town* each and every May.

Lesbian, Gay, Bisexual & Transgender Pride (☎ 212-807-7433; www.heritageofpride.org) Pride month, in June, with a packed calendar of parties and special events, culminates with a major march down Fifth Ave on the last Sunday of the month. It's a five-hour spectacle.

New York Film Festival (www.filmlinc.com) Catch major world premieres from prominent directors at this Lincoln Center event, held late September.

US Open Tennis Tournament (www.usopen.org)
The Grand Slam event in Flushing Meadows, Queens, in
September.

SLEEPING

A place to sleep over is not only going to cost
you – the average room rate in 2006 was $267
a night – it's going to force you to plan ahead
if you're at all picky about where you want to
stay, as the standard occupancy rate is 85%
and rising.

There are also some good budget options to
be found, so as long as you book in advance,
there's no reason why you can't enjoy a comfortable stay and still have enough money left
to reap the cultural benefits of the city. Keep
in mind that prices change depending on the
day of the week and the season, with spring
and fall being most expensive. Tax adds an
additional 13.25% per night. For longer stays,
an apartment rental or sublet can be the best
option (there's no tax on rentals, so you're
already that much ahead), secured with the
help of an agency like **City Sonnet** (☎ 212-614-
3034; www.westvillagebb.com; apts from $135 per night).

Lower Manhattan

Best Western Seaport Inn (Map pp142-3; ☎ 212-766-
6600, 800-468-3569; www.seaportinn.com; 33 Peck Slip btwn
Front & Water Sts; d from $215; ✖ ✖ ▢ wi-fi) Despite
its blah chain style, the Seaport Inn offers
some striking water views from its terrace
rooms, and resides among the brick lanes of
historic South Street Seaport. Plus it's got a
small on-site gym, high-speed internet and
services for assisting deaf patrons.

Battery Park City Ritz-Carlton (Map pp142-3; ☎ 212-
344-0800; www.ritz-carlton.com; 2 West St at Battery Pl; s/d/ste
from $260/450/800; ✖ ▢ wi-fi) It's hard to pick the
best amenity of this luxurious, 38-story glass-
and-brick tower, which include the sweeping
harbor and city views, in-room telescopes,
big marble baths (with 'bath-butler' service),
Bvlgari products, on-site spa and gym and two
top-notch restaurants.

Tribeca & Soho

Cosmopolitan Hotel (Map pp142-3; ☎ 212-566-1900,
888-895-9400; www.cosmohotel.com; 95 West Broadway;
d from $149; ✖) It's clean, carpeted and not so
stylish, but will save you money perhaps better spent on the prime area's chic boutiques
and eateries.

Soho Grand Hotel (Map pp142-3; ☎ 212-965-3000,
800-965-3000; www.sohogrand.com; 310 West Broadway; d

$260–360; ✖ ▢ wi-fi) The original boutique hotel
of the 'hood still reigns, with its striking glass-
and-cast-iron lobby stairway, and 367 rooms
with cool, clean lines plus Frette linens, plasma
flatscreens and Kiehl's grooming products. The
lobby's Grand Lounge buzzes with action.

Sixty Thompson (Map pp142-3; ☎ 212-431-0400;
www.60thompson.com; 60 Thompson St btwn Broome &
Spring Sts; s/d/ste $360/425/720; ✖ ▢ wi-fi) Another
minimalist charmer, rooms here have down
duvets, flatscreen TVs and cozy tweed sofas.
The rooftop Thom Bar is a stunning place to
see and be seen.

Lower East Side & East Village

ourpick East Village Bed & Coffee (Map pp142-3;
☎ 212-533-4175; www.bedandcoffee.com; 110 Ave C
btwn 7th and 8th Sts; r from $95; ✖ wi-fi) Behind the
colorfully muraled door is a heck of a find: a
cheap *and* stylish place in the heart of a very
cool 'hood. The 10 airy rooms sport different well-executed themes – Mexican (with a
bright-yellow wall and pressed-tin doodads),
Zen (with a small Buddha and icy tones) and
so on – and common areas are lovely, from
the high-ceilinged kitchen to the leafy back
garden. Note that all bathrooms are shared.

Hotel on Rivington (Map pp142-3; ☎ 212-475-2600;
www.hotelonrivington.com; 107 Rivington St btwn Essex &
Ludlow Sts; r from $295; ✖ ▢ wi-fi) New in 2005, this
shimmering 20-floor tower looms large over
LES tenement buildings, its glass-enclosed
rooms offering stunning views of the East
River and downtown's spread. Rooms vary
quite a bit – some have balconies, some have
hanging flat-screen TVs – so ask to see one
first if you're picky. The ground-floor restaurant is a hipster hotspot, natch.

Bowery Hotel (Map pp142-3; ☎ 212-505-9100; www
.theboweryhotel.com; 335 Bowery btwn 2nd & 3rd Sts; r from
$325; ✖ ✖ ▢ wi-fi) Turning around the history
of the Bowery – as a street of flophouses for
down-on-their-luck boozers – once and for
all, this new kid on the block is a stunner.
The style is airy 19th-century elegance, and
rooms come equipped with lots of light, sleek
furnishings mixed with antiques, HDTV and
iPod stereos. A lobby bar is for the stylish
only, and onsite restaurant Gemma serves
upscale Italian with preferred seating saved
for hotel guests

West (Greenwich) Village

Larchmont Hotel (Map pp142-3; ☎ 212-989-9333; www
.larchmonthotel.com; 27 W 11th St btwn Fifth & Sixth Aves; s/d

$80/109; 🚫 🖵) This European-like inn is cozy and affordable, with shared bathrooms and communal kitchens. The hotel's 52 small and basic carpeted rooms include sinks and robes and slippers, plus a plum spot on a beautiful, leafy side street.

Abingdon Guest House (Map pp142-3; ☎ 212-243-5384; www.abingdonguesthouse.com; 13 Eighth Ave at Jane St; s/d from $169/179; 🚫 🖵 wi-fi) Don't look out the window and you'll swear you've landed in a New England B&B. Elegant, comfortable rooms feature four-poster beds, (non-working) fireplaces, scads of exposed brick and billowing curtains. Plus a lovely little garden out back.

Chelsea & Meatpacking District

Chelsea International Hostel (Map pp150-1; ☎ 212-647-0010; www.chelseahostel.com; 251 W 20th St btwn Seventh & Eighth Aves; dm/r $28/70; 🚫 🖵) A festive, international crowd sleeps here, where the back patio is party central. Bunkrooms sleep four to six and amenities include communal kitchens and laundry facilities.

Chelsea Star Hotel (Map pp150-1; ☎ 212-244-7827; 300 W 30th St at Eighth Ave; dm/s/d from $30/90/110; 🚫 🖵 wi-fi) This just-renovated cheapie has really cleaned up its act, turning scruffy quarters into neat, cozy rooms with a dash of style (especially in the 'superior' and 'deluxe' options, with thicker comforters and, in some cases, four-poster beds and nice wood floors).

Chelsea Pines Inn (Map pp150-1; ☎ 212-929-1023; www.chelseapinesinn.com; 317 W 14th St btwn Eighth & Ninth Aves; r with breakfast from $150; 🚫 🐾 🖵 wi-fi) It's gay-man central, with vintage movie posters on the walls, a greenhouse and small back patio for eating and socializing. Rooms are small but homey and employees are fonts of wisdom.

Maritime Hotel (Map pp150-1; ☎ 212-242-4300; www.themaritimehotel.com; 363 W 16th St btwn Eighth & Ninth Aves; r from $325; 🚫 🖵 wi-fi) A white tower dotted with portholes, this is a marine-themed luxury inn with 120 compact, teak-paneled rooms, each with its own round window (and flatscreen TV). The most luxe quarters feature outdoor showers, a private garden and sweeping Hudson River views.

Hotel Gansevoort (Map pp142-3; ☎ 212-206-6700; www.hotelgansevoort.com; 18 Ninth Ave at 13th St; r/ste from $395/625; 🚫 🐾 🖵 wi-fi) Since opening in 2004 this 187-room luxury hotel in the trendy Meatpacking District has been a hit with its 400-thread-count linens, hypoallergenic down duvets, plasma TVs, chic basement spa and

rooftop bar with fabulous views. Down-to-earth types, beware: it's on the nauseatingly trendy side of things, and its tacky exterior billboard has really pissed off locals.

Union Square, Flatiron & Gramercy Park

our pick Gershwin Hotel (Map pp150-1; ☎ 212-545-8000; www.gershwinhotel.com; 7 E 27th St at Fifth Ave; dm/s/d from $35/43/119; 🚫 🖵) This popular and funky spot is half youth hostel, half hotel, and buzzes with original pop art, touring bands and a young and artsy European clientele. Plus, it sits right next door to the Museum of Sex (see p148). A new onsite eatery was awaiting a restaurant permit at research time.

Marcel (Map pp150-1; ☎ 212-696-3800; www.nychotels.com; 201 E 24th St at Third Ave; d from $227; 🚫 🖵) Minimalist with earth-tone touches, this 97-room inn is a poor-man's chic boutique and that's not a bad thing. Modernist rooms on the avenue have great views, and the sleek lounge is a great place to unwind from a day of touring. Visit its website for other classy affordable inns within the Amsterdam Hospitality group.

W New York – Union Square (Map pp150-1; ☎ 212-253-9119; toll-free 877-946-8357; www.whotels.com; 201 Park Ave S at 17th St; r from $400; 🖵) This hipster pad demands a black wardrobe and a platinum credit card. Like all the W hotels, everything is top of the line, comfortable and classy – rooms have somber tones and beds have leather framed headboards – and its location right on bucolic Madison Square Park is a big perk. Manhattan has several W outposts, but this is the only one downtown.

Midtown

Pod Hotel (Map pp150-1; ☎ 212-355-0300; www.thepodhotel.com; 230 E 51st St btwn Second & Third Aves; r from $99; 🚫 🚫 🖵 wi-fi) A dream come true for folks who'd like to live inside their iPod – or at least curl up and sleep with it – this new and affordable hot spot has a range of room types, most big enough for the bed and not much else, that allow you to experience sleekness without going broke. 'Pods' have bright bedding, tight workspaces, flatscreen TVs, iPod docking stations and 'rain' shower heads.

Hotel QT (Map pp150-1; ☎ 212-354-2323; www.hotelqt.com; 125 W 45th St btwn Sixth & Seventh Aves; r with breakfast from $170; 🚫 🐾 🖵 wi-fi) This affordable hipster pad, courtesy of celeb hotelier Andre Balazs, is a Times Square innovator, with a swimming pool and bar sharing space in the chic lobby, and extremely tight – but modern-cool – rooms that put you right in the center of the action.

Hudson (Map pp156-7; ☎ 212-554-6000; 356 W 58th St btwn Eighth & Ninth Aves; www.hudsonhotel.com; r $285-450; ☒ ☐ wi-fi) This delicious marriage between designer Phillipe Starck and hotelier Ian Schrager is an absolute jewel – if you're not aching for quiet, that is. Part hotel and part nightclub, the beauty has several lounge bars that are always jammin', and the teensy rooms are highly stylized, with lots of glass, bright wood and gossamer scrims.

Dream (Map pp150-1; ☎ 212-247-2000; www.dreamny .com; 210 W 55th St btwn Broadway & Seventh Ave; d from $365; ☒ ☐ wi-fi) A relative newcomer, this truly dreamy spot has plenty of surreal qualities, from an Ayurvedic spa to the lobby's two-story, Caribbean-fish aquarium. Hypersleek style and rooms outfitted with plasma TVs, loaded iPods and beds lit from below with an icy-blue glow.

Upper West Side

Jazz on the Park Hostel (Map pp156-7; ☎ 212-932-1600; www.jazzhostels.com; 36 W 106th St btwn Central Park West & Manhattan Ave; dm with breakfast $27-32, d with breakfast $85; ☒ ☐) This way-cool, trés popular hostel has small rooms with standard wood-frame bunks, a beautiful roof deck and an exposed-brick lounge that hosts local jazz acts (not to mention the espresso and cheap lasagna). Its midtown **Jazz on the Town** (Map pp150-1; 130 E 57th St btwn Lexington & Park Aves;) and new **Jazz on the City** (Map pp156-7; 201 W 95th St btwn Broadway & Amsterdam Ave) also have a fun atmosphere and great roof decks, as do outposts on 14th St and in Harlem. All Jazz hostels share the same pricing system.

Hostelling International-New York (Map pp156-7; ☎ 212-932-2300; www.hinewyork.org; 891 Amsterdam Ave at 103rd St; dm $29-40, d $135; ☒ ☐ wi-fi) It's got clean, safe and air-conditioned dorm rooms in a gorgeous landmark building, with a sprawling and shady patio and a super-friendly vibe.

On the Ave (Map pp156-7; ☎ 212-362-1100, 800-509-7598; www.ontheave.com; 2178 Broadway at W 77th St; r from $225; ☒ ☐ wi-fi) This sleek bargain boasts a design composed of warm earth tones, stainless steel and marble baths, featherbeds, flatscreen TVs and original artwork. It's near Lincoln Center, Central Park and a slew of good eats.

Upper East Side

Bentley (Map pp156-7; ☎ 212-644-6000, 888-664-6835; www .nychotels.com; 500 E 62nd St at York Ave; r/ste $135/235;

☐) You can't stay any further east than in this chic boutique hotel, boasting a swanky lobby, down comforters, slick rooms (though the mini kitchenettes are dated afterthoughts) and some of New York's most spectacular East River views.

Carlyle (Map pp156-7; ☎ 212-744-1600; www.thecarlyle .com; 35 E 76th St btwn Madison & Park Aves; r from $650) This New York classic is the epitome of old-fashioned luxury: a hushed lobby with glossy marble floors, antique boudoir chairs and framed English country scenes or Audubon prints in the rooms; some have terraces and baby grand pianos. If you can't afford to stay here, at least have a cocktail in the art-deco Bemelmans Bar.

Harlem

Harlem Flophouse (Map pp156-7; ☎ 212-662-0678; www .harlemflophouse.com; 242 W 123rd St btwn Adam Clayton Powell & Frederick Douglass Blvds; s/d $100/125; ☒ ☐ wi-fi) The four gorgeous bedrooms here conjure up the jazz era with antique light fixtures, glossed-wood floors and big beds, plus classic tin ceilings and wooden shutters. There are radios tuned to local jazz stations (and two cats) on the premises.

102 Brownstone (Map pp156-7; ☎ 212-662-4223; www.102brownstone.com; 102 W 118th St btwn Lenox Ave & Adam Clayton Powell Blvd; s/d $125/165; ☒ ☐ wi-fi) A wonderfully redone Greek Revival rowhouse on a beautiful residential street, room styles range from Zen to classy boudoir.

Brooklyn

Baisley House (Map pp142-3; ☎ 718-935-1959; 294 Hoyt St btwn Union & Sackett Sts; r with breakfast $162 & $192; ☒ ☐) This three-room inn sits among 18th-century townhouses and is overflowing with Victorian touches (wing-back chairs, period-piece landscapes) and serves a big, always-different breakfast in the back garden when it's nice out. Smith Street, aka 'restaurant row,' is a block away.

Marriott at the Brooklyn Bridge (Map pp142-3; ☎ 718-246-7000; www.mariott.com; 333 Adams St; d from $199; ☒ ☒ ☐ wi-fi) Though it's a predictable chain, it's newish and immaculate, and the only big-time hotel this side of the East River. Rates drop on weekends when the business folk go home.

EATING

In a city with 18,000 restaurants, and new ones opening every single day of the year, where are you supposed to begin? Go with whatever your belly desires, whether it's Italian, French, Israeli, Japanese, South Indian or good ol' American-diner burgers and fries. You'll find whatever it is you're after either a quick walk or subway ride away – and it's bound to be the best you've ever had, no matter what your budget.

Lower Manhattan

Ruben's Empanadas (Map pp142-3; ☎ 212-962-5330; 64 Fulton St at Gold St; empanadas $3.50; ⏲ 8am-6pm Mon-Fri, 11am-5pm Sat) A tiny storefront with no decor, this takeout shop is Argentine heaven – with greaseless empanadas in endless varieties, from the requisite beef and chicken to broccoli with mozzarella and ricotta, Argentine sausage and gooey guava.

Financier Patisserie (Map pp142-3 ; ☎ 212-334-5600; 62 Stone St at Mill Ln; mains $9-12; ⏲ 7am-9pm Mon-Fri, 9am-5:30pm Sat) A graceful French café located on the quaint and tiny Stone St, the Patisserie's fresh pastries – including almond-crusted fruit tarts and the signature madeleine-type mini cake – are truly worth raving over, as is more wholesome fare, including the lentil and celery root soup, savory chicken with goat cheese on ciabatta and the range of fresh salads.

Acqua (Map pp142-3; ☎ 212-349-4433; 21 Peck Slip at Water St; mains $12-18; ⏲ noon-11pm Mon-Thu, till 11:30pm Fri-Sat, till 10pm Sun) A sleek wine bar right near South Street Seaport, this charmer offers savory portions of cured meats and cheeses; pizzas and paninis; and fresh pastas including gnocchi with pesto and gorgonzola. Pair any choice with a carafe of wine and you'll be good to stay.

Tribeca, Soho & Noho

Soho Park (Map pp142-3; ☎ 212-219-2129, 62 Prince St at Lafayette St; mains $6-9; ⏲ 8:30am-midnight Mon-Sat, 10am-8pm Sun) It's cheap-ass, wholesome grub served in surprisingly elegant surroundings – the place is housed in a former parking garage, newly outfitted with glass walls, potted plants and blond-wood benches). Go lowbrow, with burgers, kielbasa, Belgian fries, or highbrow, with frisee salad or a sandwich of raw fennel, parmesan and arugula.

Franklin Station Café (Map pp142-3; ☎ 212-274-8525; 222 W Broadway btwn Franklin & N Moore Sts; mains $7-14; ⏲ 10am-11pm Mon-Fri, 9am-11pm Sat-Sun) This simple, airy café serves eclectic breakfasts – brioche French toast, poached eggs with caviar

and salmon and congee (rice porridge) – and Malaysian lunch and dinners, such as spicy shrimp with noodles and bean sprouts, curried squid or vegetables, and grilled salmon in turmeric ginger sauce.

La Esquina (Map pp142-3; ☎ 646-613-7100; 106 Kenmare St at Cleveland Pl; mains $12-20; ⏲ noon-4pm upstairs, 6pm-midnight upstairs & down) This Mexican hot spot, whose only marking is a huge neon sign that blares 'The Corner' (hence *la esquina*), bustles night and day for good reason. Delectable, authentic treats – served upstairs in a mellow café or downstairs in a dark, loud vault that calls for reservations made way in advance – include tacos of every stripe, mango and jicama salad, savory black beans and *huitlacoche* (corn fungus) quesadillas.

Bubby's Pie Company (Map pp142-3; ☎ 212-219-0666; 120 Hudson St at N Moore St; mains $12-20; ⏲ 8am-4pm & 6-11pm Mon-Thu, till midnight Fri, 9am-4pm & 6pm-midnight Sat, till 10pm Sun) This old Tribeca standby is *the* place for simple, big, delicious food: slow-cooked BBQ, grits, matzo-ball soup, buttermilk potato salad, fried okra and big fat breakfasts, all melt-in-your-mouth good. It's a great place to bring little kids, too.

Chinatown, Little Italy & Nolita

Bo Ky Restaurant (Map pp142-3; ☎ 212-406-2292; 80 Bayard St btwn Mott & Mulberry Sts; soup $5-7; ⏲ 9am-10pm) Incredibly cheap and bare bones (but mighty tasty), Bo Ky is home to nearly three dozen types of soup with exotic ingredients that usually feature some form of noodle, pork or chicken (vegetarians should be wary); the fishball flat noodle, curry chicken rice noodle and 'combination soup' are particularly popular.

Peasant (Map pp142-3; ☎ 212-965-9511; 194 Elizabeth St btwn Spring & Prince Sts; mains $15-30; ⏲ 6-11pm Tue-Sat, till 10pm Sun) A warm dining area of bare oak tables is structured around a brick hearth and open kitchen, which lovingly turns out hearty, pan-Italian, mostly meat-based fare. Solid stunners include gnocchi with wild mushrooms, oven-baked rabbit and *zuppa di pesce*.

Da Nico (Map pp142-3; ☎ 212-343-1212; 164 Mulberry St; mains $18-40; ⏲ noon-11pm Sun-Thu, till midnight Fri-Sat) If you're bent on a Little Italy dinner, Da Nico is a classic. It's family-run and traditional in feel – exposed-brick walls, light wood tables and chairs around a coal-fired pizza oven – and the extensive restaurant highlights both northern and southern Italian cuisine that's red-sauce predictable – shrimp scampi, chicken cacciatore, rigatoni with eggplant – but delicious.

Lower East Side

Yonah Schimmel Knish Bakery (Map pp142-3; ☎ 212-477-2858; 137 E Houston St btwn Eldridge & Forsyth Sts; knish $3; ☻ 9:30am-7pm) This spot has been selling baked, fist-sized knishes for almost 100 years and knows how it's done. Choose from varieties including potato, sweet potato, red cabbage, cheese and kasha, all stellar, plus bagels, blintzes and cookies.

Teany (Map pp142-3; ☎ 212-475-9190; 90 Rivington St btwn Ludlow & Orchard Sts; mains $7-12; ☻ 10am-11pm Sun-Thu, till 1am Fri, Sat) This teeny-tiny café, tucked below street level on a quietly hip block, is co-owned by famously vegan pop star Moby. The book-like menu boasts close to 100 teas, frothy soy-infused coffees, beer and wine, and delicious treats like muffins, salads, desserts and tea sandwiches (the cheddar-pickle and peanut butter–chocolate ones rock).

Schiller's Liquor Bar (Map pp142-3; ☎ 212-260-4555; 131 Rivington St at Norfolk St; mains $12-25; ☻ 11am-1am Mon-Wed, till 2am Thu, till 3am Fri, 10am-3am Sat, 10am-1am Sun) One of the most consistently happening spots in the 'hood, Schiller's has a stunning bohemian-antique decor, buzzing crowd and great, reasonably priced meals. It's all over the map, too – pork chops, steak frites, eggplant parm, cobb salad, spaghetti with pesto sauce. There's a wine list in three parts: 'Cheap, Decent, Good.'

WD-50 (Map pp142-3; ☎ 212-477-2900; 50 Clinton St at Stanton St; mains $40-75; ☻ 6-11pm Mon-Sat, till 10pm Sun) Chef-owner Wylie Dufresne draws VIPs and wannabes alike to his hot spot, where bamboo floors, a fireplace and exposed beams all highlight the provocative fare, like soybean gazpacho with crab, bass with artichoke and peanut brittle and pork belly with smoked yucca.

East Village

B & H Dairy (Map pp142-3; ☎ 212-505-8065; 127 Second Ave btwn St Marks Pl & 7th St; mains $4-8; ☻ 7am-10pm) This is a classic lunch counter with some of the most authentic Jewish-dairy comfort food and crusty old 'tude around. Everything is homemade, fresh and vegetarian, including the six types of soup on offer daily (try the borscht or mushroom barley), which, along with a pillowy slice of fresh-baked challah, will fill you up for hours – for less than the cost of a movie.

Counter (Map pp142-3; ☎ 212-982-5870; 105 First Ave btwn E 6th & 7th Sts; mains $15-25; ☻ 5pm-midnight Mon-Thu, till 1am Fri, 11am-1am Sat, till 4pm Sun) This unique eatery manages to mix infused-vodka martinis with organic vegetarian cuisine with outlandish success. Credit the futuristic, backlit dining room, fabulous large-scale artwork and innovative dishes, like tournedos of seitan and cauliflower 'risotto.'

Il Bagatto (Map pp142-3; ☎ 212-228-3703; 192 E 2nd St btwn Aves A & B; mains $15-25; ☻ 5:30-11:40pm Tue-Thu, 5:30pm-12:45am Fri-Sat, 5-10:30pm Sun, closed Aug) A bustling yet romantic little nook, this spot has great wine and sinfully rich Italian creations, with highlights including cheese and spinach ravioli swimming in butter and sage sauce, homemade gnocchi in gorgonzola sauce, and paper-thin beef slices sautéed in olive oil and white wine. Desserts are divine.

Hearth (Map pp142-3; ☎ 646-602-1300; 403 E 12th St at First Ave; mains $20-40; ☻ 6-10pm Sun-Thu, till 11pm Fri, Sat) One of the earliest classy dining spots to take the East Village by storm, Hearth has become a staple for finicky, deep-pocketed diners who love the warm, brick-walled interior and seasonal menu's concoctions, like roasted sturgeon with lentils and bacon, zucchini ravioli and rabbit papardelle with fava beans.

West (Greenwich) Village & Meatpacking District

Taïm (Map pp142-3; ☎ 212-691-1287; 222 Waverly Pl btwn Perry & W 11th Sts; mains $7-9; ☻ noon-10pm) Not all Middle Eastern fare is alike, and this tiny little falafel joint proves it with its smoothies, salads and sass – and even its falafel, which ranges from the traditional to those spiced up with roasted red pepper or hot harissa. Refreshing salads include carrots spiced with garlic and cumin, and a ruby-red dish of marinated beets. Excellent smoothies blend exotics from dates to tamarind.

Florent (Map pp142-3; ☎ 212-989-5779; 69 Gansevoort St btwn Greenwich & Washington Sts; mains $10-18; ☻ 9am-5am Mon-Wed, 24hr Fri-Sun) This all-night hang colonized the Meatpacking District many moons ago and it's still going strong. It's a bustling spot that draws clubbers and hungry locals at all hours with its hangar steak, burgers and breakfast selections, as well as its praiseworthy blood sausage and pork chops.

Fatty Crab (Map pp142-3; ☎ 212-352-3590; 643 Hudson St; mains $15-28; ☻ noon-4am Thu-Sat, till midnight Sun-Wed) This intimate Malaysian hot spot makes your taste buds do gymnastics with its rarities – watermelon pickle and crispy pork salad, chicken curry with a poached egg and coconut rice and skate grilled on a banana leaf. Oh – and Dungeness crab, cooked in spicy chili sauce.

Blue Hill (Map pp142-3; ☎ 212-539-1776; 75 Washington Pl btwn Sixth Ave & MacDougal St; mains $30-50; ☷ 5:30-11pm Mon-Sat, till 10pm Sun) A place for high rolling Slow Food junkies, Blue Hill is a low-key, high-class dining spot where you can be certain that everything on your plate is fresh and seasonal. Expect barely-seasoned veggies as centerpieces for dishes like cod with cauliflower and currants, pork stewed with four types of beans, and grass-fed lamb with white beans and new potatoes. The space itself, slightly below street level and housed in a landmarked former speakeasy, is sophisticated and serene.

Chelsea, Union Square, Flatiron & Gramercy Park

Maoz (Map pp150-1; ☎ 212-260-1988; 38 Union Sq East; sandwiches $5-9; ☷ noon-2am) This new branch of an Amsterdam chain has folks patiently waiting in a line that extends out the door each day. Why all the fuss? You get delicious falafel, in pita or a bowl, and get to pile on the veggie fixins – fried broccoli, Israeli carrot salad, shredded cabbage, creamy tahini – as high as you'd like.

Chennai Garden (Map pp150-1; ☎ 212-689-1999; 129 E 27th St btwn Park & Lexington Aves; mains $14-18; ☷ 11:30am-3pm & 5-10pm Tue-Fri, noon-10pm Sat-Sun) Come for South Indian faves like paper-thin dosas (rice-flour pancakes) stuffed with spicy mixtures of potatoes and peas, and a range of more expected curries. The interior is bright and bustling – especially for the popular $7 lunchtime buffet.

Tía Pol (Map pp150-1; ☎ 212-675-8805; 205 Tenth Ave; tapas plates $15-20; ☷ noon-3pm & 6pm-midnight Tue-Fri, 11am-3pm & 6pm-midnight Sat, till 10:30pm Sun) A tucked-away nook with a cool but earthy vibe, the place packs in in-the-know folks for its excellent range of authentic tapas, salads and Spanish wines.

Blossom (Map pp150-1; ☎ 212-627-1144; 187 Ninth Ave btwn 21st & 22nd Sts; mains $25-35; ☷ noon-2:45pm & 5-10:30pm Fri-Sat, noon-2:45pm & 5-10pm Sun, 5-10pm Mon-Thu) A creative and elegant vegan spot, housed in a Chelsea townhouse, where menu items span the globe and enliven the taste buds. Try the flaky seitan empanada, mojo-marinated tempeh or Portobello stuffed with cashew-tahini sauce. Desserts are so super-rich you won't miss the dairy.

Pure Food and Wine (Map pp150-1; ☎ 212-477-1010; 54 Irving Pl btwn 17th & 18th Sts; mains $30-40; ☷ 5:30pm-midnight) Pure achieves the impossible: it churns out delicious and artful concoctions, made completely from raw organics that are put through blenders, dehydrators and the capable hands of Pure's staff. Creative results include tomato-zucchini lasagne (sans cheese and pasta); mushroom, avocado and ginger sushi rolls; and the chanterelle, olive and 'ricotta' ravioli with pistachio oil and macadamia cream sauce. In warm months, don't miss the shady, oasis-like backyard.

Midtown

OMS/B (Map pp150-1; ☎ 212-922-9788; 156 E 45th St btwn Lexington & Third Aves; omusubis $4-6; ☷ 8:30am-7:30pm Mon-Fri, 11am-7pm Sat) Running from museum to architectural site to a big night out? Skip the usual fast-food options and pop in for a twist on the *omusubi*, a ubiquitous Japanese lunch food consisting of stuffed rice balls. Here the weighty treats are triangular, wrapped in a sheet of nori and stuffed with goodies like eel, edamame, fish flake, teriyaki chicken and Japanese plum.

Bouchon Bakery (Map pp156-7; ☎ 212-823-9366; 50 Columbus Circle in Time Warner Center; mains $12-20; ☷ 11:30am-5:30pm Mon-Wed, till 7:30pm Thu-Sat) One of seven restaurants in the Time Warner Center (the rest are extremely high-end), this one from Per Se owner Thomas Keller brings new meaning to 'food court.' It's an open-air (well, mall-air) café with food that is just outstanding: beet and mache salad, three-bean soup, turkey and tuna and veggie sandwiches that soar to new gourmet heights. And the pastries are to die for.

44X10 (Map pp150-1; ☎ 212-977-1170; 622 Tenth Ave at 44th St; mains $20-30; ☷ 5:30pm-midnight Mon-Fri, 11:30am-3pm & 5:30pm-midnight Sat, till 10:30pm Sun) One of the trendy Hell's Kitchen pioneers and still going strong, this sleek and airy dining room serves a little something for everyone, from buttermilk fried chicken and glazed mahimahi to flavorful chopped salad.

Hangawi (Map pp150-1; ☎ 212-213-0077; 12 E 32nd St btwn Fifth & Madison Aves; mains $20-30; ☷ noon-3pm & 5-10:30pm Mon-Thu, noon-5pm & 5-11pm Sat, 5-10pm Sun) An oasis in Koreatown, this Zen-like dining-room is strictly no-meat and no-shoes (cubbies and bathroom slippers are provided).

Unique dishes include crispy mushrooms in sweet and sour sauce, tofu stone bowl rice with sesame leaves and organic vegetable stir-fries. Desserts are creamy and dreamy.

Upper West Side & Morningside Heights

Hungarian Pastry Shop (Map pp156-7 ; ☎ 212-886-4230; 1030 Amsterdam Ave btwn W 110th & 111th Sts; pastries $2-4; ❤ 8am-11:30pm Mon-Fri, 8:30am-11:30pm Sat, till 10:30pm Sun) Join the intense Columbia students who sit for hours with laptops, cooling coffee and plates of cookies in this Morningside Heights classic. The same owners have the gourmet deli next door, so you can bring the soups and sandwiches in to eat before dessert.

Barney Greengrass (Map pp156-7; ☎ 212-724-2707; 541 Amsterdam Ave at W 86th St; mains $8-15; ❤ 8:30am-4pm Tue-Fri, till 5pm Sat-Sun) Step back in time at this century-old 'sturgeon king' gourmet shop and eatery serving a long list of traditional Jewish delicacies, from bagels and lox, a kippered salmon and whitefish platter, pastrami on rye and sturgeon scrambled with eggs and onions.

Edgar's (Map pp156-7; ☎ 212-496-6126; 255 W 84th St btwn Broadway & West End Ave; mains $10-15; ❤ 8am-1am Sun-Thu, till 2am Fri-Sat) A tucked-away neighborhood favorite, this dark and romantic café serves strong espresso drinks, creative salads and sandwiches and a vast array of tantalizing desserts, including vegan options.

Mana (Map pp156-7; ☎ 212-787-1110; 646 Amsterdam Ave btwn 91st & 92nd Sts; mains $12-18; ❤ noon-9:30pm) The clean and simple atmosphere is like a second home to many healthful locals, who come for virtuous plates of steamed vegetables, Asian-influenced stews and organic-fish options, plus vegan desserts.

Kefi (Map pp156-7; ☎ 212-873-0200; 222 W 79th St; mains $12-20; ❤ 5-10pm Sun-Thu, till 11pm Fri-Sat) This newcomer became an instant classic thanks to its elegant take on hearty, traditional Greek food and its intimate dining area decked out with billowy wall hangings. Settle into plates of moussaka, spanakopita, grilled octopus, lamb and rich, raisin-studded meatballs. And get there early – the no-reservations policy creates a constant wait.

Upper East Side

Candle Cafe (Map pp156-7; ☎ 212-472-0970; 1307 Third Ave btwn E 74th & 75th Sts; mains $12-15; ❤ 11:30am-10:30pm Mon-Sat, 11:30am-9:30pm Sun) Candle is a light at the end of a carnivorous UES cave. Offerings range from the most simplistic spreads of greens, roots, grains and soy-based protein to the more complex concoctions, such as seitan piccata with creamed spinach and a grilled potato cake. Its second, more upscale location is **Candle 79** (Map pp156-7; ☎ 212-537-7179; 154 E 79th St at Lexington Ave; mains $18-$23; ❤ noon-3:30pm & 5:30-10:30pm Mon-Sat, noon-4pm & 5-10pm Sun).

Beyoglu (Map pp156-7; ☎ 212-650-0850; 1431 Third Ave at E 81st St; mains $14-20; ❤ noon-11pm) A charismatic, Turkish loungey space, this is where you'll find excellent yogurt soup, doner kabobs and feta-flecked salads. Get in early for your pick of a good table; it's within strolling distance of the Met, making for a tasteful way to end an artistic afternoon.

Central Park Boathouse Restaurant (☎ 212-517-2233; Central Park Lake, enter Fifth Ave at 72nd St; mains $15-40; ❤ noon-4:30pm & 5:30-9:30pm Mon-Fri, 9:30am-4pm & 6-9:30pm Sat-Sun, dinner Apr-Nov only) The historic Loeb Boathouse, perched on the shores of the park's lake, is one of the city's most incredible settings for a serene and romantic meal. Food is top-notch, too – witness the lunch appetizer of yellow-fin tuna tartare arranged around mango, jicama relish and lotus root chips, or a dinner of homemade gnocchi tossed with slow-roasted cauliflower. Reserve early and aim for an outdoor table.

Daniel (Map pp156-7; ☎ 212-288-0033; 60 E 65th St btwn Madison & Park Aves; three-course prix fixe $96; ❤ Mon-Sat 5:30-11pm) This chichi French palace features floral arrangements and wide-eyed foodies who gawk over plates of peeky toe-crab and celery-root salad, foie gras terrine with gala apples and black truffle-crusted lobster – and that's just the first course. (Here's a fab secret: there's an all-veggie menu, too).

Harlem

Amy Ruth's Restaurant (Map pp156-7; ☎ 212-280-8779; 114 W 116th St btwn Malcolm X & Adam Clayton Powell Jr Blvds; mains $10-16; ❤ 8am-midnight Mon-Thu, 24hr Fri & Sat) Though Food Network coverage has amped up the tourist crowds, this place still does an exquisite job with all the standards – candied yams, smoked ham, corn pudding, chicken and dumplings, you name it – and it has a particularly hard-to-resist specialization in waffles; choose from sweet (chocolate, strawberry, blueberry, smothered in sautéed apples) or savory (paired with fried chicken, rib-eye or catfish).

Ginger (Map pp156-7; ☎ 212-423-1111; 1400 Fifth Ave at 116th St; mains $12-16; ❤ 5:30pm-10:30 Mon-Thu, till 11:30pm Fri-Sat, till 10pm Sun) This bright and happy room, with red lanterns and bamboo ceiling beams, is the stage for organic, creative treats like ginger-beer-braised short ribs with beans and cashews, house-special grilled Angus beef spare ribs, vegetarians' grilled tofu and pineapple-pork fried rice.

Brooklyn

SEA (Map pp142-3; ☎ 718-384-8850; 114 N 6th St; mains $8-15; ⏱ 11:30am-1am Sun-Thu, till 2am Fri-Sat) A massive Thai restaurant with a nightclub vibe, this is the place to hunker down with Williamsburg hipsters for traditional rice-noodle dishes, red and green curries and some of that thick, sweet Thai iced tea – or specialty cocktails, if you prefer.

Alma (Map pp142-3; ☎ 718-643-5400; 187 Columbia St at Degraw St; mains $17-25; ⏱ 10am-2:30pm & 5:30-11pm Fri-Sat, till 10pm Sun; 5:30-10pm Sun-Thu) Atop a Red Hook building that's near the waterfront, Alma packs in fans of the inventive Mexican fare (chicken enchiladas smothered in pumpkin -seed sauce, grilled duck breast in peanut sauce) and strong margaritas. Though you'll wait a while (there's a downstairs bar), it's worth holding out for a seat on the rooftop, with beautiful views of Manhattan.

Grocery (Map pp142-3; ☎ 718-596-3335; 288 Smith St; mains $30-40; ⏱ 5:30-10pm Mon-Thu, till 11pm Fri, 5-11pm Sun) Minimal and diminutive, this is one of the reigning stars of Brooklyn's restaurant row in Boerum Hill, thanks to fresh, seasonal cuisine and a lovely back garden. Reserve early to enjoy juicy sliced pork chops, goat's cheese ravioli topped with beets and excellent wines and desserts.

DRINKING

Watering holes come in many forms in this city: sleek lounges, cozy pubs and booze-soaked dives – no smoke, though, thanks to city law. Here's a highly selective sampling.

Downtown

Brandy Library (Map pp142-3; ☎ 212-226-5545; 25 N Moore St at Varick St) If you see sipping brandy as a serious sort of pastime, the Library will make you feel like you've entered nirvana. There are soothing reading lamps, beautiful bottles lining the backlit, floor-to-ceiling shelves and cozy club chairs. Choose a top-shelf liquor from the very extensive catalog and focus.

Circa Tabac (Map pp142-3; ☎ 212-941-1781; 32 Watts St btwn Sixth Ave & Thompson St) One of five places left in the city where you can still puff away (and

are encouraged to do so) while you drink, Tabac offers more than 150 types of smoke, mainly global cigars. Its specialty drinks list includes the soothing Cucumber Cocktail (gin, lemon, sugar and cukes), and the deco-style lounge, with bamboo walls and velvet lounge chairs, is as sumptuous as much of its fine-cut tobacco.

Angel's Share (Map pp142-3; ☎ 212-777-5415; 2nd fl, 8 Stuyvesant St btwn Third Ave & 9th St) Sneak through the Japanese restaurant to discover this tiny gem of a hideaway, with creative cocktails, well-suited waiters and a civilized policy that states you cannot stay and drink if there's not room enough for you to sit.

Holiday Cocktail Lounge (Map pp142-3; ☎ 212-777-9637; 75 St Marks Pl btwn First & Second Aves) You want dive bar? You've got it, right here. The old-school, battered, charming place feels as if it's from another era – and with $3 drinks and crotchety service, it might as well be.

Easternbloc (Map pp142-3; ☎ 212-420-8885; 505 E 6th St btwn Aves A & B) A popular East Village gay spot, it's home to a kitschy iron-curtain theme replete with Bettie Page videos, Communist-era posters and adorable Eastern European–looking bartenders. DJs spin on weekends.

Bar Next Door (Map pp142-3; ☎ 212-529-5945; 129 MacDougal St btwn W 3rd & 4th Sts) One of them more lovely boites in the neighborhood, this basement of a restored townhouse is all low ceilings, exposed brick and romantic lighting.

Henrietta Hudson (Map pp142-3; ☎ 212-924-3347; 438 Hudson St) All sorts of cute young girls storm this long-running lesbian spot, a former pool-and-pint joint that's now a sleek lounge with varied DJs.

Midtown

Half King (Map pp150-1; ☎ 212-462-4300; 505 W 23rd St at Tenth Ave) A unique marriage of cozy beer pub and sophisticated writers' lair, you'll often catch top-notch literary readings in this wood-accented, candlelit watering hole. In warm seasons, a front sidewalk café and mellow backyard patio open for business.

Gym (Map pp150-1; ☎ 212-337-2439; 167 Eighth Ave at W 18th St) A gay sports bar? That's right. But here the decor is classy – wide-plank wood floors, high ceilings and a long, sleek bar – the men are polite, and ice skating championships are as popular as basketball playoffs.

Therapy (Map pp150-1; ☎ 212-397-1700; 348 W 52nd St btwn Eighth & Ninth Aves) Multileveled, airy and sleekly contemporary, this is a gay Hell's Kitchen hot spot. Theme nights abound, from stand-up comedy to musical shows.

Ginger Man (Map pp150-1; ☎ 212-532-3740; 11 E 36th St btwn Fifth & Madison Aves) This high-ceilinged, handsome pub is heaven to those who take their suds seriously. It's got an extensive selection of global bottles and drafts, not to mention a range of scotches, wines and even cigars.

Morrell Wine Bar & Café (Map pp150-1; ☎ 212-262-7700; 1 Rockefeller Plaza – W 48th St btwn Fifth & Sixth Aves) One of the pioneers of the wine-bar craze in NYC was this mega grape-geeks' haven. The list here is over 2000 long, with a whopping 150 wines available by the glass. And the airy, split-level room, right across from the famous skating rink, is as lovely as the vino.

Uptown

79th Street Boat Basin (Map pp156-7 ; ☎ 212-496-5592; W 79th St in Riverside Park) A covered, open-sided party spot under the ancient arches of a park overpass, this is an Upper West Side favorite once spring hits. Order a pitcher, some snacks and enjoy the sunset view over the Hudson River.

Subway Inn (Map pp156-7; ☎ 212-223-8929; 143 E 60th St btwn Lexington & Third Aves) An old-geezer watering hole with cheap drinks and loads of authenticity, this place should truly be landmarked, as the entire scene – from the vintage neon sign outside to the well-worn red booths and old guys huddled inside – is truly reminiscent of bygone days. It's an amusing place to recover from a shopping spree at Bloomingdale's (p176), just around the corner.

Lenox Lounge (Map pp156-7; ☎ 212-427-0253; www .lenoxlounge.com; 288 Malcolm X Blvd btwn 124th & 125th Sts) The classic art-deco Lounge, which hosts frequent big names, is an old favorite of local jazz cats, though it's a beautiful and historic house for anyone who wants a nice place to imbibe. Don't miss the luxe Zebra Room in the back.

Brooklyn

Cattyshack (Map pp142-3; ☎ 718-230-5740; 249 Fourth Ave at President St, Brooklyn) Home base for the lesbians of Park Slope (and there are lots of 'em) this chic, three-level space features a rooftop deck (for smokers), hot go-go dancers, great DJs and special theme nights. Boys are welcome, too.

Brooklyn Inn (Map pp142-3; ☎ 718-625-9741; 138 Bergen St at Hoyt St) Housed in an old speakeasy, this Boerum Hill neighborhood spot is high ceilinged, with dark-oak ornate walls and a great jukebox. Perfect place to knock back pints and get to know the locals.

Spuyten Duyvil (Map pp142-3; ☎ 718-963-4140; 359 Metropolitan Ave) A homey Williamsburg spot, this is where you'll find some of the most esoteric foreign beers in the city.

ENTERTAINMENT

You should already know that you'll find every type of entertainment under the sun in this town – not only Broadway shows and jazz concerts. *Time Out New York*, *New York* and weekend editions of *The New York Times* are great guides once you arrive.

Nightclubs

Cielo (Map pp142-3; ☎ 212-645-5700; 18 Little West 12th St btwn Ninth Ave & Washington St; admission $5-20) Known for its intimate space and kick-ass sound system, this Meatpacking District staple packs in a fashionable, multi-culti crowd nightly for its blend of tribal, old-school house and soulful grooves, with a lovely little smoking patio out back.

Studio Mezmor (Map pp150-1; ☎ 212-629-9000; 530 W 28th St btwn Tenth & Eleventh Aves; admission $25) This get-lost-in-another-world mega club, formerly Crobar, caters to a largely suburban crowd on weekends, but, come weekend, holds plenty of fabulous queer-tinged bashes with super DJs. There are multiple rooms, which host simultaneous soirees with varying themes, crowds and DJs.

Pacha (Map pp150-1; ☎ 212-209-7500; 618 W 46th St btwn Eleventh Ave & West Side Hwy) A massive and spectacular place, this is 30,000 sq ft and four levels of glowing, sleek spaces and cozy seating nooks that rise up to surround the main dance-floor atrium. Big name DJs are always on tap.

Pyramid (Map pp142-3; ☎ 212-228-4888; 101 Ave A btwn 6th & 7th Sts) You'll find a happening, themed soiree on just about any night of the week at this mainly gay party cave. But Friday, offering the long-running '80s party, 1984, draws the biggest mobs.

Live Music

Though it's no Austin or Seattle, NYC does have an impressive indie music scene, and a slew of venues that vary greatly in size and crowd. More traditional sounds, of course, are constants, as the slew of jazz clubs and classical venues are rock solids here.

Madison Square Garden (Map pp150-1; ☎ 212-465-5800; www.thegarden.com; Seventh Ave btwn W 31st & W 33rd Sts) For the biggest celebs this place draws stadium-sized crowds.

Radio City Music Hall (Map pp150-1; ☎ 212-247-4777; Sixth Ave at W 51st St) In the middle of Midtown, the architecturally grand concert hall, built in 1932, hosts the likes of kd lang, Lyle Lovett, Mary J Blige and Widespread Panic. Its management is the same as for Madison Square Garden, though, so get prepared for tacky glow-in-the-dark drinks and disruptive, latecomer seating.

Beacon Theater (Map pp156-7; ☎ 212-496-7070; 2124 Broadway btwn W 74th & 75th Sts) This Upper West Side venue has a pretty cool vibe for such a large, mainstream space. It hosts big (often old-time) acts – Squeeze, the Indigo Girls – for folks who want to see shows in a more intimate environment than that of a big concert arena.

Joe's Pub (Map pp142-3; ☎ 212-539-8770; Public Theater, 425 Lafayette St btwn Astor Pl & E 4th St) Part cabaret theater, part rock and new-indie venue, this small and lovely supper club has hosted the likes of Toshi Reagon, Melissa Ferrick and Diamanda Galas.

Village Vanguard (Map pp142-3; ☎ 212-255-4037; 178 Seventh Ave at W 11th St) This basement-level venue in the West Village may be the world's most prestigious jazz club, as it has hosted literally every major star of the past 50 years. There's a two-drink minimum and a serious no-talking policy.

BB King Blues Club and Grill (Map pp150-1; ☎ 212-997-4144; 237 W 42nd St) Catch old-school blues – along with rock, folk and reggae acts – like Etta James and Merle Haggard at this two-tiered, horseshoe-shaped room in the heart of the new Times Square.

Smoke (Map pp156-7; ☎ 212-864-6662; 2751 Broadway btwn W 105th & 106th Sts) Unobstructed sight lines and plush sofas have hardcore fans of top-notch talent lining up around the block to get into this Upper West Side jazz and supper club on weekends.

Jazz at Lincoln Center (Map pp156-7 ; ☎ 212-258-9595; www.jazzatlincolncenter.org; Broadway at W 60th St) Of the center's three venues, which include the fancy Rose Theater and Allen Room, it's Dizzy's Club Coca-Cola that you'll most likely wind up in, as it's got nightly shows. And how lucky for you, since, with the exception of its awful name, the nightclub is flawless, with stunning views overlooking Central Park and excellent line-ups of both local and touring artists.

Delancey (Map pp142-3; ☎ 212-254-9920; www.thedelancey.com; 168 Delancey St at Clinton St) This LES hot spot has great indie-band bookings and a packed but airy second-floor patio deck.

Highline Ballroom (Map pp150-1; ☎ 212-414-5994; 431 W 16th St btwn Ninth & Tenth Aves) An intimate and brand-new Chelsea spot, it's already proven its chops by snagging performers like Olu Dara, Moby, KT Tunstall and Suzanne Vega.

Theater

In general, 'Broadway' productions are staged in the lavish, early-20th-century theaters surrounding Times Square. You'll choose your theater based on its production – *Wicked, Spring Awakening, Company* – but all are pretty glamorous and old-fashioned. Evening performances begin at 8pm.

'Off Broadway' simply refers to shows performed in smaller spaces (200 seats or fewer), which is why you'll find many just around the corner from Broadway venues, as well as elsewhere in town. 'Off-off Broadway' events include readings, experimental and cutting-edge performances and improvisations held in spaces with fewer than 100 seats. Some of the world's best theater happens in these more intimate venues before moving to Broadway, including *Spring Awakening* and *Rent*. Some distinguished small theaters include **Playwrights Horizons** (Map pp150-1; ☎ 212-564-1235; 416 W 42nd St btwn Ninth & Tenth Aves), **PS 122** (Map pp142-3; ☎ 212-477-5288; 150 First Ave at E 9th St), **New York Theater Workshop** (Map pp142-3; ☎ 212-460-5475; 79 E 4th St btwn Second & Third Aves) and the **Public Theater** (Map pp142-3; ☎ 212-539-8770; 425 Lafayette St btwn Astor Pl & E 4th St).

Choose from current shows by checking print publications (p139), or at a website like **Theater Mania** (www.theatermania.com). You can purchase tickets through **Telecharge** (☎ 212-239-6200; www.telecharge.com) and **Ticketmaster** (☎ 212-307-7171; www.ticketmaster.com) for standard ticket sales, or **TKTS ticket booths** Midtown (Map pp150-1; www.tkts.com; 47th St at Broadway; ☺ 10am-8pm Mon-Fri, from 11am Sun); Downtown (Map pp142-3; Front St at John St, South St Seaport; ☺ 11am-6pm) for same-day tickets to Broadway and off-Broadway musicals at up to 75% off regular prices.

Comedy

Venues range in room size – and size of booked talent – but most push the alcohol with drink minimums, so you should be laughing by the end no matter who's onstage.

Caroline's on Broadway (Map p150-1; ☎ 212-757-4100; 1626 Broadway) It's the best-known place in the city, and host to the biggest names on the circuit.

Stand-Up New York (Map pp156-7; ☎ 212-595-0850; 236 W 78th St; tickets $5-12) This spot features funny theme nights, plus gets surprise appearances from star comedians.

Gotham Comedy Club (Map pp150-1; ☎ 212-367-9000; 208 W 23rd St btwn Seventh & Eighth Aves) You'll find more innovative acts, plus a monthly gay-comedy show, at Gotham.

Upright Citizens Brigade Theatre (Map pp150-1; 307 W 26th St) Wacky, edgy and hysterical is the name of UCB's game.

Cinemas

Even though movie tickets cost at least $10, long lines on evenings and weekends are the norm. To ensure you'll get in – and not wind up watching with a stiff neck from the front row – it's pretty much imperative that you call and buy your tickets in advance (unless it's mid-week, mid-day or for a film that's been out for months already). Most theaters are handled either through **Movie Fone** (☎ 212-777-3456; www.moviefone.com) or **Fandango** (www.fandango.com). You'll have to pay an extra $1.50 fee per ticket, but it's worth it.

AMC Empire 25 (Map pp150-1; 234 W 42nd St) is a gem in the heart of Times Square. It shows a mix of mainstream and indie films in theaters with massive screens and stadium seating.

Landmark Sunshine Cinema (Map pp142-3; ☎ 212-358-7709; 143 E Houston St) Housed in a former Yiddish theater, Landmark shows first-run indies on huge screens.

Brooklyn Academy of Music Rose Cinemas (Map pp142-3; ☎ 718-777-3456; 30 Lafayette Ave) In Brooklyn, BAM is comfortable as well as popular for its new-release indies and special festival screenings.

Film Forum (Map pp142-3; ☎ 212-727-8110; 209 W Houston St) Small (well, cramped) yet beloved, it screens revivals, classics and documentaries.

IFC Center (Map pp142-3; ☎ 212-924-7771; 323 Sixth Ave at 3rd St) Formerly the Waverly, which sat in closed decrepitude in recent years, this three-screen art house has a great café and a solid line-up of new indies, cult classics and foreign films.

Performing Arts

From piano halls to ballet theaters, New York is king of the hill.

Lincoln Center (see p154) Every top-end genre has a stage at this massive complex, built in the 1960s and now undergoing a major redesign. Its **Avery Fisher Hall** is the showplace of the New York Philharmonic, while **Alice Tully Hall** houses the Chamber Music Society of Lincoln Center, and the **New York State Theater** is home to both the New York City Ballet and the New York City Opera. Great drama is found at both the **Mitzi E Newhouse** and **Vivian Beaumont** theaters; and frequent concerts at **Juilliard School**. But the biggest draw is the **Metropolitan Opera House**, home to the Metropolitan Opera and American Ballet Theater.

Carnegie Hall (Map pp150-1; ☎ 212-247-7800; www.carnegiehall.org; 154 W 57th St at Seventh Ave) Since 1891 the historic performance hall has hosted the likes of Tchaikovsky, Mahler and Prokofiev. Today it hosts visiting philharmonics, the New York Pops orchestra, piano soloists and various world-music performers, including Cesaria Evora and Bobby McFerrin.

Symphony Space (Map pp156-7; ☎ 212-864-1414; www.symphonyspace.org; 2537 Broadway at W 95th St) A multi-genre space with several facilities in one, this Upper West Side gem is home to many series, including Wall to Wall, annual free music marathons focusing on a specific composer, and Selected Shorts, which has celebrities reading from famed short stories. Theatre, cabaret, comedy, dance and world-music concerts go throughout the week.

Brooklyn Academy of Music (BAM; pp142-3; ☎ 718-636-4100; 30 Lafayette Ave) Sort of a Brooklyn version of the Lincoln Center – in its all-inclusiveness rather than its vibe, which is much edgier – this spectacular venue also hosts everything from modern dance (such as the resident Mark Morris Dance Group) to opera, cutting-edge theatre and music concerts.

Sports

Baseball fans have several choices of teams to watch: the **New York Mets** (Map p137; ☎ 718-507-8499; www.mets.com; Shea Stadium, 123-01 Roosevelt Ave, Flushing, Queens), the **New York Yankees** (Map p137; ☎ 718-293-6000; www.yankees.com; Yankee Stadium, 161st St

& River Ave, the Bronx), or the minor-league **Staten Island Yankees** (Map p137; ☎ 718-720-9200; www.siyanks .com; Richmond County Ballpark, 75 Richmond Tce, Staten Island) or **Brooklyn Cyclones** (Map p137; ☎ 718-449-8497; www .brooklyncyclones.com; Key-Span Park, Surf Ave & W 17th St, Coney Island). Don't get too attached to the current Mets or Yankees stadiums, though – both have brand new headquarters under construction that are slated to be ready for the 2009 season.

For basketball, you can get courtside with the NBA's **New York Knicks** (☎ 212-465-6741; www .nba.com/knicks; Madison Square Garden, btwn Seventh Ave & 33rd St), though when the team is doing well (not often), seats are more than scarce. The women's WNBA league **New York Liberty** (☎ 212-465-6741; www.wnba.com/liberty; Madison Square Garden) is a more laid-back time.

New York City's NFL (pro football) teams, the **Giants** (☎ 201-935-8222; www.giants .com) and **Jets** (☎ 516-560-8200; www.newyorkjets .com), share the Giants Stadium in Rutherford's Meadowlands complex.

SHOPPING

You want it? New York's got it. Marc Jacobs bag, Levis super-low 518 boot-cut jeans, cashmere socks, Tibetan decorative masks, Turkish carpets, bulk organic catnip, out-of-print books, custom-made leather chaps or an iPhone, you'll find it all here. And you can get it day or night, as it's not unusual for shops – especially downtown boutiques – to stay open until 10 or 11 at night.

Downtown

Lower Manhattan is where you'll find across-the-board bargains. Downtown's coolest offerings are in Soho and its eastern neighbor, Nolita. The East Village and the Lower East Side have funky shops selling music, gifts and clothing for a younger crowd. Count on the streets of Chinatown for knock-off designer handbags and watches.

Century 21 (Map pp142-3; ☎ 212-227-9092; 22 Cortland St at Church St) This four-level department store is an out-of-the-bag secret, beloved for clothing, shoes and housewares from top designers for at least half off normal retail.

J&R Music & Computer World (Map pp142-3; ☎ 212-238-9000; 15-23 Park Row) For all electronics known, especially computers, hit J&R, which takes up a full city block.

Citystore (Map pp142-3; ☎ 212-669-7452; Municipal Bldg, One Centre St, North Plaza) A small, little-known city-run shop, it's the perfect place

to score only-in-New-York memorabilia, including authentic taxi medallions, manhole coasters and baby onesies bearing the official 'City of New York' seal.

Babeland Lower East Side (Map pp142-3; www.babeland .com; ☎ 212-375-1701; 94 Rivington St); Soho (Map pp142-3 ☎ 212-966-2120; 43 Mercer St btwn Broome & Grand Sts) This women-run sex-toy shop takes a warm, hands-on-museum approach to selling potentially embarrassing items like blue dildos and rabbit-shaped vibrators.

Bloomingdale Soho (Map pp142-3; ☎ 212-729-5900; 504 Broadway) The smaller, younger outpost of the Upper East Side (below) legend, this Bloomie's sheds housewares and other department-store items for a clear focus on fashion. Labels cover the gamut from Ted Baker to Heatherette.

Jeffrey New York (Map p150-1; 449 W 14th St, Meatpacking District) Awesome high-end fashion temple – selling coveted labels like Versace, Pucci, Prada and Michael Kors.

Marc Jacobs (Map pp142-3; 385, 403 & 405 Bleecker St) The local fashion guru pulls in crowds (to several different shops, all of varying price levels) who love his old-fashioned-chic shoes, dresses and bags.

Midtown & Uptown

Midtown's Fifth Ave and the Upper East Side's Madison Ave have the famous high-end fashion and clothing by international designers. Times Square has many supersize stores, though they're all chains. Chelsea has more unique boutiques.

Macy's (Map pp150-1; ☎ 212-695-4400; 151 W 34th St) This grand-dame department store has long made Midtown's Herald Square one of the city's busiest shopping zones. Find everything from jeans to kitchen appliances.

Barney's New York (Map pp156-7; ☎ 212-826-8900; 660 Madison Ave) Classy and coveted emporium with spot-on choice collections of the best designer duds (Marc Jacobs, Prada, Helmut Lang, Paul Smith, Miu Miu shoes). **Barney's Co-op** Uptown (2151 Broadway); Downtown (236 W 18th St) offers hipper, less expensive versions of high-end fashion.

Bloomingdale's (Map pp156-7; ☎ 212-705-2000; 1000 3rd Ave at E 59th St). Massive 'Bloomies' is something like the Metropolitan Museum of Art to the shopping world: historic, sprawling, overwhelming and packed with bodies, but you'd be sorry to miss it.

Henri Bendel (Map pp150-1; ☎ 212-247-1100; 712 Fifth Ave) As boutique-cozy as a big-name, its European collections include curious, stylish clothing of established and up-and-coming designers, as well as cosmetics and accessories.

Tiffany & Co (Map pp150-1; ☎ 212-755-8000; 727 Fifth Ave) This famous jeweler, with the trademark clock-hoisting Atlas over the door, has won countless hearts with its fine diamond rings, watches, silver Elsa Peretti heart necklaces, and fine crystal vases and glassware

GETTING THERE & AWAY
Air
Three major airports serve New York City. The biggest is the **John F Kennedy International Airport** (☎ 718-244-4444; www.panynj.gov/aviation/jfk frame), in the borough of Queens – also home to **La Guardia Airport** (☎ 718-533-3400; www.panynj .gov/aviation/lgaframe). **Newark International Airport** (☎ 973-961-6000; www.panynj.gov/aviation/ewrframe), across the Hudson River in Newark, NJ, is a popular option, as flights here tend to be cheapest. While using online booking websites search 'NYC,' rather than a specific airport, which will allow most sites to search all three spots at once. **Long Island MacArthur Airport** (☎ 631-467-3210; www.macarthurairport.com), in Islip, is another money-saving (though time-consuming) alternative, but may make sense if a visit to the Hamptons or other parts of Long Island are in your plans.

Bus
For NYC details see p178. **Short Line** (☎ 212-736-4700; www.shortlinebus.com) runs numerous buses to towns in northern New Jersey and up-state New York, while **New Jersey Transit buses** (☎ 973-762-5100; www.njtransit.state.nj.us) serves all of New Jersey.

Car & Motorcycle
See p1144 for information about vehicle rentals. But note that renting a car in the city is mighty expensive, starting at about $75 a day for a midsize car – before extra charges like the 13.25% tax and various insurance costs.

Train
Penn Station (Map pp150-1; 33rd St btwn Seventh & Eighth Aves) is the departure point for all **Amtrak** (☎ 800-872-7245; www.amtrak.com) trains, including Acela Express service to Boston and Washington, DC. All fares vary based on the day of the week and the time you want to travel. Also arriving into Penn Station – as well as points in Brooklyn and Queens – is the **Long Island Rail Road** (☎ 718-217-5477; www.mta.nyc.ny.us/lirr), which serves several hundred thousand commuters each day. **New Jersey Transit** (☎ 973-762-5100; www .njtransit.com) also operates trains from Penn Station, with service to the suburbs and the Jersey Shore. Another option for getting into New Jersey, but strictly points north such as Hoboken and Newark, is the **New Jersey PATH** (☎ 800-234-7284; www.pathrail.com), which runs trains on a separate-fare system ($1.50) along the length of Sixth Ave, with stops at 34th, 23rd, 14th, 9th and Christopher Sts, and the reopened World Trade Center station.

The only train line that still departs from Grand Central Terminal, Park Ave at 42nd St, is the **Metro-North Railroad** (☎ 212-532-4900; www .mnr.org), which serves the northern city suburbs, Connecticut and the Hudson Valley.

GETTING AROUND
To/From the Airport
All major airports have onsite car-rental agencies. It's a hassle to drive into NYC, though, and many folks take taxis, shelling out the $45 taxi flat rate (plus toll and tip) from JFK and a metered fare of about $35 to Midtown from La Guardia.

A cheaper and pretty easy version to/from JFK is take the **AirTrain** ($5 one way) which connects to Penn Station via the Long Island Rail Road (LIRR; about $10 one-way) at Jamaica Station in Queens. You can save $3 by using the subway, rather than LIRR, though it's much slower. To/from Newark, its own **AirTrain** links all terminals to a New Jersey Transit train station which connects to Penn Station ($5 one way).

For LaGuardia, a reliable (but not super-speedy) option is the M60 bus, which heads to/from Manhattan across 125th St in Harlem and makes stops along Broadway on the Upper West Side.

All three airports are also served by shuttles, which charge about $20 one way; such companies include the **New York Airport Service Express Bus** (☎ 718-875-8200; www.nyairportservice .com), which leaves every 15 minutes for Port Authority, Penn Station and Grand Central Station; and **Super Shuttle Manhattan** (☎ 800-258-3826; www.supershuttle.com), which picks you (and others) up anywhere, on demand, with a reservation.

Car & Motorcycle

Driving within city limits is a ridiculous waste of everyone's time. Don't do it.

If you are driving out or in, however, know that the worst part is joining the masses as they try to squeeze through tunnels and over bridges to traverse the various waterways that surround Manhattan. Also be aware of local laws, such as the fact that you can't make a right on red (like you can in the rest of the state) and also the fact that every other street is one way, which can send an inexperienced driver into a series of frustrating circles.

Public Transportation

Iconic, cheap, round-the-clock and a century old in 2005, the New York City **subway system** (www.mta.info; per ride $2; ⏱ 24hr) is a remarkable example of mass transit that works in spite of itself. The 656-mile system can be intimidating at first, but dive in and you'll soon be a fan of its many virtues. Maps are available for the taking at every stop. To board, you must purchase a Metrocard, available at windows and self-serve machines, which accept change, dollars or credit/debit cards; purchasing many rides at once gets you freebies.

If you're not in a big hurry, consider taking the **bus** (per ride $2). You get to see the world go by, they run 24/7 and they're easy to navigate – going crosstown at all the major street byways (14th, 23rd, 34th, 42nd, 72nd Sts and all the others that are two-way roads) and uptown or downtown, depending which avenue they serve. You can pay with a MetroCard or exact change but not dollar bills. Transfers from one line to another are free, as are transfers to or from the subway.

Taxi

Hailing and riding in a cab are rites of passage in New York. Prices will seem reasonable or outrageous, depending on where you're from. Current fares are $2.50 for the initial charge (first one-fifth mile), 40¢ each additional one-fifth mile as well as per 60 seconds of being stopped in traffic, $1 peak surcharge (weekdays 4pm to 8pm), and 50¢ night surcharge (8pm to 6am daily). Tips are expected to be 10% to 15%. To hail a cab, it must have a lit light on its roof. Also know that it's particularly difficult to score a taxi in the rain, at rush hour and at around 4pm, when many drivers end their shifts.

NEW YORK STATE

There's upstate and downstate and never the twain shall meet. The two have about as much in common as the Upper East Side and the Bronx. And yet everyone shares the same governor and legislature in the capital, Albany. While this incompatibility produces legislative gridlock, it's a blessing for those who cherish quiet and pastoral idylls as much as Lower East side bars and the subway. Defined largely by its inland waterways, the Hudson River, the 524-mile Erie Canal connecting Albany to Buffalo, and the St Lawrence River, New York stretches to the Canadian border at world-famous Niagara Falls and the under-the-radar Thousand Islands. Buffalo is a cheap, foodies' paradise and wine aficionados can pick their favorite vintage from around the state, but especially in the Finger Lakes region close to the college town of Ithaca. From wilderness trails with backcountry camping to small town Americana, miles and miles of sandy beaches, from the historic, grand estates and artists colonies in the Hudson Valley and Catskills to the rugged and remote Adirondacks it's easy to understand why so many people leave the city never to return.

Information

New York State Tourism (☎ 800-225-5697; www .iloveny.com) Info, maps, travel advice available by phone.
New York State Travel Information (www.travelin fony.com) Weather advisories, road information and more.
New York State Office of Parks, Recreation and Historic Preservation (www.nysparks.com) Camping, lodging and general info on all state parks.
Uncork New York (www.newyorkwines.org) One-stop shop for statewide wine info.

LONG ISLAND

Private-school blazers, nightmare commutes, strip malls colonized by national chains, cookie-cutter suburbia, moneyed resorts, wind-swept dunes and magnificent beaches – and those accents. Long Island, a long peninsula contiguous with the boroughs of Brooklyn and Queens, has all of these things, which explain its somewhat complicated reputation. The site of small European whaling and fishing ports from as early as 1640, Levittown, just 25 miles east of Manhattan in Nassau County, is where builders first perfected the art of mass producing homes. But visions of suburban dystopia aside, Long Island has wide ocean and bay beaches, important historic sites, renowned vineyards, rural regions and of course the Hamptons, in all their luxuriously indulgent, sun baked glory.

North Shore

In Port Washington, the **Sands Point Preserve** (☎ 516-571-7900; www.sandspointpreserve.org; 127 Middleneck Rd; admission Mon-Fri free, Sat & Sun $2) is a wooded bayfront park that's also home to the 1923 **Falaise** (admission $6; ☷ Thu-Sun May-Oct, tours hourly noon-3pm), one of the few remaining Gold Coast mansions and now a museum. East of there is the bucolic town of Oyster Bay (hometown of Billy Joel), with an even bigger claim to fame that it's home to **Sagamore Hill** (☎ 516-922-4788; www.nps.gov/sahi; ☷ 10am-4pm Wed-Sun), a National Historic Site home where Theodore Roosevelt vacationed during his presidency.

South Shore

Despite the periodic roar of over-flying jets **Long Beach**, the closest beach to the city and most accessible by train, has a main town strip with ice-cream shops, bars and eateries, a lively surfers' scene and pale city hipsters mixing with suntanned locals.

On summer weekends the mob scene on the 6-mile stretch of pretty **Jones Beach** is a microcosm of the city's diversity, attracting surfers, wild city folk, local teens, nudists, staid families, gay men, lesbians and plenty of old-timers. Long Island Rail Rd to Wantagh makes a bus connection to Jones Beach.

Just off the southern shore is a separate barrier island, **Fire Island**, which includes **Fire Island National Seashore** (☎ 631-289-4810) and several summer-only villages accessible by ferry from Long Island. The Fire Island Pines and Cherry Grove (both car-free) comprise a historic, gay bacchanalia that attracts men and women in droves from New York City, while villages on the west end cater to straight singles and families. Beach camping is allowed in **Watch Hill** (☎ 631-567-6664; www.watchhillfi.com; campsites $20; camping from May 16–Oct 14), though mosquitoes can be fierce and reservations are a must. At the western end of Fire Island, **Robert Moses State Park** is the only spot accessible by car. Ferry terminals to Fire Island beaches and the national seashore are close to LIRR stations at Bayshore, Sayville and Patchogue (round trip $12.50, May to November). There are limited places to stay, and booking in advance is strongly advised (check www.fireisland.com for accommodations information).

The Hamptons

Achieving near iconic status along with some of its single-named celebrity denizens like Paris and Diddy, attitudes about the Hamptons are about as varied as the number of Maseratis and Land Rovers cruising the perfectly landscaped streets. But no amount of debutantes, celebrities, young Wall Street types, and wannabes can detract from the sheer beauty of the beaches, and what's left of the farms and woodland. If you can bury the envy, a pleasurable day of sightseeing can be had simply driving past the homes of the extravagantly wealthy, ranging from cutting edge modernist to faux-castle monstrosities. However, many summertime residents are

---

NEW YORK FACTS

Nicknames Empire State, Excelsior State, Knickerbocker State

Population 19.3 million

Area 54,471 sq miles

Capital city Albany (population 96,000)

Sales Tax 4%

Birthplace of Walt Whitman (1819–92), Theodore Roosevelt (1858–1919), Franklin D Roosevelt (1882–1945), Eleanor Roosevelt (1884–1962), Edward Hopper (1882–1967), Humphrey Bogart (1899–1957), Lucille Ball (1911–89), Woody Allen (b 1935), Tom Cruise (b 1962), Michael Jordan (b 1963), Jennifer Lopez (b 1969)

Home of Six Nations of the Iroquois Confederacy; first US cattle ranch (1747, in Montauk, Long Island); US women's suffrage movement (1872); Erie Canal (1825)

Famous for Niagara Falls (half of it), Hamptons, Cornell University, Hudson River

Private island owned by the Secret Society of Skull and Bones Deer Island in the Thousand Islands

partying the weekends away in much more modest group rentals and at a revolving door of clubs. While each Hampton is not geographically far from every other, traffic can be a nightmare.

SOUTHAMPTON

Though the village of Southampton appears blemish-free as if it were botoxed, it gets a face-lift at night when raucous clubgoers let their hair down. Its beaches are sweeping and gorgeous, and the **Parrish Art Museum** (☎ 631-283-2111; www.parrishart.org; 25 Jobs Lane; $5; ⏰ 11am-5pm Mon-Sat, from 1pm Sun) is an impressive regional institution. At the edge of the village is a small Native American reservation, home to the Shinnecocks, who run a tiny **museum** (☎ 631-287-4923; 100 Montauk Hwy) with unpredictable opening hours. For a quick and reasonable meal try this branch of the **Golden Pear** (☎ 631-283-8900; 99 Main St; sandwiches $9; ⏰ 7:30am- 5:00pm Fri-Sat, 7:30am- 5:30pm Sun-Thu), serving delicious soups, salads and wraps. Well-heeled revelers can down cocktails and Dom Perignon at **Pink Elephant** (☎ 631-287-9888; 281 County Rd).

BRIDGEHAMPTON & SAG HARBOR

Moving east, Bridgehampton has a more modest looking drag, but its fair share of trendy boutiques and fine restaurants. The **Bridgehampton Inn** (☎ 631-537-3660; www.bridge hamptoninn.com; 2266 Main St; r low season $195-285, high season $340-390; ⏸ wi-fi) is an attractive traditional country house. Old-fashioned diner **Candy Kitchen** (☎ 646-537-9885; Main St; mains $5-12) is as un-Hamptons as you can get; there's a luncheonette counter, filling breakfasts, burgers and sandwiches. Across the street is **World Pies** (☎ 631-537-7999; 2402 Montauk Hwy; mains from $15) which does fancy, well-dressed pizzas and a tasty lobster salad; patio seating is a bonus.

Seven miles north, on Peconic Bay, is the lovely old whaling town of Sag Harbor; ferries to Shelter Island leave a few miles north of here. Check out its **Whaling Museum** (☎ 631-725-0770; www.sagharborwhalingmuseum.org; adult/child $5/3; ⏰ 10am-5pm Mon-Sat, from 1pm Sun), or simply stroll up and down its narrow, Cape Cod–like streets. Get gourmet sustenance without going broke at **Provisions** (☎ 631-725-3636; cnr Bay & Division Sts; sandwiches $9; ⏰ 8:30am-6pm), a natural foods market with delicious take-away wraps, burritos and sandwiches.

EAST HAMPTON

Don't be fooled by the oh-so casual looking summer attire – the sunglasses alone are probably equal to a month's rent. Oozing fabulous amounts of money in a studied nonchalance is a blood sport here where Steven Spielberg, Martha Stewart and Diddy have homes. Longstanding restaurants (by Hamptons standards) like **Della Femina** (☎ 631-329-6666; 99 N Main St; dishes $20-30; ⏰ 6-11pm Fri-Sat, 6-10pm Sun-Thu) and **Nick & Toni's** (☎ 631-324-3550; 136 N Main St; dishes $20-30; ⏰ 6-10pm Mon-Wed, 6-10:30pm Thu, 6-11:30pm Fri-Sun) draw regulars from the celebrity crowd and those trolling for sightings. Catch readings and art exhibits at **Guild Hall** (☎ 631-324-0806; www.guildhall.org; 158 Main St; ⏰ summer hours 11am-5pm Mon-Sat, noon-5pm Sun, winter hours 11am-5pm Thu-Sat, noon-5pm Sun), or have a debauched night out at the **Star Room** (☎ 631-537-3332; 378 Montauk Hwy). A word to the wise: strike the phrase 'bottle service' from your vocabulary.

MONTAUK & AROUND

More Jersey Shore, less Polo Club, Montauk is the humble stepsister of the Hamptons though its beaches are equally beautiful. There's a slew of relatively reasonable restaurants and a louder bar scene. At the very eastern, wind-whipped tip of the South Fork is **Montauk Point State Park**, with its impressive, 1796 **Montauk Point Lighthouse** (☎ 631-668-2544; www.montauk lighthouse.com; adult/child $7/3; ⏰ 10:30am-5:30pm), the fourth oldest still active in the US. You can camp about 15 minutes west of here at the dune-swept **Hither Hills State Park** (☎ 631-668-2554; New York residents/nonresidents $26/50; ⏰ Apr-Nov), right on the beach. Just reserve early. Several miles to the north is the Montauk harbor, with dockside restaurants and hundreds of boats in the marinas.

You'll find a string of very basic (but beachfront) motels near the entrance to the town beach, including the **Royal Atlantic Beach Resort** (☎ 631-668-5103; www.royalatlantic.com; 126 South Edgemere Rd; r with breakfast $70-240; ⏸ 🐾). A few miles west, just across the street from the beach is **Sunrise Guesthouse** (☎ 631-668-7286; www.sunrise bandb; 681 Old Montauk Hwy; r low season $85-125, high season $130-150; ⏸), a modest and comfortable bed and breakfast. Nearby is the posh **Gurney's Inn & Spa** (☎ 631-668-2345; www.gurneys-inn.com; 290 Old Montauk Hwy; r $190-700).

Two great places to wind down the day with drinks and hearty seafood are the roadside restaurants **Clam Bar** (☎ 631-267-6348; 2025

Montauk Hwy; ☺ noon-8pm daily, weather permitting) and **Lobster Roll** (☎ 631-267-3740; 1980 Montauk Hwy; ☺ 11:30am-9:30pm Mon-Thu & Sun May-Oct, till 10pm Fri & Sat), both on the highway between Amagansett and Montauk.

North Fork & Shelter Island

Mainly, the North Fork is known for its un-spoiled farmland and wineries – there are close to 30, clustered mainly in the towns of Jamesport, Cutchogue and Southold – and the **Long Island Wine Council** (☎ 631-722-2220; www.liwines.com) provides details of the local wine trail, along Rte 25 north of Peconic Bay. **Paumanok Vineyards** (☎ 631-722-8800; www.paumanok.com; 1074 Main Rd, Aquebogue) and **Lenz Winery** (☎ 800-974-9899; www.lenzwine.com; Main Rd, Peconic) are said to produce especially high-quality wines.

The main North Fork town and the place for ferries to Shelter Island, **Greenport** (www.greenport.com) is a bit more down-to-earth and affordable than most South Fork villages. Hunker down for some excellent seafood at one of the marina restaurants, and take a free spin on the historic waterfront carousel, the gem of **Harbor Front Park**.

Between the North and South Forks, Shelter Island, accessible by ferry from North Haven to the south and Greenport to the north, is home to a cluster of Victorian buildings and the **Mashomack Nature Preserve**. It's a great spot for hiking or kayaking.

For low-key luxury book a room at **Andre Balazs's Sunset Beach** (☎ 631-749-2001; www.sunsetbeachli.com; 35 Shore Rd; r/ste from $215-500), a hip and sophisticated resort.

Getting There & Around

The most direct driving route is along I-495, aka the LIE (Long Island Expressway) though avoid rush hour, when it's commuter hell. Once in the Hamptons, there is one main road to the end, Montauk Hwy. The **Long Island Railroad** (☎ 718-217-5477; www.mta.nyc.ny.us/lirr) serves all regions of Long Island, including the Hamptons ($20 one way) and North Fork, from Penn Station, Brooklyn and Queens. The **Hampton Jitney** (☎ 631-283-4600; www.hamptonjitney.com; one way $27) and newly established **Hampton Luxury Liner** (☎ 631-537-5800; www.hamptonluxuryliner.com; one way $25) bus services connect Manhattan's Upper East Side to various Hamptons villages; the former also has new service to/from various spots in Brooklyn.

HUDSON VALLEY

Immediately north of New York City, the road rage dissipates, green becomes the dominant color and the vistas of the Hudson River and the mountains breathe life into your urban-weary body. Home to the Hudson River School of painting in the 19th century, the history of the region is preserved in the many grand estates, properties of the Vanderbilts and Roosevelts among them, and the pictur-esque villages. The Lower Valley and Mid Val-ley are more populated and suburban, while the Upper Valley has a rural feel, with hills leading into the Catskills mountain region. For region-wide information, check out the **Hudson Valley Network** (www.hvnet.com).

Lower Hudson Valley

Pristine forested wilderness with miles of hik-ing trails are available just 40 miles north of New York City: **Harriman State Park** (☎ 845-786-5003) covers 72 sq miles and offers swimming, hiking and camping; adjacent **Bear Mountain State Park** (☎ 845-786-2701) offers great views from its 1306ft peak, with the Manhattan sky-line looming beyond the river and surround-ing greenery; there's a restaurant and lodging at the inn on Hessian Lake. In both parks there are several scenic roads snaking their way past secluded lakes with gorgeous vistas.

Several magnificent homes and gardens can be found near Tarrytown and Sleepy Hollow, on the east side of the Hudson. **Kykuit**, one of the properties of the Rockefeller family, has an impressive array of Asian and European artwork and immaculately kept gardens with breathtaking views. **Lyndhurst** is the estate of railroad tycoon Jay Gould and **Sunnyside** the home of author Washington Irving. Go to the **Historic Hudson Valley** (www.hudsonvalley.org) website for info on these and other historic attractions.

West of Rte 9W and 50 miles north of New York City, the **Storm King Art Center** (☎ 845-534-3115; www.stormkingartcenter.org; Old Pleasant Rd, Mountainville; adults/students $10/9; ☺ 11am-5pm Wed-Sun Apr-Nov), is a 400-acre outdoor sculpture park with roll-ing hills that showcases stunning avant-garde sculpture by well-known artists; a free tram gives tours of the grounds. Nearby **West Point** (☎ 845-938-2638; ☺ 9am-5pm), open to visitors, is where a strategic fort became the US Military Academy in 1802. Not far from here the large, strip mall–filled town of Newburgh is the site of **Washington's Headquarters State Historic Site**

(☎ 845-562-1195; Liberty at Washington Sts; donations accepted; ⏱ 1-5pm Wed-Sat Apr-Oct), General George's longest-lasting base during the Revolutionary War; there's a museum, galleries and maps.

At Beacon, a fairly nondescript town east of Rte 9W, fashionable regulars of the international art scene stop for **Dia Beacon** (☎ 845-440-0100; www.diaart.org; ⏱ 11am-6pm Thu-Mon Apr 14–Oct 17; to 4pm Fri-Mon rest of year), featuring a renowned collection from 1960 to the present, and enormous sculptures and installation pieces.

Middle & Upper Hudson Valley

On the western side of the Hudson is **New Paltz**, home of a campus of the State University of New York, natural food stores and a liberal eco-friendly vibe. In the distance behind the town the ridge of the Shawangunk (Shon-gum or just the 'Gunks') mountains rises more than 2000 feet above sea level. **Minnewaska State Park Preserve** has 12,000 acres of wild landscape, the centerpiece of which is a usually ice-cold mountain lake.

The nearby iconic **Mohonk Mountain House** (☎ 845-255-1000; www.mohonk.com; 1000 Mountain Rest Rd; r $250-750; 🅿 🕸 🖳) looks like it's straight out of a fairy tale, a rustic castle perched magnificently over a dark lake. It's an all-inclusive resort where guests can gorge on elaborate five-course meals, stroll through gardens, hike miles of trails, canoe, swim, etc. A new luxury spa center is there to work out the kinks after all the strenuous activity. Non-overnight guests can visit the grounds (adult/child per day $21/16) – well worth the price of admission.

The largest town on the Hudson's east bank, **Poughkeepsie** (puh-*kip*-see) is famous for **Vassar**, a private liberal-arts college that admitted only women until 1969. Cheap motel chains are clustered along Rte 9, south of the Mid-Hudson Bridge, but try the **Copper Penny Inn** (☎ 845-452-3045; www.copperpennyinn.com; 2406 Hackensack Rd; r with breakfast $140-230; 🗶) a charming and cheerful B&B set on 12 wooded acres.

Hyde Park is chock-full of history, as it's long been associated with the Roosevelts, a prominent family since the 19th century. The **Franklin D Roosevelt Library & Museum** (☎ 800-337-8474; www.fdrlibrary.marist.edu; 511 Albany Post Rd/Rte 9; admission $14; ⏱ 9am-6pm May-Oct, to 5pm Nov-Apr) features exhibits on the man who created the New Deal and led the USA into WWII. First Lady Eleanor Roosevelt's peaceful cottage, **Val-Kill** (☎ 845-229-5302; www.nps.gov/elro; admission $8; ⏱ 9am-5pm), was

her retreat from Hyde Park, FDR's mother and FDR himself. The 54-room **Vanderbilt Mansion** (☎ 877-444-6777; www.nps.gov/vama; Rte 9; admission $8; ⏱ 9am-5pm), a national historic site 2 miles north on Rte 9, is a spectacle of lavish beaux-arts and eclectic architecture. A combination ticket to all three sites is $20.

Hyde Park's famous **Culinary Institute of America** (☎ 800-285-4627; www.ciachef.edu; 1964 Campus Dr) trains future chefs and can satisfy absolutely anyone's gastronomic cravings. It's home to six student-staffed eateries, including the Apple Pie Bakery Café, '50s-style Eveready Diner, and the elegant Escoffier Restaurant.

CATSKILLS

It will be decades at least before year-rounders consider the weekenders locals and not interlopers, but the introduction of fine cuisine and cute boutiques has yet to overwhelm the small town charm and pastoral atmosphere of the Catskills. For some out-of-staters this bucolic region of undulating, forest-covered mountains and picturesque farmland is still synonymous with Borscht-belt family resorts. However, that era is long past, and after some economically tough times the Catskills, though lower profile than the Hamptons, have become a popular choice for sophisticated city dwellers seeking second-home getaways.

Woodstock & Around

Shorthand for free love, free expression and the political ferment of the 1960s, world-famous **Woodstock** today still wears its counter-culture tie dye in the form of healing centers, art galleries, cafés and an eclectic mix of aging hippies and young Phish-fan types. The famous 1969 Woodstock music festival, though, actually occurred in Bethel, a town over 40 miles southwest. **Woodstock Inn on the Millstream** (☎ 845-679-8211; www.woodstock-inn-ny.com; 48 Tannery Brook Rd; r with breakfast from $119; 🕸 wi-fi), just a short walk from town, is an ideal getaway with well designed rooms, a cascading stream and truly glorious gardens. Popular **Taco Juan's** (☎ 845-679-9673; 31 Tinker St; ⏱ noon-8pm daily, noon-8:30 weekends) has casual and take-away Mexican, and homemade ice cream.

Saugerties, just 7 miles east of Woodstock, is not nearly as quaint and feels comparably like the big city, but there are two highly recommended places to sleep. For a truly romantic and unique place to lay your head, stay at the picturesque **Saugerties Lighthouse**

(☎ 845-247-0656; www.saugertieslighthouse.com; r incl breakfast $135 Nov-Mar, $160 Apr-Oct; ✗), an 1869 landmark that sits on a small island in the Esopus Creek, accessible by boat or more commonly by a half-mile long trail from the parking lot. Rooms are booked far in advance but a walk to the lighthouse is highly recommended regardless. On a verdant piece of property several miles outside town on the way to Woodstock is the five room **Villa at Saugerties** (☎ 845-246-0682; www.thevillaatsaugerties .com; 159 Fawn Rd; d with breakfast low/high season from $135/145; ❄ ☒ wi-fi), rustic and country on the outside, hip and cosmopolitan on the inside.

On the eastern side of the river is Rhinebeck, with a bustling main street, good antique shops, inns, farms and wineries. There's also an **Aerodrome Museum** (☎ 845-752-3200; www .oldrhinebeck.org) and the destination bistro **Terrapin** (☎ 845-876-3330; www.terrapinrestaurant.com; 6426 Montgomery St; lunch sandwiches $7, dinner mains from $19) which serves mouth-watering dishes like Hudson valley stone church farm French Peking duck with orange apricot sauce. Much further to the north is Hudson – a beautiful town with a hip, gay-friendly community of artists, writers and performers who fled the city.

Route 28 & Around

Scenic Route 28 cuts through the heart of the Catsills. The refreshing waters of Pine Hill Lake at nearby **Belleayre Beach** (☎ 800-942-6904; www.belleayre.com) is the summertime place to cool off. Not far from here is the **Lazy Meadow Motel** (☎ 845-688-7200; www.lazymea dow.com; 5191 Rte 28, Mt Tremper; r from $150; ☒ wi-fi) owned by Kate Pierson of the B-52s. You have your choice of retrofitted airstream trailers or more conventional rooms though all are decorated with the same distinctive nostalgia for a design era gone-by; Esopus Creek passes through the back of the property. If you continue on Rte 28, past Fleischmann's and Margaretville, you'll come to the small town of Andes. Basic rooms are available in town at the **Andes Hotel** (☎ 845-676-3980; www .andeshotel.com; s/d $65/85; ☒ wi-fi), which has a fine restaurant attached.

A destination in-and-of itself, the **Roxbury** (☎ 607-326-7200; www.theroxburymotel.com; r $100-180; ☒ wi-fi), in the tiny village of the same name, is a wonderfully creative gem of a place. Housed in a perfectly restored conventional looking country hotel are luxuriously designed rooms, each inspired by a particular '60s or '70s era

TV show; a new spa is attached. In nearby Arkville, you can take a scenic ride on the historic **Delaware & Ulster Rail Line** (☎ 800-225-4132; www.durr.org; Hwy 28; adult $10; ❂ Sat & Sun May-Aug). Skiers should head further north, where Rtes 23 and 23A lead you to **Hunter Mountain Ski Bowl** (☎ 518-263-4223; www.huntermtn.com), a year-round resort with challenging runs and a 1600ft vertical drop.

Getting There & Around

Having a car is near essential in these parts. **Adirondack Trailways** (☎ 800-776-7548; www.trail waysny.com) operates daily buses from NYC to Kingston, the Catskills' gateway town, as well as to Saugerties, Catskills, Hunter and Woodstock. Buses leave from NYC's Port Authority. The commuter rail line **Metro-North** (☎ 800-638-7646; www.mta.info/mnr) makes stops through the Lower and Middle Hudson Valley.

FINGER LAKES REGION

A bird's eye view of this region of rolling hills and eleven long narrow lakes – the eponymous fingers – reveals an outdoors paradise stretching all the way from Albany to far western New York. Of course there's boating, fishing, bicycling, hiking and cross-country skiing, but it's also the state's premier wine-growing region with more than 65 **vineyards**, enough for the most discerning oenophile.

Ithaca & Around

An idyllic home for college students and older generations of hippies who cherish elements of the traditional collegiate lifestyle – laidback vibe, café poetry readings, art-house cinemas, green quads, good eats – this city perched above Cayuga Lake, besides being a destination in-and-of itself is also a convenient halfway point between New York City and Niagara Falls. For tourist information, head to the **Visit Ithaca Information Center** (☎ 607-272-1313; www.visitithaca.com; 904 E Shore Dr; ❂ 9am-5pm Mon-Fri, from 10am Sat).

Founded in 1865, **Cornell** boasts a lovely campus, mixing traditional and contemporary architecture, and sits high on a hill overlooking the picturesque town below. The modern **Herbert F Johnson Museum of Fine Art** (☎ 607-255-6464; www.museum.cornell.edu; University Ave; admission free; ❂ 10am-5pm Tue-Sun) – designed by IM Pei – has a major Asian collection, plus pre-Columbian, American and European exhibits.

The area around Ithaca is known for its waterfalls, gorges and gorgeous parks. However, downtown has its very own – **Cascadilla Gorge** – starting several blocks from Ithaca Commons and ending, after a steep and stunning vertical climb, at the Performing Arts Center of Cornell. Eight miles north on Rte 89, the spectacular **Taughannock Falls** spill 215ft into the steep gorge below; **Taughannock Falls State Park** (☎ 607-387-6739; www.taughannock.com; Rte 89) has two major hiking trails, craggy gorges, tent-trailer sites and cabins. **Buttermilk Falls Park** (☎ 607-273-5761 summer, 607-273-3440 winter; Rte 13) has a popular swimming hole at the foot of the falls as does **Robert Treman Park** (☎ 607-273-3440; 105 Enfield Falls Rd) a few miles further out of town.

Remember to spit. That is, if you're driving. Otherwise, feel free to swallow as many glasses of Finger Lakes wine as you'd like. Dozens of wineries line the shores of Cayuga Lake, Lake Seneca and Lake Keuka. Two recommended Cayuga Lake wineries are **Sheldrake Point** (☎ 607-532-9401) and **Thirsty Owl** (☎ 607-869-5805; www.thirstyowl.com).

Around 44 miles to the southwest is the charming town of Corning, home to Corning Glass Works and the hugely popular **Corning Museum of Glass** (☎ 800-732-6845; www.cmog.org; adult/child $12.50/free; 9am-5pm, to 8pm all summer). The massive complex is home to fascinating exhibits on glass-making arts, complete with glass-blowing demonstrations, interactive items for kids and special exhibits.

SLEEPING & EATING

The gracious and grand **Henry Miller Inn** (☎ 607-256-4553; www.millerinn.com; 303 N Aurora St, Ithaca; r with breakfast $115-195; wi-fi), only a few steps from the commons, is a completely restored historic home with luxuriously designed rooms – three have Jacuzzis – and a gourmet breakfast. Nearby is the also recommended **Inn on Columbia** (☎ 607-272-0204; www.columbiabb.com; 228 Columbia St; d $150; wi-fi) with a more modern, contemporary feel.

Ithaca has a great variety of international, gourmet and vegetarian restaurants. According to locals in the know, **Glenwood Pines** (☎ 607-273-3709; burgers $5; 11am-9:30pm Sun-Thu, 11am-10:30pm Fri & Sat), a modest roadside restaurant overlooking Lake Cayuga on Rte 89 four miles north of Ithaca, serves the best burger in town. In downtown Ithaca Commons is **Just a Taste Wine and Tapas Bar** (☎ 607-277-9463;

116 N Aurora St; tapas $6; 5:30-10pm Sun-Thu, 5:30-11pm Fri & Sat, 10:30am-2:30pm Sat & Sun), featuring creative meat, seafood and vegetable dishes and a unique wine tasting option. Nearby **Moosewood Restaurant** (☎ 607-273-9610; www.moosewoodrestaurant.com; 215 N Cayuga St; mains $13; 11:30am-3pm Mon-Sat, 5:30-8:30pm Sun-Thu, 5:30-9pm Fri & Sat;) is famous for its vegetarian dishes and recipe books by founder Mollie Katzen. **Maxies Supper Club & Oyster Bar** (☎ 607-272-4136; 635 State St; mains $13; 4-11pm Sun-Thu, 4pm-1am Fri & Sat) has Southern cuisine with New Orleans specials like Jumbo Gumbo.

Seneca Falls

After being excluded from an antislavery meeting, Elizabeth Cady Stanton and her friends drafted an 1848 declaration asserting that 'all men and women are created equal,' transforming this small town into the birthplace of this country's organized women's rights movement. The inspirational **Women's Rights National Historical Park** (☎ 315-568-2991; www.nps.gov/wori; 136 Fall St; 9am-5pm) has a small but impressive museum, as well as a visitor center offering tours of Cady Stanton's house. The surprisingly tiny **National Women's Hall of Fame** (☎ 315-568-8060; www.greatwomen.org; 76 Fall St; admission $3; 10am-5pm Mon-Sat, noon-5pm Sun, May-Sep, 11am-5pm Wed-Sat Oct-Apr) honors American women such as first lady Abigail Adams, American Red Cross founder Clara Barton and civil-rights activist Rosa Parks.

ALBANY

Despite its status as the center of legislative power in the state, Albany (or 'Smallbany' to jaded locals) remains a tourism backwater. It became New York State's capital in 1797 because of its geographic centrality to local colonies and its strategic importance in the fur trade. The railroad reached town in 1851 and helped solidify the city as an important transportation crossroads and manufacturing center. Albany is an architecturally diverse city, from the ostentatiously modern to the classically Victorian, but several blocks from the city center stately government buildings give way to derelict and neglected streets and a general feeling of malaise. **Lark Street** (www.larkstreet.org), north and uphill of downtown, has several restaurants and bars popular with university students when school is in session.

Sights & Activities

The **Empire State Plaza** comprises 98 acres of land and 10 government buildings, state agencies, a modern-art sculpture display and a performing-arts center that's dubbed 'the Egg' for its oval architecture. The plaza also has the tall Corning Tower, with an **observation deck** (☎ 518-474-2418; Corning Tower; admission free; 🕙 10am-2:30pm) that overlooks the city and the Hudson River from its 42nd floor; and the **New York State Museum** (☎ 518-474-5877; www.nysm.nysed.gov; admission by donation; 🕙 9:30am-5pm), which documents the state's political, cultural and natural history. East of the plaza, **Albany Institute of History & Art** (☎ 518-463-4478; www.albanyinstitute.org; 125 Washington Ave; admission $8; 🕙 10am-5pm Wed-Sat, noon-5pm Sun) houses decorative arts and works by Hudson River–school painters. **Albany City Hall** (☎ 518-434-5075; Washington Ave & State St) is also worth a visit for its grand 19th-century architecture; call ahead for tour times.

Sleeping & Eating

To sleep downtown try **Angel's Bed and Breakfast** (☎ 518-426-4104; 96 Madison Ave; www.angelsbedandbreakfast.com; r with breakfast $115-225; 🖳 wi-fi), a historic building with an outdoor roof deck and **74 State** (☎ 518-434-7410; www.74state.com; 74 State St; r from $165; 🖳 wi-fi), a high end boutique hotel.

The majority of the restaurants are located along Pearl St and Lark St, a more eclectic and happening scene. **A Taste of Greece** (☎ 518-426-9000; 193 Lark St; dishes $9-15; 🕙 11am to 9pm Tue-Fri, 5 to 10pm Sat & Sun) does Hellenic standards in a simple setting. In one of the city's oldest buildings next to the tourism information office is **Nicole's Bistro at Quackenbush Square** (☎ 518-465-1111; 633 Broadway; mains $19-25; 🕙 11:30am-2:30pm and 5pm-10pm Mon-Fri, 5pm-10pm Sat), an elegant and upscale restaurant.

Drinking & Entertainment

One of the city's best spots for a drink is **Antica Enoteca, Old World Wine Bar** (☎ 518-463-2881; 200 Lark St; 🕙 closed Mon), a miniature maze of cozy tables with tapas and a selection of more than 50 very reasonably priced wines by the glass. **Justin's** (☎ 518-436-7008; www.justinsonlark.com; 301 Lark St; 🕙 11am-1am) has live jazz every night of the week as well as dinner and drinks. For a local coffee spot try the **Daily Grind** (204 Lark St; 🕙 6:30am-9pm Mon-Fri, 7am-9pm Sat, 7am-8pm Sun), a simple place below street level with good sandwiches, pastries, specialty drinks and wi-fi.

Getting There & Around

From the **bus terminal** (34 Hamilton St), **Trailways** (☎ 518-427-7060) and **Greyhound** (☎ 518-434-8461) head to/from New York City ($42 one way, three hours). Amtrak stops out of New York City ($57 one way, 2½ hours), as do several major airlines flying into the **Albany International Airport** (737 Albany Shaker Rd; www.albanyairport.com) about 10 miles north from downtown.

AROUND ALBANY

Cooperstown

For sports fan, **Cooperstown** (Chamber of Commerce; ☎ 607-547-9983; www.cooperstownchamber.org), 50 miles west of Albany, is instantly recognized as the home to the shrine for the national sport. But the small-town atmosphere and stunning views of the countryside around beautiful Ostego Lake make it worth visiting even for those who don't know the difference between E.R.A. and R.B.I.

The **National Baseball Hall of Fame & Museum** (☎ 607-547-7200; 25 Main St; www.baseballhalloffame.org; adult/child $14.50/5; 🕙 9am-5pm) has exhibits, a theater, library and an interactive statistical database. The old stone **Fenimore Art Museum** (☎ 607-547-1400; www.fenimoreartmuseum.org; 5798 Lake Rd; admission $11; 🕙 10am-4pm Tue-Sun Apr, May, Oct & Nov, to 5pm Jun-Sep) has an outstanding collection of Americana.

Several affordable low-slung motels line Rte 80 alongside the lake outside of town. **The Inn at Cooperstown** (☎ 607-547-5756; www.innatcooperstown.com; 16 Chestnut St; r with breakfast from $100; 🖳 wi-fi) is a beautifully restored country home blocks from Main St and **Hoffman Lane Bistro** (☎ 607-547-7055; 2 Hoffman Ln; mains $15) has an excellent and eclectic menu.

Saratoga Springs

In its heyday in the early 1800s, when 'taking the waters' was considered the equivalent of a trip to the hospital, Saratoga Springs, north of Albany, was world famous, visited once by Joseph Bonaparte, Napoleon's older brother, and the king of Spain. While a single spring still operates, these days the town is known more for its performing arts center, racetrack and the liberal-arts college Skidmore.

The only remaining bathhouse – the first was built in 1784 – is the **Roosevelt Baths and Spa** (40-min spa $25) in the 2300-acre **Saratoga Spa State Park** (☎ 518-584-2535; www.saratogaspastatepark.org; 19 Roosevelt Dr; per car $4; 🕙 dawn-dusk). The mineral and gas infused waters are pumped underground from the Lincoln Springs over a mile away. Controversially, these days very hot tap water is added to the mix though purists insist on going cold. Park grounds include golf courses, an Olympic-sized pool complex, multi-use trails, ice rinks and world-famous **Saratoga Performing Arts Center** (☎ 518-587-3330; www.spac.org; Hall of Springs), with orchestra, jazz, pop, rock and dance performances. From late July to September, horse racing fans flock to the **Saratoga Race Course** (☎ 518-584-6200; www.saratogaracetrack.com) the country's oldest thoroughbred track.

In nearby Glens Falls, the remarkable Hyde Collection, housed in the **Hyde Collection Art Museum** (☎ 518-792-1761; www.hydecollection .org; 161 Warren St; admission free; ☒ 10am-5pm Tue-Sat, from noon Sun), an impressive 1912 Florentine Renaissance–style villa, includes works by Rembrandt, Degas and Matisse.

SLEEPING & EATING

The nearest campground is **Cold Brook Campsites** (☎ 518-584-8038; www.coldbrookrvresort.com; 385 Gurn Springs Rd; campsites $30), about 10 miles north in Gansevoort. There are plenty of inns and B&Bs in town; the **Geyser Lodge Bed & Breakfast** (☎ 518-584-0389; www.geyserlodge.com; r with breakfast from $109; ☒ ☒ wi-fi) is a graceful Victorian only a mile from downtown. Eateries line Broadway and the intimate side streets include **Beverly's** (☎ 518-583-2755; 47 Phila St; mains $8; ☒ 7am-3pm), a gourmet breakfast spot, and sophisticated and friendly **Circus Cafe** (☎ 518-583-1106; 392 Broadway St; mains $15; ☒ 11:30am-10pm daily, till 11pm Fri & Sat Jul-Aug) with everything from sandwiches to American comfort food.

THE ADIRONDACKS

Majestic and wild, the Adirondacks, a mountain range with 42 peaks over 4000 feet high, rival any of the nation's wilderness areas for sheer awe-inspiring beauty. The 6 million acres of park and forest preserve that climb from central New York State to the Canadian border include towns, mountains, lakes, rivers and more than 2000 miles of hiking trails. There's good trout, salmon and pike fishing, along with excellent camping spots. The Adirondack Forest Preserve covers 40% of the park, preserving the area's pristine integrity. In colonial times settlers exploited the forests for beaver fur, timber and hemlock bark, but by the 19th century 'log cabin' wilderness retreats, both in the form of hotels and grand estates, became fashionable.

Lake George, Lake Placid & Saranac Lake

Maybe it's a blessing that the primary gateway to the Adirondacks, the village of **Lake George** (www.lakegeorgechamber.com), is a kitsch tourist town full of cotton candy, arcades and cheap souvenirs. The real reason for coming is the 32-mile-long lake itself, with its crystalline waters and forested shoreline, and once you leave the town behind the contrast is only more striking.

The state maintains wonderfully remote **campgrounds** (☎ 800-456-2267) on Lake George's islands, and one of several places for wilderness information is the **Adirondack Mountain Club** (☎ 518-523-3441; www.adk.org; 814 Goggins Rd). Small motels line the main street of Lake George.

It's something of a stretch to imagine this small mountain resort was once at the center of the world's attention – well twice. In 1932 and 1980, **Lake Placid** hosted the Winter Olympics and the facilities and infrastructure remain, and elite athletes still train here. Parts of the **Olympic sports centers** (www.orda.org) are open to visitors, including ice arenas, a ski-jumping complex and a chance to bobsled or luge with a professional driver. Hotels, inns, restaurants and shops line the main street in town, which actually fronts Mirror Lake. Skiers should head to nearby **Whiteface Mountain** (www.whiteface.com), with 76 trails and a serious 3400ft vertical drop.

South of Lake Placid town, the Adirondack Mountain Club's (ADK) **Adirondack Loj** (☎ 518-523-3441; www.adk.org; dm/r with breakfast $45/140) is a rustic retreat surrounded by mountains on the shore of peaceful Heart Lake. Wilderness campsites, lean-tos and cabins are also available.

Further north is the **Saranac Lake** region, where you'll find even more secluded wilderness areas – small lakes and ponds, ancient forests and wetlands. The town of Saranac Lake itself, once a center for tuberculosis treatments, feels a little down on its luck. However, the nearby **Porcupine Inn** (☎ 518-891-5160; www .theporcupine.com; 350 Park Ave; r with breakfast $150-300; ☒ wi-fi), housed in a classic Adirondacks-style lodge house, is run with loving care and perfection. A hike up to nearby Moody Pond and Baker Mountain affords excellent views of the area.

Getting There & Around

Both **Greyhound** (☎ 800-231-2222; www.greyhound .com) and **Adirondack Trailways** (☎ 800-776-7548) serve various towns in the region. A car is really essential to exploring the region.

THOUSAND ISLANDS REGION

Virtually unknown to downstate New Yorkers, in part because of its relative inaccessibility, this region of over 1800 islands – from tiny outcroppings just large enough to lie down on to larger islands with roads and towns – is a scenic wonderland separating the US from Canada. From its source in the Atlantic Ocean far to the north, the wide and deceptively fast moving St Lawrence River East empties into Lake Ontario at Cape Vincent. This portion of the river was once a summer playground for the very rich, who built large, stately homes here. It is still a popular vacation area known for its boating, camping and even shipwreck scuba diving.

Sackets Harbor was the site of a major battle during the War of 1812. While it is on Lake Ontario and not technically part of the Thousand Islands, it is a convenient starting point for touring the region. The centrally located and friendly **Ontario Place Hotel** (☎ 315-646-8000; 103 General Smith Dr; d from $80; ⧉ wi-fi) has comfortable, well-kept rooms. Several good restaurants line the street that runs down to the harbor front including **Tin Pan Galley** (☎ 315-646-3812; 110 West Main St; sandwiches $9; ⌚ 8am-9pm Tue-Thu, 8am-9:30pm Fri, 7am-10pm Sat, 7am-12:45pm Sun) which has a lovely outdoor garden patio.

The relaxing, French-heritage village of **Cape Vincent** is at the western end of the river where it meets the lake. Drive out to the **Tibbetts Point Lighthouse** for stunning lake views; an attractive **hostel** (☎ 315-654-3450; lighthousehostel@tds.net; dm $18) shares the property. Nearby **Burnham Point State Park** (☎ 315-654-2324; Rte 12E; campsites $25) has wooded, lakeside campsites.

Clayton, 15 miles to the east along the Seaway Trail, has more than a dozen marinas and a few good eating choices in an area generally bereft of them. **TI Adventures** (☎ 315-686-2500; www.tiadventures.com; 1011 State St; half-day kayak rental $30) rents kayaks and runs whitewater rafting trips down the Black River. Such activities are also organized by several companies in Watertown, a sizeable city half an hour's drive to the south.

The owner/chef of friendly **Bella's** (☎ 315-686-2341; 602 Riverside Dr, Clayton; mains $6; ⌚ 8am-3pm daily, 6-9pm Thu-Sat), does excellent breakfast and lunch. **Lyric Coffee House** (☎ 315-686-4700; 246 James St, Clayton; ⌚ 8am-10pm, Mon-Sat, 1-10pm Sun; wi-fi), surprisingly modern for this town, serves specialty coffee drinks, gelato and pastries.

Further east, **Alexandria Bay** (Alex Bay), an early-20th-century resort town, is still the center of tourism on the American side – its sister city is Gananoque in Canada. While it is run down and tacky, there's enough around to keep you occupied: go-karts, mini-golf and a **drive-in movie theater** (baydrivein.com) are only minutes away. It's also the departure point for ferries to Heart Island, where **Boldt Castle** (☎ 800-847-5263; www .boldtcastle.com; adult/child $5.75/3.50; ⌚ 10am-6:30pm mid-May–mid-Oct) marks the sad love story of a rags-to-riches New York hotelier who built the castle for his beloved wife, who then died before its completion. The same hotelier once asked his chef to create a new salad dressing, which was popularized as 'Thousand Island' – an unfortunate blend of ketchup, mayonnaise and relish. **Uncle Sam's Boat Tours** (☎ 800-253-9299; www.unclesam boattour.com, 45 James St; 2 Nation tour adult/child $16/8, Two Castle Tour adults/children $28/14) has several departures daily for its recommended two-nation cruise which allows you to stop at Boldt Castle and ride back on one of its half-hourly ferries for free.

Camping, especially at the **Wellesley Island State Park** (☎ 518-474-0456; www.nysparks.com; campsite $19) is probably the best sleeping option even for the raccoon averse. Many sites are almost directly on the riverfront and some have their own 'private' beaches. Reservations are recommended in the high season. The island is only accessible by crossing a toll portion ($2.50) of the Thousand Islands Bridge. There is a small convenience store/diner on the way to the campgrounds, but your best bet is to stock up on supplies at one of the large grocery stores in Alex Bay or Clayton.

There are several supposedly upscale resorts around Alex Bay, though none is especially good value. Probably the best midrange choice is **Capt. Thomson's Resort** (☎ 315-482-9961; www.captthomsons.com; 47 James St; d from $75; ⧉ ⧉ wi-fi) on the waterfront next to the office for Uncle Sam's Boat Tours.

Ogdensburg, 37 miles north of Alex Bay, is the birthplace of Frederic Remington (1861–1909), an artist who romanticized the

American West in paintings and sculpture. The **Frederic Remington Art Museum** (☎ 315-393-2425; www.fredericremington.org; 303 Washington St, Ogdensburg, NY; admission $8; ☼ 11am-5pm Wed-Sat, from 1pm Sun) has some of his sculptures, paintings and personal effects.

Getting There & Around

Jet Blue (☎ 800-538-2583) has regular daily flights to Hancock International Airport in Syracuse, an hour and a half south. Several major car rental agencies have offices in the airport. Bicyclists will enjoy the mostly flat Scenic Byway Trail.

WESTERN NEW YORK

Stabilizing somewhat after hemorrhaging industries and population for the past decade, most of the cities in this region live in the shadow of Niagara Falls, a natural wonder that attracts upwards of 12 million visitors from around the world per year. Buffalo was once a booming industrial center and the terminus of the Erie Canal, which used to serve as the transportation lifeline connecting the Great Lakes and the Atlantic Ocean; it now boasts an indigenous culinary scene and bohemian enclaves. Syracuse and Rochester are both homes to big universities; the latter is worth a visit for the **George Eastman House** (☎ 585-271-3361; 900 East Ave, Rochester; adult/student/child $8/5/3; ☼ 10am-5pm Tue-Sat, until 8pm Thu, 1-5pm Sun) and **International Museum of Photography & Film** (☎ 585-271-3361; 900 East Ave; www.eastmanhouse.org; adult/child $8/5; ☼ 10am-5pm Tue-Sat, from 1pm Sun).

Niagara Falls

It's a tale of two cities and two falls, though either side of this international border affords views of an undeniably dramatic natural wonder. There are honeymooners and heart-shaped Jacuzzis, arcades, tacky shops and kitsch boardwalk-like sights, but as long as your attention is focused nothing can detract from the majestic sight. The closer to the falls you get the more impressive they seem and the wetter you become. For good reason, the Canadian side is where most everyone visits though it's easy to stroll back and forth between the two (see opposite).

ORIENTATION & INFORMATION

The falls are in two separate towns: Niagara Falls, New York (USA) and Niagara Falls, Ontario (Canada). The towns face each other across the Niagara River, spanned by the Rainbow Bridge, which is accessible to cars and pedestrians.

On the US side the **Niagara Falls Convention & Visitors Bureau** (☎ 800-338-7890; www.nfcvb.com; cnr 4th & Niagara Sts; ☼ 8:30am-5pm) has all sorts of guides; its more helpful Canadian counterpart is located near the base of the **Skylon Tower** (☎ 905-356-6061; www.niagarafallstourism.com; 5400 Robinson St; ☼ 9am-5pm).

SIGHTS & ACTIVITIES

You can see side views of the **American Falls** and their western portion, the **Bridal Veil Falls**, dropping 180ft by simply walking across the pedestrian bridge from Canada. Take the **Prospect Point Observation Tower** (☎ 716-278-1796; admission $1, free from 5pm; ☼ 9:30am-7pm) elevator up for a vista. Cross the bridge to **Goat Island** for other viewpoints, including Terrapin Point, which has a fine view of Horseshoe Falls and pedestrian bridges to the Three Sisters Islands in the upper rapids. From the north corner of Goat Island, an elevator descends to the **Cave of the Winds** (☎ 716-278-1730; admission $8), where walkways go within 25ft of the cataracts (raincoats provided). The **Maid of the Mist** (☎ 716-284-8897; www.maidofthemist.com; tours adult/child $12.50/7.30; ☼ Apr-Oct) boat trip around the bottom of the falls has been a major attraction since 1846 and is highly recommended. Boats leave every 15 minutes from the base of the Prospect Park Observation Tower on the US side and from the bottom of Clifton Hill on the Canadian side.

For those seeking more of an adrenalin rush, check out **Niagara Helicopters** (☎ 905-357-5672; niagarahelicopters.com; 3731 Victoria Ave; $110), **Whirlpool Jet Boat Tours** (☎ 888-438-4444; www.whirlpooljet .com; adult/child $50/42) and **Rainbow Air** (☎ 716-284-2800; www.rainbowairinc.com; 45 Main St; tours $60).

SLEEPING & EATING

There's virtually no reason to spend the night on the US side of the falls. The purple glass–covered Seneca Niagara Casino & Hotel towers over the surrounding derelict blocks. Some of the hotel chains are represented – Ramada Inn, Howard Johnson, Holiday Inn – but unless you're a fugitive on the run, cross the border to Canada. There are a few restaurants near the bridge area, including several Indian take-away

---

BORDER CROSSING: CANADIAN NIAGARA FALLS

When people say they are visiting the falls they usually mean the Canadian side, which is naturally blessed with a far superior view. Canada's **Horseshoe Falls** are wider and especially photogenic from Queen Victoria Park; at night they're illuminated with a colored light show. The **Journey Behind the Falls** (US$7.50; 9am-8:30pm Mon-Fri, 9am-11pm Sat & Sun Jun-Sep, 9am-8pm Sep-Oct, 9am-7pm Nov-Dec, 9am-5:30pm Mon-Fri, 9am-7:30pm Sat & Sun Jan-Jun) gives access to a spray-soaked viewing area beneath the falls.

    Casino Niagara (☎ 905-374-3598; 5705 Falls Ave) pales in comparison to upscale **Fallsview Casino Resort** (www.fallsviewcasinoresort.com) which has a mall of expensive shops and restaurants. Niagara on the Lake, 15km to the north, is a small town full of elegant B&Bs and a famous summertime theater festival.

    Virtually every major hotel chain has at least several locations on the Canadian side of the falls. Backpackers should head to the **HI Niagara Falls Hostel** (☎ 905-357-0770; www.hostellingniagara .com; 4549 Cataract Ave; dm US$25). **Skyline Inn** (☎ 800-263-7135; Falls Ave; r US$70; P) is a good choice if you're seeking a budget place away from the noise. River Rd is lined with B&Bs but **Chestnut Inn** (☎ 905-374-7623; www.chestnutinnbb.com; 4983 River Rd; r from $100;), a tastefully decorated colonial home with a wrap-around porch stands above the rest. Highly recommended **Old Stone Inn** (☎ 905-357-1234; www.oldstoneinn.on.ca; 5425 Robinson St; r from $140; P wi-fi) has elegant and modern rooms and a richly atmospheric restaurant. Parents looking to keep the kids occupied should head immediately to the **Great Wolf Lodge** (☎ 800-605-9653; www .greatwolf.com; 3950 Victoria Ave; suites from US$229; P wi-fi), whose centerpiece is an enormous indoor water park.

    Obvious tourist traps are a dime a dozen in and around Clifton Hill. American fare and chains dominate the culinary scene, but **Tandoor Hut** (☎ 905-356-3830; 5780 Ferry St; mains US$11; 10am-11pm) and the reasonably priced Japanese restaurant, **Yukiguni** (☎ 905-354-4440; 5980 Fallsview Blvd; mains US$13; 11:30am-11pm) are good ethnic options in the Fallsview area. The Lundy's Lane area has tons of cheap eats.

---

places. See boxed text, above for sleeping and eating information.

GETTING THERE & AROUND

From the **NFTA Terminal** (Niagara Frontier Transportation Authority; www.nfta.com; 4th & Niagara Sts), No 40 buses go to Buffalo ($2.25, one hour) for air and bus connections; and there is an extensive local bus service. The **Amtrak train station** (☎ 716-285-4224) is about 2 miles northeast of downtown. And from Niagara Falls, daily trains go to Buffalo, Toronto and New York City ($63, nine hours). The **Greyhound & Trailways terminal** (☎ 905-357-2133; 4555 Erie Ave) is on the Canada side.

Parking costs $3 to $10 a day on either side of the falls. Most of the midrange hotels offer complimentary parking to guests while upscale hotels tend to charge $10 to $20 a day for the privilege.

Crossing the Rainbow Bridge to Canada costs US$3/1 for cars/pedestrians. There are customs and immigration stations at each end – carry proper papers. Because the policy is in flux it's now recommended that US citizens have their passport available (see p1127).

Buffalo

This undeservedly maligned working class city does have long, cold winters and its fair share of abandoned industrial buildings but it also has a vibrant community of college students and 30-somethings living well in cheap real estate and gorging on this city's unique and tasty cuisine. When the General Mills factory on the Buffalo River is churning out Coco Puffs, downtown even sometimes smells like chocolate. Native local hero Ani DiFranco, who has chosen her hometown as the place to base her indie music label, is in the vanguard of an ongoing effort to revitalize this former booming terminus of the Erie Canal. Settled by the French in 1758 – its name is believed to derive from *beau fleuve* (beautiful river). Just an hour south of Niagara Falls, Buffalo is about an eight-hour trip from New York City.

The helpful **Buffalo Niagara Convention & Visitors Bureau** (☎ 716-852-0511; www.buffalocvb.org; 617

Main St) has good walking-tour pamphlets and a great website.

SIGHTS & ACTIVITIES

Architecture buffs will have a field day here, starting at the **Prudential Building** (28 Church St), designed by Louis Sullivan in 1895 as the Guaranty Building, which used an innovative steel-frame construction to create the first modern skyscraper. Be sure to glimpse the stunning art-deco **City Hall** (65 Niagara Sq), built in 1931, and the neo-Gothic **Old Post Office** (121 Ellicot St) from 1894. The **M&T Bank** (545 Main St) is topped with a gilded dome of 140,000 paper-thin sheets of 23.75-karat gold leaf. Six **Frank Lloyd Wright houses** are a highlight; the 1904 **Darwin Martin House** (☎ 716-856-3858125; Jewett Parkway) and neighboring **Barton House** (118 Summit Ave) are accessible by appointment. For details about local architecture check out www.walkbuffalo.org.

North of downtown, the sprawling Delaware Park was designed by Frederick Law Olmsted. Its jewel is the **Albright-Knox Art Gallery** (☎ 716-882-8700; www.albrightknox.org; 1285 Elmwood Ave; admission $10, 3-10pm Fri free; ☒ 10am-5pm Wed-Thu, Sat & Sun, to 10pm Fri), a sizable museum including some of the best French impressionists and American masters. Buffalo also has good science, history and children's museums and a fine zoo. The **Elmwood** neighborhood, stretching along Elmwood Ave between Allen St and Delaware Park, is dotted with hip cafés, restaurants, boutiques and bookstores. Hertle Ave in North Buffalo is an up-and-coming neighborhood with several good restaurants and cafés.

The **Theodore Roosevelt Inaugural National Historic Site** (☎ 716-884-0095; 641 Delaware Ave; admission $5; ☒ 9am-5pm Mon-Fri, from noon Sat & Sun) in the Ansley-Wilcox house is where you can learn the tale of Teddy's emergency swearing-in here following the assassination of William McKinley.

This is a hardcore sports town and locals live and die with the **NFL Buffalo Bills** (☎ 716-648-1800; www.buffalobills.com) football team and the **Buffalo Sabres** (☎ 716-855-4100; www.sabres.com), the city's NHL ice-hockey team.

SLEEPING

Standard chains line the highways around the city. Budget travelers can sleep at the **Hostelling International – Buffalo Niagara** (☎ 716-852-5222; www.hostelbuffalo.com; 667 Main St; dm $25, r $60;

☒ ⬚). The **Beau Fleuve** (☎ 800-278-0245; www.beaufleuve.com; 242 Linwood Ave; r $105-160; ☒) is a historic B&B in the Linwood neighborhood. Downtown has the **Adam's Mark Hotel** (☎ 716-845-5100; www.adamsmark.com; 120 Church St; r from $120; ☒ ⬚ wi-fi), the Hyatt Regency and Holiday Inn. For truly luxurious accommodation and flawless service, head to the very special and grand **Mansion on Delaware Avenue** (☎ 716-886-3300; www.mansionondelaware.com; 414 Delaware Ave; r with breakfast from $175; ☒ wi-fi).

EATING

Buffalo is curiously blessed with an abundance of unique, tasty and cheap eats. **Ted's** (☎ 716-834-6287; Sheridan Ave; hot dog $2; ☒ 10:30am-11pm Mon-Sun) fast food specialty is hot dogs, foot-longs, any way you like 'em. **Charlie the Butcher's** (☎ 716-633-8330; 1065 Wehrle St; beef on weck sandwich $5; ☒ 11am-4:30pm) is a specialist in beef-on-weck (sliced roast beef on a crispy German kaiser roll sprinkled with caraway seeds). **Jim's Steakout** (☎ 716-886-2222; 194 Allen St; sandwiches $7.50; ☒ 10:30am-5am) is known for its chicken finger sub ($7.30) and steak hoagies. For the famous deep-fried chicken wings covered in a spicy sauce, head to the landmark **Anchor Bar** (☎ 716-886-8920; 1047 Main St; 10 wings $9; ☒ 10am-11pm Mon-Thu, 10am-1am Fri-Sat; ☒), which claims credit for inventing the 'delicacy.' Locals in the know say **Duff's** (☎ 716-834-6234; 3651 Sheridan Dr, Amherst; 10 wings $8; ☒ 11am-11pm) wings are tastier. **Bob & John's** (☎ 716-836-5411; 1545 Hertel Ave; sandwich $5, chicken wings $8; ☒ 11am-11pm) serves beef-on-weck, buffalo wings and according to some, the best pizza in Buffalo.

For slightly more upscale eats try **Betty's** (☎ 716-362-0633; 370 Virginia St; mains $12; ☒ 8am-9pm Tue, 8am-10pm Wed-Fri, 9am-10pm Sat, 9am-3pm Sun) in the Allentown neighborhood which does interpretations of American comfort food; try the huge scrambled tofu hash ($7). Nearby is **Mother's Restaurant** (☎ 716-882-2989; 33 Virginia Pl; mains $14; ☒ 4pm-4am Mon-Sat, 2pm-4am Sun) where politicians and sport figures come to be seen.

DRINKING

Bars along Chippewa St (aka The Chip Strip) are open until 4am and cater primarily to the frat-boy crowd. More eclectic neighborhoods like Elmwood, Linwood and Allentown have more than their fair share of late night options. **Faherty's** (☎ 716-881-9183; Elmwood Ave) has a wide open layout and a good selection of beers. **Nietzches** (Allen St) is a legendary dive-bar and across the street a few storefronts down is **Old Pink** (Allen St), a dark, cavernous, grungy place – both have live music. Several gay bars are clustered around the south end of Elmwood, including **Fugazi** (☎ 716-881-3588; 503 Franklin St).

GETTING THERE & AROUND

Buffalo's **Niagara International Airport** (☎ 716-630-6000), about 16 miles east of downtown, is a regional hub. Jet Blue Airways has inexpensive round-trip fares from New York City (one hour, from around $140). Buses arrive and depart from the **Greyhound terminal** (☎ 716-855-7531; 181 Ellicott St). **NFTA** (☎ 716-285-9319) local bus No 40 goes to the transit center on the American side of Niagara Falls ($2.25). From the downtown **Amtrak train station** (☎ 716-856-2075; 75 Exchange St), you can catch trains to major cities.

NEW JERSEY

New Jersey gets a bad rap. While New Yorkers like to poke fun at it for being one big highway with some malls sprinkled in, it's actually a bit more complex than first meets the eye. The tiny state is both a quarter farmland and the most densely populated state in the USA. It's got 127 miles of beautiful beaches as well as two of New York's greatest icons: the Statue of Liberty and Ellis Island. And then there are the diverse, fair-minded people, who inhabit many culturally-rich towns and cities. Even the courts are progressive: a domestic partnership law went into effect in late 2006, making New Jersey one of only four states which allow same-sex partners to have rights that are equivalent to those of a marriage.

Its gay former mayor did not fare so well – but that had more to do with Jim McGreevey's lying, cheating ways (with both his wife and matters of the government) than with his scandalous coming-out on live TV. There's been no rest for the weary voters since he stepped down, either: just over a year after Governor Jon Corzine took office in 2006, he was severely injured in a car accident – and he wasn't wearing a seatbelt, which made him a scofflaw that no one was about to let off the hook. He turned it around, though, mocking himself in a pro-seatbelt public service announcement shortly after his recovery. That's NJ for you: dichotomous, quirky and strong willed.

Lots of great malls, too.

History

The state's original residents were called *lenni lenape* (original people), and probably numbered less than 20,000 when European settlers arrived in the early 17th century. More wipeouts came during the Revolutionary War, when New Jersey saw many battles, but the population grew from 15,000 in 1700 to more than 185,000 by 1795, when industry boomed. After WWII, Newark and Jersey City saw influxes of immigrants and by the mid-1980s New Jersey had some of the country's fastest-growing metropolitan areas – a trend that still continues.

Information

Find statewide tips on sights, accommodations and festivals through the **New Jersey Tourism Commission** (☎ 800-847-4865; www.visitnj.org).

The major newspapers of record in New Jersey are the *Newark Star-Ledger* (www.nj.com/news/ledger), the *Asbury Park Press* (www.app.com) and the *Jersey Journal* (www.nj.com/jjournal). The website **www.nj.com** has statewide news from all the major dailies.

Though NJ is made up folks who love their cars, there are other transportation options: **New Jersey Transit** (www.njtransit.com) operates buses out of NYC's Port Authority and trains out of its Penn Station. The **New Jersey PATH train** (see p177) goes to northern New Jersey, as do the ferries of **New York Waterway** (☎ 800-337-7437; www.nywaterway.com).

NORTHERN NEW JERSEY

Stay east and you'll experience the Jersey urban jungle. Go west to find its opposite: the peaceful, refreshing landscape of the Delaware Water Gap and rolling Kittatinny mountains.

Hoboken & Jersey City

A sort of TV-land version of a cityscape, Hoboken is a cute little urban pocket just across the Hudson River from NYC – and, because of cheaper rents that lured pioneers over at least a decade ago, a sort of sixth city borough, too. It's no longer cheapo – a slick W Hotel set to open here in 2008 is just one of the many signs – but it's still a fun place for a jaunt. On weekends the bars and live-music venues come alive – especially the legendary **Maxwell's** (☎ 201-653-1703; 1039 Washington St), which has featured up-and-coming rock bands since 1978. But the town also has some lovely residential streets and a leafy, revitalized waterfront – a far cry from when the gritty *On the Waterfront* was filmed here. The **Hoboken Historical Museum** (☎ 201-656-2240; www.hobokenmuseum.org; 1301 Hudson St; admission free; ☽ 2-9pm Tue-Thu, 1-5pm Fri, from noon Sat & Sun) gives a great overview.

Fast-gentrifying **Jersey City** (www.destination jerseycity.com) has also been swelling with New York escapees seeking lower rents. But its biggest draw is the 1200-acre **Liberty State Park** (☎ 201-915-3403; www.libertystatepark.org; ☽ 6am-10pm), which hosts outdoor concerts with the Manhattan skyline as a backdrop and has a great bike trail, and also operates **ferries** to Ellis Island and the **Statue of Liberty** (adult/child $10/8). Also in the park is the recently expanded **Liberty Science Center** (☎ 201-200-1000; www.lsc.org; adult $12-18.50, child $9-16.50, extra for IMAX & special exhibits; ☽ 9:30am-5:30pm), which is especially great for kids.

Newark & Around

Though many NYC-bound travelers fly into Newark International Airport, few stick around to see the city they've landed in. Too bad, since **Newark** (www.gonewark.com) – long mired in images of the 1960s race riots that made it off-limits to many for so long – has been in the midst of a renaissance for years now, even more so since its young rabble-rousing mayor, Cory Booker, took office in 2006.

Many are drawn here to experience the thriving Portuguese culture of the **Ironbound District**; whose restaurant-lined Ferry St lies right outside of the city's neoclassic **Penn Station** (accessible from NYC's same-named station via NJ Transit). Also not far from here is the **Newark Museum** (☎ 973-596-6550; www .newarkmuseum.org; 49 Washington St; suggested donation $7; ☽ noon-5pm Wed-Fri, 10am-5pm Sat-Sun Oct-Jun, noon-5pm Sat-Sun Jul-Sep), which has a renowned Tibetan Collection and hosts the annual Newark Black Film Festival in June. The **New Jersey Performing Arts Center** (☽ 973-642-0404; www.njpac.org; 1 Center St) is the city's crowning jewel, hosting national orchestras, operas, dance, cabaret, theater, jazz and world-music concerts. And the new **Prudential Center**, which opened in late 2007 and has quickly become the new star in town, hosting the New Jersey Devils hockey team, plus basketball games and concerts.

Other attractions include the grand **Cathedral Basilica of the Sacred Hearts** (☎ 973-484-4600; www.cathedralbasilica.org; 89 Ridge St) and the 400-acre Frederick Law Olmstead-designed **Branch Brook Park**, with some 2700 cherry trees that blossom in April.

Delaware Water Gap

The Delaware River meanders in a tight S-curve through the ridge of NJ's Kittatinny Mountain, and its beauteous image turned this region into a resort area beginning in the 19th century. The **Delaware Water Gap National Recreation Area** (☎ 908-496-4458; www.nps .gov/dewa), which comprises land in both New Jersey and Pennsylvania, was established as a protected area in 1965, and today it's still an unspoiled place to swim, boat, fish, camp, hike and see wildlife – just 70 miles east of New York City.

The 3348-acre **Kittatinny Valley State Park** (☎ 973-786-6445; www.state.nj.us/dep) is home to lakes with boat launches, lime outcroppings and campsites, plus former railroads that have been converted into hiking and biking trails. **High Point State Park** (☎ 973-875-4700), also great for camping and hiking, has a monument which, at 1803 feet above sea level, affords wonderful views of surrounding lakes, hills and farmland.

On your way to the outdoors, stop in the otherwise missable town of Paramus to find one of the best gear stores around: **Campmor** (☎ 201-445-5000; www.campmor.com; 810 Rte 17; ☽ 9:30am-9:30pm Mon-Fri, till 7:30pm Sun), a sprawling retail space filled with every backpack, tent, sleeping bag and hiking shoe you'd ever want. Prices are good, too.

NEW JERSEY FACTS

Nickname Garden State
Population 8.7 million
Area 8722 sq miles
Capital city Trenton (population 84,639)
Sales tax 7%
Birthplace of Count Basie (1904–84), Frank Sinatra (1915–98), Meryl Streep (b 1949), Bruce Springsteen (b 1949), Queen Latifah (b 1970)
Home of The first movie (1889), first professional baseball game (1896), first drive-in theater (1933), the Statue of Liberty
Famous for The Jersey Shore, the setting for *The Sopranos*, Bruce Springsteen's musical beginnings
Official state bug Honeybee

CENTRAL NEW JERSEY

Otherwise known as the armpit (only for how it looks on a map, of course), this region is home to the state capital, Trenton, and a string of beautiful, wealthy communities including Princeton, at the eastern border of Pennsylvania.

Princeton & Around

Settled by an English Quaker missionary, the tiny town of **Princeton** (www.visitprinceton.org) is a place filled with lovely architecture and several noteworthy sites, number one of which is its Ivy League **Princeton University** (www.princeton .edu), which was built in the mid-1700s and soon became one of the largest structures in the early colonies. The town's **Palmer Square**, built in 1936, is a lovely place to shop and stroll. The **Historical Society of Princeton** (☎ 609-921-6748; www.princetonhistory.org; 158 Nassau St; tours $20) leads historical walking tours of the town and the **Orange Key Guide Service & Campus Information Office** (☎ 609-258-3603; www.princeton.edu/orangekey) offers free university tours.

Accommodations are expensive and hard to find during graduation time in May and June, but beyond that, it should be easy to arrange for a stay at one of several atmospheric inns. The **Inn at Glencairn** (☎ 609-497-1737; www.innatglen cairn.com; 3301 Lawrenceville Rd; r from $195; P ⊠ 🐾 wi-fi) is a recently renovated Georgian Manor with old-world style and modern amenities.

Trenton

It may not be the most beautiful place, but New Jersey's capital **Trenton** (www.trentonnj.com) has several historic sites worth stopping in on – especially if you can pair it up with a trip to Philly or Atlantic City.

You can tour the grand **New Jersey Statehouse** (☎ 609-633-2709; 125 West State St; free; ⏰ 10am-3pm Mon-Fri, from noon Sat) and visit the **Old Barracks Museum** (☎ 609-396-1776; www.barracks.org; Barrack St; admission $8; ⏰ 10am-5pm), built in 1758 and now the state's last remaining barracks from the French and Indian War. The **New Jersey State Museum** (☎ 609-292-6464; www.state.nj.us/state /museum; 205 W State St; admission free; ⏰ 9am-4:45pm Tue-Fri, 9am-4pm Sat), with a planetarium, is home to diverse collections from fossils to fine art. The massive **Trenton Farmers Market** (☎ 609-695-2998; www.thetrentonfarmersmarket.com; 960 Spruce St, ⏰ 9am-6pm Tue-Sat, 10am-4pm Sun, May-Sep) has vendors hawking fresh produce, baked goods and crafts.

JERSEY SHORE

Perhaps the most famous and revered feature of New Jersey is its sparkling shore, stretching from Sandy Hook to Cape May and studded with resort towns from the tacky to the sublime, with plenty of dining options for seafood fans. Towns get mobbed during summer weekends, but, come early fall, you could find yourself wonderfully alone on the sand.

Sandy Hook & Red Bank

At the northernmost tip of the Jersey shore is the **Sandy Hook Gateway National Recreation Area** (☎ 732-872-5970; www.nps.gov/gate; $10 per car 10am-4pm Memorial Day through Labor Day; ⏰ dawn-dusk), a 6-mile-long sandy barrier beach at the entrance to New York Harbor (and you can see the city skyline from your beach blanket on clear days). The ocean side of the peninsula has wide, sandy **beaches** (including a nude area at Gunnison Beach) edged by an extensive system of bike trails, while the bay side is great for fishing or wading. The brick buildings of the abandoned coastguard station, **Fort Hancock**, sits eerily empty (though it's been targeted for a controversial development project), its hulls open for quiet exploration. The **Sandy Hook Lighthouse**, which offers guided tours, is the oldest in the country.

The town next door, the **Highlands**, has seafood restaurants on the water, offering a great end to your day before hopping the **Seastreak** (☎ 800-2628-7433; www.seastreak.com; return $30), a fast ferry service that runs between here and NYC. It's also home to the **Twin Lights Historic Site** (☎ 732-872-1814; ⏰ 10am-5pm) and a swank new hotel, the **Blue Bay Inn** (☎ 732-708-7600; www.blue bayinn.com; 51 First Ave; r $159-299; P ⊠ 🐾 🖵).

About 10 miles inland is the artsy town of **Red Bank**, with a hoppin' main strip of hipster shops, galleries and cafés, plus a sizable Mexican population (and plenty of authentic Mexican-food eateries. New Jersey Transit stops here.

Asbury Park & Ocean Grove

Asbury Park experienced passing prominence in the 1970s when Bruce Springsteen 'arrived' at the **Stone Pony** (☎ 732-502-0600; 913 Ocean Ave) nightclub, which is still offering live music. After that, the town went through a major decline, followed by a recent and still-in-progress comeback – led by wealthy gay men from NYC who snapped up blocks of forgotten Victorian homes and storefronts to refurbish. Now there are a number of luxury condos in the works, and though the place still has a very unfinished quality to it (and rough pockets that should be avoided), there's still plenty to enjoy (especially if you're a gay man). The sprawling **Antique Emporium of Asbury Park** (☎ 732-774-8230; Cookman Ave) has two levels of amazing finds, while **Bistro Olé** (☎ 732-897-0048; www.bistroole.com; 230 Main St; mains $12-20; ☺ 5-9pm Mon-Thu & Sun, 5-10pm Fri-Sat), serving Spanish-influenced fare, and **Moonstruck** (☎ 732-988-0123; www.moonstrucknj.com; 517 Lake Ave; mains $17-25; ☺ 4-10pm Wed, Thu, Sun, till 11pm Sat), with eclectic Italian fare, are total scenes. The boardwalk is a lovely place for an afternoon stroll.

The town immediately to the south, **Ocean Grove**, is a fascinating place to wander. Founded by Methodists in the 19th century, the place retains what's left of a post–Civil War **Tent City** revival camp – now a historic site with 114 cottage-like canvas tents clustered together and used for summer homes. The town has well-preserved Victorian architecture and a 6500-seat wooden auditorium, and there are many beautiful, big-porched **Victorian inns** to choose from for a stay; visit www.oceangrovenj.com for guidance.

Monmouth County Beaches

In between Sandy Hook and Asbury Park sits the town of **Long Branch** – a place of fast-fading glory since the 1980s, but one which has experienced a bit of a renaissance lately. Though its elegance is gone, a new, mall-like food-and-shopping complex by the ocean called Pier Village (www.piervillage.com) packs 'em in for everything from Greek dinners to swimwear shopping. Just a bit inland from here is the famed **Monmouth Park Race Track** (☎ 732-222-5100; www.monmouthpark.com; $2; 11:30am-6pm May-Oct), where you can see thoroughbred racing in a gracious, historic setting.

Belmar (www.belmar.com) has beautiful beaches, a spirited boardwalk with some arcade games, and beachfront food shacks that can get mobbed when the bars close at 2am. Next-door **Bradley Beach** (www.bradleybeachonline.com) is its quiet, peaceful sister with row after row of adorable summer cottages and a beautiful stretch of shore, and **Spring Lake** (www.springlake.org) is a classy community once known as the 'Irish Riviera,' with lush gardens, Victorian houses, gorgeous beaches and elegant accommodations. One of the best is the **Chateau Inn and Suites** (☎ 732-974-2000; www.chateauinn.com; 500 Warren Ave; r $199-329).

Ocean County Beaches

Kids will love nearby **Point Pleasant** (www.pointpleasantbeach.com), home to **Jenkinson's Boardwalk** (☎ 732-892-0600; www.jenkinsons.com; packages adult/child $16/12.50), with an aquarium, rides, arcade games, funhouse, miniature golf and dining options.

Just below there, the narrow **Barnegat Peninsula** barrier island extends some 22 miles south from Point Pleasant. In its center, **Seaside Heights** sucks in the wild 20-something summer crowds with beaches, boardwalks, bars, arcades and two amusement piers. Occupying the southern third of Barnegat Peninsula is **Island Beach State Park** (☎ 732-793-0506; per car weekday/weekend $6/10), a 10-mile barrier island that's pure, untouched dunes and wetlands with many **naturalist-led programs** (☎ 732-793-1698 to register). **Long Beach Island** (☎ 609-361-1000; www.longbeachisland.com) is south of here, with beautiful beaches balanced by a string of summer homes, eateries and bars. The latest overnight hot spot is **Daddy O** (☎ 609-361-5100; www.daddyohotel.com; 4401 Long Beach Blvd; $195-375; Ⓟ ⓧ ⓧ wi-fi), a sleek boutique hotel and restaurant near the ocean.

SOUTH JERSEY

A mixture of kitsch and country, the state's southern region – closely identified with neighboring Philadelphia – represents the best of New Jersey's extremes.

Pine Barrens

Locals call this region the Pinelands – and like to carry on the lore about the one million acres of pine forest being home to a mythical beast known as the 'Jersey Devil.' It's also widely known as the place where Tony Soprano and his cohorts like to dump bodies. But this protected area is truly more serene than scary. The land contains several state parks and forests, and is a haven for bird-watchers, hikers, campers, canoeists and all-round nature enthusiasts. A good outfitter is **Pine Barrens Canoe Rental** (☎ 609-726-1515; www.pinebarrenscanoe.com; 3260 Route 563; kayak $37, canoe $48), which has maps and other details about all trips in the area. The **Wharton State Forest** (☎ 609-561-0024) is one good place to canoe – as well as hike and picnic – and the 40,000-acre **Edwin B Forsythe National Wildlife Refuge** (☎ 609-652-1665; www.fws.gov/northeast/forsythe) is paradise for bird-watchers.

Nestled within the Pine Barrens region is the quirky **Historic Village at Allaire** (☎ 732-919-3500; www.allairevillage.org; adult/child $3/2; ☼ noon-4pm, weekends only May-Oct), the remains of what was a thriving 19th-century village called Howell Works. You can still visit the blacksmith and tinsmith shops, the foreman's cottage, the slaughterhouse and the general store, all run by folks in period costume.

Atlantic City

'AC,' as locals call it, has been on some roller coaster ride since 1977. That's when the state approved gambling casinos in the hope of revitalizing this fast-fading resort town – known throughout the late 19th and early 20th century for its grand boardwalk and Ocean Pier, the world's first oceanside amusement pier, and later as the inspiration for Monopoly's game board. And while the sudden influx of hotel-casinos has lined the pockets of those in the biz (including the infamous Donald Trump), it hasn't necessarily done much for the rest of the town, still mired in poverty in many areas. The 2006 loss of the Miss America Pageant – hosted in Atlantic City's convention hall since 1921 – was just the latest blow to folks here.

Luckily, things have begun to shift for visitors in recent years, mainly because one new hotel-casino, the Borgata, has brought new glitz and glamour here, causing more bright spots – including a slew of nightclubs and a spiffy new shopping mall, the **Pier at Caesars** (www.thepiershopsatcaesars.com), jutting out into the Atlantic – to follow. Things are definitely looking up. And a trip here is worth it for anyone interested in a truly complex American snapshot – with some casino fun, to boot.

ORIENTATION & INFORMATION

The **Atlantic City Convention & Visitors Bureau** (☎ 609-449-7130; www.atlanticcitynj.com; Atlantic City Expressway; ☼ 9am-5pm), under the giant teepee in the middle of the Atlantic City Expressway, with another location right on the boardwalk at Mississippi Ave, can provide you with maps and accommodations deals. *Atlantic City Weekly* (www.acweekly.com) has useful info on events, clubs and eateries. The small **Atlantic City Historical Museum** (☎ 609-347-5839; cnr Boardwalk & New Jersey Aves; admission free) provides a quirky look at AC's past.

SLEEPING & EATING

The only truly destination-worthy hotel at this point is the **Borgata** (☎ 866-69267-4282; www.theborgata.com; r $149-400; P ☒ ☒ wi-fi), with high-style rooms, a full-service spa, major concert hall, four five-star restaurants and, of course, a grand casino with a pretty classy crowd. Not to be outdone, though, good ol' **Harrah's Atlantic City** (☎ 609-441-5000; www.harrahs.com; 777 Harrah's Blvd; r $149-349) is undergoing a $550 million expansion project, and the summer of 2007 saw the first of its dazzling updates: the new Elizabeth Arden Red Door Spa, plus a massive glass-domed pool that shares space with Jacuzzis, cabanas, a pool bar and deck-lounge areas that will host activities from luaus to poolside spa treatments. Note that the cheapest rates at all AC hotels will be found on weekdays.

The best in-casino dining is to be had at the Borgata, home to Specchio (Italian), Bobby Flay Steak and N.O.W. (Asian noodle bar), among other top choices, but good (and more affordable) food can be found in the 'real' part of downtown, too. **Mexico Lindo** (☎ 609-345-1880; 2435 Atlantic Ave; dishes $5-12; ☼ 8am-10pm) is a favorite among Mexican locals and serves big, cheap breakfasts – as does **Hannah G's** (☎ 609-823-1466; 7310 Ventnor Ave; dishes $6-10; ☼ 7am-2pm Mon-Sun), a family-owned, excellent breakfast and lunch spot in nearby Ventnor.

DRINKING & ENTERTAINMENT

It's the **casinos**, as you may have guessed, that are the biggest draw here. As in Las Vegas, they all have themes – Far East, Ancient Rome, Wild West – but they're superficially done. Inside they're all basically the same – clanging, flashing and non-stop, with no outside light creeping in to remind you that sunset has long come and gone while you've been planted firmly in front of the slot machines or tables for blackjack, poker, baccarat or craps.

Beyond the casino walls you'll find the wide, oceanfront **boardwalk**, the first in the world. Enjoy a walk or a hand-pushed rolling-chair ride ($25) and drop in on one of several boardwalk clubs and lounges, like **Blue Martini** (☎ 609-340-2709; Bally's, Park Place at the Boardwalk), **The Continental** (☎ 609-674-8300; the Pier at Caesars) or the new **Liquid Bar** (lobby of Trump Plaza, Boardwalk at Mississippi Ave).

You're spoiled for choice when it comes to live music, too. Check out the calendar at the **Borgata** (see above), which has a comedy club,

---

WHAT THE...?

Drive around the beach communities just south of Atlantic City and something massive, gray and kitsch will stop you in your tracks: **Lucy the Margate Elephant** (☎ 609-823-6473; www.lucytheelephant .org; Atlantic Ave, Margate, NJ; tour $5; ☺ 11am-4pm Mon-Fri, 10am-5pm Sat-Sun), a 65ft-high wooden pachyderm constructed in 1881 as a developer's truly weird scheme to attract land buyers to the area. The interior is divided into rooms – it was actually leased as a summer home in 1902 – and was used for a short time as a tavern, but rowdy patrons almost destroyed her. Now recognized on the National Register of Historic Places, Lucy is open daily in summertime for tours, which start every half hour.

---

an intimate concert hall and a massive music venue that's hosted Mary J Blige, Bob Dylan, Stevie Wonder and Diana Krall. And then there's the venerable **House of Blues** (☎ 609-236-2583; www.hob.com; 801 Boardwalk at the Showboat), home to various bars, a restaurant and a plush music hall where Steppenwolf, Eddie Griffin and Taylor Hicks have headlined recently.

GETTING THERE & AWAY

The small **Atlantic City 'International' Airport** (☎ 800-645-7895) is a 20-minute drive from the center of Atlantic City, and a great option for reaching any part of South Jersey or Philadelphia.

There are many bus options to AC, including NJ Transit (round-trip $28) and Greyhound (round-trip $31), both leaving from New York's Port Authority, and **Capitol Trailways** (www.capitoltrailways.com; round-trip $34-36), from points in Pennsylvania. A casino will often refund the fare (in chips, coins or coupons) if you get a bus directly to its door.

New Jersey Transit (☎ 973-762-5100, 800-772-2222; www.njtransit.com) trains only go to Atlantic City from Philadelphia ($8 one-way)

The Wildwoods & Ocean City

South of Atlantic City, the three towns of **North Wildwood**, **Wildwood** and **Wildwood Crest** are an archaeological find – whitewashed motels with flashing neon signs, turquoise curtains and pink doors, especially in Wildwood Crest, a kitsch slice of 1950s Americana. Wildwood, a party town popular with teens and young overseas visitors, is the main social focus. The **Greater Wildwood Chamber of Commerce** (☎ 609-729-4000; www.gwcoc.com; 3306 Pacific Ave, Wildwood) hands out information on self-guided tours around the 'doo-wop' motels. The beach is free, and the 2-mile-long boardwalk has several piers that are host to roller coasters, Ferris wheels and weekly fireworks displays

in summer. About 250 motels offer rooms for $50 to $200, making it a good option if Cape May is booked out.

Ocean City (www.oceancityvacation.com), meanwhile, is a truly kitsch and old-fashioned family holiday spot, home to duneswept beaches and a dizzying amount of kid-centric arcades and themed playlands, including **Playland's Castaway Cove** (☎ 609-399-4751; www.boardwalkfun.com; 10th St and Boardwalk; $1; ☺ noon-5pm summer), a faux pirate ship sporting bumper cars, a tilt-a-whirl and various other head-spinning rides. Motels are plentiful, cheap (average $65 a night) and old-fashioned, as are the myriad crab shacks and seafood joints.

Cape May

Founded in 1620, Cape May – the only place in the state where the sun both rises and sets over the water – is on the state's southern tip and is the country's oldest seashore resort. Its sweeping beaches get crowded in summer, but the stunning Victorian architecture is attractive year-round. Contact the **Cape May County Chamber of Commerce** (www.cmccofc.com) for details about the area.

In addition to 600 gingerbread-style houses, the city boasts antique shops and places for whale- and bird-watching, and is just outside of **Cape May Point State Park** (☎ 609-884-2159) and its 157ft **Cape May Lighthouse** (☎ 609-884-5404; admission $5). The sandy **beach** (day/week/season $5/10/15) is the main attraction in summer months.

Cape May's B&B options are endless, with the majority leaning toward the froofy end of the design spectrum. The classic, sprawling **Congress Hall** (☎ 609-884-8422; www.congresshall.com; 251 Beach Ave; r $100-465; P X X □) has a range of beautiful quarters for various budgets, plus there's a cool restaurant and bar onsite.

The tiny, eclectic **Louisa's Café** (☎ 609-884-5884; 104 Jackson St; dishes $14-23; ☺ 5-9pm Tue-Sat in summer,

Fri-Sat in fall) is the town's prize midrange eatery, and upscale diners should reserve a table at the award-winning **Ebbitt Room** (☎ 609-884-5700; 25 Jackson St; dishes $20-27; ☺ 5-11pm) in the posh Virginia Hotel.

PENNSYLVANIA

Home to the nation's original capital, Philadelphia, as well as towns and landscapes varied enough to make this massive state feel like its own country, Pennsylvania is the perfect place to get a big taste of what America's all about. Its historic sites alone – Philly's Independence Park, battle sites like Gettysburg and Valley Forge – offer a wonderful, basic understanding of the USA. But the additional aspects, both artistic and nature-based, satiate in endless other, often surprising, ways. Did you know, for example, that Philadelphia, birthplace of actor John Barrymore, is home to a thriving theater scene that's often the testing ground for Broadway-bound productions? Or that Pittsburgh, Andy Warhol's hometown, has the only Warhol museum in the country? Pennsylvania is also where you'll find artistic gems like Frank Lloyd Wright's Fallingwater, and quirky, artsy towns such as Easton, Jim Thorpe and Milford, a mint-condition Poconos gem that's been attracting New Yorkers in search of fabulous weekend homes. And then there are the majestic natural wonders – like the Allegheny National Forest, the stunning shores of Lake Erie, the glistening banks of the Schuylkill River – that really make this land shine.

History

In 1681 William Penn, a Quaker, founded his colony as a 'holy experiment' that respected religious freedom, liberal government and even indigenous inhabitants. But it didn't take long for European settlers to displace those communities, thus giving rise to Pennsylvania's status as the richest and most populous British colony in North America. It became a great influence in the independence movement and, much later, an economic leader through its major supply of coal, iron and timber, followed by raw materials and labor during WWI and WWII. In the postwar period its industrial importance gradually declined. Urban renewal programs and the growth of service and high-tech industries have boosted the economy, most notably in Philadelphia and Pittsburgh.

Quakers founded Pennsylvania on the principle of religious tolerance – a stance that attracted other minority religious sects, including the well-known Mennonite and Amish communities – and an accepting attitude still prevails in most of the state. The current governor, Edward Rendell, is a moderate Democrat.

Information

Pennsylvania Travel and Tourism (☎ 800-847-4872; www.visitpa.com) The official tourism department has a comprehensive website featuring maps, videos and suggested itineraries. It also operates 15 welcome centers scattered around the state's borders, stocked with maps, guides, regional info and well-informed staffers.

PHILADELPHIA

Located just 90 miles from New York City, Philadelphia has long lived in Gotham's overwhelming shadow. It existed as a sort of historic stage set, great for school trips to the Liberty Bell followed by lunches of Philly cheese steaks, but not much else worth traveling for, right? Wrong. In the late 1990s, then-mayor Ed Rendell (now Pennsylvania's governor), picked Philly up by its lapels and shook it, infusing it with self-confidence, and current Mayor John Street has continued in that vein by revitalizing blighted neighborhoods and introducing Wireless Philadelphia, an initiative that would create the first city to be totally wired. Experience the Philadelphia

---

PENNSYLVANIA FACTS

Nicknames Keystone State, Quaker State
Population 12.3 million
Area 46,058 sq miles
Capital city Harrisburg (population 47,472)
Sales tax 6%
Birthplace of Louisa May Alcott (1832–88), Martha Graham (1878–1948), Andy Warhol (1928–87), Grace Kelly (1929–82), Bill Cosby (b 1937)
Home of US Constitution, the Liberty Bell, first daily newspaper (1784), first auto service station (1913), first computer (1946)
Famous for Soft pretzels, Amish people, Philadelphia cheesesteak, Pittsburgh steel mills
Animal celebrity Punxsutawney Phil (of Groundhog Day)

DON'T MISS

- **Independence National Historic Park** (opposite) Home of the Liberty Bell and other historic sites.
- **Italian Market** (p208) It's a feast for the eyes – and stomach.
- **Fairmount Park** (p205) Philly's massive green oasis.
- **Society Hill** (p203) A bucolic residential 'hood.
- **Old City** (p202) History, quaintness, funky shops.
- **Philadelphia Museum of Art** (p203) The famous *Rocky* stairs (and world-class art).
- **Reading Terminal Market** (p208) Eat yourself silly – for a song.

renaissance by strolling through a series of spiffed-up neighborhoods, exploring glorious Fairmount Park, catching a play or symphony or a night of live music or clubbing. Oh – and, while you're at it, get a major dose of history, too.

History

William Penn made Philadelphia his capital in 1682, basing its plan on a grid with wide streets and public squares – a layout copied by many US cities. For a time the second-largest city in the British Empire (after London), Philadelphia became a center for opposition to British colonial policy. It was the new nation's capital at the start of the Revolutionary War and again after the war until 1790, when Washington, DC, took over. By the 19th century New York City had superseded Philadelphia as the nation's cultural, commercial and industrial center.

Orientation & Information

Philadelphia is easy to navigate. Most sights and accommodations are within walking distance of each other, or a short bus ride away. East–west streets are named; north–south streets are numbered, except for Broad and Front Sts.

Historic Philadelphia includes Independence National Historic Park and Old City, which extends east to the waterfront. West of the historic district is Center City, home

to Penn Sq and City Hall. The Delaware and Schuylkill (*skoo*-kill) rivers border South Philadelphia, which features the colorful Italian Market, restaurants and bars. West of the Schuylkill, University City has two important campuses as well as a major museum. Northwest Philadelphia includes the genteel suburbs of Chestnut Hill and Germantown, plus the hip and growing Manayunk, with plenty of bustling pubs and eateries. The South St area, between S 2nd, 10th, Pine and Fitzwater Sts, has bohemian boutiques, bars, eateries and music venues.

BOOKSTORES
Giovanni's Room (☎ 215-923-2960; 345 S 12th St) Gay and lesbian books and periodicals.
House of Our Own (☎ 215-222-1576; 3920 Spruce St) Used books, small-press publications and frequent readings.
Joseph Fox (☎ 215-563-4184; 1724 Sansom St) Good selection of architecture, design and children's books.
Robin's Bookstore (☎ 215-735-9600; 108 S 13th St) Philly's oldest independent bookstore, featuring a large African American studies section.

EMERGENCY
Philadelphia Suicide & Crisis Center (☎ 215-686-4420)
Rape Crisis Center (☎ 215-985-3333)
Traveler's Aid Society (☎ 215-523-7580; www
.travelersaid.org; 1201 Chestnut St, 12th fl) A nonprofit agency that helps with anything from stolen wallets to emergency shelter.

INTERNET ACCESS
Wireless Philadelphia is still in the planning stages, so for now you may have to pay to surf on your laptop; internet cafés charge about $10 an hour and most hotels have free access.
Central Library (☎ 215-686-5322; 1901 Vine St) Free internet access.
Intermezzo Café & Lounge (☎ 215-222-4300; 3131 Walnut St) University City café with 15 free, high-speed hook-up ports.
Philadelphia Java Co (☎ 215-928-1811; 518 S 4th St; wi-fi per hr $2).

INTERNET RESOURCES
Maneo (www.maneo.com) Philly's site for the nightlife-happy, with guest lists, DJ info and more.
Philadelphia Citysearch (www.philadelphia.citysearch .com) Restaurant, bar, club hotel and shopping listings.
Philly.com (www.philly.com) News, listings and more, courtesy of the *Philadelphia Inquirer*.

MEDIA

City Paper (www.citypaper.net) Free weekly available at street boxes around town.

HX Philadelphia (www.myspace.com/hxphilly) Free gay weekly with nightlife and culture listings, available at nightspots and Giovanni's Room (see Bookstores, p198).

Philadelphia Daily News (www.philly.com/dailynews) A tabloid-style daily.

Philadelphia Inquirer (www.philly.com/mld/inquirer) The region's top daily newspaper.

Philadelphia Magazine (www.phillymag.com) A monthly glossy.

Philadelphia Weekly (www.philadelphiaweekly.com) Free alternative weekly available at street boxes around town.

WHYY 91-FM (www.whyy.org) Local National Public Radio affiliate.

MEDICAL SERVICES

CVS (☎ 215-465-2130; 10th at Reed St; ☼ 24hr) Pharmacy in South Philadelphia; call for other locations.

Graduate Hospital (☎ 215-893-2350; 1800 Lombard St) Close to the business district.

Pennsylvania Hospital (☎ 215-829-3000; www.uphs .upenn.edu/pahosp; 8th & Spruce Sts)

MONEY

ATMs are found everywhere, especially at banks and convenience stores. Most ATMs charge a service fee of $2.50 or so per transaction, unless you are using the bank that issued your particular card.

There are exchange bureaus in every terminal of the Philadelphia International Airport, though the best rates are at banks in the city. Most banks are open 10am to 5pm Monday to Thursday, until 6pm Friday, and sometimes for a few hours on Saturday morning. Other exchange options:

American Express Travel Service (☎ 215-587-2300; 1600 JFK Blvd)

Thomas Cook (☎ 215-563-7348; 1800 JFK Blvd)

POST

B Free Franklin Post Office (☎ 215-592-1289; 316 Market St; ☼ 9am-5pm Mon-Fri) Postmarks stamps with Franklin's signature.

Philadelphia Main Post Office (☎ 215-895-8000; 2970 Market St; ☼ 6am-midnight) Impressively old and massive, occupying several city blocks; call for other branch locations.

TOURIST INFORMATION

Greater Philadelphia Tourism Marketing Corporation (www.gophila.com; 6th St at Market St) The highly developed, nonprofit visitors bureau has information about tours, attractions, hotels, package deals, special events, and gay and lesbian tourism. Its welcome center shares space with the National Park Service center.

Independence Visitor Center (☎ 215-636-1666; 6th St at Market St; ☼ 8:30am-5:30pm) Run by the National Park Service, the center distributes useful visitor guides and maps, plus sells tickets for the various official tours that depart from nearby locations, including Trolley Works & 76 Carriage Company (see p206). Staff members are helpful and knowledgeable.

Sights & Activities

While most of Philly's better-known historic sites are concentrated in the Independence National Historic Park, there's much of interest in just about every other neighborhood, too. The Old City and farther-afield Germantown are rich with history, Center City is bursting with arts and culture, South Philadelphia is home to the Italian Market, and University City, across the Schuylkill River, feels like an entirely separate college town. Manayunk, away from the city center, is a hip strip of eateries, shops and lounges.

INDEPENDENCE NATIONAL HISTORIC PARK

This L-shaped 45-acre **park** (www.nps.gov/inde), along with Old City, has been dubbed 'America's most historic square mile.' Once the backbone of the United States government, today it is the backbone of Philadelphia's tourist trade. Stroll around and you'll see storied buildings in which the seeds for the Revolutionary War were planted and the US government came into bloom. You'll also find beautiful, shaded urban lawns dotted with large groups of school children, costumed actors – and mounds of construction-zone dirt: park renovation began in 2003 with the relocation of the Liberty Bell into its own little building and has dragged on ever since. But it's expected to be completely finished, landscaping and all, by summer of 2008. Most sites are open every day from 9am to 5pm, and some are closed Monday. Note that you must call or stop in to the **Independence Visitor Center** (see left) to make a timed reservation before visiting the high-volume Independence Hall, and beware that lines for the Liberty Bell can be extremely long.

Liberty Bell Center (☎ 215-597-8974; 6th & Market Sts) is Philadelphia's top tourist attraction, commissioned to commemorate the 50th anniversary of the Charter of Privileges

PHILADELPHIA

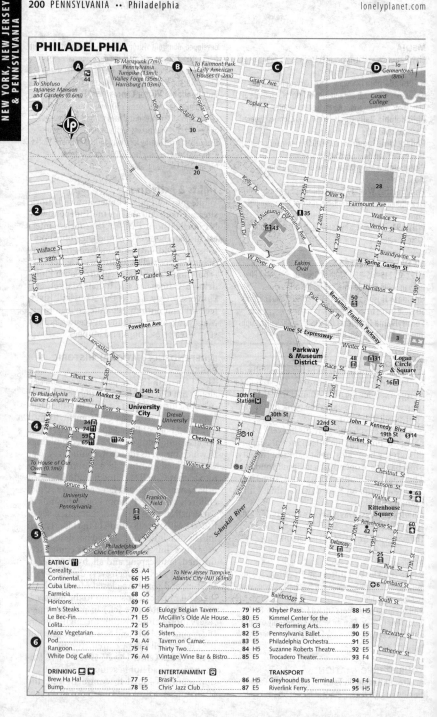

EATING 🍴

Cereality	65	A4
Continental	66	H5
Cuba Libre	67	H5
Farmicia	68	G5
Horizons	69	F6
Jim's Steaks	70	G6
Le Bec-Fin	71	E5
Lolita	72	E5
Maoz Vegetarian	73	G6
Pod	74	A4
Rangoon	75	F4
White Dog Café	76	A4

DRINKING 🍷 🍸

Brew Ha Ha!	77	F5
Bump	78	E5

Eulogy Belgian Tavern	79	H5
McGillin's Olde Ale House	80	E5
Shampoo	81	G3
Sisters	82	E5
Tavern on Camac	83	E5
Thirty Two	84	H5
Vintage Wine Bar & Bistro	85	E5

ENTERTAINMENT 🎭

Brasil's	86	H5
Chris' Jazz Club	87	E5

Khyber Pass	88	H5
Kimmel Center for the		
Performing Arts	89	E5
Pennsylvania Ballet	90	E5
Philadelphia Orchestra	91	E5
Suzanne Roberts Theatre	92	E5
Trocadero Theater	93	F4

TRANSPORT

Greyhound Bus Terminal	94	F4
Riverlink Ferry	95	H5

0 — 500 m
0 — 0.3 miles

INFORMATION
American Express Travel Service	1 E4
B Free Franklin Post Office	2 E4
Central Library	3 D3
CVS	4 F4
Giovanni's Room	5 E5
Graduate Hospital	6 D5
Greater Philadelphia Tourism Marketing Corp	(see 7)
Independence Visitor Center	7 G5
Intermezzo Café & Lounge	8 C4
Joseph Fox	9 D5
Main Post Office	10 C4
Pennsylvania Hospital	11 F5
Philadelphia Java Co	12 G6
Robin's Bookstore	13 E5
Thomas Cook	14 D4
Traveler's Aid Society	15 F5

SIGHTS & ACTIVITIES
Academy of Natural Sciences Museum	16 D4
African American Museum in Philadelphia	17 G4
Arch St Meeting House	18 G4
Betsy Ross House	19 H4
Boathouse Row	20 B2
Carpenters' Hall	21 G5
Chinese Friendship Gate	22 F4
Christ Church	23 H5
City Hall	24 E4
Civil War Library & Museum	25 D5
Clay Studio	26 H4
Congress Hall	27 G5
Eastern State Penitentiary	28 D2
Elfreth's Alley	29 H4
Elfreth's Alley Museum	(see 29)
Ethical Society	(see 42)
Fairmont Park	30 B1
Franklin Court	(see 56)
Franklin Institute Science Museum	31 D3
Independence Hall	32 G5
Independence Seaport Museum	33 H5
Institute of Contemporary Art	34 A4
Joan of Arc Statue	35 C2
Liberty Bell Center	36 G5
Library Hall	37 G5
National Constitution Center	38 G4
National Museum of American Jewish History	39 G4
National Portrait Gallery	(see 52)
Old City Hall	40 G5
Pennsylvania Academy of the Fine Arts	41 E4
Philadelphia Children's Theatre	42 D5
Philadelphia Museum of Art	43 C2
Philadelphia Zoo	44 A1
Philadelphia's Magic Garden	45 F6
Philosophical Hall	46 G5
Physick House	47 G6
Please Touch Museum	48 D3
Powel House	49 G5
Rodin Museum	50 D3
Rosenbach Museum & Library	51 D5
Second Bank of the US	52 G5
Trophy Bikes	53 G5
University Museum of Archaeology & Anthropology	54 B5
US Mint	55 G4
US Postal Service Museum	56 G5

SLEEPING
Alexander Inn	57 F5
Bank St Hostel	58 H5
Inn at Penn	59 A4
Rittenhouse 1715	60 D5
Shippen Way Inn	61 G6
Society Hill Hotel	62 G5
Sofitel Philadelphia	63 D5
Thomas Bond House	64 H5

(Pennsylvania's constitution enacted in 1701 by William Penn). The 2080lb bronze bell was made in London's East End by the Whitechapel Bell Foundry in 1751. The bell's inscription, from Leviticus 25:10, reads: 'Proclaim liberty through all the land, to all the inhabitants thereof.' The bell was secured in the belfry of the Pennsylvania State House (now Independence Hall) and tolled on important occasions, most notably the first public reading of the Declaration of Independence in Independence Square. The bell became badly cracked during the 19th century; despite initial repairs it became unusable in 1846 after tolling for George Washington's birthday.

Independence Hall (☎ 215-597-8974; Chestnut St btwn 5th & 6th Sts) is the 'birthplace of American government,' where delegates from the 13 colonies met to approve the Declaration of Independence on July 4, 1776. An excellent example of Georgian architecture, it sports understated lines that reveal Philadelphia's Quaker heritage. Behind Independence Hall is the spiffy **Independence Square**, where the Declaration of Independence was first read in public.

The **National Constitution Center** (☎ 215-409-6600; www.constitutioncenter.org; 525 Arch St; adult/child $6/5; ☉ 9:30am-5pm Mon-Fri, to 6pm Sat & Sun), right next to the visitor center, makes the United States Constitution sexy and interesting for a general audience through theater-in-the-round reenactments. There are exhibits including interactive voting booths and Signer's Hall, which contains lifelike bronze statues of the signers in action.

Other attractions in this historic park include: **Carpenters' Hall**, owned by the Carpenter Company, the USA's oldest trade guild (1724), which is the site of the First Continental Congress in 1774. **Library Hall** is where you'll find a copy of the Declaration of Independence, handwritten in a letter by Thomas Jefferson, plus first editions of Darwin's *On the Origin of the Species* and Lewis and Clark's field notes. **Congress Hall** (S 6th & Chestnut Sts), meanwhile, was the meeting place for US Congress when Philly was the nation's capital, and **Old City Hall**, finished in 1791, was home to the US Supreme Court until 1800. The **Franklin Court** complex, a row of restored tenements, pays tribute to Benjamin Franklin with a clever underground museum displaying his inventions, as well as details on his many other contributions (as statesman, author and journalist) to

society. At the **B Free Franklin Post Office** (see p199) mail receives a special handwritten Franklin postmark (Ben was also a postmaster) and there's a small **US Postal Service Museum**. **Christ Church** (☎ 215-922-1695; S 2nd St), completed in 1744, is where George Washington and Franklin worshiped.

Philosophical Hall (☎ 215-440-3400; 104 S 5th St; admission free; ☉ 10am-4pm Wed-Sun Mar–Labor Day & Thu-Sun Labor Day–Feb), south of Old City Hall, is the headquarters of the American Philosophical Society, founded in 1743 by Benjamin Franklin. Past members have included Thomas Jefferson, Marie Curie, Thomas Edison, Charles Darwin and Albert Einstein.

Second Bank of the US (Chestnut St btwn 4th & 5th Sts), modeled after the Greek Parthenon, is an 1824 marble-faced Greek Revival masterpiece that was home to the world's most powerful financial institution until President Andrew Jackson dissolved its charter in 1836. The building then became the Philadelphia Customs House until 1935, when it became a museum. Today it's home to the **National Portrait Gallery** (Chestnut St; ☉ 11am-4pm Wed-Sun; admission free), housing many paintings by Charles Willson Peale, America's top portraitist at the time of the American Revolution.

OLD CITY

Old City – the area bounded by Walnut, Vine, Front and 6th Sts – picks up where Independence National Historical Park leaves off. And, along with Society Hill, Old City was early Philadelphia. The 1970s saw revitalization, with many warehouses converted into apartments, galleries and small businesses. Today it's a quaint and fascinating place for a stroll.

The tiny, cobblestone **Elfreth's Alley** (www.elfrethsalley.org; off 2nd St btwn Arch & Race Sts;) is believed to be the oldest continuously occupied street in the USA. Its 32 well-preserved brick row houses are still inhabited with real live Philadelphians, so be considerate as you stroll along, and be sure to stop into **Elfreth's Alley Museum** (☎ 215-574-0560; No 126; adult/student $5/1; ☉ 10am-5pm Mon-Sat, from noon Sun Mar-Oct, closed Mon-Wed Nov-Feb) which was built in 1755 by blacksmith and alley namesake Jeremiah Elfreth; it's been restored and furnished to its 1790 appearance.

The nearby **Betsy Ross House** (☎ 215-686-1252; www.betsyrosshouse.org; 239 Arch St; suggested donation adult/child $3/2; ☉ 10am-5pm daily Apr-Sep, closed Mon Oct-Mar) is where it is believed that

Betsy Griscom Ross (1752–1836), upholsterer and seamstress, may have sewn the first US flag.

The cool **Clay Studio** (☎ 215-925-3453; www .theclaystudio.org; 139 N 2nd St; admission free; ☼ noon-6pm Tue-Sun) exhibits staid as well as oddball works in ceramic; it's been in Old City since 1974 and is partially responsible for the development of the area's burgeoning gallery scene. The **National Museum of American Jewish History** (☎ 215-923-5986; www.nmajh.org; 55 N 5th St; ☼ 10am-5pm Mon-Thu, 10am-3pm Fri, noon-5pm Sun) features exhibits that examine the historical role of Jews in the USA. At the nearby **US Mint** (☎ 215-408-0114; www.usmint.gov; Arch St, btwn 6th & 7th Sts; admission free; ☼ tours 9am-3pm Mon-Fri), you can line up for same-day, self-guided tours that last about 45 minutes. **Arch Street Meeting House** (☎ 215-627-2667; www.archstreetfriends .org; 320 Arch St; requested donation $1; ☼ 9am-5pm Mon-Sat, from 1pm Sun) is the USA's largest Quaker meeting house.

SOCIETY HILL

Architecture from the 18th and 19th centuries dominates the lovely residential neighborhood of Society Hill, bound by Front and 8th streets from east to west, and Walnut and Lombard streets north and south. Along the cobblestone streets you'll see mainly 18th and 19th century brick row houses, mixed in with the occasional modern highrise, like the **Society Hill Towers** designed by IM Pei. but **Washington Square** was conceived as part of William Penn's original city plan, and offers a peaceful respite from sightseeing. **Physick House** (☎ 215-925-7866; 321 S 4th St btwn Cypress & Delancey Sts; adult/child $5/4; ☼ noon-5pm Thu-Sat, from 1pm Sun), the home of surgeon Philip Syng Physick, was built in 1786 by Henry Hill – a wine importer who kept City Tavern well stocked – and is the only freestanding, Federal-style mansion remaining in Society Hill. The 18th-century **Powel House** (☎ 215-627-0364; 244 S 3rd St; adult/child $5/4; ☼ noon-5pm Thu-Sat, from 1pm Sun) was home to Samuel Powel, a mayor of Philadelphia during colonial times.

CENTER CITY, RITTENHOUSE SQUARE & AROUND

Philadelphia's center of creativity, commerce, culture and just about everything else, this region is the engine that drives the city. It contains the city's tallest buildings, the financial district, big hotels, museums, concert halls, shops and restaurants.

The leafy **Rittenhouse Square**, with its wading pool and fine statues, is the best known of William Penn's city squares. The majestic **City Hall** (☎ 215-686-9074; www.phila.gov; Broad & Market Sts; admission free; ☼ 9:30am-4:30pm Tue-Fri), completed in 1901, stands 548ft tall in Penn Square. The world's tallest masonry construction without a steel frame, and it's topped by a 27-ton bronze statue of William Penn. Just below that is an **observation deck**, where you can get a bird's eye view of the city. City Hall's park is the site of a useful oddity: an automatic public toilet, which costs 25¢, plays music while you pee and self-cleans when you are done.

Highly recommended for Civil War buffs is the comprehensive **Civil War Library & Museum** (☎ 215-735-8196; www.netreach.net/~cwlm; 1805 Pine St; admission $5; ☼ 11am-4:30pm Thu-Sat) boasting artifacts and exhibitions. **Rosenbach Museum & Library** (☎ 215-732-1600; www.rosenbach.org; 2010 Delancey Pl; admission $8, free on Tue; ☼ 10am-5pm Tue & Thu-Sun, to 8pm Wed), meanwhile, is for bibliophiles, as it features rare books and manuscripts, including James Joyce's *Ulysses*, and special exhibits.

BENJAMIN FRANKLIN PARKWAY & MUSEUM DISTRICT

Modeled after the Champs Elysées in Paris, the parkway is a center of museums and other landmarks. **Philadelphia Museum of Art** (☎ 215-763-8100; www.philamuseum.org; Benjamin Franklin Parkway & 26th St; adult/senior, student & child $10/7; Sun pay-what-you-wish; ☼ 10am-5pm Tue, Thu, Sat & Sun, to 8:45pm Wed & Fri) is the highlight. It's one of the nation's largest and most important museums, featuring some excellent collections of Asian art, Renaissance masterpieces, post-impressionist works and modern pieces by Picasso, Duchamp and Matisse. The grand stairway at its entrance was immortalized when star Sylvester Stallone ran up the steps in the 1976 flick *Rocky*.

Pennsylvania Academy of the Fine Arts (☎ 215-972-7600; www.pafa.org; 118 N Broad St; admission $5; ☼ 10am-5pm Tue-Sat, 11am-5pm Sun) is a prestigious academy that has a museum with works by American painters, including Charles Willson Peale and Thomas Eakins. The **Academy of Natural Sciences Museum** (☎ 215-299-1000; www .acnatsci.org; 1900 Benjamin Franklin Parkway; adult/child/ senior $9/8/8.25; ☼ 10am-4:30pm Mon-Fri, 10am-5pm Sat & Sun) features a terrific dinosaur exhibition

> ## WHAT THE...?
>
> **Eastern State Penitentiary** (☎ 215-236-3300; www.easternstate.org; 22nd St & Fairmount Ave; admission $9; ⏲ 10am-5pm, last entry 4pm), opened in 1829, was controversial for a program that was meant to change behavior through solitary confinement and labor. Before it was abandoned in 1971 it held some of the country's most notorious criminals, including Al Capone. Today you can wander throughout the ancient cell blocks and even take a 'haunted' night-time tour.

where you can dig for fossils on weekends. **Franklin Institute Science Museum** (☎ 215-448-1200; http://sln.fi.edu; 222 N 20th St; City Center; adult/child & senior $12.75/10; ⏲ 9:30am-5pm) is where hands-on science displays were pioneered; a highlight is the Ben Franklin exhibit. At the **Rodin Museum** (☎ 215-763-8100; www.rodinmuseum.org; Benjamin Franklin Parkway & N 22nd St; suggested donation $3; ⏲ 10am-5pm Tue-Sun), you'll find Rodin's great works the *Thinker* and *Burghers of Calais*.

SOUTH STREET
Sort of a Greenwich Village of Philly, **South Street** is where one goes to find record shops, art-supply stores tiny cheapskate eateries and college-favorites like head shops, T-shirt stores and the teenage goth chicks who populate them. A hidden gem worth seeking out is **Philadelphia's Magic Garden** (1020 South St; www .philadelphiasmagicgardens.org), a mystical, art-filled pocket of land that's the passion of mosaic muralist Isaiah Zager.

SOUTH PHILADELPHIA
The **Italian Market** (9th St btwn Wharton St and Fitzwater St; www.phillyitalianmarket.com; ⏲ 9am-5pm Tue-Sat, 9am-2pm Sun) is a highlight of South Philadelphia. The country's largest outdoor market, it's where butchers and artisans hawk produce and cheese, homemade pastas, incredible pastries and freshly slaughtered fish and meats, from lamb to pheasant. A great time to experience it in all its glory is in mid-May, for the annual **Sorrento Cheese Ninth Street Italian Market Festival** (www.9thstreet italianmarketfestival.com).

In the midst of all the foodie frenzy is the **Mummers' Museum** (☎ 215-336-3050; www.mum mersmuseum.com; 1100 S 2nd St; adult/child $3.50/2.50; ⏲ 9:30am-4:30pm Tue-Sat, from noon Sun Oct-Apr, till 9:30pm Thu May-Sep), celebrating the tradition of disguise and masquerade. It has an integral role in the famed Mummers Parade, which takes place here every New Year's Day.

CHINATOWN & AROUND
The fourth-largest Chinatown in the USA, Philly's version has existed since the 1860s. Chinese immigrants who built America's transcontinental railroads started out west and worked their way here. Today's Chinatown remains a center for immigrants, though now many of the neighborhood's residents come from Malaysia, Thailand and Vietnam in addition to every province in China. Though it does hold a few residents, the tone of Chinatown is thoroughly commercial. The **Chinese Friendship Gate** (N 10th St btwn Cherry & Arch Sts) is a decorative arch built in 1984 as a joint project between Philadelphia and its Chinese sister city, Tianjin. The multicolored, four-story gate is Chinatown's most conspicuous landmark.

Between here and Independence Park is the **African American Museum in Philadelphia** (☎ 215-574-0380; www.aampmuseum.org; 701 Arch St; admission $8; ⏲ 10am-5pm Tue-Sat, from noon Sun), housed in a foreboding concrete building but containing excellent collections on African American history and culture.

PENN'S LANDING
Back in its heyday Penn's Landing – the waterfront area along the Delaware River, between Market and Lombard Sts – was a very active port area. Eventually those trans-

> ## CHEESESTEAK WARS
>
> What's to fight about when it comes to a stack of tender, juicy, thinly sliced beef, topped with lashings of freshly fried onion rings, covered with gorgeous, gooey melted cheese, served in a soft, warm, white bread roll? Well it's the city's namesake taste sensation, and anyone who serves it up wants theirs to be the best. While many purveyors claim to have the ultimate version, the most famous – and most rivaled – ones sit right across the street from each other. Pat's and Geno's (see p208) are both brash and bright and cheap and, well, pretty much the same, though each has its diehard supporters. Be the latest judge and take a taste test.

actions moved farther south down the Delaware, and today most of the excitement is about boarding boats, like the **Riverboat Queen** (www.riverboatqueenfleet.com; from $15) or **Spirit of Philadelphia** (www.spiritcruises.com; from $30), for booze cruises, or simply strolling along the water's edge. The 1.8-mile **Benjamin Franklin Bridge**, the world's largest suspension bridge when completed in 1926, spans the Delaware River and dominates the view here. A sculpture garden is a work in progress, and a fun destination is the **Independence Seaport Museum** (☎ 215-925-5439; 211 S Columbus Blvd; www.phillyseaport.com; adult/child/senior $9/6/8, 10am-noon Sun free; ☻ 10am-5pm), highlighting Philadelphia's role as an immigration hub; its shipyard closed in 1995 after 200 years.

Just across the Delaware River in otherwise missable Camden, NJ, is the excellent **Adventure Aquarium** (☎ 856-365-3300; www.adventureaquarium.com; 1 Riverside Dr; adult/child $18/15; ☻ 9:30am-5pm), featuring globally themed creature exhibits like the West African River Experience, Penguin Island, a coral station of colorful Caribbean fish, a shark tank and an archway where you can pass under schools of fish. To get there, just hop on the **RiverLink Ferry** (☎ 856-365-1166; www.riverlinkferry.org; return $6), which runs hourly from Penn's Landing.

UNIVERSITY CITY

This neighborhood, separated from downtown Philly by the Schuylkill River, feels like one big college town. That's because it's home to both Drexel University and the Ivy League **University of Pennsylvania** (commonly called 'U Penn'), founded in 1740. The leafy, bustling campus makes for a pleasant afternoon stroll, and it's got two museums definitely worth a visit: the **University Museum of Archaeology & Anthropology** (☎ 215-898-4000; www.upenn.edu /museum; 3260 South St; adult/child/senior & student $8/5/6, Sun free; ☻ 10am-4:30pm Tue-Sat, 1-5pm Sun, closed Sun in summer) contains archaeological treasures from ancient Egypt, Mesopotamia, Mesoamerica, Greece, Rome and North America; and the heralded **Institute of Contemporary Art** (☎ 215-898-5911; www.icaphila.org; 118 S 36th St; admission $6; ☻ noon-8pm Wed-Fri, 11am-5pm Sat-Sun) is an excellent place to catch shows by folks making a big splash at the cutting-edge of the art world.

Oh, and whether you're catching a train or not, be sure to pop your head into the romantic, neoclassical **30th St Station** (☎ 215-349-3147; 30th St at Market St) while you're in the 'hood.

Flooded with sunlight during the afternoon, it's positively ethereal.

FAIRMOUNT PARK

The snaking Schuylkill River bisects this 9,200-acre greenspace – bigger than New York's Central Park and, in fact, the largest city park in the country. From the earliest days of spring every corner is thrumming with activity – ball games, runners, picnickers, you name it. The enthusiasm is catchy and you'll certainly want to join them. Runners will love the tree-lined, riverside trails, which range from 2 miles to 10 miles in length. **Philly runners** (www.phillyrunners.org) is an all-skills running club that has great maps and information

Park trails are also great for bicycling. For rentals, **Trophy Bikes** (☎ 215-222-2020; 3131 Walnut St; bike rental full/half day $25/20) stocks the latest hybrids and a couple of tandems, and staff members specialize in touring. For advice and group rides, contact the **Bicycle Club of Philadelphia** (☎ 215-843-1093; www.phillybikeclub.org), which leads rides for all skill levels.

On the east bank, **Boathouse Row** has Victorian-era rowing-club buildings that lend a lovely old-fashioned flavor to this stretch. Across the park are a number of **early American houses** (admission $3) that are open to the public, including **Laurel Hill** (☎ 215-235-1776) and **Woodford** (☎ 215-229-6115). Also, check out the **Shofuso Japanese Mansion and Gardens** (☎ 215-878-5097; www.shofuso.com), a picturesque home and tea house constructed in the traditional 16th-century style. Scattered all throughout the park are some notable monuments, including one, at the far east end, for **Joan of Arc**.

Also within park borders is the **Philadelphia Zoo** (☎ 215-243-1100; www.philadelphiazoo.org; 3400 Girard Ave; adult/child peak $17/14, off-peak $13; ☻ 9:30am-5pm Mar-Nov, 9:30am-4pm Dec-Feb), the country's oldest zoo, which has tigers, pumas, polar bears – you name it – in naturalistic habitats.

MANAYUNK

With its steep hills and Victorian row houses overlooking the Schuylkill River, Manayunk – from a Native American expression meaning 'where we go to drink' – still remains a good spot to accomplish this activity. Other than drinking, visitors are also permitted to eat (see p209) and shop. It's a lovely and bustling place for an hour or an afternoon and evening. And the towpath that runs alongside the neighborhood is an excellent place for **bicycling**.

GERMANTOWN & CHESTNUT HILL

An odd mix of blight and preserved grandeur, the Germantown historic district – a good 20-minute drive or ride north on the SEPTA 23 from central downtown Philly – has a handful of tiny museums and notable homes worth checking out. **Cliveden of the National Trust** (☎ 215-848-1777; www.cliveden.org; 6401 Germantown Ave; ☉ noon-4pm Thu-Sun) was the summer home of wealthy Benjamin Chew, built in 1760 and used as a de facto stronghold during the Battle of Germantown during the Revolutionary War in 1777. You can visit it, along with the **Deshler-Morris House** (☎ 215-596-1748; www.nps.gov/demo; 5442 Germantown Ave), where President Washington met with his cabinet in 1793 (note: closed for renovations at time of research, with plans to reopen in early 2009); the **Germantown Historical Society** (☎ 212-844-1683; www.germantownhistory.org; 5501 Germantown Ave; call for hours); and the **Johnson House** (☎ 212-438-1768; www.johnsonhouse.org; 6306 Germantown Ave; ☉ 10am-4pm Thu-Fri, tours at 1:30, 2:30 and 3:30pm), the site of a 1768 stationhouse for the Underground Railroad.

Just north of Germantown is **Chestnut Hill** (www.chestnuthillpa.com) with its quaint, small-town-like main strip of shops and eateries, and huge and historic residential homes and mansions.

Philadelphia for Children

Safe, friendly and easy to navigate, Philly is an extremely kid-friendly town.
Academy of Natural Sciences (☎ 215-299-1000; www.ansp.org; 1900 Benjamin Franklin Parkway; adult/child $10/8; ☉ 10am-4:30pm Mon-Fri, to 5pm Sat-Sun) From the dinosaur hall to the butterfly garden, there are natural wonders for everyone.
Please Touch Museum (☎ 215-963-0667; www .pleasetouchmuseum.org; 210 N 21st St; admission $10; ☉ 9am-4:30pm Sep-Jun, to 5pm Jul-Aug) Has a great array of hands-on exhibits on subjects including Maurice Sendak, *Alice in Wonderland,* baby animals and science.
Philadelphia Children's Theatre (☎ 215-528-2600; www.pctheatre.org; 2030 Sansom St; adult/child $10/12) For a bit of culture once the playing is out of their system, head here for shows like *Snow White* and *Peter Rabbit* (put on via the Philadelphia Ethical Society), accompanied by study guides so young audiences can learn about each play's major themes.
Philadelphia Zoo (p205) Lions and tigers and bears, oh my!

Tours

Ed Mauger's Philadelphia on Foot (☎ 800-340-9869; www.ushistory.org/more/mauger; tour $20) Historian and author of the book *Philadelphia Then and Now* offers walking tours with a variety of themes, including Exercise Your Rights (Conservatives Tour), Exercise Your Lefts (Liberals Tour) and Women in the Colony.
Mural Tours (☎ 215-685-0754; www.muralarts .org/tours; tour $24; ☉ tours 11am Sat Jun-Oct) Guided trolley tour of the city's diverse and colorful outdoor murals, the largest collection in the country.
Philadelphia Trolley Works & 76 Carriage Company (☎ 215-925-8687; www.phillytour.com; adult $20-70, child $4-13) Tour part of the city or just about every last corner, either on a narrated trolley ride or quieter horse-drawn carriage.

Festivals & Events

Mummers' Parade (www.mummers.com) A very Philly parade, it's an elaborate celebration of costumes every New Year's Day (Jan 1).
Annual Jam on the River (www.jamontheriver.com) Excellent music lineup, from folkies to jam bands. Memorial Day weekend.
Manayunk Arts Festival (www.manayunk.com) It's the largest outdoor arts and crafts show in the Delaware Valley, with more than 250 artists from across the country each June.
Philadelphia Live Arts Festival & Philly Fringe (www.livearts-fringe.org) Catch the latest in cutting-edge performance each September.

Gay & Lesbian Philadelphia

Philadelphia is one seriously gay-friendly town – even officially, as the city has been courting queer visitors with an extensive tourism campaign since 2004, using clever turns of phrase such as 'Get your history straight and your nightlife gay.' Things were kicked up another notch in spring of 2007, when the 'gayborhood' – an area that lies between Broad and 12th Sts and Walnut and Pine Sts – was dubbed Midtown Village and permanently decked out with rainbow-flag-festooned street signs during a special ceremony.

Although two events in particular bring a festive air to Philly – **Equality Forum** (www .equalityforum.com) in May and **Gay Pride Weekend** (www.phillypride.org) in June – there is plenty going on all the time, especially on weekends. Because nights and venues change frequently, check with www.phillygaycalendar .com. Here is just a sampling of where to see and be seen:

Brew Ha Ha! (☎ 215-893-5680; 212 S 12th St) The epicenter of the Gayborhood in the afternoon, it's a lovely place to cruise in daylight hours.

Bump (☎ 215-732-1800; 1234 Locust St) Weekend nights get going at this sleek spot, with a low-lit lounge and cozy back patio.

Sisters (☎ 215-735-0735; 1320 Chancellor St) This one's for the ladies.

Tavern on Camac (☎ 215-545-0900; 243 S Camac St) Show tunes and other old-school fun reign in the downstairs piano bar, while a small upstairs dance floor gets packed with dance-happy folks.

Sleeping

Though the majority of places are found in and around Center City, there are plenty of alternatives sprinkled throughout the other neighborhoods too – from Penn's Landing to University City. There's certainly no shortage of places to stay, but serious hotel aficionados may be disappointed, as there are, shockingly, no slick, hipster boutique properties of the sort found in most every big city these days; it's strictly national chains and B&Bs here. Note that most hotels offer some kind of parking service, usually costing about $25 per day.

BUDGET & MIDRANGE

Bank St Hostel (☎ 215-922-0222; 2 S Bank St; dm $25; ✗ 🖳) This is an excellent HI hostel in a safe neighborhood, just a short walk from the 2nd St Station and major sights. It's got 70 dorm beds and a lounge area with a pool table.

Shippen Way Inn (☎ 215-627-7266; 416-418 Bainbridge St; r incl breakfast $105-150; ✗) This hunkered-down, 1750s colonial house has nine quirky-cozy rooms with low, exposed-beam ceilings, wicker furniture and quilted beds. Enjoy breakfast in the herb garden on warm mornings and a roaring fireplace in the living room on chilly nights.

Alexander Inn (☎ 215-923-1004; www.alexanderinn .com; 301 S 12th St; r incl breakfast $109-159; 🖳) Though it's marketed as a 'boutique hotel,' the sleek image that conjures is not what you'll find at the inn – but it's a perfectly comfortable, gay-owned (and marketed) place to stay, featuring art deco-ish quarters, a friendly staff and good breakfast. Great bang for the buck, and an even better location, off Antique Row.

Society Hill Hotel (☎ 215-925-1919; 301 Chestnut St; r $100-160; P ✗) Philly's smallest hotel has a European atmosphere, friendly staff and is right near Independence Park. Its very small

but quaint rooms, used as temporary housing for longshoremen in the 1800s, feature brass beds and private bathrooms. Light sleepers note that the first floor of the place is a popular bar and restaurant.

Thomas Bond House (☎ 215-923-8523; www.win ston-salem-inn.com/philadelphia; 129 S 2nd St; r $105-190; P ✗ 🐾) If sightseeing in Independence Park has you wishing you could time travel back to the colonial days, this B&B is for you. A restored 1769 Georgian-style house has been a leather tannery, rag supplier and residence, and now it's an inn stuck in a lovely time warp, with Chippendale period furnishings and working fireplaces.

TOP END

our pick **Inn at Penn** (☎ 215-222-0200; www.theinnat penn.com; 3600 Sansom St; r $200-250; P ✗ 🐾 🖳) Away from the downtown hubbub – but quickly accessible via the nearby SEPTA – this Hilton hotel sits on the U Penn campus. Recently renovated rooms have crisp linens and fluffy comforters and are simply decorated with tasteful earth tones. Feels spiffy, updated and cozy. An excellent choice.

Sofitel Philadelphia (☎ 215-569-8300; www.sofi tel.com; 120 S 17th St; r $215-400; P 🐾 🖳 wi-fi) The French chain's local version is pretty lovely indeed. Towering up from the former site of the Philadelphia Stock Exchange, its rooms have firm beds topped with fluffy comforters and a sleek, rather masculine vibe. The cool lobby lounge is a great place to plan your day of sightseeing.

Rittenhouse 1715 (☎ 215-546-6500; www.ritten house1715.com; 1715 Rittenhouse Square; r $239-319, s $309-699; ✗ 🐾 🖳 wi-fi) Just steps from Rittenhouse Square, this is an elegant, top-notch choice (and good enough for Oprah and Baryshnikov, who have both bedded down here). Housed in a 1911 mansion and infused with old-world sophistication, it's brimming with modern amenities – iPod docking stations, plasma TVs, wi-fi throughout – juxtaposed with thoroughly old-fashioned, over-the-top decor (froofy curtains, period furniture) that makes for one unique stay.

Eating

Philly is known for its cheesesteaks and, while you shouldn't leave without a sampling, you can also find a range of international eateries – and many of them are BYOB.

OLD CITY

Cuba Libre (☎ 215-627-0666; www.cubalibrerestaurant
.com; 10 S 2nd St; dinner $15-24; ☺ 11:30am-11pm Mon-Fri,
from 10:30am Sat-Sun) This festive, multistoried
Cuban eatery and rum bar is the place for
Cuban sandwiches, guava-spiced BBQ, savory
black beans and salads tossed with smoked
fish and marinated vegetables. It has veggie
options, too.

Continental (☎ 215-923-6069; www.continental
martinibar.com; 138 Market St; dinner $16-25; ☺ 11:30am-
3:30pm Mon-Fri, 5-11pm Sun-Wed, 5pm-midnight Thu-Sat,
10:30am-4:30pm Sat-Sun, bar daily till 2am) A stylized
old-fashioned diner, the specialties here are
hip crowds, eclectic tapas and specialty martinis – as indicated by the huge speared martini
olives that hang from the ceiling.

Farmicia (☎ 215-627-6274; www.farmiciarestaurant
.com; 15 S 3rd St; mains $19-26; ☺ 11:30am-3pm & 5:30-
10pm Tue-Thu, till 11pm Fri-Sat, 11am-3pm and 5-9pm
Sun) Dedicated to simply crafted, local and
organic foods, the meals at this BYOB spot –
including an organic Angus burger with cara-
melized onions, and Alaskan salmon with
roasted beets and lentils – are creative and
soul satisfying. Vegetarians are well cared
for, with a variety of tofu, pasta and veggie-
and-grain plates to choose from. Weekend
brunch rocks, too.

CENTER CITY & AROUND

Reading Terminal Market (☎ 215-922-2317; www
.readingterminalmarket.org; 12th & Arch Sts; dishes $3-10;
☺ 8am-6pm Mon-Sat, 9am-4pm Sun) At the budget
end, this huge indoor market is the best
you'll find. Procure a map of the place inside one of the entrances and take your pick,
from fresh Amish cheeses and Thai desserts,
to falafel, cheesesteaks, salad bars, sushi,
Peking duck, great Mexican and cups of
fresh-roasted java.

Lolita (☎ 215-546-7100; 106 S 13th St; dishes $16-22;
☺ 5-10:30pm Sun-Thu, till 11pm Fri-Sat) This always-
packed BYOB offers up tasty takes on the
Mexican-fusion trend, such as *epazote* tamales
and duck breast stuffed with fat cherries, plus
a variety of margarita mixes you can pour
into your BYO tequila. A lesbian-owned establishment, it's especially popular with the
pre-nightclub gay crowd.

Le Bec-Fin (☎ 215-567-1000; www.lebecfin.com;
1523 Walnut St; prix fixe dinner $90-138; ☺ 11:30am-9pm
Mon-Fri, 6-9:30pm Sat) Totally over-the-top in its
old-world snooty splendor, many gourmets
rate Le Bec-Fin as the country's best restau-

rant for its setting, service and superb French
food. Expect top-notch service, stuffy diners
and rich and clever dishes like snail cassou-
let, poached bass with mango chutney and
roasted squab with lentils.

CHINATOWN & SOUTH STREET

Maoz Vegetarian (☎ 215-625-3500; www.maozveg.com;
248 South St; dishes $5-7; ☺ 11am-1am Sun-Wed, 11am-3am
Thu-Sat) A bright new chain from Amsterdam,
Philly's was the first outpost to hit the US. The
tiny storefront is always packed with healthy
hipsters wanting in on the cheap, fresh falafel
sandwiches which you can pile high with marinated veggies, spicy toppings and soothing
sauces from a free fixings bar.

Jim's Steaks (☎ 877-313-5467; South St at 4th St; steak
sandwiches $5-8; ☺ 10am-1am Mon-Thu, till 3am Fri-Sat,
noon-10pm Sun) If you can brave the long lines –
which bust out of the front door and snake
around the side of the shiny art-deco building –
you'll be in for a treat at this Philly institution,
which serves mouth watering cheesesteaks
and hoagies (plus soups, salads and breakfasts).

Rangoon (☎ 215-829-8939; 112 N 9th St; dishes
$6-15; ☺ 11:30am-9pm Sun-Thu, till 10pm Fri-Sat) For
something a little different, try this Chinatown Burmese spot, offering a huge array of
tantalizing specialties from spicy red-bean
shrimp and curried chicken with egg noodles
to coconut tofu.

Horizons (☎ 215-923-6117; www.horizonsphiladel
phia.com; 611 S 7th St; mains $15-20; ☺ 6-10pm Tue-Thu,
6-11pm Fri-Sat) The only truly gourmet vegan
restaurant in Philly, this is where you can
delve into healthy, guilt-free dishes made of
soy and veggies without sacrificing ambience.
Try spicy glazed tofu with edamame mashed
potatoes, hearts of palm paella and bourbon
BBQ tempeh, plus a range of creative cocktails
and vegan desserts.

SOUTH PHILADELPHIA & ITALIAN MARKET

Geno's (☎ 215-389-0659; www.genosteaks.com; S 9th St
& Passyunk Ave; sandwich $6; ☺ 24hr) and **Pat's King of
Steaks** (☎ 215-468-1546; www.patskingofsteaks.com; S 9th
St & Passyunk Ave; sandwich $6; ☺ 24hr) are two of Phil-
ly's most popular and legendary cheesesteak
places (see p204).

Sam's Morning Glory Diner (☎ 215-413-3999; www
.morningglorydiner.com; 735 S 10th St; mains $5-7; ☺ 7am-
4pm Mon-Fri, 8am-3pm Sat-Sun) With its bright indoor wall mural, sunny service and creative
fare – try the asparagus-salmon frittata, tofu

scramble or homemade pancakes – this is the perfect place to kick start your day. Fresh salads and sandwiches also make it a great lunchtime pit-stop.

Paradiso (☎ 215-271-2066; www.paradisophilly.com; 1627 E Passyunk Ave; mains $18-26; ☺ 11:30am-3pm & 5-10pm Mon-Thu, till 11pm Fri-Sat, 4-9pm Sun) One of the newest additions to South Philly's Restaurant Row is this elegant, airy, white-tablecloth dining room, turning out upscale Italian feasts like pistachio-crusted lamb chops, homemade gnocchi and New York strip steak glazed with anchovy butter.

UNIVERSITY CITY

Cereality (☎ 215-222-1162; 3631 Walnut St; cereal meals $3-6; ☺ 6:30am-7pm Mon-Sat, 8am-5pm Sun) Indulge your inner-child at this bright and whimsical snack shop, popular with students. Just pick two cereals, a topping from fruit to candy, and milk (including soy). Fun!

Pod (☎ 215-387-1803; 3636 Sansom St; dinner mains $14-23; ☺ 11:30am-11pm Mon-Thu, till midnight Fri, 5pm-midnight Sat, till 10pm Sun) This space-age-looking theme restaurant has pan-Asian treats including dumplings, sushi and big plates of teriyaki, plus plenty of quirky cocktails.

our pick White Dog Café (☎ 215-386-9224; 3420 Sansom St; dinner mains $17-26; ☺ 11:30am-2:30pm Mon-Sat, 5-10pm Mon-Thu, till 11pm Fri-Sat, 10:30am-2:30pm & 5-10pm Sun) Owned by humanitarian and sustainable-foods activist Judy Wicks, this 24-year-old institution is the kind of funky-yet-upscale place that college students have their visiting parents take them for special dinners. The local, largely organic menu offers eclectic eats like troll-caught mahimahi with avocado salsa, grilled local-pasture pork chops with apples and pears, and local seitan with pepper-anise coulis. Brunch, too, is a happening scene.

MANAYUNK, GERMANTOWN & CHESTNUT HILL

Winnie's LeBus Manayunk (☎ 215-487-2663; 4266 Main St; dinner mains $12-18; ☺ 9am-3pm Mon-Fri, 9am-10pm Sun-Thu, 9am-11pm Fri-Sat) Casual, kid-friendly and fun, LeBus offers an eclectic range of dishes, from grilled tilapia and jambalaya to black-bean quesadillas, plus crowd-pleasing brunches.

Trolley Car Diner (☎ 215-753-1500; www.trolley cardiner.com; 7619 Germantown Ave; dinner mains $12-20; ☺ 11:30am-2:30pm Tue-Sat, 5-9pm Tue-Thu, 5-10pm Fri-Sat, 10am-2pm & 5-9pm Sun) Housed in a classic art-deco diner – moved here from its former site in Wilkes Barr, PA, with much fanfare in 2000 – this old-fashioned, family-style diner serves all the comfort foods you'd ever want: club sandwiches, patty melts, fried shrimp, salads and a homemade, white-bean 'peanut-butter' sandwich.

Cresheim Cottage (☎ 215-248-4365; www.creshe imcottage.com; 7402 Germantown Ave; dinner mains $12-20; ☺ 11:30am-2:30pm Tue-Sat, 5-9pm Tue-Thu, 5-10pm Fri-Sat, 10am-2pm & 5-9pm Sun) The Cottage is a local-sustainable adherent, and you can tell by the freshness of the delicious dishes, like seafood stew and the unique chicken meatloaf muffin for dinner, and the buttermilk pancakes and 'green eggs and ham' (poached, with basil-hollandaise sauce and cheese grits).

Drinking & Entertainment

BARS & CLUBS

Eulogy Belgian Tavern (☎ 215-413-2354; 136 Chestnut St) In Old City – which boasts the highest concentration of liquor licenses in the US outside of New Orleans – it offers hundreds of beers in a laid-back vibe.

Thirty Two (☎ 215-627-3132; www.32lounge.com; 12 S 2nd St) is a luxe lounge scene with bottle service and popular DJs.

Bar Ferdinand (☎ 215-923-1313; www.barferdinand .com; 1030 N 2nd St) A romantic Spanish tapas spot, it offers endless choices of wines, global beers and specialty cocktails.

McGillin's Olde Ale House (☎ 215-735-5562; www .mcgillins.com; 1310 Drury St) Philadelphia's oldest continually operated tavern (since 1860) displays framed copies of all its liquor licenses behind the bar with empty spaces for the prohibition years, when it remained open as a speakeasy.

Vintage Wine Bar and Bistro (☎ 215-922-3095; www.vintage-philadelphia.com; 129 S 13th St) Here you can choose from 65 wines by the glass to pair with tasty little bites.

Shampoo (☎ 215-922-7500; www.shampoooonline .com; Willow St btwn 7th & 8th Sts; cover $7-12) Home to foam parties, hot tubs and velvet seating, this giant nightclub's weekly repertoire includes an immensely popular gay night on Fridays, a long-standing Wednesday goth night, and a conventional free-for-all on Saturdays.

Brasil's (☎ 215-413-1700; 112 Chestnut St; cover $10) This is the place to bump and grind to Latin, Brazilian and Caribbean sounds, with DJ John Rockwell.

LIVE MUSIC

Chris' Jazz Club (☎ 215-568-3131; 1421 Sansom St; cover $5-10) Showcasing local talent along with national greats, this intimate space features a four o'clock piano happy hour Tuesday through Friday and good bands Monday through Saturday nights.

Ortlieb's Jazzhaus (☎ 215-922-1035; 847 N 3rd St; occasional cover $5) With a jazz lineup that's among the most respected in town, the Tuesday house band has a particularly stellar reputation.

Khyber Pass (☎ 215-238-5888; 56 S 2nd St; cover $5-15) Devoted to rock, this dirty old bar has a nightly schedule of live music. The Strokes made it big while they were the Khyber's resident band.

Trocadero Theater (☎ 215-922-5483; 1003 Arch St; cover free-$12) Recent headliners at this rock & roll showcase have included Through the Eyes of the Dead, Bernie Worrell and Redeemer/Destroyer. Monday night is movie night, followed by the Monday Night Club, with a hodgepodge of musicians, spoken-word artists and comedians.

THEATER & CULTURE

Kimmel Center for the Performing Arts (☎ 215-790-5800; www.kimmelcenter.org; Broad & Spruce Sts) Philadelphia's most active center for fine music, the Kimmel Center organizes a vast array of performances, including those for many of the companies listed below.

Philadelphia Theatre Company (☎ 215-985-1400 ext 100; www.phillytheatreco.com; Suzanne Roberts Theatre, 480 S. Broad St at Lombard St; tickets $33-51) The company, which produces high-end contemporary plays with regional actors has a brand new home, the Suzanne Roberts Theatre, which opened in the heart of the arts district in late 2007.

Pennsylvania Ballet (☎ 215-551-7000; www.paballet.org; Broad & Locust Sts; tickets $10-122) Recent shows by this excellent dance company, whose home is the beautiful Academy of Music, include *Sleeping Beauty*, *Swan Lake* and *The Nutcracker*.

Philadelphia Dance Company (☎ 215-893-1999; www.philadanco.org; 9 N Preston St; tickets $25-50) This 30-something-year-old company provides top-shelf exhibitions of grace, strength and movement, blending ballet and modern as the resident dance company at the Kimmel Center.

Philadelphia Orchestra (☎ 215-790-5800; www.philorch.org; Broad & Spruce Sts; tickets $10-130) The city's orchestra, founded in 1900, plays at the Kimmel Center, where it also resides. Christoph Eschenbach's recent appointment as music director generated excitement.

SPORTS

Football is all about the **Philadelphia Eagles** (Lincoln Field; ☎ 215-336-2000; www.philadelphiaeagles.com), who play at state-of-the-art Lincoln Field. The NFL season runs from August through January, with home games occurring twice each month, usually on Sundays. The baseball team is the **Philadelphia Phillies** (Citizen's Bank Park; ☎ 215-336-2000; www.phillies.mlb.com; tickets $15-40), and the National League team plays 81 home games from April to October. Finally, basketball comes courtesy of the **Philadelphia 76ers** (Wachovia Center; ☎ 215-339-7676, ticket sales 800-462-2849; www.nba.com/sixers; 3601 S Broad St; tickets $15-62).

Getting There & Away

Philadelphia International Airport (☎ 215-937-6800, 800-745-4283; www.phl.org; 8000 Essington Ave), 7 miles south of Center City, is served by direct flights from Europe, the Caribbean, Mexico and Canada; and offers connections to Asia, Africa and South America. Domestically, it has flights to over 100 destinations in the USA.

Greyhound (☎ 800-229-9424; www.greyhound.com; 1001 Filbert St) and **Peter Pan Bus Lines** (☎ 800-237-8747; www.peterpanbus.com; 1001 Filbert St) are the major bus carriers. Greyhound connects Philadelphia with hundreds of cities nationwide, while Peter Pan concentrates on the Northeast. A return fare to New York City is about $42 (2½ hours one way), to Atlantic City $18 (1½ hours) and to Washington, DC, $43 (3½ hours). **Capitol Trailways** (☎ 800-444-2877; www.capitoltrailways.com) makes connections to Lancaster, Reading, New York City, and Washington, DC. **NJ Transit** (☎ 215-569-3752 within Philadelphia, 800-772-2222 within NJ, 973-762-5100 from out of state; www.njtransit.com) carries you from Philly to points in New Jersey.

Beautiful **30th St Station** (☎ 215-349-3196; www.30thstreetstation.com) is one of the biggest train hubs in the country. **Amtrak** (☎ 800-872-7245; www.amtrak.com) provides service from here to Boston (regional and Acela express service $97-206 one way, 5-5¾ hours) and Pittsburgh (regional service $45, 7¼ hours). A cheaper but longer (adult/child $19/13; 2½ hours) way to get to NYC is to take the SEPTA R7 suburban train to Trenton in New Jersey. There you connect with **NJ Transit** (☎ 215-569-3752 in

Philadelphia, 800-772-2222 from NJ, 973-762-5100 from out of state; www.njtransit.com) to Newark's Penn Station, then continue on NJ Transit to New York City's Penn Station.

Several interstate highways lead through and around Philadelphia. From the north and south, I-95 (Delaware Expressway) follows the eastern edge of the city beside the Delaware River, with several exits for Center City. I-276 (Pennsylvania Turnpike) runs east across the northern part of the city and over the river to connect with the New Jersey Turnpike.

Getting Around

Fare for a taxi to Center City is a flat fee of $20. The airport is also served by SEPTA's regional service using the R1 line. The R1 ($6) will drop you off in University City or in numerous stops in Center City. SEPTA's ticketing machines on the train platforms frequently don't work.

Although driving is pretty simple in central Philadelphia, parking is difficult and regulations are strictly enforced. Downtown distances are short enough to let you see most places on foot, and a train, bus or taxi can get you to places farther out relatively easily. Philly is an inexpensive place to rent cars. Typical daily rates for a compact are $30 to $50 with unlimited mileage, less on weekends or by the week. See p1144 for car-rental advice.

SEPTA (☎ 215-580-7800; www.septa.org) operates Philadelphia's municipal buses, plus two subway lines and a trolley service. Though extensive and reliable, the web of bus lines is difficult to make sense of, particularly since SEPTA's confusing website doesn't provide a comprehensive map of the 120 routes servicing Philly's 159 sq miles. To get such a map, you have to purchase SEPTA's *Official Philadelphia Transit & Street Map* ($7) either online or from a sales office (see website for directory). The one-way fare on most routes is $2, for which you'll need the exact change or a token. Many subway stations and transit stores sell discounted packages of two tokens for $2.60.

Cabs, especially around City Center, are easy to hail. Fares are $1.80 for the first one-sixth of a mile, then 30¢ for each subsequent one-sixth plus 20¢ for every minute of waiting time. The fare from University City to Penn's Landing is about $7. The flat fare from Center City to the airport is $20. Some cabs accept credit cards.

The **Phlash** (☎ 215-474-5274) shuttle bus loops downtown from Logan Circle through Center City to the waterfront and South St (one way/ all day $2/4).

AROUND PHILADELPHIA
New Hope & Lambertville

New Hope and its sister town Lambertville (across the river in NJ) sit equidistant from Philadelphia and New York City, and are a pair of quaint, artsy little towns. Both are edged with long and peaceful towpaths, perfect for runners, cyclists and strollers, and a bridge with a walking lane lets you criss-cross between the two with ease. The towns draw a large amount of gay folk, who feel comfortable here because of the rainbow flags that hang outside of various businesses – symbols of a welcoming, liberal attitude that was in place long before a gay anti-discrimination ordinance passed in 2002 in New Hope, which has its own Gay Pride festival in May.

ORIENTATION & INFORMATION

New Hope is about 40 miles north of Philadelphia, on the shore of the Delaware River. The **New Hope Visitors Center** (☎ 215-862-5030; www .newhopevisitorscenter.org; 1 W Mechanic St) is a great first stop for maps and brochures about town. The **New Hope Chamber of Commerce** (☎ 215-862-9990; www.newhopepa.com) can answer questions about local businesses, as can the **Lambertville Chamber of Commerce** (☎ 609-397-0055; www.lambert ville.org).

SIGHTS & ACTIVITIES

Strolling the quaint streets and its shops and galleries is a day within itself, but one of New Hope's most unique offerings is the mule-drawn canal boat rides in the Delaware Canal, a leftover from the canal-building era of the mid-19th century. Stop by the **New Hope Canal Boat Company** (☎ 215-862-0758; www.onthecanal.net; 149 Main St; adult/child $10/6; ☒ tours noon May-Oct) for tickets. Or spend a few picturesque hours gliding downstream in a tube, raft or canoe, courtesy of **Bucks County River Country** (☎ 215-297-5000; www.rivercountry.net; 2 Waters Lane, Point Pleasant; tube/canoe $18/20; ☒ rent 9am-2:30pm, return by 5pm), about 8 miles north of New Hope on Rte 32. The **Golden Nugget Antique Market** (☎ 609-397-0811; www.gnmarket.com; 18 River Rd; ☒ 6am-4pm Wed, Sat & Sun), one mile south of Lambertville, has all sorts of finds, from furniture to clothing, from a variety of dealers.

SLEEPING & EATING

A great day trip from either Philly or NYC, both towns have a plethora of cute B&Bs if you decide to make a weekend out of it. Try the **York Street House Bed & Breakfast** (☎ 609-397-3007; www.yorkstreethouse.com; 42 York St, Lambertville; r incl breakfast $125-260; P X X wi-fi), a 1909 mansion with cozy rooms and big breakfasts, or the **Mansion Inn** (☎ 215-862-1231; www.themansioninn.com; 9 South Main St, New Hope; r $155-275; P X X □) in the heart of town – an 1865 gingerbread mansion with elegant detailing.

When you get hungry, hit the hoppin' **Marsha Brown Creole Kitchen and Lounge** (☎ 215-862-7044; www.marshabrownrestaurant.com; 15 S Main St, New Hope; dinner mains $15-22; ☉ 5-10pm Mon-Thu, till 11pm Fri, 2-11pm Sat, till 9pm Sun) for catfish, steaks and lobster, or **DeAnna's** (☎ 609-397-8957; www.deannasrestaurant.com; 54 N Franklin St, Lambertville; dinner mains $18-24; ☉ 5-9:30pm Tue-Fri, 5-10pm Sat, 4-9pm Sun) for awesome eclectic food and a hip, romantic vibe.

Easton

The historic, picturesque and artsy town of Easton, home to Lafayette College, is in the Lehigh Valley, just over the New Jersey border and on the banks of the Delaware River. For detailed information about the town, which makes a fun day trip from either Philadelphia (75 miles away) or New York City (70 miles away), visit www.easton-pa.com.

Strolling around the quaint main streets here is a lovely way to spend the afternoon, especially if you stop into some of the many art galleries that have moved here in recent years. **Connexions** (☎ 610-250-7627; 213 Northampton St; ☉ 11am-5pm Thu-Fri, till 6pm Sat, noon-5pm Sun) showcases local artists and hosts frequent openings and gallery talks. The most popular reason to visit is the wonderful **Crayola Factory** (☎ 610-515-8000; www.crayola.com/factory; 30 Centre Sq; ☉ 9:30am-4pm Tue-Fri , to 5pm Sat, from noon Sun Sep-May, 9:30am-5pm Mon-Sat, from 11am Memorial Day–Labor Day; admission $9.50), home of the beloved crayons, where kids (and adults!) can watch the crayons and markers get made, plus enjoy hands-on exhibits such as a room where you're *supposed* to write on the walls. In the same complex with the same hours is the **National Canal Museum** (☎ 610-559-6613; www.canals.org; admission $9), with fascinating exhibits on how canals helped create a national economy.

Grab a sandwich or coffee at the **Quadrant** (☎ 610-252-1188; 20 N 3rd St), a bookstore and café

that's a hip hang for locals, and, if you just don't want to leave, grab a cozy room at the **Lafayette Inn** (☎ 610-253-4500; www.lafayetteinn.com; 525 W Monroe St; r $125-175, s $225; P X wi-fi), an 18-room Georgian-style mansion with antiques, big breakfasts and wi-fi.

Brandywine Valley

Straddling the Pennsylvania–Delaware border, the Brandywine Valley is a patchwork of rolling, wooded countryside, historic villages, gardens, mansions and museums. The **Brandywine Valley Tourist Information Center** (☎ 800-228-9933; www.brandywinevalley.com; Rte 1; ☉ 10am-6pm Apr-Sep, to 5pm Oct-Mar) sits outside the gates of the spectacular **Longwood Gardens** (☎ 800-737-5500; www.longwoodgardens.org; Rte 1; admission $14; ☉ 9am-6pm Mon, Wed, Thu & Sun, till 10pm Tue, Fri & Sat), near Kennett Sq, which has 1050 acres, 20 indoor gardens and 11,000 kinds of plant, with something always in bloom. There's also a Children's Garden with a maze, fireworks and illuminated fountains in summer, and festive lights at Christmas. The **Brandywine Valley Wine Trail** (www.bvwinetrail.com), meanwhile, is a lovely conduit between a handful of new vineyards, all with tasting rooms.

A showcase of American artwork, the **Brandywine River Museum** (☎ 610-388-2700; www.brandywinemuseum.org; Hwy 1 & Rte 100; adult/child $8/5), at Chadd's Ford, includes the work of the 'Brandywine School' – Howard Pyle, NC Wyeths and Maxfield Parrish. One of the valley's most famous attractions, though, is **Winterthur** (☎ 302-888-4600, 800-448-3883; www.winterthur.org; Rte 52, Winterthur, DE; adult/child/senior & student $20/10/18; ☉ 10am-5pm Tue-Sun), actually in Delaware, an important museum of American furniture and decorative arts that was the country estate of Henry Francis duPont until he opened it to the public in 1951.

Valley Forge

After being defeated at the Battle of Brandywine Creek and the British occupation of Philadelphia in 1777, General Washington and 12,000 Continental troops withdrew to Valley Forge. Today, Valley Forge symbolizes Washington's endurance and leadership. The **Valley Forge National Historic Park** (☎ 610-783-1077; www.nps.gov/vafo; N Gulph Rd & Rte 23; admission free; ☉ dawn-dusk) contains 5½ sq miles of scenic beauty and open space 20 miles northwest of downtown Philadelphia – a remembrance of where 2000 of George Washington's 12,000 troops perished from freezing temperatures, hunger and disease, while many others returned home.

PENNSYLVANIA DUTCH COUNTRY

The core of Pennsylvania Dutch Country lies in the southeast region of Pennsylvania, in an area about 20 by 15 miles, east of Lancaster. The Amish (*ah*-mish), Mennonite and Brethren religious communities are collectively known as the 'Plain People.' All are Anabaptist sects, persecuted in their native Switzerland, who from the early 1700s settled in tolerant Pennsylvania. Speaking German dialects, they became known as 'Dutch' (from 'Deutsch'). Most Pennsylvania Dutch live on farms and their beliefs vary from sect to sect. Many do not use electricity, and most opt for horse-drawn buggies – a delightful sight, and sound, in the area. The strictest believers, the Old Order Amish, wear dark, plain clothing, and live a simple, Bible-centered life – but have, ironically, become a major tourist attraction, thus bringing busloads of gawkers and the requisite strip malls, chain restaurants and hotels that lend this entire area an oxymoronic quality, to say the least.

Information

To escape the busloads of tourists and learn about the region, use a map to navigate the back roads, avoiding main Routes 30 and 340 at all costs. Even better, rent a bike and pack some food for your exploration. You may also consider hiring a guide for a private tour, or simply visiting in winter, when tourism is down. **Lancaster County Bicycle Tours** (☎ 717-768-8366; bicycletours@aol.com) rents bikes and leads intimate tours that visit an Amish home and grocery store ($50 per half-day). Some farm homes rent rooms for $50 to $100 – they welcome kids and offer a unique opportunity to experience farm life. The **Dutch Country Visitors Center** (☎ 800-723-8824; www.padutchcountry .com; 9am-5pm), off Rte 30 in Lancaster, offers comprehensive information. For a true overnight experience, just ask to be directed to one of the farming families that rent rooms and offer home-cooked meals.

Sights & Activities

On the western edge of the Amish country, the pleasant town of **Lancaster** – a surprising mix of hip art galleries, eateries and preserved brick rowhouses – was briefly the US capital in September 1777, when Congress stopped here overnight. The bustling **Central Market** (☎ 717-291-4739; William Henry Pl; 6am-3pm Tue, Fri & Sat) offers local produce, cheese, meats and Amish baked goods and crafts. Next door, the **Heritage Center Museum** (☎ 717-299-6440; 5 W King St; adult/child $6/4; 10am-5pm Tue-Sat, from noon Sun) has a collection of 18th- and 19th-century paintings and period furniture, plus gives an excellent overview of Amish culture. The monthly **First Friday** (www.lancasterarts.com) celebration brings out a friendly local crowd for gallery hops along artsy Prince St.

Probably named for its crossroads location, nearby **Intercourse** has heavily touristed shops selling clothing, quilts, candles, furniture, fudge and, of course, souvenirs with off-color jokes.

Bird-in-Hand has craft stores, restaurants and a farmers market. **Country Barn Quilts & Crafts**, east of town, has a good selection of souvenirs. **Abe's Buggy Rides** (☎ 717-392-1794; Mon-Sat; adult/child $10/5) does a fun but not-so-authentic 2-mile tour, and one guide even speaks Spanish. In **Lititz**, visitors come for the **Sturgis Pretzel House** (☎ 717-626-4354; www.juliussturgis.com; Rte 772; admission $3; 9:30am-4:30pm Mon-Sat), the USA's first pretzel factory. The nearby **Ephrata Cloister** (☎ 717-733-6600; www.ephratacloister.org; 632 W Main St, Ephrata; admission $7; 9am-5pm Mon-Sat, from noon Sun) gives tours of its collection of medieval-style buildings, one of the country's earliest religious communities.

Sleeping & Eating

There's a slew of inns in the Amish country, and you will find several cheap motels along the southeastern portion of Rte 462/Rte 30. The **Landis Guest Farm** (☎ 717-898-7028; www.landisfarm.com; Gochlan Rd; r with breakfast $95; P X) in Manheim puts you up in a cozy cottage, provides a country breakfast and lets you milk the cows. For a refreshingly hip and urban experience, make a beeline to the snazzy new **Lancaster Arts Hotel** (☎ 866-720-2787; www.lancasterartshotel.com; 300 Harrisburg Ave; r from $169; P X wi-fi), housed in an old brick tobacco warehouse and featuring a groovy boutique-hotel ambience. Its excellent onsite bar and eatery, **John J Jeffries** (☎ 717-431-3307; mains $14-25; 11:30am-2pm & 5:30-10pm Mon-Fri, noon-2pm & 5:30-10pm Sat, 5:30-9pm Sun), serves a local organic, seasonal menu.

To sample one of the famous family-style restaurants of Amish country, get prepared to rub elbows with lots of tourists. The experience is part of coming to Amish country, though – and it'll offer you lots of delicious dishes, including the famous, sticky-sweet dessert of shoofly pie. To avoid the biggest crush of tour buses, try the family-owned **Stoltzfus Farm Restaurant** (☎ 717-768-8156; www .stoltzfusmeats.com; 3718 E Newport Rd, Intercourse; meals $18; ☽ 11:30am-8pm Mon-Sat Apr-Oct, Fri-Sat only in Nov) tucked off the main road and offering a mouthwatering lineup (candied sweet potatoes, homemade sausage, buttered noodles) in a pretty intimate dining room.

Getting There & Around

RRTA (☎ 717-397-4246) local buses link the main towns, but a car is much better for sightseeing. The **Capitol Trailways & Greyhound terminal** (☎ 717-397-4861; Lancaster train station) has buses to Philadelphia and Pittsburgh. The **Amtrak train station** (☎ 717-291-5080; 53 McGovern Ave, Lancaster) has trains to and from Philadelphia ($13, 80 minutes) and Pittsburgh ($38, six hours).

SOUTH CENTRAL PENNSYLVANIA
Hershey

Less than two hours from Philly is the fabled kids' favorite **Hershey** (www.hersheypa.com), home to a collection of attractions that explain, hype and, of course, hawk, the many trappings of Milton Hershey's chocolate empire. The piece de resistance is **Hershey Park** (☎ 800-437-7439; www.hersheypa.com; 100 W Hersheypark Dr; adult/child $46/27; ☽ 10am-10pm Jun-Aug, closes between 6 & 8pm at other times), a seriously commercialized amusement park with more than 60 thrill rides (not chocolate themed) for everyone from tykes to serious daredevils, plus various performances and frequent fireworks displays. **Hershey's Chocolate World** (☎ 717-534-4900; www .hersheys.com/chocolateworld; 251 Park Blvd; 'Chocolate Experience' film $6/4; ☽ 9am-10pm Jun-Aug, closes between 6 and 8pm at other times) is a mock factory and massive candy story with over-stimulating features like a 3-D movie and singing characters and free chocolate galore. For a more low-key informational visit, try the **Hershey Museum** (☎ 717-534-3439; www.hersheymuseum.org; 170 W Hersheypark Dr; adult/child $7/3.50; ☽ 10am-8pm summer, till 5pm other times), which tells the story of Mr Hershey through interactive history exhibits.

Gettysburg & Hanover
GETTYSBURG

This tranquil, compact and history-laden town, 145 miles west of Philadelphia, saw one

of the Civil War's most decisive and bloody battles. It's also where Lincoln delivered his Gettysburg Address. The area is anchored by the 8-square-mile **Gettysburg National Military Park** (☎ 717-334-1124; www.nps.gov/gett; 97 Taneytown Rd; ☽ 6am-10pm Apr-Oct, 6am-7pm Nov-Mar), with a great museum, bookstore and tour dispatch center (and a big new visitor center now under construction, set for a 2008 completion). Here you can pick up a map that details a self-guided auto tour, with somber sights including the Eternal Light Peace Memorial and the Wheatfield, which was strewn with more than 4000 dead and wounded after the battle.

The **Gettysburg Convention & Visitors Bureau** (☎ 717-334-6274; www.gettysburg.com; 35 Carlisle St; ☽ 8:30am-5:30pm) also distributes a comprehensive list of town attractions, which include the **Eisenhower National Historic Site** (☎ 717-338-9114; 250 Eisenhower Farm Lane; admission $8; ☽ 9am-5pm), which is Ike's former home, and the house that served as **General Lee's Headquarters** (☽ 717-334-3141; Budford Ave; admission free; ☽ 9am-5pm mid-Mar–Nov).

The annual **Civil War Heritage Days** (recorded information ☎ 717-334-2028) festival, taking place from the last weekend of June through the first weekend of July, features living history encampments, battle re-enactments, a lecture series and book fair that draws war re-enactment aficionados from near and wide. You can find **re-enactments** (www.gettysburg.com/living history) throughout the year, as well.

For accommodations, try **Gaslight Inn** (☎ 717-337-9100; www.thegaslightinn.com; 33 E Middle St; r $105-195), a wonderful B&B right in the center of town. **Herr Tavern & Publick House** (☎ 717-334-4332; www.herrtavern.com; 900 Chambersburg Rd; mains $19-27; ☽ 11am-9pm Mon-Sat, 5-9pm

Sun) serves upscale American lunch and dinner in a historic setting, while the hip **Ragged Edge Coffee House** (☎ 717-334-4464; www .raggededgecoffeehs.com; 110 Chambersburg St; sandwiches $6; ☽ 7am-8pm Sun-Thu, 7am-11pm Fri-Sat) has great coffee, sandwiches, smoothies and live music on weekend nights.

HANOVER

A peaceful alternative base for visiting Gettysburg is the historic town of Hanover, just 10 miles east on Rte 116, and home to well-preserved Georgian, classic revival and neoclassical architecture. While you're there, visit the lively **Amish Market** (E Chestnut St) on Saturday, catch a group show at the **Hanover Area Arts Guild** (☎ 717-632-2521; 32 Carlisle St) or tour one of two snack-food factories – famous pretzel maker **Snyder's of Hanover** (☎ 800-233-7125; www.snyders ofhanover.com; 1350 York St; tours free; ☽ 10am, 11am, 1pm Tue-Thu) or **UTZ Quality Foods** (☎ 800-367-7629; www .utzsnacks.com; 900 High St; tours free; ☽ 8am-4pm Mon-Thu), best known for its potato chips.

    Beechmont (☎ 717-632-3013; www.thebeech mont.com; 315 Broadway; r $94-159; P ✕ ☒ ☐) is an absolutely charming, well-run and beautifully appointed B&B serving huge, delicious breakfasts.

PITTSBURGH

Still mired in its steelworker reputation in most Americans' minds, Pittsburgh is a surprisingly hip, fun, cultured and beautiful city – almost European in feel with its steep, settled hills and seven bridges spanning three major waterways. The people are friendly and down-to-earth, and the neighborhoods exude a historic, unique vibe that's anchored by the many architectural gems. And culture vultures will be pleased to discover top-notch museums, verdant parklands, quirky music scenes and an ever-growing clutch of clubs and eateries – mixed in with the endearing, scrappy, blue-collar element that remains among closely-knit neighborhoods that refuse to completely give way to the creep of gentrification.

History

George Washington established a British presence here in 1753, before the start of the French and Indian War, but the French wound up controlling the area until being ejected by the British, who renamed Fort Duquesne as Fort Pitt, after Prime Minister William Pitt the Elder. Eventually called Pittsburgh, the city became famous for iron and steel production during the 19th century, and the industry was furthered by the Civil War. Scottish-born immigrant Andrew Carnegie grew rich by modernizing steel production here, which dipped during the Great Depression but rose again because of mass-produced automobiles in the 1930s. An urban-renewal program in the 1990s transformed the downtown area, and today, despite lingering economic hardships, the place has had a growing 'cool' and artistic cachet, especially for folks seeking affordable urban real estate.

Orientation & Information

The city sits at the point where the Monongahela and the Allegheny Rivers join the Ohio River, spreads out over the waterways and has neighborhoods connected by picturesque bridges (all with footpaths). It's large and not easily traversed on foot unless you're exploring one neighborhood at a time. The mystical-sounding Golden Triangle, between the converging Monongahela and Allegheny Rivers, is Pittsburgh's downtown, now comprehensively (if soullessly) renovated. Just northeast of here, the Strip offers warehouses, ethnic food stores and nightclubs and, across the Allegheny River, the North Side has the big new sports stadiums plus several museums. Across the Monongahela River is the South Side, whose Slopes rise up to Mt Washington; at the Flats, E Carson St bustles with clubs and restaurants. East of downtown is Oakland,

---

DON'T MISS

- **The Strip** (p221) Industrial-chic home to cheap eats and big clubs.

- **Carnegie Museum of Art** (p218) Top-notch works.

- **Mt Washington** (p218) Ride up for sunset on the Monongahela Incline.

- **South Side Slopes** (p218) Climb up or down for cool views.

- **Cathedral of Learning** (p218) The University's pièce de résistance.

- **Lawrenceville** (p219) Go furniture shopping in the new design district.

- **Andy Warhol Museum** (p217) The works of Pittsburgh's favorite son.

the university area, and beyond that Squirrel Hill and Shadyside, residential neighborhoods with an elegant, small-town feel.

Rand McNally makes good laminated maps of Pittsburgh, available in the city's airport bookstores, while **Universal Map** (www.universalmap.com) makes an excellent paper street map of Greater Pittsburgh.

BOOKSTORES

Caliban Book Shop (☎ 412-681-9111; www.caliban books.com; 410 S Craig St) Specializes in literary first editions, fine arts, poetry & travel.

City Books (☎ 412-481-7555; 1111 E Carson St) In South Side.

Jay's Bookstall (☎ 412-683-2644; 3604 Fifth Ave) Well-stocked indie shop.

Joseph-Beth Booksellers (☎ 412-381-3600; www .josephbeth.com; 2705 E Carson St) The seventh location (first in PA) in a growing regional chain; massive selection.

University of Pittsburgh Book Center (4000 Fifth Ave) Close to 90,000 general titles, plus textbooks.

EMERGENCY

Pittsburgh Action Against Rape (☎ 412-765-2731)

Poison Emergency Hotline (☎ 412-681-6669)

INTERNET ACCESS

While wi-fi hot spots are pretty well ubiquitous, free ones are not (though the Pittsburgh International Airport has free access). Check www.wifi411.com for a list of locations. Hotels and inns usually have a computer or wi-fi available to guests.

Beehive (☎ 412-488-4483; 1327 E Carson St) Cool South Side café with free wi-fi.

Carnegie Library of Pittsburgh (☎ 412-622-3114; 4400 Forbes Ave) Main branch (plus others; call for info) has free public access at terminals.

INTERNET RESOURCES

City of Pittsburgh (www.city.pittsburgh.pa.us) Details on neighborhoods and political districts.

Citysearch (pittsburgh.citysearch.com) Nightlife, restaurants, shopping.

Hello Pittsburgh (www.hellopittsburgh.com) Comprehensive city listings.

Pittsburgh.net (www.pittsburgh.net) Listings, neighborhoods and events.

MEDIA

Pittsburgh City Paper (www.pghcitypaper.com) Free alternative weekly with extensive arts listings.

Pittsburgh's Out (www.outpub.com) Free monthly gay newspaper.

Pittsburgh Post-Gazette (www.post-gazette.com) A major daily.

Pittsburgh Tribune-Review (www.pittsburghlive .com) Another major daily.

WQED-FM: 89.3 The local National Public Radio affiliate.

MEDICAL SERVICES

Allegheny County Health Department (☎ 412-687-2243; 3333 Forbes Ave) Has a walk-in medical center.

Allegheny General Hospital (☎ 866-680-0004; 320 E North Ave) Emergency room.

CVS (☎ 412-687-4180; 3440 Forbes Ave; ☼ 24hr)

Rite Aid (☎ 412-621-4302; 209 Atwood St; ☼ 24hr)

University of Pittsburgh Medical Center (☎ 412-647-8762; 200 Lothrop St) Emergency, high-ranking medical care.

MONEY

ATMs are plentiful. You will find them in delicatessens and grocery stores (where you may be charged up to a $2 fee) as well as in banks. For currency exchange, try the following:

Citizens Bank (☎ 412-234-4215; 5th & Grant Sts)

PNC Bank (☎ 412-762-2090; 5th & Wood Sts)

POST

Post office (☎ 412-642-4476; 700 Grant St) Main branch; call for other locations.

TOILETS

Public toilet (E Carson St at 18th St) While pubs and restaurants are mellow about letting you sneak into their bathrooms, you'll be psyched to find Pittsburgh's lone automated toilet, which lets you in for a fee of 25¢.

TOURIST INFORMATION

Greater Pittsburgh Convention & Visitors Bureau (☎ 412-281-7711, 800-366-0093; www.visitpittsburgh .com; Liberty Ave); Pittsburgh International Airport (near baggage claim; ☼ 9am-5pm Mon-Fri, to 3pm Sat & Sun); the Strip (1212 Smallman St, ☼ 10am-5pm) Publishes the *Official Visitors Guide* and provides maps and tourist advice.

UNIVERSITIES

University of Pittsburgh, Carnegie-Mellon University and Duquesne University are all large presences in town, with sprawling campuses and bustling academic crowds.

Sights & Activities

Points of interest in Pittsburgh are scattered everywhere, and its spread-out nature makes it a difficult place to cover thoroughly on foot. Driving can also be troublesome, due to the oddly laid-out streets, which even confuse locals. Public buses, luckily, are quite reliable (see p222 for more information).

For pretty much any outdoor pursuit, the best option is the elaborate, 1700-acre system of the **Pittsburgh Parks Conservancy** (☎ 412-682-7275; www.pittsburghparks.org), which comprises **Schenley Park** (with a public swimming pool and golf course), **Highland Park** (with swimming pool, tennis courts and bicycling track), **Riverview Park** (sporting ball fields and horseback riding trails) and **Frick Park** (with hiking trails, clay courts and a bowling green), all with beautiful running, biking and blading trails.

Active types can find guidance at places like the **Golden Triangle Bike & Blade Shop** (☎ 412-600-0675; Eliza Furnace Trail under 1st Ave Transit Stn; rental per hr/day $8/28), which rents bikes and leads various tours of the city. **Venture Outdoors** (☎ 412-255-0564; www.wpfi.org; 304 Forbes Ave) promotes outdoor recreation in the region, and sponsors bike rides and hikes in the city. For night runs contact **People Who Run Downtown** (☎ 412-366-7458; www.pittsburghrunning.org; ☙ Tue 5:30pm), a group of folks who organize weekly evening runs, followed by drinks at a neighborhood pub.

GOLDEN TRIANGLE

Here's where you'll find the **Allegheny County Courthouse** (☎ 412-350-5410; 436 Grant St; ☙ 9am-5pm Mon-Fri), a 19th-century Romanesque stone building that fills two city blocks and was designed by Henry Hobson Richardson. At the triangle's tip is **Point State Park**, which is popular during summer with strollers, runners and loungers. Its renovated **Fort Pitt Museum** (☎ 412-281-9284; www.fortpittmuseum.com; 101 Commonwealth Pl; admission $5; ☙ 9am-5pm Wed-Sun) commemorates the historic heritage of the French and Indian War. The nicely remodeled brick warehouse that is the **Senator John Heinz Pittsburgh Regional History Center** (☎ 412-454-6000; www.pghhistory.org; 1212 Smallman Ave; adult/child $7.50/3; ☙ 10am-5pm) offers a good take on the region's past, with exhibits on the French and Indian War, early settlers, immigrants, steel and the glass industry; it's also home to the **Western Pennsylvania Sports Museum** (☎ 412-454-6000; www.pghhistory.org; 1212 Smallman Ave; ☙ 10am-5pm), focusing on champs from Pittsburgh.

Riverfront trails along the north side of the Golden Triangle are perfect for strolling, running or biking. The perimeter of the Golden Triangle's **Point State Park** is a popular short run; for a longer run, head to the 11-mile gravel-paved **Montour Trail**, accessible by crossing the 6th St bridge and catching the paved path at the Carnegie Science Center (p218).

NORTH SIDE

While this part of town feels most populated when its PNC Park is filled with sports fans for a Pittsburgh Steelers game, rest assured that its many museums are hopping, too. The **Andy Warhol Museum** (☎ 412-237-8300; www.warhol.org; 117 Sandusky St; adult/child $12/9; ☙ 10am-5pm Tue-Thu, Sat & Sun, till 10pm Fri), celebrates Pittsburgh's coolest native son, who became famous for his pop art, avant-garde movies, celebrity connections and Velvet Underground spectaculars. Exhibits include the classic Campbell's soup

---

ANDY WARHOL

Andy Warhol (1928–87), whose life works are on proud display at his namesake museum (above), was one of the most influential US artists of the 20th century. Born the son of Polish immigrants in the Oakland district of Pittsburgh, Warhol turned into one of America's favorite freaky artists. He coined the phrase about everyone having '15 minutes of fame.' Warhol, though, had more than 15 years of it.

At his mother's suggestion, he studied art at the Carnegie Institute (now Carnegie Mellon University). Come graduation in 1949 he was outta there, relocating to big, bad New York City, where he became a leading freelance commercial artist, developed his distinctive style of pop art and, by the early 1960s, was exhibiting some works that would soon be famous – silkscreen paintings of Marilyn Monroe, Mao Zhedong and Campbell's soup cans. He also produced many experimental, underground movies starring a motley crew of drag queens and models, and opened the Factory, which is when the fun really started. His studio became party central for avant-garde artists, druggies, prostitutes, tricks, poor little rich girls (and boys) and various other pals and sycophants. In 1968 he was shot by an angry feminist Valerie Solanis, who had once been part of his artistic circle. But he died of more natural causes – following a gall-bladder operation. Unglamorous but true.

cans and celebrity portraits, while the museum's theater hosts frequent film screenings and quirky performers.

Also not to be missed is the **Mattress Factory** (☎ 412-231-3169; www.mattress.org; 500 Sampsonia Way; adult/child $9/free, half-price Thu; ☷ 10am-5pm Tue-Sat, 1-5pm Sun), hosting unique installation art and frequent performances.

Carnegie Science Center (☎ 412-237-3400; www.carnegiesciencecenter.org; 1 Allegheny Ave; adult/child $14/10, IMAX & special exhibits extra; ☷ 10am-5pm Sun-Fri, till 7pm Sat), great for kids, is a cut above the average hands-on science museum, with innovative exhibits on subjects from outer space to candy.

The **National Aviary** (☎ 412-321-4364; www.aviary.org; W Commons, Allegheny Sq; adult/child $9/7.50; ☷ 9am-5pm) is another treat, with more than 600 exotic and endangered birds, many of which fly freely above you in high-ceilinged, climate-controlled aviaries. Nearby in the northwest is the **Mexican War Streets** neighborhood, named after battles and soldiers of the 1846 Mexican War. The carefully restored rowhouses, with Greek revival doorways and Gothic turrets, have finally been discovered by real-estate moguls, and are on their way to becoming trendy. For now, though, the quiet streets make for a peaceful, post-museum stroll.

The **Pittsburgh Children's Museum** (☎ 412-322-5058; www.pittsburghkids.org; Allegheny Sq; adult/child $5/4.50; ☷ 10am-5pm Mon-Sat, from noon Sun) features a climbable space sculpture, exhibits about Jim Henson and Mister Rogers and some child-friendly Warhol works.

SOUTH SIDE & MT WASHINGTON

The South Side, bursting with shops, eateries, bars and cool characters, is a great place for strolling. To see it from above, ride either the **Monongahela Incline** (☎ 412-442-2000; www.portauthority.org; each way adult/child $1.75/85¢; ☷ 5:30am-12:45am Mon-Sat, 8:45am-midnight Sun) or **Duquesne Incline** (☎ 412-381-1665; http://incline.pghfree.net; each way adult/child $1.75/85¢; ☷ 5:30am-12:45am Mon-Sat, 8:45am-midnight Sun), the historic funicular railroads that run up and down **Mt Washington**'s steep slopes and afford great city views (and along which a young Jennifer Beals rode her bicycle in the classic '80s film *Flashdance*). At the start of the Duquesne Incline is **Station Square** (☎ 412-261-9911; www.stationsquare.com; Station Sq Dr at Fort Pitt Bridge), an over-hyped group of beautiful, renovated railway buildings that now comprise what is essentially a big ol' mall.

Rising up from the bustling South Side valley is the neighborhood called the **South Side Slopes**, a fascinating community of houses that seem perilously perched on the edge of cliffs, accessible via steep, winding roads and hundreds of steep stairs; there's a popular **Step Trek** (www.steptrek.org) each fall, during which crowds clamor up the 23,982 vertical feet to the top.

OAKLAND & AROUND

The University of Pittsburgh and Carnegie Mellon University are here, and the surrounding streets are packed with cheap eateries, cafés, shops and student homes. Rising up from the center of the U Pitt campus is the soaring **Cathedral of Learning** (☎ 412-624-6000; 157 Cathedral of Learning; admission free, tours $3; ☷ 9am-3pm Mon-Fri, from 9:30am Sat, from 11am Sun), a grand, 42-story Gothic tower which, at 535ft, is the second-tallest education building in the world. It houses the elegant **Nationality Classrooms**, each representing a different style and period, with gorgeous details such as the cherry-wood chalkboard doors in the India room and the red-velvet upholstered chairs of Austria. While a few rooms are always left open to viewers, most are accessible only with a guided tour.

Nearby are two **Carnegie Museums** (☎ 412-622-3131; www.carnegiemuseums.org; 4400 Forbes Ave; admission to both $10; ☷ 10am-5pm Tue-Sat, from noon Sun) – the **Carnegie Museum of Art**, with terrific exhibits of architecture, impressionist, post-impressionist and modern American paintings; and the **Carnegie Museum of Natural History**, featuring a complete Tyrannosaurus skeleton and exhibits on Pennsylvania geology and Inuit prehistory. East of Oakland, in Point Breeze, is the wonderful **Frick Art & Historical Center** (☎ 412-371-0600; www.frickart.org; 7227 Reynolds St; museum & grounds free, Clayton tours $10; ☷ 10am-5pm Tue-Sun), which displays some of Henry Clay Frick's Flemish, French and Italian paintings in its Art Museum; assorted Frickmobiles like a 1914 Rolls Royce in the Car & Carriage Museum; more than five acres of grounds and gardens; and Clayton, the restored 1872 Frick mansion.

SQUIRREL HILL & SHADYSIDE

These upscale neighborhoods feature wide streets and Victorian mansions, excellent restaurants and both eclectic and chain shops. **Squirrel Hill** is home to Pittsburgh's large Jewish population, and features the city's best kosher eateries, butchers and Judaica shops.

Temple Sinai (☎ 412-421-9715; www.templesinaipgh .org; 5505 Forbes Ave) is a synagogue that's housed in the architecturally stunning Elizabethan-style former mansion of John Worthington. In **Shadyside**, Walnut St is the bustling main strip.

GREATER PITTSBURGH

Formerly gritty **Lawrenceville** has recently become the city's **Interior Design District** (www.1662designzone.com), comprising the stretch on and around Butler Street from 16th to 62nd Sts. It's a long and spotty strip of shops, galleries, studios, bars and eateries that's on every hipster's radar, and runs into the slowly gentrifying **Garfield** neighborhood, a good place for cheap ethnic eats. Bloomfield, a really little Little Italy, is a strip of groceries, Italian eateries and, of all things, a landmark Polish restaurant, the Bloomfield Bridge Tavern (see p221).

Folks with kids to entertain might want to seek out the **Pittsburgh Zoo & PPG Aquarium** (☎ 412-665-3640; www.pittsburghzoo.com; 1 Wild Pl; adult/child $10/8; ☯ 9am-5pm fall/spring, to 4pm winter, till 6pm summer) or, in the summer, **Sandcastle Waterpark** (☎ 412-462-6666; www.sandcastlewaterpark .com; 1000 Sandcastle Dr; admission $25; ☯ 11am-6pm Jun-Sep), Pittsburgh's water theme park. It features the Mon Tsunami tidal wave pool, Thunder Run inner-tube river and Boardwalk Blasters shotgun slides.

Tours

Alan Irvine Storyteller Tours (☎ 412-521-6406; www.alanirvine.com/walking_tour; tours $8-12) Historian Irvine brings the city's past to life in a journey through several neighborhoods.

Just Ducky Tours (☎ 412-402-3825; www.justducky tours.com; Station Sq; adult/child $19/15; ☯ Apr-Oct) General city tours in a WWII amphibious vehicle.

Pittsburgh History & Landmarks Foundation (☎ 412-471-5808; www.phlf.org; Station Sq; tours from $5) Specialized historic, architectural or cultural tours by foot or motor coach.

Festivals & Events

Hothouse (www.sproutfund.org/hothouse) This annual June night of eclectic performance, art and music supports Pittsburgh's creative side.

Pittsburgh Three Rivers Regatta (www.pghregatta .com) Sails soar on the three rivers in July or August.

Step Trek (www.steptrek.org) A community climb up the 23,982 vertical feet of steps of the South Side Slopes in early fall.

Sleeping

With a bit of searching, you can find bargain and charm all in one spot. Oakland has the straight-up chain hotels – Hampton Inn, Holiday Inn, Residence Inn and the like. For more character, check in with the **Pittsburgh Bed & Breakfast Association** (☎ 724-352-4899; www .pittsburghbnb.com).

BUDGET & MIDRANGE

HI Pittsburgh Hostel (☎ 412-431-1267; www.hipitts burgh.org; 830 E Warrington Ave; dm $22; ☐) In South Side's Allentown neighborhood, this 50-bed hostel is in a still-splendid early-20th-century building with dreary (but very cheap!) sleeping quarters and well preserved common areas.

Holiday Inn Express (☎ 412-488-1130; www.hi express.com; 20 S 10th St; d $135-200; P ✗ ✗ ✗ ☐) Sure, it's a bland chain – but it's location on the hip South Side can't be beat, and it's clean and affordable.

ourpick **Inn on the Mexican War Streets** (☎ 412-231-6544; http://hometown.aol.com/innwarst/collect; 604 W North Ave; r $139-189; P ☯ wi-fi) This historic, gay-owned mansion on the North Side is near the museums and right on the bus line that takes you downtown. Here you'll be treated to hearty homemade breakfasts, charming hosts, stunning antique furnishings and an elegant porch, plus there's a brand-new martini lounge, the RH Boggs Library Bar and a four-star restaurant, Acanthus.

Morning Glory Inn (☎ 412-431-1707; www.morn ingglorybedandbreakfast.com; 2119 Sarah St; r $145-190, ste $210-450; ✗ wi-fi) Head to this Italianate-style Victorian brick townhouse for a quiet and elegant room with (slightly froofy) character – plus big, delicious breakfasts – right in the heart of the jumpin' South Side scene.

TOP END

Inn on Negley (☎ 412-661-0631; www.theinnonnegley .com; 703 Negley Ave; r $170-235; P ✗ ✗ wi-fi) Formerly a pair of Shadyside inns, these two Victorian houses have been combined into one newly refurbished gem with a clean-line aesthetic that still bursts with romance. It features four-post beds, handsome furniture and fireplaces, large windows and, in some rooms, hot tubs.

Sunnyledge (☎ 412-683-5014; www.sunnyledge.com; 5124 Fifth Ave; r $189-275; ✗) This historic 1886 mansion in Shadyside holds eight elegant rooms with thick robes and mini-bars, plus a lovely tearoom, martini bar, library and fitness center.

Westin Convention Center (☎ 412-281-3700; www .westin.com; 1000 Penn Ave; r from $200; P ✕ ✗ 👟 wi-fi) The tallest, most imposing of the high-rise hotels in the downtown district, the Westin offers great special rates throughout the year, along with wonderfully anonymous rooms that feature comfortable beds and puffy down comforters and a sleek, sophisticated style. It's a two-minute walk to the gay-bar district, and just a slightly longer jaunt to the Strip.

Eating

While the pickings are slim compared to Philadelphia, you will find eclectic, ethnic and down-home fare, with some (though not a ton of) good vegetarian options and a preponderance of budget spots. Note that your meal will come with a side of second-hand smoke, as you can still light up in Pittsburgh eateries – a fact that could thrill Europeans but horrify folks from LA.

BUDGET

Primanti Bros (☎ 412-263-2142; www.primantibros .com; 18th St at Smallman St; sandwiches $5; ⏱ 24hrs) A Pittsburgh institution on the Strip, this always-packed place specializes in greasy and delicious hot sandwiches – from knockwurst and cheese to the 'Pitts-burger cheesesteak' – that come with extras like French fries, coleslaw and onions *between* the thick slices of bread. Other outlets can be found in Oakland, Downtown and South Side.

Original Hot Dog Shop (☎ 412-621-7388; 3901 Forbes Ave; meals $3-5; ⏱ 10am-3:30am Mon-Thu, till 5am Fri-Sat) Affectionately nicknamed 'dirty Os' by locals, it's a favorite for its cheap dogs and mounds of crispy fries – especially after a night at the bars.

Pho Minh (☎ 412-661-7443; 4917 Penn Ave; mains $5-7; ⏱ noon-9pm Wed-Thu & Sun, till 10pm Fri-Sat) A tiny and *très* popular Vietnamese spot with cheap and excellent noodles, tofu dishes and nearly 20 types of *pho*, a traditional soup.

Spice Island Tea House (☎ 412-687-8821; 253 Atwood St; mains $6-10; ⏱ 11:30am-9pm Mon-Thu, till 10pm Fri-Sat) This tiny and popular pan-Asian eatery has budget treats from Chinese noodles to Thai curries.

Quiet Storm (☎ 412-661-9355; www.quietstormcoffee .com; 5430 Penn Ave; mains $6-11; ⏱ 7:30am-10pm Mon-Fri, 9am-10pm Sat, 9am-9pm Sun) This hipster-filled, multi-use café in Garfield specializes in veggie

and vegan cuisine, but also serves killer coffee and Sunday brunch, and hosts frequent readings and musical performances.

MIDRANGE

Kaya (☎ 412-261-6565; 2000 Smallman Ave; dishes $10-14; ⏱ 11:30am-10pm Mon-Wed, till 11pm Thu-Sat, noon-9pm Sun) This is a cool and popular Caribbean place with jerk chicken, Cuban sandwiches and plenty of vegetarian options, plus a funky decor.

Abay (☎ 412-661-9736; www.abayrestaurant.com; 130 S Highland Ave; mains $11; ⏱ 11:30am-2:30pm & 5-10pm Tue-Sat, till 9pm Sun) This funky spot features great Ethiopian cuisine from chicken-to lentil-based stews, all served with that spongy, delicious *injera* bread instead of cutlery.

Lemon Grass Café (☎ 412-765-2222; 124 Sixth St; dishes $12; ⏱ 11am-9pm Mon-Fri, till 1pm Sat, 4-9pm Sun) With impressive Cambodian and Thai cuisine, including killer *phat Thai*, green curry and plenty of vegetarian options, this is the best Downtown bet.

Gypsy Café (☎ 412-381-4977; www.gypsycafe.net; 1330 Bingham St; mains $14-19; ⏱ 11:30am-midnight most days but call first, hours change) The purple floors and walls and brightly colored rugs make loyal patrons as happy as the fresh, seasonal fare. Sample menu items include a smoked trout plate, spanikopita, and a stew of shrimp, scallop and feta.

Dish Osteria Bar (☎ 412-390-2012; 128 S 17th St; mains $14-25; ⏱ 4pm-1:45am Mon-Sat) A tucked-away, intimate locals' fave, the simple wood tables and floors belie the at-times extravagant Mediterranean creations, which range from fresh sardines with caramelized onions to fettuccine with lamb *ragù*. There's a cozy and elegant bar up front.

TOP END

Eleven (☎ 412-201-5656; www.bigburrito.com/eleven; 1150 Smallman St; mains $16-25; ⏱ 11:30am-2pm & 5-10pm Mon-Fri, till 11pm Sat, 5-9pm Sun) The ubiquitous Big Burrito Restaurant Group (Kaya) has done it again with this slick, high-ceilinged eclectic eatery, with top-notch fare such as gnocchi with broccoli rabe, Alaskan halibut and an elaborate vegetarian tasting menu.

Le Pommier (☎ 412-431-1901; 2104 E Carson St; mains $19-25; ⏱ 5:30-10pm Mon-Sat) It's modern French cuisine in a frenetic bistro setting, serving fine wines and meals from veal and rabbit to duck and tofu (really!).

UUBU 6 (☎ 412-381-7695; www.uubu6restaurant.com; 178-180 Pius St; dinner mains $18-25; ⏱ 11am-11pm Mon-Sat, till 8pm Sun) The first high-end eatery to open in the rapidly gentrifying South Side Slopes, this cozy newbie is housed in a spiffed-up old union lodge, and serves delicacies such as asparagus-and-peeky-toe-crab risotto (for lunch) and, for dinner, duck meatballs with mustard greens and seared basil swordfish.

River Moon Café (☎ 412-683-4004; www.rivermooncafe.com; 108 43rd St; mains $19-27; ⏱ 5-9:30pm Tue-Sat, 11:30am-2:30pm Sun) This recent addition to the exceedingly popular Lawrenceville nabe serves creative, diverse (and beyond satisfying) fare from salmon and lemon angel hair pasta to filet mignon gorgonzola.

Drinking & Entertainment
BARS & CLUBS
Most nightlife is centered on the South Side and the Strip. **Z: Lounge** (☎ 412-481-2234; 2108 E Carson St) is a mellow, trendy pub on the South Side with specialty martinis, while **Last Chance** (2533 Penn Ave), on the Strip, is a popular neighborhood pub for guys who can hold their liquor. **Bloomfield Bridge Tavern** (☎ 412-682-8611; 4412 Liberty Ave), 'the only Polish restaurant in Lil' Italy,' is a gritty pub serving beers with excellent sides of *pierogi*, while the **Church Brew Works** (☎ 412-688-8200; www.churchbrew.com; 3525 Liberty Ave), serving handcrafted beers in a massive former church space, is a standout in Lawrenceville. Downtown, the **Prelude Wine Bar** (Pittsburgh Renaissance Hotel, 107 6th St) has a swanky vibe and more than 50 wines by the glass.

You'll find several big, frenzied dance clubs clustered at the edge of the Strip district, including **Bash Nightclub** (☎ 412-325-0499; www.bashnightclubpgh.com; 1900 Smallman St), which is rowdy, cruisy and packed on weekends – not to mention the home of a bucking mechanical bull. At Station Square is **Matrix** (☎ 412-261-2220; www.matrixpgh.com; 7 E Station Sq Dr), a sort of mall of nightclubs housing Club Exit (industrial fans), Club Liquid (young electronica fans), Club Velvet (salsa and merengue) and Club Goddess (Top 40 pop).

Most gay bars, such as **Pegasus** (☎ 412-281-2131; 818 Liberty Ave) and the **Liberty Avenue Saloon** (☎ 412-338-1533; 41 Liberty Ave), are in a concentrated stretch of Liberty Ave Downtown. They're hoppin' and plentiful, but perhaps the hippest, most frenzied gay spot is the off-the-beaten-path nightclub **Pittsburgh Eagle** (☎ 412-766-7222; www.pitteagle.com; 1740 Eckert

St; ⏱ Fri-Sat 9pm-2am), which draws internationally known DJs and porn stars alike.

LIVE MUSIC
Shadow Lounge (☎ 412-363-8722; 5972 Baum Blvd) This is *the* place for catching hot hip-hop and house DJs, plus indie bands, readings and open-mike nights.

Quiet Storm (☎ 412-661-9355; www.quietstormcoffee.com; 5430 Penn Ave) This very cool coffeehouse features frequent local indie, pop and folk bands with big followings.

Rex Theater (☎ 412-381-6811; 1602 E Carson St) It's a favorite South Side venue for touring jazz, rock and indie bands.

THEATER & CULTURE
Pittsburgh Cultural Trust (☎ 412-471-6070; www.pgharts.org; 803 Liberty Ave) Promotes all downtown arts, from the Pittsburgh Dance Council and PNC Broadway in Pittsburgh to visual art and opera; the website has links to all main arts venues.

Heinz Hall (☎ 412-392-4800; www.pittsburghsymphony.org; 600 Penn Ave) This historic venue is home to the Pittsburgh Symphony Orchestra, with a season that lasts from October to May.

Carnegie Music Hall (www.pittsburghchambermusic.org; 4400 Forbes Ave) A historic venue in Oakland, this is home to the Pittsburgh Chamber Music Society.

Benedum Center for the Performing Arts (☎ 412-456-6666; 719 Liberty Ave; tickets from $15) Benedum hosts dance, opera and Broadway shows.

Harris Theater (☎ 412-682-4111; 800 Liberty Ave) A wide variety of art-house films, often part of film festivals, screen at this restored theater.

Southside Works Cinema (☎ 412-432-5770; www.thesouthsideworks.com; 510 S 27th St) A brand-new 10-screen cinema with stadium seating, this is where to catch first-run mainstream and indie films.

SPORTS
On the North Side, just by the Allegheny River, are **PNC Park** (☎ 412-321-2827; www.pirateball.com), where the Pittsburgh Pirates major-league baseball team bases itself, and **Heinz Field** (☎ 412-323-1200; www.pittsburghsteelers.com), where the NFL Pittsburgh Steelers hold football showdowns. **Mellon Arena** (☎ 412-642-1800; www.pittsburghpenguins.com), just east of downtown, is where the NHL Pittsburgh Penguins play hockey.

Getting There & Away

Pittsburgh International Airport (☎ 412-472-3500; www.pitairport.com), 18 miles west from downtown, has direct connections to Europe, Canada and major US cities via a slew of airlines, including the new **Independence Air** (www.flyi.com), with low rates to NYC, DC and Atlanta.

Arriving in its station near the Strip, **Greyhound** (☎ 412-392-6513; 11th St & Liberty Ave) has frequent buses to Philadelphia ($44, seven hours), New York ($53, 11 hours) and Chicago, Illinois ($55, 10 to 14 hours).

Pittsburgh is easily accessible via major highways, from the north or south on I-76 or I-79, from the west on Rte 22 and from the east on I-70. It's about an eight-hour drive from New York City and about three hours from Buffalo.

Amtrak (☎ 412-471-6171; 1100 Liberty Ave) is behind the magnificent original train station, with trains heading to cities including Philadelphia ($45 to $71, seven to eight hours) and New York ($60 to $111, nine to 11 hours).

Getting Around

The excellent **28X Airport Flyer** (☎ 412-442-2000; www.ridegold.com; one way $2.25) public bus makes runs to Oakland and Downtown every 20 minutes. Taxis are readily available and cost about $35 to Downtown. Various shuttles also make downtown runs and cost $13 to $17 per person one way. Car rentals are available from the terminal, and many hotels offer courtesy-van pickup; phones are located by the baggage-claim area.

Driving around Pittsburgh can be extremely frustrating – roads end with no warning, one-way streets can take you in circles and there are various bridges to contend with. However, get a good map (see p215) and, even better, a co-pilot and you should be OK.

Port Authority Transit (☎ 412-442-2000; www .portauthority.org) operates an extensive bus system and a limited light-rail system, the 'T,' which is useful for going from Downtown to the South Side. Bus and T fares range from free to $3, depending on the zone in which you're traveling.

For taxis, call **Yellow Cab Co of Pittsburgh** (☎ 412-321-8100) or **Checker Cab** (☎ 412-664-6600), which charge by zone.

AROUND PITTSBURGH
Fallingwater & Kentuck Knob

A Frank Lloyd Wright masterpiece, **Fallingwater** (☎ 724-329-8501; www.paconserve.com; admission $16; ⏰ 10am-4pm Tue-Sun Mar-Nov, 11am-3pm winter weekends, weather permitting) is south of Pittsburgh on Rte 381. Completed in 1939 as a weekend retreat for the Kaufmanns, owners of the Pittsburgh department store, the building sports a design acclaimed for its integration with the natural setting. To see inside you must take one of the hourly guided tours and reservations are recommended. A more intensive two-hour tour, with photography permitted, is offered at 8:30am ($50). The rather attractive forested grounds open at 8:30am.

Much less visited is **Kentuck Knob** (☎ 724-329-1901; www.kentuckknob.com; weekday/weekend $16; ⏰ 10am-4pm Tue-Sun, from noon Mon), another Frank Lloyd Wright house (designed in 1953), built into the side of a rolling hill. It's noted for its natural materials, hexagonal design and honeycomb skylights. House tours last about an hour and include a jaunt through the onsite sculpture garden, with works by Andy Goldsworthy, Ray Smith and others.

To spend a night or two in the area, opt for the earthy **Country Seasons Bed & Breakfast Inn** (☎ 724-455-6825; www.countryseasonsbnb.com; Rte 381; Mill Run; r $93-113), with basic but charming rooms, a big front porch and a main fireplace. Or try the swank **Nemacolin Woodlands Resort & Spa** (☎ 412-422-2736; www.nemacolin.com; 1001 Lafayette Dr, Farmington; r from $200), with a spa, golf course and dining rooms.

NORTHERN PENNSYLVANIA

The smallest of the Great Lakes, at 241 miles across and only 62ft deep, **Lake Erie** warms quickly in the summer and frequently freezes in the winter, making it a magnet for all sorts of recreation, from swimming to ice fishing (a popular sport here).

The city of **Erie** (www.visitEriePA.com) is, for the most part, a depressed industrial center save for the touristy, redeveloped, shop-filled **Bayfront District**. But the **Presque Isle State Park** (☎ 814-838-5138; www.presqueisle.org; park office on Peninsula Dr), which shoots north and then curves back down upon itself just like Cape Cod in Massachusetts, is a stunningly beautiful place to visit, no matter what the season. It's a lovely sandy peninsula with dramatic, ocean-like vistas interspersed with wooded areas and biking trails. The **Lady Kate** (☎ 800-988-5780; www.piboat

tours.com; adult/child $16/9), a ferry that leaves from Presque Isle's south shore, gives 90-minute narrated tours of Lake Erie's shoreline.

Though there is no camping allowed on Presque Isle, the nearby **Virginia's Beach** (☎ 814-922-3261; www.virginiasbeach.com; campsite $26-37, cottage $75-115; P X ✷) has tent/RV sites and cottages right on Lake Erie. The 1960s-style **El Patio Motel** (☎ 814-838-9772; r from $70) is a clean, standard motor lodge near the park's entrance, while **A Place Inn Time** (☎ 814-734-4136; www.aplaceinntime.com; 206 Erie St; $89-135), 20 minutes away in Edinboro, is a cozy B&B with an English garden.

Occupying the northeast corner of Pennsylvania is the famed **Poconos** (☎ 800-762-6667; www.800poconos.com) region, containing 2400 sq miles of mountains, streams, waterfalls, lakes and forests, making it a beautifully natural getaway at any time during the four seasons. Among the quaint (as well as tacky) towns is

adorable **Milford** (www.pikechamber.com), home to the historic **Columns Museum** (☎ 570-296-8126; 608 Broad St; admission $3; ⏱ 1-4pm Wed, Sat & Sun) and the lovingly restored **Hotel Fauchere** (☎ 570-409-1212; www.hotelfauchere.com; 401 Broad St; r $275-350).

Further west in a tucked-away valley is **Jim Thorpe**, (named for an athletic hero of the early 1900s), which offers a slew of bike trails and rafting runs (as well as the requisite outfitters); and the **Lehigh Gorge Scenic Railway** (☎ 570-325-8485; www.lgsry.com; adult/child $12/9; ⏱ 11am, 1pm, 3pm), offering peaceful one-hour rides through the Lehigh Gorge State Park.

Nature lovers should also explore the 797-sq-mile **Allegheny National Forest** (☎ 814-723-5150; www.fs.fed.us/r9/forests/allegheny), encompassing several state parks and sprouting with acres of hemlock, maple, white ash and the valuable Allegheny black cherry. It's an excellent place for camping and hiking, canoeing and fishing.

New England

New England may look small on a map, but don't let that fool you – it harbors a wealth of sights. Yes, you could drive from one end of the region to the other in a day – albeit a very long day – but, really, why would you want to? There are simply too many enticements along the way, no matter what road you take.

Along the coast you'll find age-old fishing villages raking in the lobsters, sandy beaches begging for a dip and cities celebrating their past while reveling in their present. Revitalized gems such as Providence and Portland boast palate-pleasing dining and uncrowded sights, while busy Boston packs a wallop with history and culture aplenty.

Then there's inland New England. Vermont, New Hampshire and Maine are as rural and rugged as the mountains that run up their spines. Dramatic White Mountain National Forest is action-central for anything to do with the outdoors, from winter skiing to summer hiking and fall foliage splendor. Or take it further afield in Maine's northern wilderness, a vast frontier where black bear and moose outnumber people and white-water rafting and backcountry camping get top billing.

So take it slow. Crack open a lobster and let the sweet juices run down your fingers, stroll the cobbled streets of Nantucket, sink your toes into the sands of Cape Cod. Go to Harvard and Yale, if just for a day, and rub shoulders with Ivy Leaguers in hip campus cafés. Arm yourself with a good map and ramble along country roads past covered bridges and charming towns with white-steepled churches. The highways can wait for another day.

HIGHLIGHTS

- Grabbing a seat at Boston's venerable **Fenway Park** (p244) and joining the frenzied fanatics cheering on the Red Sox.

- Rendezvousing with acrobatic humpbacks on a whale-watching cruise from **Provincetown** (p251).

- Feasting on fresh boiled lobster at one of the **lobster shacks** (p291) along the New England coast.

- Hiking to **Franconia Falls** (p284) for the coolest swimming hole in the White Mountains.

- Digging into **Acadia National Park** (p297), bicycling and hiking its carriage roads, and relaxing over afternoon tea at Jordan Pond.

- Soaking up some sun and watching the stars at **Newport's** (p264) seaside folk and jazz festivals.

- Being dazzled by brilliant fall foliage in the **Green Mountains** (p274), **Berkshires** (p259) and **Litchfield Hills** (p270).

Acadia
National
Park ★
Maine

Vermont
★ Franconia
Falls
New ★ Lobster
Hampshire Shacks
Green
Mountains ★

Boston ★ ★ Provincetown
Massachusetts
Berkshires ★

Connecticut ★ ★ Rhode Island
Litchfield Newport
Hills

HISTORY

When the first European settlers arrived, New England was inhabited by the Algonquian peoples who lived in small tribes, raising corn and beans, hunting game and harvesting the rich coastal waters.

English captain Bartholomew Gosnold landed at Cape Cod and sailed north to Maine in 1602 but it wasn't until 1614 that Captain John Smith, who charted the region's coastline for King James I, christened the land 'New England.' With the arrival of the Pilgrims at Plymouth in 1620, European settlement began in earnest. Over the next century the colonies expanded and thrived, often at the expense of the native people.

Although subjects of the British crown, New Englanders governed themselves with their own legislative councils and they came to view their affairs as separate from those of England. In the 1770s King George III instituted policies intent on reining in the colonists' free-wheeling spirits and he imposed a series of costly taxes. The colonists, unrepresented in the English Parliament, revolted under the slogan 'no taxation without representation.' Attempts to squash the revolt resulted in the battles of Lexington and Concord, setting off the American Revolution that gave birth to the USA in 1776.

Following independence, New England established itself as an economic powerhouse, its harbors booming centers for shipbuilding, fishing and trade. New England's famed Yankee clippers plied ports from China to South America. The USA's first water-powered cotton-spinning mill was established in Rhode Island in 1793. New England's swift rivers became the engines of vast mills turning out clothing, shoes and machinery.

By the early 20th century many of the mills had moved south. The economy sprung back to life again during WWII. Today education, finance, biotechnology and tourism are linchpins of the regional economy.

LOCAL CULTURE

New Englanders are traditionally reserved, with a Yankee thriftiness of speech, which stands in marked contrast to the casual outgoing nature of Californians and other folks out West. Visitors sometimes see this reserve as unfriendliness, but it's simply a more formal regional style.

Particularly in rural areas you'll notice the pride folks take upon themselves on their ingenuity and self-sufficient character. These New Englanders remain fiercely independent, from the fishing boat crews who brave Atlantic storms to the small Vermont farmers who fight to keep operating independently within America's gobble-up agribusiness economy.

Fortunately for the farmers and fishers, buy-local and go-organic movements have grown by leaps and bounds throughout the region. From bistros in Boston to small towns in the far north the menus are greening.

One place you won't find that ol' Yankee reserve is at the ballfield. New Englanders are absolutely fanatical about sports. Attending a Red Sox game is as close as you'll come to a modern-day gladiators-at-the-coliseum scene – wild cheers and nasty jeers galore. People come from far and wide to be in attendance – one seasoned fan, horror novelist Stephen King, regularly treks some 250 miles from his home in Bangor, Maine just to watch the Red Sox play.

LAND & CLIMATE

New England's landscape has appealing variety, with verdant valleys, rolling hills and abundant forests. A spine of craggy mountains runs roughly from northeast to southwest; the highest point, Mt Washington in the White Mountains, tops out at 6288ft.

The coastline is varied as well. In the north it's largely rocky, sculpted into coves and sprinkled with the occasional sandy beach, while the southern coastline, including prized Cape Cod, is bounded by long swaths of sand and dunes.

The weather in New England is famously changeable. Muggy 90°F (32°C) days in July may be followed by a day of cool 65°F (18°C) weather. Precipitation averages about 3in per month year-round.

The beachy summer season is roughly June to mid-September. New England's world-famous fall foliage peaks from mid-September to mid-October.

PARKS

Green spaces abound. Acadia National Park (p297), which is situated on the rugged, northeastern coast of Maine, is New

NEW ENGLAND

NEW ENGLAND

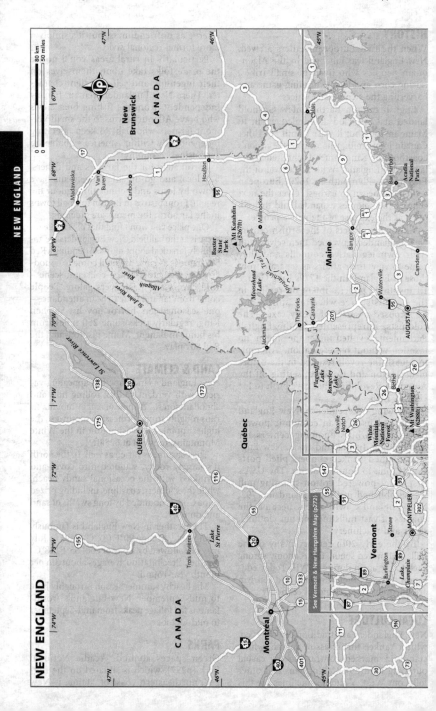

NEW ENGLAND

CANADA

Montréal

401

15

155

73

30

9N

11

Trois Rivières

Lake
St Pierre

20

10

133

15

Burlington

Lake
Champlain

87

2

89

7

Vermont

89

Stowe

MONTPELIER

302

2

93

91

55

147

See Vermont & New Hampshire Map (p272)

Québec

QUÉBEC

St Lawrence River

40

116

55

175

173

138

30

CANADA

Madawaska

Van Buren

Caribou

17

1

Jackman

St John River

Allagash River

The Forks

Caratunk

201

Moosehead
Lake

Baxter
State
Park

▲ Mt Katahdin
(5267ft)

Millinocket

95

Houlton

New
Brunswick

CANADA

3

4

6

1

9

Calais

1

1

Maine

Bangor

ALT
1

ALT
1

3

Bar Harbor

Acadia
National
Park

Camden

3

Waterville

2

95

AUGUSTA

26

Bethel

26

2

▲ Mt Washington
(6288ft)

White
Mountain
National
Forest

Dixville
Notch

26

3

Flagstaff
Lake

Rangeley
Lake

Appalachian Trail

0   80 km
0   50 miles

47°N

46°N

45°N

67°W

68°W

69°W

70°W

71°W

72°W

73°W

74°W

45°N

46°N

47°N

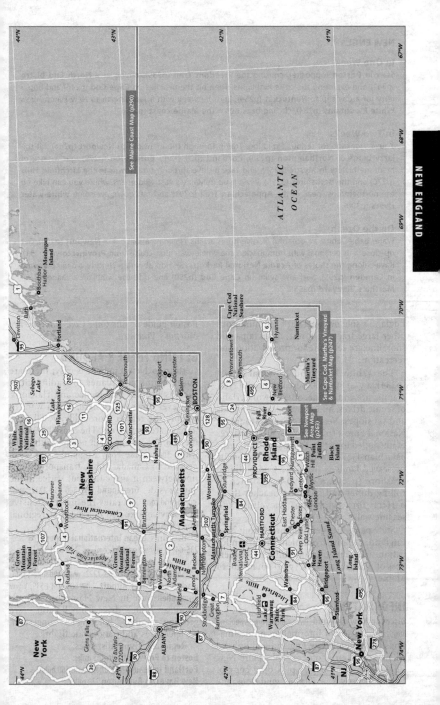

NEW ENGLAND

NEW ENGLAND

NEW ENGLAND...

In One Week

Start in **Boston** (opposite), cruising the **Freedom Trail** (p239), dining at a **North End bistro** (p241) and exploring the city's highlights. Then hit the beaches on **Cape Cod** (p246) and hop a ferry for a day trip to **Nantucket** (p254). End the week with a jaunt north to New Hampshire's **White Mountains** (p284), circling back down the **Maine coast** (p288).

In Two Weeks

You've got time for serious exploring. Tramp through the mansions in **Newport** (p264), hit the jazzy burgs of **Northampton** (p258), **Portland** (p291) and **Burlington** (p279), get a taste of maritime history in **Mystic** (p268), and take a drive through rural towns in the **Litchfield Hills** (p270) and the **Berkshires** (p259). Wrap it up in Maine's vast wilderness, where you can hike up the northernmost peak of the **Appalachian Trail** (p301) and raft down awesome **white-water rivers** (p300).

On the Ocean

Water babies unite: an oceanful of adventures awaits. Navigate a sailboat in **Newport** (p264). Get up-close and personal with humpbacks on a whale-watching cruise from **Provincetown** (p251). Kayak along the shores of **Acadia National Park** (p298). Hop aboard a century-old windjammer in **Camden** (p295). Surf and swim on **Cape Cod** (p250) and ride the wind on a sailboard on **Martha's Vineyard** (p255).

England's sole national park but numerous other large tracts of forest, mountains and shoreline are set aside for preservation and recreation.

The White Mountain National Forest (p284), a vast 800,000-acre expanse of New Hampshire and Maine, offers a wonderland of scenic drives, hiking trails, campgrounds and ski slopes. Vermont's Green Mountain National Forest (p274) covers 400,000 acres of unspoiled forest that's crossed by the Appalachian Trail. The other gem of nationally preserved lands is the Cape Cod National Seashore (p250), a 44,600-acre stretch of rolling dunes and stunning beaches that's perfect for swimming, bicycling and seaside walks.

State parks are plentiful throughout New England, ranging from niches in urban locations to the remote and untamed wilderness of Baxter State Park (p301) in northern Maine.

INFORMATION

Discover New England (www.discovernewengland .org) has all sorts of information on destinations throughout New England and links to all six state tourist offices. To explore New England in more depth, pick up a copy of Lonely Planet's *New England* guidebook, the *Boston* guide or our *Cape Cod, Nantucket & Martha's Vineyard.*

GETTING THERE & AROUND

Getting to New England is easy; there are buses, trains and planes to leading cities such as Boston, Providence and Hartford. However once you're here, if you want to explore the region thoroughly, you'll need to have access to a car. The coastal I-95 and the inland I-91, the main north–south highways, transverse New England from Connecticut to Canada. Public transportation is fine between major cities, but scarce in the countryside. **Greyhound** (☎ 800-231-2222; www .greyhound.com) operates the most extensive bus service and also books other regional bus companies.

Boston's **Logan International Airport** (☎ 800-235-6426; www.massport.com) is New England's main air hub. Providence's **TF Green Airport** (☎ 401-737-8222, 888-268-7222; www.pvdairport.com) and **Manchester Airport** (☎ 603-624-6539; www .flymanchester.com) in New Hampshire – both about an hour's drive from Boston – are growing 'minihubs' boasting less congestion, cheaper fares and nationwide flights.

Regional driving distances:
Boston to Provincetown 145 miles.
Portland to Acadia National Park: 160 miles.
New Haven to Burlington 270 miles.

MASSACHUSETTS

The history is legendary – Plymouth, where the Pilgrims landed; Boston, where the first shots of the American Revolution rang out; and Nantucket, whose whaling ships swarmed the oceans. But there's a lot more than landmark sights in this old state. Fast forward to the present: Boston and neighboring Cambridge have blossomed into spirited college towns, Provincetown's a gay-extravaganza whirl, and those whales – a major attraction in their own right – are now followed by affectionate sightseers on whale-watching cruises. By all means start in Boston, the state's busy hub, where you can mix colonial sights and museum strolls with sizzling nightlife and pub crawls. Then move further afield, to the woodsy Berkshires and the dunes and beaches of Cape Cod and Martha's Vineyard.

History

Massachusetts has played a major role in American politics since the arrival of the first colonists. In the 18th century, spurred by a booming maritime trade, Massachusetts colonists revolted against trade restrictions imposed by Great Britain. British attempts to quell the revolt resulted in the 1770 Boston Massacre, which became a rallying call to action. The Boston Tea Party followed, setting the stage for the 1775 battles between British troops and colonial militia at Lexington and Concord, which started the American Revolution.

In the 19th century Massachusetts became the center of the world's whaling industry, bringing unprecedented wealth to the islands of Nantucket and Martha's Vineyard, whose ports are still lined with grand sea captains' homes.

Information

Boston Globe (www.boston.com) The region's main newspaper has lots of useful visitor-related information online.

Massachusetts Office of Travel & Tourism
(☎ 617-973-8500, 800-227-6277; www.massvacation
.com; 10 Park Plaza, Suite 4510, Boston, MA 02116) Has information on the entire state and will mail out a free magazine-size travel guide on request.

BOSTON

Sure, it's the largest city in New England, but with just 600,000 residents Boston retains an intimate neighborhood scale that belies its stature. While it's one of America's oldest cities, with a plethora of historic sights, its heartbeat is hip and youthful. A score of colleges and universities attract students from around the world, adding to the city's cultural diversity and enriching a thriving arts, theater and entertainment scene. And thanks to its compact nature, it's a cinch to get around.

History

When the Massachusetts Bay Colony was established by England in 1630, the port of Boston became its capital. Boston is a city of firsts: Boston Latin School, the first public school in the USA, was founded in 1635, followed a year later by Harvard, the nation's first university. The first newspaper in the 13 original colonies was established here in 1704, America's first labor union organized here in 1795 and the country's first subway system opened in Boston in 1897.

Not only were the first battles of the American Revolution fought here, but Boston also was home to the first African American regiment to fight in the US Civil War. Waves of immigrants, especially Irish in the mid-18th century and Italians in the early 20th, have infused the city with European influences.

MASSACHUSETTS FACTS

Nicknames Bay State, Old Colony
Population 6.4 million
Area 10,555 sq miles
Capital city Boston (population 590,763)
Sales tax 5%
Birthplace of Benjamin Franklin (1706–90), Emily Dickinson (1830–86), presidents John Adams (1735–1826), John Quincy Adams (1767–1848), John F Kennedy (1917–63) and George Bush Sr (b 1924)
Home of Harvard University, Boston Marathon, Plymouth Rock
Famous for Boston Tea Party, Boston Red Sox, first state to allow gay marriage
Most parodied accent Bostonians' *pahk the cah in Hahvahd Yahd*

NEW ENGLAND

Today Boston remains at the forefront of higher learning and its universities have spawned world-renowned industries in biotechnology, medicine and finance.

Orientation & Information

Boston's leading neighborhoods radiate out from Boston Common, the city's central park, and the lion's share of sights are within walking distance of the Common.

Virtually all of the city's attractions and the airport are easily accessible by MBTA (the 'T') subway trains (p245). The Park St station, a 'T' hub, is beneath the Common. Harvard Sq, the epicenter of Cambridge, is about 5 miles northwest of the Common and served by the T's Red Line.

BOOKSTORES

Barnes & Noble (Map pp234-5; ☎ 617-247-6959; www .barnesandnoble.com; 800 Boylston St) This Prudential Center branch is convenient and well stocked.

Coop (Map p237; ☎ 617-499-2000; 1400 Massachusetts Ave, Cambridge) Head here for regional books, music and all sorts of Harvard-logo souvenirs.

Globe Corner Bookstore (Map p237; ☎ 617-497-6277; www.globecorner.com; 90 Mt Auburn St , Cambridge) Near Harvard Sq, specializing in travel books and maps.

Out of Town News (Map p237; ☎ 617-354-7777; Harvard Sq, Cambridge) This National Historic Landmark sells newspapers from major US and international cities.

INTERNET ACCESS

Boston Public Library (Map pp234-5; ☎ 617-536-5400; www.bpl.org; 700 Boylston St; ☽ 9am-9pm Mon-Thu, 9am-5pm Fri & Sat) Free for 15 minutes, or get a visitor card at the circulation desk and sign up for longer terminal time.

Tech Superpowers & Internet Café (Map p231; ☎ 617-267-9716; www.techsuperpowers.com; 252 Newbury St; per 15min/1hr $3/5; ☽ 9am-8pm Mon-Fri, noon-8pm Sat & Sun) Provides online computers, but if you have your own laptop wi-fi access is free throughout Newbury St.

INTERNET RESOURCES

City of Boston (www.cityofboston.gov) Official website for the city government.

iBoston (www.iboston.org) Visit this website for the scoop on Boston history, architecture and historic sites.

MEDIA

Boston Globe (www.boston.com) New England's major daily newspaper, with a handy calendar insert on Thursday.

Boston Phoenix (www.bostonphoenix.com) Free alternative weekly, available Thursday, with solid arts and entertainment coverage.

MEDICAL SERVICES

CVS Pharmacy (Map pp234-5; ☎ 617-437-8414; 587 Boylston St; ☽ 24hr)

Massachusetts General Hospital (Map pp234-5; ☎ 617-726-2000; 55 Fruit St; ☽ 24hr) Off Cambridge St.

BOSTON IN...

Two Days

Follow in the footsteps of America's revolutionary founders on the **Freedom Trail** (p238), stopping to have a pint at the **Green Dragon Tavern** (p243), a former haunt of Paul Revere himself. End your first day with a home-style Italian feast in the **North End** (p241).

Your mother always wanted you to go to Harvard, right? Begin day two in **Cambridge** (p236) poking around Harvard Sq and checking out the campus sights. In the afternoon, take a tour of historic **Fenway Park** (p236) – or better yet, catch a **Red Sox game** (p244). End the day with the beautiful people on **Newbury St** (p242).

Four Days

Start day three at one of the city's stellar museums – for classic American art, head to the **Museum of Fine Arts** (p236) or for cutting edge, the new **Institute of Contemporary Art** (p233). For sumptuous city views, paddle a kayak down the **Charles River** (p232) or take an elevator up 50 floors to the **Prudential Center Skywalk** (p233).

On your final day, head west to **Lexington** and **Concord** (p245) if you have a literary inclination, or spend the day at kid-friendly **Plimoth Plantation** (p246). When you get back into town, catch a **play** (p244) at one of Boston's renowned theaters or hit the **nightclubs** (p243) along Lansdowne St.

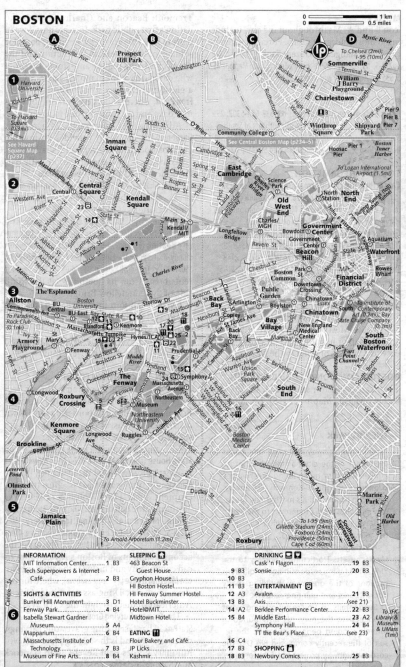

BOSTON

INFORMATION	
MIT Information Center...........	1 B3
Tech Superpowers & Internet	
Café.................................	2 B3
SIGHTS & ACTIVITIES	
Bunker Hill Monument...........	3 D1
Fenway Park.......................	4 B4
Isabella Stewart Gardner	
Museum............................	5 A4
Mapparium.........................	6 B4
Massachusetts Institute of	
Technology.......................	7 B3
Museum of Fine Arts............	8 B4

SLEEPING	
463 Beacon St	
Guest House......................	9 B3
Gryphon House...................	10 B3
HI Boston Hostel.................	11 B3
HI Fenway Summer Hostel.....	12 A3
Hotel Buckminster..............	13 B3
Hotel@MIT.........................	14 A2
Midtown Hotel....................	15 B4
EATING	
Flour Bakery and Café.........	16 C4
JP Licks.............................	17 B3
Kashmir.............................	18 B3

DRINKING	
Cask 'n Flagon....................	19 B3
Sonsie..............................	20 B3
ENTERTAINMENT	
Avalon..............................	21 B3
Axis..................................	(see 21)
Berklee Performance Center..	22 B3
Middle East........................	23 A2
Symphony Hall....................	24 B4
TT the Bear's Place.............	(see 23)
SHOPPING	
Newbury Comics..................	25 B3

MONEY

You'll find ATMs throughout the city, including at most subway stations. Foreign currency can be exchanged at **Citizens Bank** (53 State St Map pp234-5; ☎ 800-922-9999; opposite Trinity Church Map pp234-5; 535 Boylston St; Harvard Sq Map p237).

POST

Main Post office (Map pp234-5; ☎ 617-654-5302; 25 Dorchester Ave; ☯ 24hr) One block southeast of South Station. There are several other post offices around central Boston (Map pp234-5) and near Harvard Sq (Map p237).

TOURIST INFORMATION

Cambridge Visitor Information Booth (Map p237; ☎ 617-441-2884, 800-862-5678; www.cambridge-usa .org; 4 Brattle St; ☯ 9am-5pm Mon-Sat, 1-5pm Sun) This Harvard Sq kiosk has all the scoop on Cambridge.

Greater Boston Convention & Visitors Bureau (GBCVB; Map pp234-5; ☎ 617-536-4100, 888-733-2678; www.bostonusa.com); Boston Common (Map pp234-5;148 Tremont St; ☯ 9am-5pm); Prudential Center (Map pp234–5; 800 Boylston St; ☯ 10am-6pm) Distributes a free city guide.

Sights & Activities

Slip on a good pair of walking shoes, and this city's yours. Most of Boston's main attractions are found in or near the city center, making it easy to ramble from one to the next.

BOSTON COMMON & PUBLIC GARDEN

The heart of Boston since 1634, the 50-acre **Boston Common** (Map pp234-5), bordered by

---

THE BIG PARK

The hulking highway that once tore across the center of the city has morphed into a 2-mile stretch of meandering green space known as the Rose Kennedy Greenway. Named in honor of JFK's mother, the greenway stretches from Chinatown to the North End, reclaiming land from what was once the elevated section of I-93.

A variety of community groups, from the Massachusetts Horticultural Society to the YMCA, are taking responsibility for different sections of the greenway, building shady pocket parks and planting gardens.

Incidentally, if you're wondering what happened to the hwy, it's now buried in tunnels running beneath the city, the result of the recently completed Big Dig, the costliest highway project in US history.

Tremont, Beacon and Charles Sts, was the nation's first public park. In years past it was a pasture for cattle grazing, a staging ground for soldiers of the American Revolution and the site of chastising pillory-and-stocks for those who dared defy Puritan mores. These days it's a gloriously carefree scene, especially at the **Frog Pond**, where waders cool off on hot summer days and ice skaters frolic in winter.

Adjoining the Common, the 24-acre **Public Garden** (Map pp234–5) provides an inviting oasis of bountiful flowers and shady trees. Its centerpiece, a tranquil lagoon with old-fashioned pedal-powered **Swan Boats** (☎ 617-522-1966; adult/child 2-15 $2.75/1.25; ☯ 10am-4pm or 5pm mid-Apr–early Sep), has been delighting children for generations.

The nearby Charles River is action-central for joggers, cyclists, skaters and rowers. **Community Boating** (Map pp234-5; ☎ 617-523-1038; www.community-boating.org; The Esplanade; per 2 days kayak/sailboat $50/100; ☯ 1pm-dusk Mon-Fri, 9am-dusk Sat & Sun Apr-Oct) rents boats from its boathouse at the south side of the Longfellow Bridge.

Cyclists can join up with **Boston Bike Tours** (Map pp234-5; ☎ 617-308-5902; www.bostonbiketours.com; departs from Boston Common; tours $30; ☯ 11am Fri-Sun) to follow Paul Revere's ride, cruise Harvard Sq on wheels or take in a brewery tour.

BEACON HILL & DOWNTOWN

Rising above Boston Common is historic Beacon Hill, the well-heeled address of prominent Bostonian families. The bordering downtown district encompasses a mix of colonial-era sights and modern office buildings.

Crowning Beacon Hill is the golden-domed **State House** (Map pp234-5; ☎ 617-727-3676; www.state .ma.us/sec/trs; Beacon St at Park St; admission free; ☯ 8am-6pm Mon-Fri), the seat of Massachusetts' government since 1798. Volunteers lead free 30-minute tours from 10:30am to 3:30pm.

The **Museum of Afro-American History** (Map pp234-5; ☎ 617-725-0022; www.afroammuseum.org; 46 Joy St; admission free; ☯ 10am-4pm Mon-Sat) illustrates the accomplishments of Boston's African American community and includes the adjacent **African Meeting House** (☯ same as above), where former slave Frederick Douglass recruited African American soldiers to fight the Civil War.

The **Granary Burying Ground** (Map pp234-5; Tremont St at Park St) has fascinating gravestone carvings, dates to 1660 and is the resting place of Revolutionary heroes Paul Revere, John Hancock and Samuel Adams.

At the **Old South Meeting House** (Map pp234-5; ☎ 617-482-6439; www.oldsouthmeetinghouse.org; 310 Washington St; adult/child 6-18 $5/1; ⊙ 9:30am-5pm Apr-Oct, 10am-4pm Nov-Mar), colonists met in 1773 for a rousing debate on taxation without representation before throwing the Boston Tea Party.

The red-brick **Faneuil Hall** (Map pp234-5; Congress St), topped with its famed grasshopper weathervane and fronted with a statue of Samuel Adams, has been a market and public meeting place since 1740. Today the hall, Quincy Market and North and South Market buildings make up the Faneuil Hall Marketplace with lots of small shops and eateries.

NORTH END & CHARLESTOWN

An old-world warren of narrow streets, the Italian North End offers visitors an irresistible mix of colorful period buildings and mouth-watering family-run eateries. Colonial sights spill across the river into Charlestown, where America's oldest battleship lies docked.

You get two attractions in one at the **Paul Revere House** (Map pp234-5; ☎ 617-523-2338; www .paulreverehouse.org; 19 North Sq; adult/child 5-17 $3/1; ⊙ 9:30am-5:15pm mid-Apr–Oct, to 4:15pm Nov–mid-Apr), since it's not only the former home of the patriot who rang out the warning 'the British are coming' but it's also the oldest (1680) house still standing in Boston.

It was at the **Old North Church** (Map pp234-5; ☎ 617-523-6676; 193 Salem St; admission free; ⊙ 9am-5pm) that two lanterns were hung in the steeple on that fateful night of April 18, 1775, signaling to a waiting Paul Revere that British forces were setting out by sea ('one if by land, two if by sea').

Work off that North End lunch by clambering around the decks of the **USS Constitution** (Map pp234-5; ☎ 617-242-7511; admission free; ⊙ tours every 30min 10:30am-3:30pm daily Apr-Oct, Thu-Sat Nov-Mar), centerpiece of the Charlestown Navy Yard. Built in 1797, the old warship's oak-timbered hull was so thick that cannonballs literally bounced off it, earning it the nickname 'Old Ironsides.'

The 221ft granite obelisk **Bunker Hill Monument** (Map p231; (☎ 617-242-5641; Monument Sq; admission free; ⊙ 9am-4:30pm) commemorates the American Revolution's first major battle.

BACK BAY

Extending west from Boston Common this chic neighborhood boasts graceful brown-stone residences, grand buildings and the tony shopping mecca of Newbury St.

Copley Square (Map pp234–5) plaza is surrounded by historic buildings, including the ornate French-Romanesque **Trinity Church** (☎ 617-536-0944; cnr Boylston & Clarendon Sts; adult/child under 16 $5/free; ⊙ 9am-6pm Mon-Fri, 9am-5pm Sat, 12:30-5pm Sun), the masterwork of architect HH Richardson. Across the street, the Italian Renaissance-style **Boston Public Library** (☎ 617-536-5400; 700 Boylston St; ⊙ 9am-9pm Mon-Thu, 9am-5pm Fri & Sat), America's first municipal library, is adorned with grand murals by John Singer Sargent.

For a stunning 360-degree bird's-eye view of the city, head to the **Prudential Center Skywalk** (Map pp234-5; ☎ 617-859-0648; 800 Boylston St; adult/child under 12 $11/7.50; ⊙ 10am-10pm), the tower's 50th-floor observation deck.

If you've ever wanted to walk across the planet, the Christian Science Church's **Mapparium** (Map p231; ☎ 617-450-7000; 200 Massachusetts Ave; adult/child 6-17 $6/4; ⊙ 10am-4pm Tue-Sun), an enormous stained-glass globe with a bridge through its center, offers the easiest route.

WATERFRONT & SEAPORT DISTRICT

Boston's rave new waterfront museum, the **Institute of Contemporary Art** (Map p231; ☎ 617-478-3100; www.icaboston.org; 100 Northern Ave; adult/child under 18 $12/free; ⊙ 10am-5pm Tue, Wed, Sat & Sun, 10am-9pm Thu & Fri), dazzles from the avant-garde architecture to its 21st-century collection of new-wave paintings, sculptures and multimedia art. Come after 5pm on Thursday and admission's free!

A treat for the eyes, **New England Aquarium** (Map pp234-5; ☎ 617-973-5200; www.neaq.org; Central Wharf; adult/child 3-11 $18/10; ⊙ 9am-5pm Mon-Fri, 9am-6pm Sat & Sun) centers around a four-story-high tank teeming with sharks and colorful tropical fish.

Extremely popular are the aquarium's naturalist-led **whale-watching cruises** (adult/child 3-17 $36/30; ⊙ Apr-Oct) that head 30 miles out to Stellwagen Bank to watch feeding humpback whales do their acrobatic breaches.

CHINATOWN, THEATER DISTRICT & SOUTH END

Compact and easy to stroll, Chinatown offers up enticing Asian eateries cheek-to-jowl, while the adjacent Theater District is clustered with performing arts venues. The sprawling South End boasts one of America's largest concentration of Victorian row houses and a

NEW ENGLAND

NEW ENGLAND

CENTRAL BOSTON

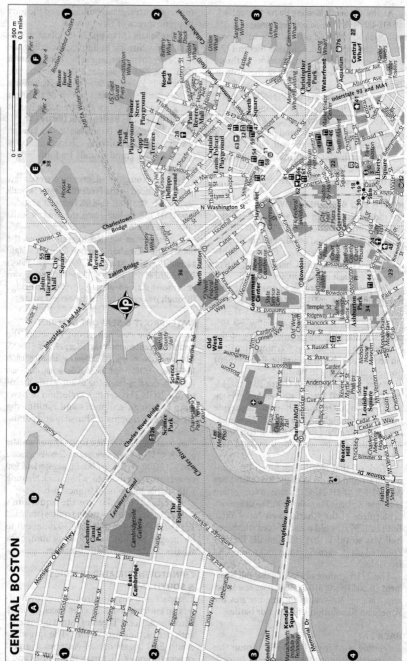

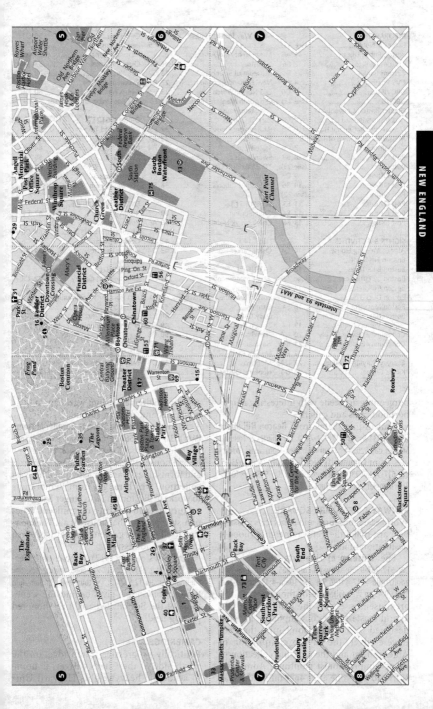

burgeoning art scene with interesting neighborhood cafés and galleries.

Rent in-line skates from **Beacon Hill Skate** (Map pp234-5; ☎ 617-482-7400; cnr Charles & Tremont Sts; per day $20; ☼ 11am-6pm Wed-Mon) and bicycles from **Community Bicycle Supply** (Map pp234-5; ☎ 617-542-8623; 496 Tremont St; per day $25; ☼ 10am-7pm Mon-Sat, noon-5pm Sun).

FENWAY & KENMORE SQUARE

World-class museums and America's classiest ballpark make the Fenway neighborhood a destination in itself.

The **Museum of Fine Arts** (MFA; Map p231; ☎ 617-267-9300; www.mfa.org; 465 Huntington Ave; adult/child 7-17 $15/6.50; ☼ 10am-4:45pm Sat-Tue, 10am-9:45pm Wed-Fri), one of the country's top art museums, covers the gamut from Old World masters to a contemporary art wing designed by IM Pei. Don't miss the Paul Revere silver, the superb compilation of American art and the amazing collection of French impressionist paintings. Admission is free to everyone after 4pm on Wednesday

and for children after 3pm weekdays, all day weekends and daily in summer.

The nearby **Isabella Stewart Gardner Museum** (Map p231; ☎ 617-566-1401; www.gardnermuseum.org; 280 The Fenway; adult/child under 18 $12/free; ☼ 11am-5pm Tue-Sun) houses priceless paintings, tapestries and furnishings. Gardner assembled her vast collection, which ranges from Rembrandts to works by Bostonian John Singer Sargent, a century ago and lived in a magnificent Venetian-style palazzo that houses it all. The mansion itself, with its garden courtyard, is worth the price of admission.

America's oldest (1912) baseball park, **Fenway Park** (Map p231; ☎ 617-226-6666; www.redsox.com; adult/child under 12 $12/10; ☼ tours every hr 9am-4pm Mon-Sat, noon-4pm Sun), gives behind-the-scenes tours of the Boston Red Sox' time-honored playing field.

CAMBRIDGE

Politically progressive Cambridge, on the north side of the Charles River, is home to academic heavyweights Harvard University and Massachusetts Institute of Technology (MIT). Some 30,000 students make for a lively scene. Its central **Harvard Square** (Map p237) overflows with cafés, bookstores and street performers. Along Massachusetts Ave, opposite the Harvard T station, lies **Harvard University** (Map p237; www .harvard.edu), which counts dozens of Nobel laureates and seven US presidents among its graduates – for other chewy tidbits join a free student-led campus tour at the **Holyoke Center** (Map p237; ☎ 617-495-1573; 1350 Massachusetts Ave; ☽ 1hr tours 10am & 2pm Mon-Fri & 2pm Sat Sep-May, 10am, 11:15am, 2pm & 3:15pm Mon-Sat mid-Jun–mid-Aug).

It should come as no surprise that Harvard, the nation's oldest (1636) and wealthiest uni-

versity, has amassed incredible collections. The **Fogg Art Museum** (Map p237; ☎ 617-495-9400; www.artmuseums.harvard.edu; 32 Quincy St; adult/child 18 & under $9/free; ☽ 10am-5pm Mon-Sat, 1-5pm Sun) showcases Western art since the Middle Ages, with a particularly strong impressionist collection; admission includes the **Busch-Reisinger Museum**, which specializes in Northern European art, and the **Arthur M Sackler Museum** (☎ 617-495-9400; 485 Broadway; ☽ 10am-5pm Mon-Sat, 1-5pm Sun), devoted to Asian and Islamic art. The **Harvard Museum of Natural History** (Map p237; ☎ 617-495-3045; 26 Oxford St; adult/child 3-18 $9/6; ☽ 9am-5pm) and the interconnected **Peabody Museum of Archaeology & Ethnology** present outstanding Native American exhibits and an exquisite collection of 4000 glass flowers.

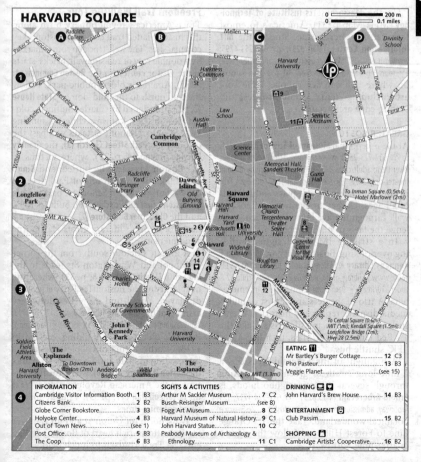

HARVARD SQUARE

NEW ENGLAND

BOSTON HARBOR ISLANDS

Now designated a National Recreation Area, **Boston Harbor Islands** (www.bostonislands.com; admission free; ☺ mid-Apr–mid-Oct) consists of 34 islands with sandy beaches, hiking trails and camping. Since the massive cleanup of Boston Harbor in the 1990s, these once-polluted islands, just a 45-minute boat ride from downtown Boston, have been transformed into sparkling natural assets.

Georges Island is the transportation hub for the islands and the site of Fort Warren, a 19th-century fort and Civil War prison. Other popular destinations are Bumpkin Island, known for its slate beaches and wildflower fields; Grape Island, a haven for bird-watchers; and Lovells Island, with dunes and a wide swimming beach.

Harbor Express (☎ 617-223-8666; round-trip adult/child under 12 $12/7) runs ferries between Boston's Long Wharf (Map pp234–5) and Georges Island. From Georges Island free shuttle boats are available to other islands in the chain.

Camping is allowed at primitive **campsites** (☎ 877-422-6762; www.reserveamerica.com; campsite $10; ☺ late Jun-early Sep) on Grape, Bumpkin and Lovells islands.

At the **Massachusetts Institute of Technology** (MIT; Map p231), America's foremost tech campus, nerds rule. Stop at the **MIT Information Center** (Map p231; ☎ 617-253-4795; www.mit.edu; 77 Massachusetts Ave; admission free; ☺ tours 10:45am & 2:45pm Mon-Fri) for the scoop on where you can see robots, some cool art (including Henry Moore bronzes) and cutting-edge architecture.

GREATER BOSTON

At the exceptional **Museum of Science** (Map pp234-5; ☎ 617-723-2500; www.mos.org; Science Park, Charles River Dam; adult/child 3-11 $16/13, planetarium or Omni theater only $9/7; ☺ 9am-5pm Sat-Thu, 9am-9pm Fri), hundreds of interactive displays enthrall kids of all ages. Go eye to eye with a dinosaur, walk through the live butterfly garden, challenge the laws of physics and more.

In a striking IM Pei–designed building overlooking Boston Harbor, the **John F Kennedy Library & Museum** (Map p231; ☎ 617-514-1600; www.jfklibrary.org; Columbia Point; adult/child 12 & under $10/free; ☺ 9am-5pm) houses JFK memorabilia. A trio of theaters and a host of multimedia displays replay key historical events such as the Cuban missile crisis. Take the T's Red Line to JFK/UMass, then hop a free 'JFK' shuttle bus.

A highlight of the Emerald Necklace, a 7-mile-long swath of green space cutting through several Boston neighborhoods, is **Arnold Arboretum** (Map p231; ☎ 617-524-1717; 125 Arborway; admission free; ☺ dawn-dusk), a 265-acre botanical wonderland. Take the T's Orange Line to Forest Hills and follow the signs a quarter-mile northwest.

Freedom Trail Walking Tour

Trace America's revolutionary birth along this history-laden trail covering Boston's key colonial sites. The well-trodden route, marked by a double row of red sidewalk bricks, starts at the visitor center on the **Boston Common** (1; p232), America's oldest public park. Follow the trail north to the gold-domed **State House** (2; p232), designed by Charles Bulfinch, colonial Boston's best-known architect. Rounding Park St onto Tremont St takes you past the colonial-era **Park Street Church** (3); the **Granary Burying Ground** (4; p232), where victims of the Boston Massacre lie buried; and **King's Chapel** (5), topped with one of Paul Revere's bells. Continue down School St, past the site of **Boston's first public school** (6), built in 1635, and the **Old Corner Bookstore** (7), a 19th-century haunt of Boston's literary greats Hawthorne and Emerson.

A minute's detour south from the corner of School and Washington Sts leads to the **Old South Meeting House** (8; p233), where the nitty-gritty on the Boston Tea Party is proudly displayed. You'll find more Revolutionary exhibits at the **Old State House** (9; ☎ 617-720-1713; 206 Washington St; adult/child 6-18 $5/1; ☺ 9am-5pm), Boston's oldest public building, erected in 1713. Nearby, a ring of cobblestones at the intersection of State and Congress Sts marks the **Boston Massacre site (10)**, where the first victims of the American Revolution died. Next up is **Faneuil Hall** (11; p233), a public market since colonial times.

Walk north on Union St and up Hanover St, the trattoria-rich heart of Boston's Italian enclave. Treat yourself to lunch before continuing to North Sq, where you can tour the **Paul Revere House** (12; p233), the Revolutionary hero's former home. Follow the trail onward to the **Old North Church** (13; p233), where a lookout in the steeple signaled to Revere that the British were coming, setting off his famous midnight gallop.

Continue northwest on Hull St, where you'll find more colonial graves at **Copp's Hill Burying Ground** (14) before crossing the

Charlestown Bridge to reach the **USS Constitution** (15; p233), the world's oldest commissioned warship. To the north lies **Bunker Hill Monument** (16; p233), the site of the first battle fought in the American Revolution, where your walk peaks with a sweeping view of Boston.

Boston for Children

The city's small scale makes it an easy city for families to explore. A good place to start is the Public Garden (p232), where fans of Robert McCloskey's classic Boston tale *Make Way for Ducklings* can visit statues of the famous mallards and cruise on the delightful Swan Boats. At the Boston Common (p232), kids can cool their toes in the Frog Pond and romp on the playground's swings and jungle gyms.

The **Boston Children's Museum** (Map pp234–5; ☎ 617-426-8855; www.bostonchildrensmuseum.org; 300 Congress St; adult/child 2-15 $10/8, 5-9pm Fri $1; ⏰ 10am-5pm Sat-Thu, 10am-9pm Fri) is especially entertaining for those under eight, while the Museum of Science (opposite) will thrill kids of all ages. Hits at the New England Aquarium (p233) include stroking cool creatures in the touch pool, watching seals being nursed back to health at the Animal Rescue Center and joining an awesome whale-watching tour.

Boston by Little Feet (Map pp234–5; ☎ 617-367-2345; www.bostonbyfoot.com; 1hr tour $8; ⏰ 10am Mon & Sat, 2pm Sun May-Oct), departing from Dock Sq at Faneuil Hall, and designed for kids aged six to 12, offers a fun slice of the Freedom Trail from a child's perspective. And those quirky, quacky Boston Duck Tours (below) are always a hit.

Tours

Boston Duck Tours (Map pp234–5; ☎ 617-723-3825; www.bostonducktours.com; adult/child 3-11 $27/18; ⏰ every half-hour 9am-dusk Apr-Nov) offers ridiculously popular land-and-water tours using WWII amphibious vehicles that cruise the downtown streets before splashing into the Charles River. Tours leave from the Prudential Center and the Museum of Science.

Knowledgeable guides from **Boston by Foot** (☎ 617-367-2345; www.bostonbyfoot.com; 90min tour $12; ⏰ May-Oct) offer all sorts of architecturally focused walking tours, including ones in the North End and Beacon Hill. Reservations aren't necessary; meeting locations and times are online.

FREEDOM TRAIL WALKING TOUR

0 ——— 200 m
0 ——— 0.1 miles

Start Boston Common
Finish Bunker Hill Monument
Distance 2.5 miles
Duration three hours

NEW ENGLAND

Freelance guides dressed in colonial garb – think Ben Franklin – lead **walking tours** (per person $12; ☺ departures on the hour) of the Freedom Trail from the information kiosk at Boston Common (p232). Or join one of the free ranger-led Freedom Trail tours provided by the **Boston National Historical Park Visitors Center** (Map pp234-5; ☎ 617-242-5642; www.nps.gov/bost; 15 State St; ☺ 9am-5pm).

Festivals & Events

Boston Marathon (www.boston-marathon.com) One of the country's most prestigious marathons takes runners up Heartbreak Hill in a 26.2-mile race ending at Copley Sq on Patriots Day, a Massachusetts holiday on the third Monday in April.

Fourth of July (www.bso.org) Boston hosts one of the biggest Independence Day bashes in the USA, with a free Boston Pops concert on the Esplanade and a fireworks display that's televised nationally.

Italian festivals (www.northendboston.com) During July and August the North End honors saints with a series of colorful weekend street fairs.

Head of the Charles Regatta (www.hocr.org) Spectators line the banks of the Charles River on a weekend in mid-October to watch international rowing teams compete in the world's largest two-day rowing event.

Sleeping

High occupancy rates translate into high prices in Boston, but advance planning can lessen the sting. You will typically find the best deals on weekends when business travelers exit town. The majority of hotels are in the downtown area and the Back Bay, both which are convenient to transportation and sightseeing.

For places that book solely through agencies try **Bed & Breakfast Agency of Boston** (☎ 617-720-3540, 800-248-9262; www.boston-bnbagency.com; r $100-180), which represents more than 100 B&Bs and apartments in greater Boston.

BUDGET & MIDRANGE

HI Boston Hostel (Map p231; ☎ 617-536-9455; www .bostonhostel.com; 12 Hemenway St; dm incl breakfast $28-45, r incl breakfast $69-99; ☒ ☐) This inviting year-round Back Bay hostel offers dorm rooms with four to six beds and lots of perks from free use of linens to organized tours.

HI Fenway Summer Hostel (Map p231; ☎ 617-267-8599; www.bostonhostel.com/fenway; 575 Commonwealth Ave; dm/r incl breakfast $35/89; ☺ Jun-Aug; ☒ ☐) A Boston University dormitory in winter, this Kenmore Sq hostel has dorms with three beds

each, as well as private rooms, and is close to nightlife.

463 Beacon Street Guest House (Map p231; ☎ 617-536-1302; www.463beacon.com; 463 Beacon St; r $89-149; **P** ☒) This 19th-century Back Bay brownstone with high ceilings and hardwood floors has 20 rooms on six floors, most with kitchenettes. The cheaper rooms can be a bit cramped but the pricier ones are commodious. Parking costs $9 and there are also apartments available by the week from $595.

Hotel Buckminster (Map p231; ☎ 617-236-7050, 800-727-2825; www.bostonhotelbuckminster.com; 645 Beacon St; r $119-149; **P** ☒) Built in 1897 by renowned architect Stanford White, this Kenmore Sq hotel is a mere baseball's toss from Fenway Park. Don't expect anything fancy – it's a faded dame, but the rooms are adequate and sport money-saving conveniences such as microwaves and refrigerators. Parking costs $18.

Midtown Hotel (Map p231; ☎ 617-262-1000; www.midtownhotel.com; 220 Huntington Ave; r $149-239; **P** ☒ ☒) A central Back Bay location, spacious rooms and affordable rates are the hallmarks of this no-frills hotel. Sure, the fittings are a bit dated but it's clean, friendly and just minutes from the Prudential Center and the throbbing heart of the city. Parking is available for $14.

Hotel@MIT (Map p231; ☎ 617-577-0200, 800-222-8733; www.hotelatmit.com; 20 Sidney St, Cambridge; r $149-300; **P** ☒ ☒) Sleek comfort is the buzzword at this state-of-the-art hotel. Rooms boast ergonomically designed furniture, T1 internet access and original artwork from the MIT collection. The guest list is thick with scientists and the place maintains a fun geek edge – among the in-room gadgets are Sony PlayStations! Parking is available for $22.

Charlesmark Hotel (Map pp234-5; ☎ 617-247-1212; www.thecharlesmark.com; 655 Boylston St; r incl breakfast $159-209; ☒ ☐ wi-fi) This smart Euro-style boutique hotel packs it all from a terrific Copley Sq location to cozy rooms graced with artwork, Italian tile and high-tech amenities. In the lobby you'll find free coffee and online computers.

Hotel 140 (Map pp234-5; ☎ 617-585-6600, 800-714-0140; www.140clarendon.com; 140 Clarendon St; r incl breakfast $169; **P** ☒ ☒ ☐) The newest boutique addition to the Back Bay, this thoroughly renovated former YWCA sports 40 clean, contemporary rooms. They're compact but if you snag an internet discount they can be a great deal. Parking is $20.

Harborside Inn (Map pp234-5; ☎ 617-723-7500; www.harborsideinnboston.com; 185 State St; r from $179; P ⚡ 🖥 wi-fi) This renovated 19th-century warehouse-turned-inn offers comfy rooms just steps from Faneuil Hall and Boston's waterfront. No two rooms are alike but period charm prevails throughout. Light sleepers should request an inside atrium room. Parking is available for a hefty $26.

TOP END

Gryphon House (Map p231; ☎ 617-375-9003; www.innboston.com; 9 Bay State Rd, r incl breakfast $189-235; P ⚡ 🖥) If you need room to stretch, the eight suites in this graceful 19th-century brownstone near Kenmore Sq won't disappoint. Each suite has its own classic personality but all have gas-log fireplaces and other cozy touches fused seamlessly with modern amenities like high-speed internet. Parking will set you back $15.

our pick Omni Parker House (Map pp234-5; ☎ 617-227-8600; www.omniparkerhouse.com; 60 School St; r $199-329; P ⚡ wi-fi) If the walls could talk this historic hotel overlooking the Freedom Trail would fill volumes. Employees have included Malcolm X and Ho Chi Minh, the guest list Charles Dickens and JFK. Despite its well-polished elegance, dark woods and chandeliers, there's nothing stodgy about the place – you can be as comfortable here in a T-shirt as in a suit and tie. And you couldn't be more in the thick of things; it's just a stroll to many of the city's top sights and best restaurants, which offsets the $38 parking fee somewhat.

Eating

No matter what your taste, Boston will tantalize your buds. Head to Chinatown for affordable Asian fare, to the South End for an up-and-coming café scene. And when the sun sets, there's no place like the North End, whose narrow streets are lined with more than 100 Italian restaurants.

BEACON HILL & DOWNTOWN

Quincy Market (Map pp234-5; off Congress & North Sts; ⏰ 10am-9pm Mon-Sat, noon-6pm Sun) Right on the Freedom Trail, this huge hall is lined with food stalls selling everything from Chinese plate lunches to New England seafood. A favorite local option is a lobster roll at Boston & Maine Fish Company.

21st Amendment (Map pp234-5; ☎ 617-227-7100; 150 Bowdoin St; mains $7-12; ⏰ 11:30am-2am) Rub shoulders with politicians at this dark-wood

pub near the Statehouse. And you don't need the deep pockets of a lobbyist to eat here – a grilled chicken sandwich or a generous Caesar salad will set you back less than $10. Great service too.

Durgin Park (Map pp234-5; ☎ 617-227-2038; 340 Faneuil Hall Marketplace; lunch mains $7-13, dinner mains $15-25; ⏰ 11:30am-10pm Mon-Sat, 11:30am-9pm Sun) Climbing the stairs to this traditional eatery is like stepping back to colonial times. It has been dishing out New England favorites like prime rib, Boston baked beans and Indian pudding to diners at long communal tables since 1827.

Ye Olde Union Oyster House (Map pp234-5; ☎ 617-227-2750; 41 Union St; mains $16-24; ⏰ 11am-9:30pm Sun-Thu, 11am-10pm Fri & Sat) Slurp up fresh-shucked oysters and a heaping of history at Boston's oldest (1826) restaurant. It's been a haunt of many prominent Bostonians including JFK who had his own booth in the upstairs dining room. Forgo the meat dishes – this place is all about seafood.

On Friday and Saturday everybody flocks to the huge open-air **Haymarket** (Map pp234-5; Blackstone & Hanover Sts) to pick up bargain-priced fruits and veggies. Prettiest strawberries you've ever seen, but don't dare touch anything until you've paid for it!

NORTH END & CHARLESTOWN

Maria's Pastry Shop (Map pp234-5; ☎ 617-523-1196; 46 Cross St; snacks $1-3; ⏰ 7am-7pm Mon-Sat, 7am-5pm Sun) Forget the big boys on pricy Hanover St – the women at this wee bakery create heavenly cannoli and cakes that are equally luscious but a fraction of the cost.

Salumeria Italiana (Map pp234-5; ☎ 617-523-8743; 151 Richmond St; sandwiches $5; ⏰ 8am-6pm Mon-Thu, 8am-7pm Fri & Sat) Pick up picnic supplies at this Italian deli selling delicious focaccia sandwiches, antipasto and cold cuts.

Rabia's (Map pp234-5; ☎ 617-227-6637; 73 Salem St; mains $14-24; ⏰ 11:30am-10:30pm) On the downtown edge of the North End, this classic trattoria rakes in office workers at lunch and a fine-dining crowd at night. Its $6 lunch specials, offered till 3pm, are hands-down the neighborhood's best deal.

Neptune Oyster (Map pp234-5; ☎ 617-742-3474; 63 Salem St; mains $16-26; ⏰ 11:30am-11pm Sun-Thu, 11:30am-midnight Fri & Sat) Barely bigger than a clam, this snappy place has the best raw bar in the North End and serves up good hot Italian-style seafood as well.

Daily Catch (Map pp234-5; ☎ 617-772-4400; 323 Hanover St; mains $18-25; ⏰ 11am-10:30pm) It's just an unassuming little joint, but you'll find superb Sicilian-style seafood as fresh as its name. Favorites include the garlicky calamari scampi and the homemade squid-ink pastas. The only difficult catch here is scoring a table – arrive early.

our pick Carmen (Map pp234-5; ☎ 617-742-6421; 33 North Sq; lunch mains $15-21, dinner mains $19-32; ⏰ 5:30-10pm Tue-Thu, 11:30am-3pm & 5:30-11pm Fri & Sat, 3-10pm Sun) Exposed red-brick walls and soft candlelight set the tone at this cozy neighborhood restaurant down the street from the Paul Revere House. Innovative Italian cuisine just doesn't get any better. House specialties include tender slow-roasted Tuscan pork, lobster risotto, fresh clam linguine in a spicy garlic sauce and savory steaks. With just 30 seats, you'd be wise to call ahead for reservations.

Olives (Map pp234-5; ☎ 617-242-1999; 10 City Sq; mains $20-32; ⏰ 5:30-10pm Mon-Sat) The original restaurant of celeb chef Todd English, Olives draws rave reviews for its innovative Mediterranean-New American menu featuring wood-grilled meats and seafood. Book early to avoid a long wait.

BACK BAY

JP Licks (Map p231; ☎ 617-236-1666; 352 Newbury St; cone $3.50; ⏰ 11am-midnight) Go ahead, spoil your dinner. Cool off with a cone of Boston's favorite homemade ice cream.

29 Newbury (Map pp234-5; ☎ 617-536-0290; 29 Newbury St; lunch mains $10-18, dinner mains $12-32; ⏰ 11:30am-10pm) This trendy sidewalk café, opposite the Armani store, is the perfect stage for watching chic shoppers parade on Newbury St. The menu, featuring the likes of grilled shrimp salad in champagne vinaigrette, makes its own tasteful statement.

Kashmir (Map p231; ☎ 617-536-1695; 279 Newbury St; lunch buffet weekdays/weekends $10/13, dinner mains $12-18; ⏰ 11:30am-11pm) The lunch buffet of savory Indian dishes, warm naan bread and homemade chutneys is one of Boston's best lunch deals.

CHINATOWN, THEATER DISTRICT & SOUTH END

Flour Bakery & Café (Map p231; ☎ 617-267-4300; 1595 Washington St; mains $6-10; ⏰ 7am-7pm Mon-Fri, 8am-6pm Sat, 9am-3pm Sun) Just follow your nose to this sweet place with a grand chalkboard menu of mouthwatering pastries and creative sandwiches. The chutney roast lamb and goat's cheese on rustic bread is a sure winner.

Xinh Xinh (Map pp234-5; ☎ 617-422-0501; 7 Beach St; mains $6-12; ⏰ 10am-10pm) This friendly Vietnamese eatery in the midst of Chinatown is delightfully different. If you're feeling inventive, order *banh hoi*, a burrito-like rice-paper wrap chock-full of fragrant goodies that you roll yourself. Wash it down with a creamy avocado shake.

Peach Farm (Map pp234-5; ☎ 617-481-3332; 4 Tyler St; mains $6-15; ⏰ 11am-2am) Be transported to Hong Kong when you walk in the door of this basement restaurant with pink tablecloths and live fish tanks. One tasty treat is clams in black bean sauce, but all the seafood here is top-notch.

Montien (Map pp234-5; ☎ 617-338-5600; 63 Stuart St; mains $9-18; ⏰ 11:30am-10pm Mon-Sat, 4pm-10pm Sun) For a zesty meal before the opening curtain, head to this classy Thai restaurant in the midst of the theater district. It has wonderfully fragrant curries and other spicy counterparts, including a whole page of vegetarian options.

Franklin Café (Map pp234-5; ☎ 617-350-0010; 278 Shawmut Ave; mains $15-20; ⏰ 5:30pm-1:30am) This South End haunt draws a loyal crowd hungry for New American comfort food with a gourmet twist. The turkey meatloaf with cinnamon fig gravy and mashed potatoes is the defining signature dish but vegetarians searching for hearty salads won't be disappointed either.

CAMBRIDGE

Veggie Planet (Map p237; ☎ 617-661-1513; 47 Palmer St at Club Passim; mains $5-11; ⏰ 11:30am-10:30pm) Vegetarian is never dull at this popular place featuring homemade soups, organic salads and pizzas topped with everything from goat's cheese to Thai curry. Come on Sunday afternoon for live jazz.

Mr Bartley's Burger Cottage (Map p237; ☎ 617-354-6559; 1246 Massachusetts Ave; burgers $8-10; ⏰ 11am-10pm Mon-Sat) Join the Ivy Leaguers at this landmark Harvard Sq burger joint serving juicy hamburgers named after local celebs. Maybe a plump Ted Kennedy with a liberal chunk of cheddah? The onion rings score an A+ too.

Pho Pasteur (Map p237; ☎ 617-482-7467; 36 John F Kennedy St; mains $8-12; ⏰ 11am-10pm) Opposite Harvard University, this inviting restaurant dishes up hearty bowls of authentic pho soup brimming with fresh herbs, as well as tasty spring rolls and other Vietnamese treats.

Drinking & Entertainment

Happening Boston offers something for everyone. For up-to-the-minute listings, pick up one of the free entertainment rags, the *Boston Phoenix* or the *Improper Bostonian*.

Half-price tickets to same-day theater and concerts are sold for cash only (beginning at 10am) at the **BosTix kiosks** (Map pp234-5; www .artsboston.org; Faneuil Hall Congress St; Copley Sq Dartmouth & Boylston Sts).

BARS

Top of the Hub (Map pp234-5; ☎ 617-536-1775; Prudential Center, 800 Boylston St; ☒ 11.30am-1am) A head-spinning city view is on tap at this chic restaurant lounge on the 52nd floor of the Prudential Center.

Sonsie (Map p231; ☎ 617-351-2500; 327 Newbury St; ☒ 7am-1am) Overlooking the action on trendy Newbury St, Sonsie is the 'it' place in Boston to sip a glass of chardonnay and spot celebs.

John Harvard's Brew House (Map p237; ☎ 617-868-3585; 33 Dunster St, Cambridge; ☒ 11:30am-12:30am Sun-Thu, 11:30am-1:30am Fri & Sat) This subterranean Harvard Sq microbrewery serves well-crafted brews in an inviting English-pub atmosphere.

Cheers (Map pp234-5; ☎ 617-227-9605; 84 Beacon St; ☒ 11am-1am) Only the exterior of this landmark bar appeared in the opening scenes of the *Cheers* sitcom and it serves far more tourists than locals, but if it's time for a cold one, why not?

Caffè Vittoria (Map pp234-5; ☎ 617-227-7606; 296 Hanover St; ☒ 8am-midnight) *The* place to enjoy a cappuccino or an aperitif in style in the North End's 'Little Italy.'

Bars line historic Union St, just north of Faneuil Hall, including the **Bell in Hand Tavern** (Map pp234-5; ☎ 617-227-2098; 45 Union St; ☒ 11.30-1am), the oldest tavern in the USA. Down the next alley you'll find the atmospheric **Green Dragon Tavern** (Map pp234-5; ☎ 617-367-0055; 10 Marshall St; ☒ 11am-1:30am) where Paul Revere is said to have met with his patriot pals to plan their revolutionary shenanigans.

Sports bars pepper the neighborhood around Fenway Park', including the venerable favorite **Cask 'n' Flagon** (Map p231; ☎ 617-536-4840; 62 Brookline Ave; ☒ 11.30-2am), which is wallpapered with classic Red Sox photos and memorabilia.

CLUBS & LIVE MUSIC

Hours vary with the season and the act – call for schedules.

Avalon (Map p231; ☎ 617-262-2424; avalonboston .com; 15 Lansdowne St; cover $15-30) This cavernous Fenway dance club features big-name rock bands and Boston's hottest Friday-night DJ scene.

Axis (Map p231; ☎ 617-262-2437; 13 Lansdowne St; cover $5-20) A favorite of the college crowd with dancing to rock and hip-hop.

Paradise Rock Club (Map p231; ☎ 617-562-8800; the dise.com; 969 Commonwealth Ave; cover $16-25) Top indie bands and the likes of Sean Lennon take to the stage at this edgy landmark club.

Club Passim (Map p237; ☎ 617-492-7679; www.club passim.org; 47 Palmer St; cover $5-35) This venerable Harvard Sq folk club has been the haunt of up-and-coming folksingers since the days of Dylan and Baez.

GAY & LESBIAN BOSTON

No surprise – the bustling hub city of the only state to legalize gay marriage welcomes gay travelers. The center of the action is Boston's South End.

Boston's most popular sleep for gay travelers is **Chandler Inn** (Map pp234-5; ☎ 617-482-3450, 800-842-3450; www.chandlerinn.com; 26 Chandler St; r $119-189), a South End hotel with 56 tidy rooms; it's also the site of **Fritz** (☎ 617-482-4428; ☒ noon-2am), a laid-back gay watering hole.

The stalwart of the gay and lesbian scene is **Club Café** (Map pp234-5; ☎ 617-536-0966; 209 Columbus Ave; ☒ 11am-2am), a convivial South End bar and restaurant. Other Boston clubs have gay nights; at Avalon (above) it's Sunday and at Axis (above) it's Monday.

Gay Pride (www.bostonpride.org) events in mid-June include a parade, festival and block parties.

Good sources of information are **Bay Windows** (www.baywindows.com), a free weekly serving the gay and lesbian community; and the online **Edge Boston** (www.edgeboston.com) with the latest on entertainment happenings.

NEW ENGLAND

TT the Bear's Place (Map p231; ☎ 617-492-2327; tthebears.com; 10 Brookline St, Cambridge; cover $8-15) Intimate, diehard rock joint played by local bands on the rise.

Middle East (Map p231; ☎ 617-864-3278; mideast club.com; 472 Massachusetts Ave; cover $8-15) At Cambridge's Central Sq, this multifloor club hosts top indie bands.

Berklee Performance Center (Map p231; ☎ 617-747-2261; berkleebpc.com; 136 Massachusetts Ave; cover $15-50) One of America's premier music schools hosts concerts by famed alumni and other renowned artists.

THEATER & CULTURE

Wang Theatre (Map pp234-5; ☎ 617-482-9393; www.citi center.org; 270 Tremont St) One of New England's largest theaters, this extravagant 1925 landmark hosts top dance and theater performances.

Symphony Hall (Map p231; ☎ 617-266-1492; www .bso.org; 301 Massachusetts Ave) The celebrated Boston Symphony Orchestra and Boston Pops perform here.

Charles Playhouse (Map pp234-5 ; ☎ 617-426-6912; 74 Warrenton St) Home to the wildly popular Blue Man Group, this dual-stage backstreet theater has an engaging underground ambience.

Two splendid historic theaters, the **Colonial Theatre** (Map pp234-5; ☎ 617-426-9366; 106 Boylston St) and **Wilbur Theatre** (Map pp234-5; ☎ 617-423-4008; 246 Tremont St), feature try-outs of Broadway-bound shows.

Free summer concerts take place at the outdoor bandstand **Hatch Memorial Shell** (Map pp234-5; Charles River Esplanade) on the banks of the Charles River, including the Boston Pops' July 4 concert, Boston's biggest annual music event.

SPORTS

From April to September (or October when they make the play-offs) Boston's major-league baseball team, **Boston Red Sox** (☎ 877-733-7699; www.redsox.com; 4 Yawkey Way), takes to the field at **Fenway Park** (Map p231; tickets $14-130).

At the **TD Banknorth Garden** (Map pp234-5; 150 Causeway St) from October to April, the NBA **Boston Celtics** (☎ 617-523-3030; www.celtics.com; tickets $10-170) play basketball and the NHL **Boston Bruins** (☎ 617-624-1900; www.bostonbruins.com; tickets $10-102) play ice hockey.

At the **Gillette Stadium** (Foxboro), 25 miles south of Boston, the NFL **New England Patriots** (☎ 800-543-1776; www.patriots.com; tickets $50-135) play football from August to January and the MLS **New England Revolution** (☎ 877-438-7387; www.revo lutionsoccer.net; tickets $18-34) play soccer from April to October.

Shopping

Fashionable Newbury St is Boston's version of New York's Fifth Ave. It is perfect for strolling and chock-a-block with chic boutiques, art galleries and offbeat shops. Starting on its highbrow east end it's all Armani, Brooks Brothers and Cartier, but by the time you reach the west end you'll find funky bookstores, craft shops and home-style ice-cream parlors.

Copley Place (Map pp234-5; 100 Huntington Ave) and the **Shops at Prudential Center** (Map pp234-5; 800 Boylston St), both in the Back Bay, are the city's main indoor malls.

Get independent music CDs at **Newbury Comics** (Map p231; ☎ 617-236-4930; 332 Newbury St), Harvard-logo sweatshirts at the **Coop** (Map p237; Massachusetts Ave, Cambridge), *Cheers*-logo anything at **Cheers** (Map pp234-5; ☎ 617-227-9605; 84 Beacon St) and Red Sox baseball caps at **Out of Left Field** (Map pp234-5; ☎ 617-722-9401; Congress St) at Faneuil Hall.

Good places to browse for arts and crafts are **Bromfield Art Gallery** (Map pp234-5; ☎ 617-451-3605; 450 Harrison Ave), Boston's oldest cooperative, and **Cambridge Artists' Cooperative** (Map p237; ☎ 617-868-4434; 59a Church St, Cambridge) at Harvard Sq. For visual arts the **Fort Point Arts Community Gallery** (Map pp234-5; ☎ 617-423-4299; 3000 Summer St) is at the center of Boston's avant-garde art scene.

Getting There & Away

Getting in and out of Boston is easy. The train and bus stations are conveniently side by side, and the airport is a short subway ride away.

Logan International Airport (☎ 800-235-6426; www .massport.com), just across Boston Harbor from the city center, is served by major US and foreign airlines and has all the expected amenities including currency-exchange booths.

South Station (Map pp234-5; 700 Atlantic Ave) is the terminal for long-distance buses including those operated by **Greyhound** (☎ 617-526-1808), **Peter Pan Bus Lines** (☎ 617-946-0960) and **Vermont Transit** (☎ 800-522-8737). In addition the Chinatown operation **Fung Wah Bus Company** (☎ 617-345-8000; www.fungwahbus.com) runs buses from South Station to New York City for just $15 each way.

MBTA Commuter Rail (☎ 617-222-3200) trains connect Boston's North Station (Map pp234-5) with Concord and Salem and Boston's South Station (Map pp234-5) with Plymouth

WHAT THE...?

In early 1692 a group of Salem girls began to act strangely. The work of the devil? The girls, pressured to blame someone, accused a slave named Tituba of witchcraft. Under torture, Tituba accused others and soon accusations were flying thick and fast. By September, 55 had pleaded guilty and 19 who wouldn't 'confess' to witchcraft were hanged. The frenzy died down when the accusers pointed at the governor's wife.

Best of Salem's 'witchy' sites is the **Witch House** (☎ 978-744-8815; 310 Essex St; adult/child 6-14 $8/4; ⏰ 10am-5pm May-Nov), the home of the magistrate who presided over the trials. To dig deeper, read Arthur Miller's *The Crucible*, which doubles as a parable to the 1950s anticommunist 'witch hunts' in the US Senate that resulted in Miller's blacklisting.

and Providence; fares vary with the distance, maxing out at $7.75.

The **Amtrak** (☎ 617-345-7460, 800-872-7245; www .amtrak.com) terminal is at South Station; trains to New York cost $78 (4¼ hours) or $109 on the speedier *Acela Express* (3½ hours).

All major car-rental companies have offices at the airport, and many have locations around the city. Bear in mind that driving in Boston is confusing – narrow, one-way streets and aggressive drivers – and parking is expensive. It's almost always better to stick to public transportation within the city. If you're traveling onward by rental car, pick up your car at the end of your Boston visit.

Getting Around

Logan International Airport is served by the MBTA's Blue Line at Airport Station ($2). Free shuttle buses connect Airport Station with all airport terminals. Taxis line up outside the terminals; expect to pay about $25 to get downtown.

The **MBTA** (☎ 617-222-3200; www.mbta.com; single ride $2, day/week pass $9/15) operates the USA's oldest subway (the 'T'), which began in 1897. Four color-coded lines – Red, Blue, Green and Orange – radiate from the downtown stations of Park St, Downtown Crossing and Government Center. 'Inbound' trains are headed for these three stations, 'outbound' trains away from them. Trains operate from around 5:30am to 12:30am.

Taxis are plentiful; expect to pay between $10 and $20 between two points within the city limits. Flag taxis on the street, find them at major hotels or call **Metro Cab** (☎ 617-242-8000) or **Independent** (☎ 617-426-8700).

AROUND BOSTON

The historic towns rimming Boston make for fine day-tripping. If you don't have your own

transportation, you can reach these places by MBTA (left) buses and rail.

Lexington & Concord

In 1775 the colonial town of Lexington, 15 miles northwest of Boston, was the site of the first battle of the American Revolution. Following the battle, the British redcoats marched 10 miles west to Concord where they fought the American minutemen at the town's North Bridge – the first American victory. You can revisit this momentous bit of history at **Minute Man National Historic Park** (☎ 978-369-6993; www.nps .gov/mima; 174 Liberty St, Concord; admission free; ⏰ 9am-5pm Apr-Oct) and along the 5.5-mile **Battle Road trail**, suitable for hiking and biking.

In the 19th century, Concord harbored a vibrant literary community. Next to the **Old North Bridge** is the **Old Manse**, former home of author Nathaniel Hawthorne. Within a mile of the town center are the **Ralph Waldo Emerson house**, Louisa May Alcott's **Orchard House** and the **Wayside**, where Alcott's *Little Women* was set.

Walden Pond, where Henry David Thoreau lived and wrote *Walden*, is 3 miles south of the town center; you can visit his cabin site and take an inspiring hike around the pond. All these authors are laid to rest in **Sleepy Hollow Cemetery** on Bedford St in the town center. Admission is free to Walden Pond and the cemetery; the homes can be visited for a small fee. **Concord Chamber of Commerce** (☎ 978-369-3120; www.concordchamberofcommerce.org; 58 Main St; ⏰ 9:30am-4:30pm) has details.

Salem

Salem, 20 miles northeast of Boston, burned its infamous place in history with the 1692 hysteria that put innocent people to death for witchcraft (see the boxed text, above). The tragedy has proven a boon for operators of several Salem witch attractions, some serious, others that make light of the events. **Destination Salem** (☎ 877-725-3662; www.salem.org; 54 Turner St) has information on town attractions.

The exceptional **Peabody Essex Museum** (☎ 978-745-9500; www.pem.org; East India Sq; adult/child under 17 $13/free; ☼ 10am-5pm) reflects Salem's rich maritime history. The museum was founded upon the art, artifacts and curios collected by Salem traders during their early expeditions to Asia. They had deep pockets and refined taste, returning with outstanding primitive art collections from island tribes in the remote Pacific as well as world-class collections from China and Japan.

Salem was the center of a thriving clipper-ship trade with China and its pre-eminent trader, Elias Derby, became America's first millionaire. For a sense of those glory days, take a walk along Derby St and out to Derby Wharf, which is now the center of the **Salem Maritime National Historic Site**.

Plymouth

It may have not been their original destination (New York was) but when the *Mayflower* Pilgrims arrived here in 1620 they realized they were in a hospitable place and settled in. The rest is history. Often referred to as 'America's hometown,' Plymouth was the first permanent European settlement north of Virginia. **Plymouth Rock**, a weather-worn chunk of granite on the harborfront, marks the place the Pilgrims came ashore. Several other sights in town elucidate the challenges the settlers had to overcome. **Destination Plymouth** (☎ 508-747-7533; www.visit-plymouth.com; 170 Water St), opposite the harbor, has details on all sights.

Today, travelers make pilgrimages to **Plimoth Plantation** (☎ 508-746-1622; www.plimoth.org; MA 3A; adult/child 6-12 $25/15; ☼ 9am-5pm Apr-Nov), an authentically re-created 1627 Pilgrim village. Everything – the houses, the crops, the food cooked over wood stoves and even the vocabulary used by the costumed interpreters – is meticulously true to the period. Equally insightful are the homesites of the Wampanoag Indians, who helped the Pilgrims through their first difficult winter. If you're traveling with kids, or if you're a history buff, don't miss it. The admission price includes entry to the *Mayflower II*, a replica of the Pilgrims' ship, at Plymouth Harbor.

When hunger strikes head to the harborside **Lobster Hut** (☎ 508-746-2270; Town Wharf; mains

KING OF THE ROAD

When exploring the Cape, eschew the speedy Mid-Cape Hwy (MA 6) and follow instead the Old King's Hwy (MA 6A), which snakes along Cape Cod Bay and is the longest continuous stretch of historic district in the USA. The Old King's Hwy is lined with gracious period homes, some converted to antique shops and art galleries, which make for good browsing en route.

$6-18; ☼ 11am-8pm) for reliably good fried clams, fresh fish and boiled lobster.

CAPE COD

Think saltwater taffy, seaside cottages, children building sandcastles and sailboats at sunset. When New Englanders want a day at the beach they head to 'the Cape.' This sandy peninsula is fringed with 400 miles of sparkling shoreline. But there's a lot more than just beaches here. The Cape boasts quaint fishing villages, excellent biking and hiking trails, and some of the freshest seafood imaginable.

Cape Cod Chamber of Commerce (☎ 508-362-3225, 888-332-2732; www.capecodchamber.org; MA 6 at MA 132, Hyannis; ☼ 8:30am-5pm Mon-Fri, 9am-5pm Sat year-round, 10am-2pm Sun in summer) provides Capewide information. Buses run between Boston and the Cape's main towns.

Sandwich

The Cape's oldest village wraps its solidly historic center around a swan-filled pond. It doesn't get much prettier than this.

Fun for kids and adults alike, the 76-acre **Heritage Museums & Gardens** (☎ 508-888-3300; www.heritagemuseumsandgardens.org; Grove St; adult/child 6-16 $12/6; ☼ 10am-5pm Apr-Oct, Sat-Sun Nov-Dec) sport a terrific vintage automobile collection, a working 1912 carousel, folk-art collections and one of the finest rhododendron gardens in America.

Get a feel for what life was like for early settlers by touring the **Hoxie House** (☎ 508-888-1173; 18 Water St; adult/child 5-12 $3/2; ☼ 10am-5pm Mon-Sat, 1-5pm Sun mid-Jun–mid-Oct), c 1640, the oldest house on Cape Cod.

The restored **Dexter Grist Mill** (☎ 508-888-5144; Water St; adult/child 5-12 $3/2; ☼ 10am-5pm Mon-Sat, 1-5pm Sun mid-Jun–Sep) dates back to 1654 and has centuries-old gears that still grind cornmeal.

And bring a camera, with its oak waterwheel and paddling swans this is perhaps the most photographed scene on the Cape.

Colorful Sandwich glass had its heyday in the 19th century, a heritage that's artfully displayed in the **Sandwich Glass Museum** (☎ 508-888-0251; www.sandwichglassmuseum.org; 129 Main St; adult/child 6-14 $4.75/1; ☼ 9:30am-5pm Apr-Dec, 9:30am-4pm Wed-Sun Feb-Mar).

A treat for kids is the **Thornton W Burgess Museum** (☎ 508-888-4668; 4 Water St; suggested donation adult/child under 13 $2/1; ☼ 10am-4pm Mon-Sat, 1-4pm Sun May-Oct), named for the Sandwich native who wrote the *Peter Cottontail* series. Story time on the lawn, overlooking the pond featured in Burgess' works, is particularly evocative – call for times.

If you're ready for the beach, head to **Sandy Neck Beach** (Sandy Neck Rd; Ⓟ), off MA 6A a 6-mile dune-backed strand that's ideal for beachcombing and a bracing swim. Parking costs $15.

SLEEPING & EATING

Shawme-Crowell State Forest (☎ 508-888-0351, 877-422-6762; www.reserveamerica.com; MA 130; campsites $14) You'll find 285 shady campsites in this 700-acre woodland, near MA 6A.

Belfry Inne & Bistro (☎ 508-888-8550, 800-844-4542; www.belfryinn.com; 8 Jarves St; r incl breakfast $145-275; dinner mains $21-32; ☼ dinner 5-9pm; ☒) Ever fall asleep in church? You'll love the rooms, some with stained glass, in this creatively restored former church, now an upmarket

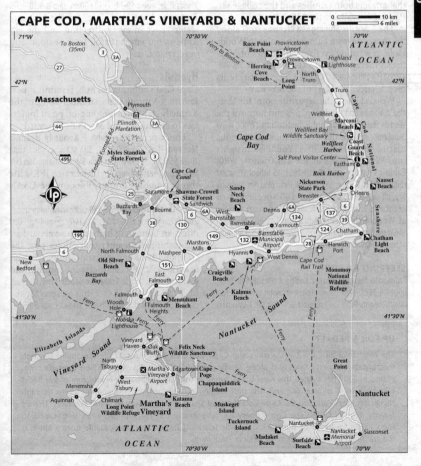

CAPE COD, MARTHA'S VINEYARD & NANTUCKET

NEW ENGLAND

B&B. Its stylish restaurant serves the finest food in town – ask about the $25 early dinner that includes enticements like crispy duck ravioli.

Seafood Sam's (☎ 508-888-4629; Coast Guard Rd; mains $8-17; ☻ 11am-8:30pm) A good family choice for fish and chips, clams and lobster. Dine at picnic tables overlooking Cape Cod Canal and watch the fishing boats sail by.

Falmouth & Woods Hole

Crowd-pleasing beaches and the quaint seaside village of Woods Hole are the hallmarks of the Cape's second-largest town.

Falmouth has 70 miles of coastline, none finer than **Old Silver Beach** (off MA 28A, North Falmouth; ℗), a long, sandy stretch with calm waters that attracts both families and the college set. Parking is available for $20.

The 3.5-mile **Shining Sea Bikeway** runs along the shoreline from Falmouth center to Woods Hole, rewarding cyclists with views of Martha's Vineyard en route. **Corner Cycle** (☎ 508-540-4195; 115 Palmer Ave; 8/24hr $15/20; ☻ 9am-6pm) rents bicycles near the start of the bikeway.

Woods Hole is the departure point for Martha's Vineyard ferries (p257) and home of the **Woods Hole Oceanographic Institution** (WHOI; www .whoi.edu), one of the world's most prestigious marine research facilities. You'll get insights into WHOI's work at the kid-friendly **WHOI Exhibit Center** (☎ 508-289-2663; 15 School St; adult/child under 10 $2/free; ☻ 10am-4:30pm Mon-Sat Jun-early Sep, off-season hours vary). See 140 species of sea creature, including a few the kids can touch, at **Woods Hole Science Aquarium** (☎ 508-495-2001; 166 Water St; admission free; ☻ 11am-4pm Tue-Sat Jun-Aug, 11am-4pm Mon-Fri Sep-May).

SLEEPING & EATING
Falmouth Heights Motor Lodge (☎ 508-548-3623, 800-468-3623; www.falmouthheightsmotel.com; 146 Falmouth Heights Rd; d incl breakfast $89-189; ☒) Within

walking distance of the beach and Vineyard ferry, the 28 rooms here are a cut above the competition and the attractive grounds harbor a picnic grove with gas barbecues.

Palmer House Inn (☎ 508-548-1230, 800-472-2632; www.palmerhouseinn.com; 81 Palmer Ave; r incl breakfast $149-295; ☒ ☐) Pamper yourself in one of the posh rooms in this 200-year-old Victorian-style inn in Falmouth center.

Laureen's (☎ 508-540-9104; 170 Main St; mains $7-20; ☻ 8:30am-8:30pm) Join the locals at this downtown bistro for healthy salads and creative sandwiches made with yummy Armenian bread that has feta cheese baked right into it. Dinner adds on grilled meat and seafood dishes.

Fishmonger Café (☎ 508-540-5376; 56 Water St, Woods Hole; mains $9-24; ☻ 11:30am-3pm & 5:30-9pm) Everyone loves this place, for the fantastic water views in every direction and the eclectic menu emphasizing fresh seafood and vegetarian fare.

Hyannis

Cape Cod's commercial hub, Hyannis is best known to visitors as the summer home of the Kennedy clan and a jumping-off point for ferries to Nantucket and Martha's Vineyard.

The worthwhile **John F Kennedy Hyannis Museum** (☎ 508-790-3077; 397 Main St; adult/child 10-16 $5/2.50; ☻ 9am-5pm Mon-Sat, noon-5pm Sun late May-Oct, off-season hours vary) celebrates JFK's life through photos and exhibits on the USA's 35th president.

Hy-Line Cruises (☎ 508-790-0696; www.hylinecruises .com; Ocean St Dock; adult/child 5-12 $14/7; ☻ mid-Apr–Oct) offers an hour-long harbor cruise aboard an old-fashioned steamer that circles past the compound of Kennedy family homes. **Kalmus Beach** (Ocean St; ℗) is popular for sunning and windsurfing, while **Craigville Beach** (Craigville Beach Rd; ℗) is the place to see and be seen for the college set; parking at both sites costs $15.

UP FOR A PEDAL?

The mother of all Cape bicycle trails, the **Cape Cod Rail Trail**, runs 22 glorious miles through forest, past cranberry bogs and along sandy ponds ideal for a dip. A $6 million upgrade completed in 2007 has turned this rural route, formerly used as a railroad line, into one of the finest bike trails in all of New England. The path begins in Dennis on MA 134 and continues through Nickerson State Park and the Cape Cod National Seashore all the way to South Wellfleet. There's a hefty dose of Olde Cape Cod scenery en route and you'll have opportunities to detour into the villages for lunch or sightseeing. Bicycle rentals ($25 per day) are available from a kiosk at the trailhead in Dennis and at Nickerson State Park.

SLEEPING & EATING

Captain Gosnold Village (☎ 508-775-9111; www.cap taingosnold.com; 230 Gosnold St; r/cottage from $100/250; ⊠) A little community unto itself and just a sandal-shuffle from the beach, choose from motel rooms or fully equipped Cape Cod–style cottages; there's a playground for the kids. The cottages sleep four.

Anchor-in (☎ 508-775-0357; www.anchorin.com; 1 South St; r $119-229; ⊠ ⊡) Bright airy rooms with harbor-view balconies separate this family-run hotel from all the chains back on the highway. And if you're planning a day trip to Nantucket the ferry is just a stroll away.

Ardeo (☎ 508-790-1115; 644 Main St; mains $6-24; ⊙ 11:30am-10pm) A perfect family choice with something for every taste. The menu ranges from burgers and pizza to traditional Greek fare.

Misaki (☎ 508-771-3771; 379 W Main St; lunch $7-12, dinner $12-22; ⊙ noon-2:30pm & 5-9pm Mon-Sat) Enjoy your fresh New England seafood served up raw as first-rate sushi and sashimi at this authentic Japanese restaurant.

RooBar (☎ 508-778-6515; 586 Main St; mains $15-30; ⊙ 4pm-1am) Hyannis' smartest restaurant serves creative New American fusion dinners, including plenty of fresh seafood, and has a lively bar scene after dark.

Brewster

A quiet, low-key town on the Cape's bay side, Brewster makes a good base for out-doorsy types. The Cape Cod Rail Trail (op-posite) cuts clear across town and there are excellent options for camping, hiking and water activities.

The 2000-acre oasis of **Nickerson State Park** (☎ 508-896-3491; 3488 MA 6A; admission free; ⊙ 8am-8pm) has ponds with sandy beaches, boating, biking and walking trails. **Jack's Boat Rentals** (☎ 508-896-8556; Cliff Pond; boat rental 1st/additional hr $20/12; ⊙ 9am-6pm), within the park, rents canoes, kayaks and sailboats. **Barbara's Bike** (☎ 508-896-7231; per day $25; ⊙ 9am-6pm) rents bi-cycles by the park entrance.

The **Cape Cod Museum of Natural History** (☎ 508-896-3867; www.ccmnh.org; 869 MA 6A; adult/child 3-12 $8/3.50; ⊙ 10am-4pm daily Jun-Sep, 10am-4pm Wed-Sun Oct-May) offers fascinating exhibits on the Cape's flora and fauna and has a wonderful boardwalk trail that tromps across a salt-marsh to a remote beach.

SLEEPING & EATING

Nickerson State Park (☎ 877-422-6762; www.reserveam erica.com; campsites $17) Head here for Cape Cod's best camping with 418 wooded campsites; it often fills, so reserve your spot early.

Isaiah Clark House (☎ 508-896-2223, 800-822-4001; www.isaiahclark.com; 1187 MA 6A; r incl breakfast $120-150; ⊡) A former sea captain's house dating to 1780, this inviting B&B has cozy guest rooms with canopied beds and fireplaces.

Cobies (☎ 508-896-7021; 3260 MA 6A; dishes $6-18; ⊙ 10:30am-9pm) Just off the Cape Cod Rail Trail, this roadside clam slack dishes out fried seafood that you can crunch and munch at outdoor picnic tables. On weekends it has lobster too.

Chatham

The Cape's most genteel town boasts old sea captains' houses, art galleries and a splendid shoreline. At the east end of town just below the historic coast guard lighthouse on Shore Rd is **Chatham Light Beach**, a lovely strand that invites strolling. The **Monomoy National Wildlife Refuge** has two adjacent islands that abound with shorebirds. **Beachcomber Boats** (☎ 508-945-5265; Crowell Rd; adult/child 3-15 $22/16) offers Monomoy birding and seal-watching excursions.

If you're in town on a Friday night, don't miss the summertime band concerts under the stars at **Kate Gould Park** (Main St; admission free), an atmospheric throwback to an earlier era.

SLEEPING & EATING

Chatham Highlander (☎ 508-945-9038; www.chatham highlander.com; 946 MA 28; r $119-199; ⊠ ⊠) Within walking distance from the town center, the rooms are straightforward but large and clean. Unlike Chatham's stodgy resorts, this motel welcomes families – kids will love the pair of pools.

Carriage House Inn (☎ 508-945-4688, 800-355-8868; www.thecarriagehouseinn.com; 407 Old Harbor Rd; r incl break-fast $140-255; ⊠ ⊠) An affordable choice by Chatham standards, the rooms are tidy, the queen beds comfy, the breakfast gourmet. Friendly touches, like the free use of beach gear, add to its popularity.

Chatham Squire (☎ 508-945-0945; 487 Main St; mains $7-20; ⊙ 11:30am-10pm) Rub shoulders with locals over classic Cape Cod fare at this boisterous tavern. The varied menu rambles from chowder and burgers to fresh seafood.

NEW ENGLAND

Impudent Oyster (☎ 508-945-3545; 15 Chatham Bars Ave; mains $8-26; ☽ 11:30am-3pm & 5-10pm) An eclectic menu, from its namesake fresh-shucked oysters to Japanese-influenced fare, makes this a real pearl – don't miss the drunken oysters in sake.

Cape Cod National Seashore

Extending some 40 miles, the **Cape Cod National Seashore** (www.nps.gov/caco) encompasses most of the shoreline from Eastham to Provincetown. It's a treasure-trove of unspoiled beaches, dunes, salt marshes and forests. Thanks to President John F Kennedy, this vast area was set aside for preservation in the 1960s, just before a building boom hit the rest of his native Cape Cod. The National Seashore's **Salt Pond Visitor Center** (☎ 508-255-3421; Nauset Rd at MA 6, Eastham; admission free; ☽ 9am-5pm) has exhibits and films on the area's ecology and can provide maps to the park's numerous trails, some which begin right at the center. Check out the daily offering of interpretive ranger walks and talks, which are free, including a tour of an old sea captain's house with an awesome whale-jawbone gate. **Coast Guard Beach**, just down the road from the visitor center, is a hot swimming and surfing spot in summer and a great place to see seals in winter. There's no camping in the park.

Wellfleet

This town lures visitors with its art galleries, lovely beaches and famous Wellfleet oysters.

Birders flock to Massachusetts Audubon Society's **Wellfleet Bay Wildlife Sanctuary** (☎ 508-349-2615; www.wellfleetbay.org; West Rd; adult/child $5/3; ☽ 8:30am-5pm late May–mid-Oct, Tue-Sun rest of year), off MA 6A, where trails cross 1000 acres of tidal creeks, salt marshes and sandy beach.

Marconi Beach has a monument to Guglielmo Marconi, who sent the first wireless transmission across the Atlantic from this site, and a grand beach backed by undulating dunes. Parking costs $15.

About two dozen Wellfleet **art galleries** host receptions on summer Saturday evenings. For an evening of nostalgia, park at **Wellfleet Drive-In** (☎ 508-349-7176; MA 6; adult/child 5-11 $7.50/4.50; ☽ Jun–mid-Oct), one of a dwindling number of drive-in cinemas surviving in the USA. **Wellfleet Flea Market** (☎ 508-349-2520; MA 6; per car $3; ☽ 7am-4pm Wed, Thu, Sat & Sun in summer, Sat & Sun only in spring & fall), held at the Wellfleet

Drive-In, hosts 300 dealers and makes an interesting diversion for bargain hunters. The acclaimed **Wellfleet Harbor Actors Theater** (☎ 508-349-6835; www.what.org; 1 Kendrick Ave; tickets from $29) produces edgy contemporary plays.

SLEEPING & EATING

Even'Tide Motel (☎ 508-349-3410, 800-368-0007; www.eventidemotel.com; 650 US 6; r $75-170, cottages per week $1200-2600; ☒) An indoor heated pool adds to the appeal of this small motel, which also has nine cottages accommodating four to eight people each.

Juice (☎ 508-349-0535; 6 Commercial St; mains $6-16; ☽ 7am-10pm) Liquids get high billing at this café serving fair-trade coffee and organic juices. The innovative menu covers the spectrum from Wellfleet shellfish to veggie fajitas.

Moby Dick's (☎ 508-349-9795; MA 6; mains $7-18; ☽ 11:30am-10pm) There's often a line out the door at this roadside eatery, but you'll be rewarded for your wait with some of the best fish, fried clams and chowder at this end of the Cape.

DRINKING & ENTERTAINMENT

Beachcomber (☎ 508-349-6055; Cahoon Hollow Beach, Ocean View Dr) A former lifesaving station right on the beach, 'Da Coma' is *the* place to have a drink or rock the night away. And some really good bands – including Weezer and They Might Be Giants – sometimes pop in.

Truro

Squeezed between Cape Cod Bay on the west and the open Atlantic on the east, narrow Truro abounds with water views and beaches. In North Truro, **Highland Lighthouse** (Cape Cod Light; ☎ 508-487-1121; Lighthouse Rd; tours $4; ☽ 10am-5:30pm May-Oct) sits at the Cape's highest elevation (a mere 120ft!), dates back to 1797 and casts the brightest light on the New England coastline. The adjacent **Highland House Museum** (☎ 508-487-3397; Lighthouse Rd; adult/child $4/free; ☽ 10am-4:30pm Jun-Sep) is a charming little place dedicated to the area's farming and fishing past.

Budget digs don't get much more atmospheric than at **HI Truro** (☎ 508-349-3889; www.capecodhostels.org; N Pamet Rd, North Truro; dm $30-35; ☽ late Jun-early Sep), a former coast guard station dramatically sited amid beach dunes. Book early to avoid disappointment.

Local artwork adorns the rustic walls of **Terra Luna** (☎ 508-487-1019; 104 MA 6, North Truro; mains $17-26; 🕐 5:30-9pm), a lively bistro that skillfully fuses contemporary American and Mediterranean cuisine.

Provincetown

When the Pilgrims landed here in 1620 they were just the first wave to seek refuge on these remote shores. Those who followed were, however, much less puritanical. Fringe writers and artists began making a summer haven in Provincetown a century ago, and in later years the gay and lesbian community turned this sandy outpost into the hottest gay vacation destination in the Northeast. Commercial St, the main waterfront drag, has a nonstop carnival atmosphere. While the action throbs from the center of town, Provincetown also has quiet dunes where you can walk without another soul in sight and an untamed coastline with glorious beaches.

ORIENTATION & INFORMATION

The town's center runs along two parallel streets, the seaside Commercial St, with the lion's share of restaurants, galleries and shops, and Bradford St one block inland. Quiet guesthouses line the narrow streets between Bradford and Commercial.

Provincetown Bookshop (☎ 508-487-0964; 246 Commercial St) Excellent owner-run bookshop.

Provincetown Chamber of Commerce (☎ 508-487-3424; www.ptownchamber.com; 307 Commercial St; 🕐 9am-5pm Jun-Aug, 10am-4pm Mon-Sat Sep-May) At MacMillan Wharf; get tourist information here.

Provincetown Public Library (☎ 508-487-7094; 356 Commercial St; 🕐 10am-5pm Mon & Fri, noon-8pm Tue & Thu, 10am-8pm Wed, 10am-2pm Sat, 1-5pm Sun) Allows 30 minutes of free internet access and is a sight in itself – occupying a former museum, it has some cool displays.

Tim's Used Books (☎ 508-487-0005; 242 Commercial St) Plenty of good reads at bargain prices.

SIGHTS & ACTIVITIES

Climb to the top of the world's tallest all-granite structure, the impressive 253ft-high **Pilgrim Monument** (☎ 508-487-1310; High Pole Rd; adult/child 5-12 $7/3.50; 🕐 9am-5pm April-Nov, to 7pm Jul & Aug), for a sweeping view of town and the surrounding coast. The monument commemorates the landing of the *Mayflower* Pilgrims and tells the story of their short stay here.

Established in 1914 to celebrate the town's thriving art community, the excellent **Provincetown Art Association & Museum** (☎ 508-487-1750; www.paam.org; 460 Commercial St; adult/child under 12 $5/free; 🕐 11am-8pm Mon-Thu, 11am-10pm Fri, 11am-5pm Sat & Sun Jun-Sep, noon-5pm Thu-Sun Oct-May) displays the works of the many artists who have found inspiration from Provincetown over the past century.

On the wild tip of the Cape, **Race Point Beach** is a beauty with crashing surf and undulating dunes extending as far as the eye can see. The west-facing **Herring Cove Beach** is typically calmer and an ideal spot for catching the sunset; nude bathers (though illegal) head to the left, families to the right.

An exhilarating way to explore Provincetown's amazing dunes and beaches is along the National Seashore's 8 miles of paved bike trail. Several shops rent bikes, including **Ptown Bikes** (☎ 508-487-8735; 42 Bradford St; per day cruiser/mountain bike $15/20; 🕐 9am-6pm). Or explore the easy way with **Art's Dune Tours** (☎ 508-487-1950; Standish St; adult/child $21/16), which arranges fun hour-long 4WD tours through the dunes.

The **Province Lands Visitor Center** (☎ 508-487-1256; Race Point Rd; admission free; 🕐 9am-5pm May-Oct) has displays on dune ecology and an observation deck with an eye-popping 360-degree view of the outermost reaches of Cape Cod; the deck stays open until midnight.

Provincetown is an ideal departure point for **whale-watching tours**, which cruise the Stellwagen Bank National Marine Sanctuary. Extending north from Provincetown, this is the major summer feeding ground for humpback whales, awesome creatures with a flair for acrobatically breaching out of the water. They come surprisingly close to the boats, and usually offer great photo opportunities. Other whales also frequent these waters, including many of the 300 remaining North Atlantic right whales, the world's most endangered whale species. The environmentally oriented **Dolphin Fleet Whale Watch** (☎ 508-240-3636, 800-826-9300; MacMillan Wharf; 3-4hr trips adult/child 5-12 $33/25; 🕐 Apr-Oct) offers several tours a day.

SLEEPING

Provincetown offers nearly 100 small guesthouses without a single chain hotel to mar the view. In summer it is certainly wise to book ahead, especially on weekends. If you arrive without a booking, the chamber of commerce (p251) keeps tabs on available rooms.

Dunes' Edge Campground (☎ 508-487-9815; www.dunes-edge.com; 386 MA 6; campsites $38) Camp amid the dunes and shady pines at this family-friendly campground.

Christopher's by the Bay (☎ 508-487-9263, 877-476-9263; www.christophersbythebay.com; 8 Johnson St; r with shared/private bath from $100/155; ⊠ wi-fi) Tucked away on a side street with a backyard koi pond, this welcoming inn is top value. The rooms located on the 2nd floor are the snazziest, but the 3rd-floor rooms, which share a bath, get the ocean view.

Fairbanks Inn (☎ 508-487-0386; www.fairbanksinn .com; 90 Bradford St; r incl breakfast $139-259; ⊠ ⊠ ⊑ wi-fi) If four-post beds and a cozy fireplace appeal then you're in for a treat at this cordial B&B occupying a restored 1776 sea captain's home. Some of the more expensive rooms have cooking facilities.

Snug Cottage (☎ 508-487-1616, 800-432-2334; www .snugcottage.com; 178 Bradford St; r incl breakfast $155-240; ⊠ ⊑ wi-fi) Cute as a button and one of the few places that has real wood-burning fireplaces rather than gas. The handsome rooms are big, bright and sunny with extra touches including a DVD library.

Carpe Diem (☎ 508-487-4242, 800-487-0132; www .carpediemguesthouse.com; 12 Johnson St; r incl breakfast $155-255; ⊠ ⊑) Warm hospitality and comfortable rooms await at this convivial guesthouse that is a favorite with European travelers. It is all very classy, from the Finnish sauna to the live orchid sprays.

Race Point Lighthouse (☎ 508-487-9930; www .racepointlighthouse.net; Race Point; r $160-195; ⊠) If unspoiled sand dunes and a 19th-century lighthouse sound like good company, stay in one of the three upstairs bedrooms in the old lightkeeper's house. Cool place – solar powered and literally on the outer tip of the Cape.

Surfside Hotel & Suites (☎ 508-487-1726, 800-421-1726; www.surfsideinn.cc; 543 Commercial St; r incl breakfast $169-299; ⊠) For those who prefer a hotel to a B&B this locally owned establishment has an enviable beachfront location and a pool that the kids can splash in.

CHOW-DAH PLEASE

Feasting on New England's homegrown specialties, especially its delicious crustaceans and shellfish, can be an event in itself. Local culinary delights include the following:

- clam chowder – or, as Bostonians say, 'chow-dah,' this New England staple combines chopped clams, potatoes and clam juice in a base of milk and cream
- clambake – a meal of lobster, clams and corn on the cob, usually steamed
- cranberries – tart red berries grown in Massachusetts bogs, usually sweetened and used in juice, sauces and muffins
- frappe – whipped milk and ice cream, pronounced 'frap'; called a 'milkshake' in other regions, but known as a 'cabinet' in Rhode Island
- Indian pudding – baked pudding made of milk, cornmeal, molasses, butter, ginger, cinnamon and raisins
- littlenecks – small hard-shell clams typically eaten raw on the half shell, or as clams casino with the meat dashed with hot sauce, wrapped in bacon and grilled
- lobster dinner – New England summer favorite that centers around a hot boiled lobster, a nutcracker for opening the claws, a crock of melted butter and a bib to keep you dry
- oysters – often served raw on the half shell or, for the less intrepid, broiled or baked; the best and sweetest are Wellfleet oysters from Cape Cod
- quahogs – large, hard-shelled clams, (pronounced ko-hogs), that are cut into strips and fried, chopped in chunks for chowder or used to make stuffing
- raw bar – a place to eat fresh-shucked live (raw) oysters and clams
- steamers – soft-shelled clams steamed and served in a bucket; extract the meat, swish it in broth to wash off any sand, then dip it in melted butter and enjoy

EATING

Whether you're in the mood for simple eats or cuisine-as-high-art, you're in the right place – Provincetown has the best dining scene this side of Boston.

Portuguese Bakery (☎ 508-487-1803; 299 Commercial St; pastries $2-3; ☯ 7am-11pm) This century-old institution is famous for its *malasadas* – fried dough served hot and sinfully drenched in sugar.

Spiritus Pizza (☎ 508-487-2808; 190 Commercial St; pizza slices/pies $3/15; ☯ 11:30am-2am) The favorite spot for a late-night bite and cruising. For something different try the White Greek – sauce-free with feta cheese, spinach and olives.

Karoo Kafe (☎ 508-487-6630; 338 Commercial St; mains $5-10; ☯ 11am-8:30pm) The South African owner serves up delicious home-style dishes, including many aromatic curries. Favorites include the ostrich satay and the spicy *peri-peri* (chili) chicken; the latter comes in a vegetarian tofu version too.

Bubala's by the Bay (☎ 508-487-0773; 183 Commercial St; mains $8-20; ☯ 11am-1am) Great people-watching and good food at this sidewalk café that bustles night and day. Omelets, fish and chips, and focaccia sandwiches are mainstays.

Pepe's Wharf (☎ 508-487-8717; 371 Commercial St; mains $9-20; ☯ 11:30am-10pm) Locals and seasoned visitors head to this seafront eatery for a million-dollar view on a paper-plate budget. A burger and fries will set you back just $10 and nothing on the menu, including fresh grilled swordfish, runs over $20.

Mews (☎ 508-487-1500; 429 Commercial St; mains $10-32; ☯ 6-10pm, Sun brunch 11am-2:30pm) A fantastic water view, the hottest martini bar in town and scrumptious food add up to P'town's finest dinner scene. Opt to dine gourmet on tuna sushi and rack of lamb downstairs or go casual with a juicy burger from the café menu upstairs.

Lobster Pot (☎ 508-487-0842; 321 Commercial St; mains $18-28; ☯ 11:30am-10pm) True to its name, this bustling fish house overlooking the ocean is *the* place for lobster and ladles up a superb lobster bisque. Best way to beat the crowd is to come in midafternoon.

If you happen to be in town on Saturday morning, stop by the **farmers market** (Town Hall; ☯ 8am-noon Sat Jul-Sep), where you can buy fish right off the boat and produce from the trucks of local farmers.

DRINKING

PiedBar (☎ 508-487-1527; 193 Commercial St; ☯ 2pm-1am) has a fine ocean view and attracts a mixed crowd. **Atlantic House** (☎ 508-487-3821; 4 Masonic Pl; ☯ noon-1am) is a hot spot for gay men. Of course all the clubs serve liquor and many dining spots have a bar; **Ross's Grill** (☎ 508-487-8878; 236 Commercial St) is one of the standouts overlooking the water, and has good chili too.

ENTERTAINMENT
Nightclubs

Provincetown is awash with gay clubs, drag shows and cabaret. And don't be shy if you're straight – everyone's welcome and many shows have first-rate performers.

Crown & Anchor (☎ 508-487-1430; 247 Commercial St) The queen of the scene, this multiwing complex has a nightclub, a leather bar and a steamy cabaret that takes it to the limit.

Boatslip Beach Club (☎ 508-487-1669; 161 Commercial St) Take a twirl at one of its famous afternoon-tea dances.

Vixen (☎ 508-487-6424; 336 Commercial St) A favorite lesbian hangout, with everything from an intimate wine bar to comedy shows and dancing.

Theater

Provincetown boasts a rich theater history. Eugene O'Neill began his writing career here and Marlon Brando and Richard Gere performed on Provincetown stages before they hit the big screen.

Provincetown Theater (☎ 508-487-7487; www.newprovincetownplayers.org; 238 Bradford St) This stellar performing arts center hosts Provincetown's leading theater troupe, the New Provincetown Players, and always has something of interest.

SHOPPING

Along Commercial St you'll find everything from sex toys and edgy clothing to the usual tourist T-shirts.

The real prizes here are dozens of art galleries, the finest this side of Boston. High-quality galleries worth browsing include **Albert Merola Gallery** (☎ 508-487-4424; 424 Commercial St), **William-Scott Gallery** (☎ 508-487-4040; 439 Commercial St) and **Tao Water Gallery** (☎ 508-487-8880; 352 Commercial St).

NEW ENGLAND

NEW ENGLAND

GETTING THERE & AWAY

Plymouth & Brockton buses (☎ 508-746-0378) operates several buses daily between Boston and Provincetown ($28, 3½ hours). In summer, **Bay State Cruise Company** (☎ 617-748-1428; www .boston-ptown.com) runs a fast ferry (one-way/round-trip $44/69, 1½ hours, three times a day) and a weekend-only slower ferry ($19/33, three hours) between Boston's World Trade Center Pier and MacMillan Wharf.

NANTUCKET

Once homeport to the world's largest whaling fleet, Nantucket's storied past is reflected in its period homes and cobbled streets. When whaling went bust in the mid-19th century the town plunged from riches to rags. The population dwindled, and its grand old houses sat idle until wealthy Bostonians and New Yorkers discovered that Nantucket made a fine place to spend the summer. High-end tourism has been Nantucket's mainstay ever since. **Nantucket Visitors Services & Information Bureau** (☎ 508-228-0925; www.nantucketchamber.org; 25 Federal St; ☉ 9am-6pm) has brochures and bus schedules.

Sights & Activities

The whole town is a virtual museum of historic homes and churches, so it's fun to just amble about and soak up the atmosphere. A top sight is the evocative **Whaling Museum** (☎ 508-228-1894; www.nha.org; 13 Broad St; adult/child 6-17 $15/8; ☉ 10am-5pm Fri-Wed, 10am-8pm Thu mid-May–mid-Oct, call for off-season hours) in a former spermaceti (whale-oil) candle factory.

At the eastern end of the island sits Nantucket's only other village, **Siasconset** ('Sconset), known for its sweet cottages and rambling rose gardens.

And then there are the gorgeous beaches. If you have young 'uns head to **Children's Beach**, right in the town of Nantucket, where the water's calm and there's a playground. **Surfside Beach**, 2 miles to the south, is where the college crowd goes for active surf. The best place to catch the sunset is **Madaket Beach**, 5.5 miles west of town.

No destination on the island is more than 8 miles from town and thanks to Nantucket's relatively flat terrain, bicycling is an easy way to explore. Rent bikes from **Young's Bike Shop** (☎ 508-228-1151; 6 Broad St; per day $25).

Sleeping & Eating

HI Nantucket (☎ 508-228-0433; nantuckethostel@yahoo .com; 31 Western Ave; dm $22-37) Known locally as Star of the Sea, this cool hostel in a former life-saving station 2 miles from town at Surfside Beach is Nantucket's sole nod to the budget traveler. Reservations are essential.

Barnacle Inn (☎ 508-228-0332; www.thebarna cleinn.com; 11 Fair St; d incl breakfast with/without bath $175/135) This is what old Nantucket is all about – folksy owners and simple accommodations that harken to earlier times. Rooms don't have TVs or air-con, but they do have good rates, particularly if you opt for shared bath.

Veranda House (☎ 508-228-0695; www.theveranda house.com; 3 Step Lane; r incl breakfast from $249) One of the most stylish inns on the island, the Veranda House puts contemporary minimalism into an old New England shell, with striking results. Frette linens, cozy comforters and orchid sprays set the tone. Request an upper-floor room for a sweeping harbor view.

Even Keel Café (☎ 508-228-1979; 40 Main St; breakfast & lunch $5-15, dinner $12-25; ☉ 7am-10pm) Walk straight through the restaurant to the shady patio out back where locals and tourists in the know order up generous omelets, innovative salads and the Keel's famous crab cakes.

Black-Eyed Susan's (☎ 508-325-0308; 10 India St; breakfast $7-10, dinner mains $16-29; ☉ 7am-1pm daily & 6-10pm Mon-Sat) Don't be fooled by the casual decor, this pint-size café serves the island's best breakfast and savory dinners, with lots of gourmet touches.

Straight Wharf Restaurant (☎ 508-228-4499; Straight Wharf; mains $25-35; ☉ 11:30am-2pm & 5:30-10pm) The best place for fresh-caught seafood served up with a harbor view. Join the yachties on the deck and order up Nantucket scallops and a homebrewed Cisco beer.

Getting There & Around

Cape Air (☎ 800-352-0714; www.flycapeair.com) flies from Boston, Hyannis, Martha's Vineyard and Providence to Nantucket Memorial Airport.

The **Steamship Authority** (☎ 508-477-8600; www .steamshipauthority.com; one-way adult/child 5-12 slow ferry $15/7, fast ferry $30/22) runs ferries throughout the day between Hyannis and Nantucket. The fast ferry takes an hour; the slow ferry 2¼ hours. The slow ferry takes cars, but the $360 round-trip fare aims to discourage visitors from adding to traffic congestion on Nantucket's narrow streets.

Hy-Line Cruises (☎ 508-228-3949; www.hyline cruises.com; one-way adult/child 5-12 $27.50/16) operates a daily boat between Nantucket and Martha's Vineyard from mid-June to mid-September (two hours). Hy-Line also runs passenger ferries between Hyannis and Nantucket at rates and schedules similar to the Steamship Authority's.

Once you're on Nantucket, getting around is a snap. The **NRTA Shuttle** (☎ 508-228-7025; www .shuttlenantucket.com; rides $1-2, day pass $7; ☉ late May-late Sep) operates buses around town and to 'Sconset and the beaches.

MARTHA'S VINEYARD

Martha's Vineyard is a world unto itself. Home to 5000 year-round residents, its population swells tenfold in summer. The island celebrates a rich diversity of landscapes and people. Rural Aquinnah is home to Wampanoag Indians and Oak Bluffs is a favored summer home for wealthy African Americans. The Vineyard is New England's largest island, so you'll need wheels to get around, but you can readily explore by bike or bus.

Martha's Vineyard Chamber of Commerce (☎ 508-693-0085; www.mvy.com; Beach Rd, Vineyard Haven; ☉ 9am-5pm Mon-Fri & 9am-4pm Sat) has visitor information. There are also summertime visitor information kiosks at the ferry terminals.

Vineyard Haven

A lovely harbor full of classic wooden sailboats, and bustling streets lined with eye-catching restaurants and shops lure visitors and islanders alike to this appealing town.

A vineyard on the Vineyard? But of course: about 3 miles southwest of town, **Chicama Vineyards** (☎ 508-693-0309; Stoney Hill Rd, West Tisbury; ☉ 11am-5pm Mon-Sat, 1-5pm Sun) offers free tasting tours at noon, 2pm and 4pm.

Wind's Up (☎ 508-693-4252; 199 Beach Rd; ☉ 9am-6pm) rents boats and boards. Rates per four hours are: windsurfing gear $50, single kayaks $45 and canoes or tandem kayaks $55.

SLEEPING & EATING

Martha's Vineyard Family Campground (☎ 508-693-3772; www.campmv.com; 569 Edgartown Rd; campsites $46, cabins $120-140) A mile and a half from the ferry terminal, this woodsy place offers the island's only camping and has basic cabins that sleep four to six people.

Clark House Inn (☎ 508-693-6550, 866-493-6550; www.clarkhouseinn.com; 20 Edgartown Rd; r incl breakfast $105-235; ☒ ☒ wi-fi) Relax in a rocker on the front porch of this homey B&B. The rooms are comfy, the hosts helpful and the rates a bargain for the Vineyard.

Crocker House Inn (☎ 508-693-1151, 800-772-0206; www.crockerhouseinn.com; 12 Crocker Ave; r incl breakfast $185-415; ☒ ☒ wi-fi) Convenient to town and the ferry, this cheery inn has eight well-appointed rooms, some with fireplaces and harbor views.

Black Dog Tavern (☎ 508-693-9223; 21 Beach St Extension; mains $6-34; ☉ 7am-9pm) More famous for its T-shirts than its food, this legendary eatery packs a crowd. Breakfast is the best deal with naughty indulgences like strawberry-and-white-chocolate pancakes.

Mediterranean (☉ 508-693-1617; 52 Beach Rd; mains $10-35; ☉ 11am-3pm Mon-Sat & 5-10pm daily) Sit on the deck overlooking the harbor and feast on grilled lamb shish kabob, Spanish fish stew and other southern-European flavors. Innovative sandwiches, some vegan, and scrumptious desserts too.

Oak Bluffs

This ferry-port village is pure fun, a place to wander with an ice-cream cone in hand, poke into souvenir shops and revel into the night.

Oak Bluffs started out in the mid-19th century as a summer retreat by a revivalist church, whose members enjoyed a day at the beach as much as a gospel service. They first camped out in tents, but soon built some 300 cottages, each adorned with whimsical gingerbread trim. These brightly painted cottages surround the open-air **Trinity Park Tabernacle** (1879), where the lucky descendants of the Methodist Campmeeting Association still gather for events.

Take a nostalgic ride on the classic **Flying Horses Carousel** (☎ 508-693-9481; Circuit Ave at Lake Ave; tickets $1.50; ☉ 10am-10pm), which has been captivating kids of all ages since 1876. It is the USA's oldest merry-go-round: the antique horses have manes of real horse hair and if you stare into their glass eyes you'll see neat little silver animals inside.

A scenic **bike trail** runs along the coast connecting Oak Bluffs, Vineyard Haven and Edgartown – it's largely flat so makes a good pedal for families. More experienced riders might want to bike the 20 miles to Aquinnah. Rent bicycles at **Anderson's Bike Rental**

NEW ENGLAND

(☎ 508-693-9346; Circuit Ave Extension; per day $15; ⏱ 9am-6pm) near the ferry terminal.

SLEEPING & EATING

Narragansett House (☎ 508-693-3627; 888-693-3627; www.narragansetthouse.com; 46 Narragansett Ave; r incl breakfast $100-275) Comprised of adjacent Victorian gingerbread-trimmed houses, this place offers old-fashioned rooms, small but atmospheric. It also has a couple of apartments for $1200 a week.

Oak Bluffs Inn (☎ 508-693-7171, 800-955-6235; www .oakbluffsinn.com; 64 Circuit Ave; r incl breakfast $145-300) If you enjoy romantic inns with antique furnishings, this cushy inn, just a stone's throw from the beach, is a beauty.

Giordano's (☎ 508-693-0184; 107 Circuit Ave; mains $8-17; ⏱ 11:30am-11pm) Established in 1930, this family-friendly eatery is famous for its fried clams and also serves good hand-tossed pizzas.

Sweet Life Café (☎ 508-696-0200; 63 Circuit Ave; mains $28-46; ⏱ 5:30-10pm) Romantic candlelight dining at its finest, this chef-driven bistro adds a gentle French accent to superbly prepared island seafood and complements it with a perfectly matched wine list.

Lampost (☎ 508-696-9352; Circuit Ave) Head to this combo bar and nightclub for the hottest dance scene on the island.

Edgartown

Perched on a fine natural harbor, Edgartown has a rich maritime history and a patrician air. At the height of the whaling era it was home to more than 100 sea captains whose fortunes built the grand old homes that line the streets today.

The **Martha's Vineyard Preservation Trust** (☎ 508-627-8619) manages several historic buildings clustered together on Main St: the **Dr Daniel Fisher House**, an 1840 mansion that once housed the island's wealthiest resident (no, he didn't make his fortune from his medical practice – he owned the whale-oil refinery); the **Old Whaling Church**, a classic Greek Revival building; and the 1672 **Vincent House**, built in a traditional Cape style. Call the Trust for tour information.

For more insight into Edgartown's past, visit the **Martha's Vineyard Museum** (☎ 508-627-4441; 59 School St; adult/child 6-14 $7/4; ⏱ 10am-5pm Tue-Sat mid-Jun–mid-Oct, shorter off-season hours), which has a fascinating collection of whaling paraphernalia and scrimshaw.

After exploring the town, hop the **ferry** (☎ 508-627-9427; round-trip bicycle & rider $6, car & driver $10; ⏱ 7am-midnight Jun–mid-Oct, off-season hours vary) for the five-minute jaunt to **Chappaquiddick Island**, where there are good beaches, including lovely **Cape Poge**, a wildlife refuge that runs along the entire east side of the island.

The Massachusetts Audubon Society's **Felix Neck Wildlife Sanctuary** (☎ 508-627-4850; Edgartown-Vineyard Haven Rd; adult/child 3-12 $4/3; ⏱ dawn-dusk) is a birder's paradise with 4 miles of trails skirting marshes and ponds. A magnificent barrier beach, **Katama Beach** (also 'South Beach'), situated off Katama Rd, stretches for 3 miles; rough surf is the norm on the ocean side but there are protected salt ponds on the inland side.

SLEEPING & EATING

Edgartown Inn (☎ 508-627-4794; www.edgartowninn .com; 56 N Water St; r $110-275; ✗ ❄) No phones or TV, and some rooms share baths, but this tidy former sea captain's home is Edgartown's best bargain.

Victorian Inn (☎ 508-627-4784; www.thevic.com; 24 S Water St; r incl breakfast $200-385; ✗ ❄ wi-fi) Four-post beds, fresh-cut flowers and private balconies are just part of the appeal at this upscale inn. And, yes, it is Victorian – listed on the National Register of Historic Places.

Espresso Love (☎ 508-627-9211; 17 Church St; mains $5-12; ⏱ 6:30am-6pm, to 11pm mid-Jun–Aug) Serves the richest cup o' Joe in town, sweet cinnamon rolls and luscious sandwiches – perhaps a curried chicken with walnuts and currants?

Newes from America (☎ 508-627-4397; 23 Kelley St; mains $9-14; ⏱ 11:30am-11pm) One of the oldest buildings in town, this dark, cozy place dishes up large portions of good pub grub. The fish and chips are made with fresh catch – wash them down with a good ale.

Up-Island

The rural western half of the island is a patchwork of rolling hills, small farms and open fields frequented by wild turkeys and deer. The main sights are the picturesque fishing village of **Menemsha** and the coastal **Clay Cliffs of Aquinnah**. Also known as the Gay Head Cliffs, the 150ft-high cliffs glow with an amazing array of colors that can be best appreciated in the late-afternoon light. You can hang out at **Aquinnah Beach**, just below the multicolored cliffs, or walk a mile north along the shore to an area that's popular with nude sunbathers. Beach parking costs $15. The cliffs themselves, which are a National Landmark, shouldn't be touched; removing clay or bathing in the mud pools is strictly forbidden.

Cedar Tree Neck Sanctuary (☎ 508-693-5207; Indian Hill Rd, West Tisbury; admission free; ☺ 8:30am-5:30pm), off State Rd, has an inviting 2.5-mile hike across native bogs and forest to a coastal bluff with views of Cape Cod. **Long Point Wildlife Refuge** (☎ 508-693-7392; adult/child under 16 $3/free; ☺ 9am-5pm; **P**), off Edgartown–West Tisbury Rd, offers good birding and a mile-long trail to a lovely remote beach. Parking costs $10.

Reserve early for one of the 72 beds at the **HI Martha's Vineyard** (☎ 508-693-2665; vineyard@usahostels.org; Edgartown-West Tisbury Rd, West Tisbury; dm $30-38; ☺ Apr-Oct; ☐), 8 miles from Vineyard Haven.

Getting There & Away
Cape Air (☎ 800-352-0714; www.flycapeair.com) has frequent flights from Boston, Nantucket, Hyannis and Providence to Martha's Vineyard Airport. One-way fares range from $56 from Hyannis (25 minutes) to $169 from Boston (40 minutes).

Car and passenger ferries operated by the **Steamship Authority** (☎ 508-477-8600; www.steamshipauthority.com; round-trip adult/child 5-12/bike/car $14/7.50/6/130) run from Woods Hole to Vineyard Haven (nine per day in summer) and to Oak Bluffs (five per day), a 45-minute voyage. If you're bringing a car book as far in advance as possible.

From Falmouth Harbor, the passenger ferry **Island Queen** (☎ 508-548-4800; www.islandqueen.com; 75 Falmouth Heights Rd; round-trip adult/child 3-12/bike $15/7/6) sails to Oak Bluffs at least seven times daily in summer.

From Hyannis, **Hy-Line Cruises** (☎ 508-778-2600, 800-492-8082; www.hylinecruises.com; Ocean St Dock; round-trip adult/child 5-12/bike slow ferry $37/19/12, fast ferry $59/43/12) operates a slow ferry (1½ hours) once daily to Oak Bluffs and a high-speed ferry (55 minutes) five times daily.

For information on ferries between Martha's Vineyard and Nantucket, see p254.

Getting Around
The **Martha's Vineyard Regional Transit Authority** (☎ 508-693-9440; www.vineyardtransit.com; 1-/3-day pass $6/15) operates a network of buses that travel frequently between all towns. It's a practical way to get around and you can even reach out-of-the-way destinations like the Gay Head Cliffs by bus.

The most convenient car-rental company is **Budget** (☎ 508-693-1911) with locations near the Oak Bluffs and Vineyard Haven ferry terminals and at the airport. **Adventure Rentals** (☎ 508-693-1959; 7 Beach Rd, Vineyard Haven) rents mopeds, 4WDs and regular cars. Car-rental rates vary with demand – expect to pay around $100 daily in midsummer; mopeds cost around $65. Be aware that Vineyarders disdain mopeds – and accidents are common.

CENTRAL MASSACHUSETTS
Poking around this central expanse of Massachusetts, between big-city Boston and the fashionable Berkshires, provides a taste of the less-touristed stretch of the state. But it's no slacker, thanks largely to a score of colleges that add a youthful face to the region. Indeed, Northampton brims with the coolest café life this side of New York.

Worcester
The state's third-largest city (pronounced wuh-ster), had its glory days in the 19th century. The industries that made the town rich went bust but the old barons left a legacy in Worcester's fine museums. The first-rate **Worcester Art Museum** (☎ 508-799-4406; www.worcesterart.org; 55 Salisbury St; adult/child under 18 $10/free, Sat mornings free; ☺ 11am-5pm Wed-Fri, 10am-5pm Sat, 11am-5pm Sun) showcases works by luminary French impressionists and American masters including Whistler and Sargent. The amazing **Higgins Armory Museum** (☎ 508-853-6015; www.higgins.org; 100 Barber Ave; adult/child 6-16 $9/7; ☺ 10am-4pm Tue-Sat, noon-4pm Sun) is a military buff's heaven. It started as the private

---

WHAT THE...?

It's no joke, though it's been the butt of a few. The **American Sanitary Plumbing Museum** (☎ 508-754-9453; 49 Piedmont St, Worcester; admission free; ☺ 10am-2pm Tue & Thu, closed Jul & Aug) contains the vintage toilet collection of a multigenerational family of plumbers. Get the scoop on all that's happened since the flush replaced the chamber pot.

NEW ENGLAND

collection of a local steel tycoon who built a fanciful art-deco armory to house thousands of military collectables including Corinthian helmets from ancient Greece and more than 100 full suits of armor.

Springfield

The city's top claim to fame is as the birthplace of the all-American game of basketball. The **Naismith Basketball Hall of Fame** (☎ 413-781-6500; 1000 W Columbus Ave; adult/child 5-15 $17/12; ☺ 10am-5pm), south of I-91, celebrates the sport with exhibits and memorabilia from all the big hoop stars. Springfield was also home to the Indian Motorcycle Company, which began making the legendary bikes in 1901; the last of its factory buildings houses the **Indian Motorcycle Museum** (☎ 413-737-2624; 33 Hendee St) but it's planning to relocate, so call for the latest.

Northampton

The region's top dining, hottest nightlife and snazziest shopping all await in this perky burg known for its liberal politics and highly visible lesbian community. Easy to explore on foot, the town center is chock-a-block with cafés, funky shops and art galleries. **Greater Northampton Chamber of Commerce** (☎ 413-584-1900; www.northamptoncommon.com; 99 Pleasant St; ☺ 9am-5pm Mon-Fri) is information central.

The **Smith College** (☎ 413-584-2700; www.smith.edu) campus, covering 127 acres with lots of greenhouses and lovely gardens, is well worth a stroll. Don't miss the **Smith College Museum of Art** (☎ 413-585-2760; Elm St at Bedford Tce; adult/child 6-12 $5/2; ☺ 10am-4pm Tue-Sat, noon-4pm Sun), which boasts an impressive collection of 19th- and 20th-century European and North American paintings, including works by John Singleton Copley, Claude Monet and Paul Cézanne.

WHAT THE...?

Life-size bronze sculptures of the Cat in the Hat and other wonky characters from the books of Springfield native Theodor Seuss Geisel will delight kids at the outdoor **Dr Seuss National Memorial Sculpture Garden** (cnr State & Chestnut Sts, Springfield; admission free; ☺ 7am-8pm).

SLEEPING & EATING

Autumn Inn (☎ 413-584-7660; 259 Elm St/MA 9; r incl breakfast $100-150; ☷ ☐ wi-fi) Despite its motel-like layout, this two-story place near Smith College sports an agreeable innlike ambience and large, comfy rooms.

Best Western Valley Inn (☎ 413-586-1500, 800-941-3066; 117 Conz St; r incl breakfast $109-159; ☷ ☷ wi-fi) Set on the south side of town, this modern hotel offers renovated rooms, the fancier ones with fireplaces and heart-shaped spa bathtubs.

Hotel Northampton (☎ 413-584-3100; www.hotelnorthampton.com; 36 King St; r $150-225; ☷ wi-fi) If you want a taste of old Northampton, the century-old Hotel Northampton in the town center is a class act with period decor, well-appointed rooms and modern conveniences.

Sylvester's (☎ 413-586-5343; 111 Pleasant St; mains $5-9; ☺ 7am-2:30pm) Follow the locals to this unassuming eatery for the best breakfast in town. Forget mixes – everything is from scratch, real maple syrup tops the pancakes, the homefries are loaded with sautéed onions and the omelets are however you like them.

Paul & Elizabeth's (☎ 413-584-4832; 150 Main St; mains $8-16; ☺ 11:30am-9:15pm Mon-Sat, 10am-9:15pm Sun) Come to Northampton's hippest café for luscious vegetarian dishes and a tempura-style fish dish served with hand-cut fries that may well be the best fish and chips you'll ever try.

Eastside Grill (☎ 413-586-3347; 19 Strong Ave; mains $10-20; ☺ 5-10pm) If a thick juicy steak, Cajun-style blackened fish and homemade desserts sound tempting, join the crowd at this award-winning dinner restaurant.

DRINKING & ENTERTAINMENT

Haymarket Café (☎ 413-586-9969; 185 Main St; ☺ 11:30am-10pm; wi-fi) If you're up for a coffee jolt or fresh-squeezed juice, head straight to this Bohemian hangout.

Northampton Brewery (☎ 413-584-9903; 11 Brewster Ct; ☺ 11:30am-1am) Tip a glass of Northampton Pale Ale at this bustling microbrewery's rooftop beer garden.

Iron Horse Music Hall (☎ 413-584-0610; 20 Center St; tickets $10-25) Nationally acclaimed folk and jazz artists line up to play in this intimate setting.

Calvin Theatre (☎ 413-584-1444; 19 King St; tickets $25-50) The venue for big-name performances for everything from hot rock and indie bands to comedy shows.

Amherst

This college town, a short drive from Northampton, is built around the mega **University of Massachusetts** (☎ 413-545-0111; www.umass.edu) and two small colleges, the liberal **Hampshire College** (☎ 413-549-4600; www.hampshire.edu) and the prestigious **Amherst College** (☎ 413-542-2000; www .amherst.edu). Contact them for campus tours and event information; there's always something happening.

The lifelong home of poet Emily Dickinson (1830–86), the 'belle of Amherst,' is open to the public as the **Emily Dickinson Museum** (☎ 413-542-8161; www.emilydickinsonmuseum.org; 280 Main St; adult/child 6-17 $8/5; ☒ 1-5pm Wed-Sat Apr, May, Sep & Oct, 10am-5:30pm Wed-Sat & 12:30-5:30pm Sun Jun-Aug). Note that the last tour starts at 4:30pm.

THE BERKSHIRES

Tranquil towns and a wealth of cultural attractions are nestled in these cool green hills. For more than a century the Berkshires have been a favored retreat for wealthy Bostonians and New Yorkers. And we're not just talking Rockefellers – the entire Boston symphony summers here as well. The **Berkshire Visitors Bureau** (☎ 413-443-9186, 800-237-5747; www.berkshires .org; 109 South St, Pittsfield; ☒ 8:30am-5pm Mon-Fri) has information on the entire region.

Great Barrington

This up-and-coming town is hands-down the best place in the Berkshires to be at mealtime. Head straight to the intersection of Main (US 7) and Railroad Sts in the town center where you'll find an artful mix of galleries and mouthwatering eateries – everything from bakeries to ethnic cuisines.

Families will love **Baba Louie's** (☎ 413-528-8100; 286 Main St; mains $8-16; ☒ 11:30am-9:30pm) for its organic wood-fired pizzas and $5 kids specials. For sophisticated dining, black-and-chrome **Pearl's** (☎ 413-528-7767; 47 Railroad St; mains $10-28; ☒ 11am-10pm) draws a crowd with savory meat dishes and chocolate martinis.

Stockbridge

This timeless New England town, sans even a single traffic light, looks like something straight out of a Norman Rockwell drawing. Oh wait...it is! Rockwell (1894–1978), the most popular illustrator in US history, lived on Main St and used many of the townsfolk as his subjects. Join the crowds at the **Norman Rockwell Museum** (☎ 413-298-4100; www.nrm .org; 9 Glendale Rd/MA 183; adult/child under 18 $12.50/free; ☒ 10am-5pm), where Rockwell's original slice-of-Americana paintings can be examined up close and personal.

Lenox

The cultural heart of the Berkshires, the refined village of Lenox hosts one of the country's premier music series, the open-air **Tanglewood Music Festival** (☎ 617-266-1492, in summer 413-637-5165; www.bso.org; admission $18-90; ☒ late Jun-Aug), featuring the Boston Symphony Orchestra and guest artists like cellist Yo-Yo Ma.

Shakespeare & Company (☎ 413-637-3353; www .shakespeare.org; 70 Kemble St; admission $10-52) performs the Bard's work throughout the summer. The renowned **Jacob's Pillow Dance Festival** (☎ 413-243-0745; admission $28-58), 10 miles east of Lenox in Becket, stages contemporary dance from mid-June through August.

The **Mount** (☎ 413-637-1899; 2 Plunkett St at US 7; adult/child under 6 $16/free; ☒ 9am-5pm May-Oct), novelist Edith Wharton's former estate, offers hour-long tours of her house and inspirational gardens.

Charming period inns abound in Lenox. The senior of them, **Birchwood Inn** (☎ 413-637-2600; www.birchwood-inn.com; 7 Hubbard St; r incl breakfast $150-300; ☒), registered its first guest in 1767 and continues to offer warm hospitality today.

You'll find several choice bistros along Church St in the town center. The perennial favorite, **Church Street Café** (☎ 413-637-2745; 65 Church St; lunch $12-15, dinner $22-30; ☒ 11:30am-2:30pm & 5-9pm), creatively fuses fresh New England fare with Asian accents.

Pittsfield

Just west of the workaday town of Pittsfield is **Hancock Shaker Village** (☎ 413-443-0188; www .hancockshakervillage.org; US 20; adult/child under 13 $15/free; ☒ 10am-5pm Jun-Nov, call for off-season hours), a fascinating museum illustrating the lives of the Shakers, the religious sect who founded this village in 1783. The Shakers believed in communal ownership, the sanctity of work and celibacy, the latter of which proved their demise. Their handiwork – graceful in its simplicity – includes wooden furnishings and 20 buildings, the most famous of which is the round stone barn.

Williamstown & North Adams

Cradled by the Berkshire's rolling hills, Williamstown is a picture-perfect New England college town centered around the campus of Williams College. Williamstown and neighboring North Adams boast three excellent art museums, each a worthy destination in itself.

SIGHTS & ACTIVITIES

The outstanding **Clark Art Institute** (☎ 413-458-2303; www.clarkart.edu; 225 South St, Williamstown; adult/child under 18 Jun-Oct $12.50/free, Nov-May free to all; ☉ 10am-5pm, closed Mon Sep-Jun) focuses on 19th-century paintings with oodles of Renoirs and other French impressionists as well as a solid collection of American paintings by Winslow Homer, John Singer Sargent and others.

Williams College Museum of Art (☎ 413-597-2429; www.wcma.org; 15 Lawrence Hall Dr, Williamstown; admission free; ☉ 10am-5pm Tue-Sat, 1-5pm Sun) showcases works by American luminaries such as Mary Cassett, Grant Wood and Andy Warhol.

Mass MoCA (☎ 413-662-2111; www.massmoca.org; 87 Marshall St, North Adams; adult/child 6-16 $10/4; ☉ 10am-6pm Jul & Aug, 11am-5pm Wed-Mon Sep-Jun) has become such a splash that it's put once-sleepy North Adams on the map. This avant-garde contemporary art museum sprawls across an amazing 222,000 sq ft, making it the largest gallery in the USA. Bring your walking shoes! MoCA is also a happening venue for music, cutting-edge theater and dance performances.

The first-rate **Williamstown Theatre Festival** (☎ 413-597-3400; www.wtfestival.org; MA 2, Williamstown; tickets $25-55) stages contemporary and classic plays in July and August, often with notable casts.

SLEEPING & EATING

You'll find the area's best eating options on Williamstown's Spring St.

River Bend Farm (☎ 413-458-3121; www.riverbendfarmbb.com; 643 US/MA 7; r with shared bath incl breakfast $120; ✗) Step back a couple hundred years in this Georgian colonial B&B furnished with antiques and boasting five fireplaces.

Williams Inn (☎ 413-458-9371, 800-828-0133; www.williamsinn.com; 1090 Main St; r $170-300; ✗ ⚇ 🖥 wi-fi) A favorite of visiting alumni, this century-old establishment on the Williamstown green is the area's top-rated hotel.

Tunnel City Coffee (☎ 413-458-5010; 100 Spring St; snacks $2-5; ☉ 6:30am-6pm; wi-fi) Come to this stu-

dent haunt for potent espressos, quiche and tempting desserts.

Sushi Thai Garden (☎ 413-458-0004; 27 Spring St; mains $6-15; ☉ 11:30am-10pm) Order from the Thai side of the menu and you're in for a treat. A good choice is the Penang curry, redolent with basil and spices.

RHODE ISLAND

America's smallest state packs plenty of wallop in a compact package, more than making up for its lack of land with 400 miles of gorgeous coastline, deeply indented bays and lovely beaches. The state's engaging capital, Providence, is small enough to be friendly but large enough to offer top-notch dining and ace attractions. And then there's the town of Newport, a summer haunt of the well-heeled, brimming with opulent mansions, fancy yachts and world-class music festivals. Should you want to take it further afield, hopping a ferry to Block Island provides an unspoiled island experience perfect for a day trip.

History

The name Roger Williams (1603–83) gave to the community he founded in 1636 – nothing less than Providence! – spoke to the optimism his followers shared. A religious outcast from Puritanical Boston, Williams established the colony on the principle that all people were entitled to freedom of conscience. He was an early advocate of separation between religion and government, a concept that later became a foundation of

---

RHODE ISLAND FACTS

Nicknames Ocean State, Little Rhody

Population 1.1 million

Area 1214 sq miles

Capital city Providence (population 176,862)

Sales tax 7%

Birthplace of Jazz trumpeter Bobby Hackett (1915–76), Broadway composer George M Cohan (1878–1942) and toy icon Mr Potato Head (b 1952)

Home of The first US tennis championships

Famous for Being the smallest state

Official state bird A chicken? Why not. The Rhode Island Red, which revolutionized the poultry industry

the US Constitution. Progressive little Rhode Island became the first American colony to abolish slavery (1774) and the first to declare independence from Britain in 1776. Despite an economic decline during much of the 20th century, Rhode Island has bounced back, re-energizing its cities, undertaking vast public works projects and establishing itself as a player in the fields of higher education, business and tourism.

Information

Rhode Island Tourism Division (☎ 401-222-2601, 800-556-2484; www.visitrhodeisland.com; 1 W Exchange Pl, Providence, RI 02903; ☼ 8:30am-4:30pm Mon-Fri) Distributes visitor information on the whole state.

Providence Journal (www.projo.com) The state's largest daily newspaper.

PROVIDENCE

Like a phoenix rising from its ashes, once dreary Providence has revitalized itself into one of the finest small cities in the country. From the historic downtown district to the café-laden streets embracing Brown University, everything about this town invites a closer look.

Orientation & Information

Exit 22 off I-95 deposits you into the heart of the city, near the State House, the Amtrak station and downtown restaurants. The university area is a short walk to the east. The colorful Italian enclave of Federal Hill centers on Atwells Ave, a mile west of the city center.

Brooks Pharmacy (☎ 401-272-3048; 1200 N Main St; ☼ 24hr)

Brown Bookstore (☎ 401-863-3168; 244 Thayer St; ☼ 9am-8pm Mon-Fri, 10am-8pm Sat, 11am-5pm Sun)

Post office (☎ 800-275-8777; 2 Exchange Tce; ☼ 8am-5pm Mon-Fri)

Providence Phoenix (www.thephoenix.com/provi dence) Free alternative weekly, with extensive entertainment coverage.

Providence-Warwick Convention & Visitors Bureau (☎ 401-274-1636, 800-233-1636; www.pwcvb .com; 1 W Exchange St; ☼ 8:30am-5pm Mon-Fri)

Rhode Island Hospital (☎ 401-444-4000; 593 Eddy St; ☼ 24hr) South of the city center, off I-95 exit 19.

Sights & Activities

The city's focal point, the **State House** (☎ 401-222-2357; 82 Smith St; admission free; ☼ 8:30am-4:30pm Mon-Fri) is crowned with one of the world's largest self-supporting marble domes and was modeled in part on St Peter's Basilica in Vatican City.

The wonderfully eclectic **Rhode Island School of Design Museum** (RISD; ☎ 401-454-6500; www.risdmu seum.org; 224 Benefit St; adult/child 5-18 $8/2; ☼ 10am-5pm Tue-Sun), showcases everything from ancient Roman art to 20th-century American paintings and decorative arts. Pop in before 1pm Sunday and admission is free. On the hillside above RISD lies **Brown University** (☎ 401-863-2378; www .brown.edu; 71 George St), with an eminently strollable campus awash in Ivy League charm.

The offbeat **Culinary Archives & Museum** (☎ 401-598-2805; www.culinary.org; 315 Harborside Blvd; adult/child 5-18 $7/2; ☼ 10am-5pm Tue-Sun) contains a half-million-item collection devoted to the history of dining – everything from ancient cookbooks to early-20th-century dining cars. It's at Johnson & Wales University; to get there, take I-95 exit 18, turn right on Allens Ave and follow the signs to the campus.

Roger Williams Park (☎ 401-785-3510; 1000 Elm-wood Ave; admission free) has so many Victorian-era touches, such as its classic carousel, it's been cited by the National Trust for Historic Preservation as one of America's top urban parks. Among its sights are botanic gardens and a **zoo** (adult/child $10/6; ☼ 9am-5pm) with polar bears and elephants. From downtown, take I-95 south to exit 17, Elmwood Ave.

Sleeping

Christopher Dodge House (☎ 401-351-6111; www .providence-hotel.com; 11 W Park St; r incl breakfast $119-179; ▣) Hardwood floors, gas fireplaces and cozy quilts on the bed set the tone at this inviting B&B overlooking the State House. If it's full ask about its other inn, the Mowry-Nicholson House, just a block away.

Providence Biltmore (☎ 401-421-0700, 800-294-7709; www.providencebiltmore.com; 11 Dorrance St; r $179, ste $209; ⊠ wi-fi) Entering the lobby of this landmark downtown hotel is like stepping back into the 1920s. The rooms retain their period charm while adding modern conveniences and comfy king beds. Suites are huge for just $30 more.

Eating

Providence brims with superb eateries. For the 'Little Italy' immersion, stroll the trattorias lining Atwells Ave on Federal Hill. For affordable eclectic eats head to Thayer St, on the hill above Brown University.

Angelo's Civita Farnese (☎ 401-621-8171; 141 Atwells Ave; mains $5-12; ☺ 11:30am-9pm Sun-Thu, 11:30am-10pm Fri & Sat) Federal Hill's favorite family eatery dishes up generous portions of pastas and traditional meat dishes. Bambinos will love the antique train set that circles the dining-room ceiling.

Le Greque (☎ 401-351-3454; 130 Westminister St; mains $6-8; ☺ 10am-6pm Mon-Fri, 11am-5pm Sat) A standout among several mom-and-pop eateries in the Arcade, Providence's vintage (circa 1828) indoor mall, this joint serves excellent falafel pita sandwiches and other Greek treats.

Café Paragon (☎ 401-331-6200; 234 Thayer St; mains $7-16; ☺ 11am-1am) This arty café bustles with students from nearby Brown University who flock here for the innovative tapas and gourmet burgers.

Hemenway's (☎ 401-351-8570; 121 S Main St; lunch $8-15, dinner $18-26; ☺ 11:30am-10pm Mon-Thu, 11:30am-11pm Fri & Sat, noon-9pm Sun) If you're in the mood for seafood head to this stylish downtown grill and order from the 'Today's Fresh Catch' menu – it doesn't get any better!

Cassarino's (☎ 401-751-3333; 177 Atwells Ave; mains $15-22; ☺ 11:30am-10pm Mon-Sat) This sexy Federal Hill ristorante scores perfecto on everything. Begin with the balsamic calamari, follow with shrimp *cappellini primavera*, add a glass of Pinot Grigio and you've got a night to remember. Good $10 lunches before 3pm too.

Drinking & Entertainment

Union Station Brewery (☎ 401-274-2739; 36 Exchange Tce) Downtown in the old train station, this atmospheric microbrewery crafts tasty lagers and serves good light eats too.

WHAT THE...?

Move over, Christo. Providence has blazed onto the public art installation scene with **WaterFire** (www.waterfire.org), set on the river that meanders through the city center. Nearly 100 braziers poke above the water, each supporting a bonfire that roars after dark. Flames dance off the water, music plays, black-clad gondoliers glide by, and party-goers pack the riverbanks. A captivating blend of art and entertainment, Water-Fire takes place about 18 times between May and September, mostly on Saturday, from sunset to 1am.

Lupo's Heartbreak Hotel (☎ 401-331-5876; www .lupos.com; 79 Washington St; cover $10-35) Providence's legendary music venue features both top rock bands and indie acts.

AS220 (☎ 401-831-9327; www.as220.org; 115 Empire St) An alternative space open to experimental bands, performance artists, offbeat films and more – you never know what you might find.

Providence Performing Arts Center (☎ 401-421-2787; www.ppacri.org; 220 Weybosset St; tickets $30-60) Concerts and Broadway musicals are highlights at this beautifully restored 1928 art-deco theater.

Getting There & Away

TF Green Airport (☎ 401-737-8222; www.pvdairport .com; I-95, exit 13, Warwick), 20 minutes south of downtown Providence, is served by major US airlines and car-rental companies.

Peter Pan Bus Lines (☎ 401-751-8800) connects Providence with Boston ($8, one hour) numerous times a day and also runs buses to Cape Cod and New York. Several daily **Amtrak** (☎ 800-872-7245) trains link Providence with Boston ($16, 50 minutes) and New York ($68, three hours). If you're traveling on weekdays, **MBTA** (☎ 617-222-3200, 800-392-6100) commuter trains between Providence and Boston ($7.75, 70 minutes) are a better deal.

The **Rhode Island Public Transit Authority** (RIPTA; ☎ 401-781-9400, 800-244-0444; www.ripta.com; one-way $1.50, day pass $6) runs old-fashioned trolley-style buses throughout the city from its downtown Kennedy Plaza hub and also links Providence with Newport.

NEWPORT

The town's very name conjures up images of Great Gatsby mansions and unbridled wealth. In the 1890s Newport became *the* place for rich New Yorkers to summer. They built opulent seaside mansions, each successive one attempting to outdo the neighbors. These mansions – dubbed 'summer cottages' – are so dazzling that people still flock to Newport just to ogle them. Newport is also famous for its legendary music festivals and its active yachting scene.

Orientation & Information

Newport is easy to navigate, with most of the action on or near the waterfront.

Bank of America (☎ 401-846-7401; 181 Bellevue Ave)

Newport County Convention & Visitors Bureau

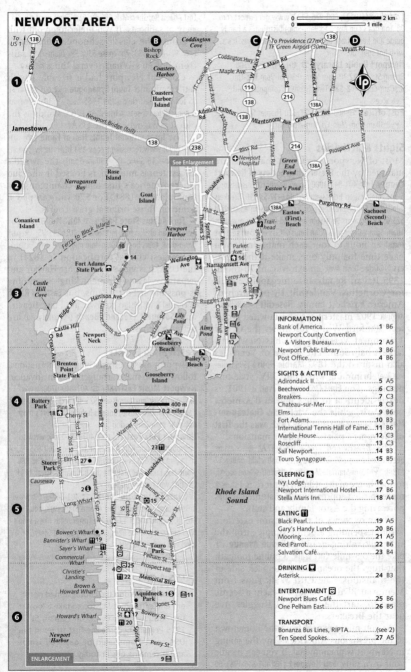

NEWPORT AREA

Rhode Island Sound

INFORMATION

Bank of America	**1** B6
Newport County Convention & Visitors Bureau	**2** A5
Newport Public Library	**3** B6
Post Office	**4** B6

SIGHTS & ACTIVITIES

Adirondack II	**5** A5
Beechwood	**6** C3
Breakers	**7** C3
Chateau-sur-Mer	**8** C3
Elms	**9** B6
Fort Adams	**10** B3
International Tennis Hall of Fame	**11** B6
Marble House	**12** C3
Rosecliff	**13** C3
Sail Newport	**14** B3
Touro Synagogue	**15** B5

SLEEPING

Ivy Lodge	**16** C3
Newport International Hostel	**17** B6
Stella Maris Inn	**18** A4

EATING

Black Pearl	**19** A5
Gary's Handy Lunch	**20** B6
Mooring	**21** A5
Red Parrot	**22** B6
Salvation Café	**23** B4

DRINKING

Asterisk	**24** B3

ENTERTAINMENT

Newport Blues Café	**25** B6
One Pelham East	**26** B5

TRANSPORT

Bonanza Bus Lines, RIPTA	(see 2)
Ten Speed Spokes	**27** A5

ENLARGEMENT

(☎ 401-845-9123, 800-976-5122; www.gonewport.com; 23 America's Cup Ave; ⊙ 9am-5pm) Distributes a handy guide and keeps track of accommodation vacancies. It's a wi-fi hot spot too.

Newport Public Library (☎ 401-847-8720; 300 Spring St; ⊙ 12:30-9pm Mon, 9:30am-9pm Tue-Thu, 9:30am-6pm Fri & Sat) Twenty online computers with free access.

Post office (☎ 800-275-8777; 320 Thames St; ⊙ 8:30am-6pm Mon-Fri, 9am-1pm Sat)

Sights & Activities

Most of Newport's grandest mansions are managed by the **Preservation Society of Newport County** (☎ 401-847-1000; www.newportmansions.org; 5-site combination tickets adult/child 6-17 $31/10, Breakers adult/child $16/4, Breakers plus 1 other mansion adult/child $23/6; ⊙ Breakers 9am-5pm Apr–mid-Oct, other mansions 10am-5pm, call for off-season hours). Give yourself at least an hour to tour each mansion. If you have time for only one, make it the **Breakers** (44 Ochre Point Ave), an extravagant 70-room, 1895 Italian Renaissance megapalace built for Cornelius Vanderbilt II, patriarch of America's richest family. **Rosecliff** (548 Bellevue Ave), a 1902 masterpiece of renowned architect Stanford White, resembles the Grand Trianon at Versailles and has Newport's largest ballroom. The palace of Versailles also inspired the 1892 **Marble House** (596 Bellevue Ave), brimming with Louis XIV–style furnishings. The **Elms** (367 Bellevue Ave), c 1901, is nearly identical to the Château d'Asnières near Paris, while the Victorian **Chateau-sur-Mer** (474 Bellevue Ave), built in 1852, was the first of Newport's palatial summer mansions.

The **Beechwood** (☎ 401-846-3772; www.astors beechwood.com; 580 Bellevue Ave; adult/child under 17 $18/8; ⊙ 10am-5pm late May-Oct, call for off-season hours), former home of the affluent Astor clan, takes a more spirited approach with costumed actors portraying the Astor family and staff.

To enjoy views of the mansion exteriors without spending a penny simply stroll the sidewalks along grand **Bellevue Avenue** or take the 3.5-mile **Cliff Walk**, a public footpath that hugs the ocean along the back side of the mansions. The Cliff Walk runs from Memorial Blvd to Bailey's Beach; a scenic place to start the walk is at Ruggles Ave near the Breakers.

As you might expect from the hometown of the prestigious America's Cup, the sailing in Newport is phenomenal. If you can handle your own sails, **Sail Newport** (☎ 401-846-1983; 60 Fort Adams Rd; 3hr rentals $96 ⊙ 9am-5pm) rents a variety of sailboats. If you prefer to go out with a group, the classic schooner **Adirondack II** (☎ 401-846-1983; 2hr cruise $30; ⊙ 10am-7pm) sails from Bowen's Wharf several times a day.

Colonial Newport had a sizeable Jewish settlement and **Touro Synagogue** (☎ 401-847-4794; 85 Touro St; adult/child under 13 $5/free; ⊙ 10am-5pm Jul & Aug, call for off-season hours), c 1763, stands as the oldest synagogue in the USA.

The **International Tennis Hall of Fame** (☎ 401-849-3990; www.tennisfame.com; 194 Bellevue Ave; adult/child under 16 $9/5; ⊙ 9:30am-5pm), the world's largest tennis museum, is housed in the club where America's first tennis championships took place in 1881. For $70 you can play a game on those original grass courts.

Fort Adams State Park (☎ 401-841-0707; Harrison Ave; park admission free, fort tours adult/child $8/5; ⊙ park dawn-dusk, tours hourly 10am-4pm mid-May–Oct), site of the largest coastal fortification (c 1824) in the USA, has views of Newport Harbor and expansive lawns for picnicking. Swimming is possible at Fort Adams, but **Easton's Beach** (Memorial Blvd), also known as 'First Beach,' and **Sachuest (Second) Beach** (Purgatory Rd) are better beaches.

Festivals & Events

Newport's music festivals have an international following, so make arrangements in advance.

Newport Music Festival (☎ 401-849-0700; www.newportmusic.org; admission $25-40) A class act, with 17 days of chamber music concerts held in Newport's most romantic mansions during July.

Newport Folk Festival (☎ 401-847-3700; www.newportfolk.com; Fort Adams State Park; adult $55-75, child under 13 $5) Everybody who's anybody in the folk world has taken the stage at this hallmark festival, held the first weekend in August.

JVC Jazz Festival/Newport (☎ 401-847-3700; www.festivalproductions.net; Fort Adams State Park; adult $65-100, child under 13 $5) The roster reads like a who's who of jazz, with the likes of BB King and Al Green, on a weekend in mid-August.

IT'S A GAS

As you stroll along the cobblestoned northern end of Thames St, stop to take a look at the antique street lamps on Pelham St. In 1805 Pelham became the first street in the USA to be illuminated by gas-fired lamps and it remains gas lit today.

WORTH THE TRIP: BLOCK ISLAND

This secluded jewel 12 miles off the coast of Rhode Island retains unspoiled charm that's hard to find on the mainland. A mere 7 miles from one end to the other, the island packs wonderful beaches and more than 25 miles of hiking and biking trails.

Ferries dock at Old Harbor, the main town, which has changed little since its gingerbread houses were built in the late 19th century. The beaches begin right at the north side of town. If you continue north 2 miles you'll come to the **Clay Head Nature Trail**, which follows high clay bluffs above the beach offering good bird-watching along the way. **Rodman Hollow**, a 100-acre wildlife refuge at the south end of the island, is also laced with interesting trails.

The island is an ideal size to explore by bicycle; you can rent one from several places near the ferry dock, including **Old Harbor Bike Shop** (☎ 401-466-2029; per day $25).

The **Block Island Chamber of Commerce** (☎ 800-383-2474; www.blockislandchamber.com), right at the ferry dock, can help with accommodations, but be aware the island's four-dozen inns typically book full in summer.

The **Block Island Ferry** (☎ 866-783-7996; www.blockislandferry.com; adult round-trip slow/high speed $21/30) runs high-speed (30 minutes, May-Oct) and slow (55 minutes, year-round) ferries from Galilee State Pier in Point Judith, each two to five times a day, as well as once-daily slow (two hours, July and August) ferries from Fort Adams State Park in Newport. Children pay half price; bring a bicycle along for $6 round-trip. Schedules are convenient for day-trippers, with morning departures and late-afternoon returns.

Sleeping

Newport International Hostel (☎ 401-369-0243; www.newporthostel.com; 16 Howard St; dm with shared bath incl breakfast $35-59; ☒) Steps from Newport's bustling Thames St, this friendly hostel has just two rooms with five beds. The manager, a world traveler, will share all sorts of tips for having a great stay without breaking the bank. Hostel prices are highest on summer weekends.

Stella Maris Inn (☎ 401-849-2862; www.stellamarisinn.com; 91 Washington St; r incl breakfast $125-225; ☒) Grab a rocking chair on the porch and watch the sailboats breeze by at this comfortably old-fashioned inn occupying a former convent. It's in quiet neighborhood but just a stroll to the city center.

Ivy Lodge (☎ 401-849-6865, 800-834-6865; www.ivylodge.com; 12 Clay St; r incl breakfast $199-349) Treat yourself to the good life at this grand Victorian inn just a stone's throw from Newport's sumptuous mansions. All rooms have antique furnishings, most have fireplaces, and if you need some more romance some have Jacuzzi tubs.

Eating

Gary's Handy Lunch (☎ 401-847-9480; 462 Thames St; dishes $3-7; ☻ 5am-3pm, to 8pm Fri) Newport's working folk kick-start their day over coffee and simple breakfast fare at this old-school diner.

Salvation Café (☎ 401-847-2620; 140 Broadway; mains $8-20; ☻ 5-11pm) Bright decor and brilliant food are in store at this quirky café. The menu is pure eclectic ranging from chicken pesto pizza to Portuguese-style clams.

Black Pearl (☎ 401-846-5264; Bannister's Wharf; mains $9-25; ☻ 11am-10pm) This friendly tavern, perched over the water, is as atmospheric as it gets. The varied menu includes burgers, seafood and an award-winning clam chowder.

Red Parrot (☎ 401-847-3140; 348 Thames St; mains $10-26; ☻ 11am-11pm) Excellent seafood in every imaginable incarnation from lobster quesadillas to grilled swordfish. Grab a window table, order a frosty Caribbean drink and enjoy the people-watching on bustling Thames St.

Mooring (☎ 401-846-2260; Sayer's Wharf; mains $10-30; ☻ 11:30am-9pm Mon-Sat, noon-9pm Sun) A harborfront location, an outdoor patio and a menu brimming with fresh seafood make an unbeatable combination for sunset dining. It also has a stellar wine list.

Drinking & Entertainment

Newport Blues Café (☎ 401-841-5510; 286 Thames St) One of the best blues and R & B scenes this side of New York City.

One Pelham East (☎ 401-847-9460; 276 Thames St) This romping place has entertainment most nights, drawing locals and tourists alike with rock bands.

Asterisk (☎ 401-841-8833; 599 Thames St) A local favorite at the less-touristed south end of Thames, this café has a stylish urban ambience and kick-ass espresso martinis.

Getting There & Away

Bonanza Bus Lines (☎ 888-751-8800), operating under the umbrella of Peter Pan Bus Lines, has several buses daily to Boston ($21, 1¾ hours). State-run **RIPTA** (☎ 800-244-0444; www .ripta.com) operates frequent buses (one-way $1.50, day pass $6) from the visitor bureau to the mansions, beaches and Providence.

Rent bicycles at **Ten Speed Spokes** (☎ 401-847-5609; 18 Elm St; per day $25; ☷ 10am-6pm Mon-Fri, 10am-5pm Sat, noon-5pm Sun) near the visitor bureau.

RHODE ISLAND BEACHES

If you're up for a day at the beach Rhode Island's southwestern coastal towns make great destinations. It is the Ocean State, after all.

The mile-long **Narragansett Town Beach** in Narragansett is the place to go for surfing. The nearby **Scarborough State Beach** is one of the most popular beaches in Rhode Island, with a wide beach, a glorious pavilion and inviting boardwalks. **Watch Hill** at the state's southwestern tip is a wonderful place to turn back the clock, with its Flying Horse Carousel and Victorian setting. Get details on the entire area from the **South County Tourism Council** (☎ 800-548-4662; www.southcountyri.com; 4808 Tower Hill Rd, Wakefield).

CONNECTICUT

Sandwiched between sexy New York City and northerly New England's quainter quarters, Connecticut typically gets short shrift by travelers. Sure the brawny I-95 coastal corridor is largely industrial, but take a closer look and you're in for pleasant surprises. New Haven, centered around Yale University, has blossomed into a happening place that fuses historic appeal with an up-and-coming cultural scene. Mystic boasts a terrific nautical museum and the Litchfield Hills area, in the state's northwestern corner, is as prettily pastoral as any place in New England.

CONNECTICUT FACTS

Nicknames Constitution State, Nutmeg State
Population 3.5 million
Area 5018 sq miles
Capital city Hartford (population 124,510)
Sales tax 6%
Birthplace of Abolitionist John Brown (1800–59), circus man PT Barnum (1810–91), actress Katharine Hepburn (1909–2003), presidential spoiler Ralph Nader (b 1934)
Home of The first written constitution in the US; the first lollipop, pay phone and helicopter
Famous for Starting the US insurance biz and building the first nuclear submarine
Quirkiest state song lyrics 'Yankee Doodle,' which manages to entwine patriotism with doodles, feathers and macaroni

---

The Connecticut River, which slices clear across Connecticut, gives the state its name. The word comes from the Mohegan Indian mouthful *quinnehtukqut*, which means 'place of the long river.'

History

In 1633 the Dutch built a small settlement at current-day Hartford, but it was the English, arriving en masse in the following years, that shaped Connecticut.

Thanks to the industriousness of the citizenry, the Connecticut Yankee peddler became a fixture in early American society, traveling by wagon from town to town selling clocks and other manufactured gadgets. Connecticut etched a leading role in the Industrial Revolution when Eli Whitney built a New Haven factory in 1798 to produce firearms with interchangeable parts – the beginning of modern mass production.

In 1810 America's first insurance company opened in Hartford and by the 1870s the city boasted the highest per capita income in the USA. Two of America's leading literary figures, Harriet Beecher Stowe (1811–96) and Mark Twain (1835–1910), were Hartford neighbors for 17 years.

Information

There are welcome centers at the Hartford airport and on I-95 and I-84 when entering the state by car.
Connecticut Tourism Division (☎ 860-270-8080;

www.ctvisit.com; 755 Main St, Hartford, CT 06103)
Distributes visitor information for the entire state.

Hartford Courant (www.ctnow.com) The state's largest
newspaper has news and visitor information online.

CONNECTICUT COAST

The long Connecticut coast is not all of a
piece. The western end is largely a bedroom
community connected by commuter rail to
New York City. But by the time you get to
hip New Haven, Connecticut's undiluted
spirit has begun to shine through. Sweet
Mystic, on the eastern end not far from
Rhode Island, is about tall ships and the
siren call of the sea.

New Haven

For visitors New Haven is all about Yale. Head
straight to New Haven Green, graced by old
colonial churches and Yale's hallowed ivy-
covered walls. In recent years this revitalized
city has emerged as a spirited cultural center.
Its top museums and best restaurants are all
within a few blocks of the Green. The oldest
planned city in America (1638), New Haven is
laid out in orderly blocks spreading out from
the Green, making it a cinch to get around.
The **Greater New Haven Convention & Visitors Bureau** (☎ 203-777-8550, 800-332-7829; www.newhavencvb
.org; 59 Elm St; ☺ 8:30am-5pm Mon-Fri) is one block
east of the Green.

SIGHTS & ACTIVITIES

Yale University is not only the prestigious alma
mater of five US presidents but it's one cool
campus thick with Gothic buildings. Most
impressive of the spires is **Harkness Tower**, from
which a carillon peals at measured moments
throughout the day. For campus tours or to
pick up a campus map, drop by Yale's **visitor
center** (☎ 203-432-2300; www.yale.edu/visitor; 149 Elm St;
☺ 9am-4:30pm Mon-Fri, 11am-4pm Sat & Sun, free 75min
tours 10:30am & 2pm Mon-Fri, 1:30pm Sat & Sun) on the
north side of the Green.

America's oldest university art museum,
the **Yale University Art Gallery** (☎ 203-432-0600;
1111 Chapel St; admission free; ☺ 10am-5pm Tue-Sat,
1-6pm Sun), boasts masterworks by Winslow
Homer, Edward Hopper and Jackson Pollock, as well as a superb European collection that includes Vincent van Gogh's *The
Night Café.*

Jurassic Park fans should head straight for
the fascinating **Peabody Museum of Natural History**
(☎ 203-432-5050; 170 Whitney Ave; adult/child 3-17 $7/5;

☺ 10am-5pm Mon-Sat, noon-5pm Sun), a great place
to see real dinosaurs.

You may also want to pop into the **Yale
Center for British Art** (☎ 203-432-2800; 1080 Chapel
St; admission free; ☺ 10am-5pm Tue-Sat, noon-5pm Sun),
which holds one of the most comprehen-
sive collections of British paintings outside
the UK.

SLEEPING & EATING

Courtyard New Haven at Yale (☎ 203-777-6221; www
.marriott.com; 30 Whalley Ave; d from $119-199; ☒ ☒ wi-fi)
Just a few minutes' walk from the Yale cam-
pus, the Courtyard offers the best value of the
city's central hotels. Rooms are standard chain
fare, but large, clean and well-equipped.

Touch of Ireland Guest House (☎ 866-787-7990;
www.touchofirelandguesthouse.com; 670 Whitney Ave;
r incl breakfast $125-140; ☒ ☒ wi-fi) Share tips
with fellow travelers in the fireplaced den at
this friendly B&B on the north side of the
city. The four guest rooms in this century-
old home have an Irish theme and comfy
down-home decor.

Louis' Lunch (☎ 203-562-5507; 261 Crown St; burgers $4; ☺ 11am-4pm Tue-Wed, noon-2am Thu-Sat, closed
Aug) This age-old hamburger joint claims to
have invented the hamburger in 1900 and
it still broils them in historic cast-iron vertical grills. Some things have changed over
the century – but you won't find them here.
Don't even think of asking for ketchup.

Atticus Bookstore Café (☎ 203-776-4040; 1082
Chapel St; mains $4-8; ☺ 7am-midnight; wi-fi) This café
in a bookstore brews strong Java, award-
winning homemade soups and tasty pastries.
Free wi-fi too.

Claire's Corner Copia (☎ 203-562-3888; 1000 Chapel
St; mains $6-10; ☺ 8am-9pm Sun-Thu, 8am-10pm Fri &
Sat) For the best vegetarian food in town,
saunter over to this cheerful chef-run restaurant opposite Yale. Claire cooks up her
own time-honored recipes using fresh, organic ingredients – it's like walking into
grandma's kitchen.

Frank Pepe's (☎ 203-865-5762; 157 Wooster St; mains
$6-16; ☺ 4-10pm Mon, Wed & Thu, 11:30am-11pm Fri &
Sat, 2:30-10pm Sun) Pepe's takes its name from
the Italian immigrant who tossed America's
first pizza a century ago. You'd best believe
they've got the recipe perfected – Pepe's
fame goes well beyond New Haven's border.
For a memorable treat order the white pizza
topped with fresh clams.

NEW ENGLAND

NEW ENGLAND

Zinc (☎ 203-624-0507; 964 Chapel St; lunch mains $10-14, dinner mains $22-30; ☻ noon-2:30pm Tue-Fri & 5-9pm Sun-Thu, 5-10pm Fri & Sat) New American fare with Asian accents are the stars at this chic bistro serving smoked duck nachos, lobster risotto and wasabi sesame-crusted tuna.

DRINKING & ENTERTAINMENT
Toad's Place (☎ 203-624-8623; www.toadsplace.com; 300 York St; admission $10-35) Everyone from Count Basie to the Rolling Stones have taken the stage here at this legendary venue.

New Haven has a first-rate theater scene. You can catch a play before it hits the big time at the venerable **Shubert Theater** (☎ 203-562-5666, 888-736-2663; www.capa.com; 247 College St; tickets $18-60), which has been hosting Broadway musicals on their trial runs since 1914. New Haven also has two award-winning repertory theaters: **Yale Repertory Theatre** (☎ 203-432-1234; www.yale.edu/yalerep; 1120 Chapel St; tickets $22-45) and **Long Wharf Theatre** (☎ 203-787-4282, 800-782-8497; www.longwharf.org; 222 Sargent Dr; tickets $26-67).

The free weekly **New Haven Advocate** (www.newhavenadvocate.com) lists current entertainment happenings.

GETTING THERE & AWAY
By train from New York City skip Amtrak and take **Metro North** (☎ 212-532-4900, 800-638-7646; one-way $14-19), which has near-hourly services and the lowest fares. **Peter Pan Bus Lines** (☎ 800-343-9999) and **Greyhound Bus Lines** (☎ 800-221-2222) connect New Haven to scores of cities including Hartford ($14, one hour) and Boston ($34, four hours).

Mystic & Around
An alluring centuries-old seaport, Mystic boasts a top-notch nautical museum, a stellar aquarium and attractive period accommodations. Yes, it gets inundated with summer tourists, but there's good reason why everyone stops here, so get off the highway and check it out. Swing by on a weekday to avoid the worst of the crowds. The **Greater Mystic Chamber of Commerce** (☎ 860-572-1102; www.mysticchamber.org; 2 Roosevelt Ave; ☻ 10am-4pm), at the old train station, has visitor information.

SIGHTS & ACTIVITIES
America's maritime history springs to life at **Mystic Seaport** (☎ 860-572-5315; www.mysticseaport

.com; 75 Greenmanville Ave/CT 27; adult/child 6-17 $17.50/12; ☻ 9am-5pm Apr-Oct, 10am-4pm Nov-Mar), where costumed interpreters ply their trades in a sprawling re-created 19th-century seaport village. You can scurry aboard several historic sailing vessels, including the *Charles W Morgan* (built in 1841), the last surviving wooden whaling ship in the USA. And if you want to experience a little voyage yourself, the 1908 steamboat **Sabino** (☎ 860-572-5351; adult/child 6-17 $5.50/4.50; ☻ 11:30am-3:30pm) departs hourly on the half-hour on jaunts up the Mystic River.

Mystic Aquarium (☎ 860-572-5955; www.mysticaquarium.org; 55 Coogan Blvd; adult/child 3-17 $17.50/12.50; ☻ 9am-6pm) is home to 6000 species of interesting sea creatures, and we're not talking just fish. The residents include penguins, sea lions and even a beluga whale! And where else can a kid pet a cownose ray?

In nearby Ledyard the extensive **Mashantucket Pequot Museum & Research Center** (☎ 800-411-9671; www.pequotmuseum.org; 110 Pequot Trail, off CT 214, Mashantucket; adult/child 6-15 $15/10; ☻ 10am-4pm) features a reconstructed 1550 Native American village. The Mashantucket Pequot Indian tribe also owns the mega-splash **Foxwoods Resort & Casino** (☎ 800-752-9244; www.foxwoods.com; CT 2, Ledyard), the largest gambling venue this side of Vegas.

SLEEPING & EATING
Whaler's Inn (☎ 860-536-1506, 800-243-2588; www.whalersinnmystic.com; 20 E Main St; r $135-255; ✗) This centrally located place offers a variety of comfy accommodations from traditionally decorated rooms in an 1865 Victorian house to modern rooms in motel-style buildings.

Mermaid Inn (☎ 860-536-6223; www.mermaidinnofmystic.com; 2 Broadway Ave; r $150-225; ✗) It's the friendly touches, like the homemade cookies and evening brandy, that separate this inviting Victorian B&B from the competition. The amenities, gourmet breakfast and central location are all spot on.

Old Mystic Inn (☎ 860-572-9422; www.oldmysticinn.com; 52 Main St, Old Mystic; r inc breakfast $155-205; ✗) Canopy beds and cozy fireplaces set the tone in the guest rooms of this romantic 1784 colonial inn near the head of the Mystic River.

S&P Oyster Co (☎ 860-536-2674; 1 Holmes St; mains $9-20; ☻ 11:30am-10pm) Dine on the waterfront at this seafood eatery, famous for oysters on the half shell and hearty portions of fish and chips. It's in the town center at the east side of the drawbridge.

Captain Daniel Packer Inne (☎ 860-536-3555; 32 Water Ave; lunch mains $9-16, dinner $26-34; ⏱ 11am-4pm & 5-9pm) This atmospheric tavern in an 18th-century house near the Mystic River has a marvelous menu that covers everything from local seafood to Jack Daniel's–glazed steak.

DRINKING & ENTERTAINMENT
Harp & Hound (☎ 860-572-7778; 4 Pearl St) This pub, in a historic building on the west side of the drawbridge, is the late-night place to grab a pint of Irish ale; decent pub grub too.

LOWER CONNECTICUT RIVER VALLEY
Several colonial-era towns grace the banks of the Connecticut River, offering up their rural charm at a delightfully unhurried pace.

Essex
Established in 1635, riverside Essex is the region's most interesting town and a good starting point for exploring the valley. The streets are lined with handsome Federal-period houses, the legacy of rum and tobacco fortunes made in the 19th century.

The **Connecticut River Museum** (☎ 860-767-8269; 67 Main St; adult/child 6-12 $7/4; ⏱ 10am-5pm Tue-Sun) exhibits regional history and includes a full-scale reproduction of the world's first submarine, built at this site in 1776. For a fun trip hop the **Essex Steam Train & Riverboat** (☎ 860-767-0103; www.essexsteamtrain.com; 1 Railroad Ave; adult/child 2-11 $17/9, with cruise $26/13; ⏱ 11am, 12:30pm, 2pm & 3:30pm mid-Jun–Aug, weekends only in spring & fall), an antique steam locomotive that runs 12 scenic miles to Deep River, where you can cruise on a Mississippi-style riverboat before returning by train.

Griswold Inn (☎ 860-767-1776; www.griswoldinn .com; 36 Main St; r incl breakfast $100-220, ste $160-370, lunch/ dinner mains from $12/25; ✕ ☷) has been providing cozy colonial comfort since 1776, making it one of the oldest inns in America. It's also a favorite place to dine on traditional New England cuisine in an historic setting.

Old Lyme
With its prime location near the mouth of the Connecticut River, Old Lyme was home to some 60 sea captains in the 19th century. Today its claim to fame is its art community. In the early 1900s art patron Florence Griswold opened her estate to visiting artists, many of whom offered paintings in lieu of rent. Her Georgian mansion, now the **Flor-**ence Griswold Museum** (☎ 860-434-5542; 96 Lyme St; adult/child 6-12 $8/4; ⏱ 10am-5pm Tue-Sat, 1-5pm Sun), exhibits 6000 works with solid collections of American impressionist paintings, sculpture and decorative arts.

A romantic place to lay your head is the classy **Bee & Thistle Inn** (☎ 860-434-1667, 800-622-4946; www.beeandthistleinn.com; 100 Lyme St; r $140-250; ✕), a 1756 Dutch Colonial farmhouse.

East Haddam
You'll find two intriguing attractions in this small town on the east bank of the Connecticut River. The medieval-style **Gillette Castle** (☎ 860-526-2336; 67 River Rd; adult/child 6-17 $5/3; ⏱ 10am-4:30pm late May–mid-Oct) is a wildly eccentric stone-turreted mansion built in 1919 by actor William Hooker Gillette, who made his fortune playing Sherlock Holmes. The classic **Goodspeed Opera House** (☎ 860-873-8668; www.goodspeed.org; CT 82; tickets $26-66), an 1876 Victorian music hall known as 'the birthplace of the American musical,' still produces a full schedule of musicals.

HARTFORD
Connecticut's capital is best known as the hometown of America's insurance industry – not exactly a 'let's-rush-to-see-the-place' endorsement. But look beyond its backbone of office buildings and you'll find some worthwhile sights offering unique slices of Americana.

Sights & Activities
The **Mark Twain House & Museum** (☎ 860-247-0998; www.marktwainhouse.org; 351 Farmington Ave; adult/child 6-16 $13/8; ⏱ 9:30am-5:30pm Mon-Sat, noon-5:30pm Sun) is where the legendary author penned many of his greatest works, including *A Connecticut Yankee in King Arthur's Court*. The house itself – a Victorian Gothic with fanciful turrets and gables – is as quirky as the author was.

Next door you'll find the **Harriet Beecher Stowe House** (☎ 860-522-9258; www.harrietbeecher stowe.org; 77 Forest St; adult/child 5-12 $8/4; ⏱ 9:30am-4:30pm Tue-Sat, noon-4:30pm Sun), home to the author of *Uncle Tom's Cabin*, which so rallied Americans against slavery that Abraham Lincoln once credited Stowe with starting the US Civil War.

America's oldest art museum, **Wadsworth Atheneum** (☎ 860-278-2670; www.wadsworthathe neum.org; 600 Main St; adult/child under 13 $10/free;

NEW ENGLAND

11am-5pm Wed-Fri, 10am-5pm Sat & Sun), show-cases outstanding collections of Hudson River School paintings and sculptures by renowned Connecticut artist Alexander Calder (1898–1976).

You can tour the **State Capitol** (860-240-0222; cnr Capitol Ave & Trinity St; admission free; 8am-5pm Mon-Fri), built in 1879 in such a hodgepodge of styles that it's sometimes dubbed 'the most beautiful ugly building in the world.' Below the capitol grounds, the 37-acre **Bushnell Park** features a working 1914 carousel, lovely gardens and summer concerts. The real prize of Connecticut's public buildings is the **Old State House** (860-522-6766; 800 Main St; adult/child 6-17 $6/3; 11am-5pm Tue-Fri, 10am-5pm Sat), designed by famed colonial architect Charles Bulfinch; erected in 1796, it's one of the oldest capitol buildings in the USA.

Sleeping & Eating

Goodwin Hotel (860-246-7500, 800-922-5006; www .goodwinhotel.com; 1 Haynes St; r $159-279;) Hartford's classiest, this elegant 1881 establishment across from the Civic Center has a historic brick exterior and a cheery updated interior.

Tapas on Ann (860-525-5988; 126 Ann St; mains $5-12; 11am-9pm Mon-Fri, 5-11pm Sat) Come to this bustling bistro for unbeatable Mediterranean fare tickled with New England touches. Start with the sherried clam chowder, move on to the souvlaki or vegetarian hummus platter, and don't miss the specialty martinis.

Café @ WA (860-278-2670; 600 Main St; mains $9-15; 11:30am-2:30pm Wed-Sun) This café inside the Wadsworth Atheneum is a fine place to break for lunch, with creative panini-bread sandwiches, chicken and brie pastries and specialty salads.

Peppercorn's Grill (860-547-1714; 357 Main St; mains $12-22; 11:30am-10pm Mon-Fri, 4pm-midnight Sat) Contemporary Italian-American fare is in store at this local favorite, with plenty of seafood options from spicy clam cakes to lobster ravioli. Save room for the tiramisu.

Getting There & Away

Bradley International Airport (860-292-2000; www .bradleyairport.com; I-91, exit 40, Windsor Locks), 12 miles north of the city, serves southwestern New England.

The conveniently central **Union Station** (860-247-5329; 1 Union Pl) links Hartford by train to cities throughout the Northeast,

including New Haven (one-way $15, one hour) and New York City (one-way $46, three hours).

LITCHFIELD HILLS

Laced with lakes, woodlands and vineyards, the rolling hill country of northwestern Connecticut attracts nature-lovers looking for quiet escapes. The **Northwest Connecticut Visitors Bureau** (800-663-1273; www.litchfieldhills .com) has information on the region.

Litchfield

Founded in 1719 as a thriving commerce center on the stagecoach route between Hartford and Albany, Litchfield is the region's sparkling centerpiece. Its many handsome period buildings are a testimony to the prosperous Colonial era. Stroll along North and South Sts to see the finest homes, including the 1773 **Tapping Reeve House & Law School** (860-567-4501; www.litchfieldhistory.org; 82 South St; adult/child 14 & under $5/free; 11am-5pm Tue-Sat, 1-5pm Sun mid-Apr–Nov), the USA's first law school (founded in 1775), which trained some 130 members of Congress. Included in the admission fee is the **Litchfield Historical Society Museum** (860-567-4501; 7 South St).

Haight-Brown Vineyard (860-567-4045; 29 Chestnut Hill Rd; 10:30am-5pm Mon-Sat, noon-5pm), off CT 118 and the state's first winery, offers free tastings (don't miss the merlot) and self-guided vineyard walks.

If you're ready to take a longer hike, Connecticut's largest wildlife preserve, the **White Memorial Conservation Center** (860-567-0857; US 202; admission free; dawn-dusk), 2.5 miles west of town, has 35 miles of inviting trails with good bird-watching.

Litchfield Hills B&B (860-567-2057; www .litchfieldhillsbnb.com; 548 Bantam Rd/US 202; r incl breakfast $95-120), in one of the town's oldest homes (1735), borders the White Memorial Conservation Center.

Lake Waramaug

Of the dozens of lakes and ponds in the Litchfield Hills area, Lake Waramaug, bordered by a state park, is the most beautiful. As you make your way around the northern shore on North Shore Rd, stop at **Hopkins Vineyard** (860-868-7954; 25 Hopkins Rd; 10am-5pm Mon-Sat, 11am-5pm Sun May-Dec) for wine tastings. It's next to the 19th-century **Hopkins Inn** (860-868-7295; www.thehopkinsinn.com; 22 Hopkins

Rd, New Preston; r $115, apt $130-220; lunch mains $13-18, dinner mains $20-26; ❌ 🅿️), which has lakeview accommodations and a well-regarded restaurant with Austrian-influenced country fare. **Lake Waramaug State Park** (☎ 860-868-0220, 877-688-2267; 30 Lake Waramaug Rd; campsites first/successive nights $22/13) has lakeside campsites, but book well in advance.

VERMONT

Artisanal cheeses, buckets of maple syrup, Ben & Jerry's ice cream…just try to get out of this state without gaining 10 pounds. Fortunately, there are plenty of ways to work it off: hike the trails of the Green Mountains, paddle a kayak on Lake Champlain or hit Vermont's snowy slopes.

Vermont gives new meaning to the word rural. Its capital would barely rate as a small town in other states and even its largest city, Burlington, has just 39,000 happy souls. The countryside is a blanket of rolling green, with some 80% of the state forested and most of the rest given over to some of the prettiest farms you'll ever see. Add a smattering of quaint villages, scores of covered bridges and those friendly, laid-back Vermonters and what's not to love?

History
Frenchman Samuel de Champlain explored Vermont in 1609 and in his ever-humble manner lent his name to Vermont's largest lake.

Vermont played a key role in the American Revolution in 1775 when Ethan Allen

---

VERMONT FACTS

Nickname Green Mountain State

Population 623,908

Area 9609 sq miles

Capital city Montpelier (population 8035)

Sales tax 6%

Birthplace of Mormon leader Brigham Young (1801–77), folk painter Anna Mary 'Grandma' Moses (1860–1961), President Calvin Coolidge (1872–1933)

Home of More than 100 covered bridges

Famous for Ben & Jerry's ice cream

Vermont grown Morgan horse, America's first unique horse breed

---

led a local militia, the Green Mountain Boys, to Fort Ticonderoga, capturing it from the British. In the years that followed Allen took a friendlier stance toward the British, and considered petitioning the crown to make Vermont an independent British state. In 1791, two years after Allen's death, Vermont was admitted to the USA.

The state's independent streak is as long and deep as a vein of Vermont marble. Long a land of dairy farmers, Vermont is still mostly rural, with the lowest population of any New England state. In 2000 Vermont became the first US state to legalize same-sex civil unions.

Information
Vermont Chamber of Commerce (☎ 802-223-3443; www.vtchamber.com; PO Box 37, Montpelier, VT 05601) Will mail out a handy magazine-size vacation guide to Vermont upon request.

Vermont Department of Tourism (☎ 802-828-3237, 800-837-6668; www.vermontvacation.com; 6 Baldwin St, Montpelier, VT 05633) Provides online information on Vermont by region, season and other user-friendly categories.

SOUTHERN VERMONT
The southern swath of Vermont holds its oldest towns, the cool trails of the Green Mountain National Forest and plenty of scenic back roads just aching to be explored.

Brattleboro
Ever wonder where the 1960s counter-culture went? It's alive and well in this riverside burg overflowing with craft shops and with more tie-dye per capita than any other place in New England.

SIGHTS & ACTIVITIES
Begin at Main St, which is lined with period buildings, including the handsome art-deco Latchis Building, which houses a hotel and theater. The **Brattleboro Museum & Art Center** (☎ 802-257-0124; www.brattleboromuseum.org; 10 Vernon St; adult/child under 6 $4/free; ⏰ 11am-5pm Wed-Mon), in the old Union Station, showcases the multimedia works of regional artists.

Windham County, surrounding Brattleboro, boasts 30 **covered bridges**. Pick up a driving guide to the bridges at the **Brattleboro Area Chamber of Commerce** (☎ 802-254-4565; www.brattleborochamber.org; 180 Main St; ⏰ 9am-5pm Mon-Fri, 10am-2pm Sat).

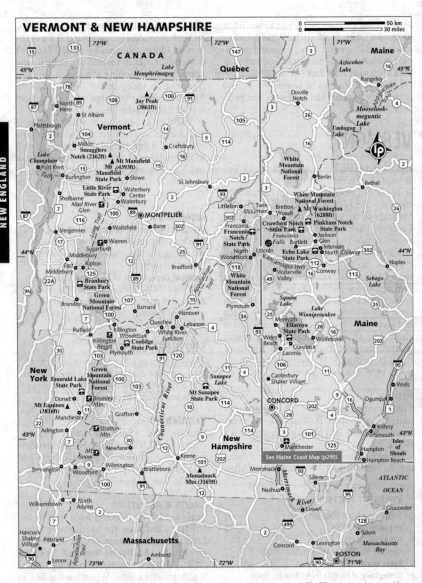

VERMONT & NEW HAMPSHIRE

SLEEPING & EATING

Latchis Hotel (☎ 802-254-6300; www.latchis.com; 50 Main St; r incl breakfast $75-125; ✗) You couldn't be more in the thick of things than at this restored art-deco hotel with 30 simply furnished rooms.

Forty Putney Road B&B (☎ 802-254-6268, 800-941-2413; www.fortyputneyroad.com; 40 Putney Rd; r/ste incl breakfast $139/199; ✗ ✗ wi-fi) Within walking distance of the town center, this estate home sports three cheery rooms and a swank suite with its own fireplace.

Mole's Eye Café (☎ 802-257-0771; 4 High St; mains $5-8; ✗ 11:30am-midnight) This hopping place not only dishes up inexpensive Mexican fare but it's the top venue in town for live music.

Riverview Café (☎ 802-254-9841; 36 Bridge St; mains $5-15; ☯ 8am-10pm) Come to this breezy riverside restaurant for wild blueberry pancakes topped with real maple syrup, luscious crab cakes and regional microbrews on tap.

Thai Garden (☎ 802-251-1010; 7 High St; mains $6-15; ☯ 11:30am-3pm & 5-10pm) The aromatic scent of fresh herbs fills the air at this authentic Thai restaurant with delicious curries, pad Thai and vegetarian fare.

Brattleboro Food Co-op (☎ 802-257-0236; 2 Main St; ☯ 8am-9pm) Naturally this town has a big-league health-food store.

Wilmington & Mt Snow

Wilmington, midway between Brattleboro and Bennington, is the gateway to **Mt Snow** (☎ 802-464-3333, 800-245-7669; www.mountsnow.com; VT 100), which is best known as a family skiing resort, but golfing and mountain biking also woo visitors in warm-weather seasons. The **Mt Snow Valley Chamber of Commerce** (☎ 802-464-8092, 877-887-6884; www.visitvermont.com; 21 W Main St; ☯ 10am-5pm) has information on accommodations and attractions.

In Wilmington the 14-room **Nutmeg Inn** (☎ 802-464-7400, 800-277-5402; www.nutmeginn.com; VT 9; r incl breakfast $109-205; ✗), an 18th-century farmhouse, offers local hospitality including a full country breakfast.

Bennington

A measure of how rural southern Vermont really is, cozy Bennington with just 15,000 inhabitants ranks as the region's largest town. You'll find an interesting mix of cafés and shops downtown, while the hillside area known as Old Bennington boasts age-old colonial homes and a trio of covered bridges (p274). A hilltop granite obelisk commemorating the 1777 Battle of Bennington towers above it all, making Bennington visible from miles around.

The friendly folks at **Bennington Area Chamber of Commerce** (☎ 802-447-3311, 800-229-0252; www.bennington.com; US 7; ☯ 9am-5pm Mon-Fri, 10am-4pm Sat), a mile north of downtown, provide visitor information.

SIGHTS & ACTIVITIES

Gracing the center of Old Bennington, the **Old First Church** (cnr Monument Ave & Rte 9) is famous for its churchyard, which holds the bones of five Vermont governors and poet Robert Frost,

who is buried beneath the inscription 'I Had a Lover's Quarrel With the World.'

Vermont's loftiest structure, the **Bennington Battle Monument** (☎ 802-447-0550; Monument Ave; adult/child $2/1; ☯ 9am-5pm Apr-Oct), offers an unbeatable 360-degree view of the countryside with peeks at covered bridges and across to New York. Best of all, you won't have to strain hamstrings climbing this 306ft obelisk – an elevator whisks you painlessly to the top.

The **Bennington Museum** (☎ 802-447-1571; www.benningtonmuseum.com; VT 9; adult/child under 18 $8/free; ☯ 10am-5pm Thu-Tue) showcases early Americana art, crafts and furniture, as well as the world's largest collection of works by famed folk artist Anna Mary 'Grandma' Moses (1860–1961), who painted Vermont farm scenes until the age of 100.

You can tour the potters workshop at **Bennington Potters** (☎ 802-447-7531; 324 County St; admission free; ☯ 9:30am-6pm Mon-Sat, 10am-5pm Sun), where quality stoneware with a distinctive mottled design has been made for more than a half-century. Should anything catch your fancy there's an on-site shop.

SLEEPING & EATING

Greenwood Lodge & Campsites (☎ 802-442-2547; VT 9; dm/campsites/r $28/22/62; ✗) Eight miles east of Bennington at Prospect Mountain ski run in Woodford, this little lodge has dorm rooms, private rooms and camping facilities set in a wooded area near swimmable ponds.

Paradise Motor Inn (☎ 802-442-8351; www.theparadisemotorinn.com; 141 W Main St; r $80-115; ✗ ☒ ☒) Attractive rooms, a quiet yet central setting and a heated outdoor pool make a winning combination. Spend the extra $35 for a premier room and enjoy your own little sauna and a Jacuzzi.

Henry House (☎ 802-442-7045, 888-442-7045; www.henryhouseinn.com; 214 Murphy Rd; r incl breakfast $85-135; ✗) Sit on the rocking chair and watch the traffic trickle across a covered bridge at this colonial home built in 1769 by American Revolution hero William Henry. This is the real deal on 25 peaceful acres and dripping with so much of its original charm that you might expect long-gone Lieutenant Henry to walk down the hall.

Izabella's (☎ 802-447-4949; 351 Main St; mains $5-8; ☯ 7:30am-4pm Tue-Fri, 8:30am-4pm Sat) This hip café in the center of town makes creative omelets, homemade soups and luscious goat's cheese and turkey panini sandwiches.

THE BRIDGES OF BENNINGTON COUNTY

A 15-minute detour from Bennington takes you across three authentic covered bridges spanning the Wallomsac River at the rural north side of town. To get started turn west onto VT 67A just north of the tourist office and continue 3.5 miles, turning left on Murphy Rd at the **Burt Henry Covered Bridge**. Smile, exhale, slow down: you're back in horse and buggy days. As you pop out the back side of this 117ft-long bridge dating to 1840, curve to the left. Murphy Rd soon loops through the **Paper Mill Bridge**, which takes its name from the 1790 mill that once sat beneath the bridge (look along the river for the old gearworks). Next turn right onto VT 67A, go half a mile and turn right onto Silk Rd where you'll soon cross the c 1840 **Silk Road Bridge**. If you continue along Silk Rd for 2 miles, bearing to the left at each turn, you'll eventually reach the **Bennington Battle Monument** (p273).

Blue Benn Diner (☎ 802-442-5140; 314 North St; mains $5-12; 🕑 6am-8pm Mon-Fri, 6am-4pm Sat, 7am-4pm Sun) It may be a 1950s-era diner, but it's no greasy spoon. The extensive menu includes breakfast all day and a healthy mix of American, Asian and Mexican fare.

Madison Brewing Co (☎ 802-442-7397; 428 Main St; mains $7-18; 🕑 11:30am-9:30pm) A family-style microbrewery? Yep, this perky pub and restaurant brews homemade root beer as well as heady malt ales. The food ranges from veggie burgers to juicy steaks and there's even a kids' menu.

Manchester

Sitting in the shadow of Mt Equinox, Manchester's been a fashionable summer retreat since the 19th century. The mountain scenery, the agreeable climate and the Batten Kill River – Vermont's best trout stream – continue to draw vacationers today.

The town has two faces, both likeable. Manchester Center, at the north end, sports cafés and upscale outlet stores. To the south lies dignified Manchester Village, lined with marble sidewalks, stately homes and the posh Equinox hotel.

The **Manchester & the Mountains Regional Chamber of Commerce** (☎ 802-362-2100, 800-362-4144; www.manchestervermont.net; 5046 Main St, Manchester Center; 🕑 9am-5pm Mon-Fri) provides visitor information.

SIGHTS & ACTIVITIES

Anglers make pilgrimages to Manchester to visit the **American Museum of Fly Fishing** (☎ 802-362-3300; VT 7A; adult/child 6-14 $5/3; 🕑 10am-4pm), where rods used by Ernest Hemingway and other famed fishers are displayed; to shop at the adjacent **Orvis** (☎ 802-361-3750; VT 7A) flagship store, which is dedicated to outfitting fisher-folk; and to fly-fish for trout in the **Batten Kill River**.

BattenKill Canoe (☎ 802-362-2800; www.battenkill.com; 6328 VT 7A, Arlington; canoes $55-65, kayaks $35-40; 🕑 9am-4:30pm mid-April–Oct), 5 miles south of Manchester, rents canoes and kayaks for paddling down the Batten Kill River. Rent a road or mountain bike from **Batten Kill Sports Bicycle Shop** (☎ 802-362-2734; US 7 & VT 11/30; per day $25; 🕑 9:30am-5:30pm).

The **Appalachian Trail**, which overlaps the **Long Trail** (p278) in Vermont, passes just east of Manchester. For trail maps as well as details on shorter day hikes, stop by the (United States Forestry Service) USFS **Green Mountain National Forest** (☎ 802-362-2307; 2538 Depot St, Manchester Center; 🕑 8am-4:30pm Mon-Fri) office.

Just south of Manchester, **Hildene** (☎ 802-362-1788; www.hildene.org; 1005 Hildene Rd/VT 7A; adult/child 6-14 $12/4; 🕑 9:30am-4:30pm Jun-Oct, 11am-3pm Thu-Mon Nov-May), a 24-room Georgian Revival mansion, was the country estate of Robert Todd Lincoln, son of President Abraham Lincoln. Visitors can tour the mansion with original Lincoln family furnishings and stroll its lovely gardens.

For a view from the top, drive to the summit of 3835ft **Mt Equinox**. Take VT 7A south of Manchester to **Skyline Drive** (☎ 802-362-1114; car & driver $8, additional passenger $2; 🕑 9am-dusk May-Oct), a private 5-mile toll road.

SLEEPING

Aspen Motel (☎ 802-362-2450; www.thisisvermont.com/aspen; 5669 Main St/VT 7A; r $80-120; ⊠ ✱ 🏊) An affordable standout, this family-run hotel set back serenely from the road has 25 comfortable rooms and a convenient location within walking distance of Manchester Center.

Inn at Manchester (☎ 802-362-1793, 800-273-1793; www.innatmanchester.com; 3967 VT 7A; r incl breakfast $155-195; ✕ ☷ ☐ ☐ wi-fi) Classic fittings blend seamlessly with modern conveniences at this pampering upscale inn between Manchester Center and Manchester Village. It's a quiet place and only accepts children 13 and older.

Equinox (☎ 802-362-4700, 800-362-4747; www.equi noxresort.com; 3567 Main St; r $255-499; ☷ ☷) Manchester's grande dame since 1769 boasts 183 rooms, its own 18-hole golf course, two pools and a luxury spa. Despite modern upgrades its handsome period character prevails.

EATING

Spiral Press Café (☎ 802-362-9944; cnr VT 11 & 7A; mains $5-9; ☷ 8am-6:30pm Mon-Sat, 9am-5pm Sun; wi-fi) Stop at this Manchester Center café attached to Northshire Bookstore for luscious scones, fresh salads and delicious panini sandwiches. Great coffee and free wi-fi too.

Up for Breakfast (☎ 802-362-4204; 4935 Main St; mains $6-10; ☷ 7am-noon) Search out this hole-in-the-wall 2nd-floor restaurant in Manchester Center for the best breakfast in town, anything from good ol' blueberry pancakes to a brie and fresh apple omelet.

Harvest Grille (☎ 802-362-1550; 4940 Main St; mains $6-12; ☷ 11:30am-9pm) New England comfort food – like a half-pound Angus burger topped with a chunk of Vermont cheddar – is the billing at this unpretentious grill in Manchester Center.

Bistro Henry (☎ 802-362-4982; cnr VT 11 & 30; mains $24-35; ☷ 5-9:30pm Tue-Sun) A good bet for a romantic dinner, this chef-driven bistro with a Mediterranean accent whips up innovative fare paired with an award-winning wine list.

CENTRAL VERMONT

Central Vermont, nestled in the Green Mountains, is classic small-town, big-countryside New England. Its time-honored villages and ski resorts have been luring travelers here for generations.

Woodstock & Quechee

The postcard-perfect Vermont town, Woodstock's streets are lined with graceful Federal- and Georgian-style houses, and a river spanned by a covered bridge meanders right through the heart of town. Quechee (pronounced *kwee*-chee), its smaller cousin 7 miles to the northeast, abounds in rural scenery and hiking trails. The whole area invites you to slow down. The **Woodstock Area Chamber of Commerce** (☎ 802-457-3555; www.wood stockvt.com; 18 Central St; ☷ 9:30am-5pm) provides visitor information.

SIGHTS & ACTIVITIES

Quechee Gorge, a 170ft craggy chasm cut by the Ottauquechee River, offers good hiking. Begin at **Quechee Gorge State Park** (☎ 802-295-2990; 5800 US 4, Quechee; admission free), where you can pick up a trail map.

VINS Nature Center (☎ 802-359-5000; www.vin snaturecenter.org; US 4, Quechee; adult/child 3-16 $8/6.50; ☷ 9am-5pm May-Oct, 10am-4pm Wed-Sun Nov-Apr), near the Quechee Gorge, rehabilitates injured falcons, bald eagles and other raptors. See these magnificent birds up close, then enjoy a nature walk on the center's 40 acres.

To learn about maple sugaring and cheese-making, and sample both, head to the family-run **Sugarbush Farm** (☎ 802-457-1757; www .sugarbushfarm.com; 591 Sugarbush Farm Rd; admission free; ☷ 8am-5pm Mon-Fri, 9am-5pm Sat & Sun). The sugaring

NEW ENGLAND

US OUT OF VERMONT?

The state that produced the stealth antiwar presidential candidate Howard Dean is now home to a grassroots movement to secede from the United States. Known as the Second Vermont Republic, the independence movement is being debated in town meetings throughout the state. Organizers hope to get the towns to convince the state government to declare a peaceable secession from Washington, returning Vermont to its pre-1791 status as an independent republic.

It's no surprise such a movement would start in Vermont, where the towns are so small that local politicians know their constituents by name. The central gripe is that the federal government, oft referred to as The Empire, has become too big and corrupt to serve ordinary citizens.

Is this the little Vermont that roared? While many Vermonters think the very idea of secession is far-fetched, they have a reputation for listening to their neighbors and that's beginning to show in the polls. In the latest tally 13% of those questioned favored secession, nearly double what it was the previous year. To follow the action log onto www.freevermont.net.

LOCAL VOICES Rob Hunter

Gallery manager, Vermont State Craft Center at Frog Hollow (opposite), age 37, Middlebury, Vermont
This Vermont native spends his working hours in a gallery filled with brilliant stained glass, handsome pottery and sensuously rubbed woods – with a wall of windows overlooking the achingly picturesque Otter Creek.

Why do you think Vermont has such a great crafts scene? In the '60s there was a big movement to get out of the city. Vermont was still raw and untamed. Hippies – for lack of a better word – and free spirits headed this way. Brattleboro, being just over the border, became a huge center for the arts, and it grew across Vermont from there.

Why is Vermont State Craft Center in the shop's name? It started as an alternative center for teenagers in 1971; they started making crafts and needed a place to sell their stuff and it grew from there. It changed over the years, and now the gallery works are chosen from among 270 juried artists. We were the first state-recognized craft center in the nation. People think that means we get state funding. We don't – but we have the state seal of approval.

You travel overseas a lot. Do you think you'll keep coming back to Vermont? I've never found anyplace like it. Vermont's got a real charm to it.

If friends came to Vermont to visit, where would you take them? The Burlington waterfront (p279) is one of the great things to do, with the bike path that goes along the water; get an ice cream, enjoy the music. And the Shelburne Museum (p279) is phenomenal. And, though it's not in Vermont, Mass MoCA (p260) over the border in North Adams, MA. But the number one place to go, really, is Frog Hollow.

season is from March to April, but you can tour the sugarhouse year-round. To get there take US 4 to Taftsville, 3.5 miles east of Woodstock, cross the Taftsville covered bridge and follow the signs.

See what 19th-century farm life was all about at **Billings Farm & Museum** (☎ 802-457-2355; www.billingsfarm.org; VT 12 at River Rd; adult/child 5-12 $10/6; ☯ 10am-5pm May-Oct), a living history museum and functioning dairy farm.

SLEEPING

Quechee Gorge State Park (☎ 888-409-7579; 5800 US 4, Quechee; campsites/lean-tos $14/25) Campers will find 47 pine-shaded campsites and seven lean-tos in this 600-acre park.

Quechee Inn at Marshfield Farm (☎ 802-295-3133, 800-235-3133; www.quecheeinn.com; 1119 Main St, Quechee; r incl breakfast $90-245; ☒ ☒) Dating to 1793 this classic country inn on the National Register of Historic Places offers cozy rooms with four-post beds and plenty of rural tranquility.

Shire Riverview Motel (☎ 802-457-2211; www .shiremotel.com; 46 Pleasant St/US 4; r $98-218; ☒ ☒) The best deal in Woodstock center: the manager's helpful, the rooms well maintained and the river views second to none. The colonial decor is similar in all 42 rooms, but you get better views and perks like fireplaces as the rates rise.

EATING

Farmers Diner (☎ 802-295-4600; 5573 Woodstock Rd/ VT 4, Quechee; mains $6-14; ☯ 6:30am-7:30pm) Grab a booth in this old-fashioned diner and feast on fresh Vermont-grown delights including creamy organic milkshakes, beefy burgers and creative omelets. This cornerstone of the buy-local, eat-local movement is well worth seeking out.

Osteria Pane e Salute (☎ 802-457-4882; 61 Central St; mains $10-22; ☯ 5-10pm Thu-Mon) This acclaimed dinner restaurant in the center of Woodstock serves mouthwatering Tuscan-style pizzas, innovative pastas and well-matched wines. Great atmosphere to boot.

Simon Pearce (☎ 802-295-1470; 1760 Main St, Quechee; lunch mains $12-15, dinner mains $25-40; ☯ 11:30am-2:45pm & 6-9pm) First watch the artisans hand-blowing glass and throwing pottery in the basement workshops, then go upstairs and enjoy a gourmet meal served on their handiwork. The riverside restaurant overlooks a waterfall and the on-site shop sells Pearce's finery.

Killington

An hour's drive west of Woodstock is **Killington Resort** (☎ 802-422-3333, 800-923-9444; www .killington.com), Vermont's premier ski destination, boasting 200 runs on seven mountains, a vertical drop of 3150ft and 33 lifts. And thanks to the world's most extensive snow-making system, Killington has one of the longest seasons in the east. Come summer when the snow melts, mountain bikers and hikers claim the slopes.

There are more than a hundred places to stay in the Killington area, from cozy ski lodges to chain hotels. Almost all are along Killington Rd, the 6-mile road that leads north off US 4 up the mountain. The **Killington Chamber of Commerce** (☎ 802-773-4181, 800-337-1928; www .killingtonchamber.com; US 4; ☙ 9am-5pm Mon-Fri year-round, 10am-2pm some Sat) has all the nitty-gritty.

Middlebury

This former factory town has converted its old water-driven mills into enticing riverside restaurants and galleries. Add the verdant campus of Middlebury College and you've got yourself a fine place to while away an afternoon. The **Addison County Chamber of Commerce** (☎ 802-388-7951; www.midvermont.com; 2 Court St; ☙ 9am-5pm Mon-Fri) has all the expected brochures.

SIGHTS & ACTIVITIES

Small but diverse, the **Middlebury College Museum of Art** (☎ 802-443-5007; S Main St; admission free; ☙ 10am-5pm Tue-Fri, noon-5pm Sat & Sun) takes you on a world twirl beginning with an Egyptian sarcophagus and ending with Andy Warhol. Don't miss the fiercesome Japanese samurai suit.

The **Vermont State Craft Center at Frog Hollow** (☎ 802-388-3177; www.froghollow.org; 1 Mill St; ☙ 10am-5:30pm Mon-Sat, noon-5pm Sun), inside a converted mill, sells a wide variety of high-quality paintings and crafts created by more than 200 Vermont artisans. Even if you're not buying, it's terrific browsing.

SLEEPING & EATING

Inn on the Green (☎ 802-388-7512, 888-244-7512; www .innonthegreen.com; 71 S Pleasant St; r incl breakfast $119-189; ☒) On the National Register of Historic Places, this gracious Federal-style inn with 11 attractive rooms overlooks the town green.

Taste of India (☎ 802-388-4856; 1 Bakery Lane; mains $6-13; ☙ 11:30am-10pm) Come here for reliable Indian fare at reasonable prices, and if you arrive before 2:30pm there are dozens of $6 lunch specials, including several vegetarian options.

Tully & Marie's (☎ 802-388-4182; 5 Bakery Lane; mains $7-20; ☙ 11:30am-10pm) Perched on the river, this smart restaurant serves New American fare with Asian influences, covering the gamut from vegetarian Thai noodles to Vermont-raised steaks. Brilliant food, service and atmosphere.

Warren & Waitsfield

The towns of Warren and Waitsfield boast two significant ski areas: **Sugarbush** and **Mad River Glen**, in the mountains west of VT 100. Opportunities abound for bicycling, canoeing, horseback riding, kayaking, gliding and other activities. Stop at the **Sugarbush Chamber of Commerce** (☎ 802-496-3409, 800-828-4748; www.madrivervalley.com; VT 100, Waitsfield; ☙ 9am-5pm Mon-Fri, 9am-noon Sat) for a mountain of details. Brochures and rest rooms are available 24 hours a day in the chamber's lobby.

NORTHERN VERMONT

The lushly green northern region of Vermont cradles the fetching state capital of Montpelier, the ski mecca of Stowe, the vibrant college town of Burlington and the state's highest mountains.

Montpelier

America's smallest capital, Montpelier is a thoroughly likeable town full of period buildings and backed by verdant hills. It speaks to its village nature that you can literally walk in the front door of the gold-domed (c 1836)

SCENIC DRIVE: VT 100

Running up the rugged backbone of Vermont, VT 100 meanders through the rural heart of the state. This quintessential country road rambles past rolling pastures speckled with cows, through tiny villages with white-steepled churches and along green mountains crossed with hiking trails and ski slopes. It's the perfect side trip for those who want to slow down, inhale pine-scented air and soak up the bucolic country life that forms the very soul of Vermont. Think farm stands, century-old farmhouses converted to small inns, pottery shops, country stores and home-style cafés. The road runs north to south all the way from Massachusetts to Canada. It has some tranquil moments but never a dull one – jump on for a taste of it at any point.

State House (☎ 802-828-2228; 115 State St; admission free; ☺ tours on the half-hr 10am-3:30pm Mon-Fri & 11am-2:30pm Sat Jul-Oct), and exit out the back onto a forested trail.

If you come through at mealtime, head for the intersection of State and Main Sts, where you'll find several restaurants. The bakery-café **La Brioche** (☎ 802-229-0443; 89 Main St; snacks $2-6; ☺ 6:30am-6pm Mon-Fri, 7am-5pm Sat), one of three eateries run by students from Montpelier's New England Culinary Institute, serves up yummy quiches, sandwiches and pastries.

Stowe & Around

With Vermont's highest peak, Mt Mansfield (4393ft), as its backdrop, Stowe ranks as Vermont's classiest ski destination. It packs all the alpine thrills you could ask for – both cross-country and downhill skiing, with gentle runs for novices and challenging stuff for pros. Biking, hiking and kayaking take center stage in the summer. Lodgings and eateries are thick along VT 108/Mountain Rd, which continues northwest from Stowe center to the ski resorts. The **Stowe Area Association** (☎ 802-253-7321, 877-317-8693; www.gostowe.com; 51 Main St; ☺ 9am-5pm Mon-Sat, 9am-8pm Jun-Aug) provides information and lodging assistance.

SIGHTS & ACTIVITIES

Wintertime's action-central, the twin-peak **Stowe Mountain Resort** (☎ 802-253-3000, 800-253-4754; www.stowe.com; 5781 Mountain Rd) has a variety of terrains with ski runs suitable for all levels. Cross-country skiing is available at several places, including the **Trapp Family Lodge** (☎ 802-253-8511, 800-826-7000; www.trappfamily.com; 700 Trapp Hill Rd), run by the family whose life inspired *The Sound of Music*.

The 5.5-mile **Stowe Recreation Path**, a greenway running along the West Branch River northwest from the village center, is a great place for walking, jogging, bicycling and skating. **AJ's Ski & Sports** (☎ 802-253-4593; 350 Mountain Rd; ☺ 9am-6pm), next to the path, rents bikes and in-line skates for $8 per hour or $27 per day.

Vermont's **Long Trail**, which passes through Stowe, follows the crest of the Green Mountains and runs the entire length of Vermont with rustic cabins, lean-tos and campsites along the way. Its caretaker, the **Green Mountain Club** (☎ 802-244-7037; www.greenmountainclub.org; 4711 Waterbury-Stowe Rd, VT 100), has full details on the Long Trail and shorter day hikes around Stowe.

Take a drive through dramatic **Smugglers Notch**, northwest of Stowe on VT 108 (the road's closed in winter). This narrow pass slices through mountains with 1000ft cliffs on either side, and there are plenty of places where you can stop along the way to ooh and aah or take a short walk.

Umiak Outdoor Outfitters (☎ 802-253-2317; 849 S Main St; ☺ 9am-6pm) rents canoes (per day $50) and kayaks ($40) and also offers two-hour guided river trips ($37).

Get the inside scoop at **Ben & Jerry's Ice Cream Factory** (☎ 802-882-1240; www.benjerry.com; VT 100, Waterbury; adult/child under 12 $3/free; ☺ 9am-9pm Jul & Aug, 9am-7pm Sep & Oct, 10am-6pm Nov-May, 9am-6pm Jun), where tours and a moo-vie about the hippie founders are topped off with a taste tease of the latest flavor.

SLEEPING & EATING

Smugglers Notch State Park (☎ 802-253-4014; 6443 Mountain Rd; campsites/lean-tos $16/25; ☺ late May–mid-Oct) Camp at the base of Mt Mansfield, 9 miles northwest of downtown Stowe on VT 108.

Mountaineer Inn (☎ 802-253-7225; www.stowe mountaineerinn.com; 3343 Mountain Rd; r incl breakfast $119-139; ☒ ☒) With an indoor pool, sauna and fireplace in the lounge, this family-run place packs all the perks of its pricier neighbors, yet oozes rustic charm with knotty-pine furniture and a homey feel. The four-bed family units cost just $20 more than standards. Ask for a room in the rear overlooking the stream.

Ye Olde England Inne (☎ 802-253-7558, 800-477-3771; www.englandinn.com; 433 Mountain Rd; r incl breakfast $139-250; mains $18-28; ☺ dinner 5-9pm; ☒ ☒) The English innkeepers here add Britannia accents like complimentary afternoon tea, an onsite pub serving UK ales and a dinner restaurant featuring beef Wellington. Rooms have canopied beds and Jacuzzis.

Harvest Market (☎ 802-253-3800; 1031 Mountain Rd; ☺ 7am-5:30pm) Stop at this gourmet market for morning coffee and delicious pastries, Vermont cheeses and sandwiches before you head for the hills.

Pie-casso (☎ 802-253-4411; 1899 Mountain Rd; mains $8-12; ☺ 11am-10pm) This pizzeria goes far beyond the simple pie: grilled chicken salads, shrimp scampi, and hand-tossed pesto pizzas are just part of the menu. Bar and live music too.

BURLINGTON

This hip college town on the shores of scenic Lake Champlain is one of those places that makes you think, wouldn't it be great to live here? The dining and entertainment scene is on par with a happening city, while the slow, friendly pace is pure small town. And where else can you walk to the end of Main St and paddle off in a kayak?

Orientation & Information

Vermont's largest city is a manageable place with most of its restaurants and pubs on or near Church St, a pedestrian mall midway between the University of Vermont and the lake.

Crow Bookshop (☎ 802-862-0848; 14 Church St; ❂ 10am-9pm Mon-Wed, to 10pm Thu-Sat, 11am-6pm Sun) Excellent selection of new and used books.

Fletcher Allen Health Care (☎ 802-847-0000; 111 Colchester Ave; ❂ 24hr)

Lake Champlain Regional Chamber of Commerce (☎ 802-863-3489; www.vermont.org) Maintains 24-hour visitor kiosks at the waterfront end of College St and on the Church St pedestrian mall.

Post office (☎ 802-863-6033; 11 Elmwood Ave; ❂ 8am-5pm Mon-Fri, 9am-1pm Sat)

Seven Days (www.sevendaysvt.com) Free weekly with event and entertainment listings.

Sights & Activities

If you're ready for outdoor adventures head to the waterfront, where options include kayaking and cruises on **Lake Champlain** and bicycling, in-line skating and walking on the 9-mile shorefront **Burlington Bike Path**. Jump-off points and equipment rentals for all these activities are within a block of each other near the waterfront end of Main St. Rent bikes and in-line skates at **Local Motion** (☎ 802-652-2453; 1 Steele St; bikes/skates per half-day $21/16; ❂ 10am-6pm). **Waterfront Boat Rentals** (☎ 802-864-4858; Perkins Pier; single kayaks per hr/day $12/56, canoes or double kayaks per hr/day $16/64; ❂ 10am-5pm) rents a variety of boats. The 17-passenger *Friend Ship* (☎ 802-598-6504; 1 College St; adult/child $35/20), a classic schooner, makes two-hour sails three times a day.

Crowning the highest hill in town is the handsome **University of Vermont** (UVM; www.uvm .edu; Main St/Rte 2), home to the **Fleming Museum** (☎ 802-656-2090; 61 Colchester Ave; adult/child 6-17 $5/3; ❂ 9am-4pm Tue-Fri, 1-5pm Sat & Sun Sep-Apr, noon-4pm Tue-Fri, 1-5pm Sat & Sun May-Aug), which contains a 2000-item Native American gallery and a diverse collection by American artists from Winslow Homer to Andy Warhol.

Got kids with you? The **ECHO Lake Aquarium & Science Center** (☎ 802-864-1848; www.echovermont.org; 1 College St; adult/child 3-17 $9.50/7; ❂ 10am-5pm), on the Burlington waterfront, will delight youngsters with its aquatic habitats wriggling with creatures and hands-on interactive exhibits illuminating Lake Champlain's ecological wonders.

At the **Lake Champlain Chocolates** (☎ 802-864-1807; 750 Pine St; admission free; ❂ tours on the hr 9am-2pm Mon-Fri) factory, you'll learn how a simple bean morphs into what critics are calling some of the finest chocolate in the country. Best of all, you'll get to sample the final product.

Magic Hat Brewery (☎ 802-658-2739; www.magichat .net; 5 Bartlett Bay Rd, South Burlington; ❂ tours on the hr 3-5pm Wed-Fri & noon-3pm Sun) offers free tours of its brew operation – and of course they'll tip the tap to let you sample the art.

On a 45-acre estate 7 miles south of Burlington the **Shelburne Museum** (☎ 802-985-3346; www.shelburnemuseum.org; US 7, Shelburne; adult/child 6-18 $18/9; ❂ 10am-5pm May-Oct, to 8pm Thu Jun-Aug) boasts a stellar collection of North American folk art and early New England architecture. The scores of period buildings include a lighthouse (1871), a covered bridge (1845) and even the side-wheeler steamship *Ticonderoga* (1906). Give yourself at least a couple of hours to enjoy this amazing place; tickets are good for two days.

Enjoy a slice of Vermont farm life at **Shelburne Farms** (☎ 802-985-8686; www.shelburnefarms. org; 1611 Harbor Rd, Shelburne; adult/child 3-17 $6/4; ❂ 10am-4pm mid-May–mid-Oct), a classic 1400-acre farm laid out by Frederick Law Olmsted, America's premier 19th-century landscape architect. Try your hand at milking a cow, feed the chickens, or hike the extensive nature trails through pastures and along Lake Champlain.

If you're ready to take your travels further afield head north on VT 2 to explore the unspoiled **Lake Champlain Islands**. Connected to the mainland by a causeway, these four islands (and a peninsula jutting down from Canada) are home to just 6500 year-round residents. Extending 30 miles from south to north they make a perfect day trip with fine rural scenery, lakeside beaches and small farms selling roadside produce. Should you want to extend your stay, information on campgrounds and B&Bs is available from **Champlain Islands Chamber of Commerce** (☎ 802-372-5683, 800-262-5226; www.champlainislands.com; VT 2,

North Hero; ☼ 9am-4pm Mon-Fri year-round & 10am-2pm Sat & Sun Jun-Aug).

Sleeping

North Beach Campground (☎ 802-862-0942, 800-571-1198; www.enjoyburlington.com; 60 Institute Rd; campsites $23) This choice lakeside campground skirts the bike path, has a sandy beach and offers on-site kayak and canoe rentals.

Inn at Shelburne Farms (☎ 802-985-8498; www .shelburnefarms.org; 1611 Harbor Rd; r $210-380, with shared bath $110-190; ✗) Vacation like a millionaire at this lakefront manor house-turned-inn at Shelburne Farms. On the National Register of Historic Places, this former summer residence of the Vanderbilts has 24 antique-filled bedrooms and the captivating air of a bygone era.

Lang House (☎ 802-652-2500, 877-919-9799; www.lang house.com; 360 Main St; r incl breakfast $135-225; ✗ ☒ wi-fi) Little extras like cozy bathrobes and a home-cooked breakfast add to the appeal of this friendly Victorian inn. Situated between downtown and the university, it makes an ideal base for exploring Burlington.

Willard Street Inn (☎ 802-651-8710, 800-577-8712; www.willardstreetinn.com; 349 S Willard St; r incl breakfast $140-230; ✗ ☒ ▯ wi-fi) With marble floors and a solarium dining room this gracious inn a short walk from UVM is a class act. The 16 rooms are comfy, some with lake views and gas fireplaces, and the gourmet breakfast will start your day in style.

Eating

Stonesoup (☎ 802-862-7616; 211 College St; mains $3-8; ☼ 7am-7pm Mon & Sat, 7am-9pm Tue-Fri) Don't let the bargain prices fool you. The food at this laid-back café is hearty and healthy, much of it organic. Sandwiches, soups, and a buffet bar of fresh salads and hot dishes shore up the menu.

Penny Cluse Café (☎ 802-651-8834; 169 Cherry St; mains $4-10; ☼ 6:45am-3pm Mon-Fri, 8am-3pm Sat & Sun) *The* place for breakfasts, this downtown café packs a perky college crowd with its south-western accented dishes like ranchero-style omelets and freshly squeezed juices.

Three Tomatoes (☎ 802-660-9533; 83 Church St; mains $7-16; ☼ 11:30am-9pm Mon-Thu, 11:30am-10pm Fri & Sat) An arched brick interior and delicious wood-fired pizzas give authenticity to this award-winning Italian trattoria on the pedestrian mall. The pastas and wine list won't disappoint either.

Adrianas (☎ 802-658-1323; 25 Church St; mains $7-22; ☼ 11:30am-10pm) The sidewalk tables at this French-inspired bistro are the place to be on a sunny day. Go with the grilled dishes – the sea scallops with red pepper glaze are heavenly.

Drinking & Entertainment

Uncommon Grounds (☎ 802-865-6227; 482 Church St; ☼ 7am-10pm Mon-Thu, 8am-11pm Fri & Sat, 9am-9pm Sun; wi-fi) Get your caffeine fix with organic coffee, prime sidewalk tables and free wi-fi.

Vermont Pub & Brewery (☎ 802-865-0500; 144 College St; ☼ 11:30am-1am Sun-Wed, 11:30am-2am Thu-Sat) This microbrewery attracts a crowd with its bustling outdoor beer garden and burly ales; good burgers and pub grub too.

Radio Bean Coffeehouse (☎ 802-660-9346; 8 N Winooski Ave; ☼ 8am-midnight) A Bohemian coffeehouse serving fair-trade coffee by day, it transforms after dark into an intimate candle-lit venue for artsy jazz and indie bands.

Club Metronome (☎ 802-865-4563; 188 Main St) attracts a hot dance crowd with DJs spinning '80s rock, while live bands takes the stage downstairs at **Nectar's** (☎ 802-658-4771), best known as the place where the jam band Phish got started.

Getting There & Away

Lake Champlain Ferries (☎ 802-864-9804; www.ferries .com; King St Dock; adult/child/car $4.70/2.05/11.80) runs ferries several times a day from mid-May to mid-October across the lake to Port Kent, NY (one hour).

NEW HAMPSHIRE

You're gonna like the scale of things in the Granite State: the towns are small and personable, the mountains majestic and rugged. The heart of New Hampshire is unquestionably the granite peaks of the White Mountain National Forest. Outdoor enthusiasts of all stripes flock to New England's highest range (6288ft at Mt Washington) for cold-weather skiing, summer hiking and brilliant fall foliage scenery. Oh, and don't be fooled by that politically conservative label that people stick on the state. The state mantra, 'Live Free or Die,' indeed rings from every automobile license plate, but truth be told residents here pride themselves in their independent spirit more

---

NEW HAMPSHIRE FACTS

Nicknames Granite State, White Mountain State

Population 1.3 million

Area 9351 sq miles

Capital city Concord (40,687)

Sales tax None

Birthplace of early astronaut Alan Shepard (1923–98), Tupperware inventor Earl Tupper (1907–83)

Home of The highest mountains in northeastern USA

Famous for Being the first to vote in US presidential primaries, giving the state hefty political power for its size

Most extreme state motto 'Live Free or Die'

---

than right-wing politics. New Hampshire, after all, is one of but a handful of states that recognize same-sex civil unions.

History

Named in 1629 after the English county of Hampshire, New Hampshire was the first American colony to declare its independence from England in 1776. During the 19th-century industrialization boom, the state's leading city, Manchester, became such a powerhouse that its textile mills were the world's largest.

New Hampshire played a high-profile role in 1944 when President Franklin D Roosevelt gathered leaders from 44 Allied nations to remote Bretton Woods for a conference to rebuild global capitalism. It was at the Bretton Woods Conference that the World Bank and the International Monetary Fund emerged.

In 1963 this antitax state found another way to raise revenue, by becoming the first state in the USA to have a legal lottery. In 1999 New Hampshire became the first in the USA to have a female governor and female leaders in both its state legislative chambers at the same time.

Information

There are handy welcome centers at major state border crossings, including ones that are open 24 hours at the north and south ends of I-93.

New Hampshire Division of Travel & Tourism Development (☎ 603-271-2665, 800-386-4664; www.visitnh.gov; 172 Pembroke Rd, Concord, NH 03302)

Distributes information on the state, as do the welcome centers.

Union Leader (www.unionleader.com) The state's largest newspaper.

PORTSMOUTH

Portsmouth wears its history on its sleeve. With roots in shipbuilding and the maritime trade, the once brawny heart of New Hampshire's sole coastal city now has a gentler appeal. The old brick warehouses along the harbor have been converted to restaurants and shops catering to visitors. A score of elegant period homes that formerly belonged to shipbuilding tycoons and naval officers graces the city center. On the docks that once bustled with merchant ships, you can now sit and munch fish and chips or hop aboard an old-fashioned cruise boat. The **Greater Portsmouth Chamber of Commerce** (☎ 603-436-3988; www.portcity.org; 500 Market St; ☷ 8:30am-5pm Mon-Fri, plus 10am-5pm Sat & Sun Jun–mid-Oct) provides visitor information.

Sights & Activities

Step back in time at **Strawbery Banke Museum** (☎ 603-433-1100; www.strawberybanke.org; cnr Hancock & Marcy Sts; adult/child 5-17 $15/10; ☷ 10am-5pm May-Oct), where an entire neighborhood of 40 period buildings comprise a living history museum. Visit the old general store, watch the potter throw his clay then treat yourself to a scoop of homemade ice cream.

Like a fish out of water, the 205ft-long **USS Albacore** (☎ 603-436-3680; Market St; adult/child 7-17 $5/3.50; ☷ 9:30am-5pm Jun–mid-Oct, 9:30am-4:30pm Thu-Mon mid-Oct–May) is now a beached museum surrounded by a grassy lawn. The decommissioned submarine, once the world's fastest, was launched from the Portsmouth Naval Shipyard in 1953.

Several of Portsmouth's grand historic houses have been beautifully preserved, including the 1758 **John Paul Jones House** (☎ 603-436-8420; cnr Middle & State Sts; adult/child under 14 $8/free; ☷ 11am-5pm), where the admiral known as 'the father of the US Navy' once lived. The 1760 **Wentworth Gardner House** (☎ 603-436-4406; 50 Mechanic St; adult/child 6-14 $5/2; ☷ 1-4pm Tue-Sun mid-Jun–mid-Oct), one of the finest examples of Georgian architecture in the Northeast, was so prized that the Metropolitan Museum of Art planned to move it to New York City before Portsmouth residents raised their voices in protest.

NEW ENGLAND

WORTH THE TRIP: CANTERBURY SHAKER VILLAGE

A traditional Shaker community from 1792, **Canterbury Shaker Village** (☎ 603-783-9511; www .shakers.org; 288 Shaker Rd, Canterbury; adult/child 6-17 $15/7; ☺ 10am-5pm mid-May–Oct) maintains the Shaker heritage as a living history museum. Interpreters demonstrate the Shakers' daily lives, artisans create Shaker crafts, and walking trails invite pondside strolls. The greening of America has deep roots here – for more than two centuries the Shakers' abundant gardens have been turning out vegetables, medicinal herbs and bountiful flowers the organic way. If you're ready for a soulful diversion you could easily spend half a day here on the farm. Take a little whole-someness home with you – there's a store selling Shaker reproductions, an organic farm stand and a superb restaurant serving the kind of food grandma used to make using heirloom veggies fresh picked from the garden. The village is 15 miles north of Concord off NH 106; take exit 18 off I-93 and follow the signs.

For those traveling with kids, the hands-on exhibits at the **Children's Museum of Portsmouth** (☎ 603-436-3853; 280 Marcy St; admission $6; ☺ 10am-5pm Tue-Sat, 1-5pm Sun, also 10am-5pm Mon mid-Jun–Aug) will pique their curiosity.

Portsmouth Harbor Cruises (☎ 603-436-8084, 800-776-0915; www.portsmouthharbor.com; Ceres St Dock; adult $12-20, child $8-13) runs several trips around the historic harbor as well as inland river cruises that are particularly scenic during fall foliage season. **Isles of Shoals Steamship Company** (☎ 603-431-5500, 800-441-4620; www.islesofshoals.com; 315 Market St; adult $17-25, child 5-13 $7-15) provides cruises aboard a replica 1900s-style ferry that harkens back to more leisurely times. Some of the cruises focus on lighthouses, others on the Isles of Shoals. For a big splurge, there's a lobster clambake dinner cruise on Friday evenings (adult/child $55/45).

Sleeping & Eating

Inn at Strawbery Banke (☎ 603-436-7242, 800-428-3933; www.innatstrawberybanke.com; 314 Court St; r incl breakfast $145-150; ✗) Friendly innkeepers, comfortable rooms and a delicious homemade breakfast are in store at this small B&B convenient to both the Strawbery Banke Museum and the city center.

Sise Inn (☎ 603-433-1200, 877-747-3466; www .siseinn.com; 40 Court St; r incl breakfast $199-279; ✗ wi-fi) Step back a century at this graceful 1881 Queen Anne–style inn. The rooms have engaging period decor but also boast modern amenities.

Muddy River Smokehouse (☎ 603-430-9582; 21 Congress St; mains $8-16; ☺ 11am-9pm Sun-Thu, 11am-10:30pm Fri & Sat) Hey y'all, this downtown restaurant has the best hickory-smoked BBQ this side of the South. Big meals are served up with baked beans and cornbread.

Portsmouth Gas Light Co (☎ 603-430-9122; 64 Market St; mains $8-20; ☺ 11:30am-10pm) There's something for everyone here. Head downstairs for wood-fired brick-oven pizza (all-you-can-eat pizza buffet at lunch on weekdays for just $6.50), upstairs for grilled seafood and steaks.

Old Ferry Landing (☎ 603-431-5510; 10 Ceres St; mains $9-25; ☺ 11:30am-8pm) Soak up Portsmouth's nautical atmosphere on the deck of this harborside restaurant overlooking the tugboat dock. The chef masters all sorts of seafood from fried clams to boiled lobster.

Drinking & Entertainment

Portsmouth Brewery (☎ 603-431-1115; 56 Market St; wi-fi) This hopping microbrewery serves specialty beers like Smuttynose Portsmouth Lager along with light eats.

Breaking New Grounds (☎ 603-436-9555; 14 Market St) Get your caffeine fix at this sunny café.

The acclaimed **Seacoast Repertory Theatre** (☎ 603-433-4472; 125 Bow St; tickets $22-32) performs *West Side Story*–type musicals in the historic 1892 Bow St Theatre.

Getting There & Away

By car, take I-95 exit 7; it takes about an hour to drive to Portsmouth from either Boston or Portland, ME. **Vermont Transit** (☎ 800-552-7837; www.vermonttransit.com) runs several daily buses to both Boston (one-way $18, 65 minutes) and Portland (one-way $17, 1¼ hours).

MANCHESTER

A couple of colleges and an art school give this old mill town vitality. New Hampshire's largest city, Manchester became a manufacturing powerhouse in the 19th century by harnessing the ripping Merrimack River. The brick **Amoskeag Mills** (1838), which stretch along the Commercial St riverbanks for more than a mile now house software companies and other 21st-century backbones of the city's economy.

Head to Elm St near the town green where you'll find the tourist office and the lion's share of eateries and pubs. The **Greater Manchester Chamber of Commerce** (☎ 603-666-6600; www .manchester-chamber.org; 889 Elm St; ☺ 8am-5pm Mon-Fri) has visitor information.

The city's highlight, the recently expanded **Currier Museum of Art** (☎ 603-669-6144; www.currier .org; 201 Myrtle Way; adult/child under 18 $5/free; ☺ 11am-5pm Sun, Mon, Wed, Fri, 11am-8pm Thu, 10am-5pm Sat), showcases works by American artists Georgia O'Keeffe and Andrew Wyeth. It also operates the 1950 **Zimmerman House** (tours $11), the only home in New England designed by famed American architect Frank Lloyd Wright (1867–1959) that's open to the public.

I-93, US 3 and NH 101 all pass through Manchester. The **Manchester Airport** (☎ 603-624-6539; www.flymanchester.com) is served by major US airlines, including discounter Southwest Airlines. **Vermont Transit** (☎ 800-451-3292; www.vermonttransit.com) and **Concord Trailways** (☎ 800-639-3317) provide bus services between Manchester and other New England cities.

CONCORD

History-laden Concord makes a refreshing break. Don't let the fact that it's a state capital throw you – think of it as a laidback little town that just happens to have a capitol building gracing Main St the way other communities this size would have a town hall. Everything radiates out from the State House – you'll find several delis and restaurants nearby.

The gold-domed, eagle-topped **State House** (☎ 603-271-2154; 107 N Main St; admission free; ☺ 8am-5pm Mon-Fri), built in 1819 of New Hampshire granite, houses the oldest legislative chamber in the US. Forget metal-detectors, this is a remarkably relaxed affair – you can walk right in, check out the intriguing lobby display of battle-tattered Civil War flags, then head up to the 2nd floor to visit the chamber. The **Museum of New Hampshire History** (☎ 603-228-6688; www.nhhistory.org; 6 Eagle Sq; adult/child 6-18 $5.50/3; ☺ 9:30am-5pm Mon-Sat, noon-5pm Sun, closed Mon Jan-Jun & Nov), opposite the State House, chronicles the history of the Granite State in more depth. **Pierce Manse** (☎ 603-225-4555; 14 Penacook St; ☺ 11am-3pm Tue-Fri mid-Jun–mid-Oct), the

home of Franklin Pierce (1804–69), the only US president to hail from New Hampshire, can be toured. The **Greater Concord Chamber of Commerce** (☎ 603-224-2508; www.concordnhchamber .com; 40 Commercial St) has visitor information.

LAKE WINNIPESAUKEE

A popular summer retreat for urban New England families looking for a break from the city, New Hampshire's largest lake stretches 28 miles in length, contains 274 islands and offers abundant opportunities for swimming, boating and fishing.

Weirs Beach

This lakeside town dishes up a curious slice of honky-tonk Americana with its celebrated video arcades, mini-golf courses and go-cart tracks. The **Greater Laconia/Weirs Beach Chamber of Commerce** (☎ 603-366-4770; www.laconia-weirs.org; 383 S Main St, Laconia) supplies information on the area.

Mount Washington Cruises (☎ 603-366-5531; www.cruisenh.com; cruises $25-51) operates scenic lake cruises, some including dinner, from Weirs Beach aboard the old-fashioned MS *Mount Washington*. For something more unusual, hop aboard the company's mailboat MV *Sophie C* on its two-hour **cruise** (adult/child 4-12 $22/12) to deliver mail to the lake islands.

Winnipesaukee Scenic Railroad (☎ 603-745-2135; www.hoborr.com; adult/child 3-11 $12/10; ☺ late May–mid-Oct) offers train rides along the shore of Lake Winnipesaukee.

Wolfeboro

On the opposite side of Lake Winnipesaukee and a world away from the ticky-tacky commercialism of Weirs Beach sits genteel Wolfeboro. The **Wolfeboro Chamber of Commerce** (☎ 603-569-2200, 800-516-5324; www.wolfeborochamber.com; 32 Central Ave; ☺ 10am-5pm Mon-Sat, 10am-3pm Sun), in the old train station, has the scoop on everything from boat rentals to lakeside beaches.

Anointing itself 'the oldest summer resort in America,' the town's awash with graceful period buildings. While strolling its pleasant streets drop by the **Hampshire Pewter Co** (☎ 603-569-5944; 43 Mill St; admission free; ☺ 9am-5pm Mon-Fri), where you can watch craftspeople work their trade.

Wolfeboro is home to the **Great Waters Music Festival** (☎ 603-569-7710; www.greatwaters.org; Brewster

---

SCENIC DRIVE: KANCAMAGUS HIGHWAY

One of New England's finest, the 35-mile Kancamagus Hwy (NH 112) is a beauty of a road cutting through the **White Mountain National Forest** between Conway and Lincoln. Laced with excellent hiking trails, scenic lookouts and swimmable streams, this is as natural as it gets. There's absolutely no development along the entire highway, which reaches its highest point at **Kancamagus Pass** (2868ft).

You can pick up brochures and hiking maps at the **Saco Ranger District Office** (☎ 603-447-5448; 33 Kancamagus Hwy; ☽ 9am-4:30pm) at the eastern end of the highway near Conway and at the **Lincoln Woods Ranger Office** (☎ 603-630-5190; Kancamagus Hwy; ☽ 8:30am-3:30pm) at the western end near the Mile 29 marker.

Coming from Conway, 6.5 miles west of the Saco ranger station, you'll see **Lower Falls** on the north side of the road – stop here for the view and a swim. No trip along this highway is complete without taking the 20-minute hike to the breathtaking cascade of **Sabbaday Falls**; the trail begins at Mile 15 on the south side of the road. The best place to spot moose is along the shores of **Lily Pond**; stop at the roadside overview at Mile 18. At the Lincoln Woods ranger station, cross the suspension footbridge over the river and continue for 3 miles to **Franconia Falls**, the finest swimming hole in the entire national forest, complete with a natural rock slide. Parking anywhere along the highway costs $3 per day (honor system) or $5 per week; just fill out an envelope at any of the parking areas.

The White Mountain National Forest is ideal for campers, and you'll find several campgrounds run by the forest service accessible from the Kancamagus Hwy. Most are on a first-come, first-served basis; pick up a list of them from one of the ranger stations that bookend the highway.

Academy, NH 28; ☽ Jul & Aug), where big-name folk, jazz and other acoustic artists perform on the banks of Lake Winnipesaukee.

Off NH 28 about 4 miles north of town is lakeside **Wolfeboro Campground** (☎ 603-569-9881; 61 Haines Hill Rd; campsites $20-22) with 50 wooded campsites.

The classic place to stay is the 44-room **Wolfeboro Inn** (☎ 603-569-3016, 800-451-2389; www .wolfeboroinn.com; 90 N Main St; r incl breakfast $190-270), the town's principal lodging since 1812. Some of the rooms have balconies overlooking the lake.

The **Yum Yum Shop** (☎ 603-569-1919; 16 N Main St; snacks $1-6; ☽ 6am-7pm), a Wolfeboro institution, is a family-run bakery which sells flaky pastries, old-fashioned doughnuts and fresh-made sandwiches. The cozy pub at the Wolfeboro Inn, **Wolfe's Tavern** (☎ 603-569-3016; 90 N Main St; mains $7-22; ☽ 8am-10pm), serves a varied menu ranging from pizza and burgers to seafood.

WHITE MOUNTAINS

What the Rockies are to Colorado the White Mountains are to New Hampshire. New England's grandest mountain range is a magnet for adventurers, with boundless opportunities for everything from hiking

and kayaking to skiing. Those who prefer to take it in from the comfort of a car seat won't be disappointed either, as scenic drives wind over rugged mountains ripping with waterfalls, sheer rock faces and sharply cut gorges.

You'll find information on the White Mountains at ranger stations throughout the **White Mountain National Forest** (www.fs.fed .us/r9/white) and chambers of commerce in the towns along the way.

Waterville Valley

In the shadow of Mt Tecumseh, Waterville Valley was developed as a resort community during the latter half of the 20th century, when hotels, condominiums, golf courses and downhill and cross-country ski trails were all laid out. It's very much a planned community and arguably a bit too groomed but there's plenty to do including tennis, indoor ice skating, bicycling, in-line skating and other family fun. The **Waterville Valley Region Chamber of Commerce** (☎ 603-726-3804, 800-237-2307; www.watervillevalleyregion.com; NH 49, Campton; ☽ 9am-5pm Wed-Mon), situated off I-93 exit 28, has all the details.

Like many New England ski mountains, the **Waterville Valley ski area** (☎ 800-468-2553; www.wa

terville.com) is open in the summer for mountain biking and hiking.

Mt Washington Valley

Stretching north from the eastern end of the Kancamagus Hwy, the Mt Washington Valley includes the towns of Bartlett, Conway, Glen, Intervale, Jackson and North Conway. All sorts of outdoor activities are available here. The area's hub and biggest town, North Conway, is also a center for outlet shopping, including some earthy stores like LL Bean. For information on the entire area contact the **Mt Washington Valley Chamber of Commerce** (☎ 603-356-5701, 800-367-3364; www.mtwashingtonvalley.org; Main St, North Conway; ☯ 9am-6pm Mon-Sat, 10am-5pm Sun).

SIGHTS & ACTIVITIES

Nostalgia at its finest, the **Conway Scenic Railroad** (☎ 603-356-5251, 800-232-5251; www.conwayscenic .com; NH 16, North Conway; adult $13-64, child 4-12 $9-40; ☯ daily mid-May–mid-Oct, weekends mid-Apr–mid-May & mid-Oct–Dec) runs an antique steam train on a variety of excursions from North Conway through the Mt Washington Valley and dramatic Crawford Notch. It's a real stunner, especially during the fall foliage season.

Two miles west of North Conway off US 302, placid **Echo Lake State Park** rests at the foot of a sheer rock wall called White Horse Ledge. The park offers lakeside hiking, swimming and a scenic road up 700ft-high Cathedral Ledge.

Skiing areas include **Attitash** (☎ 603-374-2368, 877-677-7669, lodging reservations 888-223-7669; www.attitash.com; US 302, Bartlett), 5 miles west of Glen, which also operates America's longest Alpine slide in summer; **Cranmore Mountain Resort** (☎ 603-356-5543, 800-786-6754; www.cranmore .com), 1 mile east of North Conway; and **Black Mountain Ski Area** (☎ 603-383-4490, lodging reservations 800-698-4490; www.blackmt.com; NH 16B, Jackson), a cross-country skiing mecca that offers horseback riding in summer.

If you're up for paddling, **Saco Bound** (☎ 603-447-2177; www.sacobound.com; 2561 E Main/US 302, Conway; rental per day $26-42) rents canoes and kayaks and also offers guided tours.

SLEEPING

North Conway in particular is thick with sleeping options from resort hotels to cozy inns.

HI Albert B Lester Memorial Hostel (☎ 603-447-1001; www.conwayhostel.com; 36 Washington St, Conway; dm/r $20/50; ☒ ▣) Perched on the edge of the White Mountain National Forest, off NH 16, this 45-bed hostel in a converted Conway farmhouse is well situated for outdoor adventurers.

Colonial Motel (☎ 603-356-5178, 866-356-5178; www.thecolonialmotel.com; 2431 White Mountain Hwy, North Conway; r $59-99; ☒ ▣ wi-fi) This family-run motel has a central location and 26 spotlessly clean rooms at affordable rates. For an extra $10 you can treat yourself to one with a Jacuzzi tub.

Cranmore Inn (☎ 603-356-5502, 800-526-5502; www .cranmoreinn.com; 80 Kearsarge St, North Conway; r incl breakfast $79-124; ☒ ☒ ▣ wi-fi) With a convenient in-town location, this North Conway landmark has been operating as a country inn since 1863 and good-value comfort has been its key to success.

North Conway Grand Hotel (☎ 603-356-9300, 800-522-1793; www.northconwaygrand.com; NH 16 at Settlers' Green, North Conway; r $109-219; ▣) If you are looking for all the comforts of a resort hotel, this place has commodious rooms with full amenities and extras like a free DVD library, tennis courts and a fitness center.

Camping options include **Cove Camping Area** (☎ 603-447-6734; www.covecamping.com; Cove Rd, Conway; campsites $24-50), off Stark Rd on Conway Lake with canoe rentals and a sandy beach; and **Saco River Camping Area** (☎ 603-356-3360; off NH 16, North Conway; campsites $23-33; ▣) on the Saco River.

EATING

Peach's (☎ 603-356-5860; South Main St, North Conway; mains $5-10; ☯ 7am-2:30pm) Cute as a button, this peachy place a half-mile south of the chamber of commerce serves blueberry pancakes and other breakfast delights until closing. At lunch the menu adds homemade soups that'll warm the soul on a cool day.

Café Noche (☎ 603-447-5050; 147 Main St, Conway; mains $8-14; ☯ 11:30am-9pm) For good Tex-Mex fare topped with real-deal salsas head to this festive central Conway spot. The margaritas, in a head-spinning variety of flavors, will rev up the appetite.

Shalimar (☎ 603-356-0123; 27 Seavy St, North Conway; mains $10-14; ☯ 11am-2:30pm & 5-10pm) Families take note: this Indian restaurant opposite the train station has a $5 children's menu that even fussy kids will like. For the adults it's all authentic family-style Indian dishes. Unbeatable $7 lunch deals before 2pm.

North Woodstock & Lincoln

You'll pass right through the twin towns of Lincoln and North Woodstock on your way between the Kancamagus Hwy and Franconia Notch State Park, so it's a handy place to break for a bite or a bed. The towns straddle the Pemigewasset River at the intersection of NH 112 and US 3. If you're ready for some action **Loon Mountain** (☎ 603-745-8111; www.loonmtn.com; Kancamagus Hwy, Lincoln) offers winter skiing and snowboarding and in summer has mountain-bike trails, climbing walls and New Hampshire's longest gondola ride. Or ratchet the adrenaline up a notch by zipping 2000ft down a hillside while strapped to just a cable in **Alpine Adventures** (☎ 603-745-9911; 41 Main St, Lincoln; zips $85; ☺ 9am-3pm) zipline treetop experience. For more on the area, contact the **Lincoln-Woodstock Chamber of Commerce** (☎ 603-745-6621; www.lincolnwoodstock.com; NH 112, Lincoln; ☺ 9am-5pm Mon-Fri).

SLEEPING

Country Bumpkins (☎ 603-745-8837; www.country bumpkins.com; US 3, Lincoln; campsites/RV sites $19/27, cabins $60-100) Rest in peace (late-night parties are banned) at this family-oriented place on the Pemigewasset River, with 45 campsites and six heated cabins with kitchenettes and private baths.

Wilderness Inn (☎ 603-745-3890, 800-777-7813; www.thewildernessinn.com; cnr US3 & NH 112; r incl breakfast $70-175; ☒ ☒ wi-fi) Gather round the fireplace with other guests at this century-old B&B with hardwood floors and country-style decor. Or if you're feeling romantic go for the cottage ($175) with a sleigh bed, gas fireplace and oversized Jacuzzi tub.

Woodstock Inn (☎ 603-745-3951, 800-321-3985; www.woodstockinnnh.com; US 3, North Woodstock; r incl breakfast $94-184; ☒ wi-fi) Spread across five historic houses in the heart of North Woodstock this inn offers a variety of comfortable rooms, many furnished with antiques, some with fireplaces.

EATING & DRINKING

Cascade Coffee House (☎ 603-745-2001; 126 Main St, North Woodstock; mains $4-7; ☺ 7am-3pm Mon-Fri, 7am-5pm Sat & Sun) Taking its influence from the adjacent art gallery, this creative place serves up luscious pastries, protein smoothies, iced coffees and panini sandwiches. Or perhaps a grilled portabella salad with baby greens?

Woodstock Inn Station & Brewery (☎ 603-745-3951; US 3, North Woodstock; mains $7-18; ☺ 11:30am-10pm) This brewpub satisfies a wide range of food cravings with pub grub, steaks and Mexican fare. Live entertainment on weekends in summer and frothy microbrewed ales year-round.

Franconia Notch State Park

Franconia Notch is the most celebrated mountain pass in New England, a narrow gorge shaped over the eons by a rushing stream slicing through the craggy granite. I-93, in places feeling more like a country road than a highway, runs straight through **Franconia Notch State Park** (admission free). The park **visitor center** (☎ 603-745-8391; www.franconi anotchstatepark.com; I-93, exit 34A) is 4 miles north of North Woodstock at the side of the **Flume Gorge** (adult/child 6-12 $10/7; ☺ 9am-5pm May-Oct), an awesome cleft in the granite bedrock. A 2-mile self-guided nature walk takes you right through the deep opening, which narrows to a mere 12ft.

The visitor center can give you details on other hikes in the park, ranging from short nature walks to day-long treks. For an enjoyable 20-minute stroll, stop at the **Basin** pulloff, between exits 34A and 34B, where a half-mile trail runs along a stream to a glacier-carved granite pool. The Basin is lovely, but swimming is not allowed. To take a dip, head to **Echo Lake Beach** (☎ 603-823-8800; adult/child $3/1; ☺ 10am-5:30pm), exit 34C, where you can swim and rent a kayak, rowboat or canoe.

The **Cannon Mountain Aerial Tramway** (☎ 603-823-8800; I-93, exit 34B; round-trip adult/child 6-12 $11/7; ☺ 9am-5pm mid-May–mid-Oct) whisks you to the

---

THE TENACIOUS OLD MAN

The **Old Man of the Mountain** is everywhere except on the mountain. This symbol of the Granite State – a 40ft-tall natural rock profile that graced Franconia Notch for eons until it crumbled and collapsed in 2003 – keeps appearing on brochures as if nothing has happened. His craggy face graces the commemorative New Hampshire quarter. He's plastered on state highway signs. And his proud gaze stares out from the 'Live Free or Die' license plates long after he's passed. The Old Man is dead. Long live the Old Man.

4200ft summit for some breathtaking views of Franconia Notch and the White Mountains.

Franconia Notch State Park's **Lafayette Place Campground** (☎ 603-823-9513, reservations 603-271-3628; campsites $19-24; mid-May–mid-Oct) has 99 wooded campsites, but they fill up early in summer, so it's best to reserve in advance.

A few miles north of Franconia Notch lies the **Frost Place** (☎ 603-823-5510; www.frost place.org; Ridge Rd, Franconia; adult/child 6-12 $4/2; 1-5pm Sat & Sun Jun, 1-5pm Wed-Mon Jul–mid-Oct), the farm where poet Robert Frost (1874–1963) wrote his most famous poems, 'The Road Not Taken' and 'Stopping by Woods on a Snowy Evening.'

Bretton Woods & Crawford Notch

Before 1944, Bretton Woods was known primarily as a low-key retreat for wealthy visitors who patronized the majestic Mt Washington Hotel. After President Roosevelt chose the hotel for the historic conference that established a new post-WWII economic order, the town's name took on worldwide recognition. The countryside, with Mt Washington looming above it, is as magnificent today as it was back then. The **Twin Mountain-Bretton Woods Chamber of Commerce** (☎ 800-245-8946; www.twin mountain.org; US 302 & US 3, Twin Mountain) has details on the area.

The region's largest ski area, **Bretton Woods ski station** (☎ 603-278-3320; www.brettonwoods.com; US 302) offers both downhill and cross-country winter skiing.

US 302 heads south from Bretton Woods to Crawford Notch (1773ft) through stunning mountain scenery ripe with towering cascades. **Crawford Notch State Park** (☎ 603-374-2272; adult/child 6-11 $3/1; mid-May–mid-Oct) maintains an extensive system of hiking trails, including short hikes around a pond and to a waterfall, and a longer trek up Mt Washington.

If walls could talk, the historic **Mt Washington Hotel** (☎ 603-278-1000, 800-258-0330; www.mtwash ington.com; US 302; r $195-550;) could spin quite a tale. Opened in 1902, this grande dame of New England mountain resorts boasts 2600 acres of grounds, 27 holes of golf, 12 clay tennis courts, a pair of heated pools and an equestrian center.

Cheaper but still classy digs can found at the **Bretton Arms Inn** (☎ 603-278-1000; www .mtwashington.com; US 302; r incl breakfast $149-260;

 ), an 1896 inn affiliated with the Mt Washington Hotel.

Inside Crawford Notch State Park, the **Dry River Campground** (☎ 603-271-3628; US 302; campsites $18-23; mid-May–mid-Dec) has quiet sites and good facilities.

Pinkham Notch

From Pinkham Notch (2032ft), on NH 16 about 11 miles north of North Conway, a system of hiking trails provides access to the natural beauties of the Presidential Range, including lofty **Mt Washington** (6288ft), the highest mountain east of the Mississippi and north of the Smoky Mountains. Hikers need to be prepared: Mt Washington's weather is notoriously severe and can turn on a dime. Dress warmly – not only does the mountain register New England's coldest temperatures (in summer, the average at the summit is 45°F/7°C) but unrelenting winds make it feel even colder than the thermometer reading.

For the less athletically inclined, the **Mount Washington Auto Road** (☎ 603-466-3988; www.mount washingtonautoroad.com; car & driver $20, extra passengers adult/child 5-12 $7/5; May–mid-Oct, weather permitting) offers easier summit access.

The Appalachian Mountain Club's (AMC) **Pinkham Notch Visitor Center** (☎ 603-466-2727, 800-262-4455; www.outdoors.org; NH 16; 6:30am-10pm) is the area's informational nexus for like-minded adventurers and a good place to buy hiking necessities, including topographic trail maps and the handy *AMC White Mountain Guide*. The AMC runs the adjacent **Joe Dodge Lodge** (dm with breakfast & dinner $68). **Dolly Copp Campground** (☎ 603-466-2713; NH 16; campsites $20), a USFS campground 6 miles north of the AMC facilities, has 176 simple campsites.

HANOVER

The archetypal New England college town, Hanover's town green is bordered on all four sides by the handsome brick edifices of Dartmouth College. Virtually the whole town is given over to this Ivy League school; chartered in 1769, it is the nation's ninth-oldest college. Main St, rolling down from the green, is bordered by perky pubs and cafés catering to the collegian crowd. **Hanover Area Chamber of Commerce** (☎ 603-643-3115; www.hanoverchamber .org; 216 Nugget Bldg, Main St; 9am-4pm Mon-Fri) has visitor information.

Sights & Activities

Hanover is all about Dartmouth College, so hit the campus. To join a free student-guided **campus walking tour** (☎ 603-646-2875; www.dartmouth.edu) contact the admissions office or click the calendar online for tour times. If the times don't fit your schedule pick up a map at the admissions office and head off on your own. Don't miss the **Baker-Berry Library** (☎ 603-646-2560; ☼ 8am-10pm), splashed with the grand *Epic of American Civilization*, painted by the renowned Mexican muralist José Clemente Orozco (1883–1949), who taught at Dartmouth in the 1930s.

The collections at Dartmouth's **Hood Museum of Art** (☎ 603-646-2808; Wheelock St; admission free; ☼ 10am-5pm Tue & Thu-Sat, to 9pm Wed, noon-5pm Sun) covers a wide swath from Assyrian stone reliefs dating to 883 BC to contemporary American art by heavyweights including Jackson Pollock and Edward Hopper.

Sleeping & Eating

Chieftain Motor Inn (☎ 603-643-2550; www.chieftaininn.com; 84 Lyme Rd/NH 10; r with breakfast $119-140; ☒ ☒ ☐ wi-fi) In a riverfront setting at the north side of town, this rustic inn offers complimentary use of canoes, making it a good spot to combine an outing with a night's sleep.

Hanover Inn at Dartmouth College (☎ 603-643-4300, 800-443-7024; www.hanoverinn.com; cnr Main & Wheelock Sts; r $260; ☒) Hanover's most elegant stay, a college-affiliated period hotel overlooking the town green, fills with proud parents during weekend events.

Dirt Cowboy Café (☎ 603-643-1323; 7 S Main St; snacks $1.50-5; ☼ 7am-6pm) On a sunny day grab yourself one of the sidewalk tables at this café kitty-corner from the town green and order up the best coffee in town. Tasty baguette sandwiches and smoothies too.

Lou's (☎ 603-643-3321; 30 S Main St; mains $4-8; ☼ 6am-3pm Mon-Fri, 7am-3pm Sat & Sun) A student haunt since 1947, everybody comes to this unpretentious eatery for the breakfasts served until closing. Tuck into a hearty half-pound steak-and-eggs plate or go light with low-carb options.

Molly's (☎ 603-643-2570; 43 S Main St; mains $8-16; ☼ 11:30am-10pm) Overlooking Main St, this spirited bar and grill has its finger on the pulse of the action and whips up everything from pizza and burgers to grilled salmon.

Drinking & Entertainment

Canoe Club (☎ 603-643-9660; 27 S Main St; ☼ 5pm-midnight) The place to head if you're in the mood for music, this smart café has live entertainment nightly – anything from acoustic to jazz.

Murphy's on the Green (☎ 603-643-4075; 11 S Main St; ☼ 11am-12:30am) At this classic Irish pub, students and faculty discuss weighty matters over pints of Irish ale.

Hopkins Center for the Arts (☎ 603-646-2422; 6241 www.hop.dartmouth.edu; Hinman St) The 'Hop' is Dartmouth's refined venue for string quartets, modern dance and plays.

Getting There & Away

To get to Hanover by car take exit 13 off I-91. **Vermont Transit** (☎ 603-643-2128, 800-552-8737; www.vermonttransit.com) runs buses to Hanover from major New England towns. One-way fares are $30 between Hanover and Boston (2½ hours) and $26 between Hanover and Burlington (two hours).

MAINE

New England's rugged frontier state has two distinct faces. Tiny fishing villages, seaside lobster joints and postcard-perfect summer resorts dot the coast, offering everything necessary for a relaxing beach vacation. Head inland and you'll find a land so vast that the rest of New England could fit within its boundaries with room to spare. Maine's grand interior expanse is given over to rushing rivers, dense forests and lofty mountains just begging to be explored. As a traveler in Maine, your choices are as spectacularly varied as the landscape. You can opt to sail serenely along the coast on a graceful schooner or rip through white-water rapids on a river raft, spend the night in an old sea captain's mansion-turned-B&B or camp among the moose on a quiet backwoods lake.

History

The French and English vied to establish colonies in Maine during the 1600s, but deterred by the harsh winters these settlements failed.

In 1652 Massachusetts annexed the territory of Maine to provide a front line of defense against potential attacks during the French and Indian Wars. Maine indeed did become

MAINE FACTS

Nickname Pine Tree State
Population 1.5 million
Area 35,387 sq miles
Capital city Augusta (population 18,560)
Sales tax 5%
Birthplace of Poet Henry Wadsworth Longfellow
(1807–82)
Home of Horror novelist Stephen King
Famous for Lobster, moose, blueberry pancakes,
LL Bean
State drink Maine gave the world Moxie, America's first (1884) and spunkiest soft drink

a battlefield between English colonists in New England and French forces in Canada.

In the early 19th century, in an attempt to settle sparsely populated Maine, 100-acre homesteads were offered free to settlers willing to farm the land. In 1820 Maine broke from Massachusetts and entered the Union as a state.

In 1851 Maine became the first state to ban the sale of alcoholic beverages, the start of a temperance movement that eventually took hold throughout the United States. It wasn't until 1934 that Prohibition was finally lifted.

Information

If you're entering the state on I-95 heading north, stop at the well-stocked visitor information center on the highway.

Maine Office of Tourism (☎ 888-624-6345; www
.visitmaine.com; 59 State House Station, Augusta,
ME 04330) Will send out a handy magazine on Maine
destinations.

Maine Tourism Association (☎ 207-623-0363; www
.mainetourism.com) Links chamber of commerce offices
throughout Maine.

SOUTHERN MAINE COAST

Maine's most touristed quarter, this seaside region lures visitors with its sandy beaches, resort villages and outlet shopping. The best place to stop for the latter is the southernmost town of Kittery, which is chock-a-block with outlet stores selling everything from camping gear to fine china.

Ogunquit

Aptly named, Ogunquit means 'Beautiful Place by the Sea' in the native Abenaki tongue, and its 3-mile-long beach has long

been a magnet for summer visitors. Ogunquit Beach, a sandy barrier beach, separates the Ogunquit River from the Atlantic Ocean, offering beachgoers the option to swim in cool ocean surf or in the warmer, calmer cove.

As a New England beach destination, Ogunquit is second only to iconic Provincetown for the number of gay travelers who vacation here. Most of the town lies along Main St (US 1), which is lined with restaurants, shops and motels. For waterfront dining and boating activities head to Perkins Cove at the south end of town.

The **Ogunquit Chamber of Commerce** (☎ 207-646-2939; www.ogunquit.org; 36 Main St; ⊙ 9am-5pm) has visitor information.

SIGHTS & ACTIVITIES

A highlight in town is walking the coastal footpath, the **Marginal Way**, which skirts the 'margin' of the sea from Shore Rd, near the center of town, for a mile before ending near Perkins Cove. You won't need to do much walking to reach the beach, as **Ogunquit Beach**, also called Main Beach by locals, begins right in the town center at the end of Beach St.

The **Ogunquit Playhouse** (☎ 207-646-5511; www
.ogunquitplayhouse.org; 10 Main St), which first opened in 1933, offers both flashy Broadway musicals and children's theater each summer.

Finestkind Scenic Cruises (☎ 207-646-5227; www
.finestkindcruises.com; Perkins Cove; adult/child from $12/7) offers several boat cruises, including 50-minute voyages to pull up lobster traps.

SLEEPING

Pinederosa Camping (☎ 207-646-2492; 128 North Village Rd, Wells; campsites $25; 🐾) The nearest camping is here, off US 1, a mile north of Ogunquit's center.

Ogunquit Beach Inn (☎ 207-646-1112; www
.ogunquitbeachinn.com; 67 School St; r incl breakfast $89-169; 🖳 wi-fi) A favorite among Ogunquit's gay visitors, this pleasant B&B in the town center is close to both Main St and the beach. The accommodating hosts supply little extras like complimentary use of beach chairs and a movie library.

Puffin Inn (☎ 207-646-5496; www.puffininn.com;
433 Main St; r incl breakfast $109-189; 🚫 🖳 wi-fi) This three-story Victorian has 11 rooms, each with its own character and some with private decks. Start your morning with a full home-cooked breakfast served on the porch.

NEW ENGLAND

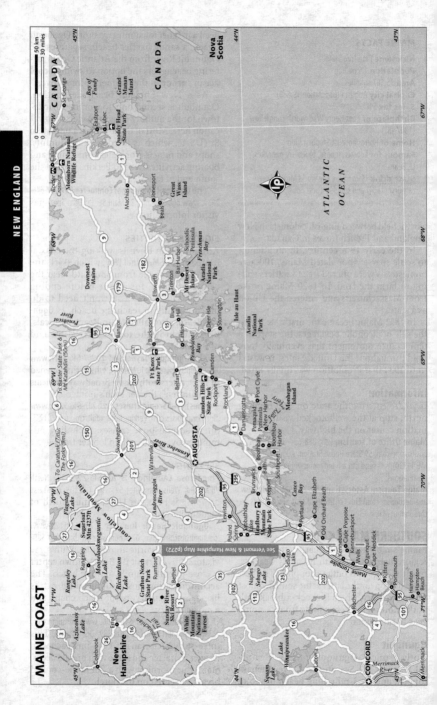

MAINE COAST

EATING

You'll find most of Ogunquit's restaurants on the south side of town at Perkins Cove, and in the town center along Main St near its intersection with Beach St.

Bread & Roses (☎ 207-646-4227; 246 Main St; items $2-7; ☺ 7am-8pm) The kind of bakery that most small towns only dream about – the raspberry croissants are heavenly, the innovative salads healthy, the panini sandwiches grilled to perfection. It's takeout, but there are café tables on the porch.

Jackie's Too (☎ 207-646-4444; Perkins Cove Rd; mains $7-27; ☺ 11am-9pm) This place packs it all in: seaside patio dining and a menu with something for everyone, from hummus wrap sandwiches to steaks and fresh seafood. Good spot for a sunset cocktail too.

Lobster Shack (☎ 207-646-2941; Perkins Cove Rd; mains $8-22; ☺ 11am-8pm) If you want good seafood and aren't particular about the view, this reliable joint serves lobster in all its various incarnations from lobster stew to lobster in the shell.

Barnacle Billy's (☎ 207-646-5575; 183 Shore Rd; mains $10-30; ☺ 11am-9pm) For lobsters with a view, this landmark restaurant overlooking Perkins Cove is the one. The lobster prices depend on the weight you choose but expect to pay around $25 to $30.

Kennebunkport

On the Kennebunk River, Kennebunkport fills with tourists in summer who come to stroll the streets, admire the century-old mansions and get their fill of sea views. Be sure to take a drive along Ocean Ave, which runs along the east side of the Kennebunk River and then follows a scenic stretch of the Atlantic that holds some of Kennebunkport's finest estates, including the summer home of former president George HW Bush.

Three public beaches extend along the west side of the Kennebunk River and are known collectively as Kennebunk Beach. The center of town spreads out from Dock Sq, which is along ME 9 (Western Ave) at the east side of the Kennebunk River bridge. The **Kennebunk/Kennebunkport Chamber of Commerce** (☎ 207-967-0857; www.visitthekennebunks.com; 17 Western Ave; ☺ 9am-5pm Mon-Fri year-round, 8:30am-3pm Sat Jul & Aug) has tourist information.

SLEEPING

Franciscan Guest House (☎ 207-967-4865; www.franciscanguesthouse.com; 26 Beach Ave; r incl breakfast $59-149; ⊠ ☺ ☺) Serenity awaits at this suitably simple but perfectly comfortable 50-room guesthouse on the grounds of St Anthony's Monastery. Enjoy the outdoor saltwater pool and 60 acres of wooded walking trails.

Green Heron Inn (☎ 207-967-3315; www.greenheroninn.com; 126 Ocean Ave; r incl breakfast $160-200; ⊠ ☺) In a fine neighborhood, overlooking a picturesque cove, this Kennebunkport inn has 10 cozy rooms and is within walking distance of a sandy beach and several restaurants. Breakfast is gourmet and multicourse.

Old Fort Inn (☎ 207-967-5353; www.oldfortinn.com; Old Fort Ave; r incl breakfast $160-395; ⊠ ☺) One block from the beach and just minutes from the presidential Bush family estate, this cushy historic inn boasts 16 rooms with antique furnishings, four-post beds and the like.

EATING & DRINKING

Clam Shack (☎ 207-967-2560; 2 Western Ave; mains $5-16; ☺ 11:30am-10pm) By the bridge at the west side of the Kennebunk River, this simple joint is justifiably famous for its fried clams, but the lobster roll overflowing with succulent chunks of lobster is the ultimate prize here.

Alisson's (☎ 207-967-4841; 11 Dock Sq; mains $6-20; ☺ 11am-10pm) In the center of town on the east side of the Kennebunk River, Kennebunkport's most popular eatery offers a varied menu that includes Maine seafood as well as burgers, chicken and pasta.

Federal Jack's Restaurant & Brew Pub (☎ 207-967-4322; 8 Western Ave; mains $6-20; ☺ 11:30am-1am) Overlooking the Kennebunk River, this bustling brewpub serves frosty mugs of handcrafted ales (try the Blue Fin Stout) along with pub fare like fried calamari and barbecued ribs.

PORTLAND

Maine's leading city is undergoing a renaissance attracting artists, trendy chefs and other energetic souls. Its happening museum and gallery scene, lively waterfront and manageable size (population 63,000) all add up to great exploring. And the city has etched out a solid reputation for the hottest dining scene north of Boston.

Orientation & Information

Portland sits on a hilly peninsula surrounded on three sides by water: Back Cove, Casco Bay and the Fore River. It's easy to find your way around. Commercial St (US 1A) runs along the waterfront through the Old Port, while the parallel Congress St is the main thoroughfare through downtown, passing the art museum, city hall and banks.

Convention & Visitors Bureau of Greater Portland (☎ 207-772-5800; www.visitportland.com; 245 Commercial St; ☻ 8:30am-5pm Mon-Fri year-round, 10am-5pm Sat Jun-Aug, to 3pm Sat Oct-May) Pick up a free Portland map here.

Maine Medical Center (☎ 207-662-0111; 22 Bramhall St; ☻ 24hr)

Portland Phoenix (www.thephoenix.com/portland) Free alternative weekly newspaper, covering arts and entertainment.

Portland Public Library (☎ 207-871-1700; 5 Monument Sq; ☻ 9am-6pm Mon, Wed & Fri, noon-9pm Tue & Thu, 9am-5pm Sat) Has 15-minute free internet access. Also a wireless hot spot.

Post office (☎ 207-871-8424; 125 Forest Ave; ☻ 7:30am-7pm Mon-Fri, 7:30am-5pm Sat)

Sights & Activities
OLD PORT

Portland's heart thumps from the **Old Port**, where salt-scented breezes, brick sidewalks and lamp-lit streets just beg for poking about. This restored waterfront district centers on the handsome 19th-century buildings lining Commercial St and the narrow side streets extending a few blocks inland. Once home to the brawny warehouses and merchant quarters of a busy port, the focus has shifted from shipping to shopping. This gentrified neighborhood now houses Portland's finest restaurants, pubs, boutiques and galleries.

Head to waterfront Commercial St for an eclectic food and drink scene. Galleries to seek out include **Maine Potters Market** (☎ 207-774-1633; 376 Fore St), a collective with works from 13 potters; **Abacus American Crafts** (☎ 207-772-4880; 44 Exchange St), which has jewelry, glass and lots of great gift items; and **Fore Street Gallery** (☎ 207-874-8084; 366 Fore St), where contemporary art rules.

MUSEUMS & HISTORIC BUILDINGS

Works of Maine painters Winslow Homer, Edward Hopper and Andrew Wyeth are showcased at the **Portland Museum of Art** (☎ 207-775-6148; www.portlandmuseum.org; 7 Congress Sq; adult/child 6-17 $10/4, 5-9pm Fri free; ☻ 10am-5pm Sat-Thu, 10am-9pm Fri, closed Mon mid-Oct–May). Maine's premier art museum also boasts solid contemporary collections and postimpressionist works by Picasso, Monet and Renoir, as well as a brilliant collection of Portland art glass.

And if you enjoy period homes be sure to stroll through the restored 1801 **McLellan House**, entered through the museum and included in the ticket price.

Folks with kids in tow should head for the **Children's Museum of Maine** (☎ 207-828-1234; www.childrensmuseumofme.org; 142 Free St; admission $6; ☻ 10am-5pm Mon-Sat, noon-5pm Sun, closed Mon Sep-Jun). This house of fun is next to the Portland Museum of Art.

The **Wadsworth-Longfellow House** (☎ 207-879-0427; 485 Congress St; adult/child 5-11 $7/3; ☻ 10am-4pm Mon-Sat, noon-4pm Sun May-Oct), the childhood home of Henry Wadsworth Longfellow (1807–82), retains its original character, complete with the poet's family furnishings. Admission includes entry to the **Maine Historical Society Museum** (☎ 207-774-1822; 489 Congress St), which has changing exhibits on the state's history.

History buffs won't want to miss the hilltop **Portland Observatory** (☎ 207-774-5561; 138 Congress St; adult/child 6-16 $6/4; ☻ 10am-5pm late May-early Oct), built in 1807 as a maritime signal station to direct ships entering the bustling harbor. Its function was roughly on par with that of an airport traffic control tower today. From the top of this unique observatory you'll be rewarded with a sweeping view of Casco Bay.

AROUND PORTLAND

Up for a picnic in an unbeatable setting? Head 4 miles south of central Portland to Cape Elizabeth and the 90-acre **Fort Williams Park** (admission free; ☻ dawn-dusk) where you'll find **Portland Head Light** (☎ 207-799-2661; 1000 Shore Rd, Cape Elizabeth; lighthouse museum adult/child 6-18 $2/1; ☻ 10am-4pm Jun-Oct), New England's most photographed lighthouse and the oldest (1791) of Maine's more than 60 lighthouses.

For a whole different angle on Portland and Casco Bay, hop one of the boats that offer narrated scenic cruises out of Portland Harbor. **Casco Bay Lines** (☎ 207-774-7871; www.cascobaylines.com; 56 Commercial St, Portland; adult $11.50-18.50, child 5-9 $5.50-8.50) tours the Portland coast and Casco Bay islands on a variety of cruises that last from 1¾ to six hours. You can also have Casco Bay Lines drop you off at Peaks Island and then hook up with **Maine Island Kayak Company** (☎ 207-766-2373; www.maineislandkayak.com; 70 Luther St, Peaks Island, Portland; tour $65; ☻ May-Nov) for a half-day kayak tour of the bay. For a classy sail, the **Portland Schooner**

Company (☎ 207-776-2500; www.portlandschooner .com; 40 Commercial St, Portland; adult/child 2-12 $30/15; ⏱ May-Oct) offers two-hour trips aboard a pair of elegant Maine-built, century-old wooden schooners.

Landlubbers can ride the rails on the antique trains of the **Maine Narrow Gauge Railroad Co & Museum** (☎ 207-828-0814; www.mngrr.org; 58 Fore St; adult/child 3-12 $10/6; ⏱ on the hour 11am-4pm mid-May–mid-Oct, shorter off-season hours) for a journey along Casco Bay.

Sleeping

In addition to in-town choices, there are several chain hotels south of the city center at I-95, exit 48.

Inn on Carleton (☎ 207-775-1910, 800-639-1779; www.innoncarleton.com; 46 Carleton St; r with breakfast $99-219; ✗ 🐾) Get a sense of Portland's roots in this restored 1869 Victorian inn with six elegant rooms furnished in antiques. It's in a fine old neighborhood, very quiet but still convenient to downtown sights.

Eastland Park Hotel (☎ 207-775-5411, 888-671-8008; www.eastlandparkhotel.com; 157 High St; r $115-165; ✗ 🐾 wi-fi) Dating to the 1920s, this period downtown hotel is a good-value place to lay your head. The rooms are large and comfortable, the staff is friendly and there are good online deals.

Inn at Park Spring (☎ 207-774-1059, 800-437-8511; www.innatparkspring.com; 135 Spring St; r incl breakfast $129-175; ✗) Friendly innkeepers, clean, well-appointed rooms, a superb breakfast and a convenient location near the Portland Museum of Art are just part of the appeal of this period B&B.

Eating

Standard Baking Co (☎ 207-773-2112; 75 Commercial St; snacks $1-4; ⏱ 7am-6pm Mon-Fri, 7am-5pm Sat & Sun) This Old Port bakery in a brick warehouse makes the best gingerbread you've ever tasted. Luscious pastries and French breads too.

Becky's Diner (☎ 207-773-7070; 390 Commercial St; mains $4-10; ⏱ 4am-9pm) Grab yourself a stool at the counter and rub shoulders with the burly locals at this bustling place favored by waterfront workers. Blueberry pancakes, haddock chowder and New England pot roast are high on the favorites list.

Duckfat (☎ 207-774-8080; 43 Middle St; mains $5-11; ⏱ 11am-8pm Mon-Sat, 9am-4pm Sun) If you have gourmet taste on a fast-food budget, this one-of-a-kind eatery won't disappoint. Try the

---

GET CRACKIN'

Eating a boiled lobster is a messy pleasure and no trip to New England is complete without experiencing this culinary delight. Lobster eateries will give you a plastic bib, a metal cracker, melted butter for dipping the meat, a dish for the shells and lots of napkins. Tear in with your hands and fingers. Suck the sweet meat out of the legs, crack the claws to reach the treat inside, then finally twist off the tail by bending it back to remove the prized tail meat in one piece.

Thai chicken panini sandwich, the duck confit salad, or the signature fries crisped in duck fat and dribbled with truffle ketchup.

Gilbert's Chowder House (☎ 207-871-5636; 92 Commercial St; mains $7-20; ⏱ 11am-10pm) Sit on the waterfront patio and enjoy a bowl of award-winning chowder, fish and chips and other briny delights from the sea.

555 (☎ 207-761-0555; 555 Congress St; mains $14-29; ⏱ 5-10pm Mon-Sat, 10:30am-2pm & 5-9:30pm Sun) The latest darling of trendy food magazines, this award-winning restaurant specializes in New England cuisine kicked up a notch. Foodies rave over the Maine peeky-toe crab risotto with smoked chili oil. The perfectly matched wine list gives hints of the chef's Napa roots.

Fore Street Restaurant (☎ 207-775-2717; 288 Fore St; mains $18-30; ⏱ 5-10pm) A perennial favorite for a dinner out, this place with its exposed brick interior and open kitchen is as inviting as the food is delicious. The menu changes nightly, but expect wood-roasted meats and seafood served with in-season Maine produce.

Drinking & Entertainment

Gritty McDuff's Brew Pub (☎ 207-772-2739; 396 Fore St) An Old Port institution, this hopping microbrewery is the place to enjoy a robust pint of Black Fly stout or a snappy ale.

Bull Feeney's (☎ 207-773-7210; 375 Fore St) There's always something happening at this Irish pub, which offers Guinness on tap, free Happy Hour (4pm to 7pm) appetizers and weekend entertainment.

Styxx (☎ 207-828-0822; 3 Spring St) Gay men and women head here for dancing and a night out on the town.

Getting There & Around

Portland International Jetport (☎ 207-774-7301; www.portlandjetport.org) is served by a half-dozen domestic carriers, with nonstop flights to several cities in the eastern US, but despite its name no international flights land here.

Coastal Maine is most easily explored by car, but **Vermont Transit** (☎ 207-772-6587; www.vermonttransit.com; 950 Congress St), inside the Greyhound terminal, runs buses between Portland and Boston (one-way $19, 2¼ hours) and also travels along the Maine coast up to Bar Harbor (one-way $46, four hours).

Amtrak's **Downeaster train** (www.amtrakdowneaster.com) makes its two-hour trip four times daily heading between Portland and Boston (one-way $19).

The local bus **Metro** (☎ 207-774-0351; www.gpmetrobus.com; fares $1.25), which runs throughout the city, has its main terminus at Monument Sq at the intersection of Elm and Congress Sts, near the public library.

CENTRAL MAINE COAST

Midcoast Maine is where the mountains meet the sea. You'll find craggy peninsulas jutting deep into the Atlantic, alluring seaside villages and endless opportunities for hiking, sailing and kayaking.

Freeport

The fame and fortune of Freeport, 16 miles northeast of Portland, began a century ago when Leon Leonwood Bean opened a shop to sell equipment to hunters and fishers heading north into the Maine wilderness. Bean's good value earned him loyal customers, and over the years the **LL Bean store** (☎ 800-341-4341; www.llbean.com; Main St; ☼ 24hr) has added stylish sportswear to its high-quality outdoor gear. Although more than 125 other stores have joined the pack, the wildly popular LL Bean is still the epicenter of town.

Ironically, this former stopover for hardy outdoor types is now devoted entirely to city-style shopping, consisting of a mile-long Main St (US 1) lined with stores that sell everything from porcelain dinnerware and fine jewelry to luggage and the latest fashions. **Freeport Merchants Association** (☎ 207-865-1212, 800-865-1994; www.freeportusa.com; 23 Depot St; ☼ 9am-5pm Mon-Fri) provides both tourist and shopping information.

SLEEPING & EATING

Although 'shop till you drop' may be the town's motto, there's no need to stay on your feet all night – this town has some inviting inns.

James Place Inn (☎ 207-865-4486, 800-964-9086; www.jamesplaceinn.com; 11 Holbrook St; r incl breakfast $135-185; ✖ ☒) Built in 1880, this sweet seven-room B&B has a great location just two blocks from LL Bean, but beyond the hustle and bustle of the main drag. Most of the rooms have a Jacuzzi; one has a fireplace.

Kendall Tavern B&B (☎ 207-865-1338, 800-341-9572; www.kendalltavern.com; 213 Main St; r incl breakfast $150-175; ✖) Friendly innkeepers make you feel right at home at this beautifully restored farmhouse at the north side of the town center. Blueberry pancakes or similar treats greet guests at breakfast.

Lobster Cooker (☎ 207-865-4349; 39 Main St; mains $5-12; ☼ 11am-7pm Sun-Fri, 11am-8pm Sat) A favorite with shoppers, this fast-food place just two blocks south of LL Bean has terrific clam chowder and good seafood sandwiches.

Harraseeket Lunch & Lobster Co (☎ 207-865-4888; 36 Main St, South Freeport; mains $9-25; ☼ 11am-8:45pm) Head to this harborside restaurant and lobster pound 3 miles south of Freeport center for its legendary lobster rolls chock-full of succulent meat. It's a great place for steamers, too.

Bath

Bath has been renowned for shipbuilding since colonial times and that remains the raison d'être for the town today. **Bath Iron Works**, one of the largest shipyards in the USA, builds steel frigates and other ships for the US Navy. The worthwhile **Maine Maritime Museum** (☎ 207-443-1316; 243 Washington St; adult/child 6-17 $10/7; ☼ 9:30am-5pm), south of the ironworks on the Kennebec River, showcases wooden boats and the town's centuries-old maritime history.

Boothbay Harbor

Set back from the open ocean on a fjordlike harbor, this fishing village packs thick with tourists in the summer. Other than eating lobster, the main activity here is hopping boats. **Balmy Days Cruises** (☎ 207-633-2284, 800-298-2284; www.balmydayscruises.com; Pier 8) runs one-hour harbor tours (adult/child under 12 $12/6) and day trips to Monhegan Island (adult/child $32/18). **Cap'n Fish's Boat Trips** (☎ 207-633-3244,

800-636-3244; www.mainewhales.com; Pier 1) offers four-hour whale-watching trips (adult/child five to 12 $35/22). The **Boothbay Harbor Region Chamber of Commerce** (☎ 207-633-2353; www.boothbayharbor. com; 192 Townsend Ave/ME 27; ☼ 9am-5pm Mon-Fri, 10am-5pm Sat) provides visitor information.

SLEEPING & EATING

Gray Homestead (☎ 207-633-4612; www.graysoceancamp ing.com; 21 Homestead Rd, Southport; campsites $32) Fall asleep to the lull of the surf at this ocean-side campground 4 miles south of Boothbay Harbor via ME 27 and 238. Kayaks for rent, too.

Brown's Wharf Inn (☎ 207-633-5440, 800-334-8110; www.brownswharfinn.com; 121 Atlantic Ave; r $119-179; ✗ ✗ wi-fi) Sit on your own private balcony and watch the fishers bring in the catch at this 70-room motel smack on the harbor.

Topside Inn (☎ 207-633-5404, 877-486-7466; www .topsideinn.com; 60 McKown St; r incl breakfast $120-165; ✗) Perched on a hilltop, this 19th-century sea captain's house turned B&B has 21 comfortable rooms and a bird's-eye view of the town and surrounding ocean.

Boothbay Harbor crawls with lobster eateries. One of the best and cheapest is the **Lobster Dock** (☎ 207-633-7120; 49 Atlantic Ave; mains $12-25; ☼ 11:30am-8:30pm). From chunky lobster stew to boiled lobster in the shell, this waterfront place perfects everything that can be done with the crusty crustacean. If you're not keen on mayonnaise try the unconventional mayo-free lobster rolls drenched in warm butter.

Pemaquid Peninsula

At the southernmost part of the Pemaquid Peninsula, **Pemaquid Point** is one of the most wildly beautiful places in Maine, its grainy igneous rock formations pounded by treacherous seas. Perched atop the rocks in the 6-acre **Lighthouse Park** (☎ 207-677-2494; Pemaquid Point; adult/child under 12 $2/free; ☼ dawn-dusk) is the 11,000-candlepower Pemaquid Light, built in 1827. A star of the 64 surviving lighthouses along the Maine coast, Pemaquid Light is the beauty featured on the back of the Maine state quarter. The keeper's house is now the **Fishermen's Museum** (admission incl park fee; ☼ 9am-5pm mid-May–mid-Oct) displaying period photos, old fishing gear and lighthouse paraphernalia.

Monhegan Island

This small granite island with high cliffs and crashing surf, 9 miles off the Maine coast, attracts summer day-trippers, artists and nature-lovers who find inspiration in the dramatic views and agreeable isolation. Tidy and manageable, Monhegan is just 1.5 miles long and a half-mile wide. The website **Monhegan Commons** (www.monhegan.com) has island information and accommodation links. Rooms typically book full in summer,

NEW ENGLAND

HOIST THE SAILS

Feel the wind in your hair and history at your side aboard the gracious, multimasted sailing ships known as windjammers. The sailing ships – both historic and replicas – gather in the harbors at both Camden and neighboring Rockland to take passengers out on either day or overnight sails.

Day sails cruise for two hours in Penobscot Bay from June to October ($30); you can usually book your place on the day. On the Camden waterfront, look for the 86ft wooden tall ship **Appledore** (☎ 207-236-8353; www.appledore2.com) and the two-masted schooner **Olad** (☎ 207-236-2323; www.maineschooners.com).

Other schooners make three- to six-day cruises, offer memorable wildlife viewing (seals, whales and puffins) and typically include stops at small coastal towns, offshore islands and Acadia National Park.

You can get information on several ships in one fell swoop through the **Maine Windjammer Association** (☎ 800-807-9463; www.sailmainecoast.com), which represents 12 traditional tall ships, seven of which have been designated National Historic Landmarks. Among them is the grand-daddy of the schooner trade, the *Lewis R French,* America's oldest (1871) windjammer. Rates range from $400 for a three-day cruise to $950 for a six-day voyage.

Reservations for the overnight sails are a must. Rates are highest in midsummer. June offers long days, uncrowded harbors and lower rates, though the weather can be cool. Late September, when the foliage begins to take on color, is a particularly scenic time.

so plan ahead if you're not just visiting on a day trip.

In addition to its 17 miles of walking trails, there's an 1824 **lighthouse** with a small **museum** (admission $2) in the former keeper's house and several artists studios that you can poke your head into.

The 31 rooms in the 1870s **Monhegan House** (☎ 207-594-7983; www.monheganhouse.com; s/d incl breakfast $81/140) have shared baths but offer cheery ocean and lighthouse views. The Novelty, at the back of Monhegan House, sells sandwiches, salads and ice cream.

Departing from Port Clyde, the **Monhegan Boat Line** (☎ 207-372-8848; www.monheganboat.com; round-trip adult/child 2-12 $30/16) runs three boats daily to Monhegan from late May to mid-October, once a day for the rest of the year. The **MV Hardy III** (☎ 800-278-3346; www.hardyboat .com; round-trip adult/child 2-12 $29/17; ☉ mid-Jun–Sep) departs for Monhegan twice daily from New Harbor, on the east side of the Pemaquid Peninsula. Both boats take approximately one hour and have both early morning departures and late-afternoon returns, perfect for day-tripping.

Camden

With rolling hills as a backdrop and a harbor full of sailboats, Camden is a gem. Home to Maine's large fleet of windjammers (see boxed text, p295), it attracts nautical-minded souls.

You can get a superb view of picturesque Camden and its surroundings by taking the 45-minute climb up Mt Battie in **Camden Hills State Park** (☎ 207-236-3109; 280 Belfast Rd/US 1; adult/child 5-11 $3/1; ☉ 7am-sunset) at the north side of Camden.

The **Camden-Rockport-Lincolnville Chamber of Commerce** (☎ 207-236-4404; www.camdenme.org; 1 Public Landing, Camden; ☉ 9am-5pm Mon-Sat, plus 10am-4pm Sun Jun-Aug) provides visitor information.

SLEEPING & EATING

Camden Hills State Park (☎ 207-624-9950; 280 Belfast Rd/US 1; campsites $22; ☉ May–mid-Oct) This popular park has hot showers and 107 forested campsites, as well as 30 miles of scenic hiking trails; reservations are advised.

Whitehall Inn (☎ 207-236-3391, 800-789-6565; www .whitehall-inn.com; 52 High St; r incl breakfast $99-199; ☒ wi-fi) Unwind in a rocking chair on the shady front porch of this century-old inn with 40 rooms and a timeless New England character.

Afternoon tea, a full breakfast and a tennis court add to the appeal.

Captain Swift Inn (☎ 207-236-8113, 800-251-0865; www.swiftinn.com; 72 Elm St/US1; r incl breakfast $119-245; ☒ ☒ wi-fi) Crème brûlée french toast? That gives you just a taste of what you're in for at this pampering B&B. Occupying an 1810 Federal-style home, the comfy rooms vary, but think hardwood floors, four-post beds and a warm fireplace.

Camden Deli (☎ 207-236-8343; 37 Main St; mains $4-9; ☉ 7am-10pm) This family-run deli with a rooftop deck overlooking Camden Harbor serves everything from Maine blueberry pancakes to Italian sandwiches piled high with salami and hot peppers. Come between 4pm and 7pm for free appetizers and $3 beers.

Cappy's (☎ 207-236-2254; 1 Main St; mains $6-15; ☉ 11am-11pm; wi-fi) The star of this place is the award-winning clam chowder, sold by the cup, bowl or pint. You can also order burgers, fresh fish sandwiches and lobster rolls but definitely start off with the rich, creamy chowder.

Blue Hill

Graced with period houses, Blue Hill is a charming coastal town that's home to many artists and craftspeople. Start your exploration at Main St and the adjoining Union St, where you'll find several quality galleries selling Blue Hill pottery, sculptures and paintings.

Since 1902 the **Kneisel Hall Chamber Music Festival** (☎ 207-374-2811; www.kneisel.org; Pleasant St/ME 15; tickets $20-30; ☉ Fri-Sun late Jun-late Aug) has attracted visitors from far and wide to its summer concert series. The **Blue Hill Chamber of Commerce** (☎ 207-374-3242; www.bluehillpeninsula .org; 28 Water St; ☉ 8:30am-4pm Tue-Thu) has visitor information.

Evening hors d'oeuvres by the fireplace and a gourmet breakfast are just two of the perks at **Blue Hill Inn** (☎ 207-374-2844, 800-826-7415; www .bluehillinn.com; Union St; r incl breakfast $138-195; ☒ wi-fi), the town's landmark B&B since 1840.

Fantastic food and atmosphere are in store at **Wescott Forge** (☎ 207-374-9909; 66 Main St; lunch mains $8-11, dinner mains $17-30; ☉ 11:30am-2:30pm & 5:30-9pm Wed-Sat), a contemporary restaurant in an old blacksmith shop. Lunch features sandwiches and quesadillas, while dinner gets fancy with the likes of Dijon duck breast.

ACADIA NATIONAL PARK

Dramatic scenery and a plethora of activities, from bird-watching to mountain climbing, makes the only national park in New England a magnet for outdoor enthusiasts. An unspoiled wilderness of coastal mountains, towering sea cliffs and quiet ponds, this century-old park owes its existence to tycoon John D Rockefeller, who donated the land to the park system to spare it from development.

Orientation & Information

Granite mountains and coastal vistas greet you upon entering **Acadia National Park** (www .nps.gov/acad). The park is open year-round, though Park Loop Rd and most facilities are closed in winter. There is an admission fee from May through to October. The fee, which is valid for seven consecutive days, is $20 per vehicle between mid-June and early October ($10 at other times), or otherwise $5 on bike or foot.

Start your exploration at the **Hulls Cove Visitor Center** (☎ 207-288-3338; ME 3; ☾ 8am-4:30pm mid-Apr–Jun & Oct, 8am-6pm Jul & Aug, 8am-5pm Sep), from where the 27-mile **Park Loop Road** circumnavigates the eastern portion of the park.

Sights & Activities

PARK LOOP ROAD

Park Loop Rd, the main sightseeing jaunt through the park, takes you to several of Acadia's highlights. If you are up for a bracing swim or you just want to walk along Acadia's longest beach, stop at **Sand Beach**, where there's a summertime lifeguard. Located about a mile beyond Sand Beach you'll come to **Thunder Hole**, where wild Atlantic waves crash into a deep narrow chasm with such force that it creates a thundering boom, loudest during incoming tides. Look to the south to see dramatic **Otter Cliffs**, a favorite rock-climbing spot that rises vertically from the sea above a rocky shoreline. At **Jordan Pond** a 1-mile nature trail loops around the south side of the pond and a longer, 3.5-mile trail skirts the entire pond perimeter. After you've worked up an appetite, reward yourself with a relaxing afternoon tea on the lawn of Jordan Pond House (p298). Situated near the end of Park Loop Rd a side road leads up to Cadillac Mountain.

CADILLAC MOUNTAIN

The majestic centerpiece of Acadia National Park is **Cadillac Mountain** (1530ft), the highest peak on the US East Coast, reached by a 3.5-mile spur road off Park Loop Rd. Four **trails** lead to the summit from four directions should you prefer hiking boots to rubber tires. The panoramic 360 degree view of ocean, islands and mountains is a winner any time of the day, but it's truly magical at dawn when visitors flock to the top to watch the sun rise over Frenchman Bay.

OTHER ACTIVITIES

Some 120 miles of **hiking trails** crisscross Acadia National Park, from easy half-mile nature walks and level rambles to mountain treks up steep and rocky terrain. One standout is the 3-mile round-trip **Ocean Trail**, which runs between Sand Beach and Otter Cliffs and takes in the most interesting coastal scenery in the park. Pick up a guide describing all the park trails at the visitor center.

The park's 57 miles of carriage roads are the prime destination for **bicycling**. You can rent quality mountain bikes, replaced new each season, at **Acadia Bike** (☎ 207-288-9605; 48 Cottage St, Bar Harbor; per day $21; ☾ 8am-8pm).

Rock climbing on the park's sea cliffs and mountains is breathtaking. Gear up with **Acadia Mountain Guides** (☎ 207-288-8186; www.aca diamountainguides.com; 198 Main St, Bar Harbor; half-day with instructor & equipment $80; ☾ 10am-6pm), Acadia's only accredited climbing school.

Scores of **ranger-led programs** including nature walks, birding talks and kids field trips are available in the park. The visitor center provides the daily schedule. For information on kayaking and other activities see the Bar Harbor section (p298).

Sleeping & Eating

The park has two campgrounds, both wooded and with running water, showers and barbecue pits. The 306-site **Blackwoods Campground** (☎ 877-444-6777; ME 3; campsites $20; ☾ year-round), 5 miles south of Bar Harbor, accepts advance reservations. The 214-site **Seawall Campground** (ME 102A; campsites $14-20; ☾ late May-Sep), 4 miles south of Southwest Harbor, operates on a first-come, first-served basis. If these are full several commercial campgrounds can be found just outside Acadia National Park.

Sit on the lawn overlooking **Jordan Pond House** (☎ 207-276-3316; afternoon tea $8.75, mains $10-24; ☾ 11:30am-at least 8pm mid-May–Oct) and have a memorable afternoon tea with popovers and strawberry jam. Lunchtime sandwiches and prime rib dinners are served too at the park's sole restaurant.

There are scores of restaurants, inns and hotels in Bar Harbor (below), just a mile beyond the park.

Getting There & Around

The convenient **Island Explorer** (☎ 207-667-5796; www.exploreacadia.com; all rides free; ☼ late Jun–early Oct) runs eight shuttle bus routes throughout Acadia National Park and to adjacent Bar Harbor, linking trailheads, campgrounds and accommodations.

For information on getting to Acadia National Park and Bar Harbor see the Bar Harbor section that follows.

BAR HARBOR

Set on the doorstep of Acadia National Park, this alluring coastal town once rivaled Newport, RI, as a trendy summer destination for wealthy Americans. Today many of the old mansions have been turned into inviting inns and the town has become a magnet for outdoor enthusiasts. The **Bar Harbor Chamber of Commerce** (☎ 207-288-5103, 888-540-9990; www .barharbormaine.com; 93 Cottage St; ☼ 8am-6pm Mon-Fri, 9am-6pm Sat & 10am-6pm Sun mid-Jun–Sep, 9am-5pm Mon-Fri Oct–mid-Jun) has visitor information.

Sights & Activities

Bar Harbor Whale Watch (☎ 207-288-2386; www .barharborwhales.com; 1 West St; adult $22-49, child 6-14 $15-26; ☼ mid-May–Oct), next to the town pier, offers a wide variety of sightseeing cruises,

including whale-watching and puffin trips. It also offers a ranger-led tour to Baker Island, a 130-acre island that's part of Acadia National Park but reachable only by boat.

For a cruise in style, hop aboard the four-mast schooner *Margaret Todd* operated by **Downeast Windjammer Cruises** (☎ 207-288-4585; www.downeastwindjammer.com; 27 Main St; adult/child under 12 $32/22), which sets sail three times a day.

Kayaking tours generally go to the islands in Frenchman Bay or the west side of Mt Desert Island, depending on which way the wind's blowing. **Coastal Kayaking Tours** (☎ 207-288-9605; www.acadiafun.com; 48 Cottage St; 2½-/4-hour tours $37/46; ☼ 8am-8pm) offers personalized tours, taking out a maximum of six kayaks at a time.

Sleeping

There's no shortage of sleeping options in Bar Harbor, ranging from lovely B&Bs to the usual chain hotels.

Bar Harbor Hostel (☎ 207-288-5587; www.barhar borhostel.com; 321 Main St; dm/r $25/80; ☒ ☐) This well-maintained hostel a mile from Acadia National Park has single-sex dorms with 10 beds each as well as a private room that can sleep up to four people. Reservations are recommended.

Quimby House Inn (☎ 207-288-5811, 800-344-5811; www.quimbyhouse.com; 109 Cottage St; r $99-199; ☒ ☒ wi-fi) A top value among Bar Harbor's small hotels, with clean, spacious rooms, helpful staff and a convenient downtown location.

A MAINE WOODS NATIONAL PARK?

The concept is as grand as Maine's vast north woods. Taking inspiration from John D Rockefeller, who donated land for Acadia National Park, Roxanne Quimby, founder of the organic personal-care company Burt's Bees, has bought 77,000 acres of Maine woods hoping to make it the cornerstone of a new national park. The goal is to grow it into a 3.2-million-acre park that would restore native ecosystems and cover a greater land area than both Yellowstone and Yosemite national parks combined. Actor Robert Redford and other Hollywood celebrities have jumped on board to support the idea but a counter-movement has managed thus far to put the proposed park on hold.

Concerned with being banned from hunting and snowmobiling on new parklands, not to mention the loss of timber jobs, many folks in the surrounding towns have become vocal opponents. Probably even more telling, some conservation groups have come out against the park, worried that the backlash will hamper their efforts in other areas where public support is essential, such as the struggle to stop a 420,000-acre resort from being developed on Moosehead Lake. Still, the vision is there and supporters are optimistic that its time will come. Check out their website at www.restore.org.

Holland Inn (☎ 207-288-4804; www.hollandinn.com; 35 Holland Ave; r incl breakfast $110-165; ✗ ✗) Nine cheery rooms, a hearty breakfast and resident innkeepers who make you feel at home are in store at this renovated 1895 farmhouse, which is situated just a short stroll from the town center.

Coach Stop Inn (☎ 207-288-9886, 800-927-3097; www .coachstopinn.com; 715 Acadia Hwy; r incl breakfast $125-155; ✗ wi-fi) Built in 1804 as a stagecoach stop, this inn makes claim to being the oldest in Bar Harbor. Run by a chef, it's justifiably famous for its fancy country breakfasts, cozy rooms and warm hosts.

Eating & Drinking

Bagel Factory (☎ 207-288-3903; 3 Cadillac Ave; items $2-7; ☯ 7am-2pm Mon-Sat) Search out this hole-in-the-wall for real New York–style bagels. Delicious homemade soups, too, should you want to dunk that bagel.

Lompoc Café & Brewpub (☎ 207-288-9392; 36 Rodick St; mains $6-15; ☯ 11:30am-1am) This friendly café features an eclectic menu with Middle Eastern fare, organic Greek salads and thin-crusted pizzas. Local brews on tap – or try the blueberry cosmo. There's live jazz, folk or blues Thursday to Saturday nights.

Rupununi (☎ 207-288-2886; 119 Main St; mains $7-25; ☯ 11am-1am) Enjoy an all-American menu of burgers, steaks and fresh seafood. Rupununi also has a rollicking night scene, with a dance floor and a trio of bars serving an amazing variety of Maine beers.

McKays (☎ 207-288-2002; 231 Main St; mains $9-18; ☯ 4:30-10pm) One of Maine's buy-local, organic-when-possible restaurants, this is a good place to come for Maine crab cakes, farm-raised chicken and good ol' beer-battered fish and chips.

Trenton Bridge Lobster Pound (☎ 207-667-2977; ME 3, Ellsworth; lobsters $10-15; ☯ 10:30am-8pm Mon-Sat) Sit at a picnic table and crack open a boiled lobster at this traditional lobster pound bordering the causeway that connects Mt Desert Island to mainland Maine. Run by the very folks who pull up the lobster traps – this is as fresh as it gets.

Getting There & Away

Colgan Air (☎ 800-428-4322; www.colganair.com) has daily flights between Bar Harbor and Boston ($159). The Hancock County-Bar Harbor Airport is at Trenton off ME 3, 12 miles northwest of Bar Harbor. **Budget** (☎ 207-667-1200) and

Hertz (☎ 207-667-5017) have car-rental booths at the airport.

Vermont Transit (☎ 800-451-3292; www.vermont transit.com) runs buses between Bar Harbor and several New England cities, including Portland (one-way $46, four hours) and Boston (one-way $64, 6½ hours).

DOWNEAST MAINE

The 900-plus miles of coastline running northeast from Bar Harbor are sparsely populated, slower-paced and foggier than southern and western Maine. Highlights include the **Schoodic Peninsula**, whose tip is a noncontiguous part of Acadia National Park; the lobster fishing villages of **Jonesport** and **Beals**; and **Great Wass Island**, a nature preserve with walking paths and good bird-watching, including the chance to see puffins.

Machias, with a branch of the University of Maine, is the center of commerce along this stretch of coast. **Lubec** is about as far east as you can go and still be in the USA; folks like to watch the sun rise at nearby **Quoddy Head State Park** so they can say they were the first in the country to catch the sun's rays.

Calais (*ka*-lus), at the northern end of US 1, is a twin town to St Stephen in New Brunswick, Canada. Southwest of Calais is the **Moosehorn National Wildlife Refuge** (☎ 207-454-7161; US1, Baring; admission free; ☯ dawn-dusk), which has hiking trails and offers opportunities to spot bald eagles, America's national bird.

INTERIOR MAINE

Sparsely populated northern and western Maine is rugged outdoor country. River rafting, hiking trails up Maine's highest mountain and the ski town of Bethel make the region popular with adventurers.

Augusta

In 1827 Augusta became Maine's capital, but it's small and, truth be told, not terribly interesting. The **Kennebec Valley Chamber of Commerce** (☎ 207-623-4559; www.augustamaine.com; 21 University Dr; ☯ 8:30am-5pm Mon-Fri) provides information on Augusta. If you're passing through, take a gander at the granite **State House** (1829), then stop at the adjacent **Maine State Museum** (☎ 207-287-2301; State House Complex, State St; adult/child 6-18 $2/1; ☯ 9am-5pm Tue-Fri, 10am-4pm Sat), which traces the state's natural and cultural history.

Bangor

A boomtown during Maine's 19th-century lumbering prosperity, Bangor was destroyed by a sweeping fire in 1911. Today it's a modern, workaday town, perhaps most famous as the hometown of horror novelist Stephen King (look for his mansion – complete with bat-and-spiderweb gate – among the grand houses along Broadway). The **Bangor Region Chamber of Commerce** (☎ 207-947-0307; www.ban gorregion.com; 519 Main St; ☺ 9am-4pm Mon-Fri) has visitor information.

Sabbathday Lake

The nation's only active Shaker community is at Sabbathday Lake, 25 miles north of Portland. Founded in the early 18th century, a handful of devotees keep the Shaker tradition of simple living, hard work and fine artistry alive. You can tour several of their buildings on a visit to the **Shaker Museum** (☎ 207-926-4597; adult/child 6-12 $6.50/2; ☺ 10am-4:30pm Mon-Sat late May–mid-Oct). To get there, take exit 63 off the Maine Turnpike and continue north for 8 miles on ME 26.

Bethel

The rural community of Bethel, nestled in the rolling Maine woods 12 miles east of New Hampshire on ME 26, offers an engaging combination of beautiful mountain scenery, outdoor escapades and good-value accommodations. **Bethel Area Chamber of Commerce** (☎ 207-824-2282, 800-442-5826; www .bethelmaine.com; 8 Cross St; ☺ 9am-5pm Mon-Sat, plus noon-5pm Sun Jul-Sep & Jan-Mar) provides information for visitors.

SIGHTS & ACTIVITIES

Bethel Outdoor Adventure (☎ 207-824-4224, 800-533-3607; www.betheloutdooradventure.com; 121 Mayville Rd/US 2; per day kayak/canoe $35/50; ☺ 8am-8pm), right on the banks of the Androscoggin River, rents canoes and kayaks and takes you by shuttle upriver – your choice of 4 or 10 miles – so you can paddle back on the 'family-friendly moving flatwater' at your own pace. It also rents bicycles, can set you up for fly-fishing and offers on-site camping.

If you're up for a hike, head to **Grafton Notch State Park** (☎ 207-824-2912; ME 26), north of Bethel, which has pretty mountain scenery, waterfalls and lots of trails of varying lengths.

Sunday River Ski Resort (☎ 207-824-3000; www .sundayriver.com; ME 26), 6 miles north of Bethel, is one of the best family-oriented ski centers in the region, with eight interconnected mountain peaks and 120 trails.

SLEEPING & EATING

White Mountain National Forest (☎ reservations 877-444-6777; www.recreation.gov; campsites $16-18) The Maine portion of this national forest has several basic campgrounds near Bethel.

Chapman Inn (☎ 207-824-2657, 877-359-1498; www .chapmaninn.com; 1 Mill Hill Rd; incl breakfast dm $33, r $79-109; ▯ wi-fi) A great place to share notes with fellow travelers, this friendly, central 1865 B&B has 10 country-style rooms as well as hostel-style dorm beds. Billiards, darts and free bicycles add to the fun.

Sudbury Inn & Suds Pub (☎ 207-824-2174, 800-395-7837; www.sudburyinn.com; 151 Main St; r incl breakfast $89-139; mains $8-26; ❄) The choice place to stay in downtown Bethel, this historic inn has 17 rooms, a pub with 29 beers on tap, pizza and live weekend entertainment. There's also an excellent dinner restaurant serving venison with wild mushrooms and other Maine-centric fare.

Caratunk & The Forks

For white-water rafting at its finest, head to the **Kennebec River**, below the Harris Dam, where the water shoots through a dramatic 12-mile gorge. With rapid names like Whitewasher and Magic Falls, you know you're in for an adventure.

The adjoining villages of Caratunk and the Forks, on US 201 south of Jackman, are at the center of the Kennebec River rafting. The river rafting options range from rolling rapids and heart-stopping drops to calmer waters where children as young as seven can join in. Rates vary with demand and which tour you choose, but range from $65 to $125 per person for a day-long outing. Multiday packages, with camping or cabin accommodations, can also be arranged.

Reliable operators include the following:
Crab Apple Whitewater (☎ 800-553-7238; www .crabapplewhitewater.com)
Magic Falls Rafting (☎ 800-207-7238; www .magicfalls.com)
Three Rivers Whitewater (☎ 877-846-7238; www .threeriverswhitewater.com)

Baxter State Park

Set in the remote forests of northern Maine, **Baxter State Park** (☎ 207-723-5140; www.baxter stateparkauthority.com; admission per car $12) centers on

Mt Katahdin (5267ft), Maine's tallest mountain and the northern terminus of the 2175-mile **Appalachian Trail** (www.nps.gov/appa). This vast 204,733-acre park is maintained in a wilderness state – no electricity and no running water (bring your own or plan on purifying stream water) – and there's a good chance you'll see moose, deer and black bear. Baxter has extensive hiking trails, several leading to the top of Mt Katahdin, which can be hiked round-trip in a day as long as you're in good shape and get an early start.

Baxter's 10 campgrounds contain 1200 campsites (per day $18) but they do fill up, so it's best to book in advance, which can be done online or by phone with a credit card.

At Millinocket, south of Baxter State Park, there are motels, campgrounds, restaurants, supermarkets and outfitters that specialize in white-water rafting and kayaking on the Penobscot River. Get information from the **Katahdin Area Chamber of Commerce** (☎ 207-723-4443; www.katahdinmaine.com; 1029 Central St, Millinocket).

Washington, DC & the Capital Region

What? Why check out the Capital Region? It's all a bunch of monuments, right?

If that's what you think you're selling this place, and yourself, short. This is America at her most diverse: physically, culturally, even historically. The grass is caked with blood from America's settlement (Jamestown), birth (the Revolution) and coming of age (the Civil War). The aristocracy of regal Georgetown sits half an hour from dope fiends slinging smack outside an Anacostia project. You can lose yourself in the flat lands of the Chesapeake Bay, a soft, sensual landscape of never-ending waterways, or drive through the flinty heart of the Appalachian Mountains in one (long) day.

The attractive, uneasy tapestry of American society is woven intensely into the landscape. Scots-Irish mountain folk populate West Virginia, while in Maryland, the nation's richest African American neighborhoods are a scant few miles from some of the poorest ghettoes in the country. Peruvians hold pick-up soccer games against Nicaraguan co-workers, while Pakistani and Bahaman neighbors set up cricket pitches not 20 miles from Capitol Hill. In Bethesda, MD, one of the largest Jewish communities in the country sits minutes from Virginia, where Saudi money funds Islamic academies and the Christian Broadcasting Network pumps its evangelism onto the nation's airwaves. And at the center of it all is the nation's capital, where the entire country is microcosmed into a glistening, crime-ridden, maddening whole.

If you want a feel for America she's all accessible here, where the country was born, where she runs herself, and where she struts her ugliest and prettiest sides for lucky visitors like you.

HIGHLIGHTS

- Visiting the USA's heart and soul at places such as the **National Archives** (p314) and the **National Mall** (p311) in Washington, DC.

- Getting drunk as a sailor in the film-noir, immigrant enclaves of the port of **Baltimore** (p325).

- Breathing in America's adolescence at Civil War battle sites such as **Manassas** (p347).

- Taking a Sunday drive along the **Blue Ridge Parkway** (p364) – breathtaking views don't get much more scenic than this.

- Getting your first taste of the New South in multicultural **Richmond's eateries** (p352).

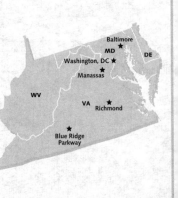

THE CAPITAL REGION IN...

One Week

Follow a version of the two-day DC itinerary (p313) and spend a day and a hard-partying night in **Baltimore** (p325) before exploring Maryland's gorgeous **Eastern Shore** (p337). Cross over the Chesapeake Bay bridge-tunnel and time-warp through Virginia's history, from her settlement and independence struggle in the **Historic Triangle** (p353) to her reconciliation with America at **Appomattox Court House** (p361). Swing north through **Richmond** (p348), where students, Dixie aristocracy and African Americans get mashed into a fascinating whole before rolling back (exhausted) into DC.

Two Weeks

Follow the above itinerary (hell, give DC and Baltimore a few more days while you're at it). Afterwards, experience Virginia's aristocratic soul in **Charlottesville** (p360) before driving down her mountainous backbone through **Staunton** (p363), **Lexington** (p364) and the **Crooked Road** (p366). Now truck through West Virginia, stopping off for hikes in the **Monongahela National Forest** (p368), before returning to Washington via the serene battlefields of **Antietam** (p340).

The American Experience Tour

Here's a one-week blitz of sites that make America...well, simply America. Follow the two-day DC itinerary (p313), making sure to see the **Supreme Court** (p314), **White House** (p315) and **National Archives** (p314); finish with a **Capitol Tour** (p314). On the third day visit **Anacostia** (p316) to see America's income disparities, and the **Eden Center** (p346) to witness immigrant success. Now for some history: take the **Civil Wargasm scenic drive** (p357) all the way to **Appomattox Court House** (p361), and turn around for the **Historic Triangle** (p353). In a week, you've visited the major centers of Federal government; rich, poor and immigrant neighborhoods; and the most important places of America's colonization, Revolution and Civil War.

HISTORY

The 108 English colonists who landed at Jamestown in 1607 had a charter from the Virginia Company of London and, apparently, not a lot of common sense. Two gentlemen brought personal tailors with them. No one thought to bring farm tools. Or farmers, for that matter. Native Americans occasionally fought the newcomers; at other times, they showed the colonists how to plant corn. Their eventual reward was disease and a choice between forcible integration or exile.

Jamestown survived, and the Royal Colony of Virginia came into being in 1624. Ten years later, fleeing the English Civil War, Lord Baltimore established the Catholic colony of Maryland at St Mary's City, where a Spanish-Jewish doctor treated a town council that included a black-Portuguese sailor and Margaret Brent, the first woman to vote in North American politics. Delaware was settled as a Dutch whaling colony in 1631, practically wiped out by Native Americans, and later resettled by the British. Celts displaced from Britain filtered into the Appalachians, where they created a persisting, fiercely independent culture. Border disputes between Maryland, Delaware and Pennsylvania led to the creation of the Mason–Dixon line, which eventually separated the industrial North from the agrarian, slave-holding South.

The Revolutionary War finished here with the British surrender at Yorktown in 1781. Then, to diffuse regional tension, central, swampy Washington, District of Columbia (DC), was made the new nation's capital. But divisions of class, race and economy were strong, and this area in particular split along its seams during the Civil War: Virginia seceded from the Union while its impoverished western farmers, long resentful of genteel plantation owners, seceded from Virginia. Maryland stayed in the Union but her white slave-owners rioted against Northern troops, while thousands of black Marylanders joined the Union Army.

LOCAL CULTURE

The North–South tension long defined this area, but the region has also jerked between

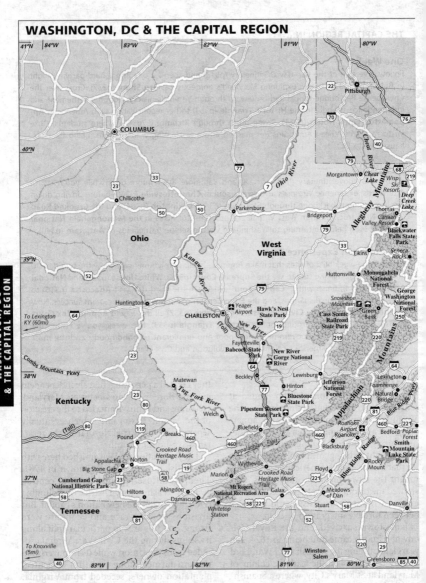

WASHINGTON, DC & THE CAPITAL REGION

the aristocratic pretensions of upper-class Virginia, miners and watermen, immigrant boroughs and the ever-changing rulers of Washington, DC. Since the Civil War, local economies have made the shift from agriculture and manufacturing to high technology and servicing and staffing the federal government.

Many blacks settled this border region either as slaves or escapees running for Northern freedom. Today African Americans still form the visible underclass of major cities, but in the rough arena of the disadvantaged they compete with Latino immigrants, mainly from Central America. On the other end of the spectrum, ivory

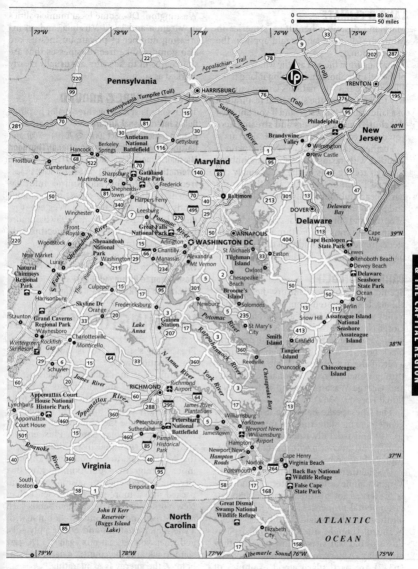

towers – in the form of world-class universities and research centers such as the National Institute of Health – attract intelligentsia from around the world. The local high schools are often packed with the children of scientists and consultants staffing some of the world's most prestigious think tanks.

All of the above has spawned a culture that is, in turns, as sophisticated as a journalist's book club; as linked to the land as bluegrass festivals in Virginia; and as hooked into the main vein of urban America as Billie Holiday, go-go, Baltimore Club and DC Hardcore. And of course, then there's politics, a subject always simmering under the surface here.

LAND & CLIMATE

Maryland describes herself as 'America in Miniature,' but the label could apply to the entire region.

Starting from the east are the windy beaches of the Atlantic Shore and just a bit inland is the Chesapeake Bay, the nation's largest estuary. Bay towns breathe the slow tidal respiration of a land married to water, and if you unfurled the clotted mass of rivers and streams here you'd get a coastline bigger than California's.

Further west the Atlantic coastal plain is studded with farms and suburbs, climbing through rolling hills to the increasingly developed Piedmont Plateau and finally, the hard, beautiful mountains of the Blue Ridge and Shenandoah.

Spring and fall are gorgeous and mild, while summer and winter suffer through thermometer extremes. The humidity of the summer in particular makes DC feel like Hanoi.

PARKS & WILDLIFE

Scenic grandeur here means the Appalachians, best explored from the Shenandoah Valley and West Virginia. The New River Gorge National River (p370) is utterly Edenesque and home to white-tailed deer and black bear. If you're fit enough, try hiking a bit of the Appalachian Trail, which runs through Shenandoah National Park (p362) and George Washington and Jefferson National Forests (p363).

The Chesapeake Bay has a user-friendly, gentle charm: state-run Assateague Island (p340) and federally run Chincoteague Island (p360) are awash with great blue herons, ospreys, blue crabs and wild horses.

Despite there being more than 30 parks in Virginia alone, a lot of protected land here is preserved for historical, rather than environmental properties. That doesn't mean all those old battlefields and houses aren't beautiful though; one of the weird paradoxes of old war sites is how peaceful they are today. Antietam (p340) and Manassas (p347) are particularly good examples of this phenomenon.

INFORMATION

A lot of conventions and conferences are held in this region and they can double or triple lodging prices; it's always best to call ahead. Smoking is banned in bars and clubs in Maryland (as of February, 2008), Delaware and Washington, DC. Some local municipalities in Virginia and West Virginia, and an increasing number of private businesses, are also going smoke free. Businesses that are smoke free in these states are usually clearly marked as such.

GETTING THERE & AROUND

The region is served by three major airports: **Dulles International Airport** (IAD; ☎ 703-572-2700), **Reagan National Airport** (DCA; ☎ 703-417-8000) and **Baltimore-Washington International/Thurgood Marshall Airport** (BWI; ☎ 410-859-7111). **Richmond International Airport** (RIC; ☎ 804-226-3000) is less frequently used. Bus and Amtrak information is under specific cities, while major roads include I-81 through Western Virginia, I-495 (DC Beltway), I-695 (Baltimore Beltway), the East Coast–connecting I-95 and I-66 (DC to Northern Virginia).

Driving distances:

Washington to Baltimore 40 miles.
Washington to Richmond 107 miles.
Wilmington to Virginia Beach 244 miles.

WASHINGTON, DC

First thing's first: DC is not a boring, bureaucratic town.

Think of it more like a funnel for the world's talented and ambitious. It's hard to imagine another American city where so many bright young things are packed together, and while the residents of this town work hard, they play harder. Plus, embassies and international institutions such as the World Bank, to say nothing of an enormous immigrant population, all give this city the spiced edge of cosmopolitanism, packed into a more manageable space than New York City (NYC). Neighborhoods such as U Street and Dupont Circle burst with Type A personalities and ethnic polyglots, and when you set that mix against a DC jazz soundtrack and the country's national symbology, the energy is exhilarating.

The intersections of DC's divides – the intellectual energy of all those think tanks, news bureaus and policy centers, the aristocratic airs of Georgetown, the streetwise cunning of Anacostia – makes for a world city with a distinctive tension. The soaring possibilities of the American dream, and the harsh realities so many dreamers awaken to, play out against a superpower capital made up of neighborhoods that are still cozy enough to care.

Come to the Mall, which symbolizes America's highest hopes, and visit Southeast DC to see her grimmest realities, and experience the warts and all that gives this city – and perhaps the nation it governs – its unique appeal.

HISTORY
Like a lot of American history, the District of Columbia (DC) story is one of compromise. In this case, the balance was struck between Northern and Southern politicians who wanted to plant a federal city between their power bases. As potential capitals such as Boston, Philadelphia and Baltimore were rejected as too urban-industrial by Southern plantation-owners, it was decided a new city would be carved at the 13 colonies' midway point, along the banks of the Potomac River. Maryland and Virginia donated the land (which Virginia took back in the 19th century).

DC was originally run by Congress, was torched by the British during the War of 1812, and lost the south bank slaveport of Alexandria to Virginia in 1846 (when abolition talk was buzzing in the capital). The capital's federally managed status led to what might lightly be called questionable spending priorities, and over the years DC evolved along diverging tracks; as a marbled temple to federal government and residential city for federal employees on the one hand, and an urban ghetto for northbound African Americans and overseas immigrants on the other.

The capitol finally got its own mayor in 1973 (Walter Washington, among the first African American mayors of a major American city). Ever under-funded, today DC residents are taxed like other American citizens, yet lack a voting seat in Congress. The educated upper class is leagues away from the neglected destitute; almost half the population has a university degree, yet a third are functionally illiterate.

ORIENTATION
The capital was designed by two planners to be perfectly navigable. Unfortunately, their urban visions have mashed up against each other. Pierre L'Enfant's diagonal state-named streets share space with Andrew Ellicott's grid (remember: letters go east–west, numbers north–south). On top of that the city is divided into four quadrants with identical addresses in

different divisions – F and 14th NW puts you near the White House, while F and 14th NE puts you near Rosedale Playground.

The lion's share of sites are in the Northwest (NW) quadrant, while the most run-down neighborhoods tend to be in the Southeast (SE). Keep your urban wits about you at night, and be prepared for crowds (and crowds and *crowds*) during events such as the Cherry Blossom Festival. The Potomac River is to your south and west; Maryland lies to the north and east; and the Beltway, the capital ring road, encircles the entire package.

INFORMATION
Bookstores
Chapters (☎ 202-737-5553; 445 11th St NW; ☽ 10am-6:30pm Mon-Fri, 11am-5pm Sat) Hosts some great evenings with authors.
Kramerbooks (☎ 202-387-1400; 1517 Connecticut Ave NW, Dupont Circle; ☽ 7:30am-1am Sun-Thu, 24hr Fri & Sat) Ground zero for the city's hip literati.
Lambda Rising (☎ 202-462-6969; www.lambdarising .com; 1625 Connecticut Ave NW; ☽ 10am-10pm, until midnight Fri & Sat) A landmark gay and lesbian bookstore.
Olsson's (☎ 202-785-1133; 1307 19th St NW; ☽ 10am-10pm Mon-Wed, 10am-10:30pm Thu-Sat, noon-8pm Sun) Beloved neighborhood independent.

Emergency & Medical Services
DC Fire and Emergency Medical Services can also be reached at ☎ 202-673-331.
CVS Pharmacy (☎ 202-785-1466; Massachusetts Ave & 20th St NW; ☽ 24hr)
George Washington University Hospital (☎ 202-715-4000; 901 23rd St NW)

WASHINGTON, DC, FACTS

Nicknames DC, Chocolate City
Population 581,530
Area 68.3 sq miles
Capital city Exactly!
Sales tax 5.75%
Birthplace of Duke Ellington, Marvin Gaye, Dave Chapelle, Al Gore and democracy, baby!
Home of The Redskins, cherry blossoms, all three branches of American government
Famous for National symbols, crime, partying interns, struggle for congressional recognition
Official motto: Justitia Omnibus (Justice for All)
Unofficial motto and license plate slogan: Taxation Without Representation

WASHINGTON, DC

Internet Access

CyberStop Café (☎ 202-234-2470; 1513 17th St NW, Dupont Circle; per hr $8; 🕑 7:30am-midnight Sun-Thu, 7:30am-2am Fri & Sat)

Kramerbooks (☎ 202-387-1400; 1517 Connecticut Ave NW, Dupont Circle; 🕑 7:30am-1am Sun-Thu, 24hr Fri & Sat)

Newsroom & International Language Center

(☎ 202-332-1489; 1753 Connecticut Ave NW; per 15/60min $3/11; 🕑 7am-9pm)

Internet Resources

Online visitor information (www.dcvisit.com)

Media
90.9 WETA-FM National Public Radio (NPR) affiliate.
93.9 WKYS-FM Hip-hop.
101.1 WIYY-FM Rawk.
1050 AM Federal News Radio, for news and policy wonks.
Newsroom & International Language Center
(☎ 202-332-1489; 1753 Connecticut Ave NW; ☿ 7am-9pm) Newspapers from all over are downstairs, plus language books and cassettes upstairs at the language center.
Washington City Paper (www.washingtoncitypaper .com) Free edgy weekly with entertainment and dining listings.
Washington Post (www.washingtonpost.com) Respected daily city (and national) paper. Its tabloid-format daily *Express* is free. Also check washingtonpost.com/cityguide for events listings.

Money
Currency exchange is available at the major airports and during weekday business hours at most banks, as well as **Travelex** (☎ 202-371-9220; Union Station, 50 Massachusetts Ave NE, Gate G booth; ☿ 9am-5pm Mon-Sat, noon-6pm Sun). Also has a location **downtown** (☎ 202-872-1428; 1880 K St NW; ☿ 9am-5pm Mon-Fri).

Post
Post office (2 Massachusetts Ave NE; ☿ 7am-midnight Mon-Fri, until 8pm Sat & Sun)

Tourist Information
DC visitor center (☎ 202-328-4748; Ronald Reagan Bldg, 1300 Pennsylvania Ave NW; ☿ 8am-6pm Mon-Sat summer, shorter hours rest of year) Hotel reservation line and a film which gives an excellent overview of DC.
International Visitors Information Desk (☎ 703-572-2536; ☿ 9am-5pm Mon-Fri) Run by the Meridian International Center, staff at this desk (at the Arrivals Terminal at Washington-Dulles Airport) can answer questions in more than 40 languages.
Washington Convention & Visitors Association (☎ 202-789-7000; www.washington.org; 901 7th St NW, 4th fl, Washington, DC, 20005; ☿ 9am-5pm Mon-Fri)
For travelers with disabilities:
General information (☎ 202-789-7000) On hotels, restaurants and attractions.
Metrorail (☎ 202-635-6434; www.wmata.com)
Smithsonian access (☎ 202-357-2700, TTY 202-357-1729)

SIGHTS
The three 'Ms' – monuments, museums and memorials – are clustered around a fourth: the Mall. The major branches of government are within walking distance of here too. The area around Chinatown also has good museums, while Georgetown, U Street and Dupont Circle are hot spots for ethnic eats, nightlife, shopping and the local gay scene.

National Mall
When someone says 'Washington, DC,' and you think of everything that symbolizes America – white buildings, big flags, Abe Lincoln and a reflecting pool – you're thinking of the National Mall. This is America's great public space, where citizens come to protest their government, chill in the sun, visit museums and soak up collective national symbolism. The 1.9-mile-long lawn is anchored on one end by the Lincoln Memorial, on the other by Capitol Hill, intersected by the reflecting pool and World War II memorial, and centered by the Washington monument.

Perhaps no other symbol has housed the national ideal of massed voice affecting radical change so much – from Martin Luther King's 1963 'I Have a Dream Speech' to anti-globalization protests in the 1990s. But hundreds of other rallies occur here every day; the Mall, framed by great monuments and museums and shot through with tourists, dog-walkers and idealists, acts as loudspeaker for any cause.

SMITHSONIAN INSTITUTION MUSEUMS
As stimulating as a (free!) good book or lecture, if America was a quirky grandfather, this would be his attic. An attic that happens to house a globally prestigious research unit, yes, but an attic nonetheless, where a rotating 1% of a staggering collection – the lunar lander, dinosaurs, great art and relics that weren't looted during the days of Empire (ahem, Europe) – is on display at one time.

Englishman James Smithson (who never came to the USA) willed $4.1 million to the country to found an 'establishment for the increase and diffusion of knowledge' in 1826. Unfortunately, his intellectual baby badly needs (and is receiving) some expensive upkeep. It has been suggested the museums start charging for admission, but the powers-that-be won't hear of it, arguing fees would fly in the face of the Smithsonian's mission. The museums will stay free if it kills them. And it just might. Currently, the **Arts & Industries Museum** (www.si.edu/ai; 900 Jefferson Dr, SW) is closed indefinitely and the **National Museum of**

American History (http://americanhistory.si.edu; 14th St & Constitution Ave, NW) is scheduled to re-open in the summer of 2008.

The red-turreted **Smithsonian Castle** (Smithsonian Institution Building; ☎ 202-357-2700; www.si.edu; 1000 Jefferson Dr SW; ☽ 10am-5pm) is the visitor center for all museums, but not that interesting in and of itself. Be prepared for lines and bag-checks. The following museums are free and open every day but Christmas from 10am to 5:30pm unless otherwise noted. Some have extended hours in summer. Note that not all Smithsonian museums are included here.

A favorite of the kids, the **National Museum of Natural History** (cnr 10th St & Constitution Ave SW) bounces between some sweet dinosaur skeletons, a fantastic archaeology/anthropology collection, the 45-carat Hope diamond and pretty damn near everything else under the sun.

The **National Air & Space Museum** (cnr 6th St & Independence Ave SW) is the most popular Smithsonian museum; everyone flocks to see the Wright brothers' flyer, Chuck Yeager's *Bell X-1*, Charles Lindbergh's *Spirit of St Louis* and the *Apollo 11* command module. An IMAX theater, planetarium and a ride simulator are all here (adult/child $8.50/7 each). Even more avionic goodness is in Virginia at the Steven F Udvar-Hazy Center (p348), an annex to hold this museum's leftovers.

The **National Gallery of Art** (☎ 202-737-4215; www.nga.gov; Constitution Ave btwn 3rd & 4th Sts NW; admission free; ☽ 10am-5pm Mon-Sat, 11am-6pm Sun) is about as cultured as you'll get outside of NYC's Met (with a très IM Pei facade). An underground passage connects the double wings: the original, neoclassical west wing is primarily stuffed with European art from the Middle Ages to the early 20th century, with works by all the greats (including the continent's only da Vinci); the east wing is a little more abstract, a lot more conceptual.

At times a grim summation of human nature, at times a fierce confirmation of basic goodness, the **US Holocaust Memorial Museum** (☎ 202-488-0400; www.ushmm.org; 100 Raoul Wallenberg Pl; ☽ 10am-5pm) is a must-see. The main exhibit (not recommended for under-11s, who can go to a separate, also-free on-site exhibit) gives visitors the identity card of a single Holocaust victim, narrowing the scope of suffering to the individual level while paying thorough, overarching tribute to its powerful subject. Only a limited number of visitors are admitted a day, so come early.

The doughnut-shaped **Hirshhorn Museum & Sculpture Garden** (cnr 7th St & Independence Ave SW; ☽ garden 7:30am until dusk, musuem 10am-5:30pm) houses a huge collection of modern sculpture, rotated regularly, including works by Rodin, Henry Moore and Ron Mueck, as well as paintings by O'Keeffe, Warhol, May Ray and de Kooning.

The **National Museum of African Art** (950 Independence Ave SW) showcases masks, textiles and ceramics from the sub-Sahara, as well as ancient and contemporary art from all over the continent.

Pouring over ancient manuscripts and Japanese silk screens is about as perfect a way to spend an afternoon as any at both the quiet **Arthur M Sackler Gallery** (1050 Independence Ave SW) and the **Freer Gallery of Art** (cnr Jefferson Dr & 12th St SW), which together comprise the National Museum of Asian Art. Slightly incongruously, they are also home to more than1300 works by the American painter James Whistler.

The **National Museum of the American Indian** (cnr 4th St & Independence Ave SW) takes on a little too much and can feel scattered, but it is still worth visiting if you want to learn about America's indigenous people. One absolute success here is the regionally specialized menu of the Native Foods café on the ground floor.

MALL MONUMENTS & ATTRACTIONS
Oldest joke in DC: 'So, what part of Washington is his monument modeled on?' Yeah, that's right, America has a bigger…obelisk than you. Just peaking at 555ft (and 5in), the **Washington Monument** (☎ 202-426-6841; ☽ 9am-4:45pm) is the tallest building in the district. It took two phases of construction to complete; note the different hues of the stone. Tickets are free but must be reserved; or you can order in advance from http://reservations.nps.gov for $1.50. They're available from the **kiosk** (15th St btwn Madison St & Jefferson Dr SW; ☽ 8am-4:30pm).

The following all have free admission unless otherwise noted.

The **Bureau of Engraving & Printing** (☎ 202-874-2330; cnr 14th & C Sts SW; ☽ 9am-2pm Mon-Fri), aka the most glorified print shop in the world, is where all the US paper currency is designed. Some $32 million of it rolls off the presses daily. Get in line early at the ticket kiosk on Raoul Wallenberg Pl.

WASHINGTON, DC, IN...

Two Days

Set the alarm and brew some coffee, son. Head for the **Capitol** (p314), feel the grandeur, then pop into the **Library of Congress** (p314). Now go Smithsonianing: try the **Air & Space Museum** (opposite), **National Museum of Natural History** (opposite) and the **National Museum of the American Indian** (opposite). Wander down the **National Mall** (p311); at the 'bottom,' soak up pride, love and loss at the **Lincoln Memorial** (below) and **Vietnam Veterans Memorial** (below). Hungry? **Dupont Circle** (p321) and **U Street** (p320) are both good for international eats.

Next day, head back to the Mall for the **US Holocaust Memorial Museum** (opposite) and the **Arthur M Sackler Gallery** (opposite) and the **Freer Gallery of Art** (opposite), then see the **National Archives** (p314) and **Reynolds Center for American Art** (p315). Catch the illuminated **White House** (p315) and **FDR Memorial** (p314) at night-time.

Four Days

Time to see the other side of DC: ride out to **Anacostia** (p316) and visit the **Frederick Douglass National Historic Site** (p317) and the **Anacostia Museum & Center for African American History & Culture** (p317). Grab dinner in **Dupont Circle** (p321). On day four pick a site you haven't seen and live la dolce vita in **Georgetown** (p316) and/or **U Street** (p316).

'Poppa Abraham' looks out on the reflecting pool from the **Lincoln Memorial** (☎ 202-426-6895; 24hr), where the inscribed Gettysburg Address speaks to all the potential hopes of a nation that weathered the Civil War.

The **Vietnam Veterans Memorial** (☎ 202-462-6842; southeast of Lincoln Memorial, Constitution Gardens; 24hr) is the opposite of DC's usual white, gleaming marble. Instead it's a black, low-lying 'V', a physical expression of the psychic scar wrought by the Vietnam War. The 58,000 names of dead soldiers chiseled into the dark, reflective wall, scattered with heartfelt left mementos, form the most powerful monument in DC (if not the nation).

The elaborate **Korean War Veterans Memorial** (southwest of Lincoln Memorial, Constitution Gardens; 8am-11:45pm) is centered around a patrol of ghostly steel soldiers marching by a wall of etched faces from that conflict; seen from a distance, the images on the wall form the outline of the Korean mountains.

Occupying one end of the Reflecting Pool (and controversially, the center of the Mall, the only war memorial to have that distinction) the **National WWII Memorial** (17th St btwn Constitution & Independence Aves; 24hr) wants to be (and pretty much is) as stirring as one of the great quotes from that war. Consequently, those quotes are inscribed all over the memorial, which manages to avoid being over the top – just.

DC's oldest art museum, the **Corcoran Gallery** (☎ 202-639-1700; cnr 17th St & New York Ave NW; adult/child under 13 $8/free; 10am-5pm Wed-Sun, until 9pm Thu), has had a tough time standing up to the free, federal competition around the block, but this hasn't stopped it from maintaining one of the most eclectic exhibitions in the country. Two-for-one admission in July and August.

Groundbreaking occurred on the **Martin Luther King Jr National Memorial** in November, 2006, in West Potomac Park. The first Mall monument to an African American is set for completion in 2008. The **Newseum** (www.newseum.org), once located in Rosslyn, VA, is being moved to 555 Pennsylvania Ave. When it reopens in late 2007 it will be the most comprehensive museum in the world dedicated to journalism and journalists.

Capitol Hill

The Capitol, appropriately, sits atop Capitol Hill (what L'Enfant called 'a pedestal waiting for a monument') across a plaza from the almost-as-regal Supreme Court and Library of Congress. Congressional office buildings surround the plaza. A pleasant residential district stretches from E Capitol St to Lincoln Park, but beyond those roads the neighborhood declines. Union Station, Capitol South and Eastern Market metro stations serve this area.

CAPITOL

Impressive Americana at its stately best, the bell of the Capitol Dome fairly screams, 'Hey! Important stuff happens here!' Since 1800, this is where the legislative branch of American government – ie Congress – has met to write the country's laws. The lower House of Representatives (438 members) and upper Senate (100) meet respectively in the south and north wings of the building.

Tours here are free and easy to join, if you're willing to wait in long lines at the temporary **Capitol Service Kiosk** (☎ 202-225-6827; cnr 1st St SW & Maryland Ave SW; ⏰ ticket distribution 9am-3:30pm Mon-Sat). Getting in line by 8am helps your chances of getting a pass. The interior of the building is as daunting as the exterior, if a little cluttered with the busts, statues and personal mementos of generations of congress members.

A huge visitor's center is still under construction (and way over budget) as of this writing, and is expected to open in 2008. To watch Congress in action, call ☎ 202-225-6827 for session dates. US citizens can request visitor passes from their representatives or senators (☎ 202-224-3121); foreign visitors show passports at the House gallery.

LIBRARY OF CONGRESS

To prove to Europeans America was cultured, John Adams plunked the world's largest **library** (☎ exhibitions 202-707-4604; www.loc.gov; 101 Independence Ave SE; admission free; ⏰ 10am-5:30pm Mon-Sat) on Capitol Hill. The LOC's motivation is simple: 'universality,' the idea that all knowledge is useful. Stunning in scope and design, the building's baroque interior and neoclassical flourishes are set off by a Main Reading Room that looks like an ant colony constantly harvesting 29 million books. The visitor center and tours of the reading rooms are both located in the Jefferson Building, just behind the Capitol building.

SUPREME COURT

Even nonlaw students are impressed by the **highest court in America** (☎ 202-479-3211; 1 1st St NE; admission free; ⏰ 9am-4:30pm Mon-Fri). Arrive early to watch arguments (Monday to Wednesday October to April) or bench sittings (Monday mid-May to June). You can visit the permanent exhibits and the building's seven-spiral staircase year-round.

UNION STATION & AROUND

Union Station (☎ 202-371-9441; 50 Massachusetts Ave) greets train visitors to the capital with a gorgeous 1908 beaux arts building; its great hall was modeled on the Roman baths of Diocletian.

Also recommended in this area:

Folger Shakespeare Library (☎ 202-544-7077; 201 E Capitol St; admission free; ⏰ 10am-4pm Mon-Sat) Houses the world's largest collection of Shakespeare materials.

National Postal Museum (☎ 202-633-5555; 2 Massachusetts Ave NE; admission free; ⏰ 10am-5:30pm) Has the planet's largest stamp collection, antique mail plane and touching war letters.

US Botanic Garden (☎ 202-225-8333; 245 1st St SW; admission free; ⏰ 10am-5pm) Hot, sticky, green and enormous: more than 26,000 different species of plants flower here.

Tidal Basin

It's magnificent to stroll around this manmade inlet and watch the monument lights wink across the Potomac, especially during the Cherry Blossom Festival (p319), the city's annual spring rejuvenation, when the basin bursts into a pink and white floral collage. Thanks for the trees, Japanese ambassador from 1912. **Paddleboat rentals** (1501 Maine Ave, SW; 2-person boat per hr $7) are available at the boathouse.

The be-domed **Jefferson Memorial** (☎ 202-426-6822; 900 Ohio Drive, SW, south side of Tidal Basin; admission free; ⏰ 8am-11:45pm), etched with the founding father's most famous writings, might win the 'Best quotes on the inside of a DC memorial' award.

The **FDR Memorial** (Memorial Park; admission free; ⏰ 24hr) is a 7.5-acre tribute to the longest-serving president in US history and the era he governed. In a thoughtful, well-laid-out path, visitors are taken through the Depression, the New Deal–era, and World War II. Best visited at night, when the interplay of rock, fountains and the lights of the Mall are enchanting.

Downtown

Downtown Washington began in what is now called Federal Triangle, but has since spread north and east, encompassing the area east of the White House to Judiciary Sq at 4th St, and from the Mall north to roughly M St. Hours of operation for the attractions below are 10am to 5:30pm daily unless otherwise noted.

It's hard not to feel a little in awe of the big three documents in the **National Archives**

(☎ 202-501-5000; www.archives.gov; 700 Constitution Ave; admission free; ⏰ 10am-9pm summer, until 5:30pm rest of year). The Declaration of Independence, the Constitution and the Bill of Rights, plus one of four copies of the Magna Carta: taken together, it becomes clear just how radical the American experiment was for its time. The Public Vaults, a bare scratching of archival bric-a-brac, are a flashy rejoinder to the main exhibit – and speaking of which, do *not* use the flash on your camera here.

Don't miss the **Reynolds Center for American Art** (☎ 202-275-1500; cnr F St & 8th St NW; http://reynoldscenter .org; admission free), which combines the **National Portrait Gallery** with the **American Art Museum**. From haunting depictions of the inner city and rural heartland to the self-taught visions of itinerant wanderers, the center has dedicated itself to capturing the relentless optimism and critical self-appraisal of American art, and succeeds in a big way.

You like those bits in the Bond movies with Q? Then you'll like the immensely popular **International Spy Museum** (☎ 202-393-7798; www .spymuseum.org; 800 F St NW; adult/child 6-11 $16/13; ⏰ 10am-6pm, slightly longer during summer and weekends); all the undercover tools-of-the-trade on display make this place great for (secret) history buffs. Get there early. Hours change seasonally, so it's best to check online or call first.

Devoted to the architectural arts, the under-appreciated **National Building Museum** (☎ 202-272-2448; www.nbm.org; 401 F St NW; donations accepted; ⏰ 10am-5pm Mon-Sat, from 11am Sun) is appropriately housed in an architectural jewel: the 1887 Old Pension Building. Four stories of ornamented balconies flank the dramatic 316ft-wide atrium, and the gold-colored Corinthian columns rise 75ft high. The various permanent and rotating exhibits on different aspects of architecture are sequestered in rooms off the atrium.

The **Science Museum of the National Academy of Sciences** (☎ 202-334-1201; cnr 6th & E Sts; adult/child 5-18 $5/3) is a big, kid-friendly complex of hands-on, educational fun.

The red-carpeted entrance and dignified Grand Salon of **Renwick Gallery** (☎ 202-357-2700; cnr 17th St & Pennsylvania Ave NW; admission free) is crammed with 19th-century paintings – a startling contrast to the wild, whimsical craftwork in the adjoining rooms. Worth a visit just for Wendell Castle's *Ghost Clock*.

Grub out at the sweet international food court in the **Old Post Office Pavilion** (☎ 202-298-

4224; 1100 Pennsylvania Ave NW; admission free; ⏰ 10am-8pm Mon-Sat, noon-7pm Sun Mar-Aug, 10am-7pm Mon-Sat, noon-6pm Sun Sep-Feb), which also happens to be an elegant 1899 Romanesque revival landmark. The 400ft observation tower gives great downtown panoramas.

On April 14, 1865, John Wilkes Booth assassinated Abraham Lincoln in his box seat at **Ford's Theatre** (☎ 202-638-2941; 511 10th St). The theater still operates today, with its threadbare basement **Lincoln Museum** (admission free; ⏰ 9am-5pm) devoted to the assassination. Across the street, **Peterson House** (516 10th St, NW; admission free; ⏰ 9am-5pm) is where Lincoln gave up the ghost the next morning.

White House & Foggy Bottom

An expansive park called the Ellipse borders the Mall; on the east side is the power-broker block of Pennsylvania Ave. Foggy Bottom was named for the mists that belched out of a local gas works; now, as the home of the State Department and George Washington University, it's an upscale (if not terribly lively) 'hood crawling with students and professionals.

WHITE HOUSE

You can practically hear the theme to the *West Wing* as you walk by 1600 Pennsylvania Ave, and at night, the grounds are so stately you'll want to snap off a salute. The White House has survived both fire (freakin' Brits) and expansions in its day. Jacqueline Kennedy redecorated with her stylish touch, Franklin Roosevelt added a pool, Clinton a jogging track and George W Bush a T-ball field. Cars can no longer pass the White House on Pennsylvania Ave, clearing the area for posing school groups and round-the-clock peace activists.

A self-guided **tour** (☎ 202-456-7041; ⏰ 7:30am-noon Tue-Sat) will lead you through the ground and 1st floors, but the 2nd and 3rd ones are off-limits. Unfortunately these tours are only available to groups of 10 or more and need to be arranged months in advance. Americans must apply via one of their state's members of Congress, and non-Americans must apply through either the US consulate in their home country or their country's consulate in DC. If that sounds like too much work, pop into the **White House visitor center** (☎ 202-208-1631; www.whitehouse.gov; Chamber of Commerce Bldg, Cnr of 15th & E; ⏰ 7:30am-4pm); it's not the real deal, but hey, there's executive paraphernalia scattered about.

The riverfront **Watergate complex** (2650 Virginia Ave NW) encompasses apartments, boutiques, and the office towers that made 'Watergate' a byword for political scandal after it broke that President Nixon's 'plumbers' had bugged the headquarters of the 1972 Democratic National Committee.

Adams Morgan, Shaw & U Street

If it's not party time in Adams Morgan, it's time to get a hangover-cure lunch from an Ethiopian or Central American diner. This multi-ethnic neighborhood (especially 18th St) becomes sin central on weekend nights. The area isn't easily metro-accessible; try and catch the bus 98 that runs between Adams Morgan and U Street Metro stations.

To the east, Shaw stretches from around Thomas Circle to Meridian Hill Park and from N Capitol St to 15th St NW. Best known for its African American heritage, back in the 1930s the **Lincoln Theatre** (☎ 202-328-6000; 1215 U St NW) was a high point on the 'chitlin' circuit' of African American entertainment, hosting celebrities such as DC native Duke Ellington. Following the 1968 assassination of Martin Luther King Jr riots devastated the commercial district. This area has since undergone a renaissance (and recently, gentrification) and in the process some excellent restaurants and bars have cropped up.

Dupont Circle

A well-heeled splice of gay community and DC diplomatic scene, this is city life at its best. Great restaurants, bars, bookstores, cafés, captivating architecture and the electric energy of a lived-in, happening neighborhood make Dupont worth a linger. The local historic mansions have largely been converted into embassies, and Embassy Row (on Massachusetts Ave), runs through DC's thumping gay heart.

The **Phillips Collection** (☎ 202-387-2151; 1600 21st St NW; free Tue-Fri, special exhibitions vary; ⏱ 10am-5pm Tue-Sat, until 8:30pm Thu summer, 11am-6pm Sun) was the first modern-art museum in the country; its main draw is whatever the special exhibition happens to be at the moment. Always first-rate.

Rotating exhibits on worldwide expeditions are found at the **National Geographic Society's Explorer Hall** (☎ 202-857-7588; 1145 17 St NW; admission free; ⏱ 9am-5pm Mon-Sat, from 10am Sun).

Know your warp from your woof? Set in a quiet neighborhood, the oft-overlooked **Textile Museum** (☎ 202-667-0441; 2320 S St NW; requested donation $5; ⏱ 10am-5pm Mon-Sat, from 1pm Sun) is the country's only museum devoted to the textile arts.

Georgetown

Georgetown is so damn regal it doesn't need public transportation. No, seriously, the metro doesn't stop here, but thousands of the bright and beautiful, from Georgetown students to ivory tower academics to diplomats call this leafy, aristocratic neighborhood home. At night, shop-a-block M St becomes congested with traffic, turning into a weird mix of high school cruising night and high street boutique.

Get a historical overview from the **visitor center** (☎ 202-653-5190; 1057 Thomas Jefferson St NW; ⏱ 8:30am-5pm Wed-Sun Apr-Nov). Costumed guides lead visitors on a history-intensive, hour-long, mule-driven barge trip along the **C&O Canal towpath** (adult/child $8/5).

The museum featuring exquisite Byzantine and pre-Columbian art housed within the historic mansion at **Dumbarton Oaks** (☎ 202-339-6401; R & 31st Sts NW) should be open when you read this, plus its 10 acres of outstanding formal **gardens** (adult/child $7/5 Apr-Oct, free Nov-Mar; ⏱ 2-6pm Tue-Sun).

Bill Clinton went to school at **Georgetown University** (☎ 202-687-5055; 37th & O Sts), which should give you an idea of the student body: smart, hard-working party people.

The **Potomac Heritage National Scenic Trail** connects Chesapeake Bay to the Allegheny Highlands in a 700-mile corridor. It includes the C&O Canal towpath, the 17-mile Mt Vernon Trail (Virginia), and the 75-mile Laurel Highlands Trail (Pennsylvania). See opposite for bike-rental information.

Anacostia

The drive from Georgetown to Anacostia takes about 30 minutes and the patience to endure a world of income disparity. The neighborhood's smack-crack-and-brick row houses sitting mere miles from the Mall form one of DC's great contradictory panoramas, yet strong communities persist. More tourists may start arriving on the first day of the baseball season in 2008, when Nationals Stadium is set to open, bringing with it no-doubt double-edged gentrification. The impact of renovation dollars can already be seen at some spruced-up intersections.

Freedom fighter and man of letters Frederick Douglass' home is now the **Frederick Douglass National Historic Site** (☎ 202-426-5960; 1411 W St SE; admission free; ☺ 9am-4pm). Despite a god-awfully cheesy intro movie, the on-site rangers are fantastically helpful, and the house, with its commanding view over crumbling Anacostia, speaks to the heights black America has reached and the wide gaps it has left to bridge.

The Smithsonian's **Anacostia Museum & Center for African American History & Culture** (☎ 202-287-3307; 1901 Fort Pl SE; ☺ 10am-5pm) is surrounded by the community that is the subject of its educational mission. Call ahead, as the museum closes for about a month between its excellent, rotating installations.

Around Washington, DC

While plenty of DC buildings take a leaf from the 'inspire reverent awe' school of design, they're rarely religious in nature (unless you consider patriotism a religion). The gothic **Washington National Cathedral** (☎ 202-537-6200; www.cathedral.org; cnr Massachusetts & Wisconsin Aves; admission free; ☺ 10am-5:30pm Mon-Sat, 8am-6:30pm Sun), as hushed and overwhelming as its European counterparts, breaks this rule. It's officially Episcopal, but serves as the 'national house of prayer for all people,' and is a common venue for First Family weddings and the like. The Bishop's Garden and the gargoyle tour are recommended. Fees vary.

ACTIVITIES

Under the auspices of the National Park Service (NPS), **Rock Creek Park's** 1755 acres follow Rock Creek as it winds through the northwest of the city. There's miles of bicycling, hiking and horseback-riding trails, and even a few coyotes. The C&O Canal offers bicycling and hiking trails in canal-side parks and the lovely 11-mile **Capital Crescent Trail** (www.cctrail.org) connects Georgetown north to Silver Spring, MD, via some splendid Potomac River views. By 2008, the **Metropolitan Branch Trail** (www.metbranchtail.com), an 8-mile trail that runs from Silver Spring to Union Station, is set to be complete. DC segments will hopefully beautify some northeastern neighborhoods and provide bridges over dangerous intersections. Fifteen miles north of DC, **Great Falls National**

Park (www.nps.gov/grfa) is a fairly outstanding slice of wilderness, great for rafting or rock climbing some of the beautiful cliffs that hang over the Potomac. Should you want to get some angling in, the boys at **G & S Bait Shop** (☎ 202-546-8163; 421 Morse St NE) can probably help you.

Thompson Boat Center (☎ 202-333-9543; cnr Virginia Ave & Rock Creek Parkway NW) at the Potomac River end of Rock Creek Park rents canoes (per hour $8), tandem kayaks (per hour $10) and bikes (per day $25). **Big Wheel Bikes** (☎ 202-337-0254; 1034 33rd St; per hr/day $7/35; ☺ 11am-7pm Tue-Fri, 10am-6pm Sat & Sun) is also a good bike-rental outfitter. The guys at the **Washington Area Frisbee Club** (www.wafc.org) are always looking for unwitting volunteers to join their madness – trust us, you haven't played Ultimate till you've played it on the National Mall. Finally, DC does have some active **Hash House Harriers**; hook up at www.dchashing.org or www.whitehousehash.com and go on, on, on.

WASHINGTON, DC, FOR CHILDREN

Museums around the city will entertain and educate children of all ages. But if you – or they – tire of indoor attractions, there are plenty of parks and playgrounds such as the **Guy Mason Playground** (3600 Calvert St NW) off Wisconsin Ave.

Many hotels offer babysitting services, but here are a few independent agencies:
Bring Along the Children (☎ 202-484-0889) Offers day and evening babysitting services and kid-oriented tours.
Mothers' Aides (☎ 703-250-0700, 800-526-2669; www.mothersaides.com)

The Mall

The wide-open spaces of the Mall are perfect for outdoor family fun, whether you want to throw a Frisbee, have a picnic, ride the world's oldest **carousel** (tickets $2) or stroll through museums.

Kids like things that go squish and/or make other things go squish, and can find both in the dinosaurs and insects of the National Museum of Natural History (p312). The John F Kennedy Center for the Performing Arts (p324) puts on entertaining shows for tots, and the National Air & Space Museum (p312), has moon rocks, IMAX films and a wild simulation ride.

The **Discovery Theater** (☎ 202-357-1500; www.discoverytheater.org; 1010 Jefferson Dr; tickets $5; ☺ performances 10am & 11:30am Jan-Jul), in the basement

WASHINGTON, DC & THE CAPITAL REGION

OFFBEAT WASHINGTON, DC

Father Karras tumbled to his cinematic death down the staircase nowadays referred to as the **Exorcist Steps** (3600 Prospect St, Georgetown).

Those of timid stock better stick to the amputation kits and the bullet that killed Lincoln on display at the **National Museum of Health & Medicine** (☎ 202-782-2200; 6900 Georgia Ave at Elder St NW; admission free; ☺ 10am-5:30pm), which remains open while its exhibits are moved to Bethesda, MD. The rest of us will be staring in horrified fascination at jars of elephantitis-stricken legs, conjoined twins and megacolons.

The **Awakening** is a spectacular statue of a man climbing out of the ground. His giant head, arm, knee and foot have delighted visitors for years. In 2007 the trapped giant finally freed himself when he was moved to National Harbor, a waterfront development project in Maryland 8 miles south of the city. From his new harbor home, developers say the giant will be clawing his way out of the banks of the Potomac.

In Anacostia, the **world's largest chair** towers over Martin Luther King Ave and V St.

The **Albert Einstein monument** (cnr Constitution Ave & 21st St NW) on the lawn of the National Academy of Sciences is a little-known statue of the frumpy physicist. His lap just begs to be climbed onto.

You may need binoculars to spot it, but that is indeed **Darth Vader's Head** on the west tower of the National Cathedral (p317). Luke's dad shares space with a pig-tailed girl, a raccoon and an umbrella-toting man, all designs sent in by children during a cathedral-sponsored contest in the 1980s.

of the Ripley Center, stages magical theatrical performances.

The National Theatre (p324) offers free Saturday-morning performances from puppet shows to tap dancers (reservations required).

The **National Children's Museum** (☎ 202-675-4120; L'Enfant Plaza, cnr D St & 9th St SW) will reopen its expanded doors in 2009.

Off the Mall

The **National Zoological Park** (☎ 202-357-2700; 3000 Connecticut Ave NW; admission free; ☺ 6am-8pm Apr 6–Oct 25, until 6pm Oct 26–Apr 5) is home to some 2000 species in natural habitats. Resident celebrities include the giant pandas Mei Xiang, Tian Tian and their enormously popular (and cute) son Tai Shan, who will remain in America until at least July 2009.

Through the **Saturday Medieval Workshop** (☎ 202-537-2934) at the Washington National Cathedral (p317) kids and parents can try their hand at making gargoyles, stained glass and limestone carvings.

Located about 15 miles east of downtown in Largo, MD, **Six Flags America** (☎ 301-249-1500; adult/child over 3 $40/29; ☺ May-Oct) offers a full array of roller coasters and tamer kiddie rides.

GAY & LESBIAN WASHINGTON, DC

Home to more than 30 national gay and lesbian organizations and more than 300 social, athletic, religious and support groups, DC is one of the most gay-friendly cities in the USA. The community is most visible in Dupont Circle and Capitol Hill. Washington is often the scene of huge gay rights marches, and gay pride is an integral part of DC's character. Although the African American community is more conservative towards gay issues, DC remains a major center for gay, black America.

Dupont Circle is by far the city's most gay-friendly neighborhood, offering the bulk of the city's nightlife options. The club and bar scene on Pennsylvania Ave SE and around Capitol Hill is easily reached by the Eastern Market Metro station. In Dupont Circle, Lambda Rising (p307) is the landmark gay and lesbian bookstore.

For places to get your club on, see the boxed text, p323.

TOURS

Bike the Sites (☎ 202-966-8662; www.bikethesites.com; adult/child under 13 $40/30; ☺ Mar-Nov) The three-hour 'Capital sites' tour is a favorite with families.

Scandal Tours (☎ 202-783-7212, 800-758-8687; www.gnpcomedy.com/ScandalTours.html; tickets $27; ☺ 1pm Sat Apr-Sep) Run by comedy troupe Gross National Product, it dishes all the gossip about DC's infamous spots, covering George Washington to George Dubya.

Tourmobile Sightseeing (☎ 202-554-5100, 888-868-7707; www.tourmobile.com) An open-air trolley runs daily between the major sights. Tons of theme tours are offered, including the spectacular 'Washington by Night' (adult/child $20/10).

FESTIVALS & EVENTS

National Cherry Blossom Festival (☎ 202-547-1500; www.nationalcherryblossomfestival.org) Held late March to early April. At her prettiest.

Smithsonian's Folklife Festival (☎ 202-357-2700; www.folklife.si.edu) This fun family event, held over two weekends in June and July, features distinctive regional folk art, crafts, food and music.

Independence Day Not surprisingly a big deal here, celebrated on July 4 with the best freakin' fireworks ever.

SLEEPING

Washington DC Accommodations (☎ 800-503-3330; www.wdcahotels.com) provides assistance with lodging. For B&Bs citywide, contact **Bed & Breakfast Accommodations** (☎ 877-893-3233; www.bedandbreakfastdc.com).

Budget

Washington International Student Center (☎ 202-667-7681; www.washingtondchostel.com; 2451 18th St NW; dm $24; 🔀 wi-fi) Well-located in the heart of Adams Morgan, this hostel is back after getting gutted by fire. Decent dorms.

HI Washington DC (☎ 202-737-2333; www.hiwashingtondc.org; 1009 11th St NW at K St; dm incl breakfast members/nonmembers $32/35; 🔀 🖳) If you're looking for an enormous (ie 270-room), friendly hostel full of fun, young international types, look no further then this budget institution.

Kalorama Guest House (☎ 202-667-6369; www.kaloramaguesthouse.com; 1854 Mintwood Pl NW; s $50-95, d $55-100, ste $100-140; P 🔀) They're a bit strict on the rules in reception, and you better like climbing stairs, but there's no doubting this is the sort of Victorian, sherry-serving place people love to deem 'quaint.' Adams Morgan's nightlife (decidedly not 'quaint') is minutes away. Parking is $15.

Midrange

Adam's Inn (☎ 202-745-3600; www.adamsinn.com; 1746 Lanier Pl, NW; r $99-140; P 🔀 🖳) It can be a struggle to get eye contact, let alone one-on-one service in DC, but this townhouse B&B provides all of the above, plus fluffy linens and a central location.

Jury's Washington Hotel (☎ 202-483-6000; 1500 New Hampshire Ave NW; r from $160; P 🔀 🖳 wi-fi) Jury's tries to be a little more buttoned-down than the glamorous embassy row it sits near, but

it can't help it: little flairs of extravagance just bubble up, from well-trained attentive staff to the bright, marble lobby. Parking is $20.

our pick Hotel Helix (☎ 800-706-1202, 202-462-9001; www.hotelhelix.com; 1430 Rhode Island Ave NW; r from $180; P 🔀 🖳 wi-fi) Modish and hi-liter bright, the Helix is playfully cool – the perfect hotel for the bouncy international set that makes up the surrounding neighborhood of Dupont Circle. Little touches suggest a youthful energy (Pop Rocks in the minibar) balanced with worldly cool, like the pop-punk decor – just camp enough to be endearing. Parking is $27.

Top End

Morrison-Clark Inn (☎ 202-898-1200; www.morrisonclark.com; 1015 L St NW; r from $200; P 🔀 wi-fi) The only hotel in town on the Register of Historic Places, this elegant inn has spacious rooms ranging from Victorian to neoclassical. Some come decked out with private balconies and marble fireplaces. Parking is $25.

Hotel Rouge (☎ 202-232-8000; www.rougehotel.com; 1315 16th St NW; r from $200; P 🔀 🖳 wi-fi) Rouge tries very hard to be very cool and very red. The Crimson and white rooms allow you to 'Chow' (at a stainless steel kitchenette), 'Chat' (flat-screen TV and computer with internet access) or 'Chill' (PlayStation2). Should you like to 'Sleep,' the hip, red-pleather-head-boarded beds, are perfectly serviceable. Parking costs $27.

Hotel Palomar (☎ 202-448-1800; www.hotelpalomar-dc.com; 2121 P St NW; r from $200; P 🔀 🖳 wi-fi) Everything seems to bend here: from the staff to your every whim to the modernist lines of the Palomar's decor, a sleekly shaped black-white-and-purple color scheme set off by sinuous furniture and lighting fixtures. Talk about stylish spoiling. Parking is $32.

Hotel Monaco (☎ 202-628-7177, 800-649-1202; www.monaco-dc.com; 700 F St NW; r from $239; P 🔀 wi-fi) The neoclassical facade has aged with considerable grace at this marble temple to stylish glamour. Free goldfish on request and a geometric, deco-inspired interior helps polish the 1930s, cool-daddy-o vibe. Parking costs $34.

Hotel Washington (☎ 202-638-5900, 800-424-9540; www.hotelwashington.com; cnr 15th St & Pennsylvania Ave; r from $300; P 🔀 wi-fi) The Washington is a grand old dame, but she's managed to accessorize (think webTV) without losing her dignity. Depending on your taste you'll find standard rooms cozy or cramped. The city's oldest continuously operating hotel is just around the corner from the White House, and its rooftop restaurant has one of the best views in town. Parking is $29.

Mandarin Oriental Hotel (☎ 202-554-8588; www .madarinoriental.com/washington; 1330 Maryland Ave SW; r from $405; P ⊠ ⊠ wi-fi) This enormous luxury complex generates a lot of buzz, and when it's on, the latest offering in the Mandarin chain is spot on: a taste of decadent self-spoiling that would satisfy a Czar on an expense account. But the Mandarin isn't always on. A gracious concierge may be off-set by a brusque front desk, and the tucked away location keeps you from walking to the city itself. If you don't mind being isolated in an expensive resort, come here, but don't expect to feel the capital at your fingertips. Parking costs $39.

EATING

As you might expect of one of the world's most international cities, DC has an eclectic palette. No one culture defines its menu, although Southern Americans, Ethiopians, Asians and Latinos all try.

Capitol Hill

Eastern Market (225 7th St SE; ⊗ 10am-6pm Tue-Fri, 8am-6pm Sat, 8am-4pm Sun) Great market, great produce, great deals – what more do you want? A fire badly damaged the market in 2007, and as of this writing most vendors are either selling their goods outside the market building or in Hine Junior High School, just across the street.

Dubliner (☎ 202-737-3773; 520 N Capitol St NW; mains $7-10; ⊗ 7am-2am Mon-Thu, 7am-3am Fri, 7:30am-3am Sat, 7:30am-2am Sun) Yes, it's the same dark-wood-paneled Irish pub you see everywhere (except Ireland), but this one is stuffed with ambitious interns blabbing about their bosses proclivities mere feet from the Capitol. Also, the pub grub is excellent.

Johnny's Half Shell (☎ 202-737-0400; 400 N Capitol St NW; lunch mains $10-16, dinner mains $18-26; ⊗ 7am-10pm Mon-Fri, 4:30-10pm Sat) Johnny's is good for classic steak and seafood fare but its main draw is engaging in DC's version of celebrity spotting – ie watching power-lunching senators and congressmen from next door.

Downtown & White House Area

Zaytinya (☎ 202-638-0800; 701 9th St NW; mezzes $4-10; ⊗ 11:30am-11:30pm Tue-Thu, until 10pm Sun & Mon, until midnight Fri & Sat) Good-looking waitstaff serve good-looking clientele Greek, Lebanese and Turkish meze (tapas by a fancier name) against a sleek, spacious white, brown and Hellenic blue backdrop.

Full Kee (☎ 202-371-2233; 509 H St NW; mains from $6; ⊗ 11am-2am, until 3am Sat & Sun) As pretty as a communist cafeteria with service to match, Full Kee remains one of the best-value Chinese places in DC. Everything is good, but the salty, crispy-skinned duck and glistening roast pork is flat-out spectacular.

Burma Restaurant (☎ 202-347-8396; 740 6th St NW; mains from $10; ⊗ 11am-3pm Mon-Fri, 6-10pm daily) Actually, the cuisine is more Shan, but since no one knows the difference and the food is still great, who cares? The mango pork is reason alone to revel in this mortal coil.

Jaleo (☎ 202-628-7949; 480 7th St NW; tapas $6-10, dinner mains $16; ⊗ 11:30am-11:30pm Tue-Thu, until 10pm Sun & Mon, until midnight Fri & Sat) The whole tapas thing has been done to death, but Jaleo helped start the trend in DC and still serves some of the best Spanish cuisine in town. The interior is an Iberian pastiche of explosive color and vintage mural-dom, which all underlines, rather than overpowers, the quality of the excellent food.

Zola (☎ 202-654-0999; 800 F St NW; lunch mains $10-23, dinner mains $16-25; ⊗ 11:30am-3pm Mon-Fri, plus 5-10pm daily, until later Fri & Sat) A playful espionage theme is carried through into the International Spy Museum restaurant, with peepholes into the kitchen and Russian documents on the walls. The lobster mac-and-cheese is worth killing for.

our pick **Georgia Brown's** (☎ 202-393-4499; 950 15th St NW; mains $16-32; ⊗ 11:30am-10pm Mon-Fri, 5-10pm Sat, 10am-2:15pm & 5-9:30pm Sun) Georgia Brown's treats the humble ingredients of the American South (shrimp, okra, red rice, grits and sausage) with the respect great French chefs give their provincial dishes. The result is consistently excellent regional American cuisine: high-class Southern food from the Carolina Lowcountry served in a warm, autumnal interior.

Adams Morgan, Shaw & U Street

Julia's Empanadas (☎ 202-328-6232; 2452 18th St NW; empanadas $3; ⊗ 10:30am-10:30pm Mon-Thu, until 8pm Sun, until 4am Fri & Sat) In Europe, you soak up your beer with a kabob. Here, you go to Julia's, where the Salvadoran owner/namesake still rolls out meat-and-cheesy pocket pastries that go down great even when you're stone-cold sober.

Florida Avenue Grill (☎ 202-265-1586; 1100 Florida Ave NW; mains $4-7; ☯ 8am-9pm Tue-Sat, until 4:30pm Sun) Your stomach will thank you, even if your heart decides to pack it in after feasting on the Grill's Southern standards of fried catfish and collard greens. This joint's been raking 'em in since 1944 and has the celebrity photos and neighborhood loyalty to prove it.

Ben's Chili Bowl (☎ 202-667-0909; 1213 U St NW; mains $4-8; ☯ 11am-2am Mon-Thu, until 4am Fri & Sat, noon-8pm Sun) Every night the lines stretch around the block from this institution, known as much for its welcoming atmosphere as its excellent food. Go for a half-smoke, DC's (better) version of your hot dog slathered in cheese and (what else?) chili.

Mixtec (☎ 202-797-1819; 1792 Columbia Rd NW; mains $5-10; ☯ 9am-10pm Sun-Thu, 10am-11pm Fri & Sat) Budget Mexican that eschews the taco/burrito/enchilada drabness of the genre, Mixtec is justifiably popular with Anglos and Latinos. The moles are freshly prepared, the meat authentically spiced (rumors say they use more than 200 seasonings) and the huevos rancheros are a great hangover cure.

Pasta Mia (☎ 202-328-9114; 1790 Columbia Rd NW; mains $10-15; ☯ 6:30-10pm Mon-Sat) Even cold weather doesn't deter the faithful from lining up for their turn at affordable, monstrously portioned Italian on checkered tablecloths. No reservations or line-jumping bribes accepted.

Reef (☎ 202-518-3800; 2446 18th St NW; dishes $10-16; ☯ from 4pm) If the name hasn't tipped you off, the giant fish tanks will – seafood stars on this slim, organic menu. Many folks come (or stay) to drink, zoned out in front of the tanks or reveling at the rooftop bar.

Oohs & Aahs (☎ 202-668-8735; 1005 U St NW; mains $10-17; ☯ 12:30-10pm Tue-Sat) Oohs & Aahs is making a strong bid for Soul Food crown of Shaw and U Street. It has hiked its prices recently, but it's still worth a stop for gut-busting amounts of traditional African American cuisine: fried chicken, BBQ, and obscenely good mac-and-cheese.

Meskerem (☎ 202-462-4100; 2434 18th St NW; mains $10-20; ☯ noon-midnight Sun-Thu, until 3am Fri & Sat) A stand-by of the local Ethiopian scene, Meskerem is three floors of communal eating goodness smack in the African heart of Adams Morgan.

Coppi's Organic (☎ 202-319-7773; 1414 U St NW; mains $12-24; ☯ 6-11pm Mon-Thu, 5pm-midnight Fri & Sat, 5-10pm Sun) One of the pioneers of the rebirth of U Street, this boisterous, bicycle-themed spot serves wood-fired pizza and calzones. Mercifully, half-portions are available.

Dupont Circle

our pick Bistro Du Coin (☎ 202-234-6969; 1738 Connecticut Ave NW; mains $8-24; ☯ 11:30am-11pm Tue, Wed & Sun, 11:30am-1am Thu-Sat) *Mon dieu!* Bistro has a reputation for serving roll-up-your-sleeves, American-sized portions of rustic French favorites such as *steak-frites* (grilled steak and French fries), cassoulet, rabbit stew, and tureens of its famous *moules* (mussels). This place is always packed, usually with happy European diplomats and other Old World expats.

Dakota Cowgirls (☎ 202-232-7010; 1337 14th St NW; mains $10-14; ☯ 11am-10:30pm Sun-Thu, 10:30am-midnight Fri-Sat) 'Gay-camp, Western, awesome burgers' aren't five words generally used in the same sentence, but all of the above come together at this rollicking homage to cowboys, kitsch and some of the best meat between two buns in town.

Afterwords (☎ 202-387-1400; 1517 Connecticut Ave NW; mains $12-16; ☯ 7:30am-1am Sun-Thu, 24hr Fri & Sat) Not your average bookstore café, this spot attached to Kramerbooks will stimulate your palate as much as the novel you just bought stimulates your mind.

Viridian (☎ 202-462-8999; www.viridianrestaurant .com; 1515 14th St NW; mains $14-32; ☯ 5:30-11pm) A little bit art gallery, a lot bit sleek proponent of New American cuisine, Viridian likes to pump itself as DC's 'Green Restaurant.' Whatever; the seasonal menu (with great vegetarian and vegan options) and locally sourced ingredients are fantastic, as is (generally) the art on display in the dining area.

Georgetown

Quick Pita (☎ 202-338-7482; 1210 Potomac St NW; mains $3-7; ☯ 11am-2:30am Sun-Thu, until 4:30am Fri & Sat) Do like the Georgetown students and come here to watch the counter guys curse each other in Arabic and serve up late-night ecstasy – oh, the falafel and cheese fries, yeessss…

Martin's Tavern (☎ 202-333-7370; 1264 Wisconsin Ave NW; lunch mains $8-15, dinner mains $12-27; ☯ from 11:30am) Martin's is a favorite with Georgetown students and US presidents, who all enjoy the old-school darkened dining room and quite possibly the best cheeseburger in town.

Cafe Milano (☎ 202-333-6183; 3251 Prospect St NW; mains $17-35; ☯ from 11:30am) Slip on your best see-and-be-seen duds before snagging a sidewalk table at this Italian bistro, with homemade ravioli that melts on the tongue and more delicious ways to prepare mushrooms than you can imagine.

DRINKING & ENTERTAINMENT

See the Washington City Paper or Washington Post weekend section (p311) for comprehensive listings. Conveniently located at the Old Post Office Pavilion, **Ticketplace** (☎ 202-842-5387; www.ticketplace.org; 1100 Pennsylvania Ave, NW; 11am-6pm Tue-Fri, 10am-5pm Sat) sells same-day concert and show tickets at half-price.

Unless noted, closing time is 2am weekdays, 3am weekends.

Bars & Clubs

CAPITOL HILL & DOWNTOWN

Hawk & Dove (☎ 202-543-3300; 329 Pennsylvania Ave SE; from 10am) The quintessential Capitol Hill bar is a hot spot for political junkies with intimate corner booths perfect for sipping pints and creating the next District scandal.

Pour House (☎ 202-546-1001; 319 Pennsylvania Ave SE; from 4pm Mon-Fri, from 11am Sat & Sun) This rowdy sports bar attracts off-shift Hillies when they're ready to doff their suits, don their baseball caps and yell obscenities at a staggering amount of blaring TV screens.

ADAMS MORGAN, SHAW & U STREET

Busboys & Poets (☎ 202-387-7638; 2021 14th St NW; 8am-midnight Mon-Thu, 10am-2:30am Fri & Sat, 10am-midnight Sun; wi-fi) Leftie-sensible bookstores cum coffee houses cum wi-fi centers are often silly cliches of themselves, which is why the ones that get the formula right, like Busboys, are so damn refreshing. It's just a genuine joy to sit here, write your novel and sip a fine macchiato. Has frequent readings and open mike nights.

Café Saint-Ex (☎ 202-265-7839; 1847 14th St NW; 11am-1:30am Tue-Fri, from 5pm Mon, 11am-2:30am Sat & Sun) Nurse a pint of Belgian-style ale at a sidewalk table or inside, where photographs of pilot and *Little Prince* author Antoine de Saint-Exupery smile down at you. Downstairs, the intimate Gate 54 is frequently the scene of live jazz and its funky derivatives.

Tryst (☎ 202-232-5500; 2459 18th St; from 6:30am Mon-Sat, 8am-12:30am Sun; wi-fi) The hodgepodge of tables and cozy sofas at this Greenwich Village–style coffeehouse–lizard lounge harbors patrons so faithful they should probably pay rent. There's wi-fi, but surfing's a no-no on weekend nights – you should be striking up a conversation with that cute stranger next to you anyway.

Chi-Cha Lounge (☎ 202-234-8400; 1624 U St NW; from 5:30pm) Slip through the double-sided mirror door, settle into a low settee and order up a hookah of fruit-flavored tobacco. In the midst of this Middle Eastern atmosphere, the trendy clientele is nibbling Ecuadorian tapas and sipping Peruvian drinks.

Tom Tom (☎ 202-518-6667; 2335 18th St NW; from 6pm Mon-Sat, from 1pm Sun) Need a meat market? Try this slaughterhouse, with its split-level, dark blue dance floor packed with DC locals, drunk interns and the international set, all trying not to slip on their sweating hormones.

Tabaq (☎ 202-265-0965; 1336 U St NW; 5pm-1am Tue-Thu & Sun, until 2:30am Fri & Sat) The top floor of this resto-club, with its glass walls and sweeping views of surrounding U Street, has the cold, clean lines of a Scandinavian lounge and the hedonistic vibe of a Greek island.

Madam's Organ (☎ 202-667-5370; 2461 18th St NW; cover weekday/weekend $3/5; 5pm-2am Sun-Thu, until 3am Fri & Sat) The Organ is a well-loved stand-by (*Playboy* named it one of the best bars in the country) and still one of the rowdiest, sweatiest, All-American-iest joints to catch some power blues, power rock and power shots.

Bukom Cafe (☎ 202-265-4600; 2442 18 St NW; 4pm-2am daily) Big with the West Africa set, Bukom is the place for Mama Africa–style pop and groovin'.

DUPONT CIRCLE

Sparky's (☎ 202-332-9334; 1720 14 St NW; 7.30am-11pm Mon-Thu, 7:30am-midnight Fri, 8am-midnight Sat, 9am-10pm Sun; wi-fi) There's admittedly a shortage of good coffee houses in DC, but Sparky's is great: Macbook-toting yuppies, an upstairs game room with an Atari 2600 (!) and to top it off: Best. Chai. Latte. Ever.

our pick **Brickskeller** (☎ 202-293-1885; 1523 22nd St NW; from 11:30am Mon-Fri, from 6pm Sat & Sun) Let's make this simple: *The Guinness Book of World Records* says the 'Skeller has the biggest variety of beer available. *In the world.* See you there.

Gazuza (☎ 202-667-5500; 1629 Connecticut Ave NW; from 5pm) A lounge that strives for the heights of hipness, Gazuza is more like the place where folks warm up for, or end up

WASHINGTON, DC & THE CAPITAL REGION

after, a good night out. Hey, it's still fun – all the pretty things eventually come here to drink on the patio and pretend they're not checking each other out.

Science Club (☎ 202-775-0747; 1136 19th St NW; ☾ from 5pm) Everyone, from the geeky types implied by the name to the DC power-set, comes here to shake a tailfeather to the blend of hip-hop, funk and house that thumps across the dim-lit floors of this excellent club.

Lucky Bar (☎ 202-331-3733; 1221 Connecticut Ave NW; ☾ from 3pm Mon-Fri, from noon Sat, from 9pm Sun) If you need a break from the slick, uber-euro-gestalt most Dupont places strive for, come to this convivial little sports bar. Lucky can be as wild as the next child but at least it's not as pretentious as its neighbors.

Eighteenth Street Lounge (☎ 202-466-3922; 1212 18th St NW; ☾ from 9:30pm Tue, Wed & Sat, from 5:30pm Thu & Fri) You know what cool is? Listening to the best DJs in the city spin while sipping a strong drink and chatting up the gorgeous clientele in this beautiful club. That's cool.

GEORGETOWN

Tombs (☎ 202-337-6668; 1226 36 St at P St NW; ☾ from 11:30am Mon-Sat, from 9:30am Sun) If it looks familiar, think back to the '80s; this was the setting for *St Elmo's Fire*. Today this cozy, windowless bar is a favorite with Georgetown students and profs boozing out under crew regalia.

Mie N Yu Lounge (☎ 202-333-6122; 3125 M St NW; ☾ from 4pm) Mie N Yu (pronounced 'Me an you' – ugh) lays snob appeal and the Asian-fusion lounge thing on pretty thick, and

the bar prices are frankly outrageous. But it's popular with the gorgeous Georgetown set, who love to look as good as the dark bamboo-and-silk interior.

COLUMBIA HEIGHTS

This neighborhood is north on the Green line, and has good emerging nightlife.

Raven (☎ 202-387-9274; 3125 Mt Pleasant Ave NW; ☾ from noon) A dive! Huzzah! A dirty, skuzzy, cheap-o DC dive! The Raven, with a jukebox full of oldies and more attitude than a pissed-off Ramone, can kick your ass. Give it some respect and you'll agree this is the best bar for warm-up drinking (and post-club beers) in the capital.

our pick **Wonderland** (☎ 202-232-5263; 1101 Kenyon St NW; ☾ from 5pm) We've got a lot of time for Wonderland, which manages to combine punk sensibility and affordable drinks with a welcoming beer garden where you can chat up strangers on some outsize wooden benches. That done, take your new friend to the upstairs dance floor, where local DJs spin and just-met couples get close.

Live Music

9:30 Club (☎ 202-393-0930; 815 V St NW; ☾ varies with gigs) This spacious dive, featuring two floors and a midsize stage, is the best place in town to see bands such as Wilco, the Pixies or Jack Johnson.

DC 9 (☎ 202-483-5000; 1940 9th St NW; ☾ from 8pm) It costs nothing to lounge and sip downstairs, but you'll have to ante up for the live rock and DJs on the 2nd floor.

GAY & LESBIAN BARS & CLUBS

Get your club on at the following places:

Phase 1 (☎ 202-544-6831; 525 8th St SE; cover free–$5; ☾ from 7pm Thu-Sun) The city's only exclusively lesbian club.

Bachelors Mill (☎ 202-544-1931; 1106 8th St SE; ☾ from 7pm) Caters to gay and lesbian African Americans.

Halo (☎ 202-797-9730; 1435 P St NW; ☾ from 5pm) Mostly male, super chic.

Club Chaos (☎ 202-232-4141; 1603 17th St at Q St NW; ☾ from 6pm) Draws gays and straights alike to its dance floor. Wednesday is ladies' night.

Annie's Paramount Steak House (☎ 202-232-0395; 1609 17th St NW; mains $8-13; ☾ 10am-11pm Mon, 10am-midnight Tue-Wed, 10am-1am Thu, 24hr Fri-Sun) Not a club, but *the* place to be seen for pre- or post-club grub.

DC Eagle (☎ 202-347-6025; www.dceagle.com; 639 New York Ave NW; ☾ 4pm-2am Mon-Fri, noon-3am Sat & Sun) Mostly a leather-and-Levi's crowd, with killer dyke nights.

Remington's (☎ 202-543-3113; 639 Pennsylvania Ave SE; ☾ from 5pm) Country-and-western cowboy fun.

Omega DC (☎ 202-223-4917; 2122 P St; ☾ from 4pm Mon-Fri, from 7pm Sun, from 8pm Sat) Meat market, serves free drinks for shirtless guys on Wednesday nights, XXX videos and hawt dancers on Saturdays.

Blues Alley (☎ 202-333-4141; 1073 Wisconsin Ave NW; ⊙ from 8pm) This classy Georgetown jazz supper club attracts some big-name artists. Entrance is through the alley just south of the intersection of Wisconsin and M.

Verizon Center (☎ 202-628-3200; 601 F St NW) DC's great big sports arena cum big-name band venue.

Performing Arts

John F Kennedy Center for the Performing Arts
(☎ 202-467-4600; www.kennedy-center.org; 2700 F St NW) One of the best places to catch a performance. It occupies a gorgeous, grandiloquent space on the Potomac. The National Symphony, Washington Chamber Symphony and Washington Opera perform here, while the center's Millennium Stage puts on free performances at 6pm daily.

Wolf Trap Farm Park for the Performing Arts (☎ 703-255-1900; www.wolftrap.org; 1645 Trap Rd, Vienna, Virginia) This outdoor park some 40 minutes from downtown DC hosts summer performances by the National Symphony and other highly regarded musical and theatrical troupes.

The **National Theatre** (☎ 202-628-6161; www.nationaltheatre.org; 1321 Pennsylvania Ave NW; tickets $40-90) is Washington's oldest continuously operating theater, though the **Shakespeare Theatre** (☎ 202-547-1122; www.shakespearedc.org; 450 7th St NW; tickets $23-70) has a more evocative venue. In summer outdoor performances are held at **Carter Barron Amphitheatre** (16th St & Colorado Ave NW).

Sports

Washington Redskins (☎ 301-276-6050) The city's football team plays at FedEx Field, east of DC in Maryland.

Washington Nationals (☎ 202-397-7328) DC's baseball team currently plays at Robert F Kennedy Memorial Stadium (RFK; which is up for a name change), but a new stadium is to be built along the Anacostia Riverfront by 2008.

Both **DC United** (☎ 202-587-5000) and the women's **Washington Freedom** (☎ 202-547-3137) play at RFK.

Washington stole Baltimore's lacrosse team in 2007; now the **Washington Bayhawks** (☎ 866-994-2957; www.washingtonbayhawks.com) play at Harbin field in Georgetown University.

The **Verizon Center** (☎ 202-628-3200, 202-432-7328; 601 F St NW) hosts the NBA Washington Wizards, the WNBA Washington Mystics and the NHL Washington Capitals ice-hockey team.

GETTING THERE & AWAY

Dulles International Airport (IAD; ☎ 703-572-2700), 25 miles west of the city, and **Reagan National Airport** (DCA; ☎ 703-417-8000), 22 miles south, are the main airports serving DC, although **Baltimore-Washington International/Thurgood Marshall Airport** (BWI; ☎ 410-859-7111), 30 miles to the northeast, is also an option. All three airports, particularly Dulles and National, are major hubs for flights from around the world. Door-to-door airport shuttles from downtown DC (www.washingtondcairportshuttles.com) cost $12 one way from National and $27 one way from Dulles. National airport has its own metro rail station, which is by far the cheapest option into the city (around $2), and pretty quick too. From Dulles, there are direct public buses to Rosslyn metro station and L'Enfant Plaza ($3), and the more cushy and timely **Washington Flyer** (☎ 888-927-4359; www.washfly.com) which runs to West Falls Church metro ($9).

Other transport options:
Greyhound bus station (☎ 800-231-2222; 1005 1st St NE)

MARC train (Maryland Rail Commuter; ☎ 800-325-7245; www.mtamaryland.com) The regional rail service for the Washington DC–Baltimore metro area. Trains frequently run to Baltimore ($7) and other Maryland towns ($4 to $9). Amtrak trains also run from here to destinations around the country, including New York City ($67), Chicago ($78) and Richmond ($26)

Peter Pan Trailways (☎ 800-343-9999; 1005 1st St NE) Buses stop opposite.

GETTING AROUND

For door-to-door van service between all three airports and downtown DC, try **SuperShuttle** (☎ 800-258-3826; www.supershuttle.com; fares around $25), **Washington Flyer** (☎ 888-927-4359; www.washfly.com; tickets $8) or the Number 5A **Metrobus** (☎ 202-962-1234; www.wmata.com; express $3) from the Dulles car-rental area to central DC (L'Enfant Plaza) once an hour. Not much room for baggage.

Car rentals include the following:
Budget (☎ Dulles airport 703-920-3360, Reagan airport 703-419-1021; www.budget.com)
Dollar (☎ Dulles airport 703-661-6888; www.dollar.com)
Thrifty (☎ 703-658-2200; www.thrifty.com)
Metrobus (☎ 202-637-7000; www.wmata.com) operates buses throughout the city and suburbs (tickets from $1.20).

Metrorail (☎ 202-637-7000; www.wmata.com) runs to most sights, hotel and business districts, and to the Maryland and Virginia suburbs. Trains operate 5:30am to midnight weekdays, 8am to 1am weekends. Machines inside stations sell computerized fare cards; fares from $1.20. All-day excursion passes cost $5.

For car and taxi try the following:

Capitol Cab (☎ 202-546-2400)
Diamond (☎ 202-387-2221)
Yellow Cab (☎ 202-544-1212)

MARYLAND

Lucky you: you've landed in the aptly named 'Land of Pleasant Living.' King Arthur's wizard to locals (ie 'Merlin') is mountains on the one end and a marsh and field checkerboard on the other – straight out of God's happiest daydream. A blend of Northern streetwise and Southern down-homeness gives this most osmotic of border states an appealing identity crisis. Her main city, Baltimore, is a sharp, demanding port; the Eastern Shore jumbles artsy yuppies, hard-nosed docks and working fishermen; the DC suburbs are packed with aristocrats seeking green space and the poor seeking lower rents. Yet it all works. Who cares about identity when you can kick back with some beer and a bushel (of bluecrabs) and experience the beauty of Chesapeake country?

History

George Calvert set Maryland up as a refuge for persecuted English Catholics in 1634 when he purchased St Mary's City from the local Piscataway, whom he initially tried to co-exist with. Puritan refugees drove both Piscataway and Catholics from control and shifted power to Annapolis; their harassment of Catholics produced the Tolerance Act, a flawed but progressive law that allowed freedom of any (Christian) worship in Maryland – a North American first.

That commitment to diversity has always characterized this state, despite a mixed record on slavery. Although her loyalties were split during the Civil War, a Confederate invasion was halted here in 1862 at Antietam. Following the war Maryland harnessed its black, white and immigrant workforce, splitting the economy between Baltimore's industry and shipping, and later Washington, DC's need for services. Today the answer to 'What makes a Marylander?' is 'All of the above:' the state mixes rich, poor, the foreign-born, urban sophisticates and rural villages like few others.

Information

Office of Tourism (☎ 866-639-3526; www.mdwelcome.com; 217 E Redwood St, Baltimore, MD 21202). Welcome centers with maps and region-specific guides are scattered throughout the state. The state parks reservation number is ☎ 888-432-2267.

BALTIMORE

B'more, Bawlmer, and the less flattering 'Body-more' (if London had this town's murder rate there'd be 3560 bodies floating in the Thames every year), Baltimore dares you to visit. Seriously, man up, yo (as they say here). A lot of cities try to be hip, stylish, on top of the trends. Baltimore says screw that, and God bless her. Like a criminal-turned-musician – timeless, hard-bitten and world-weary – Baltimore has a twinkle in the eye and a wisecrack on the lips. What other city would be the subject of *The Wire*, TV's most probing drama? It takes a town with the pathos of the docklands, grim poverty, a defiant working class and the international carnival of Fell's Point. With one foot in the Bay and the other stumbling from a pub crawl through Canton, this gritty, sly city begs visitors to come an hour north from DC to where the wild things are.

History

Although Baltimore briefly served as national capital after the Revolution, this town is defined by her port. Besieged during the War of 1812 and riot-torn during the Civil War, Baltimore weathered both, dispatching Balti-

---

MARYLAND FACTS

Nickname The Old Line State, The Free State
Population 5.62 million
Area 12,407 sq miles
Capital city Annapolis (pop 36,178)
Sales tax 5%
Birthplace of Frederick Douglass, Nancy Pelosi, Thurgood Marshall, Edgar Allen Poe, Babe Ruth
Home of Tom Clancy, the Baltimore Orioles, most of the federal government's workforce
Famous for Crabs, lacrosse, the Chesapeake Bay
State sport Jousting

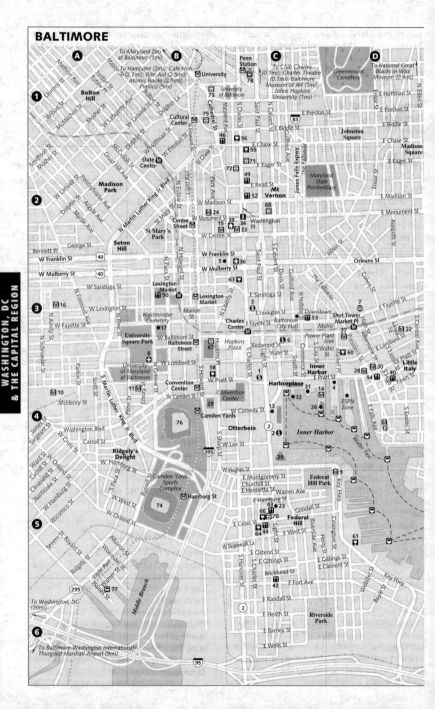

BALTIMORE

0 _____ 1 km
0 _____ 0.5 miles

INFORMATION
American Express Travel Services......**1** C4
Baltimore Area Visitor Center..........**2** C4
Bank of America..................................**3** C3
Barnes & Noble..................................**4** D4
Enoch Pratt Free Library....................**5** B3
Maryland Office of Tourism...............**6** C3
Post Office...**7** D3
University of Maryland Medical
Center...**8** B3

SIGHTS & ACTIVITIES
American Visionary Art Museum......**9** D5
B&O Railroad Museum.....................**10** A4
Babe Ruth Birthplace & Museum.....**11** B4
Baltimore Civil War Museum...........**12** D4
Baltimore Ducks...............................**13** C4
Baltimore Maritime Museum...........**14** C4
Contemporary Museum....................**15** B2
Edgar Allan Poe House.....................**16** A3

Edgar Allan Poe's Grave...................**17** B3
Fell's Point Ghost Tour.....................**18** E4
Fells Point Maritime Museum..........**19** E4
Fort McHenry National Monument &
Historic Shrine.............................**20** G6
Getaway Sailing................................**21** G5
Jewish Museum of Maryland...........**22** D3
Light Street Cycles...........................**23** C5
Maryland Historical Society.............**24** B2
Maryland Science Center.................**25** C4
National Aquarium in Baltimore.....**26** C4
Port Discovery..................................**27** D3
Reginald F Lewis Museum of Maryland
African American History &
Culture..**28** D4
Sports Legends at Camden Yards.....**29** B4
Star-Spangled Banner Flag House & 1812
Museum..**30** D4
Top of the World Observation Deck.**31** C4
USS Constellation.............................**32** C4
Walters Art Gallery..........................**33** C3
Washington Monument....................**34** C2
World Trade Center..................(see 31)

SLEEPING
Admiral Fell Inn...............................**35** E4
Baltimore Hostel..............................**36** C3
Inn at 2920......................................**37** H6
Inn at Henderson's Wharf................**38** E5
Peabody Court..................................**39** C2

EATING
Amicci's..**40** D4
Bertha's..**41** E4
Bicycle..**42** C6
Blue Agave.......................................**43** C5
Cross Street Market.........................**44** C5
Dominicano Internacional
Restaurant...................................**45** H4
Dukem...**46** B1

El Trovador.......................................**47** E4
Jimmy's Restaurant..........................**48** E4
Kumari..**49** C2
Lexington Market.............................**50** B3
Nacho Mama's..................................**51** G6
Never On Sunday..............................**52** C2
New York Fried Chicken...................**53** C3
Vaccaro's Pastry...............................**54** D4

DRINKING
13th Floor...**55** C2
Brewer's Art.....................................**56** C1
Claddagh Pub...................................**57** H6
DSX...**58** B4
Good Love Bar..................................**59** F4
Howl at the Moon............................**60** D3
Little Havana....................................**61** D5
Max's on Broadway..........................**62** E4
Mick O'Shea's...................................**63** C3
Mother's...**64** C5
One-Eyed Mike's..............................**65** E4
Owl Bar.....................................(see 55)
Thirsty Dog Pub................................**66** C5

ENTERTAINMENT
1st Mariner Arena.............................**67** B3
Center Stage.....................................**68** C2
Club Phoenix...........................(see 46)
Fletcher's..**69** C5
Funk Box...**70** C5
Grand Central...................................**71** C2
Hippo..**72** C2
Lyric Opera House............................**73** B1
M&T Bank Stadium...........................**74** B5
Meyerhoff Symphony Hall................**75** B1
Oriole Park at Camden Yards............**76** B4

TRANSPORT
Greyhound Bus Station.....................**77** A6
Penn Station.....................................**78** C1
Peter Pan Buses.......................(see 77)

Johns
Hopkins
Johns Hopkins
Hospital

Jefferson St
N Broadway
N Wolfe St
Orleans St

E Fairmont Ave   To Best Inn
(4mi)
E Baltimore St
E Lombard St
S Bethel St
S Broadway
S Ann St
S Wolfe St
S Durham St
S Castle St
S Chester St
E Pratt St
S Caroline St
S Bond St
S Regester St
Gough St
S Eden St
S Bank St

Eastern Ave
Fleet St
Aliceanna St
Lancaster St
S Chapel St
Broadway
Market
Market
Square
Thames St

Fell's
Point

Philpot
St

Water Taxi

Northwest
Harbor

Water Taxi

Patapsco River

Patterson
Park

Fleet St
Cambridge St
Foster Ave
Fait Ave
Hudson St
Boston St
Lakewood Ave
Kenwood Ave
Linwood Ave
Streeper St
Potomac St
Decker Ave
Ellwood Ave
Curley St
S Robinson St
S Boulton St
Clinton St
S Highland Ave
S Dean St
S Conkling Ave

Anchorange

Canton

Dillon St
O'Donnell St
Elliott St
Toone St

See Enlargement

Water Taxi
Lighthouse
Point

LP

Haubert St
Hull St
Beason St
Decatur St
Andre St
E Clement St
E Fort Ave

Latrobe Park

0 _____ 100 m
0 _____ 0.1 miles

57
O'Donnell St
Canton
Sq
O'Donnell St
51

Linwood St
Curley St
Potomac St

37
Elliott St

WASHINGTON, DC
& THE CAPITAL REGION

more Clippers (the fastest sailing ships in the world) across the globe in her heyday.

The slow erosion of shipping, Great Depression and the loss of the steel industry in the 1970s all gutted Baltimore. The boom and bust cycle has carved this city's character, attracting and dispersing immigrants into Baltimore's ethnic enclave neighborhoods. The city is 70% African American, mixing persistent black poverty with a African American middle class that is one of the nation's oldest and most culturally significant.

During the 1980s the Inner Harbor was spruced up into the city's centerpiece. Gentrification projects remain a double-edged sword, carving out urban rot in some places while simultaneously pricing out the urban poor.

WASHINGTON, DC
& THE CAPITAL REGION

Orientation & Information

From the Inner Harbor walk east (or water taxi) to the huddled intimacy of Little Italy and the party districts of Canton and Fell's Point (Salvadoran central these days). Baltimore St divides city streets into north and south; Charles St divides them east and west. Up north is kitschy Hampden, swish Mt Vernon, and Johns Hopkins University (surrounded by dangerous neighborhoods). The docks are to the southeast. Try not to go too far west of Martin Luther King Jr Blvd, especially at night.

BOOKSTORES

Atomic Books (☎ 410-662-4444; 1100 W 36th St; ☸ 11am-6pm, until 8pm Wed-Sat) Let's just say that John Waters loves this indie in Hampden. In fact, any John Waters fan mail should be sent care of them.
Barnes & Noble (☎ 401-385-1709; 601 E Pratt St, Power Plant, Inner Harbor; ☸ 8am-10pm Mon-Sat, 9am-9pm Sun) Will carry everything that Atomic doesn't and likely nothing Atomic does.

INTERNET ACCESS

Enoch Pratt Free Library (☎ 410-396-5430; 400 Cathedral St; ☸ 11am-8pm Mon-Wed, 10am-5:30pm Thu, 10am-5pm Fri-Sat, 1-5pm Sun, 1-5pm daily Jun-Sep)

MEDIA

89.7 FM WTMD Local Towson University station; alternative music.
97.9 FM WIYY Rocken!
Baltimore Sun (www.baltimoresun.com) Daily city newspaper.
City Paper (www.citypaper.com) Free alt-weekly.

DON'T MISS

- **American Visionary Art Museum** – where self-taught masters push the art world's boundaries (p330)

- **National Aquarium of Baltimore** – makes *Finding Nemo* look like canned tuna (opposite)

- **Fell's Point/Canton** – join the happy, alcohol-induced genocide of countless brain cells (p334)

- **The Wire** - The local show that put Baltimore back on the map has been called the best television of its time (p330)

MEDICAL SERVICES

Rite-Aid (☎ 410-467-3343; the Rotunda, 711 W 40th St) A 24-hour pharmacy.
University of Maryland Medical Center (☎ 410-328-6971; 655 W Baltimore St) Has a 24-hour emergency room.

MONEY

American Express Travel Services (☎ 410-837-3100; 100 E Pratt St; ☸ 9am-5pm Mon-Fri)
Bank of America (☎ 410-385-8310; 201 N Charles St; ☸ 9am-5pm Mon-Fri)

POST

Post office (☎ 410-347-4425; 900 E Fayette St; ☸ 8:30am-5pm Mon-Fri, until 4pm Sat)

TOURIST INFORMATION

Baltimore Area visitor center (☎ 410-837-4636, 877-225-8466; www.baltimore.org; 451 Light St; ☸ 9am-6pm Mon-Fri) Consider a Harbor Pass (adult/child $49/35), which gives admission to four major area attractions plus a one-day water-taxi pass.

Sights & Activities

Baltimore is a city of neighborhoods, and getting from one set of sites to the other requires a taxi, car or Baltimore light-rail. With that said, the Federal Hill–Inner Harbor–Little Italy–Fell's Point stretch is pretty walkable.

HARBORPLACE & INNER HARBOR

This where most tourists start and, unfortunately, end their Baltimore sight-seeing, The Inner Harbor is a big, gleaming waterfront renewal project of shiny glass, air-conditioned malls and flashy bars that manages to capture the maritime heart of this city, albeit in a safe-for-the-family kinda way. But it's also just the tip of Baltimore's iceberg.

Baltimore's **World Trade Center** is (drum-roll)…the tallest pentagonal structure in the world! Woopee. Anyways, the views from the **Top of the World observation deck** (☎ 410-837-8439; 401 E Pratt St; adult/child 3-12 $5/4; 🕙 10am-6pm Wed-Sun Sep-May, 10am-6pm Sun-Fri, until 8pm Sat Jun-Aug) are sweet.

Shipspotters should consider a visit to the **Baltimore Maritime Museum** (☎ 410-369-3453; www.baltimoremaritimemuseum.org; Piers 3 & 5 off E Pratt St; adult/child 6-14 $8/5; 🕙 10am-6pm daily Mar-Nov, 10am-5pm Fri-Sun Jan & Feb), which does ship tours aboard a Coast Guard Cutter, lightship and submarine, or the **USS Constellation** (☎ 410-539-1797; Pier 1 at 301 E Pratt St; adult/child under 15 $9/5; 🕙 10am-5:30pm Apr-Oct, until 4:30pm Nov-Mar), the last all-sail warship built by the US Navy.

National Aquarium of Baltimore

The city's greatest pride is her **aquarium** (☎ 410-576-3800; www.aqua.org; 501 E Pratt St; adult/child 3-11/child under 3 $22/13/free; 🕙 9am-6pm Sun-Thu, until 8pm Fri & Sat Jul & Aug, 9am-5pm daily, until 8pm Fri Mar-Jun & Sep-Oct, 10am-5pm daily, until 8pm Fri Nov-Feb) and it must not be missed. The huge main building, seven stories high, topped with a Louvre-esque glass pyramid and run through by a titanic spiral staircase, houses quite possibly the best exhibit on marine life in the country. If you never go to a coral reef or scuba dive or otherwise follow Jacque Cousteau's footsteps, the 16,500 species on display here are seriously the next best thing. The wetlands displays are enchanting, and the dolphin shows and gloomy shark tanks are a favorite with the kids, who will learn a lot here without ever realizing it. A 10-year expansion is currently underway; the newest addition houses a 35ft waterfall and painstaking reconstruction of the Umbrawarra Gorge in Australia.

DOWNTOWN & LITTLE ITALY

You can easily walk from Downtown to Little Italy, but follow the delineated path as there's a rough housing project along the way.

A mob of antiwar, slave-owning Marylanders rioted against Union soldiers at the start of the Civil War, and the **Baltimore Civil War Museum** (☎ 410-385-5188; 601 S President St; adult/child under 13/senior & student $4/free/3; 🕙 10am-5pm, Thu-Mon) does an excellent job of documenting

the event, the first bloodshed of America's bloodiest conflict.

The **Star-Spangled Banner Flag House & 1812 Museum** (☎ 410-837-1793; www.flaghouse.org; 844 E Pratt St; adult/child under 18 & student $7/5; 🕙 10am-4pm Tue-Sat) is where Mary Pickersgill sewed the gigantic flag that inspired America's national anthem. Today, it's haunted by creepy wax soldiers from the War of 1812.

Few states have been as defined by their African American population as Maryland, and the **Reginald F Lewis Museum of Maryland African American History & Culture** (☎ 410-333-1130; www.africanamericanculture.org; 830 E Pratt St; adult/child 6 & under/senior & student $8/free/6; 🕙 10am-5pm Tue-Sun, from noon Sun), across the street from a pre–Civil War slave market, effectively tells their complex tale. In East Baltimore, the **National Great Blacks in Wax Museum** (☎ 410-563-3404; www.ngbiwm.com; 1601 E North Ave; adult/student/child 3-11/$9/8/6; h9am-5pm Tue-Sat, from noon Sun, until 6pm Jan 15-Oct 15) surreally mixes religious leaders, activists, the Atlantic slave trade and the African American struggle for social justice with…Madame Tussaud's.

Maryland also has traditionally had one of the largest, most active Jewish communities in the country; their story is told at the **Jewish Museum of Maryland** (☎ 410-727-1539; 15 Lloyd St; adult/student/child under 12 $8/4/3; 🕙 noon-4pm Sun & Tue-Thu), worth a visit for two of the best-preserved historical synagogues in America.

The **Babe Ruth Birthplace & Museum** (☎ 410-727-1539; 216 Emory St; adult/child $6/3; 🕙 10am-6pm Apr-Oct, until 7:30pm on Orioles home games, 10am-5pm Tue-Sun Nov-Mar) celebrates the Baltimore native son who happens to be the greatest baseball player in history. Four block east, **Sports Legends at Camden Yards** (Camden Station, cnr Camden & Sharp Sts; adult/child $10/6.50) honors more Maryland athletes (Johnny Unitas, Brooks Robinson, Pam Shriver) and, with almost 40 exhibits, is basically every (American) sports fans' most lascivious fantasy. The museums share hours and tickets for $14/11.

The Baltimore & Ohio railway was (arguably) the first passenger train in America, and the **B&O Railroad Museum** (☎ 410-752-2490; www.borail.org; 901 W Pratt St; adult/child 2-12/senior $14/8/10) is a loving testament to both that line and American railroading in general. Trainspotters will be in heat among more than 150 different locomotives, the most comprehensive collection in the country.

'Where's the **Edgar Allan Poe House** (☎ 410-396-7932; 203 N Amity St; adult/child under 13 $3/1; ☷ noon-3:45pm Wed-Sat)?' 'Every house here a po' house!' That's an old Baltimore joke, but it should give you an idea of the neighborhood surrounding the macabre author's old residence, filled with his personal effects. Hours vary; call ahead. Poe's **grave** is in nearby Westminster Cemetery.

Light Street Cycles (☎ 410-685-2234; 1015 Light St; rental per day $25-45; ☷ 10am-8pm Mon-Fri, 10am-6pm Sat, 11am-3pm Sun) rents out everything from street to mountain bikes. This is a great town for chartering sailboats or learning how to pilot them; try **Getaway Sailing** (☎ 410-342-3110; 2700 Lighthouse Point; charters per day $110-685; ☷ 10am-8pm Mon-Fri, 10am-6pm Sat, 11am-3pm Sun) off Boston St for both.

MT VERNON
Don't pass up the **Walters Art Gallery** (☎ 410-547-9000; www.thewalters.org; 600 N Charles St; admission free; ☷ 11am-5pm Wed-Sun, until 8pm Fri), which spans over 55 centuries, from ancient to contemporary, with excellent displays of Asian treasures, rare and ornate manuscripts and books, and a comprehensive French paintings collection.

So modern it's probably post, the **Contemporary Museum** (☎ 410-783-5720; www.contempo rary.org; 100 W Centre St; admission free; ☷ noon-5pm Wed-Sun, until 7pm Thu) loves to ride the cutting edge of art. Auxiliary to the on-site exhibits is the museum's mission of bringing art to unexpected spots around the city. Call or check the website for the latest guerrilla art attack.

The **Maryland Historical Society** (☎ 410-685-3750; www.mdhs; 201 W Monument St; adult/student & child over 12 $4/3; ☷ 10am-5pm Wed-Sun), with some 5.4-million artifacts (including the original Star-Spangled Banner manuscript) is technically the largest museum in Maryland. The society building is part scholarly attic, part well-executed peek into the many ingredients that blend into one of America's most mixed-up states.

Baltimore's **Washington Monument** (☎ 410-396-0929; 699 Washington Pl; suggested donation $1; ☷ dawn-dusk Wed-Sun) is a big compensating Doric column that crowns regal Mt Vernon Sq. Climb 228 steps to the top for a city view or just check out the exhibits at the base.

FEDERAL HILL & AROUND
On a bluff overlooking the harbor, **Federal Hill Park** lends its name to the comfortable neighborhood that's set around Cross St Market and comes alive after sundown.

The **Fort McHenry National Monument & Historic Shrine** (☎ 410-962-4290; 2400 E Fort Ave; adult/child under 17 $5/free; ☷ 8am-7:45pm summer, 8am-4:45pm rest of year) is one of the most visited sites in Baltimore. This star-shaped fort was instrumental in saving the city from the British Navy in the Battle of Baltimore during the War of 1812. After a long night of bombs bursting in air, prisoner Francis Scott Key saw the tattered flag still waving, and the national anthem 'The Star-Spangled Banner' (set to the tune of a popular drinking song) was born.

We've got nothing but love for the **American Visionary Art Museum** (AVAM; ☎ 410-244-1900; www.avam.org; 800 Key Hwy; adult/student & senior $12/8;

GETTING TO THE WIRE

What do you get when you combine a former *Baltimore Sun* crime reporter and a former Baltimore homicide detective? Only the best damn show on American TV.

The Wire, which airs on HBO, has been hailed as television literature, a series that bridges entertainment and art and ends up exemplifying both. Set on the hard streets of West Baltimore, this brainchild of *Homicide* creators David Simon (the reporter) and Ed Burns (the cop) has evolved from a crime drama into an analysis of the American city and its perennially neglected underclass: America's poor, black ghettos.

Neither romanticizing nor demonizing its subject matter, the show's major theme is how individuals are constrained by their organizations. Much of the fervently loyal fan base is from the Baltimore/DC area, which is unsurprising given the true star of the show is Baltimore herself, in all her rough-edged grace. They say *Withnail and I* exemplifies England, and *The Castle* is crucial to understanding Australia. If so, *The Wire* is Baltimore given gritty, television voice; if you plan on visiting, try and catch a season on DVD. If not, watch a season anyways and you'll soon be B'more bound.

10am-6pm Tue-Sun). Exclusively showcasing self-taught (or 'outsider' art), AVAM is what every art museum should be: a happy celebration of unbridled creativity utterly free of arts-scene pretension. Some of the work comes from asylums, others are created by self-inspired visionaries, but it's all totally captivating and well worth a long afternoon.

FELL'S POINT & CANTON

Further east, cobblestones fill the historic maritime neighborhood of Fell's Point, where 18th-century homes have become restaurants, bars and shops. Just north of Fell's is the locus of the city's rapidly expanding Latino population. Further east, the slightly more sophisticated streets of Canton fan out, and its grassy square is surrounded by more great restaurants and bars.

The **Fell's Point Maritime Museum** (☎ 410-732-0278; 1724 Thames St; adult/student & child over 12 $4/3; 10am-5pm Thu-Mon) immerses you in the salt-blooded heritage that is Baltimore's birthright, including its seedy side, such as the smuggling outfits that once operated out of the city.

NORTH BALTIMORE

The 'Hon' expression of affection, an oft-imitated but never quite duplicated 'Bawl-merese' peculiarity, was born from **Hampden**, an urban neighborhood at the pinnacle of hipness. Spend a lazy afternoon browsing kitsch, antiques and eclectic clothing along the **Avenue** (aka W 36th St). To get to Hampden, take I-83 N, merge onto 25 N and take a right onto the Avenue.

Close by, you'll find **Johns Hopkins University** (☎ 410-516-8171; main bldgs 3400 N Charles St), famed for its medical school. The **Baltimore Museum of Art** (☎ 410-573-1700; 10 Art Museum Dr at 31st & N Charles Sts; adult/child & senior $7/3; 11am-5pm Wed-Fri, until 6pm Sat & Sun), with its massive collection (the early American, Asian and African galleries are particularly impressive) and a lovely sculpture garden, easily competes with its Smithsonian cousins to the south.

Baltimore for Children

This city loves kids and proves it with amazing museums, strollable waterfront promenades and family-friendly restaurants. Most attractions are centered on the Inner Harbor, including the National Aquarium of

Baltimore (p325) perfect for pint-sized visitors. Kids can run wild o'er the ramparts of historic Fort McHenry National Monument & Historic Shrine (opposite) too.

Swinging into a three-level jungle treehouse, producing a TV show and solving riddles in the Mystery House are a sample of the interactive adventures at **Port Discovery** (☎ 410-727-8120; www.portdiscovery.org; Power Plant Live complex, 35 Market Pl; admission $11; 10am-5pm, Mon-Sat, from noon Sun year-round, until 6pm Fri Jul-Aug), a cool kids' museum where even the adults have fun. The HiFlyer Balloon offers a bird's-eye view of Baltimore, but it's temporarily closed; tickets that include a balloon ride (summer only) are usually adult/child $19/15.

Lily-pad hopping, adventures with Billy the Bog Turtle and grooming live animals are all in a day's work at the **Maryland Zoo in Baltimore** (☎ 410-366-5466; www.marylandzoo.org; Druid Hill Park; adult/child/senior $15/10/12; 10am-4pm).

The awesome **Maryland Science Center** (☎ 410-685-5225; www.mdsci.org; 601 Light St; adult/child 3-12 $14/9.50; 10am-6pm Sun-Thu, until 8pm Fri & Sat summer, 10am-5pm Tue-Thu, 10am-8pm Fri, 10am-6pm Sat, 11am-5pm Sun, closed Mon fall-spring) features a three-story atrium, tons of interactive exhibits on dinosaurs, asteroids and the human body, and the requisite IMAX theater. Hours change seasonally and it's best to check online or call ahead first.

Tours

Baltimore Ducks (☎ 877-887-8225; www.baltimore ducks.com; Conway & Light Sts, Inner Harbor; adult/child 3-12 $24/14) The quintessential tourist activity, a ride on an amphibious former-WWII military 'Duck' shows visitors the city via land and water.

Fell's Point Ghost Tours (☎ 410-342-5000; www .fellspointghost.com; departs from 731 S Broadway; adult/ child under 13 $12/8; 7pm Fri or Sat Mar-Nov) Delve into the spooky and bizarre side of a bawdy maritime area. Also offers a haunted pub tour for $20.

Festivals & Events

Preakness (☎ 410-542-9400; www.preakness.com) Held on the 3rd Sunday of every May, the 'Freakness' is the second leg of the Tripe Crown horse race. Imagine the Royal Ascot, if the Ascot was invaded by an army of wasted, gambling Marylanders.

Honfest (www.honfest.net) In June, come learn Bawlmerese, the nation's most slurred accent, at this summer celebration of kitsch, beehive hairdos, rhinestone glasses and all of Baltimore's many other eccentricities.

WASHINGTON, DC & THE CAPITAL REGION

Sleeping

Stylish and affordable B&Bs are mostly found in the downtown 'burbs of Canton, Fell's Point and Federal Hill.

BUDGET & MIDRANGE

Baltimore Hostel (☎ 410-576-8880; www.baltimorehostel.org; 17 W Mulberry St; HI members/nonmembers dm $25/28; ☒ ▣) A community-wide effort went into the painstaking renovation of this fantabulous 1857 mansion, which became Baltimore's contribution to the Hostelling International (HI) trail in 2007. Helpful management, nice location and filigreed classical-chic make this one of the best hostels we've seen in the region.

Best Inn (☎ 410-485-7900; www.bestinnhotel.com; 6510 Frankford Ave; s $71-79, d $79-84; ▣ ☒ ☒) The Best doesn't excel in any areas, including price, which is the main reason to stay at this otherwise nondescript hotel.

our pick Inn at 2920 (☎ 410-342-4450; www.theinnat2920.com; 2920 Elliott St; r $155-225; ☒ wi-fi) Thank God: a B&B that doesn't try and plunk you into a Jane Austen–era boudoir (although the Inn was once a bordello). Instead, you get five totally individualized rooms, high thread-count sheets, sleek, avant-garde decor, beta fish roommates and the bohemian/boozapolooza neighborhood of Canton right outside your door. The Jacuzzis and the green sensibility of the owners are a nice touch.

Peabody Court (☎ 410-727-7101; www.peabodycourthotel.com; 612 Cathedral St; r from $159; ▣ ☒ wi-fi) Gay friendly and smack in the middle of Mt Vernon, the friendly staff and all-marble bathrooms at the Peabody want to give you a big, luxurious hug. Parking is $29.

Inn at Henderson's Wharf (☎ 410-522-7777; www.hendersonswharf.com; 1000 Fell St; r $179-259; ▣ ☒ wi-fi) A complimentary bottle of wine upon arrival sets the tone at this marvelously situated Fell's Point hotel, which began life as an 18th-century tobacco warehouse. Consistently one of the city's best lodgers.

TOP END

Admiral Fell Inn (☎ 410-522-7377; www.admiralfell.com; 888 S Broadway; r incl breakfast from $209; ▣ ☒ wi-fi) Must not have been much of a sailor – sorry. Overlooking Market Sq in Fell's Point, this gracious if slightly corporate-feeling hotel wants to be (and pretty much is) the cream of Baltimore's hotel crop. You know the drill: four-poster beds, the attentions of slavish staff…it's all here.

Eating

Look, this is an ethnically rich town that sits on top of the greatest seafood repository in the world, not to mention the faultline between the down-home South and cutting-edge innovation of the Northeast. Baltimore, in other words, knows how to eat. A great place to sample food is the city's famous markets; here are two favorites:

Cross Street Market (1065 Cross St btwn Light & Charles Sts; ☙ 7am-7pm Mon-Sat)

Lexington Market (400 W Lexington St; ☙ 8:30am-6pm Mon-Sat)

DOWNTOWN & LITTLE ITALY

Vaccaro's Pastry (☎ 410-685-4905; 222 Albemarle St; items $2-5; ☙ 9am-11pm Sun-Thu, until 1am Fri & Sat) Leave the gun. Take the cannoli. No, seriously, the cannoli at this Italian bakery is the best in the state. And seriously, don't bring a gun.

New York Fried Chicken (☎ 410-385-2400; 412 E Baltimore St; dishes $4-8; ☙ 11am-2:30am) We're not exactly sure why a fried chicken place south of the Mason–Dixon would associate itself with NYC, but we are sure this place (and its associated, expanding franchises) serves some of the best greasy goodness in the city.

Amicci's (☎ 410-528-1096; 231 S High St; lunch mains $7-10, dinner mains $14-19; ☙ 11:30am-midnight Mon-Fri) Amicci's may be the southernmost place in America where you can still find blinged-out Italian waitstaff serving decent gnocchi in a loud dining room. The *pane rotunda* (garlic bread with shrimp) is the stuff of local legend.

MT VERNON

Never on Sunday (☎ 410-752-0311; 806 N Charles St; mains $5-10; ☙ 24hr, closed Sun) This working-man Greek diner caters to junkies, addicts, students, writers and other assorted scum. The food won't wow anyone into submission, but people usually come here too late/hungover to care.

Kumari (☎ 410-547-1600; 911 N Charles St; mains $7-12; ☙ 11:30am-10:30pm) If you haven't had Nepalese food, think heavier and creamier (and at this place, tastier) than your average curry. Kumari's buffet is great value and a potent hangover cure to boot.

Dukem (☎ 410-385-0318; 1100 Maryland Ave; mains $10-20; ☙ 11am-2am, until later Fri & Sat) Dukem could give the Ethiopian places in DC a run for their money, except it's actually a satellite colony of a Washington joint by the same name. That's fine; the father has taught the son well in East African standards of spicy chicken and lamb sopped up with spongy flatbread.

FEDERAL HILL

Blue Agave (☎ 410-576-3938; 1032 Light St; mains $14-28; ☻ from 5pm) Agave's does hip, upscale Mexican food, but it's not pretentious; a midwestern family would feel as welcome here as a clique of New York socialites. The pork carnitas platter is heavenly, and incidentally, the margaritas could knock out a horse.

Bicycle (☎ 410-234-1900; 1444 Light St; mains $15-28; ☻ 5:30-10pm Mon-Thu, until later Fri & Sat) Striking colored walls, a spacious interior and a hip art-gallery feel accent the French-, South American– and Asian-inspired (in other words, nouvelle-Californian) offerings.

FELL'S POINT

Jimmy's Restaurant (☎ 410-675-5999; 1739 Fleet St; lunch mains $4-8; ☻ 5am-9pm) Jimmy's has been scrubbed clean as of late, but you could never scrape all the grease off this waterfront spoon. This quintessential diner serves scrapple (you don't wanna know), and lest we forget, you can take a six-pack to go. This, friends, is what it means to be Bawlmer.

Dominicano Internacional Restaurant (☎ 410-276-1117; 601 S Conkling St; mains $6-14; ☻ 11am-11pm daily) These Dominicans immigrated to the Land of Plenty to serve plenty: of chicken, pork, goat etc. It's all good. Technically in Highlandtown, bright island murals and Spanish-speaking waitstaff make this a fun place to eat on a summer afternoon, although there's no Red Stripe – damn.

El Trovador (☎ 410-276-6200; 318 S Broadway St; mains $7-19; ☻ 11am-11pm, until later Fri & Sat) Trovador is a cornerstone of the Latino community, and it does gussied up Salvadoran favorites (pork stew, grilled steak with onions and tomato sauce) with style.

Bertha's (☎ 410-327-5795; 734 S Broadway St; mains $10-21; ☻ 11:30am-11pm Sun-Thu, until later Fri & Sat) A command emblazoned on bumper stickers across the state, 'Eat Bertha's Mussels' is shorthand for 'Come to Fell's Point, get sloshed in a dark pirate's den and gorge yourself on shellfish.' Bertha's Sunday brunch is as famous as her bivalves.

CANTON

Nacho Mama's (☎ 410-675-0898; 2907 O'Donnell St; mains $7-18; ☻ 11am-late) The food is tex-mex-y decent

but really, you should come here at night for the infamous hubcap of dozen-tequila-shot-strong margarita (no, really).

HAMPDEN & NORTH BALITMORE

Cafe Hon (☎ 410-243-1230; 1002 W 36th St; brunch mains $4-8; dinner mains $9-15; ☻ 7am-9pm Mon-Fri, from 9am Sat & Sun) You don't have to be sporting rhinestone-studded glasses and an ironic bouffant to eat here, but you'll earn serious brownie points. The fare at this veggie-friendly diner is as hearty as the café's attitude. After dinner slide over to adjacent Bar Hon.

Drinking & Entertainment

On weekends, Fell's Point and Canton turn into temples to alcoholic excess that would make a Roman emperor blush. Mt Vernon and North Baltimore are a little more civilized, but any one of Baltimore's neighborhoods houses a cozy local pub. The Power Plant Live complex is filled with chain-brand clubs. Unless otherwise noted, closing time is 2am.

BARS & CLUBS
Downtown & Little Italy

Mick O'Shea's (☎ 410-539-7504; 328 N Charles St; ☻ from 11:30am) Your standard paraphernalia-festooned Irish pub, with live Irish music Wednesday through Saturday. Maryland Governor (and former Baltimore mayor) Martin O'Malley used to play here.

DSX (☎ 410-659-5844; 200 W Pratt St; ☻ 11am-9pm, later on game days) If you find American sport boring, you won't after getting silly and tanked with rabid Baltimore fans at this bar, which is within projectile-vomit distance of Camden Yards (p335).

Howl at the Moon (☎ 410-783-5111; 22 Market Pl Power Plant Live; cover Fri & Sat $7, Thu $5; ☻ from 7pm, from 5pm Fri) Howl stands out from the cookie-cutter clubs of Power Plant Live with its innovative theme: a call-in piano bar where the audience forces an ivory-masher/crooner to improvise the entertainment all night long.

Mt Vernon

Brewer's Art (☎ 410-547-9310; 1106 N Charles St; ☻ from 4pm, from 5pm Sun) This subterranean cave mesmerizes the senses with an overwhelming selection of beers. Its upstairs embodiment serves respectable dinners in its classy dining room.

our pick Club Charles (☎ 410-727-8815; 1724 N Charles St; ☻ from 6pm) Filled with hipsters displaying the breed's usual skinny jeans/vintage T-shirt plumage, normals also flock here to enjoy good tunes and cheap drinks in one of the best decorated bars in Maryland: red, red, red, heaven and hell motif, more red. If you don't look deadly cool under the Charles' lights, sorry my friend: you are lame.

13th Floor (☎ 410-347-0888; 1 E Chase St; ☽ from 5pm Wed-Fri, from 6pm Sat) This is one of the smoothest spots in the city to get your club on: atop the Gothic Belvedere Hotel, with fresh tracks, unbeatable views and a classy elevator ride waiting when you're ready to go home. Also in the Belvedere, the Owl Bar is a nostalgic throwback to '50s Baltimore, with a long wooden bar that attracts a martini-sipping crowd.

Federal Hill

Thirsty Dog Pub (☎ 410-727-6077; 20 E Cross St; ☽ from 5pm) Marylanders really love drinking with their dogs. After you've made the rounds petting the canine clientele, grab a delicious brew (or two for $3) and try to snag the cozy fireside nook in the back. Excellent pizza, too.

Mother's (☎ 410-244-8686; 1113 S Charles St; ☽ from 11am Mon-Fri, from 8am Sat & Sun) Here's a classic Baltimore neighborhood bar and grill where the drinks flow freely; you'll be called 'Hon' more than once and the Purple Patio is the meeting spot for wing specials and pre- and post-Ravens game discussions.

Little Havana (☎ 410-837-9903; 1325a Key Hwy; ☽ 4:30pm-midnight Mon-Thu, from 11am Fri-Sun) A good after-work spot and a better place to sip *mojitos* (rum- and lime-based drink), Little Havana attracts the sort of young professional who just know there's a salsa goddess deep in their soul.

Funk Box (☎ 410-625-2000; 10 E Cross St; cover $10-20) In just a few years the Box has carved out a reputation as the hippest live-music venue in Baltimore. Admirably mixes up big names with strong local talent in a (imagine that) funky concert hall that feels intimate and expansive all at once.

Fell's Point & Canton

our pick **Good Love Bar** (☎ 410-534-4588; 2322 Boston St; ☽ from 6pm) Think dark, sexy lighting; think three floors of cushy, lounge-and-flirt furniture; think music that manages to mingle black and white clubbers like few other places in Baltimore, and you've thought up Good Love.

One-Eyed Mike's (☎ 410-327-9823; 708 S Bond St; ☽ 11am-1am Mon-Sat) Yar! They be pirates at this seedy, drunk-as-a-sailor-on-shore-leave pub, and if ye want, they be stowing away a bottle of Grand Marnier for ye in a glass display case, which ye can drink from whenever ye return. Now walk the plank, or something.

Max's on Broadway (☎ 410-675-6297; 737 S Broadway; ☽ from 11am) Nothing says 'cute waterfront restoration' like the cobblestone streets of Fell's Point, and nothing says 'pesudo-Bacchanalian orgy' like the crowds that stumble down those streets into this bar. Max's enormous beer menu makes Belgium kinda jealous.

Claddagh Pub (☎ 410-522-4220; 2918 O'Donnell St; ☽ from 11am, from 9am Sat & Sun) The crowds at Claddagh work hard to confirm ugly stereotypes about the Irish by trying to consume their volume in alcohol at this Disney-fied Dublin pub.

Fletcher's (☎ 410-558-1889; 701 S Bond St; cover $5; ☽ from 4pm Mon-Thu, from 11am Fri-Sun) Inhale the dried-beer scent on the walls with the pretty youngsters and rough, amiable oldsters who come here, one of the best rock stages in town.

GAY & LESBIAN VENUES

Baltimore has one of the largest gay African American scenes in America, on the 'down low,' seeking hook-ups in anonymous settings and maintaining a straight facade, and sometimes wives and families, at home. In fact, Baltimore has a remarkably vibrant, multiracial gay scene. **Out in Baltimore** (www.outinbaltimore.com) has comprehensive listings. Plenty of straight folks go out in gay Baltimore to soak up the friendly, often outrageous vibe.

Hippo (☎ 410-547-0069; 1 W Eager St; ☽ from 4pm) This is the city's largest gay club, with ladies' and men's tea, cabaret and crazy themed dance nights.

Grand Central (☎ 410-752-7133; 1001 N Charles St; ☽ from 4pm, from 3pm Sun) More of a complex than a club, whatever your taste, one of Central's areas (dance floor, pub, video bar, and leather-and-Levi's club) is sure to suit your fancy.

Club Phoenix (☎ 410-837-3906; 1101 Cathedral St; ☽ from 4pm, noon Sat & Sun) A more laid-back (not *that* laid-back, though) spot that aims to be friendly and pretension-free.

PERFORMING ARTS & THEATER

The **Baltimore Symphony Orchestra** (☎ 410-783-8000) performs at the **Meyerhoff Symphony Hall** (1212 Cathedral St). The Baltimore Opera performs at the **Lyric Opera House** (☎ 410-685-5086; www.lyric operahouse.com; 140 W Mt Royal Ave).

Theater options:

Center Stage (☎ 410-332-0033; 700 N Calvert St) Stages Shakespeare, Wilde, Miller and contemporary works.

Charles Theatre (☎ 410-727-3456; www.thecharles .com; 1711 N Charles St) Best art-house films in the city.

SPORTS

Whether it's touchdowns, home runs, goals or monster-truck shows, Baltimoreans love their sports. The town plays hard and parties even harder, with tailgating parties in parking lots and games on numerous televisions.

Baseball

The Baltimore Orioles play at **Oriole Park at Camden Yards** (☎ 410-547-6277; http://baltimore.orioles .mlb.com; 333 W Camden St; ☿ Apr-Oct).

Football

The Baltimore Ravens play at **M&T Bank Stadium** (☎ 410-261-7283; www.baltimoreravens.com; 1101 Russell St; ☿ Sep-Jan).

Lacrosse & Soccer

Maryland is lacrosse heartland, and its residents arguably the sport's most fanatic followers. With the loss of the Bayhawks, the best place to watch 'lax' is **John Hopkins University** (☎ 410-516-7490; hopkinssports.cstv.com; stadium at cnr University Parkway & N Charles St). The Major League Soccer team **Baltimore Blast** (☎ 410-732-5278; www .baltimoreblast.com; ☿ Oct-Apr) plays at the **1st Mariner Arena** (☎ 410-321-1908; 201 W Baltimore St).

Horseracing

Racing is huge here, especially at **Pimlico** (www .pimlico.com), which hosts the Preakness (p331).

Getting There & Away

Baltimore-Washington International/Thurgood Marshall Airport (BWI) This gateway is 10 miles south of downtown via I-295.

Greyhound Bus Station & Peter Pan (☎ 410-752-7682; 2110 Haines St) Buses from Washington, DC, cost $11; from New York they cost $27 to $37.

Penn Station (1515 N Charles St; ☎ 410-291-4165) In north Baltimore. MARC operates weekday commuter trains to and from Washington, DC (one-way/round-trip $7/14).

Getting Around

Check **Maryland Transit Administration** (MTA; www .mtamaryland.com) for all schedules and fares.

Baltimore Water Taxi (☎ 410-563-3901; Inner Harbor; adult/child under 11 $8/4) Lands at all harborside attractions and neighborhoods.

Light Rail (☎ 410-539-5000; tickets $1.60) From BWI to Lexington Market and Penn Station.

MARC trains (☎ 800-325-7245) Hourly between Penn Station and BWI on weekdays for $4.

SuperShuttle (☎ 800-258-3826; www.supershuttle .com) BWI-van service to the Inner Harbor for $21.

ANNAPOLIS

Sometimes (annoyingly) dubbed 'Nap-town,' Annapolis is as charming as state capitals get. The cobblestones, flickering lamps and brick row houses are worthy of Dickens, but the effect isn't artificial; this city has preserved, rather than created, its heritage.

Besides history is water: Naval Academy 'middies' (midshipmen, or more plainly, students) stroll through the streets with ramrods up their backs while the yacht-owning hordes have overrun the docks and crammed them with floating temples to hubris. Everyone sails, the food is great, and a beer on a pier cooled by a salty headwind is even better.

There's a **visitor center** (☎ 410-280-0445; www .visitannapolis.org; 26 West St; ☿ 9am-5pm) and a seasonal information booth at City Dock. A **Maryland Welcome Center** (☎ 410-974-3400; 350 Rowe Blvd; ☿ 9am-5pm) is inside the State House, and runs tours of the building twice daily.

Sights & Activities

Think of the State House as a wheel hub from which most attractions fan out, leading down to the **City Dock** and **historic waterfront**.

US NAVAL ACADEMY

The undergraduate college of the US Navy is one of the most selective universities in America. The **Armel-Leftwich visitor center** (☎ 410-293-8125; Gate 1 at the City Dock entrance; tours adult/student $7.50/5.50; ☿ 9am-5pm, until 4pm Jan & Feb) is the place to book tours and immerse yourself in all things Academy. Come for the formation weekdays at 12:05pm sharp, when the 4000 midshipmen and midshipwomen conduct a 20-minute military marching display in the 'Yard.' Photo ID is required upon entry. If you've got a thing for American naval history, go on and revel in the **Naval Academy Museum** (☎ 410-293-2108; 118 Maryland Ave; admission free; ☿ 9am-5pm Mon-Sat, from 11am Sun).

MARYLAND STATE HOUSE

The country's oldest state capitol in continuous legislative use, the stately 1772 **State House** (☎ 410-974-3400; 25 State Circle; ☉ 9am-5pm Mon-Fri, 10am-4pm Sat & Sun) also served as national capitol from 1733 to 1734. The Maryland Senate is in action here from January to April. The upside-down giant acorn atop the dome stands for wisdom. Photo ID is required upon entry.

DOWNTOWN ANNAPOLIS

A costumed docent will lead you on a **Three Centuries Walking Tour** (☎ 410-268-7601; adult/child under 12 $14/4), a great introduction to all things Annapolis. The 10:30am tour leaves from the visitor center and the 1:30pm tour leaves from the information booth at the City Dock; there's a slight variation in sights visited by each, but both cover the country's largest concentration of 18th-century buildings, influential African Americans and colonial spirits who don't want to leave. The associated **Pirates of the Chesapeake Bay Cruise** (adult/child 3-11 $15/10; ☉ late May-Sep) is good 'yar'-worthy fun, especially for the kids.

At the City Dock, the **Kunta Kinte-Alex Haley Memorial** marks the spot where Kunta Kinte – ancestor of *Roots* author Alex Haley – was brought in chains from Africa. Haley won the Pulitzer Prize for his epic.

Annapolis brims with attractive, historical buildings, but our favorite is **St John's College** (cnr College Ave & King George St), one of the USA's most innovative colleges.

You can't walk without tripping on a sailing school, cruise or bareboat (sail-it-yourself) charter. **Watermark Cruises** (City Dock), which operates the Three Centuries Walking Tour, is one of the best of the lot. The beautiful 74ft-schooner **Woodwind** (☎ 410-263-7837; 80 Compromise St; day sail/dusk cruise $31/20; ☉ May-Oct) offers two-hour cruises and a $265 'boat and breakfast' combination, one of the more unique lodging options in town.

Sleeping

Call ☎ 800-848-4748 for free accommodation reservations.

ScotLaur Inn (☎ 410-268-5665; www.scotlaurinn.com; 165 Main St; r $95-125; P ☒ wi-fi) The folks from Chick & Ruth's Delly offer 10 simple pink-and-blue rooms with private bath at their B&B (bed and bagel) above the deli.

Country Inn & Suites (☎ 800-456-4000, 410-571-6700; www.countryinns.com; 2600 Housley Rd at Hwy 450; r from $119; P ☒ ☒) As charming as chains get, and has free shuttles to the historic district.

O'Callaghan Hotel (☎ 866-548-1446; www.ocallaghanhotels.com; 174 West St; r $150-240; P ☒ ☒ wi-fi) This Irish chain is a cushy if corporate-feeling big box that offers good luxury outside the B&B circuit.

Chez Amis B&B (☎ 410-263-6631; www.chezamis.com; 85 East St; r $165-215; P ☒) Unless you have a bunny phobia, you'll enjoy your stay at this friendly four-room B&B just steps from the capitol (which is also the name of the room with the best view). Full gourmet breakfast is served. Children over 10 welcome.

Eating & Drinking

As you might guess, the seafood here is superb. Annapolis also does excellent power grub (steaks, pizza etc), which makes sense given all the politicians running around.

Bagels And... (☎ 410-224-8686; 2019 West St; bagels 75¢; ☉ 6am-3pm Mon-Fri, 6:30am-3pm Sat, 7am-2:30pm Sun) This is a good kosher spot that serves some of the best bagels and bialys (like a flatter bagel that substitutes the center hole for a pocket of diced onions) in the state.

City Dock Café (☎ 410-269-0969; 18 Market Space; items $2-5; ☉ 6:30am-10pm) We will swear by the café mocha here, which must be the tastiest rocket-fuel we've ever imbibed.

Ninja Café 1 (☎ 410-269-0490; 118 Dock St; mains $5-12; ☉ 11am-9pm) This claustrophobic joint serves Chesapeake-inspired sushi and sashimi right off the docks.

Chick & Ruth's Delly (☎ 410-269-6737; 165 Main St; mains $6-10; ☉ 6:30am-10pm Sun-Thu, until 11:30pm Fri & Sat) A cornerstone of Annapolis, the 'delly' is bursting with affable quirkiness and a stressfully large menu. Sandwiches are named after famous local folks – Maryland Senator Barbara Mikulski is the open-faced tuna.

Galway Bay (☎ 410-263-8333; 63 Maryland Ave; mains $8-15; ☉ 11am-midnight, from 10:30am Sun) The epitome of a power-broker bar, the Galway is the dark sort of hideaway where political deals go down over Jameson, stouts and mouthwatering pub grub. Funnily enough, this Irish place is run by real Irish people.

Rams Head Tavern (☎ 410-268-4545; 33 West St; tickets $11-60; ☉ from 11am) The best bar in town serves good eats and tasty microbrews in an attractive oak-paneled setting, while hot live acts burn up the stage.

Buddy's Crabs, Ribs & Raw Bar (☎ 410-626-1100; 100 Main St; mains $14-28; ☉ 11:30am-9:30pm Mon-Thu,

---

EATING: MARYLAND BLUE CRABS

Eating at a Maryland crab shack, where the dress code stops at shorts and flip-flops and seagulls poop in your beer, is the quintessential Chesapeake Bay experience, the culinary expression of this region's comfort in casualness. Traditionally, Maryland crabs are served steamed or in crabcake form. Steamed crabs are prepared very simply, using beer and Old Bay seasoning. One of the best shacks in the state is an hour south of DC. **Captain Billy's** (☎ 301-932-4323; 11495 Popes Creek Rd, Newburg; ⏲ 11am-9pm Tue-Sun) gets everything right: brown paper tablecloths, friendly waitstaff and a view of the river your crabs were swimming in moments before. The other great Maryland recipe is crabcakes. The best have the right amount of 'filler' to balance out lump crabmeat, and our favorites are served in **Stoney's** (☎ 410-586-1888; Oyster House Rd, Broome's Island; ⏲ 11:30am-9pm Thu-Sun) 40 miles south of DC.

---

from 11am Fri & Sat, from 8:30am Sun) Buddy's does the Maryland waterfront dining thing – no pretension, big portions, heart-attack ingredients and seafood so fresh it's kicking – very well. The menu is half price for kids between 6pm and 10pm, and its weekday $12 lunch buffet is great value.

Getting There & Around

The C-60 bus route (tickets $3; service from 7am to 7pm Monday to Friday) connects Annapolis with BWI airport. Greyhound runs buses to Washington, DC ($15.50). **Annapolis Transit** (☎ 410-263-7964) provides local transport.

EASTERN SHORE

Unbroken miles of bird-dotted wetlands and serene waterscapes are hours from one of America's busiest urban corridors. Buppies (Bohemian Yuppies) are evident, but there are still dock towns where watermen live off the Chesapeake Bay. The flat topography is made for bicycling.

Easton

The historic hamlet of Easton, with its buried powerlines, is a popular artsy weekend getaway from DC and Baltimore. Get a map at the **Easton Welcome Resource Center** (☎ 410-822-0345; 11 Harrison St; ⏲ 9am-5pm), which also serves as a booking agent for the historic **Avalon Theatre** (☎ 410-822-7299; www.avalontheatre.com; 40 E Dover St). Restored to its former art-deco style, the 400-seater showcases local plays and national live music acts.

The small **Academy Art Museum** (☎ 410-822-2787; 106 South St; suggested donation $2; ⏲ 10am-4pm Mon-Sat) is the best art museum on the Eastern Shore, with a substantial collection of American and European art from the last half-century.

The **Historical Society of Talbot County** (☎ 410-822-0773; 25 S Washington St; admission free; ⏲ 10am-4pm Mon-Sat) maintains a small history museum and offers **tours** of historic house and sites associated with Shore native Frederick Douglass (tickets $5).

Tidewater Inn (☎ 410-822-1300; www.tidewaterinn .com; 101 E Dover St; r from $109; P ⛤) is a cute, colonial option near the town center. Stuffed with Australian Aboriginal art, the **Inn at Easton** (☎ 410-822-4910; www.theinnateaston.com; 28 S Harrison St; r $200-225, ste $225-445; P ✖ wi-fi) has a unique Chesapeake-meets-Dreamtime theme; the attached restaurant serves superb high-end fusion cuisine and is regularly ranked one of the best in the region.

Get your art-internet-and-coffee fix at **Coffee East** (☎ 410-819-6711; 3 Goldsborough St; ⏲ from 6am Mon-Sat, from 7am Sun; 🖳 wi-fi). Enjoy the Pacific-inspired artwork at **General Tanuki** (☎ 410-819-0707; 25 Goldsborough St; lunch mains $5-12, dinner mains $18-25; ⏲ noon-2pm & 4-9pm Mon-Thu, noon-10pm Fri & Sat) while digging into an Asian-tinged menu of curry-fried oyster sandwiches and fresh sushi.

St Michaels & Tilghman Island

St Michaels is a little more authentically tied to the water than Easton, but it's still a precious village flooded with out-of-town boaters. During the War of 1812, inhabitants rigged up lanterns in a nearby forest and blacked out the town. British naval gunners shelled the trees, allowing St Michaels to escape destruction. The building now known as the **Cannonball House** (Mulberry St) was the only structure to have been hit.

At the lighthouse, the **Chesapeake Bay Maritime Museum** (☎ 410-745-2916; Navy Point; adult/child 6-17 $13/5; ⏲ 10am-6pm summer, until 5pm spring & fall, until 4pm winter) delves into the deep ties between

Shore folk and America's largest estuary. Narrated historic cruises aboard the **Patriot** (☎ 410-745-3100; Navy Point; adult/child under 13 $20/15) leave from the Crab Claw dock thrice daily.

Laura Ashley's most lurid fantasies probably resemble the rooms in the red-brick **Parsonage Inn** (☎ 410-745-5519; www.parsonage-inn.com; 210 N Talbot St; r incl breakfast $100-195; **P** **X**), which is run by a pair of lovely, awfully hospitable inn-keepers.

At **208 Talbot** (☎ 410-745-3838; 208 N Talbot St; mains $26-33; ☽ 5-9pm Sun-Thu, until 10pm Fri & Sat), if the oysters in champagne sauce or pan-seared rockfish don't grab you, you can bring in your own waterfowl from the day's hunting and have the chef cook it.

At the end of the road over the Hwy 33 drawbridge, tiny **Tilghman Island** still runs a working waterfront where local captains take visitors out on graceful oyster skipjacks; the **Rebecca T Ruark** (☎ 410-886-2176; www.skipjack.org; 2hr cruises adult/child under 12 $30/15), is the oldest certified vessel in the country. Head to legendary **Harrison's Chesapeake House** (☎ 410-886-2121; 21551 Chesapeake House Dr; mains $8-22; ☽ 6am-9pm Mon-Fri, until 11pm Sat & Sun) for a massive, 'no apologies, lots of butter' (we love that) Eastern Shore seafood feast.

Berlin & Snow Hill

Imagine 'small-town, main street Americana,' cute that image up by a few points, and you've come close to these Eastern Shore villages. Most of the buildings here are preserved or renovated to look preserved. If you love antique shops, die before you leave, because you will never find a greater concentration of porcelain knickknacks.

In Berlin, the **Globe Theater** (☎ 410-641-0784; 12 Broad St; lunch $6-12, dinner $19-28; ☽ 11am-10pm Mon-Thu, 11am-midnight Sat, 10am-10pm Sun) is a lovingly restored main stage that serves as a restaurant, bar, art gallery and theater for nightly live music; the kitchen is known for its Asian-meets-American menu. The nearby, still-functioning **Hair Shop** (17 N Main St) was a setpiece in the 1999 film *Runaway Bride*.

There's B&B's galore overflowing with charm and doilies, but if you need an alternative try the **Atlantic Hotel** (☎ 410-641-3589; 2 N Main St; r $85-155, d $115-215; **P** **X**). This handsome, gilded-era lodger gives guests the time-warp experience with all the modern amenities, and the attached **Solstice** (lunch mains $8-15, dinner mains $21-28; ☽ 11am-3pm & 5-10pm Mon-Sat, 10am-3pm Sun)

serves excellent Spain-comes-to-the-Tidewater dishes such as chorizo and clam bake.

A few miles from Berlin, Snow Hill is even tinier and cozier. Nearby **Furnace Town** (☎ 410-632-2032; Old Furnace Rd; adult/child $4/2; ☽ 10am-5pm Apr-Oct), off Rte 12, is a living history museum that marks the old location of a 19th-century iron-smelting town. In Snow Hill itself, while away an odd, rewarding half-hour in the **Julia A Purnell Museum** (☎ 410-632-0515; 208 W Market St; adult/child under 12 $2/50¢; ☽ 10am-4pm Tue-Sat, 1-4pm Sun Apr-Oct), a tiny structure that feels like an attic for the entire Eastern Shore (Eh? The second president of Liberia was born around here?). Have a sumptuous doss at the **River House Inn** (☎ 410-632-2722; 201 E Market St; www.riverhouseinn.com; r $250-300; **P** **X**), which overlooks a breathtakingly pretty bend of the Pocomoke River.

OCEAN CITY

The OC is where you'll experience the American seaside holiday at its tacky best. Eat a sandy hot dog on the beach, buy a T-shirt with unprintably obscene slogans, drink to excess with students and watch families argue over a round of mini-golf. Did we mention the water's great and there's an awesome national park nearby?

Extending 2.5 miles from the inlet to 27th St, the boardwalk is the center of action. The **visitor center** (☎ 410-723-8600; ☽ 9am-5pm) and local **hotel-motel-restaurant association** (☎ 410-289-6733; www.ocvisitor.com), in the convention center on Coastal Hwy at 40th St, can help you find lodging. Many establishments are only open during temperate months; prices plummet off-season. Traffic is jammed and parking scarce in summer.

Sleeping

There are some 10,000 identical guest rooms (double beds, cable TV, kitchenette) in town. Waterfront views and weekends hike prices, which skyrocket near Memorial Day and July 4. Many places have two-night minimum rules on weekends, especially during the season.

MIDRANGE

King Charles Hotel (☎ 410-289-6141; www.kingcharleshotel.com; 1209 Baltimore Ave at 12th St; r $105-148; **P** **X**) This place could be a quiet summer cottage, except it happens to be within spitting distance of the best boardwalk action.

SCENIC DRIVE: MARITIME MARYLAND

Maryland and the Chesapeake Bay have always been inextricable, but few parts of the state actually live off the water today. Here's a chance to see some towns that stubbornly cling to the ebb-and-rip clock of the tides.

About 150 miles south of Baltimore, at the edge of the Eastern Shore, is **Crisfield**, the top working water town in Maryland. Get visiting details at the **visitor center** (☎ 410-968-2501; 3 9th St; 10am-4pm Mon-Sat). Any seafood you eat here will be goooood, but for a true Shore experience, try some of the strip-the-paint strong coffee at **Gordon's** (☎ 410-968-0566; 831 W Main St; from 4am), where watermen flock in the early morning hours before heading out on their boats.

From here you can leave your car overnight (or take a day trip) and board the pedestrian **ferry** (☎ 410-425-5931/4471; $20; departs noon & 5pm daily, evening service varies in winter) to **Smith Island**, the only off-shore settlement in the state. Settled by fisherfolk from the English West Country some 400 years ago, the island's tiny population still speaks with what linguists reckon is the closest thing to a 17th-century Cornish accent. Take a tour of this appealing little archipelago of marsh grass on a rented golf cart and visit the nearby **Martin National Wildlife Refuge**, one of the prettiest wetlands we've ever seen; ask about getting there at the island marina. Ferries will take you back to the mainland and the present day at 3:30pm.

Crystal Beach (☎ 410-289-7165; www.crystalbeach hotel.com; cnr 25th St & Boardwalk; r $120-250; P 🐾 🛆) The name makes this hotel sound like a tinkly princess palace; actually, it's a decently situated midrange option.

Spinnaker Motel (☎ 410-289-5444; www.pur nellproperties.com/spinnaker; cnr 18th St & Baltimore Ave; r from $180; P 🐾 🛆) Basically a bunch of boxes on the beach, but the boxes are comfy, the beach is pretty and this is a cheaper waterfront option.

TOP END

Inn on the Ocean (☎ 410-289-8894; www.innonthe ocean.com; 1001 Atlantic Ave at the Boardwalk; r $175-350; P 🐾) This six-roomed B&B is an elegant escape, especially when compared with the boardwalk's big-box blah.

Lighthouse Club Hotel (☎ 410-524-5400, 888-371-5400; www.fagers.com/hotel; 201 60th St on the Bay; r incl breakfast $225-305; P 🐾 wi-fi) You might never make it to the beach when your buff-toned suite is equipped with a double Jacuzzi and romantic views of the bay.

Eating & Drinking

Surf 'n' turf and all-you-can-eat deals are the order of the day. Dance clubs cluster around the boardwalk's southern tip.

Phillips Crab House (☎ 410-289-9121; 2004 Philadelphia Ave at 21st St; lunch mains $9-14, dinner mains $16-24; from noon) This regional chain has been around since 1956 and has an enormous menu (and venue; its neon could blind an army) of all things from the sea.

Embers (☎ 410-289-3322; 24th St & Coastal Hwy; mains $19-26; from 2pm) The awe-inspiring $27 seafood-and-steak buffet at this popular restaurant may well be the root cause of America's obesity crisis.

Fager's Island (☎ 410-524-5500; 60th St; mains $19-36; from 11am) The food is good, if expensive, but it's best for a drink – Tchaikovsky's 1812 Overture is cued up exactly 15 minutes and 34 seconds before sunset, to time the cannons with the sun hitting the horizon.

Shenanigans (☎ 410-289-7181; cnr 4th St & Boardwalk; from 11am Mar-Oct) Here's where you find hearty quasi-authentic Irish fare, live traditional music and raucous crowds.

Seacrets (☎ 410-524-4900; cnr W 49th St & the Bay; from 11am) A water-laced, Jamaican-themed restaurant-bar-club straight out of MTV's *Spring Break*, you can drift around in an inner tube while drunk and never get pulled over!

Getting There & Around

Carolina Trailways (☎ 410-289-9307; cnr 2nd St & Philadelphia Ave) runs frequent buses to Wilmington ($20) and twice a day to Washington DC ($45) and Baltimore ($35).

Ocean City Municipal Bus Service (☎ 410-723-1607; day pass $2) runs the length of the beach.

WESTERN MARYLAND

Damn, Maryland keeps getting better: try her mountainous spine here, packed with rugged scenery and Civil War battlesites.

Frederick

Halfway between the battlefields of Gettysburg, PA, and Antietam, Frederick is a popular stop along the Civil War trail. Its 50-square-block historic district is filled with 18th- and 19th-century buildings in various states of renovation. The **visitor center** (☎ 301-663-8687; 19 E Church St at Market St) conducts weekend walking tours in summer ($4.50); it validates parking from the garage next door.

The **National Museum of Civil War Medicine** (☎ 301-695-1864; www.civilwarmed.org; 48 E Patrick St; adult/student/child 10-16 $6.50/5.50/4.50; ⏱ 10am-5pm Mon-Sat, 11am-5pm Sun) gives a fascinating, sometimes gruesome look at the health conditions soldiers and doctors faced during the war, as well as important medical advancements that came out of the conflict.

Hollerstown Hill B&B (☎ 301-228-3630; www.hollerstownhill.com; 4 Clarke Pl; r $115-125; P ✿) has four pattern-heavy rooms, two resident terriers and an elegant billiards room.

The **Mudd Puddle** (☎ 301-620-4324; 124 S Carroll St; panini $5; ⏱ from 7am Mon-Fri, 8am-10pm Sat) is a warm, comfortable coffee and panini place that hosts live entertainment most weekends.

Frederick is accessible via **Greyhound** (☎ 301-663-3311; 100 S East St) and **MARC trains** (☎ 301-228-2888; 141 B&O Ave at East Ave; ⏱ weekdays only).

Antietam National Battlefield

The site of the bloodiest day in American history is, ironically, supremely peaceful, quiet and haunting, uncluttered save for plaques and statues. On September 17, 1862, General Robert E Lee's first invasion of the North was stalled here in a tactical stalemate that left 23,000 dead, wounded or missing – more casualties than America had suffered in all her previous wars combined. Poignantly, many of the battlefield graves are inscribed with German and Irish names, a roll call of immigrants who died fighting for their new homeland.

The **visitor center** (☎ 301-432-5124; State Rd 65; 3-day pass for individuals/families $4/6; ⏱ 8:30am-6pm, until 5pm low-season) offers self-guided driving-tour pamphlets and audiotapes ($6).

Ten miles after I-68 turns into I-70, the highway literally passes through **Sideling Hill**, an impressive rock exposure nearly 850ft high. Pull over to check out the **exhibit center** (☎ 301-842-2155; admission free; ⏱ 9am-5pm) and the striated evidence of some 340 million years of geologic history. Also, 10 miles away off I-67 is **Gathland State Park** (☎ 301-791-4767;

> **CAMPING WITH HORSES**
>
> Wild, wild horses, the only herd on the East Coast, roam the barrier island of Assateague, a perfect, barren sandscape fluffed with the occasional patch of dune grass. The island is a **park** (vehicle/cyclist & pedestrian $10/3) with a strict speed limit of 25mph. A **visitor center** (☎ 410-641-1441; Hwy 611) has information on two National Park Service **campgrounds** (☎ 410-641-3030, 800-365-2267; peak season campsite $20) and state **park facilities** (☎ 410-641-2120; campsites/RV sites $34/44).

admission free; ⏱ 8am-sunset), former home of Civil War journalist George Alfred Townsend and site of the country's only monument to war correspondents.

Cumberland

At the Potomac River, the frontier outpost of Fort Cumberland (not to be confused with the Cumberland Gap between Virginia and Kentucky) was the pioneer gateway across the Alleghenies to Pittsburgh and the Ohio River. Today Cumberland has expanded into the outdoor-recreation trade to guide visitors to the region's rivers, forests and mountains.

C&O CANAL NATIONAL HISTORIC PARK

A marvel of engineering, the C&O Canal was designed to stretch alongside the Potomac River from Chesapeake Bay to the Ohio River – linking commercial centers in the east with frontier resources out west. Construction on the canal began in 1828 but was halted here in 1850 by the Appalachian Mountains. By then the first railroad had made its way to Cumberland, rendering the canal obsolete.

The **C&O Canal National Historic Park visitor center** (☎ 301-739-4200; 15 Canal Pl; ⏱ 9am-5pm Mon-Fri) chronicles the importance of river trade in eastern-seaboard history. The park's protected 185-mile corridor includes a 12ft-wide towpath/hiking and bicycling trail and maintains six visitor centers, the first in Georgetown and the last one here.

Outside the **Allegheny County visitor center** (☎ 301-777-5132) passengers can catch steam-locomotive rides aboard the **Western Maryland Scenic Railroad** (☎ 800-872-4650; www.wmsr.com; adult/child $25/12), traversing forests and steep ravines to Frostburg, a three-hour round-trip.

There are plenty of reputable outfitters in the area. **Allegany Expeditions** (☎ 800-819-5170; www.alleganyexpeditions.com; 10310 Columbus Ave/Rte 2) leads tours to suit whatever adventure itch you've got, from spelunking to fly-fishing.

Deep in your heart, you know you should have been in *Grease*. The next best thing is chilling by the iconoclastic soda fountain and jukebox in the famous **Queen City Creamery & Deli** (☎ 301-777-0011; N Harrison St; mains $5-8; ☺ 7am-10pm, shorter hours in winter).

Deep Creek Lake

In the extreme west of the panhandle, Maryland's largest freshwater lake is an all-seasons playground. The crimson and copper glow of the Alleghenies attracts thousands during the annual **Autumn Glory Festival** in October, rivaling New England's leaf-turning backdrops. The **Garrett County visitor center** (☎ 301-387-4386; www.garrettchamber.com), off US 219 on the north end, has information on all outdoor activities, including the state's only ski resort, **Wisp** (☎ 301-387-4911).

DELAWARE

Delaware: the First State, mascoted by the smurfish, poultryesque Blue Hen, a blip on the American map, out-sized (or under-sized) in reputation by tinier Rhode Island. Ah, give her a break. Delaware still rides her reputation as first state to ratify the Constitution, but she's probably better known as a low-tax haven and 'headquarters' (ie mailing address) for a glut of corporations.

So you may be pleasantly surprised to find Delaware neat and attractive, home to sound little towns, cozy countryside and long, sunny beaches. Plus: Wilmington is like a safer Baltimore, Dover is twee and many towns alternate between two almost-English sensibilities: cute, compact village greens versus the magnificent (if gaudy) estates of the Brandywine Valley.

History

In colonial days Delaware was the subject of an aggressive land feud between Dutch, Swedish and British settlers. The former imported classically northern European middle-class concepts, the latter a plantation-based aristocracy, which is partly why Delaware remains a typically mid-Atlantic cultural hybrid today.

The little state's big moment came on December 7, 1787, when Delaware became the first state to ratify the US Constitution and thus the first state in the Union. It remained in that union throughout the Civil War, despite supporting slavery. During this period, as throughout much of the state's history, the economy drew on the chemical industry (originally a gunpowder factory) set up by French immigrant Charles DuPont in 1802. Low taxes drew other firms (particularly credit card companies) in the 20th century, boosting the state's prosperity.

Information

Delaware Tourism Office (☎ 302-739-4271, 866-284-7489; www.visitdelaware.com; 99 King's Hwy, Dover, DE 19903)
Visitor center (☎ 302-737-4059; I-95 btwn exits 1 & 3)

DELAWARE BEACHES

Delaware's 28 miles of sandy Atlantic beaches are the best reason to linger. All businesses and services listed here are open year-round unless otherwise noted, and all prices are for the high season (June to August). Low-season bargains abound.

Lewes

In 1631 the Dutch gave this whaling settlement the pretty name of Zwaanendael, or valley of the swans, before promptly getting massacred by local Nanticoke Indians. Today the more-boringly titled Lewes is a cute seaside gem.

The **visitor center** (☎ 302-645-8073; www.lewes chamber.com; 120 Kings Hwy; ☺ 9am-5pm Mon-Fri) directs you to sights such as the **Zwaanendael Museum** (☎ 302-645-1148; 102 Kings Hwy; admission free; ☺ 10am-4:30pm Tue-Sat, 1:30-4:30pm Sun), where the exuberantly friendly staff explain the Dutch roots of this first state settlement.

DELAWARE FACTS

Nickname The First State, Small Wonder
Population 853,476
Area 2491 sq miles
Capital city Dover (pop 32,800)
Sales tax None
Birthplace of Charles DuPont, Nylon
Home of Credit card companies, banks, chemical and pharmaceutical firms, a whole lotta chickens
Famous for Lack of taxes, not being famous (ie the 'Hi…I'm in Delaware' bit in *Wayne's World*)
State bird Blue Hen

WASHINGTON, DC & THE CAPITAL REGION

You like heart-wrenchingly cute digs? Great; come say at the **Hotel Rodney** (☎ 302-645-6466; www.hotelrodneydelaware.com; 142 2nd St; r $115-200, ste $160-315; P ⊠ ⚎ ⚎), with its 18 antique-laden rooms. **Beacon Motel** (☎ 302-645-4888; 514 Savannah Rd; r $150-200; P ⊠ ⚎ ⚎) has large, quiet rooms and easy access to Rehoboth Beach.

Do yourself a favor and get acquainted with the Reubens and friendly waitstaff at the **Blue Plate Diner** (☎ 302-644-8400; 329 Savannah Rd; dishes $5; ⚏ 8am-9pm, shorter hours in winter). Exquisite French-inspired fare is found at the town's best upscale eatery, the gingerbread-style **Buttery Restaurant** (☎ 302-645-7755; cnr 2nd Ave & Savannah Rd; mains $15-24; ⚏ 11:30am-2:30pm, dinner from 5pm daily, brunch 10:30am-2:30pm Sun). Get there between 5pm and 6:30pm for the $28 prix-fixe dinner.

The **Cape May–Lewes Ferry** (☎ reservations 800-643-3779, schedule 302-644-6030; www.capemaylewesferry .com; Nov-Mar per vehicle $23 plus per passenger $7, Apr-Oct per vehicle $29 plus per passenger $9.50) runs daily 80-minute ferries across Delaware Bay to New Jersey from the terminal a mile from downtown Lewes. Keep in mind that if you're on foot, the town of Cape May is miles away from the docks.

Cape Henlopen State Park

One mile east of Lewes, more than 4000 acres of dune bluffs, pine forests and wetlands are preserved in a lovely **state park** (☎ 302-645-8983) that's popular with bird-watchers and beachgoers ($6 per out-of-state car). You can see clear to Cape May from the observation tower. North Shores beach draws many gay and lesbian couples. **Camping** (☎ 302-645-2103; campsites $31; ⚏ Mar-Nov) includes oceanfront or wooded sites.

Rehoboth Beach & Dewey Beach

Rehoboth is an appealing if odd place: part North (subs are grinders), part South ('Git R' Done' T-shirts), part chic gay resort, part boozy family getaway. Rehoboth Ave, the main drag, is lined with restaurants, food stalls and souvenir shops, from the **visitor center** (☎ 302-227-2233; www.beach-fun.com; 501 Rehoboth Ave; ⚏ 9am-5pm) at the traffic circle to the mile-long beach boardwalk.

Further south, along Hwy 1, is Rehoboth's wild little sister, **Dewey Beach**, known for its frantic nightlife. All lodging, eating and drinking listings are in Rehoboth unless otherwise noted.

Books, coffee and internet access (wired and wireless), plus a nice lounge area, can all be found at **Booksandcoffee** (☎ 302-226-9959; 113 Dickinson St, Dewey; ⚏ 7:30am-7pm).

SLEEPING

There may be two-night minimum stays during the high season; call ahead.

Royal Rose Inn (☎ 302-226-2535; www.royalroseinn .com; 41 Baltimore Ave; r incl breakfast $130-190; P ⚎ wi-fi) This gay-friendly place can't decide if it wants to be camp or respectable or both, kinda like Rehoboth itself. Either way, the rooms are lovely.

Shore Inn (☎ 302-227-8487; www.shoreinn.com; 703 Rehoboth Ave; r $130-200, ste $175-235; P ⚎) Who likes clothing-optional sun decks? A safe bet: the guests at this fun, men-only B&B.

Corner Cupboard Inn (☎ 302-227-8553; www .cornercupboardinn.com; 50 Park Ave; r incl breakfast $160-260; P ⚎ wi-fi) Sheltered on a tree-lined street north of Lake Gerar off 2nd St, this cozy (as a cupboard, duh) house is the place to chill out from beach life while remaining within walking distance of it.

EATING & DRINKING

Do it right and eat on the Boardwalk; good beachfront food includes Thrasher's for pizza, Nicola's for fries, Gus and Gus's for fried chicken and Dollie's for saltwater taffy. Afterwards, here are some options when you're ready for a drink and a sit-down meal.

Café Solé (☎ 302-227-7107; 44 Baltimore Ave; sandwiches $4-8; ⚏ 11am-3:30pm daily, from 5:30pm Wed-Sun) Best sandwiches in town. Ever tried a fried oyster BLT?

Dogfish Head (☎ 302-226-2739; 320 Rehoboth Ave; mains $9-23; ⚏ from 4pm Mon-Fri, from noon Sat & Sun) When a place mixes its own brewery with some of the best live music on the Atlantic Shore, you know you've got a winning combination.

Planet X Café (☎ 302-226-1928; 35 Wilmington Ave; mains $20-30; ⚏ from 5:30pm, Thu-Sun only low-season) This café plays up the potential of organic ingredients and free-range poultry to create incredible, globe-spanning dishes in a space that elegantly mixes Chesapeake comfort, traces of playful camp and the spicy edge of a Southeast Asian temple complex.

La La Land (☎ 302-227-3887; 22 Wilmington Ave; mains $26-35; ⚏ from 6pm) Purple fairies and gold stars playfully hang over one of the heartiest, most innovative menus in Rehoboth: yellowfin

---

LOCAL VOICES: ERIC PAUL LEVY, ROCKIN' THE DELAWARE SCENE

Eric Paul Levy is a Wilmington-born rocker who has been playing in bands across Delaware, Maryland, New Jersey and other states for two decades.

What and where is the Delaware sound? Wilmington is great right now, and that's a sign we're stepping it up. The rock sound filters down from New York. But in this area [Southern] country pop filters up. The Mason–Dixon Line runs through the Delaware sound, and gives us more of a country influence.

What's there to do in Delaware? Besides the beaches, which are all good, Delaware is the land of poultry and adultery. It's chicken hell. Not as bad as [New] Jersey, though (laughs).

Let's get specific: what's there to do in Dover? Rehoboth Beach? Are people cool with the gay scene in Rehoboth? Dover is small-town America. Rehoboth? It's out. People wanna do their thing, let 'em. Just don't let the kids see it, and that goes for the straights too. Families been coming to Rehoboth for as long as the homosexuals, so I don't think either one has a problem with the other. I love the Dogfish Head (opposite).

What's up with George Thorogood and the Delaware Destroyers dropping the 'Delaware' from there name? I mean, Bruce Springstein's been playing up the fact he's from New Jersey for his whole career. Yeah, well, Jersey is Jersey. Delaware ? Dude. Delaware's got no street cred.

---

sushi with capers, beef fillet with Roquefort cheese…yeah, this is x-rated food porn.

GETTING AROUND

The **Jolly Trolley** (☎ 302-227-1197; 1-way $2, past midnight $3; ☼ 8am-2am summer) connects Rehoboth and Dewey and makes frequent stops along the way. **Greyhound/Carolina Trailways** (801 Rehoboth Ave) buses stop on Rehoboth Ave.

NORTHERN & CENTRAL DELAWARE

The grit of Wilmington is balanced by the rolling hills and palatial residences of the Brandywine Valley, particularly the soaring estate of Winterhur. Dover is cute, friendly, and gets a little lively after hours.

Wilmington

It's a shame Wilmington is often overlooked; a unique cultural milieu (African Americans, Jews, Caribbeans etc) and an energetic arts scene make this a town worth a visit. The central commercial district is along Market St, while Riverfront turns old warehouses and other industrial sites into shops, restaurants and museums. The **visitor center** (☎ 302-652-4088; www.visitwilmingtonde.com; 100 W 10th St; ☼ 9am-5pm Mon-Fri) is downtown.

The **Delaware Art Museum** (☎ 302-571-9590; 800 S Madison St; adult/student/child $10/5/3; ☼ 10am-4pm Tue-Sat, noon-4pm Sun) exhibits work of the local Brandywine School, including Edward Hopper, John Sloan and three generations of Wyeths. The **Delaware Center for the Contemporary Arts**

(☎ 302-656-6466; www.thedcca.org; 200 S Madison St; adult/student/child under 12 $5/3/free, Sat morning & Wed free; ☼ 10am-5pm Tue, Thu, Fri & Sat, from noon Wed & Sun) is bringing some mind-expanding culture to the burgeoning Riverfront district. Located in, of all things, an art-deco Woolworth's building, the **Delaware History Museum** (☎ 302-656-0637; www.thedcca.org; 200 S Madison St; adult/student/child under 12 $5/3/free; ☼ 10am-5pm Tue, Thu, Fri & Sat, from noon Wed & Sun) proves the First State has done loads more than earn its nickname.

The premier hotel in the state, the **Hotel du Pont** (☎ 302-594-3100; www.hoteldupont.com; cnr Market & 11th Sts, r $130-250; ste $260-750; P ❧ wi-fi) is luxurious and classy enough to satisfy its namesake (ie one of America's most successful industrialists). Parking here is $22. **Leo & Jimmy's Deli** (☎ 302-656-7151; 728 Market St; mains $4-10; ☼ 5:30am-4pm Mon-Fri) is a Wilmington standby, well-loved for its excellent sandwiches and service. For dessert, try the famously decadent chocolate at old-school **Govatos** (☎ 302-652-4082; 800 Market St; mains $4-9; ☼ 8am-5pm Mon-Fri year-round, until 3pm Sat Oct-Apr).

Wilmington is accessible via **Greyhound/ Carolina Trailways** (☎ 302-655-6111; 101 N French St) and **Amtrak** (☎ 302-429-6527; 100 S French St).

Brandywine Valley

After making their fortune the French-descended DuPonts turned the Brandywine Valley into a sort of American Loire Valley, and it remains a nesting ground for the wealthy and ostentatious to this day. The **Brandywine**

Valley Tourist Information Center (☎ 610-719-1730), outside Longwood Gardens in Kennett Square, PA, distributes information on the region's triple crown of **chateaux** and gardens: Winterthur, Longwood Gardens and Nemours (under renovation and scheduled to reopen in 2008).

Winterthur (☎ 302-888-4600; www.winterthur.org; Hwy 52; adult/student/child $20/18/10; ☽ 10am-5pm Tue-Sun), off Kennett Pike, an incredible monument to American excess, includes the 175-room country estate of Henry Francis DuPont, and a blinged-out decorative arts museum. The gardens and several child-specific attractions are visited by tram. It's 6 miles northwest of Wilmington.

Hagley Museum (☎ 302-658-2400; www.hagley.org; Hwy 141; adult/student/child $11/9/4; ☽ 9:30am-4:30pm daily, weekdays only in winter) is another fascinating shrine to the DuPont legacy. The sprawling outdoor museum includes the ruins of the original DuPont mills, craftsmith demonstrations and exhibits on cutting-edge DuPont products.

New Castle

Unlike many historic American villages, the people of New Castle decided not to pave their heritage into a strip of gas stations. Thus: New Castle, a web of cobblestone streets and 18th-century buildings that's as colonially cute as a kitten in a powdered wig. The **visitor center** (42 The Strand; ☽ 9am-5pm Mon-Fri) arranges walking tours, or you can wander the compact old town on your own. Sights include the **Old Court House** (☽ closed Mon), the **arsenal on the Green**, **churches** and **cemeteries** dating back to the 17th century, and **historic houses**.

The elderly owner of the five-room **Terry House B&B** (☎ 302-322-2505; www.terryhouse.com; 130 Delaware St; r $90-110; P) will play the piano for you while you enjoy a full breakfast. There's big, mouth-watering colonial dishes (roast duck and honey-drop biscuits, anyone?), all heavy on butter, cream and the other things that make life worth living, at **Jessop's Tavern** (☎ 302-322-6111; 114 Delaware St; mains $16-22; ☽ 11am-3pm & 5-10pm Mon-Sat) and its classier sister, the **Arsenal at Old New Castle** (☎ 302-328-1290; 30 Market St; mains around $30).

Dover

You wouldn't think it given how stately central Dover is, with her classic brick buildings and shady, tree-lined boulevards, but this little town is good fun. The 1792 Old State House,

1874 Court House, belly-stretching cheap eats and cheerful bars dot the area around the central Green, and throb with happy crowds at night.

Walk beside the State House to find the state **visitor center** (☎ 302-739-4266; 406 Federal St; ☽ 8:30am-4:30pm Mon-Sat, from 1:30pm Sun) and history exhibits at the foot of a long plaza from the capitol. The seven **Delaware State Museums** (☎ 302-736-7400) are all excellent, eccentric little temples to their respective fields. In Dover, try the **Johnson Victrola Museum** (☎ 302-739-4266; cnr Bank & New Sts; admission free; ☽ 10am-3:30pm Tue-Fri, 9am-4:30pm Sat) which honors 'talking machine' pioneer Eldridge Johnson with exhibits including the RCA Records trademark dog, Nipper.

Southeast of town, Dover Air Force Base is the country's largest air force base and the first stop for America's returning war dead. Unfortunately there's nothing (public) around to mark their homecoming; the thing to see here is the **Air Mobility Command Museum** (☎ 302-677-5938; cnr Hwys 9 & 1; admission free; ☽ 9am-4pm Tue-Sun), filled with vintage planes and other aviation artifacts.

Pay the owners of the **State Street Inn** (☎ 302-734-2294; www.statestreetinn.com; 228 State St; r incl breakfast $110-125; P ☒) a visit, because they like to bend over backwards for their guests. It helps that they rent out plush rooms in a plush-as-velveteen house.

Corner Eatery at 33 (☎ 302-735-9822; 33 W Loockerman St; mains $5-9; ☽ 10am-3pm Mon-Fri) is a townie favorite for its no-nonsense, cheap and filling fare.

our pick **WT Smithers** (☎ 302-674-8875; 140 S State St; ☽ from 11am Mon-Sat) is one of the best neighborhood bars we've hung out in, a good mix of rough-edged regulars, affable staff and statehouse types all sharing buffalo wings and excellent beer on tap.

VIRGINIA

The sheer density of this state is mind-boggling: every acre of soil is packed with some saga of national significance, be it the USA's colonization, Revolution or Civil War. Sometimes the past hits you on the head, but often it's just subtly absorbed against the cricket chorus of an ancient battlefield.

The national narrative is set against a stunning stage. Long beaches kiss the ocean,

VIRGINIA FACTS

Nickname Old Dominion

Population 7.64 million

Area 42,793 sq miles

Capital city Richmond (pop 194,729)

Sales tax 4%

Birthplace of Eight presidents, Robert E Lee, Arthur Ashe, Tom Wolfe

Home of The Pentagon, the CIA, more technology workers than any other state

Famous for History, the Shenandoah Valley, more history, being a presidential birthplace, did we mention history?

Named for The 'Virgin' Queen Elizabeth I

with pine-clad marshes, the soft curve of the Piedmont and the lush, rugged beauty of the Appalachians always laying to the west. The invisible line between the North and South is drawn here too; you'll know you've crossed when you hear the sweet drawl of a Richmond doyenne offering plates of biscuits and country ham.

History

You had a one in three shot at surviving Jamestown back in the 1600s. When the original settlers stopped dying and figured there was no gold in them thar hills, they started growing tobacco. One planter, John Rolfe, married a local princess named Pocahantas – who was incidentally 10 when she met 28-year old John Smith. The myth you've heard about their relationship is exactly that, an ego-pumping invention of Smith's.

A feudal aristocracy grew out of tobacco farming, and many gentry scions became Founding Fathers, including native son George Washington. In the 19th century the slave-based plantation system grew in size and incompatibility with the industrializing North; Virginia seceded in 1861, and became the epicenter of the Civil War. Following its defeat the state walked a tense cultural tightrope, accruing a layered identity that included older aristocrats; a rural and urban working class; waves of immigrants; and today, the burgeoning tech-heavy suburbs of DC. The state revels in its history, yet still wants to pioneer the American experiment; thus, while Virginia only reluctantly de-segregated in the 1960s,

today it houses one of the most ethnically diverse populations of the New South.

Information

Virginia's **Division of Tourism** (☎ 800-321-3244; www.virginia.org; 901 E Byrd St, Richmond, VA 23219) produces a comprehensive state guide. There are 10 welcome centers throughout the state. Many chain hotels won't let rooms to people under 21 years of age, so if that's you, check before you show up on the doorstep.

NORTHERN VIRGINIA

Half yuppie bedroom suburb, half immigrant hotpot, Northern Virginia tries – valiantly if a little unsuccessfully – to offer DC's arts and international flair without the dirt and crime.

Arlington

Just across the Potomac from DC, the 612-acre **Arlington National Cemetery** (☎ 703-692-0931; www.arlingtoncemetery.org; admission free; ☉ 8am-7pm Apr 1–Sep 30, until 5pm rest of year) is the burial ground for more than 245,000 military personnel and their dependents, with veterans from every US war since the Revolution. Leaving from the visitor center, **tourmobiles** (☎ 202-554-5100; adult/child $7/3.50) are a handy way to visit the cemetery's memorials.

The famous **Marine Corps Memorial** (☎ 703-289-2500) depicts six soldiers raising the American flag on Iwo Jima, and was built entirely on donations from former and current Marines. It's all the more poignant given the fate of the soldiers who are depicted (some were killed in combat, and those that came home suffered from survivor's guilt), to say nothing of the fate of those currently serving in the Corps. The **Air Force Memorial's** (☎ 703-247-5805; www.airforcememorial.org) three soaring arcs are meant to invoke the medium of air and the rush of air combat; this is the newest, sleekest memorial to an American service branch.

Robert E Lee's 1100-acre property, **Arlington House**, was confiscated when Lee left to command northern Virginia's army. Union soldiers were buried around the house so he could never use it again. After the Civil War, the site became the national cemetery, and the house is open to the public. The **Tomb of the Unknowns** represents soldiers killed in action who can't be identified as belonging to either side; military guards retain a

WASHINGTON, DC & THE CAPITAL REGION

WORTH THE TRIP: EDEN CENTER

If the Capital Region hasn't felt international enough, take a trip down clogged Wilson Blvd to the corner of Seven Corners in Falls Church, VA. About 11 miles from Washington is the **Eden Center**, the heart and soul of the region's Vietnamese community. Affectionately known as 'Little Saigon,' the Center is an enormous shopping plaza that has effectively mutated from a mall – that most American contribution to modern architecture – into a Southeast Asian market. If you've been traveling in Vietnam you'll feel like you're back. Clearly, this is the best place to eat Vietnamese food in the region, and the best of the best is **Huong Que** (☎ 703-538-6717; mains $8-15; ☯ 10am-10pm, until later Fri & Sat), tucked off to the west side of the plaza. Final caveat: leave Communist chic T-shirts at home. Don't forget the Center was created by South Vietnamese refugees, many of whom suffered through re-education camps.

---

round-the-clock vigil, and the changing of the guard (every half-hour, March to September, every hour October to February) is one of Arlington's most moving sights. An eternal flame marks the **grave of John F Kennedy**, next to those of Jacqueline Kennedy Onassis and two of her infant children. Other points of interest include the Pan Am Flight 103 cairn and a memorial to the astronauts of the space shuttle *Challenger*.

Ray's the Steaks (☎ 703-841-7297; 1725 Wilson Blvd; mains $15-35; ☯ 6-10pm Tue-Sat) is (way) better at serving tasty, enormous sides of cooked cow than inventing gimmicky names. Or head a few miles west to Vietnam, ie the Eden Center (above). In nearby Rosslyn you can go to the parking garage where *Washington Post* reporter Bob Woodward met with W Mark Felt, aka 'Deep Throat,' his secret source in the Nixon Whitehouse during Watergate. The **garage** is at 1401 Oak St and the pair rendezvoused at level C, space 32 (not that there's anything around to mark the spot).

Alexandria

When people say 'Alexandria' they're usually referring to Old Town: think colonial buildings, olde-timey fonts ande funnye spelling. But once you stop smelling cheesiness, you have to admit there's innovative art and dining around the red-brick corners. The **visitor center** (☎ 703-838-5005; www.funside.com; 221 King St; ☯ 9am-5pm) issues parking permits and discount tickets to historic sights. Don't miss the Torpedo Factory Art Center (opposite).

Cozy doesn't begin to describe little **Le Refuge** (☎ 703-548-4661; 127 N Washington St; lunch mains $10-16, dinner mains $18-30; ☯ 11:30am-2:30pm & 5:30-10pm). The vibe is admittedly kinda funny: lacy curtains, flower-framed menu,

ubiquitous pink alongside big manly cuts of French steak.

If you're looking to roll up your sleeves a little more, gnosh pub grub and listen to free, live Bluegrass try **Tiffany Tavern** (☎ 703-836-8844; 1116 King St; lunch mains $6-13, dinner mains $9-18; ☯ 5pm-midnight, until later Fri & Sat, 11:30am-2:30pm Wed-Fri).

To get to Alexandria from downtown DC get off at the King St Metro station. Local buses cover the mile to the visitor center. On weekends the free DASH shuttle bus connects the station with the waterfront and points in between.

Mt Vernon & Around

George Washington once hung his hat (and is now buried with his wife) at **Mt Vernon** (☎ 703-780-2000; www.mountvernon.org; adult/child 6-11 $11/5; ☯ 9am-5pm, until 4pm Nov-Feb), a 19-room country house that overlooks the Potomac. One of the most visited historic sites in the nation, it affords glimpses of 18th-century farm life and the first president as a country squire. Mt Vernon does not gloss over or demonize the Founding Father and his slave ownership, and the site explanations to that effect are worth checking out. The Washingtons lived here from 1759 to 1775, when George assumed command of the Continental Army. After the Revolution and eight years as president, he retired here in 1797, until his death in 1799.

There's great ye olde colonial dining (turkey with cornbread stuffing, mmmm) at the **Mount Vernon Inn** (☎ 703-780-0011; lunch $12-16, dinner $14-21; ☯ 11am-3:30pm daily, 5-9pm Mon-Sat), at the main gate.

America's premier folk music venue, the nearby **Birchmere** (☎ 703-549-7500; 3701 Mt Vernon Ave), looks like a warehouse that crashed into an acid-tripping, Americana-obsessed muralist.

Mt Vernon is 15 miles south of DC by an often congested road; you can Metro to Huntington, then take the Fairfax Connector bus 101. It also makes a gorgeous bike ride along the river from DC.

Great Falls National Park (☎ 703-285-2965; www.nps.gov/grfa; ☺ 7am-sunset) is one of those wild, wooly wilderness spaces that somehow survives mere minutes from a major urban nexus. It's an excellent fresh-air destination for those sick of museum crawling (or indeed, any outdoor enthusiasts period). The park is essentially a gorgeous, well-maintained forest cut through by the Potomac River, which surges over a series of local rapids and spills into the titular falls. There's excellent rock climbing on the river cliffs, and a spiderweb of trails that navigate 800 acres of lush, lovely woodland. See also p317

Manassas

Manassas exemplifies the paradox of preserved battlefields: in the effort to protect a place of violence, a space of total serenity is created. The two battles of Bull Run (known in the South as Manassas) were fought here in July 1861 and August 1862, as well as a battle against a proposed Walt Disney historical park in the 1990s. That last fight was won, and today **Manassas Battlefield Park** is a curving green hillscape, sectioned into fuzzy fields of tall grass and wildflowers by strong, split-rail wood fences. The rangers at the **visitor center** (☎ 703-361-1339; admission $3; ☺ 8:30am-5pm) are knowledgeable, helpful, and will send you on a self-guided tour. **Virginia Railway Express** (VRE; ☎ 800-742-3873; www.vre.org; 9451 West St; per person $7.20) runs weekday trains to DC's Union Station.

FREDERICKSBURG

Fredericksburg is a pretty town with a historical district modeled to look like exactly that, an almost overwrought cliché of howdya do,

small-town America. George Washington grew up here, and the Civil War exploded in the streets and surrounding fields. Today mainstreet is a pleasant amble of bookstores, gastropubs and student-y cafés.

Sights

More than 13,000Americans were killed during the Civil War in four battles fought in a 17-mile radius covered by **Fredericksburg & Spotsylvania National Military Park**, maintained by the NPS. Don't miss the burial ground of Stonewall Jackson's amputated arm near the **Fredericksburg Battlefield visitor center** (☎ 540-373-6122; 1013 Lafayette Blvd; admission free, film $2; ☺ 9am-5pm), where you can also pick up a driving-tour map that covers the area

The town's **visitor center** (☎ 540-373-1776; www.fredericksburgva.com; 706 Caroline St; ☺ 9am-5pm) offers a pass to historic Fredericksburg for nine local sights (adult/child six to 18 $29/9.50) including the ones described below. Unless otherwise noted, the following colonial attractions are open 9am to 5pm Monday to Saturday, 11am to 5pm Sunday March to November; 10am to 4pm Monday to Saturday and noon to 4pm Sunday in winter.

James Monroe Museum & Memorial Library (☎ 540-654-1043; 908 Charles St; adult/child 6-18 $5/1; ☺ 10am-5pm Mon-Sat, from 1pm Sun, slightly shorter hours in winter) The museum's namesake is the nation's fifth former president.

Mary Washington House (☎ 540-373-1569; 1200 Charles St; adult/child 6-18 $5/2) Home of George Washington's mother.

Rising Sun Tavern (☎ 540-371-1494; 1304 Caroline St; adult/child 6-18 $5/2) A museum with tavern wenches!

Sleeping & Eating

Richard Johnston Inn (☎ 540-899-7606; www.therichardjohnstoninn.com; 711 Caroline St; r $95-160; P ✷) Scores points for location, comfort and friendliness (especially from the two resident Scottie dogs). Most rooms have private bathrooms, and guests get full breakfast on weekends.

Besides serving a classy caffeine jolt, the **Griffin Bookshop & Coffee Bar** (☎ 540-899-8041; 106 Hanover St; ☺ 9am-6pm Mon-Thu, 10am-9:30pm Fri & Sat, noon-5pm Sun) may be the best bookstore between DC and Richmond.

Yeah, a Turkey Reuben is kinda yuppie, but it's sure damn tasty at the **Olde Towne Wine & Cheese Deli** (☎ 540-373-7877; 707 Caroline St; mains $5-7; ☺ 11am-4pm Mon-Sat).

WASHINGTON, DC & THE CAPITAL REGION

WHAT THE...?

What do you do with a major armaments factory when it goes offline? Turn it into a massive publicly-supported arts space with some 150 galleries and studios, duh, which is exactly what Alexandria did with the **Torpedo Factory Art Center** (☎ 703-838-4565; 105 N Union St; admission free; ☺ 10am-5pm).

WORTH THE TRIP: STEVEN F UDVAR-HAZY CENTER

How awesome is the Smithsonian's Air and Space collection? So awesome they had to create a whole new annex for it out in Chantilly, VA. Off of Hwy VA-28, 33 miles from Washington, the **Steven F Udvar-Hazy Center** (☎ 202-357-2700; ⏱ 10am-5:30pm) is a huge warehouse overflowing with enough avionic goodness to justify a day trip, especially for those who love their aerospace paraphernalia. The Center is currently the home of the Enola Gay, the Space Shuttle Enterprise and a Concorde jet, among other goodies. But Udvar-Hazy's biggest draws are its knowledgeable guides and the vast sense of space it conveys, which highlights the Center's diminished (and less kid-heavy) crowd compared to its sister in DC. While the museum is free, parking costs a ridiculous $12.

Getting There & Away

VRE connects to DC from Caroline St. Buses come into the **Greyhound/Trailways depot** (☎ 540-373-2103; 2217 Princess Ann St).

RICHMOND

Richmond, former capital of the Confederacy, now seems like a poster-city for melting-pot America. Interracial couples are everywhere, and the city balances hipster cred with one of the most vibrant African American communities in the country. Of course, the attractive veneer of diversity cracks soon enough into ugly income disparities; most African American neighborhoods seem depressed compared with upmarket areas on the East and West ends of the center. This town also grapples with memorializing its controversial history (p352). But in the end Richmond is welcoming, warm and offers the chance to witness an almost unique phenomenon: the gradual absorption of a traditional Southern city into the international milieu of the Northeast Corridor.

Orientation & Information

The James River bisects Richmond, with most attractions to its north. Uptown residential neighborhoods include the Fan district, south of Monument Ave, and Carytown, in the west end. Downtown, Court End holds the capitol and several museums. On E Cary St between 12th and 15th Sts, converted warehouses in Shockoe Slip house shops and restaurants. Once you pass under the trestlelike freeway overpass, you're in Shockoe Bottom. Just north of Court End is the historic African American neighborhood of Jackson Ward. Keep in mind that Cary St is more than 5 miles long; E Cary St is downtown while W Cary St is in Carytown.

BOOKSTORES

Carytown Books (☎ 804-359-4831; 2930 W Cary St; ⏱ 10am-7pm Mon-Sat, until 5pm Sun)
Fountain Bookstore (☎ 804-788-1594; 1312 E Cary St; ⏱ 10am-8pm Mon-Thu, until 9pm Fri & Sat, noon-5pm Sun)

MEDIA

90.1 FM WDCE University of Richmond station.
93.5 FM WBBC Country.
Richmond-Times Dispatch (www.richmondtimes dispatch.com) Daily newspaper.

MEDICAL SERVICES

Johnston-Willis Hospital (☎ 804-330-2273; 1401 Johnston-Willis Dr)
Richmond Community Hospital (☎ 804-225-1700; 1500 N 28th St)

POST

Post office (700 E Main St; ⏱ 7:30am-5pm Mon-Fri)

TOURIST INFORMATION

Richmond visitor center (☎ 804-783-7450; www .richmondva.org; 405 N 3rd St; ⏱ 9am-5pm) Get the Richmond pass (five of 20 sights for $15) here.

Sights

The Champs Elysées of Richmond, tree-lined **Monument Avenue** holds mammoth statues of such revered Southern heroes as General JEB Stuart, Robert E Lee, Matthew Fontaine Maury, Jefferson Davis, Stonewall Jackson and, er, tennis player Arthur Ashe (see p352).

Both the changing and permanent exhibits at the **Virginia Historical Society** (☎ 804-358-4901; 428 N Blvd; admission adult/concession/child under 18 $5/$3/free ⏱ 10am-5pm, Sun 1-5pm) manage to portray Virginia as the most important place ever, damnit, but don't sugar-coat the state's history of race and class conflict either. It's fun for kids, too.

It was here at **St John's Episcopal Church** (☎ 804-648-5015; 2401 E Broad St; tours adult/child $6/4; ⊙ 10am-4pm, from 1pm Sun) that firebrand Patrick Henry uttered his famous battle cry, 'Give me liberty or give me death!' (or words to that effect) during the rebellious 1775 Second Virginia Convention. His speech is reenacted at 2pm on Sunday in summer.

The Thomas Jefferson–designed, smug-and-stately **Virginia State Capitol** (☎ 804-698-1788; cnr 9th & Grace Sts, Capitol Sq; daily tours free) re-opened in May 2007 for the state's 400-year anniversary. The impressive dome, oddly enough, can only be seen from the inside.

The **Virginia Holocaust Museum** (☎ 804-257-5400; 2000 E Cary St; admission free; ⊙ 9am-5pm Mon-Fri, from 11am Sat & Sun) is structured like an attic/diorama of the Holocaust survivors who settled here after World War II. It's occasionally kitschy (like the mannequins in Nazi uniforms), but still powerful thanks to the personalized nature of the exhibits.

The **Museum & White House of the Confederacy** (☎ 804-649-1861; cnr 12th & Clay Sts; adult/child under 7/student/senior $10/free/5/9; ⊙ 10am-5pm Tue-Sat, from noon Sun) used to enshrine the Southern 'Lost Cause,' but today it is trying to evolve into an objective museum. While some exhibits still have a whiff of Confederate apologetica, others are superbly educational. The tour of the adjacent Confederate White House comes with plenty of obscure, good-for-a-round-of-trivial-pursuit facts. (See also p353.)

In contrast, the **American Civil War Center** (☎ 804-780-1865; 490 Tredegar St; adult/concession/child 7-12/child under 7 $8/$6/$2/free; ⊙ 9am-5pm) bends over backwards to divide the Civil War story fairly between Union, Confederate and African American experiences. Despite this huge mission, the center manages to feel authoritative and intimately in touch with the motivations of these three groups.

Jackson Ward, an African American neighborhood that was known as Little Africa in the late 19th century, is now a national historic landmark district. It comes off as a tough neighborhood (which it is), but there's a deep cultural legacy here as well. The **Black History Museum & Cultural Center of Virginia** (☎ 804-780-9093; 3 E Clay St; adult/child under 13/student $5/3/4; ⊙ 10am-5pm Tue-Sat, from 11am Sun) highlights the achievements of African American Virginians and displays collections of African arts, textiles and artifacts.

The tranquil **Hollywood Cemetery** (☎ 804-648-8501; entrance cnr Ablemarle & S Cherry Sts; printed guide $1; ⊙ 8am-5pm, tours 11am Mon-Sat Apr-Oct), perched above the James River rapids, contains the gravesites of two US presidents (James Monroe and John Tyler), the only Confederate president (Jefferson Davis) and more than 18,000 Confederate soldiers.

The **Virginia Museum of Fine Arts** (☎ 804-340-1400; 2800 Grove Ave; requested donation $5; ⊙ 11am-5pm Wed-Sun) has a remarkable repertoire of European works, sacred Himalayan art and one of the largest Fabergé egg collections on display outside Russia. The museum is open throughout its expansion project (to be completed in 2008); the extra space will translate into more face time for Latin and Native American holdings.

Housed in the 1919 Broad St Station, the **Science Museum of Virginia** (☎ 804-367-0000; 2500 W Broad St; adult/child 4-12 $10/9, incl IMAX adult/child $17.50/16.50; ⊙ 9:30am-5pm Mon-Sat, 11:30am-5:30pm Sun) is interactive, educational, entertaining and sure to distract your kids.

The 1.25-mile waterfront **Canal Walk** between the James River and the Kanawha (ka-naw) and Haxall Canals is a languid, lovely way of seeing a dozen highlights of Richmond history.

Sleeping

Massad House Hotel (☎ 804-648-2893; www.massadhousehotel.com; 11 N 4th St; r $75-110; P ⊠ ⊠) This is the cheapest in-city option and its location for exploring can't be beat. The small rooms are packed into a Tudor-style boardinghouse, which accentuates the place's Euro-chic.

West Bocock House (☎ 804-358-6174; 1107 Grove Ave; ste $85; P ⊠ ⊠) The gracious hostess of this B&B is the epitome of Southern class and hospitality, and the three gorgeous rooms she rents are a lovely example of Southern baroque style.

Linden Row Inn (☎ 804-783-7000; www.lindenrowinn.com; 100 E Franklin St; r incl breakfast $99-179; P ⊠) This intimate little lodge is an antebellum gem, a midsized period piece where the Southern charm doesn't feel put on.

Omni Hotel (☎ 804-344-7000; www.omnihotel.com; 100 S 12th St; r from $150; P ⊠ wi-fi) It does Southern comfort with a smile. What this place lacks in architectural character is made up for up by helpful-as-hell staff. The location also happens to be dead-on.

RICHMOND

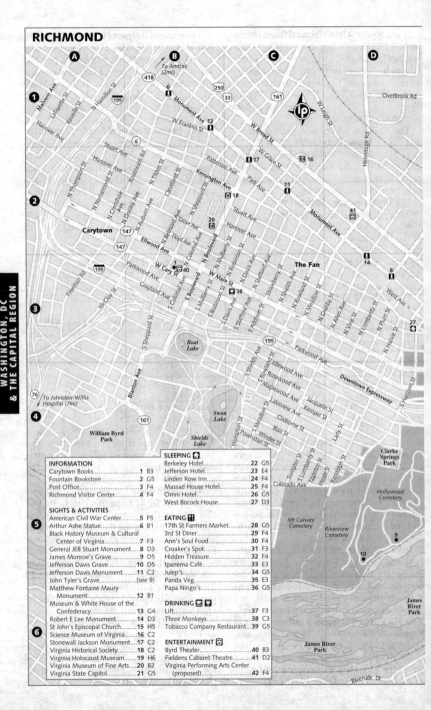

INFORMATION
Carytown Books	**1** B3
Fountain Bookstore	**2** G5
Post Office	**3** F4
Richmond Visitor Center	**4** F4

SIGHTS & ACTIVITIES
American Civil War Center	**5** F5
Arthur Ashe Statue	**6** B1
Black History Museum & Cultural Center of Virginia	**7** F3
General JEB Stuart Monument	**8** D3
James Monroe's Grave	**9** D5
Jefferson Davis Grave	**10** D5
Jefferson Davis Monument	**11** C2
John Tyler's Grave	(see 9)
Matthew Fontaine Maury Monument	**12** B1
Museum & White House of the Confederacy	**13** G4
Robert E Lee Monument	**14** D3
St John's Episcopal Church	**15** H5
Science Museum of Virginia	**16** C2
Stonewall Jackson Monument	**17** C2
Virginia Historical Society	**18** C2
Virginia Holocaust Museum	**19** H6
Virginia Museum of Fine Arts	**20** B2
Virginia State Capitol	**21** G5

SLEEPING
Berkeley Hotel	**22** G5
Jefferson Hotel	**23** E4
Linden Row Inn	**24** F4
Massad House Hotel	**25** F4
Omni Hotel	**26** G5
West Bocock House	**27** D3

EATING
17th St Farmers Market	**28** G5
3rd St Diner	**29** F4
Ann's Soul Food	**30** F4
Croaker's Spot	**31** F3
Hidden Treasure	**32** F4
Ipanema Café	**33** E3
Julep's	**34** G5
Panda Veg	**35** E3
Papa Ningo's	**36** G5

DRINKING
Lift	**37** F3
Three Monkeys	**38** C3
Tobacco Company Restaurant	**39** G5

ENTERTAINMENT
Byrd Theater	**40** B3
Fieldens Cabaret Theatre	**41** D2
Virginia Performing Arts Center (proposed)	**42** F4

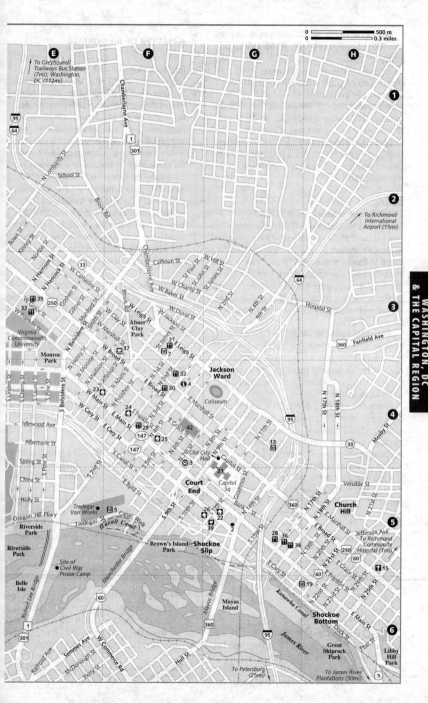

Berkeley Hotel (☎ 804-780-1300; www.berkeleyhotel .com; 1200 E Cary St; r from $190; P ✖ wi-fi) Excellently located in Shockoe Slip, this gracious, European-style hotel has spacious rooms with cherry furnishings, although the staff seems occasionally befuddled.

Jefferson Hotel (☎ 804-788-8000; www.jefferson hotel.com; 101 W Franklin St; r from $285; P ✖ ✖ wi-fi) If you want to know what it feels like to be Robert E Lee kickin' it with a mint julep, come to the city's premier hotel, a favorite haunt of Dixie nobility and visiting celebrities. Parking costs $10.

Eating

17th St farmers market (cnr 17th & E Main Sts; ✖ 9am-2pm Thu, Sat & Sun, hours may vary) A bustling market that kicks off at the beginning of May and goes through October.

3rd St Diner (☎ 804-788-4750; 218 E Main St; mains $4-10; ✖ 24hr) This diner resembles the aftermath of a pink-and-blue explosion. Bring quarters for the (loud) jukebox and lose the attitude because this dive serves it up quick, no frills, 24/7.

Ann's Soul Food (☎ 804-643-5337; 216 E Broad St; mains $4-10; ✖ 7:30am-4pm Mon-Fri, 7:30am-2pm Sat) If you must have that early heart attack, best earn it by shoveling through the excellent meatloaf and corncakes at this spartan diner in Jackson Ward.

Panda Veg (☎ 804-359-6688; 948 W Grace St; mains $5-12; ✖ 11:30am-10:30pm Mon-Thu, until later Fri & Sat, noon-11pm Sun) This dark, student-y vegetarian enclave makes a point of proving tofu can replace meat in any Chinese dish you can imagine. Vegan buffets run on weekends.

Papa Ningo's (☎ 804-344-9886; 1701 E Franklin St; mains $6-15; ✖ 10:30am-8pm Mon-Thu, until 2am Fri & Sat) The big hunks of pork and chicken at this Dominican place don't just stick to your ribs – they sort of latch on and ward off hunger for the rest of the day.

Hidden Treasure (☎ 804-225-9048; 219 E Clay St; mains $6-15; ✖ 11:30am-3pm Mon, 11:30am-5pm Tue-Sat, noon-5pm Sun) Seeing as it's right across from the city visitor center this place isn't all that hidden, which is fine considering the quality seafood (try the crab bisque) at this cozy, occasionally chaotic neighborhood joint.

our pick **Croaker's Spot** (☎ 804-421-0560; 119 E Leigh St; mains $8-17; ✖ 11am-9pm Mon-Wed, 11am-10pm Thu, 11am-11pm Fri, noon-11pm Sat, 1-7pm Sun) Everyone in Jackson Ward knows this soul and seafood joint, as do likely the heart wards of local hos-

A MATTER OF MEMORIALS

Just how race, memorials and memory intersect in Richmond can be a prickly issue. In the mid-1990s Monument Ave, the grand public parade of the city, which passes through some oligarchic real estate, lay at the center of a New South storm of controversy. At issue: whether to erect an **African American statue** tennis player, philanthropist and native son (who hated his hometown) at the end of a promenade of statues dedicated to Confederate heroes: Jeb Stuart, Robert E Lee, Jefferson Davis etc. In the end, the statue went up. It makes for an interesting drive: rows of dead guys on horses and then Ashe, in his tennis shorts, standing astride one of the wealthiest, whitest neighborhoods in the city.

pitals. The decor is proudly African American: sepia photos of the Ward and clocks timed to Johannesburg and Dakar. And the food, the *food*…angels sing on high of the 'fish boat': fried catfish drowning in spicy sauce with hunks of cornbread and creamy grits on the side.

Ipanema Café (☎ 804-213-0170; 917 W Grace St; mains $12-19; ✖ 11:30am-1pm & 5:30-11pm Mon-Fri, 5:30-11pm Sat) Join the art students and urban professionals descending into this vegetarian-oriented, Mediterranean- and Asian-angled restaurant whose playlist and wine list are as interesting as the menu.

Julep's (☎ 804-377-3968; 1719 E Franklin St; mains $15-30; ✖ 5:30-10pm Mon-Sat) Richmond's latest, and some say greatest, shrine to refined New Southern cuisine, Julep's is where you go to impress someone and have a swank, lovely meal in the process. The earth-toned, 1940s-style interior only makes that yellowfin with the wild mushroom orzo that much classier.

Drinking & Entertainment

Last call is 2am, folks.

Lift (☎ 804-344-5438; 218 W Broad St; ✖ 7am-7pm Mon-Fri, 9am-3pm Sat) Lift, with its stiff lattes and airy interior speckled with all sorts of fun culled from the local arts scene, does just that to your spirits. A cuter café we dare you to find.

Tobacco Company Restaurant (☎ 804-782-9555; 1201 E Cary St; ✖ from 11:30am) An embodiment of the era when tobacco was king, the atmosphere of this three-story, brothel-like restaurant-bar is more of a draw than the food. Have a drink instead.

Three Monkeys (☎ 804-204-2525; 2525 W Main St; ⊙ from 11am) Specialty drinks, pastel walls, Mediterranean-Asian-whatever-fusion cuisine – bah! Yeah, that stuff is all here, but at night hormonal guys and gals hang out on the heated patio and act like establishment namesakes – and so should you.

Byrd Theater (☎ 804-353-9911; 2908 W Cary St; tickets $2) You can't beat the price at this fabulous old theater, which shows recent movies. Wurlitzer-organ concerts precede the Saturday-night shows.

Fieldens Cabaret Theatre (☎ 804-346-8113; www.richmondtriangleplayers.com; 2033 W Broad St) This is the venue for the outrageous gay-themed shows of the Richmond Triangle Players.

Virginia Performing Arts Center (www.vapaf.com) Under construction at press time, this center will span the entire block of Broad St between 6th and 7th Sts and will be the area's premier venue for concerts, opera, dance and theater.

Getting There & Around

The cab fare from **Richmond International Airport** (RIC; ☎ 804-226-3000), about 10 miles east of town, is about $25.

Amtrak (☎ 800-872-7245) Stops off about 5 miles north of town at 7519 Staples Mill Rd.

Greater Richmond Transit Company (GRTC; ☎ 804-358-4782; www.ridegrtc.com) Runs local buses (base fare $1.50, exact change only). Bus 27 runs to/from downtown.

Greyhound/Trailways bus station (☎ 804-254-5910; 2910 N Blvd)

AROUND RICHMOND

Just south of Richmond in Petersburg, **Blandford Church** (☎ 804-733-2396; 111 Rochelle Lane; adult/child $5/4; ⊙ 10am-5pm) has the largest collection of Tiffany & Co windows in one place. Each exquisite pane is dedicated to one Confederate state and its war dead. Entrance to the church is only possible with a tour. The Petersburg **Siege Museum** (☎ 804-733-2404; 15 W Bank St; adult/child $5/4, combo ticket with Blandford Church adult/child $11/9; ⊙ 10am-5pm) relates the plight of civilians during the siege of 1864–65, and several miles east of town, **Petersburg National Battlefield** (US 36; vehicle/pedestrian $5/3; ⊙ 9am-5pm) is where Union soldiers planted explosives underneath a Confederate breastwork, leading to the Battle of the Crater (cinematized and novelized in *Cold Mountain*). In nearby Pamplin Historical Park, the excellent **Museum of the Civil War Soldier** (☎ 804-861-2408; adult/child 6-11 $13.50/7.50; ⊙ 9am-6pm summer, until 5pm rest of year) illustrates the privations faced by soldiers on both sides of the conflict.

HISTORIC TRIANGLE

If all the events of Virginia's past haven't done in your head yet, the Historic Triangle of Jamestown (British North America's first settlement), Yorktown (final battle of the American Revolution) and Williamsburg (colonial Virginia's capital) awaits.

LOCAL VOICES: DEAN KNIGHT, RICHMOND NATIVE & TOUR GUIDE OF THE MUSEUM & WHITE HOUSE OF THE CONFEDERACY

What's it like working for the Museum of the Confederacy? The Museum was founded at the height of the 'Lost Cause' movement. Pretty nasty things about the war were forgotten and people saw it through rose-colored glasses. But now I think we get a much higher percentage of people who are here specifically for history. I like working here. They pay me to learn this stuff. That's what's cool. I really wanted to learn about my hometown.

What do you say when people ask you about your job? Do people think you're a (Confederate) apologist? I never hide it. I'm talking about the Confederacy in a historical, rather than ideological way. I've never had anyone say they were angry my tour was slanted one way or the other.

Does the Civil War still impact this part of the country? As an adult, you'll inevitably feel it. You pick up a Richmond newspaper, and the war will be in it in some way.

Do you get many African American visitors? No, and it's a shame, because I think they'd really get something out of this.

Bad news first: the roads are clogged, the kids are loud, and in an effort to get everyone into history, some of the sites are a bit cartoonish. But there's a lot of good, too. Park rangers and costumed interpreters are enthusiastic, love to chat, and really know their stuff, especially esoteric lore you won't find in books. The quieter sites are not as immediately gripping, but give yourself a minute and the weight of what has passed will quickly sink in.

A daily free shuttle travels between the Williamsburg visitor center, Yorktown and Jamestown. A five-day open ticket to Jamestown Settlement, Historic Jamestowne, Colonial Williamsburg, Yorktown Battlefield and the Yorktown Victory Center is $70 for adults and $30 for children aged six to 17. Tickets can be bought at the Williamsburg visitor center (right) or online at www.historyisfun.org.

Williamsburg

An open-air, living history museum is the centerpiece of Williamsburg, which was capital of Virginia from 1699 to 1780. If any place is going to get your kids into history, 'Colonial Williamsburg,' with its hands-on crafts and costumed interpreters, is it. But the elegantly renovated colonial milieu is plenty appealing to adults as well, and anyways, there's grog in those taverns when you need a break. Chat with the keen guides to get into the spirit of the thing.

The actual town of Williamsburg is a stately place, and the prestigious campus of the College of William and Mary adds a decent dash of youth culture: coffee shops, cheap pubs and fashion boutiques.

SIGHTS & ACTIVITIES

The **Colonial Williamsburg Foundation** (☎ 757-229-1000, 800-447-8679; www.history.org) runs the living history museum at the heart of Williamsburg. Around 40 authentic 17th- and 18th-century buildings are open to ticket holders and staffed with costumed townsfolk, all sharing the tricks of their various trades and breaking character only long enough to snap a family photo for you. Walking around the historic district and patronizing the shops and taverns is free, but entry to building tours is restricted to ticket holders. Expect crowds, lines and petulant children, especially in summer.

To park and purchase tickets, follow signs to the **visitor center** (☎ 757-229-1000; ⏰ 8:30am-6pm), north of the historic district between Hwy 132 and Colonial Parkway, where kids can get outfitted in period costumes for $20 (tri-cornered hat sold separately). Parking is free; shuttle buses run frequently to and from the historic district, though there's a footpath you can take from the visitor center. Parking anywhere around the district is severely restricted. Exhibitions are open 9am to 5pm.

Types of passes include:

Colonial Sampler (adult/child $34/15) Covers orientation tour and all exhibition buildings minus the palace and museums, for one day.

Governor's Key to the City (adult/child $48/24) Includes all exhibition buildings, palace and museums and walking tours.

You can buy tickets at several other locations, including the **Merchants Square information booth** (⏰ 9am-5pm) at the west end of Duke of Gloucester St and the **Secretary's Office** (⏰ 9am-5pm), near the capitol, at the east end.

Recommended for those who don't scare easily is the chilling **Original Ghosts of**

WORTH THE TRIP: OLGERS STORE

Jimmy Olgers has inhabited this country store-cum-museum of generally weird stuff on the corner of Route 460 and Namozine Rd in Sutherland, 40 miles south of Richmond, ever since he was raised on a dirt floor in the back room. He is, to put it lightly, a true American eccentric. The gentle giant with a molasses drawl is happy to shoot the breeze with visitors on his front porch or show off the store interior (please donate), stuffed with photographs, 'the world's biggest bloomers' and a scrap-heap forged, gold spray-painted statue of Robert E Lee. Jimmy fights for all that is local and quirky about tiny Dinwiddie County, VA, but he faces formidable opponents: his own mortality and a Wal-mart warehouse complex just up the road. Yet if anyone is a survivor, it's Olgers, whose own grandfather surrendered with Lee at Appomattox before walking 85 miles to the store his descendant now runs.

Williamsburg tour (☎ 757-253-1058, 877-624-4678; adult/child under 7 $10/free; ⏰ 8pm & 8:45pm Jun-Aug). Tickets can also be purchased at the Williamsburg Attraction Center at Prime Outlets on Richmond Rd.

Chartered in 1693, the **College of William & Mary** (☎ 757-221-1540; www.wm.edu) retains the oldest college building in the USA, the Sir Christopher Wren Building. The school's alumni include Thomas Jefferson and James Monroe.

SLEEPING & EATING

Williamsburg Hotel & Motel Association (☎ 800-446-9244; www.gowilliamsburg.com) Located at the visitor center, this association finds accommodations at no charge.

Williamsburg & Colonial KOA Resorts (☎ 800-562-1733; www.williamsburgkoa.com; 5210 & 4000 Newman Rd respectively, I-64 exit 234; campsites $20-31, cabins $30-50; 🛖) With two campgrounds rolled into one, you'll find superb amenities such as movies and game rooms, plus free buses to area attractions.

Governor's Inn (☎ 757-229-1000; 506 N Henry St; r $70-110; P 🛗 🛖) Williamsburg's official 'economy' choice is a big box by any other name, but there's nothing to complain about and hey, it's central.

White House Inn (☎ 757-229-8580, 866-229-8580; www.awilliamsburgwhitehouse.com; 718 Jamestown Rd; r $130-205; P 🛗 ✖) This B&B with red, white and blue bunting, welcomes guests regardless of political persuasion, though Republicans and Democrats have to park at different ends. Politics makes great bedfellows, especially when it's featherbeds we're talking about.

Williamsburg Inn (☎ 757-229-1000, ext 3089; 136 E Francis St; r from $455; P 🛗 🛖 wi-fi) Queen Elizabeth II stayed here in 2007, so you know the Inn is cushy. Williamsburg's premier property is noted by its not-so-colonial price tag, but the pampering is nonstop at this beautiful property, which looks like a grand country estate.

Cheese Shop (☎ 757-220-0298; 410 Duke of Gloucester St, Merchants Sq; mains $5-6; ⏰ 10am-8pm Mon-Sat, 11am-6pm Sun) Locals swear by this deli, with its wide assortment of sandwiches and a Paris-worthy cheese selection.

Aromas (☎ 757-221-6676; 431 Prince George St; lunch mains $5-10; ⏰ 7am-10pm Mon-Thu, until 11pm Fri & Sat, 8am-8pm Sun) Dark wood, soft lights, vintage posters and crayon-bright paintings make this sandwich bar a good place to chill after a day of time traveling.

Trellis Restaurant (☎ 757-229-8610; Merchants Sq; lunch mains $8-14, dinner mains $17-32; ⏰ 11am-3pm & 5-9:30pm) A Virginia culinary landmark, the Trellis caters to burger-seeking tourists for lunch and nirvana-seeking foodies for dinner. Regional specialties shine, such as salmon fillet with country ham.

Four historic district taverns serve 'ye old vittles and grog' from costumed waitstaff. It's fun once. Reservations can be made through the visitor center or by calling ☎ 757-229-2141. **Chowning's** (Duke of Gloucester St; mains $7-18; ⏰ 11:30am-2:30pm, 5pm-late), next to Market Sq, is the best and most casual of the bunch. Attached is **Gambol's** (dishes $4-14), which is the post-5pm merrymaking spot.

GETTING THERE & AROUND

Williamsburg Amtrak Station (☎ 757-229-8750; 468 N Boundary Street) Half a mile north of the historic central district. Trains run twice a day to Washington DC ($34), Richmond ($16) and New York ($77).

Bikes Unlimited (☎ 757-229-4620; 759 Scotland St; bike rental per hr from $14; ⏰ 9:30am-6:30pm Tue-Fri, 10am-5pm Sat, noon-4pm Sun)

Greyhound/Trailways station (☎ 757-229-1460) Bus and train situated at the corner of Lafayette and N Boundary Sts.

Triangle Theme Parks

Three miles east of Williamsburg on Hwy 60, **Busch Gardens** (☎ 800-343-7946; www.buschgardens.com; adult/child 3-9 $55/48; ⏰ Apr-Oct; P) is a European-themed park with great roller coasters. Just down the road off Hwy 199 east of Williamsburg, **Water Country USA** (☎ 800-343-7946; www.watercountryusa.com; adult/child 3-9 $39/32; ⏰ May-Sep; P) is a water-lovin' kids' paradise with twisty slides, raging rapids and wave pools. A three-day, combo ticket for both parks is $70. Parking is $10 at both places.

Jamestown

The first permanent English settlement in North America almost wasn't. In 1607 Sir Walter Cope described Jamestown thus: 'in steed of mylke we fynde pearle…and gold in steede of honye.' In fact, what the English found was starvation and disease. But Jamestown was always star-crossed; a farmers' revolt a few years later torched several buildings, and the settlement never recovered. Eventually Jamestown emptied out, but not before the House of

Burgesses convened in 1619, the first Western democratic assembly in the Americas.

Historic Jamestowne (☎ 757-253-4838; adult/child under 17 $10/free; ☻ 9am-5pm), run by the NPS, is the original Jamestown site. It's pretty and quiet; deer and geese pick at the ruins (or what's left of them) and a general sense of understatement adds to the gentle appeal. An on-site museum is well put together. Tickets bought here are combo tickets for Yorktown Battlefield and good for five days.

The state-run **Jamestown Settlement** (☎ 757-253-4838; adult/child 6-12 $13.50/6.25; ☻ 9am-5pm) reconstructs the 1607 James Fort, a Native American village and full-scale replicas of the first ships to bring settlers to Jamestown, along with living-history fun. A **combo ticket** (adult/child 6-12 $17.75/8.50) that includes the Yorktown Victory Center is available.

Yorktown

British General Cornwallis surrendered to George Washington here in 1781, effectively ending the American Revolution. The event was more of a whimper than a bang; the British were cut off from the sea by the French and confronted with massive American guns on land. Cornwallis' position was hopeless, his superiors indifferent and surrender inevitable. Ironically, the struggle for Redoubt 10, one of the few pitched battles at this turning point for American independence, was almost entirely fought by European auxiliaries.

Yorktown Battlefield (☎ 757-898-3400; adult/child under 17 $10/free, 5-day ticket good for Historic Jamestowne; ☻ 9am-5pm) is the actual battlefield: green, calm and run by the NPS. The visitor center is a little cheesy and a lot informative. State-run **Yorktown Victory Center** (☎ 757-253-4838; adult/child 6-12 $8.75/4.50; ☻ 9am-5pm) focuses more on reconstruction, reenactment, and the Revolution's impact on the people who lived through it.

The actual town of Yorktown is a pleasant enough waterfront idyll. Have a swim and a doss at the functional and friendly **Duke of York Motel** (☎ 757-898-3232; 508 Water St; r from $70; P ☒ ☒).

Despite the mortifying spectacle of a grown man in a carrot hat acting as your host, **Carrot Tree** (☎ 757-246-9559; 411 Main St; mains $6-12; ☻ 8am-4pm Mon-Sat, from 10am Sun) is a good, affordably upmarket spot for lunch. Afterwards, grab a beer at the **Yorktown Pub** (☎ 757-886-9964; 112 Water St; mains $6-15; ☻ 11am-midnight Sun-Thu, 11am-2am Fri & Sat).

James River Plantations

The grand homes of Virginia's slaveholding aristocracy were a clear sign of the era's class divisions. A string of them line scenic Hwy 5 on the north side of the river, though many have closed their doors to the public. The ones listed here run from east to west.

Sherwood Forest (☎ 804-829-5377), the largest frame house in the country, was the home of 9th president William Henry Harrison (who died a month into office, having caught pneumonia after refusing to put on his overcoat) and his successor, John Tyler. It's still owned by the Tyler family, and tours are available by appointment for $35 per person. The grounds (and a touching pet cemetery) are open to **self-guided tours** (☻ 9am-5pm, adult/child $5/3).

Berkeley (☎ 804-829-6018; www.berkeleyplantation.com; adult/child 13-16/child 6-12 $11/7.50/6; ☻ 9am-4:30pm) has witnessed the first official Thanksgiving (take that, Plymouth, MA!), the composing of military melody 'taps,' the first 10 presidents as overnight guests, and the 1862 headquartering of Union General George McClellan.

Situated picturesquely on the river, **Shirley** (☎ 800-232-1613; www.shirleyplantation.com; adult/child 6-18 $11/7.50; ☻ 9am-5pm) is Virginia's oldest plantation and perhaps the best example of what a British-model plantation actually looked like, with its tidy row of brick service and trade houses – tool barn, ice house, laundry etc – leading up to the big house.

HAMPTON ROADS

The Hampton Roads (named not for asphalt, but the confluence of the James, Nansemond and Elizabeth Rivers and Chesapeake Bay) have always been prime real estate. The Powhatan Confederacy fished these waters and hunted the fingerlike protrusions of the Virginia coast for thousands of years before John Smith arrived in 1607. The pirate Blackbeard was killed here and had his head popped onto a pike, while navies from two continents littered the area with wreckage during the Revolutionary and Civil Wars. Today Hampton Roads is known for its clogged, well, roads, as well as its cultural mishmash of history, the military and the arts.

Norfolk

Norfolk, home of the world's largest naval base, consistently ranks near the bottom of 'Best Cities for Singles' lists, which is unsurprising given all the sailors around (and oddly enough, the headquarters of People for the Ethical Treatment of Animals). The city pumps the arts, but a whiff of military officiousness and rowdy, off-duty fun always lingers in the air. The waterfront is packed with bars, Hooters (natch) and the usual Anywhere, America chains, and fair enough – sailors home from Iraq are entitled to bland Americana and winsome lasses stuffed into orange hot pants, and so are you. There are two visitor centers: **Interstate** (☎ 757-441-1852; I-64 exit 273; ◷ 9am-5pm) and **Downtown** (☎ 757-664-6620; 232 E Main St; ◷ 9am-5pm). The historic Ghent district, west of the city center, is where this town's refugee population of artsy types, foodies and cappuccino lovers flocks.

SIGHTS

Yes, blowing up boats is fun, and there's no better place to (virtually) do so than the **Nauticus National Maritime Center** (☎ 757-664-1000; adult/child 4-12 $11/8.50; ◷ 10am-6pm May-Sep, 10am-5pm Tue-Sat, from noon Sun Oct-Apr), a huge naval museum that loves to get interactive. Use the Center entrance to access the more adult-oriented **Hampton Naval Museum** (☎ 757-322-2987; admission free), where you can explore the deck of the *Wisconsin*, one of the last US battleships.

The **Chrysler Museum of Art** (☎ 757-664-6200; 245 W Olney Rd; adult/child under 13 $7/free, Wed free; ◷ 10am-5pm Tue & Thu-Sat, until 9pm Wed, 1-5pm Sun)

is a glorious setting for a superb collection. Exhibits include work by Bierstadt, Renoir and Man Ray, and world-class glassware offerings. The **MacArthur Memorial** (☎ 757-441-2965; MacArthur Sq; admission free; ◷ 10am-5pm Mon-Sat, from 11am Sun) houses the general's military and personal artifacts, along with his tomb and that of his wife. **Selden Arcade** (☎ 757-664-6880; Selden Ave; ◷ 7am-6:30pm Mon-Sat, 11am-3pm Sun) is Norfolk's arts walk and home of the city's Cultural Arts Center. It's good for a pleasant stroll through some hit-and-miss galleries.

The magnificent, red-sailed **American Rover** (☎ 757-627-7245; adult/child under 12 $16/10) ◷ Apr-Oct) schooner takes you on a narrated, two-hour cruise of the Hampton Roads. Or see the country's largest Naval docks (believe us, aircraft carriers are *really* impressive) on the associated **Victory Rover** (☎ 757-627-7406; adult/child under 12 $16/10; ◷ Mar-Dec).

SLEEPING & EATING

For waterfront digs, there are tons of budget to midrange options lining Ocean View Ave (which actually borders the bay). Two of the best dining strips are downtown's Granby St and Ghent's Colley Ave.

Best Western (☎ 757-583-2621; 1330 E Ocean Ave; r from $100; P ⊠ ⊠) One of the options lining the bay.

Tazewell Hotel (☎ 757-623-6200; www.thetazewell .com; 245 Granby St; r $100-200; ⊠) Occupying prime real estate, this attractive hotel is as friendly

---

SCENIC DRIVE: THE CIVIL WARGASM

In his 1998 book *Confederates in the Attic*, Tony Horwitz sets out on a 'Civil Wargasm,' a week-long quest to visit as many Civil War sites as humanly possible. Seeing as you might be more strapped for time, we propose the one-day Wargasm: a trip that will wear you down as much as a forced march with the Army of Northern Virginia.

Wake up early (like, 6am) in Washington, DC, and head for Manassas (p347) to watch the sunrise over one of the most blessed rural panoramas in America. Now to Fredericksburg (p347), where the national park records the history of no less than four battles, including Chancellorsville and Fredericksburg, the high-water marks of the Confederacy. Get directions from a ranger to the burial site of Stonewall Jackson's arm, then proceed to Guinea Station, where Jackson himself died in a picturesque white cottage. On to Richmond for some context; try and tour the Museum & White House of the Confederacy (p349) and American Civil War Center (p349) before bouncing to Petersburg National Battlefield (p353) and, finally (phew!) following Lee's retreat route through perfect Virginia countryside to Appomattox Court House (p361).

This is a great whirlwind tour for history buffs, but it has appeal for non-hard-core Civil War fans too. As Horwtiz puts it, 'There's no place where the war feels more intact than Virginia, where you're literally walking across the graves of hundreds of thousands of people. It's like visiting parts of the western front in Europe. For foreign travelers, seeing the landscape gives a lot of insight to how vivid the war still is to a lot of people.'

as big-name, downtown hubs get. Ask about the story of the Wishing Oak.

B&B at Historic Page House Inn (☎ 757-625-5033; www.pagehouseinn.com; 323 Fairfax Ave; r $140-225; Ⓟ ☒ ☒ wi-fi) Opposite the Chrysler Museum, this luxurious B&B is a cornerstone of Norfolk elegance.

Doumar's (☎ 757-627-4163; 919 Monticello Ave at E 20th St, Ghent; mains $1.50-4; ☉ 8am-late Mon-Sat) Since 1904, this slice of Americana has been the drive-up home of the world's original ice-cream-cone machine, plus great BBQ. Counter service available too. Cash only.

456 Fish (☎ 757-625-4444; 456 Granby St; mains $17-28; ☉ 5-10pm Sun-Thu, 5-11pm Fri & Sat) In an elegant bistro setting, Fish doles out some of the best seafood in a town that knows the genre. Its handful of nonpiscatorial dishes, such as rack of lamb, are well executed too.

Todd Jurich's Bistro (☎ 757-622-3210; 150 W Main St; lunch mains $21-30, dinner mains $25-32; ☉ 11:30am-2pm Mon-Fri, 5:30-10pm Mon-Sat) Jurich's is arguably the best upscale restaurant in Hampton Roads. This swish addition to the Norfolk dining scene gets solid reviews for mixing up Tidewater and global ingredients, such as wasabi potatoes and fried spoonbread.

DRINKING & ENTERTAINMENT

Elliot's Fair Grounds Coffee (☎ 757-640-2899; 806 Baldwin Ave, Ghent; ☉ 7am-late; wi-fi) Where the hell did this place come from? Ah well, leftie students and wi-fi have a habit of popping up in the unlikeliest places…

Taphouse Grill at Ghent (☎ 757-627-9172; 931 W 21st St, Ghent) Good microbrews are served and good local bands jam at this warm little pub.

Scotty Quixx (☎ 757-625-0008; 436 Granby St; ☉ 4pm-2am Mon-Sat) What do you do with a drunken sailor? Send him to Scotty's, which is packed with shore-leave Navy guys looking for a good time.

GETTING THERE & AROUND

Greyhound/Trailways terminal (☎ 757-625-7500; 701 Monticello Ave) runs buses three to four times a day to Richmond ($23), Virginia Beach ($13) and Washington, DC ($37).

Hampton Roads Transit (☎ 757-222-6100; www.hrtransit.org) serves the entire Hampton Roads region. Buses ($1.50) run from downtown (Charlotte and Bank Waterside Drive) throughout the city and to Newport News and Virginia Beach.

Norfolk Electronic Transit Shuttle (NET) (☉ 6:30am-11pm Mon-Fri, noon-midnight Sat, noon-8pm Sun) is a free bus service that connects Norfolk's major downtown sites, including Nauticus and the Chrysler Museum.

Newport News

The city of Newport News comes off as a giant example of suburban sprawl, but it's unclear what it's sprawling from. It holds within its borders several attractions, but for charming lodgings and lively dining, head south to Norfolk. The **visitor center** (☎ 888-493-7386; 13560 Jefferson Ave, Newport News Park; ☉ 9am-5pm) is at the north end off I-64 exit 250-B.

The **Mariners' Museum** (☎ 757-596-2222; www.mariner.org; 100 Museum Dr; adult/child 6-17 $12.50/7.25; ☉ 10am-5pm Mon-Sat, from noon Sun) is one of the biggest, most comprehensive maritime museums in the world. The on-site **USS Monitor Center** (www.monitorcenter.org) houses the dredged carcass of the *Monitor*, one of the world's first ironclad warships, as well as a life-size replica of the real deal (which can be seen undergoing a long chemical bath, a single step in a lengthy preservation process). The **Virginia Living Museum** (☎ 757-247-8523; 9285 Warwick Blvd, Huntington Park; adult/child 3-12 $13/10; ☉ 9am-5pm, slightly shorter hours in winter) is an educational extravaganza that comprises a petting zoo, planetarium and other interactive science-y stuff.

The pleasant **Mulberry Inn** (☎ 757-887-3000; 16890 Warwick Blvd; r incl breakfast from $100; Ⓟ ☒ ☒) is a good alternative to legging it to Norfolk for decent lodging.

VIRGINIA BEACH

Some people like to watch loud young men drink themselves louder; some like high culture; some want a nice place to tan the family. You get all of the above in Virginia's largest city, which tries hard not to be just another hedonistic seaside escape.

I-264 runs straight into the **visitor center** (☎ 800-822-3224; www.vbfun.com; 2100 Parks Ave; ☉ 9am-5pm) and the beach. Surfing is permitted at the beach's southern end near Rudee Inlet and alongside the 14th St pier.

Sights & Activities

If you want to see an aquarium done right, come to the **Virginia Aquarium & Marine Science Center** (☎ 757-385-3474; 717 General Booth Blvd; adult/child $12/8; ☉ 9am-7pm), one of the country's best. Kids will also love **Ocean Breeze**

Water Park (☎ 757-422-4444; 849 General Booth Blvd; adult/child 3-11 $22/16; ☾ from 10am, from 11am Sun, late May–early Sep) with its 13 water slides and giant wave pool.

Mt Trashmore (☎ 757-473-5237; 310 Edwin Dr; admission free; ☾ 7:30am-dusk) is off I-64 exit 17B. Virginia Beach's only verticality was the creative solution to a landfill problem, and now serves as a prime picnicking and kite-flying venue. Tony Hawk has grinded in the renovated skatepark.

Fort Story (cnr 89th St & Pacific Ave), an active army base at Cape Henry, encompasses the First Landing site (admission free) of 1607 colonists and the first **federal lighthouse** (admission $3), dating back to 1792. Assume your car will be searched.

Edgar Cayce Association for Research & Enlightenment (☎ 800-333-4499; 215 67th St at Pacific Ave), founded by the self-proclaimed psychic of the early 20th century, has an extensive library and bookstore (with shelving categories like 'Life after Life' and 'Intuitive Arts'), a full schedule of drop-in lectures and therapies such as massages and colonies, and a meditative labyrinth.

Nearby, in a prime example of American religious diversity, are the folks at the **Christian Broadcasting Network** (☎ 757-579-2747; 977 Centerville Turnpike), founded by evangelist Pat Roberston. If you want to know what makes a certain kind of American fundamentalist tick (and see a human side that is, for all its politics, warm to visitors) come here for a free 45-minute tour; call ahead to reserve a spot.

The **Contemporary Arts Center of Virginia** (☎ 757-425-0000; 2200 Parks Ave; adult/child $8/6 ☾ 9am-5pm, until 9pm Mon) has excellent rotating exhibitions housed in a fresh, ultramodern building that lovingly focuses natural light onto an outstanding collection of local and international artwork.

WILDLIFE REFUGES

Back Bay National Wildlife Refuge (☎ 757-721-2412; www.fws.gov/backbay/; per vehicle/pedestrian $5/2 Apr-Oct, free Nov-Mar) is an 8000-acre wildlife and migratory bird marshland habitat, most stunning during the December migration season. Some 30 miles southwest of Virginia Beach, the 109,000-acre **Great Dismal Swamp National Wildlife Refuge** (☎ 757-986-3705; admission free; ☾ dawn-dusk), which straddles the North Carolina border, is rich in flora and fauna, including black bears, bobcats and more than 200 bird species.

Sleeping

All prices are for the 'season' (May 25 to September 4); rates may drop for the rest of the year.

First Landing State Park (☎ 757-412-2300; Cape Henry; campsites $29) You couldn't ask for a prettier campground than the one at this bayfront state park, though cabins have no water view.

Cutty Sark Motel (☎ 757-428-2116; 3614 Atlantic Ave; r $55-140; P ☒) Rooms at Cutty Sark have private balconies and kitchenettes, but check that the view you're promised doesn't look out onto a parking lot.

Angie's Guest Cottage B&B (☎ 757-428-4690; 302 24th St; r up to $150; P ☒ ☒) comprise some attractive tweeness near the beach, and is also an HI-AYH Hostel (members/nonmembers $17/20). Some private rooms are for members only, and there is a two-night minimum. Both of the above operations are owned by the friendly **Ocean Cove Motel** (☎ 757-491-1830; r $60-150; P ☒) next door.

Eating & Drinking

Jewish Mother (☎ 757-422-5430; cnr 31st St & Pacific Ave; mains $5-14; ☾ 8am-2am) Get your nosh on here with packed deli sandwiches, blintzes, 'penicillin soup' (ie chicken) and monster-sized pie. Excellent live music staged nightly.

Bangkok Garden (☎ 757-498-5009; 4000 Virginia Beach Blvd; mains $7-13; ☾ 11am-10pm Mon-Thu, later Fri & Sat, 4-9pm Sun) The best Thai in the area, everything is done well here, especially (not surprisingly) the seafood.

Harpoon Larry's Oyster Bar (☎ 757-422-6000; 24th St & Pacific Ave; mains $12-16; ☾ noon-2am daily) The roll of paper towels adorning each table gives you a sense of the prevailing atmosphere. Beer, friendly folks and fresh seafood comprise the perfect triumvirate. On Monday oysters are only 35¢ each.

Steinhilber's (☎ 757-340-1156; 653 Thaila Rd; mains $20-31; ☾ 5-10pm Mon-Sat) A nice upscale alternative to the beach, this Surf-'n'-turf-centered establishment sits back in a residential neighborhood on a serene tidewater pier.

A bevy of interchangeable clubs and bars sit between 17th and 23rd Sts around Pacific and Atlantic Aves.

Getting There & Around

Make sure when booking bus tickets that Virginia Beach is specified as the **Greyhound** (☎ 757-422-2998) terminus. **Hampton Roads Transit**

SCENIC DRIVE: VIRGINIA'S EASTERN SHORE

Across the 17-mile Chesapeake Bay bridge-tunnel (fee $12), Virginia's isolated Eastern Shore, dotted with fishing villages and serene, low-lying natural refuges, has the feel of a remote, maritime escape. A drive up or down the peninsula takes a little over an hour. Tucked behind windswept Assateague Island (p340), the town of **Chincoteague** (shink-o-teeg), on the island of the same name, is Virginia's principal Eastern Shore destination. Chincoteague is famous for its oysters and late-July **'wild pony swim,'** when the small horses that inhabit Assateague are led across the channel for annual herd-thinning foal auctions. The **chamber of commerce** (☎ 757-336-6161; 6733 Maddox Blvd; ☺ 9am-4:30pm) has maps of hiking and bicycling trails up to and into the incredibly relaxing **Chincoteague National Wildlife Refuge** (☎ 757-336-6122; per vehicle $10; ☺ 6am-8pm), a lovely wetland repose for migratory waterfowl.

(☎ 757-222-6100; www.hrtransit.com) runs the Virginia Beach Wave trolley (tickets $1), which plies Atlantic Ave in summer.

THE PIEDMONT

A scarp-and-plain landscape that feels simultaneously elegant and rugged, the Piedmont divides the state between its aristocratic lowlands and mountainous frontier. Monticello and the University of Virginia are on the Unesco World Heritage list.

Charlottesville

With a Confederate monument down the road from a Nepalese-Tibetan buffet, Charlottesville has the potential to be too mixed – the University of Virginia attracts Southern aristocracy and artsy lefties in equal proportion. But sometimes, when the main promenade is overflowing with attractive students, couples and professors sipping wine and coffee under a blanket of perfect blue weather (and the distant Appalachians), 'C-ville' is practically perfect.

Two **Charlottesville/Albemarle Visitor Centers** (☎ 877-386-1103; www.charlottesvilletourism.org), on Hwy 20 south near I-64 exit 121a and at 610 E Main St, sell various block passes for area attractions.

MONTICELLO & AROUND

Thomas Jefferson tried to make **Monticello** (☎ 434-984-9822; adult/child 6-11 $15/7; ☺ 8am-5pm Mar-Oct, 9am-4:30pm Nov-Feb) an architectural expression of the new America: a bit of English country manor, a foyer like a Native American longhouse, a self-sustaining agricultural system. It ended up being a temple to Jefferson himself – a worldly, eccentric building that draws off many continents and countries, a supposedly simple homage to yeoman farm-

ing built on the back of slave labor. A lot of the innovations and contradictions of America could be summed up here, but the standard tour feels too rushed – although daily specialty tours include a plantation community tour exposing the complicated past of the slave owner who declared all men equal.

Frequent shuttles run from the parking lot up the hill. Tours are also offered of the nearby 1784 **Michie Tavern** (☎ 434-977-1234) and James Monroe's estate, **Ash Lawn-Highland** (☎ 434-293-9539), 2.5 miles east of Monticello. A combo ticket for all three is $27, while yet more colonial 'fayre' can be had at the Michie **Ordinary** (meals around $14), best known for its lunch buffets.

UNIVERSITY OF VIRGINIA

At the west end of town, the grounds (never 'campus') of the **University of Virginia** (UVa), which were founded by Thomas Jefferson, revolve around the stately Rotunda, a scale replica of Rome's Pantheon. The permanent collection at UVa's **art museum** (☎ 804-924-3492; 155 Rugby Rd; admission free; ☺ 1-5pm Tue-Sun) is eclectic and its traveling exhibits always interesting.

SLEEPING

There's a good selection of budget and midrange chain motels lining Emmet St/US 29 north of town.

English Inn (☎ 434-971-9900; 2000 Morton Dr; r incl breakfast from $80-130; P ⚑) Old school Brit-chic and a Tudor-facade accent some standard rooms.

Guesthouses (☎ 434-979-7264; www.va-guesthouses .com; r from $155; ☺ 9am-2pm Mon-Fri; P ✗) This reservation service provides cottages and B&B rooms. Call within business hours ideally at least a day before you'll need a room.

Vegan pilgrims should flock to Schuyler, about 15 miles southeast of town for the **White Pig B&B** (☎ 434-831-1416; www.thewhitepig.com; 5120 Irish Rd; r $155-185; P ☒) on the 170-acre Briar Creek Farm. This B&B/animal sanctuary has one of the most innovative vegan-friendly menus in the state – who likes soy bacon?

Just across from Monticello is, appropriately enough, the **Inn at Monticello** (☎ 434-979-3593; www.innatmonticello.com; 1188 Scottsville Rd; r $195; P ☒ wi-fi), off Hwy 20 S, a Victorian B&B set off against the Piedmont's rolling hillscape. Every one of the lodge's five rooms are cozy little testaments to colonial grandeur.

In an impossible-to-beat downtown location, the **South Street Inn** (☎ 434-979-0200; www .southstreetinn.com; 200 South St; r incl breakfast $130-250; P ☒) is a warm, aged brick hotel that used to be a girl's finishing school and later, a brothel – sweet!

EATING & DRINKING

The central pedestrian drag is great for people-watching and outdoor dining when the weather is nice. At night, the bars along University Ave are packed with the world's academic elite, half of whom are stumbling into a gutter to vomit.

VaVino (☎ 434-974-9463; 401 E Main St; mains $4-12; ☒ 11am-11pm) Flash your class at Virginia's first wine bar, which caters to the all-in-black crew. The wine-oriented nibbles (ham, cheese, olives etc) are as stripped down and pretty as the minimalist dining room.

White Spot (☎ 434-295-9899; 147 University Ave; mains around $5; ☒ 8am-11pm, until 2:30am Fri & Sat) While in the commercial district, try a genuine C-ville concoction, the fried-egg-topped Gus Burger.

Bashir's Taverna (☎ 434-923-0927; 515 E Main St; tapas $6-9.50, dinner $15-23; ☒ 6-10:30pm Fri & Sat) If you've been to Morocco, you've seen every decoration in this place. Look past the Marrakech bric-a-brac; you're craving couscous, *tagine* (North African stew) and belly-dancing, and Bashir doesn't disappoint on either count.

Zocalo (☎ 434-977-4944; 201 E Main St; mains $18-26; ☒ 5:30pm-2:30am Tue-Sun) Zocalo is cooler than you and kinda lets you know it. This sharp, metallic restaurant-bar serves the world's latest fusion cuisine, Pan-Piedmont Latin, and pulls the effort off nicely. 'Course, the pretty people propping up the bar with their cocktails certainly makes the food more enjoyable.

Mudhouse (☎ 434-984-6833; 213 W Main St; ☒ 7am-11pm, until 7pm Mon; wi-fi) Do as the cool kids do and come here for bracing espresso, wi-fi and daily artsy happenings.

GETTING THERE & AROUND

A free trolley runs through the historic district.

Amtrak (☎ 434-296-4559; 810 W Main St) Trains run four times a day to Washington DC ($30), once a day to Richmond ($24) and twice a day to Williamsburg ($80).

Greyhound/Trailways terminal (☎ 434-295-5131; 310 W Main St) Runs buses three times a day to Richmond ($19.50), Washington DC ($25) and once a day to Williamsburg ($36.50).

Appomattox Court House & Around

At the McLean House in the town of Appomattox Court House, General Robert E Lee surrendered the Army of Northern Virginia to General Ulysses S Grant, in effect ending

---

VINTAGE VIRGINIA

Now the fifth-biggest wine producer in the USA, Virginia has been promoting her vineyards and associated wine trails in a big way lately. There's a glut of wineries in the pretty hills around Charlottesville; here's three goodies:

Jefferson Vineyards (☎ 800-272-3042; www.jeffersonvineyards.com) Known for consistent quality vintage, this winery harvests from its namesake's original 1774 vineyard site.

Keswick Vineyards (☎ 434-244-3341; www.keswickvineyards.com) Keswick won a wave of awards for its first vintage and has since been distilling a big range of grapes off Rte 231.

Oakencroft (☎ 434-296-4188; www.oakencroft.com) The closest vineyards to Charlottesville belong to the oldest winery in Albemarle county.

There are wine routes all across the state these days; plenty crisscross the tidewater region near Historic Triangle and run along the sides of the Shenandoah Valley. Check **www.virginiawinetour .com** (☎ 540-622-2505) for more information.

the Civil War. Instead of coming straight here, follow **Lee's retreat** (☎ 800-673-8732; www.varetreat .com) on a winding 25-stop tour that starts in Petersburg at Southside Railroad Station (River St and Cockade Alley) and cuts through some of the most attractive countryside in Virginia. Best take a detailed roadmap, as the trail is not always clearly marked. You'll finish at the 1300-acre **Appomattox Court House National Historic Park** (☎ 434-352-8987; summer $4, mid-Sep–May $3; ◷ 8:30am-5pm). Most of the 27 restored buildings are open to visitors.

SHENANDOAH VALLEY

In local parlance: damn, but it's pretty here. Arguably the most impressive landscape on the Eastern seaboard, this was the westward border of colonial America. The Scots-Irish frontiersman who settled these mountains were Highland Clearance refugees, and they and their descendants have always been suspicious of government and protective of their liberties. It's a strange valley, where folks love God, guns, local universities (Sweet Briar, Virginia Tech, Washington and Lee, Randolph-Macon, Virginia Military Institute), Shakespeare companies and the sweet-smelling galax and laurel peaks of the Appalachians in equal measure.

Shenandoah National Park

One of the most spectacular national parks in the country lays not 100 miles from Washington, DC. Every season in the **park** (☎ 540-999-2243; www.nps.gov/shen; week passes Dec-Feb per car/individual $10/5, Mar-Nov per car/individual $15/10) is like a new smile from nature: in spring and summer the wildflowers explode, in fall the leaves burn bright red and orange, and in winter a cold, starkly beautiful hibernation period sets in.

SIGHTS & ACTIVITIES

The park is cut through by **Skyline Drive**, a 105-mile-long road that redefines your idea of 'Scenic Route.' You're constantly treated to an impressive view, but keep in mind the road is bendy, slow-going (35mph limit) and in peak season, congested. On a good day it takes three hours to traverse the entire stretch; you can always detour to I-81 to go faster.

There are two visitor centers in the park. **Dickey Ridge** (☎ 540-635-3566; Mile 4.6; ◷ 8:30am-5pm Apr 6–Oct 27) in the north and **Byrd** (☎ 540-

999-3500; Mile 51; ◷ 8:30am-5pm Mar 31–Oct 27) in the south have maps, backcountry permits and information on hiking (the Appalachian Trail frequently crosses Skyline), horseback riding, hang-gliding, bicycling (only on public roads) and other wholesome goodness.

There are all sorts of good hikes around here; these are only a few, from north to south:

Old Rag Mountain This is a tough, 8.8-mile trail that culminates in a rocky scramble only suitable for the physically fit. Your reward is the summit of Old Rag Mountain and, along the way, some of the best views in Virginia.

Skyland Four easy trails here, none exceeding 1.6 miles, with a few steep sections throughout. Stony Man Trail gives great views for not-too-strenuous trekking.

Big Meadows Very popular area with four easy to midlevel difficulty hikes. The Lewis Falls and Rose River Trails run by some cascades, and the former accesses the Appalachian Trail.

Riprap Three trails of varying difficulty. Blackrock Trail is an easy 1-mile loop that yields fantastic views. You can either hike the moderate 3.4-mile Riprap Trail to Chimney Rock, or detour and make a fairly strenuous 9.8-mile circuit that connects with the Appalachian Trail.

SLEEPING

Camping is available at five **NPS campgrounds** (☎ 877-444-6777). The following prices are all per day: **Mathews Arm** (at Mile 22.1; campsites $15), **Big Meadows** (Mile 51.3; campsites late spring to early fall $17, other times $20), **Lewis Mountain** (Mile 57.5; campsites $15, no reservations accepted), **Loft Mountain** (Mile 79.5; campsites $15) and **Dundo Group** (Mile 83.7; campsites $35, min 7 people, reservations required). Camping outside these sites requires registering a free backcountry permit with a visitor center. For not-so-rough lodging, try **Skyline Lodge** (☎ 703-242-0315; Mile 41.7; r $87-200), and **Lewis Mountain** (☎ 800-999-4714; Mile 57.5; cabins from $76; ✗), both open from March 30 to November 25. It's best to bring your own food into the park if you're going camping or on extended hikes.

GETTING THERE & AROUND

Amtrak trains run to Staunton, in the Shenandoah Valley, once a day from Washington, DC ($34) and twice a day from Richmond ($17). But you'll really need your own wheels to explore the length and breadth of the park, which can be easily accessed from several exits off I-81.

Front Royal & Around

The northernmost tip of Skyline Dr initially comes off as a drab strip of gas stations, but there's a friendly enough main street and some cool caverns nearby. Stop in to the **visitor center** (☎ 540-332-3971; 414 E Main St; 🕙 9am-5pm) and the **Shenandoah Valley Travel Association** (☎ 800-847-4878; www.visitshenandoah.org; US 211 W, I-81 exit 264; 🕙 9am-5pm) before heading 'up' (a reference to altitude, not direction) the valley.

Front Royal's claim to fame is **Skyline Caverns** (☎ 540-635-4545; www.skylinecaverns.com; US 340; adult/child 7-13 $16/8; 🕙 9am-5pm Mon-Fri, until 6pm Sat & Sun & summer), which boasts rare, white-spiked anthodites – mineral formations that look like sea urchins.

Woodward House on Manor Grade (☎ 540-635-7010; www.acountryhome.com; 413 S Royal Ave/US 320; r $99-135, cottages $220; P ✗) is a cluttered B&B with eight cheerful rooms. Sip your coffee from the deck and don't let the busy street below distract from the Blue Ridge Mountain vista.

County Seat (☎ 540-636-8884; 104 S Royal Ave; mains $6-8; 🕙 7am-5pm Mon-Fri, 9am-4pm Sat) is a cuddly, colonial-style pub with Virginia ham sandwiches in the deli and Belgian beer on tap.

Jalisco's (☎ 540-635-7348; 1303 N Royal Ave; mains $8-15; 🕙 11am-10pm) has surprisingly good Mexican; the chile rellenos go down a treat.

Soul Mountain Cafe (☎ 540-636-0070; 1303 117 E Main St; mains $12-24; 🕙 noon-9pm Mon-Sat, until 4pm Sun), with its Bob Marley posters and African sculptures, is kinda incongruous, but when you're serving andouille over penne and crabmeat-stuffed salmon, that's fine by us.

Some 25 miles north, in the town of Winchester, is the **Museum of the Shenandoah Valley** (☎ 888-556-5799; 901 Amherst St; adult/student $12/10; 🕙 10am-4pm Tue-Sun), which does a good job of introducing you to Appalachian culture and history.

If you can only fit one cavern into your itinerary, head 25 miles south from Front Royal to the world-class **Luray Caverns** (☎ 540-743-6551; www.luraycaverns.com; I-81 exit 264; adult/child 7-13 $19/9; 🕙 9am-6pm, until 7pm summer, until 4pm Nov 1–Mar 31st) and hear the 'Stalacpipe Organ,' hyped as the largest musical instrument on Earth.

George Washington & Jefferson National Forests

Stretching along the entire western edge of Virginia, these two mammoth **forests** (www.fs.fed.us/r8/gwj; campsites $5-20, primitive camping free) comprise more than 1562 sq miles of mountainous terrain bordering the Shenandoah Valley, and contain challenging to easy trail networks, which include 330 miles of the **Appalachian Trail** (www.appalachiantrail.org) and mountain-biking routes. Hundreds of developed campgrounds are scattered throughout. **USDA Forest Service headquarters** (☎ 540-265-5100; 5162 Valleypointe Parkway), off the Blue Ridge Parkway in Roanoke, oversees a dozen ranger stations along the ranges. You can also pick up information at the **Natural Bridge visitor center** (☎ 540-291-2121) across from the Natural Bridge entrance.

Staunton & Around

This pretty little town jumps out of the mountains with its cozy college (Mary Baldwin), old time-y avenues, and oddly enough, one of America's premier Shakespeare companies.

The **Frontier Culture Museum** (☎ 540-332-7850; overlooking I-81 exit 222; adult/child/student $10/6/9; 🕙 9am-5pm mid-Mar–Nov, 10am-4pm Dec–mid-Mar) has authentic historic farm buildings from Germany, Ireland and England, which have been plunked here to provide a comparison to an onsite American frontier farm. Good if you're into history or farming or both. The town's **visitor center** (🕙 9am-5pm) shares space with the museum.

Woodrow Wilson Birthplace & Museum (☎ 540-885-0897; 18-24 N Coalter St; adult/child/student 6-12 $8/3/5; 🕙 9am-5pm Mon-Sat, from noon Sun, until 4pm Nov-Feb) is a scholarly peek into the life of the 28th president and founder of the League of Nations, as well as the pre– and post–WW I era he emerged from. Don't leave without catching a show at the **Blackfriars Playhouse** (☎ 540-851-1733; 10 S Market St; tickets $20-30), where the American Shakespeare Center company performs in the world's only re-creation of Shakespeare's original indoor theater.

Right downtown, the thoroughly mauve and immensely welcoming **Frederick House** (☎ 540-885-4220, 800-334-5575; www.frederickhouse.com; 28 N New St; r incl breakfast $95-190; P ✗ 🐾) consists of five historical residences with a combination of rooms and suites, all with private bathrooms and some with fireplaces and decks.

Time to happily advance closer to the grave at the famous **Mrs Rowe's** (☎ 540-886-1833; I-81 exit 222; mains $6-12; 🕙 7am-8pm Mon-Sat, until 7pm Sun), where the Southern recipes haven't budged in decades; neither will you after some fried chicken and hash browns topped with melted cheese.

Lexington & Around

This is the place to see Southern gentry at their stately best, as cadets from the Virginia Military Institute jog past the prestigious academics of Washington & Lee University. The **visitor center** (☎ 540-463-3777; 106 E Washington St; ⏰ 9am-5pm) has free parking.

You'll either be impressed or put-off by the extreme discipline of the cadets at **Virginia Military Institute** (VMI; ☎ 540-464-7230; Letcher Ave; ⏰ 9am-5pm when campus & museums open), the only university to have sent its entire graduating class into combat (plaques to student war dead are touching and ubiquitous). A full-dress parade takes place most Fridays at 4:30pm during the school year. The school's **George C Marshall Museum** (☎ 540-463-7103; adult/child $3/free) honors the creator of the Marshall Plan for post-WWII European reconstruction. The **VMI Cadet Museum** (☎ 540-464-7334; admission free) houses the stuffed carcass of Stonewall Jackson's horse, a homemade American flag made by an alumnus prisoner of war in Vietnam and a tribute to VMI students killed in the War on Terror.

Founded in 1749, colonnaded Washington & Lee University is one of the top small colleges in America. The **Lee Chapel & Museum** (☎ 540-458-8768; ⏰ 9am-4pm, from 1pm Sun), inters Robert E Lee, while his horse Traveller is buried outside. One of the four Confederate banners surrounding Lee's tomb is set in an original flagpole, a branch a rebel soldier turned into a makeshift standard.

Historic Country Inns (☎ 540-463-2044; 11 N Main St; r $75-165; P ❄) operates two inns downtown and one outside town. All of the buildings have some historical significance to Lexington, and most of the rooms are individually decorated with period antiques. The charming, ecominded **Applewood Inn & Llama Trekking** (☎ 540-463-1962, 1-800-463-1902; r $110-150; P ❄ ❄) offers a slew of outdoorsy activities on a farm a 10-minute drive away.

This far out in the mountains, you'll of course be expecting raw, Asian seafood, and **Sushi Matsumoto** (☎ 540-464-8196; 159 S Main St; mains $5-20; ⏰ 11:30am-2pm Mon-Fri & 5-9pm Mon-Sat) does not disappoint in this regard.

The **Southern Inn** (☎ 540-463-9498; 37 S Main St; lunch mains $7-12, dinner $15-30; ⏰ 5-10pm Mon & Tue, 11:30am-10pm Wed-Sat, until 9pm Sun) has a no-nonsense, classy menu (think roast duck and stuffed trout) and the perfect ambience for a

WHAT THE...?

Inspired by classic horror movies and creative genius, 'mad' professor Mark Cline has created the ultimate triage of kitsch in the hills near Natural Bridge: **Foamhenge** (a styrofoam Stonehenge), **Dinosaur Park** (watch Civil War soldiers get devoured by velociraptors!) and the spooky, kooky **Haunted Monster Museum**. All sites are clearly signposted between Staunton and Natural Bridge on Route 11.

date between a VMI cadet and Washington & Lee sorority sister.

Natural Bridge

Yes, it's kitschy, and yes, vocal creationists who insist it was made by the Hand of the Almighty are dominating the site, but the 215ft-high **Natural Bridge arch** (☎ 540-291-2121; adult/child 6-15 $10/5; ⏰ 8am-dusk), 15 miles from Lexington, is still pretty cool. It was surveyed by 16-year-old George Washington back in the day (look 23ft up on the left side to see his initials).

BLUE RIDGE HIGHLANDS & SOUTHWEST VIRGINIA

The southwestern tip of Virginia is the most rugged part of the state. Turn onto the Blue Ridge Parkway or any side road and you'll immediately plunge into dark strands of dogwood and fir, fast streams and white waterfalls. You're bound to see Confederate flags in the small towns, but there's a proud hospitality behind the fierce veneer of independence.

Blue Ridge Parkway

Where Skyline Dr ends, the **Blue Ridge Parkway** (www.blueridgeparkway.org) picks up. The road is just as pretty (if not prettier) than Skyline and runs from the southern Appalachian ridge in Shenandoah National Park at Mile 0 to North Carolina's Great Smoky Mountains National Park at Mile 469. Wildflowers bloom in spring and fall colors are spectacular, but watch out for foggy days; no guardrails can make for hairy driving. There are a dozen visitor centers scattered over the parkway, and any of them make a good kick-off point to start your trip.

SIGHTS & ACTIVTIES

There's all kinds of sights running along the Parkway; these are a handful, listed from north to south:

Sherando Lake (☎ 540-291-2188, Mile 16) In George Washington National Forest (p363), this is a pretty blue dollop of pastel scenery, and a nice place for a swim.

James River & Kanawha Canal (☎ 800-933-9535; Mile 63) A footpath here leads to the canal locks and, if you have time, a pleasant amble over local river bluffs.

Peaks of Otter (☎ 540-586-4357; Mile 86) You close a nice Capital Region circle by coming here; stones from the tops of these mountains (Sharp Top, Flat Top and Harkening Hill) are inside the Washington Monument. Shuttles run to the top of Sharp Top or you can try a fairly challenging hike to the summit.

Mabry Mill (☎ 276-952-2947; Mile 176) One of the most photographed buildings in the state, the Mill nests in such a fuzzy green vale you'd think you'd entered the opening chapter of a Tolkien novel.

SLEEPING

Get in touch with the NPS beforehand if you're planning on sleeping along the parkway. There are nine local **campgrounds** (☎ 977-444-6777), four in Virginia; all campsites are $16 (cabins extra). Every year the staggered opening date of facilities changes, but sites are generally accessible from April to November. Two NPS-approved indoor facilities are on the Parkway in Virginia: **Peaks of Otter** (☎ 540-586-1081; Mile 86, 85554 Blue Ridge Parkway; r $100; P ✹), a pretty, split-rail-surrounded lodge nestled between two of its namesake mountains, and **Rocky Knob Cabins** (☎ 540-593-5303; Mile 174, 256 Mabry Mill Rd; cabin with shared bath $59; P), set off in a secluded stretch of forest. Bring food as eating options are limited along the parkway.

Roanoke & Around

Illuminated by the giant star atop Mill Mountain, Roanoke's the big city in these parts, with a compact set of attractions based around the bustling indoor-outdoor **Historic City Market** (213 Market St; ✹ 7:30am-4:30pm Mon-Sat), a sumptuous farmers market loaded with temptations even for those with no access to a kitchen. For local information, check out the **Roanoke Valley Visitor Information Center** (☎ 540-342-6025, 800-635-5535; www.visitroanokeva.com; 101 Shenandoah Ave NE; ✹ 9am-5pm) in the old Norfolk & Western train station.

Center in the Square (☎ 540-342-5700; www.centerinthesquare.org; 1 Market Sq; ✹ 10am-5pm Tue-Sat, 1-5pm Sun) is the city's cultural bread and butter, with

a science museum and planetarium (adult/child $8/6), theater, local-history museum (adult/child $3/2) and art museum (tickets $3). The site of the **Harrison Museum of African American Culture** (☎ 540-345-4818; 523 Harrison Ave; admission free; ✹ 1-5pm Tue-Sat), was the first public high school for African Americans in America, and has displays on local African American culture and traditional and contemporary African art.

The tiny town of Bedford suffered the most casualties per capita during WWII, and hence was chosen to host the moving **National D-Day Memorial** (☎ 540-586-3329; US 460 & Hwy 122; adult/child $5/3; ✹ 10am-5pm). Among its towering arch and flower garden is a cast of bronze figures re-enacting the storming of the beach, complete with bursts of water symbolizing the hail of bullets the soldiers faced.

Mt Rogers National Recreation Area

This seriously beautiful district is well worth a visit from outdoor enthusiasts. Hike, fish or cross-country ski among ancient hardwood trees and the state's tallest peak. The **park headquarters** (☎ 276-783-5196), on Hwy 16 in Marion, offers maps and recreation directories. The NPS operates five campgrounds in the area; contact park headquarters for details.

Abingdon

You like history? You like art? Then you'll like Abingdon, which retains fine Federal and Victorian architecture in its historic district, and hosts the bluegrass **Virginia Highlands Festival** over the first half of August. The **visitor center** (☎ 800-435-3440; 335 Cummings St; ✹ 9am-5pm) has exhibits on local history.

Founded during the Depression, **Barter Theatre** (☎ 540-628-3991; www.bartertheatre.com; 133 W Main St; performances from $20) earned its name from audiences trading food for performances. Actors such as Gregory Peck and Ernest Borgnine have cut their teeth on Barter's stage.

The **Virginia Creeper Trail** (www.vacreepertrail.org), named for the railroad that once ran this route, travels 33 miles between Whitetop Station near the North Carolina border and downtown Abingdon. Several outfitters rent bikes, organize outings and run shuttles, including **Virginia Creeper Trail Bike Shop** (☎ 276-676-2552; 201 Pecan St; per 2hr $10; ✹ 9am-6pm) near the trailhead.

Martha Washington Inn (☎ 540-628-3161; 150 W Main St; r from $169; P ✹), opposite the Barter,

HOT TOPIC: GUN CONTROL & VIRGINIA TECH

On April 16, 2007, Virginia Tech student Seung-Hui Cho, murdered 32 people with handguns bought (illegally, as it turned out) from a licenced gun shop, before shooting himself on the tech campus in Blacksburg, Virginia. Gun control advocates immediately called for greater firearms restrictions, but to the shock of many, prominent gun lobbyists used the incident to call for *increased* access to firearms on universities (concealed weapons were banned on Virginia Tech in 2006). Cho, it was pointed out, had been deemed mentally unstable by a Virginia judge in 2005; his mental condition prevented him from buying firearms but had not been reported to a federal database. The point, gun advocates said, was Cho was *not* a law-abiding gun owner. Lawful gun-owners, it was argued, had stopped mass shootings in the past (Pearl High School, MS, in 1997, and Appalachian School of Law in 2002).

In the end, the loophole that kept Cho off the national Instant Criminal Background Check System was closed. Virginia Governor Tim Kaine told both sides of the debate to take their 'crusade' elsewhere, while the world scratched its head at America's relationship with cherished, sometimes deadly freedoms.

is the region's premier historic hotel, a Victorian sprawl of historical classiness and iron-wrought style.

For the boho in all of us, **Zazzy'z** (☎ 276-698-3333; 380 E Main St; sandwiches $4.25; ⊙ 7am-7pm Mon-Fri, 8am-6pm Sat, until 5pm Sun) serves cheap, filling sandwiches and kick-your-ass coffee in a lovely old bookstore whose political titles veer from the radical to reactionary. The bird at **Chick-N-Little** (☎ 276-628-6690; 401 W Main St; mains $5-10; ⊙ 6am-8pm) isn't, but it is some of the tastiest fried goodness in mountain Virginia – wash it down with some sweet tea.

The Crooked Road

When Scots-Irish fiddle-and-reel married African American banjo-and-percussion, American music, including country and its twangy cousin, bluegrass, was born. The latter genres still dominates the Blue Ridge, and the **Crooked Road** (www.thecrookedroad.org) takes you through nine sites associated with that history, and some eye-stretching mountain scenery. The trail is sad and beautiful; the traditions it tries to preserve always seem threatened by gentrification, but during a live show you'll witness the double joy of elders connecting to deep cultural roots and a new generation of musicians keeping that heritage alive and evolving. The following are only two stops on the Road.

FLOYD

Little Floyd's not much more than an intersection between Hwys 8 and 221, but life explodes on Friday nights at the **Floyd Country Store** (☎ 540-745-4563; 206 S Locust St; jamboree admission

$3; ⊙ 10am-10:30pm Fri, until 5:30pm Sat). Every Friday starting at 6:30pm, $3 gets you four bluegrass bands in four hours and the chance to watch happy crowds nod along to regional heritage. No smokin', no drinkin', but plenty of dancin' (of the jig-and-tap style) is the order of the day. Nearby **County Sales** (☎ 540-745-2001; Talley's Alley; ⊙ 9am-4:30pm Mon-Fri) claims to be the world's first, and still largest, purveyor of bluegrass music.

The **Lawson House Inn** (☎ 540-745-7829; www .lawsonhouseinn.com; 302 E Oxford St; r $100; P ⊠ 🐾 wi-fi) is a three-room B&B in 'downtown' Floyd (what part of Floyd *isn't* downtown?) that's good for your aching back: it has an on-site massage therapist and a hot tub.

When you're all jigged out head for **Odd-fella's** (☎ 540-745-3463; lunch mains $5-7, dinner mains $11-18; ⊙ 11:30am-2:30pm & 5-9pm Wed-Sat, 11am-3pm Sun), a woodsy, organic-menu kinda place that answers the question: what do you get when you cross a redneck with a hippie? Apparently, parmesan-crusted catfish – nice.

GALAX

Galax claims to be the world capital of mountain music, although it feels like anywhere-else-ville outside of the immediate downtown area (on the National Register of Historic Places). The main attraction is the **Rex Theater** (☎ 276-236-5309; www.rextheat ergalax.com; 113 E Grayson St), a musty, red-curtained belle of yore. Frequent bluegrass acts cross its stage, but the easiest one to catch is the free Friday night live WBRF 98.1 show, which pulls in crowds from across the mountains.

Tom Barr of **Barr's Fiddle Shop** (☎ 276-236-2411; 105 S Main St) is the Stradivarius of the mountains, a master craftsman sought out by fiddle and mandolin aficionados from across the world. The **Old Fiddler's Convention** (www.oldfiddlersconvention.com) is held every year in Galax; it's one of the premier mountain music festivals in the world.

HI Blue Ridge Mountains (☎ 276-236-4962; 214507 Blue Ridge Parkway; dm $17, P X 😄) is a good mountain-top place to crash with access to some awesome nearby views. The **Galax Motel** (☎ 276-236-9935; www.galaxmotel.com; 549 E Stuart Dr; s $26, d $34; X 😄 P) is pretty plain, but the price is nice and the owners are sweet, while the **Doctor's Inn** (☎ 276-238-9998; thedoctorsinnvirginia. com; 406 W Stuart Dr; r $109-129; X 😄 P wi-fi) nicely fills the local 'let's stuff a historic building full of grandma's antiques and spoil our guests rotten' B&B niche.

Yes, the rich cultural tapestry of the Appalachians is reason enough to visit Galax, but a nice additional draw is the **Galax Smokehouse** (☎ 276-236-1000; 101 N Main St; mains $5-13; 🕙 11am-9pm Mon-Sat, until 3pm Sun), which serves groaning platters of sweetly sauced Memphis-style BBQ.

WEST VIRGINIA

West Virginia's got an image problem. At best, everyone knows it from a tired John Denver song. At worst, it's the subject of every inbred, cousin-coupling joke in America.

Which is funny, since this unbroken line of green mountains is one of the prettiest states in the union. Created by secessionists from secession, the people here still think of themselves as hardscrabble sons of miners, and that perception isn't entirely off. But the Mountain State is also gentrifying and occasionally, that's a good thing: the arts are flourishing in the valleys, where some towns offer a welcome break from the state's constantly evolving outdoor activities.

History

Virginia was once the biggest state in America, divided between the plantation aristocracy of the Tidewater and the mountains of what is now West Virginia. The latter were settled by tough farmers who staked out independent freeholds across the Appalachians. Always resentful of their Eastern brethren and their reliance on cheap (ie slave) labor,

the mountaineers of West Virginia declared their independence from Virginia when the latter tried to break off from America during the Civil War.

Yet the scrappy, independent-at-all-costs stereotype was challenged in the late 19th and early 20th centuries, when miners here formed into cooperative unions and battled employers in some of the bloodiest battles in American labor history. That odd mix of chip-on-the-shoulder resentment towards authority and look-out-for-your-neighbor community values continues to characterize West Virginia today, although the creeping blandness of suburbia threatens this unique regional culture.

Information

West Virginia Division of Tourism (☎ 304-558-2200, 800-225-5982; www.callwva.com) operates welcome centers at interstate borders and in **Harpers Ferry** (☎ 304-535-2482). Check www.adventuresinwv.com for info on the state's myriad adventure tourism opportunities.

Many hotels and motels tack on a $1 'safe' fee, refundable upon request at checkout. So if you didn't use that room safe, get your dollar back.

EASTERN PANHANDLE

The most accessible part of the state has always been and continues to be a mountain getaway for DC types.

Harpers Ferry

The center of this town is a maddeningly cute conglomeration of steep cobblestone streets framed by the Shenandoah Mountains

---

WEST VIRGINIA FACTS

Nickname Mountain State
Population 1.82 million
Area 24,244 sq miles
Capital city Charleston (pop 51,400)
Sales tax 6%
Birthplace of Mary Lou Retton, Pearl S Buck, Chuck Yeager
Home of The National Radio Astronomy Observatory, much of the American coal industry
Famous for Mountains, John Denver songs ('Country Roads'), the Hatfield-McCoy feud
Actual towns Mud, Rock, Big Stick, Hoohoo, Nitro

---

and River. Exhibits narrate the town's role at the forefront of westward expansion, American industry and, most famously, the slavery debate. In 1859, old John Brown tried to spark a slave uprising here and was hung for his efforts; the incident rubbed friction between North and South into the fires of Civil War. Historic buildings and museums are accessible to those with passes, which can be found, along with parking and shuttles, north of town at the **visitor center** (☎ 304-535-2482; vehicle/pedestrian $6/4; ⏰ 9am-5pm) off Hwy 340. Parking is incredibly limited in Harpers Ferry proper.

SIGHTS & ACTIVITIES

Among the free sites in the historic district, the 1858 **Master Armorer's House** explains how rifle technology developed here revolutionized the firearms industry; the **Storer College building**, long ago a teachers' college for freed slaves, now traces the town's African American history. The laughably tacky **John Brown Museum** (168 High St; adult/child 6-12 $7/5; ⏰ 9am-5pm) tells the story of Brown's life and raid in wax.

The 2160-mile Appalachian Trail is headquartered at the **Appalachian Trail Conference** (☎ 304-535-6331; www.atconf.org; cnr Washington & Jackson Sts; ⏰ 9am-5pm Mon-Fri Apr-Oct), a tremendous resource for hikers. Day hikers also scale the Maryland Heights Trail past Civil War fortifications or the Loudoun Heights Trail for river views.

Check with the visitor center about renting bikes to explore the **C&O Canal towpath**. To arrange rafting, kayaking, canoeing and tubing excursions, contact **River Riders** (☎ 800-326-7238; www.riverriders.com; 408 Alstadts Hill Rd).

SLEEPING & EATING

Hilltop House Hotel (☎ 304-535-2132; www.hilltophousehotel.com; 400 E Ridge St; r $85-160; P 🐾) Stunning views abound from this sprawling stone inn overlooking the Shenandoah and Potomac rivers. Any of the 64 rooms make an excellent base from which to explore panhandle West Virginia and Maryland.

   Town Inn (☎ 304-702-1872, 877-489-2447; www.thetownsinn.com; 179 High St; r $120-140; 🐾) Smack in the middle of the historic district, this B&B feels like it's been built into the mountain, an illusion accented by the pretty slate bathroom in the largest room.

   Anvil (☎ 304-535-2582; 1270 Washington St; lunch mains $8-12, dinner mains $12-23; ⏰ 11am-9pm Wed-

Sun) Local trout melting in honey pecan butter and an elegant Federal dining room equals excellence at this restaurant, in next-door Bolivar.

GETTING THERE & AROUND

Amtrak (☎ 800-872-7245) and **MARC** (☎ 800-325-7245) trains run to Washington's Union Station.

Berkeley Springs

America's first spa town (George Washington and his cronies frequently relaxed here), is an odd jumble of spiritualism, artistic expression and pampering spa centers. Farmers in pickups sporting Confederate flags and acupuncturists in tie-dye smocks regard each other with bemusement on the roads of Bath (still the official name).

Don't let the locker-room appearance deter you from the Berkeley Springs State Park's **Roman Bathhouse** (☎ 304-258-2711; bath $40; ⏰ 10am-4:30pm); it's the cheapest spa deal in town. (Fill your water bottle with some of the magic stuff at the fountain outside the door.) For a more indulgent experience, try a mix-and-match of treatments across the green at the **Main Bath House** (☎ 304-258-9071; ⏰ 10am-5pm) such as a bath, shower and hour's massage ($75) or chocolate-strawberry body wrap for $90.

Inn & Spa at Berkeley Springs (☎ 304-258-2210, 800-822-6630; www.theinnandspa.com; r $69-250; P 🐾), right next to the park, offers luxurious treatment plus lodging package deals at breathtaking prices. The holistic **Coolfont Resort** (☎ 304-258-4500; 3621 Cold Run Valley Rd; campsites $20-35, r per person $69-99, chalets per person $139-179; P 🐾) is like wellness summer camp for adults (but popular with families, too).

Get a bite ($5 lunch specials on weekdays) and listen to live music at the bar-restaurant **Tari's** (☎ 304-258-1196; 123 N Washington St; dinner mains $15-25), or go gourmet at **Lot 12 Public House** (☎ 304-258-6264; 302 Warren St; mains $19-34; ⏰ from 5pm Wed-Sun), halfway up the hill.

MONONGAHELA NATIONAL FOREST

Almost the entire eastern half of West Virginia is marked green parkland on the map, and all that goodness falls under the auspices of this stunning national forest. Within its 1400 sq miles are wild rivers, caves and the highest peak in the state (Spruce Knob). More than 850 miles of trails include the 124-mile **Allegheny Trail**, for hiking and backpacking, and the 75-mile rails-to-trails **Greenbrier River Trail**, popular with bicyclists.

Elkins, at the forest's western boundary, is a good base of operations. The **National Forest Service Headquarters** (☎ 304-636-1800; 200 Sycamore St; campsites/primitive sites $5/free, RV sites $10-30) distributes recreation directories for hiking, bicycling and camping.

Fat Tire Cycle (☎ 304-636-0969; 101 Randolph Ave; ☿ 9am-5pm Mon-Fri, until 3pm Sat) rents gear and sponsors excursions. Stock up on trail mix, energy bars and hippie auras at **Good Energy Foods** (☎ 304-636-8808; 214 3rd St; ☿ 9am-5:30pm Mon-Sat).

In the southern end of the forest, **Cranberry Mountain Nature Center** (☎ 304-653-4826; Hwy 150 & Hwy 39/55; ☿ 9am-4:30pm May-Oct) has scientific information on the forest.

The surreal landscapes at **Seneca Rocks**, 35 miles southeast of Elkins, attract rock climbers up its 900ft-tall sandstone strata. **Seneca Shadows Campground** (☎ 877-444-6777; campsites $11-30; ☿ Apr-Oct) is 1 mile east.

An 8-mile portion of the Allegheny Trail links two full-service state parks 30 miles northeast of Elkins: **Canaan Valley Resort** (☎ 304-866-4121), a downhill ski resort, and **Blackwater Falls State Park** (☎ 304-259-5216), with backcountry ski touring. Further south, **Snowshoe Mountain** (☎ 877-441-4386; www.snowshoemtn.com; lift tickets $33-43) is the state's largest downhill resort and has become a mountain-biking center from spring to fall.

Nearby, the **Cass Scenic Railroad State Park** (☎ 304-456-4300; www.cassrailroad.com; excursions from $13) runs steam trains, from an old logging town to mountaintop overlooks, daily in summer and for peak fall foliage. Accommodations include cottages and (pretty cool) **cabooses** ($70-200).

The hills of rural West Virginia are the unlikely venue for some of the world's most cutting-edge radio technology. The **Green Bank Science Center & the National Radio Astronomy Observatory** (☎ 304-456-2150; www.gb.nrao.edu; Green Bank; admission & tour free; ☿ 8:30am-6pm summer, 10am-5pm Wed-Sun rest of year) was where the black hole in the center of our galaxy was detected. The observatory's star attraction, the Green Bank radio telescope, looks like an immense satellite dish and is the largest movable object on land. The whole center lies within the country's only federal radio-free zone, which is why your car won't pick up any stations within 25 miles of the center.

MORGANTOWN

Morgantown's been dubbed one of the best cities of its size in the country, and it's not hard to see why: it's nestled within a dramatic valley, has a thriving arts scene fed from local West Virginia University, drips with bars, cafés and restaurants and houses a population that runs from South Asian immigrants to Appalachian mountain folk.

The students of enormous **West Virginia University** (☎ 304-293-0111; www.wvu.edu) fuel much of the city's energy. **Mountaineer Field** (☎ 304-293-2294; 1 Rogers St) is (in)famous for housing some of the rowdiest fans in American collegiate sport; football games here are an enjoyable afternoon of tossing ice chips and car batteries at the opposing team.

As always in this state, there's outdoor activities a stone's throw away; **Cheat Lake** (www.cheatlake.com) is an 8-mile-long reservoir east of town overflowing with hiker-bicyclist trails, ski routes and scenic overlooks. Once you're outdoor-ed out you can exercise your brain in the **Monongalia Arts Center** (☎ 304-282-3325; 107 High St; admission free; 10am-6pm Mon-Fri, 10am-4pm Sat) one of the largest and best museum and gallery spaces in the mountains. Catch a show in the lovely old 1924 **Metropolitan Theatre** (☎ 304-291-4884; 369 High St), an elegant main street anchor, and see the fascinating, if mind-numbingly exhaustive glass collection of Mr Kurt Ly, a Vietnamese West Virginian (of course), at the **Morgantown Glass Museum** (☎ 304-291-2957; 1628 Mileground Rd; ☿ 2-5pm Wed-Sat).

The **Hotel Morgan** (☎ 304-291-2517; 127 High St; r $80-150; P ☒ wi-fi) is a gorgeously appointed historical building; the grand ballroom is so grandiose you'd think you'd entered the set of *The Shining* (minus psycho Jack Nicholson). Service is friendly and informal, even at the elegant attached **Montmarte** (mains $14-23; ☿ 5-10pm Mon-Sat), fabulous enough for its American cuisine and commanding view but even more appealing thanks to the modish interior, which runs from early-20th-century tycoon-chic to gentle, rounded conceptual lines. The **Blue Moose Café** (☎ 304-292-8999; 248 Walnut St; $5-7; ☿ 7am-11pm Mon-Thu, until later Fri & Sat, 8am-11pm Sun), is a student-y sandwich shop with vaguely '50s-cum-boho vibe. **Maxwell's** (☎ 304-292-0982; 1 Wall St; lunch mains $6-11, dinner mains $9-11; ☿ 11am-8:45pm Mon-Thu, until 9:45pm Fri & Sat, until 1:45pm Sun) is a warm, underground den of burgers and dinner stir-fries that run from Cajun to Pan-Asian.

> **WHAT THE...?**
>
> Oh my God, everything inside this madhouse *tilts at an angle!* See gravity and the known limits of tackiness defied at the **Mystery Hole** (☎ 304-658-9101; US 60 at Mile 44; adult/child under 11 $5/4; ☽ 10:30am-6pm, call ahead for open days), one of the great attractions of roadside America.

SOUTHERN WEST VIRGINIA

This part of the state has carved out a viable stake as adventure-sporting capital of the Eastern seaboard. The forested mountains are pretty, rugged and hell to drive over if you're car isn't up to spec.

New River Gorge National River

The New River is actually one of the oldest in the world, and the primeval forest gorge it runs through is one of the most breathtaking in the Appalachians. The NPS protects a stretch of the New River that falls 750ft over 50 miles, with a compact set of rapids up to Class V concentrated at the northernmost end.

Canyon Rim visitor center (☎ 304-574-2115; ☽ 9am-5pm), just north of the impressive gorge bridge, is the only one of five NPS visitor centers along the river that's open year-round with information on river outfitters, gorge climbing, hiking and mountain biking, as well as white-water rafting to the north on the Gauley River. Rim and gorge trails offer beautiful views. There are four free basic camping areas.

Nearby **Hawks Nest State Park** offers views from its rim-top **lodge** (☎ 304-658-5212; r $72-87); in summer it operates an aerial tram (closed Monday) to the river, where you can catch a cruising boat ride.

Fayetteville

Pint-sized Fayetteville acts as the jumping-off point for New River thrill-seekers. On the third Saturday in October, hundreds of base jumpers parachute from the 876ft-high New River Gorge Bridge for the **Bridge Day Festival**.

Still under renovation at the time of this writing, the **Beckley Exhibition Coal Mine** (☎ 304-256-1747; http://beckleymine.com), in nearby Beckley is scheduled to open in April, 2008. Visitors will be able to descend 1500ft into a former coal mine, while the rehabilitated coal town above will serve as a museum for the region's mining heritage.

Among the many state-licenced rafting outfitters in the area, **USA Raft** (☎ 800-872-7238; www.usaraft.com; packages from $50) stands out for its white-water rafting trips.

South of town off Hwy 19, lodging and camping directories can be found at the **county tourist office** (☎ 304-465-5617). **Mountain Laurel RV Park/Campground** (☎ 304-574-0188; cnr Laurel Creek Rd & US 19) is a cheap camping option.

Fill up on hefty portions served under stained-glass windows with hippie hikers at **Cathedral Café & Bookstore** (☎ 304-574-0202; 134 S Court St; mains $5-8; ☽ 8am-4pm; ▯), which also has free internet access.

The South

More than any other part of the country, the South has an identity all of its own – a sense of regional pride, a musical way of speaking, a complicated political history and a shared culture that cuts across state lines. In short, the South is a big, bawdy place that is both modernly cosmopolitan and obsessed with its own past. While slick cities such as Atlanta and Charlotte are in perpetual states of reinvention, some of the more historic cities – places like New Orleans and Savannah – are virtual shrines to their former selves, celebrating historic architecture, locally flavored language and a kind of gentility that just doesn't exist in other parts of the country.

Blessed with fertile soil and a rich mix of cultures, the South nurtures a food culture that's arguably unsurpassed in the USA: succulent barbecue, plump Gulf oysters, cheesy grits and fried green tomatoes are all regional delicacies, endlessly tweaked by modern chefs. The arts thrive here, too: the South is the only American region identified by its own strain of literature, and Southern music history runs all the way from slave spirituals through the 21st-century hip-hop of OutKast. Jazz, the blues and rock 'n' roll were all born in the South. Nashville, the world's undisputed country-music capital, will keep you honky-tonkin' deep into the Tennessee night. And the state of Louisiana remains a unique repository for Cajun and zydeco music. Shrines to Southern-born musicians are all over this part of the country.

Due to its temperate weather, the South is hospitable to outdoor play nearly 365 days a year. Sun bunnies particularly appreciate this climate and the region's terrain, as beaches run for hundreds of miles down the South's Atlantic Coast, then circle back along the Gulf of Mexico. The South caters to all incarnations of the active traveler, too, with countless paths to hike, mountains to climb, rivers to run and swamps to explore.

HIGHLIGHTS

- Supporting the post-Katrina economy (and, yes, enjoying yourself in the process) by visiting still-great, still-recovering, still-partying-hard New Orleans during **Jazz Fest** (p440).

- Sucking down oysters at **Wintzell's** (p425)in Mobile, Alabama.

- Plunging into the **Mississippi Delta** (p427) on lonesome old Hwy 61, and eventually leaving the state via the stunning **Natchez Trace Parkway** (p468).

- Telling your friends you vacationed at Cape Fear after swinging through the **North Carolina coast** (p377).

- Touring the grand antebellum homes and cotton plantations of **Charleston** (p390).

- Shopping for country music at **Ernest Tubb's record shop** (p476) in Nashville.

- Hiking, camping and jaw-dropping in the scenic **Great Smoky Mountains National Park** (p388).

Kentucky

Nashville ★   Great Smoky   North
              Mountains   Carolina
         ★ National Park   ★

Tennessee   South   North
                    Carolina   Carolina
Arkansas   Natchez   Coast
         Trace ★   ★
         Parkway   Alabama   Georgia   Charleston
              Mississippi

Mississippi ★
Delta   ★ Mobile
Louisiana
         ★ New Orleans

THE SOUTH

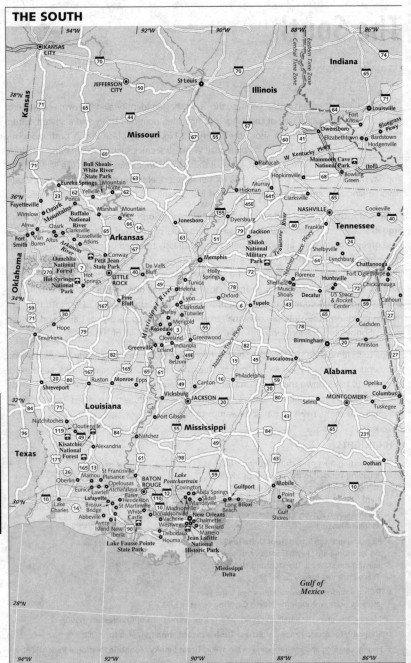

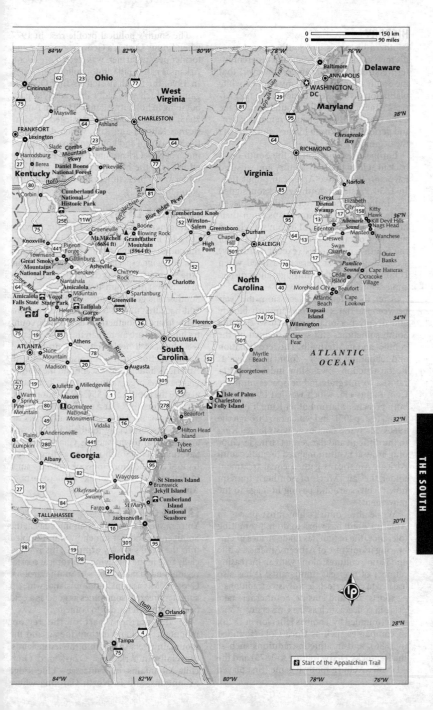

HISTORY

Southern history is like Southern cooking – it's messy, and open to radically different interpretations. All can agree, however, that the South's agrarian economy (run by white plantation owners who enslaved the first African Americans) laid the groundwork for the Civil War (1861–65), which remains a central period in Southern history. But it wasn't the beginning.

European exploration in the South dates back to at least the 16th century and wreaked havoc on the Native American population. In 1830 President Andrew Jackson signed the Indian Removal Act, which displaced some 50,000 Native Americans from their homes. When Abraham Lincoln was elected president on an antislavery platform, all of the South's nine states (except Kentucky) seceded, and most were devastated when Union soldiers blazed through and crushed confederate dreams.

After the attempted secession, the 'war between the states' became famously bloody and deeply personal, so much so that the South sometimes still seems defined by the conflict and its aftermath. The reconciliation and rebuilding process – formally known as Reconstruction – was slow indeed. Whites refused to integrate public spaces until the Civil Rights era, which was led by Atlanta-born preacher Martin Luther King Jr (see the boxed text, p407), and which ran through the 1960s. Many less famous activists joined King in the difficult and dangerous struggle, chipping away at institutionalized prejudice until African Americans gained equal treatment under the law. Much of Southern tourism now revolves around paying homage to the movement.

While the South – like most places in America – still has work to do in promoting tolerance, the region has made strides in embracing its mixture of African America, white and Latino cultures, along with an increasing number of overseas immigrants. It has also learned to celebrate its less divisive traditions – eg sports, arts and cuisine. Southerners take pride in colleges such as the University of Virginia (founded by Thomas Jefferson in 1825), in companies such as Coca-Cola (founded in 1886), and in athletic traditions such as the Kentucky Derby (dating to 1875) and the Alabama-Auburn football game (first played in 1893).

The South's political profile rose in 1977 when Jimmy Carter, a Georgia governor and former peanut farmer, was elected president. Arkansas native Bill Clinton followed in 1993. In 1996, the South hosted its first Olympic games, which was sadly marred by a park bombing in host city Atlanta. Then, in August 2005, the Gulf Coast was besieged by Hurricanes Katrina and Rita, which devastated the Mississippi and Louisiana coasts, and left much of New Orleans underwater. Rebuilding efforts (see the boxed text, p435) were still underway at press time, and could seemingly go on forever.

CULTURE & LIFESTYLE

Southerners have a reputation for moving just a bit more slowly than folks in the rest of the country, talking strangely, drinking hard and not being especially sophisticated. While little Southern towns certainly don't approximate New York's nonstop bustle, and while Southerners generally are significantly more laid-back that most US urbanites, exceptions to the image of Southerners as drawling country bumpkins are more than the norm. Atlanta is a glitzy, well-heeled city that prides itself on internationalism – it's also the home to America's hottest music scene and the world's biggest news organization, CNN. Charlotte is at once the capital of NASCAR (National Association for Stock Car Auto Racing) country and a major banking center. Southerners do love sports, especially football, but the fine arts thrive in towns such as Charleston and Savannah. The South is a sprawling, fascinating, contradictory mess of a place – and, in that way, it feels a lot like a microcosm of America itself.

LAND & CLIMATE

You can spend a sweltering summer day in the South and wonder if somehow you stumbled into the devil's sweaty armpit. This is especially true in the low-lying subtropical coastal regions and in inland areas of South Carolina, Georgia, Mississippi and Louisiana, where a summer breeze is sometimes as good as a cold beer, and much harder to come by.

In the northern part of the region, mountains cool and dry out the air and the mountain rivers trickle into the fertile lands, especially in Arkansas' Ozark and Ouachita Mountains, in Tennessee's Blue Ridge Mountains, and in North Carolina where the foothills of the Appalachian Mountains thrust northward.

Tourism in the region peaks from June to September. Mild weather and blossoming flowers make spring (May to June) a good time to visit, and fall colors decorate the landscape in September and October, especially in the mountain regions.

PARKS & WILDLIFE

The South is full of parks, monuments and historic sites. Some honor people (Martin Luther King Jr in Georgia, the Wright Brothers in North Carolina), others preserve historic and scenic passages (Natchez Trace Parkway from Mississippi to Tennessee, the Blue Ridge Parkway in North Carolina). Some sites mark significant Civil War battles (Vicksburg, MS; Chickamauga, GA; Forts Pulaski and Sumter, SC), while others honor waterways (Buffalo River, AR; Cumberland Island National Seashore, GA).

The region's bona fide 'national parks,' thus designated for their role in protecting nature and sheer beauty, include the Great Smoky Mountains National Park in Tennessee and North Carolina; Mammoth Cave National Park, KY; and Hot Springs National Park, AR.

Learn more at the National Park Service (NPS) website (www.nps.gov) or contact the states directly:

Alabama (☎ 888-252-7272; www.alapark.com)
Arkansas (☎ 888-287-2757; www.arkansasstateparks.com)
Georgia (☎ 800-864-7275; www.gastateparks.org)
Kentucky (☎ 800-255-7275; www.state.ky.us/agencies/parks)
Louisiana (☎ 888-677-1400; www.lastateparks.com)
Mississippi (☎ 800-407-2575; www.mdwfp.com)
North Carolina (☎ 919-733-4181; www.ncsparks.net)

THE SOUTH...

In One Week
Fly into the gigantic airport in **Atlanta** (p402) and stay awhile in this booming city, taking time to see the **Georgia Aquarium** (p406) and the fascinating museum at the **Center for Puppetry Arts** (p408). Then hop in the car – this is a vast region with tons to see, and you'll need a car to do it right – and drive south to **Savannah** (p415) for decadent food, jaw-dropping architecture and surrounding beaches. Then make the long trip west to the Alabama coast, rewarding yourself with oysters at **Wintzell's** (p425) when you arrive in Mobile. Continue along the Gulf Coast until you reach **New Orleans** (p433), where you can park the car and explore the city on foot with our **walking tour** (p441) before devoting your remaining time to celebrating jazz history and partying the night away on **Bourbon Street** (p446).

In Two to Three Weeks
Before leaving the Big Easy, spend some time communing with locals about how they're doing post-Katrina, or **volunteering** (see boxed text, p435) with a local organization that assists hurricane victims. Then make your way north through the haunting Mississippi Delta and visit legendary Memphis music sites, including **Graceland** (p461) and **Beale St** (p462), and then mosey on over to **Nashville** (p468) until you've got your fill of country music. Consider an outdoorsy detour to **Great Smoky Mountains National Park** (p388) before turning south to the **Birmingham Civil Rights Institute** (p422) and feasting on ribs at **Dreamland** (p423).

For Foodies
Southern food is a journey unto itself. New Orleans is foodie central, thanks to the beignets at **Café du Monde** (p444) and the *muffuletta* sandwiches at **Central Grocery** (p445). Hot dogs rarely taste better than at **Pete's Famous Hot Dogs** (p422) in Birmingham, and Alabama has multiple locations of the rib joint **Dreamland** (p423), which happens to serve a mean banana pudding for dessert. You can't beat the fried catfish (or the country ambience) at **Taylor Grocery** (p427) in the Mississippi Hill Country, but you can get terrific tamales at **Abe's** (p428) over in the Delta. Atlanta has a staggering ethnic food corridor along **Buford Highway** (p410), and **Watershed Restaurant** (p411) serves its legendary fried chicken on Tuesday nights in nearby Decatur.

South Carolina (☎ 888-887-2757; www.southcarolina parks.com)
Tennessee (☎ 888-867-2757; www.state.tn.us /environment/parks)

INFORMATION

No central tourism agency covers the entire South, but each state runs helpful visitor centers located at state borders along major highways. These places are stocked with highway maps, brochures and coupon books. (They also have cleaner restrooms than you're likely to find in off-ramp gas stations.) Visit the individual states online for specific information to help plan your trip ahead of time.

GETTING THERE & AROUND

With the world's busiest airport, Atlanta, Georgia is the main air gateway to the region. Memphis, TN, New Orleans, LA, Charlotte and Raleigh, NC, have large regional airports. **Greyhound** (☎ 800-231-2222; www.greyhound .com) buses are frequent (if sometimes slow) and can be a dependable way to get from city to city. A number of **Amtrak** (☎ 800-872-7245; www.amtrak.com) train routes traverse the South. Beyond the cities – and often within them – you really need a car to get around.

Fortunately, this region has some good drives. These include the Blue Ridge Parkway, the Natchez Trace Parkway and Hwy 12 along North Carolina's Outer Banks. I-10 runs along the Gulf Coast from Florida to New Orleans; I-20 links South Carolina with Louisiana via Georgia, Alabama and Mississippi; and I-40 goes from North Carolina to Arkansas via Tennessee. The chief north–south routes include I-95, I-75, I-65 and I-55.

NORTH CAROLINA

It's trailer parks next to McMansions in North Carolina, where the Old South stands shoulder-to-shoulder with the New South. From the ancient mountains in the west to the sandy barrier islands of the Atlantic you'll find a variety of cultures and communities not easy to stereotype.

The state is a patchwork of the progressive and the Stone Age: Asheville was named the 'New Freak Capital of the US' by *Rolling Stone,* while cohabitation was technically illegal until 2006. The Raleigh area has the highest concentration of PhDs in the country, yet North Carolina routinely ranks 48th in education. Important industries range from tobacco and hogs to banking and nanotechnology.

Most travelers tend to skirt through the business-oriented urban centers of the central Piedmont, instead choosing to stick to the scenic routes along the coast (via the islands of the Outer Banks) and those through the Appalachian Mountains, especially along the unforgettable Blue Ridge Parkway.

So come on down, ya'll, grab a plate of 'cue and watch the Duke Blue Devils and the Carolina Tar Heels battle it out on the basketball court where college hoops rival Jesus for Carolinians' souls.

History

The second territory to be colonized by the British, the state was originally part of the Province of Carolina, named in memory of King Charles I (Carolus in Latin), which included much of the southeast.

North Carolina was the first colony to vote for independence from the Crown, and

---

NORTH CAROLINA FACTS

Nickname Tar Heel State
Population 8.9 million
Area 48,711 sq miles
Capital city Raleigh (population 359,332)
Sales tax 6%, plus an additional hotel-occupancy tax of up to 6%
Birthplace of Novelist Thomas Wolfe (1900–38), evangelist Billy Graham (b 1918), actress Ava Gardner (1922–90), jazzman John Coltrane (1926–67), NASCAR driver Richard Petty (b 1937)
Home of The Blue Ridge Parkway, Research Triangle Park, Krispy Kreme donuts
Famous for Having the first state university in America; first powered airplane flight (1903), college basketball
Spookiest place The Devil's Tramping Ground, in Chatham County, a circular patch of dirt where grass won't grow; legends say it's Satan's portal to earth

THE SOUTH

several important Revolutionary War battles were fought here. The state was asleep economically during most of the 1800s, due mainly to closed-minded and indifferent leaders, leading to the nickname the 'Rip Van Winkle State.' Divided on slavery, North Carolina reluctantly seceded in 1861, and went on to provide more Confederate soldiers than any other state.

WWII brought some new industries and large military bases, and the economy continues to boom with the growth of finance in Charlotte, and of technology and medicine in the Raleigh-Durham area.

Information

The **North Carolina Division of Tourism** (☎ 919-733-8372, 800-847-4862; www.visitnc.com; 301N N Wilmington St, Raleigh, NC 27601) sends out good maps and information, including its annual *Official Travel Guide*.

NORTH CAROLINA COAST

With windswept barrier islands and vast, snake-ridden swamps, dignified Colonial towns and boardwalk bars brimming with sunburned tourists, the North Carolina coast is still undeveloped enough to have a bit of everything, whether you seek solitude or boisterous summer fun. On the isolated Outer Banks, fishermen still make their living hauling in catches of shrimp and oysters and the older locals talk in the same British-tinged brogue carried over by their English ancestors. Further south, Wilmington is known as a center of film and TV production and its surrounding beaches are popular with local spring-breakers and tourists. Estuaries, sounds and tidal lagoons teem with shorebirds and fish; ancient lighthouses watch the passing of time; and somewhere, perhaps, pirate treasure lies buried just under the shifting sands.

Outer Banks

Cut off from the mainland by the Intercoastal Waterway, the Outer Banks are fragile ribbons of sand that trace the contours of the coastline for 100 miles. From north to south, the barrier islands of Bodie, Roanoke, Hatteras and Ocracoke, essentially large sandbars, are linked by bridges and ferries. The quiet, far northern communities of **Corrola**, **Duck** and **Southern Shores** are popular with well-heeled vacationers and retirees. The nearly contiguous Bodie Island towns of **Kitty Hawk**, **Kill**

Devil Hills and **Nags Head** are heavily developed and more populist in nature, with fried fish joints, outdoor bars, motels and dozens of sandals 'n' sunblock shops. Roanoke Island, west of Bodie Island, is home to the tiny fishing village of **Wanchese** and the town of **Manteo**, home to the 'Lost Colony,' whose British settler inhabitants disappeared without a trace in the 1580s. Further south, Hatteras Island is a protected national seashore with a few small villages and a wild, windswept beauty. At the tail end of the banks, wild ponies run free and salty old Bankers shuck oysters and weave hammocks on Ocracoke Island, accessible only by ferry.

Nearly 2000 ships have run aground on hidden shoals around the Outer Banks in the past 450-odd years, giving the area the name 'The Graveyard of the Atlantic' and making it a popular destination for shipwreck divers.

The town of **Edenton**, on the west end of the Albermarle Sound, has a lovely Colonial-era waterfront and makes a nice stop off on the way to the Banks. See the **visitor center** (☎ 252-482-2637; www.edenton.org; 108 N Broad St; ☺ 9am-5pm Mon-Sat, 1-4pm Sun) for accommodations and a self-guided-tour map.

ORIENTATION & INFORMATION

Hwy 12, also called Virginia Dare Trail, or 'the coast road,' runs close to the Atlantic for the length of the Outer Banks. US 158, usually called 'The Bypass,' begins just north of Kitty Hawk and merges with US 64 as it crosses onto Roanoke Island. Most of the tourist attractions and facilities are along the 16-mile strip of Bodie Island, in the almost adjoining towns of Kitty Hawk, Kill Devil Hills and Nags Head. Locations are usually given in terms of 'Mileposts' (MP), beginning with MP 0 at the foot of the Wright Memorial Bridge at Kitty Hawk, where US 158 crosses to the mainland. Just past MP 16, US 64/264 crosses the Nags Head–Manteo Causeway ('the causeway') to Roanoke Island and from there goes to the mainland. Hwy 12 continues south to Hatteras Island and, by ferry, to Ocracoke Island.

The best sources of information are at the **visitor centers** (Kitty Hawk ☎ 252-261-4644; MP 1.5; ☺ 9am-5pm); Manteo ☎ 252-473-2138, 800-446-6262; US 64/264; ☺ 9am-5pm); Ocracoke ☎ 252-928-4531, south end of Hwy 12; ☺ 9am-5pm). Visitor centers in Nags Head, Pea Island and Buxton are open April

to October. Also useful is www.outerbanks
.org. Corolla's **public library** (1123 Ocean Trail/Hwy 12)
has free internet access and the entire Manteo
waterfront has free wi-fi.

SIGHTS

The following sights are listed in order of
north to south.

The Whalehead Club

This sunflower-yellow gabled 'cottage' (☎ 252-
453-9040; www.whaleheadclub.org; 1100 Club Way, Corolla;
tours $7; ☺ dawn-dusk) was built in the 1920s as a
getaway for Philadelphia industrialist Edward
Collings Knight Jr and his wife. The 21,000-
sq-ft mansion has been restored to its original
Art Nouveau glory and is located within the
Currituck Heritage Park, which has picnic and
fishing areas and the free **Outer Banks Center for
Wildlife Education**, with an extensive collection
of carved duck decals.

Wright Brothers National Monument

This national **monument** (☎ 252-441-7430; www
.nps.gov/wrbr; admission $4; ☺ 9am-5pm, to 6pm summer)
is located among the same Kitty Hawk dunes
where self-taught engineers Wilbur and Orville Wright launched the world's first successful airplane flight on December 17, 1903,
which lasted 12 seconds. Though the Wrights
were from Ohio, they chose Kitty Hawk for
its good winds and soft landing surfaces, and
North Carolina has stamped the words 'First
in Flight' on its license plates since 1982. The
visitor center has exhibits on aviation history
and lectures every two hours.

Fort Raleigh National Historic Site

In 1587, more than 20 years before the Pilgrims
landed at Plymouth Rock, a group of 100 English colonists settled on Roanoke Island under
the leadership of John White. Three years later,
White returned from a trip back to England to
find the settlers vanished without a trace. The
fate of the 'Lost Colony' remains a mystery, but
the **visitor center** (☎ 252-473-5772; www.nps.gov/fora;
1401 National Park Dr, Manteo; ☺ 9am-5pm, to 6pm summer) has exhibits, artifacts and a free film about
Native Americans and English settlers that will
fuel your imagination. Look for the prints based
on 1585 illustrations by John White, which are
now some of the best-known depictions of pre-
European North America. A small mound
nearby is meant to re-create the earthworks of
the original fort.

Attractions at the site include **Lost Colony
Outdoor Drama** (☎ 252-473-3414, 866-468-7630; www
.thelostcolony.org; 1409 National Park Dr, Manteo; adult/child
$16/8; ☺ show 8:30pm Mon-Sat Jun-Aug). This im-
mensely popular and long-running musical
dramatizes the fate of the colonists. It plays at
the Waterside Theater throughout summer.

The antique 16th-century **Elizabethan Gardens** (☎ 252-473-3234; www.elizabethangardens.org; 1411
National Park Dr, Manteo; adult/child $8/5; ☺ 9am-8pm daily
summer, shorter hours off-season) include a Shakespearian herb garden and rows of beautifully
manicured flowerbeds.

If underwater critters are more to your
liking, head to the **North Carolina Aquarium**
(☎ 252-473-3494, 866-332-3475; www.ncaquariums
.com/ri/riindex.htm; 374 Airport Rd, Roanoke Island; adult/
child $8/6; ☺ 9am-5pm), where you can watch tiger
sharks glide through the gloomy depths, chill
by the gator pond or stroke the slimy bellies
of (de-barbed) stingrays in the touch tank.

Cape Hatteras National Seashore

Extending some 70 miles from south of Nags
Head to the south end of Okracoke Island, this
fragile necklace of islands remains blissfully free
of overdevelopment. Three **visitor centers** (☺ 9am-
6pm summer, shorter hours rest of year; Bodie ☎ 252-441-5711;
Hatteras ☎ 252-995-4474; Ocracoke ☎ 252-928-4531) serve
the park on the main islands. The **park headquarters** (☎ 252-473-2111; www.nps.gov/caha; 1401 National
Park Dr) is in Manteo. Natural attractions include
local and migratory waterbirds, marshes, woodlands, dunes and miles of empty beaches. Other
attractions (from north to south) follow.

At the northern end of Hatteras Island,
the 5834-acre **Pea Island National Wildlife Refuge**
(☎ 252-987-8111; www.fws.gov/peaisland; admission free;
☺ 9am-4pm, to 5pm summer) is a great place for
watching the area's 365 bird species along the
nature trails and observation points.

You can't miss the 156ft horizontally
striped **Bodie Island Lighthouse** (☎ 252-441-5711,
admission free) right off the highway. It has a visitor center in the lighthouse keeper's quarters.
You can't climb this one, but there's a pretty
nature trail around it.

Chicamacomico Lifesaving Station (☎ 252-987-
1552; www.chicamacomico.net; Rodanthe village; adult/child
$5/4; ☺ noon-5pm weekdays Apr-Oct) is the most com-
plete of seven lifesaving stations in the Outer
Banks, with exhibits on the station's history
since 1874.

At 208ft tall, the iconic **Cape Hatteras Lighthouse** (☎ 252-995-4474; www.nps.gov/caha/lrp.htm; step

limb adult/child $7/3.50; 9am-4:30pm Apr-Oct, to 5:30pm ummer) is the tallest brick lighthouse in the US. Located just off the highway, you can climb the 248 steps and check out the visitor center (open year-round).

Graveyard of the Atlantic Museum (252-986-9995; www.graveyardoftheatlantic.com; 59158 Coast Guard Rd, Hatteras; admission by donation; 9am-6pm) is all about preserving the Outer Banks' maritime history, with exhibits about shipwrecks, cool 'beach finds' and salvaged cargo.

Ocracoke Island

Accessed via the free Hatteras–Ocracoke ferry, small **Ocracoke Village** (252-928-6711; www.ocra okevillage.com) sits at the south end of 14-mile-long Ocracoke Island. It's a funky little village that's crowded in summer and desolate in winter, where the older residents still speak in the 17th-century British dialect known as 'Hoi Toide' (their pronunciation of 'high tide') and refer to nonislanders as 'dingbatters.' Edward Teach, also known as Blackbeard the pirate, used to hide out in the area and was killed here in 1718. You can camp by the beach where the wild ponies run, have a fish sandwich in a local pub, ride a rented scooter around the village's narrow streets or visit the 1823 **Ocra-koke Lighthouse**, the oldest one still operating in North Carolina.

ACTIVITIES

The same strong wind that once helped the Wright brothers launch their biplane today propels numerous sailors, windsurfers, and hang gliders. Other popular outdoor activities include kayaking, fishing, cycling, horse tours and scuba diving – all well catered for in the northern resort areas. The usually calm coastal waters occasionally kick up, creating perfect conditions for bodysurfing. Surfing on the numerous beach breaks is best from August to October, with the East Coast championships in early September. Outfitters rent out a range of equipment.

Back Country Outfitters (252-453-0877; www outerbankstours.com; 107-C Corolla Light Town Center; 2hr tour adult/child $46/23) offers guided 4WD tours over the dunes and through the maritime forest to see the unique wild Mustang ponies that roam the Outer Banks.

Kitty Hawk Kites (252-441-4124, 877-359-2447; www.kittyhawkkites.com; 3933 Croatan Hwy, Nags Head; bike/ kayak rental per day $25/39) has locations all over the Banks offering beginners' kite-boarding

lessons (three hours, $200) and hang-gliding lessons at Jockey's Ridge State Park (from $89). It also rents kayaks, sailboats, bikes and in-line skates and has a variety of tours and courses.

Nags Head Diving (252-473-1356; www.nagshead diving.com; 406 Uppowoc St, Manteo; scuba class $295, open-water dives $225, beach dives $30) has NAUI-certified instructors who run everything from basic classes to guided dives of the shipwrecks of the Graveyard of the Atlantic.

SLEEPING

Crowds swarm the Outer Banks in summer, so it's best to reserve a place, rather than just show up. The area has hundreds of motels, efficiencies and B&Bs; the visitor centers offer referrals. Also check www.outer-banks.com. The following are high-season rates.

Adventure Bound Campground (252-255-1130, 877-453-2545; 1004 W Kitty Hawk Rd; campsites for 2 adults $20, for each additional adult/child $5/2.50; P) In a pleasant but out-of-the-way location, this welcoming year-round campsite has a newly renovated bathhouse with hot water and flush toilets, badminton, volleyball and shuffleboard courts, free use of fishing equipment and tent rental.

Island Inn (252-928-4351, 877-456-3466; www .ocracokeislandinn.com; 25 Lighthouse Rd, Ocracoke; r $59-139, villas per week $1200-1500; P wi-fi) In Ocracoke Village, this grand old turn-of-the-century clapboard inn has shabby-chic rooms with mismatched bedspreads, spooky oil portraits and pedestal sinks. Amenities include a heated pool, and the front porch overlooks the ocean. Open year-round.

Days Inn Orville & Wilbur Wright (252-441-7211, 800-325-2525; www.outer-banks.com/days-oceanfront; MP 8.5; r $119-239; P wi-fi) Set in a lovely 1940s white brick hotel with a fireplace in the lobby, the inn has clean, simple rooms, some with decks overlooking the ocean. Open year-round.

Days Inn Mariner I & II (252-441-2021, 800-325-2525; www.outer-banks.com/days-mariner; MP 7; r $159-269; P wi-fi) A mile and a half away from the Days Inn Orville & Wilbur Wright, this inn has slightly less charm and slightly higher prices, but is a good bet if the Wright is full. Open year-round.

Sanderling Resort & Spa (252-261-4111, 877-650-4812; www.thesanderling.com; 1461 Duck Rd; r $349-459; P wi-fi) The poshest digs in the Outer Banks, this three-building resort has airy, modern rooms, a formal restaurant serving haute American cuisine, and a spa where guests can be massaged with hot stones in a gazebo facing the ocean.

The National Park Service runs four summer-only **campgrounds** (☎ 800-365-2267; www .nps.gov/caha/camping99.htm; campsites $20; **P**) on the islands, which feature cold-water showers and flush toilets. They are located at Oregon Inlet, near the Bodie Island lighthouse, Cape Point and Frisco near the Cape Hatteras lighthouse and **Ocracoke** (☎ 800-365-2267; http://res ervations.nps.gov) on Ocracoke Island. Only sites at Ocracoke can be reserved; the others are first-come, first-served.

EATING & DRINKING
The main tourist strip on Bodie Island has the most restaurants and nightlife, but only in season. The following are all nonchain places open for lunch and dinner year-round.

Howard's Pub (☎ 252-928-4441; Hwy 12, Ocracoke Village; mains $6-16; ⊗ 11am-10pm Mon-Thu, to midnight Fri & Sat) has been around in one incarnation or another since the 1850s. In a big wooden building at the edge of the village, Howard's now serves crab cake sandwiches and baby back ribs to the hoards who come to sit on the porch to listen to live music and drink one of the 200 beers on tap.

Awful Arthur's Oyster Bar (☎ 252-441-5955; MP 6; mains $11-18; ⊗ 11am-10:30pm) Come here for the raw bar and hopping atmosphere. It serves seafood, steak, chicken and pasta dishes. Don't be shy about ordering a beer before noon; the locals aren't.

Black Pelican (☎ 252-261-3171; MP 4; mains $11-22; ⊗ 11:30am-9:30pm) The restaurant, in an old lifesaving station decorated with flags and vintage beer signs, specializes in what could be described as International Beach Cuisine: seared Tuna Nagano, Shrimp Florentine and New England clam chowder, along with steamed shellfish by the half-pound and excellent wood-fired pizzas. The bar is a popular locals hangout.

Blue Point (☎ 252-261-8090; 1240 Duck Rd, Duck; mains $20-32; ⊗ 11:30am-2pm & 5-9:30pm Tue-Sun, 5-9.30pm only Mon) Overlooking the Currituck Sound in the upscale town of Duck, this contemporary bistro serves refined Southern coastal cuisine – think seared sea scallops over arugula – and is considered by many the best fine dining on the Banks. At lunchtime, paninis and fancy salads are delicious and reasonably priced.

GETTING THERE & AWAY
If you're driving, access Hwy 12 (the main road along the cape) from Hwy 158 at Kitty Hawk or from Hwy 64/264, which leads over Roanoke Island to the park's northern entrance.

No public transportation exists to or on the Outer Banks, however the **North Carolina Ferry System** (☎ 800-293-3779; www.ncferry.org) operates several routes, including the free 40-minute Hatteras–Ocracoke car ferry, which runs at least hourly from 5am to 10pm; bookings aren't necessary. Ferries also run between Ocracoke and Cedar Island (one way $15, 2¼ hours) every two hours or so; reservations are recommended especially in summer. There are also ferries that link Ocracoke and Swan Quarter on the mainland ($15, 2½ hours).

Crystal Coast
The southern Outer Banks, composed of several coastal towns and islands, are collectively called the 'Crystal Coast,' at least for tourist offices' promotion purposes. Locals usually just call this area 'Down East.' **Cape Lookout National Seashore** has seasonal nesting sites for turtles and shorebirds and can only be reached by boat. Diamond-patterned **Cape Lookout Lighthouse** is arguably the most photogenic on the Atlantic Coast.

A rather unappealing industrial and commercial stretch of US 70 goes through **Morehead City**, with plenty of chain hotels and restaurants. Get information from the well-stocked **Crystal Coast Visitors Bureau** (☎ 252-726-8148; 340 Arendell St/Hwy 70; ⊗ 9am-5pm Mon-Fri, from 10am Sat & Sun).

Postcard-pretty **Beaufort** (*bow*-fort), the third-oldest town in the state, was originally called 'Fish Town' and still trades off its maritime heritage. The pirate Blackbeard was a frequent visitor to the area in the early 1700s – in 1996 the wreckage of his flagship, the *Queen Anne's Revenge*, was discovered at the bottom of Beaufort Inlet. The **visitor center** (☎ 252-728-5225; 138 Turner St; ⊗ 9:30am-5pm Mon-Sat summer, 10am-4pm winter) is in the Beaufort Historic Site.

Small **ferry services** (www.nps.gov/calo/planyou visit/ferry.htm; $14-25) leave regularly from the Beaufort boardwalk for the Cape Lookout Lighthouse and for **Shackleford Banks** and **Carrot Island**, uninhabited sandbars with spectacular seashells and herds of wild ponies. Camping is allowed on Shackleford Banks.

WILMINGTON-AREA BEACHES

While riverfront Wilmington doesn't have its own beach, there are plenty of sandy stretches just a few minutes away.

From north to south:

Surf City A low-key beach town with good waves.

Topsail Beach Clean, white-sand beach, home to sea turtle rehab center.

Wrightsville Beach The closest beach to Wilmington, with plenty of fried fish joints, sunglass shops and summer crowds.

Carolina Beach Warm water and boardwalk equal row upon row of beach umbrellas.

Kure Beach Popular fishing beach and home to the North Carolina Aquarium at Fort Fisher.

Southport Not a swimming beach, but a quaint town with tons of antique stores.

Bald Head Island Accessible by ferry from Southport, this secluded sea turtle sanctuary forbids cars, making travel difficult for those for don't rent a golf cart.

Caswell Beach A quiet beach with nearby golf course.

Oak Island The largest beach community in North Carolina, with three piers.

The cypress trees and crumbling gravestones of the **Old Burying Ground** on Ann St in Beaufort are the picture of Southern Gothic.

The **Bogue Banks**, across the sound, have popular public swimming beaches.

Wilmington

The largest city on the North Carolina coast, Wilmington sits at the mouth of the Cape Fear River in all its azalea-scented antebellum glory. At night the large historic downtown becomes the playground for local college students, tourists and the occasional film type from the nearby studios – the area is home to a large film industry and such movies as *Blue Velvet* and *The Crow* have been filmed here.

The **visitor center** (☎ 910-341-4030, 800-222-4757; 24 N 3rd St; 8:30am-5pm Mon-Fri, 9am-4pm Sat, from 1pm Sun), in the 1892 courthouse building, has a walking-tour map. There is a seasonal **visitor booth** (Market St; 9am-4:30pm Apr-Sep). A **free trolley** (7:20am-9:20pm Mon-Fri, from 11am Sat, 11am-6pm Sun) runs through the historic district.

SIGHTS

The **Cameron Art Museum** (☎ 910-395-5999; www.cameronartmuseum.com; 3201 S 17th St; adult/child $7/5; 11am-5pm Tue-Thu, Sat & Sun, to 9pm Fri) focuses on North Carolinian artists and American art and is known for its exceptional collection of prints by Pennsylvania-born impressionist Mary Cassatt.

Take a river taxi ($5 round-trip) or cross the Cape Fear Bridge to reach the **Battleship North Carolina** (☎ 910-251-5797; www.battleshipnc.com; adult/child $12/6; 8am-5pm, to 8pm summer).

This 45,000-ton megaship earned 15 battle stars in the Pacific Theater in WWII before being decommissioned in 1947. Today, self-guided tours of the now-empty decks take in the crew's quarters, captain's cabin, gun turrets, galleys and more.

Screen Gems Studios (☎ 910-343-3433; www.screengemsstudios.com; 1223 N 23rd St; admission $12/5; 1hr tour noon & 2pm Sat, Sun summer only) offers a behind-the-scenes tour of the working studio where shows such as *Dawson's Creek* and *One Tree Hill* were filmed.

If you don't mind keeping reptilian company, visit **Cape Fear Serpentarium** (☎ 910-762-1669; www.capefearserpentarium.com; 20 Orange St; admission $8; 11am-5pm Mon-Fri, to 6pm Sat & Sun), where you can gawk at yellow eyelash vipers, read about how it feels to die from the bite of the deadly bushmaster, and, at 3pm on Saturday and Sunday, watch gonzo herpetologist/showman Dean Ripa hand-feed mice to his 100-plus species of beasties.

SLEEPING

There are numerous budget hotels and a KOA Campground on Market St, just north of downtown.

Best Western Coastline Inn (☎ 910-763-2800, 800-617-7732; www.coastlineinn.com; 503 Nutt St; d incl breakfast weekday/weekend from $89/139;) Comfy, plain rooms, most with kitchenettes, in a quiet, newly renovated hotel overlooking the harbor.

Front Street Inn (☎ 910-762-6442, 800-336-8184; www.frontstreetinn.com; 215 Front St; r incl breakfast $135-235; wi-fi) In an old Salvation Army building only steps from the Riverwalk, this boutique B&B has 12 dreamy suites, each with its own theme – 'Hemingway' has a mosquito net canopy and a wet bar, 'Jacques Cousteau' has blue walls and a huge fish tank.

EATING

Water St Restaurant (☎ 910-343-0042; 5 S Water St; mains $9-20; ⏰ 11:30am-10pm) Bits of *Dawson's Creek* were filmed in this former peanut warehouse, which serves all kinds of sandwiches, seafood and pasta. There's sidewalk dining, and Dixieland, blues and jazz music in the evenings.

Elijah's (☎ 910-343-1448; 2 Ann St; mains $11-27; ⏰ 11:30am-10pm) The saying 'the better the view, the worse the food' doesn't hold at this riverfront joint, with ample outdoor seating and classic seafood dishes such as stuffed shrimp and oysters Rockefeller.

THE TRIANGLE

Located in the central North Carolina region known as the Piedmont, the cities of Raleigh, Durham and Chapel Hill form a rough triangle. Three top research universities – Duke, University of North Carolina, and North Carolina State are located here, as is the 7000-acre computer and biotech office campus known as Research Triangle Park. Swarming with egghead computer programmers, bearded peace activists and hip young families, each town has its own unique personality, despite being only a few miles apart. And everyone here – we mean everyone – goes crazy for university basketball.

GETTING THERE & AROUND

Raleigh-Durham International Airport (RDU; ☎ 919-840-2123; www.rdu.com), a significant hub, is a 25-minute drive northwest of downtown Raleigh. **Carolina Trailways/Greyhound** (Raleigh ☎ 919-834-8275; 314 W Jones St; Durham ☎ 919-687-4800; 820 W Morgan St) serve Raleigh and Durham.

The **Triangle Transit Authority** (☎ 919-549-9999; www.ridetta.org; adult $2) operates buses linking Raleigh, Durham and Chapel Hill, and all three to the airport.

Raleigh

A politely pretty town with some notable splashes of color, North Carolina's capital sits in the Triangle's southeastern corner. Home to North Carolina State University (NCSU), Raleigh has a handsome downtown with some neat (and free!) museums and galleries. In the past two decades, urban-renewal project have given the town a shot in the arm, wit the festive Fayetteville St pedestrian mall an a growing cultural scene.

The **Capitol Area Visitor Information Cent** (☎ 866-724-8687; 5 E Edenton St; ⏰ 9am-5pm Mon-F from noon Sun) is in the lobby of the North Caro lina Museum of History. Pick up other helpf information at the **convention & visitors burea** (☎ 919-834-5900, 800-849-8499; www.visitraleigh.com; 4 Fayetteville Mall; ⏰ 8:30am-5pm Mon-Fri).

SIGHTS

North Carolina Museum of Art (☎ 919-839-626 www.ncartmuseum.org; 2110 Blue Ridge Rd; admission fre ⏰ 9am-5pm Tue-Thu & Sat, to 9pm Fri, from 10am Sun) located on the western fringe of town and ha a fine collection including works by master from Raphael to Monet to Georgia O'Keeff It has a variety of programs, including chil dren's films, workshops and summer movie and concerts.

North Carolina Museum of History (☎ 919-71 0200; www.ncmuseumofhistory.org; 5 E Edenton St; admi sion free; ⏰ 9am-5pm Mon-Sat, from noon Sun) has a kinds of artifacts, such as Civil War photo Cherokee crafts, 19th-century costumes an a special exhibit on stockcar racing.

See Willo, the world's only dinosaur wit a heart (it's fossilized) at the modern, air **North Carolina Museum of Natural Sciences** (☎ 91 733-7450; www.naturalsciences.org; 11 W Jones St; admi sion free; ⏰ 9am-5pm Mon-Sat, from noon Sun). There also a unique and scary Acrocanthosauru skeleton, five habitat dioramas and lots o well-done taxidermy.

Exploris (☎ 919-834-4040; www.exploris.org; 20 E Hargett St; adult/child $5/5, with IMAX theater $13/1 ⏰ 10am-4pm Tue-Sat, from noon Sun) is a fun, hands on museum for kids.

SLEEPING & EATING

Downtown is pretty quiet on nights an weekends, but the Glenwood South are northwest of downtown is hopping wit cafés, bars and clubs, and NCSU students ea and party on Hillsborough St, by campus. Th surrounding suburbs have a wealth of grea ethnic dining.

Velvet Cloak Inn (☎ 919-828-0333; www.velvetcloakin .com; 1505 Hillsborough St; r from $89; P ⛽ 🏊 🖳 wi-f Business travelers and trysting students popu late the 100 flowery, carpeted rooms at thi high-end motel near campus, a much-love site for weddings and other parties.

Umstead Hotel & Spa (☎ 919-447-4000; www
.theumstead.com; 100 Woodland Pond; r from $299;
P ✗ ☒ ☎ ☐ wi-fi) Computer chips embedded in the silver room-service trays alert
bellboys to whisk away leftovers post haste at
this lavish new boutique hotel. How's that for
taking care of details? In the Raleigh suburb
of Cary, the Umstead's the final word in fan-
ciness, with huge rooms featuring imported
linen, and enormous flat-screen TV and a
Zenlike spa.

Hayes-Barton Cafe (☎ 919-856-8551; 2000 Fairview
Rd; mains $11-15; ☻ 11:30am-2pm Mon-Sat, 6-9pm Wed-
Sat) This 1940s-themed diner, attached to an
old family pharmacy in the trendy Five Points
neighborhood, is a hot spot for pimento cheese
sandwiches and a vertigo-inducing Mile
High coconut cake.

Durham

Though it currently bills itself as the 'City of
Medicine,' 100 years ago Durham could just
as easily have called itself 'City of Cigarettes.'
Built on the fortunes of the Bull Durham and
American Tobacco companies, its main industry collapsed when smoking began to go out
of style in the 1960s, leaving behind acres of
brick tobacco warehouses that are now being
turned into art galleries, cafés and condos as
part of a downtown revival project.

Today the city is home to world-class Duke
University and Duke Hospital (hence the
'City of Medicine' nickname); the Durham
Bulls minor-league baseball team (of 1988
film *Bull Durham* fame); and some nifty
restaurants, bars and theaters, if you know
where to look.

Hubs of activity include **Brightleaf Square**, a
tobacco warehouse-turned-shopping area in
the east side of downtown, and boutique-lined,
New Age-y **Ninth Street**, near Duke campus.

The **visitor center** (☎ 919-687-0288, 800-446-8604;
www.durham-nc.com; 101 E Morgan St; ☻ 8:30am-5pm Mon-
Fri, 10am-2pm Sat) has information and maps.

SIGHTS

Endowed by the Duke family's cigarette fortune, **Duke University** (☎ 919-684-2572; www.duke
.edu) has a Georgian-style East Campus and a
neo-Gothic West Campus with an impressive
1930s chapel. Heavenly **Sarah P Duke Gardens**
(☎ 919-684-3698; www.hr.duke.edu/dukegardens; 426
Anderson St; admission free; ☻ 8am-dusk) include 55
acres of koi ponds, terraced rose gardens and
magnolia groves and manicured fields, where

students and visitors lounge and play Frisbee
on warm afternoons.

The new **Nasher Museum of Art** (☎ 919-684-5135;
www.nasher.duke.edu; 2001 Campus Dr; adult/child $5/free;
☻ 10am-5pm Tue-Sat, to 9pm Thu, from noon Sun) houses
an impressive collection of Classical, European
and American art in an even more impressive
contemporary cube of a building.

The humble farmstead at **Bennett Place**
(☎ 919-383-4345; 4409 Bennett Memorial Rd; ☻ 10am-
4pm Tue-Sat) was the site of Confederate general
Joseph E Johnston's 1865 surrender of 90,000
troops to Union general William T Sherman,
effectively ending the Civil War. There are free
guided tours every half-hour.

Make your own tornado, climb in a space
ship, or ogle the alligators at the **Museum of
Life & Science** (☎ 919-220-5429; www.ncmls.org; 433
Murray Ave; adult/child $9.50/7.50; ☻ 10am-5pm Mon-Sat,
from noon Sun).

From April to September be sure to catch
an afternoon or evening ball game at the **Durham Bulls Athletic Park** (☎ 919-956-2855; www.dbulls
.com; 409 Blackwell St; tickets $6-8).

SLEEPING & EATING

Carolina Duke Motor Inn (☎ 919-286-0771, 800-438-
1158; 2517 Guess Rd; r from $37; P ☒ ☎) You can't
beat the price at this 182-room motel off I-
85. Facilities are clean and in close proximity
to some of the best classic truck-stop diners
around!

Washington Duke Inn & Golf Club (☎ 919-490-0999,
800-443-3853; www.washingtondukeinn.com; 3001 Cameron
Blvd; r from $150; P ✗ ☒ ☎ ☐ wi-fi) This huge,
pink 'English manor house' just across from
Duke campus is one of the swankest options
in town, with plush rooms and an obsessively
trimmed golf course.

Guglhupf Bakery (☎ 919-401-2600; 2706 Durham-
Chapel Hill Blvd; mains $5-10; ☻ 7am-6pm Tue-Sat, 9am-
3pm Sun) Mornings, a tart cherry Danish and a
cappuccino are the way to go at this superior
German-style bakery and café. In the afternoon, try a Westphalian ham sandwich and
a Pilsner on the sunny patio.

Magnolia Grill (☎ 919-286-3609; 1002 Ninth St; mains
$23-29; ☻ 6-10pm Tue-Sun) The exquisite upscale
Southern cuisine in this noisy little restaurant
near Duke campus has been winning raves for
20 years. Think grits soufflé topped with fois
gras. Save room for pastry chef Karen Barker's
killer desserts. Reservations are highly recommended, but the bar area sometimes has room
for walk-ins.

THE SOUTH

Chapel Hill

The ultraconservative North Carolina senator Jesse Helms famously said, 'Why build a zoo when we can just put a fence around Chapel Hill?' It's not San Francisco, but Chapel Hill (and the adjoining town of Carrboro) is certainly the most forward-thinking part of the state. The University of North Carolina (UNC), founded in 1789, was the first state university in the nation, with grassy, poplar-lined quads. Music, especially indie rock and alternative country, is huge, as is basketball – Michael Jordan leaped to fame during his tenure at UNC.

Downtown lies about 2 miles northwest of the Hwy 15/501 bypass. The main drag is Franklin St, with funky clothing shops, bars and restaurants on its north side and the UNC campus to the south; the same street enters Carrboro to the west. **Weaver Street Market** (www.weaverstreetmarket.com) grocery coop in Carrboro is an informal town square, and its front lawn is always blanketed with grad students and young families taking advantage of the free wi-fi and outdoor music.

Pick up good area information from the **Chapel Hill-Orange County Visitors Bureau** (☎ 919-968-2060, 888-968-2060; www.chocvb.org; 501 W Franklin St; ⏱ 8:30am-5pm Mon-Fri, 10am-2pm Sat).

SLEEPING & EATING

You'll find most restaurants and nightspots along Franklin St. Just to the west, Carrboro attracts postcollege hippies and hipsters.

Inn at Celebrity Dairy (☎ 919-742-5176; www.celebritydairy.com; 144 Celebrity Dairy Way; r incl breakfast $70-130; ⓟ ✛ ✗) Thirty miles west of town in rural Chatham County, this working goat dairy offers B&B accommodations in a Greek Revival farmhouse. Enjoy goat cheese omelets for breakfast then head out to the barn to pet the goat who provided the milk. You can also come for the Sunday lunch, served the third Sunday of each month.

Carolina Inn (☎ 919-933-2001, 800-962-8519; www.carolinainn.com; 211 Pittsboro St; r from $140; ⓟ ✛ ▢ ✗ wi-fi) In the center of campus but a far cry from the dorms, this Georgian-style hotel has 184 plush rooms and gracious Southern touches like Friday evening bluegrass concerts on the veranda, afternoon teas in the upscale restaurant, and fresh roses everywhere.

Allen & Son's Barbecue (☎ 919-942-7576; 6203 Millhouse Rd; mains $7-10; ⏱ 10am-5pm Tue-Wed, to 8pm Thu-Sat) Tasting the smoky, vinegary, hand-chopped barbecue here is a religious experience, enough to make up for soggy fries and cinder block ambience (or maybe that's part of the charm).

Crook's Corner (☎ 919-929-7643; www.crookscorner.com; 610 W Franklin St; mains $7-22; ⏱ 5:30-10pm Tue-Sat, brunch 10:30am-2pm Sun) Topped by a folk art sculpture of a pig, Crook's is a longtime institution for Southern food that ranges from the downhome (pit BBQ sandwiches) to the haute (T-bone with asparagus), and is always good for an elegant cocktail in the bamboo-shaded patio.

DRINKING & ENTERTAINMENT

For entertainment listings, pick up the free weekly *Independent*. A couple of places are must-visits.

Local 506 (☎ 919-942-5506; www.local506.com; 506 W Franklin St) A popular venue for alternative bands trying to make it big. Memberships ($3) must be purchased to enter, with an extra $3 charge for those over 18 but under 21.

Cat's Cradle (☎ 919-968-4345; www.catscradle.com; 300 E Main St; ✗) In Carrboro, this place has been hosting the cream of the rock, reggae, alternative and jazz worlds for 30 years. The 600-capacity venue is smoke-free and most shows are all ages.

CHARLOTTE

The largest city in North Carolina and the biggest US banking center after New York, Charlotte has the sprawling, sometimes faceless look of many New South suburban megalopolises. But although Queen City, as it's known, is primarily a business town, it's got a few good museums, stately old neighborhoods and lots of fine food.

Busy Tryon St cuts through skyscraper-filled downtown Charlotte, known as 'Uptown,' home to banks, hotels, museums and restaurants. The tiny, funky NoDa neighborhood (short for 'North Davidson;' www.noda.org), a collection of renovated textile mills 2 miles north of Uptown at N Davidson St and 36th, is the city's bohemian refuge.

The **visitor center** (☎ 704-331-2700, 800-231-4636; www.visitcharlotte.org; 330 S Tryon St; ⏱ 8:30am-5pm Mon-Fri, 9am-3pm Sat), off W 2nd St, publishes maps and a visitors guide. The **public library** (☎ 704-336-2725; 301 N College St; ⏱ 9am-9pm Mon-Thu to 6pm Fri & Sat, from 1pm Sun) has terminals for free internet access.

Sights & Activities

The **Levine Museum of the New South** (☎ 704-333-1887; www.museumofthenewsouth.org; 200 E 7th St; adult/child $6/5; 🕑 10am-5pm Tue-Sat, from noon Sun) gives an excellent look at modern Southern history covering everything from sharecropping to NASCAR racing.

Mint Museum of Art (☎ 704-337-2000; www.mintmuseum.org; 2730 Randolph Rd; adult/child $6/3; 🕑 10am-10pm Tue, 10am-5pm Wed-Sat, to 5pm Sun) is housed in the 19th-century US Mint building in the peaceful Edgewood neighborhood. The collection includes African art, historic maps, American paintings and an impressive number of Spanish Colonial bleeding saint icons. Your ticket also gets you into the **Mint Museum of Craft & Design** (200 N Tryon St), which chronicles the history of studio crafts including glass, wood and metalwork and jewelry.

Discovery Place (☎ 704-372-6261; www.discoveryplace.org; 301 N Tryon St; adult/child $10/8; 🕑 9am-5pm Mon-Sat, from 12:30pm Sun) is a hands-on science museum with an Omnimax cinema (adult/child $7.50/6). Wander through a rainforest, peer inside a huge eyeball or sample liquid-nitrogen ice cream in the chemistry lab.

Sleeping

Because so many hotels cater to the business traveler, rates at most hotels are less expensive on weekends.

Blake Hotel (☎ 704-372-4100; www.theblakehotel.net; 555 South McDowell St; r from $109; P ✂ 💻 wi-fi) Black leather, chrome and tiger-striped decor give this 308-room hotel a neo-'70s feel that extends to the restaurant and cocktail lounge. Newly renovated rooms feature flatscreen TVs and fine Belgian linens sure to please the swinging businessperson in us all.

Dunhill Hotel (☎ 704-332-4141; www.dunhillhotel.com; 237 N Tryon St; r weekend/midweek from $159/269; P ✂ 💻) Now dwarfed by skyscrapers, this 10-story hotel towered over Uptown when it was opened in 1929. The 60 rooms combine old-fashioned style, such as striped wallpaper and four-poster beds, with modern amenities such as wi-fi, minifridges and 24-hour room service. Off the lobby, the Monticello restaurant has a very Old Europe charm.

Eating

As befits a city swarming with young bankers, Charlotte has a great selection of fine restaurants.

Bar-B-Q King (☎ 704-399-8344; 2900 Wilkinson Blvd; mains $4-9; 🕑 10:30am-10:30pm Tue-Thu, 10:30am-11:30pm Fri & Sat) Follow the blinking neon arrow to this midcentury marvel, where carhops deliver BBQ platters and perfectly-fried trout sandwiches directly to the driver's side window. 'The Bar' is one of several retro joints surviving on Wilkinson Blvd, the first four-lane highway in North Carolina.

Boudreaux's Louisiana Kitchen (☎ 704-331-9898; 501 E 36th St; mains $9-15; 🕑 lunch & dinner) *'Laissez les bon temps rouler'* (Let the good times roll) is the motto at this purple-, red- and green-walled converted NoDa warehouse, featuring New Orleans standards such as gumbo, crawfish étoufée and blackened catfish.

Mimosa Grill (☎ 704-343-0700; 327 S Tryon St; mains $22-28; 🕑 11am-10pm Mon-Thu, 11am-11pm Fri, 5-11pm Sat, 5-10pm Sun) What says 'New South' like filet mignon topped with pimento cheese? This stylish-yet-relaxed Uptown eatery is equally classy for impressing a date or making a business deal.

Drinking & Entertainment

Check out the weekly *Creative Loafing* for entertainment listings.

Neighborhood Theatre (☎ 704-358-9298; www.neighborhoodtheatre.com; 511 E 36th St) This renovated movie theater in the NoDa district is an excellent live-music venue.

Lowe's Motor Speedway (☎ 704-455-3200; www.lowesmotorspeedway.com; tours $5; 🕑 tours 9:30am-3:30pm Mon-Sat, from 1:30pm Sun) Begun on dirt tracks in the Southeast, NASCAR is now the second most watched sport on American TV. Races are held at Lowe's, 12 miles northeast of town.

Getting There & Around

Charlotte-Douglas International Airport (CLT; ☎ 704-359-4027; www.charmeck.org; 5501 Josh Birmingham Parkway) is a US Airways hub that receives direct flights from Europe and the UK.

Both the **Greyhound station** (☎ 704-375-3332; 601 W Trade St) and **Amtrak** (☎ 704-376-4416; 1914 N Tryon St) are handy to Uptown.

Charlotte Area Transit (☎ 704-336-3366; 310 E Trade St) provides local bus services throughout the metro area.

NORTH CAROLINA MOUNTAINS

Seekers of all sorts have been drawn to these ancient mountains for hundreds of years: the Cherokee came to hunt, Scots-Irish immigrants came in the 1700s looking for a better life, fugitives hid from the law in the deep forests, the ill came to take in the fresh air, and naturists came to hike the craggy trails.

The Appalachians in the western part of the state include the Great Smoky, Blue Ridge, Pisgah and Black Mountain subranges. Carpeted in blue-green hemlock, pine and oak trees, these cool hills are home to cougars, deer, black bear, wild turkeys and great horned owls. Hiking, camping, climbing and rafting adventures abound, and there's another jaw-dropping photo opportunity around every bend.

Blue Ridge Parkway

Commissioned by President Franklin D Roosevelt as a Depression-era public-works project, the scenic Blue Ridge Parkway traverses the southern Appalachians from Virginia's Shenandoah National Park at Mile 0 to the Great Smoky Mountains National Park at Mile 469. North Carolina's piece of the parkway twists and turns for 262 miles of glorious alpine vistas. The National Park Service campgrounds and **visitor centers** (☎ 877-444-677; www.blueridgeparkway.org; tent sites $14) are open May to October, except for the Linville Falls campsite, which is open year-round. There is no entrance fee for the parkway; visitors can pick up free information at the visitor centers. Be aware that restrooms and gas stations are few and far between.

Highlights and campgrounds along the parkway include the following:

Cumberland Knob Mile 217.5 – NPS visitor center, easy walk to the knob.

Doughton Park Mile 241.1 – Gas, food, trails and camping.

Blowing Rock Mile 291.8 – Small tourist town, named for a craggy, commercialized cliff that offers great views, occasional updrafts and an Indian love story.

Moses H Cone Memorial Park Mile 294.1 – A lovely old estate with pleasant walks and a craft shop.

Julian Price Memorial Park Mile 296.9 – Camping.

Grandfather Mountain Mile 305.1 – A picturesque, privately run park with hiking trails.

Linville Falls Mile 316.4 – Lovely hiking trails to the falls, campsites.

Linville Caverns Mile 317- A limestone cave with neat formations and underground streams; tours $6.

Little Switzerland Mile 334 – Old-style mountain resort.

Crabtree Meadows Mile 339.5 – Camping.

Mt Mitchell State Park Mile 355.5 – Highest mountain east of the Mississippi (6684ft), hiking trails and tent camping.

Folk Art Center Mile 382 – Traditional and contemporary local crafts.

Mount Pisgah Mile 408.8 – Hiking and camping.

High Country

The northwestern corner of the state is know as 'High Country.' Its main towns are Boone Blowing Rock and Banner Elk, all short drive from the Blue Ridge Parkway. **Boone** is a lively little college town, home to Appalachian Stat University (ASU). **Blowing Rock** and **Banner El** are quaint tourist centers.

The High Country **visitor center** (☎ 828-264 1299, 800-438-7500; www.highcountryhost.com; 1700 Blowin Rock Rd, Boone; ☽ 9am-5pm Mon-Sun) has informa tion about canoeing outfitters, river raftin and parks.

At **Appalachian Heritage Museum** (☎ 828-264 2792; 129 Mystery Hill Lane, Blowing Rock; adult/child $8/6 you can get a glimpse of 19th century middle class mountain life at this well-preserve home, the highbrow side of a tourist comple that includes Mystery Hill, where a 'gravita tional anomaly' supposedly causes balls to roll uphill.

Blowing Rock Stage Company (☎ 828-295-9168 www.blowingrockstage.com; 452 Sunset Dr, Blowing Rock) ha live performances throughout the summer.

Hwy 321 from Blowing Rock to Boone i studded with tourist traps. The cutesy **Tweetsi Railroad** (☎ 828-264-9061; www.tweetsie.com; adult/chil $26/18; ☽ hours vary by season), is a much-loved Wild West–themed amusement park.

SLEEPING & EATING

Smoketree Lodge (☎ 828-963-6505, 800-422-1880, www .smoketree-lodge.com; Hwy 105N; r from $75; P ✗ ☐ wi-fi) On a secluded bend in the road between Boone and Banner Elk, this good-value getaway has a rustic, hunting-lodge vibe, cozy rooms with kitchenettes and a lovely heated pool.

Broyhill Inn & Conference Center (☎ 828-262-2204, 800-951-6048; www.broyhillinn.com; 775 Bodenheimer Dr; ▪ from $139; P ✗ ☐ wi-fi) Atop a hill, this large ASU-run hotel has amazing views of Boone from the picture windows of the sunny restaurant and lounge. Standard rooms are clean and newly renovated, with microwaves and fridges.

Black Cat (☎ 828-263-9511; 127 S Depot St, Boone; mains $5-7; ☽ 11:30am-9pm, to 10pm Fri & Sat) Down an alley off King St, this eclectically

THE SOUTH

decorated cantina is popular with students and everyone else for cheap, creative burritos and beer.

Asheville

This Jazz Age gem of a city appears like a mirage out of the mists of the Blue Ridge Mountains. Long a vacation destination for moneyed East Coasters, the city now has a large student population and a highly visible contingent of hardcore hippies.

Asheville remained unchanged from the Great Depression through the 1980s because of economic stagnation, thus the art-deco buildings of downtown remain much the same as they were in 1910. But the area is now hopping with boutiques, restaurants, vintage stores and record shops, giving it a decidedly modern vibe.

Perched at the confluence of the Swannanoa and French Broad Rivers and tucked in the middle of a loop formed by I-40/I-240, the town is relatively compact and easy to negotiate on foot. West Asheville is an up-and-coming area, still gritty but very cool.

The brand-new **visitor center** (☎ 828-258-6129; www.exploreasheville.com; 36 Montford Ave; ☼ 9am-5pm) is at I-240 exit 4C.

Malaprop's Bookstore & Cafe (☎ 828-254-6734; www.malaprops.com; 55 Haywood St; ☼ 9am-9pm Mon-Thu, to 10pm Fri & Sat, to 7pm Sun) is a downtown tradition for sipping cappuccino and perusing the used-book shelf. There's free wireless internet.

The **public library** (☎ 828-251-4991; 67 Haywood Ave; ☼ 10am-8pm Mon-Thu, to 6pm Fri, 2- 5pm Sat) offers free internet access.

SIGHTS

With 43 bathrooms, 65 fireplaces and a private bowling alley, the Gilded Age **Biltmore Estate** (☎ 828-255-1333, 800-624-1575; www.biltmore.com; adult/child under 16/child under 9 $44/22/free; ☼ 9am-5:30pm, to 4:30 winter), is America's largest private home and Asheville's biggest tourist attraction. The French-style chateau was built in 1895 for George Washington Vanderbilt II, heir to the Vanderbilt shipping and railroad fortune, who modeled it after the grand homes he'd seen on his various European jaunts. Viewing the estate and its 250 acres of manicured grounds and gardens takes several hours. The estate's winery offers tastings and sales. There are several cafés offering midpriced meals, a gift shop the size of a small supermarket, and an inn so luxurious it's practically fattening.

The yellow-gabled **Thomas Wolfe Memorial** (☎ 828-253-8304; www.wolfememorial.com; 52 N Market St; admission $1; ☼ 9am-5pm Tue-Sat, 10am-4pm winter, 1-5pm Sun) was Wolfe's mother's boardinghouse and the model for 'Dixieland' in Wolfe's 1929 novel *Look Homeward Angel*, banned in Asheville for years for its unflattering portrayal of real local citizens. The 29-room house holds artifacts from the writer's life and the adjacent visitor center shows a video on his life.

At **Chimney Rock Park** (☎ 828-625-9611; www.chimneyrockpark.com; adult/child $14/6; ☼ 8:30am-4:30pm), a 20-mile drive southeast of Asheville, the American flag flaps in the breeze atop this popular park's namesake 315ft granite monolith. An elevator takes visitors up to the chimney, but the real draw is the exciting hike around the cliffs to a 404ft waterfall.

SLEEPING

Asheville Bed & Breakfast Association (☎ 877-262-6867; www.ashevillebba.com) Handles bookings for the numerous B&Bs in the Asheville area, from gingerbread-trimmed cottages to mountain lodges.

Bon Paul & Sharky's Hostel (☎ 828-350-9929; www.bonpaulandsharkys.com; 816 Haywood Rd; campsite per person $10, dm $21; P ⊠ ⊠ ⊠ wi-fi) In a cottage in a hip West Asheville residential neighborhood, this hostel has a laid-back college-dorm vibe and sweet amenities such as a free Sno Cone machine, outdoor dog kennels and communal bikes. Guests are welcome to pitch a tent in the backyard.

ArtHaus Hostel (☎ 828-225-3278; www.aahostel.com; 16 Ravenscroft Dr; r $50; P ⊠ ⊠ ⊠ wi-fi) Right downtown, this inconspicuous green bungalow is like a backpacker's B&B, with sparely decorated private rooms, communal bathrooms and free waffles.

our pick **Grove Park Inn Resort & Spa** (☎ 828-252-2711, 800-438-5800; www.groveparkinn.com; 290 Macon Ave; r $155; P ⊠ ⊠ ⊠ wi fi) Built in 1913, this titanic stone lodge clings to the side of the mountain like a strange mushroom. Inside is a minivillage of 510 rooms, four restaurants, numerous shops and an underground grotto of a spa, complete with stone pools and an indoor waterfall. Burnished wood furniture and tapestry-covered beds fit with the building's craftsman-style grandeur.

THE SOUTH

EATING

Early Girl Eatery (☎ 828-259-9292; 8 Wall St; mains $11-15; ☽ 7:30am-3pm & 5pm-9pm Mon-Fri, brunch 9am-3pm Sat & Sun) Try a tofu scramble or a plate of free-range roast chicken in this neighborhood café's sunny, plant-filled dining room overlooking a small city park. People will stand in the rain for hours waiting for brunch.

Salsa's (☎ 828-252-9805; 6 Patton Ave; mains $13-17; ☽ 11:30am-2:30pm & 5:30-9pm) Uh oh, Mexico and Jamaica just crashed into a farmer's market cart and landed on your plate! This tiny, brightly painted joint serves amazing, mutant Latin fusion cuisine – think lamb empanadas with goat cheese and banana salsa or crab-jalapeno-saffron-fennel egg rolls. Beware huge crowds, unreasonably spicy appetizers and unannounced substitutions, and *always* order off the specials menu.

Shop for flowers, food supplies and fresh produce at the **Grove Arcade** (☎ 828-252-7799; www .grovearcade.com; 1 Page Ave), a massive, 1929 Gothic-style building containing specialty groceries, boutiques and restaurants.

DRINKING & ENTERTAINMENT

Downtown Asheville has all types of bars and cafés, from frat boy beer halls to hookah-n-sprout hippie holes in the wall. West Asheville has a more laid-back townie vibe.

Westville Pub (☎ 828-225-9782; 777 Haywood Rd; 4pm-late) A good place to bond with local 20- and 30-somethings over a bottle of organic ale.

For live music, try the warehouse-sized **Orange Peel** (☎ 828-25-5851; www.theorangepeel.net; 101 Biltmore Ave; tickets $10-25) for big-name indie, punk and reggae acts, or the **Grey Eagle** (☎ 828-232-5800; www.thegreyeagle.com; 185 Clingman Ave; tickets $8-15) for bluegrass and jazz.

GETTING THERE & AROUND

Greyhound (☎ 828-253-8451; 2 Tunnel Rd) has several buses daily to Knoxville, TN ($29, two hours), Raleigh ($60, six to nine hours), and Atlanta, GA ($48.50, from six hours). **Asheville Transit** (☎ 828-253-5691; www.ashevilletransit .com; 60 W Haywood St; tickets 75¢) has 24 local bus routes running from 6am to 11:30pm Monday to Saturday.

Great Smoky Mountains National Park

More than 10 million visitors a year come through this giant park, known for its beauty and biodiversity. The Great Smoky Mountains National Park straddles the border with Tennessee, which roughly follows the Appalachian Trail north to Virginia and the Shenandoah National Park.

Newfound Gap Road/Highway 441 is the only thoroughfare that crosses Great Smoky Mountains National Park, winding through the mountains from Gatlinburg, TN, near Sugarlands Visitor Center (p479) in the northwest, crossing the North Carolina border at Newfound Gap and descending to the gateway town of Cherokee and the **Oconaluftee Visitor Center** (☎ 423-436-1200; Hwy 441), in the southeast. The busy visitor center includes the Smokies Discovery Center, where visitors learn about the park's ecosystems and biodiversity through interactive exhibits. The Oconaluftee River Trail, one of only two in the park that allows leashed pets, leaves from the visitor center and follows the river for 1.5 miles to the boundary of the Cherokee reservation.

Nearby attractions include the 1886 **Mingus Mill** (☽ 9am-5pm Mar 15-Dec 1; self-guided tours free), 2 miles west of Cherokee, a turbine-powered mill that still grinds wheat and corn much as it always has. A pleasant path enters the woods to follow the 100yd-long board-walled canal, which delivers water to the mill from Mingus Creek. The onsite **Mountain Farm Museum** is a restored 19th-century farmstead, complete with barn, blacksmith shop and smokehouse (with real pig heads!), assembled from original buildings from different parts of the park to give visitors an idea of what life was like for early British settlers to this isolated wilderness.

Cherokee

Many of the Cherokee people, who have lived in the North Carolina mountains for more than 10,000 years, were forcibly removed from their homes by the US government in the 1830s and marched to Oklahoma in what became known as the Trail of Tears. Many died along the way, but some escaped removal by hiding in the hills, and some who did leave returned home later, on foot. Their descendants, about 12,000 members of the Eastern Band of the Cherokee, now occupy a 56,000-acre reservation, called the Qualla Boundary, at the edge of the national park. The small town has ersatz Indian souvenir shops, fast-food joints and **Harrah's Cherokee Casino** (☎ 828-497-7777; www.harrahs.com).

The high-quality **Museum of the Cherokee Indian** (☎ 828-497-3481; www.cherokeemuseum.org; Hwy 441 & Drama Rd; adult/child $9/6; ☺ 9am-5pm) has an informative exhibit on the Trail of Tears and eerily realistic dioramas.

In the hills behind the museum, the **Oconaluftee Indian Village** (☎ 866-554-4557; adult/child $13/6; ☺ 9am-5:30pm) is a replica of an 18th-century Cherokee village where Cherokees demonstrate traditional crafts.

Just around the bend, **Unto These Hills** (☎ 866-554-4557; adult/child $18/8 ☺ 8:30pm Mon-Sat summer), a musical dramatizing the Trail of Tears, has been performed at the outdoor Mountainside Theatre since 1950.

Bryson City

On the banks of the Nantahala River, a white-water mecca, quaint Bryson City is a great jumping-off point for all sorts of outdoor activities.

The excellent **Nantahala Outdoor Center** (☎ 828-488-2176, 828-586-8811; www.noc.com; guided rafting trips $41-117; 13077 Hwy 19/74), just west of Bryson City, rents equipment and does guided trips for hiking, mountain biking, canoeing and white-water rafting. In particular, it offers a large range of rafting tours on nearby rivers, such as the Nantahala, French Broad, Pigeon and Ocoee, some of which are gentle enough for children.

The **Great Smoky Mountain Railroad** (☎ 800-872-4681; www.gsmr.com; adult/child Nantahala Gorge trip $31/16) runs scenic train excursions through the dramatic river valley, departing from the Bryson City depot.

SOUTH CAROLINA

Cross the border of South Carolina and plunge back in time. For a traveler heading down the eastern seaboard, venturing into South Carolina marks the beginning of the Deep South, where the air is hotter, the accents are thicker and traditions are clung to with even more fervor.

Starting at the silvery sands of the Atlantic Coast, the state climbs westward from the Coastal Plain and up through the Sand Hills, the Piedmont, the Foothills and on into the Blue Ridge Mountains. Most travelers stick to the coast, with its glorious marshlands, white-columned colonial plantations and palm tree–studded beaches. But instate

has a wealth of sleepy old towns, wild and undeveloped state parks and spooky blackwater swamps just waiting to be explored by canoe.

Along the sea islands you hear the sweet songs of the Gullah, a culture and language created by former slaves who held onto many West African traditions through the ravages of time.

Whether you're looking for a romantic weekend in genteel, gardenia-scented Charleston or a week of riotous fun at bright, tacky Myrtle Beach, South Carolina is a lovely, affordable destination.

History

More than 28 separate tribes of Native Americans have lived in what is now South Carolina, many of them Cherokee who were later forcibly removed during the Trail of Tears.

The English founded the Carolina colony in 1670, with settlers pouring in from the royal outpost of Barbados, giving the port city known as Charles Towne a Caribbean flavor.

West African slaves were brought over to turn the thick coastal swamps into rice paddies and by the mid-1700s the area was deeply divided between the slave-owning aristocrats of the Lowcountry and the poor Scots-Irish and German farmers of the rural Backcountry.

South Carolina was the first state to secede from the Union, and the first battle of the Civil

---

SOUTH CAROLINA FACTS

Nickname Palmetto State
Population 4.3 million
Area 30,109 sq miles
Capital city Columbia (population 117,400)
Sales tax 5%
Birthplace of Jazzman Dizzy Gillespie (1917–93), political activist Jesse Jackson (b 1941), boxer Joe Frazier (b 1944), *Wheel of Fortune* hostess Vanna White (b 1957)
Home of The first US public library (1698), museum (1773), steam railroad (1833)
Famous for Firing the first shot of the Civil War, from Charleston's Fort Sumter
Smelliest festival The annual Chitlin' Strut festival in the town of Salley, a celebration of the odiferous stuffed pig's intestine dish known as chitterlings or chitlins, a dubious Southern delicacy

THE SOUTH

War occurred at Fort Sumter in Charleston Harbor. The end of the war left much of the state in ruins.

South Carolina traded in cotton and textiles for most of the 20th century. It remains a relatively poor agricultural state, though with a thriving coastal tourism business.

Information

The **South Carolina Department of Parks, Recreation & Tourism** (☎ 803-734-1700 www.discoversouth carolina.com; 1205 Pendleton St, Room 505, Columbia, SC 29201) sends out *South Carolina Smiles*, the state's official vacation guide. On top of the 5% goods and services tax, expect to pay up to 10% extra tax on accommodations.

CHARLESTON

Put on your twin set and pearls or your seersucker suit, have a fortifying sip of sherry, and prepare to be thoroughly drenched in Southern charm. Charleston is a city for strolling, for admiring antebellum architecture, for long dinners on the veranda, for stopping to smell the blooming jasmine. Tooth-achingly romantic, everywhere you turn is another blushing bride standing on the steps of yet another charming church.

The cradle of the Civil War, Charleston is also one of the most popular tourist destinations in the southeast. In the high season the scent of gardenia and honeysuckle mixes with the tang of horse from the innumerable carriage tours that clip-clop down the cobblestones day and night.

History

Well before the Revolutionary War, Charles Towne (named for Charles II) was one of the busiest ports on the eastern seaboard, the center of a prosperous rice-growing and trading colony. With influences from the West Indies and Africa, France and other European countries, it became a cosmopolitan city often compared to New Orleans.

The first shots of the Civil War rang out at Fort Sumter, in Charleston's harbor. After the war, as the labor-intensive rice plantations became uneconomical without slave labor, the city's importance declined. Natural disasters wrought more damage, with a major earthquake in 1886, several fires and storms, and devastating Hurricane Hugo in 1989. But much of the town's historic fabric remains, to the delight of four million tourists every year.

Orientation & Information

The Charleston metropolitan area sprawls over a broad stretch of coastal plains and islands, but the historic heart is very compact, about 4 sq miles at the southern tip of a peninsula between the Cooper and Ashley Rivers. I-26 goes to North Charleston and the airport. Hwy 17, the main coastal road, cuts across the Charleston peninsula as the Crosstown Expressway. Soaring bridges connect west to James Island and West Ashley, and east to Mount Pleasant.

The most important north–south streets of the downtown peninsula are King, Meeting and E Bay. Market and Broad Sts cut east–west, with lots of shops and restaurants.

BOOKSTORES

Charleston Preservation Society (☎ 843-722-4630; www.preservationsociety.org; 147 King St; ☺ 10am-5pm Mon-Sat) Has a wealth of local history and architecture books.

Waldenbooks (☎ 843-853-1736; www.waldenbooks .com; 120 Market St; ☺ 10am-6pm Mon-Sat, noon-5pm Sun) Chain with large selection of books and magazines, including regional titles.

EMERGENCY

Main police station (☎ 843-577-7434; 180 Lockwood Blvd)

INTERNET ACCESS

The City of Charleston maintains free public internet (wi-fi) access throughout downtown.
Public library (☎ 843-805-6801; www.ccpl.org; 68 Calhoun St; ☺ 9am-9pm Mon-Thu, to 6pm Fri & Sat, 2-5pm Sun) Free internet access.

MEDIA

Charleston City Paper (www.charlestoncitypaper.com) An alternative weekly that comes out on Wednesday, with good entertainment and restaurant listings.
Post & Courier (www.charleston.net) Charleston's daily newspaper.

MEDICAL SERVICES

Medical University of South Carolina (MUSC; ☎ 843-792-2300; 171 Ashley Ave)

MONEY

Bank of America (☎ 843-723-6822; 200 Meeting St) Banking services and ATM.

POST

Post office Bay St (☎ 843-722-3624; 557 E Bay St; ☺ 8:30am-5:30pm, Mon-Fri, 9am-noon Sat); Main branch (☎ 843-577-0688; 83 Broad St; ☺ 9am-5pm Mon-Fri)

CHARLESTON

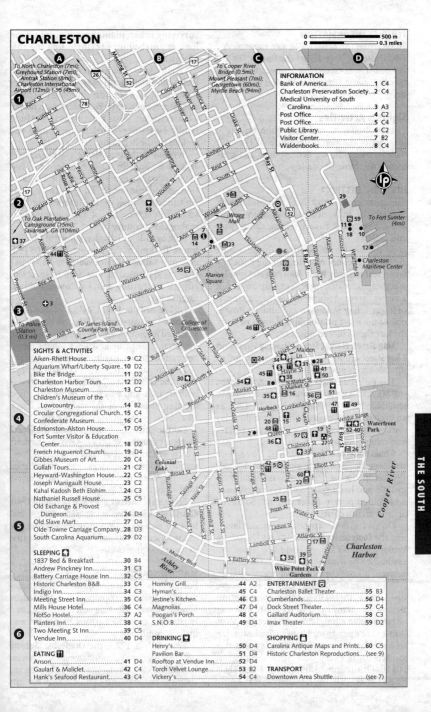

0 ____ 500 m
0 ____ 0.3 miles

INFORMATION
Bank of America..............................1 C4
Charleston Preservation Society..2 C4
Medical University of South
  Carolina....................................3 A3
Post Office....................................4 C2
Post Office....................................5 C4
Public Library................................6 C2
Visitor Center...............................7 B2
Waldenbooks...............................8 C4

SIGHTS & ACTIVITIES
Aiken-Rhett House........................9 C2
Aquarium Wharf/Liberty Square..10 D2
Bike the Bridge............................11 D2
Charleston Harbor Tours..............12 D2
Charleston Museum......................13 C2
Children's Museum of the
  Lowcountry..............................14 B2
Circular Congregational Church...15 C4
Confederate Museum...................16 C4
Edmonston-Alston House.............17 D5
Fort Sumter Visitor & Education
  Center.....................................18 D2
French Huguenot Church.............19 D4
Gibbes Museum of Art.................20 C4
Gullah Tours................................21 C2
Heyward-Washington House........22 C5
Joseph Manigault House..............23 C2
Kahal Kadosh Beth Elohim...........24 C3
Nathaniel Russell House...............25 C5
Old Exchange & Provost
  Dungeon..................................26 D4
Old Slave Mart............................27 D4
Olde Towne Carriage Company....28 D3
South Carolina Aquarium.............29 D2

SLEEPING
1837 Bed & Breakfast.................30 B4
Andrew Pinckney Inn...................31 C3
Battery Carriage House Inn...........32 C5
Historic Charleston B&B...............33 C4
Indigo Inn...................................34 C3
Meeting Street Inn.......................35 C4
Mills House Hotel........................36 C4
NotSo Hostel...............................37 A2
Planters Inn................................38 C4
Two Meeting St Inn.....................39 C5
Vendue Inn.................................40 D4

EATING
Anson..41 D4
Gaulart & Maliclet.......................42 C4
Hank's Seafood Restaurant..........43 C4

Hominy Grill...............................44 A2
Hyman's.....................................45 C4
Jestine's Kitchen.........................46 C3
Magnolias...................................47 D4
Poogan's Porch...........................48 C4
S.N.O.B......................................49 D4

DRINKING
Henry's......................................50 D4
Pavilion Bar................................51 D4
Rooftop at Vendue Inn................52 D4
Torch Velvet Lounge....................53 B2
Vickery's....................................54 C4

ENTERTAINMENT
Charleston Ballet Theater............55 B3
Cumberlands..............................56 D4
Dock Street Theater....................57 D4
Gaillard Auditorium.....................58 C3
Imax Theater..............................59 D2

SHOPPING
Carolina Antique Maps and Prints.60 C5
Historic Charleston Reproductions....(see 9)

TRANSPORT
Downtown Area Shuttle................(see 7)

THE SOUTH

TOURIST INFORMATION

Visitor center (☎ 843-853-8000; www.charlestoncvb
.com; 375 Meeting St; ☽ 8:30am-5pm Mon-Sat) This
well-stocked center can help with accommodations and
tours. Its 23-minute *Charleston Forever* video ($2) is worth
seeing.

Sights & Activities

The city itself is the main attraction, especially
the part of the peninsula south of Hwy 17,
with its magnolia-shaded avenues and genteelly crumbling back alleys.

HISTORIC DISTRICT

The quarter south of Beaufain and Hasell
Sts has the bulk of the antebellum mansions, sweetgrass basket-sellers, shops, bars
and cafés.

At the southernmost tip on the peninsula
are the antebellum mansions of the Battery –
take a seat in shady **White Point Park** and ponder
whether 'filthy rich merchant seaman' is still
a viable career. Around the corner, a stretch
of lower E Bay St known as Rainbow Row is
one of the most photographed areas of town
for its candy-colored houses.

King Street, **Market Street**, **Meeting Street** and
E Bay Street are the main tourist drags, full of
upscale shops and restaurants.

The Palladian **Old Exchange & Provost Dungeon**
(☎ 843-727-2165; www.oldexchange.com; 122 E Bay St;
adult/child $7/3.50; ☽ 9am-5pm), built in 1771 as
an exchange and customs house for the busy
port, was used as a dungeon prison for pirates
and other outlaws.

Gibbes Museum of Art (☎ 843-722-2706; www.gib
besmuseum.org; 135 Meeting St; admission adult/child $9/5;
☽ 10am-5pm Tue-Sat, 1-5pm Sun) was established
in 1905 and has a good collection of colonial
and contemporary American art, Southern
art and architecture.

On the 2nd floor of the old city market building, the **Confederate Museum** (☎ 843-723-1541; 188
Meeting St; adult/child $5/3; ☽ 11am-3:30pm Tue-Sat) was
established by the Daughters of the Confederacy, and houses copious 'rebel' memorabilia.

A number of majestic historic homes are
open to visitors. Discounted combination
tickets may tempt you to see more, but one
or two will be enough for most people. Most
houses are open from 10am to 5pm Monday
to Saturday, 1pm to 5pm Sunday and run
guided tours every half-hour. Admission
is $10. Of the most interesting, **Aiken-Rhett
House** (☎ 843-723-1159; 48 Elizabeth St) is the only

surviving urban plantation; it gives a good
look at antebellum life, including the role
of slaves.

Overlooking Charleston Harbor, the 1828
Edmonston-Alston House (☎ 843-722-7171; 21 E Battery
St) was built by a Scottish shipping merchant
and later renovated by rice-plantation mogul
Charles Alston. It has remained in the Alston
family ever since – in fact, the family still
resides on the 3rd floor.

Heyward-Washington House (☎ 843-722-0354;
87 Church St), built in 1772, belonged to Thomas Heyward Jr, a signer of the Declaration of Independence. Though the outside
isn't much to look at, the interior contains
some fine examples of Charleston-made
mahogany furniture.

Built by a Rhode Islander, known in Charleston as 'the king of the Yankees,' the 1808 Federal-style **Nathaniel Russell House** (☎ 843-724-8481;
51 Meeting St) is noted especially for its spectacular, self-supporting spiral staircase and lush
English garden.

Nicknamed the 'Holy City' for its abundance
of houses of worship, Charleston has always
practiced religious tolerance. Persecuted French
Protestants, Baptists and Jews sought refuge
here, adding diverse cultural influences.

The Romanesque Revival **Circular Congregational Church** (☎ 843-577-6400; 150 Meeting St) was
built in 1681 and was used as the city's first
meeting place, hence the name of its street.
The oldest graves in the city are here.

Gothic spires and arches mark the **French
Huguenot Church** (☎ 843-722-4385; 136 Church St),
which was founded in 1681 by French Protestant refugees. Services were once timed
with the tides to accommodate those arriving by boat.

First established in 1749 and rebuilt in 1840,
Kahal Kadosh Beth Elohim (☎ 843-723-1090; 90 Hasell
St) is the oldest continuously used synagogue
in the country and home to the nation's first
Reform congregation.

MARION SQUARE

Formerly home to the state weapons arsenal, this 10-acre greenspace is bounded by
King, Calhoun, Meeting and Hutson Sts and
is situated close to various museums and
historic buildings.

Founded in 1773, the **Charleston Museum**
(☎ 843-722-2996; www.charlestonmuseum.org; 360 Meeting
St; adult/child $10/5; ☽ 9am-5pm Mon-Sat, from 1pm Sun)
claims to be the country's oldest, with exhibits

THE SOUTH

from various periods of Charleston's long and storied history, from Washington-era silver to slave tags, as well as a collection of stuffed and mounted prehistoric animals.

Across the street from the museum, **Joseph Manigault House** (☎ 843-723-2926; 350 Meeting St) is a neoclassical-style historic home, once the showpiece of a French Huguenot family who made their fortune trading rum, sugar and rice.

Children's Museum of the Lowcountry (☎ 843-853-8962; www.explorecml.org; 25 Ann St; admission $7; ❉ 10am-5pm Tue-Sat, from 1pm Sun) has eight interactive exhibit areas, including a 30ft replica shrimp boat where kids can play captain.

AQUARIUM WHARF

The Aquarium Wharf surrounds pretty Liberty Sq and is a great place to stroll around and watch the tugboats guiding ships into the seventh-largest container port in the US. The wharf is the embarkation point for tours to Fort Sumter. Boat tours of the harbor depart from the harbor tour dock and nearby Charleston Maritime Center. Also here is the IMAX Theater (p396).

The excellent **South Carolina Aquarium** (☎ 843-720-1990; www.scaquarium.org; 100 Aquarium Wharf; adult/child $16/8; ❉ 9am-6pm, from noon Sun) covers 69,000 sq ft, almost all of which are devoted to South Carolina habitats, flora and fauna. The best part of the aquarium is the 330,000-gallon Great Ocean Tank, where sharks, massive fish and a giant loggerhead turtle swim behind a two-story window.

The first shots of the Civil War rang out at **Fort Sumter**, on a pentagon-shaped island in the center of the harbor. A Confederate stronghold, the fort was shelled by Union forces from 1863 to 1865. By the end of the war, it was a pile of rubble. A few original guns and fortifications, and the obviously strategic location, give a feel for the momentous history here. The only way to get here is by boat tour. Tours leave from the National Park Service's **Fort Sumter Visitor & Education Center** (www.nps.gov/fosu; adult/child $14/8; ❉ tours depart 9:30am, 12pm & 2:30pm summer, fewer tours in winter) or from Patriot's Point in Mt Pleasant, across the river.

Bicycling is a good way to see downtown and beyond. **Bike the Bridge** (☎ 843-853-2453; www.bikethebridgerentals.com; 360 Concord St; bike rental per 3 hr/full day $15/25), based down near Aquarium Wharf, rents bikes, jogging stroll-

---

OLD SLAVE MART

Currently closed for renovations (see www .nps.gov/history/nr/travel/charleston/osm .htm for updates of reopening), the Old Slave Mart at 6 Chalmers St is part of South Carolina's painful past. Captured Africans were once stored here in the 'barracoon' (slave jail) before being taken to the mail hall and auctioned off to the highest bidder. Slaves stood on auction blocks to be inspected by wealthy plantation owners before being taken away to work the rows of cotton, indigo and tobacco. After the Civil War the market became a tenement building, before being turned into an African American crafts museum in 1938. The city of Charleston plans to make the building into a museum of slavery.

---

ers and gives out a free bike guide to the historic district.

Tours

Listing all the walking, carriage, bus and boat tours could take up this entire book. There's an array of excellent walking tours on everything from Charleston's ghosts, to Civil War and African American history tours. Ask at the visitor center for the gamut.

Carolina FoodPros Tour (☎ 877-728-2783; www .carolinafoodpros.com/tours; tours $40-60) Offers walking and bus tours of Charleston restaurant kitchens, bakeries and chocolate shops.

Charleston Harbor Tours (☎ 800-344-4483; www .charlestonharbortours.com; 90min tours adult/child $14.50/9.50) Takes visitors on a historical tour of town aboard the *Carolina Belle* ship; departs from the Charleston Maritime Center.

Gullah Tours (☎ 843-763-7551; www.gullahtours.com; 43 John St; 2hr tour adult/child $18/12) A native Gullah speaker directs a bus exploration of the history of African American Charleston.

Olde Towne Carriage Company (☎ 843-722-1315; www.oldetownecarriage.com; 20 Anson St; 45min tours adult/child $20/10) Guides on this popular horse-drawn-carriage tour offer colorful commentary as you clickety-clack around town.

Sleeping

Staying in the historic downtown is the most attractive option, but it's the most expensive, especially at weekends and during special events. Rates in town fluctuate wildly – a $200 room in summer could be just $70 in winter – so call ahead to see if you can get a better deal. The rates below are for high season (spring and early summer). The chain hotels on the highways offer significantly lower rates.

One of the best ways to get to know Charleston is to stay at a small home where the owners serve up authentic Southern breakfasts and dole out great local information. Small places start at around $100 for doubles with breakfast, but many have only one or two rooms, so it helps to use an agency such as **Historic Charleston B&B** (☎ 843-722-6606; www.his toriccharlestonbedandbreakfast.com; 57 Broad St).

BUDGET

NotSo Hostel (☎ 843-722-8383; www.notsohostel.com; 156 Spring St; dm/r $21/60; P ✗ ✗ 📶 wi-fi) North of downtown, three old houses have been carved into dorms and private rooms, the verandas decked with hammocks. Common kitchens and baths are clean and the friendly staff knows all the best local hangouts.

Southwest of Charleston, **Oak Plantation Campground** (☎ 843-766-5936, 866-658-2500; www.oakplan tationcampground.com; 3540 Savannah Hwy; campsites & RV sites $15-20) and **James Island County Park** (☎ 843-795-7275; 871 Riverland Dr; campsites/RV sites $19/35, cottages $138) offer shuttle services downtown. Reservations are highly recommended.

MIDRANGE

1837 Bed & Breakfast (☎ 843-723-7166, 877-723-1837; www.1837bb.com; 126 Wentworth St; r incl breakfast $99-199; P ✗ ✗) Like staying at the home of your eccentric, antiques-loving aunt, 1837 has nine charmingly over-decorated rooms, including three in the old brick carriage house. In the morning, the friendly proprietress serves up hearty egg and meat dishes in the yellow dining room.

Indigo Inn (☎ 843-577-5900; www.indigoinn.com; 1 Maiden Ln; r incl breakfast $99-285; P ✗ wi-fi) Smack in the middle of the often noisy historic district, this good-value hotel encloses an oasis-like private courtyard, where guests can sip free wine and cheese by the fountain. Rooms are spacious, but slightly dark. Don't let the name fool you – the building is definitely green, not indigo. Parking costs $7.

Battery Carriage House Inn (☎ 843-727-3100; www.batterycarriagehouse.com; 20 S Battery; r $100-279; P ✗ wi-fi) Step through the iron gates and into this secluded 11-room treasure, where an interior garden filled with roses and whim-

sically trimmed topiary hedges begs you to sit down for a cup of tea. Luckily, the owners are happy to oblige – breakfast comes to the door of your simple, elegant room on a silver tray.

Vendue Inn (☎ 843-577-7970; www.vendueinn.com; 19 Vendue Range; r incl breakfast $119-369; P ✗ 📶 wi-fi) This boutique hotel, in the part of downtown known as the French Quarter, is decked out in a trendy mix of exposed brick and eccentric antiques. Rooms have a variety of cool amenities, such as deep soaking tubs and gas fireplaces. Even cooler is the rooftop bar (p396).

Andrew Pinckney Inn (☎ 843-937-8800, 800-505-8983; www.andrewpinckneyinn.com; 40 Pinckney St; r $129-189; P ✗ ✗ 📶 wi-fi) A pre-Colonial sugar baron would have been right at home breakfasting in the rooftop garden of this 32-room hotel. Sand-colored walls and botanical prints lend an upscale Caribbean vibe. The location, on a quiet bit of street right near the market, is excellent. Parking costs $12.

Meeting Street Inn (☎ 843-723-1882, 800-842-8022; www.meetingstreetinn.com; 173 Meeting St; r incl breakfast from $159; P ✗ ✗ wi-fi) Dark, antique-furnished rooms with four-post beds contrast with the sunny, pink stucco courtyard of this 56-room hotel, in the thick of the historic district. Parking's $12.

TOP END

Mills House Hotel (☎ 843-577-2400, 800-874-9600; www .millshouse.com; 115 Meeting St; r $219-340; P ✗ ✗ wi-fi) This grand old dame (150 years young, *merci*) has gotten an $11 million face lift,

---

SPOLETO USA

For 17 days in May and June **Spoleto USA** (☎ 843-722-2764; www.spoletousa.org) turns the city into an Italianate wonderland, a massive performing arts festival full of dancing, singing and jubilant brass bands. More than 130 performances take place in theaters, churches, on plantations, in parks and gardens.

Pulitzer Prize–winning composer Gian Carlo Menotti started a similar festival in Spoleto, Italy, and decided to bring it to Charleston, that most European of American cities, in 1977. Audiences so loved Spoleto that they augmented it with **Piccolo Spoleto**, another explosion of the arts that follows on the heels of Spoleto.

and is now one of the most opulent choices in the area. Gilded elevators lead from an enormous marble lobby to 214 lushly upholstered rooms. The wood-paneled cocktail lounge has a clubby, Old South charm. Parking costs $16.

Two Meeting St Inn (☎ 843-723-7322; www.twomeetingstreetinn.com; 2 Meeting St; r $219-435; **P** **⊠** **⊠**) The story goes that George W Williams left his daughter, Martha, $75,000 on a satin pillow to celebrate her marriage to Waring P Carrington. They used the cash to build this stunning Queen Anne mansion on the Battery in 1892, now a B&B with nine frilled and tasseled guest rooms. The stained glass was supposedly crafted and installed by Tiffany himself.

Planters Inn (☎ 843-722-2345, 800-845-7082; www.plantersinn.com; 112 N Market St; r from $300; **P** **⊠** **⊠** **⬚** wi-fi) This ultraluxury hotel has a fleet of concierges and white-jacketed bellboys ready to meet your every need, whether it's a chartered fishing boat or another glass of champagne. All rooms have canopy beds, oriental rugs and high ceiling; some have fireplaces and verandas. Parking costs $16.

Eating

From hearty, lard-heavy Lowcountry cuisine to nouvelle French bistros, there are enough good restaurants in Charleston for a town three times its size. On Saturday, stop by the farmers market, which sets up in Marion Sq from 8am to 1pm, April to October.

BUDGET & MIDRANGE

Jestine's Kitchen (☎ 843-722-7224; 251 Meeting St; mains $6-12; ☽ 11am-9:30pm Tue-Thu, to 10pm Fri & Sat, to 9pm Sun) Charleston housekeeper Jestine Mathews lived to be 112, though probably not by eating the glorious fried chicken, fried green tomatoes and (fried) hush puppies at the down-home café named in her honor. Order 'table wine' (sweet tea) to drink and finish up with the famous Coca-Cola cake.

Gaulart & Maliclet (☎ 843-577-9797; 98 Broad St; mains $6-15; ☽ 8am-5pm Mon, 8am-10pm Tue-Thu, to 11pm weekends) Locals crowd around the shared tables at this tiny bistro, known as 'Fast & French,' to nibble on Gallic cheeses and sausages or nightly specials ($15) that include bread, soup, a main dish and wine.

Hominy Grill (☎ 843-937-0930; 207 Rutledge Ave; mains $7-15; ☽ 7:30am-8pm Mon-Fri, 9am-3pm Sat & Sun) Slightly off the beaten path is this sunny café serving whimsical, vegetarian-friendly Southern cuisine. Breakfast and brunch are particularly popular, with overstuffed omelets and, of course, hominy grits, served on the patio.

Hyman's (☎ 843-723-6000; 215 Meeting St; mains $8-24; ☽ 11am-11pm) Crowds line up for hours outside this venerable seafood restaurant, fanning themselves with take-out menus while awaiting Hyman's famous she-crab soup, po'boy sandwiches and crispy flounder. Lines are more reasonable at lunch, and kids are always welcome.

Poogan's Porch (☎ 843-577-2337; 72 Queen St; mains $12-20; ☽ 9am-3pm & 5-9:30pm) Dine on sherried crab soup and toast points in the dim, floral-patterned environs of this supposedly haunted Victorian mansion, tucked away on a downtown side street.

Magnolias (☎ 843-577-7771; 185 E Bay St; $7-14 lunch, $15-22 dinner; ☽ 11:30am-2pm & 5:30-10pm) think 'Down South Eggroll' stuffed with collards and chicken, served with peach chutney, in a chic minimalist dining room.

TOP END

S.N.O.B. (☎ 843-723-3424; 192 E Bay St; mains $16-34; ☽ lunch Mon-Fri, dinner nightly) The cheeky name (it stands for 'slightly north of Broad,' as in Broad St) reflects the anything-goes spirit of this newcomer, which draws raves for its eclectic menu, filled with treats such as house-smoked salmon or sautéed squab breast over cheese grits. Exposed brick walls and an open kitchen lend a casual ambience.

Hank's Seafood Restaurant (☎ 843-723-3474; 10 Hayne St; mains $17-28; ☽ 5-10:30pm Sun-Thu, to 11:30pm Fri & Sat) Dark wood, tinkly piano music and fine, fine fish mark this Charleston standard, a 1940s-style fish house specializing in rich seafood classics such as Oysters Casino and shrimp linguine.

Anson (☎ 803-577-0551; 12 Anson St; mains $19-36; ☽ dinner) The most upscale Lowcountry around, in a dreamy pink-and-green carriage house straight out of central casting. Pecan-crusted lamb and grouper in champagne sauce go well with the lovely wine list.

Drinking

Balmy Charleston evenings are perfect for lifting a cool cocktail or dancing to live blues. Check out the weekly *Charleston City Paper* (published every Wednesday) and the 'Preview' section of Friday's *Post & Courier*.

THE SOUTH

Henry's (☎ 843-723-4363; 54 N Market St) The bar of choice for single, young (and not so young) professionals, with a large wood bar and sports on TV.

Pavilion Bar (☎ 843-723-0500; 225 E Bay St) The swimming pool at this fun and casual rooftop bar is for hotel guests only, but the luscious views of the Cooper River and downtown Charleston are free.

Rooftop at Vendue Inn (☎ 843-723-0486; 23 Vendue Range) This two-level rooftop bar has the best views of downtown, and the crowds to prove it. Enjoy afternoon nachos or late-night live blues.

Torch Velvet Lounge (☎ 843-723-9333; 545 King St) Slightly north of the tourist district, Torch aims for urban chic, with bed-sized couches and a DJ spinning techno.

Vickery's (☎ 843-577-5300; 15 Beaufain St) Locals flock to Vick's to heft ice-cold beers on the tiki-torch-lit patio or chow down on Cuban sandwiches in the diner-style booths.

Entertainment

Cumberlands (☎ 843-577-9469; 26 Cumberland St) This live-music venue has traditionally served local blues bands, but you can also hear local alt and grunge rock.

Dock Street Theater (☎ 843-965-4032; www.charlestonstage.com; 135 Church St) Reconstructed in 1936 from original 1736 blueprints, Dock Street is America's oldest live-performance theater. The busy venue hosts an array of community and professional music and theater groups.

Charleston Ballet Theater (☎ 843-723-7334; www.charlestonballet.com; 477 King St) The ballet puts on an eclectic mix of traditional and contemporary shows.

Charleston Symphony Orchestra (☎ 843-723-7528; www.charlestonsymphony.com; 77 Calhoun St) Since 1936, the symphony, now led by David Stahl, has performed in the Gaillard Auditorium.

IMAX Theater (☎ 843-725-4629; www.charlestonimax.com; Aquarium Wharf) Call for tickets and times.

Shopping

The historic district is clogged with overpriced souvenir shops and junk markets, but a careful shopper can find some treasures in the antiques stores and oddball boutiques. The further north on King St you go, the hipper the shopping.

Historic Charleston Reproductions (☎ 843-723-8292; 105 Broad St; �y 10am-5pm Tue-Sat) Come here for a selection of jewelry, home furnishings and furniture inspired by the city's historic homes. Earrings based on the cast-iron railings at the Aiken-Rhett House (p392) are $60.

Carolina Antique Maps & Prints (☎ 843-722-4773; 91 Church St; �y 10am-5pm Tue-Sat) Buy a vintage map of Charleston or a magnolia-blossom botanical print at this crowded little shop, tucked away on a residential street.

Getting There & Around

To reach Charleston by car from the north coast or south coast, use Hwy 17. From I-95, take I-26 southeast for about an hour to Charleston.

Charleston International Airport (☎ 843-767-7009) is 12 miles outside of town in North Charleston, with 63 daily flights to 17 destinations.

The **Greyhound station** (☎ 843-744-4247; 3610 Dorchester Rd) has regular buses to Atlanta ($63, eight hours), Savannah ($29, 2½ hours) and Myrtle Beach ($28, 2½ hours).

The **Amtrak train station** (☎ 843-744-8264; 4565 Gaynor Ave) is an inconvenient 8 miles north of downtown.

Downtown Area Shuttle (DASH; ☎ 843-724-7420; adult single/day pass $1/3) has faux streetcars doing four loop routes from the visitor center.

AROUND CHARLESTON
Mt Pleasant

Across the long Cooper River Bridge is the residential and vacation community of Mt Pleasant, originally a summer retreat for early Charlestonians, along with the slim barrier resort islands of **Isle of Palms** and **Sullivan's Island**. Though increasingly glutted with traffic and strip malls, the city's pretty charm still exists, especially in the historic downtown, called the **Old Village**. Some good seafood restaurants sit overlooking the water at **Shem Creek**, where it's fun to dine creekside at sunset and watch the incoming fishing boat crews unload their catch. This is also a good place to rent kayaks to tour the estuary. Stop by the **Mt Pleasant/Isle of Palms Visitors Center** (☎ 843-849-9172; 311 Johnnie Dodds Blvd/Hwy 17; �y 9am-5pm Mon-Fri) for information and maps.

Patriot's Point Naval & Maritime Museum (☎ 843-884-2727; www.patriotspoint.org; 40 Patriots Point Rd; adult/child $15/8; �y 9am-6:30pm) features the USS *Yorktown*, a giant aircraft carrier used extensively in WWII. You can tour the ship's flight deck, bridge and ready rooms and get a glimpse of what life was like for its sailors. There is also a small museum, submarine, naval destroyer,

Coast Guard cutter and a re-created 'fire base' from Vietnam. From Patriots Point, you can also catch the Fort Sumter Boat Tour.

Just 7 miles from Charleston on Hwy 17 N, **Boone Hall Plantation** (☎ 843-884-4371; www .boonehallplantation.com; 1235 Long Point Rd; adult/child $17.50/7.50; ☺ 9am-5pm Mon-Sat, 1-4pm Sun) is famous for its magical Avenue of Oaks, a long row of moss-dripping oak trees planted by Thomas Boone in 1743, and the magnificent house museum. Boone Hall is still a working plantation, though strawberries, tomatoes, peaches and Christmas trees long ago replaced cotton as the primary crop.

Near Boone Hall, **Charles Pinckney National Historic Site** (☎ 843-881-5516; 1254 Long Point Rd; admission free; ☺ 9am-5pm) sits on the remaining 28 acres of Snee Farm, once an expansive plantation of Charles Pinckney, a famous South Carolinian statesman. Exhibits in the 1820s cottage-turned-museum cover archaeological findings on the site, historical descriptions of slave life and information on coastal vegetation. Several walking trails meander through the magnolias. The site is 6 miles north of Charleston off Hwy 17 on Long Point Rd.

About 8 miles south of Charleston, **Folly Beach** is good for a day of sun and sand. **Folly Beach County Park** (☎ 843-588-2426; cars/pedestrians $5/free; ☺ 10am-6pm), on the west side, has public changing areas and beach-chair rentals. The other end of the island is popular with surfers.

Ashley River Plantations

Only a 20-minute veer away from Charleston, three spectacular plantations are worthy of a detour. You'll be hard-pressed for time to visit all three in one outing, but you could squeeze in two (allow at least a couple of hours for each). If you've only got time to visit one, choose Magnolia Plantation (a better bet with kids) or Middleton Place (a delight for the sheer mastery of its gardens). Ashley River Rd is also known as SC 61, which can be reached from downtown Charleston via Hwy 17.

The 1738 Palladian brick mansion of **Drayton Hall** (☎ 843-769-2600; www.draytonhall.org; 3380 Ashley River Rd; adult/child $14/8; ☺ 9:30am-4pm, to 3pm winter) was the only structure on the Ashley River to survive the Revolutionary and Civil Wars and the great earthquake of 1886. Admission includes a guided tour of the perfectly preserved house and the chance to stroll the gardens and cemetery.

The lovely **Magnolia Plantation** (☎ 843-571-1266; www.magnoliaplantation.com; 3550 Ashley River Rd; adult/child $15/9, plus house entry $7; ☺ 8am-5:30pm) sits on 500 acres that have been owned by the Drayton family since 1676. Plantation crops have included everything from indigo and rice to cotton, sugarcane, corn and potatoes, tended by hundreds of slaves. Today, the land explodes with azaleas and camellias. A great way to see the plantation is by taking the nature train (adult/child $7/5), which toots around the property.

Designed in 1741, the landscaped gardens of **Middleton Place** (☎ 843-556-6020; www.mid dletonplace.org; 4300 Ashley River Rd; adult/child $45/30; ☺ 9am-5pm) are the oldest in the US. For 125 years, the property belonged to a succession of the illustrious Middletons, including several prominent politicians. The grounds, now maintained by a nonprofit, are truly formidable, a mix of classic formal French gardens and romantic wooded settings. A flooded ricefield demonstrates rice cultivation, the giant Middleton Oak seems too incredible to be real, and marble statues studded around the grounds seem to grow out of the earth. There are various ways to tour Middleton, including by horse-drawn carriage; the price above is for the whole package, though you can pick and choose attractions once you arrive.

NORTH COAST

The coastline from the North Carolina border to the city of Georgetown is known as the Grand Strand, some 60 miles of fast-food joints, beach resorts and three-story souvenir shops. What was once a laid-back summer destination for working-class people from across the southeast has become some of the most overdeveloped real estate in the country.

Though environmentalists worry that development is taking its toll on the shores and marshes, for now, fun and easy livin' is the name of the game. Whether you're ensconced in a behemoth resort or sleeping in a tent at a state park, all you need to enjoy your stay is a pair of flip-flops, a margarita and some quarters for the pinball machine.

Myrtle Beach

Love it or hate it, Myrtle Beach means summer vacation, American-style.

Bikers take advantage of the lack of helmet laws to let their graying ponytails fly

THE SOUTH

in the wind, bikini-clad teenagers play Pac-Man and eat hot dogs in smoky arcades, and whole families roast like chickens on the white sand.

North Myrtle Beach, actually a separate town, is slightly lower-key, with a thriving culture based on the 'shag' (no, not that kind of shag) – a jitterbug-like dance invented here in the 1940s.

It ain't for nature lovers, but with enormous outlet malls and innumerable mini-golf courses, water parks, daiquiri bars and T-shirt shops, it's a rowdy good time.

There's internet access at **Chapin Memorial Library** (☎ 843-918-1275; 400 14th Ave N; ✆ 9am-6pm Mon, Wed & Fri, to 8pm Tue & Thu, to 5pm Sat) and loads of maps and brochures at the **visitor center** (☎ 843-626-7444, 800-496-8250; www.myrtle-beachinfo.com; 1200 N Oak St; ✆ 8:30am-5pm Mon-Fri, 10am-2pm Sat).

SIGHTS & ACTIVITIES

Several amusement park/shopping mall hybrids teem with people at all hours. **Broadway at the Beach** (☎ 843-444-3200; www.broadwayatthebeach.com; 1325 Celebrity Circle), with shops, restaurants, nightclubs, rides, hotels and an IMAX theater, is one of the largest.

Just south of 3rd Ave S and Ocean Blvd, **Family Kingdom** (☎ 843-626-3447; www.family-kingdom.com; all-day ride pass $29.50) is a sprawling amusement park and water park combo. Hours vary, depending on the time of year; it's closed in winter. You can also go parasailing or rent jet skis or speed boats at **Myrtle Beach Watersports** (☎ 843-497-8848; www.myrtlebeachwatersports.com; 17th Ave S, North Myrtle Beach; jet ski rental-hr/half-day $60/95).

WHAT THE...?

South of the Border, off I-95 on the North Carolina–South Carolina state line is a massively kitschy roadside attraction, promoted by hundreds of billboards along I-95. It was originally conceived in 1950 as a fireworks stand – pyrotechnics are illegal across the state line in North Carolina. Pedro, a wildly stereotypical Mexican cartoon, hawks fireworks, beer and thousands of tacky souvenirs at this combo rest stop, strip mall, motel and amusement park, capped by a giant sombrero tower visible from the highway.

Sixteen miles south of town on Hwy 17 S, magical **Brookgreen Gardens** (☎ 843-235-6000; www.brookgreen.org; adult/child $12/5; ✆ 9:30am-5pm) are home to the largest collection of American sculpture in the country, set amid 9000 acres of rice plantation turned subtropical garden paradise.

SLEEPING

Hundreds of hotels have prices that vary by the season and day; a room might cost $30 in January and more than $150 in July. The following lists high-season (mid-June to mid-August) rates.

Myrtle Beach State Park (☎ 843-238-5325; campsites $23, cabins per week $600) Most campgrounds are veritable parking lots catering to families with RVs, but the best camping is found in the shady sites of this state park, 3 miles south of central Myrtle Beach.

Beach Side Motel (☎ 843-626-9558; www.beachsidemyrtlebeach.com; 1203 S Ocean Blvd; r $92-127; P ✗ ⊠) Smack in the middle of the madness, this boxy white motel is one of the best ocean-side values, with carpeted rooms and suites, some with retro wood-paneled kitchenettes.

Landmark Resort (☎ 843-448-9441; www.landmarkresort.com; 1501 S Ocean Blvd; r $99-207; P ✗ ⊠) Didn't get to go to summer camp as a kid? This family-oriented behemoth will make up for it, with a full menu of activities from beach kickball to tie-dying, the 'South's largest indoor pool complex,' and bright, newly renovated rooms.

EATING

The thousands of restaurants are mostly high volume and middlebrow – think buffets longer than bowling alleys and 24-hour doughnut shops. Seafood, ironically, is hard to come by; locals go to the nearby fishing village of Murrells Inlet.

Duffy Street Seafood Shack (☎ 843-281-9840; 202 Main St, North Myrtle Beach; mains $7-15; ✆ from 4pm) This place has a dive-y, peanut shells-on-the-floor ambience and a raw bar 'happy hour' with 30¢ shrimp.

Lee's Inlet Kitchen (☎ 843-651-2881; 4460 Business Hwy 17; mains $15-23; ✆ from 4:30pm) A Murrells Inlet mainstay since 1948, Lee's serves massive platters of scallops, deviled crab and hush puppies in a huge cottage-style building.

Library (☎ 843-448-4527; 1212 N Kings Hwy; mains $17-37; ✆ from 5pm Mon-Sat) It could be 1957 in the wood-paneled environs of the Library, the fanciest restaurant on the Strand, which serves the most deliciously retro of French dishes – think duck *à l'orange* and theatrically flambéed desserts.

ENTERTAINMENT

Fat Harold's Beach Club (☎ 843-249-5779; 212 Main St, North Myrtle Beach; ☺ 4pm-2am) It's a gas to watch the graying beach bums groove to doo-wop and old-time rock 'n' roll at this North Myrtle institution, which calls itself 'Home of the Shag.' The dance, that is. Free shag lessons are offered at 8pm on Tuesday and Thursday.

Carolina Opry (☎ 843-913-1400; www.thecarolinaopry .com; 8901a Business 17 N; tickets from $19; ☺ shows daily at 8pm) Glittery musicals and variety shows.

GETTING THERE & AROUND

The traffic coming and going on Hwy 17 Business/Kings Hwy can be infuriating. To avoid 'the Strand' altogether, stay on Hwy 17 bypass, or take Hwy 31/Carolina Bays Parkway, which parallels Hwy 17 between Hwy 501 and Hwy 9.

Myrtle Beach International Airport (☎ 843-448-1589) is located within the city limits, as is the **Greyhound** (☎ 843-448-2472; 511 7th Ave N) station.

SOUTH COAST

South of Charleston, stretches of shimmery, oyster-gray sand and seafoam-green water are punctuated with resort towns and pretty villages. A necklace of **sea islands** runs up the coast, home to both secluded Gullah com-

munities, where descendants of African slaves maintain a unique culture, and world-famous golf courses, where the well-heeled wheel and deal.

Rental homes and golf courses abound on **Kiawah Island**, while the small coastal town of **Edisto Island** (*ed*-is-tow) is as homespun as big Sunday dinners. The picturesque town of **Beaufort** has a long colonial history and a thriving shrimp industry. Further south is **Hilton Head Island**, home to gated communities and great golf.

Beaufort

Not to be confused with Beaufort (Bow-fort), NC, Beaufort (*byoo*-furt) is an elegant little town of antebellum homes, its streets lined with magnolias and dripping with Spanish moss. Beaufort Bay sparkles like a million diamonds in the bright sun and glows like fireflies by moonlight. Locals conjecture that the area's high phosphate content is responsible for the water's uncommon reflections.

With a naval hospital, air-force base and Marine recruit center, the military provides the town's main industry, but the movie business and tourism are upcoming rivals.

The **visitor center** (☎ 843-986-5400, 800-638-3525; www.beaufortsc.org; Main 1106 Carteret St; ☺ 9am-5:30pm; Satellite John Mark Verdier House, cnr Bay & Scott Sts; ☺ 10am-5:30pm) has local information, distributes maps and organizes boat, carriage and walking tours.

In mid-July, during the **Water Festival** (☎ 843-524-0600; www.waterfestival.com) the city celebrates the river and sea bounty with music, dancing,

THE SOUTH

tournaments and air shows by the Marines. In October, the **Shrimp Festival** (☎ 843-986-5400; www.cityofbeaufort.org/visitor/shrimp.htm) celebrates the local importance of these diminutive crustaceans.

Hilton Head Island

Twelve miles long and 5 miles wide, Hilton Head is South Carolina's largest barrier island, the focal point of a low-country estuary. The entire area is a veritable temple to the worship of leisure time and the game of golf. There are dozens of courses enclosed in private residential communities called 'plantations,' and the island's great cultural events are the annual golf tournaments.

The island prides itself on being designed in concert with the natural environment, but summer traffic and miles of stoplights make it hard to see the forest (or a tree) along US Hwy 278. There are, however, some lush nature preserves. The beaches are wide, white and so hard you can ride a bike on them for miles. Right at the entrance to the island is the **visitor center** (☎ 800-523-3373; 100 William Hilton Parkway; ⏰ 9:30am-5pm), which has a small museum and can give you information on accommodations and, well, golf.

COLUMBIA

South Carolina's state capital is a quiet place, with wide, shady streets and the kind of old-fashioned downtown where pillbox hats are still on display in the windows of family-run department stores. The University of South Carolina adds a youthful vibe, and college students whoop it up over basketball wins in campus-side bars. Though Columbia is a pleasant stop, most visitors, like General Sherman's troops, charge on through to the coast.

The **visitor center** (☎ 803-545-0002; www.columbia cvb.com; 1101 Lincoln St; ⏰ 9am-5pm Mon-Sat, from 1pm Sun) has information about four historic houses open for tours, including Woodrow Wilson's boyhood home.

The grand, Corinthean-columned **State House** (☎ 803-734-2430; 1100 Gervais St; admission free; ⏰ 9am-5pm Mon-Fri, from 10am Sat) has bronze stars on its west side to mark the impacts from Northern troops' cannonballs. Around the capital, assorted memorials attest to the state's military history.

The **South Carolina State Museum** (☎ 803-898-4921; www.museum.state.sc.us; 301 Gervais St; adult/child $5/3; ⏰ 10am-5pm Tue-Sat, from 1pm Sun) is housed in an 1894 textile factory building, one of the world's first electrically powered mills. Exhibits on science, technology and the state's cultural and natural history make a nice activity for a rainy day.

Located just 17 miles southeast of town on I-77, the **Congaree National Park** (☎ 803-776-4396; www.nps.gov/cosw; 100 National Park Rd; ⏰ 8:30am-5pm) protects 22,000 acres of land, the largest contiguous area of old-growth floodplain forest in the US. You can walk along a boardwalk through primeval knobby-kneed cypress trees, camp beside frolicking river otters, or take a canoe through the swamp. The park is open year-round.

If you are after somewhere to spend the night, the pale-green **Whitney Hotel** (☎ 803-252-0845, 800-637-4008; www.whitneyhotel.com; 700 Woodrow St; r incl breakfast $129; P ⬚ ⬚ ⬚) has an old-fashioned art-deco vibe, along with 74 spacious suites with sitting areas and kitchens. A number of good restaurants and bars are within walking distance.

For eating and entertainment, head to the Five Points area in the southeast corner of

---

LOCAL VOICES

Name Lucille Akingobi

Occupation Sweetgrass basket weaver with a stand on the side of Hwy 17, north of Charleston. These stands are ubiquitous up and down the coast, and baskets often sell for hundreds of dollars.

What exactly is a sweetgrass basket? It's an old African art, started in the 1700s here in the state. They're made from four natural materials: sweetgrass, palm, bulrush and pine needles.

Where did you learn to weave? From my mom. I was seven. I was interested in it, and she would be outside under the tree, weaving. I'd pick the old ones (*Lucille shows the old palm fronds that have fallen to the ground*).

There are so many basket sellers. Are they all different? You can tell who's done it. My way is unique...you just put it together. You use your own judgment.

This art form has been passed down for generations. Do you think it will continue? My kids don't do it.

WORTH THE DRIVE: SWAMP TOURS

Tannic acid leached from decaying plant matter colors many South Carolina swamps and rivers an inky black. Canoeing among the knobby cypress trees, dripping with Spanish moss as dry and gray as witches' hair, you may just feel like a character in a Southern Gothic novel. With more than 2000 miles of navigable waterways, the state is a paddlers heaven. The **Audubon Society** (☎ 843-462-2150; www.beidlerforest.com/canoe.html; 4hr trips adult/child $25/15) offers canoe trips into the spooky depths of the Beidler Forest, off I-26 near Harleyville, about 45 minutes from Charleston. **Canoe South Carolina** (☎ 843-563-5051; www.canoesc.com; self-guided/guided day trips $30/88) does tours of the Edisto River and surrounding swamplands, leaving from the town of Canadys, off Hwy 95.

---

downtown, where Harden, Greene and Devine Sts meet Saluda Ave. Try the hidden **Rockaway Athletic Club** (☎ 803-256-1075; 2719 Rosewood Dr; mains $9-12; ☾ 11am-11pm) for killer pimento cheese burgers and lots of beer.

GEORGIA

Vastly different at each of its edges, Georgia – the largest state east of the Mississippi River – is in many ways the perfect distillation of everything the South has to offer. It's a state of wild geographic and cultural extremes: right-leaning Republican politics lean against liberal idealism, small towns merge with gaping cities, northern mountains rise to the clouds and produce roaring rivers, while coastal marshlands teem with fiddler crabs and swaying cordgrass.

Atlanta is the state capitol and the region's transportation hub, a sprawling metropolis with friendly neighborhoods alongside multinational corporations such as UPS and Coca-Cola (which celebrates itself with a glossy downtown museum). So start your trip in the city known as 'the ATL,' then road trip across the state to fall under the spell of Savannah's live oaks, seafood, antebellum homes and humid nights. From here you're close to the coastal barrier islands, a mix of ritzy resorts and nature preserves. Bring your tuxedo to Jekyll Island, and your hiking boots to Cumberland Island.

History

Permanent English settlement dates from 1733, when James Edward Oglethorpe founded Savannah. By the time of the Revolutionary War, almost half the population were slaves. Though far removed from the Civil War's early phases, Georgia held two crucial battlefronts in the latter part of the war: Chicka-

muga, where Union troops were defeated, and Atlanta, which they conquered and burned. Atlanta, the South's major transportation hub, was rebuilt with startling speed.

In the 20th century the state vaulted to national prominence on the back of an eclectic group of events and images: the wildly popular novel and film *Gone With the Wind*; Reverend Martin Luther King Jr and civil rights protests; 39th US President Jimmy Carter; and Atlanta's rise as a global media and business center, culminating in the 1996 Summer Olympics. Since then, Georgia's capital has become known as the 'Motown of the South' thanks to its sizzling hip-hop and R&B scene.

Information

To move around Georgia, you'll probably need a car. (Atlanta has a city-wide train system called Marta, but service is limited.) I-75 bisects the state running north–south; I-20 runs east–west.

You can expect to pay an additional 6% tax on hotel accommodations in Georgia.

GEORGIA FACTS

Nickname Peach State
Population 9.36 million
Area 59,441 sq miles
Capital city Atlanta (population 5 million)
Sales tax 6% to 7%
Birthplace of Baseball legend Ty Cobb (1886–1961), president Jimmy Carter (b 1924), civil rights leader Martin Luther King Jr (1929–68), singer Ray Charles (1930–2004)
Home of Coca-Cola, the world's busiest airport, the world's biggest aquarium
Famous for Peaches
State law: Statewide 'blue laws' prevent the sale of alcohol on Sundays.

The **Department of Economic Development** (☎ 404-962-4000; www.georgia.org; 75 5th Street NW, Suite 1200, Atlanta, GA 30308) has a useful website.

ATLANTA

With five million residents and counting, the so-called 'capital of the South' continues to experience explosive growth thanks to southbound Yankees and international immigrants alike. It's also booming as a tourist destination thanks to two glitzy 21st-century attractions – the Georgia Aquarium and the new World of Coca-Cola – plus the arrival of Mei Lan, a giant panda cub at the Atlanta Zoo. Beyond the attractions you'll find a constellation of superlative restaurants, two luxury megamalls, ample Civil War lore, miles of hiking trails and a plethora of African American history.

Without natural boundaries to control development, Atlanta keeps growing – sometimes up, but mostly out. Suburban sprawl has turned Atlanta into an almost endless city. Increased car dependence creates horrendous traffic, traffic creates smog, smog pollutes water and so on.

For all this suburbanization, Atlanta is a pretty city covered with trees and elegant homes. Distinct neighborhoods are like friendly small towns. Racial tensions are minimal in 'The City Too Busy To Hate,' which prides itself as hometown to the civil rights titan Martin Luther King Jr.

History

Born as a railroad junction in 1837, Atlanta became a major Confederate transportation and munitions center for General William T Sherman, whose Union forces blazed through Georgia in 1864. When they left they burned everything, leaving more than 90% of Atlanta's buildings in ruins.

After the war, Atlanta became the epitome of the 'New South,' a concept that entailed reconciliation with the North, the promotion of industrialized agriculture, and a progressive business outlook. Atlanta's relentless boosterism led to civic improvements and energetic business partnerships. Segregation ended relatively painlessly here, compared with other Southern cities, and President John F Kennedy lauded this transition as a model for other communities facing integration.

Atlanta earned a moment in the international spotlight when it hosted the 1996 Summer Olympic Games. The city put on her prettiest debutante gown, and CNN beamed her picture worldwide. People took notice, the moving trucks came rolling down the freeways and, like summer weeds, condos sprouted everywhere. Since then, the city has focused its development energy on the downtown and Midtown neighborhoods, both of which have flourished in recent years.

Orientation

The Atlanta metropolitan area sits inside a highway loop called I-285 or, locally, 'the Perimeter.' Inside the circle, I-20 travels east–west, while I-75 and I-85 run north–south. I-75 and I-85 become a single highway – 'the Downtown Connector'– as the roads pass through the city center. Atlanta's rapid transit system is known as **Marta** (Metropolitan Atlanta Rapid Transit Authority; www. itsmarta.com), and it's extremely handy for getting to and from the airport. Unfortunately, its destinations around the city aren't as plentiful as urban explorers might hope.

In the city, Ponce de Leon Ave (known in town as 'Ponce') is a key east–west surface road. Peachtree St and Piedmont Ave are the main north–south arteries, but be forewarned: you'll find lots of other streets, roads and avenues also called Peachtree. Many streets also change names suddenly. Addresses also specify NE, SE, SW or NW. W Peachtree St divides east from west and Martin Luther King Jr Dr/ Edgewood Ave divides north from south.

Business-oriented downtown Atlanta has a few worthwhile attractions, but you'll have to venture into Atlanta's sprawling neighborhoods to see the best the city has to offer. East

---

DON'T MISS

- **The Georgia Aquarium** – provides an eye-popping undersea experience (p406)

- **Watershed** – serves scrumptious Southern food (p411)

- **The Carter Presidential Library & Museum** – features an Oval Office replica (p408)

- **The Braves** – Atlanta's beloved baseball team (p412)

- **Center for Puppetry Arts** – with its mind-blowing puppet museum (p408)

of downtown, Sweet Auburn attractions pay homage to Martin Luther King Jr. Little Five Points (L5P) and East Atlanta cater to Atlanta's alternative set. Yuppie central Virginia-Highland boasts restaurants, boutique shopping and taverns. Decatur – a quaint independent city just east of Atlanta – offers several good restaurants and nightspots. Turner Field and Grant Park are south of downtown. North of downtown, Midtown is a bustling entertainment and nightlife area, with posh Buckhead further out.

Information
BOOKSTORES
A Cappella Books (☎ 404-681-5128, 866-681-5128; www.acappellabooks.com; 484c Moreland Ave NE; ⌚ 11am-9pm Mon-Thu, to 10pm Fri & Sat, noon-8pm Sun) The location is new, but the anarchist spirit remains in this L5P haunt, which hosts many readings and musical performances. The store has a particularly well-stocked music section.

Borders Books Music & Cafe (☎ 404-607-7903; www.bordersstores.com; 650 Ponce de Leon Ave NE; ⌚ 9am-11pm Mon-Sat, to 10pm Sun) Accessible location of the national chain.

EMERGENCY & MEDICAL SERVICES
Atlanta Medical Center (☎ 404-265-4000; 303 Parkway Dr NE)
Emory University Hospital (☎ 404-712-7021; 1364 Clifton Rd NE)
Grady Memorial Hospital (☎ 404-616-1000; 80 Jesse Hill Dr SE)
Main police station (☎ 404-853-3434; 675 Ponce de Leon Ave at City Hall East)
Piedmont Hospital (☎ 404-605-5000; 1968 Peachtree Rd)

INTERNET ACCESS
Maasty Computers Internet Cafe (☎ 404-294-8095; www.maastyinternetcafe.com; 736 Ponce de Leon Ave; per 15min $2.50; ⌚ 8am-11pm Mon-Thu, to midnight Fri & Sat, to 10pm Sun) Near City Hall East, Maasty supplements its wi-fi with computer repair service and hourly digital camera rentals. It's a dark little place with a vaguely industrial vibe and a menu that uses computer slang to indicate sizes.
Public library (☎ 404-730-1700; 1 Margaret Mitchell Sq; ⌚ 9am-9pm Mon-Thu, to 6pm Fri & Sat, 2-6pm Sun) Many branches of the public library offer free internet, including this main branch.

INTERNET RESOURCES
Access Atlanta (www.accessatlanta.com) A great place to find out about Atlanta news and upcoming events.

Atlanta Coalition of Performing Arts (www.atlantaperforms.com) Gives info and links about the city's music, film, dance and theater scene.
Atlanta Music Guide (www.atlantamusicguide.com) Maintains a live-music schedule, plus a directory of local venues and links to online ticketing.
Atlanta Travel (www.atlanta.net) Official site of the Atlanta Convention & Visitors Bureau with excellent links to shops, restaurants, hotels and upcoming events.

MEDIA
Atlanta (www.atlantamagazine.com) A monthly general-interest magazine covering local issues, arts and dining.
Atlanta Daily World (www.atlantadailyworld.com) The nation's oldest continuously running African American newspaper (since 1928).
Atlanta Journal-Constitution (www.ajc.com) Atlanta's major daily newspaper, with a good travel section on Sunday.
Creative Loafing (www.atlanta.creativeloafing.com) For hip tips on music, arts and theater this free alternative weekly comes out every Wednesday.

POST
For general postal information call ☎ 800-275-8777.
Post office Downtown (41 Marietta St); Federal Center (☎ 404-521-9843; 41 Marietta St NW); Little Five Points (455 Moreland Ave SE); North Highland (1190 N Highland Ave NE) Mail addressed to General Delivery, Atlanta, GA 30301 can be picked up at Federal Center.

TOURIST INFORMATION
Atlanta Convention & Visitors Bureau (☎ 404-521-6600; www.atlanta.net; 233 Peachtree St; ⌚ 8:30am-5:30pm Mon-Fri) Has an online neighborhood guide, a restaurant guide and a link to info for gay and lesbian travelers. The CVB website also lets you buy a City-Pass, a tremendous money saver that bundles admission to six attractions for the discounted price of $64.

UNIVERSITIES
Atlanta is home to many universities and colleges, including the following:
Emory University (☎ 404-727-6123; www.emory.edu; 380 S Oxford Rd NE) Between downtown and Decatur is one of the top universities in the USA.
Georgia Institute of Technology (☎ 404-894-2000; www.gatech.edu; 25 North Ave) Known as 'Georgia Tech,' this is one of the top technical colleges, with a wildly popular football team.
Morehouse College (☎ 404-681-2100; www.morehouse.edu) The traditionally African American men's school that educated Martin Luther King Jr.

ATLANTA

THE SOUTH

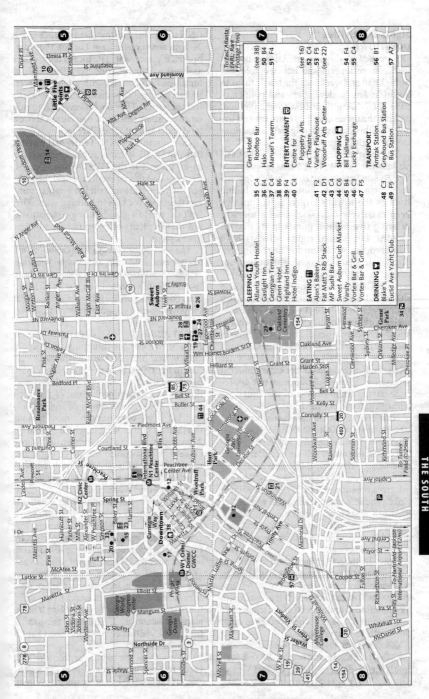

THE SOUTH

Sights & Activities

DOWNTOWN

On weekdays, downtown Atlanta bustles with conventioneers and business folk, but by nightfall and weekends the bustle turns to a shuffle. Lately, developers and politicians have been doing their best to change that, making the urban core more vibrant and livable. To this end, some big new attractions have recently come online.

The showstopper of the bunch is the **Georgia Aquarium** (☎ 404-581-4000; www.georgiaaquarium .com; 225 Baker St; adult/child $24/18; 🕑 10am-5pm Mon-Thu, 9am-6pm Fri-Sun), a colossal facility billing itself as the world's largest aquarium. It's been massively successful among tourists, drawing five million guests in its first 18 months, but animal rights activists have criticized the aquarium for displaying exotic whale sharks, two of which died not long after the attraction opened. Nevertheless, the Georgia Aquarium has other whale sharks still swimming, and it also boasts a tank of gorgeous beluga whales. Other animals on exhibit include otters and pirhana, and there's even a petting tank where guests can touch sharks and rays. Little kids may enjoy the 4-D movie, which sprinkles water on the audience and preaches environmental sensitivity. Mom and Dad may not appreciate paying $5.50 on top of the aquarium admission fee to see the film.

Next door to the Georgia Aquarium is the new **World of Coca-Cola** (☎ 404-676-5151; www.woc catlanta.com; 121 Baker St; adult/child $15/9; 🕑 9am-5pm, 8am-6pm summer), a self-congratulatory yet entertaining museum that opened in 2007, relocating from several blocks away. The climactic moment comes when guests sample Coke products from around the world. But there are also Andy Warhol pieces to view, a 4-D film to catch, company history to learn, and what seems like 20 billion promotional materials to behold.

Down by the site of the old Coke museum is **Underground Atlanta** (☎ 404-523-2311; www.under ground-atlanta.com; cnr Peachtree & Alabama Sts; 🕑 10am-9pm Mon-Sat, 11am-6pm Sun), which is an enclosed, air-conditioned multilevel maze of shops, bars and restaurants. This is where you go to catch the shuttle to Braves games.

CNN Center (☎ 404-827-2300; www.cnn.com/Studio Tour; 1 CNN Center; 50min tours adult/child $12/9; 🕑 8:30am-5pm) is the headquarters of the cable-TV news service. You might be tempted to take the CNN tour, a behind-the-scenes glance at the 24-hour news organization, but don't be heartbroken if you miss it. The tour is dark, dingy and just a little bit condescending. Except for an early encounter with a teleprompter, visitors don't get close enough to the action to feel connected. They do, however, get to ride on an enormous escalator that climbs above a food court and into the CNN facility.

Just north of CNN, **Centennial Olympic Park** (☎ 404-223-4412; www.centennialpark.com) is a 21-acre legacy to the 1996 Olympic Games. Concerts and special events are held throughout the year. The fountain is a popular summertime spot for kids in bathing suits. This isn't the world's grandest or grassiest park, but there's plenty of room to toss a ball or have a picnic.

The gold-domed **Georgia State Capitol** (☎ 404-656-2844; www.sos.state.ga.us; 206 Washington St; tours free; 🕑 8am-5:30pm Mon-Fri, guided tours at 10am, 11am, 1pm & 2pm) is Atlanta's political hub. Tours include a film about the legislative process and a glance at the government's communications facility.

SWEET AUBURN

Auburn Ave was the thumping commercial and cultural heart of African American culture in the 1900s. It takes some imagination, but if you listen closely, you can almost hear the jazz and history oozing out of the brick facades. Today, a collection of sights is associated with Sweet Auburn's most famous son: Martin Luther King Jr, who was born on Auburn and preached on Auburn and whose grave now looks on to the street. Although the neighborhood has been dilapidated, construction work and new businesses suggest an imminent Sweet Auburn revival.

The historic **Martin Luther King Jr National Historic Site** commemorates the life, work and legacy of the Civil Rights lodestar. The center takes up several blocks. A stop by the bustling **visitors center** (☎ 404-331-5190; www.nps.gov/malu; 450 Auburn Ave NE; admission free; 🕑 9am-5pm, to 6pm summer) will help you get oriented with a map and brochure of area sites and exhibits. From here, free guided tours leave for the **Martin Luther King Jr Birthplace** (501 Auburn Ave). If you miss the tour, a film in the visitors center tells about King's life in the house.

Across from the visitor center, the **King Center for Non-Violent Social Change** (☎ 404-526-8900; 449 Auburn Ave NE) has more information on

King's life and work, and a few of his personal effects, including his Nobel Peace Prize. His **gravesite**, between the church and center, is surrounded by a long, reflecting pool and can be viewed anytime.

Ebenezer Baptist Church (☎ 404-688-7263; 407 Auburn Ave NE; admission free; ☯ tours 9am-6pm Mon-Sat, from 1:30pm Sun) was the preaching ground for King Jr, his father and grandfather, who were all pastors here. This is also where King Jr's mother was murdered in 1974. You can take a free tour of the original church, but Sunday services are now held at a new Ebenezer across the street.

All of the King sites are a few blocks' walk from Marta's King Memorial station.

MIDTOWN

Midtown is like a hipper, second downtown, with pleny of great bars, restaurants and cultural venues.

Through 2009, the expanded **High Museum of Art** (☎ 404-733-4444; www.high.org; 1280 Peachtree St NE; adult/child $15/10; ☯ 10am-5pm Tue-Wed & Fri-Sat, to 8pm Thu, noon-5pm Sun), is working in partnership with the Louvre, displaying works that belong to the famous Parisian museum. But don't overlook the High's permanent collection of American art, which includes fascinating works from the turn of the 20th century, plus contemporary pieces from the likes of Gerhard Richter and folk art from Georgia treasure Howard Finster. The whole museum is done up in blinding white, making the facility itself feel quite artful.

Margaret Mitchell House & Museum (☎ 404-249-7015; www.gwtw.org; 990 Peachtree St at 10th St; adult/child $12/9; ☯ 9:30am-5pm) is a shrine to the author of *Gone With the Wind*. Mitchell wrote her epic in a small apartment in the basement of this historic house. A separate, adjacent museum includes memorabilia from the blockbuster film version of the title.

In the middle of Midtown, **Piedmont Park** (www.piedmontpark.org) is a glorious, rambling urban park and the setting of many cultural and music festivals. The park has fantastic bike paths, a Saturday Green Market, a well-loved dog area and lovely green spaces. Neighboring **Skate Escape** (☎ 404-892-1292; www.skateescape.com; 1086 Piedmont Ave NE), at 12th St, rents out bicycles (from $6 per hour) and in-line skates ($6 per hour).

In the northwest corner of Piedmont Park, the stunning 30-acre **Atlanta Botanical Garden** (☎ 404-876-5859; www.atlantabotanicalgarden.org; 1345 Piedmont Ave NE; adult/child $12/9; ☯ 9am-5pm Tue-Sun, to 7pm summer) has a Japanese garden, winding paths and the amazing Fuqua Orchid Center.

THE SHORT LIFE OF A CIVIL RIGHTS GIANT

Martin Luther King Jr, the singular figure of the American Civil Rights Movement, was born in 1929, the son of an Atlanta preacher. His lineage was significant, not only because he would follow his father to the pulpit of Ebenezer Baptist Church, but because his political speeches rang out with a preacher's inflections.

King graduated from the African American men's school Morehouse College and received his PhD from Boston University, but he was known more as a populist than as an academic. He provided the face and voice of the Civil Rights Movement, in which African Americans demanded equality, and he insisted upon achieving this goal through nonviolent means.

In 1955 King led the 'bus boycott' in Montgomery, AL. After a year of boycotting, the US Supreme Court removed laws that enforced segregated buses. From this successful beginning, King emerged as an inspiring moral voice in civil rights.

His nonviolent approach to racial equality and peace makes the irony of his death all the more cruel: he was assassinated on a Memphis hotel balcony in 1968, four years after receiving the Nobel Peace Prize and five years after giving his legendary 'I Have a Dream' speech in Washington, DC.

King remains one of the most recognized and respected figures of the 20th century. In a span of 10 years, he led a movement that essentially ended a system of statutory discrimination in existence since the country's founding. The Martin Luther King Jr National Historic Site (opposite) and the King Center for Non-Violent Social Change in Atlanta (opposite) are testaments to his moral vision, his ability to inspire others and his lasting impact on the fundamental fabric of American society.

HOT TOPIC: PARKING IN PIEDMONT PARK

In the middle of Atlanta, where green space is precious and development stakes are high, an epic battle has been waged over a proposed 800-car parking deck serving Piedmont Park and the Botanical Garden. The surrounding Midtown neighborhood has been divided between residents who wanted to preserve parkland and those who wanted to make these two popular urban attractions more accessible. (Parking for both is limited.) The debate has raged, complete with yard signs and at least one lawsuit. Contact the **Piedmont Park Conservancy** (www.piedmontpark.org), which has supported the deck, or the **Friends of Piedmont Park** (www.friendsofpiedmontpark.org), an organization that has opposed the deck, to see where the issue stands now.

GRANT PARK & OAKLAND CEMETERY

A large oasis of green situated on the edge of the city center, **Grant Park** (www.grantpark.org) is home to **Zoo Atlanta** (☎ 404-624-5600; www.zoo atlanta.org; adult/child $17/12; ☉ 9:30am-4:30pm), which features flamingos, elephants, kangaroos and the odd tiger. But the zoo's pride and joy is baby Mei Lan, the giant panda cub whose every movement is a picture of adorability. Be prepared to wait if you want to see her.

Gone With the Wind author Margaret Mitchell and golf great Bobby Jones are buried in the **Oakland Cemetery** (☎ 404-688-2107; www .oaklandcemetery.com; 248 Oakland Ave SE; guided tours/ selfguided tours $5-10/free; ☉ sunrise-sunset, tours Mar-Nov). Many interesting Victorian and neoclassical monuments are scattered throughout the site, and – if it doesn't creep you out too much – there's a nice open greenspace for picnics.

LITTLE FIVE POINTS & EAST ATLANTA

These two bohemian neighborhoods are close to one another, but miles away from mainstream Atlanta's genteel sensibilities. They're young, scruffy neighborhoods with a definite edge. Both are dominated by a main drag – **Euclid Ave** in L5P and **Flat Shoals Ave** in East Atlanta – and both are anchored by popular music venues, Variety Playhouse and the EARL, respectively (see p411). These neighborhoods offer Atlanta's most dense concentration of funky local boutiques; the stretch of Moreland Ave separating the two 'hoods is equally dense with big chain stores. Both neighborhoods are well-explored on foot, and both are jammed with restaurants. Visit one neighborhood on a sunny Saturday afternoon and then, after grabbing a bite, take a quick car trip over to the other.

VIRGINIA-HIGHLAND

Atlanta's preppiest neighborhood is populated by adorable homes (with big price tags) and beautiful boutiques (with big price tags). Highland Ave runs through the heart of the neighborhood, and makes for a pleasant stroll.

POINTS EAST & DECATUR

Located on a hilltop overlooking downtown, the **Carter Presidential Library & Museum** (☎ 404-865-7100; www.jimmycarterlibrary.org; 441 Freedom Parkway; adult/child $8/free; ☉ 9am-4:45pm Mon-Sat, from noon Sun) features exhibits highlighting Jimmy Carter's 1977–81 presidency, including a replica of the Oval Office. Carter's Nobel Prize is also on display. Don't miss the tranquil Japanese garden out back.

Fernbank Museum of Natural History (☎ 404-929-6300; www.fernbank.edu/museum; 767 Clifton Rd NE; adult/child $13/11; ☉ 10am-5pm Mon-Sat, from noon Sun) makes other museums seem hopelessly dull. It covers the natural world from seashells to giant lizards, and it has an **IMAX theater** (adult/child $11/9). On Martinis & IMAX Friday (5:30pm to 10pm January to November), the lobby turns into a cocktail lounge and live jazz echoes through the bones of a 123ft dinosaur.

Atlanta for Children

Atlanta has plenty of activities to keep children entertained, delighted and – perhaps against their will – educated. Following are some of the major sites that work at being kid-friendly.

Center for Puppetry Arts (☎ 404-873-3391; www .puppet.org; 1404 Spring St NW; museum adult/child $8/6; ☉ 9am-5pm Wed-Sat, 11am-5pm Sun) is a wonderland for visitors of all ages, and hands-down one of Atlanta's most unique and worthwhile attractions. The museum houses a treasury of puppets, some of which you get to operate yourself. There are Asian puppets, African puppets, shadow puppets, Muppets and more. Separate tickets are required for the performances (see p411).

Imagine It! Children's Museum of Atlanta (☎ 404-659-5437; www.imagineit-cma.org; 275 Olympic Centennial Park Dr NW; admission $11; ✹ 10am-4pm Mon-Fri, to 5pm Sat & Sun) is a hands-on museum geared toward kids aged eight and under. Adults aren't allowed in without a youngster in tow.

In the Fernbank Museum of Natural History (opposite), kids can gawk at the dinosaurs. Or you might like to introduce your little animals to much bigger ones at Zoo Atlanta (opposite).

Festivals & Events

Atlanta Jazz Festival (www.atlantafestivals.com) A city-sponsored month-long event culminating in live concerts in Piedmont Park on Memorial Day Weekend, end of May.

Atlanta Pride Festival (☎ 404-929-0071; www .atlantapride.org) End of June (see below).

National Black Arts Festival (☎ 404-730-7315; www.nbaf.org) Artists from across the country converge on Atlanta for this festival celebrating African American music, theater, literature and film. Held in July at various locations.

Sleeping

Rates at downtown hotels tend to fluctuate wildly depending on whether there is a large convention in town. Weekends are often cheaper, as are hotels away from downtown.

BUDGET

A cheap option is to stay somewhere along the Marta line outside downtown, and take the train into the city for sightseeing. Plenty of chain hotels have locations in Atlanta.

Atlanta Youth Hostel (☎ 800-473-9449; www.hostel -atlanta.com; 223 Ponce de Leon Ave at Myrtle St; dm/r $23/69; ✷ ✗ wi-fi) In a white brick Midtown mansion, this lively hostel has private beds and dorm rooms. It wins accolades both for its cleanliness and for its sweet location just blocks east of the Marta North Ave station. If you don't mind sharing a room, ask for room 36, which has a massive balcony.

MIDRANGE

Highland Inn (☎ 404-874-5756; www.thehighland inn.com; 644 N Highland Ave; r or ste incl breakfast $82-106; **P** ✗ ✷ wi-fi) This European-style inn has a great location in the middle of Virginia-Highland, and a shabby-chic vibe that tends to appeal to touring musicians. Rooms have private baths, and there are laundry facilities onsite.

University Inn (☎ 800-654-8591; www.univinn .com; 1767 North Decatur Rd; s & d incl breakfast $89-150; **P** ✗ ✷ ▤) The rooms aren't flashy, but it's tough to complain when you're situated on the doorstep of the Emory University campus.

GAY & LESBIAN ATLANTA

Atlanta is one of the few places in Georgia – perhaps in the South – with a noticeable and active gay and lesbian population. Midtown is the center of gay life; the epicenter is around Piedmont Park and the intersection of 10th St and Piedmont Ave. The town of Decatur, east of downtown Atlanta, has a significant lesbian community. For news and information, grab a copy of the *Southern Voice* newspaper; also check out www.gayatlanta.com.

At the prime corner of Piedmont Ave and 10th St in Midtown is the cheerful **Outwrite Bookstore & Coffeehouse** (☎ 404-607-0082; www.outwritebooks.com; 991 Piedmont Ave; ✹ 10am-11pm), which feels like an information clearinghouse for all of gay Atlanta.

In a vaguely industrial stretch of Midtown (near one of Atlanta's popular strip clubs) is **Wetbar** (☎ 404-745-9494; www.wetbaratlanta.com; 960 Spring St NW; ✹ 8pm-3am Wed-Sat), a spot with a concrete bar and concrete floor that seem to match the neighborhood's urban grit. The tank-topped bartenders will take good care of you, and the sound system will rattle your teeth.

Head upstairs to the ratty couch if you want to sit and talk at **Mary's** (☎ 404-624-4411; www .marysatlanta.com; 1287 Glenwood Ave SE), a scruffy-chic East Atlanta dive. But the action is downstairs, a narrow space with room for a bar and a campy karaoke night known, naturally, as Mary-oke.

Atlanta Pride Festival (☎ 404-929-0071; www.atlantapride.org) is a massive annual celebration of the city's gay and lesbian community. Held at the end of June in and around Piedmont Park, it attracts people from all over the country.

Just a short walk from Piedmont Park, **Blake's** (☎ 404-892-5786; www.blakesontheparkatlanta .com; 227 10th St NE; ✹ 11am-3am Mon-Sat, to midnight Sun) bills itself as 'Atlanta's favorite gay bar since 1987.'

THE SOUTH

Although this place feels like a suburban chain hotel, it's actually a family-owned B&B.

our pick **Gaslight Inn** (☎ 404-875-1001; www.gaslightinn.com; 1001 St Charles Ave NE; r incl breakfast from $115; ✗ ❄) A dandy of a B&B, this frilly but charming inn is nice enough to move into. Guests can walk to the shops of Highland Ave or can cozy up in the rooms – some of which feature a whirlpool or steam room, and all of which offer bathrobes. Beds are at least queen size.

Hotel Indigo (☎ 404-874-9200; www.hotelindigo.com; 683 Peachtree St; r $129-179; P ❄ wi-fi) A boutique-style hotel that's actually part of a chain, the Indigo has a boisterous blue color scheme and a sunny personality. More important is the outstanding Midtown location, across the street from restaurants and entertainment and within walking distance of a Marta stop. Parking costs $18.

Georgian Terrace (☎ 404-897-1991; www.thegeorgianterrace.com; 659 Peachtree St NE; r $149-169; P ❄ ❄ wi-fi) A giant hotel on the National Register of Historic Places, this grand dame across from the Fox Theater offers an absolute feast for the senses. Many of the *Gone With the Wind* stars stayed here during the film's debut in 1939 and the hotel, having undergone a massive facelift, is worth a wander whether you stay here or not. Parking costs around $22 to $25 per day.

TOP END

Glenn Hotel (☎ 404-521-2250; www.glennhotel.com; 110 Marietta St NW; r from $200; P ❄ wi-fi) Painstakingly hip, the Glenn feels more like a discreet night-club than a slick hotel, but (with a swanky rooftop bar for guests and locals alike) it's actually a bit of both. Boutique hotels are surprisingly rare in Atlanta, and this place seems to relish its exclusivity. If you were a visiting supermodel or a sexy musician performing at nearby Philips Arena, this is where you'd want to stay. Parking will cost you around $21 per day.

Eating

Food culture in Atlanta is nothing short of obsessive. Local chefs are discussed breathlessly, hot new restaurants are instantly mobbed, lines at local favorites stretch out the door. The options range from haute cuisine to humble Southern staples, and the quality can be absolutely magnificent at both ends of the spectrum.

DOWNTOWN & MIDTOWN

Varsity (☎ 404-881-1706; 61 North Ave at Spring St; dogs from $1.35; ✆ 10am-11:30pm Mon-Thu, to 12:30am Fri & Sat) The world's largest drive-in restaurant and an Atlanta institution since 1928, the Varsity is a glorified fast-food joint, but it's always packed with folks ordering walk-a-dogs (hot dogs), glorified steaks (hamburgers) and bags of rags (fries).

Fat Matt's Rib Shack (☎ 404-607-1622; 1811 Piedmont Rd NE; sandwiches from $3.95; ✆ 11:30am-11:30pm, to 12:30am Fri, from 2pm Sun) Less than a mile north of Piedmont Park, a much more down-home choice is divey Fat Matt's, a shrine to two great Southern traditions: barbecue and the blues. Take special note of the Brunswick stew, a delicious side dish best described as barbecue soup.

MF Sushi Bar (☎ 404-815-8844; 265 Ponce de Leon Ave; special rolls $7-17.50; ✆ lunch 11:30am-2:30pm Mon-Fri, dinner 5:30pm-10:30pm Mon-Thu, to 11:30pm Fri, 6-10pm Sun) Lots of trendy restaurants populate the slick Midtown neighborhood, but this place is one of the slickest (and best). The ultimate treat is to order *omakase*, an off-the-menu move that allows the chef total control over your meal. If that's too risky (or too expensive), the standard rolls and fish pieces are here – they're just better than usual. The MF, by the way, stands for Magic Fingers.

SWEET AUBURN

Sweet Auburn Curb Market (☎ 404-659-1665; www.sweetauburncurbmarket.com; 209 Edgewood Ave SE; ✆ 8am-6pm Mon-Sat) Like the Reading Terminal Market in Philadelphia or the Ferry Building in San Francisco (but, frankly, not as nice as either) the Curb Market allows foodies to browse countless stalls for cooking ingredients or hot meals served on the premises.

BUFORD HIGHWAY

Blessed with a thriving immigrant community, Atlanta has a plethora of Asian and Latin eateries, many of which can be found along this fascinating, sprawling stretch of strip malls. Adventurous diners can simply hop in the car and explore the drag, stopping at whatever looks interesting. But those who need a destination to get started should consider **Nam Chun Hong** (☎ 770-454-5640; 5953 Buford Hwy; dumplings $6.95; ✆ 11:30am-10pm Mon-Fri, to 11pm Sat & Sun), the home to scrumptious pan-fried dumplings.

BUCKHEAD

Kyma (☎ 404-262-0702; 3085 Piedmont Rd; mains $19-34; ⏰ 5-11pm Mon-Sat) This restaurant luxuriates in the sensuous simplicity of Greek food. Start with the trio of traditional spreads, then choose between fish: will it be the dorado, the pompano or the barramundi? This is a high-end place, so dress accordingly.

LITTLE FIVE POINTS

Vortex Bar & Grill (☎ 404-688-1828; burgers from $6.45; ⏰ 11am-midnight Sun-Thu, to 3am Fri & Sat); L5P (438 Moreland Ave); Midtown (878 Peachtree St) Walk through the gaping jaws of a giant skull and enter the Vortex, a scrappy joint with a snarky menu boasting '140 styles of gourmet burgers,' an ideal meal before hitting the L5P bar scene. Ages 18 and up only.

VIRGINIA-HIGHLAND

Alon's Bakery (☎ 404-872-6000; 1394 N Highland Ave; sandwiches from $6.30; 7am-8pm Mon-Fri, 8am-8pm Sat, 9am-4pm Sun) Atlanta's most revered bakery doubles is a go-to market for anyone needing a dinner-party item or picnic-basket stuffer. The goods include gourmet cheeses, wine, chicken salad, egg salad and all manner of pastry.

ourpick **Sotto Sotto** (☎ 404-523-6678; 313 N Highland Ave NE; dishes $16-32; ⏰ 5:30-11:30pm Mon-Thu, to midnight Fri & Sat, to 10pm Sun) A lively, trendy restaurant with crisp service and an ever-delighting menu of Italian dishes. The risotto is heaven on earth. Reservations suggested.

DECATUR

Watershed (☎ 404-378-4900; www.watershedrestaurant.com; mains $12-34; ⏰ 11am-10pm Mon-Sat, 10am-3pm Sun) Simply outstanding (and outstandingly simple), this is the place for traditional Southern food done up with just a touch of class. Tuesday night is fried chicken night; get there early or the birds will be gone. Any other night, order the veggie plate – you've never had a better one. The restaurant's vibe is friendly and casual, and James Beard Award–winning chef Scott Peacock is nothing less than a local hero.

Drinking

Atlanta likes to drink. The following spots, a few of many, include a local institution, a swanky hotel bar and a great dive. When all else fails, walk around Virginia-Highland (if you're feeling posh) or Little Five Points (if you're feeling grimy) to choose between several clustered establishments.

Manuel's Tavern (☎ 404-525-3447; 602 N Highland Ave) A longtime political hangout that draws a good, conversational beer-drinking crowd.

Euclid Avenue Yacht Club (☎ 404-688-2582; 1136 Euclid Ave) A divey bar ideal for grabbing a drink before a show at the nearby Variety Playhouse. Smokers and nonsmokers get separate rooms.

Glenn Hotel rooftop bar (☎ 404-521-2250; 110 Marietta St NW) If you're facing the reception desk, head through the unmarked door to the right and take the elevator to the roof. Then, feast your eyes on the skyline.

Entertainment

Atlanta has big-city nightlife, with lots of live music and cultural events. Check out the free *Creative Loafing* for weekly listings.

THEATERS

Fox Theatre (☎ 404-881-2100; www.foxtheatre.org; 660 Peachtree St NE) A spectacular 1929 movie palace with fanciful Moorish and Egyptian designs. It hosts Broadway shows, and concerts in an auditorium holding more than 4500 people.

Woodruff Arts Center (☎ 404-733-4200; www.woodruffcenter.org; 1280 Peachtree St NE at 15th St) An arts campus hosting the High Museum, the Atlanta Symphony Orchestra and the Alliance Theatre.

Center for Puppetry Arts (☎ 404-873-3391; www.puppet.org; 1404 Spring St NW; tickets $12-22) Performances range from *Beauty and the Beast* to more adult-oriented productions at this wonderful puppetry center (p408).

LIVE MUSIC & NIGHTCLUBS

Cover charges at the following vary nightly. Check their respective websites for music calendars and ticket prices.

EARL (☎ 404-522-3950; 488 Flat Shoals Ave) The indie rocker's pub of choice – a smoky restaurant with surprisingly good food; it's also a bar and a busy live-music venue.

Eddie's Attic (☎ 404-377-4976; www.eddiesattic.com; 515b N McDonough St, Decatur; ⏰) One of the city's best venues to hear live folk and acoustic music, in a nonsmoking atmosphere seven nights a week.

Halo (☎ 404-962-7333; www.halolounge.com; 817 W Peachtree St) If you can find this sexy industrial lounge, which is tucked into the north side of the Biltmore building, you're cool enough

THE SOUTH

to chill on the space-age furniture, and to drink at a glowing marble bar that resembles hot lava.

Variety Playhouse (☎ 404-524-7354; www.variety-playhouse.com; 1099 Euclid Ave NE) A smartly booked and well-run concert venue for a variety of touring artists.

SPORTS

Order tickets to sporting events through **Ticketmaster** (☎ 404-249-6400; www.ticketmaster.com).

Atlanta Braves (☎ 404-522-7630; www.atlantabraves.com; tickets $1-60) The Major League Baseball (MLB) team plays at Turner Field.

Atlanta Falcons (☎ 770-965-3115; www.atlantafalcons.com; tickets from $25) The National Football League (NFL) team plays in the Georgia Dome.

Atlanta Hawks (☎ 866-715-1500; www.hawks.com), the National Basketball Association (NBA) team, and **Atlanta Thrashers** (☎ 866-715-1500; www.atlantathrashers.com), the National Hockey League (NHL) team, play at Philips Arena.

Shopping

Atlantans love to shop. Virginia-Highland has a unique selection of boutique shops, including the supremely fashionable **Bill Hallman** (☎ 404-607-1171; 784-792 N Highland Ave; ☼ at least 11am-7pm), which clothes lads and lasses alike. Find vintage and secondhand threads in Little Five Points or at the smartly stocked **Lucky Exchange** (☎ 404-817-7715; 212 Ponce de Leon Ave; ☼ 11:30am-6pm Mon-Sat, 12-5pm Sun). The teeny East Atlanta boutique **Rare Footage** (☎ 404-215-2188; 493 Flat Shoals Ave; ☼ noon-8pm Mon-Sat, to 6pm Sun) sells limited-edition sneakers.

The two major high-end shopping malls are adjacent to each other in Buckhead – **Lenox Square** (☎ 404-233-6767; 3393 Peachtree Rd NE; ☼ 10am-9pm Mon-Sat, noon-6pm Sun) and **Phipps Plaza** (☎ 404-262-0992; 3500 Peachtree Rd NE; ☼ 10am-9pm Mon-Sat, noon-5:30pm Sun) – with upscale shops such as Barneys New York Co-Op and Giorgio Armani.

Getting There & Away

Atlanta's huge **Hartsfield-Jackson International Airport** (☎ 800-897-1910; www.atlanta-airport.com), 12 miles south of downtown, is a major regional hub and an international gateway. With nearly 85 million visitors a year, it is the busiest airport in the world in overall passenger traffic.

The **Greyhound terminal** (☎ 404-584-1728; 232 Forsyth St) is next to the Marta Garnett station.

Some sample fares and journey times include Nashville, TN ($45.50, five hours), New Orleans, LA ($77, 10½ hours), New York ($109, 20 hours), Miami, FL ($104, 16 hours) and Savannah, GA ($42.50, 4¾ hours).

The **Amtrak station** (☎ 404-881-3062; 1688 Peachtree St NW at Deering Rd) is just north of downtown.

Getting Around

The **Metropolitan Atlanta Rapid Transit Authority** (Marta; ☎ 404-848-4711; www.itsmarta.com; fare $2.25) rail line travels to/from the airport to downtown, along with a few less-useful routes used mostly by commuters.

The **Atlanta Airport Shuttle** (☎ 404-524-3400; one-way tickets $16.50-20.50) also transports passengers to hotels all over the city in a nine-passenger shuttle (from 6am to midnight). The shuttle and car-rental agencies have desks in the airport situated at the baggage-claim level.

Driving in Atlanta can be infuriating. You'll often find yourself sitting in traffic jams, and it's easy to get disoriented – a road map is invaluable.

AROUND ATLANTA
Stone Mountain

About 20 miles east of Atlanta, Stone Mountain juts into the Georgia sky – a giant mount of granite that can't, and shouldn't, be missed. You'll visit the mountain through **Stone Mountain Park** (☎ 770-498-5690; www.stonemountainpark.com; Hwy 78 E, exit 8; per car $8; ☼ park 6am-midnight, attractions from 10am), which combines natural splendor with a creepy Confederate nostalgia. (The rebel flag, for instance, still flies at

---

WHAT THE…?

Towering over Marietta like some kind of poultry Godzilla is the aptly named **Big Chicken** (cnr US 41 & Hwy 120), a skyscraping mechanical bird with a rolling eyeball and moving beak. The Big Chicken is an odd Atlanta icon dating back to the mid-'60s, and at this point it has become as much of a landmark as anything in the metro area. Today it looms over a KFC restaurant, which sells stuffed replicas for $7.99. Big Chicken history is preserved there on the wall and under glass, along with children's artwork inspired by the bird.

the mountain's base, and the trio of Robert E Lee, Stonewall Jackson and Jefferson Davis are carved into the mountain's side.) If you're up for a climb, skip the Crossroads area (a tourist trap cluster of old-timey shops) and head for the walk-up trail, a 1.3 mile hike that affords a lovely view from the summit. You can see telephone poles covered in chewing gum on the way up, and the city of Atlanta off in the distance once you get to the top. Camping and basic hotel accommodations are available in the park.

NORTH GEORGIA

The southern end of the great Appalachian Range extends some 40 miles into Georgia's far north, providing some superb mountain scenery and wild white-water rivers, a topography quite unlike anywhere else in Georgia. The fall colors emerge late here, peaking in October. Free brochures with directions for self-guided driving tours are available at most of the region's visitor centers.

A few days are warranted to see sites like the 1200ft-deep **Tallulah Gorge** (☎ 706-754-7970), the scenery and hiking trails at **Vogel State Park** (☎ 706-745-2628) and the interesting collection of Appalachian folk arts at the **Foxfire Museum** (☎ 706-746-5828; adult/child $5/free; ☼ 9am-4pm Mon-Fri) in Mountain City.

Dahlonega

In 1828 Dahlonega was the site of the first gold rush in the USA. The boom these days, though, is in tourism. It's an easy excursion from Atlanta and offers intriguing history surrounded by beautiful mountain scenery.

Walking around the historic main square is a major event itself. Many offbeat shops compete for tourist dollars. The **visitor center** (☎ 706-864-3711; www.dahlonega.org; 13 S Park St; ☼ 9am-5:30pm) has plenty of information on area sites and activities (including hiking, canoeing, kayaking, rafting and mountain biking). In the center of the square, the **Dahlonega Gold Museum** (☎ 706-864-2257; adult/child $4/2.50; ☼ 9am-5pm Mon-Sat, from 10am Sun) tells the fascinating story of gold mining in the region.

Amicalola Falls State Park (☎ 706-265-4703), 18 miles west of Dahlonega on Hwy 52, features the 729ft **Amicalola Falls**, the highest waterfall in Georgia. The park offers spectacular scenery, in addition to excellent hiking and mountain-biking trails.

Helen

Helen is the sort of town you can only find in the USA: a faux Swiss-German mountain village where the shops have names like 'Das ist Leather.' Beginning in 1968, business leaders looked for ideas to transform the dreary lumber town into a tourist attraction. Soon, the Bavarian look took hold and somehow this place has become a popular tourist destination.

The **visitor center** (☎ 800-858-8027; www.helenga .org; 726 Brukenstrasse; ☼ 9am-5pm Mon-Sat, 10am-4pm Sun) is on the southern side of town. **Oktoberfest**, from mid-September to early November is a popular event, with plenty of oompah bands and bratwurst. In summer, you'll see hundreds of folks **Shooting the Hooch** – going down the slow-moving Chattahoochee River on inner tubes. The best way to see Helen is on foot; just join the throngs of slow-moving tourists. If the crowds get too much, head to nearby **Unicoi State Park** (☎ 706-878-2201), a beautiful park with hiking trails, cabins, campsites and attractive mountain scenery.

CENTRAL GEORGIA

Georgia is a massive state, and this region is a kind of catch-all for everything that's not metro Atlanta, mountainous north Georgia or swampy Savannah-centric south Georgia. The remaining area feels rustic and Southern; it's the difference between suburban living and country living. You're apt to see open fields and red clay along the side of the road.

Athens

A beery, artsy and utterly laid-back college town roughly 70 miles east of Atlanta, Athens has an extremely popular football team (the University of Georgia Bulldogs), a worldfamous music scene (which has launched artists including the B-52's, REM and Widespread Panic) and a burgeoning restaurant culture (featuring star chef Hugh Acheson and his dynamite eatery Five & Ten). Known throughout Georgia as UGA, the university drives the culture of Athens and ensures an ever-replenishing supply of young barhoppers and concertgoers. The pleasant, walkable downtown offers a plethora of funky choices for eating, drinking and shopping. At least three routes run from Atlanta to Athens (Hwy 316, Hwy 129 and Hwy 78), each with relative pluses and minuses.

THE SOUTH

The **Athens Welcome Center** (☎ 706-353-1820; 280 E Dougherty St; ◷ 10am-6pm Mon-Sat, from noon Sun), in a historic antebellum house at the corner of Thomas St, provides maps and information on local tours – these include a Civil War tour and a 'Walking Tour of Athens Music History,' printed in conjunction with the local entertainment magazine, *Flagpole*.

SIGHTS & ACTIVITIES

With winding outdoor paths and a socio-historical edge, Athens' **State Botanical Garden of Georgia** (☎ 706-542-1244; www.uga.edu/~botgarden; 2450 S Milledge Ave; suggested donation $2; ◷ 8am-6pm, to 8pm summer) makes Atlanta's seem tacky and overpriced. Athens does it right, using signs to provide smart context for its amazing collection of plants, which runs the gamut from rare and threatened species to a tantalizing watermelon patch.

Oconee Forest Park (http://warnell.forestry.uga .edu/ofp/facilities.htm; cnr College Station Rd & Alumni Dr), located at the back of the university's expansive Recreational Sports Complex, has wooded hiking trails and an enormous off-leash dog area.

SLEEPING & EATING

Hilton Garden Inn (☎ 706-353-6800; www.stayhgi.com; 390 E Washington St; r $109-139, ste $239-259; P 🍽 🚫 🐾 wi-fi) A bright, corporate-style downtown hotel with all the trimmings. Parking's $8 per day.

Foundry Park Inn & Spa (☎ 706-549-7020; www .foundryparkinn.com; 295 E Dougherty St; r $115-145; P 🍽 🐾 wi-fi) Friendly, handsome and well-located near the thriving (and super walkable) downtown area, the Foundry Park is the ideal Athens hotel. In addition to its 119 rooms and on-site spa, the hotel campus includes the Melting Point, a cozy music venue.

Grit (☎ 706-543-6592; www.thegrit.com; 199 Prince Ave; mains $5-7; ◷ 11am-10pm Mon-Fri, from 10am Sat & Sun) A vegetarian joint serving hot noodle bowls, scrumptious brunches and tofu. Hungry morning types should belly up to a 'border patrol' breakfast of eggs, pinto beans and more slathered onto a giant flour tortilla.

Clocked (☎ 706-548-9175; 259 W Washington St; burger special $6.50; ◷ 11am-11pm Sun-Thu, to 4am Fri & Sat) Perhaps the world's hippest diner? Clocked conjures up goodies like watermelon lemonade and sweet potato chicken soup.

Big City Bread (☎ 706-543-1187; www.bigcitybread .net; 393 Finley St; ◷ 7am-6pm Mon-Sat, to 3pm Sun) A few café-style seats are available indoors, but most folks sit outside (often with dogs) to enjoy tasty breakfasts that include pastries and hot dishes. Morning rush? Get the mixed berry tart to go.

Five & Ten (☎ 706-546-7300; www.fiveandten.com; 1653 S Lumpkin St; mains $16-31; ◷ 5:30-10pm Sun-Thu, to 11pm Fri & Sat, 10:30am-2:30pm Sun) Driven by superior ingredients (as opposed to showy technique), Five & Ten ranks among the South's very best restaurants. Its menu is earthy and slightly gamey: oysters, cheese, risotto, North Carolina trout and frogmore stew. Brunch is sensational. If you want a table for dinner you'd best call ahead.

DRINKING & ENTERTAINMENT

40 Watt Club (☎ 706-549-7871; www.40watt.com; 285 W Washington St) The famous 40 Watt is still one of America's greatest rock clubs. It has lounges in the back, a tiki bar off to the side, Christmas lights overhead, $2 PBR beers behind the bar and indie rock on stage. No wonder it's legendary.

Manhattan Café (337 N Hull St) A dark, divey, decadent bar where the upholstery is ripped and the specialty cocktail is spicy Blenheim Ginger Ale with Maker's Mark whiskey.

Aroma's (☎ 706-208-0059; 1235 S Milledge Ave) A romantic retreat from the downtown hubbub, serving wine and excellent cheese plates. There's even a fireplace to warm up cool nights. Keep your eye out for shocking by-the-glass champagne specials.

Ciné (☎ 706-353-7377; www.athenscine.com; 234 W Hancock Ave) A smart two-screen art-house movie theater with a little bar in the lobby.

Macon

Macon is a pleasant little city with a few interesting sights. The town was established in 1823 and prospered as a cotton port on the Ocmulgee River. The area had a strong Unionist and peace movement before and during the Civil War, which left Macon mostly unscathed. Many antebellum houses remain today. In fact, it has more structures on the National Register of Historic Places (5500) than any other Georgian city.

The **convention & visitor's bureau** (☎ 478-743-1074; www.maconga.org; 450 Martin Luther King Jr Blvd) has a website with a downloadable visitors guide.

Georgia Music Hall of Fame (☎ 888-427-6257; www .gamusichall.com; 200 Martin Luther King Jr Blvd; adult/child $8/3.50; ◷ 9am-5pm Mon-Sat, from 1pm Sun) showcases the multitude of musical talent that has bloomed in Georgia, including REM, James

---

LET THE (REDNECK) GAMES BEGIN

Every year on a hot, steamy day in July, Southerners converge on the small town of Dublin to compete in the annual **Redneck Games** (☎ 478-272-4422; http://redneckgames .tripod.com; admission free). The festivities begin with the ceremonial lighting of the BBQ grill and, along with live music, burgers, dogs and Bud, there's plenty of action. As folks wave their Confederate flags and holler 'yee haw!' others compete in a range of events, including the mud-pit belly flop, bobbing for pig's feet, the hubcap hurl and the ever-popular armpit serenade. The event is held at Buckeye Park in East Dublin, about 55 miles east of Macon.

Brown, Little Richard, Ray Charles and the Allman Brothers.

Held the third week of March, Macon's **Cherry Blossom Festival** (☎ 478-751-7429; www .cherryblossom.com) celebrates the blossoming of 250,000 flowering Japanese Yoshino cherry trees.

Ocmulgee National Monument (☎ 478-752-8257; www.nps.gov/ocmu/; 1207 Emery Hwy; admission free; ☺ 9am-5pm), just east of town, is an archaeological site with Native American burial mounds, artifacts and an ancient earth lodge.

SAVANNAH

Like a Southern belle with a split personality, this grand historic town revolves around formal antebellum architecture and unbridled public debauchery. It sits alongside the Savannah River, about 18 miles from the coast, amid Lowcountry swamps and mammoth live oak trees dripping with Spanish moss. With its gorgeous mansions, cotton warehouses and Colonial public buildings, Savannah preserves its past with pride, grace and a slight smirk. Unlike its sister city of Charleston, SC, which retains its reputation as a dignified and refined cultural center, Savannah revels in being the bad girl – the town has been described as 'a beautiful lady with a dirty face,' and in some ways it resembles a pint-sized New Orleans. Savannah loves its sinful pleasures, be they cheese grits, cocktails, or the bump and grind of partying local students.

Savannah has a somber side, but she never takes herself too seriously. Savannah College of Art & Design – which is known locally as SCAD – has a surprisingly strong presence that keeps the city from getting too staid. The city's massive St Patrick's Day celebration is a legendary rite of spring and there is an entire cottage industry catering to those tourists who have heard that Savannah is haunted – curious ghost-hunters are able to arrange to take tours of the city in a chauffeured hearse.

Orientation & Information

Savannah's Historic District is a rectangle bounded by Savannah River, Forsyth Park, E Broad St and Martin Luther King Jr Blvd. Almost everything of interest to visitors lies either within or just outside this area, though having a street map will certainly help you to keep your bearings. In converted cotton warehouses situated along the Savannah River, you will find a commercial district of bars, restaurants and shops. City Market is an equally important district of shops and restaurants near Franklin Sq, and W Broughton St is a cosmopolitan shopping drag.

Each of the 21 of Savannah's original 24 squares marks a truly exquisite place to relax among flower gardens, shade trees and – usually – a monument to some notable person who is buried in the square.

Bull St, which runs north–south, divides the east and west branches of Savannah's streets.

BOOKSTORES
E Shaver, Bookseller (☎ 912-234-7257; 326 Bull St; ☺ 9am-6pm Mon-Sat) Shelves are stocked with tomes on local and regional history and the collected works of Paula Deen.

EMERGENCY
Main police station (☎ 912-232-4141)

INTERNET
Main Library (☎ 912-652-3600; 2002 Bull St, btwn 36th & 37th; ☺ 9am-9pm Mon-Thu, to 6pm Fri & Sat, 2-6pm Sun) Offers free internet and wi-fi access.

MEDICAL SERVICES
Candler Hospital (☎ 912-819-6000; 5353 Reynolds St)
CVS Pharmacy (☎ 912-238-1494; cnr Bull & W Broughton Sts)

MONEY
There are plenty of ATMs throughout the city. For full service, head to Johnson Sq, where there are several major banks.

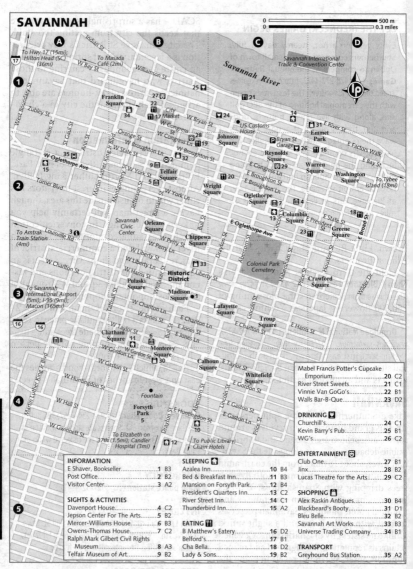

SAVANNAH

INFORMATION	
E Shaver, Bookseller................**1** B3	
Post Office...............................**2** B2	
Visitor Center.........................**3** A2	

SIGHTS & ACTIVITIES	
Davenport House.....................**4** C2	
Jepson Center For The Arts......**5** B2	
Mercer-Williams House............**6** B3	
Owens-Thomas House..............**7** C2	
Ralph Mark Gilbert Civil Rights	
Museum................................**8** A3	
Telfair Museum of Art.............**9** B2	

SLEEPING	
Azalea Inn..............................**10** B4	
Bed & Breakfast Inn................**11** B3	
Mansion on Forsyth Park.........**12** B4	
President's Quarters Inn..........**13** C2	
River Street Inn......................**14** C1	
Thunderbird Inn.....................**15** A2	

EATING	
B Matthew's Eatery................**16** D2	
Belford's................................**17** B1	
Cha Bella................................**18** D2	
Lady & Sons...........................**19** B2	

Mabel Francis Potter's Cupcake	
Emporium.............................**20** C2	
River Street Sweets.................**21** C1	
Vinnie Van GoGo's.................**22** B1	
Walls Bar-B-Que.....................**23** D2	

DRINKING	
Churchill's..............................**24** C1	
Kevin Barry's Pub...................**25** B1	
WG's......................................**26** C1	

ENTERTAINMENT	
Club One................................**27** B1	
Jinx..**28** B2	
Lucas Theatre for the Arts.......**29** C2	

SHOPPING	
Alex Raskin Antiques...............**30** B4	
Blackbeard's Booty..................**31** D1	
Bleu Belle...............................**32** B2	
Savannah Art Works................**33** B3	
Universe Trading Company.......**34** B1	

TRANSPORT	
Greyhound Bus Station............**35** A2	

POST

Post office (☎ 912-235-4653) Historic District (cnr W State & Barnard Sts; ⏱ 8am-5pm Mon-Fri); Main (2 N Fahm St at Bay St; ⏱ 8am-5:30pm Mon-Fri, 9am-1pm Sat)

TOURIST INFORMATION

Visitor center (☎ 912-944-0455; www.savannahvisit .com; 301 Martin Luther King Jr Blvd; ⏱ 8:30am-5pm

Mon-Fri, from 9am Sat & Sun) Excellent resources and services are available in this center, based in a restored 1860's train station. Many privately operated city tours start here.

Sights & Activities

One of the best ways to enjoy Savannah is to sit on a bench in one of the beautiful squares and simply watch the world go by. You'll see businessmen in seersucker suits and refined Southern ladies in sunbonnets, mixed with nose-pierced artists from the Savannah College of Art & Design as they try to capture on canvas the drama of dripping moss.

MUSEUMS & PARKS

The Central Park of Savannah is a sprawling rectangular greenspace called **Forsyth Park**, which has lots of room for jogging, tossing Frisbees and walking dogs – or ferrets, as the case may be. (We've seen it.) The park's beautiful fountain is a quintessential photo-op.

Along with silver from the 1800s and a colossal oil painting depicting a scene from the Hundred Years War, Sylvia Shaw's famous 1936 *Bird Girl* sculpture – the one on the cover of *Midnight in the Garden of Good and Evil* – stands inside the slightly musty **Telfair Museum of Art** (☎ 912-232-1177; www.telfair .org; 121 Barnard St; adult/child $10/4; 🕙 noon-5pm Mon, 10am-5pm Tue-Sat, 1-5pm Sun). A $15 multivenue pass allows discounted admission to two affiliated museums, the Jepson and the Owens-Thomas House.

The **Jepson Center for the Arts** (JCA; ☎ 912-790-8800; 207 W York St; adult/child $10/4; 🕙 noon-5pm Mon, 10am-5pm Tue-Sat, 1-5pm Sun) is fresh off a 2006 opening and is looking pretty darn space age by Savannah's standards. The JCA focuses on 20th- and 21st-century art. Its contents are modest in size, but intriguing. *Swarm*, a video piece from 2002, paints your image while you stand slack jawed before it. There's also a neat interactive area for kids.

On the outskirts of the historic district is the **Ralph Mark Gilbert Civil Rights Museum** (☎ 912-231-8900; 460 Martin Luther King Jr Blvd; 🕙 9am-5pm Mon-Sat). Leaving the larger history of the movement to the Civil Rights Institute in Birmingham, Savannah's museum focuses on the local history of segregated schools, hotels, hospitals, jobs and lunch counters.

HISTORIC HOMES

Completed in 1819 by British architect William Jay, the **Owens-Thomas House** (☎ 912-233-9743; 124 Abercorn St; adult/child $10/4; 🕙 noon-5pm Mon, 10am-5pm Tue-Sat, 1-5pm Sun) exemplifies Regency architecture, which is known for its symmetry. The guided tour is fussy, but it delivers interesting trivia about the number of coats of paint on the walls (22) and the number of years by which this mansion preceded the White House in getting running water (about 20).

You can't leave Savannah without seeing the **Mercer-Williams House** (☎ 912-236-6352; www .mercerhouse.com; 429 Bull St; adult/child $12.50/$8). Although Jim Williams, the Savannah art dealer portrayed by Kevin Spacey in the film version of *Midnight in the Garden of Good and Evil*, died back in 1990, his infamous mansion didn't become a museum until 2004. You're not allowed to see the upstairs, where Williams' family still lives, but the downstairs is an interior decorator's fantasy. Williams' sister gives lunchtime tours.

Davenport House (☎ 912-236-8097; www.daven porthousemuseum.org; 324 E State St) Federal-style architecture isn't exactly scintillating, and the house has very little original furnishing, but the tour is sweet and the attention to detail is serious enough that fake bugs crawl on the fake food in the dining room.

Sleeping

Thunderbird Inn (☎ 912-232-2661; www.thethunder birdinn.com; 611 W Oglethorpe Ave; r incl breakfast from $99; 🅿 🐾 wi-fi) Vintage chic reigns at the Thunderbird, a renovated motel with rooms starting at $99, including internet and continental breakfast. Parking is free, too. The hotel is just outside the tourist area, across from the Greyhound station – look for the humongous neon sign.

Azalea Inn (☎ 912-236-2707; www.azaleainn.com; 217 E Huntingdon St; r from $139; 🐾 🗶 🖭) Lemon yellow and located on a quiet street, the Azalea also has a lovely little pool in the back.

ourpick Bed & Breakfast Inn (☎ 912-238-0518; www.savannahbnb.com; 117 W Gordon St; r from $149; 🗶 🐾 wi-fi) Here's a B&B that puts you spittin' distance from the Mercer-Williams House and serves blueberry pancakes for breakfast. Just don't miss the place – it looks like an apartment building at first glance. Once inside, allow sweetheart manager Gussie Baker to take care of you. You've got 16 rooms and four villas from which to choose.

President's Quarters Inn (☎ 800-233-1776; www .presidentsquarters.com; 225 E President St; r from $173; 🅿 🗶 🐾 wi-fi) Built in 1855 as a duplex, it's now a B&B across the street from the Owens Thomas house. One bonus: wine from 5pm to 6pm. Another: free private parking, a rarity in the historic district.

River Street Inn (☎ 912-234-6400; www.riverstreetinn .com; 124 E Bay St; r from $189; 🐾 🗶 wi-fi) Don't

THE SOUTH

trip on the wildly uneven floors in this old-timey hotel with a plum location. When reserving, specify whether you want a view of the city or the Savannah River. Some balconies available.

Mansion on Forsyth Park (☎ 912-238-5158; www .mansiononforsythpark.com; 700 Drayton St; r from $329; P ⚡ 🐾 ✕ wi-fi) The location is choice. The design motif is bohemian chic. The rooms are absurdly expensive. But if you want luxe accommodations, the 18,000-sq-ft Mansion delivers. (The sexy bathrooms alone are practically worth the money, with their frosted-glass showers, sunken tubs and electric candlelight.) The hotel feels pretty doggone glam with art all over the walls, a spa downstairs and an adjacent cocktail lounge featuring a Bosendorfer – the Rolls-Royce of pianos. Parking costs $19 per day.

Eating
BUDGET

Mabel Francis Potter's Cupcake Emporium (☎ 912-341-8014; 6 E State St; cupcakes $1.50; ⏲ 10:30am-6pm Mon-Sat, noon-5pm Sun) Knicknacks up front, fresh-baked cupcakes in the back. Get one to go and nibble (or gobble) it up while you're walking. The place boasts dozens of flavors including a butter cream cupcake with frilly pink frosting.

River Street Sweets (☎ 912-234-4608; 13 E River St; pralines per pound $14.95; ⏲ 9am-11pm) A tip: order your pralines not at the cash register, but directly from the praline counter, where they're nice and warm. If you love them – and you will – you can ship some home.

Vinnie Van GoGo's (☎ 912-233-6394; 317 W Bryan St; slice $2.50; ⏲ 4-11:30pm Mon-Thu, to 1am Fri, noon-1am Sat, to 11:30pm Sun) OK, so the joint is cramped. And the ordering process can be intense. But the New York–style pizza rocks hard, with crust about as thin as a dollar bill.

B Matthews Eatery (☎ 912-233-1319; www.bmat thewseatery.com; 325 E Bay St; breakfast $5-10; ⏲ 8am-10pm Mon-Sat, 11:30am-3pm Sun) Located on a mellow corner of bustling Bay St, B Matthews serves locally roasted coffee, croissant sandwiches and a Savannah staple: shrimp and grits. Dinner, too.

our pick Walls Bar-B-Que (☎ 912-232-9754; 515 E York Lane; plates from $6.40; ⏲ 11am-9pm Thu-Sat) Adventurous barbecue lovers, keep looking until you find this glorious 'cue hut on tiny E York Lane, tucked behind E York St near Price St. Once you arrive, order a baseball-sized mound of deviled crab – watch out for shell bits – and the juicy smoked pork of your hog heaven dreams.

Belford's (☎ 912-233-2626; 315 St Julian St; breakfast $6.95-14.95; ⏲ 8am-10pm Mon-Sat, 11:30am-3pm Sun) You can get the standard breakfast buffet at this City Market restaurant, but that would mean passing on the cheesy blue-crab frittata, served with grits and fruit.

Masada Cafe (☎ 912-236-9499; 2301 W Bay St; plates from $7.75; ⏲ 11am-7pm Mon-Sat, to 6pm Sun) Yes, it's a church cafeteria. No, you don't need to be a member of the congregation to eat there. Just come on in and belly up to the cafeteria-style line, where you pick your meat (country fried steak, pork chop, oxtails, fried chicken) and your sides (stuffing, red rice, mac-n-cheese). Saturday is rib day.

MIDRANGE

Cha Bella (☎ 912-790-7888; 102 E Broad St; brunch $15.95; ⏲ 5:30-10pm daily, brunch 11am-3pm Sun) The patio has four charming swings in which to bide your time while waiting for your croissant French toast stuffed with peaches and covered in bourbon maple syrup. A high-end dinner – think $38 lamb chops – is also served.

Lady & Sons (☎ 912-233-2600; www.ladyandsons .com; 102 W Congress St; buffet $17; ⏲ lunch 11am-3pm Mon-Sat, dinner from 5pm Mon-Sat, 11am-5pm Sun) Savannah's irrepressible culinary doyenne Paula Deen has created a monster. Her country cookin' is indeed delicious – the fried chicken will have you begging for mercy – but you've gotta know what you're doing to get a table. Show up at 9:30am for lunch or 3:30pm for dinner to put your name on the list. One other trick: try eating alone in the bar.

TOP END

Elizabeth on 37th (☎ 912-236-5547; www .elizabethon37th.net; mains $27-34; 105 E 37th St; ⏲ from 6pm) Not as good as it should be for the price (but still darn good), Elizabeth puts diners in a lovely setting and presents ambitious cuisine without too much fuss. Specials might include lacquered quail, or potato-crusted snapper with squash and Brussels sprouts. A nice touch: eight varietals of wine by the glass. Locals warn that the neighborhood isn't safe for walking, so look for close on-street parking.

Drinking

Churchill's (☎ 912-232-8501; 13 W Bay St) A British pub serving the requisite grub. If it's warm outside, expect the rooftop terrace to be mobbed with a country clubbish crowd.

Kevin Barry's Pub (☎ 912-233-9626; www.kevinbarrys.com; 117 W River St) Harp and Guinness are on tap in the downstairs bar, which feels like a cave. The upstairs balcony has a dynamite view of the river. Irish fare served.

WG's (☎ 912-236-7696; 17 Lincoln St) Feeling more like a Hobbit house than a bar, this rustic-chic dive bar will put you in the company of thirsty locals, not rowdy tourists. Order an unusual beer (Celebrator, anyone?) and head out to the cozy veranda. Or shoot pool.

Entertainment

Club One (☎ 912-232-0200; www.clubone-online.com; 1 Jefferson St) Home to legendary drag queen The Lady Chablis, this multilevel gay club gets naughty even on her off nights with a cabaret show led by the saucy hostess Destiny.

Jinx (☎ 912-236-2281; www.thejinx.net; 127 W Congress St) Metalheads and bikers, here's your hangout. Expect live music at punishing volume, and try to get the booth with the Ms Pac Man game doubling as a drink table.

Lucas Theatre for the Arts (☎ 912-525-5040; www.scad.edu/venues/lucas; 32 Abercorn St) Hosting concerts (guitarist Jonny Lang), plays (*Guys and Dolls*) and films (*The Day the Earth Stood Still*) in a historic building dating 1921.

Shopping

Blackbeard's Booty (E River St at Lincoln St) The place to go for puzzles, kites, Jolly Roger flags, train sets and Edgar Allan Poe bobblehead dolls.

Bleu Belle (☎ 912-443-0011; www.bleubelle.com; 205 W Broughtron St; ☼ 10am-6pm Mon-Sat, noon-4pm Sun) A friendly boutique selling flirty women's clothes. Think BCBG dresses, Seven For All Mankind jeans, and lacy tanks.

Alex Raskin Antiques (☎ 912-232-8205; 441 Bull St; ☼ 10am-5pm Mon-Sat) Selling a generous selection of tables and dressers. The place even smells old.

Savannah Art Works (☎ 912-443-9331; www.savannahartworks.com; 240 Bull St; ☼ 10:30am-6pm Mon-Sat, 1-5pm Sun) Come here for folk art with a positive vibe, like a big ol' heart made from empty Coke and Pabst Blue Ribbon cans.

Universe Trading Company (☎ 912-233-1585; 27 Montgomery St) Bric-a-brac doesn't begin to cover the contents of this cluttered salvage and antiques emporium. Walking through this place is like taking the world's deepest Dumpster dive. The wares include lawn ornaments, used shoes, vinyl records, cigar store Indians, life-sized Blues Brothers statues and a fake shark head with '$185 firm' on the price tag.

Getting There & Around

The visitor center touts shuttles from the airport to Historic District hotels for $25 round-trip. Once in town, you won't need a car to enjoy Savannah. If you have one, it's best to park it and walk or take tours. **Chatham Area Transit** (CAT; ☎ 912-233-5767) operates local buses, including a free shuttle that makes its way around the Historic District and stops within a couple of blocks of nearly every major site.

The **Savannah/Hilton Head International Airport** (SAV; ☎ 912-964-0514; www.savannahairport.com) is about 5 miles west of downtown off I-16.

Greyhound (☎ 912-232-2135; 610 W Oglethorpe Ave) has connections to Atlanta ($40, about five hours), Charleston, SC ($29, about two hours), and Jacksonville, FL ($26.50, 2½ hours).

The **Amtrak station** (☎ 800-872-7245; 2611 Seaboard Coastline Dr) is just a few miles west of the Historic District.

AROUND SAVANNAH

About 18 miles east of Savannah at the end of US Hwy 80, **Tybee Island** (☎ visitor center 912-786-5444; www.tybeevisit.com; 1st St/US Hwy 80; ☼ 9:30am-5pm) is a sleepy beach community with 3 miles of wide, sandy beach, good for swimming and castle building. The 154ft-tall **Tybee Island Lighthouse** (☎ 912-786-5801; www.tybeelighthouse.org; adult/child $6/5; ☼ 9am-5:30pm Wed-Mon) is the oldest in Georgia. The strenuous 178 steps to the top reward you with magnificent views. The admission also gets you into neighboring **Tybee Island Museum**.

BRUNSWICK & THE GOLDEN ISLES

Georgia is blessed with a string of islands running down the coast. The islands have very different characters, and provide experiences ranging from the rustic to the spoiled rotten.

With its large shrimp-boat fleet and downtown historic district shaded beneath

THE SOUTH

lush live oaks, Brunswick dates from 1733 and has charms you might miss when sailing by on I-95 or the Golden Isle Parkway (US Hwy 17). During WWII, Brunswick shipyards constructed 99 Liberty transport ships for the navy. Today, a new 23ft scale model at **Mary Ross Waterfront Park** on Bay St stands as a memorial to those ships and their builders.

Brunswick-Golden Isles Visitors Bureau (☎ 912-265-0620; www.bgivb.com; Hwy 17 at St Simons Causeway; ☺ 8:30am-5pm Mon-Fri) has loads of practical information about all the Golden Isles.

St Simons Island

Famous for its golf courses, resorts and majestic live oaks, St Simons Island is the largest and most developed of the Golden Isles. It lies 75 miles south of Savannah and just 5 miles from Brunswick. While the southern half of the island is a thickly settled residential and resort area, the northern half and adjacent **Sea Island** and **Little St Simons** offer vast tracts of coastal wilderness amid a tidewater estuary.

Jekyll Island

An exclusive refuge for millionaires in the late 19th and early 20th centuries, Jekyll Island is a 4000-year-old barrier island with 10 miles of beaches. Today it's an unusual clash of wilderness, historically preserved buildings, modern hotels and a massive campground (complete with wi-fi). It's an easily navigable place – you can get around by car, horse or bicycle, but there's a $3 parking fee per day. The posh **Jekyll Island Club Hotel** (☎ 800-535-9547; www.jekyll club.com 371 Riverview Dr; ; d/ste $189/399; P ⊠ ☒ wi-fi) looms large on this island. It's a great place for a drink after a sunset seafood dinner at nearby waterfront restaurant **Latitude 31** (☎ 912-635-3800; www.crossoverjekyll.com), located right on the wharf. An endearing new attraction is the **Georgia Sea Turtle Center** (☎ 912-635-4444; www .georgiaseaturtlecenter.org; Hopkins Rd; adult/child $6/4; ☺ 10am-7pm), a conservation center and turtle hospital where the patients are on view for the public.

Cumberland Island

An unspoiled paradise, a backpacker's fantasy, a site for day trips or extended stays – it's clear why the Carnegie family used Cumberland as a retreat long ago. Most of this southernmost barrier island is now oc-cupied by the **Cumberland Island National Seashore** (☎ 912-882-4336; www.nps.gov/cuis; admission $4). Almost half of its 36,415 acres consists of marsh, mudflats and tidal creeks. On the ocean side are 16 miles of wide, sandy beach that you might have all to yourself. The island's interior is characterized by a maritime forest. Ruins from the Carnegie estate Dungeness are astounding, as is the island's wildlife population. Animals include wild turkeys, tiny fiddler crabs and beautiful butterflies. Feral horses roam the island and are a common sight.

The only public access to the island is via boat. A convenient and pleasant **ferry** (☎ 912-882-4335; adult/child $17/12; ☺ departures 9am & 11:45am) leaves from the mainland at the St Marys dock. Reservations are recommended. December through February, the ferry does not operate on Tuesday or Wednesday.

The island's only private accommodations are at the **Greyfield Inn** (☎ 904-261-6408; www.greyfieldinn.com; d & ste incl meals $350-575, 2-night min stay), a mansion built in 1900. Camping is available at **Sea Camp Beach** (☎ 912-882-4335; per person $4), a campground set among magnificent live oaks.

Note: there are no stores or waste bins on the island. Eat before arriving, and keep your trash with you.

Okefenokee National Wildlife Refuge

Established in 1937, the **Okefenokee Swamp** is a national gem, encompassing 396,000 acres of bog in a giant saucer-shaped depression that was once part of the ocean floor. The swamp is home to an estimated 9000 to 15,000 alligators, 234 bird species, 49 types of mammal and 60 amphibian species. The **Okefenokee Swamp Park** (☎ 912-283-0583; www.okeswamp.com; US1 South in Waycross; admission $12; ☺ 9am-5pm) has captive bears and gators onsite, or you can explore the swamp in a canoe or on a boat tour. The ultimate experience is a multiday canoe trip on the swamp's 120 miles of waterways. Call the US Fish & Wildlife Service's **Okefenokee National Wildlife Refuge Wilderness Canoe Guide** (☎ 912-496-7836; www.fws.gov/okefenokee/) if you're considering a trip. Guided boat trips are also available. Warning: the water level in 2006 and '07 was so low that water trips from the park were suspended indefinitely.

ALABAMA

Obsessed with football and race – two things Southerners never stop discussing – this rectangular state has a complicated and fascinating heritage. It has been home to one of the world's greatest musicians (Hank Williams Sr) and one of gridiron's most legendary coaches (Paul 'Bear' Bryant). Jefferson Davis became the first president of the Confederacy here in 1861, the year the Civil War began. Nearly 100 years later, when an African American woman named Rosa Parks refused to budge on a bus, the American Civil Rights movement was galvanized.

Known for incredible acts of activism, Alabama and the actions that happened here in the 1950s and '60s led the way for civil rights triumphs throughout the USA. All that struggle and strife came at a cost and, ever since, Alabama has had to conquer its reputation of rebels, segregation, discrimination and wayward politicians.

Alabama has a surprising diversity of landscapes, from foothills in the north and a gritty city in the middle to the subtropical Gulf Coast down south. Visitors come to see the heritage of antebellum architecture, to celebrate the country's oldest Mardi Gras in Mobile, and to learn about the civil rights struggle. Every fall, the University of Alabama Crimson Tide and the Auburn University Tigers continue one of college football's greatest rivalries.

History

Alabama was among the first states to secede in the Civil War. Montgomery was the first Confederate capital, Mobile was a major Confederate port and Selma was a munitions center. Alabama lost around 25,000 soldiers in the war, and reconstruction came slowly and painfully.

Racial segregation and Jim Crow laws survived into the mid-20th century, when the Civil Rights movement campaigned for desegregation of everything from public buses to private universities, a notion that Governor George Wallace viciously opposed. In perhaps the most famous moment in civil rights history, an African American woman named Rosa Parks refused to give up her bus seat to a white passenger and was thus arrested; the ensuing uproar sparked a bus

ALABAMA FACTS	
Nickname The Heart of Dixie
Population 4.6 million
Area 52,423 sq miles
Capital city Montgomery (pop 202,000)
Sales tax 4% but up to 11% with local taxes
Birthplace of Author Helen Keller (1880–1968), Civil Rights activist Rosa Parks (1913–2005), musician Hank Williams (1923–53)
Home of The US Space & Rocket Center
Famous for Rosa Parks and the Civil Rights movement
Bitterest rivalry The University of Alabama versus Auburn University

boycott and began to turn the tide in favor of racial equality. Alabama saw brutal repression and hostility, but federal civil rights and voting laws eventually prevailed. At a political level, reform has seen the election of dozens of African American mayors and representatives. And from funky Muscle Shoals all the way down to genteel Mobile, Alabama has contributed in positive ways to Southern culture.

Information

The **Alabama Bureau of Tourism & Travel** (☎ 334-242-4169, 800-252-2262; www.800alabama.com; PO Box 4927, Montgomery, AL 36103) sends out a vacation guide and has a slick website with extensive tourism options.

BIRMINGHAM

No one can ignore Birmingham's checkered past – civil rights violence earned it the nickname 'Bombingham,' and an industrial economy yielded another unappealing nickname, 'The Pittsburgh of the South.' But that was decades ago. Today this midsized blue-collar city has a surprising amount of culture to offer, and it has integrated its civil rights struggle into the tourist experience. The nickname these days is 'Diverse City.'

Birmingham's urban core is mostly a business district, and only a few attractions sit beneath the skyscrapers. To really capture the city's essence, you'll want to visit four neighborhoods – lively Five Points, near the University of Alabama Birmingham; funky Lakeview, home to one of the South's greatest bars; charming Homewood, an upscale shopping strip with a pedestrian-friendly

THE SOUTH

layout and a small-town vibe; and the Civil Rights District, an unforgettable cluster of attractions at the edge of downtown.

Orientation & Information

The streets in downtown Birmingham run north–south, and the avenues run east–west. (The spine is 20th St.) The primary attractions and cool neighborhoods are all relatively close, but you'll have a much easier time seeing the city with a car than without one. The hip Lakeview and Five Points neighborhoods are on the city's south side, and the civil rights attractions and main art museum are to the north.

You can find tourist information at the **Greater Birmingham Convention & Visitors Bureau** (☎ 205-458-8000, 800-458-8085; www.sweetbirmingham.com; 2200 9th Ave N; ☽ 8:30am-5pm Mon-Fri).

Sights & Activities

Birmingham Civil Rights Institute (☎ 205-328-9696, 866-328-9696; www.bcri.org; 520 16th St N; adult/child $10/free; ☽ 10am-5pm Tue-Sat, 1-5pm Sun) is the most worthwhile sight in town. Its moving audio, video and photography exhibits tell the story of racial segregation in the USA, from WWI and the Civil Rights movement to racial and human-rights issues around the world today.

Across the street in **Kelly Ingram Park**, 1960s civil rights protestors are depicted in sculptures that are both proud and harrowing.

The **16th St Baptist Church** (☎ 205-251-9402; cnr 16th St & 6th Ave N; ☽ tour ministry 10am-4pm Tue-Fri) became a gathering place for meetings and protests in the 1950s and '60s. When Ku Klux Klan (KKK) members bombed the church in 1963, killing four girls, the city was flung into a whirlwind of social change. Today, the rebuilt church is a memorial and a house of worship (services 11am Sunday).

Birmingham Museum of Art (☎ 205-254-2565; www.artsbma.org; 2000 8th Ave N; admission free; ☽ 10am-5pm Tue-Sat, noon-5pm Sun) collects work from Asia, Africa, Europe and the Americas. Don't miss Rodin's striking sculpture work in the outdoor sculpture garden.

Art-deco buildings in trendy **Five Points South** house shops, restaurants and nightspots. Equally noteworthy is the **Homewood** community's quaint commercial drag on 18th St S.

Visible from all over the city thanks to the country's second-largest statue, the nearby

Vulcan Park (☎ 205-933-1409; www.visitvulcan.com; 1701 Valley View Dr; ☽ 7am-10pm) offers fantastic views for free, and an observation tower for a price.

The Carver Performing Arts Center houses the **Alabama Jazz Hall of Fame** (☎ 205-254-2731; www.jazzhall.com; 1631 4th Ave N; self-guided/guided $2/3; ☽ 10am-5pm Tue-Sat), which celebrates jazz musicians such as Dinah Washington, Nat King Cole and Duke Ellington.

Twelve miles south of town, off I-65 exit 246, **Oak Mountain State Park** (☎ 205-620-2524; admission $3; ☽ dawn-dusk) is Alabama's largest state park, where you can hike, camp, boat or chill out on the lakeside beach.

Sleeping

Redmont Hotel (☎ 205-324-2101; www.theredmont.com; 2101 5th Ave N; r from $89; P ⊠ wi-fi) The piano and chandelier in the lobby suggest a certain old-world traditionalism, and the prices seem stuck in the past too. (But hey, that's a good thing.) Located in a weirdly quiet section of downtown, the Redmont rises into a handsome and somewhat lonely tower. Immaculate rooms are cleaned within an inch of their lives. Parking's available ($15).

Tutwiler Hotel (☎ 205-322-2100; www.thetutwilerhotel.com; 2021 Park Pl N; r/ste from $139/179; P ⊠ wi-fi) So much for tradition: this grand old landmark hotel is now officially known as the Hampton Inn & Suites-Downtown-Tutwiler. Despite the chain association, it's still nice – a recently renovated mix of historic charm and plush modern amenities. The first choice for downtown accommodations.

Sheraton (☎ 205-324-5000; www.starwoodhotels.com; 2101 Richard Arrington Jr Blvd N; r from $249; P ⊠ ⊠ wi-fi) Pet-friendly accommodations and proximity to the art museum compensate for the impersonal nature of this massive convention hotel. Deep rate discounts online. Parking costs $10.

Eating & Drinking

Pete's Famous Hot Dogs (☎ 205-252-2905; 1925 2nd Ave N; dogs $1.80) This closet-sized downtown joint has been serving since 1915 and makes a good choice for an inexpensive but tasty fare. Order more than one of the tiny (and scrumptious) dogs, and wolf them down on a nearby park bench.

Savage's Bakery (☎ 205-871-4901; 2916 18th St S; ☽ 9am-5:30pm Mon-Fri, 9am-5pm Sat) A Birmingham institution since 1939, this bakery's the perfect spot to grab a sweet snack while shopping in Homewood.

Sol Y Luna (☎ 205-322-1186; 2811 7th Ave S; tapas $9-12; ☺ 5-10pm Mon-Wed, to midnight Thu-Sat) Thirsty patrons can order tequila flights (and then a taxi) at this spunky Mexican restaurant-cantina, which specializes in small plates.

Dreamland (☎ 205-933-2133; 1427 14th Ave S; slabs $17.95; ☺ 10am-10pm Mon-Thu, 10am-11pm Fri & Sat, 11am-10pm Sun) Barbecue fiends must make the pilgrimage to Birmingham's franchise of this Alabama and Georgia minichain, a rib-lover's fantasy.

Highlands Bar & Grill (☎ 205-939-1400; 2011 11th Ave S; mains $26-40; ☺ 5:30-10pm Tue-Thu, 5:30-10:30pm Fri & Sat) One of internationally acclaimed chef Frank Stitt's eateries, and arguably Birmingham's best restaurant, the sumptuous menu features meat and seafood beautified by a flash of sophistication borrowed from both southern France and traditional Southern cuisine.

Lou's Pub & Package Store (☎ 205-322-7005; 726 29th St S; beer $3.50) After dinner, you simply must wind up at this glorious dive, with its salty proprietor who calls everybody 'baby.'

Getting There & Around

The **Birmingham International Airport** (☎ 205-595-0533) is located about 5 miles northeast of downtown. **Greyhound** (☎ 205-251-3210; 618 19th St N), north of downtown, serves cities including Atlanta, GA ($34, three hours), Huntsville ($20.50, two hours), Montgomery ($23.50, two hours), Jackson, MS ($35, about four hours), and New Orleans, LA ($71.50, 10 hours). **Amtrak** (☎ 205-324-3033; 1819 Morris Ave), downtown, has trains daily to New York ($122, 23 hours) and New Orleans ($34, about seven hours).

Birmingham Transit Authority (☎ 205-521-0101; adult $1) runs local buses.

AROUND BIRMINGHAM

The college town of **Tuscaloosa** was the state capital from 1826 to 1846, and the University of Alabama was established in 1831. The world here revolves around its successful Crimson Tide football team. The **Paul W Bryant Museum** (☎ 205-3484668; www.bryant.ua.edu; 300 Bryant Dr; adults $2; ☺ 9am-4pm) enshrines the Tide's most celebrated coach, and sells replicas of his trademark fedora.

North of Birmingham, the aerospace community of **Huntsville** had its high-tech beginnings in the 1950s when German scientists were brought in to develop rockets for the US army. The US space program took off and attracted international aerospace-related companies. **The US Space & Rocket Center** (☎ 256-837-3400; www.spacecamp.com/museum; I-565, exit 15; adult/child museum $16/11, with IMAX $20.95/15.95; ☺ 9am-5pm) is a combination science museum and theme park. It's a great place to take a kid, or to become one again. The center has IMAX films, exhibits, rides and a video presentation that answers the all-important question: how do astronauts use the toilet in space?

Four cities on the Tennessee River make up the area known as 'the Shoals': **Florence**, **Sheffield**, **Tuscumbia** and **Muscle Shoals**. To find your way around, grab one of the free and extremely useful maps located at the **Colbert County visitor center** (☎ 256-383-0783; www.colbert countytourism.org; 179 Hwy 72W, Tuscumbia; ☺ 8:30am-5pm Mon-Fri year-round, 9am-4pm Sat summer).

Famous for its music history, which has drawn Aretha Franklin among others, the area is thick with interesting spots. The cheesy-cool **Alabama Music Hall of Fame** (☎ 256-381-4417; www.alamhof.org; 617 Hwy 72 W, Tuscumbia; adult/child $8/5; ☺ 9am-5pm Mon-Sat, from 1pm Sun) immortalizes both Hank Williams and Lionel Richie. Tours are available of **Ivy Green** (☎ 256-383-4066; www .helenkellerbirthplace.org; 300 W Commons St, Tuscumbia; adults/students $6/2; ☺ 8:30am-4pm Mon-Sat, from 1pm Sun), the home of blind-deaf 'miracle worker' Helen Keller, who is celebrated with an annual summertime festival in Tuscumbia.

The **Rosenbaum House** (☎ 256-760-6379; www .wrightinalabama.com; 601 Riverview Dr, Florence; adults/ students & seniors $8/5; ☺ 10am-4pm Mon-Sat) is a fascinating home designed by architect Frank Lloyd Wright. And the **Hollywood Inn** (☎ 256-765-2142; 804 W College St, Florence; plate $6.75; ☺ 11am-5pm Mon-Wed, to 6pm Thu-Sat) serves fabulous soul food and sublime tea. The small but proud **W C Handy Birthplace, Museum & Library** (☎ 256-760-6434; www.flo-tour.org/handymus.html; 620 W College St, Florence; adults/students $2/50¢; ☺ 10am-4pm Tue-Sat) houses the piano on which Handy wrote 'Saint Louis Blues.'

MONTGOMERY

The explosion of the Civil Rights movement happened here in 1955, when an African American seamstress named Rosa Parks refused to give up her seat to a white man on a city bus, launching a bus boycott and galvanizing the Civil Rights movement nationwide. Montgomery has commemorated that incident with a museum, which (along

THE SOUTH

with an excellent Shakespeare program) is the main reason to visit.

Although it's Alabama's capital city, Montgomery feels more like a sleepy little town living mostly in the past. The odd exception is that every business in town seems to offer wi-fi access – even Burger King. To its credit, Montgomery covers both fine and folk arts well, with a terrific Shakespeare festival and a museum devoted to country-music legend Hank Williams. Get to know I-85, which runs east–west through Montgomery, as the sights tend to be near one off-ramp or another.

Sights & Activities

A tribute to Mrs Parks (who died in October 2005), the **Rosa Parks Museum** (☎ 334-241-8661; http://montgomery.troy.edu/rosaparks/museum/; 251 Montgomery St; adult/child $5.50/3.50; ☹ 9am-5pm Mon-Fri, 9am-3pm Sat) features a sophisticated video recreation of the bus-seat protest and a separate children's area that covers African American history pre-1955.

The **Scott & Zelda Fitzgerald Museum** (☎ 334-264-4222; www.fitzgerald-museum.com; 919 Felder Ave; donations requested; ☹ 10am-2pm Wed-Fri, 1-5pm Sat & Sun), the writers' home from 1931 to '32, now houses first editions, translations, and original artwork including a mysterious self-portrait of Zelda in pencil.

The superb **Alabama Shakespeare Festival** (☎ 334-271-5353, 800-841-4273; www.asf.net) delivers live summertime performances at a lovely facility in Blount Cultural Park. It's a must-see if you're here at that time.

To see local sluggers take a crack at the big leagues, support the **Montgomery Biscuits** (☎ 334-323-2255; www.biscuitsbaseball.com; 200 Coosa St; tickets $7-11), who play minor-league baseball in a handsome downtown park.

Sleeping & Eating

OK, so Montgomery may not be known for its luxurious restaurants and accommodations. But you don't need filet mignon and the Ritz every night – sometimes hot dogs and a chain hotel work alright in a pinch.

Fairfield Inn (☎ 334-270-0007; www.mariott.com; 5601 Carmichael Rd; r from $69; P ☒ ☒ ☒ wi-fi) It definitely ain't fancy, but it's cheap, clean and convenient to the Shakespeare Festival.

Chris' Hot Dog (☎ 334-265-6850; 138 Dexter Ave; dogs $2; ☹ 10am-7pm Mon-Sat, to 8pm Fri) Served on pillow-soft buns, the dogs have made this funky joint a Montgomery institution since

---

THANKS, HANK

The **Hank Williams Museum** (☎ 334-262-3600; www.thehankwilliamsmuseum.com; 118 Commerce St; adult/child $8/3; ☹ 9am-4:30pm Mon-Sat, 1-4pm Sun) pays homage to the country-music giant and Alabama native, a pioneer who effortlessly fused hillbilly music with African American blues. You'll see Hank's personal stuff, including the baby-blue 1952 Cadillac he died in at age 29. The museum provides directions to a life-size bronze statue of Hank in Lister Hill Plaza and to the gravesite where he's buried in the Oakwood Cemetery Annex.

1917. Order your dog 'all the way' and see if you can guess what's in the special house sauce.

Montgomery Brewing Co (☎ 334-834-2739; www .montgomerybrewpub.com; 12 W Jefferson St; dinner $10-16; ☹ from 11am Mon-Fri, from 4pm Sat) A lively hub of activity, the MBC is located in a neat little warehouse district by the ballpark. Try the house-made Montgomery Blonde brew. If you're hungry, the choices include burgers, nachos and alligator tail.

Getting There & Around

Montgomery Regional Airport (☎ 334-281-5040; www .montgomeryairport.org; 4445 Selma Hwy) is about 15 miles from downtown and is served by daily flights from Atlanta, Charlotte, Cincinnati, Houston and Memphis. **Greyhound** (☎ 334-286-0658; 950 W South Blvd) also serves the city. The **Montgomery Area Transit System** (☎ 334-262-7321; www.montgomerytransit.com) operates the city buses.

SELMA

On Bloody Sunday, March 7, 1965, the media captured state troopers and deputies beating and gassing African Americans and white sympathizers near the Edmund Pettus Bridge. Led by Martin Luther King Jr, the crowd was marching to the state capital (Montgomery) to demonstrate for voting rights. This was the culmination of two years of violence, which ended when President Johnson signed the Voting Rights Act of 1965. Today Selma is a quiet town, and though its attractions are few, they do provide an excellent insight into the voting rights protests that were at the crux of the Civil Rights movement.

The strangely modern **Cyber Blue** (☎ 334-876-9898; 109 Broad St), is a café that serves mocha toffee cappuccinos and charges $4 an hour for internet access. It's not far from Selma's key attraction, the **National Voting Rights Museum** (☎ 334-418-0800; 1012 Water Ave; adult/senior/student $8/6/6; ☼ 9am-5pm Mon-Fri, 10am-3pm Sat), located near the Edmund Pettus Bridge, which honors the movement's 'foot soldiers' – the unsung heroes who marched for freedom.

For local produce, including Chilton County peaches and fresh-roasted peanuts, visit **Cleckler's Produce** (☎ 334-872-3793; 301 Church St). And for peppery stew and a sloppy, delicious pork sandwich, head to the outskirts of town and visit **Old South Bar-B-Q** (☎ 334-872-2585; 4477 Hwy 80 E).

MOBILE

Wedged between Mississippi and Florida, the only real Alabama coastal town is Mobile (mo-*beel*), a seaport with green spaces, shady boulevards and four historic districts. It's ablaze with azaleas in early spring, and Mardi Gras has been celebrated here for nearly 300 years. Mobile is interesting and fun in the same sense as New Orleans, only the volume and brightness are turned way down. The Dauphin St historic district is where you'll find many bars and restaurants, and it's where much of the Mardi Gras action takes place. Unlike the Mississippi Gulf Coast, which is still devastated by Hurricane Katrina, downtown Mobile looks as though the storm never happened.

Like St Charles Ave in New Orleans, **Government St**, near downtown, makes for a lovely drive thanks to its mansions and tree canopy. The **Leinkauf Historic District** has more great homes, and you can practice kicking extra points on the American football field in **Crawford-Murphy Park**.

Stretch your legs some more at the nearby **USS Alabama** (☎ 251-433-2703, 800-426-4929; www.ussalabama.com; 2703 Battleship Parkway; adult/child $12/6; ☼ 8am-6pm Apr-Sep, 8am-4pm Oct-Mar; Ⓟ), a 207m behemoth famous for escaping nine major WWII battles unscathed. It's a worthwhile self-guided tour for its awesome size and might. While there, you can also tour a submarine and get up close and personal with military aircraft. Parking's available ($2).

For a lazy lunch, try the **Bluegill** (☎ 251-625-1998; www.bluegillrestaurant.com; 3775 Battleship Parkway; shrimp $6.95; ☼ 11am-9pm Sun-Thu, 11am-10pm Fri & Sat), a casual waterfront restaurant specializing in massive peel-'n'-eat shrimp and addictive fried crab claws. Goopy key lime pie is available for dessert.

For dinner, belly up to the oyster bar at **Wintzell's** (☎ 251-432-4605; www.wintzellsoysterhouse.com; 605 Dauphin St; ☼ 11am-10pm Sun-Thu, 11am-11pm Fri & Sat), a historic restaurant serving fresh bivalves fried, steamed, stewed or (best of all) raw on the half-shell.

Lay down your head at the **Malaga Inn** (☎ 251-438-4701, 800-235-1586; 359 Church St; r from $94; Ⓟ ✗ ✗ ✗ ▢) a 40-room spot with nicely furnished rooms that open onto balconies overlooking the courtyard or street.

MISSISSIPPI

One of the USA's most misunderstood (and yet most mythologized) states, Mississippi is home to gorgeous country roads, shabby juke joints, crispy catfish, hallowed authors and acres of cotton. Long scorned for its lamentable civil rights history and its low ranking on the list of nearly every national marker of economy and education, most people feel content to malign Mississippi without ever experiencing it firsthand. But unpack your bags for a moment and you'll glimpse the real South. It lies somewhere amid the Confederate defeat at Vicksburg, the literary legacy of William Faulkner in bookish Oxford, the birthplace of the blues in the Mississippi Delta and the humble origins of Elvis Presley in Tupelo.

The state seems proud of its rural nature, and small pleasures, like the absolute darkness of a place unspoiled by light pollution, more than compensate for the lack of urban

THE SOUTH

MISSISSIPPI FACTS

Nickname The Magnolia State

Population 2.9 million

Area 46,906 sq miles

Capital city Jackson (176, 614)

Sales tax 7%

Birthplace of Author Eudora Welty (1909–2001), musicians Robert Johnson (1911–38) and Elvis Presley (1935–77), puppeteer Jim Henson (1936–90)

Home of The blues

Famous for Cotton fields

Kitschiest souvenir Elvis Presley lunchbox in Tupelo

glitz. Yes, it's a spread-out place. But that allows for some transcendent drives through awe-inspiring cotton country and the windy, wooded Natchez Trace Parkway.

History

Stay in Mississippi long enough, and you'll hear folks refer to a time 'when cotton was king.' That time dates back at least to 1860, when Mississippi was the country's leading cotton producer and one of the 10 wealthiest states. The Civil War wrecked Mississippi's economy, and reconstruction was traumatic. And the state's racist history – from slavery through the Civil Rights era – has left deep scars. (One of the most famous incidents came in 1962, when violence erupted as student James Meredith became the first African American to attend the University of Mississippi.)

Today, though still a poor state, people have come to realize that the blues – one of America's richest and most distinctive art forms – are worth celebrating. And that Mississippi has been disproportionately blessed with literary luminaries. And so the state has developed a tourist industry revolving around its proud cultural history, as well as its waterfront casinos.

Information

The legendary north–south Hwy 61 runs the length of the Delta. I-55 is the main north–south highway down the heart of the state, and I-20 bisects Mississippi going east–west. A small portion of the state's Southern tip – the Gulf Coast – touches the Gulf of Mexico. **Mississippi Division of Tourism Development** (☎ 601-359-3297, 866-733-6477; www.visitmississippi.org; PO Box 849 Jackson, MS 39205) has a directory of visitor bureaus.

TUPELO

Unless you have an unhealthy Elvis obsession, you probably shouldn't plan to spend a long time in Tupelo. But an afternoon pop-in is rewarding indeed. If you've ever sung 'Blue Suede Shoes' in the shower, if you've ever swept your hair into a sideburned pompadour, if you've ever seen the 1968 'Comeback Special' or visited Graceland or pined for an Elvis Presley lunchbox, then the hometown of the King is probably worth a stop.

Elvis Presley's Birthplace (☎ 662-841-1245; www.elvispresleybirthplace.com; 306 Elvis Presley Blvd; all sights adult/child $7/3.50; 9am- 5:30pm Mon-Sat, 1-5pm Sun) is east of downtown off Hwy 78. The 15-acre park complex contains the two-room shack Elvis lived in as a boy, a museum displaying personal items, a modest chapel and a massive gift shop.

The **Tupelo Automobile Museum** (☎ 662-842-4242; www.tupeloautomuseum.com; 1 Otis Blvd; adult/child $10/5; 10am-6pm Tue-Sun) feels like more of a garage than a museum, but – when the vintage cars on display include a 1927 Ford Model T, a 1948 Tucker, a '57 Chevy and a 1981 DeLorean – no reasonable gearhead could complain. A bonus: you're welcome to take all the pictures you like.

Dairy Kream (☎ 662-842-7838; 796 E Main St) serves chocolate-vanilla twists in a cone for about a buck. Cash only.

OXFORD

A refreshingly sophisticated little town that's bustling and prosperous, Oxford was named by colonists after the English city in hopes it would open a school as revered as its namesake. The University of Mississippi (Ole Miss) opened in 1848, and provides Oxford's heartbeat. (You know a town has an intellectual bent when its favorite native son is a literary lion like William Faulkner. But former Ole Miss quarterback Archie Manning runs a close second; the speed limit here on campus is 18mph, in deference to his old uniform number.)

Social life in Oxford revolves around 'The Square,' a series of downtown blocks dotted with shops and eateries. It's the city's main geographical reference point, too, so if you're turned around ask somebody for directions to (or from) the Square.

Sights & Activities

Square Books (☎ 662-236-2262; www.squarebooks.com; 111 Courthouse Sq; 9am-9pm Mon-Thu, to 10pm Fri & Sat, 9am-6pm Sun), one of America's great independent bookstores, is the epicentre of Oxford's lively literary scene and a frequent stop for traveling authors. Signed copies abound. There's a café and balcony upstairs, along with an immense section devoted to Faulkner, whose likeness is sculpted a few steps away outside City Hall.

University of Mississippi Museum (☎ 662-915-7073; University Ave at 5th St; www.olemiss.edu/depts/u_museum; admission free; 9:30am-4:30pm Tue-Sat,

---

THE KING'S HUMBLE ORIGINS

Elvis and his stillborn twin, Jesse, were born in Tupelo in the front room of a 450-sq-ft shotgun shack at 4:35am on January 8, 1935. The Presleys lived there until Elvis was three, when the house was repossessed.

Elvis bought his first guitar at **Tupelo Hardware** (114 W Main St) for $12; attended grades one to five at Lawhon School; won second prize in a talent contest at the fairgrounds west of town; earned A grades in music at **Milam Junior High School** (Gloster & Jefferson Sts); and attended the **First Assembly of God Church** (909 Berry St).

When Elvis was 13, he and his family left Tupelo for Memphis. He returned at 21 to play the Mississippi-Alabama Fair, and the National Guard was called in to contain the crowds. The following year, Elvis came back for a benefit concert, with proceeds going to help the city purchase and restore his birthplace, which now attracts nearly 100,000 visitors each year.

1-4:30pm Sun) houses fine arts, folk arts, a Confederate uniform and a plethora of science-related marvels, including a microscope and electromagnet from the 19th century.

Literary pilgrims head directly to **Rowan Oak** (☎ 662-234-3284; off Old Taylor Rd; adult/child & students $5/free; 🕑 10am-4pm Tue-Sat, 1-4pm Sun), the graceful 1840s home of William Faulkner, who authored so many brilliant and dense novels set in Mississippi, and whose work is celebrated in Oxford with an annual conference in July. Tours of Rowan Oak – where Faulkner lived from 1930 until he died in 1962 – are self-guided. But ask nicely, and someone will play a tape of the author reading his Nobel Prize acceptance speech. The staff can also provide directions to Faulkner's grave, which is located in St Peter's Cemetery, northeast of the Square. Look for the historic marker.

The **Grove**, a green space on the University of Mississippi campus, comes to life during the fall football season. The tailgating here is unparalleled – it's half cocktail party, half debutante ball.

Sleeping & Eating

Super 8 (☎ 662-234-7013; 2201 Jackson Ave West; s $60; P 🐾 🖭 wi-fi) This option is a surprisingly comfortable (and pet-friendly) chain hotel. Continental breakfast.

Inn at Ole Miss (☎ 662-234-2331; Alumni Dr; www .theinnatolemiss.com; r/ste from $76/189; P 🐾 ✕ 🖭) Forget about getting a room here during football weekends – the hotel's plum location adjacent to the Grove makes it an extremely tough booking – but the rest of the year you'll enjoy accommodations right on Ole Miss campus.

Downtown Oxford Inn & Suites (☎ 662-234-3031; www.downtownoxfordinnandsuites.com; 400 N Lamar St; r from $99; P 🐾 🖭 wi-fi) Rooms can be tough

to come by in Oxford, so plan ahead and call here first – the main advantage is the choice location near the square. It can't be beat.

Ajax Diner (☎ 662-232-8880; 118 Courthouse Sq; dishes $7-12; 🕑 lunch & dinner) You can do a veggie plate, or a jambalaya special here at mealtimes. But don't miss the bar, one of the few places that underage travelers can hang with older drinking buddies. Shoot a toothpick into the ceiling before you go.

our pick **Taylor Grocery** (☎ 662-236-1716; Old Taylor Rd; dishes $7-14; 🕑 11am-2pm Mon-Fri, 6-10pm Thu-Sat) Be prepared to wait – and to tailgate in the parking lot – at this splendidly rusticated catfish haunt. You'll be glad you did. Get your cat fried or grilled, and bring a marker to sign your name on the wall. The joint is about 15-minutes' drive from downtown Oxford, south on Old Taylor Rd, in the hamlet of Taylor.

L&M (☎ 662-238-7780; 309 N Lamar; dishes $17.50-29; 🕑 5:30pm-10pm Tue-Sat, 10am-2pm Sun) Just off the town square, the casually gourmet L&M offers house-cured meats and a wicked brunch in a funky subterranean space.

MISSISSIPPI DELTA

One of the most mythical places in all of the USA, the Delta is a panoramic agricultural expanse that thrums with historic significance. Its vernacular food culture ranks as one of America's great folk arts, but even the grub is trumped by the Delta's other great cultural export: blues music.

Clarksdale

Yes, the town seems stuck in the past – but what a fascinating past it has had. Wealth, poverty, white culture, black culture and blues culture have all collided in this little Delta town, which has emerged on wobbly

THE SOUTH

VISITING JUKE JOINTS

It's believed that 'juke' is a West African word that survived in the Gullah language, the Creole-English hybrid spoken by isolated African Americans in the US. The Gullah 'juke' means 'wicked and disorderly.' Little wonder, then, that the term was applied to the roadside sweatboxes of the Mississippi Delta, where secular music, suggestive dancing, drinking and, in some cases, prostitution were the norm. The term 'jukebox' came into vogue when recorded music, spun on automated record-changing machines, began to supplant live musicians in such places, as well as in cafés and bars.

Most juke joints are African American neighborhood clubs, and outside visitors can be a rarity. Many are mostly male hangouts. There are very few places that local women, even in groups, would turn up without a male chaperone. Otherwise, women can expect a lot of persistent, suggestive attention.

For visitors of both sexes, having a friendly local with you to make some introductions can make for a much better evening. It can also help to call ahead to find out what's going on and to say you're going to stop by. If you arrive alone and unannounced, talk to people to break the ice.

Note that juke joints don't always keep regular hours. Some open only when the owner's in the mood. We recommend **Ground Zero** (☎ 662-621-9009; www.groundzerobluesclub.com; 0 Blues Alley; ☽ 11am-2pm Mon-Tue, to 11pm Wed & Thu, to 1am Fri & Sat), a huge and friendly hall with a dancefloor surrounded by tables. It's also a good starting point for disoriented Delta travelers who (for a fee) can crash in a nice furnished room upstairs. By contrast, **Red's** (☎ 662-627-3166; 395 Sunflower Ave; ☽ Fri & Sat night usually) looks a little scary to first-timers, but it is one of Clarksdale's best jukes. A faded sign out front indicates that this was once the Laverne Music Center, and only a hand-scrawled sign on the wall above the huge BBQ pit tells us it's now called Red's. If the pit's smoking, order whatever's cooking.

legs as the Delta's most well-developed tourist spot (although Greenwood is nipping at its heels).

SIGHTS & ACTIVITIES

Friendly St Louis carpetbagger Roger Stolle runs **Cat Head Delta Blues & Folk Art** (☎ 662-624-5992; 252 Delta Ave; ☽ 10am-5pm Mon-Sat), a colorful all-purpose blues emporium. The floors are hardwood and the shelves are jammed with books, face jugs and blues records. Stolle seems to know everyone in the Delta; skip the Chamber of Commerce and stop here for the lowdown.

A small but eager-to-please collection of memorabilia is on display at the **Delta Blues Museum** (☎ 662-627-6820; www.deltabluesmuseum.org; 1 Blues Alley; adult/child $7/5; ☽ 9am-5pm Mon-Sat), including Charlie Musselwhite's harmonica and BB King's guitar, Lucille. There's also a shrine to Delta legend Muddy Waters and, of course, a gift shop.

Juke Joint Festival (www.jukejointfestival.com) and **Sunflower River Blues & Gospel Festival** (www.sunflowerfest.org) are two bluesy throw-downs, the former in April and the latter in August. The juke fest is more about the venues than the headliners; Sunflower draws bigger names.

SLEEPING & EATING

Shack Up Inn (☎ 662-624-8329; www.shackupinn.com; r $50-75; P ☒) At the cheeky Hopson Plantation, 2 miles south on the west side of Hwy 49, guests stay in refurbished sharecropper cabins. The cabins have covered porches and are filled with old furniture and musical instruments. If they're full, ask for a room in the renovated cotton gin. Either way, the old commissary is an atmospheric venue for live-music performances, and the owners are fonts of information.

Abe's (☎ 662-624-9947; 616 State St; mains $3-6; ☽ 10am-9pm Mon-Thu, to 10pm Fri & Sat, 11am-2pm Sun) At the Crossroads – the famous intersection of Hwys 61 and 49, where bluesman Robert Johnson supposedly sold his soul to the devil – look for the tall sign with the happy pig in a bow tie. Abe's has served zesty pork sandwiches on cheap white buns since 1924. Get one with vinegary slaw, and an order of slow-burning tamales.

Madidi (☎ 662-627-7770; 164 Delta Ave; mains $20-33; ☽ 6-9pm Tue-Sat) Handsome and refined, just like co-founder Morgan Freeman, this upscale eatery has a menu including cornmeal oysters, rib-eye steak and blue cheese au gratin potatoes. Reservations requested.

THE SOUTH

Around Clarksdale

For such a poor, flat part of the country, the Delta has a surprisingly deep list of funky little towns with food, gambling and history to offer.

TUNICA

Smack between Clarksdale and Memphis is this little gambling mecca, which hosts a bunch of hotel-casinos. The **Gold Strike** is the biggest, a 1200-room monolith rising 31 stories into the Delta sky. Sharing a parking lot are the **Horseshoe** (a real gambler's casino with lots of table games) and the Tudor-style **Sheraton** (which has a steakhouse that will put your name on the wall if you finish its porterhouse). If you're traveling south after gambling, hit the **Blue & White** (☎ 662-363-1371; 1355 Hwy 61 N; mains from $6; ☾ 5am-10pm) – a classic greasy spoon.

GREENVILLE

The Delta's largest city, Greenville is roughly midway between Clarksdale and Vicksburg. It was here that the levee broke during the catastrophic Great Flood of 1927. Today it has some riverboat gambling and not much else. But in September, Greenville hosts the **Mississippi Delta Blues & Heritage Festival** (☎ 662-335-3523; www.deltablues.org) near the intersection of Hwy 454 and Hwy 1. And six nights a week, the James Beard Award-winning dive **Doe's Eat Place** (☎ 662-334-3315; www.doeseatplace.com; 502 Nelson St; ☾ 5-9pm Mon-Sat) serves world-class steaks in the middle of an unassuming neighborhood. The place may look sketchy from the outside, but the food is for real. Come early or make a reservation if you don't want to leave hungry and sad.

DELTA BLUES FESTIVALS

Several outdoor music festivals take place each year in the Delta. Here's a selected list; check out www.bluesfestivalguide.com for an international month-by-month guide.

Juke Joint Festival Clarksdale, mid-April (see opposite)

Mississippi Delta Blues & Heritage Festival Greenville, mid-May (see above)

BB King Homecoming Indianola, early June

Highway 61 Blues Festival Leland, early June

Sunflower River Blues & Gospel Festival Clarksdale, August (see opposite)

LELAND

East of Greenville, Hwy 82 heads out of the Delta. The **Highway 61 Blues Museum** (☎ 662-686-7646; www.highway61blues.com; 400 N Broad St; ☾ 10am-5pm Mon-Sat), in the Old Temple Theater, honors local bluesmen. Leland hosts the **Highway 61 Blues Festival** in June. A tiny visitor center honors Muppet man Jim Henson, who was born in Leland.

CLEVELAND

Home to Delta State University, this little burg has a fancy-pants restaurant, KC's (☎ 662-843-5301; www.kcsrestaurant.com; 400 Hwy 61; mains $20-32; ☾ 4-10pm Mon-Sat), that aspires to greatness and falls somewhat short. But if you're a gourmand who has tired of Mississippi catfish and tamales, you might want to stop in anyway.

GREENWOOD

Greenwood is a leafy Delta town with an old-fashioned downtown that seems on the rebound from dilapidation.

The wonderful bookstore **Turnrow** (☎ 662-453-5995; www.turnrowbooks.com; 304 Howard St) is a gorgeous space with a lovely veranda out back and a strong Southern accent on the shelves. Ask a local for directions north on Money Rd to see the hilly little cemetery where ghostly bluesman Robert Johnson is, according to a roadside marker, 'thought to be buried.' (Yes, he has a headstone.)

Just up the road from the cemetery, the **Tallahatchie Flats hotel** (☎ 662-453-1854; www.tallahatchieflats.com; 58458 County Rd 518; r from $60) is a compound of modest shacks that are rentable as private hotel rooms. Back in town, you'll be sitting pretty if you stay at the **Alluvian** (☎ 662-453-2114; www.thealluvian.com; 318 Howard St; r from $185), a boutique hotel that's almost unbelievably urbane for this part of the country. It's owned by the Viking Range Corporation, the upscale cooking supply company that has a very strong presence in Greenwood.

Vicksburg

Vicksburg is famous for its strategic location in the Civil War, thanks to its position on a high bluff overlooking the Mississippi River. General Ulysses S Grant besieged the city for 47 days, until its surrender on July 4, 1863, at which point the North gained dominance over North America's greatest river.

The major sights are readily accessible from I-20 exit 4B (Clay St). The **visitor center**

THE SOUTH

(☎ 601-636-9421; www.visitvicksburg.com; 3300 Clay St; 🕒 9am-5pm Mon-Fri) hands out indispensable free maps that mark color-coded scenic driving paths into and out of the city.

The old, slow downtown stretches along several cobblestone blocks of Washington St, and historic-house museums cluster in the Garden District, on Oak St south of Clay St, and also between 1st St E and Clay St. Vicksburg's stretch of the Mississippi River has casinos.

National Military Park (☎ 601-636-0583; www.nps.gov/vick; per car $8; 🕒 8am-5pm), north of I-20 on Clay St is this massive battlefield, Vicksburg's main attraction for Civil War buffs. A 16-mile driving tour passes historic markers explaining battle scenarios and key events. You can buy an audiotape tour on cassette or CD in the visitor center gift shop, or drive through on your own (but plan for at least 90 minutes). The cemetery contains some 17,000 Union graves, and a museum houses the ironclad gunboat USS *Cairo*. Civil War re-enactments are held in May and July.

SLEEPING & EATING

Battlefield Inn (☎ 601-638-5811; www.battlefieldinn.org; 4137 N I-20 Frontage Rd; r incl breakfast $50-80; P ⊠ ⟐) Robert E Lee meets David Lynch in this hotel, which is surreal in the extreme. The Battlefield Inn has a talking parrot in the entryway, a karaoke bar inside the hotel, a wet bar by the swimming pool and canons on the property.

Anchuca (☎ 601-661-0111; www.anchucamansion.com; 1010 1st East St; r from $125; P ⊠ ⟐ wi-fi) So lovely that it offers $6 tours to the public, this mansion was once owned by Jefferson Davis' brother, Joseph. Today it has a cozy library bar and loads of historic furnishings to be enjoyed by hotel guests and touring gawkers alike.

Walnut Hills (☎ 601-638-4910; 1214 Adams St; blue plate special $8.95; 🕒 11am-9pm Mon-Fri, to 2pm Sun) Your best bet for eating in Vicksburg is this charming old house near downtown, which serves traditional Southern favorites. Daily menus include fried chicken and country-fried steak, Southern cooked vegetables, biscuits and cornbread. Some meals are served family-style at big round tables.

JACKSON

Mississippi's capital is hardly glamorous, but the city has a handful of funky surprises to go along with a cluster of museums and historic sites. Although Jackson is Mississippi's largest city by far, most modern development has sprawled into plush suburbs leaving the downtown area – essentially a short stretch of Capitol St – something of a ghost town.

The **convention & visitors bureau** (☎ 601-960-1891; www.visitjackson.com; 111 E Capitol St, Suite 102; 🕒 9am-5pm Mon-Fri) has free information.

The one must-see attraction is the **Mississippi Museum of Art** (☎ 601-960-1515; www.msmuseumart.org; 380 South Lamar St; admission free; 🕒 10am-5pm Tue-Sat, from noon Sun), which got new digs in June 2007. The museum's collection of Mississippi art – a permanent exhibit dubbed 'The Mississippi Story' – is nothing less than superb.

Also worth a stop, though completely different in its feel and scope, is the **Agriculture & Forestry Museum** (☎ 601-713-3365; 1150 Lakeland Dr; adult/child $4/2; 🕒 9am-5pm Mon-Sat). This rustic attraction is actually spread among several buildings designed to resemble a small Mississippi town, complete with a blacksmith's shop and general store. In the main exhibit hall you can learn about catfish farming 'from the egg to the plate,' and see working model trains.

Southern literature buffs should make a reservation to tour the **Eudora Welty House** (☎ 601-353-7762; www.mdah.state.ms.us/welty; 1119 Pinehurst St; 🕒 tours 9am, 11am, 1pm & 3pm Wed-Fri). Welty, the Pulitzer Prize–winning author, lived in this Tudor Revival house for more than 75 years, and it's preserved to look as it did in the 1980s. The garden out back is lovely, too.

Tucked way back in Lefleur's Bluff State Park is the **Museum of Natural Science** (☎ 601-354-7303; www.msnaturalscience.org; 2148 Riverside Dr; adult/child $5/3; 🕒 8am-5pm Mon-Fri, from 9am Sat, from 1pm Sun), an indoor-outdoor attraction with exhibits and aquariums inside, and nice hiking trails outside.

The **Smith Robertson Museum** (☎ 601-960-1457; 528 Bloom St; adult/child $4.50/1.50; 🕒 9am-5pm Mon-Fri, 10am-1pm Sat, 2-5pm Sun), housed in Mississippi's first public school for African American kids, is the alma mater of author Richard Wright. It traces African American cultural history.

Described by a former governor as 'without question the state's most historic building,' the **Old Capitol** (☎ 601-576-6920; http://mdah.state.ms.us/museum; 100 State St; admission free; 🕒 8am-5pm Mon-Fri, 9:30am-4:30pm Sat, 12:30-4:30pm Sun) has been in the midst of a major restoration project, and is therefore closed. It's scheduled to re-open in January of 2009.

Sleeping & Eating

our pick **Old Capitol Inn** (☎ 601-359-9000; www.oldcap itolinn.com; 226 N State St; r from $95; P ⚡ ⚡ ⚡ wi-fi) Everything a B&B should be, this 24-room inn feels cozy in the cheapest room and elegant at the top end. The rooftop deck, complete with hot tub, overlooks a courtyard and pool. A full Southern breakfast with grits and eggs is complimentary in the morning. The inn's thoughtful service is exemplified by little details such as hand-written weather reports brought to your room for the next day, along with mints.

Edison Walthall (☎ 601-948-6161, www.edison walthallhotel.com; 225 E Capitol St; r/ste from $99/125; P ⚡ ⚡) A more traditional hotel, this place feels a bit outdated but has a clubby lobby and a plum location near the Governor's Mansion.

Hal & Mal's (☎ 601-948-0888; www.halandmals .com; 200 S Commerce St; dishes $7-18; ⚡ 11am-2am Mon-Sat) Has Mississippi beer on tap and, oftentimes, live music in the air. It's situated near the Old Capitol, above the Pascagoula St underpass.

One of the South's greatest (and yet most unsung) restaurants calls itself a drive-in, but it's really a gussied-up diner that serves smart twists on Southern staples. It's called **Walker's Drive-In** (☎ 601-982-2633; www.walkersdrivein.com; 3016 N State St; mains $24-32; ⚡ 11am-2pm Mon-Fri, dinner from 5:30pm Tue-Sat), and it serves heavenly tamales with *pico de gallo* (salsa) and sweet corn sauce as an appetizer, simultaneously honoring and updating the Mississippi tamale tradition. If you're there on a hot night, order the light summer salad. Dinner is more ambitious (and more expensive) than lunch.

Children and sweet-toothed adults will turn cartwheels upon discovering the **Fondren Beverage Emporium** (☎ 601-321-0806; 3030 N State St; ⚡ 10am-6pm Tue-Sat), an amazing shop specializing in rare soft drinks and strange candies. This is the place for gourmet lemonade, bacon-flavored breath mints, cucumber-flavored water and two coolers full of root beer.

Getting There & Away

At the junction of I-20 and I-55, it's easy to get in and out of Jackson. Its international **airport** (☎ 601-939-5631; www.jmaa.com) is 10 miles east of downtown. **Greyhound** (☎ 601-353-6342; 300 W Capitol St) buses serve Birmingham, AL ($40.50, 4½ hours), Memphis, TN ($40.50, four hours), and New Orleans, LA ($38.50,

5½ hours). Amtrak's *City of New Orleans* stops at the station at 300 W Capitol St.

NATCHEZ

Perched on a bluff overlooking the Mississippi, this antebellum town attracts tourists with its opulent architecture, especially during the 'pilgrimage' seasons in spring and fall, when local mansions are opened to visitors. The **visitor center** (☎ 601-446-6345; www.natchezms.com; 640 S Canal St; ⚡ 8:30am-5pm Mon-Sat, 9am-4pm Sun) shows a film about the town's history. This is also the southern end of the Natchez Trace Parkway (p468). The staff has an extensive list of B&Bs, plus information about tours.

GULF COAST

In the backyard of New Orleans, the Gulf Coast is where Southern gamblers and beach bums go to play. The economy, traditionally based on the seafood industry, got a shot of adrenaline in the 1990s when big Vegas-style casinos muscled in alongside the sleepy fishing villages. So it's an interesting mix down here: you've got Southern-speaking Vietnamese and Irish fishermen playing blackjack alongside bigwigs who have jetted in from big cities. The casinos are centered along and around Beach Blvd in Biloxi, which has rebuilt since Hurricane Katrina swept through. The nearby town of Gulfport, however, is still devastated.

Keep track of what's open for business through the **Mississippi Gulf Coast Convention & Visitors Bureau** (☎ 228-896-6699; www.gulfcoast.org; 11975 Seaway Rd, Gulfport), which has a website that lists openings and re-openings.

The charter company **Cat Island Adventures** (☎ 228-223-1650; www.mscatisland.com; Long Beach Harbor, Long Beach), was set back by the storm but is now open – it offers barrier island tours and, on land, 29 flavors of the shaved ice treats known as snow balls ($1.50). In the town of Ocean Springs, the **Shed** (☎ 228-875-5582; www.theshedbbq.com; ⚡ 11am-9pm Wed, Thu & Sun, to 10pm Fri & Sat) serves mythic barbecue alongside a campground.

Casinos

Although Hurricane Katrina devastated Biloxi's waterfront casinos, a vigorous rebuilding effort means that tourists can again try their luck on the Gulf Coast. The rebuilt **Beau Rivage** (www.beaurivage.com) is the

---

BALLAD OF THE MISSISSIPPI GULF COAST

While news cameras converged on New Orleans in the aftermath of Hurricane Katrina, which thrashed communities along the Gulf Coast in August 2005, the usually scenic and tidy towns along the Mississippi and Alabama coasts transformed into worlds of chaos and ruin. Torrential rains and violent winds lashed, splaying homes and tossing cars and buildings as if they were toys. One Biloxi fisherman described the scene as something out of a twisted Picasso painting: boats dangled like ornaments in tree branches, while slot machines from obliterated casinos floated down rivers that were yesterday's city streets. Some of the city's massive floating casinos that dominated the shoreline were simply tossed inland.

Despite the tragedy and destruction, Gulf Coast residents went to work rebuilding and rebounding. Today, much of the coastline is still desolate – you can drive down Beach Blvd and see vacant lot after vacant lot facing the now-tranquil Gulf of Mexico. And yet, some parts of the area – especially casinos – have rebuilt. Case in point: the Hard Rock Hotel & Casino was just about to open in 2005 when Katrina wiped the place out. By the summer of 2007 the casino was rebuilt and again on the brink of opening.

---

king of the strip, a glittering gold behemoth that is to Biloxi what Bellagio is to Las Vegas. The **Imperial Palace** (www.ipbiloxi .com) goes for a hip vibe, but loses some credibility by hosting a tribute to Barry Manilow. The **Isle of Capri** (www.isleofcapricasino .com/Biloxi) has a tacky tropical theme – soap in the hotel rooms is carved into the shape of a parrot.

LOUISIANA

In the words of William Faulkner: 'The past is never dead. It's not even past.' Nowhere is that as true in the US as it is in Louisiana. Nostalgia for times long gone and recognition of hardships endured are nursed and celebrated at every turn. This leads to a dynamic sense of place – natives know they are rooted here, and embrace what makes them unique. This is a state where African American cowboys strap washboards to their chests and strum the distinctive clicking sound of zydeco, where gators lurk in swamps and are hunted by French-speaking Cajuns, and where a lone sax player can redefine a day. Singular cultures coexist, knowing to leave well enough alone – after all, don't we all just want to eat well and dance till we can't remember?

In the rolling hills and pine forests of northern Louisiana, the mostly Protestant population shares similar traits with other Southern states. But the world becomes a different place amid the swamps of southern Louisiana and the debauched streets of New Orleans – where jazz and Afro-Caribbean sounds color the thick sultry air with so much history and invincibility, you just can't resist the beautiful urge to let loose.

History

The lower Mississippi River area was dominated by the Mississippian mound-building culture until around 1592 when Europeans arrived and decimated the Native Americans with the usual combination of disease, unfavorable treaties and outright hostility.

The land was passed back and forth from the Spanish to the French, to the British and back to the French. After the American Revolution, the whole area passed to the USA in

---

LOUISIANA FACTS

Nicknames Bayou State, Pelican State, Sportsman's Paradise

Population 4.3 million

Area 42,562 sq miles

Capital city Baton Rouge (population 229,553)

Sales tax 4% plus local city and county taxes

Birthplace of Jazz, naturalist John James Audubon (1785–1851), trumpeter Louis 'Satchmo' Armstrong (1901–71), author Truman Capote (1924–84), musician Antoine 'Fats' Domino (b 1928), pop star Britney Spears (b 1981)

Home of Tabasco sauce, chef Emeril Lagasse

Famous for Creole and Cajun cooking, New Orleans' Mardi Gras

Official state reptile Alligator

the 1803 Louisiana Purchase, and Louisiana became a state in 1812.

Steamboats plying the rivers opened a vital trade network across the continent. New Orleans became a major port, and Louisiana's slave-based plantation economy kept a flowing export of rice, tobacco, indigo, sugarcane and especially cotton. Louisiana seceded from the Union in 1861, but Union forces seized control of New Orleans in 1862, occupying much of the state during the war. Louisiana was readmitted to the Union in 1868, and the next 30 years saw political wrangling, economic stagnation and renewed discrimination against African Americans.

In the early 20th century oil discovery gave the economy a boost, while the devastation of cotton crops by boll weevils forced some agricultural diversification. In the 1920s, autocratic governor Huey Long was able to modernize much of the state's infrastructure. Industry and tourism developed, but the tradition of unorthodox and sometimes ruthless politics continues today. Race and economics are ongoing sources of struggle: witness the post-Katrina rebuilding process (p435). The 2005 hurricane and the flooding in its aftermath have reshaped southern Louisiana. Locals negotiate the tricky path through redevelopment, the return of displaced people, wetland restoration and outsider involvement.

Information

Thirteen Welcome Centers dot freeways throughout the state, **Louisiana Office of Tourism** (☎ 225-342-8119, 800-633-6970; www.louisianatravel.com; PO Box 94291, Baton Rouge, LA 70804-9291).

NEW ORLEANS

A heady confluence of the haughty European and the boisterous third-world, New Orleans is often referred to as the northernmost Caribbean city. Precious architecture stands alongside careening overloaded junk trucks, sumptuous delicacies tickle palates while offal in the streets offends the eyes. Never be in a hurry, and any time you step outside, be ready for a meandering conversation with a total stranger.

In August 2005 New Orleans' various strata were laid bare when Hurricane Katrina lashed the city and levee breaks left residents scrambling for their lives. But even after her hardships, the town's unofficial motto and pervading gestalt is *Laissez les bons temps rouler* (Let the good times roll). The people of New Orleans have embraced the process of rebuilding, and though the population in town has been halved by the poststorm diaspora, the areas along the river, most-frequented by visitors, never saw flooding and are rich once again with the city's trademark joyfulness.

New Orleans' vibrant, old-school panache lends a certain dignity to otherwise debauched activities. Revelers throw strings of beads from cast-iron balconies in appreciation of beautiful strangers passing below. The sonorous echoes of unbelievably sweet jazz, funky brass, R & B and blues beat from unexpected corners, and dancing becomes a reaction, not a choice. Meanwhile succulent restaurant aromas recall a history infused with African, Spanish, French, Italian and Caribbean cultural influences.

It's a great city to walk around, anchored by the beguiling French Quarter and the adjoining *faubourgs* (originally, 'suburbs'). Despite the city's bawdy reputation, it's the moment when things are quiet – late afternoon when everyone is at the hotel getting ready to go out, early morning when the light explodes on the city and work crews come out to spray away last night's sins – that New Orleans reveals its subtler charms.

History

The town of Nouvelle Orléans was founded as a French outpost in 1718 by Jean-Baptiste Le Moyne de Bienville. Early settlers arrived from France, Canada and Germany, and the French imported thousands of African slaves. The city became a central port in the slave trade; due to local laws some slaves were allowed to earn their freedom and assume an established place in the Creole community as *les gens de couleur libres* (free people of color).

The Spanish were largely responsible for building the French Quarter as it still looks today because fires in 1788 and 1794 decimated the earlier French architecture. The influx of Anglo Americans after the Louisiana Purchase led to an expansion of the city into the Central Business District (CBD), Garden District and Uptown. By 1840 New Orleans was the nation's fourth-largest city, with more than 100,000 people.

New Orleans survived the Civil War intact after an early surrender to Union forces, but

NEW ORLEANS IN...

Two Days

Start your first day with coffee and beignets at **Café du Monde** (p444) followed by a walk to Jackson Sq and the visitor center. Pick up a free map of the city. Take the leisurely **French Quarter Walking Tour** (p441) to get your bearings and soak up quintessential New Orleans. In the afternoon, sip a cocktail at a local bar, such as **Lafitte's Blacksmith Shop** (p446). At night, don good walking shoes and hit **Bourbon Street** (p446). Rock out. Drink plenty of water before bed.

Did you drink the water? If so, your hangover is well under control. Start day two with a stroll through the **French Market** (p438) to shop for souvenirs. Walk down the riverside Moonwalk and take a trip on the **Canal Street Ferry** (p439). Return to your hotel. Take a nap. At night, indulge at one of the excellent restaurants, such as **Cochon** (p445) and then head to the Faubourg Marigny district to listen to **live music** (p447) in a small local bar.

Four Days

Follow the two-day itinerary, and on the third day get out of the city and search for gators on a **swamp tour** (p451) or at the **Barataria Preserve** (p449). If reptiles aren't your thing, take a driving tour of the **Mississippi River plantations** (p449), or a guided tour of the **post-Katrina rebuilding** (p442). Pick a neighborhood club for that night's entertainment, or dance the night away at **Oz** (p444). The next day, head up to the **Garden District** (p439), ogle the mansions, and stop into **Commander's Palace** (p446) for a 25¢ lunchtime martini. Spend your evening dining on delicious **Cajun** or **Creole cuisine** (p444).

the economy languished with the end of the slavery-based plantations. In the early 1900s, New Orleans was the birthplace of jazz music. Many of the speakeasies and homes of the jazz originators have been destroyed through neglect, but the cultural claim was canonized in 1994 when the NPS established the New Orleans Jazz National Historical Park to celebrate the origins and evolution of America's most widely recognized indigenous musical art form. Oil and petrochemical industries developed in the 1950s, and today, tourism is the other lifeblood of the local economy.

Orientation & Information

New Orleans is wedged between the Mississippi River to the south and Lake Pontchartrain to the north. The historic French Quarter (Vieux Carré), encircling Jackson Sq, runs from Esplanade Ave to Canal St. Canal St separates the Quarter from the CBD and Warehouse District, which extends to the freeway.

Continuing upriver along St Charles Ave are the Lower Garden District, a ramshackle neighborhood with a bohemian enclave, and the lovely Garden District, well known for its historic mansions. St Charles Ave follows the hooked course of the river into Uptown and

the Riverbend area, anchored by Tulane and Loyola universities.

The Tremé, across N Rampart St from the French Quarter, is a historically rich, predominantly African American residential neighborhood. Downriver from the French Quarter, the streets of Faubourg Marigny, a diverse and especially gay-friendly community, form a triangle bisected by lively Frenchmen St. The artsy Bywater neighborhood lies downriver.

Though the quaint Algiers district sits across the river, it is also part of New Orleans. Neighborhoods closer to the sites of the levee breaches, suhc as Lakeview, Gentilly and the Lower 9th Ward were hard-hit by posthurricane flooding, and are best explored only by car.

Maps are available at the New Orleans Welcome Center in Jackson Sq (opposite).

BOOKSTORES

Faulkner House Books (☎ 504-524-2940; www .faulknerhousebooks.net; 624 Pirate's Alley; ☽ 10am-6pm) The erudite owner of this former residence of author William Faulkner sells rare first editions.

Maple Street Book Shop (☎ 504-866-4916; www.ma plestreetbookshop.com; 7523 Maple St; ☽ 9am-7pm Mon-Sat, 10am-6pm Sun) A mainstay independent bookstore in Uptown, with the Children's Book Shop (p442) next door.

THE SOUTH

EMERGENCY & MEDICAL SERVICES

Medical Center of Louisiana (☎ 504-903-3000; 2021 Perdido St) Has an emergency room.

New Orleans/AIDS Task Force (☎ 504-821-2601; www.noaidstaskforce.org; 2601 Tulane Ave, Suite 500) For HIV testing.

INTERNET ACCESS

The CBD and French Quarter are theoretically served by municipal wi-fi, but coverage is spotty. Libraries have free internet access for cardholders.

Bastille Computer Café (☎ 504-581-1150; www .bastille-computer-cafe.com; 605 Toulouse St; per 30min $5; ☙ 10am-11pm) In the French Quarter, with high-speed, wi-fi and photo editing.

Riverside Internet Café (☎ 504-299-1945; 1 Poydras St; per 30min $5; ☙ 9am-6pm) On the 2nd floor of Riverwalk Mall, with high-speed and a river view.

MEDIA & INTERNET RESOURCES

Gambit Weekly (www.bestofneworleans.com) Free weekly hotsheet of music, culture, politics and classifieds.

Offbeat Magazine (www.offbeat.com) Free monthly specializing in music.

Times-Picayune (www.nola.com) New Orleans' daily newspaper has an entertainment calendar and 'Lagniappe,' a more extensive guide, is included every Friday.

WWOZ (90.7FM) (www.wwoz.org) Tune in here for Louisiana music and more (p442).

POST

Post office CBD (610 S Maestri Pl; ☙ 8:30am-4:30pm Mon-Fri); French Quarter (207 N Peters St, Suite 200; ☙ 8:30am-4:30pm Mon-Fri); Main branch (☎ 800-275-8777; 701 Loyola Ave; ☙ 7am-7pm Mon-Fri, 8am-5pm Sat) Mail sent General Delivery, New Orleans, LA 70112, goes to the main branch. Postboxes in outlying areas are not necessarily reliable since Katrina.

TOURIST INFORMATION

The city's official visitors' website is www .neworleansonline.com.

Jean Lafitte National Historic Park Visitor Center (☎ 504-589-2636; www.nps.gov/jela; 419 Decatur St; ☙ 9am-5pm) Operated by the NPS, with exhibits on local history, guided walks and daily live music.

New Orleans Welcome Center (☎ 504-568-5661; www.neworleansinfo.com; 529 St Ann St; ☙ 9am-5pm) In Jackson Sq, it provide lots of free information and maps.

REBUILDING NEW ORLEANS *Jay Cooke*

Want to help with the New Orleans recovery? When visiting the Crescent City, consider volunteering a few hours of your time. Many worthwhile organizations are on the job; here's a far-from-inclusive list.

Arts Council of New Orleans (www.artscouncilofneworleans.org) Assists visual artists, writers and performers with grants, housing relief and studio space.

Audubon Nature Institute (www.auduboninstitute.org) Supporting Audubon Zoo and Aquarium animals.

Coalition to Restore Coastal Louisiana (www.crcl.org) Restoring and preserving coastal wetlands to prevent future Katrinas.

Habitat for Humanity (www.habitat-nola.org) Leading the way in New Orleans housing reconstruction, with a musicians' village and antipoverty agenda.

Greater New Orleans Foundation/Rebuild New Orleans Fund (www.gnof.org) Longtime local foundation focused on education, job training, nonprofits and racial equality.

Louisiana Disaster Recovery Foundation (www.louisianahelp.org) Supporting statewide economic redevelopment, housing, health care and legal services.

New Orleans City Park (www.neworleanscitypark.com/volunteer.html) The city's premier green space has heaps of projects needing assistance.

Preservation Resource Center of New Orleans (www.prcno.org) Promotes the preservation of New Orleans architecture and neighborhoods.

Rebuild New Orleans Public Library (www.nutrias.org) Eight of 12 New Orleans libraries were devastated by Katrina.

Save Our Cemeteries (www.saveourcemeteries.org) Restoring a unique aspect of New Orleans heritage and culture.

Tipitina's Foundation (www.tipitinasfoundation.org) Provides instruments for New Orleans students, and housing and business support for city musicians.

THE SOUTH

lonelyplanet.com

NEW ORLEANS

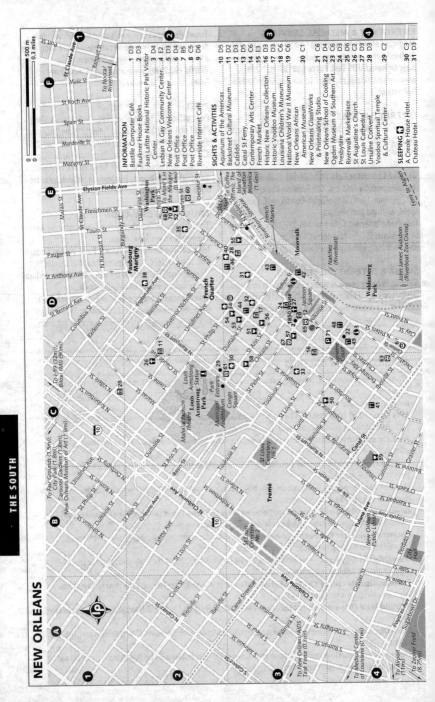

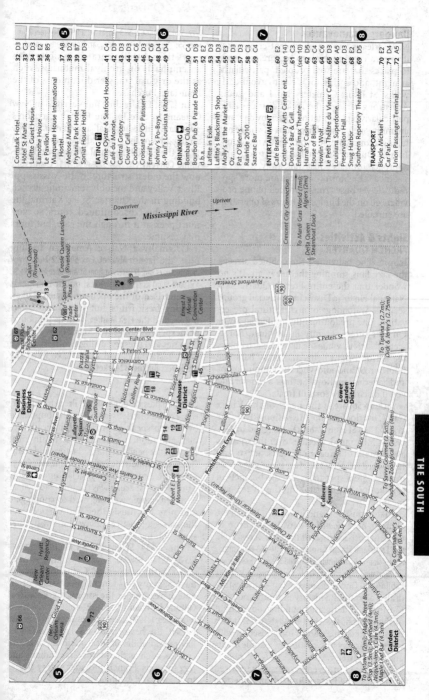

Cornstalk Hotel...................32 D3
Hôtel St Marie...................33 C3
Lafitte Guest House...............34 D3
Lamothe House....................35 E2
Le Pavillon.......................36 B5
Marquette House International
  Hostel..........................37 A8
Melrose Mansion..................38 D2
Prytania Park Hotel...............39 B7
Soniat House Hotel................40 D3

EATING 🍴
Acme Oyster & Seafood House......41 C4
Café du Monde....................42 D3
Central Grocery..................43 D3
Clover Grill.....................44 D3
Cochon..........................45 C6
Croissant D'Or Patisserie........46 C6
Emeril's.........................47 C6
Johnny's Po-Boys.................48 D4
K-Paul's Louisiana Kitchen.......49 D4

DRINKING 🍸
Bombay Club......................50 C4
Bourbon Pub & Parade Disco.
  d.b.a..........................51 D3
Lafitte in Exile.................52 E2
Lafitte's Blacksmith Shop........53 E3
Molly's at the Market............54 D3
Oz..............................55 E3
Pat O'Brien's....................56 D3
Rawhide 2010.....................57 D3
Sazerac Bar......................58 D4
                                 59 D4

ENTERTAINMENT 🎭
Cafe Brasil......................60 E2
Contemporary Arts Center ent.....(see 14)
Donna's Bar & Grill..............61 C3
Energy Imax Theatre..............(see 10)
Harrah's Casino..................62 D5
House of Blues...................63 C4
Howlin' Wolf.....................64 C6
Le Petit Théâtre du Vieux Carré..65 D3
Louisiana Superdome..............66 A5
Preservation Hall................67 D3
Snug Harbor......................68 E2
Southern Repertory Theater.......69 D5

TRANSPORT
Bicycle Michael's................70 E2
Car Park.........................71 D4
Union Passenger Terminal.........72 A5

THE SOUTH

Dangers & Annoyances

New Orleans has a high violent-crime rate; it's not a city in which to be careless. Stick to places that are well peopled, particularly at night, and spring for a cab to avoid dark walks. St Louis Cemetery No 1 and Louis Armstrong Park – in the Tremé district – have particularly bad reputations, even by day, and are more safely visited in groups (if you're not taking a tour, coincide your visit with tours). In the Quarter, street hustlers frequently approach tourists – just walk away.

Since 'The Storm,' services are more sporadic, fewer buses run, more cell phone providers go on the blink, and hours of operation are curtailed.

Sights & Activities

FRENCH QUARTER

Iconic. The balconies, the cobbled streets, the lazy fans spinning the heavy air. It's no wonder that the entire French Quarter is a National Historic District and myriad groups serve as watchdogs of architectural preservation. The predominantly residential lower Quarter offers serenity in its quiet, floral-scented streets, while the upper Quarter plays the harlot: bright lights and noisy bars line Bourbon St and idiosyncratic antique shops and galleries jam Royal St. Take a wander and you'll discover all sorts of treats.

Jackson Square is the heart of the Vieux Carré, overlooking the Mississippi River. The grand 1794 **St Louis Cathedral**, designed by Gilberto Guillemard, presides over the square's assortment of street musicians, artists and tarot-card readers. The river levee's **Moonwalk** makes a great spot to sit and dip beignets in *café au lait* while watching the river boats meander by.

Many museums and historic homes in the Quarter have been hit hard by the drop in tourism post-Katrina. At the time of research, the **Louisiana State Museum** (☎ 504-568-6968; http://lsm.crt.state.la.us; each bldg adult/child $6/free; ☽ 9am-5pm Tue-Sun) was operating only two sites. The 1911 **Cabildo** (701 Chartres St), on the left of the cathedral, is a Louisiana history museum and has a Katrina exhibit. Its sister building, on the right of the church, the 1813 **Presbytère** (751 Chartres St), is an excellent Mardi Gras museum, with vibrant displays of costumes, parade floats and royal jewelry.

Ensconced in several exquisitely restored buildings, the **Historic New Orleans Collection**

(☎ 504-523-4662; 533 Royal St; admission free, home tour $5; ☽ 9am-4:30pm Tue-Sat, from 10am Sun) displays thoughtfully curated exhibits with an emphasis on archival materials, such as the original transfer documents of the Louisiana Purchase.

In 1728, 12 Ursuline nuns arrived in New Orleans to care for the French garrison's 'miserable little hospital' and to educate the young girls of the colony. Between 1745 and 1752, the French colonial army built the **Ursuline Convent** (☎ 504-529-3040; 1112 Chartres St), now the oldest structure in the Mississippi River Valley and the only remaining French building in the Quarter. Since Katrina, the convent has discontinued tours so you must peek at it through the gate, but tours may resume.

Originally a Native American trading post, the **French Market** (☎ 504-522-2621; www.frenchmarket.org; N Peters St from St Ann St to Barracks St; ☽ 9am-5pm) is the US' oldest public market. It is comprised of the open-air **Farmers Market**, offering fresh fruits, hot sauces and cookbooks, and the **Flea Market**, with its potpourri of inexpensive souvenirs: Mardi Gras trinkets, bolo ties and preserved alligator heads. Since 1860, restaurants and shops have filled the enclosed **Butcher's Market**.

TREMÉ

On the lakeside edge of the French Quarter, the Tremé district was originally populated by French-speaking African American Creoles, and modern residents still retain great pride in the neighborhood's history and traditions. **Louis Armstrong Park** encompasses **Congo Square**, an American cultural landmark. Now a brick open space, it was the one place where enslaved people were allowed to congregate and play the music they had carried over the seas – a practice outlawed in most other slave-holding societies.

The 1824 **St Augustine's Church** (☎ 504-525-5934; 1210 Governor Nicholls St) is the second-oldest African American Catholic church in the US; many jazz funeral processions originate here. Across the street, the **Backstreet Cultural Museum** (☎ 504-522-4806; www.backstreetmuseum.org; 1116 St Claude Ave; admission $5; ☽ 10am-5pm Tue-Sat), the brainchild of Sylvester Francis, has memorabilia of local African American culture, such as the Mardi Gras Indians and jazz funerals. Francis provides savory stories to accompany exhibits.

THE SOUTH

YOU PUT A SPELL ON ME

Chicken feet don't adorn doorsteps, but the practice of voodoo does live on in New Orleans. The shadowy **Historic Voodoo Museum** (☎ 504-680-0128; www.voodoomuseum.com; 724 Dumaine St; adult/child $7/3.50; ⏰ 4-6:30pm Mon-Thu, 10am-7pm Fri & Sat) explores this exotic form of spiritual expression first brought to New Orleans by West African slaves who came via Haiti. Priestess Miriam Williams gives consultations from her **Voodoo Spiritual Temple & Cultural Center** (☎ 504-522-9627; 828 N Rampart St; ⏰ 11am-6pm Mon-Sat) and dispenses *gris-gris* (charms), incense and oils. **The Island of Salvation Botanica** (☎ 504-948-9961; www.feyvodou.com; 835 Piety St; ⏰ 10am-5:30pm Wed-Sat, from noon Sun), in the Bywater, is stocked with similar talismans and Priestess Sallie Ann Glassman is renowned for her ceremonies.

The **New Orleans African American Museum** (☎ 504-566-1138; 1418 Governor Nicholls St; adult/child $5/3; ⏰ 11am-4pm Wed-Sat) exhibits local artists in a tidy Creole cottage with terraced grounds.

St Louis Cemetery No 1 (Basin St; ⏰ 8am-3pm) received the remains of most early Creoles. The shallow water table necessitated aboveground burials, with bodies placed in the family tombs you see to this day. Don't enter the cemetery alone; if the ghosts don't get you, the muggers might.

CBD & WAREHOUSE DISTRICT

The CBD and Warehouse District comprise the commercial section established after the Louisiana Purchase. Today, several outstanding museums anchor the Warehouse District, and local art galleries cluster along **Julia St** holding openings on the first Saturday evening of each month.

Aquarium of the Americas (☎ 504-581-4629; www.auduboninstitute.org; 1 Canal St; adult/child $17/7; ⏰ 10am-5pm Tue-Sun) simulates an eclectic selection of watery habitats – look for the rare white alligator. You can buy combination tickets to the IMAX theater (p447) next door and the Audubon Zoo in Uptown (p440; boats from Woldenberg Park go there).

The **Canal Street Ferry** (pedestrian & cyclist/car free/$1; ⏰ 6am-8:45pm), departing from the foot of Canal St, is a fast and fabulous ride across the Mississippi to Algiers and back.

Extending nearly half a mile along the Mississippi on the site of the 1984 World's Fair, the **Riverwalk Marketplace** (☎ 504-522-1555; www.riverwalkmarketplace.com; at Poydras St & the river; ⏰ 10am-6pm Mon-Sat, from noon Sun) houses a shopping mall and food court.

The excellent **Ogden Museum of Southern Art** (☎ 504-539-9600; www.ogdenmuseum.org; 925 Camp St; adult/child $10/5; ⏰ 11am-4pm Thu-Sun, free live music 6-8pm Thu) displays a vast collection of modern artwork as well as definitive early outsider art, such as that of Clementine Hunter. Henry Hobson Richardson designed the intricate stone annex.

Across the street, the **Contemporary Arts Center** (☎ 504-528-3800; www.cacno.org; 900 Camp St; adult/child $5/free; ⏰ 11am-4pm Thu-Sun) maintains airy galleries filled with rotating avant-garde shows.

The extensive, heart-wrenching **National World War II Museum** (☎ 504-527-6012; www.nationalww2museum.org; 945 Magazine St; adult/child $14/6; ⏰ 9am-5pm Tue-Sun) collects the sobering eyewitness accounts of life and conflict during WWII, and houses actual planes, weaponry and landing craft, as well as excellent exhibits on all phases of the war. Many of the volunteer docents are war survivors. A multimillion-dollar expansion, in progress at the time of research, will include an interactive theater and a United Service Organization cantina.

GARDEN DISTRICT & UPTOWN

Magnificent oak trees arch over St Charles Ave, and lush gardens surround ornate mansions. The Garden District enfolds some of the most decadent of these and makes for a lovely stroll. After the Louisiana Purchase, subdivision of former plantations extended Uptown following the steam railway on St Charles Ave, where the **St Charles Avenue streetcar** ran until Katrina. The reopening of the line keeps getting pushed back, and at the time of research the route must be traversed by bus, car or Mardi Gras float (most Uptown krewes roll down St Charles – look for beads in the trees). Clusters of shops and galleries dot **Magazine St**.

Further west, Tulane and Loyola universities occupy adjacent campuses alongside expansive **Audubon Park**. Tulane was founded in 1834 as a medical college in an attempt to control repeated cholera and yellow-fever

MARDI GRAS & JAZZ FEST

During **Mardi Gras** (www.mardigrasneworleans.com) the city puts parades before paychecks, costumes before commerce. Although it began as a pagan rite of spring it has since evolved into pure, generalized bacchanalia. In the four weeks leading up to Fat Tuesday, parades roll all over town. Check the newspaper or *Arthur Hardy's Mardi Gras Guide* (www.mardigrasguide.com) for routes and schedules.

Parades season is kicked off by the highly satirical Krewe du Vieux, one of the few to march in the French Quarter. The others are Barkus, a parade of costumed dogs, and St Anne, a gorgeous, Mardi Gras–day krewe (parading club) of fabulously adorned folks. If you wear a costume, you can march with them!

A common route in Uptown, along St Charles Ave to Canal St, is quite family-friendly, and usually features a couple of krewes, each made up of a dozen or more tractor-drawn floats, marching bands and masked riders. Crowds scramble for souvenir 'throws': beads, doubloons, go-cups and stuffed animals – kids make out like bandits. Dramatic nighttime parades feature flambeaux carriers wielding flaming torches.

Before sunrise on Mardi Gras day, the entire parade corridor along St Charles Ave is staked out with chairs, ladders and coolers. The culminating parades of Zulu (starting around 8:30am) and Rex (starting about 10am) each include more than 30 floats and bands. If you are rewarded with a hand-painted Zulu coconut, you are one of the chosen few. By midafternoon it's all beer and beads on Bourbon St and at midnight on the dot, the police sweep the streets of every last reveler.

Less about debauchery, and more about sheer musical and culinary enjoyment, the **New Orleans Jazz & Heritage Festival** (☎ 504-522-4786; www.nojazzfest.com; 1205 N Rampart St, New Orleans, LA 70116; adult/child 2-11 in advance $35/5, at the gate $45/5) or 'Jazz Fest' began in 1968 as a celebration of the city's 250th birthday. Famous jazz players such as Louis Armstrong, Duke Ellington and Dave Brubeck lit up the place and it has since expanded to 10 stages at the Fair Grounds, untold musical genres and two glorious weekends in late April and early May.

Come hungry: food booths overflow with delectable treats such as softshell crab po'boys, fried *boudin* (Cajun rice-and-pork sausage) balls and white-chocolate bread pudding. Bring dancing shoes, sunscreen, a hat, some water and a blanket for chilling out between acts. The musical line-up comes out in January; make hotel reservations early.

epidemics. Today the verdant campuses offer a welcome respite from city streets, and often the universities host concerts and lectures that are worth the trip Uptown.

Among the country's best zoos, the **Audubon Zoological Gardens** (☎ 504-861-2537; www.auduboninstitute.org; 6500 Magazine St; adult/child $12/7; ◷ 9am-5pm) contains the ultracool Louisiana Swamp exhibit, full of alligators, bobcats, foxes, bears and snapping turtles. The zoo cruise from Woldenberg Park, downtown, brings you here by riverboat.

CITY PARK & MID-CITY

The **Canal streetcar** makes the run from the CBD to City Park. Acquired in 1850, the 1300-acre **City Park** (☎ 504-482-4888; www.neworleanscitypark.com) is famous for its huge moss-draped live oaks and scenic bayou lagoons. During the aftermath of Hurricane Katrina, the park sat underwater, but once again it is

back up and running. The beautiful **Botanical Garden** (☎ 504-483-9488; adult/child $5/2; ◷ 10am-4:30pm Tue-Sun) is working to rebuild its lost plant collections.

Also in City Park, the elegant **New Orleans Museum of Art** (☎ 504-658-4100; www.noma.org; 1 Collins Diboll Circle; adult/child $8/4; ◷ 10am-4:30pm Wed-Sun) was founded in 1910 and is well worth a visit. Its **sculpture garden** (admission free; ◷ 10am-4:30pm Wed-Sun) contains a cutting-edge collection in lush, meticulously planned grounds.

Besides hosting the regular horseracing season, the **Fair Grounds** are also home to the huge springtime New Orleans Jazz & Heritage Festival (above).

ALGIERS

New Orleans' historic annex on the westbank, Algiers Point is a sequestered community of restored houses, down-home restaurants and bars, and quiet streets. Best reached by the

Canal St ferry (p439), and toured on foot or by bike, it also harbors the garish and good-fun **Mardi Gras World** (☎ 504-361-7821; www.mardigras world.com; cnr Brooklyn & Newton Sts; adult/child $17/11; ☻ tours 9:30am-4:30pm). A free shuttle runs from the ferry, and after a short film on Mardi Gras history, the tour takes you through the giant workshops where artists create elaborate floats for New Orleans krewes (marching clubs), Universal Studios and Disney World.

Walking Tour: French Quarter

The Quarter's elegant 18th-century Spanish colonial architecture lines narrow streets, seducing with bright colors and minimalist beauty. A leisurely stroll, peeking inside iron gates and browsing the shops and galleries, is the best way to soak up the vibe.

Begin your walk at the **Presbytère** (**1**; p438) on Jackson Sq and head down Chartres St to the corner of Ursulines Ave and the **Ursuline Convent** (**2**; p438).

Directly across Chartres St, at No 1113, the 1826 **Beauregard-Keyes House** (**3**) combines Creole- and American-style design. Civil War General PGT Beauregard rented rooms here, and author Frances Parkinson Keyes lived here from 1942–1970.

Walk along Ursulines Ave to Royal St, perhaps stopping for a quick *café au lait* and delectable pastry at **Croissant D'Or Patisserie** (**4**; p445). The soda fountain at the **Royal Pharmacy** (**5**) is a preserved relic from halcyon malt-shop days; the owners of the pharmacy feel it's too classic to pull out.

Continue up Ursulines Ave and then left onto Bourbon St. The ramshackle one-story structure on the corner of St Philip St is a salty little tavern and National Historic Landmark called **Lafitte's Blacksmith Shop** (**6**; p446). Head down St Philip back to Royal St and take a right.

When it comes to quintessential New Orleans postcard images, Royal St takes the prize. Cast-iron galleries grace the buildings and a profusion of flowers garland the facades. Take it slowly and appreciate the details.

At No 915 the **Cornstalk Hotel** (**7**; p443) stands behind one of the most frequently photographed fences anywhere. At Orleans Ave, stately magnolia trees and lush tropical plants fill **St Anthony's Garden** (**8**), behind **St Louis Cathedral** (**9**; p438).

Alongside the garden, Pirate's Alley is an inviting, shaded walkway that calls for a lit-

tle detour. The first buildings to the right, Nos 622 to 624 Pirate's Alley, are just two of the **Labranche Buildings** (**10**). Note the original wrought-iron balconies, some of the finest in town, which date to the 1840s. At 624 Pirate's Alley, charming **Faulkner House Books** (**11**; p434), is named for its most famous resident, William Faulkner.

Turn right down Cabildo Alley and then right up St Peter St, toward Royal St. Tennessee Williams shacked up at No 632 St Peter, the **Avart-Peretti House** (**12**), in 1946–47 when he wrote *A Streetcar Named Desire*.

At the corner of Royal, the **LeMonnier Mansion** (**13**), at No 640, is commonly known to be New Orleans' first 'skyscraper.' If you kept going up St Peter, you'd reach **Pat O'Brien's** (p446) and the rustic façade of **Preservation Hall** (p447).

WALK FACTS

Start Presbytère
Finish Cabildo
Distance 1 mile
Duration About 90 minutes

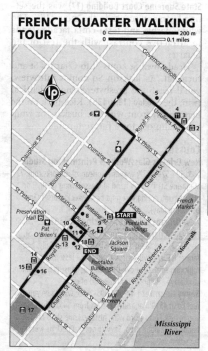

FRENCH QUARTER WALKING TOUR

0 ————— 200 m
0 ————— 0.1 miles

THE SOUTH

FUNKY, GROOVY, CHILL: WWOZ (90.7FM)

This all-volunteer radio station pumps out world-class jazz, blues and roots music 24/7. DJs are often local musicians with encyclopedic knowledge of their genre, though the emphasis is always on soaking up the sounds. Now that it is live on the web (www.wwoz.org), there's no reason to miss it. If you're in town, tune in at the top of each odd hour to catch the list of who's playing around town that night. Every city should be so lucky.

Turn left on Royal St. At the corner of Royal and Toulouse Sts stands a pair of houses built by Jean François Merieult in the 1790s. The **Court of Two Lions (14)**, at 541 Royal St, opens onto Toulouse St and next door is the **Historic New Orleans Collection (15**; p438). Across the street, at No 520, a carriageway leads to the picturesque **Brulatour Courtyard (16)**.

On the next block, the massive 1909 **State Supreme Court Building (17)** was the setting for many scenes in the movie *JFK*. The white marble and terra-cotta facade stands in attractive contrast with the rest of the Quarter.

Head down St Louis St to Chartres St and turn left. As Jackson Sq comes into view, you'll reach the Presbytère's near-identical twin, the **Cabildo (18**; p438). Kick back on the benches in front with the buskers or whip your palm out for a future foretold.

Courses

New Orleans GlassWorks & Printmaking Studio (☎ 504-529-7277; www.neworleansglassworks.com; 727 Magazine St) Try your hand at glassblowing (really!) or printmaking during weekend or six-week courses (September to May).

New Orleans School of Cooking (☎ 504-525-2665; www.neworleansschoolofcooking.com; 524 St Louis St; class $27; 🕙 10am-12:30pm) Menus rotate daily, and former NJ Jet Kevin Belton turns these lessons into a rollicking comedy show. Dine on creations such as gumbo, jambalaya and pralines at the end of class.

Savvy Gourmet (☎ 504-895-2665; www.savvygourmet.com; 4519 Magazine St; class from $45) Whether you're looking to learn wine history, knife skills or hands-on seafood prep, Savvy's got it. Check its website for schedule.

New Orleans for Children

Many of New Orleans' daytime attractions are well-suited for kids: the Audubon Zoo (p440), Aquarium of the Americas (p439) and Mardi Gras World (p441), for example. Also check out the 'kid stuff' listings in the *Times-Picayune* Living section on Monday.

Carousel Gardens (☎ 504-482-4888; www.neworleanscitypark.com; admission $2; 🕙 11am-5:30pm Sat & Sun) The 1906 carousel should reopen soon; other amusement-park rides can give the kiddies a thrill in the meantime.

Children's Book Shop (☎ 504-861-2105; 7529 Maple St; 🕙 10am-6pm Mon-Sat) Cozy storytelling next door to the Maple Street Book Shop (p434).

Louisiana Children's Museum (☎ 504-523-1357; www.lcm.org; 420 Julia St; admission $7; 🕙 9:30am-4:30pm Tue-Sat, from noon Sun) Great hands-on exploratory exhibits and toddler area. Children under 16 must be accompanied by an adult.

Tours

Tours, tours everywhere! Check the *New Orleans Official Visitors Guide* for a full selection of the myriad offerings. Some companies now give post-Katrina devastation tours. The Jean Lafitte National Historic Park Visitor Center (p435) leads free walking tours of the French Quarter at 9:30am (get tickets at 9am).

Carriage ride (Jackson Sq; 5 people per 30min from $60; 🕙 to midnight) A mule-drawn ride through the Quarter gives a relaxing glimpse of the narrow streets at a gentle pace while the driver spins fanciful yarns.

Friends of the Cabildo (☎ 504-523-3939; 1850 House Museum Store, 523 St Ann St; adult/child $12/free; 🕙 tours 10am & 1:30pm Tue-Sun) Volunteers lead excellent two-hour walking tours of the Quarter.

Historic New Orleans Tours (☎ 504-947-2120; www.tourneworleans.com; adult/child $15/7) Get a slice of the macabre on a cemetery, voodoo or haunted tour.

Steamboat Natchez (☎ 504-586-8777; www.steamboatnatchez.com) Embrace the Mississippi! Two-hour Harbor Cruises (adult/child $19.50/9.75; skip the onboard buffet lunch), evening Dinner-Jazz Cruises ($33.50/16.75 cruise only), and Aquarium-Zoo Cruises ($17.50/8.75 cruise only) depart the boat dock behind JAX Brewery at the foot of Toulouse St.

Tours by Isabelle (☎ 504-391-3544; www.toursbyisabelle.com; Hurricane Katrina Tour $58) Offers a 70-mile, 3½ hour journey through New Orleans' devastation from Hurricane Katrina; also has standard city tours.

Festivals & Events

New Orleans never needs an excuse to party – whether in commemoration of shrimp and petroleum or the mighty mirliton, there's almost always some celebration in town. Just the wee-est of listings follow; check www .neworleanscvb.com for more.

Mardi Gras In February or early March, Fat Tuesday marks the orgasmic finale of the Carnival season (p440).

St Patrick's Day March 17 and its closest weekend see parades of cabbage-wielding Irishfolk.

St Joseph's Day – Super Sunday March 19 and its nearest Sunday bring 'gangs' of Mardi Gras Indians out into the streets in all their feathered, drumming glory. The Super Sunday parade usually begins around noon at Bayou St John and Orleans Ave, but follows no fixed route.

Tennessee Williams Literary Festival (www.tennes seewilliams.net) In March, five days of literary panels, plays and parties celebrate the author's work.

French Quarter Festival (www.fqfi.org) The second weekend of April; free music on multiple stages.

Jazz Fest The last weekend of April and the first weekend of May; a world-renowned extravaganza of music, food, crafts and good-living (p440).

Essence Music Festival (www.essence.com) Independence Day weekend sees star-studded performances at the Superdome.

Southern Decadence (www.southerndecadence.net) A huge gay, lesbian and transgender festival, including a leather block party, on Labor Day weekend (first weekend in September).

Art for Arts' Sake The first Saturday of October; scores of galleries in the Warehouse District and along Magazine St kick off the season.

Sleeping

As a result of the drop in tourism after Katrina, struggling hotels have slashed prices dramatically. Luxe rooms can be had for a song. Prices below are high-season nonfestival rates; expect them to rise as tourists return. Always, rates peak during Mardi Gras and Jazz Fest, and fall in the hot summer months. Book early and call or check the internet for special deals. Hotel sales tax is 13%, plus $1 to $3 per person per night. Parking in the Quarter costs $15 to $25 per day.

BUDGET

Marquette House International Hostel (☎ 504-523-3014; www.neworleansinternationalhostel.com; 2249 Carondelet St; dm $22, s/d from $44/53; ☺ office 7am-noon & 5-10pm; ℗ ✕ ⊗) A sprawling compound of both dorms and private rooms (with refrigerators and microwaves) near the Garden District. Serviceable, but certainly not luxurious, the rooms are upstaged by the lush garden area, perfect for hanging out and meeting fellow travelers.

A Creole House Hotel (☎ 504-524-8076, 800-535-7858; www.acreolehouse.com; 1013 St Ann St; r incl breakfast from $49; ⊗) Play bohemian in this musty, no-frills townhouse smack in the gay district of the Quarter. Frumpy but comfy is the name of the game.

MIDRANGE

Lamothe House (☎ 504-947-1161; 800-367-5858; www .lamothehouse.com; 621 Esplanade Ave; r/ste incl breakfast from $80/100; ✕ ⊗ ⊡ wi-fi) Grand mansion rooms fuse royal with bordello: gilt accents and rococo carvings compete with delicate oil paintings. Starker rooms in the outbuildings adjoin easily for families, and the spacious courtyard lets you all spread out.

Chateau Hotel (☎ 504-524-9636; www.chateauho tel.com; 1001 Chartres St; r/ste incl breakfast from $80/170; ℗ ✕ ⊗) Though it's more a debauched hotel than chateau, it's tucked in a quiet corner of the lower Quarter and has consistently low prices. Slightly dingy rooms, some with balconies, surround a pretty and refreshing courtyard pool. Parking costs around $16.

Cornstalk Hotel (☎ 504-523-1515, 800-759-6112; www.cornstalkhotel.com; 915 Royal St; r incl breakfast $85-185; ℗ ✕ ⊗ wi-fi) Pass through the famous cast-iron fence and into a plush, antiqued B&B where the serenity sweeps away the whirl of the busy streets outside. Gemlike rooms are all unique and luxurious. Parking's available for $15.

Hôtel St Marie (☎ 504-561-8951; www.hotelstmarie .com; 827 Toulouse St; r from $90; ✕ ⊗ ⊡ wi-fi) A tidy operation just steps away from Bourbon St. Rooms aren't much more than basic-motel, but they're cheap and clean, and the lush courtyard offers a respite from the raucousness nearby.

Prytania Park Hotel (☎ 504-524-0427, 888-498-7591; www.prytaniaparkhotel.com; 1525 Prytania St; r from $90; ℗ ✕ ⊗ wi-fi) Really a complex of three separate hotels, the Prytania Park's small honey-colored rooms are a bit dingy. The Prytania Oaks is sleeker (rooms from $119) and the Queen Anne is an exquisite boutique hotel, newly renovated and bedecked with antiques (rooms from $130). Perfect spot for bouncing between the Quarter and the Garden District or Uptown, and parking is free.

Le Pavillon (☎ 504-581-3111, 800-535-9095; www .lepavillon.com; 833 Poydras Ave; r/ste from $100/600; ℗ ✕ ⊗ ⊡ wi-fi) Built in 1907, this elegant European-style hotel's opulent marble lobby, plush, modern rooms and rooftop pool are

---

GAY & LESBIAN NEW ORLEANS

New Orleans' dynamic gay community is concentrated around the lower French Quarter and Faubourg Marigny. The **Lesbian & Gay Community Center** (LGCC; ☎ 504-945-1103; 2114 Decatur St) is a great resource for travelers, anyone moving to the Big Easy or looking to find out about special events, the hottest bars and gay-friendly businesses. Also check out *Ambush Magazine* (www.ambushmag.com, www.gaynewonleans.com).

The delightfully scandalous annual **Southern Decadence** (www.southerndecadence.net) festival mixes mainstream corporate sponsors with events such as the legendary banana-sucking contest. For five days, beginning at midnight the Wednesday before Labor Day weekend (first weekend in September), upwards of 120,000 gay, lesbian and transgender revelers converge for a literal orgy of partying.

If you miss out on the festival, fear not. There's still plenty of nightlife left. Gay-friendly bars follow (unfortunately, there's not much of a lesbian bar scene in town).

Bourbon Pub & Parade Disco (☎ 504-529-2107; www.bourbonpub.com; 801 Bourbon St) The party spills out onto the sidewalk at this popular dance club.

Lafitte in Exile (☎ 504-522-8397; www.lafittes.com; 901 Bourbon St) Easily the most popular gay bar in the Quarter. The balcony is superb and the drink specials just keep coming.

Oz (☎ 504-593-9491; www.oznewonleans.com; 800 Bourbon St) Even Uptown debs have been seen shaking their tail feathers at this mixed dance club. The bar is manned by buff, shirtless bartenders.

Rawhide 2010 (☎ 504-525-8106; www.rawhide2010.com; 740 Burgundy St) A rocking good-time leather bar.

---

a steal. Decadent suites might prevent you from ever leaving the building. If booking a queen room, request a bay window. Parking costs $25.

our pick Melrose Mansion (☎ 504-944-2255, 800-650-3323; www.melrosemansion.com; 937 Esplanade Ave; r $100-179; ☒ ☒ ☒) If you were a millionaire with a New Orleans pied-à-terre, this could be it. It's austerely elegant with hand-selected antiques sitting alongside the freshest modern art, and during high season you'll be regaled with a home-baked breakfast and evening wine and cheese in the chic parlor. Before the storm, prices were twice the current rates.

Lafitte Guest House (☎ 504-581-2678, 800-331-7971; www.lafitteguesthouse.com; 1003 Bourbon St; r $180-230; ☐ ☒ ☒ wi-fi) Completely renovated and refurnished after Katrina, this graceful 1848 French manor house offers an exquisite hideaway just down from the partying part of Bourbon St. You

'll have to choose between lolling in the canopied bed or people-watching if you have a room with a balcony. Parking free for first seven cars – a rarity!

TOP END

Soniat House Hotel (☎ 504-522-0570, 800-544-8808; www.soniathouse.com; 1133 Chartres St; r/ste incl breakfast from $275/$525; ☐ ☒ wi-fi) If the luxury chains off Canal St are not your cup of tea, embrace old-style living with liveried servants, fresh-baked buttermilk biscuits and understated Creole elegance. You will be left alone amid the parquet floors, wrought-iron balconies and period furnishings to soak up the tranquility, unless you ring for service. No children under 10. Parking costs $25.

Eating

In New Orleans, chances are good that if you are not actually eating, you are talking about your next meal or reverentially describing one that you recently had. Embrace the sheer range of flavors available from the divey-ist po'boy joint to the 'It' restaurant of the current superstar chef. Creole cooking is deeply influenced by French cuisine and Caribbean spices, and Cajun food tends toward the fiery hot and usually involves seafood – the more heads the better. Unfortunately, since Katrina many restaurants have reduced their hours because staffing is difficult. The Advocacy Center (www.advocacyla.org/zagat.php) reviews restaurants for disabled accessibility.

FRENCH QUARTER

Café du Monde (☎ 504-525-4544; 800 Decatur St; beignets $1.75; ⏰ 24hr) Delectable deep-fried, powdered sugar–coated beignets paired with piping hot chicory *café au lait* are sure to cure almost any overindulgence. Eat in or take your treats to the levee Moonwalk overlooking the river.

Croissant D'Or Patisserie (☎ 504-524-4663; 617 Ursulines Ave; meals $3-5; ☯ 7am-2pm Wed-Mon) Newspaper-toting locals fill this simple bakery where you'll have trouble choosing amongst the myriad croissants and quiches. It's a welcome pit stop in a morning stroll through the quiet lower French Quarter.

Johnny's Po-Boys (☎ 504-524-8129; 511 St Louis St; breakfast $2-6, lunch $6-10; ☯ 9am-3pm Mon-Fri, 9am-4pm Sat & Sun) Well-worn and often crowded, Johnny's delivers superb stuffed po'boys. The fried oyster number (lightly breaded in cornmeal) recruits devotees. No credit cards.

Clover Grill (☎ 504-598-1010; 900 Bourbon St; dishes $5-8; ☯ 24hr) Compact and tidy, this '50s-style diner slangs the hash all night long. If you order a burger, the tatooed chef will cook it up under a hubcap.

Central Grocery (☎ 504-523-1620; 923 Decatur St; muffuletta half/whole $7/13; ☯ 9am-5pm Tue-Sat) A Sicilian immigrant invented the world-famous *muffuletta* sandwich here in 1906. Today, it's still the best place in town to get one: a round, seeded loaf of bread stuffed with ham, salami, provolone and marinated olive salad.

Acme Oyster & Seafood House (☎ 504-522-5973; 724 Iberville St; mains $10-12, dozen oysters $10; ☯ 11am-10pm Sun-Thu, to 11pm Fri & Sat) Out-of-towners and locals alike flock to this old-school oyster bar. Its reputation for shucking the city's best oysters, along with its seafood gumbo and po'boys, has endured since 1910. Take a seat at the mirrored bar and be mesmerized by the shuckers.

K-Paul's Louisiana Kitchen (☎ 504-596-2530; 416 Chartres St; mains $29-36; ☯ 5:30-10pm Mon-Sat) Paul Prudhomme single-handedly popularized Cajun cooking in this welcoming bricked bistro. The chefs use the very best ingredients and a loving attention to detail in preparing quintessential dishes such as jambalaya and blackened gulf fish, and the knowledgeable waiters bring it out with a smile.

CBD & WAREHOUSE DISTRICT

our pick **Cochon** (☎ 504-588-2123; www.cochonrestaurant.com; 930 Tchoupitoulas St; mains $16-19; ☯ 11am-10pm Mon-Fri, from 5pm Sat) James Beard Award–winning chef Donald Link's fabulous brasserie serves up gourmet Southern comfort food such as rabbit and dumplings and wood-fired roast oysters. Housemade *boucherie* and a fearless willingness to pair the simply succulent with the exceptionally extravagant catapult this laid-back spot into the echelons of truly unique cuisine.

Emeril's (☎ 504-528-9393; www.emerils.com; 800 Tchoupitoulas St; dinner mains $25-38; ☯ 11:30am-2pm Thu & Fri, 6-10pm nightly) Chef Emeril Lagasse's flagship restaurant lives up to all the hype. His protégés rustle up consistently scrumptious

---

LOCAL VOICES: CHEF PAUL PRUDHOMME

Chef Paul Prudhomme put Louisiana cooking on the map. A native of Opelousas, he now lives in the Faubourg Marigny neighborhood of New Orleans, and supplies the world with his unique take on local cuisine and his boundless enthusiasm for all things Louisianan.

Why should people come back to New Orleans?

New Orleans is the most fun city in the country. It's the most unique city in the country. It's got the best food – no matter where I've been around the world. It's also a great hospitality place. We all, locals, enjoy tourists, and that's unusual.

Where would you take a friend who is new to New Orleans?

Well, the French Quarter (p438), that would be important, and a tour of the devastation that still exists in some places (p442). I'd take them to restaurants – there are other fabulous places to eat, besides my place (above), and…depending on what they like…a nightclub (p446). And **Harrah's** (☎ 504-533-6000; Canal St at the river) if they like to gamble. The idea is to entertain people and it's so easy to do it here. We even do it on the street! *(Gesturing at a Dixieland jazz band on the sidewalk.)*

What's your favorite New Orleans music?

I'm from Acadiana, so my favorite music is Cajun, but I love these jazz guys. I don't think we have any bad kind of music. We have a music here for any mood there is. It's spectacular!

Bam!-worthy fare under the modern glass arch looking out on the main dining room, and an attentive staff sees to your every need.

GARDEN DISTRICT & UPTOWN

Jacques-Imo's Cafe (☎ 504-861-0886; 8324 Oak St; mains $14-21; ☼ 5:30-10pm Tue-Thu, to 10:30pm Fri & Sat) Best taken early, before the hordes descend on this funky bar–restaurant. Alligator cheesecake and ribald conversation vie for your attention, as do the hand-painted murals and an eclectic crowd.

Dick & Jenny's (☎ 504-894-9880; 4501 Tchoupitoulas St; mains $17-22; ☼ 5:30-10pm Tue-Thu, to 10:30pm Fri & Sat) Just up the street from Tipitina's (opposite), this quaint clapboard restaurant specializes in inventive, seasonal dishes such as seared sea scallops and gulf shrimp with sun-dried tomato and goat-cheese polenta and saffron chardonnay butter – at a reasonable price. Though popular, no reservations are allowed, so be prepared to sip an excellent cocktail in the courtyard as you wait for your table. There is always a vegetarian option.

Commander's Palace (☎ 504-899-8221; www.commanderspalace.com; 1403 Washington Ave; mains lunch $14-17, dinner $30-42; ☼ 11:30am-2pm Mon-Fri, to 1pm Sat, 10:30am-1:30pm Sun, 6-10pm Mon-Sat) One of New Orleans' *grande dames*, Commander's is a formal but friendly mainstay of impeccable Creole cooking and knowledgeable, friendly service. In the heart of the gorgeous Garden District, pop in for the lunchtime 25¢

THE NOLA MENU

For the uninitiated, the parlance of local cuisine can make ordering a challenge. Get a head start:

beignet – fresh, rectangular doughnuts doused in powdered sugar

boudin – Cajun rice-and-pork sausage, delicious when served in deep-fried balls

callas – fried rice-based pastry, like a beignet but harder to come by

dressed – topped with lettuce, tomato and mayo

gumbo – stewlike adventure; each one is unique!

jambalaya – rice-based dish, usually choc full of some combination of seafood, chicken and sausage

po'boy – thick sandwich made on French bread

tasso – intensely flavored smoked pork, often used as seasoning

---

martinis and a cup of the signature turtle soup ($6.50), or a *prix fixe* extravaganza ($29). Post-Katrina renovations turned the formerly elegant dining room into an odd aviary. No shorts allowed.

Drinking

New Orleans is a drinking town. Of course there's Bourbon St, and its baubles, shimmer and hustle, but each neighborhood has its favorite watering holes. You could try a new one every night and not repeat your experience. The kinder, gentler strip runs along Frenchmen St in Faubourg Marigny.

For a great cup of Joe in a laidback, artsy hang, try **Coffea** (☎ 504-342-2484; 3218 Dauphine St, in the Bywater; ☼ 7am-3pm, from 9am Sat & Sun, closed Tue; wi-fi), owned by a local painter and harmonica virtuoso.

BARS & CLUBS

Most bars open every day, often by noon, get hopping around 10pm, and can stay open all night. There's no cover charge unless there's live music. It's illegal to have open glass liquor containers in the street so all bars dispense plastic 'go cups' when you're ready to wander.

d.b.a. (☎ 504-942-3731; 618 Frenchmen St) Mellow until it fills up for live music and late-night partying; the extensive drinks menu and window seats will keep you busy while you wait.

Lafitte's Blacksmith Shop (☎ 504-523-0066; 941 Bourbon St) This idiosyncratic corner bar always has a steadfast crew of regulars propped up on its stools.

Sazerac Bar (☎ 504-529-7111; 123 Baronne St) In the Fairmont Hotel, a real classic with gorgeous art-deco murals, and it's the originator of the eponymous beverage.

Molly's at the Market (☎ 504-525-5169; 1107 Decatur St) A young, bohemian hipster crowd swills the Guinness and mingles out onto the sidewalk.

Bombay Club (☎ 504-586-0972; 830 Conti St) The most cultured place for a drink in the Quarter, it specializes in high-priced martinis.

Pat O'Brien's (☎ 504-525-4823; 718 St Peter St) The sugary sweet Hurricane was developed here, where a labyrinthine series of alcoves and courtyards hide many a reveler.

Mimi's in the Marigny (☎ 504-872-986; 2601 Royal St) Neighborhood joint with pool and tapas.

Entertainment

LIVE MUSIC

What's New Orleans without live local music? Almost any weekend night you can find something for every taste: jazz, blues, brass band, country, Dixieland, zydeco, rock or Cajun. Free shows in the daytime abound. Check *Gambit* or *Offbeat* (p435) for schedules (showtimes vary, especially post-Katrina) and get off Bourbon St to see the true breadth and creativity of local musicians.

Snug Harbor (☎ 504-949-0696; 626 Frenchmen St; cover $12-20) In the Marigny, the city's premier contemporary jazz venue is all about world-class music. Ellis Marsalis has a standing Friday-night gig.

Donna's Bar & Grill (☎ 504-596-6914; 800 N Rampart St; cover $7-10) Shoulder up to the bar, grab a plate of red beans and rice and groove to jazz, blues or brass bands in this homey room on the edge of the Quarter.

Preservation Hall (☎ 504-522-2841; 726 St Peter St; cover $8) A veritable museum of traditional and Dixieland jazz, Preservation Hall is a pilgrimage. But like many religious obligations, it ain't necessarily easy, with no air-conditioning, limited seating and no refreshments (you can bring your own water, that's it).

Tipitina's (☎ 504-895-8477; 501 Napoleon Ave; cover $10-30) Always drawing a lively crowd, this legendary Uptown club rocks out like the musical Mecca it is: local jazz, blues, soul and funk stop in, as well as national touring bands.

Howlin' Wolf (☎ 504-522-9653; 907 S Peters St; cover $5-25) This Warehouse District mainstay hosts bigger local acts as well as touring rock and alt-rock bands.

Cafe Brasil (☎ 504-949-0851; 2100 Chartres St; cover $5-10) On the corner of Frenchmen St, a hip, bohemian crowd dances to reggae, Latin jazz and acoustic bands.

Maple Leaf Bar (☎ 504-866-9359; 8316 Oak St; cover $5-10) Riverbend's pride and joy – its pressed-tin ceiling and close atmosphere get especially heated late. Rebirth Brass Band plays Tuesday.

House of Blues (☎ 504-310-4999; 255 Decatur St; cover $7-35) Specializing in big-name, touring acts, the main hall can be cavernous. The smaller upstairs Parish room offers a little more soul.

THEATER & CULTURE

As with live music, check local listings for current schedules – there are often free performances, art markets and festivals of all sorts. Many venerable venues, such as the Orpheum, Saenger and Mahalia Jackson Theatres, have been shuttered due to flood damage. As a result, performance groups use temporary homes such as Tulane University's concert halls.

Le Petit Théâtre du Vieux Carré (☎ 504-522-2081; www.lepetittheatre.com; 616 St Peter St) One of the oldest theater groups in the US, it offers classic and contemporary Southern plays.

NOCCA|Riverfront (☎ 504-940-2900; www.nocca.com; 2800 Chartres St) The New Orleans Center for the Creative Arts, a public arts academy, hosts excellent seasons of dance, literary readings and performance art through its Center Stage program, as well as student and faculty showcases.

Southern Repertory Theater (☎ 504-422-6545; www.southernrep.com; 3rd fl, Canal Pl Shopping Center, 333 Canal St) Presents classic and contemporary plays.

The **Louisiana Philharmonic Orchestra** (☎ 504-523-6530; www.lpomusic.com), one of only two musician-owned symphonies in the world, performs from September to May. **New Orleans Opera Association** (☎ 504-529-3000; www.neworleansopera.org) and **New Orleans Ballet** (☎ 504-522-0996; www.nobadance.com) are the other major classical groups. The Contemporary Arts Center (p439) is the premier venue for modern plays, dance and performance art. **Zeitgeist Multidisciplinary Arts Center** (☎ 504-827-5858; www.zeitgeistinc.net) hosts indie films and performance art at varying venues until its center on Canal St is renovated, so check websites for details.

Next to the Aquarium of the Americas, the **Entergy IMAX Theatre** (☎ 504-581-4629; 1 Canal St; adult/child $8/5) shows films on a 74ft-by-54ft screen.

SPORTS

The 60,000-seat **Louisiana Superdome** (☎ 504-587-3663; www.superdome.com; 1500 Sugar Bowl Dr), made infamous during Katrina's aftermath, has returned to housing the NFL **New Orleans Saints** (www.neworleanssaints.com), Tulane's football team, concerts and special events such as the NCAA (college) Sugar Bowl. The neighboring New Orleans Arena is part-time home to basketball team **New Orleans Hornets** (www.nba.com/hornets), though they play most of their season in Oklahoma, post-Katrina. Minor League baseball team, the **Zephyrs** (www.zephyrsbaseball.com), are based at Zephyr Field in the suburb Metairie.

Getting There & Away

Louis Armstrong New Orleans International Airport
(MSY; ☎ 504-464-0831; www.flymsy.com; 900 Airline Hwy),
11 miles west of the city, handles primarily
domestic flights.

The **Union Passenger Terminal** (☎ 504-299-1880;
1001 Loyola Ave) is home to **Greyhound** (☎ 504-524-
7571, 800-231-2222; ☽ 5:15am-1pm & 2:30-6pm) which
has regular buses to Baton Rouge ($17, two
hours), Memphis, TN ($60, 11 hours) and
Atlanta, GA ($83, 12 hours).

Amtrak (☎ 504-528-1610, 800-872-7245; ☽ ticketing
5:45am-10pm) trains also operate from the Union
Passenger Terminal. *City of New Orleans* runs
to Jackson, MS; Memphis, TN; and Chicago,
IL. *Crescent* serves Birmingham, AL; Atlanta,
GA; Washington, DC; and New York City.
Sunset Limited stops on its way between Los
Angeles, CA and Miami, FL.

Getting Around

TO/FROM THE AIRPORT

There's an information booth at the airport's
A&B concourse. **Airport Shuttle** (☎ 504-522-3500,
866-596-2699; one-way per person $13) runs to down-
town hotels. The **Jefferson Transit** (☎ 504-737-7433;
adult $1.60) Airport Route E2 picks up outside
entrance 7 on the airport's upper level; it stops
along Airline Hwy (Hwy 61) on its way into
town (final stop Tulane Ave and Loyola Ave).
After 7pm it only goes to Tulane Ave and Carrollton Ave in Mid-City; a solid 5 miles through
a dreary neighborhood to get to the CBD, from
where you must transfer to a Regional Transit
Authority (RTA) bus – a haphazard transfer at
best, especially with luggage.

Taxis downtown cost $28 for one or
two people, $12 more for each additional
passenger.

CAR & MOTORCYCLE

Bringing a car to downtown New Orleans is
a costly proposition and may actually hinder
your visit, dealing with the narrow one-way
streets and parking. During daytime, downtown street parking has a two-hour limit.
Parking garages in the upper part of the Quarter charge about $5 for the first hour and $20
for 24 hours.

PUBLIC TRANSPORTATION

The **Regional Transit Authority** (RTA; ☎ 504-248-
3900; www.norta.com) runs the local bus service.
Bus and streetcar fares are $1.25, plus 25¢
for transfers; express buses cost $1.50. Exact

change is required. RTA Visitor Passes for
one/three days cost $5/12.

The RTA also operates three streetcar lines.
The historic St Charles streetcar is still running only a short loop in the CBD due to
hurricane damage to the Uptown tracks. The
Canal streetcar makes a long journey up Canal
St to City Park, with a spur on Carrollton Ave.
The Riverfront line runs 2 miles along the
levee from the Old US Mint, past Canal St, to
the upriver convention center and back.

For a taxi, call **United Cabs** (☎ 504-522-9771) or
White Fleet Cabs (☎ 504-822-3800).

Rent bicycles at **Bicycle Michael's** (☎ 504-945-
9505; www.bicyclemichaels.com; 622 Frenchmen St; rentals per
hr/day $7.50/20; ☽ 10am-7pm Mon-Tue & Thu-Sat, to 5pm
Sun, closed Wed), in Faubourg Marigny.

AROUND NEW ORLEANS

Leaving gritty, colorful New Orleans quickly
catapults you into a world of swamps, bayous,
antebellum plantation homes and laidback
small communities. A well-planned foray
into these lesser-known environs builds the
context for New Orleans' idiosyncrasies and
the workaday life of southeastern Louisiana.
Baton Rouge, the state capital, is an easy
daytrip if you're interested in picking up some
political history.

The North Shore

Bedroom communities sprawl along **Lake
Ponchartrain's** north shore, but head north
of Mandeville, and you'll reach the bucolic
village of **Abita Springs**, which was popular in
the late 1800s for its curative waters. Today,
the springwater still flows from a fountain in
the center of the village, but the primary liquid
attraction here is the **Abita Brewery** (☎ 985-893-
3143; 21084 Hwy 36; tours free; ☽ 1pm & 2:30pm Sat, 1pm
Sun), about a mile west of town. Thirty-one-
mile **Tammany Trace trail** (www.tammanytrace.org)
connects Northshore towns, passing through
Fontainebleau State Park (☎ 504-624-4443), on the
lakeshore near Mandeville, and terminating in
Slidell. The bridge over Bayou Lacombe is still
being rebuilt post-Katrina, but the rest of the
linear trail, which was converted from an old
railroad, makes for an energizing bike ride that
drops you into each town's center.

Other worthwhile stops nearby are the hip
antique stores in downtown **Covington** and
the **Lake Ponchartrain Basin Maritime Museum**
(☎ 985-845-9200; www.lpbmaritimemuseum.org) in
Madisonville.

Barataria Preserve

This section of the Jean Lafitte National Historical Park & Preserve, south of New Orleans near the town of Marrero, provides the easiest access to the dense swamplands that ring New Orleans. Set in an area originally settled by Isleños (Canary Islanders) in 1779, the preserve is home to alligators, nutrias, tree frogs and hundreds of species of birds. It is well worth taking a ranger-led walk to learn about the many ecosystems that make up what is often lumped together as 'wetlands.'

Start at the **NPS Visitors Center** (☎ 504-589-2330; Hwy 3134; admission free; ☾ 9am-5pm), 1 mile west of Hwy 45, where you can pick up a map or join a guided walk. Rangers lead canoe trips into the swamp (most Saturday mornings and monthly on full moon nights; call to reserve a spot). To rent canoes for the tour or for an independent paddle, go to **Bayou Barn** (☎ 504-689-2663; www.bayoubarn.net; canoes per person 2hr $15; ☾ 10am-6pm Thu-Fri & Sun, from 8:45am Sat) on the Bayou de Familles just outside the park entrance. This pleasantly funky restaurant compound of tin-topped buildings hosts occasional Sunday Cajun or zydeco dances (admission $5).

River Road

Elaborate plantation homes dot the east and west banks of the Mississippi River between New Orleans and Baton Rouge. First indigo, then cotton and sugarcane brought great wealth to these plantations, many of which are open to the public. Most tours focus on the lives of the plantation owners, the restored architecture and the ornate gardens of antebellum Louisiana, and skip over the story of plantation slaves who made up the majority of the plantations' population. It's easy to explore the region by car, and organized tours are widely available from New Orleans.

Destrehan (☎ 985-764-8785; www.destrehanplantation.org) and **San Francisco** (☎ 985-535-2341; www.sanfranciscoplantation.org) plantations on the east bank are closest to New Orleans, but far and away the most dynamic and informative tour is at **Laura Plantation** (☎ 225-265-7690; www.lauraplantation.com; 2247 Hwy 18; adult/child $15/5; ☾ 9:30am-5pm) in Vacherie on the west bank. This ever-evolving and popular tour teases out the distinctions between Creole, Anglo and African American antebellum life via meticulous research and the written records of the Creole women who ran the place for generations.

Also in Vacherie, the star of **Oak Alley Plantation** (☎ 225-265-2151; www.oakalleyplantation.com; 3645 Hwy 18; adult/child $10/5; ☾ 9am-4:40pm) is its dramatic approach, with a canopy of 28 majestic live oaks lining the entry to this grand Greek Revival–style house. The tour is relatively staid, but the docents wear hoopskirts, and there are guest cottages and a restaurant onsite.

Be sure to flesh out any plantation tour with a visit to the **River Road African American Museum** (☎ 225-474-5553; www.africanamericanmuseum.org; 406 Charles St; museum $4; ☾ 10am-5pm Wed-Sat, from 1pm Sun) 25 miles further along in Donaldsonville. This excellent museum preserves the important history of African Americans in the rural communities along the Mississippi. Exhibits chronicle plantation slavery; the journey to freedom via the Underground Railroad, and the lives of free African American people, such as inventor Leonard Julien who created the sugarcane-planting machine. Donaldsonville itself was a prosperous city for African Americans after the Civil War and the site of the original African American Mardi Gras.

Closer to Baton Rouge, in White Castle, the slightly bedraggled **Nottoway Plantation** (☎ 225-545-2730; www.nottoway.com; 30970 Hwy 405; adult/child $10/5; ☾ 9am-5pm) is the largest plantation house in the South. Play make-believe when you stay overnight since you essentially get the run of the place after the last tour of the day. Rooms in the mansion proper are grandest (doubles in mansion $210, singles/doubles in outbuildings from $115/145); rates include a gigantic breakfast and a tour.

Baton Rouge

In 1699, French explorers named this area *baton rouge* (red stick) when they came upon a reddened cypress pole that Bayagoulas and Houma Native Americans had staked in the ground to mark the boundaries of their respective hunting territories. An industrial town with a bustling port and the state capital, formerly lethargic Baton Rouge has swollen in size as relocated New Orleanians settle post-Katrina. Visitors are mostly drawn to Baton Rouge for Louisiana State University (LSU) and Southern University (the largest historically African American university in the country) or a visit to the tallest capitol building in the nation.

Most attractions are downtown, off I-110 which intersects I-10 near the river. Beware:

North Blvd and North St are two different downtown roads. LSU is in the southwest quadrant of the city where Highland Rd is the main thoroughfare. The most centrally located **visitor center** (☎ 225-346-1253, 800-527-6843; www.visitbatonrouge.com; 702 River Rd; ☺ 8am-5pm) has maps and festival schedules.

SIGHTS & ACTIVITIES

The art-deco skyscraper looming over town is the **Louisiana State Capitol** (☎ 225-342-7317; tours free; ☺ 8am-4:30pm) on aptly named State Capitol Dr. Built at the height of the Great Depression to the tune of $5 million, it's populist governor 'Kingfish' Huey Long's most visible legacy. The 27th-floor **observation deck** has a great view. The neo-Gothic hulk of the **Old State Capitol** (☎ 225-342-0500; 100 North Blvd; admission free; ☺ 10am-4pm Tue-Sat, from noon Sun) houses exhibits about the state's colorful political history. Across the street, the **LSU Museum of Art** (☎ 225-389-7200; www.lsumoa.com; 100 Lafayette St; adult/child $8/4; ☺ 10am-5pm Tue-Sat, to 8pm Thu, 1-5pm Sun) exhibits old and new works alike in the sleek Shaw Center for the Arts. The **Louisiana Arts & Science Museum** (☎ 225-344-5272; www.lasm .org; 100 S River Rd; adult/child $6/5, with planetarium show $8/7; ☺ 10am-4pm Tue-Fri, to 5pm Sat, 1-5pm Sun), which houses arts and natural history installations and offers planetarium shows, rounds out central Baton Rouge's cultural offerings.

Just east of town at I-10 and Highland Rd, the kiddies will love the amusement and water parks, **Dixie Landin** (☎ 225-753-3333) and **Blue Bayou** (☎ 225-753-3333; www.bluebayou.com). North of Baton Rouge, the town of **St Francisville** (www .stfrancisville.net) and its neighboring plantations have historically been, and continue to be, a lovely respite from the heat of the delta.

SLEEPING & EATING

Chain hotels line the sides of I-10, but for a more intimate stay, try the exquisite **Stockade Bed & Breakfast** (☎ 225-769-7358; www.thestockade.com; 8860 Highland Rd; d incl breakfast $135-160; P ✕ ☺ wi-fi). One room is accessible for travelers with disabilities. Book ahead on weekends, especially during football season. **Great Oaks Plantation** (☎ 225-927-8414; www.greatoaksplantation.com; 110 N Foster Dr; d incl breakfast $145-175; P ☺ ☺ wi-fi), a verdant oasis, provides the bizarre opportunity to stay in a columned antebellum home smack in the middle of a city.

Local workers crowd the **Main Street Market** (501 Main St; mains $6; ☺ 7am-4pm Mon-Fri, to 2pm Sat) for

an array of fresh, organic sandwiches, salads, sushi and pastries. **Louie's Cafe** (☎ 225-346-8221; 209 W State St; breakfast $5-8, mains $8-10; ☺ 24hr), near LSU, has a slouchy 1950s ambience and serves everything from burgers to tuna teriyaki; lots of veggie options here, too.

ENTERTAINMENT

At the gates of LSU, the **Varsity Theatre** (☎ 225-383-7018; www.varsitytheatre.com; 3353 Highland Rd; ☺ 8pm-2am) is *the* place for live music, from local bands to big-name acts, often on weeknights. The attached restaurant boasts an extensive beer selection and a raucous college crowd.

GETTING THERE & AROUND

Baton Rouge lies 80 miles west of New Orleans on I-10. **Baton Rouge Metropolitan Airport** (☎ 225-355-0333; www.flybtr.com) is north of town off I-110. **Greyhound** (☎ 225-383-3811; 1253 Florida Blvd at N 12th St) has regular buses to New Orleans, Lafayette and Atlanta, GA. **Capitol Area Transit System** (CATS; ☎ 225-389-8282; www.brcats.com) operates buses around town.

CAJUN COUNTRY

One of the truly unique parts of the US, Acadiana is named for French settlers exiled from L'Acadie (now Nova Scotia, Canada) by the British in 1755. As they lived alongside Native Americans and Creoles, 'Acadian' eventually morphed into 'Cajun.' The harrowing journey to Louisiana and the fight for survival in its swamplands are points of cultural pride for modern-day Cajuns, and do a lot to explain their combination of toughness and absolute ease in their own skins.

Cajuns are the largest French-speaking minority in the US – prepare to hear it on radios and in the sing-song lilt of their English. While Lafayette is the nexus of Acadiana, getting out and around the waterways, villages and ramshackle roadside taverns really drops you straight into Cajun living. It's hard to find a bad meal here; jambalaya and crawfish étoufée (a thick Cajun stew) are prepared slowly with pride (and cayenne!), and if folks aren't fishing, then they are probably dancing. Don't expect to sit on the sidelines…*allons danson* (let's dance).

Lafayette

Lafayette has been blighted by sprawl and its accompanying traffic, but if you stick to the historic downtown, this friendly city opens up like an oyster. History blends with live local music and world-class cooking, and small-town Acadiana is 15 minutes away in any direction (just not at rush hour).

From I-10, exit 103A, the Evangeline Thruway (Hwy 167) goes to the center of town via the **visitor center** (☎ 337-232-3737, 800-346-1958; www.lafayettetravel.com; 1400 NW Evangeline Thruway; ☾ 8:30am-5pm Mon-Fri, from 9am Sat & Sun). Find wi-fi internet access at the **Mello Joy Cafe Downtown** (☎ 337-232-0006; 625 Jefferson St; ☾ 7am-7pm Mon-Sat, 8:30am-1:30pm Sun).

SIGHTS & ACTIVITIES

In the heart of downtown, the **Acadiana Center for the Arts** (☎ 337-233-7060; www.acadianacenterfor hearts.org; 101 W Vermilion St; adult/child/student $5/2/3; ☾ 9am-5pm Tue-Fri, 10am-6pm Sat) maintains three chic galleries and hosts dynamic theater, lecture and special events. The **Children's Museum of Acadiana** (☎ 337-232-8500; www.childrensmuseum ofacadiana.com; 201 E Congress St; admission $5; ☾ 10am-5pm Tue-Sat) encourages kids to romp through

bizarre 'real life' sets, such as an operating room, a TV studio and a bank.

The best NPS museum in Cajun Country is the **Acadian Cultural Center** (☎ 337-232-0789; 501 Fisher Rd; admission free; ☾ 8am-5pm), near the airport. Interactive displays give life to local folkways and rangers guide **boat tours** (adult/child $10/6; ☾ 10:30am Tue-Sat Mar-May & Sep-Nov) of Bayou Vermilion. Next door, tranquil **Vermilionville** (☎ 337-233-4077; www.vermilionville.org; 300 Fisher Rd; adult/student $8/5; ☾ 10am-4pm Tue-Sun), a restored/recreated 19th-century Cajun village, wends along the bayou. Friendly, costumed docents explain Cajun, Creole and Native American history; local bands perform most Sundays.

Just south of Girard Park, the sleek **University Art Museum** (☎ 337-482-1369; 710 E St Mary Blvd; adult/youth $5/3, 10am-noon Tue & Sat free; ☾ 10am-5pm Tue-Sat) hosts beautifully curated exhibits, often with an educational bent.

SLEEPING & EATING

Chains clump near exits 101 and 103, off I-10 (doubles from $60).

Blue Moon Guest House (☎ 337-234-2422, 877-766-2583; www.bluemoonguesthouse.com; 215 E Convent St; dm $18, r $70-90; ℗ ☒ wi-fi) Not for the faint of heart, a bed in this tidy old home includes admission to Lafayette's most popular nightclub, located in the back yard. The friendly owners, full kitchen and camaraderie among guests create a casual hang, within walking distance of downtown.

La Maison de Belle B&B (☎ 337-235-2520; 608 Girard Park Dr; d/ste incl breakfast $110/125; ℗ ☒ ☒) Situated on spacious grounds alongside the verdant park, it's easy to forget that you're in

---

SWAMP TOURS

You haven't experienced Louisiana unless you've been out on its waterways, and the easiest way to do it is to join a swamp tour. Arrange them from New Orleans or go on your own and contract directly with a bayou-side company.

Annie Miller's Son's Swamp & Marsh Tours (☎ 985-868-4758; www.annie-miller.com; 3718 Southdown Mandalay Rd, Houma; adult/child $15/10) The son of legendary swamp guide Annie Miller has taken up his mom's tracks.

Cajun Man's Swamp Cruise (☎ 985-868-4625; www.cajunman.com; Hwy 182; adult/child $20/10) Fifteen miles west of Houma, Black Guidry serenades passengers with his accordion.

McGee's Landing (☎ 337-228-2384; www.mcgeeslanding.com; 1337 Henderson Levee Rd, Henderson; adult/child $18/12) Drive over the Henderson levee and come down into another place and time.

Westwego Swamp Adventures (☎ 504-581-4501; www.westwegoswampadventures.com; 501 Laroussini St, Westwego; adult/child $24/12, with transport $43/24) One of the closest to New Orleans, it can pick you up in the Quarter.

the heart of the city. Louisiana novelist John Kennedy Toole shacked up in the back cottage ($150). Main-house rooms are lovingly restored.

Head to local favorite **T-Coon's** (☎ 337-232-3803; 740 Jefferson Blvd; mains $5-8; ☺ 6am-2pm Mon-Thu, to 4pm Fri) for crawfish omelets in the morning and bodacious plates of étoufée or smothered rabbit for lunch. Or try **Old Tyme Grocery** (☎ 337-235-8165; 218 W St Mary St; po'boys $6; ☺ 8am-10pm Mon-Fri, 9am-7pm Sat) for some excellent shrimp or roast beef po'boys.

If you've never dined in a barn before, now's your chance. Lafayette specializes in big ol' dancehalls that offer one-stop entertainment, dancing and local cuisine. Standouts include **Mulate's** (☎ 337-332-4648; 325 Mills Ave, Breaux Bridge) on the way to Breaux Bridge, **Randol's** (☎ 337-981-7080; www.randols.com; 2320 Kaliste Saloom Rd, Lafayette) south of town, and **Prejean's** (☎ 337-896-3247; www.prejeans.com; 3480 I-49, North Lafayette) 2 miles north of town. Markets and even gas stations keep a pot of hot *boudin* (Cajun rice-and-pork sausage) by the cash register, a sure sign you're in Cajun country.

ENTERTAINMENT
The free and fabulous **Festival International de Louisiana** rocks out six stages with hundreds of local and international artists for five days in April. During the rest of the year, in the Lafayette club scene, it's all about who's playing. To find out, pick up the free weekly *Times* (www.thetimesofacadiana.com) or *Independent* (www.theind.com).

Blue Moon Saloon (☎ 337-234-2422, 877-766-2583; www.bluemoonpresents.com; 215 E Convent St; cover $5-8) The employees are happy, the patrons are happy, the musicians are happy. What don't you love about this small, welcoming spot that seems to be everybody's first choice?

El Sid O's (☎ 337-237-1959; 1523 N St Antoine St) A cinder-block joint for zydeco at its grittiest.

Grant Street Dancehall (☎ 337-237-8513; www.grantstreetdancehall.com; 113 W Grant St) This cavernous warehouse in the heart of downtown books larger shows with larger prices.

GETTING THERE & AWAY
Greyhound (☎ 337-235-1541; 315 Lee Ave) operates from a hub beside the central commercial district, making 12 runs daily to New Orleans ($23, 3½ hours) and Baton Rouge ($15, one hour). **Amtrak's** (133 E Grant St) *Sunset Limited* goes to New Orleans three times a week.

Cajun Wetlands
In 1755, *le Grande Dérangement,* the British expulsion of the rural French settlers from Acadia, created a homeless population of Acadians who searched for decades for a place to settle. In 1785, seven boatloads of exiles arrived in New Orleans. By the early 19th century, 3000 to 4000 Acadians occupied the swamplands southwest of New Orleans. Native American tribes such as the Attakapas helped them learn to eke out a living based upon fishing and trapping, and the aquatic way of life is still the backdrop to modern living.

East and south of Lafayette, the **Atchafalaya Basin** is the preternatural heart of the Cajun wetlands. Stop in to the **Atchafalaya Welcome Center** (☎ 337-228-1094; Butte La Rose/Exit 121 from I-10; ☺ 8:30am-5pm) to learn how to penetrate the dense jungle protecting these swamps, lakes and bayous from the casual visitor. They'll fill you in on camping in **Indian Bayou** and exploring the **Sherburne Wildlife Management Area**, as well as the exquisitely situated **Lake Fausse Pointe State Park**.

ourpick **Café des Amis** (☎ 337-332-5273; 140 E Bridge St; lunch $12-15, dinner $14-22; ☺ 11am-2pm Tue, to 9pm Wed & Thu, 7:30am-9:30pm Fri & Sat, 8am-2:30pm Sun), 11 miles east of Lafayette in the sleepy town of **Breaux Bridge**, is one of southern Louisiana's most memorable culinary experiences. Relax amid funky local art, as friendly waiters trot out sumptuous breakfasts, crunchy lump crab cakes, and white-chocolate bread pudding worth fighting for. If the decadence wears you out, stay overnight in its tidy B&B, **Maison des Amis** (☎ 337-507-3399; r $80-115) right along Bayou Teche.

Tiny **St Martinville** (www.stmartinville.org), 15 miles southeast of Lafayette, packs a mighty punch. Within one block of the bayou in the town center, visit the **African American Museum & Acadian Memorial** (☎ 337-394-2250; adult/child $2/1; ☺ 10am-4:30pm) to learn about the diasporas of both Cajuns and African Americans, the old **opera house** filled with antiques, and the **St Martin de Tours Cathedral**. The bayou-side **'Evangeline Oak'** is the local embodiment of Henry Wadsworth Longfellow's 1847 epic poem *Evangeline,* which recounts the fictional story of two star-crossed Acadian lovers. The **Old Castillo B&B** (☎ 337-394-4010; 220 Evangeline Blvd; r incl breakfast $80-150; ☒) offers spare, elegant lodging.

One mile north of the town center, **Longfellow-Evangeline State Historic Site** (☎ 337-394-

3754; 1200 N Main St; adult/child $2/free; 9am-5pm) explains the nuances of Creole and Acadian history, and gives tours of its restored Creole cottage and farmstead.

Ten miles further south, bustling-but-still-quaint **New Iberia** (www.cityofnewiberia.com) prospered on the sugarcane of surrounding plantations. Today, the town's best-known native son is mystery writer James Lee Burke, whose novels are often set here. A tour of **Shadows-on-the-Teche** (337-369-6446; 317 E Main St; adult/child $7/4; 9am-4:30pm Mon-Sat, from noon Sun), a historic house-museum, captures the fluctuating fortunes of one plantation family.

Eclectic, 100-year-old **Estorge-Norton House** (337-365-7603; 446 E Main St; d incl breakfast $80-100; P) lies near the center of town. The low-key **LagniappeToo Café** (337-365-9419; 204 E Main St; dishes $5-8; 10am-2pm Mon-Thu, 10am-2pm & 6-9pm Fri, 6-9pm Sat) serves up simple food in a simple setting. **Clementine** (337-560-1007; 113 E Main St; mains $8-14; 11am-2pm Mon & Wed, 11am-2pm & 6-9pm Tue & Thu, 11am-2pm & 6-10pm Fri, 6-10pm Sat) packs in locals and tour groups alike for regional treats such as Natchitoches meat pies.

Drive southwest of New Iberia along Hwy 329 through cane fields to lush and lovely **Avery Island**, home of **McIlhenny Tabasco** (337-365-8173; tours free; 9am-5pm) and its excellent **wildlife sanctuary** (adult/child $6.25/4.50). The beautiful, manicured paths around the island actually cover a salt dome that extends 8 miles below the surface. Even though the air smells lightly of Tabasco, alligators and egrets bask in the protected sunshine – bring a lunch and mosquito repellant, and make a day of it.

Historic **Abbeville**, 21 miles southwest of Lafayette carries the mantle of best oysters in Louisiana. If you are a devotee of the fat, salty bivalve, make the pilgrimage to **Dupuy's Oyster Shop** (337-893-2339; 108 S Main St; 11am-2pm & 5-9pm Tue-Thu, to 10pm Fri & Sat) or one of its worthy rivals.

If you happen to be on Hwy 90, **Thibodaux** (ti-ba-doh) has another NPS museum, the **Wetlands Cajun Cultural Center** (985-448-1375; 314 St Mary St; admission free; 9am-8pm Mon, to 6pm Tue-Thu, to 5pm Fri-Sun). Exhibits cover virtually every aspect of wetlands life, from music to the environmental impacts of oil exploration. Musicians jam here Monday evenings (6pm to 8pm) and rangers guide seasonal boat tours.

Named for the Houma tribe of Native Americans, who were displaced in the mid-19th century by the Acadians, nearby **Houma** is the gritty, economic hub of the Cajun Wetlands.

Cajun Prairie

Think: dancing cowboys! Cajun and African American settlers to the higher, drier terrain north of Lafayette developed a culture based around animal husbandry and farming, and the 10-gallon hat still rules. It's also the hotbed of Cajun and zydeco music (and thus accordions), and crawfish farming.

Opelousas squats sleepily alongside Hwy 49, and its historic downtown is home to the esoteric **Museum & Interpretive Center** (337-948-2589; 315 N Main St; admission free; 9am-5pm Mon-Sat); check out the doll collection. The **Opelousas Museum of Art** (337-942-4991) showcases homegrown artists. On the main square, **Palace Cafe** (337-942-2142; dishes $5-13; 6am-9pm Mon-Sat) rustles up savory crawfish étoufée and shrimp bisque.

The top zydeco joints in Acadiana, **Slim's Y-Ki-Ki** (337-942-9980), a few miles north on Main St, across from the Piggly Wiggly, and **Richard's** (337-543-8223), 8 miles west in Lawtell, strike it up most weekends. Wear your dancing shoes and don't be afraid to sweat!

Plaisance, northwest of Opelousas, hosts the grassroots, fun-for-the-family **Southwest Louisiana Zydeco Festival** (337-942-2392; www.zydeco.org) in August.

Eunice (www.eunice-la.com) is Cajun music central. Musician Mark Savoy builds accordions just west of the town center at the **Savoy Music Center** (337-457-9563). Stop in to pick up a few CDs, order a bespoke accordion, or catch the Saturday-morning Cajun jam session. The Saturday-night 'Rendez-Vous des Cajuns' at the **Liberty Theater** (337-457-7389; cnr S Second St & Park Ave; adult/child $5/3) is broadcast on local radio. In fact, visitors are welcome all day at **KBON** (101.1FM; 337-546-0007; 109 S 2nd St). Ogle the DJ and browse the capacious Wall of Fame, signed by visiting musicians. Two blocks away, the **Cajun Music Hall of Fame & Museum** (337-457-6534; www.cajunfrenchmusic.org) caters to the diehard music buff, and the NPS runs the **Prairie Acadian Cultural Center** (337-457-8490; cnr 3rd St & Park Ave; admission free; 8am-5pm Tue-Fri, to 6pm Sat) with exhibits on swamp life and Cajun culture.

If all this leaves you in need of a respite, try centrally located **Potier's Cajun Inn** (337-457-0440; 110 W Park Ave; r incl breakfast $75) for a cozy room with a kitchenette, or **Ruby's Café** (337-550-7665;

221 W Walnut Ave; meals $4-7; 6am-2pm Mon-Fri, from 7am Sun) for popular plate lunches.

Though it's got a great name, **Mamou**, the main thing the town's got going for it is **Fred's Lounge** (337-468-5411; 420 6th St) with its Saturday-morning live Cajun band and charming country waltzes.

CANE RIVER COUNTRY

The central part of the state is a crossroads of Louisiana's distinct cultures, politics and religions, with bilingual French Catholic and Franco African people along the Cane River and monolingual, chiefly Protestant residents to the north. Hwy 119 meanders alongside the Cane River. You'll pass locals dipping fishing poles into the lazy water or whiling away the day on front-porch rockers.

Melrose Plantation (318-379-0055; I-49, exit 119; adult/child $7/3; noon-4pm Tue-Sun) is a complex of interesting buildings built by a family of free people of color headed by Marie Therese Co-incoin. The early-20th-century owner, Cammie Henry, housed artists and writers such as William Faulkner and Sherwood Anderson in the 1796 Yucca House. Africa House is done in Congo style and contains a vivid 50ft mural depicting plantation life by Clementine Hunter, the renowned folk artist. Hunter had been a field hand and cook at Melrose before picking up a paintbrush at age 50. The nearby **Kate Chopin House** (318-379-2233; 243 Hwy 495, Cloutierville), was the author's residence while she wrote *The Awakening*.

A bit further north you'll find charming French architecture in historic **Natchitoches** (mysteriously pronounced *nak*-id-esh), a sleepy little backwater town until Hollywood film-makers arrived in 1988 to film the blockbuster movie *Steel Magnolias*. But much of central Louisiana is a lonely place, densely forested and sparsely populated. The **Kisatchie National Forest** (318-473-7160) is 937 sq miles of Southern yellow pine and hardwood.

NORTHERN LOUISIANA

Make no mistake: the rural, oil-industry towns along the Baptist Bible Belt make northern Louisiana as far removed from New Orleans as Paris, TX is from Paris, France. Even with the commercial center of Shreveport, this is a region battling to find self-definition after decades of decline.

In the far northwest corner of Louisiana, Captain Henry Shreve cleared a 165-mile

logjam on the Red River and founded the river port town of **Shreveport**, in 1839. The city boomed with oil discoveries in the early 1900s, but the port declined after WWII. Many downtown businesses were closed and revitalization came in the form of huge Vegas-size casinos and a riverfront entertainment complex. The city is bisected by I-49 and I-20 and encircled by I-220. The **visitor center** (318-222-9391, 800-551-8682; 629 Spring St; 8am-5pm Mon-Fri, 10am-2pm Sat) is downtown.

In northeastern Louisiana, **Monroe** also used to be a prosperous oil and gas town, but ramshackle homes have replaced moneyed mansions. Greenthumbs and God-fearin' folk come to check out the **Biedenharn Museum & Garden** (318-387-5281; www.bmuseum.org; 2006 Riverside Dr; admission free; 10am-5pm Mon-Sat, from 2pm Sun). Created by Coke founder Joseph Biedenharn's daughter, the complex features a Bible museum, conservatory and garden filled with plants mentioned in the good book.

About 50 miles northeast of Monroe on Hwy 557 near the town of Epps, the **Poverty Point State Historic Site** (318-926-5492, 888-926-5492; www.lastateparks.com; adult/child $2/free; 9am-5pm) has a remarkable series of earthwork and mounds along what was once the Mississippi River. A two-story observation tower gives a view of the site's six concentric ridges. Around 1000 BC this was the hub of a civilization comprising hundreds of communities, with trading links as far north as the Great Lakes.

ARKANSAS

Tucked smack in the center of the US, hiding out between the Midwest and the Deep South, Arkansas is America's buried treasure. There is a reason its motto is 'The Natural State' – the mountains and valleys of the west and north are absolutely gorgeous. The worn slopes of the Ozarks and the Ouachita (wash-ee-tah) Mountains hide little-known lakes bridged by crenellated granite and limestone outcroppings. Tiny, empty roads crisscross dense forests that let out onto surprising, sweeping vistas and gentle pastures dotted with grazing horses. Its rivers are made for rafting, fishing and lolling about. Don't be fooled by talk of Wal-Mart, Bill Clinton or hillbilly culture. Though they all have a place here, they are only screens to keep this secret beauty a secret.

Little Rock sits in the middle of a nondescript plain that gives onto the Mississippi River's Arkansas Delta and a living home of the Delta Blues. The entire state is dotted with state parks; get off of the interstate, pick a road, and go.

History

Caddo, Osage and Quapaw Native Americans had permanent settlements here when Spaniard Hernando de Soto visited in the mid-1500s. Frenchman Henri de Tonti founded the first white settlement in 1686. After the 1803 Louisiana Purchase, Arkansas became a US territory, and slaveholding planters moved into the Delta to grow cotton. Poorer immigrants from Appalachia settled in the Ozark and Ouachita plateaus.

On the edge of the frontier, lawlessness persisted until the Civil War. From 1863 the northern part of the state was occupied by Union troops. Reconstruction was difficult, and development only came after 1870 with the expansion of railroads. Racial tension peaked in 1957, when the federal government intervened to enforce the integration of Arkansas schools. The state has one of the lowest per-capita incomes in the US, with many poor African Americans in the Delta and poor whites in the Ozarks.

Information

The state sales tax in Arkansas is 6%, plus a 2% visitors tax and local city and county taxes.
Department of Parks & Tourism (☎ 501-682-7777, 800-628-8725; www.arkansastravel.com; 1 Capitol Mall, Little Rock, AR 72201) Sends out a vacation plan kit; ask for the excellent annual State Parks Guide.

ARKANSAS FACTS

Nickname Natural State
Population 2.8 million
Area 52,068 sq miles
Capital city Little Rock (population 184,420)
Sales tax 6%, plus 2% visitors tax and local taxes
Birthplace of General Douglas MacArthur (1880–1964), musician Johnny Cash (1932–2003), former President Bill Clinton (b 1946), author John Grisham (b 1955), actor Billy Bob Thornton (b 1955)
Home of Wal-Mart
Famous for Electing the first female US senator, Hattie Caraway (1931)
Official state instrument Fiddle

LITTLE ROCK

Downtown Little Rock resembles a friendly small town with some dynamic big-city characteristics, and it's as multicultural as Arkansas gets. The burgeoning River Market district brings a level of sophistication to the staid city center. Across the river, North Little Rock, a growing enclave of shops and restaurants, stretches alongside the extensive riverfront park.

Established in 1814, Little Rock became the state capital in 1836 and boomed as the commercial and administrative center of a growing state. Development was sporadic in the 20th century, dogged by political corruption and racial segregation. In 1957, the town shot to infamy when the governor and irate whites tried to prevent nine African American students from attending Central High School. The federal government finally intervened, sending in the army.

The town's **visitor center** (☎ 501-371-0075, 877-220-2568; www.littlerock.com; 615 E Capitol Ave; ☽ 7:30am-6:30pm) is housed in 1842 Curran Hall. You can check email at the **public library** (☎ 501-918-3000; 100 Rock St; ☽ 9am-8pm Mon-Thu, to 6pm Fri & Sat, 1-5pm Sun).

Sights

The best stroll is in the **River Market district**, an area of shops, galleries, restaurants and pubs on W Markham St and President Clinton Ave along the bank of the river. **Ottenheimer Market Hall** (☎ 501-375-2553; www.rivermarket.info; btwn S Commerce & S Rock Sts; ☽ 7am-6pm Mon-Sat) houses an idiosyncratic collection of food stalls and shops. **Riverfront Park** rolls pleasantly along the Arkansas River and at its eastern end you might discern the little rock for which the city is named.

William J Clinton Presidential Center (☎ 501-537-0042; www.clintonpresidentialcenter.com; 1200 E President Clinton Ave; adult/child $7/3; ☽ 9am-5pm Mon-Sat, from 1pm Sun) houses the largest archival collection in presidential history, including 80 million pages of documents and two million photographs. Peruse the full-scale replica of the oval office, the exhibits on all stages of Clinton's life or the gifts from visiting dignitaries (such as Lance Armstrong's yellow jersey). The entire complex is built to environmentally friendly 'green' standards.

The **Old State House Museum** (☎ 501-324-9685; 300 W Markham St; admission free; ☽ 9am-5pm Mon-Sat, from 1pm Sun), the state capitol from 1836 to

THE SOUTH

1911, now holds impressively restored legislative chambers and displays on Arkansas history and culture.

Take the kids to the **Arkansas Museum of Discovery** (☎ 501-396-7050; www.amod.org; 500 President Clinton Ave; adult/child $8/7; ☽ 9am-5pm Mon-Sat, from 1pm Sun), housing interactive exhibits on dinosaurs, science and history.

Sleeping & Eating

Because of government and convention-center traffic, it's difficult to find inexpensive hotels in downtown, and rates fluctuate wildly. Budget motels lie off the interstates.

Rosemont (☎ 501-374-7456; www.rosemontofflit tlerock.com; 515 W 15th St; s/d incl breakfast from $89/99; **P** ✖ wi-fi) In an 1880s restored farmhouse near the Governor's mansion, this place drips with cozy character.

Peabody Little Rock (☎ 501-906-4000, 800-723-2639; www.peabodylittlerock.com; 3 Statehouse Plaza; r from $140; **P** ✖ ▯ wi-fi) Sister to the famous Peabody Hotel in Memphis, TN, this one boasts a sleek marble lobby and luxed-out rooms overlooking the river. The hotel also re-creates the Memphis Peabody's tradition of the Duck March (p465).

Flying Fish (☎ 501-375-3474; 511 President Clinton Ave; mains $5-15; ☽ 11am-10pm) This place gets packed with patrons fiending for its delicious seafood and funky vibe. Go for the grilled rainbow trout ($9) or a buttery tilapia po'boy ($6) and slake your thirst with a jumbo margarita ($8).

Ottenheimer Market Hall (☎ 501-375-2553; www.rivermarket.info; btwn S Commerce & S Rock Sts; ☽ 7am-6pm Mon-Sat) Trawl the stalls for some good-value breakfast or lunch – you'll find everything from fresh fruits and pastries, to sushi, burgers and BBQ.

Getting There & Around

Little Rock National Airport (LIT; ☎ 501-372-3439; www.lrn-airport.com) lies just east of downtown. The **Greyhound station** (☎ 501-372-3007; 118 E Washington St) is in North Little Rock, serves Hot Springs ($18, one to two hours), Memphis, TN ($28, 2½ hours) and New Orleans, LA ($87, 18 hours). Amtrak occupies **Union Station** (☎ 501-372-6841; 1400 W Markham St). **Central Arkansas Transit** (CAT; ☎ 501-375-1163; www.cat.org) runs local buses; a trolley makes a loop on W Markham St and President Clinton Ave (adult/child 50¢/25¢).

HOT SPRINGS

The quaint city of Hot Springs (and its not-so-quaint strip-mall and mini-golf suburbs) almost surround the **Hot Springs National Park** (www.nps.gov/hosp; admission free), a tiny preserve 55 miles southwest of Little Rock. The thermal waters in and around the park spout a million gallons of 143°F (62°C) water daily from 47 natural springs, and modern-day pilgrims bathe in it at spas or sip it from fountains. The other big draws are the horse races at **Oaklawn** (www.oaklawn.com; ☽ races Jan-Apr), scenes from Bill Clinton's boyhood and water sports on nearby **Lake Hamilton**.

Elaborate restored bathhouses line Bathhouse Row behind shady magnolias on the east side of Central Ave. Opposite, galleries, shops and restaurants pack 19th-century commercial buildings. For city information or to pick up a map of Clinton-related sites, go to the city's **visitor center** (☎ 501-321-2277, 800-772-2489; www.hotsprings.org; 629 Central Ave; ☽ 9am-6pm).

Sights & Activities

On Bathhouse Row in the 1915 Fordyce bathhouse the **NPS visitor center** (☎ 501-620-6715; 369 Central Ave; ☽ 9am-5pm) and **museum** (admission free) has exhibits about the park's history first as a Native American free-trade zone, and later as a turn-of-the-19th-century European spa.

A promenade runs through the park around the hillside behind Bathhouse Row, where some springs survive intact, and a network of trails covers Hot Springs, North and West Mountains. A scenic drive to the top of Hot Springs Mountain reaches the 216ft **Hot Springs Mountain Tower** (☎ 501-623-6035; adult/child $6/3; ☽ 9am-9pm Apr-Oct, 9am-5pm Nov-Mar) and spectacular views of the surrounding mountains covered with dogwood, hickory, oak and pine – lovely in the spring and fall.

To take a splash in the magic water, visit one of the resort hotels' spas, or **Buckstaff Bathhouse** (☎ 501-623-2308; www.buckstaffbaths.com; 509 Central Ave; thermal bath/with 20min massage $22/46; ☽ 7-11:45am & 1:30-3pm Mon-Sat, 8-11:45am Sun, closed Sun Dec-Feb), just south of the Fordyce.

National Park Duck Tours (☎ 501-321-2911; www .rideaduck.com; 418 Central Ave; adult/child $12/8) offers 75-minute amphibious boat tours and the **Belle of Hot Springs** (☎ 501-525-4438; www.belleriv erboat.com; 5200 Central Ave; adult/child $15/8) cruises Lake Hamilton. Or go by bus with **National Park Tours** (☎ 501-525-4457; 350 Central Ave; adult/child $30/15).

Sleeping & Eating

Chain motels line highways around town; the visitor center has a list of lakeside rental properties and area B&Bs. Most restaurants congregate along the Central Ave tourist strip and offer ho-hum, but cheap food.

Gulpha Gorge Campground (☎ 501-624-3383; campsites $10) Two miles northeast of downtown off Hwy 70B this campground offers attractive NPS campsites (no showers, hookups or reservations).

Alpine Inn (☎ 501-624-9164; www.alpine-inn -hot-springs.com; 741 Park Ave/Hwy 7 N; s/d from $49/55; **P** ✗ ♨ ☎) The friendly owner of this inn, less than a mile from Bathhouse Row, tidily maintains a row of themed rooms like the Golf Room or the Country-Western Room. Some have kitchenettes.

Arlington Resort Hotel & Spa (☎ 501-623-7771, 800-643-1502; www.arlingtonhotel.com; 239 Central Ave; r/ste from $80/$175; **P** ♨ ☎) This gloriously imposing hotel tops Bathhouse Row. The grand lobby sets the tone for the in-house spa and aging, but deluxe rooms. Think: *The Shining*, but cheerful.

McClard's (☎ 501-624-9586; www.mcclards.com; 505 Albert Pike; mains $5-11; ☽ 11am-8pm Tue-Sat) Southwest of the center, McClard's throngs with locals who know that Bill Clinton's favorite boyhood BBQ joint dishes up succulent ribs, slow-cooked beans and creamy slaw. This is some of the South's best BBQ.

Brick House Grill (☎ 501-321-2926; 801 Central Ave; mains $8-20; ☽ 11am-9pm Mon-Thu, to 10pm Fri & Sat, 5-9pm Sun) Downtown near the art galleries, this grill rustles up scrummy seafood, steaks and chicken dishes, and has a full bar.

Getting There & Away

Greyhound (☎ 501-623-5574; 1001 Central Ave) has buses heading to Little Rock ($16, 1½ hours, twice daily).

AROUND HOT SPRINGS

The wild, pretty **Ouachita National Forest** (☎ 501-321-5202; welcome center 100 Reserve St, Hot Springs) is studded with artificial lakes and draws hunters, fisherfolk, leaf-peepers and boaters. The small roads through the mountains unfailingly bring hidden nooks and wonderful views.

The I-30 makes a pretty straight run from Little Rock to Texarkana and the Texas border. Clinton buffs might stop at **Hope**, where the ex-Pres spent his first seven years, but there's not much to see other than the spiffy

Hope Visitor Center & Museum (☎ 870-722-2580, 800-233-4673; www.hopearkansas.net; 100 E Division St; ☽ 8:30am-5pm Mon-Sat, 1-4pm Sun), in the old depot, and his boyhood home.

ARKANSAS RIVER VALLEY

The Arkansas River cuts a swath across the state from Oklahoma to Mississippi. Folks come to fish, canoe and camp along its banks and tributaries.

The enchanting trails of **Petit Jean State Park** (☎ 501-727-5441; www.petitjeanstatepark.com), west of Morrilton, wind past a lush 95ft waterfall, expansive vistas, campgrounds and a rustic stone lodge.

Continuing upstream from Little Rock, bypass I-40 for **US 64**, and meander through quirky towns and rolling hills. **Atkins**, the 'Pickle Capital of Arkansas', **Russellville** and **Clarksville**, a college town, are just warm-ups for sweet Altus.

The center of Arkansas' Germanic winegrowing region, **Altus** had the dubious distinction of being the location for the first season of the Paris Hilton/Nicole Richie reality show, *The Simple Life*. Now that the celebs have vacated, the small town square has returned to quiet normalcy, and the **city hall** (☎ 479-468-4191; 125 W Main St; ☽ 8am-4:30pm Mon-Fri) will be happy to point you in the direction of the nearest winery or B&B.

While you're in town, don't miss a scrumptious meal at **Kelt's** (☎ 479-468-2413; 119 W Main St; mains $7-18; ☽ 11am-10pm Mon-Sat, noon-3:30pm Sun), a self-declared 'guilt-free zone.' This excellent pub, with a full line of rich beers, has a spoken menu of, among other things, homecooked rib-eye steaks with three delectable sauces ($15), shrimp *en croute* (in pastry; $7) or chocolate crepes ($5). When local bands play, the joint gets jumpin'.

Just north of the town of **Ozark** (no, you are not yet in the Ozark Mountains), spectacular **Hwy 23/Pig Trail Byway**, lined with wild echinacea and lilies, climbs up through **Ozark National Forest** (☎ 479-968-2354) and into the mountains; an excellent way to reach Eureka Springs (p458).

Van Buren boasts a six-block historic district from the town's heyday as a river port and trading post. The **Ozark Scenic Railway** (☎ 479-751-8600, 800-687-8600; www.arkansasmissouri-rr.com; adult/child from $31/16; ☽ Fri & Sat Apr-Sep, Sat Oct-Nov) offers a 70-mile trip over trestles and through tunnels to **Winslow** and back.

THE SOUTH

OZARK MOUNTAINS

Stretching from northwest and central Arkansas into Missouri, the **Ozark Mountains** (☎ 870-404-2741, 800-544-6867; www.ozarkmountainregion.com) are an ancient range, once surrounded by sea and now well-worn by time. Verdant rolling mountains give way to misty fields, and dramatic karst formations line sparkling lakes and meandering rivers. Explore the region by driving its back roads. Though some of the towns bank on kitschy hillbilly culture melded with mini-golf, scratch below the surface to the unique cultural traditions, such as acoustic folk music and home-cooked hushpuppies and catfish.

Mountain View

Detour east of US 65 or along Hwy 5 to this wacky Ozark town, known for its tradition of informal music-making at Courthouse Sq. Creeping commercialism is taking its toll, as the **chamber of commerce** (☎ 870-269-8068; www.yourplaceinthemountains.com; 107 N Peabody Ave; ⏰ 9am-4:30pm Mon-Fri, 10am-2pm Sat) promotes the place as the 'Folk Music Capital of the World,' but loads of live folk music and bizarre festivals help it fit the bill. The **public library** (☎ 870-269-3100; 326 W Washington St) offers free internet.

Ozark Folk Center State Park (☎ 870-269-3851; www.ozarkfolkcenter.com), just north of town, hosts ongoing craft demonstrations, as well as nightly live music that brings in an avid, older crowd. **Cash's White River Hoe-Down** (☎ 870-269-4161; Hwy 5/9/14; adult/child $18/free; ⏰ 7:30pm Thu-Sat Apr-Oct), just north of downtown is a heavily hyped, live country-music and comedy show.

Spectacular **Blanchard Springs Caverns** (☎ 870-757-2211; off Hwy 14), located 15 miles NW of Mountain View, were carved by an underground river and rival those at Carlsbad (see p894). Three Forest Service guided tours range from disabled accessible (adult/child $10/5) to hardcore spelunking ($75). **Country Oaks B&B** (☎ 870-269-2704; 17221 Hwy 9; s/d from $65/100; P ✗ ✗ wi-fi) is nestled in a breathtaking sweep of valley. **Jo Jo's Catfish Wharf** (☎ 870-585-2121; Hwy 5; mains $7-13; ⏰ 11am-8pm, to 9pm Fri & Sat), 6 miles north of town, overlooking the river, efficiently dishes out tasty fried catfish, green tomato pickle and hushpuppies.

Fifty miles north on Hwy 5, **Mountain Home** is known for water sports and recreation-loving retirees. **Bull Shoals-White River State Park** (☎ 870-445-3629; www.arkansasstateparks.com/bullshoalswhiteriver) makes a good jumping-off point.

Eureka Springs

Near the northwestern corner of the state, Eureka Springs perches in a steep valley. Victorian buildings line crooked streets and an earthy local population welcomes all – it is one of the most explicitly gay-friendly towns in the Ozarks. On the surface, galleries and shops compete with commercialized country music and the 70ft **Christ of the Ozarks** statue for your attention. But bend a local's ear and find out who's playing at the nearest pub or the location of their favorite swimming hole and this idiosyncratic village will take on new dimensions.

The **visitor center** (☎ 479-253-8737, 800-638-7352; www.eurekaspringschamber.com; 516 Village Circle on Hwy 62 E) has information about lodging, tours and local attractions, such as the rockin' **blues festival** (www.eurekaspringsbluesfestival.com). The old **ES & NA Railway** (☎ 479-253-9623; www.esnarailway.com; 299 N Main St; adult/child $12/6) puffs through the hills on an hour-long tour four times a day Tuesday .

If your budget can stand it, bypass the cheap motels on the rim of the canyon and splurge on lodging in the town center. **Grand Central Hotel** (☎ 479-253-6756; www.grandcentralresort.com; 37 N Main St; r from $125; P ✗ ✗ wi-fi) lives up to its name. In a splendid 125-year-old building, ornate hallways and old-world woodwork lead to cozy rooms with palatial bathrooms. **Local Color Cafe** (☎ 479-253-9522; 71 S Main St; mains $15-22; ⏰ 11am-9pm Mon-Sat, 9am-2pm & 5-9pm Sun) serves up pan-seared tilapia to cool jazz tunes as fireflies dance off the balcony. **Chelsea's** (☎ 479-253-6723; 10 Mountain St) attracts local carousers who party into the wee hours on live-music nights.

Buffalo National River

This 135-mile river flows beneath dramatic bluffs through unspoiled Ozark forest. The upriver section tends to have most of the whitewater, while the lower reaches ease lazily along – perfect for a float. The **Buffalo National River** (☎ 870-741-5443; www.nps.gov/buff) has three designated wilderness areas, the most accessible is through the **Tyler Bend visitor center** (☎ 870-439-2502; ⏰ 8am-5pm May-Sep, 8:30am-4:30pm Oct-Apr), 11 miles north of Marshall on Hwy 65.

Evidence of human occupation dates back some 10,000 years, but this wild and naturally bountiful area kept even modern Ozark settlers isolated and self-sufficient. They developed a distinct dialect, along with unique craftsmanship and musical traits. Thanks to its National River designation in 1972, the Buffalo is one of the few remaining unpolluted, free-flowing rivers in the country.

The best way to see the park is by canoe or raft. Outfitters such as **Wild Bill's** (☎ 800-554-8657; www.ozark-float.com) in Yellville and **Buffalo Outdoor Center** (☎ 800-221-5514; www.buffaloriver.com) in Ponca arrange canoes or rafting trips (from $40 per person), tubes ($5), hiking tours, fishing trips and horseback rides. For weekend trips, reserve in advance.

ARKANSAS DELTA

Roughly 120 miles east of Little Rock, the Great River Rd follows the west bank of the Mississippi River through the Arkansas Delta. **Helena** is regular small-town Arkansas until it explodes for its annual **Arkansas Blues & Heritage Festival** (www.bluesandheritage.com; admission free), formerly the King Biscuit Blues Festival, when blues musicians and 100,000 fans take over downtown for three days in early October. Food stalls sell home-cooked soul food and BBQ.

Year-round, blues fans should visit the **Delta Cultural Center** (☎ 870-338-4350; www.deltaculturalcenter.com; 141 Cherry St; admission free; ⏰ 9am-5pm Mon-Sat), where the world's longest-running blues radio program, *King Biscuit Time,* is broadcast (12:15pm Monday to Friday), and *Delta Sounds* (1pm Monday to Friday) often has live musicians. The museum displays all manner of blues memorabilia such as Albert King's and Sister Rosetta Tharpe's guitars and John Lee Hooker's signed handkerchief.

TENNESSEE

Most states have one official state song. Tennessee has seven.

Here, the folk music of the Scots-Irish mountain-dwellers in the east combined with the bluesy rhythms of the African Americans in the western Mississippi bottomlands to give birth to the modern country music that makes Nashville famous.

These three geographic regions, represented by the three stars on the Tennessee flag, have their own unique beauty: the heather-colored peaks of the Great Smoky Mountains descend into lush green valleys in the central plateau around Nashville

and then onto the hot, sultry lowlands near Memphis.

In Tennessee, you can hike shady mountain trails in the morning, and by evening be stomping your feet in a Nashville honky-tonk or walking the streets of Memphis with Elvis' ghost.

From country churches where snake handlers still speak in tongues to modern cities where record execs wear their sunglasses even at night, Tennesseans are a zesty lot.

History

Spanish settlers first explored Tennessee in 1539 and French traders were plying the rivers by the 17th century. Virginian pioneers soon established their own settlement and fought the British in the American Revolution. Taking their name from the Cherokee town of Tanasi, Tennessee joined the United States as the 16th state in 1796.

Under the administration of President Martin Van Buren, about 16,000 natives were displaced from their homes in the mid-1800s and marched west along the 'Trail of Tears', to the Indian Territory of Arkansas.

Tennessee was the last Southern state to secede during the Civil War, and many important battles were fought here. Immediately following the war, six Confederate veterans from the town of Pulaski formed the infamous Ku Klux Klan to disenfranchise and terrorize the newly free blacks.

TENNESSEE FACTS

Nickname Volunteer State
Population six million
Area 41,217 sq miles
Capital city Nashville (population 569,891)
Sales tax 7%, plus local taxes of up to about 15%
Birthplace of Frontiersman Davy Crockett (1786–1836), guitarist Chet Atkins (1924–2001), soul diva Aretha Franklin (b 1942), singer Dolly Parton (b 1946), former vice president Al Gore (b 1948)
Home of Graceland, Grand Ole Opry, Jack Daniels Distillery
Famous for 'Tennessee Waltz,' country music, Tennessee walking horses
Odd law In Tennessee, it's illegal to fire a gun at any wild game other than whales from a moving vehicle

THE SOUTH

Major industries today are textiles, tobacco, cattle and chemicals, with tourism, especially in Nashville and Memphis, raking in hundreds of millions a year.

Information

The **Department of Tourist Development** (☎ 615-741-2159, 800-462-8366; www.tnvacation.com; 312 8th Ave N, Nashville, TN 37243) has welcome centers at the state borders.

MEMPHIS

Modern-day Memphis stakes its identity on two things: musical history and BBQ pork. It delivers marvelously on both. The slick downtown area bustles with pilgrims who come to worship at the altars of Elvis, Johnny Cash, Howlin' Wolf and Isaac Hayes, to name just a few. While they're here, they can't help but stray from kosher living and indulge their inner love of slow-cooked swine. Some make a circuit, taste-testing dry versus wet, rib versus pulled.

Between sated bellies and musical dreams realized, it's easy to forget that Memphis is also a sprawling, struggling American city. Wander outside of the center and the rough and tumble reality of trying to make a living in the Mid-South becomes apparent. Radically different neighborhoods interlock: refurbished mansions sit near tumbledown shotgun shacks, college campuses lie in the middle of odd warehouse districts. So whether you are here to tour Elvis' mint caddie collection or ferret out the liveliest dive bar, embrace Memphis with all of its glitz and grit.

History

More than 1000 years ago, a Mississippian civilization built mounds on the bluffs of the eastern shore. In 1739 the French established Fort Assumption to protect their river trade. After the US took control, a treaty in 1818 edged the Chickasaw nation out of western Tennessee, and Andrew Jackson helped found the settlement of Memphis. The city was incorporated in 1826 and prospered on the expanding cotton trade of the Mississippi Delta.

Early in the Civil War, Union troops occupied the city but the postwar collapse of the cotton trade was far more devastating. A yellow-fever epidemic in 1878 claimed more than 5000 lives and many white residents abandoned the city. Memphis declared bankruptcy. The African American community revived the town, led by Robert Church, a former slave. By the 1920s Beale St was the hub of social and civic activity. Memphis became an early center of blues music, and in the 1950s local recording company Sun Records cut tracks for blues, soul, R & B and rockabilly artists.

Orientation & Information

Downtown Memphis lies along the east bank of the Mississippi. Riverside Dr runs parallel to the river. The principal tourist district is a bit inland, roughly bounded by Union Ave and Beale St, and Main and 4th Sts. Further east, cool neighborhoods such as Midtown (along Union Ave), Overton Sq and Cooper-Young (near the intersection of Cooper St and Young Ave) have shops, bars and restaurants. Graceland is 3 miles south of town on US 51, also called 'Elvis Presley Blvd.'

EMERGENCY & MEDICAL SERVICES
Methodist University Hospital (☎ 901-516-7000; 1265 Union Ave)
Police (☎ 901-543-2677; 545 S Main St)

INTERNET ACCESS
Café Francisco (☎ 901-578-8002; 400 N Main St; ☯ 6:30am-6pm Mon-Fri, from 7:30am Sat & Sun) Wi-fi for customer use.
Public library (☎ 901-526-1712; 33 S Front St; ☯ 10am-5pm Mon-Fri) Has computers and free internet access.

INTERNET RESOURCES
Blues Foundation (www.blues.org) Official site of the national Blues Foundation, based in Memphis.
Memphis Gay & Lesbian Community Center (www.mglcc.org) Find out about local rainbow-friendly businesses and events.
Memphis Websites (www.memphiswebsites.com) Links galore! Looking for anything Memphis-related, you'll likely find a link here.
Official Elvis Website (www.elvis.com) Everything you ever wanted to know about the King.

MEDIA
Commercial Appeal (www.commercialappeal.com) Daily newspaper.
Memphis Flyer (www.memphisflyer.com) Free weekly distributed Thursday; has entertainment listings.
Triangle Journal News (www.mglcc.org/trianglejournal .htm) Free monthly for the gay community.

MONEY

ATMs are widely available.

First Tennessee Bank (☎ 901-523-4883; 165 Madison Ave; ☺ 8:30am-6pm Mon-Fri, 9am-1pm Sat)

POST

Post office Main branch (☎ 901-521-2559; 555 S 3rd St; ☺ 8:30am-5pm Mon-Fri); Midtown (1520 Union Ave; ☺ 7:30am-5:30pm Mon-Fri, 10am-2pm Sat)

TOURIST INFORMATION

Tennessee State Visitor Center (☎ 901-543-5333, 888-633-9099; www.memphistravel.com; 119 N Riverside Dr; ☺ 9am-5pm Nov-Mar, to 6pm Apr-Oct) Stocked with brochures for the whole state.

Sights & Activities
GRACELAND

In the spring of 1957, at age 22, Elvis spent $100,000 on this house and 13.8 acres, called **Graceland** (☎ 901-332-3322, 800-238-2000; www.elvis .com; Elvis Presley Blvd/US 51; all attractions adult/child $30/15; ☺ 9am-5pm Mon-Sat & 10am-4pm Sun Mar-Oct, 10am-4pm Nov-Feb, mansion closed Tue Nov-Feb). He lived here until his death in 1977, and he's buried next to the swimming pool with his closest relatives. Priscilla Presley (who divorced Elvis in 1973) opened Graceland to tours in 1982, and now millions come here to pay homage to the King. Elvis himself had the place redecorated in 1974; with a 15ft couch, fake waterfall, yellow vinyl walls and green shag-carpet ceiling, it's a virtual textbook of '70s style. The rooms lined with gold records vividly illustrate Elvis' cultural impact.

You begin your tour at the 'visitor plaza' across the street, in the thicket of ticket sales, souvenir shops and cafés. A $250 million state-of-the-art rebuilding and expansion of the visitor facilities is in the works, but for the meantime they are tucked into strip malls nestled in a slightly seedy neighborhood. In busier seasons the staff will assign you a mansion tour time, or you can book ahead. The basic 1½-hour mansion tour is a recording with sound bites from Elvis, Priscilla and Lisa Marie. Buy a package to see the entire estate, or pay to see individual sights, which include the mansion (adult/child $25/10), the 'Sincerely Elvis' memorabilia collection ($7/3.50), the car museum ($9/4.50) and the aircraft collection ($9/4.50). If you want to see all the sites (Elvis buffs should), allow at least four hours. Graceland is about 3 miles from downtown Memphis. Driving, take US 51 (Bellevue Blvd, which becomes Elvis Presley Blvd). Parking costs $6. Nondrivers can take bus 43 from downtown, or hop on the free Sun Studio shuttle (below).

NATIONAL CIVIL RIGHTS MUSEUM

Housed in the Lorraine Motel, where the Reverend Dr Martin Luther King Jr was fatally shot on April 4, 1968, is the excellent **National Civil Rights Museum** (☎ 901-521-9699; www .civilrightsmuseum.org; 450 Mulberry St; adult/child $12/8.50, 3-5pm Mon free; ☺ 9am-5pm Mon & Wed-Sat, from 1pm Sun Sep-May, to 6pm Jun-Aug). Five blocks south of Beale St, this museum's extensive exhibits, detailed timeline and accompanying audio-guide tour chronicle the ongoing struggles for African American freedom and equality in the US. Both Dr King's cultural contribution and his assassination serve as prisms for looking at the Civil Rights movement, its precursors and its indelible and continuing impact on American life. The turquoise exterior of the 1950s motel and two preserved interior rooms remain much as they were at the time of King's death, and serve as pilgrimage points in their own right.

MEMPHIS MUSIC STUDIOS

Any serious Elvis or American-music fan will want to visit historic landmark **Sun Studio** (☎ 901-521-0664, 800-441-6249; www.sunstudio .com; 706 Union Ave; adult/child $10/free; ☺ 10am-6pm). Starting in the early 1950s, Sun's Sam Phillips recorded blues artists such as Howlin' Wolf, BB King and Ike Turner, followed by the rockabilly dynasty of Jerry Lee Lewis, Carl Perkins, Johnny Cash, Roy Orbison and, of course, the King of rock and roll, Elvis Presley (who started here in 1953). Sun Records moved on in 1959, but the studio reopened in 1987, and Ringo Starr, U2 and Paul Simon, among many others, have come here to record. Today packed 40-minute guided tours through the tiny studio offer a chance to hear original tapes of historic recording sessions.

The best way to tour Memphis is to hop on the Sun Studio **free shuttle** (hourly, starting 11:15am). The bus does a loop to the major music sites – Sun Studio, Beale St, Stax Museum of American Soul Music, Heartbreak Hotel and Graceland. It picks up hourly at each location, and you can get on or off the shuttle at any point.

THE SOUTH

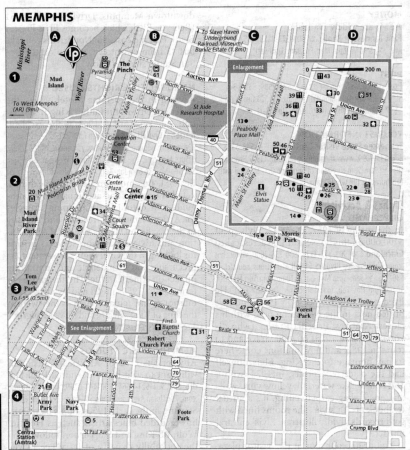

MEMPHIS

THE SOUTH

If the **Stax Museum of American Soul Music** (☎ 901-946-2535; www.staxmuseum.com; 926 E McLemore Ave; adult/child $10/7; ☽ 9am-4pm Mon-Sat, from 1pm Sun Mar-Oct, from 10am Mon-Sat, from 1pm Sun Nov-Feb) fails to give visitors goose pimples it's because the original building was demolished long ago, but today's more stable structure echoes the past with a marquee blazing the reassuring words 'Soulsville USA.' Indeed, this venerable spot was soul music's epicenter in the 1960s, when Otis Redding, Booker T and the MGs and Wilson Pickett recorded here. Dive into soul-music history with photos, displays of '60s and '70s peacock clothing and, above all, Isaac Hayes' 1972 Superfly Cadillac outfitted with shag fur carpeting and 24-karat-gold exterior trim.

BEALE STREET

The strip from 2nd to 4th Sts hops with clubs, restaurants, souvenir shops and neon signs – a veritable musical theme park – though only one of the stores is an original from Beale St's heyday in the early 1900s. It's easy and safe to walk around; police check ID in the evening.

The **Orpheum Theater** (☎ 901-525-7800; www .orpheum-memphis.com; 203 S Main St) is restored to its 1928 glory and faced by an Elvis statue. Its **Walk of Fame** features musical notes embedded in the sidewalk with the names of well-known musicians.

The original **A Schwab's** (☎ 901-523-9782; 163 Beale St; admission free; ☎ 9am-5pm Mon-Sat) dry-goods store has three floors of voodoo powders, 99¢

0   600 m
0   0.4 miles

INFORMATION
Café Francisco..........................**1** B1
First Tennessee Bank................**2** B3
Methodist University Hospital...**3** E4
Police Station...........................**4** A4
Post Office...............................**5** A4
Post Office...............................**6** F4
Post Office...............................**7** A2
Public Library...........................**8** A3
Tennessee State Visitor Center..**9** A2

SIGHTS & ACTIVITIES
A Schwab's.............................**10** C2
Blues City Tours......................**11** B3
Brooks Museum of Art.............**12** H3
Center for Southern Folklore....**13** C1
Gibson Beale St Showcase.......**14** C2
Magevney House......................**15** B2
Mallory-Neely House................**16** C3
Memphis Riverboats.................**17** A3
Memphis Rock 'n' Soul
  Museum................................**18** D2
Memphis Zoo..........................**19** H2
Mississippi River Museum.........**20** A2
National Civil Rights Museum
  (Lorraine Motel)....................**21** A4
New Daisy Theater...................**22** D2

Old Daisy Theater....................**23** D2
Orpheum Theater.....................**24** C2
Pepsi-Cola Pavilion...................**25** D2
Ride the Ducks........................**26** D2
Sun Studio..............................**27** C3
Walk of Fame...................(see 24)
WC Handy House Museum........**28** D2
Woodruff-Fontaine House.........**29** C3

SLEEPING
Best Western Benchmark Inn....**30** D1
Inn at Hunt Phelan..................**31** B3
King's Court Motel....................**32** D1
Peabody Hotel.........................**33** D1
Sleep Inn at Court Square.........**34** A2
Talbot Heirs............................**35** C1

EATING
Automatic Slim's Tonga Club....**36** C1
Blue Monkey...........................**37** H4
Blues City Cafe........................**38** C2
Huey's...................................**39** C1
King's Palace Café...................**40** C2
McEwen's...............................**41** A3
Pig on Beale...........................**42** C2
Rendezvous............................**43** D1
Tops Bar-B-Q..........................**44** E4

DRINKING
Buccaneer...............................**45** F3
Flying Saucer Draught
  Emporium.............................**46** C2
Quetzal Cafe...........................**47** C3
Side Street Grill.......................**48** H4
Silky O'Sullivan's.....................**49** D2
Swig......................................**50** C2

ENTERTAINMENT
AutoZone Park.........................**51** D1
BB King's................................**52** C2
Cannon Center for Performing
  Arts.....................................**53** B2
Circuit Playhouse.....................**54** G3
FedEx Forum...........................**55** D2
Hattiloo Theatre......................**56** C3
Hi-Tone Cafe...........................**57** H3
Kudzu's..................................**58** C3
New Daisy Theater.............(see 22)
Orpheum Theater..............(see 24)
Pyramid..................................**59** A1

TRANSPORT
Greyhound Bus
  Station.................................**60** D1
MATA Terminal.........................**61** B1

neckties and clerical collars. Between 3rd and 4th Sts, a statue of songwriter and composer WC Handy overlooks the **Pepsi-Cola Pavilion**, a park and outdoor amphitheatre where bands jam in the summertime. **WC Handy House Museum** (☎ 901-522-1556; 352 Beale St; adult/child $3/2; ☽ 10am-5pm Tue-Sat May-Aug, 11am-4pm Tue-Sat Sep-Apr) is around the corner off 4th St.

The **New Daisy Theater** (☎ 901-525-8979; www.newdaisy.com; 330 Beale St) has art-deco backdrops depicting the district's honky-tonk heyday, and continues to hold concerts. The little-used **Old Daisy Theater** stands forlornly across the road.

The Smithsonian's **Memphis Rock 'n' Soul Museum** (☎ 901-205-2533; www.memphisrocknsoul.org; cnr Lt George W Lee Ave & 3rd St; adult/child $10/7; ☽ 10am-7pm),

next to FedEx Forum, examines the social and cultural history that produced the music of the Mississippi Delta.

At the giant **Gibson Beale Street Showcase** (☎ 901-544-7998; www.gibson.com; 145 Lt George W Lee Ave; admission $10; ☽ tours on the hour 11am-4pm Mon-Sat, noon-4pm Sun) take the fascinating 45-minute tour of the guitar factory, where solid blocks of wood are transformed into legendary Gibson guitars. No kids under five admitted.

MISSISSIPPI RIVER & MUD ISLAND

A monorail (free with museum admission) and elevated walkway cross the Wolf River to **Mud Island River Park** (☎ 901-576-7241; www.mudisland.com; 125 N Front St; ☽ 10am-5pm Apr-May & Sep-Oct, to 6pm Jun-Aug, always closed Mon) where you

THE SOUTH

can rent kayaks, canoes and bikes. Mud Island was made briefly famous when singer-songwriter Jeff Buckley drowned here while swimming in 1997 and was brought to shore at the foot of Beale St. For visitors now, the **Mississippi River Museum** (☎ 901-576-7241; www.mudisland.com; adult/child $8/5; ⊗ 10am-5pm Apr-May & Sep-Oct, to 6pm Jun-Aug, always closed Mon) displays excellent exhibits depicting the cultural and physical history of the lower Mississippi River valley, including a supercool to-scale model of the river and Gulf.

MUSEUMS & HISTORIC HOUSES

In the bucolic 'Victorian Village' district on Adams Ave, east of downtown, the grand 1870 **Woodruff-Fontaine House** (☎ 901-526-1469; www.woodruff-fontaine.com; 680 Adams Ave; adult/child $10/6; ⊗ noon-4pm Wed-Sun) carefully preserves Victorian clothing and furnishings, and docents tell ghost stories.

The city of Memphis operates two houses that were closed at the time of research due to a budget shortfall, but they may re-open: the 1852 **Mallory-Neely House** (☎ 901-523-1484; 652 Adams Ave) and the smaller **Magevney House** (☎ 901-526-4464; 198 Adams Ave). If you're interested in the history of local life in the 19th century, check to see if they're open again.

Slave Haven Underground Railroad Museum/ Burkle Estate (☎ 901-527-3427; 826 N 2nd St; adult/child $6/4; ⊗ 10am-1pm Mon-Sat), in an unimposing clapboard house, is thought to have been a way station for runaway slaves on the Underground Railroad, complete with trapdoors and tunnels.

The Center for Southern Folklore (☎ 901-525-3655; www.southernfolklore.com; 119 S Main St; admission free; ⊗ 11am-6pm Mon-Sat, to 5pm in winter), in Pembroke Sq at Peabody Place Mall, has a café, books, photographic arts and crafts, and holds free music performances, local tours and film screenings.

Children's Museum of Memphis (☎ 901-458-2678; www.cmom.com; 2525 Central Ave; adult/child $7/6; ⊗ 9am-5pm Tue-Sat, from noon Sun), near Liberty Bowl Stadium, gives the kids a chance to let loose and play in, on and with exhibits such as a giant model heart, weaving loom and water wheel.

Pink Palace Museum & Planetarium (☎ 901-320-6320; www.memphismuseums.org; 3050 Central Ave; adult/child $8.25/5.75; ⊗ 9am-5pm Mon-Sat, from noon Sun) sits 3 miles east of downtown. The 1923 mansion was built as a residence for Piggly Wiggly founder Clarence Saunders and opened in 1996 as a natural- and cultural-history museum. It mixes fossils, Civil War exhibits and an exact replica of the original 1916 Piggly Wiggly, the world's first self-service grocery store. It also has an IMAX theater; tickets sold separately.

OVERTON PARK

Stately homes surround relaxing Overton Park, where the **Brooks Museum of Art** (☎ 901-544-6200; www.brooksmuseum.org; 1934 Poplar Ave; adult/child $7/3; ⊗ 10am-4pm Tue-Fri, to 5pm Sat, 11:30am-5pm Sun) offers excellent exhibits from stonework to cartoons. The permanent collection includes Renaissance and baroque paintings and sculptures, plus an extensive collection of American work.

Also within the park, the sprawling, world-class **Memphis Zoo** (☎ 901-276-9453; www.memphiszoo.org; 2000 Prentiss Pl; adult/child $13/8; ⊗ 9am-6pm Mar-Oct, to 5pm Nov & Dec), hosts two giant panda stars, Ya Ya and Le Le, in a $16-million exhibit on native Chinese wildlife and habitat. The Northwest Passage section is home to polar bears, sea lions and eagles. Other residents include the full gamut of monkeys, penguins, African wildlife, etc. Imagine an animal, they probably have it.

Tours

Blues City Tours (☎ 901-522-9229; www.bluescitytours.com; 325 Union Ave; adult/child from $24/19) A wide variety of informative bus tours.

Horse-drawn carriage rides (2-6 people per 30min from $45) Depart from Beale St or outside the Peabody Hotel.

Memphis Riverboats (☎ 901-527-5694, 800-221-6197; www.memphisriverboats.com; Riverside Dr; sightseeing cruise adult/child $18/10, music cruise with buffet $45/30) Riverboat times fluctuate so call ahead. At the foot of Monroe Ave.

Ride the Ducks (☎ 877-887-8225; www.memphisducks.com; cnr Beale & 3rd Sts; adult/child $19/10) An amphibious tour of landlubber sights and Wolf River Harbor.

Festivals & Events

International Blues Challenge (www.blues.org) Sponsored by the Blues Foundation, each January/February blues acts do battle in front of a panel of judges.

Memphis in May (www.memphisinmay.org) Every Friday, Saturday and Sunday in May, something's cookin', whether it's the Beale St Music Festival, the barbecue cooking contest or the grand finale sunset symphony.

Mid-South Fair (www.midsouthfair.org) Since 1856, folks come out each September to this combo amusement park and agricultural fair.

Sleeping

Cheaper chain motels lie off I-40, exit 279, across the river in West Memphis, Arkansas. Tax on accommodations in Memphis is 15%.

Memphis Graceland RV Park & Campground (☎ 901-396-7125; 3691 Elvis Presley Blvd; campsites/cabins from $23/42; P ⚡ wi-fi) Next to Graceland and owned by Elvis Presley Enterprises, keep Lisa Marie in business when you camp out or sleep in the no-frills log cabins (shared bathrooms).

King's Court Motel (☎ 901-527-4305; 265 Union Ave; d from $45; P ❌ ⚡) This stereotypical dive motel may be decrepit, but it's in the thick of things! It could sell your parking spot on game days, as it's across from the ballpark.

Best Western Benchmark Inn (☎ 901-527-4100; www.bestwesterntennessee.com; 164 Union Ave; d $97; P ❌) Though the unexceptional rooms are worn around the edges, the location three blocks from Beale St is unbeatable. Sit on the benches out front of this stucco tower-block and look longingly at the Peabody across the way. Parking costs $10.

Sleep Inn at Court Square (☎ 901-522-9700; www.sleepinns.com; 40 N Front St; r incl breakfast from $110; P ❌) Near the river and six blocks from Beale St, you can catch the trolley outside in leafy Court Sq. Simple, impeccably clean rooms and genial staff make this a quiet getaway in busy downtown. Parking costs $5.

Heartbreak Hotel (☎ 901-332-1000, 877-777-0606; www.heartbreakhotel.net; 3677 Elvis Presley Blvd; d from $110; P ❌ ⚡ 🖥) At the end of Lonely St, behind Graceland's parking lot, this basic hotel is tarted up with all things Elvis. A heart-shaped outdoor pool and free transportation to Beale St at night add to the frisson of excitement you get from being so close to the King's haunts.

ourpick Talbot Heirs (☎ 901-527-9772, 800-955-3956; www.talbothouse.com; 99 S 2nd St; ste from $130; P ❌) More like studio apartments than hotel rooms, each suite's furniture is individually chosen, each kitchen impeccably designed. Kilim rugs, original artwork, and warm sunlight and staff make this cheerful brownstone smack in the middle of downtown both convenient and comfy. Parking costs $10.

Inn at Hunt Phelan (☎ 901-525-8225; www.huntphelan.com; 533 Beale St; ste from $180; P ❌ ❌ wi-fi) This venerable mansion just down from the action on Beale St is oddly surrounded by warehouses and parking lots. But once you're inside the gates, you step back in time. Gorgeous antebellum rooms laden with antiques, murals and lovely touches like fresh roses in the common areas, evoke the 1800s high-life.

Peabody Hotel (☎ 901-529-4000, 800-732-2639; www.peabodymemphis.com; 149 Union Ave; r from $245; P ❌ ⚡) This *grande dame* has been Memphis' premier hotel since the 1930s. It's a social center, with a spa, superb restaurants and a classy lobby bar. It also boasts its own quirky tradition: every day for 85 years, at 11am sharp, the hotel's 10 ducks file from the elevator across the red-carpeted lobby, accompanied by their red-coated Duckmaster. The birds cavort in the fountain until 5pm, when they retire to their penthouse. Park your car here for $21.

Eating

Memphis is all about the BBQ, specifically chopped pork shoulder served in a sandwich, or dry-rubbed ribs, but other savory treats fight for room on neighborhood menus. Hip, young locals tend to congregate at the restaurants and bars near S Main St and Peabody Pl, or those near the intersection of Cooper St and Young Ave, southeast of downtown.

BUDGET

Tops Bar-B-Q (☎ 901-725-7527; 1286 Union Ave; $3-7; ⏱ 8:30am-11:45pm) With many locations, including this one in Midtown, Tops is a longtime Memphis favorite for cheap no-frills BBQ.

Brother Juniper's (☎ 901-324-0144; 3519 Walker Ave; ⏱ 6:30am-1pm Tue-Fri, 7am-12:30pm Sat, 8am-1pm Sun) Trek down to the University of Memphis for a straight-up good eatin' Southern breakfast in a kid-friendly joint. Omelets, biscuits, grits oh my!

Huey's (☎ 901-527-2700; 77 S 2nd St; mains $6-9; ⏱ 11am-3am) Pass through the graffitied foyer and under the Xmas lights to get the best burger in town, at this lively Huey's location nearest the Beale St action.

Blue Monkey (☎ 901-272-2583; 2012 Madison Ave; mains $7-12; ⏱ 11am-3am) Locals flock to this relaxed Midtown hang for savory pub food with flair (including delectable homemade potato chips), drinks specials and nightly live music.

Pig on Beale (☎ 901-529-1544; 167 Beale St; sandwich & 2 sides $8, full rib dinner $15; ⏱ 10:30am-11pm)

PULLED PORK

You haven't experienced the South until you've tried tender, succulent pulled BBQ pork. Variations on the pulled-pork sandwich reign all over; in Memphis, it's served with a tomato-based BBQ sauce and a dollop of coleslaw in a cheap white bun. Once you've tried one, you'll agree it knocks the pants off a hamburger any day of the week.

The key to good BBQ pork is the rub (seasoning mix) and the cooking technique (low temp and slow). Recipes vary from cook to cook, but the following rub will create a little taste of Southern heaven.

Pork Rub

This quantity of rub should be enough for 2lb to 3lb of pork.

- 4 tablespoons paprika
- 2 tablespoons salt
- 2 tablespoons coarsely ground black pepper
- 2 tablespoons cumin powder
- 3 tablespoons dark brown sugar
- 1 tablespoon dried oregano
- 1 tablespoon cayenne pepper
- 2 teaspoons dried sage
- 2 bay leaves, ground
- 1 teaspoon dry mustard

Mix seasonings together thoroughly. Rub mixture onto boneless pork shoulder halves (also known as Boston butt) and let it sit overnight. Barbecue or roast the meat, keeping the temperature very low (under 200°F/90°C), for about two hours per pound of meat. Do not cover the meat. Keep a roasting pan beneath the rack to catch fat drippings, which you can use to baste the meat periodically (or baste with equal parts apple cider vinegar and olive oil). Once the meat is cooked, let it cool before shredding it. Mix in BBQ sauce and slap that butt on some buns.

Slow-smoked pork ribs slide off the bone at this Beale St BBQ joint. You can get wet or dry ribs, served up with classic creamy coleslaw or corn on the cob…and plenty of napkins.

MIDRANGE

Rendezvous (☎ 901-523-2746; www.hogsfly.com; 52 S 2nd St; mains $6-17; ☒ 4:30-10:30pm Tue-Thu, 11am-11pm Fri, from 11:30am Sat) Tucked in an alleyway off Union Ave, this mainstay sells an astonishing 5 tons of its exquisite charcoal-broiled dry ribs weekly. Friendly service and genuine old-Memphis atmosphere makes eating here an event.

Blues City Cafe (☎ 901-526-3637; 138 Beale St; mains $8-15; ☒ 11am-3am) With live music Tuesday to Sunday, this is a great choice for chowing on some good old Southern fare while listening to local bands.

King's Palace Café (☎ 901-521-1851; 162 Beale St; mains $10-22; ☒ 11am-10pm, to midnight Fri & Sat) Jazz and blues filter through the tony dining room while

contented customers happily devour award-winning gumbo and other Cajun specialties.

Automatic Slim's Tonga Club (☎ 901-525-7948; 83 S 2nd St; lunch $8-14, dinner $16-25; ☒ 11am-2pm Mon-Fri, 5-10pm Sun-Thu, 5pm-midnight Fri & Sat) This sleek, artsy bistro has slow-roasted yellowfin tuna, jerk duck and a killer coconut shrimp with mango sauce.

TOP END

McEwen's (☎ 901-527-7085; 122 Monroe Ave; lunch $7-9, dinner $25-30; ☒ 11am-2pm Mon-Fri, 5:30-10pm Mon-Thu, 5:30pm-midnight Fri & Sat) Don't let the drab stucco exterior fool you: join the upper-crusty professional set for excellent eats with nary a BBQ in sight. Lunch is a steal, with treats such as oven-roasted vegetables on focaccia ($7) served up in the butter-yellow dining room lined with original landscape paintings; dinner brings pan-seared halibut in coconut ginger broth ($26).

Drinking & Entertainment

Most Memphis restaurants and bars mix food, drinks and music, so it's easy to turn a meal into a party. Beale St is the obvious spot for checking out both locals and tourists grooving to live blues, country, rock and jazz. On weekend nights, the two-block strip is closed to traffic, turning it into a full-on party zone. Cover for most clubs is free or only a few bucks. Beale St warms up early, and its bars are open all day, while neighborhood clubs tend to start filling up around 10pm. If action is heavy, bars stay open all night, otherwise expect everything to wind down around 1am. Another hip hang is the Cooper-Young District, radiating out from the intersection of Cooper St and Young Ave, southeast of downtown. To find out what live acts are playing, check www.livefrommemphis.com.

Stylish **Quetzal Cafe** (☎ 901-521-8388; 668 Union Ave; 6:30am-10pm Mon-Thu & Sun, 7:30am-11pm Fri & Sat; wi-fi), near Sun Studio, roasts its own coffee beans and has both wireless and internet access.

BARS & CLUBS

Flying Saucer Draught Emporium (☎ 901-523-7468; 130 Peabody Pl) Your head will spin, either from the 200 beer choices or the raucous crowd.

Swig (☎ 901-522-8515; 100 Peabody Pl) Bust out your cocktail togs and swill exquisite martinis with the beautiful people at this swanky bar.

Silky O'Sullivan's (☎ 901-522-9596; 183 Beale St) A bizarre propped-up facade towers above this cavernous tavern designed for nothing more than drinking, drinking, drinking.

Buccaneer (☎ 901-278-0909; 1368 Monroe Ave) Dance the night away in a popular, dingy shack.

Side Street Grill (☎ 901-274-8955; 31 Florence St) A laidback, gay-friendly crowd relaxes at this Overton Sq neighborhood watering hole and martini bar.

LIVE MUSIC

BB King's (☎ 901-524-5464; 143 Beale St) A full restaurant serving ribs and Southern favorites, BB's is better known for its friendly fun-seeking crowd and great live music.

Kudzu's (☎ 901-525-4924; 603 Monroe Ave) Near downtown, this joint gets jumping with live bands (Friday and Saturday) and Thursday-night guitar-pickin' jam sessions.

Hi-Tone Cafe (☎ 901-278-8663; www.hitonememphis.com; 1913 Poplar Ave) Near Overton Park, this funky little dive balances pool shooting with live music.

New Daisy Theater (☎ 901-525-8971; www.newdaisy.com; 330 Beale St) Groovy, all-ages venue hosting a variety of live-music shows.

Pyramid (☎ 901-521-9675; www.pyramidarena.com; Riverfront Dr) The 32-story pyramid is the world's third largest, taller than the Statue of Liberty. Big-name bands play here.

THEATER & CULTURE

Orpheum Theater (☎ 901-525-7800; www.orpheummemphis.com; 203 S Main St) A 1928-era vaudeville palace, restored as a venue for Broadway shows, ballet and major concerts.

Cannon Center for Performing Arts (☎ 901-576-1269, 800-726-0915; www.thecannoncenter.com; 255 N Main St) Home to the Memphis Symphony Orchestra, this 2100-seat theater offers incredible acoustics and an intimate setting for ballet, opera and jazz concerts.

Circuit Playhouse & Playhouse on the Square (☎ 901-726-4656; www.playhouseonthesquare.org); Circuit Playhouse (1705 Poplar Ave); Playhouse on the Square (51 S Cooper St) These wonderful affiliated theatres offer Memphis' only live theater productions of Broadway and off-Broadway plays.

Hattiloo Theatre (☎ 901-525-0009; www.hattilootheatre.org; 656 Marshall Ave) Memphis' African American repertory theatre stages musicals, Shakespeare and modern drama.

SPORTS

Memphis Redbirds (☎ 901-721-6000; www.memphisredbirds.com; tickets $5-18) This American Automobile Association (AAA) minor-league affiliate of the St Louis Cardinals baseball team plays at AutoZone Park April to August.

Memphis Grizzlies (☎ 901-888-4667, 866-648-4667; www.grizzlies.com) The NBA's Memphis Grizzlies bring on the basketball action at FedEx Forum from October to April.

Getting There & Around

Memphis International Airport (☎ 901-922-8000; www.memphisairport.org; 2491 Winchester Rd) is 12 miles southeast of downtown via I-55; a taxi to or from downtown costs $27. Try **City Wide Cab Company** (☎ 901-324-4202) or **Yellow Cab** (☎ 901-577-7777). The **Downtown-Airport Shuttle** (DASH; ☎ 901-522-1677; one-way $15) serves most downtown hotels.

Greyhound (☎ 901-523-1184; 203 Union Ave; 24hr) runs frequent buses to Nashville ($34, four hours); Little Rock, AR ($30, 2½ hours); and New Orleans, LA ($60, 10½ hours).

SCENIC DRIVE: NATCHEZ TRACE PARKWAY

About 25 miles southwest of Nashville off Hwy 100, drivers pick up the **Natchez Trace Parkway** (☎ 800-305-7417; www.nps.gov/natr/), which leads 444 miles southwest to Natchez, Mississippi (p431). This northern section is one of the most attractive stretches of the entire route, with leafy trees leaning together to form an arch over the winding road. There are three primitive campsites along the way, free and available on a first-come, first-served basis. Near the parkway entrance, stop at the landmark **Loveless Cafe** (☎ 615-646-9700; www.lovelesscafe.com; 8400 Hwy 100; dishes $6-15; ☯ 7am-9pm), a 1950s roadhouse famous for its biscuits with homemade preserves, country ham, and ample portions of Southern fried chicken.

Central Station (☎ 901-526-0052; 545 S Main St; ☯ 5:45am-11:15pm), the Amtrak terminal, has been restored to its original 1914 splendor. *City of New Orleans* goes to Chicago, IL ($174, 10½ hours) and New Orleans, LA ($61, nine hours).

Memphis Area Transit Authority (MATA; ☎ 901-274-6282; www.matatransit.com; fare $1.45) operates local buses. Schedules are available at the **MATA terminal** (444 N Main St; ☯ 7am-4pm Mon-Fri, 8am-4:30pm Sat). MATA's **Main Street Trolley** ($1, every 12 minutes) makes a loop from Amtrak to the Pyramid via Main St and Riverside Dr.

SHILOH NATIONAL MILITARY PARK

'No soldier who took part in the two day's engagement at Shiloh ever spoiled for a fight again,' said one veteran of the bloody 1862 battle, which took place among these lovely fields and forests. During the fight 3400 soldiers died, and the Confederate forces were eventually repelled by the Union.

The Shiloh National Military Park, part of the NPS, is located just north of the Mississippi border near the town of Crump, TN. The **visitor center** (☎ 731-689-5696; www.nps.gov/shil/; park entry $3; ☯ 8am-5pm year-round) gives out maps and shows a video about the battle, and sells an audio tour.

The vast park can only be seen by car. Sights along the route include the Shiloh National Cemetery, an overlook of the Cumberland River where Union reinforcement troops arrived by ship, and various markers and monuments.

NASHVILLE

So you're an aspiring country singer, arriving in downtown Nashville after days of hitchhiking, with nothing but your battered guitar on your back. Gaze up at the neon lights of Lower Broadway, take a deep breath of smoky, beer-perfumed air, feel the boot-stompin' rumble from deep inside the crowded honky-tonks, and say to yourself 'I've made it.'

This ain't no country club baby, this is Nashville.

For country-music fans and wannabe songwriters all over the world, a trip to Nashville is the ultimate pilgrimage. Think of any song involving a pickup truck, a bottle of booze, a no-good woman, or a late lamented hound dog, and chances are it came from Nashville. Since the 1920s the city has been attracting musicians who have taken the country genre from the 'hillbilly music' of the early 20th century to the slick 'Nashville sound' of the 1960s to the punk-tinged alt-country of the 1990s.

Nashville has many attractions to keep you busy, from the Country Music Hall of Fame and the revered Grand Ole Opry House to rough blues bars, historic buildings and big-name sports. It also has friendly people, a lively university community, excellent fried chicken and an unrivaled assortment of tacky souvenirs.

History

Originally inhabited by the Shawnee Indians, the city was settled by Europeans in 1779 and named Fort Nashborough after Revolutionary War hero Francis Nash.

By the beginning of the Civil War, Nashville was prospering as a river port and railway center, only to be hammered down by Union troops. The Tennessee Centennial Exposition in 1897 and its concurrent building boom signaled the city's recovery – the lovely Victorian-style brick buildings of downtown are a legacy of this period.

From 1925, Nashville became known for its live-broadcast *Barn Dance,* later nicknamed the *Grand Ole Opry.* Its popularity soared, the city proclaimed itself the 'country-music capital of the world' and recording studios sprang up in Music Row.

Today Nashville is the second most populous city in Tennessee, with more than a dozen colleges and universities and an economy based on music, tourism, healthcare and publishing.

Orientation & Information

Nashville sits on a rise beside the Cumberland River, with the state capitol situated at the highest point. The compact downtown area slopes south to Broadway, the city's central artery. Briley Parkway, which forms a ring around the city, connects to I-40 to take you out of town.

Downtown, historic commercial buildings comprise the entertainment area called 'The District,' from 2nd Ave to 5th Ave and along Broadway, where old dives and rib joints sit comfortably alongside tourist-grabbers such as the Hard Rock Cafe. Across the Cumberland River is the Coliseum where the Titans play rabble-rousing football; Music Row, Elliston Pl and Vanderbilt University are situated west of downtown, with funky restaurants along Broadway, 21st Ave and West End Ave. Off the Briley Parkway northeast of town, Music Valley is a tourist zone full of budget motels, franchise restaurants and outlet stores built around the Grand Ole Opry.

BOOKSTORES
Elder's Bookstore (☎ 615-327-1867; www.eldersbookstore.com; 2115 Elliston Pl; 10am-4:30pm Mon-Fri, to 4pm Sat) This excellent used-book shop has been around since the 1930s.

EMERGENCY
Main police station (☎ 615-862-8600; 310 1st Ave S)

INTERNET ACCESS
Caffeine (☎ 615-259-4993; www.caffeinenashville.com; 1516 Demonbreun St; 7am-9pm Mon, 7am-10pm Tue-Thu, 8am-10pm Sat, 8am-2pm Sun) A downtown coffee shop with food and free wi-fi.
Public library (☎ 615-862-5800; www.library.nashville.org; 615 Church St; 9am-8pm Mon-Thu, to 6pm Fri, to 5pm Sat, 2-5pm Sun) Free internet access, printing for 15¢ a page.

MEDIA & INTERNET RESOURCES
Nashville Scene (www.nashvillescene.com) Free alternative weekly covering local entertainment and news.
Out & About (www.outandaboutnashville.com) A monthly publication covering gay and lesbian issues throughout Tennessee.
Rage (www.nashvillerage.com) Alternative free weekly.
Tennessean (www.tennessean.com) Nashville's daily newspaper.

MEDICAL
Baptist Hospital (☎ 615-284-5555; 2000 Church St)
Vanderbilt University Medical Center (☎ 615-322-5000; 1211 22nd Ave S)

NASHVILLE IN...

Two Days
Grab lunch at the **Farmers Market** (p474) and go ogle Elvis' gold Cadillac at the **Country Music Hall of Fame** (p471). See who's stompin' the stage at **Tootsie's Wild Orchid Lounge** (p475) and wander the smoky honky-tonks of the **District** (p471) until dawn.

The next day, explore the tacky wonderland of **Music Valley** (p473) and take in a show at the venerable **Grand Ole Opry** (p476). Swing up to north Nashville for some late-night eats at deadly delicious **Prince's Hot Chicken** (p474).

Four Days
In addition to the two-day itinerary: have a bagel at **Noshville** (p474) and go check out the vintage cowboy boots at **Katy K's Ranch Dressing** (p476) in the funky 12th Ave S neighborhood. Book a table at **Bluebird Cafe** (p475) to see some of the best singer-songwriters around.

The next morning, hang out with Vandy students in Centennial Park and visit the hilarious reproduction **Parthenon** (p472). Catch the music execs in their natural habitat around **Music Row** (p472), then head over to hip **Elliston Place** (p472) for a slice of pie at all-night **Cafe Coco** (p475).

THE SOUTH

THE SOUTH

NASHVILLE

INFORMATION
AmSouth Bank...........................1 E2
Baptist Hospital........................2 B3
Caffeine...................................3 D3
Elder's Bookstore.....................4 B4
Nashville Convention & Visitors
 Bureau..................................5 E2
Nashville Visitors Information
 Center...................................6 F4
Police Station...........................7 F4
Post Office...............................8 C3
Post Office...............................9 D3
Public Library..........................10 E2

SIGHTS & ACTIVITIES
Country Music Hall of Fame &
 Museum................................11 E3
Fort Nashborough....................12 E3
Frist Center for the Visual Arts...13 D3
Parthenon...............................14 A4
Ryman Auditorium...................15 F4
State Capitol...........................16 D2
Tennessee Bicentennial Mall....17 D1
Tennessee State Museum..........18 E2

SLEEPING
Best Western Downtown..........19 D2
Courtyard by Marriott.............20 C4
Hermitage Hotel......................21 E2
Music City Hostel....................22 C3
Union Station Hotel.................23 D3

EATING
Elliston Place Soda Shop..........24 B4
Farmers Market.......................25 D1
Market Street Public House......26 E2
Merchant's.............................27 F4
Nashville.................................28 C4
Red..29 C3

DRINKING
Cafe Coco..............................30 B3
Robert's Western World...........31 F4
Tribe..................................(see 29)

ENTERTAINMENT
BB King's Blues Club...............32 E2
Bourbon St Blues & Boogie Bar.33 E2
Exit/In...................................34 B4
Gaylord Entertainment Center...35 E3
Ryman Auditorium...................36 F4
Schermerhorn Symphony Hall...37 E2
Station Inn.............................38 D3
Tennessee Performing Arts
 Center..............................(see 18)
The Coliseum..........................39 F1
The End.................................40 B4
Tootsie's Wild Orchid Lounge...41 F4

SHOPPING
Ernest Tubb's.........................42 F4
Gruhn Guitars........................43 F4
Hatch Show Print....................44 F4

TRANSPORT
Greyhound Bus Station............45 E3
MTA Transit Mall....................46 E2

MONEY

AmSouth Bank (☎ 615-748-2091; 315 Deaderick St) Banking and currency exchange.

POST

Post office (☎ 800-275-8777); Church St (1718 Church St); Frist (Frist Center for Visual Arts, 919 Broadway) All mail sent to General Delivery, Nashville, TN 37203 goes to the Church St branch.

TOURIST INFORMATION

Nashville Convention & Visitors Bureau (☎ 615-259-4730, 800-657-6910; www.nashvillecvb.com; 150 4th Avenue N) Has a great online visitors' guide and hotel booking portal.

Nashville Visitors Information Center (☎ 615-259-4747; www.visitmusiccity.com; Gaylord Entertainment Center; ⏱ 8:30am-5:30pm) Pick up free city maps here at the glass tower.

Sights & Activities

DOWNTOWN

The historic 2nd Ave N business area was the center of the cotton trade in the 1870s and 1880s, when most of the Victorian warehouses were built; note the cast-iron and masonry facades. Today it's the heart of the **District**, with shops, restaurants, underground saloons and nightclubs. Two blocks west, **Printers Alley** is a narrow cobblestone lane known for its nightlife since the 1940s. Along the Cumberland River, Riverfront Park is a shady, landscaped promenade featuring **Fort Nashborough**, a 1930s replica of the city's original outpost, and a dock from which river taxis cruise out to Music Valley.

'Honor Thy Music' is the catchphrase of the monumental **Country Music Hall of Fame & Museum** (☎ 615-416-2001; www.countrymusichalloffame .com; 222 5th Ave S; adult/child $18/11, student & AAA discounts; ⏱ 9am-5pm), reflecting the near-Biblical importance of country music to Nashville's soul. See case upon case of artifacts including Patsy Cline's cocktail gown, Johnny Cash's guitar, Elvis' gold Cadillac and Conway Twitty's yearbook picture (back when he was Harold Jenkins). There are written exhibits tracing country's roots, computer touch screens to allow access to recordings and photos from the Country Music Foundation's enormous archives and walk-in listening booths. The fact- and music-filled audio tour ($5 extra) is narrated by contemporary country musicians. From here you can also take the Studio B Tour (adult/child $13/11,

one hour), which shuttles you to Radio Corporation of America's (RCA's) famed Music Row studio, where Elvis recorded 'Are You Lonesome Tonight?' and Dolly Parton cut 'I Will Always Love You.'

Everyone who's anyone has performed at the **Ryman Auditorium** (☎ 615-889-3060; www.ryman .com; 116 5th Ave N; daytime tour adult/child $12.50/6.25, incl backstage $16.25/10; ⏱ 9am-4pm), from WC Fields to Martha Graham to Bob Dylan to the Indigo Girls. The soaring brick tabernacle was built in 1890 by wealthy riverboat captain Thomas Ryman to house religious revivals, and watching a show from one of its 2000 seats can still be described as a spiritual experience. It has been used for various performances, including the Saturday-night **Grand Ole Opry** (www.opry .com). The *Opry* stayed here for 31 years, until it moved out to the Opryland (p472) complex in 1974. The Ryman underwent massive renovations and reopened in 1994. Today, the *Opry* performs during summer months (March to November) at Opryland, and at the Ryman in the winter months (November to March).

At the northeast edge of downtown, the 1845 Greek Revival **state capitol** (☎ 615-741-2692; Charlotte Ave; tours 9am-4pm Mon-Fri free), between 6th and 7th Sts, was built from local limestone and marble by slaves and prison inmates working alongside European artisans. Around back, steep stairs lead down the northern side to the **Tennessee Bicentennial Mall**, whose outdoor walls are covered with historical facts about Tennessee's history, and the wonderful **Farmers Market** (p474).

Just south of the capitol, government buildings surround Legislative Plaza. The Performing Arts Center covers an adjacent block and houses the **Tennessee State Museum** (☎ 615-741-2692; www.tnmuseum.org; 5th Ave btwn Union & Deaderick; admission free; ⏱ 10am-5pm Tue-Sat, from 1pm Sun), a large and genuinely engaging look at the state's history, with Native American handicrafts, a life-size log cabin, 18th-century printing press, and a walk-through 'hellfire and brimstone' revival diorama, complete with sound effects. Exhibits cover the abolitionist movement from as early as 1797, as well as the KKK, which began here in 1868.

The **Frist Center for the Visual Arts** (☎ 615-244-3340; www.fristcenter.org; 919 Broadway; adult/child $8.50/6.50; ⏱ 10am-5:30pm Mon-Sat, from 1pm Sun) hosts traveling exhibitions of anything and everything, from

American folk art to Picasso. It's a clean, modern space in the grand, refurbished post office building.

WEST END

In Nashville's West End, **Music Row** is home of the production companies, agents, managers and promoters who run Nashville's country-music industry. If you're expecting to see your favorite cowboy-hat wearing crooner, think again. On today's Music Row you're more likely to see executives wolfing down power lunches. Still, it's neat to wander the streets, where icons such as Sony and RCA mix with mom-and-pop recording studios.

Elliston Place is an enclave of bohemia anchored by the ancient Elliston Place Soda Shop (p474) and Elder's Bookstore (p469).

Almost 12,000 students attend the prestigious **Vanderbilt University**, founded in 1883 by railway magnate Cornelius Vanderbilt, who wanted to give the South a world-class university. The 330-acre parklike campus buzzes with students, who eat, shop and drink along 21st Ave N, Broadway and West End Ave.

Yes, that is indeed a reproduction Athenian **Parthenon** (☎ 615-862-8431; www.parthenon .org; 2600 West End Ave; adult/child $5/2.50; ☼ 9am-4:30pm Tue-Sat, 12:30-4:30pm Sun), sitting in **Centennial Park**. Originally built in 1897 for Tennessee's Centennial Exposition and rebuilt in 1930 due to popular demand, the full-scale plaster copy of the 438 BC original now houses an **art museum** with a collection of American paintings and a 42ft statue of the Greek goddess Athena.

MUSIC VALLEY

This suburban tourist zone is about 10 miles northeast of downtown at Hwy 155/Briley Parkway exits 11 and 12B, and also reachable by bus (p477).

The **Grand Ole Opry House** (☎ 615-871-6779; www .opry.com; 2802 Opryland Dr; tours $10) seats 4400 fans in a squareish modern building for the *Grand Ole Opry* Friday and Saturday from March to November (see p471). Guided backstage tours are offered daily by reservation. The **Grand Ole Opry Museum** (☎ 615-889-3060; 2802 Opryland Dr; admission free; ☼ 10:30am-6pm Mar-Dec) across the plaza tells the story of the *Opry* with wax characters, colorful costumes and dioramas. Check out the model of Marty Robbin's 1970s Nashville office, all orange shag carpet and cowboy prints. Next door, the **Opry Mills Mall** (☎ 615-514-1100; ☼ 10am-9:30pm Mon-Sat, to 7pm Sun) houses an IMAX cinema, theme restaurants and the **Gibson Bluegrass Showcase** (☎ 615-514-2200, ext 2231; www.gibson.com; 161 Opry Mills Dr; ☼ 10am-9:30pm Mon-Sat, to 7pm Sun), a working factory and concert venue where you can see banjos, mandolins and resonator guitars being made through the glass (free).

Exit 12B goes to the massive Opryland Hotel (p474) as well as several other sights, including the **Music City Wax Museum** (☎ 615-884-7876; adult/child $8/5; ☼ 9am-5pm, to 9pm May-Sep), with eerie wax statues of costumed country stars, and the **Willie Nelson Museum** (see boxed text, below).

WILLIE NELSON MUSEUM

Call it the **everything-but-Willie-Nelson's-used-toothbrush museum** (☎ 615-885-1515; 2613 McGavock Parkway; adult/child $5/3; ☼ 9am-5pm, to 9pm May-Sep). This squat brick building holds the mother load of the Redheaded Stranger's memorabilia, much of it bought at auction when the Internal Revenue Service (IRS) seized the singer's ranch and studio in the early '90s due to $16.7 million of unpaid taxes. There are Nelson portraits, Nelson bronze busts, Nelson's Native American art collection, Nelson guitars and Nelson's old Billboard Music Awards, in addition to memorabilia from the singer's industry friends like Dolly Parton, Porter Wagoner and Faron Young.

Famous for penning songs such as 'Crazy' and 'On the Road Again,' Nelson lived in Nashville until his house burned down in 1970, at which point he moved to Austin, TX. There, he founded the 'outlaw country' genre, a heady, raw, rock 'n' roll–infused sound that refused to conform to the cleaner, softer Nashville standards of the day. Known for his long braids, bandanas and rebellious demeanor, Nelson has not softened with age. Now well into his 70s, he promotes cleaner-burning 'BioWillie' biofuel and acts as a co-chair of NORML, the National Organization for the Reform of Marijuana Laws.

THE SOUTH

Tours

Ask at the visitor center for a list of the many theme tours available in Nashville.

General Jackson Showboat (☎ 615-458-3900; www .generaljackson.com; 2812 Opryland Dr) Offers day and evening cruises on the Cumberland River, some with music and food. Departs from the Opryland Hotel (p474). Prices and trips vary widely; call for more information.

Gray Line (☎ 615-883-5555, 800-251-1864; www .graylinenashville.com) Offers a variety of bus tours, including Discover Nashville ($40, 3½ hours) or the Homes of the Stars ($35, three hours). Buses pick up from area hotels, or from the Hard Rock Cafe at 100 Broadway in the District.

NashTrash (☎ 800-342-2132, 615-226-7300; www .nashtrash.com; 900 8th Avenue N) The big-haired 'Jugg Sisters' offer a campy frolic ($32, 1½ hours) through the risqué side of Nashville history while guests sip BYO booze. At the Farmer's Market.

Festivals

CMA Music Festival (☎ 800-262-3378; www.cmafest .com) Draws tens of thousands of country music fans to town each June.

Tennessee State Fair (☎ 615-862-8980; www.tennes seestatefair.org) Nine days of racing pigs, mule-pulls and cake bake-offs every September.

Sleeping

Budget chain motels cluster on all sides of downtown, along I-40 and I-65. They all charge from around $50 to $70 for rooms. At any hotel, lower rates are available midweek, on slow weekends and during the winter. Be aware: hotel tax in Nashville adds 14.25%.

DOWNTOWN

Best Western Downtown (☎ 615-242-4311, 800-627-3297; www.bestwesterntennessee.com; 711 Union St; r $120-165; P ⊠ 🖵) With a great location near the capitol, free parking, and Ethernet in every room, this motel is one of the best values downtown. Some of the 101 tidy, smallish rooms come with microwave and fridge. An attached deli sells snacks.

our pick **Union Station Hotel** (☎ 615-726-1001; www.unionstationhotelnashville.com; 1001 Broadway; r from $159; P ⊠ 🖵 wi-fi) This soaring, Romanesque -style stone castle was once a train station and is now the city's grandest hotel. The vaulted lobby is dressed in peach and gold with inlaid marble floors and a stained-glass ceiling. Rooms are tastefully modern, with flat-screen TVs and deep soaking tubs. Parking costs $18.

Hermitage Hotel (☎ 615-244-3121, 888-888-9414; www.thehermitagehotel.com; 231 6th Ave N; r from $249; P ⊠ 🖵 wi-fi) Nashville's first million-dollar hotel was a hit with the socialites when it opened in 1910. The palatial lobby is decorated with rich tapestries and ornate carvings; rooms have mahogany furniture and deep marble soaking tubs. Parking costs $18.

WEST END

Music City Hostel (☎ 615-692-1277; www.musiccityhos tel.com; 1809 Patterson St; dm $25, r $60; P ⊠ 🖵 wi-fi) The squat bungalows may not be much to look at, but Nashville's only hostel is within walking distance of both downtown and the West End's bars and cafés, and has a welcoming atmosphere and a motley crew of international travelers ready to have fun. There's bike rental, common kitchen, a computer, and free wireless internet for those with laptops.

Courtyard by Marriott (☎ 615-327-9900, 800-245-1959; 1901 West End Ave; r from $90; P ⊠ 🚗 🖵 wi-fi) Visitors to Vanderbilt and business travelers stay in this crisp, modern hotel with large rooms (many with sleeper sofas) overlooking either Centennial Park or the university's football stadium. Parking costs $16.

Ainsworth Inn (☎ 615-383-0426; www.ainsworthinn .com; 746 Benton Ave; r from $180; P ⊠ 🚗 wi-fi) Following a bubble bath in your claw-foot tub, you can sip cocktails in the carriage house-turned-bar at this five-suite B&B, just southwest of downtown. Though full of grown-up amenities such as a private wine cellar and Victorian antiques, the 1906 mansion is child-friendly, with a backyard tree house and a game room.

MUSIC VALLEY

Nashville KOA Kampground (☎ 615-889-0282, 800-562-7789; www.koa.com; 2626 Music Valley Dr; campsite $38, cabin $60-71, lodge $115; P 🚗 wi-fi) With 460 camp- and RV sites, this campground is set back from the road and has a well-manicured, wholesome atmosphere. There are also rustic cabins, and lodges with kitchenettes. Amenities include a pool, game room, wireless internet and snack bar.

Countryside Lodge (☎ 866-615-1944, 615-316-0145; www.countryside-lodge.com; 2500 Music Valley Dr; r/ste $50/60; P 🚗 wi-fi) Though the chartreuse-and-orange color scheme may be headache-inducing, this family-run motel is one of the best values in the area, with bright, spacious rooms, some with microwaves and mini-fridges. Free wi-fi works in some rooms.

Opryland Hotel (☎ 615-889-1000, 866-972-6779; www.gaylordhotels.com; 2800 Opryland Dr; r with/without balcony $325/259; P X ❄ ☜ ☐ wi-fi) This whopping 2881-room hotel is a tourist attraction itself. It contains acres of lush indoor gardens and rivers, with boat rides, a waterfall, and an elevated walkway over the rain forest. A dozen eating options range from coffee and Danish to steak and single malt. Parking costs $12.

Eating

It's easy to eat well in Nashville, with a wide selection of terrific restaurants – from small family-run shops selling meat-and-threes to upscale bistros offering modern twists on traditional favorites. Many of the city's best eateries are situated in west of downtown, but it's easy to get a good meal anywhere.

BUDGET

The true taste of Nashville can best be found in cinder-block cabins in the industrial zone south of Broadway, where meat-and-threes come in heaping portions.

Farmers Market (☎ 615-880-2001; 900 8th Ave N at Jackson St; ❂ 9am-6pm) One of the best places in town to have lunch is at this market, where you'll find a covered food court with stalls serving tacos, gyros, jerk chicken, po'boys and more.

Elliston Place Soda Shop (☎ 615-327-1090; 2111 Elliston Pl; mains $3-6; ❂ 7am-7pm Mon-Sat) has served fountain Cokes and meat-and-threes to Vandy students since the 1930s, and the decor hasn't changed much since.

ourpick Prince's Hot Chicken (☎ 615-226-9442; 123 Ewing Dr; mains $4-8; ❂ noon-10pm Tue-Thu, noon-4am Fri & Sat) Cayenne-rubbed 'hot chicken,' fried to succulent perfection and served on a piece of white bread with a side of pickles, is Nashville's unique contribution to the culinary universe. Tiny, faded Prince's, in a north-side strip mall, is a local legend. In mild, medium, hot and death-defying extra hot, its chicken will burn a hole in your stomach and you'll come back begging for more.

Noshville (☎ 615-329-6674; 1918 Broadway; mains $5-11; ❂ 6:30am-2:30pm Mon, 6:30am-8:30pm Tue-Thu, 6:30am-9:30pm Fri, 7:30am-9:30pm Sat, to 8:30pm Sun) Misplaced Yankees adore this delightful New York–style deli, a play on the Yiddish word 'nosh,' meaning 'snack.' Customers sink their teeth into gigantic, juicy corned beef and pastrami sandwiches at the red vinyl booths, sip matzo ball soup at the modern chrome counter or get a bagel and lox to go.

MIDRANGE

Market Street Public House (☎ 615-259-9611; 134 2nd Ave N; mains $8-20; ❂ 11am-11pm Mon-Thu, to 2am Fri & Sat, 4pm-11pm Sun) This dark wood-paneled pub is a friendly refuge from the noise and lights of the District. There's a great selection of homemade microbrews and regulars' beer steins hang on the wall. The menu has salads, burgers and sandwiches as well as heartier 'pub fayre' such as shepherd's pie and fish-and-chips.

Red (☎ 625-329-3912; www.tribenashville.com; 1517 Church St; mains $9-20; ❂ 5:30-9:30pm Tue-Thu, to 10:30pm Fri & Sat, 11:30am-2pm & 5:30-9:30pm Sun) Attached to the popular West End gay and lesbian bar Tribe (opposite), Red welcomes everyone to enjoy sassed-up comfort food such as five-cheese macaroni and blackened chicken salad. A Bloody Mary–fueled Sunday brunch on the patio is popular.

Tin Angel (☎ 615-298-3444; 3201 West End Ave; mains $10-19; ❂ 11am-10pm Mon-Fri, from 5pm Sat, 11am-3pm Sun) A West Nashville corner bistro with exposed-brick walls and pressed-tin ceiling, serving eclectic, upscale Tennessee-meet-Paris dishes.

TOP END

Margot Cafe (☎ 615-227-4668; www.margotcafe.com; 1017 Woodland St; mains $14-28; ❂ 6-10pm Tue-Sat, brunch 11am-2pm Sun) This newcomer to the low-profile East Side does rustic French and Italian cuisine with great sophistication – think goat cheese ravioli, locally raised braised lamb, Riesling ice cream. The small restaurant, with exposed brick and yellow walls, is cozy and casually romantic. Menus change daily.

Merchant's (☎ 615-254-1892; www.merchantsrestaurant.com; 401 Broadway; mains $14-39; ❂ 11am-11pm Mon-Thu, 11am-midnight Fri & Sat, 4-9pm Sun) Located in a renovated 19th-century hotel in the heart of the District, this clubby bistro has gleaming parquet floors, white tablecloths and a mahogany bar overlooking Broadway. Splurge on ritzy, old-school fare such as *steak au poivre* (pepper steak) and chicken

Louis. The downstairs Grille has cheaper, more casual eats.

Drinking & Entertainment

Nashville has the nightlife of a city three times its size, and you'll be hard-pressed to find a place that *doesn't* have live music. College students, bachelor party-goers, Danish backpackers and businessmen in town for conventions all rock out downtown, where the neon lights make Broadway look like a country-themed Las Vegas. Bars and venues west and south of downtown tend to attract more locals, with many places clustered near Vanderbilt University.

BARS & CLUBS

Cafe Coco (☎ 615-321-2626; www.cafecoco.com; 210 Louise Ave; mains $6-10; ⏰ 24 hr; wi-fi) In a ramshackle old house just off Elliston Pl, hanging out at Cafe Coco is a like being at a wonderful, low-key house party that never stops. Beer, yummy coffee drinks, sandwiches, pasta, cheesecake and more are served, performers jam on the stage, people smoke on the large patio and drink at the bar, and students study on laptops using the free wi-fi, 24-hours a day.

Robert's Western World (☎ 615-244-9552; www.robertswesternworld.com; 416 Broadway; no cover; ⏰ 10am-3am) Buy a pair of boots, a beer or a burger at this unpretentious joint, a longtime favorite on the strip. Live music starts in the afternoon and lasts through the night.

Tribe (☎ 625-329-3912; www.tribenashville.com; 1517 Church St; ⏰ 4pm-midnight Mon-Thu, to 2am Fri & Sat, 11:30am-midnight Sun) Ultrafriendly Tribe caters to a largely gay and lesbian crowd, though everyone is welcome to sip martinis, watch music videos and dance the night away at this slick, modern club.

LIVE MUSIC

Nashville's opportunities for hearing live music are unparalleled. Apart from the big venues, many talented country, folk, bluegrass, Southern-rock and blues performers play smoky honky-tonks, blues bars, seedy storefronts and organic cafés for tips. Many places are free Monday to Friday or if you arrive early enough.

our pick **Bluebird Cafe** (☎ 615-383-1461; www.bluebirdcafe.com; 4104 Hillsboro Rd; cover free-$15) In a strip mall in suburban South Nashville, this ugly duckling of a café has had some of the best original singer-songwriters in country music grace

its tiny stage since 1982. Steve Earle, Emmylou Harris, and the Cowboy Junkies have all played the Bluebird, which was the setting for the 1993 Sandra Bullock and River Phoenix movie *The Thing Called Love*. Tables can be reserved up to a week in advance for the twice-nightly shows, which include a minimum charge of $7 a person, easy to spend on food or beer.

BB King's Blues Club (☎ 615-256-2727; www.bbkingbluesclub.com; 152 2nd Ave N; cover Sun-Thu $5, Fri & Sat $10; ⏰ 5pm-1am) Watch live jazz and blues in this cathedral of sound, complete with stained-glass windows and folk-art portraits of the 'saints': Johnny Cash, Miles Davis, Elvis. The kitchen serves soul food including ribs, fried chicken and catfish. Ages 21 and up after 10pm, unless accompanied by a parent.

Bourbon Street Blues & Boogie Bar (☎ 615-242-5837; www.bourbonstreetblues.com; 220 Printers Alley; cover free-$10; ⏰ 4pm-3am) This spot, in the tiny Printers Alley between 3rd and 4th Aves and Union and Church Sts, is the city's premier blues venue.

Ryman Auditorium (☎ tickets 615-458-8700, info 615-889-3060; www.ryman.com; 116 5th Ave; ticket prices vary) Often called the 'mother church of country music,' the Ryman was the home of the *Grand Ole Opry* from 1943 to 1974 and now hosts the show during the winter months. The Ryman's excellent acoustics, historic charm and large seating capacity have kept it the premier venue in town. You can also tour the Ryman during the day (p471).

Station Inn (☎ 615-255-3307; www.stationinn.com; 402 12th Ave S; ⏰ doors open 7pm, music at 9pm) In the funky but low-key 12th Ave S neighborhood, this unassuming stone building is the best place in town for serious bluegrass.

Tootsie's Wild Orchid Lounge (☎ 615-726-7937; www.tootsies.net; 422 Broadway; ⏰ 10am-2:30am Mon-Sat, from noon Sun) With a bright purple exterior and dusty walls plastered with layers of old photographs, tiny Tootsies is truly a downtown must-see. The venerated dive has appeared in several films, been written about in *Esquire* and *Playboy*, and been featured in its own TV documentary. In the 1960s, club owner and den mother 'Tootsie' Bess nurtured the careers of the likes of Willie Nelson, Kris Kristofferson and Waylon Jennings. Now, up-and-coming country musicians play the tiny stage and it is not unusual for big stars to stop by for an impromptu jam session. Pluck your heart out at open auditions which are held Friday and Saturday mornings.

THE SOUTH

WORTH THE TRIP: JACK DANIEL'S DISTILLERY

The irony of the **Jack Daniel's Distillery** (☎ 931-759-6180; www.jackdaniels.com; Rte 1, Lynchburg; tours free; ☑ 9am-4:30pm) being in a 'dry county' is lost on no one – local liquor laws dictate that no hard stuff can be sold within county lines, thus the distillery cannot give out samples of its famous whiskey. But it can give hour-long free tours, where visitors are encouraged to take long sniffs of the golden brew. The oldest registered distillery in the US, the folks at Jack Daniels have been dripping whiskey through layers of charcoal then aging it in oak barrels since 1866. The distillery is located off Hwy 55 in the diminutive town of Lynchburg, which freely admits that all visitors are either here to see the distillery or they are lost.

In the Elliston Pl neighborhood are a couple of venues that stray from hard-core country and whose cover charges vary, depending on who's playing. **Exit/In** (☎ 615-321-3340; www.exitin.com; 2208 Elliston Pl), opened in 1971, features live indie rock, with occasional helpings of reggae, metal and even country. **The End** (☎ 615-321-4457; 2219 Elliston Pl) is a tiny, deliciously dive-y alt-rock venue.

THEATER

Grand Ole Opry (☎ 615-871-6779; www.opry.com; 2802 Opryland Dr, Music Valley; adult $34.50-46.50, child $24.50-34.50; ☑ 7:30pm Fri, 6:30pm & 9:30pm Sat Mar-Nov) Though you'll find a variety of country shows throughout the week, the production Friday and Saturday evenings March through November is the *Grand Ole Opry*, a lavish tribute to classic Nashville Country music.

The **Nashville Symphony** (☎ 615-687-6500; 1 Symphony Pl; www.nashvillesymphony.org) hosts maestros and pop stars in the shiny new Schemerhorn Symphony Hall. With three great stages, the **Tennessee Performing Arts Center** (☎ 615-782-4000; www.tpac.org; 505 Deaderick St) is home to the following:
Nashville Ballet (www.nashvilleballet.com)
Nashville Opera (www.nashvilleopera.org)
Tennessee Repertory Theatre (www.tnrep.org)

SPORTS

Tennessee Titans (☎ 615-565-4200; www.titansonline.com) The NFL Tennessee Titans play in the Coliseum, across the river from downtown, from August to December.

Nashville Sounds (☎ 615-242-4371; www.nashvillesounds.com) A minor-league AAA baseball affiliate for the Pittsburgh Pirates, the Sounds play at Greer Stadium, south of town.

Nashville Predators (☎ 615-770-2300; www.nashvillepredators.com) For NHL hockey, catch the Nashville Predators at Gaylord Entertainment Center from September through April.

Shopping

Nashville's music stores are numerous and well stocked.

Ernest Tubb's (☎ 615-255-7503; www.ernesttubb.com; 417 Broadway; ☑ 9am-10pm Sun-Thu, 9am-midnight Fri & Sat) Marked by a giant neon guitar sign, this is the best place to shop for country and bluegrass records.

Gruhn Guitars (☎ 615-256-2033; www.gruhn.com; 400 Broadway; ☑ 9:30am-5:30pm Mon-Sat) This renowned vintage instrument store has an expert staff.

Hatch Show Print (☎ 615-256-2805; www.hatchshowprint.com; 316 Broadway; ☑ 9:30am-5:30pm Mon-Fri, 10:30am-5:30pm Sat) One of the oldest letter-print shops in the US. Using old-school cut-blocks, Hatch began making posters to promote early vaudeville and circus shows. The company has produced graphic ads and posters for almost every country star since.

Katy K's Ranch Dressing (☎ 615-297-4242; www.katyk.com; 2407 12th Ave S; ☑ 11am-6pm Mon-Sat, 1pm-4pm Sun) The place to go for vintage Western wear, cowboy boots and rockabilly accessories, in the funky 12th Ave S neighborhood a few miles from downtown.

Getting There & Around

Nashville International Airport (BNA; ☎ 615-275-1675; www.flynashville.com), 8 miles east of town, is not a major air hub. MTA bus 18 links the airport and downtown; the **Gray Line Airport Express** (☎ 615-275-1180; www.graylinenashville.com; one way/return $12/18; ☑ 5am-11pm) serves major downtown and West End hotels. Taxis charge a flat rate of $22 each way. Try **Nashville Cab** (☎ 615-242-7070) or **American Music City Cab** (☎ 615-742-3030).

Greyhound (☎ 615-255-3556; 200 8th Ave S) has frequent buses to Memphis ($36.50, four hours), Atlanta, GA ($45.50, five hours), Birmingham, AL ($37.50, four hours) and New Orleans, LA ($59.50, 14 hours).

The **Metropolitan Transit Authority** (MTA; ☎ 615-862-5950; www.nashvillemta.org; Transit Mall, cnr Deaderick St & 4th Ave N; adult $1.25) operates city bus services based downtown. Its express buses also go to Music Valley and back.

AROUND NASHVILLE

About 20 miles south of Nashville off I-65, the historic town of **Franklin** (www.historicfranklin.com) has a charming downtown area and beautiful B&Bs. About 50 miles south of Nashville on Hwys 41A and 231, **Shelbyville** (www.shelbyvilletn.com) is the epicenter of the high-stepping, head-bobbing Tennessee walking horse.

EASTERN TENNESSEE

Dolly Parton, Eastern Tennessee's most famous native, loves her home region so much she has made a successful career out of singing about girls who leave the honeysuckle-scented embrace of the Smoky Mountains for the false glitter of the city. They're always sorry.

Largely a rural region of small towns, rolling hills and river valleys, the eastern third of the state has friendly folks, hearty country food and pastoral charm to make most anyone feel at home.

The lush, heather-tinted Great Smoky Mountains are great for hiking, camping and rafting, while the region's two main urban areas, Knoxville and Chattanooga, are easygoing riverside cities with lively college populations and kicking music scenes.

Chattanooga

Named 'the dirtiest city in America' in the 1960s, Chattanooga was shamed into cleaning up rampant industrial pollution and focusing on downtown revitalization. Today, the riverside city has a leafy, pedestrian-friendly downtown, miles of waterfront walking trails and free electric buses.

Originally the terminus of the Western and Atlantic Railroad, the city was once a major transport hub throughout the 19th and 20th centuries, hence the 'Chattanooga Choo-Choo,' which was originally a reference to the Cincinnati Southern Railroad's passenger service from Cincinnati to Chattanooga and later the title of a 1941 Glen Miller song.

Most of Chattanooga's main sites are within a few blocks of the **visitor center** (☎ 423-756-8687, 800-322-3344; www.chattanoogafun.com; 2 Broad St; ☺ 8:30am-5:30pm) at the corner of 2nd and Broad Sts. The Bluff View Art District at High and E 2nd Sts has upscale shops and restaurants overlooking the river.

SIGHTS & ACTIVITIES

Ross's Landing, the center of the city's rejuvenated waterfront, is a good place to start a riverfront stroll. The amazing **Tennessee Aquarium** (☎ 800-262-0695; www.tnaqua.org; 1 Broad St; adult/child $19.95/10.95; ☺ 10am-6pm) is the world's largest freshwater aquarium. Exhibits mirror a large river system and give visitors a unique look at the interconnectedness of riparian areas. While here, check out a show at the attached **IMAX theater** (☎ 800-262-0695; 201 Chestnut St; adult/child $8/5.50). Next door, the **Creative Discovery Museum** (☎ 423-756-2738; www.cdmfun.org; tickets $8.95; ☺ 10am-5pm Mon-Sat, from noon Sun, closed Wed Sep-Feb) has a two-story play riverboat, a hands-on artists studio, and a climbable 42ft high spiral tower.

Chattanooga African-American Museum (☎ 423-266-8658; www.caamhistory.com; 200 ML King Jr Blvd; adult/student/child $5/2/2; ☎ 10am-5pm Mon-Fri, noon-4pm Sat) has a special exhibit on 'Empress of the Blues' singer Bessie Smith, who sang in the taverns of her native Chattanooga before reaching worldwide fame.

Some of Chattanooga's oldest and best-known attractions are 6 miles outside the city at **Lookout Mountain** (☎ 423-821-4224; www.lookoutmtnattractions.com; 827 East Brow Rd; adult/child $38/19; ☺ vary by season). Admission price includes the Incline Railway, which chugs up a steep incline to the top of the mountain; the world's longest underground waterfall, Ruby Falls; and Rock City, a garden with a dramatic clifftop overlook. The mountain is a popular hang-gliding location. **Point Park** (admission $3), at the mountain's summit, is part of the NPS' **Chickamauga & Chattanooga National Military Park** (☎ 423-866-9241; www.nps.gov/chch).

About an hour north of the city off I-75 near the town of Sweetwater, the **Lost Sea** (☎ 423-337-6616; www.thelostsea.com; 140 Lost Sea Rd; adult/child $15/7; ☺ 9am-5pm, later in spring & summer) is the largest underground lake in America, contained inside the enormous Craighead Caverns. An hour-long tour of the caverns includes a glass-bottom boat ride across the still, greenish water.

SLEEPING & EATING

You can find many budget motels around I-24 and I-75.

Econo Lodge Lookout Mountain (☎ 423-821-9000; 150 Browns Ferry Rd; r from $49; P ⊠ ⬚ wi-fi) Less than 10 minutes from downtown in a quiet location at the foot of Lookout Mountain, this clean, comfy hotel has a friendly staff and an unbeatable price.

Chattanooga Choo-Choo Holiday Inn (☎ 423-266-5000, 800-872-2529; www.choochoo.com; 1400 Market St; r from $119; railcars $169; P ⊠ ⬚ ⬚ wi-fi) This bustling hotel is housed in an imposing old railway terminal on 24 acres of manicured grounds, which include four restaurants, a swank '40s-style bar, a convention center, numerous shops and a small railroad museum. You'll sleep like a turn-of-the-century aristocrat in one of the Choo-Choo's 48 authentic Victorian railcars, outfitted for the modern age with double beds and TVs. Standard rooms and suites, in separate buildings, are clean but ordinary.

Chattanoogan (☎ 423-756-3400, 800-619-0018; www.chattanooganhotel.com; 1201 S Broad St; r/ste from $129/259; P ⊠ ⬚ ⬚ wi-fi) This 199-room downtown hotel whispers good taste. The enormous, airy lobby has three restaurants, the contemporary, earth-toned rooms have comfy beds and there's even a spa with rooftop deck.

Porkers BBQ (☎ 423-267-2726; 1251 Market St; mains $4-16; ⊙ 7am-6pm Mon-Sat) It's hog heaven in this retro-styled downtown 'cue joint, where President Bush chows down on ribs when he's in town. Booths are packed with families and the counter is perfect for solo indulgence – don't forget the banana pudding.

Aretha Frankenstein's (☎ 423-265-7685; 518 Tremont St; mains $6-9; ⊙ 7am-midnight) This turquoise cottage, tucked away on a residential street in the hip North Shore area, is tops for all-day pancakes and omelets, burritos and BLTs, or enjoying a beer on the sprawling patio.

GETTING THERE & AROUND

Chattanooga's modest airport is just east of the city. Nearby, the **Greyhound station** (☎ 423-892-1277; 960 Airport Rd) has several daily buses to Atlanta, GA ($24.50, 2½ hours), Nashville ($24.50, 2½ hours) and Knoxville ($20.50, two hours).

With an utter lack of nostalgia, Amtrak does not serve Chattanooga.

For access to most downtown sites, ride the free electric shuttle buses that ply the center. The visitor center has a route map.

Knoxville

Once known as the 'underwear capital of the world' for its numerous textile mills, Knoxville is now home to the University of Tennessee and a number of high-tech industries. Downtown is full of ornate, slightly crumbling 19th-century buildings and lovely outdoor cafés shaded by pear trees.

The **visitor center** (☎ 865-523-7263, 800-727-8045; www.knoxville.org; 301 S Gay St; ⊙ 9am-5pm Mon-Sat, from 1pm Sun) has locations downtown and near the riverfront. Most restaurants and nightlife are in the arty, renovated warehouses of **Old City**, near the train station, and **Market Square**, in central downtown. Concerts and University of Tennessee sports teams play at the **Neyland Coliseum** (☎ 615-974-0953; 1600 Stadium Dr).

The city's visual centerpiece is the **Sunsphere**, the main remnant of the 1982 World Fair. You can't miss the massive orange basketball that marks the **Women's Basketball Hall of Fame** (☎ 865-633-9000; www.wbhof.com; 700 Hall of Fame Dr; adult/child $8/6; ⊙ 10am-5pm Mon-Sat, 1-6pm Sun), a nifty look at the sport from the time when women were forced to play in full-length dresses.

SLEEPING & EATING

Hotel St Oliver (☎ 865-521-0050; 407 Union Ave; r $75-100; ⊠) This 28-room downtown gem has an eccentric rococo ambience, like staying at the home of your very rich but slightly dotty great aunt. Rooms have antique four-post beds and wet bars; the downstairs library has Victorian fainting couches and sinister-looking oil paintings.

Tomato Head (☎ 865-637-4067; www.thetomatohead .com; 12 Market Sq; mains $6-9; ⊙ 11am-10pm Tue-Sun, to 2pm Mon) A Market Sq favorite, with handmade pizzas, calzones and burritos and a cozy dining room filled with local art.

Great Smoky Mountains National Park

The Cherokee called this territory Shaconage (shah-*cone*-ah-jey), meaning roughly 'land of the blue smoke,' for the heather-colored mist that hangs over the ancient peaks. The Southern Appalachians are the world's oldest mountain range, with mile upon mile of cool, humid deciduous forest.

The 815-sq-mile park is the country's most visited, and while the main arteries and attractions can get crowded, studies have shown that 95% of visitors never venture further than 100yd from their cars, so it's easy to leave the teeming masses behind.

Popular sites include the former settlement of **Cades Cove**, the majestic peaks of **Mount Le Conte**, the dizzying heights of **Clingmans Dome** and numerous waterfalls, coves and trails, as well as nearly 2000 black bears (lock up your food).

Unlike most other national parks, Great Smoky charges no admission fee, nor will it ever; this proviso was written into the park's original charter as a stipulation for a $5 million Rockefeller family grant. Stop by a visitor center to pick up a park map and the free park newspaper, *Smokies Guide*. For more information about the North Carolina section of this park, see p388.

ORIENTATION & INFORMATION

Great Smoky Mountains National Park straddles the North Carolina–Tennessee border, which zig-zags diagonally through the heart of the park. The north–south **Newfound Gap Rd/Hwy 441** spans the park, connecting the gateway towns of Gatlinburg, TN, on the north-central border and Cherokee, NC, on the south-central border.

The park's three interior visitor centers are **Sugarlands Visitor Center** (☎ 865-436-1291; 8am-4:30pm, later in spring & summer), at the park's northern entrance near Gatlinburg; **Cades Cove Visitor Center** (☎ 877-444-6777; 9am-4:30pm, later in spring & summer) halfway up Cades Cove Loop Rd, off Hwy 441 near Gatlinburg entrance; and Oconaluftee Visitor Center, at the park's southern entrance near Cherokee, NC.

CAMPING

With 10 developed campgrounds offering about 1000 campsites, you'd think finding a place to pitch would be easy. Not so in the busy summer season: your best bet is to plan ahead. You can make **reservations** (☎ 800-365-2267; http://reservations.nps.gov) for some sites; others are first-come first-served. Camping fees are $14 to $23 per night, except for the five horse camps, which cost $20 to $25 per site. Of the park's 10 campgrounds only Cades Cove and Smokemont are open year-round; others are open March through October.

Backcountry camping is an excellent option. A (free) permit is required; you can make **reservations** (☎ 865-436-1231) and get permits at the ranger stations or visitor centers.

Gatlinburg

The best known gateway town into the Smokies is Gatlinburg, a Bavarian-flavored theme park of a town, its streets lined with souvenir shops, wedding chapels and Ye Ole pancake houses. The city has three **visitor centers** (☎ 423-436-0519, 800-343-1475; www.gatlinburg.com; 8am-6pm, to 8pm Fri & Sat, to 10pm summer), at the third and fifth stoplights and 2 miles north of town on US 441. They have separate information desks, one for city information (motels, restaurants) and one run by the park service (for campsite reservations, hiking routes etc), that are all open.

Ten miles north of Gatlinburg, **Pigeon Forge** (www.mypigeonforge.com) is a tacky complex of motels, outlet malls and country-music theaters and restaurants, all of which have grown up in the shadow of **Dollywood** (see boxed text, left).

WHAT THE...?

Dollywood (☎ 865-428-9488, 800-365-5996; www.dollywood.com; 1020 Dollywood Lane; adult/child $43.50/32.25; closed Jan-Mar) is a self-created ode to the patron saint of East Tennessee, the big-haired, bigger-bosomed country singer Dolly Parton. The park features Appalachian-themed rides and attractions, from the Mystery Mine roller coaster to the bald eagle sanctuary to the faux one-room chapel named after the doctor who delivered Dolly.

KENTUCKY

Imagine a coal miner, a fiddler, a college basketball player and a grand Southern lady in an elegant hat, all sitting on a veranda sipping mint juleps, and you're starting to get an idea of what Kentucky's all about.

A geographical and cultural crossroads, Kentucky combines the friendliness of the South, the rural frontier history of West, the industry of the North, and the aristocratic charm of the East.

KENTUCKY FACTS

Nickname: Bluegrass State

Population 4.2 million

Area 39,728 sq miles

Capital city Frankfort (pop 27,741)

Sales tax 6%

Birthplace of Frontiersman Kit Carson (1809–1868), 16th US president Abraham Lincoln (1809–1865), 'gonzo' journalist Hunter S Thompson (1937–2005), boxer Muhammad Ali (b 1942), actor Johnny Depp (b 1963)

Home of Corvette factory, Kentucky Derby, Louisville Slugger

Famous for Horses, bourbon, bluegrass music, fried chicken

Interesting place names Monkeys Eyebrow, Chicken Bristle, Shoulderblade, Hippo and Petroleum

---

In spring, the pastures of central Kentucky bloom with tiny azure buds, earning the it the moniker 'Bluegrass State.' Bluegrass music was born here too, a banjo-fueled amalgam of Appalachian folk songs, African American beats and Chicago jazz. Thoroughbred breeding is a multibillion-dollar industry, and horse country boasts a stately English countryside ambience.

The state's cities are small and elegant, with a sleepy, midcentury charm. Even the industries are nifty – a state that produces bourbon, baseball bats and Corvettes must be alright.

History

British and French forces battled for control of Kentucky in the mid-1700s, recognizing the value of the fertile land that was once used by Native Americans as a hunting ground.

Legendary frontiersman Daniel Boone blazed a trail through the Cumberland Gap and the British began pouring over the Appalachians in 1775. The state became a battleground during the Revolutionary War, with local Shawnee Indians allying with the crown.

Though a slave state, Kentucky was bitterly divided during the Civil War, with 30,000 fighting for the Confederacy and 64,000 for the Union. Both the Union president Abraham Lincoln and Confederacy president Jefferson Davis were Kentucky-born.

After the war, Kentucky built up its economy on railways, tobacco, and coal-mining. Today its motto 'Unbridled Spirit,' reflects the dominance of scenic horse country.

Information

The boundary between Eastern and Central time goes through the middle of Kentucky. If you go from Mammoth Cave to Lincoln's birthplace, you'll arrive an hour later than you thought.

Kentucky Travel (☎ 502-564-4930, 800-225-8747; www.kentuckytourism.com; Box 2011, Frankfort, KY 40602) Sends out a detailed booklet on the state's attractions.

LOUISVILLE

A major shipping center during the days of Westward Expansion, Louisville (or Looeyville, or Louahvul, or Luhvul) is still the largest city in Kentucky.

Best known as home of the Kentucky Derby, which has been drawing aristocrats to Churchill Downs since 1875, Louisville is also a nice place to stop for a day or two, with some good museums, a pretty riverfront, and interesting blue-collar neighborhoods full of corner pool halls and drive-through chili restaurants. Located just south of downtown is **Old Louisville** (www.oldlouisville.com), with the largest collection of Victorian homes in the country. A series of pretty parks (laid out by Frederick Law Olmsted in the 1890s) encircle the city, along with an inner (I-264) and outer (I-265) ring road.

The **visitor center** (☎ 502-582-3732, 888-568-4784; www.gotolouisville.com; 221 S 4th St; 10am-6pm Mon-Sat, noon-5pm Sun) has a free exhibit about that great Kentucky icon, KFC founder Colonel Sanders. Surf the web free at the **public library** (301 York St) downtown.

Sights

At the **Louisville Slugger Museum** (☎ 877-775-844; www.sluggermuseum.org; 800 W Main St; adult/child $9/4; 9am-5pm Mon-Sat, from noon Sun) look for the 120ft baseball bat leaning against the building – ya can't miss it. Hillerich & Bradsby Co have been making the famous Louisville Slugger baseball bat here since 1884. The admission fee includes a plant tour, a hall of baseball memorabilia such as Babe Ruth's bat, a batting cage and a free mini slugger. Customized bats are sold in the lobby. Note: bat production halts on Sunday, as well as on Saturday in the winter.

Located across the street, the **Frazier Museum** (☎ 502-412-2280; www.fraziermuseum.org; 829 W Main St; adult/child $12/9; ⏰ 9am-5pm Mon-Sat, from noon Sun) has a huge collection of British and American weaponry, with bloody battle dioramas realistic enough to frighten small children.

The terrific **Muhammad Ali Center** (☎ 502-584-9254; www.alicenter.org; 144 N 6th St; adult/child $9/4; ⏰ 9:30am-5pm Mon-Sat, from noon Sun) is a love offering to the city from its most famous native. Self-guided tours include a stirring film on Ali's life and video projections of his most famous fights, as well as exhibits about the racial segregation and humanitarian issues that so vexed the outspoken man once known as the 'Louisville Lip.'

Speed Art Museum (☎ 502-634-2700; www.speed museum.org; 2035 S 3rd St; admission free; ⏰ 10:30am-4pm Tue, Wed & Fri, to 8pm Thu, to 5pm Sat, noon-5pm Sun) is a handsome Greek Revival–style building with more than 12,000 pieces of art, from classical antiques to work by Kentucky artists.

Children enjoy the interactive exhibits at **Louisville Science Center** (☎ 502-561-6100; www .louisvillescience.org; 727 W Main St; adult/child $12/10; ⏰ 9:30am-5pm Mon-Thu, to 9pm Fri & Sat, noon-6pm Sun), which also houses an IMAX theater.

The Victorian-era **Old Louisville** neighborhood, just south of downtown, is well worth a drive or stroll. It has some wonderful historic homes open for tours (see www.historichomes.org).

CHURCHILL DOWNS

Home to the Kentucky Derby, **Churchill Downs** (☎ 502-636-4400, 800-283-3729; www.churchilldowns.com; 700 Central Ave), 3 miles south of downtown, is the most famous horseracing track in America. Kentucky has been a thoroughbred breeding capital since the late 1700s, and all this horsing around pays off the first Saturday in May, when the 'greatest two minutes in sports,' takes place.

Most seats at the Kentucky Derby are by invitation only or they've been reserved years in advance. On Derby Day, $40 gets you into the Paddock party scene (no seat) if you arrive early, but it's so crowded you won't see much of the race. Don't fret, however. From April

through to November, you can get a $2 seat at the Downs for many exciting races, often warm-ups for the big events.

Though the race only lasts a couple of minutes, the festivities start about three weeks before for the **Kentucky Derby Festival** (☎ 502-584-6383; www.kdf.org). After the race, the crowd sings 'My Old Kentucky Home' and watches as the winning horse gets covered in a blanket of roses. Later its name will be written on the racetrack wall.

On the grounds, the interesting **Kentucky Derby Museum** (☎ 502-637-7097; www.derbymuseum .org; Gate 1, Central Ave; adult/child $10/5; ⏰ 9am-5pm Mon-Sat, from noon Sun) has displays on the big event, where a who's who of upper-crust America wears wide-brimmed derby hats, sips mint juleps while waiting to see which horse will make its owner rich (or richer). There is a 360-degree audiovisual about the race and a tour of the track, as well as behind-the-scenes track tours ($10).

Tours

The **Belle of Louisville** (☎ 502-574-2992, 800-832-0011; www.belleoflouisville.org; adult/child $15/6), a 1914-era stern-wheeler, does scenic two-hour sightseeing cruises on the Ohio River, departing from the 4th St Wharf.

The **Ghosts of Old Louisville Tour** (☎ 502-637-2922; www.ghostsofoldlouisville.com; tickets $25) explores the macabre side of America's largest Victorian neighborhood, departing from the Old Louisville Visitor Center at 218 West Oak St.

Sleeping & Eating

Otter Creek Park (☎ 502-574-4583; http://www.louis villeky.gov/MetroParks/parks/ottercreek/; 800 Otter Creek Park Rd, Brandenburg; backcountry camping $3, campsites $16, cabins from $65) Though a good 25 miles southwest of the city, this park is part of the Louisville Metro Parks system and has rental cabins and a variety of campsites on 2600 emerald acres of fields and forest.

Rocking Horse B&B (☎ 502-583-0408, 888-467-7322; www.rockinghorse-bb.com; 1022 S 3rd St; r incl breakfast $105-195; P ✕ ✕ wi-fi) Situated on a stretch of 3rd St once known as Millionaire's Row, this 1888 Romanesque mansion has six guestrooms decorated with Victorian antiques and gorgeous stained glass. Guests can eat their two-course breakfast in the English country garden or sip complimentary port in the parlor.

Brown Hotel (☎ 502-583-1234; www.brownhotel .com; 335 West Broadway; r from $199) Opera stars, queens and prime ministers have trod the marble floors of this storied downtown hotel, built in the roaring '20s. Louisville's famous 'Hot Brown' sandwich was invented here to feed hungry guests after a 1923 dinner dance. Closed during the city's economic slump of the 1970s, the Brown has since reopened with 293 comfortable rooms, two restaurants, and a lobby restored to all its gilded glamour.

Lynn's Paradise Cafe (☎ 502-583-3447; www .lynnsparadisecafe.com; 984 Barret Ave; mains $7-15; ☺ 7am-10pm Mon-Fri, from 8am Sat & Sun) Psychedelically bright Lynn's serves up a mean Hot Brown, the open-faced turkey and bacon sandwich that is Louisville's culinary claim to fame, as well as a killer all-day breakfast – don't miss the biscuits with sorghum butter.

Lilly's (☎ 502-451-0447; 1147 Bardstown Rd; lunch $8-14, dinner $15-25; ☺ 11am-3pm Tue-Sat, 5:30-10pm Tue-Thu, 5:30-11pm Fri & Sat) Most of the good restaurants and bars are found at Bardstown Rd, including this longtime favorite for eclectic upscale fare, prepared with local ingredients by chef Kathy Cary.

Entertainment

The free weekly *Leo* (www.leoweekly.com) lists gigs and entertainment. The bulk of the drinking places can be found along funky Bardstown Rd.

Kentucky Center for the Arts (☎ 502-562-0100; www.kentuckycenter.org; 5 Riverfront Plaza) This prime performance venue hosts theater, ballet, opera, orchestra, modern dance and popular music.

Palace Theater (☎ 502-583-4555; www.louisvillepal ace.com; 625 S 4th St) The 1928 Palace Theater is a wonderfully baroque venue for big-name concerts and special events. Past performers include Tom Waits, Wilco and BB King.

Actors Theatre of Louisville (☎ 502-584-1205; www.actorstheatre.org; 504 W Main St) This highly regarded theatre performs everything from Shakespeare to contemporary musicals and has premiered several Pulitzer Prize–winning plays.

Getting There & Around

Louisville's International Airport (☎ 502-367-4636; www.flylouisville.com) is 5 miles south of town on I-65. Get there by cab (around $15) or local bus 2. The **Greyhound station** (☎ 502-585-3331; 720 W Muhammad Ali Blvd), just west of downtown, has buses to Chicago, IL, Lexington, and Memphis and Nashville, TN. Local buses are operated by **TARC** (☎ 502-585-1234; 1000 W Broadway), based at the Union Station depot.

BLUEGRASS COUNTRY

Drive through northeast Kentucky's Bluegrass country on a sunny day, and you'll get an idea of what the ancient Greeks might have been imagining when they wrote about the Elysian Fields of paradise. Horses graze in the brilliant green hills dotted with ponds, poplar trees and handsome estate houses. These once-wild woodlands and meadows have been a center of horse breeding for almost 250 years, and the area's principal city, Lexington, is known as 'Horse Capital of the World.'

Lexington

Even the prison looks like a country club in Lexington, home of million dollar houses and multimillion dollar horses. Once the wealthiest and most-cultured city west of the Allegheny Mountains, it was called 'the Athens of the West,' and today is home to the University of Kentucky and the heart of the thoroughbred racehorse industry. A handsome little city with a pedestrian-friendly downtown, stately Victorian neighborhoods and a lively youth culture, the city is well-worth a stop, though most of the attractions are in the countryside outside the metro area.

Pick up maps and area information from the **visitor center** (☎ 859-233-7299, 800-845-3959; www.visitlex.com; 301 E Vine St; ☺ 8:30am-5pm Mon-Fri, 10am-4pm Sat). The **public library** (140 E Main St; ☺ 10am-5pm Tue-Fri, from noon Sat & Sun) has free internet access and free wireless for those with laptops.

SIGHTS & ACTIVITIES

Downtown Lexington has several **historic homes** open for tours. The following are $7 each, or $15 for all four with a combination ticket – available at the visitor center or at Ashland.

Just 1.5 miles east of downtown, **Ashland** (☎ 859-266-8581; www.henryclay.org; 120 Sycamore Rd; ☺ 10am-4pm Mon-Sat) was the Italianate estate of statesman Henry Clay (1777–1852). **Hunt-Morgan House** (☎ 859-253-0362; www.bluegrasstrust .org; 201 N Mill St; ☺ 1-4pm Wed-Fri & Sun, 10am-3pm

Sat) is a fine Federal-style mansion (c 1814) with a small Civil War museum. The 1806 **Mary Todd-Lincoln House** (☎ 859-233-9999; www .mtlhouse.org; 578 W Main St; ☾ 10am-4pm Mon-Sat) has articles from the first lady's childhood and her years as Abe's wife. **Waveland** (☎ 859-272-3611; http://parks.ky.gov/findparks/histparks/wl/; 225 Waveland Museum Lane; ☾ 9am-4pm) is a 19th-century plantation.

The marvelously odd **Headly-Whitney Museum** (☎ 859-255-6653; www.headley-whitney.org; 4435 Old Frankfort Pike; adult/child $7/5; ☾ 10am-5pm Tue-Fri, from noon Sat & Sun) is the private collection of the late George Headley, a local jewelry designer and art patron whose gemstone trinkets, handmade dollhouses, Chinese ceramics and massive seashell 'grotto' are on display.

An educational theme park and equestrian sports center, the **Kentucky Horse Park** (☎ 859-233-4303, 800-678-8813; www.kyhorsepark.com; 4089 Iron Works Parkway; adult/child $15/8; ☾ 9am-5pm daily mid-Mar–Oct, Wed-Sun Nov–mid-Mar) sits on 1200 acres just north of Lexington. Horses representing 50 different breeds live in the park and participate in special live shows. Also included, the international **Museum of the Horse** has neat dioramas of the horse through history, from the tiny prehistoric 'eohippus' to the Pony Express mail carriers. Seasonal horseback riding costs $15 with park ticket, $22 without.

The adjacent **American Saddlebred Museum** (☎ 859-259-2746, 800-829-4438; www.american-saddle bred.com; 4093 Iron Works Parkway; ☾ 9am-5pm, to 6pm summer) focuses on America's first registered horse breed, horse gaits and other technical stuff – for hardcore enthusiasts.

Most farms are closed to the public, but you can visit the **Thoroughbred Center** (☎ 859-293-1853; www.thethoroughbredcenter.com/tours; 3380 Paris Pike; adult/ child $10/5; ☾ tours 9am Mon-Sat Apr-Oct, by appointment Nov-Mar). Tours of this working thoroughbred training facility take in stables, practice tracks and paddocks.

Watch 'em run at the **Keeneland Race Course** (☎ 859-254-3412, 800-456-3412; www.keeneland.com; 4201 Versailles Rd; tickets $2), which has races in April and October and horse sales throughout the year. From March to November, you can watch the champions train from sunrise to 11am. Or head to the **Red Mile** (☎ 859-255-0752; www.theredmile.com; 1200 Red Mile Rd) to see harness racing, where jockeys are pulled behind horses in special two-wheeled

carts. Live races are in the fall, but you can watch and wager on simulcasts of races from around the world year-round.

If you're itching to get back in the saddle, several working ranches around Lexington offer **horseback riding** to both newbies and experienced riders. **Whispering Woods** (☎ 502-570-9663; www.whisperingwoodstrails.com; 265 Wright Lane; trail rides per hr $20; ☾ Mar-Nov), in Georgetown, offers guided trail rides. **Deer Run Stables** (☎ 859-527-6339; 2001 River Circle Dr; www .deerrunstable.com; tours per hr $30) also offers guided trips by reservation only.

TOURS

Blue Grass Tours (☎ 859-252-5744, 800-755-6956; www.bluegrasstours.com; tours from $26) Offers tours of downtown sites and countryside horse farms, with pick-up at Lexington hotels.

Horse Farm Tours (☎ 859-268-2906; www.horsefarm tours.com; adult per hr $30; ☾ tours 9am & 1pm Mon-Sun) Picks up at Lexington hotels and offers two tours daily to working horse farms. Reservations required.

SLEEPING & EATING

For dining, the liveliest area in the evening is around E Main and S Limestone Sts.

Kentucky Horse Park (☎ 859-259-4257, 800-370-6416; www.kyhorsepark.com; 4089 Iron Works Parkway; paved/unpaved campsites from $22/13; 🖻) A campground with 260 paved sites situated next to the Horse Park farm is open year-round. There are showers, laundry, a grocery, playgrounds and more. Primitive camping is also available.

Springs Inn (☎ 859-277-5751; www.springsinn .com; 2020 Harrodsburg Rd; r from $60; 🅿 🗙 🖫) This sprawling faux-Georgian motel located a little south of downtown has been family-run since 1948. Rooms are nothing special, but the service is friendly and the sweetly old-fashioned lobby and jumbo heated pool are nice.

Gratz Park Inn (☎ 859-231-1777, 800-752-4166; www.gratzparkinn.com; 120 W 2nd St; r/ste from $169/199; 🅿 🗙 🖳 wi-fi) In an old brick building on a quiet downtown street, this 40-room hotel has dark-wood furnishings and walls painted in masculine deep reds and hunter greens. The attached restaurant, Jonathan's, serves fine regional cuisine.

Billy's Hickory Pit Bar-B-Q (☎ 859-269-9593; 101 Cochran Rd; mains $6-15; ☾ 11am-10pm Mon-Sat, 11:30am-9pm Sun) Even the green beans have meat in them at low-key Billy's, an institu-

---

THE BOURBON TOUR

Bourbon whiskey was first distilled in Bourbon County, located north of Lexington, in 1789. Today 90% of all bourbon is produced here in Kentucky (no other state is allowed to put its own name on the bottle). A good bourbon must contain at least 51% corn, and must also be stored in charred oak barrels for a mininum of two years. While in Kentucky, you must try a mint julep, the archetypal Southern drink made with bourbon, sugar syrup and crushed mint. Drink it on the veranda at dusk, wearing a seersucker suit, and then you start to get the idea of true Southern living.

The **Oscar Getz Museum of Whiskey History** (☎ 502-348-2999; 114 N 5th St; ✆ 10am-4pm Mon-Sat, from noon Sun), in Bardstown, tells the bourbon story. Most of Kentucky's distilleries, which are centered around Bardstown and Frankfort, offer free tours. Call for times.

Distilleries

Near Bardstown (exit 112 off I-65, look for signs):

Heaven Hill (☎ 502-348-3921; www.heaven-hill.com; 1311 Gilkey Run Rd, Bardstown) The largest family-run bourbon producer, runs the Bourbon Heritage Center.

Jim Beam (☎ 502-543-9877; www.jimbean.com; 149 Happy Hollow Rd, Clermont) Watch a good film about the grandson of Jim Beam with some informative bourbon-making secrets thrown in.

Maker's Mark (☎ 502-865-2099; www.makersmark.com; 3350 Burks Spring Rd, near Loretto) Where the Samuels family has been making whiskey since 1840; a National Historic Landmark.

Near Frankfort/Lawrenceburg:

Buffalo Trace (☎ 502-696-5926; www.buffalotrace.com; 1001 Wilkinson Blvd near Frankfort) Named for the ancient buffalo that led early pioneers westward, this distillery shows the whole process.

Four Roses (☎ 502-839-3436; www.fourroses.us; 1224 Bonds Mills Rd) In a Spanish hacienda-style building, this distillery gives very detailed tours; good for bourbon connoisseurs.

Rebecca Ruth Candy (☎ 502-223-7475; www.rrcandy.com; 112 East 2nd St, Frankfort) Kids and teetotalers will appreciate this old-fashioned candy factory, home of the much-loved chocolate bourbon ball.

Woodford Reserve (☎ 859-879-1812; www.woodfordreserve.com; 7855 McCracken Pike, Versailles) The historic site along a creek is restored to its 1800s glory; the distillery still uses old-fashioned copper pots.

---

tion known for its Kentucky-style smoked pork, beef and mutton and its 'burgoo,' a regional chililike stew.

Holly Hill Inn (☎ 859-846-4732; www.hollyhillinn .com; 426 N Winter St, Midway; prix-fixe lunch $15, prix-fixe dinner from $35; ☎ 11:30am-2pm & 5:30-9pm Wed-Sat, Sunday brunch 11:30am-2:30pm) Just west of Lexington in the town of Midway, a husband-and-wife team run this elegantly quirky restaurant in an old farmhouse, where guests dine in converted bedrooms and parlors. Fixed-price menus offer such bounty as Kentucky squab spring rolls, local pork in bourbon sauce and lavender ice cream.

DRINKING & ENTERTAINMENT

Applebee's Park (☎ 859-422-7867; www.lexingtonle gends.com; 1200 N Broadway) Home to Lexington Legends minor-league baseball team, it's also a great venue for outdoor concerts.

Kentucky Theater (☎ 859-231-6997; www.ken tuckytheater.com; 214 E Main St) The restored 1927 theater shows movies and is an intimate venue for occasional live music.

Rupp Arena (☎ 859-233-4567; www.rupparena .com; 430 W Vine St) The 23,000-seat venue is the home court for the UK Wildcats and also hosts any big-name rock and country acts.

For beer, bourbon and bar food, try friendly watering holes such as **Cheapside** (☎ 859-254-0046; www.cheapsidebarandgrill.com; 131 Cheapside St), with a tropical patio, and **Two Keys Tavern** (☎ 859-254-5000; 333 S Limestone St), both of which have live music.

GETTING THERE & AROUND

Lexington, at the crossroads of I-75 and I-64, is 77 miles east of Louisville. **Greyhound** (☎ 859-299-8804; 477 W New Circle Rd; ✆ 8am-11pm) is 2 miles from downtown. Regular buses go to Louisville, some by very indirect routes. There are also buses to Nashville, TN and Washington, DC. **Lex-Tran** (☎ 859-253-4636; www.lextran.com) runs local buses (bus 6 goes to the Greyhound stop).

Frankfort

A pretty little postcard of a town, all red brick and gingerbread trim, Kentucky's diminutive capital lies 26 miles west of Lexington. There are some notable historic buildings, including the 1910 domed neoclassical **capitol building** (☎ 502-564-3449; admission free; ☎ 8:30am-3:30pm Mon-Fri, 10am-2pm Sat, 1pm-4pm Sun, guided tours weekdays) and the nearby **governor's mansion**.

The older part of town is across the Kentucky River, where the **old state capitol** (☎ 502-564-1792; admission free; ☼ 10am-5pm Tue-Sat) functioned from 1827 to 1910. Nearby is the handsome **Kentucky History Center** (☎ 502-564-1792; www.history.ky.gov; 100 W Broadway St; admission free; ☼ 8am-4pm Tue-Sat), for those interested in state history.

CENTRAL KENTUCKY

The gorgeous Bluegrass Parkway runs from I-65 in the west to Rte 60 in the east, passing through some of the most luscious pasturelands in Kentucky.

About 40 miles south of Louisville is **Bardstown**, with a lovely historic downtown and enough bourbon to kill an elephant. Famous for its gaggle of distilleries (see the boxed text, opposite), the town comes alive in September for the **Kentucky Bourbon Festival** (☎ 800-638-4877; www.kybourbonfestival.com).

Follow Hwy 61 southwest and you'll hit **Hodgenville** and the **Abraham Lincoln Birthplace National Historic Site** (☎ 270-358-3137; www.nps.gov /abli; admission free; ☼ 8am-4:45pm, to 6:45pm summer), which features a replica of a Greek temple constructed around an old log cabin. Research has established that Lincoln was not actually born in the cabin, so it's referred to as his 'symbolic birthplace.'

Forty miles south of Lexington is **Berea**, known for its wealth of folk art. **The Kentucky Artisan Center** (☎ 859-985-5448; www.kentuckyartisan center.ky.gov; just off Hwy 75 at Exit 77; ☼ 8am-8pm) has a large variety of handcrafts and food.

Daniel Boone National Forest

With deep ravines and high sandstone cliffs, this vast wilderness in the eastern part of the state provides habitats for a wide variety of wildlife. The forest is divided into four districts: Cumberland, London, Stearn and Redbird, each with its own ranger station. The main **ranger station** (☎ 859-745-3100; http://www .fs.fed.us/r8/boone) is in Winchester.

The Cumberland district contains the **Red River Gorge**, whose cliffs and natural arches make for some of the best rock climbing in the country. **True North Outfitters** (☎ 888-637-6148; www.truenorthoutfitters.com; 20 Sky Bridge Rd, Pine Ridge; full -day guided climb $200) sells gear and offers guided climbing and hiking trips.

In the London district, the **Cumberland Falls State Resort Park** (☎ 859-528-4121; admission free; campsites $19; ☻) is one of the few places in the world to see a moonbow, a rainbow that sometimes forms in the fall's mist at night. The park has a rustic lodge ($60 to $80) and campgrounds. Nearby **Corbin** is the site of the original outlet of Kentucky Fried Chicken. The chicken is the same as at any KFC, but the exhibits are nostalgic for those of us who grew up lickin' our fingers.

Mammoth Cave National Park

With the longest cave system on earth, the **Mammoth Cave National Park** (☎ 270-758-2328; www.nps.gov/maca; exit 53 from I-65; ☼ 8:45am-5:15pm) has some 300 miles of surveyed passageways. Mammoth is at least three times bigger than any other known cave, with vast interior cathedrals, bottomless pits, and strange, undulating rock formations. The caves have been used for prehistoric mineral gathering, as a source of saltpeter for gunpowder and as a tuberculosis hospital. Tourists started visiting around 1810 and guided tours have been offered since the 1830s. The area became a national park in 1926 and now brings nearly two million visitors each year.

The only way to see the caves are the excellent **ranger-guided tours** (☎ 800-967-2283; adult $4-48), and it's wise to book ahead, especially in summer. Tours range from subterranean strolls to strenuous, day-long spelunking adventures; there's also a tour for those mobility impaired. The caves are in the central time zone, an hour earlier than Louisville. In addition to the caves, the park contains 70 miles of trails for hiking, horseback riding and mountain biking.

Within the park, there are three campsites with restrooms, but no electricity or water hookups ($12 to $30), 12 free backcountry campsites, and the **Mammoth Cave Hotel** (☎ 270-758-2225; www.mammothcavehotel .com; next to visitors center; r $84, cottages $74) which has standard hotel rooms and, in spring and summer, rustic cottages. There is a

THE SOUTH

gas station and convenience store near the visitor center.

WESTERN KENTUCKY

About 115 miles southwest of Louisville, **Bowling Green** is home to Western Kentucky University and the Corvette. All the world's Corvette sports cars are now produced at the Bowling Green **plant** (☎ 270-745-8019; tours $5; ☽ tours 9am, 11:30am & 1:15pm Mon-Fri) located off Hwy 65 at exit 28. Visitors wanting tours must register one day in advance. Opposite, the **National Corvette Museum** (☎ 270-781-7973, 800-538-3883; www.corvettemuseum.com; 350 Corvette Dr; adult/child $8/4.50; ☽ 8am-5pm) has more than 50 examples of this classic car.

About 107 miles west of Louisville along the Ohio River is the town of **Owensboro**, home to an International Bar-B-Q Festival in May, a bluegrass festival in October and the excellent **International Bluegrass Music Museum** (☎ 270-926-7891; www.bluegrass-museum .org; 207 E 2nd St; admission $5; ☽ 10am-5pm Tue-Sat, 1-4pm Sun). Bluegrass has its roots in the traditional ballads of British immigrants, mixed with the fast tempo of African music, flavored with gospel and spiced with lashings of American jazz. Any banjo picker or fiddle fan will appreciate the comprehensive exhibits here, including the Hall of Honor, which recognizes and profiles the genre's masters.

Florida

One thing you'll never catch Florida doing is taking itself too seriously: it's too busy basking in its nearly year-round sunshine. It's weird, delightful, wacky, wonderful. And it just wants you to have fun.

A crazy protuberance of land, Florida puts as much space between itself and the other states as it can, like a runaway teenager, or a retiree heading here to spend the kids' inheritance. It doesn't have to try to be different; it literally sticks out like a sore thumb.

And that's why we love it. We count on it for glitzy theme parks and campy roadside attractions. For alligator farms and mermaid shows. For being an endless parade of the unusual, the garish and the superlative.

But beyond the giddy delights of manmade attractions are natural wonders scattered about the state. Not just a smattering here and there, but a near constant barrage of beaches, springs and forests. Florida boasts a ridiculous amount of shoreline, and you're never more than 60 miles away from the beach. The Keys have crystal-clear water, and the only living coral reef in the continental US teems with brightly colored fish.

The Everglades is the largest subtropical wilderness in the US, and it boasts an amazing biodiversity. You might be surprised to find yourself turning into a birdwatcher, as herons, osprey, pelicans and ibis put on a constant air show. Nature preserves, wild beaches and crystal clear springs bubbling from underground caverns are liberally applied throughout the entire state.

So whether you're coming for the natural attractions or the entirely unnatural ones, the ridiculously beautiful or the beautifully ridiculous, Florida is the place.

HIGHLIGHTS

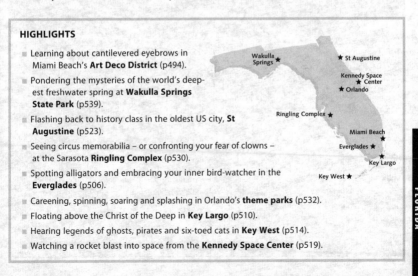

- Learning about cantilevered eyebrows in Miami Beach's **Art Deco District** (p494).
- Pondering the mysteries of the world's deepest freshwater spring at **Wakulla Springs State Park** (p539).
- Flashing back to history class in the oldest US city, **St Augustine** (p523).
- Seeing circus memorabilia – or confronting your fear of clowns – at the Sarasota **Ringling Complex** (p530).
- Spotting alligators and embracing your inner bird-watcher in the **Everglades** (p506).
- Careening, spinning, soaring and splashing in Orlando's **theme parks** (p532).
- Floating above the Christ of the Deep in **Key Largo** (p510).
- Hearing legends of ghosts, pirates and six-toed cats in **Key West** (p514).
- Watching a rocket blast into space from the **Kennedy Space Center** (p519).

FLORIDA

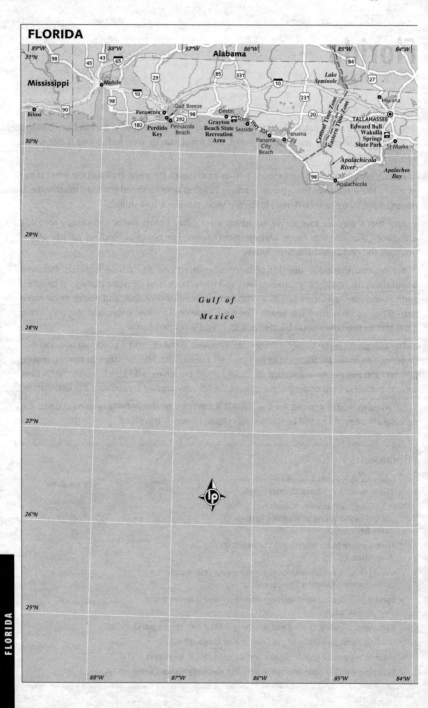

FLORIDA

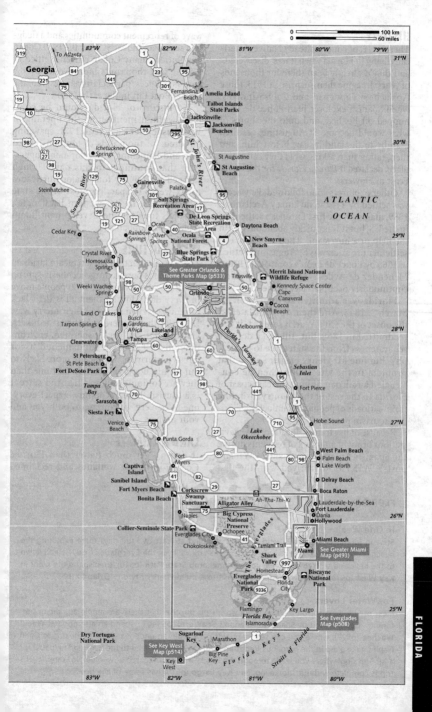

HISTORY

There were, of course, already Native Americans living in Florida when it was 'discovered,' and they'd already been there for thousands of years. Imagine their surprise in 1513, those Apalachee, Timucuan and Calusa Indians, when Spanish explorer Juan Ponce de León hopped off his boat and onto the shores of what would become St Augustine, gestured grandly to the land he saw before him, and then, rather than asking what they called this place, declared it *Pascua Florida* for the Easter Feast of Flowers.

Other explorers soon followed. Pensacola was settled by Tristán de Luna y Arellano in 1559, making it the first European settlement in the US, but it was quickly abandoned with the help of a hurricane. The first European settlement to stick was St Augustine, settled in 1565 by Ponce de León's compatriot Pedro Menéndez de Avilés – making it the oldest continuously occupied city in the US.

Florida was admitted to the Union on March 3, 1845. And then, 16 years later, at the onset of the Civil War, it seceded. It was readmitted in 1868, but still had a definite separateness from the states due to geography. But one Mr Henry Flagler solved that problem in the late 1800s when he constructed a railroad linking the east coast of Florida to the rest of the country, bringing train-carloads of people and unlocking Florida's tourism potential.

Because of its strategic location, new naval stations brought an influx of residents during the Spanish-American War and WWI, and post-WWII Florida thrived with the first wave of retirement communities and a fledgling aerospace industry. After the 1959 Cuban Revolution, many Cuban citizens settled in Miami, and thousands more would follow here as refugees, particularly as a result of the Mariel Boat Lift in the early 1980s.

No history of Florida would be complete without mentioning the opening of Walt Disney World here in 1971, spawning hundreds of thousands of tourism-related jobs and launching a development juggernaut that continues to this day. Though savaged in 2004 by four major hurricanes in six weeks (impacting most of the state but especially the far western Panhandle), Florida's tourism and development boom remains unstoppable.

LOCAL CULTURE

There is no such thing as a typical Floridian. After all, it is hard to forge a cohesive group identity when more than 1000 people move in every day. Uniting them all is their lack of unity: everyone goes on their merry way. Diversity thrives here, whether it is bikers, Cubans, retirees, gays, fishermen, environmentalists, Christian fundamentalists or circus performers. People are more likely to put on hip boots or a Goofy costume than they are to don a suit and tie. And since it is a tourism-based economy, expect everyone to be very welcoming to both you and your money.

LAND & CLIMATE

It doesn't get much flatter than Florida. Coastal lowlands, wetlands and reclaimed

---

FLORIDA ...

In One Week

Start in **Miami Beach** (p494) and plan on spending at least two full days there exploring the beaches and art deco. Take an easy day trip to Shark Valley in the **Everglades** (p507). Head down to the Keys and stop to snorkel at **John Pennekamp State Park** (p510), then spend the night in **Key West** (p514). Finish your trip with a visit to a theme park or two in **Orlando** (p532).

For Water Lovers

Most of Florida is surrounded by water, so it's no surprise that there are ample aquatic opportunities. Get splashed by Shamu at Orlando's **SeaWorld** (p534), or spend an afternoon at **Weeki Wachee** (p527), where you can see mermaids perform in an underwater amphitheatre. In Coral Gables, take a dip in the gorgeous **Venetian Pool** (p499). Then head to the **Everglades** (p507) for a 'slough slog' where you wade through the brackish water in search of wildlife. No water-lover's trip is complete without snorkeling, and **Key Largo** (p510) has some of the best.

swampland typify most of the state, and in the center and north of the state you'll find gently inclining hills. The coasts are protected by barrier islands and, in the south, coral reefs. Between the barrier islands and mainland is the stretch of water known as the Intracoastal Waterway. In Miami and south Florida, December through February is the high season with warm, dry weather, big crowds and high prices. From June to October, temperatures and rainfall rise and prices drop. Summertime is hot and muggy in Orlando, it's the main tourist season in Jacksonville, St Augustine and the Panhandle, which can be chilly in winter.

PARKS & WILDLIFE

Florida has three national parks: the mostly underwater Biscayne National Park (p510), the remote islands of Dry Tortugas National Park (p519) and the fascinating ecosystems of Everglades National Park (p507), all managed by the **Division of Recreation and Parks** (☎ 850-245-3029; www.dep.state.fl.us/parks). You can find comprehensive information on the many state parks in the **Florida Online Park Guide** (www.floridastateparks.org). Individual parks don't accept reservations; you'll need to call **Reserve America** (☎ 800-326-3521; www.reserveamerica.com; ☺ 8am-8pm). Popular parks can fill up months in advance.

As for wildlife, there is an amazing abundance and variety. The southern part of the state has lots of alligators, especially in the Everglades, and you'll see large birds – herons, osprey, pelicans and anhinga – all around the state. Then there's the sea life:

manatees, dolphins and all the fish you can snorkel.

INFORMATION

The state's tourism agency, **Visit Florida** (☎ 888-735-2872; www.flausa.com), operates welcome centers on I-95, I-75 and I-10 at exits just inside the state line, and an information center in Tallahassee's New Capitol Building (p538). Pick up Lonely Planet's *Florida* guide for more information on the state.

Note that Florida's sales tax rate is 6% but some cities and towns tack on another 9.5% to 11.5% for meals and hotel rooms.

GETTING THERE & AROUND

Miami International Airport is an international gateway, and Orlando, Tampa and Fort Lauderdale have significant numbers of US and international flights. Fort Lauderdale and Miami airports are about 30 minutes apart; it's almost always cheaper to fly into or out of Fort Lauderdale. Miami is also home to the world's busiest cruise port.

Greyhound has widespread service both within and outside the state. Amtrak's *Silver Meteor* and *Silver Star* run daily between New York and Miami, and the *Sunset Limited* crosses the south between Los Angeles and Orlando three times weekly; see p1140 and p1146 for more information.

Car-rental rates in Florida tend to be lower than in other states, though they fluctuate: expect to pay at least $200 a week for a typical economy car. Around the Christmas-holiday period, you could pay upwards of $900 a week for the same vehicle.

SOUTH FLORIDA

As varied as the state of Florida is, you'd think you'd at least be able to generalize about the regions within it. But South Florida is made up of three wildly diverse areas that bear little resemblance to each other: Miami and Fort Lauderdale represent the sophisticated cities by the sea; the Everglades are a subtropical wilderness full of wildlife; and the Keys are a chain of islands with a laid-back vibe. The fact that they're just an hour or two apart gives you a great opportunity for a multidimensional vacation.

FLORIDA

MIAMI

How does one city get so lucky? Most cities content themselves with one or two admirable attributes, but Miami seems to have it all. Let's just start with the fact that it's a world-class city, but also manages to have a perfectly gorgeous beach. It's got the sun, sand and surf you'd expect from a tropical island, but with the art, food and nightlife that only urban cities enjoy. On top of all that, Miami has arguably the best-looking people in the US. You know the glamorous model types you always see on TV but don't really exist in real life? Oh, they exist. They're just all in Miami Beach in-line skating down Ocean Ave in thongs. (Seriously, that's not just a stereotype.)

Tourism spearheaded Miami's stratospheric rise when the first passenger train service reached there in 1896, and Miami's Cuban population swelled following the 1959 Castro coup. Today, crowned by the cruiseship industry, a glittering entertainment scene and international business connections (not all of them wholly legitimate), Miami thrives almost as a nation unto itself. More than 60% of the population speaks predominantly Spanish, and in many spots you're unlikely to hear English spoken at all. Well over half the population is Latino – the vast majority Cuban – which influences everything from the political climate to cocktails and cuisine and infuses the city with a sexiness and style unlike any other.

Orientation & Information

Greater Miami is a sprawling metropolis that includes suburbs such as Coral Gables and Coconut Grove, and neighborhoods such as Little Havana and Little Haiti. Miami is on the mainland, while Miami Beach lies 4 miles east across Biscayne Bay.

Downtown Miami operates on a fairly normal grid system. Streets run east–west, and avenues and courts run north–south. Flagler St divides SE streets from SW streets – with street numbers counting up as you move away from it in either direction – and Miami Ave does the same with NW and NE avenues. (In other words, be sure to double check whether that innocent-looking address on 1st is on NE 1st Ave, NW 1st Ave, SE 1st St or SW 1st St.)

In Miami Beach, streets also run east–west and avenues north–south. South Beach (SoBe) is the heart of the action and runs from 5th St up to 21st St.

If you're planning to spend some time checking out south Florida, pick up a copy of Lonely Planet's guide to *Miami & the Keys*.

BOOKSTORES

Books & Books Coral Gables (Map p493; ☎ 305-442-4408; 265 Aragon Ave); Miami Beach (Map p495; ☎ 305-532-3222; 933 Lincoln Rd)

Downtown Book Center (Map p498; ☎ 305-377-9939; 247 SE 1st St)

Lambda Passages Bookstore (Map p493; ☎ 305-754-6900; 7545 Biscayne Blvd NE) Gay and lesbian bookstore.

MIAMI IN...

Two Days

Start your day with a walking tour through the **Art Deco Historic District** (p494), then head to the beach for swimming, sunning and people-watching. If they're in season, join the crush lining up for stone crabs at **Joe's Stone Crab Restaurant** (p502). If not, relax on the patio of the **News Café** (p502). While away the evening with swanky cocktails at **Skybar** (p503), or, for a low-key brew, head to **Playwright** (p502). Stop by the **World Erotic Art Museum** (p494), which is open till midnight. The next morning, head into the city and shop for Cuban music and clothes along Little Havana's **Calle Ocho** (p497), followed up by classic Cuban cuisine at **Versailles** (p501). Afterwards, go for a stroll at **Vizcaya** (p499) then cool off with a dip at the **Venetian Pool** (p499). End with dinner and cocktails at **Novecento** (p502).

Four Days

Follow the two-day itinerary, then head to the **Everglades** (p506) on day three, which will take up most of your day. For your last day, immerse yourself in art and design in the **Design District** (p497) followed by a visit to the **Miami Art Museum** (p496) or the **Museum of Contemporary Art** (p499), or enjoy your proximity to the ocean with **kayaking** or **windsurfing** (p500) off Key Biscayne. In the evening, check out live blues and rock and roll at Miami's oldest bar, **Tobacco Road** (p503).

GREATER MIAMI

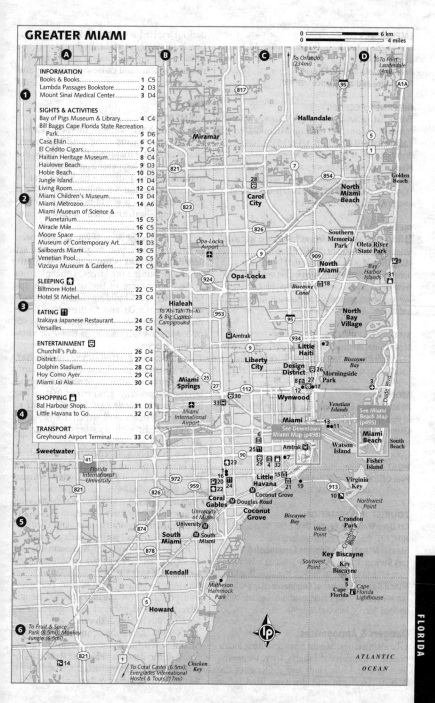

EMERGENCY

Numbers listed here operate on a 24-hour basis:

Beach Patrol (☎ 305-673-7714)
Police, fire and ambulance (☎ 911)

INTERNET ACCESS

For a list of wi-fi hot spots visit www.wi-fi hotspotlist.com and click on Miami.

Kafka's Kafe (Map p495; ☎ 305-673-9669; 1464 Washington Ave, Miami Beach; per hr $6)
Miami-Dade Public Library Downtown (Map p498; ☎ 305-375-2665; www.mdpls.org; 101 W Flagler St); Miami Beach (Map p495; ☎ 305-535-4219; 227 22nd St) Free access on a screen-available basis.

MEDIA

El Nuevo Herald (www.elnuevoherald.com in Spanish) Spanish daily published by the *Miami Herald*.
Miami Herald (www.miamiherald.com) The city's only major English-language daily. Entertainment section on Friday.
New Times (www.miaminewtimes.com) Edgy, alternative weekly with good listings of restaurants, clubs, bars and theater.

MEDICAL SERVICES

Mount Sinai Medical Center (Map p493; ☎ 305-674-2121; 4300 Alton Rd) Area's best emergency room. Also has a 24-hour visitor's medical line ☎ 305-674-2222.

MONEY

Abbot Foreign Exchange (Map p498; ☎ 305-374-2336; 230 NE 1st St, Downtown Miami)
Citibank (Map p495; ☎ 800-627-3999; 1685 Washington Ave, Miami Beach)

POST

Post Office main branch (Map p498; 500 NW 2nd Ave); Miami Beach (Map p495; 1300 Washington Ave)

TOURIST INFORMATION

Art Deco Welcome Center (Map p495; ☎ 305-672-2014; 1001 Ocean Dr; ♻ 9:30am-7pm)
Greater Miami & the Beaches Convention & Visitors Bureau (Map p498; ☎ 305-539-3000; www.gmcvb.com; 701 Brickell Ave, 27th fl; ♻ 8:30am-5pm Mon-Fri)
Miami Beach Chamber of Commerce (Map p495; ☎ 305-672-1270; www.miamibeachchamber.com; 1920 Meridian Ave; ♻ 9am-6pm Mon-Fri)

Dangers & Annoyances

Like all big cities, Miami has a few areas locals consider dangerous: Liberty City, in northwest Miami, Little Haiti and stretches of the Miami riverfront and Biscayne Blvd (after dark). Deserted areas below 5th St in South Beach are riskier at night. In downtown, use caution near the Greyhound station and the shantytowns around causeways, bridges and overpasses.

Sights

MIAMI BEACH

Miami Beach has some of the best beaches in the country, with white sand and warm, blue-green water that rivals the Bahamas. But there's so much happening on shore, it's easy to think of them more as a backdrop than as the main attraction. South Beach (or 'SoBe' if you're in a rush) is world-famous, but more for its people-watching than for its waves and sunshine.

Then there's the deco. If you've never been to Miami Beach, you might think the **Art Deco Historic District** is just a cluster of pretty buildings, but it's the largest concentration of deco anywhere in the world, with approximately 1200 buildings lining the streets around Ocean Dr and Collins Ave. Learn more at the **Art Deco Welcome Center** (Map p495; ☎ 305-672-2014; 1001 Ocean Dr; ♻ 10am-7:30pm Mon-Sat, 10am-6pm Sun).

In the evening, stroll down **Española Way**, a *trés* European strip lined with restaurants and cafés representing most of the romance-language-speaking countries. Just a few blocks north, **Lincoln Road** is blocked off to make a pedestrian mall, which draws people day and night with its stores, restaurants and bars.

You might be unfazed by the bare flesh on the beach, but there is likely to be something that will faze you at the **World Erotic Art Museum** (Map p495; ☎ 305-532-9336; 1205 Washington Ave; www.weam.com; adults over 18 $15; ♻ 11am-midnight), with an amazingly extensive collection of naughty and erotic art, decorative items and even furniture depicting all sorts of parts and acts.

Just down the street, the **Wolfsonian** (Map p495; ☎ 305-531-1001; www.wolfsonian.org; 1001 Washington Ave; adult/child $7.49/5.35; ♻ noon-6pm Sat-Tue, to 9pm Thu & Fri) has a fascinating collection that spans transportation, urbanism, industrial design, advertising and political propaganda from the late 19th to mid-20th century.

It's a bit anachronistic in sunny, carefree Miami Beach, but if you need a dose of gravitas, visit the dramatic **Holocaust Memorial** (Map p495; ☎ 305-538-1663; www.holocaustmmb.org; 1933-1945 Meridian Ave; admission free; ♻ 9am-9pm).

MIAMI BEACH

0 — 500 m
0 — 0.3 miles

INFORMATION	
Art Deco Welcome Center....	**1** D4
Books & Books....	**2** C2
Citibank....	**3** D2
Kafka's Kafe....	**4** D4
Miami Beach Chamber of Commerce....	**5** C1
Miami-Dade Public Library....	**6** D1
Post Office....	**7** D3

SIGHTS & ACTIVITIES	
Boucher Brothers Watersports....	**8** C6
Fritz's Skate Shop....	**9** C2
Holocaust Memorial....	**10** C1
Miami Beach Bike Center....	**11** C5
Wolfsonian....	**12** D4
World Erotic Art Museum....	**13** D3

SLEEPING 🏠	
Aqua Hotel & Lounge....	**14** D3
Beachcomber Hotel....	**15** D3
Clay Hotel & International Hostel....	**16** D3
Delano Hotel....	**17** D2
Pelican Hotel....	**18** D4
Tropics Hotel & Hostel....	**19** D2
Whitelaw Hotel....	**20** D4

EATING 🍴	
11th Street Diner....	**21** D4
Evolution....	**22** D2
Jerry's Famous Deli....	**23** D3
Joe's Stone Crab Restaurant....	**24** C6
La Sandwicherie....	**25** D3
Lime Fresh Mexican....	**26** B3
News Café....	**27** D4
Puerto Sagua....	**28** D4

DRINKING 🍷 🍸	
Automatic Slims....	**29** D3
Clevelander Bar....	**30** D4
Mac's Club Deuce Bar....	**31** D3
Mansion....	**32** D3
Nikki Beach Club....	**33** D6
Opium Garden & Privé....	**34** C5
Playwright....	**35** D3
Skybar....	**36** D1
Spire Bar....	**37** D4

ENTERTAINMENT 🎭	
Colony Theatre....	**38** B2
Jackie Gleason Theater of the Performing Arts....	**39** D2
Jazid....	**40** D3
Miami Beach Cinematheque....	**41** C3
Twist....	**42** D4

FLORIDA

ART DECO WALKING TOUR

There are excellent walking tours available for the Art Deco historic district – both guided and self-guided – but if you just want to hit the highlights, you can follow this quick and easy path. Start at the **Art Deco Welcome Center** (**1**; p494) at the corner of Ocean Dr and 10th St and step inside for a taste of deco style in its gift shop. Next, head north on Ocean. Between 12th and 14th Sts, you'll see three classic examples of deco hotels: the **Leslie (2)**, with classic 'eyebrows' and a typically boxy shape; the **Carlyle (3)**, which was featured in the film *The Birdcage*; and the graceful **Cardozo Hotel (4)**, featuring sleek, rounded edges. At 14th St, peek inside the **Winter Haven Hotel (5)** to see its fabulous terrazzo floors. Turn left

WALK FACTS

Start Art Deco Welcome Center
Finish Edison Hotel
Distance 1.2 miles
Duration 30 minutes

and head down 14th St to Washington Ave, and turn left again to find the **US Post Office (6)** at 13th St. Step inside to admire the domed ceiling and marble stamp tables. Two blocks down on your left is the **11th St Diner (7**; p502), a gleaming aluminum deco-style Pullman car (where you can also stop for lunch if you're hungry). At 10th St, you'll find the **Wolfsonian (8**; p494), an excellent museum with many deco-era treasures, and across the street is the beautifully restored **Hotel Astor (9)**. Turn left on 8th St and head one block to Collins Ave. On the corner, you'll see the **Hotel (10)** – originally the Tiffany Hotel and still topped by a deco-style neon spire bearing that name. Continue to Ocean Dr and turn right to see the **Colony Hotel (11)** and its famous neon sign, then double back to find the 1935 **Edison Hotel (12)**, another creation of deco legend Henry Hohauser, half a block past 9th St.

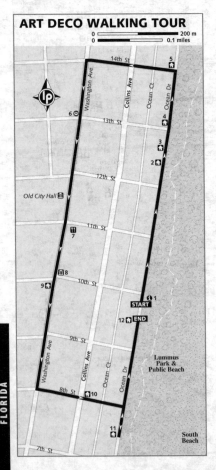

ART DECO WALKING TOUR

0   200 m
0   0.1 miles

DOWNTOWN MIAMI

Unless you're there on business, you probably won't spend a lot of time downtown among the skyscrapers, but the **Metro-Dade Cultural Center Plaza** (Map p498; 101 W Flagler St) is home to two worthwhile museums, and $6 gets you a combo ticket good for both. The **Historical Museum of Southern Florida** (Map p498; ☎ 305-375-1492; www.hmsf.org; adult/child $5/2, Sat & 3rd Thu after 5pm free; ☽ 10am-5pm Mon-Sat, noon-5pm Sun, noon-9pm 3rd Thu) has exhibits spanning Native American culture to the 1930s tourism boom. And **Miami Art Museum** (MAM; Map p498; ☎ 305-375-3000; www.miamiartmuseum.org; 101 W Flagler St; adult/child under 12 $5/free, Sun & 2nd Sat free; ☽ 10am-5pm Tue-Fri, noon-5pm Sat & Sun, noon-9pm 3rd Thu) is home to permanent and rotating exhibits, as well as the JAM at MAM happy hour on the third Thursday of each month. The MAM won't be there indefinitely; it's planning a move to Bicentennial Park, estimated at time of research for 2011.

Near the marina, **Bayside Marketplace** (Map p498; ☎ 305-577-3344; www.baysidemarketplace.com; 401 Biscayne Blvd) is a buzzy if touristy shopping and entertainment hub.

GUIDE TO MIAMI BEACHES

The beaches around Miami are some of the best in the country. The water is clear and warm and the imported white sand is relatively white. They're also informally zoned by tacit understanding into areas with their own unique crowds so that everyone can enjoy at their own speed.

Scantily-Clad Beaches
In South Beach between 5th St and 21st St, modesty is in short supply.

Nude Beaches
Nude bathing is legal at Haulover Beach Park in Sunny Isles. North of the lifeguard tower is predominantly gay; south is straight.

Gay Beaches
All of South Beach is gay-friendly, but a special concentration seems to hover around 12th St.

Family-Fun Beaches
North of 21st St is where you'll find the more family-friendly beaches, and the beach at 53rd St has a playground and public toilets.

Latino Beaches
Latino families, predominantly Cuban, congregate between 5th St and South Pointe.

Windsurfing Beaches
Hobie Beach, along the Rickenbacker Causeway on the way to Key Biscayne, is actually known as 'Windsurfing Beach.'

Surfing
In Miami Beach, South Pointe Park is your best bet, but better yet is heading up to Haulover Beach or anywhere north of 70th St.

LITTLE HAVANA

As SW 8th St heads away from downtown, it becomes **Calle Ocho** (pronounced *kah-*yeh *oh-*cho, Spanish for 'Eighth Street'). That's when you know you've arrived in Little Havana, the most prominent community of Cuban Americans in the US. But this is no Cuban theme park; it's a real neighborhood where real live people live and work. One of the best times to experience it is the last Friday of the month during **Viernes Culturales** (www.viernesculturales.com; 6:30-11pm), or 'Cultural Fridays,' a street fair showcasing Latino artists and musicians.

Pick up some Cuban-style cigars after watching *tabaqueros* (cigar makers) hand-roll them at **El Crédito Cigars** (Map p493; 305-858-4162; 1106 SW 8th St/Calle Ocho; 7am-6pm Mon-Fri, 7am-4pm Sat). You can also visit **Casa Elián** (Map p493; 2319 NW 2nd St; donations requested; 10am-6pm), the house where Elián González briefly lived in 1999 after surviving a 200-mile raft trip from Cuba. Learn more about the 2506 Bri-gade and the ill-fated Cuban invasion at **Bay of Pigs Museum & Library** (Map p493; 305-649-4719; www.bayofpigsmuseum.org; 1821 SW 9th St; admission free; 9am-4pm Mon-Sat).

DESIGN DISTRICT & WYNWOOD

Proving that SoBe doesn't hold the lease on hip, these two trendy areas north of downtown – all but deserted 20 years ago – aren't just rebounding; they're ensconcing themselves as bastions of art and design. The **Design District** (www.miamidesigndistrict.net) is mecca for interior designers, home to dozens of galleries and contemporary furniture, fixture and design showrooms. To catch the zeitgeist, stop by the experimental gallery **Moore Space** (Map p493; 305-438-1163; www.themoorespace.org; 4040 NE 2nd Ave; 10am-5pm Wed-Sat), then explore the 18-block area that goes from NE 36th St to NE 41st St, between NE 2nd Ave and N Miami Ave. Check out the **Living Room** (Map p493) at 4000 N Miami Ave, a striking work of public art that brings an inside space out.

DOWNTOWN MIAMI

Just south, Wynwood is also making a name for itself as an arts district, with myriad galleries and art studios housed in abandoned factories and warehouses. Both districts have uber-hip gallery walks the second Saturday of each month that are moveable feasts of art, wine and music.

CORAL GABLES & COCONUT GROVE

For a slower pace and more European feel, head inland. Designed as a 'model suburb' by George Merrick in the early 1920s, Coral Gables is a Mediterranean village that's centered around the shops and restaurants of the **Miracle Mile**, a four-block section of Coral Way between Douglas and LeJeune Rds.

'Swimming pool' doesn't even begin to describe the spring-fed **Venetian Pool** (Map p493; ☎ 305-460-5356; www.venetianpool.com; 2701 DeSoto Blvd; adult/child $9/5), made by filling in the limestone quarry George Merrick left behind. With waterfalls, grottos and an Italianate feel, it looks like where rich Italian mermaids would go on vacation. You can peek, but most of it's hidden behind stucco walls, wrought iron fences and bougainvillea – best just to dive right in.

Architecturally speaking, the crown jewel of Coral Gables is the **Biltmore Hotel** (Map p493; ☎ 305-445-1926; www.biltmorehotel.com; 1200 Anastasia Ave; ☑ tours Sun at 1:30pm, 2:30pm & 3:30pm), a magnificent edifice that once housed a speakeasy run by Al Capone. Even if you don't stay there, you can come for afternoon tea, a free tour or ghost stories in the lobby Thursday nights at 7pm.

In nearby Coconut Grove, immerse yourself in the loveliness of **Vizcaya Museum & Gardens** (Map p493; ☎ 305-250-9133; www.vizcayamuseum .org; 3251 S Miami Ave; adult/child $12/5; ☑ museum 9:30am-5pm, last admission 4:30pm, gardens 9:30am-5:30pm). The Italian Renaissance–style villa has 70 rooms full of centuries-old furnishings and art, and is surrounded by acres of formal gardens, fountains and grottos. It all makes a gorgeous backdrop – expect to see at least one bride with photographer in tow.

The **Miami Museum of Science & Planetarium** (Map p493; ☎ 305-646-4200; www.miamisci.org; 3280 S Miami Ave; adult/child $20/13; ☑ 10am-6pm) is a Smithsonian affiliate with a planetarium and wildlife center. Most of the museum is usually taken up with one major exhibit; call to see what's current.

GREATER MIAMI

North of downtown, the **Museum of Contemporary Art** (Map p493; ☎ 305-893-6211; www.mocanomi .org; 770 NE 125th St; adult/senior & student $5/3; ☑ 11am-5pm Tue-Sat, noon-5pm Sun) has frequently changing exhibitions focusing on international, national and emerging artists.

The home of Miami's Haitian refugees, **Little Haiti** is defined by brightly painted homes, markets and botanicas (voodoo shops). At the time of research, the **Haitian Heritage Museum** (Map p493; ☎ 305-371-5988; 3941 N Miami Ave; www.haitianheritagemuseum.org) was a 3,000-sq-ft gallery space, but a much larger space was in the works; check its website for progress.

Still in Miami – though it's 30 miles south of downtown – **Fruit & Spice Park** (☎ 305-247-5727; www.fruitandspicepark.org; 24801 SW 187 Ave; adult/child $5/1.50; ☑ 10am-5pm) shows what you can do with trees when you have a tropical climate at your disposal, which is to grow more than 500 varieties of fruit, spice, vegetable and nut. (Bet you never knew there were 125 kinds of mango.)

KEY BISCAYNE

Serene beaches and stunning sunsets are just across the Rickenbacker Causeway (toll $1) at Key Biscayne, where you'll find the boardwalks and bike trails of the beachfront **Bill Baggs Cape Florida State Recreation Park** (Map p493; ☎ 305-361-5811; 1200 S Crandon Park Blvd; bikes & pedestrians $1, vehicles with one/more occupants $3/5; ☑ 8am-dusk). From the southern shore of the park you can catch a glimpse of **Stiltsville** (see boxed text, above).

Activities

BICYCLING & IN-LINE SKATING

Skating or bicycling the strip along Ocean Dr in South Beach is pure Miami.

Fritz's Skate Shop (Map p495; ☎ 305-532-1954; 730 Lincoln Rd; per hr/day/week $10/24/69; ☼ 10am-10pm) Rent bikes and skates every day of the year.

Miami Beach Bike Center (Map p495; ☎ 305-531-4161; 601 5th St; per hr/day $8/24; ☼ 10am-7pm Mon-Sat, 10am-5pm Sun) Convenient bike rentals in the heart of SoBe.

WATER SPORTS

Boucher Brothers Watersports (Map p495; ☎ 305-535-8177; www.boucherbrothers.com; 16 Ocean Dr; ☼ 8am-4:30pm) Rentals and lessons for all sorts of water-related activities: kayaking, water-skiing, windsurfing, parasailing, waverunners and boats.

Sailboards Miami (Map p493; ☎ 305-361-7245; www .sailboardsmiami.com; 1 Rickenbacker Causeway; kayaks single/tandem per hr $15/20, windsurfing per hr $25) The waters off Key Biscayne are perfect for windsurfing, kayaking and kiteboarding; get your gear and lessons here.

Miami for Children

The best beaches for kids are north of 21st St, especially the one at 53rd St, which has a playground and public toilets, and the dune-packed one around 73rd St. Also head south to Matheson Hammock Park, which has calm artificial lagoons.

Watson Island, between downtown Miami and Miami Beach, is home to two major children's attractions. The **Miami Children's Museum** (Map p493; ☎ 305-373-5437; www.miamichildrens museum.org; 980 MacArthur Causeway, Watson Island; admission $10; ☼ 10am-6pm) is a hands-on educational museum with fun music and art studios, as well as branded work experiences that make it more corporate but keep prices reasonable. On the other side of MacArthur Causeway is **Jungle Island** (Map p493; ☎ 305-400-7270; www .jungleisland.com; 1111 Parrot Jungle Trail, Watson Island; adult/child $28/23; ☼ 10am-6pm), which used to be Parrot Jungle, but they added so many animal attractions a name change seemed in order.

Two more children's attractions are located in far South Miami: **Miami Metrozoo** (Map p493; ☎ 305-251-0400; www.miamimetrozoo.com; 12400 SW 152nd St; adult/child $11.50/6.75; ☼ 9:30am-5:30pm, last admission 4pm) has exotic elephants, tigers and Komodo dragons. The Amazon-like **Monkey Jungle** (Map p493; ☎ 305-235-1611; www.monkeyjungle.com; 14805 SW 216th St; adult/child 4-12 $18/12; ☼ 9:30am-5pm, last admission 4pm) is like an inside-out zoo, with you enclosed in screened-in trails and the simian species running free.

Tours

Learn volumes about art deco and its icons on a 90-minute walking tour with the Miami Design Preservation League. Tours leave from the **Art Deco Welcome Center** (Map p495; ☎ 305-531-3484; 1001 Ocean Dr; guided tours adult/child/senior $20/free/15, self-guided tours adult/senior $15/10) at 10:30am Wednesday, Friday, Saturday and Sunday, and at 6:30pm Thursday.

Historian extraordinaire **Dr Paul George** (☎ 305-375-1621; www.hmsf.org/programs-adult.htm; tours $22-39) leads fascinating bike, boat, coach and walking tours. Look online for a full menu of options.

Tour South Beach on two wheels with **South Beach Bike Tours** (☎ 305-673-2002; www.southbeach biketours.com; half-day tour per person $50), a three-hour exploration that covers a lot of ground.

Festivals & Events

Calle Ocho Festival (www.carnavalmiami.com) This massive street party in March is the culmination of Carnaval Miami, a 10-day celebration of Latin culture.

Winter Music Conference (www.wmcon.com) The SXSW of dance music and electronica takes place every March.

Miami Gay & Lesbian Film Festival (www.mglff. com) This early-April event screens amateur and professional films at different venues around town.

Art Basel (www.artbaselmiamibeach.com) An art show held each December that includes parties and crossover events – a sister event to Art Basel Switzerland.

Sleeping

So little time, so many great places to stay. Miami Beach is home to dozens of small boutique hotels in renovated art deco buildings. To find them and other stylish options, check out www.miamiboutiquehotels.com. Oceanfront rooms are usually the most expensive and often the noisiest. Rates vary widely by season, and the low end of the range usually applies to the slower summer months.

BUDGET

Clay Hotel & International Hostel (Map p495; ☎ 305-534-2988, 800-379-2529; www.clayhotel.com; 1438 Washington Ave; dm $26-28, r $56-150; Ⓟ ▢) Nestled right off Española Way and just blocks from the beach, this century-old Spanish-style building has an illustrious history and clean, affordable rooms.

Tropics Hotel & Hostel (Map p495; ☎ 305-531-0361; www.tropicshotel.com; 1550 Collins Ave; dm $27, r $60-105; P ☢ ☐) This friendly, sunny hostel provides a taste of that Miami vibe you came to be part of in a centrally located deco building surrounding an Olympic-size pool. Bring your passport; it's required.

MIDRANGE

Whitelaw Hotel (Map p495; ☎ 305-398-7000, 877-762-3477; www.whitelawhotel.com; 808 Collins Ave; r $75-225) With a weird (but in a good way) decor that can only be classified as 'brothel nouveau,' this deco hotel is all done up in bright red and white, from the lobby to the rooms.

Aqua Hotel & Lounge (Map p495; ☎ 305-538-4361; www.aquamiami.com; 1530 Collins Ave; r $85-220; ☢ ☐) A two-story, '50s-style building set around a central courtyard, this minimalist place has crisp, modern rooms where pets are welcome.

Miami River Inn (Map p498; ☎ 305-325-0045, 800-468-3589; www.miamiriverinn.com; 118 SW South River Dr; r $89-229; P ✗ ☢) It's hard to believe you're anywhere near downtown Miami when you're in one of the four turn-of-the-century buildings. Rooms are antique-homey and include a buffet breakfast.

Beachcomber Hotel (Map p495; ☎ 305-531-3755, 888-305-4683; www.beachcombermiami.com; 1340 Collins Ave; r $110-140; ☐) Inside the green-banana-colored exterior, the Beachcomber has 29 cozy rooms.

Hotel St Michel (Map p493; ☎ 305-444-1666, 800-848-4683; www.hotelstmichel.com; 162 Alcazar Ave; r $125-299; P ☐ ☢) You could conceivably think you're in Europe in this vaulted place at Coral Gables, with inlaid floors, old-world charm and just 28 rooms.

Biltmore Hotel (Map p493; ☎ 305-445-1926, 800-727-1926; www.biltmorehotel.com; 1200 Anastasia Ave; r $179-404; P ☢ ☐) This 1926 hotel is a National Historic Landmark, not to mention a Coral Gables landmark. Swimmers take note: it has a fabulous pool – the largest hotel pool in the country – and is just half a mile from the Venetian Pool (p499).

our pick **Pelican Hotel** (Map p495; ☎ 305-673-3373, 800-773-5422; www.pelicanhotel.com; 826 Ocean Dr; r $185-475; P ☐) The name and deco facade don't hint at anything unusual, but each room is noncornily themed, with names such as 'Best Whorehouse,' 'Executive Zebra,' and

'Big Bamboo,' and there's a retro undertone throughout. Parking is available for $22.

TOP END

Delano Hotel (Map p495; ☎ 305-672-2000, 800-848-1775; www.delano-hotel.com; 1685 Collins Ave; r off-season $205-475, Jan-Apr $325-575; P ☢ ☐) The rooms at this grand boutique are minimalist-chic, and the indoor/outdoor lobby is all billowing curtains and pillars with occasional *Alice in Wonderland* touches. Parking costs $34.

Mandarin Oriental Miami (Map p498; ☎ 305-913-8288, 866-888-6780; www.mandarinoriental.com; 500 Brickell Key Dr; r $249-1250; P ☢ ☐) Keep the glamour on the down-low at this elegant hotel set apart from downtown on exclusive Brickell Key. Its spare, Asian decor travels from the lobby to the rooms, and the spa and private beach let you enjoy your stay in relative peace. Parking will cost you $32.

Eating

As Florida's most international city, Miami has the most international food choices, with Cuban, 'Floribbean' and seafood always in abundance.

BUDGET

La Sandwicherie (Map p495; ☎ 305-532-8934; 229 14th St; mains $6-8; ☯ 9am-5am) Counter service at this casual walk-up just blocks from the beach includes salads, smoothies, shakes – and of course sandwiches.

Lime Fresh Mexican (Map p495; ☎ 305-532-5463; 1439 Alton Rd; mains $6-10; ☯ 11am-11pm) Pig out on Mexican food Miami Beach style: with the low-fat 'skinny burrito' or low-carb 'South Beach burrito.' (Regular old fattening food is also available if you don't have a thong to worry about.)

our pick **Versailles** (Map p493; ☎ 305-444-0240; 3555 SW 8th St; mains $8-15; ☯ 8am-2am Mon-Thu, 8am-3:30am Fri, 8am-4:30am Sat, 9am-2am Sun) *The* Cuban restaurant in town is not to be missed. It finds room for everybody in the large, cafeteria-style dining rooms, but be prepared either to speak Spanish or point a lot.

MIDRANGE

Puerto Sagua (Map p495; ☎ 305-673-1115; 700 Collins Ave; dishes $6-25; ☯ 7am-2am) Pull up to the counter for authentic, tasty and inexpensive *ropa vieja* (literally 'old clothes'; shredded beef), black beans and *arroz con pollo* (rice with chicken)– plus some of the best Cuban coffee in town – at this beloved Cuban diner.

FLORIDA

Izakaya Japanese Restaurant (Map p493; ☎ 305-445-2584; 159 Aragon Ave; mains & sushi $7-15; ☯ 11:30am-3pm, 6-11pm Mon-Sat) It's popular at lunch with the Coral Gables noodle-bowl crowd, but the sushi is where it really shines, served fresh, delicious and without an ounce of attitude.

Jerry's Famous Deli (Map p495; ☎ 305-532-8030; www.jerrysfamousdeli.com; 1450 Collins Ave; dishes $7-18; ☯ 24hr) Jerry's does it all – from pastrami melts to Chinese chicken salad to fettuccine alfredo – and does it all day long. It also does it big, with huge portions served in a large, open, deco space.

11th St Diner (Map p495; ☎ 305-534-6373; 1065 Washington Ave; dishes $8-16; ☯ 24hr) This deco diner housed inside a gleaming Pullman train car sees round-the-clock activity and is especially popular with people staggering home from clubs.

News Cafe (Map p495; ☎ 305-538-6397; 800 Ocean Dr; dishes $10-20; ☯ 24hr) The food and service aren't really the draw at this popular beachfront spot; it's the prime location that makes it ideal for watching the constant stream of bodies walking, skating and bicycling by.

Novecento (Map p498; ☎ 305-403-0900; 1414 Brickell Ave; mains $10-25; ☯ 11am-midnight Mon-Thu, 11am-1am Fri, 10am-1am Sat, 10am-midnight Sun) Dark wood lends an authentic ambience to this dimly-lit Argentine restaurant. It's noisy, thanks to the bar, and you'll probably be there a while – no one's in any hurry – but it's a cool downtown scene nonetheless.

TOP END
Joe's Stone Crab Restaurant (Map p495; ☎ 305-673-0365; 11 Washington Ave; mains $20-48; ☯ 5-10pm Mon, 11:30am-2pm & 5-10pm Tue-Thu, till 11pm Fri & Sat, 4-10pm Sun, closed mid-May–mid-Oct) The wait is long, the prices high. But if those aren't deal-breakers, queue up to don a bib in Miami's most famous restaurant and enjoy deliciously fresh stone crab claws.

Evolution (Map p495; ☎ 305-604-6090; 1669 Collins Ave; mains $32-45; ☯ 7-10pm Mon-Thu, 7-11pm Fri & Sat) The decor isn't understatedly elegant; it's extravagantly gorgeous. Chef David Bouley serves French-inspired cuisine in the dramatic dining room and sushi in the more casual but still chic Etoile Lounge.

Drinking & Entertainment
You'd have to try hard to be bored in Miami. The party goes on till the wee hours, with most bars staying open till 5am. There's also a cornucopia of theater and cultural performances as well as sporting events for every season. Check out www.miamiandbeaches.com for a calendar of events or www.cooljunkie.com for info on clubs, bars, galleries and more.

BARS & CLUBS
To increase your chances of getting into the major nightclubs, call ahead to get on the guest list. Having gorgeous, well-dressed females in your group doesn't hurt either (unless you're going to a gay bar).

Automatic Slim's (Map p495; ☎ 305-695-0795; 1216 Washington Ave) Rockers and rocker wannabes – tattoos are optional – come together at this rockabilly-light bar for theme nights and general rowdiness.

Mac's Club Deuce Bar (Map p495; ☎ 305-531-6200; 222 14th St) Cough, cough. Is that your lung on the floor? No matter; quaff a cheap beer and revel in the gloriously seedy vibe in this, the beach's oldest bar, which has been pouring drinks since 1926.

Clevelander Bar (Map p495; ☎ 305-531-3485; 1020 Ocean Dr) Spring break is alive and well; you can find it here at the poolside, beachside, open-air bar where bikinis are always welcome.

Mansion (Map p495; ☎ 305-532-1525; 1235 Washington Ave; cover from $20; ☯ Thu-Sun) This massive, 40,000-sq-ft nightclub complex has multiple dance floors, clubs, music styles and events. Be prepared for some quality time with the velvet rope and wear your nicest shoes.

Nikki Beach Club (Map p495; ☎ 305-538-1111; 1 Ocean Dr; cover from $25) Lounge on beds or inside your own teepee in this beach-chic outdoor space that's right on the sand.

Twist (Map p495; ☎ 305-538-9478; 1057 Washington Ave; admission free) This gay hangout has serious staying power and a little bit of something for everyone (except the religious right), including dancing, drag shows and go-go dancers.

Club Space (Map p498; ☎ 305-375-0001; 142 NE 11th St; cover $25) Thumping beats emanate nightly from this gargantuan downtown warehouse space.

Playwright (Map p495; ☎ 305-534-0667; 1265 Washington Ave) An affable Irish pub where you can actually hold a conversation, with a vast selection of imported beers.

Spire Bar (Map p495; ☎ 305-531-7700; 801 Collins Ave) The neon 'Tiffany' sign stands watch over this Todd Oldham–designed rooftop bar where you can keep an eye on most of Miami Beach.

District (☎ 305-576-7242; 35 NE 40th St) One of those 'is it a restaurant, is it a nightspot?' places in the Design District with loungey live jazz and cocktails.

Opium Garden & Privé (Map p495; ☎ 305-531-5535; 136 Collins Ave; cover from $25) An open-sky bar with a lantern-strewn Asian decor and more action upstairs. House and dance reign supreme.

Skybar (Map p495; ☎ 305-695-3900; Shore Club, 1901 Collins Ave) Sip chic cocktails on the alfresco terrace – they're too expensive to guzzle. Or, if you're 'somebody,' head for the exclusive indoor red room. Both have a luxurious Moroccan theme and beautiful people–watching.

LIVE MUSIC

Tobacco Road (Map p498; ☎ 305-374-1198; www.tobacco -road.com; 626 S Miami Ave; tickets from around $10) With a roadhouse feel and the oldest liquor license in Miami-Dade County, this rockin' joint has been around since 1912 and is often the scene of impromptu jams by well-known rockers.

Other recommendations:

Hoy Como Ayer (Map p493; ☎ 305-541-2631; www .hoycomoayer.net; 2212 SW 8th St; cover $8-25) Authentic Cuban music.

Jazid (Map p495; ☎ 305-673-9372; www.jazid.net; 1342 Washington Ave; cover Fri & Sat $10) Quality jazz in a candlelit lounge.

Churchill's Pub (Map p493; ☎ 305-757-1807; www .churchillspub.com; 5501 NE 2nd Ave; cover $10-15) The best of indie music – as well as UK football broadcasts.

THEATER & CULTURE

Colony Theater (Map p495; ☎ 305-674-1040; 1040 Lincoln Rd) Everything from off-Broadway productions to ballet and movies plays in this renovated 1934 art-deco showpiece.

Jackie Gleason Theater of the Performing Arts (Map p495; ☎ 305-673-7300; www.gleasontheater.com; 1700 Washington Ave) Miami Beach's premier showcase for Broadway shows, headliners and the Miami City Ballet.

Carnival Center for the Performing Arts (Map p498; ☎ 305-949-6722; www.carnivalcenter.org; 1300 Biscayne Blvd) Showcases jazz from around the world, theater, dance, music, comedy and more.

Miami Beach Cinematheque (Map p495; ☎ 305-673-4567; www.mbcinema.com; 512 Española Way) Plays documentaries, international films and kitschy classics.

SPORTS

Dolphin Stadium (Map p493; 2269 NW 199th St, North Dade) is home to the NFL football team **Miami**

Dolphins (☎ 305-620-2578; www.miamidolphins.com; tickets $29-108; ☉ season Aug-Dec) and the Major League baseball team **Florida Marlins** (☎ 305-626-7400; www.marlins.mlb.com; tickets $9-100; ☉ season May-Sep).

Miami Heat (☎ 786-777-4667; www.nba.com/heat; tickets $25-150; ☉ season Nov-Apr) plays NBA basketball at **American Airlines Arena** (Map p498; 601 Biscayne Blvd).

Florida Panthers (☎ 954-835-7000; http://www.pan thers.nhl.com; tickets $17-79; ☉ season mid-Oct–mid-Apr) play NHL hockey at the **Bank Atlantic Center** (Map p493; 1 Panther Parkway, Sunrise).

At **Miami Jai Alai** (Map p493; ☎ 305-633-6400; 3500 NW 37th Ave; tickets $1-5; ☉ matches noon-5pm Wed-Mon, 7pm-midnight Mon, Fri & Sat), watch and place bets on this lightning-fast court game that's a kind-of cross between lacrosse and racquetball.

Shopping

Browse for one-of-a-kind and designer items at the South Beach boutiques around Collins Ave between 6th and 9th Sts and along Lincoln Rd mall. For more unique items, try Little Havana (p497) and the Design District (p497). **Little Havana to Go** (Map p493; ☎ 305-857-9720; www .littlehavanatogo.com; 1442 SW 8th St/Calle Ocho) stocks authentic Cuban goods and clothing.

Scads of malls include Miami's most elegant, **Bal Harbour Shops** (Map p493; ☎ 305-866-0311; www.balharbourshops.com; 9700 Collins Ave).

Getting There & Away

Miami International Airport (MIA; Map p493; ☎ 305-876-7000; www.miami-airport.com) is about 6 miles west of downtown and is accessible by **SuperShuttle** (☎ 305-871-2000; www.supershuttle.com), which costs about $15 to downtown or $20 to South Beach.

Major and minor car-rental companies have booths or phones at MIA.

Greyhound destinations within Florida include Fort Lauderdale ($6.50, 45 minutes), Key West ($35, four hours) and Orlando ($45, five to six hours). Main terminals are the **Airport terminal** (Map p493; ☎ 305-871-1810; 4111 NW 27th St) and **Miami Downtown terminal** (Map p498; ☎ 305-374-6160; 1012 NW 1st Ave).

Amtrak (Map p493; ☎ 305-835-1222; 8303 NW 37th Ave) has a main Miami terminal. **Tri-Rail** (☎ 800-874-7245; www.tri-rail.com) commuter system serves Miami (with a free transfer to Miami's transit system) and MIA, Fort Lauderdale and its airport ($5 round-trip), plus West Palm Beach and its airport ($9.25 round-trip).

FLORIDA

Getting Around

Metro-Dade Transit (☎ 305-770-3131; www.miamidade .gov/transit) runs the local Metrobus and Metro-rail ($1.50), as well as the free Metromover monorail serving downtown.

FORT LAUDERDALE

It's hard to shake an image as firmly planted as the one Fort Lauderdale had for being spring break party central. But Fort Lauderd-ale – like the drunken teens who were firmly encouraged to stay away – has graduated and moved on since its *Where the Boys Are* days. It's now a stylish, sophisticated city with café-lined riverside walkways; and it's also popular among the yacht crowd for its lovely, Venice-style waterways that many people don't even realize exist. Of course, there's still a great beach; it's just settled down since its party days.

Like the rest of south Florida, Fort Lauder-dale is a major gay and lesbian destination, bringing a welcome new meaning to *Where the Boys Are*. Head to the **visitor bureau** (☎ 954-765-4466, 800-227-8669; www.sunny.org; 100 E Broward Blvd, Suite 200; ☼ 8:30am-5pm Mon-Fri), which also has information for gay and lesbian travelers (www.sunny.org/rainbow).

The **Museum of Art** (☎ 954-525-5500; www.moafl .org; 1 E Las Olas Blvd; admission adult/child $6/3; ☼ 11am-7pm Wed-Mon) is leading the revitalization of downtown, and is known for its William Gla-ckens collection (among Glackens fans) and its exciting exhibitions (among everyone else).

A 52ft kinetic-energy sculpture greets you at the also-adult-friendly **Museum of Discovery & Science** (☎ 954-467-6637; www.mods.org; 401 SW 2nd St; adult/child/senior $15/12/14; ☼ 10am-5pm Mon-Sat, noon-6pm Sun). Fun exhibits include Gizmo City and Runways to Rockets – where it actually *is* rocket science. Admission to the IMAX theater is included.

Kids can try all sorts of jobs they 'wanna do' at the superglossy **Wannado City** (☎ 954-838-7100; www.wannadocity.com; Purple Parrot Way in Sawgrass Mills Mall; person over/under 14 $29.95/15.95; ☼ varies by season), such as star in an action movie or investigate a crime scene, complete with costumes.

Nostalgic car-lovers motor over to the **Fort Lauderdale Antique Car Museum** (☎ 954-779-7300; www.antiquecarmuseum.org; 1527 SW 1st Ave; adult/child under 12 $8/free; ☼ 9am-3pm Mon-Fri, call for hours Sat & Sun) featuring 22 vintage Packards and lots of auto memorabilia.

Skip the touristy water cruises for the best unofficial tour of the city, the **Water Bus** (☎ 954-467-6677; www.watertaxi.com; day pass $11; ☼ 10:30am-midnight), whose drivers offer a lively narration of the passing scenery. Get off and on at dif-ferent stops around town; call or check online for locations.

You don't need a license to fish at the 976ft-long **Anglin's Fishing Pier** (☎ 954-491-9403; Commercial Blvd; fishing adult/child $7/3.50, walking $2/1; ☼ 24hr) which has a 24-hour bait and tackle shop, free parking and rod-and-reel rental for $5.

Sleeping

The area from Rio Mar St at the south to Vis-tamar St at the north, and from Hwy A1A at the east to Bayshore Dr, offers the highest concentration of accommodations in all price ranges. Check out Superior Small Lodgings at www.sunny.org/ssl.

Deauville Hostel & Crewhouse (☎ 954-568-5000; www.deauvillehostel.com; 2916 N Ocean Blvd; dm $22, r $55; P ⁂ ⌨) The awesome staff makes all the difference at this spiffy new beach hostel. It's cute, clean, friendly and professional – not to mention a steal.

A Little Inn by the Sea (☎ 954-772-2450; www .alittleinn.com; 4546 El Mar Dr; r $109-159, ste $189-239; P ⁂ ⌨) The bright, breezy rooms have standard Florida beach decor – tiled floors, wicker and tropical prints – but you also get breakfast, bikes and the beach, plus a quieter, out-of-the-way location in Fort Lauderdale-by-the-Sea, making this a low-key favorite.

Riverside Hotel (☎ 954-467-0671, 800-325-3280; www.riversidehotel.com; 620 E Las Olas Blvd; r $129-239; P ⌧ ⁂) This Fort Lauderdale landmark – fabulously located downtown on Las Olas – has three room types: more modern rooms in the newer tower, restored rooms in the original property and the more old-fashioned 'classic' rooms.

Pelican Grand (☎ 954-568-9431, 800-525-6232; www.pelicangrandresort.com; 2000 N Ocean Blvd; r $209-379; P ⁂ ⌨) Like staying in a comfy but upscale beach house – that just happens to be 11 stories tall. This oceanfront resort is right on the sand and includes a lazy river ride in case that's more your speed.

Gay and lesbian travelers have a plethora of gay-exclusive properties to choose from, among them the renowned, clothing-optional **Royal Palms Resort** (☎ 954-564-6444, 800-237-7256; www.royalpalms.com; 2901 Terramar St; r $199-299, ste $249-

319; **P □ ⚊**), with complimentary breakfast and a poolside cocktail hour.

Eating

Floridian (☎ 954-463-4041; 1410 E Las Olas Blvd; dishes $5-12; ☾ 24hr; wi-fi) 'The Flo' satisfies with good diner food including outstanding breakfasts served round the clock. A 1930s classic diner, it keeps up with the times by offering free wi-fi.

Lester's Diner (☎ 954-525-5641; 250 State Road; dishes $6-16; ☾ 24hr) Since the '60s Lester's has been Fort Lauderdale's favorite greasy spoon for high-powered business lunchers and late-night club-hoppers, with 24-hour breakfasts and the tallest desserts you've ever seen.

Shuck N Dive (☎ 954-462-0088; 650 N Federal Hwy; dishes $7-20; ☾ 11:30am-11pm) A cluttered shrine to Louisiana State University and the New Orleans Saints, this unassuming strip-mall restaurant is the real deal for those with a hankering for Cajun or Southern cuisine.

Sublime: World Vegetarian Cuisine (☎ 954-615-1431; 1431 N Federal Hwy; mains $10-17; ☾ 5:30-10pm Tue-Sun) Shrugging off the alfalfa-sprout image, this chic restaurant serves such inventive and delicious dishes that even carnivores won't miss the meat.

Mark's Las Olas (☎ 954-463-1000; 1032 E Las Olas Blvd; mains $24-42; ☾ 6-10pm) At one of Florida's most celebrated restaurants, watch the chefs work their magic in an open kitchen that turns out Caribbean-fusion specialties, including the legendary cracked conch with black bean mango salsa.

Chima (☎ 954-712-0580; 2400 E Las Olas Blvd; all you can eat dinner/lunch/weekend lunch $47.50/27.50/37.50; ☾ 5:30-9:30pm Mon-Wed, 5:30-10pm Thu & Fri, 5-10:30pm Sat, 2-9:30pm Sun) Gaucho-costumed servers herd a never-ending cavalcade of meats from table to table in this Brazilian *churrasco*-style steakhouse. And while that could add up to a campy dining experience, it's not: Chima's upscale locale is one of the nicest on Las Olas.

Drinking & Entertainment

Bars generally stay open until 4am on weekends and 2am during the week; check out **City Link** (www.citylinkmagazine.com) for listings. Meander the **Riverwalk Arts & Entertainment District** (☎ 954-468-1541; www.goriverwalk.com) along the New River, where you'll find the **Las Olas Riverfront** (☎ 954-522-6556; SW 1st Ave at Las Olas Blvd), with stores, restaurants, a movie theater and entertainment. During the winter season, 2nd St's periodically closed off for a giant street party.

There's live music nightly at **O'Hara's Pub & Jazz Cafe** (☎ 954-524-1764; 722 E Las Olas Blvd) and you can enjoy great microbrews and diverse live music at the **Poor House** (☎ 954-522-5145; 110 SW 3rd Ave). **Waxy O'Connors Irish Pub** (☎ 954-525-9299; 1095 SE 17th St Causeway) is good for a pint and a chat in a not-quite-authentic Irish atmosphere. Featured in the movie *Where the Boys Are*, **Elbo Room** (☎ 954-463-4615; 241 S Fort Lauderdale Beach Blvd) hangs onto its somewhat seedy reputation as one of the oldest and diviest bars around.

Getting There & Around

The **Fort Lauderdale-Hollywood International Airport** (FLL; ☎ 954-359-1200; www.broward.org/airport) is served by more than 35 airlines, some with nonstop flights from Europe; a taxi to downtown costs around $16.

The **Greyhound station** (☎ 954-764-6551; 515 NE 3rd St at Federal Hwy) is five blocks from Broward Central Terminal, with multiple daily services. The **train station** (☎ 954-587-6692; 200 SW 21st Tce) serves **Amtrak** (☎ 800-872-7245; www.amtrak.com), and the **Tri-Rail** (☎ 800-874-7245; www.tri-rail.com) has service to Miami and Palm Beach.

The **TMAX** (☎ 954-761-3543; per ride 50¢) shuttles people between downtown, the beach, Las Olas and the Riverfront Thursday through Sunday.

PALM BEACH & AROUND

Palm Beach isn't all yachts and mansions – but just about. This area 45 miles north of Fort Lauderdale is where railroad baron Henry Flagler built his winter retreat, and it's also home to Donald Trump's **Mar-a-Lago** (cnr Southern & S Ocean Blvds). In other words, if you're looking for a beach town or Florida kitsch, keep driving. Contact the Palm Beach County **visitor bureau** (☎ 561-233-3000, 800-833-5733; www.palmbeachfl.com; 1555 Palm Beach Lakes Blvd; ☾ 8:30am-5:30pm Mon-Fri) in West Palm Beach for area information and maps.

Boca Raton

Halfway between Fort Lauderdale and Palm Beach is this largely residential stretch of picturesque coast that's been preserved from major development. The main reason to stop is the outstanding **Boca Raton Museum of Art** (☎ 561-392-2500; www.bocamuseum.org; 501 Plaza Real, Mizner Park; adult/child under 12 $8/free, special exhibitions higher; ☾ 10am-5pm Tue, Thu & Fri, to 9pm Wed, noon-5pm Sat & Sun), which has a permanent collection of works by Picasso, Matisse and Warhol, and more than 1200 photographic images. The museum is in **Mizner Park** (www.miznerpark .org; cnr US 1 & Mizner Blvd), which isn't really a park so much as a ritzy outdoor mall with stores, restaurants and regular free concerts. While there, stop by the **Dubliner** (☎ 561-620-2540; mains $8-23; ☷ 4pm-2am), where you can have your beer and eat it too, thanks to the Guinness fondue appetizer.

Palm Beach

About 30 miles north of Boca Raton are Palm Beach and West Palm Beach. The two towns have flip-flopped the traditional beachland hierarchy: Palm Beach, the beach town, is more upscale, while West Palm Beach on the mainland is younger and livelier. Because Palm Beach is an enclave of the ultrawealthy, especially during its winter 'social season,' most travelers just window-shop the ocean-front mansions and boutiques lining the aptly named **Worth Avenue**. But it's worth a drive across the causeway to visit the resplendent **Henry Morrison Flagler Museum** (☎ 561-655-2826; www.flaglermuseum.com; 1 Whitehall Way; adult/child/ youth $15/3/8; ☷ 10am-5pm Tue-Sat, noon-5pm Sun) housed in the railroad magnate's winter estate, Whitehall Mansion. Admission includes the house, special exhibits, Flagler's personal train car and an excellent acoustic guide that explains it all. Call about afternoon tea, for which there is an extra charge) served in the lovely glassed-in pavilion.

Modeled after Rome's Villa Medici, Flagler's opulent oceanfront 1861 hotel, **Breakers** (☎ 561-655-6611, 888-273-2537; www.thebreakers.com; 1 S County Rd; r from $289; ☷ ☰ ☰ ☰) is a super-luxurious world unto itself, encompassing two golf courses, 10 tennis courts, a three-pool Mediterranean beach club and a trove of restaurants.

Watch the well-heeled try to navigate their messy condiments (and be sure to grab something for yourself) at the anachronistically casual **Hamburger Heaven** (☎ 561-655-5277; 314 S County Rd; mains $6-11; ☷ 7:30am-3pm Mon-Sat, 7:30am-8pm winter).

West Palm Beach

Inland from Palm Beach – and not so painstakingly tasteful – is West Palm Beach. Much of the action centers around **CityPlace** (www .cityplace.com; 700 S Rosemary Ave), a European village-style alfresco mall with splashing fountains and a slew of dining and entertainment

options. **Clematis Street** also has several worthy bars and restaurants to recommend it.

Nearby is the well-regarded **Norton Museum of Art** (☎ 561-832-5196; 1451 S Olive Ave; admission adult/child 12 & under/student $8/free/3; ☷ 10am-5pm Mon-Sat, 1-5pm Sun Oct-May, closed Mon May-Oct), housing American and European modern masters and impressionists, along with a large Buddha head presiding over an impressive Asian art collection.

By the time you read this, the planetarium, aquarium and exhibits at the **South Florida Science Museum** (☎ 561-832-1988; www.sfsm.org; 4801 Dreher Trail N; adult/child $9/6, planetarium extra $2; ☷ 10am-5pm Mon-Fri, to 6pm Sat, noon-6pm Sun) might very likely have made their big move to a grand new facility called the **Dekelboum Science Center**; check before visiting.

The retro-funky exterior of **Hotel Biba** (☎ 561-832-0094; www.hotelbiba.com; 320 Belvedere Rd; r $89-279; ☷ ☰ ☰ ☰) looks like a cute, 1950s motel in honeydew-melon green, but the rooms have a modern boutique style that would be right at home in Miami's SoBe. Try **Leila Restaurant** (☎ 561-659-7373; 120 S Dixie Hwy; lunch $8-13, dinner $17-25; ☷ 11:30-2:30pm & 6-9:30pm Mon-Wed, 11:30-2:30pm & 6-10pm Thu-Fri, 6-10:30pm Sat) for sophisticated Middle Eastern dining and evening belly dancing performances (call for schedule).

Admirably servicing its migration of snowbirds, **Palm Beach International Airport** (☎ 561-471-7420; www.pbia.org), 2.5 miles west of downtown West Palm Beach, can be a good alternative gateway to the south Florida region. The downtown **Tri-Rail station** (☎ 800-874-7245; 201 S Tamarind Ave) also serves as the **Amtrak station** (☎ 561-832-6169).

THE EVERGLADES

To the uninitiated, the Everglades might appear to be nothing more than a big swamp full of alligators and the place where they occasionally find dead bodies on *CSI: Miami*. First of all, it's not a swamp; it's a wet prairie. It may be splitting hairs, but swamps have trees, whereas the Everglades only have tree islands. It's also not stagnant, as some people believe, but creeps slowly – verrry slowly – towards the ocean. You will see alligators – lots of them – although they won't be wearing chef hats or driving airboats as the campy roadside signs will have you believe.

The Everglades is an incredibly unique ecosystem, a subtropical wilderness that supports creatures such as endangered American crocodiles, bottlenose dolphins, manatees, snowy egrets, bald eagles and ospreys. And amid the mangroves, cypress, hardwood hammocks and miles of sawgrass, there are endless opportunities for hiking, bicycling, canoeing, kayaking, boating, camping and fishing.

The Everglades has two seasons: the wet season and the dry season. And it makes a big difference which it is when you visit. The dry season is the prime time to visit – from December to April – when the weather is mild and pleasant and the wildlife is out in abundance. However, in the summer wet season – May through November – it's hot and humid and there are frequently afternoon thunderstorms. The animals disperse, but the bugs don't; they'll be looking for you. The one upside to the wet season is that you won't be sharing your experience with as many tourists.

Everglades National Park

While the Everglades have a history dating back to prehistoric times, the park wasn't founded until 1947. It's the only national park preserved not for its stunning beauty, but because someone had the foresight to recognize its ecological importance. It's considered the most endangered national park in the USA, but the Comprehensive Everglades Restoration Plan has been enacted to undo some of the damage done by draining and development.

ORIENTATION & INFORMATION

The only road taking you south into the heart of the park is Rte 9336. Rte 997 takes you north to south along the park's eastern edge. Running east–west, the Tamiami Trail (a contraction of Tampa–Miami), or Hwy 41, is a breathtaking drive between the coasts. It runs parallel to the northern (and far less scenic) Alligator Alley, or I-75.

The main park entry points have visitor centers where you can get maps, camping permits and ranger information. You only need to pay the entrance fee (per car/pedestrian $10/5 for seven days) once to access all points.

Even in winter it's almost impossible to avoid mosquitoes, but they're ferocious in summer. Bring *strong* repellent. Alligators are also prevalent: as obvious as it sounds, don't provoke them or even feed them: it's important that they don't learn to associate humans with food, and anyway, they can't tell where the food ends and a human hand begins. Although you're not likely to see them, poisonous snakes here include the diamondback and pigmy rattlesnakes, cottonmouth or water moccasin (which swims along the surface of water), and coral snakes; wear long, thick socks and lace-up boots.

SIGHTS & ACTIVITIES

If you're just driving out from Miami to take a quick peek, the best use of your time is to head straight to **Shark Valley Visitor Center** (☎ 305-221-8776; Tamiami Trail; ⏰ 8:30am-6pm), where you can take an excellent two-hour **tram tour** (☎ 305-221-8455; adult/child $14.50/8.75) along a 15-mile asphalt

---

HOT TOPIC: SAVING THE EVERGLADES

A hundred years ago, politicians occupied themselves with how to drain the Everglades. Now, environmentalists and even politicians are working hard to bring the water back.

The Everglades was once a vibrant 100-mile-long river that flowed from Lake Okeechobee to the southern tip of Florida. In order to control flooding and reclaim the land, dikes were built and canals were dug. In 1906, the thirsty, non-native melaleuca tree was even introduced to help suck up all the water.

It all worked too well. The Everglades shrank to a fraction of their original size. The delicate ecosystem – which provides fresh water to the region and supports several endangered species – was on the verge of collapse. Today, water levels are a constant concern, as is water quality.

Now, the Corps of Engineers along with federal, state, local and tribal governments are coming together to carry out the Comprehensive Everglades Restoration Plan, approved as part of the Water Resources Development Act in 2000. It will take 30 years and billions of dollars, but the plan involves filling in canals, taking out levees and restoring the water flow.

For a thorough and fascinating look at how this story has unfolded over time, visit www .theevergladesstory.org.

FLORIDA

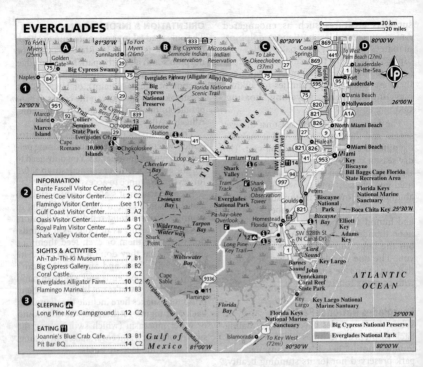

EVERGLADES

trail. Not only do you get to see the park from the shady comfort of a breezy tram, but it's narrated by knowledgeable park rangers who give a fascinating overview of the Everglades and its inhabitants. Halfway along the trail you'll come to a 50ft-high observation tower, an out-of-place concrete structure that offers a dramatic panorama of the park. You can also walk in or **bicycle** (bike rental per hr $6.25); seasonal guided full-moon bike tours are offered for $15/7 per adult/child; BYO bike.

For people who have more than a couple of hours to spare, head south to the **Ernest Coe Visitor Center** (☎ 305-242-7700; www.nps.gov/ever; Hwy 9336; ☯ 8am-5pm, from 9am in summer), which is packed with information about trails and other activities and has excellent, museum-like exhibits. Call for a schedule of fun ranger-led programs including the 'slough slog,' a two-hour wet walk through the slow-moving grassy river. Most programs start at the nearby **Royal Palm Visitor Center** (☎ 305-242-7700; Hwy 9336; ☯ 8am-4:15pm), where you can also catch two short trails. The Anhinga Trail is great for wildlife spotting, especially in winter, and the Gumbo-Limbo showcases plants and trees.

From here, you can drive 38 miles to the coast and the **Flamingo Visitor Center** (☎ 239-695-3094; ☯ 7:30am-5pm), which has maps of canoeing and hiking trails. The **Flamingo Marina** (☎ 239-695-3101; www.flamingolodge.com; ☯ 7am-7pm Mon-Fri, 6am-7am Sat & Sun) offers boat rentals and tours, plus a store where you can buy food and supplies. If you've been to the area before, you might notice the conspicuous absence of the Flamingo Lodge and the restaurant – the only lodging and eating options in the park – which were badly damaged by hurricanes in 2005. At time of research, the owners were planning to rebuild; check for updates.

For a completely different perspective, visit the park from the opposite side. At the northwestern edge of the Everglades is the **Gulf Coast Visitor Center** (☎ 239-695-3311; 815 Oyster Bar Lane off Hwy 29, Everglades City; ☯ 9am-4:30pm). From here, the **10,000 Islands** mangroves and waterways offer incredible canoeing and kayaking opportunities – including short trips to sandy beaches and shallow, brackish lagoons – and the 99-mile **Wilderness Waterway**, which runs along the park's southern edge from here to Flamingo. Rangers lead canoe trips and walks, and a **concessionaire** (☎ 239-695-2591; boat tours adult/child $26.50/13.25, canoe rental per day $25) offers 90-minute boat tours plus canoe hire.

Think of the Everglades and you think of airboats (those flat-bottom crafts with a giant fan on the back), but actually they're forbidden in the park proper. The best place to take a 30- to 45-minute ride is at the family-owned **Everglades Alligator Farm** (☎ 305-247-2628; www.everglades.com; 40351 SW 192 Ave, Homestead; adult/child $19/12; ☒ 9am-5:30pm), where you can also hold baby alligators.

SLEEPING

The National Park Service's developed **campsites** (☎ 239-695-0124; campsite Sep-May $14) inside the park and at Long Pine Key, 7 miles from the main entrance, are free during the brutally hot months but the rest of the year you'll need to make a reservation.

Camping elsewhere in the park includes beach sites, ground sites and chickees (covered wooden platforms above the water) in the backcountry along the Wilderness Waterway. **Backcountry camping** (campsite $10) is permitted throughout the park but a permit from the visitor centers is required. You should bring a hanging/hammock tent as you may not be able to pitch on underlying pinnacle rock.

AROUND THE EVERGLADES

Coming from Miami, the gateway towns of Homestead and Florida City on the east side of the park make an ideal base, especially if you're headed for the Keys. Comprehensive information about the region is available at www.evergladesonline.com.

WHERE'S ROBERT?

Hot? Hungry? Heading towards the Everglades? You must – must! – stop at **Robert is Here** (☎ 305-246-1592; 19200 SW 344th St, Homestead; ☒ 8am-7pm Nov-Aug) for a key lime milkshake (unless it's September or October, in which case you'll just have to stare longingly at the sign). This roadside fruit stand has local produce and a bevy of milkshake flavors. But it's one of the few places in the world where you'll find a key-lime-flavored milkshake, which has the perfect sweet-to-tart ratio and will have you perky and refreshed in no time.

Florida City & Homestead

A favored kitschy tourist stop in Homestead is **Coral Castle** (☎ 305-248-6345; www.coralcastle.com; 28655 S Dixie Hwy, Homestead; adult/child $9.75/5; ☒ 7am-8pm), which isn't a castle at all but a weird sculpture garden and monument to lost love.

The Homestead–Florida City area has no shortage of chain motels and fast-food restaurants, but there are some gems worth searching out, including the **Everglades International Hostel & Tours** (☎ 800-372-3874, 305-248-1122; www.evergladeshostel.com; 20 SW 2nd Ave, Florida City; dm/r $20/50; P ☒ ☐). Even if you're not staying here, one of the best ways to see the park is with the hostel's **canoe & slough slog tour** (all day/overnight including meals $95/$200), led in season by wilderness guides. You can also rent canoes ($30) and bikes ($15) to explore on your own. **Redland Hotel** (☎ 800-595-1904, 305-246-1904; www.redlandhotel.com; 5 S Flagler Ave, Homestead; ; r $99-109 P ☐) is a centrally located historic inn with clean and cozy (if not particularly fancy) rooms that include a continental breakfast.

Not just a restaurant but a bit of a social center, as well, the always-lively **White Lion Cafe** (☎ 305-248-1076; 146 NW 7th St; mains $7-10; ☒ 11am-3pm, 5pm 'till the fat lady sings' Tue-Sat) has BBQs, patio parties and karaoke, and the inside is still cute enough to bring your grandmother for lunch. The diverse menu includes a $200 peanut-butter-jelly sandwich served with a complimentary bottle of Dom Perignon. For middle-of-the-night cravings, the dependable **Mario's Latin Cafe** (☎ 305-247-2470; 1090 N Homestead Blvd; mains $5-12; ☒ 24hr) is open all night and even delivers 10am to 10pm.

Tamiami Trail

On the north edge of Everglades National Park – just across the Tamiami Trail – is the 1139-sq-mile **Big Cypress National Preserve**. Residents include alligators, snakes, Florida panthers (rarely seen), wild turkeys and many impressively large birds. Great bald cypress trees are nearly gone from the area, but dwarf pond cypress thrive. Thirty-one miles of the **Florida National Scenic Trail** (☎ 352-378-8823, 800-343-1882; www.florida-trail.org) cut through Big Cypress. Get information from the **Oasis Visitor Center** (☎ 239-695-1201; ☒ 9am-4:30pm Mon-Fri), about 20 miles west of Shark Valley. The preserve's four no-fee primitive **campgrounds** (☎ 239-695-1201) are along the Tamiami Trail and Loop Rd, and **Monument Lake Campground** (campsites $16) has nonprimitive facilities.

Half a mile east of the visitor center, drop into the **Big Cypress Gallery** (☎ 239-695-2428; www .clydebutcher.com; 52388 Tamiami Tr, Ochopee; ⊗ 10am-5pm) of Clyde Butcher , whose large-scale B&W landscape photography spotlights the region's unusual beauty.

North of Alligator Alley (Hwy 75) **Ah-Tah-Thi-Ki Museum** (☎ 863-902-1113; www.seminoletribe .com/museum; Big Cypress Seminole Indian Reservation, Hwy 8333; adult/child $6/4; ⊗ 9am-5pm Tue-Sun) has a 1.5-mile, wheelchair-accessible nature trail that takes you through a 60-acre cypress dome to a re-created Seminole village.

A good pit stop as you're heading to or from Miami is the **Pit Bar BQ** (☎ 863-226-2272; 16400 SW 8th St, Miami; mains $7-11; ⊗ 11am-10pm), a screened-in roadside place with checkered table clothes and homemade BBQ sauce.

Everglades City

This small town at the northwestern edge of the park is a good base for exploring 10,000 Islands or the Wilderness Waterway. You don't have to be a big-time hunter-gatherer to appreciate the **Rod & Gun Lodge** (☎ 239-695-2101; www.evergladesrodandgun.com; 200 Riverside Dr; r $125; Ⓟ ⓧ). Even though it was built as a hunting lodge, it still has wraparound porches, cozy rooms and a tranquil riverside setting. The **Captain's Table Hotel** (☎ 239-695-4211; www.captain stablehotel.com; 102 East Broadway; r $60-85, ste 85-170; Ⓟ ⓧ ▣) provides clean, economical rooms and one- or two-bedroom apartments.

Lightly decorated with Harley memorabilia and parts, the **Roadkill Cafe** (☎ 239-695-2369; 305 Collier Ave; mains $4-15; ⊗ 6am-8pm) fronts a motorcycle repair shop and serves excellent fish tacos. The **Everglades Seafood Depot** (☎ 239-695-0075; 102 Collier Ave; mains $4-26) is your stereotypical seafood emporium serving fresh-from-the-docks seafood in a nautical atmosphere.

East of Everglades City – and just east of Ochopee – is the quintessential 1950s-style swamp shack, **Joanie's Blue Crab Cafe** (☎ 239-695-2682; 39395 Tamiami Trail; mains $9-15; ⊗ 10am-5pm Wed-Sun), with open rafters, colorful, shellacked picnic tables and a swamp dinner of gator nuggets and fritters.

Biscayne National Park

Just south of Miami (and east of Homestead and Florida City) is this national park that's 95% water. But the 5% of land is some of the most serene and secluded waterfront you'll find. Here you can see manatees and sea turtles

in four diverse ecosystems (keys, coral reef, mangrove forest and bay). Get general park information from **Dante Fascell Visitor Center** (☎ 305-230-7275; 9700 SW 328th St, Homestead; ⊗ 9am-5pm). A park **concessionaire** (☎ 305-230-1100) runs three-hour glass-bottom-boat tours at 10am (adult/child under 12 $25/17), snorkel trips at 1:30pm ($35/30) and dive trips at 8:30am to weekends (per person $54), all of which require reservations. You can also rent canoes ($12) and kayaks ($16).

FLORIDA KEYS

Before Henry Flagler completed his railroad in 1912 connecting the Keys to the mainland, this 126-mile string of islands were just untethered bumps of land accessible only by boat. (Little surprise, then, that their early economies were built on piracy, smuggling, ship salvaging and fishing). Flagler's railroad was destroyed by a 1935 hurricane, but what remained of its bridges allowed the Overseas Hwy to be completed in 1938. Now, streams of travelers swarm down from the mainland to indulge in the alluring jade-green waters, laid-back island lifestyle, great fishing and idyllic snorkeling and diving.

The Upper Keys – from Key Largo to Islamorada - are cluttered with touristy shops and motels, and from the highway you can't even see the water. But as you go further south into the Middle Keys, the land starts to open up, offering the startling realization that you're actually driving from island to island. Trailing off like ellipses, the islands get smaller as you reach the Lower Keys, which is everything from Little Duck Key on. But far from petering out, the keys reach their grand finale at the end of the highway in Key West – many visitors' favorite key of all.

Many addresses in the Keys are noted by their proximity to mile markers (indicated as MM), which start at MM126 in Florida City and count down to MM0 in Key West. They also might indicate whether they're 'ocean-side,' which is the south side of the highway, or 'bayside,' which is north.

The **Florida Keys & Key West Visitors Bureau** (☎ 800-352-5397; www.fla-keys.com) has information on the entire area. Check www.diveflakeys .com for a full list of dive operators.

Key Largo

There are high expectations as you come over the Overseas Hwy onto Key Largo. You've heard of it your whole life. Made famous in film by Bogie and Bacall, it's been immortalized in song by musicians from the Beach Boys to Sade to Bertie Higgins. It sounds so romantic. And then you get there.

OK, it may be time to re-adjust. It's just a sleepy island and the views from the highway aren't even all that good. But there are water sports galore and some of the best snorkeling and diving around, thanks to the only living coral reef in the continental US. For maps and brochures, visit the **chamber of commerce** (☎ 305-451-1414, 800-822-1088; www.keylargo.org; MM 106; ☺ 9am-6pm).

Diving is best at **John Pennekamp Coral Reef State Park** (☎ 305-451-1202; www.pennekamppark.com; MM 102.5; vehicle with 1 person $3.50, with 2 or more $6 plus per person 50¢, pedestrian $1.50), the first underwater park in the US. In addition to a live coral reef, you can see the underwater **Christ of the Deep**, a 9ft algae-covered bronze statue that's a replica of Italy's Christ of the Abyss. If you want to stay dry, you can view the dazzling fish and coral during a 2½-hour **glass-bottom boat tour** (adult/child $22/15; ☺ 9:15am, 12:15pm & 3pm). Or you can dive right in with a **snorkeling trip** (adult/child $29/24 plus gear rental; ☺ 9am, noon & 3pm), or a two-location, two-tank **diving trip** ($50 plus gear rental; ☺ departs 9:30am & 1:30pm). You can also rent **canoes or kayaks** (per hr single/double $12/17) to journey through a 3-mile network of canoe trails. Call ☎ 305-451-6300 for all excursions.

Dozens of private outfitters take snorkelers and scuba divers out to the reef; half-day trips leave twice daily, usually around 9am and 1pm. **Horizon Divers** (☎ 305-453-3535, 866-984-3483; www.horizondivers.com; 100 Ocean Key off MM 100 oceanside; snorkel $40, scuba $70) has a friendly crew and offers rentals, dive trips and even scuba instruction.

For off-park paddling, **Florida Bay Outfitters** (☎ 305-451-3018; www.kayakfloridakeys.com; MM 104; kayak rental per half-day $35) has kayak and canoe rentals, as well as kayak tours – including a full-moon paddle – starting at $50. You can also rent camping equipment here.

SLEEPING & EATING

In addition to luxe resorts, Key Largo has loads of bright, cheery motels and camping.

John Pennekamp Coral Reef State Park (☎ 800-326-3521; www.pennekamppark.com; campsites up to 8 people $26) Sleep with the fishes – or at least near them – at one of the 47 coral-reef-adjacent sites.

Camping's poplar; reserve well in advance by phone or at www.reserveamerica.com.

Largo Lodge (☎ 305-451-0424, 800-468-4378; www .largolodge.com; MM 101.7 bayside; cottages $95-195; P) These charming, sunny cottages with their own private beach – family owned since the '50s – are surrounded by palm trees, tropical flowers and lots of roaming birds, for a taste of Florida in the good old days. (Adults over 16 only, please.)

Sunset Cove Resort (☎ 877-451-0705; www.sunset coveflorida.com; MM 99.5 bayside; rooms & cottages incl breakfast $115-175) This place provides full-size kitsch for guests, with fiberglass dinosaurs, zebras and swans living in campy harmony. Enjoy the canoes, kayaks, chickee huts and continental breakfast; all are included.

Hideout Restaurant (☎ 305-451-0128; MM 103.5 oceanside, end of Transylvania Ave; mains $6-9; ☺ 7am-2pm daily, 5-9pm Fri) Try to blend in; this place has cheap food and a suspicious attitude toward strangers. During Friday-night fish fries, eat as much as you like for $10.95.

Mrs Mac's Kitchen (☎ 305-451-3722; MM 99.4 bayside; mains $5-17; ☺ 7am-9:30pm Mon-Sat) This cute roadside diner bedecked with rusty license plates serves classic highway food such as burgers and fish baskets.

Alabama Jacks (☎ 305-248-8741; 58000 Card Sound Rd; mains $5-25; ☺ 11am-7pm) On the back road between Key Largo and Florida City, this funky open-air joint draws an eclectic crowd hungry for fish dishes washed down with local beer. Try the conch fritters; they're rave-worthy.

Fish House (☎ 305-451-4665; MM 102.4 oceanside; lunch mains $8-16, dinner mains $16-26; ☺ 11:30am-10pm) This traditional Keys seafood place is nothing fancy, but the huge variety really reels in the crowds.

Fish House Encore (☎ 305-451-0650; MM 102.3; mains $18-33; ☺ 5-10pm Wed-Mon) After one too many customers had to be turned away from the Fish House a sister restaurant was built right next door, with a slightly more upscale feel and a focus that's more broiled than fried.

Islamorada

It sounds like an island, but Islamorada is actually a string of several islands, the epicenter of which is Upper Matecumbe Key. Several little nooks of beach are easily accessible here, providing scenic rest stops. Housed in an old red caboose, the **chamber of commerce** (☎ 305-664-4503, 800-322-5397; www.islamoradachamber.com; MM

FLORIDA

83.2 bayside; ⊙ 9am-5pm Mon-Fri, 9am-4pm Sat, 9am-3pm Sun) has information about the area.

Billed as 'The Sportfishing Capital of the World,' Islamorada is a good place to catch fish, look at fish, feed the fish and eat fish – it's almost Gumplike in its variety. Catering the buffet of options is **Robbie's Marina** (☎ 305-664-8498, 877-664-8498; www.robbies.com; MM 77.5), which offers fishing charters, boat rentals, kayak rentals, jet ski tours and even houseboat rentals. Even if you don't need watercraft, stop for the tarpon, which you can hand-feed right from the dock with $2 buckets of baitfish.

You'll need a boat to visit Islamorada's two greatest treasures – neither one is accessible by car. On the ocean side a few hundred yards offshore, **Indian Key Historic State Park** (☎ 305-664-2540; www.floridastateparks.org; ⊙ 8am-dusk) is a peaceful little island with the crumbling foundations of a 19th-century settlement. On the bay side, the isolated **Lignumvitae Key Botanical State Park** (☎ 305-664-2540; www.floridastateparks.org; ⊙ 8am-5pm Thu-Mon) is named for the lignumvitae tree, nicknamed the 'tourist tree' because its shiny red bark peels like sunburned tourists. The site has virgin tropical forests and the 1919-built Matheson House. Robbie's runs shuttles to both parks; call for schedules and prices.

Dolphins and sea lions perform in an intimate, close-up setting at **Theater of the Sea** (☎ 305-664-2431; www.theaterofthesea.com; MM 84.5 oceanside; adult/child 3-12 $23.95/15.95; ⊙ 9:30am-5pm), and for an extra fee you can meet or swim with them.

Check out layer after layer of geological history in the quarry at **Windley Key Fossil Reef State Geologic Site** (☎ 305-664-2540; www.floridastateparks .org; MM 85.5; admission $1.50), with 8ft walls of fossilized coral. Pick up a self-guided booklet and look for the rangers to answer questions.

For public beach access and shaded picnic tables, try **Anne's Beach** (MM 73.5; admission free) on the oceanside boardwalk (the beach disappears at high tide); and the shallow, sheltered **Islamorada Founder's Park** (☎ 305-8531685; MM 87; park entry per adult/child $4/2, entry to pool per adult/child $3/2), which also has a dog park and Olympic-size pool. Area dive shops include **Holiday Isle Dive Shop** (☎ 305-664-3483, 800-327-7070; www.diveholi dayisle.com; MM 84.5 oceanside; snorkeling/diving $30/50, plus equipment rental $9/40), with half-day trips departing at 9am and 1pm.

SLEEPING & EATING

Long Key State Recreation Area (☎ 305-664-4815; MM 67.5; campsites $25) Book as far ahead as possible for these 60 coveted oceanfront campsites in a shady, 965-acre park.

Ragged Edge Resort (☎ 305-852-5389; www.ragged -edge.com; 243 Treasure Harbor Rd; r $62-159, ste $160-229; P ⊠) Swim off the docks at this happily unpretentious oceanfront complex off MM 86.5, with spotless motel rooms, efficiencies and two-bedroom family suites.

Lime Tree Bay Resort Motel (☎ 305-664-4740, 800-723-4519; www.limetreebayresort.com; MM 68.5 bayside; r $89-110, ste to $350; P ⊠) A plethora of hammocks and lawn chairs provide front-row seats for the spectacular sunsets at this 2.5-acre waterfront hideaway with on-site windsurfing, kayaking and boating.

Cheeca Lodge & Spa (☎ 305-664-4651, 800-327-2888; www.cheeca.com; MM 82 oceanside; r $369-699; P ⊠ 🖵) Room prices may be steep but you never have to leave the property, with activities including tennis, kayaking, golf and diving, plus a restaurant and spa.

Hungry Tarpon Restaurant (☎ 305-664-0535; MM 77.5 oceanside; mains $5-12; ⊙ 6:30am-2:30pm) After you feed the tarpon at Robbie's Marina, feed yourself a rib-sticking breakfast or lunch next door at this converted bait shop overlooking the water.

Island Grill (☎ 305-664-8400; MM 85.5 oceanside; mains $12-25; ⊙ 11am-10pm Sun-Thu, till 11pm Fri & Sat) Just under Snake Creek Bridge, this hidden spot has a lovely wooden deck made from a sunken houseboat that was raised and restored. The menu is eclectic, but, in accordance with its waterfront location, involves mostly fish.

Morada Bay (☎ 305-664-0604; MM 81.6 bayside; lunch mains $10-15, dinner mains $24-32; ⊙ 11:30am-10pm) Grab a table under a palm tree on the white-sand beach and sip a rum drink with your tapas and fresh seafood, or dance under the stars at its monthly full-moon party.

Pierre's (☎ 305-664-3225; MM 81.6 bayside; mains $34-40; ⊙ 5:30-10pm Sun-Thu, till 11 Fri & Sat) Pierre's occupies a two-story waterfront colonial house next door to Morada Bay, with attention to detail right down to the hand-cut, hand-placed wooden bar, gourmet seafood and fine wine list.

Marathon

As you drive towards Marathon, you'll start seeing some spectacular ocean views. Halfway between Key Largo and Key West, Marathon has sizable marinas and is a hub for numerous commercial fishing and lobster boats. Get local information at the **visitor center** (☎ 305-743-5417; www.floridakeysmarathon.com; MM 53.5; ☺ 9am-5pm).

SIGHTS & ACTIVITIES

At the southwest city limit, the **Seven Mile Bridge** is the longest of the 40-plus bridges that link the island chain. Running parallel on the north side are remnants of the original Seven Mile Bridge, built in the early 20th century as part of the railroad to Key West. The **Pigeon Key National Historic District** (☎ 305-289-0025, 305-743-5999; www.pigeonkey.net; adult/child $11/8.5; ☺ trams hourly from 10am-2pm) on the Marathon side of the bridge served as a camp for the workers who toiled 14 hours a day – thus the name 'Marathon' – to build the Overseas Hwy after the hurricane took down the railroad in the early 1900s. You can reach it by catching one of the choo-choo-like trams – included in your admission – or you can walk the 2.5 miles over the expanse of original bridge. Once there, you have access to the century-old buildings and a museum chronicling the lives of the men who lived and worked there.

Another escape from all the Keys' development is at the 63-acre hardwood hammock at **Crane Point Museums, Nature Center & Historic Site** (☎ 305-743-9100; www.cranepoint.net; MM 50.5 bayside; admission adult/child $7.50/4; ☺ 9am-5pm Mon-Sat, noon-5pm Sun). There's a vast system of nature trails and mangroves, a raised boardwalk, a rare early-20th-century Bahamian-style house, exhibits on pirates and wrecking, a walk-through coral reef tunnel and a small bird sanctuary that houses injured birds. You can also visit the Museum of Natural History and the Florida Keys Children's Museum.

Marathon Kayak (☎ 305-743-0561; www.mara thonkayak.com; 6363 Overseas Hwy/MM 50 oceanside; single/double half-day rentals $35/50, full day $50/65) provides kayak instruction, plus three-hour guided mangrove ecotours (per person $45), full-day mangrove ecotours ($85) and three-hour sunset tours ($45).

SLEEPING & EATING

Conch Key Cottages (☎ 305-289-1377, 800-330-1577; www.conchkeycottages.com; MM 62.3 oceanside, Conch Key; efficiency $85-139, cottages $138-349; P) This collection of cheery cottages and studios hidden

away off the road features charmingly funky decor and a mess of bougainvillea.

Rainbow Bend Fishing Resort (☎ 305-289-1505, 800-929-1505; www.rainbowbend.com; 57784 Overseas Hwy/MM58 oceanside; r incl breakfast $165-300; P ☒) A stay here includes the half-day use of a motor boat, sailboat, paddle boat, canoe or kayak. But it's more than just a manly lodge; it's painted pink and has a lovely beach, as well.

7 Mile Grill (☎ 305-743-4481; MM 47; mains $8-11; ☺ 7am-9pm) The stopping point along the Overseas Hwy when there was nothing else here, this local favorite has served up reliable family fare since 1954.

Island Fish Co (☎ 305-743-4191; MM 54 bayside; mains $10-21; ☺ 11:30am-10pm) Grab a spicy bowl of conch chowder and a seat overlooking the water at this huge, open-air tiki hut that has a raw bar and copious fish specialties.

Barracuda Grill (☎ 305-743-3314; MM 49.5 bayside; mains $14-35; ☺ 6:30am-9:00pm Mon-Sat) Right on the side of the highway you can get stylish New American cuisine in a not-quite-as-stylish setting.

Lower Keys

Key West notwithstanding, the Lower Keys (MM 46 to MM 0) are the least developed of the island chain. The **chamber of commerce** (☎ 305-872-2411, 800-872-3722; www.lowerkeyschamber .com; MM 31; ☺ 9am-5pm Mon-Fri, to 3pm Sat) is on Big Pine Key.

The Keys' most acclaimed beach – known for its shallow, warm and eminently wade-able water – is at **Bahia Honda State Park** (☎ 305-872-3210; www.bahiahondapark.com; MM 37; admission per 1/2/additional person $3.50/6/50¢), a 524-acre park with nature trails, ranger-led programs and water-sports rentals.

Drive slowly: along the highway in Big Pine Key is the 84,000-acre **National Key Deer Refuge**. Stop by or contact the **headquarters** (☎ 305-872-2239; nationalkeydeer.fws.gov; MM30.5; ☺ 8am-5pm Mon-Fri) at Big Pine Shopping Center to learn more about these endangered, dog-size deer and the trails where you can view them; they're easiest to spot at dusk and dawn.

Looe Key teems with colorful tropical fish and coral; try **Looe Key Dive Center** (☎ 305-872-2215, 800-942-5397; MM 27.5) on Ramrod Key for day trips departing at 10am and returning at 3pm. This three-tank/three-location dive is $80 plus gear for scuba divers, $40 plus gear for snorkelers, and $25 for 'bubblewatchers' who want to come along for the ride.

Camping (☎ 800-326-3521; campsites & RV sites $31.50, cabin $136) at Bahia Honda State Park is sublime, but highly sought after so book ahead; there are also six waterfront cabins. If luxury and seclusion is more your idea of paradise, try **Little Palm Island** (☎ 305-872-2524; MM 28.5 oceanside, Little Torch Key; r $760-1200; Ⓟ), 30 thatched cottages on a private island that can be reached only by boat.

The proprietors at the **No Name Pub** (☎ 305-872-9115; MM 30; mains $8-20; ☺ 11am-11pm), 1.5 miles north of US 1, know where their retirement is coming from: the approximately $60,000 in $1 bills stapled to the walls by customers; stop by for pizza and beer. At Big Pine Key Shopping Center, **Coco's Kitchen** (☎ 305-872-4495; MM 30.5 bayside; dishes $1-5; ☺ 7am-7pm Tue-Sat), off Key Deer Blvd, has cheap-as-can-be Cuban food, but typical strip-mall ambience.

Key West

Anyone will tell you Key West is a little kooky – and darn proud of it. In the words of one local: 'It's like they shook the United States and all the nuts fell to the bottom.'

The town's funky, laid-back vibe has long attracted artists, renegades and free spirits. Part of that independent streak is rooted in its physical geography: barely connected to the USA, Key West is closer to Cuba than to the rest of the States. There's only one road in, and it's not on the way to anywhere. In other words, it's an easy place to do your own thing.

Because of its handy proximity to absolutely nothing, it's been immune to corporate interference. Chickens and six-toed cats have their run of the island. Bikes are the favored means of transportation. And few people work nine to five.

Originally called 'Cayo Hueso' – Spanish for 'Bone Island' – Key West was named for all the skeletons early explorers found littering the beach. Since then, the island has enjoyed a long and colorful history that includes pirates, sunken treasures, literary legends and lots of ghosts.

These days, people flock to Key West to soak up the sun, the mellow atmosphere and more than a little booze. They listen to tales of the past. They snorkel the crystal clear water. And they find their internal clocks set to 'island time.'

But the town's popularity is like catnip to frisky developers, and they've started snapping up real estate – of which, on an island this small, there's not much. The town still clings to its funky charm, but the whole place is in danger of becoming a giant condo complex with a faint memory of mystique. In other words, go now so that in 10 years you can shake your head and say, 'You shoulda seen it 10 years ago.'

ORIENTATION & INFORMATION

When most people think of Key West, they think of Old Town, the western end of the island and the heart of the action, with inns,

---

THE CONCH REPUBLIC

Key West is known for its independent spirit, and back in 1982 they proved just how independent they could be. The US Border Patrol, eager to staunch the flow of drugs and immigrants into the states, set up a roadblock in Florida City that backed up traffic for miles both into and out of the Keys. This had an immediate and devastating impact on Key West's economy, which was dependent on the carloads of tourists driving down from the mainland. So the island did what anyone would do: they seceded.

On April 23, Key West declared independence from the USA in a highly publicized act of guerrilla theater. Mayor Dennis Ludlow, acting as the Prime Minister of the newly formed Conch Republic, declared war on the USA, breaking a loaf of stale Cuban bread over the head of a man dressed in a US Navy uniform. Moments later, knowing that Cuban bread would be no match for the US' military might, he surrendered on behalf of the Republic. Then they demanded a billion dollars in foreign aid. The event did the trick. As a result of all the ridiculous publicity, the roadblocks were removed and everything reverted back to seminormalcy.

But the Conchs still celebrate that glorious moment and consider themselves dual citizens of the US and the Conch Republic. Every April, they re-enact the secession during a week-long party that also involves bed races, parades and the auctioning off of made-up public titles (with the proceeds going to charity).

eateries and boisterous bars. The main drags are Duval St, which at the north end has a bit of a giant souvenir shop feel, and Truman Ave (US Hwy 1). New Town – known by most as the part of town you drive through to get to Old Town – is primarily residential.

A great trip-planning resource is www.fla-keys.com/keywest. Once in town, you'll find maps and brochures at the **Key West Chamber of Commerce** (☎ 305-294-2587, 800-527-8539; www .keywestchamber.org; 402 Wall St, Mallory Sq; ☺ 8am-6:30pm Mon-Fri, 9am-6pm Sat & Sun).

Gay and lesbian visitors can get information (and free internet is available for anyone) at the **Gay & Lesbian Community Center** (☎ 305-292-3223; www.glcckeywest.org; 513 Truman Ave).

The best internet café (and best coffee) in town is **Coffee Plantation** (☎ 305-295-9808; 713 Caroline St; per minute 20¢; ☺ 7am-6pm) which has free wi-fi.

SIGHTS & ACTIVITIES
On an island this small, you have to work pretty hard to avoid the over-the-top tourist action at **Mallory Square** at the northwestern end of Duval St. Near where the cruise ships vomit out their daily load, it's hardly the real Key West, but the nightly sunset celebration is a fun ritual to indulge in, however briefly, with jugglers, fire-eaters and street performers of every stripe.

Pirates and Hemingway make up much of the island's lore and legend, so it's no surprise there are museums dedicated to both. The **Ernest Hemingway Home & Museum** (☎ 305-294-1575; www.hemingwayhome.com; 907 Whitehead St; adult/child $11/6) offers tours every half-hour, during which bearded docents spin yarns of Papa. You'll see his studio, hear about his unusual pool, and witness scores of descendents of his six-toed cats – famous all on their own – languishing in the sun, on furniture, and pretty much wherever they feel like.

A new museum dedicated to all things swashbuckling, **Pirate Soul** (☎ 305-292-1113; www .piratesoul.com; 524 Front St; adult/child $14/8; ☺ 9am-7pm) has an impressive collection of authentic pirate paraphernalia, glammed up with special effects that make it either exciting or a little cheesy, depending on your perspective.

Hear an impressive tale of tenacity and treasure hunting at the **Mel Fisher Maritime Heritage Museum** (☎ 305-294-2633; 200 Greene St; adult/child $11/6; ☺ 8:30am-6pm) and gawk at the treasures salvaged from the *Atocha*, a

Spanish galleon that sank nearby almost 400 years ago.

Offering a more low-key, less swash-buckling version of Key West History, the **Museum of Art & History at the Custom House** (☎ 305-295-6616; www.kwahs.com/customhouse. htm; 281 Front St; adult/child $10/5; ☺ 9am-5pm) is a worthwhile place to spend some time, as is the **Key West Aquarium** (☎ 305-296-2051; www .keywestaquarium.com; 1 Whitehead St at Mallory Sq; adult/ child $10/5; ☺ 10am-6pm), especially if you have kids in tow.

Even if you have only the faintest interest in butterflies, you'll find yourself entranced by the sheer quantity flittering all around you at the **Key West Butterfly & Nature Conservatory** (☎ 305-296-2988; www.keywestbutterfly.com; 1316 Duval St; adult/child $10/7.50; ☺ 9am-4:30pm).

If you're coming to Key West for its beaches, don't. They range from rocky to algae-covered to funny-smelling. You'll find infinitely better just about everywhere else in Florida. That said, **Fort Zachary Taylor** (☎ 305-292-6713; admission $2.50; ☺ 8am-dusk), at the western end of Southard St, is good for sunsets and picnics. And **Smathers Beach** on S Roosevelt Blvd provides sandier shores and sunrises.

Because pollution and boating activity have damaged the inner reefs, **snorkeling** is best a little further out. Dive companies are easy to find, and **Sunny Days Catamaran** (☎ 305-292-6100; 201 Elizabeth St; www.sunnydayskeywest.com; adult/child $35/22) runs a top-notch trip.

TOURS
You might just find out your guesthouse is haunted during the **Original Ghost Tour** (☎ 305-294-9255; www.hauntedtours.com; La Concha Hotel, 430 Duval St; ☺ 8pm & 9pm nightly), and you'll hear all about the creepy antics that got Robert the haunted doll confined to East Martello.

Both the **Conch Tour Train** (☎ 305-294-5161; adult/child $27/13; ☺ tours depart 9am-4:30pm) and **Old Town Trolley** (☎ 305-296-6688; adult/child $27/13; ☺ tours depart 9am-4:30pm) offer tours leaving from Mallory Sq. The train offers an informative 90-minute narrated tour in a breezy, open car, while the trolley allows you to get on and off at its nine stops around town.

Lazy Dog Island Outfitters runs the **Mosquito Coast Kayak Tour** (☎ 305-295-9898; www.mos quitocoast.net; $60), which lets you explore the Keys' backcountry and mangrove islands.

FLORIDA

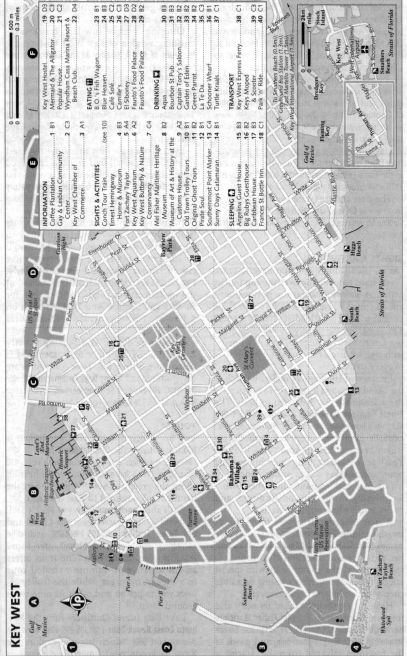

KEY WEST

0   2km
0   1 mile

To Smathers Beach (0.5ml);
Greyhound Bus Station (1.3ml);
East Martello Tower (1.5ml);
Key West International Airport (1.5ml)

MAP AREA

0   500 m
0   0.3 miles

QUIRKY KEY WEST

The much-ballyhooed **Southernmost Point Marker** (cnr Whitehead St & South St) is a large concrete buoy marking what is the most southern point in the USA. Except that it's not. Just look at the map and you'll see more southern points right there on the island.

The **East Martello Tower** (☎ 305-296-3913; 3501 S Roosevelt Blvd; adult/child $6/3; ⏱ 9:30am-4:30pm) is home to Robert the haunted doll, the inspiration for all those Chucky movies. (He's in a glass case to keep him from doing mischief to the rest of the museum.)

Residents get the last word at the **Key West Cemetery** (☎ 305-292-6715; cnr of Margaret & Angela Sts), with eccentric epitaphs such as, 'At least I know where he's sleeping tonight,' or the famous 'I told you I was sick.'

FESTIVALS & EVENTS

Key West loves a party, and in addition to the one held every night at sunset, it hosts some unique annual celebrations, too.

Conch Republic Independence Celebration (www .conchrepublic.com) A 10-day tribute to Conch Independence held every April where you can vie for (made up) public offices or watch drag queens in a footrace.

Hemingway Days Festival (www.hemingwaydays .net) Includes a bull run, marlin tournament and look-alike contest, as well as literary events, in late July.

Fantasy Fest Room rates get hiked to the hilt for this raucous, 10-day Halloween-meets-Carnivale event held in late October.

SLEEPING

Key West lodging is generally pretty expensive – especially in the wintertime and even *more* especially during special events, when room rates can as much as triple. Book ahead, or you may well end up joining the long traffic jam headed back to the mainland.

You can find chain motels in New Town, but you've got to stay in Old Town to truly experience Key West. Visit the **Key West Innkeepers Association** (www.keywestinns.com) for a lineup of the best guesthouses, pretty much all of which are gay-friendly.

Budget & Midrange

Key West Hostel (☎ 305-296-5719; www.keywesthostel .com; 718 South St; dm $34, r $115; [P]) The right price if you're traveling alone – two or more can do better – but don't expect more than a bed.

Popular House (☎ 305-296-7274, 800-438-6155; www .keywestbandb.com; 415 William St; r winter $99-285, summer

$59-175; [P] [☎]) Sunny, airy and full of artistic touches: hand-painted pottery here, a working loom there – is that a ship's masthead in the corner? There's also a range of rooms to fit every budget.

Angelina Guest House (☎ 305-294-4480; www.ange linaguesthouse.com; 302 Angela St; r winter $99-179, summer $69-119; [P] [☒] [☎]) Close – but not too close – to Duval St, this is a great value for the money. You'd never know from its yellow-and-blue country-chic decor that it was once a bordello. There are no phones or TVs; children must be over 12.

Big Ruby's Guesthouse (☎ 305-296-2323, 800-477-7829; www.bigrubys.com; 409 Appelrouth Lane; r winter $191-312, summer $112-182; [☎]) Catering to a gay clientele, this guesthouse is straight-friendly (not to mention clothing optional) with a beach-fabulous decor and lavish breakfast.

Caribbean House (☎ 305-296-0999, 877-296-0999; 226 Petronia; r summer/winter $85/105) This newly remodeled Bahamian Village inn has new owners and a fresh, bright coat of paint. Its small but cheery rooms are some of the most affordable options in town.

Frances St Bottle Inn (☎ 305-294-8530, 800-294-8530; www.bottleinn.com; 535 Frances St; r winter $199-239, summer $109-159; [☒]) This friendly inn in a peaceful part of town has a huge collection of antique glass bottles that fill every nook and cranny, from the eight comfy rooms to the two-story veranda to the small patio with a hot tub. Rental bikes are available.

Top End

Wyndham Casa Marina Resort & Beach Club (☎ 305-296-3535, 866-397-6342; www.casamarinaresort.com; 1500 Reynolds St; r $169-409; [P] [☎]) This opulent 311-room hotel was built in the 1920s by railroad magnate Henry Flagler. The lobby still retains its old-world splendor, but the recently renovated rooms are thoroughly modern.

The Mermaid & The Alligator (☎ 305-294-1894, 800-773-1894; www.kwmermaid.com; 729 Truman Ave; r winter $218-298, summer $128-168; [P] [☎]) Book way ahead: with only nine rooms, this place's charm exceeds its capacity. It's chock-a-block with treasures collected from the owners' travels, giving it a worldly flair that's simultaneously European and Zen.

EATING

You aren't technically allowed to leave the island without sampling the conch fritters – like hushpuppies, but made with conch – or the

FLORIDA

key lime pie, made with key limes, sweetened condensed milk, eggs and sugar on a Graham cracker crust.

Fausto's Food Palace (☎ 305-296-5663; dishes $4-8) Opened in 1926 by Cuban grocer Faustino 'Fausto' Castillo, this grocery store has a well-stocked deli case, making it a good stop for picnic supplies. It has two locations: 522 Fleming St and 1105 White St.

El Siboney (☎ 305-296-4184; 900 Catherine St; mains $5-13; ♥ 11am-9:30pm Mon-Sat) Key West is only 90 miles from Cuba, so this corner establishment is quite literally the closest you can get to real Cuban food. Cash only.

B.O.'s Fish Wagon (☎ 305-294-9272; 801 Caroline St; mains $7-14; ♥ 11am-8pm Mon-Sat, 11pm-5pm Sun) This looks like the backyard shed of a crazy old fisherman (but in a good way). De-lish sandwiches, conch fritters and cold beer – not to mention great prices – will win over any scaredy-cats in your group.

Blue Heaven (☎ 305-296-8666; 305 Petronia St; mains $10.50-30; ♥ 8am-10:30pm) The outdoor dining can be a bit like eating in a barnyard, but a funky, eclectic barnyard, with creative, well-executed dishes. Waiting in line to enjoy a $30 main with chickens scratching under your table? Welcome to Key West.

Camille's (☎ 305-296-4811; 1202 Simonton St; mains $14-25; ♥ 8am-3pm & 4-10:30pm) Ditch Duval St and dine with the locals at Camille's. You'll find decent prices, good food and an inventive menu that ranges from French toast with Godiva liqueur to really amazing chicken salad.

Café Solé (☎ 305-294-0230; 1029 Southard St; dishes $25-32; ♥ 5:30-10pm) A twinkle-lighted patio dining experience that's both upscale and low-key. The French approach to seafood is a welcome departure from fried grouper. Try the Angels on Horseback appetizer, which combines dates and bacon.

DRINKING

The 'Duval Crawl' – hopping (or staggering) from one bar to the next – is a favorite pastime here in the Conch Republic, and there are plenty of options for your drinking pleasure.

Former icehouse, morgue and Hemingway haunt, **Captain Tony's Saloon** (☎ 305-294-1838; 428 Greene St) is built around the town's old hanging tree and decorated with emancipated bras and signed dollar bills. Another fine purveyor of old-school Key West ambience is the **Green Parrot** (☎ 305-294-6133; 601 Whitehead

St), Key West's tenured local hangout and purported oldest bar.

You can make like Adam and Eve at the **Garden of Eden** (☎ 305-296-4565; upstairs at 224 Duval St), a clothing-optional rooftop bar where even the fig leaf is optional.

Schooner Wharf (☎ 305-292-9520; 202 William St) manages to work in three happy hours a day (8am to noon, 5pm to 7pm and 2am to 4am). And you can bet on turtle races Monday and Friday at 6pm at **Turtle Kraals** (☎ 305-294-2640; 231 Margaret St).

Among the more popular gay and lesbian hangouts are the **Bourbon St Pub** (☎ 305-296-1992; 724 Duval St) complex, **Aqua** (☎ 305-294-0555; 711 Duval St) and **La Te Da** (☎ 305-296-6706; 1125 Duval St), famous for its drag shows (around $25).

Getting There & Around

The easiest way to travel the Keys is by car, though traffic along the one major route, US Hwy 1, can be maddening during the winter high season. **Greyhound** (☎ 800-229-9424) buses serve all Key destinations along US Hwy 1, departing from downtown Miami (p503). If you fly into Fort Lauderdale or Miami, the **Keys Shuttle** (☎ 888-765-9997) provides door-to-door service to most of the Keys from around $90 one-way. Reserve at least 24 hours in advance.

You can fly into Key West International Airport (EYW) with frequent flights from major cities, most going through Miami; or **Marathon Airport** (☎ 305-743-2155), which has less frequent, more expensive flights. Or, take a fast catamaran from Fort Myers or Miami; call the **Key West Express Ferry** (☎ 888-539-2628; www .keywestshuttle.com) for schedules and fares.

Old Town in Key West is best navigated on foot or by moped, with rates from $15 per three hours. Try **Keys Moped & Scooter** (☎ 305-294-0399; 523 Truman Ave). If you need to ditch your car, finding street parking can be a challenge. Give up? Head to the 24-hour **Park 'n' Ride** garage (☎ 305-293-6426; 300 Grinnell St), where you can park for $1.50 per hour or $10 all day.

ATLANTIC COAST

Part of the allure of Florida's East Coast is things that go fast: from the rockets blasting out of Cape Canaveral to the high-energy surfing all along the coast to the NASCAR International Speedway. By contrast, St Augustine and

Amelia Island have been around for centuries, so they're in no hurry at all, and there are miles of undeveloped beaches and wetlands for a steady, get-back-to-nature pace.

SPACE COAST

They call the Titusville–Cocoa Beach–Melbourne area the Space Coast because it's home to NASA, but it could just as easily be referring to the miles of undeveloped beaches and protected national parkland, where space is one thing you can find plenty of. The highlight for techies and nontechies alike is the Kennedy Space Center, the only spot in the US from which humans have been hurled into space. Once the fictional home of NASA astronaut Major Nelson and his genie in the iconic 1960s TV series *I Dream of Jeannie*, the Space Coast is also a magnet for surfers, with Florida's best waves. Visitor information is available through **Florida's Space Coast Office of Tourism** (☎ 877-572-3224; www.space-coast.com; 430 Brevard Ave, Suite 150).

Sights & Activities

Houston, we have an attraction. It was perhaps inevitable that, considering its proximity to Orlando, the **Kennedy Space Center Visitor Complex** (☎ 321-449-4444; www.kennedyspacecenter .com; adult/child 3-11 $38/28; ☉ from 9am, closing times vary btwn 5:30pm & 7:30pm) would eventually have to come up with a ride, and so it is that Shuttle Launch Experience has officially achieved lift-off. Reaching a top 'speed' of 17,500mph – vertically – this spookily realistic simulator ride was designed by an astronaut to feel just like taking off in a space shuttle (but without all the teary goodbyes).

Your ticket to the complex – good for two days – includes a two-hour tour that departs every 15 minutes, a 45-minute IMAX film, live-action stage shows, exhibits on subjects such as early space exploration and encounters with astronauts. It also includes (or you can visit separately for $17/13) the **Astronaut Hall of Fame**, where you'll experience the G-Force Trainer and other simulator rides.

WORTH THE TRIP: DRY TORTUGAS

Seventy miles west of the Keys but feeling like the middle of nowhere, **Dry Tortugas National Park** is America's most inaccessible national park. Well, hooray for inaccessibility! Because although you can't hike or even drive to it, you get amazing snorkeling, diving, bird-watching and star-gazing as your reward.

Ponce de León – a big fan of discovering and naming places – christened the area Tortugas (tor-*too*-guzz) after the sea turtles he found here, and the 'Dry' part was added later to warn about the absence of fresh water on the island.

But this is more than just a pretty cluster of islands with no drinking water. The never-completed Civil War–era **Fort Jefferson** provides a striking hexagonal centerpiece of red brick rising up from the emerald waters on **Garden Key** – meaning along with your bottled water and seasickness pills, you should definitely bring your camera.

You can come for a half-day by seaplane, or for a full day by boat. Or if you really want to immerse yourself you can stay overnight at one of Garden Key's 13 **campsites** (per person $3). Reserve early through the **Everglades & Dry Tortugas National Park Office** (☎ 305-242-7700; www.nps.gov/drto). There are composting toilets you can use from 2:30pm till morning – during the day you go on the boat that brought you – but there are no freshwater showers. There's also no grocery store, so bring everything you need.

So how do you get there? **Sunny Days Catamaran** (☎ 305-292-6100, 800-236-7937; www .sunnydayskeywest.com; adult/children 16 & under $120/$85) leaves Key West at 8am, arrives around 10am, and gives you 4½ hours to enjoy the island before returning. Round-trip fares include continental breakfast, lunch, snorkeling gear and a 40-minute tour of the fort (but not the $5 park admission fee or sea-sickness tablets, which you might need). Round-trip fare for an overnight trip is $150/120.

Faster but more expensive, **Seaplanes of Key West** (☎ 305-294-0709, 800-950-2359; www.seaplanesofkey west.com) will get you there in 40 minutes. Half-day trips – morning and afternoon – depart from Key West International Airport, give you 2½ hours of island time and cost $199/149 adult/child under 12, and full-day trips give you 6½ hours at $345/265 (including snorkeling equipment and soft drinks).

FLORIDA

Located in a separate facility, it closes an hour later than the rest.

Add-on options abound, depending how serious you are about your astronaut experience (they're popular – book in advance). **NASA Up Close** (extra $21/15) is an in-depth tour led by an expert, and **Cape Canaveral: Then & Now** (☎ 321-449-4400; extra $21/15) is a guided tour focusing on the early days of space travel. Hungry space enthusiasts can have **Lunch with an Astronaut** (extra $23/16), and the one- or two-day **Astronaut Training Experience** (price depending on program) prepares you for spaceflight, should the opportunity ever arise.

For viewing a **rocket or space shuttle launch** up close, pay an extra $15 to get bussed to a prime viewing area. Tickets go on sale a month prior to launch and sell out fast; check the website for schedules. Viewing's also good from the Visitor Complex, or head to the popular **Jetty Park Campgrounds** (☎ 321-783-7111; 400 Jetty Park Dr, Cape Canaveral; per car $5), or Cherie Down Park, Rotary Riverfront Park or Brewer

Parkway bridge in Titusville. BYO beer and binoculars. Be prepared for inevitable launch delays – and heavy traffic after it's over.

You'll have a better chance of seeing something in the sky at the 140,000-acre **Merritt Island National Wildlife Refuge** (☎ 321-861-0667; www.fws .gov/merrittisland; SR Hwy 402, Titusville; admission free; ☺ visitor center 8am-4:30pm Mon-Fri, 9am-5pm Sat & Sun, closed Sun Apr-Oct), one of the country's best birding spots, especially from October to May (early morning and after 4pm). More endangered and threatened species of wildlife inhabit the swamps, marshes and hardwood hammocks than any other in the continental US. The best viewing is on **Black Point Wildlife Drive**, and **Village Outfitters** (☎ 321-633-7245; www.villageoutfitters.com; 113 Brevard Ave, Cocoa; single or tandem half-day trip $30) can take you on a kayak tour. Be aware that the refuge closes down in the days preceding a launch.

The 25 miles of pristine, windswept beaches at **Canaveral National Seashore & Cocoa Beach** are favored by surfers (at the south end), families (at the north end) and campers and nature

---

SURF'S UP IN THE SUNSHINE STATE

Despite all the sunshine and shoreline, Florida is no *Endless Summer*. The water around Miami tends to stay flat, blocked by the Bahamas offshore, and much of the Gulf Coast is too protected to get much of a swell. You'll find good waves – not Hawaii-good, but definitely surfable – along the mid- to north Atlantic coast, and in the Panhandle from Pensacola to St George Island. For webcams, forecasts and info on the best spots in the state (and the country), check out www .surfline.com.

Surf

- Cocoa Beach – South of Cape Canaveral, the area around the 800ft Cocoa Beach pier gets packed with space tourists and the surf crowd, but it's a good area to find a surf school. The waves are most consistent at both high and low tide.

- Sebastian Inlet – South of Melbourne, the inlet is one of the most consistent – and robust – breaks in the state, but is tide sensitive, so head there at low tide.

- New Smyrna Beach – South of Daytona, offshore rock ledges counteract the treacherous undercurrents common to the east coast. It's extremely consistent at low tide, but can get very crowded not only with humans, but with sharks.

- A St, St Augustine Beach – some mighty fine waves when they're working. For the lowdown on local surf conditions and to rent a board, make a stop at **Pit Surfshop** (☎ 904-471-4700; www.pitsurfshop.com; 18 A St, St Augustine; board rental per day $16; ☺ 9am-7pm Sun-Fri, to 8pm Sat winter, to 8pm daily summer).

Learn

The best surf school in Cocoa Beach for all ages and levels is the state's largest, **Cocoa Beach Surf School** (☎ 321-868-1980; www.cocoabeachsurfingschool.com; 3901 North Atlantic Ave; semiprivate/private lessons per hr $40/50) run by ex-pro surfer and Kelly Slater coach, Craig Carroll. Craig also teaches indoors at Walt Disney World's Typhoon Lagoon wave pool – 2½-hour group lessons held early-morning before the park opens cost $135. Book directly with **Walt Disney World** (☎ 407-939-7529).

lovers (on Klondike Beach, in the center). The seashore has a **ranger station** (☎ 321-867-4077; per person $3; 🕙 6am-8pm) at the south end, near Playalinda Beach at the end of Hwy 406/402, and a **visitor center** (☎ 904-428-3384) at the north end at Apollo Beach, on Hwy A1A east of New Smyrna Beach.

Sleeping & Eating
Rates skyrocket during space launches.

Canaveral National Seashore (☎ 321-267-1110, 386-428-3384; www.nps.gov/cana; 7611 S Atlantic Ave, New Smyrna Beach; camping permit $10; 🕙 9am-5pm) Back-country beach and island camping's available at designated sites. Permits are good for up to six people. Reservations are essential; bring everything you need including drinking water.

Fawlty Towers Motel (☎ 321-784-3870; www .fawltytowersresort.com; 100 E Cocoa Beach Causeway; r & ste $49-195; **P** 🛍 🖳) Beneath the gloriously garish and extremely pink exterior – highlighted with bright teal, no less – lie fairly straightforward rooms with an unbeatable beachside location.

Radisson Resort at the Port (☎ 321-784-0000; www.radisson.com/capecanaveralfl; 8701 Astronaut Blvd, Cape Canaveral; r $130-169; **P** 🛍 🖳) Rooms are pastel Florida-generic, but the large, lagoon-like pool is impressive, with faux ruins and tons of greenery (although 'resort' might be pushing it a bit).

Ron Jon Resort Cape Caribe (☎ 888-933-3030; www .ronjonresort.com; 1000 Shorewood Dr, Cape Canaveral; r $130-250; **P** 🛍 🖳) Activities such as mini-golf, movies, a lazy river and a 248ft water slide scream, 'Bring the family!' Its 'villas' – fancy-talk for 'condos' – sleep four to 12 and have a Santa Fe-meets-the-sea feel.

Dixie Crossroads (☎ 321-268-5000; 1475 Garden St, Titusville; mains $6-28; 🕙 11am-9pm Sun-Thu, to 10pm Fri & Sat) Smiling shrimp statues welcome you to a riot of murals, sculptures, fishponds and fountains – all garnishes for the fresh, local seafood. Want a lot? All-you-can-eat rock shrimp is $35 a person.

Coconuts on the Beach (☎ 321-784-1422; 2 Minute-men Causeway, Cocoa Beach; mains $7-17; 🕙 11am-10pm, bar open to 2am) Coconuts isn't just a name; it's a favored ingredient. The oceanfront 'party deck' hosts regular live music, so head indoors if you're seeking a family atmosphere.

Café Margaux (☎ 321-639-8343; 220 Brevard Ave, Cocoa; mains $7-24; 🕙 11am-3pm & 5-9:30pm Mon & Wed-Sat) French-inspired food, an extensive wine

list and heavy fabrics make for a sophisticated dining option in historic Cocoa village.

Corky Bell's Seafood Restaurant (☎ 321-636-1392; 4885 N US 1, Cocoa; 🕙 11am-9pm Mon-Thu, to 10pm Fri, noon-10pm Sat, noon-9pm Sun) A local favorite, this place packs 'em in, and it sure isn't because of the exquisite metal prefab it's housed in.

Getting There & Away
Driving from the south, follow Hwy A1A; from Orlando take Hwy 528 east, which connects with Hwy A1A. Greyhound has services from West Palm Beach and Orlando to Titusville.

DAYTONA BEACH
With big signs and glossy pamphlets, they bill Daytona Beach as 'The World's Most Famous Beach.' But if that sets up some sort of expectation in your head, remember that the title caught on in the 1920s and its accuracy is a matter of (not much) debate.

It certainly hasn't been the same since *Girls Gone Wild* left. Most people welcome the change, though some locals lament the decline in spring break party action. (Can't a girl find a wet T-shirt contest *anywhere*?) In fact, because of a crackdown in partying, along with efforts to position Daytona as a family destination, the college kids don't flock in for body shots, all-night dancing and doing tangible harm to their futures the way they used to. Of course, whether families will step in remains to be seen, but the bikers have, roaring into town every March for **Bike Week**.

One thing that's not going anywhere (except around in circles) is NASCAR, which was born here in 1947. As early as 1902, pioneers in the auto industry would drag race down the beach's hard-packed sands to test their inventions. That gave way to stock car racing, which paved the way for Bill France, Sr, who ran the Daytona Beach Race Course, to formalize the event and move it to the Daytona International Speedway.

The **Daytona Beach Convention & Visitors Bureau** (☎ 386-255-0415, 800-544-0415; www.day tonabeach.com; 126 E Orange Ave; 🕙 9am-5pm Mon-Fri) has a **visitor center** (☎ 386-253-8669; 1801 W International Speedway Blvd; 🕙 8.30am-7pm) in the lobby of Daytona USA. Information for gay and lesbian travelers is available at www.gaydaytona.com.

FLORIDA

Sights & Activities

During daylight hours – tide permitting – you can still drive sections of the former race track on **Daytona Beach** (☎ 386-239-7873) at a top speed of 10mph. Car access to the beach costs $5 ($3 after 3pm) and is free December and January (see boxed text, p63).

The Holy Grail of raceways is the **Daytona International Speedway** (☎ 386-947-6782, box office 888-472-2849; www.daytonaintlspeedway.com; 1801 W International Speedway Blvd; tickets from $20). Ticket prices accelerate rapidly for the big races headlined by the **Daytona 500** in February, but you can wander the massive stands for free on non-race days. Adjoining the speedway, **Daytona USA** (☎ 386-947-6530; www.daytonausa.com; adult/child 6-12 $24/19; ☺ 9am-7pm) is a superbly flashy shrine to the sport, including 3-D IMAX films, motion simulators and a 30-minute tram tour of the racetrack and pits. Real fanatics might want to indulge in the **Richard Petty Driving Experience**, where you can either ride shotgun ($134) or take the wheel ($525 to $2099) for laps around the track.

The **Museum of Arts & Sciences** (☎ 386-255-0285; www.moas.org; 352 S Nova Rd; adult/student $13/7; ☺ 9am-5pm Mon-Sat, 11am-5pm Sun) has a wonderful mishmash of everything from Cuban art to Coca-Cola relics to a 13ft giant sloth skeleton. About 6 miles south of Daytona Beach, you can walk the 203 steps to the top of **Ponce Inlet Lighthouse** (☎ 386-761-1821; www.ponceinlet.org; 4931 S Peninsula Dr; adult/child $5/1.50; ☺ 10am-5pm winter, to 9pm summer) and congratulate yourself: it's Florida's tallest. In this auto-obsessed town where cars are a religion, you can pull right up for church at the **Daytona Beach Drive-In Church** (☎ 386-767-8761; 3140 S Atlantic Ave; ☺ 8:30am & 10am Sun), a former drive-in movie theater where you attach a speaker to your car to hear the sermon.

Sleeping

The 2004 triple-hurricane action blew the roof off of properties and left the place a general shambles. Some hotels completely renovated and others shut down, with lots of condos springing up in their places. Prices soar during events; book well ahead.

Tropical Manor (☎ 386-252-4920; www.tropical manor.com; 2237 S Atlantic Ave; r $65-80, suites from $120; P ℞ 🖵) With the same owner for more than 50 years, this is one of those wonderful little gems that's disappearing way too fast. The property includes motel rooms, efficiencies and cottages, all blanketed in a frenzy of murals and bright pastels.

Sun Viking Lodge (☎ 386-252-6252; www.sunviking .com; 2411 S Atlantic Ave; r $81-339; P ℞ 🖵) With beach access, two pools and a 60ft waterslide, this viking-themed and family-owned motel is both family- and swimsuit-friendly. Most of the nicely renovated rooms have kitchenettes.

August 7 Inn (☎ 386-254-4969; www.A7Inn.com; 1209 S Peninsula Dr; r $125-250; P ✕ 🖵) The innkeepers of this gorgeous B&B have a thorough appreciation for small details and might literally bend over backwards for you.

Shores (☎ 386-767-7350; www.shoresresort.com; 2637 N Atlantic Ave; r $159-369; P ℞ 🖵) This boutique has hand-striped walls, a full-service spa and a sophisticated color palette that's a relief if you're suffering beach-decor overkill.

Eating & Drinking

Starlight Diner (☎ 386-255-9555; 401 N Atlantic Ave; dishes $4-12; ☺ 7am-midnight Mon-Thu, to 1am Fri & Sat, to 10pm Sun) Straight out of *Happy Days* – but with a little more attitude. The optimism and innocence of the '50s may not live on in this gleaming chrome diner, but the decor and food does.

Pasha Middle East Cafe (☎ 386-257-7753; 919 W International Speedway Blvd; mains $5-14; ☺ 10am-7pm Mon-Sat, noon-6pm Sun) Chow on falafel, kabob, hummus, tabouleh – and of course baklava – in a casual, family-run café and deli.

Aunt Catfish's on the River (☎ 386-767-4768; 4009 Halifax Dr; mains $8-25; ☺ 11:30am-9pm) Oh, seafood, how do I eat thee? Let me count the ways...

Billy's Tap Room & Grill (☎ 386-672-1910; 58 E Granada Blvd, Ormond Beach; mains $12-25, lunch $7-12; ☺ 11:30am-10pm Mon-Fri, 5-10pm Sat) Dating back to 1926, this tavern-style restaurant in Ormond Beach has a solid maple bar, historic photographs and grouper served 24 different ways.

Entertainment

High-octane dance clubs include **Razzles** (☎ 386-257-6236; 611 Seabreeze Blvd; ☺ 8pm-3am) and **Aqua Lounge** (☎ 386-248-3151; 640 N Grandview Ave; ☺ 9pm-3am Wed-Sun). **Rumors Nite Club & Bar** (☎ 386-252-3776; 1376 N Nova Rd; ☺ 2pm-2am) hosts drag shows, karaoke and pool for gay and gay-friendly revelers. And the **Stock Exchange** (☎ 386-255-6476; 125 Basin St, Suite 102; ☺ 11:30am-2:30am) caters to people old enough to appreciate good dance music from the '50s to the '80s.

Getting There & Around

Daytona Beach International Airport (☎ 386-248-8069; www.flydaytonafirst.com) is just east of the Speedway, and the **Greyhound bus station** (☎ 386-255-7076, 800-231-2222; 138 S Ridgewood Ave) has service around Florida.

Daytona is close to the intersection of two of Florida's major interstates. I-95 is the quickest way to Jacksonville (about 70 miles) and Miami (200 miles), and I-4 will get you to Orlando in about an hour.

Votran (☎ 386-756-7496; www.votran.com; adult/child 6-17 $1.25/50¢) runs buses and trolleys throughout the city.

ST AUGUSTINE

The first this, the oldest that… St Augustine was founded by the Spanish in 1565 and is the oldest permanent settlement in the US – which means it's chock-full of age-related superlatives. Tourists flock here to stroll the ancient streets, and horse-drawn carriages clip-clop past townsfolk dressed in period costume around the National Historic Landmark District.

At times it screams, 'Hey, everyone, look how quaint we are!' but it stops just this close from being cloying. Because underneath all those bonnets, it's the real deal. The historical significance of the town occasionally comes into sharp focus while you're walking on the cobblestone streets or standing on the (approximate) spot where Juan Ponce de León landed in 1513. The main **visitor center** (☎ 904-825-1000, 800-653-2489; www.visitoldcity.com; 10 Castillo Dr; ⏰ 8:30am-5:30pm) screens a 45-minute film ($1) on the town's history told through archival footage.

Sights & Activities

The town's two Henry Flagler buildings shouldn't be missed. His former Hotel Alcazar (1888) is now home to the wonderful **Lightner Museum** (☎ 904-824-2874; www.lightner museum.org; 75 King St; adult/child $8/2; ⏰ 9am-5pm), with a little bit of everything, from ornate Gilded Age furnishings to collections of marbles and cigar-box labels. Across the street is the gorgeous former **Hotel Ponce de León** (☎ 904-823-3378; 74 King St; tours adult/child $5/1; ⏰ 10am & 2pm, additional tours summer) which is now the world's most gorgeous dormitory, belonging to Flagler College. Take a guided tour – or at least step inside to gawk at the lobby for free.

History buffs will enjoy the oldest house in the US: the **Gonzalez-Alvarez House** (☎ 904-824-2872; www.oldesthouse.com; 14 St Francis St; adult/student $8/4; ⏰ 9am-5pm), claiming continuous occupancy from the early 17th century, as well as the **Oldest Wooden School House** (☎ 904-824-0192; 14 St George St; adult/child $3/2; ⏰ 9am-5pm), peopled by animatronic teachers and students. See how they did things back in the 18th century at the **Colonial Spanish Quarter Living History Village** (☎ 904-825-6830; 53 St George St; adult/student $6.50/4; ⏰ 9am-5:30pm Mon-Sat), a re-creation of Spanish-colonial St Augustine complete with craftspeople demonstrating blacksmithing, leather working and other trades.

Almost 500 years old (but not looking a day over 450) the **Fountain of Youth** (☎ 904-829-3168, 800-356-8222; 11 Magnolia Ave; adult/child $7/4; ⏰ 9am-5pm) was the original tourist attraction, drawing Spanish explorer Juan Ponce de León for a visit in 1513. It still serves the nasty sulfur water in tiny paper cups – and that's absolutely as much as you'll want – but this is more than a five-minute pit stop. Educational exhibits, gorgeous grounds and the approximate spot where the explorer came ashore make it more than just a tourist trap – OK, well a *little* more, anyway.

Another monument to longevity is the country's oldest masonry fort, **Castillo de San Marcos National Monument** (☎ 904-829-6506; btwn San Marcos Ave & Matanzas River; adult/child under 15 $6/free; ⏰ 8:45am-4:45pm) built by the Spanish between 1672 and 1695. Park rangers lead programs hourly and volunteers shoot off cannons most weekends.

Locals escape the tourist hordes at the nearby **Anastasia State Recreation Area** (☎ 904-461-2033; 300 Anastasia Park Rd; car/pedestrian $5/1; campsites $25) which has a terrific beach, a campground and rentals for all kinds of water sports.

Discover the town's spirited past with **Ghost Tours of St Augustine** (☎ 904-461-1009; www.ghost toursofstaugustine.com; walking tours $12; ⏰ tours 8pm daily, 9:30pm Fri & Sat winter, daily summer).

Sleeping

More than two dozen atmospheric B&Bs can be found at www.staugustineinns.com. St Augustine is a popular weekend escape; expect room rates to rise about 30% on Friday and Saturday. Inexpensive motels and chain hotels line San Marco Ave, near where it meets US Hwy 1.

Pirate Haus (☎ 904-808-1999; www.piratehaus .com; 32 Treasury St; dm $18, r $40-80; ✗ ▯) Yar, if ye don't be needing anything fancy, this family-friendly European-style guesthouse-hostel has an unbeatable location and includes a pirate pancake breakfast.

Vilano Beach Motel (☎ 904-810-0767; www.vi lanobeachmotel.com; 50 Vilano Road; r $95-105, ste $125; P ▮) Out at the beach, this 1950s motel has some kitchenettes and two-bedroom suites, making it a good-value option for longer stays.

Cedar House Inn (☎ 904-829-0079, 800-845-0012; www.cedarhouseinn.com; 79 Cedar St; r $139-229, ste $199-309; P ✗ ▯) Victorian flourishes abound, but the beds are pure modern comfort.

Casa Monica (☎ 904-827-1888, 800-648-1888; www .casamonica.com; 95 Cordova St; r $189-369; P ✗ ▯ ▮) Built in 1888, this is *the* luxe hotel in town, with turrets and fountains adding to the Spanish Moorish castle feel. Parking is available for $16.

Eating & Drinking

Eateries in St Augustine are surprisingly inexpensive. Note that restaurants often close a bit earlier or later than the hours listed.

Spanish Bakery (☎ 904-471-3046; 42½ St George St; dishes $1-3; ☽ 9:30am-3pm) Behind Whetstone Chocolates in a picnic-table-strewn courtyard, this historic stone kitchen bakes up empanadas and smoked-sausage rolls. Five dollars gets you one of the above plus a drink, roll and cookie.

Harry's Seafood, Bar & Grill (☎ 904-824-7765; 46 Avenida Menendez; mains $8-23; ☽ 11am-10pm Sun-Thu, to 11pm Fri & Sat) It may pride itself on its Cajun food, but the hopping patio and Mardi Gras atmosphere is the real draw.

Pizzalley's Pizzeria & Pizzalley's Chianti Room (☎ 904-825-2627, 904-825-4100; 117 St George St; slices $2.50-4, mains $11-22; ☽ 11:30am-9pm) Grab a slice in front, or feast on fab Italian fare in the Chianti Room in the back.

Gypsy Cab Co (☎ 904-824-8244; 828 Anastasia Blvd; mains $15-21, lunch $8-12; ☽ dinner 4:30-11pm daily, lunch 11am-3pm Sat, brunch 10:30am-3pm Sun) A local favorite, its excellent menu is all over the place, with influences from German to 'Floribbean'.

Taberna del Gallo (☎ 904-825-6830; 53 St George St; ☽ 2-7pm Thu, 2-10pm Fri & Sat, noon-7pm Sun) Flickering candles provide the only light at this 1736 stone tavern and on Saturday nights the Bilge Rats sing old sea shanties.

Stogies Jazz Club & Listening Room (☎ 904-826-4008; www.stogiesjazz.com; 36 Charlotte St; ☽ 4pm-1am Mon-Fri, 2pm-1am Sat & Sun). Be transported back to the '20s, when people weren't afraid of a little secondhand smoke.

Getting There & Around

The **Greyhound bus station** (☎ 904-829-6401; 1711 Dobbs Rd) is a few miles from the heart of things, but once you're in Old Town, you can get almost everywhere on foot.

Two companies provide convenient jump-on, jump-off tours with 20 stops on open-air trams: **Old Town Trolley Tours** (☎ 904-829-3800, 800-213-2474; www.trolleytours.com; 167 San Marco Ave; 3-day ticket adult/child 6-12 $20/7) and **St Augustine Sightseeing Trains** (☎ 800-226-6545; www.redtrains .com; 19 San Marco Ave; adult/child 6-12 $19/6).

JACKSONVILLE

Are we there yet? Have we left yet? It's hard to tell, because Jacksonville sprawls out over a whopping 840 sq miles, making it the largest city by area in the continental US (eclipsed only by Anchorage, AK). It stretches its limbs along three meandering rivers – including the St Johns River, the only river in the world besides the Nile that flows south to north. Jacksonville Beach – known locally as 'Jax Beach' – is about 17 miles east of the city center and is where you'll find white sand and most of the action. Information's available from the **convention & visitors bureau** (☎ 800-733-2668; www .visitjacksonville.com).

Sights & Activities

Enjoy a free tour (and if you're over 21, free beer) at the **Anheuser-Busch Brewery** (☎ 904-696-8373; www.budweisertours.com; 111 Busch Dr; admission free; ☽ 10am-4pm Mon-Sat). Packing kids? Maybe the **Museum of Science & History** (☎ 904-396-6674; www.themosh.org; 1025 Museum Circle; adult/child $9/7; ☽ 10am-5pm Mon-Fri, to 6pm Sat, 1-6pm Sun) is more your speed, with dinosaur fun and educational exhibits on Jacksonville's pre-Columbian history (but no beer). One of the best cultural offerings in town, the **Jacksonville Museum of Modern Art** (☎ 904-366-6911; 333 N Laura St; adult/child $6/4, Wed 5-9pm free; ☽ 10am-4pm Tue-Sun, to 9pm on Wed) focuses on 1960 to the present.

Sleeping & Eating

The cheapest rooms are along I-95 and I-10, where the lower-priced chains congregate. Beach lodging rates often rise in summer.

Omni Jacksonville Hotel (☎ 904-355-6664, 800-843-6664; 245 Water St; r $89-199; P ❋ ❐) A high-rise tower in the heart of downtown offering 354 very comfy and amenity-laden rooms.

Inn at Oak Street (☎ 904-379-5525; www.innatoakstreet.com; 2114 Oak St; r $120-180; P ✕ ❐) This place combines luscious decor, high-tech amenities and gourmet breakfast, all near downtown.

Sea Turtle Inn (☎ 800-874-6000; www.seaturtle.com; 1 Ocean Blvd, Atlantic Beach; r $129-159; P ❋) Right at the beach, and named for the sea turtles that hatch right outside in the spring.

Casa Marina (☎ 904-270-0025; www.casamarinahotel.com; 691 N 1st St, Jacksonville Beach; r $159, suites $229; P ✕) Also right on the water, this 1920s-era option is a romantic getaway.

European Street Cafe (☎ 904-398-9500; 1704 San Marco Blvd; dishes $5-8; ☾ 10am-10pm) In the San Marco historical district, it has an extensive menu, huge bakery counter, amazing prices and more than 150 beers that will all leave you with a very happy tummy. Other locations include 2753 Park St and 5500 Beach Blvd, plus 992 Beach Blvd in Jacksonville Beach.

Bistro Aix (☎ 904-398-1949; 1440 San Marco Blvd; mains $10-25; ☾ 11am-10pm Mon-Thu, to 11pm Fri, 5-11pm Sat, 5-9pm Sun) Serves a French-inspired menu in chic San Marco digs.

River City Brewing Company (☎ 904-398-2299; 835 Museum Circle; lunch $9-10, dinner $17-33; ☾ 11am-3pm & 5-10pm Mon-Thu, till 11pm Fri & Sat, 10:30am-2:30pm Sun) The perfect place to quaff a microbrew and enjoy some coconut shrimp overlooking the water.

Drinking & Entertainment

Downtown's **Jacksonville Landing** (☎ 904-353-1188; www.jacksonvillelanding.com; 2 Independent Dr) has restaurants, shops and bars, and free outdoor entertainment. At the beach, the **Freebird Live Cafe** (☎ 904-246-2473; www.freebirdlive.com; 200 N 1st St; ☾ 8pm-2am) is a rocking music venue and home of the band Lynyrd Skynyrd.

Getting There & Around

North of the city, **Jacksonville International Airport** (☎ 904-741-4902; www.jaa.aero) has rental cars. **Greyhound** (☎ 904-356-9976; 10 N Pearl St) serves numerous cities, and **Amtrak** (☎ 904-766-5110; 3570 Clifford Lane) has trains from the north and south. The **Jacksonville Transportation Authority** (☎ 904-630-3100; www.ridejta.net) runs the **Skyway monorail** (per ride 35¢) and **city buses** (per local ride 75¢, to Jax Beach $1.35).

AMELIA ISLAND

Residents are quick to tell you: Amelia Island is just as old as that braggart St Augustine – they just can't prove it. Unfortunately, no Ponce de León, no plaque, so they have to content themselves with being a pretty little island and home to **Fernandina Beach**, a shrimping village with 40 blocks of historic buildings and romantic B&Bs. Pick up walking-tour maps and information at the **visitor center** (☎ 800-226-3542; 102 Centre St; ☾ 11am-4pm Mon-Sat, noon-4pm Sun).

To learn about Amelia Island's intricate history, which has seen it ruled under eight different flags starting with the French in 1562, check out the **Amelia Island Museum of History** (☎ 904-261-7378; www.ameliaislandmuseumofhistory.org; 233 S 3rd St; adult/student $7/4; ☾ 10am-4pm Mon-Sat, 1pm-4pm Sun). Admission includes tours at 11am and 2pm. The museum also offers a Friday **ghost tour** (801 Atlantic Ave; adult/student $10/5; ☾ 6pm Fri), leaving from St Peters Episcopal church.

Take a half-hour horse-drawn carriage tour with the **Old Towne Carriage Co** (☎ 904-277-1555; www.ameliacarriagetours.com; adult/child 3-13 $15/7) or **Amelia Island Carriages** (☎ 904-556-2662; adults/child $15/7). For a romantic moonlight ride on Amelia Island's silhouetted sands, contact **Circle D Ranch** (☎ 904-556-9530; ride per hr $65, moonlight ride $90). It offers one morning and two evening rides; moonlight rides are by reservation.

Capping the north end of the island, the Spanish moss-draped **Fort Clinch State Park** (☎ 904-277-7274; pedestrian/car $1/5; ☾ 8am-dusk) has beaches, camping, bike trails and a commanding Civil War–era **fort** (admission $2; ☾ 9am-5pm), with re-enactments taking place the first weekend of every month. Amelia Island is part of the **Talbot Islands State Parks** (☎ 904-251-2320; pedestrian/car $1/4; ☾ 8am-dusk), which includes the pristine shoreline at **Little Talbot Island** and the 'boneyard beach' at **Big Talbot Island State Park**, where silvered tree skeletons create a dramatic landscape. Both are south of Amelia Island down the First Coast Hwy.

Fernandina does beat out St Augustine with two key 'oldests': Florida's oldest bar, the **Palace Saloon** (☎ 904-261-6320; 113 Centre St), and Florida's oldest hotel, **Florida House Inn** (☎ 904-261-3300, 800-258-3301; www.floridahouseinn.com; 20 & 22 S 3rd St; r $129-249; P ✕ ❐ wi-fi), which stays modern with beautifully restored rooms, wi-fi and free use of zippy, red scooters.

FLORIDA

Right on the beach, the **Elizabeth Pointe Lodge** (☎ 904-277-4851; www.elizabethpointelodge .com; 98 S Fletcher Ave; r $185-395) looks like an old Nantucket-style sea captain's house with wraparound porches, gracious service and beautifully-appointed rooms. Despite the name, the enormous **Amelia Island Plantation** (☎ 904-261-6161, 800-874-6878; www.aipfl.com; 6800 First Coast Hwy; r $186-962; P ⊠ 🖳 🛋) is a world of its own – more resort than plantation – with three golf courses, 23 tennis courts and nine restaurants.

Start your day with **Bright Mornings** (☎ 904-491-1771; 105 S 3rd St; dishes $5-9; ⏰ 7:30am-2pm Mon-Tue & Thu-Fri, 8am-2pm Sat & Sun), a supremely pleasant café serving heaping portions of breakfast and lunch. Sunset views over the marina are the star at **Brett's Waterway Cafe** (☎ 904-261-2660; 1 S Front St; lunch $10-13, dinner $20-34; ⏰ 11:30am-2:30pm & 5:30-9pm). Small plates and mains live happily side by side at the tiny, stylish bistro **29 South** (☎ 904-277-7919; 29 S 3rd St; small plates $5-12, mains $12-26; ⏰ 11am-2pm & 5:30-9pm Tue-Thu, till 10pm Fri, 9am-2pm & 5:30-10pm Sat, 9am-2pm Sun).

Hwy A1A links the island to the mainland, but there's no public transportation. Rent bikes at **Pipeline Surfshop** (☎ 904-277-3717; 2022 1st Ave; per hr/business day $5/12; ⏰ 10am-6pm).

WEST COAST

If Henry Flagler's railroad made the east coast of Florida what it is today, his nonattention to the rest of the state similarly affected the west coast. Things are calmer here, with fewer tourist hordes and more room for nature to amuse us with shelling beaches, swamp lands and nature preserves. The west coast has front-row seats to flame-red sunsets emblazoned over the Gulf of Mexico, as well as adrenaline-pumping roller coasters, hand-rolled cigars and lip-synching mermaids.

TAMPA

Florida's third-largest city is all business. Well, mostly business. Chains and oversized office parks line the highways and it's not immediately apparent what there is to do here, other than get a nine-to-five job. But Tampa's revitalized historic district Ybor City and a few downtown museums absolutely reward a stop. Information's available at the **convention & visitors bureau** (☎ 813-223-2752, 800-448-2672; www.visittampabay.com; 615 Channelside Dr; 9:30am-5:30pm Mon-Sat, 11:30am-5pm Sun).

Sight & Activities
DOWNTOWN TAMPA

Check out the **Henry B Plant Museum** (☎ 813-254-1891; www.plantmuseum.com; 401 W Kennedy Blvd; adult/child $5/2; ⏰ 10am-4pm Tue-Sat, noon-4pm Sun) if for no other reason than to wander around the landmark Victorian building it's housed in. Formerly a luxury hotel, it's easily the most beautiful building in town.

Challenge the laws of physics as well as your fear of heights at the **Museum of Science & Industry** (☎ 813-987-6100; www.mosi.org; 4801 E Fowler Ave; adult/child $20/16; ⏰ 9am-5pm), where you can ride a bike across a highwire 30ft in the air, and learn about dinosaurs, hurricanes and the human body.

The **Tampa Museum of Art** (☎ 813-274-8130; www.tampamuseum.com; 600 N Ashley Dr; adult/child $7/3; ⏰ 10am-5pm Tue-Sat) has an impressive collection, and, depending on when you read this, possibly a brand-spanking-new building next door to the old one.

At **Florida Aquarium** (☎ 813-273-4000; www .flaquarium.org; 701 Channelside Dr; adult/child $18/13; ⏰ 9:30am-5pm) you can get your hands wet with touch tanks or dive into the shark tank (scuba divers $150).

YBOR CITY

This cobblestoned 19th-century historic district preserves a strong Cuban-Spanish heritage while embracing a hip, happening nightlife scene. About two miles from downtown, Ybor (rhymes with Eeyore) City was established by the owner of a cigar factory who drew hundreds of Cuban, Spanish and Italian immigrant workers to the area, and that diversity has bestowed more charm on this area than the whole rest of Tampa put together. The **visitor center** (☎ 813-248-3712; www.ybor.org; 1600 E 8th Ave; ⏰ 10am-6pm Mon-Sat, noon-6pm Sun) provides an excellent introduction with walking-tour maps and info. Centered around a seven-block stretch of 7th and 8th Aves, everything is within walking distance.

You can still pick up a close-to-Cuban cigar and watch master cigar rollers at work at several different shops, including **La Herencia de Cuba** (☎ 800-324-9803; www.ramirezcigars.com; 1817 E 7th Ave) and **Gonzalez y Martinez** (☎ 813-248-8210; www.gonzalezymartinez.com; 2103 E 7th Ave).

LOCAL VOICES

For more than 10 years Marcy Terry has delighted audiences with underwater mermaid performances at Weeki Wachee Springs. Marcy now holds the dual title of Underwater Theatre Manager and Head Mermaid.

What's your favorite thing about being a mermaid? I just love the environment. My office is a beautiful underwater spring; I get to swim and get paid; I interact with children who believe in mermaids and they're just so happy to be here.

How long does it take to become a mermaid? First we have to get scuba certified, then we learn to breathe through air hoses, which is different from regular scuba diving. Then we start learning how to swim in a tail and learning the choreography, so it takes three to six months.

Other than Weeki Wachee, what's your favorite Florida tourist attraction? I would have to say Disney. I just love the magic there, and I have a two-year-old and she loves going there. I love seeing her little eyes light up. Everybody's happy and all the little kids believe all that stuff so you can't help but feel that way also.

If you had visitors from out of state, where would you take them? First I would bring them here. Then, the beaches are beautiful; we'd probably go to a beach. Of course we'd hit Disney. And, I don't know, I think the small roadside attractions need all the tourists they can get, so I'd probably do those.

The **Ybor City Museum State Park** (☎ 813-247-6323; www.ybormuseum.org; 1818 E 9th Ave; admission $3; 9am-5pm) chronicles the history of cigar making in interesting if text-heavy exhibits, and historic **walking tours** (incl museum admission $6) depart from the museum at 10:30am each Saturday.

BUSCH GARDENS & ADVENTURE ISLAND

Is it a theme park with animals or a zoo with rides? **Busch Gardens Africa** (☎ 813-987-5000; www.buschgardens.com; 3000 E Busch Blvd, cnr 40th St; adult/child $62/52, advance purchase all ages $52; 9am-6pm with seasonal variations; P) is both – and way more exciting than Disney's Animal Kingdom (p535), thanks to all the rides. Next door, **Adventure Island** (☎ 813-987-5660, 888-800-5447; www.adventureisland.com; 10001 McKinley Dr; adult/child $36/34; 10am-5pm with seasonal variations; P) water park has slides and rides galore. Combination tickets for one day at each park are available for $76/66 per adult/child; parking costs $9 at Busch Gardens and $6 at Adevnture Island.

WEEKI WACHEE SPRINGS

Since 1947 tourists have been lured north up the coast by the kitsch siren song of **Weeki Wachee Springs** (☎ 352-596-2062; www.weekiwachee.com; 6131 Commercial Way, Weeki Wachee; adult/child $23/16; 10am-4pm, check for seasonal variations), one of Florida's original roadside attractions. Elvis Presley and Esther Williams have been

among the guests who've flocked here to watch through glass as the glamorous long-haired mermaids perform in an underwater grotto. The mermaids are the main attraction, but there's also a wilderness river cruise, plus swimming and waterslides at the adjoining Buccaneer Bay water park. (Hint: admissions are reduced in the off-season when the water park is closed.)

Sleeping

Chains abound near Busch Gardens, along Fowler Ave/Morris Bridge Rd (Hwy 582) and Busch Blvd (Hwy 580).

Gram's Place (☎ 813-221-0596; www.grams-inn-tampa.com; 3109 N Ola Ave; campsites $15, dm $22.50, r with bath $34-68, without bath $24.50-49;) Rooms at this rockin' hostel are themed by music genre, and the jukebox spins more than 400 CDs.

Paradise Lakes Resort (☎ 813-949-9327; www.paradiselakes.com; 2001 Brinson Rd, Land O' Lakes; r $75-140; P) If you prefer an all-over tan, North America's largest 'clothing optional' resort is 17 miles north of town among its 80 secluded acres.

Don Vicente de Ybor Historic Inn (☎ 813-241-4545; www.donvicenteinn.com; 1915 Republica de Cuba; r $139; P) Built in 1895 by Ybor City's founder, this atmospheric B&B exudes history right down to its original marble staircase.

Casita de la Verdad (☎ 813-654-6087; 1609 6th Ave; house $180-250; P) Right on the fringe

FLORIDA

of Ybor City you can rent an entire two-bedroom 1908 cigar-maker's cottage that's been artfully restored with a colorful whimsy.

Eating

Downtown is a desert for dining, but Ybor City is an oasis. Keep an eye out for places popping up in Tampa's SoHo area (South of Houston Ave).

La Teresita (☎ 813-879-4909; 3246 W Columbus Dr, Ybor City; mains $5-7; ☺ 5am-midnight Mon-Thu, 24hr Fri & Sat, to 10pm Sun) Skip the restaurant and head for the horseshoe-shaped cafeteria counters to feast alongside locals from every walk of life on stuffed plantains with yellow rice and black beans plus Cuban bread and coffee.

Nicko's 1951 Diner (☎ 813-234-9301; 4603 N Florida Ave, Tampa; mains $6-11; ☺ 6am-9pm Mon-Fri, 7am-9pm Sat, 7am-2pm Sun) Diner food with lots of salads and Greek specialties have kept people coming here for decades, including Elvis back in 1956.

Four Green Fields (☎ 813-254-4444; 205 W Platt St, Tampa; dishes $6-14; ☺ 11am-3am) Feast on Irish stew, shepherd's pie or corned beef in this authentic thatched-roof cottage that looks straight out of County Killarney.

Columbia Restaurant (☎ 813-2438-4961; 2117 E 7th Ave, Ybor City; mains $18-30; ☺ 11am-10pm Mon-Thu, 11am-11pm Fri & Sat, noon-9pm Sun) This resplendent 1905 establishment occupies an entire block and seats 1600. A $6 cover gets you seating for one of its flamenco shows Monday through Sunday.

Bern's Steak House (☎ 813-251-2421; www.berns steakhouse.com; 1208 S Howard Ave, Tampa; mains $18-60; ☺ 5-11pm) This illustrious landmark serves 26 types of caviar and steaks prepared to the most exacting tastes and specifications.

Drinking & Entertainment

Find out what's happening from the *Weekly Planet*, and *Tampa Tribune*'s 'Friday Extra.' When it comes to nightlife, just head for Ybor City's 7th Ave. Start at the pirate ship–like bar **Gaspar's Grotto** (☎ 813-248-5900; 1805 7th Ave; ☺ 11:30am-3am) then wander till you find the right scene.

Tampa shows off its artier side at the elaborate 1926 **Tampa Theatre** (☎ 813-274-8981; www .tampatheatre.org; 711 N Franklin St; tickets $8.50), with independent and classic films plus occasional live performance.

Sports are big in Tampa. The area's Major League baseball franchise, the **Tampa Bay Devil**

Rays (☎ 888-326-7297; www.devilrays.com), play at **Tropicana Field** (1 Tropicana Dr, St Petersburg; tickets $8-270). The **NFL Tampa Bay Buccaneers** (☎ 800-795-2827; www.buccaneers.com) play football at **Raymond James Stadium** (4201 Dale Mabry Hwy) August to December. The **NHL Tampa Bay Lightning** (☎ 813-301-6600; http://lightning.nhl.com) play hockey October to April at the **St Pete Times Forum** (401 Channelside Dr; tickets $8-150).

Spring training for numerous Major League teams is a great way to see baseball stars up close in a spontaneous environment. Tickets are around $20. Try **Legends Field** (☎ 813-879-2244; www.legendsfieldtampa.com) to watch the New York Yankees practice.

Getting There & Around

Tampa International Airport (☎ 813-870-8700; www .tampaairport.com) has car-rental agencies inside. **Greyhound** (☎ 813-229-2174; 610 E Polk St) has numerous services. Trains run south to Miami and north through Jacksonville at the **Amtrak station** (☎ 813-221-7601; 601 Nebraska Ave). **HARTline** (☎ 813-254-4278; www.hartline.org; fare/day pass $1.50/3.25) runs the old-style streetcars.

ST PETERSBURG

You know how in some families there's a sophisticated older sibling who wears suits and has an Important Job, and then there's the younger sibling who's kind of artsy and easier to hang out with? In this particular metaphor, Tampa is the former, and St Pete's is the latter. Perched on a peninsula along the west side of Tampa Bay, St Pete's is a cultured and tourist-friendly town with easy proximity to the beaches. For the scoop on local sights, stop by the **information booth** (☎ 727-821-6164) at the over-hyped **St Petersburg Pier** (☎ 727-821-6443; www.stpetepier.com; 800 2nd Ave N; ☺ 10am-9pm Mon-Thu, to 10pm Fri & Sat, 11am-7pm Sun), which also houses tchotchke shops, restaurants and an observation deck. Advance planners can check out www.floridasbeach .com for information.

The newly expanded and twice-as-big **Museum of Fine Arts** (☎ 727-896-2667; www.fine-arts.org; 255 Beach Dr NE; adult/child $8/4; ☺ 10am-5pm Tue-Sat, 1-5pm Sun) spans pre-Columbian to impressionism to modern. **St Petersburg Museum of History** (☎ 727-894-1052; www.spmoh.org; 335 2nd Ave NE; adult/child $6/3; ☺ noon-7pm Mon, 10am-5pm Tue-Sat, 1pm-5:30pm Sun) has interesting mementos of early Florida, plus a funky 3000-year-old mummy.

Hikers, bikers and skaters can head north on the paved, 34-mile-long **Pinellas Trail** (☎ 727-464-8200; ☼ dawn-dusk), starting at 34th St and Fairfield Ave and ending in Tarpon Springs. A free booklet with mile-by-mile information is available at visitor centers.

One of the finest beaches in Florida – partly because of the excellent amenities such as plentiful, shady picnic tables – is at **Fort DeSoto Park** (☎ 727-582-2267; www.pinellascounty.org/park; 3500 Pinellas Bayway S; admission free; ☼ dawn-dusk), with a fishing pier, historic trail, water sports, camping and a fort built in 1898.

Sleeping & Eating

Fort DeSoto Park Campground (☎ 727-582-2267; www .pinellascounty.org/park; 3500 Pinellas Bayway S; campsites $28) Book way ahead for sites at the waterfront campground; the beaches here make it all worthwhile.

Grayl's Hotel (☎ 727-896-1080; www.graylshotel .com; 340 Beach Dr NE; r $99-275; ℗ ✗ 🖳) Superbly located for walking around downtown, this Mission-style inn's decor is a bit of a mishmash, but almost always appealing.

Don CeSar Beach Resort (☎ 727-360-1881, 866-728-2206; www.doncesar.com; 3400 Gulf Blvd, St Pete Beach; r from $194; ℗ 🐾 🖳) This historic behemoth out at St Pete's Beach has been providing superposh pink lodging since the 1920s.

Moon Under Water (☎ 727-896-6160; 332 Beach Dr NE; dishes $7-18; ☼ 11:30am-11pm Sun-Thu, till midnight Fri-Sat) Get your fill of fish and chips, tikka masala and cold pints at this British-style pub with a lovely front patio.

Cafe Alma (☎ 727-502-5002; 260 1st Ave S; mains $7-28; ☼ 11am-10pm Mon-Wed, till midnight Thu & Fri, 10:30am-midnight Sat) This cute subterranean café is a little hidden away but worth finding, serving sophisticated salads and sandwiches at lunch and small plates and mains at dinner.

Ted Peter's Famous Smoked Fish (☎ 727-381-7931; 1350 Pasadena Ave S; dishes $8-18; ☼ 11:30am-7:30pm Wed-Mon) The word 'institution' gets tossed around a lot, but this thriving, open-air fish joint that's been around since the 1950s wears the title well; look for it just before the causeway to St Pete Beach.

Gratzzi Ristorante (☎ 727-822-7769; Baywalk Mall; lunch $8-12, dinner $13-27; ☼ 11:30am-10pm Mon-Thu, to 11pm Fri & Sat, 4-10pm Sun) Don't be fooled by its mall location; the food is amazing, with presentation that will leave you agog.

Getting There & Around

St Petersburg-Clearwater International Airport (☎ 727-453-7800; www.fly2pie.com) has several major carriers serving the US and Canada. It also has car rentals. Widespread **Greyhound** (☎ 727-898-1496; 180 9th St N) services include Tampa ($7, 35 minutes). Amtrak trains don't go to St Pete's, but there is a bus link from Tampa.

Pinellas Suncoast Transit Authority (PSTA; ☎ 727-540-1900; www.psta.net; day pass/concession $3.50/1.50) operates PSTA buses citywide and the Suncoast Beach Trolley that links the beaches from Clearwater to Pass-a-Grille. The **Looper trolley** (per ride 25¢; ☼ 10am-5pm Sun-Thu, to midnight Fri & Sat) links the museums and St Petersburg Pier on a 30-minute narrated loop.

SARASOTA

Artists, writers, musicians, entertainers – artsy types have flocked to Sarasota since

---

WHAT THE...?

Talk about surreal. On the waterfront just outside of downtown St Petersburg is the **Salvador Dalí Museum** (☎ 727-823-3767; www.salvadordalimuseum.org; 1000 3rd St S; adult/child $14/3.50, after 5pm Thu $5; ☼ 9:30am-5:30pm Mon-Sat, to 8pm Thu, to 6:30 Fri, noon-5:30pm Sun), the largest Dalí collection outside of Spain. How did St Petersburg end up with such an illustrious collection from the eccentric Spanish artist who painted melting clocks, grew an exaggerated handlebar mustache to look like King Philip and once filled a Rolls Royce with cauliflower? In 1942 industrialist A Reynolds Morse and his wife Eleanor bought their first Dalí painting – the start of what would become the largest private Dalí collection in the world. When it came time to find a permanent home for the collection, they had one stipulation: that the collection had to stay together. Only three cities could agree to the terms – Boulder, Austin and St Petersburg – and St Petersburg won out for its waterfront location. The museum doesn't have *the* melting clocks, but it does have some melting clocks, as well as paintings with titles such as *The Ghost of Vermeer of Delft Which Can Be Used as a Table* and *Eggs on a Plate Without a Plate*.

the 1920s, with John Ringling leading the way. Today you can find cultural performances and arts venues – not to mention bookstores – all over town. The **visitor bureau** (☎ 941-957-1877, 800-522-9799; www.sarasotafl.org; 701 N Tamiami Trail; ☉ 10am-4pm Mon-Sat, noon-3pm Sun) has local information.

That big, fantastical purple building – some might say 'obnoxious' – is the **Van Wezel Performing Arts Hall** (☎ 941-953-3368, 800-826-9303; www.vanwezel.org; 777 N Tamiami Trail), purveyor of symphony, dance and theater. The **Sarasota County Arts Council** (☎ 941-365-5118; www.sarasota-arts.org; 1226 N Tamiami Tr, Suite 300) has information about a variety of upcoming local performances.

Wander about a cluster of colorful galleries and studios at **Towles Court Art District** (www.towlescourt.com; 1938 Adams Lane; ☉ 11am-4pm Tue-Sat). Independent films screen at the **Burns Court Cinema** (☎ 941-955-3456; 506 Burns Ct); call or visit www.filmsociety.org for schedules. **Gator Club** (☎ 941-366-5969; www.thegatorclub.com; 1490 Main St) has live rock, blues or alternative music nightly.

Right over the Ringling Causeway (which circus elephants helped build) on Lido Key is **St Armands Circle**, a roundabout that serves as social hub with a proliferation of stylish shops and restaurants. **Mote Aquarium** (☎ 941-388-4441; www.mote.org; 1600 Ken Thompson Parkway; adult/child 4-12 $15/10; ☉ 10am-5pm), a research center and rehabilitation facility, has touch pools, a manatee habitat, the fun Shark Attack Theater and of course fish.

Many of the beautiful beaches are private. The best public-access beach is **Siesta Key Beach**, about 5 miles south of downtown on Siesta Key, with wide, white strips of sugary quartz sand for your sunning pleasure.

Sleeping & Eating

Cypress (☎ 941-955-4683; www.cypressbb.com; 621 Gulfstream Ave; r $150-260; P ✕ ▯) This B&B on the mainland sits beneath palm and mango trees with romantic – if occasionally frilly – rooms.

Aloha Kai (☎ 941-349-5410; www.alohakai.net; 6020 Midnight Pass Rd; r $150-260; P ▨ ▯) At the bea+ch, with freestanding motel rooms, studios and apartments steps from the beach.

Broken Egg (☎ 941-346-2750; 210 Avenida Madera, Siesta Key; dishes $6-12; ☉ 7:30am-2:30pm) A breakfast institution on Siesta Key, known for its huge variety of pancakes.

Old Salty Dog (☎ 941-388-4311; 1601 Ken Thompson Parkway, City Island; mains $6-22, most under $10; ☉ 11am-9:30pm Mon-Thu, till 10 Fri & Sat, noon-9:30pm Sun) Serves drinks and munchies overlooking the water; try its batter-fried hot dog bites.

Bijou Café (☎ 941-366-8111; 1287 1st St; lunch $9-19, dinner $17-29; ☉ 11:30am-2pm & 5pm-close time Mon-Fri, 5pm-close time Sat, 5pm-close time Sun high season) French-inspired cuisine and an excellent wine list.

FORT MYERS

Just a sleepy resort town when Thomas Edison arrived in 1885, Fort Myers was pretty enough to entice him to build his winter home here. Among his many visions was palm-lined avenues, which he kicked off with a gift of more than 800 trees. This shady legacy lives on, and today 14 miles of McGregor Blvd are lined with more than 2000 palms. It's a stellar start to any visit, but the rest of the town doesn't quite live up to the introduction. The

---

CLOWNING AROUND AT THE RINGLING COMPLEX

Who doesn't love the circus? Well, people who are afraid of clowns. But a little coulrophobia isn't necessarily a deal-breaker at the **Ringling Museum Complex** (☎ 941-358-3180; www.ringling .org; 5401 Bayshore Rd; adult/student $15/5; ☉ 10am-5:30pm). On the grounds of the 66-acre complex are three separate museums, all included in your admission and each one a worthy attraction on its own. Railroad, real-estate and circus baron John Ringling and his wife Mabel put down roots here, building a Venetian Gothic waterfront mansion called **Ca d'Zan**. You can wander the ground floor at your own pace, or take a guided tour – totally worth it – which grants you access to the upstairs bedrooms. Also on the grounds, the **John & Mabel Museum of Art** is an excellent art museum with impressive high ceilings, intimidatingly large paintings and a re-created room from the Astor mansion. But the real standout here – the one you might want to sit out if you saw Stephen King's *It* – is the one-of-a-kind **Museum of the Circus** with costumes, props, posters, antique circus wagons and an extensive miniature model that let you relive the excitement of the big-top era.

FLORIDA

visitor & convention bureau (☎ 239-338-3500; www .fortmyerssanibel.com) has visitor information; call or check online.

See how the early innovators lived at the **Edison & Ford Winter Estates** (☎ 239-334-3614; www .edison-ford-estate.com; 2350 McGregor Blvd; adult/child 6-12 $20/11; ☽ 9am-5:30pm). The homes themselves are anticlimactic – you only see Edison's through the windows like a peeping Tom – but his laboratory, gardens and museum make the trip worthwhile. Check out the banyan tree at the visitor center; it's the largest in the US. Forty-minute guided tours leave every half-hour until 4pm.

Just north of Fort Myers, take a 1½-hour swamp-buggy wildlife excursion through pinewoods, freshwater marsh and cypress swamp, led by **Babcock Wilderness Adventure** (☎ 800-500-5583; www.babcockwilderness.com; 8000 SR 31, Punta Gorda; adult/child $18/11; ☽ 9am-3pm Nov-May, morning only Jun-Oct).

For American bistro food try the cute **McGregor Cafe** (☎ 239-936-1771; 4305 McGregor Blvd; lunch $8-12, dinner $15-25; ☽ 11am-3pm & 5-9pm Tue-Fri, from 8am Sat, 8am-3pm Sun), in a converted home with a shady patio under a huge live oak. Impress your date (or Mom, or client) with the regional specialties at the lovely **Veranda** (☎ 239-332-2065; 2122 Second St, Fort Myers; mains $20-33; ☽ 11am-4pm & 5:30-10pm Mon-Fri, 5:30-10pm Sat) located in a turn-of-the-century residence in downtown Fort Myers.

Getting There & Around
Regional, national and international flights service **Southwest Florida International Airport** (☎ 239-768-1000; http://flylcpa.com). **Greyhound** (☎ 239-334-1011; 2250 Peck St) has regular services.

Lee Tran's (☎ 239-533-8726; www.rideleetran.com) bus 50 leaves downtown at Daniels Rd and Hwy 41 for Fort Myers Beach (adult/child $1/50¢) every hour at 20 minutes past the hour.

FORT MYERS BEACH
Fifteen miles south of Fort Myers – and at least a half-hour drive – Fort Myers Beach is a cute if touristy party town on Estero Island. Look for blue, white and yellow flags marking beach access between houses. This is a good base from which to explore the nearby **Lovers Key State Recreation Area** (☎ 239-463-4588; pedestrian & cyclist $1, car $3-5; ☽ 8am-dusk), a bird and wildlife haven with gorgeous beaches where you can rent bikes, canoes and kayaks. Depending on

the season, you can also find **dolphin tours** or **sunset eco-tours** (☎ 239-314-0110; adult/child $25/15); call for schedules.

Catch a ferry from Fort Myers Beach for a day trip to **Key West** (p514) via the **Key West Express** (☎ 888-539-2628; www.keywestshuttle.com; 2200 Main St; adult/child $144/66, discounts for advance purchase).

The friendly, family-owned **Lighthouse Island Resort Inn & Suites** (☎ 239-463-9392; www.light houseislandresort.com; 1051 5th St; r from $99; [P] [☀] [□]) has a Caribbean feel with breezy rooms and frozen cocktails served nightly at the on-site **Tiki Bar & Grill** (mains $8-14; ☽ 8am-2am). **Silver Sands Villas** (☎ 239-463-6554; www.silversands-villas.com; 1207 Estero Blvd, Fort Myers Beach; r $89-199; [P] [☀] [□]) is a sunny cluster of beach cottages painted with fresh, bright tropical colors. Snag some terrific fresh seafood and waterfront views at **Snug Harbor** (☎ 239-463-4343; San Carlos Blvd, Fort Myers Beach; mains $8-24; ☽ 4-9pm Tue-Fri, 11:30am-9pm Sat & Sun).

SANIBEL & CAPTIVA ISLANDS
Shaped like a fish hook trying to lure Fort Myers, these two slivers of barrier island lie just across a 2-mile causeway (toll $6). Remarkably undeveloped and free from condofever, they're as lush and green as Hawaii. Even the houses are hidden by foliage, giving the islands a wild, tropical feel.

The islands are famed for shell collecting. Stop just over the causeway at the extremely helpful **chamber of commerce visitor center** (☎ 239-472-1080; www.sanibel-captiva.org; 1159 Causeway Rd) for information about the islands – including where and at what time the shells will show themselves that day (an hour before or after low tide). The **Bailey-Matthews Shell Museum** (☎ 239-395-2233; www .shellmuseum.org; 3075 Sanibel-Captiva Rd; adult/child $7/4; ☽ 10am-5pm) helps you identify your shell finds, and is a nice place to wait out an afternoon shower.

Bike trails run all over the island, and you can rent bikes and more at **Finnimore's Bike & Beach Rentals** (☎ 239-472-5577; around back at 2353 Periwinkle Way, Sanibel; ☽ 9am-5pm). This is an especially good way to see the bird-filled 6300-acre **JN 'Ding' Darling National Wildlife Refuge** (☎ 239-472-1100; www.fws.gov/dingdarling; 1 Wildlife Dr, Sanibel; ☽ 8am-4pm), which has a marvelous 5-mile **wildlife drive** (car $5, pedestrian & cyclist $1; ☽ 7:30am-5:30pm Sat-Thu). You can also experience the refuge with a guided tram, kayak

FLORIDA

or canoe tour through **Tarpon Bay Explorers** (☎ 239-472-8900; www.tarponbayexplorers.com; 900 Tarpon Bay Rd, Sanibel); call ahead for schedules.

Lodging on the islands is more expensive than on the mainland, but **Kona Kai Motel & Cottages** (☎ 239-472-1001, 800-820-2385; 1539 Periwinkle Way, Sanibel; r $99-169; P ✕ ☎) is a great value, with lush gardens and clean, cute rooms. Other unique places to stay on Sanibel include the hidden-away **Gulf Breeze Cottages** (☎ 239-472-1626; www.gbreeze.com; 1081 Shell Basket Lane, Sanibel; r $130-230, cottages $165-360; P ✕); and the lovely beachfront **Casa Ybel** (☎ 239-472-3145; www.casaybelresort.com; 2255 West Gulf Dr, Sanibel; r from $279; P ✕ ☎), which has casually elegant suites and its own bird sanctuary.

Take a break at **Island Cow** (☎ 239-472-5555; 2163 Periwinkle Way, Sanibel; mains $7-14; ☺ 7am-10pm), a colorful island café, with killer paella and tons of other options, from po'boys to steaks. Or fancy it up at **Dolce Vita** (☎ 239-472-5555; 1244 Periwinkle Way, Sanibel; mains $16-29; ☺ 5:30-10:30pm), with an eclectic international menu including wild boar saddle and Bahamian lobster tail.

On Captiva, the historic **'Tween Waters Inn Beach Resort** (☎ 239-472-5161; www.tween-waters .com; 15951 Captiva Dr, Captiva; r $175-650; P ✕ ☎) has a vast choice of room and cottage styles, plus tennis courts, spa, full-service marina and three restaurants. Don't miss the spectacularly kitsch **Bubble Room** (☎ 239-472-5558; 15001 Captiva Dr, Captiva; lunch $8-10, dinner $21-25; ☺ 11:30am-3pm & 4:30-9pm), with Christmas collectibles and memorabilia from the 1930s and '40s crammed into every corner. It's known for its desserts, but dinner diners must order an main.

CENTRAL FLORIDA

With such beautiful sand and water, it's no surprise that people gravitate to the coasts, leaving much of the middle part of the state a hollow, under-populated core. The exception is Orlando, the beating heart of tourism and largest inland city. Tourists from around the world make the pilgrimage here, drawn to the oodles of family-lovin' theme parks. Central Florida also has a slew of gorgeous natural springs bubbling up from deep beneath the earth, offering yet another reason

to leave behind the beaches for a couple of days inland.

ORLANDO

One of the top family destinations in the world, Orlando seems destined to always be mentioned in the same breath as theme parks. In fact, the parks seem to have permeated every corner, reaching their glossy, over-produced tentacles to restaurants and hotels across the city. Where are the dive bars? The hole-in-the-wall restaurants? Why are the waiters costumed and why does there always have to be something fiberglass hanging overhead? It's all Walt Disney's fault. The Magic Kingdom was so successful that it spawned a whole empire and attracted a slew of like-minded attractions; nowadays you can go to a different theme park every day of the week.

Of course there are other things to do in Orlando. Many people are surprised to find that there's a stylish downtown district, a thriving nightlife scene, and even some residents who don't dress up like pirates during the day.

Orientation & Information

So many attractions compete for tourist dollars that it's easy to get overwhelmed. Good multilingual guides and maps are available from the **visitor bureau** (☎ 407-363-5872, 800-551-0181; www.orlandoinfo.com; 8723 International Dr; ☺ 8am-7pm); also check **Go2Orlando** (www.go2orlando.com) and **Visit Orlando** (www.visitorlandoonline.com). If you're spending some time checking out the area, pick up a copy of Lonely Planet's *Orlando & Central Florida* guide.

I-4 is the main north–south connector, though it's confusingly labeled east–west. To go north, take I-4 east (toward Daytona); to go south, get on I-4 west (toward Tampa). The main east–west roads are Hwy 50 and Hwy 528 (the Bee Line Expressway, a toll road), which connect Orlando to the Space Coast. The Bee Line Expressway accesses Orlando International Airport.

Sights & Activities

DOWNTOWN ORLANDO

A good place to get 'It's a Small World' out of your head is in and around downtown's **Loch Haven Park**, a cluster of culture with nary a theme in sight. The **Orlando Museum of Art** (☎ 407-896-4231; www.omart.org; 2416 N Mills Ave; adult/child 6-18 $8/5; ☺ 10am-4pm Tue-Fri, from noon Sat & Sun) spotlights American and African art as well as unique traveling exhibits; and the **Mennello Museum of American Folk Art** (☎ 407-246-4278; www .mennellomuseum.org; 900 E Princeton St; adult/child $4/ free; ⏰ 10:30am-4:30pm Tue-Sat, to noon Sun) features fascinating traveling folk-art exhibitions. The family-friendly **Orlando Science Center & John Young Planetarium** (☎ 407-514-2000; www.osc.org; 777 E Princeton St; adult/child 3-11 $15/10; ⏰ 10am-6pm Sun-Thu, to 9pm Fri & Sat) has planetarium viewings every Friday and Saturday night. And one mile east of Loch Haven Park is the 50-acre **Harry P Leu Gardens** (☎ 407-246-2620; www.leugardens .org; 1920 N Forest Ave; adult/child 6-18 $5/1; ⏰ 9am-5pm), a tranquil escape from all the gloss.

Pre-mouse Orlando is featured at the **Orange County Regional History Center** (☎ 407-836-8500; www.thehistorycenter.org; 65 E Central Blvd; adult/child 3-12 $7/3.50; ⏰ 10am-5pm Mon-Sat, noon-5pm Sun) in a series of permanent and traveling exhibits showcasing the region.

INTERNATIONAL DRIVE

There are so many themed attractions, themed restaurants and themed hotels surrounding **International Drive** (I-Dr) that it's a quasi–theme park itself (with a theme of, well, themes). The stand-out attraction is **Titanic: Ship of Dreams** (☎ 407-248-1166; www.titan icshipofdreams.com; 8445 International Dr at the Mercado; adult/child 6-11 $20/13; ⏰ 10am-8pm), where you take on the character of a real-life Titanic passenger for a poignant tour of replicas and relics.

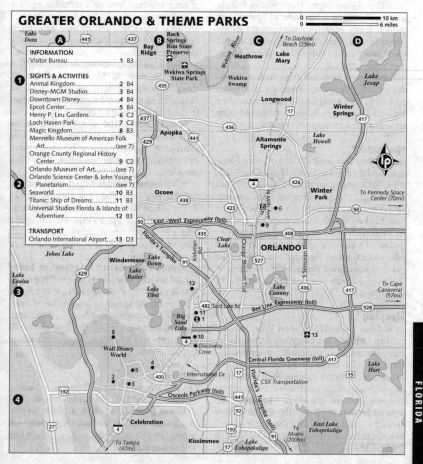

GREATER ORLANDO & THEME PARKS

0 — 10 km
0 — 6 miles

INFORMATION
Visitor Bureau.....................1 B3

SIGHTS & ACTIVITIES
Animal Kingdom.....................2 B4
Disney-MGM Studios.....................3 B4
Downtown Disney.....................4 B4
Epcot Center.....................5 B4
Henry P. Leu Gardens.....................6 C2
Loch Haven Park.....................7 C2
Magic Kingdom.....................8 B3
Mennello Museum of American Folk Art.....................(see 7)
Orange County Regional History Center.....................9 C2
Orlando Museum of Art.....................(see 7)
Orlando Science Center & John Young Planetarium.....................(see 7)
Seaworld.....................10 B3
Titanic: Ship of Dreams.....................11 B3
Universal Studios Florida & Islands of Adventure.....................12 B3

TRANSPORT
Orlando International Airport.....13 D3

FLORIDA

UNIVERSAL ORLANDO RESORT

Universal is giving Disney a run for its money with this mega-complex that features two theme parks, three hotels and an entertainment district. But where Disney is all happy and magical, Universal's shtick is 'action, thrills and excitement.'

Universal Studios Florida (☎ 407-363-8000; www.universalorlando.com; 1000 Universal Studios Plaza; adult/child 3-9 $67/56; ☺ from 9am, closing times vary; P) has a Hollywood backlot feel and is, in fact, a working studio as well as theme park with celluloid-inspired rides. Don't miss the *Back to the Future* time-travel simulator, or the fun, new 4-D *Shrek* show. Universal's **Islands of Adventure** (single-day adult/child 3-9 $67/56) is tops with coaster-lovers, and is divided into five 'islands': Marvel Super Hero Island, featuring The Amazing Adventures of Spider Man (which really is pretty amazing); the dino-happy Jurassic Park; the ersatz-mystical Lost Continent; and the kid-friendly Toon Lagoon and Seuss Landing.

Look online for ticket deals, such as multi-day park-hopper passes. Parking at the theme parks is $11. To avoid lengthy ride queues, get a Universal Express pass, which assigns a return time and has a 15 minutes or less wait.

SEAWORLD

A not-altogether-logical blend of marine animals and thrill rides, **SeaWorld** (☎ 407-351-3600, 800-327-2424; www.seaworld.com; 7007 SeaWorld Orlando Dr; adult/child 3-9 $65/54 ☺ from 9am, closing times vary; P) is home to both Shamu the killer whale and Kraken the floorless coaster. Journey to Atlantis tries to bring both concepts together: it's an oceanic water-coaster with a 60ft vertical drop. Feedings and shows take place at scheduled times, so plan out your day to make sure you don't miss out. Parking costs $10.

Sleeping

In addition to the Walt Disney World resorts (p536), Orlando has countless accommodation options. Most are clustered around International Dr, US 192 in Kissimmee and I-4. Most hotels around I-Dr are chains, but usually with amenities (and, of course, themes) you wouldn't find elsewhere. The **Central Reservation Service** (☎ 800-548-3311) operates a free service in conjunction with the visitor bureau to assist in making hotel reservations. **Universal Studios** (☎ 888-273-1311; r $209-439) has three ho-

tels, and guests zoom straight to the front of the line for rides.

Magic Castle Inn & Suites (☎ 407-396-2212, 800-446-5669; www.magicorlando.com; 5055 W Hwy 192, Kissimmee; r $37-45; P ☻ ☐) Garish exterior and serviceable rooms, but, what the heck: it's cheap, and just 3.5 miles from Walt Disney World.

Sheraton Safari Hotel (☎ 407-239-0444, 888-354-1356; www.sheratonsafari.com; 12205 Apopka Vineland Rd; r $99-139; P ☻ ☐) Families can find a happy compromise at this well-located, safari-themed hotel that's fun for kids but not annoying for adults. Lavish pool area includes a 79ft python waterslide.

Courtyard at Lake Lucerne (☎ 407-648-5188, 800-444-5289; www.orlandohistoricinn.com; 211 N Lucerne Circle E; r $99-225; P ☐) Not by Marriott, this complex of four adjacent inns in a secluded enclave near downtown is a real find. Choices include art-deco suites in a refurbished apartment building and grand Victorian rooms in the Dr Phillips House.

EO Inn & Spa (☎ 407-481-8485; www.eoinn.com; 227 N Eola Dr; r $139-229; P ☐) Sleek and understated, this downtown boutique inn overlooks Lake Eola, with neutral-toned rooms that are elegant in their simplicity. It's mostly child-free.

Peabody Orlando Hotel (☎ 407-352-4000; www.peabodyorlando.com; 9801 I-Dr; r $150-500; P ☻) More shiny-modern than its Memphis counterpart, but with the same main attraction: daily duck parades at 11am and 5pm.

Hyatt Regency Orlando Airport Hotel (☎ 407-825-1234; 9300 Airport Blvd; r from $189; P ☻ ☐) Right inside the main terminal, this hotel has balconies facing a skylit atrium where you can watch the hubbub below, with easy access to airport shopping, dining and people-watching.

Gaylord Palms Resort & Convention Center (☎ 407-586-2000; www.gaylordpalms.com; 6000 W Osceola Parkway; r $199-279; P ☻ ☐) Be sure to request a room on the inside to get a balcony overlooking the enormous, 4.5-acre atrium with themed areas depicting the Everglades, St Augustine and Key West. Amenities include live alligators.

Eating

On and around I-Dr you'll find an explosion of chains; Sand Lake Rd has upscale dining.

Rincon Criollo Cafe (☎ 407-872-1128; 331 N Orange Ave; dishes $5-7; ☺ 7am-3pm) This downtown lunch favorite has outstanding Cuban and vegetarian fare.

Race Rock Restaurant (☎ 407-248-9876; 8186 I-Dr; mains $7-15; ☼ 11:30am-11:30pm) This is a fun option for kids and racing enthusiasts. Chow down on burgers and steaks beneath ceiling-suspended NASCARs.

Dexter's (☎ 407-648-2777; 808 Washington St; mains $8-25; ☼ 11am-10pm Mon-Thu, till 11pm Fri & Sat, 10am-10pm Sun) If you're craving low-key, head for this neighborhood café on the edge of downtown.

Seasons 52 (☎ 407-354-5212; 7700 Sand Lake Rd; mains $11-27; ☼ 11:30am-2:30pm & 5-10pm Mon-Fri, till 11pm Sat & Sun) For a little *under*-indulgence, try this fresh-food grill that eschews butter, espouses low-cal and still pulls off a tasty meal.

Le Coq au Vin (☎ 407-851-6980; 4800 S Orange Ave; mains $13-29; ☼ 5:30-10pm Tue-Sat, 5-9pm Sun) Known for its namesake, this immensely popular restaurant serves superb but hard-to-pronounce French specialties.

Combine dinner with a show and you usually end up with some lesser version of both; however, a lot of people find the combination fun enough they don't mind. (Hint: you probably already have a pretty good idea if you're a dinner show type of person or not.) Good choices include the rollicking **Pirate's Dinner Adventure** (☎ 407-248-0590, 800-866-2469; www.piratesdinneradventure.com; 6400 Carrier Dr; adult/child $56/36) and the equestrian delight **Arabian Nights** (☎ 407-239-9223, 800-553-6116; www .arabian-nights.com; 6225 W Hwy 192; adult/child $53/29).

Drinking & Entertainment

The **Orlando Weekly** (www.orlandoweekly.com) is the best source for entertainment listings, but there's plenty to do downtown, which has a happening bar district around Orange Ave between Church St and Jefferson St. Find cheap drinks and a rockin' jukebox at the delightfully divey **Bar BQ Bar** (☎ 407-648-5441; 64 N Orange Ave). Check out great live music at **Social** (☎ 407-246-1419; 54 N Orange Ave; cover varies). Or unwind upstairs at **Latitudes** (☎ 407-649-4270; 35 W Church St) in a pleasant, open-air setting. Whatever else you're looking for could be found at one of the eight bars constituting **Wall St Plaza** (☎ 407-420-1515; www.wallstplaza.net; 25 Wall St) or the six gay bars that make up **Parliament House** (☎ 407-425-7571; www.parliamenthouse .com; 410 N Orange Blossom Trail; cover varies).

Universal Studio's **CityWalk** (☎ 407-363-8000; www.citywalkorlando.com; ☼ 11am-2am) has a concentration of movies, restaurants and clubs, and a $12 CityWalk Party Pass gives you access to most clubs. Venues include **CityJazz** (☎ 407-224-2189; cover $7) and **Hard Rock Live Orlando** (☎ 407-351-5483; www.hardrocklive.com; tickets from $20; ☼ box office 10am-9pm).

Getting There & Around

Orlando International Airport (☎ 407-825-2001) has buses to major tourist areas. Taxis – try **Yellow Cab** (☎ 407-422-5151) – will get you to I-Dr and the parks for about $30; **Meares Transportation** (☎ 407-423-5566) provides shuttles for around $20. **Greyhound** (☎ 407-292-3424; 555 N John Young Parkway) serves numerous cities. **Amtrak** (☎ 407-843-7611; 1400 Sligh Blvd) offers daily trains south to Miami ($34) and north to New York City ($187).

Orlando's bus network is operated by **Lynx** (☎ 407-841-5969; www.golynx.com; single rides/day pass $1.50/3.50). **I-Ride Trolley** (☎ 866-243-7483; www.iride trolley.com; adult/senior/child under 12 $1/25¢/free, exact change required; ☼ 8am-10:30pm) buses run along International Dr.

WALT DISNEY WORLD

At over 20,000 acres, Walt Disney World (WDW) is not just the Happiest Place on Earth, but the largest theme park resort in the world. It includes four parks, two water parks, six golf courses, a couple dozen hotels, numerous restaurants and even a mega-Disney entertainment district – proving that it's not such a small world, after all. At times it feels ridiculously crowded and corporate, but if you have kids in tow, you won't be able to inoculate yourself against their highly infectious enthusiasm. Even without kids, anyone who isn't scared off from coming by the thought of life-sized costumed characters will likely end up drunk on Disney and clapping their hands because they do believe in fairies – they *do*! – and wandering home with bags full of souvenirs wondering what overtook them.

Orientation & Information

Walt Disney World (☎ 407-934-7639; www.waltdisney world.com; admission adult/child per day from $67/56, Park Hopper $45) is 20 miles southwest of downtown Orlando and 4 miles northwest of Kissimmee.

To avoid lines buy your tickets in advance online, by phone or from a Disney store; tickets are cheaper per day the longer you stay. Add-on options such as the Park Hopper, which allows you to hop between all

FLORIDA

four WDW parks on any given day, are also cheaper as you go.

Disney's *Guidebook for Guests with Disabilities* (available at Guest Services, just inside each park's ticket turnstiles) has maps and ride-by-ride guides including Braille and audio options; all transportation here is wheelchair-accessible.

Crowds can sap the magic right out of the Magic Kingdom. Busy public holidays aside (see p1121), WDW is least crowded in January, February, mid-September through October and early December. During the summer, weekends are the least crowded days; the rest of the year it's the other way round. Late fall tends to have the best weather, since frequent downpours dampen the hot, humid months of June, July and August. **Gay Day** at WDW was so popular that it grew into the citywide **Gay Days** (www.gaydays.com), but the first Saturday in June is still the day to 'wear red and be seen' at the WDW resort.

Sights & Activities
MAGIC KINGDOM
It's the centerpiece of WDW and home of **Cinderella's Castle**. **Pirates of the Caribbean** has gotten some snazzed-up special effects with a dash of Johnny Depp, and **Haunted Mansion** and **Space Mountain** are still going strong. **Mickey's Toontown Fair** and **Fantasyland** are a hit with smaller kids, but anyone over 12 will want to keep walking. Fireworks displays light up the sky nightly and many nights end with a parade.

DISNEY-MGM STUDIOS
This park caters to the postfairytale crowd and is also a working studio. Hands-down the most exciting rides are the spooky and unpredictable hotel elevator in the **Twilight Zone Tower of Terror**, and the **Rock 'n' Roller Coaster**, where your stretch limo races through the streets of LA after dark. And don't miss the **Indiana Jones Epic Stunt Spectacular!**, a 35-minute show that looks a lot like the movie.

EPCOT CENTER
An acronym for 'Experimental Prototype Community of Tomorrow,' Epcot was Disney's vision of a high-tech city. It's divided into two halves: the sort-of-modern **Future World**, with corporate-sponsored journeys through not-very-cutting-edge technology,

and the not-at-all futuristic **World Showcase**, which gives you an interesting toe-dip into the culture of 11 different countries. They were originally intended to be two separate parks, which explains a lot. Epcot isn't the kids' paradise the Magic Kingdom is, but there are plenty of activities for the inquisitive tot. The new **Soarin'** ride is a winner, and **Mission: SPACE** is good for getting the adrenaline pumping after one too many educational exhibits.

ANIMAL KINGDOM
Light on attractions, bigger on animals, this park lets you see wild things in re-created 'natural' environments through assorted experiences, including the 110-acre **Kilimanjaro Safari** (best early in the day). The iconic **Tree of Life** houses the fun and interactive **It's Tough to Be a Bug!** show, and the new (and much-needed) **Expedition Everest** plummets you through an old mountain railway.

Sleeping
There are more than two dozen exceedingly family-friendly places to stay on Disney property, all offering free transportation to the parks and extended park hours. A **central reservation line** (☎ 407-934-7639) handles bookings and information.

Four properties make up Disney's 'value' segment, offering thousands of basic rooms. Beyond the themes, they're interchangeable, with over-the-top exteriors and wall-to-wall children common to all. Three **All-Star Resorts** (r $82-141; P 🛋) let you take your pick between movie, music and sports themes; and the **Pop Century Resort** (r $82-141; P 🛋) tackles pop culture by the decade, with bowling pins and Mr Potato Head living side by side.

In the 'moderate' segment, the **Port Orleans Resort** (r $145-199; P 🛋) is divided into the Southern-style Riverside Resort and the French Quarter Resort, which pulls off a pretty good facsimile of New Orleans architecture.

'Deluxe' resorts include the Yosemite-style **Wilderness Lodge** (r $215-420; P 🛋), with rustic architecture, erupting geysers, a lakelike swimming area and bunk beds for the kids. And the theme is Victorian opulence at the **Grand Floridian Resort & Spa** (r $375-720; P 🛋), a ringer for California's turn-of-the-century Hotel del Coronado with fast delivery to all parks via the Disney Monorail.

Eating

Dining with Mickey and friends is insanely popular (and only available to park guests). If your heart is set on a particular restaurant, make reservations two to six months out with **central reservations** (☎ 407-939-3463).

In the Magic Kingdom, the old-timey **Plaza Restaurant** (Main St; mains under $11) is a great option for salads, sandwiches and banana splits. **Crystal Palace** (Main St; adult $19-28, child $11-13) serves lavish buffet breakfast, lunch and dinner – tops in both quality and quantity – with special appearances from Winnie the Pooh and pals.

At Disney-MGM Studios, nostalgia rules at the **Sci-Fi Dine-In Theater** (across from Star Tours; mains $11-20, kids meals $7.50), where you dine in Cadillacs while watching B-movies (and traffic is bumper to bumper).

Each pavilion in Epcot's World Showcase has a sit-down restaurant that will set you back $14 to $30 per main, but it's more fun to snack your way around the world with the considerably cheaper counter service options. If you wish to stop and dine properly, two good choices are Morocco's **Restaurant Marrakesh** (meals $17-27, kids $7) for couscous and kebabs, and Canada's **Le Cellier** (lunch $8-22, dinner $16-37), known for its steaks. For a quick coffee, pastry or quiche, head to France's Boulangerie Patisserie.

At the entrance to Animal Kingdom, **Rain Forest Cafe** (mains $9-40, kids $6-8) is almost another park ride. Waterfalls, volcanoes, gorillas – all it needs is a tram. Although you can dine fine, there are plenty of options under $15, even at dinner.

Drinking & Entertainment

Disney wouldn't dream of leaving you with non-Disney downtime, so it built Downtown Disney as a slightly overwhelming evening entertainment complex. **Pleasure Island** (☎ 407-934-7781; admission $21) has seven dance and comedy clubs where you can Diz out till the wee hours. **Cirque du Soleil** (☎ 407-939-7600; www.cirque dusoleil.com; adult $63-112, child 3-9 $50-90; ☺ 6pm & 9pm Tue-Sat) is one of the best shows in town, and **House of Blues** (☎ 407-934-2583; www.hob.com; cover varies) hosts a Sunday gospel brunch and live music acts. Catch a movie at the 24-screen **AMC Pleasure Island** (☎ 407-298-4488) cinema or enjoy five floors of virtual reality and arcade games at **DisneyQuest Indoor Interactive Theme Park** (adult/child 3-9 $35/29; ☺ 11:30am-11pm Sun-Thu, to midnight Fri & Sat).

Getting There & Around

Most hotels in Kissimmee and Orlando – and all Disney properties – offer free transportation to WDW. Disney-owned resorts also offer free transportation from the airport.

If you're not staying in a Disney resort, you can drive to one of the four parks via I-4, which is well marked. Parking is $10 in the Disney lots, and the Magic Kingdom lot is huge; unless you get there early, you'll want to catch a tram just to get to the entrance.

Within WDW, a complex network of monorails, boats and buses can get you anywhere you want to go, including resorts and Downtown Disney. Pick up a copy of the *Walt Disney World Transportation Guide/Map* at Guest Relations just inside each park's ticket turnstiles or at your resort to understand your options.

AROUND CENTRAL FLORIDA

Hundreds of natural springs gush billions of gallons of crystal-clear water every day throughout the state, offering a plethora of outdoor pursuits. The water at **Salt Springs Recreation Area** (☎ 352-685-2048; 14152 SR 19, Salt Springs; admission $4.25, campsites/RV sites $17/24; ☺ 8am-dusk) in the Ocala National Forest is rumored to have curative powers; either way, the swimming is sublime and there are fantastic opportunities for hiking, biking, canoeing, kayaking and camping. Also near Ocala, **Silver Springs** (☎ 352-236-2121, 800-234-7458; www.silversprings.com; 5656 E Silver Springs Blvd, Silver Springs; adult/child under 10 $34/25; ☺ 10am-5pm; P) has drawn people since the late 1800s for its idyllic glass-bottom boat rides. Parking costs $24.

At **Ichetucknee Springs State Park** (☎ 386-497-2511; 12087 SW US Hwy 27, Fort White; car $5, tubing $5; ☺ 8am-dusk), you can lie back on an inner tube or raft and gently float downstream on the crystal-clear waters through unspoiled wilderness as otters swim right up beside you. Farmers rent tubes for about $5 along approach roads.

In Volusia County, **De Leon Springs State Recreation Area** (☎ 386-985-4212; 601 Ponce DeLeon Blvd, DeLeon Springs; pedestrian & cyclist $1, car $5; ☺ 8am-dusk) has a huge swimming area, and you can also explore the springs by canoe or kayak (per hour $10, per day $28 from concessions). The springs flow into the Lake Woodruff National Wildlife Refuge, with 18,000 acres of lakes, creeks and marshes.

FLORIDA PANHANDLE

The beaches up here are some of the state's best, with translucent aquamarine seas lapping against white sugar-sand formed by quartz crystal from the Appalachians. Known as the Emerald Coast, the area from Pensacola to Panama City has also earned the nickname 'Redneck Riviera' for its proximity to the southern states whose residents flock here. There is indeed a Southern feel to the area that doesn't quite trickle down to the rest of Florida. Hwy 10 – the clothesline from which the whole state is hung – is lined with wooded forest for a scenic welcome to the Sunshine State.

TALLAHASSEE

Given how little resemblance it bears to the rest of the state, Tallahassee seems like an unlikely spot for the state capital. More Southern than Floridian, more forest than beach, it's a *Gone With the Wind*–style montage of moss-draped oaks, rolling hills and sprawling plantations.

It was chosen as the capital in 1824, not so much for its representative qualities, but because, well, they just couldn't pick between St Augustine and Pensacola, the two largest cities at the time. In a King Solomon–like move, they cut the baby in half, as it were, and put the capital approximately midway between the two. Still, it's a lovely place to visit (that could save you a trip to Georgia!) and plays the gracious Southern host to anyone who drops by for a visit. Information and walking-tour maps are available from the **visitor center** (☎ 850-413-9200, 800-628-2866; www.seetallahassee.com; 106 E Jefferson St; ☯ 8am-5pm Mon-Fri, 9am-1pm Sat).

Sights & Activities

To learn about the people and events that shaped Florida, head to the museum in the **Florida Historic Capitol** (☎ 850-487-1902; 400 S Monroe St; admission free; ☯ 9am-4:30pm Mon-Fri, 10am-4:30pm Sat, noon-4:30pm Sun & holidays), a grand, columned building with an art-glass dome and candy-striped awnings. Hovering behind it with considerably less architectural charm is the current **Florida State Capitol** (New Capitol; ☎ 850-488-6167; cnr Pensacola & Duval Sts), a 22-story concrete slab where legislature meets for 60 days a year. The top floor has an observation deck and art gallery, and the ground floor has visitor information for the whole state.

The site of a 17th-century Spanish and Apalachee Indian mission, **Mission San Luis** (☎ 850-487-3711; 2020 W Mission Rd; admission free; ☯ 10am-4pm Tue-Sun) has several convincingly re-created buildings, including the impressive Council House, for a look at what the area must have been like 300 years ago.

One of the country's largest collections of African and African American artifacts and art is at the **Black Archives Research Center & Museum** (☎ 850-599-3020; Carnegie Library, cnr Martin Luther King Jr Blvd & Gamble St; admission free; ☯ 9am-5pm Mon-Fri).

A treat for runners, skaters and cyclists, **Tallahassee–St Marks Historic Railroad State Trail** (☎ 877-822-5208; admission free; ☯ 8am-dusk year-round) starts 100 yards south of the intersection of Capital Circle (Hwy 319) and Woodville Hwy (Hwy 363), and heads south for 16 flat, paved miles to the town of St Marks.

Sleeping & Eating

Accommodation rates can spike during football-game weekends and legislative sessions. Chains are clumped at exits along I-10 and along Monroe St between I-10 and downtown.

Doubletree Hotel (☎ 850-224-5000; 101 S Adams St; r $99-259; P ☙ ⚎) This downtown hotel has homogenously nice rooms and is wired for business, making it a good base for the business traveler.

Inn at Park Avenue (☎ 850-222-4024; 323 E Park Ave; r $139-179; P ✕) Half a mile from the Capitol, this historic inn built in 1838 has five homey guest rooms, hardwood floors and fireplaces galore.

Governors Inn (☎ 850-681-6855; www.thegovinn.com; 209 S Adams St; r 159-219, ste $179-309; P) In a stellar downtown location, this warm, inviting inn has two-level loft suites with open fireplace and balconies.

Po' Boys Creole Café (☎ 850-224-5400; 224 E College Ave; mains $7-15; ☯ 11am-9pm Mon & Tue, till 10pm Wed, till 11pm Thu & Fri, 10am-9pm Sat & Sun) Students and legislators alike heartily agree on this casual New Orleans–style place with an outdoor bar.

Andrew's Capital Grill & Bar (☎ 850-222-3444; 228 S Adams St; mains $8-15; ☯ 11:30am-10pm Mon-Thu, to 11pm Fri & Sat, 11am-2pm Sun) Politicians spill onto sidewalk tables for salads and burgers named after themselves, and you can fuel up at the lunch buffet for only $8.50.

Jasmine Café (☎ 850-681-6868; 109 E College Ave; mains $10-15; ⏲ 11:30am-10pm Mon-Thu, 11:30am-10:30pm Fri, noon-10:30pm Sat, noon-10pm Sun) Put a little East in your South at this cute little tucked-away sushi bar right in the heart of everything.

Andrew's 228 (☎ 850-222-3444; 228 S Adams St; mains $16-32; ⏲ 6-10pm Mon-Thu, till 11 Fri & Sat) The hottest tables in town are at this glamorous Tuscany-meets-New York place with martinis served in individual shakers.

Entertainment

Bradfordville Blues Club (☎ 850-906-0766; www .bradfordvilleblues.com; 7152 Moses Lane; tickets from $10; ⏲ call for schedule) Down the end of a dirt road lit by tiki torches, you'll find a bonfire raging under the live oaks at this hidden-away juke joint that hosts excellent national blues acts. It's off Bradfordville Rd.

Getting There & Around

The **Tallahassee Regional Airport** (☎ 850-891-7800, 800-610-1995) is about 5 miles southwest of downtown, off Hwy 263, and the **Greyhound station** (☎ 850-222-4249; 112 W Tennessee St; ⏲ 24hr) is right downtown. **Star Metro** (☎ 850-891-5200; http://talgov .com/starmetro) provides local bus service, with fares per adult/child $1.25/60¢. Rent bikes at **Great Bicycle Shop** (☎ 850-224-7461; 1909 Thomasville Rd; bikes per 24hr $30; ⏲ 10am-6pm Mon-Fri, 1-5pm Sat, noon-4pm Sun).

PANAMA CITY BEACH

There's no mistaking Panama City Beach for anything other than what it is: a beach town. Spring breakers and summer vacationers flock here for the beautiful white-sand beaches, and mile after mile of high-rise condos are cropping the view into vertical slivers. The main strip goes like this: condo, beach bar, motel, mini-golf, beach resort, seafood, condo, souvenir shop – you get the picture. Stop by the **visitor bureau** (☎ 850-233-5070, 800-722-3224; www

.thebeachloversbeach.com; 17001 Panama City Beach Parkway; ⏲ 8am-5pm) for more information.

A renowned wreck-diving site, there are dozens of natural, historic and artificial reefs. **Divers Den** (☎ 850-234-8717; 3120 Thomas Dr; ⏲ 9am-6pm Mon-Fri, 8am-6pm Sat, 8am-5pm Sun) has dives from $84 plus gear rental. Get inspiration at the **Museum of Man in the Sea** (☎ 850-235-4101; 17314 Panama City Beach Parkway; adult/child $5/2.50; ⏲ 10am-4pm) showcasing the history of diving.

St Andrews State Recreation Area (☎ 850-233-5140; 4607 State Park Lane; pedestrian or cyclist/vehicle $1/5) is graced with nature trails and swimming beaches (one of the best places to swim with children is the 4ft-deep water near the jetties area). Just offshore, **Shell Island** has fantastic snorkeling; a shuttle from St Andrews State Recreation Area departs every 30 minutes for the $20 round-trip including snorkeling gear.

Mini-golf is *big* in Panama City Beach. Nostalgic favorite **Goofy Golf** (☎ 850-234-6403; 12206 Front Beach Rd; per round $6.50; ⏲ 9am-10pm or later Mar-Sep) was built in 1959 – look for the supersize sphinx.

Sleeping & Eating

Summer is the high season for Panhandle beaches.

Flamingo (☎ 850-234-2232; www.flamingomotel.com; 15525 Front Beach Rd; r $39-189; P ☻) Most of the immaculate rooms at this family-run, very kid-friendly place on the beach have ocean views and kitchens.

Sandpiper Beacon Beach Resort (☎ 800-488-8828; www.sandpiperbeacon.com; 17403 Front Beach Rd; beachfront r $39-229; P ☻) Parents can chill at the tiki bar while kids enjoy waterslides, a lazy river and mini-golf.

Wisteria Inn (☎ 850-234-0557; wisteria-inn.com; 20404 Front Beach Rd; r $69-149; P ✗ ☻ ▢) More sophisticated than your average beach digs, the

DETOUR: WAKULLA SPRINGS

Just 15 miles south of Tallahassee is the world's deepest freshwater spring at **Edward Ball Wakulla Springs State Park** (☎ 850-224-5950; 550 Wakulla Park Drive; bike/car $1/4, boat tours per adult/child $6/4; ⏲ 8am-dusk). The springs flow from massive underwater caves that are an archeologist's dream, with fossilized bones including a mastodon that was discovered around 1850. These days you can swim in the icy springs or enjoy them from a glass-bottom boat. You can also take a boat tour of the wildlife-filled Wakulla River, which was used as a movie set for several *Tarzan* movies, as well as *The Creature from the Black Lagoon*. Overnighters can stay in the park at the **Wakulla Springs Lodge** (☎ 850-224-5950; r $85-105; P ✗), a grand Spanish-style lodge built in 1937 where an 11ft stuffed alligator named 'Old Joe' keeps an eye on things.

larger rooms are individually decorated and there are economical doubles in the back.

Mike's Diner (☎ 850-234-1942; 17554 Front Beach Rd; mains $4-12; ☺ 8am-3pm) Cheap beach fuel can be found at this friendly, accessible place with a little bit of everything.

Pineapple Willy's (☎ 850-235-0928; 9875 S Thomas Dr; mains $15-22; ☺ 11am-late) Ask for a table on the restaurant pier for breezy beachside dining. Famed for its signature drinks and its house special: Jack Daniels BBQ ribs.

Captain Anderson's Restaurant & Waterfront Market (☎ 850-234-2225; 5551 N Lagoon Dr; mains $14-36; ☺ from 4pm Mon-Fri, from 3:30pm Sat) Widely regarded as Panama City Beach's top restaurant, this behemoth packs them in. Dine early and you might get to watch the day's catch being unloaded at the adjoining marina.

Drinking & Entertainment

Billing itself as the 'last local beach club,' **Schooners** (☎ 850-235-3555; www.schooners.com; 5121 Gulf Dr; ☺ 11am-late) is good for a low-key beer on the beach. The two mega nightclubs are **Spinnaker** (☎ 850-234-7892; www.spinnakerbeachclub.com; 8795 Thomas Dr; ☺ 10am-4am) and the enormous, multiroom **Club La Vela** (☎ 850-234-3866; www.lavela.com; 8813 Thomas Dr; ☺ 10am-4am). Covers apply – and vary – at both.

Getting There & Around

The **Panama City International Airport** (☎ 850-763-6751; www.pcairport.com; 3173 Airport Rd) is served by a handful of major and minor airlines.

The **Greyhound Station** (☎ 850-785-6111; 917 Harrison Ave) is in Panama City, and the limited **Bay Town Trolley** (☎ 850-769-0557; $1/50¢) will get you around town weekdays from 6am to 6pm.

PENSACOLA

Right next door to Alabama, Pensacola is Florida's gateway from the west, welcoming visitors driving in from the rest of the country. People are drawn not just by Pensacola's relative proximity, but by its white-sand beaches made of quartz washed down from the Appalachian Mountains. But in 2004 Hurricane Ivan smashed through the city, causing untold damage and destruction, with its barrier-island beaches taking the brunt of the impact. Clean-up and regeneration is a lengthy process, but things are fairly back to normal and the local highway system got a major overhaul as an added bonus. The **visitor bureau** (☎ 850-434-1234, 800-874-1234; www.visitpensa

cola.com; 1401 E Gregory St; ☺ 8am-5pm) has maps and free internet access.

The Spanish tried to colonize this stretch of the Panhandle in 1559, but the hurricane-plagued settlement was abandoned after two years, leaving St Augustine to claim the longest continuous European settlement in the country. Pensacola's harbor and geographical position have been key in its development as a military city, and the Naval Air Station remains an intrinsic part of the city's population.

Sights & Activities

History buffs will love **Historic Pensacola Village** (☎ 850-595-5985; www.historicpensacola.org; Zaragoza St btwn Tarragona St & Adams St; adult/child 4-16 $6/2.50; ☺ 10am-4pm Mon-Sat, tours at 11am, 1pm & 2:30pm), a self-contained enclave of historic homes and museums. Admission is good for one week and includes a guided tour and entrance to each building. The nearby **TT Wentworth Museum** (☎ 850-595-5990; 330 S Jefferson St; admission free; ☺ 10am-4pm Mon-Sat) has two floors of Florida history and one floor of Wentworth's collection of oddities, including his famous (and disgusting) petrified cat.

The Pensacola Naval Air Station (NAS) is home to both the **National Museum of Naval Aviation** (☎ 850-452-3604, 800-327-5002; www.naval-air.org; 1750 Radford Blvd; admission free; ☺ 9am-5pm) and the elite **Blue Angels** squadron. You can watch the Blue Angels practice their death-defying air show at 8:30am most Tuesdays and Wednesdays through the summer and fall (check website).

To enjoy the area's lovely white sands, head to the easy-access Pensacola Beach or the neighboring **Gulf Islands National Seashore** (☎ 850-934-2600; www.nps.gov/guis; pedestrian or cyclist per 7 days $3, vehicle $8; ☺ dawn-dusk) – part of a 150-mile stretch of undeveloped beach. Hurricane Ivan ripped up a lot of road, but access has been restored to most areas. At time of research, roads to **Fort Pickens** and on **Santa Rosa Island** were still closed; check with the seashore's main **visitor center** (☎ 850-934-2600; 1801 Gulf Breeze Parkway; admission free; ☺ 9am-4:30pm), about 6 miles east of Gulf Breeze, for updates.

In 2006, a 910ft-long aircraft carrier was intentionally sunk off the coast of Pensacola to make the world's largest artificial reef. Now dubbed 'The Great Carrier Reef,' the **USS Oriskany** sits in the sand 210ft below the surface, with its flight deck at 137ft. **Viking Diving** (☎ 850-916-3483, 888-848-3483; 4612a Bellview

WHAT THE...?

Every April, locals gather around the Florida–Alabama state line on Perdido Key for the **Interstate Mullet Toss**. This probably bears some explaining. 'Interstate' refers not to an interstate, but the fact that it involves two different states. 'Mullet' refers not to a redneck hairdo, but to a type of fish. And 'Toss,' well that's pretty self-explanatory. Put them all together, and you've got contestants vying to see who can throw their dead fish furthest into Alabama. Organized by the **Flora-Bama Lounge & Package Store** (www.florabama.com), the mullet-toss has become a time-honored tradition, as well as a great excuse for a party.

Ave) and **Scuba Shop** (☎ 850-433-4319, 888-659-3483; 711 S Palafox St) can take you there.

Sleeping & Eating

Paradise Inn (☎ 850-932-2319, 800-301-5925; www.paradiseinn-pb.com; 21 Via de Luna; r $70-170; P 🕹) Bringing a boutique feel to a motel format – we'll call it 'motel nouveau' – this Pensacola Beach inn is walking distance to the beach.

Noble Manor (☎ 850-434-9544, 877-598-4634; www.noblemanor.com; 110 W Strong St; r $95-125; P ✕ 🕹 🖳) has the prettiest rooms in town, from the opulent Bacall room to the more modest Windsor.

New World Inn (☎ 850-432-4111; www.newworldlanding.com; 600 S Palafox St; r $119-149; P ✕) Good things come in weird packages, and this inn housed in a former box factory has surprisingly lovely rooms with luxe bedding and real carpeting (a beach-town luxury).

H&O (☎ 850-432-1991; 301 E Gonzalez St; dishes $2.50-11; 🕑 8:30am-5pm) Wait! Don't let the concrete-shack exterior scare you off from real-deal soul food: fried chicken or catfish with sides of candied yams, black-eyed peas or okra, finished with peach cobbler.

Jerry's Drive-In (☎ 850-433-9910; 2815 E Cervantes St; mains $6-13; 🕑 10am-10pm Mon-Fri, 7am-10pm Sat) No longer a drive-in or owned by Jerry, but this greasy spoon is always packed – possibly because you can hardly eat for less. Credit cards are not accepted.

Peg Leg Pete's Oyster Bar (☎ 850-932-4139; 1010 Fort. Pickens Rd; mains $8-19; 🕑 11am-10pm) Raw? Rockefeller? Casino? Get your oysters the way you like 'em at this popular beach hangout that also serves lunch, dinner and plenty of cold beer.

Jackson's Restaurant (☎ 850-469-9898; 400 S Palafox St; mains $28-36; 🕑 5:30-9:30pm Mon-Thu, till 10:30 Fri-Sat) Not your typical white-tablecloth restaurant; this one adds rustic touches and a stellar menu for dignified dining.

Drinking & Entertainment

Check out the *Pensacola News Journal's* Friday 'Weekender' section for entertainment listings. Downtown's **Olde Seville Square** (☎ 850-438-6505) hosts free summer concerts, and the best bars for live music are the all-ages punk bar **Sluggo's** (☎ 850-435-1541; 2403 W Cervantes St); and the tiny **Wisteria Tavern** (☎ 850-433-9222; 3808 N 12th Ave). Other good choices are **McGuire's Irish Pub** (☎ 850-433-6789; 600 E Gregory St) and gay dance club **Emerald City** (☎ 850-433-9491; 406 E Wright St).

Getting There & Around

Five miles northeast of downtown, **Pensacola Regional Airport** (☎ 850-436-5000; 2430 Airport Blvd; www.flypensacola.com) is served by major airlines.

The not-centrally-located **Greyhound station** (☎ 850-476-4800; 505 W Burgess Rd) is 9 miles north of downtown, but the **Amtrak station** (☎ 850-433-4966; 980 E Heinberg St) is just north of the visitor bureau.

Great Lakes

Here's how it's going to go down. You're planning your USA trip, you unfurl the map and gravitate immediately to the coasts. Mountains! Oceans! Metropolises! Movie stars! But the middle of the country – what's the middle ever good for? Middle management, middle child, middle of nowhere. It's nothing to strive for.

Fine. Be that way. You'll miss out on the rural–urban mash-up that plops Tibetan temples in the middle of corn fields and Janis Joplin's psychedelic Porsche near Amish women churning butter. This is surely the only region where you can sip a fresh-from-the-dairy-farm milkshake for lunch, then take part in a five-way in the city for dinner. Are you sure you want to pass it up?

Roll call for the Midwest's cities starts with soaring Chicago, which shoots up the country's mightiest skyline. Milwaukee keeps the beer-and-Harley flame burning, while Minneapolis shines a hipster beacon out over the cornfields. Detroit rocks, plain and simple.

The Great Lakes themselves are huge, like inland seas, offering beaches, islands, dunes, resort towns and lots of lighthouse-dotted scenery. Dairy farms and fruit orchards blanket the region, meaning fresh pie and ice cream await hungry road-trippers. Thirsty travelers can indulge in the Midwest's beers – the cities here have long been known for suds crafting, thanks to their German heritage, and several microbreweries maintain the tradition.

Most visitors come in summer when the weather is fine for hiking, biking, canoeing and kayaking in the local lakes and forests. Snowmobiling and cross-country skiing take over in the butt-freezing winter (as do eating and drinking in warm taverns). Whatever the season, you're guaranteed a true slice of America here in the heartland.

HIGHLIGHTS

- Absorbing the skyscrapers, museums, ethnic neighborhoods and foods of **Chicago** (p547).
- Kayaking through sea caves in the **Apostle Islands** (p622).
- Turning back the clock with a plow and buggy in Ohio's **Amish Country** (p591).
- Beach lounging, wine sipping and berry eating on **Michigan's Gold Coast** (p607).
- Soaking up the culture vibe in **Minneapolis** (p623).

HISTORY

The region's first residents included the Hopewell (around 200 BC) and Mississippi River mound builders (around AD 700). Both left behind mysterious piles of earth that were tombs for their leaders and possibly tributes to their deities. You can see remnants at Cahokia (p577) in Illinois and Mound City (p593) in Ohio.

French voyageurs (fur traders) arrived in the early 17th century and established missions and forts. The British turned up soon thereafter. The rivalry spilled over into the French and Indian Wars (Seven Years' War, 1754–61), after which Britain gained all land east of the Mississippi. Following the Revolutionary War, the Great Lakes area became the new USA's Northwest Territory, which soon was divided into states.

Settlers flocked in after the region developed its impressive canal and railroad network. But conflicts erupted between the newcomers and the Native Americans here, including the bloody 1832 Black Hawk War that forced indigenous people to move west of the Mississippi.

Industries sprang up and grew quickly, fueled by resources of coal and iron. The work available brought huge influxes of immigrants from Ireland (early and mid-19th century), Germany (mid- to late 19th century), Scandinavia (late 19th century) and southern and eastern Europe (early 20th century). For decades after the Civil War, a great number of African Americans also migrated to the region's urban centers from the South.

The area prospered during WWII and throughout the 1950s. Then came 20 years of social turmoil and economic stagnation. Manufacturing industries declined, walloping Rust Belt cities like Detroit and Cleveland with high unemployment and 'white flight' (ie white middle-class families who fled to the suburbs).

The 1980s and 90s brought urban revitalization. Growth in the service and high-tech sectors has resulted in a better economic balance. The area's population has increased again, notably with newcomers from Asia and Mexico.

LOCAL CULTURE

The Great Lakes region – aka the Midwest – is the USA's solid, sensible heartland. Folks here shrug at the brash glitz of the East Coast and flaky sex appeal of the West Coast, happy instead to be in the plain-speaking middle. It's no surprise that novelist Ernest Hemingway hailed from this part of the country, where words are seldom wasted.

Regional pride manifests at every turn in the road. It's evident in Wisconsin's freshly painted barns, the tidiness of family-owned motels in Michigan's Upper Peninsula, even in Rockford, Illinois' Sock Monkey Festival (p574).

If the Midwest had a mantra, it might be to work hard, go to church, and stick to the straight and narrow…unless there's a sports game happening, and then it's OK to slather on the body paint and dye your hair purple (or whatever team colors dictate). Baseball, football, basketball and ice hockey are all hugely popular, with the big cities sponsoring pro teams for each sport.

Music has always been a big part of local culture. Muddy Waters and Chess Records spawned the electric blues in Chicago. Motown Records started the soul sound in Detroit. Alt rock shakes both cities (think Wilco in Chicago, White Stripes in Detroit), and has come out of Minneapolis (the Replacements, Hüsker Dü) and Dayton, Ohio (Guided By Voices, the Breeders), as well.

The region is more diverse than outsiders might expect. Immigrants from Mexico, Africa, the Middle East and Asia have established communities throughout the Midwest, mostly in the cities, where they are making welcomed contributions, especially to local dining scenes.

LAND & CLIMATE

The Great Lakes possess 20% of the earth's freshwater and 95% of America's. The largest by volume is Lake Superior, followed by Lakes Michigan, Huron, Ontario and Erie – all four of which Lake Superior could contain easily.

The Ohio River and Mississippi River are the major riverways. Most of the region's larger cities lie along them or on the lakeshores.

Winters can last from late November well into April, with plenty of snow, icy winds and subfreezing temperatures (eg Chicago and Minneapolis each average about 20°F (-7°C) in January, the coldest month). By June the sun is out and temperatures start to rise, and in July and August it can be downright hot and sticky. Spring and autumn fit in around

GREAT LAKES

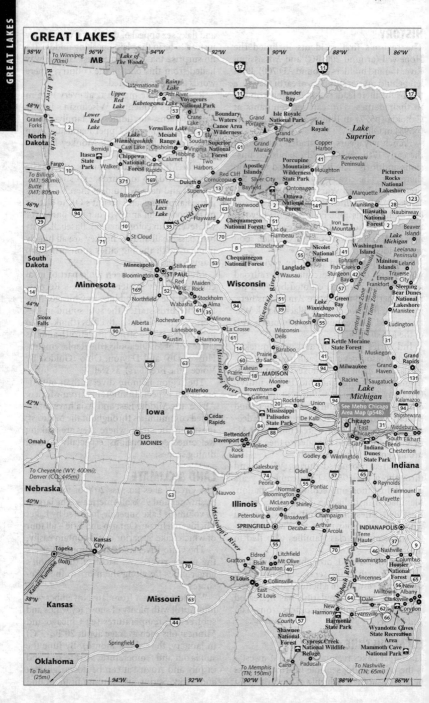

the edges, and are wonderful times to visit – particularly autumn, when leaves are at their peak of color.

PARKS & WILDLIFE

Hiking, kayaking and sand dune climbing are on tap at the region's national parks and lakeshores, including Isle Royale (p612), Sleeping Bear Dunes (p608) and Pictured Rocks (p612) in Michigan; the Apostle Islands (p622) in Wisconsin; Indiana Dunes (p584) in Indiana; and Voyageurs National Park (p635) in Minnesota.

Wide swaths of state park land also crisscross the Great Lakes; see each state's Information section for details.

Black bears, moose, beavers, elk and wolves are the wildlife stars, though you'll have to travel to the dense forests of the far north to see them. Bald eagles have made a remarkable recovery from the brink of extinction thanks to bans on certain pesticides and can be seen in huge numbers in Minnesota and along the Mississippi River. Not as fun to encounter are insects, which can be a real pain the farther north you go, specifically blackflies in the spring and mosquitoes in summer. Pack bug repellent.

INFORMATION

The **Great Lakes Information Network** (www.great lakes.net) is a web resource with info aplenty on the region's environment, economy and tourism, much of it culled from local news sources.

GETTING THERE & AROUND

Chicago's O'Hare International Airport is the main air hub for the region. Detroit, Cleveland and Minneapolis also have busy airports.

Greyhound (☎ 800-231-2222; www.greyhound. com) connects many local cities and towns. Upstart **Megabus** (☎ 877-462-6342; www.mega-bus.com/us) provides an efficient alternative between major Great Lakes cities. Note that Megabus has no bus terminals (drop-off and pick-up are at various street corners), and all purchases must be made in advance online (you cannot buy a ticket from the driver).

Southeast Michigan (including Detroit) is the least expensive place to rent cars in the region. If you are traveling on major interstate highways (such as I-80 in Ohio or

GREAT LAKES IN...

Five Days

Spend the first two days in **Chicago** (opposite). On your third day, make the 1½-hour trip to **Milwaukee** (p614) for culture, both highbrow and low. Take the ferry over to Michigan and spend your fourth day beaching in **Saugatuck** (p607). Come back via northern Indiana's **sand dunes** (p584) or **Amish communities** (p584).

Ten Days

After two days in Chicago, on day three make for **Madison** (p617) and its surrounding quirky sights. Spend your fourth and fifth days at the **Apostle Islands** (p622), then head into the Upper Peninsula to visit **Marquette** (p612) and **Pictured Rocks** (p612) for a few days, followed by **Sleeping Bear Dunes** (p608) and the wineries around **Traverse City** (p608). Return via the galleries, pies and beaches of Saugatuck.

Active Endeavors

The region offers activities to match a variety of weather moods and personal tastes. Visitors can **kiteboard** (p608) in Traverse City, **rock climb** (p592) at Hocking Hills, **kayak** (p622) in the Apostle Islands, **canoe** (p634) amid moose and wolves in the Boundary Waters, **houseboat** (p635) in remote Voyageurs National Park, **mountain bike** (p622) in Chequamegon Nation Forest, **ski** (p613) in the Porkies and **back country hike** (p612) on Isle Royale. Almost all of these are doable by beginners. So get up off your duff and get moving.

I-90 in Illinois), piles of change are useful for the tolls.

Two car/passenger ferries sail across Lake Michigan, providing a shortcut between Wisconsin and Michigan. The *Lake Express* (p607) crosses between Milwaukee and Muskegon. The older *SS Badger* (p607) crosses between Manitowoc and Ludington.

The national railroad network centers on Chicago, from where **Amtrak** (☎ 800-872-7245; www.amtrak.com) runs trains regularly to cities throughout the region and the rest of the USA.

Regional driving distances:

Chicago to Minneapolis 400 miles
Chicago to Detroit 278 miles
Milwaukee to Apostle Islands 375 miles
Minneapolis to Duluth 150 miles
Indiana Dunes to Sleeping Bear Dunes 255 miles

ILLINOIS

Chicago dominates the state with its sky-high architecture, lakefront beaches, and superlative museums, restaurants and music clubs. But venturing further afield reveals Hemingway's hometown of 'wide lawns and narrow minds,' scattered shrines to local hero Abe Lincoln, and a trail of corn dogs, pie and drive-in movie theaters down Route 66. A cypress swamp, giant ketchup bottle and prehistoric World Heritage Site make appearances in Illinois, too.

History

If you were a mound-building kind of guy or gal, looking for a place to live between AD 700 and AD 1200, Illinois was your place. The state had one of North America's largest prehistoric civilizations at Cahokia, in the south near the Mississippi River.

Illinois emerged from the Civil War as an industrial state, proficient in steel-making,

---

ILLINOIS FACTS

Nicknames Prairie State, Land of Lincoln
Population 12.8 million
Area 57,900 sq miles
Capital city Springfield (population 112,000)
Sales Tax 6.25%
Birthplace of Author Ernest Hemingway (1899–1961), animator Walt Disney (1901–66), jazz musician Miles Davis (1926–91), actor Bill Murray (b 1950)
Home of Cornfields, Route 66 start and endpoint
Famous for First skyscraper, zipper, corn dog, Ferris wheel, Twinkie, Abe Lincoln sights
Official flower Native violet

meatpacking, distilling and heavy manufacturing. This growth created great private wealth but also led to labor strife as workers – many of them European immigrants – struggled against low wages and poor conditions. Unions began forming in the mid-19th century, and violent strikes took place between 1877 and 1919. The state remains a union stronghold today.

The Prohibition era of the 1920s, when Al Capone and his gangster friends more or less ran things, corrupted the state's political system. State government has been suspect ever since, and typically pits liberal, big-city Chicago against the more conservative downstate farming and manufacturing towns.

Information

Illinois Bureau of Tourism (☎ 800-226-6632; www .enjoyillinois.com)

Illinois highway conditions (☎ 800-452-4368; www .gettingaroundillinois.com)

Illinois state park information (☎ 217-782-6752; www.dnr.state.il.us) State parks are free to visit. Campsites cost $6 to $20; some accept reservations (fee $5).

CHICAGO

Loving Chicago is 'like loving a woman with a broken nose; you may well find lovelier lovelies, but never a lovely so real.' Writer Nelson Algren summed it up well. There's something about this cloud-scraping city that bewitches. Well, maybe not during the six-month winter, when the 'Windy City' gets slapped by snowy blasts. But come May, when the weather warms and everyone dashes for the outdoor festivals, ballparks, Lake Michigan beaches and beer gardens – ahh, nowhere tops Chicago.

We mean it literally, as the Sears Tower is here, the USA's tallest building. Hard to believe all that height came compliments of a cow. That's right – Chicago 'invented' the skyscraper because of Mrs O'Leary's bovine. On October 8, 1871, the creature kicked over the lantern that started the Great Chicago Fire (or so the story goes). It torched the entire inner city and left 90,000 people homeless.

'Damn,' said the city planners. 'Guess we shouldn't have built everything from wood. It's flammable.' So they rebuilt with steel and created space for bold new structures, like the world's first skyscraper, which popped up in 1885.

Beyond its mighty architecture, Chicago is a city of Mexican, Polish, Vietnamese and other ethnic neighborhoods to eat and wander through. It's a city of blues, jazz and rock clubs any night of the week, and a full-fledged foodie scene that extends even to gourmet hot dogs. Its politics are entertaining, too. Pick up a newspaper and read about the corruption, graft and patronage that make the city tick under Da Mayor's rule (that's Mayor Richard M Daley, Chicago's leader since 1989 – not to be confused with his father, Richard J Daley, Chicago's mayor from 1955 to 1976). It's a real, old-fashioned democratic machine.

A broken nose never looked so good. Stick around awhile, and feel the love.

Orientation & Information

The central downtown area is the Loop, a hub of skyscrapers and Chicago Transit Authority (CTA) trains. Beyond this, Chicago is a city of neighborhoods. Chicago's streets are laid out on a grid and numbered; Madison and State Sts are the grid's center. As you go north, south, east or west from here, each increase of 800 in street numbers corresponds to one mile. At every increase of 400, there is a major arterial street. For instance, Division St (1200 N) is followed by North Ave (1600 N) and Armitage Ave (2000 N), at which point you're 2.5 miles north of downtown. Pick up a copy of Lonely Planet's *Chicago City Map* for details.

BOOKSTORES

Borders (Map pp552-3; ☎ 312-606-0750; 150 N State St) You name it, they've got it in this multi-floor store.

Quimby's (Map p548; ☎ 773-342-0910; 1854 W North Ave) Ground Zero for comics, zines and underground culture.

Women & Children First (Map p559; ☎ 773-769-9299; 5233 N Clark St) Women-penned fiction and other feminist tomes.

EMERGENCY & MEDICAL SERVICES

Northwestern Memorial Hospital (Map pp552-3; ☎ 312-926-5188; 251 E Erie St) Well-respected hospital that's conveniently located downtown.

Stroger Cook County Hospital (Map p548; ☎ 312-864-6000; 1969 W Ogden Ave) Public hospital serving patients low on money or sans insurance.

Walgreens (Map pp552-3; ☎ 312-664-8686; 757 N Michigan Ave; ⏰ 24hr) Chain with dozens of outlets.

Rape crisis (☎ 888-293-2080)

GREAT LAKES

METRO CHICAGO AREA

INTERNET ACCESS

Public libraries remain the best bet for free wired internet access. Walgreens pharmacies are good places to buy CDs and burn digital photos. Bars and restaurants in Lincoln Park, Bucktown and Near North often have free wi-fi; try Kitsch'n (p567), Goose Island (p568) or the Chicago Cultural Center (p550).

Screenz (Map pp556-7; ☎ 773-348-9300; 2717 N Clark St; per hr $9; ⊙ 8am-midnight Mon-Fri, from 9am Sat & Sun) Do it all here: surf, download, burn, print, scan.

INTERNET RESOURCES

The websites under Media (below), particularly the *Chicago Reader* and *Time Out Chicago*, are good restaurant and entertainment resources. Also check Tours (p564) for downloadable jaunts. Other sites include:

Gaper's Block (www.gapersblock.com) Cool info on news and events around town.

Green Maps (www.artic.edu/webspaces/greenmap/) Sustainability hot spots listed by neighborhood: from parks to organic restaurants, fair-trade shops to recycling centers; also lists bad boys like water pollutant sources.

Sustainable Chicago (www.sustainablechicago.biz) List of local green businesses.

Vegchicago (www.vegchicago.com) Vegetarian/vegan dining guide.

LIBRARIES

Harold Washington Library Center (Map pp552-3; ☎ 312-747-4300; 400 S State St; ⊙ 9am-9pm Mon-Thu, 9am-5pm Fri & Sat, 1-5pm Sun) A grand, art-filled building with free internet and wi-fi (get a temporary 'guest' card for access).

MEDIA

Chicago Reader (www.chicagoreader.com) Free alternative newspaper with comprehensive arts and entertainment listings; widely available at bookstores, bars and coffee shops.

Chicago Sun-Times (www.suntimes.com) The *Tribune's* daily, tabloidesque competitor.

Chicago Tribune (www.chicagotribune.com) The city's stalwart daily newspaper; its younger, trimmed-down version is *RedEye*.

Time Out Chicago (www.timeoutchicago.com) Hip, service-oriented magazine with all-encompassing listings.

Venus Magazine (www.venuszine.com) Arts-oriented quarterly zine for women.

Chicago's National Public Radio (NPR) affiliate is WBEZ-FM 91.5. For alternative music tune into WXRT-FM 93.1.

MONEY

ATMs are plentiful downtown, with many near Chicago and Michigan Aves. To change money, try Terminal 5 at O'Hare International or these Loop places:

Travelex (Map pp552-3; ☎ 312-807-4941; 19 S LaSalle St)
World's Money Exchange (Map pp552-3; ☎ 312-641-2151; 203 N LaSalle St)

POST

Post office (Map pp552-3) Main (☎ 312-983-8182; 433 W Harrison St; ⊙ 24hr); Fort Dearborn (☎ 312-644-0485; 540 N Dearborn St)

TOURIST INFORMATION

The **Chicago Office of Tourism** (☎ 312-744-2400, 877-244-2246; www.cityofchicago.org/exploringchicago or www.choosechicago.com) operates two well-staffed and stocked visitors centers:

Chicago Cultural Center Visitors Center (Map pp552-3; 77 E Randolph St; ⊙ 8am-7pm Mon-Thu, 8am-6pm Fri, 9am-6pm Sat, 10am-6pm Sun)
Water Works Visitors Center (Map pp556-7; 163 E Pearson St; ⊙ 8am-7pm Mon-Thu, 8am-6pm Fri, 10am-6pm Sat, 10am-4pm Sun)

Sights

Chicago's main attractions are found mostly in or near the city center, though visits to distant neighborhoods, like Andersonville, Pilsen and Hyde Park, can also be rewarding. Purchase the lump-sum **CityPass** (☎ 888-330-5008; www.citypass.com; adult/child 4-11 $49.50/39) and save on admission fees for five of Chicago's most popular attractions: the Shedd Aquarium (p551), Field Museum of Natural History (p551), Adler Planetarium (p551), Hancock Observatory (p555) and Museum of Science & Industry (p561). Students who present ID will often receive reduced museum admission.

For a more in-depth exploration of the Windy City, pick up Lonely Planet's *Chicago* city guide.

THE LOOP

The city center/financial district is named for the elevated train tracks that lasso its streets. It's busy all day, though not much happens at night other than in the Theater District, where playhouses cluster near the intersection of N State and W Randolph Sts.

Art Institute of Chicago

Chicago's premier cultural institution, the **Art Institute** (Map pp552-3; ☎ 312-443-3600; www.artic

CHICAGO IN...

Two Days

Take an architectural boat cruise and look up at the city's skyscrapers. Look down from the **John Hancock Center** (p555), one of the world's tallest buildings. See 'the Bean' reflect the skyline, and splash with Crown Fountain's human gargoyles at **Millennium Park** (opposite). Hungry after all the walking? Chow down on a deep-dish pizza at **Giordano's** (p567). Make the second day a cultural one: explore the **Art Institute** (p549), **Field Museum** (opposite) or **Adler Planetarium** (opposite). Browse boutiques and grab a stylish dinner in **Wicker Park** (p558). Head north to Al Capone's gin joint, the **Green Mill** (p571), for evening jazz.

Four Days

Follow the two-day itinerary, then on your third day rent a bicycle, dip your toes in Lake Michigan at **North Avenue Beach** (p561), and cruise through **Lincoln Park** (p558), making stops at the zoo and conservatory. If it's baseball season, head directly to **Wrigley Field** (p558) for a Cubs game. A smoky blues club, such as **Buddy Guy's Legends** (p570), is a fine way to finish the day (or start the morning).

Pick a neighborhood on your fourth day to eat, shop and soak up the culture: murals and mole sauce in **Pilsen** (p569), pagodas and Vietnamese cream puffs in **Uptown** (p559) or nuclear sights in **Hyde Park** (p560). Then see a play at one of Chicago's 200 theaters or comedy at **Second City** (p572).

.edu/aic; 111 S Michigan Ave; adult/child $12/7, admission free Thu & Fri evening; ☼ 10:30am-5pm Mon-Wed, 10:30am-9pm Thu & Fri, 10am-5pm Sat & Sun, reduced in winter) houses treasures and masterpieces from around the globe, including a fabulous selection of both Impressionist and Post-Impressionist paintings. Georges Seurat's pointillist *A Sunday on La Grande Jatte* is here; so is Grant Wood's *American Gothic*. Allow two hours to browse the highlights, but art buffs should allow much longer. A new wing for modern art is scheduled to open in 2009.

Sears Tower

Sears Tower (Map pp552-3; ☎ 312-875-9696; www.the-skydeck.com; 233 S Wacker Dr; adult/child 3-11 $12.95/9.50; ☼ 10am-10pm Apr-Sep, 10am-8pm Oct-Mar) was the world's tallest building until the end of the 20th century. Then the Malaysians built the Petronas Towers, and Sears became a has-been. Its self-esteem only got worse with Taipei, Shanghai and Dubai putting up even higher towers. Now Sears has an outright Napoleon complex. But it's still the USA's tallest building, and it's way up in the clouds. Check visibility and waiting times at the Jackson Blvd entrance before joining the queues, then persist through a security check, a series of waiting rooms, a film and more lines before the 70-second elevator ride to the 103rd-floor Skydeck. For those who prefer a drink with

their view, the John Hancock Center (p555) is a better choice.

Chicago Cultural Center

The exquisite interior of the **Cultural Center** (Map pp552-3; ☎ 312-744-6630; www.chicagoculturalcenter.org; 78 E Washington St; admission free; ☼ 8am-7pm Mon-Thu, 8am-6pm Fri, 9am-6pm Sat, 10am-6pm Sun) features rooms modeled on the Doge's Palace in Venice and Palazzo Vecchio in Florence, and is notable for its stained-glass dome and sparkling mosaics. Free exhibits and lunchtime concerts are ongoing; there's also free wi-fi.

Architecture & Public Art

Ever since it presented the world with the first skyscraper, Chicago has thought big with its architecture and pushed the envelope of modern design. The Loop is a fantastic place to roam and gawk at these ambitious structures.

The Chicago Architecture Foundation (p564) runs tours that explain the following buildings and more.

The **Chicago Board of Trade** (Map pp552-3; 141 W Jackson Blvd) is a 1930 art deco gem. Inside, manic traders swap futures and options. No one really knows what those are, other than it has something to do with corn. A small **visitors center** (☎ 312-435-3590; admission free; ☼ 8am-4pm

Mon-Fri) tries to explain it. Or stay outside and check out the mondo statue of Ceres, the goddess of agriculture, that tops the building.

The 1888 **Rookery** (Map pp552-3; 209 S LaSalle St) looks fortress-like outside, but it's light and airy inside thanks to Frank Lloyd Wright's atrium overhaul. Pigeons used to roost here, hence the name.

Architectural pilgrims get weak-kneed when they see the **Monadnock Building** (Map pp552-3; 53 W Jackson Blvd), which is two buildings in one. The north is the older, traditional design from 1891, while the south is the newer, mod half from 1893. See the difference?

Chicago has commissioned several head-scratching public sculptures throughout the decades. The Loop's triumvirate of puzzlement includes Pablo Picasso's **Untitled** (Map pp552-3; 50 W Washington St), which everyone just calls 'the Picasso'; Joan Miro's **the Sun, the Moon and One Star** (Map pp552-3; 69 W Washington St), which everyone just calls 'Miro's Chicago'; and Jean Dubuffet's **Monument with Standing Beast** (Map pp552-3; 100 W Randolph St), which everyone just calls 'Snoopy in a Blender.'

GRANT PARK

Grant Park, the green play space that forms a buffer between the Loop and Lake Michigan, has gotten lots of love over the years. The Olmsted Brothers' architectural firm was the first to convert part of the once-marshy landfill into a park. **Buckingham Fountain** (Map pp552-3; cnr Congress Parkway & Columbus Dr) became its centerpiece. It's one of the world's largest squirters, with a 1.5-million-gallon capacity. The fountain lets loose on the hour from 10am to 11pm mid-April to mid-October, accompanied at night by multicolored lights and music.

Millennium Park

Opened in 2004 and occupying Grant Park's northwest corner, **Millennium Park** (Map pp552-3; ☎ 312-742-1168; www.millenniumpark.org; Michigan Ave btwn Monroe & Randolph Sts) is the newest sight to receive Chicago's lurve. Frank Gehry's 120ft-high swooping silver band shell anchors what is, in essence, an outdoor modern design gallery. It includes Jaume Plensa's 50ft-high fountain that projects video images of locals spitting out water gargoyle-style; a Gehry-designed bridge (his first) that spans Columbus Dr and offers great skyline views; and a winter ice-skating rink (p561). But

the thing that has become the park's biggest draw is the Bean – Anish Kapoor's 110-ton, ridiculously smooth silver-drop sculpture (officially titled *Cloud Gate*). Visitors swarm it to see their reflection and that of the city skyline.

The Grant Park Orchestra (p572) plays free concerts at the band shell, and the **Millennium Park Greeter Service** (Map pp552-3; ☎ 312-742-1168; 201 E Randolph St; ⏰ 11:30am & 1pm) offers free park tours in summer.

SOUTH LOOP

Ignored for the last five decades, the South Loop – which includes the lower ends of downtown and Grant Park, along with the historic Printer's Row neighborhood of rare bookshops – has suddenly soared from dereliction to development central. The Museum Campus is the lakefront area south of Grant Park where three significant attractions sit side by side.

Field Museum of Natural History

The mammoth **Field Museum** (Map pp552-3; ☎ 312-922-9410; www.fieldmuseum.org; 1400 S Lake Shore Dr; adult/child 4-11 $12/7; ⏰ 9am-5pm) houses everything but the kitchen sink – beetles, mummies, gemstones, Bushman the stuffed ape. The collection's rock star is Sue, the largest *Tyrannosaurus rex* yet discovered. She even gets her own gift shop.

Shedd Aquarium

Top draws at the **Shedd Aquarium** (Map pp552-3; ☎ 312-939-2438; www.sheddaquarium.org; 1200 S Lake Shore Dr; adult/child 3-11 $25/18; ⏰ 9am-6pm Jun-Aug, to 10pm some Thu, reduced Sep-May) include the Oceanarium, with its beluga whales and frolicking white-sided dolphins, and the shark exhibit, where there's just five inches of Plexiglas between you and 30 or so fierce-looking swimmers.

Adler Planetarium & Astronomy Museum

Touch a 1000lb meteorite in the interactive galleries at the **Adler Planetarium** (Map pp552-3; ☎ 312-922-7827; www.adlerplanetarium.org; 1300 S Lake Shore Dr; adult/child 4-17 $10/6; ⏰ 9:30am-6pm Jun-Aug, to 4:30pm Sep-May), then view the cosmos in a digital sky show controlled from your chair's armrest. On the first Friday night of every month, the Adler's astronomers bring out their telescopes and let you view the skies with them (adult/child $20/17).

DOWNTOWN CHICAGO (THE LOOP), MUSEUM CAMPUS & NEAR NORTH SIDE

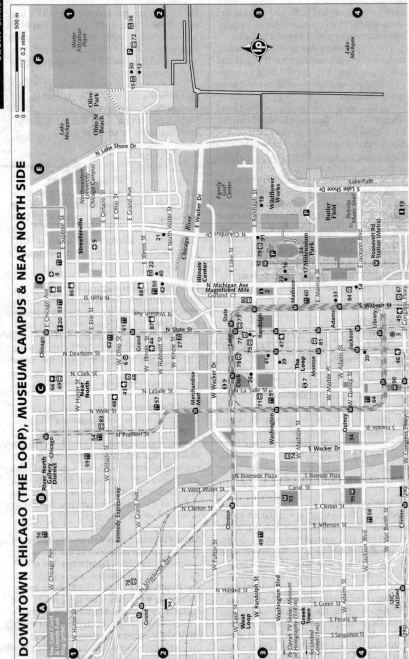

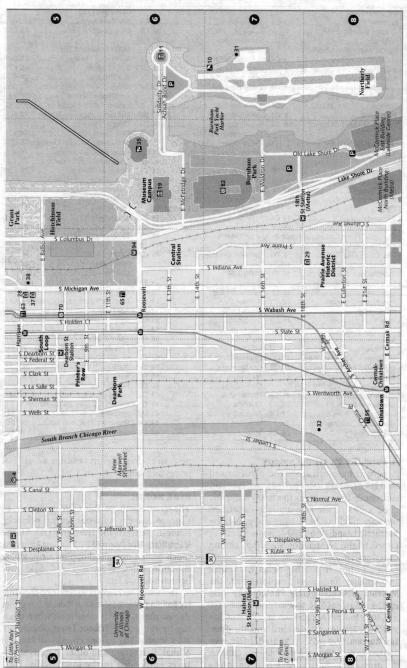

GREAT LAKES

Around the Museum Campus

A path runs south from the planetarium to **12th St Beach** (Map pp552-3), where you can climb the rocks to the breakwater for good views of the lake and the fishermen who are likely to be casting there. Nearby **Northerly Island** (Map pp552-3) hosts summer concerts and winter dog sledding, among other activities.

In addition to the big-ticket museums, two smaller ones worth exploring are the **Museum of Contemporary Photography** (Map pp552-3; ☎ 312-663-5554; www.mocp.org; Columbia College, 600 S Michigan Ave; admission free; ✆ 10am-5pm Mon-Sat, to 8pm Thu, noon-5pm Sun) and the **Spertus Museum** (Map pp552-3; ☎ 312-322-1700; www .spertus.edu; 618 S Michigan Ave) of Jewish culture. At press time, Spertus was moving into a new, next-door facility; call for admission prices and hours.

NEAR NORTH

The area north of the Chicago River to Chicago Ave encompasses several points of interest. Between the river and Oak St, the **Magnificent Mile** (Map pp552-3; N Michigan Ave) is the much-touted upscale shopping strip, where Bloomingdales, Neiman's and Saks will lighten your wallet.

The white terra-cotta exterior of the **Wrigley Building** (Map pp552-3; 400 N Michigan Ave) glows day or night. Take a close look when passing by the gothic **Tribune Tower** (Map pp552-3; 435 N Michigan Ave) to see chunks of the Taj Mahal, Parthenon and other famous structures embedded in the lower walls. Next door, the **McCormick Tribune Freedom Museum** (Map pp552-3; ☎ 312-222-4860; www.freedommuseum .us; 445 N Michigan Ave; admission $5; ☺ 10am-6pm, closed Tue) provokes thought. Hear once-banned music at the listening exhibits, or interact with computer exhibits that present actual cases testing free speech rights (ie can the Ku Klux Klan hold a rally on the community square?).

The **Museum of Broadcast Communications** (Map pp552-3; ☎ 312-245-8200; www.museum.tv; 400 N State St), filled with fascinating radio and TV nostalgia, is a newbie in the 'hood (after moving from the Loop). Call for admission prices and opening hours.

Navy Pier

Navy Pier (Map pp552-3; ☎ 312-595-7437; www.navypier .com; 600 E Grand Ave; admission free; ☺ 10am, closing times vary seasonally from 7pm-midnight) was once the city's municipal wharf. Its half-mile length is now covered with a Ferris wheel, an Imax theater, numerous shops and gimmicky chain restaurants. Locals groan over its commercialization, but its lakefront view and cool breezes can't be beat. The fireworks displays on Wednesdays (9:30pm) and Saturdays (10:15pm) are a treat, too.

The **Chicago Children's Museum** (p563) and gorgeous **Smith Museum of Stained Glass Windows** (Map pp552-3; ☎ 312-595-5024; admission free; ☺ same as pier) are also on the pier.

GOLD COAST

Starting in 1882, Chicago's wealthy flocked to this neighborhood flanking the lake between Chicago and North Aves. Within 40 years, most of the Gold Coast was covered with mansions.

Today the neighborhood giant is the 1127ft-tall **John Hancock Center** (Map pp556-7; ☎ 312-751-3681; www.hancock-observatory.com; 875 N Michigan Ave; adult/child 5-12 $11.30/7.15; ☺ 9am-11pm), which has a great 94th-floor observatory that's often less crowded than the one at Sears Tower. Better yet, skip the observatory and head straight up to the 96th-floor Signature Lounge (p569), where the view is free if you buy a drink ($6 to $12). Time it to coincide with Navy Pier's fireworks (left) and you're stylin'.

The 154ft-tall, turreted **Water Tower** (Map pp556-7; cnr Chicago & Michigan Aves) is a defining city landmark; it was the sole downtown survivor of the 1871 Great Fire.

The **Museum of Contemporary Art** (Map pp556-7; ☎ 312-280-2660; www.mcachicago.org; 220 E Chicago Ave; adult/student 12-18 $10/6, admission free Tue; ☺ 10am-8pm Tue, 10am-5pm Wed-Sun) displays head-scratching works by Franz Kline, René Magritte, Cindy Sherman and Andy Warhol.

To sample the Gold Coast's former grandeur, saunter down the 1300 and 1400 blocks of N Astor St, where gems include Frank Lloyd Wright's **Charnley-Persky House** (Map pp556-7; ☎ 312-915-0105; www.charnleyhouse.org; 1365 N Astor St; tours $5-10; ☺ Wed & Sat, call for times), which he proclaimed the 'first modern building.' One block west is a first of another kind – the **First Playboy Mansion** (Map pp556-7; 1340 N State St). Hugh Hefner began wearing his all-day jammies here, when the rigors of magazine production and heavy partying prevented him from getting dressed. The building is condos now, but a visit still allows you to boast, 'I've been to the Playboy mansion.'

THE FISH WHO ATE THE GREAT LAKES

It sounds like a bad sci-fi movie. The scary thing is it has the potential to become reality.

The ravenous fish causing all the trouble is the Asian carp. Fish farms in the southern USA imported these creatures in the 1960s and 70s to eat away pesky algae. Floods washed them into the Mississippi River and they swam north.

Though they only eat plankton, they chow phenomenal quantities – up to 40% of their body weight daily. The result is a 3ft long, 50lb bully that's wiping out the food base for native species.

The carp are now in the Illinois River, which connects to Lake Michigan and the waters beyond. The fear is if the fish enter, they'll wipe out the Great Lakes ecosystem. And since the lakes contain 20% of the world's fresh water…well, you get the scope of the problem.

So engineers built an electric barrier 50 miles southwest of Chicago that has kept the fish at bay. For now, anyway – the barrier is only a temporary model while biologists try to get funding for a permanent one. Dwindling ecofunds and safety issues regarding electrocution risk are the main hold-ups.

Meanwhile the clock ticks toward the fence's demise, and the fish wait hungrily at the gate.

GREAT LAKES

GOLD COAST & LINCOLN PARK

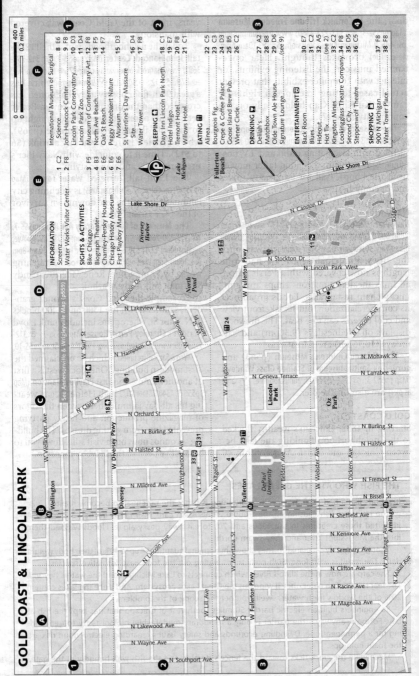

INFORMATION	
Screenz	1 C2
Water Works Visitor Center	2 F8

SIGHTS & ACTIVITIES	
Bike Chicago	3 F5
Biograph Theater	4 B3
Charnley-Persky House	5 E6
Chicago History Museum	6 E6
First Playboy Mansion	7 E6

International Museum of Surgical Science	8 E6
John Hancock Center	9 F8
Lincoln Park Conservatory	10 D3
Lincoln Park Zoo	11 D4
Museum of Contemporary Art	12 F8
North Ave Beach	13 F5
Oak St Beach	14 F7
Peggy Notebaert Nature Museum	15 D3
St Valentine's Day Massacre Site	16 D4
Water Tower	17 F8

SLEEPING 🏠	
Days Inn Lincoln Park North	18 C1
Hotel Indigo	19 E7
Tremont Hotel	20 F8
Willows Hotel	21 C1

EATING 🍴	
Alinea	22 C5
Bourgeois Pig	23 C3
Crepe & Coffee Palace	24 D3
Goose Island Brew Pub	25 B5
Wiener Circle	26 C2

DRINKING 🍷	
Delilah's	27 A2
Matchbox	28 B8
Olde Town Ale House	29 D6
Signature Lounge	(see 9)

ENTERTAINMENT 🎭	
Back Room	30 E7
Blues	31 C2
Hideout	32 A5
Hot Tix	(see 2)
Kingston Mines	33 C2
Lookingglass Theatre Company	34 F8
Second City	35 D5
Steppenwolf Theatre	36 C5

SHOPPING 🛍	
900 N Michigan	37 F8
Water Tower Place	38 F8

See Downtown Chicago (The Loop), Museum Campus & Near North Side Map (p552)

LINCOLN PARK & OLD TOWN

Lincoln Park is an urban oasis spanning 1200 leafy acres with its widest swath between North Ave and Diversey Pkwy. 'Lincoln Park' is also the name for the abutting neighborhood. Both are alive day and night with people skating, walking dogs, pushing strollers and driving in circles looking for a place to park.

The **Lincoln Park Zoo** (Map pp556-7; ☎ 312-742-2000; www.lpzoo.org; 2200 N Cannon Dr; admission free; ☽ 10am-4:30pm Nov-Mar, 10am-5pm Apr-Oct, 10am-6:30pm Sat & Sun Jun-Aug) is popular with families, who stroll by the habitats of gorillas, lions, tigers and other exotic creatures. Pick up a free map at the Gateway Pavilion (the main entrance), which provides times and locations when zoo keepers give free discussions about various animals, as well as feeding times and training demonstrations.

Near the zoo's north entrance, the magnificent 1891 **Conservatory** (Map pp556-7; ☎ 312-742-7736; 2391 N Stockton Dr; admission free; ☽ 9am-5pm) coaxes palms, ferns and orchids to flourish despite Chicago's brutal weather.

The **Peggy Notebaert Nature Museum** (Map pp556-7; ☎ 773-755-5100; www.naturemuseum.org; 2430 N Cannon Dr; adult/child 3-12 $7/4, admission free Thu; ☽ 9am-4:30pm Mon-Fri, 10am-5pm Sat & Sun) has a year-round butterfly park and other natural wonders.

The **Chicago History Museum** (Map pp556-7; ☎ 312-642-4600; www.chicagohs.org; 1601 N Clark St; adult/child 12-18 $12/10, admission free Mon; ☽ 9:30am-4:30pm Mon-Sat, to 8pm Thu, noon-5pm Sun) covers the Great Fire well, among other storied events.

Old Town rests at the southwest foot of Lincoln Park. The intersection of North Ave and Wells St is the epicenter, with restaurants, bars and Second City (p572) fanning out from here.

LAKE VIEW & WRIGLEYVILLE

North of Lincoln Park, these neighborhoods can be enjoyed by ambling along Halsted St, Clark St, Belmont Ave or Southport Ave, which are well supplied with restaurants, bars and shops. Ivy-covered **Wrigley Field** (Map p559; 1060 W Addison St) is named after the chewing-gum guy and is home to the adored but perpetually losing Chicago Cubs. If they're playing a game, you can peep in the 'knothole,' a garage-door-sized opening on Sheffield Ave, to watch the action for free. For ticket information, see p572.

WICKER PARK, BUCKTOWN & UKRAINIAN VILLAGE

West of Lincoln Park, these three neighborhoods – once havens for working-class, central European immigrants, and writers like Nelson Algren and Simone de Beauvoir – are now among Chicago's hottest properties. Aside from peeking at **Nelson Algren's house** (Map p548; 1958 W Evergreen Ave) where he wrote several gritty novels about life in Chicago (note: you can't go into the house), the neighborhoods are all about eating, drinking and shopping. Heaps of small galleries, boutiques, music clubs and martini-and-sushi lounges have shot up, especially near the

---

GANGLAND CHICAGO

The city would rather not discuss its gangster past, and consequently there are no brochures or exhibits about infamous sites. So you'll need to use your imagination when visiting the following, as most are not designated as notorious.

Two murders took place near **Holy Name Cathedral** (Map pp552-3; 735 N State St). In 1924 North Side boss Dion O'Banion was gunned down in his florist shop (738 N State St) after he crossed Al Capone. O'Banion's replacement, Hymie Weiss, fared no better. In 1926 he was killed on his way to church by bullets flying from a window at 740 N State St.

The **St Valentine's Day Massacre Site** (Map pp556-7; 2122 N Clark St) is where Capone goons dressed as cops lined up seven members of Bugs Moran's gang against the garage wall that used to be here and sprayed them with bullets. The garage was torn down in 1967.

In 1934, the 'lady in red' betrayed John Dillinger at the **Biograph Theater** (Map pp556-7; 2433 N Lincoln Ave). He was shot by the FBI outside it.

The speakeasy in the basement of the glamorous, smoky jazz bar, **Green Mill** (p571), was a Capone favorite.

Visit **Capone's Chicago Home** (Map p548; 7244 S Prairie Ave) on the South Side – although the residence was used mostly by Capone's wife, Mae, and other relatives.

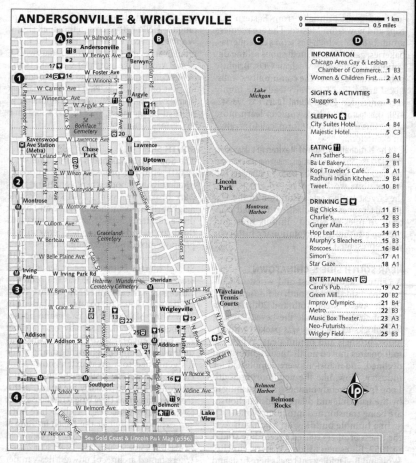

ANDERSONVILLE & WRIGLEYVILLE

0 — 1 km
0 — 0.5 miles

Milwaukee/North/Damen Ave intersection (a notoriously traffic-jammed area known as 'the Crotch'). Division St is another designer vein, which is a change from its former glory as the 'Polish Broadway' (a name that came from all the polka bars that once lined the road). Take the CTA Blue Line to Damen or Division.

ANDERSONVILLE & UPTOWN

Creative types, lesbians, gays and yuppies occupy most of this walkable, bar-filled neighborhood (Map p559), which was once heavily Swedish. Take the CTA Red Line to the Berwyn stop and walk west about a mile.

Get off one stop south at the pagoda-like Argyle St station, and you're in the heart of New Chinatown and its abundant Chinese, Vietnamese and Thai restaurants and shops.

NEAR WEST SIDE & PILSEN

Just west of the Loop is a patchwork of ethnic neighborhoods. **Greektown** (Map pp552-3) runs along S Halsted St. **Little Italy** (Map p548) extends along Taylor St. And the University of Illinois at Chicago (UIC) lies between the two. The **West Loop** (Map pp552-3) is north of Greektown along W Randolph and Washington Sts; it's akin to New York City's Meatpacking District, with hip restaurants, clubs and galleries poking out between meat-processing plants.

Southwest of Little Italy, the neighborhood of **Pilsen** (Map p548) has long been a first stop for immigrants, initially from Eastern Europe and now from Mexico. The area centers around 18th St, which has scores of taquerías, bakeries, galleries and small shops selling devotional candles and Mexican CDs. Brightly painted murals cover the community's walls. Local artist Jose Guerrero leads the highly recommended **Pilsen Mural Tours** (☎ 773-342-4191; 1½hr tour $100) where you can learn more about this traditional art form; call to arrange an excursion.

The **National Museum of Mexican Art** (Map p548; ☎ 312-738-1503; www.nationalmuseumofmexicanart.org; 1852 W 19th St; admission free; ☷ 10am-5pm Tue-Sun) exhibits work by Mexican artists. It is the largest Latino arts institution in the US. The art ranges from classical themed portraits to piles of carved minibus tires, and Mexico's turbulent, revolutionary history is well represented.

NEAR SOUTH SIDE & CHINATOWN

A century ago, the best and worst of Chicago lived side by side south of Roosevelt Rd. Prairie Ave between 16th and 20th Sts was Millionaire's Row, while the Levee District, four blocks to the west, was packed with saloons, brothels and opium dens. When the millionaires moved north, the neighborhood declined, and mansions were demolished for industry. Now, like the neighboring South Loop (p551), trendy businesses are rushing in by the truckful, and dilapidated warehouses are being transformed into luxury lofts.

In a humble building on Michigan Ave, the Chess brothers started a recording studio in 1957. Bluesmen Muddy Waters, Howlin' Wolf and Bo Diddley cut tracks here first, and paved the way for rock 'n' roll with their sick licks and amped-up sound. Chuck Berry and the Rolling Stones arrived soon thereafter. The studio is now called **Willie Dixon's Blues Heaven** (Map p548; ☎ 312-808-1286; www.bluesheaven.com; 2120 S Michigan Ave; tours $10; ☷ noon-2pm Mon-Sat) and holds a collection of blues memorabilia. Dixon was the guy who wrote most of the label's hits and the one who summed up the genre best: 'Blues is the roots, and everything else is the fruits.'

The moving **National Vietnam Veterans Art Museum** (Map pp552-3; ☎ 312-326-0270; www.nvvam.org; 1801 S Indiana Ave; adult/student $10/7; ☷ 11am-6pm Tue-Fri, 10am-5pm Sat) exhibits artworks by veterans.

Chinatown's charm is best enjoyed by going bakery to bakery and nibbling chest-nut cakes and almond cookies, then shopping for Hello Kitty items in the small shops. Wentworth Ave south of Cermak Rd is the retail heart of old Chinatown; Chinatown Sq, along Archer Ave north of Cermak, is the newer commerce district and at its wonderful noisiest on weekends. **Ping Tom Memorial Park** (Map pp552-3; 300 W 19th St) offers dramatic city-railroad-bridge views. Take the CTA Red Line to Cermak-Chinatown.

SOUTH SIDE

The South Side has had a tough time since WWII. Housing projects created impoverished neighborhoods where community ties were broken and gangs held sway. Whole neighborhoods vanished as crime and blight drove residents away. Some areas survived the damage, and redevelopment now aims to promote mixed-income communities.

The neighborhood radiating from 35th St and Martin Luther King Jr Dr is called **Bronzeville** (Map p548), and it was the center of Chicago's African American culture from 1920 until 1950, comparable to Harlem in New York. Many of the area's grand houses are being restored, especially on Calumet Ave between 31st and 33rd Sts (this was once a high-crime neighborhood, and while it's gentrified to a great extent now, some elements linger, so visitors should still use caution). Note particularly the stylish architecture of the **Frank Lloyd Wright row houses** (Map p548; 3213-3219 S Calumet Ave). Architecture buffs can explore further at the **Illinois Institute of Technology** (IIT; Map p548; ☎ 312-567-5014; www.mies.iit.edu; 3201 S State St; 90-min tour $5; ☷ 10am & 1pm), where famed architect Ludwig Mies van der Rohe designed all the modern buildings. To reach the area, take the CTA Green Line to 35th St-Bronzeville-IIT.

The **Chicago Blues Museum** (Map p548; ☎ 773-828-8118; chicagobluesmuseum@att.net; 3636 S Iron St; adult/student $10/8) displays photos, films and relics like Howlin' Wolf's guitar and the Blues Brothers' suits. It was scheduled to move at press time, but had not yet found a new site. Call or email for current details.

HYDE PARK

Hyde Park is a bookish, affluent pocket on the South Side that's home to the prestigious **University of Chicago** (Map p548; 5801 S Ellis Ave), where faculty and students have racked up 80 Nobel prizes (the economics department lays claim to one third of them). It's also where the nuclear age began. Enrico Fermi and his Manhattan Project cronies built a reactor and carried out the world's first controlled atomic reaction on Dec 2, 1942. The **Nuclear Energy sculpture** (Map p548; S Ellis Ave btwn E 56th & E 57th Sts), by Henry Moore, marks the spot where it blew its stack. The area is easily reached via Metra Electric trains from the Randolph St/ Millennium Park station to the 55th-56th-57th St station.

The vast **Museum of Science & Industry** (Map p548; ☎ 773-684-1414; www.msichicago.org; cnr 57th St & S Lake Shore Dr; adult/child 3-11 $11/7; ☉ 9:30am-4pm Mon-Sat, 11am-4pm Sun, to 5:30pm Jun-Aug) will overstimulate the serenest of souls with its myriad (and often loud) exhibits that examine everything on earth. Highlights include a WWII German U-boat nestled in an underground display ($5 extra to tour it) and the 'body slices' exhibit (two bodies cut in half-inch sections then pressed between pieces of glass).

Of the numerous buildings that Frank Lloyd Wright designed in the Chicago area, none is more famous or influential than **Robie House** (Map p548; ☎ 773-834-1847; www.wrightplus.org; 5757 S Woodlawn Ave; adult/child 11-18 $12/10). The resemblance of its horizontal lines to the flat landscape of the Midwestern prairie became known as the Prairie style. Inside are 174 art glass windows and doors. Hour-long tours are offered at 11am, 1pm and 3pm Monday to Friday (continuous from 11am to 3:30pm Saturday and Sunday).

The newly expanded **DuSable Museum of African American History** (Map p548; ☎ 773-947-0600; www.dusablemuseum.org; 740 E 56th Pl; adult/child 6-13 $3/1, admission free Sun; ☉ 10am-5pm Tue-Sat, noon-5pm Sun) has artworks and exhibits on African Americans from slavery to the civil-rights era.

Activities

Tucked away in Chicago's 552 parks are public golf courses, ice rinks, swimming pools and more. Activities are free or low cost, and the necessary equipment is available for rent in the parks. Contact the **Chicago Park District** (☎ 312-742-7529; www.chicagoparkdistrict.com); there's a separate number for **golf information** (☎ 312-245-0909).

BASEBALL BATTING CAGES

Brush up on your batting skills at **Sluggers** (Map p559; ☎ 773-472-9696; 3540 N Clark St; ☉ 3pm-

2am Mon-Thu, 11am-2am Fri-Sun), a popular bar and grill across from Wrigley Field. Ten pitches cost $1.

BICYCLING

There is some truly awesome, if somewhat crowded, cycling along the 18.5-mile lakefront path. **Bike Chicago** (☎ 312-595-9600; www.bikechicago.com; bikes per hr/day from $8/34; ☉ 9am-7pm Apr-Oct, extended hrs Jun-Aug; Navy Pier (Map pp552-3; 600 E Grand Ave; Millennium Park Bike Station Map pp552-3; 239 E Randolph St; North Ave Beach Map pp556-7; 1600 N Lake Shore Dr) rents out bicycles and offers guided, three-hour tours ($30 to $50) departing from Millennium Park/ Navy Pier at 10am/10:30am, 1pm/1:30pm and 6:30pm/7pm, respectively. If you sign up for a tour, bike rental is free. The group also provides free, do-it-yourself maps.

ICE SKATING

The Chicago Park District operates a first-class winter ice rink at **Daley Bicentennial Plaza** (Map pp552-3; ☎ 312-742-7650; 337 E Randolph St; ☉ 10am-3:30pm & 7-9:30pm Mon-Fri, 8:30am-noon Sat & Sun). Millennium Park's **McCormick Tribune Ice Rink** (Map pp552-3; 312-742-5222; 55 N Michigan Ave) is also popular. Admission is free to both; skate rental costs $5 to $7.

RUNNING & INLINE SKATING

Runners and inline skaters crowd onto the lakefront path alongside cyclists. The same places that rent bikes (above) also rent skates for identical prices.

WATER SPORTS

Chicago sits by a big lake and river, so it's no surprise that water sports rule the waves here.

Take a dip, build a sand castle or loaf in the sun at any of Chicago's 33 beaches, operated by the **Park District** (☎ 312-742-7529; www.chicago|parkdistrict.com). All are staffed with lifeguards during the summer. **North Avenue Beach** (Map pp556-7; 1600 N Lake Shore Dr) and **Oak Street Beach** (Map pp556-7; 1000 N Lake Shore Dr), both close to downtown, are particularly body-filled. Brace yourself, as the water remains butt-numbing well into July.

Chicago Sailing (☎ 773-871-7245; www.chicagosailing.com) offers all levels of instruction, including five-day beginners' classes for $445, or sailboats to rent from $45/65 per hour on weekdays/weekends. The departure point is from Belmont Harbor (Map p559).

For a remarkable view of downtown, where you'll slither through a canyon of glass and steel, kayak the Chicago River with **Wateriders** (Map pp556-7; ☎ 312-953-9287; www.wateriders.com; 900 N Kingsbury St; 3hr tours $45-55). Tours take in architectural sights and gangster spots. Beginners welcome. Call for the schedule.

Walking Tour

This tour swoops through the Loop highlighting Chicago's revered art and architecture, with a visit to Al Capone's dentist thrown in for good measure.

Start at the **Chicago Board of Trade** (1; p550), where guys in Technicolor coats swap corn (or something like that) inside a cool art deco building. Step into the nearby **Rookery** (2; p551) to see Frank Lloyd Wright's handiwork in the atrium.

Head east on Adams St to the **Art Institute** (3; p549), one of the city's most-visited attractions. The lion statues out front make a classic keepsake photo. Walk a few blocks north to avant-garde **Millennium Park** (4; p551), and saunter in to explore 'the Bean' sculpture, human-gargoyle fountains and other contemporary designs.

When you depart, head west on Washington St to the **Hotel Burnham** (5; p566). It's housed in the Reliance Building, which was the precursor for modern skyscraper design; Capone's dentist drilled teeth in what's now room 809. Just west, the **Picasso** (6; p551) – created by Mr Abstract himself – is ensconced in Daley Center Plaza. Bird, dog, woman? You decide, then go north on Clark St to **Monument with Standing Beast** (7; p551), another head-scratching sculpture.

Walk east on Randolph St through the theater district. Pop into the **Cultural Center** (8; p550) to get a soda in the café and maybe catch a free concert. Refreshed? Now go north on Michigan Ave and cross the Chicago River. Just north of the bridge you'll pass the **Wrigley Building** (9; p554), glowing as white as the Double Mint twins' teeth, followed closely by the Gothic, eye-popping **Tribune Tower** (10; p554).

So much culture can overwhelm. Clear the mind by submerging below street level to the **Billy Goat Tavern** (11; p567), a vintage Chicago dive that spawned the Curse of the Cubs. Just look around and you'll get the details, but in short: the tavern's owner, Billy Sianis, once tried to enter Wrigley Field with his pet goat. The smelly creature was denied entry,

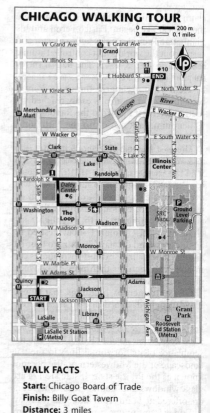

CHICAGO WALKING TOUR

WALK FACTS

Start: Chicago Board of Trade
Finish: Billy Goat Tavern
Distance: 3 miles
Duration: About 2 hours

so Sianis called down a mighty curse on the baseball team in retaliation. They've had a losing record ever since.

Chicago for Children

Chicago is a kid's kind of town. Most museums have special areas to entertain and educate wee ones. A good resource is **Chicago Parent** (www.chicagoparent.com), a free publication available at libraries, the Children's Museum and elsewhere. Also check www.chicagokids.com.

CHILDREN'S THEATER

The **Children's Theatre Company** (☎ 773-227-0180; www.chicagochildrenstheatre.org) is one of the few, full-fledged kids' theater troupes in the country, and they do a bang-up job. Performances take place at the Steppenwolf, Goodman and other theaters around town; ticket prices and times vary.

For a theatrical experience of a different kind, take the youngsters to a taping of **Chic-A-Go-Go** (www.myspace.com/chicagogoshow), a cable-access TV show that's like a kiddie version of *Soul Train* – ie it's a dance party with children and adult hipsters groovin' to eclectic tunes and live bands. Check the website for taping dates and locations, which vary.

CHICAGO CHILDREN'S MUSEUM

This **museum** (Map pp552-3; ☎ 312-527-1000; www.chichildrensmuseum.org; 700 E Grand Ave; admission $8, free Thu evening; ⏲ 10am-5pm Sun-Wed & Fri, to 8pm Thu & Sat) is on Navy Pier, and features exhibits where kids can climb a schooner, excavate dinosaur bones and generate hydroelectric power (it's fun – really). Follow up with an expedition down the pier itself, including spins on the Ferris wheel and carousel.

OTHER SIGHTS

Shedd Aquarium (p551) is drenched with whales, sharks and weird-looking fish – always young-crowd pleasers. The **Field Museum** (p551) offers lots and lots of that perennial kid favorite – dinosaurs! **Lincoln Park Zoo** (p558) has a children's area and farm where tykes can touch the animals.

Other kid-friendly activities include an El ride (see p573) around the Loop; get on the Brown Line at Merchandise Mart (Map pp552-3) and go to Clark St, which takes you on a leisurely trip through the thick of downtown's tall buildings, or try the **Loop Tour Train** (p564).

In July and August, take a lakefront swim at **North Avenue Beach** (p561), where there's soft sand, lifeguards, a snack bar and bathrooms.

Girls visiting Chicago will want to head directly to **American Girl Place** (Map pp552-3; ☎ 877-247-5223; 111 E Chicago Ave). In addition to purveying dolls from bygone eras, it has a theater with performances of a girl-oriented musical ($28 per ticket), and a café where dolls are seated and treated as part of the family.

American Childcare Services (☎ 312-644-7300; per hr $18.50, plus $20 agency fee) provides professional babysitters who will come to your hotel (four-hour minimum service).

Offbeat Chicago

Sure, your friends will listen politely as you describe your trip to the Sears Tower's tip. But you'll stop them mid-yawn when you unleash your knowledge of all things kinky culled from a Leather Museum visit, or show them the bruises amassed at a *Jerry Springer Show* fight. Chicago has a fine collection of unusual sights and activities to supplement its standard attractions.

The **International Museum of Surgical Science** (Map pp556-7; ☎ 312-642-6502; www.imss.org; 1524 N Lake Shore Dr; adult/student $8/4, admission free Tue; ⏲ 10am-4pm Tue-Sun May-Sep, closed Sun Oct-Apr) isn't necessarily the best organized, but it is the only one where you'll find a blood-letting exhibit and fine collection of 'stones' (as in kidney stone and gallstone). For those who've always wanted to see an iron lung, here's your chance.

On the **Jerry Springer Show** (Map pp552-3; ☎ 312-321-5365; www.jerryspringertv.com; 454 N Columbus Dr, 2nd

---

LOCAL VOICES

Name Kari Lydersen

Occupation: *Washington Post* reporter covering Great Lakes issues and contributor to *Dam Nation: Dispatches from the Water Underground* (Soft Skull, 2007), Chicago, Illinois

What's the biggest issue facing the Great Lakes today? Invasive species, especially the Asian carp (see box, p555). Invasive species continue to enter the Great Lakes – some of the worst are sea lampries, which suck the blood out of fish, and round gobies, which eat native mussels. The majority come in from ballast water from oceangoing ships.

Are the Great Lakes better or worse off than they were 30 years ago? Overall the lakes are better. Industrial pollution is controlled, and there's a public awareness of how critical the lakes are. Invasive species and water diversion (ie exporting water in massive quantities to other states or countries) are the two big issues currently. We're at a tipping point. We have lots of protection plans for these, but they're not implemented.

Any suggestions to travelers about how to be respectful of the local waterways? The most crucial thing is not to introduce invasive species. Boaters must clean their vessels thoroughly before entering local waters. And people who fish must use only bait that's allowable, per Fish and Wildlife guidelines.

fl, Chicago, IL 60611; tapings Mon-Wed Sep-Apr) you can bet you'll see mud-slinging, nudity, a knock-down drag-out fight or all three simultaneously. Call or write well in advance for free tickets. Far more genteel is self-help queen **Oprah** (Map pp552-3; ☎ tickets 312-591-9222, studio 312-633-1000; www.oprah.com; 1058 W Washington Blvd). Her show is extremely popular and the free tickets difficult to come by. Try the studio number if the ticket number isn't working. Last-minute tickets sometimes surface on the website.

The **Museum of Holography** (Map pp552-3; ☎ 312-226-1007; www.holographiccenter.com; 1134 W Washington Blvd; admission $5; ☯ 12:30-4:30pm Wed-Sun) contains the world's largest collection of holograms. Giant tarantulas, naked women and Michael Jordan are among the three-dimensional images. There's a school and laboratory dedicated to the science onsite, too.

Who knew Ben Franklin liked to be flogged and Egypt's Queen Hatshepsut had a foot fetish? The **Leather Archives & Museum** (Map p548; ☎ 773-761-9200; www.leatherarchives.org; 6418 N Greenview Ave; admission $5; ☯ noon-8pm Thu & Fri, noon-5pm Sat & Sun) reveals these facts and more in its displays of leather, fetish and S&M subcultures. The onsite shop sells posters, pins and other 'pervertibles.'

And Chic-A-Go-Go (p563) isn't just for kids. You, too, can shake it on the dance floor with Miss Mia and Ratso.

To Route 66 buffs: the Mother Road's starting point is across Michigan Ave on Adams St. Look for the **Route 66 sign** (Map pp552-3) on the street's north side as you head west toward Wabash Ave.

Tours

For a choice of highly recommended architectural tours by foot, boat or bus, contact the **Chicago Architecture Foundation** (Map pp552-3; ☎ 312-922-3432; www.architecture.org; 224 S Michigan Ave; tours $15-38). Tours are held year-round; departure points and times vary.

The 40-minute **Loop Tour Train** (Map pp552-3; Cultural Center Visitors Center, 77 E Randolph St; admission free; ☯ tours 10am & 10:40am Sat, May to Sep), guided by an Architecture Foundation docent, is a great way to see Chicago's buildings and learn the elevated train's history. Tickets are first-come, first-served starting at 9am.

Chicago Greeter (☎ 312-744-8000; www.chicago greeter.com; ☯ year-round) pairs you with a local city dweller who takes you on a personal free two- to four-hour tour customized by theme (architecture, history, gay and lesbian and more) or neighborhood. Travel is by foot and/or public transportation; reserve seven business days in advance. **InstaGreeter** (☯ 10am-4pm Fri & Sat, 11am-4pm Sun) is the quicker version, offering one-hour tours (free) on-the-spot from the visitors center at 77 E Randolph St. For free Millennium Park tours, see p551.

The Activities section has information on bicycle tours (p561) and kayak tours (p561).

And you can always do it yourself with free downloadable audio tours, provided you have access to an iPod and printer for maps. Try www.downloadchicagotours.com for jaunts like a Buddy Guy–narrated blues tour; or www.onscreenillinois.com, which provides a tour of Chicago's famous movie sites.

Festivals & Events

Chicago has a full events calendar year-round, but the biggies are held in the summer. **SummerDance** (Map pp552-3; ☎ 312-742-4007; www.chicagosummerdance.org; 601 S Michigan Ave; admission free) is ongoing mid-June through August, with bands playing rumba, samba and other world music preceded by fun dance lessons. It starts at 6pm Thursday to Saturday, and 4pm Sunday.

Each of the following events is free and held downtown on a weekend, unless noted otherwise. For exact dates and other details, contact the city's **Office of Special Events** (☎ 312-744-3315; www.cityofchicago.org/specialevents).

St Patrick's Day Parade (mid-Mar) After the parade, the local plumbers union dyes the Chicago River shamrock green. Then everyone drinks beer.

Blues Festival (early Jun) It's the biggest free blues fest in the world, with four days of the music that made Chicago famous.

Taste of Chicago (late Jun–early Jul) This 10-day food festival in Grant Park coincides with the Independence Day celebration. Many locals think the Taste is overrated.

Independence Day Concert (Jul 3) It features Tchaikovsky's *1812 Overture* and big-time fireworks.

Air and Water Show (mid-Aug) People flock to North Ave Beach to see daredevil displays by boats and planes.

Jazz Festival (early Sep) Chicago's longest-running music festival attracts top names on the national jazz scene over Labor Day weekend.

Gay & Lesbian Chicago

Chicago has a flourishing gay and lesbian scene; for details, check the weekly free publications of *Chicago Free Press* (www

.chicagofreepress.com) or *Windy City Times* (www.windycitymediagroup.com). The **Chicago Area Gay & Lesbian Chamber of Commerce** (Map p559; ☎ 773-303-0167; www.glchamber.org; 3656 N Halsted St; ☿ 9:30am-6pm Mon-Fri) also provides useful visitor information. **Chicago Greeter** (see Tours, opposite) offers personalized sightseeing trips.

The biggest concentration of bars and clubs is on N Halsted St between Belmont Ave and Grace St, an area known as 'Boys' Town.' **Roscoes** (Map p559; ☎ 773-281-3355; 3354 N Halsted St) is a fine place to start the night. Gay cowboy aficionados can giddyap to **Charlie's** (Map p559; ☎ 773-871-8887; 3726 N Broadway Ave).

Andersonville, aka 'Girls' Town,' is another area with many choices. Despite the name, both men and women frequent **Big Chicks** (Map p559; ☎ 773-728-5511; 5024 N Sheridan Rd) with its weekend DJs, art displays and next-door organic restaurant called **Tweet** (Map p559; ☎ 773-728-5576; 5020 N Sheridan Ave; ☿ 9am-3pm, closed Tue), where weekend brunch is a major gay scene. **Star Gaze** (Map p559; ☎ 773-561-7363; 5419 N Clark St; ☿ closed Mon & Tue) is one of the city's only all-women bars.

The late-June **Pride Parade** (☎ 773-348-8243; www.chicagopridecalendar.org; admission free) winds through Boys' Town and attracts close to 400,000 people.

Sleeping

Chicago lodging doesn't come cheap. The best way to cut costs is to reserve a room through a local hotel consolidator like **Hot Rooms** (☎ 800-468-3500; www.hotrooms.com). On weekends, and when big conventions trample through town (ie frequently), your options become much slimmer, so plan ahead to avoid unpleasant surprises. The prices we've listed are normal midweek rates in summer, the high season. Taxes add 15.4% to the rates.

B&Bs are a worthy alternative. Contact the **Chicago Bed & Breakfast Association** (www.chicago-bed-breakfast.com; r $100-229), an online service representing guesthouses throughout the city. Many properties have two- to three-night minimum stays.

Hotels in the Loop are convenient to Grant Park, the museums and business district, but are not near the best nightlife. Accommodations in the Near North/Gold Coast neighborhoods are popular for their proximity to eating, drinking, shopping and entertainment venues. Rooms in Lincoln Park, Lake View and Wicker Park entice because they're often cheaper than rooms downtown and also near hip nightlife.

All properties listed below have air conditioning unless specified otherwise.

BUDGET

HI Chicago (Map pp552-3; ☎ 312-360-0300; www.hichicago .org; 24 E Congress Pkwy; dm $27-36; P ☐) Chicago's best hostel is immaculate, centrally located in the Loop, and offers bonuses like a staffed information desk, free volunteer-led tours, discount passes to museums and shows, and luggage storage (per bag $2). The simple dorm rooms have six to 12 beds and attached bathrooms. Parking is $20 per night.

Ohio House Motel (Map pp552-3; ☎ 312-943-6000; www.ohiohousemotel.com; 600 N LaSalle St; r $90-130; P wi-fi) This throwback auto-court motel has remained unchanged since the Nixon administration. It isn't glamorous, but it is cheap, especially if you have a car (free parking!). The faded beauty is plopped right in the Near North. Wi-fi costs $10.

MIDRANGE

House of Two Urns B&B (Map p548; ☎ 773-235-1408, 877-896-8767; www.twourns.com; 1239 N Greenview Ave; r incl breakfast $119-185; P ☐ wi-fi) Artists own these two houses at mod Wicker Park's edge, so it's no surprise both places are fancifully furnished with odd antiques and original art. Amenities include free laundry, internet use, wi-fi and hot breakfast; some rooms share a bathroom. Take the CTA Blue Line to Division.

Wicker Park Inn (Map p548; ☎ 773-486-2743; www .wickerparkinn.com; 1329 N Wicker Park Ave; r incl breakfast $125-185; P wi-fi) This six-room B&B lets you stay in a classic brick row house in Wicker Park. The location puts you a few blocks from Chicago's nouveau eating, drinking and shopping epicenter, while downtown is a mere 10-minute train ride. Take the CTA Blue Line to Damen.

Days Inn Lincoln Park North (Map pp556-7; ☎ 773-525-7010, 888-576-3297; www.lpndaysinn.com; 644 W Diversey Pkwy; r incl breakfast $120-200; P ☐ wi-fi) Don't let the blah exterior put you off: this well-maintained chain hotel in Lincoln Park is a family favorite, with well-kept rooms, good service and perks like free health club access and wi-fi. It's an easy amble to the lakefront's parks and beaches, and a 15-minute bus ride to downtown. Parking costs $20.

Best Western River North (Map pp552-3; ☎ 312-467-0800, 800-727-0800; www.rivernorthhotel.com; 125 W Ohio St; r $169-226; P ♨ wi-fi) Its large, vaguely Asian-flaired rooms coupled with a sweet Near North location, indoor pool and sundeck overlooking the city are unusual benefits in this price bracket. The free parking and wi-fi seal the deal.

Hampton Inn Chicago (Map pp552-3; ☎ 312-832-0330, 800-426-7866; www.hamptonsuiteschicago.com; 33 W Illinois St; r incl breakfast $169-229; P ♨ 🖵 wi-fi) Despite fairly generic rooms, the Hampton offers good value thanks to its location near the Magnificent Mile and its array of freebies, including free wi-fi, a business center with computers, fitness facility, indoor pool, hot breakfast buffet and coin laundry. Parking is $38.

Willows Hotel (Map pp556-7; ☎ 773-528-8400, 800-787-3108; www.cityinns.com; 555 W Surf St; r/ste incl breakfast from $169/189; P wi-fi) Small and stylish, this Lake View hotel wins an architectural gold star. The chic little lobby provides a swell refuge of overstuffed chairs by the fireplace and free chocolate chip cookies and coffee. The 55 rooms, done up in shades of peach, cream and soft green, evoke a 19th-century French countryside feel. Parking is $22.

The owners have two other similarly styled and priced properties in the neighborhood: **City Suites Hotel** (Map p559; ☎ 773-404-3400, 800-248-9108; 933 W Belmont Ave), near the CTA Red Line Belmont station, which is a bit noisier than its counterparts; and the **Majestic Hotel** (Map p559; ☎ 773-404-3499, 800-727-5108; 528 W Brompton Ave), which lies east toward the lake and is more remote than its counterparts.

Tremont Hotel (Map pp556-7; ☎ 312-751-1900, 800-621-8133; www.tremontchicago.com; 100 E Chestnut St; r $169-259; P) The tasteful Tremont occupies a mannerly building near the Water Tower. The old-world-Europeanesque rooms are spacious but without many amenities. Head downstairs to the house bar and steakhouse – it's owned by Mike Ditka, mustachioed football coach of Chicago Bears, who's often imbibing onsite. Parking costs $40.

Hotel Blake (Map pp552-3; ☎ 312-986-1234; www.hotelblake.com; 500 S Dearborn St; r from $179; P 🖵 wi-fi) A relatively new addition to the lodging scene, the boutique Blake provides a sweet South Loop location midway between downtown's core and the Museum Campus. The mod, black-and-red furnishings are spread out in the amply spaced rooms; the bathrooms are flat-out huge. Parking is $39.

TOP END

Hotel Indigo (Map pp556-7; ☎ 312-787-4980, 866-246-3446; www.hotelindigo.com; 1244 N Dearborn Pkwy; r from $199; P 🖵 wi-fi) Staying at the Indigo is like staying in the guest room of your newly moneyed, Ikea-loving friend's flat: there are hardwood floors speckled with area rugs; white-washed wood furniture; bold, primary-colored walls; and oversized beds and chairs to burrow into. It's located in the Gold Coast. Parking costs $35.

Hotel Burnham (Map pp552-3; ☎ 312-782-1111, 877-294-9712; www.burnhamhotel.com; 1 W Washington St; r from $199; P wi-fi) The proprietors brag the Burnham has the highest guest return rates in Chicago; it's easy to see why. Housed in the Loop's landmark 1890s Reliance Building (precedent for the modern skyscraper), its super-cool decor woos architecture buffs. The bright rooms are lavishly furnished with mahogany writing desks and chaise longues. There's complimentary wine available each evening and free wi-fi throughout. Parking is $40.

Eating

The cultural hodgepodge that gives Chicago's neighborhoods their character translates into a mind-reeling, diverse restaurant scene. The hungry can fill up on anything from Algerian crepes to Costa Rican empanadas, from $195 multicourse meals to $2 hot dogs. And where else besides Chicago will you get the real deal for deep-dish pizza? The prices listed here are for dinner mains; lunch mains cost less.

THE LOOP

It gets lonely here come nighttime, as most Loop eateries are geared to lunch crowds of office workers.

Wow Bao (Map pp552-3; ☎ 312-334-6395; 175 W Jackson St; items $1.30-5; ☸ 6:30am-6:30pm Mon-Fri; wi-fi) In China, a 'bao' is a steamed yeast bun stuffed with meat or veggies, served mostly by street vendors. Here, it's a simple, slick chain offering egg-and-sausage, chicken curry and barbeque pork buns, plus potstickers, rice bowls and soups.

Oasis (Map pp552-3; ☎ 312-443-9534; 17 S Wabash Ave; dishes $4-7; ☸ 11am-5pm Mon-Fri, 11am-4pm Sat) Yes, you're entering a sad-looking fast food court in Jewelers Row's midst. But Oasis shines like a diamond in the rough, serving hummus and crisp falafel that are the best this side of Amman. Eat in or carry out to nearby parks.

Bombon Café (Map pp552-3; ☎ 312-781-2788; 170 W Washington Blvd; sandwiches $6-8; 🕑 7am-6pm Mon-Fri) Busy Bombon plumps its Mexican sandwiches with chicken and black beans, pork stew and habanero, and cured beef and cactus strips. The tres leches cakes and other sweets are expensive but totally, without a trace of doubt, worth it.

NEAR NORTH

Loads of restaurants and cafés pack the Near North's streets.

Billy Goat Tavern (Map pp552-3; ☎ 312-222-1525; lower level, 430 N Michigan Ave; burgers $2-4; 🕑 6am-2am Mon-Fri, 10am-2am Sat & Sun) Scruffy like the titular animal, this subterranean bar and burger joint is the legendary haunt of *Tribune* and *Sun-Times* reporters. Only the dimmest of bulbs orders fries with their cheezborger (remember John Belushi's famous *Saturday Night Live* skit: 'No fries – chips!').

Mr Beef (Map pp552-3; ☎ 312-337-8500; 666 N Orleans St; sandwiches $4-6; 🕑 8am-5pm Mon-Fri, 10:30am-2pm Sat) A Chicago specialty, the Italian Beef sandwich stacks up like this: thin-sliced, slow-cooked roast beef that's sopped in natural gravy and *giardiniera* (spicy, pickled vegetables), then heaped on a hoagie roll. Mr Beef serves the best at its picnic-style tables; just ask Jerry Springer, Jay Leno and the famous eaters shown on the walls.

Quartino (Map pp552-3; ☎ 312-698-5000; 626 N State St; mains $7-12; 🕑 11-1am) This rustic wine bar pours reasonably priced reds and whites by the bottle, glass or 'quartino' (quarter-liter carafe). For those who prefer a non-liquid dinner, it's Italian-style small plates filled with house-cured meats, pastas, pizzas, mussels, cheeses and Nutella panini.

Hop Haus (Map pp552-3; ☎ 312-467-4287; 646 N Franklin St; burgers $9-13; 🕑 11-4am) It's burgers and beer here, but not the kind you expect. Condiments like cranberries, papaya, brie and chutney top the burgers, and the meat can be kangaroo, boar or duck if beef bores you. The menu pairs boutique beers and vintage cocktails with each burger. And vegetarians need not stay away: Hop Haus makes a fantastic vegan burger.

Kitsch'n (Map pp552-3; ☎ 312-644-1500; 600 W Chicago Ave; mains $9-15; 🕑 8am-9pm Mon-Thu, to 10pm Fri & Sat, 9am-3pm Sun) Mmm, comfort food: flaky chicken or veggie pot pies, meatloaf and green bean casserole, washed down with a retro cocktail.

LINCOLN PARK & OLD TOWN

Halsted, Lincoln and Clark Sts are the main veins teeming with restaurants and bars. Parking is frightful, but it's handy to the CTA train stops at Armitage and Fullerton.

FAMED CHICAGO FARE

You can't leave town without sampling a deep-dish pizza, a hulking mass of crust that rises two or three inches above the plate and cradles a pile of toppings. One piece is practically a meal. It's hard to say which maker is the best, as they all serve gooey slices that will leave you a few pounds heavier. A large pizza averages $20 at the following places.

Pizzeria Uno (Map pp552-3; ☎ 312-321-1000; 29 E Ohio St; 🕑 11-1am Mon-Thu, 11-2am Fri & Sat, 11am-11pm Sun) Where the deep dish concept originated in 1943; sister outlet Due is one block north.

Gino's East (Map pp552-3; ☎ 312-266-3337; 162 E Superior St; 🕑 11am-10pm Mon-Sat, to 9pm Sun) Write on the walls while you wait for your pie.

Lou Malnati's (Map pp552-3; ☎ 312-828-9800; 439 N Wells St; 🕑 11am-11pm Mon-Thu, 11am-midnight Fri & Sat, noon-10pm Sun) Famous for its buttercrust.

Giordano's (Map pp552-3; ☎ 312-951-0747; 730 N Rush St; 🕑 11am-11pm Sun-Thu, 11am-midnight Fri & Sat) Perfectly tangy tomato sauce.

No less iconic is the Chicago hot dog – a wiener and bun that have been 'dragged through the garden' (ie topped with onions, tomatoes, shredded lettuce, bell peppers, pepperoncini and sweet relish, or variations thereof, but never ketchup). **Wiener Circle** (p568) and **Hot Doug's** (p568) do it right.

The city is also revered for its spicy, drippy, only-in-Chicago Italian beef sandwiches. **Mr Beef** (above) serves the gold standard.

Wiener Circle (Map pp556-7; ☎ 773-477-7444; 2622 N Clark St; items $2-4; ✷ 10:30am-4am Sun-Thu, 10:30am-5am Fri & Sat) As famous for its unruly, foul-mouthed ambience as its char-dogs and cheddar fries, the Wiener Circle is *the* place for late-night munchies. It helps to be shnockered before entering.

Crepe & Coffee Palace (Map pp556-7; ☎ 773-404-1300; 2433 N Clark St; mains $5-8; ✷ 10am-10pm) It's OK – delicious, in fact – to make a meal of pancakes. This Algerian eatery serves 'em sweet or savory (stuffed with chicken, smoked salmon or escargot).

Bourgeois Pig (Map pp556-7; ☎ 773-883-5282; 738 W Fullerton Pkwy; mains $6-7; ✷ 7am-10pm Mon-Fri, 8am-10pm Sat & Sun) An old-school lefty coffee shop with big, creaking wood tables and chairs, the Pig serves strong java and good panini sandwiches.

Goose Island Brew Pub (Map pp556-7; ☎ 312-915-0071; 1800 N Clybourn Ave; mains $8-15; ✷ 11am-10pm) Goose Island is a brew pub whose grub often incorporates specialty beer into dishes like Belgian beef stew and ale-roasted chicken. The chips make a fine accompaniment to any meal. Suds enthusiasts can take the $3 brewery tour that culminates with six samples. Crisp Honker's Ale remains a crowd favorite.

Alinea (Map pp556-7; ☎ 312-867-0110; 1723 N Halsted St; multicourse tastings $135-195; ✷ 5:30-9:30pm Wed-Sun) Mind-bending Alinea serves the kind of high-tech cuisine Jane Jetson might whip up for George, say a peanut butter and jelly sandwich toasted by a heat gun, or dishes emanating from a centrifuge or pressed into a capsule. *Gourmet* magazine recently ranked it America's No 1 restaurant.

LAKE VIEW & WRIGLEYVILLE

Clark, Halsted, Belmont and Southport are fertile streets. Parking is near impossible, so take the CTA train to the Belmont, Southport or Addison stops.

Ann Sather's (Map p559; ☎ 773-348-2378; 929 W Belmont Ave; mains $7-13; ✷ 7am-3pm Mon & Tue, 7am-9pm Wed-Sun) Try the Swedish potato sausages and cinnamon rolls.

Radhuni Indian Kitchen (Map p559; ☎ 773-404-5670; 3227 N Clark St; mains $9-16; ✷ 11am-11pm Mon-Sat, to 10pm Sun) Radhuni combines flavors from India, Pakistan and Bangladesh to create its curries, biryani dishes, spicy shrimp vindaloo and sweet, pistachio-and-almond-stuffed naan bread. A buffet ($9) is served from 11am to 3pm.

WICKER PARK, BUCKTOWN & UKRAINIAN VILLAGE

Hip restaurants open almost every day. Take the CTA Blue Line to Chicago, Damen or Western.

Irazu (Map p548; ☎ 773-252-5687; 1865 N Milwaukee Ave; mains $4-8; ✷ 10am-9pm Mon-Sat) The Costa Rican owners of Irazu dish up unusual items, like *yuca* (cassava) with garlic, empanadas and oatmeal milkshakes.

Feed (Map p548; ☎ 773-489-4600; 2803 W Chicago Ave; mains $5-8; ✷ 11am-10pm Mon-Sat) Folksy Feed serves a small menu of down-home chow such as rotisserie chicken, mac-n-cheese, mashed potatoes, corn pudding, fried okra and bulging fruit pies. Bring your own booze; cash only.

our pick **Handlebar Bar & Grill** (Map p548; ☎ 773-384-9546; 2311 W North Ave; mains $7-10; ✷ 4pm-midnight Mon-Thu, 4pm-2am Fri, 10am-2am Sat, 10am-midnight Sun) Handlebar peddles (pun intended, since the decor is bicycle-oriented) West African groundnut stew, wasabi-baked tofu and other energizing dishes; quaff the excellent beer selection on the patio.

Hot Chocolate (Map p548; ☎ 773-489-1747; 1747 N Damen Ave; mains $15-23; ✷ 11:30am-3pm Tue-Fri, 10am-2pm Sat & Sun, 5:30-10pm Tue-Sun) The pastry-chef owner whips up tasty mains, say walleye fish with pea-and-mint puree. But you're really here for dessert, so save room for the hot fudge.

LOGAN SQUARE

Several eats and drinks ring the intersection of Milwaukee, Logan and Kedzie Blvds. Take the CTA Blue Line to Logan Square.

Hot Doug's (Map p548; ☎ 773-279-9550; 3324 N California Ave; mains $2-7; ✷ 10:30am-4pm Mon-Sat) Let Doug acquaint you with a Chicago superfood: the hot dog. He serves multiple styles (Polish, bratwursts, Chicago) cooked multiple ways (char-grilled, deep-fried, steamed). Confused? Doug will explain it all. He also makes gourmet 'haute dogs' with smoked alligator and boar meat.

Lula Café (Map p548; ☎ 773-489-9554; 2537 N Kedzie Blvd; mains $14-23; ✷ 9am-10pm, to 11pm Fri & Sat, closed Tue) Slow-food lovers crowd in for Lula's locally sourced menu, which changes with the seasons. Prior dishes include striped bass with pinenut-peppered orzo, and pasta with Moroccan cinnamon and feta.

ANDERSONVILLE & UPTOWN

These northern neighborhoods burst with casual-but-edgy restaurants and bars. 'New Chinatown' is nearby on Argyle St. Take the CTA Red Line to Argyle or Berwyn.

Ba Le Bakery (Map p559; ☎ 773-561-4424; 5018 N Broadway St; sandwiches $3-4; ☻ 8am-9pm) Ba Le serves sandwiches Saigon-style, called *banh mi*, with steamed pork, shrimp cakes or meatballs on fresh baguettes made right dang here. Try the cream puffs for dessert.

Kopi Traveler's Café (Map p559; ☎ 773-989-5674; 5317 N Clark St; items $5-8; ☻ 8am-11pm Mon-Fri, 9am-midnight Sat, 10am-11pm Sun) Kopi has an Asian trekker-lodge vibe, from the pile of cushions to sit upon, to the healthy sandwiches, to the bulletin board where travelers post flyers.

NEAR WEST SIDE & PILSEN

The ethnic areas are a big draw. Greektown extends along S Halsted St, Little Italy is along Taylor St, and the Mexican Pilsen enclave centers around W 18th St. Stylish, nouveau eateries spread along W Randolph and W Washington Sts near Halsted St in an area called the West Loop or Restaurant Row. Take the CTA Blue Line to UIC-Halsted, 18th St or Clinton.

Lou Mitchell's (Map pp552-3; ☎ 312-939-3111; 565 W Jackson Blvd; mains $4-9; ☻ 5:30am-3pm Mon-Sat, 7am-3pm Sun) There's a queue to get in for the famed breakfasts, but staff give out free Milk Duds to ease the wait.

Cuernavaca (Map p548; ☎ 773-829-1147; 1160 W 18th St; mains $8-12; ☻ 9am-11pm) Family-run Cuernavaca is the real enchilada: festive atmosphere with colorful murals, soccer games on TV, full bar with bueno margaritas and roasted chicken covered in chocolatey mole sauce.

Avec (Map pp552-3; ☎ 312-377-2002; 615 W Randolph St; mains $15-25; ☻ 3:30-11:45pm Mon-Thu, 3:30pm-12:45am Fri & Sat, 3:30-9:45pm Sun) Small, rustic Avec serves Mediterranean-influenced small plates, such as chorizo-stuffed dates, and mains, like pork shoulder with green chilies. The pared-down menu also focuses on artisanal cheeses and wines. Seating is at communal tables.

SOUTH LOOP, NEAR SOUTH SIDE & CHINATOWN

Take the CTA Red Line to Harrison, Roosevelt or Cermak-Chinatown.

Yolk (Map pp552-3; ☎ 312-789-9655; 1120 S Michigan Ave; mains $5-11; ☻ 6am-3pm, from 7am Sat &

> ### DIY: HOW TO FIND A REAL CHICAGO BAR
>
> While we can't list every watering hole in town (which is too bad, because we'd enjoy the research process), we can give you the tools to go out and discover classic, character-filled bars on your own. Look for:
>
> - An 'Old Style' beer sign swinging out front.
> - A dart board and/or pool table inside.
> - Patrons wearing Cubs, White Sox or Bears-logoed ballcaps.
> - Bottles of Budweiser served in buckets of ice.
> - Sports on TV (with the latter being a 1974 Zenith, not some fancy flat-screen thing).

Sun) This egg-themed breakfast place gets busy with South Loopers thrilled over the good-value frittatas, crepes, french toast and sandwiches.

Joy Yee's Noodles (Map pp552-3; ☎ 312-328-0001; www.joyyee.com; 2159 S China Pl; drinks $3-4, mains $6-10; ☻ 11am-10:30pm) Joy Yee's roaring blenders mix more than 100 types of fruit drinks and tapioca bubble teas, which make a fine accompaniment to the slurpable bowls of udon.

Tamarind (Map pp552-3; ☎ 312-379-0970; 614 S Wabash Ave; mains $9-15; ☻ 11am-11pm) The pan-Asian menu sprawls through Chinese, Japanese, Thai and Vietnamese dishes and includes prix-fixe specials, sushi and create-your-own stir fries.

Drinking

During the long winters, Chicagoans count on bars for warmth. Usual closing time is 2am, but some places stay open until 4am or 5am. In summer many bars boast beer gardens.

THE LOOP & NEAR NORTH

Signature Lounge (Map pp556-7; ☎ 312-787-7230; John Hancock Center, 875 N Michigan Ave) Have the Hancock Observatory view without the Hancock Observatory admission price. Shoot straight up to the 96th floor and order a beverage while looking out over the city. Ladies: don't miss the bathroom view.

Billy Goat Tavern (Map pp552-3; ☎ 312-222-1525; lower level, 430 N Michigan Ave) To toss back a cold one at a character-filled dive, it's hard to beat a plunge to the Billy Goat's depths. They serve good burgers, too (see p567).

Clark Street Ale House (Map pp552-3; ☎ 312-642-9253; 742 N Clark St) It taps a massive selection of Midwestern microbrews; sample a small-pour flight for $3.

LINCOLN PARK & OLD TOWN
Olde Towne Ale House (Map pp556-7; ☎ 312-944-7020; 219 W North Ave) There are no pretenses at this long-time favorite, across from Second City (p572), where you'll mingle with beautiful people and not-so-beautiful people (they're the ones face down at the bar).

Delilah's (Map pp556-7; ☎ 773-472-2771; 2771 N Lincoln Ave) Delilah's is where underground rockers come to drink from the lengthy whiskey list.

LAKE VIEW & WRIGLEYVILLE
Ginger Man (Map p559; ☎ 773-549-2050; 3740 N Clark St) The pierced-and-tattooed patrons, pool tables and good beer selection make Ginger Man wonderfully different from the surrounding Wrigley sports bars.

Murphy's Bleachers (Map p559; ☎ 773-929-7061; 3655 N Sheffield Ave) Located across from Wrigley's fabled outfield seats, Murphy's caters to pre- and post-Cubs-game guzzlers.

WICKER PARK, BUCKTOWN & UKRAINIAN VILLAGE
Map Room (Map p548; ☎ 773-252-7636; 1949 N Hoyne Ave) At this map-and-globe-filled 'travelers' tavern,' artsy types sip coffee by day and suds from the 200-strong beer list by night.

Matchbox (Map pp556-7; ☎ 312-666-9292; 770 N Milwaukee Ave) Lawyers, artists and bums all squeeze in for the retro drinks. It's small as – you got it – a matchbox, with room for about 10 people on barstools; everyone else stands against the back wall.

California Clipper (Map p548; ☎ 773-384-2547; 1002 N California Ave) Hipsters quaff time-honored cocktails at this historic tavern. There's Monday night bingo, a tiki room and spoken word and live music shows.

ANDERSONVILLE & UPTOWN
Hopleaf (Map p559; ☎ 773-334-9851; 5148 N Clark St) You've hit the mother lode of beer selection when you walk into this beauty – there are 200 types available (30 on tap) and a Belgian eatery upstairs.

Simon's (Map p559; ☎ 773-878-0894; 5210 N Clark St) This watering hole is a fertile brooding ground for generations of underemployed musicians.

Entertainment
Check the *Reader*, *Time Out Chicago* magazine and other local media (p549). **Hot Tix** (www.hottix.org; ☯ closed Mon) sells same-day theater tickets at half-price. Buy them online, at the **Randolph branch** (Map pp552-3; 72 E Randolph St) or **Pearson branch** (Map pp556-7; 163 E Pearson St). Cover charges at music and dance clubs range from nil to $20 or more, depending on who's playing and the day of the week.

CLUBS
The club scene ranges from snooty places to casual joints where all you do is dance.

Carol's Pub (Map p559; ☎ 773-334-2402; 4659 N Clark St) A honky tonk in Chicago? Just read the sign out front – 'Live Country Music' – which results in some boot stompin' dancin' at weekends.

Funky Buddha Lounge (Map pp552-3; 312-666-1695; 728 W Grand Ave) The Buddha shakes with hip-hop and house music.

Butterfly Social Club (☎ same; 722 W Grand Ave) Located next door to the Funky Buddha is the all-natural Butterfly Social Club serving unpasteurized ciders, organic wines and spring-water ice cubes amid tropicalia and Afro beats.

Wicker Park is chockablock with clubs. **Lava** (Map pp556-7; ☎ 773-342-5282; 1270 N Milwaukee Ave) blasts music from the underground, while **Ohm** (Map p548; ☎ 773-278-5138; 1958 W North Ave; ☯ closed Mon & Tue) provides plenty of space to get jiggy to house music.

The Near North's clubs are more cavernous and luxurious (with dress codes), such as **Sound-Bar** (Map pp552-3; ☎ 312-787-4480; 226 W Ontario St; ☯ open Fri & Sat only).

LIVE MUSIC
Blues and jazz both have deep roots in Chicago, and world-class performers appear at myriad venues nightly.

Blues
Buddy Guy's Legends (Map pp552-3; ☎ 312-427-0333; 754 S Wabash Ave) This place gets the top acts in town, including the venerable Mr Guy him-

self. Rumors persist that it will be moving, so check before heading out.

Rosa's (Map p548; ☎ 773-342-0452; 3420 W Armitage Ave; ☒ closed Sun & Mon) Rosa's is a real-deal venue that brings in top local talent and dedicated fans to a somewhat dodgy Logan Square block.

Lee's Unleaded Blues (Map p548; 773-493-3477; 7401 S South Chicago Ave; ☒ closed Tue & Wed) Far off the tourist path, buried deep on the South Side, Lee's is a genuine juke joint. The local crowd dresses in their finest threads, and everyone jams until dawn.

Blue Chicago (Map pp552-3; ☎ 312-642-6261; 536 & 736 N Clark St) This is a pair of friendly clubs downtown.

New Checkerboard Lounge (Map p548; ☎ 773-684-1472; 5201 S Harper Ct) The Checkerboard was a renowned Bronzeville dive for decades. Then it moved to Hyde Park a few years ago and slicked up. But the songs remain the same: blues or jazz nightly.

Noisy, hot, sweaty and crowded are **Blues** (Map pp556-7; ☎ 773-528-1012; 2519 N Halsted St) and **Kingston Mines** (Map pp556-7; ☎ 773-477-4646; 2548 N Halsted St). Both are conveniently located in Lincoln Park and are popular drawcards for the holiday-making 4am crowd.

Jazz
Green Mill (Map p559; ☎ 773-878-5552; 4802 N Broadway Ave) Glamorous, dark and smoky, the Green Mill earned its notoriety as Al Capone's favorite speakeasy (the tunnels where he hid the booze are still underneath the bar), and you can feel his ghost urging you on to another martini. Top-flight local and national artists perform six nights per week; Sundays are for the nationally acclaimed poetry slam.

Velvet Lounge (Map p548; ☎ 312-791-9050; 67 E Cermak Rd; ☒ closed Mon) The intimate Velvet Lounge is a jazz musicians' jazz club, with avant-garde notes wafting from the saxophones.

Back Room (Map pp556-7; ☎ 312-751-2433; 1007 N Rush St) This jazz joint is so tiny it's like having a band in your bedroom.

Rock & Folk
Metro (Map p559; ☎ 773-549-3604; 3730 N Clark St) Local bands and big names looking for an 'intimate' venue play here.

Old Town School of Folk Music (Map p548; ☎ 773-728-6000; 4544 N Lincoln Ave) It's a superb room offering an eclectic line-up of world music and, yes, folk music.

Hideout (Map pp556-7; ☎ 773-227-4433; 1354 W Wabansia Ave) Tucked behind a factory, Hideout is as hard to find as the name implies, but worth it for the laid-back, indie atmosphere and nightly rock, folk and country tunes (and sometimes theater).

Phyllis' Musical Inn (Map p548; ☎ 773-486-9862; 1800 W Division St) One of the all-time great dives, this former Polish polka bar features scrappy (and quite possibly crappy) up-and-coming bands nightly.

Double Door (Map p548; ☎ 773-489-3160; 1572 N Milwaukee Ave) and **Empty Bottle** (Map p548; ☎ 773-276-3600; 1035 N Western Ave) epitomize the hard-edge Chicago rock scene.

THEATER
Chicago's reputation for stage drama is well deserved. The city's main companies:

Chicago Shakespeare Theater (Map pp552-3; ☎ 312-595-5600; www.chicagoshakes.com; 800 E Grand Ave) Will's comedies and tragedies at Navy Pier.

Goodman Theatre (Map pp552-3; ☎ 312-443-3800; www.goodman-theatre.org; 170 N Dearborn St) Known for both new and classic works.

Steppenwolf Theatre (Map pp556-7; ☎ 312-335-1650; www.steppenwolf.org; 1650 N Halsted St) Drama club of Malkovich, Sinise and other Hollywood stars.

First-rate smaller companies:

Lookingglass Theatre Company (Map pp556-7; ☎ 312-337-0665; www.lookingglasstheatre.org; 821 N Michigan Ave) Improv-based works, often incorporating acrobatics.

Neo-Futurists (Map p559; ☎ 773-275-5255; www.neofuturists.org; 5153 N Ashland Ave) Original works that make you ponder and laugh simultaneously.

Redmoon Theater (Map p548; ☎ 312-850-8440; www.redmoon.org; 1438 W Kinzie St) Puppet-oriented productions.

Major venues for touring shows are mostly clustered at State and Randolph Sts:

Auditorium Theater (Map pp552-3; ☎ 312-922-2110; 50 E Congress Pkwy)

Cadillac Palace Theater (Map pp552-3; ☎ 312-977-1700; 151 W Randolph St)

Chicago Theater (Map pp552-3; ☎ 312-462-6300; 175 N State St)

Ford Center/Oriental Theater (Map pp552-3; ☎ 312-977-1700; 24 W Randolph St)

LaSalle Bank Theater (Map pp552-3; ☎ 312-977-1700; 18 W Monroe St)

GREAT LAKES

COMEDY

Improv comedy began in Chicago, and the city still nurtures the best in the business.

Second City (Map pp556-7; ☎ 312-337-3992; www.second city.com; 1616 N Wells St) The cream of the crop – it's the place where John Belushi, Bill Murray and many others honed their wit.

Improv Olympics (Map p559; ☎ 773-880-0199; www .iochicago.net; 3541 N Clark St) Many Saturday Night Livers were fostered here.

CINEMA

Music Box Theatre (Map p559; ☎ 773-871-6604; www .musicboxtheatre.com; 3733 N Southport Ave) Patrons hear live organ music and see clouds roll across the ceiling prior to their art films at this old movie palace.

Gene Siskel Film Center (Map pp552-3; ☎ 312-846-2800; www.artic.edu/webspaces/siskelfilmcenter; 164 N State St) The small theater screens offbeat films.

PERFORMING ARTS

Symphony Center (Map pp552-3; ☎ 312-294-3000; www.cso .org; 220 S Michigan Ave) The Chicago Symphony Orchestra makes music in this beautiful facility.

Civic Opera House (Map pp552-3; ☎ 312-332-2244; www .lyricopera.org; 20 N Wacker Dr) The Lyric Opera of Chicago, one of the country's best, performs in the grand venue here.

Grant Park Orchestra (☎ 312-742-7638; www.grant parkmusicfestival.com) The orchestra puts on free classical concerts in Millennium Park (p551) throughout the summer.

Joffrey Ballet of Chicago (☎ 312-386-8905; www.jof frey.com) and **Hubbard Street Dance Chicago** (☎ 312-850-9744; www.hubbardstreetdance.com) are renowned local dance companies. They perform at the Auditorium Theater (p571) and **Harris Theater for Music and Dance** (Map pp552-3; ☎ 312-334-7777; 205 E Randolph St), respectively.

SPORTS

Wrigley Field (Map p559; 1060 W Addison St) The Cubs (☎ 773-404-2827; www.cubs.com) last won the World Series in 1908, but their fans still pack baseball's most charming stadium, dating from 1914 and known for its ivy-walled field, classic neon sign and men's trough urinals. Take the CTA Red Line to Addison; it's 4.5 miles north of the Loop.

US Cellular Field (Map p548; 333 W 35th St) The White Sox (☎ 312-674-1000; www.whitesox .com) are the Cubs' South Side rivals and play in the more modern 'Cell' (aka Comiskey Park, its name for years before corporate sponsorship). Tickets are usually cheaper and easier to get than at Wrigley. Take the CTA Red Line to the Sox-35th station; it's 4.5 miles south of the Loop.

United Center (Map p548; 1901 W Madison St) The Bulls (☎ 800-462-2849; www.nba.com/bulls) play basketball in this huge stadium, also used by the Blackhawks (☎ 312-559-1212; www .chicagoblackhawks.com) for ice hockey. It's about 2 miles west of the Loop. CTA runs special buses on game days; it's best not to walk here.

Soldier Field (Map pp552-3; 425 E McFetridge Dr) Chicago's National Football League team, the Bears (☎ 847-615-2327; www.chicagobears .com), tackles at this stadium, which stirred huge controversy when it was renovated from a classical facade to its current flying-saucer look, referred to as 'the mistake on the lake.'

Shopping

Easy-to-obtain local souvenirs include sports-logoed gear and jazz or blues CDs.

The shoppers' siren song emanates from N Michigan Ave, along the Magnificent Mile (p554). Large vertical malls here include **Shops at North Bridge** (Map pp552-3; 520 N Michigan Ave), **Chicago Place** (Map pp552-3; 700 N Michigan Ave), **Water Tower Place** (Map pp556-7; 835 N Michigan Ave) and **900 N Michigan** (Map pp556-7; 900 N Michigan Ave).

Boutiques fill Bucktown (mod), Lincoln Park (tony), Lake View (countercultural) and Andersonville (all three).

Chicago Architecture Foundation Shop (Map pp552-3; ☎ 312-922-3432; 224 S Michigan Ave) Skyscraper playing cards, Frank Lloyd Wright notecards, eyeball toilet brushes and many more unusual gifts for those with an edifice complex.

Chicago Tribune Store (Map pp552-3; ☎ 312-222-3080; 435 N Michigan Ave) For the ultimate souvenir – a Cubs ballcap.

Jazz Record Mart (Map pp552-3; ☎ 312-222-1467; 27 E Illinois St) It's thoroughly stocked on Chicago blues and jazz CDs.

Getting There & Away

O'Hare International Airport (ORD; ☎ 800-832-6352; www.flychicago.com) is the world's busiest. Most non-US airlines and international flights use Terminal 5 (except Lufthansa and flights from Canada).

The smaller **Chicago Midway Airport** (MDW; Map p548; ☎ 773-838-0600; www.flychicago.com) is used mostly by domestic carriers, like Southwest, which often have cheaper flights than airlines serving O'Hare.

The main **Greyhound station** (Map pp552-3; ☎ 312-408-5800; 630 W Harrison St) is two blocks from the CTA Blue Line Clinton stop. Buses run frequently to Cleveland ($46 to $56, 7½ hours), Detroit ($30 to $35, seven hours) and Minneapolis ($61 to $70, nine hours), as well as small towns throughout the USA.

Megabus (☎ 877-462-6342; www.megabus.com/us) departs from **Union Station** (Map pp552-3; 225 S Canal St) and travels only to major Midwestern cities. Prices are often less, and quality and efficiency better than Greyhound on these routes.

Car rental is subject to 18% tax. Many rental agencies – Avis, Hertz and others – have 24-hour desks at both airports and around town. Check the Transportation chapter (p1144) for contact details.

Chicago's classic **Union Station** (Map pp552-3; 225 S Canal St) is the hub for **Amtrak's** (☎ 800-872-7245; www.amtrak.com) national and regional service. Seven trains a day go to Milwaukee ($21; 1½ hours). Other connections:

Detroit $27, 5½ hours, three trains daily.
Minneapolis/St Paul $60 to $115, eight hours, one train daily.
New York $90 to $137, 19 hours, two trains daily.
St Louis $22 to $30, 5½ hours, five trains daily.
San Francisco (Emeryville) $130 to $245, 53 hours, one train daily.

Getting Around
TO/FROM THE AIRPORT
O'Hare International Airport is 17 miles northwest of the Loop. The cheapest, and often the quickest, way to/from O'Hare is by the CTA Blue Line ($2), but the station is a long walk from the flight terminals. At the airport, signs point variously to 'CTA,' 'Rapid Transit' and 'Trains to City.' Airport Express shuttles run between the airport and downtown hotels (per person $25). Cabs to/from downtown cost about $45.

Midway Airport is 11 miles southwest of the Loop, connected via the CTA Orange Line ($2). Other options include shuttles (per person $20) and cabs ($25 to $35).

BICYCLE
Chicago has 120 miles of bike lanes, though they aren't very well respected. Request a free map from the city's **transportation department** (☎ 312-742-2453; www.chicagobikes.org).

Bike racks are plentiful; the biggest – with showers – is at **McDonalds Cycle Center** (Map pp552-3; ☎ 888-245-3929; 239 E Randolph St). Lock it or lose it. For bike-rental information, see p561.

CAR & MOTORCYCLE
Be warned: it's difficult to find street parking and expensive to park in a lot. Rush-hour traffic is abysmal.

PUBLIC TRANSPORTATION
The **Chicago Transit Authority** (CTA; ☎ 888-968-7282; www.transitchicago.com) operates the city bus and train network, including both elevated (El) and subway trains. CTA buses go everywhere from early morning until late evening. Two of the eight color-coded train lines – the Red Line, and the Blue Line to O'Hare International Airport – operate 24 hours a day. The other lines run from about 5am to 11pm daily. During the day, you shouldn't have to wait more than 15 minutes for a train (although track renovations happening through 2009 will sometimes create lengthier lags). Get free maps at any train station.

The standard fare on a bus or train is $2; transfers cost 25¢. On buses, you can use a fare card (called a Transit Card) or pay with exact change. On the train, you must use a Transit Card, sold from vending machines at train stations. Day passes (one-/three-day pass $5/12) provide excellent savings, but can be purchased only at visitors centers or airports. At press time, CTA was threatening to raise fares by up to $1 per ride and to cut several bus routes due to budget woes. So don't be surprised if, by the time you're reading this, you have to shell out more money and wait longer for service.

Metra commuter trains (☎ 312-836-7000; www.metrarail.com) have 12 routes serving the suburbs from four terminals ringing the Loop (LaSalle St Station, Randolph St/Millennium Park Station, Richard B Ogilvie Transportation Center and Union Station – all on Map pp552–3). Some lines run daily, while others operate only during weekday rush hours. Metra fares cost $1.95 to $5 or more. An all-weekend pass costs $5.

PACE (☎ 847-364-7223; www.pacebus.com) runs the suburban bus system that connects with city transport.

TAXI

Cabs are plentiful in the Loop, north to Andersonville and west to Bucktown. In other areas, call **Yellow Cab** (☎ 312-829-4222) or **Flash Cab** (☎ 773-561-1444). Flagfall is $2.25, plus $1.80 per mile and $1 per extra passenger; a 15% tip is expected. Venture outside city limits and you'll pay one and a half times the fare.

AROUND CHICAGO

Evanston & North Shore

Evanston, 14 miles north of the Loop and reached via the CTA Purple Line, combines sprawling old houses with a compact downtown. It's also home to Northwestern University.

Beyond are Chicago's northern lakeshore suburbs, which became popular with the carriage set in the late 19th century. A classic 30-mile drive follows Sheridan Rd through various tony towns to the socioeconomic apex of Lake Forest. Attractions include the glistening white **Baha'i House of Worship** (☎ 847-853-2300; www.bahai.us; 100 Linden Ave, Wilmette; admission free; 🕐 10am-8pm May-Sep, 10am-5pm Oct-Apr) – a soaring architectural marvel – and the **Chicago Botanic Garden** (☎ 847-835-5440; www.chicagobotanic.org; 1000 Lake Cook Rd, Glencoe; admission free; 🕐 8am-dusk). Parking costs $15.

Oak Park

Located west of the Loop and easily reached on the CTA Green Line, Oak Park spawned two famous sons: novelist Ernest Hemingway was born here, and architect Frank Lloyd Wright lived and worked here from 1898 to 1908.

During Wright's 10 years in Oak Park, he designed a helluva lot of houses. Stop at the **visitors center** (☎ 888-625-7275; www.visitoakpark.com; 158 N Forest Ave; 🕐 10am-5pm) and ask for the architectural walking-tour map (usually a free, photocopied page), which gives their locations. To actually get inside a Wright-designed dwelling, you'll need to visit the **Frank Lloyd Wright Home & Studio** (☎ 708-848-1976; www.wrightplus.org; 951 Chicago Ave; adult/child 4-10 $12/5). Tours are held at 11am, 1pm and 3pm Monday to Thursday; to 6pm Friday; and continuous 11am to 3:30pm Saturday and Sunday.

Despite Hemingway calling Oak Park a 'village of wide lawns and narrow minds,' the town still pays homage to him at the **Ernest Hemingway Museum** (☎ 708-848-2222; www.ehfop.org; 200 N Oak Park Ave; adult/child $7/5.50; 🕐 1-5pm Sun-Fri, 10am-5pm Sat). Admission also includes access to **Hemingway's Birthplace** (339 N Oak Park Ave).

> **WHAT THE...?**
>
> Rockford, 85 miles northwest of Chicago, is where the sock knitting machine was invented. 'Who cares'? you say. How about if we tell you the socks from this machine became the basis for the Sock Monkey, the classic American stuffed toy? To honor the brown-and-red critters toted by generations of kiddies, Rockford holds a **Sock Monkey Festival** (☎ 815-397-9112; www.midwayvillage.com; adult/child $6/4; 🕐 early Mar), with monkey story times and monkey-making workshops. Also watch for giant fiberglass sock monkeys that pop up as decorations around town.

NORTHERN ILLINOIS

The highlight of northern Illinois is the hilly northwest, which was untouched by the last ice age and is bordered by the Mississippi River. It's an easy and popular excursion from Chicago.

En route is Union, where the **Illinois Railway Museum** (☎ 815-923-4000; www.irm.org; US 20 to Union Rd; adult $6.50-10.50, child 3-11 $4.50-8.50 depending upon season; 🕐 hrs vary Apr-Oct) sends trainspotters into fits of ecstasy with 200 acres of locomotives.

Galena

Though just a speck on the map, Galena is the area's main attraction. The town spreads across wooded hillsides and is perfectly preserved, despite a slew of tourist-oriented antique shops and restaurants.

Lead was mined in the upper Mississippi area as early as 1700, but industrial demands in the mid-19th century resulted in a boom. Galena (named after the lead sulfide ore) became a center for the industry and a major river port town, and businesses, hotels and mansions in Federal and Italianate styles shot up. The boom ended abruptly after the Civil War, and Galena was all but deserted until restoration began in the 1960s.

The main **visitors center** (☎ 815-777-4390, 877-464-2536; www.galena.org; 101 Bouthillier St; 🕐 9am-5pm Mon-Sat, 10am-5pm Sun) is on the eastern side of the Galena River, in the 1857 train depot. Get a walking guide, leave your car and explore on foot.

Elegant old Main St curves around the hillside and the historic heart of town. Among numerous sights is the **Ulysses S Grant Home** (☎ 815-777-3310; www.granthome.com; 500 Bouthillier St; adult/child $3/1; ☻ 9am-4:45pm Wed-Sun Apr-Oct, reduced hrs Nov-Mar), which was a gift from local Republicans to the victorious general at the end of the Civil War. Tours are provided (sometimes conducted by a guy who pretends he 'is' Grant).

The elaborate Italianate **Belvedere Mansion** (☎ 815-777-0747; 1008 Park Ave; adult/child $10/3; ☻ 11am-4pm Sun-Fri, to 5pm Sat late May-Oct) has the green drapes from *Gone With the Wind*.

On weekend evenings, set out on the hokey but fun **Annie Wiggins Ghost Tour** (☎ 815-777-0336; www.anniewiggins.com; 1004 Park Ave; 1hr tour $10; ☻ Fri & Sat evenings May-Oct). Yes, she wears a costume, but so does everyone it town, it seems.

Galena brims with B&Bs – you can't throw a quilt without it landing on a four-post bed at one of the zillion properties in town. Most cost at least $100 nightly, and they fill up at weekends. The visitors center does bookings; call or check the website.

Grant Hills Motel (☎ 815-777-2116; www.granthills .com; 9372 US 20; s/d $65/75; ☒ ☒) is a cozy motel 1.5 miles east of town, with fine views of the surrounding countryside and a horseshoe pitch. Or be regal like Grant and Lincoln and stay in the well-furnished rooms at the **De-Soto House Hotel** (☎ 815-777-0090; www.desotohouse .com; 230 S Main St; r $128-200; ☒ wi-fi), dating from 1855.

Clarks Again (☎ 815-777-4407; 200 N Main St; mains $3-7; ☻ 5am-1:30pm Sun-Fri, to 3pm Sat) is ideal for biscuit-and-gravy breakfasts or lunchtime sandwiches. **Log Cabin** (☎ 815-777-0393; 201 N Main St; mains $11-18; ☻ 4-10pm) is where you'll find huge dinner portions served amid Americana ambience.

Quad Cities

South of Galena along a pretty stretch of the **Great River Rd** (www.greatriverroad-illinois.org) is scenic **Mississippi Palisades State Park** (☎ 815-273-2731), a popular rock-climbing area; pick up information at the park entrance's gatehouse.

Further downstream, the **Quad Cities** (☎ 563-322-3911; www.visitquadcities.com) – Moline and Rock Island in Illinois, and Davenport and Bettendorf across the river in Iowa – make a surprisingly good stop. Rock Island has an appealing downtown (based at 3rd Ave and 18th St), with a couple of cafés, restaurants,

a lively pub and music scene, and a paddle wheeler casino. On the edge of town, **Black Hawk State Historic Site** (☎ 309-788-0177; www.black hawkpark.org; 1510 46th Ave; ☻ dawn-10pm) is a huge park with trails by the Rock River. Its **Hauberg Indian Museum** (☎ 309-788-9536; 1510 46th Ave, Watch Tower Lodge; admission free; ☻ 9am-noon & 1-5pm, reduced in winter) outlines the sorry story of Sauk leader Black Hawk and his people.

Out in the Mississippi River, the actual island of **Rock Island** once held a Civil War–era arsenal and POW camp. It now has two military museums and a Civil War cemetery.

Moline is the home of John Deere, the international farm machinery manufacturer, which has a museum/showroom in town. For Iowa-side attractions, see p659.

CENTRAL ILLINOIS

Abraham Lincoln and Route 66 sights are sprinkled liberally throughout central Illinois, which is otherwise farmland plain. East of Decatur, Arthur and Arcola are centers for the Amish.

Springfield

The small state capital has a serious obsession with Abraham Lincoln, who practiced law here from 1837 to 1861. Its Abe-related sights offer an in-depth look at the man and his turbulent times, which only some cynics find overdone. Many of the attractions are walkable downtown and cost little to nothing. Get your bearings with maps from the central **visitors center** (☎ 800-545-7300; www.visitspringfield illinois.com; 109 N 7th St; ☻ 8:30am-5pm Mon-Fri).

SIGHTS & ACTIVITIES

To visit the top-draw Lincoln Home, you must first pick up a ticket at the **Lincoln Home Visitors Center** (☎ 217-492-4150; www.nps.gov/liho; 426 S 7th St; admission free; ☻ 8:30am-5pm). The site is where Abraham and Mary Lincoln lived from 1844 until they moved to the White House in 1861. You'll see considerably more than just the home: the whole block has been preserved, and several structures are open to visitors.

The **Lincoln Presidential Library & Museum** (☎ 217-558-8844; www.alplm.org; 212 N 6th St; adult/child 5-15 $7.50/3.50; ☻ 9am-5pm) contains the most complete Lincoln collection in the world, everything from his Gettysburg Address and Emancipation Proclamation to his shaving mirror and briefcase. You'll have to wade through some Disneyesque exhibits to get to the good stuff.

After his assassination, Lincoln's body was returned to Springfield, where it lies today. The impressive **Lincoln's Tomb** sits in **Oak Ridge Cemetery** (☎ 217-782-2717; admission free; ◷ 9am-5pm Mar-Oct, to 4pm Nov-Feb), north of downtown. The gleam on the nose of Lincoln's bust, created by visitors' light touches, indicates the numbers of those who pay their respects here.

Standing a block apart are the noteworthy **Lincoln-Herndon Law Offices** (☎ 217-785-7960; cnr 6th & Adams Sts; suggested donation adult/child $2/1; ◷ 9am-5pm, closed Sun & Mon Sep–mid-Apr) and **Old State Capitol** (cnr 5th & Adams Sts; same cost & hrs). Both offer detailed tours covering Lincoln's early political life; the latter takes in his dramatic pre–Civil War debates with Stephen Douglas.

Lincoln-free attractions include the pristine 1904 **Dana-Thomas House** (☎ 217-782-6776; www.dana-thomas.org; 301 E Lawrence St; adult/child $3/1; ◷ 9am-4pm Wed-Sun), one of Frank Lloyd Wright's Prairie-style masterworks, with an insightful tour; **Shea's Gas Station Museum** (☎ 217-522-0475; 2075 Peoria Rd; admission $2; ◷ 8am-4pm Tue-Fri, to noon Sat), with Route 66 pumps and signs; and the macabre but enlightening **Museum of Funeral Customs** (☎ 217-544-3480; www .funeralmuseum.org; 1440 Monument Ave; adult/child 6-17 $4/2; ◷ 10am-4pm Tue-Sat, to 8pm Tue & Fri, 1-4pm Sun). Catch a flick under the stars at the **Route 66 Drive In** (☎ 217-698-0066; www.route66-drivein.com; 1700 Recreation Dr; adult/child 4-12 $5/3; ◷ nightly Jun-Aug, weekends mid-Apr–May, Sep).

SLEEPING & EATING

Carpenter Street Hotel (☎ 217-789-9100, 888-779-9100; www.carpenterstreethotel.com; 525 N 6th St; r incl breakfast $72; P ⊠ ⊠) It's a bland but well-priced option for downtown.

Inn at 835 (☎ 217-523-4466; www.innat835.com; 835 S 2nd St; s/d incl breakfast from $105/120; P) This 10-room B&B in an historic home offers the classiest digs in town.

Cozy Dog Drive In (☎ 217-525-1992; 2935 S 6th St; items $2-4; ◷ 8am-8pm Mon-Sat) All must stop to hail the corn dog's birthplace at the Cozy Dog. It's a Route 66 legend, with memorabilia and souvenirs, plus donuts to chase down the deeply fried main course.

ROUTE 66: GET YOUR KICKS IN ILLINOIS

America's 'Mother Road' kicks off in Chicago on Adams St just west of Michigan Ave. Before embarking, fuel up at **Lou Mitchell's** (p569) coffee shop near Union Station. After all, it's about 300 miles from the start of Route 66 to the Missouri state line.

Be aware that in Illinois, most of Route 66 has been superseded by I-55, though the old route still exists in scattered sections often paralleling the interstate.

Leave I-55 southeast of Chicago at Joliet Rd, following Hwy 53 southbound to Wilmington. Pay your respects to the 28ft fiberglass spaceman known as the **Gemini Giant** outside the **Launching Pad Drive-In** (☎ 815-476-6535; 810 E Baltimore St; ◷ 10am-9:30pm) in Wilmington. Motor down to Pontiac and on the outskirts look for the **Log Cabin Inn** (☎ 815-842-2908; 18700 Old Rte 66; ◷ 5am-4pm Mon & Tue, to 8pm Wed-Fri, to 2pm Sat). When Route 66 was realigned, the restaurant was jacked up and rotated 180° to face the new road. The **Route 66 Hall of Fame** (☎ 815-844-4566; 110 W Howard St; admission free; ◷ 11am-3pm Mon-Fri, 10am-4pm Sat) is also in town. Cruise by Bloomington-Normal and then stop off in Shirley at **Funk's Grove** (☎ 309-874-3360; ◷ call for seasonal hrs), a 19th-century maple syrup farm.

The state capital of Springfield harbors a trio of sights: **Shea's Gas Station Museum** (above), the **Cozy Dog Drive In** (above) and **Route 66 Drive In** (above).

Further south, a good section of old Route 66 parallels I-55 through Litchfield. Grab a meal and piece of pie at the 1924 **Ariston Café** (☎ 217-324-2023; N Old Rte 66; meals $6.50-15; ◷ 11am-10pm Tue-Fri, 4-10pm Sat, 11am-8pm Sun). In Mt Olive, the 1926 **Soulsby Shell Station** is the route's oldest gas pump and is in the slow process of becoming a museum.

Finally, before driving west over the Mississippi River and into Missouri, detour off I-70 at exit 3. Follow Hwy 203 south, turn right at the first stoplight and drive west to the 1929 **Chain of Rocks Bridge** (◷ dawn-dusk). Only open to pedestrians and cyclists, this mile-long bridge has a historically famous 22°-angled bend.

For more information, contact the **Route 66 Association of Illinois** (www.il66assoc.org). Detailed driving directions are at www.historic66.com/illinois.

Brewhaus (☎ 217-525-6399; 617 E Washington; sandwiches $3-6; ☯ 7am-1am) This popular pub serves the 'horseshoe,' a local specialty sandwich that consists of fried meat on toasted bread, mounded with french fries and smothered in melted cheese.

For more meal options, cruise S 6th St between Monroe and Adams Sts.

GETTING THERE & AROUND

The **Greyhound bus station** (☎ 217-544-8466; 2351 S Dirkson Pkwy), southeast of downtown, has frequent connections to St Louis ($20 to $25, 1½ hours) and Chicago ($29 to $38, 4½ hours).

The downtown **Amtrak station** (☎ 217-753-2013; cnr 3rd & Washington Sts) has five daily trains to/from St Louis ($12 to $22, two hours) and Chicago ($17 to $31, 3½ hours).

Petersburg

When Lincoln first arrived in Illinois in 1831, he worked variously as a clerk, storekeeper and postmaster in the frontier village of New Salem before studying law and moving to Springfield. In Petersburg, 20 miles northwest of Springfield, **Lincoln's New Salem State Historic Site** (☎ 217-632-4000; www.lincolnsnewsalem.com; Hwy 97; suggested donation adult/child $2/1; ☯ 9am-5pm, closed Mon & Tue Sep–mid-Apr) reconstructs the village with building replicas, historical displays and costumed performances – a pretty informative and entertaining package.

SOUTHERN ILLINOIS

A surprise awaits near Collinsville, 8 miles east of East St Louis: classified as a UNESCO World Heritage Site with the likes of Stonehenge, the Acropolis and the Egyptian pyramids is **Cahokia Mounds State Historic Site** (☎ 618-346-5160; www.cahokiamounds.com; Collinsville Rd; suggested donation adult/child $2/1; ☯ visitors center 9am-5pm; grounds 8am-dusk). Cahokia protects the remnants of North America's largest prehistoric city (20,000 people, with suburbs), dating from AD 1200. While the 65 earthen mounds, including the enormous Monk's Mound and the 'Woodhenge' sun calendar, are not overwhelmingly impressive in themselves, the whole site is worth seeing. If you're approaching from the north, take exit 24 off I-255 S; if approaching from St Louis, take exit 6 off I-55/70.

Grafton lies at the confluence of the Illinois and Mississippi Rivers. The time-forgotten

WHAT THE...?

The **World's Largest Catsup Bottle** (800 S Morrison Ave) is not a World Heritage Site like nearby Cahokia, though it certainly deserves the honor. Swing by for a look-see; it's located near Main St in downtown Collinsville.

town of **Elsah**, a few miles east, makes a worthy stop. The Great River Rd in this area is edged with cliffs and is especially scenic. Guests at **Bluffdale Vacation Farm** (☎ 217-983-2854; www.bluffdalevacationfarm.com; off Hwy 108; per person all-inclusive $99-122) help with chores like grooming horses, collecting eggs and feeding ducks. It's a kid-friendly family favorite located in Eldred, north of Grafton.

An exception to the state's flat farmland is the green southernmost section, punctuated by rolling **Shawnee National Forest** (☎ 681-253-7114) and rocky outcroppings. The area has numerous state parks and recreation areas good for hiking, swimming, fishing and canoeing, particularly around **Little Grassy Lake** and **Devil's Kitchen**. And who would think that Florida-like swampland, complete with bald cypress trees and croaking bullfrogs, would be here? But it is, at **Cypress Creek National Wildlife Refuge** (☎ 618-634-2231; www.fws .gov/midwest/cypresscreek). For guided canoe trips, contact **Peddles and Paddles** (☎ 618-658-3641; www .peddlesandpaddlesinc.com; half-day tour $25).

Union County, near the state's southern tip, has wineries and orchards. Sample the wares and stomp grapes on the 25-mile **Shawnee Hills Wine Trail** (☎ 618-893-2623; www.shawnee winetrail.com), connecting eight vineyards. At little **Cairo**, on the Kentucky border, the Mississippi and Ohio Rivers converge.

INDIANA

As Chicago newspaperman Mike Royko once wrote: 'In Indiana, a real good time consists of putting on bib overalls and a cap bearing the name of a farm equipment company and sauntering to a gas station to sit around and gossip about how Elmer couldn't get his pickup truck started that morning.' Royko was exaggerating but, er, not terribly far off the mark in describing this farm-filled state. That's not to say it doesn't hold a few

GREAT LAKES

surprises up its sleeve. Small Columbus is big on architecture, with buildings by IM Pei, Eero Saarinen and other noted designers. Breezy Bloomington fulfills with Tibetan temples and ethnic eats. The northwest holds moody sand dunes to climb, while the south has caves to explore and rivers to canoe.

History

After the usual Midwestern pattern of prehistoric mound-building natives, followed by mid-17th-century French fur traders, Indiana was settled by farmers from Kentucky (including Abraham Lincoln's family). Resulting conflicts displaced the Native Americans, the final battle being fought in 1811 at Tippecanoe.

Indiana's 'Hoosier' nickname came soon thereafter. No one is sure of its exact derivation, but it was in wide use by the 1830s. One theory is that early settlers knocking on local doors were met with a call of 'Who's here?'

Indiana is called 'the mother of vice presidents' for the five veeps it has spawned. One of the biggest political issues of the current decade has been whether or not the state should adopt daylight savings time.

Information

Indiana highway conditions (☎ 800-261-7623; www.in.gov/dot/motoristinfo)
Indiana Office of Tourism (☎ 888-365-6946; www.visitindiana.com)
Indiana state park information (☎ 800-622-4931; www.in.gov/dnr/parklake) Park entry costs $2 per day by foot or bicycle, $4 to $10 by vehicle. Campsites cost $6 to $28; reservations accepted (☎ 866-622-6746; www.camp.in.gov).

INDIANA FACTS

Nicknames Hoosier State, Crossroads of America
Population 6.3 million
Area 36,420 sq miles
Capital city Indianapolis (population 784,118)
Sales Tax 6%
Birthplace of Author Kurt Vonnegut (1922–2007), actor James Dean (1931–55), *Brady Bunch* mom Florence Henderson (b 1934), TV host David Letterman (b 1947), king of pop Michael Jackson (b 1958)
Home of Farmers, corn
Famous for Indy 500 motor race, winning basketball teams, pork tenderloin sandwich
Official flower Peony

INDIANAPOLIS

Nicknamed 'Nap Town,' Indianapolis is, truth be told, kind of snore-evoking. A notable exception is the Indy 500 Museum, where you can ogle racecars and take a spin around the renowned speedway. The art museum and White River State Park have their merits, too.

Orientation & Information

Indianapolis is geometrically laid out with diagonal avenues superimposed on a grid layout. Everything radiates from the massively impressive Monument Circle. Meridian St divides streets east from west; Washington St divides them north from south. The Broad Ripple neighborhood is 6 miles north at College Ave and 62nd St.

BOOKSTORES
Borders Books & Music (☎ 317-972-8595; 11 S Meridian St)

EMERGENCY & MEDICAL SERVICES
CVS (☎ 317-923-1491; 1744 N Illinois St; ☯ 24hr) Pharmacy.
Indiana University Medical Center (☎ 317-274-4705; 550 N University Blvd)

INTERNET ACCESS
The visitors center at the Artsgarden has free wi-fi, as do Abbey Coffeehouse and Shapiro's (see the Eating section).
Netheads Cybercafé (☎ 317-257-6635; 1011 E Westfield Blvd, Broad Ripple; per hr $6; ☯ 11am-11pm Mon-Thu, to midnight Fri & Sat, 1-9pm Sun)

MEDIA & INTERNET RESOURCES
Gay Indy (www.gayindy.org) Gay and lesbian news and entertainment listings.
Indianapolis Star (www.indystar.com) The city's daily newspaper.
Intake (www.intakeweekly.com) The *Indy Star's* free, weekly entertainment paper.
Nuvo (www.nuvo.net) Free, weekly alternative paper with the arts and music low-down.

WFBQ-FM 94.7 is the main rock channel; NPR sits on the dial at WFYI-FM 90.1.

TOURIST INFORMATION
Visitors Center (☎ 317-624-2563, 800-323-4639; www.indy.org; Artsgarden Bldg, cnr Washington & Illinois Sts; ☯ 10am-9pm Mon-Sat, noon-6pm Sun)

Sights & Activities
INDIANAPOLIS MOTOR SPEEDWAY
The Speedway, home of the **Indianapolis 500** motor race, is Indy's supersight. The **Hall of Fame Museum** (☎ 317-492-6784; www.indianapolis motorspeedway.com; 4790 W 16th St; adult/child 6-15 $3/1; 9am-5pm) features 75 racing cars (including former winners), a 500lb Tiffany trophy and a track tour ($3 extra). OK, so you're on a bus for the latter and not even beginning to burn rubber at 37mph; it's still fun to pretend. **Tickets** (☎ 317-484-6700, 800-822-4639; www.imstix.com; $20-140) are hard to come by for the big event, held on Memorial Day weekend and attended by 450,000 crazed fans. Tickets for pre-race trials and practices are more likely (and cheaper). Other races at the Speedway are the **MotoGP World Championship** in September and NASCAR **Brickyard 400** in late July. It's located 7.5 miles northwest of downtown.

The city celebrates the Indy 500 throughout May with the **500 Festival** (☎ 317-614-6400; www.500festival.com; tickets from $7). Events include a parade comprised of racecar drivers and a community shindig at the racetrack.

WHITE RIVER STATE PARK
Sprawling White River State Park, located at the edge of downtown, contains several worthwhile sights. The adobe **Eiteljorg Museum of American Indians & Western Art** (☎ 317-636-9378; www.eiteljorg.org; 500 W Washington St; adult/child 5-17 $8/5; 10am-5pm Tue-Sat, noon-5pm Sun, plus Mon in summer) features Native American basketry, pots and masks, as well as a fabulous realistic/romantic Western painting collection with works by Frederic Remington and Georgia O'Keeffe.

The **NCAA Hall of Champions** (☎ 800-735-6222; www.ncaa.org/hall_of_champions; 700 W Washington St; adult/child $3/2; 10am-5pm Tue-Sat, noon-5pm Sun, plus Mon in summer) reveals the country's fascination with college sports. You'll probably find most Hoosiers hovering around the basketball exhibits, as locals are renowned hoop-ball fanatics.

Other park highlights include gardens, a zoo, a canal walk and a military Medal of Honor Memorial.

A few miles farther west, at the **Indiana Medical History Museum** (☎ 317-635-7329; www.imhm.org; 3045 Vermont St; adult/child under 19 $5/1; 10am-4pm Thu-Sat), a guide leads visitors through century-old pathology labs. The highlight, especially for zombies, is the roomful of brains in jars.

There's also a healing herb garden to walk through.

INDIANAPOLIS MUSEUM OF ART
This **museum** (☎ 317-920-2660; www.ima-art.org; 4000 Michigan Rd; admission free; 11am-5pm Tue-Sat, to 9pm Thu & Fri, noon-5pm Sun) has a terrific collection of European art (especially Turner and some Post-Impressionists), African tribal art, South Pacific art and Chinese works. The museum is linked to **Oldfields – Lilly House & Gardens** (same as museum), the 26-acre estate of the Lilly pharmaceutical family, and **Fairbanks Art & Nature Park**, which will feature sculptures and audio installations amid 100 acres of woodlands when it opens in 2009. Added bonus: the museum houses the **Better Than New thrift shop** (☎ 317-924-4951; noon-4pm Tue-Sat & third Sun of month), with a sweet selection of jewelry and art objects.

MONUMENTS
At Monument Circle, the city center is marked by the jaw-dropping 284-ft **Soldiers & Sailors Monument**. For a bizarre, Soviet-style experience (ie cramped and dingy) take the elevator ($1) to the top. Beneath is the **Civil War Museum** (☎ 317-232-7615; admission free; 10:30am-5:30pm Wed-Sun), which neatly outlines the conflict and Indiana's abolition position. A few blocks north, the **World War Memorial** (cnr Vermont & Meridian Sts) is another impressively beefy monument.

Sleeping
Hotels cost more and are usually full during race weeks in May, June and July. Add 15% tax to the prices listed. Look for low-cost motels off I-465, the freeway that circles Indianapolis.

Indy Hostel (☎ 317-727-1696; www.indyhostel.us; 4903 Winthrop Ave; weekday/weekend dm $22/25, r $45/49; P) This small, friendly hostel offers two dorm rooms (one six-bed coed room, and one four-bed female room) and a private room. The Monon Trail runs nearby (bike rental per day $5). It's located five miles from downtown, by Broad Ripple.

Stone Soup (☎ 866-639-9550; www.stonesoupinn.com; 1304 N Central Ave; r incl breakfast $85-145; P wifi) This nine-room B&B sprawls throughout a rambling house filled with antiques and stained glass. The less-expensive rooms share a bathroom.

Hampton Inn (☎ 317-261-1200; www.hamptondt .com; 105 S Meridian St; r incl breakfast $139-169; P)

Handsome-looking public areas, good amenities (hot breakfast, internet access) and the prime downtown location add value to the cookie-cutter rooms. Parking is $13.

Canterbury (☎ 317-634-3000; 800-538-8186; www.canterburyhotel.com; 123 S Illinois St; r from $159; P ⊠ ⬚ wi-fi) Indianapolis' finest oozes class, with rooms furnished with Chippendale four-post beds, marble sinks and gold fixtures. Parking costs $20.

Eating

Central Massachusetts Ave ('Mass Ave' to locals) is bounteous when the stomach growls. The Broad Ripple area, 6 miles north at College Ave and 62nd St, has pubs and eateries representing numerous nationalities. At lunch it's hard to beat the incredible range of cheap eats at the old **City Market** (222 E Market St; ⏲ 6am-4pm Mon-Fri, 11am-3pm Sat), two blocks east of Monument Circle, filled with ethnic food stalls and local produce vendors.

Mug 'N' Bun (☎ 317-244-5669; 5211 W 10th St; mains $3-5; ⏲ 10:30am-10pm Sun-Thu, to 11pm Fri & Sat) The mugs are frosted and filled with a wonderful home-brewed root beer. The buns contain burgers, chili dogs and juicy pork tenderloins. At this vintage drive-in near the Speedway you are served – where else? – in your car.

Abbey Coffeehouse (☎ 317-663-4739; 825 N Pennsylvania Ave; mains $5-8; ⏲ 9am-midnight; wi-fi) Serene? Check. Art-filled walls? Yep. Comfy armchairs? Got 'em. The sandwiches, wraps and tempeh burritos are delicious, too.

Shapiro's Deli (☎ 317-631-4041; 808 S Meridian St; sandwiches $7-11; ⏲ 6:45am-8pm; wi-fi) Chomp into a towering corned beef or peppery pastrami sandwich on homemade bread, then chase it with fat slices of chocolate cake or fruit pie.

Bazbeaux (☎ 317-636-7662; 334 Massachusetts Ave; sandwiches $6-8, large pizza $18-21; ⏲ 11am-10pm Sun-Thu, 11am-11pm Fri & Sat) A local favorite, Bazbeaux offers an eclectic pizza selection, like the 'Tchoupitoulas,' topped with Cajun shrimp and andouille sausage. Muffalettas, stromboli and Belgian beer are some of the other unusual offerings.

Drinking & Entertainment

Downtown and Mass Ave have a few good watering holes; Broad Ripple has several.

BARS & CLUBS

Slippery Noodle Inn (☎ 317-631-6974; 372 S Meridian St) The Noodle is the oldest bar in the state, and has seen action as a whorehouse, slaughterhouse, gangster hangout and Underground Railroad station, not to mention it's one of the best blues clubs in the country. There's live music nightly, and it's cheap.

Rathskeller (☎ 317-636-0396; 401 E Michigan St) Quaff German brews at the outdoor beer garden's picnic tables in summer, or at the deer-head-lined indoor beer hall once winter strikes; located in the historic Athenaeum building.

Chatterbox Tavern (☎ 317-636-0584; 435 Massachusetts Ave; ⏲ Mon-Sat) Chill out with the varied clientele at this intimate, candlelit bar in the Mass Ave 'hood. It features live jazz nightly, and a hearty stock of beer and wine.

SPORTS

The motor races aren't the only coveted spectator events.

RCA Dome (☎ 317-262-3389; www.colts.com; 100 S Capitol Ave) Under a vast fiberglass dome 63,000 fans watch the NFL's Colts (the 2007 Super Bowl winners) play football.

Conseco Fieldhouse (☎ 317-917-2500; www.nba .com/pacers; 125 S Pennsylvania St) Basketball is huge in Indiana, and this is ground zero where the NBA's Pacers make it happen.

Getting There & Around

The **Indianapolis International Airport** (IND; ☎ 317-487-7243; www.indianapolisairport.com) is 7 miles southwest of town. The No 8 Washington bus runs between the airport and downtown ($1.25, 30 minutes). A cab to downtown costs $20 to $22.

Greyhound (☎ 317-267-3076; www.greyhound.com) shares **Union Station** (350 S Illinois St) with Amtrak. **Megabus** (☎ 877-462-6342; www.megabus.com /us) stops at 200 E Washington St. Both go to Cincinnati ($10 to $22, 2½ hours) and Chicago ($20 to $35, 3½ hours).

Avis, Hertz and other rental agencies have offices at the airport and around town. The Transportation chapter (p1144) has contact details.

IndyGo (☎ 317-635-3344; www.indygo.net; fare $1.25) runs the local buses. No 17 goes to Broad Ripple. Free Blue Line and Red Line shuttles circle the downtown sights. Service is minimal at weekends.

Amtrak (☎ 317-263-0550; www.amtrak.com) chugs into **Union Station** (350 S Illinois St). One train daily goes to Chicago ($16 to $32, 4½ hours), and three trains weekly go to Cincinnati ($17 to $30, three hours) and Washington, DC ($82 to $150, 18 hours).

For a taxi, call **Yellow Cab** (☎ 317-487-7777).

AROUND INDIANAPOLIS

Bluegrass music, architectural hot spots, Tibetan temples and James Dean all furrow into the farmland around here

Fairmount

This small town, north on Hwy 9, is the birthplace of James Dean, one of the original icons of cool. You'll know you've arrived when you see his foxy mug staring down from the huge water tower that lords it over town.

Fans should head directly to the **Historical Museum** (☎ 765-948-4555; www.jamesdeanartifacts.com; 203 E Washington St; suggested donation $1; ☺ 10am-5pm Mon-Sat, noon-5pm Sun, closed Dec-Feb) to see Dean's bongo drums, among other artifacts. This is also the place to pick up a free map that will guide you to sites like the farmhouse where Jimmy grew up and his red-lipstick-kissed grave site. The museum sells Dean posters, zippo lighters and other memorabilia, and sponsors the annual **James Dean Festival** (admission free; late Sep), when as many as 50,000 fans pour in for four days of music and rebelry.

If James Dean was considered the embodiment of cool, surely his polar opposite is Dan Quayle, who resided a mere 30 miles north on Hwy 9 in Huntington. The USA's dimwitted 44th vice president (you spell potato, he spells potatoe) is treated reverentially, along with the country's other second fid-

dles, at the **Dan Quayle Center & Vice Presidential Museum** (☎ 260-356-6356; www.quaylemuseum.org; 815 Warren St; adult/child 7-17 $3/1; ☺ 9:30am-4:30pm Tue-Sat).

Columbus

When you think of the USA's great architectural cities – Chicago, New York, Washington DC – Columbus, Indiana, doesn't quite leap to mind. But it should. Located 40 miles south of Indianapolis on I-65, Columbus is a remarkable gallery of physical design. Since the 1940s the city and its leading corporations have commissioned some of the world's best architects, including Eero Saarinen, Richard Meier and IM Pei, to create both public and private buildings. Stop at the **visitors center** (☎ 812-378-2622; www.columbus.in.us; 506 5th St; ☺ 9am-5pm Mon-Sat, noon-4pm Sun Mar-Nov, closed Sun Dec-Feb) to pick up a self-guided tour map ($2) or join a bus tour (adult/child 6-12 $10/3); tours begin at 10am Monday to Friday, 10am and 2pm Saturday, and 1pm Sunday. Over 60 notable buildings are spread over a wide area (car required), but about 15 diverse works can be seen on foot downtown. While you're here you might as well sleep in an architectural wonder, so check into the **Columbus Inn B&B** (☎ 812-378-4289; www.thecolumbusinn.com; 445 Fifth St; r from $119), which once served as city hall.

Nashville

Gentrified and antique-filled, this 19th-century town west of Columbus on Hwy 46 is now a bustling tourist center, at its busiest in fall when leaf-peepers pour in. It's also the jump-off point to **Brown County State Park** (☎ 812-988-6406; campsites $13-25), Indiana's largest, where trails give hikers and horseback riders access to the area's green hill country.

Among several B&Bs, central **Artists Colony Inn** (☎ 812-988-0600, 800-737-0255; www .artistscolonyinn.com; 105 S Van Buren St; r incl breakfast $100-170; mains $8-14) stands out for its spiffy rooms and rooftop hot tub. The inexpensive dining room offers traditional Hoosier fare, such as catfish and pork tenderloins. **Nashville House** (☎ 812-988-4554; cnr Van Buren & Main Sts; mains $16-21; ⏲ 11:30am-7pm Wed-Mon) is famous for its home-cooked meals served with fried biscuits and apple butter.

As with like-named Nashville, Tennessee (p468), Nashville, Indiana, enjoys its country music, and bands play regularly at several venues. The **Bill Monroe Museum** (☎ 812-988-6422; 5163 Rte 135 N, Bean Blossom; adult/child under 13 $4/free; ⏲ 9am-5pm Apr-Oct, 10am-4pm Tue-Sat Nov-Mar) hails the bluegrass hero 5 miles north of town.

Bloomington

Lively and lovely Bloomington, 45 miles south of Indianapolis on Hwy 37, is the home of Indiana University. The town centers on Courthouse Sq, surrounded by restaurants, bars, bookshops and the historic facade of Fountain Sq Mall. The super-stocked **visitors center** (☎ 812-334-8900; www.visitbloomington.com; 2855 N Walnut St; ⏲ 8:30am-5pm Mon-Fri, 9am-4pm Sat) is a few miles north of the town center. Nearly everything else is walkable.

On the expansive campus, the **Art Museum** (☎ 812-855-5445; www.indiana.edu/~iuam; 1133 E 7th St; admission free; ⏲ 10am-5pm Tue-Sat, noon-5pm Sun, reduced hrs summer), designed by IM Pei, has an excellent collection of African art, as well as European and US paintings.

The colorful, prayer flag-covered **Tibetan Cultural Center** (☎ 812-331-0014; www.tibetancc.com; 3655 Snoddy Rd; admission free; ⏲ 10am-4pm) and stupa, as well as the **Dagom Gaden Tensung Ling Monastery** (☎ 812-339-0857; www.ganden.org; 102 Clubhouse Dr; ⏲ call for hrs), indicate Bloomington's significant Tibetan presence. Both offer free teachings and meditation sessions; check the websites for weekly schedules.

If you arrive in mid-April and wonder why an extra 20,000 people are hanging out in town, it's for the **Little 500** (☎ 812-855-1103; www.iusf.bloomington.com; tickets $15-20). Lance Armstrong called the bike race, where amateurs ride one-speed Schwinns for 200 laps around a quarter-mile track, 'the coolest event I ever attended.'

Look for cheap lodgings along N Walnut St near Hwy 46. The limestone **Motel 6** (☎ 812-332-0820; 1800 N Walnut St; r from $44; 🅿 🖳) may be the Midwest's most attractive.

For a town of its size, Bloomington offers a mind-blowing array of ethnic restaurants – everything from Burmese to Eritrean to Mexican. Browse Kirkwood Ave and E 4th St. Charming **Anyetsang's Little Tibet** (☎ 812-331-0122; 415 E 4th St; mains $8-10; ⏲ 11am-10pm Wed-Mon) offers specialties from the Himalayan homeland, as well as Thai-influenced dishes and curries. Pubs on Kirkwood Ave close to the university cater to the student crowd (ie cheap booze).

SOUTHERN INDIANA

The pretty hills, caves, rivers and absorbing history of southern Indiana mark it as a completely different region from that of the flat and industrialized north.

Ohio River

The Indiana segment of the 981-mile-long Ohio River marks the state's southern border. From tiny Aurora, in the southeastern corner of the state, Hwys 56, 156, 62 and 66, known collectively as the **Ohio River Scenic Route**, wind through a varied landscape.

Coming from the east, a perfect place to stop is little **Madison**, a well-preserved river settlement from the mid-19th century where architectural beauties beckon genteelly from the streets. At the **visitors center** (☎ 812-265-2956; www.visitmadison.org; 601 W First St; ⏲ 9am-5pm Mon-Fri, 9am-4pm Sat, 11am-4pm Sun), pick up a walking tour brochure, which includes the James Lanier Mansion, a designated landmark overlooking the river.

Madison has motels around its edges, as well as several B&Bs; the visitors center can help with bookings. Large, wooded **Clifty Falls State Park** (☎ 812-273-8885; campsites $8-25), off Hwy 56 and a couple of miles west of town, has camping, hiking trails, views and waterfalls. Main St, with numerous antique stores, also has places for a bite. **Café Camille** (☎ 812-265-5626; 149 E Main St; mains $3-6; ⏲ 6am-4pm Mon-Fri, to 3pm Sat & Sun) is ideal for breakfast or lunch.

In Clarksville, **Falls of the Ohio State Park** (☎ 812-280-9970; www.fallsoftheohio.org; 201 W Riverside Dr) has only rapids, no falls, but is of interest for its 386-million-year-old fossil beds. The **interpretive center** (adult/child $4/1, plus $1 Fri-Sun; ☺ 9am-5pm Mon-Sat, 1-5pm Sun) explains it all. The rest of town and adjacent New Albany, the largest Indiana town in the region, aren't much, with one exception: **Rich O's Public House/New Albanian Brewing Company** (☎ 812-949-2804; 3312 Plaza Dr, New Albany; ☺ Mon-Sat) and its superlative beer selection.

Scenic Hwy 62 heads west and leads to the Lincoln Hills and southern Indiana's limestone caves. A visit to **Wyandotte Caves State Recreation Area** (☎ 812-738-2782; www.wyandotte caves.com; 7315 S Wyandotte Cave Rd; ☺ 9am-5pm Mar-Oct), near Leavenworth, is highly recommended. Tours range from 30 minutes (adult/child 4-12 $12/6) to 90 minutes (adult/child 4-12 $16/8) and take you through caves featuring ancient formations, bats and more. **Marengo Cave** (☎ 812-365-2705; www.marengocave.com; ☺ 9am-6pm), north on Hwy 66, is another stand-out. It offers both 40-minute tours (adult/child 4-12 $12.75/6.75) and two-hour tours (adult/child 4-12 $20/10). Nearby in Milltown, **Cave Country Canoes** (☎ 812-633-4806; www.cavecountry canoes.com; ☺ May-Oct) runs good half-day ($20), full-day ($24) or longer trips on the scenic Blue River; keep an eye out for river otters and rare hellbender salamanders.

Four miles south of Dale, off I-64, is the **Lincoln Boyhood National Memorial** (☎ 812-937-4541; www.nps.gov/libo; adult/child $3/free; ☺ 8am-5pm), where young Abe lived from age seven to 21. The isolated but good site also includes admission to a working **pioneer farm** (☺ 8am-5pm mid-Apr–Sep). Further west, on the Ohio River, **Evansville** is one of the state's largest cities; its Riverside Historic District retains many early 19th-century mansions.

Wabash River

In southwest Indiana, the Wabash River forms the border with Illinois. Beside it, south of I-64, captivating **New Harmony** is the site of two early communal-living experiments and is worth a visit. In the early 19th century a German Christian sect, the Harmonists, developed a sophisticated town here while awaiting the Second Coming. Later it was acquired by the British utopian Robert Owen. Learn more at the angular **Atheneum Visitors Center** (☎ 812-682-4488, 800-231-2168; www.newharmony.org; cnr North & Arthur Sts; ☺ 9:30am-5pm).

Today New Harmony retains an air of contemplation, if not otherworldliness, which you can experience at its newer attractions, such as the temple-like Roofless Church and the Labyrinth, a maze symbolizing the spirit's quest. The town has a couple of guesthouses, some pleasant eateries, and camping at **Harmonie State Park** (☎ 812-682-4821; campsites $17-25).

NORTHERN INDIANA

The truck-laden I-80/I-90 tollways cut across Indiana's northern section. Parallel US 20 is slower and cheaper, but not much more attractive. Classic car connoisseurs should detour south on I-69 to the town of **Auburn**, where the Cord Company produced the USA's favorite cars in the 1920s and '30s. The **Auburn Cord Duesenberg Museum** (☎ 260-925-1444; www .acdmuseum.org; 1600 S Wayne St; adult/child $8/5; ☺ 9am-5pm) has a wonderful display of early roadsters in a beautiful art deco setting. Next door are the vintage rigs of the **National Automotive and Truck Museum** (☎ 260-925-9100; www.natmus.com; 1000 Gordon Buehrig Pl; adult/child 6-12 $7/5; ☺ 9am-5pm).

Further west, around Shipshewana, Middlebury and Elkhart, is one of the USA's

---

TURD TOWN

The small town of Reynolds (pop 547) has a big plan to change the world – and that plan relies on pig poop, of which there is a lot in this small farming community 85 miles northwest of Indianapolis.

It's an unexpected place to lead the sustainability charge, filled with townsfolk more conservative than crunchy. But here they are, on their way toward energy independence and a cleaner environment.

The plan is simple. Reynolds built a facility that generates electricity from local waste like cornstalks, soybean stubble and hog manure. It also brews up ethanol, which the local gas station sells to the many residents who own flex-fuel vehicles. And *voilà* – the plant meets all of the town's energy needs (no more reliance on foreign oil) while it also manages pesky waste issues.

Reynolds prefers to go by the flashy nickname 'BioTown USA.' But truth be told, everyone calls it Turd Town. Learn more at the town's website at www.biotownusa.com.

largest **Amish communities**. The **Menno-Hof Visitors Center** (☎ 260-768-4117; www.mennohof.org; Hwy 5, Shipshewana; adult/child 6-14 $6/3; ☻ 10am-7pm Mon-Fri, to 5pm Sat Jun-Aug, reduced hrs Sep-May) provides thorough background information. The area holds numerous Amish and Mennonite craft outlets, bakeries and restaurants – most with hitching posts.

South Bend

The city of **South Bend** is another ex-carmaker. Stop at the **Studebaker National Museum** (☎ 574-235-9714; www.studebakermuseum.org; 201 S Chapin St; adult/child 7-18 $8/5; ☻ 10am-5pm Mon-Sat, noon-5pm Sun), with its gorgeous 1956 Packard and many other classic beauties. South Bend is better known as the home of the University of Notre Dame, famous for its 'Fighting Irish' football team. To tour the pretty campus with its gold-domed administration building, Lourdes Grotto Replica and *Touchdown Jesus* painting, start at the **visitors center** (☎ 574-631-5726; 111 Eck Center; ☻ 8am-5pm Mon-Sat, 10am-5pm Sun). US residents especially will be interested in seeing the downtown **College Football Hall of Fame** (☎ 574-235-9999; www.collegefootball.org; 111 S St Joseph St; adult/child 5-12 $11/5; ☻ 10am-5pm Sun-Thu, to 8pm Tue, 9am-6pm Fri & Sat).

Indiana Dunes

Hugely popular on summer days with sunbathers from Chicago and South Bend, **Indiana Dunes National Lakeshore** (www.nps.gov/indu) stretches along 21 miles of Lake Michigan shoreline. Beaches, dunes and woodlands are crisscrossed with hiking trails, which afford glimpses of nearby stark steel mills juxtaposed with wildlife like the regal blue heron. The lakeshore is also noted for its incredible plant variety; everything from cactus to hardwood forests and pine trees sprouts here. Beaches are usually open 7am to sunset daily. Stop at the new **Dorothy Buell Visitor Center** (☎ 219-926-7561; www.nps.gov/indu; Hwy 49; ☻ 8:30am-5pm, to 6pm summer) for details on beaches and to pick up hiking, biking, birding and eco-tourism guides. Or call the **Porter County Convention & Visitors Bureau** (☎ 800-283-8687; www.indianadunes.com) to order the guides. You can reach the area easily from Chicago via the South Shore Metra train (see p573), which stops at Dune Park (about 1.5 miles from the visitors center) among other lakeshore locations. The train departs from Randolph St/Millennium Park Station and takes 1½ hours.

Indiana Dunes State Park (☎ 219-926-1952; www.dnr.in.gov/parklake; per car $4-10, campsites $17-28; ☻ beaches 9am-sunset, park 7am-11pm, reduced hrs Sep-May) is a 2100-acre, shoreside pocket within the national lakeshore; it's located at the end of Hwy 49, near Chesterton. It has more amenities, but is also more regulated and crowded. Wintertime brings out the cross-country skiers; summertime brings out the hikers. Seven trails zigzag over the landscape; No 4 up Mt Tom rewards with Chicago skyline views.

Other than a couple of beachfront snack bars you won't find much to eat in the parks, so stop at homey, Italian **Lucrezia** (☎ 219-926-5829; 428 S Calumet Rd; mains $12-21; ☻ 11am-10pm Sun-Thu, to 11pm Fri & Sat) in Chesterton or the sophisticated foodie favorite **Miller Bakery Café** (☎ 219-938-2229; 555 Lake St; lunch mains $8-16, dinner mains $16-28; ☻ lunch 11:30am-2pm Tue-Fri, dinner 5-9pm Tue-Thu, 5-10pm Fri & Sat, 4-8pm Sun) in Miller Beach.

Near Illinois, the steel cities of **Gary** and **East Chicago** present some of the bleakest urban landscapes anywhere. Taking the train (Amtrak or South Shore line) through here will get you up close and personal with the industrial underbelly.

OHIO

All right, time for your Ohio quiz. In the Buckeye State you can 1) watch butter churn on an Amish farm; 2) party your ass off at an island resort; 3) lose your stomach on the world's fastest roller coaster; 4) rock climb among streams and caves; 5) suck down a dreamy creamy milkshake fresh from a working dairy; or 6) examine a mondo, mysterious snake built into the earth. And the answer is…all of the above. It hurts locals' feelings when visitors think the only thing to do here is tip over cows. C'mon, give Ohio a chance. Besides the above activities, you can partake in a five-way in Cincinnati and rock out in Cleveland.

History

Settlers streamed into fertile Ohio following the Revolutionary War. The state's northern part had Lake Erie, the south had the Ohio River, and there were abundant resources in between. By 1850, Ohio was the third most populous state in the nation. Industry grew (steel in the north, pork-processing in the south) and some families got rich (Rockefeller

OHIO FACTS

Nickname Buckeye State
Population 11.5 million
Area 44,825 sq miles
Capital city Columbus (population 730,657)
Sales Tax 5.5%
Birthplace of Inventor Thomas Edison (1847–1931), author Toni Morrison (b 1931), entrepreneur Ted Turner (b 1938), filmmaker Steven Spielberg (b 1947)
Home of Cows, aviation pioneers Wright Brothers
Famous for First airplane, first pro baseball team, deciding the outcome of the 2004 presidential election
Official motto With God, all things are possible

in the north, Messrs Procter and Gamble in the south). North and south still define the state today: the north is typically more liberal and pro-union, while the south is more conservative.

Seven US presidents were born in Ohio, leading to the state's sometimes-heard moniker, 'Mother of Presidents.'

Speaking of the nation's big cheese: this little ol' cow-dotted state decided the country's fate in 2004. That's when the Republicans and Democrats were tied in the presidential election. Everything had been counted except for one state's votes – Ohio's. So you can thank Ohio for Georgie Jr's second term. And it could easily play the tie-breaking role again in 2008 and beyond.

Information

Ohio Division of Travel and Tourism (☎ 800-282-5393; www.discoverohio.com)
Ohio highway conditions (www.buckeyetraffic.org)
Ohio state park information (☎ 614-265-6561; www.ohiodnr.com/parks) State parks are free to visit; some have wi-fi. Campsites cost $19 to $34; reservations accepted (☎ 866-644-6727; www.ohio.reserveworld.com; fee $8).

CLEVELAND

Does it or does it not rock? That is the question. Drawing from its roots as an industrious, working man's town, Cleveland has toiled hard in recent years to prove it does. Step One was to control the urban decay/river-on-fire thing (the Cuyahoga River was once so polluted that it actually burned). Check. Step Two was to bring a worthy attraction to town, say the Rock and Roll Hall

of Fame. Check. Step Three was to get grub beyond steak-and-potatoes. Check. So can Cleveland finally wipe the sweat from its brow? Check.

Orientation & Information

Cleveland's center is Public Sq, dominated by the conspicuous Terminal Tower. Ontario St is the east–west dividing line.

Most attractions are downtown or at University Circle (the area around Case Western Reserve University). Ohio City and Tremont, near downtown, are good neighborhoods for eating and drinking, as are Little Italy and Coventry, near the university.

BOOKSTORES

Mac's (☎ 216-321-2665; 1820 Coventry Rd, Coventry) Attached to Tommy's (p588).

EMERGENCY & MEDICAL SERVICES

MetroHealth Medical Center (☎ 216-778-7800; 2500 MetroHealth Dr)
Rape crisis (☎ 216-619-6192)

INTERNET ACCESS

Many of Cleveland's public places have free wi-fi, such as Public Sq, Playhouse Square Center and University Circle.
Lucky's Café (☎ 216-622-7773; 777 Starkweather Ave; ⏰ 7am-8pm Mon-Fri, 8am-8pm Sat, 8am-5pm Sun) Internet terminal (per hr $2) and free wi-fi.

MEDIA & INTERNET RESOURCES

Gay People's Chronicle (www.gaypeopleschronicle.com) A weekly publication with entertainment listings, distributed free throughout town.
Plain Dealer (www.cleveland.com) The city's daily newspaper, with a good Friday entertainment section.
Scene (www.clevescene.com) A weekly entertainment paper; out on Wednesday.

Tune into WCPN-FM 90.3 for NPR, or WMMS-FM 100.7 for rock.

TOURIST INFORMATION

The **Cleveland CVB** (☎ 800-321-1001; www.travelcleveland.com) operates a visitors center at **Terminal Tower** (☎ 216-621-4110; 1st fl, 50 Public Sq; ⏰ 9am-4pm Mon-Fri)

Sights & Activities

There's not a heck of a lot to do sight-wise; the Rock Hall of Fame and art museum are the big attractions.

CLEVELAND

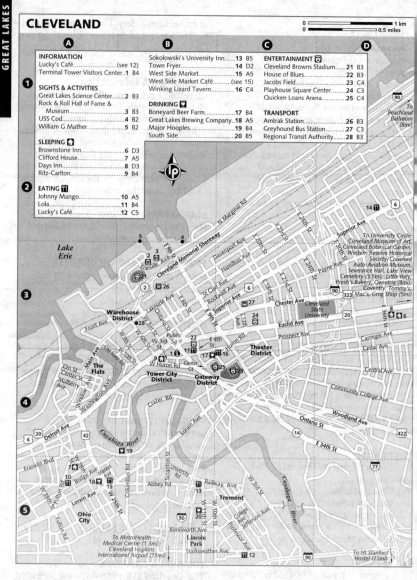

INFORMATION		
Lucky's Café.........................(see 12)		
Terminal Tower Visitors Center..**1** B4		
SIGHTS & ACTIVITIES		
Great Lakes Science Center.......**2** B3		
Rock & Roll Hall of Fame &		
Museum...............................**3** B3		
USS Cod................................**4** B2		
William G Mather...................**5** B2		
SLEEPING		
Brownstone Inn......................**6** D3		
Clifford House........................**7** A5		
Days Inn................................**8** D3		
Ritz-Carlton...........................**9** B4		
EATING		
Johnny Mango........................**10** A5		
Lola.......................................**11** B4		
Lucky's Café...........................**12** C5		

Sokolowski's University Inn......**13** B5
Town Fryer...............................**14** D2
West Side Market......................**15** A5
West Side Market Café............(see 15)
Winking Lizard Tavern...............**16** C4

DRINKING
Boneyard Beer Farm.................**17** B4
Great Lakes Brewing Company..**18** A5
Major Hooples.........................**19** B4
South Side...............................**20** B5

ENTERTAINMENT
Cleveland Browns Stadium.......**21** B3
House of Blues.........................**22** B3
Jacobs Field............................**23** C4
Playhouse Square Center.........**24** C3
Quicken Loans Arena...............**25** C4

TRANSPORT
Amtrak Station........................**26** B3
Greyhound Bus Station............**27** C3
Regional Transit Authority........**28** B3

DOWNTOWN
Rock & Roll Hall of Fame & Museum
Cleveland's top attraction, the **Rock & Roll Hall of Fame & Museum** (☎ 216-781-7625, 888-764-7625; www .rockhall.com; 1 Key Plaza; adult/child 9-12 $20/11; ☉ 10am-5:30pm, to 9pm Wed year-round, to 9pm Sat Jun-Aug) is more than a collection of memorabilia, though it does have Janis Joplin's psychedelic Porsche and Ray Charles' sunglasses. Interactive multimedia exhibits trace the history and social context of rock music and the performers who created it. Why is the museum in Cleveland? Because this is the hometown of Alan Freed, the disk jockey who popularized the term 'rock 'n' roll' in the early 1950s, and because the city lobbied hard and paid big. Be prepared for crowds.

Great Lakes Science Center

The **Science Center** (☎ 216-694-2000; www.glsc.org; 601 Erieside Ave; adult/child 3-17 $9.50/7.50; ⊙ 9:30am-5:30pm), next to the Rock Hall, gives a good account of the lakes' environmental problems. It's affiliated with the **William G Mather** (☎ 216-574-6262; http://wgmather.maritime.museum; 305 Mather Way; adult/child 3-17 $6/4; ⊙ 9:30am-5:30pm daily Jun-Aug, Fri-Sun only May, Sep & Oct, closed Nov-Apr), a freighter incarnated as a steamship museum. Also berthed nearby on the waterfront is the storied submarine **USS Cod** (☎ 216-566-8770; www.usscod .org; 1089 E 9th St; adult/child 6-18 $6/3; ⊙ 10am-4:30pm May-Sep), which saw action in WWII.

UNIVERSITY CIRCLE
Several attractions cluster around Case Western Reserve University, in an area known as University Circle, 5 miles east of downtown.

Star of the lot is the **Cleveland Museum of Art** (☎ 216-421-7340; www.clevelandart.org; 11150 East Blvd; admission free; ⊙ 10am-5pm Tue-Sun, 10am-9pm Wed & Fri), which houses an excellent collection of European paintings, as well as African, Asian and American art.

Other attractions include the lovely **Cleveland Botanical Garden** (☎ 216-721-1600; www.cbgarden .org; 11030 East Blvd; adult/child 3-12 $7.50/3; ⊙ 10am-5pm Mon-Sat, noon-5pm Sun, closed Mon Nov-Mar), with its Costa Rican cloud forest and Madagascan desert exhibits, and the **Western Reserve Historical Society/Crawford Auto-Aviation Museum** (☎ 216-721-5722; www.wrhs.org; 10825 East Blvd; adult/child 6-18 $8.50/5; ⊙ 10am-5pm Mon-Sat, noon-5pm Sun), with its collection of old cars and planes.

Beyond the circle further east, don't forget eclectic **Lake View Cemetery** (☎ 216-421-2665; www.lakeviewcemetery.com; 12316 Euclid Ave; admission free; ⊙ 7:30am-5:30pm), the 'outdoor museum' where President Garfield and John Rockefeller rest.

Sleeping
Prices listed are for summer, which is high season; rooms can be 20% less at other times (unless there is an event or convention). Prices listed do not include the 15% accommodation tax.

BUDGET
You'll have to head out of town for the cheapest digs.

HI Stanford Hostel (☎ 330-467-8711; www.stanford hostel.com; 6093 Stanford Rd; dm $11-19; ⊙ daily May-Oct, closed Tue & Wed Nov-Apr) The hostel sits peacefully in the leafy Cuyahoga Valley National Recreation Area, 22 miles south of Cleveland in Peninsula. The fine old farmhouse is surrounded by walking trails, and deer often are spotted bounding by. The office is open from 8am to 10am and 5pm to 10pm. Call for directions; it's not accessible by public transportation.

MIDRANGE
Modest motels are southwest of Cleveland's center, near the airport. The W 150th exit off I-71 (exit 240) has several options for under $100.

Brownstone Inn (☎ 216-426-1753; www.brown stoneinndowntown.com; 3649 Prospect Ave; r incl breakfast $75-135; [P] [X] [□] wi-fi) Well located between downtown and University Circle, the Brownstone is a B&B with a big personality. All five rooms in the Victorian townhouse have a private bath, and each comes equipped with robes to lounge in and an invitation for evening aperitifs in the common area.

Days Inn (☎ 216-361-8969; www.daysinn.com; 3614 Euclid Ave; r incl breakfast $85-125; [P] [X] [i] [R] [□] wi-f) The medium-sized rooms at this Days Inn have the usual ho-hum furnishings, but the raft of amenities pump up the value. It's located near the Brownstone Inn.

Clifford House (☎ 216-589-0121; www.cliffordhouse .com; 1810 W 28th St; r incl breakfast $95-135; [P] [X] [X] wi-fi) If sleeping in a leafy, Queen Anne–style house sounds appealing, this Ohio City B&B is your place. Two of the three rooms share a bathroom; the other room spreads across the third floor by itself. Jim, the owner, serves a bountiful breakfast. It's near the RTA if you're without a car.

TOP END
Ritz-Carlton (☎ 216-623-1300; www.ritzcarlton.com; 1515 W 3rd St; r from $219; [P] [X] [R] [□] wi-fi) What the heck? Stay where the rock stars stay and enjoy the perks, like marble baths, a 24-hour fitness and massage center and free shoeshines. Wi-fi costs $9.95 per day, and parking is $22.

Eating
There are more hip options and ethnic range than you might expect in a Rust Belt town.

DOWNTOWN
Places around the stadiums are busy on game days. The Warehouse District, west between W 6th and W 9th Sts, jumps the rest of the time.

Town Fryer (☎ 216-426-9235; 3859 Superior Ave; mains $5-12; ⊗ 11am-3pm Mon-Fri) It offers deeply unhealthy Cajun and Southern comfort foods, like fried catfish and maple-bacon mashed potatoes, but aren't we all really here for the fried Twinkies and Oreos? It's located between downtown and University Circle.

Winking Lizard Tavern (☎ 216-589-0313; 811 Huron Rd; mains $7-16; ⊗ 11am-midnight Mon-Thu, to 1am Fri & Sat, to 11pm Sun) This hugely popular pub-grub outlet, named for its caged iguana, is a logical downtown stop before or after a sporting event.

Lola (☎ 216-621-5652; 2058 E 4th St; lunch mains $9-16, dinner mains $24-29; ⊗ 11:30am-10pm Mon-Fri, 5pm-midnight Sat, 5-9pm Sun) Famous for his piercings, Food Channel TV appearances and multiple national awards, local boy Michael Symon has put Cleveland on the foodie map with Lola. The lunch dishes are the most fun, say coconut-and-lime-tinged scallop ceviche, macaroni and goat cheese, or the showstopper – a fried bologna sandwich with smoked Wisconsin cheddar, topped by a fried egg.

OHIO CITY & TREMONT

Ohio City and Tremont, which straddle I-90 south of downtown, are areas with lots of new establishments popping up.

Lucky's Café (☎ 216-622-7773; 777 Starkweather Ave; mains $4-8; ⊗ 7am-8pm Mon-Fri, 8am-8pm Sat, 8am-5pm Sun; wi-fi) Lucky's grows its own produce and herbs in its adjacent garden, then uses the goods in its soups and wrap sandwiches. Weekend brunch with gingerbread waffles and cheddar scallion scones wins big flavor points.

West Side Market Café (☎ 216-579-6800; 1995 W 25th St; mains $5-8; ⊗ 7am-4pm Mon & Tue, to 9pm Wed-Sat, 10am-3pm Sun) This is a smart stop if you're craving well-made breakfast and lunch fare, and cheap fish and chicken mains. The café is inside West Side Market itself, which overflows with fresh produce and prepared foods that are handy for picnicking or road-tripping.

Johnny Mango (☎ 216-575-1919; 3120 Bridge Ave; mains $5-15; ⊗ 11am-10pm Mon-Thu, 11am-11pm Fri, 9am-11pm Sat, 9am-10pm Sun) The Caribbean-influenced food and drinks are as flavorful as the interior is colorful. Mr Mango has a hearty vegetarian selection along with his meat dishes, all begging to be complemented by tropical drinks like sangria or Cuban *mojitos* (rum cocktail). Try the killer french fries made of plantains.

Sokolowski's University Inn (☎ 216-771-9236; 1201 University Rd; mains $5-13; ⊗ 11am-3pm Mon-Fri, 5-9pm Fri & Sat) The portions are huge, enough to fuel the hungriest steelworker. It's cafeteria style, so grab a tray and fill it with plump pierogi, cabbage rolls and other rib-sticking Polish fare.

LITTLE ITALY & COVENTRY

These two neighborhoods make prime stops for refueling after hanging out in University Circle. Little Italy is closest; it's along Mayfield Rd, near Lake View Cemetery (look out for the Rte 322 sign). Alternative, relaxed Coventry Village is a bit further east off Mayfield Rd.

Presti's Bakery (☎ 216-421-3060; 12101 Mayfield Rd; items $2-5; ⊗ 6am-9pm Mon-Thu, to 10pm Fri & Sat, to 6pm Sun) Try Presti's for its popular sandwiches, stromboli and divine pine-nut cookies.

Tommy's (☎ 216-321-7757; 1823 Coventry Rd; mains $4-9; ⊗ 7:30am-10pm Mon-Thu, to 11pm Fri & Sat, 9am-10pm Sun) This is a neighborhood standout, with a broad, veggie-heavy menu; don't miss the Mary Lynn spinach pie.

Drinking
BARS & CLUBS

The downtown action centers on the Warehouse District (around W 6th St), where many restaurants also have popular bars, and around E 4th St's entertainment venues. Tremont is chock-a-block with trendy bars. To imbibe on a laid-back outdoor patio, Little Italy is the place to go.

Boneyard Beer Farm (☎ 216-575-0226; 748 Prospect Ave; ⊗ closed Sun) This spot near the sports stadiums is well suited for downing a couple pre- or post-game.

Major Hooples (☎ 216-575-0483; 1930 Columbus Rd; ⊗ closed Sun) Look over the bar for Cleveland's best skyline view from this friendly, eclectic watering hole. There's free live music on weekends.

Great Lakes Brewing Company (☎ 216-771-4404; 2516 Market Ave; ⊗ closed Sun) Great Lakes wins numerous prizes for its brewed-on-the-premises beers. Added historical bonus: Eliott Ness got into a shootout with criminals here; ask the bartender to show you the bullet holes.

South Side (☎ 216-937-2288; 2207 W 11 St; wi-fi) Local athletes, blue-collar electricians and everyone in between pile into this sleek Tremont establishment to drink at the winding granite bar under its festive Italian lights.

Oenotria (☎ 216-421-9463; 12407 Mayfield Rd) Sit and sip the night away at this perfect Little Italy wine bar.

Entertainment
LIVE MUSIC
Check *Scene* and Friday's *Plain Dealer* (see p585) for listings.

House of Blues (☎ 216-523-2583; www.hob.com; 308 Euclid Ave) The chain brings in medium- and top-tier bands.

Beachland Ballroom (☎ 216-383-1124; www.beach landballroom.com; 15711 Waterloo Rd) Hip young bands play at this venue east of downtown.

Grog Shop (☎ 216-321-5588; www.grogshop.gs; 2785 Euclid Hts Blvd) Up-and-coming rockers thrash at this long-time Coventry music house.

THEATER & CULTURE
For discounted tickets (30% to 50% off), check the online service **Ctix** (www.ctix.org).

Playhouse Square Center (☎ 216-771-4444; www .playhousesquare.com; 1501 Euclid Ave) This elegant center hosts theater, opera and ballet.

Severance Hall (☎ 216-231-1111; www.clevelandorch .com; 11001 Euclid Ave) Near University Circle, Severance Hall is where the acclaimed Cleveland Symphony Orchestra holds its season (August to May). The orchestra's summer home is Blossom Music Center in Cuyahoga Valley National Park, about 22 miles south.

SPORTS
Cleveland is a serious jock town with three modern downtown venues.

Jacobs Field (☎ 866-488-7423; www.indians.com; 2401 Ontario St) Baseball's Cleveland Indians (aka 'the Tribe') hit here.

Quicken Loans Arena (☎ 800-820-2287; www.nba .com/cavaliers; 1 Center Ct) The Cavaliers play basketball at 'the Q,' as it's known, which doubles as an entertainment venue.

Cleveland Browns Stadium (☎ 440-891-5000; www .clevelandbrowns.com; 1085 W 3rd St) The NFL's Browns play football on the lakefront.

Getting There & Around
Eleven miles southwest of downtown, **Cleveland Hopkins International Airport** (CLE; ☎ 216-265-6030; www.clevelandairport.com) is linked by the Regional Transit Authority (RTA) Red Line train ($1.75). A cab to downtown costs about $28.

From downtown, **Greyhound** (☎ 216-781-0520; 1465 Chester Ave) offers frequent departures to Chicago ($48 to $55, 7½ hours) and New York ($59 to $72, 13 hours). **Megabus** (☎ 877-462-6342; www.megabus.com/us) also goes to Chicago, often for lower fares; it departs from the corner of W 3rd St and W Huron Rd.

Parking is scarce and expensive downtown during events. Avis, Hertz and other rental agencies have offices at the airport and around town. Check the Transportation chapter (p1144) for contact details.

The **Regional Transit Authority** (RTA; ☎ 216-621-9500; www.gcrta.org; 1240 W 6th St) operates the useful Red Line train that goes from downtown to Ohio City and University Circle. Fares are $1.75; day passes are $3.50.

Amtrak (☎ 216-696-5115; 200 Cleveland Memorial Shoreway) runs once daily to Chicago ($47 to $92, seven hours) and New York City ($64 to $126, 11½ hours).

For cab service, call **Americab** (☎ 216-429-1111).

AROUND CLEVELAND
Thirty miles south of Cleveland, **Akron** was a small village until Dr BF Goodrich established the first rubber factory in 1869. It was also once the country's rubber capital, and still produces more than half the country's tires and over 50,000 different rubber products. For an insight into US ingenuity, visit the **National Inventors Hall of Fame** (☎ 330-762-4463; www .invent.org; 221 S Broadway, Akron; adult/child 3-17 $8.75/6.75; ☼ 10am-4:30pm Wed-Sat).

Further south in **Canton**, birthplace of the NFL, the popular **Pro Football Hall of Fame** (☎ 330-456-8207; www.profootballhof.com; 2121 George Halas Dr; adult/child 6-14 $16/10; ☼ 9am-8pm Jun-Aug, 9am-5pm rest of year) is a shrine for the gridiron-obsessed. Look for the football-shaped tower off I-77.

West of Cleveland, attractive **Oberlin** is an old-fashioned college town, with noteworthy architecture by Cass Gilbert, Frank Lloyd Wright and Robert Venturi. Further west, just south of I-90, the tiny town of **Milan** is the birthplace of Thomas Edison. His home, restored to its 1847 likeness, is now a small **museum** (☎ 419-499-2135; www.tomedison.org; 9 Edison Dr; adult/child 6-12 $5/2; ☼ 1-4pm Wed-Sun winter, extended hrs Tue-Sun summer, closed Jan) outlining his inventions, like the light bulb and phonograph.

Still further west, on US 20 and surrounded by farmland, is **Clyde**, which bills itself as the USA's most famous small town. It got that way when native son Sherwood Anderson published *Winesburg, Ohio* in 1919. It didn't

> ## WORLD'S BIGGEST COASTERS
>
> For the world's tallest, fastest and greatest concentration of roller coasters, head to **Cedar Point Amusement Park** (☎ 419-627-2350; www.cedarpoint.com; adult/child $41.95/11.95; ☽ from 10am daily mid-May–Labor Day, from 10am Sat & Sun Sep-Oct, closing times vary), 6 miles from Sandusky. The Top Thrill Dragster drops 420ft high and whips around at 120mph (there's your tallest and fastest), while the Maverick drops at a 95° angle (that's steeper than straight down) and rolls over eight hills where riders feel weightless. If those and the 15 other coasters aren't enough, the surrounding area has a nice beach, a water park and a slew of tacky, old-fashioned attractions. Parking is $10.

take long for the unimpressed residents to figure out where the fictitious town really was. Stop at the **Clyde Museum** (☎ 419-547-9330; 124 W Buckeye St; admission free; ☽ 1-4pm Thu or by appt) in the old church for Anderson tidbits or at the library, a few doors down.

ERIE LAKESHORE & ISLANDS

In summer this good-time resort area is one of the busiest (and most expensive) places in Ohio. The seasons last from mid-May to mid-September, then everything shuts down. Pre-book accommodations.

Sandusky, long a port, now serves as the jump-off point to the Erie Islands and the world's roller coaster capital. The **visitors center** (☎ 419-625-2984; www.sanduskyohiocedarpoint.com; 4424 Milan Rd; ☽ 8:30am-5:30pm Mon-Fri, extended to evenings & Sat in summer) provides lodging and ferry information. Scads of chain motels line the roads heading into town. The web resource **Lake Erie Coastal Ohio** (www.coastalohio.com) provides good maps and event and bird-sighting information for the region.

Bass Islands

In the war of 1812's Battle of Lake Erie, Admiral Perry met the enemy English fleet near **South Bass Island**. His victory ensured that all the lands south of the Great Lakes became US, not Canadian territory.

While that's nice, history is all but forgotten on a summer weekend in packed Put In Bay, the island's main town and a party place full of restaurants and shops. Move beyond it, and you'll find a winery and opportunities for camping, fishing, kayaking and swimming. A singular attraction is the 352ft Doric column commemorating Perry's victory in the Battle of Lake Erie – you can climb up to the observation deck ($3) for views of the battle site and, on a good day, Canada.

The **Chamber of Commerce** (☎ 419-285-2832; www.put-in-bay.com; cnr 148 Delaware Ave; ☽ 10am-5pm

Mon-Sun summer, Mon-Fri rest of year) has information on activities and lodging, which starts at $70 in summer and often is booked up. **Ashley's Island House** (☎ 419-285-2844; www.ashleysislandhouse.com; 557 Catawba Ave; r weekday $70-110, weekend $120-175) is a 13-room B&B, where naval officers stayed in the late 1800s. The **Beer Barrel Saloon** (☎ 419-285-2337; 1618 Delaware Ave; ☽ 11-1am) has plenty of space for imbibing – its bar is 406ft long.

Cabs and tour buses serve the island, though bicycling is a fine way to get around. **Jet Express** (☎ 800-245-1538; www.jet-express.com) leaves Port Clinton on the mainland for Put In Bay (one way adult/child 6-12 $12/2, no cars), and also departs from Sandusky (one way adult/child 6-12 $16/5, no cars). **Miller Boatline** (☎ 800-500-2421; www.millerferry.com) from Catawba is cheapest (one way adult/child 6-11 $6/1.50, car $14).

Middle Bass Island, a good day trip by ferry from South Bass, offers nature and quiet; Miller Boatline will get you there.

Kelleys Island

Quiet and green, Kelleys is a popular weekend escape, especially for families. It has pretty 19th-century buildings, Native American pictographs, a good beach and glacial grooves – even its old limestone quarries are scenic.

The **Chamber of Commerce** (☎ 419-746-2360; www.kelleysislandchamber.com; cnr Division & Chappell Sts; ☽ 10am-4pm Mon-Sat, noon-4pm Sun summer) has activity and accommodation information. The Village, the small commercial center of the island, has places to eat, drink, shop and rent bicycles – a good way to sightsee.

Kelleys Island Ferry Boat Line (☎ 419-798-9763; www.kelleysislandferry.com) departs frequently from the Marblehead dock (one way adult/child 6-11 $7/3.50, car $13). The crossing takes about 20 minutes and leaves hourly (more frequently in summer). Jet Express (left) makes the inter-island trip to Put In Bay on South Bass Island.

Pelee Island

Pelee, the largest Erie island, is a quiet wine-producing and bird-watching destination that belongs to Canada. **Pelee Island Transportation** (☎ 800-661-2220) runs a ferry (one way adult/child 6-12 $13.75/6.75, car $30) from Sandusky to Pelee and onward to Ontario's mainland.

AMISH COUNTRY

The Amish have resisted modernity for centuries, and visiting here is like entering a time warp. Wayne and Holmes counties, between Cleveland and Columbus (immediately east of I-71), have the USA's densest Amish concentration, followed by areas in Pennsylvania and Indiana.

Descendants of conservative Dutch–Swiss religious factions who migrated to the USA during the 18th century, the Amish continue to follow the *ordnung* (way of life), in varying degrees. Many adhere to rules prohibiting the use of electricity, telephones and motorized vehicles. They wear traditional clothing, farm the land with plow and mule, and go to church in horse-drawn buggies. Others are not so strict.

Unfortunately, what would surely be a peaceful country scene is often disturbed by behemoth tour buses. Many Amish are happy to profit from this influx of outside dollars, but don't equate this with free photographic access – the Amish typically view photographs as taboo. Drive carefully, as roads are narrow and curvy and there's always the chance of pulling up on a slow-moving buggy just around the bend. Many places are closed Sunday.

Near Berlin, east of Millersburg, is the **Amish & Mennonite Heritage Center** (☎ 330-893-3192; 5798

CHILLIN' WITH ICE WINE

Hey, if the guys across the border in Canada can do it, so can Ohio. Ten state wineries, most along Lake Erie, began making ice wine a few years ago, and they're reaping big praise. The local weather – long autumns, followed by winters cold enough to freeze the grapes but not so cold that the vines die – results in a sweet dessert wine with hints of melon and apricot. Tour and try samples at **Debonne Vineyards** (☎ 440-466-3485; www.debonne.com; 7743 Doty Rd; 8-sample tasting $4; ☻ Tue-Sun) in Madison, east of Cleveland.

County Rd 77; adult/child 6-12 $7/3.50; ☻ 9am-5pm Mon-Sat year-round, to 8pm Fri & Sat Jun-Oct), which offers concise explanations of the history and life of Amish.

Kidron, on Rte 52 just north of US 250, is worth a stop on Thursday, when the **Kidron Auction** takes place at the livestock barn. Hundreds of buggies line up along the roadside, and an interesting flea market rings the barn. Across the street, **Lehman's Store** is an absolute must-see. It's the Amish community's main purveyor of modern-looking products that use no electricity.

In quiet Walnut Creek, between Sugarcreek and Berlin just north of Hwy 39, check out the amazing **Amish Flea Market** (☻ 9am-5pm Fri & Sat), where you can find new or used knick-knacks, crafts, quilts, produce, antiques and delicious baked goods. Just north of Walnut Creek, along Hwy 515, **Yoder's** (☎ 330-893-2541; ☻ 10am-5pm Mon-Sat mid-Apr–Oct) is an Amish farm that's open to visitors. Tours (per adult/child $10/6) include a buggy ride.

In the town of Millersburg, west of Berlin on US 62, the historic **Hotel Millersburg** (☎ 330-674-1457; www.hotelmillersburg.com; 35 W Jackson St; r $50-139) has very basic, reasonably priced rooms (ask for an economy or twin room for the lowest rates). There's a modern, brightly lit tavern and dining room on the ground floor.

Boyd & Wurthmann Restaurant (☎ 330-893-3287; Main St; mains from $7; ☻ 5:30am-8pm Mon-Sat) is Berlin's most atmospheric eatery and serves home-style cooking, attracting locals and tourists alike. Amish specialties, like ham loaf and wedding steak (ground meat in mushroom sauce), join familiar American fare on the menu.

COLUMBUS

Columbus is like the blind date your mom arranges – average looking, restrained personality, but solid and affable. Better yet, she's easy on the wallet, an influence from Ohio State University's 50,000-plus students (the uni is the nation's largest).

There is a **visitors center** (☎ 614-221-2489, 800-345-4386; www.experiencecolumbus.com; 90 N High St; ☻ 8am-5pm Mon-Fri) downtown.

The *Columbus Dispatch* (www.dispatch.com) is the city's daily newspaper. The free, weekly *Alive* (www.columbusalive.com) has entertainment listings. *Outlook* (www.outlooknews.com) is a weekly gay and lesbian publication.

Sights & Activities

The remarkably large, all-brick **German Village**, a half mile south of downtown, is a restored 19th-century neighborhood with cobbled streets and Italianate and Queen Anne architecture. The **German Village Society** (☎ 614-221-8888; www.germanvillage.com; 588 S 3rd St; ☺ 9am-4pm Mon-Fri, 10am-2pm Sat) has self-guided walking-tour information. Just north of downtown, the browseable **Short North** is a redeveloped strip of High St that holds contemporary art galleries, restaurants and jazz bars.

North of downtown, the university area has many casual storefronts. The campus's **Wexner Center for the Arts** (☎ 614-292-3535; www.wexarts.org; cnr 15th & N High Sts; gallery admission free; ☺ 11am-6pm Tue, Wed & Sun, to 8pm Thu-Sat) offers cutting-edge art exhibits, films and performances.

Sleeping & Eating

Add 16.75% tax to hotel rates. German Village and the Short North provide fertile grazing and guzzling grounds. The Arena District (the area around the Nationwide Arena hockey stadium) is also bursting, mostly with midrange chains and brewpubs. Around the university and along N High St from 15th Ave onward, you'll find everything from Mexican to Ethiopian to sushi, plus quality coffee shops.

Red Roof Inn (☎ 614-224-6539; 111 E Nationwide Blvd; r incl breakfast $65-129; P) Located in the Arena District, it's one of the classiest-looking Red Roofs you'll ever see. Parking is $10.

50 Lincoln B&B (☎ 614-299-5050, 800-516-9664; www.columbus-bed-breakfast.com; 50 E Lincoln St; r incl breakfast $119; P wi-fi) These eight well-maintained rooms are steps away from the Short North.

Blue Danube (☎ 614-261-9308; 2439 N High St; mains $5-9; ☺ 11-2:30am) The D'ube's smoky, neon-lit booths (and cheap beer) endure as a campus favorite. Meals are late-night booze-absorbers, like gravy-smothered fries and gyros.

Katzinger's Deli (☎ 614-228-3354; 475 S 3rd St; sandwiches $8-12; ☺ 8:30am-8:30pm Mon-Fri, from 9am Sat & Sun) Prepare for a mind-boggling array of huge, scrumptious sandwiches, from beefy to vegan.

Schmidt's (☎ 614-444-6808; 240 E Kossuth St; mains $8-14; ☺ 11am-10pm Tue-Sat, to 9pm Sun & Mon) Shovel in succulent German staples, like sausage, schnitzel and potato salad. The pièce de résistance are the half-pound cream puffs, best exemplified by the 'Buckeye,' pumped up with peanut butter. The beer flows freely to the strains of an oompah band (Fridays and Saturdays).

Drinking & Entertainment

The Ohio State Buckeyes football team packs a rabid crowd into legendary, horseshoe-shaped **Ohio Stadium** (☎ 800-462-8257; www.ohiostatebuckeyes .com; 411 Woody Hayes Dr) for its games, held on Saturdays in the fall. The National Hockey League's Columbus Blue Jackets slap the puck at the downtown **Nationwide Arena** (☎ 614-246-2000; www.bluejackets.com; 200 W Nationwide Blvd). The popular Columbus Crew pro soccer team plays in **Crew Stadium** (☎ 614-447-2739; www.thecrew .com; 2121 Velma Ave), north off I-71 and 17th Ave, from March to October.

Getting There & Around

The **Port Columbus Airport** (CMH; ☎ 614-239-4000; www.port-columbus.com) is 10 miles east of town. There is no direct public bus. A cab to downtown costs $20 to $24.

Greyhound (☎ 614-221-4642; www.greyhound.com; 111 E Town St) buses run at least six times daily to Cincinnati ($17 to $25, two hours) and Cleveland ($19 to $27, 2½ hours). Often cheaper, **Megabus** (☎ 877-462-6342; www.megabus.com/us) runs once daily to Cincinnati and twice daily to Chicago. It departs from downtown and the university; check the website for exact locations. There is no Amtrak train service.

SOUTHEASTERN OHIO

Ohio's southeastern corner cradles most of its forested areas, as well as rolling hills and scattered farms.

Around Lancaster, southeast of Columbus, the hills lead gently into **Hocking County**, which contains more than half a dozen state parks. This region of streams and waterfalls, sandstone cliffs and cave-like formations is a splendid area to explore in any season. It has miles of trails for hiking and rivers for canoeing, as well as abundant campgrounds and cabins at **Hocking Hills State Park** (☎ 740-385-6165; www.hockinghillspark.com; 20160 Hwy 664; campsites/cottages from $19/101). **Old Man's Cave** is a scenic winner for hiking. **Earth-Water-Rock: Outdoor Adventures** (☎ 740-664-5220; www.ewroutdoors.com; half-day tour $100) provides guided rock climbing and rappelling trips, and even beginners can get in on the thrills.

Athens makes a lovely base for seeing the region. Situated where US 50 crosses US

33, it's set among wooded hills and built around the Ohio University campus (which comprises half the town). The **visitors center** (☎ 740-592-1819, 800-878-9767; www.athensohio.com; 667 E State St; ⊙ 9am-5pm Mon-Sat, reduced in winter) has good regional information. Inexpensive motels – including friendly **Budget Host** (☎ 740-594-2294; 100 Albany Rd at Rte 50 W; s/d from $45/55) – dot the outskirts, and numerous student cafés and pubs line Court St, the main road. **Court Street Diner** (☎ 740-594-8700; 18 N Court St; mains $6-10; ⊙ 7am-10pm, reduced in winter) piles on breakfast, lunch and dinner platters in '50s style.

Further south, the Ohio River marks the state boundary and flows through many scenic stretches. It's a surprisingly quiet, undeveloped area.

The area south of Columbus was a center for the fascinating prehistoric Hopewell people, who left behind huge geometric earthworks and burial mounds from around 200 BC to AD 600. For a fine introduction visit the **Hopewell Culture National Historical Park** (☎ 740-774-1126; www.nps.gov/hocu; Hwy 104 north of I-35; admission free; ⊙ 8:30-6pm Jun-Aug, to 4:30pm Sep-May), 3 miles north of Chillicothe. The visitors center has a film and excellent interactive exhibit; then you can wander about the variously shaped ceremonial mounds spread over 13-acre **Mound City**, a mysterious town of the dead. **Serpent Mound** (☎ 937-587-2796; www.ohiohistory.org; 3850 Hwy 73; per vehicle $7; ⊙ 10am-5pm Wed-Sun), southwest of Chillicothe and 4 miles northwest of Locust Grove, is perhaps the most captivating site of all. The giant, uncoiling snake stretches over 0.25 miles and is the largest effigy mound in the USA.

DAYTON & YELLOW SPRINGS

Dayton has the aviation sights, but little Yellow Springs (18 miles northeast on US 68) has much more personality for accommodation and places to eat.

Sights & Activities

The huge **National Museum of the US Air Force** (☎ 937-255-3286; www.nationalmuseum.af.mil; 1100 Spaatz St; admission free; ⊙ 9am-5pm) is at the Wright Patterson Air Force base, 6 miles northeast of Dayton. It's got everything from a Wright Brothers exhibit, a Sopwith Camel (WWI biplane) and a Stealth bomber, to astronaut ice cream and military propaganda. Expect a visit to take three or more hours. Don't miss the annex with its collection of presidential planes; a free shuttle bus takes you over to the hangar (which you'll need a passport or driver's license to enter).

There are numerous Wright attractions. Among them, **Carillon Historical Park** (☎ 937-293-2841; www.daytonhistory.org; 1000 Carillon Blvd; adult/child 3-17 $8/5; ⊙ 9:30am-5pm Mon-Sat, noon-5pm Sun) has the 1905 Wright Flyer III biplane and a replica of the Wright workshop. The **Dayton Aviation Heritage National Historical Park** (☎ 937-225-7705; www.nps.gov/daav; 16 S Williams St; admission free; ⊙ 8:30am-5pm, to 6pm Jun-Aug), which includes Wright Cycle Company Complex, is where the brothers developed bikes and aviation ideas.

Sleeping & Eating

The following listings are located in Yellow Springs, a top-notch place to experience down-home Ohio.

John Bryan State Park (☎ 937-767-1274; www.johnbryan.org; 3790 Hwy 370; campsites $13-22) You can fish, hike, rock climb or camp among the limestone cliffs here.

Morgan House B&B (☎ 937-767-1761; www.arthurmorganhouse.com; 120 W Limestone St; r $95-115; wi-fi) The six comfy rooms have super-soft linens and private bathrooms. Breakfasts are organic and the coffee locally roasted.

Young's Jersey Dairy (☎ 937-325-0629; www.youngsdairy.com; 6880 Springfield-Xenia Rd) This working dairy farm has two restaurants: the **Golden Jersey Inn** (mains $8-13; ⊙ lunch & dinner Mon-Fri, plus breakfast Sat & Sun), serving dishes like buttermilk chicken; and the **Dairy Store** (sandwiches $2.50-5.50; ⊙ 6am-10pm Sun-Thu, to 11pm Fri & Sat), serving sandwiches, dreamy ice cream and Ohio's best milkshakes. There's also a coffee shop with wi-fi onsite.

Winds Café (☎ 937-767-1144; 215 Xenia Ave; mains $20-25; ⊙ lunch & dinner Tue-Sat, brunch only Sun) A hippie co-op 30 years ago, the Winds has grown up to become a sophisticated foodie favorite plating organic, seasonal dishes like fig-sauced asparagus crepes and rhubarb halibut.

CINCINNATI

Cincinnati has such a colorful past for such a fogyish city (Mark Twain said he wanted to be here when the world ends, as the city is always 20 years behind the times). The 1970s saw Jerry Springer become mayor, elected after he was caught paying for a hooker with a check. Going back further, the town was known as Porkopolis because of its salted-pork-packing plants. It was also an important center for the antislavery movement and the Underground Railroad.

So what's here now? Well, it's a good place to catch a baseball game and ride a paddle wheel boat on the swift-moving Ohio River. Mt Adams, whose twisting streets lead to one of the city's best hilltop views, is a great old neighborhood to explore. So are über-cool Northside and cobblestoned Covington. And if you're feeling frisky, Cincy's the city to join in a five-way (see boxed text, p597). Yeah, baby!

Orientation & Information

Downtown streets are laid out on a grid radiating from Fountain Square. Vine St is the east–west dividing line; east- and west-bound streets are numbered, while north- and south-bound streets are named. The snaking Ohio River forms the city's southern boundary, and Kentucky is just across the water. The Northside neighborhood, north of where I-74 and I-75 intersect, is 5 miles north of downtown.

BOOKSTORES
Barnes & Noble (☎ 859-581-2000; Newport on the Levee; ⏱ 10am-11pm)

EMERGENCY & MEDICAL SERVICES
University Hospital (☎ 513-584-1000; 234 Goodman St)

INTERNET ACCESS
@The Kafe (☎ 513-241-1343; www.atthekafe.com; Carew Tower, 441 Vine St; per ½ hr $3; ⏱ 7am-6pm Mon-Fri, 9am-6pm Sat) Internet terminals, wi-fi and you can burn photo CDs, too.

MEDIA & INTERNET RESOURCES
Cincinnati Arts (www.cincinnatiarts.com) Website for gallery, theater and music happenings.
Cincinnati Enquirer (www.enquirer.com) Daily morning newspaper.
Cin Weekly (www.cinweekly.com) *Enquirer/Post*'s weekly entertainment freebie.
CityBeat (www.citybeat.com) Free alternative weekly paper with good entertainment listings.

TOURIST INFORMATION
Cincinnati USA Regional Tourism Network (☎ 800-344-3445; www.cincinnatiusa.com) There is no bricks-and-mortar building to get information; call for a visitor's guide or go online for it.

Sights & Activities
DOWNTOWN
The elegant 1876 **Roebling Suspension Bridge** was a forerunner of John Roebling's famous Brooklyn Bridge in New York. At its foot is the **National Underground Railroad Freedom Center** (☎ 513-333-7500; www.freedomcenter.org; 50 E Freedom Way; adult/child 6-12 $12/8; ⏱ 11am-5pm Tue-Sun), with exhibits on how slaves escaped to the north; Cincinnati was a prominent stop on the railroad and a center for abolitionist activities led by residents, such as Harriet Beecher Stowe.

The city recently slicked up its centerpiece, **Fountain Square** (cnr 5th & Vine Sts), and added an ice rink to keep the fancy old 'Spirit of the Waters' fountain company. Just north, the **Rosenthal Center for Contemporary Arts** (☎ 513-721-0390; www.contemporaryartscenter.org; 44 E 6th St; adult/child 3-13 $7.50/4.50, admission free Mon evening; ⏱ 10am-9pm Mon, 10am-6pm Wed-Fri, 11am-6pm Sat & Sun) displays modern art in a new, avant-garde building designed by Iranian architect Zaha Hadid. The structure and its artworks are a pretty big deal for traditionalist Cincy. Nearby **Carew Tower** (☎ 513-241-3888; 441 Vine St; adult/child 5-11 $2/1; ⏱ 9am-5:30pm Mon-Thu, 9am-6pm Fri, 10am-7pm Sat & Sun) has a great view from its 49th-floor observation deck and a fine art deco interior. East of the square is the postmodern **Procter & Gamble world headquarters** (cnr 6th & Broadway Sts), often called the 'Dolly Parton Towers' due to its resemblance to the country singer's most prominent features.

A stroll along the riverfront will take you through several parks; one of them, **Bicentennial Commons at Sawyer Point**, features whimsical monuments and flying pigs. The pedestrian-only **Purple People Bridge** provides a unique crossing from Sawyer Point to Newport, Kentucky.

COVINGTON & NEWPORT
Covington and Newport, Kentucky, are sort of suburbs of Cincinnati. Newport, known mainly for its massive **Newport on the Levee** restaurant and shopping complex, is directly over the river at the foot of the Purple People Bridge. The development also contains the well-regarded **Newport Aquarium** (☎ 859-491-3467; www.newportaquarium.com; adult/child 2-12 $18/11; ⏱ 10am-6pm), where you can meet Sweet Pea the shark ray, parading penguins and more. **BB Riverboats** (☎ 859-261-8500; www.bbriverboats.com; 101 Riverboat Row; 1-hour tour adult/child $14/8) takes off from a dock near the aquarium

CINCINNATI

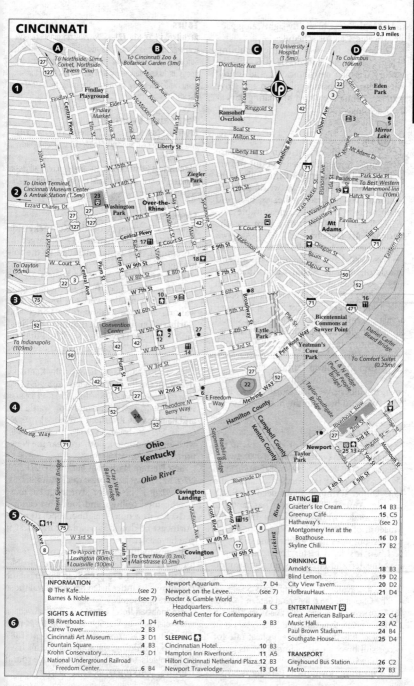

and plies the river in a nifty sightseeing paddle wheeler. Call for schedules.

Covington lies west of the Roebling Bridge. Its lively **MainStrasse** was a 19th-century German neighborhood, and is now full of shops, pubs and places to eat. Covington Landing is an area of floating bars at the Roebling's foot.

MT ADAMS

It might be a bit of a stretch to compare Mt Adams, immediately east of downtown, to Paris's Montmartre, but this hilly 19th-century enclave of narrow, twisting streets, Victorian townhouses, galleries, bars and restaurants is certainly a pleasurable surprise. Two big attractions here are the **Cincinnati Art Museum** (☎ 513-721-5204; www.cincinnatiartmuseum.org; 953 Eden Park Dr; admission free; 🕙 11am-5pm Tue-Sun, to 9pm Wed), with an emphasis on Middle Eastern and European arts as well as local works, and the **Krohn Conservatory** (☎ 513-421-4086; www.cincinnati-oh.gov/parks; 1501 Eden Park Dr; admission free; 🕙 10am-5pm), a vast greenhouse with a rainforest, desert flora and glorious seasonal flower shows. Most visitors just ascend the hill for a look around, a drink and a pause to enjoy the view from the hilltop Catholic church.

To get here, follow 7th St east of downtown to Gilbert Ave, bear northwest to Elsinore Ave, and head up the hill.

AROUND CINCINNATI

Two miles northwest of downtown, the **Cincinnati Museum Center** (☎ 513-287-7000; www.cincymuseum.org; 1301 Western Ave; adult/child 3-12 $7.25/5.25; 🕙 10am-5pm Mon-Sat, 11am-6pm Sun) occupies the 1933 Union Terminal, an art deco jewel still used by Amtrak. The interior has fantastic murals made of Rookwood tiles. Inside, the Museum of Natural History is more geared to kids, but does have a limestone cave with real bats inside. A history museum, Omnimax theater and children's museum round out the offerings. Discounted combination tickets are available. Parking costs $5.

The **Cincinnati Zoo & Botanical Garden** (☎ 513-281-4700; www.cincyzoo.org; 3400 Vine St; adult/child 2-12 $13/8; 🕙 9am-5pm), aka the 'Sexiest Zoo in America,' has the country's highest rate for successful breeding. It's famous for its gorillas, white lions and rhinos, and is located 3 miles north of downtown. Parking is $6.50.

Tours

Architreks (☎ 513-721-4506; www.cincinnatipreservation.org/architreks.html; tours adult/child $10/5; 🕙 Sat & Sun, May-Oct) Guided walking tours of various neighborhoods, including downtown and Mt Adams. Departure points and times vary, so contact the group for further details.

Festivals & Events

Riverfest (☎ 513-352-4000; admission free) Concerts and fireworks; held Sunday of Labor Day weekend (early September).

Oktoberfest (www.oktoberfest-zinzinnati.com; admission free) German beer, brats and mania; held mid-September.

Sleeping

Hotel tax is cheaper on the Kentucky side at 11.24%, rather than the 17% charged in Cincinnati. Tax is not included in the following prices.

Newport Travelodge (☎ 859-291-4434; 222 York St; r incl breakfast $65-80; P 🐾) Other properties with this prime riverfront location (it's walking distance to downtown Cincy and Northern Kentucky's entertainment districts) can't touch the Travelodge's prices. But then, it's pretty dumpy compared to those other properties.

Two good, similar options on the Kentucky riverfront are the **Comfort Suites** (☎ 859-291-6700; www.choicehotels.com; 420 Riverboat Row; r incl breakfast $95-130; P 🐾 wi-fi) with a morning waffle bar, and **Hampton Inn Riverfront** (☎ 859-581-7800; 200 Crescent Ave; r incl breakfast $99-149; P 🐾 🛗 wi-fi), with an indoor pool. Both are near the Newport/Covington attractions.

Best Western Mariemont Inn (☎ 513-271-2100, 877-271-2111; www.mariemontinn.com; 6880 Wooster Pike; s/d $89/99; P) This Tudor-style lodge has massive beamed ceilings and four-post canopy beds. It's in a quiet neighborhood 10 miles northeast of downtown, and works best if you have a car.

Room quality soars when you move to the top-end bracket, yet prices remain reasonable. The weekend rates (especially in winter) of the downtown beauties listed here can rival those of midrange hotels.

Cincinnatian Hotel (☎ 513-381-3000; www.cincinnatianhotel.com; 601 Vine St; r $129-225; P 🐾 wi-fi) The Cincinnatian is in a magnificent 1882 Victorian building; the spacious rooms have fluffy towels, silk-soft sheets and huge round bathtubs. Parking costs $25.

Hilton Cincinnati Netherland Plaza (☎ 513-421-9100; www.cincinnatinetherlandplaza.hilton.com; 35 W 5th St; r $159-214; **P** **☒** **☒** wi-fi) The 1920s-era Netherland is an art deco monument. Its opulent Palm Court Bar sports fan-shaped couches and Baroque-style murals. The rooms are swell, too. Parking is $21.

Eating

In addition to downtown, good dining options are concentrated in Mt Adams, along the riverfront and in Northside.

Graeter's Ice Cream (☎ 513-381-0653; 41 E 4th St; dishes $2-4; ☽ 7am-6pm Mon-Fri, until 3pm Sat) Another local delicacy, Graeter's is the place for dessert. The flavors that mix in chocolate chips (which are gargantuan chunks) top the list. Other branches are located around the city.

Hathaway's (☎ 513-621-1332; Carew Tower, 441 Vine St; mains $5-8; ☽ 6:30am-4pm Mon-Fri, 8am-3pm Sat) Hathaway's hasn't changed its retro dinette tables, or apron-wearing waitresses, since it started feeding hungry businesspeople 30-plus years ago. Try the goetta (pork, oats, onions and herbs) for breakfast; it's a Cincy specialty. The milkshakes will please sweet tooths.

Greenup Café (☎ 859-261-3663; 308 Greenup St; mains $10-21; ☽ 7:30am-2:30pm Mon, 7:30am-9:30pm Tue-Fri, 9am-9:30pm Sat, 9am-2pm Sun) Greenup's French chef has imported the flavors of his homeland to this cheerfully colored bistro located in an old brick warehouse. Get your croissants, brie, baguettes, crepes, pastries and killer coffee in the bohemian inner rooms, or chow in the outdoor garden when weather permits. Dinner mains focus on chicken and seafood dishes.

Chez Nora (☎ 859-491-8027; 530 Main St; mains $12-20; ☽ 11-1am) Its tables sprawl throughout a quaint multistory building, while its menu sprawls from chicken-and-goetta spring rolls to chilled mussels to walleye sandwiches to vegetarian pesto pasta. The

rooftop bar provides views of Cincinnati's skyline (especially nice on Tuesdays with half-price bottles of wine).

Slims (☎ 513-681-6500; 4046 Hamilton Ave; mains $17-18; ☽ 5:30-9:30pm Thu-Sun) This bright, simple Northside restaurant serves organic and seasonal dishes – maybe a Chilean vegetarian stew or citrus-braised pork belly – at long communal tables from 5:30pm 'until the food runs out.' Credit cards not accepted; bring your own vino.

Montgomery Inn at the Boathouse (☎ 513-721-7427; 925 Eastern Ave; small/large slab of ribs $13/22; ☽ 11am-10pm Mon-Thu, 11am-11pm Fri, 3-11pm Sat, 3-10pm Sun) Almost as renowned and addictive as Cincinnati chili are Montgomery Inn's barbecued ribs. There are a couple of outlets, but this riverside one is the best, taming carnivores with 13.5 tons of meat weekly.

Drinking

Scope for free publications like *CityBeat* and *Cin Weekly* for current listings. The free *GLBT News* (www.greatercincinnatiglbtnews.com) has a bar and club guide.

BARS & CLUBS

The city's German influence meant Cincinnati was once a beer drinkers' paradise – in the 1890s there were 1800 saloons for 297,000 people, guzzling two-and-a-half times more than the rest of the country. Mt Adams and Northside are still busy nightspots. Covington Landing has places on the river (in moored boats) that are refreshing on hot nights when there's a breeze.

Blind Lemon (☎ 513-241-3885; 936 Hatch St, Mt Adams) Head down the passageway to enter this atmospheric old speakeasy. It has an outdoor courtyard in summer, with a fire pit added in winter, and there's live music nightly.

Arnold's (☎ 513-421-6234; 210 E 8th St, Downtown; ☽ closed Sun) Arnold's is a downtown oldie but goodie dating from 1861. There's live music

---

JOIN IN A FIVE-WAY

Don't worry – you can keep your clothes on for this experience, though you may want to loosen your belt. A 'five-way' in Cincinnati has to do with chili, which is a local specialty. It comprises meat sauce (spiced with chocolate and cinnamon) ladled over spaghetti and beans, garnished with cheese and onions. You can get it three-way (minus onions and beans) or four-way (minus onions or beans), but go the whole way; life's an adventure. **Skyline Chili** (☎ 513-721-4715; 1007 Vine St; items $3-6; ☽ 10am-6pm Mon-Fri) has a cult-like following devoted to its version. There are outlets throughout town. This downtown one is an experience weekdays at noon.

nightly from the front porch-like stage – often bluegrass.

Comet (☎ 513-541-8900; 4579 Hamilton Ave, Northside) The casual Comet has the city's best jukebox and bar food (try the burrito).

City View Tavern (☎ 513-241-8439; 403 Oregon St, Mt Adams) The city sparkles out in front of you at this unassuming boozer.

HofbrauHaus (☎ 859-491-7200; 200 E 3rd St, Newport) The legendary Munich beer hall fills steins in Newport.

Entertainment
LIVE MUSIC
Southgate House (☎ 859-431-2201; www.southgate house.com; 24 E 3rd St, Newport; ☺ from noon) Big and small, touring and local bands alike play in this 1814 haunted mansion, which also happens to be the birthplace of the tommy gun.

Northside Tavern (☎ 513-542-3603; www.northside tavern.com; 4163 Hamilton Ave, Northside) Up-and-coming indie bands plug in their amps here.

THEATER & CULTURE
Music Hall (☎ 513-721-8222; www.cincinnatiarts.org; 1241 Elm St) The acoustically pristine Music Hall is the city's classical music venue, where the symphony orchestra, pops orchestra, opera and ballet hold their seasons. This is not the best neighborhood, so be cautious and park nearby.

SPORTS
Great American Ballpark (☎ 513-765-7000; www .cincinnatireds.com; 100 Main St) Home to the Reds (pro baseball's first team), Cincy is a great place to catch a game thanks to its modern riverside ballpark.

Paul Brown Stadium (☎ 513-621-3550; www .bengals.com; 1 Paul Brown Stadium) The Bengals pro football team scrimmages a few blocks west of the ballpark.

Getting There & Around
The **airport** (CVG; ☎ 859-767-3501; www.cvgairport.com) is actually in Kentucky, 13 miles south. To get downtown, take the TANK bus ($1.25) from Terminal 1 or 3; a cab costs about $25.

Greyhound (☎ 513-352-6012; www.greyhound.com; 1005 Gilbert Ave) buses travel daily to Louisville ($20 to $30, two hours), Indianapolis ($17 to $28, 2½ hours) and Columbus ($17 to $25, two hours). Often cheaper, **Megabus** (☎ 877-462-6342; www.megabus.com/us) runs once daily to Columbus and twice daily to Chicago. It de-

parts from downtown Cinci; check online for departure points.

Metro (☎ 513-621-4455; 120 E 4th St; www.go-metro .com) runs the local buses ($1) and links with the **Transit Authority of Northern Kentucky** (TANK; ☎ 859-331-8265; www.tankbus.org), which charges $1.25 per trip.

Amtrak (☎ 513-651-3337; www.amtrak.com) choo-choos into **Union Terminal** (1301 Western Ave) thrice weekly en route to Chicago ($33 to $79, eight hours) and Washington, DC ($50 to $121, 14½ hours). Trains depart in the middle of the night.

MICHIGAN

Haven't you piddled around in these other states long enough? Head to Michigan to kick it up a notch. It sports more beaches than the Atlantic seaboard. More than half the state is covered by forests. And more cherries and berries get shoveled into pies here than anywhere else in the USA. Plus its gritty city Detroit is the Midwest's rawest of all – and we mean that in a good way.

Michigan occupies prime real estate, surrounded by four of the five Great Lakes (Superior, Michigan, Huron and Erie). Islands freckle its coast – Mackinac, Beaver and Isle Royale – and make top touring destinations. Other highlights include lazing on Lake Michigan's golden beaches; cruising the colored sandstone cliffs of Pictured Rocks; and playing in the sand at Sleeping Bear Dunes.

The state consists of two parts split by water: the larger Lower Peninsula, shaped like a mitten, and the smaller, lightly populated Upper Peninsula (UP), shaped like a slipper. They are linked by the gasp-worthy Mackinac Bridge, which spans the Straits of Mackinac (*mac*-in-aw).

History
Jesuit Père Jacques Marquette sailed over from France and staked the first European claim in Michigan in 1668 (ignoring, of course, the natives already here). He named his settlement Sault Ste Marie, and it became the USA's third-oldest town. In 1763 the British swiped all of France's settlements and used Michigan as a base for conducting Indian raids against the Americans during the Revolutionary War. The Brits also built

---

MICHIGAN FACTS

Nicknames Great Lakes State, Wolverine State

Population 10.1 million

Area 96,700 sq miles

Capital city Lansing (population 115,500)

Sales Tax 6%

Birthplace of Industrialist Henry Ford (1863–1947), filmmaker Francis Ford Coppola (b 1939), musician Stevie Wonder (b 1950), singer Madonna (b 1958), tennis player Serena Williams (b 1984)

Home of Auto assembly plants, freshwater beaches

Famous for Cars, Cornflakes, the Motown sound, the typewriter, the Model T Ford

Official motto If you seek a pleasant peninsula, look about you

---

a fort on Mackinac Island in 1780. Its location in the straits between Lake Michigan and Lake Huron made it one of the most important ports in the North American fur trade, and a site the British and Americans battled over many times.

Starting in the 1920s, car-making became inextricably linked to Michigan's economy, although that hasn't been a good thing in recent years as the industry sputters. General Motors (GM), Ford and Chrysler all maintain their headquarters in or near Detroit.

Information

Michigan highway conditions (☎ 800-381-8477; www.michigan.gov/mdot)

Michigan state park information (☎ 800-447-2757; www.michigandnr.com/parksandtrails) Park entry requires a vehicle permit (per day/year residents $6/24, nonresidents $8/29). Campsites cost $10 to $33; reservations accepted (☎ same; www.midnrreservations.com; fee $8). Some parks have wi-fi.

Travel Michigan (☎ 800-644-2489; www.michigan.org)

DETROIT

Tell any American you're planning to visit Detroit, then watch their eyebrows shoot up quizzically. 'Why?' they'll ask, and warn you about the off-the-chart homicide rates, boarded-up buildings with trash swirling at their bases, and plummeting population (down from 1.8 million in 1950 to 886,000 today). 'Detroit's a crap-hole. You'll get killed there.'

Clearly, the Motor City has an image problem. While the aforementioned attributes are true, and while the city does waft a sort of bombed-out early East Berlin vibe, it's these same qualities that fuel a raw urban energy you won't find anywhere else. And that manifests in the city's arts and music scene. They shred a mean guitar in 'the D.' Very mean.

Once the pride of the nation for its car-making savvy, the city fell to pieces when the auto industry tanked. Now it's struggling to reclaim its place. It's a grim but fascinating destination.

Orientation & Information

Downtown revolves around the riverfront Renaissance Center and nearby Hart Plaza. Woodward Ave, the city's main boulevard, heads north from here to the Cultural Center and its many museums. The Mile Roads are the Detroit's major east–west arteries; 8 Mile (which entered the national consciousness thanks to local boy Eminem) forms the boundary between the city and suburbs. Across the Detroit River lies Windsor, Canada.

The area between the sports arenas north to around Willis Rd is pretty deserted and best avoided on foot come nighttime.

BOOKSTORES

John King Books (☎ 313-961-0622; 901 Lafayette Blvd; ◷ 9:30am-5:30pm Mon-Sat)

EMERGENCY & MEDICAL SERVICES

Crisis hotline (☎ 313-224-7000)

CVS (☎ 313-833-0201; 350 E Warren Ave; ◷ 24hr) Pharmacy.

Detroit Receiving Hospital (☎ 313-745-3370; 4201 St Antoine Ave)

DON'T MISS

- **Detroit Institute of Arts** – Diego Rivera murals and more (p601)

- **Motown Museum** – birthplace of soul music (p601)

- **Heidelberg Project** – Polka-dotted neighborhood (p602)

- **Lafayette Coney Island** – chili-slathered hot dogs (p603)

- **Henry Ford Museum** – American history's greatest hits (p605)

GREAT LAKES

DETROIT

0 ——— 1 km
0 ——— 0.5 miles

INTERNET ACCESS

The Bronx tavern (p603) and Renaissance Center (RenCen; right) lobby have free wi-fi.

Detroit Main Library (☎ 313-833-1000; 5201 Woodward Ave; ⏰ noon-8pm Tue & Wed, 10am-6pm Thu-Sat) Free internet terminals for visitors.

INTERNET RESOURCES

Detroit Yes (www.detroityes.com) An artist-run website that examines Detroit's 'ruins' (ie decaying buildings).

Forgotten Detroit (www.forgottendetroit.com) Another website devoted to crumbling architecture.

Look Up Detroit (www.lookupdetroit.com) Loads of links to all things Motor City.

MEDIA

Detroit News (www.detnews.com) Daily.

Detroit Free Press (www.freep.com) Daily.

Metro Times (www.metrotimes.com) Free alternative weekly that is the best guide to the entertainment scene.

Between the Lines (www.pridesource.com) Free, weekly gay and lesbian paper.

WDET-FM 101.9 is the local NPR affiliate. WCSX-FM 94.7 blasts rock.

MONEY

ATMs are plentiful in and near the RenCen. Metro Airport's McNamara Terminal has a couple of currency exchanges.

POST

Post office (☎ 313-226-8075; 1401 W Fort St; ⏰ 24hr)

TOURIST INFORMATION

Affirmations Lesbian/Gay Community Center (☎ 248-398-7105; www.goaffirmations.org; 290 W 9 Mile Rd; ⏰ 9am-9pm Mon-Thu, 9am-11pm Fri & Sat) In Ferndale, northwest of downtown, near several gay-friendly venues.

Detroit Convention & Visitors Bureau (☎ 313-202-1800, 800-338-7648; www.visitdetroit.com; 10th fl, 211 W Fort St; ⏰ 9am-5pm Mon-Fri)

Sights & Activities

Don't forget: top-notch attractions are also in Detroit's suburbs, like the Henry Ford Museum (p605) in Dearborn. Sights are commonly closed on Monday and Tuesday.

MOTOWN MUSEUM

The **Motown Museum** (☎ 313-875-2264; www.motownmuseum.com; 2648 W Grand Blvd; adult/child 4-11 $8/5; ⏰ 10am-6pm Tue-Sat) is a string of unassuming houses that became known as 'Hitsville USA' after Berry Gordy launched Motown Records here with an $800 loan in 1959. Stars that rose from the Motown label include Stevie Wonder, Diana Ross, Marvin Gaye, Gladys Knight and Michael Jackson. Gordy and Motown split for the glitz of Los Angeles in 1972, but you can still step into humble Studio A and see where the Four Tops and Smokey Robinson recorded their first hits.

CULTURAL CENTER

Several museums cluster in the area known as the Cultural Center, by Woodward and Warren Aves. Cream of the crop is the recently expanded **Detroit Institute of Arts** (☎ 313-833-7900; www.dia.org; 5200 Woodward Ave; adult/child 6-17 $6/3; ⏰ 10am-4pm Wed & Thu, 10am-9pm Fri, 10am-5pm Sat & Sun), lauded for its American collection. The centerpiece is Diego Rivera's mural *Detroit Industry*, which fills an entire room and reflects the city's blue-collar labor history.

The **Wright Museum of African American History** (☎ 313-494-5800; www.maah-detroit.org; 315 E Warren Ave; adult/child 3-12 $8/5; ⏰ 9am-3pm Tue-Thu, to 5pm Fri & Sat, 1-5pm Sun) holds less than it would seem from the impressive exterior, though it's worth a look inside. The full-scale model of slaves chained up on a dark, creaking slave ship will leave you chilled.

The **Museum of Contemporary Art Detroit** (MOCAD; ☎ 313-832-6622; www.mocadetroit.org; 4454 Woodward Ave; admission free; ⏰ noon-6pm Wed & Sun, to 8pm Thu-Sat) opened in 2006 in an abandoned, graffiti-slathered auto dealership. Heat lamps hang from the ceiling over peculiar exhibits that change every few months. On summer Saturdays, it hosts art films drive-in style in its back parking lot.

DOWNTOWN & AROUND

Downtown, the glossy **Renaissance Center** (RenCen; 330 E Jefferson Ave), GM's headquarters, is a fine place to grab a bite (in the Wintergarden), peruse vintage cars (on the lower level) or embark on the riverfront walkway. You can take the path to **Hart Plaza** (cnr Jefferson and Woodward Aves), the site of many free, summer weekend festivals and concerts. While there, check out the sculpture of Joe Louis's mighty fist.

Campus Martius (www.campusmartiuspark.org; 800 Woodward Ave) is another communal hot spot downtown, with an outdoor ice rink in winter, and eating areas, concerts and films in summer.

Busy **Greektown** (centered on Monroe St) has restaurants, bakeries and a casino. Early each day, the large halls at the **Eastern Market** (Gratiot Ave & Russell St) fill with a melting pot of bartering shoppers and vendors. Specialty shops, delis and restaurants surround the site.

Belle Isle, located 2.5 miles northeast of downtown at E Jefferson Ave and E Grand Blvd, is a good spot for a picnic and walkabout. Eventually the riverfront path from Hart Plaza will extend all the way here.

The **People Mover** (☎ 313-962-7245; www.thepeoplemover.com) looks like the monorail in the classic *Simpsons* episode. As mass transit, its 3-mile loop on elevated tracks around downtown is pretty impractical. As a tourist attraction, it's cheap (50¢) and provides great views of the city and riverfront.

Polka-dotted streets, houses covered in Technicolor paint blobs, strange sculptures in yards – this is no acid trip, but rather an art installation that covers an entire neighborhood. Welcome to the **Heidelberg Project** (www.heidelberg.org; Heidelberg St; admission free; ⊙ 24hr), the brainchild of street artist Tyree Guyton, who wanted to beautify his run-down community. Get here by taking Gratiot Ave northwest to Heidelberg St; the project spans from McDougall to Mt Elliott Sts.

Oddly, Detroit is one of the premier places to get a taste of the North Pole without having to dogsled for it. The Arctic Ring of Life at the **Detroit Zoo** (☎ 248-398-0900; www.detroitzoo.org; 8450 W 10 Mile Rd; adult/child 2-12 $11/7; ⊙ 10am-5pm May-Oct, 10am-4pm Nov-Apr) is the world's largest polar exhibit. It includes first-rate displays on Inuit culture and a 'polar bear tube,' where the huge white creatures swim overhead. The Penguinarium is also a highlight, as is the National Amphibian Conservation Center. It's located just north in Royal Oak. Parking costs $5.

Border junkies will find it easy to pop over to **Windsor, Canada** (see p604), where there are bars, restaurants and a huge casino.

Festivals & Events
North American International Auto Show
(☎ 248-643-0250; www.naias.com; 1 Washington Blvd; tickets $12) It's autos galore for two weeks in mid-January at the Cobo Center.

Movement/Detroit Electronic Music Festival
(www.demf.com; day pass $26) The world's largest electronic music festival congregates in Hart Plaza over Memorial Day weekend in May.

Woodward Dream Cruise (☎ 888-493-2196; www.woodwarddreamcruise.com; admission free) Thousands of classic cars cruise down Woodward Ave on the third Saturday in August; 1.5 million people watch them.

Sleeping
Add 9% tax to the rates listed here.

BUDGET & MIDRANGE
Affordable motels abound in the Detroit suburbs. If you're arriving from Metro Airport, follow the signs for Merriman Rd when leaving the airport and take your pick. In the city try:

Shorecrest Motor Inn (☎ 313-568-3000, 800-992-9616; www.shorecrestmi.com; 1316 E Jefferson Ave; s/d from $79/99; Ⓟ ☒ wi-fi) Looking for downtown's lowest-priced digs? The Shorecrest is a classic, no-frills motor lodge with super-helpful staff; check the website for reduced-rate coupons.

Comfort Inn (☎ 313-567-8888; www.choicehotels.com; 1999 E Jefferson Ave; r incl breakfast $89-139; Ⓟ ☒ wi-fi) Similar to the Shorecrest, though a few blocks further east, Comfort's prices reach the higher end of the spectrum when it's busy, usually in summer.

ourpick Inn on Ferry Street (☎ 313-871-6000; www.innonferrystreet.com; 84 E Ferry St; r incl breakfast from $124; Ⓟ ☒ ☒ ▢ wi-fi) Forty guestrooms fill a row of Victorian mansions right by the art museum. The lower-cost rooms are small but with deliciously soft bedding on antique, four-post frames. The CD players and stack of local music discs are a nice touch, as is the free internet, wi-fi, hot breakfast and shuttle to downtown.

Hilton Garden Inn (☎ 313-967-0900; www.hiltongardeninn.com; 351 Gratiot Ave; d from $169; Ⓟ ☒ ▢ wi-fi) The Hilton is nothing special, but it's newish, clean and close to Comerica Park, Ford Field and Greektown. Parking is $20.

TOP END
Detroit Marriott (☎ 313-568-8000; www.marriott.com; Renaissance Center; r from $179/279 weekend/weekday; Ⓟ ☒ ▢ wi-fi) This is a mondo, 72-floor convention hotel, but it is kind of cool to be in the Renaissance Center, especially if you get a view-worthy room (request when booking; extra charges apply for floors 62 to 72, but not for rooms right below). Wi-fi costs $8.99 per day, and parking is $20.

Eating

Note that many of the recommended drinking and live music establishments also serve good food.

DOWNTOWN

Monroe St in Greektown has an abundancy of Greek restaurants, as has the RenCen fast-food court.

Lafayette Coney Island (☎ 313-964-8198; 118 Lafayette Blvd; items $2.35-3.25; 🕑 7:30-4am Mon-Thu, to 5am Fri & Sat, 9:30-4am Sun) The 'coney' – a hot dog smothered with chili and onions – is a Detroit specialty. When the craving strikes (and it will) take care of business at Lafayette. The minimalist menu consists of burgers, fries, pies, donuts and beer, in addition to the signature item. Bring the antacid.

New Parthenon (☎ 313-961-5111; 547 Monroe St; mains $9-12; 🕑 11am-3am) Flaming cheese and the cry of 'Opa!' are a Detroit tradition at this Greektown restaurant. The grape leaves reign supreme.

Southern Fires (☎ 313-393-4930; 575 Bellevue Rd; mains $9-14; 🕑 11am-7pm Mon, 11am-9pm Tue-Fri, noon-9pm Sat, noon-8pm Sun) You can choose from cornmeal-encrusted catfish, braised short ribs and the 3in-thick slab of meatloaf at this soul food restaurant. Sides are succulent collard greens, sweet potatoes and buttered cornbread. It's located near Belle Isle.

CULTURAL CENTER

Avalon International Breads (☎ 313-832-0008; 422 W Willis St; items $1.50-5; 🕑 6am-6pm Tue-Sat) Detroit's earthy types huddle round the hearth at Avalon, where its fresh-baked bread (like Greektown olive, scallion dill or country Italian) makes an excellent sandwich base. There's organic coffee, cookies and muffins, too.

Cass Café (☎ 313-831-1400; 4620 Cass Ave; mains $5-9; 🕑 11am-11pm Sun-Thu, 11am-1am Fri & Sat) The Cass is a bohemian art gallery fused with a bar and restaurant serving soups, sandwiches and veggie beauties like the lentil-walnut burger.

Traffic Jam & Snug (☎ 313-831-9470; 511 W Canfield St; sandwiches $8-10, mains $14-18; 🕑 11am-10:30pm Mon-Thu, 11am-midnight Fri, noon-midnight Sat, noon-8pm Sun) Detroit's best brewpub food is all over the map – Ethiopian lentils, Indian curries and Vietnamese noodles, among others.

MEXICANTOWN & AROUND

Xochimilco (☎ 313-843-0179; 3409 Bagley St; mains $5-12; 🕑 11am-2am) Xochimilco is one of many places in Mexicantown, along Bagley St, which offers inexpensive, authentic Mexican food. Its solid menu of burritos and other standards has been pulling in crowds for years.

The walkable Ferndale area at 9 Mile Rd and Woodward Ave has many good restaurants and bars, as does Royal Oak just north of Ferndale on 10 Mile Rd.

Drinking

BARS & CLUBS

The Bronx (☎ 313-832-8464; 4476 2nd Ave; wi-fi) There isn't much there beyond a pool table, dim lighting and a couple of juke boxes filled with local garage rock. But that's the way the professors, hipsters, slackers and rockers like their dive bars. They also like the beefy burgers, free wi-fi and swell selection of beers.

Motor City Brewing Works (☎ 313-832-2700; 470 W Canfield St) Motor City brews its own beer and serves Michigan wines, along with snacks and sandwiches. It's small, intimate and has a great rooftop patio.

Union Street Saloon (☎ 313-831-3965; 4145 Woodward Ave) This place has been around since the early 1900s and attracts a mod crowd.

Contemporary Art Institute of Detroit (CAID; ☎ 313-899-2243; www.thecaid.org; 5141 Rosa Parks Blvd; admission $5; 🕑 midnight) We've listed this gallery under 'Clubs' because on Friday nights it throws off-the-hook dance parties with DJs who spin rare funk, soul and disco 45s. The events provide a social outlet for locals and bring a lot of pride to this not-so-great neighborhood. Note this is not the same place as MOCAD (p601).

Entertainment

LIVE MUSIC

St Andrew's Hall (☎ 313-961-6358; www.standrewshall.com; 431 E Congress St) It's a legendary alternative band venue; downstairs is Shelter, a smaller music/dance club.

Lager House (☎ 313-961-4668; www.lagerhousedetroit.com; 1254 Michigan Ave) This punk/underground rock pub is dingy in an atmospheric way, with scrappy bands or DJs on stage several nights a week.

Baker's Keyboard Lounge (☎ 313-345-6300; www.bakerskeyboardlounge.com; 20510 Livernois Ave) Baker's is the gold standard of Detroit's jazz and blues clubs, complete with a full-on soul food menu. It's in Hamtramck, north of downtown.

Bert's Marketplace (☎ 313-567-2030; www.berts entertainment.com; 2727 Russell St) Wynton Marsalis has sat in at this tiny jazz bar near the Eastern Market. Snap your fingers to the beat, or use them to shovel in the ribs, catfish and other soul food from the menu.

Magic Stick (☎ 313-833-9700; www.majesticdetroit .com; 4120 Woodward Ave) and the larger **Majestic Theater** (☎ same; 4140 Woodward Ave) are side-by-side concert halls where indie rockers and rap DJs perform. The complex also has bowling, billiards, a pizza joint and café.

THEATER & CULTURE

Fox Theatre (☎ 313-983-6611; 2211 Woodward Ave) It's a gloriously restored 1928 venue that large touring shows occupy.

Puppet ART/Detroit Puppet Theater (☎ 313-961-7777; www.puppetart.org; 25 E Grand River Ave; adult/child $7/5) Soviet-trained puppeteers perform beautiful shows in this 70-person theater; a small museum displays puppets from different cultures. Shows are often held on Saturday afternoon; call for the schedule.

Detroit Film Theatre (☎ 313-833-4005; 5200 Woodward Ave; tickets $7.50) Watch art flicks in the Detroit Institute of Arts (p601).

SPORTS

Palace of Auburn Hills (☎ 248-377-0100; www.nba .com/pistons; 5 Championship Dr) The Palace hosts the mighty Pistons pro basketball team. It's about 26 miles northwest of the city; take I-75 to exit 81.

Joe Louis Arena (☎ 313-396-7444; www.detroitred wings.com; 600 Civic Center Dr) The much-loved Red Wings play pro ice hockey at this arena where,

---

WHIPLASH ROCK 'N ROLL

Motown Records and soul music put Detroit on the map, but in recent years it's been hard-edged rock – aka whiplash rock 'n roll – that has pushed the city to the forefront of the music scene. Homegrown stars include the White Stripes, Von Blondies and Dirtbombs, led by their led by their crazy-ass punk forefathers the Stooges and high-energy MC5. Rap (thank you, Eminem) and techno are Detroit's other renowned genres. Scope the free publications like the *Metro Times* and *Real Detroit Weekly* for current show and club listings.

---

if you can wrangle tickets, you can witness the strange octopus-throwing custom.

Ford Field (☎ 313-262-2003; www.detroitlions.com; 2000 Brush St) The Lions pro football team plays here.

Comerica Park (☎ 313-471-2255; www.detroittigers .com; 2100 Woodward Ave) Next door to Ford Field, the Tigers (in case you hadn't guessed from the giant stone animals roaring over the entrance) play pro baseball here. The park is particularly kid friendly, with a small Ferris wheel and carousel inside.

Shopping

Pure Detroit (☎ 313-259-5100; www.puredetroit.com; 2nd fl of Wintergarden; 11am-5:30pm Mon-Fri, to 5pm Sat) Products from local fashion house Pure Detroit reflect the city's culture and are created by local artists. This auto-centric outlet in the Renaissance Center offers clocks made out of pistons, belts tailored from seatbelts and handbags cut from Camaro upholstery.

People's Records (☎ 313-831-0864; 615 W Forest Ave; 11am-7pm Tue-Sat) Calling all crate-digging record collectors: this subterranean, shoe-box-sized shop is your vinyl Valhalla. It's bound to have whatever jazz, R&B or soul album you seek.

Getting There & Around

It is best to have your own wheels to get around the Motor City; public transportation is lacking, much to the automakers' delight. Avis, Hertz and other rental agencies have offices at Metro Airport (call from the courtesy phones) and around town. The Transportation chapter (p1144) has contact details.

Detroit Metro Airport (DTW; ☎ 734-247-7678; www .metroairport.com) is 15 miles southwest of Detroit. Transport options from the airport to the city are few: you can take a cab for about $45, or you can take the No 125 SMART bus ($1.50), but it takes 1½ hours to get downtown.

Greyhound (☎ 313-961-8005; 1001 Howard St) runs to various cities in Michigan and beyond, while **Megabus** (☎ 877-462-6342; www.megabus .com/us) runs to and from Chicago daily; call for departure points.

Amtrak (☎ 313-873-3442; 11 W Baltimore Ave) trains go thrice daily to Chicago ($27 to $67; 5½ hours). You can also head east – to New York ($75 to $142; 16 hours) or destinations en route – but you'll first be bused to Toledo.

Transit Windsor (☎ 519-944-4111; www.citywindsor .ca/transitwindsor) operates the Tunnel Bus to

---

CLASSIC CARS IN MICHIGAN

More than sand dunes, Mackinac Island fudge or even the Great Lakes, Michigan is synonymous with cars. You won't have to drive far to see a fleet of beauties, particularly around Detroit:

Henry Ford Museum (below) This Dearborn museum is loaded with vintage cars, including the first one Henry Ford ever built. In adjacent Greenfield Village you can ride in a Model T that rolled off the assembly line in 1923.

Automotive Hall of Fame (☎ 313-240-4000; www.automotivehalloffame.org; 21400 Oakwood Blvd, Dearborn; adult/child 5-18 $6/3; ☻ 9am-5pm May-Oct, closed Mon Nov-Apr) Also in Dearborn, the Auto Hall is stocked with classic cars as well as a replica of the first gasoline automobile.

Motorsports Hall of Fame (☎ 800-250-7223; www.mshf.com; Novi Rd, Novi; adult/child under 12 $4/2; ☻ by appt) In the Novi Expo Center just off I-96, the Motorsports Hall has three dozen vehicles that were driven by legendary racers.

Walter P Chrysler Museum (☎ 248-944-0001; www.chryslerheritage.com; 1 Chrysler Dr, Auburn Hills; adult/child 6-12 $6/3; ☻ 10am-6pm Tue-Sat, noon-6pm Sun) This museum, in the Chrysler Technical Center Campus, has 70 vehicles on display, including rare models of Dodge, DeSoto, Nash and Hudson.

Sloan Museum (☎ 810-237-3450; www.sloanmuseum.com; 1221 E Kearsley St, Flint; adult/child 3-11 $6/4; ☻ 10am-5pm Mon-Fri, noon-5pm Sat & Sun) The Sloan has two buildings housing more than 60 cars, including the oldest production-model Chevrolet in existence and a 1910 Buick 'Bug' raced by Louis Chevrolet.

Gilmore Car Museum (☎ 269-671-5089; www.gilmorecarmuseum.org; Hickory Rd at Hwy 43, Hickory Corners; adult/child 7-15 $8/6; ☻ 9am-5pm Mon-Fri, to 6pm Sat & Sun, closed Nov-Apr) North of Kalamazoo along Hwy 43, this museum complex offers 22 barns filled with 120 vintage autos, including 15 Rolls Royces dating back to a 1910 Silver Ghost.

RE Olds Transportation Museum (☎ 517-372-0529; www.reoldsmuseum.org; 240 Museum Dr, Lansing; admission $5; ☻ 10am-5pm Tue-Sat year-round, noon-5pm Sun Apr-Oct) In the old Lansing City Bus Garage are 20 vintage cars, from the first Oldsmobile, built in 1897, to an Indy 500 pace car.

Windsor, Canada. It costs $2.75 (American or Canadian) and departs from Detroit–Windsor Tunnel (on Randolph St, across from the Renaissance Center) as well as other spots downtown. Bring your passport.

The not-so-reliable **Detroit Department of Transportation** (DDOT; ☎ 888-336-8287; www.ridedetroit transit.com) handles the pokey local bus service ($1.50). The **Suburban Mobility Authority for Regional Transportation** (SMART; ☎ 866-962-5515; www.smartbus.org) handles service to the 'burbs ($1.50 to $2). The public library has schedules.

For cab service, call **Checker Cab** (☎ 313-963-7000).

AROUND DETROIT

Like Detroit, the towns nearby are entwined with the auto industry. When the carmakers feel the pinch – which is often these days – so do towns like Flint and Dearborn.

Dearborn

Dearborn is 10 miles west of downtown Detroit and home to two of the USA's finest museums. The indoor **Henry Ford Museum** (☎ 313-982-6001; www.thehenryford.org; 20900 Oakwood Blvd; adult/child 5-12 $14/10; ☻ 9:30am-5pm) contains a fascinating wealth of American culture, such

as the chair Lincoln was sitting in when he was assassinated, Edgar Allan Poe's writing desk and the bus on which Rosa Parks refused to give up her seat. Don't worry: you'll get your vintage car fix here, too. Parking is $5. The adjacent, outdoor **Greenfield Village** (☎ 313-982-6001; adult/child 5-12 $20/14; ☻ 9:30am-5pm daily mid-Apr–Oct, 9:30am-5pm Fri-Sun Nov & Dec) features historic buildings shipped in from all over the country, reconstructed and restored, such as Thomas Edison's laboratory from Menlo Park and the Wright Brothers' airplane workshop. Plus you can add on the **Rouge Factory Tour** (☎ 313-982-6001; adult/child 5-12 $14/10; ☻ 9:30am-2:30pm mid-Apr–Aug, closed Sun Sep–mid-Apr) and see F-150 trucks roll off the assembly line where Ford first perfected his self-sufficient, mass-production techniques.

All three attractions are separate, but you can get a combination ticket for Henry Ford and Greenfield Village (adult/child 5-12 $30/22). Ask about other discounted combinations, and check the website for coupons beforehand.

Dearborn has the greatest concentration of Arabs in the country, so it's no surprise the **Arab American National Museum** (☎ 313-582-2266; www.arabamericanmuseum.org; 13624 Michigan Ave; adult/

child 6-12 $6/3; 10am-6pm Wed-Sat, to 8pm Thu, noon-5pm Sun) popped up here. It's a noble concept, but not terribly exciting, unless actor Jamie Farr's *MASH* TV show script wows you. The thousand and one Arabian eateries lining Michigan Ave provide a more engaging feel for the culture. **La Shish** (313-562-7200; 22039 Michigan Ave; sandwiches $3.75-4, mains $12-17; 10am-11pm, to midnight Fri & Sat) reigns as the local favorite.

Ann Arbor

Forty-one miles west of Detroit, liberal and bookish Ann Arbor is home to the University of Michigan. The walkable downtown is loaded with coffee shops, bookstores, brewpubs and cheap places to grab a bite.

The university provides the town's main attractions. The **Matthei Botanical Gardens** (734-998-7061; www.lsa.umich.edu/mbg; 1800 Dixboro Rd; outdoor gardens admission free, conservatory adult/child 5-18 $5/2; 8am-dusk) offers 300 acres crisscrossed by walking paths, plus a cacti-filled greenhouse; it's about 5 miles east of downtown. The 'Arb' – **Nichols Arboretum** (734-998-7061; 1610 Washington Hts; admission free; 8am-dusk) – is another oasis of greenery for walking, jogging and Frisbee throwing; it's right by campus. The university also has free art and archaeology museums.

Ann Arbor's biggest events are the school's football games, a fall tradition attracting 115,000 fans per game. Tickets are nearly impossible to purchase, especially when nemesis Ohio State is in town. You can try, or obtain tickets to other sporting events, by calling the **U of M Ticket Office** (734-764-0247; www.mgoblue.com/ticketoffice).

Fleetwood Diner (734-995-5502; 300 S Ashley St; mains $5-7; 24hr) is an atmospheric round-the-clock greasy spoon that attracts the studious and down at heel. **Jerusalem Garden** (734-995-5060; 307 S 5th Ave; mains $4-9; 11am-9pm Mon-Thu, to 9:30pm Fri & Sat, noon-8pm Sun) plates Middle Eastern dishes. Nationally lauded **Zingerman's Delicatessen** (734-663-3354; 422 Detroit St; sandwiches $9.50-12; 7am-10pm) piles local, organic and specialty ingredients onto towering sandwiches.

When darkness falls, head to the **Blind Pig** (734-996-8555; www.blindpigmusic.com; 208 S 1st St) or the **Ark** (734-761-1800; www.a2ark.org; 316 S Main St), both nationally acclaimed venues for rock, blues and more. Handcrafted beer is found at **Arbor Brewing Company** (734-213-1393; 114 E Washington St).

The town has several B&Bs; check with the **Ann Arbor CVB** (800-888-9487; www.annarbor.org).

CENTRAL MICHIGAN

Michigan's heartland, plunked in the center of the Lower Peninsula, alternates between fertile farms and highway-crossed urban areas.

Lansing

Smallish Lansing is the state capital; a few miles east lies East Lansing, home of Michigan State University. Between downtown and the university is Lansing's **River Trail**, which extends 7 miles along the shores of Michigan's longest river, the Grand. The paved path is popular with cyclists, joggers and inline skaters, and links a number of attractions, including a children's museum, zoo and salmon ladder.

Downtown, the **Michigan Historical Museum** (517-373-3559; 702 W Kalamazoo St; admission free; 9am-4:30pm Mon-Fri, 10am-4pm Sat, 1-5pm Sun) features 26 permanent galleries, including a replica UP copper mine you can walk through and a three-story relief map of the state. The **RE Olds Transportation Museum** (see boxed text, p605) will please car buffs.

Budget motels with rooms between $50 and $70 are found around Cedar St at exit 104 off I-96; you get what you pay for here. Far nicer is the **Wild Goose Inn** (517-333-3334; www.wildgooseinn.com; 512 Albert St; r incl breakfast $109-159;), a six-room B&B one block from Michigan State's campus; all rooms have fireplaces and most have Jacuzzis. The downtown hotels feed off politicians and lobbyists, and are considerably more expensive.

Most of Lansing's best restaurants are clustered around the head of Michigan Ave. For meals try **Clara's** (517-372-7120; 637 E Michigan Ave; mains $12-18; 11am-11pm Mon-Thu, 11am-midnight Fri & Sat, 10am-10pm Sun), in the historic railroad depot, or **Kewpee's** (517-482-8049; 118 S Washington Sq; mains $3-7; 8am-6pm Mon-Fri, 11am-4pm Sat), renowned for its olive burgers. The area north of campus also has abundant restaurants, pubs and nightclubs.

Grand Rapids

The second-largest city in Michigan, Grand Rapids is known for office-furniture manufacturing, a conservative Dutch Reform attitude and the fact that it's only 30 miles from Lake Michigan's Gold Coast. The **visitors center** (800-678-9859; www.visitgrandrapids.org; 171 Monroe Ave NW, Suite 700; 8:30am-5pm Mon-Fri) is downtown, with two better-than-you'd-think museums nearby.

The **Gerald R Ford Museum** (☎ 616-254-0400; www
.fordlibrarymuseum.gov; 303 Pearl St NW; adult/child 6-18
$7/3; ☺ 9am-5pm) is dedicated to the country's
only Michigander president (though he was
born with a different name in Nebraska). Ford
stepped into the Oval Office after Richard
Nixon and his vice president, Spiro Agnew,
resigned in disgrace. It's an intriguing period
in US history, and the museum does an excellent job of covering it, right down to displaying the burglary tools used in the Watergate
break-in. Ford died in 2006 and is buried on
a hillside on the museum's grounds.

Nearby the striking **Van Andel Museum Center**
(☎ 616-456-3977; www.grmuseum.org; 272 Pearl St NW;
adult/child 3-17 $8/3; ☺ 9am-4pm Mon-Fri, 10am-4pm Sat,
noon-4pm Sun) reveals the history of Grand Rapids (including its role as a furniture-maker)
and west Michigan.

The 118-acre **Frederik Meijer Gardens** (☎ 616-
957-1580; www.meijergardens.org; 1000 E Beltline NE;
adult/child 5-13 $12/6; ☺ 9am-5pm Mon-Sat, to 9pm Tue,
noon-5pm Sun) features impressive blooms and
sculptures.

Days Inn (☎ 616-235-7611; 310 Pearl St NW; r from $79;
Ⓟ ☒), downtown, is a good sleeping option.
Peaches B&B (☎ 866-732-2437; www.peaches-inn.com; 29
Gay St SE; r incl breakfast $109; Ⓟ wi-fi) is in a comfy
house a short walk from the city center.

At night, head to **Cottage Bar** (☎ 616-454-9088;
18 LaGrave St SE; mains $6-10; ☺ 11am-midnight Mon-Sat),
a hip place downtown that serves hamburgers
and has outdoor seating when it's warm, or
Grand Rapids Brewing Company (☎ 616-285-5970;
3689 28th St SE; mains $7-13; ☺ 11am-10pm Sun-Thu, to
11pm Fri & Sat).

LAKE MICHIGAN SHORE

Michigan's west coast – aka its Gold Coast –
is the place to come to watch incredible sunsets while waves tickle your toes. The 300-
mile shoreline features endless stretches of
beach, coastal parks, wineries, orchards and
small towns down during the summer
tourist season. Note all state parks listed here
take **campsite reservations** (☎ 800-447-2757; www
.midnrreservations.com; fee $8) and require a vehicle
permit (per day/year $8/29), unless specified
otherwise.

Saugatuck

Saugatuck is one of the Gold Coast's most
popular resort areas, known for its strong arts
community, numerous B&Bs and gay-friendly
vibe. The virtual **visitors center** (☎ 269-857-1701;

www.saugatuck.com) provides detailed information on attractions and accommodations,
plus maps.

The best thing to do in Saugatuck is also the
most affordable. Jump aboard the **Saugatuck
Chain Ferry** (Water St; $1; ☺ 9am-9pm), and the oper-
ator will pull you across the Kalamazoo River.
On the other side you can huff up the stairs to
the grand views atop **Mt Baldhead**, a 200ft-high
sand dune. Then race down the north side to
beautiful **Oval Beach**. The **Saugatuck Dune Rides**
(☎ 269-857-2253; www.saugatuckduneride.com; 6495 Blue
Star Hwy; adult/child 3-10 $16/10; ☺ 10am-7:30pm Mon-Sat,
noon-7:30 Sun Jul & Aug, to 5:30pm Apr-Jun & Oct) provide
a half-hour of good, cheesy fun.

Galleries and shops proliferate downtown
near Water and Butler Sts; galleries and antique shops also line the Blue Star Hwy running south from Saugatuck.

Several B&Bs are tucked into century-old
Victorian homes, with most ranging from
$100 to $300 a night per couple in the summer
high season. Try the **Bayside Inn** (☎ 269-857-4321;
www.baysideinn.net; 618 Water St; r incl breakfast $100-190),
a 10-room former boathouse with an outdoor
tub, or the 15-room **Twin Gables Inn** (☎ 269-
857-4346, 800-231-2185; www.twingablesinn.com; 900 Lake
St; r incl breakfast $126-220), which overlooks Lake
Michigan. Mom-and-pop motels on the edge
of the city, like the **Pines Motorlodge** (☎ 269-
857-5211; www.thepinesmotorlodge.com; 56 Blue Star Hwy;
r $95-165), have comfortable rooms.

For eats, **Marro's Italian Restaurant** (☎ 269-857-
4248; 147 Water St; pizzas $16-23; ☺ 5-10pm Tue-Sun) gets
props for its pizzas. Scarf down bulging fruit
pies at **Crane's Pie Pantry** (☎ 269-561-2297; 6054 124th
Ave; ☺ 9am-8pm Mon-Sat, 11am-8pm Sun May-Oct, reduced
hrs Nov-Apr), located a few miles south of Saugatuck off Hwy 89 in Fennville. It's smack dab in
the middle of a peach-apple-cherry orchard.

Muskegon & Ludington

These towns are jump-off points for the two
ferries that sail across the lake, providing a
shortcut between Michigan and Wisconsin.
The **Lake Express** (☎ 866-914-1010; www.lake-express
.com; ☺ mid-Apr–Oct) crosses between Muskegon
and Milwaukee (one way adult/child 5-17
$62/34.50, car/bicycle $72/10, 2½ hours). The
older **SS Badger** (☎ 888-337-7948; www.ssbadger.com;
☺ mid-May–mid-Oct) crosses from Ludington to
Manitowoc (one way adult/child 5-15 $59/26,
car/bicycle $62/5, four hours). Other than the
ferries, there's not much reason to hang out
in either town.

Heading beyond city limits you'll come to **Ludington State Park** (☎ 231-843-8671; campsites $27-29; ☼ year-round), on M-116, which is one of Michigan's largest state parks and a popular lakeside retreat. It has a top-notch trail system, a renovated lighthouse to visit and miles of beach. To its north is **Nordhouse Dunes**, a 3000-acre federally designated wilderness with its own trail system. You enter Nordhouse Dunes through the Lake Michigan Recreation Area, a US Forest Service campground several miles south of Manistee.

Sleeping Bear Dunes National Lakeshore

This national park stretches from north of Frankfort to just before Leland, on the Leelanau Peninsula. Stop at the park **visitors center** (☎ 231-326-5134; www.nps.gov/slbe; 9922 Front St; ☼ 9am-4pm winter, 8am-6pm summer) in Empire for information, trail maps and vehicle entry permits (week/annual $10/20).

Attractions here include the famous **Dune Climb** along Hwy 109, where you trudge up the 200ft-high dune and then run or roll down. Gluttons for leg-muscle punishment can keep slogging all the way to Lake Michigan, a strenuous 1.5-hour trek one way; bring water. Taking the 7-mile, one-lane **Pierce Stocking Scenic Drive** is an easier way to absorb the stunning Lake Michigan vistas.

Those seeking an overnight wilderness adventure should head to **North Manitou Island** or day-trip to **South Manitou Island** on the **ferry** (☎ 231-256-9061; www.leelanau.com/manitou; Leland). A round-trip costs $29/15 per adult/child under 13, with three to seven departures per week from May to mid-October. The trip takes about 1½ hours.

Feeling lazy? Plop your butt in an inner tube and float down the Platte River with **Riverside Canoe Trips** (☎ 231-325-5622; www.canoemichigan .com; 5042 Scenic Hwy, Honor; tube/kayak/canoe $17/26/36; ☼ May–mid-Oct).

Traverse City

Michigan's 'cherry capital' is the largest city in the northern half of the Lower Peninsula. It's got a bit of urban sprawl, but it's still a sweet base from which to see the Sleeping Bear Dunes, Mission Peninsula wineries, U-pick orchards and other area attractions.

Two blocks from downtown along US 31 is Clinch Park, with a pretty beach, while nearby **Traverse City State Park** (☎ 231-922-5270; 1132 US 31 N;

campsites $27) has 700ft of sugary sand. Between the two parks are dozens of resorts, motels, jet ski rental shops and parasail operators.

Wineries are all over, but the most popular drive is to head north from Traverse City on Hwy 37 for 20 miles to the end of Mission Peninsula. Stop at **Chateau Grand Traverse** (☎ 231-223-7355; www.cgtwines.com; ☼ 10am-7pm Mon-Sat, noon-6pm Sun Jun-Aug, reduced Sep-May) or **Chateau Chantal** (☎ 800-969-4009; www.chateauchantal .com; ☼ 11am-8pm Mon-Sat, noon-5pm Sun mid-Jun–Aug, reduced Sep–mid-Jun) and sample their Chardonnay or Pinot Noir. If you purchase a bottle, you can take it out to Lighthouse Park beach, on the end of the peninsula, and enjoy it with the waves licking your toes.

Back in the city, **Brick Wheels** (☎ 231-947-4274; www.brickwheels.com; 736 E 8th St; bike per day $15-30; ☼ 9am-6pm Mon-Fri, 9am-4:30pm Sat, 11am-3pm Sun) rents bicycles; visitors can immediately jump onto the **Traverse Area Recreation Trail** (TART), an 11-mile paved path along the bay. Those with more ambition (and money) can learn to kiteboard with the outfitter **Broneah** (☎ 231-392-2212; www.broneah.com; 207 Grandview Pkwy; full-day lesson $399).

If you arrive in mid-July, be sure to drive north on US 31 to Elk Rapids and beyond for roadside stands selling cherries and pies, and farms where you can pick your own fruit.

Traverse City has plentiful lodgings, but they are often full (and more expensive) at weekends. Stop at the downtown **visitors center** (☎ 800-872-8377; www.visittraversecity.com; 101 W Grandview Pkwy; ☼ 9am-6pm Mon-Sat, 11am-3pm Sun Jun–mid-Oct, 9am-5pm Mon-Fri, 9am-3pm Sat mid-Oct–May) for an accommodations list. Most resorts overlooking the bay cost $150 to $250 per night. The aforementioned wineries also double as B&Bs and fit into this price range.

Guests can rent jet skis and enjoy nightly bonfires at **Park Shore Resort** (☎ 877-349-8898; www.parkshoreresort.com; 1401 US 31 North; r weekday/weekend from $150/190; ☒). Motels on the other side of US 31 (away from the water) are more moderately priced, such as **Mitchell Creek Inn** (☎ 231-947-9330, 800-947-9330; www.mitchellcreek.com; 894 Munson Ave; r/cottage from $74/124), near the state park beach.

After a day of fun in the sun, refresh with sandwiches at foodie favorite **Folgarelli's** (☎ 231-941-7651; 424 W Front St; sandwiches $6-9; ☼ 9:30am-6:30pm Mon-Fri, 9:30am-5:30 Sat) and cold, handcrafted beer and root beer at **North Peak Brewing Company** (☎ 231-941-7325; 400 W Front St).

WORTH THE TRIP: BEAVER ISLAND

Those looking for an alternative to Mackinac Island's fudgey hullabaloo can sail from downtown Charlevoix to **Beaver Island** (www.beaverisland.org), a quiet, Irish-influenced enclave of 600 people. The **ferry** (☎ 231-547-2311, 888-446-4095; www.bibco.com) makes one to four trips daily from April through December; the two-hour journey costs $21/70 one way per person/car. Once on the island, **Inland Seas Kayaking** (☎ 231-448-2221; www.inlandseaskayaking.com; half-day tour $60-70) offers rewarding kayaking or snorkeling trips; the latter visit shipwrecked schooners. The island has a handful of hotels and B&Bs. You'll need to stay overnight if you go kayaking or snorkeling. The **Emerald Isle Hotel** (☎ 231-448-2376; www.emeraldislehotel.com; 37985 Kings Hwy; d $104-130, ste $149-169) is basic but pleasant.

Charlevoix & Petoskey

These two towns provide Hemingway sights and island excursions. They're also where Michigan's upper-crusters maintain summer homes. The downtown areas of both places have gourmet restaurants and high-class shops, and the marinas are filled with yachts.

In Petoskey, **Stafford's Perry Hotel** (☎ 231-347-4000; www.staffords.com; Bay at Lewis St; r from $85) is a grand historic place to stay. **Petoskey State Park** (☎ 231-347-2311; 2475 M-119; campsites $27-29; ☉ mid-Apr–mid-Oct) is north along M-119 and has a beautiful beach. Look for indigenous Petoskey stones, which are honeycomb-patterned fragments of ancient coral.

STRAITS OF MACKINAC

This region, between the Upper and Lower Peninsulas, features a long history of forts and fudge shops. Car-free Mackinac Island is Michigan's premier tourist draw.

One of the most spectacular sights in the area is the 5-mile long **Mackinac Bridge** (known locally as 'Big Mac'), which spans the Straits of Mackinac. The $2.50 toll is worth every penny, as the views from the bridge, which include two Great Lakes, two peninsulas and hundreds of islands, are second to none in Michigan.

Remember: despite the spelling, it's pronounced *mac*-in-aw.

Mackinaw City

At the south end of Mackinac Bridge, bordering I-75, is Mackinaw City, a tacky tourist town with a gift shop and fudge kitchen on every corner (fudge is northern Michigan's most famous product). Mackinaw City is best known as one of two departure points for Mackinac Island, but it does have a couple of interesting attractions of its own.

Right next to the bridge (its visitors center is actually beneath the bridge) is **Colonial Michilimackinac** (☎ 231-436-5563; www.mackinacparks.com; adult/child 6-17 $10/6; ☉ 9am-6pm summer, 9am-4pm May–mid-Oct), a National Historic Landmark that features a reconstructed stockade first built in 1715 by the French. Some 3 miles southeast of the city on US 23 is **Historic Mill Creek** (☎ 231-436-4226; www.mackinacparks.com; adult/child 6-17 $7.50/4.50; ☉ 9am-5pm summer, 9am-4pm May–mid-Oct), which has an 18th-century sawmill, historic displays and nature trails. A combination ticket for both sights, along with Fort Mackinac (p610), is available at a discount.

The only things that outnumber fudge shops in Mackinac City are motels, which line I-75 and US 23. Thanks to the popularity of Mackinac Island and a nearby casino, it's almost impossible to find a room for less than $100 during the summer. Exceptions include **Days Inn** (☎ 231-436-8961; www.daysinnbridgeview.com; 206 N Nicolet St; r incl breakfast weekday/weekend from $55/89; P ⚲) and **Rainbow Motel** (☎ 231-436-5518; www.rainbowmotel.net; 602 S Huron St; r weekday/weekend from $45/77; ☉ mid-May–mid-Oct; P ⚲).

St Ignace

At the north end of Mackinac Bridge is St Ignace, the other jumping-off point for Mackinac Island, and the second-oldest settlement in Michigan – Père Jacques Marquette founded a mission here in 1671. As soon as you've paid your bridge toll you'll pass a huge **Michigan Welcome Center** (☎ 906-643-6979; I-75N; ☉ 8am-6pm summer, 9am-5pm rest of year), which has racks of brochures and lodging help.

Mackinac Island

From either St Ignace or Mackinaw City you can catch a ferry to Mackinac Island, Michigan's first tourist destination. The British built a fort atop the famous limestone cliffs in 1780

PAPA'S FOOTPRINTS

A number of writers have ties to northwest Michigan, but none are as famous as Ernest Hemingway, who spent the summers of his youth at his family's cottage on Walloon Lake. Hemingway buffs often tour the area to view the places that made their way into his writing.

In Petoskey, you can see the Hemingway collection at the **Little Traverse History Museum** (☎ 231-347-2620; www.petoskeymuseum.org; 100 Depot Ct; admission $1; 🕑 10am-4pm Mon-Fri, 1-4pm Sat Jun-Sep, 1-4pm Thu-Sat May & Oct-Dec), including rare 1st-edition books that the author autographed for a friend when he visited in 1947. Afterward, visit **City Park Grill** (☎ 231-347-0101; 432 E Lake St; 🕑 11:30am-10pm Mon-Fri, to 11pm Sat & Sun), where Hemingway, with his famous drinking habit, was a regular.

Next, head south on US 31 toward Charlevoix. Just before entering that town, turn east onto Boyne City Rd, which skirts beautiful Lake Charlevoix and eventually arrives at the **Horton Bay General Store**. Built in 1876 with a high false front, the store's most prominent feature is its large porch, with benches and stairs at either end. Hemingway idled away some youthful summers on that porch and fished nearby Horton Creek for trout. He was married in Horton Bay's Congregational Church, and the general store appeared in the opening of his short story 'Up in Michigan.'

The **Michigan Hemingway Society** (www.northquest.com/hemingway; PO Box 922, Petoskey, MI 49770) provides further information for self-guided tours. It also hosts a **Hemingway festival** for a weekend every October.

and then fought the Americans for control of it during the War of 1812.

The most important date on this 2000-acre island was 1898 – the year cars were banned to encourage tourism. Today all travel is by horses or bicycles; even the police use bikes to patrol the town. The crowds of tourists (called Fudgies by the islanders) can be crushing at times, particularly at summer weekends. If at all possible, spend a night on Mackinac Island; the real charm of this historic place emerges after the last ferry leaves in the evening.

SIGHTS & ACTIVITIES

Overlooking the downtown area is **Fort Mackinac** (☎ 906-847-3328; www.mackinacparks.com; adult/child 6-17 $10/6; 🕑 9:30am-8pm in summer, 9:30am-4:30pm May–mid-Oct), one of the best-preserved military forts in the country. The admission price is also good for six other museums in town, including the Dr Beaumont Museum (where the doctor performed his famous digestive tract experiments) and Benjamin Blacksmith Shop. Edging the shoreline of the island is Hwy 185, the only state highway in Michigan that doesn't permit cars. The best way to view the incredible scenery along this 8-mile road is by bicycle; bring your own on the ferry or rent one in town at any of almost a dozen bike shops for $7 to $8 per hour plus a hefty deposit. You can make it all the way around the flat road in about an hour.

The two best attractions – **Arch Rock** (a huge limestone arch that sits 150ft above Lake Huron) and **Fort Holmes** (the island's other fort) – are both free. You can also ride past the **Grand Hotel**, which boasts a veranda stretching halfway to Detroit. Unfortunately if you're not staying at the Grand (minimum $220 per night per person), it costs $12 to stroll its long porch and step inside the lobby. Not worth it. However, if you purchase a ticket to Fort Mackinac, you can eat lunch at the Fort Mackinac Tea Room. The outdoor tables feature a million-dollar view of downtown and the Straits of Mackinac.

SLEEPING

Rooms are booked far in advance at summer weekends. Call or stop by the **visitors center** (☎ 800-454-5227; www.mackinacisland.org; Main St; 🕑 9am-5pm) for help with lodging reservations. The lodging and restaurants listed here are open mid-May to mid-October only, unless noted otherwise.

Camping is not permitted anywhere on Mackinac Island. That means you have to spend a wad to spend the night. Most hotels and B&Bs charge at least $150 for two people. Exceptions include the nine-room **McNally Cottage** (☎ 906-847-3565; www.mcnallycottage.net; Main St; r incl breakfast $70-120 🕑 late May-early Sep), the four-room **Bogan Lane Inn** (☎ 906-847-3439;

www.boganlaneinn.com; Bogan Lane; r incl breakfast $85-125; 🕐 year-round; ✗); and the eight-room **Hart's B&B** (☎ 906-847-3854; www.hartsmackinac.com; Market St; r incl breakfast $115-155; ✗). All are walkable to downtown.

EATING & DRINKING

The best-known eateries on Mackinac Island are the dozen fudge shops, which use fans to blow the tempting aroma of the freshly made confection out onto Huron St. Hamburger and sandwich shops abound downtown.

JL Beanery Coffeehouse (☎ 906-847-6533; Huron St; mains $6-13; 🕐 7am-9pm; wi-fi) Read the newspaper, sip a steaming cup of joe and gaze at the lake at this waterside café. It serves dandy breakfasts, sandwiches, soups and light dinners.

Astor St Café (☎ 906-847-6031; Astor St; mains $9-15; 🕐 11am-8pm Mon-Sat, to 3pm Sun) Astor St fires up Midwestern specials, such as pasties (meat/veggie pot pies), whitefish, roast turkey and meatloaf.

Horn's Bar (☎ 906-847-6154; Main St; mains $11-17; 🕐 11-2:30am) Horn's Bar serves traditional American dishes and features live entertainment nightly.

GETTING THERE & AROUND

Three ferry companies operate out of both Mackinaw City and St Ignace – **Arnold Line** (☎ 800-542-8528; www.arnoldline.com), **Shepler's** (☎ 800-828-6157; www.sheplersferry.com) and **Star Line** (☎ 800-638-9892; www.mackinacferry.com) – and charge the same rates: round-trip adult/child 5-12/bicycle $21/10.50/7.50. The ferries run several times daily from May to October; Arnold Line runs longer, weather permitting. The trip takes 15 minutes. Once you're on the island, horse-drawn cabs will take you anywhere, or you could rent a bicycle.

UPPER PENINSULA

Rugged and isolated, with hardwood forests blanketing 90% of its land, the Upper Peninsula (UP) is a Midwest highlight. Only 45 miles of interstate highway slice through the trees, punctuated by a handful of cities (of which Marquette is the largest). Between them lie miles of undeveloped shoreline on Lakes Huron, Michigan and Superior; scenic two-lane roads; small rural towns; and pasties, the local meat/vegetable pot pies brought over by Cornish miners 150 years ago. Michigan's two best wilderness areas – Isle Royale and the Porcupine Mountains – are here, at the UP's west end.

You'll find that it's a different world up north. Residents of the UP, aka 'Yoopers,' consider themselves distinct from the rest of the state – they've even threatened to secede in the past.

Sault Ste Marie & Around

Founded in 1668, Sault Ste Marie (Sault is pronounced 'soo') is the oldest city in Michigan and the third oldest in the USA. The town is best known for its locks that raise and lower 1000ft-long freighters between the different lake levels. **Soo Lock Park** is at the end of Water St in the heart of downtown. It features an interpretive center and observation decks from which you can watch the boats leap 21ft from Lake Superior to Lake Huron.

Most of Sault Ste Marie's motels are along the I-75 Business Loop and Ashmun St. Try the **Plaza Motor Motel** (☎ 906-635-1881, 888-809-1881; www.plazamotormotel.com; 3901 I-75 Business; r $49-81), or the spiffy **Askwith Lockview Motel** (☎ 906-632-2491, 800-854-0745; www.lockview.com; 327 W Portage Ave; r $70-76; 🕐 May–mid-Oct), across from Soo Locks.

To enjoy a carnivorous feast amid a gallery of stuffed animal heads, make your way to **Antlers** (☎ 906-632-3571; 804 E Portage Ave; mains $8-20; 🕐 11am-9pm). Huge steaks, burgers and ribs anchor the menu; animal rights enthusiasts and vegetarians beware. **Cup of the Day** (☎ 906-635-7272; 406 Ashmun St; mains $5-7; 🕐 7am-6pm Mon-Fri, 8am-3pm Sat) serves breakfast and lunch.

An hour's drive west of Sault Ste Marie, via Hwy 28 and Hwy 123, is the eastern UP's top attraction: lovely **Tahquamenon Falls**, with tea-colored waters tinted so by upstream hemlock leaves. The Upper Falls in **Tahquamenon Falls State Park** (☎ 906-492-3415; campsites $19-21, per vehicle $8) are 200ft across with a 50ft drop, making them the third-largest falls east of the Mississippi River. The Lower Falls are a series of smaller cascades best viewed by renting a boat (per person $3) and rowing across the river to an island. The large state park also has camping and great hiking, and there's a brewpub near the park entrance.

North of the park, beyond the little town of Paradise, is the fascinating **Great Lakes Shipwreck Museum** (☎ 906-635-1742; www.shipwreckmuseum.com; 18335 N Whitefish Point Rd; adult/child 6-17 $10/7; 🕐 10am-6pm May-Oct), where the intriguing displays include items trawled up from sunken ships. More than 300 vessels – including the *Edmund Fitzgerald* that Gordon Lightfoot crooned about – have sunk in the area's congested sea lanes and unpredictable weather, earning it such nicknames as the 'Shipwreck Coast' and 'Graveyard of the Great Lakes.'

Hwy 123 leads to Paradise, where family-owned **Curley's Paradise Motel** (☎ 906-492-3445; www.superiorsights.com/curleys; Hwy 123; r $80-99) sits right on the lake. There are numerous other well-kept mom-and-pop motels along this stretch of highway.

Pictured Rocks National Lakeshore

Sitting roughly mid-peninsula on the Lake Superior shoreline, Munising is the gateway to **Pictured Rocks National Lakeshore** (www.nps.gov/piro), a 110-sq-mile national park just to the east that holds the namesake colored sandstone bluffs. Most people view the 200ft-high cliffs on a 2½-hour boat tour with **Pictured Rock Boat Cruises** (☎ 906-387-2379; www.picturedrocks.com; adult/child 6-12 $31/13). Boats depart from downtown Munising hourly between 9am and 5pm (except for 10am and 4pm) in July and August; they go less often in June, September and October. You also can drive to **Miners Castle Overlook**, 12 miles east of Munising off Rte 58, for a good view. The most scenic backpacking adventure in the state is the **Lakeshore Trail**, a four- to five-day, 43-mile trek from Grand Marais to Munising through the heart of the park. Stop in at the **Hiawatha National Forest/Pictured Rocks Visitors Center** (☎ 906-387-3700; www.nps.gov/piro; 400 E Munising Ave; ☾ 8am-6pm mid-May–mid-Oct, 9am-4:30pm Mon-Sat rest of year) at the corner of Hwy 28 and Rte 58 for maps, backcountry permits and other details.

Just offshore is **Grand Island**, part of the Hiawatha National Forest. Hop aboard the **Grand Island Ferry** (☎ 906-387-3503; www.grandislandmi.com; ☾ late May–mid-Oct) to get there (round-trip adult/child 6-12 $15/10), and rent a mountain bike (per day $30) from the ferry company to zip around, or take the three-hour bus tour ($20).

Munising has lots of motels, such as the recommended **Alger Falls Motel** (☎ 906-387-3536; www.algerfallsmotel.com; Hwy 28 E; r $48-68). **Falling Rock Café & Bookstore** (☎ 906-387-3008; 104 E Munising Ave; sandwiches $5-9; ☾ 7am-8pm Sun-Fri, to 10pm Sat) has sandwiches, pasties and live music.

Marquette

From Munising, Hwy 28 heads west and hugs Lake Superior. This beautiful stretch of highway has lots of beaches, roadside parks and rest areas where you can pull over and enjoy the scenery. Within 45 miles you'll reach Marquette, a city that abounds with outdoor-recreation opportunities. Stop at the **Michigan Welcome Center** (☎ 906-249-9066; US 41/Hwy 28; ☾ 9am-5pm), in an impressive log lodge as you enter the city, and pick up brochures on hiking trails and waterfalls in the area.

Panoramic views are enjoyed on the easy **Sugarloaf Mountain Trail** or the harder, wilderness-like **Hogsback Mountain Trail**. Both are reached from County Rd 550, just north of Marquette. In the city, the high bluffs of **Presque Isle Park** make a great place to catch the sunset.

The **Noquemanon Trail Network** (www.noquetrails.org) is highly recommended for mountain biking and cross country skiing. Check the website for equipment rental and day pass (per day $9) purchase locations.

Marquette is the perfect place to stay put for a few days to explore the central UP. **Value Host Motor Inn** (☎ 906-225-5000; 1101 US 41 W; r $55-65), with a sauna, is a few miles west of town. The alpine-like **Nordic Bay Lodge** (☎ 800-892-9376; www.nordicbay.com; 1880 US 41 S; r incl breakfast $75-99; ☒ wi-fi), overlooking Lake Superior a few miles south of downtown, is in the woods with access to trails; it has a ski wax/bike maintenance room for winter/summer.

Sample the local meat/veggie pie specialty at **Jean Kay's Pasties & Subs** (☎ 906-228-5310; 1639 Presque Isle Ave; items $3-4; ☾ 10am-9pm Mon-Fri, 10am-8pm Sat & Sun).

Sit on the porch at **Gophers Café** (☎ 906-226-0900; 910 N Third St; mains $4-8; ☾ 7am-8pm Mon-Fri, to 5pm Sat) and munch crepes, quiche, soups and sandwiches. Better yet, make a meal out of the Belgian chocolates crafted onsite.

UpFront and Company (☎ 906-228-5200; 102 E Main St; mains $13-18; ☾ 11am-11pm Mon, 11-2am Tue-Fri, 2pm-2am Sat, closed Mon in winter) fires up the wood oven for pizzas, the taps for hearty beers and the amps for live music.

Isle Royale National Park

Totally free of vehicles and roads, **Isle Royale National Park** (www.nps.gov/isro; user fee per day $4; ☾ mid-Apr–Oct), a 210-sq-mile island in Lake Superior, is certainly the place to go for peace and quiet. It gets fewer visitors in a year than Yellowstone National Park gets in a day, which means the packs of wolves and moose creeping through the forest are all yours to spot and howl along with.

The island is laced with 165 miles of hiking trails that connect dozens of campgrounds along Superior and inland lakes. You must be totally prepared for this wilderness adventure, with a tent, camping stove, sleeping bags, food and water filter. Or say 'to hell with that crap,' and shell out the dough for the **Rock Harbor Lodge** (☎ 906-337-4993; www .isleroyaleresort.com; r/cottage $209-239). The **park headquarters** (☎ 906-482-0984; 800 E Lakeshore Dr; ⏰ 8am-6pm Mon-Fri, 11am-6pm Sat Jun & Jul, 8am-4:30pm Mon-Fri Aug-May) in Houghton can provide information.

From the dock outside the headquarters in Houghton, the **Ranger III** (☎ 906-482-0984) departs at 9am on Tuesday and Friday for the six-hour boat trip (one way adult/child 7-12 $56/20) to Rock Harbor, at the east end of the island. **Royale Air Service** (☎ 877-359-4753; www.royale airservice.com) offers a quicker trip, flying from Houghton County Airport to Rock Harbor in 30 minutes (one way $180). Or head 50 miles up the Keweenaw Peninsula to Copper Harbor (a beautiful drive) and jump on the **Isle Royale Queen** (☎ 906-289-4437; www.isleroyale.com) for the 8am three-hour crossing (one way adult/child under 12 $62/31). Days of departure vary, so call for the schedule. You also can access Isle Royale from Grand Portage, Minnesota (p634). Bringing a kayak or canoe on the ferry costs an additional $20.

Porcupine Mountains Wilderness State Park

Michigan's largest state park, with 90 miles of trails, is another wilderness highlight of the Upper Peninsula, and it's a lot easier to reach than Isle Royale. 'The Porkies,' as they're called, are so rugged that loggers bypassed most of the range in the early 19th century, leaving the park with the largest tract of virgin forest between the Rocky Mountains and Adirondacks.

From Silver City, head west on Hwy 107 to reach the **Porcupine Mountains visitors center** (☎ 906-885-5208; 412 S Boundary Rd; ⏰ 10am-8pm mid-May–mid-Oct), where you buy vehicle entry permits (per day/annual $8/29) and backcountry permits (per night for one to four people $14). Continue to the end of Hwy 107 and climb 300ft for the stunning view of **Lake of the Clouds**.

Winter is also a busy time at the Porkies, with downhill skiing (a 640-ft vertical drop) and 26 miles of cross-country trails; check

with the **ski area** (☎ 888-937-2411; www.skitheporkies .com) for conditions and costs.

The **Sunshine Motel** (☎ 888-988-2187; www .ontonagonmi.com/sunshine; 24077 Hwy 64; r $55, cabins $60-75), 3 miles west of Ontonagon, is near the park and makes a good base.

WISCONSIN

Wisconsin is cheesy and proud of it. The state pumps out a total of 2.4 billion pounds of cheddar, gouda and other smelly goodness from its cow-speckled farmland per year. Local license plates read 'The Dairy State' with udder dignity. Folks here even refer to themselves as 'cheeseheads' and emphasize it by wearing novelty foam rubber cheese-wedge hats for special occasions (most notably during Green Bay Packers football games).

So embrace the cheese thing, because there's a good chance you may be here for a while. Wisconsin has heaps to offer: exploring the craggy cliffs and lighthouses of Door County, kayaking through sea caves at Apostle Islands National Lakeshore, cow chip throwing along US 12, mountain biking in Chequamegon National Forest and soaking up beer, art and festivals in Milwaukee. The state does a nice job in the ecotourism department, too – keep an eye out for 'Travel Green' certified businesses.

History

During the 1820s lead-mining boom, the many miners who came from nearby states were called 'badgers' for their subterranean activities. Following statehood in 1848 and the Civil War, immigrants poured in – from Germany and Scandinavia most notably. The Badger State was soon known for its beer, butter, cheese and paper.

While Wisconsin still leads the nation in the number of dairy farms and clings to the 'top cheesemaker' title, its role is under threat. Midsize farms here, as throughout the country, are having a tough time: almost a third of Wisconsin's dairies have shut down in the past 10 years.

Information

Wisconsin markets itself well:
Bicycle Federation of Wisconsin (☎ 608-251-4456; www.bfw.org) Produces detailed maps ($3.95) for cyclists.

WISCONSIN FACTS

Nicknames Badger State, America's Dairyland

Population 5.6 million

Area 65,500 sq miles

Capital city Madison (population 221,551)

Sales Tax 5%

Birthplace of Author Laura Ingalls Wilder (1867–1957), architect Frank Lloyd Wright (1867–1959), painter Georgia O'Keeffe (1887–1986), Senator Joseph McCarthy (1908–57), actor Orson Welles (1915–85)

Home of 'Cheesehead' Packer fans, dairy farms, water parks

Famous for Breweries, artisanal cheese, first state to legislate gay rights

Official motto Forward

Wisconsin B&B Association (☎ 715-539-9222; www.wbba.org)

Wisconsin Department of Tourism (☎ 800-432-8747; www.travelwisconsin.com) Produces loads of free guides on subjects like bird-watching, biking, golf and rustic roads.

Wisconsin highway conditions (☎ 800-762-3947; www.dot.wisconsin.gov)

Wisconsin Milk Marketing Board (☎ 608-836-8820; www.wisdairy.com) Provides free statewide map of cheese and beer-related businesses to visit.

Wisconsin state park information (☎ 608-266-2181; www.wiparks.net) Park entry requires a vehicle permit (per day/year residents $7/25, nonresidents $10/35). Campsites cost $12 to $20; reservations accepted (☎ 888-947-2757; www.reserveamerica.com; fee $10).

MILWAUKEE

Here's the thing about Milwaukee: it's cool, but for some reason everyone refuses to admit it. The town was built on beer, for crissake – Pabst and Schlitz – need we say more? Massive Miller Brewery is still here and worth the tour, as are various microbreweries (including one with polka band entertainment). Harley-Davidson's tour lets you sit on vintage motorcycles. And the art museum reaches beyond the norm with its folk and outside art galleries.

In summertime, a slew of festivals lets loose revelry by the lake. Speaking of which: the Lake Express ferry makes Milwaukee a perfect jumping-off point before heading elsewhere in the Midwest. But before leaving, please go see the racing sausages at Miller Park.

Orientation & Information

Lake Michigan sits to the east of the city, and is rimmed by parkland. The inspired Riverwalk is a system of redeveloped walking paths along both sides of the Milwaukee River downtown. Wisconsin Ave divides east–west streets. North–south streets are usually numbered and increase as they head west from the lake.

BOOKSTORES

Harry Schwartz Books (☎ 414-332-1181; 2559 N Downer Ave)

EMERGENCY & MEDICAL SERVICES

Froedtert Hospital (☎ 414-805-3000; 9200 W Wisconsin Ave)

Walgreens (☎ 414-272-2171; 1400 E Brady St; ☻ 24hr) Pharmacy.

INTERNET ACCESS

The East Side neighborhood near the University of Wisconsin-Milwaukee boasts coffee shops with free wi-fi. Pier Wisconsin (opposite) also offers free wi-fi.

Milwaukee Central Library (☎ 414-286-3000; 814 W Wisconsin Ave; ☻ 9am-8:30pm Mon-Wed, to 5:30pm Thu-Sat) Free internet terminals for visitors.

MEDIA & INTERNET RESOURCES

Milwaukee Journal Sentinel (www.jsonline.com) The local daily newspaper.

On Milwaukee (www.onmilwaukee.com) Traffic and weather updates, plus restaurant and entertainment reviews.

Shepherd Express (www.shepherd-express.com) The free weekly entertainment paper; available at bookstores, coffee shops and entertainment venues.

Tune into WUWM-FM 89.7 for NPR, or WLZR-FM 102.9 for rock.

GOIN' GREEN

Wisconsin leads the ecotourism pack among US states. Its **Travel Green Wisconsin** (☎ 608-280-0360; www.travelgreenwisconsin.com) program certifies restaurants, lodgings and attractions as environmentally responsible by grading them on nine different categories including waste reduction, energy efficiency and landscaping. Check the website for a list of businesses that have received the seal of approval.

MONEY
US Bank (☎ 414-765-4035; 777 E Wisconsin Ave) ATM and foreign currency exchange available.

POST
Post office (☎ 800-275-8777; 345 W St Paul Ave)

TOURIST INFORMATION
Milwaukee LGBT Community Center (☎ 414-271-2656; www.mkelgbt.org; 315 W Court St, Suite 101; ☼ 10am-10pm Mon-Fri, 6-10pm Sat) Has information on happenings; or search www.outinmilwaukee.com.

Visitors center (☎ 800-554-1448; www.visitmilwaukee.org; 1st fl, 500 N Harbor Dr; ☼ 9am-5pm) Pick up maps and *A Taster's Guide to Wisconsin Cheese, Beer and Wine*; located in the Discovery World building.

Sights & Activities
Sights are spread out, but usually accessible by public buses.

MILWAUKEE ART MUSEUM
Even those who aren't usually museum-goers will be struck by this lakeside **museum** (☎ 414-224-3200; www.mam.org; 700 N Art Museum Dr; adult/child 13-18 $8/4; ☼ 10am-5pm, to 8pm Thu), which features a stunning wing-like addition by Santiago Calatrava. It soars open and closed every day at noon, which is wild to see. There's a permanent display on architect Frank Lloyd Wright, and fabulous folk and outsider art galleries.

HARLEY-DAVIDSON PLANT
In 1903 William Harley and Arthur Davidson, local schoolmates, built and sold their first Harley-Davidson motorcycle. A century later the big bikes are a symbol of American manufacturing pride, and this **Harley-Davidson plant** (☎ 414-343-7850, 877-883-1450; www.harley-davidson.com; 11700 W Capitol Dr; admission free; ☼ usually 9:30am-1pm Mon-Fri), in the suburb of Wauwatosa (20 minutes' drive west of downtown) is where engines are built. (Body assembly goes on in York, Pennsylvania, and Kansas City, Missouri.) The one-hour tours are kind of technical, but the ultimate payoff comes when you get to sit in the saddle of a vintage bike. No open shoes are permitted.

More bikes (including Elvis's!) will be displayed downtown at the new **Harley-Davidson Museum** (www.h-dmuseum.com; cnr Canal & 6th Sts). It was under construction at press time, but is slated to open in 2008; check the website for updates.

BREWERIES
Pabst and Schlitz have moved on, but **Miller Brewing Company** (☎ 414-931-2337; www.millerbrewing.com; 4251 W State St; admission free; ☼ 10:30am-3:30pm Mon-Sat) preserves Milwaukee's beer legacy. Join the legions of drinkers lined up for the free tours. Though the watery beer may not be your favorite, the factory impresses by its sheer scale: you'll visit the packaging plant where 2000 cans are filled each minute, and the warehouse where a half-million cases chill while awaiting shipment. And then there's the generous tasting session at the tour's end, where you can down three full-size samples. Don't forget your ID.

For more swills, head to **Sprecher Brewing Company** (☎ 414-964-2739; www.sprecherbrewery.com; 701 W Glendale Ave; tours $3; ☼ 4pm Fri, noon-2pm Sat). The small microbrewery's tour includes a museum of memorabilia from long-gone Milwaukee suds-makers and a beer garden replete with oom-pah music. It's 5 miles north of downtown; reservations required.

Lakefront Brewery (☎ 414-372-8800; www.lakefrontbrewery.com; 1872 N Commerce St; tours $5; ☼ 2pm & 3pm Mon-Sat) offers afternoon tours, but the swellest time to visit is on Friday nights when there is a fish fry, 16 brews on tap and a polka band in the attached banquet hall.

MUSEUMS
The **Eisner Museum of Advertising and Design** (☎ 414-847-3290; www.eisnermuseum.org; 208 N Water St; adult/child 12-18 $5/3; ☼ 11am-5pm Wed-Fri, to 8pm Thu, noon-5pm Sat, 1-5pm Sun) presents excellent exhibits on how the media influence today's culture.

Discovery World at Pier Wisconsin (☎ 414-765-9966; www.discoveryworld.org; 500 N Harbor Dr; adult/child 3-17 $16.95/12.95; ☼ 9am-5pm Tue-Sun) is the city's mondo, lakefront science and technology museum. It's primarily a kid pleaser, with freshwater and saltwater aquariums (where you can touch sharks and sturgeon) and a dockside, triple-masted Great Lakes schooner to climb aboard.

America's Black Holocaust Museum (☎ 414-264-2500; www.blackholocaustmuseum.org; 2233 N 4th St; adult/student $5/3; ☼ 9am-5pm Tue-Sat) outlines the consequences of racism from slavery onward.

LAKEFRONT PARK
The parkland edging Lake Michigan is prime for walking, bicycling and rollerblading. For the latter, try **Milwaukee Bike & Skate Rental**

(☎ 414-273-1343; www.milwbikeskaterental.com; Veteran's Park; per hr skates/bicycle $8/10; ☉ 10am-7pm Jun-Aug), just north of the art museum. Also here is Bradford Beach, good for swimming and lounging.

Festivals & Events

Summerfest (☎ 800-273-3378; www.summerfest.com; day pass $15) is dubbed 'the world's largest music festival,' and indeed hundreds of rock, blues, jazz, country and alternative bands swarm its 10 stages over 11 days in late June/early July. The scene totally rawks.

There's also **PrideFest** (www.pridefest.com; mid-Jun), **Polish Fest** (www.polishfest.org; late Jun), **Irish Fest** (www.irishfest.com; mid-Aug), **German Fest** (www.germanfest.com; late Jul) and a host of others. Call the visitors center for details.

Sleeping

Rates listed here are for summer, when you should book ahead; rooms can be 15% to 30% less in winter. The 14.6% tax is not included in the listed rates. For cheap chain lodging, try Howell Ave, south near the airport.

Best Western Inn Towne Hotel (☎ 414-224-8400; www.inntownehotel.com; 710 N Old World 3rd St; s/d from $89/99; P ⚡ 🖵 wi-fi) It's operated by a chain, but this old hotel, in the heart of downtown, has good quality rooms with a vintage ambience. Parking is $10.

Astor Hotel (☎ 800-558-0200; www.theastorhotel.com; 924 E Juneau Ave; r incl breakfast $99-129; P ⚡ 🖵) The Astor, dating from 1918, has bright, spacious rooms, some with cool old furnishings, plus perks like free internet and a shuttle bus to nearby sights. It's located near the lake, east of downtown's core. Parking costs $4.

Comfort Inn & Suites Downtown Lakeshore (☎ 414-276-8800, 800-328-7275; www.choicehotels.com; 916 E State St; r incl breakfast from $110; P ⚡ wi-fi) Check in here and you'll be laying low in the same digs as touring indie bands who come to town. Free wi-fi and breakfast, a lake-view deck and local shuttle bus supplement the contemporary rooms. It's located by the Astor (see above). Parking is $10.

Hotel Metro (☎ 414-272-1937, 877-638-7620; www.hotelmetro.com; 411 E Mason St; r from $189; P ⚡ wi-fi) Suites fill the mod, restored-deco Metro. Each room has a curved wall that separates the bedroom and its downy linens from the sitting area. The rooftop bar and spa add to the relaxed vibe. It's located in the heart of downtown. Parking costs $19.

Eating

Good places to scope for eats include N Old World 3rd St downtown; the fashionable East Side by the University of Wisconsin-Milwaukee; hip, Italian-based Brady St by its intersection with N Farwell Ave; and the gentrified Third Ward, anchored along N Milwaukee St south of I-94.

The Friday night fish fry is a highly social tradition observed throughout Wisconsin and all over Milwaukee. Try it at Lakefront Brewery (p615), which complements its fish with microbrews and a polka band.

Another Milwaukee specialty is frozen custard, like ice cream only smoother and richer. **Leon's** (☎ 414-383-1784; 3131 S 27th St; ☉ 11am-midnight) and **Kopp's** (☎ 414-961-2006; 5373 N Port Washington Rd, Glendale; ☉ 10:30am-11:30pm) are popular purveyors.

Milwaukee Public Market (☎ 414-336-1111; 400 N Water St; ☉ 10am-7pm Mon-Fri, 8am-5pm Sat & Sun) Browse this Third Ward market for fresh and prepared foods, cheeses and chocolates – everything is local.

Trocadero (☎ 414-272-0205; 1758 N Water St; mains $7-17; ☉ 11am-midnight Mon-Fri, from 9am Sat & Sun) Let's see – a glorious wine list, cheese plates, crepes, baguettes with jam, mussels and frites. We're in Paris, *oui?* Nope, we're near Brady St at Trocadero, a romantic coffee house–restaurant–bar with a year-round patio (it's heated in winter).

African Hut (☎ 414-765-1110; 1107 N Old World 3rd St; mains $9-14; ☉ 11:30am-10pm Mon-Thu, to 11pm Fri & Sat) Long-standing African Hut is a wonderful place to go for exotic meat and vegetarian dishes with ingredients like pounded yam, cassava and cooked-down peanuts blended with herbs.

Saki Tumi (☎ 414-224-7253; 714 N Milwaukee St; mains $8-20; ☉ 11am-10pm Mon-Thu, to midnight Fri, 5pm-midnight Sat, 4-9pm Sun) Sleek, Buddha-laden Saki Tumi mixes it up with Japanese sushi, traditional Korean grilled meats and Asian fusion dishes like *gyoza* ravioli and sesame-coated sea bass.

Drinking & Entertainment

BARS

The beer legacy guarantees that a thirst-quenching array of golden nectar is available. Over a dozen bars and restaurants lie around N Water and E State Sts. More bars can be found in Walker's Point on 1st and 2nd Sts, and along Brady St between Astor and Farwell

Sts. Drinkeries open around 4pm or 5pm and stay open to 2am.

Von Trier (☎ 414-272-1775; 2235 N Farwell Ave) The German Von Trier is a long-standing, real-deal favorite, with plenty of good stuff on tap and a biergarten.

Palm Tavern (☎ 414-744-0393; 2989 S Kinnickinnic Ave) Located in the blossoming south side neighborhood of Bay View, this warm, jazzy little bar has a mammoth selection of unusual beers and single-malt scotches.

John Hawk's (☎ 414-272-3199; 100 E Wisconsin Ave) Hawk's is a 'British' pub with a big choice of beers, fish fries, sandwiches and live jazz on Saturday. It occupies a prime spot on the riverfront.

SPORTS

Miller Park (☎ 414-902-4000; www.milwaukeebrewers .com; 1 Brewers Way) The Milwaukee Brewers play baseball at top-notch Miller Park, which has a retractable roof, real grass and racing sausages (see below). It's located near S 46th St.

Bradley Center (☎ 414-227-0400; www.nba.com/ bucks; 1001 N 4th St) The NBA's Milwaukee Bucks dunk here.

Getting There & Around

General Mitchell International Airport (MKE; ☎ 414-747-5300; www.mitchellairport.com) is 8 miles south of downtown. Take public bus No 80 ($1.75) or a cab ($25).

The **Lake Express ferry** (☎ 866-914-1010; www .lake-express.com) sails from downtown (the terminal is located a few miles south of the city center) to Muskegon, Michigan, and provides easy access to Michigan's beach-lined Gold Coast. See p607 for details.

Greyhound (☎ 414-272-2156; 606 N James Lovell St) runs frequent buses to Chicago ($13 to $20, two hours) and Minneapolis ($52 to $65, seven hours). Across the street, **Badger Bus**

WHAT THE...?

It's common to see strange things after too many stadium beers. But a group of giant sausages sprinting around Miller Park's perimeter – is that for *real*? It is if it's the end of the 6th inning. That's when the famous 'Racing Sausages' (actually people in meat costumes) waddle onto the field to give the fans a thrill. Folks here take their sausage seriously.

(☎ 414-276-7490; www.badgerbus.com; 635 N James Lovell St) goes to Madison ($17, 1½ hours). **Megabus** (☎ 877-462-6342; www.megabus.com/us) runs express to Chicago and Minneapolis, often for lower fares than Greyhound.

National car-rental agencies have offices at the airport and around town; Hertz has one at the downtown train station. Check the Transportation chapter (p1144) for contact details.

The **Milwaukee County Transit System** (☎ 414-344-6711; www.ridemcts.com; 1942 N 17th Ave) provides efficient local bus service ($1.75) as well as a free trolley that runs downtown in summer. Bus 31 is a useful route, as it goes to Miller Brewery.

Amtrak (☎ 414-271-0840; 433 W St Paul Ave) runs the *Hiawatha* train seven times per day to/from Chicago ($21, 1½ hours); catch it downtown or at Amtrak's airport train station.

For cab service, call **Yellow Cab** (☎ 414-271-1800).

MADISON

Madison gets a lot of kudos – most walkable city, best road-biking city, most vegetarian friendly, gay friendly, environmentally friendly, and just plain all-round friendliest city in the USA. Ensconced on a narrow isthmus between Mendota and Monona lakes, it's a pretty combination of small, grassy state capital and liberal, bookish college town. To get an indication of the hipness factor at work here, consider this is the place that birthed the cheeky, farcical newspaper *The Onion* (www.theonion.com).

The **visitors center** (☎ 608-255-2537, 800-373-6376; www.visitmadison.com; 615 E Washington Ave; ☯ 8am-5pm Mon-Fri) is six blocks east of Capitol Sq, though you'll likely find all you need at the university's Memorial Union (see p618). *Isthmus* (www.thedailypage.com) is the free entertainment paper.

Sights & Activities

The heart of town is marked by the X-shaped **State Capitol** (☎ 608-266-0382; admission free; ☯ 8am-6pm Mon-Fri, to 4pm Sat & Sun), the largest outside Washington, DC. Tours are available on the hour most days. On Saturday, Capitol Sq is overtaken by the **Dane County Farmers' Market** (www.dcfm.org; ☯ 6am-2pm May-Nov), a good place to sample the Wisconsin specialties of cheese curds and beer-cooked bratwursts.

By all means, take advantage of the city's lakes and 200 miles of trails. For rentals, try **Yellow Jersey** (☎ 608-257-4737; www.yellowjersey.org;

GREAT LAKES

419 State St; per day bikes $9.50; 10am-6pm Tue, Wed & Fri, to 8pm Mon & Thu, 9am-5pm Sat, noon-5pm Sun) for two-wheelers, and the **Paddlin' Shop** (608-284-0300; www.paddlin.com; 202 S Dickinson St; per day canoe/kayak $35/45; 10am-6pm Mon-Fri, to 5pm Sat & Sun) for waterfaring craft. Both are situated near Capitol Sq (three blocks and 10 blocks, respectively).

State St runs from the capitol west to the University of Wisconsin. The lengthy avenue is lined with free-trade coffee shops, parked bicycles and incense-wafting stores selling hackey sacks and flowy Indian skirts. An anomaly is the **House of Wisconsin Cheese** (608-255-5204; www.houseofwisconsincheese.com; 107 State St; 9am-8pm), which sells state-shaped cheddar blocks and foam rubber cheese-wedge hats among its pungent stock.

State St also holds the impressive **Museum of Contemporary Art** (608-257-0158; www.mmoca .org; 227 State St; admission free; 11am-5pm Tue & Wed, to 8pm Thu & Fri, 10am-8pm Sat, noon-5pm Sun), with works by Frida Kahlo, Claes Oldenburg and others, plus a rooftop cinema that screens art films on summer Friday nights; and the **Overture Center for the Arts** (608-258-4973; www .overturecenter.com; 201 State St), home to a variety of performing arts venues.

The campus has its own attractions, including the 1240-acre **Arboretum** (608-263-7888; 1207 Seminole Hwy; admission free; 7am-10pm), dense with lilac, and the **Memorial Union** (608-265-3000; 800 Langdon St), with its festive lakeside terrace perfect for an outdoor drink. The Union additionally offers free live music, films and internet access.

The **Monona Terrace Community Center** (608-261-4000; www.mononaterrace.com; 1 John Nolen Dr; admission free; 8am-5pm), two blocks from the square, has a fabulous rooftop garden overlooking Lake Monona. It finally opened in 1997, 59 years after Frank Lloyd Wright designed it. Tours (adult/student $3/2) are offered at 1pm daily. Parking costs $3.

Sleeping & Eating

Moderately priced motels can be found off I-90/I-94 (about 6 miles from the town center), off Hwy 12/18 and along Washington Ave.

A global smorgasbord of restaurants peppers State St amid the pizza, sandwich and cheap-beer joints; many places have inviting patios. Cruising Williamson ('Willy') St turns up good Lao, Jamaican, Caribbean and other eateries.

HI Madison Hostel (608-441-0144; www.madison hostel.org; 141 S Butler St; dm $23, r $47; P) The convenient hostel is a short walk from the capitol. The office is open from 8am to 11am and 5pm to 9pm, with continuous hours in summer. Parking is $5.

University Inn (608-285-8040, 800-279-4881; www .universityinn.org; 441 N Frances St; r $89-129; P wi-fi) The rooms are fine though nothing special; the inn's greatest asset is its handy location right by the State St and university action. Rates are highest at weekends.

Arbor House (608-238-2981; www.arbor-house.com; 3402 Monroe St; r incl breakfast weekday $110-175, weekend $150-230) Arbor House was an old tavern back in the day. Now it's a wind-powered, energy-efficient-appliance-using, vegetarian-breakfast-serving B&B. It's located about 3 miles southwest of the capitol but accessible to public transportation. The owners will lend you mountain bikes, too.

Michelangelo's (608-251-5299; 114 State St; mains $2-5; 7am-11pm) Pop in and try Michelangelo's fair-trade coffees, sweets and sandwiches.

Himal Chuli (608-251-9225; 318 State St; mains $8-13; 11am-9pm Mon-Sat, noon-8pm Sun) This cheerful and cozy place serves up homemade Nepali fare, including vegetarian dishes.

Café Soleil & L'Etoile (608-251-0500; 25 N Pinckney St; café mains $8-10, restaurant mains $29-35; closed Sun) The chefs here are slow food pioneers, creating their menu from local, seasonal ingredients for 30-plus years. Dishes at L'Etoile (the restaurant, open from 5:30 to 8pm) might include red snapper with summer squash or eggplant napoleon. But the best chow is found in the attached café (open 7am-2:30pm), serving scrumptious sandwiches like trout salad with fresh-baked honey oat bread and Wisconsin grilled cheeses on whole grain bread.

Drinking & Entertainment

Bars stay open to 2am.

Memorial Union (608-265-3000; 800 Langdon St) For a beer, join the fun atmosphere at this university bar.

Great Dane Pub (608-284-0000; 123 E Doty St) Big, friendly and rambling like its namesake dog, the Dane is a popular brewpub with occasional live music.

Getting There & Around

The central **Greyhound station** (608-257-3050; 2 S Bedford St) is also used by **Badger Bus** (414-276-

7490; www.badgerbus.com) for trips to Milwaukee ($17, 1½ hours).

SOUTHERN WISCONSIN

This part of Wisconsin has some of the prettiest landscapes, particularly the hilly southwest. Architecture fans can be unleashed at Taliesin, the Frank Lloyd Wright über-sight, and Racine, where a couple of his other works stand. Dairies around here cut a lot of cheese.

Racine

Racine is an unremarkable industrial town 30 miles south of Milwaukee, but it has two key Frank Lloyd Wright sights, both of which offer tours that must be pre-booked. The first, the **Johnson Wax Company Administration Building** (☎ 262-260-2154; 1525 Howe St; admission free; ☽ tours at 9am, 10am, 11am, 1:45pm & 3pm Fri), dates from 1939 and is a magnificent space with tall, flared columns. The other is the lakeside **Wingspread** (☎ 262-681-3353; 33 E Four Mile Rd; admission free; ☽ 9:30am-3pm Tue-Thu), the last and largest of Wright's Prairie houses.

The **Racine Art Museum** (☎ 262-638-8300; www.ramart.org; 441 Main St; adult/child 12-18 $5/3; ☽ 10am-5pm Tue-Sat, noon-5pm Sun) houses one of the continent's most significant craft collections, focusing on ceramics, fibers, glass, metals and wood.

Spring Green

Forty miles west of Madison and 3 miles south of the small town of Spring Green, **Taliesin** was the home of native son Frank Lloyd Wright for most of his life and is the site of his architectural school. It's now a major pilgrimage destination for fans and followers. The house was built in 1903, the Hillside Home School in 1932, and the **visitors center** (☎ 608-588-7900; www.taliesinpreservation.org; Hwy 23; ☽ 9am-5:30pm May-Oct) was built in 1953. A wide range of guided tours ($16 to $80) cover various parts of the complex; reservations are required for the more lengthy ones. The one-hour Hillside Tour ($16, no reservation needed) is a good introduction to Wright's work.

A few miles south of Taliesin is the **House on the Rock** (☎ 608-935-3639; www.thehouseontherock .com; 5754 Hwy 23; adult/child 4-17 $11.50/7.50; ☽ 9am-6pm summer, reduced rest of year), one of Wisconsin's busiest attractions. The strange 'house,' one man's obsession, was built atop a rock column and sprawled to become a monument of the imagination. The house is broken into three parts with a different tour exploring the objects and wonderments of each. Or you can

---

WORTH THE TRIP: QUIRKY US 12

Unusual sights huddle around US 12, all easy to experience on a northerly day trip from Madison.

Eleven miles up the road is Dr Evermor's **Sculpture Park** (admission free; ☽ 9am-5pm Mon & Thu-Sat, noon-5pm Sun). The doc welds old pipes, carburetors and other salvaged metal into a hallucinatory world of futuristic creatures and structures. The crowning glory is the giant, egg-domed Forevertron, cited by *Guinness World Records* as the world's largest scrap metal sculpture. The good doctor himself – aka Tom Every – is often around and happy to chat about his birds, dragons and other pieces of folk art. Look for sculptures along the highway that mark the entrance to the park.

Nearby is the town of Prairie du Sac. If you happen to be driving through the first weekend in September you can watch the annual **Cow Chip Throw** (☎ 608-643-4317; www.wiscowchip.com; admission free), where 800 competitors fling dried manure patties as far as the eye can see; the record is 248ft.

Baraboo, 40 miles northwest of Madison, was once the winter home of the Ringling Brothers Circus. **Circus World Museum** (☎ 608-356-8341, 866-693-1500; www.wisconsinhistory.org/circusworld; 550 Water St; adult/child 5-11 summer $15/8, winter $7/3.50; ☽ 9am-6pm summer, reduced hrs winter) preserves a nostalgic collection of wagons, posters and equipment from the touring big-top heyday. In summer, admission includes clowns, animals and acrobats doing the three-ring thing.

Continue north another 12 miles to the **Wisconsin Dells** (www.wisdells.com), a mega-center of kitschy diversions, including family theme parks, water-skiing thrill shows and super-minigolf courses. It's a jolting contrast to the natural appeal of the area with its scenic limestone formations carved by the Wisconsin River. To appreciate the original attraction, take a boat tour or walk the trails at Mirror Lake or Devil's Lake state parks.

experience the whole shebang for adult/child $26.50/15.50 (but it's a bit overwhelming, to be honest).

Spring Green has a B&B in town and half a dozen motels strung along Hwy 14, north of town. Small **Usonian Inn** (☎ 877-876-6426; www.uso nianinn.com; E 5116 Hwy 14; r incl breakfast $75-89; ❃ ✗) was designed by a Wright student; **Prairie House** (☎ 800-588-2088; www.theprairiehousemotel.com; E 4884 Hwy 14; r weekday/weekend $69/79) is larger, with a whirlpool and game room.

The **Spring Green General Store** (☎ 608-588-7070; 137 S Albany St; items $5-7; ☺ 9am-6pm Mon-Fri, 8am-6pm Sat, 8am-4pm Sun) serves sandwiches and earthy lunch specials.

The **American Players Theatre** (☎ 608-588-2361; www.playinthewoods.org) stages classical productions at an outdoor amphitheater by the Wisconsin River.

Monroe

It's cheese-making country around these parts, and Monroe is a fine place to start sniffing. Follow your nose to **Roth Käse** (☎ 608-328-2122; www.rothkase.com; 657 Second St; ☺ 9am-6pm Mon-Fri, to 5pm Sat, 10am-5pm Sun), which creates unusual varieties like 'buttermilk blue.' Buy it up at the onsite store, or watch 'em make it from the observation area (weekday mornings only).

For serious R&R, spend the night at **Inn Serendipity** (☎ 608-329-7056; www.innserendipity.com; 7843 County P; r incl breakfast $100-115) on a five-acre working organic farm in Browntown, just west of Monroe. This two-room B&B is about as green as it gets. It's powered by solar and wind systems, the owners compost all food waste, and they've built their bathroom using recycled windshield glass for the tile.

ALONG THE MISSISSIPPI RIVER

The Mississippi River forms most of Wisconsin's western border, and alongside it run some of the most scenic sections of the **Great River Rd** (www.wigreatriverroad.org) – the designated route that follows Old Man River from Minnesota to the Gulf of Mexico.

From Madison, head west on US 18. You'll hit the River Rd (aka Hwy 35) at **Prairie du Chien**. Founded in 1673 as a French fur trading post, the town's name quaintly honors the prairie dogs that once populated the area.

North of Prairie du Chien, the hilly riverside wends through the scene of the final battle in the bloody Black Hawk War. Historic markers tell part of the story, which finished at the Battle of Bad Ax when Native American men, women and children were massacred trying to flee across the Mississippi.

Upstream, **La Crosse** is a fine riverside town with a historic center nestling restaurants and pubs. Grandad Bluff offers grand views of the river. It's east of town along Main St (which becomes Bliss Rd); follow Bliss Rd up the hill and then turn right on Grandad Bluff Rd. For area information, stop by the **visitors center** (☎ 608-782-2366, 800-658-9424; www.explorelacrosse .com; 410 Veteran's Memorial Dr; ☺ 8am-5pm Mon-Fri, extended hrs summer). To bed down, try the friendly, English-owned **Guest House Motel** (☎ 608-784-8840, 800-274-6873; www.guesthousemotel.com; 810 S 4th St; r $60-100; ☒).

EASTERN WISCONSIN

Rocky, lighthouse-dotted Door County draws crowds in summer, while Green Bay draws crazed football fans in the freakin' freezing winter.

Green Bay

Founded in the 1660s as a fur-trading post, Green Bay boomed as a Lake Michigan port and later a terminus for Midwest railroads. Processing and packing agricultural products became a major industry, and gave name to the city's legendary pro football team: the Green Bay Packers. The franchise is unique as the only community-owned non-profit team in the NFL; perhaps pride in ownership is what makes the fans so die-hard (and wear foam rubber cheese wedges on their head).

The **visitors center** (☎ 920-494-9507, 888-867-3342; www.packercountry.com; 1901 S Oneida St; ☺ 8am-4:30pm Mon-Fri) is by the football stadium, just off Lombardi Ave, south of downtown. The town core is on the east side of the Fox River around Walnut St.

While tickets are nearly impossible to obtain, you can always get into the spirit by joining a pre-game tailgate party, where fans fire up grills and set up tables by their cars. The generous flow of alcohol has led to Green Bay's reputation as a 'drinking town with a football problem.' Or visit the **Green Bay Packer Hall of Fame** (☎ 920-569-7512; www.packers.com; Lambeau Field; adult/child 6-11 $10/5; ☺ 9am-6pm, hrs vary during home games), which is indeed packed with memorabilia. It has football movies and interactive exhibits, plus tours of the stadium.

Other sights of interest include the **National Railroad Museum** (☎ 920-437-7623; www.national

rrmuseum.org; 2285 S Broadway; adult/child 4-12 May-Sep $9/6.50, Oct-Apr $8/5; 9am-5pm Mon-Sat, 11am-5pm Sun), which features some of the biggest steam and diesel locomotives ever to haul freight into Green Bay's vast yards; train rides are offered in summer. The **Oneida Nation Museum** (920-869-2768; www.oneidanation.org; W 892 Cty Rd EE; adult/child $3/2; 9am-5pm Tue-Sat summer, 9am-5pm Tue-Fri winter), 7 miles west of downtown, outlines the matrilineal tribe's past and present.

Tidy, independent **Bay Motel** (920-494-3441; www.baymotelgreenbay.com; 1301 S Military Ave; r incl breakfast $45-75; wi-fi) is a mile from Lambeau Field.

Door County

With its rocky coastline, picturesque lighthouses, orchards and small 19th-century villages, you have to admit Door County is pretty damn lovely. The county is spread across a narrow peninsula jutting 60 miles into Lake Michigan. Despite considerable crowds in summer and increasing numbers of wealthy newcomers, development has remained essentially low-key and the atmosphere retains a certain highbrow gentility.

Visitors usually make a loop around the peninsula on its two highways. Hwy 57 runs beside Lake Michigan, and goes through Jacksonport and Bailey's Harbor. Hwy 42 borders Green Bay and passes through (from south to north) Egg Harbor, Fish Creek, Ephraim and Sister Bay. Gills Rock is perched at the peninsula's tip, decorated by a string of islands. No public buses serve the peninsula, and not much stays open from November to April.

The most attractive part of the loop begins at **Sturgeon Bay**, the peninsula's main town. As you enter it stop at the knowledgeable **Chamber of Commerce** (920-743-4456, 800-527-3529; www.doorcounty.com; 1015 Green Bay Rd; 8:30am-5pm Mon-Fri, 10am-4pm Sat & Sun mid-May–mid-Oct, reduced hrs rest of year); on the porch a kiosk with lodging information is accessible 24 hours a day .

The best accommodation choices are along the Green Bay shoreline. Prices listed are for July and August, the most expensive months; many places fill up early and have minimum-stay requirements. Camping and sunset-watching are available at **Peninsula State Park** (920-868-3258; campsites $10-12) by Fish Creek. Also in Fish Creek, **Julie's Park Café and Motel** (920-868-2999; www.juliesmotel.com; 4020 Hwy 42; r $79-120; meals $7-14; wi-fi) is tidy and well run. In Ephraim, **Trollhaugen Lodge** (800-854-4118;

www.trollhaugenlodge.com; 10176 Hwy 42; motel $79-110, B&B $89-149; wi-fi) is an excellent option; it's close to the action and has a hot tub.

Many restaurants have a 'fish boil,' a regional specialty started by Scandinavian lumberjacks, in which whitefish, potatoes and onions are cooked in a cauldron. It's sedate, until the chef douses the flames with kerosene, and then whoosh! A fireball creates the requisite 'boil over' (which gets rid of the fish oil), signaling dinner is ready. Finish with Door's famous cherry pie.

Summer Kitchen (920-854-2131; Hwy 42, Ephraim; mains $6-17; 8am-8:30pm) serves tasty breakfast, lunch and dinner. At **Shipwrecked** (920-868-2767; 7791 Egg Harbor Rd, Egg Harbor; mains $12-17; 11am-10pm) you can wash down a good dinner with the housemade brew; try the cheese curds. Also, sample the smoked fish available around Gills Rock.

From the tip of the peninsula, daily **ferries** (920-847-2546; www.wisferry.com; Northport Pier) go every half hour to **Washington Island** (round-trip adult/child 6-11/bike/car $10/5/4/24), which has 700 Scandinavian descendants, a couple of museums, beaches, bike rentals and carefree roads for cycling. Accommodations and camping are available. More remote is lovely **Rock Island**, a state park with no cars at all. It's a wonderful place for walking, swimming and camping. Get there via the eponymous **ferry** (920-535-0122), which departs Jackson Harbor on Washington Island (round-trip adult/child $9/5).

Returning on the peninsula's quiet east side, secluded **Newport State Park** offers trails, camping and solitude. **Whitefish Dunes State Park** has sandscapes and a wide beach (beware of riptides). At adjacent **Cave Point Park**, watch the waves explode into the caves beneath the shoreline cliffs.

TALK LIKE A LOCAL

Admit it: you're puzzled by how to pronounce town names like Prairie du Chien and Lac du Flambeau. Lucky for you, the website **www.misspronouncer.com** provides recordings of how to say it in Wisconsinese. The site covers 190 cities, 1260 towns and heaps of famous locals' names. Soon you'll be chattering on about football legend Brett Favre (that's *'farve'*) or your visit to Chequamegon (*'sheh wom again'*) with confidence.

NORTHERN WISCONSIN

The north is a thinly populated region of forests and lakes, appreciated for camping and fishing in summer, and skiing and snowmobiling in winter. Scenic Hwy 70 cuts east–west. The entire region has abundant mom-and-pop motels, resorts and rental cottages.

Northwoods & Lakelands

Nicolet National Forest is a vast, wooded district ideal for outdoor activities. The simple cross-roads of **Langlade** is a center for white-water river adventures. **Wolf River Guides** (☎ 715-882-3002; www.wolfriverguides.com) provides half-day kayak paddling classes followed by a half-day trip on the water (per person $110), while **Wolf River Lodge** (☎ 715-882-2182; www.wolfriverlodge .com; r incl breakfast $100) provides accommodation where you can dry off, get warm and celebrate your accomplishments in the onsite bar.

In winter, **Granite Peak Ski Resort** (☎ 715-845-2846; www.skigranitepeak.com; day pass adult/child $52/38) in **Wausau** perks up, offering 265 skiable acres and a 700ft vertical drop.

West on Hwy 70, **Chequamegon National Forest** offers exceptional mountain biking with 300 miles of off-road trails. Contact the **Chequamegon Area Mountain Bike Association** (☎ 715-798-3599; www.cambatrails.org) for trail maps and bike rental information. The season culminates in mid-September with the **Chequamegon Fat Tire Festival** (☎ 715-798-3594; www.cheqfattire.com), when 1700 strong-legged men and women peddle 40 grueling miles through the woods.

Apostle Islands

Wisconsin ends at the rugged, glaciated littoral of awesome Lake Superior, fringed by a sprinkling of unspoiled islands.

Access to the emerald Apostle Islands is from **Bayfield**, a humming resort town with narrow, hilly streets, Victorian-era buildings, lake vistas, apple orchards and not a fast-food restaurant in sight. The **Chamber of Commerce** (☎ 715-779-3335; www.bayfield.org; 42 Broad St; 8:30am-5pm Mon-Fri) has an attached visitors center, accessible at all times, with lodging information and a free phone. Storefront outfitters renting kayaks and bikes are easily found throughout town.

Bayfield has loads of B&Bs, cottages and other lodging, but reserve ahead in summer. Most rooms at **Seagull Bay Motel** (☎ 715-779-5558; www.seagullbay.com; cnr 7th St & Hwy 13; r summer $70-100, winter $40-70) have decks. **Artesian House**

SCENIC DRIVE: HWY 13

After departing Bayfield, Hwy 13 takes a fine route around the Lake Superior shore, past the Ojibwa community of **Red Cliff** and the Apostle Islands' mainland segment, which has a beach. Tiny **Cornucopia**, looking every bit like a seaside village, has great sunsets. The road runs on through a timeless countryside of forest and farm reaching US 2 for the final miles back to civilization at Superior.

(☎ 715-779-3338; www.artesianhouse.com; 84100 Hatchery Rd; r incl breakfast $115) is a four-room B&B with private bathrooms and a deck. **Old Rittenhouse Inn** (☎ 800-779-2129; www.rittenhouseinn.com; 301 Rittenhouse Ave; r $115-205) offers by far the classiest digs in town.

Kitschy, flamingo-themed **Maggie's** (☎ 715-779-5641; 257 Manypenny Ave; mains $7-16; 11:30am-9pm Sun-Thu, to 10pm Fri & Sat) is the place to sample local lake trout and whitefish; it serves pizzas and burgers, too.

The **Big Top Chautauqua** (☎ 888-244-8368; www .bigtop.org) is a major regional summer event with big-name concerts and musical theater; call for schedule and prices.

Before exploring the 21 islands of **Apostle Islands National Lakeshore**, drop by the **visitors center** (☎ 715-779-3397; www.nps.gov/apis; 410 Washington Ave, Bayfield; 8am-4:30pm daily Jun-Sep, 8am-4:30pm Mon-Fri Oct-May). Campers can pick up the required camping permit here (it costs $10 per night). The islands have no facilities, and walking is the only way to get around. Various companies offer seasonal charter, sailing and ferry trips to and around the islands, and kayaking is very popular. Try **Living Adventure** (☎ 715-779-9503; www.livingadventure.com; Hwy 13; half-day/full-day tour $55/93; Jun-Sep) for a guided paddle through arches and sea caves; beginners are welcome. If you prefer a motor to power your explorations instead of your arms, try **Apostle Islands Cruise Service** (☎ 715-779-3925; www.apostleisland.com; mid-May–mid-Oct). It departs at 10am from Bayfield's City Dock for a three-hour narrated trip past sea caves and lighthouses (adult/child $38/23). Other trips call at islands to drop off/pick up campers and their kayaks, which avoids the long, possibly rough paddle.

Inhabited **Madeline Island** (☎ 715-747-2801; www.madelineisland.com), a fine day trip, is also reached by **ferry** (☎ 715-747-2051; www.madferry .com) from Bayfield (round-trip adult/child/bi-cycle/car $10/5/5/22). Its walkable village of La Pointe has some mid-priced places to stay and restaurants for a nosh. Bus tours are available, and you can rent bikes and mopeds – everything is near the ferry dock. **Big Bay State Park** (☎ 715-747-6425; campsites $15-17, vehicle $10) has a beach and trails.

MINNESOTA

Is Minnesota really the land of 10,000 lakes, as so often advertised? You betcha. Actually, in typically modest style, the state has under-marketed itself – there are 11,842 lakes. Which is great news for travelers. Intrepid outdoors-folk can wet their paddles in the Boundary Waters, where nighttime brings a blanket of stars and lullaby of wolf howls. Those wanting to get further off the beaten path can journey to Voyageurs National Park, where there's more water than roadway. The scenic south-east flaunts eagles and historic B&Bs along the Mississippi River. If that all seems a bit too far-flung, stick to the Twin Cities of Min-neapolis and St Paul, where you can't swing a moose without hitting something cool or cultural. And for those looking for middle ground – ie a cross between the big city and the woods – the dramatic, freighter-filled port of Duluth beckons.

History

Timber was the territory's first boom industry, and soon water-powered sawmills arose at Minneapolis, St Paul and Stillwater. Wheat

---

MINNESOTA FACTS

Nicknames North Star State, Gopher State

Population 5.2 million

Area 86,940 sq miles

Capital city St Paul (population 275,150)

Sales Tax 6.5%

Birthplace of Author F Scott Fitzgerald (1896–1940), songwriter Bob Dylan (b 1941), filmmakers Joel Coen (b 1954) and Ethan Coen (b 1957)

Home of Funny accents, snowy weather, walleye fish

Famous for Introducing Spam, Lucky Charms cereal and Greyhound buses to the masses

Official bird Common loon

---

from the prairies also needed to be processed, so the first flour mills were built along the river in the 1820s.

The population boomed in the 1880s, with mass immigration (especially from Scandi-navia), development of the iron mines and expansion of the railroads. Since the 1920s depleted forests and larger farms have meant a declining rural population, but industry and urban areas have grown steadily.

Information

Minnesota highway conditions (☎ 800-542-0220; www.511mn.org)

Minnesota Office of Tourism (☎ 800-657-3700; www.exploreminnesota.com)

Minnesota state park information (☎ 888-646-6367; www.dnr.state.mn.us/state_parks) Park entry requires a vehicle permit (per day/year for residents & nonresidents $5/25). Campsites cost $11 to $23; reserva-tions accepted (☎ 866-857-2757; www.stayatmnparks .com; fee $8.50).

MINNEAPOLIS

Minneapolis is the artiest town on the prairie, with all the trimmings of progressive prosper-ity – a cache of coffee shops, organic and eth-nic eateries, swank art museums, and enough theaters to be nicknamed Mini-Apple (second only to the Big Apple, New York City). It's always happenin', even in winter.

But there's no attitude to go along with the abundance. It's the kind of place where home-less people are treated kindly at the coffee shops, where the buses are kept immaculately clean, and where the public workers tell every-one to 'Have a nice day,' rain or shine (or snow). No wonder the city recently topped the list as the most charitable place in America.

Orientation & Information

Downtown Minneapolis is a modern grid of glassy high-rise buildings, many linked by enclosed overhead walkways called 'skyways' (very welcome in winter). The Mississippi River flows northeast of downtown. Despite the name, Uptown is actually southwest of downtown, with Hennepin Ave its main axis. Minneapolis' twin city, St Paul, is 10 miles east.

BOOKSTORES

Booksmart (☎ 612-823-5612; 2914 Hennepin Ave S; ◷ 10am-midnight Mon-Sat, 11am-11pm Sun) In Uptown.

EMERGENCY & MEDICAL SERVICES

Fairview Health Services (☎ 612-273-6402; 2450 Riverside Ave)

Victim crisis line (☎ 612-340-5400)

Walgreens (☎ 612-377-3308; 2426 Hennepin Ave S; ⏰ 24hr)

INTERNET ACCESS

Many local coffee shops have free wi-fi, like Spyhouse Coffee (p628).

Minneapolis Public Library (☎ 612-630-6000; www .mplib.org; 300 Nicollet Mall; ⏰ 10am-8pm Tue & Thu, to 6pm Wed, Fri & Sat) Log on for free with a picture ID at this mod, fantastic-looking facility.

MEDIA & INTERNET RESOURCES

City Pages (www.citypages.com) Weekly entertainment freebie.

Pioneer Press (www.twincities.com) St Paul's daily.

Star Tribune (www.startribune.com) Minneapolis's daily.

Vita.MN (www.vita.mn) The *Star Tribune*'s weekly entertainment freebie.

KNOW-FM 91.1 broadcasts NPR. Community station KFAI-FM 90.3 provides eclectic music and talk.

MONEY

Wells Fargo Bank (☎ 612-667-7990; cnr 6th St S & Marquette Ave) Offers foreign exchange, as well as an ATM and regular bank services.

POST

Post office (☎ 800-275-8777; 100 1st St S)

TOURIST INFORMATION

Visitors Center (☎ 612-335-6000, 888-676-6757; www.minneapolis.org; 1301 2nd Ave S; ⏰ 8am-4:30pm Mon-Fri) In the Convention Center by the spiral staircase.

Sights & Activities

Most attractions are closed Monday; many stay open late Thursday.

DOWNTOWN & LORING PARK

Nicollet Mall is the pedestrian-friendly portion of Nicollet Ave in the heart of downtown, dense with stores, bars and restaurants. It's perhaps most famous as the spot where Mary Tyler Moore (of 70s TV fame) threw her hat into the air during the show's opening sequence. A cheesy **MTM statue** (8th St S & Nicollet Mall) depicts our girl doing just that.

The first-class, recently expanded **Walker Art Center** (☎ 612-375-7622; www.walkerart.org; 725 Vineland Pl; adult/child 12-18 $10/6, admission free Thu evening; ⏰ 11am-5pm Tue-Sun, to 9pm Thu & Fri) has a strong permanent collection of 20th-century art and photography, including big-name US painters and great US pop art.

Beside the Walker is the 7-acre **Minneapolis Sculpture Garden** (admission free; ⏰ 6am-midnight), studded with contemporary works, like the oft-photographed spoon and cherry. The garden is connected to attractive Loring Park by a sculptural pedestrian bridge over I-94.

RIVERFRONT DISTRICT

At the north edge of downtown at the foot of Portland Ave is the **St Anthony Falls Heritage Trail**, a recommended 2-mile path that provides both interesting history (markers dot the route) and the city's best access to the banks of the Mississippi River. View the cascading falls from the car-free **Stone Arch Bridge**. On the north side of the river, Main St SE has a stretch of redeveloped buildings housing restaurants and bars.

You can pick up a free trail map at the **Mill City Museum** (☎ 612-341-7555; www.millcitymuseum .org; 704 2nd St S; adult/child 6-17 $8/4; ⏰ 10am-5pm Tue-Sat, to 9pm Thu, noon-5pm Sun). To learn more about the era when Minneapolis led the world in flour milling, pay the admission price and descend the stairs. The building is actually a former mill, and the highlight is a ride inside an eight-story grain elevator ('the Flour Tower'). There are also Betty Crocker exhibits and a baking lab that gives out free samples. Honestly, the whole thing is a bit dull unless you're really into milling history. On Thursday evenings and Saturday mornings, the **Mill City Farmer's Market** (www .millcityfarmersmarket.org) takes place in the museum's attached train shed.

Definitely head next door to the cobalt-blue Guthrie Theater (p629) and make your way up to its **Endless Bridge** – a cantilevered walkway overlooking the river. You don't need a theater ticket – it's intended as a public space – though see a show if you can, as the Guthrie is one of the Midwest's finest companies. Next door is spiraling **Gold Medal Park**.

UNIVERSITY AREA

The **University of Minnesota**, by the river southeast of Minneapolis' center, is one of the USA's largest campuses, with over 50,000 students. Most of the campus is in the **East Bank** neighborhood. A uni highlight is the **Weisman Art Museum** (☎ 612-625-9494; www.weisman .umn.edu; 333 E River Rd; admission free; ⏰ 10am-5pm Tue-Fri, to 8pm Thu, 11am-5pm Sat & Sun), which occupies a swooping silver structure by architect Frank Gehry. Works inside include early 20th-century American paintings. **Dinkytown**, based at 14th Ave SE and 4th St SE, is dense with student cafés and bookshops. A small part of the university is on the **West Bank** of the Mississippi River, near the intersection of 4th St S and Riverside Ave. This area has a few restaurants, some student hangouts and a big Somali community.

UPTOWN, LYN-LAKE & WHITTIER

These three neighborhoods are south of downtown. The fabulous **Minneapolis Institute of Arts** (☎ 612-870-3131; www.artsmia.org; 2400 3rd Ave S; admission free; ⏰ 10am-5pm Tue-Sat, 10am-9pm Thu, 11am-5pm Sun) houses a veritable history of art. A new wing has enabled the museum to bring out its whopping modern and contemporary collection. The Prairie School and Asian galleries are also highlights.

Uptown, based around the intersection of Hennepin Ave S and Lake St, is a punk-yuppie collision of shops and restaurants that stays lively until late. **Lyn-Lake** abuts Uptown to the east and sports a similar urban-cool vibe; it's centered at Lyndale and Lake Sts (get the name?).

Uptown is a convenient jump-off point to the '**Chain of Lakes**' – ie Lake Calhoun, Lake of the Isles, Lake Harriet and Cedar Lake. It seems all of Minneapolis is out frolicking by the water – not surprising, really, since this is known as the 'city of lakes.' Paved cycling paths (which double as cross-country ski trails in winter) meander around the four lakes, where you can go boating in summer or ice-skating in winter. Rent bikes and blades at **Calhoun Rental** (☎ 612-827-8231; 1622 W Lake St; per hr $7.50; ⏰ 10am-6pm Mon-Thu, to 8pm Fri-Sun Apr-Oct) in Uptown; credit card and driver's license required. A few blocks west, the **Lake Calhoun kiosk** (☎ 612-823-5765; base of Lake St; per hr $15; ⏰ 10am-6pm late May-Aug, weekends only Sep & Oct) rents canoes, kayaks and paddleboats. Thomas Beach, also on Lake Calhoun, is popular for swimming.

Minneapolis for Children

Check the **Minneapolis-kids.com** (www.minneapolis -kids.org) website for the latest on kids' offerings. The local **Children's Theatre Company** (☎ 612-874-0400; www.childrenstheatre.org; 2400 3rd Ave S) is so good it has won a Tony award for 'outstanding regional theater.'

Note that many of the top sights for wee ones are in St Paul (p631), at the Mall of America (p632) and at Fort Snelling (p632). You'll also have to travel a ways to get to the respected **Minnesota Zoo** (☎ 952-431-9500; www.mnzoo.org; 13000 Zoo Blvd; adult/child 3-12 $12/7; ⏰ 9am-6pm summer, 9am-4pm winter), in suburban Apple Valley, 20 miles south of town. It has naturalistic habitats for its 400-plus species, with an emphasis on cold-climate creatures. Parking is $5. And if the rides at the Mall of America aren't enough, drive out to **Valleyfair** (☎ 952-445-7600; www.valleyfair.com; 1 Valleyfair Dr; adult/child $36/12; ⏰ from 10am daily Jun-Aug, weekends only May & Sep, closing times vary), a full-scale amusement park 25 miles southwest in Shakopee. Parking costs $9.

Festivals & Events

Minneapolis Aquatennial (☎ 612-376-7669; www .aquatennial.org; admission free) Ten days celebrating the ubiquitous lakes in mid-July.
Holidazzle (☎ 612-376-7669; www.holidazzle.com; admission free) Parades, lights and lots of good cheer downtown throughout December.

Gay & Lesbian Minneapolis

Minneapolis has the country's second-highest percentage of gay, lesbian, bisexual and transgender (GLBT) residents – only San Francisco has more – and the city enjoys strong GLBT rights. **Outfront Minnesota** (☎ 612-822-0127; www.out front.org) provides information on GLBT-friendly local businesses; check the website for bar and restaurant information. Or pick up the free, biweekly *Lavender* (www.lavendermagazine.com) magazine at coffee shops around town.

GREAT LAKES

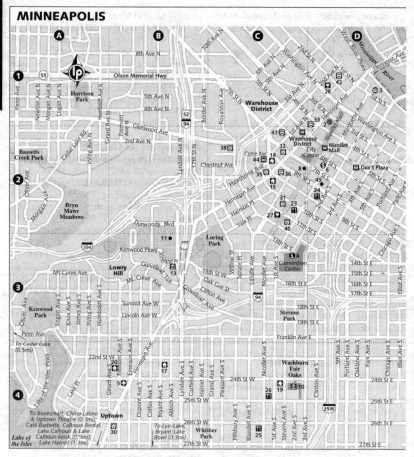

MINNEAPOLIS

For sleeping, the European-style **Hotel Amsterdam** (☎ 612-288-0459; www.gaympls.com/hotel; 828 Hennepin Ave S; r $55-70; 🖥) bills itself as 'the inn that's out.' Rooms are located above a busy bar; they are utilitarian but clean, and all share a bathroom.

For nightlife, **Gay Nineties** (☎ 612-333-7755; www.gay90s.com; 408 Hennepin Ave S, Minneapolis) has dancing, dining and drag shows that attract both a gay and a straight clientele.

The late-June **Pride Festival** (☎ 952-852-6100; www.tcpride.com; admission free), one of the USA's largest, draws about 400,000 revelers.

Sleeping

It's mostly ho-hum convention hotels downtown. B&Bs offer the best value – they've got budget prices but are solidly midrange in quality. The 13% tax is not included in the following prices.

BUDGET

Minneapolis International Hostel (☎ 612-522-5000; www.minneapolishostel.com; 2400 Stevens Ave S; dm/r $26/36; 🅿) This homey hostel beside the Institute of Arts has antique furniture, wood floors and fluffy quilts on the beds. Reservations recommended. Parking is $10.

MIDRANGE

All the B&Bs include breakfast.

Wales House (☎ 612-331-3931; www.waleshouse.com; 1115 5th St SE; r with/without shared bathroom $55/65; 🅿 ✖ 🐾 wi-fi) This cheery 10-bedroom B&B

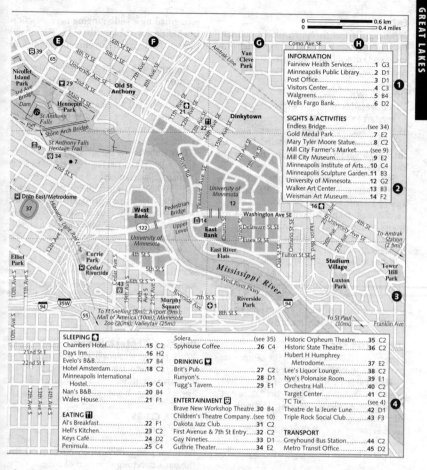

often houses scholars from the nearby University of Minnesota. Curl up with a book on the season-round porch or lounge by the fireplace. Two-night minimum stay required.

Nan's B&B (☎ 612-377-5118; 800-214-5118; zosel@mcad.edu; 2304 Fremont Ave S; r with shared bathroom $60-70; P ☒ ☒) Nan's three rooms near Lake of the Isles offer fresh-washed quilts on soft beds, sturdy wood furniture and the finest folksy hospitality the Midwest has to offer.

Days Inn (☎ 612-623-3999; www.daysinn.com; 2407 University Ave SE; r incl breakfast $69-129; P ☒ ☐ wi-fi) This slides toward the higher end for a Days Inn, catering to groups in town for special events. Rooms are standard but the amenities (free parking, breakfast and local shuttle bus) add value.

Evelo's B&B (☎ 612-374-9656; 2301 Bryant Ave S; r with shared bathroom $85; P ☒ ☒) Evelo's is in a quiet neighborhood between the Walker Art Center and Uptown. The Victorian home has beautiful woodwork, lots of windows and light, and three comfy rooms.

TOP END
Chambers Hotel (☎ 612-767-6900, 877-767-6990; www .chambersminneapolis.com; 901 Hennepin Ave S; r weekend/ weekday from $189/212; P ☒ wi-fi) It's an art gallery – no, it's a hotel. Actually, it's both, with 200 artworks (including Damien Hirst's floating bull's head at the front desk) spread throughout and 60 minimalist rooms with luxury touches like heated bathroom floors. There's also a majorly hip bar on the roof.

Eating

Minneapolis has shrugged off its culinary backwater status, and ripened into a rich dining scene known for its many restaurants that use locally sourced ingredients.

DOWNTOWN

Nicollet Mall is plastered with eateries.

Keys Café (☎ 612-339-6399; 821 Marquette Ave S; mains $5-11; ⏰ 6:30am-10pm Mon-Fri, 7am-10pm Sat, 8am-10pm Sun) Bustling Keys, a local chain, dishes up luscious breakfasts and sandwiches; try the caramel rolls or pies.

Solera (☎ 612-338-0062; 900 Hennepin Ave S; tapas $6-10; ⏰ 5pm-1am Mon-Thu, to 2am Fri & Sat, 11pm Sun, to 1am Mon-Thu, to 2am Fri & Sat) Curving booths, art deco furnishings and mosaics fill out Solera's three floors, where tapas and sangria (especially when served on the rooftop patio) keep the hipsters flocking in.

Hell's Kitchen (☎ 612-332-4700; 89 10th St S; mains $9-14; ⏰ 6:30am-2pm Mon-Fri, 8am-2pm Sat & Sun) Spirited chefs and naughty waitstaff bring you uniquely Minnesotan foods, like the walleye bacon-lettuce-tomato sandwich or bison burger, plus lemon-ricotta hotcakes for breakfast.

UNIVERSITY AREA

Low-priced eateries cluster in the campus area by Washington Ave and Oak St.

Al's Breakfast (☎ 612-331-9991; 413 14th Ave SE; mains $3-6; ⏰ 6am-1pm Mon-Sat, 9am-1pm Sun) It's the ultimate hole-in-the-wall: 15 stools at a tiny counter. Whenever a customer comes in, everyone picks up their plates and scoots down to make room for the newcomer. Fruit-full pancakes are the big crowd-pleaser.

UPTOWN, LYN-LAKE & WHITTIER

Nicollet Ave S between 14th and 29th Sts – otherwise known as 'Eat Street' – is lined with Vietnamese, Mexican and other ethnic restaurants.

Spyhouse Coffee (☎ 612-871-3177; 2451 Nicollet Ave S; items $2-5; ⏰ 6:30am-midnight Mon-Fri, 8am-midnight Sat & Sun; wi-fi) Join the artists, business types and cabbies who are here for the coffee and baked goods.

our pick **Bryant-Lake Bowl** (☎ 612-825-3737; 810 W Lake St; sandwiches $6-9, mains $9-15; ⏰ 8am-12:30am) The BLB has a divey interior (hey, it's a bowling alley, what do you expect?) but the food is high-class. Artisanal cheese plates, mock duck rolls, cornmeal-crusted walleye strips and organic oatmeal melt in the mouth, com-plemented by a wide-ranging beer selection (including several local brews). The onsite theater always has something intriguing and odd going on, too.

Peninsula (☎ 612-871-8282; 2608 Nicollet Ave S; mains $9-15; ⏰ 11am-10pm Sun-Thu, to 11pm Fri & Sat) Malaysian dishes, including *achat* (tangy vegetable salad in peanut dressing), red curry hot pot, spicy crab and fish in banana leaves, rock the palate in this contemporary restaurant.

Café Barbette (☎ 612-827-5710; 1600 W Lake St; mains $9-18; ⏰ 8am-1am Sun-Thu, 8am-2am Fri & Sat) Intimate, Parisian-style Barbette welcomes with low booths and art-filled walls. It's good for wine, cheese and appetizers with friends, or for a romantic dinner with a date, but whatever you do, don't miss the warm chocolate cake.

Chino Latino (☎ 612-824-7878; 2916 Hennepin Ave S; shared plates $18-29; ⏰ 4:30pm-1am Sun-Thu, to 2am Fri & Sat) This shiny, spangled place is the Uptown scenester hangout. The food is Latin-Asian fusion, with novelties such as a satay bar and the large, shared *pupu* (Polynesian-influenced appetizer) platter.

Drinking & Entertainment

With its large student population and thriving performing arts scene, Minneapolis has an active nightlife. Check *Vita.MN* and *City Pages* for current goings on.

BARS & CLUBS

Bars stay open until 2am.

Brit's Pub (☎ 612-332-3908; 1110 Nicollet Mall) A lawn bowling green carpets Brit's roof, and the bar's sweeping selection of Scotch, ports and beer is sure to unleash skills in the sport you never knew you had.

Runyon's (☎ 612-332-7158; 107 Washington Ave N) Runyon's is one of many busy places in the Warehouse District that pours a fine brew. Nosh on chicken wings, easily the best in town.

Tugg's Tavern (☎ 612-379-4404; 219 Main St SE) Tugg's draw is its swell outdoor patio on the Mississippi River's revitalized north-side strip.

LIVE MUSIC

Minneapolis rocks; everyone's in a band, it seems. Acts such as Prince and post-punk bands, like Hüsker Dü and the Replacements, cut their chops here.

First Avenue & 7th St Entry (☎ 612-338-8388; www
.first-ave.com; 701 1st Ave N) This is the bedrock of
Minneapolis' music scene, and it still pulls in
top bands and big crowds.

Triple Rock Social Club (☎ 612-333-7499; www.triple
rocksocialclub.com; 629 Cedar Ave) Triple Rock is a
popular punk/alternative club.

Lee's Liquor Lounge (☎ 612-338-9491; www.lees
liquorlounge.com; 101 Glenwood Ave) Rockabilly and
country-tinged alt bands twang here.

Dakota Jazz Club (☎ 612-332-1010; www.dakota
cooks.com; 1010 Nicollet Mall) The Dakota is a classy
venue that gets big-name jazz acts.

Nye's Polonaise Room (☎ 612-379-2021; 112 E Hennepin Ave) The World's Most Dangerous Polka
Band lets loose Thursday through Saturday.
It's smashing fun, and enhanced if you find
yourself an old-timer to twirl you around
the room.

THEATER & CULTURE

They don't call it Mini-Apple for nothing.
Check **TC Tix** (www.tctix.com) for same-day discounts; the purchase counter is in the visitor
information center (p624).

Brave New Workshop Theatre (☎ 612-332-6620;
www.bravenewworkshop.com; 2605 Hennepin Ave S) An
established venue for musical comedy, revue and satire.

Guthrie Theater (☎ 612-377-2224; www.guthrie
theater.org; 818 2nd St S) Minneapolis' top gun theater
troupe, with the jumbo facility to prove it.

Historic Orpheum Theatre (☎ 612-339-7007; www
.hennepintheatredistrict.org; 910 Hennepin Ave S) The
main venue for Broadway shows and touring acts.

Historic State Theatre (☎ 612-339-7007; www
.hennepintheatredistrict.org; 805 Hennepin Ave S) Another
Broadway show venue.

Orchestra Hall (☎ 612-371-5656; www.minnesota
orchestra.org; 1111 Nicollet Mall) Superb acoustics for
recitals and concerts by the acclaimed Minnesota Symphony Orchestra.

Theatre de la Jeune Lune (☎ 612-333-6200; www
.jeunelune.org; 105 1st St N) Features experimental
French-American collaborations.

Uptown Theatre (☎ 612-825-6006; 2906 Hennepin
Ave S) Art-house movies screen at this old theater.

SPORTS

Minnesotans love their sports teams. Note
that ice hockey (p631) happens in St Paul.

Hubert H Humphrey Metrodome (900 5th St S)
Both the Vikings (☎ 612-338-4537; www
.vikings.com) pro football team and the Twins
(☎ 612-338-9467; www.minnesotatwins.com)
pro baseball team play in the Metrodome.

Target Center (☎ 612-337-3865; www.nba.com/timber
wolves; 600 1st Ave N) This is where the Timber-
wolves pro basketball team lays 'em up.

Getting There & Around

The **Minneapolis-St Paul International Airport** (MSP;
☎ 612-726-5555; www.mspairport.com) is between the
two cities to the south. It's the home of Northwest Airlines, which operates several direct
flights to/from Europe.

The cheapest way to Minneapolis is via
the Hiawatha light-rail line ($1.50 to $2, 25
minutes). To reach St Paul, take bus No 54
($2, 25 minutes).

Greyhound (☎ 612-371-3325; www.greyhound.com;
950 Hawthorne Ave) runs frequent buses to Milwaukee ($52 to $65, seven hours), Chicago
($61 to $70, nine hours) and Duluth ($25 to
$35, three hours). **Megabus** (☎ 877-462-6342; www
.megabus.com/us) runs express to Milwaukee and
Chicago, often for lower fares. It departs from
both downtown and the university; check the
website for exact locations.

National car-rental agencies have offices at
the airport and around town. The Transportation chapter (p1144) has contact details.

Metro Transit (☎ 612-373-3333; www.metrotransit
.org) runs frequent, spic-n-span buses ($1.50
to $2) throughout the area, as well as the ex-
cellent Hiawatha light-rail line (same fare)
between downtown and the Mall of America.
Express bus No 94 connects Minneapolis to
St Paul; it departs from the corner of 6th St N
and Hennepin Ave A day pass ($6) is available;
pick it up with route maps at the downtown
Metro Transit Office (719 Marquette Ave S; ⌚ 7:30am-
5:30pm Mon-Fri).

The **Amtrak station** (☎ 651-644-6012; 730 Transfer
Rd), off University Ave SE, is between Minneapolis and St Paul. Trains go daily to Chicago ($59 to $105, eight hours) and Seattle
($205 to $270, 37 hours). The ride east to
La Crosse, Wisconsin, is beautiful, skirting
the Mississippi River and offering multiple
eagle sightings.

For cab service, call **Yellow Taxi** (☎ 612-
824-4444).

ST PAUL

Smaller and quieter than its twin city Minneapolis, St Paul has retained more of a historic
character. Walk through F Scott Fitzgerald's
old stomping grounds, trek the trails along
the mighty Mississippi River, or why not go
curling?

The **visitors center** (☎ 651-265-4900, 800-627-6101; www.visitstpaul.com; 175 W Kellogg Blvd, Suite 502; ⏰ 8am-4:30pm Mon-Fri), in the RiverCentre, makes a good first stop, not only for maps but also for the free 'fun card' that provides discounts at attractions.

Sights & Activities

The **Cathedral of St Paul** (☎ 651-228-1766; www.cathedralsaintpaul.org; 239 Selby Ave; admission free; ⏰ 7:30am-6pm Mon-Thu, to 4pm Fri, 8am-8pm Sat, 8am-6pm Sun) presides over the city from its hilltop perch and marks the attractive **Summit-Selby** neighborhood. This wealthy 19th-century district, now ethnically mixed, is well worth an afternoon stroll. Follow **Summit Ave**, which has a fine string of Victorian houses, including the palatial **James J Hill House** (☎ 651-297-2555; www.mnhs.org/hillhouse; 240 Summit Ave; adult/child 6-17 $8/4; ⏰ 10am-3:30pm Wed-Sat, 1-3:30pm Sun), a railroad magnate's former mansion, now open for tours.

Writer F Scott Fitzgerald once lived at the privately owned **599 Summit Avenue**, and authors Garrison Keillor and Sinclair Lewis have also called the area home. Literature buffs can pick up the *Fitzgerald Homes and Haunts* map at the St Paul visitors center.

A visit to the privately owned **Julian H Sleeper House** (☎ 651-225-1505; www.julianhsleeperhouse.com; 66 S St Albans St; tours $7; ⏰ by appt) lets you see how the upper crust really lived. The place is filled with chandeliers, oriental carpets and decorative arts from the late 19th century. The owner is a colorful storyteller and will show you his antique postcard collection and other weird stuff.

Downtown, the turreted 1902 Landmark Center contains several small museums. The winner is the **Schubert Club Museum** (☎ 651-292-3267; www.schubert.org; basement, 75 W 5th St; admission free; ⏰ 11am-3pm Mon-Fri, 1-5pm Sun), which has a brilliant collection of old pianos and harpsichords, some tickled by Mozart, Beethoven and the like. A woodturning museum (it's a decorative form of woodworking) and a WWII museum are also inside.

The **Science Museum of Minnesota** (☎ 651-221-9444; www.smm.org; 120 W Kellogg Blvd; for exhibits only adult/child 4-12 $10/7.50; ⏰ 8:30am-10pm Mon-Sat, to 7pm Sun) has the usual hands-on kids' exhibits and Omnimax theater. Adults will be enter-

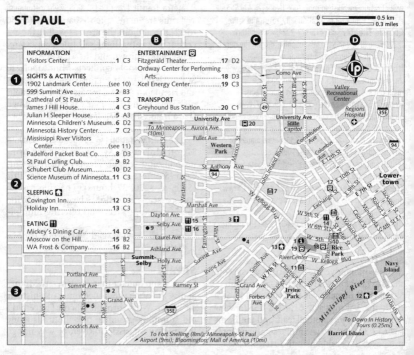

ST PAUL

INFORMATION	
Visitors Center	1 C3

SIGHTS & ACTIVITIES	
1902 Landmark Center	(see 10)
599 Summit Ave	2 B3
Cathedral of St Paul	3 C2
James J Hill House	4 C3
Julian H Sleeper House	5 A3
Minnesota Children's Museum	6 D2
Minnesota History Center	7 C2
Mississippi River Visitors Center	(see 11)
Padelford Packet Boat Co	8 D3
St Paul Curling Club	9 B2
Schubert Club Museum	10 D2
Science Museum of Minnesota	11 C3

SLEEPING	
Covington Inn	12 D3
Holiday Inn	13 C3

EATING	
Mickey's Dining Car	14 D2
Moscow on the Hill	15 B2
WA Frost & Company	16 B2

ENTERTAINMENT	
Fitzgerald Theater	17 D2
Ordway Center for Performing Arts	18 D3
Xcel Energy Center	19 C3

TRANSPORT	
Greyhound Bus Station	20 C1

tained by the wacky quackery of the fourth floor's 'questionable medical devices.' In the museum lobby is the National Park Service's **Mississippi River Visitors Center** (☎ 651-293-0200; www.nps.gov/miss; ⏰ 9:30am-5:30pm, noon-5pm Sun). Definitely stop by to pick up trail maps and see what sort of free ranger-guided walks and bike rides are going on.

Revitalized **Harriet Island**, running south off Wabasha St, is a lovely place to meander; it has a park, river walk, concert stages and fishing dock. **Padelford Packet Boat Co** (☎ 651-227-1100; www.riverrides.com; adult/child five to 12 $15/7.50) operates 1½-hour paddleboat tours from the dock. Tours begin at noon and 2pm from June to August every day except Monday, and at 2pm Saturday and Sunday only in May and September.

From November through March stop in and watch the action at the **St Paul Curling Club** (☎ 651-224-7408; www.stpaulcurlingclub.org; 470 Selby Ave). For those uninitiated in northern ways, curling is a winter sport that involves sliding a hubcap-sized 'puck' down the ice toward a bull's-eye.

St Paul for Children

The **Minnesota Children's Museum** (☎ 651-225-6000; www.mcm.org; 10 W 7th St; admission $8; ⏰ 9am-5pm Tue-Sun, to 8pm Thu, open Mon Jun-Aug) has the usual gamut of hands-on activities, as well as a giant anthill to burrow through, and the 'One World' intercultural community where kids can shop and vote.

The **Minnesota History Center** (☎ 651-296-6126; www.mnhs.org/historycenter; 345 W Kellogg Blvd; adult/child 6-17 $8/4; ⏰ 10am-8pm Tue, 10am-5pm Wed-Sat, noon-5pm Sun, open Mon Jun-Aug) educates with its 'A to Z' treasure hunt and climbable boxcar, while the Science Museum of Minnesota (opposite) pleases kids with its laser show and Omnimax.

Tours

Down In History Tours (☎ 651-292-1220; www.wabashastreetcaves.com; 215 S Wabasha St) One tour walks you through St Paul's underground caves ($5), which gangsters once used as a speakeasy. The company offers several other fun, offbeat tours, too. Call for the tour schedule.

Festivals & Events

St Paul Winter Carnival (☎ 651-223-4700; www.winter-carnival.com; admission varies depending on event) Ten days of ice sculptures, ice skating and ice fishing in January.

Sleeping

You'll find more options (and usually better value) in Minneapolis.

Holiday Inn (☎ 651-225-1515; www.holiday-inn.com/stpaulmn; 175 W 7th St; r $99-159; P ⊠ ☎) The rooms are the usual decent quality you expect from the Holiday Inn chain; the perks are the location adjacent to the RiverCentre, a small pool and an onsite Irish pub. Parking is $14.

Covington Inn (☎ 651-292-1411; www.covingtoninn.com; 100 Harriet Island Rd; r $150-235; P ⊠) This four-room, Harriet Island B&B is on a tugboat floating in the Mississippi River; watch the river traffic glide by while sipping your morning coffee.

Eating & Drinking

Grand Ave between Dale and Victoria Sts is a worthy browse, with Algerian, Nepalese, Japanese and other eateries in close proximity.

Mickey's Dining Car (☎ 651-222-5633; 36 W 7th St; mains $3-7; ⏰ 24hr) Mickey's is a downtown classic, the kind of place where the friendly waitress calls you 'honey' and satisfied regulars line the bar with their coffee cups and newspapers. The food has timeless appeal, too: burgers, malts and apple pie.

Moscow on the Hill (☎ 651-291-1236; 371 Selby Ave; mains $13-20; ⏰ 5:30-10pm Mon-Thu, to 11pm Fri, 4:30-11pm Sat, 4:30-10pm Sun) On cold gray days, come to Moscow for Eastern European comfort food (ie stews). Start with a traditional shot of Stoli and a little sweet-pickle garnish.

WA Frost & Company (☎ 651-224-5715; 374 Selby Ave; sandwiches $8-10, mains $16-28; ⏰ 11am-10pm Sun-Thu, to 11pm Fri & Sat) Frost's tree-shaded, ivy-covered, twinkling-light patio is right out of a Fitzgerald novel, perfect for a glass of wine, beer or gin. The restaurant locally sources many ingredients for dishes like the artisanal cheese plate, smoked tofu strudel and cardamom-glazed duck.

Entertainment

Fitzgerald Theater (☎ 651-290-1221; www.fitzgeraldtheater.org; 10 E Exchange St) Where Garrison Keillor tapes his *Prairie Home Companion* radio show.

Ordway Center for Performing Arts (☎ 651-224-4222; www.ordway.org; 345 Washington St) Chamber music and the Minnesota Opera fill the hall here.

Xcel Energy Center (☎ 651-222-9453; www.wild.com; Kellogg Blvd) The Wild pro hockey team skates at Xcel.

Getting There & Around

St Paul is served by the same transit systems as Minneapolis; see p629 for details. Greyhound bus routes serving Minneapolis usually stop at the **St Paul station** (☎ 651-222-0507; 166 W University Ave), too.

AROUND MINNEAPOLIS–ST PAUL
Mall of America

In Bloomington, the **Mall of America** (☎ 952-883-8800; www.mallofamerica.com; off I-494 at 24th Ave; ◷ 10am-9:30pm Mon-Sat, 11am-7pm Sun) is the USA's largest shopping center. Yes, it's just a mall, filled with the usual stores, movie theaters and eateries. But there's also an **amusement park** (☎ 952-883-8600; www.theparkatmoa.com) inside that features 30 rides, including a little roller coaster. To walk through will cost you nothing; a one-day, unlimited-ride wristband is $25, or you can pay for rides individually ($2.50 to $5). What's more, the state's largest aquarium – **Underwater Adventures** (☎ 952-883-0202; www.sharky.tv; adult/child 3-12 $17/10) – where children can touch sharks and stingrays, is in the mall. The Hiawatha light-rail runs from downtown to the mall.

Fort Snelling

East of the mall, **Fort Snelling** (☎ 612-726-1171; www.mnhs.org/fortsnelling; cnr Hwys 5 & 55; adult/child 6-17 $8/4; ◷ 10am-5pm Mon-Sat, noon-5pm Sun Jun-Aug, Sat & Sun only May, Sep & Oct) is the state's oldest structure, established in the early 19th century as a frontier outpost in the remote Northwest Territory. Guides in period dress show restored buildings and re-enact pioneer life.

SOUTHERN MINNESOTA

Some of the scenic southeast can be seen on short drives from the Twin Cities. Better is a loop of a few days' duration, following the rivers and stopping in some of the historic towns and state parks.

A few miles east of St Paul, the **St Croix River** forms the border with Wisconsin. Northeast of the city along US 61, then east on US 8, attractive Taylors Falls marks the upper limit of navigation. Take a walk along the gorge in Interstate Park. Due east of St Paul, on Hwy 36, touristy **Stillwater**, on the lower St Croix, is an old logging town with restored 19th-century buildings, river cruises and antique stores. It's also an official 'booktown,' an honor bestowed upon a few small towns worldwide that possess an extraordinary number of antiquarian

bookshops. What's more, the town is filled with classy historic B&Bs; the **chamber of commerce** (☎ 651-439-4001; www.ilovestillwater.com) provides listings online and in its print guide.

Larger **Red Wing**, to the south on US 61, is a similar but less-interesting restored town, though it does offer its famous Red Wing Shoes (actually more like sturdy boots) and salt glaze pottery.

The prettiest part of the **Mississippi Valley** area begins south of here. To drive it and see the best bits, you'll need to flip-flop back and forth between Minnesota and Wisconsin.

So from Red Wing, cross the river on US 63. **Maiden Rock**, on Wisconsin Hwy 35 (aka the Great River Rd), is downstream and offers views from its 400ft Indian-legend namesake. A bit further south, a great stretch of Hwy 35 edges beside the bluffs around **Stockholm** (population 90).

Continuing south, cross back over the river to **Wabasha** in Minnesota, which has a historic downtown and large population of bald eagles that congregate in winter. To learn more, visit the **National Eagle Center** (☎ 651-565-4989; www.nationaleaglecenter.org; 50 Pembroke Ave; adult/child $4/2; ◷ 10am-5pm). To really soak up Old Man River, spend the night at **Anderson House** (☎ 651-565-2500; www.historicandersonhouse.com; 333 Main St W; r incl breakfast $69-169). Not only does this grand old hotel have river views, you can also reserve one of its five cats for the night (no extra charge; and allergy sufferers fear not, the cats are only allowed in certain rooms). **Rivertown Café** (☎ 651-565-2202; 119 Pembroke St; dinners from $7; ◷ 7:30am-2pm Mon-Fri, to 8pm Sat, to 3pm Sun) provides a taste of small-town America.

On the Wisconsin side again, Hwy 35 is scenic heading south to **Alma**, offering superlative views from Buena Vista Park. Cross back to Minnesota further downstream at **Winona**. This former port offers river cruises from Levee Park downtown. Landlubbers can enjoy river views from Garvin Heights Park, with eagle sightings an added bonus in winter.

Inland and south, the Bluff Country is dotted with limestone bluffs, southeast Minnesota's main geological feature. **Lanesboro** is a gem and acts as an activity center. Cycling on rails-to-trails and canoeing are popular. Seven miles westward on County Rd 8 (call for directions) is **Old Barn Resort** (☎ 507-467-2512; www.barnresort.com; dm/r $23/44, campsite/RV site $24/34; ◷ Apr–mid-Nov; 🍴), a pastoral hostel cum campground/restaurant/outfitter. **Harmony**, south of Lanesboro, is the center of an Amish community, and another welcoming town.

Head north on US 52 to **Rochester**, home of the famed **Mayo Clinic** (☎ 507-284-2511; 200 1st St SW), which attracts medical patients and practitioners from around the world. Free morning tours (at 10am weekdays) and a film outline the Mayo brothers' story and describe how the clinic developed its cutting-edge reputation.

NORTHERN MINNESOTA
Duluth
At the westernmost end of the Great Lakes, Duluth (with its neighbor, Superior, Wisconsin) is one of the busiest ports in the country, sporting over 40 miles of wharf and waterfront. The town's dramatic location spliced into a cliff makes it a fab place to see changeable Lake Superior in action. One minute it's shimmering like a cut diamond, the next it's sending off ferocious, ice-capped waves. Attractions here naturally revolve around the water.

There is a **visitors center** (☎ 218-722-6024, 800-438-5884; www.visitduluth.com; 350 Harbor Dr; ⏰ 11am-7pm Sun-Fri, 9am-7pm Sat mid-Jun–Aug, reduced hrs mid-May–mid-Jun & Sep–mid-Oct) in the Duluth Entertainment Convention Center (DECC), opposite the Vista dock.

SIGHTS & ACTIVITIES
The waterfront area is distinctive; mosey along the Lakewalk trail and the Canal Park/Lake St District. Look for the Aerial Lift Bridge, which rises to let ships into the port. About a thousand ships a year pass through here. Check the computer screens outside the **Maritime Visitors Center** (☎ 218-720-5260; www.lsmma.com; 600 Lake Ave S; admission free; ⏰ 10am-9pm Jun-Aug, reduced hrs Sep-May) to learn when the big ones come and go. The first-rate center also has exhibits on Great Lakes shipping and shipwrecks.

To continue the nautical theme, walk the **William A Irvin** (☎ 218-722-7876; www.williamairvin.com; 350 Harbor Dr; adult/child $9/free; ⏰ 9am-6pm Jun-Aug, 10am-4pm May, Sep & Oct), a 610ft Great Lakes freighter. The interesting hour-long tour also includes a look aboard a Coastguard ice cutter.

The impressive **Great Lakes Aquarium** (☎ 218-740-3474; www.glaquarium.org; 353 Harbor Dr; adult/child 3-11 $13/7; ⏰ 10am-6pm May-Nov, to 5pm Dec-Apr) is one of the country's few freshwater aquariums. Highlights include the daily stingray feedings at 1pm, and the otter tanks.

The 1½-hour harbor cruises from **Vista Fleet** (☎ 218-722-6218; www.vistafleet.com; 323 Harbor Dr; adult/child $12/6; ⏰ mid-May–Oct) will get you out on the water. Or do it yourself by paddling a kayak with **Midnight Sun Adventure Company** (☎ 218-727-1330; www.midnightsunsports.com; 100 Lake Place Dr; 2½-hr tour $40). It also offers rock climbing, snowshoe and ski tours; beginners are welcome for all activities.

Skiing and snowboarding are big pastimes come winter, and **Spirit Mountain** (☎ 218-628-2891; www.spiritmt.com; 9500 Spirit Mountain Pl; per day adult/child 7-12 $45/35; ⏰ 10am-9pm Mon-Fri, 9am-9pm Sat & Sun mid-Nov–Mar), 10 miles south of Duluth, is the place to go; rentals available.

For a spectacular view of the city and harbor, climb the rock tower in **Enger Park** (Skyline Pkwy), located by the Enger Park Golf Course.

Finally, it's not every town where you can visit a paper mill, so take advantage of the opportunity in Duluth at **Stora Enso Paper Mills** (☎ 218-722-6024; 100 N Central Ave; admission free). It offers free tours on Monday, Tuesday and Friday from June to August; get tickets at the visitors center (left).

SLEEPING & EATING
Duluth has several B&Bs; rooms cost at least $100 in the summer. Check **Duluth Historic Inns** (www.duluthbandb.com) for listings. The town's accommodations fill up fast in summer, which may mean you'll have to try your luck across the border in Superior, Wisconsin (where it's cheaper, too). Note most restaurants and bars reduce their hours in winter.

Spirit Mountain (☎ 218-310-0833; www.spiritmt .com; 9500 Spirit Mountain Pl; campsites $15-25) Camping is available at Spirit Mountain, 10 miles south of town, where the best sites are the walk-ins.

WHAT THE...?

Lookin' for a little sweet pork magic? Hop on I-90 heading southwest from Rochester and pull off in Austin. Here, friends, lies the **Spam Museum** (☎ 800-588-7726; www.spam .com; 1101 N Main St; admission free; ⏰ 10am-5pm Mon-Sat, noon-4pm Sun May-Aug, closed Mon Sep-Apr), an entire institution devoted to the peculiar, revered tins of meat. Who knew canned hog could be so much fun? This place is, quite simply, fantastic.

Voyageur Lakewalk Inn (☎ 218-722-3911, 800-258-3911; www.voyageurlakewalkinn.com; 333 E Superior St; s/d peak weekends $69/74; wi-fi) Right downtown with rooftop views, Voyageur Lakewalk Inn is a real find with cozy rooms.

Willard Munger Inn (☎ 218-624-7408, 800-982-2453; www.mungerinn.com; 7408 Grand Ave; r peak weekends $70-111; wi-fi) Family-owned Munger Inn offers a good variety of rooms (budget to Jacuzzi suites), along with perks for outdoor enthusiasts such as hiking and biking trails right outside the door, free use of bikes and kayaks and a fire pit. It's near Spirit Mountain.

The Canal Park waterfront area has eateries of all price ranges in restored commercial spaces. In the **DeWitt-Seitz Marketplace** (394 Lake Ave S), **Amazing Grace** (☎ 218-723-0075; sandwiches $3-7; ☼ 6am-11pm) serves sandwiches in a comfortable café with folk music some evenings, while **Taste of Saigon** (☎ 218-727-1598; mains $6-10; ☼ 11am-8:30pm Sun-Thu, to 9:30pm Fri & Sat) creates scrumptious Vietnamese meals, including vegetarian dishes like mock duck.

Fully licensed **Pizza Luce** (☎ 218-727-7400; 11 E Superior St; large pizza $20; ☼ 11-2am Sun-Thu, to 3am Fri & Sat) is renowned for its gourmet pizzas, vegetarian options and late-night vibe. It's also plugged into the local music scene and hosts bands.

GETTING THERE & AROUND
Greyhound (☎ 218-722-5591; 4426 Grand Ave) has a couple of buses daily to Minneapolis ($25 to $35, three hours) and Milwaukee ($50 to $85, 12 hours).

North Shore
Heading northeast, Hwy 61 is a wonderfully scenic strip of pavement along Lake Superior's shore. On its way to the Canadian border, the route passes numerous state parks, waterfalls, hiking trails (notably the long-distance Superior Hiking Trail) and low-key towns. Lots of weekend, summer and fall traffic make reservations essential.

Two Harbors has a museum, lighthouse and B&B. Actually, the latter two are one and the same, with the **Lighthouse B&B** (☎ 218-834-4814, 888-832-5606; www.lighthousebb.org; r incl breakfast $125-145) being a unique place to spend the night if you can snag one of its four rooms. Just beyond town is the **Houle Information Center** (☎ 800-777-7384; www.twoharborschamber.com; 1330 Hwy 61; ☼ 9am-5pm Mon-Fri, to 6pm Sat, 10am-5pm Sun), with area information.

Route highlights north of Two Harbors are Gooseberry Falls, Split Rock Lighthouse and Palisade Head. About 110 miles from Duluth, agreeable little **Grand Marais**, a burgeoning arts town, is a good base for exploring Superior National Forest, Boundary Waters Canoe Area Wilderness (see below) and the rest of the region. For information on the Boundary Waters, visit the **Gunflint Ranger Station** (☎ 218-387-1750; ☼ 7am-5pm May-Sep), just south of town. The **visitors center** (☎ 218-387-2524; www.grandmarais.com; 13 N Broadway St; ☼ 9am-5pm Mon-Sat Jul-Sep, reduced hrs rest of year) is also a good resource.

Lodging options include camping, resorts and motels, like the **Harbor Inn** (☎ 218-387-1191; www.bytheharbor.com; 207 Wisconsin St; r $95-135). **Sven and Ole's** (☎ 218-387-1713; 7 Wisconsin St; sandwiches $3-7; ☼ 11am-9pm) is nearby for sandwiches; pizza and beer are at the attached Pickled Herring Pub.

Hwy 61 continues to **Grand Portage National Monument**, beside Canada, where the early voyageurs had to carry their canoes around the Pigeon River rapids. This was the center of a far-flung trading empire, and the reconstructed 1788 trading post is well worth seeing. **Isle Royale National Park** in Lake Superior is reached by daily **ferries** (☎ 218-475-0024; www.isleroyaleboats.com; one-way adult/child 4-11 $57/43) from May to October. (The park also is accessible from Michigan; see p612.)

Boundary Waters
From Two Harbors, Hwy 2 runs inland to the legendary **Boundary Waters Canoe Area Wilderness (BWCAW)**. This pristine region has more than a thousand lakes and streams in which to dip a paddle. It's possible to go just for the day, but most people opt for at least one night of camping. If you're willing to dig in and canoe for a while, you'll lose the crowds. Camping then becomes a wonderfully remote experience where it will be you, the howling wolves, the moose who's nuzzling the tent and a sky full of stars. Beginners are welcome, and everyone can get set up with gear from local lodges and outfitters. **Permits** (☎ 877-550-6777; www.bwcaw.org; adult/child under 18 $10/5, plus $12 reservation fee) are required for overnight stays. Day permits, though free, are also required; call **Superior National Forest** (☎ 218-626-4300) for details. Try to plan ahead, if possible, as permits are quota-restricted and sometimes run out.

Many argue the best BWCAW access is via the engaging town of **Ely**, northeast of the Iron Range area, which has accommodations, restaurants and scores of outfitters. The **Chamber of Commerce** (☎ 800-777-7281; www.ely.org; 1600 E Sheridan St; ♾ 9am-5pm Mon-Fri) has general information and accommodation assistance. Don't miss the **International Wolf Center** (☎ 218-365-4695; www.wolf.org; 1369 Hwy 169; adult/child 3-12 $7.50/4; ♾ 9am-6pm mid-Jun–early Sep, reduced hrs rest of year), which offers intriguing exhibits and wolf-viewing trips. Also in the Wolf Center is **Kawishiwi Wilderness Station** (☎ 218-365-7561; ♾ 7am-5:30pm May-Aug, 8:30am-4:30pm Sep), which offers expert camping and canoeing details, trip suggestions and required permits.

Iron Range District

An area of red-tinged scrubby hills rather than mountains, Minnesota's Iron Range District consists of the Mesabi and Vermilion Ranges, running north and south of Hwy 169 from roughly Grand Rapids northeast to Ely. Iron was discovered here in the 1850s, and at one time more than three-quarters of the nation's iron ore was extracted from these vast open-pit mines. Visitors can see working mines and the terrain's sparse, raw beauty all along Hwy 169.

In **Calumet**, a perfect introduction is the **Hill Annex Mine State Park** (☎ 218-247-7215; 880 Gary St; open-pit tours adult/child 5-12 $9/6; ♾ 9am-4pm Mon-Thu, 9am-5pm Fri-Sun), with its open-pit tours and exhibit center; tours are held in summertime only, from Friday to Sunday at 10am, 12:30pm and 3pm.

There's an even bigger pit in **Hibbing**, where a must-see **viewpoint** (admission free; ♾ 9am-6pm mid-May–mid-Sep) north of town overlooks the 3-mile-long Hull-Rust Mahoning Mine. Bob Dylan lived at 2425 E 7th Ave as a boy and teenager; the **Hibbing Public Library** (☎ 218-262-1038; www.hibbing.lib.mn.us; 2020 E 5th Ave; ♾ 9am-8pm

Mon-Thu, to 5pm Fri & Sat, closed Sat in summer) has well-done Dylan displays and a free walking tour map that takes you past various sites like the place where Bobby had his bar mitzvah. **Zimmy's** (☎ 218-262-6145; 531 E Howard St; sandwiches $6-8; ♾ 11-1am) has more memorabilia, plus drinks and pub grub. For a bed, try **Hibbing Park Hotel** (☎ 218-262-3481; www.hibbingparkhotel.com; 1402 E Howard St; r $72-88; 🐾).

Chisholm has **Ironworld Discovery Center** (☎ 218-254-7959; www.ironworld.com; Hwy 169; adult/child 6-18 $8/6; ♾ 10am-5pm Tue-Sun, to 9pm Thu), a theme park featuring open-pit mine tours and area ethnic displays.

Further east is **Virginia**, with more mine sites plus a giant loon, Minnesota's state bird. The **Pine View Inn Motel** (☎ 218-741-8918; www.pineviewinnmotel.com; 903 N 17th St; s/d $45/59) could be the cleanest in the state. The Virginia area has the Range's best restaurant selection. The **Whistling Bird Café** (☎ 218-741-7544; 101 N Broadway Ave; ♾ 4-9pm Sun-Thu, to 10pm Fri & Sat), a few miles south in Gilbert, serves Jamaican food.

Soudan has the area's only **underground mine** (☎ 218-753-2245; www.soudan.umn.edu; 1379 Stuntz Bay Rd; adult/child 5-12 $10/6; ♾ 10am-4pm late May-early Sep) available for touring; wear warm clothes.

Voyageurs National Park

In the 17th century French Canadian fur traders, or voyageurs, began exploring the Great Lakes and northern rivers by canoe. **Voyageurs National Park** (www.nps.gov/voya) covers part of their customary waterway, which became the border between the USA and Canada.

It's all about water up here. Most of the park is accessible only by hiking or motorboat (the waters are mostly too wide and too rough for canoeing, though kayaks are becoming popular). A few access roads lead to campgrounds and lodges on or near Lake Superior,

---

THE ROOTBEER LADY

So you've been hanging out in the remoter portions of the Boundary Waters, thinking you're a real wilderness stud. Sorry, that honor belongs to Dorothy Molter, who lived for 56 years in a cabin smack in the middle of nowhere, 18 miles from the nearest road. Dorothy paddled, hiked, fished, skied and snowshoed around the Boundary Waters – and served her homemade root beer to anyone who happened to drop by – cementing her reputation as a colorful north woods character. She died at age 79, and her friends hauled her homestead by dogsled to Ely. It's now a **museum** (☎ 218-365-4451; www.rootbeerlady.com; adult/child 6-12 $5/3; ♾ 10am-4:45pm Mon-Sat, noon-4:45pm Sun Jun-Aug, weekends only May & Sep) located on the south side of Hwy 169; a guided tour is included in the admission and is well worth your time.

but these are mostly used by people putting in their own boats.

The visitors centers are car-accessible and good places to begin your visit. Twelve miles east of International Falls on Hwy 11 is **Rainy Lake visitors center** (☎ 218-286-5258; ◷ 9am-5pm Jun-Sep, closed Mon & Tue Oct-May), the main park office. Ranger-guided walks and boat tours are available here. Seasonal visitors centers are at **Ash River** (☎ 218-374-3221; ◷ 9am-5pm Jun-Sep) and **Kabetogama Lake** (☎ 218-875-2111; ◷ 9am-5pm Jun-Sep). These areas have outfitters, rentals and services, plus some smaller bays for canoeing.

A big ta-do up here is **houseboating**. Outfitters such as **Ebel's** (☎ 888-883-2357; www.ebels.com; 10326 Ash River Trail, Orr) and **Voyagaire Houseboats** (☎ 800-882-6287; www.voyagaire.com; 7576 Gold Coast Rd, Crane Lake) can set you up. Rentals range from $250 to $530 per day, depending on boat size. Novice boaters are welcome and receive instruction on how to operate the vessels.

For sleeping, your choices are pretty much camping or resorts. The 12-room, shared-bathroom **Kettle Falls Hotel** (☎ 218-240-1724; www.kettlefallshotel.com; r incl breakfast from $50-70; ◷ May–mid-Oct) is an exception, located in the park's midst and accessible only by boat; make arrangements with the owners for pick-up (per person round-trip $45). **Nelson's Resort** (☎ 800-433-0743; www.nelsonsresort.com; 7632 Nelson Rd; cabins from $175) at Crane Lake is a winner for hiking, fishing and relaxing under blue skies.

Granted, this is a remote and wild area, but those seeking wildlife, canoeing and forest camping in all their glory are best off in the Boundary Waters (see p634).

Chippewa National Forest Area

This area is synonymous with outdoor activities and summer fun. Campsites and cottages abound, and almost everybody is fishing-crazy.

Attractive **Walker** has a beach and makes a good spot for a break. For information on hiking, canoeing and camping, check in at the **Chippewa National Forest office** (☎ 218-547-1044; 201 Minnesota Ave E; ◷ 8am-4:30pm Mon-Fri) either here, or in the town of Cass Lake, to the north.

Northwest of Walker, **Itasca State Park** (☎ 218-266-2100; off Hwy 71 N; campsites $15-19) is an area highlight. You can walk across the tiny headwaters of the mighty Mississippi, rent canoes or bikes, hike the trails and camp. The log **HI Mississippi Headwaters Hostel** (☎ 218-266-3415; www.himinnesota.org; dm $16-23, r from $36) is in the park; winter hours vary, so call ahead. Or if you want a little rustic luxury, try the venerable **Douglas Lodge** (☎ 866-857-2757; r $69-115), run by the park, which also has cabins and two good dining rooms.

On the western edge of the forest, neat and tidy **Bemidji** is an old lumber town with a well-preserved downtown and a giant statue of legendary logger Paul Bunyan and his faithful blue ox, Babe. The **visitors center** (☎ 800-458-2223; www.visitbemidji.com; 300 Bemidji Ave N; ◷ 8am-6pm Mon-Fri, 9:30am-6pm Sat, noon-5pm Sun Jun-Aug, reduced hrs Sep-May) displays Paul's toothbrush. Stay by the lake and fish at **Taber's Log Cabins** (☎ 218-751-5781; www.taberslogcabins.com; 2404 Bemidji Ave N; cabins $59-69; ◷ May-Oct). **Raphael's Bakery Café** (☎ 218-759-2015; 319 Minnesota Ave; items $3-5; ◷ 6am-5:30pm Mon-Fri, 6am-2pm Sat) has fine light lunches, coffee and wild-rice bread.

Great Plains

Sure, you can blow through the Plains on the Interstate. Most of the region is flat as a board and known to induce curses of 'enough wheat already!' But turn up your nose and you'll miss hearty bits of America such as South Dakota's ear-bedecked Corn Palace, the inimitable outsider art in Lucas, Bobby Vinton crooning in Branson and the stony faces of Mt Rushmore. The Plains' remote and wild parks top most must-see lists, offering eerie Badlands, bold Black Hills and the wildflower-carpeted Washita Mountains. The region is also the USA's best place to learn about Native America: here you can make arrowheads and shoot a blow gun at Oklahoma's Cherokee Heritage Center, or take in the sobering history of massacre sites like Wounded Knee.

The area retains its raw, frontier edge. This is, after all, the land where cowboys became cowboys, 60 million bison ran wild, covered wagon trains blazed trails west and the heroic Plains Indians fought overpowering forces. These days the mantle's been passed to Stetson-hatted locals lassoing steers, cowgirls cursing over football and farmers grimacing at the sky (More rain? Another tornado?) when they're not rattling along in their pickup trucks.

Though the weather can be cause for concern for locals, it's one of the region's hidden charms for visitors. Summer storms roll in on short notice, instantly darkening the sky and painting drama all over previously unimpressive landscapes.

St Louis, Kansas City and Oklahoma City slake visitors' big-city fix, but it's the anonymous dinky towns where you can truly take the country's pulse. Pull up a plate of chicken-fried steak and a slice of pie along Route 66 or any other twisting two-lane and you'll probably make a new friend before the check comes. Locals here may tell you they prefer their land wide and open so they can 'see if anyone's coming.' Why not let that someone be you?

HIGHLIGHTS

- Scratching your head trying to decide how you'll find enough time to do everything you want to do in the beautiful **Black Hills** (p667).

- Gaping at the bizarre and beautiful landscapes of **Theodore Roosevelt National Park** (p663).

- Discovering the ingenious, inimitable and inspired outsider art in **Lucas** (p679).

- Drinking beer, bowling and watching baseball, baby – all under one tall arch in **St Louis** (p645).

- Veering off the interstates to view the **Corn Palace** (p665) in Mitchell, South Dakota; **Carhenge** (p674) in Alliance, Nebraska; and other Americana.

- Framing bison, wildflowers and mountains in one perfect photo at the **Wichita Mountains Wildlife Refuge** (p686).

GREAT PLAINS

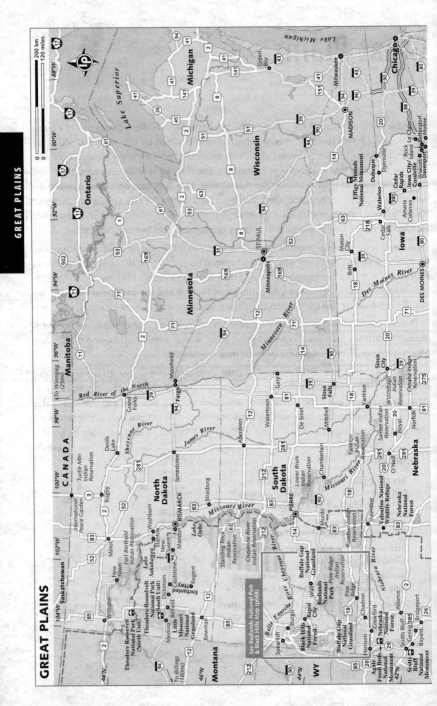

See Badlands National Park
& Black Hills Map (p666)

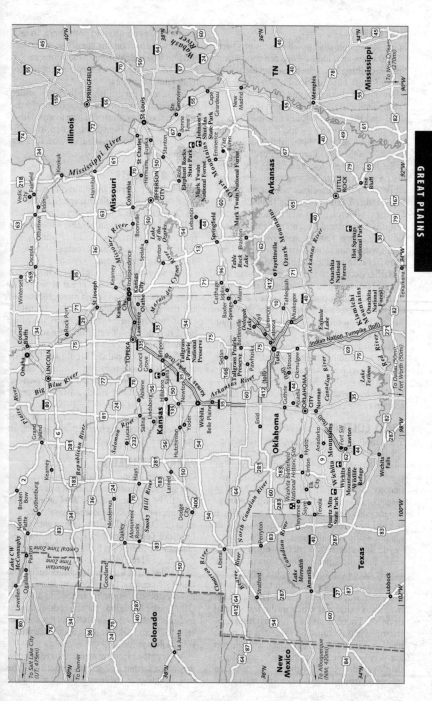

HISTORY

Spear-toting nomads hunted mammoths here 11,000 years ago, long before cannon-toting Spaniards introduced the horse (accidentally) around 1630. Fur-frenzied French explorers, following the Mississippi and Missouri Rivers, claimed most of the land between the Mississippi and the Rocky Mountains for France. The territory passed to Spain in 1763, the French got it back in 1800 and then sold it to the USA in the 1803 Louisiana Purchase.

Settlers' hunger for land pushed resident Native American tribes westward, often forcibly, as in the notorious relocation of the Five Civilized Tribes along the 1838–39 'Trail of Tears,' which led to Oklahoma from back east. Pioneers blazed west on trails such as the Santa Fe across Kansas, and cowboys made their myth on the cattle-drivin' Chisholm Trail from Texas to wild towns like Dodge City.

Earlier occupants, including the Osage and Sioux, had different, but often tragic, fates. Many resettled in pockets of Oklahoma (the Osage luckily found their plots to be above the world's richest oil wells), while others fought for lands once promised.

Railroads, barbed wire and oil all brought change as the 20th century hovered. The 1930s Dust Bowl ruined farms and spurred many residents to say: 'I've had enough of this crap – I'm heading west.' Even today, many regions remain eerily empty.

LOCAL CULTURE

The people who settled the Great Plains usually faced difficult lives of scarcity, uncertainty and isolation; and it literally drove many of them crazy. Others gave up and got out. Only fiercely independent people could thrive in those conditions and that born-and-bred rugged individualism is the core of Plains culture today. Life here is a whole lot easier now, but it's not without challenges.

All that staring out across empty space tends to make a person look inward a little. People here keep their thoughts close to the vest, and most are confident and content with their own way of doing things. High fashion here hasn't changed much in the last several decades. There is also an underlying skepticism which, it must be said, can manifest itself as a suspicion of outsiders, though you are very unlikely to experience it; and if you think you do, you're probably just not used to being around such quiet and restrained

people – traits considered polite here. In fact, sit yourself down on any small-town barstool and you'll be welcomed into the conversation. Brace yourself for a very wry sense of humor from your bar mates.

These traits get diffused in the cities, which host the same diversity and opportunity found in the rest of the country's large towns. However, here in the Heartland, urban life definitely remains less hustled and hectic than on the coasts.

LAND & CLIMATE

Astonishing but true: the Plains are not completely flat. Rolling hills characterize Missouri's Ozark Plateau, while South Dakota's Black Hills and some spots in southern Oklahoma sport real mountains. Another bumpy exception is the convoluted, below-the-plains Badlands of the Dakotas.

Thunderstorms, drought, blizzards and hailstorms all brew with equal abandon in these parts. As Dorothy can attest, tornadoes are the region's wildest weather manifestation and if you hear a tornado warning, heed it. They don't call this 'tornado alley' for nothing.

Winter can be painfully cold (well below 0°F/–17°C) in the north and summer can be painfully hot (above 90°F/32°C) everywhere. Spring and fall are mild, with an average maximum of about 50°F (10°C), so these are good seasons to visit. Many attractions cut back hours, or close up altogether, in the winter.

PARKS & WILDLIFE

Despite the Plains' abundance of open land and sparse population, the region is home to only three national parks – **Wind Cave** (p671), **Badlands** (p666) and **Theodore Roosevelt** (p663) – all in the Dakotas. The latter, along with South Dakota's **Custer State Park** (p670), is the best place to see bison (aka buffalo), creatures that once roamed the Plains 60-million strong but were killed off in wanton slaughters during the mid-19th century. Recent conservation efforts have restored the number to around 350,000. Other notable wildlife-watching destinations include South Dakota's **Black Hills National Forest** (p667) and Oklahoma's **Wichita Mountains Wildlife Refuge** (p686).

Most of the prairie grasslands have gone by way of the farmer's plow: only about 1% of the original tallgrass survives. Great places to see what's left are Kansas's **Tallgrass Prairie National Preserve** (p680), Oklahoma's **Tallgrass Prairie Preserve** (p688), Wind Cave National Park and Wichita Mountains Wildlife Refuge.

See individual state introductory sections for state park details.

GETTING THERE & AROUND

The region's main airport is **Lambert-St Louis International** (☎ 314-426-8000; www.lambert -stlouis.com), but it has few direct international flights. Visitors from abroad may be better off flying to Chicago (p572) or Dallas (p728).

The car- or motorcycle-less brave will miss most of the best of the Plains. **Greyhound** (☎ 800-231-2222; www.greyhound.com) buses only cover the interstates and don't enter much of the region at all, but **Jefferson Lines** (☎ 800-451-5333; www.jeffersonlines.com) and **Burlington Trailways**

GREAT PLAINS IN...

One Week

Spend your first two or three days in the big cities, hitting the highlights of **St Louis** (p643) and **Kansas City** (p652) and the next two or three exploring the small town standouts of Kansas and Nebraska – like **Lawrence** (p677), **Lucas** (p679) and everything along **US 20** (p674) – en route to South Dakota where the gorgeous **Black Hills** (p667) and **Badlands National Park** (p666) will fill your remaining time.

Two Weeks

With two weeks behind the wheel, you can take a big bite out of the Plains. Give yourself two days in **St Louis** (p643) and then meander through **The Ozarks** (p650) on your way to Oklahoma where you'll hook up with historic **Route 66** (p684). **Totem Pole Park** (p684), the **Will Rogers Memorial Museum** (p688) and the **Blue Whale** (p684) are all Mother Road must-sees before rolling into **Tulsa** (p686) for some artistic exploration. Move west for a day of memorials, museums and more in **Oklahoma City** (p681). On day 6, swing down to see the **Wichita Mountains Wildlife Refuge** (p686), then backtrack north to gorgeous **Guthrie** (p685).

Catch I-35 north into Kansas, heading west on I-70 a bit to **Lucas** (p679) and then east to **Lawrence** (p677) where Massachusetts St is the perfect place to stretch your road-weary legs. Fountain-filled **Kansas City** (p652) fills your next day, but consider heading north that evening to take a bite out of day nine's long drive, which takes you up to **Omaha** (p672), down Iowa's **Loess Hills Scenic Byway** (p660) and back west along **US 20** (p674). Cross into South Dakota and spend your next day contemplating the tragedy of **Wounded Knee** (p666) and the oddity of **Badlands National Park** (p666). After that, make the mandatory stop in **Wall** (p665) before rolling into the fun-filled **Black Hills** (p667), which deserve a few days. Finish your journey in North Dakota at **Theodore Roosevelt National Park** (p663).

For Nature-lovers

Skip straight out of Oklahoma City for the mixed-grass prairie and wildlife of the **Wichita Mountains Wildlife Refuge** (p686) and the **Tallgrass Prairie Preserve** (p688). Leave the fields for the forest to paddle and hike in **The Ozarks** (p650) in Missouri and then head up to Nebraska, stopping in Kansas' Flint Hills to see the **Tallgrass Prairie National Preserve** (p680) on the way.

If you're here between February and April, break out the binoculars along the **Platte River** (p674) near Grand Island where half a million sandhill cranes gather. Head northwest through the awesome **Sandhills** (p674) to the **Valentine National Wildlife Refuge** (p674). Take a canoe trip on the **Niobrara River** (p674) and then drive through more Sandhills scenery on the **Bridges to Buttes Byway** (p674), turning north to see some of the county's largest fossil finds at the **Hudson-Meng Bison Bonebed** (p675) and the **Mammoth Site** (p671).

Now you're on the edge of South Dakota's spectacular **Black Hills** (p667). Zip east to eerie **Badlands National Park** (p666) and then bounce back west following **Spearfish Canyon** (p669) north out of the Black Hills. Continue on to North Dakota's **Theodore Roosevelt National Park** (p663) where the badlands are less bizarre but even more beautiful than South Dakota's.

GREAT PLAINS

(☎ 800-992-4618; www.burlingtontrailways.com), a smaller carrier that specializes in Great Plains routes, take up the slack, getting you to most major towns and many smaller ones. They both honor Greyhound's Discovery passes and share Greyhound's depots.

A few other companies have limited service including **Megabus** (☎ 877-462-6342; www .megabus.com), linking Kansas City to Chicago via St Louis for as little as $8.

Unlike the rest of the US, you can actually get somewhat of a feel for the region from the interstate, since the wide-open spaces know no bounds. Of course, we don't recommend this. Substantial stretches of Route 66 survive and are covered in the Missouri (p653), Kansas (p679) and Oklahoma (p684) sections. The Great River Road, a well-signed network of roads and highways along the entire Mississippi River, is stunning in Iowa.

Regional driving distances:

St Louis to Dodge City: 595 miles
Des Moines to Rapid City: 625 miles
Oklahoma City to Fargo: 880 miles

Numerous daily **Amtrak** (☎ 800-872-7245; www .amtrak.com) routes across the Plains make getting here by train easy, but getting around by rail is impractical.

Ann Rutledge Between Chicago and Kansas City via St Louis.
California Zephyr Between Chicago and San Francisco via Iowa (including Osceola, south of Des Moines) and Nebraska (including Omaha and Lincoln).
Empire Builder Between Chicago and Seattle via North Dakota.
Heartland Flyer Between Fort Worth and Oklahoma City.
Kansas City Mule Between St Louis and Kansas City.
Southwest Chief Between Chicago and Los Angeles via Missouri (including Kansas City) and Kansas (including Topeka and Dodge City).
Texas Eagle Between Chicago and San Antonio via St Louis.

MISSOURI

Missouri likes to mix things up; serving visitors ample portions of both sophisticated city life and splendid country sights. Home of the Great Plains' two largest cities (St Louis and Kansas City) this is the region's most densely populated state. But, with more forest and less farm field than the others, it also cradles plenty of wild places and wide-open spaces, most notably the rolling Ozark Mountains

where the winding valleys invite adventurous exploring or just some laid-back meandering behind the steering wheel. And, if you happen to tire of culture and nature and suddenly develop the urge to see Yakov Smirnoff and eat a funnel cake, then Branson awaits.

History

Claimed by France as part of the Louisiana Territory in 1682, Missouri had only a few small river towns by the start of the 19th century when the land passed to American hands and Lewis and Clark pushed up the Missouri River. Missouri was admitted to the Union as a slave state in 1821, per the Missouri Compromise (which permitted slavery in Missouri but prohibited it in any other part of the Louisiana Territory above the 36°30′ parallel), but abolitionists never compromised their ideals and bitter feelings were stoked along the Missouri–Kansas border by Civil War time.

The state's 'Show-Me' nickname is attributed to Congressman Willard Duncan Vandiver, who said in an 1899 speech, 'I come from a state that raises corn and cotton and cockleburs and Democrats, and frothy eloquence neither convinces nor satisfies me. I am from Missouri. You have got to show me.' The name now implies a stalwart, not-easily-impressed character.

Information

Bed & Breakfast Inns of Missouri (☎ 800-213-5642; www.bbim.org)
Missouri Division of Tourism (☎ 800-519-2100; www.visitmo.com)
Missouri state parks (☎ 800-334-6946; www .mostateparks.com) State parks are free to visit.

MISSOURI FACTS

Nickname Show-Me State
Population 5.8 million
Area 69,710 sq miles
Capital city Jefferson City (population 39,600)
Sales Tax 4.225%
Birthplace of author Samuel Clemens (Mark Twain; 1835–1910), scientist George Washington Carver (1864–1943), author William S Burroughs (1914–1997), journalist Walter Cronkite (b 1916), author Maya Angelou (b 1928)
Home of world's largest BBQ contest, rapper Nelly
Famous for Gateway Arch, Budweiser
Official aquatic animal Paddlefish

IF YOU HAVE A FEW MORE DAYS IN THE GREAT PLAINS

- **Effigy Mounds National Monument** (☎ 563-873-3491; www.nps.gov/efmo; carload $5) Hundreds of Native American burial mounds sit in the bluffs high above the Mississippi River in northeast Iowa.

- **Hobo Museum** (☎ 641-843-9104; www.hobo.com; 51 Main Ave S; ☉ 10am-5pm Mon-Fri summer) The only museum of its kind and located in Britt, Iowa; hosts the National Hobo Convention the second weekend in August.

- **International Peace Garden** (☎ 888-432-6733; www.peacegarden.com; carload $10) 150,000 flowers and several monuments sit symbolically on the North Dakota–Manitoba border.

- **Sainte Genevieve, Missouri** This petite, French-founded Mississippi River town oozes history. Many of the restored 18th- and 19th-century buildings are now B&Bs and gift shops.

- **Scotts Bluff** (☎ 308-436-4340; www.nps.gov/scbl; carload $5) The most impressive Oregon Trail landmark in Nebraska is just off Hwy 26, three miles west of Gering, deep into the state's panhandle.

ST LOUIS

Slide into St Louis and sip on some Americana. Beer, bowling and baseball are some of the top attractions, but history and culture also ride high. And, of course, there's the iconic Gateway Arch that you have seen in a million pictures; it's even more impressive in person. Many music legends, including the likes of Scott Joplin, Chuck Berry, Tina Turner and Miles Davis got their start here and the bouncy live music venues keep the flame burning.

History

Fur-trapper Pierre Laclede knew prime real estate when he saw it, so he put down stakes at the junction of the Mississippi and Missouri rivers in 1764. The hustle picked up considerably when prospectors discovered gold in California in 1849 and St Louis became the jump-off point (aka 'Gateway to the West') for get-rich-quick dreamers.

St Louis became known as a center of innovation after hosting the 1904 World's Fair. Aviator Charles Lindbergh furthered the reputation in 1927 when he flew the first nonstop, solo transatlantic flight in the 'Spirit of St Louis,' named for the far-sighted town that funded the aircraft. The city retains its forward-thinking status today, with several aerospace and high-tech companies based here.

Orientation & Information

The landmark Gateway Arch rises right along the Mississippi River. Downtown runs west of the arch while the Laclede's Landing entertainment district sits just to the north.

Neighborhoods of interest radiate out from this core, including the posh Central West End abutting Forest Park; the buzzing-all-night Loop northwest of the park; the Hill, an Italian-American neighborhood; Bohemian but gentrifying Grand South Grand; Soulard, the city's Irish-Cajun-blues entertainment quarter; and nearby, historic Lafayette Square.

BOOKSTORES

Left Bank Books (Map p644; ☎ 314-367-6731; 399 North Euclid, Central West End; ☉ 10am-10pm Mon-Sat, 11am-6pm Sun) A good independent bookstore stocking new and used titles.

INTERNET ACCESS

Coffee Cartel (Map p644 ; ☎ 314-454-0000; 2 Maryland Plaza, Central West End; ☉ 24/7) Has terminals ($5 for 50 min) and free wi-fi for customers.

MEDIA

KDHX FM 88.1 (www.kdhx.org) Community-run radio playing folk, blues, odd rock and local arts reports.
Riverfront Times (www.riverfronttimes.com) The RFT is the city's alt-weekly.
St Louis Post-Dispatch (www.stltoday.com) St Louis' daily newspaper; its *Get Out* entertainment section is published each Thursday.
Vital Voice (www.thevitalvoice.com) A free, bi-weekly gay and lesbian paper.

MEDICAL SERVICES

Barnes Jewish Hospital (Map p644; ☎ 314-747-3000; N Kingshighway Blvd) Next to Forest Park.

GREAT PLAINS

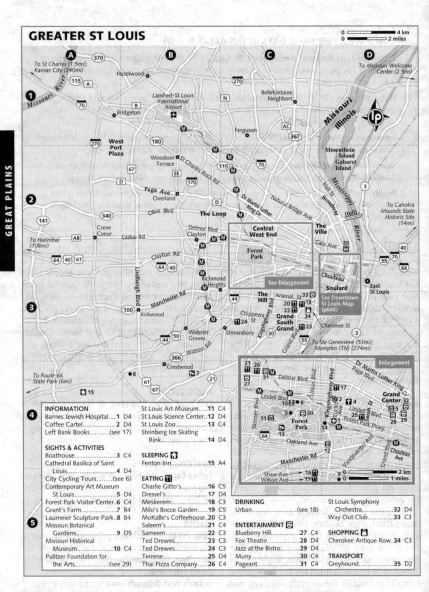

GREATER ST LOUIS

INFORMATION
Barnes Jewish Hospital....**1** D4
Coffee Cartel.................**2** D4
Left Bank Books............(see 17)

SIGHTS & ACTIVITIES
Boathouse...................**3** C4
Cathedral Basilica of Saint
Louis......................**4** D4
City Cycling Tours.........(see 6)
Contemporary Art Museum
St Louis..................**5** D4
Forest Park Visitor Center..**6** C4
Grant's Farm...............**7** B4
Laumeier Sculpture Park..**8** B4
Missouri Botanical
Gardens..................**9** D5
Missouri Historical
Museum..................**10** C4
Pulitzer Foundation for
the Arts.................(see 29)

St Louis Art Museum......**11** C4
St Louis Science Center...**12** D4
St Louis Zoo..............**13** C4
Steinberg Ice Skating
Rink......................**14** D4

SLEEPING
Fenton Inn.................**15** A4

EATING
Charlie Gitto's............**16** C5
Dressel's..................**17** D4
Meskerem.................**18** C3
Milo's Bocce Garden......**19** C5
MoKaBe's Coffeehouse....**20** C3
Saleem's..................**21** C3
Sameem..................**22** C3
Ted Drewes...............**23** C3
Ted Drewes...............**24** C3
Terrene...................**25** D4
Thai Pizza Company......**26** C4

DRINKING
Urban.....................(see 18)

ENTERTAINMENT
Blueberry Hill.............**27** C4
Fox Theatre...............**28** D4
Jazz at the Bistro.........**29** D4
Muny......................**30** C4
Pageant..................**31** C4

St Louis Symphony
Orchestra...............**32** D4
Way Out Club............**33** C3

SHOPPING
Cherokee Antique Row..**34** C3

TRANSPORT
Greyhound................**35** D2

MONEY
US Bank (Map p646; ☎ 314-418-2803; 721 Locust St; ☼ exchange dept 8:30am-4pm Mon-Fri) Best bet, after the airport, for foreign-currency exchange.

POST
Post office (Map p646; ☎ 314-436-6853; 1720 Market St; ☼ 8am-8pm Mon-Fri, 8am-1pm Sat)

TOURIST INFORMATION
Explore St Louis (Map p646; ☎ 800-607-2683; www .explorestlouis.com; 7th St & Washington Ave; ☼ 8:30am-5pm Mon-Fri, 9am-2pm Sat) There's another branch in Kiener Plaza at 6th and Chestnut.
Missouri Welcome Center (☎ 314-869-7100; www .visitmo.com; I-270 exit 34; ☼ 8am-5pm closed Sun Nov-Mar)

Sights & Activities
JEFFERSON NATIONAL EXPANSION MEMORIAL (Map p646)
The centerpiece of this National Park Service property, the striking **Gateway Arch**; (Map p646; ☎ 877-982-1410; www.gatewayarch.com; ☯ 8am-10pm Jun-Aug, 9am-6pm Sep-May) is the Great Plains' own Eiffel Tower. Completed in 1965 the Arch stands 630ft high and symbolizes St Louis' historical role as 'Gateway to the West.' The **tram ride** (adult/child $10/7) to the observatory is a bit disappointing considering the cost.

The subterranean **Museum of Westward Expansion** (Map p646; admission free; ☯ 8am-10pm Jun-Aug, 9am-6pm Sep-May), under the Arch, chronicles the Lewis and Clark expedition. Two theaters here show **films** (adult/child $7/4) throughout the day.

Churn up the Big Muddy on replica 19th-century steamboats with **Gateway Arch Riverboats** (Map p646; ☎ 877-982-1410; 1hr tour adult/child $12/6; ☯ 10:30am-6pm). A park ranger narrates the midday cruises and those after 3pm sail subject to availability. There are also numerous dinner and drinking cruises. Various combo tickets are available.

Facing the Arch, the 1845 **Old Courthouse & Museum** (Map p646; ☎ 877-982-1410; 11 N 4th St; admission free; ☯ 8am-4:30pm) is where the famed Dred Scott slavery case was first tried. Galleries depict the trial's history, as well as that of the city.

FOREST PARK (Map p644)
New York City may have Central Park, but St Louis has the even bigger (by 528 acres) **Forest Park** (Map p644; ☯ 6am-10pm). The superb, 1371-acre spread was the setting of the 1904 World's Fair. The **visitor center** (Map p644; ☎ 314-367-7275; www.forestparkforever.org; 5595 Grand Dr; ☯ 6am-8pm Mon-Fri, 6am-7pm Sat-Sun) is in an old street car pavilion and has a café.

In warm weather, beeline to the **Boathouse** (Map p644; ☎ 314-367-2224; 6101 Government Dr; boat rental per hr $15; ☯ 10am-sunset) to paddle over Post-Dispatch Lake. In cooler weather, make for the **Steinberg Ice Skating Rink** (Map p644; ☎ 314-367-7465; off N Kingshighway Blvd; adult/child $6/5, skates $2; ☯ 10am-9pm Sun-Thu, 10am-midnight Fri-Sat Nov-Mar).

In the grounds is the impressive **St Louis Art Museum** (Map p644; ☎ 314-721-0072; www.slam.org; 1 Fine Arts Dr; admission free; ☯ 10am-5pm Tue-Sun, to 9pm Fri), originally built for the fair and today holding works from just about all nations and historical eras.

Though the building is more impressive than the permanent displays – which cover the fair, Charles Lindbergh and city history – it's worth your while to step into the **Missouri Historical Museum** (Map p644; ☎ 314-746-4599; www.mohistory.org; 5700 Lindell Blvd; admission free; ☯ 10am-6pm summer, 10am-5pm rest of year, until 8pm Tue year-round).

Also in the park is the **St Louis Zoo** (Map p644; ☎ 314-781-0900; www.stlzoo.org; 1 Government Dr; admission free, fee for some exhibits; ☯ 8am-7pm summer, 9am-5pm rest of year) and the kid-savvy **St Louis Science Center** (Map p644; ☎ 314-289-4400; www.slsc.org; 5050 Oakland Ave; admission free; ☯ Mon-Sat 9:30am-5:30pm, until 9:30pm Fri, 11:30am-4:30pm Sun, closing at 4:30pm Sat-Thu rest of year), which also has a planetarium and an IMAX theater for additional fees.

City Cycling Tours (☎ 314-616-5724; www.citycyclingtours.com; 3hr-tour $30; ☯ daily year-round, call for times) offers narrated rides through the park (bicycles and helmets included) starting at the visitor center. Bike rental costs $20 for 2 hours.

MUSEUMS, GARDENS & CHURCHES
Part jungle gym, part art installation, much of the ingenious **City Museum** (Map p646; ☎ 314-231-2489; www.citymuseum.org; 701 N 15th St; admission $12; ☯ 9am-5pm Mon-Thu, 9am-1am Fri, 10am-1am Sat, 11am-5pm Sun, closed Mon & Tue Sep-May) is made from recycled industrial castoffs. Kids of all ages will love to explore it. The World Aquarium costs $6 extra.

Nobody knows if they designated beer frames, but there is some evidence the ancient Romans and Egyptians bowled. Learn this and much more at the **International Bowling Museum** (Map p646; ☎ 314-231-6340; www.bowlingmuseum.com; 111 Stadium Plaza; adult/child $7.50/6; ☯ 9am-5pm Apr-Sep until 6:30pm during Cardinals games, 11am-4pm Tue-Sat Oct-Mar) and then bowl free frames at the lanes below. The museum shares space with the **Cardinals Hall of Fame** (admission incl in museum fee).

Under the big green dome of the stunning **Cathedral Basilica of Saint Louis** (☎ 314-373-8200; 4431 Lindell Blvd; admission free; ☯ 7am-5pm), three

---

DON'T MISS

- **Gateway Arch** – so simple, but so beautiful (left)
- **City Museum** – feel like a kid again (above)
- **Dinner on The Hill** – more than just a meal (p648)
- **A Cardinals game** – sip beers in the bleachers (p649)

GREAT PLAINS

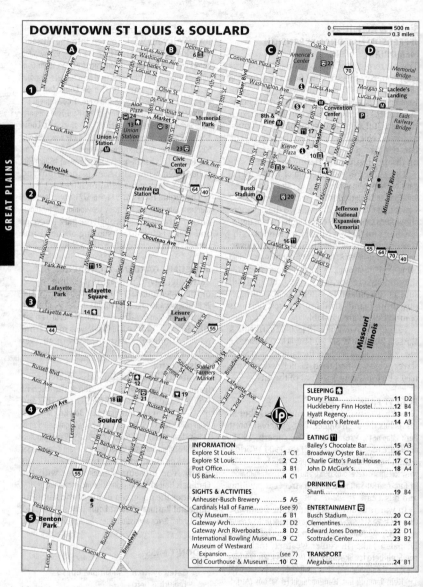

DOWNTOWN ST LOUIS & SOULARD

INFORMATION	
Explore St Louis	1 C1
Explore St Louis	2 C2
Post Office	3 B1
US Bank	4 C1

SIGHTS & ACTIVITIES	
Anheuser-Busch Brewery	5 A5
Cardinals Hall of Fame	(see 9)
City Museum	6 B1
Gateway Arch	7 D2
Gateway Arch Riverboats	8 D2
International Bowling Museum	9 C2
Museum of Westward Expansion	(see 7)
Old Courthouse & Museum	10 C2

SLEEPING	
Drury Plaza	11 D2
Huckleberry Finn Hostel	12 B4
Hyatt Regency	13 B1
Napoleon's Retreat	14 A3

EATING	
Bailey's Chocolate Bar	15 A3
Broadway Oyster Bar	16 C2
Charlie Gitto's Pasta House	17 C1
John D McGurk's	18 A4

DRINKING	
Shanti	19 B4

ENTERTAINMENT	
Busch Stadium	20 C2
Clementines	21 B4
Edward Jones Dome	22 D1
Scottrade Center	23 B2

TRANSPORT	
Megabus	24 B1

blocks east of Forest Park, you'll find a Byzantine interior draped with 83,000 sq ft of mosaics – that's 41.5 million pieces. You can learn about mosaic styles and creation downstairs in the church's **museum** (entry $1; ⏰ 10am-4pm).

The first-rate **Missouri Botanical Garden** (Map p644; ☎ 800-642-8842; www.mobot.org; 4344 Shaw Ave; adult/child $8/free; ⏰ 9am-5pm, until 8pm Wed summer) holds a 14-acre Japanese garden, carnivorous plant bog and Victorian-style hedge maze.

Though they are separate entities, the side-by-side **Contemporary Art Museum St Louis** (Map p644; ☎ 314-535-4660; www.contemporarystl.org; 3750 Washington Blvd; adult/student $5/free; ⏰ 10am-5pm Tue-Sat, until 8pm Thu, 11am-4pm Sun) and **Pulitzer**

Foundation for the Arts (Map p644; ☎ 314-754-1850; www.pulitzerarts.org; 3716 Washington Blvd; admission free; 🕑 noon-5pm Wed, 10am-4pm Sat) are a perfect pair. Both showcase thought-provoking contemporary works.

Over 80 large sculptures are spread across **Laumeier Sculpture Park** (Map p644; ☎ 314-821-1209; www.laumeier.org; I-44 exit 277B; admission free; 🕑 8am-sunset; tours 2pm 1st & 3rd Sun May-Oct), a convenient stop on your way out of town along Route 66.

Grant's Farm (Map p644; ☎ 314-843-1700; www.grantsfarm.com; 10501 Gravois Rd; admission free; 🕑 9am-3:30pm Tue-Fri, 9am-4pm Sat, 9:30am-4pm Sun mid-May–mid-Aug, reduced hrs spring & fall, closed Nov-mid-Apr; P) thrills kids with its Clydesdale horses and 1000 other animals from six continents; a tram takes you through the preserve where the beasts roam free. Parking costs $8.

Cross the river to see **Cahokia Mounds State Historic Site** (p577).

Festivals & Events

Big Muddy Blues Festival (www.bigmuddyblues.com; admission free) Five stages of riverfront blues on Labor Day weekend.

Sleeping

Motels are found all along city-encircling I-270, but the best place to look for budget motels is out along I-44.

BUDGET

Huckleberry Finn Hostel (Map p646; ☎ 314-241-0076; 1908 S 12th St, Soulard; dm $20, 1 private r $50; 🕑 closed Jan & Feb; 🌐) In a chaotic old townhouse, this independent hostel is rather rough around the edges (upgrades were ongoing when we last stopped by), but it's a friendly gathering spot with a piano in the lounge/kitchen and free lockers. It's well-sited near pubs and restaurants.

Fenton Inn (Map p644; ☎ 636-343-5710; I-44 exit 275, Fenton; r from $49; P 🌐) With a mini refrigerator and large television in each room, this is a good budget option.

MIDRANGE

Drury Plaza (Map p646; ☎ 314-231-3003, 800-378-7946; www.druryhotels.com; 2 S 4th St; r/ste from $95/155; P 🌐 🛗 🖥 wi-fi) Looking at the lovely lobby and scanning the roster of freebies, you'd never suspect this for one of downtown's cheapest digs. The rooms themselves are fairly ordinary, unless you can snag one with an Arch view. Parking costs $15.

Napoleon's Retreat (Map p646; ☎ 314-772-6979, 800-700-9980; www.napoleonsretreat.com; 1815 Lafayette Ave; r $99-150, 2-night min weekends; 🍴 🌐 🖥 wi-fi) A lovely 2nd French Empire home in lovely Lafayette Square, this B&B has five bold and beautiful rooms, each with private bath and antique furnishings. Michael and Jeff are superb hosts.

Hyatt Regency (Map p646; ☎ 314-231-1234, 800-233-1234; 1820 Market St; r from $109; P 🌐 🛗 🖥 wi-fi) This huge hotel (539 rooms) in entertaining and attractive Union Station is a mix of modern and historic structures, but it all adds up to luxurious. You'll have to book well in advance to get the lowest rates, but even if you pay more, this hotel serves up good value. Parking is an extra $14.

Eating

St Louis boasts the region's most diverse selection of food, but is particularly proud of its Italian offerings. The monthly magazine **Sauce** (www.saucemagazine.com) is full of reviews.

DRINK & DINE ST LOUIS STYLE

The city cooks and brews several local specialties:

▪ **Toasted ravioli** They're filled with meat, coated in breadcrumbs, then deep fried. **Charlie Gitto's** (p648) probably started it all, but practically every restaurant on the Hill serves them.

▪ **St Louis pizza** Its thin-crusted, square-cut, Provel cheese–based and sticks to the roof of your mouth. Local chain **Imo's** (large one-topping pizza $12), with over 70 locations across the metro, bakes 'the square beyond compare.'

▪ **Frozen custard** Don't dare leave town without gorging on this super-creamy ice cream–like treat at **Ted Drewes** (Map p644; ☎ 314-481-2652; 6726 Chippewa St; cone $0.50-2.50; 🕑 11am-11pm or so Feb-Dec). There's a smaller summer-only branch at 4224 S Grand Blvd.

▪ **Schlafly beer** Look behind bar taps for this local microbrew.

DOWNTOWN

Laclede's Landing along the riverfront next to the historic Eads Railway Bridge has several restaurants, though generally people pop down here for the atmosphere – cobblestone streets, converted brick buildings and free-flowing beer – rather than the food.

Broadway Oyster Bar (Map p646; ☎ 314-621-8811; 736 S Broadway; mains $7-12; ⌚ 11am-1:30am Sun-Thu, 11am-3am Fri-Sat) serves lots of the namesake mollusks, plus Cajun food, beer and blues nightly in a fun outdoor garden.

SOULARD & LAFAYETTE SQUARE

Restaurants and pubs occupy most corners in Soulard, with plenty of live blues and Irish music. Lafayette Square, a few miles northwest, has a growing number of chichi spots.

Bailey's Chocolate Bar (Map p646; ☎ 314-241-8100; 1915 Park Ave, Lafayette Square; desserts $5-11, pizzas $7-8; ⌚ 4pm-1am Mon-Sat, 4-10pm Sun; ⊠) It's pure brilliance. Bailey's specializes in chocolate desserts and alcoholic beverages (with some brilliant combos: white chocolate raspberry martini, anyone?), with cheese plates and pizzas thrown in to conceal the decadence.

John D McGurk's (Map p646; ☎ 314-776-8309; 1200 Russell Blvd, Soulard; mains $7-20; ⌚ 11am-1:30am Mon-Sat, 3pm-midnight Sun) The city's favorite pub oozes charm inside, where Irish bands play nightly, but you can't beat the backyard garden.

GRAND SOUTH GRAND

Running along South Grand Blvd, this young, Bohemian area is best known for its Vietnamese restaurants, but it has a whole world of flavors.

Meskerem (Map p644; ☎ 314-772-4442; 3210 S Grand Blvd; mains $7-11; ⌚ 11:30am-11pm Mon-Fri, noon-11pm Sat-Sun; ⊠) This stand-out Ethiopian restaurant gives service with a smile.

Sameem (Map p644; ☎ 314-664-3940; 3191 S Grand Blvd; mains $7-16; ⌚ 11:30am-9pm Sun-Thu, 11:30am-10pm Fri-Sat; ⊠) Sameem serves traditional Afghan dishes like lamb kabobs plus fusion meals like the spicy chicken pasta. The chutney is divine.

THE HILL

This trim, tiny-housed Italian neighborhood features innumerable pasta places. Even if you don't eat here, come take a look around.

Milo's Bocce Garden (Map p644; ☎ 314-776-0468; 5201 Wilson Ave; mains $6-14; ⌚ 11am-1am) Enjoy the outdoor courtyard to eat sandwiches, pizzas and pastas, drink and play bocce ball with old Italian guys.

Charlie Gitto's (p644 ☎ 314-772-8898; 26 Shaw Ave; mains $16-40; ⌚ 5-10pm Mon-Thu, 5-11pm Fri-Sat, 4-10pm Sun) Legendary Charlie Gitto's makes a strong claim to having invented St Louis' famous toasted ravioli. It's classy but casual with dim lighting and at-a-snap service. There's a more casual branch downtown at 207 North 6th St.

CENTRAL WEST END & THE LOOP

Sidewalk cafés rule Euclid Ave in this dignified old neighborhood. 'The Loop,' near Washington University, runs along Delmar Blvd (embedded with the St Louis Walk of Fame) and has many bars and international restaurants catering to a youthful crowd.

Thai Pizza Company (p644; ☎ 314-862-4429; 608 Eastgate; mains $6-7; ⌚ 11:15am-10pm Sun-Thu, 11:15am-1am Fri-Sat; ⊠) Try one of the creative East-meets-West 'zas or sample some real Thai off their mix-and-match menu.

Dressel's (Map p644; ☎ 314-361-1060; 419 N Euclid Ave, Central West End; mains $6-16; ⌚ 11am-1:30am Mon-Sat, 11am-midnight Sun, kitchen closes around 11:30pm) This classic Welsh pub serves rarebit, fish and chips and sandwiches in an atmosphere celebrating Wales' literary and drinking heritages.

Saleem's (Map p644; ☎ 314-721-7947; 6501 Delmar Blvd, The Loop; mains $8-17; ⌚ 11:30am-2:30pm & 5-10pm Mon-Sat, until 11pm Fri-Sat) 'Where garlic is king' is the motto, and the favoured flavour shows up in bright-orange Saleem's kabobs, kofte, hummus and other Persian dishes.

Terrene (Map p644; ☎ 314-535-5100; 33 N Sarah St, Central West End; mains $12-21; ⌚ 5-10pm Tue-Thu, 5-11pm Fri-Sat, 5-8:30pm Sun) This bright, contemporary space defines itself both through its food (pan roasted chicken with wilted spinach, chick peas, roasted garlic, natural *jus* and chive butter, for example) and its dedication to environmentalism. It serves meat, but Terrene is also a vegetarian favorite.

Drinking

Laclede's Landing and Soulard are chock full o' drinkeries, many with live music. Most bars close at 1:30am, though some have 3am licenses.

Boathouse (p645) is a lovely outdoor place to sit, sip and sunset-watch.

SLAP ME A BUD

Admittedly it's highly commercialized, but…it's still cool. The world's largest beer plant, the historic **Anheuser-Busch Brewery** (Map p646; ☎ 314-577-2626; www.budweisertours.com; 12th & Lynch Sts; admission free; ⏰ 9am-4pm Mon-Sat, 11:30am-4pm Sun, to 5pm Jun-Aug, start 10am Nov-Feb), gives super-slick tours. Would you expect less from the company that makes Budweiser and controls 50% of the domestic market? View the bottling plant and famous Clydesdale horses. Note the tanks in the aging house: each one holds 200,000 six-packs. Bring ID for free samples at the end.

---

ourpick **Shanti** (Map p646; ☎ 314-241-4772; 825 Allen Ave, Soulard; ⏰ 10am-1:30am Mon-Sat), meaning 'peace' in Sanskrit, is the Bohemian heart of Soulard. It hosts a popular Tuesday open mike and folk-bluegrass-rock acts most other nights.

Lounge on pillows, play Ping-Pong and sample exotic cocktails like lemongrass *mojitos* at **Urban** (Map p644; ☎ 314-772-3308; 3216 S Grand Blvd). It draws a diverse crowd.

Broadway Oyster Bar, Bailey's Chocolate Bar, John D McGurk's, Milo's Bocce Garden and Dressel's – all listed in the Eating section (p647) are good places to drink as well as eat.

Entertainment

Check the **Riverfront Times** (www.riverfronttimes.com), free around town, for entertainment updates.

JAZZ, BLUES & ROCK

Blueberry Hill (Map p644; ☎ 314-727-0880; www.blueberryhill.com; 6504 Delmar Blvd, The Loop) St Louis native Chuck Berry still rocks the small basement bar here at least once a month. The $25 tickets sell out very quickly. The venue hosts smaller-tier rock, reggae, blues and hip-hop bands on the other nights.

Way Out Club (Map p644; ☎ 314-664-7638; 2525 S Jefferson Ave) Way Out is a worthy venue with punk, rockabilly and alt rock bands.

Jazz at the Bistro (Map p644; ☎ 314-531-1012; www.jazzatthebistro.com; 3536 Washington Ave; ✗) Big names often play this little club.

Pageant (Map p644; ☎ 314-726-6161; www.thepageant.com; 6161 Delmar Blvd, The Loop) Many touring bands perform here.

PERFORMING ARTS

Grand Center, west of downtown, is the heart of St Louis' theater scene and home of the **St Louis Symphony Orchestra** (Map p644; ☎ 800-232-1880; www.slso.org; 718 N Grand Blvd), which has 50 free tickets for most performances.

Fox Theatre (Map p644; ☎ 314-534-1678; www.fabulousfox.com; 527 N Grand Blvd) Catch a concert or Broadway show at this 1929 ornate beauty.

Muny (Map p644; ☎ 314-361-1900; www.muny.com) The Municipal Opera (aka 'Muny') hosts nightly summer musicals outdoors in Forest Park; some of the 12,000 seats are free.

Purchase tickets for most venues through **MetroTix** (☎ 800-293-5949; www.metrotix.com).

GAY & LESBIAN VENUES

The Central West End is the community's hub, but Soulard and Grand South Grand also have hang-outs. Women can find company at **MoKaBe's Coffeehouse** (Map p644; ☎ 314-865-2009; 3606 Arsenal St; ⏰ 8am-midnight Mon-Sat, 9am-midnight Sun). Men will find friends at **Clementines** (Map p646; ☎ 314-664-7869; 2001 Menard St; ⏰ 10am-1:30am Mon-Sat, 11am-midnight Sun). Peruse the **Vital Voice** (www.thevitalvoice.com) or **St. Louis Gay Guide** (www.stlouisgayguide.com) for more.

SPORTS

Busch Stadium (Map p646; ☎ 314-345-9000; www.stlcardinals.com; Broadway & Clark Ave) The 2006 World Series–champion Cardinals baseball team plays here.

Edward Jones Dome (Map p646; ☎ 314-425-8830; www.stlouisrams.com; 901 N Broadway) This is where the NFL's Rams go deep.

Scottrade Center (Map p646; ☎ 314-241-1888; www.stlouisblues.com; 1401 Clark Ave) The St Louis Blues play NHL hockey here.

Shopping

The Loop is the neighborhood with the best mix of shops; the Central West End is good too. If you love antiques, you'll love **Cherokee Antique Row** (Map p644; Cherokee St east of Jefferson Ave) in the appropriately historic Cherokee-Lemp neighborhood. The shops in the resorted **Union Station** (Map p646; 1820 Market St) are an ordinary lot, but it's one of the most beautiful shopping malls you'll ever meet.

Getting There & Around

Lambert-St Louis International Airport (Map p644; ☎ 314-426-8000; www.lambert-stlouis.com) is the Great Plains' hub, with flights to all major regional and US cities. The airport is 12 miles northwest of downtown and is connected by the light-rail MetroLink ($3.50), taxi (about $35) or **Trans Express** (☎ 800-844-1985; $15) shuttles, which can drop you off at downtown hotels.

Greyhound (Map p644; ☎ 314-231-4485; 1450 N 13th St) buses depart several times daily to Chicago ($48, five to seven hours), Memphis ($53, 5½ to 7½ hours), Kansas City ($43, 4½ hours) and many more cities from a rough neighborhood north of downtown.

The low-cost **Megabus** (☎ 877-462-6342) runs services to Chicago and Kansas City from as little as $8 one-way; it stops next to Union Station.

Metro (☎ 314-231-2345; www.metrostlouis.org; day-pass $4.50) runs local buses and the MetroLink light-rail system. Bus No 93 connects most points of interests, including Soulard, downtown and the Central West End. Ride free between Union Station and Laclede's Landing weekdays 11:30am to 1:30pm.

For a taxi call **St Louis County Cabs** (☎ 314-993-8294).

Amtrak (Map p646; ☎ 314-331-3304; 551 S 16th St) travels six times daily to Chicago ($22, 5½ hours). There are also daily trains to Kansas City ($25, six hours) and Dallas ($86, 16¼ hours). For those using a railpass, a connecting bus service to Memphis costs $35.

AROUND ST LOUIS

Several attractive river towns north and south of St Louis on the Mississippi and just west on the Missouri make popular weekend excursions for St Louisans, including this historic pair.

St Charles

This Missouri River town, founded in 1769 by the French, is just 20 miles northwest of St Louis. The cobblestone Main Street anchors a well-preserved downtown where you can visit the **first state capitol** (☎ 636-940-3322; 200 S Main St; admission free, tours adult/child $2.50/1.50; 9am-4pm Mon-Sat, 11am-5pm Sun, closed Mon Jan-Mar). Ask at the **visitor center** (☎ 800-366-2427; www.historicstcharles .com; 230 S Main St; 8am-5pm Mon-Fri, 10am-5pm Sat, noon-5pm Sun) about the free trolley rides, which pass some rare French colonial architecture in the **Frenchtown neighborhood** to the north.

Lewis and Clark began their epic journey in St Charles on May 21, 1804 and their encampment is reenacted annually at that time. The **Lewis & Clark Boathouse and Nature Center** (☎ 636-

947-3199; www.lewisandclarkcenter.org; 1050 Riverside Dr; adult/child $2/1; 10am-5pm Mon-Sat, noon-5pm Sun) has a handful of displays about the duo.

For cyclists, St Charles is the eastern gateway to **Katy Trail State Park** (☎ 800-334-6946; www.katytrail statepark.com), a superb 225-mile trail that cuts across Missouri to Clinton, 65 miles southeast of Kansas City, along the former Missouri–Kansas–Texas railroad (the 'Katy'). The trail's eastern two-thirds snake between high bluffs and the Missouri River. **Momentum Cycles** (☎ 636-946-7433; 104 S Main St; hr/day $6/30) rents bikes.

Hotels are spread along St Charles' four I-70 exits. St Charles also has several good B&Bs, including **Boone's Lick Trail Inn** (☎ 636-947-7000, 888-940-0002; www.booneslick.com; 1000 S Main St; r weekday $125-160, weekend $145-215; wi-fi), a class act with antique furnishings.

Hannibal

Mark Twain's boyhood home, 100 miles north of St Louis, isn't as inspiring as it must have once been. Still, you need not be a big-time fan to find the scenes of Tom Sawyer and Huck Finn's great adventures – like the white fence Tom didn't paint and the cave where he and Becky Thatcher got lost – enjoyable. The **Mark Twain Boyhood Home & Museum** (☎ 573-221-9010; www.marktwainmuseum.org; 415 N Main St; adult/child $8/4; 8am-6pm, reduced in winter) presents seven buildings, including two homes Twain lived in and that of Laura Hawkins, the real-life inspiration for Becky Thatcher. Afterward, float down the Mississippi on the **Mark Twain Riverboat** (☎ 573-221-3222; www.marktwainriverboat.com; Center St; 1-hr sightseeing cruise adult/child $13/10, 2-hr dinner cruise $35/20; Apr-Nov, schedule varies). **National Tom Sawyer Days** (around July 4th weekend) features frog jumping and fence painting contests and much more.

Many of Hannibal's historic homes are now B&Bs. The **Hannibal Visitors Bureau** (☎ 866-263-4825; www.visithannibal.com; 505 N 3rd St; 8am-5pm Mon & Wed, 8am-6pm Tue, Thu & Fri, 9am-6pm Sat, 10am-5pm Sun) keeps a list. **Hotel Clemens** (☎ 573-248-1150, 877-248-1155; www.hotelclemens.us; 401 N 3rd St; r from $65; wi-fi), an older but well-maintained property popular with families, is the only hotel downtown.

THE OZARKS

Ozark hill country spreads across southern Missouri and extends into northern Arkansas and eastern Oklahoma.

One of the best Ozark escapes is the **Ozark Trail** (☎ 573-786-2065; www.ozarktrail.com), a 350-

GREAT PLAINS

LOCAL VOICE: RAMONA LEHMAN

Co-owner of Munger Moss Motel (p653) in Lebanon, Missouri since 1971

What's the appeal of Route 66 today? I've always felt that Route 66 is a romantic road; it's a nostalgic road. It's a getting-off-the-fast-pace, take-your-time type of road. Europeans tell me they love it because it is so wide open. The baby boomers, some have childhood memories of traveling on it. People many times are trying to retrace steps of days gone by. And I think for a lot of us, it reminds us of the fifties, which were just plain good old days. The road can give you shivers. In Springfield there's a part of the road that's never been covered and the first time I went there I put my foot on it and I felt it come up my bones.

Who's traveling Route 66 today? I say we've probably had people from just about every country in the world. Europeans and Asians really get caught up in it, they have fun on it. And I'm seeing more and more Americans. I remember a boy from Finland whose father came over here after the Second World War and he remembered him tell stories of traveling Route 66 on a motorcycle, and he came over to do what his father did. This year I've got six big groups coming from Norway. They ride their Harleys from end to end. And the foreigners that travel it, they love our history. They enjoy everything about it.

What's Route 66's future? It will be here forever. Route 66 will not die. I look for bigger and better things to come once the government stops dragging its feet and puts up all the scenic byway signs, and when more grants are available again. Way back, people that lived along the road made their living from the road. I once asked a friend: 'What is Route 66?' He said the road is just a thing that goes from one place to another, but the people who live and work on the road are what make the road special, and what keeps it alive and going.

mile hiking route mostly through the Mark Twain National Forest.

At massive **Johnson's Shut-Ins State Park** (☎ 573-546-2450), 8 miles north of Lesterville on Hwy N, the swift Black River swirls through canyon-like gorges ('shut-ins'). The park has been closed for repairs following a devastating flood in December 2005, but is expected to reopen in the summer of 2008. Little **Elephant Rocks State Park** (☎ 573-546-3454), next to Graniteville on Hwy 21, has enormous billion-year-old rocks – most far larger than any pachyderm. Some stand end-to-end like circus elephants.

North of US 60, midway between Cape Girardeau and Springfield, the **Ozark National Scenic Riverways** (☎ 573-323-4236; www.nps.gov/ozar) – the Current and Jack's Fork Rivers – boast 134 miles of splendid canoeing and inner-tubing. Weekends often get busy and boisterous. The headquarters, along with outfitters and motels, is in **Van Buren**. Eminence also makes a good base. There are many campgrounds along the rivers.

Branson

Hokey Branson is a love-it-or-hate-it tourist town. The main attractions are the 49 theaters hosting 100-plus country music, magic and comedy shows. The neon-lit '76 Strip' (Hwy 76) packs in miles of motels, restaurants, wax museums, shopping malls, fun parks and theaters. As Bart Simpson once said: 'It's like Vegas; if it were run by Ned Flanders.'

During the summer and again in November and December, traffic often crawls. It's often faster to walk than drive. If you're going from one end to the other, follow the color-coded routes that bypass the Strip.

The **Branson Lakes Area Convention & Visitors Bureau** (☎ 800-214-3661; www.explorebranson.com; 269 Hwy 248; ✆ 8am-5pm Mon-Sat, 10am-4pm Sun) just west of the US 65 junction, has town and lodging information. It has a second location north of town at the junction of US 65 and Hwy 160. The scores of 'Visitor Information' centers around town (even the 'official' ones) are just plugging time-shares, though sitting through a high pressure sales presentation will get you free tickets to some show.

Popular **theater shows** featuring performers like Andy Williams, the Gatlin Brothers and Fabian give Branson the 'Has-been Heaven' title, but the Acrobats of China and Breakfast with Mark Twain add some variety. Theaters usually run afternoon and evening shows, and sometimes morning ones. Prices range from about $25 to $50 a head, but you rarely need to pay full price. Pick up any of the many coupon books around town or stop by **Branson 2 for 1 Tickets** (☎ 417-336-0241; www.branson2for1tickets.com; 1100 W Hwy 76), which does business with, as the sign says, 'No Bull.' Reserve a week in advance during peak seasons.

Two attractions, opened in 1959 and 1960 respectively, spurred the Branson boom. The **Baldknobbers Jamboree** (☎ 888-734-1935; www.bald knobbers.com; 2835 W Hwy 76; adult $25-27, child $13.50-15.50), a cornball country music and comedy show; and **Silver Dollar City** (☎ 800-831-4386; www .silverdollarcity.com; adult/child $46/36; ☽ 9:30am-7pm summer, reduced hrs in winter), a huge amusement park west of town. **Branson Landing** (www.bransonlanding .com) an upscale pedestrian shopping mall downtown on Lake Tanycomo is Branson's attempt to diversify its appeal.

There are dozens of budget hotels (starting at around $23) along Hwy 76 in the heart of the Branson action, including the ultra-friendly **Stonewall West Motor Inn** (☎ 417-334-5173; 1030 W Hwy 76; r from $29; ☒ ☒ wi-fi). Nicer places tend to be in slightly quieter locations off the Strip. **Table Rock Lake**, snaking through the hills southwest of town, is a deservedly popular destination for boating, fishing, camping and other outdoor activities, and it also has good value lodging. Try **Indian Trails Resort** (☎ 417-338-2327; www.indiantrailsresort.com; Indian Point Rd; cottages $88-175; ☒ ☒ ☒), on the lake and just a few miles out of Branson.

Branson cuisine consists almost entirely of fast food, junk food and all-you-can-eat buffets (most priced $5-10). For something different, savor the family recipes at little **Casa Fuentes** (☎ 417-339-3888; 1107 W Hwy 76; mains $5-14; ☽ 11am-9pm Mon-Thu, 11am-10pm Fri-Sat, 11am-8pm Sun; ☒).

KANSAS CITY

Big, open and inviting, Kansas City (KC) is famed for its BBQ (100-plus joints slather it on), fountains (over 200; on par with Rome) and jazz. While the latter doesn't swing as it did when hometown hero Charlie Parker was around blowing notes, there are still plenty of places getting into the groove. These days, KC has sobered up to become more tax town than sax town – the Internal Revenue Service and H&R Block have huge headquarters here – but visitors have no problem finding fun.

History

KC began life in 1821 as a trading post but really came into its own once westward expansion began. The Oregon, California and Santa Fe trails all met steamboats loaded with pioneers here.

Jazz exploded in the 1930s under Mayor Tom Pendergast's Prohibition-era tenure, when he allowed alcohol to flow freely. At its peak, KC had more than 100 nightclubs, dance halls and vaudeville houses swinging to the beat (and booze). The roaring good times ended with Pendergast's indictment on tax evasion and the scene had largely faded by the mid-1940s.

KC was a bustling farm-distribution and industrial center for generations – a serious cowtown, though its giant stockyards closed in 1991.

Orientation & Information

State Line Rd divides KC Missouri and KC Kansas (which has little to offer travelers). KC Missouri has some distinct areas, including the fun and historic River Market (still home to a large farmers market) immediately north of downtown; the gallery-filled Crossroads Arts District around Baltimore and 20th Sts; and the historic 18th and Vine Historic Jazz District (this is on the upswing, but still pretty rough); Westport, on Westport Rd just west of Main St; 39th St West, just west of Westport by the Kansas border; and the chain-store-laden Country Club Plaza (often shortened to 'the Plaza'), with Seville-inspired architecture based on Broadway and 47th Sts, are ideal for eating, drinking and shopping.

BOOKSTORES
Barnes & Noble (☎ 816-753-1313; 420 W 47th St; ☽ 9am-10pm Sun-Thu, 9am-11pm Fri-Sat) At the Plaza.

INTERNET ACCESS
Westport Coffeehouse Computers (per hr $5) and free wi-fi for customers (p655).

INTERNET RESOURCES
Arts Council of Metropolitan Kansas City (www.art skc.org) Provides the performing and visual arts low-down.
Bar Scoop (www.barscoop.com) Helps dedicated drinkers plot their evening.

MEDIA
Jam (www.jazzkc.org) A free bi-monthly covering KC's jazz scene.

ROUTE 66: GET YOUR KICKS IN MISSOURI

The Show-Me state will show you a fat slice of Mother Road. Meet the route in **St Louis** (p643), where roadies rank **Ted Drewes Frozen Custard** (p647) more of a must-see than the **Gateway Arch** (p645). There are a couple of well-signed historic routes through the city.

Follow I-44 (the interstate is built over most of Route 66 in Missouri) west to **Route 66 State Park** (☎ 636-938-7198; exit 266; ✆ 7am-½hr after sunset), with its visitor center and **museum** (admission free; ✆ 9am-4:30pm) inside a 1935 roadhouse. Back on the interstate, detour at Eureka to the folk-art **Black Madonna Shrine** (☎ 636-938-5361; admission free; ✆ 9am-7pm May-Sep, 9am-6pm Apr & Oct, 9am-4pm Nov-Mar).

Speed southwest again on I-44 to Stanton, then follow the signs to family-mobbed **Meramec Caverns** (☎ 800-676-6105; www.americascave.com; adult/child $15/8; ✆ 8:30am-7:30pm summer, reduced hours rest of year), as interesting for the Civil War history and hokey charm as for the stalactites; and the conspiracy-crazy **Jesse James Wax Museum** (☎ 573-927-5233; adult/child $6/2.50; ✆ 9am-6pm Jun-Aug, 9am-5pm Sat-Sun Sep-Oct). Further west, roll through Rolla to gawk at the mini **Stonehenge replica** on the University of Missouri's campus.

The **Route 66 Museum and Research Center** (☎ 417-532-2148; 915 S Jefferson St; admission free; ✆ 8am-8pm Mon-Thu, 8am-5pm Fri-Sat) at the library in Lebanon has memorabilia past and present. Ready for a snooze? Head to the 1940s **Munger Moss Motel** (☎ 417-532-3111; www.mungermoss.com; 1336 E Rte 66; s/d from $33/41; ✆ ✆). It's got a classic neon sign and Mother Road-loving owners.

Ditch the interstate west of Springfield, taking Hwy 96 to Civil War-era **Carthage**'s historic town square and **66 Drive-In Theatre** (☎ 417-359-5959; www.66drivein.com; 17231 Old 66 Blvd; adult/child $6/3; ✆ Fri-Sun Apr-Oct). In **Joplin** get on State Hwy 66, turning onto old Route 66 (the pre-1940s route), before the Kansas state line.

For more information, contact the **Route 66 Association of Missouri** (www.missouri66.org).

Kansas City Star (www.kansascity.com) KC's daily paper; its *Preview* entertainment section comes out on Thursday.

Pitch (www.pitch.com) The free alt-weekly newspaper.

MEDICAL SERVICES

Kansas University Medical Center (☎ 913-588-5000; 3901 Rainbow Blvd) In Kansas, just across the border from 39th St West.

POST

Post office (☎ 816-374-9180; 30 W Pershing; ✆ 7am-6pm Mon-Fri, 8:30am-3:30pm Sat) In Union Station.

TOURIST INFORMATION

Greater Kansas City Visitor Center (☎ 800-767-7700; www.visitkc.com; 22nd fl, 1100 Main St in City Center Sq; ✆ 8:30am-5pm Mon-Fri) City- oriented information.

Country Club Plaza Visitor Center (☎ 816-691-3866; 4709 Central St; ✆ 10am-6pm Mon-Sat, noon-5pm Sun) Another city outlet. Pick up a free 'The Plaza Art & Architecture Guide' here.

Missouri Welcome Center (☎ 816-889-3330; www.visitmo.com; I-70, exit 9; ✆ 8am-5pm) Statewide maps and information.

Sights & Activities

The **Museums at 18th & Vine** (☎ 816-474-8463; 1616 E 18th St; adult for 1/2 museums $6/8, child $2.50/4; ✆ 9am-6pm Tue-Sat, noon-6pm Sun) are well worth visiting. You'll learn about different styles, rhythms, instruments and musicians – including KC native Charlie Parker – at the interactive **American Jazz Museum** (www.americanjazzmuseum.org). Visit the **Negro Leagues Baseball Museum** (www.nlbm.com) to learn about African American teams (eg the KC Monarchs and New York Black Yankees) that flourished until baseball became fully integrated.

Giant badminton shuttlecocks (the building represents the net) absurdly surround the encyclopedic **Nelson-Atkins Museum of Art** (☎ 816-751-1278; www.nelson-atkins.org; 4525 Oak St; admission free; ✆ 10am-5pm Tue, Wed & Sun, 10am-9pm Thu-Sat; Ⓟ) with standout European painting, photography and Asian art collections. Its new luminescent Bloch Building, designed by Steven Holl, has earned rave reviews. The nearby **Kemper Museum of Contemporary Art** (☎ 816-753-5784; www.kemperart.org; 4420 Warwick Blvd; admission free; ✆ 10am-4pm Tue-Thu, 10am-9pm Fri-Sat, 11am-5pm Sun) is smaller, but edgier. The museums are near Country Club Plaza.

GREAT PLAINS

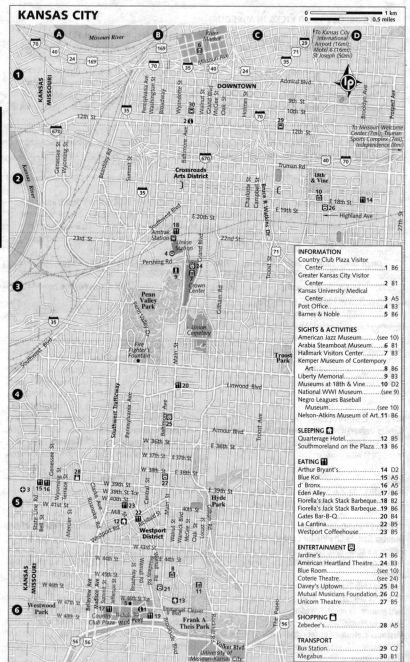

KANSAS CITY

Home to 200 tons of salvaged 'treasure' from a riverboat that sunk in 1856, the **Arabia Steamboat Museum** (☎ 816-471-1856; www.1856.com; 400 Grand Blvd; adult/child $12.50/4.75; ☽ 10am-5:30pm Mon-Sat, noon-5pm Sun) in River Market offers insight to the crafty Missouri River, which claimed some 400 steamboats.

The solemn **National WWI Museum** (☎ 816-784-1918; www.nww1.org; 100 W 26th St; adult/child $8/4; ☽ 10am-5pm Tue-Sun) sits under the towering **Liberty Memorial** (observation deck adult/child $4/3; last ticket sold 4:15pm).

Across Main St, the **Hallmark Visitors Center** (☎ 816-274-3613; www.hallmarkvisitorscenter.com; admission free; ☽ 9am-5pm Tue-Fri, 9:30am-4:30pm Sat) features not-terribly-interesting exhibits on the greeting card giant's history, but hey, Hallmark is one of KC's biggest employers, so cut it some slack.

Harley Davidson Motorcycles hail from Milwaukee, but some are made right here, and you can take a free **factory tour** (☎ 816-270-8286; 11401 N Congress; ☽ 8am-2pm Mon-Fri summer, until 1pm rest of year), at the assembly plant which is 20 minutes north of downtown. No open-toed shoes or children under 12 allowed.

Festivals & Events

American Royal Barbecue (www.americanroyal.com) The world's largest BBQ contest takes place the first weekend in October.

Sleeping

Downtown accommodations are costly and not well suited for optimal eats and drinks. Westport and the Plaza are better options. For something cheap, you'll need to head out on the interstate: north on I-35 and I-29 and east on I-70 are good places to look.

Motel 6 (☎ 816-741-6400, 800-466-8356; I-29 exit 8; s/d $40/46; ☒ ☒) Near the airport, this is your ordinary cheapie.

Quarterage Hotel (☎ 816-931-0001, 800-942-4233; www.quarteragehotel.com; 560 Westport Rd; r from $109; ℗ ☒ ☒ wi-fi) The locally owned Quarterage is centrally located in Westport. All rooms have sofas and flat-screen TVs and there are many nice extras like hot breakfast and open-bar cocktails from 5pm to 7pm.

Southmoreland on the Plaza (☎ 816-531-7979; www.southmoreland.com; 116 E 46th St; r $135-200, ste $250; ℗ ☒ ☒ wi-fi) Southmoreland is an exceptionally nice, 13-room B&B in a big old mansion between the art museums and the Plaza.

Eating & Drinking

Westport, 39th St West and Country Club Plaza are your best bets for clusters of food and drink. There are many small ethnic restaurants in River Market, but most open for lunch only. Be sure to try a locally brewed Boulevard Beer. Bars close between 1:30am and 3am.

d' Bronx (☎ 816-531-0550; 3904 Bell St; sandwiches $4-7; ☽ 10:30am-9pm Mon-Thu, 10:30am-11pm Fri-Sat, noon-8pm Sun; ☒) It's a classic deli with 50 whopping hot and cold sandwiches to choose from, though the shining star is the crispy pizza.

Westport Coffeehouse (☎ 816-756-3222; 4010 Pennsylvania St; sandwiches $5.50-6.50; ☽ 7:30am-11pm Mon-Thu, 7:30am-1am Fri, 10am-1am Sat, 10am-10pm Sun; ☒ ☐ wi-fi) This peaceful place off the main drag has good coffee and specialty teas. There is live music on weekends.

Blue Koi (☎ 816-561-5003; 1803 W 39th St; mains $5-10; ☽ 11am-9:30pm Mon-Thu, 11am-10:30pm Fri, noon-10:30pm Sat; ☒) This Asian noodle shop doles out dumplings, soups and bubble teas (many of them spiked with alcohol) with West Coast panache.

La Cantina (☎ 816-531-1616; 419 Westport Rd; mains $6-9; ☽ 11am-9:30pm Mon-Thu, 11am-10:30pm Fri-Sat) This narrow place makes a mean *salsa tomatillo* and has a pretty good bar. Brick walls and a press-tin ceiling lend a friendly feel.

Eden Alley (☎ 816-561-5415; 707 W 47th St; mains $6-16; ☽ 11am-2:30pm Mon-Tue, 11am-9pm Wed-Sat; ☒) Those seeking respite from KC's BBQ will find vegetable-rich dishes like vegan fondue and spinach-mushroom loaf. Located in Unity Temple's no-frills basement.

Entertainment

The **Pitch** (www.pitch.com) has the top cultural calendar.

LIVE MUSIC

Venues are scattered across the city.

Blue Room (☎ 816-474-8463; www.americanjazz museum.com; 1616 E 18th St) This slick club, part of the American Jazz Museum, hosts shows on Monday, Thursday, Friday and Saturday nights. Weekday shows usually have no cover charge.

Mutual Musicians Foundation (☎ 816-471-5212; 1823 Highland Ave) Also at 18th & Vine, this little spot has hosted after-hours jams since 1930. Nowadays they take place on Friday and Saturday nights and don't kick off until about 1am.

Jardine's (☎ 816-561-6480; www.jardines4jazz.com; 4536 Main St) This respected club near the Plaza has jazz seven nights a week, plus Saturday afternoons.

Davey's Uptown (☎ 816-753-1909; www.daveysuptown.com; 3402 Main St) Local and regional alternative acts play nearly nightly.

THEATER

KC's theater scene is more happening than you'd expect.

Unicorn Theatre (☎ 816-531-7529; www.unicorntheatre.org; 3828 Main St) The Unicorn stages contemporary, thought-provoking works.

American Heartland Theatre (☎ 816-842-9999; www.ahtkc.com; 2450 Grand Blvd) The American Heartland Theatre, in Crown Center, mounts Broadway-style shows.

Coterie Theatre (☎ 816-474-6552; www.coterietheatre.org; 2450 Grand Blvd) This acclaimed children's theater also calls Crown Center home.

SPORTS

Major League Baseball's **Royals** (☎ 816-921-8000; www.kcroyals.com), Major League Soccer's **Wizards** (☎ 913-387-3400; www.kcwizards.com) and the NFL's **Chiefs** (☎ 816-931-3330; www.kcchiefs.com), the top ticket in town, play at side-by-side stadiums in the **Truman Sports Complex** (I-70 exit 9).

Shopping

Country Club Plaza is KC's top shopping destination, though there is little here you won't find in any American city. Westport and 39th St West have more eclectic shops. Over 60 galleries call Crossroads Art District home.

Zebedee's (☎ 816-960-6900; 1208 W 39th St; ☺ 11am-8pm Mon & Wed-Sat, noon-5pm Sun) has a great vinyl collection, including many old jazz records.

Getting There & Around

KC International Airport (☎ 816-243-5237; www.flykci.com) is 16 miles northwest of downtown. A taxi to downtown/Plaza costs about $40/45; call **Yellow Cab** (☎ 888-471-6050). Or take the cheaper **KCI Shuttle** (☎ 800-243-5000; downtown/Plaza $17/18).

Greyhound (☎ 816-221-2835; 1101 Troost St) sends buses daily to St Louis ($43, 4½ hours), Chicago ($71, 10¼ to 12¾ hours) and Denver ($91, 11¼ hours) while **Jefferson Lines** heads to Omaha ($32, 3¼ to 4¼ hours) and Minneapolis ($85, 9½ to 10 hours). Both use the city's inconveniently located main bus station. **Megabus** (☎ 877-462-6342; 10th & Main Sts) goes to St Louis and Chicago right from downtown for as low as $8.

Amtrak (☎ 816-421-3622), in lovely Union Station, has daily service to St Louis ($25, six hours), Chicago ($40, 7½ hours) and Albuquerque ($200, 18¼ hours).

Local transport is with **Metro buses** (☎ 816-221-0660; www.kcata.org; adult fare $1.25). A 1-/3-day unlimited ride-pass costs $3/8. The convenient MAX line runs regularly between River Market and Country Club Plaza.

AROUND KANSAS CITY
Independence

Just east of Kansas City, Independence was the home of Harry S Truman, US president from 1945 to 1953. The **Truman Presidential Museum & Library** (☎ 800-833-1225; www.trumanlibrary.org; 500 W US 24; adult/child $7/3; ☺ 9am-5pm Mon-Sat, noon-5pm Sun, to 9pm Thu May-Sep) exhibits thousands of objects, including the famous 'The BUCK STOPS here!' sign, from the man who led the US through one of its most tumultuous eras.

See the simple life Harry and Bess lived following their life in the White House at the **Truman Home** (219 N Delaware St; www.nps.gov/hstr;

'CUEING IT UP

Savoring hickory-smoked brisket, pork, chicken or ribs at one of the BBQ joints around town is a must for any meat eater. KC's own style of BBQ is pit-smoked and slathered with heavily-seasoned vinegar-based sauces. A juicy slab of ribs costs about $18 throughout the city.

Calvin Trillin calls hole-in-the-wall **Arthur Bryant's** (☎ 816-231-1123; 1727 Brooklyn Ave; ☺ 10am-9:30pm Mon-Thu, 10am-10pm Fri-Sat, 11am-8pm Sun) 'the single best restaurant in the world.'

Another famous KC sauce shack is **Gates Bar-B-Q** (☎ 816-753-0828; 3205 Main St; ☺ 10am-midnight Sun-Thu, 10am-1am Fri-Sat), where it is assumed you'll want a frosted mug of beer with your beef.

Fiorella's Jack Stack Barbeque (☎ 816-531-7427; 4747 Wyandotte St; ☺ 11am-10pm Mon-Thu, 11am-10:30pm Fri-Sat, 11am-9pm Sun); Crossroads Arts District (☎ 816-472-7427; 101 W 22nd St) in Country Club Plaza is for people who'd rather dress up before dripping sauce on their pants.

WHAT THE...?

The remarkable **Leila's Hair Museum** (☎ 816-833-2955; www.hairwork.com/leila; 1333 S Noland Rd; adult/child $5/2.50; ⏰ 9am-4:30pm Tue-Sat) in Independence holds the world's largest (and only public) collection of wreaths and jewelry made from hair, a popular 19th century art form.

adult/child $4/free), furnished with original belongings. Tour tickets are sold at the **visitor center** (☎ 816-254-9929; 223 N Main St; ⏰ 8:30am-5pm, no tours Mon winter).

The 2.7-mile **Truman Historic Walking Trail**, starting at the visitor center, leads to dozens of other Truman-related sites, including the courthouse where he began his political career and **Clinton's Soda Fountain** (☎ 816-833-2046; 100 W Maple Ave; mains $4-8; ⏰ 8:30am-6pm Mon-Thu, 8:30am-8pm Fri-Sat; ☒) where he landed his first job.

The **National Frontier Trails Museum** (☎ 816-325-7575; www.ci.independence.mo.us/nftm; 318 W Pacific St; adult/child $5/3; ⏰ 9am-4:30pm Mon-Sat, 12:30-4:30pm Sun) gives a good look at life for the pioneers along the Santa Fe, California and Oregon Trails; many began their journey in Independence.

You'll also notice a huge, spiraling temple: Independence is the center of the Community of Christ, a Mormon splinter group.

St Joseph

The first Pony Express set out, carrying mail from 'St Jo' 2000 miles west to California, in 1860. The service, making the trip in as little as 8 days, lasted just 18 months before telegraph lines reached the coast rendering the riders redundant. The **Pony Express National Museum** (☎ 800-530-5930; www.ponyexpress.org; 914 Penn St; adult/child $4/2; ⏰ 9am-5pm Mon-Sat, 1-5pm Sun) tells the story of the Express and its brave riders, who were mostly orphans due to the dangers.

St Jo was also home to outlaw Jesse James and he finally met justice in what is now the **Jesse James Home Museum** (☎ 816-232-8206; 12th & Penn; adult/child $2/1; ⏰ 10am-5pm Mon-Sat, 1-5pm Sun summer, closing 4pm rest of year). The fateful bullet hole is still in the wall.

Housed in the former 'State Lunatic Asylum No 2,' the **Glore Psychiatric Museum** (☎ 816-364-1209; 3406 Frederick Ave; adult/child $3/1; ⏰ 10am-5pm Mon-Sat, 1-5pm Sun) gives a frightening and fascinating look at the history and treatment of mental illness. Simple displays tell how lobotomies accidentally began and how 'treatment' has advanced from the 'bath of surprise' to occupational therapy, such as painting. The stomach contents display is alone worth a visit. Your ticket also includes entrance to the **St Joseph Museum** and the **Knea-Von Black Archives** with a variety of historical displays next door.

Get details on nine other museums at the **visitor center** (☎ 800-785-0360; www.stjomo.com; 502 N Woodbine Rd; ⏰ 9am-4pm Mon-Sat) near I-29 exit 47, where most hotels are located.

IOWA

Iowa, home to eight pigs for every one person, is the butt of many jokes, including some stingers from native son Bill Bryson. But, in fact, Iowa holds a host of quirks and charms up its sleeve. The towering bluffs on the Mississippi River and the soaring Loess Hills lining the Missouri River bookend the state; in between you'll find the writers' town of Iowa City; the commune-dwelling refrigerator builders of the Amana Colonies; and the Sanskrit-speaking yogic-flying meditators of Vedic City. And you thought it would be dull here.

History

After the 1832 Black Hawk War pushed local Native Americans westward, immigrants flooded into Iowa from all parts of the world and hit the ground farming. Some established experimental communities such as the Germans of the Amana Colonies (p660). Others spread out and kept coaxing the soil (95% of the land is fertile) until Iowa attained its current status as 'Food Capital of the World' and US leader in hogs and corn. Iowa is also the state that makes or breaks presidents: ever since the early 1970s, the Iowa Caucus has opened the national election battle.

Information

Iowa Bed & Breakfast Guild (☎ 800-743-4692; www.ibbg.com)

Iowa state parks (☎ 515-281-5918; www.iowadnr.com) State parks are free to visit.

Iowa Tourism Office (☎ 888-472-6035; www.traveliowa.com)

GREAT PLAINS

IOWA FACTS

Nickname Hawkeye State

Population 3 million

Area 56,275 sq miles

Capital city Des Moines (population 196,900)

Sales Tax 5%

Birthplace of actor John Wayne (1907–79), author Bill Bryson (b 1951), actor Ashton Kutcher (b 1978)

Home of Madison County's bridges

Famous for Iowa Caucus that jumpstarts the presidential elections

Official rock Geode

DES MOINES

Des Moines, meaning 'of the monks' not 'in the corn' as the surrounding fields might suggest, is Iowa's often-mocked capital. The town really is rather dull, but has a few good attractions. You must see the capitol, if nothing else. A fact not mentioned in the tourist brochures: before Ozzy Osbourne married Sharon and she started cooking for him, he bit the head off a bat here in 1982.

Orientation & Information

The Des Moines River slices through downtown. The Court Ave Entertainment District sits just west, while East Village, at the foot of the capitol, and (yes) east of the river, is home to some up-and-coming art and design galleries, eateries and a few gay bars.

There is a **visitor center** (☎ 800-451-2625; www.seedesmoines.com; 400 Locust St, Suite 265; ☼ 8:30am-5pm Mon-Fri) downtown.

Sights & Activities

The **State Capitol** (☎ 515-281-5591; E 9th St & Grand Ave; ☼ 8am-4:30pm Mon-Fri, 9am-4pm Sat) must have been Liberace's favorite government building. Its every detail, from the sparkling gold dome to the spiral staircases and stained glass in the law library, seems to strive to outdo the other. Join a free tour and you can climb halfway up the dome.

Most of the displays at the **State Historical Museum** (☎ 515-281-5111; 600 E Locust St; admission free; ☼ 9am-4:30pm Mon-Sat, noon-4:30pm Sun), at the foot of the capitol, feature first person accounts from people who lived through that particular historical era or event.

The **Des Moines Art Center** (☎ 515-277-4405; www.desmoinesartcenter.org; 4700 Grand Ave; admission free; ☼ 11am-4pm Tue, Wed & Fri, 11am-9pm Thu, 10am-4pm Sat, noon-4pm Sun), south of the I-235 42nd St exit, features a good contemporary collection. It also has a one-room **downtown branch** (☎ 515-557-6109; 800 Walnut St; admission free; ☼ 11am-4pm Mon-Fri).

Much more than just country music and butter sculpture, the **Iowa State Fair** (www.iowastatefair.org; adult/child $10/4) draws a million visitors over its ten-day mid-August run.

Sleeping

Several budget chain motels are bunched at I-35/I-80 exit 136 north of town, such as **Motel 6** (☎ 515-266-5456, 800-466-8356; 4940 NE 14th St; r from $41; 🐾 🖧).

Everyone from Mae West to JFK has spent the night in the old-world **Hotel Fort Des Moines** (☎ 515-243-1161, 800-532-1466; www.hotelfortdesmoines.com; 1000 Walnut St; r/ste weekend $99/119, weekday $139/159; 🅿 🐾 🖧 🖳 wi-fi). Amenities include a business center and parking ($7), and it's conveniently located next to the Raccoon River Brewing Company.

Eating & Drinking

Downtown's Court Ave and East Village each have some worthy restaurants.

Java Joe's (☎ 515-288-5282; 214 4th St; mains $3-7; ☼ 7am-11pm Mon-Thu, 7am-midnight Fri-Sat, 9am-10pm Sun; 🗵 wi-fi) The small menu covers a lot of ground: sandwiches (corned beef, chicken salad), Indian dishes (Madras lentils), vegetarian sausage and, of course, cupfuls of coffee. Live music on weekends.

Cookry (☎ 515-369-2665; 2314 University Ave; mains $6-9; ☼ 11am-8:30pm Mon-Sat; 🗵 wi-fi) This friendly Sierra Leonean-owned place near Drake University offers some West African staples like cassava leaves and goat curry stew, plus some more familiar flavors.

Lift (☎ 515-288-3777; 222 4th St; ☼ 5pm-2am Mon-Tue, 4pm-2am Wed-Fri, 7pm-2am Sat-Sun; 🗵) The Lift is an artsy bar popular for its good beers and sassy martinis.

AROUND DES MOINES
Madison County

This scenic county, about 30 miles southwest of the capital, slumbered for half a century until Robert James Waller's block-buster, tear-jerking novel *The Bridges of Madison County* and its movie version brought in scores of fans to check out the covered bridges where Robert and Francesca fueled their affair. Pick up a map to all six bridges and other movie sets at the **Chamber of Commerce** (☎ 800-298-6119; www.madisoncounty.com; 73 Jefferson St; ☽ 9am-5pm Mon-Fri, 10am-4pm Sat, noon-4pm Sun) in Winterset.

The humble **birthplace of John Wayne** (☎ 515-462-1044; www.johnwaynebirthplace.org; 216 S 2nd St, Winterset; adult/child $4/1; ☽ 10am-4:30pm), aka Marion Robert Morrison, is now a museum.

Eldon

Grab a 'tool' out of your trunk and make your very own parody of Grant Wood's iconic painting *American Gothic* (1930) in tiny Eldon, about 90 miles southeast of Des Moines. The original house is at 301 American Gothic St, though it's not open to the public. An **interpretive center** (☎ 641-652-3352; admission free; ☽ 10am-4pm Tue-Sat, 1-4pm Sun-Mon summer, 10am-4pm Mon-Fri, 1-4pm Sat rest of year) sits across the street. The actual painting is in the Art Institute of Chicago (see p549).

Fairfield & Vedic City

Hmm; where to go to meditate for world peace and practice 'yogic flying' (where people cross their legs and bounce on their asses like children) with like-minded masses – San Francisco? LA? Try the cornfields of southern Iowa. Anchored by the golden domes of Maharishi University of Management, founded by the Maharishi Mahesh Yogi (he who taught the Beatles transcendental meditation in India), these neighboring towns host an unusual (by Iowa standards) array of vegetarian restaurants and incense-wafting shops. In hippie-trippy Vedic City all homes face east and have small domes on top.

The historic **Landmark Inn** (☎ 641-472-4152; www.fairfieldlandmarkinn.com; 115 N Main St, Fairfield; s $44-49, d $49-54; ☒ wi-fi) is good value compared to Vedic City's spa resorts. Pick up locally grown foodstuffs at **Everybody's** (☎ 641-472-5199; 501 N 2nd St; ☽ 8:30am-9:30pm; ☒), an organic grocery store with attached café. The gallery-hopping **Artwalk** draws crowds the first Friday night of each month.

ALONG I-80

Most of Iowa's attractions are within an easy drive of I-80, which runs east–west across the state's center. Des Moines is midway along the road.

Quad Cities

Four cities straddle the Mississippi River by I-80: Davenport and Bettendorf in Iowa and Moline and Rock Island in Illinois. See above for Illinois-side details. The **visitor center** (☎ 800-747-7800; www.visitquadcities.com; 102 S Harrison St, Davenport; ☽ 8:30am-5pm year-round, 10am-4pm Sat-Sun summer) has bike rentals ($7 per hour) for a ride along the Big Muddy.

The **Iowa 80 Truckstop** (☎ 563-284-6961; www.iowa80truckstop.com; I-80 exit 284 in Walcott; ☽ 24hr) is the world's biggest, baby, complete with a Hall of Fame (Monday, Wednesday and Friday 10am to 2pm) displaying actual rigs, dentist office and chrome-laden store to supplement the usual eateries and gas pumps.

A more refined experience awaits at the **Figge Art Museum** (☎ 563-326-7804; www.figgeartmuseum.org; 225 W 2nd St, Davenport; adult/child $7/4; ☽ 10am-5pm Tue-Sun, to 9pm Thu), with world-class Haitian and Mexican Colonial collections.

You can cruise up to Dubuque on the Victorian-style riverboat **Twilight** (☎ 800-331-1467; www.riverboattwilight.com; $290 per person double, triple or quad occupancy) which runs overnight trips up the gorgeous Mississippi River from nearby Le Claire.

The **Abbey Hotel** (☎ 563-355-0291, 800-438-7535; www.theabbeyhotel.com; 1401 Central Ave, Bettendorf; r $104-129, ste $169; ☒ ☒ ☒ ☒ wi-fi) has taken over a gorgeous converted monastery. Today you get marble bathrooms instead of straw beds like the nuns had.

Iowa City

The former state capital bustles with a youthful, artsy vibe. The University of Iowa campus (home to good art and natural history museums) spills across both sides of the Iowa River; to the east it mingles with downtown restaurants and bars. In summer (when the student-to-townie ratio evens out) the city mellows somewhat, but there is always something fun happening. The **visitor center** (☎ 800-283-6592; www.iowacitycoralville.org; 900 1st Ave; ☽ 8am-5pm Mon-Fri) is in neighboring Coralville.

The cute gold-domed building at the heart of campus is the **Old Capitol** (☎ 319-335-0548; admission free; ☽ 10am-3pm Tue-Wed & Fri, 10am-5pm Thu & Sat, 1-5pm Sun). Built in 1840, it was the seat of government until 1857 when Des Moines grabbed the reins. It's now a museum with furnishings from back in its heyday.

Several cheap hotels line 1st Avenue in Coralville (I-80 exit 242) including the not-

GREAT PLAINS

GREAT PLAINS

too-bad **Big Ten Inn** (☎ 866-424-4836; 707 1st Ave; r from $35; ✷ wi-fi). Four-poster beds and other antiques adorn Mark and Bob's 1913 Dutch Colonial **Brown Street Inn** (☎ 319-338-0435; www .brownstreetinn.com; 430 Brown St; r $75-130; ✕ ✷ ▣ wi-fi), an easy walk from downtown.

It's food and beer galore around downtown. **Z'Mariks Noodle Café** (☎ 319-338-5500; 19 S Dubuque St; mains $5-6; ◷ 11am-9pm; ✕) serves yummy noodle and rice bowls in a world of flavors. Iowa City's favorite grill, the classic **Hamburg Inn** (☎ 319-337-5512; 214 N Linn St; mains $5-7; ◷ 6am-11pm; ✕) speeds out heaping sandwich platters and all-day breakfast. Many members of the revered Iowa Writers' Workshop gravitate to closet-sized **Dave's Foxhead Tavern** (☎ 319-351-9824; 402 E Market St).

Amana Colonies

These seven villages, just northwest of Iowa City, are stretched along a 17-mile loop. All were established as German religious communes between 1855 and 1861 by inspirationists who, until the Great Depression, lived a Utopian life with no wages paid and all assets communally owned. Unlike the Amish and Mennonite religions, Inspirationists embrace modern technology, evident in their booming refrigerator business (note the plant in Middle Amana).

Today the seven well-preserved villages, completely devoid of chain businesses, offer a glimpse at this unique culture, and there are lots of arts, crafts, cheeses, baked goods and wines to buy. Stop at the grain-elevator–shaped **visitor center** (☎ 800-579-2294; www.amana colonies.com; 622 46th Ave, Amana; ◷ 9am-5pm Mon-Sat, 10am-5pm Sun Apr-Oct, 10am-4pm rest of year) for the essential guide-map. It also has audio tours on CD ($10) and bike rental ($15 per day).

Six museums are sprinkled throughout the villages, including the insightful **Amana Heritage Museum** (☎ 319-622-3567; 4310 220th Trl, Amana; ◷ 10am-5pm Mon-Sat, noon-4pm Sun Apr-Oct, 10am-5pm Sat Nov-Dec & Mar). The others are open summers only. An $8/15 combo ticket/family pass gets you into them all. Another popular stop is the privately-owned **Barn Museum** (☎ 319-622-3058; 220th Trl, South Amana; adult/child $3.50/1.25-1.75; ◷ 9am-5pm Apr-Oct), which has miniature versions of buildings found across rural America.

The villages have many good-value B&Bs and historic inns including **Zuber's** (☎ 319-622-3911, 888-623-3911; 2206 44 Ave, Homestead; r from $69;

✕ ✷ wi-fi) with 15 individually decorated rooms in an 1890s brick building.

One of the Amanas' top draws is the hefty-portioned, home-cooked German cuisine. One of the colonies' oldest (serving since 1940) and most renowned restaurants, **Ox Yoke** (☎ 319-622-3441; 4420 220th Trl, Amana; mains $8-18; ◷ 11am-8:30pm Mon-Sat, 9am-7pm Sun summer) fills a former communal kitchen. Keep an eye out for Millsteam wheat beer, brewed in Amana.

ALONG US 20

US 20 stretches from Dubuque on the Mississippi River to Sioux City on the Missouri River. It's not exactly scenic, but it beats I-80.

Dubuque

Dubuque makes a great stop: 19th-century Victorian homes line its narrow and surprisingly urban streets between the Mississippi River and seven steep hills. Get information from the **visitor center** (☎ 800-798-4748; www .traveldubuque.com; 300 Main St; ◷ 9am-5pm Mon-Sat, 9am-3pm Sun summer, 9am-4pm Mon-Sat, 9am-1pm Sun rest of year).

The **4th Street Elevator** (☎ 563-582-6496; 4th St & Fenelon; adult/child round-trip $2/1; ◷ 8am-10pm Apr-Nov), built in 1882, climbs a steep hill for huge views. Ring the bell to begin the ride. Learn about life (of all sorts) on the Mississippi at the impressive **National Mississippi River Museum & Aquarium** (☎ 563-557-9545; www.rivermuseum.com; 350 E 3rd St; adult $10, child $4-7.50; ◷ 10am-6pm summer, 10am-5pm rest of year). Nearby, the **Spirit of Dubuque** (☎ 563-583-8093; www.dubuqueriverrides.com; 3rd St at Ice Harbor; adult/child from $14.30/8.75; ◷ Apr-Oct, call for

---

SCENIC DRIVE: LOESS HILLS SCENIC BYWAY

The well-signed Loess Hills Scenic Byway is an inviting 220-mile network of roads running along Iowa's western edge. It's named for the rare loess (rhymes with Gus), a wind-blown glacier-ground soil that began piling up about 24,000 years ago. Steep, terraced bluffs are the result today. Nowhere else but China do loess hills reach these heights.

The most dramatic scenery is between Council Bluffs and Sioux City. Pick up a detailed guide booklet with maps at the **Western Historic Trails Center** (☎ 712-366-4900; I-29/80 exit 1B; ◷ 9am-6pm May-Sep, 9am-5pm rest of year) in Council Bluffs.

schedule) offers a variety of Mississippi sightseeing and dining cruises on a mock-paddleboat. You might see the national bird, especially in winter, at **Eagle Point Park**, north of downtown (take Rhomberg to Shiras).

The historic **Julien Inn** (☎ 563-556-4200, 800-798-7098; www.julieninn.com; 200 Main St; r $55-85, ste $75-95; ⊠ wi-fi) is fun. Built in 1914 and once owned by Al Capone, the current owners successfully mix the old and the new.

The scrumptious sandwiches and pizzas at **Café Manna Java** (☎ 563-588-3105; 269 Main St; mains $5-14; ☷ 7am-2pm Mon, 7am-9pm Tue-Sat, 8am-2pm Sun; ⊠ wi-fi) are built from breads cooked in its wood-fired oven.

Waterloo & Around

Home to five **John Deere tractor factories**, Waterloo is the place to get one of those prized green-and-yellow caps you've seen all over middle America. Fun and free tractor-driven **assembly division tours** (☎ 319-292-7697; 3500 E Donald St; ☷ 8am, 10am, 1pm Mon-Fri) and **engine works tours** (☎ 319-292-5347; 3801 Ridgeway Ave; ☷ 9:30am, 1pm Mon-Fri) show how these vehicles are made ('with pride'). Minimum age is 13 and reservations are required.

NORTH DAKOTA

It's flat, cold and *way* up there; but North Dakota is definitely not the same old ordinary vacation everybody else is doing. It's reputed to be the least-visited state in the US, though that has more to do with location than appeal. Hunting is a primary draw, but North Dakota lends itself equally well to other outdoor pursuits including windsurfing and birdwatching. The more time you spend in the vast, wide-open landscapes, the more surprised you'll be by the pockets of sophistication in Fargo, the state's only significant city.

History

During their epic journey, Lewis and Clark spent more time in what is now North Dakota than any other state, meeting up with Shoshone guide Sacagawea on their way west. In the mid-19th century, smallpox epidemics came up the Missouri River, decimating the Arikara, Mandan and Hidatsa tribes, who affiliated and established the Like-a-Fishhook Village around 1845. When the railroad arrived in North Dakota in the 1870s,

---

NORTH DAKOTA FACTS

Nickname Peace Garden State
Population 636,000
Area 70,705 sq miles
Capital city Bismarck (population 55,500)
Sales Tax 6%
Birthplace of cream of wheat (1893), bandleader Lawrence Welk (1903–92), singer-writer of westerns Louis L'Amour (1908–88) singer Peggy Lee (1920–2002)
Home of world's largest bison, turtle and Holstein statues
Famous for Teddy Roosevelt's retreat
Official fruit Chokecherry

---

thousands of settlers flocked in to take up allotments under the Homestead Act. By 1889 the state population was more than 250,000, half foreign-born (one in eight were from Norway).

Young Theodore Roosevelt came here to ditch his city-slicker image and get himself roughened up. As president, inspired by his time in North Dakota, he earned the title 'The Father of Conservation' for his work creating national forests and parks.

Information

North Dakota Bed & Breakfast Association (☎ 888-271-3380; www.ndbba.com)
North Dakota states (☎ 701-328-5357; www.ndparks.com) Vehicle permits cost $5/25 per day/year.
North Dakota Tourism Division (☎ 800-435-5663; www.ndtourism.com)

ALONG I-94

The quickest, if not exactly the most scenic, route across North Dakota, I-94 provides easy access to most of the state's top attractions.

Fargo

Named for the Fargo of Wells Fargo Bank, North Dakota's biggest city has been a fur-trading post, a frontier town, a quick-divorce capital and a haven for folks in the Federal Witness Protection Program; not to mention the namesake of the Coen Brothers' film *Fargo* – though the movie took place across the Red River in Minnesota. These days its emerging arts scene is drawing notice.

The grain elevator-shaped **visitor center** (☎ 800-235-7654; www.fargomoorhead.org; 2001 44th St; ☷ 7:30am-6pm Mon-Fri, 10am-4pm Sat-Sun summer,

8am-5pm Mon-Fri, 10am-4pm Sat-Sun rest of year) is off I-94 exit 348.

The modern, ambitious **Plains Art Museum** (☎ 701-232-3821; www.plainsart.org; 704 1st Ave N; adult/child $5/free; ☺ 10am-5pm Tue-Sat, 1-5pm Sun, to 8pm Thu) features sophisticated programming in a renovated warehouse. The permanent collection includes contemporary work by Native American artists.

Across the river in Moorhead, Minnesota, the **Heritage Hjemkomst Interpretive Center** (☎ 218-299-5511; www.hjemkomst-center.com; 202 1st Ave; adult/child $6/4; ☺ 9am-5pm Mon-Sat, 9am-8pm Tue, noon-5pm Sun) has a Norwegian stave church and 76ft replica of a 9th-century Viking ship that local high school guidance counselor Robert Asp built; his family sailed it to Norway in 1982 after his death.

ourpick Hotel Donaldson (☎ 701-478-1000, 888-478-8768; www.hoteldonaldson.com; 101 Broadway; r $170-185; ☒ ☒ ☐ wi-fi) is not the kind of digs you'd expect to find in these parts. Its 17 suites feature work from regional artists, Bose stereos, heated floors, plush linens – the works. The chic restaurant and rooftop bar are worth stopping in for a dine or a drink. Cheap motels line the freeways.

Atomic Coffee (☎ 701-478-6160; 222 Broadway; snacks $1-5; ☺ 6:30am-11pm Mon-Fri, 7am-11pm Sat, 8am-10pm Sun; ☒ wi-fi) has soups, smoothies and comfy chairs.

Bismarck

Bismarck, North Dakota's capital, has a solid downtown core that makes it feel larger than it really is. Several sights in town and around make it a nice stopover.

The Bismarck-Mandan **Visitor Center** (☎ 800-767-3555; www.discoverbismarckmandan.com; 1600 Burnt Boat Dr, Bismarck; ☺ 7:30am-7pm Mon-Fri, 8am-6pm Sat, 10am-5pm Sun summer, 8am-5pm Mon-Fri rest of year) is just off I-94.

The impressive 1930s **State Capitol** (☎ 701-328-2480; N 7th St; ☺ 8am-5pm Mon-Fri, tours hourly except noon plus 9am-4pm Sat and 1-4pm Sun summer) is often referred to as the 'skyscraper of the prairie' and looks something like a Stalinist school of dentistry from the outside, but has lovely art-deco flourishes inside. There's an observation deck on the 18th floor. Behind the Sacagawea statue, the huge **North Dakota Heritage Center** (☎ 701-328-2666; Capitol Hill; admission free; ☺ 8am-5pm summer, 8am-5pm Mon-Fri, 9am-5pm Sat, 11am-5pm Sun rest of year) does an excellent job summarizing state history.

On River Road, below the I-94 bridge, there's a replica of the 55-foot **keelboat** Lewis and Clark used on this part of their journey.

Fort Abraham Lincoln State Park (☎ 701-667-6340; $5 carload, plus $6 per person to tour historical sites), 7 miles south of Mandan on SR 1806, is well worth the detour. Its **On-A-Slant Indian Village** has five re-created Mandan earth lodges, while the fort, with several replica buildings, is where Custer departed from for the Battle of Little Bighorn.

In Bismarck, motels congregate around I-94 exit 159. Closer to downtown is the Alphaville-esque **Expressway Inn** (☎ 701-222-2900, 800-456-6388; www.expresswayhotels.com; 200 Bismarck Expressway Ave; s/d $49/59; ☒ ☒ wi-fi), with business-like rooms.

For a sampling of old-time America, saddle up to the lunch counter at **Lindy Sue's** (☎ 701-663-5311; 316 W Main St, Mandan; sandwiches $3-5; ☺ 9am-6pm Mon-Sat; ☒) for a grape phosphate or root beer float. **East 40 Chophouse** (☎ 701-258-7222; I-94 & Hwy 83; mains $14-43; ☺ 11am-9pm Mon-Fri, 3-9:30pm Sat) creates an upscale Roadhouse vibe and serves dishes like bison meat loaf and Thai shrimp pizza.

Around Bismarck

North of Bismarck are several worthwhile attractions near the spot where Lewis and Clark wintered with the Mandan in 1804–05. The best is the **North Dakota Lewis & Clark Interpretive Center** (☎ 701-462-8535; www.fortmandan.com; adult/child $7.50/5; ☺ 9am-7pm summer, 9am-5pm rest of year), 38 miles away in Washburn, where you can learn about the duo's epic expedition and the Native Americans who helped them. The same ticket gets you into **Fort Mandan** (CR 17), a replica of the fort built by Lewis and Clark, 2.5 miles west (10 miles downstream from the flooded original site). Just north of Stanton, the **Knife River Indian Villages** (☎ 701-745-3300; www.nps.gov/knri; CR 37; admission free; ☺ 8am-6pm summer, 8am-4:30pm rest of year) feature the sites of three Hidatsa and Mandan villages that were occupied for at least 900 years and a re-created earth lodge. Sacagawea joined Lewis and Clark from here.

West of Bismarck on I-94, stop and see **Sue, the World's Largest Holstein Cow** at New Salem. At Gladstone, 55 miles west of Sue, turn south along the **Enchanted Highway**, which has eight ginormous metal sculptures between the interstate and Regent, 32 miles south. In Dickinson, a bit further west, the **Dakota Dinosaur**

Museum (☎ 701-225-3466; www.dakotadino.com; I-94 exit 61; adult/child $7/4; ☜ 9am-5pm May-Sep) has dinosaur fossils and statues including a Triceratops guarding the doorway.

Theodore Roosevelt National Park

Undoubtedly North Dakota's highlight, **Theodore Roosevelt National Park** (☎ 701-623-4466; www .nps.gov/thro; 7-day pass person/carload $5/10) near the state's western border protects colorful badlands with its bizarre rock formations and healthy prairie. Most visitors take a spin on the 36-mile scenic drive in the South Unit, near I-94 at Medora. The more rugged North Unit, 68 miles north on US 85, offers a 14-mile drive and fewer visitors. An extensive area around the units is protected as the **Little Missouri National Grassland**.

The park has three visitor centers, including the **Medora visitor center** (☎ 701-623-4466; ☜ 8am-6pm Mon-Thu, 8am-8pm Fri-Sun summer, 8am-4:30pm rest of year), with Theodore Roosevelt's old cabin out back. Roosevelt described this area as 'a land of vast, silent spaces, of lonely rivers, and of plains where the wild game stared at the passing horsemen,' and it's hard to describe the place better even today.

Wildlife is still everywhere: mule deer, wild horses, bighorn sheep, elk, bison, around 200 species of bird and, of course, sprawling subterranean prairie dog towns.

Hikers can explore 85 miles of backcountry trails. For a good adventure, hike or cycle the 96-mile **Maah Daah Hey Trail** between the park units.

Accommodations in Medora (all of it overpriced during the summer) include the massive **Badlands Motel** (☎ 701-623-4444, 800-633-6721; 501 Pacific Ave; s $75-115, d $85-125, Apr-Oct; ✂ ❄ ❑ wi-fi), which has a variety of simple rooms. The park itself has two simple **campgrounds** ($10 per site) and free backcountry camping (permit required).

Medora's main claim to fame is the **Pitchfork Fondue** (☎ 800-633-6721; mains $12-22.50; ☜ 6:30pm summer), a touristy but fun steak diner.

ALONG US 2

US 2 has a wilder profile than I-94. Surprisingly there is a lot of water between **Grand Forks**, whose downtown sits on the Red River (It sat underneath it during the 1997 flood.), and **Devils Lake**, one of the top waterfowl hunting destinations in the country.

Rugby

Rugby is about halfway down the highway, but its more notable location identity is as the **geographical center of North America**. The **Prairie Village Museum** (☎ 701-776-6414; www.prairievillage museum.com; 102 US 2 SE; adult/child $5/1; ☜ 8am-7pm Mon-Sat, 1-7pm Sun May-Sep) holds everything from antique washing machines to an impressive fleet of classic cars. Out front is the **Northern Lights Tower**, which attempts to simulate the aurora borealis each night. You can watch a video of the real thing in the adjacent **gazebo** (admission free; ☜ 9am-5pm summer).

Minot

North Dakota's fourth largest city seriously celebrates its Scandinavian roots. **Scandinavian Heritage Park** (admission free; ☜ 24/7) contains northern European icons like a Norwegian stave church and Finnish sauna plus Minot's **visitor center** (☎ 800-264-2626; www.visitminot.org; 1020 S Broadway; ☜ 8am-7pm Mon-Fri, 10am-4pm Sat, noon-4pm Sun summer, 8am-5pm Mon-Fri rest of year; ❑). October's **Norsk Høstfest** is promoted as the world's largest Scandinavian festival.

The **Dakota Inn** (☎ 701-838-2700, 800-862-5003; 2401 US 2 W; s/d from $50/61; ❑ ❑ wi-fi) offers good value. Cheaper hotels sit along US 83/Broadway and Burdick Expressway.

10 North Main (☎ 701-837-1010; 10 N Main St; mains $13-25; ☜ 4-9pm Tue-Sat; ✗) is a big art-filled space with Dakota-inspired meals like elk steak and squash ravioli.

West to Montana

West of Minot the bleak horizon is dotted with attractively decrepit little prairie settlements slipping toward ghost-town status. Twenty-two miles southwest of Williston along SR 1804, **Fort Buford** (☎ 701-572-9034; adult/child $5/2.50; ☜ 8am-6pm Mon-Fri May-Sep) was the Army outpost where Sitting Bull surrendered; both he and Chief Joseph were held here at times. The ticket also gets you into the adjacent **Missouri-Yellowstone Confluence Interpretive Center** (☜ 8am-6pm Mon-Fri May-Sep, 9am-4pm Wed-Sat & 1-5pm Sun rest of year). Swing by the boat landing in May to see anglers reeling in paddlefish.

About 2 miles west, on the Montana–North Dakota border, the far more interesting **Fort Union Trading Post** (☎ 701-572-9083; www.nps.gov/fous; admission free; ☜ 8am-8pm summer, 9am-5:30pm rest of year) is a reconstruction of the American Fur Company post built in 1828.

SOUTH DAKOTA

Some of the most arresting scenery in the entire country is found here, tucked away in this remote and wild state. The weirdly lunar formations of the Badlands, like an inverted Grand Canyon, are unmissable. Then there's the Black Hills, full of forests, mountains, creeks, canyons, wildlife and two of the country's most recognizable monuments: Mount Rushmore and Crazy Horse. Elsewhere there are important Native American sites and some pleasant cities to explore.

History

When the USA acquired South Dakota with the 1803 Louisiana Purchase, the region was the domain of the Sioux and a few fur trappers. It wasn't until the 1850s that the rich Dakota soil attracted the interest of settlers.

The 1868 Fort Laramie Treaty between the USA and the Sioux promised the Sioux a 60-million-acre reservation that stretched from the Missouri River in the east to the Bighorn Mountains in the west. The treaty was broken in 1874 after Lt Col George Custer led an expedition into the Black Hills in search of gold. Unfortunately for the Sioux, he found it.

Miners and settlers soon streamed in illegally and the Sioux retaliated in the biggest of the Indian Wars. The Battle of Little Bighorn in 1876, in which the great Crazy Horse defeated Custer and killed every last soldier, was the Plains Indians' last major victory over the invaders. Faced with overwhelming force, the tribes split up. Sitting Bull fled to Canada, Crazy Horse turned in his gun in 1877, and the railroads and settlers continued the march west. The final decimation of Sioux resistance came at Wounded Knee in 1890 (see p666). Much later, in 1973, Oglala Sioux loyal to the American Indian Movement and opposed to their tribal leaders occupied Wounded Knee and kept federal officers at bay for 71 days.

Information

Bed & Breakfast Innkeepers of South Dakota (☎ 888-500-4667; www.southdakotabnb.com)
South Dakota Dept of Tourism (☎ 800-732-5682; www.travelsd.com)
South Dakota state parks (☎ 605-773-3391; www.sdgfp.info) Vehicle permits cost $5/23 per day/year.

SIOUX FALLS

South Dakota's largest city (population 139,520) has some attractive historic buildings and a sculpture walk downtown, but it's never going to be much of a tourist destination.

The city's namesake splashes along the Big Sioux River at **Falls Park** off Phillips Ave north of downtown. The park has a **light show** (☼ 9:30pm summer) and a **visitor center** (☎ 605-367-7430; www.siouxfallscvb.com; ☼ 9am-9pm daily Apr-Oct, reduced winter hours) with city-wide information and an observatory. The free **Sioux Falls Trolley** (☼ 10am-8pm Mon-Sat Apr-Sep) links the park to downtown every half-hour. The huge pink quartzite **Old Courthouse Museum** (☎ 605-367-4210; www.siouxlandmuseums.com; 200 W 6th St; admission free; ☼ 8am-5pm Mon-Fri, 9am-5pm Sat, noon-5pm Sun, until 9pm Thu), a restored 1890s building, has three floors of rotating exhibits on the region.

Sioux Falls has a wide variety of hotels and the broadest spectrum of cuisine in the Dakotas, as exemplified by the Ethiopian flavors at **Lalibela** (☎ 605-331-4595; 1001 W 11th St; mains $6-9; ☼ 10am-10pm; ✗).

Around Sioux Falls

Dedicated *Little House on the Prairie* fans should head to Laura Ingalls Wilder's former home, **De Smet**. You can pick up a free drive-by tour-map of various sites from her and her family's life at the **Laura Ingalls Wilder Memorial Society** (☎ 800-880-3383; www.discoverlaura.org; 105 Olivet Ave; ☼ 9am-5:30pm Mon-Sat & 10am-5:30pm Sun summer, 9am-4pm Mon-Sat May, 9am-4pm Mon-Fri Sep-Apr) office and gift shop. The society also leads hour-long tours inside two original **Wilder homes** (adult/child $8/4) – the one where the Wilders spent the first winter and the home 'Pa' built. An **outdoor play**

(☎ 800-776-3594; www.desmetpageant.org; adult/child $8/5) is performed each weekend in July.

ALONG I-90
Along the journey from Sioux Falls to Rapid City there's very little to interfere with your view of the horizon, but there are several must-stops along the way.

Mitchell
Every year, half a million people pull off the interstate to see the Taj Mahal of agriculture, the must-be-seen-to-be-believed **Corn Palace** (☎ 866-273-2676; www.cornpalace.org; 604 N Main St; admission free; ☺ 8am-9pm daily summer, reduced hours rest of year). Incredibly, the murals decorating the Moorish-style building are redone annually with 275,000 ears of corn. It serves as Mitch-ell's civic center, active all year.

If you're here in the evening, step back in time with a double feature at the **Starlite Drive-In Theatre** (☎ 605-996-4511; 4601 N Main St; adult/child $5/free; ☺ Apr-Sep).

Chamberlain
In a picturesque site where I-90 crosses the Missouri River, Chamberlain is home to the excellent **Akta Lakota Museum & Cultural Center** (☎ 800-798-3452; www.aktalakota.org; 1301 N Main St; admission free; ☺ 8am-6pm Mon-Sat, 9am-5pm Sun summer, 8am-5pm Mon-Fri rest of year) at St Joseph's In-dian School. It has Lakota cultural displays and contemporary art from numerous tribes. History buffs should pop into the hilltop rest stop, south of town, where the **Lewis & Clark Information Center** (☎ 605-734-4562; admis-sion free; ☺ 8am-6pm May-Oct) has some exhibits on the duo.

It's well worth taking time for a detour onto the **Native American Scenic Byway**, which begins on Hwy 50 and meanders 100 crooked miles to Pierre, following the Missouri River through rolling, rugged countryside, includ-ing the Crow Creek and the Lower Brule Indian reservations.

Pierre
Even with the black copper **State Capitol** (☎ 605-773-3765; 500 E Capitol Ave; ☺ 8am-10pm) dome ris-ing in the background, Pierre (pronounced 'peer') is just too small (population 14,050) and ordinary to feel like a seat of power. The best reason to detour off I-90 here is because it lies along the **Native American Scenic Byway** (see above).

Exhibits at the subterranean **South Dakota Cultural Heritage Center** (☎ 605-773-3458; www .sdhistory.org; 900 Governor's Dr; adult/child $4/free; ☺ 9am-6:30pm Mon-Sat, 1-4:30pm Sun summer, closes at 4:30pm rest of year) include a bloody Ghost Dance shirt from Wounded Knee.

At a bend on the Missouri River, **Framboise Island** has several hiking trails and plentiful wildlife. It's across from where the Lewis and Clark expedition spent four days and was nearly derailed when they inadvertently of-fended members of the local Brule tribe. The Pierre **visitor center** (☎ 800-962-2034; www.pierre.org; 800 W Dakota Ave; ☺ 8am-5pm Mon-Fri) is nearby.

For genuine Americana, visit South Dako-ta's largest **livestock auction** (☎ 800-280-7210; www .ftpierrelivestock.com), across the river in Ft Pierre. The cattle go under the hammer every Friday and many Saturdays.

Most hotels lie along US 83, including the **Budget Host State Motel** (☎ 605-224-5896; 640 N Euclid St; s/d from $44/49; ⚏ ⚑ wi-fi). It has basic rooms but many extras like a recliner in most rooms and a sauna.

Minuteman Missile National Historic Site
At the height of the Cold War, 450 Minute-men II intercontinental ballistic missiles, al-ways at the ready in underground silos, were just 30 minutes from their targets in the Soviet Union. The warheads have since been retired, though the Delta-09 silo, along with its under-ground launch facility, have been preserved at this young park (Map p668).

Tours inside the sites depart from the temporary **headquarters** (☎ 605-433-5552; www .nps.gov/mimi; I-90 exit 131; ☺ 8am-4:30pm Mon-Fri) daily at 10am throughout the year, plus additional times each summer. Reservations are advised. If you can't make the tour, you can watch a short film. The silo (near exit 116) also has drive-up visitation (8-11am Mon-Fri) during the summer.

Wall
You have to stop at **Wall Drug** (☎ 605-279-2275; www.walldrug.com; 510 Main St; ☺ 6:30am-6pm, extended summer hours). Not because it's interesting, but because the billboards have been beckoning since all the way back in Minnesota. The can't-miss tourist trap – still serving 5¢ cof-fee and free ice water – dominates the town, but it's scarcely more than an 'Olde West' facade and a block-long souvenir shop selling

Wild West toys, rocks, fudge, Western wear and Black Hills gold. Kids will get a kick out of the animatronic dinosaurs and fortune-telling cowboys.

The **Wounded Knee Museum** (☎ 605-279-2573; www.woundedkneemuseum.org; I-90 exit 110; adult/child $5/free; ☻ 8:30am-5:30pm Apr-Oct, extended summer hours), which tells the story of the massacre from the Lakota perspective using photos and narratives, is more insightful than anything at the actual site (see right).

Badlands National Park

If Peter Jackson had decided New Zealand wasn't right for the evil realm of Mordor (for *The Lord of the Rings* movies), he could've filmed here instead. The otherworldly landscape, with barren walls and spikes stabbing the dry air and evil crevices plunging into oblivion, was understandably named *mako sica* ('badland') by Native Americans. Looking over the bizarre formations from the corrugated walls surrounding the Badlands is like seeing an ocean someone burned all the water out of. Today Badlands National Park (Map p668) along with the surrounding **Buffalo Gap National Grassland** protects the country's largest prairie grasslands, several species of Plains mammal (including bison and black-footed ferret), prairie falcons and lots of snakes.

The park's north unit packs the most punch; the Hwy 240 loop road is easily reached from I-90 and you can drive it in an hour if you're in a hurry. The gravel Sage Creek Rim Rd goes west of the loop, above the Badlands Wilderness Area, which is where most backcountry hikers and campers go. There is nearly no water or shade here, so don't strike out into the wilderness unprepared. The less-accessible south units are in the Pine Ridge Indian Reservation and see few visitors.

The **Ben Reifel Visitor Center** (☎ 605-433-5361; www.nps.gov/badl; Hwy 240; ☻ 8am-6pm summer, 8am-5pm Apr-May & Sep-Oct, 9am-4pm rest of year) is open all year, but the **White River Visitor Center** (☎ 605-455-2878; Hwy 27; ☻ 10am-4pm summer), in the southern section, is summer-only. A seven-day pass costs $15 for cars and $7 for cyclists.

Neither the developed **Cedar Pass Campground** ($10) or primitive **Sage Creek Campground** (free) takes reservations. Hotels can be found on I-90 in Kadoka and Wall, or stay at a cozy cabin in the park at **Cedar Pass Lodge** (☎ 605-433-5460; www.cedarpasslodge.com; Hwy 240; cabins $70-95; ☻ May-Oct). Drop by the lodge's **restaurant** (mains

$3-15; ☻ 7am-8:30pm summer, 7:30am-7pm May & Sep-Oct) for an 'Indian taco' made with fry bread and bison meat.

Pine Ridge Indian Reservation

A journey through Pine Ridge is sure to be an emotional one. Home to the Lakota Oglala Sioux, this reservation south of the Badlands is one of the nation's poorest 'counties,' with over half the population living below the poverty line. Still, despite the problems, a spirit of community is palpable and locals are friendly and welcoming to visitors.

In 1890 the new Ghost Dance religion, which the Lakota followers believed would bring back their ancestors and eliminate the white man, became wildly popular. This struck fear into the area's soldiers and settlers and the frenetic circle dances were outlawed. The 7th US Cavalry rounded up a band of Lakota under Chief Big Foot and brought them to the small village of Wounded Knee. On December 29, as the soldiers began to search for weapons, a shot was fired (nobody knows by who) leading to the massacre of more than 250 men, women and children, most of them unarmed; one of the most infamous atrocities in US history. Twenty-five soldiers also died. Today, the **Wounded Knee Massacre Site**, 16 miles northeast of Pine Ridge town, is marked by a faded roadside sign and craft vendors. The mass grave, usually frequented by young men looking for handouts, sits atop the hill. The nearby visitor center has little to offer: stop at the museum in Wall (p665) instead.

Four miles north of Pine Ridge town at the Red Cloud Indian School is the **Red Cloud Heritage Center** (☎ 605-867-5491; www.redcloudschool.org; Hwy 18; admission free; ☻ 8am-6pm Mon-Fri, 9am-6pm Sat-Sun summer, 8am-5pm Mon-Fri rest of year), a good art museum with traditional and contemporary work and a craft shop. Chief Red Cloud is buried here.

The farmhouse **Wakpamni B&B** (☎ 605-288-1800; www.wakpamni.com; r from $70; ✗ ⊠ wi-fi), 21 miles east of Pine Ridge town, has regular rooms and teepees. The knowledgeable owners have a superb Lakota craft shop and can arrange horseback-riding (from $50), sweatlodge ceremonies and other cultural activities.

Tune in to what's happening on the rez by listening to local radio station KILI (90.1 FM), 'the voice of the Lakota nation,' which broadcasts community events and sometimes plays traditional music.

BLACK HILLS

This stunning region on the Wyoming–South Dakota border lures visitors with its winding canyons and wildly eroded 7000ft peaks. The region's name – the 'Black' comes from the dark Ponderosa pine-covered slopes – was conferred by the Lakota Sioux. In the 1868 Fort Laramie Treaty, they were assured that the hills would be theirs for eternity, but the discovery of gold changed that and the Sioux were pushed out into smaller reservations on flatter land.

You'll need several days to explore the area. Throughout are incredible back-road drives, caves, bison herds, Mount Rushmore and Crazy Horse monuments, outdoor activities (ballooning, cycling, rock climbing, boating, fishing, hiking, downhill skiing and panning for gold) and tons of tourist traps in between.

Orientation & Information

I-90 skirts the north of the Black Hills providing access to the gateway towns of Rapid City, Sturgis, Spearfish and Deadwood. US 385 (initially US 85), the Black Hills Parkway, runs north–south the length of the hills; along with east–west US 16 (and US 16A) out of Rapid City, it provides access to the more scenically situated, but also more touristy and expensive, south Hills towns of Keystone, Hill City and Custer, plus most of the top attractions like Mount Rushmore and Custer State Park. No matter where you stay, nothing is more than a few hours away.

There are hundreds of hotels and campgrounds across the hills; still, during the summer, room rates skyrocket (often 300% above low-season rates) and reservations are essential. Try to avoid visiting during the Sturgis motorcycle rally (p668). In winter, some lodgings and most attractions are closed.

Visitor centers and reservations:

Black Hills Central Reservations (☎ 866-601-5103; www.blackhillsvacations.com; 68 Sherman St, Deadwood; ◷ 7am-7pm Mon-Fri, 8am-4pm Sat-Sun) Last-minute hotel and cabin vacancies.

Black Hills Visitor Center (☎ 605-355-3700; www .blackhillsbadlands.com; I-94 exit 61, Rapid City; ◷ 8am-8pm summer, reduced hours rest of year)

Black Hills National Forest

The majority of the Black Hills lie within this 1875-sq-mile mixture of protected and logged forest, perforated by pockets of private land along most roads. The scenery is fantastic whether you get deep into it along the 450 miles of hiking trails or just drive the many scenic byways and gravel 'fire roads.' For cycling, the 109-mile **George S Mickelson Trail** ($2 daily fee) cuts through much of the forest, running from Deadwood through Hill City and Custer to Edgemont on an abandoned railway line. There are bike rentals at the trailhead in Deadwood and at several other trailside towns.

The forest **Headquarters** (☎ 605-673-9200; 25041 US 16; ◷ 7:30am-5pm Mon-Fri) is in Custer and a summer-only **visitor center** (☎ 605-343-8755; US 385 near Hwy 44; ◷ 8:30am-6pm) sits on the Pactola Reservoir between Hill City and Rapid City.

Good camping abounds in the forest. There are 30 basic (no showers or electricity) **campgrounds** (☎ 877-444-6777; campsites free-$23) and backcountry camping is allowed just about anywhere (free; no open fires). Reservations are recommended during the summer.

Rapid City

'Rapid' is the main gateway to the Black Hills, but its foot-friendly downtown core of well-preserved brick buildings, filled with quality shopping and dining, makes it a good destination on its own. The **visitor center** (☎ 866-727-4324; www.rapidcitycvb.com; 444 Mt Rushmore Rd; ◷ 8am-5pm Mon-Fri) is in the civic center.

The fortress-like **Journey Museum** (☎ 605-394-6923; www.journeymuseum.org; 222 New York St; adult/child $7/free; ◷ 9am-5pm summer, 10am-5pm Mon-Sat, 1-5pm Sun rest of year) takes you on a trip through 2½ billion years of the history of the Black Hills with lots of space given to the Lakota Sioux and dinosaurs.

You can see more dinosaur bones in the **Museum of Geology** (☎ 605-394-2467; 501 E St Joseph St, O'Harra Bldg; free admission; ◷ 9am-4pm Mon-Fri, 10am-5pm Sat, noon-5pm Sun summer, 9am-4pm Mon-Fri, 10am-4pm Sat rest of year) at the South Dakota School of Mines and Technology.

Two sure-fire hits with kids are the life-size concrete statues at **Dinosaur Park** (940 Skyline Dr; free admission; ◷ 6am-10pm) and the character filled playground at **Storybook Island** (off Hwy 44 W; admission free; ◷ 9am-7pm summer).

Family-owned budget motels line North Street between I-90 and downtown. The friendly **Avanti Motel** (☎ 605-348-1112, 888-819-7298; 102 N Maple Ave; s/d $45/60; ☒) is better than the budget average. For something special downtown, try the historic **Hotel Alex Johnson**

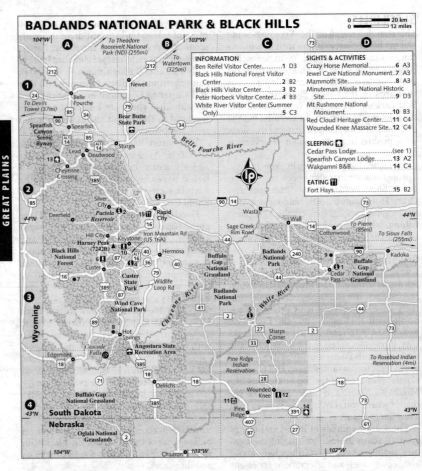

BADLANDS NATIONAL PARK & BLACK HILLS

INFORMATION
Ben Reifel Visitor Center.............1 D3
Black Hills National Forest Visitor
 Center...............................2 B2
Black Hills Visitor Center............3 B2
Peter Norbeck Visitor Center......4 B3
White River Visitor Center (Summer
 Only)..............................5 C3

SIGHTS & ACTIVITIES
Crazy Horse Memorial................6 A3
Jewel Cave National Monument...7 A3
Mammoth Site............................8 A3
Minuteman Missile National Historic
 Site......................................9 D3
Mt Rushmore National
 Monument..........................10 B3
Red Cloud Heritage Center......11 C4
Wounded Knee Massacre Site..12 C4

SLEEPING
Cedar Pass Lodge..................(see 1)
Spearfish Canyon Lodge.........13 A2
Wakpamni B&B.......................14 C4

EATING
Fort Hays................................15 B2

(☎ 605-342-1210, 800-888-2539; www.alexjohnson.com; 523 6th St; r $129; ✷ ☐ wi-fi), whose overwhelming design is based on a blend of Germanic Tudor architecture and traditional Lakota Sioux symbols – note the lobby's painted ceiling and the chandelier made of war lances.

The Black Hills' foodie favorite, the **Corn Exchange** (☎ 605-343-5070; 727 Main St; mains $13-21; ⏱ 5am-9pm Tue-Sat; ✗), uses local and organic ingredients and espouses a 'slow food' philosophy. If you prefer corny to classy, try one of the area's chuckwagon suppers, where a meat-and-potatoes meal is followed by a country music and comedy show: **Fort Hays** (☎ 605-394-9653; US 16; adult/child $18/9; ⏱ 6:30-8:15pm May-Oct; ✗), five miles south of Rapid City, shares space with a *Dances With Wolves* film set.

Sturgis

This unassuming little town revs up big time for the annual **Sturgis Motorcycle Rally** (☎ 605-720-0800; www.sturgismotorcyclerally.com; ⏱ early Aug), a gathering of around 500,000 riders, fans and curious onlookers. During the rally, you can't swing a dead cat without hitting someone in leather fringe and the streets resemble rows of giant dominoes. (Ogle all you want, but touch the bikes at your own risk.) Temporary campsites are set up around town and motels across the region boost rates to hundreds of dollars a night. Check the rally website for vacancies. The **chamber of commerce** (☎ 605-347-2556; www.sturgis-sd.org; 2040 Junction Ave; ⏱ 8am-5pm Mon-Fri) has information about everything else in town.

The **Sturgis Motorcycle Museum** (☎ 605-347-2001; www.sturgismuseum.com; 999 Main St; adult/child $5/free; ⌚ 9am-5pm summer, 9am-4pm Mon-Fri, 11am-3pm Sat-Sun rest of year) houses dozens of bikes, including many antique Harleys and Indians, and a basement room dedicated to women in motorcycling.

Sturgis is near the northern end of the **Centennial Trail**, a 111-mile route open to hikers and mountain-bike riders across the Black Hills to Wind Cave National Park (p671).

Spearfish

A good base on I-90 is Spearfish, at the mouth of gorgeous **Spearfish Canyon Scenic Byway** (US 14A). The helpful **chamber of commerce** (☎ 800-626-8013; www.spearfishchamber.org; 106 W Kansas; ⌚ 8am-5pm Mon-Fri) has a self-guided tour of the byway and hiking trail maps. The **'76 Trail** is a rewarding ascent of the canyon wall.

The church-like building overlooking the interstate east of downtown is the **High Plains Western Heritage Center** (☎ 605-642-9378; www.westernheritagecenter.com; I-90 exit 14; adult/child $7/3; ⌚ 9am-5pm). Displays are a tad scattershot, but include many that feature cowboys and a big barbed wire collection.

Chain hotels cluster around I-90 exit 14 and aging family-owned motels are downtown. For a plush, 'rustic' treat in a wilder setting, try the **Spearfish Canyon Lodge** (☎ 605-584-3435, 877-975-6343; www.spfcanyon.com; US 14A; r/ste from $149/275; ✗ ✗ wi-fi), 13 miles south of Spearfish near trails and streams, with a massive lobby fireplace and 55 modern piney rooms. Winter rates are far less.

Vegetarians will appreciate the healthy cooking at **Bay Leaf Café** (☎ 605-642-5462; 126 W Hudson St; mains $7-23; ⌚ 11am-9pm summer, 11am-4pm Mon, 11am-8pm Tue-Sat rest of year; ✗) while carnivores can sample elk sirloin and other native game dishes.

Deadwood

Like Vegas meets Bonanza, Deadwood juxtaposes the bright neon jangling of slot machines with Wild West storefronts, reenacted gunfights and eternal devotion to Wild Bill Hickock, who was shot in the back of the head here in 1876 while gambling. Settled illegally by eager gold rushers in the 1870s, Deadwood (inspiration for the hit HBO series) is now a National Historic Landmark. Its Main Street is lined with restored gold rush–era buildings. The town's hell-raisin' days are long gone,

replaced by a gentler crowd of tour-bus poker players taking advantage of limited-stakes gambling, which jump-started the town's tourist appeal in the 1990s. In winter, skiers come to hit nearby slopes.

The **Deadwood History & Information Center** (☎ 800-999-1876; www.deadwood.org; Pine St; ⌚ 9am-8pm summer, 9am-5pm rest of year), in the old train depot, has brochures on area attractions, plus exhibits and photos of the town's history. Downtown is walkable, but the historic-looking **trolley** (per ride 50¢) can be handy for getting between attractions, hotels and parking lots. If you want to head out of town on the Mickelson Trail (p667), rent a ride at **Deadwood Bicycles** (☎ 605-578-1345; www.deadwoodbicycles.com; 180 Sherman St; adult/child $25/15), right at the trailhead.

Calamity Jane (born Martha Canary) and Hickok rest side by side up on Boot Hill at **Mount Moriah Cemetery** (adult/child $1/50¢; ⌚ 8am-8pm summer, 8am-5pm rest of year). Actors stage old-style **shootouts** (2pm, 4pm and 6pm daily) on Main Street during the summer. In the nearby town of Lead (pronounced *leed*), peek at the 1250ft-deep **Homestake gold mine** (☎ 605-584-3110; 160 W Main St; admission free; ⌚ 24hr) to see what open-pit mining can do to a mountain.

Lead is also home to surely the homiest hostel you've ever stayed in (it is, in fact, the owner's home), the **Main Street Manor Hostel** (☎ 605-717-2044; 515 W Main St; www.mainstreetmanorhostel.com; dm $20-25; closed Dec-Jan; P ✗ wi-fi). Guests get use of the kitchen, garden and laundry.

Back in Deadwood, the cute little **Penny Motel** (☎ 605-578-1842, 877-565-8140; www.pennymotel.com; 818 Upper Main St; r from $56; P ✗) is simple, but offers good value. For sleeping downtown, you can't beat the **Historic Franklin Hotel** (☎ 605-578-2241, 800-688-1876; www.silveradofranklin.com; 700 Main St; r from $105; P), with its antique furnishings and cocktail-hour balcony overlooking Main St. Rooms are named for celebrities who've stayed in them, including Teddy Roosevelt and John Wayne.

You can load up on salad and greasy chicken wings at the casino buffets while saloons offer cheap pub grub to soak up the brews. For something different, there's the lemon chicken at **Chinatown Café** (☎ 605-578-7778; 649 Main St; mains $8-15; ⌚ 11:30am-2pm & 5-10pm; ✗).

Saloon No 10 (☎ 605-578-3346; 657 Main St; ⌚ 8am-2am) is hands-down the best saloon in Deadwood, with dark paneled walls and sawdust on the floor (though slot machines have slipped in to detract from the atmosphere). The original Saloon No 10, where Wild Bill took a serious loss at the gambling table, stood across the street, but the building burned to the ground and the owners brought the bar over here. They now recreate the shooting at 1pm, 3pm, 5pm and 7pm from May-Sep. That original spot is now home to **Wild West Winners** (☎ 605-578-1100; 622 Main St), with a small basement display on Hickok, but the current Saloon No 10 does a better job of re-creating the atmosphere. The other notable hooch house in town is **Midnight Star** (☎ 605-578-1555; 677 Main St), owned by actor Kevin Costner and his brother. Costumes and photos from his movies fill the building.

Mount Rushmore

Looking like they're either emerging from or being absorbed by the mountain, the stony faces of past presidents George Washington, Thomas Jefferson, Abraham Lincoln and Theodore Roosevelt – carved 60ft tall in the granite of a Black Hills outcrop – are one of the most famous images in the USA and the top attraction in the state; the monument gets nearly three million visitors each year. You can't help but be impressed by its sheer scale and the massive physical effort of the team (led by sculptor Gutzon Borglum) that created it between 1927 and 1941.

You pass through an avenue of all 50 state flags before reaching the Grand View Terrace, underneath which is the **visitor center** (☎ 605-574-3198; www.nps.gov/moru; ☺ 8am-10pm summer, 8am-5pm rest of year). The **Presidential Trail** loop leads near the monument for some fine nostril views and past the sculptors' studio. The monument is 3 miles south of Keystone via US 16A. Admission is free, but parking costs $8.

Keystone

The nearest lodging and restaurants to Mount Rushmore are in Keystone, a one-time mining town now solely devoted to the monument. Keystone is the eastern terminus of the **1880 Train** (☎ 866-367-1880; www.1880train.com; 103 Winter St; adult/child round-trip $21/12; ☺ May-Oct, call for schedule), a classic steam train running through rugged country to Hill City – there are more round-trip options from that end.

For lodging in town, try the **Keystone Boardwalk Inn** (☎ 605-666-4990, 800-252-2119; www

.keystoneboardwalk.com; 250 Winter St; r from $79; ☒ wi-fi) an ordinary, though decent motel with Jacuzzis in some rooms. Just north of town is the comfortably rustic **Powder House** (☎ 605-666-4646, 800-321-0692; www.powderhouselodge.com; 24125 US 16A; r $110, cabins $70-170; ☺ May-Sep; ☒ ☒ ☒ wi-fi), so named because it originally served as a cache for explosives and bootleg hooch. Reservations are crucial at both.

Crazy Horse Memorial

The world's largest monument, the **Crazy Horse Memorial** (☎ 605-673-4681; www.crazyhorse.org; US 385; person/carload $10/25; ☺ 7am-dusk summer, 8am-4pm rest of year) is, as author Ian Frazier describes, 'a ruin, only in reverse.' Onlookers at the 563ft-tall work-in-progress can gawk at what will be the Sioux leader astride his horse, pointing to the horizon saying, 'My lands are where my dead lie buried.'

Never photographed or persuaded to sign a meaningless treaty, the great Crazy Horse was the obvious choice for a 'monument for all Native Americans.' Lakota Sioux elders hoped a monument would balance the presidential focus of Mount Rushmore and in 1948 Boston-born sculptor Korczak Ziolkowski started blasting granite. His family continued the work after his death in 1982. Ziolkowski was no less of an indomitable spirit as Crazy Horse, as demonstrated in a movie shown at the visitor center.

No one is predicting when the sculpture will be complete. You can see (and hear) blasts several days a week and twice a year at night. A **laser-light show** that tells the story of the monument and what it represents is splashed across the rock face on summer evenings. It is worth planning your trip around it.

The huge **visitor center** includes a viewing deck, Native American museum, cultural center where you can see artisans at work, Ziolkowski's studio and the home in which his widow still lives. A bus ($4) takes you to the base of the mountain and during the Volksmarch (first weekend of June) you can climb up to the face.

You can sleep in a teepee in view of Crazy Horse's profile at the hokey but friendly **Heritage Village** (☎ 605-673-5005; www.heritage-village.com; tent/teepee/cabin $16/23/42), 1 mile south.

Custer State Park

The superb 111-sq-mile **Custer State Park** (☎ 605-255-4515; www.custerstatepark.info; 7-day pass per person/

carload $5/12) is one of the state's highlights. The only reason it isn't a national park is the state grabbed it first. It boasts one of the largest free-roaming bison herds in the world (about 1500), the famous 'begging burros' (donkeys seeking handouts) and more than 200 species of bird. Elk, pronghorns, mountain goats, bighorn sheep, coyotes, prairie dogs, mountain lions and bobcats might also be seen along the 18-mile Wildlife Loop Rd and the incredible 14-mile Needles Hwy (SD 87).

The **Peter Norbeck Visitor Center** (☎ 605-255-4464; US 16A; ☀ 8am-8pm summer, 8am-6pm Sep; 9am-5pm rest of year), on the east side of the park, has exhibits and offers activities like gold-panning demonstrations and guided nature walks. The nearby **Black Hills Playhouse** (☎ 605-255-4141; www.blackhillsplayhouse.com; $20-25) hosts summer theater.

Hiking through the pine-covered hills and prairie grassland (keep an eye out for rattlesnakes) is a great way to see wildlife and rock formations. The Sylvan Lake Shore, Sunday Gulch, Cathedral Spires and French Creek Natural Area trails are all highly recommended. Another rewarding hike is up the state's tallest mountain, **Harney Peak** (7242 ft). Swimming, fishing and boating on the park's lakes and climbing on its jagged rock spires are also popular.

You can pitch a tent in eight **campgrounds** (☎ 800-710-2267; www.campSD.com; campsites $13-18, no hookups) around the park. Reservations are recommended in summer. **Backcountry camping** ($2 per person per night) is allowed in the French Creek Natural Area. The park also has four impressive **resorts** (☎ 800-658-3530; www.custerresorts.com) with a mix of lodge rooms and cabins starting at $95 and going much higher. Book well ahead. The town of Custer, the main gateway into the park, has plenty of hotels and restaurants.

Wind Cave National Park

This park, protecting 44 sq miles of grassland and forest sits just south of Custer State Park. The central feature is, of course, the cave, which is known to be 124 miles long and new tunnels are frequently discovered. The cave's foremost feature is its 'boxwork' calcite formations (95% of all that are known exist here), which look like honeycomb and date back 60 to 100 million years. The strong gusts, felt at the entrance, but not inside, give the cave its name. Call the **visitor center** (☎ 605-745-4600; www

.nps.gov/wica; ☀ 8am-7pm summer, reduced hours rest of year) for details on the variety of **tours** (adult $7-23, child $3.50-4.50) offered, including spelunking adventures.

Hiking is a popular activity in the park, where you'll find the southern end of the 111-mile **Centennial Trail** (see p668). The **campground** (per site $6-12) rarely fills and backcountry camping (free with permit) is allowed in limited areas.

Jewel Cave National Monument

Another of the Black Hills' many fascinating caves is Jewel Cave, 13 miles west of Custer on US 16; so named because calcite crystals line nearly all of its walls. Currently 139 miles have been explored, making it the second longest known cave in the world, but it is presumed to be the longest. **Tours** (adult $4-27, child free-$4) range in length and difficulty; reservations are recommended. Make arrangements at the **visitor center** (☎ 605-673-2288; www.nps.gov/jeca; ☀ 8am-4:30pm). If you'll only visit one Black Hills cave, this would be a good choice.

Hot Springs

This attractive town, south of the main Black Hills circuit, boasts beautiful 1890s sandstone buildings and warm mineral springs feeding the Fall River.

The water at **Evans Plunge** (☎ 605-745-5165; www.evansplunge.com; 1145 N River St; adult/child $10/8; ☀ 5:30am-10pm Mon-Fri, 8am-10pm Sat-Sun summer, 5:30am-8pm Mon-Fri, 10am-8pm Sat-Sun rest of year), a giant indoor geothermal springs waterpark, is always 87°F (30.5°C). You can fill your waterbottles at **Kidney Springs**, just south of the **visitor center** (☎ 800-325-6991; www.hotsprings -sd.com; 630 N River St; ☀ 7am-7pm summer) or swim at **Cascade Falls**, which is 71°F (22°C) all year, 11 miles south on US 71.

The remarkable **Mammoth Site** (☎ 605-745-6017; www.mammothsite.com; 1800 US 18 bypass; adult/child $7.50/5.50; ☀ 8am-8pm May 15-Aug 15, reduced hrs rest of year) is the country's largest left-as-found mammoth fossil display. Hundreds of animals perished in a sinkhole here about 26,000 years ago. Most of the 55 mammoths found so far are adolescents (and all are male!). The museum has good displays about life in that era and in July you can join paleontologists digging for more bones.

Red Rock River Resort (☎ 605-745-4400, 800-306-8921; www.redrockriverresort.com; 603 N River St; s/d $65/75) has cozy rooms in an 1891 downtown building plus spa facilities (day passes for hotel guests/non-guests $10/20) like a sand heat room and massage.

NEBRASKA

Though it comes as a surprise to most people, Nebraska holds a lot of appeal for nature-lovers. Birders come from all over to witness the sandhill crane migration, there are some incredible fossil finds left *in situ* and the unique Sandhills is the Plains' most intact ecoregion. If you're more in tune to the urban beat, Nebraska's two major cities, Omaha and Lincoln, both have historic town centers with well-preserved brick structures buzzing with new life.

The state's main thoroughfare is I-80; efficient but often dull. Instead, take US 20, a seldom used back-door route into South Dakota, if you have the time.

History

Lewis and Clark followed the Missouri along Nebraska's eastern fringe and met with Native Americans here in 1804. Some 20 years later, trappers latched onto the Platte River. Then in 1841, the first covered wagon passed through on its way to Oregon. The Platte Valley was soon swarming with hopeful settlers (around 400,000) all looking to start a new life in the mythical West.

Transcontinental railroads such as the Union Pacific made covered wagons irrelevant and the trail ruts succumbed to pasture as more settlers rushed in after the 1862 Homestead Act. The rich soils and abundant

---

NEBRASKA FACTS

Nickname Cornhusker State
Population 1.8 million
Area 77,360 sq miles
Capital city Lincoln (population 225,600)
Sales Tax 5.5%
Birthplace of dancer Fred Astaire (1899–1987), actor Marlon Brando (1924–2004), civil rights leader Malcolm X (1925–65), actress Hilary Swank (b 1974)
Home of Gazillionaire Warren Buffett
Famous for only unicameral state legislature, college football
Official tree Cottonwood

---

grasslands helped Nebraska develop into a productive agricultural state.

Information

Nebraska Association of Bed & Breakfasts
(☎ 877-223-6222; www.nabb1.com)
Nebraska state parks (☎ 800-826-7275; www.out doornebraska.org) Vehicle permits cost $4/20 per day/year.
Nebraska Travel & Tourism Division (☎ 877-632-7275; www.visitnebraska.org)

OMAHA

Be careful if you're planning a quick pit-stop in Omaha. Home to the vibrant brick-and-cobblestone Old Market neighborhood, a lively music scene and several quality museums, this town can turn a few hours into a few days. It's not all spurs and steaks here these days; no ma'am.

Omaha grew to prominence as a transport hub. Its location on the Missouri River and proximity to the Platte made it an important stop on the Oregon, California and Mormon Trails, and later the Union Pacific Railroad marched west from here. These days Omaha is in the nation's top 10 for billionaires and Fortune 500 companies per capita.

Information

City Weekly (www.omahacityweekly.com) Free weekly newspaper with a good entertainment calendar.
Visitor center (☎ 866-937-6624; www.visitomaha .com; 1001 Farnam St; ⏰ 9am-4:30pm Mon-Sat, 1-4:30pm Sun summer, 9am-4:30pm Mon-Sat rest of year)

Sights & Activities

You'll probably spend much of your Omaha visit in **Old Market** on the edge of downtown. This revitalized warehouse district, full of nightclubs, restaurants and funky shops, easily holds its own when it comes to aesthetics, energy and sophistication.

Located north of Old Market is **Gene Leahy Mall**, a water-filled park that you can follow to **Heartland of America Park** where you can take a **gondola ride** (☎ 402-884-5677; person/couple $10/15; ⏰ 7-10pm Thu-Sun and by appointment) around the lagoon.

The striking art-deco **Joslyn Art Museum** (☎ 402-342-3300; www.joslyn.org; 2200 Dodge St; adult/child $7/4; ⏰ 10am-4pm Tue-Sat, noon-4pm Sun), clad in Georgia pink marble, houses a great collection of 19th- and 20th-century European and American art, including much with a Western theme.

Another art-deco landmark, the old Union Station train depot, is now the **Durham Western Heritage Museum** (☎ 402-444-5071; www.dwhm.org; 801 S 10th St; adult/child $7/5; ☺ 10am-8pm Tue, 10am-5pm Wed-Sat, 1-5pm Sun). It covers local history from the Lewis and Clark expedition to the Omaha stockyards. The soda fountain still serves hot dogs and phosphates.

One of Nebraska's top attractions owes its fortune to the state's location smack-dab in the center of the USA, which helped it become the headquarters of the Strategic Air Command (SAC). Midway between Omaha and Lincoln, the fascinating **Strategic Air & Space Museum** (☎ 402-827-3100, www.strategicairand space.com; I-80 exit 426; adult/child $7/5; ☺ 9am-5pm) boasts two massive hangars housing dozens of historic airplanes and rockets, including a B-36 Peacemaker, the largest production aircraft ever.

Sleeping
There is a good mix of midrange and budget hotels along Hwys 92 and 275, at I-80 exit 445 and across the river in Council Bluffs, Iowa.

Econo Lodge (☎ 402-345-9565, 877-424-6423; 2211 Douglas St; r from $59; P ☒ wi-fi) Just a stone's throw to downtown, this friendly place has microwaves and refrigerators in each room.

Redick Plaza Hotel (☎ 402-342-1500, 888-342-5339; www.redickplazaomaha.com; 1504 Harney St; r $90-129; P ☒ wi-fi) A stylish art-deco lobby sets the tone at this aging but adequate hotel two blocks from Old Market. Stay here for the feel, not the frills. Parking is $4.

Eating & Drinking
Asian Mongolian BBQ (☎ 402-991-9330; 1215 Howard St; lunch $6.25, dinner $8.25; ☺ 11am-3pm & 4:30pm-10pm Mon-Thu, 11am-3pm & 4:30-11pm Fri-Sat, noon-8pm Sun; ☒) You choose the food; they fry it up. Makes for a fast, tasty meal.

V. Mertz (☎ 402-345-8980; 1022 Howard St; mains $24-51; ☺ 11:30am-1:30pm Tue-Sat & 5:30-9pm daily; ☒) Spilling out into a plant-filled, skylit passageway, this is hands down the loveliest Old Market warehouse rejuvenation. The long-winded mains, as lovely as the dining room, make copious use of locally grown organic food.

Mister Toad's (☎ 402-345-4488; 1002 Howard St; ☺ noon-1am) Walking into this old wood-lined pub is like putting on clothes right out of the dryer. There's live music most nights and a cozy back room full of books and stained glass.

LINCOLN
Home to the historic Haymarket District and a lively bar scene, Lincoln makes a good overnight stop. Named for 'Honest Abe' (the former US president), Nebraska's capital city has a friendly feel thanks to a negligible crime rate, low cost of living and more parks per capita than any other similarly sized US city.

The **visitor center** (☎ 800-423-8212; www.lincoln .org; 201 N 7th St, Haymarket; ☺ 9am-8pm Mon-Fri, 8am-2pm Sat, noon-4pm Sun) is inside Lincoln Station.

Sights & Activities
From the outside, Nebraska's remarkable 400ft-high **State Capitol** (☎ 402-471-0448; 1445 K St; hourly tours free; ☺ 8am-5pm Mon-Fri, 10am-5pm Sat, 1-5pm Sun) represents the apex of phallic architecture (like many tall buildings in the Plains, it's often called the penis on the prairie) while the symbolically rich interior curiously combines classical and art-deco motifs. A 14th-floor observation deck is open to the public.

The **Museum of Nebraska History** (☎ 402-471-4754; www.nebraskahistory.org; 131 Centennial Mall N; admission free; ☺ 9am-4:30pm Mon-Fri, 1-4:30pm Sat-Sun) offers an excellent run-down of the Cornhusker State's story, starting with a large First Nebraskans room.

Lincoln's leading art house, the **Sheldon Memorial Art Gallery** (☎ 402-472-2461; www.sheldon .unl.edu; N 12th & R Sts; admission free; ☺ 10am-5pm Tue-Thu, 10am-8pm Fri, 10am-5pm Sat, noon-5pm Sun) focuses on American art back to the 19th century. A block away, the petite **Great Plains Art Museum** (☎ 402-472-3082; 1155 Q St; admission free; ☺ 1-5pm Tue-Sat, 1:30-5pm Sun) should motivate you to get off the Interstate.

The **University of Nebraska State Museum** (☎ 402-472-2642; www.museum.unl.edu; N 14th & Vine Sts, Morrill Hall; adult/child $5/3; ☺ 9:30am-4:30pm Mon-Sat, 1:30-4:30pm Sun) covers natural history and anthropology with many hands-on exhibits for children.

Sleeping
Most hotels are near I-80. Those around exit 403 are mostly midrange, while there are budget motels aplenty at exit 399, including **Economy Lodge & Suites** (☎ 402-474-1311; 2410 NW 12th St; s/d from $40/50; P ☒ wi-fi).

Embassy Suites Hotel (☎ 402-474-1111, 800-362-2779; 1040 P St; ste incl breakfast from $129; P ☒ ☒ ☒ wi-fi) This Haymarket-handy hotel has luxurious rooms around a nine-story skylit atrium. Your breakfast is cooked to order and parking is available for $6.

Eating & Drinking

Lincoln's Haymarket District, a rejuvenated six-block warehouse area dating from the early 20th century, has a good variety of grub and several cozy coffeehouses. If you're after beer and body shots, follow the college crowd down O Street.

Maggie's (☎ 402-477-3959; 311 N 8th St; mains $4-7; ☺ 8am-8pm Mon-Fri year-round, 11am-3pm Sat May-Oct; ☒ wi-fi) This casual hangout serves veggie wraps, soups and more, usually rolled with locally grown, organic ingredients.

Oven (☎ 402-475-6118; 201 N 8th St; mains $9-26; ☺ 11:30am-2pm Mon-Sat, 5:30-9:30pm Sun-Thu, 5:30-10:30pm Fri-Sat; ☒) Reasonable prices and a good wine list boost this upscale Indian restaurant above the crowd.

ALONG I-80

Shortly after Lincoln, I-80 runs an almost razor-straight 83 miles before hugging the Platte River near **Grand Island**, a top train-spotting spot and home of the colossal **Stuhr Museum of the Prairie Pioneer** (☎ 308-385-5316; www.stuhrmuseum.org; I-80 exit 312; adult/child $8/6; ☺ 9am-5pm Mon-Sat, noon-5pm Sun) with a slew of living-history exhibits.

At Grand Island, Hwy 2 branches northwest through Broken Bow to Alliance in the panhandle. It crosses the lovely **Sandhills** – 19,000 sq miles of sand dunes covered in grass – one of the country's most isolated areas.

Upstream of Grand Island, the Platte hosts 500,000 sandhill cranes (80% of the world population) and 15 million waterfowl during the spring migration (mid-February to early April). **Crane Meadows Nature Center** (☎ 308-382-1820; www.cranemeadows.org; I-80 exit 305; visitor center free, grounds $4; ☺ 9am-5pm Mon-Fri, extended hours during migration) is a good place to break out the binoculars.

Causing no small amount of driver confusion, the **Great Platte River Road Archway Monument** (☎ 877-511-2724; www.archway.org; adult $10, child $3-6; ☺ 9am-6pm summer, 9am-4pm rest of year) hangs unexpectedly over I-80 east of Kearney. The multimedia exhibits tell an engaging story of the people who've passed this way, from those riding wagon trains to those zipping down the Interstate.

North Platte, another railfan mecca, is home to the **Buffalo Bill Ranch State Historical Park** (☎ 308-535-8035; $4 carload; ☺ 9am-5pm daily summer, 9am-4pm Mon-Fri Apr-May & Sep-Oct), two miles north of town, once the home of, and now a museum about, Bill Cody, the father of rodeo and the famed Wild West Show. Look west as you cross the bridge on your way to the ranch and you'll see **Bailey Yard**, the world's largest rail classification yard, where trains are put into order.

ALONG US 20

The further west you go on US 20, the more space you'll see between towns, trees and pickup trucks. The western side of the drive, known as the **Bridges to Buttes Byway**, is very beautiful.

Royal

At **Ashfall Fossil Beds** (☎ 402-893-2000; www.ashfall.unl.edu; 86930 517th Ave; adult/child $5/3 plus $4 vehicle permit; ☺ 9am-5pm Mon-Sat, 11am-5pm Sun, reduced hours May, Sep & Oct), 8 miles northwest of town, you can see unearthed prehistoric skeletons of hundreds of animals, including rhinoceroses, buried 12 million years ago by ash from a Pompeii-like explosion in what is now Idaho.

Valentine

'America's Heart City,' sits on the edge of the Sandhills and is a great base for canoeing, kayaking and inner-tubing the federally protected **Niobrara River** (☎ 402-376-1901; www.nps.gov/niob). The river crosses the **Fort Niobrara National Wildlife Refuge** (☎ 402-376-3789), home to hundreds of bison and elk. You can also cycle the **Cowboy Trail**, a rails-to-trails conversion presently open between Valentine and Norfolk – the final gap of this 191-mile run

---

WORTH THE TRIP: CARHENGE

Rural Alliance may seem like an unlikely home for **Carhenge** (☎ 308-762-1520; www.carhenge.com; admission free), but really, is there anyplace you wouldn't be surprised to find a Stonehenge replica assembled from 38 discarded cars? The faithful reproduction, along with other car-part art, rises out of a field 3 miles north of town along Hwy 87 (catch it at the east end of town).

should be completed by summer 2008 – and due to stretch west to Chadron.

The hearts-and-flowers-themed **visitor center** (☎ 402-376-2969; www.visitvalentine.com; 253 N Main St; ☺ 9am-7pm Mon-Sat summer, 9am-5pm Mon-Fri rest of year) can give you a list of outfitters and direct you to waterfalls in the area.

Twenty miles south of town, the **Valentine National Wildlife Refuge** (☎ 402-376-1889; Hwy 83) has some superb Sandhills scenery and lots of lakes.

The throwback red-brick **Valentine Motel** (☎ 402-376-2450, 800-376-2450; Hwy 20; s/d $45/50; ✖ wi-fi) has oddly cute rooms and a 1953 Ford parked out front.

Northern Panhandle

The **Museum of the Fur Trade** (☎ 308-432-3843; www.furtrade.org; adult/child $5/free; ☺ 8am-5pm summer), three miles east of Chadron, includes the restored Bordeaux Trading Post, which swapped pelts for guns, blankets and whiskey from 1837 to 1876. Try to plan a stop, if only just for a beer, at Chadron's friendly **Olde Main Street Inn** (☎ 308-432-3380; 115 Main St; s/d from $45/60; ✖ ✖). The 1890 building is furnished with a mix of old and new, but it completely recreates the feel of bygone days.

Quiet, little Crawford has several worthy detours around it. Eighteen miles north on some pretty rough roads, **Toadstool Geologic Park** (☎ 308-432-4475; admission $3) is a mini-badlands with a wide variety of fossils, a sod house and a simple **campground** (per site $5). Nearby, and connected by a three-mile hiking trail, **Hudson-Meng Bison Bonebed** (☎ 308-665-3900; www .hudson-meng.org; adult/child $5/3; ☺ 9am-5pm summer), displays the site where hunters slaughtered hundreds of bison 10,000 years ago. **Fort Robinson State Park** (☎ 308-665-2900; admission per vehicle $4; ☺ dawn-dusk), four miles west, is where Crazy Horse was killed in 1877 while in captivity. Tours are given by horse-drawn wagon. The **Trailside Museum of Natural History** (☎ 308-665-2929; adult/child $3/1; ☺ 9am-6pm summer, 10am-5pm Apr-May & Sep-Oct), at the park, houses skeletons of a pair of mammoths who died battling each other.

At Harrison, drive 23 miles south on Hwy 29 to reach **Agate Fossil Beds National Monument** (☎ 308-668-2211; www.nps.gov/agfo; person/carload $3/5; ☺ 8am-6pm summer, 8am-4pm rest of year), a rich source of unusual fossils dating back 20 million years ago. The Native American artifact display is small but excellent.

KANSAS

Kansas conjures up visions of wicked witches and yellow-brick roads, hot-air balloons over fields of sunflowers and tornadoes powerful enough to crush entire towns. On the other hand, it's best known for wheat – 90% of the land is devoted to agriculture – hardly the most glamorous tourist attraction.

Kansas is probably the most mocked travel destination in the nation, but it's not without charms; widespread as they may be. From the vibrant indie music scene in Lawrence to quaint little villages like Lindsborg, and from Hutchinson's high-tech space center to the ancient, otherworldly Monument Rocks, there are hidden gems just waiting to be discovered. And surely nothing will surprise and amaze you as much as the oddball art community of Lucas, which is worth going way out of your way to see.

History

Kansas' history has been pretty tumultuous. The state played a key role in sparking the Civil War when the Kansas–Nebraska Act of 1854 allowed settlers in these territories to vote on whether slavery would exist in each state. Immediately, swarms of settlers on both sides of the question flooded the territories, hoping to swing the vote in their favor. Election fraud ran rampant and clashing views led to widespread violence. Known as 'Bleeding Kansas,' this volatile era lasted until January 1861, when Kansas was admitted as a free state. The Civil War began 10 weeks later.

Growing pains continued: early settlers wiped out herds of bison and expelled the Native Americans (even the state's namesake Kansa relocated to Oklahoma in 1873). Before long – partly due to prohibitionist Carrie Nation, who swept through Kansas in 1900 wielding her axe against the evils of drink – the Sunflower State was transformed from rip-roaring open range into some of the world's most productive wheatlands. The children of Mennonites who emigrated from the steppes of Russia during the 1870s brought with them handfuls of the now-famous 'Turkey Red' wheat, which made itself thoroughly at home.

Over the last decade Kansas has repeatedly embarrassed itself as religious fanatics

GREAT PLAINS

KANSAS FACTS

Nickname Sunflower State

Population 2.8 million

Area 82,282 sq miles

Capital city Topeka (population 122,400)

Sales Tax 5.3%

Birthplace of aviator Amelia Earhart (1897–1937), silent film star Buster Keaton (1895–1966), writer Langston Hughes (1902–67), Pizza Hut (established 1958), singer-songwriter Melissa Etheridge (b 1961)

Home of fictional residents Dorothy and Toto (of *Wizard of Oz* fame)

Famous for wheat

Official state song 'Home on the Range'

---

fight to teach creationism in schools instead of evolution. For the time being, biology curriculums still only contain science.

Information

Kansas Bed & Breakfast Association (☎ 888-572-2632; www.kbba.com)

Kansas state parks (☎ 620-672-5911; www.kdwp .state.ks.us) Per vehicle $4.20/24.35 per day/year Apr-Sep, $3.70/19.35 per day/year Oct-Mar.

Kansas Travel & Tourism (☎ 800-252-6727; www .travelks.com)

WICHITA

From its early cowtown days at the head of the Chisholm Trail in the 1870s to its current claim as Air Capital of the World (thanks to about half the world's general aviation aircraft being built here) Kansas' largest city has always been a prosperous place. It's hardly a hotbed of culture, but there's usually something fun happening.

Orientation & Information

Wichita's historic, all-brick Old Town, good for shopping, eating and drinking, is on the east side of downtown while the park-like Museums on the River district (home to all but one of the following sights) fills a triangle of green space between the Big and Little Arkansas Rivers to the west. Old Town has a fun **Farmers Market** (☉ 7am-noon Sat May-Oct).

The **visitor center** (☎ 800-288-9424; www.visitwichita .com; 100 S Main; ☉ 7:45am-5:15pm Mon-Fri) offers limited help.

Sights & Activities

Guarded by Wichita artist Blackbear Bosin's 44-foot statue 'Keeper of the Plains,' the **Mid-America All-Indian Center** (☎ 316-262-5221; www .theindiancenter.org; 650 N Seneca St; admission $6; ☉ 10am-4pm Tue-Sat) has exhibits of Native American art and artifacts and a traditional Wichita-style grass lodge.

The **Wichita Art Museum** (☎ 316-268-4921; www .wichitaartmuseum.org; 1400 W Museum Blvd; adult/child $5/2, admission free Sat; ☉ 10am-5pm Tue-Sat, noon-5pm Sun) is home to a good collection of American art, including pieces by Frederick Remington, Dale Chihuly and Mary Cassatt, and hosts frequent traveling exhibits.

The sleek, modern **Exploration Place** (☎ 316-263-3373; www.exploration.org; 300 N McLean Blvd; adult $8, child $3-6; ☉ 10am-8pm Tue-Sat, noon-5pm Sun-Mon) has lots of kid-friendly science exhibits, including a touchable tornado, and the CyberDome Theater.

Stroll through **Botanica, The Wichita Gardens** (☎ 316-264-0448; www.botanica.org; 701 N Amidon Ave; adult/child $6/3; ☉ 9am-5pm Mon-Sat, 1-5pm Sun, until 8pm Tue Jun-Sep, closed weekends Nov-Mar), an attractively arranged ring of 24 themed gardens, including wildflowers and a butterfly house.

Old Cowtown (☎ 316-660-1871; www.oldcowtown.org; 1865 Museum Blvd; adult/child $7.75/6; ☉ 10am-5pm Fri-Sat & Mon, noon-5pm Sun Jun-Oct) is an open-air museum that recreates the Wild West, complete with pioneer-era buildings, staged gunfights and guides in cowboy costumes. It's cheesy but great for kids.

With dinosaur fossils, Egyptian mummies, Roman mosaics, Greek pottery, Abraham Lincoln's walking cane, military relics, a sports hall of fame and much more, Old Town's **Museum of World Treasures** (☎ 888-700-1311; www.worldtreasures.org; 835 E 1st St; adult/child $9/7; ☉ 10am-5pm Mon-Sat, noon-5pm Sun) has something for everyone.

Sleeping

The usual range of motels line all major approaches to town.

Scotsman Inn Mark 8 (☎ 316-265-4679, 888-830-7268; www.scotsmaninnwichita.com; 1130 N Broadway; r $33-37; **P** **☒**) This basic budget inn near downtown is considerably better than most of the other cheapies in this area. The tidy rooms have mini-refrigerators.

Hotel at Old Town (☎ 316-267-4800, 877-265-3869; www.hotelatoldtown.com; 830 1st St; r $129-185; **P** **☒** **▯** wi-fi) The lobby can't quite pull off the building's 1900s vibe, but the piano bar gets it close; and the location is second to none. All suites have kitchenettes and some have Jacuzzis.

Eating & Drinking

Wichita is the home of Pizza Hut, but that's far from the pinnacle of the city's dining options. For some real-deal Mexican or Vietnamese, drive north on Broadway and take your pick.

Old Mill Tasty Shop (☎ 316-264-6500; 604 E Douglas Ave; malts $3.50, mains $5-7; ☒ 11am-3pm Mon-Fri, 8am-3pm Sat; ☒) Get an old-fashioned banana split or blue plate special at this 1936 soda fountain.

Anchor (☎ 316-260-8989; 1109 E Douglas; mains $5-9; ☒ 7am-2am Mon-Fri, 8am-2am Sat, 10am-2am Sun; wi-fi) An excellent artist-run bar-cum-café, the Anchor serves yummy sandwiches and a variety of beers in brick-lined rooms with pressed-tin ceilings. Bands liven things up on weekends.

River City Brewing Co (☎ 316-263-2739; 150 N Mosley; mains $7-19; ☒ 11am-10pm Mon-Tue, 11am-2am Wed-Sat, noon-10pm Sun) This classy Old Town renovation serves five of its own microbrews along with a variety of pub fare such as mac-and-cheese and BBQ salmon. It also has pool tables and live music in an upstairs cocktail lounge.

Mosley Street Melodrama (☎ 312-263-0222; 234 N Mosley St; adult/child $24/18, show only $14; ☒ 6pm Thu-Sat, nightly in Dec; ☒) After your BBQ buffet (veggie version available), boo and hiss the villains at this wacky dinner theater.

ALONG I-70

What it lacks in glamour, Kansas' 'Main Street' makes up for in efficiency, quickly shuttling you from Kansas City in Missouri to the Colorado border. The scenery can be monotonous, but there are many interesting stops along the way. West of Salina, the landscape around I-70 stretches into rolling, wide-open plains, with winds sometimes strong enough to knock over 18-wheelers.

Lawrence

Lawrence, 40 miles west of Kansas City, has been an oasis of progressive politics from the start. Founded by abolitionists in 1854 and an important stop on the Underground Railroad, it became a battlefield in the clash between pro- and anti-slavery factions. In 1863, the Confederate guerrillas of William Clarke Quantrill raided Lawrence, killing nearly 200 people and burning much of it to the ground.

The city survived, however, and so did its free-thinking spirit, making this a vibrant and entertaining destination today.

INFORMATION

Mirth Café (☎ 785-841-3282; 745 New Hampshire St; ☒ 7am-10pm; ☒ wi-fi) Has Internet terminals (per hr $4) plus free wireless for customers.

Visitor center (☎ 888-529-5267; www.visitlawrence .com; 402 N 2nd St; ☒ 8:30am-5:30pm Mon-Sat, 1-5pm Sun summer, 9am-5pm Mon-Sat, 1-5pm Sun rest of year)

SIGHTS & ACTIVITIES

Lawrence is home to the **University of Kansas** (KU) and **Haskell Indian Nations University**. KU's **Spencer Museum of Art** (☎ 785-864-4710; www.spencer art.ku.edu; 1301 Mississippi St; admission free; ☒ 10am-5pm Tue-Sat, noon-5pm Sun, to 9pm Thu) isn't large, but has a collection encompassing work by glass sculptor Dale Chihuly, Western artist Frederic Remington and many European masters.

The walkable downtown, where townies and students merge, centers on **Massachusetts St**, one of the most pleasant streets in this part of the country for a stroll.

SLEEPING

Lawrence's cheapest hotels are north of town along I-70.

Halcyon House B&B (☎ 785-841-0314, 888-441-0314; www.thehalcyonhouse.com; 1000 Ohio St; r $55-99, without bathroom $49, cottage from $129; ☒ ☒ ☒ wi-fi) The cute, oddly shaped bedrooms here have lots of natural light, and there's a landscaped garden and homemade baked goods for breakfast. It's just a short walk to downtown.

The Eldridge Hotel (☎ 785-749-5011, 800-527-0909; www.eldridgehotel.com; 701 Massachusetts St; r from $135; ☒ ☒ ☒ ☒ wi-fi) The cozy two-room suites at this historic downtown hotel, built in 1926 and renovated in 2005, have plush antique furnishings, plus room service is always on hand. It boasts a hip lounge and classy restaurant. Parking is $10.

EATING & DRINKING

ourpick Local Burger (☎ 785-856-7827; 714 Vermont St; mains $4-8; ☒ 11am-9pm Mon-Sat, 11am-8pm Sun; ☒) The 'next generation of burger joints' is all about promoting healthy dining, protecting the environment and supporting the local economy…and the food is damn good too. Try the grass-fed elk burger or the patented veggie burger. It's just a block off Massachusetts.

HOT TOPIC: WHISKEY AND WATER

'Whiskey's for drinking and water's for fighting,' they say on the Plains and this arid region is gearing up for major battles. Scientists and government officials now talk about when the looming water crisis will begin, rather than if it will come, and some say it will rock the region worse than the Dust Bowl did. Two-thirds of the irrigated farmland in Kansas, for example, could lose its water supply by 2020.

Towns are already spending millions of dollars to pipe in water, and rivers and aquifers are drying up. The Ogallala Aquifer, which stretches from South Dakota to Texas, is one of the world's largest, but it shrinks four to six feet per year in some places. And global warming, which will increase drought and evaporation, only figures to makes the problems worse.

There are solutions, but few are easy and none are cheap. In coming years expect to see more farmers switch to crops like cotton that require less water, states to pay farmers to stop watering their fields and marginal lands being given back to the prairie. These measures will do no more than slow the tide, but anyone who has future generations in mind knows that the sooner talk turns to action, the better.

Zen Zero (☎ 785-832-0001; 811 Massachusetts St; mains $6-16; ⊙ 11am-9pm Sun-Mon, 11am-10pm Tue-Sat; ✗) Some fine Thai curries and stir-fries compose most of the menu, but Japanese and Nepali dishes mix things up. The food is good and prices are surprisingly low.

Teller's (☎ 785-843-4111; 746 Massachusetts St; mains $12-29; ⊙ 11am-10pm Mon-Thu, 11am-11pm, Fri-Sat, 9am-10pm Sun, bar closes later; ✗) Long one of the city's top options, Teller's serves Italian dishes in a converted bank, with a good wine list and a 'vault' bathroom.

ENTERTAINMENT

Lawrence's music scene is excellent and the **Bottleneck** (☎ 785-841-5483; www.bottleneck live.com; 737 New Hampshire) has long been solid with scenesters.

The beaux-arts **Liberty Hall** (☎ 785-749-1972; www.libertyhall.net; 644 Massachusetts St), where Beat writer and longtime Lawrence resident William S Burroughs' funeral was held in 1997, gets some big-name bands and screens good films.

Topeka

Though most Kansans cringe when its name is mentioned, the state's aesthetically challenged capital city has some worthwhile attractions. Start your exploration at the **visitor center** (☎ 800-235-1030; www.visittopeka .travel; 1275 SW Topeka Blvd; ⊙ 8am-5pm Mon-Thu, 8am-4:30pm Fri).

The **Brown vs Board of Education National Historic Site** (☎ 785-354-4273; www.nps.gov/brvb; 1515 SE Monroe St; admission free; ⊙ 9am-5pm) is at the Monroe Elementary School, one of Topeka's African American schools at the time of the landmark 1954 Supreme Court decision that banned segregation in US schools. It has films and displays about the whole Civil Rights movement.

With a dome 11 feet higher than the one in Washington, DC, the **State Capitol** (☎ 785-296-3966; 300 SW 10th St; ⊙ 8am-5pm daily, bldg tours 9am-3pm Mon-Fri, free dome tours 11:45am-2:45pm Mon-Sat Jan-May & 10:30am-2:30pm Mon-Sat Jun-Dec) houses a fiery must-see John Steuart Curry mural of abolitionist John Brown.

From a Cheyenne teepee to Carrie Nation's hammer, the **Kansas History Center** (☎ 785-272-8681; www.kshs.org; 6425 SW 6th Ave; adult/child $5/3; ⊙ 9am-5pm Tue-Sat, 1-5pm Sun) is packed with artifacts.

Abilene

In the late 19th century, Abilene was a rowdy cowtown at the end of the Chisholm Trail. Today it's an all-American city with a compact core of historic brick buildings and well-preserved residential neighborhoods. Abilene is best known for liking Ike – former president Dwight D Eisenhower, who grew up here.

The **visitor center** (☎ 800-569-5915; www .abilenekansas.org; 201 NW 2nd St; ⊙ 8am-6pm Mon-Sat, 10am-4pm Sun summer, reduced hours rest of year) has free samples of Mamie Eisenhower's sugar cookies.

The **Eisenhower Center** (☎ 785-263-6700; www .eisenhower.archives.gov; 200 SE 4th St; museum adult/child $8/1, other sites free; ⊙ 8am-4:45pm, opens 9am Sep-May) includes Ike's boyhood home, a museum and library; and his and Mamie's graves, which are housed in a meditation center where you can contemplate the dullness of mainstream life in the Eisenhower era (1953–61).

The **American Indian Art Center** (☎ 785-263-0090; 206 S Buckeye Ave; ☯ 9:30am-5pm Mon-Sat, 10am-4pm Sun, extended summer hours) across the railroad tracks from the Eisenhower Center sells high-quality work at similarly high prices.

The **Kirby House Restaurant** (☎ 785-263-7336; 205 NE 3rd St; dinner mains $11-23; ☯ 11am-2pm & 5-8pm Mon-Sat; ☒) has a lace-curtained dining room in a historic home and a menu of staples like pork chops and country-fried steak. It also does lighter lunches and has an espresso bar at the back.

Lucas

Believe it or not, little Lucas is one of the world's foremost centers for outsider art. Samuel Dinsmoor began it all in 1907 by filling his yard with enormous concrete sculptures espousing his eccentric philosophies. His **Garden of Eden** (☎ 785-525-6395; www .garden-of-eden-lucas-kansas.com; 301 2nd St; adult/child $6/1; ☯ 10am-5pm May-Oct, 1-4pm Mar-Apr, 1-4pm Sat-Sun Nov-Feb) is visible from the sidewalk, but paid admission lets you hear some wonderful stories and see his decomposed body in a glass-topped coffin.

The phenomenal **Grassroots Art Center** (☎ 785-525-6118; www.grassrootsart.net; 213 S Main St; adult/child $6/1.25; ☯ 10am-5pm Mon-Sat, 1-5pm Sun May-Sep, 10am-4pm Mon & Thu-Sat, 1-4pm Sun Oct-Apr) has gathered works made of materials such as buttons, barbed wire, pull-tabs and chew-ing gum by self-taught, self-motivated artists from around Kansas. Admission to the galleries includes a look at a couple of other sites in town.

The **World's Largest Collection of World's Smallest Versions of World's Largest Things** (☎ 785-760-0826; www.worldslargestthings.com) traveling museum is usually parked just south of the Garden.

The best way to reach Lucas is along the **Post Rock Scenic Byway**, a scenic 18-mile jaunt past Wilson Lake starting at exit 206.

Hays

The town of Hays grew up around its namesake fort, built in the 1860s to protect railroad workers from Native Americans, but most people stop today for a look much further into the past at the domed **Sternberg Museum of Natural History** (☎ 877-332-1165; www.fhsu.edu /sternberg; 3000 Sternberg Dr; adult/child $6/4; ☯ 9am-7pm Tue-Sat, 1-7pm Sun). It houses many unusual fossils, including its famous fish-within-a-fish, and animated dinosaurs.

Monument Rocks

The startling **Monument Rocks**, 80ft-tall chalk formations that look like a Jawa hangout in *Star Wars*, are 25 miles southeast of Oakley via US 83. If you find any fossils (not uncommon) leave them where they are.

ALONG US 50 & US 56

More attractive alternatives to I-70 across Kansas are US 50 and US 56. Both pass through

---

ROUTE 66: GET YOUR KICKS IN KANSAS

Only 13 miles of Route 66 pass through the southeast corner of Kansas, but it's a very evocative drive.

The first town you hit, Galena, has been on the decline since even before the last of the area's lead and zinc mines closed in the 1970s. The **Galena Museum** (☎ 620-783-2192; 319 W 7th St; admission free; ☯ 9am-3:30pm Mon-Fri summer, Wed-Fri rest of year) includes mining displays.

Three miles down the road is Riverton, home of **Eisler Brothers Old Riverton Store** (☎ 316-848-3330; ☯ 8am-8pm Mon-Sat, 11am-7pm Sun). The 1920s general store, now selling food, flowers and souvenirs, predates Route 66.

Cross US 400 and stay on old Route 66 to the 1923 **Marsh Rainbow Arch Bridge**, the last of its kind.

From the bridge, it's less than 3 miles south to **Baxter Springs**, the site of a Civil War massacre and numerous bank robberies. The multifaceted **Baxter Spring Heritage Center** (☎ 620-856-2385; 740 East Ave; admission free; ☯ 10am-4:30pm Mon-Fri (closed Sat), 1-4:30pm Sun Apr-Oct, closed Mon-Fri Nov-Apr) is planning to open a new Route 66 gallery and has also helped restore a 1939 Phillips 66 gas station into the **Kansas Route 66 Visitor Center** (☎ 316-856-2385; www.ksrt66association.us) with a gift shop and old photos. Military Avenue (US 69A) takes you into Oklahoma.

the Flint Hills in the east, then meet out west and mosey into Dodge City arm-in-arm.

Along US 50

Fabled US 50 pairs up with I-35 southwest from Kansas City; after crossing I-135, it heads out on its own as it passes through Chase County, which William Least Heat-Moon examined in his book *Prairyerth*.

Two-thirds of the nation's remaining tallgrass prairie lies in the Flint Hills, and the 10,894-acre **Tallgrass Prairie National Preserve** (☎ 620-273-8494; www.nps.gov/tapr; free admission), two miles northwest of Strong City is a great place to explore it. Either hike the trails or take a **ranger-guided bus tour** (adult/child $5/3; ⏱ 11am, 1pm and 3pm May-Oct).

Learn about the race into outer space in, of all places, Hutchinson, home of the amazing **Cosmosphere & Space Center** (☎ 800-397-0330; www.cosmo.org; 1100 N Plum St; all-day pass adult/child $13/10.50, museum only $8/7.50; ⏱ 9am-9pm Mon-Sat, noon-9pm Sun summer, closing 6pm Sun-Thu rest of year) where you can see several real spacecraft, including the Apollo 13 command module and a space shuttle replica. Hutchinson's newest attraction heads in the other direction. At the **Kansas Underground Salt Museum** (☎ 866-755-3450; www.undergroundmuseum.org; Ave G & Airport Rd; adult/child $13.50/8.50; ⏱ 9am-6pm Tue-Sat, 1-6pm Sun) you'll journey 650 feet toward the center of the earth to get a look at how the still-working mine operates.

Yoder, four miles south of Hutchinson on Hwy 96, serves a large Amish community.

Along US 56

US 56 follows the old Santa Fe Trail. The large Mennonite communities around **Hillsboro** are descendants of Russian immigrants who brought the Turkey Red strain of wheat to the Plains, where it thrived despite harsh conditions. The **Mennonite Settlement Museum** (☎ 620-947-3775; www.hillsboro-museums.com; 501 S Ash St; adult/child $3/1; ⏱ 10am-noon & 1:30-4pm Tue-Fri, 2-4pm Sat-Sun, closed Jan-Feb) preserves a Russian clay brick house, one-room schoolhouse and replica windmill.

Cute **Lindsborg**, about 16 miles north of US 56, flaunts its Swedish roots with themed festivals, restaurants, shops and lodgings, and a collection of public-art Dala horse sculptures. Brick streets and lots of art galleries boost the appeal. The **visitor center** (☎ 888-227-2227; www.lindsborg.org; 104 E Lincoln; ⏱ 9am-4pm Mon-Fri)

can answer all your questions. You can grab brochures anytime at a booth on Main Street. The **Old Mill Museum** (☎ 785-227-3595; 120 Mill St; adult/child $2/1; ⏱ 9am-5pm Mon-Sat, 1-5pm Sun) is inside an 1898 flour mill that's in good enough shape it's still fired up the first weekend in May. There's a WPA-built 'castle' and some pretty vistas atop **Coronado Heights** hill, 4 miles northwest of town.

Back on US 56 in **Larned** you can see the **Santa Fe Trail Center Museum** (☎ 620-285-2054; www.santafetrailcenter.org; 1349 Hwy 156; adult $4, /child $1.50-2.50; ⏱ 9am-5pm, closed Mon Sep-May), a multicultural exploration of the world that developed in the 19th century along the trail linking the US and Mexico following the latter's independence from Spain. There is a sod house outside. Further west is the restored **Fort Larned National Historic Site** (☎ 620-285-6911; www.nps.gov/fols; per person $3; ⏱ 8:30am-4:30pm), the only fort along the Santa Fe Trail.

Dodge City

Dodge City, where famous lawmen Bat Masterson and Wyatt Earp tried, sometimes successfully, to keep law and order, was known as 'Queen of the Cowtowns' and the 'Wickedest Little City in America' for much of the 1870s and 1880s. The TV series 'Gunsmoke' (1955–75) revived interest in the hell-raisin' past and big crowds have got the heck *into* Dodge ever since.

Historic Trolley Tours (⏱ 9:30am, 10:45am, 1:30pm & 3pm; adult/child $6/4 summer), starting at the **visitor center** (☎ 800-653-9378; www.visitdodgecity.org; 400 W Wyatt Earp Blvd; ⏱ 8am-6:30pm summer, 8:30am-5pm Mon-Fri Sep-Apr), spin some good tales as they lead you past notorious landmarks. Self-guided audio tours ($3) and free maps let you visit on your own schedule.

The cartoon-movie-set tourist draw of **Boot Hill Museum** (☎ 620-227-8188; www.boothill.org; adult/child summer $8/7.50, rest of year $7/6.50; ⏱ 8am-8pm summer, 9am-5pm Sep-Apr) includes a cemetery, jail and saloon, where gunslingers re-enact high-noon shootouts all summer long while Miss Kitty and her dancing gals do the cancan.

You can see **Santa Fe Trail wagon-wheel ruts** about 9 miles west of town on US 50. The site is well marked.

All hotels and most restaurants, are along Business 50 (aka Wyatt Earp Blvd). **Thunderbird Motel** (☎ 620-225-4143; 2300 W Wyatt Earp Blvd; s/d $33/43; wi-fi) is a friendly, well-maintained joint where each room has a mini-refrigerator and microwave.

OKLAHOMA

Oklahoma, which means 'Red People' in Choctaw, elicits images of cowboys and Indians riding across the plains. They're mostly in pickup trucks these days, but if you're looking to absorb some Native American history and culture, you've come to the right place. Thirty-nine tribes are headquartered here, and many operate excellent museums to showcase the past and host powwows to celebrate the present.

But the Sooner State is no one-trick-pony. Oklahoma and Tulsa will surprise and delight art lovers and Oklahoma's 426 miles of Route 66 (see p684) link some of Mother Road's most memorable moments. And, with mountains rising in the south and forest shading a quarter of the land, it's often quite a lovely state too.

History
Early on, Wichita, Arapaho, Comanche and Osage people populated or used this land. By 1834 it (minus the panhandle) had been declared autonomous Indian Territory and Tribes from across the nation were relocated here, often at gunpoint. In one of the most dramatic examples, more than 4000 of 15,000 Cherokee perished of cold and hunger while marching the 'Trail of Tears' to the territory in the winter of 1838–39.

In the 1880s, before the US gave the go-ahead to parcel out former Native American lands, eager homesteaders ('Sooners') crossed territory lines to stake claims. That's right:

OKLAHOMA FACTS

Nickname Sooner State

Population 3.6 million

Area 69,900 sq miles

Capital city Oklahoma City (population 506,100; metro area 1.1 million)

Sales Tax 4.5%

Birthplace of humorist Will Rogers (1879–1935), athlete Jim Thorpe (1888–1953), folk musician Woody Guthrie (1912–67), parking meters (invented 1935), actor Brad Pitt (b 1963)

Home of the band Flaming Lips

Famous for 1930s dust bowl, 1995 Oklahoma City bombing

Official musical instrument fiddle

---

the Sooner State is named for lawbreakers. In April of 1889 settlement to non-Indians was officially opened and towns emerged overnight in the Great Land Rush.

Statehood in 1907 was followed by another boom when oil was discovered in the 1920s, but the Depression and soil erosion hurt the state badly. Thousands of 'Okie' farmers migrated west on Route 66 to find a better life. The state's agricultural industry eventually rebounded, due to greater care for the fragile Plains environment. Oil continues to play a role in the state's development.

Information
Oklahoma Bed & Breakfast Association (☎ 866-676-5522; www.oklabedandbreakfast.com)

Oklahoma Dept of Tourism (☎ 800-652-6552; www.travelok.com)

Oklahoma state parks (☎ 800-654-8240; www.touroklahoma.com) Most parks are free to visit.

OKLAHOMA CITY
Often abbreviated to OKC, Oklahoma City is known around the world for the tragic 1995 bombing of the Alfred P Murrah Federal Building by domestic terrorists. It has worked hard over the years to become more than just a cowtown, all without turning its back on its cowboy heritage. It's a manageable, friendly city with a well-rounded roster of attractions. A botanic garden in the heart of downtown and a renovated warehouse entertainment district further boost the town's appeal. Plan on making it more than just a Route 66 pit stop: if you've got the time, you'll want to stay a few days.

History
Oklahoma City literally sprang up overnight after unassigned Indian Territory lands were opened to white settlement on April 22, 1889. More than 10,000 land claimants rushed into the wilderness and staked out their piece of the pie around the Santa Fe railroad station. The city yanked capital honors out from under Guthrie in 1910 and was catapulted into wealth in 1928 when OKC's first gusher erupted above a vast oil field.

Information
Full Circle Bookstore (☎ 405-842-2900; in 50 Penn Pl mall; ⊗ 10am-9pm Mon-Thu, 10am-10pm Fri-Sat, noon-5pm Sun) Independent bookstore that stocks many Route 66 books and has free wi-fi in its café.

GREAT PLAINS

OKLAHOMA CITY

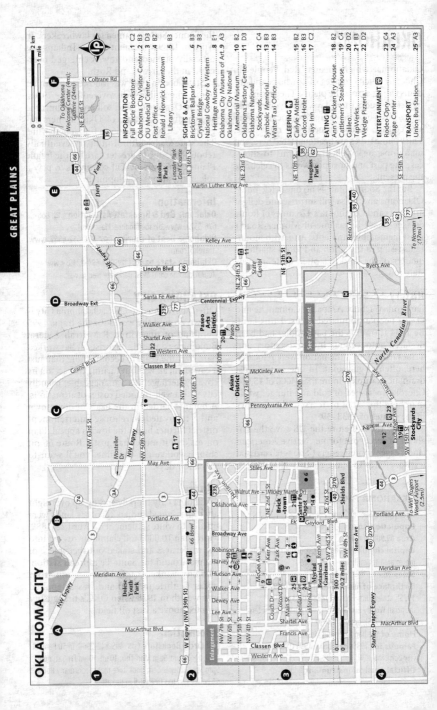

INFORMATION		
Full Circle Bookstore......................1	C2	
Oklahoma City Visitor Center.......2	B3	
OU Medical Center.......................3	D3	
Post Office...................................4	B2	
Ronald J Norwick Downtown		
Library.......................................5	B3	
SIGHTS & ACTIVITIES		
Bricktown Ballpark........................6	B3	
Crystal Bridge..............................7	B3	
National Cowboy & Western		
Heritage Museum........................8	E1	
Oklahoma City Museum of Art...9	A3	
Oklahoma City National		
Memorial Museum.....................10	B2	
Oklahoma History Center............11	D3	
Oklahoma National		
Stockyards................................12	C4	
Symbolic Memorial......................13	B3	
Water Taxi Office.......................14	B3	
SLEEPING		
Carlyle Motel..............................15	B2	
Colcord Hotel.............................16	B3	
Days Inn....................................17	C2	
EATING		
Ann's Chicken Fry House............18	B2	
Cattlemen's Steakhouse..............19	C4	
Galileo......................................20	D2	
TapWerks..................................21	B3	
Wedge Pizzeria..........................22	D2	
ENTERTAINMENT		
Rodeo Opry...............................23	C4	
Stage Center..............................24	A3	
TRANSPORT		
Union Bus Station.......................25	A3	

Oklahoma City Visitor Center (☎ 800-225-5652; www.visitokc.com; 189 W Sheridan Ave; ◷ 8:30am-5pm Mon-Fri)

Oklahoma Welcome Center (☎ 405-478-4637; www.travelok.com; 1-35 exit 137; ◷ 8:30am-5pm) Has city info too.

OU Medical Center (☎ 405-271-4700; 700 NE 13th St) Has a 24hr emergency room.

Post office (☎ 405-232-2198; 305 NW 5th St; ◷ 7am-9pm Mon-Fri, 8am-5pm Sat)

Ronald J Norwick Downtown Library (☎ 405-231-8650; 300 Park Ave; ◷ 9am-9pm Mon-Thu, 9am-6pm Fri, 9am-5pm Sat, 1-6pm Sun) One hour free Internet with photo ID.

Sights & Activities

The stories of the bombing's victims – of the 168 people that died, 16 were children at daycare – and survivors are told at the touching, high-tech **Oklahoma City National Memorial Museum** (☎ 888-542-4673; www.oklahomacitynational memorial.org; 620 N Harvey Ave; adult/student $8/6; ◷ 9am-6pm Mon-Sat, 1-6pm Sun, box office closes 1hr earlier). The outdoor **Symbolic Memorial** (N Harvey Ave; admission free; ◷ 24hr) is mostly made up of large, empty chair sculptures next to a reflecting pool in the former building's footprint. People still tie memorials to the fence on Harvey St.

Also downtown, the **Oklahoma City Museum of Art** (☎ 405-236-3100; www.okcmoa.com; 415 Couch Dr; adult/child $9/7; ◷ 10am-5pm Tue-Sat, until 9pm Thu, noon-5pm Sun) focuses on mid-20th century American art. The museum's pride and joy, a 55ft-tall Dale Chihuly glass tower, sits in the lobby. **Crystal Bridge** (☎ 405-297-3995; www .myriadgardens.com; adult/child $6/3; ◷ 9am-6pm Mon-Sat, noon-6pm Sun), a seven-story conservatory, contains plants from every continent except Antarctica amid the 17-acre **Myriad Botanical Gardens** (admission free; ◷ 6am-11pm).

To make a complete night of it in the entertaining **Bricktown District**, just east of the center, watch the Triple A Redhawks play at **Bricktown Ballpark** (☎ 405-218-1000; www.oklahomaredhawks.com; 2 Mickey Mantle Dr) and take a narrated **Water Taxi** (☎ 405-234-8294; www.watertaxi.com; 11 Mickey Mantle Dr; all-day pass $6.50; ◷ 10am-10pm Apr-Oct, reduced hrs winter) ride along the canal.

The phenomenal **National Cowboy & Western Heritage Museum** (☎ 405-478-2250; www.national cowboymuseum.org; 1700 NE 63rd St; adult/child $8.50/4; ◷ 9am-5pm) covers both art and history; and even if you come for just one, you're sure to be enthralled by the other. The excellent collection of Western painting and sculpture features many works by Charles M Russell

and Frederic Remington while the historical galleries cover everything from barbed wire to rodeos to cowboy hats.

You'll brush up against real cowboys in **Stockyards City** (www.stockyardscity.org; Agnew Ave & Exchange Ave), southwest of downtown, either in the shops and restaurants that cater to them or at the **Oklahoma National Stockyards** (auctions 8am Mon-Tue & sometimes Wed), the world's largest stocker and feeder cattle market.

The huge **Oklahoma History Center** (☎ 405-522-5248; www.okhistorycenter.org; 2401 N Laird Ave; adult/child $5/3; ◷ 9am-5pm Mon-Sat, noon-5pm Sun) makes people the focus as it tells the story of the Sooner state. It's across the street from the **State Capitol** (☎ 405-522-0836; 2300 N Lincoln Blvd; ◷ 7am-7pm Mon-Fri, 9am-4pm Sat-Sun), which was built in 1917, but only got its dome in 2002.

Festivals & Events

Red Earth Native American Cultural Festival (☎ 405-427-5228; www.redearth.org; adult/child $10/7.50) Native Americans come from across the nation to celebrate and compete in early June.

State Fair Park (☎ 405-948-6704; www.okstate fairpark.com; I-44 & NW 10th St) The fairgrounds host frequent horse- or rodeo-related events.

Sleeping

Many older motels line I-35 south of town; newer chain properties stack up along I-44 and the NW Expressway.

Carlyle Motel (☎ 405-946-3355; 3600 NW 39th St; r $33; P ✿) This simple place has seen better days, but it's generally clean and the little brick buildings are a part of Route 66 history.

Days Inn (☎ 405-946-0741, 800-329-7466; 2801 NW 39th; r from $45; P ✿ ✚ wi-fi) You can't miss this striking green hotel along I-44 (exit 124). Rooms are well appointed for the price and breakfast is included.

Colcord Hotel (☎ 405-601-4300, 866-781-3800; www .colcordhotel.com; 15 N Robinson Ave; r from $149; ste $279; P ✕ ✿ ▢ wi-fi) OKC's first skyscraper, built in 1910, is now an upscale downtown hotel. Many original flourishes, like the chandelier in the lobby, survive while the rooms and restaurant have a stylish, contemporary touch. Parking costs $9 and the hotel is walking distance to Bricktown.

Eating & Drinking

Bunches of eateries cluster in Bricktown, line Western Ave between 41st and 82nd Sts, and anchor a scattered **Asian District** (around 23rd St &

ROUTE 66: GET YOUR KICKS IN OKLAHOMA

Oklahoma's connection with America's Main Street runs deep: the road's chief proponent, Cyrus Avery, came from here; John Steinbeck's *Grapes of Wrath* told of the plight of depression-era Okie farmers fleeing west on Route 66; and Oklahoma has more miles of the original alignment than any other state. The **Oklahoma Route 66 Association** (www.oklahomaroute66.com) puts out a 62-page booklet/map that you can pick up from most visitor centers along the road. It's helpful because so many of the brown-and-white Historic Route 66 signs have been stolen for souvenirs.

Shortly after you enter the state from Kansas you'll come to Miami. Continue south through town on Main St and 2.5 miles after crossing the Neosho River turn right at the T-intersection. This will take you to the first of two original and very rough 9-foot wide alignments. The second, E 140 Rd (turn west) comes soon after the first, just before I-44.

You'll cross I-44 twice before rolling into Foyil where a 4-mile detour on Hwy 28A takes you to the massive and colorful concrete sculptures of **Totem Pole Park** (☎ 918-342-9149; www.rchs1 .org/totem.htm; admission free; ☷ 24/7)

Ten miles further on is Claremore (see p688), former home of Will Rogers.

Next up at the port city of Catoosa, just before Tulsa, is one of the most photographed Route 66 landmarks, the 80ft-long **Blue Whale** (2680 N Hwy 66).

East 11th St takes you into and right through art deco–rich Tulsa, passing near the **New Atlas Grill** (see p687) on the way. Southwest Blvd takes you across the river and out of town.

The rural route from Tulsa to Oklahoma City is one of the longest continuous stretches of Mother Road remaining (110 miles) and it sure beats the I-44 tollway that it snakes around. The food at the 1939 **Rock Café** (☎ 918-968-3390; 114 W Main St; breakfasts $3-6, mains $2-10; ☷ 6am-9pm; ☒) in

Classen Blvd) with reasonable Vietnamese, Chinese and Thai noodle houses.

Ann's Chicken Fry House (☎ 405-943-8915; 4106 NW 39th St; mains $4-12; ☷ 11am-8:30pm Tue-Sat; ☒) One of the few remaining Route 66 eateries, Ann's milks it for all it's worth with old cars, gas pumps and road signs outside and a 1950's theme inside.

Cattlemen's Steakhouse (☎ 405-236-0416; 1309 S Agnew Ave; breakfasts $3-6, lunch $4-25, dinners $10-25; ☷ 6am-10pm Sun-Thu, 6am-midnight Fri-Sat) OKC's most storied restaurant (it was once lost in a game of dice), this Stockyards City institution has been feeding cowpokes and city slickers slabs of beef and lamb's fries (that's a mannerly way of saying testicles) since 1910. The old-fangled booths, dark paneling and bold cow art suit the place.

Galileo (☎ 405-415-7827; 3009 Paseo Dr; mains $5-20; ☷ 11am-2am Tue-Sat, 11am-midnight Sun; ☒) This funky Paseo Arts District gathering spot has a menu spanning sea bass baked with lemon and cinnamon to meatloaf sandwiches to some tasty pizzas and it attracts just as diverse a crowd. There's art on the walls and the bar itself is a thing of beauty. Listen to music or poetry most nights.

TapWerks (☎ 405-319-9599; 121 E Sheridan Ave; mains $7-21, beer sample tray $7; ☷ 11am-2pm; wi-fi) Bad at making decisions? Then don't come here. This

comfy place in Bricktown serves over 150 bottled beers and has another 100 on tap. The food's not bad either and there's live music on weekends.

Wedge Pizzeria (☎ 405-602-3477; 4709 N Western Ave; pizzas $10-14; ☷ 11am-2pm & 5-10pm Mon-Thu, until 11pm Fri, 11am-11pm Sat, 5-10pm Sun; ☒) Whenever possible, this colorful little spot uses organic and locally grown ingredients on its brick-oven 'zas.

Entertainment

For listings, pick up the free weekly **Oklahoma Gazette** (www.okgazette.com) or just head to the renovated warehouses in the Bricktown district, which contain many restaurants and bars. The heart of gay Oklahoma is the **39th Street Strip** (west of Pennsylvania Ave).

Rodeo Opry (☎ 405-297-9773; www.ohfo.org; 2221 Exchange Ave; ☷ 7:30pm) Catch country-and-western wannabes weekly in Stockyards City.

Stage Center (☎ 405-270-4800; www.stagecenter .com; 400 W Sheridan Ave) This funky, hamster-house-looking building has two theaters and a cabaret room hosting contemporary plays, musicals and other events.

Shopping

The **Paseo Arts District** isn't much more than Paseo Dr itself, but there are several art gal-

GREAT PLAINS

Stroud, 50 miles west of Tulsa, ranges from chili-cheese dogs to jagersnitzel, but the souvenir menus are the most beloved item.

In Arcadia, 23 miles northeast of downtown OKC, stop at the cavernous, red **Round Barn** (☎ 406-396-0824; admission free; ☼ 10am-5pm daily summer, closed Mon winter); inside are photos of other round barns from around the world and sometimes barn dances are held in the loft.

Route 66 follows US 77 into Oklahoma City and beyond that, it's unmarked. Take Kelley Ave south, head over to Lincoln Blvd at 50th St and turn west on NW 23rd St at the capitol. You'll leave OKC by turning north on May Ave and west on NW 39th St where **Ann's Chicken Fry House** (see opposite) and the **66 Bowl** (☎ 405-946-3966; 3810 NW 39th St) are fun and photogenic. Beyond this, the route essentially hugs I-40, mostly on Business 40.

Lucille's, a gas station fronting the freeway just west of Hydro, 50 miles west of OKC, is a lonely Mother Road classic.

In Clinton walk through six decades of history, memorabilia and music at the entertaining **Route 66 Museum** (☎ 580-323-7866; www.route66.org; 2229 W Gary Blvd; adult/child $3/1; ☼ 9am-7pm Mon-Sat, 1-6pm Sun summer, closed at 5pm rest of year, closed Sun-Mon Jan-Feb).

Thirty miles further west in Elk City, the **National Route 66 Museum** (☎ 580-225-6266; adult/child $5/4; ☼ 9am-7pm Mon-Sat, 1-5pm Sun summer, 9am-5pm Mon-Sat, 2-5pm Sun rest of year) is barely more than a few old cars, but the ticket includes a re-created pioneer town and a farm museum.

The original kitschy neon sign at the **Western Motel** (☎ 580-928-3353; 315 NE Hwy 66; r $30; ❷) in Sayre, 23 miles before the border, is quite photogenic. Rooms are clean.

Route 66 spills into Texas at **Texola**, which is just a whisker away from being a ghost town.

leries and boutiques in the Spanish colonial buildings. You can buy a belt buckle or bridle in **Stockyards City**.

Getting There & Around

Will Rogers World Airport (☎ 405-680-3200; www.fly okc.com) is 5 miles southwest of downtown. The **Airport Express Shuttle** (☎ 405-681-3311) charges $17 to get downtown; in a **Yellow Cab** (☎ 405-232-6161) it costs about $20.

The Amtrak *Heartland Flyer* train goes from OKC's **Santa Fe Depot** (☎ 800-872-7245; 100 S EK Gaylord Blvd) to Fort Worth ($29, 4¼ hours). Buy your ticket on the train; there's no office here.

Greyhound buses depart daily from the **Union Bus Station** (☎ 405-235-6425; 427 W Sheridan Ave) for Dallas ($50, 5 hours) and Wichita ($38, 2¾ hours) among other destinations.

Oklahoma Spirit (☎ 405-235-7433; www.gometro .org) trolleys connect downtown and Bricktown sights for a quarter per ride. Regular city bus fares are $1.25.

AROUND OKLAHOMA CITY
Guthrie

Brick-and-stone Victorian buildings line street after street of Oklahoma's first capital, 25 miles north of Oklahoma City. The well-preserved downtown contains shops, muse-

ums and eateries, and during the summer you might catch the **Guthrie Gunfighters** stage Saturday shootouts.

The **Guthrie Information Center** (☎ 405-282-1947; www.guthrieok.com; 212 W Oklahoma Ave; ☼ 9am-5pm Mon-Fri) can point out the small museums (banjo, frontier drugstore, art, history and more) in town. Let the **Bed & Breakfast Association of Guthrie** (www.guthriebb.com) put you in one of a dozen historic inns. **Katie's Diner** (☎ 405-282-2462; 120 W Cleveland; mains $3-10; ☼ 6am-2pm Mon-Sat, 7am-2pm Sun; ❷) serves breakfast all day and the best fluffy homemade biscuits around.

WESTERN OKLAHOMA

West of Oklahoma City toward Texas the land opens into expansive prairie fields; nowhere as beautifully as in the Wichita Mountains, which, along with some Route 66 (see opposite) attractions and Native American sites, make good day trips from OKC.

Anadarko

Sixty miles southwest of OKC, Anadarko and the surrounding area are home to 64 Native American tribes. The town hosts powwows and other events almost monthly. Get a schedule from the Anadarko Visitor Center inside the **National Hall of Fame for Famous American**

Indians (☎ 405-247-5555; www.anadarko.org; Hwy 62 east of town; admission free; ☻ 9am-5pm Mon-Sat, 1-5pm Sun), which has a park with 42 bronze busts. The friendly people here enjoy answering questions. Next door is the **Southern Plains Indian Museum** (☎ 405-247-6221; Hwy 62; admission free; ☻ Tue-Sat 9am-5pm) with crafts from Kiowa, Cheyenne, Wichita and other western Oklahoma tribes.

Take a guided tour of seven typical tribal lodgings (Navajo, Apache, Wichita, Kiowa, Caddo, Pawnee and Pueblo) re-created on a hillside at **Indian City USA** (☎ 800-433-5661; www.indiancityusa.com; Rte 8, 2 miles south of town; tours adult/child $8.50/4.50; ☻ 9am-5pm). Dancers perform daily during the summer and weekends the rest of the year. The Kiowa tribe recently bought the museum and plans some changes, including the addition of a restaurant.

Keep your eye out for signs advertising church suppers and benefits; these are the best places to get Native American food in town.

Lawton to Fort Sill

Established in 1869 as an outpost against Native Americans, Fort Sill remains an active army base. The original stone structures, which were built by buffalo soldiers, are remarkably well preserved and the **Fort Sill Museum** (☎ 580-442-5123; 437 Quanah Rd; admission free; ☻ 8:30am-4:30pm) fills several of them, including a barracks furnished as it was in the 1870s and the guardhouse where Geronimo was detained after he had celebrated a little too much in nearby Lawton. Many old weapons are displayed nearby. Ask for a map to **Geronimo's grave**, which is located a couple of miles away.

The stockaded Red River Trading Post at the **Museum of the Great Plains** (☎ 580-581-3460; www.museumgreatplains.org; 601 NW Ferris Ave; adult/child $5/2.50; ☻ 10am-5pm Mon-Sat, 1-5pm Sun) in Lawton is a faithful reproduction of those found in the area from the 1830s to 1840s. There are living history encampments here in September and November. There's a prairie dog town in front and the Cherokee tribe is planning to open a museum at the back.

Hotels line up along I-44 and Cache Rd.

Wichita Mountains

Some 600 bison and a herd of longhorns roam the **Wichita Mountains Wildlife Refuge**

(☎ 580-429-3222; http://wichitamountains.fws.gov; visitor center Hwy 49 & Hwy 115; ☻ 8am-6pm), 15 miles northwest of Lawton. The mixed-grass prairie and lake areas are superb for hiking and wildlife spotting. Drive up Mt Scott (2464ft) for great views and listen for coyotes and screech owls while sleeping at the refuge's first-come, first-served **campground** ($8-16, without electricity $6) or in the backcountry (permit required).

Washita Battlefield

Take a 25-mile detour north of Route 66 to the **Washita Battlefield National Historic Site** (www.nps.gov/waba; Hwy 47A, 2 miles west of Cheyenne; admission free; ☻ dawn-dusk), where George Custer's troops launched an 1868 attack on the slumbering (and peaceful) village of Chief Black Kettle. The new **visitor center** (☎ 580-497-2742; ☻ 8am-5pm; free admission) has a museum, but the site's scenery is as appealing as its history.

TULSA

A downtown that is usually eerily empty and highways with some serious chain store-itis make Tulsa (population 382,500) seem less than stellar. The green rolling hills to the south, filled with oil money-bought mansions, paint a prettier picture. T-Town was billed as the 'Oil Capital of the World' in the early to mid-20th century, but the town actually didn't have much black gold: just oil companies reaping the rewards of statewide wells.

The staff at the **Tulsa Visitor Center** (☎ 800-558-3311; www.visittulsa.com; William Center Towers II, 2 W 2nd St; ☻ 8am-5pm; 💻) are very helpful.

Sights & Activities

Downtown Tulsa has so much art-deco architecture it was once known as the 'Terra-Cotta City.' The **Philcade Building** (511 S Boston), with its glorious T-shaped lobby, and **Boston Avenue United Methodist Church** (☎ 918-583-5181; 1301 S Boston; ☻ 8:30am-5pm Mon-Fri, 8am-5pm Sun, sometimes open Sat; guided tour noon Sun), rising at the end of downtown, are two exceptional examples. The *Downtown Tulsa Self-Guided Historic Walking Tour* map, free from the visitor center, will lead you to dozens more.

Northwest of downtown, off Hwy 64, the excellent **Gilcrease Museum** (☎ 888-655-2278; www.gilcrease.org; 1400 Gilcrease Museum Rd;

admission free; ⊙ 10am-5pm) sits on the estate of a Native American who discovered oil on his allotment. The impressive collection of American Western, Native American, and Central and South American fine art and archaeology is surrounded by some fine formal gardens.

South of town, another oil magnate's converted Italianate villa, also ringed by fabulous foliage, houses the **Philbrook Museum of Art** (☎ 918-749-7941; www.philbrook.org; 2727 S Rockford Rd, east of Peoria Ave; adult/child $7.50/5.50; ⊙ Tue-Sun 10am-5pm, to 8pm Thu). It is filled with European, Asian and African art, but the Native American works stand out.

Greenwood Cultural Center (☎ 918-596-1020; www.greenwoodculturalcenter.com; 322 N Greenwood Ave; admission free; ⊙ 9am-5pm Mon-Fri) displays photos of the historic African American Greenwood District, once known as the 'Black Wall Street', before and after a 1921 race riot. There's also pictures comprising the **Oklahoma Jazz Hall of Fame** (www.okjazz.org). The hall holds occasional concerts.

With a 200ft UFO-like **Prayer Tower** (☎ 918-495-6262; 7777 S Lewis Ave; admission free; ⊙ 10am-3:30pm Tue-Sat, 12:30-3:30pm Sun) at its heart, the campus of **Oral Roberts University** is as wacky as the televangelist who founded it.

Sleeping

Chain motels aplenty line Hwy 244 and I-44.

ourpick **Desert Hills Motel** (☎ 918-834-3311; www .deserthillsmotel.com; 5220 E 11th St; s/d $35/40; P ⊗ wi-fi) One of several low-cost Route 66 classics on the east side of town, but the neon cactus sign sets this one apart. The spotless rooms have a microwave and mini-refrigerator.

Super 8 Motel (☎ 918-438-7700, 800-900-8000; 11525 E Skelly Dr, r from $49; P ⊗ ⊛ wi-fi) Near Route 66 as you come into town, and convenient to the airport, this place has a touch of a Southwestern style outside and your usual chain hotel rooms inside.

Hotel Ambassador (☎ 918-587-8200, 888-408-8282; www.hotelambassador-tulsa.com; 1324 S Main St; r $164-204, ste $244-304; P ⊗ ⊛ 🖵) Look in the hallway for the photos of this 1929 hotel before the renovation. A location just south of downtown and a top-notch restaurant make the place ideal even if the neoclassical, boutique rooms are a bit small by today's standards.

Eating

Look for dining options in the Brookside neighborhood, on Peoria Ave between 31st and 51st Sts; on Historic Cherry St (now 15th St) just east of Peoria Ave; and the artsy Brady District, centered on Brady and Main Sts immediately north of downtown.

ourpick **Gypsy Coffee House** (☎ 918-295-2181; 303 N Cincinnati Ave; snacks & sandwiches $1-6; ⊙ noon-midnight Sun-Thu, noon-3am Fri-Sat; ⊗ 🖵 wi-fi) An all-around great hang-out in the Brady District with couches, board games, fair trade coffee and music on many nights.

New Atlas Grill (☎ 918-583-3111; 415 S Boston Ave; mains $5-6; ⊙ 7-9:30am & 11am-2:30pm Mon-Fri; ⊗) This great little lunch counter is off the lobby of the art-deco Atlas Life Building. Turkey sandwiches and 'mom's' chicken noodle soup hark back to the day.

Be Le Vegetarian Restaurant (☎ 918-499-1414; 6634 S Lewis Ave; mains $5-11; ⊙ 11am-2:30pm & 5-9pm Mon-Fri, 11am-9pm Sat; ⊗) The biggest surprise on the Tulsa dining scene, this simple mini-mall spot serves mock-meat versions (some of which are pretty good) of Chinese and Vietnamese meals.

Jamil's (☎ 918-742-9097; 2833 E 51st St; mains $10-28; ⊙ 4-11pm Sun-Thu, 4pm-midnight Fri-Sat) Each hickory-grilled steak and seafood dish comes with 'Lebanese' appetizers: tabbouleh, hummus, a cabbage roll, ribs – and fried bologna. Little has changed since it opened in 1945.

Entertainment

Pick up the free **Urban Tulsa Weekly** (www.urbantulsa .com) around town to learn what's going on.

Full Moon Café (☎ 918-583-6666; www.eatfullmoon .com; 1525 E 15th St; ⊙ 11am-midnight Mon & Wed-Thu, 11am-2am Tue & Fri, 9am-2am Sat-Sun; ⊗) Casual food and dueling pianos Thursday through Saturday; live music other nights too.

Cain's Ballroom (☎ 918-584-2306; www.cainsball room.com; 423 N Main St) Today's rockers perform on the same floor where Bob Wills played Western swing in the 1930s and the Sex Pistols caused confusion in 1978.

Discoveryland! (☎ 918-245-6552; www.discovery landusa.com; 19501 W 41st St, Sand Springs; adult/child $19/free; ⊙ 7pm Mon-Sat summer) Ten miles west of Tulsa there's a dandy outdoor production of *Oklahoma!* A Western musical revue and Native American dancers kick things off, and a pre-show dinner is available.

GREAT PLAINS

Getting There & Around

Tulsa International Airport (☎ 918-838-5000; www.tulsaairports.com), situated off Hwy 11, is northeast of downtown. **Greyhound** (☎ 918-584-4428; 317 S Detroit Ave) has daily buses bound for Oklahoma City ($20, two hours) and St Louis ($89, eight hours). Almost all local **Tulsa Transit** (☎ 918-582-2100; www.tulsatransit.org; one-day pass $3) buses originate downtown at 319 S Denver Ave.

GREEN COUNTRY

Subtle forested hills interspersed with lakes cover Oklahoma's northeast corner, aka **Green Country** (www.greencountryok.com), which includes Tulsa. The area has a strong Native American influence as it is where several of the Five Civilized Tribes (Cherokee, Choctaw, Chickasaw, Creek and Seminole) were relocated in the 1820s and 30s.

Don't miss Totem Pole Park and the Blue Whale along Route 66 (see p684).

Bartlesville

Oklahoma's first commercial oil well was dug in Bartlesville, 50 miles north of Tulsa, and soon after Frank Phillips, of Phillips 66 fame, arrived to dig more. His vast county estate, **Woolaroc** (☎ 918-336-0307; www.woolaroc .org; Rte 123, 11 miles south of town; adult/child $8/free; 10am-5pm Wed-Sun, open Tue summer), is now an outstanding museum of southwestern art and culture, and a wildlife refuge with both local and exotic animals.

Thirty miles west of Bartlesville, some 2500 bison roam across 44,645 acres at the **Tallgrass Prairie Preserve** (☎ 918-287-4803) the world's largest patch of protected tallgrass prairie.

You can tour the only Frank Lloyd Wright–designed skyscraper ever built, the stunning, 221ft **Price Tower Arts Center** (☎ 918-336-4949; www.pricetower.org; 510 Dewey Ave; adult/child $4/free, tours $10/5; 10am-5pm Tue-Sat, noon-5pm Sun; tours 11am & 2pm Tue-Sat plus noon & 1pm Fri-Sat, 2pm Sun). Even better, stay in one of the 21, upper-floor, Wright-inspired rooms that are the **Inn at Price Tower** (☎ 918-336-1000, 877-424-2424; s/d from $125/145, ste from $225;). Breakfast is included. **Copper** (☎ 918-336-1000; mains $15-20; 11am-2pm and 5-9pm Tue-Sat;) serves chichi American fare inside and out on the 16th floor.

Claremore

Born in a log cabin just north of town in 1879, Will Rogers was a cowboy, a hilarious homespun philosopher, star of radio and movies, and part Cherokee. The hilltop **Will Rogers Memorial Museum** (☎ 918-341-0719; www.willrogers.com; 1720 W Will Rogers Blvd; admission free; 8am-5pm), 30 miles northeast of Tulsa off Route 66, is a loving and entertaining tribute.

If you like guns, you'll love the **J M Davis Arms and Historical Museum** (☎ 918-341-5707; 333 N Lynn Riggs Blvd; admission free; 8:30am-5pm Mon-Sat, 1-5pm Sun, open 10am-4pm Sun summer) which has over 13,000 of them on display – not to mention the 1,200 beer steins.

Grab one of the few seats at **Dot's Café** (☎ 918-341-9718; 310 W Will Rogers Blvd; breakfasts $3-9; 7am-2pm Mon-Sat, to 8pm Thu) and enjoy good pie and a healthy dose of local gossip.

Trail of Tears Country

The area southeast of present-day Tulsa was, and to some degree still is, Creek and Cherokee land. For anyone interested in learning about Native American culture, this is a good place to start.

You may remember Merle Haggard singing 'Okie from Muskogee?' Well, **Muskogee**, 49 miles southeast of Tulsa, is home to the **Five Civilized Tribes Museum** (☎ 877-587-4237; www .fivetribes.org; Agency Hill, Honor Heights Dr; adult/student $3/1.50; 10am-5pm Mon-Sat, 1-5pm Sun) inside an 1875 Union Indian Agency house. Bacone College's **Ataloa Lodge Museum** (☎ 918-781-7283; www.bacone.edu/ataloa; 2299 Old Bacone Rd; admission free; 8am-5pm Mon-Sat, 1-5pm Sun), east of town on US 62, has a diverse collection of Native American artifacts, ancient and modern, from across the Americas. The Hopi and Navajo kachina dolls and pottery are standouts. You can also tour the **USS Batfish** (☎ 918-682-6294; www.ussbatfish.com; adult/child $5/2; 9am-4pm Mon & Wed-Sat, noon-4pm Sun Mar-Oct), a WWII submarine. It's off Hwy 165 even further east.

Twenty miles east on Hwy 62 is **Tahlequah** (tal-*ah*-quaw), the Cherokee capital since 1839. A knowledgeable native guide at the excellent **Cherokee Heritage Center** (☎ 888-999-6007; www.cherokeeheritage.org; 21192 Keeler Rd, Park Hill; adult/child $8.50/5; 10am-5pm Mon-Sat, 1-5pm Sun, closed Jan) leads tours through a re-creation of a pre-European contact woodland village (no teepees here), where you can learn to shoot a blow gun or play stick ball. A log cabin town represents Cherokee life during the mid-19th century and the museum focuses on the Trail of Tears. During the summer there are **historical dinner theater** (adult/child with dinner $25/15, without dinner $15/10; ☺ vary from year to year) performances. Take scenic Rte 10 north to where canoe outfitters line the Illinois River. Try **War Eagle Floats** (☎ 800-722-3834; www.wareagleresort.com; 13020 N Hwy 10) for two-hour to two-day trips.

Downtown **Okmulgee**, off US 75 south of Tulsa, looks a bit like the set of a 1950s film. Smack in the heart of it all is the **Creek Council House Museum** (☎ 918-756-2324; 106 W 6th St; admission free; ☺ 10am-4:30pm Tue-Sat), the former capital of the Muscogee (Creek) Nation, built in 1878. In August, the town hosts the **Okmulgee Invitational Rodeo** (☎ 918-758-1015; www.okmulgeetourism.com), an African American rodeo.

Texas

If you thought, 'Screw You, We're from Texas' was the state motto, not just the refrain in a Ray Wylie Hubbard song, you'd be forgiven for misunderstandin'. A certain chest-puffin' pride does seem to go with being from the Lone Star State. It probably has as much to do with leftover independent spirit (locals are mighty proud of Texas having been its own country) as it does with all that bigness (the state *is* larger than Germany, England, Scotland, Ireland, Northern Ireland, Belgium and the Netherlands combined). Nevertheless, the Wild West lives on today mostly in attitude. If you're expectin' to see a buncha cowboys dusty from the trail, you're about as sharp as a heapa mashed potaters. Computer-geek millionaires outnumber rich cattlemen, and you're as likely to see a Dallas fashionista as a good ol' gal in her tight-fittin' jeans.

Sure you can (and might oughta) do some two-steppin' in a 100-year-old dance hall, but you should also rock out at the hundreds of live-music venues in Austin or pulse to the mariachi beat in ol' San Antone. If you imagine the nature of Texas is tumblin' tumbleweeds, a walk along miles of undeveloped Gulf Coast beach or the sight of snow in the 8000ft-plus Guadalupe Mountains will change your mind right quick.

Of course there's also them bright lights 'n big cities – Houston and Dallas, with their culture and such. And if what you really want to see is ropers and riders, they'll oblige ya. Mosey on over to Fort Worth's historic stockyards, attend a small-town rodeo, or get your giddy-up on at Bandera's dude ranches. Wherever you go, most folks are just as friendly as pie. Can you blame 'em? They're from Texas.

HIGHLIGHTS

- Diving into some hard-rockin' blues at Austin's original live-music bar, the **Continental Club** (p701)
- Ogling the true Texana artworks that are handmade **Rocketbuster Boots** (p739) in El Paso
- Photographing brilliant cactus blooms – bright fuchsia choyo, flaming orange ocotillo – in **Big Bend National Park** (p734).
- Going country at the National Cowgirl Museum by day and the Stockyards rodeo by night in **Fort Worth** (p729).
- Marveling at the slabs of meat on massive outdoor BBQ pits at **Salt Lick Barbecue** (p701) outside Austin.
- Trying a *tripas* (tripe) taco while listening to a conjunto band during **Fiesta San Antonio** (p708)
- Boot-scooting the night away at **John T Floore's Country Store** (p709), where Wylie used to play, in Helotes.
- Watching for the **Marfa Lights** (p737) – aliens or anomalies, you decide.

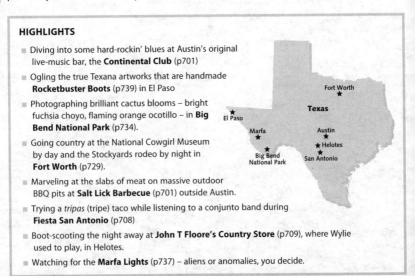

HISTORY

Given that the conquerors' diseases wiped out much of the indigenous population, it seems a bit ironic that the Spaniards named their new territory Tejas (*tay*-has), a corruption of the Caddo word for 'friend.' Caddo, Apache and Karankawa were among the tribes that Spanish explorers encountered when they arrived to map the coast in 1519.

Mexico won its independence from Spain in 1821. At first Texans supported Mexican general Antonio López de Santa Anna, until he eliminated the state federation system. That didn't sit well with many independent-minded 'Texians' (US- and Mexico-born Texans) who had been given cheap land grants and Mexican citizenship. Slavery was outlawed and immigration curtailed, and clashes escalated into the Texas War for Independence. A month after Santa Anna's forces massacred surviving combatants at the battle of the Alamo and the battle of Goliad, Sam Houston's rebels routed the Mexican troops at San Jacinto with the cry – let's all say it – 'Remember the Alamo! Remember Goliad!' Thus the Republic of Texas was born. It ended nine years later when by treaty Texas opted to become the 28th state of the Union.

Cattle ranching formed the core of Texas' post–Civil War economy, but the black gold that spewed up from Spindletop, near Beaumont, in 1910 changed everything. From then on, for better or worse, the state's economy has run on oil. During the energy crisis of the 1970s, when gasoline prices quadrupled, Texans – who were the biggest domestic oil supplier and had many of the nation's largest refineries – laughed all the way to the bank. Boom time was big, but the bust in the 1980s was just as spectacular. A worldwide glut devastated the oil industry and towns were deserted overnight.

The 1990s buzzword was diversification. South-central Texas became a high-tech corridor, and the North American Free Trade Agreement (Nafta) encouraged trade south of the border with neighboring Mexico. Former Texas governor George W Bush was elected to two terms as president of the United States, which must have made his father, George Bush Sr (the 41st US president), mighty proud. Those still involved in the oil industries have long joked, 'Lord, give me just one more boom and I promise

TEXAS FACTS
Nickname Lone Star State
Population 23.5 million
Area 261,797 sq miles
Capital city Austin (population 690,252)
Sales tax 6.25%
Birthplace of Buddy Holly (1936–59), Howard Hughes (1905–76), Janis Joplin (1943–70), George Strait (b 1952), Matthew McConaughey (b 1969)
Home of Dr Pepper, corny dogs and two President Bushes
Famous for The Cowboys and cowboys, great BBQ
Best souvenir 'Don't mess with Texas' toilet paper

I won't piss it away.' With crude oil prices continuing to rise late into the 2000s, it looks like their dreams just may have come true.

LOCAL CULTURE

Trying to typify Texas culture is like tryin' to wrestle a pig in mud – it's awful slippery. In vast generalization, Austin is alternative Texas, where environmental integrity and quality of life are actually discussed. Dallasites wallow in the shallow, spending more on silicon implants than anywhere but LA. Conservative, casual Houston has a good bit of wealth, spent nightly by good ol' boys at clubby steakhouses. San Antonio is the most Tex-Mexican of the bunch, a showplace of Hispanic culture. All across the state, two things seem to be true: football is sacred and, for boys and men, peeing outdoors is a God-given right and privilege.

LAND & CLIMATE

What ecosystem doesn't Texas have? The Rio Grande forms the southern border with Mexico in the Rio Grande Valley (known as the Valley), where palm trees, citrus and vegetables are grown in tropical heat. The Gulf of Mexico's coastal climate and sugar-sand beaches typify the semi-arid southeast; verdant hills and meandering rivers make up central Hill Country. There are pine forests and swamps in the northeast, and wide, flat desert valleys alternate with mountain ranges (Guadalupe Peak, at 8749ft, is the highest) in the way-far west.

It's said that the state has four seasons: heat, drought, hurricane and flood. July to September Texas can be hotter 'n nine

TEXAS

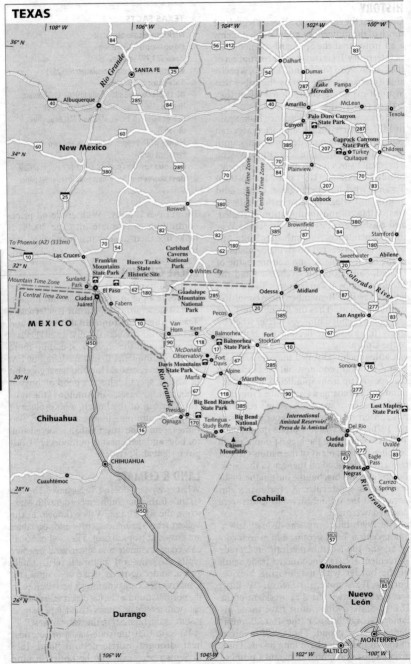

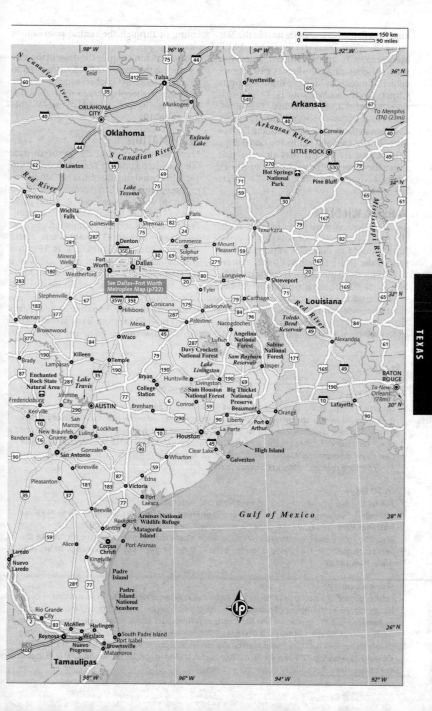

kinds a hell: temperatures are least in the '90s statewide. West Texas and Big Bend – 102°F average (39°C) – are best avoided, unless you stay in the mountains, where it's 10 degrees cooler. Winter is mild in the south – Corpus Christi rarely gets below 40°F (4°C; though there was that freak Christmas Eve snowstorm back in 2004). Ice and snow are more common in the Panhandle Plains, the Dallas–Fort Worth area and up in the Guadalupe Mountains. By far the best time to visit statewide is spring (late February to April), when the humidity is low and wildflowers are in bloom.

PARKS & WILDLIFE

Texas has two national parks in West Texas, Big Bend National Park (p734) and Guadalupe Mountains National Park (p739), as well as the Padre Island National Seashore (p720) on the Gulf Coast. **Texas Parks & Wildlife** (☎ 800-792-1112, central reservations 512-389-8900; www.tpwd.state.tx.us) puts out a free guide to the 125 wonderful state parks. Reservations for campsites ($4 to $16) and cabin rental ($40 to $90), where available, can be made online or through the central reservations number.

Bird watching is quite the draw in the Valley during the spring (March to April) and fall (September to October) migrations. The endangered whooping crane winters (November to March) in Aransas National Wildlife Refuge (p719).

INFORMATION

Local taxes usually add 2% on top of state sales tax. Hotel taxes in Texas rack up 14% to 17%. Every lodging listed has air-conditioning and parking. In San Antonio, Dallas and Houston, unless you see the Ⓟ, hotel parking ain't free (it's usually $15 to $25 a night). For attractions, a child's admission price refers to ages four to 12, except where noted; there's no charge for toddlers. In Houston and Dallas, you must dial all 10 digits in a telephone number, even for local calls. Otherwise, you can drop the area code if you're calling locally.

Request the free, booklike annual *Texas State Travel Guide* from **Texas Tourism** (☎ 800-452-9292; www.traveltex.com) or get it at one of

---

TEXAS...

In Five Days

Book two nights at the funky **Austin Motel** (p700) and arrange to listen to as much live music in the capital as you can, maybe catching an acoustic set under the live oaks at **Shady Grove** (p701). The next day drive out to a small country town like **Gruene** (p704), where you can tube down the river or boot-scoot the state's oldest dance hall. Moving on to San Antonio, you have two days to revere the **Alamo** (p707), imbibe at **Riverwalk** (p707) cafés and bargain-hunt for Mexico-made trinkets in **Market Square** (p708).

In 10 Days

Follow the five-day itin, then drive west from San Antonio to the Big Bend area (approximately 400 miles). Stay a night at the Old West–era **Gage Hotel** (p736) before driving south to **Big Bend National Park** (p734) to hike or raft among deep canyons and craggy mountains. You might also stop to see some stunning avant-garde art in **Marfa** (p735), stargaze at the **McDonald Observatory** (p736) in Fort Davis, or go for a dip in the spring-fed swimming hole at **Balmorhea State Park** (p736).

Gone Country

Outfit yourself in a new pair of boots and straw hat at **Allen Boots** (p702) in Austin before going honky-tonkin' at the **Broken Spoke** (p702). The classic cowboy bars and dude ranches a-plenty in **Bandera** (p705) are worth a few days' diversion. Then, get along little doggies, you're driving north to **Fort Worth's Stockyard District** (p729), where you'll watch the Saturday-night rodeo before trying your hand (and your rear) on the mechanical bull at **Billy Bob's** (p731). The **National Cowgirl Museum** (p729) and Frederick Remington's Western art at the **Amon Carter Museum** (p729) are the other country must-sees in town.

DON'T MISS

- **Continental Club** – live music central (p701)

- **Barton Springs** – dip in a real cool pool (p699)

- **Lamberts** – not your mama's BBQ (p700)

- **Bats** – more than a million of them (p698)

- **SoCo shopping** – Allen Boots, great vintage shops (p702)

---

its 12 Texas Travel Information Centers. Its extensive website has lodging and sights listings.

Read more about the state in these glossy mags:

Shout Texas (www.shouttexas.com) Gay and lesbian entertainment.

Texas Highways (www.texashighways.com) Road trip through the state's landscape, history and culture.

Texas Monthly (www.texasmonthly.com) In-depth features on personalities, food and current events.

Texas Parks & Wildlife Magazine (www.tpwmagazine.com) All things outdoorsy.

GETTING THERE & AWAY

The busiest international gateways to the state are Houston's George Bush Intercontinental Airport (IAH) and Dallas–Fort Worth International Airport (DFW). Austin, San Antonio and El Paso also have major airports.

Amtrak (☎ 800-872-7245; www.amtrak.com) runs the *Sunset Limited* train between Orlando, Florida, and Los Angeles three times a week, with stops including Houston, San Antonio and El Paso. The *Texas Eagle* runs between Chicago and San Antonio daily, with stops in Dallas–Fort Worth and Austin. Note that trains often have late-night arrivals or departures in Texas.

Starting in 2009, passports will be required for all people (US citizens included) crossing the border with Mexico.

GETTING AROUND

Given the distances, traveling by car is all but necessary in Texas – make sure you opt for unlimited rental mileage. To avoid one-way drop-off fees, you could catch a cheap inter-Texas flight between cities, where it's

easy to rent a car. Cut-rate carrier **Southwest Airlines** (☎ 800-435-9792; www.iflyswa.com) serves Houston, Dallas, San Antonio, Austin, El Paso, Midland-Odessa, Lubbock, Corpus Christi and Harlingen (South Padre Island). In-Texas hops can be as little as $39 to $99 one way if you book ahead. Houston-based Continental and Dallas-based American Airlines often match Southwest's sales.

Greyhound (☎ 800-231-2222; www.greyhound.com) and its partner **Kerrville Bus Lines** (☎ 800-231-2222; www.iridekbc.com) serve all but the tiniest towns, though it may take several transfers and twice as long as by car.

Regional driving distances:

Austin to San Antonio 78 miles
San Antonio to Houston 196 miles
Houston to Dallas 237 miles
Dallas to El Paso 622 miles
Brownsville to Houston 350 miles

SOUTH-CENTRAL TEXAS

OK, although the hills in south-central Texas are more like molehills than mounts, they – and the rivers that flow through – are the defining factor in the region. Dotting Hill Country are small Texasy towns that show the influence of early German and Czech settlers. Here you can eat great BBQ, dance across an old wooden floor or spend a lazy day floating on the river. To the north is the state capital of Austin, where music, music and more music is on the bill. Eighty miles south, major metropolitan centre San Antonio is home of the Alamo, and the festive Riverwalk bars and restaurants. If you want to get to the heart of Texas in a short time, south-central is the way to go.

AUSTIN

An eclectic pick-and-mix of retro funk and new-age entrepreneurial spirit, Austin's best side is a mystic soup of social consciousness and capitalist development, tattoo-covered artists and internet millionaires. Quality of life reigns supreme. Here even the buttoned-down businessmen are likely to take a day off to go swimming in spring-fed pools, jogging along Town Lake or kayaking on the river. Almost any night here you can listen to live indie rock, jazz-funk, alt country, punk ska, acoustic rhythms, Latin sambas, Tejano trumpets, world

TEXAS

beat…shall I go on? All this coolness has not gone unnoticed. Locals are concerned that too many cooks are spoiling the broth as more people continue to migrate here and suburbs spread further north. 'Keep Austin Weird' extol local bumper stickers, and so far the town isn't overly gentrified – and the restaurant selection has noticeably improved.

The Texas capital, founded on a bend in the Colorado River in 1839, in large part took shape because of the University of Texas (UT), founded in 1883. All those longhorn

tattoos and car-window stickers you see? Those are Bevo, the mascot: 'Hook 'em horns!' In the 1960s and '70s, local beer joints launched the likes of rock diva Janis Joplin and cosmic cowboy Willie Nelson; a league of performers carry on the tradition today.

Orientation & Information

Downtown centers on north–south Congress Ave, below Martin Luther King Jr Blvd. E 6th St between Congress Ave and I-35 is notorious for nighttime entertainment. Town Lake, really a dammed stretch

---

LOCAL VOICES: AUSTIN LOUNGE LIZARDS

For more than 20 years, the Austin Lounge Lizards have been poking some serious fun at subjects from passion to politics – in a bevy of musical genres: folk, country, bluegrass, surfers' rock and roll… Though they travel countrywide, you can still see them quite often in hometown Austin clubs like Cactus Cafe (p702) and other Lonestar venues, like Mucky Duck (p716) in Houston. Native Texan Conrad Deisler plays guitar, and Boo Resnick plays bass – they both contribute to the wacky, wordsmithy lyrics.

A lot of your songs, such as the repetitively redundant ballad 'Big Rio Grande River' ('In the pass they call El Paso, back in 1921…'), deal with Texas topics; what do you think of this state as source material?

Conrad: Texas is so rife with outrages both legendary and banal that a whole raft of songwriters could mine its veins for decades without bumping into each other.

Boo: Texas is also an incredible cultural crossroads for food and music – black, white, Mexican, Southern, Cajun, blues, conjunto, Tejano, rock, blues, bluegrass, country – it's all there.

Immigration is a hot topic right now – thoughts?

Conrad: Our song 'Teenage Immigrant Welfare Mothers on Drugs' gets timelier by the moment. We didn't write it, but we enhanced it with Lee Goland's permission. After one show, a Mexican immigrant approached me – his wife and friend were quite upset. He said he'd been in this country for seven years and thought he understood the song as satire. I told him that, indeed, we were depicting those who express bitter opposition to the influx of foreign workers while profiting from their labor. He seemed relieved. We shook hands.

What do you think is best/worst about Texas? Does your 'Stupid Texas Song' ('Our accents are the drawliest, our howdies are the y'alliest, our Lone Star flag's the waviest, our fried steak's the cream-graviest…') have anything to do with it?

Boo: We were in a club in Arlington, TX, and heard a song on the jukebox that was a typical Texas kind of C&W song – bragging about all these wonderful things – my hat, my boots, my truck, my girl. So we decided to take the TX bragging thing to the extreme and brag about things the other songs don't cover. We are really making fun of all those Texas songs, not Texas itself. I suppose my favorite things about Texas are the food, the music and Austin. The worst things about Texas are the Wild West redneck attitudes so many people still cling to and, of course, state government.

Conrad: If you spend a little time here, you'll quickly learn to place the hype in proper perspective. It's almost like an inside joke – everybody knows that Texas is huge, hot, flat, and prone to natural disasters and venomous snakes, but come on down and we will show you a good time!

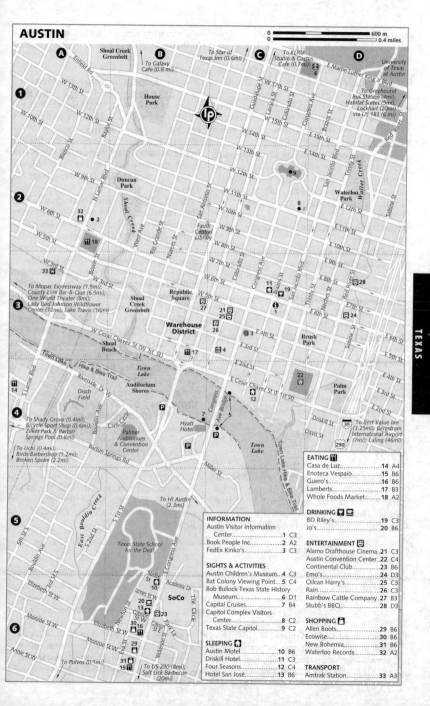

TEXAS

EATING 🍴
Casa de Luz..................	14	A4
Enoteca Vespaio..........	15	B6
Guero's........................	16	B6
Lamberts......................	17	B3
Whole Foods Market......	18	A2

DRINKING 🍷 🍺
BD Riley's....................	19	C3
Jo's..............................	20	B6

ENTERTAINMENT 🎭
Alamo Drafthouse Cinema.	21	C3
Austin Convention Center.	22	C4
Continental Club...........	23	B6
Emo's...........................	24	D3
Oilcan Harry's...............	25	C3
Rain.............................	26	C3
Rainbow Cattle Company.	27	B3
Stubb's BBQ..................	28	D3

SHOPPING 🛍
Allen Boots..................	29	B6
Ecowise.......................	30	B6
New Bohemia...............	31	B6
Waterloo Records.........	32	A2

INFORMATION
Austin Visitor Information		
Center......................	1	C3
Book People Inc...........	2	A2
FedEx Kinko's..............	3	C3

SIGHTS & ACTIVITIES
Austin Children's Museum..	4	C3
Bat Colony Viewing Point...	5	C4
Bob Bullock Texas State History		
Museum...................	6	D1
Capital Cruises.............	7	B4
Capitol Complex Visitors		
Center......................	8	C2
Texas State Capitol.......	9	C2

SLEEPING 🛏
Austin Motel................	10	B6
Driskill Hotel...............	11	C3
Four Seasons...............	12	C4
Hotel San José.............	13	B6

TRANSPORT
Amtrak Station.............	33	A3

of the Colorado River, is the southern edge of downtown and the northern boundary of South Austin. Quirky stores, cool restaurants and hip hotels line S Congress Ave (SoCo). North of downtown is UT. Guadalupe St, or 'the Drag', with its cheap eats, bars and bookstores, parallels Congress Ave alongside the university. Mopac Expressway (Loop 1) is west of downtown, and area lake roads lead off that.

Austin indoors is nonsmoking, period (bars, too). A vast wi-fi network blankets downtown. For other hot spots check out www.austinwirelesscity.org. City of Austin libraries (www.ci.austin.tx.us) have free internet.

Austin American-Statesman (www.statesman.com) Daily newspaper.

Austin Visitor Information Center (☎ 512-478-0098; www.austintexas.org; 209 E 6th St; ☯ 9am-5pm Mon-Fri, to 6pm Sat & Sun) Tour and performance tickets sold; general info on hand.

Birds Barbershop (☎ 512-442-8800; 2110 S Lamar Blvd; ☯ 9am-11pm) Some of the hippest haircuts in town; a Mohawk is only $15.

Book People Inc (☎ 512-472-4288; 603 N Lamar Blvd; ☯ 9am-11pm) A bookstore as independent as Austin.

FedEx Kinko's (☎ 512-472-4448; 327 Congress Ave; ☯ 7am-11pm Mon-Fri, 10am-7pm Sat & Sun) Internet access 20¢ a minute.

KLRU TV (www.klru.org) PBS affiliate with local programming that includes the popular music show *Austin City Limits.*

Sights

Don't limit yourself to the sights, most of which are downtown. Austin is more about the experience, man. Bars, restaurants, even grocery stores and the airport have live music. There are outdoor activities galore, or a full day might include shopping for some groovy vintage clothes and getting a Mohawk haircut.

DOWNTOWN

Wander along the hoof-marked ground of a cattle drive, look through rough-hewn slave cabins or duck into a movie theater beneath a 1930s-era marquee. High-tech interactive exhibits and fun theatrics characterize the superb (and superbly humongous) **Bob Bullock Texas State History Museum** (☎ 512-936-8746; www.thestoryoftexas.com; 1800 Congress Ave; adult/child $5.50/3, Texas Spirit film $5/3.50; ☯ 9am-6pm Mon-Sat, 11am-6pm Sun).

Yes, the 1888, stunning, pink-granite **Texas State Capitol** (☎ 512-463-0063; cnr 11th St & Congress Ave; admission free; ☯ 7am-10pm Mon-Fri, 9am-8pm Sat & Sun) really is 15ft taller than the US Capitol. For an echoing ovation, stand dead center under the dome and clap – the state senators don't mind, really. The nearby **Capitol Complex Visitors Center** (☎ 512-305-8400; www.tspb.state.tx.us; 112 E 11th St; ☯ 9am-5pm Mon-Sat, noon-5pm Sun) is the place to book tours.

Kids can play toy guitars in staged videos as part of Kiddie City Limits (a take on the famous local TV show) at the **Austin Children's Museum** (☎ 512-472-2499; www.austinkids.org; 210 Colorado St; adult/child under 2yr $5.50/3.50; ☯ 10am-5pm Tue-Sat, noon-5pm Sun).

UNIVERSITY OF TEXAS AT AUSTIN

Local PBS affiliate **KLRU Studio** (☎ 512-471-4811; www.pbs.org/klru/austin; cnr 26th & Guadalupe Sts, 6th fl) records the super-cool *Austin City Limits*, a Texas music-TV program (aired 9:30pm Friday). Tickets for tapings are hard to come by since they're given away at radio-announced locations and run out fast. Call the **hotline** (☎ 512-475-9077) for schedule information, or you can tour the studio for free Friday at 10:30am.

GOING BATTY

Up to 1.5 million Mexican free-tailed bats swarm out nightly from their roost on a platform beneath the Congress Ave Bridge. It's become an Austin tradition to watch around sunset from late March to early November as the little critters (mothers and babies only – this is a mating colony) go out to dinner. The best bat-colony viewing points are the lawns on the riverbanks to the east of the bridge, though watching from the balcony of the Four Seasons hotel bar (p700) has an appeal. **Capital Cruises** (☎ 512-480-9264; www.capitalcruises.com; 208 Barton Springs Rd; adult/child $8/5), behind the Hyatt, runs bat-watching cruises on Town Lake, departing 30 minutes before sunset. Reservations required. For more batty info, check with the **Bat Conservation International** (☎ 512-416-5700 category 3636; www.batcon.org) hotline.

MUSIC MECCA

Nearly 10,000 musicians and fans converge on Austin five days mid-March for **South by Southwest** (SXSW; ☎ 512-467-7979; www.sxsw.com), the mecca of new music festivals. The roughly 1700 acts that play around town represent every genre of music – metal funk to indie punk, jazz quartets to acoustic sets. And there are scads more unofficial bands playing at unofficial venues. Then there are the parties – both private and public (some listed at www.austinist.com). This is the best (for indie music-lovers) or worst (for crowd-haters) time to be in Austin. Hotels are booked up to a year in advance.

Buying a Platinum Badge ($650 to $950, depending how far ahead you buy) allows access to all three trade shows (music, film, internet), conferences, talks, film screenings, clubs and VIP lounges. A Music Badge ($425 to $600) gains entry to the music conference, trade show and nightly gigs (both sold online starting in September). The cheapest way to get into the clubs is to buy a wristband ($140 to $175), sold at Waterloo Records (p702). The surprise sale date – usually in late February or early March – is announced by same-day text message. (To receive festival text alerts, follow the instructions on the website under 'SXSW toolbox'.) Be warned: those with badges gain entry before those with wrist bands, and capacity controls are strictly enforced, so everyone may not get in. If your heart's set on seeing a certain group, go early and wait through a couple of acts. Research pays: the same showcase bands that sell out nights also play day parties and in-store gigs; check the *Austin Chronicle* (www.austinchronicle.com) for SWSW event listings.

SOUTH AUSTIN

Go Kodak crazy in the gardens and along the nature trails of **Lady Bird Johnson Wildflower Center** (☎ 512-292-4200; www.wildflower.org; 4801 La Crosse Ave; adult/child $6/2.50; ☉ 9am-5:30pm Tue-Sat, noon-5:30pm Sun), 12 miles south on Mopac Expressway. April is bluebonnet season…

Activities

At dusk bazillions of bats fly out from under Congress Ave Bridge – it's quite a spectacle. See the boxed text, opposite.

To the west of downtown, dive into the chilly, spring-fed, sparkly-clear waters of **Barton Springs Pool** (☎ 512-476-9044; 2201 Barton Springs Rd; adult/child $3/1; ☉ 9am-8pm late May-Aug) – seems like everyone else in Austin does. The banks of the dammed river are left pretty natural; don't mind the turtles. Barton Springs forms the centerpiece of 351-acre **Zilker Park** (☎ 512-472-4914; www.ci.austin.tx.us/zilker; 2201 Barton Springs Rd), which has trails, a nature center and botanical gardens. Creekside just north of the pool, from April to November you can rent kayaks from **Zilker Boats** (☎ 512-478-3852; www.zilkerboats.com; Zilker Park; per hour/day $10/40; ☉ 11am-dark Mon-Fri, 9am-dark Sat & Sun).

Town Lake hike and bike trail runs along the northern and southern shore of Town Lake – downtown and beyond. Park near the Congress Ave Bridge and take a walk; or reserve ahead and rent a bike (from $18 a day) at

Bicycle Sport Shop (☎ 512-477-3472; 517 S Lamar Blvd; ☉ 10am-8pm Mon-Fri, 9am-6pm Sat, 11am-5pm Sun).

Festivals & Events

South by Southwest (SXSW; ☎ 512-467-7979; www.sxsw.com) One of the American music industry's biggest gatherings (see the boxed text, above).

Austin City Limits Music Festival (☎ 512-389-0315; www.aclfestival.com; 3-day pass $105) More than 130 bands on eight stages during three days in September.

Sleeping

Hotels downtown are high rent, but you don't have to go far to find reasonable digs. SoCo has some interesting places, and there are plenty of motels on I-35.

BUDGET

HI Austin (☎ 512-444-2294; www.hiaustin.org; 2200 S Lakeshore Blvd; dm members/nonmembers $19/22; ✗ ▢ wi-fi) Two-story views of the lake from the sunny orange, yellow and red great room – complete with fish tank, guitar and comfy couches – are enough to make even nonhostelers consider a stay. Rent a bike or kayak ($10 a day) and ride the 2.5 miles to downtown (there's also a bus stop nearby). Cat on-site; recycling friendly.

Best Value Inn (☎ 512-441-0143; www.bestvalueinn.com; 2525 S I-35; r $46-54; ▢ wi-fi) Of the eight basic budget motels on S I-35 near the Oltorf St exit, a short drive from SoCo, Best Value isn't the newest, but there are a lot of little

TEXAS

perks. These include hot eggs and waffles, in-room coffee and iron, and a playground.

MIDRANGE

our pick Austin Motel (☎ 512-441-1157; www.austin motel.com; 1220 S Congress Ave; r $65-101; P 🐾 wi-fi) A waterfall mural or retro polka dots: each room is individually fun and funky, and constantly being redecorated. The random furniture resembles savvy thrift-shopper finds, which makes this place all the more appealing in that quirky, grandmotherly kind of way. The least expensive rooms are shoeboxes, but the pool-side pads seem palatial. You can't be more central in SoCo than here.

our pick Hotel San José (☎ 512-444-7322; www .sanjosehotel.com; 1316 S Congress Ave; r with shared bath $90-100, with private bath $195-240; ✗ 🐾 wi-fi) Zen-inspired Hotel San José oozes sleek and simple sophistication: cherry platform beds and pendant light fixtures, native Texas gardens and meditation nooks. In the evening nibble on appetizers in the hip courtyard wine bar (known for celebrity-spotting potential). At breakfast order a bento box of granola, organic fruit and fresh juice; health of body and mind are primary concerns of this former motor-court motel in SoCo.

Also recommended:

Star of Texas Inn (☎ 512-472-6700; www.starof texasinn.com; 611 W 22nd St; r $85-165; ✗ 🖥 wi-fi) A great, big, rambling B&B near UT. Rooms are a little old-fashioned, considering the hip young owners and friendly dog and cats. (Sister property is pet-free.)

Habitat Suites ☎ 512-467-6000; www.habitatsuites .com; 500 E Highland Mall Blvd; r $127; ✗ 🐾) Austin's green hotel – no pesticides or chemical cleaners used; solar-powered; vegetarian breakfast included.

TOP END

Driskill Hotel (☎ 512-474-5911; www.driskillhotel.com; 604 Brazos St; r $200-350; 🖥 wi-fi) Tin ceilings hang above the wood-paneled public spaces of this 1886 hotel. 'Historic' rooms have period reproductions; ask for a larger one if you want breathing room.

Four Seasons (☎ 512-478-4500; www.fourseasons .com; 98 San Jacinto Blvd; r $305-415; 🐾 🖥 wi-fi) An oil tycoon would feel right at home here with all the local limestone, rough-hewn wood tables and oversized leather chairs. This is luxury as its most rustic. From lakeside rooms (or the pool or the bar) you can watch the bats depart from under Congress Ave bridge.

Eating

Fresh and local ingredients are part of the growing focus on food in Austin – thank goodness. S Congress Ave (south of Nellie St/Academy Dr) and Barton Springs Rd (east of Lamar Blvd) have a number of interesting eateries. Some great meat-market BBQ is to be had in nearby Lockhart and Luling; see the boxed text, p703.

DOWNTOWN

Whole Foods Market (☎ 512-476-1206; www.whole foods.com; 525 N Lamar Blvd; sandwiches $6-9, mains $6-15; 🕙 8am-10pm; wi-fi) The flagship of the Austin-founded Whole Foods Market is a gourmet grocery, but it's also a seafood restaurant, pasta trattoria, sushi bar and coffee shop. Be waited on at restaurant counters or eat in after loading up from the staggering take-away buffet: self-made salads, global mains, mezze, meat loaf, deli sandwiches, sushi, smoothies…

Lamberts (☎ 512-494-1500; 401 W 2nd St; mains lunch $10-16, dinner $12-24; 🕙 11am-2pm & 5:30-11pm) Cornmeal fried shrimp, brown sugar-and-coffee-rubbed BBQ: Lamberts has a novel take on traditional Texas tastes. Don't miss the Dr Pepper cake. Local, mostly acoustic, musicians play nightly in the upstairs bar.

SOUTH AUSTIN

Polvos (☎ 512-441-5446; 2004 S 1st St; breakfast $5-8, mains $8-15; 🕙 8am-11pm) Fun, festive and just a little divey: Polvos offers central-Mexican food that always packs in a crowd. Try some of the dozen or so salsas with the fierce margaritas.

Casa de Luz (☎ 512-476-2535; www.casadeluz.org; 1701 Toomey Rd; breakfast $7, lunch & dinner $12; 🕙 7-9am, 11:30am-2pm & 6:30-8pm) A peaceful commune feel wafts from Casa de Luz, where the set macro-biotic, organic, gluten-free – yet somehow tasty – meal changes at each sitting (daily menu posted on web).

Uchi (☎ 512-916-4808; 801 S Lamar Blvd; small dishes $9-14, mains $18-27; 🕙 5:30-10pm Sun-Thu, to 11pm Fri & Sat) The beautiful people who dine on artisanal Japanese-fusion foods and slap-your-face fresh sushi here are in the know – this modern restaurant rivals those in New York. Book well ahead if you hope to experience the wonder.

Also recommended:

Guero's (☎ 512-447-7688; 1412 S Congress Ave; mains $6-15; 🕙 11am-10pm) Good Tex-Mex; bad service. But it is an Austin classic.

Enoteca Vespaio (☎ 512-441-7672; 1610 S Congress Ave; mains $9-20; 🕑 11am-10pm Mon-Sat, 10am-3pm Sun) Local ingredients (often from its own garden); homemade pasta.

AROUND TOWN

Galaxy Cafe (☎ 512-478-3434; 1000 W Lynn St; breakfast $4-6, mains $6-8; 🕑 7am-10pm) Oh, that flourless chocolate cake. Or is it the sweet-potato french fries with the blue cheesey burger? Maybe it's the mod, retro self-serve diner decor in a former laundromat that keeps 'em coming back. Who cares? Just try it.

Shady Grove (☎ 512-420-8200; 614 W 34th St; mains $8-15; 🕑 11am-11:30pm) This 1940s state-park replica, complete with Airstream trailer and metal-lawn-chair kitsch, makes a great place to hang out. Munch on black-bean burritos under lights strung between pecan trees. Thursday night April to November unplugged musicians play.

County Line Bar-B-Que (☎ 512-327-1742; 6500 Bee Caves Rd; mains $11-20; 🕑 11am-2pm & 5-9pm Mon-Fri, 11am-9pm Sat & Sun) The original BBQ joint, in a wood-shack roadhouse off Hwy 360, serves a helluva hunka beef – its barbecued 12oz rib-eye steak beats all.

Salt Lick Barbecue (☎ 512-894-3117; www.salt lickbbq.com; 18300 FM 1826, Driftwood; mains $10-15; 🕑 11am-10pm) It's worth the 20-mile drive just to see the massive barbecue pits at this park-like place off US 290. Its BBQ is mighty impressive, too (weekend crowds show it). Bring your own beer and wine.

Drinking

The frat-boy brawl that is **E 6th St** (www.6thstreet .com) gets started evenings when middle-aged tourists fill the bars; as the night goes on, the crowd gets younger and more raucous than a pig in heat. It's not the best Austin has to offer, but it is something to see. Start at **BD Riley's** (☎ 512-494-1335; 204 E 6th St), the quintessential American Irish pub, and crawl your way east.

S Congress Ave caters to the more fun and funky, off-beat Austin. Grab a table and a coffee at **Jo's** (☎ 512-444-3800; 1300 S Congress Ave; 🕑 7am-9pm; wi-fi) outdoor café and study local tattoo art as the world walks by.

Entertainment

Now you're talking – music is the reason to come to Austin. More than 150 clubs and restaurants host live jam sessions throughout the week. The free weekly **Austin Chronicle** (www.austinchronicle.com) and the XL entertainment section in Thursday's **Austin American-Statesman** (www.statesman.com) newspaper both have listings. **Tune to Austin** (www.tunetoaustin.com) publishes a widely available illustrated map that pinpoints most venues. Remember, clubs are non-smoking.

LIVE MUSIC

Clubs in Austin are generally open from 6pm to 2am Tuesday through Sunday; exceptions are noted below.

Continental Club (☎ 512-441-2444; www.continental club.com; 1315 S Congress Ave) Vintage-wearing

TEXAS

THIS IS TEXAS COUNTRY

Forget Nashville, think Austin as the new capital of country. At its best, Texas music brings country back to its roots, with an earthy grit that eschews the commercial pop stylings so seemingly popular in Tennessee. You've heard of the big-name Texans – George Strait, Willie Nelson – and maybe even some of the second tier – Cory Morrow, Pat Green, Robert Earl Keen, Jack Ingram, Jerry Jeff Walker. But it's the musicians who primarily play around Austin who are the ones to give a listen. Austinite Kelly Willis' achy alt country, and her husband Bruce Robison's songwriting skills, are not to be missed. James Hand has old-time country down to an art. Up-and-comer Sunny Sweeney's strong East Texas twang and heartfelt lyrics belie her youth. And then there's Dale Watson, Tish Hinojosa, Guy Clark, David Ball…

The Broken Spoke (p702) and the Continental Club (above) are good places to start in your musical quest. But branch out: there are dance halls all across Hill Country. Start at Gruene Hall (p704) or John T Floore's Country Store (p709), or plot your own course. *Dance Halls and Last Calls*, by Geronimo Trevino, is a great resource, as is www.honkytonktx.com/dancehalls. And there's no shortage of info on the music itself: look for **Texas Music Magazine** (www.txmusic.com) and **Best in Texas Music Magazine** (www.bestintexasonline.com), or shop at Waterloo Records (p702) and **Lonestar Music** (www.lonestarmusic.com). You'll discover a whole different kind of country.

hipsters, suburban housewives, backpack-toting tourists, day laborers and beret-wearing beatniks come together at the granddaddy of all Austin clubs. Two shows a night include rockabilly, jazz, classic country, indie funk – just about any kinda music, so check the schedule.

Broken Spoke (☎ 512-442-6189; www.broken spokeaustintx.com; 3201 S Lamar Blvd) Sand-covered wooden floors and wagon-wheel chandeliers George Strait used to hang from: Broken Spoke is a true Texas honky-tonk. Go for local acts Cornell Hurd and artist Dale Watson, who play regularly.

Stubb's BBQ (☎ 512-480-8341; www.stubbsaustin.com; 801 Red River St) A huge backyard amphitheater – which underwent a million-dollar makeover in 2007 – regularly attracts big-name concerts (hard rock, blues, roots); lesser star power plays in the downstairs theater-bar.

Emo's (☎ 512-477-3666; www.emosaustin.com; 603 Red River St) The hardcore punk, indie and alternative scene can be found at the clubs along Red River St, and Emo's leads the pack.

There are a few more alternative clubs popping in Eastside Austin (east of I-35, west of Hwy 83, between Manor Rd and Riverside Dr), where you can also find Tejano music venues.

More music:

One World Theater (☎ 512-330-9500; www .oneworldtheater.com; 7701 Bee Caves Rd) World-beat bands and Latin percussion at a green-built theater-cum-villa in the hills.

Cactus Cafe (☎ 512-480-8341; www.stubbsaustin.com; Texas Union, cnr 24th & Guadalupe Sts; ☼ 3pm-midnight Mon-Thu, to 1am Fri & Sat) Acoustic up close and personal on the UT campus.

CINEMA
Alamo Drafthouse Cinema (☎ 512-867-1839; www.orig inalalamo.com; 409 Colorado St; admission $7) Eat dinner, down a brewski, and watch cult classics and independent films at this downtown theater. Interactive events like the quote-along *Princess Bride* showing are pretty hilarious.

Sports
Get ready to rumble – it's roller-derby night and the Hellcat women skaters are expected to kick some Cherry Bomb ass. No matter who wins, the **TXRD Lonestar Rollergirls** (www.txrd.com) league always puts on a good show, usually at the **Austin Convention Center** (☎ 512-404-4000; www .austinconventioncenter.com; 500 E Cesar Chavez St).

Shopping
Find something fun at the kitsch shops, vintage-clothing stores and cool boutiques on S Congress Ave. The first Thursday of every month stores stay open late and restaurants host bands on the patios.

Allen Boots (☎ 512-447-1413; 1522 S Congress Ave) Need new fire-red lizard boots with orange flames licking up the side? You've come to the right place. Allen Boots stocks thousands of pairs of attention-grabbing boots; snazzy snap-front Western shirts, too. Local celebrities like Sandra Bullock have been known to shop here.

Waterloo Records (☎ 512-474-2500; www.water loorecords.com; 600 N Lamar Blvd; ☼ 9am-10pm) Austin's music central, Waterloo is one-stop shopping for new and used CDs. The store hosts concerts, sells tickets and generally acts as *the* source for local music info.

New Bohemia (☎ 512-326-1238; 1606 S Congress Ave; ☼ noon-10pm) Probably the best of the bunch

TEXAS

TEXAS BBQ TRAIL

People take their BBQ pretty personal 'round here. Every few years *Texas Monthly* stirs the pot by publishing its picks for the best 'Q, but the authority remains Robb Walsh's *Legends of Texas Barbecue Cookbook*. BBQ – a noun in Texas – is brisket, ribs, sausage and other meats smoked on huge pits (don't call 'em grills unless you want to be laughed outta town). And don't expect many side dishes, or sauce necessarily – the tradition stems from the dry barbecue of German and Czech meat markets in the 1800s.

Arguably the BBQ capital of Texas, Lockhart (20 miles southeast of Austin on US 183) has four places to get your fix. The two best are the modern, barnlike **Kreuz Market** (☎ 512-398-2361; 619 N Colorado St; 10:30am-8pm Mon-Sat), where the ribs taste like peppery jerky on the outside and juicy tenderloin inside. Ham, beans and such are also served. **Smitty's** (☎ 512-398-9344; 208 S Commerce St; 7am-6pm Mon-Sat, 9am-3pm Sun) is the real deal: the blackened pit room and homely dining room are all original (knives used to be chained to the tables). Ask them to trim off the fat on the brisket if you're particular about that.

But it's Luling's **City Market** (☎ 830-875-9019; 633 E Davis; 7am-6pm Mon-Sat) that wins all-round best BBQ on US 183 in our unscientific but extensive tasting. The sausage is made on premises, the brisket is always succulent, and tart and tangy sauce adds a lot. Besides, everybody knows everybody here – it's a real slice of small-town life. Don't ask for utensils or plates; there haven't been any since it opened in the 1930s. Why fix what ain't broke?

when it comes to retro thrift shops, New Bohemia is the place to look for vintage jewelry and clothing.

Ecowise (☎ 512-326-4474; 1110 W Elizabeth St) Buy earth-friendly gifts, toys and housewares.

Getting There & Around

AIR
Bergstrom International Airport (☎ 512-530-2242; www.ci.austin.tx.us/austinairport) is off Hwy 71, southeast of downtown. The Airport Flyer (bus 100, $1) runs to downtown (7th St and Congress Ave) and UT (Congress Ave and 18th St) every 40 minutes or so. **SuperShuttle** (☎ 512-258-3826; www.supershuttle.com) charges $13 from the airport to downtown. A taxi between the airport and downtown costs from $20 to $25. Most of the national rental-car companies are represented at the airport.

BUS
The **Greyhound Bus Station** (☎ 512-458-4463; www.greyhound.com; 916 E Koenig Lane) is located on the north side of town off I-35; take bus 7 (Duval) to downtown. More than 10 buses a day leave for San Antonio ($14, one to two hours).

Capital Metro (☎ 512-474-1200; www.capmetro .org) runs the extensive, free, tourist-oriented 'Dillo, or trolley-bus, service. The five daytime and two nighttime color-coded routes connect downtown, SoCo and UT.

TRAIN
The *Texas Eagle*, heading from San Antonio to Chicago, stops at Austin's **Amtrak Station** (☎ 512-476-5684; www.amtrak.com; 250 N Lamar Blvd). Take the silver 'Dillo east into downtown.

AROUND AUSTIN
Northwest of Austin along the Colorado River are the six Highland Lakes. One of the most popular for recreation is the 19,000-sq-acre **Lake Travis**. Rent boats and jet skis at the associated marina, or overnight in the lake's posh digs at **Lakeway Inn** (☎ 512-261-6600; www.lakewayinn .com; 101 Lakeway Dr; r $180-229; wi-fi), off Hwy 71. The premier pampering place in the state is the **Lake Austin Spa Resort** (☎ 512-372-7300; www .lakeaustin.com; 1705 S Quinlan Park Rd; 3-night packages from $1570;), off Rte 2222. Texas' only official nude beach, **Hippie Hollow** (www.hippiehollow .com; day pass $10; 9am-dusk Sep-May, 8am-dusk Jun-Aug) at Lake Travis is also a popular gay hangout. From FM 2222, take Rte 620 south 1.5 miles to Comanche Trail and turn right. The entrance is 2 miles ahead on the left.

HILL COUNTRY
Detour down dirt roads in search of fields of wildflowers, check into a dude ranch to get the feel of the cowboy life, float along the Guadalupe River, and twirl around a dancehall floor. Most of the small towns in the rolling hills and valleys to the west and between Austin and San Antonio are easy day-trips,

TEXAS

TEXAS

SCENIC DRIVE: WILDFLOWER TRAILS

You know spring has arrived in Texas when you see cars pulling up roadside and families climbing out to take the requisite picture of their kids surrounded by bluebonnets, the state flower. Orange Indian paintbrushes, deep-purple winecups and white-to-blue bluebonnets are at their peak March through April in Hill Country. Check with TXDOT's **Wildflower Hotline** (☎ 800-452-9292) to find out what's blooming when. You might follow Rte 16 and FM 1323, north from Fredericksburg, east to Willow City, where a riot of color lies round every corner. Or just set to wandering; most backroads host their own shows.

---

from either city. More than a century ago, German and Czech immigrants settled these towns; look for their influence in the local names and food offerings.

Gruene

If you're not going to any other rustic Texas town, stop here in Gruene (pronounced *green*) – the whole place is on the National Historic Register. Summer weekends especially, it gets busy with day-trippers wandering among the arts-and-crafts and knickknack shops in search of the perfect straw cowboy hat. **Gruene Hall** (☎ 830-606-1281; www.gruenehall.com; 1280 Gruene Rd; ☼ 11am-9pm Mon-Wed, 10am-midnight Thu & Fri, 10am-1am Sat, 10am-9pm Sun) stakes a claim to being Texas' oldest dance hall (c 1878). Country, Cajun or folk-rock bands play nightly in summer, and at least three nights a week the rest of the year. Go in the day, when you don't have to pay a cover. At night, you can hear the concert all over town because of the screened walls.

Launch here to float lazily downriver in an inner tube. Rent what you need at **Rockin' R River Rides** (☎ 888-883-5628; www.rockinr.com; 1405 Gruene Rd; per tube with/without bottom $16/14; ☼ 8am-2:30pm). The outfitter buses you up the Guadalupe and you float the three to four hours back to base. Put a plastic (not Styrofoam) cooler full of adult beverages (cans, no bottles) in a bottom-fortified tube next to you and you have a day. You won't be alone; river floating is a wildly popular summer pastime in Hill Country.

Afterwards, dine out on the decks overlooking the river at **Gristmill Restaurant** (☎ 830-625-0684; 1287 Gruene Rd; mains $10-20; ☼ 11am-11pm), a sprawling open-air place grown out of an old mill ruin. BBQ pits, volleyball nets and a riverfront location outside town make the rustic, homey **Green Outpost River Lodge** (☎ 830-625-7772; www.grueneoutpostlodge.com; 1273 River Tce; r $85-125; ☒ ☻) feel a bit like summer camp. A Victorian house and a compound of cottages make up the flowery, but couldn't-be-more-central **Gruene Mansion Inn** (☎ 830-629-2641; www.gruenemansioninn.com; r incl breakfast $155-275; ☒).

Forty-five miles south of Austin and 25 miles northeast of San Antonio, Gruene is just off I-10 and Rte 46.

Fredericksburg

Hordes of retirees parade through Victorian townhouse boutiques in the region's largest old German town (c 1870). Six-lane US 290 is the main street, which detracts from the quaintness but doesn't seem to deter visitors. Not much German is spoken (or food cooked well) here any more. But if you like precious B&Bs and cute craft shops, you've found your spot; just ask the **Fredericksburg Convention & Visitors Bureau** (☎ 830-997-6523; www.fredericksburg-texas.com; 302 E Austin St; ☼ 9am-5pm Mon-Sat, noon-5pm Sun).

World War II Pacific fleet commander Admiral Chester Nimitz grew up here and his family's old hotel contains part of the detailed **National Museum of the Pacific War** (☎ 830-997-4379; www.nimitz-museum.org; 100 Legacy Dr; adult/child $7/4; ☼ 9am-5pm), with some larger artillery as well as tons of soldiers' mementos.

In and around the area are 15 wineries; pick up a **wine-trail map** (www.texaswinetrail.com) at the visitor center or stop at **Fredericksburg Winery** (☎ 830-990-8747; www.fbgwinery.com; 247 W Main St; ☼ 10am-5:30pm Mon-Thu, to 7:30pm Fri & Sat, noon-5:30pm Sun) for an in-town tasting.

Color bursts forth from the spectacular wildflower displays at **Wildseed Farms** (☎ 800-848-0078; www.wildseedfarms.com; 100 Legacy Dr; general admission free, botanical garden $5; ☼ 9am-6:30pm), 7 miles east on US 290. Walk along nature trails near the planted fields or buy seeds and giftware in the shop.

Eighteen miles north of Fredericksburg, at **Enchanted Rock State Natural Area** (☎ 325-247-3903; www.tpwd.state.tx.us; Rte 965; adult/child $5/free; ☼ 8am-10pm), you can climb a giant pink rock. The 425ft-tall chunk of granite sure looks out of place. Go early; gates close when the daily quota is reached.

Nearly 300 B&Bs do business in the county; **Gastehaus Schmidt Reservation Service** (☎ 830-997-5612; www.fbglodging.com) helps sort them out. National newsman Dan Rather comes from Fredericksburg; his star-chef daughter Rebecca runs **Rather Sweet Bakery & Café** (☎ 830-990-0498; 249 E Main St; sandwiches $5-9, sweets $2-4; ☻ 8am-5pm Mon-Sat).

Fredericksburg is 78 miles west of Austin on Hwy 281, and 70 miles north of San Antonio (via I-10 and US 87). **Kerrville Bus Co** (☎ 800-231-2222; www.iridekbc.com; Golden Convenience Store, 1001 S Adams St) sends two daily buses to and from San Antonio ($20, two hours). None runs directly from Austin.

Luckenbach

Calling Luckenbach a town is a bit of an overstatement. The handful of creaky wooden buildings here includes a dance hall, a concession stand, a hat shop and the **General Store & Luckenbach Bar** (☎ 830-997-3224; www.luckenbach texas.com; ☻ 10am-9pm Mon-Sat, noon-10pm Sun). Part fun Western mercantile, part post office, part beer joint, this oddball place has been a country-music shrine ever since Hondo Crouch bought the 'town' in 1970 and invited friends like Waylon and Willie to hang out. Weekend afternoons the bar hosts pickers and singers out under the oak trees (or inside if it's cold). From Fredericksburg, take US 290 east to FM 1376 and turn south about 3 miles.

Bandera

Cowboy up! Horses tied up on the main street, local saloons goin' strong: Bandera's worked hard to keep its Old West character (no McDonald's allowed in town). Wannabe cowpokes can saddle up at the dozen or so outlying dude ranches. From the false-front buildings, stores sell Western duds or rustic antiques, and a few cafés serve up hearty grub.

The friendly folks at **Bandera County Visitors Bureau** (☎ 800-364-3833; www.banderacowboycapital .com; 1206 Hackberry St; ☻ 9am-5pm Mon-Sat) will gladly help figure out which dude ranch suits you. At most, lodging (cabins or rooms), meals (cookouts or buffets) and at least a one-hour horseback ride per day are included for $95 to $125 per person, per night. There may also be hay rides, kids programs, ropin' lessons, swimming and such, depending on the place. Not interested in overnightin'? At **Silver Spur Guest Ranch** (☎ 830-796-3037; www.ssranch.com; FM 1077),

10 miles south of Bandera, you get one hour on horseback plus a campfire-cooked breakfast for $40. **Twin Elm Ranch** (☎ 830-796-3628; www .twinelmranch.com; cnr Rte 470 & Hwy 16; nonguests/guests $6/free; ☻ 8pm Tue & Fri) hosts local rodeos June through August.

Digging into a big steak-and-eggs breakfast at **OST Restaurant** (☎ 830-796-3836; 305 Main St; breakfast $4-7, mains $6-14; ☻ 6am-10pm) just seems right. When the sun goes down, mosey over to the patio at **11th Street Cowboy Bar** (☎ 830-796-4849; 307 11th St; ☻ 10am-midnight Mon-Fri, to 1am Sat, noon-midnight Sun). Hank Williams Sr used to play at **Arky Blue's Silver Dollar Saloon** (☎ 830-796-8826; 308 Main St; ☻ 10am-2am); look for the table he carved his name in. Both bars have live country crooners Friday through Sunday.

From Austin, Bandera is about 100 miles (via I-35 and Rte 46); it's 27 miles northwest of San Antonio's outskirts on Rte 16 (or Bandera Rd).

SAN ANTONIO

'Remember the Alamo' three million tourists a year cry as they stampede ol' San Antone's central mission, site of the infamous battle/massacre. Crowds come for the history and to party along the tree-shaded Riverwalk, which has more cafés and clubs than a dog has fleas. The visitor volume is daunting (as is the commercial crap that's developed around the Alamo – Davy Crockett's wild amusement ride?) But the lively Tex-Mex culture (about 60% of the 1.3 million residents have Hispanic heritage) is worth experiencing. Sure, see the Alamo and the Riverwalk, but explore beyond. Drink an *aguas frescas* (fruit-infused water) at the *mercado* (marketplace) and then hear country music at an old country store Willie Nelson helped establish – here you can *fiesta* one day and rodeo the next.

San Antonio de Bexar was the territory's largest Spanish settlement when it became the seat of Tejas state government in an independent Mexico. With US statehood came a large influx of German immigrants. The city's growth in the 20th century is due in large part to local military bases – and your tourist dollars.

Orientation & Information

The intersection of Commerce and Losoya Sts is the very heart of downtown and the Riverwalk, which runs in a U shape below

SAN ANTONIO

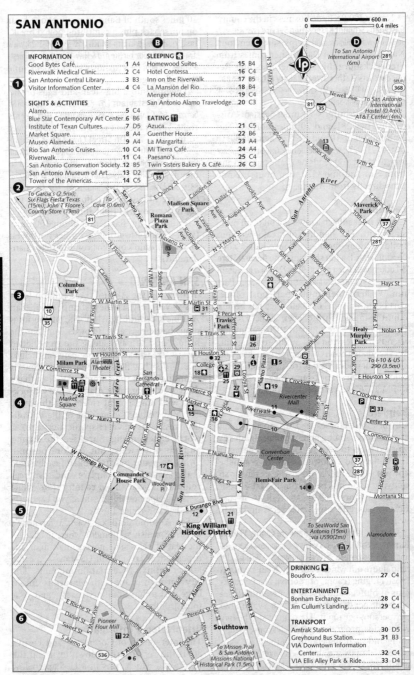

INFORMATION
Good Bytes Café.........................**1** A4	
Riverwalk Medical Clinic..............**2** C4	
San Antonio Central Library.........**3** B3	
Visitor Information Center............**4** C4	

SIGHTS & ACTIVITIES
Alamo.....................................**5** C4	
Blue Star Contemporary Art Center.**6** B6	
Institute of Texan Cultures..........**7** D5	
Market Square..........................**8** A4	
Museo Alameda.........................**9** A4	
Rio San Antonio Cruises..............**10** C4	
Riverwalk................................**11** C4	
San Antonio Conservation Society.**12** B5	
San Antonio Museum of Art........**13** D2	
Tower of the Americas...............**14** C5	

SLEEPING
Homewood Suites.....................**15** B4	
Hotel Contessa.........................**16** C4	
Inn on the Riverwalk..................**17** B5	
La Mansión del Rio....................**18** B4	
Menger Hotel...........................**19** C4	
San Antonio Alamo Travelodge....**20** C3	

EATING
Azuca.....................................**21** C5	
Guenther House........................**22** B6	
La Margarita.............................**23** A4	
Mi Tierra Café...........................**24** A4	
Paesano's................................**25** C4	
Twin Sisters Bakery & Café..........**26** C3	

DRINKING
Boudro's..................................**27** C4	

ENTERTAINMENT
Bonham Exchange......................**28** C4	
Jim Cullum's Landing..................**29** C4	

TRANSPORT
Amtrak Station..........................**30** D5	
Greyhound Bus Station...............**31** B3	
VIA Downtown Information	
Center.................................**32** C4	
VIA Ellis Alley Park & Ride...........**33** D4	

0 — 600 m
0 — 0.4 miles

street level. Signs point out access stairways, but a 3-D map bought at the info center is the best way to get oriented. Southtown and the King William Historic District lie south along the river.

Good Bytes Café (☎ 210-444-2233; 418 W Commerce St; ☷ 7am-7pm Mon-Fri, 11am-5pm Sat) Good food; free internet for a cause (proceeds go to Goodwill).

Riverwalk Medical Clinic (☎ 210-272-1741; 408 Navarro St; ☷ 24hr)

San Antonio Central Library (☎ 210-207-2500; 600 Soledad St; ☷ 9am-9pm Mon-Thu, to 5pm Fri & Sat, 11am-5pm Sun) Free internet access.

San Antonio Express-News (www.mysa.com) Daily news, travel info on web.

Visitor Information Center (☎ 210-207-6748; www .sanantoniovisit.com; 317 Alamo Plaza; ☷ 8:30am-6pm) Loads of free pamphlets and souvenirs for sale, but don't expect restaurant recommendations – they aren't allowed to make 'em.

Sights & Activities

Although San Antonio is the nation's seventh-largest city, most attractions are quite centralized – either easy strolling distance from the Riverwalk or a short trolley-bus ride away.

THE ALAMO

The mission church and a few barrack-wall fragments are all that remain of the **Alamo** (☎ 210-225-1391; www.thealamo.org; 300 Alamo Plaza; admission free; ☷ 9am-5:30pm Mon-Sat, 10am-5:30pm Sun, to 7pm daily Jun-Aug), moved to the present sight as the Mission San Antonio de Valero in 1724. (The well-recognized church façade dates from 1846.) A 17-minute film and exhibits in the Long Barrack Museum, as well as a Wall of History timeline, tell the full story of the 13 days in 1836 when Mexican general Santa Anna laid siege to occupying US and Mexican Texians. Today the church serves as a shrine to the fallen, including several Wild West luminaries of the day – James Bowie, William Travis and Davy Crockett. For more on the history, see the boxed text, below.

RIVERWALK

Whether you stroll past landscaped hotel gardens, eat at riverside café tables or cruise on down the waterway, seeing the **Riverwalk** is an essential part of the San Antonio experience. Restaurant after restaurant after bar after restaurant vies for your tourist buck from the sides of the waterfront path (a flood canal

---

REMEMBERING THE REAL ALAMO

Frontiersman Davy Crockett stands atop the rock wall swinging his empty rifle as he fights to his dying breath…at least, that's how it happened in the 1955 Disney movie version. Problem is, there are at least two translated eyewitness accounts that place Crockett among the surrendered prisoners who were executed. Sorting out what's fact and what's fiction can be a challenge, given sketchy survivor accounts and pervasive movie myths.

Some of what we know: after 12 days of continual artillery bombardment, Santa Anna quieted his guns so Texian forces could get some sleep and he could attack. The battle lasted only an hour and a half, starting at 5am on the morning of March 3, 1836. Among the Alamo defenders were Europeans, recently arrived US citizens grabbing for land, Tejanos (Texans of Mexican birth), Anglo Texan settlers and two slaves (Sam and Joe, who were the only fighters confirmed to have survived).

Alamo defender James Bowie, a US-born Mexican citizen married to the vice-governor's daughter (and who had a nasty-looking knife named after him), was sick in bed with tuberculosis and may not have gotten off a shot. Despite 26-year-old commander William Travis' eloquent 'Victory or Death' signatures, his numerous dispatches sent during the siege pleaded for help (only 30 reinforcements showed up). There's no evidence that he ever drew a line in the sand and asked those who crossed to die with him.

Although only 189 have been identified, about 250 Texian rebels (and from 120 to 500 Mexican troops out of 1500-plus) died that day, according to historians' estimates. Gregorio Esparza was the only Texas fighter to be buried (his brother was battling across the wall as a Mexican soldier); the rest of the bodies were burned – an abomination at the time. Santa Anna spared the dozen or so women and children who had taken refuge behind the fortified walls. He may have won the battle, but he gave the enemy – with this and the subsequent massacre at Goliad – a strong motivation to win the war.

diverted in the 1950s). Weekend mobs in summer are common. A **Rio San Antonio Cruises** (☎ 210-244-5700; www.riosanantonio.com; adult/child under 5yr $7.50/2; ⏰ 9am-9pm) narrated boat tour takes about 40 minutes. Buy tickets waterfront at the Rivercenter Mall (corner Commerce and S Alamo Sts) or across the water from the Hilton (near Market and S Alamo Sts).

MARKET SQUARE

If you're not going to make it down to Mexico, a trip to **Market Square** (☎ 210-207-8600; www .marketsquaresa.com; 514 W Commerce St; ⏰ 10am-8pm Jun-Aug, to 6pm rest of yr) is *necessito*. Talavera pottery, paper flowers, authentic Mexican vanilla: booths at this *mercado* sell all the handicrafts and foods you can find in a border town. Buy a Tecate beer or a pineapple *aguas frescas* and be prepared to bargain. Don't miss the **Museo Alameda** (☎ 210-207-8600; www.thealameda .org; 318 W Houston St; adult/child $8/3; ⏰ 10am-6pm Tue-Sat, noon-6pm Sun). Opened in spring 2007, this one-and-only Smithsonian Institute affiliate hosts Latino-related exhibits from the different museums in DC – Air & Space, American History, Natural History… The tourist trolley purple line runs right by the square.

MISSION TRAIL

Spain's missionary presence – and the dual purpose of territorial defense and religious conversion for the natives – can probably best be felt at the ruins of the four missions south of town. Together, Missions Concepción (1731), San José (1720), San Juan (1731) and Espada (1745–56) make up **San Antonio Missions National Historical Park** (☎ 210-932-1001; www.nps.gov/saan; Mission San José, 6701 San José Dr; admission free; ⏰ 9am-5pm). Stop first at San José, the most beautiful, and host to the national park visitor center, where you can learn what life was like here from an informative film and a few exhibits. Free tours are offered at each mission. From the Alamo, take S St Mary's St to Mission Rd. Bus 42 serves some of the Mission Trail from downtown (Navarro and Villita Sts).

OTHER DOWNTOWN ATTRACTIONS

Explore the 30 cultures, including Native American and Mexican, that made Texas what it is at the museum of the **Institute of Texan Cultures** (☎ 210-458-2300; www.texancultures.utsa.edu; 801 S Bowie St; adult/child $7/4; ⏰ 10am-6pm Tue-Sat, noon-5pm Sun). Nearby you can ride up to the observation deck of the 750ft **Tower of the Americas**

(☎ 210-207-8615; www.sanantonio.gov/sapar/hemisfair.asp; HemisFair Park; adult/child $4/1.50; ⏰ 9am-10pm Sun-Thu, to 11pm Fri & Sat), or the Landry's group–owned restaurant on top.

Late-19th to early-20th-century colonial-revival mansions and Queen Anne cottages inhabit the **King William Historic District**, south of the center, near E Durango Blvd and St Mary St. Pick up a walking-tour map outside the **San Antonio Conservation Society** (☎ 210-224-6163; 107 King William St).

Across S Alamo St to the east is **Southtown** (www.southtown.net), a small arts district. The first Friday of every month, galleries stay open late and restaurants host entertainment. A 1920s warehouse contains the **Blue Star Contemporary Art Center** (☎ 210-227-6960; www.bluestarartspace.org; 116 Blue Star; admission free; ⏰ noon-6pm Wed-Sun) and its few avant-garde studio spaces.

More traditional and way older, the **San Antonio Museum of Art** (SAMA; ☎ 210-978-8100; www .samuseum.org; 200 W Jones Ave; adult/child $8/3; ⏰ 10am-5pm Tue-Sat, noon-6pm Sun) has a noteworthy collection of Spanish Colonial, folk-Mexican and pre-Columbian works.

Got kids in tow? Take them to **SeaWorld San Antonio** (☎ 210-523-3611; www.seaworld.com; 105000 SeaWorld Dr; adult/child $44/34; ⏰ 10am-9pm Sun-Fri, to 10pm Sat), off US 90, for tons of fishy fun, or ride the rides at **Six Flags Fiesta Texas** (☎ 210-697-5050; www.sixflags.com; 17000 I-10; ⏰ 10am-9pm Jun-Aug) amusement park.

Festivals & Events

Fiesta San Antonio (☎ 210-227-5191; www.fiesta-sa.org) is a mammoth citywide party mid- to late April. For 10 days there are river parades, carnivals, Tejano music, dancing, tons of food and a 10km run to work it off.

The **San Antonio Stock Show & Rodeo** (☎ 210-225-5851; www.sarodeo.com) comes to town for 16 days starting mid-February. Big concerts follow each night's rodeo, and there's a carnival and animal shows during the day.

Sleeping

San Antonio has at least 10 million hotel rooms, so you have plenty of choices right downtown. Unlike other, more business-oriented Texas towns, the high rates here are at weekends, not weekdays.

BUDGET

San Antonio International Hostel (☎ 210-223-9426; 621 Pierce St; dm $18, r $59-89; P ☎ ▣) The musty barracks-like bunk rooms mean this place wouldn't be worth mentioning, except it's the only hostel in town. The attached B&B rooms are better, but not worth it. Pierce St is off Grason St.

San Antonio Alamo Travelodge (☎ 210-222-1000; www.travelodge.com; 405 Broadway; r $59-99; P ☻ wifi) This is a pretty typical motel – outdoor corridors surrounding a pool courtyard – in a great location. Free guest parking here means easy walking to the Alamo and access to trolley-bus routes.

MIDRANGE

Inn on the Riverwalk (☎ 210-225-6333; www.innonriver .com; 129 Woodward Pl; r $119-139; P ✗ wi-fi) Cottage rooms with whirlpool tubs, riverview rooms, multiroom rooms: all 16 decorator-designed digs are different, spread among three old houses-turned-B&Bs. This peaceful stretch of the river is a five-minute walk from the party.

Menger Hotel (☎ 210-223-4361; www.historic menger.com; 204 Alamo Plaza; r $129-175; ☻ wi-fi) President Teddy Roosevelt gathered his Rough Riders in the bar, and Confederate General Robert E Lee rode his horse into the lobby of the Menger Hotel, 300ft from the Alamo. This living-museum-cum-luxury-hotel is so welcoming that several spirits have never left.

Homewood Suites (☎ 210-222-1515; www.home woodsuites.com; 432 W Market St; r $169-219; ✗ ☻ ▢ wi-fi) Free breakfast and light happy-hour meals and drinks (Monday to Thursday) come standard at this all-suite property. The two-story gathering-room windows frame the Riverwalk beautifully.

TOP END

Hotel Contessa (☎ 210-227-9700; 306 W Market St; r $200-279; ☻ ▢ wi-fi) Wow. Fabulous, funky and design-driven, this Spanish castle–inspired hotel opened to acclaim in 2006 (think red zebra-print chairs, chenille throws and stone walls). A rooftop pool makes up for the fact that only four suites have water-front balconies.

La Mansión del Rio (☎ 210-518-1000; www.lamansion .com; 112 College St; r $200-339; ☻ ▢) Spanish-colonial élan drips from every fountain here. Rustic beams adorn ceilings, dark-wood French doors open to riverfront patios and balconies... The restaurant, Las Canarias, serves the best brunch in town.

Eating

Garcia's (☎ 210-735-4525; 842 Fredericksburg Rd; tacos $1-3, plates $4-6; ☖ 7am-2:45pm Mon-Sat) This is our top pick for hole-in-the wall Tex-Mex. The pork chop and *carne guisada* (beef stew) tacos are especially worth the drive.

Twin Sisters Bakery & Cafe (☎ 210-354-1559; 124 Broadway; breakfast $2-7, lunch $5-9; ☖ 8am-3pm Mon-Fri; ✗) Tofu *ranchero* (with hot salsa) for breakfast and turkey burgers for lunch – Twin Sisters keeps it light and fresh.

Azuca (☎ 210-225-5550; 713 S Alamo St; mains lunch $7-10, dinner $19-28; ☖ restaurant 11am-3pm & 5-10pm, bar 4pm-11pm Mon-Thu & 4pm-2am Fri & Sat) Here, a hip, stylish clientele lounges beneath blown-glass chandeliers sipping mojitos and nibbling fabulous New Latin cuisine. Eat at the bar between 4pm and 7pm, when small plates like smoky-pork *sofrito* (a Puerto Rican sweet-pepper sauce) on cloudlike corncakes are half off (usually $5 to $9).

Mi Tierra Café (☎ 210-225-1262; 218 Produce Row, Market Sq; breakfast $7-10, mains $7-13; ☖ 24hr) Red-velvet booths, colorful streamers, guitar-playing troubadours – go to this 50-year-old Market Square veteran for pageantry *à la Mexicana*.

La Margarita (☎ 210-227-7140; 108 Produce Row, Market Sq; mains $9-15; ☖ 11am-9pm Sun-Thu, to 11pm Fri & Sat) Near Mi Tierra, La Margarita has slightly better food with less show.

Also recommended:

Guenther House (☎ 210-227-1061; 205 E Guenther St; breakfast $4-7, lunch $5-8; ☖ 7am-3pm) Bakery-café.

Paesano's (☎ 210- 227-2782; 111 W Crockett St; pastas $10-16, mains $18-29; ☖ 11am-10pm) Artistic Italian; local fave.

Entertainment

Dick's Last–Hard Rock, Poly Ester's–Ugly Coyote. Along the Riverwalk entertainment district, the chain clubs and pubs seem to blur together. Pick up the free weekly **San Antonio Current** (www.sacurrent.com) for listings of local music and cultural events.

CLUBS & LIVE MUSIC

our pick **John T Floore's Country Store** (☎ 210-695-8827; www.liveatfloores.com; 14492 Bandera Rd, Helotes; tickets $8-30; ☖ 11am-9pm Sun & Tue-Thu, to 12:30am Fri & Sat) You gotta travel a little to get to this terrific old bar and dance hall, first opened in 1942 as a store by a friend of Willie Nelson's. (Willie used to play here nightly; the sign still says so.) Whether in the outdoor

TEXAS

FOLLOW THAT MARGARITA

The real way to see the Riverwalk is through margarita- (or mojito-, or martini-) colored glasses. Start with a slightly sweet prickly-pear margarita (yes, there's cactus-flower nectar in it) at **Boudro's** (☎ 210-224-8484; 421 E Commerce St; ⏰ 11am-11pm). From there, can you track down the three other establishments that serve a prickly pear? Or which place offers the 42oz margarita? The horni margarita? After you walk back to your hotel responsibly, let us know which you think was the best…you can wait till you've recovered, of course.

---

stage yard or by the fire in the rustic building, this is the true way to hear Texas country music on a Friday or Saturday night. Bandera Rd is off Hwy 16.

Cove (☎ 210-227-2683; 606 W Cypress St; ⏰ 11am-11pm Tue-Thu, to midnight Fri, to 1am Sat) Jazz, bluegrass, roots rock: they play it all at this bar–food stand–laundry–car wash (you heard right).

Jim Cullum's Landing (☎ 210-223-7266; www.landing.com; 123 Losoya St) Listen to area jazz legends evenings (7:30pm Monday through Saturday) and everyone will think you're a local.

Bonham Exchange (☎ 210-271-3811; www.bonhamexchange.com; 411 Bonham St) A stalwart brick building conceals San Antonio's premier gay dance club.

SPORTS

Four-time NBA champions the **San Antonio Spurs** (☎ 210-554-7787; www.nba.com/spurs) shoot hoops at the **AT&T Center** (☎ 210-444-5000; 1 AT&T Center Parkway & Walters St), off I-35. Purchase tickets through **Ticketmaster** (☎ 210-224-9600; www.ticketmaster.com).

Getting There & Around

AIR

You can reach 28 US and Mexican cities nonstop from **San Antonio International Airport** (☎ 210-207-3411; www.sanantonio.gov/airport), 8 miles north of downtown off I-410, east of Hwy 281. VIA city bus 2 ($1) runs from the airport to downtown about every 30 minutes, or you can take a **SATrans** (☎ 210-281-9900; www.saairportshuttle.com) shuttle bus for $14. A taxicab ride will cost about $20.

BUS

From the **Greyhound Bus Station** (☎ 210-270-5824; www.greyhound.com; 500 N St Marys St), you can get to all the big cities in the state (and lots of the small ones). For example, Houston is 3½ hours and $24 away.

VIA Downtown Information Center (☎ 210-362-2020; www.viainfo.net; 260 E Houston St; ⏰ 9am-6pm Mon-Fri, to 2pm Sat) is the place to buy a $3 day bus pass. That includes the extremely tourist-friendly downtown trolley-bus routes ($1 one way) – the best way to travel around downtown. Park at the **VIA Ellis Alley Park & Ride** (☎ 210-362-2020; btwn E Crockett & Center Sts; ⏰ ticket office 7am-6pm Mon-Fri, Sat 9am-2pm), a quick two stops from the Alamo. If you buy any VIA ticket, parking's free; ask for a parking transfer on the bus and put it in the slot when you exit.

CAR & MOTORCYCLE

Parking-garage fees in San Antonio really add up. It's better to use the metro transit buses in the center. Major car-rental agencies all have offices at the airport.

TAXI

Taxi rates are $1.70 flag fall ($2.70 after 9pm) plus $1.80 per mile. The biggest company in town is **Yellow-Checker Taxi** (☎ 210-222-2222).

TRAIN

The *Sunset Limited* (Florida–California) and *Texas Eagle* (San Antonio–Chicago) trains stop a few days a week (usually late at night) at the **Amtrak Station** (☎ 210-223-3226; www.amtrak.com; 350 Hoefgen Ave).

HOUSTON

A sprawl of concrete and superhighway? Intense summer heat? Yeah, Houston has some of that. But the nation's fourth-largest city (5 million in the metro area) is also a multicultural, zoning-free hodgepodge where in one strip mall there might be a Vietnamese grocery, a Venezuelan empanada stand and a big-beef meat market. Eat at great ethnic restaurants or shop in arts-and-antique neighborhoods. See world-class paintings and funky folk car parades. Then just down the road a bit you can walk the beaches of Galveston island and visit the astronauts at Space Center Houston. The interest's here; you just have to look a little.

Locally produced oil and gas products exported from the Houston Ship Channel have long fueled the city. In 1958, President Lyndon Johnson (a Texan) located the National Aeronautics and Space Administration (NASA) here. Houston absorbed approximately 250,000 new residents when Hurricane Katrina pummeled neighboring Louisiana in 2005. A month later Hurricane Rita missed Houston, but spooked millions into evacuating in what may be have been the world's largest traffic jam.

Orientation & Information

Houston's downtown centre is surprisingly free of traffic – because the metro area sprawls out 50 miles in each direction. Where I-45 (northwest–southeast), I-59 (southwest–northeast) and I-10 (east–west) meet forms downtown. The route for the light-rail system starts along Main St downtown and zooms south to the Museum District, Hermann Park, the Texas Medical Center and on to the behemoth Reliant Stadium.

Westheimer (local street names don't always have modifiers like Rd or Dr) starts southeast of the center in the trendy Montrose area and runs west through wealthy River Oaks. I-610 (the Loop) and the Sam Houston Tollway (Beltway 8) circle round the town.

BOOKSTORES

Brazos Bookstore (Map p712; ☎ 713-523-0701; 2421 Bissonnet St) Independent bookseller; hosts events.

EMERGENCY

Police Station (Map p712; ☎ 713-529-3100; 802 Westheimer; ☾ 24hr)

DON'T MISS

- **Space Center Houston** – Apollo rockets and spaceman fun (p718)
- **Breakfast Klub** – wings and waffles, catfish 'n grits (p715)
- **Orange Show Center for Visionary Art** – funky folk art and beer-can house (p713)
- **Museum District** – fine art, modern art, Byzantine art…(right)

INTERNET ACCESS

Houston Public Library (Map p714; ☎ 713-236-1313; 500 McKinney St; ☾ 9am-6pm Mon-Sat) Free internet computers and wi-fi.

FedEx Kinko's (Map p712; ☎ 713-520-9753; 2200 I-59 S; ☾ 24hr) Internet access 20¢ per minute.

MEDIA

88.7 KUHT Classical music and NPR (National Public Radio) from the University of Houston.

91.7 KTRU Rice University college and indie rock.

Houston Chronicle (www.chron.com) The city's daily newspaper.

Houston Press (www.houstonpress.com) Houston's free weekly.

MEDICAL SERVICES

Memorial Hermann Hospital (Map p712; ☎ 713-704-4000; 6411 Fannin St) Part of the Texas Medical Center megacomplex.

CVS Pharmacy (Map p712; ☎ 713-897-8491; 1003 Richmond Ave; ☾ 24hr)

MONEY

Chase Bank (Map p714; ☎ 713-216-4865; 712 Main St) Currency exchange and ATM.

POST

Post office (Map p714; ☎ 713-226-3161; 401 Franklin St)

TOURIST INFORMATION

Greater Houston Convention & Visitors Bureau (Map p714; ☎ 713-437-5200; www.visithoustontexas.com; cnr Walker & Bagby Sts; ☾ 9am-4pm Mon-Sat, 11am-4pm Sun) Free parking on Walker St.

Sights & Activities

Two of Houston's biggest attractions – Johnson Space Center and Galveston Island – aren't in the city proper (see p717). The Museum District and Hermann Park hold the biggest collections of museums. In addition to what's listed, around town there are small museums on the Holocaust, printing history, funerary tradition and fire fighters.

French impressionism and post-1945 European and American painting is particularly well represented at the wide-ranging **Museum of Fine Arts, Houston** (Map p712; ☎ 713-639-7300; www.mfah.org; 1001 Bissonnet St; adult/child $7/3.50, Thu free; ☾ 10am-5pm Tue-Thu, to 7pm Fri & Sat, 12:15-7pm Sun). Across the street, admire the talents of luminaries like Rodin and Matisse in the **Cullen Sculpture Garden** (Map p712; cnr Montrose Blvd & Bissonnet St; admission free).

TEXAS

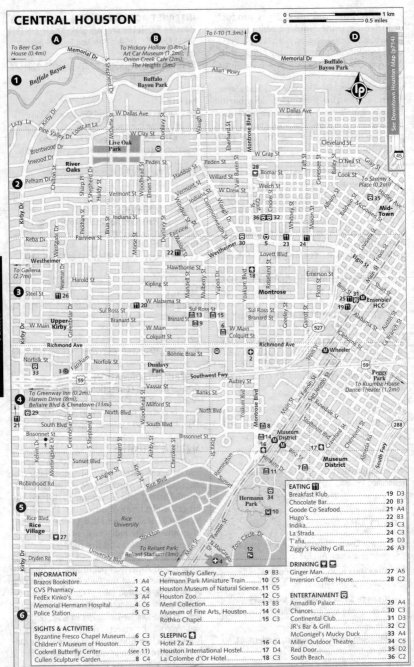

CENTRAL HOUSTON

TEXAS

INFORMATION
Brazos Bookstore	1 A4
CVS Pharmacy	2 A4
FedEx Kinko's	3 A4
Memorial Hermann Hospital	4 C6
Police Station	5 C3

SIGHTS & ACTIVITIES
Byzantine Fresco Chapel Museum	6 C3
Children's Museum of Houston	7 C5
Cockrell Butterfly Center	(see 11)
Cullen Sculpture Garden	8 C4

Cy Twombly Gallery	9 B3
Hermann Park Miniature Train	10 C5
Houston Museum of Natural Science	11 C5
Houston Zoo	12 C5
Menil Collection	13 C3
Museum of Fine Arts, Houston	14 C4
Rothko Chapel	15 C3

SLEEPING
Hotel Za Za	16 C5
Houston International Hostel	17 D4
La Colombe d'Or Hotel	18 C3

EATING
Breakfast Klub	19 D3
Chocolate Bar	20 B3
Goode Co Seafood	21 A4
Hugo's	22 B3
Indika	23 C3
La Strada	24 D3
T'afia	25 D3
Ziggy's Healthy Grill	26 A3

DRINKING
Ginger Man	27 A5
Inversion Coffee House	28 C2

ENTERTAINMENT
Armadillo Palace	29 A4
Chances	30 C2
Continental Club	31 D3
JR's Bar & Grill	32 C2
McGonigel's Mucky Duck	33 A4
Miller Outdoor Theatre	34 C5
Red Door	35 D2
South Beach	36 C2

WHAT THE...?

Beer cans, welded-steel oranges and plastic flowers as folk art? Conservative Houston has a wacky art streak. The late Jeff McKissack molded his house into a junk-art tribute to his favorite fruit until his passing. Today it's the **Orange Show Center for Visionary Art** (☎ 713-926-6368; www .orangeshow.org; 2402 Munger St; admission free; ☼ 9am-1pm Wed-Fri, noon-5pm Sat & Sun Jun-Aug, noon-5pm Sat & Sun rest of yr), off I-45 S, which fosters the folk-art vision by offering tours and keeping up the 50,000-can exterior of the **Beer Can House** (222 Malone St), off Memorial Dr. The center can give directions to other arty houses around town.

Local philanthropists John and Dominique de Menil's 15,000 artworks form the core of the **Menil Collection** (Map p712; ☎ 713-525-9400; www.menil.org; 1515 Sul Ross St; admission free; ☼ 11am-7pm Wed-Sun). The couple's taste ran from the medieval to the surreal – several rooms are devoted to the likes of René Magritte and Max Ernst. The **Cy Twombly Gallery** (Map p712; ☎ 713-525-9450; 1501 Branard St; admission free; ☼ 11am-7pm Wed-Sun) annex contains very abstract art.

Dominique's acquisition of a 13th-century Cypriot fresco almost caused an international incident; in the end, she built the custom **Byzantine Fresco Chapel Museum** (Map p712; ☎ 713-521-3990; 4011 Yupon Dr; admission free; ☼ 11am-6pm Fri-Sun) to safely protect the treasure for 99 years. Fourteen large abstract-expressionist Mark Rothko paintings anchor the more modern nondenominational sanctuary **Rothko Chapel** (Map p712; ☎ 713-524-9839; www.rothkochapel.org; 3900 Yupon Dr; admission free; ☼ 10am-6pm).

Delve into excellent traveling shows – often with shiny themes (treasures of Tsarist Russia, gold of Afghanistan) – at the **Houston Museum of Natural Science** (Map p712; ☎ 713-639-4629; www.hmns.org; 1 Hermann Circle; adult/child $9/7; ☼ 9am-5pm Mon-Sat, 11am-5pm Sun). Dinosaurs, fossils, gems and mineral exhibits, chemistry and interactive experiments are all part of the permanent collections on display here. At the onsite **Cockrell Butterfly Center** (adult/child $8/6) you can walk through a tropical garden among thousands of butterflies.

And now for something more funky: the **Art Car Museum** (☎ 713-861-5526; www.artcarmuseum.com; 140 Heights Blvd; admission free; ☼ 11am-6pm Wed-Sun) is a repository for more than 15 of the psychedelic, buglike and Mad Max–esque vehicles that have taken part in the annual Art Car Parade over the past years.

Houston for Children

Young 'uns gettin' restless? **Hermann Park** (Map p712; ☎ 713-524-5876; www.hermannpark.org; 600 Fannin St) has playgrounds, a lake with paddle boats, the **Herman Park Miniature Train** (Map p712; ☎ 713-529-5216; per ride $2.35; ☼ 10am-5pm) and the **Houston Zoo** (Map p712; ☎ 713-533-6500; www.houstonzoo.org; 1513 N MacGregor Dr; adult/child $7/3; ☼ 9am-5pm, to 6pm Jun-Aug).

Walking distance from the park is the activity-filled **Children's Museum of Houston** (Map p712; ☎ 713-522-1138; www.cmhouston.org; 1500 Binz St; admission $5; ☼ 9am-5pm Tue-Sat, to 8pm Thu, noon-5pm Sun). Little ones can make tortillas and learn some Spanish in a Mexican village, or they can learn to draw in an open-air art studio.

Tours

Houston Greeters (☎ 713-473-3837; www.houston greeter.org) will meet you at an attraction, like one of the museums, and show you around for free. If you're time constrained, take one of the **Houston Tours** (☎ 713-988-5900; www.houstontours .com; city tours $40) hitting all the major districts in town, or Space Center Houston ($60) or Galveston ($65).

Festivals & Events

Houston Livestock Show & Rodeo (☎ 832-667-1000; www.hlsr.com; Reliant Park, I-610 S at Kirby Dr; tickets $20) Twenty days of fried candy bars, midway rides, prize bulls and a nightly rodeo followed by a big-name concert (think George Strait or Beyoncé).

Art Car Parade (www.orangeshow.org; Allen Parkway) Über-augmented automobiles roll on by the second Sunday in May.

International Quilt Festival – Houston (☎ 713-781-6864; www.quilts.com; George R Brown Convention Center, 1001 Avenida de las Americas; admission $10) Last weekend in October.

Sleeping

Downtown hotels are close to transport, and rates usually drop at weekends. Chain

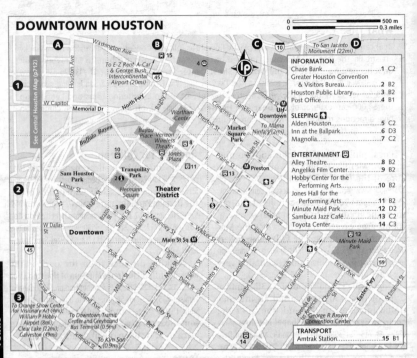

DOWNTOWN HOUSTON

INFORMATION	
Chase Bank	1 C2
Greater Houston Convention	
& Visitors Bureau	2 B2
Houston Public Library	3 B2
Post Office	4 B1

SLEEPING	
Alden Houston	5 C2
Inn at the Ballpark	6 D3
Magnolia	7 C2

ENTERTAINMENT	
Alley Theatre	8 B2
Angelika Film Center	9 B2
Hobby Center for the	
Performing Arts	10 B2
Jones Hall for the	
Performing Arts	11 B2
Minute Maid Park	12 D2
Sambuca Jazz Café	13 C2
Toyota Center	14 C3

TRANSPORT	
Amtrak Station	15 B1

motels line all the major freeways; if you are visiting the Space Center and Galveston, consider staying on I-45 south, where rooms are less.

BUDGET

Houston International Hostel (Map p712; ☎ 713-523-1009; www.houstonhostel.com; 5302 Crawford St; dm $15; ☐ ☐ wi-fi) Permanent residents, oddball staff and extreme lockout hours (10am to 5pm and midnight to 8am) give this shabby hostel house a weird vibe. But you can't beat being walking distance from museums and the light rail (seven blocks) for this price.

Greenway Inn (Map p712; ☎ 713-523-1009; www .greenwayinnsuites.com; 2929 I-59 S; r incl breakfast $69; ☐ ☐ wi-fi) Stay near Montrose restaurants and not far from the Museum District. The basic motel bed-and-desk rooms at least got an update in 2006. Solo travelers may be able to bargain.

MIDRANGE

Magnolia (Map p714; ☎ 713-221-0011; www.magnolia hotelhouston.com; 1100 Texas Ave; r $113-139; ☐ ☐ wi-fi) Dressed in deep woods and modern neu-

trals, rooms at the Magnolia both stylish *and* comfortable. Wrap up in the complimentary robe and head to the rooftop pool for a downtown panorama.

Inn at the Ballpark (Map p714; ☎ 713-228-1520; www.innattheballpark.com; 1520 Texas Ave; r $119-169; ☐) Get yourself an 11th- or 12th-floor room and, if your timing is right, you can peer into the stadium and watch the Astros play. Robert Redford in *The Natural* would feel right at home with the updated 1940s clubbiness.

Alden Houston (Map p714; ☎ 832-200-8800; www .aldenhotels.com; 1117 Prairie St; r $155-175; ☐) Flat-screen TVs with a complimentary DVD library are part of the urbane downtown luxury. Choose a 'giving room' and 10% of the proceeds go to charity.

TOP END

Hotel Za Za (Map p712; ☎ 713-526-1991; www.hotel zaza.com; 5701 Main St; r $205-270; ☐ ☐ wi-fi) Simply fabulous, darling. It's see-and-be-seen at this flamboyantly hip Museum District hotel that opened in 2007. Think silk brocade and lots of leather.

La Colombe d'Or Hotel (Map p712; ☎ 713-524-7999; www.lacolombedor.com; 3410 Montrose Blvd; r $205-475; ☒) Museum-quality antiques and rare oil paintings fill this 1923 Montrose mansion. Each of the six suitelike rooms, with sitting and dining areas, exude opulence. Of course there's a library and a French restaurant on site.

Eating

Montrose and Upper Kirby are two of the principal inside-the-Loop eating enclaves. Downtown isn't the best for restaurants, but there are a few clustered around Market St light-rail station. Head way out west to Bellaire (near Beltway 8) to find Chinatown, and look for small Vietnamese noodle houses around Mid-town. Steak is huge in Houston; the national heavy hitters – Ruth's Chris, the Palm etc – are on Westheimer near the Galleria.

MID-TOWN

Breakfast Klub (Map p712; ☎ 713-528-8561; www.the breakfastklub.com; 3711 Travis St; mains $4-8; ☒ 7am-2pm Mon-Fri, 8am-3pm Sat) Down-home cookin' with soul. Whether it's wings 'n' waffles or a breakfast sandwich with eggs, turkey, bacon and tomato, you gotta eat here. Expect to wait and wait at weekends.

T'afia (Map p712; ☎ 713-524-6922; 3701 Travis St; mains $15-20; ☒ 5-10pm Tue-Thu, 11:30am-1pm & 5-10pm Fri, 5-10pm Sat) Celebrity chef Monica Pope has been touted by Oprah for her new American cuisine. Top-quality local and organic ingredients are what do the trick.

RIVER OAKS, UPPER KIRBY & MONTROSE

Indika (Map p712; ☎ 713-524-2170; 516 Westheimer; lunch $10-16, dinner mains $17-25; ☒ 11:30am-2:30pm & 6-10pm Tue-Fri, 6-10pm Sat, 11am-3pm Sun) Inventive Indian. Expect everything from upscale versions of street food to sublime vindaloo (one of the hotter curries) – all made with the environment in mind (unbleached flour in the naan, free-range chicken...).

Hugo's (Map p712; ☎ 713-524-7744; 1600 Westheimer; lunch $12-15, dinner mains $15-26; ☒ 11am-10pm Sun-Thu, to 11pm Fri & Sat) No Tex-Mex here. Chef Hugo Ortega is known for his interior-Mexican regional cuisine.

Also recommended:

Chocolate Bar (Map p712; ☎ 713-520-8699; 1835 W Alabama St; cakes $2-10; ☒ 11am-9pm Sun-Thu, to midnight Fri & Sat) Decadent dessert café.

Ziggy's Healthy Grill (Map p712; ☎ 713-526-6888; 2002 W Alabama St; mains $6-12; ☒ 11am-9pm Sun-Thu, to 10pm Fri & Sat; ☒) Vegetarian and beyond.

Goode Co Seafood (Map p712; ☎ 713-523-7154; 2621 Westpark Dr; sandwiches $8-10, mains $17-22; ☒ 11am-10pm)

DOWNTOWN

Mama Ninfa's (☎ 713-228-1145; 2704 Navigation Blvd; mains $8-15; ☒ 11am-10pm) This is the original off-neighborhood hole-in-the-wall that spawned a Tex-Mex empire. Waiters in *guayaberas* (white embroidered shirts) are sincere when they say they're 'at your service.'

Kim Son (☎ 713-222-2461; 2001 Jefferson St; mains $10-18; ☒ 11am-11pm) Run by the La family, who escaped in a boat from Vietnam in 1979, Kim Son is a local legend with a booklike menu.

THE HEIGHTS

Hickory Hollow (☎ 713-869-6300; 101 Heights Blvd; mains $10-18; ☒ 11am-9pm Mon-Fri, to 9:30pm Fri & Sat) Drink out of Mason jars and dig into some real rib-stickin' grub – BBQ, chicken-fried steak, fried catfish – ordered counterside. Live bluegrass music Friday and Saturday night.

Drinking

The corner of White Oak and Studemont in the Heights has a few funky little bars including a roadhouse, a tiki bar, and a live music club in an old house.

Ginger Man (Map p712; ☎ 713-526-2770; Rice Village, 5607 Morningside Dr) A homey pub with 69 beers on tap, Ginger Man has a nice yard for hanging out with students from nearby Rice U. (There are similar sister pubs in Austin and Dallas, too.)

Onion Creek Cafe (☎ 713-880-0768; 3106 White Oak; ☒ 7am-2am) This place fits the neighborhood bar–late-night eatery–early-morning café bill.

Entertainment

Downtown's entertainment district has had more ups and downs than a two-bit whore on a Saturday night. Light-rail development caused a nightclub boom, but subsequent law-enforcement woes had city officials chasing the bad-boy club owners out of town. There's still a fair bit of nightlife around the Preston and Main St Sq stops. Montrose and Mid-town have clubs, but they're spread around. Look for listings in the independent weekly **Houston Press** (www.houstonpress.com).

TEXAS

TEXAS

NIGHTCLUBS & LIVE MUSIC

McGonigel's Mucky Duck (Map p712; ☎ 713-528-5999; www.mcgonigels.com; 2425 Norfolk St; ✗) Smoke-free music; how refreshing. Listen to live acoustic, Irish, folk and country performers nightly.

Continental Club (Map p712; ☎ 713-529-9899; www.continentalclub.com; 3700 Main St) This is the number-two location of Austin's famed live-music venue. It hasn't missed a beat, with top-notch blues, rock and rockabilly at least five nights a week.

Sambuca Jazz Cafe (Map p714; ☎ 713-224-5299; www.sambucarestaurant.com; 900 Texas Ave) A swanky supper club, Sambuca serves live jazz accompanied by an eclectic menu.

Yet more choices:

Armadillo Palace (Map p712; ☎ 713-529-9899; www.thearmadillopalace.com; 5015 Kirby Dr; 11am-midnight Sun-Thu, to 2am Fri & Sat) Texas country bands and sawdust on the floor.

Red Door (Map p712; ☎ 713-526-8181; www.reddoorhouston.com; 2416 Brazos St) Young beautiful things DJ it up.

Sammy's Place (☎ 713-751-3101; www.sammysat2016main.com; 2016 Main St) Motown music and '70s and '80s nights.

THEATER & CLASSICAL PERFORMANCE

Miller Outdoor Theatre (Map p712; ☎ 713-284-8350; www.milleroutdoortheatre.com; 100 Concert Dr) Hermann Park's outdoor theater is a great place to lay out a blanket on a summer night and enjoy a free play, musical or concert.

Kuumba House Dance Theater (☎ 713-524-1079; www.kuumbahouse.org; 3001 Cleburne St) Performance art and drum circles celebrate African American culture.

The Houston Grand Opera, the Society of the Performing Arts, the Houston Ballet, Da Camera chamber orchestra and the Houston Symphony all perform downtown in the **Theater District** (www.houstontheaterdistrict.org). The district's website has ticket purchase and all schedules. Venues:

Alley Theatre (Map p714; ☎ 713-228-8421; 615 Texas Ave)

Hobby Center for the Performing Arts (Map p714; ☎ 713-315-2525; 800 Bagby St)

Jones Hall for the Performing Arts (Map p714; ☎ 713-227-3974; 615 Louisiana St)

CINEMA

Angelika Film Center (Map p714; ☎ 713-225-5232; www.angelikafilmcenter.com; Bayou Pl, 510 Texas Ave) See a mix of first-run, foreign and independent films at this downtown art theater.

SPORTS

Reliant Stadium (☎ 832-667-1400; www.reliantpark.com; 1 Reliant Park, I-610 S at Kirby Dr) is home to the NFL **Houston Texans** (☎ 877-635-2002; www.houstontexans.com).

The **Houston Astros** (☎ 713-259-8000; www.astros.com) play pro baseball downtown at **Minute Maid Park** (Map p714; 501 Crawford St). The **Toyota Center** (Map p714; 1510 Polk St) is home to three pro teams:

Houston Aeros (☎ 713-627-2376; www.aeros.com) IHL hockey, sort of like Triple A in baseball.

GAY & LESBIAN HOUSTON

Montrose has been the town's gathering place for gay men and women for decades. That's not to say the town isn't conservative; public displays of affection will probably turn heads. Every June, the **Pride Committee of Houston** (☎ 713-529-6979; www.pridehouston.org) sponsors a huge gay-pride parade; related events take place all month. KPFT 90.1 FM is the home of Queer Voices radio. The **Houston Voice** (www.houstonvoice.com) is the gay and lesbian newspaper, and **Out Smart Magazine** (www.outsmartmagazine.com) has loads of local info.

Though not gay-exclusive, Sunday brunch at **La Strada** (Map p712; ☎ 713-521-2519; 322 Westheimer; ☺ brunch 11am-6pm Sat & Sun) is quite the scene – patrons show up in their PJs and proceed to get soused on bellinis until the DJ arrives at 3pm, and they can dance it off. Enjoy a tasty cup o' Joe with the boys at industrial warehouse–like **Inversion Coffee House** (Map p712; ☎ 713-523-4866; 1953 Montrose Blvd; ☺ 6:30am-midnight Mon-Sat, 7:30am-10:30pm Sun; wi-fi).

High-tech sound and lights help make **South Beach** (Map p712; ☎ 713-529-7623; www.southbeachthenightclub.com; 810 Pacific St) the top gay dance club. Next door, **JR's Bar & Grill** (Map p712; ☎ 713-521-2519; www.jrsbarandgrill.com; 808 Pacific St) is a more laid-back hangout. Go-go girls shake it at the popular lesbian dance bar **Chances** (Map p712; ☎ 713-523-7217; www.chancesbar.com; 1100 Westheimer), where parking's limited (avoid Hollywood Video across the street; they tow).

Houston Comets (☎ 713-627-9622; www.houston comets.com) WNBA basketball.
Houston Rockets (☎ 713-627-3865; www.houston rockets.com) NBA basketball.

Shopping

A huge conglomeration of shops collides in and near the mazelike **Galleria** (☎ 713-622-0663; www.simon.com; 5075 Westheimer), off I-610. Macy's, Foley's and Nordstrom anchor more than 375 mall stores, and there is even an ice-skating rink.

The **Heights** (www.heightsfirstsaturday.com), Houston's first neighborhood, is filled with Arts and Crafts bungalows. Browse 19th St (between Yale and Shepherd) for unique antiques, clever crafts, artsy furniture – anything out of the common way. The first Saturday of every month the street takes on a carnival-like air with outdoor booths and entertainment. North of I-10, Waugh Dr turns into Heights Blvd.

If you're looking for an Indian sari, head to **Harwin Drive** (Southwest Fwy), southwest of town off I-59; Houston's **Chinatown** (www.chinatownmap .com), and its scattered shops and restaurants, surround Bellaire Blvd, at Beltway 8.

Getting There & Away
AIR
Houston Airport System (www.fly2houston.com) has two airports. Twenty-two miles north of the city center, **George Bush Intercontinental** (IAH; ☎ 281-230-3100; btwn I-45 & I-59 N) is served by many major domestic and international carriers, and is home base for Continental Airlines. Twelve miles southeast of town, **William P Hobby Airport** (HOU; ☎ 713-640-3000), off I-45 S, is a major hub for Southwest Airlines and domestic travel. Read your ticket closely; some airlines, like Delta, fly out of both airports. Wi-fi is available at both airports.

BUS
Long-distance buses arrive at the **Greyhound Bus Terminal** (Map p714; ☎ 713-759-6565; www.greyhound .com; 2121 Main St), located between downtown and the Museum District, and two blocks from the Downtown Transit Center light-rail stop.

TRAIN
The Orlando–Los Angeles train (via San Antonio, Big Bend and El Paso), the *Sunset Limited*, stops at the **Amtrak Station** (Map p714;

☎ 713-224-1577; www.amtrak.com; 902 Washington Ave) three times a week.

Getting Around
Sprawling, spread-out Houston is all about superhighways and racinglike speeds (or parking lot–like traffic). Use the light rail and it's possible to visit town car-free; most of the sights are on the downtown–Museum District–Reliant Park corridor. If you want to venture further, you'll need to rent a car; the bus system is wholly inefficient for visitors' needs.

TO/FROM THE AIRPORT
The Hobby Airport Express bus (101) connects to downtown (and to the Downtown Transit Center light-rail stop) Monday through Saturday ($1). Bus 102 is the Bush IAH Express that will take you from Bush Intercontinental to downtown or the transit center. **SuperShuttle** (☎ 800-258-3826; www.super shuttle.com) provides service from both Bush IAH ($23) and Hobby ($18) airports. A taxi to IAH/HOU airports from downtown is about $37/20.

LIGHT RAIL
Houston's **Metropolitan Transit Authority** (Metro; ☎ 713-635-4000; www.ridemetro.org) runs the convenient light-rail system; $1 gets you a one-way ride.

CAR
Every major national rental agency can be found at either airport and at offices throughout town. The independent **E-Z Rent-A-Car** (☎ 281-442-7733; www.e-zrentacar.com; 2700 Greens Rd) is off-off airport, but its shuttle picks up from the Rental Center and it undercuts the big guys' prices. It operates out of the Holiday Inn; take the hotel's shuttle from the airport.

TAXI
Cab rates are $3 flag fall and $1.50 for each additional mile. Note that Houston's breadth means your cab tab can quickly surpass car-rental rates. Companies include **United** (☎ 713-699-0000) and **Yellow** (☎ 713-236-1111).

AROUND HOUSTON
Don't miss the day-trips, some of the best Houston has to offer.

TEXAS

Clear Lake

Dream of a moon landing? You can't get any closer (without years of training) than **Space Center Houston** (☎ 281-244-2100; www .spacecenter.org; 1601 NASA Rd 1; adult/child $19/15; ☯ 10am-5pm Mon-Fri, 10am-7pm Sat & Sun), off I-45 S, the official visitor center and museum of Johnson Space Center, NASA headquarters. Interactive and virtual exhibits let you try your hand at picking up an object in space or landing the shuttle. Be sure to watch the short theater film because you exit past Apollo capsules and history exhibits. The free tram shows the center at work – shuttle training facilities, zero-gravity labs, the original mission control ('Houston, we have a problem'). Space-travel enthusiasts should book ahead for a Level 9 Tour ($62, 16 and older), which gets you into areas the general tour doesn't.

Clear Lake's marinas, 22 miles from downtown, are Houston's boating playground. **NASA/Clear Lake Convention & Visitors Bureau** (☎ 281-338-0333; www.nasaclearlaketexas.com; 20710 I-45, Webster; ☯ 9am-5pm Mon-Fri) lists water sports operators on its website.

East on Galveston Bay, the **Kemah Boardwalk** (☎ 877-285-3624; www.kemah.com; cnr Bradford & 2nd Sts) is a kid-savvy waterfront, with theme restaurants, shops, amusement rides, carnival games and a jet-boat ride. For the freshest shrimp and fish, without all the glitz, head to the northern side of Kemah Bridge and turn either direction onto Shipyard Dr off Hwy 146. Shrimp shacks and dive bars line the waterfront side streets.

IF YOU HAVE A FEW MORE DAYS...

History buffs should head over to see where Texas nationhood was won on April 21, 1836. The 570ft **San Jacinto Monument** (☎ 281-479-2421; www.tpwd.state.tx.us; 3523 Hwy 134, La Porte; museum & grounds free, observation deck adult/child $7/free; ☯ 8am-6pm) looks like the Washington Monument but has a cement star on top (which makes it 12ft taller). From the top of the monument you are able to look over the 1000-acre battlefield where Texan forces under General Sam Houston shouted 'Remembered the Alamo' and gave Mexican general Santa Anna a whipping.

Galveston

Part genteel Southern lady, part sunburned beach bum, Galveston island will woo your heart. Gingerbread-covered homes line historic districts, shops and soda fountains fill the brick buildings on the Strand, and surf and sand abound on the Gulf of Mexico side. After you're done shopping or surfing, eat at one of the many seafood restaurants inside the intercoastal canalfront warehouses.

The island (at the southeastern end of I-45, 49 miles from Houston) is 30 miles long and no more than 3 miles wide. From the highway, 61st St leads to Seawall Blvd along the Gulf. The Mechanic and 22nd Sts intersection centers the Strand. **Galveston Island Visitors Center** (☎ 409-763-4311; www.galveston.com; 2027 61st St; ☯ 9am-5pm) has tons of dining info and shows a film about the island.

In 1921, a killer hurricane hit Galveston, submerging the island and claiming 8000 victims – still the country's worst natural disaster in terms of lives lost. (By comparison, the US's costliest hurricane, Katrina at $80-plus billion, took 1300 lives.) Experience the Great Storm in a multimedia presentation at **Pier 21 Theatre** (☎ 409-763-8808; www.galveston.com/pier21theatre; cnr Pier 21 & Harborside Dr; adult/child $5/4; ☯ 11am-6pm Sun-Thu, to 8pm Fri & Sat), narrated with entries from survivors' diaries. Next door, tour the *Elissa*, a beautiful 1877 Scottish tall ship and explore the town's 19th-century shipping heyday at the **Texas Seaport Museum** (☎ 409-763-1877; www.tsm -elissa.org; cnr Harborside Dr & 21st St; adult/child $6/4; ☯ 10am-5pm).

You can rent a bicycle and surrey from shops along Sewall Blvd, across from a paved path flanking the sand. Families head to **Stewart Beach Park** (6th St & Seawall Blvd; per car $8; ☯ 8am-7pm Mar-Sep) for the organized activities and beach rentals. Serious partiers go further, to the end of Seawall and **East Beach** (1923 Boddeker Dr; per car $8; ☯ 8am-7pm Mar-Sep), where alcohol is not only allowed but also sold. **Galveston Island State Park** (☎ 409-737-1222; www.tpwd.state.tx.us; FM 3005 and 13 Mile Rd; admission $3; ☯ day use 8am-10pm) is on the quieter western end and has camping ($20).

Kids will love **Moody Gardens** (☎ 409-744-4673; www.moodygardens.com; 1 Hope Blvd; day pass $31, under 3yr free; ☯ 10am-6pm Sun-Fri, to 8pm Sat, to 9pm daily Jun-Aug), with its 2-million-gallon aquarium and butterfly rain forest stuffed into giant glass pyramids. The huge **Schlitterbahn Waterpark** (2026 Lockheed St; day pass adult/child $34/27; ⊗ 10am-8pm Jun-Aug) further adds to the island's amusements. Off-season hours vary.

It's easy to make Galveston a day-trip from Houston. If you decide to stay over, know that hotels are uniformly overpriced for what you get – and completely booked at summer weekends. The **Beachcomber Inn** (☎ 409-744-7133; www.galvestoninn.com; 2825 61St St; r $55-80; ⊗ wi-fi), a block off-beach, is a neat and clean bargain. Bask in palm-fringed Spanish-colonial luxury at **Hotel Galvez** (☎ 409-765-7721; www.galveston.com/galvez; 2024 Seawall Blvd; r $179-249; ⊗). The pool deck has a great view of the gulf.

The **Landry's Restaurant group** (www.landrysrestaurants.com) has several chain seafood eateries on the piers by the Strand that are actually quite good. For a more independent experience, and the freshest red snapper on the island, head west to **Waterman** (409-632-0203; 14302 Stewart Rd; breakfast $6-10, mains $13-20; ⊗ 4pm-9pm Tue-Fri, 10am-9pm Sat & Sun). The removed waterfront-cove local is great. Want something lighter? Homemade breads form the foundation of super sandwiches at **Sunflower Bakery** (☎ 409-763-5500; 1527 Church St; pastries $1-3, sandwiches $5-7; ⊗ 7am-6pm Mon-Fri, 7:30am-4pm Sat).

Kerrville Bus Co (☎ 800-231-2222; www.iridekbc.com; 3825 Broadway) runs a morning bus and an evening bus ($16 to $20, one hour) to the Greyhound Bus Terminal in Houston. The **Galveston Island Rail Trolley** (☎ 409-763-4311; www.islandtransit.net) loops around the Strand and along Seawall Blvd via 25th St ($1 one way).

Piney Woods

In the Piney Woods of northeast Texas, 100ft-plus trees outnumber people. Nature is the attraction, but don't expect sublime vistas; here you'll find quiet trails and varied ecosystems. At **Big Thicket National Preserve** (☎ 409-246-2337; www.nps.gov/bith; cnr US 69 & Rte 420; ⊗ visitor center 9am-5pm), coastal plains meet desert sand dunes, and cypress swamps stand next to pine and hardwood forests. If you're lucky, you may run across one of 20 species of small wild orchids while hiking the 45 miles of trail. The eight park units are 100 miles northwest of Houston.

SOUTHERN GULF COAST

Sparkling bays, small harbors filled with shrimp boats, more than 60 miles of protected beaches: a trip to the Southern Gulf Coast can't help but focus on the water. You'll want to anyway, because the scrubby mesquite trees and prickly-pear cactus here don't make the prettiest of landscapes. In the region's largest town, Corpus Christi (population 283,000), you can tour a huge aircraft carrier and visit the National Seashore. Further south, the climate becomes a bit more tropical and you can party spring-break style. Once you're in the Valley, you're almost to Mexico, so at least pop over the border for a day-trip.

ARANSAS NATIONAL WILDLIFE REFUGE

Back in 1951 only 31 whooping cranes remained in the world. Today there are more than 500, thanks in large part to the preservation efforts at their wintering ground, the 70,504-acre **Aransas National Wildlife Refuge** (☎ 361-286-3559; FM 744; www.fws.gov/southwest/refuges/texas/aransas.html; per car $5; ⊗ park dawn-dusk, visitor center 8:30am-4:30pm), off Hwy 35. These giant white birds can stand 5ft tall (with a 7ft wingspan). From the observation tower you can usually see one or two. Otherwise, you have to board a boat tour in the artsy fishing village of **Rockport** (www.rockport-fulton.org), 35 miles south of the refuge, to see the cranes. **Rockport Birding & Kayak Adventures** (☎ 877-892-4737; www.rockportadventures.com; tickets $35; ☎ tours 7:30am & 1:30pm Mar-Nov) has one of the smallest boats, so it can get you closer to the magnificent creatures.

CORPUS CHRISTI

The salt breezes and palm tree–lined bay are quite pleasant: downtown sits right on the waterfront, and there's a promenade where you can stroll or ride a rented bicycle surrey. There's not a whole heck of a lot to entice visitors (and the city council seems to like it that way). Padre Island and the National Seashore are good diversions if you want a relaxing seaside break, and don't expect Mediterranean blue waters. Port Aransas is a bustling little fishing town with tons of restaurants and boat charters.

TEXAS

Corpus Christi Convention & Visitors Bureau (☎ 361-881-1888, 800-678-6232; www.corpuschristi-tx-cvb .org; 1823 N Chaparral; ☺ 9am-5pm Tue-Sat) is of limited use. Just across the harbor bridge from downtown, the 900ft aircraft carrier **USS Lexington Museum** (☎ 361-888-4873; www.usslexington .com; 2914 N Shoreline Blvd; adult/child $12/7; ☺ 9am-6pm Jun-Aug, to 5pm rest of yr) sits in the harbor, complete with foldable airplanes. Exhibits at the **Texas State Aquarium** (☎ 361-881-1200; www .texasstateaquarium.org; 2710 N Shoreline Blvd; adult/child $14/9; ☺ 9am-6pm) focus on the Gulf of Mexico and more.

On the other side of Corpus, 20 miles east off Hwy 358 (SPID), the sugar-sand beaches of **Padre Island** call. (Technically, this is 'North' Padre Island, but locals know it as 'the island'.) Public access is easy – you can drive and park on the packed sand at the water's edge that's been designated a road (not on the dunes behind). No environmental groups seem to be protesting, but there is a parking lot at **Bob Hall Pier** (15820 Park Rd 22) that you can use instead.

All the usual chain motel suspects line SPID. Downtown, the **Bayfront Inn** (☎ 361-883-7271; www.bayfrontinncc.com; 601 N Shoreline Blvd; r $60-80; ☒) is your best deal with a view of the bay. On the island, there's a cluster of three hotels on the beach. **Bahia Mar Suites** (☎ 361-949-8041; www.holidayinns.com; 15201 Windward Dr; r $113-149; wi-fi), opened in 2006, has handy kitchens and beachy colors but no pool. Chaparral and Water Sts are the hub of food and fun downtown (there are few restaurants on the island). Eat a shrimp wrap from a surfboard table or listen to live rock, folk and country in the yard at the **Executive Surf Club** (☎ 361-884-7873; www.executivesurfclub.com; 309 N Water St; ☺ 11am-11pm).

Padre Island National Seashore

The 60 miles south of Padre Island that lies outside Corpus Christi city limits is all a protected part of the windswept dunes of **Padre Island National Seashore** (☎ 361-949-8068; www.nps .gov/pais; Park Rd 22; per car $10; ☺ visitor center 8:30am-4:30pm, to 6pm Jun-Aug). In the off-season, it's easy to find yourself alone if you hike just a short distance from the visitor center (which has the only potable water in the park). The constant wind attracts kite and windsurfers to the Bird Island Basin area. Report any Kemp Ridley sea turtles you see; the endangered species nests in the park and is closely protected. If you're visiting in late summer, you might be able to take part in a turtle release; call the **Hatchling Hotline** (☎ 361-949-7163) for information. Camp at the semi-developed, paved Malaquite campground ($8), or go primitive – beach camping is free with a permit.

Port Aransas

Driving north, Padre Island morphs imperceptibly into Mustang Island, at the tip of which (20mi north) is **Port Aransas** (www .portaransas.org). This bustling little fishing and vacation village is worth a stop. From divey to divine, there are a load of places to eat seafood (Fin's, Hook's, Trout Street...), and Gulf fishing charters depart from here. **Fisherman's Wharf** (☎ 361-749-5448; www.wharfcat.com; 900 N Tarpon St) has regular deep sea fishing excursions (five hours, $50) and runs jetty boats to outer islands ($10).

THE VALLEY

Way down here in the Rio Grande Valley (known simply as 'the Valley'), you're spittin' distance from Mexico. Citrus tree plantations are gradually giving way to new subdivisions, but there are enough remaining to stock roadside stands where you can pick up fresh local grapefruits and oranges (harvested November through May).

Weslaco (www.weslaco.com), a farming community known for its sweet onions, is the closest US town with services to the preferred Mexico crossing. Both the **Best Western Palm Aire** (☎ 956-969-2411; www.bestwesternpalmaire.com; 415 Rte 1015; ☒ ☐), a pleasant place to sleep, and the **Blue Onion** (☎ 956-447-0067; 423 Rte 1015; ☺ 11am-9pm), with homemade meals and flatbread, are on the road to Mexico.

The town's walkable size and lack of violent crime, unlike some others (we're not naming any names, are we, Laredo?), make midvalley **Nuevo Progreso** (www.shop-progreso .com) the best place to border-jump for the day. Park on the US side and walk across the bridge (35¢ each way). A cacophony of bartering children, hawkers passing out dentists' cards, and street vendors accosts you immediately – the main street's one big marketplace. Silver jewelry and platters are some of the best bargains. And of course there're always tequila and other crafts to buy. (Yes, you can buy prescription drugs, but all the obvious painkillers and such are banned from US re-entry.) Stop for lunch at landmark **Arturo's** (☎ 52-899-937-0127; cnr Sonora & Ave Benito Juarez; mains $6-14; ☺ 10am-10pm), opened 1953, or at one of the fajita taco stands along the side streets.

Birders flock to the area parks associated with the **World Birding Center** (www.worldbirding center.org). Migrating masses (including thousands of hawks) pass through this natural corridor along the main North–South American fly route March to April and September through October. The visitor center and educational center at **Bentsen-Rio Grande Valley State Park** (☎ 956-585-1107; 2800 FM 2062, Mission; adult/child $5/3; ☺ park 6am-10pm, gift shop 8am-5pm) are a model of sustainable, green-driven architecture and rainwater collection. Rent a bike ($5 a day) or take the tram the 2 miles into the park, where alligators as well as birds roam the wetlands, and you may spot a javelina (wild pig) or a horny toad on your way to the hawk-observation tower.

Down in **Brownsville** (www.brownsville.org), the southernmost town in Texas, **Gladys Porter Zoo** (☎ 956-546-2177; 500 Ringgold St; adult/child $9/6; ☺ 9am-dusk) is a lush tropical botanical garden with a conservation bent. It specializes in breeding endangered animals like Komodo dragons and Philippine crocodiles.

Both Harlingen (30 miles from Weslaco, 50 miles from South Padre) and Brownsville (50 miles from Weslaco, 30 miles from South Padre) have regional airports and national car rental.

South Padre Island

Want to parasail, bungee jump and drink yourself silly? This condo-crammed island has restaurants, bars and beach activities galore – most aimed at families and the college-age party crowd. At least the tours and feeding presentations (10am) at **Sea Turtle Inc** (☎ 956-761-4511; www.seaturtleinc.com; 6617 Padre Blvd; ☺ 10am-4pm Tue-Sun) rescue facility are educational. **South Padre Island Visitor Center** (☎ 956-761-6433; www.sopadre.com; 600 Padre Blvd; ☺ 9am-5pm) website has a comprehensive list of condo rentals and beach hotels. But if you want to experience a hardcore fisherman's life, stop in Port Isabel (before you cross the bridge) to eat or stay at **White Sands Motel, Marina & Restaurant** (☎ 956-943-2414; www .the-white-sands.com; 418 W Hwy 100; breakfast $4-8, mains $8-16; ☺ 7am-10pm Tue-Sat, to 2pm Mon; ☻). Rooms are $47 to $65.

DALLAS–FORT WORTH

Dallas and Fort Worth are as different as a Beemer-driving yuppie and a rancher in a Dodge dually pick-up: the proverbial city slicker and the country cousin. Just 30 miles apart, the two towns anchor a giant megalopolis of six million people known as the Metroplex. Sure you want to see Dallas, but don't miss at least a day-trip to Fort Worth – the cowboy and Western sights and museums might be the state's best-kept secret.

DALLAS

Big hair, big egos and big guns. Flashy TV-show millionaires and heroic/criminal football players are what outsiders see of Dallas. The reality is not unrelated. OK, while the hairstyles have been tamed, the 'Big D' is still highly image-conscious. That's all right,

TEXAS

HOT TOPIC: BUILDING FENCES

Funding from Homeland Security for the Secure Fence Act gave the go-ahead for 153 miles of two-layer reinforced fence to be built along the Texas–Mexico border by 2009. Most of the fence would bisect the Rio Grande Valley from Del Rio to Brownsville. No one is particularly happy about this. Proponents argue that illegal immigration laws have not been properly enforced – the fence hasn't been built fast enough and won't go far enough. Immigration advocates insist rights are being violated. Local officials point out that the plan threatens to cut off parts of university campuses and access to key bridges. Local ranchers, who may like to stem the flow, don't hold much stock in the idea since they see the damage already done to their fences by *coyotes* (illegal-immigrant guides) in the night. Environmentalists point out that a fence will disrupt wildlife habitats in the almost 100,000 acres of preserve and parks along the border. According to congressional reports, a million illegal immigrants have been apprehended and 250,000kg of cocaine seized per annum along the southwestern border; officials estimate that they catch only 10% to 30% of the traffic. Will the fence be a solution or a setback? Time will tell.

DALLAS–FORT WORTH METROPLEX

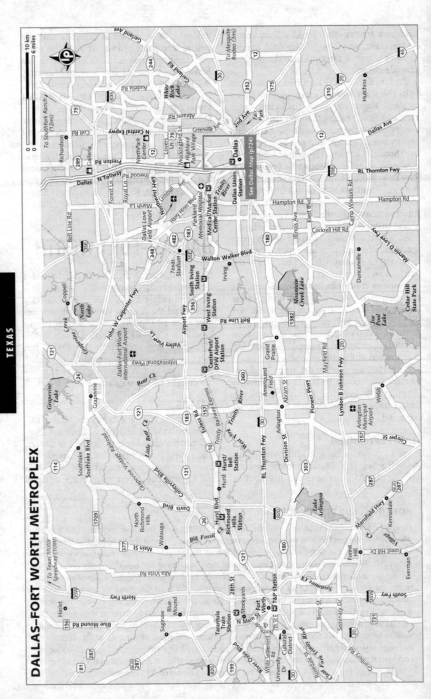

DON'T MISS

- **JFK sights** – multimedia museum and memorials (right)

- **Southfork Ranch** – the home of *Dallas* (right)

- **Bishop Arts District** – bohemian neighborhood; good eats (p726)

- **Fort Worth** – the Old West next door (p728)

he upscale ethos in this town of 1.2 million makes for a great dining scene – you can tell which place is hot by the caliber of cars the valet leaves out front. Then there's all that shopping. Oh, and some folks come for the history of JFK's assassination (and memories of JR Ewing being shot). Visit for a couple days, but don't try to scratch the surface too deep – you'll come up empty.

Orientation & Information

Downtown Dallas is east of the junction of I-30 and I-35 E; take the Commerce St exit off I-35. Uptown – with smart, trendy bars, restaurants and hotels – is north of downtown; follow Harwood St (or St Paul St, if you're taking the trolley) to McKinney Ave. Bars line Greenville Ave, northeast of downtown off Ross Ave. Deep Ellum, at the eastern end of Elm St, has become a bit scary, but it's the nucleus of Dallas' live-music scene. Oak Cliff is just west of downtown, south of I-20, which connects to Fort Worth, 30 miles to the west.

Bank of America (☎ 214-508-6881; 1401 Elm St) Foreign currency exchange.

Borders Books (☎ 214-219-0512; 3600 McKinney Ave; ☯ 10am-10pm)

Central Library (☎ 214-670-1700; 1515 Young St; ☯ 9am-9pm Mon-Thu, to 5pm Fri & Sat, noon-5pm Sun) Get a free internet card at the desk.

Dallas CVB Visitor Center (☎ 214-571-1300; www.visitdallas.com; 100 S Houston St; ☯ 8am-5pm Mon-Fri, 9am-5pm Sat & Sun) Occupies the Old Red Courthouse. Free internet access.

Dallas Morning News (www.dallasnews.com) The city's daily newspaper.

Parkland Memorial Hospital (Map p722; ☎ 214-590-8000; 5201 Harry Hines Blvd)

Police station (☎ 214-670-4413; 334 S Hall St)

Post office (☎ 214-468-8270; 400 N Ervay St)

Sights

All things JFK-related are downtown, as are the city's art museums and symphony center. Thursday night Dallas museums stay open with free entry from 5pm to 9pm.

DOWNTOWN

President John F Kennedy's downtown assassination sent the city reeling in November 1963. The shooting was followed by a chaotic manhunt and gunman Lee Harvey Oswald's eventual assassination. The fascinating and highly audiovisual **Sixth Floor Museum** (☎ 214-747-6660; www.jfk.org; Book Depository, 411 Elm St; adult/child under 5yr $10/free; ☯ 10am-6pm Tue-Sat, noon-6pm Sun & Mon) narrates in minute-by-minute detail what happened there. Eyewitness video and audio clips add depth to the experience. Even the myriad twisted conspiracy theories are succinctly summarized. From Dealey Plaza, walk along Elm St beside the infamous grassy knoll and look for the white 'X' in the road that marks the exact spot where the president was shot. Turn around and look up at the top floor of the Texas School Book Depository (now the museum) where Oswald pulled the trigger. Across N Market St is the **Kennedy Memorial**, a simple but profound sculpture by the architect Phillip Johnson.

Modern-art installations shine both outside and in at the fabulous glass-and-steel **Nasher Sculpture Center** (☎ 214-242-5100; www.nashersculpture center.org; 2001 Flora St; adult/child $10/free; ☯ 11am-5pm Tue-Sun) and gardens. The **Dallas Museum of Art** (☎ 214-922-1200; www.dallasmuseumofart.org; 1717 N Harwood St; adult/child under 12yr $10/free; ☯ 11am-5pm Tue-Sun) is a high-caliber world tour of decorative and fine art befitting a big city.

Explore the watery Mayan world of a Central American jungle at the **Dallas World Aquarium** (☎ 214-720-2224; 1801 N Griffin St; www.dwazoo.com; adult/child under 12yr $17/10; ☯ 10am-5pm). There's also a rain forest exhibit with an unusual collection of underwater critters.

SOUTHFORK RANCH

Who shot JR? Locals certainly no longer care (the TV drama *Dallas* was cancelled in 1992), but that doesn't stop interstate and international visitors from driving 30 miles north from Dallas to **Southfork Ranch** (☎ 972-442-7800; www.southfork.com; 3700 Hogge Rd/FM 2551, Plano; adult/child $9.50/7; ☯ 9am-5pm). If you are expecting to see Miss Ellie's kitchen or JR's

TEXAS

lonelyplanet.com

TEXAS

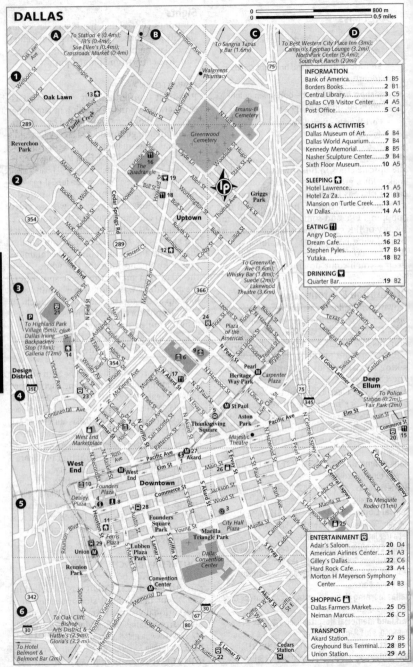

DALLAS

INFORMATION	
Bank of America	1 B5
Borders Books	2 B1
Central Library	3 C5
Dallas CVB Visitor Center	4 A5
Post Office	5 C4

SIGHTS & ACTIVITIES	
Dallas Museum of Art	6 B4
Dallas World Aquarium	7 B4
Kennedy Memorial	8 B5
Nasher Sculpture Center	9 B4
Sixth Floor Museum	10 A5

SLEEPING	
Hotel Lawrence	11 A5
Hotel Za Za	12 B3
Mansion on Turtle Creek	13 A1
W Dallas	14 A4

EATING	
Angry Dog	15 D4
Dream Cafe	16 B2
Stephen Pyles	17 B4
Yutaka	18 B2

DRINKING	
Quarter Bar	19 B2

ENTERTAINMENT	
Adair's Saloon	20 D4
American Airlines Center	21 A3
Gilley's Dallas	22 C6
Hard Rock Cafe	23 A4
Morton H Meyerson Symphony Center	24 B3

SHOPPING	
Dallas Farmers Market	25 D5
Neiman Marcus	26 C5

TRANSPORT	
Akard Station	27 B5
Greyhound Bus Terminal	28 B5
Union Station	29 A5

bedroom, you are bound to be disappointed. The ranch was used for exterior filming only (and then mirrors were employed to make it look bigger). All interior shots were filmed on a set in Hollywood. The original ranch owners, the Duncans, allowed filming in summer months only because they actually lived there with growing kids. That lasted until the show became so popular they started waking up to 200 rabid fans camped around their pool every morning. Then they sold out. You have to take the tour to see the small museum (yes, it has the gun that shot JR and Lucy's wedding dress) and the house, which today is an event center, decorated in classic '80s style.

FAIR PARK

Home to the state fair and Cotton Bowl stadium, **Fair Park** (☎ 214-421-9600; www.fairpark.org; 1300 Cullum Blvd; adult/child passport $24/14), off 2nd Ave S, was created for the 1936 Texas Centennial Exposition. Today art-deco buildings contain seven museums, focusing on science, railroad history, African Americans, women's history… This is not in the best neighborhood, but they're trying to revitalize the place, and it's perfectly safe during the day.

Tours

Hit Dallas' highlights – historical sights plus shopping with a five-hour limo tour by **Big D Shopping Spree** (☎ 214-244-2594; www.bigdshoppingspree.com; tours $125). Dramatic and committed conspiracy theorist–historian **John Nagle** (☎ 214-674-6295; www.jfktours.com; tours $20; ☽ Sat & Sun) guides 1¼-hour walking tours of JFK assassination sights.

Festivals

The 52ft Big Tex statue towers over Fair Park from late September through October during the **State Fair of Texas** (☎ 214-565-9931; www.bigtex.com; Fair Park, 1300 Cullum Blvd). Come ride the tallest Ferris wheel in North America, eat corny dogs (this is where they were invented), and browse among the prize-winning cows, sheep and quilts.

Sleeping

The best area to stay is Uptown, but hotels there can get pricey. The further you sleep from the center, the cheaper the highway chain motels get.

BUDGET

Dallas Irving Backpackers Stop (☎ 214-682-9636; 214 W 6th St, Irving; dm $20; P ☒ ▣ wi-fi) Suburbia special. This big, clean, family-run house is a pleasant place to stay – big kitchen, living room, four-bed rooms, super owners. But it is way out in a dry town (no alcohol sold), and the trains (20 minutes or less to Dallas, about 40 to Fort Worth) don't run after 10pm or on Sunday.

Best Western City Place Inn (☎ 214-827-6080; www.bestwestern.com; 4150 N Central Expressway; r $67-80; P ☳ ▣ wi-fi) The value-to-Uptown-proximity ratio is high here; the McKinney Ave trolley is just a 15-minute walk away. A funky diner gives soul to this otherwise standard motel.

MIDRANGE

Hotel Lawrence (☎ 214-761-9090; www.hotellawrencedallas.com; 302 S Houston St; r $129-174; ▣) Neoclassical earth-tone designs can't make the downtown hotel rooms seem bigger (ask for a corner room). But packages help with the cost – a Gas & Go includes a $10 gas card and discounted valet parking.

Hotel Belmont (☎ 866-870-8010; www.belmontdallas.com; 901 Fort Worth Ave; r $179-200; ☒ ☳ ▣ wi-fi) You could imagine Marlene Dietrich walking down the terracotta stairs in this stylish 1940s bungalow hotel. The garden rooms – with soaking tubs, Moroccan-blue tile work, kilim rugs and some city views – are tops.

W Dallas (☎ 214-397-4100; 2440 Victory Park Lane; www.starwood.com; r $179-269; ☳ ▣ wi-fi) Urban sophistication has come to Dallas. Lobby and guest rooms ooze minimalist edge. A mid-high-rise open-air floor (no walls) houses the trendy pool and spa.

> **IF YOU HAVE A FEW MORE DAYS…**
>
> The Conspiracy Museum may have closed, but you can still delve deeper into Kennedy assassination history. Have pizza at dark and dated **Campisi's Egyptian Lounge** (☎ 214-827-0355; 5610 E Mockingbird Lane; pizza & pasta $6-16; ☽ 11am-10pm), where Jack Ruby (Lee Harvey Oswald's assassin) used to hang out (with mob friends). Or buy veteran TV reporter Eddie Barker's *Eddie Barker's Notebooks* and read more about the places and people involved that November. (He also provides great insight into Dallas at the time.)

TEXAS

TOP END

Hotel Za Za (☎ 214-468-8399; www.hotelzaza.com; 2332 Leonard St; r $229-395; ✗ ⊠ ⊠ wi-fi) Colorful, exotic silks and whimsical shapes characterize guest rooms, and the hip, themed suites – the Shag-a-delic, the Zen, the Medusa – are pure fun ($500 to $1000). Lounge poolside or eat at the Dragonfly restaurant; you're among the 'in' crowd.

Mansion on Turtle Creek (☎ 214-559-2100; www .rosewoodhotels.com; 2821 Turtle Creek Blvd; r $200-490; ⊠ ⊠ wi-fi) Step into a life of ease, where for every two guests there's one staff member attending. Fresh flowers sit atop hand-carved European guest-room furnishings. And dinner is served in the original, 1925 marble-clad Italianate villa.

Eating

Eating out nightly is de rigueur for those living in chi-chi **Uptown** (www.uptowndallas.net) and adjacent Knox-Henderson, so you can do pretty well foodwise there. Oak Cliff's Bishop Arts District, one of the few arty enclaves, has a few interesting eateries. Greenville Ave and Deep Ellum both have cafés and restaurants, though the areas are known more for nightlife.

UPTOWN & KNOX-HENDERSON

Dream Cafe (☎ 214-954-0486; 2800 Routh St; mains $6-12; ✓ 7am-9pm Sun-Thu, to 10pm Fri & Sat) Imagine a healthy, brown-rice-and-veggies kind of diner; one with quirky decor, a huge patio and a playground for kids – you've got the picture.

Yutaka (☎ 214-969-5533; 2633 McKinney Ave; sushi $7-14; ✓ 5:45-10pm Mon, 11:45am-2pm & 5:45-10pm Tue-Thu, 11:45am-2pm & 5:45-11pm Fri & Sat) Industrial loft meets minimalism at tiny Yutaka, where you can get some of the freshest sushi in town.

Sangria Tapas y Bar (☎ 214-520-4863; 4524 Cole Ave; lunch $15, tapas $5-12; ✓ 11am-11pm Sun-Thu, until midnight Fri & Sat) The small plates and controlled chaos here are currently hot, but the several blocks around Knox Blvd and McKinney Ave seem to sprout new restaurants daily.

BISHOP ARTS DISTRICT

Gloria's (☎ 214-948-3672; 600 W Davis St; lunch specials $7-9, mains $9-15; ✓ 11:30am-10pm) Plantains, black beans and yucca are big players on the El Salvadorian–Mexican menu. Gloria's has done so well it's expanded to several local locales.

Hattie's (☎ 214-942-7400; 418 Bishop Ave; lunch $7-12, dinner mains $12-18; ✓ 11:30am-2:30pm Mon, 11:30am-

2:30pm & 5-10pm Tue-Sun) Oooo-eee *cher*, shrimp 'n' grits with Tabasco and bacon? It doesn't get more down-home Louisiana than that. The upscale white tablecloths make for a nice contrast.

DOWNTOWN & DEEP ELLUM

Angry Dog (☎ 214-741-4406; 2726 Commerce St; mains $5-9; ✓ 11am-midnight Sun-Thu, to 2am Fri & Sat) Workers crowd in at lunchtime for the unbeatable burgers.

Stephen Pyles (☎ 214-580-7000; 1807 Ross Ave; lunch $8-14, dinner mains $28-35; ✓ 11am-2pm & 6-10:30pm Mon-Fri, 6-10:30pm Sat) Local superstar chef Stephen Pyles has another creative hit on his hands. The ceviche bar is quite popular; try the one with shrimp, oranges and popcorn.

Drinking

The restaurant indoor-smoking ban doesn't affect stand-alone bars.

Quarter Bar (☎ 214-754-4940; 3301 McKinney Ave) Well-dressed but friendly Uptown patrons wander among three levels and a patio.

Belmont Bar (☎ 866-870-8010; www.belmontdallas .com; Hotel Belmont, 901 Fort Worth Ave) Sip your adult beverage on a stylish terrace overlooking the city. Sometimes it screens B-grade flicks outdoors on the white stucco wall.

Entertainment

For entertainment listings check the weekly alternative newspaper **Dallas Observer** (www.dallas observer.com) or **Guide Live** (www.guidelive.com) in Friday's *Dallas Morning News*.

LIVE MUSIC & NIGHTCLUBS

A rise in alleged gang activity keeps a few people away, but **Deep Ellum** (www.deepellumtx.com) is still live-music central. Most of the clubs are hard core – just pick one and wear black.

Gilley's Dallas (☎ 214-421-2021; www.gilleysdallas .com; 1135 S Lamar St; ✓ 6pm-2am Fri & Sat; ✗) Boot-scoot around the floor or ride the mechanical bull from the movie *Urban Cowboy*. Half the place has been sold off and made into Palladium Ballroom for pop concerts – what a shame.

House of Blues (☎ 214-978-2583; www.houseofblues .com; 220 N Lamar St) Almost nightly, bands rock the House of Blues, opened mid-2007 in the developing Victory Park area. Sunday's gospel brunch is a big hit.

Adair's Saloon (☎ 214-939-9900; www.adairssaloon .com; 2624 Commerce St) Texas graffiti–covered

GAY & LESBIAN DALLAS

Dallas' gay and lesbian scene centers on Cedar Springs Rd and Oak Lawn Ave, north of Uptown. Independent bookstore and café **Crossroads Market** (☎ 214-521-8919; 3930 Cedar Springs Rd; ☿ 10am-8pm Sun-Thu, to 10pm Fri & Sat) sits at its heart. The Dallas Gay & Lesbian Alliance's **Resource Center of Dallas** (☎ 214-528-9254; www.resourcecenterdallas.org) can refer you to points of interest and gay-owned businesses in town. The **Dallas Voice** (www.dallasvoice.com) newspaper is the town's gay and lesbian advocate.

Within a few steps of each other are a bunch of different clubs: **Station 4** (☎ 214-559-0650; 3911 Cedar Springs Rd) dance club hosts the Rose Room drag show nightly at 11pm. **JR's** (☎ 214-528-1004; 3923 Cedar Springs Rd; ☿ 11am-2am) is a fun boys' bar with darts and pool, food and wi-fi. And **Sue Ellen's** (☎ 214-559-0650; 3903 Cedar Springs Rd) is Dallas' biggest lesbian club.

Adair's hosts alt country and roots music in addition to the prevailing hard-core Deep Ellum scene.

Whisky Bar (☎ 214-828-0188; www.whisky-bar.com; 1930 Greenville Ave) Here DJs groove Friday and Saturday, and it's live acoustic Wednesdays.

Suede (☎ 214-823-1518; www.suedebardallas.com; 1518 Greenville Ave) This place has a huge rooftop patio and recorded or live country tunes.

SPORTS

'America's Team', the **Dallas Cowboys** (☎ 972-579-5000; www.dallascowboys.com; 2401 E Airport Fwy, Irving), which won three championships in the 1990s, plays NFL football at Texas Stadium (Map p722), off Hwy 183 – at least until its new Arlington stadium, to be the largest in the NFL, is finished around 2009. You can tour the old stadium ($12, on the hour) or browse the pro shop from 10am to 4pm Monday through Sunday.

The **Texas Rangers** (☎ 817-273-5100; www.texasrangers.com) play pro baseball at Ameriquest Field (Map p722) in Arlington, between Dallas and Fort Worth.

The **American Airlines Center** (☎ 214-222-3687; www.americanairlinescenter.com; 2500 Victory Ave) in Victory Park hosts mega concerts and is home to the **Dallas Stars** (☎ 214-467-8277; www.dallasstars.com) hockey team and the **Dallas Mavericks** (☎ 972-988-3865; www.dallasmavericks.com) pro basketball team.

Mesquite Rodeo (☎ 972-222-2855; www.mesquiterodeo.com; 1818 Rodeo Dr; tickets $12-30; ☿ 8pm Fri & Sat Apr-Sep) Bronc-bustin', bull-ridin' cowboys square off at a weekend rodeo broadcast nationwide. Take I-30 15 miles east to Hwy 80.

THEATER & CLASSICAL PERFORMANCES

Lakewood Theater (☎ 214-821-9084; www.lakewoodtheater.com; 1825 Abrams Parkway) This renovated 1938 art-deco cinema off Greenville Ave holds film festivals and stages concerts, musicals and plays.

At the time of writing a new performance center was under construction, but for now the **Dallas Symphony Orchestra** (☎ 214-692-0203; www.dallassymphony.com) performs at **Morton H Meyerson Symphony Center** (☎ 214-670-3600; www.meyersonsymphonycenter.com; 2301 Flora St) in the Arts District.

Shopping

The granddaddy of all area malls, the **Galleria** (☎ 972-702-7100; www.galleriadallas.com; 13355 Noel Rd), at I-635 and Dallas North Tollway, is being overshadowed by up-and-comer **NorthPark Center** (☎ 214-361-6345; www.northparkcenter.com; 1030 Northpark Center, Northwest Hwy at US 75), which has almost 2 million sq ft of retail space.

Shopping neighborhoods include the small but quirky **Bishop Arts District** (www.bishopartsdistrict.com; Bishop Ave & W Davis St; ☿ shops closed Mon), where you can find some interesting gifts and homewares, and the sprawling Design District (bounded by Oak Lawn Ave, Industrial Blvd and Hi-Line Dr), where you can prowl for all things interior-decorator related: handmade lamps, French antiques, mod furnishings…

Neiman Marcus (☎ 214-741-6911; www.neimanmarcus.com; 1 Marcus Sq) A downtown landmark, this six-story behemoth is the original Neiman Marcus store.

Highland Park Village (www.hpvillage.com; cnr Mockingbird Lane & Preston Rd) Shop at Kate Spade, Prada, Jimmy Choo and other high-end boutique stores – just a light-rail stop away.

Dallas Farmers Market (☎ 214-670-5880; www.dallasfarmersmarket.org; cnr Marilla Blvd & S Harwood St; ☿ 7am-6pm) Buy produce directly from the growers, or shop for flowers and antiques at this multibarn market.

TEXAS

Getting There & Away

AIR

American Airlines' home port is **Dallas–Fort Worth International Airport** (Map p722; DFW; ☎ 972-574-4420; www.dfwairport.com), 16 miles northwest of the city via I-35 E. Great Britain and Mexico are among the nonstop international destinations. Southwest Airlines uses smaller, more convenient **Dallas Love Field** (Map p722; DAL; ☎ 214-670-6073; www.dallas-lovefield.com), just northwest of downtown (take Inwood Rd northeast from Harry Hines Blvd and turn left on Cedar Springs).

BUS

Greyhound buses make runs all over the country from the **Greyhound Bus Terminal** (☎ 214-655-7085; www.greyhound.com; 205 S Lamar St). Direct Greyhound buses connect Dallas with cities such as Austin ($32, 3½ hours) and Houston ($37, 4½ hours).

CAR & MOTORCYCLE

Every major rental-car company has an office at DFW, and many are at Love Field too.

TRAIN

Amtrak's San Antonio–Chicago *Texas Eagle* stops at downtown's **Union Station** (☎ 214-653-1101; www.amtrak.com; 401 S Houston St).

Getting Around

TO/FROM THE AIRPORT

Catch the Monday–Saturday **Trinity Railway Express** (www.trinityrailwayexpress.org) train to downtown's Union Station ($2.25). The CenterPort/DFW Airport stop is actually in a parking lot; shuttle buses take you to the terminals. On weekdays, DART express bus 202 ($2.25) runs downtown from DFW, and bus 39 ($1.25) heads downtown from Love Field.

It's easier to take a shuttle, especially on Sunday when there's no train. **Yellow Checker Shuttle** (☎ 817-267-5150; www.yellowcheckershuttle.com) and **SuperShuttle** (☎ 817-329-2000; www.supershuttle.com) run shuttles from DFW or Love Field to downtown for around $18. A taxi between DFW and central Dallas will cost $40 to $50.

BUS & LIGHT RAIL

Dallas Area Rapid Transit (DART; ☎ 214-979-1111; www.dart.org) operates buses and an extensive lightrail system that connects Union Station and other stops downtown with outlying areas (single trip $2.25). Day passes ($4.50) are available from the store at the **Akard Station** (1401 Pacific Ave; ☺ 7:30am-5:30pm Mon-Fri); maps are also online. Travel Uptown from down on the free McKinney Ave trolley, which runs daily from the corner of Ross Ave and St Paul St, near the Dallas Museum of Art, up McKinney Ave to Hall St.

CAR & MOTORCYCLE

If you do rent a car, be warned that rush-hour freeway traffic is bad and there's little free parking downtown; parking garages cost from $10 per day.

TAXI

Yellow Cab (☎ 214-426-6262) and **Checker Cab** (☎ 972-222-2000) charge an initial $2 for each person that gets into the cab and 40¢ every quarter mile after that.

AROUND DALLAS

East Texas is full of small towns organized around the courthouse square, where spring and fall festivals and rodeos are big doggone deals. Check the **Texas Highways** (www.texashighways.com) listings to find one that suits you. **Tyler** (www.tylertexas.com; I-20 & US 69), 100 miles east of Dallas, is known for its 14-acre municipal garden (in bloom April through November) and the October rose festival.

FORT WORTH

Yee-haw, Fort Worth is a big Texas town that still has its twang. See a mini cattle drive in the morning and a rodeo on Saturday night. Don't forget to go honky-tonkin' at Billy Bob's after all that ropin' and ridin'. Down in the Cultural District, tour the Cowgirl Museum and others, including three amazing art collections. Then, after you meditate on minimalism, downtown's Sundance Sq restaurants and bars beckon. At population 500,000, the town is a far more user-friendly size than Dallas, not to mention greener and cleaner. There's a lot to do here, without a whole lotta pretense.

History

Fort Worth became famous during the great open-range cattle drives of the late 19th century, when more than 10 million head of cattle tramped through the city on the Chisholm Trail. This Old West outpost attracted some infamous desperados: Butch Cassidy and the Sundance Kid hid out in town, as did Great

Depression–era holdup artists Bonnie Parker and Clyde Barrow. During the 1920s, nearby oil-field finds turned the city into an important industry operation center. Amon Carter, oilman and early publisher of the *Star-Telegram*, put the city on the arts map when his will provided resources for local museums.

Orientation & Information

Fort Worth is fairly compact and easy to drive around; I-30 runs south of downtown and I-35 W to the east. Downtown, the Cultural District and the Stockyards form a lopsided triangle. North Main St runs between downtown and the Stockyards, 7th St E Ave connects downtown to the Cultural District, and University Dr and Northside Dr connect the Cultural District to North Main St near the Stockyards.

Central Library (☎ 817-871-7701; 500 W 3rd St; ☻ 9am-9pm Mon-Thu, 10am-6pm Sat, noon-5pm Sun) Free internet access.

Fort Worth Convention & Visitors Bureau (www.fortworth.com) downtown (☎ 817-336-8791; 415 Throckmorton St; ☻ 8:30am-5pm Mon-Fri, 10am-4pm Sat) Cultural District (☎ 817-882-8588; 3401 W Lancaster Ave; ☻ 10am-5pm Mon-Sat) Stockyards (☎ 817-624-4741; 130 E Exchange Ave; ☻ 9am-6pm Mon-Sat, noon-5pm Sun) Spiffy 3-D maps – free.

Sights & Activities

Most area museums call the leafy Cultural District home. The Stockyards are cowboy central.

STOCKYARDS NATIONAL HISTORIC DISTRICT

Cowboy-wear stores and knickknack shops, saloons and steakhouses crowd into the Old West–era buildings of the **Stockyards** (www

---

DON'T MISS

- **Billy Bob's Texas** – live bull riding and Texas two-stepping (p731)
- **National Cowgirl Museum** – ride 'em, cowgirl! (right)
- **Amon Carter Museum** – wild Western art (right)
- **Love Shack** – Food Network chef; low, low prices (p731)

.fortworthstockyards.org). What used to be a livestock industry center has turned tourist trade. City-paid cowboys on horseback roam the district, answering questions and posing for photos. Twice a day, at 10am and 4pm, they drive a small herd of Texas longhorns (about 16 to 20) down the block in front of the visitor center. It's a *goll-dang* Kodak moment, pardner. See a real live rodeo at **Cowtown Coliseum** (☎ 817-625-1025; www.stockyardsrodeo.com; 121 E Exchange Ave; adult/child rodeo $15/10, Wild West Show $9/5) Friday and Saturday nights year round at 8pm. June to August, horses and riders show off at Pawnee Bill's Wild West Show (2:30pm and 4:30pm Saturday and Sunday).

The former sheep and hog pens of **Stockyards Station** (140 E Exchange Ave; www.stockyardsstation.com) house a mall of sorts and the depot of the **Grapevine Vintage Railroad** (☎ 817-625-7245; www.tarantulatrain.com). There's an hour-long tourist train run but the scenery's dismal. It's more fun to put your penny on the track by the round house and pick it up after you watch the steam locomotive smash it.

CULTURAL DISTRICT

Five major museums and the Will Rogers Memorial Center are part of the parklike **Cultural District** (www.fwculture.com). At the **Amon Carter Museum** (☎ 817-738-1933; www.cartermuseum.org; 3501 Camp Bowie Blvd; admission free; ☻ 10am-5pm Tue-Sat, noon-5pm Sun), you can see displays of pre-1945 American art, including one of the country's best compilations of work by Western artists Frederic Remington and Charles M Russell. There's also an extensive photography collection.

At the **Modern Art Museum of Fort Worth** (☎ 817-738-9215; www.themodern.org; 3200 Darnell St; adult/child $8/free; ☻ 10am-5pm Tue-Sat, 11am-5pm Sun) you round a corner from womblike, concrete galleries to be confronted by a two-story wall of glass looking out on the city skyline. Noteworthy art in the collection includes work by Picasso and Mark Rothko. European, pre-Colombian and other international art are in focus at the **Kimbell Art Museum** (☎ 817-332-8451; www.kimbellart.org; 3333 Camp Bowie Blvd; admission free; ☻ 10am-5pm Tue-Thu & Sat, noon-8pm Fri, noon-5pm Sun).

The **National Cowgirl Museum** (☎ 817-336-3375; www.cowgirl.net; 1721 Gendy St; adult/child $6/4; ☻ 9am-5:30pm Mon-Thu, to 8pm Fri & Sat, 11:30am-5:30pm Sun) rides high with state-of-the-art exhibits.

IF YOU HAVE A FEW MORE DAYS...

Have yourself a NASCAR experience at **Texas Motor Speedway** (☎ 817-215-8565; www.texasmotorspeedway.com; Hwy 114 & I-35; tours adult/child $8/6; ⏲ 9am-5pm Mon-Fri, 10am-5pm Sat & Sun). The annual stock-car race here is in November, but you can ride along at more than 150mph (four laps, $125) or go to driving school (10 laps, $345) with **Team Texas** (☎ 940-648-1043; www.teamtexas.com) year round. The speedway is 20 miles north of downtown, on I-35 W.

Mount a slow-mo electronic bucking bronc and video magic makes it look like you're in a high-action rodeo. Four small theaters on site focus on different women – one video is about Jessie in Pixar's *Toy Story* – but the museum overall is more rugged frontiers people than anything 'girly.'

The **Museum of Science & History** (☎ 817-255-9300; www.fwmuseum.org; 1501 Montgomery St; adult/child $15/10; ⏲ 9am-5:30pm Mon-Thu, to 8pm Fri & Sat, 11am-5:30pm Sun) brims with fossils, dinosaurs and kid-friendly stuff to do – like the planetarium and an Omni Imax theater. A cattle raisers' exhibit is in the works at this writing, and entry also gets you into the Cowgirl Museum next door.

DOWNTOWN

Colorful architecture, an art gallery or two, and a host of bars, restaurants and hotels make the 14-block **Sundance Square** (www.sundancesquare.com), near Main and 3rd Sts, supremely strollable. The area is more than safe, it's downright friendly day or night – parking garages are free after 5pm and at weekends.

The works at the **Sid Richardson Collection of Western Art** (☎ 817-332-6554; www.sidrmuseum.org; 309 Main St; admission free; ⏲ 9am-5pm Mon-Sat, noon-5pm Sun) were once privately held.

Festivals & Events

The town's biggest event is the **Fort Worth Stock Show & Rodeo** (☎ 817-877-2400; www.fwstockshowrodeo.com; grounds adult/child $8/6, rodeo tickets $22), held late January or early February each year at **Will Rogers Coliseum** (1 Amon Carter Sq) in the Cultural District.

Sleeping

It's also easy to day-trip here from Dallas...

BUDGET

Days Inn (☎ 817-336-9823; www.daysinn.com; 1551 S University Dr, off I-30; r $49-60; 🐾 wi-fi) Tucked back off the highway, this motel is pretty quiet. And there's a pretty big pool, too. Stay here and you're 4 miles from downtown and less from museums.

MIDRANGE

Residence Inn (☎ 817-885-8250; www.residenceinn.com; 2500 Museum Way; ste $142-169; ✖ 🐾 💻 wi-fi) Even the smallest rooms at this Marriott Cultural District property, off W 7th St, have full kitchens and free hot breakfasts.

If you don't mind revelers and passing freight trains, you could stay stumbling distance from the action in the Stockyards.

Stockyards Hotel (☎ 817-625-6427; www.stockyardshotel.com; 109 E Exchange Place; r $169-189; wi-fi) First opened in 1907, this place clings to its cowboy past with Western-theme art, lots of leather and a steak house on site. (No nonsmoking rooms.)

Amerisuites Stockyards (☎ 817-626-6000; www.amerisuites.com; 132 E Exchange Ave; r $149-200; ✖ 🐾 💻 wi-fi) The rooms at Amerisuites are more modern than those at the Stockyards Hotel, yet they are rustic too, with heavy, dark woods.

TOP END

Ashton Hotel (☎ 866-327-4866; www.theashtonhotel.com; 610 Main St; r $195-290; ✖ wi-fi) An 1890 and a 1915 building seamlessly blend into this 39-room boutique hotel. Details like elaborate moldings and built-in bookshelves create an expensive residential feel.

Eating

Steak prices around town are weighty, but then so's the beef. Put on the feed bag downtown or in the Stockyards; there's not much to eat in the Cultural District.

DOWNTOWN

8.0 Restaurant & Bar (☎ 817-336-0880; 111 E 3rd St, Sundance Sq; mains $6-10; ⏲ 11am-11pm Tue-Sat, 3-10pm Sun) Take your choice from burgers, pasta and more. This casual café has tables under the trees and live outdoor music nightly from spring through fall. It is like a free concert for all downtown.

Reata (☎ 817-336-1009; 310 Houston St; mains $16-36; ⏲ 11am-10pm) Steaks and Southwestern specialties – tenderloin tamales, jalapeño-cheddar grits – pack the menu. Makes sense; the proprietors also own their own cattle ranch.

STOCKYARDS

Food Network iron chef Tim Love (what a name!) has almost as many restaurants as he does accolades.

Love Shack (☎ 817-740-8812; 110 E Exchange Ave; burgers $4-6; ☟ 11:30am-8pm Sun-Wed, to 11pm Thu, to 1am Fri & Sat) A real bargain, here you can enjoy Tim's tenderloin-and-brisket burgers, topped with a quail egg, and parmesan chips and double thickshakes. Live music with lunch daily and with dinner at weekends.

Esperanza's Panaderia y Café (JoTs Bakery; ☎ 817-626-4356; 2122 N Main St; breakfast $5-7, mains $7-15; ☟ 6am-7pm) Breakfasts here are real Mexican – pulled chicken tops the breakfast *migas* (eggs scrambled with tortilla strips), or you could have *machacado* (spiced dried beef) with those sunny side ups.

Joe T Garcia's (☎ 817-626-4356; 2201 N Commerce St; lunch & brunch mains $6-12, dinner $11-12; ☟ 11am-10pm Mon-Thu, to 11pm Fri & Sat, 10am-10pm Sun) Eat inside, or out where Mexican-tile fountains bubble among the tropical foliage in the walled courtyard. Lunch is à la carte, but for dinner you choose between chicken or beef enchiladas and fajitas served family style. Weekends the line to get in (no reservations) often stretches around the block.

Lonesome Dove Western Bistro (☎ 817-740-8810; 2406 N Main St; mains $28-33; ☟ 11:30am-2:30pm Tue-Sat & 5pm-10pm Tue-Thu, to 11pm Fri & Sat) Tim Love's flagship, the Lonesome Dove serves food that's been called 'urban Western' – think quail quesadillas.

AROUND TOWN

Angelo's Barbecue (☎ 817-332-0357; 2533 White Settlement Rd; plates $7-12; ☟ 10am-10pm Mon-Sat) They've been smokin' brisket, ribs and sausage at this place north of the Cultural District since 1958.

Drinking

Flying Saucer Emporium (☎ 817-336-7470; 111 E 4th St; ☟ 11am-1am Mon-Wed, to 2am Thu-Sat, noon-midnight Sun) Barmaids and men pull pints from 77 taps at this vast drinkery.

Rahr & Sons Brewing Co (☎ 817-810-9266; www .rahrbrewing.com; 701 Galveston Ave at S Main St) While out on the town, ask for local microbrews from here, or take a tour of the place 1pm to 3pm Saturday – free tasting included.

Entertainment

All the restaurants around downtown's Sundance Sq have bars, and most of the bars have music. **Fort Worth Weekly** (www.fwweekly .com) lists entertainment goings-on.

LIVE MUSIC

`our pick` **Billy Bob's Texas** (☎ 817-624-7117; www.billy bobstexas.com; 2520 Rodeo Plaza, Stockyards; ☟ 11am-2am Mon-Sat, noon-2am Sun) Top country-and-western stars, house bands and country DJs play on two stages at Texas' largest honky-tonk. Just having a mechanical bull isn't good enough here – on Friday and Saturday night a live bull-riding competition takes place at an indoor arena. Pool tables and games help make this a family place; under 18s are welcome with a parent.

ROUTE 66 – TEXAS

The Mother Road shuttles across Texas for a mere 178 miles, most of which is under I-40. The state's claim to Route 66 fame is that it contains the road's center point. It probably also has the greatest number of cars stuck in the dirt as art.

On the road from Oklahoma, McLean is about 35 miles west of Texola. The **Devil's Rope Museum** (☎ 806-779-2225; www.barbwiremuseum.com; 100 Kingsley St, McLean; admission free; ☟ 10am-4pm Tue-Sat) has Route 66 and barbed-wire exhibits, and posts a Route 66 map online.

Take a detour north on Hwy 207 in Conway (45 miles west of McLean) to spray-paint your name on one of the VW Beetles planted nose down at **Bug Ranch** (Hwy 207, off I-40). As you approach Amarillo, it's hard to miss the giant cowboy waving from the Big Texan Steak Ranch & Motel (p732). The place opened in 1959 on Route 66 but moved to I-40 in 1970. West 6th St is a short, but original, Mother Road segment. More car art is buried at Cadillac Ranch (see the boxed text, p732) on what's now the southern I-40 access road, west of Loop 335.

Fifty miles later, when you reach Adrian, you're halfway between Chicago and Los Angeles (though nearby Vega contests this).

WHAT THE...?

The late local eccentric Stanley Marsh planted 10 Cadillacs headlights down in a deserted stretch of dirt now known as **Cadillac Ranch** (I-40 btwn exits 60 & 62). He said he did it in a salute to Route 66. Visitors are always welcome to spray-paint on their own contributions to the art; the cars have even been painted pink in honor of breast-cancer awareness. Park along the south feeder road, a couple of miles west of Loop 335, and walk the well-worn path. As cool as it sounds, there's a sort of forlorn feel to the place.

The ground 'round here seems to be fertile for cars – 18 miles east of Amarillo in Conway, there are five VW bugs growing on **Bug Ranch** (Hwy 207, off 1-40).

White Elephant Saloon (☎ 817-624-1887; www .whiteelephantsaloon.com; 106 E Exchange Ave; ☎ 2pm-midnight Mon-Thu, to 2am Fri, noon-2am Sat, noon-midnight Sun) Stockyards cowboys have been bellying up to this bar since 1887 (now Tim Love owns it, too). Live country music nightly and weekend days.

THEATER & CLASSICAL PERFORMANCES

Bass Performance Hall (☎ 817-212-4325; www .basshall.com; 555 Commerce St) The glittery Bass Hall's theaters host everything from Mingo Fishtrap to the Will Rogers Follies. The symphony, ballet and opera also make their home here.

Getting There & Around

For more information about airport arrival, see p728.

BUS

Eleven buses a day make the one-hour trip ($9) from the downtown **Greyhound Bus Terminal** (☎ 817-429-3089; www.greyhound.com; 901 Commerce St) to Dallas.

The **Fort Worth Transit Authority** (The T; ☎ 817-215-8600; www.the-t.com) runs bus 1 to the Stockyards and bus 2 to the Cultural District, departing from the Transfer Center at Jones and 9th Sts. The fare costs $1.50 one way.

TRAIN

The *Texas Eagle* stops at the **Amtrak Station** (☎ 817-332-2931; www.amtrak.com; 1501 Jones St) en route to San Antonio or Chicago. Monday through Saturday the **Trinity Railway Express** (TRE; ☎ 817-215-8600; www.trinityrailwayexpress.com; T&P Station, 1600 Throckmorton St) connects downtown Fort Worth with downtown Dallas ($2.25, 1¼ hours).

PANHANDLE PLAINS

Angry black clouds gather on the horizon and seemingly seconds later hail, thunder and lightning are flashing down in a darn good imitation of judgement day. The endless, flat landscape, punctuated only by utility poles and windmills, produces some phenomenal weather, oil, and not much else. What's left of Route 66 scoots through Amarillo on the way west.

AMARILLO

Little remains of this once fabled stop on Route 66 – but there are a few quirky sights and the Big Texan steakhouse is as kitsch as they come. And the town is a convenient overnight for those driving across the US. To the south, Palo Duro Canyon is as surprising in this flat land as it is deep. Remember that this is cattle country; if the wind is blowing just right, that's the stockyards you smell.

Get oriented at the **visitor information center** (☎ 806-374-8474; www.visitamarillotx.com; cnr 4th Ave & Buchanan St; ☺ 9am-6pm Mon-Fri, 10am-4pm Sat & Sun). Old Route 66 here is most character filled along **W 6th Avenue**, also known as the San Jacinto District. Shopfronts from the 1920s sell everything from burgers and beer to books, hardware and antiques.

Stretch-Cadillac limos with steer-horn hood ornaments wait out front, marquee lights blink above, a shooting arcade pings inside the saloon, and a big tall Tex road sign welcomes you to **Big Texan Steak Ranch & Motel** (☎ 800-657-7177; www.bigtexan.com; 7700 I-40 E, exit 74; breakfast $6-17, lunch $9, mains $13-25; ☻). This cheesy roadside attraction first built on Route 66 is a love-it-or-hate-it kinda place. Billboards advertising the free 72oz steak contest start in Oklahoma (if you can't eat it – and all the side dishes – in an hour, the free steak costs $50). Cowboy troubadours serenade you while you eat, and the beef is surprisingly tender. A Texas-shaped cement pond (aka swimming pool) completes the over-the-top Old West theme at the motel (singles $45, doubles $60 to $65).

South on Rte 1541, 25 miles south of downtown Amarillo, the earth breaks away and really shows off in the **Palo Duro Canyon State Park** (☎ 806-488-2227; www.paloducanyon.com; Hwy 217; campsites $10-15, cabins $45-95, day pass $3). A fork of the Red River carved its way through multicolor caprock to create the second largest canyon in the US. A good paved road leads down to the floor and around a scenic 16-mile loop with hiking trails.

Amarillo has every chain hotel and restaurant you can think of, and then some, along I-40 (those west of town are newer). Faux painting and whimsical touches grace the rooms of the 1926 Spanish-colonial B&B **Casita del Sol** (☎ 806-342-3444; www.lacasitadelsol.com; 1607 S Harrison; r $105, ste $135;).

Greasy-spoon **Golden Light Café** (☎ 806-374-0097; 2908 W 6th Ave; mains $4-7; 11am-10pm Mon-Wed, to 11pm Thu-Sat) has been serving burgers, home-cut fries and cold beer to crowds on Route 66 since 1956.

Coaches leave from the **Greyhound Bus Terminal** (☎ 806-374-5371; www.greyhound.com; 700 S Tyler St) for Lubbock ($26, 2½ hours). Southwest and Continental Airlines fly into Amarillo International Airport, located on the eastern edge of town north of I-40 via exit 76.

WEST TEXAS

Tumbleweeds roll across dusty dry ground, cacti bloom in desert sands, endless skies contain blazing heat: West Texas is the stuff of Hollywood dreams. Drive along I-10 and there's a whole lotta nothin' to see.

Go south or north and it's a different story. Big Bend National Park – a moonscape of desert mountains and deep arroyos – is a river-running, mountain-hiking paradise. Outside the park, small-town surprises, like cutting-edge art installations and historic hotels, await. The state's tallest peaks rise from Guadalupe Mountains National Park, to the north. And in the far west, El Paso is a town in a whole different time zone from the rest of Texas.

BIG BEND

See the elbow of land poking into Mexico on the Texas map? That's the Big Bend area following the curve of the Rio Grande, and consequently the border. Mountains and valleys, Chihuahuan desert and limestone canyons make up the state and the national park that flank the river. You can tell you are in the middle of nowhere because gasoline is expensive, cell-phone coverage is minimal, and internet access is hard to find. About an hour and a half to the north of here there are towns with more services, thriving art colonies, Old West hotels, an astronomical observatory and several more state parks with great old Civilian Conservation Corps (CCC) lodgings.

This area has been likened to the devil's playground because of the summer heat – 102°F (39°C) average in July. The best times to visit are February to April and October to November. Midland-Odessa (150 miles northeast of Alpine) and El Paso (220 miles to the northwest) are the closest major airports to the area. Cheap sleeps are hard to find near Big Bend National Park. Alpine, 95 miles north of the park entrance, is the main base for gas and groceries. Marfa, Marathon and Alpine all have interesting places to stay. For more info, check out **Visit Big Bend** (www.visitbigbend.com).

TEXAS

IF YOU HAVE A FEW MORE DAYS...

And you're a big fan of rock and roll, head on out to Buddy Holly's birth (and burial) place, Lubbock. The **Buddy Holly Center** (☎ 806-767-2686; www.buddyhollycenter.org; 1801 Ave G; adult/child $5/3; 10am-5pm Mon-Fri, 11am-6pm Sat) details the career of the rocker whose plane went down in an Iowa snowstorm in 1959. Fans leave guitar picks at **Buddy Holly's grave** (Lubbock City Cemetery, cnr 31st St & Teak Ave). To get there, take a right when you get into the cemetery, and the modest headstone is on the left by the side of the road.

Otherwise, maybe Mac Davis had it right when he sang 'Happiness is Lubbock in my rearview mirror...'.

DON'T MISS

■ **Santa Elena Canyon** – Big Bend by foot or raft (below)

■ **McDonald Observatory** – almost touching the stars (p736)

■ **Marfa** – *Giant*, aliens and art (opposite)

■ **Gage Hotel** – out of an Old West novel (p736)

■ **Balmorhea State Park** – spring-fed swimming hole (p736)

Big Bend National Park

The Chisos Mountains rise up at the center of **Big Bend National Park** (☎ 432-477-2251; www.nps.gov/bibe; 7-day pass per vehicle $15, per motorcycle $5). To the west, the dramatic mesas and rock formations are the result of ancient volcanic activity. To the east of the mountains stretches desert habitat. The diverse geography in the 800,000 acres supports mountain lions and black bears, though you're more likely to see some of the 56 species of reptiles and more than 100 bird types. The park runs along the Rio Grande, but there's no legal access to Mexico here. River-rafting and other outdoor outfitters are based outside the park (see the boxed text, p736). The **Panther Junction Visitors Center** (☎ 915-477-2251; 8am-6pm) is along the main park road, 29 miles from the Persimmon Gap entrance gate south of Marathon, and 26 miles from the Maverick entrance at Study Butte. Gasoline is sold nearby.

Most of the 150-plus miles of hiking trails are in the Chisos Mountains, where the 14-mile **Rim Trail** has some challenging ascents, rewarded by mountain panoramas. Down in the desert, the 1.5-mile **Santa Elena Canyon Trail**, 40 miles southwest of Panther Junction, is one of the most popular treks because of the stunning rock and river views. It's rated easy, but you have to wade through a stream and climb stairs in the canyon wall. The adventurous (and ecoconscious) might seek out the trail that's left off maps. Hint: there are falls and lots of vegetation for the desert. Near Rio Grand Village, 20 miles southeast of the main visitor center, you can hike around some old bathhouses to the shallow **hot springs**.

The stone-and-wooden-beam cottages at **Chisos Mountain Lodge** (☎ 432-477-2291; http://chisos mountainslodge.com; lodge & motel r $94-99, cottages $115) are the most secluded of several lodging options (No 103 has the best view). Restaurant food here is so-so; better to pack a cooler ahead of time. The complex has a **visitor center** (8am-5pm) and a **camp store** (9am-9pm) with basic supplies. Nearby, **Chisos Basin Campground** (☎ 877-444-6777; www.recreation.gov; campsites $14) is the most popular in the park (it's cooler in summer and winter). No generators are allowed at **Cottonwood Campground** (☎ 877-444-6777; www.recreation.gov; campsites $14), on the desert road to Santa Elena, making it the quietest camping option.

Terlingua–Study Butte

Three miles east of the park boundary are two dusty little towns that run together at the junction of Hwy 118 and Route 170. Outfitters, a couple motels and a few restaurants line the roads. **Terlingua Ghost Town** (Rte 170 W) is a long-gone mining village where former stucco shanties have been converted into minihomes. The old general store sells a walking-tour map, arts and crafts, and books on sustainable living (most residents don't have electricity or running water). Buy a beer inside the store and hang out on the porch with locals at sunset.

Chisos Mining Company Motel (☎ 432-371-2554; www.cmcm.cc; Rte 170; s $49, d $62-80), about a mile west of Hwy 118, is the cheapest choice around, though it's really basic (no TV in some rooms). You can sleep in exquisite little self-contained rooms constructed brick by handmade brick at **La Posada Milagro** (☎ 432-371-3044; www.laposadamilagro.com; r $145-165;) in the ghost town, off Ivey St, up from the store. Nearby, the **Starlight Theatre** (☎ 432-371-2326; Ivey St; mains $15-2; 5-10pm) has been resurrected as a lively restaurant.

Part food stand, part roadside attraction, the bright-pink **Kathy's Kosmic Kowgirl Kafe** (☎ 432-371-2164; Rte 170; meals $3-7; 6:30am-5:30pm Thu-Sun), about a mile west of Hwy 118, sometimes shows movies and has campfires at night.

Lajitas to Presidio

Leaving Terlingua, you first come to **Lajitas** (☎ 877-525-4827; www.lajitas.com; r $195-330;), which looks like a town but is actually all one resort that you never have to leave. On-site outfitters arrange adventures, and you can rejuvenate at the spa, then choose between six dining outlets. Play golf here and the '19th hole' is Mexico across the river (no, you won't get your ball back). There's even a private runway for your jet. **Lajitas Stables** (☎ 432-371-2212; www.lajitasstables.com; Rte 170; 2hr rides $60), 3 miles west of town, guides riders along mesas and mountains outside area parks.

Big Bend Ranch State Park (☎ 432-229-3416; www.tpwd.state.tx.us; off Rte 170; day pass $3, campsites $3) is much less explored than its big brother. But the easily accessed turnouts for hiking or picnicking along the river road shouldn't be ignored. Make the easy 0.7-mile trek into narrow **Closed Canyon**, where the cliffs rise above you, blocking out the sun. Camping is off Casa Piedra Rd; you have to register at the **Fort Leaton State Historic Site** (☎ 432-229-3613; www.tpwd.state.tx.us; Rte 170; camping $3, fort admission $2; ⏱ 8:30am-4:30pm). Past the park, **Presidio** is a dreary border town with not much else to do other than cross into Mexico. From there, Marfa is 60 miles north on US 67.

Alpine

There ain't much to see in Alpine (population 6000), but it's the biggest town in Big Bend – and the only one with chain motels, numerous restaurants, grocery stores and public transportation. From here, the national park is 90 miles south, Marfa is 20 miles west, Marathon 18 miles east and Fort Davis 17 miles northwest. Tall tales are told at Sul Ross State University's **Cowboy Poetry Gathering** (☎ 432-364-2490; www.cowboy-poetry.org) in February. You can get regionwide information at the **Alpine Chamber of Commerce** (☎ 432-837-2326; www.alpinetexas.com; 106 N 3rd St; ⏱ 9am-5pm Mon-Fri, 10am-2pm Sun).

White-stucco-and-red-tile cottages circle around a grassy lawn in true '50s motorcourt style at **Antelope Lodge** (☎ 432-837-2451; 2310 W Hwy 90; s $36-49, d $41-59; wi-fi) – the best

bargain in Big Bend (say that five times). **Maverick Inn** (☎ 432-837-0628; www.themaverickinn.com; 1200 E Holland Ave; r $85-135) also has adobe but is a bit more upscale, dressed in its New Mexico–style Southwestern flair. Dig into super-fresh pizzas and pastas or just order a coffee and use the wi-fi at the friendly **La Trattoria** (☎ 432-837-2200; 202 W Holland; mains $7-14; ⏱ 11am-3pm Mon, Wed, Thu & Sun, 11am-3pm & 6-9pm Tue, Fri & Sat).

The town has limited **Greyhound** (☎ 800-231-2222; www.greyhound.com) bus service. The Florida–California *Sunset Limited* stops at the **Amtrak Station** (☎ 800-872-7245; www.amtrak.com; 102 W Holland St). Buy tickets on board; there's no ticket office. Arrivals are often delayed until the middle of the night by freight traffic. If you want to rent a car, you're stuck with **Alpine Auto Rental** (☎ 432-837-3463; www.alpineautorental.com; 414 E Holland Ave; from $35 a day).

Marfa

The unlikely home to art and aliens (maybe), Marfa was named by a settler after a character in the book she was reading when she arrived, Dostoevsky's *Brothers Karamazov*. The town's fame came when James Dean, Elizabeth Taylor and Rock Hudson filmed *Giant*, a Texas classic, here in 1955. The cast and crew stayed at the 1930s-era **Hotel Paisano** (☎ 866-729-3669; www.hotelpaisano.com; cnr N Highland & West Sts; r $99-149). There's movie memorabilia around the lobby and a high-class dinner-only restaurant on site. Ask the nice desk clerks; they'll probably let you poke around upstairs if the housekeepers are cleaning.

In 1986, New York artist Donald Judd created the sprawling **Chinati Foundation** (☎ 432-729-4362; www.chinati.org; off Hwy 67; adult/child $10/5; ⏱ tours 10am & 2pm Wed-Sat) complex of minimalist art half a mile south of town. The installation morphed this small desert town into an artists' enclave.

And then there are those lights so many have claimed to see off US 90 (see p737).

Marfa Gliders (☎ 800-667-9464; www.flygliders.com; Marfa airport, Hwy 17; glider rides $110) takes you soaring near the Davis Mountains. On clear days you can see Mexico. Reservations required.

If mod is your mode, you'll want to stay at the **Thunderbird** (☎ 432-729-1984; www.thunderbirdmarfa.com; US 90 W; r $125-175; ✕ 🐾 ⚟). The hip motel lures you in with retro appeal that has been likened to 'cowboy Zen' – platform beds and

---

SCENIC DRIVES: ROUTE 170

West of Lajitas, Rte 170 hugs the Rio Grande through some of the most spectacular and remote scenery in Big Bend country. This river road takes you through a lunar landscape of low desert arroyos, sweeping vistas and rugged mountains (at one point there's a 15% grade, the maximum allowable).

OUTDOOR ACCESS

Most people see Big Bend from a road or a trail. But there are some captivating perspectives you can only get with an outfitter's help. Several companies lead multihour to multiday river-rafting (in high enough water) or canoeing trips through the canyons. (The river flows principally in fall and winter; in the summer it can be just a trickle.) The guides at **Big Bend River Tours** (☎ 432-371-3033; www.bigbendrivertours.com; Rte 170), just west of Hwy 118, have floated the river more than a time or two themselves. For a short trip, choose Santa Elena Canyon (half-day $125). If you have four days, take the remote, 33-mile Bouquillas Canyon trip ($580) – no other people, just great rock formations and hiking.

Active, do-it-yourself types should check out **Desert Sports** (☎ 432-371-2727; www.desertsportstx .com; Rte 170), 5 miles west of Hwy 118; it rents canoes ($45 per day), bikes ($30) and tents ($10). Staff will also shuttle you in your car or theirs to river-launch and pick-up points ($45 to $60). Hike and bike tours are available.

The **Far Flung Outdoor Center** (☎ 432-371-2633; www.farflungoutdoorcenter.com; Rte 170 at Hwy 118) staff isn't always the most helpful, but the place does rent Jeeps ($125 per day) and have tons of guided expeditions.

faux-cowskin rugs. Pop into **Marfa Book Company** (☎ 429-729-2906; 105 S Highland Ave; ⏰ 9am-9pm) to look for local titles or to have a coffee.

Fort Davis

False-front wooden buildings, an old fort and a stellar observatory make Texas' tallest town (elevation 5000ft) a Big Bend must-see. The temperature can be a delightful 10°F to 20°F (6°C to 12°C) cooler here than in the national park, 120 miles to the south.

Atop Mt Locke (6791ft), **McDonald Observatory** (☎ 432-426-3640; www.mcdonaldobservatory.org; Hwy 118; daytime pass adult/child $8/7; ⏰ 10am-5:30pm) has a perfect vantage point for seeing stars. Take a daytime tour and do some solar viewing, or attend an evening **star party** (adult/child $10/8; ⏰ 7:30pm Tue, Fri & Sat Apr-Aug, 9:30pm Nov-Mar). The observatory is 16 steep miles northwest of town. On the way, 2 miles west of town, 24 intact buildings from the 1880s make up **Fort Davis National Historic Site** (☎ 432-426-3224; www.nps.gov/foda; Hwy 118; 7-day pass $3; ⏰ 8am-5pm). You can hike (or drive) the 3 miles further west from there to **Davis Mountains State Park** (☎ 432-426-3337; www.tpwd.state.tx.us; Hwy 118; day pass adult/child $3/free, campsites $9-16). Here the 1930s adobe buildings at **Indian Lodge** (☎ 432-426-3254; www.tpwd.state.tx.us; Hwy 118; r $75-90; ☒ ☄) were built as part of a Depression-era CCC project. Rooms have been renovated, with pine-log ceilings complementing burgundy and green Southwestern hues.

A few shops line the main street in town, and **Hotel Limpia** (☎ 432-426-3237; www.hotellimpia .com; Town Sq, Hwy 118; r $69-110; ☒ ☄ wi-fi) sprawls across several of the buildings. Across from the courthouse, **Murphy's Pizzeria & Cafe** (☎ 432-426-2020; Hwy 118; mains $5-9; ⏰ 11am-9pm Mon-Sat) serves light meals as well as personal-size pizzas.

Native Americans have known about the springs at modern-day **Balmorhea State Park** (☎ 432-375-2370; Hwy 17, off I-10; www.tpwd.state .tx.us; day pass $7; ☒ ☄ wi-fi), 37 miles north of Fort Davis, since ancient times. In the 1930s the CCC came along and created a mighty-fine swimming hole by walling off some of the flow to make a 72°F to 76°F (22°C to 24°C) pool. More water was diverted to create a desert wetland. The CCC also built an adobe motel (rooms $55 to $70) that is still in operation.

Marathon

The historic rooms at the **Gage Hotel** (☎ 432-386-4205; www.gagehotel.com; 101 US 90, Marathon; r $99-182; ☒ ☄) come straight out of Old West pulp fiction. Wide wooden blinds cover the windows, and saddle blankets drape across the raised log beds. There are ear plugs for the 1st-floor, shared-bathroom rooms ($76, no TV or phone) for a reason. Old wood reverberates, and the rich and ranchlike lobby is just down the hall. Newer cabana-style adobe suites have Mexican-tile floors, fireplaces and outdoor patios facing a lush courtyard. A few doors down, associated **Café Cenzio** (mains $17-20; ⏰ 6pm-10pm) whips up gourmet renditions of Texas faves – chicken-fried venison, anyone? This is roughing it luxury style. Marathon is 58 miles north of Big Bend National Park and isn't much more than the hotel and **Front Street Books** (☎ 915-386-4249; 145 US 90), where you can procure some of those Western novels. It has a large selection of area history, too.

EL PASO

Well, you've made it. You're just about as far west in Texas as you can go. Here you're closer to Santa Fe than Austin; and Mexico – New and old – holds more sway than the Texas capital. The pass for which the city is named, El Paso del Norte, has for centuries been a key route across the Americas. (Mexican revolutionary Pancho Villa holed up here for a time.) There's still a lot of commerce of people and goods; across the Rio Grande from this town of 609,000, almost two million more people live in Ciudad Juárez, Mexico. Developers have spiffed up much of downtown El Paso, though derelict areas do remain. The Franklin Mountains rise from desert flatlands to form a dramatic backdrop to the city. Take advantage of all the biculturalness and beauty by day-tripping to Mexico, shopping for handcrafted boots, riding the cable car and, by all means, eating some enchiladas.

Orientation & Information

The Franklin Mountains pin the downtown area against the border and cleave the rest of the city along I-10 into the eastern, airport area and the western side near the University of Texas at El Paso (UTEP) and New Mexico. Note that El Paso is in the Mountain time zone, one hour behind the rest of the state. Downtown, **El Paso Public Library** (☎ 915-544-6772; 501 N Oregon; ☺ 9am-8pm Mon-Thu,

---

WHAT THE...?

It's a bird! It's a plane! It's an alien encounter! No one really knows what the famous Marfa lights are (or aren't, for that matter). The mysterious glowballs in the sky appear occasionally to dance in the distance. The first sighting was recorded in 1883, and scientists have been tracking the phenomenon to no avail ever since. Attempt to check it out at the Marfa Lights Viewing Site, 8 miles east of town on US 90. Come prepared to wait all night; there's no schedule (the lights have been spotted between dusk and dawn) and no promises.

---

to 6pm Fri & Sat, 1-5pm Sun) has free internet access. The **El Paso Visitors Center** (☎ 915-534-0601, 800-351-6024; www.visitelpaso.com; Civic Center, Santa Fe St; ☺ 8am-5pm Mon-Fri) is small, but the staff's quite helpful.

Sights & Activities

The soul of El Paso is downtown by the border, where the streets are crowded with discount clothing stores (shoppers come *in* from Mexico, too) and people waiting for buses. The core also has a couple art and history museums, and the Plaza Theatre is once again beating at its heart.

Across the border, **Ciudad Juárez** is no tiny tourist town. The best way not to get lost (and to rest your legs) is to hop on the Border Jumper run by the **El Paso-Juárez Trolley Co** (☎ 915-544-0061; www.borderjumper.com; 1 Civic Center Plaza; adult/child $12.50/9; ☺ 10am-4pm by reservation). Buses depart from near the visitor center and make seven stops (get off and on at will). That way you get to see the cathedral and some of the town – leather factories, meat markets – in addition to shopping. The other option is to park and walk across the Santa Fe St bridge (25¢ each way for pedestrians) onto Av Juárez, the city's main tourist strip. Taking a car across the border is not recommended; theft is common.

Ride the **Wyler Aerial Tramway** (☎ 915-566-6622; www.tpwd.state.tx.us; 1700 McKinley Ave; adult/child $7/4; ☺ noon-6pm Mon, Thu & Sun, to 8pm Fri & Sat) to the top of 5632ft Ranger Peak for a panorama of sprawling Juárez, the Franklin Mountains and on into New Mexico. Threading through the desert hills are 118 miles of hiking trails in **Franklin Mountains State Park** (☎ 915-566-6441; www.tpwd.state.tx.us; Transmountain Rd; day pass $3; ☺ 8am-5pm Mon-Fri, to 8pm Sat & Sun Apr-Oct), 4 miles east of I-10.

It's not really set up for tourists, but diehard history buffs might enjoy the lower valley's **Mission Trail**. A driving route southeast of town connects the shells of several early Spanish missions on the Tigua reservation. Take I-10 east to the Zaragoza exit, turn right and follow signs.

Sleeping

La Hacienda Travelodge (☎ 915-772-4231; www .travelodge.com; 6400 Montana Ave; r $53-60; ☒ ☐ wifi) Barrel-tile roofs, courtyard greenery and wooden-plank doors provide loads of Spanish character at this motel. Street noise leaks into some rooms; all have microwaves and minifridges.

Hilton Garden Inn (☎ 915-351-2121; 111 W University Ave; r $89-94; ☒ ☒ ☐ wi-fi) Opened at the edge of UTEP, the Garden Inn was built to blend with campus architecture. So of course it resembles a Bhutanese *dzong*, or religious fortress (architects thought the style fit the Southwestern mountain landscape). The inside is more nice chain hotel than exotic monastery.

Camino Real (☎ 915-534-3000; www.caminoreal.com/elpaso; 101 S El Paso St; r $99-159; ☒ ☐) A stained-glass, two-story dome soars above the bar, and a pool graces the rooftop in this 1912 landmark hotel. Maintenance could be a bit better, though.

Eating & Drinking

Clearly, Mexican is the food of choice in El Paso; the town's known for a special bright-red chili-and-tomato sauce used on enchiladas. El Paso's mini entertainment district is two blocks of restaurants and bars around Cincinnati St between Mesa and Stanton, not far from UTEP.

L&J Café & Bar (☎ 915-566-8418; 3622 E Missouri; mains $5-12; ☽ kitchen 10am-8pm, bar to 2am) The town's best salsa and fresh chips start you off, but everything served at this friendly Tex-Mex bar is tasty.

Casa Jurado (☎ 915-532-6435; 226 Cincinnati Ave; lunch $5-7, dinner mains $6-15; ☽ 11am-10pm) Modern Mexican: choose from different sauces and stuffings, including vegetarian options like *calabacita* (Mexican squash), on the mixed enchilada plate.

Geo Geske (☎ 915-772-0066; Kern Pl, 2701 Stanton; mains lunch $9-16, dinner $16-31; ☽ 11am-2:30pm & 5-10pm Mon-Sat, 5-10pm Sun) Hot and hip: Geo Geske's salads are topped with ingredients

like lobster sashimi. G2 bar next door is a happenin' hangout.

Also recommended:

H&H Car Wash (☎ 915-533-1144; 701 E Yandell Ave; mains $3-7; ☽ 7am-3pm) Tiny hole-in-the-wall diner attached to a hand car wash.

Ardovino's Desert Crossing (☎ 505-589-0653; 1 Ardovino Dr, Sunland Park, NM; mains $10-20; ☽ 5-10:30pm Wed-Fri, 11am-3pm & 5-10:30pm Sat, 3-9pm Sun) Vintage landmark restaurant (and bar, and farmers market) across the other border.

Entertainment

Live music is pretty limited. For cultural and event listings, pick up the free weekly **What's Up** (www.whatsup-ep.com) or the Friday *Tiempo* supplement to the **El Paso Times** (www.elpasotimes.com).

Plaza Theatre (☎ 915-534-0600; www.theplazatheatre.org; 125 Pioneer Plaza) Tiny twinkling lights replicate stars and faux vines cling to Spanish courtyard walls: this elaborate theater under the stars is all indoors. The Plaza was open originally from 1930–70, and it was restored and reopened in 2007. You can once again see plays, concerts and shows at this downtown landmark.

Shopping

Cross the border for Mexican art, craft and alcohol shopping in Juárez. El Paso is also known for boot making (see the boxed text, opposite).

Getting There & Around

El Paso International Airport (☎ 915-780-4749; www.elpasointernationalairport.com), 8 miles northeast of downtown off I-10, services 16American and two Mexican cities. Chain rental-car companies are on site (you really need a car here).

BORDERLANDS

Que paso? Nada, man. All across the state Mex mixes with Tex culture and gringos use Mexican phrases. But the chance to cross into Mexico proper is a bonus if you're visiting El Paso or the Southern Gulf Coast. It may only be $5 cheaper to buy a woven blanket or silver earrings in Mexico, but the experience – the colorful commotion, the more-sour-than-sweet margaritas – is worth a detour. Just don't expect to delve deep into the culture along the border.

The tragedy of Mexican women disappearing in Ciudad Juárez has not affected travelers. (*The Daughters of Juarez*, by Teresa Rodriguez, is a provocative read.) Gang violence continues in Nuevo Laredo, which should be avoided. As early as mid-2008, US regulations could require anyone walking or driving across the border (both US citizens and foreign nationals) to have a passport. Prior to that, citizens need only have an official picture ID. You can't bring fruit into the US, or most drugs, and only 1L of alcohol per person is duty free.

GIVE 'EM THE BOOT

Savvy shoppers from around the world (not to mention Julia Roberts and Dwight Yoakam) fly in to get their feet custom fitted for some fine-feeling leather. You may not be able to round up the $800 to $3000 a pair costs, but make an appointment to visit **Rocketbuster Boots** (☎ 915-541-1300; 115 S Antony St; www.rocketbuster.com) and you'll see what all the fuss is about. The creative concordance of vintage-inspired art – '50s-era pin-up cowgirls, smiling Day of the Dead skeletons – with fine hand-tooling is stunning. This is no shop; it's a multihued museum of Americana (with the record-holding 'World's Biggest Boots' on display). Owner-designer Nevena Christi gladly shows you around. You can pick up leather pillows and boot-shaped Christmas stockings for just $75 to $300.

Numerous other custom bootmakers work around town (and in Juárez); **Caboots** (☎ 915-544-1855; www.caboots.com; 501 S Cotton St; ⊙ 9am-5pm Mon-Fri) has a few premade pairs for around $300. Or you could bargain-shop at the several megamanufacturers' local outlet centers, such as **Justin Boots** (☎ 915-779-5465; I-10 at Hawkins).

Amtrak's Florida–California *Sunset Limited* stops at **Union Depot** (☎ 915-545-2247; www.amtrak.com; 700 San Francisco Ave). The **Greyhound Bus Station** (☎ 915-532-2365; www.greyhound.com; 200 W San Antonio St) sends coaches to Albuquerque, NM ($38, six to eight hours), daily.

Sun Metro (☎ 915-533-3333; www.sunmetro.org) runs two entertainment trolley routes (25¢) to transport folks around downtown and up to Cincinnati St.

HUECO TANKS STATE HISTORIC SITE

About 32 miles east of El Paso off US 62/180, the Hueco Tanks (pronounced *wey*-co) have attracted humans for as many as 10,000 years – as evidenced by area pictographs. Three small granite mountains are pocked with depressions (*hueco* is Spanish for 'hollow') that hold rainwater, creating an oasis in the barren desert. Today the 860-acre park is a magnet for rock climbers. **Park Headquarters** (☎ 915-849-6684, central reservations 512-389-8900; www.tpwd.state.tx.us; Rte 2775; day pass $4, campsites $10-12; ⊙ 8am-6pm) has a small gift shop, a nearby interpretive center and 20 campsites (17 with electricity and water). To minimize human impact, a daily visitor quota is enforced; make reservations 24 hours in advance to gain entry. You can explore the North Mountain area by yourself, but to hike deeper into the park – where the more interesting pictographs are – you have to reserve and join one of the free **pictograph tours** (⊙ 9am & 11am Wed-Sun May-Sep, 10:30am & 2pm daily Oct-Apr).

GUADALUPE MOUNTAINS NATIONAL PARK

At 8749ft, remote Guadalupe Peak is the highest point in Texas. Winter photos of snow-covered succulents seem incongruous and amazing. McKittrick Canyon has the state's best autumn foliage and impressive spring wildflower displays. That said, it's not easy to get here. The closest motels are in Whites City, near Carlsbad Caverns National Park (p894), about 35 miles to the north in New Mexico. El Paso is 120 miles to the west.

The **Headquarters Visitors Center** (☎ 915-828-3251; www.nps.gov/gumo; 7-day pass $5, campsites $8; ⊙ 8am-6pm Jun-Aug, to 4:30pm rest of yr), off US 62/180 at Pine Springs, has RV and tent camping. The strenuous trek from the visitor-center parking lot to **Guadalupe Peak** is an 8.5-mile round trip that gains 3000ft in elevation. Of the 80 miles of trails, the best easy day hike is **McKittrick Canyon Trail** (⊙ 8am-4:30pm), off US 62/180, a 6.8-mile round trip. The trailhead is 11 miles northeast of the visitor center.

To get to the park's northern segment, **Dog Canyon**, you have to take Hwy 137 into New Mexico. Ten backcountry campsites dot the park, and overnight hikers must obtain a free permit there. No water is available in the backcountry. No gasoline, dump stations, food or beverages are available anywhere in the park.

TEXAS

Rocky Mountains

One hundred years ago a vacation to the Rocky Mountains was the doctor's tonic of choice when it came to treating everything from tuberculosis to fatigue and depression. Perhaps today's practitioners should learn a lesson from their predecessors, and start writing prescriptions for 'Going West' rather than Zoloft.

Colorado, Wyoming, Montana and Idaho are so gorgeous, so packed with adventures, so bright and sunny and blue it's impossible to stay bummed inside their borders. The region is fat with wildlife and towering mountains (think black bear in suburban swimming pools, an elk traffic jam heading into Rocky Mountain National Park). And there are enough adrenalin sports to satiate the most hard-core fanatic (think rafting Idaho's untamed Salmon River or driving cattle on horseback and sleeping under star-studded Montana skies).

The local population's eccentricities alone are enough to leave a sociologist salivating: Evangelical Christians, patriotic militiamen, ranchers, new-age hippies, movie stars, ski-bums, pot-heads and even aliens (so swear the hard-core UFO recorders), all share the same high, alpine air. Throw in a couple good ghost stories (Mesa Verde's sun bleached ruins are a good place to start); add a few history lessons (ride the cog railroad to Pike's Peak's summit, the inspiration behind 'America the Beautiful'); and you'll quickly discover why these mountain states, where the brews, bear and bike trails are as big as the snowcapped peaks and raging rivers, are so all-around irresistible.

HIGHLIGHTS

- Discovering **Silverton** (p771); Colorado's best kept secret is a true Wild West town where streets are unpaved and the 4WDing is stupendous.

- Scouting for geysers and grizzlies in magnificent **Yellowstone National Park** (p781).

- Going cowboy in lively **Missoula** (p792), which is bursting with outdoor adventures.

- Wild rafting down Idaho's untamed **Salmon River** (p800).

- Tuning into **Boulder's** (p753) yuppie crunch, a place where bikes and brews rule and locals seem not to bother with work.

- Chilling in a hot mineral spring amid Colorado's most gorgeous scenery in **Ouray** (p772).

- Rock climbing (then rocking out at the Lander Bar) in Wyoming's up-and-coming adventure destination **Lander** (p780).

- Hiking past ice-blue lakes in pristine and remote **Glacier National Park** (p795).

- Listening to the ancestors whisper at **Mesa Verde National Park's** (p776) ancient cliff dwellings.

HISTORY

Before the late 18th century when French trappers and Spaniards stepped in, the Rocky Mountain area was a land of many tribes, including the Nez Percé, the Shoshone, the Crow, the Lakota and the Utes.

Meriwether Lewis and William Clark claimed their enduring fame after the USA bought almost all of present-day Montana, Wyoming and eastern Colorado in the Louisiana Purchase in 1803. The two explorers set out to survey the land, covering 8000 miles in three years. Their success urged on other adventurers, and soon the migration was in motion. Wagon trains voyaged to the mountainous lands into the 20th century, only temporarily slowed by the completion of the Transcontinental Railroad across southern Wyoming in the late 1860s.

To accommodate settlers, the USA purged the western frontier of the Spanish, British and, in a truly shameful era, most of the Native American population. The government signed endless treaties to defuse Native American objections to increasing settlement, but always reneged and shunted tribes onto smaller reservations. Gold miners' incursions into Native American territory in Montana and the building of US Army forts along the Bozeman Trail ignited a series of wars with the Lakota, Cheyenne, Arapaho and others.

Gold and silver mania preceded Colorado's entry to statehood in 1876. Statehood soon followed for Montana (1889), Wyoming (1890) and Idaho (1890). Along with miners, white farmers and ranchers were the people with power in the late 19th century.

Mining, grazing and timber played major roles in the area's economic development, sparking the growth of cities and towns to provide financial and industrial support. They also subjected the region to boom-and-bust cycles by unsustainable use of resources and left a legacy of environmental disruption.

After the economy boomed post-WWII, the national parks started attracting vacationers. Tourism is now a leading industry in all four states, with the military – there is a major presence in Colorado especially – trailing not far behind.

LOCAL CULTURE

The Rocky Mountain states are the kind of places where die-hard, bleeding red, pistol toting Republicans down pints with stoned-out trustafarians. In Aspen's and Jackson's trendy après-ski boozing holes you'll find plenty of rich kids decked out in Burton's latest snow gear, toting Chanel and Vuitton on their gym-toned shoulders, sipping microbrews and swapping ski stories. But in blue-collar Billings and patriotic Colorado Springs, the talk is all about the war – the sons, wives and buddies fighting in Iraq. The clientele in Montana and Wyoming's Wild West saloons (where the smell of two centuries young gunpowder lingers amid the stench of cigarette smoke and hamburger grease) is a mix of leathery old cowboys and new agers – heavy on the crystal pendants and karmic evolutionary talks.

The locals here can be a finicky crew. Some are as friendly as mom's apple pie. Others are more wary, worried about the gringo or the California transplant maybe out to steal the family plot of harsh, sweat-stained ranch land.

When it comes to the Rockies, there's some local lingo you just must know: ask what kind of microbrew (a locally produced beer, usually made in small batches) is on tap at the pub. Be careful before ordering the Rocky Mountain Oysters – that's Old West talk for fried bull testicles, something we still can't appreciate after more than a decade in the region!

LAND & CLIMATE

While complex, the physical geography of the region divides conveniently into two principal features: the Rocky Mountains proper and the Great Plains. Extending from Alaska's Brooks Range and Canada's Yukon Territory all the way to Mexico, the Rockies sprawl northwest to southeast, from the steep escarpment of Colorado's Front Range westward to Nevada's Great Basin. Their towering peaks and ridges form the Continental Divide: to the west, waters flow to the Pacific; to the east, toward the Atlantic and the Gulf of Mexico.

For many travelers, the Rockies are a summer destination, and it starts to feel summery around June. The warm weather generally lasts until about mid-September. The winter, which brings in packs of powder hounds, doesn't usually hit until late November, though snowstorms can start in the mountains as early as September. Winter usually lasts until March or early April. In the mountains, the weather is constantly changing (snow in summer is not uncommon), so always be prepared. Fall, when the aspens flaunt their fall gold, or spring, when wildflowers bloom, are wonderful times to visit.

ROCKY MOUNTAINS

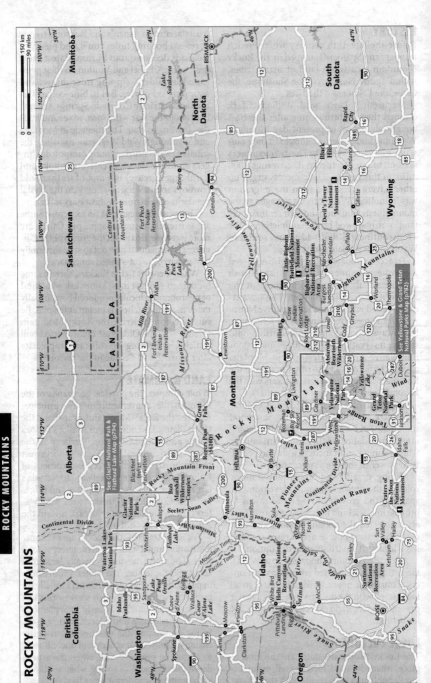

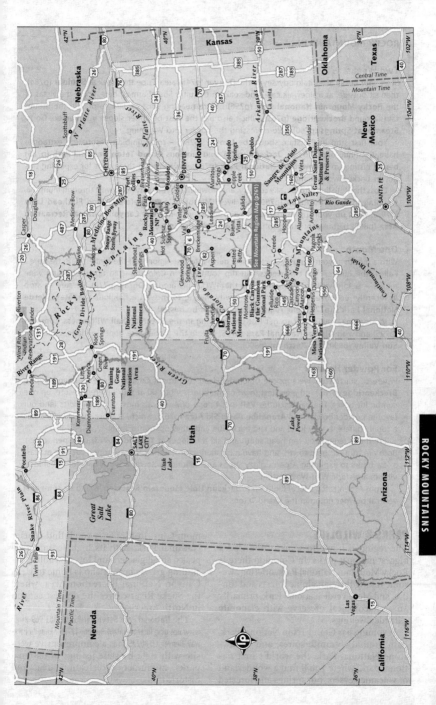

ROCKY MOUNTAINS IN...

Two Weeks

Start your Rocky Mountain odyssey in the **Denver** (p746) area. Tube the creek at **Boulder** (p754), then sit outside, at a sidewalk café, and soak up the ultra-liberal atmosphere. Enjoy the vistas of the **Rocky Mountain National Park** (p756) before heading west on I-70 to play in the mountains around **Breckenridge** (p763), which also has the best beginner slopes in Colorado. Go to **Steamboat Springs** (p760) before crossing the border into Wyoming.

Your first stop in the state should be **Lander** (p780) – rock-climbing destination extraordinaire. Continue north to chic **Jackson** (p786) and fabulous **Grand Teton National Park** (p785) before hitting up **Yellowstone National Park** (p781). Save at least three days for exploring this geyser-packed wonderland.

Cross the state line into 'big sky country' and slowly make your way northwest through Montana, stopping in funky **Bozeman** (p789) and lively **Missoula** (p792) before visiting **Flathead Lake** (p793). Wind up your trip in Idaho. Get your outdoor fix in **Hells Canyon National Recreation Area** (p802) before continuing to up-and-coming **Boise** (p798).

One Month

With a month at your hands, you can really delve into the region's off-the-beaten-path treasures. Follow the itinerary for two weeks, but dip southwest in Colorado – an up-and-coming wine region – before visiting Wyoming. Ride the 4WD trails around **Ouray** (p772). Be sure to stop in recently rediscovered **Rico** (p776), a rowdy mining town with a fabulous spa. **Mesa Verde National Park's** (p776) eerie ruins also should not be missed.

In Montana, you'll want to get lost backpacking in the **Bob Marshall Wilderness Complex** (p795) and visit **Glacier National Park** (p795) before the glaciers are gone. In Idaho, check out **Sun Valley** (p800) and **Ketchum** (p800).

For Powder Hounds

Where to start? Well, we suppose Colorado. Head to Summit County, where you can sleep in **Breckenridge** (p763) – the liveliest town of the bunch – but ski at four different resorts on one combo lift ticket. The pass includes **Vail** (p764), one of America's most famous resorts (and our favorite powder bowls); and **Arapahoe Basin Ski Area** (p763), which, at more than 13,000ft, has a totally different, very local and laid-back vibe and stays open into June!

From this region you can head south and ski the slopes at **Telluride** (p773) or **Aspen** (p765). Both are true old gold towns, and have a bit more attitude than Vail. Be sure to devote at least a few hours to exploring Aspen's glitzy shops and Telluride's down-to-earth bars for a real local vibe in a historic Wild West setting.

From Aspen catch a local flight up to **Jackson Hole Mountain Resort** (p787) to do some real vertical powder riding in the Grand Tetons.

PARKS & WILDLIFE

The region is home to some of the USA's biggest national parks. In Colorado there is Rocky Mountain National Park, offering awesome hiking through alpine forests and tundra, and Mesa Verde National Park, primarily an archaeological preserve with elaborate cliffside dwellings.

Wyoming has Grand Teton National Park, with dramatic granite spires, and Yellowstone National Park, the world's first national park, where you'll find a wonderland of volcanic geysers, hot springs and forested mountains. In Montana you'll find Glacier National Park, with its high sedimentary peaks, small glaciers and lots of wildlife, including grizzly bear. Idaho is home to Hells Canyon National Recreation Area, where the Snake River carves the deepest canyon in North America.

The **National Park Service** (NPS; ☎ 303-969-2500; www.nps.gov; Intermountain Region, 12795 Alameda Parkway, Denver, CO 80225) has a comprehensive website with state-by-state listings of national parks, monuments, recreation areas and historic trails.

The **US Forest Service** (☎ 303-275-5350; www .fs.fed.us; Rocky Mountain Regional Office, 740 Simms St, Box 25127 Lakewood, CO 80225) has visitors information on its website. Reserve Forest Service camp-sites at www.reserveusa.com, or by calling ☎ 877-444-6777; a reservation fee ($9) is charged.

The Rockies are home to all the USA's big animals – grizzly, black bear, mountain lion, buffalo and even the elusive wolf and lynx all roam the mountains. You will also find bighorn sheep, mountain goats and plenty of deer. The larger animals tend to stick to the parks and wild areas, but with the rapid human encroachment into their homeland, more and more hungry bear and even moun-tain lion are showing up in urban backyards, poaching from suburban dumpsters.

INFORMATION

For information on state parks check out the following web sites. Online camping reserva-tions can be made for Colorado, Wyoming and Idaho state parks, but no reservations are taken for Montana's state parks.

Colorado State Parks (☎ 303-470-1144, 800-678-2267; www.parks.state.co.us)

Idaho State Parks & Recreation (☎ 208-334-4199; www.idahoparks.org)

Montana Fish, Wildlife & Parks (☎ 406-444-2535; www.fwp.state.mt.us)

Wyoming State Parks & Historic Sites (☎ 877-996-7275; www.wyo-park.com)

GETTING THERE & AROUND

Denver International Airport (DIA; www.flydenver.com; 8500 Peña Blvd) is the main hub – and the popular budget favorite Southwest Airlines now flies

out of here. From Denver you can fly to the small airports dotting the area. Salt Lake City (p859) also has connections with destinations in all four states.

Greyhound (☎ 800-231-2222; www.greyhound.com) has fixed bus routes throughout the Rockies. **TNM&O** (Texas New Mexico Coaches Inc; ☎ 719-635-1505; www.greyhound.com) is affiliated with Greyhound, and serves the same lines through Colorado and parts of Wyoming. **Powder River Coach USA** (☎ 800-442-3682) primarily serves eastern Wyoming, but also goes to Denver, Billings and Rapid City, SD. **Rimrock Stages** (☎ 800-255-7655; www.rimrocktrailways.com) serves Montana destinations.

The following **Amtrak** (☎ 800-872-7245; www .amtrak.com) services run to and around the region:

California Zephyr Daily between Emeryville, CA (in San Francisco Bay Area), and Chicago, IL, with six stops in Colorado, including Denver, Fraser-Winter Park, Glenwood Springs and Grand Junction.

Empire Builder Runs daily from Seattle, WA, or Portland, OR, to Chicago, IL, with 12 stops in Montana (including Whitefish and East and West Glacier) and one stop in Idaho at Sandpoint.

Southwest Chief Links Los Angeles and Chicago; stops in the southern Colorado towns of Trinidad, La Junta and Lamar.

The Rockies are vast and public transpor-tation is limited, so it's most convenient to have your own wheels. Following are some examples of distances:

Denver to Durango, CO 338 miles.

Denver, CO, to Yellowstone National Park, WY 590 miles.

Boise, ID, to Bozeman, MT 477 miles.

HOT TOPIC: WATER

Water is the hottest topic in the West these days. Sit around the town breakfast joint long enough and you're bound to hear the word sliding off someone's tongue. Where is it going? And how little of it is there? These are the two main questions. The region as a whole has been in a severe drought for years now, and water rationing is no joke. While the winter of 2007 saw the highest snowfall tallies in years for much of the region, the drought, environmentalists say, is far from over. There are less lawn watering restrictions now than two years ago, but that could change at any moment. Locals understand water is a precious commodity in this rugged region, and restrictions are no joke and bound to be put back in place in the future – many restaurants still serve water only upon request.

On top of a drought, the Rocky Mountain states also have to cope with the fact that much of the water they do manage to collect isn't sticking around. Due to centuries-old laws, much of the water in the Colorado River – a major regional waterway – and other large rivers is being diverted to quench the thirst of folks in desert communities as far away as Las Vegas and Los Angeles.

COLORADO

Colorado was cool with the college crowd long before MTV's cameras caught on. No, the seven strangers on the hit reality show *The Real World Denver* weren't the first to dig this funky Rocky Mountain High. Their contemporaries have been flocking to the Centennial State for decades to participate in a uniquely Colorado coming-of-age ritual: the act of ski-bumming (definition: living in a mountain ski resort town such as Breckenridge, working in the service industry and riding as much fresh powder as possible in between). And it's not just the college crowd. Colorado has been catching Californians, New Yorkers and Washingtonians faster than a fly-fisher can snare a cutthroat trout on the Platte River.

Simply said, Colorado is a great place to live and play, and common knowledge among the locals is that once you taste that 'Rocky Mountain High' John Denver used to croon about you'll get so addicted to the atmosphere, altitude and attitude you'll never leave. Where else can you spend the morning in an office, the afternoon on the mountain bike and the evening sipping a hopped-up, local beer at a brewpub with friends?

History

Six bands of Utes once resided in a vast area stretching between the Yampa and San Juan Rivers. When white miners entered their lands, the Utes did not give in so easily. Chief Ouray (1833–80), remembered for paving the way to peace between the two parties, actually had little choice but to eventually give up most of the Utes' territory.

The mining era was launched with the discovery of gold west of Denver in 1859, but by the 1870s silver had taken center stage. Mountain smelter sites, such as Leadville and Aspen, turned into thriving population centers almost overnight.

The state relied heavily on its abundant natural resources, and the 20th century was economically topsy-turvy. Tourism and the high-tech industry have come to the rescue and made Colorado the most prosperous of the Rocky Mountain states.

Information

Colorado Road Conditions (☎ 877-315-7623; www .state.co.us) Highway advisories.

Colorado Travel & Tourism Authority (☎ 800-265-6723; www.colorado.com; PO Box 3524, Englewood, CO 80155) State-wide tourism information.

Denver Post (www.denverpost.com) Major newspaper; available state-wide.

Rocky Mountain News (www.rockymountainnews .com) Second major Colorado newspaper.

DENVER

Where in the country does the city's mayor also own some of the state's most popular microbreweries? Well, Denver, of course. Mayor John Hickenlooper was famous for owning Front Range brewpubs long before he got into politics. Denver is the only metropolis in this region and also happens to sit at exactly 5280ft – or 1 mile high (hence its nickname, 'Mile High City'). The city even boasts its own brand of weird American food. Try the Rocky Mountain Oysters once, but be aware before ordering that these are fried bulls testicles!

Although it's not the coolest city in the world (we think Boulder is more personal and just as easy to get to from Denver International Airport), Denver is a good place to get your bearings (or recover from jet-lag) before exploring the region. Set against a brilliant Rocky Mountain backdrop, Denver effortlessly blends Old West with cosmopolitan hip.

Orientation & Information

Most of Denver's sights are in the downtown district, which comprises a square defined to the south and east by Colfax Ave and

---

ROCKY MOUNTAINS

COLORADO FACTS

Nickname Centennial State

Population 4.9 million

Area 104,247 sq miles

Capital city Denver (pop 566, 974)

Sales tax 2.9% state tax plus individual city taxes

Birthplace of Florence Sabin (1871–1953), one of the first prominent female scientists; Douglas Fairbanks (1883–1939), star of silent films; Paul Whiteman (1890–1967), the 'King of Jazz'

Home of Ski slopes, hot springs, bighorn sheep

Famous for MTV's *The Real World Denver, The Bachelorette's* Trista and Ryan

Weird food Rocky Mountain Oysters (fried bulls testicles)

DON'T MISS

The Mile High City has a couple joints you just can't leave without experiencing.

- **Grizzly Rose** – one of the best honky-tonks in America, plus it's the best place to spot cowboys in town (p751)
- **16th Street Mall** – Denver's favorite pedestrian mall is perfect for strolling (below)
- **Tattered Cover Bookstore** – a bibliophile's dream, with thousands of titles, gorgeous journals and plenty of couches for armchair-travel reading (below)
- **Great American Beer Festival** – beer drinkers unite and toast microbrews from around the country at this revered early September festival (p749)
- **LoDo** – visit in the early evening for boutique browsing and happy hour (below)
- **Denver Art Museum** – visit the new $110-million Frederic C Hamilton wing, which is receiving rave reviews for its stellar design (below)
- **Red Rocks Park & Amphitheater** – the acoustics are as good as the views at this world-famous outdoor music venue (p749)

Broadway. The 16th St Mall is the focus of most retail activity, while Lower Downtown (LoDo), which includes historic Larimer Sq, is the heart of Denver's nightlife scene. To access LoDo and the 16th St Mall exit I-25 at Speer Blvd.

If you're arriving in Denver by bus, you'll be dropped off at Denver Bus Station on 19th St. From here it's an easy walk to the 16th St Mall. Turn right on Curtis St and follow it to 16th St.

BOOKSTORES

Book Garden (☎ 303-399-2004; 2625 E 12th Ave) Books for women, and gay and lesbian readers.
Tattered Cover Bookstore (☎ 303-436-1070; 1628 16th St) Denver's most loved bookstore.

EMERGENCY & MEDICAL SERVICES

In the event of a city-wide emergency, AM radio station 850 KOA is a designated point of information.
Denver Health Medical Center (☎ 303-436-6000; 777 Bannock St)
Denver Police/Fire/Paramedics Communications Center (☎ 720-913-2000)
Police Headquarters (☎ 720-913-2000; 1331 Cherokee St)
University Hospital (☎ 303-399-1211; 4200 E 9th Ave)

MEDIA

The mainstream newspapers are the *Denver Post* and the *Rocky Mountain News*. The best source for local events is the free weekly *Westword*. Monthly glossy mag *5280* has a comprehensive dining guide.

POST

Post office (☎ 303-296-4692; 951 20th St) Main branch.

TOURIST OFFICES

Denver Visitor Center (☎ 303-892-1505; www .denver.org; 918 16th St; ⏱ 9am-5pm Mon-Fri) Invaluable resource for both city and state information.

Sights & Activities

The best way to experience Denver is on foot. The **16th Street Mall**, a pedestrian-only strip of downtown, is lined with shops, restaurants and bars, and is a great place to stretch your legs or people-watch from an outdoor café. Another not-to-be missed area is funky **LoDo**, around Larimer Sq. This is the place to have a drink or browse the boutiques.

The $110-million Frederic C Hamilton wing at the **Denver Art Museum** (☎ 720-865-5000; www. denverartmuseum.org; 100 W 14th Ave; adult/student $8/6; ⏱ 10am-5pm Tue & Thu-Sat, 10am-9pm Wed, noon-5pm Sun), designed by Daniel Libeskind (best known for his humiliating disgrace when it came to the future World Trade Center memorial design) is at once a failure and a triumph. We won't lie: the shape of the new wing is rather torturous on the eyes. Yet at the same time this angular, fanlike edifice (which resembles the Sydney Opera House on speed) is mesmerizing. If you think the place looks weird from the outside, it gets downright eerie when you step inside. Here shapes shift with every direction you turn thanks to a combination of design and uncanny natural light tricks. The museum houses a great collection of Asian, European and Western American departments, as well

ROCKY MOUNTAINS

ROCKY MOUNTAINS

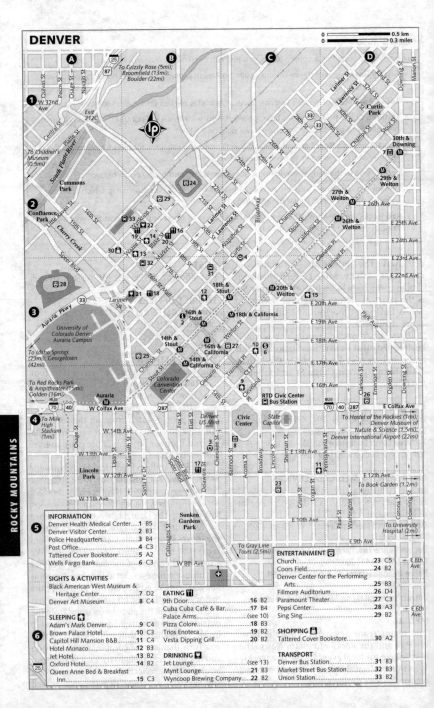

DENVER

0 .... 0.5 km
0 .... 0.3 miles

INFORMATION
Denver Health Medical Center....**1** B5
Denver Visitor Center................**2** B3
Police Headquarters..................**3** B4
Post Office.............................**4** C3
Tattered Cover Bookstore..........**5** A2
Wells Fargo Bank......................**6** C3

SIGHTS & ACTIVITIES
Black American West Museum &
Heritage Center.....................**7** D2
Denver Art Museum..................**8** C4

SLEEPING
Adam's Mark Denver..................**9** C4
Brown Palace Hotel..................**10** C4
Capitol Hill Mansion B&B..........**11** C4
Hotel Monaco........................**12** B3
Jet Hotel.............................**13** B2
Oxford Hotel.........................**14** B2
Queen Anne Bed & Breakfast
Inn..................................**15** C3

EATING
9th Door.............................**16** B2
Cuba Cuba Café & Bar...............**17** B4
Palace Arms.........................(see 10)
Pizza Colore.........................**18** B3
Trios Enoteca.......................**19** B2
Vesta Dipping Grill..................**20** B2

DRINKING
Jet Lounge..........................(see 13)
Mynt Lounge.........................**21** B2
Wyncoop Brewing Company.....**22** B2

ENTERTAINMENT
Church...............................**23** C5
Coors Field.........................**24** B2
Denver Center for the Performing
Arts...............................**25** B3
Fillmore Auditorium.................**26** D4
Paramount Theater..................**27** C3
Pepsi Center........................**28** A3
Sing Sing...........................**29** B2

SHOPPING
Tattered Cover Bookstore..........**30** A2

TRANSPORT
Denver Bus Station..................**31** B3
Market Street Bus Station..........**32** B3
Union Station.......................**33** B2

as one of the largest Native American art collections in the USA.

For something different, try the excellent **Black American West Museum & Heritage Center** (☎ 303-292-2566; 3091 California St; admission $5; ⏰ 10am-2pm Mon-Fri, 10am-5pm Sat & Sun, closed Mon & Tue winter). It chronicles the explorations of African Americans in the West during the 1800s. You'll be introduced to many intriguing characters – from African American cowboys to rodeo riders. The museum offers a glimpse at often overlooked contributions of African Americans during this era.

Red Rocks Park & Amphitheatre (☎ 303-640-2637; 16352 County Rd 93; park admission free; ⏰ 5am-11pm) is set between 400ft-high red sandstone rocks 15 miles southwest of Denver. Acoustics are so good that many artists record live albums here. The 9000-seat theater offers stunning views and draws big-name bands all summer. Even if you can't take in a show (concerts from $30), visit the park to hike through the bizarrely placed rocks.

If you've got the kids, check out the **Children's Museum** (☎ 303-433-7444; 2121 Children's Museum Dr; admission $6; ⏰ 9am-4pm Mon-Fri, 10am-5pm Sat & Sun), which is full of excellent exhibits that allow parents to interact with their kids. A particularly well-regarded section is the kid-size grocery store, where your little consumerists can push a shopping cart of their very own while learning about food and health. In the 'Arts à la carte' section kids can get creative with crafts that they can take home – all use recycled materials.

The **Denver Museum of Nature & Science** (☎ 303-322-7009; 2001 Colorado Blvd; museum adult/child $9/6, museum & IMAX $13/9; ⏰ 9am-5pm) has an IMAX theater and absorbing exhibits for all ages.

Tours

A variety of city and mountain tours (adult/child $25/12.50) are available with **Gray Line Tours** (☎ 303-289-2841; www.coloradograyline.com; 3000 E 1st Ave). The 3½-hour Denver City Tour is a favorite, stopping at popular sights. Hotel pick-up can be arranged.

Festivals & Events

These are just a few highlights of Denver's festival-laden year. Ask the visitor center for a complete schedule.

Cinco de Mayo (☎ 303-534-8342; www.newsed.org) Salsa music and margaritas at one of the country's biggest Cinco de Mayo celebrations; first weekend in May.

Great American Beer Festival (☎ 303-447-0816; www.beertown.org) A whole gamut of brew served in early September.

Taste of Colorado (☎ 303-295-6330; www.ataste ofcolorado.com) More than 50 restaurants cook up their specialties at various food stalls. In addition there's booze, live music, and arts and crafts vendors at this Labor Day festival.

Sleeping

Besides the places mentioned here, there are various chain and independent motels scattered throughout the city with rooms starting at $50. The closest campground is 15 miles north of the city in Broomfield. Speaking of Broomfield, it isn't a bad option for hotels either – you get more bang for your buck and are halfway between Denver and Boulder. Check out Lonely Planet Hotels & Hostels (www.lonelyplanet.com/hotels) internet bookings for sleeping reviews in the Denver 'burbs.

BUDGET

Unfortunately, most of Denver's hostels don't have the best reputations – the cheapest ones resemble dirty flop-houses and sometimes appear to double as shelters. Consider the places listed below, or trying staying at the very clean Boulder International Youth Hostel (p754) in nearby Boulder.

Hostel of the Rockies (☎ 303-861-7777; www.inn keeperrockies.com; 1717 Race St; dm $20, r $40; P 🖳) The Hostel of the Rockies is in a safe part of town, and across the street from a coffee shop and bar with wi-fi. Dorms and amenities are basic, but the hostel goes out of its way to encourage mingling with events such as Friday evening cook-outs. Ask for a dorm on the upper floor to score a private balcony with your bunk. There's plentiful free street parking and free internet.

Adam's Mark Denver (☎ 303-893-3333; www.adams mark.com; 1550 Court Pl; r Sun-Thu from $80, Fri & Sat $120; ❌ ☎ P) Adam's Mark boasts a great downtown location, a fitness room and sauna and budget midweek rates.

MIDRANGE

There's no need to stay in a hotel if you don't want to; Denver has fantastic B&Bs – our top two are listed following. If you do want the

ROCKY MOUNTAINS

charms of a big-name chain hotel, the city has plenty of these too; rates at these places are best if you book online.

our pick Capitol Hill Mansion B&B (☎ 303-839-5221; www.capitolhillmansion.com; 1207 Pennsylvania St; r incl breakfast $114-195; P ⊠ ❄) Stained-glass windows, original 1890s woodwork and turrets all make this gorgeous Romanesque mansion a special place to stay. Even better, the place is a virtual steal – even the most expensive suite costs under $200! And the location is fabulous. Plus, rooms are elegant, uniquely decorated and not too frilly. Some of the special features, which vary by room, include a solarium, a canopy bed and Jacuzzi tubs. The included breakfast is sumptuous; and there's evening wine and refreshments. Need we say more?

Queen Anne Bed & Breakfast Inn (☎ 303-296-6666; www.queenannebnb.com; 2147 Tremont Pl; r incl breakfast $115-185; P ⊠ ❄) In two late-1800s Victorian houses, this romantic B&B is a great choice. Chamber music plays softly in the public areas, and fresh flowers abound. Rooms are decorated with period antiques; some boast fantastic hand-painted murals. Rates include a full breakfast and evening wine tasting. In the winter, prices drop by about $20, making it the best value in town.

Jet Hotel (☎ 303-572-3300; www.thejethotel.com; 1612 Wazee St; r from $170; P ❄ ▯ wi-fi) This newly renovated minimalist boutique joint is excellent value considering its central LoDo location and swank party scene. Rooms are very posh and modern with thick white down comforters and glass tables. Past guests have complained, however, about the noise from the nightclub below. Jet has just 19 rooms (well, there are really 20 rooms, but the last one has been turned into a private club named Twenty). Parking is $21.

Oxford Hotel (☎ 303-628-5400; www.theoxfordhotel.com; 1600 17th St; r from $180; P ⊠ ❄ wi-fi) Marble walls, stained-glass windows, frescos and sparkling chandeliers adorn the public spaces of this classy hotel in a red sandstone building. Rooms are large and decked out with imported English and French antiques. The Art Deco Cruise Room Bar is one of Denver's swankiest cocktail lounges. Rates vary dramatically based on season and demand; check the website for the best rates and for well-priced packages in the off-season. Parking is $21.

TOP END

Hotel Monaco (☎ 303-296-1717; www.monaco-denver.com; 1717 Champa St; r from $210; P ❄ ▯ wi-fi) An ultra-stylish boutique joint that's a favorite with the celebrity set. Modern rooms blend French and art-deco styles – think bold colors and those fabulous European-style feather beds. Don't miss the evening 'Altitude Adjustment Hour,' when guests enjoy free wine and five-minute massages. The place is 100% pet friendly; staff will even deliver a named goldfish to your room upon request. Discounts are routinely offered online. Parking costs $21.

Brown Palace Hotel (☎ 303-297-3111; www.brownpalace.com; 321 17th St; r from $235; P ❄) This distinguished historic landmark is *the* place to stay in Denver. Within walking distance of restaurants and nightlife, the Brown Palace is elegantly decorated and provides old-world atmosphere and excellent service. It has hosted everyone over the years, from the Beatles to Winston Churchill. Parking is $22.

Eating

Denver has restaurants for all tastes and budgets. Cheap street meals can be found on the 16th St Mall.

Pizza Colore (☎ 303-534-6884; 1512 Larimer St; mains from $6; ⏱ 11.30am-10pm) Big portions of inexpensive pasta and wood-oven pizzas are served at this casual Italian restaurant. The food is delicious (especially considering the price). There's ample outdoor seating if the weather cooperates.

9th Door (☎ 303-292-2229; 1808 Blake St; tapas $6-8; ⏱ 4.30pm-2am Mon-Fri, 5.30pm-2am Sat) The decor is as juicy as the Spanish tapas at this hot Denver restaurant. The ambience is intimate, with low-lights, beaded glass chandeliers and booths you can disappear into – great for groups as they easily fit six. After dinner it becomes a popular lounge with live music.

Trios Enoteca (☎ 303-293-2887; 1730 Wynkoop St; mains $8-10; ⏱ 11.30am-late) Denver's best jazz joint keeps the noise low enough to carry on a conversation. Art-glass lampshades, bare brick walls and old pin-ups from the 1920s create the atmosphere at this sleek LoDo wine bar. Trios not only serves up great music, it also offers a bar menu – including awesome pizzas – that fill you up without breaking the budget. Even better, arrive between 5pm and 7pm Tuesday to Friday, for deals on food and drink.

Cuba Cuba Café & Bar (☎ 303-605-2882; 1173 Delaware St; mains $10-22; ⏰ 11am-11pm) We get dreamy just thinking about the mango *mojito* (rum-based cocktail) at this swanky Cuban joint serving finger-lickin' BBQ spareribs, flavor-packed fried yucca and a sumptuous coconut-crusted tuna. The back patio offers fantastic sunset city views; the bright blue-walled environs emit an island vibe.

Vesta Dipping Grill (☎ 303-296-1970; 1822 Blake St; mains $15-25; ⏰ 5-10:30pm) Pick a type of meat, then choose from 30 different sauces to dip it into. It's a simple concept that works exceedingly well. The melt-in-your mouth quality of the creative dishes – many Asian inspired – makes Vesta one of Denver's favorite restaurants. The atmosphere is relaxed yet funky.

Palace Arms (☎ 303-297-3111; Brown Palace Hotel, 321 17th St; mains from $20; ⏰ 5.30pm-late) The patriotic pioneer decor inside the Brown Palace's award-winning restaurant dates back to the 1700s – check out the silver centerpiece the British royal family commissioned. The food is as impressive as the old-world ambience, and the wine list features 900 bottles. Signature dishes include Kobe rib-eye and seared bison tenderloin.

Drinking

Most bars and nightspots are in LoDo and around Coors Field. The biweekly gay newspaper *Out Front*, found in coffee shops and bars, has entertainment listings. Many of the venues listed under Eating (opposite) are also bars.

Wynkoop Brewing Company (☎ 303-297-2700; 1634 18th St) We love the breezy ambience at the big Wynkoop, arguably the city's most rocking brewery. It offers an interesting selection of beers and more than 20 pool tables upstairs.

Jet Lounge (☎ 303-572-3300; Jet Hotel, 1612 Wazee St) Designed to blend into the Jet Hotel's lobby, this lounge is the place to see and be seen in Denver. There is a bedroom-meets-house-party vibe – candles, cozy couches, a weekend DJ and lots and lots of beautiful people. Jet Lounge was a favorite with the *Real World Denver* housemates.

Mynt Lounge (☎ 303-825-6968; 1424 Market St) This offers one of the best happy hours in town – from 3pm to 9pm the martinis are just $3, and there is a massive list to choose from. Mynt is a white-themed minimalist lounge with a very sexy vibe.

Entertainment

To find out what's happening with music, theater and other performing arts pick up a free copy of *Westword*.

our pick Grizzly Rose (☎ 303-295-1330; 5450 N Valley Hwy; cover $5-10) This is one kick-ass honky-tonk, attracting real cowboys from as far as Cheyenne – the Country Music Association (CMA) has called it the best country bar in America. If you've never experienced line dancing, there's no better place to put on the boots, grab the Stetson and let loose. Just north of the city limits off I-25 (you'll have to drive or cab it), the Grizzly is famous for bringing in huge industry stars – Willie Nelson, Lee Ann Rimes – and only charging $10 per ticket.

Church (☎ 303-832-3538; 1160 Lincoln St; cover $10) There's nothing like ordering a stiff drink inside an old cathedral. Yes, this club, which draws a large and diverse crowd, is in a former house of the Lord. Lit by hundreds of altar candles and flashing blue strobe lights, the Church has three dance floors, a couple of lounges and even a sushi bar! Arrive before 10pm Friday through Sunday to avoid the cover charge.

Sing Sing (☎ 303-291-0880; 1735 19th St; cover $7) This lively dueling piano bar is very popular with bachelorette parties. Sing Sing fills quickly, arrive around 6.30pm to score a table near the pianos. It's pretty noisy (don't expect much talking) but the atmosphere is really fun. Song requests are taken (and usually accompanied by $5) but as many folks request the same songs, you could just sit back, sip from the famous Long Island ice-tea buckets and listen. Beware when drunken brides-to-be get up on stage to dance.

WHAT THE …?

So you just get into Denver and you have a few beers at the pub and suddenly your head is swirling. What the heck is going on? You're not that much of a lightweight, right? Wrong. In the Rocky Mountains, where the elevation is usually at least a mile high, your body takes in less oxygen. This means that until you get adjusted, you will get drunk much quicker! This may be a good thing, especially if you come from a country with a weaker currency… But locals sure do like to laugh at those not smart enough to heed our warning.

Denver Center for the Performing Arts (☎ 303-893-4100; www.denvercenter.org; 1245 Champa St) Occupying four city blocks, this complex is the world's second-largest performing-arts center. It hosts resident Colorado Symphony Orchestra, Opera Colorado, Denver Center Theater Company, Colorado Ballet and touring Broadway shows.

In town, the main venues for national acts are **Paramount Theater** (☎ 303-534-8336; 1621 Glenarm Pl) and **Fillmore Auditorium** (☎ 303-837-0360; 1510 Clarkson St).

Denver is a city known for manic sports fans, and boasts five pro teams. The **Colorado Rockies** (☎ 303-762-5437) play baseball at the highly rated **Coors Field** (2001 Blake St). The **Pepsi Center** (☎ 303-405-1111; 1000 Chopper Pl) hosts the Denver Nuggets basketball team and the Colorado Avalanche hockey team. The much-lauded **Denver Broncos football team** (☎ 720-258-3333) and the **Colorado Rapids soccer team** (☎ 303-299-1599) play at **Mile High Stadium** (☎ 720-258-3000; 1805 S Bryant St), 1 mile west of downtown. Public Regional Transit District (right) buses run from points around Denver and Boulder directly to the sports stadiums and back on game nights. The cost is $3 one-way. Check RTD's website for details.

Shopping
Denver's first main shopping strip is the pedestrian-only 16th St Mall. It features a lot of T-shirt venues, mega-record shops and popular American chains such as Gap, with a few interesting Western boutiques, galleries and five-and-dime shops mixed in for good measure.

Denver's most loved bookstore, the **Tattered Cover Bookstore** (☎ 303-436-1070; 1628 16th St), is also in this neighborhood. By far the coolest shop in Denver, it's massive and bursting with books. We love the armchair-travel section – curl into the comfy chairs scattered around the shop and read about Kathmandu. And if you need a new writing journal, well this is where we come to stock up before our research trips. The selection is fabulous!

Getting There & Away
AIR
The **Denver International Airport** (DIA; www.flydenver.com; 8500 Peña Blvd) is served by around 20 airlines and offers flights to nearly every major US city. Located 24 miles east of downtown,

DIA is connected with I-70 exit 238 by the 12-mile-long Peña Blvd.

Tourist and airport information is available at a **booth** (☎ 303-342-2000) in the terminal's central hall.

BUS
Greyhound buses stop at the **Denver Bus Station** (☎ 303-293-6555; 1055 19th St), which runs services to Cheyenne ($20, three hours) and Billings ($95, 14 hours). **Powder River Coach USA** (☎ 800-442-3682) and **TNM&O** (☎ 806-763-5389) also stop here.

TRAIN
Amtrak's *California Zephyr* runs daily between Chicago and San Francisco via Denver. Trains arrive and depart from **Union Station** (☎ 303-825-2583; cnr 17th & Wynkoop Sts). For recorded information on arrival and departure times, call ☎ 303-534-2812. **Amtrak** (☎ 800-872-7245) can also provide schedule information and train reservations.

Denver's **Ski Train** (☎ 303-296-4754; www.skitrain.com) to Winter Park operates at weekends throughout the ski season, as well as in July and August. Same-day round-trip tickets cost $49. The train departs Denver's Union Station at 7:15am arriving in Winter Park at 9:30am. It departs Winter Park at 4:15pm.

Getting Around
TO/FROM THE AIRPORT
All transportation companies have booths near the baggage-claim area. **Public Regional Transit District** (RTD; ☎ 303-299-6000; www.rtd-denver.com) runs a SkyRide service to the airport from downtown Denver hourly ($8, one hour). RTD also goes to Boulder ($10, 1½ hours) from the **Market Street Bus Station**. Taxis to downtown Denver charge a flat $45, excluding tip. **Super Shuttle** (☎ 303-370-1300, 800-258-3826) offers van services (from $18) from downtown Denver and around to the airport, and vice versa.

CAR & MOTORCYCLE
Street parking can be a pain, but there are slews of pay garages in downtown and LoDo. Nearly all the major car-rental firms have counters at DIA, though a few have offices in downtown Denver; check the Yellow Pages.

PUBLIC TRANSPORTATION
RTD provides public transportation throughout the Denver and Boulder area. Local buses

cost $1.15 for local services, $2.50 for express services. Useful free shuttle buses run along the 16th St Mall.

RTD also operates a light-rail line serving 16 stations on a 12-mile route through downtown. Fares are the same as for local buses.

TAXI

For 24-hour cab service, call:

Freedom Cab (☎ 303-292-8900)

Metro Taxi (☎ 303-333-3333)

Yellow Cab (☎ 303-777-7777)

FRONT RANGE

This is the most densely populated region in Colorado, and likely the area you'll begin your Rocky Mountain odyssey. Rapid development of the I-25 and US 36 corridor has led to the creation of many microcities serving solely as satellite communities for commuters working in Colorado Springs, Denver and Boulder. You'll also find fabulous Rocky Mountain National Park here.

Boulder

Long known for its outrageous liberalism, the university town of Boulder has a yuppie crunch attitude and a mad crush on the outdoors. The main roads are always packed with cyclists, and the endless city parks bustle with hikers and dogs. The pedestrian-only Pearl St Mall, bursting with shops, sidewalk cafés and street performers, is perfect for strolling. At night, head up to the Hill, home of the 30,000-student University of Colorado, a legendary American party school.

In many ways it is Boulder, not Denver, establishing itself as the region's tourist hub. The city is about the same distance from Denver International Airport, plus staying in Boulder puts you 45 minutes closer to the big ski resorts west on I-70 and Rocky Mountain National Park.

ORIENTATION

Boulder's two areas to see and be seen are the downtown Pearl St Mall and the University Hill district (next to campus), both off Broadway. Overlooking the city from the west are the Flatirons, an eye-catching rock formation. Boulder is north of Denver. From I-25 exit at Hwy 36 (it's a left-hand exit), follow this road for about 20 miles into town.

INFORMATION

Boulder Bookstore (☎ 303-447-2074; 1107 Pearl St) Lots of travel guides and recent fiction.

Boulder Visitor Center (☎ 303-442-2911; www .bouldercoloradousa.com; 2440 Pearl St; ☷ 8:30am-5pm Mon-Thu, 8:30am-4pm Fri) Offers information and internet access.

SIGHTS & ACTIVITIES

Shop, hike, bicycle and drink until you drop. The main feature of downtown Boulder is the **Pearl Street Mall**, a vibrant pedestrian zone filled with bars, galleries and restaurants.

Hiking and mountain biking are both huge in Boulder, and luckily there's plenty of space for everyone to practice both (the city has dedicated huge chunks of land to public open space).

From the popular Chautauqua Park, at the west end of Baseline Rd, **hiking** trails head in many directions, including up to the Flatirons. Locals and their canine companions dig the 3.2-mile (round-trip) calf-buster up **Mt Sanitas**. Rocky outcroppings grace the summit and make great focal points for pictures. The views across Boulder and onto the plains to the east are stupendous. To reach the trailhead, take Broadway Ave to Mapleton Ave and head west toward the mountains for about five blocks. You can park just past the hospital in a lot on the north side where the trail begins.

The 16-mile **Boulder Creek Trail** is the main **bicycling** route in town and leads west on an unpaved streamside path to Four Mile Canyon. Challenge-seekers can also ride 4 miles up Flagstaff Rd to the top of Flagstaff Mountain. Bike rentals, maps and information are available from **University Bicycles** (☎ 303-444-4196; 839 Pearl St) and **Full Cycle** (☎ 303-440-7771; 1211 13th St).

Eldorado Canyon State Park (☎ 303-494-3943; ☷ visitor center 9am-5pm) is one of the country's most favored rock-climbing areas, offering Class 5.5 to 5.12 climbs. The park entrance is on Eldorado Springs Dr, west of Hwy 93. Information is available from **Boulder Rock Club** (☎ 303-447-2804; 2829 Mapleton Ave).

During winter, city buses leave from the corner of 14th and Walnut Sts (round-trip $7) and take you to **Eldora Mountain Resort** (☎ 303-440-8700; www.eldora.com; Hwy 130; lift ticket $50), where you can spend the day skiing and snowboarding on decent terrain – it's not as big as some of Colorado's resorts, but it is cheaper.

ROCKY MOUNTAINS

SLEEPING

Boulder has numerous lodging options, although most are on the pricey side.

Boulder Mountain Lodge (☎ 303-444-0882; www .bouldermountainlodge.com; 91 Four Mile Canyon Rd; campsites $17, r winter/summer from $69/79; ✗ ☎) Set in a shady canyon 4 miles west of Boulder on Hwy 119, this lodge is gorgeously placed amid pines and cottonwood trees. It offers shady camping, as well as clean, motel-style rooms.

Boulder International Youth Hostel (☎ 303-442-0522; www.boulderhostel.com; 1107 12th St; dm $20, r with shared bath from $45; ☐) Rooms are kept clean and warm, and the facilities here are better than many places in Denver. Located amid the fraternity houses on hip University Hill, there are plenty of cheap places to eat and drink just minutes' walk away. This is a good thing, because the hostel itself is skint on entertainment – booze is forbidden on the premises, and the sole TV only gets a few channels. If you can afford it grab a private room. Dorm dwellers are forced to endure a 10am to 5pm lockout.

Boulder Outlook Hotel & Suites (☎ 303-443-3322; www.boulderoutlook.com; 800 28th St; r from $99; ✗ ☎ ☐ wi-fi) It boasts it's the 'cure for the common hotel.' And we have to say, the Outlook is pretty unique. We dug the big rooms, the funky paint job and best of all, the large indoor pool with rocks for scrambling and a Jacuzzi!

Hotel Boulderado (☎ 303-442-4344, 800-433-4344; www.boulderado.com; 2115 13th St; r from $150; ✗) The charming Boulderado is in an exquisitely restored 1909 brick building with antique-furnished digs. Choose from small but quaint historic rooms or more spacious, wheelchair-friendly, modern abodes. This hotel offers some very reasonable packages – often cheaper than booking a room directly – via its website that include gift certificates and discounts or spa treatments. Rates vary wildly based on occupancy.

St Julien Hotel & Spa (☎ 720-406-9696; www .stjulien.com; 900 Walnut; r from $269; ✗ ☎ ☐ wi-fi) Boulder's newest hotel is its swankiest. Smack in the center of town, with fabulous Flatirons views, the St Julien offers pimped-out rooms with a mod masculine decor, big soaking tubs and plush robes. The place boasts a great gym and indoor pool (free for guests) and a lovely terrace bar with mountain views and a fantastic happy hour – it has fast become the local choice for after-work cocktails. Skip the spa; there are better options in town. Rates can drop in the winter – check the internet for specials.

EATING

It's hard to beat Boulder when it comes to happy hour. If you're on a budget, eat between 3pm and 7pm to score some amazing drink and food specials at many restaurants – we're talking a full meal of appetizers and a couple

---

LOCAL SECRET: TUBING BOULDER CREEK

There is nothing more uniquely Boulder in summertime than riding the rapids down the Boulder Creek at the west end of town. In fact it just might be the best urban do-it-yourself float trip in the country! Rapids range from mild to slightly wild – there are a few small waterfalls sure to flip your tube – plus good swimming holes and even a rope swing! The water is highest in May and June, but it's also too cold for many to tolerate. July and August offer milder rapids and warmer temperatures.

Most people start to the north of the parking lot at Eben G Fine Park between Arapahoe and Canyon Aves – head west on Canyon until you see the pull-off. There are usually vendors renting tubes ($6) here, but if you want to purchase your own rubber hit the **Conoco Gas Station** (☎ 303-442-6293; 1201 Arapahoe Ave; tubes $14). If the water seems a little too rough, the creek gets milder the further south you go. Try riding the stretch from the picnic tables in Eben G Fine down to the library.

If you'd rather paddle the rapids, the stretch of creek running parallel to the bike path and Canyon Rd (just north of the park) doubles as one of Colorado's holiest of white-water kayak parks. Built by a local, Gary Lacy, who has made quite a name for himself in the quickly growing white-water kayaking industry, the highlight is a steep drop below the last bridge before you hit Eben G Fine – it leads into a sticky hydraulic. The park is perfect for kayakers looking to practice eddy turns and cartwheels.

of top-shelf martinis for less than $20, and that's with the tip!

Lucille's Creole Cafe (☎ 303-442-4743; 2142 14th St; mains $4-8; ☼ 8am-2pm) Boulder's favorite breakfast spot – lines form early, but the wait is worth it. There's a Creole lunch menu, but everyone orders breakfast. Try the Eggs Sardou ($7) or the daily special.

Sink (☎ 303-444-7465; 1165 13th St; mains $5-10; ☼ 11.30am-10.30pm) The Sink is a Hill classic. It's been around since 1923, and there's no place quite like it. A burger dive with the most amazing graffiti art all over its dim-lit cavelike interior, it's worth coming here just to check out the writing on the walls. But since you're already seated, join the college kids and their professors in a round of beer and nachos, or sink your teeth into one of the legendary burgers or pizzas. And with $2 brews and appetizers it's got the best happy hour on the hill.

Sherpa's Adventurers Restaurant & Bar (☎ 303-440-7151; 825 Walnut St; mains $5-15; ☼ 11.30am-10pm) Part restaurant, part travel adventure center, this place, run by a Nepalese sherpa, has a large menu consisting of bits of Tibet, portions of Nepal and a few pinches of India. Plates are enormous; the *saag* (creamed spinach) appetizer ($5) alone can make a meal.

Boulder Dushanbe Teahouse (☎ 303-442-4993; 1770 13th St; mains $8-17; ☼ 8am-10pm) Incredible Tajik craftsmanship envelops the phenomenal interior of the teahouse presented by Boulder's Tajikistan sister city, Dushanbe. The international fare ranges from Amazonian to Mediterranean to, of course, Tajik.

Bacaro Ristorante (☎ 303-444-4888; 921 Pearl St; mains $8-20; ☼ 11am-late) Bacaro serves flavor-packed Italian food inside and out – in summer the rooftop bar fills quickly. Pizzas here are cheap and particularly delicious, made with thin crust and real mozzarella. Locals dig the daily happy hour when tapas start at just $1. Late night, Bacaro turns into a pumping dance club.

Boulder Cafe (☎ 303-444-4884; 1247 Pearl St; mains $8-25; ☼ 11.30am-10.30pm) Score a sidewalk table and check out the street performers on the Pearl St Mall while waiting for your oysters and ice-cold beer. The perennially popular Boulder Cafe does a great raw bar, along with a host of eclectic appetizers such as classic Swiss fondue. Entrees include pastas, steaks, sandwiches and salads. From 3pm to 6pm, all appetizers (including the raw bar) and

drinks are half-price. We think it's the best deal in town.

Mediterranean Restaurant (☎ 303-444-5355; 1002 Walnut St; mains from $12; ☼ 11.30am-10pm) Boulderites never get tired of dining at the Med, one of the city's most revered restaurants. It offers a varied European-influenced menu – from tapas to flavor-packed pasta – and a long wine list. There's also wonderful outdoor garden area for warm weather dining. Many argue that the Med's happy hour is the best in town.

DRINKING

Boulder likes to party, and there are plenty of bars to keep you lubricated well through the night. See also Eating (opposite) for restaurant-bar combos.

Mountain Sun Pub & Brewery (☎ 303-546-0886; 1535 Pearl St) Boulder's favorite brewery is always packed with an eclectic crowd of yuppies, hippies and everyone in between. The place serves a gamut of brews from chocolaty to fruity, and manages to feel relaxed despite the small, cluttered space. Walls are lined with tapestries, the booths are cozy and the pub grub is delicious – we love the burgers. At night there's usually live music of the bluegrass and jam-band variety.

Pearl Street Pub (☎ 303-939-9900; 1108 Pearl St) Sorrows are drowned with multiple pints at the scarred wooden bar upstairs, where the vibe is shabby chic meets Old West. Downstairs, 20-something locals pound shots by the pool tables, soaking up the beer-drenched atmosphere at this town's favorite trendy dive. Come for Friday night happy hour, when there is often a local acoustic folk guitarist playing the tiny, packed upstairs bar.

West End Tavern (☎ 303-444-3535; 926 Pearl St) Most people it seems end up on this place's rooftop come the end of a summer night. The top deck has its own bar, lots of seating and a covered awning on the off chance it rains. When the weather's colder, the multilevel restaurant and long wooden bar fill quickly. The West End serves high-end, imaginative pub grub including Gouda grits and a BLT with 'ahi tuna.

Catacombs Bar (☎ 303-443-0486; 2115 13th St) This cavernous pool and beer joint beneath the Boulderado Hotel attracts a young and rowdy crowd with offers of ultra-cheap drink specials. The dimly lit rooms are perfect for mingling, and the place is frequented by singles looking to hook up. Locals tend to be a respectful and friendly lot, however, so you won't feel intimidated if you just want to get drunk without the pick-up lines.

GETTING THERE & AROUND

Boulder has fabulous public transportation, with services extending as far away as Denver and its airport. The ecofriendly busses are run by **RTD** (☎ 303-299-6000; www.rtd-denver.com) and cost $1.25 per ride. Maps are available at **Boulder Station** (14th & Walnut Sts). RTD buses (route B) operate between Boulder Station and Denver's Market St Bus Station ($3.50, one hour). RTD's SkyRide bus (route AB) heads to Denver International Airport ($10, 1½ hours, hourly). **Super Shuttle** (☎ 303-444-0808) provides hotel ($19) and door-to-door ($25) shuttle service from the airport.

Rocky Mountain National Park

Teeming with stunning natural beauty, from towering peaks to wide-open alpine tundra, Rocky Mountain National Park is a Colorado must-do for visitors. It's so alluring, in fact, that more than three million visitors mosey in annually. Breathe in crisp mountain air, hike through grassy meadows, gasp at snow-capped peaks and keep an eye out for elk, bighorn sheep, moose, marmots and bear. Most visitors stay near Trail Ridge Rd (open last Monday in May to mid-October), which winds through spectacular alpine tundra environments. Those who prefer communing with nonhuman nature should venture on foot away from the road corridor; the reward is quiet, superlative scenery.

Late-19th-century hotel and road construction in the settlement of Estes Park prompted naturalist Enos Mills to campaign in 1909 to protect the area. He faced opposition from private grazing and timber interests, but in early 1915 Congress approved the bill creating Rocky Mountain National Park.

ORIENTATION

Trail Ridge Rd (US 34) is the only east–west route through the park; the US 34 eastern approach from I-25 and Loveland follows the Big Thompson River Canyon. From Boulder, the most direct route follows US 36 through Lyons to the east entrances. Another approach from the south, mountainous Hwy 7, provides access to campsites and trailheads (including

Longs Peak) on the east side of the Continental Divide. Winter closure of US 34 through the park makes access to the west side dependent on US 40 at Granby.

Two entrance stations are on the east side: at Fall River (US 36) and Beaver Meadows (US 34). The Grand Lake station (US 34) is the sole entry on the west side.

INFORMATION

There are five visitor centers associated with Rocky Mountain National Park, although only two are actually inside the park's boundaries. All are well sign-posted. You'll find the park headquarters at the **Beaver Meadows Visitor Center** (☎ 970-586-1206; US 36; ☼ 8am-6pm Jun-Aug, 8am-5pm rest of year), on US 36 just east of the entrance.

Entry to the park (vehicles $25, hikers and cyclists $15) is valid for seven days. Backcountry permits ($25) are required for overnight trips. The **Backcountry Office** (☎ 970-586-1242; Rocky Mountain National Park, Estes Park, CO 80517; ☼ 7am-7pm) is east of the Park Headquarters. Reservations can be made by mail or in person from March to the end of December, or by phone from March to mid-May and November to April.

ACTIVITIES

The bustling Bear Lake Trailhead offers easy **hikes** to several lakes and beyond. Another busy area is Glacier Gorge Junction Trailhead. The free Glacier Basin–Bear Lake shuttle services both.

Forested Fern Lake, 4 miles from the Moraine Park Trailhead, is dominated by craggy Notchtop Peak. You can complete a loop to the Bear Lake shuttle stop in about 8.5 miles for a rewarding day hike, or head into the upper fern creek drainage to explore the backcountry. The strenuous **Flattop Mountain Trail** is the only cross-park trail, linking Bear Creek on the east side with either Tonahutu Creek Trail or the North Inlet Trail on the west side.

Families might consider the moderate hikes to **Calypso Cascades** in the Wild Basin or to **Gem Lake** in the Lumpy Ridge area.

Trail Ridge Rd crosses the Continental Divide at Milner Pass (10,759ft), where trails head 4 miles (and up 2000ft!) southeast to Mt Ida, which offers fantastic views.

Trails on the west side of the park are quieter and less trodden than those on the east side. Try the short and easy East Inlet Trail to **Adams Falls** (0.3 miles) or the more moderate 3.7-mile Colorado River Trail to the **Lulu City** site.

Before July, many of the trails are snowbound, and high water runoff makes passage difficult.

All **bicycling** is restricted to paved surfaces, such as Trail Ridge Rd and the Horseshoe Park/Estes Park Loop. The only exception is the 9-mile, 3000ft climb up Fall River Rd (head back down on Trail Ridge Rd).

On the east side, the Bear Lake and Glacier Gorge Junction Trailheads offer good routes for **cross-country skiing** and **snowshoeing**. **Backcountry skiing** is also possible; check with the visitor centers.

SLEEPING & EATING

The only overnight accommodations in the park are at campgrounds; the majority of motel or hotel accommodations are around Estes Park (p758) or Grand Lake (p758).

The park has five formal campgrounds. All have a seven-day limit during summer and all but Longs Peak take RVs (no hookups). Fees are $18 ($10 in winter, when the water supply is off).

Aspenglen (54 sites) Five miles west of Estes Park on US 34.

Glacier Basin (150 sites) Seven miles west of Beaver Meadows Visitor Center.

Longs Peak (26 sites) Twelve miles south of Estes Park on Hwy 7; provides Longs Peak hikers with an early trail start.

Moraine Park (247 sites) Two and a half miles from Beaver Meadows Visitor Center.

Timber Creek (100 sites) Seven miles north of Grand Lake.

When it comes time for eating, you'll need to head to Estes Park (p758) or Grand Lake (p758).

GETTING AROUND

A free shuttle bus provides frequent summer service from the Glacier Basin parking area to Bear Lake. Another shuttle operates between Moraine Park campground and the Glacier Basin parking area. Shuttles run daily from mid-June to early September, and thereafter at weekends only until mid-October.

Estes Park

Estes Park is the primary gateway to Rocky Mountain National Park, and has enough cheesy T-shirt shops and ice-cream parlors to prove it. In the summer season the population skyrockets, and the place is filled with camera-toting tourists and meandering elk (yes, they do just wander down the street sometimes).

Try the **Estes Park Visitor Center** (☎ 970-586-4431; www.estesparkresort.com; 500 Big Thompson Ave; ⏱ 9am-8pm Jun-Aug, 8am-5pm Mon-Fri, 9am-5pm Sat, 10am-4pm Sun Sep-May), just east of the US 36 junction, for help with lodging; note that many places close in winter.

From Denver International Airport, **Estes Park Shuttle** (☎ 970-586-5151; www.estesparkshuttle.com) runs four times daily to Estes Park ($39, 1¾ hours).

SUMMIT THIS!

Colorado has 52 fourteeners (mountains over 14,000ft), and many residents make it a mission to summit all of them. We don't expect you to be quite so fierce, but climbing to the top of at least one should earn you some major bragging rights back home.

Longs Peak, in Rocky Mountain National Park, stands at 14,255ft and is one of Colorado's most popular climbs. There is only one nontechnical (meaning you don't need ropes and climbing experience) route to the summit, the Keyhole Route, and it usually doesn't open until July. You'll want to begin your hike around 3am so you can get off the summit by 10am, which should allow enough time to reach the bottom before afternoon thunderstorms roll in. The trailhead begins at the Longs Peak ranger station. The first 6 miles aren't technical, but save some reserves for the final 1½ miles, which is an intense 4850ft scramble through a field of small boulders to the summit.

Do not attempt this hike if you are not used to the altitude, don't have enough water or have little hiking experience – the terrain is harsh, and you can expect sudden snowstorms in any month. That said, when it comes to trying your first fourteener, Long's Peak is a good starter mountain (it's in a national park, which means you can register with the rangers before setting out, and if you get into trouble, help comes a lot faster).

SLEEPING

Estes Park has dozens of hotels; we have space for only a special few. Most of the budget and midrange motels are east of town along US 34 or Hwy 7.

Allenspark Lodge Bed & Breakfast (☎ 303-747-2552; www.allensparklodge.com; 184 Main St; r incl breakfast $75-150) A stay at this classic Colorado lodge, built from polished ponderosa pine logs, is a real treat. Rooms are elegant with views and handmade 1930s pine furniture. There's a library, large sunroom, hot tub, and beer and wine bar. The included hot breakfast is served family style. No children under 14.

our pick YMCA of the Rockies Snow Mountain Ranch (☎ 970-586-3341; www.ymcarockies.org; 2515 Tunnel Rd; r/cabin from $110/130; ☒) Snow Mountain Ranch is a great place for families. The center sits on a peaceful 860-acre plot just outside town and offers roomy cabins sleeping up to 10 people along with motel-style rooms. It also runs quality, affordable weekend or week-long family camps. Kids and adults are separated by day to participate in age appropriate activities (or so mom and dad can just take a little down time) that teach conservation in a fun way. Check the website for specific info, as there are too many options to list.

Stanley Hotel (☎ 970-586-4964; www.stanleyhotel .com; 333 Wonderview Ave; r from $150; ☒ ☒) Stephen King was inspired to write *The Shining* after staying here. The grand dame of northern Colorado historic resort hotels, it has great mountain views, splendid dining, and ghost tours of the building at weekend nights. Speaking of which, you should book room 401 if you want to increase your chances of ghost spotting – staff consider it the 'most haunted.'

EATING

Notchtop Bakery & Cafe (☎ 970-586-0272; 457 E Wonderview Ave; mains $5-7; ☒ 7.30am-2pm) In the Stanley Village shopping center, this is one of the best spots in town for tasty and healthy meals. Fill up on fair-trade coffee and scrumptious baked goods.

Dunraven Inn (☎ 970-586-6409; 2470 Colorado 66; dishes $9-30; ☒ 5-10pm) This place has a very eclectic decor showcasing many versions of the *Mona Lisa*. The Italian menu offers loads of pasta, seafood and vegetarian plates to choose from, along with a children's menu. It's an intimate restaurant perfect for a special evening.

Grand Lake

The other gateway to Rocky Mountain National Park, Grand Lake is less chaotic and more charming than Estes Park – although it still rakes in tourists by the thousands during summer. The downtown is pleasant, the namesake lake handsome. The **Grand Lake Visitor Center** (☎ 970-627-3402; www.grandlakechamber .com; ☒ 9am-5pm) is at the junction of US 34 and W Portal Rd.

The **Arapaho National Forest**, to the west of town, has some good mountain-biking trails; get a map from the **Grand Lake Metro Recreation District** (☎ 970-627-8328; 928 Grand Ave, Suite 204; ☒ 8am-5pm Mon-Fri). **Rocky Mountain Sports** (☎ 970-627-8124; 900 Grand Ave) rents and sells outdoor equipment. Several Rocky Mountain National Park **hiking** trailheads are just outside the town limits, including those to the Tonahutu Creek Trail and the Cascade Falls/North Inlet Trail, both near Shadowcliff Lodge.

Overlooking Grand Lake, the nonprofit **HI Shadowcliff Lodge** (☎ 970-627-9220; www.shadow cliff.org; 405 Summerland Park Rd; dm/d/cabin $20/90/125; ☒ Jun-Sep) is an ecofriendly mountain resort in a beautiful setting. Cabins, which accommodate six to eight people, have kitchen, fireplace and porch. Rooms and dorms are simple, but clean and affordable. Reservations are essential.

EG's Garden Grill (☎ 970-627-8404; 1000 Grand Ave; dishes $10-20; ☒ 11:30am-10pm) serves good grub from salads to seafood; its fish tacos make for a very satisfying lunch.

Home James Transportation Services (☎ 970-726-5060; www.homejamestransportation.com) runs door-to-door shuttles to Denver International Airport ($58, 2½ hours); reservations are a must.

Colorado Springs

Evangelical conservatives, tourists and military installations comprise the bizarre demographics of Colorado's second-largest city. Home to a large military base, the US Air Force Academy and the North American Radar Air Defense (the command center monitoring US and Canadian airspace; it's located in a hollowed-out mountain and is where the president would weather a nuclear missile strike), it's also the city where bibles were recently distributed with the Sunday paper! In a picture-perfect location below the famous Pikes Peak, Colorado Springs offers a runaway train of listed attractions: hike through Garden of the Gods' strange red rock formations, take a ride on the cog railway or browse the shops in the low-key downtown area.

I-25 bisects the sprawling metropolitan area. To the east is the central business on Tejon St between Kiowa St and Colorado Ave. Here you will find restaurants, bars, clubs and shops. To the west of the I-25 are Old Colorado City, Garden of the Gods and Manitou Springs.

The **Colorado Springs Visitor Center** (☎ 719-635-7506; www.coloradosprings-travel.com; 515 S Cascade Ave; ☑ 8:30am-5pm) has all the usual tourist information.

SIGHTS & ACTIVITIES

The bewitching red sandstone formations at the **Garden of the Gods** (the rocks are smack in the middle of town and seem so out of place you won't quite believe your eyes) draw around two million visitors each year to see highlights such as Balanced Rock, High Point and Central Garden. Soak up the beauty on one of the park hiking trails.

Travelers have been making the trip on the **Pikes Peak Cog Railway** to the summit of Pikes Peak (14,110ft) since 1891. Katherine Lee Bates was so impressed by her 1893 trip to the summit that she was inspired to write 'America the Beautiful.' Swiss-built trains smoothly make the round-trip in 3¼ hours, which includes 40 minutes at the top. Trains depart from the **Manitou Springs depot** (☎ 719-685-5401; www.cograilway.com; 515 Ruxton Ave, Manitou Springs; admission $26; ☑ Apr-Jan). The depot is 6 miles from downtown Colorado Springs. Take US 24 west to Manitou Ave; head westward on Manitou Ave, from where you'll make a left onto Ruxton Ave. The small town of **Manitou Springs** is well known for its nine soda-water springs and historic downtown area.

The tough 12.5-mile **Barr Trail** to the summit is a local favorite. From the trailhead, just above the Manitou Springs depot, the path climbs 7300ft. Fit hikers should reach the top in about eight hours. Leave in the early morning, as afternoon thunderstorms can prove deadly. Make sure your body is acclimatized to the altitude before setting out. It's easy to hitch a ride down the mountain once you reach the top.

From the town of Divide, west of Manitou Springs on US 24, you can drive the **Pikes Peak Toll Road** (per person/car $10/35; ☑ 9am-3pm winter, 7am-7pm summer) to the summit. Due to weather, it's sometimes closed in winter.

SLEEPING

Garden of the Gods Campground (☎ 719-475-9450; www.coloradocampground.com; 3704 W Colorado Ave; campsites $33, cabins from $45, r from $60; ☑) For camping close to town you could do worse than here. There are only a few trees, and most of the area is paved, but the pool is refreshing and the basic cabins and bunkhouse rooms are quite good value. Rates drop by about $10 in the cooler seasons.

Garden of the Gods Motel (☎ 719-636-5271; 2922 W Colorado Ave; r winter/summer from $60/95; ☒ ☑) With spacious rooms, an indoor pool and a sauna, this motel is good value. Conveniently situated within walking distance of Old Colorado shops and restaurants, it's popular with families.

El Colorado Lodge (☎ 719-685-5485; www.pikes-peak.com/elcolorado; 23 Manitou Ave; cabins from $70; ☒) Located in Manitou Springs, El Colorado is a Southwestern-style lodge built in 1926. Accommodations are in comfortable adobe cabins set among blue spruce and pine trees. Most come with fireplaces.

Broadmoor (☎ 719-634-7711; www.broadmoor.com; 1 Lake Ave; r from $270; ☒ ☑ wi-fi) One of the top five-star resorts in the USA, the Broadmoor sits in a picture-perfect location against the blue-green slopes of Cheyenne Mountain. Everything about the property is exquisite: acres of lush grounds and a shimmering lake to stroll past, world-class golf, ornately decorated grandiose public spaces, a myriad of bars and restaurants, a fantastic spa and uber-comfortable European-style guest rooms.

EATING & DRINKING

The Tejon strip downtown is the place to eat and drink in Colorado Springs.

Western Omelette (☎ 719-636-2286; 16 S Walnut St; mains $4-8; ☑ 7am-2pm) If you're hungover after a big night, do as the locals do and head here for a green chili cure. The Mexican breakfast dishes, such as *huevos rancheros* (with green chili, of course), are greasy spoon fare. It's a big place completely lacking in character, which oddly gives it its charm.

Tony's (☎ 719-228-6566; 311 N Tejon St; dishes $4-8; ☑ 11am-late) For greasy sandwiches or mac and cheese, you can't get much cheaper than Tony's (and the quality is not bad either). Pretty much an institution since it opened, Wisconsin-themed Tony's is a neighborhood bar that serves the cheapest pitchers in town. There's often live music at night.

WORTH THE TRIP: GOING DOWN TO CRIPPLE CREEK

Just an hour from Colorado Springs, yet worlds away, a visit to Cripple Creek is like stepping back into the Wild West of lore. The booze still flows and gambling still thrives, but yesteryear's saloons and brothels have been converted into tasteful casinos. Despite the flashing neon signs, Cripple Creek manages to retain a lot of its old charm, with most casinos tucked inside original century-old buildings.

At the turn of the 20th century the city was one of the most important in the state – producing $340 million worth of gold between 1891 and 1916, and a staggering $413 million worth by 1952.

If nothing else, Cripple Creek is a wonderful day trip from Colorado Springs. The road climbs quickly as you head west into the mountains and the last 18 miles, especially in the fall when the trees turn golden, are quite breathtaking.

Cripple Creek is 50 miles southwest of Colorado Springs on Hwy 67. Catch the **Ramblin' Express** (☎ 719-590-8687; www.ramblinexpress.com) from Colorado Springs ($22). The bus departs hourly between 7am and 10pm from the 8th St Depot and leaves from JP McGills casino hourly between 8:30am and 2:10pm.

Phantom Canyon Brewing Co (☎ 719-635-2800; 2 E Pikes Peak Ave; mains $7-18; ⏰ 11am-late) In an old exposed warehouse building, this local brewery serves a variety of pints and American cuisine in a casual atmosphere. The appetizers can be large enough for a meal. Locals flock to the upstairs bar for pool and socializing at night.

Hotel Bar (☎ 719-577-5733; Broadmoor Hotel, 1 Lake Ave) On a warm summer afternoon there's no better spot for a drink with a view than this bar overlooking a private lake. Order a chilled glass of wine and a cigar, and sit back and watch the ducks pass by. When the weather turns cool the outdoor stone fireplaces are lit.

ENTERTAINMENT
Rum Bay (☎ 719-634-3522; 20 N Tejon St; cover $5) There are seven clubs in one at Colorado Springs' long-standing favorite club. You can dance to pulsating techno in one room, sing karaoke on a stage in another or two-step the night away in a third. There's even a mellow lounge with live jazz!

GETTING THERE & AROUND
The **Colorado Springs Municipal Airport** (☎ 719-550-1900; 7770 Drennan Rd) offers a viable alternative to Denver International Airport. The **Yellow Cab** (☎ 719-634-5000) fare from the airport to the city center is between $20 and $25.

TNM&O buses between Cheyenne, WY, and Pueblo, CO, stop daily at the **depot** (☎ 719-635-1505; 120 Weber St). The **transportation center** (☎ 719-385-7433; 127 E Kiowa St; ⏰ 8am-5pm Mon-Fri)

offers schedule information and route maps for all 31 city bus lines.

CENTRAL MOUNTAIN REGION
Colorado's central and northern mountains are well known for their plethora of ski resorts – including world-famous Aspen and Vail. In summer this region offers numerous opportunities for hiking and white-water rafting.

Steamboat Springs
Steamboat has always been, and remains, a ranchers' town at heart. Its historic area features restaurants serving tasty, down-home American cooking, and plenty old mountain bars where the twang of live rockabilly rattles old wood dance floors well into the night. It doesn't have the looks of Aspen or the soul of Telluride, but what Steamboat lacks in Wild West charm, she more than compensates for in snow – and lots of it.

Steamboat Springs' two major areas are Old Town and, 5 miles south, the curving streets at Steamboat Village, centered on the ski resort. US 40 is called Lincoln Ave through town.

The **Steamboat Springs Visitor Center** (☎ 970-879-0880; www.steamboat-chamber.com; 1255 S Lincoln Ave; ⏰ 8am-5pm Mon-Fri, 10am-3pm Sat) can set you up with information.

Steamboat is known for its skiing and its springs. To check out the town's consistently rocking powder, head to the **Steamboat Ski Area** (☎ 970-879-6111; www.steamboat.com; lift ticket adult/child $64/39). With a 3600ft vertical drop, it offers trails for all levels.

MOUNTAIN REGION

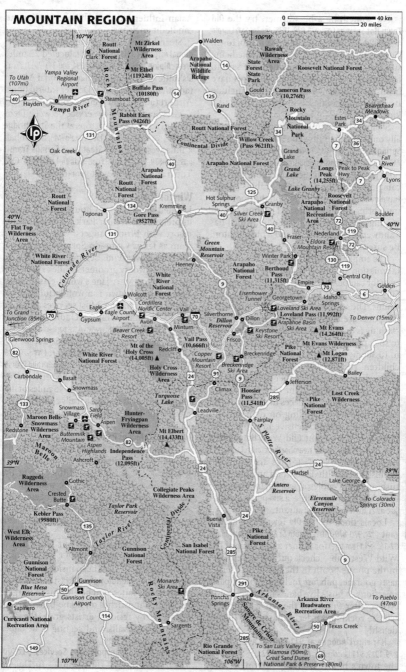

ROCKY MOUNTAINS

For something a bit warmer, try the **Old Town Hot Springs** (☎ 970-879-1828; cnr 3rd St & Lincoln Ave; adult/child $7.50/3) smack in the center of town. Known by the Ute Indians as the 'medicine springs,' the mineral waters here are said to have special healing powers. The pools have been recently renovated and now include two new water slides, a fitness centre and a kiddie pool.

Steamboat's favorite hot springs are actually outside city limits. The **Strawberry Park Hot Springs** (☎ 970-879-0342; www.strawberryhotsprings.com; 44200 County Rd; campsites/cabins/caboose $50/65/105; ☒) offer great back-to-basics relaxation. You can camp or stay in the very simple cabins – these have gas lanterns and futons on the floor (you must bring your own linen). The most luxurious digs are in the single caboose, which has a shower, solar electricity and a bigger futon. Be sure to reserve.

The emphasis here is really on the hot pools (admission included if you stay overnight, even for campers). There is a cool creek, waterfalls and massage therapists to tend to your whims. The sandy-bottomed, rock-lined soaking pools are fantastic on moonlit evenings; clothing is optional after dark. If you just want to soak the springs are open daily from 10am to 10:30pm; admission is $10 for adults, $5 for children. Vehicles without 4WD are required to use chains from November to April for the 3-mile steep road up to the resort.

There are plenty of places to sleep in town, and rates vary depending on demand and season – it's more expensive in winter. Our favorite is the elegant Old West **Hotel Bristol** (☎ 970-879-3083; www.steamboathotelbristol.com; 917 Lincoln Ave; r from $100; ☒). Digs are small but sophisticated, with dark-wood and brass furnishings and Pendleton wool blankets on the beds. There's a ski shuttle, a six-person indoor Jacuzzi and a cozy restaurant.

Locals flock to the **Old Town Pub & Restaurant** (☎ 970-879-2101; cnr 6th St & Lincoln Ave; mains $7-16; ☒ 11am-late) for dinner and dancing. The Wild West pub – check out the bullet holes in the phone booth in the bar area – serves tasty gourmet pub fare including lots of pasta selections. It hosts live bands most weekends. Arrive after 9pm and the old wood floors will be rocking. Order a margarita; they're delish!

Harwigs/L'Apogee at 911 Lincoln Ave (☎ 970-879-1919; 911 Lincoln Ave; mains from $22; ☒ 5-10pm) is the town's best fine-dining option, serving Asian-influenced French fare in elegant, candle-lit environs.

Steamboat is served by the **Yampa Valley Regional Airport** (☎ 970-276-3669), located 22 miles west. **Alpine Taxi** (☎ 970-879-8294, 800-343-7433) runs a shuttle to the Yampa Valley Regional Airport (adult/child $35/18) and Denver International Airport (adult/child $85/40, four hours).

Greyhound's US 40 service between Denver and Salt Lake City stops at the **Stockbridge Center** (☎ 970-870-0504; 1505 Lincoln Ave), about half a mile west of town. **Steamboat Springs Transit** (☎ 970-879-3717) runs free buses between Old Town and the ski resort year-round.

Winter Park

Located less than two hours from Denver, unpretentious Winter Park is a favourite ski resort with Front Rangers, who flock here from as far as Colorado Springs to ski fresh tracks each weekend. Beginners can frolic on miles of powdery groomers while experts test their skills on Mary Jane's world-class bumps. The congenial town is a wonderful base for year-round romping. Most services are along US 40 (the main drag), including the **visitor center** (☎ 970-726-4118; www.winterpark-info.com; 78841 Hwy 40; ☒ 8am-5pm Mon-Fri, 9am-5pm Sat & Sun).

South of town, **Winter Park Resort** (☎ 970-726-5514; www.skiwinterpark.com; lift ticket adult/child $80/50) covers four mountains and has a vertical drop of more than 2600ft. It also has 45 miles of lift-accessible **mountain-biking** trails connecting to a 600-mile trail system running through the valley. Other fine rides in the area include the road up to **Rollins Pass**.

The **Vintage Resort & Conference Center** (☎ 970-726-8801; www.vintagehotel.com; 100 Winter Park Dr; r from $99; ☒ ☒ ☒) is right at the base of the mountain. Standard rooms are smallish, but have high ceilings, big windows and comfortable decor. The on-site restaurant and bar serves decent food. Service is efficient and very friendly.

Locals park their dogs out front of the funky **Base Camp Bakery** (☎ 970-726-5530; 78437 Hwy 40; mains $5-12), then head inside the packed little joint for delicious breakfast sandwiches, rich, creamy lattes, and healthy bison burgers or veggie sandwiches on home-baked bread. Paintings by resident artists grace the cozy stonewashed walls, and seating is at tables with benches.

Home James Transportation Services (☎ 970-726-5060, 800-359-7535) runs shuttles to Denver

International Airport ($40, two hours). Amtrak's *California Zephyr* stops daily in Fraser (near Winter Park), while the scenic **Ski Train** (☎ 303-296-4754; ◷ 9am-4pm Tue-Fri) links Denver with Winter Park (see p752). Greyhound buses stop at the Winter Park Visitor Center and at the Amtrak station in Fraser.

Breckenridge & Around

With its 19th-century mining feel, it is hard to resist fun-loving 'Breck.' It's as appealing to family vacationers as it is to university grads partaking in that great Colorado coming-of-age ritual affectionately known as 'ski-bumming.' Breck has a reputation for partying, but boozing aside, it also makes a great base for regional explorations. Four of Colorado's best ski resorts are less than an hour's drive away.

The **visitor center** (☎ 970-453-6018; www.gobreck .com; 309 N Main St; ◷ 9am-5pm) has information on accommodations.

ACTIVITIES

In winter, it's all about the snow. **Breckenridge Ski Area** (☎ 800-789-7669; www.snow.com; lift ticket $80) spans four mountains and features some of the best beginner and intermediate terrain in the state (the green runs are flatter than most in Colorado), as well as killer steeps and chutes for experts, and a renowned snowboard park.

North America's highest resort, **Arapahoe Basin Ski Area** (☎ 970-468-0718; www.arapahoebasin .com; lift ticket $65) is smaller and less commercial, and you can often ride A-Basin until mid-June. Full of steeps, walls and backcountry terrain, it's a local favorite because it doesn't draw herds of package tourists. The outdoor bar is a great place to kick back with a cold microbrew, and people are always grilling burgers and socializing at impromptu tailgate parties in the parking lot (known as 'the beach').

Keystone Ski Resort (☎ 970-496-2316; www .keystoneresort.com; lift ticket $80) is another option and has night skiing.

In summer there are loads of **hiking** and **mountain-biking** opportunities. Ride up and bike down the trails at Breckenridge (single chairlift/day pass $14/32). The resort rents bikes (half-/full day $24/32).

SLEEPING

Check the major internet hotel consolidators for deals on Breck hotels and condos.

Fireside Inn B&B & Hostel (☎ 970-453-6456; www .firesideinn.com; 114 N French St; dm summer/winter $27/40, r summer/winter from $65/100; ☐) This welcoming hostel and B&B offers a very comfortable stay, as well as ski and bike storage and a hot tub. The owners are super friendly and breakfast is free for private-room guests, $3 for dorm dwellers.

Abbett Placer B&B (☎ 970-453-6489, 888-794-7750; www.abbettplacerbnb.com; 205 S French St; r $85-170) In a restored Victorian home, this is another personable choice. It is well run and has a hot tub, and most rooms have fireplaces. A hearty breakfast is included and free public transportation to the lifts and town stops less than half a block from its door.

EATING & DRINKING

Downstairs at Eric's (☎ 970-453-1401; 111 S Main St; mains from $6; ◷ 11am-10.30pm) Eric's is a Breckenridge institution. And locals flock to this basement joint with a game room for pitchers of microbrews, juicy burgers and delicious mashed potatoes. There are more than 120 beers to choose from.

Fatty's (☎ 970-453-9802; 106 S Ridge Rd; pizza from $7.50; ◷ 11am-10pm) Fatty's is true to its moniker: even the 10in pizza can feed two. Known for the best pizzas in town, including one with a Sicilian-style crust, it is a local dive with a bar that gets rowdy come dark. In summer sit outside on the patio and people-watch.

Cecilia's (☎ 970-453-2243; 520 S Main St) Breckenridge's long loved late-night hangout, Cecilia's packs in crowds all week long. There's a large dance floor with mostly DJ-spun groove (there are occasional live acts), loads of martini types, pool tables and even a corner couch or two. Arrive between 5pm and 8pm for half-price martinis – a great way to start your night.

GETTING THERE & AROUND

Breckenridge is off I-70, 104 miles west of Denver. The **Resort Express** (☎ 970-468-7600) offers service between Breck and Denver International Airport ($60, two hours, multiple trips daily). To get between the resorts hop on the free **Summit Stages** (☎ 970-668-0999) buses; they also go to Vail.

It's easy to hitchhike during the ski season. While this is never entirely safe and we don't recommend it, most people don't have a problem in this region.

ROCKY MOUNTAINS

Vail

Synonymous with swank, Vail is a favorite winter playground for the world's rich and famous. This is where the movie stars ski. And it's not odd to see Texans in 10-gallon hats and ladies in mink coats zipping down the slopes. A resort town in every sense of the word, the compact Vail Village offers restaurants, bars and boutiques of high standard. The glitz factor is certainly up there, but the place is more laid-back and less pretentious than Colorado's other high-octane resort, Aspen. For terrain, Vail is our favorite mountain in the state. Wide open and immense, the back bowls (which cater to intermediate and expert skiers) are nothing short of spectacular, especially on a powder day. Locals must agree, because they flock here by the SUV-load each weekend. Those not shopping and skiing can hike, bike and explore the surrounding alpine country.

ORIENTATION & INFORMATION

Vail Village is the principal center of activity. Motorists must park at the Vail Transportation Center & Public Parking garage before entering the pedestrian mall area near the chairlifts. About half a mile to the west, Lionshead is a secondary center and lift.

Check out the **Vail Visitor Center** (☎ 970-479-1385; www.visitvailvalley.com; Transportation Center; ⏰ 9am-5pm).

ACTIVITIES

Vail Mountain (☎ 970-476-9090; vail.snow.com; lift ticket adult/child $90/60) has more than 5200 skiable acres, 193 trails and extraordinarily high prices. But if you have never skied Colorado it's worth paying the extra bucks to ski here, especially on a fresh powder day. Experts will go gaga over the shoots, tree glades and wide open back bowls, but other ability levels are well taken care of, too. Kids will dig the resort's mountaintop **Adventure Ridge** (☎ 970-476-9090) where they can enjoy mountain biking, disc golf, volleyball and tramp lining in summer, and tubing, snowmobiling, snowshoeing and laser tag in winter.

Cross-country skiers can get their fix at the **Cordillera Nordic Center** (☎ 970-926-5100; www.cordillera-vail.com; 650 Clubhouse Dr, Edwards), 15 miles west of Vail. Check with the White River National Forest Holy Cross Ranger District for details on nearby backcountry ski routes such as Shrine Pass.

The Holy Cross Wilderness Area is rich with **hiking** opportunities. Try the strenuous Notch Mountain Trail that affords great views of Mt of the Holy Cross. The Half Moon Pass Trail leads up Mt of the Holy Cross.

On the south side of I-70, a paved **bicycling** route extends through town to the east, where it links with the Ten Mile Canyon Trail, which takes you over Vail Pass and into Frisco, the hub of Summit County bike trails.

SLEEPING

Apart from the campground, don't expect any budget lodgings near Vail.

Gore Creek Campground (campsites $13) This United States Forest Service (USFS) campground, located 6 miles from Vail Village at the east end of Bighorn Rd, has 25 first-come, first-served campsites open from June to September.

ourpick Tivoli Lodge (☎ 970-476-5615; www.tivolilodge.com; 386 Hanson Rd; r $129-390; ⛄ 🐕 🖳 wi-fi) If you visit in the off-season (i.e. when there's no snow; the fall is cheapest and prettiest), then even the rack rates at this place are the most fantastic deal – meaning you'll probably score something even lower over the internet. Resembling a Swiss or Austrian castle, it's a palatial place that caters to the Euro crowd. Rooms are understated, but incredibly posh with luxurious rich-colored duvets and white walls trimmed in deep brown wood.

Vail Cascade Resort & Spa (☎ 970-476-7111; www.vailcascade.com; 1300 Westhaven Dr; r from $260; ⛄ 🐕 wi-fi) An award-winning swanky property, this is the place to go for luxurious pampering. Rooms feature lots of cherry-wood furnishings and marble vanities. Two movie theaters show first-run films, and a restaurant, athletic club and full spa complete the package. Child care and a children's program are also available. Rates drop dramatically in summer, and parking is $12.

EATING & DRINKING

Joe's Famous Deli (☎ 970-479-7580; 288 Bridge St; dishes $5-8; ⏰ 8am-9.30pm) A casual, counter-service joint, Joe's does a great sandwich – if you don't like one of the 20 grilled and cold varieties, create your own. Kids will delight in the ice-cream possibilities.

Sweet Basil (☎ 970-476-0125; 193 E Gore Creek Dr; lunch $15, dinner $30) Sweet Basil is still churning out what many critics argue is the best food in the state. The menu changes seasonally, but the eclectic American fare, which usually includes favorites such as Colorado leg of lamb with white bean ratatouille, is consistently good. The ambience is also fantastic – big picture windows face out to the alpine scenery, while contemporary art graces the walls.

Billy's Island Grill (☎ 970-476-8811; Lionshead Mall; mains $22-35; ⏱ 11am-10pm) This well-respected restaurant brings the ocean to the mountains with a handsome selection of seafood, as well as aged steaks. It's not the best spot for veggies, but the gourmet cuisine is delicious if you're a carnivore. If you just want to sip drinks on the fabulous deck, check out the less expensive appetizer, soup and salad menu (around $8 per dish).

Tap Room & Sanctuary (☎ 970-479-0500; 333 Bridge St) A favorite stop with hipsters on the bar-hopping circuit, the Tap Room has a giant selection of beers, fabulous margaritas and a cigar lounge. Upstairs, the Sanctuary is a hot club that's popular with a fashionable, younger crowd.

GETTING THERE & AROUND

From December to early April only, the **Eagle County Airport** (☎ 970-524-9490), 35 miles west of Vail, has direct jet services to destinations across the country.

Colorado Mountain Express (☎ 970-926-9800; www.cmex.com) shuttles to/from Denver International Airport ($62, 2½ hours). Greyhound buses stop at the **Vail Transportation Center** (☎ 970-476-5137; 241 S Frontage Rd) en route to Denver ($23, 2¼ hours) or Grand Junction ($18, 3¼ hours).

Vail's free **buses** (☎ 970-477-3456; http://vailgov.com/transit) stop in West Vail, East Vail and Sandstone; most have bike racks.

Aspen

Unbashfully posh Aspen is Colorado's glitziest high-octane resort, playing host to some of the wealthiest skiers in the world. The handsome historic red-brick downtown is as alluring as the glistening slopes, but Aspen's greatest asset is its scenery. The magnificent alpine environment, especially in fall when the aspen trees put on a spectacular display, adds extra sugary eye candy to an already glittering jewel.

Aspen Visitor Center (☎ 970-925-1940; www.aspenchamber.org; 425 Rio Grande Pl; ⏱ 8am-5pm Mon-Fri) has all the usual information.

ACTIVITIES

OK, the top winter activity is pretty much a given: snow riding, and lots of it. The **Aspen Skiing Company** (☎ 970-925-1220; www.aspensnowmass.com; lift ticket $90) operates the area's four ski resorts. **Aspen** (or Ajax) is an athlete's mountain, offering more than 3000ft of steep vertical drop. **Aspen Highlands** has outstanding extreme skiing and breathtaking views. **Buttermilk Mountain** provides gentle slopes for beginners and intermediate skiers. **Snowmass** offers mixed terrain and boasts the longest vertical drop in the USA (4400ft).

The best cross-country skiing in the area is at **Ashcroft** (☎ 970-925-1971), in the beautiful Castle Creek Valley, with 20 miles of groomed trails passing through a ghost town.

In spring, summer and especially fall, Aspen is less crowded and there are some great lodging deals on offer. These are the seasons to experience Aspen's other best outdoor pursuit: **hiking**. September and October are particularly stunning when the yellow leaves of the aspen trees provide a fantastic contrast to the purple hues of the Maroon Bell mountains.

The Hunter Valley Trail leads through wildflower meadows and into the Hunter-Fryingpan Wilderness Area. Hot springs are the reward after 8.5 miles of moderate climbing on the Conundrum Creek Trail. The stunningly beautiful Maroon Bells–Snowmass Wilderness Area is another awesome area to hike.

Mountain biking is also popular, with loads of routes plying Aspen and Smuggler Mountains. The Montezuma Basin and Pearl Pass rides offer extreme bicycling experiences, well above timberline, south of town from Castle Creek Rd. The **Hub** (☎ 970-925-7970; 315 E Hyman Ave) rents bikes.

SLEEPING

St Moritz Lodge (☎ 970-925-3220; www.stmoritzlodge.com; 334 W Hyman Ave; dm $35, r from $80; ⏱ ☐) Neat and congenial, this European-style lodge offers a wide variety of options, from nice dorms to two-bedroom condos. Continental breakfast is served, and the pool and steam room are for all guests. The cheapest rooms share baths.

our pick **Annabelle Inn** (☎ 970-925-3822; www.annabelleinn.com; 232 W Main St; r incl breakfast from $200; ☐ wi-fi) Personable and unpretentious, the newly renovated Annabelle Inn resembles

ROCKY MOUNTAINS

an old-school European-style ski lodge. The location, right on the main street through town, is central, and the place offers rooms that are cozy without being too cute. We liked the two hot tubs – ski videos are shown by the upper one after dark. The included buffet breakfast and 3rd floor observation deck are other pluses.

Little Nell (☎ 970-920-4200; www.thelittlenell .com; 675 E Durant Ave; r from $260; ☒ ☒) Beautiful and relaxing, Little Nell exudes elegant European ambience. Gas-burning fireplaces, high-thread-count linens and rich color schemes make up the bedroom decor. The Greenhouse Bar is perfect for some après-ski unwinding.

Hotel Jerome (☎ 877-412-7725; www.hoteljerome .com; 330 E Main St; r from $270; ☒ ☒ wi-fi) Superb service and relaxed elegance are the trademarks of the historic Hotel Jerome. Rooms feature period antiques, marble baths with big tubs and thick down comforters on the beds. A classic Old West bar, ski concierge and a heated outdoor pool are extra perks.

The **USFS White River National Forest's Aspen Ranger District** (☎ 970-925-3445; 806 W Hallam; ☒ 8am-4:30pm Mon-Fri winter, plus 8am-4:30pm Sat summer) operates nine **campgrounds** (campsites $14).

EATING
Main St Bakery (☎ 970-925-6446; 201 E Main St; mains $6-10; ☒ 7am-3pm) It's a hit, especially at breakfast time, for its gamut of sweet and savory goods – from granola and pancakes to chicken pot pie – in its convivial room and outdoor patio.

Mezzaluna Aspen (☎ 970-925-5882; 624 E Main St; dishes $10-20; ☒ 11.30-10pm) Known for its delicious wood-fired pizzas and serious Italian grub, Mezzaluna is a favorite with Aspen's locals. The après-ski happy hour – from 3.00pm to 5.30pm – is usually packed. Check out the horseshoe-shaped Italian marble bar in the center of the modern dining room with art-heavy walls.

DRINKING & ENTERTAINMENT
Woody Creek Tavern (☎ 970-923-4285; 2 Woody Creek Plaza; ☒ 5-11pm) If you can make it down valley about 8 miles, do so. This local hangout was the favorite watering hole of late gonzo journalist Hunter S Thompson, and quite a few other celebrities, too. There's cheap beer on tap, walls jam-packed with stuff, and a vibe that's just like the bar back home.

J-Bar (☎ 877-412-7725, 330 E Main St; ☒ 11.30am-1am) Inside the Jerome Hotel, this historic old saloon has been a happening watering hole for more than a century now. Popular with both locals and the Hollywood crowd, it is where to see and be seen in town. Order the signature cocktail, the Aspen Crud – a blend of bourbon and ice cream! – or try the delicious J-Rita. The menu (mains $8 to $15) has enough to fill you up, and it goes down really well too. Choose from appetizers, sandwiches and a few filling mains.

Double Diamond (☎ 970-920-6905; 450 S Galena St; admission from $5) When live-music acts – from rock and blues to salsa and reggae – come to town they play at this spacious club. It's seen George Clinton, G-Love and many others. Shows generally get rocking at 10pm.

GETTING THERE & AROUND
Four miles north of Aspen on Hwy 82, **Sardy Field** (☎ 970-920-5380) has commuter flights from Denver, and nonstops to Phoenix, Los Angeles, San Francisco, Minneapolis and Memphis. **Colorado Mountain Express** (☎ 970-947-0506; www.cmex.com) offers frequent services to Denver International Airport ($100, four hours).

Roaring Fork Transit Agency (☎ 970-920-1905; www.rfta.com) buses connect Aspen with the ski areas.

Buena Vista & Salida
Buena Vista and Salida won't stick in your mind after you leave, but shooting the rapids of the Arkansas River or soaking in hot springs under the stars sure will. A bit of a jumping-off point, the area, south of Leadville on US 24, is certainly worth at least a day of your time.

For rafting, stop by **Wilderness Aware Rafting** (☎ 719-395-2112; www.wildernessaware.com; trips from $79). You'll want to run Brown's Canyon (Class III to IV), the Narrows (III to IV) or the Numbers (IV to V), and the earlier in the season the better (try for late April or early May when the river is bloated with snow run-off and the rapids are much more intense). The company is located at the junction of Hwys 285 and 24 at Johnson Village, 2 miles south of Buena Vista.

After a day on the river, forget the soreness with a soak at **Cottonwood Hot Springs Inn & Spa** (☎ 719-395-6434; www.cottonwood-hot-springs.com; 18999 County Rd 306; admission $15). The five pools are rustic with fantastic views (the stars can be amazing). Clothing is optional after dark between October and May, and the resort discourages children. The hot springs are about 6 miles south of Buena Vista. You can spend the night in one of the simple dorms ($35), rooms (from $97) or cabins (from $165) – the latter come with a private soaking pool, but even campsite rates ($35) include use of the public pools.

In Buena Vista and Salida you'll find a string of motels and lodges with rooms from about $80 in summer, less in winter. Rates are usually posted on big signs outside, so you can scope out prices from the car. Speaking of cars, you'll need one to get here. There is no public transportation.

Crested Butte

Remote and beautiful, Crested Butte feels real. Despite being one of Colorado's best ski resorts (some say *the* best), it doesn't put on airs. There's nothing haughty, or even glossy, about the town – just lovely fresh mountain air, a laid-back attitude and friendly folk.

Most everything in town is on Elk Ave, including the **visitor center** (☎ 970-349-6438; www .crestedbuttechamber.com; 601 Elk Ave; ⊗ 9am-5pm).

Crested Butte Mountain Resort (☎ 970-349-2333; www.skicb.com; lift ticket $70) sits 2 miles north of the town at the base of the impressive mountain

of the same name. Surrounded by forests, rugged mountain peaks, and the West Elk, Raggeds and Maroon Bells–Snowmass Wilderness Areas, the scenery is wet-your-pants beautiful. It caters mostly to intermediate and expert riders.

Crested Butte is also a **mountain-biking** mecca, full of excellent high-altitude single-track trails. For maps, information and mountain-bike rentals visit the **Alpineer** (☎ 970-349-5210; 419 6th St).

If you are looking for the privacy of a hotel with the lively ambience of a hostel, then grab a room at the attractive **Crested Butte International Hostel** (☎ 970-349-0588; www.crestedbuttehostel .com; 615 Teocalli Ave; dm $25-38, r $65-95; ⬛), one of Colorado's nicest. The best private rooms have their own baths. Dorm bunks come with reading lamps and lockable drawers. The communal area is mountain rustic with a stone fireplace and comfortable couches. Rates vary dramatically by season, with fall being cheapest.

Certainly not a secret, the **Secret Stash** (☎ 970-349-6245; 21 Elk Ave; pizza $13-17; ⊗ 5-9pm) is an enticing pizza place with a joyful interior. Sit on the floor upstairs, or park yourself on a velvety chair.

Crested Butte has an interesting music scene year-round. Check out the lively **Eldo** (☎ 970-349-6125; 215 Elk Ave), one of the town's

---

LOCAL VOICES: VISITING CONUNDRUM HOT SPRINGS

When I first moved to Colorado from Louisiana, I came in search of things truly Colorado, from hiking trails deep in the mountains to fly-fishing on a secluded creek, mountain biking, kayaking, backpacking and camping. The list could go on. A few years ago I hit Colorado gold with a backpacking trip to the secluded mountaintop Conundrum Hot Springs.

Just about 7 miles outside Aspen in the Maroon Bells–Snowmass Wilderness Area, the hot springs seem to be at the top of the world. To reach them, you have to endure a 9-mile strenuous hike each way. The hike itself is long but bearable, and the trail is well marked. Starting at around 9000ft and ending at nearly 12,000ft, it's the elevation that'll make you work for your prize.

The hot springs themselves appear like a mirage after you stumble and climb your way up the 3000ft, ford a river, and cross logs that circumnavigate a beaver dam. There is a scattering of small individual or two-person pools as well as a larger pool that holds many more. The water temperature seems tepid, but in late June there is still ice and snow covering some of the campsites. Regardless, it was warm enough to sit in for hours and watch the stars streak through the sky. Camping is your only option – other than the not recommended run to reach the beginning of the trailhead (and car) before dark.

We choose the former and enjoyed the hot springs the next morning as well, before heading down. After recovering from my blisters and sore muscles, I look back on the experience and realize I am so grateful I made the trip to Conundrum Hot Springs, because it is one of those truly Colorado experiences!

Danielle Marshall, elementary school teacher and Colorado transplant

most popular microbreweries that doubles as the club at which most out-of-town bands play. Peep at street life below from the great outdoor deck to escape the noise.

Crested Butte's air link to the outside world is **Gunnison County Airport** (☎ 970-641-2304), located 28 miles south of the town. **Alpine Express** (☎ 970-641-5074) meets all commercial flights in winter, but requires reservations in summer. The fare to Crested Butte is $25.

The free **Mountain Express** (☎ 970-349-7318) connects Crested Butte with Mt Crested Butte every 15 minutes in winter, less often in other seasons; check times at bus stops.

SOUTHWESTERN COLORADO

The Southwestern corner of the state boasts stunning alpine scenery and charming old mining towns brimming with Wild West lore. The mysterious Ancient Puebloan ruins, preserved as Mesa Verde National Park, are also here.

Great Sand Dunes National Park & Preserve

Landscapes collide in a shifting sea of sand at **Great Sand Dunes National Park & Preserve** (☎ 719-378-2312; www.nps.gov/grsa; 11999 Hwy 150; admission $3; ☻ visitor center 9am-5pm), making you wonder whether a space ship has whisked you to another planet. The 30-sq-mile dune park – the tallest sand peak rises 700ft above the valley floor – is squeezed between the jagged 14,000ft peaks of the Sangre de Cristo and San Juan Mountains and flat, arid scrub-brush of the San Luis Valley.

Plan your visit to the USA's newest national park (which remains a bargain in the park world by retaining its $3 admission fee) around a full moon. Stock up on supplies, stop by the visitor center for your free backcountry camping permit, then hike into the surreal landscape and set up your tent in the middle of nowhere. You won't be disappointed.

There are numerous **hiking trails,** or the more adventuresome can try **sandboarding** (where you ride a snowboard down the dunes). You'll need your own equipment, but Colorado is jam-packed with snowboard rental shops. Spring is the best time for boarding, when the dunes are at their most moist. For the slickest boarding arrive a few hours after it rains – when the dunes are wet underneath, but dry on top. Try riding down Star Dune, roughly 750ft high. It's a strenuous 3-mile

hike from the Dunes parking lot. The High Dune, about 650ft tall, is another option. Be sure to bring lots of water. Walking in loose sand is difficult, and summer temperatures on the dunes can exceed 130°F (54°C).

There is a **campground** (campsites $12) in the preserve. Otherwise, just south of the entrance you'll find the **Great Sand Dunes Oasis** (☎ 719-378-2222; 5400 Hwy 150; campsites $23, cabins with shared bath $45; ☻ May-Oct). Cabins are rustic one-room affairs with shared facilities. The place has a restaurant and grocery store.

The sand dunes are about 35 miles northeast of Alamosa and 250 miles south of Denver. From Denver, take I-25 south to Hwy 160 west and turn onto Hwy 150 north. There is no public transportation.

Durango

Summer or winter, Durango is nothing short of delightful. It's one of those archetypal old Colorado mining towns, filled with graceful hotels, Victorian-era saloons and mountains as far as the eye can see. If the town alone doesn't whet your appetite, dip into Durango's goody bag of adventures to get the glands really salivating. Meander through the historic district and listen for a shrill whistle, then watch the steam billow as the old train pulls in. Rent a bicycle and explore the trails, or get out the skis and head up the road for mile upon mile of powdery white bowls and tree-lined glades.

ORIENTATION & INFORMATION

Most visitor facilities are along Main Ave, including the 1882 Durango & Silverton Narrow Gauge Railroad Depot (at the south end of town). Motels are mostly north of the town center, which is easily walkable.

The **visitor center** (☎ 800-525-8855; www.durango .org; 111 S Camino del Rio) is south of town at the Santa Rita exit from US 550.

SIGHTS & ACTIVITIES

Taking a ride on the steam-driven **Durango & Silverton Narrow Gauge Railroad** (☎ 970-247-2733, 888-872-4607; www.durangotrain.com; trips from $89) is a Durango must. Rates vary on class, although the cheapest ticket is really just as good as a more expensive one – you're paying for the gorgeous scenery, not how plush your coach is.

These vintage locomotives have been making the scenic 45-mile (3½ hours each way)

WORTH THE TRIP: UFO WATCHTOWER & CAMPGROUND

The sand dunes may have you thinking you've left the planet, but to really keep an eye out for outer space visitors you should stop by the **UFO Watchtower & Campground** (☎ 719-378-2271; www.ufowatchtower.com; admission by donation; campsites $10; 11am-10pm) on Hwy 17, 2.5 miles north of Hooper.

Judy Messoline built the watchtower and opened her property up to UFO fanatics in 2000 after her cattle-ranching endeavors failed. The San Luis Valley is known for its high levels of UFO activity. Those who believe in the paranormal say the area is a giant antenna that attracts alien life forms, while Native American legend says it's a window to other worlds. There have been hundreds of unexplained sightings – everything from mile-long crafts to fireballs filling the night sky.

Today people from all over the country make the pilgrimage to Judy's humble dome with a 2nd-floor viewing deck. The place is becoming more popular each year – now if you ring ahead you can arrange a camping package that includes meals! Ever dreamed of getting married on a UFO watchtower? Well that can be arranged too – Judy happens to be a notary.

In August hundreds gather for an annual night of close encounters with the third kind. A visit is definitely a unique and, if you're lucky, otherworldly, experience. If nothing else, the sunsets are phenomenal.

Of course if you just want to donate, Messoline's website says the place is in need of a black helicopter, night vision goggles, biohazard suits and a phone booth.

---

trip north to Silverton for more than 125 years. The dazzling journey relives the sights and allows two hours for exploring Silverton. This trip operates only from May through October; in winter the train runs to Cascade Canyon (trips adult/child $69/22) – a gorgeous winter-wonderland trip.

Durango Mountain Resort (☎ 970-247-9000, 800-693-0175; www.durangomountainresort.com; lift ticket $64), 25 miles north on US 550, is the town's other drawcard. The resort, also known as Purgatory, offers 1200 skiable acres of varying difficulty and boasts 260in of snow per year. Lift tickets are cheaper here than in the central mountains, and the snow is just as good. Two terrain parks offer plenty of opportunities for snowboarders to catch big air.

In summer the mountain becomes a giant playground. An **alpine slide**, **llama trekking**, **bungee trampoline** and **horseback riding** are just a start. Check the website for packages and pricing. We like the half-day adventure tickets ($29, four hours), which include unlimited rides on the slide and chairlifts, plus one bungee and a try on the rock wall.

Mild to Wild Rafting (☎ 970-247-4789; 50 Animas View Dr; trips from $55) is one of numerous companies offering Animas river-rafting trips. Beginners should check out the one-hour introduction to rafting, while the more adventurous (and experienced) might run the upper Animas, which boasts Class III to V rapids.

SLEEPING

Durango's best sleeping deals are found at the independent motels just north of town on Hwy 550 (Main Ave), with the greatest concentration between 18th and 32nd Sts. Most places are very similar, with clean boxy rooms and swimming pools. Look for rates posted on big signs out front. Rooms go for around $40 in winter, $65 in summer.

General Palmer Hotel (☎ 970-247-4747; www.generalpalmer.com; 567 Main Ave; r from $105;) A Victorian landmark from 1898, the hotel features pewter four-post beds, quality linens and even a teddy bear for snuggling. Rooms are small but elegant, and if you tire of TV there's a collection of board games at the front desk. Check out the cozy library or the relaxing solarium.

Rochester House (☎ 970-385-1920; www.rochesterhotel.com; 721 E 2nd Ave; r winter/summer from $119/159; wi-fi) Influenced by old Westerns (movie posters and marquee lights adorn the hallways), the Rochester is a little bit of old Hollywood in the New West. Rooms are spacious with high ceilings. Two formal sitting rooms serving cookies and a breakfast room in an old train car are other perks at this pet-friendly establishment. If Rochester is full, try the Leland House across the street – owned by the same folks, it has the same rates.

ourpick Strater Hotel (☎ 970-247-4431; www.strater.com; 699 Main St; r $200;) The interior of this lovely, old-world hotel is museum worthy – check out the Stradivarius violin or the gold-plated commemorative Winchester in the lobby. Romantic rooms feature antiques, crystal and lace. Beds are super comfortable with impeccable linens. It's a fantastic deal in winter, when king rooms can go for as little as $89. The hot tub is a major romantic plus – it can be reserved by the hour – as is the summertime melodrama (theater) the hotel runs.

EATING

From the budget diner to the top-end steak house to mouth-watering microbreweries, Durango offers a surprisingly diverse collection of restaurants for a town its size.

Jean Pierre Bakery (☎ 970-385-0122; 601 Main Ave; mains $5-12; ⏱ 8am-9pm) Visit this charming patisserie for a taste of France in Colorado. The mouth-watering delicacies are made from scratch. Don't miss the soup and sandwich lunch special ($12), which includes a sumptuous French pastry chosen from the large counter display. Well worth at least one meal.

Steamworks (☎ 970-259-9200; 801 E 2nd Ave; mains $9-15; ⏱ 11am-late) Industrial meets ski lodge at this popular microbrewery, with high sloping rafters and metal pipes. There's a large bar area, as well as a separate dining room with a Cajun-influenced menu. At night there are DJs and live bands.

Ore House (☎ 970-247-5707; 147 E College Dr; dishes $20-30; ⏱ 5-10pm; ✗) The best steak house in town, food is served in casual and rustic environs. Order a hand-cut aged steak, or try the steak, crab leg and lobster combo known as the Ore House Grubsteak ($40). It's easily big enough for two people. There's also a large wine cellar.

Also recommended:

Olde Tymers Cafe (☎ 970-259-2990; 1000 Main Ave; mains $4-10; ⏱ 11am-10pm) Monday is $5 burger night. Olde Tymers is popular with the college crowd.

Carver Brewing Co (☎ 970-259-2545; 1022 Main Ave; dishes $5-15; ⏱ 11am-late) A local institution, this relaxed brewery is one of the town's favorites.

BREWS & BIKES IN DURANGO

Coloradoans take their beer drinking seriously, but you won't catch locals drinking any of that hopped-up water local beer giant Coors produces. No, Coloradans think of beer the way the French think of wine, and the state has a reputation for producing some mean micro (or small batch) brews. These can range from hoppy to fruity, but all tend to be strong on flavor. For serious punch, order barley wine. The alcohol content can be as high as 9%!

Durango has become a microbrew mecca of sorts. Beer connoisseurs dig that this small town boasts four breweries serving and bottling more than two dozen local beers (many of which are sold in liquor stores across the state and country). Brewers from around the state gather at the Durango Mountain Resort for the **San Juan Brewfest** in September. Check the resort website (www.durangomountainresort.com) for details. The festival includes food, music and of course lots of beer. If you're in the neighborhood, this is a great way to experience Colorado mountain life during a brilliantly beautiful season.

For info on individual breweries, see specific listings in the Eating (above) and Drinking (opposite) sections. The fourth brewery, the **Durango Brewing Co**, doesn't have a tasting room, but you can sample its brews at most local restaurants and liquor stores.

Mountain biking goes hand in hand with beer drinking in Colorado, so it's little surprise a town that supports such a lively microbrew community would also be considered paradise to mountain bikers. Bike geeks take note: Durango is home to some of the world's best bikers including Ned Overend and Travis Brown. From steep single-track to scenic road rides, Durango has hundreds of trails to choose from. Some are well advertised, others locals like to keep secret (much in the manner of surf spots), and you'll have to do a bit of snooping if you want to hit pay dirt. For an easy ride try the **Old Railroad Grade Trail**, a 12.2-mile loop that uses both US Hwy 160 and a dirt road following the old railway tracks. From Durango take Hwy 160 west through the town of Hesperus. Turn right into the Cherry Creek Picnic Area, where the trail starts.

For something a bit more technical, try **Dry Fork Loop**, accessible from Lightner Creek just west of town. It has some great drops, blind corners and vegetation.

There are quite a few sports shops on Main Ave that rent mountain bikes.

DRINKING

With a lively mix of college students and ski-bums, it is little surprise that Durango has an active night scene. Carver Brewing Co (opposite) and Steamworks (opposite) microbreweries are both popular after-dark watering holes. Live and DJ music is featured nightly at Steamworks.

Ska Brewing Company (☎ 970-247-5792; 545 Turner Dr) Big on flavor and variety, we think these are the best beers in town. Mainly a production facility, this small, friendly place has a tasting-room bar usually jam-packed with locals catching up on gossip over an end-of-the-day pint. Ask about weekly BBQs with free food and music (donations are greatly appreciated).

Diamond Belle Saloon (☎ 970-376-7150; 699 Main Ave) An elegant and cozy period place right down to the waitress dressed in Victorian-era fishnets and garter with a feather in her hair. The piano player pumps out ragtime tunes and takes requests. There are half-price appetizers and drink specials from 4pm to 6pm.

Lady Falconburgh's (☎ 970-582-9664; 640 Main Ave) With the largest selection of microbrews and imports in the Four Corners region, it's no secret that this place is popular. There's a brick and brass theme with original murals on the walls and more than 100 beers on offer – 38 of which are on tap. Voted Durango's best pub by locals, it's a great place for mingling. You won't feel out of place alone.

GETTING THERE & AROUND

The **Durango-La Plata County Airport** (☎ 970-247-8143) is 18 miles southwest of Durango via US 160 and Hwy 172. Greyhound/TNM&O buses run daily from the **Durango Bus Center** (☎ 970-259-2755; 275 E 8th Ave), north to Grand Junction and south to Albuquerque, NM.

Durango lies at the junction of US 160 and US 550, 42 miles east of Cortez, 49 miles west of Pagosa Springs and 190 miles north of Albuquerque.

Silverton

A dozen odd years ago, when the last mine shut down, it seemed Silverton was destined to become just another Colorado ghost town. And for a while it was: tourists riding the Durango & Silverton Narrow Gauge Railroad were greeted with long-abandoned storefronts and shabby restaurants. You'd hardly believe that today.

Silverton, with in-your-face mountains covered in blankets of aspens, is Colorado's best rediscovered vintage gem and definitely worth visiting. Whether you're into snowmobiling, mountain biking, fly-fishing or just basking in sunshine, Silverton delivers. Plus it's literally in the middle of nowhere.

Silverton is a two-street town, and only one of these is paved. The main drag is called Greene St, on which you'll find most businesses. Blair St, still unpaved, runs parallel to Greene and is a blast from the past. During the silver rush, Blair St was considered 'notorious' and home to thriving brothel and boozing establishments.

Although Silverton is a tourist town by day in summer, once the final choo-choo departs it turns back to local turf. Visit in the middle of the winter for a real treat – only the most hard-core residents stick around, and you'll find many of the T-shirt shops, and even hotels and restaurants, board up come first snowfall. Snowmobiles become a main means of transportation, and Silverton turns into a winter adventure playground for intrepid travelers.

In summer most people rent jeeps to explore the fabulous 4WD trails in the region (see the boxed text p772). Try the **Red Mountain Motel & RV Park** (☎ 970-382-5512; www.redmtnmotelrvpk.com; 664 Greene St; cabins from $58, r $68), which rents jeeps for $130 per day. The pet-friendly place stays open year-round, and runs snowmobile tours in the winter. The micro log cabins (they really are tiny, especially if you try to sleep four) stay warm and cozy and make good use of their limited space – ours came with a double bed, a bunk, tiny TV with HBO and even a fully outfitted little kitchenette. The river, with good fishing, is just a few minutes' walk away.

For something a bit more upscale, and smack in the middle of town, visit the **Bent Elbow** (☎ 970-387-5775; 1114 Blair St; r $50-100), which also stays open year-round. Each of the quaint, good-sized guest rooms is decorated slightly differently, but all feature a Wild West style. Locals say the restaurant (mains $6 to $12) has the best chef in town. It's a cheerful dining room with a gorgeous old wood shotgun bar that serves Western American fare. In winter the Bent Elbow arranges snowmobiling, guided ice-climbing and dog-sledding trips on nearby Molas Pass, a pristine wilderness area.

ROCKY MOUNTAINS

SCENIC DRIVE: THE MILLION DOLLAR HIGHWAY & OVERTON PASS FOUR-WHEEL DRIVE ROUTE

To really get a feel for the rugged majesty of this region – we would argue it's one of the state's most dramatic areas – take a drive from Ouray to Telluride. Fall is particularly brilliant, when the aspen trees turn the mountainsides into yellow seas.

The following drive starts in Ouray, loops through Silverton and ends in Telluride. If you have at least a Subaru (keep reading and you'll understand) you can make the entire journey in summer, but know that Overton Pass is not paved and is considered a 4WD route.

If you don't feel comfortable, or don't have the right vehicle, it is still worth driving the Million Dollar Hwy (US 550) between Ouray and Silverton (the pass is paved and open all year). This 24-mile stretch of pavement gets its name because the roadbed fill contains valuable ore.

The road is only a silver lining in this golden cloud. This is easily one of the most spectacular drives in America, and would qualify as heaven in John Denver's book. The road clings to the side of the crumbly mountains – it can be scary when raining or snowing – and passes old mine head-frames and larger-than-life alpine scenery. At some points, in fact, the jagged peaks seem close enough to snatch you.

Five miles south of Ouray town limits, on the way to Silverton, you'll pass the **Alpine Loop Backcountry Byway** (www.co.blm.gov/gra). If you have a properly equipped vehicle, it's definitely worth detouring to ride at least a portion of this classic 4WD trail. The path leads through ghost towns such as Animas Forks, forgotten stagecoach stops and trails to five fourteeners. It's worth stopping at the trailhead, regardless of your vehicle, to snap a picture. Canyons are juxtaposed against mountains that remain snowcapped even in July.

Spend a night in Silverton and then get an early start on Overton Pass to Telluride. Silverton local Doug Wall says they call it Subaru pass because 'going from Silverton to Ouray in the summer you can get by in a Subaru. Coming back's a bit more technical, but it's a beautiful drive.'

It sure is. If you're into exhilarating 4WD tracks, this is arguably one of the best (and certainly the most famous) in the state. It's especially appealing because it doesn't require super expertise, and relative beginners can conquer it when starting in Silverton.

The pass is open only in summer, despite the directions internet sites spit out.

'You wouldn't believe the number of people who come in here in the dead of winter…when half the buildings are boarded up because of snow…asking how they can get to Overton pass because they are heading to Telluride. Even though it's a steep 4WD track, Mapquest keeps sending people this way. Oh well, it's good for business,' chuckles Wall, who owns the town's only real bar, the Pride of the West (or POW as the locals say).

Even if you have an SUV of your own, renting a jeep for the trip is well worth your money. There's just something about experiencing that Rocky Mountain high, smelling the pine, tasting the grit of dirt that can only be experienced in an open-air vehicle.

To start the day with a morning latte and a breakfast burrito visit **Mobius Cycles & Café** (☎ 970-387-0770; 1321 Greene St; coffee & mains $3-5; ☻ 8am-5pm), which does the best espresso drinks – we especially like the frozen ones – in town. Ask the proprietor, a young man named Winston Churchill, about the best mountain biking in the area. He also does bicycle repairs.

Right next door to Mobius Cycles & Café, the **Pride of the West** (☎ 970-387-5150; 1323 Greene St) is Silverton's best bar. A gigantic creaking old no-frills place, it is the kind of spot where locals gather late into the night, shooting the shit at the long bar, or playing a game of pool upstairs.

Silverton has about half a dozen hotels and around the same number of restaurants if none of the above places sound appealing – although you'll be hard pressed to find food after 8pm even in the summertime (not even the gas station stays open).

Silverton is 50 miles north of Durango and 24 miles south of Ouray off US 550.

Ouray

No matter how many times you visit, Ouray's views slam you in the face every time. Sandwiched between imposing peaks, tiny Ouray just might be that little bit of paradise John Denver waxes lyrical about in 'Rocky Mountain High.' Here the mountains don't just tower over you, they actually embrace you – the peaks leave barely quarter of a mile of valley floor in town!

The **visitor center** (☎ 970-325-4746; www.ouray colorado.com; 1220 Main St; ☼ 9am-5pm) is at the hot-springs pool.

SIGHTS & ACTIVITIES

Ouray's stunning scenery isn't the only ace up the town's sleeve. For a healing soak, try the **Ouray Hot Springs** (☎ 970-325-4638; 1220 Main St; admission $9; ☼ 10am-10pm Jun-Aug, call for hours rest of year). The crystal-clear natural spring water is free of the sulphur smells plaguing other hot springs around here, and the giant pool features a variety of soaking areas at temperatures from 96°F (36°C) to 106°F (41°C). It is definitely one of the nicest public mineral springs that you will find in the region.

Climbing the face of a frozen waterfall can be a sublime experience. Head to the **Ouray Ice Park** (☎ 970-325-4061; www.ourayicepark .com; admission free; ☼ 7am-5pm mid-Dec–Mar) to try it yourself. This park spans a 2-mile stretch of the Uncompagre Gorge that has been dedicated to public ice climbing. The park is the world's first, and draws enthusiasts from around the globe to try their hand at climbs for all skill levels. For information on its festival, see below. **San Juan Mountain Guides** (☎ 970-325-4925; www.ourayclimbing.com; 2-day courses from $320) offers a weekend two-day introduction course. All equipment is included, but check out the website for dates. If you already know your stuff and just need to pick up gear, stop by **Ouray Mountain Sports** (☎ 970-325-4284; 722 Main St).

FESTIVALS & EVENTS

The **Ouray Ice Festival** (☎ 970-325-4288; www .ourayicefestival.com) is held in January each year and features four days of climbing competitions, dinners, slide shows and clinics. You can watch the competitions for free, but to check out the various evening events you will need to make a $15 donation to the ice park. Once inside you'll get free brews from popular Colorado microbrewer New Belgium.

SLEEPING

Some of Ouray's lodges are destinations in themselves.

Box Canyon Lodge & Hot Springs (☎ 970-325-4981; www.boxcanyonouray.com; 45 3rd Ave; s/d from $70/80) Offers geothermal heated rooms that are spacious and accommodating. The real treat here is four wooden springs-fed hot tubs perfect for a romantic stargazing soak.

Beaumont Hotel (☎ 970-325-7000; www.beau monthotel.com; 505 Main St; r $180-350) Ouray's classiest lodging option, this small hotel offers 12 rooms elegantly appointed with period furnishings. Established in 1886, the hotel was closed for more than 30 years before undergoing extensive renovations and reopening in 2002. It also boasts a spa and three unique boutiques.

Also recommended:

Amphitheater Forest Service Campground (☎ 877-444-6777; US 550; campsites $12) Located a mile south of town.

Historic Western Hotel, Restaurant & Saloon (☎ 970-325-4645; www.historicwesternhotel.com; 210 7th Ave; r $35-95) A range of rooms and stunning views from the open-air 2nd-floor verandah. It serves affordable food.

Wiesbaden (☎ 970-325-4347; www.wiesbadenhot springs.com; cnr 6th & 5th Aves; r from $120; ☻) Guests can use the natural indoor vapor cave for free. Plus it's cozy and romantic.

EATING

Silver Nugget Café (☎ 970-325-4100; 746 Main St; dishes $7-20; ☼ 8am-9pm) A busy, contemporary eatery in a historic building, Silver Nugget features a very large breakfast menu as well as deli-style sandwiches at lunch. Dinner offerings include deep-fried Rocky Mountain rainbow trout, and liver and onions.

Tundra Restaurant at the Beaumont (☎ 970-325-7040; 505 Main St; dishes from $20; ☼ 5-10pm) This elegant restaurant has won several awards for its wine cellar and does Thursday evening tastings. Billing itself as serving 'High Altitude' cuisine, it focuses on regional specialties with great results.

GETTING THERE & AROUND

Ouray is 24 miles north of Silverton along US 550 and best reached by private vehicle.

Telluride

It's hard not to dig Telluride. Once an old Ute hunting ground and then a saloon-swinging mining town, Telluride offers great skiing, great mountain biking and great festivals. She's a good-looking babe; an archetypical Wild West mountain village with a well-preserved Victorian downtown, laid-back residents and fabulous mountain views.

ORIENTATION

Colorado Ave, also known as Main St, is where you'll find most businesses. The town's small size means you can get everywhere on foot, so leave your car at the intercept parking lot at the south end of Mahoney Dr (near the visitor center) or wherever you are staying.

From town you can reach the ski mountain via two lifts and the gondola. The latter also links Telluride with Mountain Village, the true base for the Telluride Ski Area. Located 7 miles from town along Hwy 145, Mountain Village is a 20-minute drive east, but only 12 minutes away by gondola (free for foot passengers).

INFORMATION

Bookworks (☎ 970-728-0700; 191 S Pine St) The town's biggest bookstore.

Telluride Medical Center (☎ 970-728-3848; 500 W Pacific Ave)

Visitor center (☎ 970-728-3041; www.telluride.com; 398 W Colorado Ave; ♡ 9am-5pm)

SIGHTS & ACTIVITIES

Covering three distinct areas, **Telluride Ski Resort** (☎ 970-728-6900; www.tellurideskiresort.com; lift ticket $68) is served by 16 lifts. Much of the terrain is for advanced and intermediate skiers, but there's still ample choice for beginners.

Experienced cross-country skiers will appreciate the **San Juan Hut Systems'** (☎ 970-626-3033; www.sanjuanhuts.com; hut per night $25) series of crude huts along a 206-mile route stretching from Telluride west to Moab, UT. In summer these huts, which are equipped with bunks and cooking facilities, are popular with mountain bikers. Book well in advance, as huts fill quickly.

While on the subject, **mountain biking** is big news in Telluride. The surrounding peaks offer awesome single-track routes and, of course, stupendous scenery. Beginners should try the easy and smooth gravel **River Trail** that connects Town Park with Hwy 145 for a total trail distance of about 2 miles. If you want a bit more of a workout, continue up **Mill Creek Trail**, west of the Texaco gas station near where the River Trail ends. After the initial climb, the trail follows the contour of the mountain and ends at the Jud Wiebe Trail (hikers only) where you'll have to turn back. To rent some gear, visit **Easy Rider Mountain Sports** (☎ 970-728-4734; 101 W Colorado Ave), which has a variety of bikes to choose from, as well as maps and information.

Hiking is also popular. The **Bear Creek Trail** is slightly more than 2 miles and ascends 1040ft to a beautiful cascading waterfall. From here you can access the strenuous **Wasatch Trail**, a 12-mile loop that heads west across the mountains to **Bridal Veil Falls** – Telluride's most impressive waterfalls. The Bear Creek trailhead is at the south end of Pine St, across the San Miguel River.

FESTIVALS & EVENTS

Telluride has two giant festivals each year. **Telluride Bluegrass Festival** (☎ 800-624-2422; www.planetbluegrass.com; admission per day $55) Held in late June, this festival attracts thousands for a weekend of top-notch rollicking al fresco bluegrass. Stalls sell all sorts of food and local microbrews to keep you happy, and acts continue well into the night. Camping out for the four-day festival is very popular. Check out the website for info on sites, shuttle service and combo ticket-and-camping packages – it's all very organized!

Telluride Film Festival (☎ 603-433-9202; www .telluridefilmfestival.com; admission $20-650) Held in early September. National and international films are premiered throughout town, and the event attracts big-name stars. For more information on the relatively complicated pricing scheme, visit the film festival website.

SLEEPING

Telluride's lodging can fill quickly, and for the best rates it's best to book online. Unless you're planning to camp, however, don't expect much in the budget category. Telluride's activities and festivals keep it busy year-round.

Telluride Town Park Campground (☎ 970-728-2173; 500 W Colorado Ave; campsites $10; ♡ mid-May–mid-Sep) Right in the center of town, it has 20 sites with shower access ($1.50 for a hot shower). It fills up quickly in the high season. There are many other campgrounds within 10 miles of town; check at with the visitor center for more info.

Victorian Inn (☎ 970-728-6601; www.tellurideinn .com; 401 W Pacific Ave; r from $99; wi-fi) One of Telluride's better deals, it offers comfortable rooms (some with kitchenettes) and a hot tub and dry sauna. Kids 12 and under stay free, and you can't beat the downtown location. A

BARGAIN BASEMENT HELI-SKIING

Heli-skiing is no longer reserved solely for the Richard Bransons of the adventure world. Thanks to a new trip by **Telluride Helitrax** (☎ 970-728-8377; www.helitrax.net; guided trips $285; ☺ Jan-May), even backpackers can afford the thrill of riding virgin powder above the treeline. Called the Bear Creek Descent, this guided trip is affordable – heli-skiing can cost into the thousands for a single day – because it makes use of a remote yet easily accessible area right outside town. Plus, the trip only includes a single lift in the chopper.

One's all you need, though. After the bird leaves you hovering at 13,200ft on a ridge of Silver Mountain, take a few minutes to admire the views around you – you'll be able to see nine four-teeners in Colorado and mountains as far away as Utah. Then it's time to take the plunge. The guided 4300-vertical-foot descent takes you on an exhilarating ride – this an expert-only trip – that flies into an alpine bowl, over a sheer face, down two couloirs and through the glades before dropping you directly into downtown Telluride. Rates include the rental of extra fat skis, which allow you to cut through waist-high powder with ease. Snowboarders will need their own gear – you'll definitely want to bring a wide powder board or you'll be sure to get stuck. The best snow is usually found in April – strange we know, but typical of Colorado. Helitrax usually begins trips in January, but this varies depending on snow levels and avalanche danger, so check the website.

A powder hound's wildest dream.

continental breakfast is included. Stay here from mid-November through December 20 and get $48 lift tickets. The Victorian offers $58 lift tickets (still a deal) for most of the rest of the season.

Hotel Columbia (☎ 970-728-0660; www.columbia telluride.com; 300 San Juan Ave; r from $140;) Each room at this charismatic place has a balcony, fireplace and a mountain view. Baths are larger than average, and breakfast is included. Other highlights include a rooftop hot tub and fitness room. Plus, the hotel is right across the street from the gondola and it's pet friendly.

Inn at Lost Creek (☎ 970-728-5678; www .innatlostcreek.com; 119 Lost Creek Lane, Mountain Village; r from $189; wi-fi) A boutique luxury hotel that manages to feel unpretentious and as comfortable as your own home. The Inn is perfectly poised at the bottom of Telluride's main lift and, despite the foot traffic outside, remains private. Service is personalized, the rooms impeccably decorated. Be sure to visit the two rooftop spas. Rates are reasonable value – check the website for packages.

EATING & DRIKING

Telluride's main street (Colorado Ave) is packed with bars and eateries.

Baked in Telluride (☎ 970-728-4775; 127 S Fir St; mains $6-10; ☺ 5.30am-10pm) It has become a Telluride institution over the last 25 years, and this is where everyone now heads for a fill-up on pizza, sandwiches, salads and calzones. The front deck is where to sit if you're looking to see or be seen; the atmosphere is more than casual.

221 South Oak (☎ 970-728-9505; 221 S Oak St; mains $19-25; ☺ 5-9.30pm) This is an intimate restaurant in a historic home, with a small but innovative menu mixing world flavors with excellent results. Dishes are meat, fish and seafood based with lots of fresh vegetables. A veggie menu is available upon request.

Cosmopolitan (☎ 970-728-0660; www.columbia telluride.com; 300 San Juan Ave; mains from $20) The on-site restaurant at the Hotel Columbia is one of Telluride's most respected for fine modern dining with a twist.

Smugglers Brewpub & Grille (☎ 970-728-0919; 225 South Pine St) Beer-lovers will feel right at home at casual Smugglers, a great place to hang out in any season. With at least seven beers on tap, this brewpub is big on variety. Try the chocolaty Two Plank Porter or the Smuggler's Scottish Strong Ale. It also serves American pub food (mains $5 to $10).

Fly Me to the Moon Saloon (☎ 970-728-6666; 132 E Colorado Ave) Let your hair down and kick up your heels to the tunes of live bands at this saloon, the best place in Telluride to groove.

GETTING THERE & AROUND

Commuter aircraft serve the mesa-top **Telluride Airport** (☎ 970-778-5051; www.tellurideairport.com), 5 miles east of town – weather permitting. At

ROCKY MOUNTAINS

other times planes fly into Montrose, 65 miles north. **Telluride Express** (☎ 970-728-6000; www.tellu rideexpress.com) runs shuttles to Montrose airport (adult/child $42/20); call to arrange pick-up.

Mesa Verde National Park

Shrouded in mystery, Mesa Verde is a fascinating, if slightly eerie, national park to explore. It is here that a civilization of Ancestral Pueblo Indians appears to have vanished in AD 1300, leaving behind a complex civilization of cliff dwellings. Mesa Verde is unique among parks for its focus on preserving this civilization's cultural relics so that future generations may continue to interpret the puzzling settlement, and subsequent abandonment, of the area.

Mesa Verde rewards travelers who set aside a day or more to take the ranger-led tours of Cliff Palace and Balcony House, explore Wetherill Mesa or participate in one of the campfire programs. But if you only have time for a short visit, check out the Chapin Mesa Museum and walk through the Spruce Tree House, where you can climb down a wooden ladder into the cool chamber of a kiva.

The park entrance is off US 160, midway between Cortez and Mancos. From the entrance it is 21 miles to the **park headquarters** (☎ 970-529-4461; www.nps.gov/meve; 7-day park entry per vehicle $10, bicyclists, hikers & motorcyclists $5), which has road information and the word on park closures (many areas are closed in winter).

The **Chapin Mesa Museum** (☎ 970-529-4631; admission free; ☼ 8am-6:30pm, 8am-5pm winter) is near the park headquarters. Along the way are panoramic **Park Point** (10 miles from the entrance) and the **Far View Visitor Center**

(☎ 970-529-5034; ☼ 8am-5pm), 15 miles from the entrance, where visitors must buy tickets ($2.50) for tours of the magnificent Cliff Palace or Balcony House.

The largest concentration of Ancestral Puebloan sites is at **Chapin Mesa**, where you'll see the densely clustered Far View Site and the large Spruce Tree House. At **Wetherill Mesa**, the second-largest concentration, visitors may enter stabilized surface sites and two cliff dwellings, including the Long House, open late May through August. South from Park Headquarters, the 6-mile **Mesa Top Road** connects excavated mesa-top sites, accessible cliff dwellings and vantages of inaccessible dwellings from the mesa rim.

The park concessionaire, **Aramark Mesa Verde** (☎ 970-529-4421; www.visitmesaverde.com; PO Box 277, Mancos, CO 81328; adult/child from $36/25), offers guided tours to excavated pit homes, cliff dwellings and the Spruce Tree House daily from May to mid-October.

The nearby towns of Cortez and Mancos have plenty of midrange places to stay. Within the national park, visitors must choose between camping or a lodge.

The **Far View Lodge** (☎ 970-529-4421; r $100; ☼ mid-Apr–Oct; ☒) is the perfect spot to watch the sun set over Ute Mountain – it is perched directly on the mesa top, 15 miles from the park entrance. Rooms have Southwestern furnishings, private balconies and the same outstanding views.

Campers can head to **Morefield Campground** (☎ 970-529-4421; campsites/RV sites $19/25; ☼ May–mid-Oct), 4 miles from the park entrance. With 445 campsites, this place has plenty of capacity for the peak season. Grassy campsites at Navajo Loop are conveniently

---

WORTH THE TRIP: RICO

Check out Colorado's last frontier town, tiny **Rico**, an old mining haunt that refused to go bust after the gold ran dry. With a population of just 200, Rico is one of the state's last true Wild West towns. Visit in summer for fabulous fishing along the Dolores River (which conveniently runs through town). Anglers score big with cutthroat, rainbow and brown trout. You can also hike the 9-mile loop from the top of Lizard Head Pass to the base of Lizard Head Peak (check out www. fs.fed.us/r2/sanjuan for more on this hike), a crumbling 13,113ft tower of rock.

You can grub and catch some shut-eye at the **Rico Hotel Mountain Lodge** (☎ 970-967-3000; www.ricohotel.com; 124 S Hwy 145; r incl breakfast $80), which offers comfortable rooms in a refurbished miners boardinghouse. The on-site Argentine Grille serves delicious beef tenderloin tacos with mango, chili and cilantro (around $12). At night, unwind in the hot tub.

Rico is 40 miles north of Durango in Colorado's southwest corner. It is best reached by private vehicle.

IF YOU HAVE A FEW MORE DAYS IN COLORADO

Colorado packs a lot of punch, and we just don't have space for everything. We'll leave you with some tasters, however....

Black Canyon of the Gunnison National Park A fantastic 2000ft-deep chasm that's as eerie as it is spectacular – the combination of depth, narrow openings and sheer walls is dizzying.

Colorado National Monument Magnificent colorful sandstone canyons perfect for hiking, camping and mountain biking around.

Fruita Some of Colorado's finest mountain biking is found on the slick rocks around Fruita, 13 miles west of Grand Junction.

Glenwood Springs Fantastic hot springs and dramatic white-water rafting through a canyon.

Grand Junction A good stopping point if you're heading west on I-70. Western Colorado's main urban hub, Grand Junction has lots of sleeping options.

Leadville A scenically refreshing town with a dramatic mining legacy.

---

located near Morefield Village (which offers a general store, gas station, restaurant, showers and laundry). Free evening campfire programs take place nightly from Memorial Day to Labor Day at the Morefield Campground Amphitheater.

The **Metate Room** (☎ 970-529-4421; Far View Lodge; dishes $15-25; ☯ dinner) features an innovative menu inspired by Native American food and flavors. Palates are titillated by such mains as oven-roasted chicken breast with green chili stuffing and buffalo fajitas.

WYOMING

Galloping with rodeos and pageants, the pioneer past is alive and kicking in the 'Cowboy State.' With much of its beauty derived from its romantic emptiness, sparsely populated Wyoming is the kind of place you'd expect to find that lonesome cowboy riding the range, whistling a melancholy tune and embracing the solitude.

Wyoming's greatest bounty lies in its northwestern corner, which is home to two of the USA's most magnificent national parks: geyser-packed Yellowstone and the majestic Grand Tetons. Gateway towns, such as chic Jackson and progressive Lander, are ideal launch pads for epic hiking, camping, climbing and skiing adventures in the region. To really get off the beaten path, spend a few days wandering through Wyoming's less touristy towns and windswept prairies – places such as Laramie and Cheyenne are hardly on many travelers' radar, but do give a taste of modern Wyoming reality. Be warned: it can feel a bit isolated and depressing.

History

Home to Native American tribes, including the Arapaho and Shoshone who now reside on the 1.7-million-acre Wind River Indian Reservation, Wyoming was opened up to settlers in the 1860s after the construction of the Transcontinental Railroad.

In 1869 legislators granted women 21 years and older the right to vote and hold office – 50 full years before anyone else in the USA! Although Wyoming was later dubbed the 'Equality State,' we're not sure the lawmakers cared all that much about the women's rights movement. Many state officials instead saw it as a clever ploy to attract much-needed female settlers!

In the late 19th century, disputes that sometimes erupted into shoot-outs arose between big cattle barons and the small-time ranchers on the frontier. The Johnson County Cattle War of 1892 remains one of the most contemplated events in the region's history. In 1903 infamous range detective Tom Horn (who worked for the cattle companies) was hanged in Cheyenne for a murder that many still say he did not commit.

The 20th century saw economic development for the state based largely on extractive industries, such as mining. Uranium was discovered in 1918; trona was found in 1939. An economic mainstay for Wyoming and its surrounding states has long been Yellowstone National Park, which has lured large wads of tourist dollars since the end of WWII.

Today Wyoming remains a rural state where most folk either work on the family ranch or have jobs in the energy agency. One of the hottest issues in the state today pertains to trying to keep the younger generation in

> **WYOMING FACTS**
>
> **Nicknames** Equality State, the Cowboy State
> **Population** 506,500
> **Area** 97,914 sq miles
> **Capital city** Cheyenne (population 51,507)
> **State tax** 7%
> **Birthplace of** Abstract expressionist artist
> Jackson Pollock (1912–56)
> **Home of** Dick Cheney
> **Famous for** Yellowstone, homes where buffalo
> roam, agriculture, dude ranches
> **Best Souvenir** A piece of coal – the state is the
> USA's biggest producer

the state following university – and recent census numbers show Wyoming's under-50-year-old population is quickly declining. To entice people to stay, or to interest other 20-somethings to move to the state, politicians are offering cheap plots of land if residents agree to live and work in small towns for a set number of years. The state is also concentrating on boosting tourism revenues.

Information

Wyoming Road Conditions (☎ 307-772-0824, 888-996-7623)
Wyoming Travel & Tourism (☎ 800-225-5996; www .wyomingtourism.org; cnr I-25 & College Dr, Cheyenne, WY 82002)

CHEYENNE

Many a country tune has been penned about the cowboy town of Cheyenne, which doubles as Wyoming's state capital and largest city. With the exception of July's Cheyenne Frontier Days festival (right), this town on the edge of the prairie doesn't offer much for visitors (it's the kind of place people live in, rather than travel to). But its location at the junction of I-25 and I-80 makes it an obvious pit stop.

The **Cheyenne Visitor Center** (☎ 307-778-3133; www.cheyenne.org; 1 Depot Sq; ☼ 8am-5pm Mon-Fri, 9am-5pm Sat, 11am-5pm Sun, closed Sat & Sun winter) is a great resource.

Sights & Activities

The **Cheyenne Gunslingers** (☎ 307-635-1028; cnr Lincolnway & Carey Ave; admission free; ☼ Jun & Jul) are a nonprofit group of actors that put on a lively, if not exactly accurate Old West show – from near hangings to slippery jailbreaks. Stars include corrupt judges, smiling good guys and,

of course, the bad-ass villains. Show times are 6pm daily as well as noon on Saturdays.

For a peek into what life was like in the old days, visit the lively **Frontier Days Old West Museum** (☎ 307-778-7290; 4601 N Carey Ave; adult/child $5/free; ☼ 8am-6pm Mon-Fri, 9am-5pm Sat & Sun summer, 9am-5pm Mon-Fri, 10am-5pm Sat & Sun winter) at I-25 exit 12. It is chock-full of rodeo memorabilia – from saddles to trophies.

Festivals & Events

Beginning late July, the city stages Wyoming's largest celebration, **Cheyenne Frontier Days** (☎ 307-778-7222; 4501 N Carey Ave). It is 10 days of rodeos (admission $10 to $25), concerts, dances, air shows, chili cook-offs and other shindigs that draw big crowds from across the Rockies.

Sleeping

Reservations are a must during Frontier Days, when rates double and everything within 50 miles is booked. Rates drop during winter. A string of cheap motels line noisy Lincolnway (I-25 exit 9).

Lincoln Court (☎ 307-638-3302; 1720 W Lincolnway; r from $50; ☒ ☒ wi-fi) It has decent rooms and is the best-value motel in summer, when it shares facilities with the pricier Best Western next door, including an indoor pool, fitness room and Jacuzzi.

Nagle Warren Mansion Bed & Breakfast (☎ 307-637-3333; www.naglewarrenmansion.com; 222 E 17th St; r from $125; ☒) This lavish spread is a fabulous find. In a quickly going hip neighborhood, it offers very luxurious abodes decked out with late-19th-century regional antiques. Spacious and elegant, the mansion also boasts a small health club, Jacuzzi and massage treatments. Considering the glitz factor, it's a great deal. It also does mystery dinner packages – check the website.

Also recommended:

AB Camping (☎ 307-634-7035; abcamping@juno.com; 1503 W College Dr; campsites/RV sites $14/23; ☼ Mar-Oct) The closest camping to Cheyenne, off I-25 at exit 7.
Little America Hotel (☎ 307-775-8400; www.little america.com; 2800 W Lincolnway; r from $75; ☒ ☒) This sprawling chain hotel west of I-25 has a golf course and large rooms. You can't miss its adverts.

Eating

Albany (☎ 307-638-3507; 1506 Capitol Ave; mains $6-14; ☼ 11am-late) This classic Wyoming country restaurant has been serving locals hand-cut steaks and home-roasted meats for more than half a century. The family-run establishment makes most of its sauces and salad dressings from scratch, and features a long bar as well as leather dining booths. Portions are large, and plates are simple Old West American fare.

Sanford's Grub & Pub (☎ 307-634-3381; 115 E 17th St; mains $7-16; 🕐 11am-10pm) The walls are aflutter with sports bric-a-brac and road signs, and this fun place has a novella-length menu of tasty eats, including burgers, chicken and even a range of 'porker' dishes. Beer is served in ice-cold glasses.

Getting There & Around

The **Cheyenne Airport** (☎ 307-634-7071; www.cheyenneairport.com; 200 E 8th Ave) has daily flights to Denver. Greyhound and Powder River buses depart the **bus depot** (☎ 307-634-7744; 222 E Deming Dr) daily for Billings, MT ($80, 11 hours), and Denver, CO ($19, three hours), among other destinations.

On weekdays, the **Cheyenne Transit Program** (CTP; ☎ 307-637-6253; 🕐 8am-5pm Mon-Fri) operates six local bus routes ($1).

LARAMIE

Laramie is home to Wyoming's only four-year university and when school is in session, the town radiates the kind of boisterous, fun-loving vibe missing from most Wyoming prairie towns. Arrive when the students are away, however, and the place feels a bit too sad and faded to be fun.

For an infusion of culture, check out one of the museums on the **University of Wyoming** (UW; ☎ 307-766-4075) campus. If you're traveling with the kids (or just feel like one), stop by the **Wyoming Territorial Prison & Old West Park** (☎ 307-745-616; www.wyoprisonpark.org; 975 Snowy Range Rd; adult/child $11/free; 🕐 9am-6pm May-Oct, 10am-5pm Sat & Sun Nov-Mar, closed Apr). It's a curious restoration of an early prison and frontier town. The on-site **Horse Barn Theater** (adult/child $30/20) presents nightly melodramas and music revues at 6pm that include dinner.

There are numerous budget sleeping options off I-80 at exit 313. In town, the **Gas Lite Motel** (☎ 307-742-6616; 960 N 3rd St; r $65; ✱ wi-fi) relies on outrageous kitsch set up to sell its well-priced digs. Plastic horses keep watch over the lawn, while plastic roosters languish on the roof. A greenhouse encloses a swimming pool adorned with cowboy murals. The spic-and-span rooms in a U-shaped log-cabin–style building are pet friendly and dressed with playful Wild West touches.

Everyone eats at **Jeffrey's Bistro** (☎ 307-742-7046; 123 Ivinson Ave; dishes $6-14; 🕐 11am-8pm Mon-Wed, 11am-9pm Thu-Sat), which manages to remain packed even in summer. It's a long-established place with a zesty menu of fresh and innovative salads, sandwiches and pasta dishes.

For live country music and beers, you'll want to head to the **Old Buckhorn Bar** (☎ 307-742-3554; 114 Ivinson St) with the college kids.

Located 4 miles west of town via I-80 exit 311, **Laramie Regional Airport** (☎ 307-742-4164) has daily flights to Denver. **Greyhound** (☎ 307-742-5188) and **Powder River** (☎ 800-442-3682) buses stop at the **Tumbleweed Express gas station** (4700 Bluebird Lane) at the east end of town (I-80 exit 316).

BIGHORN MOUNTAINS

With vast grassy meadows, seas of wildflowers and peaceful conifer forests, the Bighorn Mountains are truly awe-inspiring. Factor in gushing waterfalls and abundant wildlife and you've got a stupendous natural playground.

Hundreds of miles of marked trails offer boundless opportunities for **hiking**, **mountain biking**, **snowshoeing** and even **snowmobiling**. Three scenic east–west roads cross the mountains: US 16 (Cloud Peak Skyway), between Buffalo and Worland via Powder River Pass (9666ft), skirts the pristine Cloud Peak Wilderness Area; US 14 (Bighorn Scenic Byway), between Ranchester and Greybull, conquers Granite Pass (8950ft); and US 14 Alternate (Medicine Wheel Passage) traverses Baldy Pass (9430ft), connecting Burgess Junction with Lovell. Along the way, you'll pass **Medicine Wheel National Historic Landmark**, a mysterious and sacred site for Native Americans.

Along all three routes you'll find hiking trails, picnic areas, scenic vistas, fishing streams, and dozens of inviting USFS and Bureau of Land Management (BLM) campgrounds. Check with the **Bighorn National Forest Headquarters** (☎ 307-674-2600; 2013 Eastside 2nd St, Sheridan; 🕐 8am-5pm Mon-Fri) for details.

CODY

Raucous Cody likes to capitalize on its Wild West image (it's named after legendary William F 'Buffalo Bill' Cody). With a streak of yeehaw, the town happily relays yarns (not always the whole story, mind you) about its past. Summer is high season, and Cody puts on quite an Old West show for the throngs of visitors making their way to Yellowstone National Park, 52 miles to the west. From Cody, the approach to geyserland is dramatic to say the least. President Teddy Roosevelt once said this stretch of pavement was 'the most scenic 50 miles in the world.'

The **visitor center** (☎ 307-587-2777; 836 Sheridan Ave; ☯ 8am-6pm Mon-Sat, 10am-3pm Sun Jun-Aug, 8am-5pm Mon-Fri Sep-May) is the logical starting point.

Cody's major tourist attraction is the superb **Buffalo Bill Historical Center** (☎ 307-587-4771; www.bbhc.org; 720 Sheridan Ave; adult/child $15/6; ☯ 7am-8pm Jun-Aug, 10am-3pm Tue-Sun Sep-May). A sprawling complex of five museums, it showcases everything Western: from posters, grainy films and other lore pertaining to Buffalo Bill's world-famous Wild West shows, to galleries showcasing frontier-oriented artwork to museums dedicated to Native Americans. Its Draper Museum of Natural History explores the Yellowstone region's ecosystem with excellent results. Also popular is the **Cody Nite Rodeo** (☎ 307-587-2992; Stampede Park, 421 W Yellowstone Ave; adult/child from $12/6), which giddy-ups nightly from June to August.

A great range of accommodations is offered at the pleasing **Gateway Campground** (☎ 307-587-2561; www.gatewaycamp.com; 203 Yellowstone Ave; campsites/RV sites $12/22, r & cabins from $65; ☒ ▯). There are shady sites for camping, cozy cabins (with air con and TVs!) and motel rooms.

Built by ol' Mr Bill in 1902, **Irma Hotel** (☎ 307-587-4221; www.irmahotel.com; 1192 Sheridan Ave; r from $95; ☒) offers historic rooms in the main building or more modern, less expensive motel-style rooms. Don't miss the on-site Silver Saddle Saloon; the ornate cherry-wood bar was a gift from Queen Victoria. Gun fights break out nightly at 6pm in front of the hotel from June through September.

The **Silver Dollar Bar** (☎ 307-527-7666; 1313 Sheridan Ave; mains $5-10) is a historic watering hole with lots of TV screens and live music nightly. It serves yummy burgers and has pool tables.

Yellowstone Regional Airport (☎ 307-587-5096; www.flyyra.com) is 1 mile east of Cody and runs daily flights to Salt Lake City and Denver. **Powder River** (☎ 800-442-3682) buses stop at **Palmer's Outpost** (1521 Rumsey Ave) en route to Casper or Billings, MT.

LANDER

Lander just might be the coolest little one-street town in Wyoming. Just a stone's throw from the Wind River Indian Reservation, it's a rock-climbing and mountaineering mecca attracting folks the region over.

Despite its growing popularity, Lander remains refreshingly unpretentious. Playing in the outdoors is of paramount importance to locals, and when the day's climbing festivities finish, impromptu celebrations take place over brews at the town's only bar.

The **Lander Visitor Center** (☎ 307-332-3892; www.landerchamber.org; 160 N 1st St; ☯ 9am-5pm Mon-Fri) is a good source of general information. If you've come to hike, camp or climb you're best popping into **Wild Iris Mountain Sports** (☎ 307-332-4541; 333 Main St). The shop has the inside scoop on Lander's best spots for all three. If you want to check out the single-track trails outside town, head down the street to **Freewheel Ski & Cycle** (☎ 307-332-6616; 378 W Main St).

Sinks Canyon State Park, 6 miles south of Lander on Sinks Canyon Rd (Hwy 131), is a beautiful park with perplexing natural features. The Middle Fork of the Popo Agie River

---

ROCKY MOUNTAINS

DUDE RANCHING IN THE COWBOY STATE

If you've ever watched the Billy Crystal classic *City Slickers*, you've probably dreamed of spending a week at a dude ranch. If you're in the neighborhood make the fantasy a reality and spend some time at the **Vee Bar Guest Ranch** (☎ 307-745-7036; www.vee-bar.com; 2081 Hwy 130; r per day/week $150/1450; ☒). This gorgeous property, sitting on 800 acres 21 miles west of Laramie, serves up the true Wyoming cowboy experience. Free activities include state staples such as horseback riding, fishing or tubing rivers and overnight campouts under the stars. Although most guests stay for a full week, Vee Bar offers the rather unique (for dude ranches) option of single-night visits when it is not full. This is wonderful option for folks short on time and money who still want a taste of ranch life. Rates also include meals (dinners are steak and seafood affairs; call ahead if you're a veggie to make sure there's something you can eat). Expect digs in comfortable, rustic and old-fashioned cabins.

flows through the narrow canyon, disappears into the soluble Madison limestone called the Sinks, and pops up faster and warmer a quarter of a mile downstream in a pool called the Rise. The summer-only **visitor center** (☎ 307-332-3077; 3079 Sinks Canyon Rd; ☺ 9am-6pm Jun-Aug) is near two scenic **campgrounds** (campsites $8), which come highly recommended by the locals.

For lodging, one of the better returns for your money is **Pronghorn Lodge** (☎ 307-332-3940; www.pronghornlodge.com; 150 Main St; r from $60; ☒), which has faultless and spacious rooms, plus a hot tub.

Pizza, sandwiches and salads go down well on the outdoor deck or inside the big wooden barnlike structure called the **Lander Bar** (☎ 307-332-8228; 126 Main St; dishes $5-8; ☺ 11am-late). A Lander institution, it not only serves filling fare (although ask for your sandwiches with the dressing on the side), it's also the place to go for climbing and mountain-biking gossip. There's live music many nights.

Wind River Transportation Authority (☎ 307-856-7118; www.wrtabuslines.com) provides scheduled Monday-to-Friday service between Lander, Riverton, Dubois, Rock Springs and Riverton Regional Airport ($15).

YELLOWSTONE NATIONAL PARK

They grow their mammals and geysers big up in Yellowstone, America's first national park and Wyoming's flagship attraction. From shaggy grizzlies to giant moose, this park boasts the lower 48's most motley concentration of wildlife. Plus, it is home to half the world's geysers. And when you factor in the plethora of alpine lakes, rivers and waterfalls you'll quickly realize you've stumbled across one of Mother Nature's most fabulous creations. This natural cornucopia attracts up to 30,000 visitors daily in summer and three-million gatecrashers annually. To escape the crowds, take a hike.

When John Colter became the first white man to visit the area in 1807, the only inhabitants were Tukadikas, a Shoshone Bannock people who hunted bighorn sheep. Colter's reports of the soaring geysers and boiling mud holes (at first dismissed as tall tales) brought in expeditions and tourism interest. The park was established in 1872 to preserve Yellowstone's spectacular geography: the geothermal phenomena, the fossil forests and Yellowstone Lake.

Orientation

The 3472-sq-mile park is divided into five distinct regions (clockwise from the north): Mammoth, Roosevelt, Canyon, Lake and Geyser Countries.

Of the park's five entrance stations, only the North Entrance, near Gardiner, MT, is open year-round. The others, typically open May to October, are the Northeast Entrance (Cooke City, MT), the East Entrance (Cody), the South Entrance (north of Grand Teton National Park) and the West Entrance (West Yellowstone, MT). The park's main road is the 142-mile Grand Loop Rd scenic drive.

Information

The park is open year-round, but most roads close during winter. Park entrance permits (hiker/vehicle $12/25) are valid for seven days for entry into both Yellowstone and Grand Teton National Parks. Summer-only visitor centers are evenly spaced every 20 to 30 miles along Grand Loop Rd. The **Albright Visitors Center & Park Headquarters** (☎ 307-344-2263; www.nps.gov/yell; Mammoth; ☺ 8am-7pm Jun-Aug, 9am-5pm Sep-May) serves as park headquarters.

Sights & Activities

Just sitting on the porch of the Old Faithful Lodge with a cocktail in one hand and a book in the other waiting for the geyser to erupt could be considered an activity by itself. While it's perfectly acceptable – and really quite encouraged – this better not be the only thing you do in this fabulous national park. No, get your butt off the bench and go for a hike.

Yellowstone is split into five regions, representing the five distinct ecosystems found inside the park's boundaries. And we encourage you to explore them all. You'll be given a map upon entering the national park (and your admission to Grand Teton is good here, so you can go back and forth at leisure without paying twice), and all the lodges have helpful information desks. Don't be scared to ask a park ranger for a trail recommendation; many will go out of their way to help you tailor a hike to your tastes – from great photo spots to best chance at spotting bear.

Geyser Country has the most geothermal features in the park. Upper Geyser Basin contains 180 of the park's 200 to 250 geysers. The most famous is **Old Faithful**, which spews from 3700 to 8400 gallons of water 100ft to 180ft into the air every 1½ hours or so. The Firehole

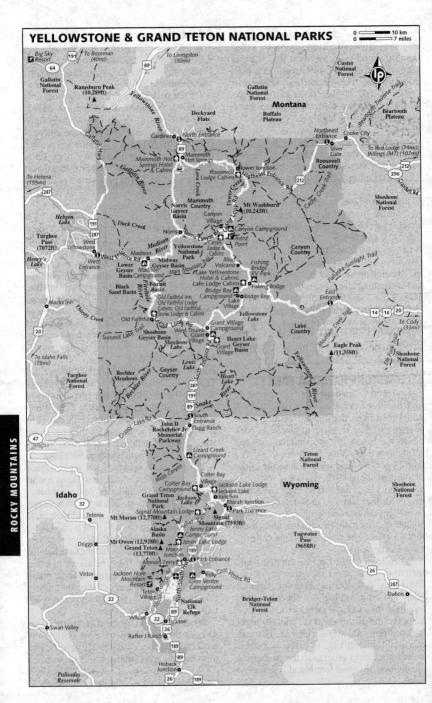

and Madison Rivers offer superb fishing and wildlife viewing. For an easy walk, check out the well-marked, very easy gravel and paved walking trail around Old Faithful and other smaller geysers that begins just outside Old Faithful Lodge.

Known for its fossil forests and geothermal areas at Mammoth Hot Springs and Norris Geyser Basin, **Mammoth Country** is North America's most volatile and oldest-known continuously active (115,000 years) thermal area. The peaks of the Gallatin Range rise to the northwest, towering above the area's lakes, creeks and numerous hiking trails.

Fossil forests, the commanding Lamar River Valley and its tributary trout streams, Tower Falls and the Absaroka Mountains' craggy peaks are the highlights of **Roosevelt Country**, the park's most remote, scenic and undeveloped region. Several good hikes begin near Tower Junction.

A series of scenic overlooks and a network of the Grand Canyon of the Yellowstone rim trails highlight the beauty of **Canyon Country**. South Rim Dr leads to the canyon's most spectacular overlook, at Artist Point. Mud Volcano is Canyon Country's primary geothermal area. Notable trails include the Seven Mile Hole Trail, which descends from the north rim into the canyon and tracks up Mt Washburn (10,243ft), the park's second-highest highest peak. Eagle Peak (11,358ft), just scraping by inside the park boundaries, is the highest mountain in Yellowstone.

Yellowstone Lake, the centerpiece of **Lake Country** and one of the world's largest alpine lakes, is also home to the country's largest inland population of cutthroat trout. Rising east and southeast of the lakes, the oft snowcapped Absaroka Mountains make for a dramatic picture – capture their reflection in the water at sunrise for something really unique.

Hikers can explore Yellowstone's backcountry from more than 85 trailheads that give access to 1200 miles of **hiking** trails. A free backcountry-use permit, available at visitor centers and ranger stations, is required for overnight trips. Backcountry camping is allowed in 300 designated sites, 60% of which can be reserved in advance by mail; a $20 fee applies regardless of the number of nights.

Bicycling is best from April to October, when the roads are usually snow-free. Cyclists can ride on public roads and a few designated service roads, but not on the backcountry trails.

ROCKY MOUNTAIN SAFARI: THE PLACES WHERE BEAR & BISON STILL ROAM

Who says safari can only happen in Africa? North America also has some fabulous megafauna. And there is nowhere better to seek out the USA's 'big five' – grizzly, black bear, moose, mountain lion and lynx – than the country's first national park.

Along with the big mammals, Yellowstone is also home to elk, pronghorn antelope and bighorn sheep. Despite some grumblings from worried farmers just outside park boundaries, wolves and bison have been reintroduced into the national park with great success. Both species are native to the area, but by the end of the last century hunting and human habitation had sent their populations spiraling toward extinction. In the last decade, the numbers have once again risen, which has ecologists and rangers alike excited.

Hayden Valley, in Yellowstone's heart, is your best all-round bet for wildlife-viewing. Check along the Yellowstone River between Yellowstone Lake and Canyon Village. For the best chances of seeing wildlife, get up early or stay out late (dawn and dusk are the best times to see the furry creatures). You can pull over anywhere off Grand Loop Rd and stage a stakeout. Have enough patience (and a pair of binoculars handy) and a bear just might wander into your viewfinder, or perhaps you'll spy a rutting elk or hear the bugle of a solitary moose before it dips its mighty head into the river for a drink.

If wolves are your thing, **Lamar Valley**, in the northern part of the park, is ground zero for spotting these magnificent beasts (it's where the animals are being reintroduced). Ask rangers where the action is at the moment; at the time of research wolves were often seen between Tower Junction and Yellowstone's northeast entrance. Catching even a fleeting glimpse of these wild and shaggy giant dogs, once almost gone forever, is a refreshing and magical experience that reminds us there are parks in the USA wild enough to just get lost looking for wolves and to take a poop with the bear in the wilderness.

Most park trails are not groomed, but unplowed roads and trails are open for **cross-country skiing**. The rapids of Yankee Jim Canyon on the Yellowstone River host white-water rafting day-trippers. **Yellowstone Raft Company** (☎ 800-858-7781; www.yellowstoneraft.com) offers a range of guided adventures out of Gardiner starting in late May.

Sleeping

NPS and private campgrounds, along with cabins, lodges and hotels, are all available in the park. Reservations are essential in summer. Contact the park concessionaire **Xanterra** (☎ 307-344-7311; www.travelyellowstone.com) to reserve a spot at its campsites, cabins or lodges.

Plentiful accommodations can also be found in the gateway towns of Cody (p780), Gardiner and West Yellowstone.

CABINS & LODGES

Xanterra-run cabins, hotels and lodges are spread around the park and open from May or June to October. Mammoth Hot Springs Hotel and Old Faithful Snow Lodge are the exceptions; these lodges are also open mid-December through March. All places are nonsmoking and none have air con, TV or internet hook-ups.

Roosevelt Lodge Cabins (Roosevelt Country; cabins $64-104) These cabins are good for families. With a cowboy vibe, the place offers nightly 'Old West dinner cookouts.' Guests travel by horse or wagon to a large meadow 3 miles from the lodge for open-air buffets.

Lake Lodge Cabins (Lake Country; cabins $64-121) The main lodge boasts a large front porch with lakeside mountain views and a cozy great room with two fireplaces. Choose from rustic 1920s wooden cabins or more modern motel-style modules.

Grant Village (Lake Country; r $91-121) Near the southern edge of the park, it offers attractive motel-style rooms. Two nearby restaurants have fabulous lake views and provide easy access to sustenance.

Old Faithful Snow Lodge & Cabins (Geyser Country; r $91-175) The newest sleeping option in the park is built to resemble a great Old Western lodge (think lots of timber). Wildlife-themed, the place tries to incorporate classic park motifs. Rooms are stylish and modern.

our pick **Old Faithful Inn** (Geyser Country; r $97-200) Built right next to the signature geyser, it's little surprise Old Faithful is the most requested lodging in the park. A national historic landmark, it embodies everything a national park lodge should. The immense timber lobby, with its huge stone fireplaces and sky-high knotted pine ceilings, is the sort of place you'd imagine Teddy Roosevelt lingering. Rooms come in all price ranges – the cheapest share baths – which is wonderful as even staying in a room without a toilet is worth the splurge here (hint: stay two nights to really get a feel and your money's worth). Even if you're in one of the lovely 'premium rooms,' don't count on spending much time in it – the public areas are just too alluring!

Lake Yellowstone Hotel & Cabins (Lake Country; cabins $111, r $139-211) Oozing grand 1920s Western ambience, this historic hotel is a classy option. It has Yellowstone's most divine lounge, which was made for daydreaming; it offers big picture windows with lake views, lots of natural light and a live string quartet serenading in the background. Rooms are well appointed, cabins more rustic.

Also recommended:

Canyon Lodge & Cabins (Canyon Country; cabins $40-115, r $145) Clean and tidy in a central local.

Old Faithful Lodge Cabins (Geyser Country; cabins $64-104) Views of Old Faithful; simple, rustic cabins.

Mammoth Hot Springs Hotel & Cabins (Mammoth Country; cabins $64-104, r $70-280) Wide variety of sleeping options; elk are often seen grazing on the front lawn.

CAMPING

The best budget options are the seven NPS-run campgrounds (campsites $14), in Mammoth (open year-round), Roosevelt and Geyser Countries, which are first-come, first-served. Xanterra runs five campgrounds (reservations accepted, per night for up to six people $18), all with cold-water bathrooms, flush toilets and drinking water. RV sites ($23) are also available.

Bridge Bay Campground (Lake Country) Near the west shore of Yellowstone Lake. There are 431 sites.

Canyon Campground (Canyon Country) Centrally located, with pay showers and coin laundry nearby. There are 272 sites.

Fishing Bridge RV Park (Lake Country) Full hook-ups for hard-shell RVs only ($33). Pay showers and coin laundry. There are 346 sites.

Grant Village Campground (Lake Country) On Yellowstone Lake's southwest shore. Pay showers and coin laundry nearby. There are 425 sites.

Madison Campground (Geyser Country) Generator-free, tent-only area. There are 280 sites.

ROCKY MOUNTAINS

Eating

Snack bars, delis, burger counters and grocery stores are scattered around the park. In addition, most of the lodges offer breakfast buffets, salad bars, and lunches and dinners in formal dining rooms. Food, while not always exceptional, is quite good considering how many people the chef is cooking for and not too over-priced for the exceptional views. Dinner reservations are required at Lake Yellowstone Hotel (☎ 307-242-3899), Grant Village (☎ 307-242-3499) and the Old Faithful Inn (☎ 307-545-4999).

We like the restaurant at the **Old Faithful Inn** (lunch $6-9, dinner $22-30; ☯ 11am-2pm & 6-10pm) best for its super reasonable lunches and its more daring than usual American menu. The Bear Pit next door is where to head if you are famished between meals (maybe after a geyser hike). It serves a couple of appetizers – including a yummy baked brief ($7) – that will tide you over until dinner is served.

Getting There & Away

The closest year-round airports are: Yellowstone Regional Airport in Cody (52 miles); Jackson Hole Airport in Jackson (56 miles); Gallatin Field Airport (Bozeman, MT, 65 miles); and Idaho Falls Regional Airport (107 miles) in Idaho. The airport in West Yellowstone, MT, is usually open June to September. It's often more affordable to fly into Salt Lake City, UT (390 miles), or Denver, CO (563 miles), and then rent a car.

No public transportation exists to or within Yellowstone National Park. During summer commercial buses operate from Jackson and Cody. Buses operate to West Yellowstone and Gardiner from Bozeman year-round.

GRAND TETON NATIONAL PARK

It's hard to stop gawking at the jagged granite spires of the Teton Range, the centerpiece of spectacular Grand Teton National Park. Twelve glacier-carved summits rise above 12,000ft, crowned by the singular Grand Teton (13,770ft). The park is less crowded and more intimate than neighboring Yellowstone, offering boundless opportunities to get off the beaten track. Numerous hiking trails wind through alpine scenery, past rushing streams and around translucent lakes that mirror the soaring peaks. Bear, elk and moose roam this 40-mile-long range; the chance of spotting wildlife is good.

Orientation

The park has two entrance stations: Moose (south), on Teton Park Rd west of Moose Junction; and Moran (east), on US 89/191/287 north of Moran Junction. The park is open year-round, although some roads and entrances close from around November to May 1, including part of Moose–Wilson Rd, restricting access to the park from Teton Village.

Information

Park entrance permits (hiker/vehicle $12/25) are valid for seven days for entry into both Yellowstone and Grand Teton National Parks. It's easy to stay in one park and explore the other in the same day.

The **Park Headquarters** (☎ 307-739-3600; www.nps.gov/grte; ☯ 8am-7pm Jun-Aug, 8am-5pm rest of year) shares a building with **Moose Visitor Center** (☎ 307-739-3399, for backcountry permits 307-739-3309; Teton Park Rd; ☯ 8am-7pm Jun-Aug, 8am-5pm rest of year), half a mile west of Moose Junction.

Activities

Upon entering the park you'll be given a packet with info about what to do in it – including lodging options. The park has 200 miles of hiking trails; pick up maps at the visitor centers. A free backcountry-use permit, also available at visitor centers, is required for overnight trips. The north–south Teton Crest Trail, which runs just west of the main summits, can be accessed from trailheads that wind up steep canyons.

The Tetons offer great rock climbing. Excellent short routes abound, as well as classic longer summits, such as Grand Teton, Mt Moran and Mt Owen. The **Jenny Lake Ranger Station** (☎ 307-739-3343; ☯ 8am-6pm Jun-Aug) is ground zero for climbing information. For instruction and guided climbs, contact **Exum Mountain Guides** (☎ 307-733-2297; www.exumguides.com).

Fishing is also a draw – several species of whitefish and cutthroat, lake and brown trout thrive in the park's rivers and lakes. Get a license at the Moose Village store, Signal Mountain Lodge or Colter Bay Marina. **Cross-country skiing** and **snowshoeing** are the best ways to take advantage of winter in the park. Pick up a brochure at Moose Visitor Center detailing routes.

Park concessionaire **Grand Teton Lodge Company** (☎ 307-543-3100; www.gtlc.com) has activity desks at each of its lodges. Options include scenic Snake River float trips (adult/child from $49/29), horseback trail rides ($33, one hour) and guide fishing on Jackson Lake ($65 per hour, two-hour minimum).

Sleeping

Most of the Grand Teton's private lodges and cabins are run by ecofriendly Grand Teton Lodge Company. The park concessionaire pushes sustainable energy, water conservation and recycling – you'll see bins around the park. It's best to reserve ahead, as the most popular rooms fill up a year in advance. Nearly everything is completely booked by the beginning of June. Call ahead for last-minute cancellations if you don't have a reservation.

Note that in keeping with the natural theme, none of the rooms in the park have air con or TVs – although you will find land-line telephones now and free wi-fi in the Jackson Lake Lodge lobby (anyone can use this).

Colter Bay Village (☎ 307-543-3100; www.gtlc.com; canvas tents $41, cabins $44-140; ☽ Jun-Sep) Cozy log and tent cabins on the shores of Jackson Lake. Rustic, yet comfortable, this is a good choice for families and budget travelers. There are two restaurants, a marina and grocery store on the premises.

Signal Mountain Lodge (☎ 307-543-2831; www.signalmtnlodge.com; r $120-150, cabins $160; ☽ May–mid-Oct) At the edge of Jackson Lake, this spectacularly located place offers a variety of accommodation options including cozy well-appointed cabins and rather posh rooms with stunning lake and mountain views.

Jackson Lake Lodge (☎ 307-543-3100; www.gtlc.com; r $189; ☽ Jun-Sep; ☒ wi-fi) The grand lobby, with its sky-high ceilings and 60ft picture windows showcasing perfect Teton views, is the centrepiece of this full-service resort with 365 guest rooms perched on a bluff overlooking Jackson Lake. Rooms are large and Western-themed; most are in cabin blocks around the property. This is the most popular lodge in the park, and fills quickly – definitely reserve in advance.

Jenny Lake Lodge (☎ 307-543-3100; www.gtlc.com; s/d $425/525; ☽ Jun-Sep) Sitting a quiet location amid the pines, Jenny Lake Lodge is the Grand Teton's most exclusive lodging option. Digs are in 37 historic Western-styled cabins. Each is beautifully decorated with thick down comforters and handmade quilts. Rates include breakfast, a five-course dinner, horseback riding and mountain biking.

CAMPING

The **NPS** (☎ 307-739-3603) operates the park's five **campgrounds** (campsites $12), all first-come, first-served. Demand for sites is high from early July to Labor Day. Most campgrounds fill by 11am (Jenny Lake fills much earlier; Gros Ventre rarely fills up). Colter Bay and Jenny Lake have tent-only sites reserved for backpackers and cyclists.

Eating

Several reasonably priced restaurants are in and around Colter Bay Village, Jackson Lake Lodge and Moose Junction. The lodges all have restaurants of some sort.

Pioneer Grill (☎ 307-543-1911; Jackson Lake Lodge; mains $5-10; ☽ 7am-9pm) This 1950s-style soda fountain offers service at counter-tops that snake around the room in a serpentine. The food is nothing special – burgers and grilled cheese – but reasonably priced. Kids will love the ice-cream sundaes ($6).

Mural Room (☎ 307-543-1911; Jackson Lake Lodge; mains $15-36; ☽ 7am-9pm) The butter comes shaped like a moose and the in-your-face Teton views justify the buffalo tenderloin's $36 price tag. A moderately priced wine list, stellar service and linen table cloths round out the Jackson Lake Lodge's most upscale dining option.

Jenny Lake Lodge Dining Room (☎ 307-543-3352; 5-course meal per person $60; ☽ 7am-9pm) Dinner is an intimate five-course experience served in a quaint log dining room. Breakfast is also fixed-price menu. Lunch is a more casual à la carte affair. Dinner and breakfast reservations required; jackets suggested for men at dinner. The porch is perfect for cocktails.

JACKSON

Jackson is as jet-setting as Wyoming gets. The handsome town – which many people incorrectly call Jackson Hole (the 'Hole' actually refers to the entire valley) – is set against a stellar Teton backdrop. It's the kind of place where cowboy meets couture, where moose, elk and bison cruise the valley floor and powder hounds swish down world-class ski slopes. The vibe is playful and slightly glam, but never pretentious. Wander into the Mangy Moose Saloon, packed with ski-bums, tourists, hipsters, ranchers and even the occasional movie star, and you'll get the idea. Jackson buzzes year-round, and summer visitors can hike, bike, raft and roam to their heart's content.

Orientation & Information

Most of the area's amenities are concentrated in the town of Jackson. Teton Village, 12 miles northwest of Jackson, is home to the wintertime mecca of Jackson Hole Mountain Resort.

Jackson Hole Wyoming (www.jacksonholenet.com) A good website for information on the area.

Valley Bookstore (☎ 307-733-4533; 125 N Cache St) Has a superb selection of books, as well as regional maps.

Visitor center (☎ 307-733-3316; www.jacksonhole chamber.com; 532 N Cache Dr; ◷ 9am-5pm)

Sights

Downtown Jackson has a handful of **historic buildings** and, in summer, the **town square shoot-out** (admission free) is a hokey tourist draw; it takes place at 6:15pm Monday to Saturday. For more substance, visit the **National Elk Refuge** (☎ 307-733-9212; www.nationalelkrefuge .fws.gov/; Hwy 89; admission free; ◷ 8am-5pm Sep-May, 8am-7pm Jun-Aug), about 2 miles northeast of town via Elk Refuge Rd. The refuge protects thousands of wapiti from November to March. A highlight of a winter visit is taking a 45-minute **horse-drawn sleigh ride** (adult/ child $13/9; ◷ 10am-4pm mid-Dec–Mar). The rides weave between the elk and offer great photo opportunities.

Activities

One of the USA's top ski destinations, **Jackson Hole Mountain Resort** (☎ 307-733-2292; www .jacksonhole.com; lift ticket $77), known as 'the Village,' boasts the USA's greatest continuous vertical rise – from the 6311ft base at Teton Village to the 10,450ft summit of Rendezvous Mountain. The terrain is mostly advanced, boasting lots of fluffy powder and rocky ledges made for jumping. When the snow melts the resort offers a host of summer-time activities – check the website.

If you're interested in mountain biking, head to **Teton Cyclery** (☎ 307-733-4386; 175 N Glenwood St) for advice and bike rentals.

Rendezvous River Sports (☎ 307-733-2471; www .jhkayakschool.com; 945 W Broadway) offers kayak instruction. For rig rentals, try **Leisure Sports** (☎ 307-733-3040; 1075 S US 89).

Sleeping

Jackson has plenty of other lodging options, both in town and around the ski hill. Reservations are essential in summer and winter, when the place fills quickly.

Anvil Motel & Bunkhouse (☎ 307-733-3668; www .anvilmotel.com; 215 N Cache Dr; dm $25, r $54-117; ✗) The Anvil Motel's 25-bed hostel is the only in-town budget option. The basement-level space has clean dorm beds, laundry, ski lockers, a TV lounge and a basic kitchen. It's quiet most of the year, but becomes party central when the powder is fresh. Hostellers can use the motel's hot tub. Speaking of the motel, it offers clean but generic rooms at good-value rates in a super central local.

Virginian Lodge (☎ 307-733-2792; www.virginian lodge.com; 750 W Broadway; winter/summer r from $55/104; ✗ ☐) This cheerful place is one of the best-value motels in town. It's not exactly posh, but rooms are clean and comfortable, and the big grassy pool area is a real plus. Push through the swinging doors of the smoky old saloon and you're in for a fun night.

Snake River Lodge (☎ 307-732-6000; www.snake riverlodge.com; 7710 Granite Loop Rd; r $175-400; ✗ ☐) Gorgeously situated at the bottom of Jackson

---

IF YOU HAVE A FEW MORE DAYS IN WYOMING

Wyoming is full of great places to get lost, sadly too many for us to elaborate on in this guide, but we'll prime you with a taster.

Devil's Tower National Monument Rising a dramatic 1267ft above the Belle Fourche River, this nearly vertical monolith is an awesome site. Known as Bears Lodge by some of the 20-plus Native American tribes who consider it sacred, it's a must-see if you are traveling between the Black Hills (on the Wyoming–South Dakota border) and the Tetons and Yellowstone.

Medicine Bow Mountains & Snowy Range West of Laramie, the lofty national forest stretching across both mountain ranges is a wild and rugged place, perfect for multinight hiking and camping trips.

Sheridan Nestled in the shadow of the Bighorn Mountains, Sheridan boasts century-old buildings, once home to Wyoming cattle barons, and is popular with adventure fanatics who come to play in the Bighorns.

Hole Mountain Resort, it has a beautiful pool, spa facilities and a fitness room with a view. Wooden walls, stone slab floors and big fireplaces create the vibe. Rooms are well stocked with down comforters, exposed wood-beamed ceilings and lots of other luxury trappings.

Eating & Drinking

Jackson is home to Wyoming's most sophisticated food. Many of our favorite restaurants here double as bars.

Snake River Brewing Co (☎ 307-739-2337; 265 S Millward St; dishes $5-12; ⏱ 11.30am-midnight; ⊗) Popular with the local ski crowd, its pub grub (think wood-fired pizza and juicy burgers) stands up well to the smooth homemade microbrews. Happy-hour pints ($2.50) and lunch specials ($6) make it a local favorite day or night.

Bubba's Bar-B-Que (☎ 307-733-2288; 515 W Broadway Ave; dishes $5-15; ⏱ 7am-10pm) Get the biggest, fluffiest breakfast biscuits for miles at this friendly and energetic bring-your-own-bottle (BYOB) eatery. Later on, it's got a decent salad bar, and serves up a ranch of ribs and racks.

Silver Dollar Bar & Grill (☎ 307-733-2190; cnr Glenwood & Broadway Aves; mains $15-25; ⏱ 11.30am-late) Inside the historic Wort Hotel, this bordello-style bar and restaurant features original Old West art and an old roulette wheel. The recently remodeled restaurant serves much better than expected pub grub – tenderloin anyone? There is live music many nights, and enough room for dancing.

Rendezvous Bistro (☎ 307-739-1100; 380 S Broadway; dishes $15-25; ⏱ 5.30-10pm Mon-Sat) Locals love this bustling, unpretentious bistro with a smart interior that serves the best-value top-end food in town – from steak to lobster. Environs are intimate, the service excellent.

Mangy Moose Saloon (☎ 307-733-9779; Teton Village) This lively Jackson institution hosts a wide variety of live shows, from free local bands to big-name name artists. A favorite après-ski spot, it attracts hordes of locals and tourists. It's an intimate venue where the stage is visible from two levels.

Million Dollar Cowboy Bar (☎ 307-733-2207; 25 N Cache Dr) There's no way you can miss the entrance to this town landmark – the neon sign is too big. It's kitschy West all right, but it is also pretty entertaining for at least one drink and a nibble.

Getting There & Around

The **Jackson Hole Airport** (☎ 307-733-7682) is 7 miles north of Jackson off US 26/89/191 within Grand Teton National Park. Daily flights serve Denver, Salt Lake City, Dallas and Houston, while weekend flights connect Jackson with Chicago.

Alltrans' Jackson Hole Express (☎ 307-733-1719; www.jacksonholebus.com) buses depart at 6:30am daily from Jackson's Exxon Station (cnr Hwy 89 S and S Park Loop Rd) for Salt Lake City ($56, 5½ hours). **Southern Teton Area Rapid Transit** (☎ 307-733-4521; www.startbus.com) buses connect Jackson and Teton Village.

MONTANA

Warning: Montana is addictive. Once you've gotten drunk on her soul-soothing nectar – a signature blend of wild beauty, passionate patriotism and new-age sex appeal – there is no way you won't return for a second slurp.

Called the 'Live and Let Live' state, Montana is a beautiful amalgamation of big skies, big bear and big rivers, made for fly-fishing (or Robert Redford movie sets – who can ever forget Brad Pitt's red bum in *A River Runs Through It*?). It's a wild, untamed state, where even the biggest tourist attractions, Glacier and Flathead Lake, never feel crowded.

Freedom is a big deal in Montana, and the state takes its patriotism seriously. Although you'll find a number of trendy boutiques, new-age shops, art galleries and wine bars in cool transplant towns such as Bozeman and Missoula, you'll also see plenty of American flags and pro-war bumperstickers.

History

Montana has seen many a historical conflict between white settlers and Native American tribes, including battles of the Big Hole and Rosebud. The gold frenzy hit in 1863, with a discovery near Bannack. Marcus Daly struck the world's largest and purest copper vein in Butte, which was mined for the next hundred years.

In 1889 Montana became the 41st state of the Union. Though tourism began to sweep through the Rockies in the late 19th century, the boom didn't really hit Montana until the 1980s. More than 25 years later the state's tourist attractions are now the major backbone of the local economy.

Information

Montana Road Conditions (☎ 800-226-7623, within Montana 511; www.mdt.state.mt.us)

Travel Montana (☎ 800-847-4868; www.visitmt.com; PO Box 200533, Helena, MT 59620)

BOZEMAN

Bozeman is kind of like Montana's version of Los Angeles – a hip place to hang – and US Census data from 2006 proves it: Bozeman's population has grown by nearly 28% in six years! Bozeman's small town agricultural roots still show, however, but today ranchers rub shoulders with hipster college students and mom-and-pop shops share space with trendy boutiques and funky restaurants on Main St. Bumped up against the Bridger Mountains, Bozeman is blessed with famous Montana beauty and a slightly bohemian air.

The **visitor center** (☎ 406-586-5421; www.boze manchamber.com; 1003 N 7th Ave; ⏱ 8am-5pm Mon-Fri) can provide information on lodging and attractions in the area.

Montana State University's **Museum of the Rockies** (☎ 406-994-2251; www.museumoftherockies.org; 600 W Kagy Blvd; adult/child $9.50/6.50; ⏱ 8am-8pm) is the most entertaining natural history museum in Montana, with dinosaur exhibits, early Native American art and laser shows.

South of town, **Hyalite Canyon** is great for climbing, trail running and mountain biking. North of town, the community-owned **Bridger Bowl Ski Area** (☎ 406-587-2111; www.bridgerbowl.com; 15795 Bridger Canyon Rd; lift ticket full/half-day $41/33) offers excellent skiing at unbeatable prices. In summer you can hike here. For maps, trail guides and gear rental drop by **Barrel Mountaineering** (☎ 406-582-1335; 240 E Main St).

MONTANA FACTS

Nickname Treasure State

Population 930,800

Area 147,045 sq miles

Capital city Helena (population 27,340)

Sales tax Montana has no state sales tax

Birthplace of Gary Cooper (1901–61), Hollywood star of 1930s to '50s; Evel Knievel (1938–2007), legendary motorcycle daredevil

Famous for Big sky, fly-fishable rivers, snow, rodeos, bear

Random fact Some Montana highways didn't have a set speed limit until the 1990s!

WHAT THE...?

Did you know that livestock out number people in Montana by 12 to 1!

Soak away your aches and pains in the pools, sauna and steam room at **Bozeman Hot Springs** (☎ 406-586-6492; admission $5; ⏱ 8am-1pm Sun-Thu, 8am-midnight Fri & Sat), 8 miles west of Bozeman off US 191.

Sleeping

The full gamut of chain motels lies north of downtown on 7th Ave, near I-90. There are also a few options east of downtown on Main St.

Bozeman Backpackers Hostel (☎ 406-586-4659; www.bozemanbackpackershostel.com; 405 W Olive St; dm/d $20/42) In a beautiful Victorian house built in 1890 (trivia: it was once home to actor Gary Cooper when he attended school in town), this independent hostel's casual approach means a relaxed vibe, friendly folk and no lockout. It's *the* place to rendezvous with active globestompers.

Lewis & Clark Motel (☎ 406-586-3341; www .lewisandclarkmotel.net; 824 W Main St; r $75; 🐾 📶 wi-fi) For a drop of Vegas in your Montana, stay at this flashy motel with casino games and cold beers in the lobby. The large rooms have floor-to-ceiling front windows, and there's a pool, Jacuzzi and sauna on-site.

Voss Inn (☎ 406-587-0982; www.bozeman-vossinn .com; 319 S Wilson St; s/d $120/140; ✗) Offering six carefully restored rooms, this Victorian-era B&B is a charming place to stay. Big beds, old-fashioned charm and terry cloth robes heighten its appeal.

Eating & Drinking

As a college town, Bozeman has no shortage of student-oriented cheap eats and enough watering holes to quench an army's thirst.

O'Brien's (☎ 406-587-3973; 312 E Main St; mains $8-20; ⏱ 7:30am-10pm) This place serves the best breakfasts in town – try the cinnamon French toast – and very reasonably priced lunches in congenial downtown environs. At dinner the place gets spruced up, white linen graces the tables and the menu becomes more upmarket, including beef tenderloin and shrimp with garlic cream sauce. Meals come with soup and lots of hot bread.

John Bozeman's Bistro (☎ 406-537-4100; 125 W Main St; mains $10-25; ⏱ 11.30am-10pm) The

ROCKY MOUNTAINS

innovative menu at this Bozeman institution changes constantly, but always remains eclectic. Offerings circumnavigate the globe, include lots of veggie options and are consistently delicious.

Mint Bar & Cafe (☎ 406-388-1100; Belgrande, 27 E Main St; mains $10-30; ✆ 5pm-10pm) Boasting a fabulous wine list, this local landmark offers more sophistication than the typical Montana roadhouse. Located 8 miles west of town, the menu is meat-oriented with juicy steaks featured prominently. Sleek booths, old cowboy photos and a mounted longhorn head create the ambience. Those on a budget will appreciate the cheaper bar menu; veggies can chow on a daily meatless plate.

Molly Brown (☎ 406-586-9903; S 8th St) Popular with students, this noisy dive bar offers 20 beers on tap and eight pool tables for getting your game on.

Zebra Cocktail Lounge (☎ 406-585-8851; 15 N Rouse St) Inside the Bozeman Hotel, this place is the epicenter of the local live music scene.

Getting There & Away

The **Gallatin Field Airport** (☎ 406-388-6632) is 8 miles northwest of downtown. **Karst Stage** (☎ 406-388-2293; www.karststage.com) runs buses daily, December to April, from the airport to Big Sky ($27, one hour) and West Yellowstone ($37, two hours); summer service is by reservation only.

Greyhound and Rimrock Trailways depart from the **bus depot** (☎ 406-587-3110; 1205 E Main St), half a mile from downtown, and service all Montana towns along I-90.

GALLATIN & PARADISE VALLEYS

Outdoor enthusiasts can explore the expansive beauty around the Gallatin River for days. **Big Sky Resort** (☎ 800-548-4486; www .bigskyresort.com; lift ticket $75), with multiple mountains, 400in of annual powder and Montana's longest vertical drop (4350ft), is the valley's foremost destination for skiing. In summer it offers gondola-served hiking and mountain biking. For backpacking and backcountry skiing, head to the **Lee Metcalf Wilderness Complex**. It covers 389 sq miles of Gallatin and Beaverhead National Forest land west of US 191. Numerous scenic USFS campgrounds snuggle up to the Gallatin Range on the east side of US 191.

Fisherfolk will prefer to tie their flies in the Paradise Valley, which is full of blue-ribbon

fishing access sites. Rafts, kayaks and canoes take to the river June to August.

Twenty miles south of Livingston, off US 89 en route to Yellowstone, unpretentious **Chico Hot Springs** (☎ 406-333-4933; www.chicohot springs.com; r from $89; ✆ 8am-midnight; wi-fi) has garnered quite a following in the last few years – now attracting celebrity guests from Hollywood. They, along with many normal folk, come to this relaxed place to soak in the two suave open-air mineral pools (admission for nonguests $8.50). The larger pool is the perfect temperature for floating (93°F or 34°C); the smaller pool is hotter (103°F or 54°C); but still not too hot to stay in long enough for wrinkles. The lively bar hosts swinging county-and-western dance bands on weekends. The on-site restaurant (mains $20 to $30) is known around the region for its fine steak and seafood fare.

ABSAROKA BEARTOOTH WILDERNESS

The fabulous, vista-packed Absaroka Beartooth Wilderness covers more than 943,377 acres and is perfect for a solitary adventure. Thick forests, jagged peaks and marvelous, empty stretches of alpine tundra are all found in this wilderness, saddled between Paradise Valley in the west and Yellowstone National Park in the south. The thickly forested Absaroka Range dominates the area's west half and is most easily reached from Paradise Valley or the Boulder River Corridor. The Beartooth Range's jagged peaks are best reached from Hwy 78 and US 212 near Red Lodge. Because of its proximity to Yellowstone, the Beartooth portion gets two-thirds of the area's traffic.

A picturesque old mining town with fun bars and restaurants and a good range of places to stay, **Red Lodge** offers great day hikes, backpacking and, in winter, skiing right near town. The **Red Lodge Visitor Center** (☎ 406-446-1718; 601 N Broadway Ave; ✆ 9am-5pm Jun-Aug, 9:30am-4:30pm Mon-Fri Sep-May) has accommodation information, while the **Beartooth Ranger Station** (☎ 406-446-2103; 6811 Hwy 212 S; ✆ 8am-4:30pm Mon-Fri), about a mile south of Red Lodge, has maps and outdoor info.

The awesome **Beartooth Highway** (US 212; ✆ Jun–mid-Oct) connects Red Lodge to Cooke City and Yellowstone's north entrance by an incredible 68-mile journey that passes soaring peaks and wildflower-sprinkled tundra. There are five USFS campgrounds (reservations accepted) along the highway, within 12 miles of Red Lodge.

BILLINGS

A friendly ranching and oil center, Billings offers big city conveniences without big city stress – it is hard to believe this small town is Montana's largest city. Though it's not an absolute must-see, it's a worthwhile place to break your journey. The historic downtown, with squat brown buildings, wide streets, cozy cafés and interesting little knick-knack shops, is hardly cosmopolitan, but emits a certain endearing charm.

Despite a slightly corporate feel to its rooms, travelers love the **Billings Hotel & Convention Center** (☎ 800-537-7286; www.billingshotel.net; 1223 Mullowney Lane; r from $90; ☒ ☒ 🖳 wi-fi). Not only does it have smiling staff, it also features super-clean rooms, a restaurant and bar, and best of all (especially if you have kids), two big waterslides at the pool!

Fuel up at the chipper **McCormick Cafe** (☎ 406-255-9555; 2419 Montana Ave; meals $4-7; ☒ 7am-4pm Mon-Fri, 8am-3pm Sat; 🖳), where you can get a steaming cup of coffee and heaped plates of bacon and eggs. Soups, salads and pizza are served at lunch. It's a down-home no-frills dining experience.

Logan International Airport (☎ 406-238-3420), 2 miles north of downtown, has direct flights to Salt Lake City, Denver, Minneapolis, Seattle, Phoenix and destinations within Montana. The **bus depot** (☎ 406-245-5116; 2502 1st Ave N; ☒ 24hr) has services to Bozeman ($30, three hours) and Missoula ($55, eight hours).

HELENA

Luring politicians, outdoor enthusiasts and artists, Montana's state capital is an agreeable city at the foot of the Rockies boasting trendy galleries and interesting restaurants. During the week it's a bustling place where politicos and lobbyists pound out legislation. At weekends it becomes a veritable ghost town, as almost everyone seems to take to the mountains for a little playtime.

For information, visit the **Helena Visitor Center** (☎ 406-442-4120; www.helenachamber.com; 225 Cruse Ave; ☒ 8am-5pm Mon-Fri).

Many of Helena's sites are free, including the neoclassical **state capitol** (☎ 406-444-4789; cnr Montana Ave & 6th St; ☒ 8am-6pm Mon-Fri); the elegant old buildings along Last Chance Gulch (Helena's pedestrian shopping district); and the

Holter Museum of Art (☎ 406-442-6400; 12 E Lawrence; ☒ 10am-5pm Mon-Sat Jun-Aug, 11:30am-5pm Tue-Fri, noon-5pm Sat & Sun Sep-May), which exhibits modern pieces by Montana artists.

Nine **hiking** and **mountain-biking** trails wind through Mt Helena City Park, including one that takes you to the 5460ft-high summit of Mt Helena.

East of downtown near I-15 is a string of chain motels – most have free continental breakfast, pool and Jacuzzi for $60 to $85.

Our favorite place to stay in town, **Sanders** (☎ 406-442-3309; www.sandersbb.com; 328 N Ewing St; d $130; ☒) is a beautiful B&B. It boasts exquisite vintage furnishings, much of them from the late-19th-century original owners. Each bedroom is unique and thoughtfully decorated.

Fire Tower Coffee House (☎ 406-495-8840; 422 Last Chance Gulch; mains $7; ☒ 7am-late; 🖳) is where to go for coffee, light meals and live music on Friday evening. The breakfast menu features a couple of different types of egg-based burritos, while lunch has a wholesome, and interesting, sandwich selection.

The **Helena Regional Airport** (☎ 406-442-2821; www.helenaairport.com), 2 miles north of downtown, operates flights to most other airports in Montana, as well as to Salt Lake City, Spokane and Minneapolis. Rimrock Stages leave from Helena's **bus depot** (☎ 406-442-5860; 3100 E Hwy 12), 7 miles east of town on US 12, where at least daily buses go to Missoula ($21, 2¼ hours), Billings ($37, 4¾ hours) and Bozeman ($18, two hours).

WORTH THE TRIP: LITTLE BIGHORN BATTLEFIELD

Ensconced within the boundless prairies and pine-covered hills of Montana's southwest plains, the Crow Indian Reservation is home to the **Little Bighorn Battlefield National Monument** (☎ 406-638-3224; admission per car $12; ☒ 8am-6pm). One of the USA's best-known Native American battlefields, this is where General George Custer made his famous 'last stand.' Custer, and 272 soldiers, messed one too many times with Native Americans (including Crazy Horse of the Lakota Sioux), who overwhelmed the force in a frequently painted massacre. A visitor center tells the tale. The entrance is a mile east of I-90 on US 212.

MISSOULA

Missoula is a hip college town (home to the University of Montana) that's growing more popular with each year (and that's not just our opinion; transplants are flocking here by the bus load). The dreadlocks, global import shops and veggie restaurants near the university add a great dash of cultural flavor to this intellectually stimulating place. A milder-than-usual climate and a gorgeous location along the Clark Fork River make Missoula the perfect outdoor playground. It's within spittin' distance of the Rattlesnake Recreation Area and the Bitterroot Range, and a river actually runs through it!

Information

Tune in to University of Montana stations KUFM (89.1FM) and KUKL (89.9FM) for National Public Radio (NPR), quirky local news and groovy free-form alternative music mixes.

Trail Head (☎ 406-543-6966; www.trailheadmontana .net; 110 E Pine St; ☼ 9.30am-8pm Mon-Fri, 9am-6pm Sat, 11am-6pm Sun) Maps, abundant advice, camping and kayaking rental gear.

USFS Northern Region Headquarters (☎ 406-329-3511; 200 E Broadway; ☼ 8:30am-4:30pm Mon-Fri)

Visitor center (☎ 406-532-3250; www.missoulacvb .org; 1121 E Broadway; ☼ 8am-5pm Mon-Fri)

Sights & Activities

Downtown, the contemporary installations at the **Art Museum of Missoula** (☎ 406-728-0447; 335 N Pattee St; admission free; ☼ 10am-7pm Tue, 10am-6pm Wed-Fri, 10am-4pm Sat) are worthy of a wander. Seven miles west of downtown, the **Smokejumper Center** (☎ 406-329-4900; W Broadway; admission free; ☼ 10am-4pm Jun-Aug) is the active base for the heroic men and women who parachute into forests to combat raging wildfires. Its visitor center has thought-provoking audio and visual displays that do a great job illustrating the life of the Western firefighter.

One of the area's most accessible **hikes** is along the south side of Clark Fork from Mc-Cormick Park (west of the Orange St bridge) into Hellgate Canyon. At sunset join the steep pilgrimage from the football stadium to the 'M' on 5158ft Mt Sentinel for spectacular views.

Advanced skiers love **Snowbowl Ski Area** (☎ 406-549-9777; www.montanasnowbowl.com; lift ticket $35), 17 miles north of Missoula, for its 2600ft vertical drop. **10,000 Waves** (☎ 406-549-6670; www.10000-waves.com; 1311 E Broadway; trips from $40) runs a range of rafting and kayaking trips on the Class III and IV rapids of Alberton Gorge (of the Clark Fork River), as well as scenic trips on the gentler Blackfoot and Bitterroot Rivers.

Sleeping & Eating

Most lodging is on Broadway between Van Buren and Orange Sts, within walking distance of the campus and downtown.

Campus Inn (☎ 406-549-5134; www.campusinn missoula.com; 744 E Broadway; r from $85; ☒ ☒ wi-fi) This solid-value place has spacious rooms with ample amenities. Some rooms are inside the main building; others are motel-style. There are two hot tubs.

Goldsmith's Bed & Breakfast (☎ 406-728-1585; www.goldsmithsinn.com; 809 E Front St; r $110-150; ☒) This delightful B&B, with comfy rooms, is a pebble's toss from the river. The outdoor deck overlooking the water is the perfect place to kick back with a good novel. Rooms are attractive, featuring Victorian furniture. Some come with private sitting rooms, fireplaces and reading nooks.

Bernice's Bakery (☎ 406-728-1358; 190 S 3rd St; mains $2-5; ☼ 7am-midnight) Fabulous organic coffee and tea, sink-your-teeth-into-'em sweets and yummy breakfasts are all staples at this revered Missoula institution. Don't miss the homemade granola.

Food For Thought (☎ 406-721-6033; 540 Daly Ave; mains $4-7; ☼ 7am-10pm) This crunchy joint, across from the University of Montana, packs in lots of college students for heaped portions of health-conscious food, including very large sandwiches.

Tipu's (☎ 406-542-0622; 1151/2 S 4th St; mains $8-13; ☼ 11.30am-9pm) Missoula's only all-vegetarian restaurant offers some of the most flavorful chai in the West and East Indian chow that's tasty and filling. Don't miss the fresh chutneys. It gets consistently good reviews.

Drinking & Entertainment

In Missoula, bar-hopping ranks right up there with hiking, rodeo, disco dancing and cow-tipping. For live music listings, browse the *Independent* (www.missoulanews.com) or the Entertainment section of Friday's *Missoulian*.

Iron Horse Brewpub (☎ 406-728-8866; 501 N Higgins St) It's undergone a multimillion-dollar expansion, and now includes a swank, smoke-free upstairs bar known as 501. Students flock to the outdoor patio to sip microbrews and chow on American pub food.

Top Hat (☎ 406-728-9865; 134 W Front St) This place rocks out with live jam bands, usually of the bluegrass and blues variety, most nights. It also offers billiards and table tennis and plenty of open space.

Getting There & Around

Missoula County International Airport (☎ 406-728-4381) is located 5 miles west of Missoula on US 12 W.

Greyhound buses serve most of the state, and stop at the **depot** (☎ 406-549-2339; 1660 W Broadway), 1 mile west of town.

FLATHEAD LAKE

Thanks to picture-pretty bays and 128 miles of wooded shoreline, fish-filled Flathead Lake is one of Montana's most favored attractions. The **Flathead Lake Marine Trail** makes paddling from one access point to another a fun way to travel; two marine **campsites** (☎ 406-751-4577; campsites $10) are available. You can easily drive around the lake in four hours. Be sure to spend time lingering along the shores and stopping at roadside fruit stands.

On the Indian Reservation at the lake's south end, quick-growing **Polson** (☎ visitor center 406-883-5969; www.polsonchamber.com; 4 2nd Ave E; 🕑 8am-4pm Mon-Fri, 9am-4pm Sat, 10am-3pm Sun Jun-Aug, 10am-2pm Sep-May Mon-Fri) is the region's biggest service center, with several gas stations, fast-food restaurants and motels.

The mind-boggling **Miracle of America Museum** (☎ 406-883-6804; 58176 Hwy 93; adult/child $3/1; 🕑 8am-8pm Jun-Aug, 8:30am-5pm Mon-Sat, 1:30-5pm Sun Sep-May), located just 2 miles south of Polson, is definitely worth seeing. By turns random and fascinating, its cluttered Americana includes motorcycles, military displays and the largest buffalo ever recorded in the state.

At the opposite end of the lake, **Bigfork** (☎ visitor center 406-837-5888; www.bigfork.org; 8155 Hwy 35; 🕑 9am-5pm Jun-Aug, 10am-2pm Mon-Fri Sep-May) is an artsy village with good grub and funky shops. The **Swan Lake Ranger District Station** (☎ 406-837-5081; 200 Ranger Station Rd; 🕑 8am-4:30pm Mon-Fri), west of Bigfork, has camping details.

Between Polson and Bigfork are lakefront campgrounds, summer camp–style resorts, and, on the lake's east side, orchards festooned with plump cherries. In either town you can join a boat tour to visit **Wild Horse Island**, where wild mares and steeds roam. Watch for Flathead Nessie, said to be a distant cousin to the Loch Ness Monster, who has been lurking around since the 1930s. **Flathead Raft Co** (☎ 406-883-5838; www.flatheadraftco.com) runs kayaking and river-rafting trips (from $42). Call for directions.

WHITEFISH & KALISPELL

With hip bars, slick restaurants and oh-so-cool boutiques, Whitefish has perfected the hip New West look. It's also got a lot going for it: it's a fabulous gateway to Glacier National Park and sits in the shadow of one of Montana's premier year-round resorts, **Big Mountain** (☎ 406-862-2900; www.bigmtn.com; lift ticket around $55), with winter downhill skiing, and gondola-served hiking and mountain biking in summer. To rent some wheels, visit **Glacier Cyclery** (☎ 406-862-6446; 326 2nd St). Though not as charming, Kalispell, 13 miles south, is Flathead Valley's cheapest place to resupply.

Whitefish Visitor Center (☎ 406-862-3501; www.whitefishrvpark.com; 520 E 2nd St; 🕑 9am-5:30pm Mon-Sat Jun-Aug, 9am-5pm Mon-Fri Sep-May) has all the usual information. **Tally Lake Ranger Station** (☎ 406-862-2508; 1335 Hwy 93 N; 🕑 8am-4:30pm Mon-Fri) has camping details and maps.

Places fill fast in both towns, so reservations are recommended. A string of chain motels lines US 93 south of Whitefish. Here you'll also find the cheerful **Chalet Motel** (☎ 406-862-5581; www.whitefishlodging.com; 6430 Hwy 93 S; r $85; 🔲🔲🔲), about a mile from town. It offers spacious rooms and has a hot tub.

The **Downtowner Motel** (☎ 406-862-2535; www.downtownermotel.cc; 224 Spokane Ave; r from $55; 🔲), in Whitefish, offers slightly cheaper rooms. Rates include use of the adjacent gym and sauna.

In Kalispell, the **Kalispell Grand Hotel** (☎ 406-755-8100; www.kalispellgrand.com; 100 Main St; r 85-125; 🔲) has smallish modern rooms. The nicest come with jetted tubs and a warm atmosphere – fresh baked cookies in the afternoon and an included home-cooked breakfast in the morning. Rooms don't have wi-fi, but there is high-speed internet access for those with laptop in tow.

Glacier Park International Airport (☎ 406-257-5994; 4170 Hwy 2) is halfway between Whitefish and Kalispell on US 2 and has flights to various destinations around the USA. The **Airport Shuttle Service** (☎ 406-752-2842) serves Whitefish ($20) and Kalispell ($9.50).

ROCKY MOUNTAINS

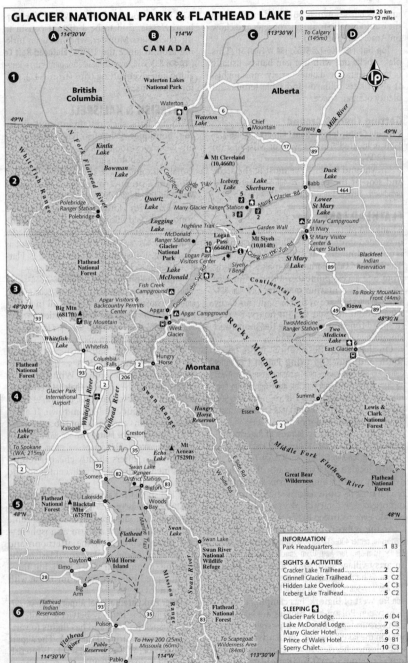

GLACIER NATIONAL PARK & FLATHEAD LAKE

INFORMATION	
Park Headquarters	1 B3

SIGHTS & ACTIVITIES	
Cracker Lake Trailhead	2 C2
Grinnell Glacier Trailhead	3 C2
Hidden Lake Overlook	4 C3
Iceberg Lake Trailhead	5 C2

SLEEPING	
Glacier Park Lodge	6 D4
Lake McDonald Lodge	7 C3
Many Glacier Hotel	8 C2
Prince of Wales Hotel	9 B1
Sperry Chalet	10 C3

Amtrak stops at Whitefish's **railroad depot** (☎ 406-862-2268; 500 Depot St) en route to West Glacier ($12) and East Glacier ($26). Intermountain Transport connects the **Kalispell bus station** (☎ 406-755-4011; 1301 S Main St) to Whitefish's railroad depot; buses also run to Missoula, Helena, Bozeman and Seattle, WA.

The free Shuttle Network of Whitefish (SNOW) runs between Whitefish and Big Mountain during ski season.

BOB MARSHALL WILDERNESS COMPLEX

Let's just say, if the state had a perfume, its essence would be bottled from the wilds around Bob Marshall. Running roughly from the southern boundary of Glacier National Park in the north to Rogers Pass (on Hwy 200) in the south, three designated wilderness areas hum within the complex. A medley of geology, plants and wildlife, Great Bear, Bob Marshall and Scapegoat are scintillating. National forest lands girding the complex offer campgrounds, road access to trailheads and quieter country when 'the Bob' hosts hunters in fall. The core lands encompass 2344 sq miles, with 3200 miles of trails and sections that are a 40-mile slog from the nearest road.

Accessing the Bob Hwy 200 in the south just got a heck of a lot easier, thanks to a four-year renovation; the park service has opened rustic **Monture Guard Station Cabin** (cabin $60), on the Bob's perimeter, to the public. To reach it you'll need to drive 7 miles north of Ovando and snowshoe or hike the last mile to your private abodes at the edge of the gorgeous Lewis and Clark Range. Contact the forest service about reservations.

Other Bob access points include the Seeley-Swan Valley in the west, Hungry Horse Reservoir in the north and the Rocky Mountain Front in the east. The easiest (and busiest) access routes are from the Benchmark and Gibson Reservoir trailheads in the Rocky Mountain Front.

Trails generally start steep, reaching the wilderness boundary after around 7 miles. It takes another 10 miles or so to really get into the Bob's heart. Good day hikes run from all sides. Two USFS districts tend to the Bob:

Flathead National Forest Headquarters (☎ 406-758-5204; www.fs.fed.us/r1/flathead; 1935 3rd Ave E, Kalispell; ☺ 8am-4:30pm Mon-Fri)
Lewis & Clark National Forest Supervisors (☎ 406-791-7700; www.fs.fed.us/r1/lewisclark; 1101 15th St N, Great Falls; ☺ 8am-4:30pm Mon-Fri)

GLACIER NATIONAL PARK

You better visit soon, because this park might have to change its name in the near future. Home to 150 glaciers in 1850, today the park only has 26 named icefields left. And those that do remain are shells of their former selves, climatologists say, and melting quickly. Yes, Montana's most beautiful and revered attraction has now become another victim of global warming.

For now, however, the park's beauty supersedes its seemingly doomed future. Dramatic, rugged and desolate alpine terrain is filled with lush valleys, clear crystal lakes and rushing waterfalls. Wildlife enthusiasts will have a field day in Glacier. Spotting animals, from cougars, grizzlies, black bear to elk, is common. Most visitors tend to stick to developed areas and short hiking trails,

ROCKY MOUNTAINS

WORTH THE HIKE

Considering the rate at which Glacier is losing its glaciers, the five- to six-hour 9-mile day **Iceberg Lake hike**, a classic favorite, is more important to undertake now than ever.

Enclosed by stunning 3000ft vertical headwalls on three sides, it's one of the most impressive glacial lakes in North America. The 1200ft ascent is gentle and the approach is mostly at or above treeline, affording awesome views. Wildflower fiends will delight in the meadows around the lake.

Iceberg Lake was named in 1905 by George Grinnell, who saw icebergs calving from the glacier at the foot of the headwalls. The glacier is no longer active, but surface ice and avalanche debris still provide sizeable flotillas of bergs as the lake melts in early summer. Scientists predict that if global climate-warming trends continue, all of the park's 50-some moving ice masses will be completely melted by 2030, so there's no better time than the present to see this ancient ice. The hike begins and ends at Iceberg Lake trailhead near the Many Glacier Ranger Station.

which is a shame. This is one park where you should definitely explore off the beaten path.

Created in 1910, Glacier's spectacular landscape continues uninterrupted north into Canada, where it is protected in less crowded Waterton Lakes National Park. Together the two parks comprise Waterton–Glacier International Peace Park. In 1995 the parks were declared a World Heritage Site for their vast cross-section of plant and animal species. Although the name evokes images of bi-national harmony, in reality each park is operated separately, and entry to one does not entitle you to entry to the other.

The park is open year-round; however, most services are open only from mid-May to September.

Orientation

Glacier's 1562 sq miles are divided into five regions, each centered on a ranger station: Polebridge (northwest); Lake McDonald (southwest), including the West Entrance and Apgar village; Two Medicine (southeast); St Mary (east); and Many Glacier (northeast). The 50-mile Going-to-the-Sun Rd is the only paved road that traverses the park.

Information

Visitor centers and ranger stations in the park sell field guides and hand out hiking maps. Those at Apgar and St Mary are open daily May to October; the visitor center at Logan Pass is open when Going-to-the-Sun Rd is open. The Many Glacier, Two Medicine and Polebridge Ranger Stations close at the end of September. **Park headquarters** (☎ 406-888-7800; www.nps.gov/glac; ✆ 8am-4:30pm Mon-Fri), in West Glacier between US 2 and Apgar, is open year-round.

Entry to the park (hiker/vehicle $12/25) is valid for seven days. Day hikers don't need permits, but overnight backpackers do (May

to October only). Half of the permits (per person per day $4) are available on a first-come, first-served basis from the Apgar Backcountry Permit Center (which is open May 1 to October 31), St Mary Visitor Center, and the Many Glacier, Two Medicine and Polebridge Ranger Stations.

The other half can be reserved at the Apgar Backcountry Permit Center, St Mary and Many Glacier Visitor Centers and Two Medicine and Polebridge Ranger Stations.

Sights & Activities

Starting at Apgar, the phenomenal **Going-to-the-Sun Road** skirts shimmering Lake Mc-Donald before angling sharply to the Garden Wall – the main dividing line between the west and east sides of the park. At Logan Pass you can stroll 1.5 miles to **Hidden Lake Overlook**; heartier hikers can try the 7.5-mile **Highline Trail**. About halfway between the pass and St Mary's Lake, the **Continental Divide Trail** crosses the road at Siyeh Bend, a good starting point for multiday hikes.

Busier routes include the 5-mile **Grinnell Glacier Trail**, which climbs 1600ft to the base of the park's most visible glacier, and the 6-mile **Cracker Lake Trail**, a 1400ft climb to some of the park's most dramatic scenery. For more solitude, try trails in the North Fork or Two Medicine areas. North of the Canadian border, the approaches to spectacular hikes are much shorter.

Mountain bikes are prohibited on park trails. Road bikes can ply the park's pavement, but they are banned from parts of Going-to-the-Sun Rd from 11am to 4pm in summer.

Glacier Park Boat Co (☎ 406-257-2426; www.glacierparkboats.com) rents kayaks and canoes, and runs popular guided tours ($11 to $17) from five locations in Glacier National Park. For rafting excursions, guided day hikes and backpacking trips, contact **Glacier Wilderness**

SOMETHING DIFFERENT

It's worth trekking nearly 7 miles one-way to the reach the 17-room **Sperry Chalet** (☎ 888-345-2649; www.sperrychalet.com; r incl meals $160; ✆ Jul 7-Sep 8) for the views alone. This is the heart of the high country, where wildflower-strewn meadows, jagged peaks and babbling brooks make the place feel like nirvana. Factor in a chance to sleep away from it all in a rustic Swiss-style chalet (which just happens to serve hot meals) on the edge of a ridge starring down at Lake McDonald, and the deal gets even sweeter. Rates include meals, and you can hire a mule to carry your gear for an extra $130 – check out www.mule-shoe.com for reservations.

Guides (☎ 406-387-5555; www.glacierguides.com) in West Glacier.

Young naturalists (aged six to 12) should request the *Junior Ranger Newspaper* at the Apgar or St Mary Visitor Centers or the Many Glacier or Two Medicine Ranger Stations.

Sleeping

Within the park, campgrounds and lodges are mainly open from mid-May to the end of September. East Glacier and West Glacier offer overflow accommodations year-round.

LODGES

Dating from the early 19th century, Glacier's seven historic lodges are now operated by **Glacier Park, Inc** (☎ reservations 406-892-2525; www .glacierparkinc.com) All are completely nonsmoking, and rooms do not have air con or TV.

Lake McDonald Lodge (☎ 406-888-5431; www .lakemcdonaldlodge.com; Lake McDonald Valley; cottage $120, r $100-150; ☽ Jun-Sep; ☒) Built in 1913, this old hunting lodge is adorned with stuffed animal trophies and exudes relaxed ambience. The 100 rooms are in lodge-, chalet- or motel-style digs. Nightly park ranger talks and lake cruises are popular activities.

Many Glacier Hotel (☎ 406-732-4411; www.many glacierhotel.com; Many Glacier Valley; r $120-200; ☽ mid-Jun–mid-Sep; ☒) Modeled after a Swiss chalet, Many Glacier is the park's largest hotel with 208 rooms. Panoramic mountain views and a pretty location on the edge of Swiftcurrent Lake add to its appeal.

Glacier Park Lodge (☎ 406-226-5600; www .bigtreehotel.com; East Glacier; r from $130; ☽ late May-Sep; ☒) The park's flagship lodge is a graceful, elegant place featuring interior balconies supported by Douglas fur timbers and a massive stone fireplace in the lobby. It's an aesthetically appealing, historically charming and very comfortable place to stay. Pluses include nine holes of golf and cozy reading nooks.

Prince of Wales Hotel (☎ 403-859-2231; www .princeofwaleswaterton.com; Prince of Wales Rd, Waterton townsite, Waterton Lakes National Park; r from C$300; ☽ mid-May–Sep; ☒) On the Canadian side, the venerable Prince of Wales Hotel is a national historic site perched on a rise overlooking the lake. Though photogenic from a distance (we're talking cover-model material), up close the hotel looks smaller and much more genteel. Nevertheless, the views alone are worth the price.

CAMPING

Of the 13 **NPS campgrounds** (☎ 406-888-7800; http://reservations.nps.gov; campsites $12-17), only sites at Fish Creek and St Mary can be reserved in advance (up to five months). Sites fill by midmorning, particularly in July and August. Only Apgar campground and St Mary campground offer winter camping ($7.50).

Eating

In summer there are grocery stores with limited camping supplies in Apgar, Lake McDonald Lodge, Rising Sun and at the Swiftcurrent Motor Inn. Most lodges have on-site restaurants, although the quality of food varies.

Dining options in West Glacier are unexciting. If you can, head to Whitefish.

Serrano's Mexican Restaurant (☎ 406-226-9392; 29 Dawson Ave; dishes $7-12; ☽ 7am-10pm) In East Glacier, Serrano's serves good Mexican food in casual environs both inside and outside on its deck.

Getting There & Around

Amtrak's Empire Builder stops at East Glacier (Glacier Park Station) and West Glacier (Belton Station). **Glacier Park, Inc** (☎ 406-892-2525) runs shuttles over Going-to-the-Sun Rd, including the unreservable Hiker's Shuttle ($8 to $24), which originates in West Glacier or Many Glacier.

IDAHO

ROCKY MOUNTAINS

There's more to Idaho than big potatoes, neo-Nazis, Demi Moore and Evel Knievel.

The southern section of this jigsaw puzzle–shaped state, sandwiched between the Pacific Northwest and the Rockies, serves enough activities to keep you smiling for weeks. There's mad five-day rafting trips (think sleeping under the stars at the edge of the water) down the world-class Snake River to join. And kick-ass shoots to ride at glitzy Sun Valley and Ketchum ski resorts, which attract a movie-star crowd. When you need to return to modernity, there's Boise. The low-key state capital is filled with funky coffee shops and increasingly trendy nightlife.

It's easy to get lost in Idaho, if you want to. The state is second only to Alaska when it comes to national forests and wilderness areas, has more lakes than anywhere else in

North America and is home to one of the USA's deepest gorges, dramatic Hells Canyon National Recreation Area.

OK, we're not going to lie. The Idaho panhandle did once attract a greater than average number of white supremacists, when the neo-Nazi group Aryan Nations was operating out of a 20-acre compound north of Cour d'Arlene. And the state claims the dubious honor of hosting one of Evel Kneivel's more infamous stunts – his unsuccessful attempt to jump his rocket propelled motorcycle across the Snake River Canyon in 1974.

But Idaho's state-wide wild beauty, endearing towns and outdoor adventure buffet are as much a part of this state's soul as the clichés and eccentric residents associated with it – and a much better part at that.

History

Idaho was not settled by whites – although the Shoshone people, along with the Bannock, have lived on this land for centuries – until gold was struck at Pierce in 1860. Miners rushed to Idaho's mountains, establishing gold camps and trade centers, such as Boise and Lewiston. Rich silver and lead veins spurred further growth, and by the late 19th century a homesteading boom had begun.

The biggest news out of Idaho in the last 20 years involved a man named Richard G Butler, founder of the white supremacist group Aryan Nations.

Butler moved to northern Idaho from Colorado in the 1970s, and claimed he chose the location to spew his hate because he was impressed by the high percentage of white residents. The devoted began flocking to Idaho's panhandle, and Butler's church and the area became home to gangs of skinheads, ex-convicts and other shady characters. Over the years, Butler's disciples included some of the most notorious figures in the neo-Nazi movement – many have since been imprisoned.

Butler's demise began in 1998, when Aryan Nation security guards fired at local resident Victoria Keenen's car. Keenen, and her son, Jason, a passenger, sued Butler. In 2000 they won. Today northern Idaho is trying to put its legacy of white supremacy to rest.

Idaho attracts more than 20 million visitors each year, and tourism is one of the state's top three industries – manufacturing and agriculture are the other two.

IDAHO FACTS

Nickname Gem State
Population 1.41 million
Area 83,575 sq miles
Capital city Boise (population 193,000)
Sales tax 6%, plus up to 3% city tax
Birthplace of Sacagawea (1787–1812), Shoshone woman on Lewis and Clark expedition; Gutzon Borglum (1867–1941), sculptor of Mt Rushmore; Picabo Street (b 1971), Olympic skiing medalist
Home of Bruce Willis, Demi Moore, Ashton Kutcher
Famous for Spuds, wilderness, white water, hunting
Movie trivia The smash indie flick *Napoleon Dynamite* was set and filmed in eastern Idaho

---

Information

Idaho Road Conditions (☎ 208-336-6600, within Idaho 888-432-7623)
Idaho Tourist Information (☎ 800-635-7820; www.visitid.org)
Idaho Travel Council (☎ 800-635-7820; www.visitid.org; PO Box 83720, Boise, ID 83720)

BOISE

Boise is positively buzzing these days. Not only is it Idaho's largest city and capital, it's also young, hip and fun. With an outdoors slant and hassle-free vibe, this city where the desert meets the mountains is more than a gateway to Idaho's wilder climes – it holds its own as a destination. Much of its late-19th-century architecture remains, cafés and restaurants stay open late, and crowds from nightspots spill onto the streets on hot summer nights. Locals consider Boise a gay-friendly city, and it has an active gay and lesbian community. And in recent years more than a few magazines have named it as one of America's top places to live.

Orientation & Information

Delve into the main business district, bounded by State, Grove, 4th and 9th Sts. Restaurants and nightspots are found downtown in the brick-lined pedestrian plaza of the Grove, the gentrified former warehouse district at 8th St Marketplace and in Old Boise, just east of downtown.

Stop by the **visitor center** (☎ 208-344-5338; www.boise.org; 850 Front St; ⌚ 10am-5pm Mon-Fri, 10am-2pm Sat Jun-Aug, 9am-4pm Mon-Fri Sep-May).

Sights

Boise has the largest population of Basque descendents outside Europe's Basque country. Along Grove St between 6th St and Capitol Blvd, the Basque Block has sites commemorating early Basque pioneers. You can learn about Basque ancestry at the **Basque Museum & Cultural Center** (☎ 208-343-2671; www.basquemuseum .com; 611 Grove St; admission free; ☷ 10am-4pm Tue-Fri, 11am-3pm Sat).

Built in 1905, the architecturally impressive **state capitol** (☎ 208-334-5174; 700 W Jefferson St) is the only US statehouse heated by geothermal water. It is worth strolling past. Riverfront Julia Davis Park contains the **Idaho Historical Museum** (☎ 208-334-2120; 610 N Julia Davis Dr; admission $2; ☷ 9am-5pm Mon-Sat, 1-5pm Sun), which is great for a real look into the Old West.

Activities

Boise is bursting with outdoor adventures, from hiking to skiing to swimming. In the foothills above town hit the **Ridge to Rivers Trail System** (www.ridgetorivers.org), offering 75 miles of scenic to strenuous hiking and mountain-biking routes.

In summer everyone loves to float down the Boise River. Rent tubes or rafts at **Barber Park** (☎ 208-343-6564; Warm Spring Rd; tube rental $6) and float 5 miles downstream. Parking here costs $5. A shuttle bus ($3) runs from the take-out point.

Sleeping

Hostel Boise (☎ 208-467-6858; 17322 Canada Rd, Nampa; www.hostelboise.com; dm/s/d $18.50/31/35; ☐) Located just outside town, this country-style hostel's rooms have a maximum of four beds each. There's a BBQ on the back patio, and lots of yard space for lying around and digesting after grilling up those tasty Boca Burgers. Lifts from the airport cost $15.

Idaho Heritage Inn (☎ 208-342-8066; www.idheritage inn.com; 109 W Idaho St; r $75-120; ☒) This wonderfully charming, family-run B&B offers six cozy rooms with varying amenities. The private baths run geothermal heated water.

Grove Hotel (☎ 208-333-8000; www.grovehotelboise .com; 245 S Capital Blvd; r from $115; ☒ ☒ wi-fi) Its outside looks bland, but Boise's only four-star hotel feels more than classy inside. The European-influenced decor features cherry-paneled walls, warm color tones and neoclassical chandeliers. With cocktail lounges, restaurants and cozy public areas, this is one of Boise's best bets for upscale accommodations.

Eating & Drinking

Renovations of Boise's oldest warehouses in the newly renovated BoDo district has led to a flourish of eclectic food and drink offerings. Have a wander.

River City Bagel & Bakery (☎ 208-338-1299; 908 Main St; mains $2-6; ☷ 6.30am-3.30pm) A good place for morning fuel, this amiable eatery offers a range of bagels and sandwiches, plus espresso, chai and more. It has sidewalk seating and an attached bookstore.

our pick **8th Street Wine Co** (☎ 208-426-9463; 405 S 8th St; mains $8-15; ☷ 11am-11pm) This trendy BoDo warehouse wine bar is gaining national attention – *Food & Wine Magazine* recently called it one of America's best wine experiences. There are more than 1000 bottles to choose from, including 50 by the glass. Along with wine, there are hand-crafted beers, sweet cocktails and delicious food in light and airy environs.

Angell's Bar & Grill (☎ 208-342-4900; cnr 9th & Main Sts; mains $10-30; ☷ 11.30am-11pm) One of Boise's most revered restaurants, it offers sophisticated fine dining downtown. Residents swear it has the freshest steak and seafood in town. For something lighter try a specialty salad or dish of pasta. Live country, folk and rock music at nondeafening levels lends a great vibe starting at 8pm Wednesday through Saturday.

Emerald Club (☎ 208-342-5446; 415 S 9th St) Proud to be 'straight friendly,' this gay bar is a convivial spot to swill some drinks and live a little on the dance floor. DJs spin nightly except Saturday, when a show gets the spotlight.

Bardenay (☎ 208-426-0538; 610 Grove St) One of Boise's most unique watering holes, Bardenay was the USA's very first 'distillery-pub,' and remains a one-of-a-kind. Today it serves its own homebrewed vodka, rum and gin in casual, airy environs. It gets consistently good reviews.

Getting There & Around

The **Boise Municipal Airport** (☎ 208-383-3110; I-84 exit 53) has daily flights to Denver, Las Vegas, Phoenix, Portland, Salt Lake City, Seattle and Spokane. Greyhound and Northwestern Trailway services depart from the **bus station** (☎ 208-343-3681; 1212 W Bannock St) and travel along three main routes: I-84, US 95 and I-15/20/287/91.

ROCKY MOUNTAINS

CLASSIC IDAHO: RAFTING THE SALMON

If you only have time for one Idaho adventure, save your pennies and take a multiday white-water rafting trip down either the Grand Canyon or Middle Form of the Salmon River.

The Grand Canyon trip traverses 90 miles in four nights, with much of the trip running through the pristine Frank Church–River of No Return Wilderness Area. You'll sleep on sandy beaches under the stars at night, and stop to check out a grotto and Anazazi ruins. The rapids are fun, but not too intense, and children are definitely not shunned. Many companies run this stretch and trips cost around $1300 for adults and $900 for kids. This includes all meals and transportation to the take-in and pick-up points. Trips run every week from late June through early September, but you'll need to check your respective company's website for exact dates.

If you want to experience Idaho at its most wild and raw, you'll need to join a trip down the Middle Fork of the Salmon. The fast-moving river is strained through a series of boulders creating technical white-water that's as thrilling as it is terrifying. Plus the location is super remote – at some points the closest road to the canyon is 100 miles away.

The experience is supreme, plus the Middle Fork is often rated as one of the world's top 10 white-water and fly-fishing trips. Trips usually last between five and eight days, and sail through more than 100 rapids (Class II to IV plus). Along the way you'll get to soak in hot springs, watch for wildlife and even take day hikes to well-preserved rock-art sites. Bring your fishing license to try your hand at blue-ribbon catch-and-release trout angling.

Even though you pay a bundle for these trips, don't expect luxury abodes. Still, once on the river, few folks complain about being served coffee in their sleeping bag or having guides whip up eggs Benedict and Dutch-oven desserts while they float, fish, soak and dream their cares away.

Early season (late May to mid-June) features peak flow and thrilling, chilly white water, while midseason (mid-June to August) means warmer water and better fishing. Late season trips (mid-August to September) offer lower water and specialized fishing and hiking itineraries.

For details about Middle Fork trips, contact Idaho's premier river outfitter, Coeur d'Alene–based **River Odysseys West** (ROW; ☎ 208-765-0841; www.rowinc.com). All-inclusive rates (excluding pre- and post-trip transportation to and from the put-in and take-out) start at $200 per day.

Boise Urban Stages (BUS; ☎ 208-336-1010) operates local buses, including an airport route (No 13).

KETCHUM & SUN VALLEY

Thanks to the highly rated Sun Valley ski resort, Ketchum and Sun Valley are Idaho's premier destinations and the most happening cluster of towns in Idaho. A longtime favorite with highfliers, Sun Valley frequently takes top honors as the best ski resort in the USA. Trophy homes of the truly rich and famous dot the hilltops and it's not uncommon to see a shining Hollywood face cruising down a slope. But despite the swank appeal, this is no LA. These year-round destinations, nestled among resplendent natural beauty, are also places to get away from it all.

Ketchum is the main commercial hub, with many restaurants, hotels and boutiques. Nobel-prize winning author (and avid sportsman) Ernest Hemingway (1899–1961) was a frequent visitor to the area, and spent his last years in Ketchum, where he's buried. Twelve miles south on Hwy 75, Hailey (lived in and half-owned by Bruce Willis) is where most seasonal workers and ski-bums live.

Information

Sun Valley/Ketchum Visitor Center (☎ 208-726-3423; www.visitsunvalley.com; 411 Main St; ☉ 9am-6pm)
USFS Sawtooth National Forest Ketchum Ranger Station (☎ 208-622-5371; 206 Sun Valley Rd; ☉ 8am-5pm Mon-Fri)

Activities

Famous for its prime powder and excellent slopes, **Sun Valley Resort** (☎ 800-786-8259; www.sunvalley.com; lift ticket $79) is west of Ketchum. In summer it offers **hiking** and **mountain biking**.

These activities are also popular along the well-maintained **Wood River Trail System** (WRTS), winding 20 miles through Ketchum and Sun Valley. Other excellent trails near Ketchum, which also permit mountain biking, include the 5.5-mile **Adams Gulch loop** and **Fox Creek**, a 5-mile loop with mountain views.

Sleeping

Lift Tower Lodge (☎ 208-726-5163; ltowerl@micron.net; 703 S Main St; r $70-100) This friendly small motel in downtown Ketchum offers free continental breakfasts and a hot tub. It sits next to a landmark exhibition chairlift, c 1939.

Tamarack Lodge (☎ 208-726-3344; www.tamarack sunvalley.com; 500 E Sun Valley Rd; r from $115; ⬛ ⬛) Tasteful rooms complete with fireplace, balcony and many amenities are offered at this well-maintained lodge. The Jacuzzi and indoor pool are definite assets. Discounts are often available midweek and off-season.

Sun Valley Lodge (☎ 208-622-2001; www.sunvalley .com; r from $180; ⬛) Hemingway completed *For Whom the Bell Tolls* in this lodge, which offers comfy rooms, the cheapest of which are smallish in size. Amenities include a fitness facility, games room, bowling alley and sauna.

Camping recommendations:

Boundary Campground (campsites $15) USFS site off Trail Creek Rd, 3 miles east of the Ketchum Ranger Station; no reservations accepted.

Meadows RV Park (☎ 208-726-5445; 13 Broadway Run, Hwy 75; campsites/RV sites $19/33) About 2 miles south of Ketchum.

Eating & Drinking

Bigwood Bread (☎ 208-726-2034; 270 Northwood Way; mains $4-9; ⏱ 7am-5pm Mon-Fri) With a cheery and upbeat atmosphere, this art-lined café creates hearty breads, baked goods, sandwiches, salads and healthy-start offerings, such as organic muesli.

Desperado's (☎ 208-726-3068; 211 4th St; mains $7-11; ⏱ 11:30am-10pm Mon-Sat) Despo's is a bright, busy and colorful eatery specializing in reasonably priced Mexican food. Fill up on burritos, chimichangas, tacos and quesadillas and a pitcher of margaritas.

Ketchum Grill (☎ 208-726-4660; 520 East Ave; mains $10-20; ⏱ 5.30-10pm) A local favorite, Ketchum Grill boasts a creative menu bursting with fresh fare. The elegant offerings include plenty of seafood and veggie options.

Whiskey Jacques (☎ 208-726-5297; 251 Main St) Make a night of it at this spacious, no-frills local institution: catch the game on TV, play a round of pool or Foosball, cut loose to live bands and DJs, or just drink until the cows come home.

Getting There & Around

The region's airport is Hailey's **Friedman Memorial Airport** (☎ 208-788-4956), 12 miles south of

Ketchum. **A-1 Taxi** (☎ 208-726-9351) offers rides to the airport from Ketchum ($22).

Ketchum Area Rapid Transit (KART; ☎ 208-726-7576; ⏱ 8am-6pm Mon-Fri) operates a free daily bus service between Ketchum and Sun Valley.

AROUND KETCHUM

A one-hour drive southeast of Ketchum, **Craters of the Moon National Monument** (☎ 208-527-3257; admission per vehicle $7; ⏱ 8am-4:30pm Sep-May, 8am-6pm Jun-Aug) is an 83-sq-mile volcanic showcase. Lava flows and tubes and cinder cones are found along the 7-mile **Crater Loop Road**, accessible by car or bicycle from April to November. In winter it's popular with skiers and snowshoers. Short trails lead from Crater Loop Rd to crater edges, onto cinder cones and into tunnels and lava caves. A surreal **campground** (campsites $12) near the entrance station has running water only in summer.

North of Ketchum, Hwy 75 follows the Salmon River and winds past timbered slopes for 30 miles before ascending Galena Summit (8701ft), which offers truly breathtaking views. The 1180-sq-mile **Sawtooth National Recreation Area** spans the Sawtooth, Smoky, Boulder and Salmon River mountains and has 40 peaks over 10,000ft, more than 300 high-alpine lakes, 100 miles of streams and 750 miles of trails. Though most tourists come in summer and winter, boundless recreation is possible year-round.

The **area headquarters** (☎ 208-727-5000; Hwy 75; ⏱ 8am-4:30pm Sep-May, 8am-5pm Jun-Aug), 8.5 miles north of Ketchum, refers visitors to guides for climbing, fishing and backcountry skiing, and has information on yurt rentals and camping. It also sells Trailhead Parking Passes (three-day/year passes $5/15), required for parking in the recreation area.

MCCALL

More rustic than glitzy, wonderfully scenic McCall sits along Payette Lake's southern shore at the northern end of Long Valley. It's a year-round community with an air of seclusion. Residents enjoy a relaxing pace of life, and visitors take advantage of great skiing at nearby **Brundage Mountain** (☎ 208-634-4151; www .brundage.com; lift tickets winter/summer $44/22) in winter. In summer, ride the chairlift to the top and mountain bike down.

The **McCall Visitor Center** (☎ 208-634-7631; 102 N 3rd St; ⏱ 8am-5pm Mon-Fri) is one block south of W Lake St. Detailed recreation information is

ROCKY MOUNTAINS

available from the USFS Payette National Forest offices: **McCall Ranger District** (☎ 208-634-0400; 102 W Lake St; ⏱ 7:30am-4:30pm Mon-Fri) and **Forest Krassel Ranger District** (☎ 208-634-0600; 500 N Mission St; ⏱ 7:30am-4:30pm Mon-Fri).

The fabulous **Whitetail Club** (☎ 208-634-2244; www.whitetailclub.com; 501 W Lake St; r from $250; 🅟 🅡) is a swanky sleeping option. Blending with the natural environment, buildings are made from lodgepole pine, stone and shiny marble. Old B&W photos, antiques, deep couches and picture windows with lake views provide a classy, yet rustic ambience. The 70-plus suites are lavish affairs with private decks, deep mahogany furniture and thick tapestries. All sorts of activities can be arranged, and two on-site restaurants offer innovative menus.

HELLS CANYON NATIONAL RECREATION AREA

Plunging down 8913ft from Mt Oore's He Devil Peak on the east rim to the Snake River at Granite Creek, awe-inspiring Hells Canyon is North America's deepest gorge – thousands of feet deeper than the Grand Canyon. The remote 652,488-acre Hells Canyon National Recreation Area is one of the state's premier natural attractions, a must-see on any Idaho itinerary. Fishing, swimming, camping and dramatic views of the gorge and surrounding mountains are just a few of the highlights.

The **Snake National Wild & Scenic River** winds through the canyon, and is a favorite spot for rafting and jet-boat trips. Nearly 900 miles of hiking trails traipse by riverbanks, past mountain peaks and along canyon walls decorated with ancient petroglyphs. Wildflowers color meadows, and much wildlife resides here.

The Hells Canyon National Recreation Area spans the Idaho–Oregon state line, but the Oregon section is not readily accessible from Idaho. US 95 runs parallel to its eastern boundary. A few unpaved roads lead from US 95 between the tiny towns of Riggins (a big rafting center) and White Bird into the NRA. Only one road leads from US 95 to the Snake River itself, at Pittsburg Landing.

The **Hells Canyon NRA Riggins** (☎ 208-628-3916; ⏱ 8am-5pm Mon-Fri) has maps and information on campgrounds, roads, trails and fishing. The unstaffed **Salmon River Visitor Center** (☎ 208-628-3778; www.rigginsidaho.com; Riggins City Park, Hwy 95; ⏱ 9am-5pm Mon-Sat) has brochures on the area's outfitters; the narrow strip of land called Riggins prides itself on being Idaho's white-water capital and is the base for rafting on the Lower Salmon River.

Travelers with time (and high-clearance vehicles) can drive to the canyon rim on unpaved roads for dramatic views. USFS Rd 517 (open July to October), a quarter of a mile south of the Hells Canyon Riggins office on US 95, climbs 17 miles to the rim and ends 2 miles later at the breathtaking **Heaven's Gate Lookout**.

IDAHO PANHANDLE

Tipping up toward Canada, this alluring region is speckled with resorts, lakes, old mining haunts and, unfortunately, some really racist bastards. **Coeur d'Alene** is the regional hub. **Kellogg** and **Sandpoint** are prime destinations for skiers, anglers and water-sports enthusiasts, while the old silver-mining town of **Wallace** exudes preserved Western flavor. Sixty lakes lie within 60 miles of Coeur d'Alene, including Hayden, Priest and Pend Oreille, all surrounded by campgrounds. Outdoor activities are ubiquitous: white-water rafting the Class III run of the St Joe National Wild and Scenic River, jet-skiing on Lake Coeur d'Alene, backpacking through the primeval forest around Priest Lake.

The Panhandle has a reputation, often inflated by the media, as a base for neo-Nazi, white-supremacist groups. However, these days you're far more likely to meet wildlife than wildly irrational people. The **Coeur d'Alene Visitor Center** (☎ 208-665-2350; 115 Northwest Blvd; ⏱ 10am-5pm Jun-Aug, 10am-3pm Tue-Sat rest of year) is a good regional information starting point.

In Sandpoint, **Lakeside Inn** (☎ 208-263-3717; lakeside@televar.com; 106 Bridge St; r $65-95; 🅟) has a good waterfront location, plus a Jacuzzi and comfortable rooms.

ROCKY MOUNTAINS

Southwest

Welcome to iconic America, the luscious backdrop of movie Westerns and the red-rock land of limitless horizons. Time has etched itself on these yawning landscapes, carving white-water canyons, soaring buttes and formations of psychedelic sandstone beyond compare. Chunky rusted jewels of mile-long freight trains hark back to a distant era, and insane art houses dot lonely rural routes. From ghost towns to spa towns, mysterious space aliens to Route 66 Americana, so many themes invite exploration that road trips barely seem to scratch the surface, never lasting long enough to experience its breadth.

Ranging from the Grand Canyon to the Mexican border, the Southwest can seem like one enormous park, alternately inhabited by saguaro cacti, high-elevation evergreens and barren tumbleweed desert. Its human population has the same variety, with Anglo, Native American and Hispanic residents forming a unique tri-cultural mix. There's plenty of small-town quirk but rarely any big-city smirk – people take it slow and always have time to stop and chat. And of course there's Las Vegas, the neon-clad desert oasis that never bothers to sleep.

It's impossible to see it all, despite all frenzied attempts. So pull up a patio chair at sunset, shuck your shoes and savor the film-finale sky.

HIGHLIGHTS

- Gaping at the unquestionably **Grand Canyon** (p835)
- Exploring Utah's drop-dead scenic **Monument Valley** (p843)
- Living the high life on the **Las Vegas Strip** (p812)
- Climbing and playing on the brilliant **White Sands dunes** (p891)
- Slicing down the slopes of **Park City** (p860)
- Watching bats fly out for a dusky dinner at **Carlsbad Caverns National Park** (p894)
- Swooning over red rocks at sunset in **Sedona** (p833)
- Rafting the turbulent spray of the **Colorado River** (p839)
- Hiking and splashing through a water-smoothed slot canyon in **Canyonlands** (p867), **Zion** (p871) or **Antelope Canyon** (p842)
- Soaking away all earthly cares at New Mexico's classic **Ojo Caliente** (p886) or the luxe digs at **Sierra Grande Lodge & Spa** (p890) in Truth or Consequences

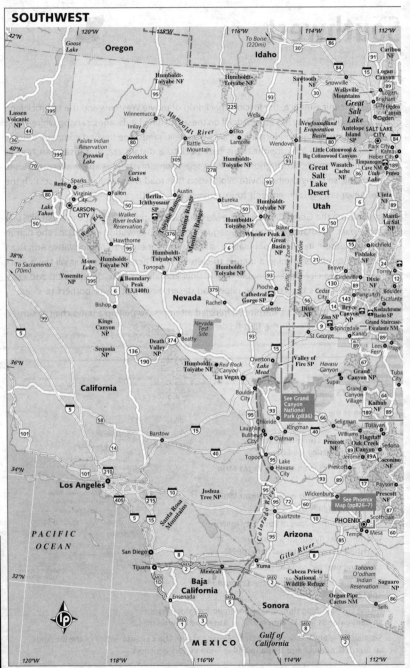

SOUTHWEST

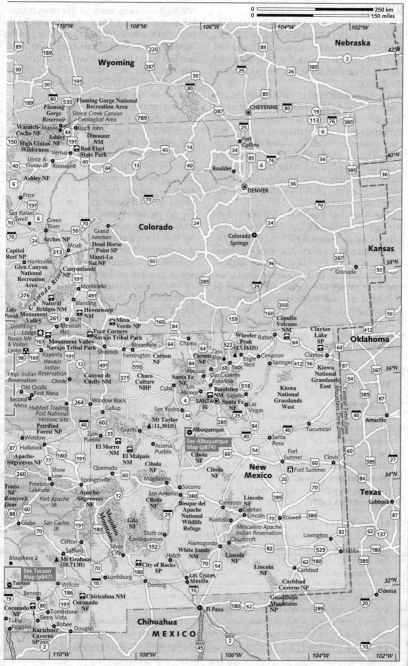

HISTORY

The history of human habitation in the Southwest dates back 12,500 years. But by AD 100, three dominant and fascinating cultures had emerged: the Hohokam, the Mogollon and the Ancestral Puebloans (formerly known as the Anasazi).

The Hohokam lived in the Arizona deserts from 300 BC to AD 1450, and created an incredible canal irrigation system, earthen pyramids and a rich heritage of pottery. But they mysteriously disappeared in the mid-15th century. From 200 BC to AD 1450 the Mogollon people lived in the central mountains and valleys of the Southwest, and left behind the Gila Cliff Dwellings National Monument (p891).

The Ancestral Puebloans left the richest heritage of archaeological sites, like that at Chaco Culture National Historic Park (p889). Today descendants of the Ancestral Puebloans are found in the Pueblo groups throughout New Mexico. The Hopi are descendants, too, and their village Old Oraibi (p844) may be the oldest continuously inhabited settlement in North America.

In 1540 Francisco Vásquez de Coronado led an expedition from Mexico City to the Southwest. Instead of riches, his party found Native Americans, many of whom were then killed or displaced. More than 50 years later, Juan de Oñate established the first capital of New Mexico at San Gabriel. Great bloodshed resulted from Oñate's attempts to control Native American pueblos, and he left in failure in 1608. Santa Fe (p879) was established as a new capital the following year.

Development in the Southwest expanded rapidly during the 19th century, mainly due to railroad and geological surveys. As the US pushed west, the army forcibly removed whole tribes of Native Americans in often horrifyingly brutal Indian Wars. Gold and silver mines drew fortune seekers, and practically overnight the lawless mining towns of the Wild West mushroomed. Capitalizing on the development, the Santa Fe Railroad lured an ocean of tourists fascinated by the West's rugged beauty and Native American culture.

Modern settlement is closely linked to water use. Following the Reclamation Act of 1902, huge federally funded dams were built to control rivers, irrigate the desert and encourage development. Rancorous debates and disagreements over water rights continue today, especially with the phenomenal boom in residential development.

THE SOUTHWEST...

In One Week

Swoop down on **Phoenix** (p824) for a sampling of the Southwest's best nightlife and shopping. Continue north to experience a perfect sunset in **Sedona** (p833) after splashing in the local swimming holes. Let someone else do the driving as you ride the rails from **Williams** (p833) to the ethereal depths of the **Grand Canyon** (p835). Detour onto the largest surviving stretch of Arizona's **Route 66** (p845), and then brave the jarring road to the Hualapai Nation's spectacular **Grand Canyon Skywalk** (p840). For your last few days, indulge your fantasies in **Las Vegas** (p812), or earmark one day for the high life and spend the rest on an out-and-back visit to **Zion National Park** (p871).

In Two Weeks

Try your luck in **Las Vegas** (p812) before kicking back in funky **Flagstaff** (p831) and peering into the abyss at **Grand Canyon National Park** (p835). Check out collegiate **Tucson** (p846) or frolic among the cacti at **Saguaro National Park** (p850). Watch the high-noon gunslinging in **Tombstone** (p851) before settling into Victorian **Bisbee** (p852).

Head east to the blinding dunes of **White Sands National Monument** (p891), then sink into **Santa Fe** (p879), a magnet for art lovers. Sing the praises of solar energy in **Taos** (p886) and watch the sunrise at awesome **Monument Valley** (p843).

Head into Utah for the red-rock national parks, including **Canyonlands** (p867) and **Arches** (p866). Munch on summer fruit at **Capitol Reef** (p868), and do the hoodoos at **Bryce Canyon** (p870). Pay your respects at glorious **Zion** (p871), before returning to Las Vegas.

LOCAL CULTURE

More than just a pretty face, the Southwest is one of the most multicultural regions of the country, encompassing a rich mix of Native American, Hispanic and Anglo populations. These groups have all had a hand in influencing the area's cuisine, architecture and the arts, but the Southwest's vast Native American reservations offer exceptional opportunities to learn about Native American culture and history. Visual arts are a strong force as well, from the art colonies dotting New Mexico to the roadside kitsch on view in small towns everywhere.

LAND & CLIMATE

The Southwest is jam-packed with one of the world's greatest concentrations of remarkable rock formations. Thanks to the area's soft and widespread sedimentary layers, rain and erosion readily carve them into fantastic shapes. The rich colors that imbue the landscape come from the unique mineral compositions of each rock type.

Although the Colorado Plateau encompasses a series of plateaus of between 5000ft and 8000ft in elevation and separated by deep canyons, the greatest among them is the Grand Canyon (p835).

While mountains are snowcapped in winter, most of the Southwest receives little annual rainfall. During the summer, temperatures can soar over 90°F (32°C); although it's dry heat, it's still uncomfortable. Nights are cooler, and spring and fall can be pleasant.

Southwestern summer rainstorms, often accompanied by lightning, can come out of nowhere, and flash floods occur regularly, sometimes from a storm many miles away. A dry riverbed or wash can become a raging torrent within minutes. Never camp in washes, and always inquire about conditions before entering canyons.

PARKS

The Southwest has *the* most fabulous concentration of national parks and monuments in North America. But keep in mind that a number of less crowded state parks are worth visiting.

One of the national park system's most deservedly popular destinations is the Grand Canyon National Park (p835) in Arizona. Other Arizona parks include Monument Val-

---

TOP FIVE PARKS IN THE SOUTHWEST

■ Monument Valley Navajo Tribal Park
■ Grand Canyon National Park
■ Carlsbad Caverns National Park
■ Bryce Canyon National Park
■ Arches National Park

---

ley Navajo Tribal Park (p843), a desert basin with towering sandstone pillars and buttes; Canyon de Chelly National Monument (p843), with ancient cliff dwellings; Organ Pipe Cactus National Monument (p850), in the pristine Sonoran Desert; the odd mix of Painted Desert and fossilized logs at Petrified Forest National Park (p844); and the pristine desert and giant cactus at Saguaro National Park (p850).

The southern red-rock canyon country in Utah includes Arches (p866), Canyonlands (p867), Zion (p871) and Bryce (p870). Grand Staircase–Escalante National Monument (p869) is a mighty region of undeveloped desert, while Capitol Reef National Park (p868) offers exceptional wilderness solitude.

New Mexico boasts both Carlsbad Caverns National Park (p894) and the mysterious Chaco Culture National Historic Park (p889). Nevada's only national park is Great Basin (p822), a rugged and remote mountain oasis.

For further information, check out the **National Park Service** (NPS; www.nps.gov) website. For information on the region's state parks, see p808 for Nevada, p853 for Utah, p873 for New Mexico and p824 for Arizona.

INFORMATION

American Southwest (www.americansouthwest.net) Arguably the most comprehensive site for national parks and natural landscapes of the Southwest.
American West Travelogue (www.amwest-travel.com) A selective reading list, photographs and more.
Notes from the Road (www.notesfromtheroad.com) Click on 'Desert Southwest' for travel writing on the region.

GETTING THERE & AROUND

Air

Phoenix's Sky Harbor International Airport and Las Vegas' McCarran International Airport are the region's busiest airports, followed by the airports serving Salt Lake City, Albuquerque and Tucson. America West, Southwest and Delta are the region's main carriers.

Bus

Long-distance buses can get you to major points within the region but don't serve all national parks or important, off-track tourist towns such as Moab. Be aware that bus terminals can be in less safe areas of town.

Car & Motorcycle

Private vehicles are often the only means to reach out-of-the-way towns, trailheads and swimming spots. For information on renting a car, see p1144.

Driving distances:

Flagstaff–Monument Valley: 170 miles
Las Vegas–Grand Canyon (South Rim): 280 miles
Las Vegas–Zion National Park: 150 miles
Phoenix–Santa Fe: 525 miles
Salt Lake City–Arches National Park: 240 miles

Train

Amtrak's train service is much more limited than the bus system, although it does link many major Southwestern towns and offers bus connections to other towns (including Santa Fe and Phoenix). The *California Zephyr* traverses Utah and Nevada; the *Southwest Chief* stops in Arizona and New Mexico; and the *Sunset Limited* cuts through southern Arizona and New Mexico.

NEVADA

Various vices can come to mind when you free-associate on Nevada, but that's only a fraction of the story. It's a sparsely populated state strewn with restless tumbleweeds and limitless tracts of desert; some perceive a barren wasteland, while others discern a faint patchwork of natural jewels.

The first state to legalize gambling, Nevada is loud with the chime of slot machines singing out from gas stations, supermarkets and hotel lobbies without fail, and pockets of licensed brothels dot the landscape. But more recent generations look at the chapped endless mesas and lonely roads and see blank canvases instead of potential mining claims. Witness the art-fueled insanity of Burning Man, and the state never feels quite the same.

The azure shore of Lake Tahoe entices hikers and snow demons, and the Truckee River

---

NEVADA FACTS

Nicknames Silver State, Sagebrush State
Population 2.5 million
Las Vegas population 600,000
Area 109,826 sq miles
Capital city Carson City (population 55,500)
Sales tax 6.5%
Birthplace of First Lady Thelma 'Pat' Nixon (1912–93); Andre Agassi (b 1970)
Home of Nevada Test Site, Burning Man festival
Famous for Las Vegas, the Comstock Lode at Virginia City, legal prostitution
Best souvenir 'Dam Proud to Be American' bumper sticker, Hoover Dam

---

makes downtown Reno a big summer beach party. The glitzy pleasure palace of Las Vegas is the shrill siren song of the south, and many have happily lost themselves in its nonstop neon world.

History

Nevada's first inhabitants were the Paiute and Ancestral Puebloan people. Though claimed by Spain, Nevada was scarcely touched by Europeans until the 1820s, when trappers ventured into the Humboldt River Valley. Most 19th-century emigrants passed straight through Nevada to the California goldfields. But in 1859 the Comstock Lode – the largest silver deposit ever mined – was discovered south of Reno.

As the Comstock Lode was mined out, Nevada's population declined. In the early 20th century, new mineral discoveries temporarily revived the state's fortunes, but the Great Depression brought an end to those dreams. So in 1931 the state government legalized gambling and created agencies to tax it, turning an illegal activity into a revenue source and tourist attraction. Today the state thrives on tourism, with most revenues coming from the ubiquitous casinos.

Information

Nevada Commission on Tourism (☎ 800-638-2328; www.travelnevada.com; 401 N Carson St, Carson City, NV 89701) Sends free books, maps and information on accommodations, campgrounds and events.
Nevada Division of State Parks (☎ 775-684-2770; www.parks.nv.gov; 901 S Stewart St, 5th Fl, Ste 5005, Carson City, NV 89701-5248) Information about Nevada state parks.

Prostitution is illegal in Clark County (which includes Las Vegas) and Washoe County (which includes Reno), though there are legal brothels in many smaller counties.

Nevada is on Pacific Standard Time and has two areas codes: Las Vegas and vicinity is ☎ 702, while the rest of the state is ☎ 775.

LAS VEGAS

America's legendary city of 24/7 hedonism, two-fisted debauchery and bacchanalian revelry floodlit by blinding neon, Las Vegas more than lives up to its tarty reputation. Whether you're channeling the singsong burbles of the slot machines or sweating down a stack of $500 blackjack chips, the cavernous hotel casinos have got your number.

A schizophrenic metropolis catering to the unruffled high roller, the hyperventilating conventioneer and everyone in between, Sin City aims to infatuate, and its reaches are all-inclusive. Hollywood bigwigs gyrate at A-list ultralounges, while elderly grandparents from Nowheresville whoop it up at the Elvis commemorative penny slots. You can sip designer martinis as you sample the apex of world-class cuisine, or wallow in a trough of deep-fried Oreo cookies washed down with gulps from a three-foot-high cocktail. Everyone finds their niche and thrills to the ride.

It's easy to lose yourself in the Strip resorts, the self-contained and climate-controlled orbits devoid of clocks and marked exits. Booze flows like water, and since it's a desert, spirits seem easier to come by. Outside, the city's geography can slap you in the face, with summer temperatures melting the thermometers.

May your luck run strong and your inhibitions be damned. Welcome to Vegas, baby.

History

Contrary to Hollywood legend, there was much more at the dusty crossroads than a gambling parlor and some tumbleweeds the day mobster Ben 'Bugsy' Siegel rolled in and erected a glamorous tropical-themed casino, the Flamingo, under the searing sun.

Speared into the modern era by the completion of a railroad that linked up Salt Lake City to Los Angeles in 1902, Las Vegas boomed in the 1920s thanks to federally sponsored construction projects. The legalization of gambling in 1931 then carried Vegas through the Great Depression. WWII brought a huge air-force base and big aerospace bucks, plus a paved highway to Los Angeles. Soon after, the Cold War justified the Nevada Test Site. It proved to be a textbook case of 'any publicity is good publicity': monthly above-ground atomic blasts shattered casino windows downtown, while the city's official Miss Mushroom Cloud mascot promoted atomic everything in tourism campaigns.

A building spree sparked by the Flamingo in 1946 led to mob-backed tycoons upping the glitz ante at every turn. Big-name entertainers, like Frank Sinatra, Liberace and Sammy Davis Jr, arrived on stage at the same time as topless French showgirls.

The high-profile purchase of the Desert Inn in 1966 by eccentric billionaire Howard Hughes gave the gambling industry a much-needed patina of legitimacy. The debut of the MGM Grand in 1993 signaled the dawn of the era of the corporate 'megaresort.'

An oasis in the middle of a final frontier, Sin City continues to exist chiefly to satisfy the needs and desires of visitors. Hosting over 39 million a year, Las Vegas is the engine of North America's fastest-growing metropolitan area and a fabled destination for countless people seeking their fortune.

Orientation & Information

Downtown Las Vegas is the original town center and home to the city's oldest hotels and casinos. Its main drag is Fremont St, four blocks of which are now a covered multimedia pedestrian mall.

DON'T MISS

- **Bellagio fountains** – dancing spurt and spray in the evening (p812)
- **Stratosphere Tower** – views to scream over (p813)
- **Fremont Street Experience** – street canopy of sound and art (p813)
- **Cirque du Soleil** artsy acrobatic circus (p817)
- **Star Trek Experience** – go boldly (p814)
- **Mandalay Bay pool** – splash in the surf (p815)
- **Ghostbar** – party with a dreamy view (p816)

SOUTHWEST

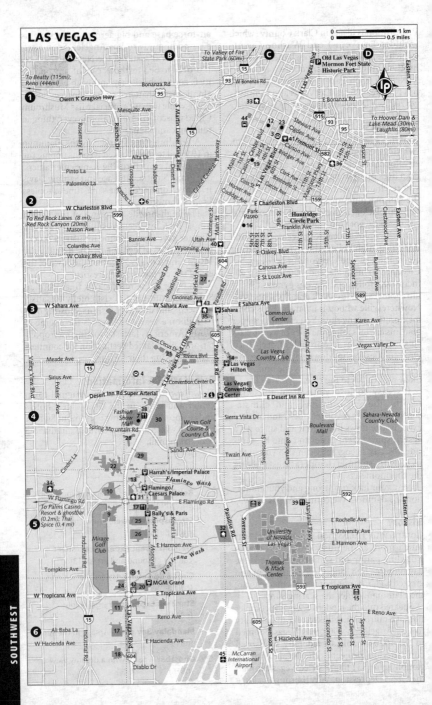

LAS VEGAS

SOUTHWEST

Las Vegas Blvd is the main north–south drag, running from North Las Vegas south toward the airport. South of the city limits, this boulevard is famously known as 'the Strip,' where you'll find most of the gargantuan hotel-casinos. It can take more than 15 minutes to drive from one end to the other, and even longer in traffic.

More casinos are found east of the Strip along Paradise Rd, and just west of I-15 near the intersection of Flamingo Rd and Valley View Blvd. The Chinatown district is west of the Strip on Spring Mountain Rd.

Major tourist areas are safe. However, Las Vegas Blvd between downtown and the Strip gets shabby, and Fremont St east of downtown is rather unsavory.

BOOKSTORES
Reading Room (☎ 702-632-9374; Mandalay Place, 3930 Las Vegas Blvd S)
Waldenbooks (☎ 702-733-1049; 3200 Las Vegas Blvd) Inside the Fashion Show Mall.

EMERGENCY & MEDICAL SERVICES
Gamblers Anonymous (☎ 702-385-7732) Assistance with gambling concerns.
Police Department (☎ 702-828-3111)
Sunrise Hospital & Medical Center (☎ 702-731-8000; 3186 S Maryland Parkway)

University Medical Center (☎ 702-383-2000; 1800 W Charleston Blvd)

INTERNET ACCESS
Cyber Stop (☎ 702-767-8803; Hawaiian Marketplace, Polo Towers Plaza, 3743 Las Vegas Blvd S; per hr $12)

INTERNET RESOURCES
City of Las Vegas (www.ci.las-vegas.nv.us) City of Las Vegas website.
Las Vegas.com (www.lasvegas.com) Travel services.
Vegas.com (www.vegas.com) Travel information with booking service.

MEDIA
Las Vegas Review-Journal (☎ 702-383-0211; www .lvrj.com) Daily paper with a weekend guide, *Neon*, on Friday.
Las Vegas Weekly (☎ 702-990-2550; www.lasvegas weekly.com) Free weekly with good entertainment and restaurant listings.

MONEY
Every hotel-casino and bank and most convenience stores have an ATM.
American Express (☎ 702-739-8474; Fashion Show Mall, 3200 Las Vegas Blvd S; ⏰ 10am-9pm Mon-Fri, to 8pm Sat, noon-6pm Sun) Changes currencies at competitive rates.

POST
Post office (☎ 702-735-8677; 3100 S Industrial Rd)
Post office (☎ 702-382-5779; 201 Las Vegas Blvd S)

SOUTHWEST

TOURIST INFORMATION

Las Vegas Visitor Information Center (☎ 702-892-0711; www.visitlasvegas.com; 3150 Paradise Rd; ☷ 8am-5pm) Free local calls and internet access.

Sights

CASINOS

The Strip's famous skyline has had a different look since 2005, thanks to the $2.7 billion **Wynn Las Vegas** (☎ 702-770-7100; www.wynnlasvegas.com; 3131 Las Vegas Blvd). The most expensive hotel–casino built to date, it upholds the city's decadent reputation. With a 50-story curved tower covered in bronze glass, the facility is as swanky as it gets. The entire place exudes an air of secrecy – the entrance is obscured from the Strip by a $130-million artificial mountain, which rises seven stories tall in some places. Inside, the Wynn resembles a natural paradise – with mountain views, tumbling waterfalls, fountains and other special effects. Acclaimed director Franco Dragone has created a water-themed production show, **Le Rêve**, in a specially constructed theater-in-the-round, which includes a million-gallon pool doubling as the stage.

Opulent, yet elegant, the **Bellagio** (☎ 702-693-7111, 877-987-6667; www.bellagio.com; 3600 Las Vegas Blvd S) was built to dazzle. Its Tuscan architecture and 8-acre artificial lake, complete with choreographed dancing fountains (3pm to midnight weekdays, noon to midnight weekends; on the half-hour until 8pm and then every 15 minutes), are riveting. The hotel's lobby features an 18ft ceiling adorned with a backlit glass sculpture composed of 2000 hand-blown flowers in brilliant colors. The **Bellagio Gallery of Fine Art** (☎ 702-693-7871; admission $17; ☷ 10am-6pm Sun-Thu, to 9pm Fri & Sat) showcases temporary exhibits by top-notch artists.

Quintessentially Las Vegas, **Caesars Palace** (☎ 702-731-7110; www.caesarspalace.com; 3570 Las Vegas Blvd S) is a Greco-Roman fantasyland featuring marble reproductions of classical statuary, including a not-to-be-missed 4-ton Brahma shrine near the front entrance. Towering fountains, goddess-costumed cocktail waitresses and the swanky, haute-couture **Forum Shops** all ante up the glitz.

Hand-painted ceiling frescoes, roaming mimes and full-scale reproductions of famous Venice landmarks are found at the romantic **Venetian** (☎ 702-414-4500; www.venetian.com; 3355 Las Vegas Blvd S; gondola rides adult/private $12.50/60). A gondola ride down the Grand Canal is a highlight. So is a visit to the stunning **Guggenheim Hermitage Museum** (☎ 702-414-2440; www.guggenheimlasvegas.org; adult/child $19/12.50; ☷ 9:30am-7:30pm).

Not trying to be any one fantasy, the tropically themed **Mandalay Bay** (M-Bay; ☎ 720-632-7777; www.mandalaybay.com; 3950 Las Vegas Blvd S) really feels likes a classy resort. Standout attractions include the multilevel **Shark Reef** (☎ 702-632-4555; adult/child $16/11; ☷ 10am-11pm), an aquarium complex home to thousands of submarine beasties with a shallow pool where you can pet pint-sized sharks.

Though traces of the original swashbuckling skull-and-crossbones theme linger at **Treasure Island** (TI; ☎ 702-894-7111; www.treasureisland.com; 3300 Las Vegas Blvd S), the new-look terra cotta–toned resort now strives for an elegant adults-only Caribbean-hideaway feel. The spiced-up **Sirens of Treasure Island** (admission free) is a mock sea battle pitting sultry temptresses against renegade freebooters. You can see it every 90 minutes from 7pm to 11:30pm.

The captivating **Mirage** (☎ 702-791-7111; www.mirage.com; 3400 Las Vegas Blvd S) is tropically themed, replete with a giant jungle-foliage atrium, meandering creeks and soothing cascades. At the casino's south entrance, the **royal white tiger habitat** permits a glare-free view of the big cats. Out front, the fiery trademark **faux volcano** erupts frequently.

Staying true to its Hollywood roots (it's owned by movie mogul Metro Goldwyn Mayer), the **MGM Grand** (MGM; ☎ 702-891-7777; www.mgmgrand.com; 3799 Las Vegas Blvd S) is a gigantic, glitzy 'City of Entertainment.' Out front is the USA's largest bronze statue, a 45ft-tall, 100,000lb lion perched atop a 25ft pedestal, ringed by lush landscaping, fountains and Atlas-themed statues.

Evoking the gaiety of the City of Light, **Paris-Las Vegas** (☎ 702-946-7000; www.parislasvegas.com; 3655 Las Vegas Blvd S) strives to capture the essence of the *grande dame* by re-creating her landmarks. Fine likenesses of the Opéra, the Arc de Triomphe, the Champs-Élysées and even the Seine frame the property. The signature attraction is the ersatz Eiffel Tower.

New York-New York (☎ 702-740-6969; www.nyny hotelcasino.com; 3790 Las Vegas Blvd S) is a mini megapolis featuring scaled-down replicas of the Empire State Building (47 stories or 529ft); the Statue of Liberty, ringed by a September 11 memorial; a mini version of the Brooklyn

Bridge; and renditions of the Chrysler, AT&T and CBS buildings.

The focus at **Luxor** (☎ 702-262-4444; www .luxor.com; 3900 Las Vegas Blvd S), perhaps the most impressive resort on the Strip, is its 30-story pyramid, cloaked in black glass from base to apex. The interior is stuffed full of enormous Egyptian statues and a stunning replica of the Great Temple of Ramses II. The **King Tut Museum** (☎ 702-262-4000; admission $10; ☯ 10am-11pm) features exquisite reproductions of ancient artifacts.

At 1149ft, the white, three-legged $550-million **Stratosphere** (☎ 702-380-7777; www.strato sspherehotel.com; 2000 Las Vegas Blvd S) is the tallest building west of the Mississippi. Situated atop the elegantly tapered tower you'll find indoor and outdoor viewing decks, offering the most spectacular 360-degree panoramas in town.

The **Hard Rock Hotel & Casino** (☎ 800-473-7625; www.hrhvegas.com; 4455 Paradise Rd) is home to one of the world's most impressive collections of rock-and-roll memorabilia. The pool complex is a sexy, see-and-be-seen scene that's perfect for entourage wannabes.

OTHER ATTRACTIONS

Atomic Testing Museum (☎ 702-794-5161; www.atomic testingmuseum.com; 755 E Flamingo Rd; adult/child $12/9; ☯ 9am-5pm Mon-Sat, 1-5pm Sun) During the atomic heyday of the 1950s, gamblers and tourists watched mushroom clouds rising behind downtown's Fremont St, and the city even crowned a Miss Atomic Bomb. Don't skip the deafening Ground Zero Theater, which mimics a concrete test bunker.

A four-block pedestrian mall topped by an arched steel canopy and filled with computer-controlled lights, the **Fremont Street Experience** (www.vegasexperience.com; Fremont St; ☯ hourly 7pm-midnight), between Main St and Las Vegas Blvd, has brought life back to downtown. Every evening, the canopy is transformed into a jaw-dropping six-minute light-and-sound show enhanced by 550,000 watts of wraparound sound.

The crown jewel of a downtown redevelopment effort, the **Neonopolis** (☎ 702-477-0470; www .neonopolis.com; 450 Fremont St; ☯ 11am-9pm) shopping and entertainment complex is most notable for its collection of vintage neon signs. At the alfresco **Neon Museum** (☎ 702-387-6366; www.neon museum.org; cnr Fremont & 3rd Sts; admission free; ☯ 24hr), plaques explain their history.

Activities

At the **Stratosphere Tower** (☎ 702-380-7777; www .stratospherehotel.com; Stratosphere, 2000 Las Vegas Blvd S; elevator adult/child $11/7, admission per ride $9; ☯ 10am-1am Sun-Thu, to 2am Fri & Sat), the Big Shot straps riders into completely exposed seats that zip up and down the tower's pinnacle for 12 seconds. The view is amazing, and pedestrians below recoil at the blood-curdling screams.

If the idea of luxury bowling sounds – ahem – right up your alley, hotfoot it to **Red Rock Lanes** (☎ 702-797-7467; www.redrocklanes.com; Red Rock Casino, Resort & Spa; 11011 W Charleston Blvd; games per person from $3; ☯ 24hr). A brand spanking new bowling palace with 72 lanes, shuffleboard, pool tables and VIP pampering galore, it gives the sport newfound class.

The Indy car simulators with 20ft wraparound screens are so authentic at the **Las Vegas Cyber Speedway & Speed** (☎ 702-734-7223; www.nas carcafelasvegas.com; Sahara, 2535 Las Vegas Blvd S; admission Cyber Speedway $10, Speed $10, daily unlimited for both $20; ☯ Cyber Speedway 10am-midnight Sun-Thu, to 1am Fri & Sat, Speed 11am-midnight Sun-Thu, to 1am Fri & Sat) that they excite real Formula One drivers. Speed is an electromagnetic rollercoaster that slingshots passengers at 70mph.

Feel your life flash before you on the **Manhattan Express Rollercoaster** (☎ 702-740-6969; www .nynyhotelcasino.com; New York-New York, 3790 Las Vegas Blvd S; admission $12.50, re-ride $6; ☯ 11am-11pm Sun-Thu, 10:30am-midnight Fri & Sat), where a twist-and-dive maneuver produces a (rather violent) sensation similar to what a pilot feels during a barrel roll in a fighter plane.

Join the local downtown scenesters for **First Friday** (☎ 702-384-0092; www.firstfriday-lasvegas.org; admission free; ☯ 6-10pm 1st Fri of month), a mobbed monthly block party of live music, art openings and street performers. Check the website for event venues.

Las Vegas for Children

Now that sin is in again, few places in Vegas bill themselves as family-friendly. State law prohibits people under 21 from loitering in gaming areas.

The Circus Circus hotel complex is all about the kids, and its **Midway** (☎ 702-734-0410; www.circuscircus.com; Circus Circus, 2880 Las Vegas Blvd S; admission free; ☯ 11am-midnight) features animals, acrobats and magicians performing on center stage; shows are held every 30 minutes. The **Excalibur** (☎ 702-597-7777; www.excalibur.com; 3050 Las Vegas Blvd S) weighs in as well, with a Fantasy

SOUTHWEST

Faire Midway and a multimedia ride starring SpongeBob SquarePants.

Offbeat Las Vegas

For connoisseurs of over-the-top extravagance, the **Liberace Museum** (☎ 702-798-5595; www.liberace.org; 1775 E Tropicana Ave; adult/child over 10 $12.50/8.50; ❤ 10am-5pm Tue-Sat, noon-4pm Sun) is a must-do. The home of 'Mr Showmanship' houses the flamboyant art cars, ornate pianos and the most outrageous costumes concocted outside a Halloween parade.

Geeks will go ga-ga over the **Star Trek Experience** (☎ 888-462-6535; Las Vegas Hilton, 3000 Paradise Rd; admission $38-42), where you can ride the Klingon Encounter and thrill to a museum of props and costumes.

Time your visit to coincide with the evening shift change of the **Imperial Dealertainers** (☎ 702-731-3311; Imperial Palace, 3535 Las Vegas Blvd S; ❤ noon-4am), celebrity impersonators who do double duty as blackjack dealers. Elvis, Janet Jackson, Gwen Stefani and others belt out hits between hands.

For a lowbrow, high-cholesterol culinary adventure, downtown's **Fremont St** covers all bases.

Sleeping

With over 130,000 hotel rooms, from penthouse villas commanding the Strip to filthy east-of-downtown fleapits aging into oblivion, there's something for everyone's budget or credit card–bruising splurge. Rates rise and fall dramatically depending on demand, with weekends and convention traffic driving up rates. Downtown hotels are generally less expensive than the Strip. Most hotel websites have handy calendars with day-by-day room rates listed. Options are categorized here by lowest possible standard room rates, but prices can easily be double that.

BUDGET

Circus Circus (☎ 702-734-0410, 800-634-3450; www.circuscircus.com; 2880 Las Vegas Blvd S; r from $42; P ⊠ ⚑ ▢ wi-fi) At this family-oriented casino mega-hotel, the no-frills rooms are pleasant and the prices hard to beat. Kids will froth at the mouth over the indoor theme park as well as the constant feed of carnival games and acrobatic acts. Pass on the Manor motel rooms – its best hand played out long ago.

Bill's Gamblin' Hall & Saloon (☎ 702-737-2100, 866-245-5745; www.billslasvegas.com; 3595 Las Vegas Blvd S; r $60-120; P ⊠ ▢ wi-fi) With cheap rooms smack bang mid-Strip, Bill's is great value and it's often hard to book a bed. Rooms feature attractive Victorian-themed decor, and guests can use the pool next door at the Flamingo without charge.

Also recommended:

USA Hostels Las Vegas (☎ 702-385-1150, 800-550-8958; www.usahostels.com/lasvegas; 1322 Fremont St; dm/r incl breakfast from $20/46; ⊠ ⚑ ▢ wi-fi)

Sahara (☎ 702-737-2111, 866-382-8884; www.saharavegas.com; 2535 Las Vegas Blvd S; r from $43; P ⊠ ⚑ ▢)

Main Street Station (☎ 702-387-1896, 800-713-8933; www.mainstreetcasino.com; 200 N Main St; r from $50; P ⊠)

GOING TO THE CHAPEL, GOING TO GET MARRIED

Spontaneous weddings have always been a Vegas trademark. It must be part of that slightly naughty, lose-your-inhibitions, what-happens-in-Vegas-stays-in-Vegas theme, because more than 100,000 couples choose to say their vows here each year! Whether it's a planned affair or a spur-of-the-moment decision, Las Vegas offers more than 30 different places to tie the knot. There's no waiting period and you don't need a blood test. You just have to be at least 18 years old and show up at the **Marriage Bureau** (☎ 702-671-0600; 201 Clark Ave; license $55; ❤ 8am-midnight). Once you have the certificate, it's off to the chapel.

For an out-of-this world marriage experience, beam up to the **Las Vegas Hilton** (☎ 702-697-8750; 3000 Paradise Rd), where you'll be tying the knot *Star Trek*–style. Intergalactic music plays as you cross the bridge of the USS *Enterprise*, and you'll even have a Klingon or Ferengi for your witness. Warp-speed weddings start at $500, and more elaborate packages cost $1000 to $3000.

For something more mainstream, try the **Little White Wedding Chapel** (☎ 702-382-5943; www.littlewhitechapel.com; 1301 Las Vegas Blvd S; ❤ 24hr). It's welcomed thousands of couples since opening in 1946, and is a favorite spot for celebs to say 'I do.' You can have an Elvis impersonator officiate or have the affair broadcast over the internet. They'll marry you in a helicopter ($750), an air balloon ($1500) – you name it. Drive-through rates start at $40, with full ceremony packages averaging around $800.

MIDRANGE

Luxor (☎ 702-262-4444, 888-777-0188; www.luxor.com; 3900 Las Vegas Blvd S; r from $70; P ⊠ ⚲ ▢ wi-fi) Featuring art deco and Egyptian furnishings and marble bathrooms, Luxor's rooms are one of Vegas' best midrange deals. Rooms in the newer tower have better views than pyramid digs.

Paris-Las Vegas (☎ 702-946-7000, 877-796-2096; www.parislasvegas.com; 3655 Las Vegas Blvd S; r from $99; P ⊠ ⚲ ▢) Bed down in the City of Light, even if the streets blare neon. Rooms have floral-print bedspreads and Versailles-style furniture.

Hard Rock Hotel & Casino (☎ 800-473-7625; www.hrhvegas.com; 4455 Paradise Rd; r from $109; P ⊠ ⚲ ▢ wi-fi) French doors reveal expansive views, and portraits of rockers grace the stylish Euro-minimalist rooms. Standard rooms have plasma TVs, and suites have snazzy whirlpool tubs. The action revolves around the lush pool area, with a sexy sandy beach and private cabanas.

Caesars Palace (☎ 702-731-7110, 800-634-6001; www.caesarspalace.com; 3570 Las Vegas Blvd S; r from $130; P ⊠ ⚲ ▢) Send away the centurions and decamp in style – Caesars' standard rooms are some of the most luxurious you will find in town. A vision of Roman conquest amassed with marble and murals awaits your command.

Mandalay Bay (☎ 702-632-7777; www.mandalaybay.com; 3950 Las Vegas Blvd S; r from $140; P ⊠ ⚲ ▢ wi-fi) The ornately appointed rooms have a South Seas theme; amenities include floor-to-ceiling windows and luxurious bathrooms. Swimmers will swoon over the sprawling pool complex, with a sand-and-surf beach and wave machine and the adults-only Moorea Beach Club.

Also recommended:

New York-New York (☎ 866-815-4365; www.nyny hotelcasino.com; 3790 Las Vegas Blvd S; r from $80; P ⊠ ⚲ ▢)

Rio (☎ 702-777-7777, 800-752-9746; www.playrio.com; 3700 W Flamingo Rd; ste from $90; P ⊠ ⚲ ▢ wi-fi)

Mirage (☎ 702-791-7111; www.mirage.com; 3400 Las Vegas Blvd S; r from $109; P ⊠ ⚲ ▢ wi-fi)

TOP END

True luxury comes cheaper here than almost anywhere else in the world. If you rain fistfuls of cash around the casino, expect to be comped a sumptuous suite.

Palms Casino Resort (☎ 702-942-7777, 866-942-7777; www.palms.com; 4321 W Flamingo Rd; r $179-300; P ⊠ ⚲ ▢ wi-fi) Off-Strip and originally aimed at young locals, the post–*Real World* Palms now attracts a flashier, MTV-influenced crowd and is a favorite with celebrity partiers like Paris Hilton and Britney Spears. Standard rooms are generous, and upper floors have a Strip view. For true luxury, trade in your car (or college savings) for the $10,000 Real World Suite, where the gang lived during filming. The 2900-sq-ft suite looks just like it did in the TV show.

ourpick Bellagio (☎ 702-693-7111, 888-987-6667; www.bellagio.com; 3600 Las Vegas Blvd S; r $179-700; P ⊠ ⚲ ▢) If anything in Vegas is truly 'spectacular,' this luxe five-diamond destination has a strong claim. Oversize, lavish bathrooms feature Italian marble, plush robes and deep soaking tubs. For a romantic evening, treat yourself and your sweetie to a fountain view room, and you'll have front-row seats for the mesmerizing whale-spout spectacular.

THEhotel (☎ 702-632-7777, 877-632-7800; www .thehotelatmandalaybay.com; Mandalay Bay, 3950 Las Vegas Blvd S; ste $190-400; P ⊠ ⚲ ▢ wi-fi) From the moment you enter the intimate lobby, you feel a world away from the Strip's hustle and bustle. It's a chic all-suite boutique hotel inside the M-Bay with a contemporary NYC vibe, and the spacious rooms come tricked out with wet bars and large plasma TVs.

Wynn Las Vegas (☎ 702-770-7100, 877-321-9966; www.wynnlasvegas.com; 3131 Las Vegas Blvd; r from $239; P ⊠ ⚲ ▢) The newest and most opulent Wynn creation is all about exclusivity – getting inside is the goal, so that you can then scoff at the hoi polloi, secure in your lavish retreat. If you reserve a suite you'll even get to use a private VIP entrance.

Eating

Sin City is an unmatched eating adventure. Since Wolfgang Puck brought Spago to Caesars in 1992, celebrity Iron Chefs have taken up residence in nearly every megaresort. Cheap buffets and loss-leader meal deals still exist, mostly downtown, but the gourmet quotient is high, with prices to match. Reservations are a must for fancier restaurants; book as far in advance as possible, especially at weekends. Every major casino has a 24-hour café and at least a couple of restaurants.

BUDGET

Just west of the Strip, the Asian restaurants on Spring Mountain Rd in Chinatown are also good budget options, with lots of vegetarian choices.

'Wichcraft (☎ 702-891-3199; MGM Grand, 3799 Las Vegas Blvd S; sandwiches $7-9; ☯ 10am-6pm) Conveniently located beside the Monorail entrance, this design-y little sandwich shop can set you up with a breakfast bite on the fly. Or order a hot panini and lounge about in the acid-green chairs.

Thai Spice (☎ 702-362-5308; 4433 W Flamingo Rd; dishes $10-14; ☯ 11:30am-10pm Mon-Thu, to 10:30pm Fri, 11am-10:30pm Sat) Locals salivate over this excellent eatery not far from the Strip. Voted best Thai restaurant in town for over a decade.

Paymon's Mediterranean Café & Hookah Lounge (☎ 702-731-6030; 4147 S Maryland Parkway; dishes $10-15; ☯ restaurant 11am-1am Mon-Thu, to 3am Fri & Sat, to 5pm Sun) One of the city's few easy-to-be-veggie spots, it serves yummies like baked eggplant with fresh garlic, baba ganoush, tabouleh and hummus. Chill with a water pipe and fig-flavored cocktail at the adjacent Hookah Lounge.

MIDRANGE

Cafe Ba-Ba-Reeba! (☎ 702-258-1211; Fashion Show Mall, 3200 Las Vegas Blvd S; tapas $2-12; ☯ 11:30am-11pm Sun-Thu, to midnight Fri & Sat) In this Spanish bar and bistro, attentive servers present paella for two and a parade of hot and cold authentic tapas and imported artisanal cheeses. Linger over uniquely flavored sangrias and bite-sized desserts.

House of Blues (☎ 702-632-7600; Mandalay Bay, 3950 Las Vegas Blvd S; dishes $13-20; ☯ 7:30am-midnight Sun-Thu, to 1am Fri & Sat) The swampy bayou atmosphere and down-home Southern cuisine at this homey roadhouse (think BBQ, burgers and salads) is enhanced by funky folk art. The Sunday Gospel Brunch ($39) is uplifting, and the hefty buffets of biscuits, creole chicken and shrimp jambalaya can be a spiritual experience.

Il Fornaio (☎ 702-740-6403; New York-New York, 3790 Las Vegas Blvd S; dishes $15-20; ☯ 7:30am-10:30am & 11:30am-midnight Sun-Thu, 7:30am-10:30am & 11:30am-1am Fri & Sat) Feast on wood-fired pizzas, seasonal salads and pastas, or make a meal of the antipasti platter, with scallops wrapped in pancetta, baked eggplant, truffled cheeses and more ($14 per person).

TOP END

Todai (☎ 702-892-0021; Miracle Mile Shops, 3663 Las Vegas Blvd S; lunch $18-20, dinner $28-30; ☯ 11:30am-2:30pm &

5:30-9:30pm Sun-Thu, 11:30am-2:30pm & 5:30-10pm Fri & Sat) A magnificent all-you-can-gorge 160ft spread of Japanese, Chinese and Korean fare features 15 salads and 40 types of sushi. Lobster and shellfish added to the mix at dinnertime.

Buffet at Bellagio (☎ 702-693-7111; Bellagio, 3600 Las Vegas Blvd S; breakfast $15, lunch $22, dinner $28-36; ☯ 8am-10pm Mon-Thu & Sun, to 11pm Fri & Sat) The Bellagio rightfully takes top honors for Vegas' best live-action buffet. The sumptuous all-you-can-eat spread at casino level includes such crowd pleasers as smoked salmon, sushi, and innumerable creative Chinese and Italian dishes.

Fix (☎ 702-693-8400; Bellagio, 3600 Las Vegas Blvd S; mains $25-40; ☯ 5pm-midnight Sun-Thu, to 2am Fri & Sat) A boisterous place to rendezvous with your crew, quaff habañero mango margaritas ($14) and nibble small plates. Kick back under the trippy roof pitched like an undulating wave, and dig into stylish platters of classic American cuisine.

Red Square (☎ 702-632-7407; Mandalay Bay, 3960 Las Vegas Blvd S; dishes $25-40; ☯ 5-11pm) How post-*perestroika*: a headless Lenin invites you to join your comrades for a tipple behind the red curtain in this postmodern Russian restaurant. Imbibers here have got rubles to spare for exquisite chicken Kiev, salmon *kulebyaka* or clams topped with caviar.

Bally's Steakhouse (☎ 702-967-7999; Bally's, 3645 Las Vegas Blvd S; dinner dishes $25-40, brunch $65; ☯ 5:30-10:30pm daily, 9:30am-2:30pm Sun) Indulge in the best – and most expensive – Sunday brunch in town. Ice sculptures and lavish flower arrangements abound at the Sterling Brunch, as do food stations featuring roast duckling, beef tenderloin and fresh sushi.

Drinking

Art Bar (☎ 702-437-2787; 1511 S Main St; ☯ 24hr) A happening downtown hipster bar, Art Bar is owned by none other than the mayor's personal Elvis impersonator. This creative haunt often hosts live bands, and crowds throng here after the First Friday art walk (see p813).

ghostbar (☎ 702-942-6832; Palms Casino Resort, 4321 W Flamingo Rd; admission $10-25; ☯ 8pm-late) Think sleek, space age and saucy. The 55th floor aerie casts an otherworldly glow, with industrial chain-mail drapes and radiant purple-tinted banquettes. Mix it up with the bold-face names and admire the drop-dead views from the outdoor patio prow.

Griffin (☎ 702-382-0577; 511 E Fremont St) A gothic *Phantom of the Opera* setting meets the cool downtown wine and martini scene. Add atmospheric gas fireplaces, vaulted brick ceiling and eclectic jukebox. Stir and sip.

Entertainment

Las Vegas has no shortage of entertainment on any given night. For tickets to many major concerts and sports events (including fights), contact one of these outlets:

Coca-Cola Tickets 2Nite (☎ 888-484-9264; Showcase Mall, 3785 Las Vegas Blvd S; ☺ noon-9pm)

Ticketmaster (☎ 702-474-4000; www.ticketmaster.com)

CLUBS & LIVE MUSIC

House of Blues (☎ 702-632-7600; Mandalay Bay, 3950 Las Vegas Blvd S; cover free-$80) Blues is the tip of the hog at this Mississippi Delta juke joint. Seating is limited, so arrive early (shows from 6pm). Sight lines are good and the outsider folk-art decor is übercool.

Kräve (☎ 702-836-0830; www.kravelasvegas.com; 3663 Las Vegas Blvd S; admission $5-20; ☺ 10pm-3am Sun-Thu, 11pm-3am Fri & Sat) The Strip's only gay club is a glam place packed wall-to-wall with hard bodies, plush booth seating and VIP cabanas – even 'airotic' flyboys. The side lounge has karaoke, salsa and girls-only nights. Enter off Harmon Ave outside Desert Passage.

Pure (☎ 702-731-7873; Caesars Palace, 3570 Las Vegas Blvd S; cover $20) A decadent see-and-be-seen superclub splashed white-on-white, virginal it is not. The upscale young hotties are practically taking up arms to get in and shimmy on the sheer-draped VIP stage.

Tao (☎ 702-388-8588; Venetian, 3355 Las Vegas Blvd S; cover $20-30) Modeled after the Asian-themed NYC nightclub, here svelte go-go girls covered only by strategically placed flowers splash in bathtubs while another in yogi garb assumes the lotus position on a pedestal high above the risqué dance floor, where Paris Hilton lookalikes forgo enlightenment to bump and grind to earthy hip-hop instead.

PRODUCTION SHOWS

There are hundreds of shows to choose from in Vegas.

Perpetually popular is Cirque du Soleil's aquatic show, **O** (☎ 702-796-9999; admission $99-150), performed at the Bellagio. Cirque du Soleil also presents **Mystère** (☎ 702-796-9999; admission $60-95) at Treasure Island (aka TI) and the adult-themed **Zumanity** (☎ 702-740-6815; admission $79-129), at New York-New York.

Stomp Out Loud (☎ 702-785-5555; Planet Hollywood, 3663 Las Vegas Blvd S; admission $50-110) has energetic percussion and acrobatics with found objects.

Shopping

Bonanza Gifts (☎ 702-385-7359; 2440 Las Vegas Blvd S) Only-in-Vegas kitsch souvenirs.

Fashion Show Mall (☎ 702-369-0704; 3200 Las Vegas Blvd S) Nevada's biggest and flashiest mall.

Grand Canal Shoppes (☎ 702-414-4500; Venetian, 3355 Las Vegas Blvd S) Italianate indoor luxury mall with gondola rides.

Mandalay Place (☎ 702-632-9333; 3930 Las Vegas Blvd S) On the skybridge between the Mandalay Bay and the Luxor. An airy promenade with unique, fashion-forward boutiques.

Miracle Mile Shops (☎ 702-888-800-8284; Planet Hollywood, 3663 Las Vegas Blvd S) A staggering 1.5 miles long.

Via Bellagio (☎ 702-693-7111; Bellagio, 3600 Las Vegas Blvd S) Swish indoor promenade.

Wynn Esplanade (☎ 702-770-7000; Wynn Las Vegas, 3131 Las Vegas Blvd S) A 75,000-sq-ft showcase of upscale consumer bliss.

LOCAL VOICES

Kelly Tucker
Performer in Cirque du Soleil's Mystère, Las Vegas

What exactly do you do? My main two acts are the bungee trapeze and Chinese poles, which is kind of like a fireman's pole but a little bit skinnier, and we do tricks with it. We fall off the trapeze and bounce back up and do flips and tricks and some choreographed stuff. We're at about 70ft.

What are some of your favorite things to do in Las Vegas? Mt Charleston's not too far from here, with amazing hiking places. If I am on the Strip, I like to do the roller-coaster ride at New York-New York (p813) and the rides at the Stratosphere (p813).

What are some of your favorite other shows on the strip? I love Le Rêve at the Wynn (p812) and O (above) at the Bellagio. Sometimes you forget how good Mystère is when you're performing in it. You kind of go in, do your job and flip around, and you forget how wonderful the show is.

Getting There & Around

Just south of the major Strip casinos and easily accessible from I-15, **McCarran International Airport** (☎ 702-261-4636) has direct flights from most US cities, and some from Canada and Europe. **Bell Trans** (☎ 702-739-7990) offers a shuttle service ($5) between the airport and the Strip. Fares to downtown destinations are slightly higher.

The **Greyhound bus station** (☎ 702-384-9561; 200 S Main St), downtown, has regular buses to and from Los Angeles ($36 to $42, six hours), San Diego ($36 to $46, eight hours) and San Francisco ($45 to $75, 15 hours). **Amtrak** (☎ 800-872-7245) does not run trains to Las Vegas, although it does offer a connecting bus service from Los Angeles ($38, six hours).

Fast, fun and fully wheelchair accessible, the **Monorail** (☎ 702-699-8299; www.lvmonorail.com) connects the Sahara to the MGM Grand, stopping at major Strip megaresorts along the way, and operating from 7am to 2am Monday to Thursday and until 3am Friday through Sunday. A single ride costs $5; a 24-hour pass is $15. The **Deuce** (☎ 702-228-7433; www.thedeucelasvegas.com), a local double-decker bus, runs frequently 24 hours daily between the Strip and downtown ($2). For up-to-date road conditions, check with the **Nevada Department of Transportation** (☎ 877-687-6237; www.nvroads.com).

AROUND LAS VEGAS

Red Rock Canyon

This dramatic **park** (☎ 702-515-5350; admission $5; 🕒 6am-dusk) is the perfect anecdote to Vegas' artificial brightness. A 20-mile drive west of the Strip, the canyon is actually more like a valley, with the steep, rugged red-rock escarpment rising 3000ft on its western edge. There's a 13-mile, one-way scenic loop with access to hiking trails and camping (campsites $10) 2 miles east of the visitor center.

Lake Mead & Hoover Dam

Lake Mead and Hoover Dam are the most-visited sites within the **Lake Mead National Recreation Area** (☎ 702-293-8906; www.nps.gov/lame), which encompasses 110-mile-long Lake Mead, 67-mile-long Lake Mohave and many miles of desert around the lakes. The excellent **Alan Bible Visitors Center** (☎ 702-293-8990; 🕒 8:30am-4:30pm), on Hwy 93 halfway between Boulder City and Hoover Dam, has information on recreation and desert life. From there, North Shore Rd winds around the lake and makes a great scenic drive. The combined forces of long-term drought, global warming and the diversion of water to thirsty Las Vegas have deposited curious and dramatic bathtublike rings on the rocky shoreline. This evidence of a rapidly receding water level is of great concern to many in the region.

Straddling the Arizona–Nevada border, the graceful curve and art-deco style of the 726ft **Hoover Dam** contrasts superbly with the stark landscape. Originally called Boulder Dam, this New Deal project was completed in 1935 at a cost of $175 million and the lives of 110 workers. Its original intent was flood control, but it now helps supply Colorado River water (and hydroelectric power) to thirsty cities, including Las Vegas. Visitors are limited to surface tours (adult/child $11/6), and tickets are sold at the **visitor center** (☎ 702-494-2517, 866-730-9097; 🕒 9am-5pm). Note that commercial trucks and buses are not allowed to cross the dam, and pedestrians cannot walk on the dam after dark. A highway that will bypass the dam traffic choke-point is in the works, with a scheduled opening date of 2010.

Valley of Fire State Park

A masterpiece of desert scenery filled with psychedelically shaped sandstone outcroppings, this **park** (admission $6) makes for another great Vegas escape. Near the northern end of Lake Mead National Recreation Area, it's easily accessible from Las Vegas. Hwy 169 runs right past the **visitor center** (☎ 702-397-2088; www.parks.nv.gov/vf.htm; 🕒 8:30am-4:30pm), which has hiking information and excellent desert-life exhibits. The winding side road to **White Domes** is especially scenic. The valley is at its most fiery at dawn and dusk, so consider staying overnight in one of the park's two year-round **campgrounds** (campsites $8).

Laughlin

On the banks of the Colorado River, Laughlin is the poor man's Vegas. The casinos lining the strip sport familiar names – Flamingo, Harrah's – but the look is more blue jeans than bling-bling. Laughlin's a down-home gambling type of place – think burgers, Budweiser and penny slots. It attracts an older, more sedate crowd – the kind of folks looking to gamble in the city without all the sin.

One reason Laughlin has become so popular is that it boasts some of the cheapest hotel rates in the West – and while rooms are fairly bland, these are no fleapits. Try the very pleasant **Colorado Belle** (☎ 702-298-4000, 866-352-3553; www.coloradobelle.com; 2100 S Casino Dr; r from $23; ❄ ☒ 🖥 wi-fi), a replica of a 19th-century Mississippi riverboat. Right on the river, the **River Palms** (☎ 702-298-2242, 800-835-7904; www.rvrpalm.com; r $24-65; ❄ ☒ wi-fi) has half a dozen eateries to choose from.

WESTERN NEVADA

A vast and mostly undeveloped sagebrush steppe, the western corner of the state is carved by mountain ranges and parched valleys. It's also the place where modern Nevada began. It was the site of the state's first trading post, first farms and the famous Comstock silver lode in and around Virginia City, which spawned towns, financed the Union side in the Civil War and earned Nevada its statehood. For information about the Nevada side of Lake Tahoe, see p988.

Reno

A soothingly schizophrenic city of big-time gambling and top-notch outdoor adventures, Reno resists pigeonholing. 'The Biggest Little City in the World' has something to raise the pulse of adrenaline junkies, hardcore gamblers and city people craving easy access wide-open spaces. In the past, the bulk of Reno's visitors flocked to its smorgasbord of casinos, but the construction of a white-water park has raised the interest of kayakers and daredevil surfers.

Reno's downtown is north of the Truckee River and south of I-80. Most of the casino action is along N Virginia St, between 1st and 6th Sts. The River Walk district along W 1st St is the best place for noncasino entertainment and food.

South of downtown, you'll find a **visitor center** (☎ 775-827-7600, 800-367-7366; www.visitrenotahoe.com; Reno Town Mall, 401 S Virginia St; ⏰ 8am-5pm Mon-Fri); there's an additional one at the airport baggage claim area (open the same hours).

SIGHTS & ACTIVITIES
Casinos

Few of Reno's casinos have the flash of Vegas, though some do try.

Eldorado (☎ 775-786-5700; 345 N Virginia St) A small city under one roof.

Grand Sierra Resort (☎ 775-789-2000; 2500 E 2nd St) Huge resort east of downtown near Hwy 395.

John Ascuaga's Nugget (☎ 775-356-3300; 1100 Nugget Ave) A legendary pioneer, located in nearby Sparks.

Peppermill (☎ 775-826-2121; 2707 S Virginia St) Away from downtown and a flashy local favorite.

Siena (☎ 775-327-4362; 1 S Lake St) One of the city's newest, and nicest, casinos, with Tuscan styling and a more subdued upscale atmosphere.

Silver Legacy (☎ 775-329-4777; 407 N Virginia St) A 19th-century streetscape plus sound-and-light shows inside a 120ft dome.

Other Attractions

The **Truckee River Whitewater Park** (☎ 775-334-2262; www.cityoffreno.com/res/com_service/whitewaterpark) injects action into the middle of downtown, with year-round kayaking and excellent tubing (and all-around splashing) in summer. Right on the river, **Wild Sierra Adventures** (☎ 866-323-8928; 254 W 1st St) rents tubes and kayaks (from $19 per hour) and leads guided river-rafting trips.

In winter, Lake Tahoe (p988) ski resorts are close by, and **Mt Rose** (☎ 775-849-0704; www.mtrose.com; lift tickets adult/child $62/17) is a mere 25 minutes away.

The **National Automobile Museum** (☎ 775-333-9300; 10 S Lake St; adult/child $9/3; ⏰ 9:30am-5:30pm Mon-Sat, 10am-4pm Sun; 🅿) has an impressive collection of one-of-a-kind vehicles, including James Dean's 1949 Mercury from *Rebel Without a Cause*, a 1938 Phantom Corsair and a 24-karat gold-plated DeLorean.

SLEEPING

Wildflower Village (☎ 775-747-8848; 4395 W 4th St; www.wildflowervillage.com; r from $50; 🖥) Perhaps more of a state of mind than a motel, this artists' colony on the edge of town has a tumbledown yet creative vibe. Individual murals decorate the facade of each room, and you can hear the freight trains rumble on by.

Silver Legacy (☎ 775-329-4777, 800-687-7733; www.silverlegacyreno.com; 407 N Virginia St; r from $80; 🅿 ❄ ☒ 🖥 wi-fi) All trimmed up in leather and lace, this large, central hotel-casino has Victorian-themed rooms that are classy and comfortable. Topped by a huge dome, the casino is a local landmark. For a mountain view, ask for a room high in the tower.

Siena Hotel Spa Casino (☎ 775-337-6260, 877-743-6233; 1 S Lake St; www.sienareno.com; r from $130; 🅿 ❄ ☒ 🖥 wi-fi) Reno's only contemporary boutique hotel is also one of its most luxurious addresses, with cozy, nicely appointed riverside rooms. Guests don't need to navigate the casino action in order to check in.

SOUTHWEST

EATING & DRINKING

Pho 777 (☎ 775-323-7777; 201 E 2nd St; dishes $5-6; ⏱ 10am-9pm) A popular Vietnamese noodle shop just off the strip serving up bowls and bowls of steamy soup. The basic decor is a welcome reprieve from the glitz and glare a block away.

Jungle Java & Jungle Vino (☎ 775-329-4484; 246 W 1st St; sandwiches $6; ⏱ 6am-midnight) A side-by-side coffee shop and wine bar with a cool mosaic floor, an internet café and free wi-fi all rolled into one. The café serves breakfast bagels and lunchtime sandwiches, and the wine bar has Monday movie nights and Tuesday wine tastings. Why would you ever leave?

Pneumatic Diner (☎ 775-786-8888; 501 W 1st St, 2nd fl; dishes $6-8; ⏱ 11am-11pm Mon-Fri, 9am-11pm Sat, 8am-11pm Sun) Consume a garden of vegetarian delights under salvaged neon lights. This groovy little place near the river has meatless and vegan comfort food and desserts to tickle your inner two-year-old, like the ice cream–laden Cookie Bomb. Enter on Ralston St.

Peg's Glorified Ham & Eggs (☎ 775-329-2600; 420 S Sierra; dishes $7-10; ⏱ 6:30am-2pm) Locally regarded for serving the best breakfast in town, Peg's offers tasty grill food that's not too greasy. It's the perfect place to sit outside and read the Sunday paper while munching on an over-stuffed omelet. Very kid-friendly.

Imperial Bar & Lounge (☎ 775-324-6399; 150 N Arlington Ave; dishes $9-14; ⏱ 4pm-2am Thu-Sat, to midnight Sun-Wed) A brand-new watering hole inhabiting a relic of the past, this building was once an old bank, and in the middle of the wooden floor you can see cement where the vault once stood. Sandwiches and pizzas go with 16 beers on tap and a buzzing weekend scene.

Harrah's Steakhouse (☎ 775-788-2929; 219 N Center St; dinner dishes $25-32; ⏱ 11am-2:30pm & 5-9:30pm Mon-Fri, 5-10:30pm Sat & Sun) This elegant restaurant has amazing service and a romantic atmosphere – think roses, linen and low lighting. The recipient of numerous local awards for fine dining, it serves the requisite big juicy steaks along with other meat and seafood options.

210 North (☎ 775-786-6210; www.210north.com; 210 N Sierra St; free before 10pm, cover $10-20; ⏱ Thu-Sat) When Reno folk want to flaunt it, they end up here. A pulsing-hot dance club and downtempo lounge that would feel right at home in Vegas, this is the glam spot for throwing your moves. Trip out to the mesmerizing LED chandelier in the Divinity Lounge.

GREAT BALLS OF FIRE!

For one week at the end of August, **Burning Man** (www.burningman.com; admission $195-280) explodes onto the sun-baked Black Rock Desert, and Nevada sprouts a third major population center – Black Rock City. An experiential art party (and alternative universe) that climaxes in the immolation of a towering stick figure, Burning Man is a whirlwind of outlandish theme camps, dust-caked bicycles, bizarre bartering, costume-enhanced nudity and a general relinquishment of inhibitions. And when the last wig-wearing Burner heads home, volunteers make sure to leave no trace, picking up every last hot-pink sequin.

GETTING THERE & AROUND

The **Reno-Tahoe International Airport** (☎ 775-328-6870) is a few miles southeast of downtown and has free wi-fi. **Greyhound** (☎ 775-322-2970; 155 Stevenson St) has frequent buses to San Francisco ($33, six hours) and Los Angeles ($66, 10½ to 15 hours), and two daily to Las Vegas ($72, 18 to 20 hours). **Amtrak** (☎ 775-329-8638; 280 N Center St) has one daily run to Sacramento; note that this route often has major delays and uses buses. One train leaves daily for Salt Lake City ($57, 13 hours) and Denver ($117, 29 hours).

Many hotels offer free shuttles to and from the airport. Local bus system **Citifare** (☎ 775-348-7433) covers the metropolitan area (adult/child $1.70/1.25); the main transfer station is at E 4th and Center Sts. The free yellow Sierra Spirit bus plies Virginia St from the University of Nevada to the river, and is a roving wi-fi hot spot.

Pyramid Lake

A piercingly blue expanse in an otherwise barren landscape, Pyramid Lake, 25 miles north of Reno on the Paiute Indian Reservation, is a stunning sight. Popular for recreation and fishing, the shores are lined with beaches and interesting tufa formations (a porous rock formed by water deposits). Near the lake's eastern shore, Anaho Island is a bird sanctuary for the American white pelican. Permits for **camping** (primitive campsites per vehicle per night $9) and **fishing** (per person $9) are available at the **ranger station** (☎ 775-476-1155; ⏱ 8am-6pm Mon-Thu & 10am-8pm Fri & Sat summer, varied hr winter), on Hwy

446 in Sutcliffe. Permits can also be purchased at area gas stations.

Carson City

Handsome old buildings and pleasant tree-lined streets abound in Nevada's state capital, a small but fast-growing town. It's a refreshing, underwhelming place offering a quiet retreat from big-city clutter. The casinos are sedate, and there are a few worthwhile historical museums to discover.

Hwy 395/Carson St is the main drag. The **visitor center** (☎ 775-882-1565; www.carson-city.org; 1900 S Carson St; ☷ 8am-5pm Mon-Fri), a mile south of downtown, gives out a local map with interesting historical walking and driving tours. For hiking and camping information, stop by the United States Forest Service (USFS) **Carson Ranger District Office** (☎ 775-882-2766; 1536 S Carson St; ☷ 8am-4:30pm Mon-Fri).

Housed inside the 1869 US Mint building, the excellent **Nevada State Museum** (☎ 775-687-4810; 600 N Carson St; admission $5; ☷ 8:30am-4:30pm) has dioramas showing Native American life, a gallery of antique guns and, in the basement, a re-created gold mine. Train buffs shouldn't miss the **Nevada State Railroad Museum** (☎ 775-687-6953; 2180 S Carson St; admission $4; ☷ 8:30am-4:30pm), which displays some 30 train cars and engines from the 1800s to the early 1900s.

Just south of downtown, keep your eyes peeled for the green plastic cacti at the **Desert Hills Motel** (☎ 775-882-1932; www.deserthillsmotel.com; 1010 S Carson St; s/d $61/69; ☒), a clean, family-owned spot. In the leafy historic district, the restored 1913 **Bliss Bungalow** (☎ 775-883-6129; www.blissbungalow.com; 408 W Robinson St; r incl breakfast from $115; ☒ ☒ wi-fi) oozes genteel charm in each of its five rooms and living spaces. The huge, art-filled restaurant and music venue of **Comma Coffee** (☎ 775-883-2662; www.commacoffee.com; 312 S Carson St; ☷ 7am-6pm Mon-Sat; wi-fi) invites lingering – whether it's over your meal, the weekend jams or the weekly salsa lessons. Despite the official hours, it's often open until 10pm.

RTC Intercity (☎ 775-348-7433; www.rtcwashoe.com) has a weekday commuter service between Carson City and Reno ($3.35, 30 minutes to one hour). The buses have free wi-fi and some service the Reno airport.

Virginia City

During the 1860s gold rush, Virginia City was a high-flying, rip-roaring Wild West boomtown. Newspaperman Samuel Clemens, alias Mark Twain, spent some time in this raucous place during its heyday; years later his eyewitness descriptions of mining life were published in a book called *Roughing It*. Good times came to an end in 1875, when a fire destroyed more than 2000 buildings. Virginia City was miraculously rebuilt within a year but never again achieved its former rough-and-tumble glory.

The high-elevation town is a National Historic Landmark, with a main street of Victorian buildings, wooden sidewalks and some hokey but fun 'museums.' The main drag is C St, with the **visitor center** (☎ 775-847-4386; www.virginiacity-nv.org; 86 S C St; ☷ 10am-4pm) in the historic Crystal Bar.

It might have started as a practical joke, but the **Virginia City International Camel Races** have now been going on for 50 years. Watch the hopeful dromedaries galumphing towards the finish line, and expect enormous crowds for this popular September event. Contact the visitor center for dates.

Many of the town's attractions are seriously silly, though some are true gems, such as the quirky **Way It Was Museum** (☎ 775-847-0766; 113 N C St; admission $3; ☷ 10am-6pm). It's a fun, old-fashioned place offering good background information on mining the lode. The half-hour tour of the **Chollar Mine** (☎ 775-847-0155; adult/child $7/2; ☷ noon-5pm May-Oct), at the southern end of F St (hours vary, call to confirm), is also worthwhile. To see how the mining elite lived, stop by the **Mackay Mansion** (D St) and the **Castle** (B St).

Virginia City has a number of places to sleep, including a large RV park. A more luxurious choice, the historic **Chollar Mansion B&B** (☎ 775-847-9777, 877-246-5527; www.chollarmansion.com; 565 S D St; r incl full breakfast $125; ☒) used to be the town mine office. It's now filled with antiques, and the views seem to go on forever. The vegetarian-friendly **Mandarin Garden** (☎ 775-847-9288; 51 N C St; dishes $6-9; ☷ 11am-9:30pm) serves cheap and tasty noodle-and-rice plates.

NEVADA GREAT BASIN

Outside Nevada's major cities, the land is largely empty, textured with range after range of mountains and arid valleys. It's big country out here – wild, remote and quiet. A trip across Nevada's Great Basin is a serene, almost haunting, experience. But those on the quest of the 'Great American Road Trip' will relish the fascinating historic towns and quirky diversions tucked away along lonely desert highways.

Along I-80

This is the old fur trappers' route, which followed the Humboldt River from northeast Nevada to Lovelock, near Reno. Heading east from Reno, **Winnemucca** is the first worthwhile stop. It boasts a vintage downtown, shops, and numerous motels and restaurants. Situated some 50 miles north, the Santa Rosa Mountains offer rugged scenery and ghost towns. For information, stop by the **chamber of commerce** (☎ 775-623-2225; 30 W Winnemucca Blvd; ☽ 8am-5pm Mon-Fri, 9am-4pm Sat, 11am-4pm Sun summer) or the USFS **Santa Rosa Ranger Station** (☎ 775-623-5025; 1200 E Winnemucca Blvd; ☽ 8am-4:30pm Mon-Fri).

Southwest of Winnemucca is the folk-art sculpture garden **Thunder Mountain**, directly off I-80 in Imlay. Built by WWII veteran Chief Rolling Mountain Thunder as a monument to the injustices against Native Americans, it's full of curious figures, buildings and other structures. Free self-guided tours are available during the day.

The culture of the American West is most diligently cultivated in **Elko**. Aspiring cowboys and cowgirls should visit the **Western Folklife Center** (☎ 775-738-7508; www.westernfolklife.org; 501 Railroad St; admission free; ☽ 10am-5:30pm Mon & Wed-Fri, 10:30am-5:30pm Tue, 10am-5pm Sat), which offers art and history exhibits, and also hosts the popular **Cowboy Poetry Gathering** each January. There's also a **National Basque Festival**, held every 4th of July, with games, traditional dancing and a 'Running of the Bulls' event. At the town center, **Stockmen's Casino & Hotel** (☎ 775-738-5141, 800-648-2345; www.stockmenscasinos.com; 340 Commercial St; r/ste from $40/70; ☒ ☐) is a good place to stay, with clean, remodeled rooms.

To the south of Elko, the **Ruby Mountains** are a superbly rugged range. The picture-perfect village of **Lamoille** has food and lodging, and one of the most photographed rural churches in the USA.

Along Highway 50

On 'the loneliest road in America' barren brown desert hills collide with big blue skies. The highway goes on forever, crossing solitary Great Basin terrain. Towns are few and far between, the only sounds the hum of the engine or the whisper of wind. Once part of the Lincoln Hwy, lonesome Hwy 50 follows the route of the Overland Stagecoach, the Pony Express and the first transcontinental telegraph line.

Fallon is an agricultural and military town, home to a naval air base. **Fallon Lodge** (☎ 775-423-4648; www.fallonlodge.com; 390 W Williams Ave; ☐) has clean, simple rooms with kitchenettes.

Heading east, the next substantial town is **Austin**, run-down since its 1880s heyday but still interesting. The mountainous area around it is lovely, and Austin's **USFS office** (☎ 775-964-2671; 100 Midas Rd; ☽ 7:30am-4:30pm Mon-Fri), just off Hwy 50, can recommend hikes and driving loops. **Mountain biking** is especially popular, and the website of the **chamber of commerce** (☎ 775-964-2200; www.austinnevada.com) lists good bike routes.

To the southwest of Austin, the **Berlin-Ichthyosaur State Park** (☎ 775-964-2440; www.parks.nv.gov/bi.htm; admission $4) features the ghost town of Berlin and the fossil remains of half a dozen ichthyosaurs (carnivorous marine reptiles that lived here 225 million years ago). Daily fossil tours are offered in summer (adult/child $3/2), and there's a good year-round **campground** (campsites $12).

During the late 19th century, $40 million worth of silver was extracted from the hills near **Eureka**. The town is now fairly well preserved, possessing a handsome courthouse, the interesting **Eureka Sentinel Museum** (☎ 775-237-5010; 10 S Bateman St; admission free; ☽ 10am-6pm daily May-Oct, to 6pm Tue-Sat Nov-Apr), a beautifully restored 1880 opera house and a few well-kept motels.

Larger **Ely**, another silver- and copper-mining town, is worth a stop. The downtown has beautiful murals of regional history and great old neon signs, along with some decent motels.

Near the Nevada–Utah border is the awesome, uncrowded **Great Basin National Park**. It encompasses 13,063ft Wheeler Peak, rising abruptly from the desert. Hiking trails near the summit take in superb country with glacial lakes, ancient bristlecone pines and even a permanent ice field. Admission is free; the park **visitor center** (☎ 775-234-7331; www.nps.gov/grba) arranges guided tours of **Lehman Caves** (admission $8-10), which are richly decorated with rare limestone formations. There are four developed **campgrounds** (campsites $12) within the park.

Along Highway 95

Hwy 95 goes roughly north–south through the western part of the state; the southern section is starkly scenic as it passes the Nevada Test Site (where more than 720 nuclear weapons were exploded in the 1950s). Five miles north of Beatty, **Bailey's Hot Springs & RV Park** (☎ 775-553-2395; campsites/RV sites $15/18), a 1906 former railroad depot, has three private hot springs in antique bath houses, open from 8am to 8pm daily. Overnight guests get complimentary usage, and day-trippers can pay $5 per person for a 30-minute soak.

Off of Hwy 374, a few miles southwest of Beatty, the **Goldwell Open Air Museum** (☎ 702-870-9946; www.goldwellmuseum.org; admission free; ⊙ 24 hr) is a rather mysterious 8-acre outdoor sculpture site surrounded by desert.

Along Highways 375 & 93

Hwy 375, dubbed the 'Extraterrestrial Hwy,' intersects Hwy 93 near top-secret **Area 51**, part of Nellis Air Force Base and a supposed holding area for captured UFOs. In the tiny town of **Rachel**, on Hwy 375, **Little A'Le'Inn** (☎ 775-729-2515; www.aleinn.com; r $40) accommodates earthlings and aliens alike, and sells extraterrestrial souvenirs.

Continuing east, Hwy 93 passes through a gorgeous Joshua-tree grove before arriving in **Caliente**, a former railroad town with a 1923 mission-style depot. Area attractions include **Cathedral Gorge State Park**, with campsites amid badlands-style cliffs. Twenty miles north, **Pioche** is an attractive mining town overlooking beautiful Lake Valley.

ARIZONA

The Grand Canyon state contains all the varied puzzle pieces of the contemporary Southwest, taking in the spires of Monument Valley and the upscale nightlife of Scottsdale. A big tent state of libertarian cowboys and shopaholic suburbanites, cacti canyons and desert golf courses, Arizona still embraces an Old West flavor.

Staking out opposite ends of the state, it claims the cool college towns of Tucson and Flagstaff. Victorian mining towns like Bisbee and Jerome exude rough-cut character, and New Agers in Sedona revel in its unseen energy. Travelers pass back and forth through the busy border hub of Nogales, and Wild

> **ARIZONA FACTS**
>
> **Nickname** Grand Canyon State
> **Population** 6.2 million
> **Area** 114,006 sq miles
> **Capital city** Phoenix (population 1.4 million)
> **Sales tax** 5.6%
> **State reptile** Arizona ridge-nosed rattlesnake
> **Famous for** Grand Canyon, saguaro cacti
> **Home of** Apache chief Geronimo (1829–1909), César Chávez (1927–93), Linda Ronstadt (b 1946, Tucson)
> **Best souvenir** Saguaro cactus car antenna ornament

West tourists flock to the shoot 'em up town of Tombstone. But in the end, the Grand Canyon is always Arizona's showy jewel.

History

Native American tribes inhabited Arizona for centuries before Spanish explorer Francisco Vásquez de Coronado launched a Southwest expedition here from Mexico City in 1540. Settlers and missionaries followed in his wake, and by the mid-19th century the US controlled Arizona. The Indian Wars, in which the US Army battled Native Americans to 'protect' settlers and claim land for the government, officially ended in 1886 with the surrender of Apache warrior Geronimo.

Railroad and mining expansion grew. In 1912 President Theodore Roosevelt's support for damming the territory's rivers led to Arizona's becoming the 48th state.

Today Arizona is in transition. Fifty years of rapid growth have taken a toll on the state's limited natural resources. Scarcity of water remains among the foremost issues for Arizona lawmakers, who continue the desperate search for water needed to supply the burgeoning cities.

Information

Arizona is on Mountain Standard Time but is the only western state that does not observe daylight saving time from spring to early fall. The exception is the Navajo Reservation, which *does* observe daylight saving time.

Generally speaking, lodging rates in southern Arizona (including Phoenix, Tucson and Yuma) are much higher in winter and spring, which are considered the state's 'high season.'

Arizona Office of Tourism (Map pp826-7; ☎ 602-364-3700, 866-891-3640; www.arizonaguide.com; 1110 W Washington, Ste 155, Phoenix, AZ 85007) Free state information.

Arizona Public Lands Information Center (Map pp826-7; ☎ 602-417-9300; www.publiclands.org; 1 N Central Ave, Ste 800, Phoenix, AZ 85004) Information about USFS, NPS, Bureau of Land Management (BLM), and state lands and parks.

PHOENIX

Covering almost 2000 sq miles, Phoenix is easily the largest metropolis in the Southwest. At first blush, it can feel like a limitless sprawl, incorporating dozens of bedroom communities, including Scottsdale, Mesa and Tempe. Reveling in more than 300 days of sunshine a year, Phoenix is searing hot in summer – think above 110°F (43°C) – but balmy days prevail in winter.

Building on its size, Phoenix has a lot to offer. There are major museums, top-notch professional sports, a cornucopia of excellent restaurants, nonstop nightlife, superlative shopping and – oddly for a desert – world-class golf (where do they get that water?). The city is also a major transportation hub, and is often used as a jumping-off point for further-flung adventures.

History

The Hohokam people lived here as early as 300 BC and developed a complex system of irrigation canals, only to mysteriously abandon them around AD 1450. Until the 1911 completion of the Theodore Roosevelt Dam, northeast of town on the Salt River, Phoenix

---

DON'T MISS

- **Heard Museum** – Native American culture exhibits (opposite)
- **Mystery Castle** – outsider art house (opposite)
- **Taliesin West** – Frank Lloyd Wright legacy (opposite)
- **Desert Botanical Garden** – prickly but perfect stroll (opposite)
- **Scottsdale nightlife** – high heels and long nights (p830)

---

didn't amount to much more than a desert outpost. Once this was built, however, the region boomed. The Central Arizona Project (CAP), a controversial $4 billion undertaking completed in the early 1990s, brought more water to the region from the Colorado River via a series of canals and pipelines that runs 336 miles from Lake Havasu to Tucson.

Orientation

Most of the valley sits approximately 1100ft above sea level, though it's ringed by mountains that range from 2500ft to more than 7000ft in elevation. Central Ave runs north–south through Phoenix, dividing west addresses from east addresses; Washington St runs west–east, dividing north addresses from south addresses.

Scottsdale, Tempe and Mesa are east of the airport. Scottsdale Rd runs north–south between Scottsdale and Tempe. The airport is 3 miles southeast of downtown.

Avoid the grungy stretch of Van Buren St between downtown and the airport; motels here are run-down and popular with prostitutes.

Information
BOOKSTORES
Bookman's (☎ 602-433-0255; 8034 N 19th Ave) Aisle after aisle of used books; free in-store wi-fi.
Wide World of Maps (☎ 602-279-2323; 2626 W Indian School Rd) Dedicated to maps and guidebooks.

EMERGENCY & MEDICAL SERVICES
Banner Good Samaritan Medical Center (☎ 602-239-2000; 1111 E McDowell Rd; ☉ 24hr emergency)
Phoenix Police Department (☎ 602-262-6151; 620 W Washington St)

INTERNET ACCESS
Central Phoenix Library (☎ 602-262-4636; 1221 N Central Ave; ☉ 10am-9pm Mon-Thu, to 6pm Fri & Sat, noon-6pm Sun) Free internet access.

MEDIA & INTERNET RESOURCES
Arizona Republic (☎ 602-444-8000; www.azcentral .com) Arizona's largest newspaper; publishes a free entertainment guide, *Calendar*, every Thursday.
craigslist (www.phoenix.craigslist.org) The active local branch of the popular bulletin board, with info on ride shares, events etc.
Phoenix New Times (☎ 602-271-0400; www.phoenix newtimes.com) The major Phoenix free weekly; lots of event and restaurant listings.

MONEY
Foreign exchange is available at the airport and major bank branches.

POST
Post office (☎ 602-253-9648; 522 N Central Ave)

TOURIST INFORMATION
Downtown Phoenix Visitor Information Center
(☎ 602-254-6500, 877-225-5749; www.visitphoenix
.com; 125 N 2nd St, Ste 120; ☼ 8am-5pm Mon-Fri) Main
tourist office of the Phoenix Convention & Visitors Bureau.
Mesa Convention & Visitors Bureau (☎ 480-827-
4700, 800-283-6372; www.mesacvb.com; 120 N Center St;
☼ 8am-5pm Mon-Fri)
Scottsdale Convention & Visitors Bureau (☎ 480-
421-1004; www.scottsdalecvb.com; 4343 N Scottsdale Rd,
Ste 170; ☼ 8am-5pm Mon-Fri)

Sights
The **ShowUp Now Pass** (☎ 602-971-2223 www.showup
nowpass.com; 1 day adult/child $18/10) includes admission to 15 area attractions; it can be purchased on-line and at all local visitors bureaus.

PHOENIX
The **Heard Museum** (☎ 602-252-8840; www.heard.org;
2301 N Central Ave; adult/child $10/3; ☼ 9:30am-5pm) is the city's best, offering outstanding presentations on Native American history and culture. Don't miss the fascinating kachina doll room.

Stroll among the succulents and a crazy forest of cacti at the **Desert Botanical Garden** (☎ 480-941-1225; 1201 N Galvin Parkway; admission adult/child $10/4; ☼ 8am-8pm Oct-Apr, 7am-8pm May-Sep). A gorgeous Monarch butterfly exhibit is the highlight of spring and fall.

Eight late 19th- and early 20th-century houses are preserved in **Heritage Square** (☎ 602-262-5029; cnr N 6th St & W Monroe St), which features a number of museums and craft shops and great places to grab lunch.

The popular **Arizona Science Center** (☎ 602-716-2000; www.azscience.org; 600 E Washington St; adult/child $9/7; ☼ 10am-5pm) has 350 hands-on exhibits, from computers to bubbles, weather, physics and biology. Live demonstrations are held throughout the day.

SCOTTSDALE
Scottsdale's main draw is its popular shopping district, known as **Old Town** for its early 20th-century buildings (and others built to look old). Another highlight is **Taliesin West** (☎ 480-860-2700; www.franklloydwright.org; 12621 Frank

---

WHAT THE...?
Equal parts Mexican hacienda, Native American cliff dwelling and psychedelic sand castle, the 18-room **Mystery Castle** (☎ 602-268-1581; 800 E Mineral Rd; adult/child $5/3; ☼ 11am-4pm Thu-Sun Oct-May or by appointment) dodges traditional labels. Constructed in the 1930s and '40s by Boyce Luther Gulley, the bizarre art house is made of stone, recycled telegraph poles, adobe and whatever else he could scavenge, and held together by a mix of sand, cement, calcium and goat's milk.

Lloyd Wright Blvd; tours adult $18-35, child $10-12; ☼ variable). Built by Frank Lloyd Wright (he also taught and lived here) in the mid-20th century, the environmentally organic buildings are spread over 600 acres.

TEMPE
Founded in 1885 and home to some 46,000 students, **Arizona State University** (ASU) is the heart and soul of Tempe. The **Gammage Auditorium** (cnr Mill Ave & Apache Blvd) was Frank Lloyd Wright's last major building.

Mill Avenue, Tempe's main drag, is packed with restaurants, bars and other collegiate hangouts. It's a fun place to wander and look for old records or vintage dresses.

MESA
Animated dinosaurs, dioramas, a territorial jail, gold panning and changing art shows are some of the displays and interactive exhibits at the **Mesa Southwest Museum** (☎ 480-644-2230; 53 N MacDonald St; adult/child $8/4;
☼ 10am-5pm Tue-Fri, 11am-5pm Sat, 1-5pm Sun).

Activities
Mountains ring the city, and there are numerous city and regional parks to hike and bike. **Phoenix South Mountain Park** (☎ 602-495-0222; 10919 S Central Ave) offers more than 40 miles of trails, great views and dozens of Native American petroglyph sites.

For fabulous desert views, especially at sunset, head to **Piestewa Peak Recreation Area** (☎ 602-262-7901; Piestewa Peak Dr). The trek to the 2608ft summit of Piestewa Peak is one of Phoenix's most popular outdoor endeavors.

Mountain and road biking is possible in both parks, with many designated trails. If

PHOENIX

SOUTHWEST

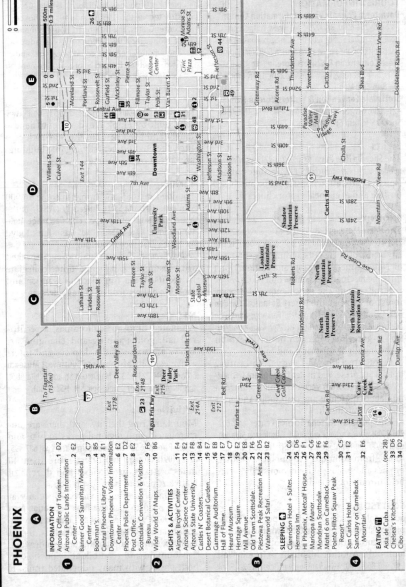

INFORMATION
Arizona Office of Tourism...................1 D2
Arizona Public Lands Information
  Center.......................................2 E2
Banner Good Samaritan Medical
  Center.......................................3 C7
Bookman's....................................4 B5
Central Phoenix Library...................5 E1
Downtown Phoenix Visitor Information
  Center.......................................6 E2
Phoenix Police Department..............7 D2
Post Office....................................8 E2
Scottsdale Convention & Visitors
  Bureau.......................................9 F6
Wide World of Maps......................10 B6

SIGHTS & ACTIVITIES
Airpark Bicycle Center..................11 F4
Arizona Science Center.................12 E2
Arizona State University................13 F8
Castles N' Coasters.......................14 B4
Desert Botanical Garden................15 E7
Gammage Auditorium...................16 E8
Hall of Flame...............................17 E7
Heard Museum.............................18 C7
Heritage Square...........................19 E2
Mill Avenue..................................20 E8
Old Town Scottsdale......................21 F6
Piestewa Peak Recreation Area......22 D5
Waterworld Safari.........................23 B2

SLEEPING
Clarendon Hotel + Suites................24 C6
Hermosa Inn.................................25 D6
HI Phoenix, Metcalf House.............26 F1
Maricopa Manor...........................27 C6
Mondrian Scottsdale.....................28 F6
Motel 6 on Camelback...................29 F6
Pointe Hilton Squaw Peak
  Resort.......................................30 C5
San Carlos Hotel...........................31 E2
Sanctuary on Camelback
  Mountain...................................32 E6

EATING
Asia de Cuba.............................(see 28)
Chelsea's Kitchen.........................33 D6
Cibo...34 D2

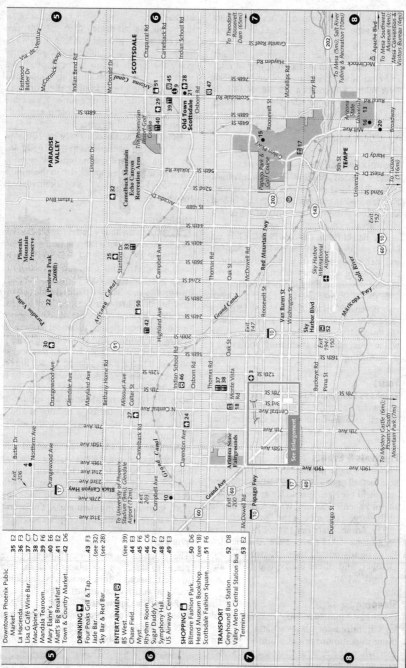

Downtown Phoenix Public

Market.........................35	E2
La Hacienda.................36	F3
Lisa G Café Wine Bar....37	C7
MacAlpine's..................38	C7
Mandala Tearoom.........39	F6
Mary Elaine's................40	E6
Matt's Big Breakfast......41	E2
Town & Country Market..42	D6

DRINKING 🍺

Four Peaks Grill & Tap..43	F3
Jade Bar......................(see 32)
Sky Bar & Red Bar........(see 28)

ENTERTAINMENT 🎭

BS West......................(see 39)
Chase Field.................44	E3
Myst...........................45	F6
Rhythm Room..............46	C6
Sugar Daddy's.............47	F7
Symphony Hall............48	E2
US Airways Center........49	E3

SHOPPING 🛍

Biltmore Fashion Park....50	D6
Heard Museum Bookshop..(see 18)
Scottsdale Fashion Square..51	F6

TRANSPORT

Greyhound Bus Station...52	D8
Valley Metro Central Bus
Terminal......................53	E2

you need to pick up pedals, try the **Airpark Bicycle Center** (☎ 480-596-6633; 8666 E Shea Blvd; per day from $35).

Floating down the Salt River in an inner tube is loads of fun and a great way to relax and cool down in summer. Near Mesa, **Salt River Tubing & Recreation** (☎ 480-984-3305; cnr Bush Hwy & Usury Pass Rd; tubes $14) rents tubes and provides van shuttles to good starting points. Tubing season is mid-April through September.

Phoenix for Children

Castles N' Coasters (☎ 602-997-7575; www.castlesncoast ers.com; 9445 Metro Parkway E; admission $23; ☺ 10am-10pm daily Sep-May, noon-9pm Sun-Thu, to 11pm Fri & Sat Jun-Aug) has bumper boats, miniature golf, a video arcade and tons of rides.

The **Hall of Flame** (☎ 602-275-3473; 6101 E Van Buren St; adult/child $6/4; ☺ 9am-5pm Mon-Sat, noon-4pm Sun), exhibiting more than 90 fully restored fire-fighting machines from 1725 to the present day, is another kiddy favorite.

If the wee ones are wilting in the heat, visit **Waterworld Safari** (☎ 623-581-8446; 4243 W Pinnacle Peak Rd; adult/child under 3/child $24/3/19; ☺ 10am-8pm Mon-Sat, 11am-7pm Sun), with a six-story-high water slide, acres of swimming pools and a wave-making machine.

Tours

Vaughan's Southwest (☎ 602-971-1381; www.south westtours.com) offers 4½-hour city tours ($50), as well as a 14-hour Grand Canyon tour ($125) for people with very limited time.

Festivals & Events

Phoenix's most popular event is the **Fiesta Bowl football game** (☎ 480-350-0911; www.fiestabowl .com), held on New Year's Day at the University of Phoenix Stadium. It's preceded by one of the largest parades in the Southwest.

The **Arizona State Fair** (☎ 602-252-6771; www .azstatefair.com) takes place at the Arizona State Fairgrounds during the first two weeks of October, and offers the typical rodeo and midway action.

Sleeping

From basic motels to ritzy resorts, the valley's hundreds of places to stay have one thing in common: prices plummet in summer when the mercury rises. Peak-season rates are quoted here.

BUDGET

HI Phoenix, Metcalf House (☎ 602-254-9803; www .home.earthlink.net/~phxhostel; 1026 N 9th St; dm $18-25, s/d 30/40; ☒ ☒ wi-fi) Chalked thank-you notes grace the facade of this homey hostel in a working-class residential neighborhood, and relaxing garden nooks buffer the front and back yards. Kitchen and common areas close during the day, and the whole place shuts down for July and August.

Motel 6 on Camelback (☎ 480-946-2280; www .motel6.com; 6848 E Camelback Rd; s/d $49/56; P ☒ ☒) Yes, it's a standard chain, but this motel is conveniently located smack dab in the middle of upscale Scottsdale, only a quick drive from the Old Town.

MIDRANGE

our pick **Clarendon Hotel + Suites** (☎ 602-252-7363; www.theclarendon.net; 401 W Clarendon Ave; r/ste incl breakfast $110/140; P ☒ ☒ ☒ ☒ wi-fi) Modern yet lusciously retro, this blue pin-striped boutique hotel features cool contemporary art and groovy touches like painted sliding window blinds. Throw in the free limited-area chauffeur service, complimentary phone use (including domestic long distance) and a swell central pool annex, and you're living large.

San Carlos Hotel (☎ 602-253-4121; www.hotelsan carlos.com; 202 N Central Ave; r $140; ☒ ☒ ☒) Big on character, this 1928 downtown property is an Italian Renaissance–inspired beauty that's been nicely restored. Rooms are small but atmospheric, and there's a restaurant and a coffee shop off the chandelier-strung lobby. Parking is $10.

Maricopa Manor (☎ 602-274-6302; 800-292-6403; www.maricopamanor.com; 15 W Pasadena Ave; r incl breakfast from $130; P ☒ ☒ ☒ wi-fi) This small, elegant place has seven beautiful suites, many with French doors onto a deck overlooking the pool, garden and fountain areas. You won't find a more intimate resort experience.

TOP END

The resorts are the most elegant and expensive places to stay. Not just places to sleep, they are destinations within themselves, and some make an entire vacation out of it.

Pointe Hilton Squaw Peak Resort (☎ 602-997-2626, 800-947-9784; www.pointehilton.com; 7677 N 16th St; r from $279; P ☒ ☒ ☒ wi-fi) With 9 acres of pools – including water slides and a 'river' tubing area – as well as a concierge for kids' activities, this all-suite resort is the most family-friendly spot in town. Request one of its recently remodeled rooms.

Sanctuary on Camelback Mountain (☎ 480-948-2100; www.sanctuaryoncamelback.com; 5700 E McDonald Dr; r from $495; P ✕ ✕ ⬛ ⬛ wi-fi) A night at this swanky spa resort leaves you spoiled for choice – a massage under the stars or a mountain-view dip in one of three pools? A trendy and romantic choice, the modern rooms and casitas coddle guests with scented candles, fluffy robes and ultra-comfy slippers.

Hermosa Inn (☎ 602-955-8614; 800-241-1210; www.hermosainn.com; 5532 N Palo Cristi Rd; r incl breakfast $330-700; P ✕ ✕ ⬛ ⬛ wi-fi) At this Spanish hacienda–style resort decked out with Mission furniture and festooned with potted cacti many of the rooms have fireplaces, and most have sumptuous king-size beds. There's always fresh cold lemonade in the adobe 1930s-era lobby.

Mondrian Scottsdale (☎ 480-308-1113; www.mondrianscottsdale.com; 7353 E Indian School Rd; r $465, ste $665; P ✕ ⬛ ⬛ wi-fi) This unsigned and überhip boutique hotel has an esoteric Garden of Eden theme (look for the ruby-red apple in the rooms) and a lobby that propels you into a white-hot wonderland of floating cotton clouds and horned steer skulls. The luxe pool bar has cushy bed seating and underwater speakers.

Eating

Phoenix has the largest selection of restaurants in the Southwest.

BUDGET

MacAlpine's (☎ 602-252-5545; 2303 N 7th St; dishes from $5; ☽ 11am-7pm Sun-Thu, to 8pm Fri & Sat) Phoenix's oldest and possibly most atmospheric diner, with cozy wooden booths and loads of antique soda fountain bric-a-brac as decoration. Burgers are its standard fare (including a yummy veggie black-bean patty), and you can perch on a counter stool and drool over the milk shakes and old-fashioned egg creams.

Matt's Big Breakfast (☎ 602-254-1074; 801 N 1st Ave; ☽ 6:30am-2:30pm Tue-Sun; dishes $6-8) This fine little downtown diner is souped up with orange retro tables and swingin' classic chairs. As the name implies, the waffles, griddlecakes and grill sandwiches don't come small. Enjoy omelets from cage-free chicken eggs and a bounty of local organic produce.

Year-round farmers markets demonstrate the bounty of the blazing sun:

Downtown Phoenix Public Market (www.phoenixpublicmarket.com; 721 N Central Ave; ☽ 8am-noon Sat) Specialty gourmet foods and local bands are highlights.

Town & Country Market (2021 E Camelback Rd; ☽ 10am-2pm Wed) Primarily seasonal produce.

MIDRANGE

Lisa G Café Wine Bar (☎ 602-253-9201; 2337 N 7th St; dishes $9-12; ☽ 11am-2pm Mon & Tue, 11am-2pm & 5-10pm Wed & Thu, 11am-2pm & 5pm-midnight Fri & Sat) Lisa Giungo wanted to have her own restaurant since she was little, and when she opened her café, she hung her childhood portraits on the walls. It adds a fun touch to this sleek and contemporary space serving primarily salads and sandwiches. Even quirkier is the name of her meatball extravaganza – 'Lisa's Bowl of Balls.'

Mandala Tearoom (☎ 480-423-3411; 7027 E 5th Ave; dishes $9-13; ☽ 11am-3pm & 5-9pm Mon-Fri, 10am-9pm Sat & Sun) An organic vegan café in cheerful minimalist surroundings, it serves up rockin' baked ziti, dozens of organic teas, and a weekend brunch with filling tofu scrambles. In addition to the creative international-inspired menu, treats include vegan truffles from Cosmic Cacao, herbal elixirs ($7) and free wi-fi.

our pick **Cibo** (☎ 602-441-2697; 603 N 5th Ave; pizzas $9-13; ☽ 11am-2pm & 5-9pm Mon-Thu, 11am-2pm & 5-11pm Fri, 5-11pm Sat) The wooden floors creak in this restored 1913 house, and the exposed-brick interiors seem to ooze history. The chef hails from just outside Naples, and his gourmet pizzas – with two sauce options, *rosse* and *bianche* – fire over a wood oven. The Italian wine selection is broad and the patio seating delightful.

Chelsea's Kitchen (☎ 602-957-2555; 5040 N 40th St; dishes $12-25; ☽ 11am-10pm Mon-Sat, 10am-9pm Sun) A casual though upscale American eatery, Chelsea 's is popular with the young professional crowd and located canal-side for a beachy feel. The menu includes lots of burgers and tacos, and it does a buzzing Sunday brunch.

TOP END

La Hacienda (☎ 480-585-4848; 7575 E Princess Dr; dishes $28-39; ☽ 6-10pm Thu-Tue) Upscale Mexican cuisine is enhanced by gorgeous surroundings, strolling mariachis and top-notch service at this restaurant inside the Fairmont Scottsdale Princess Resort. The food and setting are superb.

Asia de Cuba (☎ 480-308-1131; 7353 E Indian School Rd; dishes $32-40; 🕑 6:30am-11pm Sun-Thu, to midnight Fri & Sat) At this fusion of Cuban heat, Asian spice and the preeningly hip Mondrian Scottsdale hotel scene, you'll be licking your lips, gyrating those salsa-loving hips and puzzling about how they keep that white dining room so damn clean. Loaded with plates meant to be shared, the fun fusion menu includes such dishes as miso-glazed butterfish and Cuban-spiced chicken with Thai coconut sticky rice.

Mary Elaine's (☎ 480-423-2530; 6000 E Camelback Rd; dishes from $45; 🕑 5:30-10pm Tue-Sat) Posh and very elegant, this restaurant inside the Phoenician Resort has a well-deserved stellar reputation for delicious and creative modern-French cuisine. New tasting menus appear every season. Jackets are recommended for men.

Drinking

Scottsdale has the greatest concentration of trendy bars and clubs, while Tempe attracts the student crowd.

Four Peaks Grill & Tap (☎ 480-991-1795; 15730 N Pima Rd; 🕑 11am-2am) There's always room for a laid-back brewpub, even in high-energy Scottsdale. Hang out and sample some of its 10 draft specialties in the semi-industrial space that gets mobbed on football nights.

Jade Bar (☎ 480-948-2100; 5700 E McDonald Dr) A luscious place inside the Sanctuary on Camelback Mountain, the bar overlooks sparkling Paradise Valley. Order a cantaloupe martini as the sun sinks low on the horizon.

Sky Bar & Red Bar (☎ 480-308-1100; 7353 E Indian School Rd) The pulsing core of the Mondrian Scottsdale, and a study in opposites, these two scene-y bars are fun and out-of-control trendy. The Red Bar has the crushed blood-red velvet walls of a bordello, and the colorless black Sky Bar imagines a hell as dark as your cold, cold heart. Whichever way you head, expect high-spirited company and an elbow-wielding crowd at weekends.

Entertainment

BS West (☎ 480-945-9028; 7125 E 5th Ave; 🕑 2pm-2am) A gay high-energy video bar and dance club in the Old Town area, it hosts karaoke nights on Thursday and Sunday and a monthly drag show. There're two floors of fun and two patios.

Myst (☎ 480-970-5000; 7340 E Shoeman Lane; cover $10-40; 🕑 10pm-2am Wed, Fri & Sat) If you want to get wild in the Old Town, this mega-club and its adjoining sister club, Ballroom, are calling your name. DJs from all over the world flaunt their stuff in this stylized space, and VIP skyboxes entice the flush young things. Dress code enforced for men.

Rhythm Room (☎ 602-265-4842; 1019 E Indian School Rd; cover $4-6) Live blues and jazz are spotlighted at this local favorite. It attracts an eclectic crowd looking for a good time.

Sugar Daddy's (☎ 480-970-6556; 3102 N Scottsdale Rd; cover $2) Live music rocks this casual, and often rowdy, local pick nightly. If your ears are ringing, make your way outside; Sugar Daddy's has one of the best patios in town.

Symphony Hall (☎ 602-262-7272; 75 N 2nd Ave) Both the Arizona Opera (☎ 602-266-7464; tickets $30 to $130) and the Phoenix Symphony Orchestra (☎ 602-495-1999; tickets $20 to $70) perform here.

SPECTATOR SPORTS

The men's basketball team, the **Phoenix Suns** (☎ 602-379-7867), and the women's team, the **Phoenix Mercury** (☎ 602-252-9622), play at the US Airways Center. Football team the **Arizona Cardinals** (☎ 602-379-0102) plays at the new University of Phoenix Stadium in Glendale. The **Arizona Diamondbacks** (☎ 602-514-8400) play baseball at Chase Field.

Shopping

The **Heard Museum bookshop** (☎ 602-252-8840; www.heard.org; 2301 N Central Ave) has the best range of books about Native Americans, and the most reliable, excellent and expensive selection of Native American arts and crafts.

The valley has several notable shopping malls. For more upscale shopping, visit the **Scottsdale Fashion Square** (cnr Camelback & Scottsdale Rds) and the even more exclusive **Biltmore Fashion Park** (cnr Camelback Rd & 24th St).

Getting There & Around

Phoenix's **Sky Harbor International Airport** (☎ 602-273-3300) is 3 miles southeast of downtown. Valley Metro's Red Line operates buses from the airport to Tempe, Mesa and downtown Phoenix ($1.25).

Greyhound (☎ 602-389-4200; 2115 E Buckeye Rd) runs regular buses to Tucson ($30, two hours), Flagstaff ($27, three hours), Los Angeles ($44, seven hours) and other destinations.

Valley Metro (☎ 602-253-5000; www.valleymetro.org) operates buses ($1.25) all over the valley. On weekdays it also runs the free Flash service around the ASU area and free Dash service around downtown Phoenix. A new **light rail system** (☎ 602-254-7245; www.metrolightrail.org) is expected to open during 2008.

The free and frequent **Scottsdale Trolley** (☎ 480-421-1004; www.scottsdaletrolley.com) covers the Old Town area and runs to a number of good shopping areas. Catch it from 11am to 9pm.

CENTRAL ARIZONA

The gateway to the Grand Canyon, this region offers cool relief from summer heat amid mountains and forests. The fun college town of Flagstaff is here. So is funky, artsy Jerome. Beautiful Sedona, with its stunning red-rock scenery, is a center for the New Age and a major tourist hub.

Flagstaff

A very aural reminder of Flagstaff's history, approximately 100 freight trains barrel through this fine mountain city each day, blowing their horns with spirited abandon. A funky, vibrant town filled with students attending Northern Arizona University (NAU), Flagstaff boasts cool mountain air, ponderosa pines and even a mountain to ski, and is the favored summer retreat for the folks in Phoenix. Microbreweries, interesting hotels and hip restaurants are housed in historic brick buildings a hop, skip and jump from historic Route 66. There are plenty of outdoorsy adventures, and hiking and biking trails are abundant. Less than a two-hour drive from the Grand Canyon, Flagstaff makes a great regional base.

The **visitors center** (☎ 928-774-9541, 800-842-7293; www.flagstaffarizona.org; 1 E Route 66; 🕑 8am-5pm Mon-Sat, 9am-4pm Sun) is inside the historic Amtrak train station.

SIGHTS

If you have time for only one sight in Flagstaff, head to the **Museum of Northern Arizona** (☎ 928-774-5213; www.musnaz.org; 3101 N Fort Valley Rd; adult/student/senior $7/4/6; 🕑 9am-5pm). It features exhibits on local Native American archaeology, history and customs, as well as geology, biology and the arts.

The **Lowell Observatory** (☎ 928-774-2096; www.lowell.edu; 1400 W Mars Hill Rd; adult/child $6/3; 🕑 9am-5pm Apr-Oct, noon-5pm Nov-Mar) witnessed the first sighting of Pluto in 1920. Weather permitting, visitors can stargaze through the telescope in the evenings.

The Sinagua cliff dwellings at **Walnut Canyon National Monument** (☎ 928-526-3367; www.nps.gov/waca; admission $5; 🕑 9am-5pm Nov-Apr, 8am-5pm May-Oct) are set in the nearly vertical walls of a small limestone butte amid a forested canyon. A short hiking trail descends past many cliff-dwelling rooms. The monument is 11 miles southeast of Flagstaff off I-40 exit 204.

The 1000ft-tall volcano cone at the **Sunset Crater Volcano National Monument** (☎ 928-526-0502; www.nps.gov/sucr; admission $5; 🕑 9am-5pm Nov-Apr, 8am-5pm May-Oct), located on a loop road 12 miles north of Flagstaff along Hwy 89, was formed by volcanic eruptions in AD 1064. An interpretive trail grants visitors a firsthand look at volcanic features. Follow the loop road from the crater to nearby **Wupatki National Monument** (☎ 928-679-2365; www.nps.gov/wupa; admission $5, free if already paid at Sunset Crater; 🕑 sunrise-sunset), which has hundreds of Ancestral Puebloan historic sites, a handful of which are easily accessible.

ACTIVITIES

If you want to say you've skied Arizona, head to the small, but lofty, **Arizona Snowbowl** (☎ 928-779-1951; www.arizonasnowbowl.com; Snowbowl Rd; half/full day $38/46). Four lifts service 30 runs at elevations between 9200ft and 11,500ft. The skiing is not world class, but this is a state known for its deserts, not its snow. You can also ride the chairlift (adult/child $10/6) in summer. For a snow report, call ☎ 928-779-4577.

Arizona's highest mountain, the 12,663ft **Humphreys Peak**, is a reasonably straightforward, though strenuous, hike in summer. The trail begins at the Arizona Snowbowl and winds through forest, eventually coming out above the timberline. The total distance is 4½ miles one way; allow six to eight hours round-trip.

Absolute Bikes (☎ 928-779-5969; 18 N San Francisco St; half-/full-day rental from $30/40) rents mountain, road and children's bikes, and has trail maps and information.

SLEEPING

Flagstaff provides the best budget and midrange lodging in this region. Unlike in southern Arizona, summer is high season here. Take note that Route 66 is right next to the train tracks, and those freight trains run all night long.

Grand Canyon International Hostel (☎ 928-779-9421, 888-442-2696; www.grandcanyonhostel.com; 19 1/2 S San Francisco St; dm/d from $17/34; ✕ ☐) Housed in a historic building with hardwood floors and southwestern decor, dorms are clean and small. There's a kitchen, laundry facilities, and a host of backpacker-geared tours, and they'll fetch you from Greyhound for free.

Monte Vista Hotel (☎ 928-779-6971, 800-545-3068; www.hotelmontevista.com; 100 N San Francisco St; r $70-140; P ✕ ☒ wi-fi) Scenes from the movie *Casablanca* were filmed at this 1927 hotel, where many of the 50 rooms and suites are named after the film stars who slept in them. Rooms are comfortable and old-fashioned, but not luxurious (John Wayne and Humphrey Bogart handled it just fine).

our pick Weatherford Hotel (☎ 928-779-1919; www.weatherfordhotel.com; 23 N Leroux St; r $65-79, ste $125; ✕) Flagstaff's most historic hotel is fantastic value, keeping its rates year-round. A charming place with a turn-of-the-19th-century feel in its eight rooms and two suites (with no TVs or telephones), it boasts numerous high-ceilinged Victorian lounges and classy period furnishings. Its Zane Grey Bar can be a tad noisy, but its wood and stained-glass bar (from the glory days of Tombstone) is gorgeous.

Inn at NAU (☎ 928-523-1616; www.inn.nau.edu; San Francisco & McCreary Sts, Northern Arizona University; d incl full breakfast $99-109; P ✕ ☒ ☐ wi-fi) NAU's hotel and restaurant management program runs this wonderful 19-room hotel right on campus, and it gets straight As across the board. Though the building hints at institutional cinderblock, the very large rooms have oodles of amenities, and standard rooms have a low partition between two queen beds, so they're super-handy for three to four people. Extra credit: since it's a school, it charges no sales tax.

Inn at 410 (☎ 928-774-0088, 800-774-2008; www .inn410.com; 410 N Leroux St; r incl full breakfast $165-230; P ✕ ☒ ☐ wi-fi) A consistent local favorite, this elegant and very romantic 1907 house offers nine spacious and beautiful bedrooms. Most have a fireplace or whirlpool bath, and two have adjoining rooms suitable for families with children. The breakfast is all-the-way gourmet and the afternoon tea a lovely treat.

EATING

MartAnne's (☎ 928-773-4701; 10 N San Francisco St; dishes $4-8; ⊗ 8am-2pm Mon-Sat, 8:30am-2pm Sun) Small and funky MartAnne's does Mexican food and it does it well. Gulp down coffee and *chilaquiles* (even vegan ones with seitan) under a ceiling mural of the blue sky and tap the black-and-white checkerboard at your feet. Everything's dripping with color, including the crayons doled out to kids.

Karma (☎ 928-774-6100; 6 E Route 66; sushi rolls $7-9; ⊗ 11am-2pm & 5-10pm) A trendy sushi bar with low lights, black-shellacked tables and scented bar candles, it has lots of yummy rolls and combos to choose from, as well as noodle dishes and tempuras. You can *feel* the trains rumbling past across the street.

Flagstaff Brewing Company (☎ 928-773-1442; 16 E Route 66; dishes $8-10; ⊗ 11am-10pm) A low-key brewpub with a fun outdoorsy vibe, the Flagstaff offers food of the bar-staple variety – pizza, burgers, soup and salads – but it's quite tasty. There's a large selection of delicious microbrews (the best in town) and a daily happy hour from 4:30pm to 6:30pm.

Pasto (☎ 928-779-1937; 19 E Aspen Ave; dishes $11-20; ⊗ 5-9pm Tue-Sun) Enjoy rustic Italian cuisine fashioned from local, regional and seasonal foods and served in an upscale old world dining room with yellow walls, glittery chandeliers and aging wood floors.

our pick Brix Restaurant & Wine Bar (☎ 928-213-1021; 413 N San Francisco St; dishes $23-30; ⊗ 11am-2pm & 5-9:30pm Mon-Fri, 5-9:30pm Sat) Housed in a gently modernized early 1900s building, this contemporary and casual American eatery showcases fresh food from local farms and ranches and wine from small producers. Craft a cheese plate from the dozen-item selection, savor the steak *frites* with hints of truffles and shallots, and top it off with a plate of profiteroles. Delightful.

DRINKING & ENTERTAINMENT

San Felipe (☎ 928-779-6000; 103 N Leroux St; ⊗ 11am-2pm Mon-Sat, 11am-11pm Sun-Thu) A more mellow Mexican restaurant by day, by night the sharks-and-surfboards space is taken over by the college crowd, washing down fish tacos with voluminous amounts of tequila. Don't blame us if you end up dancing on the bar.

Museum Club (☎ 928-526-9434; 3404 E Route 66; ⊗ 11am-2am) A popular, barnlike place, Museum Club is the place to come for country music and kick-up-yer-heels roadhouse dancing. Built in the 1920s, it used to house a taxidermy museum, which may account for its local nickname, 'the Zoo.'

SOUTHWEST

Uptown Billiards (☎ 928-773-0551; 114 N Leroux St; ☺ 1pm-1am Mon-Wed, to 2am Thu-Sat, to midnight Sun) Start chalking ($7 per hour) and take your pick from 34 draft beers and 43 types of single-malt whisky. The daily happy hour runs from 5pm to 7pm, with both drink and game discounts.

Orpheum Theater (☎ 928-556-1580; www.orpheum presents.com; 15 W Aspen Ave) A grand old-style movie house from 1911, the theater is now a fine-looking music venue with occasional movie nights.

GETTING THERE & AROUND

From the **Greyhound bus station** (☎ 928-774-4573; www.greyhound.com; 399 S Malpais Lane) buses run frequently to Las Vegas ($54, six hours), Los Angeles ($56, 11 hours) and Phoenix ($27, three hours). **Open Road Tours** (☎ 928-226-8060; www.openroadtours.com; 1 E Route 66) has shuttles from its office in the Amtrak station to the Grand Canyon ($27), Phoenix Sky Harbor International Airport ($42) and Sedona ($25). Call to reserve.

Operated by **Amtrak** (☎ 928-774-8679; www .amtrak.com), the *Southwest Chief* stops in Flagstaff on its daily runs between Chicago and Los Angeles.

Williams

Bisected by Old Route 66, Williams epitomizes Main Street America. Literally a two-street town, it seems like nothing much has changed here over the decades. Most tourists visit to ride the turn-of-the-19th-century **Grand Canyon Railway** (☎ 800-843-8724; www.thetrain .com; Railway Depot, 233 N Grand Canyon Blvd; round-trip adult/child from $60/25) to the South Rim (departs 10am). Even if you're not a train buff, a trip on this historic steam locomotive can be lots of fun. Characters in period costumes provide historical and regional narration, and banjo folk music sets the tone. There's also a wildly popular *Polar Express* service (adult/child $26/14) from November through January, ferrying pajama-clad kids to the 'North Pole' to visit Santa.

One of the most fun sleeping options is the **Red Garter Bed & Bakery** (☎ 928-635-1484; 800-328-1484; www.redgarter.com; 137 Railroad Ave; r incl breakfast $120-145; ☒ ☒ wi-fi), an 1897 bordello-turned-B&B, where the ladies used to hang out the windows to flag down customers. The four rooms have nice (nonbawdy) period touches, and some have claw-foot tubs. The funky little

Grand Canyon Hotel (☎ 928-635-1419, 877-635-1419; www.thegrandcanyonhotel.com; 145 W Route 66; dm $20, r with shared/private bath $60/70; ☐ ☒ ☒ ☐ wi-fi) claims to be the oldest hotel in Arizona; it has small themed rooms and a cool big-screen movie space with comfy couches.

Route 66 fans will dig the eclectic decor at **Cruiser's Café 66** (☎ 928-635-2445; 233 W Route 66; dishes $8-16; ☺ 11am-10pm Mon-Thu & 8am-10pm Fri-Sun summer, variable hr winter), with its vintage gas pumps and old signs and murals eulogizing America's most famous highway. It's a fun place, serving BBQ and other American fare inside a 1930s filling station. The **World Famous Sultana Bar** (☎ 928-635-2021; 301 W Route 66) served as a basement speakeasy during prohibition. Today it's a saloon from another era. It sometimes hosts live music.

Open Road (☎ 928-226-8060, 800-766-7117; Railway Depot, 233 N Grand Canyon Blvd) offers two daily shuttles to the Grand Canyon ($27, plus $6 park entrance fee) and Flagstaff ($17).

Sedona

There's something about Sedona that goes beyond the ordinary. With its spindly towers, grand buttes and flat-topped mesas carved in crimson sandstone, it could enter a geography beauty contest and hold its own against the national parks. It's unquestionably one of the most beautiful places in Arizona, and one of the most scenic cities in the Southwest. Though Sedona was founded in the 19th century, the discovery of energy 'vortexes' here in the 1980s turned this once modest settlement into a bustling New Age destination. Today the combination of mysticism and red-rock majesty attracts throngs of tourists year-round. You'll find all sorts of alternative medicine practices in town, along with art galleries, gourmet restaurants and top-end resorts, not to mention numerous businesses available to read (and photograph) your aura.

In the middle of town, the 'Y' is the landmark junction of Hwys 89A and 179. Businesses are spread along both roads. The **chamber of commerce** (☎ 928-282-7722, 800-288-7336; www.visitsedona.com; Singagua Plaza, 320 N Highway 89A; ☺ 8:30am-5pm Mon-Sat, 9am-3pm Sun) has tourist information and vortex maps. (This location is temporary – they will eventually move to Forest Rd at Hwy 89A.) For free internet access, visit the **library** (☎ 928-282-7714; 3250 White Bear Rd).

SIGHTS & ACTIVITIES

New Agers believe Sedona's rocks, cliffs and rivers radiate electromagnetic energy. The earth's four best-known vortexes are here, and include **Bell Rock** near Village of Oak Creek east of Hwy 179, **Cathedral Rock** near Red Rock Crossing, **Airport Mesa** along the Airport Rd and **Boynton Canyon**. Airport Rd is also a great location for watching the spectacular red-rock sunsets.

The best way to explore the area is by hiking, biking or horseback riding in the surrounding **Coconino National Forest** (☎ 928-282-4119; www.redrockcountry.org/recreation). The website lists a huge range of recreational activities and trail information. Most day use and parking areas require a Red Rock Pass ($5 per day, $15 per week), which can be purchased at most hotels and visitor areas.

Another way to experience Sedona's stunning scenery is from the back of a Jeep. Many companies offer 4WD Jeep tours, but **Pink Jeep Tours** (☎ 928-382-5000, 800-873-3662; www.pinkjeep.com; 204 N Hwy 89A) is the most esteemed. Tours (from $68) take you alongside adrenaline-pumping drop-offs and past panoramic vistas and archeological sites.

SLEEPING

Sedona hosts many beautiful B&Bs, creekside cabins and full-service resorts.

On Hwy 89A, north of town in Oak Creek Canyon, are four nice **USFS campgrounds** (☎ 877-444-6777; www.recreation.gov; campsites $18-20); sites can be reserved in advance, though some are kept on a first come, first served basis.

Sky Ranch Lodge (☎ 928-282-6400, 888-708-6400; www.skyranchlodge.com; Airport Rd; r $75-160; ⊠ ▨ ▢) On 6 landscaped acres, the lodge has spacious motel rooms, some with balconies, fireplaces, and kitchenettes or refrigerators. Cottages ($190) with vaulted ceilings, kitchenettes and

private decks are also available. The Rim View rooms are fantastic for watching the sunset.

Inn on Oak Creek (☎ 928-282-7896, 800-499-7896; www.innonoakcreek.com; 556 Hwy 179; r incl full breakfast $195-290; ⊠ ▨ ▢ wi-fi) Casual elegance on the water is the theme at Sedona's most charming and intimate sleeping option. The Angler's Retreat room has a spectacular creek view, the Bunkhouse is all cowboy and the Duck Pond has a scenic whirlpool tub. The breakfast is as gourmet as it gets, and there's early-evening hors d'oeuvres and home-baked cookies to boot.

EATING & DRINKING

Coffeepot Restaurant (☎ 928-282-6626; 2050 W Hwy 89A; dishes $6-8; ⊙ 6am-2pm) For breakfast and lunch, this has been the place to go for decades. The menu is voluminous, offering more types of omelets than most restaurants have menu items (it lists 101, including peanut butter and jelly!).

Red Planet Diner (☎ 928-282-6070; 1655 W Hwy 89A; dishes $9-14; ⊙ 10am-11pm) A super-kitsch outer-space experience awash in hot-pink neon, this '50s-themed diner features a spaceship landing from the heavens, with pasty aliens floating through the air and decorative busts of Mr Spock and Obi-Wan Kenobi. Grill food (with a fair number of vegetarian choices) rules this Roswellian roost.

Heartland Café (☎ 928-282-0785; 1610 W Hwy 89A; dishes $16-25; ⊙ 11am-3pm & 5-9pm) An American bistro with fresh and creative seasonings, it serves wonderful meats and seafood – like pecan-crusted trout – as well as a large selection of pasta and veggie dishes. The outdoor patio is an intimate and very romantic dinner spot.

Shugrue's Hillside Grill (☎ 928-282-5300; 671 Hwy 179; mains lunch $11-15, dinner $27-32; ⊙ 11:30am-3pm & 5-9pm) A drop-dead scenic choice for an upscale

---

SCENIC DRIVE: OAK CREEK CANYON

For a blissful summer plunge, take Hwy 89A northeast of Sedona into Oak Creek Canyon. The canyon is at its narrowest here, and the red, orange and white cliffs at their most dramatic. Giant cottonwoods crowd the creek sides, providing a scenic shady backdrop for trout fishing and swimming. About 2 miles in, stop at **Grasshopper Point** (admission $8) and walk down to a narrow swimming hole amidst red rocks. Dry off and drive for 5 miles to **Slide Rock State Park** (☎ 928-282-3034; admission per vehicle $10; ⊙ 8am-6pm, to 7pm summer), a natural rock slide flushed by a chilly creek.

Head back into town around sunset and turn off at Airport Road. The setting sun makes for a trippy picture – the rocks blaze psychedelic red and orange against a bright pink and purple sky.

meal, Shugrue's serves excellent food with a heaping panoramic side of Sedona's heart-stopping views. The menu offers everything from steak to ravioli, but the seafood gets the spotlight. Reservations are recommended; dine early to ensure a window seat.

GETTING THERE & AROUND

The **Sedona-Phoenix Shuttle** (☎ 928-282-2066; www.sedona-phoenix-shuttle.com) runs between Phoenix Sky Harbor International Airport and Sedona eight times daily ($45). Call to make reservations. The free city-run **Sedona Roadrunner** (☎ 928-282-0938; www.sedonaroadrunner.com) shuttles between Hillside and the Uptown area north of the 'Y' from 9am to 6:30pm daily; trolleys arrive three to six times hourly.

Jerome

Precariously perched on a steep hillside, tiny Jerome has a European feel – as if someone took a French country village and plopped it down in the Arizona desert. Shabby chic and eclectically enticing, the old mining town and resurrected ghost town exudes an untouristy and altogether romantic feel. Known as the 'Wickedest Town in the West' during its late 1800s mining hey-day, today Jerome's historic buildings have been lovingly restored and turned into galleries, restaurants, saloons and B&Bs.

The **chamber of commerce** (☎ 928-634-2900; www.jeromechamber.com; 310 Hull Ave; ☼ 11am-3pm) offers tourist information.

A restored 1898 building with 12 rooms, the **Connor Hotel** (☎ 928-634-5006, 800-523-3554; www.connorhotel.com; 164 Main St; r $90-165; wi-fi) has nice Victorian decor, and many rooms have cool vintage wallpaper. The popular **Spirit Room Bar** (☎ 928-634-5006; 164 Main St), the town's liveliest watering hole, is downstairs, and makes hotel rooms 1 to 4 a trifle noisy.

The **Asylum Restaurant** (☎ 928-639-3197; 200 Hill St; lunch mains $10, dinner mains $18-22; ☼ 11am-3pm & 5-9pm) serves scrumptious nouveau-American fare inside the Jerome Grand Hotel, with great vegetarian options to boot. Deep-red walls, lazy fans, gilded artwork, jazz music and views, views, views provide a knockout ambience. A lengthy wine list makes the experience even sweeter.

Prescott

With a historic Victorian-era downtown and a colorful Wild West history, Arizona's first territorial capital now has a bohemian feel.

Residents are a diverse mix of hippies, retirees, cowboy-style conservatives, artsy types and outdoor enthusiasts. The town boasts over 500 buildings on the National Registry of Historic Places. Along the plaza is **Whiskey Row**, an infamous strip of old saloons that still serve up their fair share of booze.

The **chamber of commerce** (☎ 928-445-2000; www.prescott.org; 117 W Goodwin; ☼ 9am-5pm Mon-Fri, 10am-2pm Sat & Sun) has tourist information.

Right in the thick of Whiskey Row, the historic **Hotel St Michael** (☎ 928-776-1999, 800-678-3757; www.stmichaelhotel.com; 205 W Gurley St; r incl full breakfast $59-119; ☐) has basic rooms, though in a dynamite location. The restored **Hassayampa Inn** (☎ 928-778-9434, 800-322-1927; www.hassayampainn.com; 122 E Gurley St; r incl full breakfast $129-229; ☒ wi-fi) features a vintage hand-operated elevator, original furnishings, hand-painted wall decorations and a lovely dining room.

The tiny **Rose Restaurant** (☎ 928-777-8308; 234 S Cortez; dishes $20-34; ☼ 5-9pm Wed-Sun) boasts Prescott's most celebrated chef. Seafood, meat and pasta dishes tantalize from the gourmet menu. Try a Petrified Porter or a Lodgepole Light microbrew at the crowded and charismatic **Prescott Brewing Company** (☎ 928-771-2795; 130 W Gurley St; ☼ 11am-10pm Sun-Thu, 11am-11pm Fri & Sat), which also serves decent English- and American-style pub food (dishes $10 to $14).

The **Prescott Transit Authority** (☎ 928-445-5470, 800-445-7978; 820 E Sheldon St) has shuttles to Phoenix and the Sky Harbor airport ($30, two hours, 16 daily).

GRAND CANYON NATIONAL PARK

For many, the Grand Canyon epitomizes the ultimate American travel destination. Cleaving a mile deep into the earth and averaging 10 miles across, it compels even the most jaded traveler to pause and draw breath. Snaking along its floor are 277 miles of the Colorado River, which has carved the canyon over the past six million years and exposed rocks up to two billion years old – half the age of the Earth.

Initially dismissed as little more than an obstacle to exploration, the canyon first drew 19th-century miners bent on exploiting its rich natural resources. Native American resistance and the lack of water slowed development, but by the time Frederick Jackson Turner declared the end of the American frontier in 1893, entrepreneurs had transformed the canyon into one of the country's

SOUTHWEST

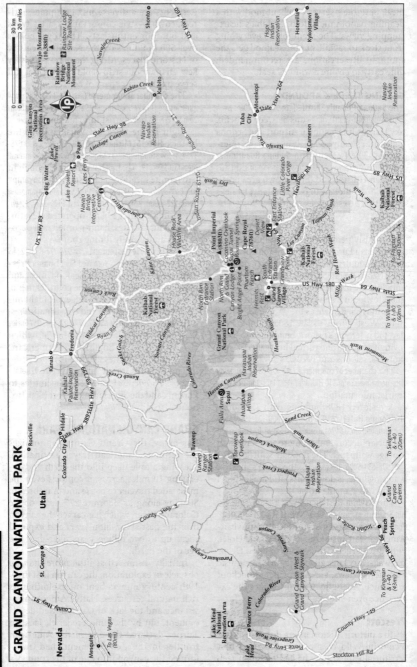

GRAND CANYON NATIONAL PARK

most celebrated destinations. At the dawn of the industrial revolution, people flocked here in search of the romanticized wilderness ideal and embraced its sublime beauty. They still do. Today the park attracts five million visitors yearly from around the world.

The two rims of the Grand Canyon offer quite different experiences and, as they lie more than 200 miles apart by road, are rarely visited on the same trip. Most visitors choose the South Rim, which boasts easy access, the bulk of services and the panoramic vistas for which the park is famous. The quieter North Rim has its own charms; at 8200ft elevation (1000ft higher than the South Rim), its cooler temperatures support wildflower meadows and tall, thick stands of aspen and spruce.

In 2007, the Grand Canyon Skywalk debuted on a remote section of the western canyon owned by the Hualapai Nation. A fascinating and controversial addition to the landscape, it's certain to change the way visitors experience the canyon.

Orientation & Information

The park's most developed area is Grand Canyon Village, 6 miles north of the South Entrance Station. The only entrance to the North Rim lies 30 miles south of Jacob Lake on Hwy 67. The North Rim and South Rim are 220 miles apart by car, 21 miles on foot through the canyon, or 10 miles as the condor flies.

Most visitor facilities are clustered around Grand Canyon Lodge (p841). The entrance ticket for the **park** (vehicles/bicyclists & pedestrians $25/12) is valid for seven days and can be used at both rims.

Canyon View Information Plaza (☎ 928-638-7644; www.nps.gov/grca; Grand Canyon Village; ⏰ 7:30am-6:30pm) At the village's northeast end, this is the main visitor center.

North Rim Visitor Center (☎ 928-638-9864; www .nps.gov/grca; ⏰ 8am-6pm) Adjacent to the Grand Canyon Lodge.

There's a free wi-fi hot spot inside the South Rim's park headquarters courtyard.

WHEN TO GO

June is the driest month, July and August the wettest. January has average overnight lows of 13°F (-11°C) to 20°F (-7°C) and daytime highs around 40°F (4°C). Summer temperatures inside the canyon regularly soar above 100°F (38°C). While the South Rim is open

year-round, most visitors come between late May and early September. The North Rim is open from mid-May to mid-October.

BACKCOUNTRY PERMITS

All overnight hikes in the park require a permit. The **Backcountry Information Center** (☎ 928-638-7875; www.nps.gov/grca; ⏰ 8am-noon & 1-5pm, phone staffed 1-5pm Mon-Fri) accepts applications for backpacking permits ($10, plus $5 per person per night) for the current month and following four months only. Your chances are decent if you apply early (four months in advance for spring and fall) and provide alternative hiking itineraries. If you arrive without a permit, don't despair. Head to their office, by Maswik Lodge, and get on the waiting list. You must show up daily at 8am to remain on the list. You'll likely get a permit within one to four days, depending on the season and itinerary. The center also has a handy scale for weighing your bulging backpack.

South Rim

Every summer, camera-toting tourists throng the park's most popular rim, though most stay only long enough to ogle from the easily accessible scenic viewpoints. So why is this rim so popular? One reason is that it's easier to access from the cities. But the main reason is that the majority of the park's infrastructure is here, and the dramatic, sweeping canyon views are endless and usually unobscured. To dodge the crowds, visit during fall or winter.

SIGHTS & ACTIVITIES

Two **scenic drives** follow the rim on either side of the village – **Hermit Road** to the west and **Desert View Drive** to the east. The rim dips in and out of view as the road passes through the piñon-juniper and ponderosa stands of Kaibab National Forest. Pullouts along the way offer spectacular views, and interpretive signs explain canyon features and geology.

Hiking along the South Rim is among park visitors' favorite pastimes, with options for every skill level. The **Rim Trail** is the most popular, and easiest, walk in the park. It connects a series of scenic points and historical sights over 13 miles, and portions are paved. Every viewpoint is accessed by one of the three shuttle routes.

The most popular of the corridor trails is the beautiful **Bright Angel**. The steep and scenic 8-mile descent to the Colorado is punctuated

---

SAFE CANYON HIKING

Hiking into the canyon is a chance to experience this majestic natural wonder from a different perspective. But while hiking below the rim can be a sublime experience, it can also be dangerous. Summer heat can quickly be crippling. Attempting to hike from the rim to the Colorado River and back in one day is *stupid*, and should not be attempted by even the fittest hikers – people have died down here before, and more will die in the future. However, if you follow a few simple rules, your hike will likely be a highlight of your Grand Canyon trip. First, water is vital. Carry at least 4 quarts of water per person per day; double that on super-hot days. Even if you're just going for a 'short jaunt' on the Bright Angel Trail, take water. A wide-brimmed hat and waterproof sunscreen are always recommended. Second, pace yourself. You may not feel tired on the way down, but remember you still have to come *up*. Before hitting the trail, visit a ranger station for hiking suggestions to match your fitness level.

---

with four logical turnaround spots. Summer heat can be crippling; day hikers should either turn around at one of the two resthouses (a 3- to 6-mile round-trip) or hit the trail at dawn to safely make the longer hikes to Indian Garden and Plateau Point (9.2 and 12.2 miles round-trip, respectively). Hiking to the river in one day is not an option. The trailhead is at Grand Canyon Village.

The **South Kaibab** is arguably one of the park's prettiest trails, combining stunning scenery and unobstructed 360-degree views with every step. Steep, rough and wholly exposed, summer ascents can be dangerous, and during this season rangers discourage all but the shortest day hikes. Turn around at **Cedar Ridge**, perhaps the park's finest short day hike. It's dazzling, particularly at sunrise, when the deep, ruddy ambers and reds of each canyon fold seem to glow from within.

Individuals and groups who want a more in-depth experience of the park while giving something back can apply for programs with **Grand Canyon Volunteers** (☎ 928-774-7488; www.gcvolunteers.org). One- and multi-day programs include wildlife monitoring, native plant restoration and forest surveying.

TOURS

Park tours are run by **Xanterra** (☎ 303-297-2757, 888-297-2757; www.xanterra.com), which has information desks at the visitor centers and Bright Angel, Maswik and Yavapai Lodges. Various daily **bus tours** (tickets from $15) are offered.

Mule trips into the canyon depart daily from the corral west of Bright Angel Lodge (right). Choose from the seven-hour daytrip ($149) or the overnight trip ($400), which includes lodging at Phantom Ranch and all meals. Riders must be at least 4ft

7in tall, speak fluent English and weigh less than 200lbs. Keep in mind that this is no carnival ride – these journeys are hot, dusty and bumpy.

SLEEPING

The South Rim's six lodges are operated by **Xanterra** (☎ 888-297-2757; www.grandcanyonlodges.com) – use this phone number to make advance reservations (highly recommended) at any of the places (including Phantom Ranch) listed here. For same-day reservations, call the **South Rim switchboard** (☎ 928-638-2631). If you can't find accommodations in the national park, try Tusayan (at South Entrance Station), Valle (31 miles south), Cameron (53 miles east) or Williams (about 60 miles south).

Desert View Campground (campsites $12; ☒ mid-May–mid-Oct) Near the East Entrance, 25 miles east of Grand Canyon Village, this first come, first served campground is a quieter alternative to Mather. A small cafeteria–snack shop serves meals.

Mather Campground (☎ 877-444-6777; www.recreation.gov; Grand Canyon Village; campsites $18-50; ☒ year-round) Offers well-dispersed, relatively peaceful sites amid piñon and juniper trees. There are pay showers and laundry facilities nearby, drinking water, toilets, grills, and a small general store.

Bright Angel Lodge (Grand Canyon Village; dm $52, r & cabins $70-143; ☒ ☒) Built in 1935, the log-and-stone Bright Angel offers historic charm and refurbished rooms. The least expensive doubles are simple, with shared baths, and there's also a convenient dorm for hikers. Rim cabins have awesome views.

Phantom Ranch (dm/cabins $34/92) At the bottom of the canyon, the ranch offers basic cabins sleeping four to 10 people, and segregated dorms. Most cabins are reserved for overnight mule tours, but hikers may make reservations if space is available. The ranch serves hearty family-style meals ($22 to $35) at dinner and breakfast ($18) and box lunches ($10). If you lack a reservation, show up at the Bright Angel Lodge transportation desk at 6am to snag any canceled bunks.

ourpick **El Tovar Hotel** (Grand Canyon Village; d/ste $142/322; ✕ ⚅) Built by Hopi craftsmen and filled with Arts and Crafts–style chairs, stained glass and exposed beams, this quintessential 1905 national park lodge attracts visitors seeking more than a roadside motel. Wide inviting porches wreathe the rambling wooden structure, offering pleasant spots to people-watch and admire canyon views. Even if you're not a guest, stop by to relax with a book on the porch swing or a drink on the patio. The public spaces hint at the genteel elegance of the park's heyday. The standard rooms here are on the small side but offer high standards of comfort. Suites are fantastic.

Also recommended:

Kachina Lodge & Thunderbird Lodge (Grand Canyon Village; r $132-152; ✕ ⚅) Nice motel-style rooms, some with canyon views.

Maswik Lodge (Grand Canyon Village; r $77-138, cabins $79; ✕ ⚅) Variety of options, including rooms with private patios, high ceilings and forest views.

Trailer Village (Grand Canyon Village; campsites & RV sites $28; ⚘ year-round) Camp here if everywhere else is full.

Yavapai Lodge (Grand Canyon Village; r $97-126; ⚘ mid-Feb–mid-Nov; ✕) Basic lodging amid peaceful piñon and juniper forest.

EATING & DRINKING

El Tovar and Bright Angel Lodge offer creative menus and surprisingly good food.

El Tovar Dining Room (☎ 928-638-2631; El Tovar Hotel, Grand Canyon Village; dishes $12-25; ⚘ 6:30am-2pm & 5-10pm) White linen–covered tables set with china and huge picture windows with canyon views create a memorable ambience. The service is excellent, the menu creative, the portions big and the food very good. Reservations required for dinner.

RUNNING THE COLORADO

The King Kong of rivers, the Colorado is an epic, adrenaline-pumping adventure. While 'normal' rapids are rated I through V (with five being pretty damn tuff), the 160-plus rapids on the Colorado merit their own scale, I to X, with many rapids a V or higher and two classified as X. This is not a river to take for granted – people die here. You should always wear your life vest, listen closely to your guide and give this river the respect it deserves. If you do, you'll likely emerge unscathed.

Unless you're already on the waiting list for a permit (see www.nps.gov/grca/planyourvisit/whitewater-rafting.htm), you can't run the Colorado on a private trip and you'll need to join a commercial one. Here the biggest decision is picking a boat – oar-, paddle- or motor-driven. Motorized trips are generally the least scary option. The huge inflatable boats go twice as fast and tend to be more stable. Oar boats are the most common vessels on the river. They give you the excitement of riding a smaller raft, but the guide does all the rowing – thus retaining control on the big rapids. For heart-attack fun, join a paddle trip (meaning everyone in the boat rows). Flipping is pretty much guaranteed, and you're completely dependent on fellow shipmates' paddling skills (depending on your attitude, it's either bad news or the ultimate rush).

River nights are spent camping (gear provided) under the stars on sandy beaches. It's not as primitive as it might sound – guides are legendary for their combination of white-water abilities, gastronomy and information.

Given two or three weeks, you can run the entire 279 miles of river through the canyon. Three shorter sections (each 100 miles or less) take four to nine days. Trip costs vary significantly, depending on luxury level and transfer options, but figure about $200 to $300 per day. Book six to 12 months in advance. Recommended outfitters:

■ **Arizona River Runners** (☎ 800-477-7238; www.raftarizona.com)

■ **OARS** (☎ 209-736-4677; www.oars.com)

■ **Outdoors Unlimited** (☎ 928-526-4511; www.outdoorsunlimited.com)

Arizona Room (Bright Angel Lodge, Grand Canyon Village; dishes $8-26; ☻ 11:30am-3pm & 4:30-10pm Mar-Oct, 4:30-10pm Nov & Dec) With a wonderful balance between casual and upscale, this restaurant is another fantastic option. Antler chandeliers hang from the ceiling, and picture windows overlook the canyon. Mains include steak, chicken and fish dishes. No reservations, and there's often a wait.

Bright Angel Restaurant (Bright Angel Lodge, Grand Canyon Village; dishes $8-13; ☻ 6:30am-10pm) This family-style restaurant serves burgers, fajitas, lasagne and other simple dishes. With few windows and no canyon views, it's a bit dark and the least inviting full-scale dining restaurant.

Also:

Canyon Café at Yavapai Lodge (Yavapai Lodge, Grand Canyon Village; dishes $5-9; ☻ 6am-10pm) Cafeteria food, service and seating.

Deli at Marketplace (Grand Canyon Village; dishes $6; ☻ 8am-7pm, 7am-8pm summer) Fresh takeaway sandwiches and hot dishes.

Maswik Cafeteria (Maswik Lodge, Grand Canyon Village; dishes $5-9; ☻ 6am-10pm) Another cafeteria-style place.

GETTING THERE & AROUND

Most people arrive at the canyon in private vehicles or on a tour. **Open Road Tours** (☎ 928-226-8060, 800-766-7117; www.openroadtours.com) runs shuttles from Phoenix Sky Harbor International Airport ($75, one daily) and Flagstaff ($27, two daily).

Free shuttles operate along three routes: around Grand Canyon Village, west along Hermits Rest Route and east along Kaibab Trail Route. Buses run at least twice per hour.

Havasu Canyon

In the heart of the Havasupai Indian Reservation, about 195 miles west of the South Rim, the hidden valley around Havasu Canyon has four gorgeous spring-fed waterfalls and enchanting azure swimming holes. The falls lie 10 miles below the rim, accessed via a moderately challenging hiking trail, and trips require an overnight stay in the village of Supai (near the falls). Do not try to hike down and back in one day – not only is it dangerous but also it doesn't allow time to see the falls.

Supai offers two sleeping options, and reservations must be secured before starting out. The **Havasupai Lodge** (☎ 928-448-2111; www.havasupaitribe.com/lodge.html; r $145; ✂ ✂) has motel rooms with canyon views and no phones or TVs. A village café serves meals and accepts credit cards. The **Havasupai Campground** (☎ 928-448-2121; per person adult/child $17/8.50), 2 miles past Supai, has primitive campsites along a creek. There's a $35 entrance fee ($17 for children) for all overnight guests. In addition, every camper must pay a $5 environmental fee, which is refunded if you pack out trash.

After a night in Supai, continue through Havasu Canyon to the waterfalls and sparkling blue-green swimming holes. If you don't want to hike to Supai, call the lodge or campground to arrange for a mule or horse ($150 round-trip) to carry you there. Rides depart from Hualapai Hilltop, where the hiking trail begins. The road to Hualapai Hilltop is 7 miles east of Peach Springs off Route 66. Look for the marked turnoff and follow the road for 62 miles.

Grand Canyon West

A highly controversial yet fascinating case of 'if you build it, they will come,' the **Grand Canyon Skywalk** (☎ 702-878-9378, 877-716-9378, www.destinationgrandcanyon.com; Diamond Bar Rd; admission incl lunch $75; ☻ 8am-4:30pm winter, 7am-8pm summer) is a slender see-through glass horseshoe bridge that levitates over a 4000ft chasm of the Grand Canyon.

The Hualapai tribe owns a million acres of the Grand Canyon, and the Skywalk is their bid to attract tourism by giving visitors a novel canyon experience. The remote site is 70 miles northeast of Kingman, and the last 14 miles are rough, unpaved and unsuitable for RVs. To prevent scuffing of the five-layer glass floor, visitors must wear surgical overshoes, and all personal effects (including cameras and phones) are forbidden on the glass (in case you drop them). Looking down into the abyss, the Skywalk's shadow appears like a partial halo.

Environmentalists have decried the Skywalk as an eyesore desecrating an otherwise pristine landmark. There have been disagreements within the tribe over building the attraction, but most of its members now back it as a viable means of self-support.

North Rim

Far from the parade of tour buses down south, the North Rim retains a sense of solitude. If the crowds on the South Rim make you cringe, this is where to head for wild isolation.

In fact, the area is so remote it sees only 10% of park visitors. Meadows are thick with wildflowers and dense clusters of willowy aspen and spruce trees, and the air is often crisp, the skies vast and blue.

Facilities on the North Rim are closed from mid-October to mid-May, although you can drive into the park and stay at the campground until the first snow closes the road from Jacob Lake.

SIGHTS & ACTIVITIES

The short and easy paved trail (0.3 miles) to **Bright Angel Point** is a canyon must. Beginning from the back porch of Grand Canyon Lodge, it goes to a narrow finger of an overlook with fabulous views. It's popular for sunrise and sunset walks, but visit after dusk for unparalleled stargazing.

The **North Kaibab Trail** is the North Rim's only maintained rim-to-river trail and connects with trails to the South Rim. The first 4.7 miles are the steepest, dropping well over 3000ft to **Roaring Springs** – a popular all-day hike. If you prefer a shorter day hike below the rim, walk just 0.75 miles down to **Coconino Overlook** or a mile to the **Supai Tunnel** to get a flavor for steep inner-canyon hiking.

Canyon Trail Rides (☎ 435-679-8665; www.canyon rides.com; Grand Canyon Lodge) offers one-hour mule trips ($30) along the rim and half- or full-day trips into the canyon. The full-day, seven-hour trip ($125, minimum age 12 years) departs at 7:30am. Lunch and water are provided. Half-day trips ($65, minimum age 10 years) leave at 7:30am and 12:30pm.

SLEEPING

Accommodations within the North Rim are limited to one lodge and one campground. If these are booked, try your luck 80 miles north in Kanab, UT, or 84 miles northeast in Lees Ferry. There are also campgrounds in the Kaibab National Forest north of the park.

our pick **Grand Canyon Lodge** (☎ 928-638-2611; www.grandcanyonnorthrim.com; r & cabins $103-148; ☻ mid-May–mid-Oct; ✗) By far our favorite sleeping option in the park (perhaps in any US national park), this lodge made of wood, stone and glass is the kind of place you imagine should be perched on the rim. The canyon views from the Sun Room are stunning, the lobby regal. Rustic, yet modern, cabins make up the majority of accommodations. Reserve far in advance.

North Rim Campground (☎ 877-444-6777; www .recreation.gov; campsites $18) This campground, 1.5 miles north of Grand Canyon Lodge, offers pleasant sites on level ground blanketed in pine needles. There is water, a store, a snack bar, and coin-operated showers and laundry facilities, but no hookups. Reservations accepted.

EATING & DRINKING

Grand Canyon Lodge Dining Room (☎ 928-638-2611; Grand Canyon Lodge; dishes $9-20; ☻ 6:30am-10am, 11:30am-2:30pm & 4:45-9:45pm) Some people get downright belligerent if they can't get a window seat at this wonderful spot with panoramic views. The windows are so huge, however, that it really doesn't matter where you sit. The solid menu includes several vegetarian options. Dinner reservations are required.

Rough Rider Saloon (☎ 928-638-2611; ☻ 5:30-10:30am & 11:30am-11pm) For a drink and a browse of the Teddy Roosevelt memorabilia, visit this popular watering hole adjacent to the Grand Canyon Lodge. Take your drink to the stone patio behind the lodge, where rough-hewn rocking chairs face the rim and a blazing fire on chilly nights. Rangers offer talks (sometimes even providing telescopes for stargazing). Espresso drinks and breakfast pastries ($2 to $3) are served in the morning.

GETTING THERE & AROUND

The **Transcanyon Shuttle** (☎ 928-638-2820; tickets 1-way/round-trip $70/130; ☻ 7am mid-May–mid-Oct) departs daily from Grand Canyon Lodge for the South Rim (five hours). Credit cards are not accepted; reserve at least one or two weeks in advance. A hikers' shuttle (from $2) to the North Kaibab Trail departs at both 5:20am and 7:20am from Grand Canyon Lodge. You can sign up the night before at the front desk.

NORTHEASTERN ARIZONA

Some of Arizona's most beautiful and photogenic landscapes lie in the northeastern corner of the state. Between the fabulous buttes of Monument Valley, the shimmering blue waters of Lake Powell and the fossilized logs of the Petrified Forest National Park are lands locked in ancient history. Inhabited by Native Americans for centuries, this region is largely made up of reservation land belonging to the Navajo and Hopi.

SOUTHWEST

Lake Powell

An enormous lake tucked into a landlocked swath of desert? You can guess how popular it is to play at Lake Powell. The country's second-largest artificial reservoir and part of the **Glen Canyon National Recreation Area** (☎ 928-608-6200; www.nps.gov/glca; admission vehicle/boat $15/16), the lake stretches between Utah and Arizona. Set amid striking red-rock formations, sharply cut canyons and dramatic desert scenery, it's water sports heaven. South of the lake and looking out over a scenic stretch of the Colorado River, **Lees Ferry** (campsites $12) is a pleasant stopover.

The region's central town is **Page**, and Hwy 89 forms the main strip. The **Carl Hayden Visitor Center** (☎ 928-608-6404; 8am-7pm late May-early Sep, to 4pm rest of yr) is located at the dam, 2 miles north of Page. Free one-hour tours (occurring multiple times daily) take you inside the dam.

To visit photogenic **Antelope Canyon** (www .navajonationparks.org/htm/antelopecanyon.htm), the stunning sandstone slot canyon in all the regional picture books, you must join a tour. The Navajo-owned and -operated **Antelope Canyon Tours** (☎ 928-645-9102; www.antelopecanyon .com; 22 S Lake Powell Blvd) is recommended.

Chain hotels line Hwy 89 in Page. One inexpensive and welcoming indie choice is **Bashful Bob's Motel** (☎ 928-645-3919; www.bashful bobsmotel.com; 750 S Navajo Dr; r $39;), which was constructed to house Glen Canyon dam builders. All 13 rooms are more like apartments, with full kitchens.

Six miles north of Page and with a direct view of the lake, the **Lake Powell Resort** (☎ 928-645-2433, 800-528-6154; www.lakepowell.com; 100 Lake Shore Dr; d $132-182, RV sites $32; wi-fi) offers basic rooms, camping, houseboat rentals and a dining room with panoramic views.

For breakfast in Page, the **Ranch House Grille** (☎ 928-645-1420; 819 N Navajo Dr; dishes $6-11; 6am-3pm) has good food, huge portions and fast service. BBQ dinners are featured at the cavernous **Dam Bar & Grille** (☎ 928-645-2161; 644 N Navajo Dr; lunch $6, dinner mains $18-20; 11am-10pm), which becomes a popular bar at night.

Navajo Indian Reservation

The wounds are healing, but the scars remain, a testament to the nastiest, most devastating chapter of US history – the uprooting and forced relocation of thousands of Native Americans to reservations. After a prolonged and merciless campaign in Canyon De Chelly, Colonel Kit Carson defeated the Navajo Nation, or Diné, in 1864. Banished to the Bosque Redondo reservation in Fort Sumner, New Mexico (p893), between 8000 and 9000 people made a grueling 300-mile death march now know as the Long Walk. After four disastrous years of near-starvation and military control, they were finally permitted to return.

The evidence of hard times can be seen everywhere, from the rusting tumbledown trailers to social services buildings in small nowhere towns. And amid all the isolation is some of North America's most spectacular scenery, including Monument Valley. In the 250,000-strong Nation, culture and pride remain strong, and many still speak Navajo as their first language. The Navajo rely on the tourist economy to survive; help keep their heritage alive by choosing to stay on reservation land or purchasing their renowned crafts.

Unlike Arizona, the Navajo Reservation observes Mountain daylight saving time. During summer, the reservation is one hour ahead of Arizona.

WINDOW ROCK

The tribal capital is at Window Rock, a bustling little place at the intersection of Hwys 264 and 12. Information about the whole reservation is available from the **Navajo Tourism Office** (☎ 928-810-8501; www.discovernavajo .com; 8am-5pm Mon-Fri) in the center of town. The **Navajo Nation Council Chambers** (☎ 928-871-6417), where the legislature holds session, are painted with murals depicting Navajo history and culture.

The **Navajo Nation Museum & Library** (☎ 928-871-7941; cnr Hwy 264 & Post Office Loop Rd; admission by donation; 8am-5pm Mon, to 8pm Tue-Fri, 9am-5pm Sat) features permanent collections, changing shows and the tribal library.

The **Annual Navajo Nation Fair**, held for several days in early September, is one of the world's largest Native American events, with an intertribal powwow, Native American rodeo, and traditional song and dance displays.

Rooms at the **Quality Inn Navajo Nation Capital** (☎ 928-871-4108, 800-662-6189; www.quality innwindowrock.com; 48 W Hwy 264; r incl breakfast $73-88;) feature Southwestern motifs. The on-site restaurant serves Navajo and American fare.

SOUTHWEST

The **Navajo Transit System** (☎ 928-729-4002; www.nts.navajo.org) runs buses from Window Rock to Gallup, NM ($2.55, one hour, four daily weekdays) and Tuba City ($13, four hours, 3pm weekdays), via the Hopi Indian Reservation.

HUBBELL TRADING POST NATIONAL HISTORIC SITE

Thirty miles west of Window Rock in the town of Ganado, this is the oldest operating **trading post** (☎ 928-755-3475; www.nps.gov/hutr; admission free; ☺ 8am-6pm May-Sep, to 5pm Oct-Apr) on the Navajo Nation. It looks much as it would have after John Lorenzo Hubbell established it in 1878, and you can tour ($2) his former home. Local artisans sell local crafts and jewelry, including top-quality Navajo weavings.

CANYON DE CHELLY NATIONAL MONUMENT

This many-fingered canyon contains several beautiful Ancestral Puebloan sites important to Navajo history. Families still farm the land, wintering on the rims, then moving to hogans on the canyon floor in spring and summer. The canyon is private Navajo property administered by the NPS. Enter hogans only with a guide and don't photograph people without their permission.

Most of the bottom of the canyon is off-limits to visitors unless you hire a guide. Find out more at the **visitor center** (☎ 928-674-5500; www.nps.gov/cach; ☺ 8am-5pm) in the small village of Chinle. **Justin Horseback Tours** (☎ 928-674-5678), near the visitor center, has horses available for $15 per person per hour, plus $15 an hour for the guide.

Also near the visitor center, **Cottonwood Campground** (campsites free) has 93 large sites on a first come, first served basis, with water but no showers. The **Thunderbird Lodge** (☎ 928-674-5841; www.tbirdlodge.com; d $106-145; ☒) has comfortable rooms, an on-site ATM, and an inexpensive cafeteria serving tasty Navajo and American meals ($6 to $12).

FOUR CORNERS NAVAJO TRIBAL PARK

Don't be shy, do a spread-eagle for the folks at home. Put a foot into Arizona and plant the other in New Mexico. Slap a hand in Utah and place the other in Colorado. This is the only place in the USA where four states come together at one point – well worth the $3 admission fee.

MONUMENT VALLEY NAVAJO TRIBAL PARK

It's just an opinion, but this park might have the most stunning scenery in America. Period. With flaming-red buttes and impossibly slender spires bursting to the heavens, the landscape has starred in countless Hollywood Westerns and looms large in all of your wildest road-trip fantasies.

Great views can be had from along Hwy 163, but to really get up close and personal, you'll need to visit the **Monument Valley Navajo Tribal Park** (☎ 435-727-5870; admission per person $5; ☺ 6am-9pm May-Sep, 8am-5pm Oct-Apr). The visitor center houses exhibits and has a blissfully cold water fountain and a restaurant. From the visitor center, a rough and unpaved **scenic drive** (☺ 6am-8:30pm May-Sep, 8am-4:40pm Oct-Apr) loop covers 17 miles of stunning valley views. You can drive it in your own vehicle or take a tour ($55, 2½ hours). One advantage here is that tours enter areas private vehicles can't. If you want to mosey through at a more relaxed gait, join a horseback ride ($55). Tour company kiosks are located in the parking area.

At the time of research, the closest hotel was Goulding's Lodge (see p868), just inside Utah. However, the tribe is building a new resort hotel, The **View at Monument Valley** (☎ 435-727-3470), which is slated to open in 2008. For the time being, visitors can overnight in its primitive de facto **campground** (per vehicle $5). It's basically just a parking lot, but the awesome sunrise more than makes up for the lack of amenities. Don't sleep in.

WORTH THE TRIP – NAVAJO NATIONAL MONUMENT

The exceptionally well-preserved Ancestral Puebloan sites of Betatkin and Keet Seel in the **Navajo National Monument** (☎ 928-672-2700; Hwy 564; admission free; ☺ 8am-5pm) don't attract busloads of tourists, probably because it's a 5-mile round-trip hike to Betatkin and a 17-mile round-trip slog to Keet Seel. Daily hiking permits are free but limited. Call to reserve one in advance or stop by the visitor center, 9 miles north of Hwy 160 along Hwy 564. Both sites can be visited only on ranger-guided tours. There's a **campground** (campsites free) at the visitor center.

Hopi Indian Reservation

The oldest, most traditional and religious tribe in Arizona (if not the entire continent), the Hopi are a private people who have received less outside influence than most other tribes. Villages, many built between AD 1400 and AD 1700, dot the isolated mesas. **Old Oraibi**, inhabited since the early 12th century, vies with Acoma Pueblo in New Mexico for the title of oldest continuously inhabited town in North America.

Hwy 264 runs past the three mesas (First, Second and Third Mesa) that form the heart of the reservation. There are no banks, and cash is preferred for most transactions. Photographs, sketching and recording are not allowed – *don't even ask*.

At the end of First Mesa, the tiny village of **Walpi** (c 1600) juts out into space from the top of a spectacularly narrow mesa; it's the most dramatic of the Hopi villages. The friendly **tourist office** (☎ 928-737-2262) can arrange guided walking tours (adult/child $8/5) several times daily. To reach Walpi, look for signs to First Mesa from Hwy 264 (around Mile 392), and follow the road to the parking area at the top of the mesa.

The Hopi are known for their kachina dolls, and these and other crafts can be purchased from individual artists in the villages and at roadside galleries.

The **Hopi Cultural Center Restaurant & Inn** (☎ 928-734-2401; www.hopiculturalcenter.com; r $90-95; dishes $7-9; ☺ 7am-8pm winter, 6am-9pm summer; ⚉), in Second Mesa, is the reservation's only hotel. The restaurant serves burgers, salads and Hopi dishes, such as *noqkwivi* (lamb and hominy stew). The Cultural Center's **museum** (☎ 928-734-6650; adult/child $3/1; ☺ 8am-5pm Mon-Fri) next door is a good first stop, with informative exhibits on Hopi history.

Winslow

'Standing on a corner in Winslow, Arizona, such a fine sight to see…' Sound familiar? Thanks to the Eagles' twangy '70s tune 'Take It Easy,' otherwise nonmemorable Winslow has earned its wings in pop culture heaven. A small plaza on Route 66 at Kinsley Ave, in the heart of old downtown, pays homage to the band with a life-sized bronze statue of a hitchhiker backed by a trompe l'oeil mural of the girl in a flatbed Ford.

Just 60 miles south of the Hopi mesas, Winslow makes a good regional base. About a dozen old motels are found along Route 66. The 1929 hacienda-style **La Posada** (☎ 928-289-4366; www.laposada.org; 303 E 2nd; r $99-149, ste $175; ⚉) is a dreamy choice. It was built as a railway hotel, and rooms are named for some of its renowned guests.

Petrified Forest National Park

Strewn with broken, horizontal fossilized logs predating the dinosaurs, this **national park** (☎ 928-524-6228; www.nps.gov/pefo; per vehicle $10) is an extraordinary site. The petrified-wood fragments are quite exquisite, and many are infused with startlingly deep color. The park's appeal is heightened by the stunning landscape of the Painted Desert, which changes hue as the sun shifts across the sky. The kaleidoscope of reds, pinks and oranges combined with the 225-million-year-old pieces of wood is a beautiful, almost haunting, sight.

The park straddles I-40 at exit 311, 25 miles east of Holbrook. From this exit, a 28-mile paved park road offers a splendid **scenic drive**. Apart from short trails at some of the pullouts, there are no maintained trails, campsites or accommodations.

WESTERN ARIZONA

The Colorado River is alive with sun-worshippers at Lake Havasu City, while Route 66 offers well-preserved stretches of classic highway near Kingman. South of I-10, the wild, empty landscape is among the most rugged in the West.

Kingman & Around

Back when Route 66 was still the Mother Road, Kingman was a bigger deal. Today it's just another fast-fading relic, a few decades past its prime. Run-down motels, ugly billboards and gas stations galore grace its main drag. But several turn-of-the-19th-century buildings remain. If you're following the Route 66 trail, or looking for cheap lodging, it's worth a stroll.

Pick up self-guided walking-tour maps at the **Powerhouse Visitor Center** (☎ 928-753-6106; 120 W Andy Devine Ave; ☺ 9am-6pm, to 5pm Dec-Feb), which has a **Route 66 museum** (admission $3) opposite Locomotive Park.

The atmospheric 1909 **Hotel Brunswick** (☎ 928-718-1800; www.hotel-brunswick.com; 315 E Andy Devine Ave; r incl breakfast $35-66; ⚉ 💻) has rock-bottom-budget cowboy/girl rooms with single beds and shared baths, as well as nicer digs with larger beds, TVs and private baths. Its on-site restaurant, the **Hubbs Brunswick Bistro** (dishes $20-30; ☽ 11am-2pm & 5-9pm Mon-Fri, 5-9pm Sat), is a fabulous gourmet bistro serving pasta, steaks and seafood.

A former gold-mining town, **Oatman**, southwest of Kingman, is now a hokey but spirited tourist haunt, with gunfights at high noon and wild burros roaming the streets. It puts on wacky annual events like a 4th of July Sidewalk Egg Fry and an International Burro Biscuit Toss for Labor Day.

Lake Havasu City

When the city of London auctioned off its 1831 bridge in the late 1960s, developer Robert McCulloch bought it for $2.5 million, disassembled it into 10,276 granite slabs, transported the 10,000 tons of stone and then reassembled it at Lake Havasu City, which sits along a dammed-up portion of the Colorado River. The place attracts hordes of young spring breakers and weekend warriors who come to play in the water and party hard. An 'English Village' of pseudo-British pubs and tourist gift shops surrounds the bridge.

The **visitors bureau** (☎ 928-453-3444; www.golake havasu.com; 314 London Bridge Rd) has information on tours and boat rentals.

With pools, nightclubs, hot tubs and restaurants, **London Bridge Resort & Convention Center** (☎ 928-855-0888, 866-331-9231; www .londonbridgeresort.com; 1477 Queens Bay; ste $179-359; ✷ ❧ ▯ wi-fi) attracts a playful crowd. Units feature either one or two bedrooms with kitchenettes.

Fresh seafood is the main draw at popular **Shugrue's** (☎ 928-453-1400; 1425 McCulloch Blvd; dishes lunch $8-12, dinner $23-27; ☽ 11am-3pm & 4:30-9pm). **Mudshark Brewing Co** (☎ 928-453-2981; 210 Swanson Ave; dishes $8-20; ☽ 11am-10pm Sun & Mon, to 10:30pm Fri & Sat) serves excellent handcrafted brews like a light Up River Lager, and has classic pizza and burger choices.

Yuma

In the blazing-hot birthplace of farmworker organizer César Chávez, the sun is always out. This is Arizona's sunniest, driest and third largest metropolitan area. With winter temperatures around 70°F (20°C), Yuma lures retirees by the thousands to the scores of trailer parks around town. But despite its popularity with snowbirds (retired winter visitors), Yuma doesn't offer much for travelers. However, if it's freezing in Tucson, you might just want to shack up here for a few days.

The **visitors center** (☎ 928-783-0071; www.visit yuma.com; 377 S Main St; ☽ 9am-5pm Mon-Fri, to 2pm Sat May-Oct, 9am-6pm Mon-Fri, to 4pm Sat, 10am-2pm Sun Nov-Apr) has all the area information. The town's number-one tourist attraction is the **Yuma Territorial Prison State Historic Park** (☎ 928-783-4771; www.pr.state.az.us; 1 Prison Hill Rd; adult/child $4/free; ☽ 8am-5pm). Between 1876 and 1909, it housed 3069 of Arizona's most feared criminals, including 29 women. Today it's a slightly gruesome, mildly historic, offbeat attraction and museum suitable for the whole family.

For sleeping, try **La Fuente Inn & Suites** (☎ 928-329-1814, 877-202-3353; www.lafuenteinn.com; 1513 E 16th St; r incl full breakfast $87-119; ✷ ❧ ▯). In a modern, Spanish colonial–style building surrounded by gardens, the spacious rooms with kitchenettes are mainly one- or two-room suites. There's an evening social hour with complimentary cocktails, as well as a fitness room.

A chic and funky gourmet eatery, the **River City Grill** (☎ 928-782-7988; 600 W 3rd St; dishes $15-22; ☽ 11:30am-2pm & 5-10pm Mon-Fri, 5-10pm Sat & Sun) has scrumptious dishes like crab cakes and brie-stuffed chicken, as well as half a dozen exceptional vegetarian entrées.

SOUTHWEST

TUCSON

A bustling college town where freight trains rumble and old West meets south of the border, Tucson is Arizona's second-largest city, but it still exudes a small town feel. Distinct neighborhoods and 19th-century buildings give it a rich sense of community and history not found in the more modern and sprawling Phoenix, which boasts a more cosmopolitan (though disputably soulless) energy.

Attractive, fun and one of the most culturally invigorating places in the Southwest, Tucson is set in a flat valley surrounded by craggy, oddly shaped mountains. The place is rich in Hispanic heritage (more than 20% of the population is of Mexican or Central American descent), so Spanish slides easily off most tongues and high-quality Mexican restaurants abound. The eclectic shops touting vintage garb, scores of funky restaurants and dive bars don't let you forget Tucson is a college town at heart, home turf to the 35,000-strong University of Arizona (U of A).

Orientation & Information

Downtown Tucson and the historic district are east of I-10 exit 258. About a mile northeast of downtown is the U of A campus; 4th Ave is the main drag here, packed with cafés, bars and interesting shops.

Though the highway will remain open, a number of I-10's on- and off-ramps in Tucson will be closed for construction through spring 2010. The **Arizona Department of Transportation** (www.i10tucsondistrict.com) posts traffic updates.

BOOKSTORES

Bookman's (☎ 520-325-5657; 1930 E Grant Rd) Great selection of used books, music and magazines.

EMERGENCY & MEDICAL SERVICES

Police (☎ 520-791-4444; 270 S Stone Ave)
Tucson Medical Center (☎ 520-327-5461; 5301 E Grant Rd; ⏰ 24hr emergency)

INTERNET ACCESS

Main library (☎ 520-791-4393; 101 N Stone Ave) Free internet access.

MEDIA

The local newspapers are the morning *Arizona Daily Star*, the afternoon *Tucson Citizen* and the free *Tucson Weekly*, full of great entertainment and restaurant listings.

MONEY

ATMs are abundant. Foreign exchange is available at most banks; $5 is charged if you don't have an account. The Tucson International Airport doesn't exchange currency.

POST

Post office (☎ 520-903-1958, 800-275-8777; 141 S 6th Ave)

TOURIST INFORMATION

Tucson Convention & Visitors Bureau (☎ 520-624-1817; www.visittucson.org; Ste 7199, 110 S Church Ave; ⏰ 9am-5pm Mon-Fri, to 4pm Sat & Sun)

Sights & Activities

The 19th-century buildings and craft stores in the **Presidio Historic District**, between Court and Main Aves and Franklin and Alameda Sts, are worth a wander.

The **Santa Catalina Mountains** are the best-loved and most visited of Tucson's many mountain ranges. Head to Sabino Canyon, where you'll find the **USFS ranger station** (☎ 520-749-8700; 5700 N Sabino Canyon Rd; per vehicle $5; ⏰ 8am-4:30pm Mon-Fri, 8:30am-4:30pm Sat & Sun). Maps, hiking guides and information are available.

The internationally renowned **Center for Creative Photography** (☎ 520-621-7968; www.creativephotography.org; 1030 N Olive Ave; admission free; ⏰ 9am-5pm Mon-Fri, noon-5pm Sat & Sun), on the University of Arizona campus, has a great collection of works by American photographers, interesting gallery shows and a remarkable archive (including most of Ansel Adams' and Edward Weston's work).

The Pima Air and Space Museum leads tours through the almost 5000 military airplanes mothballed at **Davis-Monthan Air Force Base** (☎ 520-574-0462; www.pimaair.org; 6000 E Valencia Rd; adult/child $6/3; ⏰ Mon-Fri), also known as AMARC or simply 'the Boneyard.' Call for tour times.

To go **horseback riding** amid cacti and scrub brush, visit one of several stables offering excursions by the hour, half-day or longer. Summer trips tend to be short breakfast or sunset rides. One of the most reputable companies is **Pusch Ridge Stables** (☎ 928-825-1664; 13700 N Oracle Rd; rides from $30), which also offers overnight pack trips.

Festivals & Events

The **Tucson Gem and Mineral Show** (☎ 520-332-5773; www.tgms.org), in early February, is the largest

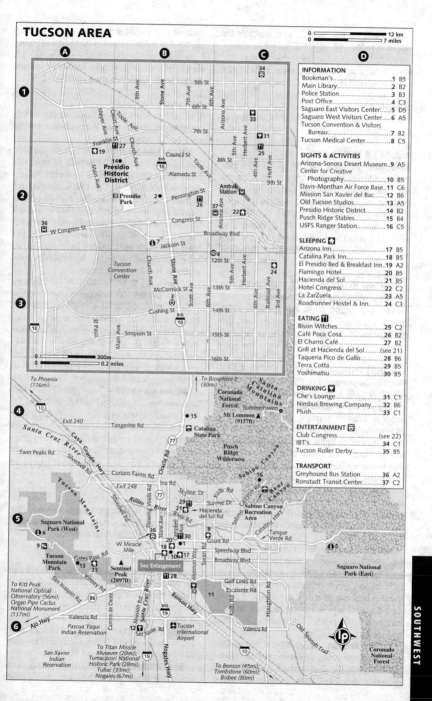

TUCSON AREA

0	12 km
0	7 miles

INFORMATION

Bookman's.....................................**1** B5	
Main Library...............................**2** B2	
Police Station..............................**3** B3	
Post Office...................................**4** C3	
Saguaro East Visitors Center.....**5** D5	
Saguaro West Visitors Center.....**6** A5	
Tucson Convention & Visitors	
Bureau.....................................**7** B2	
Tucson Medical Center...............**8** C5	

SIGHTS & ACTIVITIES

Arizona-Sonora Desert Museum..**9** A5	
Center for Creative	
Photography...........................**10** B5	
Davis-Monthan Air Force Base..**11** C6	
Mission San Xavier del Bac......**12** B6	
Old Tucson Studios...................**13** A5	
Presidio Historic District...........**14** B2	
Pusch Ridge Stables..................**15** B4	
USFS Ranger Station.................**16** C5	

SLEEPING

Arizona Inn...............................**17** B5	
Catalina Park Inn......................**18** B5	
El Presidio Bed & Breakfast Inn.**19** A2	
Flamingo Hotel..........................**20** B5	
Hacienda del Sol.......................**21** B5	
Hotel Congress..........................**22** C2	
La ZarZuela..............................**23** A5	
Roadrunner Hostel & Inn...........**24** C3	

EATING

Bison Witches...........................**25** C2	
Café Poca Cosa........................**26** B2	
El Charro Café..........................**27** B2	
Grill at Hacienda del Sol...........(see 21)	
Taqueria Pico de Gallo..............**28** B6	
Terra Cotta..............................**29** B5	
Yoshimatsu...............................**30** B5	

DRINKING

Che's Lounge...........................**31** C1	
Nimbus Brewing Company........**32** B6	
Plush.......................................**33** C1	

ENTERTAINMENT

Club Congress..........................(see 22)	
IBT's..**34** C1	
Tucson Roller Derby..................**35** B5	

TRANSPORT

Greyhound Bus Station..............**36** A2	
Ronstadt Transit Center.............**37** C2	

SOUTHWEST

of its kind in the world. The **Fiesta de los Vaqueros rodeo** (☎ 520-741-2233; www.tucsonrodeo .com) is held during the last week of February, and the huge nonmotorized parade is a locally famous spectacle.

Sleeping

Lodging prices vary considerably, with lower rates in summer and fall.

BUDGET & MIDRANGE

Roadrunner Hostel & Inn (☎ 520-628-4709; www .roadrunnerhostelinn.com; incl breakfast dm $20, r with shared bath $38; ✗ ✗ ▢ wi-fi) Located in a quiet residential neighborhood within walking distance of the arts district, this comfortable hostel has a large kitchen, free coffee and DIY waffles in the morning, and a big-screen TV for watching movies. Look for the mini-railroad outside. Note that dorms close for afternoon cleaning.

Flamingo Hotel (☎ 800-300-3533, 520-770-1910; www.flamingoholteltucson.com; 1300 N Stone Ave; r incl breakfast $49-69; P ✗ ✗ ✗ ▢ wi-fi) A classic 1950s motel festooned with old film posters, this place is an affectionate homage to Tucson's movie history. Elvis fans pay heed: the King stayed in room 102.

ourpick Hotel Congress (☎ 520-622-8848, 800-722-8848; www.hotelcongress.com; 311 E Congress St; r $79-99; P ✗ ▢ wi-fi) A groovy historic hotel with a hip rock-and-roll flavor, the Congress is a nonstop buzz of activity, mostly because of its popular bar and nightclub downstairs. In 1934, infamous bank robber John Dillinger was captured after a fire broke out while he was holed up here under an alias. Many of its rooms have period furnishings, like old wooden radios and rotary phones. The place rocks out in the evenings, so ask for a room at the far end of the hotel if you plan to turn in early. Bands playing across the street at the Rialto often stay here.

El Presidio Bed & Breakfast Inn (☎ 520-635-6151; 800-349-6151; www.bbonline.com/az/elpresidio; 297 N Main Ave; r incl full breakfast $130-150; P ✗ ✗ ▢ wi-fi) In Tucson's most attractive historic district, the inn boasts a mix of Victorian and adobe architectural styles. Rooms feature antique furniture and original art. Afternoon drinks and treats are included.

Catalina Park Inn (☎ 520-792-4541, 800-792-4885; www.catalinaparkinn.com; 309 E First St; r incl full breakfast $136-166; P ✗ ✗ ▢ wi-fi) Much time was spent restoring this 1927 home, which has many

unique and creative touches and stunning gardens of native plants. The basement-level Catalina room is sprawling – it resembles a classic adobe and has a whirlpool in a former cedar closet. Children over 10 only.

TOP END

Tucson's ranches and resorts are often destinations in themselves. Rates drop dramatically in the summer.

Hacienda del Sol (☎ 520-299-1501, 800-728-6514; www.haciendadelsol.com; 5601 N Hacienda del Sol Rd; r/ste from $195/355; P ✗ ✗ ✗ ▢) An elite hilltop girls' school built in the 1920s, this refuge contains special touches like carved ceiling beams and louvered exterior doors to catch breezes from the Spanish-colonial courtyard. Spencer Tracy, Katharine Hepburn and other legendary stars overnighted here, and artists have individually styled each of the Mexican- and Southwest-chic rooms.

La ZarZuela (☎ 520-884-4824, 888-848-8225; www .zarzuela-az.com; 455 N Camino del Oeste; s/d incl full breakfast $275/325; P ✗ ✗ ✗ ▢ wi-fi) If you entertain fantasies of escaping to a remote artsy hide-away, this is your place. A gorgeous mansion in the foothills west of the city, it has five colorful casitas with wide-open terrace and porch views. Adults only; closed from mid-June through mid-September.

Arizona Inn (☎ 520-325-1541, 800-933-1093; www .arizonainn.com; 2200 E Elm St; r from $320; P ✗ ✗ ▢) The *grande dame* of Tucson hotels, this sedate and beautiful pink-stucco place provides tranquil respite from city life. Exuding grace and old-Arizona charm, rooms are spacious and decorated with original antiques or well-done reproductions.

Eating

Tucson has a well-deserved reputation for Sonoran Mexican food, and you'll be pleasantly surprised by the caliber of cooking.

BUDGET

Taqueria Pico de Gallo (☎ 520-623-8775; 2618 S 6th Ave; dishes $2-8; ⊙ 8am-9pm Mon-Thu & Sun, to 10pm Fri & Sat) A cheap and popular south-side institution, with huge *burros* (burritos) and mouth-watering shrimp tacos. The Paleteria Diana popsicle shop beckons just across the parking lot, with dozens of fruity Mexican favorites like guayaba and tamarind ($1.50).

Bison Witches (☎ 520-740-1541; 326 N 4th Ave; sandwiches $7; ⊙ 11am-midnight) Dive into a bread bowl at this lively hangout for college students and sports fans. The draw? Mongo sandwiches (with potato chips) served up on mini cafeteria trays. The music is boisterous, there are myriad TVs, and drinks are served till 2am.

Yoshimatsu (☎ 520-320-1574; 2660 N Campbell Ave; dishes $8-11; ☯ 11:30am-2:30pm & 5-9pm Sat-Thu, 11:30am-2:30pm & 5-10pm Fri) Billing itself as a 'healthy Japanese eatery,' Yoshimatsu uses no MSG and offers lots of vegetarian and vegan options, including fish-free soup stock. Order a bento box, rice bowl or curry at the counter and eat in the casual wooden dining room, or get table service at the separate and more intimate sushi bistro.

MIDRANGE & TOP END

El Charro Café (☎ 520-622-1922; 311 N Court Ave; dishes $8-18; ☯ 11am-9pm) The oldest place in town, with a charming courtyard patio, they say it has been in the same family since 1922. Its *carne seca* (dried beef) used to be dried on the roof in the old days. Today the Mexican food is innovative, mouth-watering and fresh, making it popular with tourists and locals alike.

Terra Cotta (☎ 520-577-8100; 3500 E Sunrise Dr; dishes $16-22; ☯ 10am-3pm Sun year-round, summer 4-9pm daily, winter 11:30am-3pm & 4-9pm Mon-Thu, 11:30am-3pm & 4-10pm Fri & Sat) This restaurant gets consistently high ratings for its wood-fired pizza, spicy pork tenderloin and other upscale Southwestern fare. The small-plate starters sound so appetizing that many people order two and forgo a main dish.

ourpick Café Poca Cosa (☎ 520-622-6400; 110 E Pennington St; dinner mains $16-25; ☯ 11am-9pm Tue-Thu, to 10pm Fri & Sat) This award-winning downtown bistro serves Nuevo-Mexican to rabidly rave reviews. A bilingual Spanish–English chalkboard menu circulates between tables because the dishes change twice daily. The excellent food incorporates many regions of Mexico, and it's freshly prepared, innovative and beautifully presented. Try the chef's choice; it changes with each plate and features three different entrees. The *mole* (classic Mexican chocolate sauce) and margaritas are also superb.

Grill at Hacienda del Sol (☎ 520-529-3500; 5601 N Hacienda del Sol Rd; Sunday brunch $32, dishes $30-36; ☯ 10:30am-1:30pm Sun, 5:30-10pm) Sunsets are the best time to appreciate the superb views of Tucson and the Santa Catalina Mountains from this formal dining room. An extensive wine list draws from a 20,000-bottle cellar,

and the first-class American fare changes seasonally. Reservations required for dinner.

Drinking & Entertainment

Downtown 4th Ave, near 6th St, is the happening barhop spot, and there are a number of nightclubs on downtown Congress St. Clubs showcase everything from DJs to live music.

Che's Lounge (☎ 520-623-2088; 346 N 4th Ave; ☯ noon-2am) If Comandante Che was still in our midst, he wouldn't have charged a cover either. A popular bar with $1 drafts, a huge wraparound bar and local art gracing the walls, it rocks out with live music Saturday nights.

Club Congress (☎ 520-622-8848; 311 E Congress St; cover $3-10) Live and DJ music are found at this very popular dance club. It attracts everyone from college kids to natty professionals to guests staying at Hotel Congress upstairs.

IBT's (☎ 520-882-3053; www.ibts.net; 616 N 4th Ave) At Tucson's best gay dance club, the theme changes nightly – from drag shows to dance mixes to karaoke.

Nimbus Brewing Company (☎ 520-745-9175; 3850 E 44th St; ☯ 11am-11pm Mon-Thu, to 1am Fri & Sat) A cavernous purple warehouse space southeast of downtown, here the tanks are just behind the bar and dining room, and you can see tap lines. It has a good selection of grill food to munch on, and though it's known for ales, the oatmeal stout is great. Rock and bluegrass bands play in the evenings Thursday through Sunday.

Plush (☎ 520-798-1298; 340 E 6th St; cover $5-10) A balm to the manic 4th Ave scene, the front of this club has a down-tempo scene with hipsters lounging on funky furniture. Secrete yourself in the back space for throbbing live-music sets.

Tucson Roller Derby (☎ 520-390-1454; www.tucson rollerderby.com; Bladeworld, 1065 W Grant Rd; tickets $8-10) Here there are badass women slamming on skates, and a fun time for all.

Getting There & Around

The **Tucson International Airport** (☎ 520-573-8000) is 10 miles south of downtown. The taxi fare from the airport to downtown is around $25. **Greyhound** (☎ 520-792-3475; 471 W Congress St) runs buses to Phoenix ($19, two hours, daily) among other destinations. **Amtrak** (☎ 520-623-4442, 800-872-7245; 400 E Toole Ave) has trains to Los Angeles ($37, 10 hours, three weekly).

SOUTHWEST

The **Ronstadt Transit Center** (cnr Congress St & 6th Ave) is the major local transit hub. From here **Sun Tran** (☎ 520-792-9222; www.suntran.com) buses serve metropolitan Tucson ($1).

AROUND TUCSON

The places listed here are less than an hour's drive from town and make great day trips.

Arizona-Sonora Desert Museum & Old Tucson Studios

Javelinas, coyotes, bobcats, snakes and just about every other local desert animal are displayed in natural-looking outdoor settings at this excellent **museum** (☎ 520-883-2702; www.desertmuseum.org; 2021 N Kinney Rd; adult $9-12, child $2-4; ⌚ 7:30am-5pm Mar-Sep, to 10pm Jun-Aug, 8:30am-5:30pm Oct-Feb) off Hwy 86, about 12 miles west of Tucson. A perennial local favorite, it's one of Tucson's crown jewels. The grounds are thick with desert plants, and docents can answer questions.

A few miles southeast of the museum, the **Old Tucson Studios** (☎ 520-883-0100; www.oldtucson .com; 201 S Kinney Rd; adult/child $17/11; ⌚ 10am-6pm) were once an actual Western film set. Today the popular studios have been converted into a Western theme park (a must for kids) complete with shootouts and stagecoach rides.

Saguaro National Park

Although you see these towering succulents throughout the region, large stands of the majestic saguaro and its associated habitat and wildlife are protected in this **national park** (☎ 520-733-5158; www.nps.gov/sagu; admission $10; ⌚ 7am-sunset).

The park has two separate units, east and west of Tucson. The Saguaro East Visitors Center is 15 miles east of downtown. It has information on day hikes, horseback riding and park camping (free permits must be obtained by noon on the day of your hike). This section of the park boasts about 130 miles of trails, including the **Tanque Verde Ridge Trail**, which climbs to the summit of Mica Mountain (8666ft).

Two miles northwest of the Arizona-Sonora Desert Museum is the Saguaro West Visitors Center. Although night hiking is permitted in this portion of the park, camping is not. The **Bajada Loop Drive** is an unpaved 6-mile loop that begins 1½ miles west of the visitor center and provides fine views of cactus forests, several picnic spots and access to trailheads. The **King Canyon trailhead**, just outside the park boundary (almost opposite the Arizona-Sonora Desert Museum), stays open until 10pm and is a great sunset or stargazing hike.

Mission San Xavier del Bac

Dating back to 1692, **Mission San Xavier del Bac** (☎ 520-294-2624; 1950 W San Xavier Rd; admission by donation; ⌚ 8am-5pm) is Arizona's oldest European building still in use. A graceful blend of Moorish, Byzantine and late Mexican Renaissance architecture, the building has been restored, but work is always continuing on the frescoes inside.

Biosphere 2

Built to be completely sealed off from Biosphere 1 (that would be earth), **Biosphere 2** (☎ 520-838-6200; www.bio2.com; Hwy 77; adult/child $20/13; ⌚ 9am-4pm) is a 3-acre glassed dome housing seven separate microhabitats designed to be self-sustaining. In 1991, eight bionauts entered Biosphere 2 for a two-year tour of duty, during which they were physically cut off from the outside world. They emerged thinner, but in fair shape. Although this experiment could be used as a prototype for future space stations, it was privately funded and controversial. Heavy criticism came after the dome leaked gases and was opened to allow a bionaut to emerge for medical treatment. Columbia University now operates the facility, and gives public tours.

WEST OF TUCSON

From Tucson, Hwy 86 heads west into some of the driest and emptiest parts of the Sonoran Desert. West of Sells, the **Kitt Peak National Optical Observatory** (☎ 520-318-8726; www.noao.edu/kpno; Hwy 86; admission $2; ⌚ 9am-3:45pm) is the largest optical observatory in the world, featuring 22 telescopes, one of which is used to study the sun. Guided tours (10am, 11:30am and 1:30pm) last about an hour. The three-hour nightly stargazing sessions ($39) are a real treat. These are very popular and should be booked weeks in advance.

If you want solitude in stark, quiet and beautiful desert surroundings, visit **Organ Pipe Cactus National Monument** (☎ 520-387-6849; www.nps .gov/orpi; Hwy 85; admission $8; ⌚ visitor center 8am-5pm, park 24hr). Two unpaved loop drives (21 and 53 miles) and six hiking trails take you through the park, which has three types of large

---

HOT TOPIC: IMMIGRATION FROM MEXICO

Immigration issues continue to fan the flames in the Southwest, especially in southern Arizona. High unemployment at home and higher wages in the US mean that Mexican immigrants continue to come north in large numbers. Increased border enforcement in California and Texas and vigilante groups like the Minutemen have driven this human traffic to the most inhospitable and dangerous portions of the Sonoran desert, with a subsequent spike in fatalities from hyperthermia and exposure. When people are ill-prepared for the journey, or *coyotes* (paid smuggling guides) abandon them, the heat kills quickly yet painfully.

Distraught over a death toll of more than 100 a year, regional humanitarian and religious groups have approached it as an issue of human rights. Working within the law, they maintain emergency water stations in known crossing areas, in the hope that no one will die to cross a border.

---

columnar cacti and an excellent variety of other desert flora and fauna. There is a **campground** (campsites $12) by the visitor center.

SOUTH OF TUCSON

South of Tucson, I-19 is the main route to Nogales and Mexico. Along the way are several interesting stops.

At exit 69, the **Titan Missile Museum** (☎ 520-625-7736; 1580 W Duval Mine Rd; adult/child $8.50/5; ☼ 9am-5pm) features an underground launch site for Cold War–era intercontinental ballistic missiles. Tours are informative and leave frequently.

If history and/or shopping for crafts interest you, visit the small village of **Tubac** (I-19 exit 34), with more than 80 galleries.

At exit 29, **Tumacácori National Historic Park** (☎ 520-398-2341; www.nps.gov/tuma; admission $3; ☼ 8am-5pm) is the well-preserved ruin of a never-completed Franciscan church started in 1800.

Nogales

Arizona's most important gateway into Mexico sees a constant flow of foot and vehicle traffic sliding across the border separating Nogales, Arizona, from Nogales, Sonora, Mexico. There can be delays for cars crossing into the US; check online (http://apps.cbp.gov/bwt) for wait times updated hourly.

The **chamber of commerce** (☎ 520-287-3685; www.nogaleschamber.com; 123 W Kino Park Way; ☼ 9am-4pm Mon-Fri) has all the usual tourist information. There is also a **Mexican Consulate** (☎ 520-287-3381, 520-287-3386; 571 N Grand Ave; ☼ Mon-Fri).

Chain motels are found off I-19 at exit 4. Mariposa Rd has the usual assortment of fast-food restaurants and a supermarket.

Crucero/Greyhound (☎ 520-287-5628; 35 N Terrace Dr) is located less than a mile from the border

and has regular service to Tucson ($16, one hour). Five daily buses go to Hermosillo, Mexico ($19, 3½ hours), where there are frequent connections to Guadalajara ($73 to $84, 20 hours) and Mexico City ($129, 29 hours) with **Estrella Blanca** (www.estrellablanca.com.mx).

Drivers into Mexico can obtain car insurance from friendly, helpful **Sanborn's** (☎ 520-281-1865, 800-222-0158; www.sanbornsinsurance.com; 850 W Shell Rd; ☼ 8am-5pm Mon-Fri, varies Sat & Sun). The cost is determined by the value of the car and the length of your stay, but there's a $25 minimum charge.

SOUTHEASTERN CORNER

Cochise County is a land rich with cowboys, Native Americans, ranchers, miners, gunslingers and all manner of Western lore. It's also an area of rugged, scenic beauty.

Small **Benson** is a quiet travelers' stop with a few motels, RV parks and markets. Don't miss the fantastic **Kartchner Caverns State Park** (☎ 502-586-4100; Hwy 90; admission $5; ☼ 7:30am-6pm), 9 miles south of town. It's a 2.5-mile-long wet limestone cave, touted as one of the world's best 'living' caves. Two tours (adult/child from $19/10) are offered and these can sell out months in advance, so reserve ahead.

Small and remote **Chiricahua National Monument** (☎ 520-824-3560; adult/child $5/free), in the Chiricahua Mountains, offers strangely eroded volcanic geology and abundant wildlife. The **Bonita Canyon Scenic Drive** takes you 8 miles to Massai Point at 6870ft, and there are numerous hiking trails. The monument is 40 miles southeast of Willcox off Hwy 186.

Tombstone

This 19th-century silver-mining town was a formerly rip-roaring place, the site of the famous 1881 shootout at the OK Corral. Now a National Historic Landmark, it attracts hordes of tourists to its old Western buildings, stagecoach rides and nonstop gunfight reenactments. The town's name is probably its best asset – the place is hokey beyond belief, though kids will think it's cool. The **Visitor & Information Center** (☎ 520-457-3929; www.tombstone.org; cnr 4th & Allen Sts; ◷ 9am-4pm) lists the daily gunfight schedule and has good walking maps.

Bisbee

Built into the steep walls of Tombstone Canyon, Bisbee is one of Arizona's best-preserved historic towns. Oozing old-fashioned ambience, its elegant Victorian buildings line narrow twisting streets and house classy galleries, sumptuous restaurants and charming hotels.

Most businesses are found in the Historic District (Old Bisbee), along Subway and Main Sts. The **Visitor Center** (☎ 520-432-3554, 866-224-7233; www.discoverbisbee.com; 2 Copper Queen Plaza; ◷ 9am-5pm Mon-Fri, 10am-4pm Sat & Sun).

Bisbee owes its existence to the ore found in the surrounding hills, and the immense stair-stepped **Lavender Pit** on the edge of town testifies to its valuable bounty. To learn how it was collected, visit the **Queen Mine** (☎ 520-432-2071; 478 Dart Rd; adult/child $12/5; ◷ 9am-3:30pm). Retired miners give the hour-long tours, which descend deep underground – it's a chilly 47°F (8°C), so bring warm clothes. **Lavender Jeep Tours** (☎ 520-432-5369) also does amazing 4WD tours ($25 to $45) of area backroads and mining areas.

ourpick Shady Dell RV Park (☎ 520-432-3567; www.theshadydell.com; 1 Douglas Rd; trailers $45-145; ✗) So stylin' and so damn cute – find out why every movie star wants their own Airstream. A kitschy trailer park extraordinaire, it's full of classic 1950s tin cans as well as a converted yacht and a turquoise tiki-theme bus. Everything's done up with retro furnishings and stocked with period movies.

A centenarian with style, the **Copper Queen Hotel** (☎ 520-432-2216; www.copperqueen .com; 11 Howell Ave; r $80-200; ✗ ☎ ✶ wi-fi) boasts 52 rooms and halls bewitched by lovely copper lamps.

For casual fare, the **Bisbee Grille** (☎ 520-432-6788; 2 Copper Queen Plaza; dishes $8-15; ◷ 11am-9pm) serves salads, pastas and burgers; kids get coloring materials and their own menu.

UTAH

Go outside and play. Isn't that what parents used to say? In Utah, it could well be a marketing slogan. The rugged terrain of this little-populated state really does beg to be biked, hiked, skied and otherwise actively explored. Its dazzling display of geographic grandeur leaves visitors a bit awestruck and dumbfounded. The panoply of colors, colors everywhere, as far as the eye can see, is more varied than a 64-pack of crayons. The temptation to simply sit still and watch the ever-changing kaleidoscope runs in opposition to hiking where no one (literally) has hiked before. This haunting topography is *that* vast.

The southern Utah landscape is defined by five national parks, featuring towering mountain peaks, plunging canyons, sweeping sandstone domes and seemingly endless expanses of undulating desert. Northern Utah is marked by the Great Salt Lake, forested mountains in the snow-covered Wasatch Range (where the 2002 Olympic Winter Games were held) and the wild Uinta Mountains.

Utah is also defined by modern Mormons, whose social and political influence reverberates throughout the state. When the Mormon pioneers reached the area in 1847, they, too (like the Native Americans 7000 years before them), felt a spiritual response and claimed it as their new home (their Zion). No matter what your belief system, the magical landscape of Utah will feel like heaven on earth.

UTAH FACTS

Nicknames Beehive State, Mormon State

Population 2.5 million

Area 82,144 sq miles

Capital city Salt Lake City (population 180,000)

Sales tax 4.75%

Birthplace of Donny (b 1957) and Marie (b 1959) Osmond; beloved bandit Butch Cassidy (1866–1908)

Home of Winter Olympic Games 2002

Famous for Mormons, red-rock canyons

Best souvenir T-shirt for Wasatch Brewery's Polygamy Porter – 'Why have just one?'

SOUTHWEST

DRINKING IN UTAH

Can you get a drink in Utah? Absolutely. The state's so-called 'private clubs' are full bars selling all manner of alcoholic drinks; they stop serving nightly at 1am. Becoming a temporary 'member' costs $5 for two weeks and entitles you to bring up to five guests. You can also get 'sponsored' by another member; don't worry, it's common practice, and anyway, there's usually a watchful doorman or bartender who'll do the asking for you.

Restaurants can serve wine, beer or liquor with food. 'Taverns' sell low-alcohol (3.2%) beer only. This same 3.2% beer can be purchased at grocery and convenience stores, while hard alcohol and wine can only be purchased at state liquor stores.

For the most part, you won't even notice these laws. That's because Utah has a huge range of bars, taverns and brewpubs – and no shortage of folks to keep the doors swinging and the stools warm.

History

Utah gets its name from the nomadic Ute people who, along with the Paiute and Shoshone, lived in the Great Basin desert more than 8000 years ago. Europeans arrived as early as 1776, but Native Americans inhabited the region freely until the mid-19th century. Led by Brigham Young, the Mormons fled to Utah to escape religious persecution, establishing Salt Lake City on July 24, 1847. They called their state Deseret, meaning 'honeybee,' according to the Book of Mormon.

After the US acquired the Utah Territory from Mexico, the Mormons petitioned Congress for statehood six times. Their petitions were consistently rejected because of Mormon polygamy (the practice of having more than one spouse at the same time), which was outlawed by the US government. Tensions grew between the Mormons and the federal government until 1890, when Mormon Church President Wilford Woodruff announced that God had told him that Mormons should abide by US law. Polygamy was discontinued and, soon afterward, Utah became the 45th state in 1896. Today Mormons remain in the majority in Utah and continue to exert a powerful conservative influence on life in the state.

Information

Note: it's difficult to change currency outside Salt Lake City; see p854.

Natural Resources Map & Bookstore (www.maps .state.ut.us) Has detailed maps of all the stellar places to explore.

Utah Office of Tourism (☎ 801-538-1030, 800-200-1160; www.utah.travel; Council Hall, 300 N State St, Capitol Hill, Salt Lake City, UT 84114; ☺ 8am-5pm Mon-Fri, 10am-5pm Sat & Sun) Links on lodging, camping and outdoor activities. The companion site (www.utah.com) has information in six languages. Publishes the free *Utah Travel Guide*. The council's bookstore (☎ 801-538-1398) sells guides and maps.

Utah Pride Center (☎ 801-539-8800, 888-874-2743; www.utahpridecenter.org; 361 N 300 West, Salt Lake City, UT 84103) This helpful gay and lesbian center offers advice, activities and classes.

Utah State Parks & Recreation Department (Map p855; ☎ 801-538-7220, 877-887-2757; www.state parks.utah.gov; 1594 W North Temple, Salt Lake City, UT 84114) Sells multiple-park permits (annual fee vehicle/ senior $70/35) and arranges camping reservations.

SALT LAKE CITY

Ushered into the spotlight by the 2002 Winter Olympics, Salt Lake City (SLC) has been building on the momentum ever since. It's a modern city with charming anachronisms and a stunning mountain setting – its location prompted pioneer Mormon leader Brigham Young to inform his weary band of emigrant settlers, 'This is the place.'

SLC is the headquarters of the Mormon Church, though only about half its citizens are Latter-day Saints (LDS; see p854). It surprises many that the city is politically progressive (compared to the rest of the state) and has a sizable gay and lesbian community.

The proximity of the Wasatch Mountains is a huge lure for outdoor enthusiasts year-round. World-class hiking, climbing and snow sports await less than an hour away, and it seems like the soaring peaks loom over you from all points in the city. Add in a thriving university, wildly eclectic restaurants and a flourishing arts scene, and you might second Brigham Young's pronouncement.

Orientation & Information

SLC is laid out in a spacious grid with streets aligned north–south or east–west. Everything radiates from Temple Sq: the corner of S Temple St (running east–west) and Main St (running north–south) is the zero point for streets and addresses. Eight blocks equals one mile. The streets were originally built 132ft wide so that four oxen pulling a wagon could turn around. Because streets are so wide, there are mid-block pedestrian crossings downtown. Carry the orange flags, available at these crossings, for increased visibility.

Two major interstates cross at SLC. I-15 runs north–south, I-80 east–west and I-215 loops the city.

BOOKSTORES

Sam Weller Books (☎ 801-328-2586, 800-333-7269; 254 S Main; ✌ 10am-8pm Mon-Sat, to 4pm Sun) The city's biggest independent bookstore, with the best selection of new and used travel books, guides and maps.

EMERGENCY & MEDICAL SERVICES

Police (☎ 801-799-3000; 315 E 200 South)
Salt Lake Regional Medical Center (☎ 801-350-4111; 1050 E South Temple; ✌ 24hr emergency)
University Hospital (☎ 801-581-2121/291; 50 N Medical Dr; ✌ 24hr emergency)

INTERNET ACCESS

Main library (☎ 801-524-8200; www.slcpl.lib.ut.us; 210 E 400 South; ✌ 9am-9pm Mon-Thu, to 6pm Fri & Sat, 1-5pm Sun) Free internet access and excellent periodicals.

THIS IS THE PLACE

The members of the Church of Jesus Christ of Latter-Day Saints (LDS; www.lds.org or www.mormon.org) – or Mormons – prize family above all else, and Mormon families tend to be large. Hard work and strict obedience to church leaders are very important. Smoking, and drinking alcohol, tea or coffee, are forbidden. Women are forbidden to take leadership roles, as were African Americans until 1978.

The faith considers missionary service important, and many young adults travel the world spreading the word. Women are called Sisters during their service, and the men are called Elders. There are now around 11 million Mormons worldwide.

INTERNET RESOURCES

Downtown SLC (www.downtownslc.org) Arts, entertainment and business information about the downtown core.
Salt Lake City Arts Council (www.slcgov.com/arts) Cultural-events listings.
Salt Lake Convention & Visitors Bureau (www.visitsaltlake.com) SLC's official tourist-information website.
TravelWest (www.travelwest.net/cities/saltlake) Information on camping, parks, lodging, area attractions and more.

MEDIA

City Weekly (☎ 801-573-7003; www.slweekly.com) Free alternative weekly with good restaurant and entertainment listings.
QSaltLake (☎ 801-649-6663; www.qsaltlake.com) SLC's free gay and lesbian newspaper.
Salt Lake Tribune (☎ 801-257-8742; www.sltrib.com) Utah's largest-circulation paper; not Mormon owned, but conservative.

MONEY

Wells Fargo (☎ 801-246-2677; 79 S Main) Currency-exchange services.

POST

Post office (☎ 800-275-8777; www.usps.com; 230 W 200 South)

TOURIST INFORMATION

Public Lands Information Center (☎ 801-466-6411; 3285 E 3300 South; ✌ from 10:30am Tue-Sat) Recreation information on the Wasatch-Cache National Forest; located inside the REI store. Note that closing times vary.
Salt Lake City International Airport (☎ 801-575-2800; Terminals 1 & 2 baggage-claim areas; ✌ 9am-9pm) Visitor information at the airport.
Visitor Information Center (☎ 801-543-4900, 800-541-4955; www.visitsaltlake.com; 90 S West Temple; ✌ 8am-6pm Mon-Fri summer, 8am-6pm rest of year, 9am-5pm Sat & Sun year-round) The center, within the Salt Palace Convention Center, publishes the free Salt Lake Visitors Guide.

Sights
TEMPLE SQUARE

The city's most famous sight, **Temple Square** (☎ 801-240-2534, 800-537-9703; www.visittemplesquare.com; admission free; ✌ 9am-9pm) occupies a 10-acre block and is surrounded by 15ft-high walls. Docents at the visitor centers inside the two entrances (on S and N Temple) give free 30-minute tours.

The egg-shaped 1867 **Tabernacle** (admission free; ✌ 9am-9pm) is again the highlight after the completion of an extensive seismic retrofit

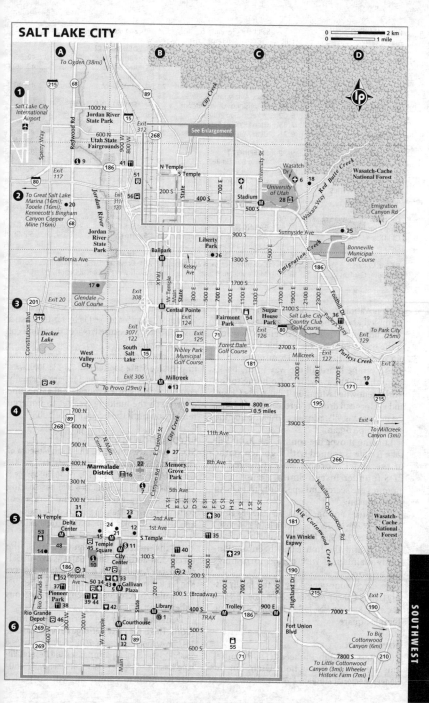

SALT LAKE CITY

INFORMATION

Main Library	**1** B6
Police	**2** B5
Post Office	**3** A5
Public Lands Information Center	(see 19)
Salt Lake Regional Medical Center	**4** C2
Sam Weller Books	**5** B6
University Hospital	**6** C2
Utah Office of Tourism	**7** B5
Utah Pride Center	**8** A5
Utah State Parks & Recreation Department	**9** A2
Visitor Information Center	**10** A5
Wells Fargo	**11** B5

SIGHTS & ACTIVITIES

Beehive House	**12** B5
City Sights	**13** B4
Discovery Gateway	**14** A5
Family History Library	**15** A5
Old Deseret Village	(see 25)
Pioneer Memorial Museum	**16** B5
Raging Waters	**17** A3
Red Butte Gardens	**18** D2
REI	**19** D4

Salt Lake City Parks & Recreation Department	**20** A2
Salt Lake Temple	**21** B5
State Capitol	**22** B4
Tabernacle	**23** B5
Temple Square	**24** B5
This is the Place Heritage Park	**25** D2
Tracy Aviary	**26** C3
University of Utah Outdoor Recreation Program	(see 6)
Utah Heritage Foundation	**27** B4
Utah Museum of Fine Arts	**28** C2

SLEEPING 🛏

Anton Boxrud B&B	**29** C5
Avenues Hostel	**30** C5
City Creek Inn	**31** A5
Grand America	**32** B6
Hotel Monaco	**33** B6
Peery Hotel	**34** A6

EATING 🍴

Avenues Bakery	**35** C5
Bombay House	**36** D3
Cucina Toscana	**37** A6
Downtown Farmers Market	**38** A6
Metropolitan	**39** A6
One World Café	**40** B5

Red Iguana	**41** B2

DRINKING 🍷

Port O' Call	**42** B6
Red Door	**43** B6
Squatter's Pub Brewery	**44** A6

ENTERTAINMENT 🎭

Abravanel Hall	**45** A5
Area 51	**46** A6
Capitol Theater	**47** B5
EnergySolutions Arena	**48** A5
E Center	**49** A4
Rose Wagner Performing Arts Center	**50** A6
Trapp Door	**51** B2

SHOPPING 🛍

Artspace	**52** A6
Gateway	**53** A5
Sugarhouse	**54** C3
Trolley Square	**55** C6

TRANSPORT

Greyhound	**56** B2
Union Pacific Rail Depot (Amtrak station)	(see 56)

and renovation in 2007. Some preservationists grumbled about the replacement of its pine pews, but a few rows of the originals were left in the back. To show off its fabled acoustics, pin drops are held every 15 minutes – the sound can be heard all the way in the back, more than 200ft away. It's also home to the world-renowned Mormon Tabernacle Choir, and visitors can drop in on **rehearsals** (7:30pm Thu, choir broadcast 9:15am Sun) accompanied by the 11,000-pipe organ.

Lording it over the square, the 210ft **Salt Lake Temple** is topped with a golden statue of the angel Moroni, who appeared to LDS founder Joseph Smith. Temple ceremonies are secret and open only to LDS 'in good standing.'

Brigham Young lived in the **Beehive House** (☎ 801-240-2671; 67 E South Temple; admission free; ☻ tours 9am-9pm Mon-Sat) until his death in 1877, and the house has been meticulously maintained with period furnishings and artwork.

Research your genealogy at the **Family History Library** (☎ 801-240-2584, 866-406-1830; 35 N West Temple; ☻ 8am-5pm Mon, to 9pm Tue-Sat), adjoining Temple Square.

DOWNTOWN

Daughters of Utah Pioneers (DUP) museums are located throughout Utah, but the **Pioneer Memorial Museum** (☎ 801-532-6479; 300 N

Main; admission free; ☻ 9am-5pm Mon-Sat yr-round, 9am-5pm Mon-Sat, 1-5pm Sun summer) is by far the best, a vast four-story treasure trove of thousands of pioneer artifacts.

Just north of Temple Sq, the walls of the impressive **State Capitol** (☎ 801-538-3000; www .utahstatecapitol.utah.gov; ☻ 8am-5pm) are normally covered with historical murals, but at the time of research the building was set to undergo renovation until the beginning of 2008.

BEYOND DOWNTOWN

SLC's best art museum, the **Utah Museum of Fine Arts** (☎ 801-581-7332; www.umfa.utah.edu; 410 Campus Center Dr; adult/child $5/3; ☻ 10am-5pm Tue & Thu-Fri, to 8pm Wed, 11am-5pm Sat & Sun) has soaring galleries, cherry-wood floors, and permanent collections of tribal, Western and modern art; it also books important international traveling shows.

In the nearby Wasatch Foothills, the lovely 150-acre **Red Butte Gardens** (☎ 801-581-4747; Wakara Way; adult/child & senior $6/4; ☻ 9am-9pm Mon-Sat, to 5pm Sun May-Aug, shorter varying hr Sep-Apr) has trails, 25 acres of gardens and gorgeous valley views.

Dedicated to the 1847 arrival of the Mormons, **This is the Place Heritage Park** (☎ 801-582-1847; www.thisistheplace.org; 2601 E Sunnyside Ave/800 South; ☻ 9am-6pm) encompasses **Old Deseret Village** (adult/child $8/6; ☻ 9am-5pm summer), a 450-acre living-history museum, with costumed docents depicting life in the mid-19th century. Some of the 41 buildings are replicas, others originals, including Brigham Young's farmhouse. In the nonsummer months, the self-guided tours cost $5/3 for adults/children.

Activities

Millcreek, Big Cottonwood and Little Cottonwood canyons, all on the east side of the Wasatch Mountains and within easy reach of SLC, offer excellent opportunities for hiking, mountain biking, camping and cross-country skiing. The **Salt Lake City Parks & Recreation Department** (☎ 801-972-7800; www.slcgov.com; 1965 W 500 South; ☻ 8am-5pm Mon-Fri) has tons of information about city parks.

REI (☎ 801-486-2100; 3285 E 3300 South) rents camping equipment, climbing shoes, kayaks and most winter-sports gear, as does the **University of Utah Outdoor Recreation Program** (☎ 801-581-8516; www.utah.edu/campusrec; 2140 E Red Butte Rd; ☻ 8am-6pm Mon-Fri), which also rents mountain bikes ($18 per day).

Salt Lake City for Children

SLC has oodles of fun things for kids to explore. Consider purchasing a one- to three-day **Visit Salt Lake Connect Pass** (www.visitsaltlake.com/what_to_do/connect.html) if you plan to visit a few attractions.

Discovery Gateway (☎ 801-456-5437; 400 W 100 South; admission $9.50; ☻ 10am-9pm Mon & Fri, to 6pm Tue-Thu & Sat, noon-6pm Sun) is a fantastic hands-on children's museum and possibly the best city attraction for families.

Wheeler Historic Farm (☎ 801-264-2241; www.wheelerfarm.com; 6351 S 900 East; admission free, wagon rides $2, tours $2; ☻ dawn-dusk, visitor center 9am-5pm), in South Cottonwood Regional Park, dates from 1886. Kids can help farmhands milk cows, churn butter and feed animals. There's also blacksmithing, quilting and wagon rides in summer.

When it gets hot, careen down the water slides at **Raging Waters** (☎ 801-972-3300; www.ragingwatersutah.com; 1200 W 1700 South; adult/child $20/16; ☻ 10:30am-7:30pm Mon-Sat, noon-7:30pm Sun Jun-Sep).

The **Tracy Aviary** (☎ 801-322-2473, 801-596-8500; 589 E 1300 South; adult/child $5/3; ☻ 9am-6pm Mar-Oct, to 4:30pm Nov-Feb) delights bird lovers with displays of winged creatures from all over the world. Kids can feed ducks, colorful lories and parrots.

Tours

City Sights (☎ 801-534-1001; www.saltlakecitytours.org; 3359 S Main, Ste 804) Offers tours of SLC and the Great Salt Lake.

Utah Heritage Foundation (☎ 801-533-0858; www.utahheritagefoundation.com; 485 N Canyon Rd) Gives tours of SLC's historic landmarks and distributes free self-guided walking-tour brochures.

Festivals & Events

Crowds come for the **Utah Arts Festival** (www.uaf.org) in late June, and **Days of '47** (☎ 801-254-4656; www.daysof47.com), the 'Mormon Mardi Gras,' from mid- to late July, which has everything from a rodeo to an enormous parade.

Sleeping

SLC's lodgings are primarily chain properties, many clustered on W North Temple near the airport and along S 200 West near 500 South and 600 South. Rates are lowest during the spring and fall, and spike when there's a convention. At top-end hotels, rates are lowest at weekends. Summertime prices plunge at ski resorts (p860), about 45 minutes' drive from downtown. High-season rates are listed below.

BUDGET

Avenues Hostel (☎ 801-359-3855; 107 F St; www.saltlakehostel.com; dm $14, s/d with shared bath $27/33, with private bath $30/35; Ⓟ ✗ 🐾 🖳 wi-fi) This standard hostel is in a quiet residential neighborhood and chock-a-block with great amenities, including free international phone calls and a hot tub. A significant proportion of guests are international exchange students.

City Creek Inn (☎ 801-533-9100, 866-533-4898; www.citycreekinn.com; 230 W North Temple; r $65-75; Ⓟ ✗ 🐾 wi-fi) One of SLC's best budget choices is located right downtown, next to Temple Sq. In the same family for three generations, it's a simple but attractive motel with a lush garden. Two-bedded rooms are pleasantly larger than average.

MIDRANGE & TOP END

Anton Boxrud B&B (☎ 801-363-8035, 800-524-5511; www.antonboxrud.com; 57 S 600 East; r incl full breakfast $75-170; Ⓟ ✗ wi-fi) You'll feel like a guest in a friend's home at this seven-room, meticulously restored 1901 Victorian on a tree-lined street, walkable to downtown. The charming innkeeper always has cookies and drinks on hand.

SOUTHWEST

Peery Hotel (☎ 801-521-4300, 800-331-0073; www .peeryhotel.com; 110 W 300 South; r $110-200; ✗ ✗ ⬜ wi-fi) This stately historic hotel is modernized with grace. The E-shaped building ushers in tons of natural light, and the impeccably maintained rooms have thick bedspreads, gilt-framed mirrors, heavy wooden furniture, and up-to-date bathrooms with pedestal sinks and aromatherapy soaps. Parking is $9.

ourpick Hotel Monaco (☎ 801-595-0000, 877-294-9710; www.monaco-saltlakecity.com; 14 W 200 South; r $120-250; ✗ ⬜ wi-fi) In this fun boutique hotel, circus tent meets beach cabaña in a conflagration of color, stripes and plush leopard-print bathrobes. It throws a killer complimentary wine and microbrew hour in the evening, made even sweeter with free chair massages. Pushing the frontiers of pet-friendliness, it'll even loan out goldfish for a little guppy love. Parking is $12.

Grand America (☎ 801-258-6000, 800-621-4505; www .grandamerica.com; 555 S Main; r $260-310; ✗ ✗ ✗ ⬜) SLC's only true luxury hotel towers over the city like a 24-story wedding cake. The retro-fancy lobby sports over-the-top custom fixtures, including Murano glass chandeliers. Rooms are decked out with Italian marble bathrooms, English wool carpeting, tasseled damask draperies and other cushy touches. Afternoon high tea ($16 to $30) is a decadent treat. Parking is $10.

Eating

Foodies will love SLC. Almost anything you crave can be found here, and there's a bountiful assortment of ethnic and vegetarian restaurants.

BUDGET

In the warmer months, the **Downtown Farmers Market** (Pioneer Park, cnr 300 South & 300 West; ✌ 8am-1pm Sat Jun-Oct) showcases locally grown produce and tasty ready-to-eat goodies.

One World Cafe (☎ 801-519-2002; 41 S 300 East; ✌ 11am-9pm) The revolution will be sliding scale: welcome to this organic cafeteria where there's no set menu and pay-what-you-wish (or can) prices, and diners decide the portion sizes of the quasi-hippie meat or vegetarian entrees. Purists can show up to volunteer an hour in exchange for a meal.

Avenues Bakery (☎ 801-746-5626; 481 E South Temple; dishes $6-9; ✌ 6:30am-7pm Mon-Fri, 7am-3pm Sat & Sun) For a crash course in SLC geography, bring a city map to breakfast and find the

neighborhoods named for the Sugar House oatmeal or the Rose Park *huevos rancheros*. For lunch, fill up on a sandwich swaddled in fresh-baked bread.

MIDRANGE & TOP END

Red Iguana (☎ 801-322-1489; 736 W North Temple; dishes $7-12; ✌ 11am-10pm Mon-Thu, to 11pm Fri, 10am-11pm Sat, 10am-9pm Sun) The locals swoon over the *mole* dishes at this exceptional family-run Mexican restaurant. The chili-packed *mole amarillo* will reduce you to happy tears.

Bombay House (☎ 801-581-0222; 2731 Parleys Way; mains $9-14; ✌ 4-10pm Mon-Sat) Flanked by the skyscraper mountains east of downtown, Bombay's Indian cooking is vibrant and fiery. Arrive early; it gets packed.

ourpick Cucina Toscana (☎ 801-328-3463; 307 W Pierpont Ave; dishes $16-25; ✌ 5:30-9:30pm Mon-Thu, to 10pm Fri & Sat) Be seated at a convivial Tuscan trattoria and possibly the best dinner party you've ever unwittingly attended. Charismatic owner–manager Valter Nassi flits between the tables in the elegant yellow room, making sure your gnocchi is delightful and your evening is one to remember.

Metropolitan (☎ 801-364-3472; 173 W Broadway; mains $25-30; ✌ 6-9pm Mon-Sat) If Salt Lake had celebs, they'd hang out at Metropolitan, where the culinary craftsmanship is so good and the flavors so sparkling they merit comparison with big-city restaurants in California. The sexy concrete-and-velvet dining room complements the chef's artistry. You can always order small plates from the bistro menu ($8 to $12) while swilling martinis at the bar.

Drinking & Entertainment

Area 51 (☎ 801-534-0819; www.area51slc.com; 451 S 400 West; ✌ Tue-Sat) Pay your respects to the alien just inside this two-story dance warehouse. DJs spin a mix of gothic-industrial, techno, rap and hip-hop on two dance floors, with a good straight and gay crowd and a section for clubgoers over 18.

Port O' Call (☎ 801-521-0589; 78 W 400 South) If it's booze you're after, this large, full-service bar colonizes four floors in a cool 1912 building. It's quiet during the day, but at night crowds can pack in for DJs and bands.

Red Door (☎ 801-363-6030; 57 W 200 South; ✌ Mon-Sat) Stir, sip and repeat at this slick industrial martini bar enveloped by deep-red walls. DJs take up residence on Friday and a three-piece jazz band wows the house on Saturday night.

Squatter's Pub Brewery (☎ 801-363-2739; www
.squatters.com; 147 W Broadway) Squatter's has some
great microbrews to choose from; try the
smooth Vienna Lager or the lighter St Provo
Girl.

Trapp Door (☎ 801-533-0173; www.trappdoor.com; 615
W 100 South) SLC's largest gay dance club shakes
its stuff five nights a week, with super-steamy
Latin grooves on Sunday.

The historic **Capitol Theater** (☎ 801-355-2787;
www.finearts.slco.org/facilities/capitol/capitol.html; 50 W
200 South), dramatic **Rose Wagner Performing Arts
Center** (☎ 801-355-2787; www.finearts.slco.org/facilities
/rose/rose.html; 138 W 300 South) and acoustically rich
Abravanel Hall (☎ 801-533-6683; www.finearts.slco.org
/facilities/abravanel/abravanel.html; 123 W South Temple) are
primary venues. For tickets call **ArtTix** (☎ 801-
355-2787, 888-451-2787; www.arttix.org).

SPORTS

Utah Jazz (www.nba.com/jazz), the men's professional basketball team, plays at the **EnergySolutions Arena** (☎ 801-325-2000; www.energysolutionsarena
.com; 301 W South Temple). The International Hockey
League's **Utah Grizzlies** (☎ 801-988-7825; www.utah
grizzlies.com) play at the **E Center** (☎ 801-988-8888;
www.theecenter.com; 3200 S Decker Lake Dr, West Valley City),
which hosted most of the men's ice hockey
competitions during the Olympics.

Shopping

The best downtown major-label shopping is
at the diverse indoor-outdoor **Gateway** (☎ 801-
456-0000; www.shopthegateway.com; 200 South to 50 North,
400 West to 500 West; ☼ 10am-9pm Mon-Thu, to 10pm Fri
& Sat, noon-5pm Sun). Nearby, you'll find artists'
studios, indie boutiques and funky second-
hand stores at **Artspace** (Pierpont Ave, btwn 300 West
& 400 West) in SLC's warehouse district. The
Sugarhouse neighborhood (2100 South, btwn 900 East &
1300 East) looks like Main Street, USA, and has a
good mix of indie shops and mall stores. For
more brand names, head to the 100 stores
inside the converted trolley barns at **Trolley
Square** (☎ 801-521-9877; btwn 600 South & 700 East).

Getting There & Around

AIR

Salt Lake City International Airport (☎ 801-575-
2400, 800-595-2442; www.slcairport.com; 776 N Terminal
Dr) is 6 miles west of downtown. Numerous
door-to-door shuttle vans are available at the
airport; a trip downtown costs $10 to $15.
Call the airport's **transportation desk** (☎ 801-
575-2477) for details.

BUS

There are several daily buses with **Greyhound**
(☎ 801-355-9579; www.greyhound.com; 300 S 600 West)
south through Provo and St George to Las
Vegas, Nevada ($55, 8½ hours); west to San
Francisco ($82, 16 hours); east to Denver
($66, 10 to 16 hours); and north to Seattle
($106, 20 to 24 hours).

UTA (☎ 801-743-3882, 888-743-3882; www.rideuta
.com; fares $1.60) buses serve SLC and the
Wasatch Front area until about midnight
(there's limited service on Sunday). TRAX,
UTA's light-rail system, runs east from the
EnergySolutions Arena to the university
and south to Sandy. The center of downtown SLC is a free-fare zone. UTA buses
also go to Provo, Tooele, Ogden and other
Wasatch Front–area cities and suburbs
($3); during ski season they serve the four
local resorts and Sundance, near Provo (all
$6.50 round-trip).

TRAIN

Amtrak's *California Zephyr* stops daily at
the **Union Pacific Rail Depot** (☎ 801-322-3510,
800-872-7245; www.amtrak.com; 340 S 600 West) going
east to Chicago ($126 to $247, 35 hours) and
west to Oakland, California ($66, 18 hours).
Schedule delays can be substantial.

AROUND SALT LAKE CITY

Once part of prehistoric Lake Bonneville, the
Great Salt Lake today covers 2000 sq miles and
is far saltier than the ocean; you can easily
float on its surface.

The pretty, 15-mile-long **Antelope Island
State Park** (☎ 801-773-2941; I-15 exit 332; per vehicle
$9; ☼ 7am-sunset), 40 miles northwest of SLC,
has the best beaches for lake swimming, as
well as nice hiking. It's also home to one of
the largest bison herds in the country, and
the fall corralling of these animals is a great
wildlife spectacle. A basic **campground** (campsites
$12) is open year-round.

Century-old **Kennecott's Bingham Canyon
Copper Mine** (☎ 801-252-3234; www.kennecott.com;
Hwy 111; per vehicle $5; ☼ 8am-8pm Apr-Oct) is the
world's largest factitious excavation and,
still operational, it's only getting bigger. The
2.5-mile-wide and 0.75-mile-deep gash, in
the Oquirrh Mountains west of SLC, is the
only artificial sight on Earth, other than the
Great Wall of China. It's visible from space
shuttles orbiting the US.

Ski Resorts

Within 40 minutes' drive of SLC are four world-class resorts in Little Cottonwood and Big Cottonwood Canyons. Consider purchasing a **Super Pass** (☎ 877-752-4386; www.ski-saltlake.com) for access to all four resorts plus round-trip transportation from SLC.

Alta Ski Area (☎ 801-359-1078; www.alta.com; Little Cottonwood Canyon; adult/child $52/23) A laid-back choice for skiers.

Brighton Ski Area (☎ 801-532-4731, 800-873-5512; www.brightonresort.com; Big Cottonwood Canyon; adult/child 7-10yr & senior $47/10).

Snowbird Ski Area (☎ 801-933-2222, 800-232-9542; www.snowbird.com; Little Cottonwood Canyon; adult/child 6yr & under/child 7-12yr $64/15/25) has excellent snowboarding.

Solitude Ski Area (☎ 801-534-1400; www.skisolitude.com; Big Cottonwood Canyon; adult/senior/child $53/25/32).

WASATCH MOUNTAINS & NORTH

Utah has awesome skiing, some of the best anywhere in North America. Its fabulous low-density, low-moisture snow – between 300in and 500in annually – and thousands of acres of high-altitude terrain helped earn Utah the honor of hosting the 2002 Winter Olympics. This mountainous region, within 55 miles of SLC, is home to 11 ski resorts, and offers abundant hiking, camping, fly-fishing and mountain biking.

Park City

A mere 30 miles east of SLC via I-80, Park City (elevation 6900ft) skyrocketed to international fame when it hosted the downhill, jumping and sledding events at the 2002 Winter Olympics. Not only is Park City the Southwest's most popular ski town, it's also home to the US ski team. Come spring, the town gears up for hiking and mountain-biking season in the high peaks nearby.

A silver-mining community during the 19th century, the city has an attractive and remarkably well-preserved Main St, lined with upscale galleries, shops, hotels, restaurants and bars. And despite the sea of prefab housing that has spread across the valley and surrounding hills, the town remains relatively charming.

The biggest and most star-studded event here is the annual **Sundance Film Festival** (☎ 801-328-3456; www.sundance.org) each January. Independent films and their makers, stars and fans fill the town to bursting for two weeks, and tickets often sell out in advance.

One **Visitor Information Center** (☎ 435-658-9616; www.parkcityinfo.com; Kimball Junction, Hwy 224 & Olympic Blvd; ☼ 9am-6pm) is in the northern Kimball Junction area, but a second office is at the **Park City Historic Museum** (☎ 435-649-7457; www.parkcity history.org; 528 Main St; admission free; ☼ 11am-5pm Mon-Sat, noon-6pm Sun). The museum has interesting mining and history exhibits and a dungeonlike former territorial jail in the basement.

ACTIVITIES

Park City boasts three of Utah's pre-eminent ski resorts. An in-town chairlift whisks skiers to **Park City Mountain Resort** (☎ 435-649-8111, 800-222-7275; www.parkcitymountain.com; adult/child under 6yr $70-80/free), host of the 2002 Winter Olympics giant slalom and snowboarding events. In the summer it has zip line rides ($19). Posh **Deer Valley Resort** (☎ 435-649-1000, 800-558-3337; www.deervalley.com; adult/child/senior $79/47/56) is for skiers only, and **Canyons** (☎ 435-649-5400; www.thecanyons.com; adult/child & senior $75/49) is Utah's largest resort. All three host summer activities like mountain biking and hiking.

Olympians may be long gone from **Utah Olympic Park** (☎ 435-658-4200; www.utaholympicpark.com; Hwy 224; adult/child & senior $8/6), but you can tour the facilities where it all happened and, if you're lucky, watch the pros practice (call for rates, schedules and reservations). From mid-November to mid-March, Park City's most thrilling offering is an 80mph **bobsled ride** (tickets $200) with an incredible 4Gs of centrifugal force. Visitors can also take classes in **ski jumping** and **luge riding**.

If you want to enjoy some free outdoor events in summer, **Mountain Town Stages** (☎ 435-901-7664; www.mountaintownstages.com) puts on music shows around town almost every night of the week, and the **Sundance Institute** (☎ 801-328-3456; www.sundance.org) holds movie screenings on Friday.

SLEEPING

There are more than 100 condo complexes, up-scale hotels and B&Bs in Park City, and while winter rates quoted here are very high, prices drop by half in summer. Rates go through the roof for the Sundance Film Festival.

Chateau Après Lodge (☎ 435-649-9372, 800-357-3556; www.chateauapres.com; 1299 Norfolk Ave; dm $35, r incl breakfast $100-150; ℗ ✗ wi-fi) Located near the ski lifts, this reasonably priced 1963 lodge is deservedly popular with budget travelers. Rooms are basic and comfortably sleep from one to four people. Mostly groups stay here outside wintertime.

Park City Peaks Hotel (☎ 435-649-5000, 800-649-5012; www.parkcitypeaks.com; 2121 Park Ave; r $179-359, ste $229-409; P ⊠ ⋇ ⋐ ⊡ wi-fi) Formerly a Radisson, this well-run 131-room hotel has comfortable contemporary rooms, most with gorgeous Wasatch Mountains views. There are a dynamite swim-through indoor-outdoor pool, hot tubs and an on-site grill restaurant.

Washington School Inn (☎ 435-649-3800, 800-824-1672; www.washingtonschoolinn.com; 543 Park Ave; r incl breakfast $305-515; ⋇ ⋈ wi-fi) These sumptuous rooms are located in a restored schoolhouse that survived the infamous Park City fire of 1898. In the evenings it has fresh house-baked cookies and a spread of hors d'oeuvres in the winter months.

EATING
Park City has more than enough dining options to suit any palate, with lots of upscale choices.

Uptown Fare (☎ 435-615-1998; 227 Main St; dishes $7; ⋈ 11am-4pm Mon-Fri) Only your own mom could fix a more comforting meal than you'll find at this cozy mother-and-daughter-operated spot. Try the homemade soups, sandwiches (the turkey is house-roasted daily) and chocolaty scratch brownies. One vegan soup and sandwich choice is always available.

Morning Ray Café & Bakery (☎ 435-649-5686; 255 Main St; mains $8; ⋈ 7am-1pm summer, to 3pm winter) A popular breakfast and lunch place, it serves strong coffee, veggie scrambles, homemade granola and bona fide New York bagels, flown in par-boiled and baked on-site. Be prepared to wait during peak season.

Wasatch Brew Pub (☎ 435-649-0900; 250 Main St; mains lunch $8-10, dinner $11-18; ⋈ 11am-close) The Polygamy Porter and First Amendment Lager go down easy with hearty pub grub. There's a full restaurant downstairs and a busy cantina upstairs with billiards and darts.

Café Terigo (☎ 435-645-9555; 424 Main St; mains lunch $12-15, dinner $22-28; ⋈ 11:30am-2:30pm & 5:30pm-close Mon-Sat, 5:30pm-close Sun) Tops for lunch (especially on the flower-festooned patio in summer), Terigo makes terrific salads and homemade pasta, meats and seafood.

our pick Purple Sage (☎ 435-655-9505; 434 Main St; dishes $19-25; ⋈ 5:30pm-close) Enjoy an intimate dining experience in a restored 1895 telephone office right in the middle of historic Main St. The warmly lit booths are separated by languidly painted silk screens, with patio seating out back for warm summer nights. Foodies love the American Western dishes like butternut-squash ravioli and buttermilk fried chicken, and fun desserts like pecan pie made with purple sweet potatoes.

Ghidotti's (☎ 435-658-0669; 6030 Market St, dishes $18-30; ⋈ 5-9pm Sun-Thu, to 10pm Fri & Sat) Located in the Redstone area, this super-romantic Italian restaurant feels like a rustic aristocratic villa, its high-ceiling and chandeliered rooms filled with pillars and fireplaces and awash in fresh flowers. Chef Bill White lives up to all expectations, with uncomplicated but delicious dishes like filet mignon and shrimp scampi Florentine.

ENTERTAINMENT
Main St's where it's at, with a half-dozen swinging nightclubs and bars.

O'Shucks (☎ 435-645-3999; 427 Main St; ⋈ 11am-1am) Dude, this dive bar is so totally rad. They pack 'em in on Tuesday with $3 schooners (32oz beers), and there's always a carpet of peanut shells crunching underfoot.

Cisero's (☎ 435-649-6800; 306 Main St; ⋈ 4pm-2am) Cisero's basement nightspot is happening seven days a week, with live music, karaoke and a dance floor tricked out with lasers. No smoking inside; there's an outside patio for puffing.

Spur Bar & Grill (☎ 435-615-1618; 3501/2 Main St; ⋈ 5pm-1am) Live bands play on weekends here, a favorite of fresh-faced 30- and 40-somethings. It's also smoke free.

Egyptian Theatre Company (☎ 435-649-9371; www .egyptiantheatrecompany.org; 328 Main St) The restored 1926 theater is a primary venue for Sundance; the rest of the year it hosts plays, musicals and concerts.

GETTING THERE & AROUND
Several companies run vans from Salt Lake City International Airport and hotels to Park City; make reservations. **Park City Transportation** (☎ 435-649-8567, 800-637-3803; www.parkcitytransporta tion.com) operates frequent shared rides ($34), while **Powder for the People** (☎ 435-649-6648, 888-482-7547; www.powderforthepeople.com) has private-charter vans ($80 for one to three people, $30 each additional passenger); reservations required.

SOUTHWEST

Park City Transit (☎ 435-615-5350; www.parkcity
.org/citydepartments/transportation) runs free trolleys three to six times an hour from 8am to
11pm, with diminished service from 6am
to 8am and 11pm to 2am. The excellent
system covers most of Park City, including
the three ski resorts, and makes it easy not
to need a car.

Heber City & Around

About 45 miles southeast of SLC, Heber City
is fairly utilitarian, but it's an affordable base
for exploring the Wasatch Mountains. Most
businesses are along Hwy 40 (Main St).

The 1904 **Heber Valley Historic Railroad** (☎ 435-
654-5601; www.hebervalleyrr.org; 450 S 600 West; adult/
child $30/20) offers family-friendly scenic trips
through gorgeous **Provo Canyon**.

About 15 miles southwest of Heber City,
scenic Hwy 189 squeezes through the steep-
walled canyon on its way to Provo, home to
clean-cut Brigham Young University, but not
really worth a stop. For information on camping and hiking in the Uinta National Forest,
contact the **Heber Ranger Station** (☎ 435-654-0470;
2460 S Hwy 40; ☼ 8am-5pm Mon-Fri).

Consider driving the attractive 20-mile
route known as the **Alpine Scenic Loop**. From
Hwy 189, head north onto narrow and twisting Hwy 92, which leads to Robert Redford's
Sundance Resort (☎ 801-225-4107, 800-892-1600; www
.sundanceresort.com; 9521 Alpine Loop Rd, Provo; r from
$282, 3-/4-bedroom house from $1089/1304; ☒ ☐ wi-
fi), an elegant, rustic and environmentally
conscious getaway located in a wilderness
setting, with excellent skiing, a year-round
arts program, spa and summer hiking, and
mountain biking.

Three beautiful caves in **Timpanogos Cave National Monument** (☎ 801-756-5238; www.nps.gov/tica;
Alpine Scenic Loop; per vehicle $3; ☼ May-Sep) are acces-
sible on ranger-led tours (adults $7, children
$3 to $5); call ahead to reserve.

SLEEPING & EATING

Heber City motels are basic but far cheaper
than accommodations in Park City. You
can also camp in the surrounding forest and
nearby state parks.

Swiss Alps Inn (☎ 435-654-0722; www.swissalpsinn
.com; 167 S Main; r $70-80; ☒ ☒ wi-fi) This quaint
motel is one of the best in town.

Snake Creek Grill (☎ 435-654-2133; 650 W 100
South; mains $17-20; ☼ 5:30-9:30pm Wed-Sun) One of
northern Utah's best restaurants looks like

a saloon from an old Western. But the all-
American Southwest-style menu features
dishes like blue-cornmeal-crusted trout and
finger-lickin' ribs.

Ogden

After the completion of the first transcontinental railway in 1869, Ogden became an
important railway town. Today its restored
mid-19th-century downtown is a major draw.
During its heyday, historic 25th St between
Union Station and Grant Ave was lined with
brothels and raucous saloons; now it has
the city's nicest selection of restaurants and
bars. Ogden lies about 38 miles north of SLC.
And since people in SLC and Park City look
down their noses at Ogden, the slopes here
are luxuriously empty.

The restored **Union Station** houses the **visitor
center** (☎ 801-778-6250, 800-255-8824; www.ogden.travel;
cnr 25th St & Wall Ave; ☼ 8am-5pm Mon-Fri); it's also
home to several worthy **museums** (☎ 801-393-
9886; www.theunionstation.org; adult/child $5/3; ☼ 10am-
5pm Mon-Sat), with vintage trains, firearms, cars
and more.

The steep-walled **Ogden Canyon** heads 40
miles northeast through the Wasatch Mountains to Monte Cristo Summit (9148ft), passing
two ski areas: **Snowbasin Ski Area** (☎ 801-620-1000,
888-437-5488; www.snowbasin.com; Hwy 226; adult/child
$62/39), a 3200-acre resort that hosted downhill
and super-G skiing events in the 2002 Winter Olympics; and the appropriately named
Powder Mountain Ski Area (☎ 801-745-3772; www
.powdermountain.net; adult/child/senior $50/30/40).

Millstream Motel (☎ 801-394-9425; 1450 Washington Blvd; r $40-45; ℗) retains the flavor of its
1940s heyday.

Logan & Around

Logan, founded in 1859, is a quintessential
old-fashioned American community with
strong Mormon ties and home to Utah State
University. Situated in bucolic Cache Valley, it
offers year-round outdoor activities – hiking,
camping, snowmobiling and cross-country
skiing. Get oriented at the **Cache Valley Visitors
Bureau** (☎ 435-755-1890, 800-882-4433; www.tourcache
valley.com; 199 N Main St; ☼ 8am-5pm Mon-Fri & 9am-1pm
Sat summer).

The **Wellsville Mountain range**, one of the
world's highest to rise from such a narrow
base, is best explored with information and
maps from the **Logan Ranger Station** (☎ 435-755-
3620; 1500 E Hwy 89; ☼ 8am-4:30pm Mon-Fri).

The 40-mile drive through **Logan Canyon** (Hwy 89 to Garden City) is beautiful any time of year, but in the fall it's jaw-dropping. You'll enjoy hiking and biking trails, rock climbing, fishing spots, and seasonal campgrounds.

Perhaps the best of its kind, the **American West Heritage Center** (☎ 435-245-6050; www.awhc .org; 4025 S Hwy 89; adult/child/senior $5/3/4; ⌚ 10am-4pm Tue-Sat May-Sep) recreates 19th-century frontier communities with plenty of hands-on activities.

SLEEPING & EATING

Beaver Creek Lodge (☎ 435-946-3400, 800-946-4485; www.beavercreeklodge.com; Hwy 89, Mile 487; r summer $89-99, winter $129-139; ✗ wi-fi) This lodge has TVs (but no phones), and offers horseback riding and snowmobiling packages.

Caffe Ibis (☎ 435-753-4777; 52 Federal Ave; dishes under $6; ⌚ 6am-6pm Mon-Thu, to 9pm Fri, to 6:30pm Sat, 8am-6pm Sun) Popular with the university crowd, this café serves gourmet coffees and sandwiches.

Bluebird Restaurant (☎ 435-752-3155; 19 N Main St; dishes $7-9; ⌚ 11am-9:30pm Mon-Fri, to 10pm Sat & Sun) The 1920s-style Bluebird is classic; check out the old ice-cream fountain.

NORTHEASTERN UTAH

Despite being hyped as 'Utah's Dinosaurland,' the main attraction is actually the high wilderness terrain. All towns are a mile above sea level, and the rugged Uinta Mountains make for great trips.

Mirror Lake Highway

This alpine route (Hwy 150) begins in **Kamas**, about 12 miles east of Park City, and covers 65 miles as it climbs to elevations of more than 10,000ft into Wyoming. The highway provides breathtaking vistas of the western Uinta Mountains, while passing by scores of lakes, campgrounds and trailheads. Contact the **ranger station** (☎ 435-783-4338; 50 E Center St, Kamas; ⌚ 8am-4:30pm Mon-Fri) for general information on the Wasatch-Cache National Forest.

Uinta Mountains

The only way to access the 800-sq-mile, east–west trending High Uintas Wilderness Area is by foot or horse – it's tough going, but the rewards are great. The high country has hundreds of lakes, most of which are stocked annually with trout and whitefish. Come for the excellent fishing and the rare experience of

wild, remote wilderness. The Ashley National Forest's **Roosevelt Ranger Station** (☎ 435-722-5018; www.fs.fed.us/r4/ashley/recreation; 650 W Hwy 40, Roosevelt; ⌚ 8am-5pm Mon-Fri) has information.

In addition to wilderness **campgrounds** (campsites $8-10), you can stay at **Defa's Dude Ranch** (☎ 435-848-5590; www.defasduderanch.com; Hwy 35, Hanna; cabins s $25-35, d $35-45; ⌚ May-Oct), which has rustic cabins in a beautiful, remote setting; bring your own bedding (or request it). There's also a café, a saloon and horseback riding ($25 per hour).

Vernal

The capital of Utah's dinosaur country, Vernal welcomes visitors with a large pink dino-buddy and plenty of services. The **travel board** (☎ 800-477-5558; www.dinoland.com) can provide information, and the good **natural history museum** (☎ 435-789-3799; 496 E Main St; ⌚ 9am-5pm yr-round, 8am-7pm summer) helps walk-ins and has driving-tour brochures. The Red Cloud Loop and Petroglyphs tour is a highlight. Check out the museum's garden full of life-size dinosaurs. The **Vernal Ranger Station** (☎ 435-789-1181; 355 N Vernal Ave; ⌚ 8am-5pm Mon-Fri) has details on camping and hiking.

Twelve miles northeast of Vernal, **Red Fleet State Park** (☎ 435-789-4432; www.stateparks.utah.gov; Hwy 191; per vehicle $5; campsites $11) offers boating, camping and an easy hike to a series of fossilized dinosaur tracks (best visited when the reservoir isn't full).

The Green and Yampa Rivers have satisfying rapids for white-water enthusiasts, as well as calmer areas for gentler float trips. **Hatch River Expeditions** (☎ 435-789-4316, 800-342-8243; www .hatchriver.com; 221 N 400 East) runs a variety of one- to five-day trips.

Sage Motel (☎ 435-789-1442, 800-760-1442; www .vernalmotels.com; 54 W Main St; s/d incl breakfast from $70/80; wi-fi) is a simple but friendly and welcoming place to stay.

Flaming Gorge National Recreation Area

Named for its fiery red sandstone, the gorge area (day use $2) has 375 miles of reservoir shoreline, fly-fishing and rafting on the Green River, trout fishing, hiking, and cross-country skiing. Visit the **Flaming Gorge Headquarters** (☎ 435-784-3445; www.fs.fed.us/r4/ashley/recreation; 25 W Hwy 43; ⌚ 8am-5pm Mon-Fri) or **Flaming Gorge Dam Visitors Center** (☎ 435-885-3135; Hwy 191; ⌚ 8am-6pm summer, 10am-4pm winter).

SOUTHWEST

DON'T BUST THE CRUST!

Only in recent years have cryptobiotic crusts begun to attract attention and concern. These living crusts cover and protect desert soils, literally gluing sand particles together so they don't blow away. Cyanobacteria, one of the earth's oldest life forms, start the process by extending mucus-covered filaments into the dry soil. Over time these filaments and the sand particles adhering to them form a thin crust that is colonized by algae, lichen, fungi and mosses. This crust plays a key role in desert food chains, as well as absorbing tremendous amounts of rainwater and reducing erosion.

Unfortunately, this thin crust is easily fragmented under heavy-soled boots and tires. Once broken, the crust takes 50 to 250 years to repair itself. In its absence, winds and rains erode desert soils, and much of the water that would nourish desert plants is lost. Many sites in Utah, in particular, have cryptobiotic crusts. Visitors to the Southwest have an important responsibility to protect these crusts by staying on established trails.

Sheep Creek Canyon, a dramatic 13-mile paved loop through the Sheep Creek Canyon Geological Area, leaves Hwy 44 about 15 miles west of Greendale Junction.

The **campgrounds** (☎ 877-444-6777; www.recreation .gov; campsites $15-18) in and around Flaming Gorge are mostly open mid-May to mid-October; reserve ahead. **Red Canyon Lodge** (☎ 435-889-3759; www.redcanyonlodge.com; 2450 W Red Canyon Lodge, Dutch John; cabins $99-139; wi-fi) provides rustic and luxury cabins without TVs. **Flaming Gorge Resort** (☎ 435-889-3773; www.flaminggorge resort.com; 1100 E Flaming Gorge Resort, Dutch John; r/condos $97/137; ✗ wi-fi) rents motel rooms and modern condominiums.

Dinosaur National Monument

One of the largest dinosaur fossil beds in North America was discovered here in 1909. The **dinosaur quarry** was enclosed and hundreds of bones were exposed but left in the rock. Unfortunately, it closed in 2006 because of dangerous structural problems, and will not reopen for three to five years.

The **monument** (☎ 435-781-7700; www.nps.gov/ dino; per vehicle $10; ◷ 8:30am-5:30pm summer, to 4:30pm winter) itself is still accessible, with a scaled-back visitors center, and you can drive, hike, backpack and raft through its dramatic and starkly eroded canyons. The monument straddles the Utah–Colorado state line. The Utah portion of the park is about 15 miles east of Vernal via Hwys 40 and 149.

SOUTHEASTERN UTAH

Nicknamed Canyon Country, this desolate corner of Utah is home to soaring snow-blanketed peaks towering over plunging red-rock river canyons. The terrain is so inhospi-table that it was the last region to be mapped in the continental US.

Over 65 million years, water carved serpentine, sheer-walled gorges along the course of the Colorado and Green Rivers, which define the borders of Canyonlands National Park, Utah's largest. Nearby Arches National Park encompasses more rock arches than anywhere else worldwide. Between the parks lies Moab, the state's premier destination for mountain biking, river-running and 4WD-ing. South of Moab, ancestral Puebloan sites are scattered among wilderness areas and parks, most notably Monument Valley, which extends into Arizona (p843).

This section is organized roughly north to south, beginning with Green River, on I-70, and following Hwy 191 into the southeastern corner of the state.

Green River

The 'world's watermelon capital,' Green River offers a good base for river running on the Green and Colorado Rivers, or exploring the nearby San Rafael Swell.

The Colorado and Green Rivers were first explored in 1869 and 1871 by the legendary one-armed Civil War veteran, geologist and ethnologist John Wesley Powell. Learn about his amazing travels at the **John Wesley Powell River History Museum** (☎ 435-564-3427; www.jwprhm .com; 1765 E Main St; adult/child $3/1; ◷ 8am-8pm Apr-Oct, to 4pm Tue-Sat Nov-Mar), which also has exhibits on the Fremont Native Americans, geology and local history. The museum also serves as the local visitor center.

Local outfitters run **white-water rafting day-trips** (adult/child $60/49), including lunch and transportation; ask about multiday excursions. Call **Holiday Expeditions** (☎ 435-564-3273, 800-624-6323; www.holidayexpeditions.com; 2075 E Main St) or **Moki Mac River Expeditions** (☎ 435-564-3361, 800-284-7280; www.mokimac.com; 100 Silliman Lane).

SLEEPING & EATING

Budget choices include the first two options, then the choices slide up the fee scale. Ray's Tavern is far and away the best place to eat in town.

Robbers Roost Motel (☎ 435-564-3452; www .rrmotel.com; 325 W Main St; r $27-60; ✖ wi-fi)

Best Western River Terrace (☎ 435-564-3401, 800-528-1234; www.bestwestern.com; 880 E Main St; r incl breakfast $80-100; ✖ ✖ ✖ wi-fi)

Holiday Inn Express (☎ 435-564-4439, 877-531-5084; www.holidayinn.com; 965 E Main St; r incl breakfast $89-104; ✖ ✖ ✖ wi-fi)

Ray's Tavern (☎ 435-564-3511; 25 S Broadway; steaks $11-20; ✖ 10am-10pm)

GETTING THERE & AWAY

There are buses through **Greyhound** (☎ 435-564-3421, 800-231-2222; www.greyhound.com; 525 E Main St) to SLC ($37, 3½ hours) and Las Vegas ($75, 7½ hours); buses stop at the Rodeway Inn. **Amtrak** (☎ 800-872-7245; www.amtrak.com; 250 S Broadway) runs daily to Denver, Colorado ($45 to $70, 11 hours). It's the only stop in southeastern Utah.

Moab

In this active and outdoorsy town with legendary slickrock mountains, it seems as though every pedestrian clutches a Nalgene water bottle and every car totes a few dusty mountain bikes. Encircled by stunning orange mountains and the snow-topped La Sal Mountains, Moab is southeastern Utah's largest town and an often-mobbed gateway for alfresco adventures. Moab bills itself as Utah's recreation capital, and it delivers.

INFORMATION

Most businesses are along Hwy 191, also called Main St.

Moab Information Center (Main & Center; ✖ 9am-5pm winter, 8am-9pm summer) This incredibly helpful place serves walk-in visitors only. It carries books and maps, and comprehensive information on everything from area campgrounds and permits to current river conditions. There's a fantastic series of free activities brochures highlighting 4WD, hiking and mountain-biking trails, river rafting, auto tours, and movie locations.

Moab Area Travel Council (☎ 435-259-8825, 800-635-6622; www.discovermoab.com; ✖ 8am-5pm Mon-Fri) Dispenses visitor information over the phone and through the mail.

BLM office (☎ 435-259-2100; www.blm.gov/utah/ moab; 82 E Dogwood; ✖ 7:45am-4:30pm Mon-Fri) Has camping information and takes reservations for group campsites. Processes river permits from 8am to noon.

Back of Beyond (☎ 435-259-5154; 83 N Main; ✖ 9am-10pm) Excellent downtown bookstore with an extensive regional selection.

ACTIVITIES

Outfitters take care of everything, from permits to food to setting up camp to transportation. Among the best:

Adrift Adventures (☎ 435-259-8594, 800-874-4483; www.adrift.net; 378 N Main)

Canyon Voyages (☎ 435-259-6007, 800-733-6007; www.canyonvoyages.com; 211 N Main)

OARS (☎ 435-259-5919, 800-342-5938; www.oars.com; 2540 S Hwy 191)

Sheri Griffith Expeditions (☎ 435-259-8229, 800-332-2439; www.griffithexp.com; 2231 S Hwy 191)

SLEEPING

Despite tons of hotels, B&Bs and campgrounds, the town is packed from spring to fall; reservations are advised. Individual **BLM campsites** (www.blm.gov/utah/moab/campgrounds .html; campsites $5-10) in the area are first come,

---

THE BARD OF MOAB

Edward Abbey (1927–89), one of America's great Western prose writers, worked as a seasonal ranger at Arches National Monument in the 1950s, before it became a national park. In his essay collection *Desert Solitaire: A Season in the Wilderness*, Abbey wrote of his time here and describes the simple beauty and subtle power of the vast landscape. In perhaps the book's most famous essay, he bemoaned what he dubbed 'Industrial Tourism,' the exploitation of the natural environment by big business acting in cahoots with government, turning the National Monument into a 'Natural Money-Mint.' Many of Abbey's predictions have come true – you need only arrive at Arches on a busy weekend and get stuck in a line of SUVs to know that he was, in his way, a prophet. After reading his book, you'll comprehend the desert in new, unexpected ways.

first served. In peak season, check with the Moab Information Center to see which sites are full.

Adventure Inn Moab (☎ 435-259-6122, 866-662-2466; www.adventureinnmoab.com; 512 N Main; s/d incl breakfast $60/80; ✕ 🐾 wi-fi) Family owned and incredibly friendly, this standard motel has a homey feel and a nice shaded yard out front to sit and relax. Room 10 is a smidgen larger than the rest.

Rodeway Landmark Inn (☎ 435-259-6147, 800-441-6147; www.landmarkinnmoab.com; 168 N Main; d incl breakfast $90-100; ✕ 🐾 wi-fi) Kids might refuse to come in once they start playing on the awesome water flume, and adults love that hot tub. An older motel, it has very clean, slightly kitschy rooms, with scenic Western murals over the beds and '70s-style furniture.

Gonzo Inn (☎ 435-259-2515, 800-791-4044; www.gonzoinn.com; 100 W 200 South; r/ste incl breakfast $145/189-315; ✕ 🐾 🐾 🖥 wi-fi) A fun and funky boutique hotel with a gecko theme and retro splashes of color. The ample suites can comfortably sleep four, with the kitchenettes and spacious patio or balcony areas to boot.

EATING

There's no shortage of places to fuel up in Moab, from backpacker coffeehouses to gourmet dining rooms. Some restaurants close earlier in winter, so call ahead.

Red Rock Bakery & Net Café (☎ 435-259-5941; 74 S Main; sandwiches $4-7; ⊙ 7am-5pm Mon-Sat, to 4pm Sun summer, 7am-4pm Mon-Sat, to 3pm Sun winter) A cheerful and sunny breakfast and lunch nook accompanied by the faint rat-a-tat-tat of laptops grooving on the free wi-fi. The fresh scones are perfectly dense, and the bagels are the real damn deal.

Eddie McStiff's (☎ 435-259-2337; 59 S Main St; dishes $7-16; ⊙ 4:30pm-10:30pm Mon-Thu, 11:30am-11pm Fri-Sun) A mammoth restaurant right in the middle of town, it serves pizza, steaks, pasta, salads, burgers and bar food, and there's free wi-fi. Set yourself up with a growler (half-gallon) of the tasty microbrew – the bar stays open later.

Moab Brewery (☎ 435-259-6333; 686 S Main; mains $8-12; ⊙ 11:30am-10pm Mon-Thu, to 11pm Fri & Sat summer, 11:30am-9pm Mon-Thu, to 10pm Fri & Sat winter) At Moab's only on-site microbrewery restaurant you can see the vats just behind the bar area. It serves a range of burgers, seafood, steak and chicken, all to better accompany a pint of its Derailleur or Dead Horse Ale.

Miguel's Baja Grill (☎ 435-259-6546; 51 N Main; dishes $9-17; ⊙ 5-10pm) Dine on Baja fish tacos ($12) in the sky-lit breezeway patio lined with brightly painted walls. Fajitas, *chilis rellenos* and seafood entrees are good sized, and the portabello salad is excellent.

Center Café (☎ 435-259-4295; 60 N 100 West; mains $26-30; ⊙ from 3:30) Consistently named southern Utah's best restaurant, the Center Café is what you'd expect of Mendocino, not Moab. The chef–owner cooks with confidence, drawing inspiration from regional American and Mediterranean cuisines – there's everything from grilled prawns with cheddar-garlic grits to pan-roasted lamb with balsamic-port reduction. The desserts are truly superb. Note that there's no specified closing time.

GETTING THERE & AROUND

There are two daily flights from SLC with **US Airways Express** (☎ 800-235-9292; www.usairways.com) to **Canyonlands Airport** (www.moabairport.com), 16 miles north of town, via Hwy 191. Planes can even transport a few bicycles.

Bighorn Express (☎ 801-746-3023, 888-655-7433; www.bighornexpress.com) operates a scheduled van service to and from SLC and Green River, while **Roadrunner Shuttle** (☎ 435-259-9402; www.roadrunnershuttle.com) operates an on-demand service as well as hiker-biker and river shuttles. **Coyote Shuttle** (☎ 435-259-8656; 55 W 300 South) also does the full range of recreational shuttles.

Arches National Park

One of the Southwest's most gorgeous parks, **Arches** (☎ 435-719-2299; www.nps.gov/arch; per vehicle $20; ⊙ visitor center 7:30am-6:30pm Apr-Oct, 8am-4:30pm Nov-Mar) boasts the world's greatest concentration of sandstone arches. Just 5 miles north of Moab on Hwy 191, the park is always packed in summer. Consider a moonlight exploration, when it's cooler and the rocks feel ghostly. Many arches are easily reached by paved roads and relatively short hiking trails. Highlights include **Balanced Rock**, the oft-photographed **Delicate Arch** (best captured in the late afternoon), the spectacularly elongated **Landscape Arch**, and popular, twice-daily ranger-led trips into the **Fiery Furnace** (adult/child $10/5), for which reservations are recommended.

As you casually stroll beneath these monuments to nature's power, listen carefully, especially in winter, and you may hear spontaneous popping noises in distant rocks – the sound of arches forming. (If you hear popping noises *overhead*, move it!)

Because of water scarcity and the heat, few visitors backpack, though it is allowed with free permits (available from the visitor center). The scenic **Devils Garden Campground** (☎ 877-444-6777, 518-885-3639; www.recreation.gov; Hwy 191; campsites $20) is 18 miles from the visitor center and fills up from March to October. Reservations must be made at least four days in advance, though half the sites are assigned first come, first served each morning; to snag one, be at the visitor center when it opens.

Dead Horse Point State Park

A tiny but stunning **state park** (☎ 435-259-2614; www.stateparks.utah.gov; Hwy 313; per vehicle $7; ☿ dawn-dusk), it's been the setting for numerous movies, including the opening scene from *Mission Impossible II* and the finale of *Thelma and Louise*. Located just off Hwy 313 (the road to Canyonlands), the park has canyons rimmed with white cliffs and walloping, mesmerizing views of the Colorado River, Canyonlands National Park and the distant La Sal Mountains. If you only have time for one major viewpoint, this is it. The 21-site **Kayenta Campground** (☎ 801-322-3770, 800-322-3770; www.stateparks.utah.gov; Hwy 313; campsites $20) provides limited water and RV facilities.

Canyonlands National Park

Covering 527 sq miles, **Canyonlands** (☎ 435-719-2313; www.nps.gov/cany; per vehicle $20) is Utah's largest and wildest park. Indeed, parts of it are as rugged as almost anywhere on the planet. Arches, bridges, needles, spires, craters, mesas, buttes – Canyonlands is a crumbling, decaying beauty, a vision of ancient earth.

You can hike, raft and 4WD (Cataract Canyon offers some of the wildest white water in the West), but be sure that you have plenty of gas, food and water before leaving Moab.

Difficult terrain and lack of water render this the least developed and visited of the major Southwestern national parks.

The canyons of the Colorado and Green Rivers divide the park into three districts. **Island in the Sky** is most easily reached and offers amazing views. There's a helpful **visitor center** (☎ 435-259-4712; www.nps.gov/cany/island; Hwy 313; ☿ 8am-4:30pm, extended hr spring-fall) and some excellent short hikes (the mile-long trail to Grand View Overlook takes you right along the canyon's edge). This park section is 32 miles south of Moab; head north along Hwy 191 and then west on Hwy 313.

Needles is on Hwy 211, which heads west from Hwy 191, 40 miles south of Moab; you'll find more great views here and a smaller **visitor center** (☎ 435-259-4711; www.nps.gov/cany/needles; Hwy 211; ☿ 9am-4:30pm, extended hr Mar-Oct). And then there's the **Maze**, one of the wildest and most remote areas in the Southwest, accessible by 4WD only. Within **Horseshoe Canyon**, along the 32-mile road from Hwy 24 to the Maze, you'll find Great Gallery, with superb life-size rock art left by prehistoric Native Americans.

In addition to entrance fees, permits are required for overnight backcountry and mountain biking camping, 4WD trips, and river trips. Reserve at least two weeks ahead, by fax or mail only, with the **Canyonlands NP Reservations Office** (☎ 435-259-4351; fax 435-259-4285; www.nps.gov/cany/permits.htm; 2282 S West Resource Blvd, Moab, UT 84532), or just show up, although reservations are recommended in spring and fall.

Natural Bridges National Monument

Forty miles west of Blanding via Hwy 95, this **monument** (☎ 435-692-1234; www.nps.gov/nabr; Hwy 275; per vehicle $10; ☿ 7am-dusk) became Utah's first NPS land in 1908. The highlight is a dark-stained, white-sandstone canyon containing three easily accessible natural bridges. The oldest, the Owachomo Bridge, spans 180ft but

---

SCENIC DRIVE: MOKI DUGWAY & MULE POINT

The Moki Dugway (Hwy 261) heads south from Hwy 95 to connect with Hwy 163 at Mexican Hat. Along the way is a turnoff to Mule Point Overlook – don't miss this cliff-edge viewpoint, one of the country's most sweeping, encompassing Monument Valley and other landmarks.

Back on Hwy 261, the pavement ends and the Moki Dugway suddenly descends a whopping 1100ft along a series of fist-clenching hairpin turns. At the bottom, a dirt road heads east into the Valley of the Gods, a 17-mile drive through mind-blowing sandstone monoliths. Near the southern end of Hwy 261, a 4-mile paved road heads west to Goosenecks State Park, a small lookout with memorable views of the San Juan River, 1100ft below.

is only 9ft thick. The flat 9-mile Scenic Drive loop is ideal for biking. Basic **camping** (campsites $10) is also available.

Hovenweep National Monument

Beautiful, little-visited **Hovenweep** (☎ 970-560-4282; www.nps.gov/hove; Hwy 262; per vehicle $10; ☼ visitor center 8am-4:30pm, to 6pm summer), meaning 'deserted valley' in the Ute language, contains six sets of prehistoric Ancestral Puebloan sites, five of which require long hikes to reach. You'll find a visitor center, a ranger station and a basic **campground** (campsites $10), but no facilities. The main access is east of Hwy 191 on Hwy 262 via Hatch Trading Post, more than 40 miles from Bluff or Blanding.

Bluff

Surrounded by red rock, tiny Bluff was founded by Mormon pioneers in 1880 and makes a comfortable, laid-back base for regional exploring. It sits at the junction of Hwys 191 and 163, along the San Juan River. **Wild Rivers Expeditions** (☎ 435-672-2244; www.riversandruins.com; 101 Main St) has been guiding trips since 1957 (day-trips adult/child $150/125). **Far Out Expeditions** (☎ 435-672-2294; www.faroutexpeditions.com; 7th & Mulberry Sts) arranges off-the-beaten-track trips to Monument Valley and other locations.

Bluff has good lodgings, including the favored and hospitable **Recapture Lodge** (☎ 435-672-2281; www.bluffutah.org/recapturelodge; Hwy 191; r $50-70; ☒ ☒ wi-fi), a rustic, cozy property pleasantly shaded between the highway and the river.

Stop by friendly **Cow Canyon Trading Post** (☎ 435-672-2208; Hwys 191 & 162; mains $12-16; ☼ 6-9pm Thu-Sun Apr-Oct), with terrific regionally inspired meat and vegetarian dinners, good salads and a coveted liquor license. The trading post has rugs, baskets, pottery, jewelry and good books.

Monument Valley

From the village of **Mexican Hat** (named after a sombrero-shaped rock), Hwy 163 winds southwest and enters the Navajo Indian Reservation and, after about 30 miles, Monument Valley Navajo Tribal Park (p843).

Just inside the Utah border, **Goulding's Lodge** (☎ 435-727-3231; www.gouldings.com; Hwy 163; r $175; ☒ ☒ wi-fi) is the only hotel near Monument Valley; each room has a balcony with a million-dollar view of the colossal red buttes. A full-service outpost, Goulding's also has a restaurant, a museum, a store, gas and a **campground** (RV/campsites $36/22). It also offers tours.

SOUTH-CENTRAL & SOUTHWESTERN UTAH

Locals call it 'color country,' but the cutesy label hardly does justice to the eye-popping hues that saturate the landscape. The deep-crimson canyons of Zion National Park, the delicate pink-and-orange minarets at Bryce Canyon, the swirling yellow-white domes of Capitol Reef – the land is so spectacular that it encompasses three national parks and the gigantic Grand Staircase-Escalante National Monument.

This section is organized roughly northeast to southwest: from Hanksville, along Hwy 24 through Capitol Reef National Park and southwest along Hwy 12, which passes the Grand Staircase-Escalante National Monument and Bryce Canyon. Quite simply, it's one of the most scenic roads in the country. From Hwy 12, Hwy 89 goes south to Kanab (and continues to the North Rim of the Grand Canyon). Further west are Cedar City, St George and gorgeous Zion National Park.

Hanksville

Conveniently situated at the junction of Hwys 95 and 24, Hanksville offers up a **BLM office** (☎ 435-542-3461; 406 S 100 West; ☼ 8am-4:30pm Mon-Fri), with information on the **Henry Mountains**, a remote, 11,000ft-high range. **Goblin Valley State Park** (☎ 435-564-3633; Hwy 24; per vehicle $6; ☼ 7am-10pm), full of delightful and alien rock formations, has **camping** (☎ 800-322-3770; www.stateparks.utah.gov; campsites $5). About 20 miles west, near Caineville, **Luna Mesa Oasis** (☎ 435-456-9122; Hwy 24; dishes $5-15; ☼ 8am-8pm Mon-Sat) is a friendly spot to grab a meal.

Capitol Reef National Park

Not as crowded as its fellow parks but equally scenic, Capitol Reef contains much of the 100-mile **Waterpocket Fold**, created 65 million years ago when the earth's surface buckled up and folded, exposing a cross-section of geologic history that is downright painterly in its colorful intensity. Hwy 24 cuts grandly through the park, but take the park's own scenic drive ($5) starting from the **visitor center** (☎ 435-425-3791; www.nps.gov/care; Hwy 24 & Scenic Dr; ☼ 8am-4:30pm, extended hr summer), where there's grassy **camping** (campsites $10). A legacy of the Mormon settlement of Fruita, the park also encompasses

SOUTHWEST

amazing **orchards** (www.nps.gov/care/historyculture/orchardscms.htm) where visitors can pick cherries, peaches and apples in season.

Torrey

This little village makes a good stopping point for lodging, as well as providing surprisingly great meals. The **travel council** (☎ 435-425-3365, 800-858-7951; www.capitolreef.org) has good information.

Capitol Reef Inn & Cafe (☎ 435-425-3271; www.capitolreefinn.com; 360 W Main St; r $48; ✗ ☼) These 10 comfortable rooms are outfitted with hand-crafted wood furniture. Climb the giant kiva to watch the sunset and then hop into the hot tub.

Pine Shadows Bungalows (☎ 435-425-3939, 800-708-1223; www.pineshadowcabins.net; 195 W 125 South, Teasdale; cabins from $69; ✗) Tucked between piñon pines beneath white cliffs, these six spacious cabins have vaulted ceilings and kitchenettes. They make for a great hideaway and excellent value just outside town.

Cafe Diablo (☎ 435-425-3070; 599 W Main St; mains $20-28; ☼ 5-10pm Apr-Oct; ✗) One of southern Utah's best eateries, Diablo serves outstanding highly stylized Southwestern cooking – including succulent vegetarian dishes – bursting with flavor and towering on the plate.

Boulder

Tiny Boulder is 32 miles south of Torrey on Hwy 12. From here, the attractive **Burr Trail** heads east as a paved road across the northeastern corner of the Grand Staircase-Escalante National Monument, winding up at Bullfrog Marina on Lake Powell. Consider taking a one-day, child-friendly excursion with knowledgeable **Earth Tours** (☎ 435-691-1241; www.earth-tours.com), which offers half-/full-day tours for $75/100, or a multiday backcountry trek with the equally recommended **Escalante Canyon Outfitters** (☎ 435-691-3037, 888-326-4453; www.ecohike.com; ☼ spring-fall), which offers four- to six-day all-inclusive treks for $1070 to $1445.

The comfortable, modern rooms (with hot tub) at **Boulder Mountain Lodge** (☎ 800-556-3446; www.boulder-utah.com; Hwy 12; r $90-168; ✗ ☼ wi-fi) are among the nicest accommodations along Hwy 12.

If you've given up on eating well in southern Utah, take heart: the must-visit **Hell's Backbone Grill** (☎ 435-335-7464; Boulder Mountain Lodge, Hwy 12; mains breakfast $5-8, dinner $13-18; ☼ 7-11:30am & 5:30-9:30pm) serves soulful, earthy preparations of locally raised meats and organically grown produce from its own garden.

Escalante

This quiet, small town provides gateway access to the Grand Staircase-Escalante National Monument. With a whopping population of about 750 people, it's the largest outpost for almost 75 miles in any direction.

The **Escalante Interagency Office** (☎ 435-826-5499; www.ut.blm.gov/monument; 775 W Main St; ☼ 7:30am-5:30pm) is a superb resource center with complete information on all area public lands. Fifteen miles east on Hwy 12, **Calf Creek Recreation Area** (☎ 435-826-5499; www.ut.blm.gov/monument; per vehicle $2, campsites $7; ☼ yr-round) has pleasant, basic camping and a recommended 3-mile hike to Lower Calf Creek Falls.

Escalante Outfitters, Inc (☎ 435-826-4266; 310 W Main St; ☼ 8am-9pm) is a great travelers' oasis, selling maps, books, camping supplies, liquor, espresso and the best homemade pizza ($12 to $22) you'll find in Utah – no kidding. Overnighters stay in cute, cozy, clean **cabins** ($50) out back.

Grand Staircase-Escalante National Monument

This 2656-sq-mile **monument** (www.ut.blm.gov/monument), established in 1996, is tucked between Bryce Canyon NP, Capitol Reef NP and Glen Canyon National Recreation Area. Tourist infrastructure is minimal, leaving a vast, remote desert for adventurous travelers who have the time and necessary outdoor equipment to explore.

Three unpaved roads, Skutumpah/Johnson Canyon Rd (the least used and most westerly route), Cottonwood Canyon Rd and Smoky Mountain Rd – cross the monument roughly north to south between Hwys 12 and 89. A fourth unpaved road (the Hole-in-the-Rock Rd) begins from Hwy 12 and dead-ends at the Glen Canyon National Recreation Area. Roads get slick and impassable when wet. Wilderness camping is allowed with a required free permit. Before heading out, obtain current road and travel information from the Escalante Interagency Office (above), the visitor centers in Kanab (p870) or **Cannonville** (☎ 435-826-5640; 10 Center St, Cannonville; ☼ 8am-4:30pm, closed winter).

Kodachrome Basin State Park

Dozens of red, pink and white sandstone chimneys highlight this colorful **state park**

(☎ 435-679-8562; www.stateparks.utah.gov; Cottonwood Canyon Rd; per vehicle $6), named for its photogenic landscape by the National Geographic Society. The Grand Parade Trail has the best views of sand pipes and other formations; there's also a **campground** (☎ 801-322-3770, 800-322-3770; campsites $15).

Bryce Canyon National Park

The Grand Staircase, a series of steplike uplifted rock layers stretching north from the Grand Canyon, culminates at this very popular **national park** (☎ 435-834-5322; www.nps.gov/brca; Hwy 63; per vehicle $25; ☺ visitor center 8am-8pm May-Sep, to 4:30pm Nov-Mar, to 6pm Oct & Apr) in the Pink Cliffs formation. It's full of wondrous pinnacles and points, steeples and spires, and odd formations called 'hoodoos.' The 'canyon' is actually an amphitheater eroded from the cliffs. During fall rains, the hoodoos peeping out of fog look otherworldly.

From Hwy 12, Hwy 63 heads 4 miles south to Rim Road Dr (8000ft), an 18-mile dead-end road that follows the rim of the canyon, passing the visitor center, lodge, viewpoints (don't miss Inspiration Point) and trailheads, ending at Rainbow Point at 9115ft elevation. You can whisk in and out in a few hours, but for a richer experience, numerous trails will take you out among the spires and deeper into the heart of the landscape. There is a free (voluntary) shuttle system from Hwy 12.

The park's only licensed outfitter is **Canyon Trail Rides** (☎ 435-679-8665; www.canyonrides.com; Hwy 63; 2hr/half-day $40/65), which operates out of Bryce Canyon Lodge (below); horse and mule rides head past dramatic hoodoos into Bryce Amphitheater.

The two campgrounds, **North Campground** (☎ 877-444-6777; www.recreation.gov; Bryce Canyon Rd; campsites $10) and **Sunset Campground** (campsites $10; ☺ late spring-fall), both have toilets and water; Sunset is more wooded, but has fewer amenities and doesn't accept reservations. For laundry, showers and groceries, visit North Campground. During summer, sites fill by noon.

The 1920s **Bryce Canyon Lodge** (☎ 435-834-5361, 888-297-2757; www.brycecanyonlodge.com; Hwy 63; r $115-140, cabins $149; ☺ Apr-Oct; ✗) exudes rustic mountain charm. Rooms are in satellite buildings and range from modern hotel-style units with up-to-date furnishings and balconies to romantic, slightly dated, freestanding cabins with gas fireplaces and front porches. If you can secure a reservation, it's worth every penny.

Panguitch & Around

Simple little Panguitch is a popular stop on Hwy 89. It's surrounded by knockout scenic drives, has several good motels and is convenient to both Bryce Canyon (24 miles) and Zion (70 miles) National Parks. The **travel council** (☎ 435-676-1160, 800-444-6689; www.brycecanyoncountry .com; 55 S Main St; ☺ 9am-5pm Mon-Fri) has regional information. **Panguitch Lake** lies southwest on Hwy 143.

Situated at 10,400ft, **Cedar Breaks National Monument** (☎ 435-586-9451; www.nps.gov/cebr; Hwy 148; per vehicle $4; ☺ visitor center 8am-6pm summer) is an absolutely stunning amphitheater featuring wonderfully eroded, almost neon-colored spires; there's **camping** (campsites $14) in summer. South of the park, scenic Hwy 14 crosses the beautiful Markagunt Plateau between I-15 and Hwy 89.

The cute little **Blue Pine Motel** (☎ 435-676-8197, 800-299-6115; 130 N Main St; r $48-55; ✗) is open year-round.

Kanab

Vast expanses of rugged desert extend everywhere around the remote outpost of Kanab, and until the advent of roads, Kanab was an isolated Mormon community. Don't be surprised if it all looks familiar now, though. Hollywood Westerns were shot here, and John Wayne and other gun-slingin' legends helped earn Kanab the nickname 'Utah's Little Hollywood.'

Hwy 89 snakes through town, and a good selection of motels and restaurants lie along it, making it a popular travelers' stopover.

The **Kanab Visitor Center** (☎ 435-644-4680; www .ut.blm.gov/monument; 745 E Hwy 89; ☺ 8am-5pm Nov-Mar, to 4:30pm Dec-Feb) provides road, trail and weather updates for Grand Staircase-Escalante National Monument (p869). The **Kane County Office of Tourism** (☎ 435-644-5033, 800-733-5263; www .kaneutah.com; 78 S 100 E; ☺ 9am-7pm Mon-Fri, to 5pm Sat summer, to 5pm Mon-Sat winter) is the main source for area information.

The historic and centrally located **Parry Lodge** (☎ 435-644-2601, 800-748-4104; www.parrylodge .com; 89 E Center St; r incl breakfast $51-73; ☺ ☺ wi-fi), the finest property around, is beautifully landscaped. Back in the day, all the actors stayed here, but the rambling motel has become a faded wallflower of the leading lady she once was. Rooms are clean and well kept, and the lodge has a hot tub, a restaurant and a bar onsite. **Laid Back Larry's** (☎ 435-644-3636; 98 S 100 East; sandwiches $3-5; ☷ 7am-4pm Mon-Fri, 8am-4pm Sat & Sun, closed Wed) can set you up with lunch and breakfast sandwiches, and it has good coffee.

Cedar City

Less than an hour's drive northeast of Zion on I-15, Cedar City is a natural stopping place. Offering free internet access, the **tourism bureau** (☎ 435-586-5124, 800-354-4849; www.scenicsouthernutah .com; 581 N Main St; ☷ 9am-5:30pm Mon, to 6pm Tue-Fri, to 1pm Sat) shares space with the **chamber of commerce** (☎ 435-586-4484). From June to September, the nationally renowned **Shakespearean Festival** (☎ 435-586-7878, 800-752-9849; www.bard.org) keeps the town buzzing.

For basic accommodations, **Abbey Inn** (☎ 435-586-9966, 800-325-5411; www.abbeyinncedar.com; 940 W 200 N; r $86-100; ☒ ☒) offers nice decor and full breakfast.

St George

A spacious Mormon town with wide streets, an eye-catching temple and pioneer buildings, St George is popular with retirees and visitors to Zion and other nearby parks. The main source for town information is the **chamber of commerce** (☎ 435-628-1658; www.stgeorgechamber .com; 97 E St George Blvd; ☷ 9am-5pm Mon-Fri). The **Interagency Information Center** (☎ 435-688-3246; 345 E Riverside Dr; ☷ 7:45am-5pm Mon-Fri, 10am-3pm Sat) provides information on USFS and BLM lands, state parks and the Arizona Strip.

Nine miles north of town, **Snow Canyon State Park** (☎ 435-628-2255; www.stateparks.utah.gov; Hwy 18; per vehicle $5) has volcanic landscapes, petroglyphs and hiking trails to lava caves.

St George has the biggest selection of accommodations in southern Utah; most are chains, though, and many line St George Blvd. For a nicer abode, try **Green Gate Village** (☎ 435-628-6999, 800-350-6999; www.greengatevillageinn.com; 76 W Tabernacle St; r incl full breakfast $79-500; ☒ ☒ ☒). Grassy lawns separate nine historic buildings that compose this attractive B&B inn. All rooms feature lovely antiques, TVs, refrigerators and private baths.

Painted Pony (☎ 435-634-1700; 2 W St George Blvd, Ancestor Sq; sandwiches $8, dinner mains $17-25; ☷ 11:30am-10pm Mon-Sat, 4-9pm Sun), with Southwestern-style dishes marked by subtlety and nuance, offers the best dining in St George. Standouts include rib-eye steak, pan-roasted

escolar and the grilled portobello sandwich. The decor complements the cooking, with Navajo prints, tin sconces and colorful contemporary art.

Greyhound (☎ 435-673-2933, 800-231-2222; www .greyhound.com; 1235 S Bluff) departs from the local McDonald's, with buses to SLC ($52, 5½ hours) and Las Vegas ($29, two hours).

Springdale

Many travelers to Zion National Park pass through here, as Springdale sits along Hwy 9 just outside the park's southern entrance. It's a pleasant, relaxed community, catering mostly to park visitors; the **visitors bureau** (☎ 888-518-7070; www.zionpark.com) can answer questions.

Springdale has an abundance of good restaurants and nice lodging options, including the basic and pleasant **Terrace Brook Lodge** (☎ 435-772-3932, 800-342-6779; www.terracebrooklodge .com; 990 Zion Park Blvd; 1-/2-bed r incl breakfast $69/89, family units $129-149; ☒ ☒ ☒ wi-fi).

Families like the order-at-the-counter **Zion Pizza & Noodle Company** (☎ 435-772-3815; 868 Zion Park Blvd; dishes $10-16; ☷ 4-10pm) and its Utah microbrews. The **Bit & Spur Restaurant & Saloon** (☎ 435-772-3498; 1212 Zion Park Blvd; mains $10-17, specials $18-24; ☷ 5-10:30pm) is a local institution and the liveliest spot in town, offering up a large selection of microbrews and occasional live music. Southwest-influenced seafood and steak specials are well worth the price.

Zion National Park

The white, pink and red rocks of **Zion** (☎ 435-772-3256; www.nps.gov/zion; Hwy 9; per vehicle $25) are huge, overpowering and magnificent – you're guaranteed to be awed. More than 100 miles of trails offer everything from leisurely strolls to wilderness backpacking and camping. The most famous backpacking trip is through the **Narrows**, 16 miles of walking and wading in the Virgin River through dramatic canyons (June to September). Prepare to get yourself wet or your spirits dampened if there's a flash-flood warning. The **Angels Landing Trail** is a strenuous vertigo-inducer, but the views of Zion Canyon are phenomenal.

From April through October, the park operates very frequent Zion Shuttles (powered by propane). Two free, linked shuttle loops depart from the visitor center from at least 6:45am to 10pm daily, and (except for guests at the lodge) are the only vehicles permitted into the canyon.

The **Zion Canyon Visitor Center** (☎ 435-772-3256; www.nps.gov/zion; ☉ 8am-7pm summer, to 6pm spring & fall, to 5pm winter) has lots of books, maps, and park recreation information. Ask about ranger-led activities, which include nature walks and interpretive talks on flora, fauna, ecology and geology. The center also houses the **backcountry desk** (☎ 435-772-0170; ☉ 7am-7pm summer, to 6pm fall, 8am-4:30pm or 5pm spring), which dispenses permits the day before your hike.

At the south gate, two **campgrounds** (☎ 877-444-6777; www.recreation.gov; campsites $16-20) have almost 300 campsites. Less than half of these campsites can be reserved, so come early for the first come, first served spots. Smack in the middle of Zion Canyon, **Zion Lodge** (☎ reservations same day 435-772-7700, advance 888-297-2757; www.zionlodge.com; r/cabins/ste $150/160/$170; ☉ yr-round; ✗ ✗ ▢) has 81 well-appointed motel rooms and 40 cabins with gas fireplaces. All have wooden porches with stellar views. There are no TVs, but there's a good restaurant. Reservations are accepted up to 13 months in advance, or try your luck with a same-day booking.

NEW MEXICO

Strewn with earth-tone adobes and decorated with boughs of blood-red ristras, New Mexico has an undeniable style. It's a sparsely populated state, and there's perhaps nowhere else in the US where three cultures – Native American, Hispanic and Anglo – intersect so pointedly. Ancient Pueblos, 300-year-old haciendas and modern buildings stand in close proximity, surrounded by wild open spaces. For centuries, Native American markets have drawn thousands lured by famed black-on-black pottery or Navajo weavings. Silhouetted crosses top centuries-old Spanish Catholic and missionary churches, and the landscape was burned into memory by the legendary Georgia O'Keeffe.

When you think you've finally pinned it down, New Mexico always turns to show a completely different side. Creatures from outer space lurk in Roswell. Bats plumb the ethereal corners of Carlsbad Caverns. Art lovers cruise the galleries of Santa Fe. Whether it's cosmopolitan, untamed or cross-cultural, New Mexico has something to show you.

NEW MEXICO FACTS

Nickname Land of Enchantment

Population 1.9 million

Area 121,356 sq miles

Capital city Santa Fe (population 66,500)

Sales tax 5%

Birthplace of Outlaw William Bonney, aka Billy the Kid (1859–81); Smokey Bear

Home of International UFO Museum (Roswell), Julia Roberts

Famous for Chilies, ancient pueblos, the first atomic bomb (1945)

Best souvenir 'Get a half life' mug, National Atomic Museum, Albuquerque

History

People roamed the land here as far back as 10,500 BC, but by Coronado's arrival in the 16th century, Pueblos were the dominant communities found here. Santa Fe was established as the colonial capital in 1610, after which Spanish settlers and farmers fanned out across northern New Mexico, and missionaries began their often violent efforts to convert the area's Puebloans to Catholicism. Following on from a successful revolt, Native Americans then occupied Santa Fe until 1692, when Diego de Vargas recaptured the city.

In 1851 New Mexico became US territory. Native American wars, settlement by cowboys and miners, and trade along the Santa Fe Trail further transformed the region, and the arrival of the railroad in the 1870s created an economic boom.

Painters and writers set up art colonies in Santa Fe and Taos in the early 20th century. In 1943 a scientific community descended on Los Alamos and developed the atomic bomb (see p893). Big issues include water rights (whoever owns the water has the power) and immigration.

Information

New Mexico Culture (www.nmculture.org) For statewide information.

New Mexico Kids! (www.newmexico-kids.com) Free bimonthly magazine with calendar of children's activities in Albuquerque and Santa Fe.

New Mexico Magazine (www.nmmagazine.com) Good guide to the state; excellent info on Native American pueblos.

New Mexico Net (www.nmnet.org)

New Mexico Route 66 Association (☎ 505-852-2995; www.rt66nm.org) Website has archives, news and event calendars.

New Mexico Tourism Department (Map p880; ☎ 505-827-7400, 800-545-2040; www.newmexico.org; 491 Old Santa Fe Trail, Santa Fe, NM 87503) Statewide visitor information and a free *Vacation Guide*.

Public Lands Information Center (Map p880; ☎ 505-438-7542, 877-276-9404; www.publiclands.org; 1474 Rodeo Rd, Santa Fe, NM 87507) Camping and recreation information.

ALBUQUERQUE

Albuquerque may not knock your socks off with sparkle, but it has an earnest, upbeat charm. Depending on your perspective, New Mexico's most populous city is simply another dot on the map of Route 66 as it snakes its way from Los Angeles to Chicago, or it's a distinctive and vibrant mix of university students, Native Americans, Hispanics, gays and lesbians.

Centuries-old adobes line its lively Old Town district, and downtown Central Ave has a densely packed nightlife district that's easy to navigate on foot. You'll find square dances and yoga classes flyered with equal enthusiasm, and ranch hands and real-estate brokers chowing down at hole-in-the-wall taquerias and retro cafés.

Orientation & Information

Albuquerque's major boundaries are Paseo del Norte Dr to the north, Central Ave to the south, Rio Grande Blvd to the west and Tramway Blvd to the east. Central Ave is the city's main artery. Also known as old Route 66, it passes through Old Town, downtown, the university and Nob Hill.

DON'T MISS

- **Rattlesnake Museum** – fine slithery friends (p874)
- **National Atomic Museum** – it's the bomb (p874)
- **Old Town** – centuries-old adobe neighborhood (p874)
- **International Balloon Fiesta** – up, up and away! (p876)
- **Central Ave nightspots** – bar- and club-hopping galore (p877)

The city is divided into four quadrants (NW, NE, SW and SE), and the intersection of Central Ave and the railroad tracks just east of downtown serves as the center point of the city.

BOOKSTORES

Page One (Map p874; ☎ 505-294-2026; www.page1book.com; 11018 Montgomery Blvd NE; 9am-10pm Mon-Sat, to 8pm Sun) Huge and comprehensive.

EMERGENCY & MEDICAL SERVICES

Police (Map p874; ☎ 505-242-2677)

Presbyterian Hospital (Map p874; ☎ 505-841-1234; 1100 Central Ave SE; 24hr emergency)

UNM Hospital (Map p874; ☎ 505-272-2411; 2211 Lomas Blvd NE; 24hr emergency) Head here if you don't have insurance.

INTERNET ACCESS

FedEx/Kinko's (Map p874; ☎ 505-255-9673; 2706 Central Ave SE; per min 20¢; 24hr Sun-Thu, closed 11pm Fri & Sat)

Library (Map p876; ☎ 505-768-5141; 501 Copper Ave NW; 10am-6pm Mon & Thu-Sat, to 7pm Tue & Wed) Free internet access after purchasing a $3 library card.

INTERNET RESOURCES

Albuquerque Online (www.abqonline.com) Exhaustive listings and links for local businesses.

Albuquerque.com (www.albuquerque.com) Attraction, hotel and restaurant information.

City of Albuquerque (www.cabq.gov) Information on public transport, area attractions and more.

MEDIA

Alibi (☎ 505-346-0660; www.alibi.com) Free weekly with good entertainment listings; available in coffee shops and bookstores around town.

POST

Post office (Map p876; ☎ 505-346-1256; 201 5th St SW)

TOURIST INFORMATION

The **Albuquerque Convention & Visitors Bureau** (☎ 505-842-9918, 800-284-2282; www.itsatrip.org) has two visitor centers:

Old Town Information Center (Map p876; ☎ 505-243-3215; 303 Romero St NW; 10:30am-5:30pm Dec-Mar, 10am-6pm Thu-Tue, to 8pm Wed Apr-Nov)

Sunport Information Center (Albuquerque International Airport; 9:30am-8pm) At the lower level baggage claim.

Sights

OLD TOWN

From its foundation in 1706 until the arrival of the railroad in 1880, the Plaza was the hub of Albuquerque; today Old Town is the city's most popular tourist area.

The **Rattlesnake Museum** (Map p876; ☎ 505-242-6569; www.rattlesnakes.com; 202 San Felipe St NW; adult/child $3.50/2.50; ⌚ 11:30pm-5:30pm Mon-Fri, 10am-6pm Sat, 1-5pm Sun, Oct-Jun, 10am-6pm Mon-Sat, 1-5pm Sun Jul-Sep), is Old Town's coolest attraction, with 65 live snakes strutting their stuff behind glass. Visitors get a 'certificate of bravery' with admission, and a forked-tongue fellow on the front door quips, 'We love tourists…they taste just like chicken.'

The **Albuquerque Museum** (Map p876; ☎ 505-243-7255; www.albuquerquemuseum.com; 2000 Mountain Rd NW; adult/child $4/1; ⌚ 9am-5pm Tue-Sun) exhibits New Mexican artists, and explores the city's tricultural Native American, Hispanic and Anglo history.

Located across the street, the **National Atomic Museum** (Map p876; ☎ 505-245-2137; www.atomicmuseum.com; 1905 Mountain Rd NW; adult/child $6/4; ⌚ 9am-5pm) has some interesting exhibits on the development of the Manhattan Project, the history of arms control and naturally occurring radiation. A display on Nagasaki and Hiroshima prompts provocative and soul-searching comments in the visitors' journal.

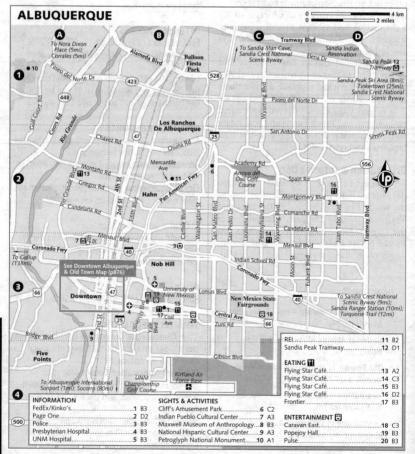

SCENIC DRIVE: TURQUOISE TRAIL

The Turquoise Trail, a National Scenic Byway, has been a major trade route since at least 2000 BC. Today it's the scenic back road between Albuquerque and Santa Fe, lined with quirky communities and other diversions. Stop in Cedar Crest at Tinkertown, an inspiring assortment of towns, circuses and other folk-art scenes. Continue through Golden, with an art gallery and lots of gorgeous desert scenery.

Madrid (pronounced MAA-drid), a bustling coal-mining company town in the 1920s and '30s, was all but abandoned after WWII. Now the town attracts more cyclists than New Agers, and it was the backdrop for the movie *Wild Hogs*. Check out the Old Coal Mine Museum, with preserved old mining equipment pretty much right where the miners left it. Next stop: Cerrillos, a photographers' dream, relatively unchanged since the 1880s. The town includes the first mine in North America, built to extract turquoise around AD 100.

Continue north on Hwy 14 until you hit I-25, which takes you into Santa Fe.

AROUND TOWN

Operated by New Mexico's 19 pueblos, the **Indian Pueblo Cultural Center** (Map p874; ☎ 505-843-7270; www.indianpueblo.org; 2401 12th St NW; adult/child $6/1; ☺ 9am-4:30pm) is a must for anyone visiting pueblos. The museum traces the development of Pueblo cultures, exhibits customs and crafts, and features changing exhibits. The restaurant serves Pueblo fare.

The University of New Mexico (UNM) area has loads of good restaurants, casual bars, offbeat shops and hip college hangouts. The main drag is Central Ave between University and Carlisle Blvds. The university's **Maxwell Museum of Anthropology** (Map p874; ☎ 505-277-4405; admission free; ☺ 9am-4pm Tue-Fri, 10am-4pm Sat), off University Blvd, has an interesting 'People of the Southwest' exhibit depicting 11,000 years of the region's cultural history.

The huge adobe-style **National Hispanic Cultural Center** (Map p874; ☎ 505-246-2261; www.nhccnm.org; 1701 4th St SW; adult/child $3/free; ☺ 10am-5pm Tue-Sun) houses a visual arts building, a performance center, and three galleries of Hispanic art, history and culture.

Northwest of downtown, the **Petroglyph National Monument** (Map p874; ☎ 505-899-0205; www.nps.gov/petr; per vehicle Mon-Fri $1, Sat & Sun $2) offers three trails of varying degrees of difficulty that encircle upwards of 15,000 rock etchings dating from AD 1300. Head west on I-40 across the Rio Grande and take exit 154 north.

The 2.7-mile **Sandia Peak Tramway** (☎ 505-856-7325; www.sandiapeak.com; Tramway Blvd; adult/child $17.50/10; ☺ 9am-8pm Wed-Sun, 5-8pm Tue) starts in the desert realm of cholla cactus and soars to the pines atop 10,678ft Sandia Peak. The High Finance Restaurant & Tavern is a popular, albeit touristy, destination at the top.

Activities

The omnipresent Sandia Mountains and the less crowded Manzano Mountains offer outdoor activities, including **hiking**, **skiing** (downhill and cross country), **mountain biking** and camping. The **Sandia Ranger Station** (☎ 505-281-3304; 11776 Hwy 337, Tijeras; ☺ 8am-5pm, closed Sun Oct-Apr), off I-40 exit 175 south, has maps and information. For equipment, try **REI** (Map p874; ☎ 505-247-1191; 1550 Mercantile Ave NE).

Reach the top of the Sandias via the eastern slope along the lovely **Sandia Crest National Scenic Byway** (I-40 exit 175 north), which passes several trailheads. Alternatively, take the Sandia Peak Tramway (left), or Hwy 165 from Placitas (I-25 exit 242), a dirt road through Las Huertas Canyon that passes the prehistoric dwelling of **Sandia Man Cave**.

Atop the Sandia Peak Tramway, the **Sandia Peak Ski Area** (☎ 505-242-9052; www.sandiapeak.com; half-/full-day lift tickets adult $32/43, child $24, senior $32) remains open during summer weekends and holidays (May to October) for mountain bikers.

Several companies offer rides over the city and the Rio Grande, including **Discover Balloons** (☎ 505-842-1111; www.discoverballoons.com; adult/child under 12yr $150/100).

Albuquerque for Children

The **¡Explora! Children's Museum** (Map p876; ☎ 505-224-8300; www.explora.mus.nm.us; 1701 Mountain Rd NW; adult/child under 12yr $7/3; ☺ 10am-6pm Mon-Sat, noon-6pm Sun) has hands-on demonstrations involving light, electricity, sound, motion, anatomy and more.

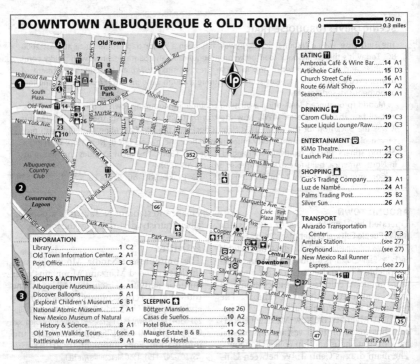

DOWNTOWN ALBUQUERQUE & OLD TOWN

EATING 🍴	
Ambrozia Café & Wine Bar	**14** A1
Artichoke Café	**15** D3
Church Street Café	**16** A1
Route 66 Malt Shop	**17** A2
Seasons	**18** A1

DRINKING 🍷	
Carom Club	**19** C3
Sauce Liquid Lounge/Raw	**20** C3

ENTERTAINMENT 🎭	
KiMo Theatre	**21** C3
Launch Pad	**22** C3

SHOPPING 🛍	
Gus's Trading Company	**23** A1
Luz de Nambé	**24** A1
Palms Trading Post	**25** B2
Silver Sun	**26** A1

TRANSPORT	
Alvarado Transportation	
Center	**27** C3
Amtrak Station	(see 27)
Greyhound	(see 27)
New Mexico Rail Runner	
Express	(see 27)

INFORMATION	
Library	**1** C2
Old Town Information Center	**2** A1
Post Office	**3** C3

SIGHTS & ACTIVITIES	
Albuquerque Museum	**4** A1
Discover Balloons	**5** A1
¡Explora! Children's Museum	**6** B1
National Atomic Museum	**7** A1
New Mexico Museum of Natural	
History & Science	**8** A1
Old Town Walking Tours	(see 4)
Rattlesnake Museum	**9** A1

SLEEPING 🛏	
Böttger Mansion	(see 26)
Casas de Sueños	**10** A2
Hotel Blue	**11** C2
Mauger Estate B & B	**12** C2
Route 66 Hostel	**13** B2

The teen-friendly **New Mexico Museum of Natural History & Science** (Map p876; ☎ 505-841-2800; www.nmnaturalhistory.org; 1801 Mountain Rd NW; adult/child under 13yr/student & senior $7/4/6; �am 9am-5pm) features an Evolator (evolution elevator), which transports visitors through 38 million years of New Mexico's geologic and evolutionary history. The museum also houses the huge-screen **DynaTheater** (adult/child 3-12 $7/4).

Cliff's Amusement Park (Map p874; ☎ 505-881-9373; www.cliffsamusementpark.com; 4800 Osuna Rd NE; adult/child $24/20; ☉ Apr-Sep), a great reward for the kids, has about 25 rides, including a roller-coaster, the Water Monkey, a play area and other traditional favorites. Opening hours vary.

Tours

From mid-March to mid-December, the Albuquerque Museum (p874) offers informative, free and guided **Old Town walking tours** (☉ 11am Tue-Sun) of 17 historically significant structures.

Festivals & Events

A million spectators are drawn to magical hot-air balloon ascensions at the **International Balloon Fiesta** (☎ 505-821-1000, 888-422-7277; www.balloonfiesta.com) in early October. The **New Mexico Gay Rodeo Association** (www.nmgra.com) hosts the **Zia Regional Rodeo** on the second weekend of August.

Sleeping

BUDGET

Route 66 Hostel (Map p876; ☎ 505-247-1813; www.myspace.com/route66hostel; dm $18, r with shared/private bath $24/30; ☐ ☒) Within easy walking distance of downtown, this basic hostel is rather creaky and worn, but it is both the cheapest and most sociable option in town. Some of the private rooms can hold up to five people ($5 for each person over double rate). Simple chores are required here for guests.

Hotel Blue (Map p876; ☎ 505-924-2400; 877-878-4868; www.thehotelblue.com; 717 Central Ave NW; s/d/ste incl breakfast $77/87/110; ☐ ☒ ☒ wi-fi) Well-positioned on a park, the modern 135-room Hotel Blue has new Temper-pedic beds and a free airport and Old Town shuttle. Bonus points awarded for the good-sized pool and fresh cookies in the lobby all day.

MIDRANGE

Mauger Estate B & B (Map p876; ☎ 505-242-8755, 800-719-9189; www.maugerbb.com; 701 Roma Ave NW; r incl full breakfast $89-189; P ✕ wi-fi) This restored Queen Anne mansion (Mauger is pronounced 'major') has comfortable rooms with down comforters, stocked fridges and freshly cut flowers. Kids are welcome, and staff swear to treat every guest like a celebrity.

Nora Dixon Place (☎ 505-898-3662, 888-667-2349; www.noradixon.com; 312 Dixon Rd, Corrales; r incl full breakfast $99-119; wi-fi) In nearby Corrales, a charming farming village 8 miles north of downtown Albuquerque, this friendly B&B has three lovely rooms nestled in the Rio Grande Bosque. They all face an enclosed courtyard with views of the Sandias. The architecture is pure adobe New Mexican territorial style.

Böttger Mansion (Map p876; ☎ 505-243-3639, 800-758-3639; www.bottger.com; 110 San Felipe St NW; r incl breakfast $115-179; P wi-fi) Built in 1912, this friendly place retains its original Victorian style – there's no Old West or Southwestern feel here!

ourpick Casas de Sueños (Map p876; ☎ 505-247-4560, 800-665-7002; www.casasdesuenos.com; 310 Rio Grande Blvd SW; r incl full breakfast $129-169; P ✕ wi-fi) An artists' colony in the 1930s and '40s, this lovely enclosed garden compound has 21 peaceful adobe casitas featuring handcrafted furniture and fine art murals. Some rooms have a kitchenette, kiva fireplace and/or a private hot tub. A mosaic and stained-glass courtyard gazebo is popular for weddings, and the romantic Ivy Cottage – with a cloistered outdoor fountain – is always in demand.

Eating

Frontier (Map p874; ☎ 505-266-0550; 2400 Central Ave SE; dishes $3-7; 24hr) An Albuquerque tradition, the Frontier boasts enormous cinnamon rolls and the best *huevos rancheros* ever. The food and people-watching are outstanding, and students love the low prices on the 24/7 breakfast, burgers and Mexican food.

Route 66 Malt Shop (Map p876; ☎ 505-242-7866; 1720 Central Ave SW; dishes $5; 11am-6pm Mon-Fri, noon-6pm Sat) This nostalgic and friendly place started small but recently got a little wiggle room, enough for 10 tables and four stools. It serves great green-chili cheeseburgers, and the house-made root beer is wonderful on its own or as a float.

Flying Star Café (dishes $7-10; 6am-11pm Sun-Thu, to 11:30pm Fri & Sat) Central Ave (Map p874; ☎ 505-255-6633;

3416 Central Ave SE); Juan Tabo Blvd (Map p874; ☎ 505-275-8311; 4501 Juan Tabo Blvd NE); Rio Grande Blvd (Map p874; ☎ 505-344-6714; 4026 Rio Grande Blvd NW); Menaul Blvd (Map p874; ☎ 505-293-6911; 8001 Menaul Blvd NE) With a half-dozen constantly packed locations, this is the place to go for homemade soups, muffins, bread, innovative main dishes, desserts and ice cream.

Church Street Café (Map p876; ☎ 505-247-8522; 2111 Church St NW; dishes $7-12; 8am-9pm Mon-Sat, to 4pm Sun) A cozy café in the middle of Old Town, it serves New Mexican fare in the historic Casa de Ruiz, an adobe built in the 1700s. The dining room features heavy wooden beams, mosaic tables and lace curtains.

Seasons (Map p876; ☎ 505-766-5100; 2031 Mountain Rd NW; lunch $7-15, dinner $17-23; 11:30am-2:30pm & 5-10:30pm Mon-Thu, 5pm-11pm Fri & Sat, 5-10:30pm Sun) With refreshingly warm yellow walls, high ceilings, fresh flowers and a creative menu, this contemporary place provides a welcome change from the adobes of Old Town. Try the hearty red-chili-dusted chicken burgers or Baja tacos either inside or in the rooftop cantina, where there's live jazz on Saturday and Sunday night.

Artichoke Café (Map p876; ☎ 505-243-0200; www.artichokecafe.com; 424 Central Ave SE; lunch $10, dinner dishes $19-29; 11am-2:30pm & 5:30-10pm Mon-Sat, 5-9pm Sun) Voted an Albuquerque favorite many times over, it takes the best from Italian, French and American cuisine. The back outdoor patio offers relief from Central Ave traffic, and the ginger crab cakes and the fresh pumpkin ravioli are amazing.

ourpick Ambrozia Cafe & Wine Bar (Map p876; ☎ 505-242-6560; 108 Rio Grande Blvd NW; dishes $20-25; 5-9pm Tue-Sat, 11am-2:30pm Sun) A gourmet Old Town cafe, Ambrozia creates scrumptious contemporary global delicacies with local ingredients. Chef–owner Sam Etheridge whips up his signature lobster corn dogs year-round, and the four-course Sunday brunch ($20) is dynamite, with delicious options like granola-crusted French toast, crab cake *huevos rancheros,* and tequila and red chili salmon.

Drinking & Entertainment

Caravan East (Map p874; ☎ 505-265-7877; 7605 Central Ave NE; nightly) The perfect place to practice your two-step or line dancing with live country-and-western bands.

Carom Club (Map p876; ☎ 505-242-1966; 301 Central Ave NW, 2nd fl; Mon-Sat) A quieter and more upscale entertainment option, this dining and billiards club has more than a dozen full-sized pool tables, as many beers on draft, and classy contemporary decor. The patio overlooking Central Ave is prime for people-watching.

Launch Pad (Map p876; ☎ 505-764-8887; www.launch padrocks.com; 618 Central Ave SW) Indie, reggae, punk and country bands rock the house most nights (though not at the same time). This is one of the best live venues in town, with an upstairs overlook for a bird's-eye stage view. Look for the spaceship on Central Ave.

Pulse (Map p874; ☎ 505-255-3334; www.pulseandblu .com; 4100 Central Ave SE; ⏰ Wed-Sat) A hip and popular queer dance club with suggested 'dress to impress' and 'undress to impress' nights.

Sauce Liquid Lounge/Raw (Map p876; ☎ 505-242-5839; 405 Central Ave NW; no cover; ⏰ Wed-Sat) Sister nightclubs joined at the hip, Raw leans toward hip-hop while Sauce Liquid Lounge works a Top 40 groove. They have overstuffed sofas for chilling, VIP tables if you want 'em, and hot, hot salsa on Wednesday.

Popejoy Hall (Map p874; ☎ 505-277-4569; www .unmtickets.com; cnr Central Ave & Cornell St SE) and the historic **KiMo Theatre** (Map p876; ☎ 505-768-3544; 423 Central Ave NW) are the primary venues for big-name national acts, local opera, symphony and theater.

Shopping

For Native American crafts and informed salespeople, stop by the **Palms Trading Post** (Map p876; ☎ 505-247-8504; 1504 Lomas Blvd NW; ⏰ Mon-Sat) or **Gus's Trading Company** (Map p876; ☎ 505-843-6381; 2026 Central Ave SW).

Luz de Nambé (Map p876; ☎ 505-242-5699; 328 San Felipe St NW; ⏰ Mon-Sat) Sells discounted and famed Nambeware.

Silver Sun (Map p876; ☎ 505-246-9692; 2011 Central Ave NW) A reputable spot for turquoise.

Getting There & Around

AIR

Though the **Albuquerque International Sunport** (☎ 505-244-7700; www.cabq.gov/airport; 2200 Sunport Blvd SE) is New Mexico's biggest airport, it's still relatively small. Most major US airlines service Albuquerque, though **Southwest** (☎ 800-435-9792) has the largest presence. Cabs to downtown cost about $25.

BUS

The **Alvarado Transportation Center** (Map p876; 1st St & Central Ave) houses **ABQ RIDE** (☎ 505-243-7433;

www.cabq.gov/transit; ⏰ 6am-10pm), the public bus system. It covers most of Albuquerque on weekdays and hits the major tourist spots daily (adult/child $1/35¢). Most lines run until 6pm. ABQ RIDE Route 50 connects the airport with downtown (last bus at 8:30pm; no weekend service).

Greyhound (Map p876; ☎ 505-243-4435, 800-231-2222; www.greyhound.com; 320 1st St SW) is next door, and serves destinations throughout New Mexico. **Twin Hearts** (☎ 505-751-1201, 800-654-9456) leaves four times daily for Santa Fe ($25), Taos ($50), Red River ($55) and Angel Fire ($55).

Sandia Shuttle (☎ 505-474-5696, 888-775-5696; www .sandiashuttle.com) runs daily shuttles to many Santa Fe hotels between 9am and 11pm ($25).

TRAIN

The *Southwest Chief* stops daily at Albuquerque's **Amtrak station** (Map p876; ☎ 505-842-9650, 800-872-7245; www.amtrak.com; 1st St & Central Ave), heading east to Kansas City, Missouri ($160, 18 hours) and beyond, or west through Flagstaff, Arizona (from $54, five hours), to Los Angeles (from $61, 16½ hours). Service to Santa Fe ($34, 1½ hours) involves transferring to a bus in Lamy, 18 miles south of Santa Fe.

A commuter line, the **New Mexico Rail Runner Express** (Map p876; www.nmrailrunner.com), shares the station, with service scheduled to reach Santa Fe in 2008.

ALONG I-40

Although you can zip between Albuquerque and Flagstaff, AZ, in less than five hours, the national monuments and pueblos along the way are well worth a visit. For a scenic loop, take Hwy 53 southwest from Grants, which leads to all the following sights, except Acoma. Hwy 602 brings you north to Gallup.

Acoma Pueblo

The dramatic mesa-top 'Sky City' sits 7000ft above sea level and 367ft above the surrounding plateau. One of the oldest continuously inhabited settlements in North America, this place has been home to pottery-making people since the later part of the 11th century. Guided **tours** (adult/child 6-17yr $12/9) focusing on their craft leave from the **visitor center** (☎ 505-469-1052, 800-747-0181; photo permit $10) at the bottom of the mesa. From I-40 take exit 108, about 50 miles west of Albuquerque.

El Malpais National Monument

Meaning 'bad land' in Spanish, eerie El Malpais encompasses about 200 sq miles of lava flows. The **information center** (☎ 505-783-4774; www.nps.gov/elma; Hwy 53; ⏰ 8:30am-4:30pm), 22 miles southwest of Grants, has hiking and primitive (free) camping details.

El Morro National Monument

The 200ft sandstone outcropping at this **monument** (☎ 505-783-4226; www.nps.gov/elmo; adult/child $3/ free; ⏰ 8am-7pm summer, 9am-6pm fall, 9am-5pm winter), also known as 'Inscription Rock,' has been a travelers' oasis for millennia. Thousands of carvings – from petroglyphs in the pueblo at the top (c 1250) to elaborate inscriptions by the Spanish conquistadors and the Anglo pioneers – offer a unique means of tracing history. It's about 38 miles southwest of Grants via Hwy 53.

Zuni Pueblo

The Zuni are known worldwide for their delicately inlaid silverwork, which is sold in stores lining Hwy 53. Walk past stone houses and beehive-shaped mud ovens to the massive **Our Lady of Guadalupe Mission**, featuring impressive kachina murals. The **Ashiwi Awan Museum & Heritage Center** (☎ 505-782-4403; www.ashiwi-museum .org; Ojo Caliente Rd; admission by donation; ⏰ 9am-5pm Mon-Fri) displays early photos and other tribal artifacts.

The friendly, eight-room **Inn at Halona** (☎ 505-782-4547, 800-752-3278; www.halona.com; 23B Pia Mesa Rd; r incl breakfast $79; ✕ ☷ wi-fi), decorated with local Zuni arts and crafts, is the only place to stay on the pueblo and located right in the middle of it.

Gallup

Because Gallup serves as the Navajo and Zuni peoples' major trading center, you'll find many trading posts, pawn shops, jewelry stores and crafts galleries in the historic district. It's arguably the best place in New Mexico for top-quality goods at fair prices. Gallup is another classic Route 66 town, with loads of vintage motels and businesses.

The **Gallup Cultural Center** (☎ 505-863-4131; www.southwestindian.com; 201 E Hwy 66; ⏰ 8am-5pm Mon-Fri) houses a small but well-done museum with Native American art, including excellent collections of both contemporary and old kachina dolls, pottery, sand painting and weaving. A tiny theater screens films about

Chaco Canyon and the Four Corners region. Contact the **chamber of commerce** (☎ 505-863-3841, 800-242-4282; www.thegallupchamber.com; 103 W Hwy 66; ⏰ 8am-5pm Mon-Fri) for details.

The town's lodging jewel is **El Rancho** (☎ 505-863-9311, 800-543-6351; www.elranchohotel.com; 1000 E Hwy 66; s/d/ste $60/70/105). Many of the great actors of the '40s and '50s stayed here, including Humphrey Bogart, Katharine Hepburn and John Wayne. El Rancho features a superb Southwestern lobby, a restaurant, a bar and an eclectic selection of simple rooms.

The small, casual **El Metate Tamale Factory** (☎ 505-722-7000; 610 W Mesa Ave; dishes $7-9; ⏰ 9am-8pm Mon-Fri, 10am-6pm Sat) makes flavorful (and affordable) tamales and other specialties.

SANTA FE

In Santa Fe, it's all about the art. A sizable number of painters, sculptors and photographers live in the area, hundreds of galleries have set up shop here, and more than a dozen museums thrive. The renowned Indian Market has been celebrated for more than 80 years. Without a doubt, the creative and cultural community holds court in New Mexico's small capital city.

Against the dramatic backdrop of the Sangre de Cristo range, Santa Fe oozes sophistication, its cosmopolitan stature belying its size. It boasts gourmet restaurants, spas, an opera company and even a ski resort. Centuries-old adobes stand proud, and live-work spaces sprout in the newly redeveloped Railyard district.

Orientation & Information

Cerrillos Rd (I-25 exit 278), a 6-mile strip of hotels and fast-food restaurants, enters town

---

DON'T MISS

- **Georgia O'Keeffe Museum** – legendary artist's largest repository (p881)
- **Indian Market** – huge Indian art gathering (p882)
- **10,000 Waves** – meditative soaks (p882)
- **Santa Fe Opera** – arias in adobe land (p884)
- **Canyon Road** – serious art and collectors' mecca (p881)

SOUTHWEST

SANTA FE

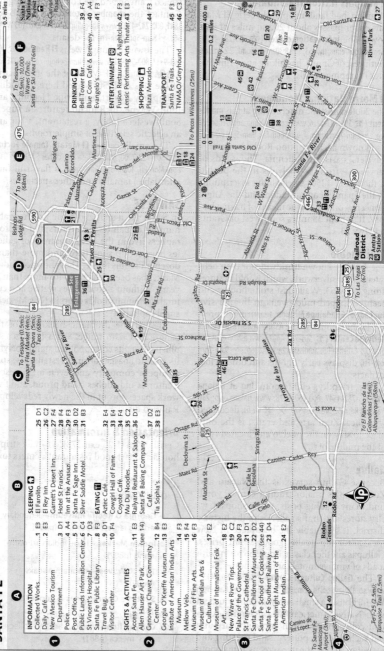

from the south; Paseo de Peralta circles the center of town; St Francis Dr (I-25 exit 282) forms the western border of downtown and turns into Hwy 285, which heads north toward Española, Los Alamos and Taos. Alameda St follows the canal east–west through the center of town, and Guadalupe St is the main north–south street through downtown. Most downtown restaurants, galleries, museums and sites are either on or east of Guadalupe St and are within walking distance of the plaza, in the center of town.

BOOKSTORES

Collected Works (☎ 505-988-4226; 208B W San Francisco St) A good selection of regional travel books.
Travel Bug (☎ 505-992-0418; www.mapsofnewmexico .com; 839 Paseo de Peralta) More travel books and maps.

EMERGENCY & MEDICAL SERVICES

Police (☎ 505-428-3710; 2515 Camino Entrada)
St Vincent's Hospital (☎ 505-820-5247; 455 St Michael's Dr; ☤ 24hr emergency)

INTERNET ACCESS

Daily Café (☎ 505-986-0735; 301 N Guadalupe St; per hr $10) Slurp and surf.
New Mexico Tourism Department (☎ 505-827-7400; www.newmexico.org; 491 Old Santa Fe Trail; ☤ 8am-5pm) Free internet access.
Santa Fe Public Library (☎ 505-955-6781; 145 Washington Ave) Reserve up to an hour of free access.

INTERNET RESOURCES

Santa Fe Chamber (www.santafechamber.com) Listings and links for local businesses.
Santa Fe Information (www.santafe.org) Official online visitors' guide to the city of Santa Fe.

MEDIA

New Mexican (☎ 505-983-3303; www.santafenew mexican.com) Daily paper with breaking news.
Santa Fe Reporter (☎ 505-988-5541; www.sfreporter .com) Free alternative weekly; Friday section has thorough listings of what's going on.

POST

Post office (☎ 505-988-2239; 120 S Federal Pl)

TOURIST INFORMATION

New Mexico Tourism Department (☎ 505-827-7400, 800-545-2070; www.newmexico.org; 491 Old Santa Fe Trail; ☤ 8am-5:30pm summer, to 5pm winter) has brochures, a hotel reservation line, free coffee and free internet access.

Public Lands Information Center (☎ 505-438-7542; www.publiclands.org; 1474 Rodeo Rd; ☤ 8:30am-4:30pm Mon-Fri) This helpful place has lots of maps and information.
Visitor Center (☎ 505-955-6200, 800-777-2489; www .santafe.org; 60 W San Francisco St, Ste 133; ☤ 8am-5pm Mon-Fri) Inside the Santa Fe arcade.

Sights

Possessing the world's largest collection of her work, the **Georgia O'Keeffe Museum** (☎ 505-946-1000; www.okeeffemuseum.org; 217 Johnson St; adult/child $8/free; ☤ 10am-5pm, to 8pm Fri, closed Wed Nov-May) features the artist's paintings of flowers, bleached skulls and adobe architecture. Tours of O'Keeffe's house (p886) require advance reservations.

Canyon Road (www.canyonroadarts.com) was once a dusty street lined with artists' homes and studios; now it's the epicenter of the city's up-scale galleries, with over 90 displaying Santa Fe School masterpieces, rare Native American antiquities and wild contemporary work. The narrow street buzzes with activity for early-evening art openings on Friday.

The four museums administered by the **Museum of New Mexico** (☎ 505-827-6463; www .museumofnewmexico.org; one museum $8, 4-day pass to all four $18, children under 16yr free; ☤ 10am-5pm, closed Mon winter) are recommended: the **Palace of the Governors** (☎ 505-476-5100; 105 Palace Ave), with regional history inside one of the country's oldest buildings; the **Museum of Fine Arts** (☎ 505-476-5059; 107 Palace Ave); the **Museum of Indian Arts & Culture** (☎ 505-476-1269; 710 Camino Lejo); and the **Museum of International Folk Art** (☎ 505-476-1200; 706 Camino Lejo).

The **St Francis Cathedral** (☎ 505-982-5619; 131 Cathedral Pl; ☤ 8am-5pm) houses the oldest Madonna statue in North America.

Primarily showing student and faculty work, the esteemed four-year **Institute of American Indian Arts Museum** (☎ 505-983-8900; 108 Cathedral Pl; adult/child $4/2; ☤ 10am-5pm Mon-Sat, noon-5pm Sun) features the finest offerings of Native American artists from around the country. The attached **Allen Hauser Art Park** contains a sculpture garden.

In 1937, Mary Cabot established the **Wheelwright Museum of the American Indian** (☎ 505-982-4636; www.wheelwright.org; 704 Camino Lejo; admission free; ☤ 10am-5pm Mon-Sat, 1-5pm Sun) to showcase Navajo ceremonial art. While its strength continues to be Navajo exhibits, it now includes contemporary Native American art and historical artifacts as well.

Activities

The Pecos Wilderness and Santa Fe National Forest, east of town, have over 1000 miles of **hiking** trails, several of which lead to 12,000ft peaks. Summer storms are frequent, so prepare for hikes by checking weather reports. For maps and details, contact the Public Lands Information Center (p881).

The **Santa Fe Ski Area** (☎ 505-982-4429, snow report 505-983-9155; www.skisantafe.com; lift tickets adult/child $51/37; ☼ 9am-4pm) is a half-hour drive from the plaza up Hwy 475. From the 12,000ft summit you can admire 80,000 sq miles of desert and mountains.

Busloads of people head up to the Taos Box (p887) for white-water river running, but there are also mellow float trips throughout New Mexico and overnight guided rafting trips. Contact **New Wave River Trips** (☎ 505-984-1444, 800-984-1444; www.newwaverafting.com; 1101 Cerrillos Rd). Stay cool on day-trips through the **Rio Grande Gorge** (adult/child half day $50/45, full day $96/77) or Taos Box ($115), or go for a three-day Rio Chama float ($357).

The Japanese-style **10,000 Waves** (☎ 505-982-9304; www.tenthousandwaves.com; 3451 Hyde Park Rd; communal tubs $19, private tubs per person $25-59; ☼ 9am-10:30pm Wed-Mon, 3:45-10:30pm Tue Jun-Oct, 10am-9:30pm Wed-Mon, 3:45-9:30pm Tue Nov-May), with landscaped grounds concealing eight attractive tubs in a smooth Zen design, offers waterfalls, cold plunges, and hot and dry saunas.

If you develop a love for New Mexican cuisine, try cooking lessons at the **Santa Fe School of Cooking** (☎ 505-983-4511; www.santafeschoolofcooking.com). Classes, with over 20 options including traditional New Mexican and Southwestern breakfast, are 2½ hours long and cost $40 to $78, including the meal.

Mellow Velo (☎ 505-982-8986; 102 E Water St) rents bikes, has information about regional trails and does guided rides.

Santa Fe for Children

Check 'Pasatiempo' (the Friday section of the free daily *New Mexican* newspaper) for its 'Bring the Kids' column, with a rundown on area events for children.

The **Santa Fe Children's Museum** (☎ 505-989-8359; www.santafechildrensmuseum.org; 1050 Old Pecos Trail; admission $8; ☼ 10am-5pm Wed-Sat, noon-5pm Sun) features hands-on exhibits on science and art for young children. The museum runs daily programs that tackle subjects like solar energy and printmaking.

The **Santa Fe Southern Railway** (☎ 505-989-8600; www.thetraininsantafe.com; 401 S Guadalupe St) runs excursions on restored railcars. Its day-trips (adult/child from $32/18, four hours) venture through the high desert, and are pulled by working freight trains.

In La Cienega, about 15 miles south of Santa Fe, **El Rancho de las Golondrinas** (☎ 505-471-2261; www.golondrinas.org; 334 Los Pinos Rd, La Cienega; adult/child $5/3; ☼ 10am-4pm Wed-Sun Jun-Sep) shows off Spanish Colonial history made real, with hands-on demonstrations of rope-making and yarn spinning, and lots of animals.

You'll want to take the **Genoveva Chavez Community Center** (☎ 505-955-4000; www.gc communitycenter.com; 3221 Rodeo Rd) home with you. With its ice rink, pool and water slide, there's something for kids of most ages. It even has a **PlayZone** (☎ 505-955-4084, 2hr admission $3) for two-to six-year olds if parents want a bit of on-site private recreating.

Tours

Access Santa Fe (☎ 505-988-2774; www.accesssantafe.com) departs from the lobbies of the El Dorado Hotel and Hotel St Francis for a two-hour walking tour of the city. The tours are held at 9:30am and 1:30pm and cost $10 (under 12s free). It also does a mystery/ghost tour of town.

Festivals & Events

Santa Fe's biggest festivals:

Santa Fe Fiestas (☎ 505-988-7575) Two weeks of events in early September, including concerts, a carnival, parades and a candlelight procession.

Santa Fe Indian Market (☎ 505-983-5220; www.swaia.org) On the weekend after the third Thursday in August, the plaza is packed with the finest Native American artisans from all over North America.

Spanish Market (☎ 505-982-2226; www.spanish market.org) In late July, traditional Spanish colonial arts, from retablos and bultos to handcrafted furniture and metalwork, make this juried show an artistic extravaganza.

Sleeping

The **visitor center** (www.santafe.org) website lists helpful reservation services. Cerrillos Rd is lined with lots of chains and independent motels.

BUDGET

Silver Saddle Motel (☎ 505-471-7663; 2810 Cerrillos Rd; r incl breakfast from $45; P ☒ ☐) Shady wooden arcades outside and inspired Southwestern comfy rustic decor within, including some rooms with attractively tiled kitchenettes. There's loads of kitschy appeal, revealing Americana at its finest.

MIDRANGE & TOP END

El Rey Inn (☎ 505-982-1931, 800-521-1349; www. elreyinnsantafe.com; 1862 Cerrillos Rd; r incl breakfast $95-155, ste $155; P ☒ ☒) This is a highly recommended classic courtyard hotel, with super rooms, a great pool and hot tub, and even a kids' playground scattered around 5 acres of greenery. The inn recycles and takes a lot of green-friendly steps to conserve resources.

Garrett's Desert Inn (☎ 505-982-1851, 800-888-2145; www.garrettsdesertinn.com; 311 Old Santa Fe Trail; r $119-169, ste $139-179; ☒ wi-fi) Centrally located jut two blocks from the plaza, the hotel has rooms and spacious suites that are far more attractive than their counterparts on Cerrillos Rd. Parking is $8.

Santa Fe Sage Inn (☎ 505-982-5952; www.santa fesageinn.com; 725 Cerrillos Rd; r incl breakfast $135-160; P ☒ ☒ ☐ wi-fi) Though cloaked in a standard motel shell, the 157 rooms have interesting accents like tin art, wrought-iron lamps and lace curtains. And even though they're situated on a major intersection, the buildings are set back from the road and surprisingly quiet.

Hotel St Francis (☎ 505-983-5700, 800-529-5700; www.hotelstfrancis.com; 210 Don Gaspar Ave; r $165-350; ☒ ☒ ☐ wi-fi) Built as a luxury property in 1923, this great plaza hotel is elegant in a decadently decrepit sort of way. Basic rooms are small, but you can upgrade for a few dollars, and the lobby does a famous afternoon tea. Parking is $5.

El Farolito (☎ 505-988-1631, 888-634-8782; www .farolito.com; 514 Galisteo St; r incl breakfast $180-250; ☒ wi-fi) Intimate and elegant, each of the eight comfy adobe casitas (some including private patio) comes with a stocked fridge, VCR and all the amenities you expect from a fine B&B. Whether it's through the use of folk art, Native American detailing or lodge decor, the feel is luxe Southwest par excellence. Farolitos, by the way, are warm little lights that line walkways and rooftops.

Inn at the Anasazi (☎ 505-988-3030, 800-688-8100; www.innoftheanasazi.com; 113 Washington Ave; r $349-399; ☒ ☒ ☐ wi-fi) At this chic full-service boutique hotel, the public spaces – including a large living room and library – are done up

in dark wood and sultry lighting. The rooms, with step-up four-post beds, have a nowhere-but-the-Southwest feel, with beamed ceilings and gas-lit kiva fireplaces. Parking is $17.

Eating
BUDGET

Tia Sophia's (☎ 505-983-9880; 210 W San Francisco St; dishes $4-7; ☽ 7am-2pm Mon-Sat) The plaza workforce joins knowledgeable collectors for this top spot's fabulous lunch specials and other great New Mexican offerings.

Santa Fe Baking Company & Café (☎ 505-988-4292; 504 W Cordova; dishes $6-8; ☽ 6am-8pm Mon-Sat, to 6pm Sun) An upbeat café serving burgers, sandwiches and hearty breakfasts all day. Place your order at the counter and tuck into Southwestern-style specialties drenched in red, green or 'Christmas' chili sauce (a combination of both).

Aztec Café (☎ 505-820-0025; 317 Aztec St; sandwiches $7; ☽ 7am-dark Mon-Thu & Sat, to 3am Fri, 8am-dark Sun) This airy multiroom café keeps the tattoos-and-climbing-gear crowd well fed with sandwiches and malteds. It features free wi-fi and local bands playing electronica and indie rock for an all-ages crowd Friday night.

MIDRANGE

Cowgirl Hall of Fame (☎ 505-982-2565; 319 S Guadalupe St; dishes $8-13; ☽ 11am-midnight Mon-Sat, 8:30am-11pm Sun, bar to 2am Mon-Sat & to midnight Sun) Two-step up to the cobblestone courtyard and try the salmon tacos, butternut-squash casserole or steaks by the pound – all served with Western-style feminist flair. Youngsters are welcome, with a great playground out back and buckets of coloring crayons to draw on the lengthy kids' menu. It also has a perennially popular bar with live music and DJs.

Mu Du Noodles (☎ 505-983-1411; 1494 Cerrillos Rd; dishes $15-20; ☽ 5:30-9pm Tue-Sat) Pan-Asian organic dishes, like salmon dumplings, Vietnamese spring rolls and tofu laksa, inspire lines out the door of this cozy contemporary spot; the noodles and specials are recommended, and almost everything has a vegan version.

Railyard Restaurant & Saloon (☎ 505-989-3300; 530 S Guadalupe St; dishes $15-22; ☽ 11:30am-2:30pm & 5:30-9:30pm Mon-Thu, 11:30am-2:30pm & 5:30-10pm Fri & Sat, 5:30-9:30pm Sun) An upscale American meat-and-potatoes menu is served in this historic railyard warehouse. Save space for dessert, 'cuz the German chocolate cake is divine.

TOP END

Geronimo (☎ 505-982-1500; 724 Canyon Rd; dishes $30-35; ⏲ 5:45-10pm Mon-Thu, 5:45-11pm Fri & Sat) Housed in a 1756 adobe, Geronimo is among the finest and most romantic restaurants in town. For a splurge you won't soon forget, come in famished and order the five-course tasting menu ($85).

Coyote Café (☎ 505-983-1615; 132 Water St; dishes $30-40; ⏲ 5:30-9pm) Chef Mark Miller's seasonal interpretations of New Mexican cuisine – try the savory bread puddings or pecan wood–grilled sirloin drizzled with *mole* – remain a highlight of any foodie's visit. For more casual open-air dining, there's also the Rooftop Cantina.

Drinking & Entertainment

Bell Tower Bar (☎ 505-982-5511; 100 E San Francisco St) Five floors atop La Fonda, you can enjoy a cold beer or killer margarita while watching one of those patented New Mexico sunsets. Open from late spring until the cold starts nipping at your toes.

Blue Corn Café & Brewery (☎ 505-438-1800; 4056 Cerrillos Rd; ⏲ 11am-10pm) This cavernous brewpub has won awards for its Atomic Blonde Ale and Cold Front Coffee Stout, served alongside tapas, burgers and Chuy's chalupas (dishes $9 to $12).

Evangelo's (☎ 505-982-9014; 200 W San Francisco St) Here there's foot-stompin' live music nightly, with rock, blues, jazz and Latin combos heating up the floorboards. The place has been run by the same family for over 30 years; check out the 2002-issued postal stamp with Evangelo's WWII portrait.

Fusion Restaurant & Nightclub (☎ 505-955-0400; 135 W Palace Ave; cover $7; ⏲ club Tue, Fri & Sat) A dramatically draped multimedia experience, the nightclub is packed with three levels of eye candy and two spaces for dancing and live music.

Lensic Performing Arts Theater (☎ 505-988-1234; www.lensic.com; 211 W San Francisco St) This beautifully renovated 1930s movie house is the city's premier venue for performing arts. Continuing its film history, it also holds $5 classic-movie screenings.

Santa Fe Opera (☎ 505-986-5900, 800-280-4654; www.santafeopera.org; tickets $25-170; ⏲ late Jun-late Aug) You can be a decked-out socialite or show up wearing cowboy boots and jeans; it doesn't matter. Opera fans (and those who've never seen or heard an opera in their lives) come to Santa Fe for this alone: an architectural marvel, with views of wind-carved sandstone wilderness crowned with sunsets and moonrises, and at center stage (and what a stage!) internationally renowned vocal talent performing masterworks of aria and romance.

Shopping

Offering carved howling coyotes, turquoise jewelry and fine art, Santa Fe attracts shoppers of all budgets.

Plaza Mercado (112 W San Francisco St) A swish spot packed with art galleries, antique stores and Santa Fe–style clothing.

Tesuque Flea Market (Hwy 84/285; ⏲ 8am-4pm Fri-Sun Mar-Nov) This outdoor market a few minutes' drive north of Santa Fe at Tesuque Pueblo offers deals on high-quality rugs, jewelry, art and clothing.

Getting There & Around

The **Santa Fe Municipal Airport** (☎ 505-955-2908; Aviation Dr) has regional commuter service only; most air passengers fly to Albuquerque.

TNM&O/Greyhound (☎ 505-471-0008; www.greyhound.com; 858 St Michael's Dr) has three daily buses to Albuquerque ($15, 80 minutes) and one daily bus to Taos ($17, two hours). **Twin Hearts Shuttle** (☎ 800-654-9456; www.twinheartstransportation.com) runs between Santa Fe and the Albuquerque Sunport ($25), Taos ($40), Española ($25), Red River ($45) and Questa ($45) daily; make reservations in advance.

Amtrak (☎ 800-872-7245; www.amtrak.com) stops at Lamy; buses continue 17 miles to Santa Fe.

Santa Fe Trails (☎ 505-955-2001; http://santafetrails.santafenm.gov; ⏲ 6am-11pm Mon-Fri, 8am-8pm Sat, 10am-7pm Sun) provides a local bus service (adult/child $1/50¢ per ride; day pass $2/1).

AROUND SANTA FE

Don't get too comfy in Santa Fe, because there's lots to see nearby. The red rocks, pine forest and streams of this region offer an embarrassment of hiking riches, natural hot springs and pueblos. Within miles of each other, Bandelier National Monument and Los Alamos evidence the iconographic geological, human and atomic history of the American West.

Pueblos

North of Santa Fe is the heart of Puebloan lands. The **Eight Northern Pueblos** (ENIPC; ☎ 505-747-1593) publish the excellent and free *Eight*

Northern Indian Pueblos Visitors Guide, available at area visitor centers.

Eight miles west of Pojoaque along Hwy 502, the ancient **San Ildefonso Pueblo** (☎ 505-455-3549; per vehicle $5, camera/sketching/video permits $10/25/20; ☾ 8am-5pm) was the home of Maria Martinez, who in 1919 revived a distinctive traditional black-on-black pottery style. Several exceptional potters (including Maria's direct descendants) work in the pueblo; stop at the **Maria Poveka Martinez Museum** (admission free; ☾ 8am-4pm Mon-Fri), which sells the pueblo's pottery.

Española

In some ways Española is the gateway to the real New Mexico, separating the tourist-choked wonderland of Santa Fe from the reality of the rural. Much of the surrounding area is farmland, and much has been deeded to Hispanic land-grant families since the 17th century. Though the town itself doesn't offer much beyond a strip with fast-food restaurants and a disproportionate number of hair salons, it has a couple of stars. Contact the **chamber of commerce** (☎ 505-753-2831; www.espanolanmchamber.com; 710 Paseo de Oñate; ☾ 9am-5pm Mon-Fri) for more information.

Just northwest of town, on the road to Ojo Caliente (p886), **Rancho de San Juan** (☎ 505-753-6818; www.ranchodesanjuan.com; Hwy 285; r & ste $275-675; ☒) is a small gem with first-class rooms, a spa, great service and a spectacular setting for dining on New Mexican classics, at two nightly seatings.

Ranchito San Pedro B&B (☎ 505-753-0583; www.janhart.com; Hwy 581; cabins $98; ☒), an adobe 'art dude ranch,' in a surprisingly pastoral neighborhood, is pet-friendly and about as relaxing as they come. Note there's a three-night minimum stay.

Las Vegas

Not to be confused with the glittery city to the west, this Vegas is one of the loveliest towns in New Mexico, and one of the largest and oldest towns east of the Sangre de Cristo Mountains. Its eminently strollable downtown has a pretty Old Town Plaza and some 900 historic buildings listed in the National Register of Historic Places. Its architecture is a mix of Southwestern and Victorian. Ask for a walking-tour brochure from the **chamber of commerce** (☎ 505-425-8631, 800-832-5947; www.lasvegasnewmexico.com; 701 Grand Ave; ☾ 9am-5pm Mon-Fri).

Built in 1882 and carefully remodeled a century later, the renovated **Plaza Hotel** (☎ 505-425-3591, 800-328-1882; www.plazahotel-nm.com; 230 Old Town Plaza; r/ste incl breakfast $135/185; ☐ wi-fi) is Las Vegas' most celebrated and historic lodging. The elegant building now offers 37 comfortable accommodations in antique-filled rooms.

Indulge in a good New Mexican meal at **Estella's Café** (☎ 505-454-0048; 148 Bridge St; lunch $5-8, dinner $10-14; ☾ 11am-3pm Mon-Wed, 11am-8pm Thu & Fri, 7am-3pm Sat). Estella's devoted patrons treasure their homemade red chili, *menudo* (tripe and grits) and scrumptious enchiladas.

From the plaza, Hot Springs Blvd leads 5 miles north to Gallinas Canyon and the massive **Montezuma Castle**, an eye-popping structure on the flanks of the Sangre de Cristo Mountains; once a hotel, it's now the United World College of the West. Along the road there, you can soak in a series of natural **hot spring pools**.

Los Alamos

Los Alamos, hugging the national forest and perched on mesas overlooking the desert, offers a fascinating dynamic in which souvenir T-shirts emblazoned with atomic explosions and 'La Bomba' wine are sold next to books on pueblo history and wilderness hiking.

You can't actually visit the **Los Alamos National Laboratory**, where the first atomic bomb was conceived, but you can visit the well-designed **Bradbury Science Museum** (☎ 505-667-4444; www.lanl.gov/museum; cnr Central Ave & 15th; admission free; ☾ 10am-5pm Tue-Sat, 1-5pm Sun & Mon), which covers atomic history. The **Los Alamos Historical Museum** (☎ 505-662-6272; ww.losalamoshistory.org; 1921 Juniper St; admission free; ☾ 9:30am-4:30pm Mon-Sat, 1-5pm Sun) features atomic-age popular culture artifacts and exhibits on the social history of life 'on the hill' during the secret project. Pick up one of its great self-guided downtown walking tour pamphlets or download it from the website.

Bandelier National Monument

Because of its convenient location and spectacular landscape, **Bandelier** (☎ 505-672-3861; www.nps.gov/band; per vehicle $6, campsites $12; ☾ dawn-dusk) is an excellent choice for folks interested in ancient pueblos. Rio Grande Puebloans lived here until the mid-1500s. Although none of the sites are restored, there are almost 50 sq miles of protected canyons offering backpacking trails and camping at Juniper Campground, set among the pines near the monument entrance. It has about 100 campsites and is first come, first served, though rarely full.

Abiquiu

The tiny community of Abiquiu (sounds like 'barbecue'), on Hwy 84 about 45 minutes' drive northwest of Santa Fe, is famous because the renowned artist Georgia O'Keeffe lived and painted here permanently from 1949 until her death in 1986. With the Chama River flowing through farmland and spectacular rock landscape, the ethereal setting continues to attract artists, and many live and work in Abiquiu. O'Keeffe's adobe house is open for limited visits, and the Georgia O'Keeffe Museum offers one-hour **tours** (☎ 505-685-4539; www.okeeffemuseum.org) on Tuesday, Thursday and Friday from April to November ($30), often booked months in advance.

Ghost Ranch (☎ 505-685-333, 877-804-4678; www .ghostranch.org; campsites $16, RV sites $19-26, dm incl breakfast $45, r with private/shared bath incl breakfast from $63/87) A retreat center at the foot of the Sangre de Cristo Mountains (and a shooting location for the movie *City Slickers*), this spectacular spot has basic lodging and cafeteria-style meals.

An area institution, the peaceful and lovely **Abiquiú Inn** (☎ 505-685-4378, 800-447-5621; www .abiquiuinn.com; Hwy 84; RV sites $18, s $79-199, d $139-199, 4-person casitas $199; ✗ ✗ wi-fi) is a sprawling collection of shaded adobes; the spacious casitas have kitchenettes. The very professional staff also runs the on-site **Abiquiú Cafe** (dishes $7-18; ✆ 7:30am-9pm). Stick to the Middle Eastern menu – falafel, dolmas and gyros are all winners – and you can't go wrong.

Ojo Caliente

Billed as America's oldest health resort, **Ojo Caliente** (☎ 800-222-9162; www.ojocalientesprings.com; 50 Los Baños Rd; r $109-249, cottages $179; ✗), which means 'hot eye' in Spanish, offers five springs, plus a family-owned resort with pleasant if not luxurious rooms and casitas. The on-site **Artesian Restaurant** (dishes $10-25; ✆ 8am-10:30am, 11:30am-2:30pm & 5-8:30pm) prepares organic and local ingredients with aplomb, including chicken with green-chili pesto and herbed cheese. It's about 40 miles north of Santa Fe on Hwy 285.

Cuba

Set in 360 beautiful acres in the Nacimiento Mountains, the friendly and recommended **Circle A Ranch Hostel** (☎ 505-289-3350; www.circle aranchhostel.com; dm $20, r $35-60; ✆ May–mid-Oct), just off Hwy 550, is a gem. The lovely old adobe lodge, with exposed beams, grassy grounds, hiking trails and a classic kitchen, is a peaceful and relaxing place to hang out. Choose between private bedrooms (some with quilts and iron bedsteads), shared bunkrooms and a yurt. It also offers work exchanges.

TAOS

Nestled in the snow-peaked Sangre de Cristo Mountains, this small town has a big reputation. Isolated Taos boasts – with a pleasant but ever-so-disinterested tone – a long history of luring artists with its fabled clear light, a stunning multistory adobe pueblo and a magnificent mountain setting.

It's an eccentric place, full of bohemians and mainstream dropouts, alternative-energy aficionados, fine chefs, acculturated B&B owners and old-time Hispanic families who still farm hay fields. It's rural and worldly, a place where grazing horses and a disproportionate number of artists hold equal sway.

Information

Taos Guide (www.taosguide.com) Great links.
Taos Vacation Guide (www.taosvacationguide.com) Good site with some sections in French, German and Spanish.
Visitor center (☎ 505-758-3873, 800-732-8267; www .taoschamber.com; 1139 Paseo Del Pueblo Sur; ✆ 9am-5pm)
Wired? (☎ 505-751-9473; 705 Felicidad Lane; ✆ 7am-7pm) Coffee shop with internet access ($7 per hour) and wi-fi.

Sights

Four miles south of Taos in Ranchos de Taos, the oft-photographed **San Francisco de Asís Church** (☎ 505-758-2754; St Francis Plaza; ✆ 9am-4pm Mon-Fri) was built in the mid-18th century but didn't open until 1815. It's been memorialized in numerous Georgia O'Keeffe paintings and Edward Weston photographs.

At 650ft above the Rio Grande, the steel **Rio Grande Gorge Bridge** is the second-highest suspension bridge in the US; the view down is eye-popping. Just west of the bridge is a fascinating community of **Earthships** (☎ 505-751-0462; www.earthship.net; Hwy 64; admission $5; ✆ 10am-4pm), self-sustaining, environmentally savvy houses built with recycled materials that are completely off the grid. You can also stay overnight in one (see right).

Taos Historic Museums (☎ 505-758-0505; www .taoshistoricmuseums.com; adult/child $7/3; ⏰ 9am-5pm summer, shorter hr winter) runs two great houses: the **Blumenschein Home** (222 Ledoux St), with spectacular art, and the **Martínez Hacienda** (Ranchitos Rd), a colonial trader's former home.

The **Millicent Rogers Museum** (☎ 505-758-2462; www.millicentrogers.org; 1504 Millicent Rogers Museum Rd; adult/child $10/6; ⏰ 110am-5pm daily, closed Mon from Nov-Mar), is filled with pottery, jewelry, baskets and textiles, and has one of the best collections of Native American and Spanish-colonial art in the US.

Housed in a historic mid-19th-century adobe compound, the **Harwood Foundation** (☎ 505-758-9826; www.harwoodmuseum.org; 238 Ledoux St; admission $8; ⏰ 10am-5pm Tue-Sat, noon-5pm Sun) features paintings, drawings, prints, sculpture and photography by northern New Mexico artists, both historical and contemporary.

Activities

During the summer, **white-water rafting** is popular in the Taos Box, the steep-sided cliffs that frame the Rio Grande. Day-long trips begin at around $100 per person; contact the visitor center for local outfitters. **Hiking** options are plentiful; trailheads line the road to the ski valley.

With a peak elevation of 11,819ft and a 2612ft vertical drop, **Taos Ski Valley** (☎ 866-968-7386; www.skitaos.org; adult/child $63/38) offers some of the most challenging skiing (no snowboarding) in the US and yet remains low-key and relaxed.

Sleeping

Abominable Snowmansion (☎ 505-776-8298; www .abominablesnowmansion.com; 476 Hwy 150, Arroyo Seco; dm $20, r with shared/private bath $48/52, teepees $32;

DON'T MISS: TAOS PUEBLO

Built around AD 1450 and continuously inhabited ever since, the streamside Taos Pueblo (☎ 505-758-1028; www.taospueblo.com; Taos Pueblo Rd; adult/child $10/5, photography or video permit $5; ⏰ 8am-4pm winter, to 5pm summer, closed for 6 weeks around Feb & Mar) is the largest existing multistoried pueblo structure in the US and one of the best surviving examples of traditional adobe construction.

⊠ 💻 wi-fi) About 9 miles northeast of Taos, this well-worn and welcoming hostel is a cozy mountainside alternative to central Taos. A big, round fireplace warms guests in wintertime, and kitschy teepees are available in summer. There's a $3 discount for HI members.

Adobe Wall Motel (☎ 505-758-3972; 227 Kit Carson Rd; r $56-66; ⊠) For almost 100 years, this shady courtyard motel has accommodated travelers in big, slightly tattered rooms with wonderful fireplaces.

Laughing Horse Inn (☎ 505-758-8350, 800-776-0161; www.laughinghorseinn.com; 729 Paseo del Pueblo Norte; r with shared bath incl breakfast $65-160; ⊠ wi-fi) Georgia O'Keeffe kept a room here for her lovers, and the small 1880s adobe still radiates an artsy *joie de vivre*. The rooms vary from narrow-and-nifty bunks to a huge, funky penthouse suite, and some have traditional kiva fireplaces. The inn emphasizes community, with guests encouraged to use the homey kitchen, socialize over tea in the living room and lounge in the hot tub under the stars.

Historic Taos Inn (☎ 505-758-2233, 800-826-7466; www.taosinn.com; 125 Paseo del Pueblo Norte; r $70-275; P ⊠ wi-fi) Even though it's not the plushest place in town, it's fabulous, with a cozy lobby, a greenhouse Jacuzzi, heavy wooden furniture, a sunken fireplace and lots of live local music at its famed Adobe Bar. Parts of this landmark date to the 17th century.

our pick **Earthship Rentals** (☎ 505-751-0462; Hwy 64; r $125-175) Experience an off-grid overnight in a boutique-chic and solar-powered dwelling. A cross between organic Gaudí architecture and space-age fantasy, these sustainable dwellings are put together using recycled tires, aluminum cans and sand, with rain catchment and gray-water systems to minimize their footprint. Half-buried in a valley surrounded by mountains, they *could* be hastily camouflaged alien vessels – you never know.

Eating

Taos Pizza Out Back (☎ 505-758-3112; 712 Paseo del Pueblo Norte; slices $3-7, medium pies $18-23; ⏰ 11am-9pm) Warning: these pizza pies may be cruelly habit-forming. Located behind another business (no, it's not Australian), it uses organic ingredients and serves epicurean combos like a Portabella Pie with sun-dried tomatoes and camembert. Slices are the size of a small country.

Bent Street Deli & Café (☎ 505-758-5787; 120 Bent St; breakfast $7, sandwiches $7; ⏰ 8am-4pm Mon-Sat, 10am-3pm Sun) Choose from 21 sandwiches with silly names like 'Power Steering' (roast beef on an onion roll) and 'All Hens on Deck' (chicken salad on wheat), or stop in for a gourmet comfort-food dinner.

Orlando's (☎ 505-751-1450; 1114 Don Juan Valdez Ln; dishes $7-11; ⏰ 10am-3pm & 5-9pm) This is it: the best New Mexican food in town, period. Those chicken enchiladas and huge burritos are all dressed to perfection and served up in the beautiful dining room.

Joseph's Table (☎ 505-751-4512; 108 A S Taos Plaza; mains $28-32; ⏰ 11:30am-2:30pm Sun & 5:30-10pm) Inside the Hotel La Fonda, Chef Joseph Wrede doles out unique and creative Southwestern dishes with an emphasis on local farms, and the dining room sprouts pussywillow chandeliers and a lush flowery mural painted by his wife and his mother. Couples should go for a 'loveshack,' one of the cozy, romantic window booths.

Drinking

Adobe Bar (☎ 505-758-2233; Historic Taos Inn, 125 Paseo del Pueblo Norte) Sidle up to the margarita menu and relax in 'the living room of Taos.' There's something about this place: the chairs, the Taos Inn's history, the casualness, the tequila. The packed streetside patio has some of the state's finest margaritas, along with an eclectic lineup of great live music, and never a cover.

Alley Cantina (☎ 505-758-2121; 121 Teresina Lane) The oldest building in Taos is an out-of-the-way bar. Catch live rock, blues, hip-hop or jazz almost nightly. Pub grub (dishes $6 to $14) is also on offer.

Eske's Brew Pub & Eatery (☎ 505-758-1517; 106 Des Georges Lane) In the mood for an Artist Ale? Maybe a Taos Green Chile Beer? (To wash down the bar food, perhaps? Dishes are $7 to $10.) This crowded hangout rotates more than 25 microbrewed ales and spotlights local bands, from acoustic guitar to jazz.

Shopping

Taos has historically been a mecca for artists, demonstrated by the huge number of galleries and studios in and around town.

Twining Weavers (☎ 505-758-9000; 133 Kit Carson Rd) Features handwoven rugs, tapestries and pillows.

El Rincón Trading Post (☎ 505-758-9188; 114 Kit Carson Rd) Even if you're not looking to buy anything, stop in here to browse through the dusty museum of artifacts, including Native American crafts, jewelry and Old West memorabilia.

Getting There & Around

From Santa Fe, take either the scenic 'high road' along Hwy 76 and Hwy 518, with galleries, villages and sites worth exploring, or follow the lovely unfolding Rio Grande landscape on Hwy 68.

Greyhound (☎ 505-758-1144, 800-231-2222; www .greyhound.com; 729A Paseo del Pueblo Sur) has a daily bus service to Albuquerque ($30, three hours) and Santa Fe ($18, 1½ hours).

Faust (☎ 505-758-3410, 888-830-3410) leaves the Albuquerque Sunport Monday through Saturday at 1:30pm; the return shuttle leaves Taos for Albuquerque at 7:30am ($40 to $50, three hours). Reservations required.

NORTHWESTERN NEW MEXICO

Dubbed 'Indian Country' for good reason – huge swaths of land fall under the aegis of the Navajo, Pueblo, Zuni, Apache and Laguna tribes – this quadrant of New Mexico showcases remarkable ancient Indian sites alongside modern, solitary Native American settlements. There are excavated dwellings at Chaco Culture National Historical Park and unexcavated ones at Aztec Ruins National Monument – the mysteries of the land are carried on the wind. It's not all Native Americans, though. In Chama, it's all aboard. The Cumbres & Toltec Scenic Railroad transports travelers to the mid-19th century on a classic locomotive train trip through the mountains.

Farmington & Around

The largest town in New Mexico's northwestern region, Farmington makes a good base from which to explore the Four Corners area. The **visitors bureau** (☎ 505-326-7602, 800-448-1240; www.farmingtonnm.org; Farmington Museum at Gateway Park, 3041 E Main St; ⏰ 8am-5pm Mon-Sat) has more information.

Shiprock, a 1700ft-high volcanic plug that rises eerily over the landscape to the west, was a landmark for the Anglo pioneers and is a sacred site to the Navajo. The Navajo community of Shiprock hosts an annual **Northern Navajo Nation Fair**, in late September or early

October, featuring a rodeo, powwow and traditional dancing.

An ancient pueblo, **Salmon Ruin & Heritage Park** (☎ 505-632-2013; adult/child $3/1; ☽ 8am-5pm Mon-Fri, 9am-5pm Sat & Sun) features a large village built by the Chaco people in the early 1100s. Abandoned, resettled by people from Mesa Verde and again abandoned before 1300, the site includes the remains of a homestead, petroglyphs, a Navajo hogan, an early Puebloan pithouse, a teepee and a *wickiup* (a rough brushwood shelter). To reach it, take Hwy 64 east toward Bloomfield.

Fourteen miles northeast of Farmington, the 27-acre **Aztec Ruins National Monument** (☎ 505-334-6174; www.nps.gov/azru; adult/child 15yr & under $5/free; ☽ 8am-5pm Sep-May, to 6pm Jun-Aug) features the largest reconstructed kiva in the country, with an internal diameter of almost 50ft. Let your imagination wander as you sit inside the Great Kiva. During the summer months rangers give early-afternoon talks at the c 1100 site about ancient architecture, trade routes and astronomy. They're very informative.

Located about 35 miles south of Farmington along Hwy 371, the undeveloped **Bisti Badlands & De-Na-Zin Wilderness** is a trippy, surreal landscape of strange, colorful rock formations – it's like stepping onto a science-fiction film set; desert enthusiasts shouldn't miss it. The Farmington **BLM office** (☎ 505-599-8900; 1235 La Plata Hwy; ☽ 8am-4:30pm Mon-Fri) dispenses information.

SLEEPING & EATING

Silver River Adobe Inn B&B (☎ 505-325-8219, 800-382-9251; www.silveradobe.com; 3151 W Main St; r incl breakfast $105-175; ✗) This lovely three-room place offers a peaceful respite among the trees on the San Juan River. Fall asleep to the sound of the river, wake to organic blueberry juice and enjoy a morning walk to the prairie dog village.

Three Rivers Eatery & Brewhouse (☎ 505-324-2187; 101 E Main St; dishes $8-11) Managing to be both trendy *and* kid-friendly, this hippish place has good food and its own microbrews. Try the homemade potato skins, but keep in mind that the steaks are substantial. Spiffy sandwiches and soups are served at lunchtime.

Chama

Nine miles south of the Colorado border, Chama's **Cumbres & Toltec Scenic Railway** (☎ 505-756-2151, 888-286-2737; www.cumbresandtoltec.com) is both the longest (64 miles) and highest (over the 10,015ft-high Cumbres Pass) authentic narrow-gauge steam railroad in the US. It's a beautiful trip, particularly in September and October during the fall foliage, through mountains, canyons and high desert.

Chaco Culture National Historic Park

Featuring massive Ancestral Puebloan buildings set in an isolated high-desert environment, intriguing **Chaco** (per vehicle $8; ☽ dawn-dusk) contains evidence of 5000 years of human occupation. In its prime, the community at Chaco Canyon was a major trading and ceremonial hub for the region – and the city the Puebloan people created here was masterly in its layout and design. Pueblo Bonito is four stories tall and may have had 600 to 800 rooms and kivas. Apart from taking the self-guided loop tour, you can hike various **backcountry trails**.

The **visitor center** (☎ 505-786-7014; www.nps.gov/chcu; ☽ 8am-5pm) is in a remote area approximately 80 miles south of Farmington. **Gallo Campground** (campsites $10, no RV sites) is 1.5 miles from the visitor center.

NORTHEASTERN NEW MEXICO

East of Santa Fe, the lush Sangre de Cristo Mountains give way to high and vast rolling plains. Dusty grasslands stretch to infinity and further – to Texas. Cattle and dinosaur prints dot the landscape, a land of extremes with formerly fiery volcanoes in Capulin and hot springs in Montezuma (p885). Ranching is an economic mainstay, and on many stretches of the road you'll see more cattle than cars.

The Santa Fe Trail, along which pioneer settlers rolled in wagon trains, ran from New Mexico to Missouri. You can still see the wagon ruts in some places off I-25 between Santa Fe and Raton. If you're looking for a bit of the Old West without a patina of consumer hype, this is the place.

Cimarron

Cimarron was a Wild West town following Anglo settlement; today it's very quiet. Driving here to or from Taos, you'll pass through gorgeous **Cimarron Canyon State Park**, a steep-walled canyon with several hiking trails, excellent trout fishing and camping.

The **Cimarron Inn & RV Park** (☎ 505-376-2268, 800-546-2244; www.cimarroninn.com; Hwy 64; campsites

$10, RV sites $25, s/d from $45/55, 6-person/12-person cabins $135/240) has 15 spotless adobe motel rooms – some with kitchenettes – and larger units that can bunk the extended family.

Capulin Volcano National Monument

Rising 1300ft above the surrounding plains, **Capulin** (☎ 505-278-2201; www.nps.gov/cavo; per vehicle $5) is the most accessible of several volcanoes in the area. From the visitor center, a 2-mile road spirals up the mountain to a parking lot at the crater rim (8182ft), where trails lead around and into the crater. The entrance is 3 miles north of the Capulin village, which itself is 30 miles east of Raton on Hwy 87.

SOUTHWESTERN NEW MEXICO

The Rio Grande Valley unfurls from Albuquerque down to the bubbling hot springs of funky Truth or Consequences. Crops, while plentiful, often grow on a wing and a prayer. Residents are few and far between, except in lively Las Cruces, the state's second largest city.

I-10 cuts through the Chihuahua Desert, dominated by yucca and agave. This is ranching country, though the cattle are sparse. North of the desert and west of I-25, the rugged Gila National Forest is wild with backpacking and fishing adventures.

Socorro & Around

Socorro means 'help' or 'aid' in Spanish, and the city was named for the assistance given to Spanish explorer Juan de Oñate (p806) and his party by the local Piro people in 1598. For a short time during the 19th century, Socorro was New Mexico's biggest town, thanks to gold and silver mining, and today its Victorian buildings are testament to that brief boom period. The **chamber of commerce** (☎ 505-835-0424; www.socorro-nm.com; 101 Plaza; ⊙ 9am-5pm Mon-Fri, to noon Sat) has area information.

At the **Economy Inn** (☎ 505-835-4666; 400 N California St; r $40-44; ✖ ⚛ wi-fi), clean and reasonably well-kept rooms have microwaves and small refrigerators. The **Socorro Springs Brewing Company** (☎ 505-838-0650; 1012 N California St; dishes $7-10; ⊙ 7am-10pm Mon-Fri, 8am-10pm Sat & Sun) is a fun place, dishing up calzones, pizzas and grill food and a choice of a half-dozen brews on tap.

Endangered whooping cranes winter in the 90 sq miles of fields and marshes at **Bosque del Apache National Wildlife Refuge** (☎ 505-835-

1828; per vehicle $3; ⊙ dawn-dusk), south of Socorro near San Antonio. There's a visitor center and driving tour. Refuge visitors often stop by the **Owl Bar Cafe** (☎ 505-835-9946; 215 San Antonio St; dishes $7-10; ⊙ 8am-8pm Mon-Sat), half a mile east of I-25 near San Antonio, for acclaimed green-chili cheeseburgers.

For those heading west into Arizona from Socorro, Hwy 60 makes a remote, scenic alternative to I-40. Past the town of Magdalena, and 47 miles west of Socorro, is the **Very Large Array** (VLA; www.vla.nrao.edu; admission free; ⊙ 8:30am-dusk) radio telescope facility, a complex of 27 huge antenna dishes sprouting like giant mushrooms in the high plains. To get there, drive 4 miles south of Hwy 60 off Hwy 52.

Truth or Consequences

Built on the site of natural hot springs in the 1880s, this funky little town once known as Hot Springs was renamed Truth or Consequences (or 'T or C') in 1950, after a popular radio program of the same name. Wander around the little hole-in-the-wall cafés, check out the junk shops and definitely take a dip in one of the town's hot-spring spas. The **visitor center** (☎ 505-894-1968, 800-831-9487; www.truthorconsequencesnm.net; 211 Main St; ⊙ 9am-5pm Mon-Fri, 11am-4pm Sat) has local listings.

Many local motels double as spas. **Riverbend Hot Springs** (☎ 505-894-6183; www.riverbendhotsprings.com; 100 Austin St; dm $25, r $40-100; ✖ ⚛ wi-fi), a riverside hostel, offers dormitory-style accommodations in cabins, trailers and teepees. Hot-spring tubs are available morning and evening ($10 to $15 per person hourly), and are free for guests.

The **Sierra Grande Lodge & Spa** (☎ 505-894-6976; www.sierragrandelodge.com; 501 McAdoo St; r $129-169, ste $270-425; ✖ ⚛ wi-fi) is an oasis, not a mirage. It's real and refined, and occupies a masterfully renovated 1920s lodge. Guest rooms and suites are luxe and tranquil; mineral-bath privileges are included with the room. Spa treatments radiate real warmth.

Las Cruces & Around

The second largest city in New Mexico is home to New Mexico State University (NMSU), which keeps things somewhat lively with about 15,000 students. The **visitors bureau** (☎ 505-541-2444, 800-343-7827; www.lascrucescvb.org; 211 N Water St; ⊙ 8am-5pm Mon-Fri) has information.

For many, a visit to neighboring **Mesilla** is the highlight of their time in Las Cruces. Wander a few blocks beyond the plaza to gather the essence of a mid-19th-century Southwestern town of Hispanic heritage

White Sands Missile Test Center Museum (☎ 505-678-8824; www.wsmr-history.org; admission free; ☺ 8am-4pm Mon-Fri, 10am-3pm Sat & Sun), about 25 miles east of Las Cruces along Hwy 70, has been a major military testing site since 1945, and it still serves as an alternative landing site for the space shuttle. Look for the crazy outdoor missile park.

In Las Cruces, **Lundeen Inn of the Arts** (☎ 505-526-3326, 888-526-3326; www.innofthearts.com; 618 S Alameda Blvd; incl breakfast s/d $77/85, ste $95-115; ✗ ✗ wi-fi), a large turn-of-the-19th-century Mexican territorial-style inn, has 20 guest rooms (all wildly different), an airy living room with soaring ceilings (made of pressed tin) and a 300-piece fine art gallery.

Join the student crowd at **Spirit Winds Coffee Bar** (☎ 505-521-1222; 2260 S Locust St; dishes $6; ☺ 7am-7pm Mon-Fri, 8am-6pm Sat & Sun) for excellent cappuccino, good sandwiches, salads, soups and pastries. **Nellie's Cafe** (☎ 505-524-9982; 1226 W Hadley Ave; dishes $7; ☺ 8am-2pm) is the favored local Mexican restaurant.

Greyhound/TNM&O (☎ 505-524-8518; www.greyhound.com; 304 Wyatt Dr) has buses traversing the two interstate corridors (I-10 and I-25), as well as buses to Roswell and beyond.

Silver City & Around

Silver City's downtown streets are dressed with lovely old brick and cast-iron buildings, some Victorian ones, a few adobes and a Wild West air. Billy the Kid spent some of his boyhood here, and a few of his haunts can be seen. Silver is also the gateway to outdoor activities in the Gila National Forest, which is rugged country suitable for remote cross-country skiing, backpacking, camping, fishing and other activities.

The **visitor center** (☎ 505-538-3785, 800-548-9378; www.silvercity.org; 201 N Hudson St; ☺ 9am-5pm Mon-Fri, 10am-2pm Sat) and the **Gila National Forest Ranger Station** (☎ 505-388-8201; www.fs.fed.us/r3/gila; 3005 E Camino Del Bosque; ☺ 8am-4:30pm Mon-Fri) have area information. To learn about the town's contentious mining history, watch the blacklisted 1954 movie *Salt of the Earth*.

Two hours north of Silver City up a winding 42-mile road, the **Gila Cliff Dwellings National Monument** (☎ 505-536-9461; admission $3; ☺ 8am-6pm summer, 9am-4pm rest of yr) was occupied in the 13th century by Mogollons. Mysterious, relatively isolated and accessible, these remarkable cliff dwellings look very much as they would have at the turn of the first millennium.

Rounded volcanic towers make up the **City of Rocks State Park** (☎ 505-536-2800; Hwy 61; campsites $10-14), where you can camp among the towers in secluded campsites with tables and fire pits. Head 24 miles northwest of Deming along Hwy 180, then 3 miles northeast on Hwy 61.

For a smattering of Silver City's architectural history, the **Palace Hotel** (☎ 505-388-1811; www.zianet.com/palacehotel; 106 W Broadway; incl breakfast d $44-57, ste $72; ✗ wi-fi) has 18 rooms with Victorian detailing. On the corner, the lofty **Javalina** (☎ 505-388-1350; 201 N Bullard; pastries $2-5; ☺ 6am-10pm) offers the three major food groups: coffee, snacks and free wi-fi. **Diane's Restaurant & Bakery** (☎ 505-538-8722; 510 N Bullard St; dishes lunch $7-8, dinner $14-22; ☺ 11am-2pm & 5:30-9pm Tue-Fri, 9am-2pm & 5:30-9pm Sat, 9am-2pm Sun) has an elegant indoor space with white tablecloths, though the latticework and canvas awnings make it feel like a romantic outdoor patio.

SOUTHEASTERN NEW MEXICO

With the exception of the forests surrounding the resort towns of Cloudcroft and Ruidoso, southeastern New Mexico is marked by seemingly endless horizons and grassy plains. It's also marked by awesome White Sands National Monument and magnificent Carlsbad Caverns National Park. Spend dusk at both places if you can. It's all here: alien sightings in Roswell, Billy the Kid at Fort Sumner and, in Lincoln, Smokey Bear and oil rigs the further east you go.

White Sands National Monument

Slide, roll and slither through brilliant, towering sand hills. Sixteen miles southwest of Alamogordo (15 miles southwest of Hwy 82/70), gypsum covers 275 sq miles to create a dazzling white landscape at this crisp, stark **monument** (☎ 505-679-2599; www.nps.gov/whsa; adult/child 16yr & under $3/free; ☺ park 8am-7pm Jun-Aug, 7am-sunset Sep-May). These captivating windswept dunes are a highlight of any trip to New Mexico. Check the park calendar for occasional moonlight bicycle rides and monthly full-moon talks. Backcountry campsites, with no water or toilet facilities, are a mile from the scenic drive. Pick up one of the limited permits ($3, issued first come, first served) in person at the visitor center at least one hour before sunset.

Alamogordo & Around

Alamogordo is the center of one of the most historically important space- and atomic-research programs in the country. The four-story **New Mexico Museum of Space History** (☎ 505-437-2840, 877-333-6589; www.nmspacemuseum .org; Hwy 2001; adult/child 4-12yr $3/2.50; � 9am-5pm) has excellent exhibits on space research and flight. Its **Tombaugh IMAX Theater & Planetarium** (adult/child $6/4.50) shows outstanding films on a huge wraparound screen on anything from dolphins to exploring Mars.

Numerous motels stretch along White Sands Blvd, including **Best Western Desert Aire Motor Inn** (☎ 505-437-2110; www.bestwestern.com; 1021 S White Sands Blvd; r $66-76; ☒ ☐ wi-fi), with standard-issue rooms and suites (some with kitchenettes), along with a sauna and whirlpool. The **Wok Inn** (☎ 505-434-4388; 1010 S White Sands Blvd; dishes $6-9; � 11am-10pm) has good Chinese food and inexpensive lunch specials ($4 to $6). The menu includes a number of veggie dishes, and it stays open later than most places in town.

The **TNM&O/Greyhound Bus Station** (☎ 505-437-3050, 800-231-2222; www.greyhound.com; 601 N White Sands Blvd) has several daily buses to Albuquerque ($41, four hours), Roswell ($27, 2½ hours), Carlsbad ($9, nine hours) and El Paso ($23, 2½ hours).

Cloudcroft

Pleasant Cloudcroft, with turn-of-the-19th-century buildings, offers lots of outdoor recreation, a good base for exploration and a low-key feel. Situated high in the mountains, it provides welcome relief from the lowlands heat to the east. The **chamber of commerce** (☎ 505-682-2733, 866-874-4447; www.cloudcroft .net; 1001 James Canyon Hwy; � 10am-5pm Mon-Sat) is on Hwy 82.

The **Lodge Resort & Spa** (☎ 505-682-2566, 800-395-6343; www.thelodgeresort.com; 1 Corona Pl; r from $125, ste $185-315; ☒ ☒ ☒ ☐ wi-fi) is one of the Southwest's best historic hotels. Rooms in the main Bavarian-style hotel are furnished with period and Victorian pieces. Within the lodge, **Rebecca's** (☎ 505-682-3131; breakfast $6-11, lunch $7-17, dinner $18-34; � 11:30am-2:30pm & 5:30-9pm) offers by far the best food in town.

Ruidoso

You want lively? For these parts? You want Ruidoso. (In Spanish, it means 'noisy'.) Downright bustling in the summer and big

with racetrack bettors, resorty Ruidoso has an utterly pleasant climate thanks to its lofty and forested perch near Sierra Blanca (12,000ft). It's spread out along Hwy 48 (known as Mechem Dr or Sudderth Dr), the main drag. The **chamber of commerce** (☎ 505-257-7395, 877-784-3676; www.ruidosonow.com; 720 Sudderth Dr; � 9am-5pm Mon-Fri, to 3pm Sat, to 3pm Sun late May-late Aug) has visitor information.

Serious horse racing happens at the **Ruidoso Downs Racetrack** (☎ 505-378-4431; www.ruidoso downsracing.com; Hwy 70; grandstand seats free, boxes $28; � races Thu-Sun late May-early Sep, casino 11am-11pm year-round). The fine **Hubbard Museum of the American West** (☎ 505-378-4142, www.hubbardmuseum.org; 841 Hwy 70 W; adult/child $6/2; � 9am-5pm) displays more than 10,000 Western-related items, including Old West stagecoaches, saddles and Native American pottery.

The best ski area south of Albuquerque is **Ski Apache** (☎ 505-336-4356, snow conditions 505-257-9001; www.skiapache.com; all-day passes adult $45-54, child $26-35; � 8:45am-4pm), 18 miles northwest of Ruidoso on the slopes of beautiful Sierra Blanca Peak (about 12,000ft). To get there, take exit 532 off Hwy 48.

Circle the wagons and ride over to **Flying J Ranch** (☎ 505-336-4330; Hwy 48 N; adult/child $22/12; � 6pm Mon-Sat May-Aug, Fri & Sat Sep-Oct), about 1.5 miles north of Alto, for a meal. This 'Western village' stages gunfights and offers pony rides with its cowboy-style chuckwagon.

SLEEPING & EATING

Numerous motels, hotels and cute little cabin complexes line the streets.

Sitzmark Chalet (☎ 505-257-4140, 800-658-9694; www.sitzmark-chalet.com; 627 Sudderth Dr; r $75-89; ☒ ☒ wi-fi) The chalet offers 17 simple but nice rooms. The hot tub comes in handy after a day of hiking.

Ruidoso Lodge Cabins (☎ 505-257-2510, 800-950-2510; www.ruidosolodge.com; 300 Main Rd; cabins $129-209; ☒ wi-fi) Attractively set along the river, the cabins have wood-burning fireplaces.

Cornerstone Bakery (☎ 505-257-1842; 359 Sudderth Dr; dishes under $8; � 7:30am-2pm) Stay around long enough and this eatery may become your touchstone. Everything on the menu, from the omelets to croissant sandwiches, is worthy.

Casa Blanca (☎ 505-257-2495; 501 Mechem Dr; dinner dishes $7-12; � 11am-9pm) Dine on Southwestern cuisine in a renovated Spanish-style house. The *chilis rellenos* are to die for.

Lincoln & Capitan

Fans of Western history won't want to miss little Lincoln. Twelve miles east of Capitan along the **Billy the Kid National Scenic Byway** (www .billybyway.com), this is where the gun battle that turned Billy the Kid into a legend took place. The whole town is beautifully preserved in close to original form; modern influences (such as neon-lit motel signs, souvenir stands, fast-food joints) are not allowed.

At the **Anderson Freeman Visitors Center & Museum** (☎ 505-653-4025; Hwy 380; admission to 4 sites adult/child $5/free; ☯ 8:30am-4:30pm), exhibits on the Buffalo soldiers, Apaches and the Lincoln County War explain the town's history.

For overnighters, the **Ellis Store Country Inn** (☎ 505-653-4609, 800-653-6460; www.ellisstore.com; Mile 98, Hwy 380; r incl breakfast $89-119; ☒) offers three antique-filled rooms (complete with wood stove) in the main house; five additional rooms are located in a historic mill on the property. From Wednesday to Saturday the host offers a six-course dinner ($70 per person), served in the lovely and cozy dining room.

Like Lincoln, cozy Capitan is surrounded by the beautiful mountains of **Lincoln National Forest**. The main reason to come is so the kids can visit **Smokey Bear Historical State Park** (☎ 505-354-2748; admission $2; ☯ 9am-5pm), where Smokey (yes, there actually was a real Smokey Bear) is buried.

Fort Sumner State Monument

Take a moment at Fort Sumner. The little village that sprang up around old Fort Sumner gets more than a footnote in the history books for two reasons: the disastrous Bosque Redondo Indian Reservation and Billy the Kid's last showdown with Sheriff Pat Garrett. The area is brimming with Native American and outlaw history. The **monument** (☎ 505-355-2573; www.nmmonuments.org; Hwy 272; adult/child $5/free; ☯ 8:30am-5pm) interprets the Bosque Redondo tragedy.

Roswell

If you've ever thrilled to *The X-Files*, the Roswell Incident is already filed away in your memory banks. In 1947, a mysterious object crashed at a nearby ranch. No one would have skipped any sleep over it, but the military made a big to-do of hushing it up, and for a lot of folks, that sealed it: the aliens had landed! International curiosity and local ingenuity have transformed the small city into a thriving extraterrestrial-wannabe zone. Bulbous white heads glow atop the downtown street lamps and busloads of tourists come to find good souvenirs.

Stop by the **visitors bureau** (☎ 505-624-0889, 888-767-9355; www.roswellmysteries.com; 912 N Main St; ☯ 8:30am-5:30pm Mon-Fri, 10am-3pm Sat & Sun) for local information.

Believers and kitsch-seekers must check out the **International UFO Museum & Research Center** (☎ 505-625-9495; www.roswellufomuseum.com; 114 N Main St; adult/child $5/2; ☯ 9am-5pm), displaying documents supporting the cover-up as well as lots of far-out art and exhibitions. The annual **Roswell UFO Festival** (www.roswellufofestival.com)

ATOMIC SOUTHWEST

In 1943, remote Los Alamos, NM (p885), was chosen as the top-secret headquarters of the Manhattan Project – the code name for the atomic bomb. Accessed by dirt roads, the site had no gas or oil lines and only one wire service, and was surrounded by thick forest.

On July 16, 1945, Manhattan Project scientists first detonated an atomic bomb at the Trinity Site in southern New Mexico, now part of the White Sands Missile Range (p891). After atomic bombs destroyed Hiroshima and Nagasaki, Los Alamos was finally exposed to the public. Today the lab is still the backbone of the town, and tourism embraces the town's atomic history. Albuquerque's National Atomic Museum (p874) tells the story of the workers and the development of the bomb.

Although the US government stopped exploding nuclear bombs underground at the Cold War–era Nevada Test Site (p823) in 1992, the end of a possible nuclear future for state residents isn't so clear-cut. In 1998, a US Department of Energy report recommended Yucca Mountain, near the test site and 100 miles northeast of Las Vegas, as the best possible location for the nation's only long-term high-level nuclear waste repository. Nevada officials have fought the proposed waste dump tooth and nail; contract fraud and lack of funds have prolonged the debate.

In Las Vegas, the Atomic Testing Museum (p813) recounts Nevada's atomic history.

beams down over the July 4 weekend, with an otherworldly costume parade, alien motorcycle rally and all kinds of UFO-crazy high jinks.

Ho-hum chain motels line N Main St. About 36 miles south of Roswell, the **Heritage Inn** (☎ 505-748-2552, 866-207-0222; www.artesiaheritageinn.com; 209 W Main St, Artesia; r incl breakfast from $84; ✄ 🖵 wi-fi) offers 11 Old West–style rooms and is the nicest lodging in the area.

The hopping **Nuthin' Fancy Café** (☎ 505-624-5399; 2103 N Main St; dishes $6-10; ☩ 6am-8:30pm Mon-Sat, to 2pm Sun) serves fabulous diner food with a Southwestern twist, and super-hero themed **Farley's** (☎ 505-627-1100; 1315 N Main St; dishes $7-9; ☩ 11am-11pm, to 1am weekends), has pub food and pizza in a huge industrial space, with 25 beers on tap.

The **TNM&O/Greyhound Bus Depot** (☎ 505-622-2510; www.greyhound.com; 1100 N Virginia Ave) has daily buses to Carlsbad ($19, two hours), Albuquerque ($39, four hours) and Santa Fe ($50, eight hours). Buses also go to El Paso, Texas ($47, five hours).

Carlsbad

Travelers use Carlsbad as a base for visits to nearby Carlsbad Caverns National Park and the Guadalupe Mountains (see p739). The **chamber of commerce** (☎ 505-887-6516, 866-822-9226; www.carlsbadchamber.com; 302 S Canal St; ☩ 9am-5pm Mon, 8am-5pm Tue-Fri, 9am-3pm Sat May-Sep) has information on both.

On the northwestern outskirts of town, **Living Desert State Park** (☎ 505-887-5516; 1504 Miehls Dr; adult/child 7-12yr $5/3; ☩ 8am-8pm May-Aug, 9am-5pm Sep-Apr) is a great place to see and learn about cacti, coyotes and wildlife. The park has a good 1.3-mile trail that showcases different habitats of the Chihuahuan Desert. Miehls Dr is off Hwy 285.

Most Carlsbad lodging consists of chain motels on S Canal St or National Parks Hwy.

The **Octillo Inn** (☎ 505-887-2861, 866-822-9226; www.octilloinn.com; 3706 National Parks Hwy; s/d incl breakfast $60/65; ✄ ☍ 🖵 wi-fi) has attractively landscaped grounds, a courtyard patio and hot tub, and live entertainment and dancing in the lounge.

The **NazzBarr** (☎ 505-887-6299; 1208 W Pierce; sandwiches $7; ☩ 6am-10pm Mon-Fri, 7am-10pm Sat, 7am-9pm Sun) restaurant and internet café offers tasty sandwiches and pizzas, free wi-fi and computer use, and lots of magazines to read. Locals and visitors crowd **Lucy**'s (☎ 505-887-7714; 701 S Canal St; dishes under $10; ☩ 11am-8pm Mon-Thu, to 9:30pm Fri & Sat) for cheap, tasty New Mexican meals.

TNM&O/Greyhound (☎ 505-887-1108; www.greyhound.com; 1000 S Canyon St) buses depart daily for Albuquerque ($56, six hours) and El Paso, Texas ($40, three hours).

Carlsbad Caverns National Park

Reminiscent of a sci-fi flick, this wondrous **national park** (☎ 505-785-2232, bat information 505-785-3012; www.nps.gov/cave; 3225 National Parks Hwy; adult/child $6/free; ☩ caves 8:30am-3:30pm summer, to 2pm rest of yr) covers 73 sq miles and includes almost 100 caves. The cavern formations are an ethereal wonderland of stalactites and fantastical geological features. Visitors can take a 2-mile subterranean walk from the cave mouth to an underground chamber 1800ft long, 255ft high and over 800ft below the surface. Guided tours of additional caves are available, and should be reserved well in advance (call ☎ 877-444-6777, or otherwise go to www.recreation.gov). It's best to bring along long sleeves and closed shoes; it gets chilly.

The cave's other claim to fame is the 250,000-plus Mexican free-tail bat colony that roosts here from April to October. Be here by sunset, when they cyclone out for an all-evening insect feast.

California

There's been a movie unspooling in your head ever since you first heard about California. Perhaps it has scenes of you hugging Mickey Mouse, walking across the Golden Gate Bridge or scaling big-shouldered mountains. Perhaps you're sashaying along a red carpet, craning your neck toward giant trees, tracking pathways once trod by indigenous people or rolling around velvety dunes. *Your* California depends solely on your expectations, and you're quite likely to find them all true.

The Golden State can be seen as the greatest social laboratory in existence. If humans develop an appetite, it will be fed here. If technology identifies a new useful gadget, it will be built here at light speed. If pseudo-stars such as Paris Hilton make a fashion statement, its ripples will be felt across the planet. The California 'nation state' is worlds apart from most of the rest of America, and perhaps no other culture anywhere has as enormous an effect on how the rest of us work, play, learn and consume.

So now it's up to you to make your own movie of memories. Will it be a noir mystery? A romantic comedy? An action adventure? Only you can decide. California provides the set. You bring the vision.

HIGHLIGHTS

- Rocking and rolling along Hwy 1 through **Big Sur** (p944)

- Trying to grasp the grandeur of **Yosemite National Park** (p989)

- Hot-rodding it down to Malibu along breathtaking **Pacific Coast Highway** (p910) in a convertible in Malibu.

- Feeling like an ant beneath the dense canopy of giant trees in **Redwood National Park** (p981).

- Surfing sand dunes and motoring through Titus Canyon in **Death Valley National Park** (p939).

- Indulging in a mud bath in **Calistoga** (p975).

- Hiking, biking and camping in the dramatic **Marin Headlands** (p972).

- Whooping it up in the **Gaslamp Quarter** (p925), San Diego's equivalent of Bourbon St.

- Hurtling into the creepy darkness of Space Mountain at **Disneyland** (p922), then sticking around for the fireworks.

- Following the *Sideways* roads and wineries of the **Santa Barbara Wine Country** (p942).

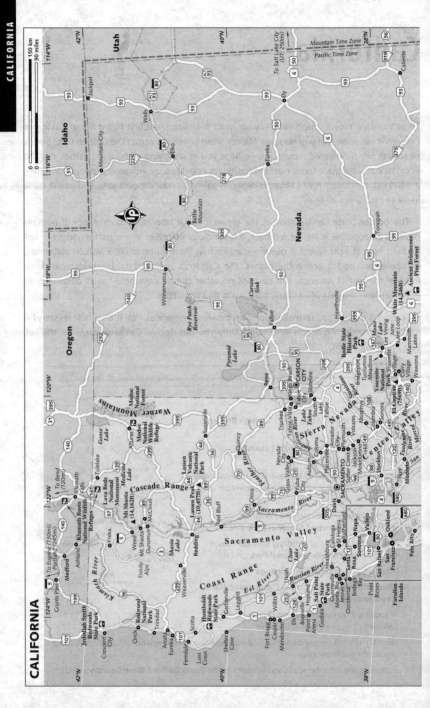

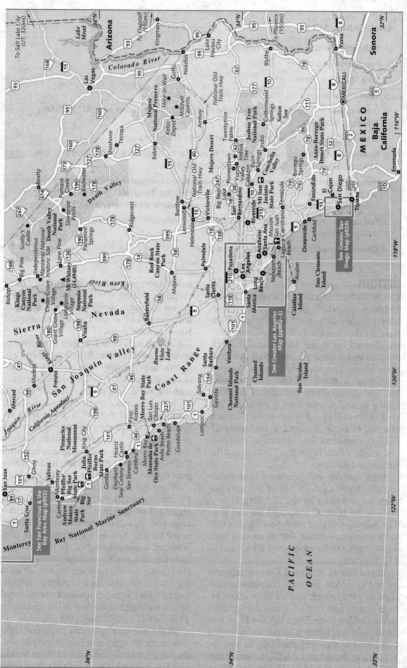

CALIFORNIA

CALIFORNIA FACTS

- **Nicknames** Golden State, Bear Flag Republic
- **Population** 36.5 million
- **Area** 155,959 sq miles
- **Capital city** Sacramento (population 458,000)
- **Other cities** Los Angeles (4.02 million), San Diego (1.26 million), San Jose (957,915), San Francisco (800,099)
- **Sales tax** 7.25%, additional local taxes can raise to this up to 8.25%
- **Birthplace of** John Steinbeck (1902–68), Ansel Adams (1902–84), Richard Nixon (1913–94), Marilyn Monroe (1926–62), Leonardo DiCaprio (b 1974)
- **Home of** Home of the highest and lowest points in the contiguous US (Death Valley and Mt Whitney, respectively); world's oldest, tallest and biggest living trees (Ancient Bristlecone Pine Forest, Redwoods National Park and Sequoia National Park, respectively).
- **Famous for** Disneyland, protests and earthquakes, Hollywood, hippie tree-huggers, Silicon Valley, surfing
- **Kitschiest souvenir** Golden Gate fridge magnet

HISTORY

California has sung its siren song for at least 25,000 years, when the first settlers began arriving via a long-gone land bridge from Asia. By the time the first European explorers showed up in the 16th century, about 300,000 indigenous people called this land their home. The Spanish combed through California in search of a fabled 'city of gold' but left the territory virtually alone after failing to find it. Not until the Mission Period (1769–1810) did Spain make a serious attempt to settle the land, establishing 21 Catholic missions for conversion purposes and military forts (presidios) to keep out the British and Russians.

After winning independence from Spain in 1821, Mexico briefly ruled California but then got trounced by the fledgling United States in the 1846–47 Mexican American War. The discovery of gold the following year sent California's population figures soaring from 15,000 to 90,000 by 1850 when it became the 31st US state.

Thousands of imported Chinese laborers helped complete the transcontinental railroad in 1869, which opened up markets on both coasts and further spurred migration to the Golden State. The 1906 San Francisco earthquake was barely a hiccup as California continued to grow exponentially in size, diversity and importance. Mexican immigrants arrived during the 1910–21 Mexican Revolution and again during WWII to fill labor shortages. During WWII, important military-driven industries developed, and anti-Asian sentiments lead to the internment of many Japanese Americans.

California has always been a pioneer in social trends thanks to its size, confluence of wealth, heavy immigration and lack of tradition. Since the 1930s, Hollywood has mesmerized the world with its dreams and fashions, while San Francisco reacted against the banal complacency of post-WWII suburbia by spreading beat poetry, hippie free love and gay pride. The internet revolution, initially spurred by the high-tech visionaries in Silicon Valley, rewired the country and led to a 1990s gold rush in overspeculated stocks.

When the stock bubble burst, plunging the state's economy into chaos, Californians blamed their governor, Gray Davis (Democrat) and, in a controversial recall election, voted to give Arnold Schwarzenegger (Republican) a shot at fixing things. Despite some early fumbles, the 'Governator' surprised just about everyone when distancing himself from the Bush administration and putting environmental issues, stem cell research and universal health insurance at the top of his agenda. In 2006, he was handily reelected.

Meanwhile, California's all-important high-tech sector struggles to regain its momentum, the need for public education reform builds, and the conundrum of immigration from

Mexico – which, though illegal, fills a critical cheap labor shortage for agriculture – continue to bedevil the state.

LOCAL CULTURE

California is a state of extremes. Grinding poverty shares urban corridors with fabulous wealth; the state is the world's seventh largest economy and has nearly 400,000 homeless people. Waves of immigrants continually arrive, and their enclaves remain striking miniversions of their homelands. Extreme tolerance for others is the norm, and so is intolerance, which you'll encounter on the freeways or if you smoke. The confluence of wealth, size, immigration and lack of tradition has made California a trendsetter by nature. After all, this is the state that invented the internet and the iPod, power yoga and reality TV. Image is important, appearances are stridently youthful and outdoorsy, and the automobile defines who you are and how important you consider yourself.

LAND & CLIMATE

Deserts, forests, high alpine zones, river deltas, coastal wetlands, valleys – you want 'em, California's got 'em. The highest mountain in the contiguous USA (Mt Whitney, 14,494ft) is here and so is the lowest point in the nation (Badwater in Death Valley, 282ft below sea level). And those earthquakes? There isn't a day without one, but don't worry, most are so small, that you won't notice even a quiver.

The northern and eastern mountain regions get inundated with snow in winter, while in summer the mercury can soar as high as 120°F (49°C) in the Central Valley and the deserts. At the same time, inland heat pulls chilly blankets of fog over the coast from Big Sur north, so don't forget that sweater. Fog also hovers briefly over SoCal (Southern California) in late spring, but by July the coast is clear, so to speak.

PARKS & WILDLIFE

Yosemite (p989) and Sequoia (p993) became California's first national parks in 1890, and today there are five more: Death Valley (p939), Joshua Tree (p936), Channel Islands (p940), Redwood (p981) and Lassen Volcanic (p987). The National Park Service also manages 23 other historic sites, preserves and other areas.

Lest we give the feds too much credit, California also has 278 state parks. It's a diverse bunch that includes everything from underwater marine preserves to giant redwood forests, protecting nearly a third of the coastline and more than 3000 miles of trails. Currently, day-use fees per vehicle range from $2 to $14, while camping fees run $9 to $25. About 50 state parks offer wi-fi access.

CALIFORNIA IN...

One week
California in a nutshell: Start in **Los Angeles** (LA; p900), perhaps making a side trip to **Disneyland** (p922), then head up the breathtaking Central Coast, stopping in **Santa Barbara** (p940) and **Big Sur** (p944), before soaking up a dose of city culture in **San Francisco** (p950). From here head inland to **Yosemite** (p989) and **Death Valley** (p939) before returning to LA. It's a whirlwind tour that'll introduce you to the best the state has to offer.

Two weeks
Follow the one-week itinerary at a saner pace and add a jaunt to the **Wine Country** (p974) and **Tahoe** (p987) to the mix.

It's Kiddy Time
Rug rats will be head over heels with all the treasures waiting in the Golden State. Few can resist the magic of **Disneyland** (p922), but speed-crazed teens might prefer the rollercoaster thrills at nearby **Knott's Berry Farm** (p922) and **Six Flags Magic Mountain** (p922). Movie magic awaits at **Universal Studios** (p908) in LA, while San Diego is all about animal magnetism with its famous **zoo** (p928), **wild animal park** (p933) and **SeaWorld** (p928). In Northern California, be sure to hit the **Monterey Bay Aquarium** (p946) and the **Santa Cruz Boardwalk** (p949). Of the national parks, **Yosemite** (p989) is the most kid-friendly.

Here are some useful contacts:

California State Park camping reservations
(☎ 800-444-7275; www.reserveamerica.com)
California State Parks (☎ 916-653-6995, 800-777-0369; www.parks.ca.gov)
National Park Service (NPS; www.nps.gov)
National Park camping reservations (☎ 518-885-3639, 877-444-6777; www.recreation.gov)

When it comes to animals in California, think big. As big as a school bus, in fact. That's the size of the gray whales who migrate Alaska to northern Mexico and back between December and April. Year-round you'll see pods of bottle-nosed dolphins and porpoises frolicking just offshore and barking seals and sea lions lazing under piers and on beaches.

The California grizzly survives only on the state flag, but black bears are quite common, especially in the Sierra Nevada.

Almost half of the bird species found in North America – including avocets, green-winged teals and northern pintails – use coastal and inland refuges for rest and re-fueling. Also keep an eye out for the regal bald eagle, which happily soared off the en-dangered species list in 2007. Ambitious zoo breeding programs have also reintroduced condors into the wild, although they're still exceedingly rare.

And so, you might think, are animals in the desert. Wrong. Most critters are simply too smart to hang out in the daytime heat. Roadrunners can often be spotted on the side of the road, and other desert inhabitants in-clude burrowing kit foxes, tree-climbing grey foxes, jackrabbits, kangaroo rats and various snakes, lizards and spiders. Desert bighorn sheep and birds flock to watering holes in palm oases.

INFORMATION

California Division of Tourism (www.visitcalifornia.com)
Statewide highway conditions (☎ 916-445-7623, 800-427-7623; www2.dot.ca.gov/hq/roadinfo)

GETTING THERE & AROUND

Los Angeles (LA) and San Francisco (SF) are major international airports, while smaller ones such as Sacramento, Oakland, San Jose, Orange County and San Diego handle prima-rily domestic travel.

Greyhound (☎ 800-231-2222) goes to just about every corner in the state.

Car-rental stations are ubiquitous, but rates are generally lowest in Los Angeles, San Diego and San Francisco. See p1144.

Four main **Amtrak** (☎ 800-872-7245; www .amtrak.com) routes connect California with the rest of the USA: *California Zephyr* (Chi-cago–San Francisco/Emeryville), *Coast Starlight* (Seattle–Los Angeles), *Southwest Chief* (Chicago–Los Angeles), *Sunset Lim-ited* (Orlando–Los Angeles). Useful intra-state routes are the *Pacific Surfliner* (San Diego to San Luis Obispo via Los Angeles), the *Capitol Corridor* (San Jose to Auburn via Oakland and Sacramento) and the *San Joaquins* (Bay Area to Bakersfield with bus link to Yosemite).

A sampling of regional driving distances:
Crescent City to San Diego 870 miles.
San Francisco to Los Angeles 380 miles.
Los Angeles to San Diego 120 miles.

LOS ANGELES

Buff, bronzed and beautiful, LA is a sly se-ductress who tempts you with her beaches, bosoms and beemers. She's a bon vivant, passionately feasting on the smorgasbord of life, never taking things – or herself – too seriously. She's a beacon of hope for count-less dreamers and daredevils. But she's also a cranky broad, a mistress of misery who'll chew up and spit out anyone who isn't quite A-list material.

Right now is an exciting time to visit LA. Hollywood and Downtown are in the midst of an unstoppable urban renaissance; a climate of openness and experimentation energizes the art, music and fashion scenes; and innovative chefs have kicked local cuisine into high gear.

So if you think you've already figured out what LA is all about – smog, traffic, celebrity murders, Botox babes and Paris wannabes – think again. The city's truths aren't delivered in broad swath in headlines or on a movie screen. Rather, they are doled out in small portions at the local street, personal and expe-riential levels. Be sure to explore and enjoy.

Orientation

Los Angeles may be vast and amorphous, but the areas of visitor interest are fairly well de-fined. About 12 miles inland, downtown com-bines high-brow culture with global-village pizzazz, a growing loft scene and an up-and-coming arts district. Euro-flavored Pasadena lies northeast of downtown, while hip-again Hollywood is to the northwest. Urban designer chic and lesbi-gays rule West Hollywood. Located south of here, Museum Row is Mid-City's main draw, while further west are ritzy Beverly Hills; Westwood, home to UCLA; mansion-studded Bel-Air; and Brentwood with the hilltop Getty Center. Santa Monica is the most tourist-friendly beach town; others include swish but low-key Malibu, boho Venice and hopping Long Beach.

Getting around is easiest by car, although public transport is usually adequate within specific neighborhoods. For information on traveling to and from Los Angeles International Airport (LAX), see p920.

Information
BOOKSTORES
Book Soup (Map p909; ☎ 310-659-3110; 8818 W Sunset Blvd, West Hollywood) Frequent celeb sightings.
Distant Lands (Map pp902-3; ☎ 626-449-3220; 56 S Raymond Ave, Pasadena) Treasure chest of travel books, guides and gadgets.

EMERGENCY & MEDICAL SERVICES
Cedars-Sinai Medical Center (Map p909; ☎ 310-423-3277; 8700 Beverly Blvd, West Hollywood; 🕑 24hr emergency)
Rape & battering hotline (☎ 800-656-4673; 🕑 24hr)
Rite-Aid pharmacies (☎ 800-748-3243; 🕑 some 24hr) Call for the branch nearest you.
Venice Family Clinic (Map p911; ☎ 310-392-8636; 604 Rose Ave, Venice) Good for general health concerns, with means-based fees.

INTERNET ACCESS
Cyber Java (Map p907; ☎ 323-466-5600; 7080 Hollywood Blvd, Hollywood; per 15min/hr/wi-fi $1.75/6/free; 🕑 7am-11:30pm)
Interactive Café (Map p911; ☎ 310-395-5009; 215 Broadway, Santa Monica; per 10min/wi-fi $1/free; 🕑 6am-midnight Sun-Thu, until 2am Fri & Sat)

INTERNET RESOURCES
At LA (www.at-la.com) Web portal to all things LA.
Daily Candy LA (www.dailycandy.com) Little bites of the stylish LA scene.
Flavorpill (www.flavorpill.com) Hip city culture guide.
Gridskipper LA (www.gridskipper.com/travel/los-angeles) Urban travel guide to the offbeat, naughty and nice.
LA.com (www.la.com) Clued-in guide to shopping, dining, nightlife and events.

Visit Los Angeles (www.visitlosangeles.info) Official tourist office site.

MEDIA
KCRW 89.9 FM (www.kcrw.org) World music, intelligent talk, BBC and NPR.
LA Weekly (www.laweekly.com) Free alternative news and listings magazine.
Los Angeles Magazine (www.lamag.com) Monthly gossipy lifestyle glossy.
Los Angeles Times (www.latimes.com) Main daily newspaper.

MONEY
American Express (Amex; Map p909; ☎ 310-659-1682; 8493 W 3rd St, Mid-City; 🕑 9am-6pm Mon-Fri, 10am-3pm Sat)
TravelEx Beverly Hills (Map p909; ☎ 310-247-0892; 9595 Wilshire Blvd; 🕑 9:30am-5:30pm Mon-Fri); West Hollywood (Map p909; ☎ 310-659-6093; 8901 Santa Monica Blvd; 🕑 9:30am-5:30pm Mon-Fri, 9am-1pm Sat) The West Hollywood branch is inside US Bank.

POST
Post offices abound in Los Angeles. Call ☎ 800-275-8777 for the nearest branch.

TOURIST INFORMATION
Beverly Hills visitor center (Map p909; ☎ 310-248-1015, 800-345-2210; www.lovebeverlyhills.org; 239 S Beverly Dr, Beverly Hills; 🕑 8:30am-5pm Mon-Fri)
Downtown LA visitor center (Map p905; ☎ 213-689-8822; www.visitlosangeles.info; 685 S Figueroa St; 🕑 8:30am-5pm Mon-Fri)
Hollywood visitor center (Map p907; ☎ 323-467-6412; Hollywood & Highland complex, 6801 Hollywood Blvd; 🕑 10am-10pm Mon-Sat, 10am-7pm Sun) In the Kodak Theatre entrance.
Santa Monica (☎ 800-544-5319; www.santamonica .com); Visitor Center (Map p911; ☎ 310-393-7593; 1920 Main St; 🕑 9am-6pm); Information Kiosk (☎ 310-393-7593; 1400 Ocean Ave; 🕑 9am-5pm Jun-Aug, 10am-4pm Sep-May)

Sights
Each of LA's neighborhoods has its own unique appeal. For great museums and architecture head to Downtown, Mid-City or Pasadena. West Hollywood has the legendary Sunset Strip and trendy shopping, while the beach towns are great for soaking up the laid-back SoCal vibe.

DOWNTOWN
If the ballet of cranes is any indication, things are finally looking up in Downtown LA. An

GREATER LOS ANGELES

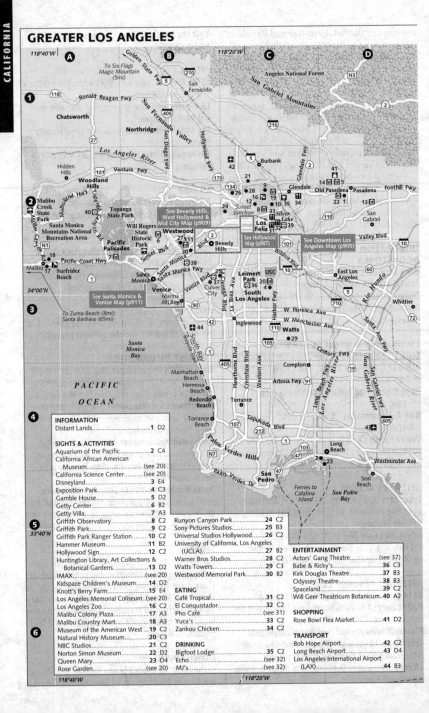

INFORMATION
Distant Lands.................................1 D2

SIGHTS & ACTIVITIES
Aquarium of the Pacific.................2 C4
California African American
　Museum...................................(see 20)
California Science Center............(see 20)
Disneyland...................................3 E4
Exposition Park............................4 C3
Gamble House...............................5 D2
Getty Center.................................6 B2
Getty Villa....................................7 A3
Griffith Observatory.......................8 C2
Griffith Park.................................9 C2
Griffith Park Ranger Station.........10 C2
Hammer Museum.........................11 B2
Hollywood Sign............................12 C2
Huntington Library, Art Collections &
　Botanical Gardens.....................13 D2
IMAX..(see 20)
Kidspace Children's Museum.......14 D2
Knott's Berry Farm.......................15 E4
Los Angeles Memorial Coliseum..(see 20)
Los Angeles Zoo...........................16 C2
Malibu Colony Plaza.....................17 A3
Malibu Country Mart.....................18 A3
Museum of the American West ...19 C2
Natural History Museum...............20 C3
NBC Studios.................................21 C2
Norton Simon Museum................22 D2
Queen Mary.................................23 D4

Runyon Canyon Park....................24 C2
Sony Pictures Studios...................25 B3
Universal Studios Hollywood........26 C2
University of California, Los Angeles
　(UCLA)......................................27 B2
Warner Bros Studios.....................28 C2
Watts Towers...............................29 C3
Westwood Memorial Park.............30 B3

EATING
Café Tropical................................31 C2
El Conquistador............................32 C2
Pho Café....................................(see 31)
Yuca's...33 C2
Zankou Chicken...........................34 C2

DRINKING
Bigfoot Lodge...............................35 C2
Echo..(see 32)
MJ's..(see 32)

ENTERTAINMENT
Actors' Gang Theatre..................(see 37)
Babe & Ricky's.............................36 C3
Kirk Douglas Theatre....................37 B3
Odyssey Theatre...........................38 B3
Spaceland....................................39 C2
Will Geer Theatricum Botanicum...40 A2

SHOPPING
Rose Bowl Flea Market.................41 D2

TRANSPORT
Bob Hope Airport.........................42 C2
Long Beach Airport.......................43 D4
Los Angeles International Airport
　(LAX)...44 B3

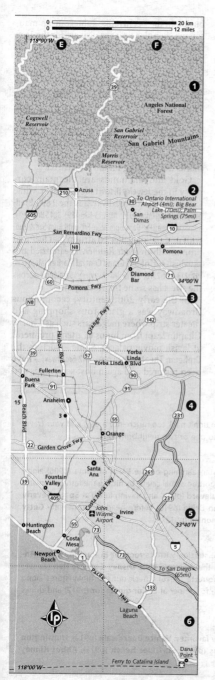

entire entertainment district is springing up around the Staples Center, while on Grand Ave, Frank Gehry is masterminding a snazzy retail and residential strip. But the real changes are more subtle. Thousands of young professionals, college kids and artists have moved into newly created lofts. Bars, restaurants, a big supermarket and a movie theater have followed in their wake. And the growing gallery district along Main and Spring Sts draws scores to its monthly art walks. Of course, things don't change overnight, so don't expect Manhattan. But the momentum is undeniably there, and for adventurous urbanites, now is an exciting place to be Downtown.

Park the car, then explore on foot or via a DASH minibus (p921). Parking is cheapest (about $6 all day) around Little Tokyo and Chinatown.

El Pueblo de Los Angeles & Around

Compact, colorful and car-free, this historic district is an immersion in LA's Spanish–Mexican roots and protects the city's oldest buildings, most notably the 1818 **Avila Adobe** (Map p905; ☎ 213-680-2525; admission free; ☒ 10am-3pm). It's right on **Olvera Street**, a festive tack-o-rama where you can chomp on tacos and stock up on handmade candy and folkloric trinkets. The **visitor center** (Map p905; ☎ 213-628-1274; Sepulveda House, Olvera St; ☒ 10am-3pm) has free self-guided tour pamphlets.

LA's original Chinatown was razed to make way for the majestic 1939 **Union Station** (Map p905; 800 N Alameda St; ℗), the last of America's grand rail stations whose glamorous art deco interior can be seen in *Blade Runner*, *Bugsy* and many other movies. The Chinese, meanwhile, were forced to resettle a few blocks north along Broadway and Hill St. The community's trials and triumphs are documented in the small **Chinese American Museum** (Map p905; ☎ 213-485-8567; www.camla.org; 425 N Los Angeles St; adult/student/senior $3/2/2; ☒ 10am-3pm Tue-Sun).

Today's **Chinatown** (Map p905) is still a cacophonous community hub crammed with dim sum parlors, exotic temples, herbal apothecaries and curio shops. On once rundown **Chung King Road**, an edgy gallery scene now lures hipsters from around town.

Civic Center

Until 1966 no other LA building stood taller than the 1928 **City Hall** (Map p905; ☎ 213-978-1995; 200 N Spring St; admission free; ☒ 9am-5pm Mon-Fri, free

CALIFORNIA

tours 10am & 11am Mon-Fri), which cameoed in the *Superman* TV series and the sci-fi thriller *War of the Worlds*. There's some cool views of Downtown and the mountains from the observation deck.

Architect Frank Gehry pulled out all the stops for his landmark **Walt Disney Concert Hall** (Map p905; ☎ 323-850-2000; www.laphil.com; 111 S Grand Ave; audio tours adult/student/senior $12/10/10, guided tours $15; ✆ audio tours most days 10am-2pm, call for guided-tour times; Ⓟ), a gravity-defying sculpture of curving and billowing stainless-steel walls that's the home base of the Los Angeles Philharmonic. Parking here is $8. Nearby, works by Mark Rothko, Dan Flavin, Joseph Cornell and other big-shot contemporary artists give **MOCA Grand Avenue** (Map p905; ☎ 213-626-6222; www.moca.org; 250 S Grand Ave; adult/child/student/senior $8/free/5/5, 5-8pm Thu free; ✆ 11am-5pm Mon & Fri, 11am-8pm Thu, 11am-6pm Sat & Sun) an edge in the art world. The postmodern building by Arata Isozaki offers additional eye candy.

José Rafael Moneo mixed Gothic proportions with bold contemporary design for his 2002 **Cathedral of Our Lady of the Angels** (Map p905; ☎ 213-680-5200; www.olacathedral.org; 555 W Temple St; admission free; ✆ 6am-6pm Mon-Fri, 9am-6pm Sat, 7am-6pm Sun; Ⓟ), which teems with art and sparkles with serenity achieved by soft light filtering in through alabaster panes. Gregory Peck is buried in the beehivelike subterranean mausoleum. Popular times to visit are for the 1pm weekday tours and the recitals at 12:45pm on Wednesday, both free.

Pershing Square & Around

The hub of Downtown's historic core, **Pershing Square** (Map p905) was LA's first park in 1866 and is now a postmodern concrete patch enlivened by public art, summer concerts and the grand old **Millennium Biltmore Hotel** (p914). The forest of office high-rises just north of here marks the bustling Financial District.

Gold and diamonds are the main currency in the **Jewelry District** along Hill St, while Latino-flavored Broadway has the 1893 **Bradbury Building** (Map p905; ☎ 213-626-1893; 304 S Broadway; admission free; ✆ 9am-6pm Mon-Fri, until 5pm Sat & Sun) with its dazzling galleried atrium that featured prominently in *Blade Runner*. The frenzied and sawdust-sprinkled **Grand Central Market** (Map p905; ☎ 213-624-2378; 317 S Broadway; ✆ 9am-6pm) across the street has some fun nosh spots.

In the early 20th century, cacophonous Broadway was a glamorous shopping and theater strip where megastars such as Charlie Chaplin leapt from limos to attend premieres at lavish movie palaces. Some – such as the **Orpheum Theater** (Map p905; 842 Broadway) – have been restored and again host screenings and

---

LOS ANGELES IN...

Distances are ginormous in Los Angeles (LA), so don't pack too much into a day, pad your travel time for traffic and confine your explorations to one or two neighborhoods.

One Day

Fuel up for the day at **Toast** (p917), then go star-searching on the **Walk of Fame** (p906) along revitalized Hollywood Blvd. Up your chances of spotting actual celebs by hitting the fashion-forward boutiques on paparazzi-infested **Robertson Boulevard** (p920) and having lunch at **Spago Beverly Hills** (p917). Take a digestive stroll along **Rodeo Drive** (p910) before heading to the lofty **Getty Center** (p910). Wrap up with dinner in **Santa Monica** (p917).

Two days

Keep a tab on rapidly evolving Downtown LA, starting with its roots at **El Pueblo de Los Angeles** (p903), catching up with the present at the dramatic **Walt Disney Concert Hall** (above) and peeking into the future over latte at **Banquette** (p916). Check out the funky stores along **Sunset Junction** (p920), and stay in Silver Lake for dinner at **El Conquistador** (p917) and drinks at the **Good Luck Bar** (p918).

More days

If you can squeeze them in, here are some other favorites: **Venice Boardwalk** (p912), **Huntington Library, Art Collections & Botanical Gardens** (p912), **Surfrider Beach** (p911), **Abbot Kinney Boulevard** (p912) and **Spaceland** (p918).

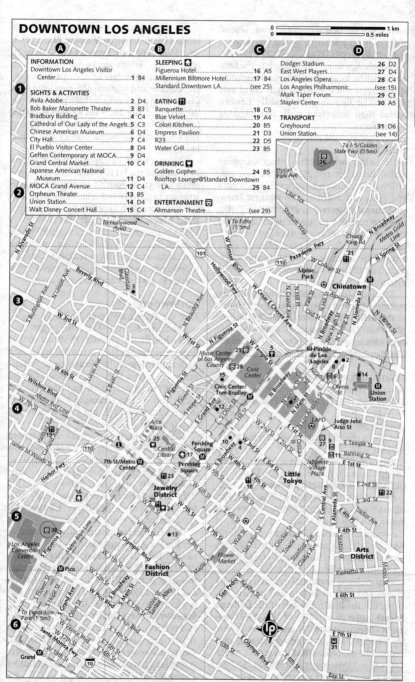

DOWNTOWN LOS ANGELES

0 ——————— 1 km
0 ——————— 0.5 miles

A

INFORMATION
Downtown Los Angeles Visitor
Center..**1** B4

SIGHTS & ACTIVITIES
Avila Adobe...................................**2** D4
Bob Baker Marionette Theater.....**3** B3
Bradbury Building.........................**4** C4
Cathedral of Our Lady of the Angels.**5** C3
Chinese American Museum............**6** D4
City Hall..**7** C4
El Pueblo Visitor Center................**8** D4
Geffen Contemporary at MOCA....**9** D4
Grand Central Market..................**10** C4
Japanese American National
Museum.....................................**11** D4
MOCA Grand Avenue..................**12** C4
Orpheum Theater.........................**13** B5
Union Station...............................**14** D4
Walt Disney Concert Hall.............**15** C4

B

SLEEPING 🏠
Figueroa Hotel.............................**16** A5
Millennium Biltmore Hotel...........**17** B4
Standard Downtown LA............(see 25)

EATING 🍴
Banquette....................................**18** C5
Blue Velvet..................................**19** A4
Colori Kitchen..............................**20** B5
Empress Pavilion..........................**21** D3
R23..**22** D5
Water Grill...................................**23** B5

DRINKING 🍷
Golden Gopher.............................**24** B5
Rooftop Lounge@Standard Downtown
LA..**25** B4

ENTERTAINMENT 🎭
Ahmanson Theatre....................(see 29)

C / D

Dodger Stadium...........................**26** D2
East West Players.........................**27** D4
Los Angeles Opera.......................**28** C4
Los Angeles Philharmonic.........(see 15)
Mark Taper Forum.......................**29** C3
Staples Center.............................**30** A5

TRANSPORT
Greyhound...................................**31** D6
Union Station............................(see 14)

parties, but the best way to get inside several of them is on tours run by the Los Angeles Conservancy (p914).

Shopaholics should head south to the **Fashion District** to forage for designer knockoffs, sample sales and original designs at cut-rate prices. The flair is more Middle Eastern bazaar than American mall, and haggling is ubiquitous.

Little Tokyo

Little Tokyo swirls with outdoor shopping malls, Buddhist temples, public art, traditional gardens and authentic sushi bars and *izakaya* (taverns). The **Japanese American National Museum** (Map p905; ☎ 213-625-0414; www.janm.org; 369 E 1st St; adult/child/student/senior $8/free/4/5, 5-8pm Thu free; ☉ 11am-5pm Tue, Wed & Fri-Sun, 11am-8pm Thu), is a great place to get a feel for the Japanese immigrant experience, including the painful chapter of the WWII internment camps.

Arty types can pop next door to gawk at the cutting-edge and often provocative exhibits at the **Geffen Contemporary at MOCA** (Map p905; ☎ 213-626-6222; www.moca.org; 152 N Central Ave; adult/child/student/senior $8/free/5/5, Thu free; ☉ 11am-5pm Mon & Fri, 11am-8pm Thu, 11am-6pm Sat & Sun).

EXPOSITION PARK & AROUND

A quick jaunt south of Downtown LA by DASH bus (p921), **Exposition Park** (Map pp902-3; ☉ 24hr; ℗) is filled with enough kid-friendly museums, historic sports facilities and green spaces to keep you busy for a day. Parking is $6.

Dinos to diamonds, bears to beetles, hissing roaches to an ultrarare megamouth shark – the old-school **Natural History Museum** (Map pp902-3; ☎ 213-763-3466; www.nhm.org; 900 Exposition Blvd; adult/child/senior/student $9/2/6.50/6.50; ☉ 9:30am-5pm Mon-Fri, from 10am Sat & Sun) will take you around the world and back millions of years in time. Kids love digging for fossils in the Discovery Center and making friends with creepy crawlies in the Insect Zoo.

A simulated earthquake, hatching baby chicks and a giant techno-doll named Tess bring out the kid in all of us at the **California Science Center** (Map pp902-3; ☎ 323-724-3623; www .californiasciencecenter.org; 700 State Dr; admission free; ☉ 10am-5pm), a great hands-on science museum. The next-door **IMAX** (Map pp902-3; ☎ 213-744-7400; adult/child/senior/student $8/4.50/5.75/5.75) is ideal for capping off an action-filled day.

More grown-up attractions are the **California African American Museum** (Map p902-3; ☎ 213-744-7432; www.caamuseum.org; 600 State Dr; admission free; ☉ 10am-5pm Tue-Sat, 11am-5pm Sun), a handsome showcase of African American art, culture and history; the romantic **Rose Garden** (Map pp902-3; admission free; ☉ 9am-dusk mid-Mar–Dec); and the 1923 **Los Angeles Memorial Coliseum** (Map pp902–3), site of the 1932 and 1984 Summer Olympic Games and other key events.

The area south of Exposition Park, along both sides of the I-110 (Harbor Fwy), is generally known as South Los Angeles and no stranger to poverty and crime. One good reason to venture out here is the world-famous **Watts Towers** (Map pp902-3; ☎ 213-847-4646; 1765 E 107th St; adult/child/senior/teen $7/free/3/3; ☉ tours 11am-3pm Fri, 10:30am-3pm Sat, 12:30-3pm Sun), a huge and fantastical free-form sculpture cobbled together from found objects – green 7-Up bottles to seashells and pottery shards.

HOLLYWOOD

Like the Terminator, you can't keep Hollywood down forever. The land of grit and grime has finally cleaned up its act and is giving the Sunset Strip a run for its money with shiny new clubs, theaters and restaurants. It's a faux Vegas-type glamour, to be sure, but most people are just happy to see locals and visitors returning in droves. Box office results aren't in, but a possible blockbuster awaits.

The spark plug for the rebirth was **Hollywood & Highland** (Map p907; ☎ 323-467-6412; www.holly woodandhighland.com; 6801 Hollywood Blvd; admission free; ☉ 24hr; ℗), a big mall that's a perfect marriage of kitsch and commerce. Parking is $2. It's right on the **Hollywood Walk of Fame** (Map p907), which honors more than 2000 celebrities with stars embedded in the sidewalk.

Real-life celebs sashay along the red carpet for the Academy Awards and other big parties held at the **Kodak Theatre** (Map p907; ☎ 323-308-6363; www.kodaktheatre.com; tours adult/child/senior/student $15/10/10/10; ☉ 10:30am-4pm Jun-Aug, 10:30am-2:30pm Sep-May). They also turn out for movie premieres at the adjacent 1927 **Grauman's Chinese Theatre** (Map p907; ☎ 323-463-9576; 6925 Hollywood Blvd), famous for its forecourt where screen legends from Judy Garland to George Clooney have left their imprint in cement: feet, hands and – in the case of Jimmy Durante – his nose.

Across Hollywood Blvd you can spot the sparkly marquee of another famous movie palace: the flamboyant 1926 **El Capitan Theatre** (Map p907; ☎ 323-467-7674; 6838 Hollywood Blvd), which shows Disney blockbusters. Another one, the exotic 1922 **Egyptian Theatre** (Map p907; ☎ 323-466-3456; 6712 Hollywood Blvd), is just down the street. It presents arty retrospectives and postscreening Q&As with directors, writers and actors.

Museums around here generally fall into the tourist-trap category, but we quite like the slightly musty **Hollywood Museum** (Map p907; ☎ 323-464-7776; www.thehollywoodmuseum.com; 1660 N Highland Ave; adult/student/senior $15/12/12; ⏰ 10am-5pm Wed-Sun). It's a shrine to the stars, crammed with kitsch, knickknacks and props from classic films and the latest smash hits. Han-

nibal Lecter's original jail cell in the basement, though, may creep you out.

Above the bustle, in its dignified hillside perch, looms LA's most recognizable landmark, the **Hollywood Sign** (Map pp902–3) built in 1923 as an advertising gimmick for a real-estate development called Hollywoodland. East of Hwy 101 (Hollywood Fwy), the neighborhoods of **Los Feliz** (loss *fee*-les; Map pp902–3) and **Silver Lake** (Map pp902–3) are boho-chic enclaves with shopping, funky bars and a hopping cuisine scene.

The Metro Red Line (p921) links central Hollywood and Los Feliz with Downtown LA and the San Fernando Valley. There's validated parking ($2 for four hours) at Hollywood & Highland.

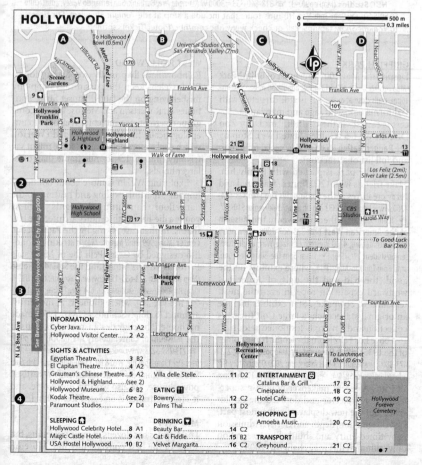

HOLLYWOOD

INFORMATION		
Cyber Java	1	A2
Hollywood Visitor Center	2	A2

SIGHTS & ACTIVITIES		
Egyptian Theatre	3	B2
El Capitan Theatre	4	A2
Grauman's Chinese Theatre	5	A2
Hollywood & Highland	(see 2)	
Hollywood Museum	6	B2
Kodak Theatre	(see 2)	
Paramount Studios	7	D4

SLEEPING		
Hollywood Celebrity Hotel	8	A1
Magic Castle Hotel	9	A1
USA Hostel Hollywood	10	B2

Villa delle Stelle	11	D2

EATING		
Bowery	12	C2
Palms Thai	13	D2

DRINKING		
Beauty Bar	14	C2
Cat & Fiddle	15	B2
Velvet Margarita	16	C2

ENTERTAINMENT		
Catalina Bar & Grill	17	B2
Cinespace	18	C2
Hotel Café	19	C2

SHOPPING		
Amoeba Music	20	C2

TRANSPORT		
Greyhound	21	C2

CALIFORNIA

TOURING THE STUDIOS: MOVIE MAGIC REVEALED

Half the fun of visiting Hollywood is hoping you might see a star. Up the odds by being part of the studio audience of a sitcom or game show, which usually tape between August and March. To nab free tickets, check with **Audiences Unlimited** (☎ 818-753-3470, ext 812; www.tvtickets.com) or stop by its booth at **Universal Studios Hollywood** (Map pp902-3; ☎ 818-622-3801; www.universal studioshollywood.com; 100 Universal City Plaza; admission over/under 48in $50/40; ☒ hours vary; **P**), one of the world's largest movie studios (parking is $10). Its movie-based theme park offers an entertaining mix of thrill rides, live action and audience participation shows, plus a studio backlot tram tour peppered with special effects. It's fun, but chances of actually seeing a star are practically nil.

For the most authentic behind-the-scenes look, take a tour of **Warner Bros Studios** (Map pp902-3; ☎ 818-972-8687; www2.warnerbros.com/vipstudiotour; 3400 Riverside Dr, Burbank, San Fernando Valley; tours $45; ☒ 8:30am-4pm Mon-Fri, longer in spring and summer; **P**) or **Sony Pictures Studios** (Map pp902-3; ☎ 323-520-8687; 10202 W Washington Blvd, Culver City; tours $25; ☒ 9:30am, 10:30am, 12:30pm, 1:30pm & 2:30pm Mon-Fri; **P**). Both whisk you to sound stages, outdoor sets and into such departments as wardrobe and make-up. Reservations are required; bring photo ID. **Paramount Studios** (Map p907; ☎ 323-956-1777; 5555 Melrose Ave, Hollywood; tours $35; ☒ Mon-Fri; **P**) has also resumed tours.

NBC Studios (Map pp902-3; ☎ 818-840-3537; 3000 W Alameda Ave, Burbank, San Fernando Valley; adult/child $8.50/5.50; ☒ 9am-3pm Mon-Fri) runs tours that include a stop at the *Tonight Show* set. For tickets to *Tonight Show* tapings, call or check www.nbc.com/nbc/footer/Tickets.shtml.

GRIFFITH PARK

Despite the May 2007 fire, most of **Griffith Park** (Map pp902-3; ☎ 323-913-4688; admission free; ☒ 6am-10pm, trails close at dusk; **P**) is still carpeted with California oak, wild sage and manzanita. Access is easiest via the Griffith Park Dr or Zoo Dr exits off I-5 (Golden State Fwy). Stop by the **Ranger Station** (4730 Crystal Springs Dr) for a map and full list of attractions.

The hilly park is packed with family fun. Make friends with 1200 finned, feathered and furry creatures at the **Los Angeles Zoo** (☎ 323-644-4200; www.lazoo.org; 5333 Zoo Dr; adult/child/senior $10/5/7; ☒ 10am-5pm; **P**), then hop over to the **Museum of the American West** (☎ 323-667-2000; www.autry nationalcenter.org; 4700 Western Heritage Way; adult/child/senior/student $9/3/5/5; ☒ 10am-5pm Tue-Sun year-round, until 8pm Thu Jun-Aug; **P**), where exhibits on the good, the bad and the ugly of America's westward expansion rope in even the most reluctant of cowpokes. Star exhibits include an original stagecoach, a large Colt firearms collection and a nymph-festooned saloon.

Above Los Feliz loom the iconic triple domes of the 1935 **Griffith Observatory** (Map pp902-3; ☎ 213-473-0800; www.griffithobservatory.org; 2800 Observatory Rd; adult/child/senior $8/4/4; ☒ noon-10pm Tue-Fri, 10am-10pm Sat & Sun). A recent makeover bought a super-techie star projector and doubled the exhibit space, but the new displays, for the most part, lack imagination, depth and clarity. Admission is by timed-entry and shuttle bus reservation only, although this may change in 2008.

WEST HOLLYWOOD

Rainbow flags fly proudly over Santa Monica Blvd. Celebs keep the gossip rags happy by misbehaving on the fabled Sunset Strip. Boutiques on Robertson and Melrose have become ground zero of sass and chic. Welcome to unapologetically hip West Hollywood (WeHo), which packs more personality (some might say frivolity) into its 1.9-sq-mile frame than most larger hoods.

Exploring WeHo is more about boutique-hopping, martini-swilling and heating up the dancefloor than hitting the sights – unless you're a die-hard 20th-century architecture fan, that is. In that case, swing by the **Pacific Design Center** (Map p909; 8687 Melrose Ave), a striking monolith designed by Cesar Pelli (he of Malaysia's Petronas Towers fame), and the **Schindler House** (Map p909; ☎ 323-651-1510; www.makcenter.com; 835 N Kings Rd; adult/senior/student $7/6/6, 4-6pm Fri free; ☒ 11am-6pm Wed-Sun; **P**), where pioneering modernist architect Rudolph Schindler (1887–1953) made his home. The edgy design-related exhibits at the **Museum of Contemporary Art** (MOCA; Map p909; ☎ 213-289-5223; www.moca.org; 8687 Melrose Ave; admission free; ☒ 11am-5pm Tue, Wed & Fri, 11am-8pm Thu, 11am-6pm Sat & Sun), a small offshoot of Downtown's artistic powerhouse, are also worth a quick ogle, and it's free. Entrance is on San Vicente Blvd.

MID-CITY

Los Angeles has dozens of great museums, but some of the best conveniently line Museum

BEVERLY HILLS, WEST HOLLYWOOD & MID-CITY

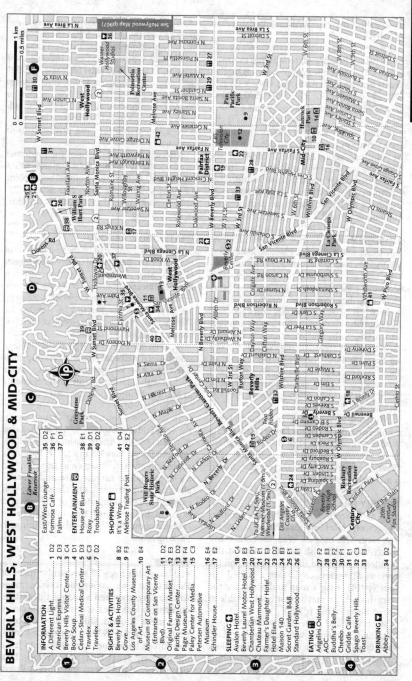

INFORMATION
A Different Light..........................1 D2
American Express.........................2 D3
Beverly Hills Visitor Center............3 C4
Book Soup...................................4 D1
Cedars-Sinai Medical Center..........5 D3
Travelex......................................6 C3
Travelex......................................7 D2

SIGHTS & ACTIVITIES
Beverly Hills Hotel........................8 B2
Grove..9 F3
Los Angeles County Museum
  of Art.....................................10 E4
Museum of Contemporary Art
  (Entrance on San Vicente
  Blvd)......................................11 D2
Original Farmers Market...............12 E3
Pacific Design Center...................13 D2
Page Museum..............................14 F4
Paley Center for Media.................15 C3
Petersen Automotive
  Museum...................................16 E4
Schindler House...........................17 E2

SLEEPING
Avalon Hotel...............................18 C4
Beverly Laurel Motor Hotel..........19 E3
Chamberlain West Hollywood......20 D1
Chateau Marmont.......................21 E1
Farmer's Daughter Hotel..............22 E3
Hotel Elan..................................23 D2
Maison 140................................24 B3
Secret Garden B&B......................25 E1
Standard Hollywood....................26 E1

EATING
Angelini Osteria...........................27 F2
AOC...28 E3
Buddha's Belly.............................29 F1
Cheebo......................................30 F1
Griddle Café...............................31 E3
Spago Beverly Hills......................32 C3
Toast..33 E3

DRINKING
Abbey..34 D2

East/West Lounge.......................35 D2
Formosa Cafe.............................36 F1
Palms...37 D1

ENTERTAINMENT
House of Blues...........................38 E1
Roxy...39 D1
Troubadour.................................40 D2

SHOPPING
It's a Wrap..................................41 D4
Melrose Trading Post...................42 E2

Row, a short stretch of Wilshire Blvd just east of Fairfax.

Ancient Chinese pottery to Japanese wood-block prints, Rembrandt to Magritte to Ansel Adams' Yosemite photographs, the **Los Angeles County Museum of Art** (Lacma; Map p909; ☎ 323-857-6000; www.lacma.org; 5901 Wilshire Blvd; adult/child/senior/student $9/free/5/5, after 5pm free; ☯ noon-8pm Mon, Tue & Thu, noon-9pm Fri, 11am-8pm Sat & Sun) has it all, and then some. Ranked among the country's top art museums, it's an Aladdin's cave of paintings, sculpture and decorative arts stretching across the ages and borders. A much-anticipated major revamp masterminded by Renzo Piano will visually unify the various buildings and add a new one dedicated to contemporary art by 2008.

A four-story ode to the auto, the **Petersen Automotive Museum** (Map p909; ☎ 323-930-2277; www .petersen.org; 6060 Wilshire Blvd; adult/child/senior/student $10/3/5/5; ☯ 10am-6pm Tue-Sun; P) has shiny vintage cars galore, plus a fun LA streetscape showing how the city's growth has been shaped by the automobile. Parking is $6.

Between 10,000 and 40,000 years ago, tar-like bubbling crude oil trapped saber-toothed cats, mammoths and other extinct Ice Age critters, which are still being excavated at the La Brea Tar Pits. Check out their fossilized remains at the **Page Museum** (Map p909; ☎ 323-934-7243; www.tarpits.org; 5801 Wilshire Blvd; adult/child/senior/student $7/2/4.50/4.50; ☯ 9:30am-5pm Mon-Fri, 10am-5pm Sat & Sun; P). Parking is $6.

Museum Row is easily combined with a romp around the **Original Farmers Market** (6333 W 3rd St; P), where you can fill up on gumbo, tacos or crepes before hitting the adjacent **Grove**, a pleasant open-air shopping mall with a musical fountain.

BEVERLY HILLS

The mere mention of Beverly Hills conjures images of Maseratis, manicured mansions and mega-rich moguls. Well, the reality isn't much different. Stylish and sophisticated, this is indeed a haven for the well-heeled and the famous. Stargazers could take a guided bus tour (p914), snag a map and scout for the stars' homes, or maybe just book a table at Spago Beverly Hills (p917).

It's pricey and pretentious, but no trip to LA would be complete without a saunter along **Rodeo Drive** (Map p909), the famous three-block ribbon of style where sample-size fembots browse for Prada and Gucci in killer-design stores. If the price tags make you gasp, head over to Beverly Dr, which has more budget-friendly boutiques and mainstream chains.

TV and radio addicts can indulge their passion at the **Paley Center for Media** (Map p909; ☎ 310-786-1000; www.mtr.org; 465 N Beverly Dr; suggested donation adult/child/senior/student $10/5/8/8; ☯ noon-5pm Wed-Sun), a mind-boggling archive of broadcasts going back to 1918. Pick your faves from a huge list, grab a seat at a private console and enjoy.

Afterwards, a suitable spot for predinner drinks is the **Beverly Hills Hotel** (Map p909; ☎ 310-887-2887; 9641 Sunset Blvd), the unofficial hobnobbing headquarters of the industry elite since 1912.

Several city-owned garages offer two hours of free parking.

WESTWOOD & AROUND

Westwood is dominated by the vast campus of the prestigious **University of California, Los Angeles** (UCLA, Map pp902–3). The university-run **Hammer Museum** (Map pp902-3; ☎ 310-443-7000; www. hammer.ucla.edu; 10899 Wilshire Blvd; adult/child/senior $5/free/3; ☯ 11am-7pm Tue, Wed, Fri & Sat, 11am-9pm Thu, 11am-5pm Sun; P) has cutting-edge contemporary art exhibits. Parking is $3.

Tucked among the high-rises, postage stamp-sized **Westwood Memorial Park** (Map pp902-3; 1218 Glendon Ave; admission free; ☯ 8am-dusk; P) is packed with such famous 6ft-under residents as Marilyn Monroe, Burt Lancaster and Rodney Dangerfield.

In its billion-dollar, in-the-clouds perch, the **Getty Center** (Map pp902-3; ☎ 310-440-7300; www .getty.edu; 1200 Getty Center Dr; admission free; ☯ 10am-6pm Sun & Tue-Thu, 10am-9pm Fri & Sat; P) presents triple delights: a stellar art collection, Richard Meier's fabulous architecture and seasonally changing gardens. On clear days, you can add breathtaking views of the city and ocean to the list. A great time to visit is in the late afternoon after the crowds have thinned. Parking is $8.

MALIBU

Malibu, which hugs 27 spectacular miles of Pacific Coast Hwy, has long been synonymous with surfing, stars and a hedonistic lifestyle, but actually looks far less posh than the glossy mags make it sound. Still, it's been celebrity central since the 1930s when money troubles forced landowner May Rindge to lease out property to her Hollywood friends. Leo, Brangelina, Marin Sheen and other A-listers

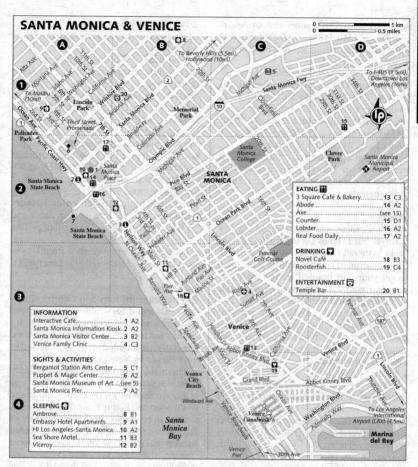

SANTA MONICA & VENICE

0 ———— 1 km
0 ———— 0.5 miles

INFORMATION
Interactive Café.................................1 A2
Santa Monica Information Kiosk..2 A2
Santa Monica Visitor Center.........3 B2
Venice Family Clinic........................4 C3

SIGHTS & ACTIVITIES
Bergamot Station Arts Center......5 C1
Puppet & Magic Center..................6 A2
Santa Monica Museum of Art...(see 5)
Santa Monica Pier...........................7 A2

SLEEPING
Ambrose...8 B1
Embassy Hotel Apartments...........9 A1
HI Los Angeles-Santa Monica.....10 A2
Sea Shore Motel.............................11 B3
Viceroy...12 B2

EATING
3 Square Café & Bakery................13 C3
Abode...14 A2
Axe..(see 13)
Counter..15 D1
Lobster...16 A2
Real Food Daily...............................17 A2

DRINKING
Novel Café.......................................18 B3
Roosterfish......................................19 C4

ENTERTAINMENT
Temple Bar.......................................20 B1

have homes here and can often be spotted shopping at the villagelike **Malibu Country Mart** (Map pp902-3; 3835 Cross Creek Rd; P) and the more utilitarian **Malibu Colony Plaza** (Map pp902-3; 23841 W Malibu Rd; P).

Despite its wealth and star quotient, Malibu is best appreciated through its twin treasures: the **Santa Monica Mountains National Recreation Area** (Map pp902–3; for car-free access, see www.parklinkshuttle.com) and the beaches, including the aptly named **Surfrider**.

Malibu's cultural star is the **Getty Villa** (Map pp902-3; ☎ 310-440-7300; www.getty.edu; 17985 Pacific Coast Hwy; admission free; P), a replica Roman villa that's a fantastic showcase of Greek, Roman and Etruscan antiquities. Admission is by timed ticket only (no walk-ins), and parking is $8.

SANTA MONICA

Santa Monica is the belle by the beach, the poshest among LA's seaside cities, hemmed in by luxe beachfront hotels and sprinkled with kobe-burger restaurants and $100-T-shirt boutiques. It wasn't always so. A few years ago, that person talking to himself was probably an unhinged homeless guy, not some exec barking into his Bluetooth.

Tourists and loitering teens make car-free and chain-lined **Third Street Promenade** (Map p911) the most action-packed zone, but for more local flavor head on over to celeb-favored **Montana Avenue** (Map p911) and down-homey **Main Street** (Map p911). Kids love the venerable **Santa Monica Pier** (Map p911), where diversions include a quaint carousel, a

CALIFORNIA

solar-powered Ferris wheel and an aquarium with touch tanks. There's free two-hour parking in public garages on 2nd and 4th Sts.

Art fans gravitate inland toward the avant-garde **Bergamot Station Arts Center** (Map p911; 2525 Michigan Ave; ☉ 10am-6pm Tue-Sat; **P**), a former trolley stop with 35 galleries and the progressive **Santa Monica Museum of Art** (Map p911; ☎ 310-586-6488; www.smmoa.org; 2525 Michigan Ave; suggestion donation $5; ☉ 11am-6pm Tue-Fri, 11am-8pm Sat).

Note that smoking is forbidden almost everywhere in Santa Monica, including the beach, outdoor restaurants and Third St Promenade.

VENICE

It's a freak show, a human zoo and a wacky carnival, but as far as LA experiences go, the **Venice Boardwalk** (Map p911) is truly essential. This cauldron of counter-culture is the place to get your hair braided, your karma corrected or your back massaged *qi gong*–style (Chinese physical exercises completed in a meditative state). Encounters with wannabe Schwarzeneggers, hoop dreamers, a Speedo-clad snake charmer and a roller-skating Sikh minstrel are pretty much guaranteed, especially on hot summer days. Alas, the vibe gets a bit creepy after dark.

To escape the hubbub, simply meander inland to the **Canalwalk** (Map p911), a vestige of Venice's early days as an amusement park when Italian *gondolieri* (gondolier drivers) poled visitors along quiet waterways. Today, ducks preen and locals lollygag in row boats in this serene, flower-festooned neighborhood.

Currently the hippest Westside strip is funky yet sophisticated **Abbot Kinney Boulevard** (Map p911), where you will find a palm-lined mile of cafés, restaurants, yoga studios and eclectic shops selling surf memorabilia and handmade perfumes.

There's street parking on Abbot Kinney and parking lots ($6 to $15) on the beach.

LONG BEACH

LA's southernmost seaside town is home to Worldport LA, the world's third-busiest container port after Singapore and Hong Kong. But Long Beach's industrial edge has worn smooth in its humming downtown and along the restyled waterfront. Pine Ave in particular is chockablock with restaurants and clubs popular with everyone from coiffed conventioneers to the testosterone-fuelled frat pack.

Long Beach's 'flagship' is the grand and supposedly haunted British ocean liner **Queen Mary** (Map pp902-3; ☎ 562-435-3511; www.queenmary.com; 1126 Queens Hwy; adult/child/senior from $23/12/20; ☉ 10am-6pm; **P**). Larger and fancier than the *Titanic*, it transported royals, dignitaries, immigrants and troops during its 1001 Atlantic crossings between 1936 and 1964. Parking is $10. Kids will probably have a better time at the **Aquarium of the Pacific** (Map pp902-3; ☎ 562-590-3100; www.aquariumofpacific.org; 100 Aquarium Way; adult/child/senior $21/12/17; ☉ 9am-6pm; **P**), a high-tech romp through an underwater world where sharks dart, jellyfish dance and sea lions frolic. Imagine the thrill of petting a shark! Parking is $6.

Long Beach is easily reached from Downtown LA via the Metro Rail Blue Line (p921).

PASADENA

Resting below the lofty San Gabriel Mountains, Pasadena drips wealth and gentility and feels like a world apart from urban LA. It's famous for its art museums, grand estates, fine craftsman architecture and, of course, the Rose Parade on New Year's Day (p914).

The main fun zone is **Old Pasadena** (Map pp902–3) situated along Colorado Blvd west of Arroyo Seco Parkway. Keep strolling and you'll soon see Rodin's *The Thinker*, who's a mere overture to the full symphony of European art awaiting at the **Norton Simon Museum** (Map pp902-3; ☎ 626-449-6840; www.nortonsimon.org; 411 W Colorado Blvd; adult/child/student/senior $8/free/free/4; ☉ noon-6pm Wed-Thu & Sat-Mon, until 9pm Fri; **P**). Don't skip the basement, which has fabulous Indian and Southeast Asian sculpture.

A masterpiece of craftsman architecture, the 1908 **Gamble House** (Map pp902-3; ☎ 626-793-3334; www.gamblehouse.org; 4 Westmoreland Pl; adult/child/student/senior $8/free/5/5; ☉ noon-3pm Thu-Sun; **P**) by Charles and Henry Greene was Doc Brown's home in *Back to the Future*.

There's great British and French art and lots of rare books, including a Gutenberg Bible, but it's the exquisite gardens that make the **Huntington Library, Art Collections & Botanical Gardens** (Map pp902-3; ☎ 626-405-2100; www.huntington.org; 1151 Oxford Rd; adult/child/student/senior $15/6/10/12; ☉ 10:30am-4:30pm Tue-Sun Jun-Aug, Sat & Sun Sep-May, noon-4:30pm Tue-Fri Sep-May; **P**) such a special place. The Rose Garden is redolent with more than 1200 varieties (and a lovely tea room; make reservations early), the Desert Garden has a Seussian quality and the new Chinese garden has a small lake crossed by a stone bridge. The interactive Children's Garden yields lots of surprises.

Activities

Kitesurfing to hang-gliding, there isn't a sport you can't pursue in LA, but these are the most popular.

BICYCLING & IN-LINE SKATING

Get a scenic exercise kick skating or riding along the paved **South Bay Bicycle Trail** that parallels the beach for most of the 22 miles between Santa Monica and Torrance Beach. Rental outfits are plentiful in all beach towns. Mountain bikers should head to the Santa Monica Mountains. Check www.labikepaths .com for details.

HIKING

Turn on your celeb radar while strutting it with the hot bods along the trails of **Runyon Canyon Park** (Map pp902–3) right above Hollywood. **Griffith Park** (Map pp902–3) is also laced with trails. For longer rambles head to the Santa Monica Mountains, where **Will Rogers State Historic Park**, **Topanga State Park** and **Malibu Creek State Park** (all Map pp902–3) are all excellent gateways to beautiful terrain. Parking costs $8, but riding the ParkLINK Shuttle (www.parklinkshuttle.com) is free.

SWIMMING & SURFING

Water temperatures become tolerable by June and peak at about 70°F (21°C) in August and September. Water quality varies; for updated conditions check the 'Beach Report Card' at www.healthebay.org. Top beaches for swimming are Malibu's **Zuma** (off Map pp902–3), **Santa Monica State Beach** (Map p911) and **Hermosa Beach** (Map pp902–3). **Surfrider**

LOCAL VOICES: JIM MARSHALL

Jim is an actor who works as a stand-in for Charlie Sheen on the Emmy-nominated television sitcom *Two and a Half Men*, which has been airing since 2003. Other major accomplishments include a stint as associate director on the sitcom *Growing Pains* from the late '80s to early '90s where he got work alongside a teenaged Leonardo DiCaprio. We caught up with Jim just before shooting resumed after the three-month summer hiatus.

How long does it take to shoot an episode of Two and a Half Men? It takes five days to shoot a single show. We table-read on Monday, rehearse on Tuesday and Wednesday, then Thursday is camera blocking and Friday we shoot with the audience. **What's it like to work on the show?** I work four days a week, Tuesday to Friday. It's our fifth season and we're a hit show. It's just so nice to work on a show that is popular, and that cracks me up every time I happen to catch an episode on TV at home. **What do you love about your job?** I love that it's a crash course in writing, directing and acting and that I get to watch very funny, talented and creative people at the top of their game make comedy. I spend most of my days laughing. It's never boring. **Do you have any tips for studio audiences?** Remember that you're an integral part of the process, not just a passive observer. Bring a sweater or a jacket because the studio is pretty cold. Leave cameras and cell phones in the car. And eat before you come to the taping because you'll be in there for about 4½ hours, although on *Two and a Half Men* we give everyone pizza and sodas about halfway through. **Are there any places in LA with particular star-spotting potential?** I've actually run into celebs anywhere I go, even at holes-in-the-walls such as **Zankou Chicken** (Map pp902–3; ☎ 818-244-2237; 1415 E Colorado St, Glendale; mains $3.70-8.50; ☻ 10am-11pm; ℗ ♿) where they make this really delicious shwarma and garlic chicken. I've seen Beck, Heather Graham and Leonardo DiCaprio there. And I just saw Jackson Browne at a Patti Smith concert at the Roxy (Map p909; ☎ 310-276-2222; www.roxyonsunset.com; 9009 W Sunset Blvd, West Hollywood; all ages; ℗). **What's your favorite place to catch a movie?** I think the best deals are the programs at the Academy of Motion Picture Arts & Sciences (www.oscars.org/events), the home of the Oscars. It's such a treat to see a beautiful, brand-new print of a classic film in a state-of-the-art theater. Screenings are only $5, and there are always filmmakers or other speakers talking about the film.
Interview conducted by Andrea Schulte-Peevers

Beach (Map pp902–3) in Malibu is a legendary surfing spot.

Los Angeles for Children

Keeping the rug rats happy should be child's play in LA. Many museums and attractions have kid-oriented exhibits, activities and workshops, but the excellent **Kidspace Children's Museum** (Map pp902-3; ☎ 626-449-9144; www .kidspacemuseum.org; 480 N Arroyo Blvd, Pasadena; admission $8; ☯ 9:30am-5pm; ℗) specifically lures the single-digit set with hands-on exhibits, outdoor learning areas and gardens. It's best after 1pm when the field-trip crowd has left.

Kids love animals, of course, making the sprawling Los Angeles Zoo (p908) in family-friendly Griffith Park a sure bet. Dinosaur fans gravitate to the Natural History Museum (p906), while budding scientists love the California Science Center (p906) next door.

The Santa Monica Pier (p911) has carnival rides and a small aquarium, but for a full 'fishy' immersion head south to the Aquarium of the Pacific (p912) in Long Beach, where teens might get a kick out of the ghost tours of the *Queen Mary* (p912).

The adorable singing and dancing marionettes at **Bob Baker Marionette Theater** (Map p905; ☎ 213-250-9995; www.bobbakermarionettes.com; 1345 W 1st St, near Downtown; admission $12, reservations required; ☯ 10:30am Tue-Fri, 2:30pm Sat & Sun; ℗) have enthralled generations of wee Angelenos. A similarly magical experience awaits at **Puppet & Magic Center** (Map p911; ☎ 310-656-0483; www.puppet magic.com; 1255 2nd St, Santa Monica; admission $7.50; ☯ 1pm Wed, 1pm & 3pm Sat & Sun).

Tours

Esotouric (☎ 323-223-2767; www.esotouric.com; walking/bus tours $10/55) Hip, offbeat, insightful and entertaining walking and bus tours themed around famous crime sites (Black Dahlia anyone?), literary lions (Chandler to Bukowski) and historical neighborhoods.

Los Angeles Conservancy (☎ 213-623-2489; www .laconservancy.org; tours $10) Thematic walking tours, mostly of Downtown LA, with an architectural focus. Reservations required.

Red Line Tours (☎ 323-402-1074; www.redlinetours .com; tours $22) 'Edutaining' walking tours of Hollywood and Downtown using headsets that cut out traffic noise.

Starline Tours (☎ 323-463-333, 800-959-3131; www .starlinetours.com; tours from $37) Narrated bus tours of the city, stars' homes and theme parks.

Festivals & Events

Rose Parade (☎ 626-449-4100; www.tournamentof roses.com) New Year's Day cavalcade of flower-festooned floats along Pasadena's Colorado Blvd, followed by the Rose Bowl football game.

Cinco de Mayo (☎ 213-485-8372; www.cityofla .org/elp) Free festivities in Downtown LA's El Pueblo de Los Angeles from late April to early May.

Sunset Junction Street Fair (☎ 323-661-7771; www.sunsetjunction.org) Silver Lake street party with grub, libations and edgy bands in mid-August.

West Hollywood Halloween Carnival (☎ 323-848-6400; www.visitwesthollywood.com) Free rambunctious street fair with eccentric, and often X-rated, costumes on Santa Monica Blvd in West Hollywood on October 31.

Hollywood Christmas Parade (☎ 323-469-8311; www.hollywoodchamber.net) On the Sunday after Thanksgiving, celebs ring in the season by waving at fans from flashy floats along Hollywood Blvd.

Sleeping

For the beach life, base yourself in Santa Monica or Venice. Cool-hunters and party people will be happiest in West Hollywood, culture-vultures in Downtown and the posh lot in Beverly Hills. Central Hollywood is another major party zone and has easy access to the Metro Red Line. Room rates are pretty steep and further swelled by a lodging tax of 12% to 14%. Hotel parking is free unless noted otherwise.

DOWNTOWN

Figueroa Hotel (Map p905; ☎ 213-627-8971, 800-421-9092; www.figueroahotel.com; 939 S Figueroa St; r $134-174, ste $195-245; ℗ 🐾 🖳 wi-fi) A rambling oasis near the Staples Center, the Fig welcomes guests to a richly tiled Spanish-style lobby segueing to a sparkling pool and buzzy outdoor bar. The Moroccan-themed rooms are comfy and exotic but vary in size and configuration. Parking is $8.

Standard Downtown LA (Map p905; ☎ 213-892-8080; www.standardhotel.com; 550 S Flower St; r from $140; ℗ 🐾 🖳) This design-savvy hotel goes for a young, hip and shag-happy crowd, so don't come here with kids or to get a solid night's sleep (the upper floors are quieter). Mod, minimalist rooms have platform beds and peek-through showers. Parking is $25.

Millennium Biltmore Hotel (Map p905; ☎ 213-624-1011, 800-245-8673; www.thebiltmore.com; 506 S Grand Ave; r $160-360, ste $460-3000; ℗ 🐾 🖳 🖳) Drenched in tradition and gold-leaf, this palatial hotel has bedded stars, presidents and royalty in rooms with all the trappings, although some lack elbow space. The gorgeous art deco health club takes the work out of workout. Parking is $32.

HOLLYWOOD

USA Hostel Hollywood (Map p907; ☎ 323-462-3777, 800-524-6783; www.usahostels.com; 1624 Schrader Blvd; incl breakfast & tax dm $27-29, r $64; ☐ wi-fi) Not for introverts, this energetic hostel puts you within steps of the Hollywood party circuit. Make new friends during staff-organized BBQs, comedy nights and tours or during free pancake breakfast in the recently redone guest kitchen.

Hollywood Celebrity Hotel (Map p907; ☎ 323-850-6464, 800-222-7017; www.hotelcelebrity.com; 1775 Orchid Ave; r incl breakfast $110-190; P ⊠ ☐ wi-fi) The art deco–style lobby is a sleek overture to this good-value property behind Hollywood & Highland. Rooms, while large and comfortable, can't quite carry the tune, but the fall-over-backwards staff, free breakfast and clean steam room still get our thumbs up.

Magic Castle Hotel (Map p907; ☎ 323-851-0800, 800-741-4915; www.magiccastlehotel.com; 7025 Franklin Ave; r $160-330; P ⊠ ⊠ wi-fi) Walls are a bit thin (bring earplugs), but otherwise this is a charming base of operation with large and modern rooms (the full-kitchen suites sleep up to six), exceptionally helpful staff and a petite courtyard pool where fresh pastries and gourmet coffee get days off to a good start. Parking is $9.

Villa delle Stelle (Map p907; ☎ 323-876-8100; www .villadellestelle.com; 6087 Harold Way; ste $150-285; P wi-fi) This quiet four-suite gem flaunts sophisticated golden age glamour and plenty of space in units inspired by such icons as Humphrey Bogart and Grace Kelly. Wine, cheese and a cheerful live-in manager greet your arrival.

WEST HOLLYWOOD & MID-CITY

Beverly Laurel Motor Hotel (Map p909; ☎ 323-651-2441, 800-962-3824; 8018 W Beverly Blvd; r $95-120; P ⊠ ⊠ wi-fi) Ride the retro wave on the cheap at this slicked up 1950s motel near the Farmers Market and Grove. Rooms are just above basic and the pool tiny, but the attached Swingers diner (mains $5 to $11) makes colossal burgers and wicked Bloody Marys.

Secret Garden B&B (Map p909; ☎ 323-656-3888, 877-732-4736; www.secretgardenbnb.com; 8039 Selma Ave; r incl breakfast $125-170; P ⊠ ⊠ ☐ wi-fi) This gay-friendly B&B has a romantic Rapunzel tower

tucked away in a dreamy garden and a charismatic owner–chef who whips up magical meals on an antique stove. All five rooms bulge with character and eclectic furnishings.

our pick **Farmer's Daughter Hotel** (Map p909; ☎ 323-937-3930, 800-334-1658; www.farmersdaughterhotel .com; 115 S Fairfax Ave; r $160-250; P ⊠ ⊠ ☐ wi-fi) Opposite the Farmers Market and Grove mall, this perennial pleaser gets high marks for its sleek 'urban cowboy' look and great location. Adventurous love birds should ask about the No Tell Room… Parking is $12.

Hotel Elan (Map p909; ☎ 323-658-6663, 888-203-2212; www.elanhotel.com; 8435 W Beverly Blvd; r $195-260; P ⊠ ⊠ wi-fi) The Elan flaunts an uncluttered urban feel and offers reliably good service and cloud-soft bedding. Light sleepers should request a room on the upper floor and away from the street. There are some great restaurants and boutiques nearby. Parking is $19.

Chamberlain West Hollywood (Map p909; ☎ 310-657-7400, 800-201-9637; www.chamberlainwesthollywood .com; 1000 Westmount Dr; ste $260-290; P ⊠ ⊠ ☐ wi-fi) This sassy lifestyle hotel scores points with design-minded travelers. Each of its 112 gadget-filled studios and suites has a gas fireplace, a balcony and sumptuous bedding perfect after cavorting on the nearby Sunset Strip. Nice rooftop pool, too. Parking is $24.

Chateau Marmont (Map p909; ☎ 323-656-1010, 800-242-8328; www.chateaumarmont.com; 8221 W Sunset Blvd; r $350-785; P ⊠ ⊠ wi-fi) Its French-flavored indulgence may look dated, but this faux-chateau has long attracted A-listers – Greta Garbo to Bono – with its legendary discretion. The garden cottages are the most romantic, but not everyone is treated like a star. Parking is $28.

Still a hip standby but no longer cutting edge, the **Standard Hollywood** (Map p909; ☎ 323-650-9090; www.standardhotel.com; 8300 W Sunset Blvd; r $150-275, ste $500; P ⊠ ⊠ ☐ wi-fi) has an Astroturf-fringed pool and condoms in the minibars. Parking is $24.

BEVERLY HILLS

Maison 140 (Map p909; ☎ 310-281-4000, 800-503-1395; www.maison140beverlyhills.com; 140 S Lasky Dr; r incl breakfast $240-270; P ⊠ ⊠ wi-fi) Parisian boudoir meets the Far East at this sensuous gem in the former home of silent-movie siren Lillian Gish where rooms skimp on size but not on luxury. Rates include pool privileges at the Avalon (p916). Parking is $21.

CALIFORNIA

Avalon Hotel (Map p909; ☎ 310-277-5221, 800-535-4715; www.avalonbeverlyhills.com; 9400 W Olympic Blvd; r $280-410; P ❄ ♨ ☐ wi-fi) Midcentury modern gets a 21st-century twist at this high-octane hot spot where the moneyed and metrosexual vamp it up by the hourglass-shaped pool and snazzy Blue on Blue restaurant–bar. Parking costs $28.

SANTA MONICA & VENICE

Sea Shore Motel (Map p911; ☎ 310-392-2787; www.seashoremotel.com; 2637 Main St; r $100-140, ste $150-250; P ❄ wi-fi) These friendly, family-owned lodgings put you steps from the beach and right on happening Main St. The tiled rooms are basic but attractive enough, and the lofty kitchen suites ideal for families.

Embassy Hotel Apartments (Map p911; ☎ 310-394-1279; www.embassyhotelapts.com; 1001 3rd St; r $170-385; ❌) This hushed hideaway delivers charm by the bucket. A rickety elevator takes you to units oozing old-world flair but equipped with kitchens. The relative paucity of hotel services, though, makes this place better suited to do-it-yourselfers.

our pick **Ambrose** (Map p911; ☎ 310-315-1555, 877-262-7673; www.ambrosehotel.com; 1255 20th St; r incl breakfast $220-270; P ❄ ❌ ☐ wi-fi) This sustainable boutique hotel beautifully blends craftsman and Asian aesthetics and has spic-and-span rooms where amenities include recycling containers along with the gamut of electronic gadgets. Breakfast is an organic gourmet affair.

Also recommended:

HI Los Angeles-Santa Monica (Map p911; ☎ 310-393-9913, 800-909-4776, ext 137; www.lahostels.org; 1436 2nd St; dm members/nonmembers $28/31, r with shared bath $70; ❌ ☐) Institutional, but clean, safe and handily near the beach and Third St Promenade.

Viceroy (Map p911; ☎ 310-260-7500, 800-622-8711; www.viceroysantamonica.com; 1819 Ocean Ave; r $390-475, ste $470-680; P ❄ ♨ ☐ wi-fi) Designer hotel brings Hollywood glamour to the seaside. Parking costs $20.

Eating

With great produce, innovative chefs and beautiful locales, LA's cuisine scene is as exciting, varied, fun and adventurous as the city itself. The best of California cooking makes creative use of local, seasonal and fresh ingredients and flirts with foreign influences, be they Mexican spices, Asian cooking techniques or Mediterranean flavor pairings.

Meanwhile, a bustling immigrant population is bringing the world's food to LA, from Ethiopian *watt* (stew) to Mexican *pozole* (stew) and Vietnamese pho (soup).

DOWNTOWN

our pick **Colori Kitchen** (Map p905; ☎ 213-622-5950; 429 W 8th St; mains $6-10; 🕙 11am-3pm Mon-Sat, 6pm-10pm Fri & Sat) Everybody feels like family in this Euro-flavored eatery where owner–chef Luigi kicks Italian comfort food into high gear. Bring your own bottle (BYOB) or hit the nearby Golden Gopher (p918) for postprandial libations.

Banquette (Map p905; ☎ 213-626-2708; 400 S Main St; $6-10; 🕙 7am-11pm Mon-Fri, 9am-midnight Sat, 9am-3pm Sun) This darling wine bistro feels plucked straight from Paris' Left Bank and is a preferred sipping, relaxing and grazing grounds for boho locals. Try its killer chocolate croissants (breakfast is served all day), lively panini sandwiches and 20 wines by the glass.

R23 (Map p905; ☎ 213-687-7178; 923 E 2nd St; mains lunch $9-13, dinner $12-30; 🕙 11:30am-2pm Mon-Fri, 5:30-10pm Mon-Sat) Not even the bold art and bizarre Frank Gehry–designed cardboard chairs can distract sushi lovers from the exquisite piscine treats prepared in this industrial-flavored hideaway.

Blue Velvet (Map p905; ☎ 213-239-0061; 750 Garland Ave; mains lunch $9-19, dinner $24-32; 🕙 11:30am-2:30pm & 5:30-10:30pm) The views are magical, the pool sleek, the decor ecofriendly and the market-driven menu divine, especially at night when compelling options may include slow-poached ocean trout and venison loin with bacon–onion puree.

Other culinary treats:

Empress Pavilion (Map p905; ☎ 213-617-9898; 3rd fl, 988 N Hill St; dim sum per plate $2-6, most mains $10-25; 🕙 10am-2:30pm & 5:30-9pm, until 10pm Sat & Sun) Dim sum and then some.

Water Grill (Map p905; ☎ 213-891-0900; 544 S Grand Ave; mains $21-49; 🕙 11:30am-9:30pm Mon-Fri, 5-9:30pm Sat & Sun) The best fish in town – enough said…

HOLLYWOOD

Palms Thai (Map p907; ☎ 323-462-5073; 5900 Hollywood Blvd; mains $6-19; 🕙 11am-2am) It's in a new location but the food's as sharp as ever if the steady stream of Thai families, tattooed scenesters and cops is anything to go by. The huge menu has all the usual favorites, but adventurous eaters should go for the wild boar curry or the garlic-pepper frog. It ain't easy bein' green…

Bowery (Map p907; ☎ 323-465-3400; 6268 W Sunset Blvd, Hollywood; mains $8.50-18.50; ⏲ noon-2am Mon-Fri, 6pm-2am Sat & Sun) This New York–ish gastropub draws a crowd that's like a two-inch heel: chic but sensible. There's Chimay on tap and comfort food on the menu. The cooked-to-order burger is great and the roast chicken French dip sandwich an interesting twist.

El Conquistador (Map pp902-3; ☎ 323-666-5136; 3701 W Sunset Blvd, Silver Lake; mains $10-17; ⏲ 11am-10pm Sun-Thu, 11am-11pm Fri & Sat) Halloween meets Margaritaville at this campy cantina that's a perfect launch-pad for a night on the razzle. One cocktail may suffice to drown your sorrows, so be sure to fill up on yummy nachos, quesadillas, enchiladas and other above-average classics.

And let's not forget the following:

Yuca's (Map pp902-3; ☎ 323-662-1214; 2056 Hillhurst Ave, Los Feliz; mains $1.40-4; ⏲ 11am-6pm Mon-Sat) Award-winning snack shack with Mexican faves.

Café Tropical (Map pp902-3; ☎ 323-661-8391; 2900 Sunset Blvd, Silver Lake; sandwiches $3.50-5.50; ⏲ 6am-10pm Mon-Fri, 7am-10pm Sat & Sun; wi-fi) Strong coffee and addictive guava-cheese pie.

Pho Café (Map pp902-3; ☎ 213-413-0888; 2841 W Sunset Blvd; mains $6-8; ⏲ 11am-midnight) Pho-nomenal Vietnamese soups at signless hipster hangout.

WEST HOLLYWOOD, MID-CITY & BEVERLY HILLS

Griddle Café (Map p909; ☎ 323-874-0377; 7916 W Sunset Blvd, West Hollywood; dishes $6-9; ⏲ 8am-4pm) If you've greeted the day with bloodshot eyes, get back into gear at this tasty breakfast joint favored by Hollywood's young and tousled. The high-octane coffee, wagon-wheel-sized pancakes and yummy egg dishes might just do the trick.

Cheebo (Map p909; ☎ 323-850-7070; 7533 W Sunset Blvd, West Hollywood; mains $7-16, dinner $10-23; ⏲ 8am-11:30pm) Cheap and cheerful, this joint makes heaping salads and bulging sandwiches but, it's the organic pizzas that truly have pizzazz. Kids love the free paper and crayons and special afternoon menu.

Buddha's Belly (Map p909; ☎ 323-931-8588; 7475 Beverly Blvd, Mid-City; mains $8.50-16; ⏲ noon-10pm Mon-Thu, noon-11pm Fri & Sat, 3-10pm Sun) This place is always busy as a beehive thanks to a light, inventive and fresh pan-Asian menu that has few false notes. Grab a seat on the bamboo-fringed parking-lot patio to escape the noisy dining room.

Toast (Map p909; ☎ 323-655-5018; 8221 W 3rd St, Mid-City; mains $9-13; ⏲ 7:30am-10pm) Sitcom stars to dolly grips, the Hollywood crowd loves its Toast. Not to mention its hefty sandwiches, crunchy salads and frothy lattes. Avoid the crush on weekend mornings.

AOC (Map p909; ☎ 323-653-6359; 8022 W 3rd St, Mid-City; dishes $9-18; ⏲ 6-11pm) At this jewel of a wine bar Suzanne Goin feeds a feistily flavored small-plate menu to friends, lovebirds and trendy families. There are more than 50 wines by the glass and an entire page of artesanal cheeses.

Angelini Osteria (Map p909; ☎ 323-297-0070; 7313 Beverly Blvd, Mid-City; mains $10-38; ⏲ noon-2:30pm Tue-Fri, 5:30-10:30pm Tue-Sun) Conversation flows as freely as the wine at this convivial eatery whose die-hard regulars share a passion for chef Gino's soulful risottos, pungent pastas and rustic trattoria classics.

Spago Beverly Hills (Map p909; ☎ 310-385-0880; 176 N Cañon Dr, Beverly Hills; mains lunch $19-48, dinner $32-66; ⏲ 11:30am-2:15pm Mon-Sat, 5:30-10:30pm daily) Wolfgang Puck's flagship emporium is still tops for celebrity-spotting and fancy eating. Book early if you want to scan the power crowd for famous faces while nibbling on expertly crafted global fusion fare.

SANTA MONICA & VENICE

Axe (Map p911; ☎ 310-664-9787; 1009 Abbot Kinney Blvd, Venice; mains lunch $6-12, dinner $16-26; ⏲ 11:30am-3pm Tue-Fri, 9am-3pm Sat & Sun, 6-10pm Tue-Sun) It's good vibes all around at this industrial-chic space (pronounced 'a-shay') where artsy bohos tuck into sharp-flavored dishes woven together from whatever is local, organic and in season.

Counter (Map p911; ☎ 310-399-8383; 2901 Ocean Park Blvd, Santa Monica; burgers from $6.50; ⏲ 11am-10pm) Get creative at this postmodern patty joint where you can build your own gourmet burger by mixing and matching your favorite bread, meat, cheese, topping and sauce. Some nerd figured out that this adds up to 312,120 permutations.

3 Square Café & Bakery (Map p911; ☎ 310-399-6504; 1121 Abbot Kinney Blvd, Venice; mains $8-20; ⏲ 8am-3pm Mon-Fri, 5-10pm Tue-Sat, 9am-4pm Sun) Hans Röckenwagner is back with a tiny café where newbies and loyalists devour his famous pretzel burgers, gourmet sandwiches and apple pancakes. Bakery shelves are piled high with rustic breads, fluffy croissants and jam-oozing doughnuts called *Berliners*.

our pick **Lobster** (Map p911; ☎ 310-458-9294; 1602 Ocean Ave, downtown; mains $12-38; ☑ 11:30am-10pm) The ocean views impress as much as the food at this lively seafood shrine that's always packed to the gills thanks to dock-fresh ingredients and Allyson Thurber's flawlessly crafted plates.

Abode (Map p911; ☎ 310-394-3463; 1541 Ocean Ave, Santa Monica; small plates $10-22, mains $26-39; ☑ 11:30am-2:30pm Mon-Fri, 10am-2pm Sat & Sun, 5:30-10pm daily) With chocolate booths, tangerine chairs and walnut tables, Abode's design is as tastefully composed as its fabulous contemporary American cuisine. Organic, sustainable and artisanal ingredients find their destiny in such plates as arctic char with truffle berry guacamole or vegetarian eggplant chorizo.

Those tempted by tempeh and *seitan* (wheat-based meat substitute) should also check out **Real Food Daily** (Map p911; ☎ 310-451-7544; 514 Santa Monica Blvd, Santa Monica; mains $8-13; ☑ 11:30am-10pm).

Drinking

Bigfoot Lodge (Map pp902-3; ☎ 323-662-9227; 3172 Los Feliz Blvd, Silver Lake) Smokey the Bear presides over this alt-lounge perfect for camping out with a minty Girl Scout Cookie martini or two. After 10pm DJs hit the decks with Brit faves, rockabilly and surf punk.

Golden Gopher (Map p905; ☎ 213-614-8001; 417 W 8th St, Downtown) Campy gopher lamps give even pasty-faced hipsters a healthy glow at this dark drinking den with a smoking patio and in-store liquor store for postclosing revelries.

Formosa Café (Map p909; ☎ 323-850-9050; 7156 Santa Monica Blvd, Hollywood) Bogart and Gable used to knock 'em back at this bat cave of a watering hole that's so authentically noir that scenes from *LA Confidential* were filmed here. Skip the Chinese food.

Cat & Fiddle (Map p907; ☎ 323-468-3800; 6530 w Sunset Blvd, Hollywood) Morrissey to Frodo, you never know who might be popping by for a Boddingtons on the fountain courtyard. Fortunately, this Brit-pub staple is more about friends and conversation than faux-hawks and working the deal.

Good Luck Bar (off Map p907; ☎ 323-666-3524; 1514 Hillhurst Ave, Los Feliz) The clientele is cool, the music loud and the drinks seductively strong at this well-established watering hole with Shanghai gangster-bar looks.

Velvet Margarita (Map p907; ☎ 323-469-2000; 1612 N Cahuenga Blvd, Hollywood) Sombreros, velvet Elvises, cheesy Mexican cult movie projections and margarita-swilling scenesters – it's Cabo San Lucas meets Graceland at this dark palace of kitsch on the Cahuenga Corridor party drag.

Also recommended:

Beauty Bar (Map p907; ☎ 323-468-3800; 1638 N Cahuenga Blvd, Hollywood) Beautilicious martinis and manicures.

Rooftop Lounge@Standard Downtown LA (Map p905; ☎ 213-892-8080; 550 S Flower St, Downtown) Libidinous rooftop bar with sexy waterbed pods and an infinity pool for cooling down.

Novel Café (Map p911; ☎ 310-396-8566; 212 Pier Ave) Low-key indie java shop favored by writers, beach bums and Main St shoppers.

Entertainment

LA Weekly (www.laweekly.com) and the Los Angeles *Times* (www.calendarlive.com) have extensive entertainment listings, while **Flavorpill** (www.flavorpill.com) highlights offbeat happenings. Snag tickets online, at the box office or through **Ticketmaster** (☎ 213-480-3232; www.ticketmaster.com).

LIVE MUSIC & NIGHTCLUBS

Troubadour (Map p909; ☎ 310-276-6168; 9081 Santa Monica Blvd, West Hollywood; ☑ Mon-Sat) This legendary rock hall did its part in catapulting the Eagles and Tom Waits to stardom and is still great for catching tomorrow's headliners. A beer-drinking crowd serious about its music keeps attitude to a minimum.

Cinespace (Map p907; ☎ 323-817-3456; 6356 Hollywood Blvd, Hollywood) DJ-to-the-stars Steve Aoki has a Tuesday residency at this upstairs playground of skinny-jeansters who favored eyeliner long before certain pirates made it fashionable. The dinner-and-a-movie nights (Thursday to Saturday) are perfect if you're not into switching venues halfway through the night.

our pick **Spaceland** (Map pp902-3; ☎ 323-661-4380; 1717 Silver Lake Blvd, Silver Lake) Beck and the Eels played some early gigs at what is still LA's best place for indie and alterna-sounds. Big-name talent such as Pink has been known to pop by and hit the mike for quick and dirty impromptu sessions. Mondays are free.

Hotel Cafe (Map p907; ☎ 323-461-2040; 1623.5 N Cahuenga Blvd) The 'it' place for handmade music sometimes features big-timers such as Suzanne Vega, but it's really more of a stepping stone for message-minded newbie balladeers. Get there early and enter from the alley.

Temple Bar (Map p911; ☎ 310-393-6611; 1026 Wilshire Blvd, Santa Monica) Drenched in crimson like a Chinese opium den, this relaxed Westside club gets a crowd that defines the word eclectic. Same goes for the music, which covers the spectrum from jazz to electronica, hip-hop to world.

Babe & Ricky's (Map pp902-3; ☎ 323-295-9112; 4339 Leimert Blvd, Leimert Park; ☿ Thu-Mon) This legendary blues joint is great any time, but Mondays are cult: $8 buys the inimitable vocals of octogenarian crooner Ms Mickey Champion and Mama Laura's late-night soul food buffet.

Other party dens:

Catalina Bar & Grill (Map p907; ☎ 323-466-2210; 6725 W Sunset Blvd, Hollywood; ☿ Tue-Sun) LA's premier jazz club.

Echo (Map pp902-3; ☎ 213-413-8200; 1822 W Sunset Blvd, Silver Lake) Divey hangout for Eastside hipsters craving an eclectic alchemy of sound.

House of Blues (Map p909; ☎ 323-848-5100; www.hob.com; 8430 W Sunset Blvd, West Hollywood) The original branch.

CLASSICAL MUSIC & OPERA

Los Angeles Philharmonic (Map p905; ☎ 323-850-2000; www.laphil.org; 111 S Grand Ave; tickets $15-120) The world-class LA Phil performs classics and cutting-edge works at the Walt Disney Concert Hall. In 2009, music director Esa-Pekka Salonen will be handing the baton to Venezuelan wunderkind Gustavo Dudamel.

<u>our pick</u> **Hollywood Bowl** (off Map p907; ☎ 323-850-2000; www.hollywoodbowl.com; 2301 N Highland Ave, Hollywood; tickets $1-105; ☿ late Jun-Sep) This historic natural amphitheater is the LA Phil's summer home and also a stellar place to catch big-name rock, jazz, blues and pop acts. Come early for a preshow picnic (alcohol is allowed).

Los Angeles Opera (Map p905; ☎ 213-972-8001; www.laopera.com; Dorothy Chandler Pavilion; 135 N Grand Ave, Downtown; tickets $20-222) Helmed by Plácido Domingo, this renowned opera ensemble plays it pretty safe with crowd-pleasers.

THEATER

Half-price tickets to selected shows are available online through **LAStageTIX** (www.theatrela.org) and in person at the visitor centers in Hollywood and Downtown LA (p901).

Center Theatre Group (☎ 213-628-2772; www.taperahmanson.com) The big daddy of SoCal's resident ensembles gives you new and classic plays and musicals in – count 'em – three venues: the Ahmanson Theatre (Map p905) and Mark Taper Forum (Map p905) in Downtown LA and the Kirk Douglas Theatre (Map pp902–3) in Culver City.

Actors' Gang Theatre (Map pp902-3; ☎ 310-838-4264; www.theactorsgang.com; 9070 Venice Blvd, Culver City) Cofounded by Tim Robbins, this socially mindful troupe has won many awards for its bold and offbeat interpretations of classics and new works pulled from ensemble workshops.

Odyssey Theatre (Map pp902-3; ☎ 310-477-2055; www.odysseytheatre.com; 2055 S Sepulveda Blvd, near Westwood) This well-respected ensemble delivers the

---

'OUT' & ABOUT IN LOS ANGELES

Los Angeles is one of the country's gayest cities, with the rainbow flag flying especially proudly along Santa Monica Blvd in West Hollywood (WeHo). Other big gayborhoods are Silver Lake and Long Beach, and there are smaller, mellow scenes in Santa Monica and Venice. To plug in, scan the freebie mags in bars, restaurants and gay-friendly establishments, including **A Different Light** (Map p909; ☎ 310-854-6601; 8853 Santa Monica Blvd, West Hollywood), *the* bastion of queer lit, nonfiction and magazines.

Here's our Top Five to get you started:

Abbey (Map p909; ☎ 310-289-8410; 692 N Robertson Blvd, West Hollywood) WeHo's funnest, coolest and most varied club, bar and restaurant.

East/West Lounge (Map p909; ☎ 310-360-6186; 8851 Santa Monica Blvd, West Hollywood) Chic and chichi venue for sophisticated mingling.

Palms (Map p909; ☎ 310-652-6188; 8572 Santa Monica Blvd, West Hollywood) Lesbian scene staple with legendary Beer Bust Sunday.

Roosterfish (Map p911; ☎ 310-392-2123; 1302 Abbot Kinney Blvd, Venice) Timeless, friendly, been-there-forever neighborhood bar.

MJs (Map pp902-3; ☎ 323-660-1503; 2810 Hyperion Ave, Silver Lake) Manly high-octane haunt with '80s videos, hot go-go guys and cheap, stiff drinks.

CALIFORNIA

classics and its own plays in a ho-hum space of three 99-seat theaters under one roof.

Other thespian venues:

East West Players (Map p905; ☎ 213-625-7000; www .eastwestplayers.org; 120 N Judge John Aiso St, Downtown) Pioneering Asian American ensemble.

Will Geer Theatricum Botanicum (Map pp902-3; ☎ 310-455-3723; www.theatricum.com; 1419 N Topanga Canyon Blvd, north of Santa Monica) Enchanting summer repertory in the woods.

SPECTATOR SPORTS

Dodger Stadium (Map p905; ☎ 866-363-4377; www .dodgers.com; 1000 Elysian Park Ave, Downtown; tickets $10-225) LA's Major League Baseball team plays from April to September in this legendary stadium.

Staples Center (Map p905; 213-742-7340; www.staple scenter.com; 1111 S Figueroa St, Downtown) This state-of-the-art venue is home base for all three of LA's professional basketball teams – the LA Lakers, LA Sparks and LA Clippers – as well as the LA Kings NHL ice hockey team.

Shopping

No matter whether you're a penny-pincher or a power shopper, you'll find plenty of opportunity to drop some cash in LA. Fashionistas flock to **Robertson Boulevard** (Map p909; btwn Beverly & 3rd St) and **Melrose Avenue** (Map p909; btwn San Vicente & La Brea), while bargain hunters haunt Downtown's Fashion District (Map p905). Hollywood is ground zero for groovy tunes, most notably at **Amoeba Music** (Map p907; ☎ 323-245-6400; 6400 W Sunset Blvd). East of here, Silver Lake has cool kitsch, collectibles and emerging LA designers, especially around **Sunset Junction** (cnr Hollywood & Sunset Blvds). Other 'chain-gang-free' strips are ritzy Montana Ave and Main St in Santa Monica (Map p911), funky Abbot Kinney Blvd in Venice (p911) and Larchmont Blvd in Hollywood (Map p907).

Good flea markets include the weekly **Melrose Trading Post** (Map p909; 7850 Melrose Ave, West Hollywood; admission $2; ☉ 9am-5pm Sun), which brings out hipsters in search of retro treasure, and the monthly **Rose Bowl Flea Market** (Map pp902-3; Rose Bowl, 1001 Rose Bowl Dr, Pasadena; admission $7-20; ☉ 5am-4:30pm 2nd Sun of the month), the 'mother' of all flea markets with more than 2200 vendors.

Getting There & Away

AIR

The main LA gateway is **Los Angeles International Airport** (LAX; Map pp902-3; ☎ 310-646-5252;

www.lawa.org), a U-shaped, bilevel complex with nine terminals linked by the free Shuttle A, which leaves from the lower (arrival) level. Hotel and car-rental shuttles stop here as well.

Long Beach Airport and Burbank's Bob Hope Airport handle mostly domestic flights.

BUS

The main bus terminal for **Greyhound** (Map p905; ☎ 213-629-8401; 1716 E 7th St) is in an unsavory part of Downtown, so avoid arriving after dark. Some buses go directly to the **Hollywood terminal** (Map p907; ☎ 323-466-6381; 1715 N Cahuenga Blvd).

CAR

The usual international car-rental agencies have branches at LAX and throughout Los Angeles (see p1144 for central reservation numbers). If you don't have a prebooking, use the courtesy phones in the arrival areas at LAX. Free shuttles to off-airport offices leave from the lower level.

TRAIN

Amtrak trains roll into Downtown's historic **Union Station** (Map p905; ☎ 800-872-7245; 800 N Alameda St). The *Pacific Surfliner* travels daily to San Diego ($34, 2¾ hours), Santa Barbara ($25, 2½ hours) and San Luis Obispo ($36, 5½ hours).

Getting Around

TO/FROM THE AIRPORT

All services mentioned below leave from the lower terminal level. Door-to-door shuttles, such as those operated by **Prime Time** (☎ 800-733-8267) and **Super Shuttle** (☎ 800-258-3826), charge $18, $23 and $14 for trips to Santa Monica, Hollywood or Downtown, respectively.

IT'S A WRAP

Dress like a movie star – in their actual clothes! Packed-to-the-rafters **It's a Wrap** (Map p909; ☎ 310-246-9727; 1164 S Robertson Blvd, Mid-City) sells wardrobe castoffs from TV and film studios – mostly small-size designer duds – at steep discounts. We've seen stuff from *CSI Miami*, *Law & Order* and *Alias*. Tags are coded (there's a list at the check-out counter), so you'll know whose clothing you can brag about wearing.

Curbside dispatchers will summon a taxi for you. The flat rate to Downtown is $44.50, while going to Santa Monica costs about $30, to Hollywood $42 and to Disneyland $90.

Public transportation has become a lot easier since the arrival of **LAX FlyAway** (☎ 866-435-9529; adult/child 2-12 $4/2; ☽ 5am-1am) shuttle buses. They travel nonstop to Downtown's Union Station (Map p905; 45 minutes) and Westwood Village near UCLA (off Map p909; 30 minutes). To get to Hollywood, connect to the Metro Red Line subway at Union Station (total $5.25, 1¼ hours). For Santa Monica or Venice, catch the free Shuttle C bus to the LAX Transit Center, then change to the Santa Monica Rapid 3 (75¢, one hour).

CAR & MOTORCYCLE

Unless time is no factor or money is extremely tight, you'll to want to spend some time behind the wheel, although this means contending with some of the worst traffic in the country. Avoid rush hour (roughly 7am to 9am and 3:30pm to 6pm).

Parking at motels and cheaper hotels is usually free, while fancier ones charge anywhere from $8 to $25 for the privilege. Valet parking at nicer restaurants and hotels is commonplace with rates ranging from $2.50 to $10.

For local parking recommendations, see the individual neighborhoods in the Sights section.

PUBLIC TRANSPORTATION

Los Angeles' main public transportation agency is **Metro** (☎ 800-266-6883; www.metro.net), which operates about 200 bus lines as well as five rail lines:

Blue Line Downtown to Long Beach.
Gold Line Union Station to Pasadena.
Green Line Norwalk to Redondo Beach.
Purple Line Downtown to Koreatown.
Red Line Union Station to North Hollywood, via central Hollywood and Universal Studios.

A useful bus line is Metro Rapid bus 720, which travels along Wilshire Blvd between Santa Monica and eastern LA via Westwood, Beverly Hills, Mid-City, Koreatown and Downtown LA.

Tickets cost $1.25 per boarding or $5 for a day pass with unlimited rides. Bus drivers sell single tickets and day passes (exact fare required), while train tickets are available from vending machines at each station. Trip planning help is available at ☎ 800-266-6883 or online at www.met ro.net.

Some neighborhoods, including Downtown and Hollywood, are served by local **DASH** minibuses (☎ your area code + 808-2273; www.ladot transit.com; 25¢). Santa Monica–based **Big Blue Bus** (☎ 310-451-5444; www.bigbluebus.com) serves much of western LA, including Santa Monica, Venice, Westwood and LAX (75¢). Its Line 10 Freeway Express runs from Santa Monica to Downtown LA ($1.75, one hour).

TAXI

Except for those lined up outside airports, train stations, bus stations and major hotels, cabbies respond only to phone calls. Fares are metered and cost $2.65 at flag fall plus $2.45 a mile. Some companies:

Checker (☎ 800-300-5007)
Independent (☎ 800-521-8294)
Yellow Cab (☎ 800-200-1085)

AROUND LOS ANGELES
Catalina Island

Mediterranean-flavored **Catalina Island** (www .visitcatalina.org, www.catalinachamber.com) is a popular getaway for harried Angelenos, but seems to sink under the weight of day-trippers in summer. Commercial activity concentrates in the pint-sized port town of **Avalon** where the tourist office on the Green Pier has maps and information on sights and activities.

Catalina isn't famous for its beaches, but it does have some excellent snorkeling at Descanso Beach, Lovers' Cove and Casino Point Marine Park, a marine reserve that is also the best shore dive. Gear rentals cluster on the Green Pier. Other ways to escape the throngs are by kayaking to the quiet coves of Catalina's rocky coastline or by taking a tour of the nature-protected backcountry, such as those offered by **Catalina Adventure Tours** (☎ 310-510-2888; www.catalinaadventuretours .com; from $33). You'll enjoy memorable views of the rugged coast and sandy coves and may even run into a herd of bison. The only other way to access the inland areas is either by foot, boat or mountain bike (permit required; call ☎ 310-510-1421).

Catalina Express (☎ 310-519-1212, 800-481-3470; www.catalinaexpress.com; round-trip $60) operates ferries to Avalon from San Pedro, Long Beach and Dana Point (in Orange County). Reservations are recommended in summer.

Six Flags Magic Mountain

Velocity is king at **Six Flags** (off Map pp902-3; ☎ 661-255-4111; www.sixflags.com/parks/magic mountain; 26101 Magic Mountain Parkway, Valencia; adult/child under 4ft/senior $60/30/30; ☺ from 10am daily mid-Mar–Aug, Fri-Sun Sep & Oct, Sat & Sun Nov-Mar, closing times vary from 6pm-midnight; P), the ultimate roller-coaster park, where you can go up, down and inside out faster and in more baffling ways than anywhere aside from a space shuttle. Check the website for discounts. It's about 30 miles north of central LA off the I-5 (Golden State Fwy). Parking is $15.

SOUTHERN CALIFORNIA COAST

ORANGE COUNTY

You know you've joined the big leagues when they start making a TV series about you. That's just what happened to Orange County, that giant quilt of suburbia wedged between LA and San Diego. Disneyland may have put the place on the map more than 50 years ago, but from 2003 to 2007 every installment of the hit show *The OC* beamed fresh images of local affluence, aspirations and anxieties across the globe. Indeed, Orange County is all about living large. Shopping is a major passion, and it's not surprising that the country's single biggest grossing mall is ritzy South Coast Plaza in Costa Mesa. But don't forget, when too much commercialism gets you down, there are always the beaches – all 42 glorious miles of them – to restore the spirit.

Disneyland Resort

The mother of all theme parks, **Disneyland** (Map pp902-3; ☎ 714-781-4000 or 714-781-7290; www .disneyland.com; 1313 Harbor Blvd, Anaheim; 1-day pass either park adult/child 3-9 $63/53, both parks $83/73; P) lures you into a parallel world that's as enchanting as it is freaky and frenzied. Prepare to wait an hour or more for the most popular rides and attractions, including the wildly creative Indiana Jones Adventure, the white-knuckle Space Mountain and the new Pirate's Lair where Jack Sparrow welcomes wanna-be swashbucklers. The Finding Nemo Submarine Voyage is a new gentle adventure for little ones. Parking is $10.

Bigger and less crowded, **Disney's California Adventure** celebrates the natural and cultural glories of the Golden State but lacks the density of attractions and depth of imagination. The best rides are Soarin' over California, a virtual hang-glide, and the Twilight Zone Tower of Terror that drops you 183ft down an elevator chute.

Nearby, **Downtown Disney** is essentially a 21st-century version of Disneyland's Main Street with plenty of opportunities to drop even more cash in its stores, restaurants and entertainment venues.

You can see either park in a day, but going on all the rides requires at least two days (three if visiting both parks). To minimize wait times, especially in summer, come midweek and get there before the gates open. Also take advantage of the Fastpass system, which preassigns specific boarding times for selected attractions.

A variety of multiday passes are available. Check the website for online discounts and seasonally changing park hours. In July and August they're both usually open from 8am to midnight.

Chain properties are a dime a dozen in the surrounding city of Anaheim, but a recommended indie is flowery **Candy Cane Inn** (☎ 714-774-5284, 800-345-7057; www.candycaneinn.net; 1747 S Harbor Blvd; r $100-190; P ☒ ☒). If you're tired of the run-of-the-mill eateries in Disneyland Resort, nab a table at the **Anaheim White House** (☎ 714-772-1381; 887 S Anaheim Blvd; mains lunch $12-20, dinner $23-39; ☺ 11:30-2:30 Mon-Fri, 5-10pm daily) for seafood and Italian in a baronial setting.

Knott's Berry Farm

Smaller and less commercially frenzied than Disney, Old West–themed **Knott's Berry Farm** (Map pp902-3; ☎ 714-220-5200; www.knotts.com; 8039 Beach Blvd, Buena Park; adult/child 3-11/senior $49/19/19; ☺ from 10am; P) often teems with packs of speed-crazed adolescents testing their mettle on an intense line-up of thrill rides. Gut-wrenchers include the wooden Ghost Rider and the '50s-themed Xcelerator, while the single-digit-aged find tamer action at Camp Snoopy. If your stomach's up for it, wrap up with a visit with Mrs Knott's classic fried-chicken dinner (mains $15 to $20). Save time and money by printing your tickets online. Parking costs $10 and closing times vary from 6pm to 1pm; check the website.

Orange County Beaches

Hummer-driving hunks and Botoxed beauties mix it up with surfers and artists to give Orange County's beach towns their distinct vibe. Just across the LA–OC county-line, **Seal Beach** is refreshingly noncommercial with its pleasantly walkable downtown, while gentrified **Huntington Beach** (aka Surf City, USA) epitomizes the California surfing lifestyle. Next up is the ritziest of the OC's beach communities: **Newport Beach**, portrayed in *The OC*, and nirvana for luxe shoppers. Families should steer toward Balboa Peninsula for its beaches, vintage wooden pier and quaint amusement center.

Laguna Beach is the OC's most cultured and charming seaside town, where secluded beaches, glassy waves and eucalyptus-covered hillsides create a Riviera-like feel. Art is huge here, especially in July when three festivals come to town.

Mission San Juan Capistrano (☎ 949-234-1300; cnr Ortega Hwy & Camino Capistrano; adult/child/senior $7/5/6; ☼ 8:30am-5pm), about 10 miles south and inland from Laguna, is one of California's most beautiful missions, featuring lush gardens and the charming Serra Chapel.

SAN DIEGO

San Diegans shamelessly, yet endearingly, promote their hometown as 'America's Finest City.' Smug? Maybe, but it's easy to see why. The weather is practically perfect, with coastal high temperatures hovering around 72°F (22°C) all year. Beaches or forests are rarely more than 10 minutes drive away. Its population (about 1.26 million) makes it America's eighth largest city (or about 1.5 times the size of San Francisco), yet San Diego is considerably more laid back than the city by that *other* bay, not to mention throbbing Los Angeles.

San Diego was originally the home of the indigenous Kumeyaay Native Americans and was settled by Spanish missionaries and Anglo immigrants in the 18th and 19th centuries. Yet despite its natural harbor and agreeable climate, it languished as a relative backwater until WWII, when the Japanese attack on Pearl Harbor prompted the US Navy to relocate the US Pacific Fleet here from Hawaii. Growth has been phenomenal ever since in military, tourism, educational and research institutions (especially in medicine and oceanography), alongside high-tech

companies in the inland valleys and businesses involved in cross-border trade. It all makes San Diego seem more All American than its California compadres, despite its borderland location.

For visitors, San Diego bursts with world-famous attractions: the zoo, Sea World, Legoland and the museums of Balboa Park for starters. The ritzy, picturesque enclave of La Jolla has pride of place on San Diego's coast. Conventions are big business too, and next to the convention center is the always buzzing Gaslamp Quarter. And San Diego's beach cities make for 'hanging 10' or dipping in the world's largest pool (aka the Pacific).

Orientation

San Diego's compact downtown revolves around the historic Gaslamp Quarter, a beehive of restaurants, bars and boutiques with the convention center just to its south. Southwest of here, Coronado is reached via a stunning bridge, while Little Italy and museum-rich Balboa Park (home of the San Diego Zoo) are to the north. The park segues into Hillcrest, the city's les-bi-gay hub. West of here are tourist-oriented Old Town, and the water playground around Mission Bay.

Heading north along the coast, Ocean Beach, Mission Beach and Pacific Beach epitomize the laid-back SoCal lifestyle while La Jolla sits pretty and privileged. The I-5 Fwy cuts through the region north–south, while the I-8 Fwy is the main east–west artery. The CA163 Fwy heads north from downtown through Balboa Park.

Information

BOOKSTORE

Le Travel Store (Map p926; ☎ 619-544-0005; 745 4th Ave, Downtown)

EMERGENCY & MEDICAL SERVICES

Mission Bay Hospital (Map p924; ☎ 858-274-7721; 3030 Bunker Hill St, Mission Bay)

Police (☎ 619-531-2000)

Rite-Aid pharmacies (☎ 800-748-3243) Call for the branch nearest you.

Scripps Mercy Hospital (Map p924; ☎ 619-294-8111; 4077 5th Ave, Hillcrest; ☼ 24hr emergency room)

INTERNET ACCESS

For wi-fi hot-spot locations, check www.jiwire.com.

CALIFORNIA

GREATER SAN DIEGO

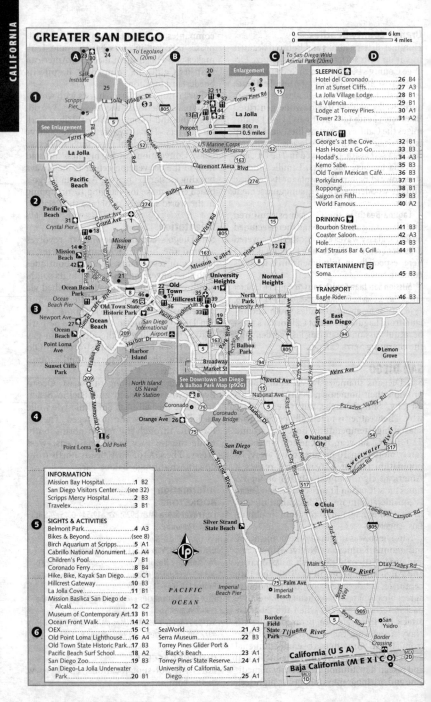

See Downtown San Diego
& Balboa Park Map (p926)

San Diego Public Library (Map p926; ☎ 619-236-5800; www.sandiego.gov/public-library; 820 E St, Downtown; wi-fi access free) Call or check the website for branch locations.

INTERNET RESOURCES

Access San Diego (www.accessandiego.com) Excellent source for barrier-free travel around San Diego.
Gaslamp.org (www.gaslamp.org) Everything you need to know about the bustling Gaslamp Quarter, including parking secrets.
San Diego Convention & Visitors Bureau (www.sandiego.org) Search hotels, sights, dining, rental cars and more, and make reservations.
San Diego.com (www.sandiego.com) Comprehensive ad-based portal to all things San Diegan, from fun stuff to serious business.

MEDIA

Gay & Lesbian Times (www.gaylesbiantimes.com) Free weekly.
KPBS 89.5 FM (www.kpbs.org) National public radio.
San Diego Magazine (www.sandiegomagazine.com) Glossy monthly.
San Diego Reader (www.sdreader.com) Free tabloid-sized listings magazine.
San Diego Union-Tribune (www.signonsandiego.com) The city's major daily.

MONEY

Travelex (🕙 10am-6pm Mon-Fri, until 4pm Sat, 11am-4pm Sun); Downtown (Map p926; ☎ 619-235-0901; Horton Plaza); La Jolla (Map p924; ☎ 858-457-2412; University Towne Centre mall, 4417 La Jolla Village Dr) Foreign currency exchange services.

POST

Post offices abound in San Diego. Call ☎ 800-275-8777 or log onto www.usps.com for the nearest branch.

TOURIST INFORMATION

Balboa Park Visitors Center (Map p926; ☎ 619-239-0512; www.balboapark.org; 1549 El Prado; 🕙 9:30am-4:30pm) In the House of Hospitality. Sells park maps and the Passport to Balboa Park (adult/child $35/19, with zoo admission $59/33), which allows one-time entry to 13 of the park's museums within one week.
San Diego Visitors Centers (☎ 619-236-1212, 800-350-6205; www.sandiego.org); Downtown (Map p926; cnr W Broadway & Harbor Dr; 🕙 9am-5pm Jun-Sep, 9am-4pm Oct-May); La Jolla (Map p924; 7966 Herschel Ave; 🕙 11am-7pm Mon-Sat, 10am-6pm Sun mid-Jun–Aug, shorter hours rest of year)

Sights
DOWNTOWN

In 1867, creative real estate wrangling by developer Alonzo Horton created the so-called 'New Town' that is today's downtown San Diego. Downtown's main street, 5th Ave, was once a notorious strip of saloons, gambling joints and bordellos known as Stingaree.

These days, Stingaree has been beautifully restored as the thumping heart of downtown San Diego and rechristened the **Gaslamp Quarter** (Map p926), a playground of restaurants, bars, clubs, shops and galleries. For the full historical picture, peruse the exhibits inside the 1850 **William Heath Davis House** (Map p926; ☎ 619-233-4692; www.gaslampquarter.org; 410 Island Ave; adult/senior $5/4; 🕙 10am-6pm Tue-Sat, 11am-3pm Sun), which also offers guided walking tours (adult/senior and student $10/8; tours 11am Saturday) of the quarter.

Just a quick stroll southeast of the Gaslamp is Downtown's newest landmark, **Petco Park** (Map p926; ☎ 619-795-5011; www.petco parkevents.com; 100 Park Blvd; tours adult/child/senior $9/5/6; 🕙 tours 10:30am, 12:30pm & 2:30pm Tue-Sun subject to game schedule), home of the San Diego Padres baseball team. Take an 80-minute behind-the-scenes tour.

Downtown's commercial focal point is the colorful, mazelike shopping mall **Westfield Horton Plaza** (Map p926; Broadway & 4th St; 🅿). West of here, the **Museum of Contemporary Art** (Map p926; ☎ 619-234-1001; www.mcasd.org; 1001 Kettner Blvd; adult/student/senior $10/free/5; 🕙 11am-9pm Thu & Fri, 11am-6pm Sat-Tue) emphasizes minimalist and pop art, as well as conceptual works and cross-border art. A new **annex** (Map p926; 1100 Kettner Blvd) is across the street at the historic Santa Fe Depot railroad station, and a third branch in La Jolla (p929; one ticket is good for all three venues).

The museum is little more than a Frisbee toss away from the Embarcadero waterfront, where you can catch a harbor cruise or the Coronado Ferry (p926). The main attraction, though, is the **San Diego Aircraft Carrier Museum** (Map p926; ☎ 619-544-9600; www.midway.org; Navy Pier; adult/child/senior/student $15/8/10/10; 🕙 10am-5pm; 🅿) aboard the decommissioned USS *Midway*, the Navy's longest-serving aircraft carrier (1945–91). A self-guided audio tour takes in berthing spaces, galley, sick bay and, of course, the flight deck with its restored aircraft, including an F-14 Tomcat. Allow at least two hours. Parking costs from $5.

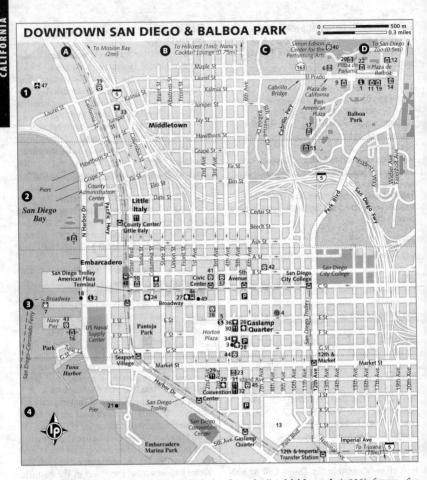

DOWNTOWN SAN DIEGO & BALBOA PARK

Other salty Embarcadero sights include the historic sailing vessels of the **Maritime Museum** (Map p926; ☎ 619-234-9153; www.sdmaritime.com; 1492 N Harbor Dr; adult/child/senior $12/8/9; ☑ 9am-8pm, until 9am late May-early Sep), most notably the 1863 *Star of India*. Further south, **Seaport Village** (☑ 10am-9pm) is a tourist-geared cluster of novelty shops, gift stores and snack bars.

In northern downtown, **Little Italy** (Map p926; www.littleitalysd.com) has evolved into one of the city's hippest places to live, eat and shop. India St is the main drag.

CORONADO

Coronado Island (technically a peninsula) is joined to the mainland by a soaring, boomerang-shaped bridge. The main draw

here the **Hotel del Coronado** (p930), famous for its buoyant Victorian architecture and illustrious guest book, which includes Thomas Edison, Brad Pitt and Marilyn Monroe (its exterior stood in for a Miami hotel in the classic film *Some Like it Hot*). The hourly **Coronado Ferry** (☎ 619-234-4111; www.sdhe.com; 1 way/round-trip $3/6; ☑ 9am-10pm) shuttles between the Broadway Pier on the Embarcadero (Map p926) to the ferry landing at the foot of Orange Ave (Map p924), where **Bikes & Beyond** (Map p924; ☎ 619-435-7180; rental per hr/day from $7/30; ☑ 9am-7.30pm) rents bicycles.

BALBOA PARK

Balboa Park is an urban oasis brimming with more than a dozen museums, gorgeous gardens and architecture, performance spaces and the famous zoo. Early 20th-century beaux arts and Spanish colonial buildings (the legacy of world's fairs) are grouped around plazas along the east–west El Prado promenade. Balboa Park (parking free) is easily reached from downtown on bus 7. A free tram shuttles visitors around.

The Balboa Park Visitors Center sells park maps and the Passport to Balboa Park; see p925 for details. Some museums occasionally have free admission on Tuesday – check with visitor center.

The scenic park approach from the west across Cabrillo Bridge drops you at Plaza de California, dominated by the flamboyant **California Building** (Map p926). Inside, the **Museum of Man** (Map p926; ☎ 619-239-2001; www.museumofman.org; Plaza de California; adult/child/senior $8/4/6; ☉ 10am-4:30pm) exhibits world-class pottery, jewelry, baskets and other artifacts. Behind the museum are the **Old Globe Theaters** (p933).

Further east, a trio of museums rings Plaza de Panama, including the **San Diego Museum of Art** (Map p926; ☎ 619-232-7931; www.sdmart.org; Plaza de Panama; adult/child/student/senior $10/4/7/8; ☉ 10am-6pm Tue-Sun, until 9pm Thu), which gets accolades for its European old masters and good collections of American and Asian art. The **Mingei International Museum** (Map p926; ☎ 619-239-0003; www.mingei.org; 1439 El Prado, Plaza de Panama; adult/student/senior $6/3/4; ☉ 10am-4pm Tue-Sun) exhibits folk art from around the globe, while the small but exquisite **Timken Museum of Art** (Map p926; ☎ 619-239-5548; www.timkenmuseum.org; 1500 El Prado;

admission free; ☉ 10am-4:30pm Tue-Sat, from 1:30pm Sun, closed Sep) showcases European and American heavies, from Rembrandt to Cézanne and John Singleton Copley.

East along El Prado, the **Museum of Photographic Arts** (Map p926; ☎ 619-238-7559; www.mopa.org; adult/child/student/senior $6/free/4/4; ☉ 10am-5pm, until 9pm Thu) exhibits fine-art photography and hosts an ongoing film series. The **San Diego Model Railroad Museum** (Map p926; ☎ 619-696-0199; www.sdmrm.org; adult/senior/student $6/3/5; ☉ 11am-4pm Tue-Fri, 11am-5pm Sat & Sun) is one of the largest of its kind with brilliantly 'landscaped' train sets.

Next up is Plaza de Balboa, flanked by the **Reuben H Fleet Science Center** (Map p926; ☎ 619-238-1233; www.rhfleet.org; adult/child/senior $7/6.25/6.25; ☉ 9:30am-varies), a family-oriented hands-on museum cum **Imax theater** (adult/child $11.75/9.75 incl Science Center admission, $7 on Friday nights, additional films $4; ☉ 11am to close of museum). Opposite is the **Natural History Museum** (Map p926; ☎ 619-232-3821; www.sdnhm.org; adult/child/student/senior $9/4/6/7; ☉ 10am-5pm), with dinosaur skeletons, an impressive rattlesnake collection, an earthquake exhibit and nature-themed movies in a giant-screen cinema.

Buildings around Pan-American Plaza in the park's southern section date from the 1935 Pacific-California Exposition. It's all about polished chrome and cool tailfins at the **San Diego Automotive Museum** (Map p926; ☎ 619-231-2886; www.sdautomuseum.org; 2080 Pan American Plaza; adult/child/senior $7/5/6; ☉ 10am-5pm). The **San Diego Air & Space Museum** (Map p926; ☎ 619-234-8291; www

CALIFORNIA

DON'T MISS

- **San Diego Zoo** – One of the world's best (below)
- **Hotel del Coronado** – Long may it host (p930)
- **Gaslamp Quarter** – I love the nightlife (p925)
- **Balboa Park museums** – Something for every interest (p927)
- **La Jolla** – The 'jewel' by the sea (opposite)

.aerospacemuseum.org; adult/child/student/senior $15/ 9/12/12; 🕙 10am-5:30pm Jun-Aug, until 4:30pm Sep-May) offers a fun-filled look at the history and mystique of flight. Highlights include an original Blackbird SR-71 spy plane and a replica of Charles Lindbergh's *Spirit of St Louis*.

If it slithers, crawls, stomps, swims, leaps or flies, chances are you'll find it in the **San Diego Zoo** (Map p924; ☎ 619-231-1515; www.sandiego-zoo.org; adult/child $21/14, with guided bus tour & aerial tram ride $33/22; 🕙 hours vary) in northern Balboa Park. It's one of the world's great zoos, with 3000-plus animals representing 800-plus species in a beautifully landscaped setting. Arrive early, when the animals are most active. Attractions include animal shows and an aerial tram. See also the affiliated San Diego Wild Animal Park (p933); combination tickets available.

North of Balboa Park, **Hillcrest** (Map p924) is queer central, but everyone's welcome in its buzzing restaurants, boutiques, bookstores, bars and cafés. Start your stroll at the **Hillcrest Gateway** (Map p924), a neon arch near 5th and University Ave.

OLD TOWN & MISSION VALLEY

In 1769, a band of missionaries led by the Franciscan friar Junípero Serra founded the first of the 21 California missions, on San Diego's Presidio Hill, and a small village (pueblo) grew around it. The spot turned out to be less than ideal for a mission, however, and in 1774 the mission was moved about seven miles upriver, closer to a steady water supply and fertile land. Today the mission is secluded in a corner of Mission Valley, a district best known for three massive shopping malls and an unlovely freeway, while the original pueblo is now called Old Town, with a historical park and good restaurants.

Mission Basilica San Diego de Alcalá (Map p924; ☎ 619-281-8449; www.missionsandiego.com; 10818 San Diego Mission Rd at Friars Rd; adult/child $3/2; 🕙 9am-4:45pm) is a modest rectangle embracing a tranquil garden.

Back above Old Town in place of the original now stands the handsome **Serra Museum** (Map p924; ☎ 619-297-3258; 2727 Presidio Dr; adult/child/ student/senior $5/2/4/4; 🕙 10am-4:30pm), which is less about the man himself than about life during the city's rough-and-tumble early period.

Head downhill to **Old Town State Historic Park** (Map p924; ☎ 619-220-5422; San Diego Ave at Twiggs St; 🕙 visitor center 10am-5pm; P), which preserves five original adobe buildings and several recreated structures from the first pueblo, including a schoolhouse and a newspaper office. Most now contain museums, shops or restaurants. A visitor center operates free tours.

POINT LOMA

This peninsula wraps around the entrance to crescent-shaped San Diego Bay like an arm around a shoulder. Enjoy stunning bay panoramas from the **Cabrillo National Monument** (Map p924; ☎ 619-557-5450; www.nps.gov/cabr; per car $5 or per person $3; 🕙 9am-5pm; P), which honors the leader of the first Spanish exploration of the West Coast. In winter enjoy whale-watching and tide-pooling. The nearby 1854 **Old Point Loma Lighthouse** helped guide ships until 1891 and is now a museum.

MISSION BAY & BEACHES

After WWII, coastal engineering turned the mouth of the swampy San Diego River into a 7-sq-mile playground of parks, beaches and bays. Amoeba-shaped Mission Bay sits just inland. Surfing is popular in Ocean Beach and Mission Beach, and all the beaches are naturals for swimming, kite flying and bicycling along miles of paved bike paths.

Mission Bay's four-star attraction is **SeaWorld** (Map p924; ☎ 800-257-4268, 619-226-3901; www .seaworld.com/seaworld/ca; 500 SeaWorld Dr; adult/child 3-9 $57/47; 🕙 9am-11pm Jul–mid-Aug, shorter hr rest of year; P). It's easy to spend a day here, shuttling among shows, rides and exhibits. The biggest draws are live animal shows, particularly *Believe*, featuring Shamu, the world's most famous killer whale, and his killer whale amigos leaping, diving and gliding. Some may find the presentation a little, well, awww, but the animals induce awe. Dolphin shows are also popular. Avoid marked 'soak zones' near the tanks unless you want to get wet. There are also zoolike animal exhibits and a few amusement-park-style rides, such as the Journey to Atlantis flume. Lines can be long in summer and around holidays. Parking is $10.

San Diego's three major beaches are ribbons of hedonism where armies of tanned, taut bodies frolic in the sand and surf. South of Mission Bay, hippie-flavored **Ocean Beach** (OB; Map p924) has a fishing pier, beach volleyball, sunset BBQs and good surf. Newport Ave is chockablock with bohemian bars, eateries and shops selling beachwear, surf gear and antiques.

West of Mission Bay, **Mission Beach** (MB; Map p924) and its northern neighbor, **Pacific Beach** (PB; Map p924), are connected by the car-free **Ocean Front Walk** (Map p924), which swarms with skaters, joggers and cyclists year-round. The small **Belmont Park** amusement park in MB beckons with a historic wooden roller coaster and large indoor pool. PB has the better-quality restaurants and nightlife.

LA JOLLA

Snuggling against one of Southern California's loveliest sweeps of coast, La Jolla (Spanish for 'the jewel;' say la-*hoy*-ah, if you please) is a ritzy suburb with shimmering beaches and a tight, upscale downtown. Noteworthy sights include the **Children's Pool** (Map p924; no longer a kids' swim area but now home to sea lions), kayaking at **La Jolla Cove** (Map p924), exploring **sea caves**, and snorkeling the **San Diego-La Jolla Underwater Park** (Map p924). The **Museum of Contemporary Art** (Map p924; ☎ 858-454-3541; www.mcasd.org; 700 Prospect St; adult/student/senior $10/free/5; ☼ 11am-7pm Thu, until 5pm Fri-Tue) is sister venue of the Downtown branch (p925; same ticket for both locations).

Outside central La Jolla is the **University of California, San Diego** (UCSD), with its renowned research facilities. The **Birch Aquarium at Scripps** (Map p924; ☎ 858-534-3474; http://aquarium.ucsd.edu; 2300 Exhibition Way; adult/child/student/senior $11/7.50/8/9; ☼ 9am-5pm; P) has a spectacular oceanfront setting. Up the coast, the **Torrey Pines State Reserve** (Map p924; ☎ 858-755-2063; www.torreypine.org; 12600 N Torrey Pines Rd; ☼ 8am-dusk; P) protects the endangered Torrey pine and is perfect for leisurely ocean-view strolls on 2000 acres. Parking here costs $8. Hang-gliding at Torrey Pines State Beach takes you by **Black's Beach** (Map p924), legendary among naturalists.

Activities

San Diegans live for the water. Surfing and windsurfing (for a surf report, call ☎ 619-221-8824) are both excellent, although in some areas territorial locals are a major irritation. Learn to hang 10 at the **Pacific Beach Surf School** (Map p924; ☎ 858-373-1138; www.pacificbeachsurfschool.com; 4150 Mission Blvd; private lessons $70-85). The best snorkeling and scuba diving is in the **San Diego-La Jolla Underwater Park** (Map p924), where you'll encounter glowing orange garibaldi flitting around giant kelp forests. For gear or instruction, try **OEX** (Map p924; ☎ 858-454-6195; www.oeexpress.com; 2158 Avenida de la Playa) in La Jolla.

Tours

Hike, Bike, Kayak San Diego (Map p924; ☎ 858-551-9510, 866-425-2925; www.hikebikekayak.com; 2246 Avenida de la Playa, La Jolla) Just what it says.

Old Town Trolley Tours (☎ 619-298-8687; www.trolleytours.com; adult/child $30/15) Hop-on, hop-off loop tour to the main attractions; also land-and-water SEAL tours with military emphasis.

San Diego Harbor Excursion (Map p926; ☎ 619-234-4111; www.sdhe.com; 1050 N Harbor Dr; adult/child from $17/8.50) A variety of bay and harbor cruises.

Sleeping

Rates skyrocket downtown during big conventions and the summer peak. The San Diego Conventions & Visitor Bureau runs a **room reservation line** (☎ 800-350-6205; www.sandiego.org).

DOWNTOWN

USA Hostel San Diego (Map p926; ☎ 619-232-3100, 800-438-8622; www.usahostels.com; 726 5th Ave; dm/d incl breakfast $25/61; ✗ ☐ wi-fi) In a former Victorian-era hotel, this convivial Gaslamp hostel has cheerful rooms, a full kitchen and a lounge for chilling. Rates include linen, lockers and a pancake breakfast.

500 West Hotel (Map p926; ☎ 619-234-5252, 866-500-7533; www.500westhotel.com; 500 W Broadway; s/d/tw with shared bath $59/69/79; P ✗ ☎ ☐) Rooms are shoebox-sized and baths down the hallway in this 1920s YMCA building (renovated 2004), but hipsters on a budget love the bright decor, flat-screen TVs, communal kitchen (or diner-style restaurant) and fitness studio.

Sofia Hotel (Map p926; ☎ 619-234-9200, 800-826-0009; www.thesofiahotel.com; 150 W Broadway; r from $175; P ✗ ☐ wi-fi) San Diego is in the midst of a boom of historic hotels receiving contemporary redos. Steps from Horton Plaza and the business district, the Sofia has 212 stylish rooms, in-room spa services and a yoga studio. Parking is $25.

Horton Grand Hotel (Map p926; ☎ 619-544-1886, 800-542-1886; www.hortongrand.com; 311 Island Ave; r $179; P ☒ ☐ wi-fi) Some rooms in this 1886 brick hotel in the Gaslamp have street-facing wrought-iron balconies, so for quiet get one facing the inner courtyard. All are individually decorated with Victoriana and have gas fireplaces. Parking costs $24.

Ivy (Map p926; ☎ 619-814-1000; www.ivyhotel.com; 600 F St; r from $350; P ☒ ☒ ☐ wi-fi) The newest of the razzle-dazzle hotels to illuminate the Gaslamp Quarter. Ineffably chic and sexy (glass-enclosed shower with bed views, anyone?), and guests get access to some of the city's most styling nightspots, on site. Parking costs $30.

BEACHES

La Jolla Village Lodge (Map p924; ☎ 858-454-0791, 800-454-4361; www.lajollavillagelodge.com; 1141 Silverado St; r incl breakfast $120-210; P wi-fi) Situated right at the edge of downtown La Jolla, it looks cookie-cutter on the outside but rooms here have custom-built '50s-modern-style furniture and teak headboards.

Inn at Sunset Cliffs (Map p924; ☎ 619-222-7901, 866-786-2543; www.innatsunsetcliffs.com; 1370 Sunset Cliffs Blvd, Ocean Beach; r $150-250, ste from $240; P ☒ ☒ ☐ wi-fi) Wake up to the sound of surf crashing onto the rocky shore at this charmer wrapped around a flower-bedecked courtyard. Breezy rooms are on the small side (and may have the occasional cracked tile), but it's still tops in Ocean Beach. Some larger suites have full kitchens. It's worth asking about discounts.

ourpick Tower 23 (Map p924; ☎ 866-869-3723; www.t23hotel.com; 723 Felspar St, Pacific Beach; r from $199; P ☐) Tops for a contempo-cool beach stay. This once-blah hotel has been transformed into a mod and modernist showplace, with minimalist decor, lots of teals and mint blues and a sense of humor.

Hotel del Coronado (Map p924; ☎ 619-435-6611, 800-468-3533; www.hoteldel.com; 1500 Orange Ave, Coronado; r $280-505; P ☒ ☒ ☐) San Diego's iconic hotel, the Del provides more than a century of history, tennis courts, spa, shops, restaurants, manicured grounds and a white-sand beach. Some rooms are in a 1970s seven-story building; book the original building.

Also recommended:

La Valencia (Map p924; ☎ 858-454-0771, 800-451-0772; www.lavalencia.com; 1132 Prospect St, La Jolla; r $275-575; P ☒ ☒ ☐ wi-fi) This William Templeton Johnson–designed edifice (1926) is La Jolla's signature hotel. Parking $17.

Lodge at Torrey Pines (Map p924; ☎ 858-453-4420, 800-995-4507; www.lodgetorreypines.com; 11480 N Torrey Pines Rd, La Jolla; r from $350; P ☒ ☒ ☐ wi-fi) Genteel craftsman-style property overlooking the famed Torrey Pines Golf Course. It costs $17 to park your car here.

Eating

With more than 6000 restaurants, San Diego's dynamic dining scene will please everyone from fast-food junkies to serious gourmets. Reservations are advised at dinnertime, especially on weekends.

DOWNTOWN

Café 222 (Map p926; ☎ 619-236-9902; 222 Island Ave; mains $6-12; ⏰ 7am-1:45pm) Downtown's favorite breakfast place for pumpkin waffles, buttermilk, orange-pecan or granola pancakes, and eggs in scrambles or benedicts. There are lunchtime sandwiches and salads, but we can't get enough of breakfast (available until closing).

Croce's Restaurant & Jazz Bar (Map p926; ☎ 619-233-4355; 802 5th Ave; mains breakfast & lunch $7-19, dinner $23-35; ⏰ 5:30pm to midnight Mon-Fri, 10am-midnight Sat & Sun) Empty tables are a rare sight at this sizzling restaurant, a pioneer of the Gaslamp and Ingrid Croce's tribute to her late husband, singer Jim Croce. The contemporary American menu has few false notes, nor have the musicians who perform nightly at the jazz bar.

Gaslamp Strip Club (Map p926; ☎ 619-231-3140; 340 5th Ave; mains $14-24; ⏰ kitchen 5pm-10pm Sun-Thu, 5pm-midnight Fri & Sat, bar open later) Pull your own bottle from the wine vault, then char your own favorite cut of steak, chicken or fish on the open grills in this retro-Vegas dining room. Fab, creative martinis, 'pin-up' art by Alberto Vargas, and reasonable prices. No one under 21 allowed.

ourpick Oceanaire (Map p926; ☎ 619-858-2277; 400 J St; most mains $20-35; ⏰ 5pm-10pm Sun-Thu, 5pm-11pm Fri & Sat) The look is art deco ocean liner, and the service is just as refined. Chef Brian Malarkey was named San Diego's chef of the year for the oyster bar and such creations as Maryland blue crab cakes and horseradish crusted Alaskan halibut. The 'stealing home' menu (available 5pm to 7pm) lives up to its name; $30 for three courses.

OLD TOWN & HILLCREST

our pick **Old Town Mexican Cafe** (Map p924; ☎ 619-297-4330; 2489 San Diego Ave, Old Town; dishes $3-14; ⏱ 7am-midnight) Watch the staff turn out fresh tortillas in the window while waiting for a table. Besides breakfast (great *chilaquiles* – soft tortilla chips covered with mole), there's a big bar (try the Old Town ultimate margarita) and dining room serving famous *machacas* (shredded pork with onions and peppers).

Hash House a Go Go (Map p924; ☎ 619-298-4646; 3628 5th Ave, Hillcrest; breakfast mains $5-15; ⏱ 7.30am-2pm Mon-Fri, 7.30am-2.30pm Sat & Sun, 5.30pm-9pm Tue-Fri, 5.30pm-10pm Sat & Sun) This busy, youthful place makes biscuits and gravy straight outta Carolina, towering benedicts, large-as-your-head pancakes and, of course, hash seven different ways. Come hungry.

Saigon on Fifth (Map p924; ☎ 619-220-8828; 3900 5th Ave, Hillcrest; mains $7-16; ⏱ 11am-midnight; Ⓟ) This Vietnamese place tries hard and succeeds, with dishes such as fresh spring rolls, fish of Hue (with garlic, ginger and lemongrass) and rockin' 'spicy noodles'. Elegant but not overbearing. Note: entrance on University Ave.

Kemo Sabe (Map p924; ☎ 619-220-6802; 3958 5th Ave, Hillcrest; mains $14-30; ⏱ from 5.30pm) Send your tastebuds on a bold journey to where Asia meets the American Southwest, both in the decor and on the plate. Thai jerk smoked duck salad and 10-spice honey chicken are typical of chef Deborah Scott's audacious fusion fare.

BEACHES

Porkyland (Map p924; ☎ 858-459-1708; 1030 Torrey Pines Rd; dishes $3-8; ⏱ 8am-8pm) *Ay, caramba!* This tiny Mexican joint just outside central La Jolla has no atmosphere, but the burritos and fish tacos have a devoted following. The *habanero* (hot round chili) burrito ($4.50) will make your taste buds roar (in a good way) and still leave you money for beer.

Hodad's (Map p924; ☎ 619-224-4623; 5010 Newport Ave, Ocean Beach; burgers $4-9; ⏱ 11am-9pm Sun-Thu, 11am-10pm Fri & Sat) OB's legendary burger joint serves great shakes, massive baskets of onion rings and succulent hamburgers wrapped in paper. The walls are covered in license plates, grunge/surf-rock plays (loud!) and your bearded, tattooed server might sidle in to your booth to take your order.

World Famous (Map p924; ☎ 858-272-3100; 711 Pacific Beach Dr, Pacific Beach; mains breakfast & lunch $7-12, dinner $10-23; ⏱ 7am-11pm) Watch the surf while enjoying 'California coastal cuisine,' an ever-changing menu of inventive dishes from the sea (banana rum mahi, bacon-and-spinach–wrapped scallops), plus steaks, salads, lunchtime sandwiches and burgers and occasional specials, such as fish or lobster taco night. Popular at breakfast, too.

Roppongi (Map p924; ☎ 858-551-5252; 875 Prospect St, La Jolla; tapas $10-25, mains $18-32; ⏱ 11:30am-9:30pm) Tapas-style Asian-fusion really shines at this gorgeous eatery with clever lighting that makes everyone look good. The Polynesian crab stack, piled high and tossed at table, is a killer choice, and the 'ahi tuna with watermelon a surprising flavor bomb. Great wines and sakes, too.

George's at the Cove (Map p924; ☎ 858-454-4244; 1250 Prospect St, La Jolla; mains $26-44; ⏱ 11am-11pm; Ⓟ) The Euro-Cal cooking is as dramatic as the oceanfront location thanks to the bottomless imagination and restless palate of champion chef Trey Foshee. George's has been on just about every list of top restaurants in California, and indeed the USA. Three venues allow you to enjoy it at different price points: the Ocean Terrace, George's Bar and George's California Modern.

Drinking

Onyx Room & Thin (Map p926; ☎ 619-235-6699; 852 5th Ave, Downtown) The candle-lit Onyx is a downstairs jazz lounge with a dancefloor; Thin is an ultra-cool, industrial-look upstairs bar, great for cocktails and conversation. Wear nice shoes.

Bitter End (Map p926; ☎ 619-338-9300; 770 5th Ave, Gaslamp) The crowd wears khakis and drinks martinis at this former brothel that has been turned into an atmospheric watering hole. There's an extensive selection of beers on tap. Dancing downstairs.

Karl Strauss Brewery & Grill Downtown (Map p926; ☎ 619-234-2739; 1157 Columbia St); La Jolla (Map p924; ☎ 858-551-2739; cnr Wall St & Herschel Ave) Local microbrewery serving surprisingly decent pub grub (most mains $9 to $19). Hours vary, so phone ahead. Pitchers cost $10 during happy hour (4pm to 6:30pm Monday to Friday).

Nunu's Cocktail Lounge (off Map p926; ☎ 619-295-2878; 3537 5th Ave, Hillcrest) Dark and divey, this hipster haven started pouring when JFK was president and still looks the part with its curvy booths, big bar and lovably kitsch decor. Smoking patio.

Airport Lounge (Map p926; ☎ 619-685-3881; 2400 India St, Little Italy) The clientele is cool, the DJs

---

TIJUANA: CHAOS, CLASS & CULTURE CLASH

The border crossing between San Diego and Tijuana is the world's busiest. More than 50 million people and 17 million vehicles enter the US annually, and Tijuana, that grubby, noisy, frenzied, yet oddly tantalizing city of two million, has long been a draw for Americans.

During Prohibition in the 1920s, Tijuana (TJ, for short) was the darling of the Hollywood crowd. These days, tequila and beer entice college students, Navy boys and other revelers on weekend trips to the rollicking bars and nightclubs of **Avenida Revolución** (La Revo), the main tourist strip a 15-minute walk from the border. By day, shops lure bargain hunters in search of everything from cheap liquor to shoes to pharmaceuticals; nearly all businesses accept US dollars.

Once you've 'done' La Revo, pick up a map from a **visitor center** (www.tijuanaonline.org) and discover the often sophisticated side of Tijuana. There are branches right by the **pedestrian border crossing** (☎ 52-664-607-3097; 9am-6pm Mon-Thu, 9am-7pm Fri & Sat, 9am-3pm Sun) and on **La Revo** (☎ 52-664-685-2210; 10am-4pm Mon-Thu, 10am-7pm Fri-Sun) between Calles 3 and 4. The excellent **Museo de las Californias** (☎ 52-664-687-9600; Paseo de los Héroes & Miña; admission $2; 10am-6pm Tue-Fri, until 7pm Sat & Sun) chronicles Baja California's often intriguing history. It's part of the **Centro Cultural de Tijuana**, which also offers classical concerts, theater and dance recitals. Nearby, **Mercado Hidalgo** is a fun indoor/outdoor market where locals stock up on rice, beans and chili,

---

hot, the design mod, the drinks strong and the servers dressed like flight attendants at this buzzy watering hole in the flight path of San Diego Airport.

Coaster Saloon (Map p924; ☎ 858-488-4438; 744 Ventura Pl, Mission Beach) This old-fashioned neighborhood bar has front-row views of the Belmont Park roller coaster and draws an unpretentious crowd with its beer selection and good margaritas.

Bourbon Street (Map p924; ☎ 619-291-4043; www .bourbonstreetsd.com; 4612 Park Blvd, Hillcrest) This gay bar's warren of bars, courtyards and dance-floor makes for easy mingling. Look for bingo nights, guest DJs and wicked-cheap martini happy hours.

Hole (Map p924; ☎ 619-225-9019; 2820 Lytton St, Ocean Beach) Out of the way dive (surrounded by auto repair shops). Head down the stairs to find manly men enjoying Sunday beer bust, wet underwear contests and more. It's also near military housing, so you might ask, but please don't tell, OK?

Entertainment

Check the San Diego *Reader* or the Night and Day section in the Thursday edition of the San Diego *Union-Tribune* for the latest happenings around town. **Arts Tix** (3rd Ave & Broadway, Downtown; 11am-6pm Tue-Thu, 10am-6pm Fri & Sat, 10am-5pm Sun), in a kiosk on Broadway outside Horton Plaza, has half-price tickets for same-day evening or next-day matinee performances and discounted tickets to all types of other events. **Ticketmaster** (☎ 619-220-

8497; www.ticketmaster.com) and **House of Blues** (www .hob.com) sell other tickets.

LIVE MUSIC & NIGHTCLUBS

Casbah (Map p926; ☎ 619-232-4355; 2501 Kettner Blvd; cover free-$15) Liz Phair, Alanis Morissette and the Smashing Pumpkins have all rocked this funky Casbah on their way up the charts, and it's still a good place to catch local acts and tomorrow's headliners.

Shout House (Map p926; ☎ 619-231-6700; 655 4th Ave, Downtown; cover free-$10) Dueling pianos entertain at this rowdy but innocent Gaslamp bar. Pianists have an amazing repertoire: standards, rock and more; we recently heard the cult comedy number 'D*ck in a Box'.

4th & B (Map p926; ☎ 619-231-4343; 345 B St, Downtown; cover varies) This midsized venue has music lovers head-bobbing with an eclectic mix of talent, from unsigned hopefuls to Macy Gray, Psychedelic Furs and the Last Comic Standing tour. Rest your feet and eardrums in the lounge.

Stingaree (Map p926; ☎ 619-544-0867; www.sting sandiego.com; 454 6th Ave, Downtown; cover varies) Vegas in the Gaslamp. Superslinky decor provides the backdrop for San Diego's most-likely-to-spot-a-celebrity club. Table service for your drinks and cabanas on the roof.

Soma (Map p924; ☎ 619-226-7662; www.somasd .com; 3350 Sports Arena Blvd, near Old Town; cover $8-23) This all-ages venue (no booze) spotlights up-and-coming local bands of the alterna-rock and punk persuasion. Electric and edgy, with fiercely loyal crowds.

from pussycat mild to hellishly hot. The **Catedral de Nuestra Señora de Guadalupe** (Avenida Niños Héroes & Calle 2a) is Tijuana's oldest church.

TJ has an excellent cuisine scene. Good choices on or near La Revo include the casual **Café La Especial** (☎ 52-664-685-6654; Avenida Revolución 718; breakfast $5-12, lunch & dinner $6-17 (most under $12); ☻ 9am-10pm Sun-Thu, 9am-11:30pm Fri & Sat), in the basement below Hotel Lafayette, for *carne asada* (roast meat), enchiladas, tacos and some of the best margaritas on the strip. To taste a Caesar salad at its birthplace, head to the restaurant at the venerable though shopworn **Hotel Caesar** (☎ 52-664-685-1606; Av Revolución 827; ☻ 9am-midnight; caesar salad $6, $8 with chicken). Wash it down with beer. Beyond La Revo, take a taxi to the gracious, upscale **La Diferencia** (☎ 52-664-634-3346; Blvd Sánchez Taboada 1061; mains around US$15; ☻ noon-10:30pm Mon-Sat, noon-8pm Sun) in the Zona Rio for sumptuous dishes like out of *Like Water for Chocolate* (poblano pepper stuffed with beef and fruit – salmon with mango and habanero sauce).

Tijuana is easiest reached via the San Diego Trolley (below) and a walk across the border and via Mexicoach shuttle (one way/round-trip $5/8, every 30 minutes) from the Border Station Parking lot. Expect long lines when returning to the US. See Visas (p1127) and Customs (p1116) for entry requirements.

CLASSICAL MUSIC & THEATER

San Diego Opera (Map p926; ☎ 619-570-1100; www.sdopera.com; Civic Theatre, 3rd & B St) High-quality, eclectic programming is the hallmark of the city's opera ensemble, which occasionally draws international guest stars such as Cecilia Bartoli.

Old Globe Theaters (Map p926; ☎ 619-234-5623; www.theglobetheaters.org; Balboa Park) High-caliber theater is performed in three venues, including a replica of Shakespeare's eponymous stage.

San Diego Symphony (Map p926; ☎ 619-235-0804; www.sandiegosymphony.com; 750 B St) presents classical and family concerts in Copley Symphony Hall. In summer, it moves to **Navy Pier** (Map p926; 960 N Harbor Dr) for more light-hearted fare.

Getting There & Away

San Diego International Airport (Lindbergh Field; Map p926; ☎ 619-231-2100; www.san.org) sits about 3 miles west of Downtown; plane-spotters will thrill watching jets come in for a landing over Balboa Park.

Greyhound (Map p926; ☎ 619-515-1100; 120 W Broadway, Downtown) has hourly direct buses to Los Angeles (one way/round-trip $17/28, 2½ to four hours).

Amtrak (☎ 800-872-7245; www.amtrak.com) runs the *Pacific Surfliner* several times daily to Los Angeles ($34, three hours) and Santa Barbara ($37, 6½ hours) from the **Santa Fe Depot** (Map p926; 1055 Kettner Blvd, Downtown).

All major car-rental companies have desks at the airport, or call the national toll-free numbers (p1144). **Eagle Rider** (Map p924; ☎ 619-222-8822, 877-437-4337; 3655 Camino del Rio W, Old Town) rents motorcycles from $75 per day.

Getting Around

Bus 992, nicknamed the Flyer ($2.25), operates at 10- to 15-minute intervals between the airport and Downtown, with stops along Broadway. Airport shuttle services (from about $10 to Downtown) include **Cloud 9 Shuttle** (☎ 800-974-8885; www.cloud9shuttle.com) and **Xpress Shuttle** (☎ 800-900-7433; www.xpressshuttle.com). A taxi to Downtown from the airport costs between $8 and $13.

Local buses and the San Diego Trolley, which travels south to the Mexican border, are operated by **Metropolitan Transit System** (MTS; ☎ 619-233-3004; www.sdcommute.com). The **Transit Store** (Map p926; ☎ 619-234-1060; Broadway & 1st Ave) has available route maps, tickets and one-/two-/three-/four-day Day Tripper passes for $5/9/12/15, respectively. Taxi flag fall is $1.70, plus $2 for each additional mile.

AROUND SAN DIEGO
San Diego Wild Animal Park

Take a walk on the 'wild' side at this 1800-acre **open-range zoo** (off Map p924; ☎ 760-747-8702; www.sandiegozoo.org; 15500 San Pasqual Valley Rd, Escondido; general admission adult/child $28.50/$17.50, including tram adult/child $33/22; ☻ 9am-9pm mid-Jun–early Sep, to 5pm early Sep–mid-Jun; **P**). Giraffes graze, lions lounge and rhinos romp more or less freely on the valley floor. For that instant safari feel, board the Journey to Africa tram ride, taking you around the world's second-largest continent in less than half an hour. Combination tickets with the San Diego Zoo are $59/39. Parking is $8.

The park is in Escondido, about 35 miles north of downtown San Diego. Take the I-15 Fwy to the Via Rancho Parkway exit, then follow the signs. Parking is $8.

Legoland

This enchanting **fantasy park** (off Map p924; ☎ 760-918-5346; www.lego.com/legoland/california; 1 Legoland Dr, Carlsbad; adult/child $57/44; ☻ 10am-5pm, extended hours Jul & Aug, closed Tue & Wed Sep-May; **P**) of rides, shows and attractions is mostly suited to the elementary-school set. Tots can dig for dinosaur bones, pilot helicopters and earn their driver's license. Mom and dad will probably get a kick out of Miniland, recreating such American landmarks as the White House, the Golden Gate Bridge and Las Vegas entirely of Lego blocks. From Downtown San Diego (about 32 miles), take the I-5 Fwy north to the Cannon Rd E exit. Parking costs $10.

CALIFORNIA DESERTS

The desert is a land of contradictions: vast yet intimate, remote yet sophisticated, searing yet restorative. Over time, you may find that what first seemed barren and boring will transform in your mind's eye to harrowing beauty: weathered volcanic peaks, subliminally erotic sand dunes, purple-tinged mountains, groves of cacti, tiny wildflowers pushing up from caramel-colored soil for their brief lives, lizards scurrying beneath colossal boulders, uncountable stars. Locales such as swanky Palm Springs and desolate Death Valley will help you understand why so many people find California's deserts spiritual, chic and irresistible.

PALM SPRINGS

The Rat Pack is back, or at least the Rat Pack's hangout is. In the 1950s and '60s, Palm Springs, some 100 miles east of LA, was the swinging getaway of Sinatra, Elvis and other big stars. The Coachella Valley subsequently gave over to retirees in golf clothing and grew, well, a little dull...until the mid-1990s, when a new generation latched onto the city's retro-chic charms: kidney-shaped pools, midcentury modernist steel-and-glass bungalows, boutique hotels with vintage decor and piano bars serving perfect martinis. In today's Palm Springs, retirees mix with hipsters and a significant gay and lesbian contingent.

Even if in-and-out-and-in-again grooviness leaves you cold, there's plenty to do in and around Palm Springs. Hike palm-studded canyons or ski through silky snow (or both in the same day), play golf, explore museums, shop at massive malls or high-toned boutiques, sample a date milk shake, tour a windmill or straddle a fault line.

High season is October to April, but Palm Springs stays reasonably busy even in summer when hotel rates drop and temperatures rise above 100°F (38°C). Some establishments close down for part of the summer or keep irregular hours. If traveling off-season, phone ahead to avoid disappointment.

Orientation

Palm Springs is the principal city of the Coachella Valley, south of the I-10 Fwy. In Palm Springs, compact downtown, Palm Canyon Dr (aka Hwy 111, the main road through the valley), runs north–south. The parallel Indian Canyon Dr runs one-way south to north. The main east–west thoroughfare, Tahquitz Canyon Way, takes you toward Palm Springs' airport.

Information

Access the internet for free at the **public library** (☎ 760-322-7323; www.palmspringslibrary.org; 300 S Sunrise Way; ☻ 9am-8pm Mon & Tue, 9am-5.30pm Wed, Thu & Sat, 10am-5.30pm Fri).

In town are **Desert Regional Medical Center** (☎ 760-323-6511; 1150 N Indian Canyon Dr; ☻ 24hr) and a **post office** (333 E Amado Rd).

Tramway Visitors Center (☎ 760-778-8418, 800-347-7746; www.ps-springs.org; 2901 N Palm Canyon Dr; ☻ 9am-5pm, seasonal variations possible) is north of town, at the tramway turnoff, in a 1965 Albert Frey–designed gas station. Look for specialty guides (mobility, impaired, gay and lesbian travelers, etc) and *A Map of Palm Springs Modern* ($5) for architecture fans.

Sights & Activities

The **Palm Springs Aerial Tramway** (☎ 888-515-8726, 760-325-1449; www.pstramway.com; 1 Tramway Rd; adult/child/senior $21.95/14.95/19.95, after 3pm $18.95/11.95/18.95; ☻ 10am-10.30pm Mon-Fri, from 8am Sat & Sun) features gently rotating cars that whisk you 2.5 miles from sunbaked desert to pine-scented Alpine wonderland in 10 minutes. Temperatures can be up to 40°F lower than at the base. The mountain station at 8516ft offers sweeping views and access to 54 miles of hiking trails through the wilderness of **Mt San Jacinto State Park**, including a 5.5-mile trek to the summit. In winter, you can comb through the forest on snowshoes or cross-country skis, available for rent at the **Adventure Center** (Thu-Sun) near the mountain station.

Another chilling-out option is **Knott's Soak City** (☎ 760-327-0499; www.knotts.com/soakcity/ps; 1500 S Gene Autry Trail; adult/child $27.95/16.95, after 3pm $16.95/16.95; hours vary), a water park with rides including Pacific Spin 'river rafting,' slides, tube rides and wave pools.

In the cooler months, especially during the spring wildflower season, don't miss a ramble around the lands owned by the native Cahuilla people: **Indian Canyons** (☎ 760-325-3400; www.indian-canyons.com; adult/child/student/senior $6/2/4.50/4.50; 8am-5pm daily Oct-Jul, Fri-Sun Jul-Sep) is rare veins of green; picnic by a palm-shaded stream or beneath towering rock formations. **Tahquitz Canyon** (☎ 760-416-7044; www.tahquitzcanyon.com; 500 W Mesquite; adult/child $12.50/6; 7:30am-5pm Oct-Jul, Fri-Sun only Jul-Sep) is famous for its 60ft waterfall and ancient rock art.

The **Palm Springs Art Museum** (☎ 760-325-7186; www.psmuseum.org; 101 Museum Dr; adult/child/senior $12.50/5/10.50; 10am-5pm Tue, Wed & Fri-Sun, noon-8pm Thu) features contemporary painting and sculpture and pre-Columbian antiquities, plus temporary exhibits. Free admission Thursday 4pm until 8pm.

At the airport, the **Palm Springs Air Museum** (☎ 760-778-6262; www.air-museum.org; 745 N Gene Autry Trail; adult/student 13-17/child/senior $10/8.50/5/8.50, Sat senior $10; 10am-5pm) shows off some great vintage planes, including the amazing WWII-era B-17 (the 'Flying Fortress').

Tours

Celebrity Tours (☎ 760-770-2700; Rimrock Shopping Center, 4751 E Palm Canyon Dr; 1hr tour adult/child/senior $30/12/28, 2½hr tour $35/14/33) Local gossip – past and present.

Desert Adventures (☎ 888-440-5337, 760-324-5337; www.red-jeep.com; 3/3½/4hr tours $129/139/149) Snappily narrated and information-packed jeep tours through shake, rattle and roll country along the San Andreas Fault. Inquire about discounts.

PS Modern Tours (☎ 760-318-6118; psmoderntours@aol.com; tour $65) Fact-filled three-hour tour for fans of Albert Frey, Richard Neutra, John Lautner and other midcentury architects.

PS Windmill Tours (☎ 760-320-1365; www.bestofthebesttours.com; 90min tours adult/child/senior $23/10/20) Learn about the grove of whirring windmills surrounding Palm Springs. Tours are at 9am, 11am, 2pm.

Sleeping

Rates at desert hotels vary wildly from season to season. We're quoting high-season rates (generally December to May); look for discounts at other times. Hotel reservations can be made via www.palm-springs.org or ☎ 760-322-6368 or ☎ 800-325-6875.

Alpine Gardens Hotel (☎ 760-323-2231, 888-299-7455; www.alpinegardens.com; 1586 E Palm Canyon Dr; r $65-130; P ☒ ☎ ☐) If the yeah-baby groove leaves you cold, all 10 rooms at this impeccably kept motel, c 1954, have redwood-beamed ceilings, refrigerators, and slightly kitsch but extra-charming furnishings. Some have kitchens.

Casa Cody (☎ 760-320-9346, 800-231-2639; www.casacody.com; 175 S Cahuilla Rd; r incl breakfast $99-179, ste $199-389; P ☒ ☎ wi-fi) Charlie Chaplin once stayed in this country inn tucked behind billowing bougainvillea. Units have desert-themed decor, including some with full kitchens, wood-burning fireplaces and private patios.

Inndulge (☎ 760-327-1408, 800-833-5675; www.inndulge.com; 601 Greenfall Rd, Warm Sands; r incl breakfast $129-199; P ☒ ☎ ☐ wi-fi) Small, clothing-optional hotels for gay men are the name of the game in the Warm Sands neighborhood (just outside central Palm Springs). This midrange option has a 1950s shell, a variety of rooms and suites (updated with mission furniture and gay-themed photo posters), pool and hot tub that encourage mingling and summer specials. Sexual temperature: six out of 10.

Orbit In (☎ 760-323-3585, 877-996-7248; www.orbitin.com; 562 W Arenas Rd; r incl breakfast $179-309; P ☒ ☐ wi-fi) It's back to the '50s at Palm Springs' retro property of record, with high-end original midcentury furniture (think Eames, Noguchi and more) around a quiet pool.

our pick **Parker Palm Springs** (☎ 760-770-5000, 888-450-9488; www.theparkerpalmsprings.com; 4200 E Palm Canyon Dr; r from $300; P ☎ ☐) Posh full-service resort with whimsical decor by designer-du-jour Jonathan Adler. The Palm Springs Yacht Club spa is to die for.

Also recommended:

Caliente Tropics (☎ 760-327-1391, 866-468-9595; www.calientetropics.com; r $65-107; P ☒ ☎ wi-fi)

Polynesian-style motor lodge where Elvis once splashed poolside. Kid-friendly.

Chase Hotel (☎ 760-320-8866, 877-532-4273; www .chasehotelpalmsprings.com; 200 W Arenas Rd; r incl breakfast from $129, ste $139-209; P ⊠ ⊠ ⊒) Downtown midcentury motel complex. Top marks for uncluttered, oversized rooms (some with kitchenettes).

Eating

Tyler's Burgers (☎ 760-325-2990; 149 S Indian Canyon Dr; dishes $4-7; ⊙ 11am-4pm Mon-Sat, closed mid-Jul–Aug & sometimes Mon in warmer months) The city's favorite burger stand has a magazine rack stocked with the *Robb Report* and financial magazines. It's at La Plaza, a sort of drive-thru shopping street in the town center. Expect a wait.

El Mirasol (☎ 760-323-0721; 140 E Palm Canyon Dr; mains $7-19; ⊙ 11am-10pm) There are showier Mexican places in town, but everyone ends up back here for the informal vibe, copious margaritas and snappy dishes from tacos to chicken mole. Indoor and outdoor seating available.

Wang's (☎ 760-325-9264; 424 S Indian Canyon Dr; mains $10-15; ⊙ 5.30-9.15pm Sun-Thu, 5.30-10.30pm Sat & Sun, closed 3 weeks in Aug) The menu may sound like standard-issue upscale Chinese, but the atmosphere is anything but. This swank outpost, mood-lit, with indoor koi pond and giant cocktails, is the darling of the in-crowd. Kiss, kiss.

our pick **Copley's on Palm Canyon** (☎ 760-327-1196; 445 N Palm Canyon Dr; mains $25-35; ⊙ 5.30pm-late nightly & 10am-2pm Sun Jan–mid-May, 6pm-late Tue-Sun mid-May–Dec, closed late Jul-late Aug) On the former Cary Grant estate, Andrew Manion Copley gets seriously inventive: think prosciutto-wrapped duck breast and 'Oh my lobster pie'. Bring your sweetie and your credit card.

Also recommended:

Native Foods (☎ 760-416-0070; 1775 E Palm Canyon Dr; mains $8-15; ⊙ 11:30am-9:30pm Mon-Sat, closed Jul–mid-Aug) Tasty vegan fare in a rather fancy strip mall.

Hadley Fruit Orchards (☎ 888-854-5655; www .hadleyfruitorchards.com; 48980 Seminole Dr, Cabazon; date shakes from $3.50; ⊙ 9am-7pm Mon-Thu, 8am-8pm Fri-Sun) Claims to have invented trail mix. Stop for a date milk shake on your drive to LA.

Drinking

Melvyn's (☎ 760-325-0046; 200 W Ramon Rd) The likes of Sinatra and McQueen were among the early customers at this swanky watering hole at the Ingleside Inn. You can still quaff excellent martinis at its burnished bar.

Village Pub (☎ 760-323-3265; 266 S Palm Canyon Dr; wi-fi) A casual place for kicking back with your buds, the pub has live music, darts and beer on tap.

Entertainment

Blue Guitar (☎ 760-327-1549; 120 S Palm Canyon Dr) Hear live jazz and blues upstairs Friday to Sunday nights, at this venue next door to the Plaza Theater; call for the current schedule. It's owned by Kal David, the celebrity guitarist.

Toucans (☎ 760-416-7584; 2100 N Palm Canyon Dr) Swinging gay and lesbian venue, with a semitropical vibe, dancefloor and occasional drink specials. Other gay nightspots are concentrated on Arenas Rd east of Indian Canyon Dr.

Getting There & Around

Palm Springs International Airport (☎ 760-318-3800; www.palmspringsairport.com; 3400 E Tahquitz Canyon Way) is served directly from US cities, including Chicago, Dallas, Los Angeles and San Francisco; the airport is five minutes' drive from downtown. **Amtrak** (☎ 800-872-7245; www.amtrak .com) serves North Palm Springs Station, on a desolate stretch of desert 4 miles north of downtown Palm Springs. *Sunset Limited* trains run to and from Los Angeles ($34, 2½ hours) on Sunday, Wednesday and Friday and continue to New Orleans. Slow-moving local bus service is provided by **SunBus** (☎ 760-343-3451; www.sunline.org; ticket/day pass $1/3).

JOSHUA TREE NATIONAL PARK

Like images from a Dr Seuss book, the whimsical Joshua trees (actually tree-sized yuccas)

THE CAST FROM THE PAST

Palm Springs' historic Plaza Theater, dating from 1936, hosts the **Palm Springs Follies** (☎ 760-327-0225; www.psfollies.com; 128 S Palm Canyon Dr; tickets $48-90; ⊙ late Oct–mid-May), a Ziegfeld Follies–style revue of music, dancing, showgirls and comedy. The twist? Many of the performers are as old as the theater – all are over 50, and some into their 80s. But this is no amateur hour; in their heyday, many of these old-timers hoofed it alongside Hollywood and Broadway's biggest, who occasionally guest-star. High-energy shows deliver flash, splash, inspiration and patriotism.

WHAT THE...?

You may do two double takes in Cabazon, 17 miles' drive west of Palm Springs: the first when you see a giant **T-Rex & Apatosaurus** (☎ 951-922-8700; www.worldsbiggestdinosaurs.com; 50800 Seminole Dr, Cabazon; ☻ gift shop 10am-dusk; T-Rex hours vary), north of the I-10 Fwy, and the second when you see how they're being marketed. Claude K Bell, a sculptor for Knott's Berry Farm in Orange County, spent 1964 to 1975 creating these concrete behemoths (55ft and 45ft tall, respectively). They remained a temple of tourist kitsch until 2005, when they were purchased by a group of creation scientists, who contend that God created the original dinosaurs on the sixth day of Creation along with the other animals. In the gift shop in the Bronto belly, alongside the sort of dino-swag you might find at other science museums, you can read about hoaxes and fallacies of evolution and Darwinism, biblical quotes purporting to refer to dinosaurs, and evidence that dinosaurs and man existed at the same time.

---

welcome visitors to this 794,000 acre park at the convergence of the Sonora and Mojave deserts. It's popular with rock climbers and day hikers, especially in spring when many trees dramatically send up a huge single cream-colored flower. The mystical quality of this stark, boulder-strewn landscape has inspired many artists, most famously the band U2, which named its 1987 album *The Joshua Tree*.

Park highlights include **Hidden Valley** with its dramatic piles of golden boulders; **Keys View**, with vistas as far as Mexico (best at sunset); and the **Cholla Cactus Garden**. An excellent short hike is the 1.2-mile **Barker Dam loop trail**, which takes in all that makes Joshua Tree special: weathered rock piles, a historic dam, Native American petroglyphs and, of course, the trees themselves. For a more strenuous hike, head to **49 Palms Oasis** (3 miles) or **Lost Palms Oasis** (7.2-mile round-trip); these are best avoided in summer.

Three of the parks **visitor centers** (☎ 760-367-5500; www.nps.gov/jotr; Oasis Utah Trail & National Park Dr, Twentynine Palms; ☻ 8am-5pm; Joshua Tree Park Blvd; ☻ 8am-5pm; Cottonwood 8 miles north of I-10, Cottonwood Springs; ☻ 8am-4pm), are open daily. In emergencies call ☎ 909-383-5651.

Park admission is $15 per vehicle, good for seven days and including a map/brochure and the useful, seasonal *Joshua Tree Guide*. There are no facilities besides rest rooms, so gas up and bring food and plenty of water.

Sleeping & Eating

Of the park's nine **campgrounds** (☎ 877-444-6777; www.recreation.gov; sites $10-15, reservations available at some campgrounds), only Black Rock Canyon and Cottonwood have shared-use water, flush toilets and dump stations. Check www.nps.gov/jotr for more information about individual sites.

Backcountry camping is permitted as long as it's a mile from the road and 500ft from any trail; registration is required at one of the 12 backcountry boards throughout the park.

If camping is not your thing, base yourself in Twentynine Palms (home of the largest US Marine base), Joshua Tree or Yucca Valley, all north of the park. Standouts from the run-of-the-mill motels along 29 Palms Hwy:

Twentynine Palms Inn (☎ 760-367-3505; www.29palmsinn.com; 73950 Inn Ave, Twentynine Palms; most rooms & suites incl breakfast $85-225, mid-Jun–mid-Sep $70-180; P ✗ ✦ ✦) Historic adobe-and-wood cabins and respected restaurant (mains lunch $6 to $14, dinner $15 to $23) around an oasis.

Spin & Margie's Desert Hideaway (☎ 760-366-9124; www.deserthideaway.com; 64491 29 Palms Hwy, Joshua Tree; ste $125-160; P ✗ ✦) Charming Southwestern-style cabins with kitchen and private patio; sleep two to six people.

For inventive sustenance, drop by the funky-cool **Crossroads Café** (☎ 760-366-5414; 61715 29 Palms Hwy, Joshua Tree; dishes $6-10; ☻ 7am-8pm Thu-Tue, shorter hours in summer). Coffee, sandwiches, salads, live music, films and internet access are on the menu at the nearby **Beatnik Cafe** (☎ 760-366-2090; 61597 29 Palms Hwy, Joshua Tree; meals under $10; ☻ 11am-11pm, until midnight Wed & Sat).

AROUND JOSHUA TREE NATIONAL PARK

North of the park, **Pioneertown** (www.pioneertown.com; Hwy 247) was built in 1946 as a Western movie set. Visit Mane St, try the old bowling alley, or enjoy BBQ, cheap beer and live music at the legendary honky-tonk **Pappy & Harriet's Pioneertown Palace** (☎ 760-365-5956; www.pappyandharriets.com; mains lunch $5-11, dinner $9-25; ☻ from 11am Thu-Sun, from 5pm Mon, closing time varies with shows).

ANZA-BORREGO DESERT STATE PARK

Shaped by an ancient sea and tectonic forces, Anza-Borrego is the largest state park in the USA outside Alaska. Framing the park's only settlement – tiny Borrego Springs (pop 2535) – are 600,000 acres of mountains, canyons and badlands; a fabulous variety of plants and wildlife; and intriguing relics of native tribes, Spanish explorers and gold-rush pioneers. Wildflower season (usually March to May; updates at ☎ 760-767-4684) is a great time to visit, right before the Hades-like heat makes exploring dangerous.

Borrego Springs has stores, restaurants, motels and a public library with free internet access. The park's excellent **visitor center** (☎ 760-767-4205; www.anzaborrego.statepark .org; 200 Palm Canyon Dr; ☾ 9am-5pm Oct-May, Sat & Sun only Jun-Sep) is 2 miles west. Look also for new field programs by the **Anza-Borrego Foundation** (www.theabf.org/programsfield.htm).

You'll need your own wheels to explore the park. A passenger car will get you to many interesting spots, but only a 4WD can tackle many of the 500 miles of backcountry dirt roads. Better yet, hike (pack plenty of water). Good – and fairly easy – options include the **Borrego Palm Canyon Trail** (3-mile round-trip) to a native palm grove and waterfall; the **Cactus Loop Trail** (1 mile) with great views; and the **Pictograph Trail** (2 miles) for close-ups of native rock art and a restored stagecoach stop.

The park's three developed and eight primitive campgrounds rarely fill up, but you can also camp for free anywhere you wish as long as you keep at least 100ft away from water. Open ground fires and gathering vegetation (dead or alive) are prohibited.

Accommodations in Borrego Springs include the well-kept **Palm Canyon Resort** (☎ 760-767-5341, 800-242-0044; www.palmcanyonresort.com; 221 Palm Canyon Dr; r $70-195; P ✖ ✑), a hotel and RV park with country-style rooms and a good restaurant (mains $10 to $20); the adobe-style **Borrego Valley Inn** (☎ 760-767-0311, 800-333-5810; www.borregovalleyinn.com; 405 Palm Canyon Dr; r incl breakfast $200-230; P ✖ ✑ ✑ wi-fi), which has lovely rooms with Southwestern decor; and the luxe **La Casa del Zorro** (☎ 760-767-5323; 3845 Yaqui Pass Rd; r from $295) and restaurant (dinner mains $30 to $40).

For a casual yet stylish meal, **Red Ocotillo** (☎ 760-767-7400; 818 Palm Canyon Dr; mains breakfast $6-13 & dinner $6-15; ☾ 7am-9pm; P wi-fi), in a re-furbished Quonset hut, serves breakfast all day (think Benedicts and skillet omelets) as well as hulking sandwiches and cold beer. Pet friendly.

MOJAVE NATIONAL PRESERVE

If you're on a quest for the 'middle of nowhere,' you'll find it in the desert wilderness of the **Mojave National Preserve** (www.nps.gov/moja; admission free), a 1.6-million-acre jumble of sand dunes, mountains, Joshua trees, volcanic cinder cones and sculpted rock formations. No services or facilities are available within the preserve.

From Baker, Kelbaker Rd crosses a ghostly landscape of cinder cones before arriving at **Kelso Depot**, a handsome Spanish mission revival-style railroad station built in 1924. It houses a **visitor center** (☎ 760-252-6108; ☾ 9am-5pm) with interesting desert-demystifying exhibits. From here it's another 10 miles south to the majestic **Kelso Dunes** that rise up to 700ft and, when conditions are right, emanate a low 'booming' sound caused by shifting sands. The dunes' quiet and graceful presence is nothing short of magical. The trip to the top of the tallest one takes two to three hours round-trip; it's strenuous because the sand is so fine.

At Kelso Depot, Kelbaker Rd intersects with the northeast-bound Kelso–Cima Rd. After about 19 miles, take Cima Road toward I-15, which takes you over the almost perfectly symmetrical **Cima Dome**, a 75-square-mile, 1500ft hunk of granite whose slopes are smothered in one of the world's largest and densest **Joshua tree forests**. For a close-up look, hike up the Teutonia Peak Trail (4 miles round-trip).

East of Kelso–Cima Rd, Mojave Rd takes you to the preserve's two first-come, first-served **campgrounds** (campsites $12) set amid a volcanic landscape at Mid Hills and Hole-in-the-Wall. The latter also has a small **visitor center** (☎ 760-928-2572; ☾ 10am-4pm Wed-Sun Oct-Apr, Fri-Sun May-Sep). Roads in this area are unpaved but well maintained. South of Hole-in-the-Wall, **Mitchell Caverns** (☎ 760-928-2586; adult/child $4/2; ☾ tours 1:30pm Mon-Fri, 10am, 1:30pm & 3pm Sat & Sun early Sep-late May, 1:30pm Sat & Sun late May-early Sep) is a subterranean world of quirky limestone formations.

Free backcountry and roadside camping is permitted throughout the preserve in areas that have been previously used for this purpose. If you need a roof over your head, there are a few grotty motels in Baker (around $60 per room). Much better, albeit a bit off the beaten path, is the B&B-style **Nipton Hotel** (☎ 760-856-2335; www.nipton.com; tent cabins $68 with your own bedding, plus $7 per person for bedding, d $79, all incl breakfast; ✗ ℞ wi-fi), in a century-old adobe villa in the railroad outpost of Nipton northeast of the preserve. The owners also offer tent cabins, a café and a well-stocked trading post.

DEATH VALLEY NATIONAL PARK

The name itself evokes all that is harsh and hellish – a punishing, barren and lifeless place of Old Testament severity. Yet closer inspection reveals that nature is putting on a truly spectacular show in Death Valley with water-fluted canyons, singing sand dunes, palm-shaded oases, scuttling rocks, sculpted mountains and plenty of endemic wildlife. It's truly a land of superlatives, holding the US records for hottest temperature (134°F, or 56°C, measured in 1913), lowest point (Badwater, 282ft below sea level) and being the largest national park outside Alaska (4687 sq miles). Peak tourist season is during the spring wildflower bloom.

Orientation & Information

Centrally located Furnace Creek has a general store, restaurants, lodging, post office, gas station, ATM and a **visitor center** (☎ 760-786-3200; www.nps.gov/deva; ℞ 8am-5pm), whose website is an excellent pretrip planning resource. Stovepipe Wells, about 24 miles northwest, has a store, gas station, ATM, motel–restaurant and ranger station. Gas and sustenance are also available at Scotty's Castle, in the north, and Panamint Springs, on the park's western edge. The park entrance fee ($20 per vehicle; valid for seven days) must be paid at self-service pay stations located throughout the park. For a free map and newspaper present your receipt at the visitor center.

Sights & Activities

Start out early in the morning by driving up to **Zabriskie Point** for spectacular valley views across golden badlands eroded into waves, pleats and gullies. Further south, at **Dante's View**, you can simultaneously see the highest (Mt Whitney) and lowest (Badwater) points in the contiguous USA. The drive there takes about 1½ to two hours round-trip, but the 5000ft elevation makes this area attractive for escaping the summer heat.

Badwater itself, a foreboding landscape of crinkly salt flats, is a 17-mile drive south of Furnace Creek. Attractions along the way include narrow **Golden Canyon**, easily explored on a 2-mile round-trip walk, and **Devil's Golf Course**, where salt has piled up into saw-toothed miniature mountains. A 9-mile detour along **Artists Drive** is best done in the late afternoon when the hills erupt in fireworks of color.

Near Stovepipe Wells, north of Furnace Creek, you can scramble along the smooth marble walls of **Mosaic Canyon** or roll down powdered sugar at the undulating **Sand Dunes** (magical during a full moon). Another 36 miles north is the fantastical **Scotty's Castle** (☎ 760-786-2392; adult/child/senior $11/6/9; ℞ 9am-5pm), where costumed guides bring to life the strange tale of lovable con-man Death Valley Scotty. About 8 miles west of here, giant **Ubehebe Crater** is the result of a massive volcanic eruption. Hiking to the bottom and back takes about 30 minutes. It's slow going for another 27 miles on a tire-shredding dirt road (high clearance required) to reach the eerie **Racetrack**, where you can ponder the mystery of faint tracks etched into the dry lakebed by slow-moving rocks.

The most spectacular backcountry adventure, though, is the 27-mile trip along unpaved **Titus Canyon Road**, which climbs, curves and plunges through the Grapevine Mountains past a ghost town, petroglyphs and dramatic canyon narrows. It's a one-way road accessible only from Hwy 374 near Beatty; the entrance is about 2 miles outside park boundaries.

Sleeping & Eating

During wildflower season accommodations are often booked solid and campgrounds fill by midmorning, especially on weekends.

Stovepipe Wells Village (☎ 760-786-2387; www .stovepipewells.com; r $91-111; ✗ ☕ 🖥) Rooms are a bit long in the tooth, but this roadside motel still offers the most bang for the buck in the park. The pool, though small, is a refreshing asset, and the quirky restaurant (breakfast and lunch mains $5 to $8, dinner mains $10 to $23) delivers above-par cowboy cooking.

Furnace Creek Inn (☎ 760-786-2345; www.furnace creekresort.com; r $275-405; ℞ mid-Oct–mid-May; ✗ ☕) At this elegant, mission-style hotel you can count the colors of the desert while unwind-

CALIFORNIA

ing by the spring-fed pool, but the restaurant (lunch mains $10 to $14, dinner mains $21 to $29) isn't quite as gourmet as advertised. Nice Sunday brunch, though.

Campers will find public showers ($5) at Furnace Creek Ranch and Stovepipe Wells Village; the fee includes pool access. Free backcountry camping permits are available from the visitor center.

Campgrounds are first-come, first-served, except for Furnace Creek, which accepts reservations from October to April. Here are some central camping options:

Sunset (Furnace Creek area; sites $12; ☾ Oct-Apr) Huge and RV-oriented.

Stovepipe Wells (Stovepipe Wells Village; sites $12; ☾ Oct-Apr) Parking-lot style, but close to the sand dunes.

Furnace Creek (☎ 877-444-6777; www.recreation.gov; Furnace Creek area; campsites $12-18; ☾ year-round) Pleasant grounds, including some shady sites.

Texas Spring (Furnace Creek area; sites $14; ☾ Oct-Apr) Small and best for tents; nice hillside location.

Furnace Creek Ranch (☎ 760-786-2345; www.furnace creekresort.com; r $116-193; ✿ ◙) is a rambling 224-unit resort with cramped cabins and slightly larger motel-type rooms. They're dated but comfortable, and the best ones have patios or balconies. Its **Wrangler Restaurant** (mains breakfast buffet $10, lunch $10-12, dinner $19-29; ☾ 6am-9:30pm) puts out unexciting but belly-filling buffet breakfasts and turns into a pricey steak house at night. Better stick with the **Forty-Niner Café** (mains $6-19; ☾ 7am-9pm) next door, which cooks up American standards, although the juiciest burgers are at the **19th Hole Bar & Grill** (burgers $10; ☾ 11am-4pm).

AROUND DEATH VALLEY

Your accommodation choices widen if you're willing to overnight outside the park. The pit stops of Beatty, NV, and Ridgecrest are your best bets for budget and midrange motels. En route to the latter, the ghost town of **Rhyolite** and the **Goldwell Open-Air Museum** are intriguing roadside attractions.

CENTRAL COAST

No trip to California is worth its salt without a jaunt along the almost surreally scenic Central Coast. One of the US' most iconic roads, Hwy 1, skirts past the cultivated perfection of Santa Barbara and its wine country, the towering sand dunes of Guadalupe, fantastical Hearst Castle, soul-stirring Big Sur and hippie-haunt Santa Cruz. Slow down – this region wants to be savored, not gulped.

VENTURA & THE CHANNEL ISLANDS

Ventura has a charming downtown teeming with cafés, restaurants and antique shops. But it's also the main gateway to the remote and rugged **Channel Islands National Park**, nicknamed 'California's Galápagos' for its unique flora and fauna. Boat trips leave from Ventura Harbor, southwest of Hwy 101, where you can pester the friendly rangers at the **NPS visitor center** (☎ 805-658-5730; www.nps.gov/chis; 1901 Spinnaker Dr; ☾ 8:30am-5pm) for insider tips and information.

The islands are preserved as virtual wilderness with few facilities but offer incomparable snorkeling, diving, swimming, kayaking, hiking and bird-watching. Primitive **campgrounds** (☎ 877-444-6777; www.recreation.gov; $15) are your only overnight option; bring food and water.

Anacapa, the closest island to the mainland, is best for half- or single-day trips, with short, easy trails and unforgettable views. Santa Cruz, the largest island, is also convenient for single-day trips, though its longer, more strenuous hikes invite extended explorations. The other three islands require longer channel crossings and are best visited as three-day camping trips. San Miguel is often shrouded in fog; Santa Barbara island supports a sizable elephant seal colony; and Santa Rosa is home to many bird species and indigenous archaeological sites.

The main operator offering day trips and camper transportation is harbor-based **Island Packers** (☎ 805-642-1393; www.islandpackers.com; 1691 Spinnaker Dr, Ventura). Rates begin at $42/25 per adult/child for the Anacapa day trip and $27/18 for a nonlanding three-hour gray whale watch (January to March).

SANTA BARBARA

Life is sweet in Santa Barbara, a picture-perfect coastal Shangri-La where the air is redolent with citrus and jasmine, bougainvillea drapes whitewashed buildings and it's all hemmed in by seemingly endless pearly white beaches. Oprah Winfrey and Kevin Costner like it here. And so does Sue Grafton whose novels are set in a fictionalized beach town not unlike Santa Barbara. You won't regret slowing down for the fabulous Mediterranean architecture, fine museums and exceptional food and local wines.

State St is the main drag with bars and cafés clustering south of Ortega St, while attractive shops and museums are further north.

Information

Green Santa Barbara (http://greensantabarbara.com) Tips and tricks on minimizing your footprint during your stay in Santa Barbara.

Outdoors Santa Barbara visitor center (☎ 805-884-1475; http://outdoorsb.noaa.gov; 4th fl, 113 Harbor Way; ☑ 11am-5pm, until 6pm summer) Comprehensive public lands information, including the Channel Islands.

Visitor center (☎ 805-965-3021; www.santabarbaraca.com; 1 Garden St; ☑ 9am-5pm, until 6pm Jul & Aug, until 4pm Nov-Jan) Lots of free maps and brochures; ask for the excellent *Sideways* and 'Film Tour' booklets.

Sights & Activities

The **Santa Barbara County Courthouse** (☎ 805-962-6464; 1100 Anacapa St; admission free; ☑ 8:30am-4:30pm Mon-Fri, 10am-4:30pm Sat & Sun) is an absurdly beautiful place to be on trial. Marvel at the hand-painted ceilings, kaleidoscopic tiles and intricate murals and definitely wheeze your way up the clock tower for panoramic views of city and mountains.

The soul of the city is the 1786 **Mission Santa Barbara** (☎ 805-682-4149; www.sbmission.org; 2201 Laguna St; adult/child $4/free; ☑ 9am-5pm), justifiably nicknamed the 'Queen of the Missions'. There are some fabulous Chumash wall decorations inside the church, a moody cemetery and exhibits on life during the Mission period.

Santa Barbara Botanic Garden (☎ 805-682-4726; www.sbbg.org; 1212 Mission Canyon Rd; adult/child 2-12/student/senior $8/6/6/4; ☑ 9am-6pm Mar-Oct, 9am-5pm Nov-Feb) is a lush place for a picnic, but for a quirkier garden experience book early to visit **Lotusland** (☎ 805-969-9990; www.lotusland.org; adult/

child $35/10; ☑ tours 10am & 1:30pm Wed-Sat mid-Feb–mid-Nov), the legacy of the eccentric late Madame Ganna Walska. Tours take in rare botanical species and enchanting corners, including the dramatic Blue Garden.

Back in town, **Santa Barbara Museum of Art** (☎ 805-963-4364; www.sbma.net; 1130 State St; adult/child/student/senior $9/6/6/6, Sun free; ☑ 11am-5pm Tue-Sun) has a well-edited collection of European and American hot shots – think Monet, Matisse and O'Keefe – and also puts on sophisticated special exhibits.

Down on the waterfront, the focus is on **Stearns Wharf**, a rough wooden pier with restaurants, shops and the small and tot-friendly **Ty Warner Sea Center** (☎ 805-962-2526; www.sbnature.org; adult/child/senior/student $7/4/6/6; ☑ 10am-5pm), created by the Beanie Baby tycoon. Fun activities include petting baby sharks, crawling through a surge channel and studying water samples collected from the ocean floor.

A paved trail skirts the beach for miles, passing the harbor where **Paddle Sports** (☎ 805-899-4925; www.kayaksb.com; 117b Harbor Way; per 2hr from $20) rents kayaks and operates Channel Island kayak tours (from $170). **Sea Landing** (☎ 805-963-3564; www.sealanding.net; 301 W Cabrillo Blvd) runs whale-watching (per adult/child from $40/20) and other trips and has watersports rentals.

Sleeping

When it comes to lodging, prepare for sticker shock, because even basic rooms can command $200 in summer. Bargains can sometimes be found along motel row several miles north on State St near Las Positas Rd.

Presidio Motel (☎ 805-963-1355; www.thepresidiomotel.com; 1620 State St; r midweek $60-160, weekend $90-230; ℗ wi-fi) Steps from downtown, this is a motel with panache and personality thanks to buzzy art, dreamy bedding, and hip and helpful owners. Noise can be an issue but breakfast and bikes are free. Check-in is between 8am and 10pm.

Hotel Santa Barbara (☎ 805-957-9300, 888-259-7700; www.hotelsantabarbara.com; 533 State St; r $140-270; ℗ ✕ ✦ wi-fi) Walk to shopping and restaurants from this downtown charmer with a pedigree going back to 1926. Some of the yellow-and-blue Cal-Med rooms can be on the small side.

Brisas del Mar (☎ 805-966-2219, 800-468-1988; www.brisasdelmarinn.com; 223 Castillo St; midweek $180-326, weekend $200-346; ℗ ✦ ▯ wi-fi) Big kudos for the copious freebies (DVDs, wi-fi, breakfast, wine and cheese, milk and cookies) and new Mediterranean-style front section. End up in the dated motel wing in back, though, and you'll be in floral wallpaper hell.

Four Seasons Biltmore (☎ 805-969-2261, 800-332-3442; www.fourseasons.com; 1260 Channel Dr; r $550-900, ste $100-4600; P 🞕 🞕 🖵 wi-fi) A delightful symphony of tile and wood, this historic seaside estate gets laid-back luxe right. Price tag too steep? Savor the refined ambience wandering around the oh-so-soothing gardens, or by enjoying sunset cocktails or a gourmet meal.

Eating & Drinking

La Super Rica (☎ 805-963-4940; 622 N Milpas St; dishes $1.50-6.50; 🕙 11am-9pm) Wow! Julia Child said it first and made this picnic-table shack famous. It's great Mexican, albeit served on paper plates. Don't fret the line – get into it.

Sojourner (☎ 805-965-7922; 134 E Canon Perdido; mains $5.50-12.50; 🕙 11am-11pm) Locals' favorite Soj has been doing its mostly meatless magic since 1978 and infuses each dish with a unique twist. The vegetable nut burger and gingered tofu wonton pillows are recommended.

Brophy Brothers (☎ 805-966-4418; mains $8-20; 🕙 10am-10pm) The fish and seafood at this always bustling harbor hangout are so fresh that you half expect them to leap straight out of the ocean. Awesome place at sunset.

Quantum Kitchen (☎ 805-962-5999; 201 W Carrillo St; burgers $10-16; 🕙 11am-3pm Mon-Fri, 5pm-midnight Wed-Sat) One of the few joints in town to satisfy late-night munchies, this contempo eatery is famous for its build-your-own-burgers and delectable skinny fries.

our pick **Bouchon** (☎ 805-730-1160; www.bouchon santabarbara.com; 9 W Victoria St; mains $24-34; 🕙 dinner) Every ingredient sings with freshness at this unhurried, rustically romantic foodie favorite. The servers are a treat and will capably find the perfect wine match for your pomegranate-bathed lamb or maple-glazed duck.

Entertainment

Santa Barbara's fun zone revolves around Lower State St where crowds usually pack the Guinness-soaked and peanut-shell-covered planks of the **James Joyce** (☎ 805-962-2688; 513 State St) pub. For urban flair, fancy cocktails and dancing, head to the white-and-blue **EOS Lounge** (☎ 805-564-2410; 500 Anacapa St; 🕙 Tue-Sat).

Getting There & Around

Greyhound (☎ 805-965-7551; 34 W Carrillo St) has daily buses to Los Angeles and San Francisco, while **Amtrak** (209 State St) runs direct train and coach services to Los Angeles and San Luis Obispo.

The electric **Downtown-Waterfront Shuttle Bus** (☎ 805-683-3702; 25¢; 🕙 10am-6pm year-round, 10am-10pm Fri & Sat Jun-Aug) hums along State St to Stearns Wharf; a second route goes along Cabrillo Blvd paralleling the beach.

SANTA BARBARA TO SAN LUIS OBISPO

Just north of Santa Barbara on Hwy 101 are two recommended state beaches, **El Capitan** and **Refugio**, both with ridiculously popular **campgrounds** (☎ 800-444-7275; www.reserveamerica .com; day-use/camping $8/25). Further north, mock-Danish village **Solvang** (www.solvangusa.com) is a kitsch lovers' dream with its nonfunctioning windmills and Hansel-and-Gretel bakeries. A scenic back-country route north from Santa Barbara is via Hwy 154 where you can go for the grape in the **Santa Barbara wine country**. Retrace the misadventures of Miles and Jack of *Sideways* fame with the help of a free map available at the Santa Barbara visitor center; its general wine country booklet is also useful. For all-day winery tours with an eco-angle, check out **Sustainable Vine** (www.sustainablevine.com).

Less famous but definitely up-and-coming is the **Edna Valley/Arroyo Grande Valley wine country** (www.slowine.com) further north. Most wineries are along Hwy 227 and its side roads, which eventually take you to San Luis Obispo.

Staying on Hwy 101, **Pismo Beach** has a nice long stretch of sand, but there's actually a prettier beach in tiny and sunny **Avila Beach** (avoid the summer weekend crowds), which had its act cleaned up following a decades-long oil leak from a nearby Unocal refinery.

our pick **Avila La Fonda Hotel** (☎ 805-595-1700; www.avilalafondahotel.com; 101 San Miguel St; r $200-400; P 🖵 wi-fi) is a memorable place to spend the night; its cheerful decor evokes Old Mexican charm. With in-room Jacuzzis for two, a giant plasma TV and a free snack basket, you may find it hard to leave.

SAN LUIS OBISPO

San Luis Obispo (SLO) is lively yet low-key with a high quality of life and community spirit. Like so many other California towns, it grew up around a mission, founded in 1772

WORTH THE TRIP: COASTAL DUNES

Heading north on Hwy 101, consider a detour along Rte 166 to tiny, hard-scrabble **Guadalupe**, the gateway to the largest coastal dunes on the continent. Pop by the **Dunes Center** (☎ 805-343-2455; www.dunescenter.org; ☼ usually 10am-4pm Tue-Sun, confirm hours) for basic but intriguing displays on the mysterious Dunites, who lived in the sand in the 1930s, and on the Lost City of DeMille (www.lostcitydemille.com), the entire movie set of Cecil B DeMille's 1923 version of *The Ten Commandments* that still lies buried somewhere beneath the velvety mounds. More recently, scenes from *Pirates of the Caribbean* were filmed here. The best dune access is via the **Rancho Guadalupe Dunes Preserve** (admission free) about 3 miles west of town.

Back in town, dig into some of the juiciest steaks ever at the genuine Old West–flavored **Far Western Tavern**. And yes, Johnny and Keira ate here.

---

by Junípero Serra. There's not much to see, tourist-wise, but it makes an enjoyable base for area explorations. The **visitor center** (☎ 805-781-2777; www.visitslo.com; 1039 Chorro St; ☼ 10am-5pm, until 7pm Fri & Sat) is off Higuera St. The best day to visit is Thursday, when the local **farmers market** (☼ 6-9pm) turns Higuera St into a fantastic street party, complete with rock and roll and sidewalk BBQs.

Sights & Activities

San Luis Obispo's main historical draw is the endearingly simple **Mission San Luis Obispo De Toloso** (☎ 805-543-6850; suggested donation $2; ☼ 9am-5pm Apr-Oct, 9am-4pm Nov-Mar), established in 1772, made more cheerful by recently added floral embellishments. It's on **Mission Plaza**, a shady oasis with restored adobes overlooking San Luis Creek, where kids can splash.

Other sights are considerably more low-brow. In town, **Bubblegum Alley** (btwn 733 & 737 Higuera St) is a narrow passageway plastered with wads of chewed gum arranged in arbitrary artistry vaguely reminiscent of a Jackson Pollock painting. Outside town, the fantastically campy **Madonna Inn** (☎ 805-543-3000; www.madonnainn.com; 100 Madonna Rd) is famous for its themed rooms (including the exotic Oriental Fantasy and hot-pink Sugar & Spice) and the bizarre waterfall urinal in the men's room.

Sleeping & Eating

San Luis Obispo's motel row is north of downtown along Monterey St.

HI Hostel Obispo (☎ 805-544-4678; www.hostelobispo.com; 1617 Santa Rosa St; dm $20-23, r $45-60; ☼ closed 10am-4:30pm; P ⌨ wi-fi) The motherly Elaine presides over this gem of an ecohostel in a converted Victorian one block from the train station. Rates include a pancake breakfast and Fairtrade coffee and tea.

Sanitarium (☎ 805-544-4124; www.thesanitariumspa.com; 1716 Los Osos St; r $190-290; P ✗ wi-fi) This seven-room 'sanitarium' in a converted 19th-century medical office is likely to cure whatever ails you. The vibe is relaxed, the flair artsy and the freestanding Moroccan metal tubs add a quirky touch.

Big Sky Café (☎ 805-545-5401; www.bigskycafe.com; 1121 Broad St; mains $8-18; ☼ 7am-9pm Mon-Sat, 8am-9pm Sun) This feel-good café gets top marks all around for its imaginative market-fresh menu, choice wines by the glass and a staff that doesn't chintz with the smiles.

Novo (☎ 805-543-3986; www.novorestaurant.com; 726 Higuera St; mains $12-30; ☼ 11am-10pm) It's hard to decide what's more special about this place: the enchanting creekside setting or the eclectic tapas menus with inflections of Brazil, the Med and Asia.

Getting There & Away

Greyhound (☎ 805-543-2121; 150 South St) has frequent buses to Los Angeles, Santa Barbara and San Francisco. **Amtrak** (1011 Railroad Ave) has daily service aboard the *Pacific Surfliner* to Santa Barbara, LA and San Diego and to points north on the Seattle-bound *Coast Starlight*.

MORRO BAY TO HEARST CASTLE

North of San Luis Obispo on Hwy 1, the first town you meet is **Morro Bay**. Its namesake **Morro Rock**, a 578ft volcanic peak, is the first hint of the coast's upcoming drama, though Morro Bay itself won't make you linger.

There are some fantastic state parks here, though, with marvelous hiking and **camping** (☎ 800-444-7275; www.reserveamerica.com). South of town, **Morro Bay State Park** (☎ 805-772-2560; campsites $20-25; wi-fi) has a natural history museum and a heron rookery reserve. Further south, and even better, is the largely undeveloped

Montaña de Oro State Park (☎ 805-528-0513; campsites $11-15), featuring coastal bluffs, sand dunes and a 4-mile sand spit separating Morro Bay from the Pacific. North of town, **Morro Strand State Beach** (☎ 805-772-2560; campsites $20-25) is a nice sweep of sand.

About 20 miles north of Morro Bay, the self-proclaimed artists' village of **Cambria** is the best town to lay off the gas. The cute-as-a-button **HI Bridge Street Inn** (☎ 805-927-7653; www .bridgestreetinncambria.com; 4314 Bridge St; dm $22-25, r $40-70; ℗ ✗) sleeps like a hostel but acts like a B&B. It's bright but tiny, rooms share baths, and the friendly owners make you feel at home. Check-in is between 5pm and 9pm. One of the best eateries in town is **Robin's** (☎ 805-927-5007, 4095 Burton Dr; lunch $7-10, dinner $13-24; ☻ 11am-9pm) where you can savor eclectic, pan-Asian dishes on a wisteria-draped patio.

For no-frills, midrange motels, head further north to San Simeon, gateway to the hilltop **Hearst Castle** (☎ 800-444-4445; www.hearstcastle.org; adult/child mid-May–mid-Sep 6-17 $24/12, mid-Sep–mid-May $20/10, night tours $30/15; ☻ 8:20am-3:20pm, later in summer), California's most famous monument to wealth and ambition. William Randolph Hearst, the newspaper magnate, entertained real and Hollywood royalty at this fantasy estate dripping with European antiques, accented by shimmering pools and surrounded by lush gardens. Of the four tours offered, Tour 1 includes a film about Hearst's life and is recommended for first-timers. All tours last about 1¾ hours, including the round-trip bus ride from the shiny new visitor center (don't miss the Hearst exhibit). Reservations are recommended in summer. Evening tours led by guides in period garb run in spring and fall.

Point Piedras Blancas, about 4.5 miles north of Hearst Castle, is home to California's largest **elephant-seal colony**, which breed, molt, sleep, frolic and, occasionally, go aggro on the beach. The main viewpoint has interpreta-

---

WHAT THE...?

Cutesy Cambria goes quirky at **Nitt Witt Ridge** (☎ 805-927-2690; 881 Hillcrest Dr; adult $10/5; ☻ tours 10am-6pm Jun-Aug, 10am-4pm Sep-May), a three-story folk-art antithesis to Hearst Castle. Made entirely from abalone shells, beer cans, toilets seats and other detritus, it took a local eccentric some 50 years to build. Reservations preferred.

---

tive panels. The seals are here year-round, but the pups are born between December and March.

BIG SUR

The famous 90-odd miles of coastline between Cambria and the Monterey Peninsula are an awe-inspiring symphony of nature, and at times Hwy 1 seems to clutch at the cliffs as if in desperation above a ravenous sea. Lodging, food and services are scarce, but demand is high year-round, which generally translates into high prices and poor service. To truly experience the Big Sur mystique, consider overnight camping, but book sites as early as possible. An excellent pretrip planning source is www.bigsurcalifornia.org. Note that the $8 parking fee at any of the state parks (Julia Pfeiffer Burns, Pfeiffer Big Sur and Andrew Molera) is good for same-day access to all three.

It's about 25 miles from Hearst Castle to blink-and-you-miss-it **Gorda**, home to the **Treebones Resort** (☎ 877-424-4787; www.treebonesresort .com; campsite $60, yurt incl breakfast $145-270; ℗ ☻ wi-fi), a set of 16 cliff-top yurts (essentially circular tent cabins with a skylight) with hotel-standard amenities and ocean-view decks. It's unique but hardly luxurious considering bathrooms are in the main lodge. There are also seven campsites. Dinner is $17 to $28.

About 24 miles further north is the New Age-y **Esalen Institute** (☎ 831-667-3000; www.esalen .org), famous for its esoteric workshops and ocean-view hot springs. With a reservation you too can frolic in the latter – but only from 1am to 3am ($20; clothing optional).

Next up is **Julia Pfeiffer Burns State Park** and it's a gem, thanks to the 80ft McWay Falls, California's only coastal waterfall, reached after an easy quarter-mile hike. Nearby, two small and popular walk-in campgrounds sit secluded above the surging waves.

Partington Cove, 2 miles along, is a raw and breathtaking spot where crystalline waters engulf thick kelp forest, star fish and anemones pose in tide pools, and crashing surf salts your skin. A 15-minute trail leads down from a gate inside a large hairpin turn. Everybody ignores the warning signs to scamper around the rocks at trail's end.

Seven miles further is **Deetjen's Big Sur Inn** (☎ 831-667-2377; www.deetjens.com; r $130-200, with shared bath $80-95; ℗), a quirky and rustic homestead with rooms and a cutesy restaurant serving gourmet country meals daily (breakfast $5 to $12, dinner $24 to $34).

Nearby, the funky and artistic **Henry Miller Memorial Library** (☎ 831-667-2574; www.henrymiller .org; 11am-6pm Wed-Mon;) is the heart and soul of Big Sur bohemia and a cultural center with concerts, open-mike nights and an outdoor film series. Stop by anytime for free coffee and wi-fi (donations appreciated) or browse through the bookstore crammed with the work of Miller and his friends.

The food takes a backseat to the dramatic views that make cliff-top **Nepenthe** (☎ 831-667-2345; lunch $12-20, dinner $14-35; 11:30am-10pm) such a celebrated restaurant. The Ambrosia burger is quite good, or go downstairs to the outdoor self-service **Café Kevah** (mains $7-14; 9am-2:30pm) for cheaper eats and the same views.

About a mile up, the friendly staff at the **United States Forest Service Big Sur Ranger Station** (☎ 831-667-2315; 8am-4:30pm, 8am-6pm Jun-Aug) will happily clue you in about hiking and camping options and supply you with overnight parking ($4) and fire permits (free) for the **Ventana Wilderness**, which is superb backpacking turf. The most popular adventure is the 10-mile hike to Sykes hot springs.

Backing up onto the ranger station, idyllic **Pfeiffer Big Sur State Park** is crisscrossed by sun-dappled trails cutting through the redwoods; an easy favorite is the 1.4-mile round-trip to Pfeiffer Falls. You can camp or stay in the rambling **Big Sur Lodge** (☎ 831-667-3100, 800-424-4787; www.bigsurlodge.com; r $160-300;), a quiet complex of renovated, single-story attached buildings.

Across the highway, take an unmarked road with a sign saying 'narrow road'. Two miles later it drops you at the crescent-shaped **Pfeiffer Beach** (separate entry fee $5) whose towering offshore granite outcrops – one with a tunnel carved through it – will have you burning up the pixels. Unfortunately it's often superwindy here, and strong currents make the water too dangerous for swimming.

Most of Big Sur's commercial activity is concentrated along the next 6 miles in the 'Village'. Here, you'll find the post office, gas stations, motels, grocery stores and restaurants, including the **Big Sur Bakery & Restaurant** (☎ 831-667-0520; pizza $14-19, mains $23-37; 8am-3pm Tue-Sun, and until 9.30pm Tue-Sat), home of the $5 latte, yummy pastries, wood-fired pizzas and steaks.

Further on, **Big Sur River Inn** (☎ 831-667-2700; www.bigsurriverinn.com; s/ste $135/250) offers

extremely basic and noisy motel rooms, slightly better family suites and a popular restaurant overlooking a creek. Alternatively, pick up a burrito at the Burrito Bar in the adjacent store and stake out a picnic spot right by the water. Also here is the **Maiden Pub** (☎ 831-667-2355), Big Sur's biggest party den (as far as that goes) with reasonably priced pub grub, live music and an encyclopedic beer menu.

Visitors often overlook **Andrew Molera State Park**, about 4.5 miles further north, but locals love this trail-laced pastiche of gentle meadows, shrub-covered ocean bluffs, rich wildlife and velvety beaches. From the parking lot, a half-mile trail leads to a small first-come, first-served walk-in **campground** (campsites $9).

For an intriguing side trip, turn off Hwy 1 onto the unpaved but graded **Old Coast Road** opposite the Andrew Molera entrance (4WD not necessary). It serpentines through the Santa Lucia Mountains, opening up sweeping ocean vistas, dipping into shady dales with soaring redwood groves and cutting across ranchland where cattle roam freely. Allow one hour for the 11-mile trip, which deposits you right by scenic Bixby Bridge. From here, you'll be in Carmel in about a half-hour, tops.

CARMEL & AROUND

Ritzy **Carmel-by-the-Sea** has the genteel, manicured and exclusive feel of a country club. Simply plop down in any downtown café (Ocean Ave is the main drag) and watch the parade of behatted ladies toting fancy-label shopping bags, dapper gents tooling around in top-down beemers and frazzled nannies admonishing their pampered charges. There are some great restaurants, and beach sunsets are a dream on rare fog-free days, but unless you're into shopping there isn't much here to make you stick around for long. Just soak up Carmel's idiosyncratic charms and keep moving.

Sights

If you're going to see only one California mission, make it **San Carlos Borroméo de Carmelo Mission** (☎ 831-624-1271; www.carmelmission.org; 3080 Rio Rd; adult/child under 17/senior $5/1/4; 9:30am-5pm Mon-Sat, 10:30am-5pm Sun) in a gorgeous setting about 1 mile south of downtown. An oasis of calm and solemnity, its great old stone basilica is filled with original art, including a carved and painted main altar. A separate chapel holds the masterful memorial tomb to mission founder Junípero Serra who is buried in the sanctuary. Two small museums yield plenty of dusty surprises.

They bark, they bray, they bathe and they're fun to watch. Sea lions are the stars of **Point Lobos State Reserve** (☎ 831-624-4909; http://ptlobos .org; per car $8; ☒ 9am-5pm, 9am-7pm during daylight saving time), 4 miles south of Carmel. Its dramatically rocky coastline also makes for some excellent tide-pooling. The full perimeter hike is 6 miles, but even shorter walks let you experience this extraordinary meeting of land and sea. Come early at weekends as parking is limited.

Carmel and Monterey are linked by Hwy 1 and by the scenic **17-Mile Drive** (www.pebble beach.com; cars $9.50, bicycle free; ☒ sunrise-sunset), which meanders past exclusive mansions, crumbling coastline with the trademarked Lone Cypress and peerless golf courses in the community of Pebble Beach. The most scenic stretch is between the Pacific Grove gate and the Carmel Gate.

Sleeping & Eating

Pine Inn (☎ 831-624-3851, 800-228-3851; www.pineinn .com; cnr Ocean Ave & Lincoln St; r $150-300; ☒ ☒) Fine antiques and cozy lighting lend an old-school gravitas to this historic inn in the heart of town. The cheaper rooms won't fit a ton of luggage but lack none of the plush comforts. Steinbeck met his third wife, Elaine Scott, here in 1949.

Bruno's Market & Deli (☎ 831-624-3821; cnr 6th & Junípero; sandwiches $3-6.50; ☒ 7am-8pm) Makes a mean tri-trip beef sandwich and has all the other accoutrements for a kick-ass picnic.

Rio Grill (☎ 831-625-5436; mains $9-25; ☒ 11:30am-10pm) At this jazzy bistro near the mission local ingredients find their destiny in wickedly flavored Southwestern dishes. The fire-roasted artichokes will have you licking your fingers.

Forge in the Forest (☎ 831-624-2233; cnr of 5th & Junípero; mains $10-25; ☒ 11:30am-9pm Sun-Thu, until 10pm Fri & Sat) This darling bistro is built around a crusty old forge, serves inspired American cuisine and has one of the loveliest patios in town.

MONTEREY & AROUND

Monterey's allure is all about fish and the sea. The one-time capital of the sardine-canning industry now lures visitors with a world-class aquarium that is a veritable temple to the bay's underwater universe. A National Marine Sanctuary since 1992, Monterey Bay itself screams for exploration by water, be it by kayak, boat, scuba or snorkel. The city also delivers a window on the state's Spanish and Mexican roots with numerous restored period buildings open for touring. Don't waste time, on the much-hyped tourist ghettos of Fisherman's Wharf and Cannery Row.

The **visitor center** (☎ 831-657-6400; www.monterey info.org; ☒ 9am-6pm Mon-Sat, 9am-5pm Sun Apr-Oct, 9am-5pm Mon-Sat 10am-4pm Sun Nov-Mar) is at Camino El Estero and Franklin St. There's a smaller **branch** (150 Olivier St; ☒ 8am-5pm Mon-Fri) near the Monterey State Historic Park. Free pamphlets include the excellent *Literary & Film Map*.

Sights
MONTEREY BAY AQUARIUM

We dare you not to be charmed, amazed and enriched by this glorious **aquarium** (☎ 831-648-4800, tickets 800-756-3737; www.montereybay aquarium.org; 886 Cannery Row; adult/child 3-12/student/senior $25/16/23/23; ☒ 9:30am-6pm Mon-Fri, 9:30am-8pm Sat & Sun Jun-Aug, 10am-6pm Sep-May). Give yourself at least half a day to watch sharks and sardines play hide and seek in fast-growing kelp forests, observe the smile-inducing antics of frisky otters, meditate upon ethereal jellyfish and get touchy-feely with sea cucumbers, bat rays and other tide-pool creatures. Feeding times are best; see the schedule in the lobby. To avoid the worst crowds, get tickets in advance, be there when doors open and stick around during lunchtime.

MONTEREY STATE HISTORIC PARK

Old Monterey is a cluster of lovingly restored 19th-century brick and adobe buildings covered on a 2-mile self-guided walking tour called the **Path of History**. Admission to the buildings is free but opening hours vary seasonally. Pick up a free brochure and find out what's open at the **park headquarters** (☎ 831-649-7118; Custom House Plaza; ☒ 10am-5pm), which has a few period exhibits.

Opposite, the **Maritime Museum** (☎ 831-372-2608; adult/child $8/5; ☒ 10am-5pm Thu-Tue) illuminates Monterey's salty past, including the rollercoaster-like rise and fall of the local sardine business. Nearby **Fisherman's Wharf** is not a bad place for a bowl of rib-sticking clam chowder.

> ### WORTH THE TRIP: NATIONAL STEINBECK CENTER
>
> About 17 miles east of Monterey, Salinas is the birthplace of John Steinbeck (1902–68), a Stanford dropout who went on to win a Nobel Prize for Literature. Tough, funny and brash, he sensitively captured the troubled spirit of rural and working-class America in such novels as *Grapes of Wrath* and *Of Mice and Men*.
>
> Smack in the middle of the flat, fertile valley that was Steinbeck's home and passion, the **National Steinbeck Center** (☎ 831-775-4721; www.steinbeck.org; 1 Main St; adult/child 6-12 $11/6; ☼ 10am-5pm) brings his novels to life with interactive, kid-accessible exhibits and short movie clips. One cherished possession is Rocinante, the camper Steinbeck drove across America while writing *Travels with Charley*.
>
> Also here is the surprisingly interesting **Rabobank Agricultural Museum**, where you'll learn the ins-and-outs of modern agriculture. There are video interviews with local farmers and activities such as 'The Produce Game' that take you from the field to the supermarkets.

CANNERY ROW

Immortalized in Steinbeck's eponymous novel, **Cannery Row** (www.canneryrow.com) was the hectic, smelly epicenter of the sardine-canning industry, Monterey's lifeblood until the 1950s. Nowadays it nets only tourists with its cheesy souvenir shops and mediocre restaurants. Come here for the aquarium, then move on.

MONARCH SANCTUARY

Just in time for Halloween, millions of pumpkin-colored monarch butterflies arrive at this fragrant pine grove to spend the winter months. It's in Pacific Grove; follow the signs from Lighthouse Ave.

Activities

A favorite activity is walking or bicycling the paved 18-mile **Monterey Peninsula Recreation Trail**, which edges the coast through Monterey and ends at Lovers Point beach in Pacific Grove. Maps and rentals are available from **Bay Bikes** (☎ 831-655-2453; www.baybikes.com; 585 Cannery Row; per hr/day from $8/32).

Kayaking is especially magical at sunset. Rent one from the friendly folks at **Monterey Bay Kayaks** (☎ 831-373-5357, 800-649-5357; www.montereybaykayaks.com; 693 Del Monte Ave; per day $30). Guided tours start at $50, lessons at $75.

Diving and snorkeling are supreme here, although the water is rather frigid. Rent a full get-up, including wet suit, at **Monterey Bay Dive Center** (☎ 831-656-0454; www.montereyscubadiving.com; 225 Cannery Row; snorkel/scuba per day $39/75), which also runs guided tours (from $60) and PADI certification courses ($325).

Fisherman's Wharf is the launch pad for whale-watching trips year-round. We recommend **Monterey Bay Whale Watch** (☎ 831-375-4658; http://gowhales.com; adult $32-43, child 3-12 $21-33, reservations required), whose guides are trained marine biologists.

For an affordable taste of the peninsula's world-famous golf, tee up at the public **Pacific Grove Golf Links** (☎ 831-648-5777; www.ci.pacific-grove.ca.us; 77 Asilomar Blvd; $20-40), but even here you need to reserve at least one week ahead.

Festivals & Events

AT&T Pebble Beach National Pro-Am golf tournament (www.attpbgolf.com) February

Monterey Wine Festival (www.montereywine.com) June

Monterey Jazz Festival (www.montereyjazzfestival.org) September

Sleeping

Monterey's room rates fluctuate wildly by season and soar sky-high during special events.

HI Monterey Hostel (☎ 831-649-0375; www.montereyhostel.org; 778 Hawthorne St; dm $22-28; P ☐) Only four blocks from Cannery Row, this simple, clean hostel is just the ticket for backpackers. Reservations strongly recommended.

Monterey Hotel (☎ 831-375-3184, 800-727-0960; www.montereyhotel.com; 406 Alvarado St; r incl breakfast $110-150, ste $200-300; P wi-fi) Right on happening Alvarado, this 1904 edifice is grand in a traditional manner with reproduction Victorian furniture but no elevator. Rooms in back are quieter but probably not if a planned expansion gets under way. Check ahead. Parking is $15.

Old Monterey Inn (☎ 831-375-8284, 800-350-2344; www.oldmontereyinn.com; 500 Martin St; r $240-480; P ✗) This B&B is as welcoming as a friend's home; a very rich friend with good taste, that is. All rooms are classily decorated in subdued English-country style and have

WILD THINGS

Now this is service! After a good night's sleep in your breezy safari tent and surrounded by the nocturnal growling of lions, tigers and other jungly things, your breakfast is delivered by an elephant named Ruby. Salinas meets Serengeti at **Vision Quest Safari** (☎ 831-455-1901, 800-228-7382; www.wildthingsinc.com; 400 River Rd, Salinas; r $195-225), a unique B&B attached to a facility that trains rescued and retired wild animals to become 'stars' in film and TV. Even if you're not staying, you can meet Ed the hyena, Joseph the lion and dozens of other critters on guided one-hour tours held daily at 1pm (adult/child $10/8, additional tour 3pm June to August).

wood-burning fireplaces. Meet fellow guests over wine and cheese in the late afternoon.

Skip the frills and save a bunch at the chain and indie motels along Munras Ave in downtown Monterey and N Fremont St, east of Hwy 1. Two consistently pleasant options are the **Cypress Gardens Inn** (☎ 831-373-2761, 877-922-1150; www.cypressgardensinn.com; 1150 Munras Ave; r $50-160; P ☻ ☑) and the diver-friendly **Lone Oak Lodge** (☎ 831-372-4924, 800-283-5663; www.lone oaklodge.com; 2221 N Fremont; r $55-110; P), which even has a spa and sauna.

Eating

Montrio (☎ 831-648-8880; 414 Calle Principal; tapas $5-8, mains $9-25; ☺ 4:30pm-10pm, 4:30pm-11pm Fri & Sat) It's a five-alarm crowd at this hip and artsy former firehouse with an open kitchen where busy chefs give organic and market-fresh products a creative, international spin. It's fun, but noise can be an issue.

Old Monterey Cafe (☎ 831-646-1021; 489 Alvarado St; meals $6-12; ☺ 7am-2:30pm) Homey and inexpensive, this eatery usually bulges with locals fortifying themselves on plate-warping breakfast, salads and sandwiches.

Monterey's Fish House (☎ 831-373-4647; 2114 Del Monte Ave; mains $9-20; ☺ 11:30am-2:30pm & 5-9:30pm) Here it is. You found it. The perfect, family-owned seafood restaurant where the fish is dock-fresh, every preparation divine and the bill affordable! Ignore the menu and wait for the specials, though the crab cakes and crab ravioli deserve some sort of prize. Reservations essential.

Passionfish (☎ 831-655-3311; 701 Lighthouse Ave, Pacific Grove; mains $14-20; ☺ 5-9:30pm Sun-Thu, 5-10:30pm Fri & Sat) The name says it all, so don't come to this classy and intimate dining shrine looking for steak and ribs.

Getting Around

Monterey-Salinas Transit (MST; ☎ 831-899-2555; www.mst.org; tickets from $2, day pass $4.50) oper-

ates buses around the peninsula to Carmel and Pacific Grove, north to Salinas and Watsonville, and south to Big Sur. The Monterey Transit Plaza is at the south end of Alvarado St.

From June to August, free trolleys cruise between downtown and Cannery Row from 10am to 7pm.

SANTA CRUZ

SoCal beach culture meets North California (NoCal) counterculture in Santa Cruz (SC), where it is such a party town all the time that, you wonder how the University of California Santa Cruz students ever actually study. The 13,000-strong student population makes SC way more youthful, hip and lefty-political than touristy Monterey. If you get sick of being a beach bum, head to the redwoods – state parks make up more than one-sixth of the county.

While some locals worry that SC's weirdness quotient is dropping, judging by attendance at Wednesday's **Farmers Market** (☎ 831-454-0566; www.santacruzfarmersmarket.org; Cedar & Lincoln Sts; ☺ 2:30-6:30pm), it's OK, dude.

Orientation & Information

Pacific Ave, the main drag, is a little mall-ish but also has some fun eateries and boutiques. For the beach and honky-tonk Boardwalk, head south on parallel Front St and turn left on Beach St. The on-the-ball **visitor center** (☎ 831-425-1234, 800-833-3494; www.santacruz.org; 1211 Ocean St; ☺ 9am-5pm Mon-Fri, 10am-4pm Sat, 11am-3pm Sun) has accommodations availability; book online through the website.

Bookshop Santa Cruz (☎ 831-423-0900; 1520 Pacific Ave; ☺ 9am-10pm Sun-Thu, until 11pm Fri & Sat) is as busy on a Friday night as any bar, as is **Logos Books & Records** (☎ 831-427-5100; 1117 Pacific Ave; ☺ 10am-10pm Sun-Thu, until 11pm Fri & Sat).

Sights

There's free admission to the supercool, vintage 1906 **Boardwalk** (☎ 831-426-7433; www .beachboardwalk.com; 400 Beach St; rides $2-5, all-day ticket $28; ☼ daily mid-Apr–mid-Nov, Sat & Sun mid-Nov–mid-Apr). Alternate between the beach and the oldest beachfront amusement park on the West Coast, with a 1923 Giant Dipper coaster and a 1911 Looff carousel; hours vary weekly.

Definitely check out the tiny **Surfing Museum** (☎ 831-420-6289; www.santacruzsurfingmuseum .org; 1305 E Cliff Dr; admission free, suggested donation $1; ☼ noon-4pm Thu-Mon), in the old Mark Abbott Memorial Lighthouse, which has vintage redwood boards and is packed with surfing paraphernalia and memorabilia.

Past the huge cement gray whale is the worthwhile **Santa Cruz Museum of Natural History** (☎ 831-420-6289; www.santacruzmuseums.org; 1305 E Cliff Dr; admission $2.50; ☼ 10am-5pm Tue-Sun) on the east side of the San Lorenzo River. Inside, the natural history collection includes a touch-friendly tidepool explaining the many critters living along the shore right across the street.

Big Basin Redwoods State Park (☎ 831-338-8860; www.bigbasin.org; per car $6; ☼ 6am-10pm), 23 miles north of Santa Cruz via Hwys 9 and 236, is where California's conservation movement all started. It's got 20,000 acres of redwood forest and 80 miles of trails, one of which drops to the Pacific.

A funky old-fashioned tourist trap, the **Mystery Spot** (☎ 831-423-8897; www.mysteryspot.com; off Branciforte Dr; admission $5; ☼ 9am-5pm, until 7pm in summer) has hardly changed from the day it opened in the 1940s. On the sloping hillside, compasses seem to point in crazy directions, mysterious forces push you around and buildings lean at silly angles. All this nonsensical fun is located 3 miles north of town. Don't forget your bumper sticker.

Finally, meditate on local weirdness at the oriental-style **Tea House Spa** (☎ 831-426-9700; www.teahousespa.com; 112 Elm St; private hot tub r per person per hr $10-15; ☼ 11am-midnight).

Activities

Gorgeous W Cliff Dr is fun for hiking and biking, especially at sunset. Check Beach St for bike-rental shops. **Kayak Connection** (☎ 831-479-1121; 413 Lake Ave; kayak per 4hr $35) has kayak rentals.

SURFING

Recommended beginner breaks are Cowell's – next to famous, experts-only Steamer Lane – and 38th Avenue, which is near several popular intermediate breaks, like 26th Avenue and the Hook.

If you're dying to bleach your hair blond and join the wave-skimmers, the **Richard Schmidt Surf School** (☎ 831-423-0928; www.richard schmidt.com; 236 San Jose Ave; per 2hr lesson $80) can get you out there, all equipment included.

For stellar rentals from in-the-know staff, head to nearby Capitola. Women-owned **Paradise Surf Shop** (☎ 831-462-3880; www.paradisesurf .com; 3961 Portola Dr; boards $20) has board rentals and lessons ($100). Dudes can get suited up at **O'Neill Surf Shop** (☎ 831-475-4151; www.oneill.com; 1115 41st Ave; boards $20, wet suits $10).

Sleeping & Eating

Hotel prices creep up in summer. For midrange motels and chains, try Riverside Ave and Ocean St.

Santa Cruz Hostel (☎ 831-423-8304; www.hi -santacruz.org; 321 Main St; dm/d $23-55) Budget overnighters dig this cute hostel at the Carmelita Cottages. In a pretty garden setting, it's just two blocks from the beach and five from downtown. One bummer: the 11pm curfew. Make reservations.

Camping (☎ 800-444-7275; campsites $25) Pitch a tent among the redwoods in nearby Henry Cowell and Big Basin State Parks, north of town off Hwy 9, or at New Brighton State Beach, about 4 miles south of Santa Cruz near Capitola. Reservations are advised. Big Basin also has excellent, simple tent cabins (☎ 831-338-4745, 800-874-8368; www.big-basintentcabins.com; cabin $50), if you didn't bring gear.

Brookdale Lodge (☎ 831-338-6433; www.brookdale lodge.com; 11570 Hwy 9; r midweek/weekend from $79/99; P ☼ wi-fi) In the mountains, 14 miles north, this is an escape from the crazy boardwalk scene. Fantastic for families (huge pool); rooms are plain but tidy. Its restaurant sits by a burbling stream.

Sea & Sand Inn (☎ 831-427-3400; www.santacruzmotels .com; 201 W Cliff Dr; r $99-199; P wi-fi) With insane views of ocean and boardwalk (from every room) this is a quiet motel on a cliff. Some upstairs rooms have fireplaces and patio hot tubs.

Saturn Cafe (☎ 831-429-8505; 145 Laurel St at Pacific Ave; mains $6-9; ☼ 11:30am-3am) A Santa Cruz classic, the decor of the late-night Saturn Cafe is

CALIFORNIA

WHAT THE...?

Some locals swear Bigfoot lives in the Santa Cruz Mountains, and the **Bigfoot Discovery Museum** (☎ 831-335-4478; www.bigfootdis coveryproject.org; 5497 Hwy 9, Felton; ⏲ 11-6pm, closed Tue) has gathered the facts and the *National Enquirer* covers to prove it. Give him 20 minutes, and Mike Rugg will make you a believer.

---

an evolving pop-culture freak show, while the menu could pass for a greasy-spoon diner if it wasn't entirely vegetarian and vegan.

Attic (☎ 831-460-1800; www.theatticsantacruz.com; 931 Pacific Ave; mains $8-11; ⏲ 10am-9pm) A self-described 'art lounge' with healthy eats, an arm-long list of teas and various artful happenings.

Downtown Santa Cruz, especially Pacific Ave and Front St, is chockablock with eateries of all stripes.

Entertainment

Red Bar (☎ 831-425-1913; www.redsantacruz.com; 200 Locust St) A young, funky dive with a swankier bar and restaurant upstairs (observe hipsters breakdancing between the velvet couches).

Ask around or check *Metro Santa Cruz* for schedules. **Kuumbwa Jazz Center** (☎ 831-427-2227; www.kuumbwajazz.org; 320 Cedar St) books big-name big-band sounds, while **Catalyst** (☎ 831-423-1336; www.catalystclub.com; 1011 Pacific Ave) is a huge club that often hosts rock concerts. **Club Dakota** (☎ 831-454-9030; www.clubdakota.net; 1209 Pacific Ave) is the hip spot for gay and lesbian dancing, DJs, and events.

Getting There & Away

Santa Cruz Metropolitan Transit (☎ 831-425-8600; www.scmtd.com) operates from the **Santa Cruz Metro Transit Center** (920 Pacific Ave; ticket/day pass $1.50/4.50) and serves the greater Santa Cruz region. The Hwy 17 Express ($4) connects to the train station in San Jose. At the Transit Center, **Greyhound** (☎ 831-423-1800) runs daily buses to/from San Francisco ($13) and Los Angeles ($44).

SANTA CRUZ TO SAN FRANCISCO

Far more scenic than either freeway is narrow, coastal Hwy 1, along which beaches are strung like pearls. North of Montara State Beach, unsigned **Gray Whale Cove State Beach** is notable as a clothing-optional strand.

Just south, the **HI Point Montara Lighthouse Hostel** (Map p952; ☎ 650-728-7177; dm from $20, r from $55), on Hwy 1 at 16th St, is a scuffed, clean and popular hostel with a private beach. Follow signs to **Moss Beach Distillery** (☎ 650-728-5595; 140 Beach Way; sandwiches & mains $12-16; ⏲ noon-8pm), a historic spot with good fish-and-chips and an ocean-view deck that's da bomb at sunset.

Quiet **Half Moon Bay** is rimmed by a long, attractive state beach ($6 day-use), and its Pillar Point Harbor has several good restaurants and a brewpub.

Ten miles south and a mile east on Hwy 84, the friendly **San Gregorio General Store** (☎ 650-726-0565; Hwy 84 & Stage Rd; ⏲ 9am-7pm) has cowboy hats, crockery, and even a full bar, but provisions are limited to chips and soda. Check out live-music weekends.

Five miles south, tiny **Pescadero** is home to the locally renowned **Duarte's Tavern** (☎ 650-879-0464; www.duartestavern.com; 202 Stage Rd; lunch $6-11; ⏲ 7am-9pm), where creamy artichoke soup and olallieberry pie are crowd-pleasers. The freshest authentic tacos and hibiscus sodas are ready to go at the tasty, popular **Taqueria y Mercado de Amigos** (☎ 650-879-0232; 1999 Pescadero Creek Rd; ⏲ 9:30am-10pm), an unassuming gas station minimart.

Situated another 5 miles south, beds at **HI Pigeon Point Lighthouse Hostel** (Map p952; ☎ 650-879-0633; dm from $23, r from $55) are popular yet well managed. It's a quiet, windswept coastal perch.

Año Nuevo State Reserve (☎ 650-879-0227; day-use $6; ⏲ 8am-dusk, closed Dec 1-14), 3 miles south of Costanoa, is home base to hundreds of elephant seals that took over abandoned Año Neuvo Island; you can view them from a distance December to March. Call ahead to reserve space on one of the popular 2½-hour, 3-mile guided **walking tours** (☎ reservations 800-444-4445; per person $5).

SAN FRANCISCO & THE BAY AREA

SAN FRANCISCO

Somewhere between waking and sleeping, there's a costumed pug parade already in progress past candy-colored Victorian houses, a street-corner prophet reciting beat poetry through a megaphone, and skateboarders grinding to an awed halt to see an orange bridge poking through a blanket of fog. This dreamscape is an actual city called San Francisco, where East meets West and fact meets fiction.

If you've ever wondered where the envelope goes when it's pushed, here's your answer. Psychedelic drugs, newfangled technology, gay liberation, green ventures, free speech, and culinary experimentation all became mainstream long ago in San Francisco. Not afraid to go for broke, the city has lost fortunes but never its cheeky spirit in gold rush panics and dot-com crashes, not to mention earthquakes and fires. Losing your shirt is now a favorite local pastime with the clothing-optional Bay to Breakers race, Pride Parade and hot Sundays on the nude north end of Baker Beach. This is no place to be shy: out here among eccentrics of every stripe, no one's going to notice a few tan lines. So long, inhibitions; hello, San Francisco.

History

Oysters and acorns would have been your main dinner options in the Mexico-run Ohlone settlement of San Francisco c 1847 – but a year and some gold nuggets later, and beer and steak were the order of the day. By 1849, gold found in the nearby Sierra Nevada foothills had turned a waterfront village of 800 into a port city of 100,000 prospectors, card sharks, con men, prostitutes and honest folk trying to make an honest living – good luck telling which was which. That friendly bartender might drug your drink, and you'd wake up a mile from shore, shanghaied into service on some ship bound for Argentina. (No wonder San Franciscans still prefer their bartenders surly.)

By 1850, California had been nabbed from Mexico and fast-tracked for US statehood, presenting San Francisco with the problem of introducing public order to 200 saloons and an untold number of brothels and gambling dens. Panic struck when Australia glutted the market with gold in 1854, and ire turned irrationally on the city's Chinese community, who from 1877 to 1945 were restricted to living and working in Chinatown by anti-Chinese laws and race riots. The main way out of debt was dangerous work building railroads for the city's robber barons, who used dynamite

and lumber to carve out commerce and entertainment empires beyond the waterfront fleshpots.

But the city's lofty ambitions and 20-plus theaters came crashing down in 1906, when earthquake and fire left 3000 dead, 100,000 homeless and much of the city reduced to rubble. Theater troupes and opera divas performed for free amid smoldering ruins, reviving a performing arts tradition that continues to this day. Ambitious public works projects continued through the 1930s, when Diego Rivera, Frida Kahlo and federally funded muralists began the tradition of leftist politics in paint visible in 250-plus Mission murals.

World War II brought seismic shifts to San Francisco's community, as women and African Americans working in San Francisco shipyards created a new economic boom, and President Franklin Delano Roosevelt's Executive Order 9066 mandated the internment of the city's historic Japanese American community. A 40-year court battle ensued, ending in an unprecedented apology from the US government. San Francisco became a testing ground for civil rights and free speech, with beat poet Lawrence Ferlinghetti and City Lights Bookstore winning a landmark 1957 ruling against book banning with the publication of Allen Ginsberg's splendid, incendiary *Howl*.

The Central Intelligence Agency (CIA) hoped an experimental drug called LSD might turn San Francisco test subject Ken Kesey into the ultimate fighting machine, but instead the author of *One Flew Over the Cuckoo's Nest* served it up in Kool-Aid and kicked off the psychedelic '60s. The Summer of Love brought free food, love and music to the Haight; an out and proud gay community to the Castro; and back-to-nature California cuisine to tastebuds nationwide in the '70s.

The 1980s meant bloated stock market gains and devastating losses from AIDS, but the city had rallied from recession in the early '90s to become a model for disease treatment and prevention. When other California cities systematically shut out homeless people by closing clinics and forbidding sitting on sidewalks, San Francisco absorbed homeless Vietnam veterans, runaways and addicts, and continues the work of repairing shattered lives today.

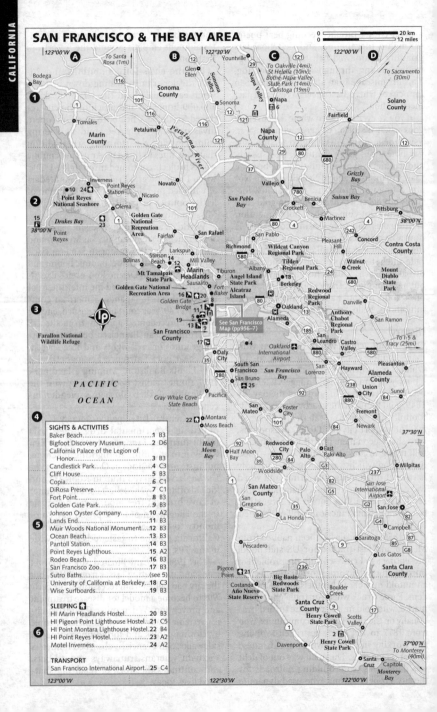

SAN FRANCISCO & THE BAY AREA

The city's arty cyberpunk crowd introduced wild ideas to Silicon Valley in the 1990s, spawning a dot-com tech bubble that popped in 2000 – after displacing many tattooed creative types with buttoned-down venture capitalists. But rents and hopes were never entirely deflated, and San Francisco's quintessential bohemians are clutching their leases for dear life as real estate prices climb, Web 2.0 takes off and a biotech boom begins. This is where you come in, just in time for San Francisco's next wild ride.

Orientation

The tongue of land that sticks out into the Pacific mocking the rest of the continental US is San Francisco. The 7x7-mile city is laid out on a staid grid, but its main street downtown is a diagonal contrarian streak called Market St. South of Market are the warehouses, galleries and rampant hedonism of South of Market (SoMa), and North of Market you'll find pinstriped Financial District (FiDi) with the wild parrots of North Beach on its shoulders.

From here on out to the ocean, the scenery gets weirder and wilder. The decor choices shift from the Tuscan faux-finish of North Beach to exuberant pagoda-topped Chinatown deco along Columbus St, which points north toward the sea lions bellyflopped on Fisherman's Wharf. To the West it's a steep slide from swanky Nob Hill and Russian Hill through the shopping and entertainment gauntlet that is Union Square, all the way downhill to seedy Tenderloin back alleys.

Alongside the squalor of the 'Loin are the grandiose ambitions of Civic Center and the east/west dividing line of Van Ness Ave. Follow Van Ness south until you see taco trucks and graffiti art, and you'll know you've arrived in the funky Mission. Further west is witty, pretty and gay Castro, and north of the Castro the freak flags fly high in the hippie Haight. Keep heading north and you'll rub shoulders with old money in Pacific Heights and wonder how everyone suddenly got so blonde in the Marina. Westward, ho: the Richmond and Sunset districts flank Golden Gate Park, where the city gets back to nature.

Keep your city smarts and wits about you, especially at night in the Tenderloin, SoMa and the Mission. Expect to be asked for spare change often, but don't feel obliged – donations stretch further at nonprofit Haight Ashbury Food Program (p961).

From San Francisco International Airport, take Hwy 101 north. See p971.

Information

BOOKSTORES

A Different Light Bookstore (Map pp956-7; ☎ 415-431-0891; www.adlbooks.com; 489 Castro St; ☷ 10am-11pm) The USA's largest gay bookseller: raucous readings; gay, lesbian, bisexual and transgender (GLBT) resources; and literary cruising.

Adobe Books (Map pp956-7; ☎ 415-864-3936; 3166 16th St ☷ 11am-10pm Mon-Thu & Sun, 11am-11pm Fri & Sat) Every book you never knew you needed used and cheap, if you can find it in the obstacle course of sofas, cats, art books and German philosophy.

Books Inc (Map pp956-7; ☎ 415-864-6777; www .booksinc.net; 2275 Market; ☷ 9am-9pm) Travel books, mainstream titles and a local bestseller section that tells you everything you need to know about the mental state of San Francisco.

Bound Together Anarchist Book Collective (Map pp956-7; ☎ 415-431-8355; 1369 Haight St; ☷ 11:30am-7pm) All-volunteer nonprofit bookstore stocked with conspiracy theory comics, organic farming manuals and other radical notions.

City Lights Bookstore (Map pp956-7; ☎ 415-362-8193; www.citylights.com; 261 Columbus Ave; ☷ 10am-midnight) Landmark bookseller, publisher, free-speech champion. Trust excellent staff picks, browse Muckraking and Stolen Continents downstairs and find Nirvana upstairs in Poetry.

Green Apple (Map pp956-7; ☎ 415-387-2272; www.greenapplebooks.com; cnr Clement St & 6th Ave; ☷ 10am-10:30pm) Three-story mother lode of new releases, used books and remaindered titles.

Kayo Books (Map pp956-7; ☎ 415-749-0554; www.kayobooks.com; 814 Post St; ☷ 11am-6pm Wed-Sun) Pulp fiction, and proud of it: vintage noir novels, trashy romances and features an entire Bizarre Nonfiction section.

EMERGENCY & MEDICAL SERVICES

American College of Traditional Chinese Medicine (Map pp956-7; ☎ 415-282-9603; 450 Connecticut St; ☷ 8:30am-9pm Mon-Thu, 9am-5:30pm Fri & Sat) Acupuncture, herbal remedies and other traditional Chinese medical treatments.

Fire department (☎ 415-558-3200)

Pharmaca (Map pp956-7; ☎ 415-661-1216; www .pharmaca.com; 925 Cole St; ☷ 8am-8pm Mon-Fri, 9am-8pm Sat & Sun) Pharmacy plus naturopathic remedies and weekend chair massage)

SAN FRANCISCO IN...

Limber up and ditch the car: calf muscles and a bus fare are all you'll need to see SF at its best.

One day

Since the Gold Rush, great San Francisco adventures have started in **Chinatown** (p145), where you can still wander back alleys in search of hidden fortunes – in cookies, that is. Beat it to **City Lights Bookstore** (p953) to revel in Beat poetry and free speech, then walk past the **Transamerica Pyramid** (p959) to **City View** (p967Eating/Chinatown) for scrumptious dumplings. Hit **SFMOMA** (oppositeSights/SoMa) and the downtown **gallery scene** (p959), then head over to the **Asian Art Museum** (opposite) for an easy stroll across oceans. Two blocks from the wonders of ancient Korea and ultra-mod Japanese fashion is **Davies Symphony Hall** (p970) where Michael Tilson Thomas & co dish up delectable Mahler best washed down with pitchers of white sangria and Nuevo Latino cuisine at **Destino** (p968). End the night with cocktails and standup at Café du Nord (p969), film festival premieres at the **Castro Theatre** (p970) or Castro-boy-cruising at **Cafe Flore** (p968).Two days

Start your day amid the unlikely splendors of mural-covered **Balmy Alley** (p960), then window-shop up to **826 Valencia** (p960) to load up on pirate supplies and literary mags and watch icthyoid antics in the Fish Theater. By the time you walk to 16th and Valencia, you should be hungry enough to eat a horse – maybe even a burrito at **Pancho Villa** (p967). If you still can move post-burrito, hoof it up to the Haight for flashbacks at vintage clothing boutiques and follow starry-eyed hippies to the Summer of Love site: **Golden Gate Park** (p961). Head to the **MH de Young Museum** (p961) for far-out tower views and farther-out art, then bus it down to Land's End for a coastal stroll to work up your appetite for organic Cal-Moroccan feasts at **Aziza** (p969).

For Foodies

Graze your way across San Francisco, starting with the farmers market at the **Ferry Building** (p966). Then head through the gamut of local temptations indoors – sourdough baguettes, artisanal chocolate, sustainable farmed caviar, organic goat blue cheese – while keeping an eye out for tastings, demos and classes. Your crash course in dim sum awaits along Chinatown's **Stockton Street** (p959), where florescent-lit mom-and-pop shops dole out shrimp and chive dumplings, crowd-pleasing barbecue pork buns and sweet lotus-root mooncakes. From here it's a BART ride to 24th Street and Mission, where **La Taquería** (p967) provides Cal-Mex revelations in the form of classic burritos and bodegas revive tired palates with fragrant corn tortillas and jalapeño-spiked salsa. Cross town to shop Clement Street's restaurant supply stores for fearsome cleavers and adorable *amuse-bouche* plates, and scour **Green Apple** (p953) for remaindered California cuisine cookbooks. Then hit **Jardinière** (p967) for a mood-enhancing and quite possibly libido-stimulating meal by chef Traci des Jardins, James Beard's 2007 Best West Coast Chef.

Police, fire & ambulance (☎ 311)
San Francisco General Hospital (off Map pp956-7; ☎ 415-206-8000, emergency room 415-206-8111; 1001 Potrero Ave)
SF Rape Treatment Center (☎ 415-206-3222)
Walgreens (Map pp956-7; ☎ 415-861-6276; 498 Castro at 18th; ☷ 24hr) Pharmacy and over-the-counter meds; dozens of locations citywide.

INTERNET ACCESS

More than 370 free wi-fi hot spots citywide: connect for free in Union Sq, most cafés, hotel lobbies or the Metreon (p958). Walgreens (above) can burn digital photos onto a CD for $2.99.

Apple Store (Map pp956-7; ☎ 415-392-0202; 1 Stockton St; free wi-fi access & internet terminal usage; ☷ 10am-9pm Mon-Sat, 11am-6pm Sun)

INTERNET RESOURCES

Chowhound (www.chowhound.com/boards/1) Bossy, informed foodies explain exactly where to eat what in SF.
Craigslist (http://sfbay.craigslist.org) Jobs, dates, free junk, tango lessons, Buddhist babysitters, you name it.
SF Station (www.sfstation.com) Local picks for SF events: music, lectures, openings, galas, good times.
Yelp (www.yelp.com) Locals trade verbal fisticuffs over SF's best shopping, bars, spas and restaurants.

LAUNDRY

Bernal Bubbles (off Map pp956-7; ☎ 415-821-9530; www.bernalbubbles.com; 397 Cortland near Bocana St; ⏲ 7am-10pm) Free wi-fi, coin laundry, wash and fold service, video games, bulletin board for stray socks, and free lecture series the first Saturday of every month at 10pm.

Brain Wash (Map pp956-7; ☎ 415-255-4866; www .brainwash.com; 1122 Folsom; ⏲ 7am-11pm) Come with laundry, stay for breakfast all day, cheap beer, live entertainment, pinball, free wi-fi and internet terminals ($3 per 20 minutes).

MEDIA

KALW 91.7 FM Local National Public Radio (NPR) affiliate.

KPFA 94.1 FM Alternative news and music.

KPOO 89.5 FM Community radio with jazz, R & B, blues and reggae.

KQED 88.5 FM Local NPR affiliate.

San Francisco Bay Guardian (www.sfbg.com) Free weekly; alternative news and entertainment listings.

San Francisco Chronicle (www.sfgate.com) Main daily newspaper; news, entertainment and event listings on website (no registration required).

SF Weekly (www.sfweekly.com) Free weekly; local gossip and entertainment.

MONEY

Bank of America (Map pp956-7; ☎ 415-262-4760; www.bankamerica.com; downstairs, 1 Powell St; ⏲ 9am-6pm Mon-Fri, 9am-2pm Sat)

POST

Rincon Center post office (Map pp956-7; ☎ 800-275-8777; www.usps.com; 180 Steuart; ⏲ 8am-6pm Mon-Fri, 8am-2pm Sat)

TOURIST INFORMATION

San Francisco's Visitor Information Center (Map pp956-7; ☎ 415-391-2000; www.onlyinsanfrancisco.com; lower level, Hallidie Plaza, cnr Market & Powell Sts; ⏲ 9am-5pm Mon-Fri, 9am-3pm Sat & Sun, closed Sun Nov-Apr)

Sights

Let San Francisco's 43 hills and more than 80 arts venues stretch your legs and imagination, and take in some (literally) breathtaking views. When your knees go weak with the workout and/or sheer romance of it all, hop a bus, tram or cable car.

UNION SQUARE

The paved square is nothing special, but look around: this is front-row seating for the non-stop drama of bejeweled theater-goers dodging clanging cable cars, fly girls camped out

overnight for limited-edition sneakers and business travelers heading into the Tenderloin for entertainment too scandalous to include on expense reports. The action begins with shoppers clustered around the Powell St **cable-car turnaround**, gets dramatic along the Geary St **Theater District**, and switches on the red lights south of Geary.

CIVIC CENTER

Skateboarders, world-class violinists and career protesters hop off the bus at Civic Center, where lofty ambitions hit the ground running. The beaux arts **City Hall** (Map pp956-7; ☎ docent tours 415-554-6032; 400 Van Ness Ave; ⏲ 8am-8pm Mon-Fri, noon-4pm Sat) rose from the ashes of the 1906 earthquake to house the city's signature mixture of graft, corruption and radical politics under a splendid rotunda. The view looking out to the Pacific and beyond is even more sublime at the **Asian Art Museum** (Map pp956-7; ☎ 415-581-3500; www.asianart.org; 200 Larkin St; adult/child 13-17 $12/7; ⏲ 10am-5pm Tue, Wed, Fri-Sun, until 9pm Thu), where you can cover the territory from racy ancient Persian miniatures to cutting-edge Japanese fashion in an hour. Moving along next door you can check out an assortment of books, lectures and 6th floor historical exhibits, as well artist Ann Chamberlain's card catalog wallpaper, at San Francisco's **Main Library** (Map pp956-7; ☎ 415-557-4400; http://sfpl.lib.ca.us; cnr Larkin & Grove Sts; ⏲ noon-5pm Sun, 10am-6pm Mon, 9am-8pm Tue-Thu, 10am-6pm Fri & Sat).

Classical music fans need no introduction to **War Memorial Opera House** (p970), home of the city's opera and dance scene, and **Davies Symphony Hall** (p970), where conductor Michael Tilson Thomas' baton prods Beethoven to new heights and whips Berlioz into shape.

The symphony crowd chows down and spiffs up a couple blocks away in Hayes Valley. Beyond the local designers and brasseries is a Buddhist home away from home: San Francisco's landmark **Zen Center** (Map pp956-7; ☎ 415-863-3136; http://sfzc.org; 300 Page St; ⏲ 9:30am-12:30pm & 1:30-4pm Mon-Fri, 9am-noon Sat), spiritual retreat for the largest Buddhist community outside Asia.

SOMA

Don't let the high rises and warehouses fool you: SoMa is packed with outrageous art venues, adventurous dining and anything-goes after-hours clubs. Check out original

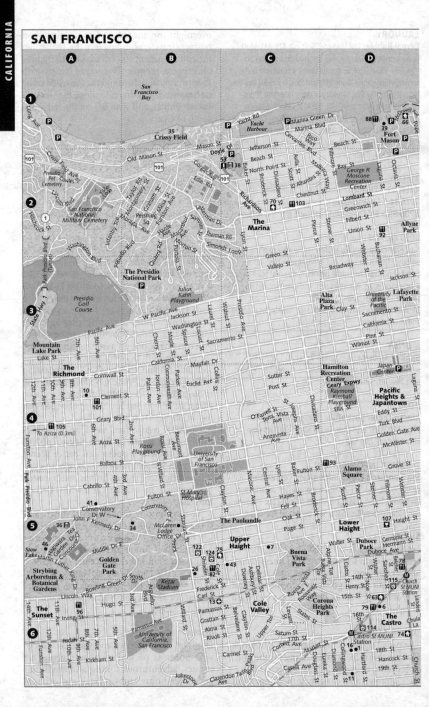

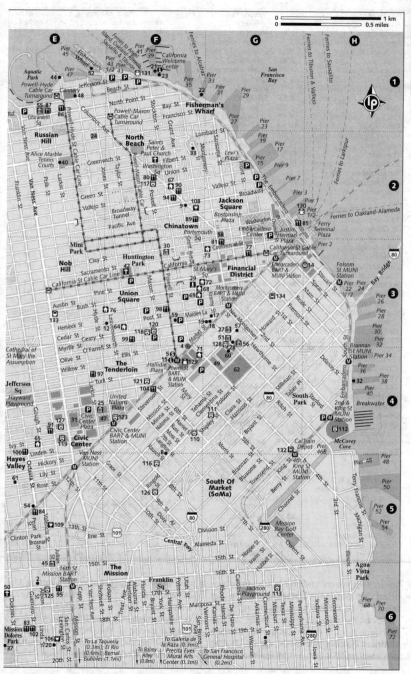

Spiderman covers and too-hot-to-print po-litical cartoons at the **Cartoon Art Museum** (Map pp956-7; ☎ 415-227-8666; www.cartoonart.org; 655 Mission St; adult/child 6-12 $6/2; ☯ 11am-5pm Tue-Sun). On this same block is the always moving **Museum of African Diaspora** (Map pp956-7; ☎ 415-358-7200; www.moadsf.org; 685 Mission; ☯ 10am-6pm Mon & Wed-Sat,

noon-5pm Sun), tracing connections among Afri-can communities through art, storytelling and technology. Hit the high-tech video arcade at the **Metreon** (Map pp956-7; ☎ 415-369-6000; www .portal1arcade.com; 101 4th St, 2nd fl; ☯ 10am-10pm Sun-Thu, 10am-11pm Fri & Sat). Ready for an art attack? See the boxed text, opposite.

THE FINANCIAL DISTRICT

Back in its Barbary Coast heyday, loose change would buy you time with loose women in this neighborhood – now you'd be lucky to see a loose tie during happy hour. But the area still has redeeming quirks: a redwood grove has taken root in the remains of old whaling ships below the funky **Transamerica Pyramid** (Map pp956-7; 600 Montgomery St), and colorful flocks of eccentric art collectors descend from hilltop mansions for First Thursday gallery openings at **14, 49 and 77 Geary** (Map pp956-7; www.sfada .com; San Francisco Art Dealers Association; most galleries 10:30am-5:30pm Tue-Fri, 11am-5pm Sat). Hedonism is still alive and well at the **Ferry Building** (p966), where foodies happily miss their ferries slurping local oysters and bubbly.

CHINATOWN

More than pagoda rooftops and deco dragon street lamps, it's astounding resilience that defines these 22 blocks and 40 alleyways. Since the 1840s, this community has survived riots, discrimination, fires, bootlegging gangsters and politicians' attempts to relocate it down the coast – the amazing-but-true story unfolds before your eyes at the landmark **Chinese Historical Society of America Museum** (Map pp956-7; ☎ 415-391-1188; www.chsa .org; 965 Clay St; adult/child 6-17 $3/1; noon-5pm Tue-Fri, until 4pm Sat & Sun).

In the 1930s, Chinatown merchants rallied to oust the back-alley brothels and opium dens, and gave **Grant Avenue** its signature Chinatown deco look. One block uphill, **Stockton Street** is lined with dim sum dives, vegetable sellers and apothecaries with walls of wooden drawers. But since you'll never really know Chinatown until you roam its alleys, take our Walking Tour (p962) or reserve your spot on a Chinatown Alleyways Tour (p964).

NORTH BEACH

Parrots and poetry make the air of North Beach seem rarified – or maybe that's just the aroma of espresso brewing and pizza baking. beat writers Jack Kerouac, Allen Ginsberg and Lawrence Ferlinghetti made this Italian neighborhood the proving ground for free spirits and free speech in the 1950s, and the escaped parrots who've flocked here lately make it an unlikely urban jungle. But some things stay the same: in cafés and pizzerias lining Columbus, you'll still hear Italian spoken.

For a 360-degree view of the neighborhood and superb 1930s murals, head up the **Filbert Street steps** and brave the occasional parrot's insult to reach **Coit Tower** (Map pp956-7; ☎ 415-362-0808; admission free, elevator rides adult $3.75; 10am-6:30pm).

SAN FRANCISCO ART ATTACK

Think you can keep up with San Francisco's creative masterminds? Get mind-boggled, bug-eyed and slack-jawed with this mini–walking tour:

Start picturing the world differently at **SFCamerawork** (Map pp956-7; ☎ 415-512-2020; www .sfcamerawork.org; 657 Mission St, 2nd fl; 11-6pm Tue-Sat)

Next, get your art while it's hot and controversial at **Catharine Clark Gallery** (Map pp956-7; ☎ 415-399-1439; www.cclarkgallery.com; 657 Mission St, ground fl; 10:30am-5:30pm Tue-Fri, 11am-5:30pm Sat).

Follow the steady stream of hipsters into **Yerba Buena Center for the Arts** (Map pp956-7; ☎ 415-978-2787; www.ybca.org; 701 Mission St; art gallery admission $6; noon-5pm Tue-Sun, until 8pm Thu-Sat) for avant-garde art year-round, openings that pack in thousands of art freaks and free events in the Yerba Buena Gardens May to October.

Dash over to Yerba Buena Lane for the celebration of busy hands, bright ideas and simple materials already in progress at the **Museum of Craft & Folk Arts** (Map pp956-7; ☎ 415-227-4888; www.mocfa.org; 51 Yerba Buena Lane; adult/child under 18 $5/free; 11am-6pm Tue-Fri, 11am-5pm Sat & Sun).

Cross the street to **San Francisco Museum of Modern Art** (SFMOMA; Map pp956-7; ☎ 415-357-4000; www.sfmoma.org; 151 3rd St; adult/child under 12 $10/free; 11am-6pm Fri-Tue, until 9pm Thu). Inside Mario Botta's light-washed treasure box the history of photography is illuminated, and you can see the future coming – SFMOMA was first to show breakthrough new media artists Matthew Barney, Kiki Smith, Olafur Eliasson and Bill Viola.

RUSSIAN HILL & NOB HILL

Gardeners, fitness freaks and suckers for sunsets all brave the dizzying climbs west of North Beach up Russian and Nob Hills. Drivers test their mettle on the crooked 1000 block of **Lombard Street** (Map pp956–7), but many roll past without realizing they're missing one of the city's best sunset vistas at **George Sterling Park** (Map pp956–7) and a splendid Diego Rivera mural at the nearby **Art Institute** (☎ 415-771-7020; 800 Chestnut St; ☻ 8am-9pm).

Stairways lead urban hikers past hidden cottages and secret gardens, but wheezers and geezers may prefer to hop the cable car uphill to **Grace Cathedral** (Map pp956–7; ☎ 415-749-6300; www.gracecathedral.com; 1100 California St; ☻ 7am-6pm Mon-Fri, 8am-6pm Sat, 7am-7pm Sun; services with choir at 8:15 & 11am). The quiet awe of the place settles in as you contemplate Keith Haring's triptych for the AIDS Interfaith Memorial Chapel and the stained-glass tributes to Human Endeavors, including a window showing Albert Einstein in a halo of atomic particles. No contemplation of life's meaning would be complete without a meander through the indoor or outdoor labyrinths.

FISHERMAN'S WHARF

With the notable exception of sea lions belching up their fresh fish dinners over at **Pier 39** (Map pp956–7; ☎ 415-981-7437; www.pier39.com), most of the piers are packed with landlubbers attempting to digest sourdough bread bowls of gloppy clam chowder (don't bother; it can't be done). For a real taste of the city's seafaring past, head to the **San Francisco Maritime National Historical Park** (Map pp956–7; ☎ 415-561-7100; Beach St, the Cannery; ☻ 9:30am-5pm) for a peek at the 19th-century ships moored at **Hyde Street Pier** (boarding pass $5, national park passes accepted) and scale models boats and unbreakable knots at the **museum** (900 Beach St, Aquatic Park; admission free; ☻ 10am-5pm). Nearby at Pier 45 you can guillotine a man for a quarter at the **Musée Mécanique** (Map pp956–7; ☎ 415-346-2000; admission free; ☻ 10am-7pm), where such 19th-century arcade games as the macabre French Execution and eerily accurate glass-eyed Fortune Teller compete for your spare change with original Space Invaders and Ms Pacman.

THE MARINA & PRESIDIO

Army sergeants would surely be scandalized by all the frolicking going on in the former army bases in the Marina and Presidio. Comedy improv, environmental nonprofits and kiddie art classes are the order of the day at **Fort Mason** (Map pp956–7; ☎ 415-441-3400; www.fortmason.org). Mad scientists and ducklings feel right at home alongside the Presidio Army Base at the weird and wonderful **Exploratorium** (Map pp956–7; ☎ 415-561-0360; www.exploratorium.edu; 3601 Lyon St; adult/child 4-12 $12/8; ☻ 10am-5pm Tue-Sun) science museum, which overlooks a duck pond and Bernard Maybeck's 1915 **Palace of Fine Arts** (Map pp956–7).

The Presidio's coastal airstrip has been stripped of asphalt and brought back to teeming life as **Crissy Field** (Map pp956–7; ☎ 415-561-7690; www.crissyfield.org), a haven for coastal birds, kite-fliers and urban beachgoers. From here, take your pick of spectacular views of Golden Gate Bridge: see it from below like Alfred Hitchcock for a thrilling case of *Vertigo* at **Fort Point** (Map p952; ☎ 415-561-4395; www.nps.gov/fopo), or see it *au naturel* on the Presidio's west side at clothing-optional **Baker Beach** (Map p952; ☻ sunrise-sunset).

THE MISSION

Art trawls, bar crawls, political protests, and authenticity trips inevitably lead to the Mission. The Mission would have you believe every underground movement started here first, and that's not entirely untrue. Before SF graffiti art became an international hit through such galleries as **Jack Hanley** (Map pp956–7; ☎ 415-522-1623; www.jackhanley.com; 395 Valencia St; ☻ 11am-6pm Tue-Sat), there were 1970s political murals lining Mission side-streets and **Balmy Alley** (off Map pp956–7; off 24th St near Folsom) – for tours, see p964. Politics come with the territory: protests are still held almost every weekend at **Dolores Park**, and Chicano Pride finds new expression at **Galería de la Raza** (off Map pp956–7; ☎ 415-206-9242; www.galeriadelaraza.org; 2857 24th St; ☻ noon-6pm Wed-Sat).

Given a steady Mission diet of burritos, margaritas, coffee and California cuisine priced to move, creative types seem to thrive – hence all the local design boutiques, 'zines, bookstores and nonprofit arts venues clustered around Valencia and Mission Sts. When a Pirate Supply Store landed at **826 Valencia** (Map pp956–7; ☎ 415-642-5905; www.826valencia.com; 826 Valencia; ☻ 2:30-5:30pm Mon-Thu, 2:30-4:30pm Sat & Sun) selling eye patches and McSweeney's publications to fund writing workshops for local youth, it just seemed to make sense. Ever since the local Ohlone painted pulsating hearts behind the altar at **Mission Dolores** (Map pp956-7; ☎ 415-621-8203; cnr Dolores & 16th Sts; admission adult/child $3/$2; ☯ 9am-4pm) around 1795, the Mission has been making bizarre, beautiful visions real.

THE CASTRO

Sure, San Francisco's other neighborhoods have their fair share of gays – but here in the landmark gay Castro district they're extra-strength, like superheroes or condoms. This is one neighborhood where they don't just get mad about discrimination and half-ass drag, they get organized: hence the historic **Human Rights Campaign** (Map pp956-7; ☎ 415-431-2200; www.hrc.org; 600 Castro St) and annual **Halloween** cross-dressing extravaganza (see p964).

You'll know you're entering the Castro from downtown when you see that glorious Victorian painted aqua and glassed in on one side, so that even when people are inside the **San Francisco Lesbian, Gay, Bisexual, Transgender Community Center** (Map pp956-7; ☎ 415-865-5555; www.sfcenter.org; 1800 Market St) they can still be out and proud. Check here for open mike poetry nights, stitch-n-bitch knitting sessions, GLBT parenting groups, protests, parades and worthy causes. But you've officially arrived when you see the marquee of the **Castro Theatre** (p970), where every film begins with the rise of a mighty organ…that's right, an actual organ rises from the orchestra pit to keep the audience humming along to show tunes until the movie starts.

THE HAIGHT

This legendary neighborhood is better known as the G-spot of the Summer of Love, and certain habits seem to have stuck since the swinging '60s – only a very mysterious, very local illness could explain the suspicious number of medical marijuana clubs packed into these few blocks. Like tie-dyes, ideals have never gone out of fashion here – hence the **Anarchist Book Collective** (p953), the cooperative indie **Red Vic Movie House** (p970) and the **Haight Ashbury Food Program** (Map pp956-7; ☎ 415-566-0366; www.thefoodprogram.org; 1525 Waller St).

North of Divisadero St, the **Upper Haight** features head shops, cafés, boutiques, vintage clothes and used CDs. Across Divisadero,

Lower Haight is big on hairdressers, record stores, bars, skate shops and, um, gardening supply shops. Anywhere you go on Haight you'll find punks, artistes, aesthetes, oddballs and misfits, all fitting right into the scenery.

GOLDEN GATE PARK & AROUND

San Francisco was way ahead of its time in 1866, when the city decided to turn 1017 acres of sand dunes into the world's largest city park. This was a green scheme so ambitious and unprecedented, that it scared off Frederick Law Olmstead, the celebrated architect of New York's Central Park, and led to a fight with real estate speculators who wanted to turn Golden Gate Park into a theme-park resort. The park does have its attractions, including the carnivorous plants and outer-space orchids in the historic 1879 **Conservatory of Flowers** (Map pp956-7; ☎ 415-666-7017; www.conservatory offlowers.org; adult/child 5-11 $5/1.50; ☯ 9am-4:30pm Tue-Sun). But instead of roller rinks, hotels and a kitschy Eskimo village, park architect William Hammond Hall opted for tasteful botanical gardens, a **Japanese Tea Garden** (☎ 415-752-4227; Hagiwara Tea Garden Dr; adult/child 6-12 $3.50/1.25; ☯ 8:30am-6pm) with a bonsai grove, and boating on scenic **Stow Lake** (☎ 415-752-7869; per hr boats $13-17, surreys/bikes/in-line skates $20/8/6).

The latest addition is the sleek, sensational copper-clad **De Young Fine Arts Museum** (Map pp956-7; ☎ 415-863-3330; www.thinker.org/deyoung; adult/student over 13 $10/$6; ☯ 9:30am-5:15pm Tue-Sun), which is oxidizing green to blend into the park. The shows are as unexpected as the architecture, including theatrical retrospectives of Vivienne Westwood's fashion, Oceanic masks and Hiroshi Sugimoto's time-lapse photographs of drive-in movies.

Toward the Western edge of the park things get quixotic, with actual bison stampeding in their paddock toward dilapidated windmills. The park ends in blustery **Ocean Beach** (Map p952; ☎ 415-556-8371 ☯ sunrise-sunset), less amenable to bikini-clad clambakes than wet-suited surfers willing to take on notorious rip tides (casual swimmers beware). At the north end of Ocean Beach is the recently rebuilt and sadly soulless **Cliff House** (Map p952; ☎ 415-386-3330; www.cliffhouse .com; 1090 Point Lobos) restaurant, overlooking the splendid ruin of **Sutro Baths** (Map p952), where Victorian dandies once converged for a bracing bath and workout.

Follow the trail above Sutro Baths around **Lands End** (Map p952) for postcard-worthy views of the Marin Headlands and the Golden Gate Bridge. The trail leads to the **California Palace of the Legion of Honor** (Map p952; ☎ 415-863-3330; www.thinker.org/legion/index.asp; adult/student over 13 $10/6, Tue free; ⊙ 9:30am-5pm Tue-Sun), which mixes blockbuster exhibits of Fabergé eggs with highly unusual paintings by folk-art visionary Howard Finster.

SAN FRANCISCO BAY

Imagine looking toward the Pacific to see a squat concrete bridge striped black and caution yellow: that's what the US Navy initially had in mind for the bridge spanning the Bay. Luckily chief engineer Joseph B Strauss and architects Gertrude and Irving Murrow insisted on a soaring deco design and International Orange paint that harmonized with the natural environment, and the result is the 1937 engineering marvel and aesthetic triumph known as the **Golden Gate Bridge** (Map p952; ☎ 415-921-5858). Cars pay a $5 toll to cross from Marin to San Francisco; pedestrians and cyclists stroll the east sidewalk for free.

There is one impressive hunk of concrete in the Bay: the notorious island prison Al Capone called home, better known as **Alcatraz** (Map p952). Prison authorities boasted it was inescapable, but since importing guards and all other necessities cost the state more than putting up prisoners at the Ritz, it was closed in 1963. Native American leaders took over the island from 1969–1971 to protest US occupation of Native lands, and their standoff with the FBI is commemorated in a small museum and 'Red Power' signs near the ferry dock. Ferry tickets must be reserved in advance from **Alcatraz Cruises** (Map pp956-7; ☎ 415-981-7625 from 8am-7pm; www .alcatrazcruises.com; adult/child 5-11 day $21.75/13.75, adult $28.75/17.25; ⊙ tours depart from Pier 33 about every half-hour 9am-4pm, 6:10pm & 6:40pm). The 2½-hour visit includes a fascinating audio tour with prisoners, guards, and families recalling life on the Rock.

Activities

Rent your wheels at **Avenue Cyclery** (Map pp956-7; ☎ 415-387-3155; 756 Stanyan St) on the eastern edge of Golden Gate Park or **Blazing Saddles** (Map pp956-7; ☎ 415-202-8888; www.blazingsaddles .com; per hr/day $7/28), conveniently located on Fisherman's Wharf.

Grab a disc-golf bag at **Golden Gate Bike & Skate** (Map pp956-7; ☎ 415-668-1117; 3038 Fulton St) and head to Marx Meadow at Golden Gate Park to fling away on the free course.

To get *into* the bay – and maybe spot a sea lion – rent kayaks at **City Kayak** (Map pp956-7; ☎ 415-357-1010; www.citykayak.com; Pier 38, cnr Embarcadero & Townsend Sts; per hr $15-25) or take a 1½-hour catamaran cruise with **Adventure Cat** (Map pp956-7; ☎ 415-777-1630; www.adventurecat.com; Pier 39; adult from $25).

Hard-core surfer dudes and chicks head to **Ocean Beach** (Map p952), where cold swells rise 12ft or higher. The dudes at **Wise Surfboards** (☎ 415-750-9473; www.wisesurfboards.com; 800 Great Hwy) give you the whole scoop; they even update a surf report (☎ 415-273-1618).

For whale-watching and trips to the Farallon Islands, contact **Oceanic Society Expeditions** (Map pp956-7; ☎ 800-326-7491; www.oceanic-society.org; Fort Mason, bldg E; adult $80-85).

Walking Tour

Limber up and look sharp: you never know what you'll see just over the next hill in San Francisco. On this walk, you'll discover revolutionary plots, find hidden fortunes, meet birds that swear like sailors, shimmy up a giant fire hose and go gourmet with Gandhi.

Starting at **Chinatown's Dragon Gate** (1; Grant Ave at Bush St), head north one block past the gilded deco lamps and trinket shops of Grant St and hang a right on Pine St. On your left, **Old St Mary's Park (2)** marks the spot of a notorious brothel leveled in the 1906 fire, but now the only tricks here are performed by renegade skateboarders under the watchful eye of Beniamino Bufano's 1929 statue of revolutionary leader Sun Yat-sen. Backtrack onto Grant; you'll walk one block past Old St Mary's Church and turn left on Sacramento to find the colorfully painted, flag-festooned temple balconies of **Waverly Place (3)** on your next right. Pay your respects at **Tien Hou Temple** (4; 125 Waverly Place, 4th fl; free, but offering appreciated; ⊙ hours vary), or hang your next left onto Clay St. One block up is the **Chinese Historical Society of America Museum** (5; p959), in the majestic Chinatown YWCA built by Julia Morgan, California's first female architect and the only person William Randolph Hearst trusted to build his castle (p943).

Walk back down Clay past Stockton, and the first lane on your left is **Spofford Alley (6)**, where you'll hear the click of mah-jongg tiles, a Chinese orchestra warming up and beauticians gossiping indiscreetly over their blow-driers. Long ago you might have overheard the whisper of Sun Yat-sen and his conspirators here plotting the 1911 overthrow of China's last dynasty, or gunfire blasts during 1920s bootlegger turf wars. At Washington St, jog right and left to enter **Ross Alley (7)**,

---

WALK FACTS

Start Chinatown's Dragon Gate
Finish Ferry Building
Distance 2 miles
Duration a half-day

SAN FRANCISCO WALKING TOUR

---

once packed with brothels and more recently pimped as the picturesque setting for forgettable sequels such as *Karate Kid II* and *Indian Jones and the Temple of Doom*. At the end, you can get your fortune while it's hot, folded into warm cookies on vintage machines at **Golden Gate Fortune Cookie Factory** (**8**; 56 Ross Alley).

Head right back to Grant, and turn left; up a block and a half on your right is **Jack Kerouac Alley (9)**. The spot where many beat writers once passed out is now marked with poetry on the sidewalk and murals on the walls. At the end is **City Lights Bookstore** (**10**; p953), home of beat poetry and defender of free speech. Get some lit to read over coffee a block and a half away at **Caffe Trieste** (**11**; ☎ 415-982-2605; www.caffe trieste.com; 601 Vallejo; ☘ 6:30am-10pm, until midnight Fri & Sat), beloved since the '50s for its opera jukebox, accordion jams and ink-stained, paint-daubed regulars. Cross Columbus on Vallejo to check out the **Good Luck Parking Garage** (**12**; 735 Vallejo), where every parking spot comes with stenciled fortunes by artist Harrell Fletcher such as 'You are not a has-been.'

Back on Columbus, head north, take a right at Stockton and another right at Filbert St, and pace yourself for the climb up Telegraph Hill to **Coit Tower** (**13**; p959). The tower was built by eccentric millionaire Lillie Hitchcock Coit to honor firefighters and resemble a giant hose – not that many fire hoses have splendid murals painted inside, but hey, you can't argue with this view. Take the **Filbert Steps (14)** downhill past sculpture gardens, trees full of wild parrots and hidden cottages, onward to Sansome St. Cut through **Levi's Plaza (15)**, named for San Francisco's most famous inventor, to the Embarcadero. Turn right and from here it's just a few blocks south to the gourmet delights of the Ferry Building (p966) – enjoy your lunch on a Bayside bench out back, with the bronze statue of Gandhi peeking rather hungrily over your shoulder.

San Francisco for Children

Although these days there are more dogs than children in SF, there's still plenty for kids to do.

American Child Care (☎ 415-285-2300; www.amer icanchildcare.com; 580 California St, Suite 1600) The cost is $20 per hour plus gratuity; four-hour minimum.

Aquarium of the Bay (Map pp956-7; ☎ 415-623-5301; www.aquariumofthebay.com; Pier 39; adult/child

SAN FRANCISCO FOR CHILD PRODIGIES

Zoo too elementary for your little Einstein? Inventive young minds thrive at these SF attractions:

Exploratorium (p960) Discover scientific answers to all those crazy kid questions, and sharpen your senses in the Tactile Dome (book ahead).

Fort Mason (p960) Tai chi, theater and hands-on art classes for young talents.

Zeum Art & Technology Center (Map pp956-7; ☎ 415-777-2800; www.zeum.org; 221 4th St; adult/child 4-18 $7/5; ⏰ 11am-5pm Wed-Sun, plus Tue in summer) Technology that's too cool for school: robots, live-action video games, hands-on workshops on claymation and music videos.

$14/$7.50; ⏰ 9am-8pm daily summer, 10am-6pm Mon-Fri & 10am-7pm Sat & Sun rest of year) Glide through glass tubes underwater while sharks prowl overhead.

Fire Engine Tours (Map pp956-7; ☎ 415-333-7077; www.fireenginetours.com; Beach St at the Cannery; adult/child under 12/teen $45/30/25) Hot stuff: a 75-minute, open-air vintage fire engine ride over Golden Gate Bridge. Tours depart at 1pm Wednesday to Monday.

Golden Gate Park (p961) Kid heaven: buffaloes, a carousel, playgrounds, miniature trees, pedal boats and a beach.

Metreon (p955) Movies and video games for hyperactive kids, including virtual bowling and Dance Dance Revolution.

San Francisco Zoo (Map p952; ☎ 415-753-7080; www.sfzoo.org; cnr Sloat Blvd & 47th Ave; adult/child 3-11 $11/5; ⏰ 10am-5pm) Well-kept habitats, with a minisavannah and a cuddly Lemur Forest.

Tours

California Historical Society (Map pp956-7; ☎ 415-357-1848; www.californiahistoricalsociety.org; 678 Mission St) When eccentric urban planner Gary Holloway isn't dressing in monk's robes or rearranging his tea tin collection, he leads enlightening Historical Walkabouts through obscure San Francisco neighborhoods.

Chinatown Alleyway Tours (☎ 415-984-1478; www.chinatownalleywaytours.org; adult/child under 5/child 6-9/student $15/free/5/10) Teens who grew up here lead two-hour tours for an up-close-and-personal peek into Chinatown's past. Tours depart 11am Saturday or by appointment.

Precita Eyes Mission Mural Tours (☎ 415-285-2287; www.precitaeyes.org; for public tour, adult $10-12, child under 17 $5) Local artists lead two-hour walking tours covering more than 60 murals in a six-block radius of mural-bedecked Balmy Alley. Tours depart 11am weekdays and 1:30pm weekends.

Public Library City Guides (☎ 415-557-4266; www.sfcityguides.org; public tours free) Local historians lead tours by neighborhood and theme: Art Deco Marina, Gold Rush Downtown, Summer of Love Treasure Hunt in the Haight. See website for meeting times and locations.

Festivals & Events

Chinese New Year Parade (☎ 415-391-9680; www.chineseparade.com) Chase the 200ft dragon, lion dancers and toddler kung-fu classes through Chinatown in late January/early February.

Cherry Blossom Festival (☎ 415-563-2313; www.nccbf.org) Japantown gets flower-powerful with *taiko* drums, shrines and sunshine mid-April.

SF International Film Festival (☎ 415-561-5000; www.sffs.org) Sunglasses and paparazzi are must-have accessories at the nation's oldest film festival in late April.

Cinco de Mayo (☎ 415-256-3005; www.cincodemayosf.com) Lowriders rumble and skirts twirl to celebrate Mexican independence in Civic Center; first weekend in May.

Bay to Breakers (☎ 415-359-2800; www.baytobreakers.com; race registration $30-40) Many run costumed, others naked, some scared from Embarcadero to Ocean Beach the third Sunday in May.

Carnaval (☎ 415-826-1401; www.carnavalsf.com) Brazilian, or just faking it with a wax and a tan? Come shake your tail feathers in the Mission the last weekend of May.

SF Gay Pride Month (☎ 415-864-3733; www.sfpride.org) A day isn't enough to do SF proud: June begins with the Gay & Lesbian Film Festival, and goes out in style the last weekend with the Dyke March (☎ 415-241-8882; www.dykemarch.org) and the frisky, fun, half-million-strong Lesbian, Gay, Bisexual and Transgender Pride Parade.

SF AIDS Walk (☎ 415-615-9255; www.aidswalk.net/sanfran) Until AIDS takes a hike, you can: this pioneering 6.2-mile fundraiser benefits 43 AIDS organizations the third Sunday in July.

Folsom Street Fair (☎ 415-861-3247; www.folsomstreetfair.com) Work that leather look and enjoy public spankings for local charities the last weekend of July.

SF Shakespeare Fest (☎ 415-422-2221; www.sfshakes.org) The play's the thing in the Presidio, outdoors and free of charge on sunny September weekends.

LitQuake (www.litquake.org) Authors spill true stories and trade secrets over drinks at the legendary Lit Crawl, held the second weekend in October.

SF Jazz Festival (☎ 415-788-7353; www.sfjazz.org) Old-schoolers and hot new talents blow horns and minds in late October.

Halloween (www.halloweeninthecastro.com) Killer drag and conceptual costumes rock the Castro street party on the last Saturday of October.

Diá de los Muertos (☎ 415-821-1155; www.dayofthedeadsf.org) The dead party means a parade, sugar skulls and fabulous altars in the Mission on November 2.

Dance Along Nutcracker (☎ 415-255-1355; www .sflgfb.org/show.html) Do you tutu? Dance to the Nutcracker Suite performed by the Lesbian/Gay Freedom Band the first weekend in December.

Sleeping

San Francisco is the birthplace of the oh-so-cool boutique hotel; you can find one just about anywhere, for a price: in SF, rooms from $100 to $200 are 'midrange.' The **San Francisco Visitor Information Center** (p955), which speaks 12(!) languages, runs a **reservation line** (☎ 888-782-9673; www.sfvisitor.org) or you can book online. **Bed & Breakfast SF** (☎ 415-899-0060; www.bbsf.com) is a local B&B–apartment service. Lombard St (Hwy 101) is packed with chains and motels. The city's hotel tax is 14%.

UNION SQUARE & CIVIC CENTER

our pick Hotel des Arts (Map pp956-7; ☎ 415-956-3232; www.sfhoteldesarts.com; 447 Bush St; r without/with bath $69/100; P ☒ wi-fi) Contemporary artists have individually designed each room, and hallways are chockablock with art – it's like living in a gallery where you're the installation. Unforgettable. Parking $24.

Zen Center (Map pp956-7; ☎ 415-863-3136; www .sfzc.org; 300 Page St near Laguna; s $76-108, d $96-132; ☒) Relaxing for singles, the comfortable rooms (some with shared bath) here are simplicity itself. Zen participation is not expected, but you can join residents for the 5am prayer bell.

Hayes Valley Inn (Map pp956-7; ☎ 415-431-9131, 800-930-7999; www.hayesvalleyinn.com; 417 Gough St; s $84-105; wi-fi) The kind of modest, attractive budget stay you hope for but don't expect in SF. The resident dog and mothering staff make it feel like home. Good-sized rooms share tiny, clean bathrooms and a kitchen.

Mosser (Map pp956-7; ☎ 415-986-4400, 800-227-3804; www.themosser.com; 54 4th St; r $99-189, with shared bath $49-89; P ☒ ☐ wi-fi) Quirky contemporary small rooms; opt for the bargains with sparkling shared bath. Homemade muffins. Parking $29.

York Hotel (Map pp956-7; ☎ 415-885-6800; www .yorkhotel.com; 940 Sutter St; r $99-189; P ☐ wi-fi) Hitchcock's Vertigo was filmed here, and the York's subdued, retro-modern stylings look equally good today. Management often works a deal, and the swanky Plush Room (☎ 415-885-2800; www.empireplushroom.com) has cabaret shows nightly. Parking $25. Internet $2 per 15 minutes.

Halcyon Hotel (Map pp956-7; ☎ 415-929-8033, 800-627-2396; www.halcyonsf.com; 649 Jones St; d per night/week from $99/590; P wi-fi) These 25 crisp little efficiencies (with microwaves and wet bars) still have sweet 1912 building details. Seven-night minimum October to April. Parking costs $15.

Hotel Triton (Map pp956-7; ☎ 415-394-0500, 800-800-1299; www.hoteltriton.com; 342 Grant Ave; r $109-239; P ☐) Funky designer hotel with a cheeky sense of humor – upholstered headboards, crushed velvet spreads and blown-glass chandeliers, ecocelebrity suites and a rubber-duck mascot. Parking $33.

Orchard Garden Hotel (Map pp956-7; ☎ 415-399-9807; www.theorchardgardenhotel.com; 466 Bush St; r $179-239; wi-fi) Chic, nongranola, ecoconscious design with rooftop garden views and chilled staff.

THE FINANCIAL DISTRICT & NORTH BEACH

Pacific Tradewinds (Map pp956-7; ☎ 415-433-7970, 888-734-6783; www.sanfranciscohostel.org; 680 Sacramento St; dm $24-26; ☒ ☐ wi-fi) With unshakable bunks (no private rooms) and nautical trim, this is the city's smallest hostel, situated high above street noise. Egregiously nice, travel-savvy staff.

our pick Hotel Bohème (Map pp956-7; ☎ 415-433-9111; www.hotelboheme.com; 444 Columbus Ave; r $159-174; ☒ wi-fi) Gangster-swank decor and ceiling lights covered by Oriental paper umbrellas create a beat-era, moody atmosphere.

FISHERMAN'S WHARF & THE MARINA

HI San Francisco Fisherman's Wharf (Map pp956-7; ☎ 415-771-7277; Fort Mason Bldg 240; dm/s $28/75 P ☒ ☐ wi-fi) Superbig dorms and communal showers lack privacy, but otherwise this hostel has it all: an unmatched setting in a national park, no curfew, great social rooms and a café.

Marina Motel (Map pp956-7; ☎ 415-921-9406, 800-346-6118; www.marinamotel.com; 2576 Lombard St; r $75-129; P ☒ ☒ wi-fi) Italian-themed 1930s motor court that loves backpackers and families; a standout from the choices on Lombard St.

THE MISSION

Elements Hotel (Map pp956-7; ☎ 415-647-4100; www.elementssf.com; 2524 Mission St; dm/d $20/60; ☐ wi-fi) A new, popular cheapie with stylish bright rooms and a rooftop bar. Central to hipster neighborhood.

FIVE TASTY REASONS TO MISS THAT FERRY

When it comes to fine dining, you'll be missing the boat unless you stop and taste the treats on offer at the Ferry Building:

- Today's catch at **Hog Island Oyster Company** (☎ 415-391-7117; www.hogislandoysters.com; half-dozen $10-15; ☾ 11:30am-8pm Mon-Fri & 11am-6pm Sat-Sun; happy hour 5-7pm)

- Free-range beef burgers at **Taylor's Automatic Refresher** (☎ 866-328-3663; www.taylorsrefresher.com; burgers $7-9 ☾ 10:30am-8:30pm Mon-Sun)

- James Beard Award–winning chef Traci des Jardins' *nuevo* Mexican street eats at **Mijita** (☎ 399-0814; www.mijitasf.com; menu items under $10; ☾ 11am-7pm Mon-Wed, 11am-8pm Thu-Fri, 9am-8pm Sat, 10am-4pm Sun).

- Cal-Vietnamese sugarcane prawn at Charles Phan's family-run **Slanted Door** (☎ 415-861-8032; http://slanteddoor.com; mains $12-25; ☾ 11am-10:30pm)

- The Ferry Building weekend **farmers market** (☎ 415-291-3276; www.cuesa.org; ☾ 10am-2pm Tue, 8am-5pm Sat year-round; also 4-8pm Thu & 10am-2pm Sun in summer).

THE CASTRO

Beck's Motor Lodge (Map pp956-7; ☎ 415-621-8212, 800-227-4360; www.becksmotorlodgesf.com; 2222 Market St; r $93-135; ✗ wi-fi) The pastels are a tad overdone but it's centrally located; free parking sweetens the deal. During gay events, it can get cruisey.

Parker Guest House (Map pp956-7; ☎ 415-621-3222, 888-520-7275; www.parkerguesthouse.com; 520 Church at 17th St; r $150-199, with shared bath from $119; P ✗ 🖳 wi-fi) SF's best gay (but hetero- and parent-friendly) B&B has luxurious decor, a steam bath and gardens. Limited parking ($15); reserve ahead.

THE HAIGHT

Red Victorian (Map pp956-7; ☎ 415-864-1978; www.redvic.com; 1665 Haight St; r $129-229; ✗ wi-fi) Idiosyncratic and heartfelt, Sami Sunchild's remarkable B&B transcends every Summer of Love cliché. Each comfy room is a work of art, and shared facilities are wild. Breakfast included. The wi-fi is in the lobby.

Eating

Hope you're hungry – there's one restaurant for every 28 people in San Francisco, and every red-blooded resident has an opinion on which one you absolutely, positively, cannot miss. The city even has a monument to gourmet glory: the **Ferry Building** (Map pp956-7; ☎ 415-693-0996; www.ferrybuildingmarketplace.com) – see the boxed text, above.

UNION SQUARE & THE FINANCIAL DISTRICT

Sears Fine Foods (Map pp956-7; ☎ 415-956-9662; www.searsfinefood.com; 439 Powell St; breakfast $7-10; ☾ 6:30am-10pm) Cures hangovers with silver-dollar pancakes, golden hash browns, slabs of grilled ham and a bottomless mug of coffee.

Shalimar (Map pp956-7; ☎ 415-928-0333; 532 Jones St; mains under $10; ☾ 11:30pm-3pm & 5pm-midnight) Follow your nose to tandoori chicken straight off the skewer and naan bread still bubbling from the oven; vegetables are leaden, so don't hold back on the roasted meats.

Aqua (Map pp956-7; ☎ 415-986-1160; www.aqua-sf.com; 252 California St; lunch mains $18-30, dinner mains from $30; ☾ 11:30am-2:30pm Mon-Fri, 5:30-10:30pm Mon-Thu, plus 5:30-11pm Fri & Sat, 5:30-9:30pm Sun) Dinner here is a major investment, but the $35 three-course business lunch is a solid bet: tiny, jewel-like dishes so fresh and delicately handled you can almost taste the sun in a cherry tomato and that wild salmon's last smirk.

CIVIC CENTER

Saigon Sandwich Shop (Map pp956-7; ☎ 415-474-5698; 560 Larkin St; sandwiches $2.50; ☾ 6:30am-5pm Mon-Sat, 7am-4:30pm Sun) No wonder there's a line: Vietnamese *banh mi* (baguettes piled with roast meat, tofu or meatballs), plus pickled carrots, thin onion, chilis and cilantro – all for $2.50.

Stacks (Map pp956-7; ☎ 415-241-9011; 501 Hayes St; breakfast $8-12; ☾ 9am-5pm Tue-Sun) The decor is more Branson-Missouri-motel than Cali-chic, but the fluffy-crispy wheat-germ pancakes and stuffed crabmeat omelets add a fresh California twist on brunch.

Tu Lan (Map pp956-7; ☎ 415-626-0927; 8 6th St; menu items under $10; ☾ 11am-9:30pm Mon-Sat) Sidewalks don't get skankier than the one you'll be waiting on, but try complaining after your heap of velvety Vietnamese chicken curry or tangy tomato-onion prawns.

our pick **Jardinière** (Map pp956-7; ☎ 415-861-5555; www.jardiniere.com; 300 Grove St; mains $22-40; ☯ 5-10:30pm Sun-Wed, 5-11:30pm Thu-Sat) Iron Chef champ Traci Des Jardins has a way with organic vegetables, free-range meats and sustainably caught seafood that's slightly naughty; bedding a rack of lamb on roasted eggplant, and scallops with melon and caviar.

CHINATOWN

House of Nanking (Map pp956-7; ☎ 415-421-1429; 919 Kearny St; mains $7-12; ☯ 11am-10pm Mon-Fri, from noon Sat, noon-7:30pm Sun) Give your server a general idea what interests you, and accept whatever fresh, Shanghai-style dishes land on the table: meltaway scallops, fragrant sautéed hollow-heart greens, lettuce-wrapped chicken.

City View (Map pp956-7; ☎ 415-398-2838; 662 Commercial; meals $10-25; ☯ 11am-2:30pm Mon-Fri, 10am-2:30pm Sat & Sun) Dim sum aficionados used to cramped quarters and surly service are wowed by impeccable shrimp and leek dumplings, savory pork spare ribs and garlicky Chinese broccoli graciously served in this spacious, sunny room.

NORTH BEACH

Molinari (Map pp956-7; ☎ 415-421-2337; 373 Columbus Ave; sandwiches $5-8; ☯ 8am-6pm Mon-Fri, 7:30am-5:30pm Sat) This must be what the pope gets when he orders a sandwich: crusty Italian bread with slabs of salami, translucent sheets of prosciutto and milky buffalo mozzarella.

Cinecittà (Map pp956-7; ☎ 415-291-8830; 663 Union St; pizzas $9-12; ☯ 11am-10pm Sun-Thu, 11am-midnight Fri & Sat) That aroma you followed into this 18-seat eatery is thin-crust Roman pizza, probably the crowd-pleasing Capricciosa: artichoke hearts, olives, fresh mozzarella, prosciutto, and egg.

Ideale (Map pp956-7; ☎ 415-391-4129; 1309 Grant Ave; mains $10-22; ☯ 6-10:30pm Tue-Sun) Expat Italian regulars are stunned that a restaurant this authentic borders the Pacific, with *al dente* pasta, risotto made with superior Canaroli rice and wisecracking Tuscan waitstaff.

FISHERMAN'S WHARF

Ghirardelli Ice Cream (Map pp956-7; ☎ 415-474-3938; www.ghirardellisq.com; 900 North Point St; ice cream $3-8;

☯ 9am-11pm Sun-Thu, 9am-midnight Fri &Sat) Chocolate milk shakes are for sharing and making moony eyes over, and the Cable Car comes with Rocky Road ice cream, marshmallow topping and enough hot fudge to pave Kerouac Alley.

Gary Danko (Map pp956-7; ☎ 415-749-2060; www.garydanko.com; 800 North Point St; set-price menu $60-80; ☯ dinner) Smoked-glass windows prevent passersby from tripping over their tongues at the sight of exquisite roasted lobster with morels, blushing duck breast with rhubarb compote and the lavish cheese cart. Ladies get tiny cakes as parting gifts.

THE MARINA

La Boulange (Map pp956-7; ☎ 415-440-4450; www.baybread.com; 1909 Union St; lunch deal $7; ☯ 7am-7pm Mon-Sat) La Combo is a $7 lunchtime deal to justify your next boutique purchase: half a tartine (open-faced sandwich) with soup or salad, plus all the cornichons and Nutella you can grab from the condiment bar.

Greens (Map pp956-7; ☎ 415-771-6222; www.greensrestaurant.com; Fort Mason Center, bldg A; mains $7-20; ☯ noon-2:30pm Tue-Sat, 5:30-9pm Mon-Sat, 10:30am-2pm Sun) Career carnivores won't realize there's no meat in the hearty black bean chili with *crème fraiche* and pickled jalapenos, or that roasted eggplant panino. On weekends, book ahead or get yours to go.

Taste of the Himalayas (Map pp956-7; ☎ 415-674-9898; 2420 Lombard St; mains $9-15; ☯ 11am- 2:30pm & 5-10pm Wed-Mon) Even more heart-warming than a *momo* (a dumpling-samosa hybrid) or the nutty-creamy chicken tikka masala is the sweetly sincere owner, who's often moved to sing a song of welcome.

THE MISSION

La Taquería (off Map pp956-7; ☎ 415-285-7117; 2889 Mission St at 25th; burritos $4-6; ☯ 11am-9pm) No debatable tofu, saffron rice, spinach tortilla or mango salsa – just classic tomatillo or mesquite salsa, perfectly grilled meats and flavorful beans inside a flour tortilla.

Pancho Villa (Map pp956-7; ☎ 982-2182; panchovillasf.com; 3071 16th St; burritos $4-6; ☯ 10am-midnight) The Mission burrito wars rage on, with Pancho Villa militants claiming victory for grilled chicken and pork burritos served to lines out the door.

Tartine Bakery (Map pp956-7; ☎ 415-487-2600; www.tartinebakery.com; 600 Guerrero; sandwiches $7-8; ☯ 8am-7pm, until 8pm Thu-Sun) Gluttony and vats of butter are the obvious explanations for *pain au chocolat* (chocolate croissant), rich enough for millionaires, and *croque monsieurs*, turbo-loaded with ham, two kinds of cheese and bechamel.

Delfina (Map pp956-7; ☎ 415-552-4055; www.delfinasf.com; 3621 18th St; mains $17-22; 5:30-10pm Sun-Thu, 5:30-11pm Fri & Sat) Simple yet sensational seasonal California cuisine: steelhead trout graced with caramelized endive, roast chicken and mashed spuds trumped with royal trumpet mushrooms. Reservations required, like, yesterday.

THE CASTRO

Burgermeister (Map pp956-7; ☎ 415-437-2874; www.burgermeistersf.com; 138 Church St; burgers $5-8; 11am-midnight Mon-Sat) Personal ads may promise hot and beefy, but Burgermeister delivers with a half-pound free-range burger loaded with grilled onions, local blue cheese and organic mesclun greens.

Cafe Flore (Map pp956-7; ☎ 415-621-8579; http://cafeflore.com; 2298 Market St at Noe; mains $7-11; 7am-11pm Sun-Thu, 7am-midnight Fri & Sat) Mind your soup slurping: this all-glass corner venue maximizes opportunities to see and be seen. Repartee is so quick it seems scripted, and calls for a double cappuccino to keep up.

Destino (Map pp956-7; ☎ 415-552-4451; www.destinosf.com; 1815 Market St; small plates $8-12; 5-10pm Mon-Thu, 5-11pm Fri & Sat, 11am-2pm & 5-10pm Sun) Your tastebuds will think tectonic plates have shifted at this Peru-meets-California bistro, starring 'ahi ceviche with mango and achiote oil, skewered beef hearts and scallop risotto cake atop greens with ancho dressing.

THE HAIGHT

Rosamunde Sausage Grill (Map pp956-7; ☎ 415-437-6851; 545 Haight St; sausages $4; 11:30am-10pm) Here's a stroke of genius for you: load up classic Brats or chicken-cherry links with complimentary roasted peppers, grilled onions, mustard and mango chutney, and enjoy at Toronado (opposite) next door with a cold beer.

Cole Valley Cafe (Map pp956-7; ☎ 415-668-5282; www.colevalleycafe.com; 701 Cole St; sandwiches $5.75; 7am-8pm; wi-fi) Powerful coffee, free wi-fi and hot gourmet sandwiches that are a bargain at any price, let alone $5.75 for lipsmacking thyme-marinated chicken with lemony avocado spread.

GAY/LES/BI/TRANS SAN FRANCISCO

Singling out the best places to be queer in San Francisco (SF) is almost redundant. Though the Castro is a major gay center and the Mission is a magnet for lesbians, the entire city is known for being gay-friendly – hence the number of out elected representatives in City Hall at any given time. Nightlife is fabulous here. New York Marys may label SF the retirement home of the young – indeed, the sidewalks roll up early – but when it comes to sexual outlaws and underground weirdness, SF kicks New York's ass. Dancing queens and slutty boys head South of Market (SoMa), the location of most thump-thump clubs and sex venues. There was a time when bars would euphemistically designate Sunday afternoons as 'tea dances,' appealing to gay crowds to make money at an otherwise slow time. The tradition now makes Sundays one of the busiest times for SF's gay bars.

Of course it's all gay all day in the Castro, but here are some other GLBT faves:

San Francisco Lesbian, Gay, Bisexual, Transgender Community Center (Map pp956-7; ☎ 415-865-5555; www.sfcenter.org; 1800 Market St) 'The Other City Hall' is home to nonprofits and host to comedy nights, political rallies, drag showcases and other pursuits of happiness – it even provides childcare services to visiting proud parents.

Sisters of Perpetual Indulgence (☎ 415-820-9697; www.thesisters.org) For guerrilla antics, see what the self-described 'leading-edge order of queer nuns' is up to. It's a charitable organization and a San Francisco institution.

Lexington Club (Map pp956-7; ☎ 415-863-2052; 3464 19th St; 3pm-2am) SF's most attractive lesbian bar.

Stud (Map pp956-7; ☎ 415-252-7883; www.studsf.com; 399 9th St; admission $5-8; 5pm-3am) Rocking the SF gay scene for 40-plus years yet brimming with youthful vigor, this is the bar equivalent of Viagra.

AsiaSF (Map pp956-7; ☎ 415-255-2742; www.asiasf.com; 201 9th St; dinner 6-10pm Sun-Thu, from 5pm Sat, club 10pm-2am Mon-Sun) Oddly, this all-Asian tranny lounge has decent food. Respectable drinks are served by waitresses who'll make you look thrice and still you aren't sure.

Little Star Pizza (Map pp956-7; ☎ 415-441-1118; www
.littlestarpizza.com; 846 Divisadero St; pizza serving 2-3 $17-
23; ☺ 5-10pm Tue-Thu & Sun, 5-11pm Fri & Sat) Midwest
weather patterns reveal Chicago's thunder
has been stolen by Little Star's deep-dish pie,
with California additions of cornmeal, fresh
veggies and premium meats.

THE RICHMOND

Park Chow (Map pp956-7; ☎ 415-665-9912; 1240 9th
Ave; mains $8-18; ☺ 11am-10pm Mon-Thu, 11am-11pm Fri,
10am-11pm Sat, 10am-10pm Sun) Shake that fog-belt
chill with reliable, California comfort food
such as mild curry Smiling Noodles, stalwart
spaghetti with meatballs and caramel gingerbread with pumpkin ice cream.

Wooden Charcoal BBQ (Map pp956-7; ☎ 415-751-
6336; 4609 Geary Blvd; meals $8-22; ☺ 11am-2am) Serious
late-night munchies deserve marinated short
ribs and chicken, thinly sliced and grilled to
perfection at your table. All orders come with
rice, soup and an assortment of *sundubu* (Korean side dishes).

Taiwan (Map pp956-7; ☎ 415-387-1789; 445 Clement
St; meals $10; ☺ 11am-10pm Sun-Thu, 11am-midnight Fri,
10am-midnight Sat) Feast for days on stellar dishes
under $8, including dumplings made fresh to
order, smoky dry braised green beans, feisty
black bean chicken and housemade Shanghai
sesame hot sauce noodles.

Aziza (off Map pp956-7; ☎ 415-752-2222; www.aziza
sf.com; 5800 Geary Blvd; mains $18-24; ☺ 5:30-10:30pm
Mon & Wed-Sun) Mourad Lahlou's modern Middle Eastern makes the most of California's organic produce and free-range meats: quail gets
the royal treatment with cumin-orange glaze
and brandied currants, and the prawn *tagine*
(stew) with Meyer lemons is pizzazz in a pot.

Drinking

Hit the Mission, the Haight and North Beach
for killer bars and pubs.

Zeitgeist (Map pp956-7; ☎ 415-255-7505; 199 Valencia St) The back beer garden (with evening
BBQ) is the in spot for city bikers and
punk hipsters.

Toronado (Map pp956-7; ☎ 415-863-2276; www
.toronado.com; 547 Haight St) A venerable Haight
watering hole. Beer mavens dig the 50-plus
microbrews on tap; punks love the jukebox.

Tosca Cafe (Map pp956-7; ☎ 415-391-1244; 242 Columbus Ave) Red vinyl booths and an all-opera
jukebox: this self-assured Italian joint is classic
North Beach. Good luck getting into the back
room, which hosts celebs such as Bono.

Entertainment

Like the nightlife, baby? Don't just scan
the listings in the *SF Weekly* – hit up locals for hot spots. For half-price tickets to
the theater, big music acts and other shows,
go online or head to **TIX Bay Area** (Map pp956-7;
☎ 415-433-7827; www.theatrebayarea.org; ☺ Tue-Sun),
at Union Sq. Or scan the daily discounts at
www.goldsta revents.com.

NIGHTCLUBS & LIVE MUSIC

Pick up a copy of *SFWeekly* (www.sfweekly
.com) or online at www.sfgate.com or www
.sfstation.com for upcoming events.

Café du Nord (☎ 415-861-5016; www.cafedunord
.com; 2170 Market St) The '30s Swedish American
Music Hall and former speakeasy rocks regular crowds nightly.

El Rio (off Map pp956-7; ☎ 415-282-3325; www.elriosf
.com; 3158 Mission St at Cesar Chavez) Diverse in every
aspect, from music to patrons, El Rio is quintessential Mission hip.

Annie's Social Club (Map pp956-7; ☎ 415-974-
1585; www.anniessocialclub.com; 917 Folsom St) Live
punk shows that'll do wonders for your
flagging street cred include local and
international names.

Bottom of the Hill (Map pp956-7; ☎ 415-621-4455;
www.bottomofthehill.com; 1233 17th St) Oddballs, newcomers and punks crowd the nightly lineup.
Worth the trek off the beaten path.

DANCE CLUBS

Cat Club (Map pp956-7; ☎ 415-703-8965; www.cat
clubsf.com; 1190 Folsom St) Thursday's '1984' lures a
mix of lipstick lesbians, goth boys and other
'80s lovers.

1015 Folsom (Map pp956-7; ☎ 415-431-7444;
www.1015.com; 1015 Folsom St) Bring a posse. A very
happening, multilevel club with five dancefloors and a 500ft 'water wall.'

Milk (Map pp956-7; ☎ 415-387-6455, www.milksf
.com; 1840 Haight St) Hip-hop gets stylish 20-
somethings down on the dancefloor at this
tiny, narrow club (thankfully there are high
ceilings to let off some people-steam). White
plastic booths are forgiving of spilled drinks.
Get there before 9pm to avoid the cover, and
hang in through the short wait at weekends:
the scene is worth it.

CLASSICAL MUSIC & OPERA

Yerba Buena Center for the Arts (Map pp956-7; ☎ 415-
978-2787; www.ybca.org; 701 Mission St) Yerba Buena hosts
first-class modern music, dance and theater.

CALIFORNIA

Davies Symphony Hall (Map pp956-7; ☎ 415-864-6000; www.sfsymphony.org; 201 Van Ness Ave) The famed San Francisco Symphony performs here from September to May.

For a dose of high culture, San Francisco Opera and the **San Francisco Ballet** (☎ 415-861-5600; www.sfballet.org) perform at the **War Memorial Opera House** (Map pp956-7; ☎ 415-864-3330; www.sfopera.com; 301 Van Ness Ave).

THEATER
You know SF is full of drama seekers. The city's sprinkled with small theater companies and one major daddy, the **American Conservatory Theater** (ACT; www.act-sf.org).

Geary Theater (Map pp956-7; ☎ 415-749-2228; 415 Geary St) Shows destined for New York or London must first pass muster at this turn-of-the-century theater, which has hosted ACT's (American Conservatory Theater) landmark productions of Tony Kushner's *Angels in America* and Robert Wilson's *Black Rider*.

Club Fugazi (Map pp956-7; ☎ 415-421-4222; www.beachblanketbabylon.com; 678 Green St; seats $25-78) This theater showcases the ribald, hilarious *Beach Blanket Babylon* – a totally SF theater-comedy extravaganza.

Catch touring Broadway productions:

Curran Theatre (Map pp956-7; ☎ 415-551-2000; 445 Geary St)

Golden Gate Theatre (Map pp956-7; ☎ 415-551-2000; 1 Taylor St)

Orpheum Theatre (Map pp956-7; ☎ 415-551-2000; 1192 Market St)

CINEMA
Castro Theatre (Map pp956-7; ☎ 415-621-6120; www.thecastrotheatre.com; 429 Castro St) Grand old-style cinema with the city's best calendar of art, independent and foreign films.

Also recommended for funky, whacked celluloid:

Red Vic (Map pp956-7; ☎ 415-668-3994; www.redvicmoviehouse.com; 1727 Haight St)

Roxie Cinema (Map pp956-7; ☎ 415-863-1087; www.roxie.com; 3117 16th St)

SPORTS
San Francisco 49ers (☎ 415-656-4900; www.sf49ers.com) For garlic fries, beer and SF's NFL football team, head to Candlestick Park (Map p952).

San Francisco Giants (☎ 415-478-2277; http://san francisco.giants.mlb.com) The major-league baseball club plays at the stunning AT&T Park (Map pp956-7).

Shopping
So much for traveling light: San Francisco is clearly out to sabotage your grand carry-on-only plans. The accumulation begins innocently enough in Chinatown with silk slippers, maybe a dragonfly kite – but then you hit City Lights, and pile on so many great books. Further up Grant Ave from Bush to Filbert Sts you will find custom zoot suits, local designer dresses, and rare vinyl. In Hayes Valley, locally designed earrings and underwear are easy enough to pack, though beware the siren call of gourmet sake, handmade felt rugs and mod chandeliers along Hayes St from Franklin to Laguna Sts. Foot fetishists, CD hoarders and vintage clotheshounds are in serious trouble in the Upper Haight, while bookworms and bric-a-brac collectors can't resist Valencia St between 16th and 24th Sts. Mall rats may never escape from the 400 stores of **Westfield San Francisco Shopping Center** (Map pp956-7; 865 Market St; ⊙ most shops 9:30am-9pm Mon-Sat, 10am-7pm Sun).

Designer addicts will be fashion victimized along Fillmore between Bush and Clay, and should avoid downtown altogether. Then again, you could just buy another suitcase...

Getting There & Away
AIR
San Francisco International Airport (SFO; Map p952; ☎ 650-821-8211; www.flysfo.com) is 14 miles south of downtown off Hwy 101. Most domestic and international carriers fly in and out of SFO. SFO's AirTrain connects the terminals with parking garages, rental-car centers and Bay Area Rapid Transit (BART).

BUS
The **Transbay Terminal** (Map pp956-7; 425 Mission St), is the major intercity bus station, located on the corner of 1st St in SoMa. Take **AC Transit** (☎ 510-891-4777; www.actransit.org) buses to the East Bay, **Golden Gate Transit** (☎ 415-455-2000; www.goldengate.org) buses north to Marin and Sonoma Counties and **SamTrans** (☎ 800-660-4287; www.samtrans.com) buses south to Palo Alto and the Pacific coast.

Greyhound (☎ 415-495-1569, 800-231-2222; www.greyhound.com) has several buses that leave here daily for Los Angeles ($39 and up, from eight hours), Truckee near Lake Tahoe ($58 round-trip, 5½ hours), and other destinations.

TRAIN

CalTrain (☎ 800-660-4287; www.caltrain.com) connects San Francisco with towns along the Peninsula to San Jose. From the depot at 4th and King Sts in San Francisco, it links to Millbrae (connecting to BART and SFO, 30 minutes), Palo Alto (one hour) and San Jose (1½ hours). **Amtrak** (☎ 800-872-7245; www .amtrakcalifornia.com) runs free shuttle buses to San Francisco's Ferry Building and CalTrain station from its terminals in Emeryville and Oakland's Jack London Sq.

Getting Around

Operated by the Metropolitan Transportation Commission, www.511.org shows you transit options with departure and arrival times for the entire Bay Area; call ☎ 511 for automated transit information.

TO/FROM THE SAN FRANCISCO AIRPORT

BART (Bay Area Rapid Transit; ☎ 415-989-2278; www.bart .gov; one-way $4.95) offers a cheap, fast, direct ride from the airport to downtown San Francisco. A slower option is **SamTrans** (☎ 800-660-4287) express bus KX ($3.50, 30 minutes) to San Francisco's Transbay Terminal.

The **SFO Airporter** (☎ 650-246-2768; www .sfoairporter.com; adult $15) bus departs from the baggage-claim areas and stops at major hotels. Door-to-door shuttles cost $14 to $17 and take 20 to 45 minutes; try **Super-Shuttle** (☎ 415-558-8500; www.supershuttle.com) or **Lorrie's** (☎ 415-334-9000).

Taxis to downtown San Francisco cost $35 to $50, plus tip.

TO/FROM THE OAKLAND AIRPORT

The most comprehensive door-to-door shuttle service is with **Super Shuttle** (☎ 800-258-3826) – a shared ride to downtown SF averages $25. There's a scheduled shuttle operated by **Airport Express** (☎ 800-327-2024; www.airportexpress-inc.com) that leaves every two hours from 6am to midnight between Oakland Airport and Sonoma ($28) and Marin ($22) counties.

There's a professional taxi rank just outside. Fares average $25 to Oakland, $50 to SF – ask for a flat rate to or from the airport.

There are two public transportation options for getting into San Francisco: BART (the subway system) is cheaper and more reliable than Amtrak. An AirBART shuttle ($3) runs every 10 minutes to Coliseum station; from there it's a 25-minute ride into SF downtown ($3.35 to Powell St station).

BOAT

Blue & Gold Ferries (Map pp956-7; ☎ information 415-773-1188, sales 415-705-5555; www.blueandgoldfleet.com) runs the Alameda–Oakland ferry from Pier 41 and the Ferry Building. **Golden Gate Ferry** (☎ 415-455-2000; www.goldengate.org) has regular service from the Ferry Building to Larkspur and Sausalito in Marin County.

CAR & MOTORCYCLE

If you can, avoid driving in San Francisco: street parking is harder to find than true love, and meter readers are ruthless. The most convenient downtown parking lots are at the Embarcadero Center, at 5th and Mission Sts, under Union Sq, and at Sutter and Stockton Sts.

National car-rental agencies have 24-hour offices at the airport and offices downtown. See p1144 for toll-free contact information. **City Rent-a-Car** (Map pp956-7; ☎ 415-359-1331; www .cityrentacar.com; 1433 Bush St) is a competitively priced independent city agency.

Zipcar lets you rent a Prius Hybrid or Mini by the hour for flat rates starting at $7.88 per hour, including gas and insurance, or by day for $58.50. Zipcar's Extra Value Plan requires a $25 application fee and $50 prepaid usage in advance. Anyone without a US driver's license will need to fax a copy of their driving record in English to Zipcar at 617-995-4300 (instructions at www.zipcar.com/apply/foreign-drivers). Once approved, you can reserve a car online at www.zipcar.com or by phone at 866-4ZIPCAR. These are located all over the city.

PUBLIC TRANSPORTATION

San Francisco's **Municipal Transit Agency** (MUNI; ☎ 415-673-6864; www.sfmuni.com) operates comprehensive bus and streetcar lines and three cable-car lines; two cable-car lines leave from Powell and Market Sts, and one leaves from California and Markets Sts. A detailed *MUNI Street & Transit Map* ($2.50) is available at newsstands and the Powell St MUNI kiosk. The standard fare for buses or streetcars is $1.50; cable-car fare is $5. A MUNI Passport (one-/three-/seven-days $11/18/24) allows unlimited travel on all MUNI transport, including cable cars; it's sold at San Francisco's Visitor Information Center (p955) and at the TIX Bay Area kiosk at Union Sq. A seven-day City Pass ($43) includes transit and admission to six attractions.

The **BART system** (☎ 415-989-2278; www.bart .gov; tickets $1.25-7.45) is the commuter train system linking San Francisco with the East Bay. In the city, BART runs beneath Market St, down Mission St and south to SFO and Millbrae, where it connects with CalTrain.

TAXI
Fares run about $2.25 per mile; meters start at $3.30. Here are some of the major cab companies:
DeSoto Cab (☎ 415-970-1300)
Green Cab (☎ 415-626-4733; www.greencab.com)
Hybrid, fuel-efficient vehicles; worker-owned collective.
Veteran's Taxicab (☎ 415-648-1313)
Yellow Cab (☎ 415-626-2345)

MARIN COUNTY
Majestic redwoods cling to green coastal hills just across the Golden Gate Bridge in wealthy, laid-back **Marin** (www.visitmarin.org). **Sausalito**, the first town you encounter, is a cute, touristy bayside town that makes a good destination for bike trips over the bridge (take the ferry back). At the harbor, the **San Francisco Bay-Delta Model** (☎ 415-332-3871; www.spn.usace.army.mil/bmvc/; 2100 Bridgeway Blvd; admission free; ❂ 9am-4pm Tue-Fri, 10am-5pm Sat & Sun, closed Sun winter) is a geeky fun, 1.5-acre hydraulic re-creation of the entire bay and delta.

Marin Headlands
These hilly, windswept, rugged headlands are laced with hiking trails and offer striking views of the city. To reach the **visitor center** (☎ 415-331-1540; ❂ 9:30am-4:30pm), take the Alexander Ave exit from the Golden Gate Bridge and head west on Conzelman Rd. Attractions include the **Point Bonita lighthouse** (❂ Sat-Mon), the Cold War–era **Nike missile site** (❂ Wed-Fri) and **Rodeo Beach**, plus there's *free* walk-in camping on the cliffs at Bicentennial. At Fort Baker, the **Bay Area Discovery Museum** (☎ 415-339-3900; www .baykidsmuseum.org; 557 McReynolds Rd, Sausalito; adult/child

1-17 $8.50/7.50; ❂ 9am-5pm Mon-Fri) is a cool destination for kids.

Near the visitor center, the **HI Marin Headlands Hostel** (Map p952; ☎ 415-331-2777, 800-909-4776; dm from $20, r from $60; ℗ ▢ wi-fi) occupies two historic 1907 buildings on a sunny green hill. Private rooms in the commanding officer's house are sweet.

Mt Tamalpais State Park
Majestic 2571ft 'Mt Tam' is where kick-ass mountain bikers head, and hikers too. **Mt Tamalpais State Park** (Map p952; ☎ 415-388-2070; www .mttam.net; per car $6) encompasses 6300 acres of wilderness plus more than 200 miles of trails; get a map, and don't miss East Peak. Panoramic Hwy climbs from Hwy 1 through the park to Stinson Beach, itself a relaxed town with a pretty beach. **Park headquarters** are at **Pantoll Station** (801 Panoramic Hwy; campsites $15), where there are trailheads and a first-come, first-served campground. Or you can pack in food, linens and towels to the rustic **West Point Inn** (☎ 415-646-0702; cabins $35), reached on foot and without electricity.

Near park headquarters, **Mountain Home Inn** (☎ 415-381-9000; www.mtnhomeinn.com; 810 Panoramic Hwy; ❂ 11:30am-3pm Wed-Sun, 5:30-8pm Wed, Thu & Sun, until 9pm Fri & Sat; lunch $10-17, 3-course dinner $38; ☒ ▢ wi-fi) occupies a secluded perch. Appealing, outdoorsy rooms ($175 to $325) bring in the view, while the restaurant's open-air deck offers gourmet meals Wednesday to Sunday.

Muir Woods National Monument
You might need a neck brace after gazing at a glorious stand of the world's tallest trees in 550-acre **Muir Woods** (☎ 415-388-2595; www.nps .gov/muwo; per car $3). A national monument since 1908, it was named after Sierra Club founder John Muir. The easy (sometimes crowded) 1-mile Main Trail Loop leads past the splendor of the thousand-year-old trees at Cathedral Grove and returns via Bohemian Grove. Muir Woods is 12 miles north of the Golden Gate Bridge via Hwy 101 (take the Hwy 1 exit and follow signs). No camping or picnicking allowed, though.

Point Reyes National Seashore
Wind-tousled and sun-exposed, the triangular peninsula of **Point Reyes National Seashore** (Map p952) comprises 110 sq miles of blustery beaches, lagoons and forested cliffs. The

westernmost point of the peninsula, Point Reyes Headlands, is crowned by the **Point Reyes Lighthouse** (🕙 Thu-Mon), where you can watch for whales, or be surprised by the tule elk appearing on the peninsula's northern tip. The **Bear Valley Visitors Center** (☎ 415-464-5100; www.nps .gov/pore) is just past Olema and has trail maps and park displays. Point Reyes has four hike-in **campsites** (☎ reservations 415-663-8054; campsites $15), two near the beach.

The **West Marin chamber of commerce** (☎ 415-663-9232; www.pointreyes.org) can point out loads of cozy inns and cottages. **Motel Inverness** (Map p952; ☎ 415-669-1081; www.motelinverness.com; 12718 Sir Francis Drake Blvd; r $99-200) is an appealing, nicely managed midrange motel; its 24-hour lodge is warmed by a great fireplace. The economy-minded can bunk at **HI Point Reyes Hostel** (Map p952; ☎ 415-663-8811; dm from $18), off Limantour Rd, 8 miles from the Bear Valley Visitors Center.

Oyster-lovers, head to **Johnson Oyster Company** (☎ 415-669-1149; 1 dozen oysters $9-12; 🕙 8am-4:30pm), off Sir Francis Drake Blvd in the park. This is where they farm them, so just pluck, shuck and suck. Nearby, Point Reyes Station is a pleasant small town for a meal or picnic supplies.

BERKELEY

Not much has changed in Berkeley since the 1960s heyday of anti–Vietnam War protests: the 'Make Love Not War' bumper stickers on VW vans of yore have been replaced with 'No Blood For Oil,' and hemp-wearing men and women both still sport a single classic long gray braid down their back. It's no longer legal to walk around nude, but 'Berserkeley' remains the radical hub of the Bay Area, full of university students, professors and hippies, and strolling its attractive university and surrounding streets is a constant source of fascination and political, um, enlightenment.

Sights & Activities

The **University of California at Berkeley** (Map p952) – 'Cal' – is one of the country's top universities and home to 33,000 diverse, politically conscious students. The university's **Visitor Services center** (☎ 510-642-5215; www.berkeley .edu; 101 University Hall, 2200 University Ave at Oxford St; 🕙 8:30am-4:30pm Mon-Fri, tours 10am Mon-Sat, 1pm Sun) has info and leads free campus tours. Cal's landmark is the 1914 Sather Tower (also called the 'Campanile'), with rides ($2) to the top. The Bancroft Library displays the small gold nugget that started the California gold rush in 1848.

Other campus highlights include the **Berkeley Art Museum** (☎ 510-642-0808; www.bampfa.berkeley .edu; 2626 Bancroft Way; admission $8; 🕙 11am-5pm Wed-Sun, until 7pm Thu), east of Telegraph Ave. It may resemble a concrete bunker, but its galleries help sharpen the cutting edge of modern art. Also here, the highly respected **Pacific Film Archive** (☎ 510-642-1124) screens little-known independent and avant-garde films.

Leading to the campus's main south gate, **Telegraph Avenue** is as far-out and gritty as San Francisco's Haight St, and even more crowded with cafés, cheap eats, record stores and bookstores – including beatnik-era **Moe's** (☎ 510-849-2087; www.moesbooks.com; 2476 Telegraph Ave).

If you've had enough brain stimulation, relax in **Tilden Regional Park** (☎ 510-562-7275; www.ebparks.org) in the Berkeley hills, which has hiking trails, picnic areas, swimming at

---

IF YOU HAVE A FEW MORE DAYS: OAKLAND

Just across the bay, gritty-urban Oakland's got Attitude, the A's and deep African American roots that come through in world-celebrated music, lit and art. It kicks SF's fog with daily sunshine and has a lovely historic downtown, a saltwater lake and small clusters of fun clubs and restaurants.

Oakland Museum of California (☎ 510-238-2200; www.museumca.org; cnr 10th & Oak Sts; adult/child 6-17 $8/5; 🕙 10am-5pm Wed-Sat, from noon Sun) is a must-see. Relevant, fascinating exhibits have included amazing Yosemite photography and interactive Great Quake rooms.

Heinhold's First & Last Chance Saloon (☎ 510-839-6761; 48 Webster), in Jack London Sq, is a lopsided quake survivor and National Literary Landmark; it's open daily for inspirational drinking. Yes, your beer really *is* sliding off the counter.

Yoshi's (☎ 510-238-9200; www.yoshis.com; 510 Embarcadero West; mains $15-20; 🕙 5:30-10pm Mon-Thu, until 10:30pm Fri & Sat, 5-9pm Sun) is one of the country's top jazz clubs; the sushi's OK too.

CALIFORNIA

Lake Anza, and plenty of kid stuff, such as pony rides and a steam train. Most activities charge a small fee.

Sleeping

Basic and midrange motels are clustered west of campus along University Ave.

Bancroft Hotel (☎ 510-549-1000, 800-549-1002; www .bancrofthotel.com; 2680 Bancroft Way; r $119-159; P ✕ wi-fi) Across from campus, this old-fashioned 22-roomer is on three floors (no elevator). Parking $10. There's wi-fi in the lobby.

Hotel Durant (☎ 510-845-8981, 800-238-7268; www .hoteldurant.com; 2600 Durant Ave; r $135-180; P ▢ wi-fi) The 140-room Durant is more modern and polished in decor and service, with the popular Henry's Publick House and Grille downstairs. Parking $10. There's wi-fi in the lobby.

Eating & Drinking

Chez Panisse (☎ 510-548-5525; www.chezpanisse.com; 1517 Shattuck Ave; set-price menu $50-85, café mains $18-25; ☽ seatings at 6pm & 8:30pm Mon-Thu, closed Sun) Genuflect at the birthplace of California cuisine; Alice Waters' formal restaurant downstairs is open only for set-price dinners. Upstairs, a more relaxed café serves lunch and dinner. Why all the fuss over fresh, organic, local produce? Reserve a table (up to a month ahead) and find out.

Also in the Gourmet Ghetto, which is along Shattuck Ave north of University Ave, are **Cheese Board Pizza** (☎ 510-549-3055; 1512 Shattuck Ave; $18 a pie or $2.25 a slice; ☽ 11:30am-2pm & 4:30-7pm Tue-Sat) and the adjacent **Cheese Board Collective** (☎ 510-549-3183; 1504 Shattuck Ave; $18 a pie or $2.25 a slice; ☽ 10am-6pm Tue-Fri, until 5pm Sat). The rich smell of goat-cheese pizzas lures most folks in from the sidewalk.

Still, gourmet doesn't have to empty your wallet. **Vik's Chaat Corner** (☎ 510-644-4412; 726 Allston Way at 4th St; items $3.50-6; ☽ 11am-6pm Tue-Sun) is off-the-chart good, but nothing more than a warehouse-district Indian cafeteria.

A prime student pick is **Café Intermezzo** (2442 Telegraph Ave; meals $5-7; ☽ 8am-10pm).

For the best social introduction to Berkeley's bar scene, head to the back patio at **Jupiter** (☎ 510-843-8277; 2181 Shattuck Ave).

Getting There & Around

AC Transit (☎ 510-817-1717; www.actransit.org) runs local buses in Berkeley as well as between Berkeley and Oakland ($2) and Berkeley and

San Francisco ($3.50). From San Francisco, it's a short trip on **BART** (www.bart.gov) to the Downtown Berkeley station ($3.25), which is four blocks from the main Cal campus gate.

NORTHERN CALIFORNIA

Green and mild, with fog seeping in from the coast and burning off over vineyards and mountains, Northern California is where things seem to grow and change and take shape in every awesome way imaginable. The Coastal Range in the west and the mighty Sierra Nevada cradle the vast, sea-level Central Valley, filled with fruit trees. Along the coast are soft redwoods and fabled Wine Country; in the Sierra you'll find stunning Yosemite and Lake Tahoe.

WINE COUNTRY

Wine Country is bliss realized. A patchwork of vineyards covers toast-colored hills, stretching from the cool, foggy Pacific coast to the hot, inland Sonoma and Napa Valleys. More than 500 wineries exist in Napa and Sonoma Counties, but with its history of winning blind taste-tests in France, quality, not quantity, sets the region apart.

It's an easy day trip from San Francisco, but stay overnight if you can; the heavy afternoon summer traffic is a buzz-kill. Free tastings exist no more in fancy Napa; a 'flight' of several varieties runs $5 to $15, but as high as $30. In down-to-earth Sonoma, tastings are sometimes free, and you'll probably meet the vintner's family dog. Wineries are open 10am to 4pm or 5pm daily. Some reduce hours in winter; call ahead. A cushy, if touristy, way to see Wine Country is on the **Napa Valley Wine Train** (☎ 707-253-2111, 800-427-4124; www.winetrain .com; adult/child under 12 $50/25, plus lunch $39.50/23 or dinner $48/23), which offers three-hour trips daily.

Napa Valley

More than 200 wineries crowd 30-mile-long Napa Valley along two main arteries: busy St Helena Hwy (Hwy 29) and curvy Silverado Trail, a mile or two east.

Downtown Napa is decidedly plain. Follow signs for the **Napa Valley Visitors Bureau** (☎ 707-226-7459; www.napavalley.com; 1310 Napa Town Center; ☽ 9am-5pm), which has brochures, lodging updates and the free *Inside Napa Valley*, with a comprehensive winery guide. Check email at **Napa Library** (☎ 707-253-4241; www.co.napa.ca.us/library; 580 Coombs St; ☺ 10am-9pm Mon-Thu, until 5:30pm Fri, until 5pm Sat, 2-9pm Sun).

SIGHTS

Cabernet Sauvignon is what Napa's about; seek out the boutique wineries. The following are listed south to north.

Sample tiny-scale-production cult wines at supercool **Vintners' Collective** (☎ 707-255-7150; www.vintnerscollective.com; 1245 Main St; ☺ 11am-6pm Wed-Mon).

Don't miss **Copia** (Map p952; ☎ 707-259-1600; www.copia.org; 500 1st St; adult/child under 12 $5/free; ☺ 10am-5pm Wed-Mon) – everything Wine Country in one heady package. From the interactive exhibits about America's culinary habits to the primer on wine tasting, to cooking demonstrations, to a restaurant and café, to films and concerts: you'll be sated.

Just north, popular, kosher-vegan **Hagafen Cellars** (☎ 888-424-2336; www.hagafen.com; 4160 Silverado Trail) supplies the White House for Israeli VIPs.

West of town in the Carneros district, see modern art at 217-acre **DiRosa Preserve** (Map p952; ☎ 707-226-5991; www.dirosapreserve.org; 5200 Carneros Hwy; admission $3; ☺ 9:30am-3pm Tue-Fri, tours by appointment Tue-Sat), then visit the **Artesa Winery** (☎ 707-224-1668; www.artesawinery.com; 1345 Henry Rd) for top-of-the-world vistas, stunning architecture and bubbly.

North of town, wine and art merge at **Hess Collection** (☎ 707-255-1144; www.hesscollection.com; 4411 Redwood Rd). Works by Francis Bacon, Louis Soutter and others are spread over three floors, with the tasting room downstairs. For earthy Sangiovese and fruit-forward pinot grigio, visit **Luna Vineyards** (☎ 707-255-2474; www.lunavineyards.com; 2921 Silverado Trail). Chef-owned **Robert Sinskey** (☎ 707-944-9090; www.robertsinskey.com; 6320 Silverado Trail) does wine-and-cheese pairings (call ahead).

In Rutherford, visit ever-so-fun **Frog's Leap** (☎ 707-963-4704; www.frogsleap.com; 8815 Conn Creek Rd) – free, but you *must* call ahead. Francis Ford Coppola's **Rubicon Estate** (☎ 707-968-1100; www.niebaum-coppola.com; 1991 St Helena Hwy; $25) has a movie 'museum,' including a Tucker car and Coppola's *Godfather* Oscars; the tour focuses on the dramatic 1887 Inglenook chateau.

St Helena is the Beverly Hills of Napa. The **Culinary Institute of America** (☎ 707-967-2320; 2555 Main St; cooking demonstration $15; ☺ 10am-6pm), a grad school for chefs, occupies the Christian Brothers' 1889 chateau and features twice-daily cooking demos. The attached, well-regarded **Wine Spectator Greystone restaurant** (☎ 707-967-1010; mains $19-32; ☺ 11:30am-9:30pm Sun-Thu, until 10pm Fri & Sat) serves less-pricey appetizers in its bar and lovely garden.

Near Calistoga, surrealist art and wine make your head spin at **Clos Pegase** (☎ 707-942-4981; www.clospegase.com; 1060 Dunaweal Lane). Don't miss it.

Linger in **Calistoga**, particularly in its famous **thermal spas** or mud baths. **Indian Springs** (☎ 707-942-4913; 1712 Lincoln Ave) and Golden Haven (p976) are both good picks; packages last an hour and start around $75, not including extras such as massages. For the complete Northern California, clothing-optional experience, head for **Harbin Hot Springs** (☎ 707-987-2477; www.harbin.org; day-use midweek/weekend $25/35, dm $35/50, d $90/140), 4 miles north of Middletown, which is 12 miles north of Calistoga. There's a vegetarian restaurant; bring linens for dorms.

IF YOU HAVE A FEW MORE DAYS: PALO ALTO & SAN JOSE

Once abuzz with dot-com start-ups, **Palo Alto** has settled into being a cool college town – most of the laptop-toters you'll see are Stanford University students. Check out the campus and the gorgeous **Cantor Arts Center** (☎ 650-723-4177; admission free; ☺ 11am-5pm Wed-Sun, 11am-8pm Thu), on Museum Way; its Rodin sculpture garden is both horrific and beautiful. **Palo Alto Creamery Fountain & Grill** (☎ 650-323-3131; 566 Emerson St; mains $9-18; ☺ 7am-11pm Mon-Thu, 7am-midnight Fri, 8am-midnight Sat, 8am-11pm Sun) delivers 1923-style Americana with foot-high apple pie and malteds too thick for a straw.

If you've got kids, take 'em to the museums in **San Jose**. Especially fun is the **Technology Museum of Innovation** (☎ 408-294-8324; www.thetech.org; 201 S Market St; admission $8; ☺ 10am-5pm, Tue-Sun winter), where interactive exhibits sell the computer revolution. Don't tell slack-jawed adults this was built for the kids.

SLEEPING & EATING

Napa lodgings are pricey unless you opt for midrange chain-style motels. Your best bet for sleeping is Calistoga.

Bothe-Napa Valley State Park (☎ 707-942-4575; reservations 800-444-7275; www.reserveamerica.com; campsites $15-20; 🐾) For camping; gorgeous hiking beneath redwoods to the Bale Grist Mill.

Calistoga Inn (☎ 707-942-4101; www.calistogainn .com; 1250 Lincoln Ave, Calistoga; r with shared bath midweek/ weekend $65/125) No TVs or phones. Downstairs is a brewery-restaurant.

Golden Haven (☎ 707-942-6793; www.goldenhaven .com; 1713 Lake St, Calistoga; r midweek/weekend from $85/99) Nothing-special rooms at great prices.

El Bonita Motel (☎ 707-963-3216, 800-541-3284; www.elbonita.com; 195 Main St; r $135-189) Book in advance to secure a room at this sought-after St Helena motel.

Oakville Grocery (☎ 707-944-8802; www.oakville grocery.com; 7856 St Helena Hwy at Oakville Crossroad; 🕙 9am-6pm) *The* place for stinky cheeses, crusty breads, sandwiches and picnics.

Gordon's Cafe & Wine Bar (☎ 707-944-8246; 6770 Washington St, Yountville; sandwiches & salads $6-12; 🕙 to 3pm) Hang with locals at this unpretentious midvalley breakfast and lunch spot.

Wappo Bar & Bistro (☎ 707-942-4712; 1226 Washington St, Calistoga; lunch mains $9-14; dinner mains $14-24 🕙 11:30am-2:30pm & 6-9:30pm, closed Tue) For eclectic world-influenced bistro fare; winemakers eat here.

French Laundry (☎ 707-944-2380; www.frenchlaundry .com; 6640 Washington St, Yountville; fixed-price menu $240; 🕙 5:30-9:30pm daily, 11am-1pm Fri-Sun) The pinnacle of California dining, the French Laundry is epic, a high-wattage culinary experience on par with the world's best. Book two months ahead at 10am sharp.

Sonoma Valley

Way-fun Sonoma Valley is less commercial than Napa and has about 60 wineries, most just off Hwy 12. Unlike Napa, most Sonoma wineries welcome picnicking.

Kick-back-casual Sonoma anchors the valley's southern end. The **visitor center** (☎ 707-996-1090, 800-576-6662; www.sonomavalley; 453 1st St E; 🕙 9am-5pm) is on historic Sonoma Plaza, surrounded by restaurants, shops and galleries.

SIGHTS & ACTIVITIES

Sonoma State Historical Park (☎ 707-938-1519; www .parks.ca.gov; adult/child under 17 $2/free; 🕙 10am-5pm) includes the 1823 Sonoma Mission; Sonoma

Barracks; Vallejo home, a half-mile away; and Petaluma Adobe (15 miles west near suburban Petaluma), for a little 19th-century California.

Down a quiet country road in Sonoma, **Gundlach-Bundschu** (☎ 707-938-5277; www.gunbun .com; 2000 Denmark St) feels like a storybook castle, with its own lake, picnicking and hiking.

Taste Syrah in a garage at tiny, Aussie-owned **Loxton Cellars** (☎ 707-935-7221; www.loxtonwines.com; 11466 Dunbar Rd). In Kenwood, meet the interesting winemaker at **Kaz Winery** (☎ 707-833-2536; www.kazwinery.com; 233 Adobe Canyon Rd; 🕙 11am-5pm Fri-Mon).

Santa Rosa, at the valley's northern end, is nothing special, but convenient and affordable. A quirky, fun stop is the **Charles M Schulz Museum** (☎ 707-579-4452; www.schulzmuseum.org; 2301 Hardies Lane; adult/child $8/5; 🕙 11am-5pm Mon-Fri, 10am-5pm Sat & Sun), dedicated to Santa Rosa's native son and his creation, Charlie Brown and the Peanuts gang.

SLEEPING

The town of Sonoma makes a convenient base.

Sugarloaf Ridge State Park (☎ 707-833-5712, reservations 800-444-7275; www.reserveamerica.com; campsites $15-20) North of Kenwood on Adobe Canyon Rd. Fifty sites (no hookups) are nestled in two meadows, close to strenuous hiking and wineries: take your pick.

Hillside Inn (☎ 707-546-9353; www.hillside-inn.com; 2901 Fourth St; s/d $70/78; 🅿 🐾 wi-fi) Town's best-kept motel is closest to Sonoma Valley, too; add $4 for kitchens.

Sandman Hotel (☎ 707-544-8570; 3421 Cleveland Ave; s/d $84/90; 🅿 🐾 wi-fi) This is one of several chain motels on Cleveland Ave. It's a good option if you're conserving cash.

Jack London Lodge (☎ 707-938-8510; www.jack londonlodge.com; 13740 Arnold Dr, Glen Ellen; r midweek/ weekend $120/180; 🅿 🐾 🐾 wi-fi) Saloon-style, antique-filled motel rooms.

Sonoma Hotel (☎ 707-996-2996, 800-468-6016; www .sonomahotel.com; 110 W Spain St, Sonoma; r incl breakfast midweek/weekend from $140/198; 🐾) On Sonoma Plaza, it's historic and stylish. Several small rooms are cheaper.

El Pueblo Inn (☎ 707-996-3651, 800-900-8844; www .elpuebloinn.com; 896 W Napa St, Sonoma; r old/new midweek $154/184, weekend $219/249; 🅿 🐾 🐾) One mile west of downtown Sonoma, El Pueblo has comfy older motel rooms and posher newer ones.

EATING

Cafe la Haye (☎ 707-935-5994; www.cafelahaye.com; 140 E Napa St, Sonoma; mains $16-33; ⏲ from 5:30pm Tue-Sat) Attached to an arts center, it serves big-city cooking in a tiny bistro.

Other options:

Sonoma Market (☎ 707-996-3411; 500 W Napa St, Sonoma; ⏲ 6am-9pm) Get picnic supplies here.

Fig Cafe (☎ 707-938-2130; www.thegirlandthefig.com; 13690 Arnold Dr, Glen Ellen; mains $10-20; ⏲ 5:30-9pm, brunch 9:30am-2pm Sat & Sun) Euro-Cal comfort food in a casual café.

Russian River Valley

The Russian River Valley is so hip just because it doesn't care. In western Sonoma County, it's two hours north of San Francisco (via Hwys 101 and 116), and has its own vineyards, redwoods and small, honky-tonk vacation towns. **Guerneville** is the biggest. Gays and lesbians love it, as do young families and Harley riders. Everyone digs canoeing. The **visitor center** (☎ 707-869-3533; www.russianriver.com; 16209 1st St; ⏲ 10am-5pm, until 4pm Sun) has maps and lodging updates.

The 805-acre **Armstrong Redwoods State Reserve** (☎ 707-869-2015; per car $6, campsites $15), 2 miles north of Guerneville, protects magnificent old-growth redwoods. Camp at nearby Austin Creek.

For lazy down-river floats, everyone rents canoes from **Burke's Canoe Trips** (☎ 707-887-1222; www.burkescanoetrips.com; 8600 River Rd; canoes $58), 7 miles east of town; call ahead, and stash a six-pack and sunscreen.

South of town, taste bubbly in a hilltop barn at **Iron Horse Vineyards** (☎ 707-887-1507; www.ironhorsevineyards.com; 97786 Ross Station Rd; $10 tasting; ⏲ 10am-3:30pm).

Nine miles west of Guerneville, tiny, über-quaint **Duncans Mills** has kayak rentals and the always-good **Cape Fear Café** (☎ 707-865-9246; 25191 Hwy 116; breakfast & lunch $8-15, dinner $16-24; ⏲ 9am-2:30pm & 5-9pm).

The **Bohemian Highway**, south of Monte Rio, winds south to some cool finds in **Occidental**, with funky shops (think found-object designs and consignment lingerie), cafés and creative bistro fare.

Healdsburg to Ukiah

Healdsburg's getting posher but is full of spunky, fun-loving locals. The foodie paradise centers on a green, Spanish-style plaza. More than 90 wineries within a 30-mile radius dot the Rus-

DON'T MISS

- **J Vineyards** – Gourmet pairings with tastings…mmm (below)
- **Roshambo Winery** – Ultra-hip winery fighting the establishment (below)
- **Canoeing** the Russian River at Burke's Canoes (left)
- **Soaking** in Calistoga at Indian Springs (p975)
- **Thermal spa bliss** (p975)

sian River, Dry Creek and Alexander Valleys. The **Healdsburg Visitors Center** (☎ 707-433-6935, 800-648-9922; www.healdsburg.org; 217 Healdsburg Ave; ⏲ 9am-5pm Mon-Fri, until 3pm Sat, 10am-2pm Sun) has *Wine Country* maps; **Spoke Folk Cyclery** (☎ 707-433-7171; www.spokefolk.com; 201 Center St; per hr/day $10/30) rents bikes.

Near the Russian River, pop art, zin and breakbeat music collide at gimmicky **Roshambo Winery** (☎ 707-433-7165; www.roshambowinery.com; 3000 Westside Rd). At the north end of Dry Creek Valley, it's a fun bike trip to **Bella Vineyards** (☎ 707-473-9171, 866-572-3552; www.bellawinery.com; 9711 W Dry Creek Rd) – big reds served in a hillside cave. At **J Vineyards** (☎ 888-594-6326; www.jwine .com; 11447 Old Redwood Hwy) the $25 tasting flight comes paired with delectable offerings from the on-site chef.

Pastoral **Anderson Valley** is studded with vineyards and apple orchards; detour via Hwy 128 northwest to tiny **Booneville**. If you feel inspired, stop here and play a round of disc golf at the **Mendocino Brewing Company** (☎ 707-895-2337; www.mendobrew.com; 17700 Hwy 253), then return via Hwy 253 northeast to Ukiah. Cute **Hopland**, 15 miles south of Ukiah on Hwy 101, has Old West–style buildings and wine-tasting rooms. Get lost in (and eat your way through) the **Fetzer Vineyards Organic Estates** (☎ 800-846-8637; www.fetzer.com; 13601 Eastside Rd; ⏲ 9am-5pm), a series of gorgeous meandering gardens; drop by **Real Goods Solar Living Center** (☎ 707-744-2017; www.solarliving.org; 13771 S Hwy 101; admission by donation $1-5; ⏲ 8:30am-5pm) for 12 acres of demos on permaculture and alternative energy.

SLEEPING & EATING

Healdsburg's budget options include the not-half-bad **L&M Motel** (☎ 707-433-6528; www.landm motel.com; 70 Healdsburg Ave; r $75-99; ✕ ✕ ✕) and the nicer **Best Western Dry Creek** (☎ 707-433-0300, 800-222-5784; www.drycreekinn.com; 198 Dry Creek Rd; r $115-135; ✖ ■).

Foodies: the venerable French Laundry (p976) now has competition in swanky **Cyrus** (☎ 707-433-3311; www.cyrusrestaurant.com; fixed-price menus $68-92; ⏱ 5:30-9:30pm), an ultrachic dining room in the great tradition of the French-country auberge. **Bovolo** (☎ 707-431-2962; 106 Matheson St; lunch mains $9-16; 3-course supper $27; ⏱ in summer 9am-9pm Fri-Tue, to 6pm Thu, in winter 9am-6pm Mon, Tues & Thu, untill 9pm Fri-Sun) at Plaza Farms is a delicious Slow Food takeout-café.

The **Hopland Brewery Tavern** (☎ 707-744-1361; ⏱ noon-7pm Thu-Mon, until 9pm Fri & Sat) is the nation's oldest brewpub and has awesome beer by the Mendocino Brewing Company, but no food.

Getting There & Around

Wine Country is 90 minutes north of San Francisco via Hwy 101 or I-80. Buses get you to the valleys but aren't ideal for vineyard-hopping. For transit information, dial ☎ 511. **Greyhound buses** (☎ 800-231-2222; www.greyhound.com) run from San Francisco to Santa Rosa ($19.75). **Golden Gate Transit** (☎ 415-923-2000; www.goldengate.org) runs from San Francisco to Petaluma ($7.60) and Santa Rosa ($8.40), where you connect with **Sonoma County Transit** (☎ 707-576-7433; www.sctra nsit.com).

For Napa, take BART trains (p972) from San Francisco to El Cerrito, and transfer to **Vallejo Transit** (☎ 707-648-4666; www.vallejotransit.com) to Vallejo; **Napa Valley Vine** (☎ 707-255-7631, 800-696-6443; www.napavalleyvine.net) buses run between Vallejo, Napa and Calistoga.

Bicycles cost about $30 to $40 per day. Rent in Yountville (and book tours) at **Napa Valley Bike Tours** (☎ 707-944-2953, 800-707-2453; www.napavalleybiketours.com; 6488 Washington St), in Calistoga at **Calistoga Bike Shop** (☎ 707-942-9687, 866-942-2453; www.calistogabikeshop.com; 1318 Lincoln Ave) and in Sonoma at **Sonoma Valley Cyclery** (☎ 707-935-3377; 20093 Broadway).

NORTH COAST

Forget everything you've learned about California from the movies – unless you're a Hitchcock fan. The moody, isolated North Coast shatters the sunny Cali myth, but it is staggeringly beautiful in its own right. There are towering redwoods, deep-green mosses, craggy cliffs and lazing sea lions, but hardly any people: if you're looking for someplace

to set down your yurt or escape the law, look no further.

Bodega Bay to Fort Bragg

Winding above crashing surf, along narrow, cascading cliffs and grassy flatlands, Hwy 1 along the Sonoma and Mendocino coast may be the most beautiful – and challenging – stretch of main road in Northern California. When your sunglasses start sliding all over the dashboard, know to take it easy. At the gorgeous beaches, swimming's not a good idea (frigid water and rip tides), but watch for gray whales migrating down the coast from November to April. Budget four hours without stops, and good luck finding a radio station.

Bodega Bay is a cool little fishing town; follow along the fantastic state beaches extending north to Jenner. Head inland 3 miles to tiny Bodega – recognize it from Hitchcock's 1963 thriller *The Birds*? It looks far less ominous. Here, **Bodega Bay Sportfishing** (☎ 707-875-3495; 1410 Bay Flat Rd) runs whale-watching trips and **Bodega Bay Surf Shack** (☎ 707-875-3944; www.bodegabaysurf.com; surfboards per day $13, kayaks per 4hr $45) rents surfboards and kayaks.

From **Jenner**, perched atop pretty coastal hills at the mouth of the Russian River, you can catch glimpses of a resident harbor seal colony. Look for seals from Hwy 1 turnouts north of town.

The centerpiece of **Fort Ross State Park** (☎ 707-847-3286, 707-847-3708; www.parks.ca.gov; per car $6, campsites $15) is an 1812 Russian trading post with cool historical exhibits and reconstructed barracks and blockhouses. There's also drive-in, first-come, first-served camping.

Salt Point State Park (☎ 707-847-3221, reservations 800-444-7275; www.reserveamerica.com; per car $6, campsites $25) has hiking trails, tide pools, two campgrounds and Gerstle Cove Marine Reserve and Kruse Rhododendron State Reserve, where pink blooms spot the green, wet woods in springtime. Cows dot the rock-strewn fields on the bluffs; look for organic dairy cooperatives.

Gualala (wah-*la*-la), founded in 1858 as a lumber mill, has a breathtaking coastal location. It's expensive to stay in town, but a mile south, **Gualala Point Regional Park** (☎ 707-785-2377, reservations 707-565-2267; www.sonoma-county.org/parks; per car $5, campsites $19) has a redwood-forested campground, windswept beach and hiking trails down to the Pacific.

Pretty **Point Arena** has a cute main street and an ugly fishing pier. Just north, if you want to pay the whopping entrance fee, ascend the 1908 **Point Arena Lighthouse & Museum** (☎ 707-882-2777; www.pointarenalighthouse.com; admission $7) for knockout coastal views. Access is only from 10am to 3:30pm.

Eight miles north of Elk, **Van Damme State Park** (☎ 707-937-5804, reservations 800-444-7275; www.reserveamerica.com; per car $6, campsites $25) has popular **Fern Canyon Trail**, passing through a pygmy forest, and good camping.

No North Coast vista compares to **Mendocino**. Walk the headland among berry bramble, lilies and wildflowers, with cypress jutting out onto dizzying cliffs. Driftwood atop wild fields and cave tunnels hewn from the rock is evidence of nature's force, and the sea is blue even when the sky isn't. The town itself is full of cutesy shops and B&Bs – no chains – and has earned the nickname 'Spendocino,' but you won't find Prada sunglasses here. At **Mendocino Twist** (☎ 707-937-1717; 45140 Main St) you can choose from bamboo, hemp, organic cotton and even *soy* clothing. The **visitor center** (☎ 707-937-5397; www.gomendo.com; ⏰ 11am-4pm) is in the Ford House on Main St.

Fort Bragg is where you'll find cheap gas, a trailer park on the bluff, sprawling motels and a large Latino working population. Gems include **Cowlick's Ice Cream** (☎ 707-962-9271; 250 N Main St; $2.75 regular cone, $1.75 small cone; ⏰ 11am-9pm) – cool flavor: candy-cap 'shrooms – and thick, hearty brews at **North Coast Brewing Co** (☎ 707-964-2739; 455 N Main St). Fort Bragg's pride and joy is the 1885 **Skunk Train** (☎ 800-866-1690; www.skunktrain.com; adult/child 3-11 $45/20), whose diesel and steam engines make half-day trips into the woods.

SLEEPING & EATING

Sleeping and Eating options following are listed south to north.

The **Bodega Harbor Inn** (☎ 707-875-3594; www.bodegaharborinn.com; 1345 Bodega Ave; r $70-150; ✖), in Bodega Bay, has affordable cottage-style rooms. BBQ oysters and local rock cod are faves at the **Boathouse** (☎ 707-875-3495; 1445 N Hwy 1; mains $11-15; ⏰ noon-8pm), a little buoy-strung shack with a sloping floor.

Jenner's **River's End Cabins** (☎ 707-865-2484; www.ilovesunsets.com; 11048 Hwy 1; cabins $115-185) is peaceful and rustic (no TV/phone) with a restaurant. **Wright's Beach campsites** (☎ 800-444-7275; www.reserveamerica.com; campsites $25-35) are nestled

in the bushes on a spectacular white sandy beach; $35 sites have the best views.

In Gualala, gorgeous and quirky **St Orres** (☎ 707-884-3303; www.saintorres.com; Hwy 1; r with shared bath incl breakfast $90-130, cottages from $135) has a hand-hewn Russian-style redwood main hotel, secluded cottages and a dramatic Cal-cuisine restaurant (dinner mains $40). Or sample from the in-house bakery and char-cuterie at **Pangaea** (☎ 707-884-9669; www.pangaeacafe.com; 39165 S Hwy 1; mains $23-25; ⏰ from 5:30pm Wed-Sun). Just north, ever-so-charming **Mar Vista Cottages** (☎ 707-884-3522, 877-855-3522; www.marvistamendocino.com; 35101 S Hwy 1; cottages from $155; ✖) is the sweetest stay on this route.

Lovely Mendocino is an expensive stay. **Sweetwater Spa & Inn** (☎ 800-300-4140, 707-937-4076; www.sweetwaterspa.com; 44840 Main St; r $75-275) runs dozens of attractive lodgings; all rates include use of the spa, which can also be enjoyed on its own.

Jughandle Creek Farm (☎ 707-964-4630; http://jughandle.creek.org; r & cabins adult $38, student $30, child $13, camping $12) is an educational center in Caspar, opposite Jug Handle State Reserve. Hostel-like private rooms and cabins share baths (bring sleeping bags); the farmhouse has a kitchen. Call ahead for work-stay discounts.

Fort Bragg has many nondescript midrange motels. The most unbelievable bargain is the **Colombi Motel** (☎ 707-964-5773; www.colombimotel.com; 647 Oak St; r $35-55). Local musicians play at always-fun **Headlands Coffeehouse** (☎ 707-964-1987; 120 E Laurel St; panini sandwiches $7-8; ⏰ 7am-10pm Sun-Thu, to 11pm Fri-Sat).

GETTING THERE & AWAY

Mendocino Transit Authority (MTA; ☎ 800-696-4682; www.4mta.org) operates bus 65 daily from Fort Bragg south to Santa Rosa via Willits and Ukiah ($20, 3 hours); at Santa Rosa, catch San Francisco–bound bus 80 ($8.40), operated by **Golden Gate Transit** (☎ 415-923-2000; www.goldengate.org). Neither Greyhound nor Amtrak serves towns along Hwy 1.

Ukiah to Scotia

Ukiah doesn't have a lot going on, but nearby is the **Vichy Hot Springs Resort** (p980).

North of tiny **Leggett** on Hwy 101, lose yourself under giant redwoods at **Standish-Hickey State Recreation Area** (☎ 707-925-6482, 69350 Hwy 101; per car $6). It has river swimming and fishing as well as 9 miles of hiking trails in virgin and second-growth redwoods (look for the 225ft-tall Miles Standish tree). Fourteen miles further north is **Richardson Grove State Park**, for 1400 acres of more virgin redwoods.

Garberville and its ragged sister Redway, 2 miles away, became famous in the 1970s for the sinsemilla (potent, seedless marijuana) grown in the surrounding hills. Today Garberville is a quiet, one-street town with cheap motels and diners, and fisher-logger types and hippies.

The **Lost Coast** became 'lost' when the state's highway system bypassed the rugged mountains of the King Range, which rise 4000ft within several miles of the ocean. The region is largely undeveloped, and the scenery is stunning. From Garberville it's 23 miles along a rough road to Shelter Cove, a seaside subdivision with a deli, restaurant and motels. Talk to locals before venturing along back roads.

Along Hwy 101, 80-sq-mile **Humboldt Redwoods State Park** (☎ 707-946-2409, reservations 800-444-7275; www.reserveamerica.com; campsites $15-20) protects some of the world's oldest redwoods. Feel like you're driving a Matchbox car underneath the canopy of the awe-inspiring **Avenue of the Giants**, a 32-mile, two-lane road running parallel to Hwy 101. Book ahead for magnificent campsites near the informative **visitor center** (☎ 707-946-2409; ☙ 9am-5pm).

Scotia is a rarity in the modern world: a 'company town' entirely owned and operated by the Pacific Lumber Company. It's a creepy place (smile: you're being watched). Stop by the **Scotia Museum & Visitors Center** (☎ 707-764-2222; www.palco.com; admission free; ☙ 8am-4:30pm Mon-Fri summer only), on Main St, and see if it's offering mill tours.

SLEEPING & EATING

The following sleeping and eating listings run south to north.

In Ukiah, chain motels, such as Motel 6, Super 8 Motel and Discovery Inn, line S State St. The best value is **Sunrise Inn** (☎ 707-462-6601; www.sunriseinn.net; 650 S State St; r $48-68; ☒). Seven hundred-acre **Vichy Springs Resort** (☎ 707-462-9515; www.vichysprings.com; 2605 Vichy Springs Rd, Ukiah; RV campsites $20, lodge s/d $120/165, creekside r $170/215, cottages $295; ☒ ☒) has the only warm-water, naturally carbonated mineral baths in North America; two-hour day-use costs $25, all-day use runs to $38. For eats that are alone worth the detour to Ukiah, enjoy organic, seasonal

Euro-Cal plates at **Patrona** (☎ 707-462-9181; www.patronarestaurant.com; dinner mains $15-25; ☙ 5:30-9pm Tue-Sat, plus 11:30am-2pm Thu & Fri).

The historic Tudor-style **Benbow Inn** (☎ 707-923-2124, 800-355-3301; www.benbowinn.com; r $130-200; wi-fi), just south of Garberville off Hwy 101, indulges guests with complimentary decanted sherry in each lovely room; consider a riverside room if you're splurging. The white-tablecloth restaurant and wood-paneled bar are particularly inviting on foggy evenings.

Along the Avenue of the Giants, tiny Miranda has several eateries and **Miranda Gardens Resort** (☎ 707-943-3011; www.mirandagardens.com; cottages without kitchen $105-135, with kitchen $145-185; ☒). Stand-alone, redwood-paneled cottages are a tad musty, but ideal for families and long stays.

In Phillipsville, the **Vacation House in the Redwoods** (☎ 707-722-4330; www.redwoodvisitor.org; 31117 Ave of the Giants; house $135) is a lovely one-bedroom cottage in a sunny flower farm. It also has a hammock, deck and hot tub, and sleeps up to five.

GETTING THERE & AROUND

Greyhound (☎ 800-231-2222; www.greyhound.com) operates from San Francisco to Ukiah ($31.50). The **Redwood Transit System** (☎ 707-443-0826; www.hta.org) operates buses Monday through Saturday between Scotia and Trinidad ($1.95, 2½ hours).

Eureka to Crescent City

While it doesn't inspire shouting its name, sleepy **Eureka**, strip-mallish on the outside, does have its Old Town with fine Victorians and inviting shops and restaurants. The **Eureka visitor center** (☎ 707-442-3738, 800-356-6381; www.eurekachamber.com; 2112 Broadway; ☙ 8:30am-5pm Mon-Fri, 10am-4pm Sat) has maps and information. In Old Town, **Going Places** (☎ 707-443-4145; 328 2nd St) is a fabulous travel bookstore.

The **Clarke Memorial Museum** (☎ 707-443-1947; 3rd & E Sts; admission by donation; ☙ 11am-4pm Tue-Sat) has impressive Native American collections. Don't miss **Blue Ox Millworks** (☎ 707-444-3437; www.blueoxmill.com; adult/child 6-12 $7.50/3.50; ☙ 9am-4pm Mon-Sat), one of only seven of its kind in the nation that hand-mills Victorian detailing using traditional carpentry and authentic 19th-century equipment. Fascinating, self-guided tours let you watch the craftsmen work. Cruise the harbor aboard the blue-

and-white 1910 **Madaket** (☎ 707-445-1910; www .humboldtbaymaritimemuseum.com; adult/child 5-12/senior & teen $15/7.50/13; ☼ May-Oct), which departs from the foot of C St.

Nine miles north of Eureka, don't let **Arcata's** quaint facade fool you: this is a patchouli-dipped, far-left leaning college town, where trucks run on biodiesel and recycling gets picked up by tandem bicycle. On the northeast side of town, **Humboldt State University** (☎ 707-826-3011; www.humboldt.edu) has a pretty campus and a provocative art gallery.

At the junction of Hwys 299 and 101 is a **California Welcome Center** (☎ 707-822-3619; www.arcata chamber.com; ☼ 9am-5pm), with tons of area info.

Trinidad, a working fishing town about 12 miles north of Arcata, sits on a bluff overlooking a glittering blue-water harbor. There are lovely sand beaches and short hikes on Trinidad Head. Nearby Luffenholtz Beach is popular (but unpatrolled) for surfing, and north of town, Patrick's Point Rd is dotted with lodging and campgrounds tucked into the forest. **Patrick's Point State Park** (☎ 707-677-3570; reservations 800-444-7275; www.reserveamerica.com; day-use $6, campsites $15-20) has stunning rocky headlands, tide pools and camping.

On Hwy 101 a mile south of tiny **Orick** is the **visitor center for Redwood National & State Parks** (☎ 707-464-6101, ext 5265; www.nps.gov/redw; ☼ 9am-5pm). Together, Redwood National Park and Prairie Creek, Del Norte and Jedediah Smith State Parks are a designated World Heritage Site and contain almost half of the remaining old-growth redwood forests in California. The national park is free; the state parks have a reciprocal $6 day-use fee in some areas. Only the state parks have developed campsites ($20), all highly recommended. The visitor center has info about all the parks and free permits for backcountry camping and to visit Tall Trees Grove.

The highlights at **Redwood National Park** are **Lady Bird Johnson Grove** and **Tall Trees Grove**, home to several of the world's tallest trees, as well as roaming elk herds.

Prairie Creek Redwoods State Park (☎ 707-464-6101, ext 5301) has famous Fern Canyon, a sheer 60ft fissure overgrown with ferns. It's free to drive the 8-mile **Newton B Drury Scenic Parkway**, which passes through virgin redwood forests and runs parallel to Hwy 101.

But for the giant cast-metal golden bears at the bridge, you could drive right past **Klamath** and never know it existed. Isolated amid trees

and water, it's ideal for outdoor adventures. Several miles north, **Del Norte Coast Redwoods State Park** (☎ 707-464-6101, ext 5120) contains redwood groves and 8 miles of unspoiled coastline.

Sprawling over a crescent-shaped bay, **Crescent City** with its ticky-tacky-box architecture is the only sizable coastal town north of Arcata. More than half the town was destroyed by a tidal wave in 1964, hence the '60s kitsch effect. When the tide's out, you can check out the 1865 **Battery Point Lighthouse** (☎ 707-464-3089; admission $3; ☼ 10am-4pm Wed-Sun Apr-Oct), at the south end of A St.

Jedediah Smith Redwoods State Park (☎ 707-464-6101, ext 5112), 5 miles northeast of Crescent City, is less crowded than the other parks but no less beautiful and lush. The redwood stands are so dense that there are few trails, but the outstanding 11-mile **Howland Hill Scenic Drive** is the best way to see the forest if you can't hike.

SLEEPING & EATING

The sleeping and eating options following are listed south to north.

Plain Jane motels line Hwy 101 in Eureka; the cheapest are south of downtown. On a hill above the highway is the family-run **Bayview Motel** (☎ 707-442-1673, 866-725-6813; www.bayview motel.com; 2844 Fairfield St; r $90-95; ☒ wi-fi), a bright, clean midrange choice (some rooms *do* have a bay view). In Old Town, luxurious **Carter House Inns** (☎ 707-444-8062, 800-404-1390; www.carterhouse .com; 301 L St; r incl breakfast $185-213; ☒ wi-fi) runs a cushy hotel and several Victorian properties across the street. Its fashionable Restaurant 301 is famous for New French–Cal cuisine and magnificent wines.

On the nearby Samoa Peninsula, the ever-popular **Samoa Cookhouse** (☎ 707-442-1659; all-you-can-eat meals $10-15; ☼ 7am-9pm) is the dining hall of an 1893 lumber camp. Lumberjack-sized grub with all the fixin's is served on long, oilcloth-covered tables.

In Arcata, the 1915 **Hotel Arcata** (☎ 707-826-0217, 800-344-1221; www.hotelarcata.com; 708 9th St; r $84-90; wi-fi) is a little stuffy, but the rooms are comfy and it's on the square.

In Klamath, the hiker-catering 1914 **Requa Inn** (☎ 707-482-1425, 866-800-8777; www.requainn.com; 451 Requa Rd; r $85-155; ☒ wi-fi) has country-style rooms overlooking the river. Pioneer homestead **HI Redwood Hostel** (☎ 707-482-8265; www .norcalhostels.org; 14480 Hwy 101; dm/r $20/45), 8 miles north of Klamath, occupies a stunning spot.

CALIFORNIA

Crescent Beach Motel (☎ 707-464-5436; www.cres centbeachmotel.com; 1455 Hwy 101 S, Crescent City; ocean view s/d $92/98, nonview r $70) has plain rooms with ugly bedspreads, no phones, but wow! – million-dollar ocean views.

GETTING THERE & AROUND

Greyhound (☎ 800-231-2222; www.greyhound.com) serves Arcata; from San Francisco budget $39 and seven hours. **Redwood Transit buses** (☎ 707-443-0826; www.hta.org) serve Arcata and Eureka on their Monday through Saturday Trinidad–Scotia routes ($1.95, 2½ hours).

SACRAMENTO

Gold-diggers will be disappointed. In the flat, agricultural Central Valley, Sacramento, with its blandly alphabetical streets, is nothing flash. But if it's the gold-rush history and not the gold you're after, start in the state capital. Its Old Sacramento, touristy-kitsch at times, is otherwise an authentic patch of the dusty Old West with raised wooden sidewalks, hitching posts for parking meters, and real steam trains. Check out the museums (well worthwhile), but know that the city isn't exactly pedestrian friendly. Its creative attempts at connecting walkways from Old Sac to downtown, over and under roaring freeways, doesn't quite work. But it tries hard!

In 1839, Swiss immigrant John Sutter built a fort and pioneer community in present-day Sacramento – making it the area's first European settlement. After the shiny stuff was found in the nearby foothills in 1848, the fort was quickly overrun by fortune-hungry miners. In 1854, after several years of legislative waffling, the riverfront settlement became California's capital.

The **visitor center** (☎ 916-442-7644; www.discover gold.org; 1004 2nd St; ☼ 10am-5pm) in Old Sacramento can recommend hotels.

Sights

The pristine white 19th-century **state capitol** is at 10th St and Capitol Mall; inside, it's stunning. The **Capitol Museum** (☎ 916-324-0333; www .statecapitolmuseum.com; admission free; ☼ 9am-5pm), gives tours through period-furnished chambers. Don't miss the Assembly and Senate rooms, which are open to the public even when in session.

Along the Sacramento River, **Old Sacramento** (Old Sac; www.oldsacramento.com) clusters California's largest concentration of historic buildings on the National Register, decent restaurants and three superb museums. The **California State Railroad Museum** (☎ 916-323-9280, 916-445-6645; www.californiastaterailroadmuseum.org; 125 I St; adult/child 6-17 $8/3; ☼ 10am-5pm) is the locomotive mother lode. It lets you get into and under more than 20 meticulously restored black beasts of steam and diesel; ride a steam train ($8) at summer weekends. Next door, the **Discovery Museum** (☎ 916-264-7057; www.the discovery.org; 101 I St; adult/child 13-17/child 4-12 $5/4/3; ☼ 10am-5pm, closed Mon in winter) brings to life gold-rush-era Sacramento.

Nearby, Judge Edwin B Crocker's jaw-dropping Victorian home contains his visionary collection of 19th-century paintings, now the eponymous **Crocker Art Museum** (☎ 916-264-5423; www.crockerartmuseum.org; 3rd & O Sts; adult/child 7-17 $6/3; ☼ 10am-5pm Tue-Sun, until 9pm Thu). There's free admission Sunday from 10am to 1pm.

Restored to its 1850s appearance, **Sutter's Fort** (☎ 916-445-4422; cnr 27th & L Sts; adult/child 6-16 $4/2; ☼ 10am-5pm) fills with costumed 'reenactors' daily in summer and sometimes Saturday the rest of the year. Adjacent to the fort, the well-done **California State Indian Museum** (☎ 916-324-0971; adult/child under 16 $2/free; ☼ 10am-5pm) is small but informative, and has Ishi artifacts.

Sleeping & Eating

Downtown has a glut of midrange chain hotels, including Quality Inn, Holiday Inn, Travelodge and Best Western. For restaurants, try Old Sac and J St north of 16 St.

our pick **HI Sacramento Hostel** (☎ 916-443-1691; 925 H St; dm $22, r $34.50; ℗ ✕ 🖳) This is a *hostel*? Sweet! The public areas in this restored Victorian mansion are B&B quality, spacious dorms are clean, and staff are superfriendly, plus it's convenient to Old Sac. Parking $5. Internet $1 per five minutes.

Delta King (☎ 916-444-5464, 800-825-5464; www.delta king.com; r incl breakfast midweek/weekend from $119/169; ℗ ✕ 🐾) The idea might be cheesy, but the teeny-tiny cabins are gorgeous in this refurbished 1927 paddlewheeler docked on the river in Old Sac. Riverside rooms (add $15) are best. Three ghosts included. Parking $12.

Firehouse (916-442-4772; www.firehouseoldsac .com; 1112 2nd St; lunch mains $11-18, dinner $19-39; ☼ 11:30am-2:30pm Sun-Fri & 5-10:30pm Mon-Sat) Ignore the elevator music and enjoy the tree-canopied courtyard, notable wine list and gourmet tweaks to the Old Sac fave's steak-and-seafood menu.

For award-winning beer (try the IPA) and decent pub grub, join the locals at **Rubicon** (916-448-7032; www.rubiconbrewing.com; 2004 Capitol Ave; sandwiches $6-9; 11am-11:30pm Mon-Thu, until 12:30am Fri & Sat, until 10pm Sun).

Getting There & Around

Sacramento is 91 miles east of San Francisco via I-80 and 386 miles north of LA via I-5. **Sacramento International Airport** (916-929-5411; www.sacairports.org), 15 miles north of downtown off I-5, is serviced by most major airlines.

Greyhound (800-231-2222; 7th & L Sts) serves San Francisco ($14, two hours), Los Angeles ($52.50, nine hours), Seattle ($82, 17½ hours) and other major towns.

Sacramento's **Amtrak** (800-872-7245; cnr 5th & I Sts) depot is near downtown. Trains leave daily for Oakland ($18, two hours) and Los Angeles ($56, 14 hours).

Sacramento Regional Transit (916-321-2877; www.sacrt.com) runs a bus system (fare $2), a free downtown DASH trolley and a light-rail commuter line.

GOLD COUNTRY

Fools rushed in once. These days, wiser settlers keep it nice 'n' slow. Hugging the western Sierra Nevada, California's Gold Country, with its string of little nugget towns, winds 300 lazy, scenic miles north to south along Hwy 49. The most interesting route is from Nevada City to Sonora. As some ramshackle mining towns decay into the foothills, others have discovered a new mother lode in tourism, restoring magnificent 19th-century hotels and saloons. Sunbaked in the summer and snow-shrouded in winter, these hills are where the proud working West drinks hard, raises a family, and knows everyone in town and perhaps the county.

A gold nugget half the size of a pea started it all – by the end of 1848 more than 30,000 people had come, and by 1849 the gold rush was on, with an additional 60,000 people (known as the 49ers) scrambling to California in search of the 'Mother Lode.'

On golden summer days, rafting trips start here for the American, Tuolumne, Kings and Stanislaus Rivers. **Whitewater Connection** (800-336-7238; www.whitewaterconnection.com), on Hwy 49 in Coloma, offers half-day trips (from $94) and longer excursions. **Wolf Creek Wilderness** (530-477-2722; www.wolfcreekwilderness.com; 595 E Main St, Grass Valley; kayaks per day from $40) has kayak rentals and lessons ($40 to $150).

Outside of Auburn off I-80, exit 121, is a **California Welcome Center** (530-887-2111; www.visitplacer.com; 13411 Lincoln Way; 9:30am-4:30pm Mon-Fri, 9am-3pm Sat, 11am-3pm Sun) with statewide information, or contact the **Gold Country Visitors Association** (800-225-3764; www.calgold.org).

Northern Mines

Highway 50 divides the Southern and Northern Mines; the latter stretch south from Nevada City to Placerville.

Shiny as a silver dollar, **Nevada City** has polished up its once-rough streets with organic cafés and boutiques. For self-guided walking tours, visit the **chamber of commerce** (530-265-2692, 800-655-6569; www.nevadacitychamber.com; 132 Main St; 9am-5pm Mon-Fri, 11am-4pm Sat) or roam Broad and surrounding narrow, humpy streets for saloons and fur traders. The **Tahoe National Forest Headquarters** (530-265-4531; 8am-4:30pm Mon-Fri, plus Sat in summer), on Hwy 49 at the north end of Coyote St, has hiking and backcountry info – a bike race is held here each year and, with 18-plus trail routes, the surrounding forest is ripe for exploring by foot or pedal.

About 5 miles southwest, **Grass Valley** is a self-sufficient trading post with hardware and fabric stores – local artists, hippies and ranchers come here to buy groceries. Two miles east of town off Hwy 49, the landscaped grounds of **Empire Mine State Historic Park** (530-273-8522; www.empiremine.org; adult/child 6-16 $3/1; 9am-6pm summer, 10am-5pm winter) sit atop 367 miles of mine shafts that, from 1850 to 1956, produced six million ounces of gold. In summer, living-history weekends are popular; an underground tour of the main shaft is due to open in July 2010.

Past Auburn, the road swerves often and opens up to glorious green hills. Catch a summer swim where the North and South Forks of the American River join up, 3 miles south of Auburn on Hwy 49.

Coloma is eye-catching from the road with its **Marshall Gold Discovery State Historic Park** (530-622-3470; per car $5; 8am-dusk). There's a replica of Sutter's Mill, restored buildings, a museum (hours vary) and short hikes.

SLEEPING & EATING

The following sleeping and eating options are listed north to south.

CALIFORNIA

In Nevada City, the **Outside Inn** (☎ 530-265-2233; www.outsideinn.com; 575 E Broad St; r $75-145; ✹ ✗ ✷ wi-fi) caters to outdoorsies; themed rooms are funky-rustic (one has a rock-climbing wall). It's dog- and kid-friendly. Just outside town, **Northern Queen Inn** (☎ 530-265-5824; www.northernqueeninn.com; 400 Railroad Ave; r $94-99; ✹ ✷ wi-fi) is an affordable, well-kept 86-room motel, and has separate cottages with kitchens.

Park next to the pickups at the **Northridge** (☎ 530-478-0470; 773 Nevada St; pizza $9-22; ✹ 11am-9pm Mon-Thu & Sun, until 12:30am Fri & Sat), an unkempt roadside bar and pizza joint that's a plain ole good time. For downtown nosh, **Citronée** (☎ 530-265-5697; www.citroneebistro.com; 320 Broad St; dinner mains $16-35; ✹ from 5:30pm, closed Tue) is where local chefs eat at shift-end. Seared 'ahi, tapas and *coq au vin* is cheaper upstairs in the wine shop, fancier downstairs.

In Grass Valley, the 1852 **Holbrooke Hotel** (☎ 530-273-1252, 800-933-7077; www.holbrooke.com; 212 W Main St; r midweek/weekend from $90/105; ✹ ✗) has 28 Victorian-style rooms, with exposed brick, iron bed frames, claw-foot tubs and elaborate wallpapers. Its restaurant and bar are recommended; other good eats are nearby.

Also in Grass Valley, the coolest renovation of a historic property is the **Swan Levine House** (☎ 530-272-1873; www.swanlevinehouse.com; 328 S Church St; r $95-110; ✹ ✷), a rambling 19th-century hospital turned into a modern-art gallery with four huge, funky rooms. An attached print-making studio is open for guests' use.

Along I-80 near Auburn, at exit 121, is **Ikedas** (☎ 530-885-4243; www.ikedas.com; 13500 Lincoln Way; ✹ 8am-7pm, until 8pm weekends), a market with yummy homemade pies, burgers and fresh peach shakes. It's a fave of Tahoe-bound travelers.

Southern Mines

Descend into the Southern Mines – from Placerville to Sonora – to lose sight of civilization as you know it. Here are the raw, real prospecting towns. Some, such as **Plymouth** (Ole Pokerville) and **Mokelumne Hill** (Moke Hill), are virtual ghost towns – a line of abandoned shopfronts slowly crumbling into photogenic oblivion. Others, such as **Jackson**, **Murphys** and **Sutter Creek**, are doing just fine and are un-hurriedly planning the next town rodeo or jumping frog jubilee.

For an antidote to gold-rush fever, take Hwy 88 north to **Chaw'Se Indian Grinding Rock State Historic Park** (per car $6, campsites $15; ✹ dawn-dusk), which remains sacred ground for the local Miwok Indians. The magnificent 'grinding rock' is covered with ancient petroglyphs and mortar holes called chaw'Ses.

On the way to Grinding Rock, **Black Chasm Cavern** (☎ 866-762-2837; www.caverntours.com; adult/child 3-13 $12.95/6.50; ✹ 9am-6pm summer, 10am-5pm winter) is so stunning that *The Matrix* used it for a set, while 9 miles east of San Andreas, the granddaddy of the area's caves is the spectacular **California Cavern** (☎ 209-736-2708, 888-818-7462; www.caverntours.com; admission adult/child 3-13 $12.95/6.50; ✹ 10am-6pm mid-Apr–Nov), described by John Muir as 'graceful flowing folds deeply pleated like stiff silken drapery.'

Columbia (☎ 209-536-1672; www.columbiacalifornia .com) is now a state historic park, with four square blocks of authentic 1850s buildings and concessionaires in period costumes conjuring the Old West. It's crazy with kids panning for gold. The park itself doesn't close, but most businesses are open 10am to 5pm.

SLEEPING & EATING

Sleeping and eating listings following are ordered north to south.

our pick **St George Hotel** (☎ 209-296-4458; www .stgeorgehotel.com; 16104 Main St, Volcano; r incl breakfast $92-121; ✗ ✹ ▢) Dating from 1862, this hotel is enough reason for driving to Volcano – or even the Gold Country. Attractive rooms in the grand main building share baths, while six bungalows have private baths. Locals crowd the renowned dinner-only restaurant and its vintage saloon (open Thursday to Sunday) – a favorite watering hole serving burgers.

Hotel Leger (☎ 209-286-1401; www.hotelleger .com; 8304 Main St; r from $55) In Moke Hill. This is an authentic saloon–hotel where weeknight rates are a steal, but you might be the ghost town's lone guest in a room furnished with crumbling settees.

In Murphys, stay in the same room as Mark Twain or Ulysses S Grant at **Murphys Historic Hotel & Lodge** (☎ 209-728-3444, 800-532-7684; www.murphyshotel.com; 457 Main St; r midweek $69-89, add $20 weekends; ✹ ✗). With shared bath, no phone or telly, and an antler-festooned saloon, it's like you've just stepped off a stagecoach. Can't live without TV? Adjacent motel rooms are available. Cheap, fresh tacos and wood-fired pizzas are at **Firewood** (☎ 209-728-3248; 420 Main St; mains $5-10; ✹ 11am-9pm) across the street, which has six brews on tap to cap the deal.

In Columbia, the co-run **City Hotel & Fallon Hotel** (☎ 209-532-1479, 800-532-1479; www.cityhotel .com; Fallon Hotel r incl breakfast from $80-145, City Hotel r incl breakfast $115-145) have the most authentic Victorian restorations. The 24 stunning rooms are museum-worthy. The City Hotel has an acclaimed **restaurant** (meals $14-30; ✆ 5-9:30pm Tue-Sun, plus 9am-2pm Sun), and Fallon Hotel hosts a repertory theater. Ask about packages.

Busy Sonora has lots of midrange hotels, but for the same price, stay at the **Gunn House Hotel** (☎ 209-532-3421; www.gunnhousehotel.com; 286 S Washington St; r $79-119; P ⊠ ⊠ ⊠). Its historic, character-laden rooms are a work of love; owner Shirley bakes goodies for the breakfast room by the pool.

GETTING THERE & AROUND

About 26 miles northeast of Sacramento, Hwy 49 intersects I-80 in the town of Auburn. Local bus systems include **Gold Country Stage** (☎ 530-477-0103), which links Nevada City, Grass Valley and Auburn (fare $1 to $2), and **Placer County Transit** (☎ 530-885-2877). No public transit serves the Southern Mines on Hwy 49.

NORTHERN MOUNTAINS

In the eerily beautiful, other-worldly Northern Mountains, take a deep breath and understand that places like this still exist. Sparsely populated, it's a little-explored wonder of lakes, alps, rivers and desert. From the heights of Lassen Peak and snowcapped Mt Shasta to the scorched badlands of Lava Beds National Monument, the area captivates with landscapes of drama and grace. Working towns dotted along the way keep it real and bring you back to earth.

Redding to Yreka

Redding, something of a sprawling pit stop on the way to the scenic stuff, is suddenly getting hip. In part it's due to its new **Sundial Bridge**, a sleek glass-deck pedestrian overpass with a sky-spearing sundial designed by Spanish architect Santiago Calatrava. Locals joke that it's 'the $23 million bridge that goes nowhere,' but it spans the Sacramento River and draws walkers to the greater **Turtle Bay Exploration Park** (☎ 800-887-8532; www.turtlebay.org; 840 Auditorium Dr; adult/child 4-12 $12/7; ✆ 9am-5pm; closed Tue in winter). For a fun break, kerplunk a few golf balls into the river at **Aqua Golf** (☎ 530-244-4653; 2275 Park Marina Dr; ✆ 10am-7pm, until 6pm Sun). Visitor info for the whole area is available at **Shasta-Cascade Wonderland Association** (☎ 530-365-1180, 800-474-2782; www.shastacascade.com; ✆ 9am-5pm Mon-Fri, 10am-4pm Sat & Sun) located 10 miles south of Redding in the Shasta Factory Outlets Mall off I-5.

Weaverville, 45 miles west on Hwy 299 (the Trinity Scenic Byway), is a cool detour from Redding: you'll find the gold-rush-era Taoist temple **Joss House** here, a blacksmith and the lovingly restored **Weaverville Hotel** (☎ 530-623-2222, 800-750-8986; www.weavervillehotel.com; 203 Main St). **Weaverville Ranger Station** (☎ 530-623-2121; 210 N Main St; ✆ 8am-5pm Mon-Fri, until 4:30pm Sat) issues backcountry permits to surrounding **Trinity Alps**, a barely touched wilderness of mountain lakes and rivers.

North of Redding, I-5 crosses deep-blue **Shasta Lake**, California's biggest reservoir. Hiking trails lace the shore's 365 (!) miles. Rundown RV parks abound, but the **Lakehead Campground** (☎ 530-238-8443; www.lakehead campgroundandrv.com; campsites $19) is decent. The lake exists solely because of colossal **Shasta Dam** (☎ 530-275-4463; www.usbr.gov; ✆ 8am-5pm, free tours 9am-3pm); if you visit, be aware of high-security precautions (no electronics). High in the limestone megaliths at the north end of the lake are the prehistoric caves of **Lake Shasta Caverns** (☎ 530-238-2341, 800-795-2283; www.lakeshastacaverns .com; adult/child 3-11 $20/12; ✆ tours 9am-3pm).

Teensy **Dunsmuir**, a historic railroad town, differentiates itself via music, theater, art, and cuisine while keeping its rusticity. If for no other reason, stop to fill your water bottle from the public fountains; Dunsmuir claims it's got the best H2O on earth.

Gorgeous **Mt Shasta town** lures not only climbers but also spiritual trekkers who believe the majestic mountain imbues the region with numinous power. Apparently, locals seem to be on a perpetual high from it – they're all smiles. **Mt Shasta visitor center** (☎ 530-926-4865, 800-926-4865; www.mtshastachamber .com; 300 Pine St; ✆ 9am-5:30pm Mon-Thu, until 6pm Fri & Sat, until 4pm Sun) is a useful info hub. Tiny, white-clapboard **Sisson Museum** (☎ 530-926-5508; www .mountshastasissonmuseum.org; admission free; ✆ 1-4pm Apr-Dec, from 10am Jun-Aug, closed Jan-Mar) shows off macho mountaineering history.

Don't have an accident when you round the bend of I-5 and first see **Mt Shasta** (14,162ft)! Stark and startling, the snow-charged volcanic peak is undeniably king of the horizon. Over everything else, it's the reason to visit Mt Shasta city.

Everitt Memorial Hwy climbs the mountain to 7900ft; to access it, simply head east from town on Lake St and keep going. Take rangers' advice on good hiking trails – according to both your condition and the weather's. Ten-thousand-foot-plus climbs require a $15 Summit Pass from the **Mt Shasta Ranger Station** (☎ 530-926-4511; 204 W Alma St; ☼ 8am-4:30pm Mon-Sat). Campers note: even in summer, temperatures on and around the mountain drop below freezing. Ski or board its south slope, off Hwy 89, at **Mt Shasta Board & Ski Park** (☎ 530-926-8610, 800-754-7427; www.skipark.com) or hop on a mountain bike or chairlift ride in summer.

McCloud, a square-dancin' mill town tucked below Shasta's southern slope, is 10 miles east of I-5 on Hwy 89. Creeks and waterfalls are refreshing surprises along McCloud's serene trails; the **Heritage Junction Museum** (☎ 530-964-2604; 320 Main St; admission free; ☼ 11am-3pm Mon-Sat, from 1pm Sun) is a fun jumble of curios, better than grandma's attic.

In **Yreka** (y-ree-kuh. Think 'Eureka!'), a sleepy old Trappist town at the very top of inland California, you can chug through lovely Shasta Valley on the **Blue Goose** (☎ 530-842-4146, 800-973-5277; www.yrekawesternrr.com; 300 E Miner St; adult/child $20/10; ☼ departures 11am Wed-Sun in summer, weekends only in winter), a 1915 open-air passenger steam train.

SLEEPING & EATING
Sleeping and Eating listings are ordered south to north.

Clustered near major thoroughfares, lodgings in Redding tend to be noisy. Situated north of downtown on N Main are a few clean, quiet motels. Try simple **Value Inn & Suites** (☎ 530-241-2252; 533 N Market St; d from $60; ☒ wi-fi) or quaint **Tiffany House B&B** (☎ 530-244-3225; www.tiffanyhousebb.com; 1510 Barbara Rd; d from $110).

For something different (and kitsch) sleep in a vintage caboose at **Railroad Park Resort** (☎ 530-235-4440, 800-974-7245; www.rrpark.com; d from $95; ☒ ☒), off I-5 just south of Dunsmuir. Among Dunsmuir's gourmet eateries is Thai restaurant **Sengthongs** (☎ 530-235-4770; www.sengthongs.com; 5855 Dunsmuir Ave; dinner mains $16-24; ☼ 5pm-9pm Thu-Mon).

For its tiny size, McCloud has a disproportionate number of B&Bs – all charming. Most celebrated is **McCloud Bed & Breakfast Hotel** (☎ 530-964-2822, 800-964-2823; www.mccloudhotel.com;

408 Main St; d from $120; ☒), a regal, block-long Victorian property. The on-site restaurant serves breakfast (free to guests) and dinner. The intensely scenic three-hour **Shasta Sunset Dinner Train** (☎ 800-733-2141; www.shastasunset.com; set-price meals $89, tax/drinks extra; ☼ 6pm) departs at weekends from McCloud.

Mt Shasta town's serene **Strawberry Valley Inn** (☎ 530-926-2052; 1142 S Mt Shasta Blvd; d incl breakfast from $99; ☒ ☒ wi-fi) has tastefully understated, spacious rooms. Get wired (on caffeine and internet) at **Seven Suns Coffeehouse** (☎ 530-926-9700; 1011 S Mt Shasta Blvd; lunch items $6.50-8.50; ☼ 6am-4pm; ☐ wi-fi).

Comfy motels line Yreka's Main St, including the **Klamath Motor Lodge** (☎ 530-842-2751, 800-551-7255; 1111 S Main St; d $64; ☒ ☒). Ask for the crunchy crust at popular **Brickhouse Bakery & Pizzeria** (☎ 530-841-0553; 313 W Miner St; dinner mains from $8; ☼ 6:30am-9pm).

GETTING THERE & AROUND
Amtrak trains (☎ 800-872-7245; www.amtrak.com) service Redding and Dunsmuir; **Greyhound buses** (☎ 800-231-2222; www.greyhound.com) serve Redding and Yreka. **Stage buses** (☎ 530-842-8295, 800-2478243) cover Siskiyou County from Dunsmuir to Yreka, weekdays only. By car, San Francisco to Redding is 215 miles (four hours); Redding to Yreka is 98 miles (one hour 45 minutes). For updated road conditions call **Siskiyou County** (☎ 530-842-4438).

Northeast Corner
Eerily quiet after a turbulent past, beautiful **Lava Beds National Monument** represents the wrath of recent geologic and ancient human history. This volcanic park's got it all: lava flows, craters, cinder and spatter cones, and more than 500 lava tubes. This charred land was site of the Modoc War, one of the last major Indian Wars, and the Native Americans maintain a strong presence here today – their ancestors' petroglyphs adorn some of the park's cave walls. Info, good maps and free flashlights (for cave exploring) are available at the **visitor center** (☎ 530-667-8113; www.nps.gov/labe; 1 Indian Well; ☼ 8am-6pm May-Oct, until 5pm Nov-Sep). Coming from the north on Hwy 161, turn south on Hill Rd (which is the park's north entrance.) Nearby is the park's only **campground** (campsite $10). The simple sites (no showers) are suitable for tents and small RVs. Free wilderness camping is available; ask at the visitor center.

Winged migrants find a safe haven just north at **Klamath Basin National Wildlife Refuges** – a reserve consisting of six separate refuges. This is a prime stopover on the Pacific Flyway and an important wintering site for bald eagles. The **visitor center** (☎ 530-667-2231; http://klamathbasinrefuges.fws.gov; 4009 Hill Rd; ⏰ 8am-4:30pm Mon-Fri, 10am-4pm Sat & Sun) is along the road to Lava Beds Monument on Hwy 161. Self-guided 10-mile auto tours (free) of the Lower Klamath and Tule Lake reserves provide excellent viewing; better still are the self-guided canoe tours ($30). Inquire at visitor center.

Overall, this area has few commercial services, though there is the friendly, tidy **Ellis Motel** (☎ 530-667-5242; r $40-45, with kitchen extra $5), 1 mile north of Tulelake on Hwy 139. One of the most popular (and one of the only) restaurants around is **Captain Jack's Stronghold** (☎ 530-664-5566; mains $8-14; ⏰ Tue-Sun), located 5 miles south of Tulelake on Hwy 139.

Modoc National Forest blankets almost 3125 sq miles of California's northeast corner. **Medicine Lake**, 14 miles south of Lava Beds Monument on Hwy 49, is a pristine, blue, gleaming crater lake surrounded by pine forest, hulking volcanic formations and cool, secluded campgrounds.

Alturas, at the junction of Hwys 299 and 395, is the Modoc County seat, and mostly for local ranchers. The Modoc National Forest **Supervisor's Headquarters** (☎ 530-233-5811; www.fs.fed.us/r5/modoc; 800 W 12th St; ⏰ 8am-4:30pm Mon-Fri) provides hiking info and maps. The **Modoc National Wildlife Refuge** (☎ 530-233-3572; http://modoc.fws.gov; ⏰ 7:30am-4pm Mon-Fri) is 3 miles southeast of Alturas. Just 24 miles east of Alturas, on the California–Nevada border, is the high desert of **Surprise Valley**, gateway to the wild **Warner Mountains**.

The region's impressive, Yellowstone-like **Lassen Volcanic National Park** (per car $10, campsites $16-18) is further south. Steaming hydrothermal sulfur pools (pee-ew!) and cauldrons with such names as 'Devil's Kitchen' can be visited at some distance, plus there's Lassen Peak, at 10,457ft the world's largest plug-dome volcano. The park has two entrances, both with visitor centers: the smaller on Hwy 44 at Manzanita Lake, and the main one south off Hwy 89, where **park headquarters** (☎ 530-595-4444; www.nps.gov/lavo; ⏰ 8am-4:30pm daily Jul-Sep, Mon-Fri Oct-Jun) is located. Hwy 89 through the park is open to cars June to October (and to cross-country skiers in winter). All camping is first-come, first-served. Outside the park lodges and cabins line Hwy 89 between Hat Creek and Old Station.

SIERRA NEVADA

In the mighty Sierra Nevada – dubbed the 'Range of Light' by John Muir – nature has been as prolific and creative as Picasso in his prime. This 400-mile phalanx of craggy peaks, chiseled and gouged by glaciers and erosion, is a patchwork of landscapes that welcomes and challenges outdoors fans. Cradling no fewer than three national parks (Yosemite, Sequoia and Kings Canyon), the Sierra is a wonderland of superlatives, home to the contiguous USA's highest mountain, North America's tallest waterfall and the world's biggest tree.

LAKE TAHOE

Shimmering softly in myriad Technicolor shades of blue and green, Lake Tahoe is the nation's second deepest lake and has an average depth of 1000ft. Generally speaking, the north shore is quiet and upscale, the west shore rugged and old-timey, the east shore undeveloped and the south shore busy and tacky with aging motels and flashy casinos. The horned peaks surrounding the lake are a recreational heaven.

Tahoe gets packed in summer, around holidays and at winter weekends when reservations are essential. **Lake Tahoe Central Reservations** (☎ 530-583-3494, 888-434-1262; www.mytahoevacation.com) is among the agencies that can help with rooms and packages. Overall, room rates tend to be lowest in South Lake Tahoe. There's also lots of camping in the state parks and at United States Forest Service (USFS) sites.

North Shore & East Shores

As the north shore's commercial hub, **Tahoe City** is great for grabbing supplies at supermarkets and information at the **visitor center** (☎ 530-581-6900; 380 N Lake Tahoe Blvd; ⏰ 9am-5pm Mon-Fri, until 4pm Sat & Sun). It's also the closest lake town to **Squaw Valley USA** (☎ 530-583-6985; www.squaw.com; off Hwy 89; adult/child/teen $62/5/31), a megasized ski resort that hosted the 1960 Winter Olympic Games. The après-ski crowd gathers for beer 'n' burgers at the venerable **Bridgetender** (☎ 530-583-3342; 65 W Lake Blvd; dishes $8-10; ☼ 11am-2am).

But the little towns east of here are way cuter. In summer, swim or kayak at **Tahoe Vista** and **Kings Beach**. For a taste of old Tahoe, spend a night at **Rustic Cottages** (☎ 530-546-3523, 888-778-7842; www.rusticcottages.com; 7449 N Lake Blvd, Tahoe Vista; cabins incl breakfast $64-209; ✗), whose storybook cabins blend seamlessly into the pine forest. Kings Beach has some great eats, including satisfying pastas at **Lanza's** (☎ 530-546-2434; 7739 N Lake Blvd; mains $10-19; ☼ 5-10pm) and unpretentious American fare at **Jason's Beachside Grille** (☎ 530-546-3315; 8338 N Lake Blvd; mains lunch $8-11, dinner $8-20; ☼ from 11am), whose lakeview deck is perfect for sunset drinks. Worth the price is **Spindleshanks** (☎ 530-546-2191; 6873 N Lake Blvd, Tahoe Vista; mains $21-30; ☼ from 5:30pm).

Further east, Hwy 28 barrels into Nevada at Crystal Bay, where you can try your luck at any of its casinos, including the **Cal-Neva Resort** (☎ 775-832-4000, 800-225-6382; www.calnevaresort.com; 2 Stateline Rd; r $149-169; 🖳 wi-fi), whose onetime owner Frank Sinatra entertained Kennedy, Monroe and mobsters in the early 1960s.

A popular playground with pristine beaches, lakes and miles of trails, **Lake Tahoe-Nevada State Park** (☎ 775-831-0494; http://parks.nv.gov /lt.htm) is the biggest draw on the eastern shore. In summer, crowds splash around in the brilliant turquoise water of **Sand Harbor**.

Truckee & Donner Lake

Don't miss Truckee, which is not in fact a truck stop but a thriving little mountain town. It's got an upscale main street, hip organic coffee shops and superb dining in the historical downtown near the Amtrak train depot. The sophisticated bistro–lounge **Moody's** (☎ 530-587-8688; 10007 Bridge St; lunch mains $10-16, dinner mains $22-30; ☼ 11am-4pm & 5-10pm) is a fave of Paul McCartney. Ski bunnies can hit several resorts, including **Sugar Bowl** (☎ 530-426-9000; www .sugarbowl.com; Hwy 40 near Soda Springs/Norden exit off I-80; adult/teen $59/44), cofounded by Walt Disney. It's near Donner Summit, where the Donner Party pioneers became trapped during the fierce winter of 1846. More than half of the group's 89 members died; the rest survived by eating the dead bodies. The grisly tale is chronicled at the **Emigrant Trail Museum** (☎ 530-582-7892; ☼ 9am-4pm), on the eastern shore of Donner Lake, which has great swimming and boating.

South Lake Tahoe & West Shore

With clustered motels, eateries and stores lining busy Hwy 50, South Lake Tahoe is oddly urban, unlike your typical back-to-nature lake town. Gambling in Stateline, just across the Nevada border, attracts thousands, as does the world-class ski resort of **Heavenly** (☎ 775-586-7000; www.skiheavenly.com; tickets adult/child lift $65/29, gondola $22/14). A trip to the top aboard the sleek gondolas guarantees fabulous views of the lake and the **Desolation Wilderness** (www.fs.fed.us/r5/ltbmu/recreation/wilder ness/desowild). This stark and beautiful landscape of raw granite peaks, glacier-carved valleys and alpine lakes extends south and west of the lake – hikers love it. Get maps, information and wilderness permits (required for overnight trips) at the **USFS Visitors Center** (☎ 530-543-2674; Hwy 89; ☼ 8am-4:30pm May & Oct, until 5pm daily in summer). It's about 3 miles north of the 'Y' (the intersection of Hwys 50 and 89) right at the **Tallac Historic Site** (☎ 530-541-5227; admission by donation; ☼ 10am-4:30pm Jun-Sep), which preserves several early 20th-century estates now containing exhibits.

North of here, Hwy 89 sinuously threads along the densely forested western shore to **Emerald Bay State Park** (☎ 530-541-3030; day-use fee $6; ☼ late May-Sep), where granite cliffs and pine trees frame a fjordlike inlet, truly sparkling green. A steep 1-mile trail leads down to **Vikingsholm Castle** (adult/child $5/3; ☼ 10am-4pm), a 1928 Scandinavian-style mansion open for touring. The castle also marks one end of the gorgeous **Rubicon Trail**, which ribbons north along the lakeshore for 4.5 mostly gentle miles to **DL Bliss State Park** (☎ 530-525-7277; day-use fee $6), famous for its sandy beaches. There's **camping** (☎ reservations 800-444-7275; www .reserveamerica.com; sites $20-35) in both parks. Also, check out the darling cabins of **Tahoma Meadows B&B Cottages** (☎ 530-525-1553, 866-525-1533; www.tahomameadows.com; 6821 W Lake Blvd; cottages $129-179; ✗).

Getting There & Around

Major commercial airlines serve **Reno-Tahoe International Airport** (☎ 775-328-6400), from where **South Tahoe Express** (☎ 866-898-2463) runs frequent shuttles to South Tahoe (one-way/ return $24/43, 1½ hr).

Greyhound has daily buses from Truckee to Reno ($15, 50 minutes), Sacramento ($31, three hours) and San Francisco ($37, five to six hours). Amtrak stops in Truckee.

Local buses operated by **Tahoe Area Rapid Transit** (TART; ☎ 530-581-3922; www.laketahoetransit.com) run between Tahoma on the western shore to Incline Village on the northern shore as well as to Truckee. South Lake Tahoe is served by **BlueGO** (☎ 530-541-7149; www.bluego.org), which, in summer, also operates the Nifty Fifty Trolley to Camp Richardson and Emerald Bay.

In winter, Hwy 89 (Emerald Bay Rd) is usually closed, and tire chains are often required on I-80 and Hwy 50; for road information, call ☎ 800-427-7623.

YOSEMITE NATIONAL PARK

There's a reason why everybody's heard of it. But is it for real? In America's third largest park, the heights are dizzying, the mist from the falls drenching, the majestic, hulking silhouettes of El Capitan and Half Dome almost shocking against a crisp blue sky. Green meadows and mirror-pools balance it all somehow with serenity and depth, and the whole effect is like a drug for photographers, who seem to forget anything else exists. It's a landscape of dreams, relentlessly surrounding us oh-so-small people on all sides. But just when 'four million visitors a year' is starting to make sense, the hiss and belch of another tour bus, disgorging dozens, rudely breaks the spell. While crowds can't be ignored, these rules-to-live-by will shake most of them:

- Avoid summer. Spring's best, when the waterfalls are in full gush and the dogwoods are in bloom.
- Park your car and leave it – simply by biking or hiking a mile and a half up any trail, you'll lose the car-dependent majority.
- To hell with jet lag. Get up early.

Orientation

So worth it, Yosemite's entrance fee ($20 per vehicle, $10 for those on bicycle or foot) is valid for seven days. Four primary entrances include South Entrance (Hwy 41), Arch Rock (Hwy 140), Big Oak Flat (Hwy 120 west) and Tioga Pass (Hwy 120 east). Hwy 120 traverses the park as Tioga Rd (see the boxed text, p993), connecting Yosemite Valley with Mono Lake via the 9945ft Tioga Pass.

The people-traffic glut occurs mostly in overrun Yosemite Village, home to the main visitor center; a post office; an excellent, newly redone museum; and eateries. Curry Village is another hub. Less-busy Tuolumne

(twol-uh-mee) Meadows, toward the eastern end of Tioga Rd, draws primarily hippie backpackers and climbers. Remote Wawona, near the southern entrance, has a hotel, golf course, pioneer-history demo village and giant sequoias.

For a price (whew!), gas up year-round at Wawona and Crane Flat inside the park or at El Portal on Hwy 140 just outside its boundaries. In summer, gas is also sold at Tuolumne Meadows.

Information

The stores in Yosemite Village, Curry Village and Wawona have ATMs. Extended summer hours may apply.

Big Oak Flat Information Station (☎ 209-379-1899; 🕙 9am-5pm Apr-Oct)

Post office (Yosemite Village; limited branch at Yosemite Lodge, 🕙 12:30-2:45pm Mon-Fri)

Public library (☎ 209-372-4552; Girls' Club Bldg; Yosemite Valley; 🕙 hours vary; 🖳)

Tuolumne Meadows visitor center (☎ 209-372-0263; 🕙 9am-5pm late spring-early autumn)

Wawowa Information Station (☎ 209-375-9531; 🕙 8:30am-4:30pm late May-early Oct)

Yosemite Lodge at the Falls (☎ 559-253-5635; Yosemite Valley) Wireless internet is free but limited and sporadic.

Yosemite Medical Clinic (☎ 209-372-4637; 🕙 hours vary) Also has a dental clinic.

Yosemite Valley visitor center (☎ 209-372-0299; www.nps.gov/yose; 🕙 9am-5pm year-round)

Yosemite Wilderness Centre (☎ 209-372-0740; www.nps.gov/yose/wilderness/)

Sights

YOSEMITE VALLEY

If you get to the top of Yosemite Falls and the guy next to you breaks into a heartfelt rendition of 'America the Beautiful,' don't be surprised. For 7 miles of valley, from the ground up, it's song-inspiring – rippling meadow-grass; gleaming green-black tortoiseshell waters under pine; cool, impassive pools reflecting strangely shaped, looming monoliths of granite and their cascading, glacier-cold whitewater ribbons. You can't ignore monumental **El Capitan** (7569ft), one of the world's largest mountains and an El Dorado for rock climbers, and **Half Dome** (8842ft), a perfectly rounded dome and the park's spiritual centerpiece. Many try to capture it in a photo; the classic spot is up Hwy 41 at **Tunnel View**. Sweat it out and you'll get better views

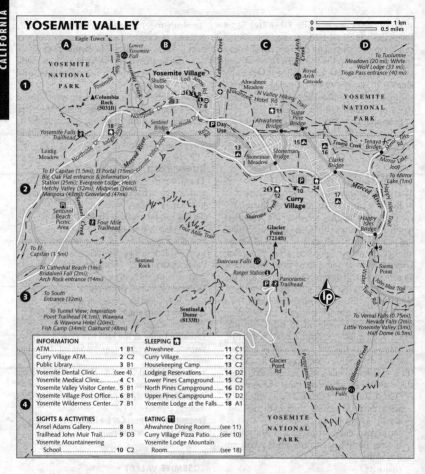

YOSEMITE VALLEY

INFORMATION	
ATM	**1** B1
Curry Village ATM	**2** C2
Public Library	**3** B1
Yosemite Dental Clinic	(see 4)
Yosemite Medical Clinic	**4** C1
Yosemite Valley Visitor Center	**5** B1
Yosemite Village Post Office	**6** B1
Yosemite Wilderness Center	**7** B1

SIGHTS & ACTIVITIES	
Ansel Adams Gallery	**8** B1
Trailhead John Muir Trail	**9** D3
Yosemite Mountaineering School	**10** C2

SLEEPING	
Ahwahnee	**11** C1
Curry Village	**12** C2
Housekeeping Camp	**13** C2
Lodging Reservations	**14** D2
Lower Pines Campground	**15** C2
North Pines Campground	**16** D2
Upper Pines Campground	**17** D2
Yosemite Lodge at the Falls	**18** A1

EATING	
Ahwahnee Dining Room	(see 11)
Curry Village Pizza Patio	(see 10)
Yosemite Lodge Mountain Room	(see 18)

– sans the crowds – from the **Inspiration Point Trail** (2.6 miles round-trip), which starts at the tunnel. If you fancy yourself the next Ansel Adams, head up the 1-mile paved trail to **Mirror Lake** early or late in the day to catch the ever-shifting reflection of Half Dome in the still waters.

Astounding waterfalls are made more frightening when snowmelt turns them into thunderous cataracts, though most are reduced to a mere trickle by late summer. **Yosemite Falls** is considered the tallest in North America, dropping 2425ft in three tiers. A slick wheelchair-accessible trail leads to the bottom of this cascade or, for solitude and different perspectives, you can also clamber up the grueling trail to the top of the falls

(6.8 miles round-trip). No less impressive are nearby **Bridalveil Fall** and others scattered throughout the valley. A strenuous staircase climb up **Vernal Falls** leads you, gasping, right to the top edge of the falls for a vertical-drop view; look for rainbows in the mist clouding off the wall.

HETCH HETCHY

Yep, it's the site of the most controversial dam in history – but whether restored to its natural state or not, Hetch Hetchy Valley remains gloriously pretty and mostly crowd-free. Its Wapama Falls, approached via a 2.2-mile wildflower-dotted hike, sends a scary 1000ft avalanche of whitewater crashing from shelf to shelf over the sparkling reservoir. In spring, prepare to be drenched. Forty minutes from Yosemite Valley, Hetch makes a decent alternative home base for enthusiastic adventurers.

GLACIER POINT & WAWONA

Soaring 3200ft above the valley floor, **Glacier Point** offers one of the park's most glorious views and practically puts you at eye level with Half Dome. It's about an hour's drive up Glacier Point Rd off Hwy 41 or a strenuous hike along the **Four-Mile Trail** (9.2 miles round-trip). If you don't want to backtrack, reserve a seat on the hikers' shuttle bus (p992).

In Wawona, the park's historical center and a half-hour drive from the valley, the main attraction is the **Mariposa Grove of Giant Sequoias**, where the 2700-year-old Grizzly Giant and other gargantuan trees make their home.

TUOLUMNE MEADOWS

Approximately 55 miles from Yosemite Valley, Tuolumne Meadows, at 8600ft, is the largest subalpine meadow in the Sierra. It provides a dazzling contrast to the valley, with lush, open fields, clear blue lakes, ragged granite peaks and domes, and cooler temperatures. Hikers and climbers will find a paradise of options, and campgrounds are less crowded. Access is via the Tioga Rd (Hwy 120; see the boxed text, p993), where you'll find a store, lodge and visitor center.

Activities

HIKING

With the 800 miles of varied-level hiking trails, even your five-year-old brother can trek in Yosemite. Easy valley-bottom trails can get as jammed as a U2 concert; escape the teeming masses by heading up. The ultimate hike is to the top of **Half Dome** (17 miles

---

DARKROOM SHOW

Not everyone knows this, but *original* Ansel Adams prints are shown every Saturday at 3pm in the tiny back room of the **Ansel Adams Gallery** (☎ 209-372-4413; www.ansel adams.com) in Yosemite Village. The 'Fine Print' tour is limited to five people due to space, but you can call up to three days in advance to book a spot.

---

round-trip), but be warned: it is strenuous, difficult and best tackled in two days. Challenging enough is to follow the same trail as far as **Vernal Falls** (2.6 miles round-trip), the top of **Nevada Falls** (6.5 miles round-trip) or idyllic **Little Yosemite Valley** (8 miles round-trip). The route partly follows the famous John Muir Trail.

Free wilderness permits are required year-round for overnight trips, and a quota system limits the number of people leaving from each trailhead. You can make **reservations** (☎ 209-372-0740; www.nps.gov/yose/wilderness/permits .htm; per person $5) from 24 weeks to two days before your trip, or try grabbing a permit at a park wilderness center on the day of your planned hike.

ROCK CLIMBING

With sheer spires, polished domes and soaring monoliths, Yosemite is rock-climbing nirvana. **Yosemite Mountaineering School** (☎ 209-372-8344; www.yosemitemountaineering.com; all-day class from $117), in Curry Village, offers topflight instruction for rock hounds from novice to advanced, plus guided climbs and equipment rental.

WINTER SPORTS

In winter the action converges on **Badger Pass** (☎ 209-372-1000; www.badgerpass.com), whose gentle slopes are perfect for beginning skiers and snowboarders. Cross-country skiers can schuss around the forest on 40km of groomed tracks and another 140km of marked trails. There are additional trails at Crane Flat and the Mariposa Grove. Equipment rental is available at the ski schools and the Yosemite Mountaineering School (see above).

Sleeping & Eating

One sole concessionaire, Delaware North Companies, has a monopoly on all lodging and eating establishments in Yosemite; the result is overpriced rooms often in need of updating and cleaning. Stay outside the park for better value; picnic to save up for dinner. In-park **lodging reservations** (☎ 559-252-4848; www .yosemitepark.com) can be made up to 366 days in advance and are critical from May to early September. Rates – and demand – drop from mid-November to mid-March. Unless noted, all lodging listed is in-valley.

Curry Village (canvas cabins $77, cabins without/with bath $90/120; r $147; 🖳) Curry's hundreds of units, sometimes rowdy at night, are squished together beneath towering evergreens. Tent cabins resemble army barracks with scratchy wool blankets; opt for a real cabin (small but cozy). The outdoor Pizza Patio turns into a chatty après-hike hangout in the evenings (breakfast/dinner buffets $10/12, patio mains $6 to $20).

Yosemite Lodge at the Falls (r $113-177; 🍴 💻) Musty-smelling, motel-style rooms have patios or balconies overlooking Yosemite Falls, meadows or the parking lot. Fine dining is hit or miss at the Mountain Room (mains $16 to $30); the livelier lounge sells snacks and has an open-pit fireplace for toasting marshmallows.

Wawona Hotel (r without/with bath $123/192; 🕐 mid-Mar–Nov, Dec holidays; 🍴 🍴) Filled with ghosts and character, this Victorian-era throwback has wide porches, manicured lawns and a golf course. Half the 104 thin-walled rooms share baths and need some paint and attention. The romantic dining room with vintage details serves Southwest-inspired dishes (dinner mains $14 to $25).

Ahwahnee (r $408; ste $499-893; 🍴) The aloof Ahwahnee, a forested historic property with little signage, has sumptuous rooms where the rich, royal and renowned stay. The rest of us can taste the ambience in the grand medieval dining room – gourmet fare (dinner mains $25 to $39) below soaring sugar-pine timbers and wrought-iron candelabras.

From May to September, most **campgrounds** (☎ 800-436-7275; www.recreation.gov) are crammed, noisy and booked to bulging, especially **Upper Pines** (sites $20), **Lower Pines** (sites $20) and **North Pines** (sites $20) in the valley. All three require reservations, which can be made months in advance; check the website for details. Alternatively, try camping in Wawona or Tuolomne, outside the valley but still inside the park.

Overnighters looking for a quieter, more rugged experience are better off in smaller, nonvalley spots such as **Bridalveil Creek** (sites $20), **Yosemite Creek** (sites $20) and **Porcupine Flat** (sites $20). These are first-come, first-served and usually full by noon. All campgrounds have bear boxes, picnic tables, fire rings, water and either flush or vault toilets. The Yosemite Mountaineering School (p991) rents camping gear.

Simple canvas tent cabins sleeping up to four people are in the valley at cramped **Housekeeping Camp** (cabins $74) and, in summer,

at **Tuolumne Meadows Lodge** (cabins $80) and **White Wolf Lodge** (cabins $75) in the high country. The latter two have dining halls serving breakfast and dinner (mains from $7 to $20).

OUTSIDE YOSEMITE NATIONAL PARK

Popular gateway towns with lodging include Fish Camp, Mariposa, Oakhurst, Midpines, El Portal and Groveland.

Yosemite Bug Lodge & HI Hostel (☎ 209-966-6666, 866-826-7108; www.yosemitebug.com; dm $18, tent cabins $45, r $55-115, r with shared bath $40-70; 💻) Tucked into a leafy dell in Midpines, about 20 miles from the park on Hwy 140, the funky Bug hosts people from all over the globe who dig the clean rooms and delicious meals. If you don't have a car, you might feel too secluded.

Evergreen Lodge (☎ 209-39-2606; www.evergreen lodge.com; 33160 Evergreen Rd, Groveland; prefurnished tents for 1-4 people $50-80, cabins $99-199; 🍴) One mile from Yosemite's western edge and the entrance to Hetch Hetchy, summer-campy Evergreen lets roughing-it guests cheat with comfy, prefurnished tents; guided rec activities abound, and there's a fun bar, store and excellent restaurant.

our pick **Narrow Gauge Inn** (☎ 559-683-7720, 888-644-9050; www.narrowgaugeinn.com; 48571 Hwy 41, Fish Camp; r incl breakfast Nov-Mar $79-179, Apr-Oct $129-225; 🍴 🍴) Nonhokey Swiss chalet–style done to the nines, with 26 comfy rooms, each with balcony or patio, and the excellent Sugar Pine steam railroad just next door. The 'buffalo bar' is authentic, and boar, antelope and elk are on the very fine menu (mains $16 to $36; open Wednesday to Sunday May to October). The inn's about 4 miles south of the park.

Getting There & Around

The nearest Greyhound and Amtrak stations are in Merced, where you can transfer to buses operated by **Yarts** (☎ 877-989-2787; www.yarts.com), which travel to the park along Hwy 140, stopping in towns along the way. In summer, another Yarts route runs from Mammoth Lakes (p995) along Hwy 120 via the Tioga Pass (see the boxed text, opposite). Tickets are $25 one-way from Merced and $30 from Mammoth Lakes, less if boarding in between.

In winter, valley roads are plowed and the highways to the parks are kept open (except Tioga Rd/Hwy 120), although snow chains may be required.

Free hybrid shuttle buses loop around Yosemite Valley and the Tuolumne Mead-

IMPASSABLE TIOGA PASS

Hwy 120 is the only road connecting Yosemite National Park with the Eastern Sierra, and it climbs through the mountains' highest pass, Tioga Pass at 9945ft. Most California maps mark this road 'closed in winter,' which while literally true is also misleading. Tioga Rd is usually closed from the first heavy snowfall in October until May or even June. If you are planning a trip through Tioga Pass in the spring, you're likely to be out of luck. According to the park's official policy, the earliest date that the road through the pass will be plowed is April 15, yet the pass has only been open in April once since 1980. So call ahead (☎ 209-372-0200) for road and weather conditions before heading for Tioga Pass.

ows and Wawona areas. There are also hikers' buses from the valley to Glacier Point (one way/round-trip $20/32.50) and Tuolumne Meadows (round-trip $23).

Bike rentals (per hour/day $7.50/24.50) are available at Yosemite Lodge and Curry Village.

SEQUOIA & KINGS CANYON NATIONAL PARKS

Neck braces might be needed after gawking at the giant – 29 stories high! – rust-red sequoias in this twin park. Here, the famous trees are bigger and mightier and more numerous than anywhere else. Tough and fire-charred, they'd easily swallow three freeway lanes and keep growing. Giant, too, are the mountains here – try Mt Whitney, at 14,494ft the tallest in the lower 48 states. Finally, there is giant Kings Canyon, gored out of granite by the powerful Kings River. These are what lure the vast majority of the 1.5 million annual visitors here, but for quiet, solitude, and close-up sightings of unskittish animals, hit the trail to quickly lose yourself in breathtakingly beautiful wilderness.

Orientation & Information

Sequoia was designated a national park in 1890 (the second in the USA after Yellowstone), Kings Canyon in 1940. The two parks, though distinct, are operated as one unit with a single admission (valid for seven days) of $20 per carload or $10 for individuals arriving on bicycle or foot. For the latest updates and general info, call the park at ☎ 559-565-3341 (24-hour recorded information) or check the website at www.nps .gov/seki.

From the west, Hwy 180 leads to the parks' Big Stump Entrance before plunging down into Kings Canyon. Coming from the south, Hwy 198 enters Sequoia at the Ash Mountain Entrance from where it ascends as the incredibly narrow and zigzagging Generals Hwy.

Grant Grove Village (☎ 559-565-4307), in Kings Canyon, and **Lodgepole Village** (☎ 559-565-4436), in Sequoia, are the two hubs. Each has a year-round **visitor center** (◷ 8am-8pm mid-Jul–Sep, shorter hours winter), market, showers, a post office and ATM. Also open all year is the **Foothills Visitors Center** (☎ 559-565-3135; ◷ 8am-5pm), at the Ash Mountain Entrance. **Cedar Grove Visitors Center** (☎ 559-565-3793) and the **Mineral King Ranger Station** (☎ 559-565-3768) are open only in summer.

Gas is available at Hume Lake (year-round) and Stony Creek (summer), both outside park boundaries on national forest land.

Sights
SEQUOIA NATIONAL PARK

We dare you to try hugging the trees in **Giant Forest**, a 5-sq-mile grove protecting the park's most gargantuan ones; the world's biggest is the **General Sherman Tree**. With sore arms and sticky sap fingers, lose the crowds by venturing on any of the many forested trails (bring a map).

Two miles south is the well-done **Giant Forest Museum** (☎ 559-565-4480; admission free; ◷ 9am-4:30pm). More trails are there, one of them wheelchair accessible. For 360-degree views of the Great Western Divide, climb the steep quarter-mile staircase up **Moro Rock**.

Discovered in 1918, **Crystal Cave** (☎ 559-565-3759; www.sequoiahistory.org; adult/child/senior $11/6/9; ◷ 11am-4pm mid-May–Oct) has limestone formations estimated to be 10,000 years old. The 45-minute tour covers half a mile of chambers; tickets are available at the Lodgepole and Foothills visitor centers, *not* at the cave.

KINGS CANYON NATIONAL PARK

North of Grant Grove Village, **General Grant Grove** brims with majestic giants. Beyond here,

Hwy 180 begins its 36-mile descent into **Kings Canyon**, serpentining past violently chiseled rock walls tinged by moss and decorated with waterfalls. Near **Boyden Cavern** (☎ 209-736-2708; adult/child/senior $10/5/9; ◷ May-Oct) the road meets the Kings River, its thunderous roar ricocheting off granite cliffs soaring up to 4000ft high, making Kings Canyon one of the deepest canyons in North America.

Offering camping, simple lodging and food, friendly **Cedar Grove Village** is the last outpost of civilization before the rugged grandeur of the backcountry. A popular day hike climbs for 5 miles to roaring **Mist Falls** from Roads End; continue into the aspens for 2 miles to **Paradise Valley**. An easier, 1.5-mile fern-fringed trail loops around **Zumwalt Meadow**. Watch for rattlesnakes, bear and deer, surprisingly unfazed by humans.

Activities

Hiking is why people come here – there are 800 miles of marked trails to prove it. Cedar Grove and Mineral King offer the best backcountry access. Trails are usually open by mid-May, although there's hiking year-round in the Foothills area. Overnight backcountry trips require wilderness permits ($15), subject to a quota system. For details, see www.nps.gov/seki/bcinfo.htm. You can also rent a naturalist for a half-day through the **Natural History Association** (☎ 559-565-4251). Horseback riding is offered at Grant Grove Village and the **Cedar Grove Pack Station** (☎ 559-565-3464; per hr/half-day $30/$65).

In winter, you can **cross-country ski** or **snowshoe** among the snow-draped trees of Grant Grove and the Giant Forest. Equipment rental is available at Grant Grove Village and the Wuksachi Lodge, but the best cross-country skiing and snowboarding is at the affordable Montecito Lake Resort in the Sequoia National Forest.

Sleeping & Eating

Outside Sequoia's southern entrance, several independent and chain motels line Hwy 198 in the town of Three Rivers.

Grant Grove Cabins (☎ 559-335-5500, 866-522-6966; www.sequoia-kingscanyon.com; cabins $62.50-129; ⊠ wi-fi) Various cabin types dotted around Grant Grove Village range from tent cabins to nicely furnished historical cottages with private bathrooms.

Cedar Grove Lodge (☎ 559-335-5500, 866-522-6966; www.sequoia-kingscanyon.com; Cedar Grove Village; r $119-135; ◷ May-Oct; ⊠ wi-fi) The 21 motel-style rooms with common porches overlooking Kings River are simple and comfy, with affable staff.

Montecito Sequoia Resort (☎ 800-843-8677, reservations 800-227-9900; www.mslodge.com; 63410 Generals Hwy btwn Sequoia & Kings Canyon National Parks; r incl meals $129-159) Basic, newly renovated rooms include all (hearty) meals, cross-country-ski/snowboard lessons and access to 50 miles of groomed trails.

John Muir Lodge (☎ 559-335-5500, 866-522-6966; www.sequoia-kingscanyon.com; Grant Grove Village; r $170; ⊠) Quiet, classy and modern, this woodsy lodge has good-sized, if somewhat generic, rooms and a lovely lobby with stone fireplace, books and board games.

Wuksachi Lodge (☎ 559-253-2199, 888-252-5757; www.visitsequoia.com; near Lodgepole Village; r $174-220; wi-fi) A conference center with modern, spacious rooms, TV and telephone (a rarity in either park).

Camping reservations (☎ 301-722-1257, 800-365-2267; http://reservations.nps.gov) are accepted only at Dorst and Lodgepole in Sequoia with the other dozen or so campgrounds being first-come, first-served (they rarely fill up). Most have flush toilets; sites cost $10 to $20. Cedar Grove and Foothills campsites are best in spring and autumn when the ones at the higher elevations

---

GIANT SEQUOIAS: KINGS OF THE FOREST

In California you can stand under the world's oldest trees (in the Ancient Bristlecone Pine Forest, opposite) and its tallest (the coastal redwoods in Redwood National Park, p981), but the record for biggest in terms of volume belongs to the giant sequoias (*Sequoiadendron giganteum*). They grow only on the Sierra's western slope and are most abundant in Sequoia, Kings Canyon and Yosemite National Parks. John Muir called them 'Nature's forest masterpiece,' and anyone who's ever craned their neck to take in their soaring vastness has done so with the awe usually reserved for Gothic cathedrals. Trees can grow to 300ft tall and 40ft in diameter with bark more than 2ft thick. The Giant Forest Museum (p993) in Sequoia National Park has excellent exhibits about the trees' fascinating history and ecology.

get nippy at night. Only Lodgepole, Azalea and Potwisha are open year-round.

There's a limited, pricey selection of food to choose from at the markets in Grant Grove Village, Lodgepole Village and Cedar Grove Village. The latter two also have snack bars serving burgers, sandwiches, hot dogs and other no-nonsense food for less than $10. The pricey restaurant at **Wuksachi Lodge** (☎ 559-253-2199, 888-252-5757; dinner mains $18-28; ⏰ 7am-9pm) is hit or miss.

EASTERN SIERRA

Vast, empty and majestic, the Eastern Sierra is where jagged peaks plummet down into the arid expanse of the Great Basin desert, a dramatic juxtaposition that creates a potent cocktail of scenery. Hwy 395 runs the entire length of the range, with turnoffs leading to pine forests and shaggy meadows, alpine lakes, simmering hot springs and glacier-gouged canyons. Hikers, cyclists, fishers and skiers love to escape and chill-out here. The main towns are Bridgeport, Mammoth Lakes and Bishop.

Be sure to detour, if you can, to **Bodie State Historic Park** (☎ 760-647-6445; admission $3; ⏰ 8am-7pm Jun-Aug, 8am-4pm Sep-May), where a gold-rush ghost town is preserved in a state of 'arrested decay.' Weathered buildings, still stocked with provisions, sit frozen in time on a dusty, wind-swept plain. To get there, head east for about 13 miles (the last three unpaved) on Hwy 270 about 7 miles south of Bridgeport. Although the park is open year-round, the road is often closed in winter.

South of here, quiet and mysterious **Mono Lake** (moan-oh) is famous for its unearthly tufa towers, which rise from the alkaline water like drip sand castles. The best photo ops are at the **South Tufa Reserve** (admission $3), on the lake's southern rim. The **Mono Basin Scenic Area Visitors Center** (☎ 760-647-3044; ⏰ 8am-5pm Mon-Fri, until 7pm Sat & Sun) has excellent exhibits.

From the nearby town of Lee Vining, Hwy 120 heads west into Yosemite National Park via the Tioga Pass, although the road is only open in summer (see the boxed text, p993).

Continuing south, you can detour around the scenic 16-mile **June Lake Loop** or head on to **Mammoth Lakes**, a fast-growing four-season resort town framed by exhilarating scenery and guarded by 11,053ft **Mammoth Mountain** (☎ 760-934-0745, 800-626-6684; www.mammothmountain.com; ski-lift tickets $57), a top-notch

ski area. The slopes morph into a mountain-bike park in summer, when there's also wonderful camping, fishing and day hiking in the Mammoth Lakes Basin and the Reds Meadow area. While here, swing by the near-vertical, 60ft-high basalt columns of the **Devil's Postpile National Monument**, which were formed by volcanic activity. Hot-springs fans can soak in the roiling pools of the **Hot Creek Geological Site** (admission free; ⏰ dawn-dusk) south of town. Be sure to pay attention to posted signs to avoid getting scalded. The **Mammoth Lakes Visitor Center & Ranger Station** (☎ 888-466-2666; www.visitmammoth.com; Hwy 203; ⏰ 8am-5pm Mon-Fri) has maps and information about all of these sites.

South of Mammoth, Hwy 395 descends into the Owens Valley, soon arriving in charismatic **Bishop**, where sights include an interesting railroad museum and a Paiute-Shoshone cultural center. Covered sidewalks and vintage neon signs adorn the busy main street. Bishop provides access to the best fishing and rock climbing in the entire Eastern Sierra, and it's the main gateway for horse-pack trips.

To check out some of the earth's oldest living things – seriously – budget a half-day or so for a trip up to the **Ancient Bristlecone Pine Forest** (☎ 760-873-2500). These gnarled, otherworldly looking trees are found above 10,000ft on the slopes of the parched White Mountains, where you'd think nothing could grow. The oldest tree – called Methuselah – is estimated to be more than 4700 years old. The road (closed November to April) is paved to the top, where there are hikes of varying length, primitive camping and a visitor center. From Hwy 395 take Hwy 168 east for 13 miles, then head uphill for another 10 miles at the marked turnoff.

Hwy 395, meanwhile, barrels on south to Independence and the **Manzanar National Historic Site** (☎ 760-878-2194; www.nps.gov/manz; admission free; ⏰ 9am-4:30pm Nov-Apr, until 5:30pm May-Oct), which commemorates the war relocation camp where some 10,000 Japanese Americans were interned during WWII following the attack on Pearl Harbor. Exhibits and a short film shown at the interpretive center vividly chronicle life at the camp.

South of here, in Lone Pine, you can finally catch a glimpse of **Mt Whitney**, at 14,494ft the highest mountain in the lower 48. Climbing to its peak is hugely popular but requires

CALIFORNIA

DON'T MISS

- **Bodie State Historic Park** – A real gold-rush ghost town (p995)

- **Mono Lake** – Unearthly, mysterious formations (p995)

- **Manzanar National Historic Site** (p995)

- **Whoa Nellie Deli** (right) – comfort food, such as wild buffalo meatloaf

a permit issued on a lottery basis. For full details, consult www.fs.fed.us/r5/inyo. West of Lone Pine, the bizarrely shaped coyote-colored boulders of the **Alabama Hills** have enchanted filmmakers who used them as a backdrop for such classics as *How the West Was Won*. For information, stop by the **Interagency Visitor Center/Mt Whitney Ranger Station** (☎ 760-876-6222; ☼ 8am-5pm winter, until 6pm summer) at the Hwy 395/136 junction.

Sleeping & Eating

The Eastern Sierra is freckled with camp-grounds. Backcountry camping requires fire permits, even for a camp stove, available for free at any ranger station. Mammoth Lakes and Bishop are your best bet for chain motels.

Redwood Motel (☎ 760-932-7060, 888-932-3292; www .redwoodmotel.net; 425 Main St, Bridgeport; d $60-99; ☼ mid-Mar–Nov; ✖ wi-fi) A cow in a Hawaiian shirt and other wacky farm animal sculptures provide a cheerful welcome to this spotless motel. Your host will shower you with local area tips.

Winnedumah Hotel (☎ 760-878-2040; www.winne dumah.com; 211 N Edwards St, Independence; r $85-150; ✖) This 1927 country-style inn was once a popular movie-star hangout when the cameras were rolling in the nearby Alabama Hills. Some rooms have shared bath.

Mammoth Country Inn (☎ 760-934-2710, 866-934-2710; www.mammothcountryinn.com; 75 Joaquin Rd, Mammoth Lakes; r incl breakfast $99-199; ✖ wi-fi) Seven-room B&B with artist-designed beds, fluffy robes and sparkling new baths.

Erick Schat's Bakkery (☎ 760-873-7156; 763 N Main St, Bishop; sandwiches $6-8; ☼ 6am-6pm) The best place along Hwy 395 to feed cravings for freshly made sandwiches – served on their own breads – or tasty cookies and pastries.

Whoa Nellie Deli (☎ 760-647-1088; mains $7-18; ☼ 7am-9pm late Apr-Oct) Great food in a gas station? Come on... No, really, you gotta try this amazing kitchen where chef Matt 'Tioga' Toomey feeds delicious fish tacos, wild buffalo meatloaf and other tasty morsels to clued-in passers-by. It's near the junction of Hwys 120 and 395, in Lee Vining.

Pacific Northwest

Located on America's rain-lashed Pacific Rim and characterized by its vibrant, dot-com–fuelled economy, the Pacific Northwest region has stamped its mark on modern world culture like an errant 21st-century Cinderella. Culturally speaking, the manifestations are everywhere. You don't have to be a guitar-wielding caffeine junkie to have heard of Starbucks coffee or grunge music, while other ingenious northwestern innovations such as Microsoft and Amazon.com have hijacked the technological superhighways everywhere from Beijing to Bratislava.

But it's not all computer gadgetry and tall dark-roast skinny lattes. Immortalized by their spectacular mountains and vast primeval forests, the states of Washington and Oregon are as spectacular as they are economically vibrant. While some regions exhibit their past glories in buildings and architecture, the Pacific Northwest measures out its history in ancient trees (Washington's red cedars are older than most of Europe's medieval castles) and rugged mountain peaks – the snowcapped Cascades, which run like a spine from Canada to California are punctuated by a string of magnificent but menacing volcanoes.

Elsewhere, this robust and famously rainy northwest pocket has embellished the nation with a host of eye-catching and unique geographical features. Encased in four splendid national parks is one of the world's only temperate rain forests, more glaciers than anywhere else in the lower 48 states and some of America's most mystical and awe-inspiring mountain peaks.

It's no small wonder that armies of hard-working Seattleites and Portlanders often switch off their ubiquitous laptops a couple of hours early and head hedonistically for the great outdoors.

HIGHLIGHTS

- Bicycling around the serendipitous **San Juan Islands** (p1021) and exchanging salutations with the congenial locals.

- Washing down bratwurst with beer in the quirky Bavarian-themed Washington town of **Leavenworth** (p1023).

- Diving into the mix with wannabe rock stars, dot-com billionaires and aging fetish freaks in cool and trendy **Seattle** (p1003).

- Supping a hand-crafted microbrew beer in hip **Portland** (p1028).

- Exploring the gusty **Oregon Coast** (p1049) in search of whales, wild weather, hidden beaches and rugged capes.

PACIFIC NORTHWEST

HISTORY

Native American societies including the Chinook and the Salish had long-established coastal communities by the time Europeans arrived in the Pacific Northwest in the 18th century. Inland, on the arid plateaus between the Cascades and the Rocky Mountains, the Spokane, Nez Percé and other tribes thrived on seasonal migration between river valleys and temperate uplands.

Three hundred years after Columbus landed in the New World, Spanish and British explorers began probing the northern Pacific coast, seeking the fabled Northwest Passage. In 1792, Capt George Vancouver was the first explorer to sail the waters of Puget Sound, claiming British sovereignty over the entire region. At the same time, an American, Capt Robert Gray, found the mouth of the Columbia River. In 1805 the explorers Lewis and Clark crossed the Rockies and made their way down the Columbia to the Pacific Ocean, extending the US claim on the territory.

In 1824 the British Hudson's Bay Company established Fort Vancouver in Washington as headquarters for the Columbia region. This opened the door to waves of settlers but had a devastating impact on the indigenous cultures, assailed as they were by the double threat of European diseases and alcohol.

In 1843 settlers at Champoeg, on the Willamette River south of Portland, voted to organize a provisional government independent of the Hudson's Bay Company, thereby casting their lot with the USA, which formally acquired the territory from the British by treaty in 1846. Over the next decade, some 53,000 settlers came to the Northwest via the 2000-mile-long Oregon Trail.

Arrival of the railroads set the region's future. Agriculture and lumber became the pillars of the economy until 1914, when the opening of the Panama Canal and WWI brought increased trade to Pacific ports. Shipyards opened along Puget Sound, and the Boeing aircraft company set up shop near Seattle.

Big dam projects in the 1930s and '40s provided cheap hydroelectricity and irrigation. WWII offered another boost for aircraft manufacturing and shipbuilding, and agriculture continued to thrive. In the postwar period Washington's population, especially around Puget Sound, grew to twice that of Oregon. But hydroelectricity production and the massive irrigation projects along the Columbia have nearly destroyed the river's ecosystem. Logging has also left its scars, especially in Oregon. The environment remains a contentious issue in the Northwest; flash points are the logging of old-growth forests and the destruction of salmon runs in streams and rivers.

In the 1980s and '90s, the economic emphasis shifted again with the rise of the high-tech industry, embodied by Microsoft in Seattle and Intel in Portland. The region has also reinvigorated its ecocredentials and stands at the forefront of US efforts to offset climate change.

LOCAL CULTURE

The stereotypical image of a Pacific Northwesterner is of a casually dressed, latte-supping urbanite who drives a hybrid car, votes Democrat and walks around with an unwavering diet of Nirvana-derived indie rock programmed into their iPod. But, as with most fleeting regional generalizations, the reality is far more complex.

Noted for their sophisticated café culture and copious microbrew pubs, the urban hubs of Seattle and Portland are the northwest's most emblematic cities. But head east into the region's dryer and less verdant interior and the cultural affiliations become increasingly more traditional. Here, strung out along the Columbia River Valley or nestled amid the arid steppes of southeastern Washington, small towns host raucous rodeos, tourist centers promote cowboy culture, and a cup of coffee is served 'straight up' with none of the fancily fashioned chai lattes and icy frappés that are par for the course in Seattle.

In contrast to America's hardworking eastern seaboard, life out west is more casual and less frenetic than in New York or Boston. Idealistically, Westerners would rather work to play than live to work. Indeed, with so much winter rain, the citizens of Olympia or Bellingham will dredge up any excuse to shun the nine-to-five treadmill and hit the great outdoors a couple of hours (or even days) early. Witness the scene in late May and early June when the first bright days of summer will prompt a mass exodus of hikers and bikers making enthusiastically for the national parks and wilderness areas for which the region is justly famous.

Creativity is another strong northwestern trait, be it redefining the course of modern rock music or reconfiguring the software on the latest Microsoft computer program. No longer content to live in the shadow of Hong Kong or California, the Pacific Northwest has redefined itself internationally in recent decades through celebrated TV shows (*Frasier* and *Grey's Anatomy*), iconic global personalities (Bill Gates) and a groundbreaking music scene that has spawned everything from grunge rock to riot grrrl feminism.

Tolerance is widespread in Pacific Northwestern society from recreational drug use to physician-assisted suicide. Commonly voting Democrat in presidential elections, the population has also enthusiastically embraced the push for 'greener' lifestyles in the form of car clubs, recycling programs, organic restaurants and bio-diesel whale-watching tours. An early exponent of ecofriendly practices, Seattle mayor Greg Nickels is currently advocating himself as a leading spokesman on climate change, while salubrious Portland regularly features high in lists of America's most sustainable cities.

LAND & CLIMATE

The Pacific Northwest is cut in half both physically and climatically by the looming Cascade Range, which runs like a rugged spine from Canada down to California. Thanks to this substantial geographic barrier, the region's vegetation and terrain are extremely varied.

The area to the west of the Cascades receives an enormous amount of precipitation (up to 200in a year in the Hoh River Rainforest) and hence boasts numerous glaciers, record-breaking snowfalls and a lush temperate

---

PACIFIC NORTHWEST IN...

Four Days

Kick off on day one in **Seattle** (p1003), the northwest's self-proclaimed capital, with a morning latte in Pike's Place Market and a quick gawp at the new exhibits in the recently expanded art museum. If it's summer, take a car or bus to **Mt Rainier National Park** (p1025) on day two for a hike in the alpine meadows of aptly named Paradise. Start day three with a sortie down I-5 to the **Mt St Helens Visitor Center** (p1026) at Silver Lake before branching off in Vancouver toward the magnificent **Columbia River Gorge** (p1042). Take your time on day four with a scenic drive back to **Portland** (p1028), where you can grab an appetizing beer and gourmet meal before hitting one of the city's cheap and quirky hotels.

One Week

Follow the four-day itinerary, before heading out to **Cannon Beach** (p1050) on day five to enjoy a breath of fresh air on the gusty Oregon Coast. Track north after lunch via **Astoria** (p1049) and the Megler Bridge back into Washington. If you hurry you should make it up to collegiate **Olympia** (p1017) before dark and a feast of indie-orientated nighttime music. On the morning of day six – hangover permitting – tackle the **Olympic National Park** (p1017), via one of the eastern entrances if you're short on time, or by circumnavigating the whole perimeter if you want to get a real feel for one of America's most exotic wilderness areas. Spend the night in a hotel in historic **Port Townsend** (p1019) before sallying forth on your final day on a whale-watching tour in the **San Juan Islands** (p1021) or a quiet sojourn over to pastoral **Whidbey Island** (p1020).

Two Weeks

Follow the one-week itinerary before chugging east on the Empire Builder train across the Cascades to understated **Spokane** (p1024), where you can jog with the locals along the scenic Centennial Trail. Track south next to the **Yakima** (p1026) for some authentic Native American culture before moving onto **Walla Walla** (p1027) for America's classiest wine tasting outside of California's Napa Valley. Transfer over to the Idaho–Oregon border next for a heart-in-your-mouth, white-knuckle white-water rafting experience amid jaw-dropping scenery in **Hells Canyon** (p1048) before geologically acquainting yourself with the **John Day Fossil Beds National Monument** (p1048) a few clicks south. You'll kick yourself if you miss out on the adventures of activity-obsessed **Bend** (p1044), but leave enough time at the end of your trip to fully appreciate the eerily still, cool waters of **Crater Lake National Park** (p1045).

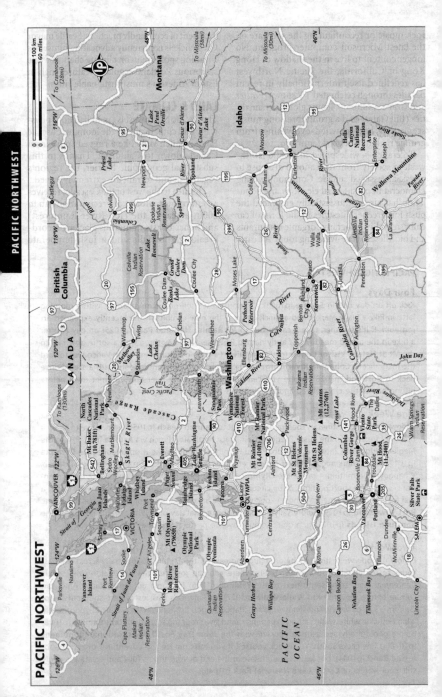

PACIFIC NORTHWEST

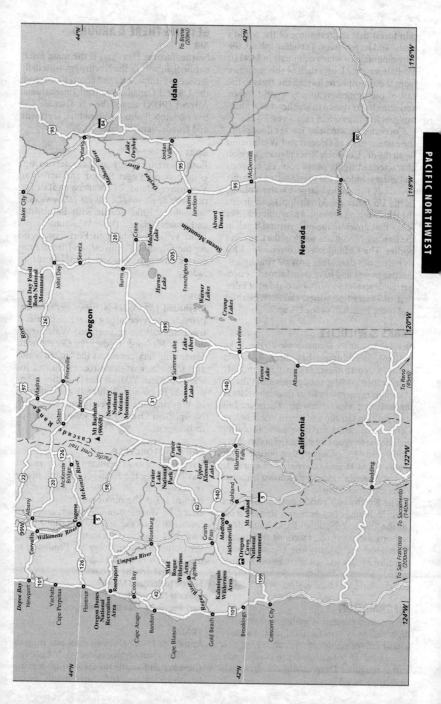

rain forest that shelters some of the world's oldest and largest trees. Traveling inland, the lofty mountains – which culminate in 14,411ft Mt Rainier – suck up much of this moisture from the atmosphere, leaving the areas to the east of the range languishing in arid steppe and semidesert (Pasco in southeast Washington gets less than 6in of rain a year).

Cocooned on a massive ice-age floodplain, the eastern parts of Oregon and Washington lie on the dry Columbia River plateau, a region characterized by its many coulees, canyons and gorges. Indeed, the spectacular Columbia River has the second-largest water volume in the US (after the Mississippi) and drains the whole region through a magnificent river gorge that provides the only natural break in the Cascade Mountains south of the Canadian border. The Columbia is also renowned for its numerous dams that provide vital hydroelectric power and have transformed a once-barren desert into a veritable Garden of Eden that produces fine wines, classic vegetables and more than half of the US apple crop.

PARKS & WILDLIFE

Oregon has one national park, Crater Lake (p1045); Washington has three: Olympic (p1017), North Cascades (p1023) and Mt Rainier (p1025). Maps and passes are available at various ranger stations or through **Nature of the Northwest** (www.naturenw.org). There are 240 state parks in Oregon and 215 in Washington. Other areas noted for their natural beauty include the Oregon Coast, the Columbia River Gorge and Hell's Canyon that borders with Idaho. Mt St Helens offers visitors a unique look at America's most well-known National Volcanic Monument.

The Northwest's parks contain numerous fauna including black bear, rare Roosevelt elk (in the Olympic National Park), mule deer, bighorn sheep, coyote, raccoons and pronghorn antelope. Meanwhile the seas boast plentiful whales and sea lions. Resident birds include herons, kingfishers, loons, ospreys, meadowlarks and bald eagles.

INFORMATION

Oregon and western Washington have a 10-digit dialing system for local calls. To make a local call within the ☎ 206, ☎ 253, ☎ 425, ☎ 360 and ☎ 564 area codes in Washington, and throughout Oregon, dial the area code first (without a 1).

GETTING THERE & AROUND

AIR

Seattle-Tacoma (Sea-Tac) is the main international airport in the Northwest, with daily service to Europe, Asia and points throughout the US and Canada. Portland International Airport (PDX) serves the US, Canada and has nonstop flights to Frankfurt, Germany and Guadalajara, Mexico.

BOAT

Both passenger-only and car ferries operate around Puget Sound and across to Vancouver Island, BC. **Washington State Ferries** (WSF; ☎ 206-464-6400, 888-808-7977; www.wsdot.wa.gov/ferries) links Seattle with Bainbridge and Vashon Islands. Other WSF routes cross from Whidbey Island to Port Townsend on the Olympic Peninsula, and from Anacortes through the San Juan Islands to Sidney, BC.

BUS

Greyhound (☎ 800-229-9424; www.greyhound.com) provides service along the I-5 corridor from Bellingham in northern Washington down to Medford in southern Oregon with connecting services across the United States and Canada. East–west routes fan out toward Spokane, Yakima, the Tri-Cities (Kennewick, Pasco and Richland) and Pullman in Washington, and Pendleton, Bend and Newport in Oregon with numerous stops in between.

CAR & MOTORCYCLE

Driving your own vehicle is a convenient way of touring the Pacific Northwest. Major rental agencies can be found throughout the region. I-5 is the major north–south road artery. In Washington I-90 heads east from Seattle to Spokane and into Idaho. In Oregon I-84 branches east from Portland along the Columbia River Gorge via Pendleton to link up with Boise in Idaho.

Regional driving distances:

Seattle to Portland 174 miles.
Spokane to Pendleton 205 miles.
Port Angeles to Astoria 217 miles.

TRAIN

Amtrak (☎ 800-872-7245; www.amtrak.com) runs an excellent train service north (to Vancouver, Canada) and south (to California) linking Seattle, Portland and other major urban centers with the Cascades and Coast Starlight service. The famous *Empire Builder* heads east to Chicago from Seattle and Portland (joining in Spokane, Washington).

WASHINGTON

Washington is a state of two distinct halves. To the west lie the snow-capped volcanoes and evergreen forests of the spectacular Cascade Range juxtaposed against the urban cool of glittering Seattle, while in the east hard-working fruit pickers and traditional rural farmers contribute just as much to the booming economy that has become famous the world over for everything from computers to Kurt Cobain. For most visitors, Seattle is the region's obvious launching pad, with its cosmopolitan café culture and its handy proximity to the outdoor delights of Mt Rainier and the Olympic National Park. Few Washingtonians will forgive you, however, if you overlook sophisticated Olympia with its laidback collegiate charm, the pastoral San Juan Islands and their resident army of back-to-the-landers, or Johnny-come-lately Walla Walla, the next big thing in the international wine world (if the rumors are to be believed).

History

The first US settlement in Washington was at Tumwater, on the southern edge of Puget Sound, in 1845. Both Seattle and Port Townsend were established in 1851 and quickly became logging centers. Lumber was shipped at great profit to San Francisco, the boomtown of the California gold rush.

In 1853, Washington separated from the Oregon territory. Congress reduced the amount of land open to native hunting and fishing, and opened up the eastern part of the state to settlement. The arrival of rail links in the last decades of the century created a readily accessible market for the products of the Pacific Northwest and brought in floods of settlers.

Washington was admitted to the union in 1889, and Seattle began to flourish in 1897, when it became the principal port en route to the Alaska and Yukon goldfields. The construction of the Bonneville Dam (1937) and Grand Coulee Dam (1947) accelerated the region's industrial and agricultural development by providing cheap hydroelectric power and irrigation.

WASHINGTON FACTS
Nickname Evergreen State
Population 6.4 million
Area 71,342 sq miles
Capital city Olympia (population 43,000)
Sales tax 6.5%
Birthplace of Singer and actor Bing Crosby (1903–77), guitarist Jimi Hendrix (1942–70), computer geek Bill Gates (b 1955), Denver Broncos quarterback John Elway (b 1960), saxophonist Kenny G (b 1956), grunge icon Kurt Cobain (1967–94)
Home of Mt St Helens, Microsoft, Starbucks, Nordstrom, Evergreen State College
Famous for Grunge rock, coffee, *Frasier*, *Twin Peaks*, volcanoes, apples, wine, precipitation
State vegetable The Walla Walla sweet onion

The rapid postwar urbanization of the Puget Sound region created an enormous metropolitan area linked by perpetually jammed freeways that mar some of the waterfront vistas. Industry switched from lumber to computer technologies as Seattle rode the dot-com boom, suffered a small recession and emerged to fight another day. Placed firmly on the world map through the work of homegrown global giants such as Starbucks and Microsoft, Washington is looking to the future with a greener face. Popular Seattle mayor Greg Nickels has been instrumental in rallying more than 400 American cities to reduce carbon emissions in line with the Kyoto protocol and the knock-on effect in other towns is palpable.

Information

Washington road conditions (☎ Seattle 206-368-4499, elsewhere in the state 800-695-7623)

Washington State Parks & Recreation Commission (☎ 360-902-8844, 800-233-0321; www.parks .wa.gov; PO Box 42650, Olympia, WA 98504)

Washington State Tourism Office (☎ 360-725-5052; www.tourism.wa.gov; ⏱ 7am-7pm) Useful website; 'travel counselors' offer travel-related advice over the phone.

SEATTLE

Practically everything you think you know about Seattle has changed. It's a city that has outgrown its own stereotype. No longer the slacker haven where flannel-clad musicians and artists mope in cafés all day and basements rent for $80 a month, the city has caught the scent of success and turned giddy. It is a thriving urban core amid spectacular natural beauty; people here have it good, and they know it.

Seattle is also a city of contradiction: its roots as a logging town versus its progressive ecofriendliness; its growth in business versus resistance to the global marketplace. It can build empires (Starbucks, Microsoft) and then shun them (World Trade Organization; WTO). But these are all signs of a city struggling to define itself, a dynamic place on the cusp of maturity and an exciting entry point to any exploration of the Pacific Northwest.

History

Seattle was named for Chief Sealth, leader of the Duwamish tribe that inhabited the Lake Washington area when David Denny led the first group of white settlers here in 1851. The railway came through in 1893, linking Seattle with the rest of the country. For a decade, prospectors headed for the Yukon gold territory would stop in Seattle to stock up on provisions.

The boom continued through WWI, when Northwest lumber was in great demand and the Puget Sound area prospered as a shipbuilding center. In 1916 William Boeing founded the aircraft manufacturing business that would become one of the largest employers in Seattle, attracting tens of thousands of newcomers to the region during WWII.

In November 1999, the city drew attention as protesters and police clashed violently outside a WTO summit. Two of the city's biggest business successes, Starbucks and Microsoft, are loved and loathed almost equally. Boeing has relocated its headquarters to Chicago, though it's still a major presence in Seattle.

Infrastructure is the latest hot topic. The Alaskan Way Viaduct, the eyesore of a traffic channel between downtown and the Waterfront, will be torn out and replaced (plans were still being formulated at the time of research). Light-rail transit is expanding, and a hub of biotech companies and residences in south Lake Union will be served by the city's first streetcar in 65 years.

Orientation

Seattle's Sea-Tac Airport is 13 miles south of the city. Amtrak trains use the King St Station, north of the new Seahawks Stadium, just south of Pioneer Sq. Greyhound's bus terminal is at 8th Ave and Stewart St, on the north edge of downtown.

Seattle is neighborhood-oriented: Capitol Hill and the U District are east of I-5, while downtown, Seattle Center, Fremont and Ballard lie to the west. To reach Fremont from downtown, take 4th Ave to the Fremont Bridge; from here, hang a left on NW 36th Ave (which becomes Leary) to reach Ballard. Eastlake Ave goes from downtown to the U District.

Information

BOOKSTORES
Bulldog News & Espresso (☎ 206-632-6397; 4208 University Way NE) A very thorough newsstand.
Elliott Bay Book Company (☎ 206-624-6600; 101 S Main St) Labyrinthine store in historic Pioneer Sq has readings almost nightly.
Metsker Maps (☎ 206-623-8747; 1511 1st Ave) New location, same great selection of maps and travel guides.

EMERGENCY & MEDICAL SERVICES
45th St Community Clinic (☎ 206-633-3350; 1629 N 45th St, Wallingford) Medical and dental services.
Harborview Medical Center (☎ 206-731-3000; 325 9th Ave) Full medical care, with emergency room.
Seattle Police (☎ 206-625-5011)
Seattle Rape Relief (☎ 206-632-7273)
Washington State Patrol (☎ 425-649-4370)

INTERNET ACCESS
Practically every bar and coffee shop in Seattle has free wi-fi, as do most hotels. For laptop-free travelers, internet cafés include:
Cyber-Dogs (☎ 206-405-3647; 909 Pike St; dogs $2-5; 1st 20min free, then per hr $6; ☺ 10am-midnight) A veggie hotdog stand, espresso bar, internet café and youngster hangout/pickup joint.
Online Coffee Co (www.onlinecoffeeco.com; per min 14¢; ☺ 7:30am-midnight); Olive Way (☎ 206-328-3731; 1720 E Olive Way); Pine St (☎ 206-323-7798; 1404 E Pine St) The Olive Way location is in a cozy former residence, while the Pine St shop is more utilitarian-chic. The first hour is free for students.

INTERNET RESOURCES
hankblog.wordpress.com Insider art-related news and views from the folks at the Henry Art Gallery.

www.historylink.org Loads of essays and photos on local history.

www.seattlediy.com Information on underground events and house shows.

www.seattlest.com A blog about various goings-on in and around Seattle.

slog.thestranger.com A frequently updated blog by the staff of *The Stranger*.

www.visitseattle.org Seattle's Convention and Visitors Bureau site.

MEDIA

KEXP 90.3 FM Legendary independent music and community station.

KUOW 94.9 FM National Public Radio (NPR) news.

Seattle Gay News Weekly.

Seattle Post-Intelligencer (www.seattlepi.com) Daily.

Seattle Times (www.seattletimes.com) The state's largest daily paper.

Seattle Weekly (www.seattleweekly.com) Free weekly with news and entertainment listings.

The Stranger (www.thestranger.com) Irreverent weekly edited by Dan Savage of 'Savage Love' fame.

MONEY

American Express (Amex; ☎ 206-441-8622; 600 Stewart St; ☷ 8:30am-5:30pm Mon-Fri)

Travelex-Thomas Cook Currency Services Airport (☎ 206-248-6960; ☷ 6am-8pm); Westlake Center (☎ 206-682-4525; Level 3, 400 Pine St; ☷ 9:30am-6pm Mon-Sat, 11am-5pm Sun) The booth at the main airport terminal is behind the Delta Airlines counter.

POST

Post office Broadway Station (☎ 206-324-5474; 101 Broadway E); Main branch (☎ 206-748-5417; 301 Union St); University Station (☎ 206-675-8114; 4244 NE University Way, U District)

TOURIST INFORMATION

Seattle/King County Visitors Center (☎ 206-461-5840; www.seeseattle.org; cnr 7th Ave & Pike St; ☷ 9am-5pm) Inside the Washington State Convention and Trade Center; it also operates a useful Citywide Concierge service.

Sights

Most of Seattle's sights are concentrated in a fairly compact core area. The historic downtown, Pioneer Sq, includes the area between Cherry and S King Sts, along 1st to 3rd Ave. The main shopping area is along 4th and 5th Aves from Olive Way down to University St. Just north of downtown is Seattle Center, with many of the city's cultural and sporting facilities, as well as the Space Needle and the Experience Music Project. Across busy Alaskan Way from the Pike Place Market is the Waterfront, Seattle's tourist mecca.

DOWNTOWN

The heart of downtown Seattle is **Pike Place Market**, on Pike St between Western and 1st Aves. The buzzing warren of fruit stands, cafés and little shops is excellent street theater, although claustrophobically crowded on the weekends. Go early on a weekday morning to avoid the crush. The Main and North Arcades are the most popular areas, with bellowing fishmongers, arts and crafts, and precarious stacks of fruits and vegetables. Don't miss the oddball shops on the lower levels.

Newly renovated and expanded, the **Seattle Art Museum** (☎ 206-654-3100; 1300 1st Ave; adult/child/student/senior $13/free/7/10, 1st Thu of month admission free; ☷ 10am-5pm Tue, Wed & Fri-Sun, to 9pm Thu & Fri) now has 118,000 extra square feet. Some have criticized the new section for having a clinical feel, but it's difficult not to be struck by a sense of excitement upon entering. Above the ticket counter hangs Cai Guo-Qiang's *Inopportune: Stage One*, a series of white cars exploding with neon. Between the two museum entrances (one in the old building and one in the new) is the 'art ladder,' a free space with installations cascading down a wide stepped hallway. And the galleries themselves are much improved. The museum's John H Hauberg Collection is an excellent display of masks, canoes, totems and other pieces from Northwest coastal tribes.

North of Pike Place Market is **Belltown**, the birthplace of grunge. One famous club is still here, but the area has gone seriously upscale, with fancy restaurants and designer boutiques in converted lofts. Still, it remains one of the liveliest parts of town for nightlife.

PIONEER SQUARE

This enclave of red-brick buildings, the oldest part of Seattle, languished for years and was almost razed to build parking lots, until a wave of public support led to Historic Register status followed by an influx of art galleries, antique shops and cafés. It can be seedy at night, but trendy nightclubs perpetrate more crimes than individuals do.

Yesler Way was the original 'skid road' – in Seattle's early days, loggers in a camp above town would send logs skidding down the road to Henry Yesler's pierside mill. With the slump

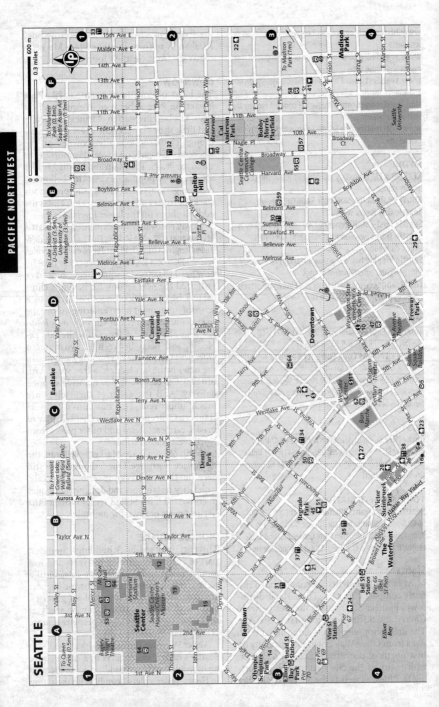

PACIFIC NORTHWEST

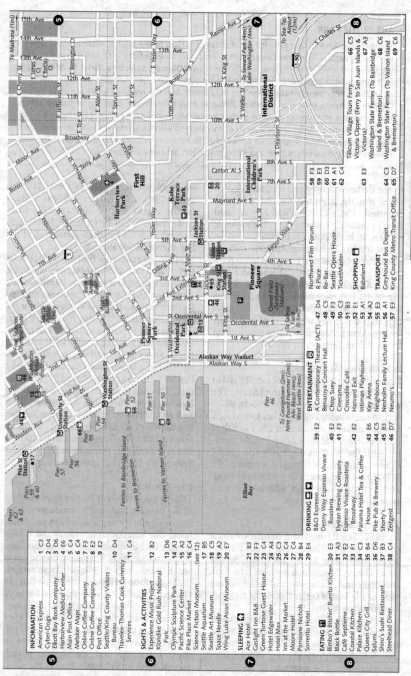

ART IN THE PARK

The eagle has landed. Or maybe it's about to take off. Hard to say, but it's certainly impossible to ignore: The *Eagle* is Alexander Calder's 39ft-tall red steel creation from 1971, and it happens to be the crowning jewel of the Seattle Art Museum's new **Olympic Sculpture Park** (☎ 206-654-3100; 2901 Western Ave; admission free; ☷ 6am-9pm May-Sep, 7am-6pm Oct-Apr). Hovering over train tracks in an unlikely oasis between the water and busy Elliott Ave, the brand-new, 8.5-acre, $85 million Olympic Sculpture Park is an excellent lesson in how to make the most out of limited urban space. Worth a visit just for its views of the Olympic Mountains across Elliott Bay, the park is still in that awkward youthful phase – much of the planned vegetation has yet to fill in – but it has a lot of potential. Its Z shape slinks back and forth between Belltown and the edge of the bay, rescuing unused parcels of land and filling them with art and plant life.

PACIFIC NORTHWEST

in the timber industry and resulting decline of the area, the street became a haven for the homeless. The nickname Skid Rd (or 'Skid Row') eventually came to mean the opposite of 'Easy St' in cities across the US.

Just south of Pioneer Square Park, on Occidental Ave S, **Occidental Park** contains totem poles carved by Chinookan artist Duane Pasco.

The **Klondike Gold Rush National Historic Park** (☎ 206-553-7220; cnr Jackson St & 2nd Ave S; admission free; ☷ 9am-5pm) has exhibits, photos and news clippings describing what kind of provisions you would've needed were you to stake a claim in the Yukon Territory in 1897.

INTERNATIONAL DISTRICT

East of Pioneer Sq (take S Jackson St), Asian shops and restaurants line the streets. The **Wing Luke Asian Museum** (☎ 206-623-5124; 407 7th Ave S; adult/child/student $4/2/3; ☷ 11am-4:30pm Tue-Fri, noon-4pm Sat & Sun) documents the city's wealth of Asian cultures and their often fraught meeting with the West through artwork, special exhibits, historic photographs, a replica of a WWII Japanese American internment camp and recorded interviews with people who were forced into the camps.

SEATTLE CENTER

In 1962, Seattle hosted a World's Fair, a summer-long exhibition that enticed nearly 10 million visitors to view the future, Seattle style. The vestiges, which 45 years later look simultaneously futuristic and retro, are on view at the **Seattle Center** (☎ 206-684-8582; www.seattlecenter.com; 400 Broad St).

Sticking out of the skyline and impossible to ignore, the emblematic **Space Needle** (☎ 206-905-2100; adult/child/senior $16/8/14; ☷ 9am-midnight) is a 605ft-high observation station with a revolving restaurant. The **monorail** (☎ 206-905-2600;

www.seattlemonorail.com; adult/child/senior $4/1.50/2; ☷ 9am-11pm), a 1.5-mile experiment in mass transit, runs every 10 minutes daily from downtown's Westlake Center right through a crumple in the smashed-guitar hull of the Experience Music Project.

Microsoft cofounder Paul Allen's **Experience Music Project** (EMP; ☎ 206-367-5483; www.emplive.com; 325 5th Ave N; adult/child/student & senior $19.95/14.95/15.95; ☷ 9am-6pm Sun-Thu, to 9pm Fri & Sat summer, 10am-5pm Sun-Thu, to 9pm Fri & Sat winter) is worth a look for the architecture alone. Whether it's worth the admission price depends on how old and music-obsessed you are. The Frank Gehry building houses 80,000 music artifacts, including handwritten lyrics by Nirvana's Kurt Cobain and a Fender Stratocaster demolished by Jimi Hendrix. Attached to the EMP is the **Science Fiction Museum** (☎ 206-724-3428; www.sfhomeworld.org; 325 5th Ave N; adult/child $15/12; ☷ 10am-8pm summer, 10am-5pm Wed-Mon winter), a nerd paradise of costumes, props and models from sci-fi movies and TV shows. Admission is free between 5pm and 8pm on the first Thursday of the month.

CAPITOL HILL

This stylish, irreverent part of town displays all the panache and vitality you'd expect from Seattle's primary gay and lesbian neighborhood. The junction of Broadway and E John St is the core of activity, with restaurants, bars, shops and plenty of interesting characters to watch. Further north, in stately **Volunteer Park**, the **Seattle Asian Art Museum** (☎ 206-654-3100; 1400 E Prospect St, Volunteer Park; adult/child/student & senior $5/free/3; ☷ 10am-5pm Tue-Sun, 10am-9pm Thu; **P**) houses the extensive art collection of Dr Richard Fuller, who donated this severe art moderne–style gallery to the city in 1932. Admission is free on the first Thursday and first Saturday of each month. Also in Volunteer Park is the glass-sided Victorian **conservatory** (admission free), filled with palms, cacti and tropical plants.

FREMONT

Fremont, about 2 miles north of Seattle Center, is known for its lefty vibe, farmers market and wacky public sculpture, including a rocket sticking out of a building and a statue of Lenin shipped over from Slovakia. People come from all over town for the **Fremont Sunday Market** (☎ 206-781-6776; www.fremontmarket.com/fre mont; Stone Way & N 34th St; 10am-5pm Sun summer, to 4pm Sun winter). The market features fresh fruits and vegetables, arts and crafts and all kinds of people getting rid of junk.

Another piece of public art, **Waiting for the Interurban** (N 34th St at Fremont) is a cast-aluminum statue of people awaiting a train that never comes: the Interurban linking Seattle and Everett stopped running in the 1930s (it started up again in 2001 but the line no longer passes this way). Check out the human face on the dog; it's Armen Stepanian, once Fremont's honorary mayor, who made the mistake of objecting to the sculpture.

THE U DISTRICT

The 700-acre University of Washington campus sits at the edge of Lake Union in a commercial area about 3 miles northeast of downtown. The main streets are University Way, known as the 'Ave,' and NE 45th St, both lined with coffee shops, restaurants and bars, cinemas and bookstores. The core of campus is **Central Plaza**, known as Red Sq because of its brick base. Get information and a campus map at the **visitor center** (☎ 206-543-9198; 4014 University Way; 8am-5pm Mon-Fri).

Near the junction of NE 45th St and 16th Ave is the **Burke Museum** (☎ 206-543-5590; adult/student/senior $8/5/6.50, 1st Thu each month free; 10am-5pm, 1st Thu of month 10am-8pm), with an excellent collection of Northwest-coast Native American artifacts. At the corner of NE 41st St and

---

LOCAL VOICE: DAREK MAZZONE

KEXP world-music DJ Darek Mazzone was born in Poland, where he lived until age nine; after that he lived in Boston. He ended up in Seattle by accident, when a van broke down after a road trip in 1992. 'The funny thing is I was listening to KEXP when it happened,' he says.

How has the music scene changed over the years? Well, it's always got an eyeball on it, internationally. There's always something new that's bubbling up in Seattle. Right now it's Modest Mouse and Death Cab for Cutie. But it's interesting to see it from a perspective of being *in* the city, because right now the most interesting thing that's bumping in Seattle is hip-hop. There are some phenomenal bands. Like Blue Scholars – they're conscious, they sing about the war and about what's really going on. But there's other stuff, too. We've got a great jazz scene; we've got a really funky reggae scene; one of the best Balkan groups in the world, Kultur Shock. There's always something interesting going on. It's a good town for collaboration.

What's your favorite thing about your neighborhood (Capitol Hill)? I love being in the center of everything. I love walking. I'm desperate for the light-rail, which is going to transform the city dramatically. This is my favorite city in the world, and I love coming back to it. But I would love to take off for five years and come back and just see it transform.

Where do you take visitors? If they're hip, I take them to Georgetown, which I love. It's such a cool neighborhood. I take friends to places that I know there's no way they would experience otherwise. I take them to farmers markets. This is a foodie kind of town, it's amazing. Fremont's always fun; that's changed, too, but it still has that commie/hippie vibe.

Any only-in-Seattle moments? There are a lot of only-in-Capitol Hill moments. This is where the freaks live. This is where you're gonna see a 60-year-old fetish couple walking down the street with leashes. You're going to see a wide range of really interesting fashion choices. I know millionaires, billionaires who live here, so, you know, you're at the espresso stand, and there's the billionaire, there's the rock star, there's the crusty, and there's the tourist. And there really isn't the separation that you'd find in other cities, because nobody gives a fuck. That really is the definitive Seattle moment.

15th Ave is the **Henry Art Gallery** (☎ 206-543-2280; adult/student/senior $10/free/6, Thu free; ☺ 11am-5pm Tue, Wed & Fri-Sun, to 8pm Thu), a sophisticated space centered on a remarkable permanent exhibit by light-manipulating sculptor James Turrell, and featuring various temporary and touring collections.

BALLARD

Ballard, despite its recent veneer of hipness, still has the feel of an old Scandinavian fishing village – especially around the locks, the marina and the Nordic Heritage Museum. The old town has become a nightlife hot spot, but even in the daytime its historic buildings and cobblestone streets make it a pleasure to wander through.

Northwest of Seattle, the waters of Lake Washington and Lake Union flow through the 8-mile-long Lake Washington Ship Canal and into Puget Sound. Construction of the canal began in 1911; today 100,000 boats a year pass through the **Hiram M Chittenden Locks** (☎ visitors center 206-783-7059; 3015 NW 54th St; ☺ 24hr), about a half-mile west of Ballard off NW Market St. Take bus 17 from downtown at 4th Ave and Union St. On the southern side of the locks, you can watch from underwater glass tanks or from above as salmon navigate a **fish ladder** on their way to spawning grounds in the Cascade headwaters of the Sammamish River, which feeds Lake Washington.

Activities
HIKING

There are great hiking trails through old-growth forest at Seward Park, which dominates the Bailey Peninsula that juts into Lake Washington, and longer but flatter hikes in 534-acre Discovery Park northwest of Seattle. The **Sierra Club** (☎ 206-523-2019) leads day-hiking and car-camping trips on weekends; most day trips are free.

BICYCLING

A cycling favorite, the 16.5-mile **Burke-Gilman Trail** winds from Ballard to Log Boom Park in Kenmore on Seattle's Eastside. There, it connects with the 11-mile **Sammamish River Trail**, which winds past the Chateau Ste Michelle winery in Woodinville before terminating at Redmond's Marymoor Park.

More cyclists pedal the oft-congested loop around **Green Lake**. Closer in, the 2.5-mile **Elliott Bay Trail** runs along the waterfront.

DON'T MISS:

- **Fremont Sunday Market** – browse for produce and crafts, or just people-watch (p1009)
- **Olympic Sculpture Park** – impressive outdoor sculpture garden with a backdrop of mountains (p1008)
- **Ballard** – just wandering this former Scandinavian fishing village gives you a good taste of Seattle's varied neighborhoods (left)
- **Brouwer's** – an enormous beer hall with an epic bar and cool industrial decor (p1013)

Get a copy of the *Seattle Bicycling Guide Map*, published by the City of Seattle's **Transportation Bicycle & Pedestrian Program** (☎ 206-684-7583; www.cityofseattle.net/transportation/bikemaps.htm) online or at bike shops.

The following are recommended for bicycle rentals and repairs:

Bicycle Center (☎ 206-523 8300; 4529 Sand Point Way; rentals 1/24hr $3/15) A longstanding bike shop that does rentals and repairs; it's right off the Burke-Gilman Trail.

Gregg's Cycles (☎ 206-523-1822; 7007 Woodlawn Ave NE) Here since 1932, Gregg's is a higher-end shop with two new storefronts in Bellevue and Lynwood; rentals are still out of the Green Lake shop. Fancy road bikes rent for $30 to $56 per hour, or you can get a more standard model for $18 per hour or $135 per week.

Recycled Cycles (☎ 206-547-4491; 1007 NE Boat St; bike rental 6/24hr $20/40) Also in the U District, toward the water at the lower end of the 'Ave.'

ON THE WATER

On Lake Union, **Northwest Outdoor Center Inc** (☎ 206-281-9694, 800-683-0637; www.nwoc.com; 2100 Westlake Ave N; kayaks per hr $10-15) rents kayaks and offers tours and instruction in sea and whitewater kayaking.

The **UW Waterfront Activities Center** (☎ 206-543-9433; canoe & rowboat per hr $7.50; ☺ approx 10am-7pm, closed Nov-Jan), at the southeast corner of the Husky Stadium parking lot off Montlake Blvd NE, rents canoes and rowboats. Bring ID or a passport.

The **Agua Verde Paddle Club** (☎ 206-545-8570; 1303 NE Boat St; s kayak per 1/2hr $15/25, double kayak $18/30; ☺ 10am-dusk Mon-Sat & 10am-6pm Sun Mar-Oct), near the university on Portage Bay, rents kayaks.

Seattle for Children

The whole of Seattle Center will fascinate youngsters, but they'll get the most out of the **Pacific Science Center** (☎ 206-443-2001; www .pacsci.org; 200 2nd Ave N; adult/child 3-5/child 6-12 $11/6/8, IMAX Theater & Laserium with general admission extra $3, without general admission $8/6/7; ⏱ 10am-6pm; P). It entertains and educates with virtual-reality exhibits, laser shows, holograms, an IMAX theater and a planetarium – parents won't be bored either. Parking costs between $5 and $10.

Downtown on Pier 59 is the newly reno-vated **Seattle Aquarium** (☎ 206-386-4300; 1483 Alaskan Way at Pier 59; adult/child $15/10; ⏱ 9:30am-5pm), another fun way to learn all about the natural world of the Pacific Northwest. 'Window on Washington Waters' is a look at the sea floor of the Neah Bay area, where rockfish, salmon, sea anemones and more than 100 other fish and invertebrate spe-cies live. The centerpiece of the aquarium is a glass-domed room where sharks, octopi and other deepwater denizens lurk in the shadowy depths.

Tours

Argosy Cruises Seattle Harbor Tour (☎ 206-623-1445, 800-642-7816; www.argosycruises.com; adult/child $18.61/7.81) Argosy's popular Seattle Harbor Tour is a one-hour narrated tour of Elliott Bay, the Waterfront and the Port of Seattle. It departs from Pier 55.

Bill Speidel's Underground Tour (☎ 206-682-4646; 608 1st Ave; adult/child/senior $14/7/12) This famous 'underground' tour, though corny at times, delivers the goods on historic Seattle as a rough and rowdy industrial town. The tour operates from 11am to 5pm but the schedule varies.

See Seattle Walking Tours (☎ 425-226-7641; www .see-seattle.com; $20) See Seattle runs a variety of theme tours, from public-art walks to scavenger hunts. Tours run from 10am from Monday to Saturday.

WHAT THE...?

The **Fremont Troll** lurks beneath the north end of the Aurora Bridge at N 36th St. The troll's creators – artists Steve Badanes, Will Martin, Donna Walter and Ross Whitehead – won a competition sponsored by the Fre-mont Arts Council in 1990. The 18ft-high cement figure snacking on a Volkswagen Beetle is now a favorite place for late-night beer drinking.

Festivals & Events

Northwest Folklife Festival (☎ 206-684-7300; www.nwfolklife.org) Memorial Day weekend in May. International music, dance, crafts, food and family activi-ties at Seattle Center.

Seafair (☎ 206-728-0123; www.seafair.com) Late July and August. Huge crowds attend this festival on the water, with hydroplane races, a torchlight parade, an air show, music and a carnival.

Bumbershoot (☎ 206-281-8111; www.bumbershoot .com) Labor Day weekend in September. A major arts and cultural event at Seattle Center, with live music, author readings and lots of unclassifiable fun.

Sleeping

From mid-November through March 31, most downtown hotels offer Seattle Super Saver Packages – generally 50% off rack rates, with a coupon book for savings on dining, shop-ping and attractions. Call the **Seattle Hotel Hotline** (☎ 800-535-7071). You can make reservations on its website at www.seattlesupersaver.com.

BUDGET

Green Tortoise Guest House (☎ 206-340-1222; www .greentortoise.net; 105 Pike St; dm $24-29, r $77-80; 🖳) The only hostel in the city center now that HI Seattle has closed, this once-super-grungy place has moved around the corner from its old home and is right across the street from Pike Place Market. There are 30 bunk rooms and 16 European-style rooms (shared bath and shower). Prices include breakfast.

Moore Hotel (☎ 206-448-4851, 800-421-5508; 1926 2nd Ave; s/d $67/79, s/d with shared bath $52/64, ste $104-156; ✗ 🖳 wi-fi) Rooms at this once-grand hotel next to the elegant Moore Theater are noth-ing fancy, but they have plenty of old-world charm.

our pick **College Inn** (☎ 206-633-4441; www.college innseattle.com; 4000 University Way NE; s/d with breakfast from $55/75; ✗ 🖳 wi-fi) The pretty, half-tim-bered building in the U District, left over from the 1909 Alaska–Yukon Exposition, has 25 European-style guestrooms with sinks and shared baths. Note there are four flights of stairs and no elevator. Pub in the basement!

MIDRANGE

Gaslight Inn B&B (☎ 206-325-3654; www.gaslight-inn .com; 1727 15th Ave; r $88-158; ✗ 🖳) The Gaslight Inn has 15 rooms available in two neighboring homes, 12 of which have private bathrooms. In summer, it's refreshing to dive into the out-door pool or just hang out on the sun deck.

Pensione Nichols (☎ 206-441-7125; www.pensione nichols.com; 1923 1st Ave; s/d/ste $98/125/230; P 💻) Ideally situated between Pike Place Market and Belltown, this charming haven has 10 European-style rooms and a common room overlooking the market. Parking costs $12.

our pick Ace Hotel (☎ 206-448-4721; www.acehotel .com; 2423 1st Ave; r without/with bath $99/190; P 💻) One of Seattle's hippest hotels, the Ace sports minimal, futuristic decor (everything's white or stainless steel, even the TV), antique French army blankets, condoms instead of pillow mints and a Kama Sutra in place of the Bible. Parking costs $15.

Hotel Max (☎ 206-441-4200, 800-426-0670; www .hotelmaxseattle.com; 620 Stewart St; s/d from $179/199; P 💻) Original artworks hang in the (small but cool) guest rooms, and it's tough to get any hipper than the Max's supersaturated color scheme – not to mention package deals such as the Grunge Special or the Gaycation. Rooms feature menus for your choice of pillows and spirituality services. Parking costs $15.

TOP END

Inn at the Market (☎ 206-443-3600, 800-446-4484; www.innatthemarket.com; 86 Pine St; r $175-300, r with water views $230-400; P) The elegant Inn at the Market is the only lodging in the venerable Pike Place Market. This 70-room boutique hotel has large rooms, many of which enjoy grand views onto market activity and Puget Sound. Parking costs $20.

Hotel Edgewater (☎ 206-728-7000, 800-624-0670; www.edgewaterhotel.com; 2411 Alaskan Way, Pier 67; r with city/water views from $299/439; P) This luxury hotel on Pier 67 is the only one that faces onto Elliott Bay. You're no longer allowed to fish from the windows, but you can sit by the fireplace and reel in the salty air and views of Puget Sound. Valet parking is available for $26.

Sorrento Hotel (☎ 206-622-6400, 800-426-1265; www.hotelsorrento.com; 900 Madison St; r from $339; ✗ P 💻) William Howard Taft, 27th US president, was the first registered guest at the Sorrento, an imposing Italian-style hotel known since its birth in 1909 as the jewel of Seattle. Parking is $19.

Eating
BUDGET

The most fun way to assemble a budget meal is by foraging in Pike Place Market for fresh produce, baked goods, deli items and take-out ethnic foods.

Bimbo's Bitchin' Burrito Kitchen (☎ 206-329-9978; 506 E Pine St; tacos $2.95; burritos $5.50-7.50; ☯ noon-11pm Mon-Thu, to 2am Fri & Sat, 2pm-10pm Sun) Bimbo's slings fat tacos, giant burritos and juicy quesadillas until closing time. The tiny space is crammed with kitschy knick-knacks, including velvet matador portraits, oil paintings with neon elements, and a hut-style thatched awning.

Chaco Canyon Cafe (☎ 206-522-6966; 4761 Brooklyn Ave NE; juices $3-5, mains $5-10; ☯ 8am-8pm Mon-Fri, 9am-4pm Sat, 10am-4pm Sun) The menu at this comfy Southwestern-style nook in the U District is all vegan, 90% organic and almost half raw-food. There's a long list of melty sandwiches, smoothies and juices, coffee and tea.

Agua Verde Cafe (☎ 206-545-8570; 1303 NE Boat St; 3 tacos $6.50; ☯ 11am-9pm Mon-Sat, takeout 7:30am-2pm Mon-Fri) Overlooking the water, Agua Verde serves mouth-watering, garlic-buttery tacos of fish, shellfish or portabella mushrooms. You can also rent kayaks downstairs.

our pick Salumi (☎ 206-621-8772; 309 3rd Ave S; sandwiches $7-10, plates $11-14; ☯ 11am-4pm Tue-Fri) The line waiting at Mario Batali's dad's place is like its own little community. People chat, compare notes, talk about sandwiches they've had and loved…it's nice. Sandwiches come with any of a dozen types of cured meat and fresh cheese. There aren't many seats, so plan to picnic.

MIDRANGE

Shiro's Sushi Restaurant (☎ 206-443-9844; 2401 2nd Ave; sushi $2-9, specials $9-13, mains $20-21; ☯ 5:30-9:45pm) Get a seat at the bar and watch the maestro prepare some of the freshest sushi rolls in town.

Sitka & Spruce (☎ 206-324-0662; www.sitkaand spruce.com; 2238 Eastlake Ave E; lunch $5-11, dinner $5-18; ☯ 11:30am-1:30pm Tue-Fri, 5:30-10:30pm Wed-Sat, 10am-2pm Sat & Sun) In a strip mall next to a Subway, this restaurant has won acclaim for its casual vibe, good wine selection and all-local ingredients.

Café Septieme (☎ 206-860-8858; 214 Broadway E; starters $5-9, breakfast & lunch mains $7-9, dinner mains $15-18; ☯ 9am-midnight) A pretty, Euro-style restaurant-bar with red walls and white-clothed tables, Septieme serves filling but sophisticated burgers, salads, pastas and fish dishes; the bacon-provolone cheeseburger is great.

Palace Kitchen (☎ 206-448-2001; 2030 5th Ave; salads $7-9, mains $12-25; ☯ 5pm-1am) Owned by celebrity chef Tom Douglas, Palace Kitchen is a late-night hot spot that fills up when the cocktail crowd gets peckish. Its bar snacks are anything but ordinary; try the king-crab omelet.

Coastal Kitchen (☎ 206-322-1145; 429 15th Ave E; lunch mains $8-12, starters $8-10, dinner mains $14-20; ⏱ 8am-11pm) This longtime favorite turns out some of the best food in the neighborhood – it has an eclectic mix of Cajun, Mayan and Mexican inspirations, and an Italian-language instruction tape running in the bathroom, if that gives a clue toward influences.

Black Bottle (☎ 206-441-1500; blackbottleseattle.com; 2600 1st Ave; mains $8-9; ⏱ 4:30pm-1:30am) The crowd outside the front door of this new Belltown restaurant is your first clue that something interesting is happening inside. The menu offers further clues: octopus carpaccio, lemon squid salad, saffron risotto cakes.

TOP END

Tilth (☎ 206-633-0801; 1411 N 45th St; small plates $6-14, large plates $10-29; ⏱ 5:30-10pm Tue-Thu & Sun, 5:30-10:30pm Fri & Sat, 10am-2pm Sat & Sun) The only ingredients on chef Maria Hines' menu that aren't organic are those found in the wild; everything else is carefully selected to meet certified-organic standards, and prepared in a manner that preserves its essence.

Queen City Grill (☎ 206-443-0975; 2201 1st Ave; starters $9-17, salads $6, mains $12-33; ⏱ 5pm-2am) This longtime Belltown favorite serves daily seafood specials and menus that change to reflect the use of seasonal ingredients. The room is warmly lit and cozy, yet sophisticated, and service is all class.

ourpick Steelhead Diner (☎ 206-625-0129; www .steelheaddiner.com; 95 Pine St; starters $9-14, sandwiches $9-13, mains $15-33; ⏱ 11am-10pm Tue-Sat, 10am-3pm Sun) Homey favorites such as fish and chips, grilled salmon or braised short ribs and grits become fine cuisine when they're made with the best of what Pike Place Market has to offer.

Drinking

You'll find cocktail bars, dance clubs and live music on Capitol Hill. The main drag in Ballard has brick taverns old and new, filled with the hard-drinking older set in daylight hours and indie-rockers at night. Belltown has gone from grungy to fratty, but has the advantage of many drinking holes neatly lined up in rows. Industrial Georgetown is an up-and-coming barfly's paradise, still rough around the edges. And, this being Seattle, you can't walk two blocks without hitting a coffee shop.

COFFEEHOUSES

Seattle gave us Starbucks, and the home-grown-turned-overgrown chain is hard to avoid. But small independent coffeehouses abound.

B&O Espresso (☎ 206-322-5028; 204 Belmont Ave E) Full of understated swank, this is the place to go for Turkish coffee – if you can get past the pastry case up front.

Café Allegro (☎ 206-633-3030; 4214 University Way NE) Supposedly the city's first espresso bar, located in the U District, Allegro keeps students and professors wired.

Espresso Vivace Roasteria (☎ 206-860-5869; Denny Way 901 E Denny Way; Broadway 321 Broadway E) Asked what's the best coffee in Seattle, most people will mention Vivace. There's also a walkup window on Broadway.

Panama Hotel Tea & Coffee House (☎ 206-515-4000; 607 S Main St) The Panama, a historic 1910 building that contains the only remaining Japanese bathhouse in the US, doubles as a memorial to the neighborhood's Japanese residents forced into internment camps during WWII.

Zeitgeist (☎ 206-583-0497; 171 S Jackson St; wi-fi) A lofty, brick-walled café, the pretty Zeitgeist has great coffee and sandwiches.

BARS

ourpick Brouwer's (☎ 206-267-2437; 400 N 35th St; ⏱ 11am-2am) This dark cathedral of beer in Fremont has rough-hewn rock walls and a black metal grate in the ceiling. Behind an epic bar are tantalizing glimpses into a massive beer fridge. A replica *Mannequin Pis* statue at the door and the Belgian crest everywhere clue you in to the specialty.

Shorty's (☎ 206-441-5449; 2222 2nd Ave) An unpretentious oasis in a block of *très-chic* lounges, Shorty's has cheap beer and hot dogs, alcohol slushies and a back room that's pure pinball heaven.

Blue Moon (☎ 206-633-626; 712 NE 45th St) Legendary haunt of literary drunks, the Blue Moon is exactly a mile from campus, thanks to an early zoning law. Be prepared for impromptu poetry recitations, jaw-harp performances and inspired rants.

Copper Gate (☎ 206-706-3292; 6301 24th Ave NW) Formerly one of Seattle's worst dives, the Copper Gate in Ballard is now an upscale bar-restaurant focused on meatballs and naked ladies. A Viking longship forms the bar, with a peepshow pastiche for a sail and a cargo of helmets and gramophones.

Nine Pound Hammer (☎ 206-762-3373; 6009 Airport Way S) This darkened beer hall in Georgetown is generous with the pours and the peanuts, and the mixed crowd of workers, hipsters, punks and bikers vacillates between energetic and rowdy.

BREWPUBS
Jolly Roger Taproom (☎ 206-782-6181; 1514 NW Leary Way; pints $4, pitchers $10; ☽ closed Sun) Less scurvy-barnacle than placid-yachtsman, Maritime Pacific Brewing's Jolly Roger Taproom in Ballard is a tiny, pirate-themed bar with a nautical chart painted onto the floor, good seafood and about 15 taps.

Hale's Ales Brewery (☎ 206-706-1544; www .halesales.com; 4301 Leary Way NW) Hale's makes fantastic beer, notably its ambrosial Cream Ale. Its flagship brewpub in Fremont feels like a business-hotel lobby, but it's worth a stop. There is a self-guided tour near the entrance.

Pike Pub & Brewery (☎ 206-622-6044; 1415 1st Ave) This pub in Pike Place Market serves great burgers and brews in a funky neoindustrial multilevel space.

Elysian Brewing Co (☎ 206-860-1920; 1221 E Pike St) On Capitol Hill, the Elysian's huge windows are great for people-watching – or being watched, if your pool game's good enough.

Entertainment
Consult the *Stranger, Seattle Weekly* or the daily papers for listings. Tickets for big events are available at **TicketMaster** (☎ 206-628-0888), which operates a **discount ticket booth** (☎ 206-233-1111) at Westlake Center.

LIVE MUSIC
our pick Crocodile Cafe (☎ 206-441-5611; 2200 2nd Ave) A beloved institution in Belltown and famous as a launching pad for the grunge scene, the Croc still hosts great local and touring bands.

Neumo's (☎ 206-709-9467; 925 E Pike St) The 'new Moe's' fills the big shoes of its long-gone namesake in booking some of the best local and touring rock shows in town.

Chop Suey (☎ 206-324-8000; 1325 E Madison St) Chop Suey is a dark, high-ceilinged space with a ramshackle faux-Chinese motif and eclectic bookings.

Tractor Tavern (☎ 206-789-3599; 5213 Ballard Ave NW, Ballard) This spacious, amber-lit venue in Ballard mainly books folk and acoustic acts.

CINEMAS
The biggest event of the year for Seattle cinephiles is the **Seattle International Film Festival** (SIFF; ☎ 206-464-5830; www.seattlefilm.com/siff; tickets $5-10, passes $300-800). The festival uses a half-dozen cinemas but also has its own dedicated cinema, in McCaw Hall's **Nesholm Family Lecture Hall** (321 Mercer St, Seattle Center), and typically starts in mid-May.

The **Seattle Lesbian & Gay Film Festival** (☎ 206-323-4274; admission $6-8), a popular festival in October, shows new gay-themed films from directors worldwide.

Cool cinemas include:
Cinerama (☎ 206-441-3653; 2100 4th Ave) One of the very few Cineramas left in the world, it has a fun, sci-fi feel.
Harvard Exit (☎ 206-781-5755; 807 E Roy St at Harvard) Built in 1925, Seattle's first independent theater.
Northwest Film Forum (☎ 206-329-2629; www .wigglyworld.org; 1515 12th Ave) – Impeccable programming, from restored classics to cutting-edge independent and international films.

THEATER & PERFORMING ARTS
Check local newspapers for reviews and schedules.

A Contemporary Theatre (ACT; ☎ 206-292-7676; 700 Union St) One of the three big companies in the city, ACT fills its $30 million home at Kreielsheimer Place with performances by Seattle's best thespians and occasional big-name actors.

Intiman Playhouse (☎ 206-269-1900) The Intiman Theatre Company, Seattle's oldest, takes the stage at this theater.

Pacific Northwest Ballet (☎ 206-441-9411) The ballet is the foremost dance company in the Northwest and does more than a hundred performances a season from September through June at McCaw Hall.

Seattle Opera (☎ 206-389-7676) The Seattle Opera, also at McCaw Hall, features a program of four or five full-scale operas every season, including a summer Wagner's *Ring* cycle that draws sellout crowds.

Seattle Symphony (☎ 206-215-4747) The symphony is a major regional ensemble; it plays at the Benaroya Concert Hall, downtown at 2nd Ave and University St.

SPORTS
Seattle Mariners (☎ 206-628-3555; www.mariners.org; admission $7-60) The beloved baseball team plays in Safeco Field just south of downtown.

Seattle Seahawks (☎ 425-827-9777; www.seahawks .com; admission $42-95) The Northwest's only National Football League (NFL) franchise plays in the 72,000-seat Seahawks Stadium.

Supersonics (☎ 206-283-3865; www.nba.com/sonics; admission $10-235) Seattle's National Basketball Association (NBA) franchise draws huge crowds at Seattle Center's Key Arena.

Huskies (☎ 206-543-2200; www.gohuskies.com; admission $6-65) The University of Washington Huskies football and basketball teams are another Seattle obsession.

GAY & LESBIAN VENUES

Re-bar (☎ 206-233-9873; 1114 Howell St) This storied dance club, where many of Seattle's defining cultural events happened (such as Nirvana album releases etc), welcomes gay, straight, bi or undecided revelers to its lively dance floor.

Neighbours (☎ 206-324-5358; 1509 Broadway Ave E) For the gay club scene and its attendant glittery straight girls, check out this always-packed dance factory.

R Place (☎ 206-322-8828; 619 E Pine St) Three floors of dancing to hip-hop/R & B DJs and plenty of sweaty body contact make this club a blast for pretty much everyone who isn't terribly uptight.

Shopping

The main big-name shopping area is downtown from 3rd to 6th Aves and University to Stewart Sts. Pike Place Market is a maze of arts-and-crafts stalls, galleries and small shops. Pioneer Sq and Capitol Hill have locally owned gift and thrift shops.

Some only-in-Seattle shops to seek out:

Archie McPhee (☎ 206-297-0240; 2428 NW Market St, Ballard; 🕙 10am-7pm Mon-Sat, 11am-7pm Sun) Famous for its mail-order catalog, Archie McPhee is a browser's heaven, and you'll almost certainly wind up buying something you never realized you needed – like bacon air fresheners or a ninja lunchbox.

Babeland (☎ 206-328-2914; 707 E Pike St; 🕙 11am-10pm Mon-Sat, noon-7pm Sun) The answer to the question 'Where can I buy pink furry handcuffs and a glass dildo?'

Sonic Boom (☎ 206-568-2666; www.sonicboom records.com; 514 15th Ave E; 🕙 10am-10pm Mon-Sat, to 7pm Sun) A local institution, Sonic Boom now has several locations and frequently hosts in-store performances by bands coming through town.

Getting There & Away

AIR

Seattle's airport, **Seattle-Tacoma International Airport** (Sea-Tac; ☎ 206-433-5388; www.portseattle.org), 13 miles south of Seattle on I-5, has daily service to Europe, Asia, Mexico and points throughout the USA and Canada, with frequent flights to and from Portland, OR, and Vancouver, BC.

BOAT

Victoria Clipper (☎ 800-888-2535, 206-443-2560; www.vic toriaclipper.com) operates several high-speed passenger ferries to Victoria, BC, and to the San Juan Islands. It also organizes package tours which can be booked in advance through the website. Victoria Clipper runs from Seattle to Victoria up to six times daily; round-trips cost from $117 for adults and $58 for children.

The **Washington State Ferries** (☎ 206-464-6400, in Washington 888-808-7977; www.wsdot.wa.gov/ferries) website has maps, prices, schedules, trip planners, and weather updates, plus estimated waiting time for popular routes. Fares depend on the route, vehicle size and trip duration, and are collected either for round-trip travel or one-way travel, depending on the departure terminal.

Bellingham links the contiguous US with Alaska via the **Alaska Marine Hwy Ferry** (☎ 360-676-8445), which travels once a week up the Inside Passage to Juneau, Skagway and other southeast Alaskan ports.

BUS

A **biodiesel bus** (☎ 503-502-5750; www.sharedroute.org) runs from Portland and Olympia to Seattle and back once daily Friday to Sunday. A one-way trip from Portland to Seattle costs $20, while a round-trip will set you back $50.

Greyhound (☎ 800-231-2222, in Seattle 206-628-5561, baggage 206-628-5555; www.greyhound.com; 811 Stewart St; 🕙 6am-midnight) connects Seattle with cites all over the country, including Chicago, IL ($195 one-way, two days, three daily), Spokane ($38, five to seven hours, three daily), San Francisco, CA ($95, 20 hours, four daily), and Vancouver, BC ($25, three to four hours, six daily).

TRAIN

Amtrak (☎ 800-872-7245; www.amtrak.com) serves Seattle's **King Street Station** (303 S Jackson St; 🕙 6am-10:30pm, ticket counter 6:15am-8pm). Three main routes run through town: the *Amtrak Cascades* (connecting Vancouver, BC, Seattle, Portland and Eugene), the very scenic *Coast*

Starlight (connecting Seattle, Oakland and Los Angeles) and the *Empire Builder* (connecting Seattle, Spokane, Fargo and Chicago).

Some examples of one-way ticket prices from Seattle:

Chicago, IL From $309, 46 hours, daily.

Oakland, CA $135, 23 hours, daily.

Portland, OR $28 to $31, three to four hours, five daily.

Vancouver, BC $28 to $43, three to four hours, five daily.

Getting Around

TO/FROM THE AIRPORT

There are a number of options for making the 13-mile trek from the airport to downtown Seattle.

Shuttle Express (☎ 800-487-7433; shuttleexpress.com; $26-53) has pickup and dropoff on the third floor of the airport garage. Gray Line's **Airport Express** (☎ 206-626-6088; graylineseattle.com; one way adult $10-13, child $7-10) fetches passengers in the parking lot outside door 00 at the south end of the baggage-claim level.

Taxis and limousines (about $35 and $40, respectively) are available at the parking garage on the 3rd floor. Rental car counters are located in the baggage claim area.

Catch **Metro buses** (one-way $1.25-1.75) outside door 6 by baggage carousel 5, on the baggage claim level. Buses 194 Express and 174 go downtown. From there, the free 99 bus goes to the Waterfront, Pioneer Sq and the International District, or use the online **trip planner** (☎ Rider Information system 206-553-3000; www .transit.metrokc.gov).

CAR & MOTORCYCLE

Seattle traffic has been among the worst in the country for years and isn't improving. If you do drive, take a friend: some Seattle freeways have High-Occupancy Vehicle lanes for vehicles carrying two or more people. National rental agencies have offices at the airport and around town.

PUBLIC TRANSPORTATION

Buses are operated by **Metro Transit** (☎ schedule info 206-553-3000, customer service 206-553-3060; www .transit.metrokc.gov; fares $1.25-1.75), part of the King County Department of Transportation.

TAXI

All Seattle taxi cabs operate at the same rate, set by King County; at the time of research the rate was $2.50 at meter drop, then $2 per mile.

Any of the following offer reliable taxi service:

Orange Cab Co (☎ 206-444-0409; www.orangecab.net)

Redtop Taxi (☎ 206-789-4949; yellowtaxi.net)

Yellow Cab (☎ 206-622-6500; yellowtaxi.net)

AROUND SEATTLE

Puget Sound

Bainbridge Island is a popular destination with locals and visitors alike; it's the quickest and easiest way to get out on the water from Seattle, and the ferry ride provides stunning views of Seattle and the Sound. Prepare to stroll around lazily, tour some waterfront cafés, taste unique wines at the **Bainbridge Island Winery** (☎ 206-842-9463; Hwy 305; ☼ tastings 11am-5pm Fri-Sun), 4 miles north of Winslow, and maybe rent a bike and bicycle around the invitingly flat countryside.

Another easy way to get onto the Sound from Seattle is with **Tillicum Village Tours** (☎ 206-933-8600, 800-426-1205; www.tillicumvillage.com; adult/child/senior $79/30/72), which operates from March and December, departing from Pier 55. The four-hour trip to Blake Island – the birthplace of Seattle's namesake, Chief Sealth – includes a salmon bake, a native dance and a movie at an old Duwamish Indian village.

Washington State Ferries (☎ 206-464-6400, in Washington 888-808-7977; www.wsdot.wa.gov/ferries; Seattle to Bainbridge, adult/child/car & driver $6.70/5.40/14.45, bicycle surcharge $1) runs many times daily.

Tacoma

Tacoma gets a bad rap as a beleaguered mill town known mostly for its distinctive 'Tacom-aroma,' a product of the nearby paper mills. Its nickname, 'City of Destiny,' because it was the Puget Sound's railroad terminus, once seemed like a grim joke. But destiny has started to come through for Tacoma. A renewed investment in the arts and significant downtown revitalization make it a worthy destination on the Portland–Seattle route.

Find information at the **visitor center** (☎ 253-305-1000, 800-272-2662; www.traveltacoma.com; 1001 Pacific Ave; ☼ 8:30am-5pm Mon-Fri).

Tacoma's tribute to native son Dale Chihuly, the **Museum of Glass** (☎ 253-396-1768; 1801 E Dock St; adult/child $10/4; ☼ 10am-5pm Mon-Sat, noon-5pm Sun, plus 10am-8pm Thu in summer), with its slanted tower called the Hot Shop Amphitheater, has art exhibits and glassblowing demonstrations. Chihuly's characteristically elaborate and colorful **Bridge of Glass** walkway connects the museum with downtown's enormous copper-domed neobaroque **Union Station** (1911).

Take Ruston Way out to **Point Defiance** (☎ 253-591-5337; zoo admission adult/child $10/8; ☺ 9:30am-5pm), a 700-acre park complex with free-roaming bison and mountain goats, a logging museum, zoo, aquarium and miles of trails.

The **Antique Sandwich Company** (☎ 253-752-4069; 5102 N Pearl St; lunch & snacks $5-8) is a funky luncheonette and coffee shop near Point Defiance.

For B&Bs, call the **Greater Tacoma B&B Reservation Service** (☎ 253-759-4088, 800-406-4088). Moderately priced hotels are scattered south of the center between I-5 exits 128 and 129.

Sound Transit bus routes 590 and 594 use the station behind the **Tacoma Dome** (510 Puyallup Ave); the fare to Tacoma city center is $3. The free Downtown Connector service makes a loop between the station and Seattle city center every 15 minutes. **Amtrak** (☎ 253-627-8141; 1001 Puyallup Ave) links Tacoma to Seattle and Portland.

Olympia

Characterized by its cool urban energy and revered for its close proximity to the scenic wonders of Mt Rainier and the Olympic National Park, Olympia has been attracting both indoor artists and outdoor adventurers for decades. Grunge pioneers Nirvana originally hailed from here and played some of their earliest gigs in the bars and pubs of downtown; creator of *The Simpsons* Matt Groening once edited the campus newspaper at progressive Evergreen College; while pioneering brewer Leopold Schmidt chose the artesian water of nearby Tumwater to craft his smooth and flavorful Olympia beer. The **State Capitol Visitor Center** (☎ 360-586-3460; cnr 14th Ave & Capitol Way) offers information on the capitol campus, the Olympia area and Washington State.

At the Washington State Capitol campus is the vast, domed 1927 **Legislative Building**. Free tours are offered hourly between 8am and 4:30pm every day except Christmas and Thanksgiving. Visitors can also tour the **campus** and see the Temple of Justice and the Capitol Conservatory, which houses a large collection of tropical plants. The campus is open between 8am and 4pm Monday to Friday and admission is free.

The **State Capital Museum** (☎ 360-753-2580; 211 W 21st Ave; admission $2; ☺ 10am-4pm Tue-Fri, noon-4pm Sat)

has exhibits on the Nisqually Indians. The fun **Olympia Farmers Market** (☎ 360-352-9096; ☺ 10am-3pm Thu-Sun Apr-Oct, Sat & Sun Nov-Dec), at the north end of Capitol Way, has fresh local produce, crafts and food booths.

The **Olympia Inn** (☎ 360-352-8533; 909 Capitol Way S; s/d $50/57) is an unpretentious downtown motel. A little more upmarket is the modern **Phoenix Inn Suites** (☎ 360-570-0555; 415 Capitol Way N; s/d $99/109; ☒ ☒ ☒ wi-fi) adjacent to the water at Percival Landing.

ourpick **Batdorf & Bronson** (☎ 360-786-6717; 513 Capitol Way S; ☺ 6am-7pm Mon-Fri, 7am-6pm Sat & Sun) is a local roaster offering ethical coffee. The famous Olympia oysters can be sampled at the **Oyster House** (☎ 360-753-7000; 320 W 4th Ave; seafood dinners $15-20; ☺ 11am-11pm Sun-Thu, to midnight Fri & Sat). The **Spar Bar** (☎ 360-357-6444; 114 4th Ave E; breakfast $4-5, lunch $5-8; ☺ 7am-9pm) is a stylish old café and cigar store with a purple-glazed facade and a cozy back-room bar called the Highclimber.

The city's still-happening music scene is showcased at the **4th Avenue Tavern** (☎ 360-786-1444; 210 4th Ave E) with its retro-fitted bar or **Le Voyeur** (☎ 360-943-5710; 404 4th Ave E), a bohemian, vegan-friendly chattering house.

OLYMPIC PENINSULA

Cut off from the rest of the state by water on three sides, the remote Olympic Peninsula is insular and lightly populated. Dominated by the Olympic National Park, the region's main urban centers are located in the northeast and include the gateway town of Port Angeles, historic Port Townsend and the drier, balmier settlement of Sequim, now a budding retirement community. Protected climatically by the Olympic Mountains, Sequim plays host to abundant outdoor activities.

Exempt from strict wilderness regulations, the parts of the peninsula outside of the Olympic National Park are largely given over to the lumber industry. Further west, clinging to the wild Pacific coast, are a handful of large Native American Indian reservations.

Olympic National Park

Declared a national monument in 1909 and a national park in 1938, the 1406-sq-mile Olympic National Park shelters a unique rainforest, copious glaciated mountain peaks and a 57-mile strip of Pacific coastal wilderness that was added in 1953. Existing as one of North America's last great wilderness areas, most of the park remains relatively untouched by human habitation with 1000-year-old cedar trees juxtaposed with pristine alpine meadows, clear glacial lakes and a largely roadless interior. Opportunities for independent exploration in this huge and remote backcountry region abound with visitors enjoying such diverse activities as hiking, fishing, kayaking and skiing.

INFORMATION

Park entry fee is $5/15 per person/vehicle, valid for one week, payable at park entrances. Many park visitor centers double as United States Forestry Service (USFS) ranger stations, where you can pick up permits for wilderness camping ($5 per group, valid up to 14 days, plus $2 per person per night).

Forks Visitor Information Center (☎ 360-374-2531, 800-443-6757; 1411 S Forks Ave; 🕑 10am-4pm) Suggested itineraries and seasonal information.

Olympic National Park Visitor Center (☎ 360-565-3130; 3002 Mt Angeles Rd; 🕑 9am-5pm) The best overall center is situated at the Hurricane Ridge gateway, a mile off Hwy 101 in Port Angeles.

Wilderness Information Center (☎ 360-565-3100; 3002 Mt Angeles Rd; 🕑 7:30am-6pm Sun-Thu, 7:30am-8pm Fri & Sat in summer, 8am-4:30pm daily in winter) Directly behind the visitor center, you'll find maps, permits and trail information.

EASTERN ENTRANCES

The graveled Dosewallips River Rd follows the river from US 101 for 15 miles to **Dosewallips Ranger Station**, where the trails begin; call ☎ 360-565-3130 for road conditions. Even hiking smaller portions of the two long-distance paths – with increasingly impressive views of heavily glaciated **Mt Anderson** – is reason enough to visit the valley. Another eastern entry for hikers is the **Staircase Ranger Station** (☎ 360-877-5569; 🕑 summer only), just inside the national park boundary, 15 miles from Hoodsport on US 101. Two state parks along the eastern edge of the national park are popular with campers: **Dosewallips State Park** and **Lake Cushman State Park** (☎ 888-226-7688; campsites/RV sites $17/24). Both have running water, flush toilets and some RV hookups.

NORTHERN ENTRANCES

At **Hurricane Ridge**, perched precipitously 18 miles south of Port Angeles, you're often above the weather. At road's end there's an interpretive center in a flower-strewn meadow from which you can see Mt Olympus and dozens of other peaks. Aside from various trailheads, you'll also find one of only two national-park-based ski runs in the US. For more information contact the **Hurricane Ridge Winter Sports Club** (☎ 360-417-1542; www.hurricaneridge.net).

Popular for boating and fishing is **Lake Crescent**, the site of the park's oldest and most reasonably priced **lodge** (☎ 360-928-3211; 416 Lake Crescent Rd; lodge r with shared bath $68-85, cottages $132-211; 🕑 May-Oct; 🖳 wi-fi). Sumptuous and sustainable food is served in the lodge's ecofriendly restaurant. From **Storm King Information Station** (☎ 360-928-3380; 🕑 summer only) on the lake's south shore, a 1-mile hike climbs through old-growth forest to Marymere Falls. Along the Sol Duc River, the **Sol Duc Hot Springs Resort** (☎ 360-327-3583; www.northolympic.com/sol duc; 12076 Sol Duc Hot Springs Rd, Port Angeles; r $115-169, RV sites $23; 🕑 late Mar-Oct; 🖳 🖳) has lodging, dining, massage and, of course, hot-spring pools (adult/child $10/7.50), as well as great day hikes.

WESTERN ENTRANCES

Isolated by distance and one of the US' rainiest microclimates, the Pacific side of the Olympics remains its wildest. Only US 101 offers access to its noted temperate rain forests and untamed coastline. The **Hoh River Rainforest** lies at the end of the 19-mile Hoh River Rd and offers visitors one of the region's strangest natural treasures (opposite).

our pick **Lake Quinault Lodge** (☎ 360-288-2900, www.visitlakequinault.com; 345 S Shore Rd; lodge r $134-167, cabin $125-243; 🖳 🖳), a luxury classic of 1920s 'parkitecture' on South Shore Rd, boasts a heated pool and sauna, a crackling fireplace and a memorable dining room noted for its sweet-potato breakfast pancakes. A number of short trails begin just below the lodge, leading to **Lake Quinault**, a beautiful glacial lake surrounded by forested peaks. It's popular for fishing, boating and swimming and is punctuated by some of the nation's oldest trees.

The photogenic **Enchanted Valley Trail** climbs up to a large meadow (a former glacial lakebed) that's resplendent with wildflowers and copses of alder trees. The 13-mile hike to the aptly named valley begins from the Graves Creek Ranger Station at the end of the South Shore Rd, 19 miles from US 101.

THE HOH RIVER RAINFOREST

Cocooned in a Tolkeinesque maze of dripping ferns and moss-draped trees, the Hoh River Rainforest has no earthly counterpart. Its uniqueness is primarily a result of abnormally high annual rainfall (between 12ft and 14ft) along with its carefully protected status within the Olympic National Park. Classified as one of the world's few remaining temperate rain forests, the Hoh is also the planet's largest. Hidden in a dense, dark-green 'cold jungle,' huge colonies of ghostly epiphytes compete with armies of teeming insects, myriad endangered fauna (such as the Roosevelt elk) and 1000-year-old Douglas fir and western hemlock trees.

You can get better acquainted with the area's complex yet delicate natural ecosystems at the **Hoh visitor center & campground** (☎ 360-374-6925; ☼ 9am-4:30pm, to 6pm Jul & Aug), 19 miles east of Hwy 101 from a turnoff on the park's western perimeter. A number of backcountry hikes start from the parking lot, including the short, interpretive **Hall of Moses trail** (0.8 miles). Ask about the twice-daily guided ranger walks in the summer.

Port Townsend

Port Townsend is one of the architectural showpieces of the Pacific Northwest and contrasts substantially with the urban sprawl of Puget Sound. It is also a North American rarity in that it has successfully managed to evade the onslaught of modern commercialization and survive into the 21st century with its historical legacy firmly intact. To get the lowdown on the city's 1890s architectural boom call in at the **visitor center** (☎ 360-385-2722; www.ptchamber.org; 2437 E Sims Way; ☼ 9am-5pm Mon-Fri, to 4pm Sat & Sun). Further enlightenment can be gleaned at the **Jefferson County Historical Society Museum** (☎ 360-385-1003; 210 Madison St; adult/child 12 & under $4/1; ☼ 11am-4pm Mon-Sat, 1-4pm Sun, closed Jan & Feb).

Historic **Fort Worden State Park** (☎ 360-344-4400; www.parks.wa.gov/ftworden; 200 Battery Way; ☼ 6:30am-dusk Apr-Oct, 8am-dusk Nov-Mar), located 2 miles north of the ferry landing (take Cherry St from uptown), was featured in the film *An Officer and a Gentleman*. Within the complex are the **Commanding Officer's Quarters** (☎ 360-385-4730; admission $1; ☼ 10am-5pm Jun-Aug, 1-4pm Sat & Sun only Mar-May & Sep-Oct), a restored Victorian-era home, and the **Coast Artillery Museum** (☎ 360-385-0373; admission $2; ☼ 11am-4pm Jun-Aug, Sat & Sun only Mar-May & Sep-Oct).

Within **Fort Worden State Park**, the **HI Olympic Hostel** (☎ 360-385-0655; olyhost@olympus.net; 272 Battery Way; dm $17-20, r from $50) has impeccable if spartan quarters in a former barracks; it's up the hill behind the park office. Downtown has a plethora of old restored hotels – try the **Palace Hotel** (☎ 360-385-0773; 1004 Water St; r $55-109; ☒), a former brothel reincarnated as an attractive period piece. The turreted, Prussian-style **Manresa Castle** (☎ 360-385-5750, 800-732-1281; www.manresacastle.com; cnr 7th & Sheridan Sts; r from $99) is a 40-room mansion built in 1892, that is light on fancy gimmicks but heavy on period authenticity.

Port Townsend is a pleasurable place to eat, drink and be merry. For breakfast head to the **Salal Café** (☎ 360-385-6532; 634 Water St; breakfast $7-8, lunch $8-9; ☼ 7am-2pm) for eggs: scrambled, poached, fried or stuffed into a burrito. Lunch is best enjoyed at **Bread & Roses Eatery** (☎ 360-379-3355; 230 Quincy St; ☼ 7am-7pm Wed, Thu, Sun & Mon, to 9pm Fri & Sat) whose pièce de résistance is a delicious rosemary roast-lamb sandwich on fig bread. The **Silverwater Cafe** (☎ 360-385-6448; 237 Taylor St; lunch $6-10, dinner $10-17; ☼ 11:30am-10pm Sun-Thu, to 11pm Fri & Sat) provides a romantic atmosphere for a creatively prepared dinner.

Port Townsend can be reached from Seattle in a ferry/bus connection via Bainbridge Island and Poulsbo (bus 90 followed by bus 7). **Washington State Ferries** (☎ 206-464-6400) goes to and from Keystone on Whidbey Island (car and driver/passenger $11.15/2.60, 35 minutes).

Port Angeles

Larger than Port Townsend but less historically interesting, Port Angeles is a solid fishing and lumber town which, by right of geography, acts as the main headquarters for the nearby Olympic National Park. The **visitor center** (☎ 360-452-2363; 121 E Railroad Ave; ☼ 8am-8pm May-Oct, 10am-4pm Nov-Apr) is adjacent to the ferry terminal. Rent outdoor gear at **Olympic Mountaineering** (☎ 360-452-0240; 140 W Front St).

Cheap and cheerful budget accommodation can be found at the **Thor Town** (☎ 360-452-0931; www.thortown.com; 316 N Race St; per person $14), a congenial hostel. For a convenient central hotel adjacent to the ferry dock, check out the **Downtown Hotel** (☎ 360-565-1125; 101 E Front St; d/ste $65/85; ☒ ☒).

Bella Italia (☎ 360-457-5442; 118 E 1st St; mains $11-19; ☺ from 4pm) boasts a comprehensive wine list and offers a last splurge for hikers heading for the Olympic wilderness. The **Crab House** (☎ 360-457-0424; 221 N Lincoln St; mains $15-30; ☺ 5:30am-11pm) in the Red Lion hotel serves fresh Dungeness crabs a stone's throw from the region's eponymous spit.

Two ferries run from Port Angeles to Victoria, BC: the **Coho Vehicle Ferry** (☎ 360-457-4491; passenger/car $11.50/44), taking 1½ hours, and the passenger-only **Victoria Express** (☎ 360-452-8088; adult/child $12.50/7; ☺ May-Sep), which runs between May and December and takes one hour.

Olympic Bus Lines (☎ 360-417-0700) runs twice daily to Seattle from the public transit center at the corner of Oak and Front Sts ($39). **Clallam Transit buses** (☎ 360-452-4511) go to Forks and Sequim where they link up with other transit buses, enabling you to circumnavigate the whole peninsula.

Northwest Peninsula

Several Native American reservations cling to the extreme northwest corner of the continent and they welcome respectful visitors. Hit hard by the decline in the salmon-fishing industry, the small settlement of Neah Bay on Hwy 12 is characterized by its weather-beaten boats and craning totem poles. This is home to the Makah Indian Reservation, whose **Makah Museum** (☎ 360-645-2711; 1880 Bayview Av; admission $5; ☺ 10am-5pm Apr-Aug, closed Mon-Tue Sep-May) displays artifacts from one of North America's most significant archaeological finds. Exposed by tidal erosion in 1970, the 500-year-old Makah village of Ozette quickly proved to be a treasure trove of native history, unearthing a huge range of materials including whaling weapons, canoes, spears and combs. Seven miles beyond the museum, a short boardwalk trail leads to **Cape Flattery**, a 300ft promontory that marks the most northwesterly point in the lower 48 states.

Convenient to the Hoh River Rainforest and the Olympic coastline is **Forks**, 57 miles from Neah Bay. Good overnight accommodation can be found at the amiable **Forks Motel** (☎ 360-374-6243; 432 S Forks Ave; s/d $65/70; ☒ ☒ wi-fi).

NORTHWEST WASHINGTON

Wedged between escarpment and sea, northwest Washington is an attractive mixture of undulating hills, emerald-green islands and sparkling ocean. Its urban hub is laidback Bellingham with its collegiate coffee bars and organic ethnic restaurants, while its dazzling highlight is the pastoral San Juan Islands, an extensive archipelago accessible only by ferry and air that glimmers like a sepia-toned snapshot from another era. Equally verdant, and simpler to reach, Whidbey Island contains beautiful Deception Pass State Park and the quaint, oyster-rich village of Coupeville. Situated on Fidalgo Island and attached to the mainland via a bridge, the settlement of Anacortes is the main hub for ferries to the San Juan Islands and Victoria in Canada. If your boat's delayed you can chill out in expansive Washington Park or sample the local halibut and chips in a couple of classic downtown restaurants.

Whidbey Island

Measuring 41 miles north to south, Whidbey Island is one of the largest contiguous islands in the United States. It is also quite possibly one of the greenest. Endowed with six state parks, a unique National Historical Reserve, a budding artists and writers community, plus a free – yes, free – island-wide public bus service, there's more to this lush oasis than meets the eye.

Deception Pass State Park (☎ 360-675-2417; 41229 N State Hwy 20) straddles the eponymous steep-sided water chasm that flows between Whidbey and Fidalgo Islands, and incorporate lakes, islands, campsites and 27 miles of hiking trails.

Ebey's Landing National Historic Reserve (☎ 360-678-3310; admission free; ☺ 8am-5pm Oct 16-Mar 31, 6:30am-10pm Apr 1-Oct 15) comprises 17,400 acres encompassing working farms, sheltered beaches, two state parks and the town of **Coupeville**. This small settlement is one of Washington's oldest towns and boasts an attractive seafront, antique stores and a number of old inns. Call by at the **visitor center** (☎ 360-678-5434; www.centralwhidbeychamber .com; 107 S Main St; ☺ 10am-5pm) for more details. Whidbey is famous for its inns and B&Bs and you'll do well to check out the unique **Captain Whidbey Inn** (☎ 360-678-4097; 2072 W Captain Whidbey Inn Rd; s/d/cabins/cottages $85/95/175/275, incl full breakfast) built entirely from rust-colored madrona wood. For fresh local clams and hand-crafted microbrews look no further than **Toby's Tavern** (☎ 360-678-4222; 8 Front St; ◷ 11am-9pm Sun-Thu, to 10pm Fri & Sat).

Washington State Ferries link Clinton to Mukilteo (car and driver/passenger $8.60/3.95, 20 minutes, every 30 minutes) and Keystone to Port Townsend (car and driver/passenger $11.15/2.60, 30 minutes, every 45 minutes). Free **Island Transit buses** (☎ 360-678-7771) run the length of Whidbey every hour daily except Sunday, from the Clinton ferry dock.

Bellingham

Mild-mannered Bellingham – or the 'City of Subdued Excitement,' as it is sometimes (humorously) known – is Washington's 10th-largest population center and widely lauded by real-estate agents as being one of the Pacific Northwest's most livable communities. Embellishing the sidewalks of the revitalized city center you'll find second-hand bookstores, cozy coffee bars, myriad ethnic restaurants and a bustling and vibrant farmers market that sells everything from Bavarian pretzels to organic furniture. The best downtown tourist information can be procured at the **Visitor Info Station** (☎ 360-527-8710; 1304 Cornwall St; www .downtownbellingham.com; ◷ 9am-6pm).

Victoria/San Juan Cruises (☎ 360-738-8099, 800-443-4552) has whale-watching trips to Victoria, BC, via the San Juan Islands. Boats leave from the Bellingham Cruise Terminal in Fairhaven.

The **Val-U Inn** (☎ 360-671-9600; 805 Lakeway Dr; s/d $79/89; ✵ wi-fi) is a clean, well-managed motel just off I-5 and an easy walk from downtown Bellingham. The Vancouver–Seattle Airporter Shuttle stops here. The **Hotel Bellwether** (☎ 360-392-3100, 1 Bellwether Way; r $129-229, lighthouse $399; ✵ ✵ wi-fi), Bellingham's finest and most charismatic hotel, is positioned on the waterfront with views over the harbor toward the whale-like hump of Lummi Island.

The **Old Town Cafe** (☎ 360-671-4431; 316 W Holly St; mains $5-7; ◷ 8am-3pm) is a classic bohemian breakfast haunt where you can get to know the locals over fresh pastries and espresso. The **Swan Cafe** (☎ 360-734-0542; 1220 N Forest St; dishes $5-7; ◷ 8am-9pm) is a Community Food Co-op with an on-site café-deli that sells fresh, organic, fair-trade and guilt-free food. For strangely flavored but scrumptious ice cream try **Mallards** (☎ 360-734-3884; 1323 Railroad Ave; ◷ 8:30am-10pm Mon-Wed, to 11pm Thu & Fri, 11am-11pm Sat & Sun), a Bellingham institution. The **Mt Baker Thea-**

tre (☎ 360-734-6080; 106 N Commercial St) showcases everything from live music to dance and plays, and regularly draws in top-name acts.

San Juan Islands Shuttle Express (☎ 360-671-1137) offers daily summer service to Orcas and San Juan Islands ($20). **Alaska Marine Highway Ferries** (☎ 360-676-0212; www.state.ak.us/ferry/) goes to Skagway and other southeast Alaskan ports (from $363 without car). The **Bellair Airporter Shuttle** (☎ 800-423-4219; www.airporter.com) runs to Sea-Tac airport ($34) with connections en route to Anacortes and Whidbey Island.

SAN JUAN ISLANDS

Free from the big-city hustle of Seattle and the tainting influences of street crime, big-box supermarkets or anything resembling a coffee franchise, the idyllic San Juan Islands float like tree-carpeted time capsules amid the sparkling waters of Upper Puget Sound.

There are over 450 landfalls in this expansive archipelago if you count every rock, sandbar, islet and eagle's perch between Anacortes and the Canadian border, though only about 200 of these islands are named, and of these, only a handful are inhabited. Washington State Ferries services the four largest – San Juan, Orcas, Shaw and Lopez Islands – while others are only accessible to the select few lucky enough to have a private boat or seaplane.

For good general information about the San Juans, contact the **San Juan Islands Visitor Information Center** (☎ 360-468-3663; www.guidetosan juans.com; ◷ 10am-2pm Mon-Fri).

The best way to explore the San Juans is by sea kayak or bicycle. Kayaks are available for rent on Lopez, Orcas and San Juan Island. Expect a guided half-day trip to cost $30 to $45. Note that most beach access is barred by private property, except at state or county parks. Bicyling-wise Lopez is flat and pastoral, San Juan Island worthy of an easy day loop, while Orcas offers the challenge of undulating terrain and the steep 5-mile ride to the top of Mt Constitution.

Airlines serving the San Juan Islands include **Harbor Air Lines** (☎ 800-359-3220; www .harborair.com), **Kenmore Air** (☎ 800-543-9595) and **West Isle Air** (☎ 800-874-4434). Public transport is pretty much nonexistent, but most motels will pick up guests at the ferry landing with advance notice.

Washington State Ferries (☎ 206-464-6400, in Washington 800-843-3779; www.wsdot.wa.gov/ferries) leaves

Anacortes for the San Juans; some continue to Sidney, BC, near Victoria. Ferries run to Lopez Island (45 minutes), Orcas Landing (60 minutes) and Friday Harbor on San Juan Island (75 minutes). Fares vary by season; the cost of the entire round-trip is collected on westbound journeys only (except those returning from Sidney, BC). To visit all the islands, it's cheapest to go to Friday Harbor first and work your way back through the other islands.

Lopez Island

Lopez – or 'Slow-pez,' as locals prefer to call it – is the archetypal friendly isle, a bucolic blend of pastoral farmland and forested state parks where motorists wave congenial greetings and the pace of life hasn't changed much since Capt George Vancouver first sauntered by in 1792. South of the ferry landing (1.3 miles) **Odlin County Park** (☎ 360-468-2496; campsites from $15) provides a cheap night's stopover in a serene rural setting.

San Juan Island

San Juan Island is the archipelago's unofficial capital, a verdant mix of low forested hills and small rural farms that resonate with a dramatic and unusual 19th-century history. The main settlement is Friday Harbor, where the **chamber of commerce** (☎ 360-378-5240; 135 Spring St) is situated inside a small arcade off the main street.

San Juan Island National Historical Park (☎ 360-378-2240; 8:30am-4pm), commemorating a mid-19th-century British–US territorial conflict, consists of two former military camps on opposite ends of the island. Both of these day-use sites contain remnants of the old officers' quarters; the American Camp, on the island's southeast end, features a splendid hike up Mt Finlayson, from which three mountain ranges can be glimpsed on a clear day. On the western shore, **Lime Kiln Point State Park** (8am-5pm 15 Oct-30 Mar, 6:30am-10pm Apr 1-Oct 15) is devoted to whale-watching.

Wayfarer's Rest (☎ 360-378-6428; www.rockisland .com/~wayfarersrest; 35 Malcolm St; dm/cabins $30/60) in Friday Harbor is a backpackers hostel. **Roche Harbor Resort** (☎ 800-451-8910; www.rocheharbor .com; Roche Harbor; r $79-99, 2-bedroom townhouse $375-425, condo $143-205;) is a splendid seaside village on the island's northwest corner. Friday Harbor has several great places to eat near the ferry landing.

Orcas Island

Precipitous, unspoiled and ruggedly beautiful, Orcas Island is the San Juan's emerald jewel. The ferry terminal is at Orcas Landing, 13.5 miles south of the main population center, Eastsound. On the island's eastern lobe is **Moran State Park** (☎ 360-376-2326; 6:30am-dusk Apr-Sep, 8am-dusk Oct-Mar), dominated by Mt Constitution (2409ft), with 40 miles of trails and an awe-inspiring 360-degree mountain-top view.

Orcas has some stellar accommodation options from cheap cottages to luxury resorts. At the top end of the market is the exquisite **Rosario Resort & Spa** (☎ 360-376-2222; www .rosario-resort.com; Rosario Way; r $188-400; wi-fi), a magnificent seafront mansion built by former shipbuilding magnate Robert Moran in 1904 and now converted into an upscale resort. On the northern coast the **Smuggler's Villa Resort** (☎ 360-376-2297; www.smuggler.com; N Beach Rd; r Jun-Sep $129-225, Oct-May $259-325;) offers family-friendly facilities and an outdoor pool, while the quaint **Orcas Hotel** (☎ 360-376-4300; www.orcashotel.com; Orcas Landing; r $89-208;) offers good old-fashioned hospitality at a reasonable price. Campers will find solace at **Moran State Park** (☎ 360-376-2326; standard sites $13, hiker & biker sites $6), which has more than 150 campsites (no hookups).

Cafe Olga (☎ 360-376-5098; 11 Point Lawrence Rd, Olga; mains $9-11; 9am-6pm Mon-Fri, 9am-8pm Sat & Sun, closed Wed Mar-Apr), in the village of the same name, is tucked inside a barn alongside a crafts gallery. It specializes in pie and seafood and provides a good tonic if you've just burnt 2000 calories cycling up and down Mt Constitution. For *fuerte* Mexican flavors hit **Bilbo's Festivo** (☎ 360-376-4728; 310 A St, Eastsound; dinner mains from $14; 4-9pm).

NORTH CASCADES

Geologically different from their southern counterparts, the North Cascade Mountains are peppered with sharp, jagged peaks, copious glaciers and a preponderance of complex metamorphic rock. Thanks to their virtual impregnability, the North Cascades were an unsolved mystery to humans until relatively recently. The first road was built across the region in 1972 and, even today, it remains one of the Northwest's most isolated outposts.

Mt Baker

Rising like a snowy sentinel above the sparkling waters of upper Puget Sound, Mt Baker

(10,781ft) possesses a luminous ethereal beauty that has been mesmerizing visitors to the northwest for centuries.

Well-paved Hwy 542 – known as the Mt Baker Scenic Byway – climbs 5100ft to the aptly named **Artist Point**, 56 miles from Bellingham. Near here you'll find the **Heather Meadows Visitor Center** (MP 56 Mt Baker Hwy; ⏱ 8am-4:30pm May-Sep) and a plethora of varied hikes.

Boasting the greatest annual snowfall of any ski area in North America, Mt Baker is a skier's paradise and the **Mt Baker Ski Area** (☎ 360-734-6771; www.mtbakerskiarea.com) has 38 runs, eight lifts and a vertical rise of 1500ft. Due to its rustic facilities, ungroomed terrain and limited après ski options, the resort has gained something of a cult status among skiers and boarders, who flock here for the Legendary Baker Banked Slalom, held every January.

In true Baker-esque style the **Glacier Creek Lodge** (☎ 360-599-2991; 10036 Mt Baker Hwy; r $60, 4-person cabin $135; ⊠) is rustic but friendly, with a choice between 12 cozy cabins or 10 tiny motel rooms.

Leavenworth

Leavenworth is Washington's very own themed Bavarian 'village,' a former lumber town that went Teutonic back in the 1960s in order to stop an economic rot of catastrophic proportions from putting it permanently out of business. Rather amazingly, the ploy worked. Leavenworth's reincarnation as a quintessential Romantische Strasse village has transformed a once-dull Cascadian pit stop into a thriving and surprisingly authentic tourist haven. If you're not immediately sold on the town's rather unusual German makeover, head to the **Leavenworth Chamber of Commerce & Visitor Center** (☎ 509-548-5807; 940 US 2; www .leavenworth.org; ⏱ 8am-5pm Mon-Thu, to 6pm Fri & Sat, 10am-4pm Sun). The **Leavenworth Ranger Station** (☎ 509-548-6977; 600 Sherbourne St; ⏱ 7:30am-4:30pm daily Jun 15-Oct 15, 7:45am-4:30pm Mon-Fri rest of year) can advise on a whole host of local outdoor activities.

Authentic Bavarian hospitality can be found at **Hotel Pension Anna** (☎ 509-548-6273; www .pensionanna.com; 926 Commercial St; r $99-149, ste $199-249; ⊠), which harbors Austrian-style furniture and a European-inspired breakfast. The **Bavarian Lodge** (☎ 509-548-7878; 810 Hwy 2; r $99-119, ste $145-189; ⊠ ⊠ ⊠ wi-fi) takes the German theme to luxury levels in a plush, clutter-free

establishment with modern – but definably Bavarian – characteristics.

For bratwurst, Wiener schnitzel and Jäger schnitzel served with sauce, red cabbage and spätzle, head to **Cafe Christa** (☎ 509-548-5074; upstairs 801 Front St; lunch $7-9, dinner $14-18; ⏱ 11am-10pm), where you can wash down your meal with an accompanying stein of Hofbräuhaus Munich lager.

Lake Chelan

Long, slender Lake Chelan is central Washington's playground. **Lake Chelan State Park** (☎ 509-687-3710), on South Shore Rd, has 144 campsites; a number of lakeshore campgrounds are accessible only by boat. The town of **Chelan**, at the lake's southeastern tip, is the primary base for accommodations and services, and it has a **USFS ranger station** (☎ 509-682-2549; 428 Woodin Ave). **Link Transit buses** (☎ 509-662-1155; www.link transit.com) connect Chelan with Wenatchee and Leavenworth ($1).

Beautiful **Stehekin**, on the northern tip of Lake Chelan, is accessible only by **boat** (☎ 509-682-4584; www.ladyofthelake.com; round-trip $39), **seaplane** (☎ 509-682-5555; round-trip from Chelan $159) or a long hike across Cascade Pass, 28 miles from the lake. Most facilities are open mid-June to mid-September.

Methow Valley

The Methow's (met-how) combination of powdery winter snow and abundant summer sunshine has transformed the valley into one of Washington's primary recreation areas with unlimited opportunities to bike, hike, fish and cross-country ski.

The USFS maintains the **Methow Valley Visitor Center** (☎ 509-996-4000; 24 West Chewuch Rd; ⏱ 8am-5pm May-Oct), on Hwy 20 at the west end of Winthrop. For classic accommodations and easy access to cross-country skiing and hiking trails, decamp at the exquisite **Sun Mountain Lodge** (☎ 509-996-2211; www.sunmountainlodge.com; Box 1000, Winthrop, WA 98862; lodge r $160-620, cabin $160-345; ⊠ ⊠ ⊠ wi-fi), 10 miles west of the town of Winthrop.

North Cascades National Park

With no settlements, no overnight accommodations and only one unpaved road, the North Cascades National Park is off the radar as far as standard tourist facilities are concerned. But for the backcountry hiker and adventurer, therein lies the beauty.

IF YOU HAVE A FEW MORE DAYS IN THE WASHINGTON CASCADES...

Washington's Cascades are full of latent surprises – both natural and constructed. If you're keen to get off the main tourist routes and fly by the seat of your pants, try taking in some of the following treats.

- **Ross Lake Resort** is a cluster of floating cabins on the west side of Ross Lake just north of the Ross Dam. There's no road in, so guests either hike the 2-mile trail from Hwy 20 or take the resort's tugboat-taxi-and-truck shuttle from the parking area near Diablo Dam.

- Hike the trail up to **Desolation Peak** (6102ft) overlooking Ross Lake and ponder the hut where Beatnik novelist Jack Kerouac once spent two months alone as a fire lookout in 1956. The hike is 6.8 miles one-way and pretty strenuous, although you'll be richly rewarded with the same stunning vistas that inspired Kerouac. The trailhead is best accessed via water taxi from the Ross Lake Resort (above).

- The twin Western Washington towns of **Snoqualmie** and **North Bend** are famous as the setting for David Lynch's surrealistic 1990s TV drama *Twin Peaks*. But you don't have to be a trivia-obsessed TV geek to appreciate the majesty of stunning 268ft Snoqualmie Falls, the luxury of the Salish Lodge & Spa or the historical value of Snoqualmie's Northwest Railway Museum.

The **North Cascades Visitor Center** (☎ 206-386-4495; 502 Newhalem St, near Newhalem; ☏ 9am-4:30pm daily mid-Apr–Oct, Sat & Sun Nov-Mar, extended hours mid-Jun–Labor Day) in the small settlement of Newhalem on Hwy 20 is an essential orientation point for visitors and is staffed by expert rangers who can enlighten you on the park's highlights.

NORTHEASTERN WASHINGTON

Bordered by Canada to the north and Idaho to the east, Northeastern Washington is dominated by the understated yet populous city of Spokane and is internationally famous for producing one of the 20th century's greatest engineering marvels, the gargantuan Grand Coulee dam.

Grand Coulee Dam

The colossal Grand Coulee Dam is the country's largest hydroelectric project and one of the great engineering marvels of the modern world. While many people visit the area to admire the dam itself, an equal number are drawn by the fishing, hunting and swimming opportunities that the structure and the adjoining 150-mile-long Lake Roosevelt have inadvertently created.

Visitors can orientate themselves at the **Grand Coulee Visitor Arrival Center** (☎ 509-633-9265; ☏ 9am-5pm), an interactive exhibit center that details the history of the dam, offers free guided tours and showcases a spectacular nightly laser show.

Spokane

In the cultural wilderness of Central and Eastern Washington, Spokane is a hidden gem. Nestled among the modern skywalks and kitschy relics of the much-lauded 1974 World's Fair you'll find lovingly restored steam mills, classic art-deco skyscrapers and the Davenport, one of Washington's – and America's – most intricately decorated hotels. Stop by the **Spokane Area Visitor Information Center** (☎ 509-747-3230; www.visitspokane.com; 201 W Main Ave at Browne St) for a raft of information.

The former site of Spokane's 1974 World's Fair & Exposition, the **Riverfront Park** (☎ 509-456-4386; www.spokaneriverfrontpark.com) provides a welcome slice of urban greenery in the middle of downtown. It has been redeveloped in recent years with a 17-point **sculpture walk**, along with plenty of bridges and trails to satisfy the city's plethora of amateur runners. The park's centerpiece is **Spokane Falls**, a gushing combination of scenic waterfalls and foaming rapids. There are various viewing points over the river, including a short **gondola ride** (admission $7; ☏ 11am-6pm Sun-Thu year-round, to 10pm Fri & Sat Apr-Sep), which takes you directly above the falls. Walkers and joggers crowd the interurban **Spokane River Centennial Trail** (☎ 509-624-7188), which extends for 37 miles to the Idaho border and beyond.

Encased in a striking state-of-the-art building in the historic Browne's Addition neighborhood, the **Northwest Museum of Arts & Culture** (☎ 509-456-3931; www.northwestmuseum.org; 2316 W 1st

Ave; adult/child/senior & student $7/free/5; ☻ 11am-5pm Tue-Sun, to 8pm Wed & Fri) has – arguably – one of the finest collections of indigenous artifacts in the Northwest.

our pick **Davenport Hotel** (☎ 509-455-8888; 10 S Post St; r standard/deluxe $219/239; ☒ ☒ ☒ wi-fi), a historic Spokane landmark, is highly lauded and great if you fancy a splurge. Equally charming is the smaller but similarly polished **Montvale Hotel** (☎ 509-747-1919; 1005 W 1st Ave; r queen/king $139/179; ☒ ☒ wi-fi). If price is your main preoccupation try the centrally located **Rodeway Inn** (☎ 509-747-1041, 901 W 1st Ave; s/d $43/45; ☒). OK, it's a chain (of sorts): a family-run motel.

Frank's Diner (☎ 509-747-8798; 1516 W 2nd Ave; breakfast $6-8; ☻ 6am-8pm), inside a vintage railway car, is a must for breakfast. The **Steam Plant Grill** (☎ 509-777-3900; 159 S Lincoln; wraps & sandwiches $7-9, mains $15-23; ☻ 11:30am-9:30pm Mon-Thu & Sun, to 11pm Fri & Sat) serves everything from Thai wraps to New Zealand lamb chops in the neoindustrial confines of a once-legendary old steam plant.

With a vibrant student population based at Gonzaga University, Spokane has a happening nighttime scene. You can sample the local hand-crafted ales at the **Northern Lights Brewing Company** (☎ 509-242-2739; 1003 E Trent Av), an enticing microbrewery near the university campus. For an alternative gay-friendly nighttime establishment try **Dempsey's Brass Rail** (☎ 509-747-5362; 909 W 1st). For concerts, plays, film festivals and the Spokane Opera check out the **Metropolitan Performing Arts Center** (☎ 509-455-6500; www.metmtg.com/themet; 901 W Sprague Ave).

Buses and trains depart from the **Spokane Intermodal Transportation Station** (221 W 1st Ave). **Amtrak** (☎ 509-624-5144) has a daily service on the esteemed *Empire Builder* to Seattle ($56, 7½ hours), Portland ($56, 9½ hours) and Chicago ($237, 14½ hours).

SOUTH CASCADES

The South Cascades split Washington climatically in two and extend from Snoqualmie Pass in the north down to the mighty Columbia River on the border with Oregon. The preserve of wilderness seekers, hikers and backcountry campers, these lofty mountains have long, wet winters, while a short but intense summer season transforms the snowy alpine meadows into a riot of huckleberries and wildflowers.

Mt Rainier National Park

Majestic Mt Rainier (14,411ft), the US' fourth-highest peak (outside Alaska), is also one of its most beguiling. Encased in a 368-sq-mile national park (the world's fifth national park when it was inaugurated in 1899), the mountain's snow-capped summit and forest-covered foothills harbor numerous hiking trails, huge swaths of flower-carpeted meadows and an alluring conical peak that presents a formidable challenge for aspiring climbers. The park has four entrances. Nisqually, on Hwy 706 via Ashford, near the park's southwest corner, is the busiest and most convenient gate, being close to the park's main nexus points and remaining open year round. The other entrances are Ohanapecosh, via Hwy 123; White River, off Hwy 410; and Carbon River, the most remote entryway, at the northwest corner. Call ☎ 800-695-7623 for road conditions.

For information on the park check out the National Park Service (NPS) website at www.nps.gov/mora, which includes downloadable maps and descriptions of 50 park trails.

Park entry is $15 per car or $5 per pedestrian. For overnight trips, get a wilderness camping permit (free) from ranger stations or visitor centers. The six campgrounds in the park have running water and toilets, but no RV hookups. **Reservations** (☎ 800-365-2267; www.mount.rainier.national-park.com/camping.htm; reserved campsites summer/rest of year $15/12, unreserved campsites $10) are strongly advised during summer months and can be made up to two months in advance by phone or online.

The park's two main nexus points are Longmire and Paradise. Longmire, 7 miles inside the Nisqually entrance, boasts a **Museum/Information Center** (☎ 360-569-2211, ext 3314; admission free; ☻ 9am-6pm Jun-Sep, 9am-5pm Oct-May), a number of important trailheads and the cozy **National Park Inn** (☎ 360-569-2411; www.guestservices.com/rainier; 1-bed r with shared/private bath $104/139, 2-room unit $191; ☻ year-round; ☒), which also contains a homey restaurant. More hikes and interpretive walks can be found 12 miles further east at Paradise, which is served by the flying-saucer-shaped **Henry M Jackson Visitor Center** (☎ 360-569-2211, ext 2328; ☻ 9am-7pm daily May-Sep, 10am-5pm Sat & Sun Oct & Apr). Climbs to the top of Rainier leave from here and can be organized through the **American Alpine Institute** (☎ 360-671-1505; www.aai.cc; 1515 12th St, Bellingham, WA 98225), which offers guided five-day climbs from $1540.

The **Wonderland Trail** is a 93-mile path that completely circumnavigates Mt Rainier via a well-maintained unbroken route. The hike is normally tackled over 10 to 12 days with walkers staying at one of 18 registered campsites along the way. Before embarking, you'll need to organize a free backcountry permit from the **Wilderness Information Center** (☎ 877-617-9950; www.nps.gov/mora; 55210 238th Av E, Ashford WA 98304-9751); forms are available online.

The remote Carbon River entrance gives access to the park's inland rain forest. The **ranger station** (☎ 360-829-9639), just inside the entrance, is open daily in summer.

Gray Line (☎ 206-624-5077; www.graylineseattle.com) runs tours from Seattle ($59, 10 hours).

Mt St Helens National Volcanic Monument

Thanks to a 1980 eruption that set off an explosion bigger than the combined power of 21,000 atomic bombs, Washington's 87th-tallest mountain needs little introduction. What it lacks in height Mt St Helens makes up for in fiery infamy; 57 people perished on the mountain on that fateful day in May 1980 when an earthquake of 5.1 on the Richter scale sparked the biggest landslide in human history and buried 230 sq miles of forest under millions of tons of volcanic rock and ash.

Mt St Helens makes an interesting day trip from Seattle either by car or on a bus tour with **Gray Line of Seattle** (☎ 206-626-5208; www.graylineofseattle.com) available from June through September. Your first port of call should be the **Mt St Helens Visitor Center** (☎ 360-274-2100; 3029 Spirit Lake Hwy; admission $3; ☻ 9am-5pm), situated 5 miles east of Castle Rock on Hwy 504, which showcases films, exhibits and free information on the mountain, and serves as an excellent introduction to the monument. For a closer view of the destructive power of nature, venture to the **Coldwater Ridge Visitor Center** (☎ 360-274-2131; ☻ 10am-6pm May-Oct, 9am-5pm Nov-Apr) with views over toward Mt Helens' gaping northern crater. Exhibits focus on how animal and plant life survived the explosion and track their regeneration in the years since.

Mt Adams

Further from Seattle than Mts Rainier and St Helens, and covered on its eastern flanks by the Yakama Indian Reservation, Mt Adams receives nowhere near as many visitors as its more famous neighbors. Yet it is enchantingly beautiful. Protected in the 66 sq-mile **Mt Adams Wilderness**, Adams sports plenty of picturesque hikes including the much-loved **Bird Creek Meadow Trail**, a 3-mile loop that showcases the best of the mountain's meadows, wildflowers and waterfalls. Another unique activity in the area is blue-huckleberry picking in the high meadows around the Indian Heaven Wilderness. For huckleberry permits and information on hiking and climbing, consult the **Mt Adams Ranger District USFS office** (☎ 509-395-3400; 2455 Hwy 141; ☻ 8am-4:30pm Mon-Sat, plus Sun in summer) in Trout Lake.

The most enticing local accommodation option can be found at **Serenity's** (☎ 509-395-2500; www.serenitys.com; 2291 Hwy 141; cabin $99-129; wi-fi), a mile south of Trout Lake on Hwy 141, which offers four beautifully presented cabins in the woods in the shadow of snow-sprinkled Mt Adams.

CENTRAL & SOUTHEASTERN WASHINGTON

Parched, remote and barely served by public transportation, Southeastern Washington is the state's loneliest corner. Further west, around Yakima and Wenatchee, the dramatic peaks of the Cascade Mountains fold imperceptibly into a barren steppelike desert broken only by the Nilelike presence of the Columbia River and its irrigating artificial dams.

Yakima & Around

Yakima is the trading center of an immense and rather bleak agricultural area. The main reason to stop is the excellent **Yakima Valley Museum** (☎ 509-248-0747; 2105 Tieton Dr; adult/senior $5/3; ☻ 10am-5pm Mon-Fri, noon-5pm Sat & Sun), with exhibits on native Yakama culture, tons of artifacts and a hands-on learning center for kids.

Numerous wineries lie between Yakima and Benton City; pick up a map at the **Yakima Valley Visitors & Convention Bureau** (☎ 509-575-3010; www.visityakima.com; 10 N 8th St).

This valley is home to the Yakama Indian Reservation, the state's largest. The huge **Yakama Indian Nation Cultural Center** (☎ 509-865-2800; adult/child $4/1; ☻ 8am-5pm), off Hwy 97 at Toppenish, has displays on traditional life. Toppenish is also known for its murals depicting events from Yakima and Northwest history, visible on many buildings around town.

WASHINGTON WINE

A relative newcomer to the viticultural world, Washington's position as the US' second-largest wine-producing region (after California) is no longer in question. In 2006 the state opened up an average of three new wineries a week and, thanks to unrestrictive growing practices and liberal irrigation laws, even experienced French growers were heading out West to sow their vines in such unlikely places as Walla Walla and the Yakima Valley.

The secret, for aficionados, is in the soil. Enriched more than 15,000 years ago when the destructive Missoula floods deposited a thick layer of muddy sediment around the rugged Columbia River Gorge, the grape-growing potential in this arid region is second only to France. Add in dry climate (allowing farmers to control the amount of water the grapes receive), plenty of annual sunshine and a northerly latitude that ensures long hours of daylight during the summer, and you've got a formula favorable enough to satisfy even the fussiest of wine connoisseurs.

The Washington wine industry now boasts more than 500 private wineries in nine different American Viticultural Areas (AVAs), producing an eclectic mix of different wines – 80% of which are red – including Merlot, Cabernet Sauvignon and the much-vaunted Syrah.

Excellent wineries can be found in Walla Walla, the Yakima Valley, the Columbia River Valley and Spokane.

Walla Walla

Over the last decade, Walla Walla has converted itself from an obscure agricultural backwater, famous for its sweet onions and large state penitentiary, into the hottest wine-growing region outside of California's Napa Valley. While venerable Marcus Whitman College is the town's most obvious cultural attribute, you'll also find zany coffee bars here, along with cool wine-tasting rooms, fine Queen Anne architecture and one of the state's freshest and most vibrant farmers markets.

For information on wine tasting and maps of a quartet of 4 fascinating urban walking tours call in at the **Chamber of Commerce** (☎ 509-525-0850, www.wallawalla.org; 29 E Sumach St; ⏰ 8:30am-5pm Mon-Fri, 9am-4pm Sat & Sun summer).

The remains of the 1836 **Whitman Mission** are 7 miles west of Walla Walla off US 12. Marcus Whitman and 14 other missionaries died when, in 1847, after a measles epidemic killed half their tribe, a band of Cayuse Indians attacked the 11-year-old mission. When news of the uprising reached Washington, DC, Congress established the Oregon Territories, the first formal government west of the Rockies. The **visitor center** (☎ 509-522-6357; adult/family $3/5; ⏰ 8am-4:30pm) has exhibits and maps.

Walla Walla's best-known landmark and most salubrious hotel is the independently run **Marcus Whitman Hotel & Conference Center** (☎ 509-525-2200, www.marcuswhitmanhotel.com; 6 W Rose St; r/ste $139/279; ⊠ wi-fi). For a cheap sleep call in at the **City Center Motel** (☎ 509-529-2660, 627 W Main St; s/d $55/60; ⊠ ⊠).

The wine boom has lured a number of notable restaurateurs to the area. One of the newest fine-dining experiences can be found at **26 Brix** (☎ 509-526-4075; 207 W Main St; mains $15-27; ⏰ 5-10pm Mon & Thu-Sat, 9am-2pm & 5-9pm Sun), which takes fresh local ingredients and turns them into cordon bleu food. For a tasty cheaper snack and top-class beers, try the **Mill Creek Brew Pub** (☎ 509-522-2440; 11 S Palouse; burgers $6-8; ⏰ 11am-midnight).

OREGON

It's hard to slap a single characterization onto Oregon's geography and people. The landscape mixes rugged coastline and thick evergreen forests with barren, fossil-strewn deserts, volcanoes and glaciers. And as for its denizens, you name it – Oregonians run the full gamut from prologging, antigay conservatives to tree-hugging, dope-growing, ex-hippie liberals. The one thing they all have in common is an independent spirit – and a fierce devotion to where they live.

History

Oregon started as an ad hoc collection of New England missionaries and French and British trappers, officially becoming a US territory in 1848 and a state in 1859. Settlers populated most of the coastal and central region by the 1860s, many having made the

OREGON FACTS

Nickname Beaver State

Population 3.7 million

Area 95,997 sq miles

Capital city Salem (population 150,000)

Sales tax Oregon has no sales tax

Birthplace of Scientist, antinuclear activist and double Nobel laureate Linus Pauling (1901–94); chef James Beard (1903–85); children's writer Beverly Cleary (b 1916); The Simpsons creator Matt Groening (b 1954); notorious ice princess Tonya Harding (b 1970)

Home of The Oregon Shakespeare Festival, the 'Bottle Bill,' Nike, spotted owls

Famous for The Oregon Trail, forests, rain, not being able to pump your own gas

State beverage Milk (dairy's big here)

arduous six-month journey across the continent on the Oregon Trail.

The new Oregonians proceeded to appropriate the homelands of the various Native American groups. In what came to be called the Rogue River Wars, one such group – the Takelma, dubbed *coquins*, or 'rogues,' by French beaver trappers early in the 19th century – attacked immigrant parties and refused to negotiate with the army to allow passage through their land. Consequently, tensions mounted, and butchery escalated on both sides. Eventually the Takelma retreated into the canyons of the western Rogue Valley, but they surrendered after several winter months of skirmishing with little food or shelter. They were sent north to the Grand Ronde Reservation on the Yamhill River, and they weren't alone. By the late 1850s, most of the Native Americans in the region had been confined to reservations.

The railroad reached Portland in 1883, and by 1890 the city was one of the world's largest wheat-shipment points. The two world wars brought further economic expansion, much of it from logging. In the postwar era, idealistic baby boomers flooded into Oregon from California and the eastern states, seeking alternative lifestyles and natural surroundings. These arrivals brought pace-setting policies on many environmental and social issues.

Since the 1960s, Portland and western Oregon have been particularly influenced by the new, politically progressive settlers, while small towns and rural areas have remained mostly conservative. Its ballot-initiative system gives Oregonians the opportunity to advance citizen-proposed laws to the ballot box, and Oregon has become a stage for political dramas on divisive issues – such as physician-assisted suicide and gay marriage – in which the whole country has an interest.

Information

Nature of the Northwest (☎ 503-872-2750, 800-270-7504; www.naturenw.org/forest-directory.htm; Suite 177, 800 NE Oregon St, Portland, OR 97232; ☾ 9am-5pm Mon-Fri) Recreational information on national forests and state parks of the region; sells the Northwest Forest Pass (per day/year $5/30), required at many parks, trailheads, visitor centers and boat launches.

Oregon road conditions (☎ 800-977-6368, from out of state 503-588-2941)

Oregon State Parks & Recreation Dept (☎ 503-378-6305, 800-551-6949; www.oregonstateparks.org; 1115 Commercial St NE, Salem, OR 97310)

Oregon Tourism Commission (☎ 503-986-0000, 800-547-7842; www.traveloregon.com; 775 Summer St NE, Salem, OR 97301; ☾ 8am-5pm Mon-Fri) Sends out information and brochures on accommodations, camping, state parks and recreation outfitters.

PORTLAND

Call it what you want – PDX, P-town, Stumptown, City of Roses, Bridge City or Beervana – Portland positively rocks. It's a city with a vibrant downtown, pretty residential neighborhoods, ultragreen ambitions and zany characters. Here liberal idealists outnumber conservative stogies, Gortex jackets are acceptable in fine restaurants and everyone supports countless brewpubs, coffeehouses, knitting circles, lesbian potlucks and book clubs. Portland is an up-and-coming destination that has finally found itself, and an appealing, can't-miss stop on your adventures in the Pacific Northwest.

History

The Portland area was first settled in 1844 when two New Englanders bought a claim on the Willamette's west bank. They tossed a coin to decide the new settlement's name – 'Portland' won over 'Boston.'

Portland's location near the confluence of the Columbia and Willamette Rivers helped drive the young city's growth. The California gold rush clamored for Oregon lumber, while the growing population of settlers in the Willamette Valley demanded supplies. The Northern Pacific Railroad (which arrived in 1883) and the WWII shipbuilding boom didn't hurt the local economy either.

Today more than half-million people live in the greater Portland area. Shipping operations have since moved north of downtown, the Old Town's been revitalized and the once-industrial Pearl District now brims with expensive lofts and boutiques. Outdoor-clothing manufacturers Nike, Adidas and Columbia Sportswear help drive the economy, along with high-tech companies such as Intel and Tektronix.

Despite its economic ups and downs, Portland continues to attract new settlers to this day, each with their own hopes and dreams for a new life.

Orientation

Portland lies just south of the Washington border and about an hour's drive from the Pacific Coast. The Willamette River flows through the center of town, dividing the city into east and west. Burnside St divides north from south, organizing the city into four quadrants: Northwest, Southwest, Northeast and Southeast. Make sure you understand this, as the same address could exist on both NE Davis St and NW Davis St, which are on opposite sides of the river!

Downtown is in Southwest Portland. The historic Old Town, rough-and-tumble Chinatown, trendy 23rd Ave, chic Pearl District and exclusive West Hills are in Northwest Portland. Close to the center but across the river is the Lloyd District, an extension of downtown.

Northeast and Southeast Portland are mostly tree-lined, late-19th-century residential neighborhoods, each with its own trendy cluster of shops and restaurants. Popular commercial streets include N Mississippi Ave, NE Alberta St, SE Hawthorne Blvd and SE Division St. Sellwood is furthest south and a pretty neighborhood with antique stores and yuppies.

Information

BOOKSTORES

CounterMedia (☎ 503-226-8141; 927 SW Oak St) Liberally minded books on fringe culture and vintage erotica.
In Other Words (☎ 503-232-6003; 8 NE Killingsworth St) Feminist bookstore and resource center, just north of the Lloyd District.

Powell's City of Books (☎ 503-228-4651; www .powells.com); Burnside St (1005 W Burnside St); SE Hawthorne St (3723 SE Hawthorne) The USA's largest independent bookstore, with a whole city block of new and used titles at the Burnside St store. Other branches around town.
Reading Frenzy (☎ 503-274-1449; 921 SW Oak St) Emporium of indie 'zines, comics and books that supports Portland writers and artists.

EMERGENCY & MEDICAL SERVICES

Legacy Good Samaritan Hospital & Medical Center (☎ 503-413-7711; 1015 NW 22nd Ave)
Portland Police (☎ 503-823-0000)
Walgreens (☎ 503-238-6053; 940 SE 39th Ave) Offers a 24-hour pharmacy; to the city's west.

INTERNET ACCESS

Backspace (☎ 503-248-2900; www.backspace.bz; 115 NW 5th Ave) Youth-oriented hangout with arcade games, coffee and long hours.
Urban Grind Coffeehouse (☎ 503-546-0649; www .urbangrindcoffee.com; 2214 NE Oregon St) Slick café with computers and free wi-fi. Also at 911 NW 11th.

INTERNET RESOURCES

City of Portland (www.portlandonline.com) Stumptown's official website.
Gay Oregon (www.gaypdx.com) A resource for Portland's gay and lesbian communities.
PDX Guide (www.pdxguide.com) Fun and spot-on food and drink reviews by a guy who knows, plus other happenings around town.
Portland Independent Media Center (www.port land.indymedia.org) Community news and lefty activism.

MEDIA

Just Out (www.justout.com) Free biweekly serving Portland's gay community.
KBOO 90.7 FM Progressive local station run by volunteers; alternative news and views.
Portland Mercury (www.portlandmercury.com) The local sibling of Seattle's the *Stranger*, this free weekly is published on Thursday.
Portland Monthly (www.portlandmonthlymag.com) Excellent subscription magazine focusing on the city's happenings.
Willamette Week (www.wweek.com) Free alt-weekly covering local news and culture, published on Wednesday.

MONEY

Travelex (☎ 503-281-3045; ⏱ 5:30am-4:30pm); Portland International Airport (main ticket lobby); downtown (900 SW 6th Ave) Foreign-currency exchange.

PORTLAND

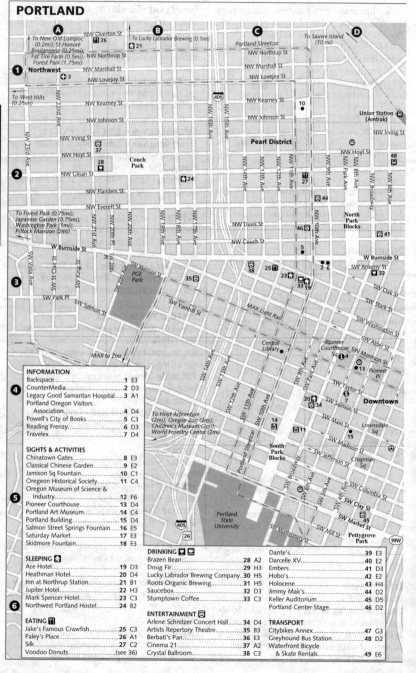

PACIFIC NORTHWEST

INFORMATION
Backspace	1 E3
CounterMedia	2 D3
Legacy Good Samaritan Hospital	3 A1
Portland Oregon Visitors	
Association	4 D4
Powell's City of Books	5 C3
Reading Frenzy	6 D3
Travelex	7 D4

SIGHTS & ACTIVITIES
Chinatown Gates	8 E3
Classical Chinese Garden	9 E2
Jamison Sq Fountain	10 C1
Oregon Historical Society	11 C4
Oregon Museum of Science &	
Industry	12 F6
Pioneer Courthouse	13 D4
Portland Art Museum	14 C4
Portland Building	15 D4
Salmon Street Springs Fountain	16 E5
Saturday Market	17 E3
Skidmore Fountain	18 E3

SLEEPING
Ace Hotel	19 D3
Heathman Hotel	20 D4
Inn at Northrup Station	21 B1
Jupiter Hotel	22 H3
Mark Spencer Hotel	23 C3
Northwest Portland Hostel	24 B2

EATING
Jake's Famous Crawfish	25 C3
Paley's Place	26 A1
Silk	27 C2
Voodoo Donuts	(see 36)

DRINKING
Brazen Bean	28 A2
Doug Fir	29 H3
Lucky Labrador Brewing Company	30 H5
Roots Organic Brewing	31 H5
Saucebox	32 D3
Stumptown Coffee	33 C3

ENTERTAINMENT
Arlene Schnitzer Concert Hall	34 D4
Artists Repertory Theatre	35 B3
Berbati's Pan	36 E3
Cinema 21	37 A2
Crystal Ballroom	38 C3
Dante's	39 E3
Darcelle XV	40 E2
Embers	41 D3
Hobo's	42 E2
Holocene	43 H4
Jimmy Mak's	44 D2
Keller Auditorium	45 D5
Portland Center Stage	46 D2

TRANSPORT
Citybikes Annex	47 G3
Greyhound Bus Station	48 D2
Waterfront Bicycle	
& Skate Rentals	49 E6

POST
Post office main branch (☎ 503-294-2564; 715 NW Hoyt St); University Station (☎ 503-274-1362; 1505 SW 6th Ave)

TOURIST INFORMATION
Portland Oregon Visitors Association (☎ 503-275-8355, 877-678-5263; www.travelportland.com; 701 SW 6th Ave; ⏱ 8:30am-5:30pm Mon-Fri, 10am-4pm Sat, 10am-2pm Sun) A small theater shows a 12-minute film about the city. Tri-Met bus and light-rail offices are also here. Located in Pioneer Courthouse Sq.

Sights
Most of Portland's sights are close together in the downtown area and the nearby Old Town–Chinatown nexus. The city's main parks – and best views – are in the lofty West Hills.

DOWNTOWN
The heart of downtown Portland, **Pioneer Courthouse Square** is nicknamed 'Portland's living room' and is the most visited public space in the city. When it isn't full of hacky-sack players, sunbathers or lunching office workers, the square hosts concerts, festivals and rallies. Across 6th Ave is the **Pioneer Courthouse** (1875), the legal center of 19th-century Portland.

Built in 1980, the **Portland Building** (cnr SW 5th Ave & Main St) was designed by Michael Graves and has been a focus of controversy for its gift-box appearance and user unfriendliness (the windows are tiny). It nevertheless holds the distinction of being the world's first major postmodern structure. Above its main doors crouches **Portlandia**, an immense statue representing the Goddess of Commerce.

Along the tree-shaded **South Park Blocks** sits the state's primary history museum, the **Oregon Historical Society** (☎ 503-222-1741; www.ohs.org; 1200 SW Park Ave; adult/child 6-18 $10/5; ⏱ 10am-5pm Tue-Sat, noon-5pm Sun). As well as temporary exhibits and several objects from Oregon's history on permanent display, there's a research library and a bookstore.

Just across the park is the **Portland Art Museum** (☎ 503-226-2811; www.portlandartmuseum.org; 1219 SW Park Ave; adult/child 5-18 $10/6; ⏱ 10am-5pm Tue, Wed & Sat to 8pm Thu & Fri, noon-5pm Sun). Excellent exhibits include Native American carvings, Asian and American art and English silver. The museum also houses the Whitsell Auditorium, a first-rate theater that frequently screens rare or international films.

DON'T MISS

- **Amnesia Brewing** – Mississippi neighborhood's unforgettable microbrewery (p1037)

- **Hawthorne Boulevard** – trendy neo-bohemian hippie street (opposite)

- **International Rose Test Gardens** – great views and awesome smells opposite)

- **Kennedy School** – hotel, theatre, restaurant and bar in one (p1035)

- **Powell's City of Books** – largest independent bookstore in the world (p1029)

- **Saturday Market** – weekend fun with crafts and performers (opposite)

Two-mile-long **Tom McCall Waterfront Park** flanks the west bank of the Willamette River, hosting summer festivals and concerts. In warm weather, the **Salmon Street Springs Fountain** swarms with frolicking kids. Across the river is another great walking strip, the **Eastbank Esplanade**.

OLD TOWN & CHINATOWN
The core of rambunctious 1890s Portland, once-seedy **Old Town** was once the domain of assorted unsavory characters lurking among rundown brick buildings and smelly alleyways. These days, though, disco queens outnumber drug dealers; several of the city's music clubs are in this area. Running beneath Old Town's streets are the **shanghai tunnels** (☎ 503-622-4798; adult/child $11/6), a series of underground corridors through which unscrupulous people would kidnap or 'shanghai' drunken men and sell them to sea captains looking for indentured workers. Tours are available by appointment.

The ornate **Chinatown Gates** (cnr Burnside St & SW 4th Ave) define the southern edge of Portland's so-called Chinatown – you'll be lucky to find any Chinese people here at all (most are on 82nd Ave, over to the east). There are a few token Chinese restaurants, but the main attraction is the **Classical Chinese Garden** (☎ 503-228-8131; www.portlandchinesegarden.org; cnr NW 3rd Ave & Everett St; adult/child under 5/senior $7/free/6; ⏱ 10am-5pm). It's a one-block haven of tranquility, reflecting ponds and manicured greenery. Free tours are available with admission.

Victorian-era architecture and the lovely **Skidmore Fountain** give the area beneath the Burnside Bridge some flair. Hit it on a weekend to catch the **Saturday Market** (☎ 503-222-6072; www.portlandsaturdaymarket.com; ⏰ 10am-5pm Sat, 11am-4:30pm Sun, closed Jan & Feb), a fun outdoor crafts fair (also open Sunday) with street entertainers and food carts.

NORTHWEST

Fashionable NW 23rd Ave brims with clothing boutiques, home decor shops and cafés. Restaurants – including some of Portland's finest – lie mostly along NW 21st Ave. This is a great neighborhood for strolling, window-shopping and people-watching.

Just east of Northwest, the **Pearl District** is an old industrial precinct that has transformed itself into Portland's swankiest neighborhood. It's a great place to walk around, full of expensive lofts, upscale boutiques and trendy restaurants. On the first Thursday of every month, art galleries extend their evening hours and the area turns into a fancy street party of sorts. The Pearl is bordered by NW 9th Ave, NW 14th Ave, W Burnside St and NW Lovejoy St.

WEST HILLS & WASHINGTON PARK

Behind downtown Portland are the West Hills, known for its exclusive homes, windy streets and huge **Forest Park**.

The grand **Pittock Mansion** (☎ 503-823-3623; ww.pittockmansion.com; 3229 NW Pittock Dr; adult/child 6-18/senior $7/4/6; ⏰ 11am-4pm; Ⓟ) was built in 1914 by Henry Pittock, who revitalized the *Oregonian* newspaper. It's worth visiting the (free) grounds just to check out the spectacular views – bring a picnic.

The huge Washington Park complex contains the **International Rose Test Gardens** (☎ 503-823-3636; admission free; ⏰ dawn-dusk; Ⓟ) with 400 types of roses and good views. Further uphill is the tranquil **Japanese Garden** (☎ 503-223-1321; www.japanesegarden.com; adult/child 6-17 $8/5.25; ⏰ 10am-7pm Tue-Sun, noon-7pm Mon; Ⓟ). Prettiest in the fall, **Hoyt Arboretum** (☎ 503-228-8733; 4000 Fairview Blvd; admission free; ⏰ trails 6am-10pm, visitor center 9am-4pm Mon-Fri, 9am-3pm Sat; Ⓟ) is home to more than 1000 species of both native and exotic trees and has 12 miles of walking trails.

NORTHEAST & SOUTHEAST

Across the Willamette River from downtown is the **Lloyd Center**, America's first full-blown shopping mall, along with the glass-towered **Oregon Convention Center** and the **Rose Garden Arena**.

Further up the Willamette, **N Mississippi Avenue** used to be full of run-down buildings, but they've been transformed into trendy shops and restaurants. Northeast is artsy **NE Alberta Street**, a ribbon of art galleries, boutiques and cafés. Don't miss the summertime street party that takes place every last Thursday of the month – it's a hoot. For a dose of hippie-hipster culture, visit **Hawthorne Boulevard** (near 39th Ave). It's a bohemian string of bookstores, cutesy shops and cafés.

Activities

Hiking and **mountain biking** are two of the most popular and easily enjoyable outdoor activities in Portland.

Hikers will find more than 70 miles of trails in **Forest Park**, the country's largest urban park. The **Wildwood Trail** starts at the Hoyt Arboretum and winds through 30 miles of forest, with many spur trails allowing for loop hikes. Other trailheads into Forest Park are at the western ends of NW Thurman and NW Upshur Sts.

Cyclists have the riverside **Springwater Corridor**, which starts near the Oregon Museum of Science & Industry and goes all the way to the suburb of Gresham – over 21 miles long. Mountain bikers shouldn't miss **Leif Erikson Drive**, a great old logging road leading 11 miles into Forest Park and offering occasional peeks over the city. Avoid riding on hiking paths here, as you'd be poaching the trails.

For scenic farm country, head to **Sauvie Island**, 10 miles northwest of downtown Portland. This island is prime bicycling land – it's flat, has relatively little traffic and much of it is wildlife refuge. For bike rentals, see p1039.

ON THE WATER

Summer in Portland means finding cool things to do on hot days, and fortunately there's a few.

For simple pleasures, visit the **Salmon Street Springs Fountain** or the **Jamison Square Fountain** (cnr NW Johnson & 10th), both of which attract splashing kids.

Swim indoors at **Matt Dishman Community Center** (☎ 503-823-3673; 77 NE Knott St; admission $2-3.25). For an outdoor experience, try the pool at **US Grant Park** (☎ 503-823-3674; cnr NE 33rd Ave & US Grant St; admission $2-3.25), north of the Lloyd district. Hours at both pools vary for different activities, so call beforehand.

About 10 miles south of central Portland are the water slides and indoor wave pool of **North Clackamas Aquatic Park** (☎ 503-557-7873; 7300 SE Harmony Rd, Milwaukee; adult $10, child $5-7). Hours vary widely, so call ahead.

Kayakers have **Portland River Company** (☎ 503-229-0551; www.portlandrivercompany.com) or **Scappoose Bay Kayaking** (☎ 503-397-2161, 877-272-3353; www.scappoosebaykayaking.com; 57420 Old Portland Rd), both with tours and rentals.

Portland for Children

Kids and their parents both love **Oregon Museum of Science & Industry** (OMSI; ☎ 503-797-6674; www.omsi.edu; 1945 SE Water Ave; adult $9, senior & child 3-13 years $7; ⏰ 9am-9pm), which offers hands-on science exhibits for kids. There's also an Omnimax theater, planetarium shows and a submarine tour (all separate charge).

In summer, the Zoo Train connects the Washington Park rose garden with the **Oregon Zoo** (☎ 503-226-1561; www.oregonzoo.org; 4001 SW Canyon Rd; adult/child $9.75/8.25; ⏰ 8am-6pm Apr-Sep; P). Don't miss 'zoolights' during the holiday season, when the zoo becomes a winter wonderland filled with lit-up trees and animal figures. In summer there are concerts on the zoo's lawns. Parking costs $1.

Parents also love the nearby **Children's Museum** (☎ 503-223-6500; www.portlandcm.org; 4015 SW Canyon Rd; admission $7; ⏰ 9am-5pm Mon-Sat, 11am-5pm Sun; P), a great place to keep the kids busy with hands-on learning activities and exhibits. Next door, the **World Forestry Center** (☎ 503-228-1367; www.worldforestry.org; 4033 SW Canyon Rd; adult/child 3-18/senior $7/5/6; ⏰ 10am-5pm; P), offers similar experiences but with a woodsy twist. Parking is available at both venues for $1.

For rides and go-karts, head south to **Oaks Amusement Park** (☎ 503-233-5777; www.oakspark.com; SE Oaks Park Way; admission free, ride bracelets $11.25-14; P). Hours vary widely, so call ahead.

Tours

For kayak tours, see p1033.

Ecotours of Oregon (☎ 503-245-1428, 888-868-7733; www.ecotours-of-oregon.com) Naturalist tours of northwest Oregon and Washington, including the Columbia River Gorge, Mt St Helens and the wine country.

Portland Spirit (☎ 503-224-3900, 800-224-3901; www.portlandspirit.com) Tour Portland from the water; cruises offer sightseeing, historical narratives and/or meal combinations.

Portland Walking Tours (☎ 503-774-4522; www.portlandwalkingtours.com) Art, food, neighborhood, history, underground and even ghost-oriented tours.

Festivals & Events

Portland International Film Festival (☎ 503-221-1156, www.nwfilm.org) Oregon's biggest film event highlights nearly 100 films from over 30 countries. Held mid-late February.

Portland Rose Festival (☎ 503-227-2681; www.rosefestival.org) Rose-covered floats, dragon-boat races, fireworks, roaming packs of sailors and the crowning of a Rose Queen all make this Portland's biggest celebration. Held late May to early June.

Queer Pride Celebration (☎ 503-295-9788; www.pridenw.org) Keep Portland queer in mid-June: enjoy a kick-off party, take a cruise or join the parade.

Waterfront Blues Festival (☎ 503-973-3378, www.waterfrontbluesfest.com) Enjoy top blues acts music and partying at Tom McCall Waterfront Park in early July.

Oregon Brewers Festival (☎ 503-778-5917; www.oregonbrewfest.com) Quaff microbrews during the summer (late July) in Tom McCall Waterfront Park and during the winter (early December) at Pioneer Courthouse Sq.

Sleeping

Reserve ahead in summer.

BUDGET

Hawthorne Portland Hostel (☎ 503-236-3380; www.portlandhostel.org; 3031 SE Hawthorne Blvd; member/nonmember dm $22/25, d $48/54; ✗ ⌨ wi-fi) With good vibes and a great Hawthorne location (1 mile east of the city on SE Hawthorne Blvd), this ecofriendly hostel offers artsy atmosphere, good rooms and a grassy garden. Check out its planted ecoroof. Computer and bike rentals available.

Northwest Portland Hostel (☎ 503-241-2783; 425 NW 18th Ave; dm $28, d $44-89; ✗ P ⛺ ⌨ wi-fi) Perfectly located between the Pearl District and NW 21st and 24th Aves, this friendly hostel takes up two buildings and features plenty of common areas (including a small deck), good rooms and bike rentals. Non–Hostelling International (HI) members pay $3 extra.

White Eagle (☎ 503-335-8900, 866-271-3377; www.mcmenamins.com; 836 N Russell St; dm $34, d $45-68; P) A legendary musicians' haunt that may actually be haunted, the White Eagle's 11 basic rooms (shared baths) are a top choice for music fans and heavy sleepers. The hotel was opened in 1905 and had all the amenities a gentleman might need – brothel upstairs, opium den below. It's north of the Lloyd district.

LOCAL VOICES: MIKE MCMENAMIN

A Portland native, Mike is one of two McMenamin brothers who started the quirky Pacific Northwest McMenamin empire that includes more than 50 brewpubs, hotels, restaurants, music venues and movie theaters – most located in historic buildings and decorated in highly eclectic style. They're all very fun places to visit, stay at and have a drink at (or three). See www.mcmenamins .com for a taste.

What are the best things about Portland?
I think the neighborhoods here are fabulous; there're dozens of them that feel good and have their own life. Portland is charming: rolling hills, proximity to a lot of stuff; it's a good spot, small-town feel…but it's getting faster, or I'm getting slower.

How did go about finding buildings to restore?
In the early days, we used to have to drive around and snoop stuff out. But now we get piles of suggestions, photos, brochures and calls from people that like that we preserve things. It's rewarding that they think of us like that, but it's also kind of unfortunate because we can't do everything.

What role did you play in starting Portland's microbrew movement?
There was a group of people – Portland Brewing, Widmer, us and Bridgeport…that were instrumental in getting that whole thing going. In 1985 [pubs could legally brew their own beer] and it's been a great thing. You tend to think of a brewery as a vast thing, but it can be in the corner of the kitchen.

ourpick **McMenamins Edgefield** (☎ 503-492-3086; www.mcmenamins.com; 2126 SW Halsey St, Troutdale; dm $35, d $120, with shared bathroom $58-108; ✗ ✗ ☐ wi-fi) This former county poor farm, restored by the McMenamin Brothers, is now a one-of-a-kind, 38-acre hotel complex with a dizzying variety of services. Taste wine and home-made beer, play golf, watch movies, shop at the gift store, listen to live music, walk the extensive gardens and eat at one of its restaurants. It's about a 20-minute drive east from downtown.

MIDRANGE

Jupiter Hotel (☎ 503-230-9200; www.jupiterhotel.com; 800 E Burnside St; d Sun-Thu from $100-145, Fri & Sat $128-178; ℗ ✗ ✗ ☐ wi-fi) The hippest hotel in town, this slick, remodeled motel is within walking distance of downtown and right next to Doug Fir (p1037), a top-notch live music venue. Standard rooms are tiny – go for the Deluxe Metro instead, and ask for a pad away from the bamboo patio if you want some shut-eye. Check in after midnight for a discount.

Ace Hotel (☎ 503-228-2277; www.acehotel.com; 1022 SW Stark St; d with shared/private bath from $107/147; ℗ ✗ ✗ ☐ wi-fi) Currently Portland's trendiest sleep is this unique hotel fusing classic, industrial, minimalist, retro and eclectic styles together. From the photo booth and sofa lounge in its lobby to the recycled fabrics and furniture in its rooms, the Ace makes the warehouse feel work. Parking costs $20.

Kennedy School (☎ 503-249-3983, 888-249-3983; www.mcmenamins.com; 5736 NE 33rd Ave; d $112-140; ℗ ✗ ☐ wi-fi) Portland's most eclectic institution, this former elementary school, located a few miles from the center, is now home to a hotel (sleep in old classrooms), restaurant (great garden courtyard), several bars, a microbrewery and movie theater. There's a soaking pool, and the whole school is decorated in McMenamin's funky art style – mosaics, fantasy paintings and historical photographs.

Mark Spencer Hotel (☎ 503-224-3293, 800-548-3934; www.markspencer.com; 409 SW 11th Ave; d from $125; ℗ ✗ ✗ ☐ wi-fi) A no-nonsense, downtown option is this simple yet slightly refined choice, hosting spacious unmemorable rooms – all with kitchens. Continental breakfast is included, and there's complimentary tea with cookies in the afternoon. Parking costs $16.

Portland's White House B&B (☎ 503-287-7131, 800-272-7131; www.portlandswhitehouse.com; 1914 NE 22nd Ave; d $140-253; ✗ ✗ ☐ wi-fi) Portland's most gorgeous B&B looks like the DC landmark and boasts fine art (antique porcelains and bronze statues), eight luxurious rooms and a relaxing garden patio. Expect flat-screen TVs and truffles in your room. It's just east of the Lloyd district.

Inn at Northrup Station (☎ 503-224-0543, 800-224-1180; www.northrupstation.com; 2025 NW Northrup St; d from $156; P X X 및 wi-fi) Almost over the top with its bright color scheme and funky decor, this supertrendy hotel boasts huge artsy suites, many with a patio or balcony. There's a cool rooftop patio with plants, and continental breakfast is included.

TOP END

Heathman Hotel (☎ 503-241-4100; 800-551-0011; www.heathmanhotel.com; 1001 SW Broadway; d from $200; P X 및 wi-fi) A Portland institution, the Heathman has top-notch service and one of the best restaurants in the city. It also boasts high tea in the afternoons, jazz in the evenings and a library stocked with signed books by authors who have stayed here. Rooms are elegant, stylish and luxurious. Parking costs $30.

Eating

Portland is rapidly becoming a gourmand's dream, with hot new restaurants opening all the time. Most of the upscale joints are in Northwest and the Pearl District, and even at the snootiest you can wear casual duds. For international food carts, visit SW 5th Ave at Stark St. If it's raining, there's a food court in the basement of Pioneer Place shopping center.

St Honoré Boulangerie (☎ 503-445-4342; 2335 NW Thurman; light meals $5-7; ⊙ 7am-8pm) Insanely popular for its luscious breads and pastries, this modern-rustic bakery also serves tasty panini sandwiches, vegetarian soups and oven-fired pizzas. Snag a sidewalk table on a sunny day.

Silk (☎ 503-248-2172; mains $7-10; Pearl District (1012 NW Glisan St); Hawthorne District (☎ 503-230-1474; 3404 SE Hawthorne Blvd); 82nd Ave (☎ 503-230-1474; 1919 SE 82nd Ave) Vietnamese-food lovers will love this gorgeous restaurant. Everything is delicious, from the banana-blossom salad and lemongrass shrimp to the pho noodle soups. The original restaurant (called Pho Van) can be found on SE 82nd Ave.

Lovely Hula Hands (☎ 503-445-9910; 4057 N Mississippi; mains $10-21; ⊙ 5-10pm) This neighborhood favorite has that elegant yet homey

> **WHAT THE...?**
>
> Truly unique is the **Velveteria** (☎ 503-233-5100; www.velveteria.com; 518 NE 28th; admission $3; ⊙ noon-5pm Fri-Sun), a treasure trove full of stunning velvet paintings that will make you appreciate the art form; don't miss the 'nudes' room. It's run by a wacky couple who have been combing thrift stores and estate sales for years.

feel, serving up wide-ranging dishes such as North African vegetable stew and green garlic soufflé. Those in the know go for the luscious hamburgers – some of the best in Portland.

Pambiche (☎ 503-233-0511; 2811 NE Glisan St; mains $11-17; ⊙ 11am-10pm Sun-Thu, to midnight Fri & Sat) Portland's best and most popular Cuban food, with riotously colorful atmosphere. Lunch is a good deal, but happy hour is even better (2pm to 6pm Monday to Friday, 10pm to midnight Friday and Saturday). Leave room for dessert.

Lauro (☎ 503-239-7000; 3377 SE Division St; mains $16-21; ⊙ 5-9pm Sun-Thu, to 10pm Fri & Sat) Renowned owner-chef David Machado opened his Southeast Division restaurant in 2003, beginning a neighborhood revitalization that continues today. Expect Mediterranean-inspired dishes such as chicken tagine and stuffed lamb shoulder.

Jake's Famous Crawfish (☎ 503-226-1419; 401 SW 12th Ave; mains $17-32; ⊙ 11am-11pm Mon-Thu, to midnight Fri, noon-midnight Sat, 3-11pm Sun) Portland's best seafood lies within this elegant old-time venue. The oysters are divine, the crab cakes a revelation – and the horseradish salmon your ticket into heaven. Come at 3pm and praise the lord for (cheap) happy hour.

our pick Paley's Place (☎ 503-243-2403; 1204 NW 21st; mains $20-32; ⊙ 5:30-10pm Mon-Thu, to 11pm Fri & Sat, 5-10pm Sun) Vitaly and Kimberly Paley have established one of Portland's premiere restaurants, offering a creative blend of French and Pacific Northwest cuisines. Whether it's the duck confit, Kobe burger or veal sweetbreads, you can count on fresh ingredients, excellent service and a memorable experience.

Also recommended:

Noble Rot (☎ 503-233-1999; 2724 SE Ankeny St; small plates $5-16; ⊙ 5pm-midnight Mon-Sat) Upscale wine bar whipping up small creative plates and daily wine-sampling flights.

Paradox Café (☎ 503-232-7508; 3439 SE Belmont; mains $6-9; 🕙 8am-9pm Mon-Wed, to 10pm Thu-Sat, to 3pm Sun) Small, funky retro café with mostly vegan and veg fare; a few burgers also available.

Pok Pok (☎ 503-232-1387; 3226 SE Division St; mains $8-11; 🕙 11.30am-10pm Mon-Fri, 5-10pm Sat) Popular Thai hole-in-the-wall with some of Portland's best Thai food.

Drinking

Check www.barflymag.com for eclectic, spot-on reviews. As of 2009, Oregon bars and pubs will be nonsmoking.

BARS

Brazen Bean (☎ 503-234-0636; 2075 NW Glisan St) Located in a sweet Victorian house, this very popular bar is known for its martinis – more than 25 different kinds. During happy hour (5pm to 8pm weekdays) the prize drinks are $4 and service slows to molasses.

Saucebox (☎ 503-241-3393; 214 SW Broadway) Metro-sleek restaurant with pretty bar staff serving upscale Asian-fusion cuisine, but also very popular for its wide selection of drinks, including creative cocktails. DJs fire up at 10pm.

Horse Brass Pub (☎ 503-232-2202; 4534 SE Belmont) Portland's most authentic English pub, cherished for its dark-wood atmosphere, smoke-filled air, excellent fish and chips, and 50 beers on tap. Play some darts, watch soccer on TV or just take it all in.

Doug Fir (☎ 503-231-9663; 830 East Burnside) Paul Bunyan meets the *Jetsons* at this ultratrendy venue with edgy, hard-to-get talent, drawing crowds from tattooed youth to suburban yuppies. Sample its restaurant (open 21 hours), then stumble next door to the rock-star quality Jupiter Hotel.

Crush (☎ 503-235-8150; 1400 SE Morrison St) Slip into this sexy lounge with all the pretty people and order one of the exotic cocktails. The menu's gourmet (try brunch) and there's a 'vice' room just for smokers. Great for a girls night out, straight or lesbian.

Laurelthirst Pub (☎ 503-232-1504; 2958 NE Glisan) Crowds sometimes spill onto the sidewalk at this dark, funky and sometimes smoky neighborhood joint. Almost-nightly music is free until the evening, when you'll likely cough up just a $3 cover. Good beer and wine selection (but no liquor), along with fine breakfasts.

Back Stage Bar (☎ 503-236-9234; 3702 SE Hawthorne) Hidden gem behind the Bagdad Theater with a seven-story-high space, pool tables galore and tons of personality.

BREWPUBS

It's crazy, but Portland has about 30 brewpubs within its borders – more than any other city on earth. This makes choosing difficult, so here's a starting list.

Amnesia Brewing (☎ 503-281-7708; 832 N Beech St) Hip Mississippi St's main brewery, with a casual feel and picnic tables out front. Excellent beer – try the Desolation IPA or Wonka Porter. Outdoor grill offers burgers and sausages.

Widmer Gasthaus (☎ 503-281-3333; 929 N Russell St) Yuppified brewery-restaurant with tasty beers – some available only here. The Hefeweizen is a good choice. Weekend tours, sports on TV and close to live music at the White Eagle.

Lucky Labrador Brewing Company (☎ 503-236-3555); Hawthorne Blvd (915 SE Hawthorne Blvd); Pearl District (1945 NW Quimby St) Large, no-nonsense beer hall with a wide selection of brews and dog-friendly back patio, where movies are shown in summer.

New Old Lompoc (☎ 503-225-1855; 1616 NW 23rd Ave) Eclectic pub offering more than a dozen taps with treats such as Condor Pale Ale, Sockeye Cream Stout and Bald Guy Brown. The leafy back patio is a must on warm days.

Roots Organic Brewing (☎ 503-235-7668; 1520 SE 7th Ave) Relative newcomer on the scene focusing on fully organic brews.

COFFEEHOUSES

Portland is full of good coffee shops, and everyone has their neighborhood favorite – including these:

Stumptown Coffee (☎ 503-230-7797; 3377 SE Division St; 🖳 wi-fi) Generally considered Portland's best coffee. Also at 3356 SE Belmont and 128 SW 3rd.

Pied Cow Coffeehouse (☎ 503-230-4866; 3244 SE Belmont St) Colorful and bohemian Victorian house with atmosphere and a lovely garden patio. Hookahs available.

Albina Press (☎ 503-282-5214; 4637 N Albina Ave; 🖳 wi-fi) Pure nirvana for its delicious cups of coffee, artistically constructed by competition-winning baristas.

Red & Black Cafe (☎ 503-231-3899; 2138 SE Division; 🖳 wi-fi) Worker-owned/-run spot with progressive ideals; enjoy live music, art exhibits and even the occasional genderqueer puppet show.

Anna Bannanas (☎ 503-274-2559; 1214 NW 21st; 📶 wi-fi) Funky hangout in an old renovated house with a comfortable feel, gourmet food and a good crowd.

Entertainment

Check the *Mercury* or *Willamette Week* for schedules and cover charges.

LIVE MUSIC

See also Doug Fir (p1037), Laurelthirst Pub (p1037) and Holocene (right).

Dante's (☎ 503-226-6630; www.danteslive.com; 1 SW 3rd Ave) This steamy red bar books vaudeville shows along with national acts including The Dandy Warhols and Concrete Blonde. Drop in on Monday night for the ever-popular Karaoke from Hell.

Berbati's Pan (☎ 503-248-4579; www.berbati.com; 10 SW 3rd Ave) This established rock club nabs some of the more interesting acts in town. Expect big band, swing, acid rock and R & B music. Outdoor seating and pool tables a plus.

Crystal Ballroom (☎ 503-225-0047; www.mcmenamins.com/crystal; 1332 W Burnside St) Major bands play at this historic ballroom, from the Grateful Dead to Steve Earl. The 'floating' dance floor bounces at the slightest provocation.

Mississippi Studios (☎ 503-288-3895; www.mississippistudios.com; 3939 N Mississippi Ave) Intimate venue perfect for budding acoustic talent, along with more established musical groups. Excellent sound system.

Jimmy Mak's (☎ 503-295-6542; www.jimmymaks.com; 221 NW 10th Ave) Stumptown's premier jazz venue, serving excellent Mediterranean food; casual smoking bar-lounge in the basement. Music starts at 8pm.

Hawthorne Theatre (☎ 503-233-7100; www.hawthornetheatre.com; 1507 SE 39th) All-ages music venue, good for live rock, reggae, punk, pop, metal and country music. Intimate stage, high balcony and 21-and-over section for legal boozehounds.

GAY & LESBIAN VENUES

For current listings see *Just Out*, Portland's free gay biweekly. Or grab a *Gay and Lesbian Community Yellow Pages* (www.pdxgayyellowpages.com) for other services.

For an upscale, mixed-crowd bar, see Crush (p1037).

Darcelle XV (☎ 503-222-5338; 208 NW 3rd) Portland's premiere drag show, featuring queens in big wigs, fake jewelry and over-stuffed bras. Male strippers perform at midnight on weekends.

Holocene (☎ 503-239-7639; 1001 SE Morrison St) Best for lesbians on 'Tart Night,' which takes place every second Sunday of the month. Otherwise it's your typical hipster crowd dance scene in a modern industrial space.

Embers (☎ 503-222-3082; 110 NW Broadway) Regulars come to meet up for the music (from '80s tunes to techno and pop), amateur drag shows, a fun dance floor and friendly camaraderie. Mixed crowd.

Egyptian Room (☎ 503-236-8689; 3701 SE Division St) Portland's main lesbian hangout, where guys are (barely) tolerated and girls are (mostly) butch. It's heavy on the hip-hop and full of chain-smokers, with karaoke and pool tables to distract.

Hobo's (☎ 503-224-3285; 120 NW 3rd Ave) Past the old historic storefront is a classy restaurant-piano bar popular with older gay men. It's a quiet, relaxed place for a romantic dinner or drink.

CINEMAS

Portland's great selection of old renovated cinemas – often selling beer, pizza and $3 tickets – makes going to the movies a joy.

Bagdad Theater (☎ 503-236-9234; www.mcmenamins.com; 3702 SE Hawthorne Blvd) Another awesome McMenamin venue with bargain flicks.

Cinema 21 (☎ 503-223-4515; www.cinema21.com; 616 NW 21st Ave) Portland's premiere art- and foreign-film theater.

Clinton Street Theater (☎ 503-238-8899; www.clintonsttheater.com; 2522 SE Clinton St) Portland's coolest and weirdest films, from Japanese horror to provocative documentaries.

Kennedy School (☎ 503-249-3983; www.mcmenamins.com; 5736 NE 33rd) The McMenamin Brothers' premiere Portland venue. Watch movies in the old school gym.

Hollywood Theatre (☎ 503-281-4215; www.hollywoodtheatre.org; 4122 NE Sandy Blvd) Historic art-deco spot playing classic, foreign and quirky independent movies.

THEATER & PERFORMING ARTS

Arlene Schnitzer Concert Hall (☎ 503-228-1353, 800-228-7343; www.pcpa.com/events/asch.php; 1037 SW Broadway) The Oregon Symphony performs in this beautiful, if not acoustically brilliant, downtown venue.

Artists Repertory Theatre (☎ 503-241-1278; 1516 SW Alder St) Some of Portland's best plays, including regional premieres, are performed in this intimate space.

Keller Auditorium (☎ 503-248-4335; www.pcpa.com/events/keller.php; 222 SW Clay St) The Portland Opera, Oregon Ballet Theatre and Oregon Children's Theatre all stage performances here.

Portland Center Stage (☎ 503-445-3700; www.pcs.org; 128 NW 11th Ave) The city's main theater company, now performing in the Portland Armory – a newly renovated Pearl District landmark that boasts state-of-the-art features.

SPORTS

Portland's only major-league sports team is the **Trail Blazers** (www.nba.com/blazers), who play basketball at Rose Garden Arena. The **Winter Hawks** (www.winterhawks.com), Portland's minor-league hockey team, and the **LumberJax** (www.portlandjax.com), the city's lacrosse team, both play here too.

PGE Park hosts the Portland's minor-league baseball team, the **Portland Beavers** (www.portlandbeavers.com), along with the A-League soccer team, the **Portland Timbers** (☎ 503-553-5555).

Shopping

Portland's downtown shopping district extends in a two-block radius from Pioneer Courthouse Sq. Pioneer Place, an upscale mall, is between SW Morrison and SW Yamhill St, east of the square. The Pearl District is dotted with high-end galleries, boutiques and home-decor shops – don't miss Powell's City of Books (see p1029). On the first Thursday of each month galleries stay open longer and people fill some of the Pearl's streets amid a party atmosphere. And on weekends, visit the quintessentially Portland Saturday Market (p1033).

Eastside has lots of trendy shopping streets that also host a few restaurants and cafés. SE Hawthorne Blvd is the biggest, N Mississippi Ave is the most recent and NE Alberta is the most artsy and funky. Down south, Sellwood is known for its antique shops.

Getting There & Away
AIR

Portland International Airport (PDX; ☎ 877-739-4636; www.flypdx.com) has daily flights all over the US, as well as to seven international destinations. Amenities include money changers, restaurants, bookstores (including three Powell's branches) and business services like free wi-fi.

BUS

Greyhound (☎ 503-243-2357; www.greyhound.com; 550 NW 6th Ave) connects Portland with cities along I-5 and I-84. Destinations include Chicago, Boise, Denver, San Francisco, Seattle and Vancouver.

If you're traveling between Portland, Olympia and Seattle, consider patronizing **Shared Route** (☎ 503-502-5750; www.sharedroute.org), which provides service three times weekly on a biodiesel bus.

TRAIN

Amtrak (☎ 503-241-4290; www.amtrak.com; NW 6th Ave & Irving St) serves the following destinations:
Chicago $237, two days, two daily.
Oakland $69, 18 hours, one daily.
Seattle $28, 3½ hours, four daily.
Vancouver, BC $42, four hours, two daily.

Getting Around
TO/FROM THE AIRPORT

Tri-Met's MAX light-rail train runs between the airport and downtown ($2, 45 minutes). If you prefer a bus, **Blue Star** (☎ 503-249-1837; www.bluestarbus.com) offers a shuttle service between PDX and several downtown stops ($14, 30 minutes). Taxis from the airport cost about $30.

BICYCLE

It's easy to get around Portland on a bicycle (see p1033). Rent bikes from **Citybikes Annex** (☎ 503-239-6951; www.citybikes.coop; 734 SE Ankeny), **Fat Tire Farm** (☎ 503-222-3276; 2714 NW Thurman St) or **Waterfront Bicycle & Skate Rentals** (☎ 503-227-1719; 315 SW Montgomery St).

CAR & MOTORCYCLE

Major car-rental agencies have outlets at PDX airport and around town. Oregon law prohibits you from pumping your own gas. Most of downtown is metered parking; a free option is to park along an inner-Southeast street and walk across a bridge to the city center. If you use a SmartPark garage ($1.25 per hour), remember to move your car after four hours (even if just around the block and back in) or your costs will double.

PUBLIC TRANSPORTATION

Local buses and the MAX light-rail system are run by Tri-Met, which has an **information center** (☎ 503-238-7433; www.trimet.org; �·ᯅ 8:30am-5:30pm Mon-Fri) at Pioneer Courthouse Sq. A streetcar runs from Portland State University, south of downtown, through the Pearl District to NW 23rd Ave. Within the downtown core, public transportation is free; outside downtown, fares run $1.70 to $2. If you're a night owl, be aware that buses and light-rail both stop running at 1:30am.

TAXI
Cabs are available 24 hours by phone. Downtown, you can often just flag them down.
Broadway Cab (☎ 503-227-1234)
Radio Cab (☎ 503-227-1212)

AROUND PORTLAND
A short and scenic drive from Portland are some of the best wineries in the state, mostly scattered around the towns of Dundee and McMinnville along Hwy 99W. To get started, contact **Willamette Valley Wineries Association** (☎ 503-646-2985; www.willamettewines.com).

Meandering through plush green hills on winding country roads from one wine-tasting room to another is a delightful way to spend an afternoon (just make sure you designate a driver). Many well-signed wineries are dotted along Hwys 99W and 18. If you only have time for a quick sampling, head for the **Oregon Wine Tasting Room** (☎ 503-843-3787; ☯ 11am-6pm), 9 miles south of McMinnville on Hwy 18, where you'll find around 70 of the area's wineries represented. **Grape Escape** (☎ 503-282-4262; www .grapeescapetours.com) specializes in wine-country tours.

For something different, head to McMinnville's **Evergreen Aviation Museum** (☎ 503-434-4180; www.sprucegoose.org; 500 NE Captain Michael King Smith Way; adult/child 3-17/senior $13/11/12; ☯ 9am-5pm) and check out Howard Hughes' **Spruce Goose**, the world's largest wood-framed airplane. There's also a replica of the Wright brothers' Flyer, along with an IMAX theater (movie admission separate).

There are several fine restaurants in the area, but for something spectacular consider the **Joel Palmer House** (☎ 503-864-2995; www .joelpalmerhouse.com; 600 Ferry St, Dayton; mains $20-37; ☯ 5-9pm Tue-Sat); its dishes are peppered with wild mushrooms collected by hand from the surrounding woods. And if you need an interesting place to stay, consider **McMenamins Hotel Oregon** (☎ 503-472-8427; 310 NE Evans St, McMinnville; d $60-130; ✗ ✗ ☐ wi-fi), an older building renovated into a charming hotel. It boasts a pub with an awesome rooftop bar.

WILLAMETTE VALLEY
The Willamette Valley, a fertile 60-mile-wide agricultural basin, was the holy grail for Oregon Trail pioneers who headed west more than 150 years ago. Today it's the state's breadbasket, producing more than 100 kinds of crops – including renowned Pinot Noir grapes. Salem, Oregon's capital, is about an hour's drive from Portland at the northern end of the Willamette Valley, and most of the other attractions in the area make easy day trips as well. Toward the south is Eugene, a dynamic college town worth a few days of exploration.

Salem
Salem's main draws are the capitol building and Willamette University. Find information at the **visitor center** (☎ 503-581-4325; 1313 Mill St SE; ☯ 8:30am-5pm Mon-Fri, 10am-5pm Sat).

The city's highlight is Willamette University's **Hallie Ford Museum of Art** (☎ 503-370-6300; 900 State St; adult/senior $3/2; ☯ 10am-5pm Tue-Sat, 1-5pm Sun), boasting Oregon's best collection of Pacific Northwest art, including an impressive Native American gallery.

The 1938 **Oregon State Capitol** (☎ 503-986-1388; 900 Court St NE) looks like a sci-fi film director's vision of an Orwellian White House. Free tours run hourly between 9am and 4pm in summer. Rambling 19th-century **Bush House** (☎ 503-363-4714; 600 Mission St SE; adult/child 6-12/senior $4/2/3; ☯ noon-5pm Tue-Sun) is an Italianate mansion now preserved as a museum with historic accents, including original wallpapers and marble fireplaces.

Silver Falls State Park (☎ 503-873-8681; car per day $3) is 26 miles east of Salem on Hwy 214 (via Hwy 22). South Falls, a 177ft waterfall, is just a few feet from the main parking lot. For something longer, hike a 7-mile loop trail that covers 10 waterfalls – including a few you can walk behind. There's also camping, swimming and a 4-mile paved bike path.

Fifteen miles northeast of Salem on Hwy 213 (Silverton Rd) is the **Oregon Garden** (☎ 503-874-8100; www.oregongarden.org; 879 W Main St; adult/child under 8/student 8-17/senior $10/free/8/9; ☯ 7am-6pm Wed & Sat, 9am-6pm Sun-Tue & Thu). It's prettiest in late May and nurtures more than 20 smaller specialty gardens, along with many rare and native plant species. It's also home to Oregon's only building designed by architect Frank Lloyd Wright, the **Gordon House** (☎ 503-874-6606) – call ahead for tours ($5). The garden's off-season hours and admissions vary.

Eugene

Full of youthful energy, liberal politics, alternative lifestyles and fun-loving atmosphere, Eugene also offers fine restaurants, riverside bike paths and several lovely parks. Nicknamed 'Tracktown,' the city is the birthplace of Nike and famous for its track-and-field champions. Environmental issues are a big deal here, and Eugene was a hotbed of hippie counterculture in the 1960s, hosting major protests during the Vietnam War (Ken Kesey grew up in the area). Today, many local radicals have found new careers as business owners in upscale developments around town.

The region around Eugene has plenty of outdoor recreation and several world-class wineries. For more information there's the **Convention & Visitors Association of Lane County** (☎ 541-484-5307, 800-547-5445; www.visitlanecounty.com; 754 Olive St; ⌚ 8am-5pm Mon-Fri, 10am-4pm Sat & Sun).

SIGHTS & ACTIVITIES

At E 5th Ave and Pearl St is the **5th St Public Market** (www.5stmarket.com), an old mill that now anchors several dozen restaurants, cafés and boutiques around a pretty courtyard. Performers occasionally entertain here.

For great fun and a quintessential introduction to Eugene's peculiar vitality, don't miss the **Saturday Market** (☎ 541-686-8885; www.eugene saturdaymarket.org), held on Saturdays from March through November at E 8th Ave and Oak St.

Housed in a replica of a Native American longhouse, the **University of Oregon Museum of Natural History** (☎ 541-346-3024; natural-history.uoregon .edu; 1680 E 15th Ave; adult $3, senior & child 3-18 $2; ⌚ 11am-5pm Wed-Sun) contains the state's best display of fossils, Native American artifacts and geologic curiosities.

The renowned **Jordan Schnitzer Museum of Art** (☎ 541-346-3027; jsma.uoregon.edu; 1430 Johnson Lane; adult/ senior $5/3; ⌚ 11am-8pm Wed, to 5pm Thu-Sun) offers a rotating permanent collection of world-class art, from Korean scrolls to Rembrandt paintings.

SLEEPING

Prices can rise sharply during key football games and graduation.

Eugene Kamping World (☎ 541-343-4832, 800-343-3008; www.woodalls.com; 90932 S Stuart Way; campsites/RV sites $18/30) Large, tidy campground 6 miles north of Eugene (I-5 exit 199).

Eugene International Hostel (☎ 541-349-0589; www.eugenehostel.com; 2352 Willamette St; dm/s/d $19/30/40; ⌑ wi-fi) A laid-back and friendly hostel located in an old house with just a handful of rooms. Closed 1pm to 4pm for cleaning.

Timbers Motel (☎ 541-343-3345, 800-643-4167; www .timbersmotel.net; 1015 Pearl St; d $60; ⌧ ⌑ wi-fi) Centrally located motel with spacious but generic rooms (the cheapest are in the basement but can't be reserved).

River Walk Inn (☎ 541-344-6506, 800-621-2904; www .ariverwalkinn.com; 250 N Adams St; d $78-111; ⌧) Dutch colonial B&B with four simple, pretty rooms (two with private bathroom) and a casual, homey atmosphere. Close to the river.

Campbell House (☎ 541-343-1119, 800-264-2519; www.campbellhouse.com; 252 Pearl St; d incl breakfast from $132; ⌧ ⌧ ⌑ wi-fi) Large inn with 19 rooms, suites and a cottage; lovely common spaces and garden too.

EATING & DRINKING

Papa's Soul Food Kitchen (☎ 541-342-7500; 400 Blair Blvd; mains $6-9; ⌚ noon-2pm & 5-9pm Tue-Fri, 2-9pm Sat) Line up with the locals at this outrageously popular Southern-food spot, which grills up awesome fried catfish and seafood gumbo. The best part is the live blues music, which keeps the joint open late on weekends.

Beppe & Gianni's Trattoria (☎ 541-683-6661; 1646 E 19th Ave; mains $14-16; ⌚ 5-9pm Sun-Thu, to 10pm Fri & Sat) One of Eugene's most beloved restaurants. Homemade pastas are the real deal here and the desserts excellent. Expect a wait.

McMenamins (⌚ 11am-11pm Sun-Thu, to midnight Fri & Sat) North Bank (☎ 541-343-5622; 22 Club Rd); High St (1243 High St); E 19th St (1485 E 19th St) Gloriously located on the banks of the mighty Willamette, the North Bank pub-restaurant boasts riverside patio tables. The other two locations lack water views but offer similar fare.

Beanery (☎ 541-342-3378; 152 W 5th Ave; ⌚ 6am-11pm Mon-Sat, 7am-11pm Sun) Warm, modern loft space hosting a great organic coffeehouse. Enter through the alley in back.

Sam Bond's (☎ 541-343-2635; 407 Blair Blvd) Eugene's favorite live-music venue. Nightly entertainment from 4pm on, with good organic pizza, free bluegrass jams on Tuesday and a nice outdoor patio for those sweltering summer nights.

GETTING THERE & AROUND

Eugene is serviced by the **Eugene Airport** (☎ 541-682-5430; www.eugeneairport.com), **Amtrak** (☎ 541-687-1383; www.amtrak.com; cnr E 4th Ave & Willamette St) and **Greyhound** (☎ 541-344-6265; www.greyhound.com; 987 Pearl St).

Local bus service is provided by **Lane Transit District** (LTD; ☎ 541-687-5555; www.ltd.org). For bike rentals there's **Paul's** (☎ 541-344-4150; 152 W 5th St; ☻ 9am-7pm Mon-Fri, 10am-5pm Sat & Sun).

McKenzie River Valley

The single name 'McKenzie' identifies a beautiful river, a high mountain pass and a spectacular historic highway. Premiere recreational opportunities abound, from fantastic fishing and exceptional hiking to racy rafting trips. The **McKenzie Ranger Station** (☎ 541-822-3381; www.fs.fed.us/r6/willamette; 57600 McKenzie Hwy; ☻ 8am-4:30pm) can help with finding trails and campgrounds.

The scenic, 26-mile **McKenzie National Recreation Trail** follows the river north from near the ranger station to Fish Lake; access the trail via several entry points from Hwy 126. In summer, take the hair-raising **Old McKenzie Highway** (Hwy 242, closed November to June) over the 5325ft, lava-laden mountain pass to the **Dee Wright Observatory** for spectacular views of the area's many volcanoes. The **Obsidian Trail** is a very popular access point into the nearby Three Sisters Wilderness, but requires a free limited-entry permit (available at ranger stations).

The little community of McKenzie Bridge, 50 miles east of Eugene on Hwy 126, offers a few cabins and a market. Along Hwy 126 are other scattered accommodations, including **Harbick's Country Inn** (☎ 541-822-3805; www.harbicks-country-inn.com; 54791 McKenzie Hwy; d $72-99; ✕ ✕ ☐ wi-fi), an attractive motel; **Belknap Hot Springs Lodge** (☎ 541-822-3512; www.belknaphotsprings.com; 59296 Belknap Springs Rd; campsites/RV sites $22/27, cabins $95-440, d $105-205; ℗ ✕ ✕ ☐ wi-fi), a large spalike mountain resort with something for everyone; and **Clear Lake Resort** (☎ 541-967-3917; www.clearlakeresort-oregon.org; Hwy 126; cabins $60-110), with both rustic and more modern lakeside cabins (bring bedding). The resort is 4 miles south of Hwy 20. Reserve all rooms in summer.

There are many lovely summer **campgrounds** (campsites $12) in the area, which include Paradise (old-growth grove near white water), Delta (scenic and enchanting) and Ice Cap Creek (clifftop location near reservoir and waterfalls).

Lane Transit District (☎ 541-687-5555; www.ltd.org) bus 91 from Eugene provides service along Hwy 126 to the McKenzie Ranger Station.

COLUMBIA RIVER GORGE

Cleanly dividing Oregon and Washington is the spectacular Columbia River Gorge, carved some 15,000 years ago by cataclysmic floods. Driving east on I-84 (or the slower but more scenic Columbia River Hwy, US 30) has you passing high waterfalls and nearly vertical mountain walls, all while paralleling the mighty Columbia. There are lovely hikes, bewitching waterfalls and fine wine-tasting possibilities, and windsurfers and kiteboarders will be awed by the gorge's fierce and famous winds.

Hood River & Around

The town of Hood River, 63 miles east of Portland on I-84, is a slender wedge of bike and ski shops, cafés, restaurants and a few hotels. The Columbia River here is famous as a windsurfing hot spot, and there's great mountain biking south of town off Hwy 35 and Forest Rd 44. For information there's the **chamber of commerce** (☎ 541-386-2000; www.hoodriver.org; 405 Portway Ave; ☻ 9am-5pm Mon-Fri, 10am-5pm Sat & Sun), across I-84 from the city center.

SCENIC DRIVE: HISTORIC COLUMBIA RIVER HIGHWAY

Finished in 1915, this gorgeous winding highway between Troutdale and the Dalles was the first paved road in the Northwest and America's first scenic highway. It was also part of the Oregon Trail and the last leg of Lewis and Clark's expedition. There are gushing waterfalls in spring, wildflower displays in summer and awe-inspiring views all year round. Hikers have plenty of trailheads to choose from, and cyclists can cruise two stretches of the old highway renovated for nonvehicle use (cars 'detour' onto I-84).

Be sure to stop at the interpretive center **Vista House** (☎ 503-695-2230; ☻ 9am-6pm), boasting an amazing view. Must-see **Multnomah Falls** is a 642ft waterfall – Oregon's tallest – with a one-hour hike to the top. There's a **visitor center** (☎ 503-695-2372; ☻ 9am-5pm) here with plenty of area information. Finally, hikers will appreciate the **Eagle Creek Trail**, the gorge's premier trail.

To reach the historic highway, take exit 17 or 35 off I-84.

PACIFIC NORTHWEST

Camping in the area includes **Viento State Park** (☎ 541-374-8811; campsites/RV sites $14/16), 8 miles west of town and popular with windsurfers. The **Columbia River Gorge Hostel** (☎ 509-493-3363; www.bingenschool.com; cnr Cedar & Humbolt Sts; dm/r from $19/49, dm linens $3), across the Columbia in Bingen, WA, has simple and affordable lodging in an old schoolhouse. The **Inn at the Gorge** (☎ 541-386-4429; www.innatthegorge.com; 1113 Eugene St; d $108-152; ✕ 🐾 💻 wi-fi) is an attractive B&B with five rooms (some with kitchenette) and wide porches.

Full Sail Brewery (☎ 541-386-2247; 506 Columbia St; mains $9-23; ☯ 11:30am-8pm) has a cozy tasting-room bar with a small pub menu. Free 20-minute brewery tours end up here. **Celilo Restaurant & Bar** (☎ 541-386-5710; 16 Oak St; mains $15-25; ☯ 11:30am-3pm & 5-9:30pm) offers excellent gourmet cuisine with a conscience; ingredients are organic and local where possible, they compost and recycle, and vegetable oil is converted into biodiesel.

OREGON CASCADES

Snowy peaks are scattered all around this beautiful region, offering an outdoors smorgasbord of recreational adventures. Think skiing, mountaineering, hiking, camping, bicycling, golfing, rafting, kayaking, fishing and rock climbing – it's all here, along with a healthy dose of sunshine in which to enjoy it all. Don't miss majestic Crater Lake, which started life as a 12,000ft volcano before blowing its top. And when it's time for a break, the booming metropolis of Bend is there to provide travelers with plenty of fine food, civilization and rest.

Mt Hood

Oregon state's highest peak, Mt Hood (11,240ft), pops into view over much of northern Oregon on sunny days, exerting a magnetic tug on skiers, hikers and sightseers. In summer wildflowers bloom on the mountainsides and hidden ponds shimmer in blue, making for unforgettable hikes; in winter, downhill and cross-country skiing dominate. Timberline Lodge (right), a beautiful wood gem from the 1930s, offers glorious shelter and refreshments to both guests and nonguests.

Mt Hood is accessible year-round on US 26 from Portland (56 miles), and from Hood River (44 miles) on Hwy 35. Together with the Columbia River Hwy, these routes comprise the Mt Hood Loop, a popular scenic drive. Government Camp is the center of business on the mountain.

For information visit ranger stations **Hood River** (☎ 541-352-6002; 6780 Hwy 35, Parkdale; ☯ 8am-4:30pm Mon-Sat) and **ZigZag** (☎ 503-622-3191; 70220 E Hwy 26, Zigzag; ☯ 7:45am-4:30pm Mon-Sat). The weather changes quickly here; carry chains in winter. For road conditions, dial ☎ 800-977-6368.

HIKING

A Northwest Forest Pass ($5) is required at most trailheads.

Loop 7 miles to beautiful **Ramona Falls**, which tumbles down mossy columnar basalt. Or head 1.5 miles up from US 26 to **Mirror Lake**; continue a half-mile around the lake, then 2 miles beyond to a ridge.

The 40.7-mile **Timberline Trail** circumnavigates Mt Hood along a scenic wilderness. Noteworthy portions of it include the hike to McNeil Point and the short climb to Bald Mountain. From Timberline Lodge, Zigzag Canyon Overlook is a 4.5-mile round-trip.

After Japan's Mt Fuji, Mt Hood is the world's most-climbed peak over 10,000ft. Climbing it should be taken seriously – deaths do occur. Contact a ranger station for details.

SKIING

Mt Hood Meadows (☎ 503-337-2222; www.skihood .com; lift tickets adult/child 7-14 $52/30) The largest ski area on Mt Hood, with the best conditions.

Timberline Lodge (☎ 503-622-0717; www.timber linelodge.com; lift tickets adult/child 7-14/child 15-17 $52/30/40) Boasts skiing in summer. Its legendary lodge is a must for refreshments.

Mt Hood SkiBowl (☎ 503-272-3206; www .skibowl.com; lift tickets adult/child 7-12 $38/20) The USA's largest night-ski area and the closest skiing to Portland.

Nordic Center (☎ 503-337-2222, ext 262; day pass $10) Ten miles of groomed wooded trails. Several other free (ungroomed) trails start here too.

SLEEPING & EATING

Mazama Lodge (☎ 503-272-9214; www.mazamas.org; Westlake Rd; dm members/nonmembers $15/20, d $45-60) Run by mountaineering group Mazamas, this lodge has mostly dorms (bring bedding). There are decks with mountain views, plus a restaurant. Open weekends mostly; in winter trek 10 minutes from the parking lot.

Huckleberry Inn (☎ 503-272-3325; www.huckleberry -inn.com; 88611 E Government Camp Loop; d $92-168; ☒) Small, simple and rustic rooms available, plus a 'bunk' room that sleeps up to 14. Located in Government Camp.

ourpick Timberline Lodge (☎ 800-547-1406; www .timberlinelodge.com; d $115-270; ☒ ☒ ☐ wi-fi) This gorgeous historic lodge offers everything from rustic bunks to luxury suites. Enjoy views of Mt Hood, hiking trails, bars and an exceptional restaurant. Bring your swimsuit.

Backyard Bistro (☎ 503-622-6302; 67898 E US 26; mains $6-9; ☻ 11am-8pm Tue-Sat, 10am-4pm Sun) This tiny but elegant bistro serves up awesome soups, salads and sandwiches; there's a great patio for warm days.

Rendezvous Grill & Tap Room (☎ 503-622-6837; 67149 E US 26; mains $20-30; ☻ 11:30am-9pm) Outstanding dishes such as porterhouse steak and Dungeness crab linguine are served here. Great desserts and wine list also.

Reserve **campsites** (☎ 877-444-6777; www.reserve usa.com) in summer. On US 26 are streamside campgrounds Tollgate and Camp Creek. Large and popular Trillium Lake has great views of Mt Hood. Find RV hookups at **Mt Hood Village** (☎ 800-255-3069; www.mthoodvillage.com; 65000 E US 26; RV sites $42-49, cabins $59-200; ☒).

Sisters

Straddling the Cascades and high desert lies the darling town of Sisters. Once a stagecoach stop for loggers and ranchers, the town is now a hot spot full of boutiques and art galleries. All around are mountain scenery, spectacular hiking and awesome climate. For help, see the **chamber of commerce** (☎ 541-549-0251; www.sisters chamber.com; 291 Main St; ☻ 9am-5pm) or the **ranger station** (☎ 541-549-7700; www.fs.fed.us/r6/centraloregon; 207 N Pine St; ☻ 8am-4pm).

At the southern end of Sisters, the city park has **campsites** ($10, no showers). For more comfort there's the **Sisters Inn** (☎ 541-549-7829; www.sistersinnandrvpark.com; 540 US 20 W; d $87-109, RV sites $35-38; ☒ ☒ ☒ ☐ wi-fi), with great rooms and an indoor pool. Or try the **Sisters Motor Lodge** (☎ 541-549-2551; www.sistersmotorlodge.com; 511 W Cascade St; d $98-159; ☒ ☒ ☐ wi-fi), offering 11 homey rooms, some with kitchenettes.

Bend

Everyone wants to live in Bend. Where else can you can ski in the morning, kayak in the afternoon and golf into the evening? More

---

HIKING IN THE THREE SISTERS WILDERNESS

This beautiful 283,400-acre region spans the Cascade Range and is highlighted by the glaciered Three Sisters, three recent volcanic peaks each topping 10,000ft. The area is traversed by scenic trails, including the glorious Pacific Crest Trail, easily accessed from Hwy 242 at McKenzie Pass.

Strong hikers should consider climbing South Sister. It's Oregon's third-highest peak, but during the summer the southern approach doesn't demand any technical equipment. The steep 5.6-mile trail begins near Devils Lake (just off the Cascade Lakes Hwy) and is passable only in late summer. Get advice at the Sisters Ranger Station.

---

outdoor adventures abound – there's also exceptional bicycling, hiking, mountaineering, fly-fishing and rock climbing close by. With the lovely Deschutes River winding through the heart of the city, Bend offers an attractive downtown area full of boutiques, galleries and upscale dining. It's no wonder Bend is booming.

Don't miss the extraordinary **High Desert Museum** (☎ 541-382-4754; www.highdesertmuseum .org; 59800 S US 97; adult/child 5-12/senior $15/9/12; ☻ 9am-5pm), 6 miles south of Bend. It charts the settlement of the West, along with the region's natural history. The sea otter exhibit and trout pool are highlights.

Just 22 miles southwest of Bend is Oregon's best skiing – glorious **Mt Bachelor** (9065ft). With 370in of snow a year, the season begins in November and can last until May. A one-day lift ticket is $52 per adult, $44 per senior and $32 per child aged six to 12; holiday tickets cost a bit more. Check on ski conditions at ☎ 541-382-7888 or www .mtbachelor.com. Cross-country skiing is also possible.

Get information at the **visitor & convention bureau** (☎ 541-382-8048; www.visitbend.com; 917 NW Harriman St; ☻ 9am-5pm Mon-Fri, 10am-4pm Sat) and the **Bend–Fort Rock Ranger District** (☎ 541-383-5300; www.fs.fed/us/r6/centraloregon; 1230 NE 3rd St; ☻ 7:45am-4:30pm Mon-Fri).

SLEEPING & EATING

There's a countless supply of cheap motels and services on 3rd St (US 97).

Tumalo State Park (☎ 541-388-6055, 800-551-6949; www.oregonstateparks.org; 64120 OB Riley Rd; campsites/RV sites/yurts $17/22/29) Located 5 miles northwest of Bend off US 20.

Cascade Lodge (☎ 541-382-2612, 800-852-6031; 420 E 3rd St; d $60; ✷ ⊠ ⬛ wi-fi) One of the better motels on this strip, with good spacious rooms set away from busy 3rd St. Jacuzzi suites and kitchenettes are available. There's an outdoor pool

McMenamins Old St Francis School (☎ 541-382-5174; www.mcmenamins.com; 700 NW Bond St; d $145-175, cottages $190-330; ✕ ⬛ ⬛ wi-fi) Awesome old schoolhouse remodeled into a classy 19-room hotel. The fabulous saltwater Turkish bath alone is worth the stay (nonguests pay $5). Also on the premises are a restaurant-pub, three bars and a movie theater.

Blacksmith (☎ 541-318-0588; 211 NW Greenwood Ave; mains $17-27; ⏱ 5:30-10pm) Renowned restaurant offering cowboy comfort food with a twist: think lobster enchiladas or wild mushroom bread pudding. Creative desserts too.

Deschutes Brewery & Public House (☎ 541-382-9242; 1044 NW Bond St; ⏱ 11am-11pm Mon-Thu, to midnight Fri & Sat, to 10pm Sun) Bend's first microbrewery, gregariously serving up plenty of food and handcrafted beers.

Newberry National Volcanic Monument

This volcanic region (day use $5) showcases 500,000 years of volcanic activity. Start your visit at the **Lava Lands Visitor Center** (☎ 541-593-2421; ⏱ 9am-5pm Jul-Sep, limited hours spring & fall, closed winter), located 13 miles south of Bend. Nearby attractions include **Lava Butte**, a perfect cone rising 500ft, and **Lava River Cave**, a lava tube. Four miles west of the visitor center is **Benham Falls**, a good picnic spot on the Deschutes River.

Newberry Crater was once one of the most active volcanoes in North America, but after a large eruption a caldera was born. Close by are **Paulina Lake** and **East Lake**, deep lakes rich with trout, while looming above is 7985ft **Paulina Peak**.

Cascade Lakes

Hwy 46, also called the Cascade Lakes Hwy, loops roughly 100 miles between high mountain peaks, linking together lovely alpine lakes. There are several trailheads in the area, along with campgrounds at most lakes. Beyond Mt Bachelor the road is closed from November to May.

Many lakes have cabins ranging from rustic to upscale. These include **Twin Lakes Resort** (☎ 541-382-6432; www.twinlakesresortoregon.com), **Elk Lake Resort** (☎ 541-480-7378; www.elklakeresort.net) and **Crane Prairie Resort** (☎ 541-383-3939; www.crane-prairie-resort-guides.com). Reserve ahead.

Crater Lake National Park

The gloriously still waters of Crater Lake reflect surrounding mountain peaks like a giant dark-blue mirror, making for spectacular photographs and breath-taking panoramas. Most people just cruise the 33-mile rim drive (open approximately June to mid-October), but there are also exceptional hiking and cross-country skiing opportunities. In summer, a $10 vehicle fee is charged to enter the park; in winter, admission is free but only the south entrance is open, and just to the rim. It's best to top off your gas tank before arriving at Crater Lake. For information head to **Steel Visitor Center** (☎ 541-594-3100; ⏱ 9am-5pm in summer, 10am-4pm in winter).

Most travelers do a day trip from Medford, Roseburg or Klamath Falls. In the park, choose between the **Cabins at Mazama Village** (☎ 541-830-8700, 888-774-2728; www.craterlakelodges.com; d $130; ✕), open June to early October, and the majestic old **Crater Lake Lodge** (☎ 541-594-2255, 888-774-2728; www.craterlakelodges.com; d $148-278; ✕ ✷), open from late May to mid-October. Nearby campgrounds include the large **Mazama Campground** (campsites/RV sites $19/22), open mid-June to early October, and the tiny **Lost Creek Campground** (campsites $10), open mid-July to mid-September; neither take reservations. There are many USFS campgrounds around Union Creek and Prospect, west on Hwy 62.

SOUTHERN OREGON

With a warm and sunny climate that belongs in nearby California, Southern Oregon is the state's banana belt. Rugged landscapes, scenic rivers and a couple of attractive towns top the highlights list, while breathtaking Crater Lake (above) isn't too far away. Centrally located between Seattle and San Francisco, Southern Oregon is certainly worth more than a short gas break as you cruise I-5.

Ashland

People come from all over the world for Ashland's famous Shakespeare festival (OSF; see p1046) which attracts 100,000 playgoers over nine months. These crowds help to support the city's plethora of fancy hotels, upscale B&Bs and fine restaurants, but even without OSF Ashland is a pleasant place to visit. There's lovely, 93-acre Lithia Park, which winds along Ashland Creek above the center of town, and in the surrounding areas are a few good wineries and plenty of activities. For detailed information visit the **chamber of commerce** (☎ 541-482-3486; www.ashlandchamber .com; 110 E Main St; ☺ 9am-5pm Mon-Fri, 11am-3pm Sat, noon-3pm Sun).

ACTIVITIES

Powdery snow is abundant at **Mt Ashland Ski Resort** (☎ 541-482-2897; www.mtashland.com), 16 miles southwest on 7533ft Mt Ashland. Pedal-pushers can rent a bike at **Siskiyou Cyclery** (☎ 541-482-1997; 1729 Siskiyou Blvd; per day $35; ☺ 10am-5:30pm Tue-Sat) and explore the countryside on Bear Creek Greenway.

Kokopelli (☎ 541-201-7694, 866-723-8874; www.koko pelliriverguides.com; 2475 Siskiyou Blvd) and **Adventure Center** (☎ 541-488-2819, 800-444-2819; www.raftingtours .com; 40 N Main St) both offer rafting trips on the Rogue River.

For a good soak check out **Jackson Wellsprings** (☎ 541-482-3776; www.jacksonwellsprings.com; 2253 Hwy 99), a casual New Age–style place which boasts an 85°F (29°C) mineral-fed swimming pool ($6) and 103°F (39°C) private Jacuzzi tubs ($20 to $30 for 75 minutes). It's 2 miles north of town.

SLEEPING

Reserve in summer. Jackson Wellsprings, above, has camping, RV sites and teepees.

Glenyan Campground (☎ 541-488-1785, 877-453-6929; www.glenyanrvpark.com; 5310 Hwy 66; campsites/RV sites $22/28; ☒ ☐ wi-fi) Pleasant campground 4 miles southeast; go for a creek-side spot.

Ashland Hostel (☎ 541-482-9217; www.theashland hostel.com; 150 N Main St; dm $25, d from $59; ☒ ☒ ☐) A bit too upscale for a true hostel but conveniently located near downtown.

Columbia Hotel (☎ 541-482-3726, 800-718-2530; www.columbiahotel.com; 262-1/2 E Main St; d $78-136; ☒ ☒ ☐ wi-fi) Awesome European-style hotel – which means some rooms share baths. Quaint vintage rooms (no TVs) and historic feel; located right downtown.

Palm (☎ 541-482-2636, 877-482-2635; www.palmcot tages.com; 1065 Siskiyou Blvd; d $96-175; ☒ ☒ ☒ ☐ wi-fi) A fabulous motel remodeled into charming garden cottage rooms (some of which have a kitchen). It's a green oasis on a busy avenue, complete with both pool and sundeck in back.

Country Willows (☎ 541-488-1590, 800-945-5697; www.countrywillowsinn.com; 1313 Clay St; d $135-265; ☒ ☒ ☒ ☐ wi-fi) Luxurious B&B in the 'country-side', but only minutes from the center. Fabulous rooms and suites, some huge and creatively designed.

EATING

Morning Glory (☎ 541-488-8636; 1149 Siskiyou Blvd; breakfast $9-12; ☺ 8am-2pm) Colorful and eclectic café with creative dishes such as Alaskan crab omelet, tandoori tofu scramble and shrimp cakes with poached eggs.

ourpick **New Sammy's Cowboy Bistro** (☎ 541-535-2779; 2210 S Pacific Hwy; mains $23-36; ☺ 5-8:30pm Thu-Sun) Some consider this funky spot, run by an eclectic couple, Oregon's best restaurant. Located in Talent, about 3 miles north of Ashland. Reserve weeks in advance; limited winter hours.

Peerless on 4th (☎ 503-488-6067; 265 4th St; mains $24-38; ☺ 5:30-9pm) Fine Northwest cuisine is the star attraction at this upscale spot that uses only the freshest ingredients, resulting in

---

OREGON SHAKESPEARE FESTIVAL

Highly respected and wildly popular, the OSF repertoire is rooted in Shakespearean and Elizabethan drama, but also features revivals and contemporary theater from around the world. Eleven productions run February through October in three theaters near Main and Pioneer Sts: the outdoor **Elizabethan Theatre**, the **Angus Bowmer Theatre** and the intimate **New Theatre**.

Performances sell out quickly; obtain tickets in advance at www.osfashland.org. You can also try the **box office** (☎ 541-482-4331; 15 S Pioneer St; tickets $30-75). Backstage tours (adult/youth $11/8.25) also need to be booked well in advance.

Check the OSF Welcome Center for other events, which may include scholarly lectures, play readings, concerts and preshow talks.

PACIFIC NORTHWEST

some of Ashland's best food. There's a patio area out front for warm nights.

Jacksonville

Small but endearing, this ex-gold-prospecting town is the oldest settlement in southern Oregon and a National Historic Landmark. The main drag is lined with well-preserved buildings dating from the 1880s, now converted into boutiques and galleries. Music lovers can't miss the **Britt Festival** (☎ 541-773-6077; www.brittfest.org), a world-class musical experience with top-name performers. Seek more enlightenment at the **chamber of commerce** (☎ 541-899-8118; www.jacksonvilleoregon.org; 185 N Oregon St; ☺ 10am-5pm Mon-Fri, 11am-4pm Sat & Sun).

Jacksonville is full of fancy B&Bs; for budget motels head 6 miles east to Medford. **Jacksonville Stage Lodge** (☎ 541-899-3953, 800-253-8254; www.stagelodge.com; 830 N 5th St; d $102-113; ✕ ✱ 🖵 wi-fi) is a modern hotel with 27 spacious and fine contemporary rooms, while **Magnolia Inn** (☎ 541-899-0255, 866-899-0255; www.magnolia-inn.com; 245 N 5th St; d $138-165; ✕ ✱ 🖵 wi-fi) has pleasant rooms and a guest kitchen with nearby veranda.

Wild Rogue Wilderness

Just northwest of Ashland, the Wild Rogue Wilderness lives up to its name, with the turbulent Rogue River cutting through 40 miles of untamed, roadless canyon. The area is known for turbulent white-water rafting (classes III and IV) and long-distance hikes.

Grants Pass is the gateway to adventure along the Rogue. The **chamber of commerce** (☎ 541-476-7717, 800-547-5927; www.visitgrantspass.org; 1995 NW Vine St; ☺ 8am-5pm Mon-Fri) is right off I-5 exit 58. For raft permits and backpacking advice, contact the Bureau of Land Management's (BLM) **Smullin Visitors Center** (☎ 541-479-3735; www.blm.gov/or/resources/recreation/rogue/index.php; 14335 Galice Rd; ☺ 7am-3pm) in Galice.

Rafting the Rogue is not for the faint of heart; a typical trip takes three days and costs upward of $650. Outfitters include **Raft The Rogue** (☎ 800-797-7238; www.rafttherogue.com; 21171 Hwy 62), **Rogue Rafting Company** (☎ 888-236-3096; www.upperrogue.org/roguerafting; 7725 Rogue River Dr) and **Orange Torpedo Trips** (☎ 541-476-5061, 800-635-2925; www.orangetorpedo.com).

A highlight of the region is the 40-mile **Rogue River Trail**, once a supply route from Gold Beach. The full trek takes four to five days; day hikers might aim for Whiskey Creek Cabin, a 6-mile round-trip from the Grave Creek trailhead. The trail is dotted with rustic lodges ($110 to $140 per person with meals; reservations required). Try **Black Bar** (☎ 541-479-6507; www.blackbarlodge.net), **Paradise** (☎ 888-667-6483; www.paradiselodge.us) and **Half Moon Bar** (☎ 888-291-8268; www.halfmoonbarlodge.com). There are also primitive campgrounds along the way.

North Umpqua River

This 'Wild and Scenic' river boasts world-class fly-fishing, fine hiking and serene camping. The 79-mile **North Umpqua Trail** begins near Idleyld Park and passes through Steamboat en route to the Pacific Crest Trail. A popular sideline is pretty **Umpqua Hot Springs**, east of Steamboat near Toketee Lake. Not far away, stunning, two-tiered **Toketee Falls** flows over columnar basalt, while **Watson Falls** (272ft) is one of the highest waterfalls in Oregon. For information stop by Glide's **Colliding Rivers Information Center** (☎ 541-496-0157; 18782 N Umpqua Hwy; ☺ 9am-5pm May-Oct). Adjacent is the **North Umpqua Ranger District** (☎ 541-496-3532; ☺ 8am-4:30pm Mon-Fri).

Between Idleyld Park and Diamond Lake are dozens of riverside campgrounds; these include lovely **Susan Creek** and primitive **Boulder Flat** (no water). A few area accommodations fill up quickly in summer; try the log-cabin-like rooms at **Dogwood Motel** (☎ 541-496-3403; www.dogwoodmotel.com; 28866 N Umpqua Hwy; d $65-70; ✕ ✱).

Oregon Caves National Monument

This very popular cave (there's only one) lies 19 miles east of Cave Junction on Hwy 46. Three miles of passages are explored via 90-minute **walking tours** (☎ 541-592-2100; www.nps.gov/orca; adult/child 16 & under $8.50/6; ☺ 10am-4pm Apr-May & Oct-Nov, 9am-5pm Jun-Sep, closed Dec-Mar) that include 520 rocky steps and dripping chambers running along the River Styx. Dress warmly, wear shoes with good traction and be prepared to get dripped on.

Cave Junction, 28 miles south of Grants Pass on US 199 (Redwood Hwy), provides the region's services. Here you'll find the decent **Junction Inn** (☎ 541-592-3106; 406 Redwood Hwy; d from $65; 🕭), along with a few restaurants. For fancy lodgings right at the cave there's the impressive **Oregon Caves Chateau** (☎ 541-592-3400, 877-245-9022; www.oregoncaveschateau.com; d from $90-137; ☺ May-Oct); grab a milkshake at the old-fashioned soda fountain here. Campers should head to **Cave Creek Campground** (☎ 541-592-2166; 14 miles up Hwy 46; campsites $10), about 4 miles from the cave.

EASTERN OREGON

Eastern Oregon hoards some of the state's most diverse, unusual and spectacular highlights. While much of it is extensive farmlands or desert plateaus, there are also stunning mountains, painted hills, alkali lakebeds and the country's deepest river gorge. Some smaller towns might whisk you back in time with their still-palpable spaghetti-Western touches, but that's part of the charm of this underrated but highly worthwhile region.

John Day Fossil Beds National Monument

Within the soft rocks and crumbly soils of John Day country lies one of the world's greatest fossil collections, laid down between six and 50 million years ago. Roaming the forests at the time were saber-toothed nimravids, pint-sized horses, bear-dogs and other early mammals.

The national monument includes 22 sq miles at three different units: Sheep Rock Unit, Painted Hills Unit and Clarno Unit. Each has hiking trails and interpretive displays. To visit all of the units in one day requires quite a bit of driving, as more than 100 miles separate the fossil beds.

Visit the excellent **Thomas Condon Paleontology Center** (☎ 541-987-2333; www.nps.gov/joda; 32651 Hwy 19, Kimberly; ⊙ 9am-5:30pm) 2 miles north of US 26 at the Sheep Rock Unit. Displays include a three-toed horse and petrified dung-beetle balls, along with many other fossils and geologic history exhibits. If you feel like walking, take the short hike up the **Blue Basin trail**, which will make you feel like you've just landed on the sunny side of the moon.

The Painted Hills Unit, near the town of Mitchell, consists of low-slung, colorfully banded hills formed about 30 million years ago. The Clarno Unit exposes mud flows that washed over an Eocene-era forest and eroded into distinctive, sheer-white cliffs topped with spires and turrets of stone.

Several campgrounds are in the area: Lone Pine and Big Bend (sites $8) are nice riverside ones on Hwy 402, north of the Sheep Rock Unit and 2 to 3 miles east of Kimberly. Every little town in the area has at least one hotel;

these include the charming **Historic Hotel Oregon** (☎ 541-462-3027; 104 E Main St; dm $15, d $29-79; ☒) in Mitchell and the fine **Service Creek Lodge** (☎ 541-468-3331; www.servicecreekstagestop.com; 38686 Hwy 19; d $75; ☒ ☒), which also has raft rentals for the placid John Day River. The town of John Day itself has several good accommodation choices.

Wallowa Mountains

The Wallowa Mountains, with their glacier-hewn peaks and crystalline lakes, are among the most beautiful natural areas in Oregon. The only drawback is the large number of visitors who flock here in summer, especially to the pretty **Wallowa Lake** area. Escape them all on one of several long hikes into the nearby **Eagle Cap Wilderness Area**, such as the 6-mile one-way jaunt to **Aneroid Lake** or the 9-mile trek on the **West Fork Trail**. From the upper Lostine Valley, or from the Sheep Creek Summit of USFS Rd 39, there is easier day-hike access to the Eagle Cap's high country.

Just north of the mountains, in the Wallowa Valley, **Enterprise** is a homely backcountry town with several motels such as the **Ponderosa** (☎ 541-426-3186; 102 E Greenwood St; d $67-74; ☒ ☒ ▢ wi-fi). If you like beer, don't miss the town's microbrewery, Terminal Gravity. Just 6 miles south is Enterprise's fancy cousin, the upscale town of **Joseph**. Expensive bronze galleries and artsy boutiques line the main strip, and accommodations comprise mostly B&Bs.

Hells Canyon

Dramatic landscapes can be found at Hells Canyon, where the Snake River has been carving out an 8000ft-deep trench for about 13 million years beneath the highest surrounding peaks, making it the USA's deepest river gorge.

For perspective, drive 30 miles from Joseph to Imnaha, where a 24-mile slow gravel road leads up to the excellent lookout at **Hat Point** (USFS Rd 4240). From here you can see the Wallowa Mountains, Idaho's Seven Devils, the Imnaha River and the wilds of Hells Canyon. This road is open from late May until snowfall; give yourself two hours each way for the drive. In Enterprise, the **Wallowa Mountains Visitor Center** (☎ 541-426-5546; www.fs.fed.us/r6/w-w; 88401 Hwy 82; ⊙ 8am-6pm Mon-Sat) has a wealth of information on road conditions and area details.

For white-water action and spectacular scenery, head down to **Hells Canyon Dam**, 25 miles north of the small community of Oxbow. **Hells Canyon Adventures** (☎ 541-785-3352, 800-422-3568; www.hellscanyonadventures.com; 4200 Hells Canyon Dam Rd) runs raft trips and noisy **jet-boat tours** from May through September (reservations required). Just past the dam the road ends at the **Hells Canyon Visitor Center** (☎ 541-785-3395; ☽ 8am-4pm summer only), which has good advice on the area's campgrounds and hiking trails.

The area has many campgrounds. Just outside Imnaha is the fine **Imnaha River Inn** (☎ 541-577-6002, 866-601-9214; www.imnahariverinn.com; d $128), while Oxbow has the awesome-value **Hells Canyon B&B** (☎ 541-785-3373; www.hells-canyon-bed-and-breakfast.com; d $60). For more services head to the towns of Enterprise, Joseph and Halfway.

Steens Mountain & Alvord Desert

Steens Mountain, the highest peak in southeastern Oregon (9670ft), is part of a massive, 30-mile fault-block range. On the west slope of the range, Ice Age glaciers bulldozed massive U-shaped valleys into the flanks of the mountain. To the east, delicate alpine meadows and lakes flank the Steens, dropping off dizzyingly into the Alvord Desert 5000ft below.

Beginning in Frenchglen, the 66-mile gravel **Steens Mountain Loop Road** offers access to Steens Mountain Recreation Area; it's open from late June to October (depending on the weather) and requires a high-clearance vehicle in parts. Call the **Bureau of Land Management** (BLM; ☎ 541-573-4400; ☽ 7:45am-4:30pm Mon-Fri) for information. If you happen to be in the area outside these months or have a low-clearance vehicle, consider seeing the Steens via the flat eastern gravel road through the scenic Alvord Desert. Take a full gas tank and prepare for weather changes year-round.

There are campgrounds on the Steens Mountain Loop, such as the BLM's pretty Page Springs and fine South Steens Campgrounds (campsites $6 to $8, water available). Free 'dispersed' camping is allowed in the Steens and Alvord Desert (bring water). The historic **Frenchglen Hotel** (☎ 541-493-2825; fghotel@yahoo.com; 39184 Hwy 205, Frenchglen; d $67-100; ☽ Mar 15-Oct 31; ✗) has small, cute rooms with shared bath, plus five modern rooms. Dinners are available (reserve ahead). South of the Alvord Desert, Fields has a small **inn** (☎ 877-225-9424; www.alvordinn.com; d $60-70).

OREGON COAST

Beaches, rocky headlands, amazing vistas, hidden hikes and whale-watching – all are highlights along Oregon's 362 miles of gorgeous coastline. While the bigger, better-known resort cities lie to the north, once you cross Florence heading south the towns get smaller and the scenery is more pristine. Summer camping at the over 70 state parks and wilderness areas is a great way to go and is a popular pastime among Oregonians.

Astoria

Named after America's first millionaire, John Jacob Astor, Astoria sits at the wide mouth of the Columbia River and was the first US settlement west of the Mississippi. It's grown rapidly in the last 10 years, attracting new developments and renovating its historical houses, including many beautiful Victorians. The can't-miss 4.1-mile-long **Astoria–Megler Bridge** crosses into Washington state and is the world's longest continuous truss bridge. Find information at the **visitor center** (☎ 503-325-6311; www.oldoregon.com; 111 W Marine Dr; ☽ 9am-5pm).

PACIFIC NORTHWEST

WORTH THE TRIP: SUCCOR CREEK BYWAY

The wildly eroded Owyhee River country is off the beaten path, but sections of this 35-mile gravel road are unforgettable. It runs between Adrian and a junction with US 95, 18 miles north of Jordan Valley.

Follow the road south from near Adrian, and after 12 miles you'll drop into a canyon with volcanic-tuff walls hundreds of feet high. The **Succor Creek State Recreation Area** is near here, with primitive campsites and stunning scenery.

Views are even more spectacular at **Leslie Gulch**, further south on a 16-mile side road. You'll see colorful volcanic rock eroded into amazing pinnacles, and eventually reach a reservoir. Rock climbing is possible and there's primitive camping in the area (beware of rattlesnakes).

Driving on gravel roads is slow going, so leave yourself plenty of time and take food and water.

Astoria's 150-year-old seafaring heritage is well interpreted at the fine **Columbia River Maritime Museum** (☎ 503-325-2323; www.crmm.org; 1792 Marine Dr; adult/child 6-17/senior $8/4/7; ⏰ 9:30am-5pm). The less flashy **Heritage Museum** (☎ 503-338-4849; www.cumtux.org; 1618 Exchange St; adult/child 6-17/senior $4/2/3; ⏰ 10am-5pm) has historical exhibits which include Ku Klux Klan (KKK) paraphernalia.

The extravagant **Flavel House** (☎ 503-325-2203; www.cumtux.org; 441 8th St; adult/child 6-17/senior $5/2/4; ⏰ 10am-5pm) is a Queen Anne Victorian built by Capt George Flavel, one of Astoria's leading citizens during the 1880s. For a good view, head uphill to the **Astoria Column**, a 125ft tower painted with scenes from the westward sweep of US exploration and settlement.

Five miles south of Astoria, the **Lewis & Clark National Historical Park** (☎ 503-861-2471; www.nps .gov/lewi; adult/child 2-15 $5/2; ⏰ 9am-6pm Jun-Aug, to 5pm Sep-May) offers a reconstructed fort similar to one the Corps of Discovery occupied during their miserable winter of 1805–06. And 10 miles west of Astoria off US 101 is **Fort Stevens State Park** (☎ 503-861-1671; campsites/RV sites/yurts $18/22/30), which commemorates the historic military reservation that guarded the mouth of the Columbia River. There's beach access, camping and bike trails.

Hideaway Inn & Hostel (☎ 503-325-6989; www .hideawayinnandhostel.com; 443 14th St; dm $20, r $33-88; ⏹ wi-fi) has cheap bunks and private rooms; call ahead as there's no doorbell. **Rose River Inn B&B** (☎ 503-325-7175, 888-876-0028; www.rose riverinn.com; 1510 Franklin Ave; d $99-176; ✗ ⏹ wi-fi) is a country-style home with four pretty rooms.

Wet Dog Cafe (☎ 503-325-6975, 144 11th St; mains $9-17; ⏰ 11am-10pm Sun-Thu, to 2am Fri & Sat) is a quirky pub-restaurant which brews its own beer and has live music on weekends. **Baked Alaska** (☎ 503-325-7414; 1 12th St; mains $18-24; ⏰ 11am-10pm) is one of Astoria's finer restaurants, with great water views.

Cannon Beach

Immense basalt promontories and sandy beaches make attractive Cannon Beach a fun, touristy and upscale coastal destination. Highly photogenic **Haystack Rock** is a popular landmark just offshore, while stunning views grace the Oregon Coast Trail over Tillamook Head in nearby Ecola State Park. For more area goodies ask the **chamber of commerce** (☎ 503-436-2623; www.cannonbeach.org; 207 N Spruce St; ⏰ 10am-5pm Mon-Sat, 11am-4pm Sun).

The lovely **Cannon Beach Hotel** (☎ 503-436-1392, 800-238-4107; www.cannonbeachhotel.com; 1116 S Hemlock St; d from $132-242; ✗ ⏹ wi-fi) has small but tasteful rooms. For budget lodgings you're better off in Seaside, 9 miles north; try the **Seaside International Hostel** (☎ 503-738-7911, 888-994-0001; www.seasidehostel.net; 930 N Holladay Dr; dm/r from $23/47; ⏹ wi-fi), with a grassy backyard overlooking a river. Campers have **Sea Ranch RV Park** (☎ 503-436-2815; www.cannon-beach.net/searanch; 415 Fir St; campsites/RV sites/cabins $26/30/80).

There are plenty of eateries in town; try the sandwiches and pasta at **Gower Street Bistro** (☎ 503-436-2729; 1116 S Hemlock St; mains $14-22; ⏰ 9am-3pm & 5-9pm, to 10pm Fri & Sat) or the burgers and pizza at **Lumberyard** (☎ 503-436-0285; 264 3rd St; mains $9-23; ⏰ 11am-10pm).

Newport

Oregon's second-largest commercial port, Newport is a lively tourist city with several fine beaches and a world-class aquarium. Good restaurants – along with some tacky attractions, gift shops and barking sea lions – abound in the historic Bayfront area, while bohemian Nye Beach offers art galleries and friendly village atmosphere. Get information at the **visitor center** (☎ 541-265-8801, 800-262-7844; www.newportchamber.org; 555 SW Coast Hwy; ⏰ 8am-5pm Mon-Fri, 10am-3pm Sat).

The top-notch **Oregon Coast Aquarium** (☎ 541-867-3474; www.aquarium.org; 2820 SE Ferry Slip Rd; adult/child 3-13/senior $13.25/7.75/11.25; ⏰ 9am-6pm) is a must for families, featuring a sea otter pool, surreal jellyfish tanks and Plexiglas tunnels through a shark tank. A less expensive alternative is the nearby **Hatfield Marine Science Center** (☎ 541-867-0271; www.hmsc.orst.edu/visitor; 2030 S Marine Science Dr; ⏰ 10am-5pm) with more modest exhibits; it's free, but donations help run its programs.

Campers can head to **South Beach State Park** (☎ 541-867-4715, 800-452-5687; www.oregonstateparks .org; campsites/RV sites/yurts $22/22/29), 2 miles south on US 101, which has 227 campsites and 27 yurts. Book-lovers shouldn't miss the **Sylvia Beach Hotel** (☎ 541-265-5428; www.sylviabeachhotel .com; 267 NW Cliff St; d $105-208; ✗), with simple but comfy rooms, each named after a famous author. Breakfast is included; reservations are mandatory. A good deal in a great neighborhood is **Rogue Ales Public House** (☎ 541-265-3188; 740 SW Bay Blvd; apt $100-143), offering just three modern apartments above its pub-restaurant. Rather than breakfast, two 22oz beers come with the package – making it a true 'Bed and Beer.'

For a fancy meal, try **Saffron Salmon** (☎ 541-265-8921; 859 SW Bay Blvd; mains $22-30; ⏰ 11:30am-2:30 & 5-8:30pm Thu-Tue). Once you get past the stellar wall-to-wall view, dig into grilled Chinook salmon or herb-crusted rack of lamb. Reserve for dinner.

Yachats

One of the Oregon coast's best-kept secrets, this neat and friendly little town lies at the base of beautiful **Cape Perpetua**. Volcanic intrusions to the south form a beautifully rugged shoreline, with dramatic features such as the Devil's Churn and the Spouting Horn. Ten miles south is the much-photographed **Heceta Head Lighthouse**, built in 1894 and perched above the churning ocean. Five miles further south on US 101 is the almost tourist trap but fun **Sea Lion Caves** (☎ 541-547-3111; www.sealioncaves .com; adult/child 6-12/senior $9/5/8; ⏰ 8am-6pm Jul & Aug, 9am-5:30pm Sep-Jun), a smelly grotto filled with groaning sea lions. Get more tips at the **visitor center** (☎ 800-929-0477; www.yachats.org; US 101 & 3rd St; ⏰ 10am-5pm).

Camp at **Beachside State Park** (☎ 541-563-3220, 800-452-5687; www.oregonstateparks.org; campsites/RV sites/ yurts $17/21/29), 5 miles north on US 101. In town, the large rooms with kitchens at **Ya'Tel Motel** (☎ 541-547-3225; www.yatelmotel.com; US 101 & 6th St; d $64-108; ✗) are a great deal. For something special, head 7 miles south on US 101 to **Sea Quest B&B** (☎ 541-547-3782, 800-341-4878; www .seaquestinn.com; d from $184; ✗ 🖳 wi-fi), a gorgeous B&B with stunning ocean views.

Oregon Dunes National Recreation Area

Stretching for 50 miles between Florence and Coos Bay, the Oregon Dunes form the largest expanse of coastal dunes in the USA. The dunes tower up to 500ft and undulate inland as far as 3 miles to meet coastal forests, harboring curious ecosystems that sustain an abundance of wildlife. Hiking trails, bridle paths, and boating and swimming areas are available, but avoid the stretch south of Reedsport as noisy dune buggies (or OHVs) dominate this area. Inform yourself at the Oregon Dunes National Recreation Area's **headquarters** (☎ 541-271-3495; www.fs.fed/us/r6/sius law; 855 Highway Ave; ⏰ 8am-4:30pm Mon-Fri, to 4pm Sat & Sun) in Reedsport.

State parks include popular **Jessie M Honeyman** (☎ 541-997-3641; US 101; campsites/RV sites/yurts $17/21/29), 3 miles south of Florence, and pleasant **Umpqua Lighthouse** (☎ 541-271-4118; US 101; campsites/RV sites/yurts/cabins $16/20/27/35), 6 miles south of Reedsport. USFS campgrounds include **Eel Creek** (☎ 877-444-6777; US 101; campsites $17), 10 miles south of Reedsport.

Bandon

Optimistically touted as Bandon-by-the-Sea, this little town happily sits at the bay of the Coquille River. Its harbor has gentrified into a picturesque shopping district, while south of town are vacation resorts and occasional beach access points. **Coquille Point**, at the end of 11th St, is a popular place to spot migrating whales in winter and spring. For details harass the **chamber of commerce** (☎ 541-347-9616; www .bandon.com; cnr 2nd St & Chicago Ave; ⏰ 10am-5:30pm).

Camp at **Bullards Beach State Park** (☎ 541-347-2209, 800-452-5687; US 101; campsites/yurts $20/27), 2 miles to the north. At the harbor is **Sea Star Guesthouse** (☎ 541-347-9632; www.seastarbandon.com; 370 1st St; d $80-115; ✗), offering pleasant homey rooms, some with loft and kitchenette. Just outside town is **Lighthouse B&B** (☎ 541-347-9316; www.lighthouselodging.com; 650 SW Jetty Rd; d $150-263; ✗ 🖳 wi-fi), boasting fine river views and excellent rooms.

For fancy food head to **Wild Rose Bistro** (☎ 541-347-4428; 130 Chicago St; mains $18-24; ⏰ 5-10pm Wed-Mon), which uses fresh ingredients to whip up some of the coast's best dishes. Fine views and a busier atmosphere are found at **Lord Bennett's** (☎ 541-347-3663; 1695 Beach Loop Rd; mains $16-26; ⏰ 11am-2:30pm & 5-9pm Mon-Fri, 10am-2:30pm & 5-9pm Sat & Sun).

WHALE-WATCHING

Each year, the longest migration of any mammal takes place in the Pacific Ocean, when approximately 20,000 gray whales make their annual 10,000-mile round-trip journey between the Arctic Sea and the lagoons of Baja California. The migration along the Oregon coast peaks in late December, but whales can also be spotted from March to May as they meander back north.

During the peak migration season, viewpoints are sometimes staffed with volunteers who can help identify and interpret gray whale behavior. For a close-up view take one of the two-hour boat tours, accessible from Depoe Bay or Newport.

Port Orford

Sleepy Port Orford, located on a scenic stretch of coastline, is just a blip on the map. It has a great laid-back feel, but signs of gentrification loom on the horizon. Two nearby state parks offer panoramic seascapes; **Port Orford**, with short walking loops, and **Cape Blanco**, the second-most-westerly point of the continental USA. The **visitor center** (☎ 541-332-8055; www.discoverportorford.com; ☻ 8am-5pm) is in the middle of town.

You can camp on the rocky headland at **Cape Blanco** (☎ 541-332-6774, 800-452-5687; www.oregonstateparks.org; US 101; campsites & RV sites/cabins $16/35), 4 miles north of Port Orford. For a luxurious woodsy retreat head inland to **Wildspring Guest Habitat** (☎ 541-322-0977, 866-333-9453; www.wildspring.com; 92978 Cemetery Loop; d $245-278; ☒ 🖳 wi-fi).

Gold Beach

Situated at the mouth of the fabulous Rogue River, Gold Beach attracts anglers, and folks looking to zip upstream via jet boat into the Wild Rogue Wilderness Area. Hikers can appreciate the area's spectacular coastline; visit **Cape Sebastian State Park**, a rocky headland 7 miles south, for a panorama stretching from California to Cape Blanco. Get details at the **Gold Beach Chamber of Commerce** (☎ 541-247-7526, 800-525-2334; www.goldbeachchamber.com; 29279 S Ellensburg Ave; ☻ 9:30-5:30pm Tue-Sun).

For rustic, modern or beach cabins (along with RV sites) head to **Ireland's Rustic Lodges** (☎ 541-247-7718; 29346 Ellensburg Ave; www.irelandsrusticlodges.com; d $108-162; 🖳 wi-fi) There's a glorious garden area in front and beach views in back. Awesome food can be had at **Patti's Rollin 'n Dough bistro** (☎ 541-247-4438; 94257 N Bank Rogue Rd; mains $7-14; ☻ 10:30am-3pm Tue-Sat), one of the coast's best eateries, though it only serves lunch (reserve ahead).

Brookings

Just 6 miles from the California border is this balmy and bustling commercial town. Other than great fishing and the scenic coastline, visitors come to visit the remote and unique vegetation of the **Kalmiopsis Wilderness Area**. North of town is **Samuel H Boardman State Park**, with 11 miles of Oregon's most beautiful coastline. Oregon's only redwood forests, along with old-growth myrtle, are found in **Alfred A Loeb State Park** (☎ 541-469-2021, 800-452-5687; www.oregonstateparks.org; N Bank Chetco River Rd; tents/cabins $16/35), 10 miles east. The **chamber of commerce** (☎ 541-469-3181; www.brookingsor.com; 16330 Lower Harbor Rd; ☻ 9am-5pm Mon-Fri) is at the harbor.

Alaska

Big, beautiful and wildly bountiful. Far away, rurally isolated and very expensive. Alaska is a traveler's dilemma.

There are few places in the world with the grandeur and breathtaking beauty of Alaska. Not only is Mt McKinley the highest peak in North America, it's also a stunning sight when you catch its alpenglow in Wonder Lake. A 900lb brown bear catching a leaping salmon in its jaws is not something seen in Iowa. A 5-mile-wide glacier shedding chunks of ice the size of small cars is not something you'll see anywhere else in the USA.

Alaska is also an out-of-the-way and costly destination for anybody tripping through the rest of the country. It takes a week on the road to reach the 49th state, two to three days on a ferry or, from any region outside the Northwest, a $600-to-$800 airline ticket. Once there you'll find accommodations expensive, bus and train options meager and much of the state roadless and inaccessible.

But for those who have a strong sense of adventure, a little extra time and a love for life on the grand scale, whether it's kayaking through a sea of icebergs and seals or witnessing a 40-ton humpback whale breaching, Alaska is a hard place to pass up. And once there, even on a short side trip, you'll marvel at this amazing land and begin plotting your return.

ALASKA

HIGHLIGHTS

- Kayaking among icebergs while whale-watching at **LeConte Glacier** (p1061)
- Photographing brown bears feast on salmon at **Pack Creek** (p1065) in Admiralty Island National Monument
- Following the Klondike gold rush into the mountains with a ride on the historic **White Pass & Yukon Railroad** (p1067)
- Riding the tram to enjoy dinner and an amazing top-of-the-world view from Seven Glaciers Restaurant at **Alyeska Resort** (p1075)
- Hiking along Resurrection Bay to view the WWII artifacts at **Caines Head State Recreation Area** (p1075)
- Exploring the **Kennecott Copper Mine** and spending the night in the funky town of McCarthy (p1079)
- Looking for brown bears and Mt McKinley, the tallest peak in North America, from the shuttle bus in **Denali National Park** (p1081)
- Enjoying a strenuous mountain hike and then a soothing hot soak at **Chena Hot Springs** (p1083)
- Panning for gold and mingling with miners on the legendary **Golden Sands Beach** (p1084)

ALASKA

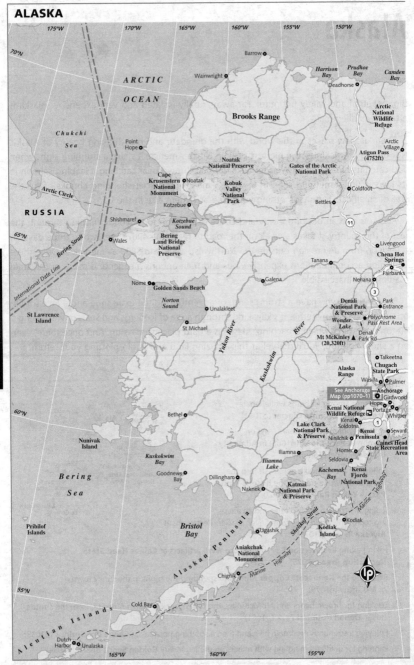

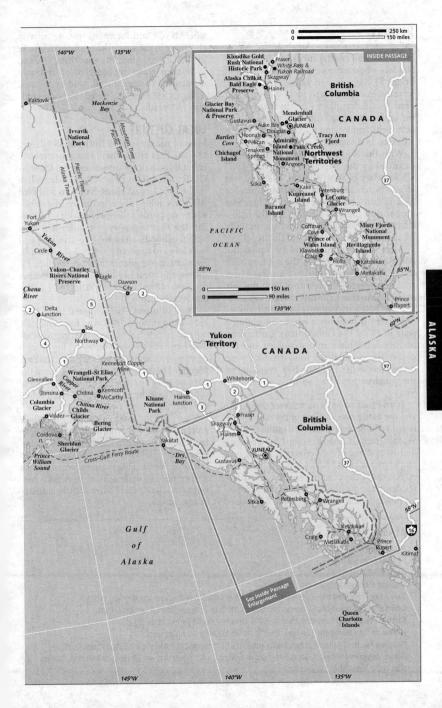

HISTORY

Indigenous Alaskans – Athabascans, Aleuts and Inuit, and coastal tribes of Tlingits and Haidas – migrated over the Bering Strait land bridge 35,000 years ago. In the 18th century, waves of Europeans arrived: first British and French explorers, then Russian whalers and fur traders, naming land formations, taking otter pelts and leaving the cultures of Native Alaskans in disarray.

With the Russians' finances badly overextended by the Napoleonic Wars, in 1867 US Secretary of State William H Seward was able to purchase the territory from them for $7.2 million – less than 2¢ an acre. There was uproar over 'Seward's Folly,' but the land's riches soon revealed themselves: initially whales, then salmon, gold and finally oil.

After Japan bombed and occupied the Aleutian Islands in WWII, the military built the famous Alcan (Alaska–Canada) Hwy, which connected the territory with the rest of the USA. The 1520-mile Alcan was constructed in less than nine months and contributed greatly to postwar Alaska becoming a state in 1959. The Good Friday Earthquake in 1964 left Alaska in a shambles, but recovery was boosted when oil deposits were discovered under Prudhoe Bay, resulting in the construction of a 789-mile pipeline to Valdez.

With Prudhoe Bay's oil reserves drying up and the battle over drilling in the Arctic National Wildlife Refuge (ANWR) still raging in Washington, DC, Alaska suffers from budget deficits and one of the country's highest unemployment rates. An escalating price for oil has eased the pain in recent years, while residents are pinning their economic hopes on possible new North Slope oil fields outside ANWR and increased mining activity elsewhere in the state. The future is still fuzzy in the Last Frontier, but one thing is clear. With their economy centered on resource extraction, whether it's oil, gold or salmon, Alaskans will always be mired in a boom-and-bust way of life.

LOCAL CULTURE

Most of Alaska is rural Bush, small villages and roadless areas where transportation is either by boat or on snowmobiles in the winter. Yet more than 60% of the residents live in the four largest cities. You can still find Alaskans in log cabins in the middle of nowhere supporting themselves with traplines. But the vast majority of residents live in neighborhoods, work nine-to-five jobs and look forward to playing softball at weekends. Even in remote villages there are satellite TV dishes, the latest hip-hop CDs and internet access to the rest of the world, including eBay and Amazon.com.

Rural or urban, Alaskans tend to be individualistic in their lifestyles, following few outside trends but rather adhering to what their harsh environment dictates. They are also very opportunistic. In the summer Alaskans play hard because the weather is nice and the days are long. In the winter they linger at the office because the temperature is often below 0°F (-15°C).

They love the outdoors and cherish their great parks. But the majority of Alaskans have few problems with drilling the pristine wilderness of the ANWR or clear-cutting Tongass National Forest. They want to live in Alaska so they need to make a living in Alaska, surviving in a land where there is little industry or agriculture.

ALASKA FACTS

Nickname Last Frontier

Population 670,053

Area 591,004 sq miles

Capital city Juneau (population 30,737)

Sales tax There is no state sales tax in Alaska, but many cities have their own and they vary widely

Official state symbols forget-me-not (flower), North to the Future (motto), mushing (sport)

Birthplace of Singer and poet Jewel (b 1974), cartoonist Virgil F Partch (1916–84)

Home of The Iditarod; the 'Last Great Race' is the world's longest dogsled event

Famous for Its size (if split in half, Alaska would still be the largest two states in the USA), Eskimos (Inuit)

Giant Veggies The largest cabbage ever grown in Alaska, a 105.6lb-er that was 6ft across and 4ft high, won top prize in the Alaska State Fair in 2000

ALASKA IN...

One Week

From Washington state, hop on one of the Alaska Marine Highway ferries for a cruise through **Southeast Alaska** (p1059). Spend a day in **Petersburg** (p1061) for whale-watching and three days in **Juneau** (p1063) to check out its great hiking and glaciers. Jump back on the Alaska Marine Highway to Skagway and relive the **Klondike gold rush** (p1067).

Two Weeks

Fly to **Anchorage** (p1068), rent a car and beat it out of town. Head south and follow the beautiful Seward Hwy to **Seward** (p1075) and go kayaking in Resurrection Bay. Continue the road trip by driving to artsy **Homer** (p1076). Begin the second week in Anchorage exploring Alaska's biggest city, then jump on the Alaska Railroad for charming **Talkeetna** (p1080). Continue north on the train to spend three days in **Denali National Park** (p1081), viewing wildlife and hopefully Mt McKinley.

Wilderness Cabins

Explore the Southeast wilderness by reserving rustic **National Forest cabins** (☎ 877-444-6777; www.reserveusa.com). The Anan Bay Cabin near Wrangell includes an observatory where you can watch bears feed on salmon. A short flight from Juneau delivers you to West Turner Lake Cabin, a classic log structure overlooking the lake. At the White Sulphur Springs Cabin near Sitka, you can spend the evenings sipping wine and soaking in hot springs

---

LAND & CLIMATE

Be prepared for a big state – Alaska is huge. Or, as residents love to point out: if Alaska was divided in half it would become the largest two states in the country, dropping Texas to third. At latitudes spanning the Arctic Circle, the main body of Alaska is about 800 sq miles, with the arc of the Aleutian Islands chain stretching some 1600 miles south and west, and a 'panhandle' strip running 600 miles southeast down the North American coast.

The coastal regions, such as Southeast and Prince William Sound, have lush coniferous forests, while the Interior is dominated by boreal forest of white spruce, cottonwood and birch. Further north is a taiga zone – a moist, subarctic forest characterized by muskeg, willow thickets and stunted spruce – then the treeless Arctic tundra, with grass, mosses and a variety of tiny flowers thriving briefly in summer.

Alaska's size is the reason for its extremely variable climate. The Interior can top 90°F (32°C) during the summer, while the Southeast and Southcentral maritime regions will average 55°F (13°C) to 70°F (21°C). In the Southeast it rains almost daily from late September through October, while even a week of good weather in the summer will include a day or two when you need to pull out your rain gear. In winter, residents experience long nights, -50°F (-55°C) temperatures and the mesmerizing northern lights.

The peak tourist season is early July to mid-August, when the best-known parks are packed and it's essential to make reservations for ferries and accommodations. May and September still have mild weather, it's less crowded and prices are lower.

PARKS & WILDLIFE

Alaska has land to roam and plenty of parks to do it in. Within the state the National Park Service (NPS) administers 54 million acres as national parks, preserves and monuments. The most popular national parks are Klondike Gold Rush National Historical Park in Skagway (p1067), Denali National Park in the Interior (p1081) and Kenai Fjords National Park near Seward (p1076).

Various agencies administer Alaska's parks, refuges and forests. The US Forest Service administers Tongass National Forest; US Fish & Wildlife Service manages Kenai National Wildlife Refuge; while the Bureau of Land Management is responsible for White Mountains National Recreation Area. State parks account for another 3 million acres, and most offer camping, hiking and paddling. At 773 sq miles, Chugach State Park (on the edge of Anchorage) is the country's third-largest state park.

ALASKA

All the above agencies have wilderness cabins you can rent (see Information below) and plenty of places to watch wildlife. On land, Alaska's most popular species to view are moose, bears and bald eagles. Harder to spot are caribou, which inhabit the Interior in large herds; mountain goats and Dall sheep, which also live in remote areas; and wolves, which are reclusive by nature. Marine life includes seals, porpoises, whales, sea otters and walruses. During summer, millions of spawning salmon fill rivers and streams.

INFORMATION

The **Alaska Travel Industry Association** (www.travel alaska.com) is the official tourism marketing arm for the state and publishes a vacation planner with listings of B&Bs, motels, tours and more. Another source for statewide tourist information is the **Alaska Information Resource Center** (www.stateofalaska.com), which has weather reports, links to state newspapers and ferry, air and train schedules online.

The best place for information on national parks, state parks and all public land agencies along with their cabin rental programs is one of the four Alaska Public Lands Information Centers (APLICs) scattered around the state. Anchorage has the largest **APLIC** (☎ 907-271-2737; www.nps.gov/aplic/center) and is the best one to contact in advance of your trip.

ACTIVITIES

Alaska is many things, but first and foremost it is the great outdoors. Travelers go there for the mountains, the trails, the wildlife, the camping – the adventure. Hiking trails are boundless and they're the best way to escape the summer crowds in places like Juneau and the Kenai Peninsula. Mountain biking is allowed on many trails, and bikes can be rented throughout the state. You can also rent kayaks in coastal towns like Ketchikan, Sitka, Juneau, Seward and Valdez, where paddlers enjoy sea kayaking in protective fjords, often within view of glaciers. Other popular outdoor activities are white-water rafting, wildlife watching, canoeing, fishing and just pulling over on the road and admiring the scenery.

GETTING THERE & AROUND
Air

The vast majority of visitors to Alaska, and almost all international flights, fly into **Ted Stevens Anchorage International Airport** (www.dot .state.ak.us/anc). **Alaska Airlines** (AS; ☎ 800-426-0333; www.alaskaair.com) has direct flights to Anchorage from Seattle, Chicago and many West Coast cities. Other airlines also offer direct flights, including **Northwest** (NW; ☎ 800-225-2525; www.nwa.com) from Minneapolis, **Delta** (DL; ☎ 800-221-1212; www.delta.com) from Atlanta and New York, and **American Airlines** (AA; ☎ 800-443-7300; www.aa.com) from St Louis and Dallas. Within the state, Alaska Airlines serves many towns, while 'bush planes' can be chartered to the most remote areas.

Boat

The **Alaska Marine Highway** (☎ 800-642-0066; www .ferryalaska.com) connects Bellingham, WA, with 14 towns in Southeast Alaska and is a very popular way to travel to this roadless region. The ferries also service six towns in South-central Alaska, and make six runs a year from Kodiak to Unalaska in the Aleutian Islands and from Whittier to Juneau.

Bus

Bus services link all the main towns in Alaska, with connections to the lower 48. Traveling by bus is not that much cheaper than flying, but you do get to experience the Alaska Hwy. From Seattle, WA, **Greyhound** (☎ 206-628-5526; www.greyhound.com; cnr 8th Ave & Stewart St) can get you to Whitehorse, Canada, via Vancouver. From Whitehorse, **Alaska Direct** (☎ 800-770-6652; www.alaskadirectbusline .com; 509 Main St) leaves three days a week for Anchorage.

Car

Be sure to allow at least a week to drive from northern USA through Canada to Fairbanks on the mostly paved Alcan Hwy. It's not worth the time it takes unless you can make some stops along the way and spend a few weeks in Alaska. Local rental cars are handy to get around the countryside; they start at $45 a day, with 100 miles free.

Train

The **Alaska Railroad** (☎ 907-265-2494, 800-544-0552; www.akrr.com) offers service between Seward and Anchorage and from Anchorage to Denali, before ending in Fairbanks. Book seats early on this popular train.

SOUTHEAST ALASKA

The Southeast is as close as Alaska comes to continental USA, but most of it is inaccessible by road. It's possible to fly to the panhandle for a quick visit, but a better option if you can spare a week or two is to cruise the Inside Passage, a waterway made up of thousands of islands, glacier-filled fjords and a mountainous coastline. You can jump on a state ferry and stop at a handful of ports for hiking, kayaking and whale-watching.

Getting There & Around

AIR

Alaska Airlines (☎ 800-426-0333; www.alaskaair.com) has daily northbound and southbound flights year-round, with stops at all main towns. Round-trip advance-purchase fares include Seattle–Ketchikan, Anchorage–Juneau and Ketchikan–Juneau. Smaller airlines serving the region include **LAB Flying Service** (☎ 907-789-9160; www.labflying.com), **Taquan Air** (☎ 907-225-8800, 800-770-8800; www.taquanair.com) and **Wings of Alaska** (☎ 907-789-0790; www.wingsofalaska.com).

BOAT

Alaska Marine Highway (☎ 800-642-0066; www.ferry alaska.com) calls on the main towns almost daily in summer. The complete trip, from Bellingham, WA, to Haines ($353 per person) stops at ports along the way and must be scheduled in advance. Trips within the Inside Passage include Ketchikan–Petersburg ($60), Sitka–Juneau ($45) and Juneau–Haines ($37). Alaska Marine Highway ferries are equipped to handle cars (Bellingham–Haines $797), but space must be reserved months ahead.

You can also pick up the state ferries from Prince Rupert, British Columbia, to Ketchikan ($60), or twice a month join the special runs across the Gulf of Alaska from Juneau to Whittier ($221).

TRAIN

The narrow-gauge 1890s **White Pass & Yukon Railroad** (☎ 800-343-7373; www.whitepassrailroad.com) links Skagway and Fraser, British Columbia, with a bus connection to Whitehorse, which is situated on the Alcan Hwy ($106).

KETCHIKAN

Ketchikan, the first stop of the Alaska Marine Highway, is a thin town: several miles long, never more than 10 blocks wide and crammed with Alaskan character, adventure and the scenery you came looking for.

Ketchican Visitors Bureau (☎ 907-225-6166, 800-770-3300; www.visit-ketchikan.com; 131 Front St; 🕑 7am-5pm) Helpful staff will book tours and accommodations.

Seaport Cyberstation (☎ 907-247-4615; 5 Salmon Landing; per hr $6; 🕑 8am-7pm) Access the internet here.

Southeast Alaska Discovery Center (☎ 907-228-6220; 50 Main St; adult/child $5/free; 🕑 8am-5pm) Houses an impressive exhibit hall; provides details of outdoor activities.

Sights & Activities

Learn about all things salmon from the observation decks of the **Deer Mountain Tribal Hatchery & Eagle Center** (☎ 907-225-5158, 800-252-5158; 1158 Salmon Rd; adult/child $9/free; 🕑 8am-4:30pm). The eagle center allows you to get up close and personal with a pair of injured eagles who can no longer fly.

The star of the former red-light district of Creek St is **Dolly's House** (☎ 907-225-6329; 24 Creek St; adult/child $5/free; 🕑 8am-5pm), the parlor of Ketchikan's most famous madam, Dolly Arthur. The **Totem Heritage Center** (☎ 907-225-5900; 601 Deermont St; adult/child $5/free; 🕑 8am-5pm) features a collection of 19th-century totems in a spiritual setting.

The 3-mile **Deer Mountain Trail** begins near the city center and provides access to the alpine world above the timberline and wonderful views of the town. There are more trails in the **Ward Lake Recreation Area**. **Southeast Sea Kayaks** (☎ 907-225-1258, 800-287-1607; www.kayakketchikan .com; 1007 Water St; single/double kayak per day $45/60, day trip $89-199) offers rentals and guided trips.

Sleeping

Ketchikan Hostel (☎ 907-225-3319; 400 Main St; dm $15; ✗) A friendly, clean hostel that is always bustling in the summer.

New York Hotel (☎ 907-225-0246, 866-225-0246; www.thenewyorkhotel.com; 207 Stedman St; s/d $114/129; ✗ 🖳) A historic inn in the heart of town but far enough from the cruise-ship crowds for a quiet setting.

Gilmore Hotel (☎ 907-225-9423, 800-275-9423; www .gilmorehotel.com; 326 Front St; d $120-160; 🖳) Built in 1927, the Gilmore has 38 rooms that still retain a historical flavor but include cable TV, coffeemakers and hair dryers.

Cape Fox Lodge (☎ 907-225-8001, 866-225-8001; www.westcoasthotels.com/capefox; 800 Venetia Way; r $190-200) Ketchikan's splashiest lodging comes with hilltop views.

ALASKA

IF YOU HAVE A FEW MORE DAYS

Real Alaska is only a three-hour ferry ride away from the cruise-ship madness of Ketchikan. Prince of Wales Island, the third-largest island in the USA, features Native Alaskan villages, the Southeast's most extensive road network and a lot of clear-cuts, but no cruise ships. For information, **Prince of Wales Chamber of Commerce** (☎ 907-755-2626; www.princeofwalescoc.org; Klawock Bell Tower Mall, Craig-Klawock Hwy; ☺ 10am-3pm Mon-Fri) is in Klawock and a **USFS office** (☎ 907-826-3271; 900 9th St; ☺ 8am-5pm Mon-Fri) is in Craig.

Bring a mountain bike and you can spend a week exploring the 300 miles of paved and graded gravel roads or the 1800 miles of shot-rock logging roads. Bring a kayak and you can do the same along 990 miles of contorted coastline. Or rent either one from **A5 Outdoor Recreation** (☎ 907-329-2399; www.a5outdoorrec.com; 103A Sea Otter Dr, Coffman Cove; bike per day $35, single/double kayak $50/60).

In Craig, stay at **Ruth Ann's Hotel** (☎ 907-826-3378; cnr Main & Water Sts; r $90-125; ☒) or the delightful **Inn of the Blue Heron** (☎ 907-826-3608; 406 9th St; s $79-99, d $94-114; ☒).

The **M/V Prince of Wales** (☎ 866-308-4848; www.interislandferry.com; adult/child $32/18) makes the Hollis–Ketchikan run twice a day. The main communities of Klawock and Craig are 25 miles and 31 miles southwest of Hollis respectively. Sister ship **M/V Stikine** (adult/child $32/18) provides service between Wrangell and Coffman Cove at the northern end of the island.

Eating & Drinking

Good Fortune (☎ 907-225-1818; 4 Creek St; lunch specials $7, dinner $8-14; ☺ 9am-9pm) Head upstairs in Ketchikan's best Chinese restaurant to feast on double mushroom pork while watching the cruise-ship crowds on Creek St.

our pick **That One Place** (207 Stedman St; breakfast $7-10, lunch $8-13; ☺ 8am-4pm; ☒) A wonderful café at the New York Hotel, where practically everything on the lunch menu is seafood-related. Locals rave about the halibut tacos.

Bar Harbor Restaurant (☎ 907-225-2813; 2813 Tongass Ave; lunch $9-12, dinner $16-22; ☺ 11am-2pm & 5-9pm Mon-Sat; ☒) A cozy place between downtown and the ferry terminal with a menu that is intriguingly eclectic – from halibut burritos to coconut prawns with a marmalade sauce. For the three days it's not raining, there's an outdoor deck.

First City Saloon (☎ 907-225-1494; 830 Water St) A sprawling place with giant-screen TVs, 20 beers on tap, pool tables and live music.

Getting There & Around

Alaska Airlines and Alaska Marine Highway ferries service Ketchikan (see p1059). For wheels, try **Alaska Car Rental** (☎ 907-225-5123, 800-662-0007; 2828 Tongass Ave; per day $53).

AROUND KETCHIKAN

Ten miles north of Ketchikan, **Totem Bight State Historical Park** (☎ 907-247-8574; admission free; ☺ 6am-10pm) contains 14 restored totem poles and a historic **longhouse** (admission free; ☺ 8am-8pm).

Misty Fjords National Monument begins 22 miles east of Ketchikan, offering wildlife-watching and spectacular views of 3000ft sheer granite walls that rise from the ocean. **Alaska Travel Adventures** (☎ 907-225-6044, 800-228-1905; www.mistyfjord.net; adult/child $139/86) runs a six-hour trip around the monument. **Island Wings** (☎ 907-225-2444, 888-854-2444; www.islandwings.com; tour $325) combines flightseeing and hiking in the monument's lush old-growth forests.

WRANGELL

Wrangell already had strong ties to the Tlingit, the Russians and the British when the Americans took over the fort in 1868. Today Wrangell is one the few ports where the state ferries dock downtown, so at the very least jump off the boat for a quick look around town.

The **visitor center** (☎ 907-874-3901, 800-367-9745; www.wrangell.com; 296 Outer Dr; ☺ 10am-4pm Mon-Fri) is in the Nolan Center. Also at the center is the impressive **Wrangell Museum** (☎ 907-874-3770; 296 Outer Dr; adult/child/family $5/3/12; ☺ 10am-5pm Mon-Sat), where you can learn about gold-rush Wrangell or why Wyatt Earp filled in as the town's deputy marshal for 10 days. In the middle on the harbor is **Chief Shakes Island**, with six totems and a tribal house.

Sleeping & Eating

The **City Park Campground** (Zimovia Hwy; campsite free), 1.75 miles south of the ferry terminal, is a delightful place to pitch a tent, while **Wrangell Hostel** (☎ 907-874-3534; 220 Church St; dm $18; ✗) is in the Presbyterian church.

Hardings Old Sourdough Lodge (☎ 907-874-3613, 800-874-3613; www.akgetaway.com; 1104 Peninsula St; s/d $94/104; ✗) This is the nicest place to stay, with its home-style meals, attentive hosts and a sauna and steam bath to mellow out in before dinner.

Stikine Inn (☎ 907-874-3388, 888-874-3388; 107 Stikine Ave; s/d $101/114; ✗) The largest hotel in town, conveniently located near the ferry dock. All 33 rooms have private bathrooms and many have a view of the water ($10 extra).

Diamond C Café (☎ 907-874-3677; 223 Front St; breakfast $4-10; ☺ 6am-3pm; ✗) Where locals head for breakfast or to satisfy their deep-fried, deep-sea craving.

Stikine Inn Restaurant (☎ 907-874-2353; 107 Stikine Ave; lunch $8-13, dinner $12-22; ☺ 7am-9pm; ✗) Offers local seafood right off the boats and a panoramic view of Zimovia Strait.

PETERSBURG

At the north end of spectacular Wrangell Narrows lies the picturesque community of Petersburg, a town known for its Norwegian roots and home to Alaska's largest halibut fleet.

The **Petersburg Chamber of Commerce** (☎ 907-772-4636; www.petersburg.org; cnr Fram & 1st Sts; ☺ 9am-5pm Mon-Sat, noon-4pm Sun) has B&B and USFS information. You can also visit the **USFS office** (☎ 907-772-3871; Federal Bldg, Nordic Dr; ☺ 8am-5pm Mon-Fri).

Sights & Activities

The center of old Petersburg was **Sing Lee Alley**, which winds past weathered homes and boathouses perched on pilings above the water. The **Clausen Memorial Museum** (☎ 907-772-3598; 203 Fram St; adult/child $3/free; ☺ 10am-5pm Mon-Sat) features local artifacts and fishing relics, and a small but excellent museum store.

There are kayaking opportunities, ranging from day paddles to week-long adventures. **Tongass Kayak Adventures** (☎ 907-772-4600; www.tongasskayak.com; single/double kayak $55/65) offers rentals and drop-off transportation, as well as several guided paddles, including a day paddle at **LeConte Glacier** ($225), North America's southernmost tidewater glacier and often a spectacular scene of falling ice and breaching whales.

ALASKA

HOT TOPIC: THE CANARIES OF THE ARCTIC

Many environmentalists contend that the Arctic is global warming's 'canary in the mine'. If that is so, the small bird itself is the largest bear in the world. Scientists say the earth's rising temperature, due in a large part to human activities such as driving cars and burning coal, has had an immediate and profound effect on the Arctic.

Studies have shown that the average winter temperature in the Arctic has increased 7°F (13°C) in the last 50 years. Permafrost – ground that is continually frozen for at least two years – is thawing, and the Arctic sea ice is melting. The US National Center for Atmospheric Research estimates that by 2040 the Arctic Ocean will be ice-free in the summer.

All this is bad news for the world's 20,000 polar bears. In short, their home is melting.

Polar bears are the world's largest terrestrial carnivore, with some males reaching a height of 12ft and weighing more than 1,400lbs. The bears depend on sea ice for their survival. They hunt their primary prey, the ringed seal, from the ice. They travel, mate and sometimes even give birth on the ice.

The fast retreat of Arctic ice has already greatly affected this species. The delay in freeze-up causes polar bears to lose critical fat reserves, affecting reproduction and the ability of pregnant females to produce enough milk for their cubs. Canadian scientists documented a 15% drop in birth rates in the Hudson Bay area, while in Alaska the US Minerals Management Service has concluded that polar bears are drowning as they try to swim increasingly long distances between the ice and land. In Barrow bears are wandering into town like never before.

The facts are indisputable: in 2006, the US Department of the Interior proposed that polar bears be added to the endangered species list. If the bears receive such federal protection, they would be the first US mammals officially deemed to be in danger of extinction because of global warming. Still, some scientists say this is too little to late, claiming that in 10 to 15 years the world's only polar bears will be living in zoos.

Sleeping & Eating

Alaska Island Hostel (☎ 907-772-3632, 877-772-3632; www.alaskaislandhostel.com; 805 Gjoa St; dm $23; ✗ ☐) A friendly place, 1.5 miles from the ferry terminal. It offers four-person dorm rooms, a laundry, a kitchen and an outdoor grill in case you hook a big one.

Tides Inn (☎ 907-772-4288, 800-665-8433; www.tidesinnalaska.com; 307 1st St; s/d $80/90; ☐) The town's longtime, centrally located motel, offering 45 rooms. A small continental breakfast is included.

Scandia House (☎ 907-772-4281, 800-722-5006; www.scandiahousehotel.com; 110 N Nordic Dr; s/d $100/120; ☐) Petersburg's most upscale hotel, offering a view of the harbor, a courtesy van to pick you up and freshly baked muffins in the morning.

Coastal Cold Storage (☎ 907-772-4177, 306 Nordic Dr; lunch $7-9; ✆ 6am-5:30pm Mon-Sat, 7am-2pm Sun) Has the best seafood salads, chowders and halibut sandwiches in this seafood town.

Rooney's Northern Lights Restaurant (☎ 907-772-2900; 203 Sing Lee Alley; breakfast $5-10, dinner $16-30; ✆ 6am-10pm; ✗) Overlooks a bustling harbor; all the crab, halibut and shrimp on its seafood platter are locally caught.

Kito's Kave (☎ 907-772-3207; 11 Sing Lee Alley; dinner $10-12) Serves Petersburg's best Mexican and later at night live music and dancing.

SITKA

Russians established Southeast Alaska's first nonindigenous settlement here in 1799, and the town flourished on fur. Today Sitka sees itself as both the cultural center of the Southeast and its most beautiful city, because it's the only one facing the Pacific Ocean.

The **Sitka Convention & Visitors Bureau** (☎ 907-747-5940; www.sitka.org; 330 Harbor Dr; ✆ 8am-5pm Mon-Fri) is located across the street from St Michael's Cathedral, and also staffs a desk in the Centennial Building. The **USFS office** (☎ 907-747-6671; 204 Siginaka Way; ✆ 8am-4:30pm Mon-Fri) can provide hiking and kayaking information for the area.

Sights & Activities

Sitka National Historical Park has a gorgeous trail that winds past 15 totem poles, while its **visitor center** (☎ 907-747-0110; Lincoln St; adult/child $4/free; ✆ 8am-5pm) features Russian and indigenous artifacts and traditional carving demonstrations. For an eye-to-eye encounter with a bald eagle, head to the nearby **Alaska Raptor Center**

(☎ 907-747-8662, 800-643-9425; www.alaskaraptor.org; 101 Sawmill Creek Rd; adult/child $12/6; ✆ 8am-4pm) where injured birds relearn to fly in its flight training center.

St Michael's Cathedral (☎ 907-747-8120; 240 Lincoln St; admission $2; ✆ 9am-4pm Mon-Fri) is a replica of the original 1840s Russian Orthodox cathedral destroyed by fire in 1966; priceless treasures were salvaged by residents. Castle Hill is the site of **Baranof's Castle**, where Alaska was officially transferred from Russia to the USA. Built in 1842, the **Russian Bishop's House** (☎ 907-747-6281; Lincoln St; adult/child $4/free; ✆ 9am-5pm) is Sitka's oldest intact Russian building. **Sheldon Jackson Museum** (☎ 907-747-8981; 104 College Dr; adult/child $4/free; ✆ 9am-5pm), on the college campus, houses an excellent indigenous culture collection.

Sitka has superb hiking, and the **Gaven Hill Trail** into the mountains is accessible from the downtown area. There are also many kayaking trips around Baranof and Chichagof Islands. **Sitka Sound Ocean Adventures** (☎ 907-747-6365; www.ssoceanadventures.com; single/double kayak $52/62) rents kayaks and runs guided day trips; its office is in a blue bus at the Centennial Building. Thanks to Sitka's ocean location, marine-wildlife boat tours have mushroomed in the town. **Allen Marine Tours** (☎ 907-747-8100, 888-747-8101; www.allenmarinetours.com; adult/child $79/49; ✆ 8:30-11:30am Sat & Sun) offers three-hour tours that often include spotting otters and whales.

Sleeping

The Sitka area has almost 30 B&Bs; the visitor center keeps an updated list.

Sitka HI-AYH Hostel (☎ 907-747-8661; 303 Kimsham St; dm $19; ✗) This church basement facility has a kitchen, a lounge, an eating area and an unbeatable price for a cot.

Karras B&B (☎ 907-747-3978; 230 Kogwanton St; s/d $55/86; ✗) A few blocks from downtown, there are four cozy rooms with shared bath in this private home overlooking picturesque Katlian St.

Sitka Hotel (☎ 907-747-3288; www.sitkahotel.com; 118 Lincoln St; s/d $85/90, with shared bath $65/70; ☐) This venerable hotel is in the heart of downtown and has 60 rooms, which are small but well kept.

Shee Atiká Totem Square Inn (☎ 907-747-3693, 866-300-1353; www.sheeatika.com; 201 Katlian St; r $149; ✗ ☐) Along with 66 rooms, this inn offers free continental breakfast, a full kitchen on the 4th floor and high-speed internet. Its best

---

WORTH THE TRIP: SMALL PORTS IN SOUTHEAST ALASKA

The **LeConte ferry** (☎ 800-642-0066) services a handful of small ports between Sitka and Juneau, offering a chance to experience a Southeast Alaska not overrun by cruise-ship passengers. Stay for a day or two and then hop on a **Wings of Alaska** (☎ 907-789-0790; www.wingsofalaska.com) or **LAB Flying Service** (☎ 907-766-2222; www.labflying.com) flight to return to either city.

On Kupreanof Island, the Native Alaskan beachfront community of **Kake** boasts Alaska's tallest totem pole. Rustic **Tenakee Springs** is known for its relaxed pace, alternative lifestyle and public bathhouse, built around a 108°F (42°C) hot spring. Twice monthly, the *LeConte* travels to the lively fishing town of **Pelican**, on Chichagof Island, a unique day trip from Juneau ($100). Built on pilings over tidelands, Pelican's main street is a mile-long wooden boardwalk.

---

feature, however, is the view from the rooms, which overlook either the historic square or the ocean.

Eating & Drinking

Back Door Café (☎ 907-747-8856; 104 Barracks St; meals under $6; ☽ 6:30am-5pm Mon-Sat, 9am-2pm Sun; ✗) Escape the downtown cruise-ship storm in this hide-away coffeehouse that serves homemade bagels, pastries, soups and sandwiches.

Bayview Restaurant (☎ 907-747-5440; 407 Lincoln St; breakfast $6-10, lunch $8-11, dinner mains $19-27; ☽ 5am-8pm Tue-Sat, 5am-3pm Sun-Mon; ✗) Serves gourmet hamburgers and offers a view of the boat harbor.

Little Tokyo (☎ 907-747-5699 315; Lincoln St; lunch $8-10, fish & tempura rolls $7-12; ☽ 11am-9pm; ✗) Even crew members from the commercial fleet, who know a thing or two about raw fish, say Sitka's only sushi bar is a good catch.

our pick **Ludvig's Bistro** (☎ 907-966-3663; 256 Katlian St; dinner mains $20-33; ☽ 2-10pm Tue-Sat; ✗) A bit of European atmosphere on scenic Katlian St with only seven tables and a handful of stools at a brass-and-blue-tile bar. The women who run it describe their seafood-laden menu as 'rustic Mediterranean fare', and it's by far the most innovative cooking in Sitka.

Pioneer Bar (☎ 907-747-3456; 212 Katlian St) This is the most interesting place to have a beer in Sitka, and is one of Alaska's classic bars. The walls are covered with photos of boats, their crews and big fish, while hanging over the bar is a ship's brass bell. Don't ring it unless you're ready to buy a round.

Getting There & Away

Sitka Airport, on Japonski Island, is served by **Alaska Airlines** (☎ 800-426-0333; www.alaskaair .com). **Northstar Rental** (☎ 907-966-2552, 800-722-6927; Sitka Airport; ☽ 8am-6pm) has compacts for $55 per day. **Alaska Marine Highway** (☎ 907-747-8737, 800-

642-0066; www.ferryalaska.com) ferries stop almost daily at the terminal, which is 7 miles north of town. **Ferry Transit Bus** (☎ 907-747-8443; one-way /round-trip $6/8) will take you into town.

JUNEAU

There's no prettier capital in the country than Alaska's Juneau, whose historic downtown clings to a mountainside beneath snowcapped peaks and its narrow streets lead you past a bustling waterfront. The rest of the city spreads north into the Mendenhall Valley. Juneau is also Alaska's cruise-ship capital and the gateway to many attractions, including Glacier Bay National Park (p1065) and Admiralty Island National Monument (p1065).

Information

Juneau Convention & Visitors Bureau (☎ 907-586-2201, 800-587-2201; www.traveljuneau.com; 101 Egan Dr; ☽ 8am-5pm) In Centennial Hall.

Juneau Ranger Station (☎ 907-586-8751; 8461 Old Dairy Rd; ☽ 8am-5pm Mon-Fri) Has information on cabins, Glacier Bay, Admiralty Island and Tongass National Forest.

Juneau Library (☎ 907-586-5249; 292 Marine Way; ☽ 11am-9pm Mon-Thu, noon-5pm Fri-Sun) Provides internet access.

Sights & Activities

The **Alaska State Museum** (☎ 907-465-2901; 395 Whittier St; adult/child $5/free; ☽ 8:30am-5:30pm) has historical displays and indigenous artifacts, plus a full-size eagles' nest atop a two-story tree.

The **Juneau-Douglas City Museum** (☎ 907-586-3572; 114 W 4th St; adult/child $3/free; ☽ 9am-5pm Mon-Fri, 10am-5pm Sat & Sun) highlights the area's gold-mining history. The **Last Chance Mining Museum** (☎ 907-586-5338; 1001 Basin Rd; admission $5; ☽ 9:30am-12:30pm & 3:30-6:30pm) is an impressive complex of railroad lines, ore cars and repair sheds. The

ALASKA

short hike to **Treadwell Mine ruins**, just south of Douglas, is also very interesting.

About 3 miles north of downtown, the **Macaulay Salmon Hatchery Visitor Center** (☎ 907-463-4810, 877-463-2468; 2697 Channel Dr; adult/child $3.25/1.75; �% 10am-6pm Mon-Fri, 10am-5pm Sat & Sun) has underwater viewing windows that allow you to see fish spawning. Displays explain the salmon life cycle and the operations of the hatchery.

The area's numerous glaciers include **Mendenhall Glacier**, the famous 'drive-in' glacier; the informative **USFS Visitor Center** (☎ 907-789-0097; Glacier Spur Rd; admission $3; �%8am-7:30pm) is 13 miles from the city. **Mendenhall Glacier Transport** (☎ 907-789-5460; one-way $5) runs a bus from downtown to the visitor center.

our pick **West Glacier Trail**, which sidles along Mendenhall Glacier, has the most stunning scenery. Hiking is the most popular activity in the area, and some trails access USFS cabins. **Juneau Parks & Recreation** (☎ 907-586-5226; 155 S Seward St; �%8am-4:30pm) offers free organized hikes. The **Mt Roberts Trail** is the most popular hike to the alpine country above Juneau.

Or skip the hike – the **Mt Roberts Tram** (☎ 907-463-3412, 888-461-8726; 490 S Franklin St; adult/child $22/13; �%9am-9pm) takes passengers from the dock to the timberline, where there is a nature center and a restaurant.

The area is wonderful for kayaking and whale-watching. **Alaska Boat & Kayak** (☎ 907-789-6886; www.juneaukayak.com; 11521 Glacier Hwy; single /double kayak $50/70; �%9am-6pm) rents boats and offers guided day paddles. **Four Seasons Tours** (☎ 907-790-6671, 877-774-8687; www.4seasonsmarine .com; adult/child $139/59) combines whale-watching with a stop for a salmon feast.

The steep-sided Tracy Arm fjord, 50 miles southeast of Juneau, makes an excellent day trip. **Adventure Bound Alaska** (☎ 907-463-2509, 800-228-3875; 215 Ferry Way; adult/child $130/90) runs day cruises.

Sleeping

Downtown accommodations are heavily booked during summer, but Juneau has more than 50 B&Bs; stop at the visitor center to find one.

our pick **Juneau International Hostel** (☎ 907-586-9559; www.juneauhostel.org; 614 Harris St; dm adult/child $10/5; ☒ ▣) Alaska's best hostel is a five-minute walk from the state capitol.

Alaskan Hotel (☎ 907-586-1000, 800-327-9347; www .thealaskanhotel.com; 167 S Franklin St; r with/without bath $60/80; ☒) This lovely historic hotel is located in the heart of the Franklin St nightlife district – great news if you want to party, less so if you're a light sleeper.

Driftwood Lodge (☎ 907-586-2280, 800-544-2239; www.driftwoodalaska.com; 435 Willoughby Ave; r $94; ☒ ▣) The rooms are no-frills but clean, and most have kitchenettes. There's a courtesy airport and ferry van, a coin laundry and bike rental.

Pearson's Pond Luxury Inn (☎ 907-789-33772, 888-658-6328; www.pearsonspond.com; 4541 Sawa Cr; d $300-400; ☒ ▣) One of Juneau's finest places to stay is this small, luxurious inn near the Mendenhall Glacier. For the weary traveler there are fireplace suites, hot tubs and even a spa for an end-of-the-road massage.

Eating & Drinking

Rainbow Foods (☎ 907-586-6476; 224 4th St; sandwiches $8-11; �%9am-7pm Mon-Sat, 9am-6pm Sun; ☒) A cool natural-foods store with a deli that makes a happening lunch spot.

Pel'Meni (Merchant's Wharf on Marine Way; dumplings $5; �%11:30am-1:30am Sun-Thu, 11:30am-3:30am Fri & Sat) Serves one thing and one thing only – bowls of authentic homemade Russian dumplings, filled with either potato or sirloin. Nightowls will like the hours.

Island Pub (☎ 907-364-1595; 1102 2nd St; �%11:30am-10pm Sun-Thu, 11:30am-midnight Fri & Sat; large pizza $13-16) Across the channel in Douglas is the capital city's best pizzeria, serving good focaccias and gourmet pizza accompanied by a mountain view.

Doc Water's Pub (☎ 907-586-3627; 2 Marine Way, Merchant's Wharf; dinner $13-27; �%10:30am-11pm; ☒) If the sun is shining, grab a table outside, watch floatplanes take off and enjoy the best beer-battered halibut in town.

Wild Spice (☎ 907-523-0344; 140 Seward St; dinner $16-28; �%11am-9pm; ☒) Hungry enough for a Mongolian BBQ? Fill your own plate here with fresh veggies, meats, seafood and spices and watch a chef cook it to perfection on an open grill.

Thane Ore House (☎ 907-586-3442; 4400 Thane Rd; dinner mains $23; ☒) Juneau's best salmon bake, 4 miles south of town, is an all-you-can-eat affair in a rustic setting. There's courtesy-van transportation and a small mining museum.

South Franklin St is Juneau's drinking sector. The (in)famous **Red Dog Saloon** (☎ 907-463-3658; 278 S Franklin St) has a sawdust floor and relic-covered walls. Hidden in the **Alaskan Hotel**

(☎ 907-586-1000, 800-327-9347; 167 S Franklin St) is a unique bar with historic ambience and occasional live music.

Getting There & Around

The main airline serving Juneau is **Alaska Air** (☎ 800-426-0333; www.alaskaair.com). Smaller companies like **Wings of Alaska** (☎ 907-789-0790; www.wingsofalaska.com) provide service to isolated communities.

The ferry terminal is located 14 miles from downtown; **M/V LeConte** (☎ 907-465-3941) runs to Hoonah ($33), Angoon ($37), and Tenakee Springs ($35), while the high-speed **M/V Fairweather** (☎ 907-465-3941) connects to Skagway ($50) and Haines ($37).

Juneau's public bus system, **Capital Transit** (☎ 907-789-6901), can take you from the airport to the city center ($1.50), but not the ferry terminal; buses run from 8am to 5pm Monday to Friday. Numerous car-rental places offer pick up/drop off and unlimited mileage. Compacts at **Rent-A-Wreck** (☎ 907-789-4111, 888-843-4111; 2450 C Industrial Blvd) are $40, while **Evergreen Ford** (☎ 907-790-1340; 8895 Mallard St) rents them for slightly more.

ADMIRALTY ISLAND NATIONAL MONUMENT

Fifteen miles southeast of Juneau, this island has 1406 sq miles of designated wilderness, featuring brown bears, eagles, whales, harbor seals and sea lions. Stock up on supplies in Juneau and go to the **Juneau Ranger District office** (☎ 907-586-8790; 8465 Old Dairy Rd; ☉ 8am-5pm Mon-Fri) in Mendenhall Valley for information.

The single settlement on Admiralty Island, **Angoon**, is a dry community with only one café. It's the starting point for the 32-mile Cross Admiralty Canoe Rte to Mole Harbor.

Favorite Bay Inn (☎ 907-788-3123, 800-423-3123; www.favoritebayinn.com; s/d $99/139; ✕) has rooms with shared bath, and will pick up from the ferry terminal.

The best bear-viewing area in Southeast Alaska is at **Pack Creek**, on the eastern side of Admiralty Island. The bears are most abundant from July to August, when the salmon are running, and visitors can watch them feed from an observation tower. The tower is reached by a mile-long trail, usually as part of a guided tour. **Alaska Discovery** (☎ 800-586-1911; www.akdiscovery.com; 5310 Glacier Hwy, Juneau) offers a one-day tour from Juneau ($590 per person) and a three-day trip ($1090).

GLACIER BAY NATIONAL PARK & PRESERVE

Sixteen tidewater glaciers spill from the mountains and fill the sea with icebergs around the famous wilderness of **Glacier Bay National Park & Preserve**. To see the glaciers, most visitors board the **Baranof Winds** (☎ 888-229-8687; www.visitglacierbay.com; $184) for an eight-hour cruise up the West Arm of Glacier Bay.

The only developed hiking trails are in Bartlett Cove, but there is excellent kayaking; rent equipment from **Glacier Bay Sea Kayaks** (☎ 907-697-2257; www.glacierbayseakayaks.com; single/double kayak per day $40/50). **Alaska Discovery** (☎ 800-586-1911; www.akdiscovery.com) and **Spirit Walker Expeditions** (☎ 907-697-2266, 800-529-2937; www.seakayakalaska.com) offer day paddles for $135.

The **park headquarters** (☎ 907-697-2230; www.nps.gov/glba; 1 Park Rd; ☉ 8am-4:30pm Mon-Fri) in Bartlett Cove maintains a free campground and a **visitor center** (☎ 907-697-2627; ☉ 7am-9pm) at the dock, which provides backcountry permits and maps. The park is served by the settlement of **Gustavus** (www.gustavusak.com), which has lodging, restaurants and supplies.

Glacier Bay Lodge (☎ 888-229-8687; www.visitglacierbay.com; 199 Bartlett Cove Rd; r $150-170; ✕) is the only hotel and restaurant at Bartlett Cove.

Gourmet meals with locally caught seafood and homegrown veggies are included with your stay at **Gustavus Inn** (☎ 907-697-2254, 800-649-5220; www.gustavusinn.com; 1 Mile Gustavus Rd; r $185; ✕), while **Puffin B&B** (☎ 907-697-2260; www.puffintravel.com; Wilson Rd; s/d $125; ✕) is the place to rent a cozy cabin in the woods.

A quarter-mile south of the Salmon River Bridge is **Beartrack Mercantile** (☎ 907-697-2358; Dock Rd; ☉ 9am-7pm Mon-Sat, 10:30am-6pm Sun), which has groceries and a deli counter. On a budget? Bring all your own supplies.

Alaska Airlines (☎ 800-252-7522; www.alaskaair.com) has daily flights between Gustavus and Juneau. The Glacier Bay Lodge bus meets flights for $12. **Glacier Bay Tours** (☎ 888-229-8687; www.visitglacierbay.com), which operates the park lodge, also runs a high-speed catamaran between Auke Bay and Bartlett Cove ($140 round-trip) and will carry kayaks at no extra charge.

HAINES

Haines is Southeast Alaska's most scenic departure point and a crucial link to the Alcan Hwy for thousands of RVers every summer on their way to Canada's Yukon Territory and Interior Alaska. The Northwest Trading

Company arrived here in 1878, followed by missionaries, gold prospectors and the US Army, which built its first permanent post in Alaska, Fort Seward, in 1903. The events of WWII – and the resulting construction of Haines Hwy and the Alcan – meant that Haines was finally connected to the rest of America.

Collect information from the **Haines Convention & Visitors Bureau** (☎ 907-766-2234, 800-458-3579; www.haines.ak.us; cnr 2nd Ave & Willard St; ⊙ 8am-6pm Mon-Fri, 9am-5pm Sat & Sun).

Sights & Activities

Haines has the most affordable museums in Alaska, with no admission over $3. The **Sheldon Museum** (☎ 907-766-2366; 11 Main St; adult/child $3/free; ⊙ 10am-5pm Mon-Fri, 1-4pm Sat & Sun) features indigenous artifacts and a gift shop upstairs, and gold-rush relics downstairs. The **American Bald Eagle Foundation** (☎ 907-766-3094; 113 Haines Hwy; adult/child $3/1; ⊙ 10am-6pm Mon-Fri, 1-5am Sat-Sun) displays more than 100 species of animals, including almost two dozen eagles, in their natural habitat. For something quirky, hit the **Hammer Museum** (☎ 907-776-2374; 108 Main St; adult/child $3/free; ⊙ 10am-5pm Mon-Fri), a 1200-hammer monument to owner Dave Pahl's obsession with the tool.

Get walking-tour maps of the **Fort Seward** national historical site from the visitor center. Within the fort, the **Alaska Indian Arts Center** (☎ 907-766-2160; Historical Bldg 13; admission free; ⊙ 9am-5pm Mon-Fri) has carving and weaving demonstrations.

Haines offers two major hiking-trail systems (the visitor center has details) and numerous rafting trips. **Chilkat Guides** (☎ 907-766-2491; www.raftalaska.com; adult/child $79/62) runs a four-hour Chilkat River raft float, while **Alaska Mountain Guides** (☎ 907-766-3366, 800-766-3396; Portage St; single or double per day $50) rents kayaks and offers guided kayaking trips.

Sleeping

Bear Creek Cabins & Hostel (☎ 907-766-2259; www.bearcreekcabinsalaska.com; Small Tract Rd; campsites/dm/cabins $14/18/48; ✕) To escape the metropolis of Haines head a mile out of town to this pleasant hostel on the edge of the woods.

Hotel Hälsingland (☎ 907-766-2000, 800-542-6363; www.hotelhalsingland.com; 13 Fort Seward Dr; d $119, with shared bath $69; ✕) This classic building in Fort Seward combines historic rooms with an excellent restaurant and a friendly bar.

On the Beach Inn (☎ 907-766-3992; www.onthebeachinn.com; 6.5 Mile Lutak Rd; r $75-125, cabins $65; ✕) After a day of climbing the mountains relax on a porch overlooking Lynn Canal at this B&B near the ferry terminal.

Fort Seward Bed & Breakfast (☎ 766-2856, 800-615-6676; www.fortsewardalaska.com; s & d $85-135; ✕) In the restored former home of the army's surgeon, this B&B has a colorful innkeeper, lots of rooms, free bikes and wonderful sourdough pancakes in the morning.

Captain's Choice Motel (☎ 907-766-3111, 800-478-2345; www.capchoice.com; 108 2nd Ave; s/d $110/120; ✕ 🖳) Nicest motel in town, with a huge sun deck that overlooks the bay.

Eating & Drinking

Chilkat Restaurant & Bakery (☎ 907-766-3653; Dalton St at 5th Ave; breakfast $6-8, lunch $7-8; ⊙ 7am-3pm Mon-Tue & Thu-Sat; ✕) A popular place that has been baking goodies and serving breakfast for 25 years. Skip the eggs and toast and try the homemade granola with blueberries.

Mountain Market & Deli (☎ 907-766-3340; 151 3rd Ave S; sandwiches $7; ⊙ 7am-7pm Mon-Fri, 7am-6pm Sat & Sun; ✕) Great coffee, innovative wraps, cool atmosphere.

Fireweed Restaurant (☎ 907-766-3838; Blacksmith St; pasta $14-20, pizza $10-22; ⊙ 11am-10pm Tue-Sat; ✕) A bright, laid-back bistro with produce straight from the restaurant's own garden. Try the grilled halibut burger.

Grizzly Greg's Pizzeria (☎ 907-766-3622; 126 Main St; small pizzas $12; ⊙ 11am-9pm; ✕) The best pizza in town; try the Grizzly Combo calzone stuffed with eight toppings. Big enough to feed a grizzly.

Haines is a hard-drinking town. Get lively with the locals at **Fogcutter Bar** (☎ 907-766-2555; Main St) or **Harbor Bar** (☎ 907-766-2444; 2 Front St).

Getting There & Away

Several air-charter companies service Haines, the cheapest being **Wings of Alaska** (☎ 907-789-0790; www.wingsofalaska.com). Also check with **LAB Flying Service** (☎ 907-766-2222, 800-426-0543; www.labflying.com), which offers an hour of Glacier Bay National Park flightseeing for $140 (minimum two people).

Chilkat Cruises (☎ 907-766-3395, 888-766-2103; www.chilkatcruises.com; one-way adult/child $30/15) will get you to and from Skagway.

Eagle Nest Car Rentals (☎ 907-766-2891, 800-354-6009; 1183 Haines Hwy), in the Eagle Nest Motel, has cars available for $50 with 100 miles included.

AROUND HAINES

The 75-sq-mile **Alaska Chilkat Bald Eagle Preserve**, along the Chilkat River, protects the world's largest-known gathering of bald eagles. The greatest numbers of birds are spotted in December and January, but you can see eagles here any time during summer. Lookouts on the Haines Hwy between Miles 18 and 22 allow motorists to glimpse the birds. **Alaska Nature Tours** (☎ 907-766-2876; www.kcd.com/aknature; 103 2nd Ave S) offers a three-hour tour of the preserve (adult/child $60/45).

SKAGWAY

The northern terminus of the Alaska Marine Highway, Skagway was a gold-rush town infamous for its lawlessness. In 1887 the population was two; 10 years later it was Alaska's largest city, with 20,000 residents. Today, Skagway survives entirely on tourism and gets packed when a handful of cruise ships pull in and thousands passengers converge on the town as if the Klondike gold rush was still on.

Information

Skagway Convention & Visitors Bureau (☎ 907-983-2854, 888-762-1898; www.skagway.com; cnr Broadway St & 2nd Ave; ☼ 8am-6pm Mon-Fri, 8am-5pm Sat, 9am-6pm Sun) In the Arctic Brotherhood Hall – just look for the thousands of driftwood pieces tacked on to its front.

Klondike Gold Rush National Historical Park Visitors Center (☎ 907-983-9223; www.nps.gov/klgo; 154 Broadway St; ☼ 8am-6pm) Provides information on the Chilkoot Trail (Alaska's most popular hiking trail because it was used by stampeders during the Klondike gold rush), local trails and camping.

Sights & Activities

The **Klondike Gold Rush National Historical Park** is a seven-block corridor along Broadway St that features 15 restored buildings, false fronts and wooden sidewalks from Skagway's golden era as a boom town. Thanks to the cruise ships, it's the most popular national park in Alaska. To best appreciate this amazing moment in Skagway's history, join a free, ranger-led walking tour that begins at the park visitor center on the hour from 9am to 3pm, except at noon.

The **Skagway Museum** (☎ 907-983-2420; Skagway City Hall, cnr 7th Ave & Spring St; adult/child $2/1; ☼ 9am-5pm Mon-Fri, 10am-5pm Sat, 10am-4pm Sun) is one of the best in Southeast, and its gold-rush relics are some of the most interesting exhibits in

a town filled with museums. **Moore's Cabin** (cnr 5th Ave & Spring St; admission free; ☼ 10am-5pm) is the town's oldest building, while **Mascot Saloon** (290 Broadway St; admission free; ☼ 8am-6pm) is a museum devoted to Skagway's heyday as the 'roughest place in the world.'

our pick **White Pass & Yukon Railroad** (☎ 907-983-2217, 800-343-7373; www.wpyr.com; 231 2nd Ave; adult/child $98/49) offers the best tour: the three-hour Summit Excursion climbs the high White Pass in a historic narrow-gauge train.

Sleeping

Skagway Home Hostel (☎ 907-983-2131; www.skagwayhostel.com; 456 3rd Ave; dm $15-20, r $50; ☒ ☐) A half-mile from the ferry terminal, this is a relaxed if somewhat cluttered hostel with kitchen and laundry facilities.

Cindy's Place (☎ 907-983-2674, 800-831-8095; www.alaska.net/~croland; Mile 1 Dyea Rd; cabin $49-120) Two miles from town are Cindy's cabins, three log units tucked away in the forest, each with a fridge, a microwave and a coffeemaker. At night you can soak in a hot tub among the towering pines. Ahhhh!

Sgt Preston's Lodge (☎ 907-983-2521, 866-983-2521; 370 6th Ave; d $80-150; ☒ ☐) A quiet, single-level motel just far enough from Broadway St to escape most of the cruise-ship crush.

At the White House (☎ 907-983-9000; www.atthewhitehouse.com; cnr Main St & 8th Ave; r $125-150; ☒) Step into the past with a night at this 10-room inn, built in 1902 and filled with antiques. The rooms are comfortable, and every morning begins with a delicious breakfast buffet.

Eating & Drinking

Haven Café (☎ 907-983-3553; 9th Ave at State St; breakfast $3-7, salads $7.50, panini $8; ☼ 6am-8pm; ☒) A great place to kick back and plan your next move. A bulletin board in the foyer provides insight into local life while the espresso is potent and the panini sandwiches and salads large.

Glacial Smoothies & Espresso (☎ 907-983-3223; 336 3rd Ave; breakfast $4-7; ☼ 6am-6pm; ☒) Serves lattes and great Belgian waffles, and has internet access.

Stowaway Café (☎ 907-983-3463; 205 Congress Way; dinner $16-25; ☼ 4-10pm ☒) Near the Harbor Master's office, this funky and fantastic café serves better fish and seafood gumbo than anywhere else in the Southeast.

Skagway Fish Company (☎ 907-983-3474; Congress Way; lunch $10-14, dinner $17-35; ☼ 11am-10pm) Located

---

DON'T MISS: THE CHILKOOT TRAIL

The **Chilkoot** is the most famous trail in Alaska and often the most popular. It was the route used by the Klondike gold miners in the 1898 gold rush, and walking it is not so much a wilderness adventure as a history lesson. The 34-mile trek takes three to four days and includes the Chilkoot Pass – a steep climb up to 3525ft that has most hikers scrambling on all fours. The highlight of the hike for many is riding the historic White Pass & Yukon Route Railroad (p1067) from Lake Bennett back to Skagway. There are cheaper ways to return, but don't pass up the train. Experiencing the Chilkoot and returning on the WP&YR is probably the ultimate Alaska trek, combining great scenery, a historical site and an incredible sense of adventure.

Interested? Stop at the **Chilkoot Trail Center** (☎ 907-983-3655; Broadway St; ☷ 8am-5pm) to obtain backpacking permits and set up the hike. Then cross the street to WP&YR depot to book a seat on the train.

---

next to the Stowaway Café, Skagway's newest restaurant is arguably its best. Despite a menu loaded with seafood, what locals rave about are its ribs – great barbecue even if you weren't in Alaska.

Red Onion Saloon (☎ 907-983-2222; 205 Broadway St) This former brothel is now Skagway's liveliest bar. Naturally.

Getting There & Away

LAB Flying Service (☎ 907-983-2471; www.labflying .com), **Wings of Alaska** (☎ 907-983-2442; www.wingsof alaska.com) and **Skagway Air** (☎ 907-983-2218; www .skagwayair.com) have regular flights between Skagway and Juneau ($100), Haines ($50) and Glacier Bay ($130).

Alaska Marine Highway (☎ 907-983-2941, 800-642-0066; www.ferryalaska.com) has ferries departing every day in summer, and **Chilkat Cruises & Tours** (☎ 888-766-2103; www.chilkatcruises.com; one-way adult/ child $30/15) runs twice daily to Haines.

Sourdough Car Rentals (☎ 907-983-2523; cnr Broadway St & 6th Ave; ☷ 8am-5pm) has both cars ($50) and bikes ($10).

Alaska Direct (☎ 800-770-6652; www.alaskadirect busline.com) connects Skagway with Fairbanks three times a week ($230), with buses stopping at Whitehorse along the way ($50).

The **White Pass & Yukon Railroad** (☎ 800-343-7373; www.whitepassrailroad.com) goes to Fraser, British Columbia, where there's a bus connection to Whitehorse (adult/child $106/53).

SOUTHCENTRAL ALASKA

Southcentral Alaska is where Alaskans and travelers alike come to play. There are mountains, glaciers, good fishing, great hiking and kayaking and lots of campgrounds to stay at. Even better, there are roads between towns and other regions of the state, making Southcentral Alaska one of the most accessible places to visit.

ANCHORAGE

Anchorage offers the comforts of a large US city but is only a 30-minute drive from the Alaskan wilderness. Founded in 1914 as a work camp for the Alaska Railroad, the city was devastated by the 1964 Good Friday earthquake but quickly rebounded as the industry headquarters for the Prudhoe Bay oil boom. Today almost half the state's residents live in or around the city, as Anchorage serves as the economic and political heart of Alaska. Sorry, Juneau.

Orientation

A surveyor was obviously in charge of laying out Anchorage. Its downtown is pedestrian-friendly, with numbered avenues running east–west and lettered streets north–south. East of A St, street names continue alphabetically, beginning with Barrow.

MAPS

The best free city map is the *Alaska Activities Map*, distributed all over town. For more detail there's Rand McNally's *Anchorage* ($4). The best selection of maps is at Title Wave Books (below) or the Alaska Public Lands Information Center (opposite).

Information
BOOKSTORES

Title Wave Books (☎ 888-598-9283) Northern Lights Center (1360 W Northern Lights Blvd); W 5th Ave (415 W 5th Ave) The best bookstore in Anchorage with two stores offering used and bargain books.

INTERNET ACCESS

Title Wave Books (☎ 888-598-9283) Northern Lights Center (1360 W Northern Lights Blvd); W 5th Ave (415 W 5th Ave) Both stores feature internet cafés.

ZJ Loussac Public Library (☎ 907-343-2975; 3600 Denali St) Free internet access.

Cyber City (☎ 907-277-7601; 1441 W Northern Lights Blvd; per hr $4; ☺ 11am-1pm Mon-Thu, 11am-2am Friday and Saturday, noon-1pm Sun) Open to 2am on Friday and Saturday for late-night gamers.

EMERGENCY

Anchorage Police (☎ 907-786-8500; 4501 S Bragaw St)
Crisis hotline (☎ 907-276-7273) This is a 24-hour sexual-assault hotline.

MEDIA

Anchorage Daily News (www.adn.com) This top-rate paper has the largest daily circulation in the state.
Anchorage Press (www.anchoragepress.com) A fabulous free weekly with events listings and social commentary.
KNBA 90.3 For Native Alaskan music and current events.
KRUA 88.1 For local news.

MEDICAL SERVICES

Alaska Regional Hospital (☎ 907-276-1131; 2801 DeBarr Rd) For emergency care.
Physician referral service (☎ 800-265-8624) Free service.
Providence Alaska Medical Center (☎ 907-562-2211; 3200 Providence Dr)

MONEY

Key Bank (☎ 257-5500, 800-539-2968; 601 W 5th Ave) Downtown.
Wells Fargo (☎ 800-869-3557; 301 W Northern Lights Blvd) The main bank is in midtown and one of 12 in the city.

POST

Post office (344 W 3rd Ave) Downtown in the village at Ship Creek Center.

TOURIST INFORMATION

Alaska Public Lands Information Center (☎ 907-271-2737; www.nps.gov/aplic/center; 605 W 4th Ave, Suite 105; ☺ 9am-5pm) Has park, trail and cabin information as well as excellent displays.
Log Cabin Visitor Center (☎ 907-274-3531 for recorded event information, 907-276-3200; www.anchorage .net; 524 W 4th Ave; ☺ 7:30am-7pm Jun-Aug, 8am-6pm May & Sep) Distributes a visitor guide and walking-tour map.

Sights & Activities

The **Alaska Native Heritage Center** (☎ 800-315-6608; www.alaskanative.net; 8800 Heritage Center Dr; adult/child

$23.50/16; ☺ 9am-5pm) is spread over 26 acres, and has a theater and exhibition space devoted to the history, lifestyle and arts of Native Alaskans. In open studios, artists carve baleen or sew skin-boats, and surrounding a small lake in the center are five replica village settings – Athabascan, Yupik, Inupiat, Aleut and Tlingit/Haida.

Please excuse the dust. **Anchorage Museum of History & Art** (☎ 907-343-4326; 121 W 7th Ave; adult/child $8/2; ☺ 9am-6pm), the largest museum in Alaska with a collection of 17,500 objects, is expanding but is still worth a visit during the upgrade. The much smaller **Heritage Library Museum** (☎ 907-265-2834; 301 W Northern Lights Blvd; admission free; ☺ noon-5pm Mon-Fri) displays Native Alaskan costumes, weapons and artwork.

The **Cadastral Survey Monument** (cnr E St & W 2nd Ave) traces Anchorage's development as a city. Nearby, **Captain Cook Monument** (Resolution Park) marks the 200th anniversary of Cook's visit to Cook Inlet and offers great views of the water. The wood-framed **Oscar Anderson House** (☎ 907-274-2336; Elderberry Park, 420 M St; adult/child $3/1; ☺ noon-4pm) was built in 1915, a year after Anchorage was founded, and its guided tours are an interesting look into the early days of Alaska.

Ideally located on the south shore of Lake Hood, the world's busiest floatplane lake, is the **Alaska Aviation Heritage Museum** (☎ 907-248-5325; 4721 Aircraft Dr; adult/child $9/6; ☺ 9am-5pm), a tribute to Alaska's colorful bush pilots and their faithful planes. Housed inside are 25 planes along with historic photos and displays of pilots' achievements, from the first flight to Fairbanks (1913) to the early history of Alaska Airlines.

The city is a cyclist's dream, with 122 miles of paved paths; the 11-mile **Tony Knowles Coastal Trail**, which begins at the west end of 2nd Ave, is the most scenic. Rent bikes at **Downtown Bicycle Rental** (☎ 907-279-5293; cnr W 4th Ave & C St; per day $32).

ourpick Flattop Mountain is Alaska's most-climbed peak: a three- to five-hour, 3.4-mile round-trip from a trailhead on the outskirts of Anchorage. Maps are available at the Alaska Public Lands Information Center (left).

Anchorage Historical Tours (☎ 907-274-3600; adult/child $5/1) takes visitors on hour-long downtown walking tours beginning at 1pm from the **Old City Hall** (W 4th Ave). For three-hour city tours ($47), try **Gray Line** (☎ 907-277-5581; 745 W 4th Ave). Its 10-hour tour includes the city and a trip out to Portage Glacier ($105).

ALASKA

ALASKA

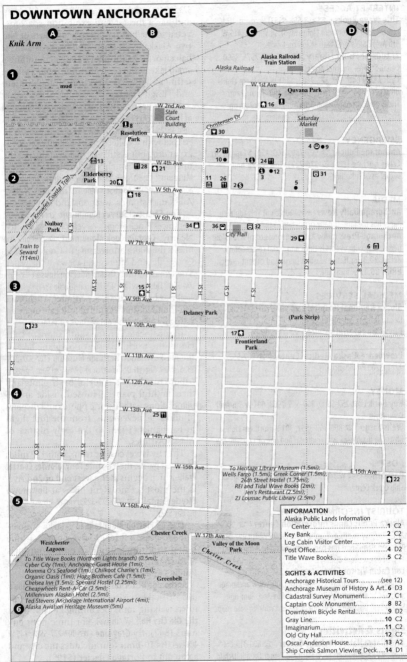

DOWNTOWN ANCHORAGE

Knik Arm

mud

Alaska Railroad Train Station

Alaska Railroad

Port Access Rd

W 1st Ave
Quvana Park

W 2nd Ave
State Court Building

Christensen Dr

Saturday Market

Resolution Park

W 3rd Ave

W 4th Ave

Elderberry Park

W 5th Ave

W 6th Ave

City Hall

Tony Knowles Coastal Trail

Nulbay Park

Train to Seward (114mi)

W 7th Ave

W 8th Ave

W 9th Ave

Delaney Park

(Park Strip)

W 10th Ave

Frontierland Park

W 11th Ave

W 12th Ave

W 13th Ave

W 14th Ave

W 15th Ave
E 15th Ave

To Heritage Library Museum (1.5mi);
Wells Fargo (1.5mi); Greek Corner (1.5mi);
26th Street Hostel (1.75mi);
REI and Tidal Wave Books (2mi);
Jen's Restaurant (2.5mi);
ZJ Loussac Public Library (2.5mi)

W 16th Ave

Westchester Lagoon

Chester Creek

W 17th Ave
Valley of the Moon Park

To Title Wave Books (Northern Lights branch) (0.5mi);
Cyber City (1mi); Anchorage Guest House (1mi);
Momma O's Seafood (1mi); Chilkoot Charlie's (1mi);
Organic Oasis (1mi); Hogg Brothers Café (1.5mi);
Chelsea Inn (1.5mi); Spenard Hostel (2.25mi);
Cheapwheels Rent-A-Car (2.5mi);
Millennium Alaskan Hotel (2.5mi);
Ted Stevens Anchorage International Airport (4mi);
Alaska Aviation Heritage Museum (5mi)

Greenbelt

Chester Creek

INFORMATION

Alaska Public Lands Information Center	**1** C2
Key Bank	**2** C2
Log Cabin Visitor Center	**3** C2
Post Office	**4** D2
Title Wave Books	**5** C2

SIGHTS & ACTIVITIES

Anchorage Historical Tours	(see 12)
Anchorage Museum of History & Art	**6** D3
Cadastral Survey Monument	**7** C1
Captain Cook Monument	**8** B2
Downtown Bicycle Rental	**9** D2
Gray Line	**10** C2
Imaginarium	**11** C2
Old City Hall	**12** C2
Oscar Anderson House	**13** A2
Ship Creek Salmon Viewing Deck	**14** D1

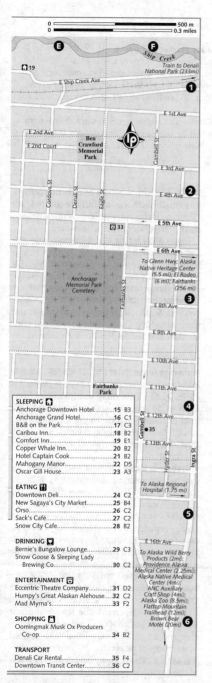

'Flightseeing' – touring in a small plane – is popular in Anchorage. Tours are short and expensive, but if time is limited they offer a glimpse into Alaska's grandeur. More than a dozen charter companies peddle flightseeing: **Rust's Flying Service** (☎ 907-243-1595, 800-544-2299; www.flyrusts.com) has 30-minute tours ($95), a three-hour flight to view Mt McKinley in Denali National Park ($295) and a full day of fly-in fishing ($425).

Anchorage for Children

Anchorage is exceptionally kid-friendly – a third of the city's 125 free parks boast playscapes. Close to downtown, **Frontierland Park** (corner of 10th Ave & E St) is a local favorite. **Valley of the Moon Park** (corner of Arctic Blvd & W 17th Ave) makes a delightful picnic spot. If the Flattop Mountain hike (p1069) is overly ambitious for your kids, head to **Alaska Wild Berry Products** (☎ 907-562-8858; 5525 Juneau St; admission free; 10am-11pm). Inside the sprawling gift shop is a chocolate waterfall; outside there's a short nature trail that leads to a handful of reindeer that kids can feed and pet.

To add some science to Alaska's nature, check out the **Imaginarium Science Discovery Center** (☎ 907-276-3179; 737 W 5th Ave; adult/child $5.50/5; 10am-6pm Mon-Sat, noon-5pm Sun). This award-winning center features creative, hands-on exhibits that explain the northern lights, earthquakes, oil exploration and other Alaskan topics.

The unique wildlife of the Arctic is on display at the **Alaska Zoo** (☎ 907-346-1088; 4731 O'Malley Rd; adult/child $10/6; 9am-6pm Sat-Mon, Wed-Thu, 9am-9pm Tue & Fri), the only zoo in North America that specializes in northern animals, including three species of Alaskan bears, snow leopards, Amur tigers and Tibetan yaks.

Sleeping
BUDGET

Spenard Hostel (☎ 907-248-5036; www.alaskahostel.org; 2845 W 42nd Pl; dm/r $20/75;) This friendly, independent hostel is near the airport and has 24-hour check-in – great for red-eye arrivals to Alaska. Free coffee in the morning, bike rentals available and a ride board to find a lift to other locations.

26 Street Hostel (☎ 907-274-1252; www.26streethostel .com; 1037 W 26th St; dm/r $25/60;) Anchorage's newest hostel is in Midtown and is trying hard

---

DON'T MISS IN ANCHORAGE...

If it's Saturday or Sunday head over to the **Saturday Market** (W 3rd Ave & E St; ☽ 10am-6pm Sat & Sun) for live music, cheap food and great souvenirs from birch steins to birch syrup.

The **Wild Salmon On Parade**, an annual event (early June to September) in which local artists turn fiberglass fish downtown into an Elvis Presley salmon, 'Uncle Salmon' painted in red, white blue or 'Fish & Chips', a poker-playing halibut. To see them all pick up a fish tour map at the Log Cabin Visitors Center.

View thousands of salmon spawning up Ship Creek – and anglers trying to catch them – from the **Ship Creek Salmon Viewing Deck**. It's reached by following C St north from the Alaska Railroad Depot. King salmon arrive in early June; silvers follow in August. So many fish it's mind-boggling.

---

with clean rooms, free internet and continental breakfast, and a TV room with loads of videos.

[our pick] Anchorage Guest House (☎ 907-274-0408; www.akhouse.com; 2001 Hillcrest Dr; dm $35, r from $85; ✗ ▭) This beautiful place feels more like a B&B than a hostel, and the prices reflect that. Rent a bike ($2.50 per hour) for the nearby Tony Knowles Coastal Trail, or soak up the midnight sun in the sunroom.

Brown Bear Motel (☎ 907-653-7000; Mile 103 Seward Hwy; r from $52; ✗) Cheap and clean rooms, but the motel is 14 miles from town and can get noisy when the adjacent Brown Bear Saloon is hopping. Tip a few with the locals and then hit the sack.

MIDRANGE

Chelsea Inn (☎ 907-276-5002; 3836 Spenard Rd; s/d $79/99, with shared bath $69/79; ℗ ▭) This small European-style inn has comfortable rooms with a communal kitchen, internet access, continental breakfast and free transportation from the airport. What more could you want?

Oscar Gill House (☎ 907-279-1344; www.oscargill.com; 1344 W 10th Ave; r $99-135; ✗) This historic home features sinfully good sourdough blueberry pancakes in the morning and free bikes.

Caribou Inn (☎ 907-272-0444, 800-272-5878; www .cariboubnb.com; 501 L St; s/d $109/119, with shared bath $89/99; ✗ ℗) Ideal downtown location, and the rooms, though small and a bit worn around the edges, are definitely acceptable.

[our pick] B&B on the Park (☎ 907-277-0878, 800-353-0878; www.bedandbreakfastonthepark.net; 602 W 10th Ave; r $125; ✗) All five rooms in this beautifully restored 1946 log church have their own private bath. Family-style breakfast is served at 8am sharp, so no lollygagging in bed!

Anchorage Downtown Hotel (☎ 907-258-7669; www.anchoragedowntownhotel.com; 826 K St; s or d $130-

150; ✗ ▭) Although not exactly downtown, this small hotel was recently renovated. All 17 rooms feature private baths, coffeemakers, small refrigerators and microwaves.

Copper Whale Inn (☎ 907-258-7999; www.copperwhale .com; cnr W 5th Ave & L St; r $165-195; ✗) Just blocks from the city center, the rooms are no-frills but tidy, and your view of Cook Inlet and the Alaska Range is the highlight of breakfast.

Comfort Inn (☎ 907-277-6887; 111 W Ship Creek Ave; d or s $190; ☂ ▭) Right by the train station and so close to Ship Creek you can look out your window and see anglers hooking salmon.

TOP END

Anchorage Grand Hotel (☎ 907-929-8888, 888-800-0640; www.anchoragegrandhotel.com; 505 W 2nd Ave; s or d $199; ✗ ▭) This small but luxurious hotel features 30 spacious suites that include full kitchens and separate living and bedroom areas. Many overlook Ship Creek and Cook Inlet, and its downtown location is convenient to everything.

Mahogany Manor (☎ 907-278-1111, 888-777-0346; www.mahoganymanor.com; 204 E 15th Ave; d $199-249, ste $249-349; ✗ ▭) Perched above the city, the manor is surrounded by woods that obscure the city's skyline in summer. The common areas – replete with floor-to-ceiling windows, numerous decks, huge fireplaces and a 19ft Jacuzzi – are a tad more impressive than the rooms themselves.

Millennium Hotel (☎ 907-243-2300, 866-866-8086; www.millenniumhotels.com; 4800 Spenard Rd; r $270-300; ✗ ☂ ▭) Four miles from downtown and right on Lake Spenard, the world's busiest floatplane base, this sprawling hotel has rustic-chic rooms and a lobby filled with stuffed bears. Babysitting service, 24-hour room service, even a private floatplane dock, are a few of the countless perks.

Hotel Captain Cook (☎ 907-276-6000, 800-843-1950; www.captaincook.com; cnr W 4th Ave & K St; r $245-430; ☒ ☐) The swanky *grande dame* of Anchorage pampers guests with hot tubs, fitness clubs, a beauty salon, Web TV and the famed Crow's Nest Bar, where you gaze upon Cook Inlet in one direction and the Chugach Mountains in the other. For the price, the standard rooms aren't all that swanky though.

Eating

Anchorage boasts a variety of international cuisines you'll be hard-pressed to find in the Bush. Fill up while you can!

BUDGET

New Sagaya's City Market (☎ 907-274-6173; W 13th Ave; ☒ 6am-10pm Mon-Sat, 8am-9pm Sun) Specializing in Asian fare, this eclectic upscale grocery store stocks lots of organic goodies and has a great deli.

Hogg Brothers Café (☎ 907-276-9649; 1049 W Northern Lights Blvd; breakfast & lunch $6-12; ☒ 6:30am-4pm; ☒) This bizarre, pig-obsessed joint serves all-day breakfasts, including 20 kinds of omelettes.

Momma O's Seafood (☎ 907-278-2216; 2636 Spenard Rd; mains $7-13; ☒ 11am-8pm Mon-Fri; ☒) The place for a halibut fix – have it fried or, better, Cajun style – but don't discount the excellent onion rings or udon noodles.

our pick **Snow City Café** (☎ 907-272-2489; 1034 W 4th Ave; breakfast $7-12; lunch $7-10; ☒ 7am-3pm Mon-Fri, 7am-4pm Sat & Sun; ☒) Locals love this place for its healthy grub. For breakfast skip the usual eggs and toast and try a bowl of Snow City granola with dried fruit, honey and nuts instead.

MIDRANGE

El Rodeo (☎ 907-338-5393; 385 Muldoon Rd; lunch & dinner $8-17; ☒ 11am-9:30pm Mon-Thu, 11am-10pm Fri, 11:30am-10pm Sat, 11:30am-9pm Sun; ☒) This little Mexican restaurant gets packed at night but the wait for a table is well worth it. For more than 10 years this has been the best and most affordable Tex-Mex in Anchorage.

Greek Corner (☎ 907-276-2820; 302 W Fireweed; lunch $7-12, dinner $12-22; ☒ 11am-10pm Mon-Fri, noon-10pm Sat, 4pm-10pm Sun; ☒) Best moussaka and stuffed grape leaves in Alaska. So what are they doing serving pizza and pasta? Trying to make a living.

Moose's Tooth Pub & Pizzeria (☎ 907-258-2537; 3300 Old Seward Hwy; pizza $9-26; ☒ 11am-11pm Mon-Thu, 11am-1pm Fri & Sat, noon-11pm Sun; ☒) Take your pick from the impressive menu of veggie, meat or seafood pizzas. Wash your pizza down with one of the award-winning brews on tap.

Downtown Deli (☎ 907-276-7116; 525 W 4th Ave; dinner $12-17; ☒ 6am-10:30pm; ☒) This fabulous spot, owned by former governor Tony Knowles, is famed for its reindeer stew and Philly cheesesteak.

TOP END

Sack's Café (☎ 907-274-4022; 328 G St; lunch $9-13, dinner $18-40; ☒ 11am-2:30pm & 5-9:30pm Mon-Thu, 11am-2:30pm & 5-10:30pm Fri & Sat, 10:30am-3pm Sun; ☒) Call it Asian-Mediterranean-Alaskan fusion. Lunch items include chicken curry and sandwiches with tiger prawns and avocado. For dinner try the popular chicken and Alaskan scallops with shiitake mushrooms and Asian black-bean salsa.

Orso (☎ 907-222-3232; 737 W 5th Ave; lunch $9-16, dinner $17-28; ☒ 11am-10:30pm; ☒) This restaurant is like a stepping into a Tuscan country inn only there's modern art all around and soft jazz floating into both dining levels and the bar. Its entrees are Mediterranean grill with an Alaskan twist, its pasta is made fresh daily and everything is served by waitstaff who know how the chef prepares it.

Jen's Restaurant (☎ 907-561-5367; 701 W 36th Ave; lunch $10-22; dinner $18-36; ☒ 11:30am-2pm Mon-Fri, 6-10pm Tue-Sat; ☒) Innovative, Scandinavian-accented cuisine emphasizing fresh ingredients and elaborate presentation. There's also a tapas bar.

Drinking

Organic Oasis (☎ 907-277-7882; 2610 Spenard Rd; mains $7-12; ☒ 11am-7pm Mon, 11am-9pm Tue-Thu, 11am-10pm Fri-Sat) Anchorage's hippest juice bar. Not into purified carrots? They also serve beer, wine and burgers with loads of veggie choices and often have live music.

Snow Goose & Sleeping Lady Brewing Co (☎ 907-277-7727; 717 W 3rd Ave) If the sun is setting over Cook Inlet and the Alaska Range, head to the rooftop deck of this brewpub. Only the beer is better than the view.

Bernie's Bungalow Lounge (☎ 907-276-8808; 626 D St) Absolutely fabulous, dahlings, with pink flamingoes, colorful leather couches and extravagant, brightly colored mixed drinks.

Entertainment

Check the *Anchorage Press* and Friday's *Anchorage Daily News* for the latest entertainment listings.

ALASKA

Mad Myrna's (☎ 907-276-9762; 530 E 5th Ave; cover Sat & Sun $5-10; ✗) A fun, cruisy bar with line-dancing Thursday, drag shows on Friday and dance music most other nights after 9pm.

our pick **Chilkoot Charlie's** (☎ 907-272-1010; 2435 Spenard Rd) 'Koots,' as locals call this beloved landmark, is big and brash, with 10 bars, four dance floors and sawdust everywhere. It's amazing the bands that have played here: Doobie Brothers, Blue Oyster Cult and Green Day among others.

Humpy's Great Alaskan Alehouse (☎ 907-276-2337; 610 W 6th Ave) Live music nightly from around 9pm, running the gamut from acoustic folk and ska to disco retrospective. All of it can be enjoyed with more than 40 beers on tap, the most of any bar in Anchorage.

Eccentric Theatre Company (☎ 907-274-2599; 413 D St) This may be the best live theater in town, staging everything from Hamlet to a Mel Brooks' jazz musical based on the poetry of Don Marquis. Only in Anchorage…

Shopping

Oomingmak Musk Ox Producers Co-op (☎ 272-9225; www.qiviut.com; 604 H St; ☾ 10am-6pm Mon-Sat) Handles a variety of very soft, very warm and very expensive garments made of arc-tic musk-ox wool, hand-knitted in isolated Inupiaq villages.

REI (☎ 907-272-4565; 1200 W Northern Lights Blvd; ☾ 10am-9pm Mon-Sat, 10am-6pm Sun) There are scores of wilderness outfitters, but this shop has a huge selection of backpacking, kayaking and camping gear.

ANC Auxiliary Craft Shop (☎ 907-729-1122; 4315 Diplomacy Dr; ☾ 10am-2pm Mon-Fri, 11am-2pm 1st & 3rd Sat of month) On the 1st floor of the Alaska Native Medical Center; has some of the finest Native Alaskan arts and crafts available to the public.

Getting There & Around

Ted Stevens Anchorage International Airport (☎ 907-266-2525; www.dot.state.ak.us/anc/index.shtml) has fre-quent inter- and intrastate flights. Terminals are off International Airport Rd. **Alaska Air-lines** (☎ 800-252-7522; www.alaskaair.com) flies to 19 Alaskan towns, including Fairbanks, Juneau, Nome and Barrow. **Era Aviation** (☎ 800-866-8394; www.flyera.com) flies to Cordova, Valdez, Kodiak and Homer. **Pen Air** (☎ 800-448-4226; www.penair.com) serves southwest Alaska.

Alaska Shuttle (☎ 907-338-8888) offers door-to-door transportation between the airport and downtown (one to three people $14) and out-lying areas of Anchorage (one to three people $22). The city's bus service (People Mover) picks up from both terminals (bus 7A) on a route that heads back downtown.

Cheapwheels Rent-A-Car (☎ 907-561-8627; 3811 Spenard Rd) has compacts (daily/weekly $50/300) and unlimited mileage for rentals three days or longer. **Denali Car Rental** (☎ 907-276-1230; 1209 Gambell St) has subcompacts (daily/weekly $55/330) with 150 miles included. Avoid picking up a car at the airport as you will be hit with a 32% rental tax, as opposed to 18% in the city.

Alaska/Yukon Trails (☎ 800-770-7275; www.alaskashuttle.com) goes to Denali ($65, five hours) and Fairbanks ($91, nine hours). **Seward Bus Lines** (☎ 907-563-0800; www.sewardbuslines.net) goes to Se-ward ($45, 2½ hours), while **Homer Stage Lines** (☎ 907-868-3914; www.homerstageline.com) will take you to Homer ($60, five hours).

Alaska Railroad (☎ 907-265-2494, 800-544-0552; www.alaskarailroad.com) goes south to Whittier ($58, 2½ hours) and Seward ($65, four hours), and north to Denali ($135, eight hours) and Fairbanks ($189, 12 hours).

People Mover (☎ 907-343-6543; www.peoplemover .org; adult/child $1.75/1) is the local bus service; its main terminal is at the **Downtown Transit Center** (cnr W 6th Ave & G St).

AROUND ANCHORAGE

Seward Hwy runs south of Anchorage, squeezed between the mountains and Turn-again Arm, where motorists often pull over to watch beluga whales. At Portage, a short railroad and toll road runs to Whittier for the ferry to Valdez. Portage Glacier Access Rd leads to the **Begich-Boggs Visitors Center** (☎ 907-783-2326; ☾ 9am-6pm), 5 miles south of Portage, and **Portage Glacier**. **Gray Line** (☎ 907-277-5581) offers hour-long cruises ($29), the only way to see the entire glacier. There are two USFS campgrounds along Portage Glacier Access Rd: **Black Bear Campground** (campsites $10) and **Williwaw Campground** (1/2 people $13/20).

North of Anchorage, Glenn Hwy runs 13 miles to Eagle River Rd – a beautiful moun-tainside trip. The **Eagle River Nature Center** (☎ 907-694-2108; 32750 Eagle River Rd; ☾ 10am-5pm; **P**) offers wildlife displays and scenic hik-ing. Parking costs $5. Near Palmer, 42 miles north, **Hatcher Pass** is an alpine paradise, with hiking, parasailing, gold-rush artifacts and panoramas of the Takeetna Mountains. Stay at **Hatcher Pass Lodge** (☎ 907-745-5897; www.hatcherpass lodge.com; Mile 17.5 Hatcher Pass Rd; r $110, cabins $165; ✗)

or **Motherlode Lodge** (☎ 907-745-6171, 877-745-6171; www.motherlodelodge.com; Mile 14 Hatcher Pass Rd; d $135; ✗). Both have restaurants.

KENAI PENINSULA

This wonderful region, broken up by mountains, fjords and glaciers and laced with hiking trails and salmon-filled rivers, is a popular playground for both tourists and locals. More than half the population of the state lives within a two-hour drive of Kenai Peninsula. Even if you despise crowds, there are easy escapes into the wilderness that seem to lie just outside every town.

Seward

This scenic town is flanked by rugged mountains and overlooks Resurrection Bay. Founded in 1903 as an ice-free port at the southern end of the Alaska Railroad, Seward prospered as the beginning of the gold-rush trail to Nome and was later devastated by the 1964 Good Friday earthquake.

The downtown **visitor center** (www.seward.com; cnr Jefferson St & 3rd Ave; ☼ 9am-5pm) is in a Pullman railroad car. There's also a **USFS office** (☎ 907-224-3374; cnr 4th Ave & Jefferson St; ☼ 8am-5pm Mon-Fri). The **Seward Library** (☎ 907-224-3646; 238 5th Ave; ☼ 10-9pm Mon-Fri, 10-7pm Sat) offers free internet access. The **Kenai Fjords National Park Visitor Center** (☎ 907-224-7500; www.nps.gov/kefj; 1212 4th Ave; ☼ 8:30am-7pm) has information on hiking and paddling.

SIGHTS & ACTIVITIES

our pick **Alaska SeaLife Center** (☎ 800-224-2525; www.alaskasealife.org; 301 Railway Ave; adult/child $15/12; ☼ 8am-7pm) is the only cold-water marine science facility in the western hemisphere. It's home to a thousand fish, nearly all from Alaskan waters,

and is the top attraction on the Kenai Peninsula. Plan to spend an afternoon here watching puffins, otters and 1000lb Steller sea lions glide past the giant viewing windows.

Six miles south of town is **Caines Head State Recreation Area**, which was fortified during WWII to guard the entrance of Resurrection Bay after the Japanese bombed the island of Unalaska. Exploring the bunkers, gun emplacements and surrounding alpine country makes for an intriguing way to spend a day. You can access the area on foot at low tide along the Coastal Trail, or paddle to it with **Kayak Adventures Worldwide** (☎ 907-224-3960; www.kayakak.com; 328 3rd Ave; single/double kayak per day $60/75, day trip $120; ☼ 8am-7pm), which offers guided day trips and kayak rentals. **Miller's Landing Campground** (☎ 907-224-5739, 866-541-35739; www.millerslandingak.com; Lowell Point Rd; one-way/round-trip $38/48) also runs a water taxi to the state park.

Seward's other great hike is the **Mt Marathon Trail**, a 3-mile walk (round-trip) to spectacular views on the mountain overlooking Seward.

SLEEPING

Snow River Hostel (☎ 907-440-1907; www.snowriverhostel.org; Mile 16 Seward Hwy; dm/d $15/40; ✗) Out of town, but highly recommended for its wooded tranquility.

Breeze Inn (☎ 907-224-5237, 888-224-5237; 1306 Seward Hwy; s/d $129/139; ✗ ☐) The most affordable motels are at the Boat Harbor, and this one has the largest and cleanest rooms.

Van Gilder Hotel (☎ 800-204-6835; www.vangilderhotel.com; 308 Adams St; d/ste $155/195, d with shared bath $109; ✗) A 1916 historic hotel, which means two things: tiny rooms and brass beds. Victorian charm is the most endearing aspect of this hotel, Seward's oldest.

WORTH THE DRIVE...GIRDWOOD

Enfolded into mighty peaks famed for skiing, and overlooking the beauty of Turnagain Arm, Girdwood is a magnet for epicurean urbanites, artists and hippies successful in spite of themselves. With fine restaurants, great hiking, a colorful town center and not one but two trams, it's a must.

At **Alyeska Resort** (☎ 907-754-1111; www.alyeskaresort.com; 1000 Arlberg Ave; r $279-309; ✗ ☒ ☐ ☐) in Girdwood, you can ride a tram to explore the alpine area, and then enjoy its mountaintop restaurant, **Seven Glaciers** (dinner $30-69; ☼ 5:30-9:30pm), before heading back down.

The Crow Pass Trail, 5.8 miles north of Alyeska Hwy on Crow Creek Rd, is a short but beautiful alpine hike that features gold-mining relics, an alpine lake and usually Dall sheep on the slopes above. It's 4 miles to Raven Glacier, the traditional turnaround point of the trail. Refuel after the hike at **Maxine's Glacier City Bristol** (☎ 907-783-2888; Crow Creek Rd; dinner $15-22; ☼ 5pm-midnight; ✗), which features a Mediterranean-theme menu of roasted leg of lamb and seared ahi tuna accompanied by acoustic music on Friday and Saturday nights.

Seward Windsong Lodge (☎ 907-224-7116, 888-959-9590; www.sewardwindsong.com; Mile 0.5 Exit Glacier Rd; r/ste $215/265; ✗ ☐) Snowcapped mountains rise above Seward's most luxurious lodge, while just down the road is a glacier. Sure, you're 4 miles from Seward, but there's free shuttle transportation whenever you want to go downtown.

EATING & DRINKING

Terry's Fish & Chips (☎ 907-224-8807; cnr 4th Ave & North Harbor St; mains $8-13; ☽ 10am-midnight) If it swims, Terry batter-fries it, throws it in a basket and serves it with fries.

Resurrection Roadhouse (☎ 907-224-7116; Exit Glacier Rd; lunch $9-14, dinner $18-46; ☽ 6am-10pm) This local favorite is home to 'halibut tsunami,' Thai seafood cakes and the best nachos in town. They also have a vast range of on-tap brews.

Ray's Waterfront (☎ 224-5606; breakfast & lunch $10-16, dinner $19-31; ☽ 11am-11pm) Hands down, this is Seward's culinary high point, with attentive service, picture-postcard views and the finest seafood above water.

Yukon Bar (☎ 907-224-3063; cnr 4th Ave & Washington St) and **Tony's Bar** (☎ 907-224-3045; 135 4th Ave) have live music and can get loud at night. Head to **Resurrect Art Gallery & Coffee House** (☎ 907-224-7161; 320 3rd Ave; ☽ 8am-5pm Mon-Fri, 8am-4pm Sat-Sun; ✗) for a latte and a quieter atmosphere.

GETTING THERE & AWAY

Sadly, there are no ferries to Seward as the Alaska Marine Highway eliminated service in 2006. **Seward Bus Lines** (☎ 907-224-3608; www.sewardbuslines.net) runs daily to Anchorage ($45, 2½ hours). **Alaska Railroad** (☎ 800-544-0552; www.alaskarailroad.com) takes a spectacular daily route to Anchorage ($65, four hours).

Kenai Fjords National Park

South of Seward is Kenai Fjords National Park. The park's main features are the 917-sq-mile **Harding Icefield** and the tidewater glaciers that calve into the sea. Even though it's making a fast retreat, **Exit Glacier**, at the end of Exit Glacier Rd, is still the most popular attraction. There's a visitor center and a paved 0.25-mile trail to a glacier overlook. Hikers can climb a difficult 5 miles to the edge of the ice field – worth it for spectacular views. The park visitor center is in Seward (p1075).

The best marine-wildlife cruises in the state are the tour boats that run into Kenai Fjords. **Major Marine Tours** (☎ 907-224-8030, 800-764-7300; www.majormarine.com) offers a half-day Resur-

rection Bay tour (adult/child $59/29) and a full-day tour viewing Holgate Arm ($119/59), both of which include a national park ranger on every boat. The latter tour is the best way to view seals, whales and other marine wildlife.

Sterling Hwy

Paved Sterling Hwy makes an arc around the Kenai Peninsula, passing **Kenai National Wildlife Refuge**, where you might see moose, bears, eagles, salmon and a plague of anglers. Head to **Kenai**, which has good views and some Russian history, and continue on to Captain Cook Strait Recreation Area, which is off the fishing circuit. South of Soldotna, the scenic highway hugs the coastline, passing through small villages with campgrounds and great clamming beaches. Picturesque **Ninilchik** has a Russian accent, and **Eagle Watch Hostel** (☎ 907-567-3905; Mile 3 Oil Well Rd; dm/r $13/35; ✗) is 3 miles east in a gorgeous rural setting where you can see eagles.

Homer

Charming, colorful Homer, at the end of Sterling Hwy, sits on beautiful Kachemak Bay amid awe-inspiring mountains. The town began attracting alternative types in the 1960s, and is now home to artists and aging hippies. The **visitor center** (☎ 907-235-7740; www.homeralaska.org; 201 Sterling Hwy; ☽ 9am-7pm Mon-Fri, 10am-6pm Sat & Sun) has courtesy phones to book rooms or tours. Homer's new **library** (☎ 907-235-3180; 500 Hazel Ave; ☽ 10am-6pm Mon, Wed, Fri & Sat, 10am-8pm Tue & Thu) is impressive and has internet access.

SIGHTS & ACTIVITIES

Inside the **Pratt Museum** (☎ 907-235-8635; 3779 Bartlett St; adult/child $6/3; ☽ 10am-6pm) are exhibits on the history and marine life of Kachemak Bay; outside there is a botanical garden and a forest trail to explore. More intriguing wildlife exhibits are found at the **Alaska Islands and Ocean Visitor Center** (☎ 907-235-6961; 95 Sterling Hwy; ☽ 9am-6pm).

Homer Spit is a 4.5-mile sand bar with clamming, beach camping and a small boat harbor. The best hiking is along the beaches, particularly the Shoreline Rte west of Main St, and at Kachemak Bay State Park, located across Kachemak Bay.

SLEEPING

Karen Hornaday Memorial Campground (campsites/RV sites $8/15) Below the bluffs just north of downtown, this campground is less busy than those on the Spit.

Homer Hostel (☎ 907-235-1463; www.homerhostel
.com; 304 W Pioneer Ave; dm $23, r s/d $47/60) Superclean,
very well run, perfectly located right downtown
and operated with unbridled ebullience by a
gung-ho, welcome-to-Homer enthusiast.

Driftwood Inn (☎ 907-235-8019, 800-478-8019;
www.thedriftwoodinn.com; cnr Main St & Bunnell Ave; d $72-
175; ☒ ▣) Quiet yet centrally located, it has
rooms ranging from tiny 'ship quarters' to
large rooms with all the amenities. Fall asleep
to the sound of the waves.

Old Town B&B (☎ 907-235-7558; www.oldtownbedand
breakfast.com; 106 W Bunnell Ave; d $95-115) Has beauti-
ful rooms, great views and lots of antiques;
breakfast is served at Panarelli's Café next
door.

Skyline B&B (☎ 907-235-3832; www.skylinebb.com;
60855 Skyline Dr; r $98-127; ☒) Above the city, this
classy B&B has five rooms with beautiful
views of Grewingk Glacier.

Heritage Hotel (☎ 907-235-7787, 800-380-7787; www
.alaskaheritagehotel.com; 147 E Pioneer Ave; d $119-165) This
1948 log cabin has a newly remodeled older
section with small, ultra-adorable rooms, plus
a newer wing with Jacuzzi suites.

EATING & DRINKING

Two Sisters Bakery (☎ 907-235-2280; 233 W Bunnell Ave;
light meals $5-9; ☯ 7am-6pm Mon-Sat, 9am-4pm Sun; ☒)
One of Homer's many excellent coffee houses,
with tables on a porch overlooking the bay.

Cosmic Kitchen (☎ 907-235-6355; 510 E Pioneer Ave;
burritos & sandwiches $7-9; ☯ 9am-6pm Mon-Fri, 9am-3pm
Sat-Sun) A hippie twist on the standard diner:
on one hand, they have burgers and Budweiser; on the other, you can pay 50 cents
extra to have bee pollen added to your $4
mango smoothie.

Fat Olives (☎ 907-235-8488; 276 Ohlson Ln; dinner
$16-26; ☯ 11am-9:30pm) In this chic and hyper-
popular pizza joint and wine bar, you could
gorge affordably on appetizers like pro-
sciutto-wrapped Alaska scallops or spend a
bit more for mains like wood-oven-roasted
game hen.

our pick **Café Cups** (☎ 907-235-8330; 162 W Pioneer
Ave; lunch $8-10, dinner $16-21; ☯ 11am-10pm Mon-Sat)
Has a wacky exterior (think Antoni Gaudi)
and an equally fun, eclectic yet refined menu,
including offerings like the 'cosmic-halibut-
by-the-sea-wich.'

Salty Dawg Saloon (Homer Spit Rd) Maybe the
most-colorful bar on the Kenai Peninsula,
the Salty Dawg is one of those places that's
famous for being famous.

GETTING THERE & AWAY

Era Aviation (☎ 907-235-7565, 800-866-8394; www.flyera
.com) flies frequently from Anchorage. The ferry
M/V Tustumena (☎ 907-235-8449; www.ferryalaska.com)
goes twice weekly to Seldovia ($33, 1½ hours)
and Kodiak ($74, 9½ hours). **Polar Car Rental**
(☎ 800-876-6417; Homer airport terminal; ☯ 24hr) rents
subcompacts for $65 a day. **Homer Stage Line**
(☎ 907-235-2252; www.homerstageline.com) provides a
bus service to Anchorage ($60, five hours).

PRINCE WILLIAM SOUND

The glaciers may be melting but Prince William Sound, the northern extent of the Gulf
of Alaska, is still flanked by mountains and
features abundant wildlife, from whales and
harbor seals to eagles and bears. Don't pass
through without splurging on a marine-
wildlife boat tour or a kayak adventure.

Whittier

At the western end of Prince William Sound,
Whittier was built by the military as a WWII
warm-water port. Rail tunnels were drilled
west through solid rock to connect with the
main line of the Alaska Railroad. The tunnel
was recently converted to handle vehicles as
well, and the first luxury hotel opened up
shortly after that.

Alaska Sea Kayakers (☎ 907-472-2534, 877-472-
2534; www.alaskaseakayakers.com; Whittier Boat Harbor; 2-
day single/double rental $80/110, trip $79-300) has rentals
and guided trips for paddlers to explore the
fjords and glaciers near Whittier.

If you're looking for a place to stay, **June's
B&B** (☎ 907-472-2396, 888-472-2396; www.breadnbutter
charters.com; office in the Triangle; condos $115-145) offers
insight into the local lifestyle by putting you
up in swanky suites atop Begich Towers. The
Inn at Whittier (☎ 907-472-7000, 866-472-5757; www
.innatwhittier.com; 1 Harbor Loop Rd; r $219-269; ☒) has
luxury suites and a grand view of the boat
harbor from its restaurant and lounge.

A train leaves Whittier daily for Anchorage ($58, 2½ hours). The ferry M/V *Bartlett*
travels east to Valdez ($89, 2¾ hours) and
Cordova ($89, 3¼ hours) daily.

Valdez

Just 25 miles east of Columbia Glacier, the ice-
free port of Valdez is the southern terminus of
the Trans-Alaska Pipeline. Valdez first boomed
when 4000 gold seekers passed through, heading for the Klondike. After the 1964 earthquake,
the city was rebuilt 4 miles further east.

The **Valdez Convention & Visitors Bureau** (☎ 907-835-4636; www.valdezalaska.org; 200 Fairbanks Dr; ☺ 8am-7pm Mon-Sat, 9am-6pm Sun) has information about the area and courtesy phones to book accommodations. The **library** (☎ 907-835-4632; 212 Fairbanks St; ☺ 10am-6pm Mon & Fri, 10am-8pm Tue-Thu, noon-5pm Sat) has free internet access.

SIGHTS & ACTIVITIES

Though the *Exxon Valdez* oil spill was an environmental disaster, the cleanup created a cash bonanza when Exxon hired fishing boats and locals to clean beaches. Many opportunists became known as the 'spillionaires.' The **Valdez Museum** (☎ 907-835-2764; 217 Egan Dr; adult/child $5/free; ☺ 9am-6pm) is packed with displays, including oil-spill exhibits and a model of the pipeline. Bustling **Small Boat Harbor** has a scenic mountain backdrop and pleasant boardwalk where you can watch charter fishing boats unload catches of halibut in the evening.

The magnificent **Columbia Glacier** is retreating, but its 3-mile-wide face can still be seen from Alaska Marine Highway ferries going to or from Whittier. For a longer and much closer look, **Stan Stephens Glacier & Wildlife Cruises** (☎ 907-835-4731, 866-867-1297; www.stanstephenscruises .com; 112 N Harbor Dr) runs seven-hour boat tours to Columbia Glacier (adult/child $95/47) and a nine-hour tour that also includes Meares Glacier (adult/child $130/65).

Although not blessed with the hiking that Anchorage and Juneau possess, Valdez still offers a number of scenic trails. **Shoup Bay Trail** is a 12.8-mile hike to its namesake bay that includes walk-in campsites halfway there. For white-water enthusiasts, **Keystone Raft & Kayak Adventures** (☎ 907-835-2606, 800-328-8460; www .alaskawhitewater.com; half-day $75) runs raft trips on the Class IV Tsaina River, while kayakers can explore the icebergs, seals and kittiwake colony of Shoup Bay.

ourpick Anadyr Adventures (☎ 907-835-2814, 800-865-2925; www.anadyradventures.com; 225 Harbor Dr; single/double kayak per day $45/65) offers rental kayaks, water taxi service and guided day trips.

SLEEPING

Bear Paw RV Campground (☎ 907-835-2530; 101 N Harbor Dr; campsites/RV sites $18/32) Conveniently located right downtown; has showers and laundry – and a great little wooded glade just for tents!

Downtown B&B Inn (☎ 907-835-2791; 800-478-2791; www.alaskan.com/downtowninn; 113 Galena Dr; r $100, with shared bath $85) More hotel than B&B,

though you do get breakfast with your clean, basic room.

Blueberry Mary B&B (☎ 907-835-5015; 810 Salmonberry Way; r $100-110; ✗) A mile from downtown, this B&B has a gorgeous view of the bay, a sauna for after the hike and, yes, blueberries on your waffles at breakfast.

Aspen Hotel (☎ 907-835-4445, 800-478-4445; www .aspenhotelsak.com; 100 Meals Ave; r $159-189; 💺 ✗ 💻) Valdez's newest hotel is also its largest and nicest, with wi-fi and an indoor pool and spa.

EATING

Fu Kung (☎ 907-835-5255; 207 Kobuk Dr; lunch $7-10, dinner $12-18; ☺ 11am-11pm Mon-Sat, 4pm-11pm Sun) In a structure that wonderfully fuses Asian and Alaskan themes, this restaurant has fantastic Chinese food and lunch specials including egg roll and quality wonton soup.

Ernesto's Taqueria (☎ 907-835-2519; 328 Egan Dr; fast food $7-9; ☺ 5:30am-10pm) Locally loved, this place serves large portions of serviceable Mexican food on the cheap.

Totem Inn Restaurant (☎ 907-835-4443; 144 E Egan Dr; breakfast & lunch $7-10, dinner $12-32; ☺ 5am-11pm; ✗) The best breakfast in town; you can find decent burgers and seafood here the rest of the day.

GETTING THERE & AWAY

Era Aviation (☎ 907-266-8394, 800-866-8394; www .flyera.com) makes the 40-minute flight daily to Anchorage. **Alaska Marine Highway** (☎ 907-835-4436; www.ferryalaska.com) ferries sail regularly to Whittier ($89, 2¾ hours), Homer ($202, 34 hours) and Cordova ($50, 2¾ hours).

Cordova

At the eastern end of the sound, this beautiful little town's population of 2600 doubles in summer with fishery and cannery workers. First settled by the nomadic Eyak, who lived on the enormous salmon runs, Cordova became a fish-packing center in 1889.

The **Cordova Library** (☎ 907-424-6667; 622 1st Ave; ☺ 10am-8pm Tue-Fri, 1-5pm Sat) has visitor information, including B&B listings, and internet access. The **USFS office** (☎ 907-424-7661; 612 2nd St; ☺ 8am-5pm Mon-Fri) has free maps to hiking trails accessible from the road.

SIGHTS & ACTIVITIES

The **Cordova Museum** (☎ 907-424-6665; 622 1st Ave; admission $1; ☺ 10am-6pm Mon-Sat, 2-4pm Sun) has a small but intriguing collecting that ranges from when the Russians arrived in the area to a heart-wrenching display on the *Exxon Valdez* oil spill. It also offers cassettes for self-guided town tours and will store your pack during the day. It has displays on history, marine life and mining.

Activity centers on the small boat harbor during summer.

our pick Childs Glacier calving into the Copper River is a magnificent sight – it's part of the stunning scenery to be found along the 50-mile Copper River Hwy. **Alaska River Expeditions** (☎ 907-424-7238, 800-776-1864; www.alaskarafters.com; Mile 13 Copper River Hwy) offers a full-day bus tour to Childs Glacier ($60/30 adult/child) or a half-day raft and hike adventure to **Sheridan Glacier** ($95/75 adult/child).

SLEEPING & EATING
Prince William Motel (☎ 907-424-3201, 888-796-6835; 501 2nd St; s/d $90/100) Though nothing fancy, it has huge, clean rooms, and for $20 extra you get a full kitchen.

Reluctant Fisherman Inn (☎ 907-424-3272, 800-770-3272; cnr Railroad & Council Aves; r $130-155) As close to luxurious as Cordova gets, this place overhangs Orca Inlet and has a restaurant and lounge.

Baja Taco Wagon (☎ 907-424-5599; Harbor Loop; dinner $7-12; ☼ 8am-8pm) Don't pass up this funky converted school bus across from the harbor; this is the place to enjoy some of the best tacos north of San Diego.

Ambrosia (☎ 907-424-7175; 413 1st St; dinner $11-18; ☼ 4pm-10pm) On the hillside downtown; serves Italian standards like veal parmigiana and chicken Marsala, and its wine list is not too shabby.

Powder House Bar (☎ 907-424-3529; Mile 1.5 Copper River Hwy; dinner $9-11; ☼ 10am-late Mon-Sat, noon-late Sun) Features folk and country music along with its grub and drinks.

GETTING THERE & AWAY
Alaska Airlines (☎ 907-424-7151, 800-252-7522; www.alaskaair.com) flies daily from Anchorage and Juneau. In summer, the ferry M/V *Bartlett* arrives every couple of days from Valdez ($50, 2¾ hours) or Whittier ($89, 3¼ hours). Rent a car at **Cordova Auto Rentals** (☎ 907-424-5982, Smith Airport, Mile 12 Copper River Hwy) for $85.

Wrangell–St Elias National Park
Part of a 31,250-sq-mile wilderness area, this park is a crossroad of mountain ranges: Wrangell, Chugach and St Elias. Extensive ice fields and 100 major glaciers spill from the

peaks, including one bigger than the state of Rhode Island. This park is more difficult to visit than Denali National Park but, to those who make the effort, no less impressive due to its mountainous scenery and numerous opportunities for wilderness adventure whether on foot or in a raft.

From Valdez, the Richardson Hwy is a jaw-dropping scenic route to Glennallen, past canyons, mountain passes and glaciers. The **Wrangell–St Elias National Park Visitor Center** (☎ 907-822-5234; www.nps.gov/wrst; Mile 106.8 Richardson Hwy; ☼ 8am-6pm) is in Copper Center.

A side road at Tonsina goes southeast to Chitina, which has the last place to fill up your tank. From there, the rugged Mt McCarthy Rd follows former railroad tracks 60 miles east through the stunning Chugach Mountains and across the mighty Copper River to the Kennicott River. Here a footbridge is used to cross the river and access historic McCarthy and the abandoned copper-mining town of Kennicott.

McCarthy & Kennecott
Scenic and funky little McCarthy was the Wild West counterpart of the Kennicott company town and, to a degree, still is today. The historic buildings in McCarthy are inns, restaurants and bars that serve visitors arriving from the other side of the Kennicott River. The company town of Kennecott is the remains of what was one of the greatest and richest copper mines in the USA.

In 1900 miners discovered the rich Kennecott copper deposit, and a syndicate built 196 miles of railroad through the wilderness to take the ore to Cordova. For 30 years Kennecott worked around the clock, but in 1938 management closed the mine, giving workers two hours to catch the last train out. Despite some pilferage, Kennecott remains a remarkably preserved piece of US mining history. The **Kennecott Visitor Center** (☎ 907-960-1027; Kennicott Railroad Depot; ☼ 9am-5:30pm) is staffed by the NPS during the summer (June to August), and has displays and maps of the company town.

There's some good hiking around the glaciers, peaks and mines, as well as rafting on the Kennicott River. **St Elias Alpine Guides** (☎ 907-544-4445, 888-933-5427; www.steliasguides.com) offers historical walking tours of Kennecott ($25) and a half-day hike on Root Glacier ($60). For flightseeing there's **Wrangell Mountain Air** (☎ 907-554-4411, 800-478-1160; www.wrangellmountainair.com).

ALASKA

Kennicott River Lodge & Hostel (☎ 907-554-4441; www.kennicottriverlodge.com; dm/cabin/ste $28/100/150; ☒) is a beautiful log lodge on the west side of the river with a 12-person sauna. **Ma Johnson's Hotel** (☎ 907-554-4402; www.mccarthylodge.com; s/d $109/159; ☒), in a renovated 1916 building, offers round-trip transportation from the footbridge and a wholesome breakfast. The same people who own Ma Johnson's also have **Lancaster's Backpacker Hotel** (s/d $48/68), offering fewer amenities and the lowest rates in McCarthy.

Backcountry Connection (☎ 907-822-5292, within Alaska 866-582-5252; www.alaska-backcountry-tours.com) buses leave Glennallen most days for McCarthy via Chitina ($79). In McCarthy there's a four-hour layover to visit Kennicott; this long day trip costs $99. **McCarthy Air** (☎ 907-554-4440; www.mccarthyair.com) can fly you into McCarthy from Valdez or Chitina for $550 for three people.

KODIAK ISLAND

Southwest of Kenai Peninsula, Kodiak Island is most famous for Kodiak brown bears, which grow huge gorging on salmon. Accommodations and transportation are expensive, but camping gear and a mountain bike can make Kodiak affordable.

The **Kodiak Island Convention & Visitors Bureau** (☎ 907-486-4782, 800-789-4782; www.kodiak.org; 100 Marine Way; ☼ 8am-6pm Mon-Sat, 10am-4pm Sun) has lists of accommodations (including 20 B&Bs). The **Homes Johnson Library** (☎ 907-486-8686; 319 Lower Mill Rd; ☼ 10am-9pm Mon-Fri, 10am-5pm Sat, 1-5pm Sun) has free internet access.

Bear-watching is best from July to September, but usually involves a charter flight to a remote salmon stream through a company like **Sea Hawk Air** (☎ 800-770-4295; www.seahawkair .com; per person $440). **Orcas Unlimited** (☎ 907-481-1121; www.orcasunlimited.com) has a half-day kayak outing ($160) and a full-day paddle ($200) that's supported by a mother ship.

Bev's Bed & Make Your Own Darn Breakfast (☎ 907-486-0834; www.bevsbedandbreakfast.com; 1510 Mission Rd; r $70-80; ☒) You have to admire the attitude of this B&B proprietor and love the price.

Kodiak Inn (☎ 907-486-5712, 888-563-4254; www.kodiak inn.com; 236 W Rezanof Dr; r $149-179; ▢). Kodiak's largest and most upscale motel is located downtown; it has a fine restaurant, an outdoor hot tub and an airport shuttle service.

Alaska Airlines (☎ 800-252-7522; www.alaskaair.com) has two flights and **Era** (☎ 907-487-4363, 800-866-8394; www.flyera.com) has five flights daily from Anchorage. The ferry **M/V Tustumena** (☎ 907-486-3800; www.ferryalaska.com) connects Kodiak with Homer ($74, 9½ hours) three times weekly.

THE INTERIOR

A grand expanse of forest and alps sweeping from Anchorage to Fairbanks and Canada, the Interior has been immortalized by poets, picked over by miners and popularized in the quirky 1990s TV series *Northern Exposure*. Here is Alaska's heartland: dogsleds and gold pans, roadhouses and fish wheels, moose on the side of the road and a seemingly endless stretch of pavement disappearing into the mountains.

The main route into this region is George Parks Hwy (Hwy 3), which winds 358 miles from Anchorage to Fairbanks, passing Denali National Park. The Richardson Hwy (Hwy 4) extends 366 miles south from Fairbanks to Valdez while the Glenn Hwy (Hwy 1) completes this Interior triangle by extending 189 miles from Anchorage to Glennallen. All the Interior roads are lined with turnoffs, campgrounds and hiking trails serviced by small towns with limited facilities and high prices.

GEORGE PARKS HWY

North of Anchorage, George Parks Hwy passes through the commuter town of Wasilla, just past the Glenn Hwy (Hwy 1) turnoff. A dramatic detour, the Fishook-Willow Rd between Palmer and Willow goes through **Hatcher Pass** (see p1074), an alpine paradise with foot trails, gold-mining artifacts and panoramas of the Talkeetna Mountains.

Talkeetna

At Mile 98.7, a side road heads north to this interesting town. It was a miners supply center in 1901, and later a riverboat station and a railroad-construction headquarters. Since the 1950s, Mt McKinley mountaineers have made Talkeetna their staging post, and today the town is the most interesting along the George Parks Hwy by far. The **Talkeetna/Denali Visitors Center** (☎ 907-733-2688, 800-660-2688; www .talkeetnadenali.com; George Parks Hwy; ☼ 7am-8pm) has information about the area.

The **Mountaineering Ranger Station** (☎ 907-733-2231; cnr 1st & B Sts; ☼ 8am-6pm) handles expeditions to Mt McKinley and has displays that will interest even those who have no desire to stand on North America's highest peak. The four restored buildings of the **Talkeetna Historical Society Museum** (☎ 907-733-2487; admission $3; ☉ 10am-5:30pm) are a block south of Main St and house exhibits on bush pilots and McKinley climbs.

For scenic flights to view Mt McKinley ($170 to $250), check out **Hudson Air Service** (☎ 907-733-2321, 800-478-2321; www.hudsonair.com) or **K2 Aviation** (☎ 907-733-2291, 800-764-2291; www.flyk2.com). If the day is clear, be prepared for a long wait, made worth it by an unforgettable flight.

SLEEPING & EATING

Talkeetna Hostel International (☎ 907-733-4678; www.talkeetnahostel.com; I St; dm/s/d $23/55/75; ☒ ☐) This well-loved but not-too-worn hostel has coed dorm rooms, private rooms, a shared kitchen and great advice about what to do in Talkeetna.

Latitude 62 Lodge/Motel (☎ 907-733-2262; Mile 13.5 Talkeetna Spur Rd; s/d $63/74) If downtown Talkeetna is just too hippie-dippy for you, there's always this place, with hunting-lodge decor.

Talkeetna Alaskan Lodge (☎ 907-733-9500, 888-959-9590; www.talkeetnalodge.com; Mile 12.5 Talkeetna Spur Rd; s or d $265-395; ☐) A newish and luxurious Native-corporation–owned place with 153 rooms and suites, a restaurant and a lounge. The hillside setting offers great views of Mt McKinley.

Mountain High Pizza Pie (☎ 907-733-1234; Main St; pizza slice $4, sandwiches $6-12; ☉ 11:30am-11pm) This arty, airy restaurant makes fabulous pizza that is served with a mug of Alaska's favorite microbrews.

Talkeetna Roadhouse (☎ 907-733-1351; Main St; breakfast $10-13; ☉ 6am-3pm & 5-9pm; ☒) This is the best spot for a hearty breakfast, and in the evening it serves soup and light fare.

Café Michele (☎ 907-733-5300; Talkeetna Spur Rd & 2nd St; dinner $18-30; ☉ 11am-10pm; ☒) Too pricey for some, but without question this café serves the town's best food and has the most upscale atmosphere.

GETTING THERE & AWAY

The **Alaska Railroad** (☎ 800-544-0552; www.akrr.com) from Anchorage stops at Talkeetna daily in summer ($82, 3½ hours) and heads north to Denali National Park ($79, four hours) and Fairbanks ($103, 8½ hours). **Talkeetna Shuttle Service** (☎ 907-733-1725, 888-288-6008) has a daily

run between Anchorage and Talkeetna ($65, three hours).

Denali National Park

This breathtaking wilderness area, which includes North America's highest mountain, attracts a million visitors a year. A single road curves 91 miles through the heart of the park, leading to off-trail hiking opportunities, wildlife and stunning panoramas. The Denali Park Rd can be used only by official shuttle buses, which have limited seating. Numbers of overnight backpackers in the wilderness zones are also strictly limited. This means Disneyland-like crowds at the entrance but relative solitude once you're inside.

Wildlife, including mammals such as marmot and moose, is easy to spot. Caribou, wolves and brown bears are crowd favorites. However, the main attraction is magnificent Mt McKinley, a high pyramid of rock, snow and glaciers rising from the valley floor. Clouds will obscure McKinley more often than not, so be prepared to wait for the big picture.

INFORMATION

The park entrance is at Mile 237.3 George Parks Hwy. Entry costs $10 per person or $20 per vehicle, and is good for a week. The highway north and south of the park entrance is 'Glitter Gluch,' a touristy strip of private campgrounds, lodges, restaurants and facilities.

Begin your trip to Denali at the **Wilderness Access Center** (WAC; ☎ 907-683-9274; Mile 1 Denali Park Rd; ☉ 5am-8pm) to obtain shuttle-bus tickets, campsites and backcountry permits or to purchase a map. Then head to the new **Denali Visitor Center** (☎ 907-683-2294; www.nps.gov/dena; ☉ 8am-6pm) to learn what makes this park so special. If possible, plan the exact days you will be at Denali and reserve bus seats and campsites through **Denali National Park Reservations** (☎ 907-272-7275, 800-622-7275; www.reservedenali.com).

Shuttle buses provide access for day hiking and sightseeing, and can be reserved from late February for that summer. In the backcountry you can get on or off buses along their routes. Buses leave the WAC regularly (5:30am to 4pm) for various stops, including Polychrome Pass Rest Area ($22.50, three hours) and Wonder Lake ($39.75, 6½ hours). Special camper shuttle buses, with space for backpacks and mountain bikes, charge $28.75 to any point on the road.

ALASKA

ACTIVITIES

For day hiking, get off the shuttle bus at any valley, riverbed or ridge that takes your fancy (no permit needed). For a guided walk, book at the WAC one or two days ahead.

For backcountry camping, you must get a backcountry permit from the WAC one day in advance. The park is divided into 43 zones, each with a regulated number of visitors. Some are more popular than others. Watch the Backcountry Simulator Program video at the WAC – it covers bears, rivers and backcountry safety – and check the quota board for an area you can access. You then go to the counter to book a camper shuttle bus and buy your maps.

Most cyclists book campsites at the VAC and then carry their bikes on the camper shuttle. Cycling is only permitted on roads. Rent bikes from **Denali Outdoor Center** (☎ 907-683-1925, 888-303-1925; www.denalioutdoorcenter.com; Mile 238.5 Parks Hwy; per day for two days or more $35).

Several rafting companies offer daily floats on the Nenana River. **Denali Raft Adventures** (☎ 907-683-2234, 888-683-2234; www.denaliraft.com; Mile 238 Parks Hwy; $72) offers a wild canyon run through the gorge, as well as a milder Mt McKinley float ($72).

SLEEPING & EATING

Campsites inside the park cost $9 to $20, and most can be reserved for a $4 fee. That includes Riley Creek, just inside the park entrance, which is usually overrun by RVers. Other campgrounds are spaced along the park road, the most popular being Wonder Lake (Mile 85 Park Rd; campsites $16), overlooking Mt McKinley, while Sanctuary River (Mile 23 Park Rd; campsites $9) makes a great base for day hikes.

Denali Mountain Morning Hostel (☎ 907-683-7503; www.hostelalaska.com; Mile 224 George Parks Hwy; dm/r $25/75, cabins $75-130; ✉ ▢) A great place to get a bunk, stash your gear (or rent some) and catch a shuttle to the park. Make reservations!

McKinley/Denali Salmon Bake Cabins (☎ 907-683-2733; www.denaliparksalmonbake.com; Mile 238.5 Parks Hwy; cabins $140, shared bath $74) 'The Bake' has 12 cabins, including a couple of bare-bones shared-bath tent cabins that are by far the cheapest digs in Glitter Gulch.

Carlo Creek Lodge (☎ 907-683-2576; www.alaskaone.com/carlocreek; Mile 224 George Parks Hwy; cabins shared bath/private $85-115) About 13 miles south of the park entrance, this lodge offers a variety of creek-side accommodations.

our pick **Earthsong Lodge** (☎ 907-683-2863; www.earthsonglodge.com; Mile 4 Stampede Rd, off Mile 251 Parks Hwy; s or d $145-185) North of Healy; rents out 12 private-bathroom cabins above the timberline at 1900ft – just a short climb away from stunning views of Mt McKinley. Even has a log coffeehouse.

Overlook Bar & Grill (☎ 907-683-2641; Mile 238.5 George Parks Hwy; dinner $12-42; ✉ 11am-11pm) This is a cozy place for a meal of steak, seafood or pasta at the Crow's Nest Inn; it's also the best bar in the greater Denali area.

Just outside the park, **Lynx Creek Pizza & Pub** (☎ 907-683-2547; Mile 238.6 George Parks Hwy; pizza $14-24; ✉ 11am-midnight) has excellent offerings, including beer on tap and huge pizzas.

GETTING THERE & AWAY

From the VAC inside the park, **Alaska/Yukon Trails** (☎ 800-770-7275; www.alaskashuttles.com) bus departs for Anchorage ($65, six hours) and Fairbanks ($53, three hours).

The **Alaska Railroad** (☎ 907-265-2494, 800-544-0552; www.akrr.com) departs from a depot near Riley Creek campground; it's expensive (Anchorage $135, Fairbanks $59) but very scenic.

FAIRBANKS

A spread-out, low-rise city, Fairbanks features extremes of climate, colorful residents and gold fever. In a city that can hit -60°F (-70°C) in the winter, summer days average 70°F (21°C) and occasionally top 90°F (32°C). Downtown is roughly centered on Golden Heart Park, and Cushman St is more or less the main street.

Fairbanks was founded in 1901, when a trader could not get his riverboat any further up the Chena River. A gold strike made Fairbanks a boom town, with 18,000 residents by 1908, but by 1920 it had slumped to 1000. WWII, the Alcan Hwy and military bases produced minor booms, but the town took off as a construction base for the Trans-Alaska Pipeline in 1973 and still serves as a gateway to the North Slope. Just north of the city is Fort Knox, Alaska's largest gold mine.

Information

The **Log Cabin & Downtown Visitor Information Center** (☎ 907-456-5774; www.explorefairbanks.com; 550 1st Ave; ✉ 8am-8pm), overlooking the Chena River, has courtesy phones to motels and B&Bs, and free internet access. The **Alaska**

Public Lands Information Center (☎ 907-456-0527; 250 Cushman St; ☼ 9am-6pm) has maps, information and displays on parks, wildlife refuges and recreation areas.

Sights & Activities

Pioneer Park (☎ 907-459-1087; cnr Airport Way & Peger Rd; admission free; ☼ 11am-9pm) is a 44-acre park and the city's biggest attraction. The historical displays are impressive and include an old stern-wheeler, the railroad car that carried President Warren Harding, and giant gold dredgers.

our pick **Museum of the North** (☎ 907-474-7505; 907 Yukon Dr; adult/child $10/5; ☼ 9am-7pm) at the University of Alaska is now Alaska's most impressive museum. A recent $32 million expansion added a Native art gallery and a sound-and-light theatre that features the Northern Lights. But the most popular exhibit is still Blue Babe, a 36,000-year-old bison found preserved in the permafrost.

Canoeing options range from afternoon paddles to overnight trips; ask at **7 Bridges Boats & Bikes** (☎ 907-479-0751; www.7gablesinn.com/7bbb; 4312 Birch Lane; canoe per day $35), at 7 Gables Inn. Alternatively, cruise the calm Chena River with a 3½-hour tour on the historic stern-wheeler **Riverboat Discovery** (☎ 907-479-6673; www.riverboatdiscovery.com; 1975 Discovery Dr; adult/child $50/35; ☼ 8:45am & 2pm).

Sleeping

Go North Hostel (☎ 907-479-7272; 866-236-7272; 3500 Davis Rd; dm $24, tents $12; ▢) Fairbanks' best hostel houses backpackers in four comfortable tent cabins, offers communal cooking in a bright kitchen cabin and boasts a dazzling array of services, including canoe-trip shuttles and guided backcountry expeditions.

Ah, Rose Marie (☎ 907-456-2040; www.akpub.com/akbbrv/ahrose.html; 302 Cowles St; d $80; ✕) This perpetually recommended B&B, just west of downtown, has four homey rooms and great breakfasts.

Golden North Motel (☎ 907-479-6201, 800-447-1910; www.goldennorthmotel.com; 4888 Old Airport Rd; s/d $80/99; ▢) This friendly, helpful place may be the cheapest respectable motel in town. Rooms tend to be on the small side.

Super 8 Motel (☎ 907-451-8888, 800-800-8000; 1909 Airport Way at Wilbur St; s/d $135/145) Corporate and characterless but clean and efficient. It's near Pioneer Park and offers a free shuttle service to the airport and train station.

All Seasons Inn (☎ 907-451-6649; 888-451-6649; www.allseasonsinn.com; 763 7th Ave; r $150-220; ✕ ▢) On a quiet residential street downtown, All Seasons Inn has a great sun porch and nine lovingly furnished rooms that can accommodate a variety of sleeping arrangements.

Eating & Drinking

Cookie Jar (☎ 907-479-8319; 1006 Cadillac Ct; breakfast $5-10; ☼ 6:30am-8:30pm Mon-Thu, 6:30am-9pm Fri-Sat, 8am-4pm Sun) Bizarrely situated behind a pair of car dealerships off Danby St, this place attracts flocks of locals for the all-day breakfast.

Sourdough Cafe (☎ 907-479-0523; University Ave at Cameron St; breakfast $7-11, burgers & sandwiches $7-10; ☼ 6am-10pm) Considered by many to be the town's best diner, this place, just down University Ave from campus, serves up sourdough pancakes all day long.

Gambardella's Pasta Bella (☎ 907-457-4992; 706 2nd Ave; lunches $8-12, dinners $12-22; ☼ 11am-10pm Mon-Sat, 4-10pm Sun) *The* place for Italian food in Fairbanks, with luscious pasta dishes, pizza and homemade bread. There's an outdoor café that's a delight during Fairbanks' long summer days.

Soapy Smith's (☎ 907-451-8380; 543 2nd Ave; lunch $10-13, dinner $12-25; ☼ 11am-9pm Mon-Sat) Though Smith was a Skagway character who died before Fairbanks even existed, this place has good burgers in saloon-style environs.

Lavelle's Bistro (☎ 907-450-0555; 575 1st Ave; mains $17-35; ☼ 11am-2pm & 4:30-10pm Mon-Sat, 4:30-10pm Sun) Chic, urbane and blessedly devoid of Last Frontier kitsch, Lavelle's has a wine list as long as your arm and mains that include potato-crusted salmon.

WORTH THE DRIVE…CHENA HOT SPRINGS

Start the morning hiking in Chena River State Recreational Area, which has a variety of walks, including the impressive Granite Tors Trail, a 15-mile loop. Then end the day at **Chena Hot Springs Resort** (☎ 907-451-8104, 800-478-4681; www.chenahotsprings.com; Mile 56.5 Chena Hot Springs Rd; campsites/yurts/r $20/65/160-195), where you can soak away those sore feet or have a cold one in its Aurora Ice Museum, the world's only year-round ice palace. The resort also offers economical yurts, a good restaurant and a bar where you can belly up and drink as if you were a local.

Palace Theatre & Saloon (☎ 907-456-5960; www
.akvisit.com; adult/child $18/9) At Pioneer Park, this
saloon comes alive at night with honky-tonk
piano, can-can dancers and other acts in the
Golden Heart Revue.

Getting There & Around

Alaska Airlines (☎ 907-474-0481, 800-252-7522; www
.alaskaair.com) has nine daily flights to Anchorage
with occasional bargains. **Frontier Flying Service**
(☎ 907-450-7200, 800-478-6779; www.frontierflying.com)
also flies to Anchorage as well as throughout
Arctic Alaska.

Rent-A-Wreck (☎ 907-452-1606, 800-478-1606;
2105 S Cushman St) will rent you a compact for
$39 a day.

Alaska Direct Bus Lines (☎ 800-770-6652; www
.alaskadirectbusline.com) runs from Fairbanks to Tok
($70, five hours) where you can pick up a bus to
Whitehorse ($180, 15 hours). **Alaska/Yukon Trails**
(☎ 800-770-7275; www.alaskashuttles.com) offers daily
connections to Denali National Park ($46, 2½
hours) and Anchorage ($91, eight hours). It
also services Dawson City ($162, 10 hours).

The **Alaska Railroad** (☎ 800-544-0552; www.akrr
.com) departs at 8:15am daily for Denali National Park ($54, three hours) and Anchorage
($179, 12 hours).

The **Metropolitan Area Commuter Service**
(☎ 907-459-1011) provides a local, weekday bus
service (single fare/day pass $1.50/3).

THE BUSH

The Bush is the vast area of Alaska that is
not readily accessible by road or ferry. It includes Arctic Alaska, the Brooks Range, the
Alaska Peninsula–Aleutian Islands chain and
the Bering Sea coast. Traveling to the Bush
usually involves small, expensive chartered
aircraft. Facilities for travelers are also pricey
and very limited.

To visit **Arctic Alaska**, take the Dalton Hwy,
a rough gravel road that goes 490 miles north
from Fairbanks to Deadhorse, near Prudhoe
Bay. You can tour the oil complex at Prudhoe, but you can't camp on the shores of the
Arctic Ocean. The highlight of the long drive
is the **Arctic Circle** and **Atigun Pass** (4752ft) in
the Brooks Range, 300 miles from Fairbanks,
for the views of the North Slope. **Dalton Hwy
Express** (☎ 907-474-3555; www.daltonhighwayexpress
.com) makes the run to Prudhoe Bay three times
a week. It's $140 round-trip from Fairbanks
to the Arctic Circle (six hours one way), and
$392 to Prudhoe Bay (16 hours one way).
Arctic Outfitters (☎ 907-474-3530; www.arctic-outfitters
.com) offers a self-drive package to Prudhoe
Bay for $1,197, which includes a car, three
nights' lodging for two people and an Arctic
Ocean tour.

The Dalton Hwy passes the remote **Gates of
the Arctic National Park**, which has great hiking
and paddling, but the park is best accessed
from the town of **Bettles**, which can be reached
only by air. For information, contact the **National Park Ranger Station** (☎ 907-692-5494; wwwnps
.gov/gaar). For guided and unguided trips into
the park as well as accommodations in Bettles,
contact **Bettles Lodge** (☎ 800-770-5111, 907-692-5111;
www.bettleslodge.com).

On the Bering Sea coast, the legendary
gold-rush town of **Nome** is friendly and an
intriguing place to visit, whether you want to
explore the still-visible links to its golden past
or have a go panning for nuggets yourself.
The **visitor center** (☎ 907-443-6624; www.nomealaska
.org; ⏲ 9am-9pm) has information about accommodations and trips in the surrounding area.
You can camp on **Golden Sands Beach** (campsite
free), where gold is still being sought after
by a small band of miners who set up their
sluice boxes and other equipment every summer. You can talk to them, see the nuggets
they find and then give panning a whirl for
yourself. No need to stake a claim at Golden
Sands Beach. **Alaska Airlines** (☎ 800-252-7522;
www.alaskaair.com) offers non-stop flights from
Anchorage.

Hawaii

So many states claim uniqueness, and Hawaii does too. But this string of emerald islands in the cobalt-blue Pacific Ocean, over 2000 miles from any continent, takes a little more work to get to. So it's reasonable to wonder: will that be time and money well spent?

Glad you asked. Have a brochure, and watch these classic movies and TV shows. See Elvis singing on tropical beaches. Admire surfers skating thunderous waves. Memorize the galloping *Hawaii Five-0* theme music.

Hawaii, as tourist bureaus and Hollywood constantly remind us, is 'paradise.' Push past the hype and what do you find? Darned if they're not right. Hawaii is hiking sculpted cliffs or diving coral-reef cities in the afternoon and drinking mai tais to slack-key guitar at sunset. It's slurping chin-dripping papayas with hibiscus flowers in your hair; it's Pacific Rim cuisine, fiery volcanoes and cavorting whales. By serendipity and design (and popular consensus), Hawaii is an almost flawless destination. It's an enchanting multicultural society whose roots lie in Polynesia, Asia, North America and Europe, and it's an expression of nature at its most luscious and divine.

Over seven million visitors come to experience paradise annually, but the islands are not as crushed with sun-baked tourists and cooing honeymooners as that makes it sound. If you want a cushy resort vacation, head for Oahu's Waikiki or West Maui. For something cheaper or more adventurous, aim for the Big Island or Kaua'i. If time is short, stick to one island and make the most of it. Honolulu is a teeming cultural and economic powerhouse, but in under an hour you can be alone in the rain forest or snoozing on white sand.

Locals know that Hawaii isn't really paradise, but on any given day it can sure feel like it.

HAWAII

HIGHLIGHTS

- Discovering Hawaiian history and culture in **Honolulu's museums** (p1092)
- Snorkeling with tropical fish in Maui's **Molokini Crater** (p1105)
- Hiking the smoldering crust of a living volcano at **Hawai'i Volcanoes National Park** (p1102)
- Driving over the 54 bridges of Maui's jaw-dropping **Road to Hana** (p1106)
- Exploring the canyons and sea cliffs of Kaua'i's **Waimea Canyon** and **Koke'e State Park** (p1109)

Waimea Canyon & Koke'e State Park ★

Honolulu ★

Molokini Crater ★ ★ Road To Hana

Hawaii

Hawai'i Volcanoes National Park ★

HISTORY

Little is known about Hawaii's first settlers, who arrived around AD 500. Tahitians arrived around AD 1000 and for the next 200 years navigated thousands of miles back and forth across the ocean in double-hulled canoes. Ruled by chiefs, ancient Hawaiian society was actually matriarchal, and its religion followed strict laws known as *kapu*.

By accident, famed British explorer Captain James Cook 'discovered' the islands in 1778. The first white Westerner to arrive, Cook was mistaken for the god Lono and treated like a deity. He stayed several weeks and then resumed his journey. When he returned to Hawaii a year later, his less-than-godlike behavior led to fighting and he was killed.

Beginning in the 1790s, King Kamehameha, chief of the Big Island, conquered and united all the Hawaiian islands. He is credited with bringing peace and stability to a society that was often in flux due to wars and the power struggles of the ruling class. However, after his death in 1819 his son inherited the throne and, in a stunning repudiation of their religion, deliberately violated the *kapu* and destroyed the temples.

As fate would have it, Christian missionaries arrived not long after, and in the midst of Hawaii's social and spiritual chaos they found it relatively easy to 'save souls.' New England whalers also arrived, seeking different quarry, and by the 1840s Lahaina and Honolulu were the busiest whaling towns in the Pacific. Meanwhile, foreigners made a grab for Hawaii's fertile land, turning vast tracts into sugarcane plantations. As there weren't enough Hawaiians to work the fields, immigrants were brought in from China, Japan, Portugal and the Philippines, giving rise to Hawaii's multiethnic culture but also displacing Native Hawaiians, most of whom became landless.

In 1893 a group of American businessmen overthrew the Hawaiian monarchy. The US government was initially reluctant to support the coup, but it soon rationalized its colonialism by citing the islands' strategic importance and annexed Hawaii in 1898. Hawaii played an infamous role in US history when a surprise attack on Pearl Harbor vaulted America into WWII. Hawaii became the 50th US state in 1959.

HAWAII FACTS

Nickname Aloha State

Population 1.3 million

Area 10,930 sq miles

Capital city Honolulu (population 372,000)

Sales tax 4.16% (plus 7.25% room tax)

Birthplace of Don Ho (1930–2007), Barack Obama (b 1961), Nicole Kidman (b 1967), Michelle Wie (b 1989)

Home of ukuleles, America's only royal palace

Famous for surfing, hula, mai tais, the world's most active volcano

Most famous unofficial state fish: humuhumunukunukuapua'a (or, 'fish with a nose like a pig')

LOCAL CULTURE

Compared to 'the mainland' – the blanket term for the rest of the USA – Hawaii may as well be another country. In fact, some Native Hawaiians would like to restore Hawaii's status as an independent nation. It makes sense. Geologically, historically and culturally, Hawaii developed in isolation, and, like its flora and fauna, its society is unique, endemic and even fragile. Locals treasure their customs and sensibilities and constantly guard them against the diluting influence of *haole* (white or mainland) ways – which arrive like so many invasive species.

In Hawaii, no ethnicity claims a majority, but this diversity is also distinct from typical American multiculturalism. Hawaii has large Asian populations and very small African American and Mexican Hispanic communities, with about 20% of residents identifying themselves as full or part Native Hawaiian.

As befits a tropical paradise, Hawaii has a decidedly casual personality. Except in cosmopolitan Honolulu, aloha shirts and sandals ('rubbah slippahs') are acceptable attire for any occasion, socializing revolves around food and family (major celebrations can involve entire communities and take days), and fun means sports and the outdoors. In local and Hawaiian sensibilities, caring for the land and caring for the community are integral and intertwined.

Then there is aloha – or alooooooohaa, as they say at the luau. It is of course a greeting, but, more than that, it describes a gentle, everyday practice of openness, hospitality and loving welcome – one that's extended to everyone, local and visitor alike.

Language

Hawaii has two official state languages, English and Hawaiian, and one unofficial language, pidgin. In recent years, the Hawaiian language has experienced a renaissance that has saved it from extinction, but outside of a formal setting (a classroom, museum, or performance) you are unlikely to hear it spoken. It wasn't until the arrival of the Christian missionaries in the 1820s that Hawaiian was translated into a written language. Written Hawaiian has only 13 letters, and it is generally pronounced exactly as written, with glottal stops marked by an okina (reverse apostrophe).

All residents speak English, but when locals 'talk story' with each other, they reach for the relaxed, fun-loving cadences of pidgin. Pidgin developed as the lingua franca of the sugar plantations, a common tongue for diverse foreign workers. It can sound like broken English, but it has its own syntax and grammar; it is (somewhat controversially) considered its own language. The most well-known (and hilarious) introduction is the *Pidgin to Da Max* series by Douglas Simonson, but mind the non-local's caution, okay brah?

LAND & CLIMATE

The Hawaiian Islands exist because of a hot spot beneath the earth's slow-moving Pacific Plate, which has been spewing lava and creating islands for 70 million years. Today, the state of Hawaii contains eight main islands, only six of which are populated.

Measure for measure, the Hawaiian islands are as diverse as it gets. Their flora and fauna are a textbook case of Darwinian evolution. Time and time again, single migratory species blossomed into dozens of variations, as isolated individuals adapted to arid coastal deserts, rain forests and snow-capped subarctic mountaintops. As a result, the majority of Hawaiian plants and animals are endemic, and nearly as often, endangered.

All the islands have similar climates: southwestern coasts are sunny, dry and lined with sandy beaches, while the northeastern sides have lush rain forests, cascading waterfalls and pounding surf. Hawaii enjoys warm weather year-round, with coastal temperatures averaging a high of 83°F (28°C) and a low of 68°F (20°C). Summer and fall are the driest seasons, winter the wettest.

HAWAII IN...

Four Days

Those on a trans-Pacific stopover will land at Honolulu. With only a few days, spend them all on **O'ahu** (p1090). In between surfing and sunning on **Waikiki Beach** (p1092), check out **Honolulu's museums** (p1092), walk around **Chinatown** (p1092), hike up **Diamond Head** (p1097) and snorkel **Hanauma Bay** (p1097). Don't leave without admiring the monster waves of the **North Shore** (p1098).

One Week

With a week, fit in another island – say, **Maui** (p1103). Explore the old whaling town of **Lahaina** (p1103), head to **Haleakala National Park** (p1107) to see the sunrise above the crater, take a **whale-watching cruise** (p1104), snorkel **Molokini Crater** (p1105), and drive the **Road to Hana** (p1106).

Two Weeks

With two weeks, be more leisurely and visit two or three islands. If you choose the **Big Island** (p1098), visit the ancient Hawaiian **Pu'uhonua O Honaunau National Historical Park** (p1100), hike into **Waipi'o Valley** (p1101), catch the farmers market and museums in **Hilo** (p1101), and say aloha to Pele at **Hawai'i Volcanoes National Park** (p1102). If you choose **Kaua'i** (p1107), kayak the **Wailua River** (p1108), hike **Waimea Canyon** and **Koke'e State Park** (p1109), surf **Hanalei Bay** (p1108), snorkel **Ke'e Beach** (p1108) and don't miss hiking the Kalalau Trail on the **Na Pali Coast** (p1108).

HAWAII

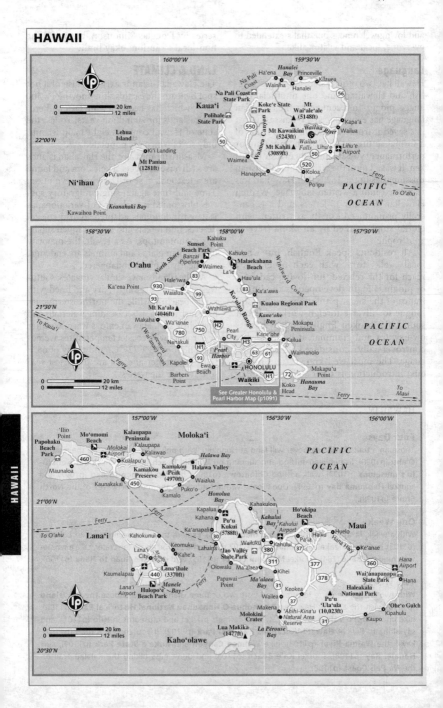

Kaua'i

160°00'W — 159°30'W
22°00'N

Na Pali Coast
Ha'ena • Princeville
Hanalei Bay • Wainiha • Kilauea
Na Pali Coast State Park • Hanalei
Koke'e State Park • 56
Polihale State Park • Mt Wai'ale'ale (5148ft)
550 • Mt Kawaikini (5243ft)
Waimea Canyon • Wailua River • Wailua
50 • Mt Kahili (3089ft) • Kapa'a
Waimea • Wailua Falls • Lihu'e
Hanapepe • 520 • Koloa • Lihu'e Airport
Po'ipu
PACIFIC OCEAN
To O'ahu

Lehua Island
Ki'i Landing
Mt Paniau (1281ft)
Ni'ihau
Pu'uwai
Kawaihoa Point • Keanahaki Bay

Ferry

O'ahu

158°30'W — 158°00'W — 157°30'W

Kahuku Point
Sunset Beach Park
Banzai Pipeline • Kahuku
Waimea • Malaekahana Beach
North Shore
Hale'iwa • 83 • La'ie
930 • Waialua • Hau'ula
Ka'ena Point • 99 • 83 • Ka'a'awa
93 • Wahiawa • Kualoa Regional Park
Mt Ka'ala (4046ft) • Ko'olau Range
Makaha • H2 • Kane'ohe Bay
Wai'anae • 750 • Pearl City • Mokapu Peninsula
Nanakuli • H3 • Kane'ohe
Leeward (Wai'anae) Coast • H1 • 63 • 61 • Kailua
Kapolei • Pearl Harbor • Waimanalo
Ewa Beach • HONOLULU • Makapu'u Point
Barbers Point • Waikiki • 72
Koko Head • Hanauma Bay
To Kaua'i
Ferry
Koko Crater
21°30'N
PACIFIC OCEAN
Ferry • To Maui
Windward Coast

See Greater Honolulu & Pearl Harbor Map (p1091)

157°00'W — 156°30'W — 156°00'W

Moloka'i
'Ilio Point
Papohaku Beach Park • Mo'omomi Beach • Kalaupapa Peninsula
Molokai Airport • Kalaupapa • Kalawao
460 • Kualapu'u • Halawa Bay
Maunaloa • Kamakou Preserve • Halawa Valley
450 • Kamakou Peak (4970ft) • Waialua
Kaunakakai • Puko'o
Kamalo
PACIFIC OCEAN
21°00'N
Honolua Bay
Kapalua • Kahakuloa
Lana'i
Kahana • Pu'u Kukui (5788ft) • Ho'okipa Beach
Ka'anapali • Waihe'e • Kahului Bay • Pa'ia
30 • Iao Valley State Park • Kahului Airport • Haiku • Huelo
Lana'i City • Lahaina • Wailuku • 37 • **Maui** • Ke'anae
Keomuku • Olowalu • Ma'alaea • 380 • 360
Kahe'a • Lana'ihale (3370ft) • Papawai Point • 311 • 377 • Hana Airport
Kaumalapau • Manele Bay • 31 • Kihei • Wai'anapanapa State Park
Lana'i Airport • Hulopo'e Beach Park • Ma'alaea Bay • Keokea • Hana
To O'ahu • Ferry • Wailea • 37 • Haleakala National Park
Ferry • Makena • Pu'u 'Ula'ula (10,023ft)
'Ahihi-Kina'u Natural Area Reserve • 'Ohe'o Gulch
Molokini Crater • Kipahulu
Lua Makika (1477ft) • La Pérouse Bay • 31 • Kaupo
Kaho'olawe
20°30'N

0 — 20 km
0 — 12 miles

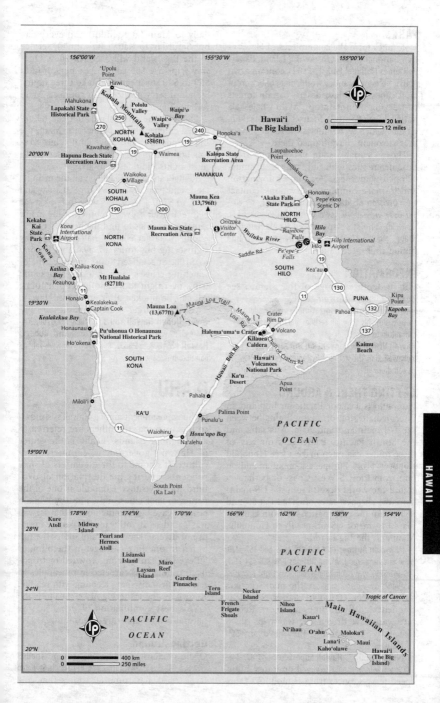

PARKS

Volcanoes form the centerpieces of Hawaii's two national parks. On the Big Island, **Hawai'i Volcanoes National Park** (p1102) contains two active volcanoes and a wondrous collection of landscapes, from lava deserts to rain forests to freezing mountaintops. Maui's **Haleakala National Park** (p1107) focuses on Haleakala Crater, which so resembles the lunar surface that astronauts have trained there.

Hawaii's many state parks range from beachfront sites with full facilities to undeveloped wilderness. For more information and to make camping reservations, contact the **Division of State Parks** (Map p1093; ☎ 808-587-0300; www.hawaii.gov/dlnr/dsp; 1151 Punchbowl St, Honolulu). The state-sponsored **Na Ala Hele** (Map p1091; ☎ 808-973-9782; www.hawaiitrails.org) has hiking-trail information.

INFORMATION

For in-depth coverage of the islands, see Lonely Planet's *Hawaii* guide.

Hawaii Ecotourism Association (www.hawaiiecotourism.org) This nonprofit certifies and lists businesses committed to ecotourism.

Hawaii Visitors & Convention Bureau (www.gohawaii.com) The state's official tourism site covers Hawaii thoroughly.

GETTING THERE & AROUND

Honolulu is a major Pacific air hub and an intermediate stop on many flights between the US mainland and Asia, Australia and the South Pacific. Passengers on any of these routes can often make a free Honolulu stopover. From Europe, ask about an add-on fare from the US West Coast or perhaps a round-the-world ticket. From the US mainland, the cheapest fares often start at around $600 from the east coast, $400 from California. Most major US airlines fly to Honolulu, Maui and the Big Island.

Hawaiian Airlines (☎ 808-838-1555, 800-367-5320; www.hawaiianair.com), **Aloha Airlines** (☎ 808-484-1111, 800-367-5250; www.alohaairlines.com), and **go!** (☎ 888-435-9462; www.iflygo.com) are the main carriers flying between Hawaiian islands. Service is frequent and flight times are short. Recent fare wars have driven one-way trips down to $30 to $40; typically, they have run $60 to $100.

New in 2007, **Hawaii Superferry** (☎ 877-443-3779; www.hawaiisuperferry.com) operates high-speed ferry services from Honolulu, O'ahu,

daily to Maui (at Kahului) and every day but Saturday to Kaua'i (at Lihu'e); service to the Big Island will begin in 2009. One-way trips are $55 to $65 per person (add $60 to $70 for a car) and take three hours. Standard ferry services also connects Maui to Lana'i and Moloka'i.

O'ahu is the only island that can be explored extensively by public bus. Maui, the Big Island and Kaua'i have limited bus services between major towns but no service to most sightseeing destinations.

Rental cars are available on all the main islands and typically cost $35 to $50 a day and $175 to $250 a week. It's wise to book a car before arrival; browse websites of the major rental companies to find the best price.

On the larger islands, half- and full-day sightseeing bus tours are available for $60 to $100. Specialized tours include whale-watching cruises, bicycle tours, snorkeling trips, overnight tours and helicopter tours. All can be booked after arrival in Hawaii. Two of the larger tour companies are **Discover Hidden Hawaii Tours** (☎ 808-737-3700, 800-946-4432; www.discoverhawaiitours.com) and **Roberts Hawaii** (☎ 808-954-8652, 866-898-2519; www.robertshawaii.com).

O'AHU

O'ahu is preeminent among Hawaii's islands – so much so that the others are referred to as 'Neighbor Islands.' O'ahu is the center of Hawaii's government, commerce and culture. It's home to three-quarters of state residents, and it's the destination of two-thirds of all visitors. Honolulu is one of the nation's major cities, and its nearby Waikiki beaches gave birth to the notion that Hawaii was paradise. If you want to take the measure of diverse Hawaii, O'ahu offers the full buffet in one tidy package: in the blink of an eye you can go from crowded metropolis to rolling hills carpeted in pineapples to remote turquoise bays teeming with sea life. Known as 'the gathering place,' O'ahu is the USA's best combination of urban living, natural beauty and rural community.

Getting Around

O'ahu's extensive public bus system, **TheBus** (☎ 808-848-5555; www.thebus.org; 811 Middle St, Kalihi Transit Center), has some 80 routes that col-

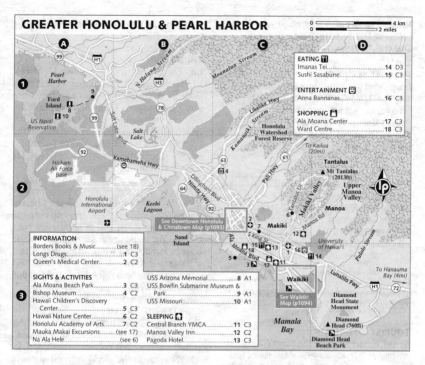

GREATER HONOLULU & PEARL HARBOR

EATING 🍴
Imanas Tei..14 D3
Sushi Sasabune................................15 C3

ENTERTAINMENT 🎭
Anna Bannanas..................................16 C3

SHOPPING 🛍️
Ala Moana Center..............................17 C3
Ward Centre.......................................18 C3

INFORMATION
Borders Books & Music.............(see 18)
Longs Drugs...1 C3
Queen's Medical Center.....................2 C2

SIGHTS & ACTIVITIES
Ala Moana Beach Park........................3 C3
Bishop Museum...................................4 C2
Hawaii Children's Discovery
  Center..5 C3
Hawaii Nature Center.........................6 C2
Honolulu Academy of Arts.................7 C2
Mauka Makai Excursions...........(see 17)
Na Ala Hele...............................(see 6)

USS Arizona Memorial.........................8 A1
USS Bowfin Submarine Museum &
  Park...9 A1
USS Missouri......................................10 A1

SLEEPING 🛏️
Central Branch YMCA........................11 C3
Manoa Valley Inn...............................12 C2
Pagoda Hotel......................................13 C3

lectively cover most of O'ahu; all fares are $2. From Honolulu International Airport to Waikiki, take bus 19 or 20. Buses 2, 19 and 20 connect Waikiki with downtown Honolulu and Chinatown.

The major car-rental companies are at the airport, and several also have branches in Waikiki. Another option for getting between Honolulu and Waikiki is the **Waikiki Trolley** (☎ 808-593-2822; www.waikikitrolley.com; all-day pass adult/child $25/12).

HONOLULU & WAIKIKI

More Asian than American, Honolulu is a delightful blend of ethnicities, a cacophonous mixture of language, custom and cuisine served with generous helpings of Hawaiian hospitality. Among its many museums and cultural offerings, it has the only royal palace in the USA, and has become a foodie heaven of cheap noodle joints and fancy Pacific Rim cuisine. Then, when city life is all too much, you can saunter over to gorgeous Waikiki to lounge on the sand, play in the water and listen to splendid Hawaiian music in the evening.

Orientation & Information

The airport is on the outskirts of Honolulu; airport buses pass through Honolulu's city center on their way to Waikiki. Diamond Head, the extinct volcano looming above the eastern side of Waikiki, is such a major landmark that islanders typically say 'go Diamond Head' when they give directions.

BOOKSTORES
Bestsellers (Map p1094; ☎ 808-953-2378; Hilton Hawaiian Village, 2005 Kalia Rd, Waikiki; 🕐 8am-10pm)
Borders Books & Music (Map p1091; ☎ 808-591-8995; Ward Centre, 1200 Ala Moana Blvd, Honolulu; 🕐 9am-11pm, to midnight Fri & Sat)

INTERNET ACCESS
Kuhio Ave has lots of internet shops; average surfing costs $6 to $7 an hour.
Daily Buzz Internet Cafe (Map p1094; ☎ 808-924-2223; 150 Kaiulani Ave, Waikiki; per hr $6; 🕐 6am-8pm Mon-Fri, to 2pm Sat & Sun)

MEDIA
Honolulu Advertiser (www.honoluluadvertiser.com) Hawaii's largest daily newspaper.

HAWAII

Honolulu Weekly (www.honoluluweekly.com) Progressive free paper with extensive entertainment section.
KINE (105.1 FM) Hawaiian music.

MEDICAL SERVICES

Longs Drugs (Map p1091; ☎ 808-949-4781; www
.longs.com; 2220 S King St, Honolulu; ◑ 24hr) Honolulu
has numerous Longs with varying hours.
Queen's Medical Center (Map p1091; ☎ 808-538-
9011; 1301 Punchbowl St, Honolulu; ◑ 24hr) A major
full-service hospital.

MONEY

The following financial institutions have
islandwide branches.
Bank of Hawaii (Map p1094; ☎ 808-543-6900, 888-
643-3888; www.boh.com; 2228 Kalakaua Ave, Waikiki)
First Hawaiian Bank (Map p1093; ☎ 808-525-6888;
www.fhb.com; 2 N King St, Honolulu)

POST

Post office downtown (Map p1093; ☎ 800-275-8777;
335 Merchant St); Waikiki (Map p1094; ☎ 808-973-7515;
330 Saratoga Rd)

TOURIST INFORMATION

Hawaii Visitors & Convention Bureau (Map p1094;
☎ 808-923-1811, 800-464-2924; www.gohawaii.com;
Waikiki Shopping Plaza, 2270 Kalakaua Ave, Suite 801)
O'ahu Visitors Bureau (☎ 877-525-6248; www.visit
-oahu.com) Stock up on brochures at the airport counter.

Sights & Activities

DOWNTOWN HONOLULU

At the heart of downtown Honolulu, the
19th-century 'Iolani Palace (Map p1093; ☎ 808-
522-0832; www.iolanipalace.org; cnr S King & Richards
Sts; tours $20; ◑ 9am-3pm Tue-Sat) offers a unique
glimpse of Hawaii's intriguing history. At
the adjacent **State Capitol** (Map p1093), visitors
can wander through the rotunda without
charge. Built of coral slabs, the nearby 1842
Kawaiaha'o Church (Map p1093; ☎ 808-522-1333; 957
Punchbowl St; admission free; ◑ 8am-4pm Mon-Fri) is
O'ahu's oldest church.

A central piece of the island art scene,
the **Hawai'i State Art Museum** (Map p1093; ☎ 808-
586-0300; www.hawaii.gov/sfca; 250 S Hotel St; admission
free; ◑ 10am-4pm Tue-Sat) showcases the work of
Hawaiian artists.

The **Hawai'i Maritime Center** (Map p1093;
☎ 808-523-6151; www.holoholo.org/maritime; Pier 7; admission $7.50; ◑ 8:30am-5pm) offers an evocative
look at Hawaii's maritime history, from the

arrival of the first Polynesian settlers to the
whaling era.

CHINATOWN

Immediately north of downtown Honolulu,
Chinatown is an intriguing quarter that lends
itself to exploring. Bring an appetite, since
grazing the superb Asian food is a prime activity as you wander among the herbalists,
temples and tattoo parlors. Get started at the
colorful **O'ahu Market** (Map p1093; cnr Kekaulike & N
King Sts) – the bustling heart of Chinatown for
more than a century.

WAIKIKI

Waikiki is all about that loooong beach.
Catamarans and outriggers pull up onto the
sand offering rides, and at regular intervals
concession stands rent surfboards, boogie
boards, kayaks and windsurfing gear at reasonable prices. If you need just a *little* help
perfecting your technique, lessons are readily
available as well.

GREATER HONOLULU

Bishop Museum (Map p1091; ☎ 808-847-3511; www.bishop
museum.org; 1525 Bernice St; admission $16; ◑ 9am-5pm),
considered the finest Polynesian anthropolog-
ical museum in the world, offers impressive
displays on Hawaii's multiethnic history, as
well as a Science Adventure Center that puts
you inside an erupting volcano.

The exceptional **Honolulu Academy of Arts** (Map
p1091; ☎ 808-532-8701; www.honoluluacademy.org; 900
S Beretania St; admission $7; ◑ 10am-4:30pm Tue-Sat, 1-
5pm Sun) has must-see collections of Asian,
European and Pacific art.

There are several hiking trails and lookouts with sweeping city views in the Tantalus
area, the lush Upper Manoa and Makiki Valleys, and in the hills above the University of
Hawai'i. Some trailheads are accessible by
bus. Run by the state Division of Forestry &
Wildlife, **Na Ala Hele** (Map p1091; ☎ 808-973-9782;
www.hawaiitrails.org; 2135 Makiki Heights Dr; ◑ 7:45am-
4:30pm Mon-Fri) distributes free trail maps.

For a great place to swim without the tourist crowds, head to **Ala Moana Beach Park** (Map
p1091; 1201 Ala Moana Blvd), between downtown
and Waikiki.

Honolulu & Waikiki for Children

O'ahu spills over with activities for *keiki* (children). To check out the wild side, head to the
petting area of the **Honolulu Zoo** (Map p1094; ☎ 808-

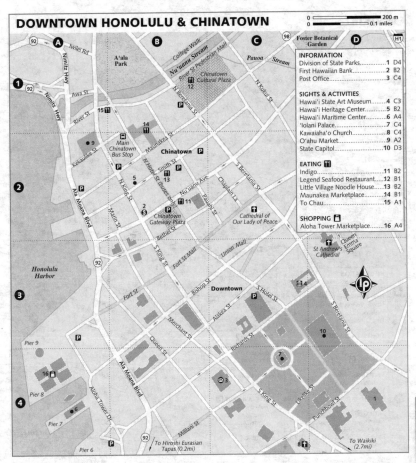

DOWNTOWN HONOLULU & CHINATOWN

INFORMATION	
Division of State Parks	1 D4
First Hawaiian Bank	2 B2
Post Office	3 C4

SIGHTS & ACTIVITIES	
Hawai'i State Art Museum	4 C3
Hawai'i Heritage Center	5 B2
Hawai'i Maritime Center	6 A4
'Iolani Palace	7 C4
Kawaiaha'o Church	8 C4
O'ahu Market	9 A2
State Capitol	10 D3

EATING	
Indigo	11 B2
Legend Seafood Restaurant	12 B1
Little Village Noodle House	13 B2
Maunakea Marketplace	14 B1
To Chau	15 A1

SHOPPING	
Aloha Tower Marketplace	16 A4

971-7171; www.honoluluzoo.org; 151 Kapahulu Ave; adult/
child $8/1; 9am-4:30pm). Across the street, the
Waikiki Aquarium (808-923-9741; www.waquarium
.org; 2777 Kalakaua Ave; adult/child $9/2; 9am-5pm) has
a touch tank geared for kids.

The kid-centered **Hawaii Nature Center** (Map
p1091; 808-955-0100; www.hawaiinaturecenter.org; 2131
Makiki Heights Dr) conducts family programs and
hikes on most weekends; see the website for
a schedule.

Of course, kids love Waikiki Beach as much
as anyone. And when the sun fails to shine,
the hands-on **Hawaii Children's Discovery Center**
(Map p1091; 808-524-5437; www.discoverycenterhawaii
.org; 111 Ohe St; adult/child $8/6.75; 9am-1pm Tue-Fri,
10am-3pm Sat & Sun) is the perfect place to spend
an afternoon.

Tours

For something more interesting than the typical bus tour, try one of the following:
Hawaii Food Tours (800-926-3663, 800-715-2468;
www.hawaiifoodtours.com; tours $100-200) From holes-
in-the-wall to gourmet temples.
Hawai'i Heritage Center (Map p1093; 808-521-
2749; 1140 Smith St; tours $10; 9:30-11:30am Wed &
Fri) Chinatown walking tours.
Mauka Makai Excursions (866-896-0596; www
.hawaiianecotours.net; 350 Ward Ave, Ste 106; tours $52-
85) Hawaiian-run cultural ecotours; some hiking.

Festivals & Events

King Kamehameha Day (808-586-0333), a state
holiday in early June, is celebrated with festivities at 'Iolani Palace. Across the state from

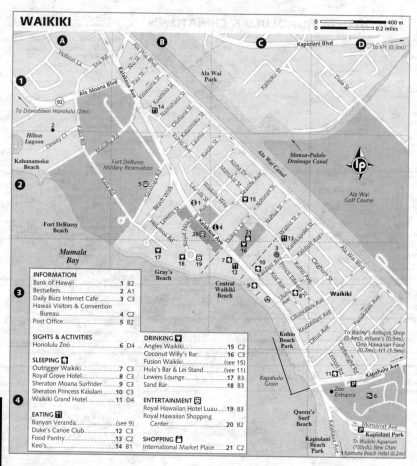

WAIKIKI

INFORMATION
Bank of Hawaii..........................**1** B2	
Bestsellers..................................**2** A1	
Daily Buzz Internet Cafe.........**3** C3	
Hawaii Visitors & Convention	
Bureau...................................**4** C2	
Post Office................................**5** B2	

SIGHTS & ACTIVITIES
Honolulu Zoo...........................**6** D4

SLEEPING
Outrigger Waikiki......................**7** C3	
Royal Grove Hotel....................**8** C3	
Sheraton Moana Surfrider.......**9** C3	
Sheraton Princess Kaiulani....**10** C3	
Waikiki Grand Hotel...............**11** D4	

EATING
Banyan Veranda.......................(see 9)	
Duke's Canoe Club..................**12** C3	
Food Pantry.............................**13** C2	
Keo's.......................................**14** B1	

DRINKING
Angles Waikiki..........................**15** C2	
Coconut Willy's Bar.................**16** C3	
Fusion Waikiki.........................(see 15)	
Hula's Bar & Lei Stand.............(see 11)	
Lewers Lounge........................**17** B3	
Sand Bar...................................**18** B3	

ENTERTAINMENT
Royal Hawaiian Hotel Luau......**19** B3	
Royal Hawaiian Shopping	
Center................................**20** B2	

SHOPPING
International Market Place......**21** C2

August into October, **Aloha Festivals** (http://aloha
festivals.com) inspires two months of cultural
performances and celebrations. The North
Shore comes alive for the **Triple Crown of Surfing**
(www.triplecrownofsuring.com) from November to
December. See www.gohawaii.com for more
festivals and events.

Sleeping
As a rule, the best selection of hotels is in
Waikiki, while Honolulu has far better eats.

HONOLULU
Central Branch YMCA (Map p1091; ☎ 808-941-3344; www
.ymcahonolulu.org; 401 Atkinson Dr; r with shared/private bath
from $37/57; ✗ ☜) Opposite a lovely beach just
outside Waikiki, the YMCA has 114 straight-

forward rooms. Those with private bath are
open to men and women; shared-bath rooms
are for men only. Guests have access to Y facilities. Parking ($5) is occasionally available.

Pagoda Hotel (Map p1091; ☎ 808-941-6611, 800-367-
6060; www.pagodahotel.com; 1525 Rycroft St; r from $120;
☜) Return visitors flock to this place for its
good-value, comfortable digs. Midway between Waikiki and downtown, it's best suited
to visitors with a car. Check out the hotel's
namesake pagoda-style restaurant and surrounding koi pond. Parking is $5.

Manoa Valley Inn (Map p1091; ☎ 808-947-6019;
www.manoavalleyinn.com; 2001 Vancouver Dr; r with shared/
private bath from $130/160; P ✗) This restored,
atmospheric Victorian exudes colonial
charm. It's a satisfying stay as long as you

don't mind being near the university rather than the beach.

WAIKIKI

Waikiki is the center of the action, and the closer to the beach, the pricier it gets. Kalakaua Ave, the main beachfront strip, is lined with swanky high-rise hotels with equivalent decor. For better value, look off the beach and along Kuhio Ave.

Royal Grove Hotel (Map p1094; ☎ 808-923-7691; www .royalgrovehotel.com; 151 Uluniu Ave; r $50-80; ✕ 🐾 🖭) This classic, family-run, low-rise hotel satisfies the thrifty with spacious if worn rooms (all with kitchenette, some with AC) and genuine aloha. Central location.

Waikiki Grand Hotel (Map p1094; ☎ 808-923-1814, 800-321-2558; www.queenssurf.com; 134 Kapahulu Ave; r from $100, ste $150-250; 🐾 🖭) Cleanliness and decor vary among these decent condo units, but at least they're not cookie-cutter. The hotel is also known for Hula's, a popular gay bar. Parking is $14.

New Otani Kaimana Beach Hotel (☎ 808-923-1555, 800-356-8264; www.kaimana.com; 2863 Kalakaua Ave; r $170-375, studios $200, ste $270-680; 🐾) For a little more privacy and seclusion, the New Otani offers well-kept, small rooms and its own beach about a half mile from the throbbing heart of Waikiki. Parking is $15.

Sheraton Princess Kaiulani (Map p1094; ☎ 808-922-5811, 866-716-8109; www.princess-kaiulani.com; 120 Kaiulani Ave; r $205-400; 🐾 🖭 🖵) Rooms aren't special, but the location is great and being *just* off the beach means better rates. Parking is $15.

Outrigger Waikiki (Map p1094; ☎ 808-923-0711, 800-688-7444; www.outrigger.com; 2335 Kalakaua Ave; r from $360; ✕ 🐾 🖭 🖵) This is the Outrigger chain's flagship hotel in Waikiki, meaning its beach spot is absolutely prime even if the good rooms are ho-hum similar. Parking is $25.

our pick **Sheraton Moana Surfrider** (Map p1094; ☎ 808-922-3111, 866-716-8109; www.moana-surfrider .com; 2365 Kalakaua Ave; r from $380; 🐾 🖭 🖵 wi-fi) Hawaii's first beachfront hotel (since 1901), this grand establishment has been authentically restored; even guest rooms retain their period appearance. Avoid noisier 'city view' rooms; online deals significantly lower the rate. Parking is $15.

Eating

Honolulu is a culinary delight – abundant with every sort of ethnic Asian eatery you could name. If this were the mainland, the scene would get much more press.

HONOLULU

To Chau (Map p1093; ☎ 808-533-4549; 1007 River St; soups $4-7; ⏱ 8:30am-2:30pm) Most say this Chinatown staple serves Honolulu's best *pho*, a delicious, steamy Vietnamese soup spiced with heaps of fresh basil.

Maunakea Marketplace (Map p1093; N Hotel St; meals $5; ⏱ 7am-3:30pm) This Chinatown food court serves the ultimate local grinds, with mom-and-pop vendors whipping up homestyle Chinese, Filipino and Thai fare.

Imanas Tei (Map p1091; ☎ 808-941-2626; 2626 S King St; mains $5-15; ⏱ 5-11:30pm Mon-Sat) At this *izakaya* (a Japanese pub serving food), enjoy world-class sake while grazing on sushi and crowd-pleasing *nabemono* (do-it-yourself meat and vegetable soups). It's a great time.

Little Village Noodle House (Map p1093; ☎ 808-545-3008; 1113 Smith St; mains $7-15; ⏱ 10:30am-10:30pm Sun-Thu, to midnight Fri & Sat) A quiet, air-conditioned restaurant in Chinatown? That's only the beginning. The kitchen sets a gold standard, particularly for black-bean sauce and noodles.

Legend Seafood Restaurant (Map p1093; ☎ 808-532-1868; Chinatown Cultural Plaza; mains $8-20; ⏱ 10:30am-2pm & 5:30-9pm Mon-Fri, 8am-2pm & 5:30-9pm Sat & Sun) Bright, busy and a tad impersonal, Legend Seafood is best known for its extensive dim sum – observe what savvy patrons grab from the wheeled carts and follow suit.

Sushi Sasabune (Map p1091; ☎ 808-947-3800; 1419 S King St; mains $10-15; ⏱ noon-2pm & 5:30-10pm Tue-Fri, 5:30-10pm Sat & Mon) Sushi lovers, get ready to be dazzled at this *omakase* (chef's choice)

BE YOUR OWN TOUR GUIDE

No car? No worries, brah! You can make a fun, easy day excursion circling the island by public bus. Routes 52 and 55 combine, taking you in four nonstop hours from Honolulu's Ala Moana Center, up H1 to Haleiwa, past the North Shore, down the Windward Coast, and back to Honolulu via the Pali Hwy. Stop as many times as you like and simply catch the next bus; they run every 30 to 60 minutes daily. Each bus ride costs $2, which for a five-break journey comes to a whopping $10. Or buy a four-day visitor pass ($20) and have unlimited usage for a multiday trip. What a deal!

restaurant – whether familiar or unrecognizable, the sushi is never less than exquisite. Reserve ahead.

Indigo (Map p1093; ☎ 808-521-2900; 1121 Nu'uanu Ave; mains $16-26; ⊗ 11:30am-2pm & 6-9:30pm Tue-Fri, 6-9:30pm Sat) A cheery open-air courtyard, creative dim sum and contemporary Eurasian cuisine keep Indigo hopping with locals and visitors alike. It also has a popular nightclub.

ourpick Hiroshi Eurasian Tapas (☎ 808-533-4476; 500 Ala Moana Blvd; mains $18-22; ⊗ 5:30-9:30pm) The Honolulu culinary scene is all about East-West fusions, and chef Hiroshi Fukui adds his own personal stamp with his subtle, unlikely, delicious creations.

WAIKIKI

Food Pantry (Map p1094; ☎ 808-923-9831; 2370 Kuhio Ave; ⊗ 6am-1am) The best place to get groceries in Waikiki.

Ono Hawaiian Food (☎ 808-737-2275; 726 Kapahulu Ave; meals $8-11; ⊗ 11am-7:45pm Mon-Sat) Come here to try traditional fare – go for the kalua pig plate, served with several Hawaiian side dishes.

Irifune's (☎ 808-737-1141; 563 Kapahulu Ave; mains $10-15; ⊗ 11:30am-1:30pm & 5:30-9:30pm Tue-Sat) Follow the locals to this bustling Japanese eatery where fresh fish is artistically prepared – the *tataki 'ahi* (seared tuna) is to die for.

Keo's (Map p1094; ☎ 808-951-9355; 2028 Kuhio Ave; mains $12-18; ⊗ 7am-2pm & 5-10pm) A favorite of visiting celebs, this Thai restaurant has a full page of vegetarian options as well as all the usual fish and meat versions.

Duke's Canoe Club (Map p1094; ☎ 808-922-2268; 2335 Kalakaua Ave; breakfast & lunch buffet $12, dinner mains $15-27; ⊗ 7am-10pm) Named after surfing legend Duke Kahanamoku, this waterfront restaurant packs in a crowd for its island atmosphere, live music and reliable food.

Banyan Veranda (Map p1094; ☎ 808-922-3111; 2365 Kalakaua Ave; 3-course meals $57; ⊗ 5:30-9pm) This courtyard veranda at the Sheraton Moana Surfrider offers classic Pacific Rim and French cuisine in a thoroughly romantic setting.

Drinking

Coconut Willy's Bar (Map p1094; ☎ 808-923-9454; International Market Place, 2330 Kalakaua Ave; ⊗ 11:30am-midnight) Willy's tends to be loud, but it's a great people-watching spot.

Sand Bar (Map p1094; ☎ 808-922-4422; Sheraton Waikiki Hotel, 2255 Kalakaua Ave; ⊗ music 6-8:30pm)

This cabana-like bar has views of Diamond Head and live Hawaiian music nightly, including '*keiki* hula', when a children's hula group displays its stuff.

Lewers Lounge (Map p1094; ☎ 808-923-2311; Halekulani Hotel, 2199 Kalia Rd; ⊗ music 7:30pm-1am) This sophisticated lounge is old-school Waikiki, with top-shelf, fresh-juice cocktails and smooth live jazz music.

Entertainment

The free *Honolulu Weekly* has full details on what's happening around Honolulu and Waikiki.

Waikiki abounds in Hawaiian-style entertainment. Bask in the aloha with performances by local hula troupes at the city-sponsored **Kuhio Beach Torch Lighting & Hula Show** (☎ 808-843-8002; admission free; ⊗ 6:30-7:30pm) at Kuhio Beach Park (Map p1094). Many beachfront hotels offer evening Hawaiian music at their outdoor bars. Two excellent places to start are the beachside Sheraton Moana Surfrider (p1095) and Duke's Canoe Club (left).

Anna Bannanas (Map p1091; ☎ 808-946-5190; 2440 S Beretania St; ⊗ 9pm-2am Thu-Sun) Near the university, this is a hot weekend dance venue.

Royal Hawaiian Hotel Luau (Map p1094; ☎ 808-921-4600; www.royal-hawaiian.com/de_luau.htm; 2259 Kalakaua Ave; adult/child 5-12yr $100/55; ⊗ 6-8:30pm Mon & Thu) Yup, this luau is touristy, but the pretty oceanfront setting is scenically ideal. It's in the heart of Waikiki, the food is decent and the performances are professional.

Royal Hawaiian Shopping Center (Map p1094; ☎ 808-922-0588; 2201 Kalakaua Ave; ⊗ 6:30pm Tue-Sun) Odd setting that it is, this mall hosts interesting musical and hula performances on the 2nd floor and sponsors various classes in hula, lei making and the ukulele.

Shopping

International Market Place (Map p1094; ☎ 808-971-2080; 2330 Kalakaua Ave; ⊗ 10am-10pm) All the kitschy, tacky souvenirs you ever wanted spread among a hundred stalls under a sprawling banyan tree in central Waikiki.

Bailey's Antique Shop (☎ 808-734-7628; 517 Kapahulu Ave; ⊗ 10am-6pm) An overwhelming collection of vintage and used aloha shirts – all styles and prices.

You'll also find Hawaiian crafts, food and clothing in Honolulu's main shopping centers:

GAY & LESBIAN WAIKIKI

Waikiki is the heart of Honolulu's well-developed gay scene. Two free monthly magazines, **DaKine** (www.dakinemagazine.com) and **Odyssey** (www.odysseyhawaii.com), have full details. Queen's Surf Beach (Map p1094) is the destination for the sun-worshipping gay crowd.

Waikiki's top gay venue, **Hula's Bar & Lei Stand** (Map p1094; ☎ 808-923-0669; 134 Kapahulu Ave; ⏰ 10am-2am), is a cheery open-air bar and the place to meet. Other good spots include **Angles Waikiki** (Map p1094; ☎ 808-926-9766; 2256 Kuhio Ave; ⏰ 10am-2am), a bar by day and a nightclub after dark; and **Fusion Waikiki** (Map p1094; ☎ 808-924-2422; 2260 Kuhio Ave; ⏰ 10pm-4am Sun-Thu, 8pm-4am Fri & Sat), which features karaoke and female-impersonator shows.

Ala Moana Center (Map p1091; ☎ 808-955-9517; 1450 Ala Moana Blvd; ⏰ 9:30am-9pm Mon-Sat, 10:30am-7pm Sun)

Aloha Tower Marketplace (Map p1093; ☎ 808-566-2337; 1 Aloha Tower Dr; ⏰ 9am-9pm)

Ward Centre (Map p1091; ☎ 808-591-8411; Ward Ave; ⏰ 10am-9pm Mon-Sat, to 6pm Sun) Adjacent to Ward Warehouse.

PEARL HARBOR

On December 7, 1941, a Japanese attack on Pearl Harbor took 2500 lives, sank 21 ships and fatefully catapulted the US into WWII. Today more than 1.5 million people a year 'remember Pearl Harbor' by visiting the **USS Arizona Memorial** (Map p1091).

From the memorial, which sits directly over the sunken *Arizona*, visitors can look down at the shallow wreck that became a tomb for 1177 sailors. The **visitor center** (☎ 808-422-0561; www.nps.gov/usar; admission & tour free; ⏰ 7:30am-5pm) runs 1¼-hour tours that include a documentary on the attack and a boat ride out to the memorial. Tours run on a first-come, first-served basis; arrive early to beat the queues. No purses, fanny packs or large cameras are allowed; storage ($2) is available in the parking lot.

If you have to wait for your tour to start, walk over to the adjacent **USS Bowfin Submarine Museum & Park** (Map p1091; ☎ 808-423-1341; www.bowfin.org; admission free, submarine tours $10; ⏰ 8am-5pm), where you can poke around grounds dotted with WWII relics or clamber down into a retired submarine. Bowfin is also the departure point for a shuttle bus to the **USS Missouri** (Map p1091; ☎ 808-973-2494; www.ussmissouri.org; tours $16; ⏰ 9am-5pm), whose deck hosted the Japanese surrender that ended WWII.

From Waikiki, bus 42 goes to Pearl Harbor ($2) or take the **VIP Trans** (☎ 808-839-0911; round trip $10), which picks up from Waikiki hotels.

SOUTHEAST O'AHU

The southeast coast abounds in dramatic scenery and offers plenty of activities. For a sweeping view of the area make the 1.5-mile climb up **Diamond Head** (Map p1091; Diamond Head Rd; per person/car $1/5; ⏰ 6am-6pm), the 763ft extinct volcano that forms the famous backdrop to Waikiki.

The best place on O'ahu to go eyeball to eyeball with tropical fish is at **Hanauma Bay Nature Preserve** (☎ 808-396-4229; Hwy 72; admission $5; ⏰ 6am-7pm Wed-Mon Apr-Oct, to 6pm rest of year), a gorgeous turquoise bathtub set in a rugged volcanic ring. For the best conditions head to the outer reef; you can rent snorkel gear on site. Parking costs $1.

Long and lovely **Sandy Beach**, along Hwy 72 about a mile north of Hanauma, offers challenging bodysurfing with the kinds of punishing shorebreaks and strong rips that make it a favorite of pros – exhilarating action even for spectators!

To get to these places from Waikiki, take bus 22 ($2).

WINDWARD COAST

The deeply scalloped Ko'olau mountains form a scenic backdrop for the entire windward coast. Trade winds whipping in from the northeast rebound off the mountains, creating ideal conditions for windsurfing.

The reef-protected **Waimanalo Bay** contains O'ahu's longest beach (5.5 miles of gleaming white sand), and it's great for swimming. From Hwy 72, make a detour south on Hwy 61 to reach the **Nu'uanu Pali Lookout** (1200ft) and its stunning panoramic coastal view.

Beneath the windswept *pali* (cliffs) sits beautiful **Kailua Beach**, the island's top **windsurfing** spot. Just beyond the beach, the bird sanctuary of **Popoia Island** is a popular destination for kayakers. Gear rental and windsurfing lessons are available weekdays on the

HAWAII

HOT TOPIC: O'AHU'S HOMELESS

Homelessness is a problem in every big city in the US, and it's grown dramatically on O'ahu, due largely to a galloping real-estate market that has doubled rents and sometimes tripled home prices in recent years. The most dramatic evidence of this problem is along the Wai'anae Coast, west of Honolulu, where many of the city-managed beach parks now contain semipermanent homeless encampments. Some estimate that there are over 1000 homeless people on the beaches and perhaps as many as 10,000 islandwide.

Unlike on the mainland, most of O'ahu's homeless are low-income families and the working poor, whose low-wage jobs haven't kept pace with the economy. In 2006 the governor announced plans for the construction of new subsidized-housing projects, but most observers doubt that more housing alone will solve the problem. Tourism and real estate, the main drivers of the state's boom, both tend to gentrify neglected, inexpensive communities (like Wai'anea), marginalizing the poor even further. Until the structure of Hawaii's economy changes, homelessness will likely persist as the unintended consequence of creating 'paradise.'

beach. **Kailua** has plenty of sleeping and eating options, and makes a good place to stay. For area B&Bs and condos, check the **Bed & Breakfast Association of O'ahu** (☎ 808-262-8286; www.stayoahu.com).

Other notable beaches on the windward coast are **Kualoa Regional Park**, which has a scenic setting and an ancient stone fishpond, and **Malaekahana Beach**, a sandy beach good for swimming and surfing.

The **Polynesian Cultural Center** (☎ 808-293-3333, 800-367-7060; www.polynesia.com; Hwy 83, La'ie; admission $55; ☺ noon-9pm Mon-Sat) is a Polynesian theme park (and all that implies) with villages, performances and luau buffets. It draws more visitors than anyplace else on O'ahu except Pearl Harbor and is run by the Mormon Church.

NORTH SHORE

O'ahu's North Shore is legendary for the massive 30ft winter swells that thunder against its beaches. In the 1960s, surfers first learned to ride these deadly waves, and today the North Shore hosts some of the most awesome surf competitions in the world, particularly December's famed Triple Crown.

The gateway to the North Shore, **Hale'iwa** is the only real town in this region – along its main road you'll find a funky surf museum, shops selling surfing paraphernalia, and rusty pickup trucks with surfboards tied to the roof. When the surf's up, folks really do drop what they're doing and hit the waves. And they don't have to go far, as **Hale'iwa Ali'i Beach Park**, right in town, sees towering north swells.

The North Shore's most popular beach, **Waimea Bay Beach Park**, in the town of Wai-

mea, flaunts a dual personality. In summer the water can be as calm as a lake and ideal for swimming and snorkeling, while in winter it rips with the highest waves on the island.

A few miles to the north, the **Banzai Pipeline** breaks over a shallow reef, creating a death-defying ride for the pros hitting the action here. Next up is **Sunset Beach Park**, O'ahu's classic winter surf spot, famous for its incredible surf and tricky breaks; it's also a fashionable sunbathing locale.

Hale'iwa Joe's (☎ 808-637-8005; www.haleiwajoes .com; 66-011 Kamehameha Ave, Hale'iwa; appetizers $7-10, lunch $8-15, dinner $18-26; ☺ 11:30am-9:30pm), a North Shore institution, serves up hearty seafood-inspired meals. Emma's Poke (marinated raw 'ahi) and coconut shrimp are some of the favorites.

HAWAI'I (THE BIG ISLAND)

Diverse in every way, and twice the size of all the other Hawaiian islands combined, the Big Island earns its nickname. Most thrillingly, it's still growing. Hawai'i contains two active volcanoes, one of which – Kilauea – has been erupting almost nonstop for the last 25 years. Along with red-hot lava, the Big Island offers stargazing from subarctic mountaintops, ancient Hawaiian places of refuge, an artistic working-class city, well-preserved plantation towns, horse riding in cowboy country, rugged hikes through deserts and rain forests, and a full range of soporific beaches, from bone-white strands to green to tan to black and cratered with lava-rock tide pools. Considering it contains a whole continent's worth of adventures, Hawai'i is actually quite accessibly small.

Getting There & Around

Mainland flights arrive at both Kona and Hilo International **airports** (www.hawaii.gov/dot/airports/hawaii), and both have taxi stands and car-rental booths. You'll want to rent a car, as the public bus system, **Hele-On** (☎ 808-961-8744; www.co.hawaii.hi.us/mass_transit/heleonbus.html), is geared to commuters and has a very limited Monday-to-Saturday service, though it's free and circles the island.

KAILUA-KONA

At first glance, Kailua-Kona seems the sort of overbright tourist town where you sit in open-air cafés and count sunburnt vacationers for amusement. But past the kitschy shops lie the remains of old temples and other historical treasures from when this was the summer home of Hawaiian royalty. Plus, with sun-drenched beaches north and south, and stacks of activities at hand, this condo-rich area makes a great base for wider explorations.

Sights & Activities

The grounds of King Kamehameha's Kona Beach Hotel at **Kamakahonu Beach** were once the site of Kamehameha the Great's royal residence. They include the **Ahu'ena Heiau**, a temple Kamehameha once used for human sacrifice.

Minutes away on Ali'i Dr is the lava-rock **Moku'aikaua Church** (☎ 808-329-0655; Ali'i Dr; admission free; 🕑 8am-5pm), built in 1836 by Hawaii's first Christian missionaries. Across the street, get

---

WHAT THE...?

You see first one. Then a few in small groups. Then a whole line: spandex-bright cyclists peddling like wild beasts beneath a brutal sun. Check the calendar. Is it September or October? Of course – they're simply some of the 1500 triathletes readying themselves for the Big Island's **Ironman Triathlon World Championship** (www.ironmanlive.com), in which they'll bike 112 miles, run 26.2 miles and swim 2.4 miles. Call us crazy, but we'll just watch, thanks.

---

a peek at how royalty used to live at **Hulihe'e Palace** (☎ 808-329-1877; www.daughtersofhawaii.com; 75-5718 Ali'i Dr; admission $6; 🕑 9am-4pm), built in 1838 and packed with curious Hawaiian artifacts. For great easy-access snorkeling, head to **Kahalu'u Beach** on Ali'i Dr in Keauhou at the south side of Kailua; inexpensive gear rental is available on site.

Sleeping

For more condos, check the listings with **ATR Properties** (☎ 808-329-6020, 888-311-6020; www.konacondo.com) or **Kona Hawaii Vacation Rentals** (☎ 808-329-3333, 800-244-4752; www.konahawaii.com).

Kona Tiki Hotel (☎ 808-329-1425; www.konatiki.com; 75-5968 Ali'i Dr; r $65-88; 🏊) It's all about the price, the location and the surf outside your window; rooms are straightforward to the point of being tired. Some have kitchenettes.

Hale Kona Kai (☎ 808-329-2155, 800-421-3696; www.halekonakai-hkk.com; 75-5870 Kahakai Rd; 1-bedroom units $155-175; 🏊 ❄ wi-fi) It's hard to find fault with these well-kept oceanfront condo units, which have kitchens and all the modern comforts. Three-night minimum.

Eating

Island Lava Java (☎ 808-327-2161; 75-5799 Ali'i Dr; light eats $7-14; 🕑 6am-10pm; 🖥) It's the irresistible combo of any good café: fresh local coffee, good food and fascinating people-watching. There's internet access ($4 for 20 minutes) too.

Kona Brewing Company (☎ 808-329-2739; www.konabrewingco.com; 75-5629 Kuakini Hwy; sandwiches & salads $7-12, pizza $15-22; 🕑 11am-10pm Sun-Thu, to 11pm Fri & Sat) The Big Island's first microbrewery makes top-notch ales with a Hawaiian touch, in addition to serving decent sandwiches and pizzas. As a result, the place packs, so reserve ahead.

Kanaka Kava (☎ 808-327-1660; www.kanakakava.com; Coconut Grove Marketplace, 75-5803 Ali'i Dr; kava $4, salads $12-14; 🕑 10am-10pm Sun-Wed, to 11pm Thu-Sat) At this tiny spot, join locals for some mildly intoxicating kava (juice of the *'awa* plant) and *poke* (cubed, marinated raw tuna), plus salads and other well-made Hawaiian fare.

Fujimamas (☎ 808-327-2125; www.fujimamas.com; 75-5719 Ali'i Dr; meals $16-25; 🕑 11:30am-2:30pm & 5-11pm Mon-Sat, 5-11pm Sun) A chic, hip newcomer, Fujimamas immediately stands out in Kailua's restaurant scene. The fun, inventive Japanese meals and sushi will, as the menu promises, 'make you go ummm.'

SOUTH KONA COAST

Don't let yourself become so blinded by beaches you fail to explore South Kona's verdant hillsides and laid-back towns, its coffee farms and ancient Hawaiian sites, and, of course, its exquisite snorkeling.

A side road off Hwy 11 leads to the sparkling waters of mile-wide **Kealakekua Bay**. **Kealakekua Bay State Historical & Underwater Park** is at the bay's southern end, while an obelisk at its northern end marks the spot where Captain Cook was killed. The bay's northern end has the island's best **snorkeling**, which can be reached only by sea. For kayak rentals and tours, try the Hawaiian-owned **Aloha Kayak Company** (☎ 808-322-2868, 877-322-1444; www.alohakayak.com; Hwy 11, Honalo; kayak rentals $25-60, half-day tours $50-65). For snorkel and dive cruises, and nighttime manta-ray trips, try **Sea Paradise** (☎ 808-322-2500, 800-322-5662; www.seaparadise.com; adult/child snorkel cruise $95/59, manta snorkel $79/59).

In the town of Captain Cook, **Manago Hotel** (☎ 808-323-2642; www.managohotel.com; 82-6155 Hwy 11; r with shared/private bath $35/61), run by the same family since 1917, offers simple, well-kept rooms; 3rd-floor rooms snag a view.

Luana Inn (☎ 328-2612; www.luanainn.com; incl breakfast r $150-180, ste with kitchen $200; ⬛ ⬛) is a modern, spacious, tastefully decorated B&B that benefits immensely from the careful attention of its hosts. Breakfast is a buffet.

South of Kealakekua Bay, the incredible **Pu'uhonua O Honaunau National Historical Park** (☎ 808-328-2288; www.nps.gov/puho; per car $5; ⏰ 7am-8pm) is an ancient place of refuge that includes several temples and a *pu'uhonua* (a sanctuary where defeated warriors could have their lives spared). There's terrific snorkeling at nearby 'Two-Step,' at the boat ramp immediately north of the park.

NORTH KONA COAST

Beautiful secluded beaches lie on the north Kona Coast. Some are accessible only by foot, but visitors can reach the sparkling sands of pristine **Kekaha Kai State Park** (Hwy 19; admission free; ⏰ closed Wed) by car. The Big Island's fanciest resorts are further north, in the Waikoloa area of the South Kohala district. South Kohala was an important area in Hawaiian history, and it shelters *heiau* (ancient stone temples), fishponds, petroglyphs and ancient trails. The island's most popular beach, **Hapuna Beach State Recreation Area** (Hwy 19; admission free), is renowned for swimming, bodysurfing and generally lounging life away. To make it yours for a song, rent one of Hapuna's simple, screened **A-frame cabins** (☎ 808-974-6200; www.hawaii.gov/dlnr /dsp; cabins $20).

To go the other way, consider the **Hilton Waikoloa Village** (☎ 808-886-1234, 800-221-2424; www .hiltonwaikoloavillage.com; 425 Waikoloa Beach Dr, Waikoloa; r $280-430; ⬛ ⬛ ⬛ ⬛ wi-fi), which blurs the line between resort and theme park. It's huge, chock-full of amenities and extravagant.

WAIMEA

Waimea is the epicenter of the USA's largest cattle ranch, and you can learn all about Hawai'i's unusual cowboy history at the **Parker Ranch Museum** (☎ 808-885-7655; www.parkerranch.com; Parker Ranch Center, 67-1185 Mamalahoa Hwy; adult/child

---

WORTH THE TRIP: KONA COFFEE FARMS

Commercial coffee is grown on the other Hawaiian islands, but none yet has the gourmet cachet of 100% Kona coffee, which is the most successful coffee grown in the USA. The region's fertile volcanic soil and climate – sunny mornings, cloudy afternoons, cool nights – make for ideal conditions. But also there are no large plantations. About 600 small coffee farms, most family-run, dot the Kona district; harvesting by hand occurs several times during the season, and roasting is always in small batches.

For a free tour, stop by **Greenwell Farms** (☎ 888-592-5662; www.greenwellfarms.com; ⏰ 8am-5pm Mon-Sat, tours until 4pm). It's one of Kona's oldest coffee farms, in Kealekekua on Hwy 11 between the 110- and 111-mile markers. Then, just down the road, check out the **Kona Coffee Living History Farm** (☎ 808-323-2006; www.konahistorical.org; adult/child $15/7.50; ⏰ tours on the hr 9am-1pm Mon-Fri), which recreates rural Japanese-immigrant life in the early 20th century. In November, catch the 10-day **Kona Coffee Cultural Festival** (☎ 808-326-7820; www.konacoffeefest.com).

Since 100% Kona coffee runs $22 to $30 a pound, don't be fooled by imitations (or by 'cheap' Kona coffee, which typically contains only 10% Kona beans): look for the **Kona Coffee Council** (www.kona-coffee-council.com) seal of approval on the bag.

$7/5.50; 🕑 9am-5pm Mon-Sat, last entry 4pm). Suitably inspired, book a horseback ride with the Hawaiian-owned **Dahana Ranch Roughriders** (☎ 808-885-0057, 888-399-0057; www.dahanaranch .com; rides per 1½/2hr $60/100; 🕑 9am, 11am, 1pm & 3pm, reservations required).

Waimea is oddly flush with gourmet restaurants, and none is more famous than **Merriman's** (☎ 808-885-6822; www.merrimanshawaii .com; Opelo Plaza, 65-1227 Opelo Rd; dinner mains $30-45; 🕑 11:30am-1:30pm & 5:30-9pm Mon-Fri, 5:30-9pm Sat & Sun), an early innovator of Hawaii Regional Cuisine. Service is perfect, and the proof is on the plate.

MAUNA KEA

Measured from its base beneath the sea, this sacred **mountain** (13,796ft) is the tallest on earth, and its summit, nearly touching the sky, is clustered with world-class astronomical observatories. Partway up the mountain, the **Onizuka Center for International Astronomy** (☎ 808-961-2180; www.ifa.hawaii.edu/info/vis; admission free; 🕑 9am-10pm) offers displays, free astronomy presentations, awesome stargazing and summit tours (BYO 4WD). Continuing to the summit for sunset is unforgettable, but it requires a 4WD or a grueling 6-mile, high-altitude hike that takes 10 hours round trip; contact the center for advice and weather conditions.

Getting to the Onizuka Center means driving the 50-mile Saddle Rd (Hwy 200), which cuts across the 'saddle' between Mauna Kea and Mauna Loa, Hawai'i's other towering mountain. The views are majestic, but the paved road is accident prone, so most car-rental contracts prohibit travel on it; ask when renting.

The easiest way to experience Mauna Kea? Book a good guided tour, such as one with **Hawaii Forest & Trail** (☎ 808-331-8505, 800-464-1993; www.hawaii-forest.com; tours $170).

HAMAKUA COAST

The Hamakua Coast offers some of the Big Island's most spectacular scenery – it's a *Lost*-worthy show of deep ravines, lush jungle valleys and cascading waterfalls.

Most scenic of all is **Waipi'o Valley**, the largest of seven magnificent amphitheater valleys on the windward coast. Hwy 240 dead-ends at a dramatic overlook; the road down is so steep only 4WDs can make it. It's worth the 30-minute hike down (and 60 minutes back

up) to meditate on the black-sand beach, admiring the wild horses and thunderous ocean, and surrounded by ribbony waterfalls feeding ancient taro patches.

Another moody stop is beautiful **Laupahoehoe Point**, where in 1946 Hawaii's worst tsunami swept away half the town as well as dozens of children on their way to school. **'Akaka Falls State Park** (Hwy 220) contains two stunning waterfalls that are easily accessed along a short rain-forest loop trail. **Pepe'ekeo Scenic Dr** makes for a delightful 4-mile detour, cutting through a thick forest of flowering tulip trees on the way south to Hilo.

HILO

The island capital, Hilo has been dubbed the 'rainiest city in the US,' and that soggy reputation tends to keep tourists away. It's their loss, because Hilo is one of the most interesting cities in the state. Ethnically diverse, largely working class, with a walkable, historic downtown, it provides visitors with an evocative slice of real Hawaii. Browse its vibrant farmers market and its wealth of galleries and museums, and you find a sense of community undampened by mass tourism. Besides, the rain isn't all bad. It's usually short-lived, and it's responsible for the heart-stopping landscape cradling you on all sides.

Sights & Activities

With its waterfront of century-old buildings, downtown Hilo brims with weather-beaten charm. Pick up a walking-tour map at the **Big Island Visitors Bureau** (☎ 808-961-5797; www.gohawaii .com/bigisland; 250 Keawe St; 🕑 8am-4:30pm Mon-Fri).

One of Hawaii's most fascinating museums, **'Imiloa Astronomy Center of Hawai'i** (☎ 808-969-9700; www.maunakeaastronomycenter.com; 600 'Imiloa Pl; adult/child $14.50/7.50; 🕑 9am-4pm Tue-Sun) explores Native Hawaiian culture and mythology, Hawaiian ecology and environment, and astronomical discoveries about our universe – all filtered through the lens of Mauna Kea. It's an eye-popping, thought-provoking journey.

The **Lyman Museum** (☎ 808-935-5021; www .lymanmuseum.org; 276 Haili St; admission $10; 🕑 9:30am-4:30pm Mon-Sat) provides an excellent overview of Hawaii's natural and cultural history. Hilo has survived several major tsunami, and the dramatic **Pacific Tsunami Museum** (☎ 808-935-0926; www.tsunami.org; 130 Kamehameha Ave; adult $7; 🕑 9am-4pm Mon-Sat) brings these chilling events to life.

If possible, time your visit for Hilo's twice-weekly **farmers market** (www.hilofarmersmarket.com; cnr Mamo St & Kamehameha Ave; 🕑 6am-3pm Wed & Sat), an islandwide event that's equal parts gossip and shopping. The produce is first rate, and craft and clothing stalls abound.

Sleeping

Hilo Bay Hostel (☎ 808-933-2771; www.hawaiihostel.net; 101 Waianuenue Ave; dm $22, r with/without bathroom $65/55; 🖳) Put simply, this hostel is great. Perfectly situated downtown, it's well maintained and welcoming; private rooms are a great deal.

Dolphin Bay Hotel (☎ 808-935-1466, 877-935-1466; www.dolphinbayhilo.com; 333 Iliahi St; r $100-160) This is a perennial favorite with volcanoes-bound travelers who like to settle in. Rooms aren't snazzy, but they're clean and comfortable and have kitchens.

Inn at Kulaniapia (☎ 808-935-6789, 866-935-6789; www.waterfall.net; d $120, cottages $175; 🖳) If romance means having your own private waterfall, then book one of the cozy roosts in this secluded B&B.

Shipman House B&B (☎ 808-934-8002, 800-627-8447; www.hilo-hawaii.com; 131 Kaiulani St; r incl breakfast $205-225; ✖ wi-fi) Hilo's most gracious B&B occupies a historic Victorian mansion packed with museum-quality Hawaiiana. Queen Lili'uokalani once entertained on the grand piano.

Eating

Miyo's (☎ 808-935-2273; Waiakea Villa, 400 Hualani St; mains $8-15; 🕑 11am-2pm & 5:30-8:30pm Mon-Sat) Overlooking Waiakea Pond, evocative Miyo's serves tasty homemade Japanese meals in a rustic teahouse setting.

Café Pesto (☎ 808-969-6640; 308 Kamehameha Ave; pizzas $11-18, dinner mains $16-30; 🕑 11am-9pm Sun-Thu, to 10pm Fri & Sat) A buzzing, friendly downtown choice with a varied menu; pizzas and seafood are noteworthy.

Restaurant Kaikodo (☎ 808-961-2558; www.restaurantkaikodo.com; 60 Keawe St; dinner mains $20-35; 🕑 11am-2pm & 5:30-9pm Mon-Fri, 5:30-9pm Sat) Stylish, artistic, romantic and gourmet – the scene is much more San Francisco than Hilo, but impeccable food, service and decor make for a memorable night wherever you are.

HAWAI'I VOLCANOES NATIONAL PARK

Despite Hawaii's many wonders, this **national park** (☎ 808-985-6000; www.nps.gov/havo; week pass per car $10) stands out: its two active volcanoes testify to the ongoing birth of the islands. Majestic Mauna Loa (13,677ft) looms like a sleeping giant, while young Kilauea – the world's most active volcano – has been erupting almost continually since 1983. With luck, you'll witness the primal event of molten lava tumbling into the sea. But the park contains much more – overwhelming lava deserts, steaming craters, lava tubes, ancient rain forests – and hikers will always wish for more time.

Near the park entrance, **Kilauea Visitor Center** (☎ 808-985-6017; 🕑 7:45am-5pm) makes a great introduction, and rangers provide updates on trail conditions, volcanic activity and guided walks. The **Volcano Art Center** (☎ 808-967-7565, 866-967-7565; www.volcanoartcenter.org; 🕑 9am-5pm) coordinates special events.

Sights & Activities

The 11-mile **Crater Rim Dr** circles Kilauea Caldera, offering almost nonstop views of the goddess Pele's scorched, smoldering home. If time is short, drive this, making sure to stop at the overlook for **Halema'uma'u Crater**; the **Thurston Lava Tube**, an enormous cave left by flowing lava; and the **Jaggar Museum** (☎ 808-985-6049; admission free; 🕑 8:30am-5pm), with working seismographs, lava displays and a stupendous vista.

The best two-hour hike is the 4-mile **Kilauea Iki Trail**, which crosses the top of steaming Kilauea Iki Crater; this hike can be easily extended by joining up with the **Halema'uma'u Trail**, a 7-mile loop. For an all-day or overnight adventure, **Napau Crater Trail** (18 miles round trip) leads right up to the tremendous, smoke-belching Pu'u O'o vent.

The park's equally scenic, 18-mile **Chain of Craters Road** leads down to the coast, ending abruptly where recent lava flows have buried it. Rangers here can advise you on how or if it's possible to hike to the active flow; a tell-tale steam plume marks the spot where lava enters the water. Stay for sunset, as darkness brings out the fiery glow. This road contains no facilities, but several nice hikes lead from it, including a short one to a petroglyph field.

Sleeping & Eating

Below, all but Volcano House and the campgrounds are in the nearby village of Volcano, which has many nice B&Bs and vacation homes. **Volcano Gallery** (☎ 800-908-9764; www.volcanogallery.com) is a locally managed rental agency.

The national park maintains two excellent, free, first-come, first-serve campgrounds: Namakanipaio, off Hwy 11 outside the park entrance, and Kulanaokuaiki, along Hilina Pali Rd inside the park. Backcountry camping is limited; register at the visitor center no more than one day ahead. Also, Namakanipaio has 10 simple, A-frame **cabins** (☎ 808-967-7321; cabins $50).

Holo Holo In (☎ 808-967-7950; www.enable.org/holoholo; 19-4036 Kalani Honua Rd; dm $19, r $45-60; 💻) This friendly hostel is a great budget choice.

our pick **My Island B&B** (☎ 808-967-7216; www.myislandinnhawaii.com; 19-3896 Old Volcano Rd; r incl breakfast $75-110, house $150) From the landscaped gardens to the historic 1886 house to the gracious, gregarious hosts, it doesn't get a lot better or friendlier than this European-style B&B. Breakfast is delightful.

Volcano House (☎ 808-967-7321; www.volcanohousehotel.com; 1 Crater Rim Dr; r $95-225) Unfortunately, the park's only hotel and restaurant define ordinary – though the views of the steaming caldera are anything but.

Kilauea Lodge (☎ 808-967-7366; www.kilauealodge.com; Old Volcano Rd; r incl breakfast $155-195; ✕ wi-fi) This cozy lodge offers a variety of well-appointed, snuggly rooms, and it runs the area's best restaurant (mains $25 to $35; open 5:30pm to 9pm), serving hearty steaks and German comfort food (*hassenpfeffer*, anyone?).

Thai Thai Restaurant (☎ 808-967-7969; 19-4084 Old Volcano Rd; mains $12-17; ⏲ 4:30-9pm) Inspired by Pele, perhaps, the Thai cuisine here is satisfyingly hot and authentic; leftovers make a great trail lunch.

MAUI

According to some, you can't have it all. Perhaps those folks haven't been to Maui, which consistently lands atop travel-magazine reader polls as one of the world's best, most romantic islands. Why? Most start with its wealth of glorious beaches and go from there: luxe resorts, friendly B&Bs, gourmet cuisine, fantastic luau, and world-class windsurfing, whale watching, snorkeling, diving and hiking. Need adventure? Drive the jungly road to Hana or traverse the moonlike volcanic crater of Haleakala. Want pampering? West Maui awaits your call. Need more? Maui is the gateway to its sister islands of Moloka'i (p1109) and Lana'i (p1110), which are conveniently reached by ferry. But is Maui *really* all that? Well, it does weave a gauzy spell that leaves most visitors more in love than when they arrived, so you'll just have to excuse those who, when the magazines call, wax a little enthusiastic.

Getting There & Around

Most travelers to Maui arrive at **Kahului International Airport** (OGG; ☎ 808-872-3830), the busiest airport in Hawaii outside Honolulu. From the airport, shuttle buses service the main tourist destinations. **Executive Shuttle** (☎ 808-669-2300, 800-833-2303) has the best prices, charging $26 to Kihei and $36 to Lahaina.

From Honolulu, Hawaii Superferry makes one round trip daily to Maui; for information, see p1090.

The island's public bus system, **Maui Bus** (☎ Roberts Hawaii 808-871-4838, Maui County 808-270-7511; www.mauicounty.gov/bus), operates several daily routes (fares $1) that service the main towns, including Kahului, Lahaina, Wailuku, Kihei and Wailea. However, to really explore Maui you need your own wheels; in addition to the major car-rental companies at the airport, consider the ecofriendly, biodiesel-fueled cars at **Bio-Beetle** (☎ 808-873-6121, 877-873-6121; www.bio-beetle.com), which start at $50/230 a day/week.

LAHAINA & KA'ANAPALI

For cook-it-yourself condo life, head to Kihei (p1105). For the megahotel and resort experience, bunk down in Ka'anapali, which also has prime beaches. And for atmosphere, entertainment and fine dining, make time for Lahaina, a 19th-century whaling town rich with well-preserved period architecture. Maui's best festivals occur in Lahaina and, for romantics, it's tough to beat the town's combination of history, gourmet restaurants and dazzling Pacific Ocean sunsets.

Sights & Activities

The focal point of Lahaina is its bustling small-boat harbor, backed by the historic **Pioneer Inn** and Banyan Tree Sq – the latter is home to the largest **banyan tree** in the US. The main drag and tourist strip is Front St, which runs along the ocean and is lined with shops, galleries and restaurants.

All of Lahaina's main sightseeing attractions are within walking distance of

HAWAII

the waterfront. They include the former homes of early missionaries, prisons built for rowdy sailors and the remains of a royal palace. Pick up a free walking-tour map at the **Lahaina Visitor Center** (☎ 808-667-9193, 888-310-1117; www.visitlahaina.com; 648 Wharf St; ☼ 9am-5pm), inside the old courthouse at Banyan Tree Sq.

When you're ready for the beach, head 3 miles north to Ka'anapali, which is fronted by one sandy strand after another; between them, all watersports are possible, and eager outfitters abound. The gem may be **Kahekili Beach Park**, boasting swaying palms and fantastic snorkeling and swimming. In Ka'anapali, visit the evocative **Whaling Museum** (☎ 808-661-4567; 2345 Ka'anapali Parkway; admission free; ☼ 9am-10pm) in the Whalers Village mall.

Sleeping

Makai Inn (☎ 808-662-3200; www.makaiinn.net; 1415 Front St; r $100-175; ✺ wi-fi) On the northern outskirts of Lahaina, this family-run gem sports a waterfront location, full kitchens and lots of aloha.

House of Fountains (☎ 808-667-2121, 800-789-6865; www.alohahouse.com; 1579 Lokia St; r incl breakfast $140-170; ✺ ✎ ☐) The visitors bureau named this the state's most Hawaiian B&B. In addition to museum-quality Hawaiiana, you'll find well-equipped, modern rooms and a great breakfast. It's near Wahikuli Beach Park between Lahaina and Ka'anapali.

Ka'anapali Beach Hotel (☎ 808-661-0011, 800-262-8450; www.kbhmaui.com; 2525 Ka'anapali Parkway; r incl breakfast from $230; ℙ ✺ ☎) Not the fanciest, newest or biggest, this low-key Ka'anapali resort hotel has an enviable beach location and real Hawaiian aloha. There are free guest lessons in ukulele, hula and lei-making.

Eating & Drinking

Pioneer Inn (☎ 808-661-3636; 658 Wharf St; ☼ 7am-10pm) With its whaling-era atmosphere and harborside veranda, this is unquestionably the most popular place for a drink in Lahaina.

Aloha Mixed Plate (☎ 808-661-3322; 1285 Front St; plates $4-14; ☼ 10:30am-10pm) This fun Hawaiian beach shack is the best place to go local with a Hawaiian plate lunch or to catch sunset with a tropical drink, a few pupu (don't miss the coconut prawns) and Hawaiian music.

Sansei Seafood Restaurant (☎ 808-669-6286; www.sanseihawaii.com; 600 Office Rd; sushi $4-15; mains $17-40; ☼ 5:30-10pm Sat-Wed, to 1am Thu & Fri) In Lahaina, this place is trendy and packed, with out-of-this-world sushi and intriguing Japanese-Hawaiian fare; karaoke nights on Thursday and Friday have half-price food after 10pm.

Hula Grill & Barefoot Bar (☎ 808-667-6636; Whalers Village; grill menu $8-18, dinner mains $19-30; ☼ 11am-10:30pm) Watch the swimsuit parade in Ka'anapali as you dine under coconut-frond umbrellas on creative pupu and robust dinner mains like kiawe wood–grilled steaks.

Pacific'O (☎ 808-667-4341; 505 Front St; lunch $13-16, dinner mains $26-36; ☼ 11:30am-4pm & 5:30-9:30pm) A top Lahaina choice that pairs bold and innovative Pacific Rim cuisine with an unbeatable beachside setting and live jazz on weekends.

David Paul's Lahaina Grill (☎ 808-667-5117; 127 Lahainaluna Rd; mains $28-41; ☼ 6-10pm, bar stays open later) This award-winning Lahaina restaurant expertly mixes Hawaiian and continental influences, with the likes of seared tuna crusted in Maui onions and Kona coffee–roasted rack of lamb.

Entertainment

ourpick Old Lahaina Lu'au (☎ 808-667-1998, 800-248-5828; www.oldlahainaluau.com; 1251 Front St; adult/child

---

WHALES IN LOVE

Every winter from November through May, some 10,000 humpback whales crowd the shallow waters along the western coast of Maui for breeding, calving and nursing. These awesome creatures are easy to spot from shore, particularly when they perform their acrobatic breaches. It's one of nature's grandest spectacles.

To get an even closer look, take a whale-watching cruise with the nonprofit **Pacific Whale Foundation** (☎ 808-249-8811, 800-942-5311; www.pacificwhale.org; adult/child $32/17; ☼ Dec-Apr), which sails out of both Lahaina and Ma'alaea harbors. Another place to get acquainted with these creatures is in Kihei at the **Hawaiian Islands Humpback Whale National Marine Sanctuary Headquarters** (☎ 808-879-2818, 800-831-4888; www.hawaiihumpbackwhale.noaa.gov; 726 S Kihei Rd; ☼ 10am-3pm Mon-Fri). Think the whales aren't happy to be in Maui? Listen to them singing at www.whalesong.net.

$90/60; 5:15-8:15pm) For a night to remember, this beachside luau is unsurpassed for its authenticity and all-around aloha – the hula troupe is first rate and the feast superb. Book far ahead. Have kids? Consider the morning luau (adult/child $70/50; 9am to noon Wednesday and Friday), which includes hands-on Hawaiian activities.

Feast at Lele (808-667-5353, 866-299-5353; www.feastatlele.com; 505 Front St; adult/child $105/75; 6-9pm) No half-hearted buffet, this gourmet luau is a delicious culinary tour of Pacific cultures, accompanied by an excellent music-and-dance performance.

MA'ALAEA BAY

Ma'alaea Bay runs along the low isthmus separating the mountain masses of western and eastern Maui. Prevailing winds from the north funnel between the mountains, creating strong midday gusts and some of the best **windsurfing** conditions on Maui.

The superb **Maui Ocean Center** (808-270-7000; www.mauioceancenter.com; 192 Ma'alaea Rd, Ma'alaea; adult/child $23/16; 9am-6pm Jul & Aug, to 5pm rest of year), the largest tropical aquarium in the USA, offers a feast for the eyes. The aquarium is dedicated to Hawaiian marine life, and the variety and brilliance of the fish and coral is nothing short of dazzling. It's as close as you can get to being underwater without donning dive gear!

A fantastic harbor view, attentive service and excellent seafood make **Ma'alaea Grill** (808-243-2206; Ma'alaea Harbor; lunch $7-15, dinner $17-33; 10:30am-9pm) one of Maui's best seafood restaurants.

KIHEI

Sun-kissed, gleaming beaches run for miles and miles south of Kihei, which is less ritzy than West Maui. Vacationers flock to this coast for the excellent swimming, snorkeling, windsurfing and kayaking, and abundant condos keep prices reasonable.

For kayak rentals and adventurous tours, try **South Pacific Kayaks** (808-875-4848, 800-776-2326; www.southpacifickayaks.com; 95 Hale Kuai St; 1-/2-person kayaks per day $40/50, tours $65-99). The kayak paddle to **Molokini Crater** (per person $140) is a workout that leads to Maui's best snorkeling and diving spot. Or opt for a two-hour Molokini Express boat trip with **Blue Water Rafting** (808-879-7238; www.bluewaterrafting.com; Kihei Boat Ramp; tours $45-115).

Sleeping

To begin sorting through Kihei's condo possibilities, check out **Bello Realty** (808-879-3328, 800-541-3060; www.bellomauivacations.com) or **Condominium Rentals Hawaii** (808-879-2778, 800-367-5242; www.crhmaui.com).

Nona Lani Cottages (808-879-2497, 800-733-2688; www.nonalanicottages.com; 455 S Kihei Rd; r $115, cottages $130) The scent of plumeria fills the air at this little cottage cluster, whose friendly hosts make leis from the flowers grown out back.

Two Mermaids on Maui B&B (808-874-8687, 800-598-9550; www.twomermaids.com; 2840 Umalu Pl; studio/1-bedroom units incl breakfast $110/135;) For a more personal touch, try the two kitchenette units at this friendly, cheerful B&B.

Kihei Kai Nani (808-891-0049, 800-473-1493; www.kiheikainani.com; 2495 S Kihei Rd; 1-bedroom units $139;) This inviting low-rise complex has roomy, well-equipped one-bedroom units. Good off-season discounts.

Eating

Da Kitchen Express (808-875-7782; Rainbow Mall, 2439 S Kihei Rd; meals $7-10; 9am-9pm) This quintessential Hawaiian diner dishes up tasty plate lunches; it's a good place to try *laulau*, loco moco and other local staples.

Alexander's (808-874-0788; Kihei Kalama Village, 1913 S Kihei Rd; meals $8-13; 11am-9pm) *The* place for fish and chips, made with either mahi-mahi, 'ahi or *ono*. Fried fare can be greasy, but the grilled fish is perfection.

Entertainment

Hapa's Night Club (808-879-9001; 41 E Lipoa St; admission $5-8;) Maui's hottest dance spot has something for everyone. It hosts the gay community on 'ultra-fab' Tuesday, does an aloha jam on Wednesday and has top live bands other nights.

WAILEA & MAKENA

As Maui's most upscale seaside community, Wailea boasts million-dollar homes and extravagant resorts with four-figure room rates – all because this stretch of coastline cradles golden-sand beaches of absolutely dreamy perfection. The mile-long **Wailea Beach Path** is a superb place to enjoy shoreline whale watching in winter.

South of Wailea, Makena has two knockout undeveloped beaches – **Big Beach** and the secluded **Little Beach** – as well as the **'Ahihi-Kina'u Natural Area Reserve**, which encompasses

HAWAII

trails, historic ruins and hidden coves ideal for snorkeling.

KAHULUI & WAILUKU

Kahului and Wailuku, Maui's two largest communities, flow together in one urban sprawl. Kahului hosts Maui's windsurfing shops, whose employees give lessons at breezy **Kanaha Beach**. The **Maui Arts & Cultural Center** (☎ 808-242-7469; www.mauiarts.org; 1 Cameron Way) is Maui's premier concert venue, which also runs an excellent **art gallery** (☎ 808-242-2787; admission free; ☼ 11am-5pm Tue-Sun).

The more historic Wailuku makes for a good stroll and lunch break. On the outskirts of Wailuku, **'Iao Valley State Park** ('Iao Valley Rd; admission free; ☼ 7am-7pm) centers on the picturesque 'Iao Needle rock pinnacle, which rises 1200ft from the valley floor.

Information

Maui Memorial Medical Center (☎ 808-244-9056; 221 Mahalani St, Wailuku; ☼ 24hr) The island's main hospital.

Maui Visitors Bureau (☎ 808-872-3893; www.visit maui.com; Kahului Airport; ☼ 7:45am-9:45pm) Operates a staffed booth in the airport's arrivals area.

Sleeping & Eating

Old Wailuku Inn (☎ 808-244-5897, 800-305-4899; www .mauiinn.com; 2199 Kaho'okele St, Wailuku; r $150-190; 🅿) Step back into the 1920s in this elegant period home, built by a wealthy banker and authentically restored by the friendly innkeepers. Rooms are large and comfy, with traditional Hawaiian quilts warming the beds.

Mañana Garage (☎ 808-873-0220; 33 Lono Ave, Kahului; lunch $10-15, dinner $19-30; ☼ 11am-9:30pm, to 2am Mon and every other Sat) A local favorite, this sizzling place sports a splashy Caribbean decor and delicious Latin-influenced dishes. Late-

night salsa and tango happen Monday and every other Saturday.

Drinking

Wow-Wee Maui's Kava Bar & Grill (☎ 808-871-1414; 333 Dairy Rd, Kahului; ☼ 10am-9pm Sun-Thu, to 10pm Fri & Sat) This hip café is the place to try kava. Mildly intoxicating, this spicy elixir was a favored ceremonial drink in ancient Hawaii.

PA'IA

But for the incessant winds, Pa'ia would be a forgotten former sugar town. Instead, it's become the Windsurfing Capital of the World and draws an eclectic, international crowd and a burgeoning selection of superb restaurants. To admire the windsurfing and kitesurfing action, head to **Ho'okipa Beach.**

Pa'ia Fish Market Restaurant (☎ 808-579-8030; 100 Hana Hwy; meals $9-15; ☼ 11am-9:30pm) is the place to go for fresh fish sandwiches. With a French chef, **Moana Bakery & Café** (☎ 808-579-9999; 71 Baldwin Ave; breakfast & lunch $7-15, dinner $12-29; ☼ 8am-9pm) has terrific croissants and a creative fusion of French and Hawaiian offerings. **Mama's Fish House** (☎ 808-579-8488; www.mamas fishhouse.com; 799 Poho Pl; mains $34-50; ☼ 11am-2pm & 4:30-9pm) is Maui's most celebrated seafood restaurant, which pairs beachside romance with impeccably prepared fish. Reservations are essential.

HANA & AROUND

The mainland influences so evident everywhere else on Maui are missing in Hana, where many residents are Native Hawaiian, and they treasure the town's relaxed pace and quiet isolation. Surfers head to **Waikoloa Beach**, while sunbathers favor **Kaihalulu (Red Sand) Beach**, reached by a trail at the end of Uakea Rd.

SCENIC DRIVE: ROAD TO HANA

The most spectacular coastal drive in all Hawaii, the Hana Hwy (Hwy 360) winds its way deep into jungle valleys and back out above a rugged coastline. Not for the faint of heart, the road is a real cliff-hugger with 54 one-lane bridges, roadside waterfalls and head-spinning views. Gas up and pack a lunch in Pa'ia, and bring your swimsuit.

For a cosmic getaway, consider a night at the Edenlike **Hale Akua Shangri-La** (☎ 808-572-9300; 888-368-5305; www.haleakua.com; Huelo Rd, Huelo; r $60-300; 🅿 🈳), where romance is vegetarian and the hot tub is clothing optional.

Definitely pull over to explore the lava tubes and black-sand beach at Wai'anapanapa State Park, where the camping ($5) and cabins ($45) are inviting. For permits, contact the **Division of State Parks** (☎ 808-984-8109; www.hawaii.gov/dlnr/dsp).

The road south from Hana is incredibly beautiful. 'Ohe'o Stream cuts its way through **'Ohe'o Gulch** as a gorgeous series of wide pools and waterfalls, each tumbling into the one below. Just past the gulch is the sleepy village of **Kipahulu**, burial site of aviator Charles Lindbergh.

Maintenance at this Hana condo complex can be uneven, but **Hana Kai-Maui** (☎ 808-248-8426, 800-346-2772; www.hanakai.com; 1533 Uakea Rd; studios $145-195, 1-bedroom units $165-295) has an ideal oceanfront spot and great views from upper-floor rooms. With an atmospheric beachside setting, **Bamboo Inn** (☎ 808-248-7718; www.bambooinn.com; Uakea Rd; ste $175-185, villas $240; ⊠ wi-fi) makes a relaxing Hana retreat. Two suites and one two-story villa have kitchenettes and include breakfast.

Hana isn't known for great eats, so satisfy your hunger with the mammoth, fresh burgers at the beachfront **Hana Ranch Restaurant Takeout** (☎ 808-248-8255; Hana Ranch Center, Mill Rd; meals $6-12; ☾ 6:30-10am, 11am-4pm & 6-8:30pm Wed, Fri & Sat).

HALEAKALA NATIONAL PARK

No trip to Maui is complete without visiting this **national park** (www.nps.gov/hale; 3-day entry pass per car $10), containing the mighty volcano that gave rise to East Maui. The volcano's floor measures a whopping 7.5 miles wide, 2.5 miles long and 3000ft deep – more than enough to swallow the entire isle of Manhattan. From its towering rim there are dramatic views of its lunarlike surface. But the adventure needn't stop at the viewpoints – with a good pair of hiking boots you can walk down into the crater on trails that meander around eerie cinder cones, and peer up at towering walls.

For an unforgettable experience, arrive in time to see the sunrise – an event that Mark Twain called the 'sublimest spectacle' he'd ever seen. Check on weather conditions and sunrise times (☎ 808-877-5111) before driving up. **Park headquarters** (☎ 808-572-4400; ☾ 8am-4pm) can give you details on free guided hikes and nature talks.

Free tent camping is allowed at Hosmer Grove, near the main entrance (three-night maximum); no permit required. Permits (first come, first served, from the park headquarters) are required for the two backcountry campgrounds on the crater floor. There are primitive cabins in the crater, but demand is so high they hold a monthly lottery (write to Cabin Lottery Request, Haleakala National Park, Box 369, Makawao, HI 96768 two months in advance).

KAUA'I

Lush, rural Kaua'i is the Pacific Ocean's magnificent jade temple. On Hawaii's oldest major island, nature's fingers have had time to dig deep – carving the unbelievable fluted cliffs of the Na Pali Coast and the tremendous ragged gash of Waimea Canyon. A mecca for hikers and kayakers, Kaua'i is beloved by outdoor enthusiasts of all stripes, and it has been the darling of honeymooners ever since Elvis tied the knot here in *Blue Hawaii*. Forget coddling resorts, decadent shopping or bustling nightlife. Come to Kaua'i for its heavenly art gallery – the one you find outdoors. The price for these works? Just a pair of boots and a little sweat.

Getting There & Around

All commercial flights land at **Lihu'e Airport** (LIH; ☎ 808-246-1448; www.hawaii.gov/dot/airports/kauai/lih). The major car-rental companies maintain booths there, and taxis line up outside the arrival area. The new Hawaii Superferry runs between Honolulu and Kaua'i once a day from Monday through Friday and on Sunday; for information, see p1090. Kaua'i has a limited public **bus service** (☎ 808-241-6410; ☾ Mon-Sat), which serves most towns but doesn't go to tourist destinations like Kilauea Point and Koke'e State Park. Fares are $1.50.

LIHU'E

This former plantation town is Kaua'i's capital and commercial center. Seek information at the **Kaua'i Visitors Bureau** (☎ 808-245-3971, 800-262-1400; www.kauaidiscovery.com; 4334 Rice St; ☾ 8am-4:30pm Mon-Fri). The insightful **Kaua'i Museum** (☎ 808-245-6931; www.kauaimuseum.org; 4428 Rice St; admission $7; ☾ 9am-4pm Mon-Fri, 10am-4pm Sat) traces the island's intriguing history.

Garden Island Inn (☎ 808-245-7227, 800-648-0154; www.gardenislandinn.com; 3445 Wilcox Rd; r from $95; ⊠ ⊠) offers comfortable rooms just minutes from the beach. Rub shoulders with the locals at **Hamura Saimin** (☎ 808-245-3271; 2956 Kress St; noodle soups $4; ☾ 10am-10pm Sun-Thu, to midnight Fri & Sat), which has been serving homemade noodles since the 1920s.

WAILUA & AROUND

You wouldn't know it from the shopping strip–lined Kuhio Hwy, but the Wailua area contains great outdoor opportunities. Families should head to **Lydgate Beach Park** (www .kamalani.org), with the best kids' playground in Hawaii and safe swimming at a well-protected beach. The mountains above Wailua hold some recommended **hikes**, such as the Kuilau Ridge Trail, the Moalepe Trail and the Nounou Mountain Trails.

However, most come to kayak the **Wailua River**. The easy, bucolic 5-mile kayak – which can include the famous Fern Grotto, swimming holes and hikes to waterfalls – is so popular it's restricted almost completely to guided tours. Book a day ahead with **Kayak Kaua'i** (☎ 808-826-9844, 800-437-3507; www.kayakkauai .com; double kayaks per day $75, tours adult/child $85/60) and **Outfitters Kaua'i** (☎ 808-742-9667, 888-742-9887; www.outfitterskauai.com; kayaks per person per day $40, tours adult/child $98/78). For a unique experience, take a Native Hawaiian–led Wailua River trip in an outrigger canoe with **Kamokila Hawaiian Village** (☎ 808-823-0559; www.kamokila.com; tours adult/child $30/20).

NA PALI COAST & NORTH SHORE

Unspoiled and unhurried, Kaua'i's mountainous north shore features otherworldly scenery and enough outdoor adventures for a lifetime. Be sure to stop at **Kilauea Point National Wildlife Refuge** (☎ 808-828-0383; www.fws.gov/pacificislands /wnwr/kkilaueanwr.html; Kilauea Rd, Kilauea; admission $3; ☺ 10am-4pm) to enjoy its historic lighthouse and thriving seabird sanctuary.

Gentle **'Anini Beach Park** is spacious, with calm water perfect for kids, lazy kayaking, easy snorkeling and the best beginner windsurfing on the island. Camping is recommended (and quieter midweek); get permits from the **Division of Parks & Recreation** (☎ 808-241-4463; www .kauai.gov; campsites per person $3).

The most glamorous resort on Kaua'i is **Princeville Resort** (☎ 808-826-9644, 866-716-8110; www.princevillehotelhawaii.com; 5520 Ka Haku Rd; r online/ rack from $415/565; ☒ ☒ ☒). Definitely stop at sunset to admire the glorious view of Hanalei Bay, either from the resort's grassy lawn, from the magnificent if tiny **Pali Ke Kua Beach**, or from a table at the elegant **Café Hanalei** (☎ 808-826-9644; breakfast $8.50-14.50, lunch $18-25, dinner $29-40; ☺ 6:30am-2:30pm & 5:30-9:30pm), where the good Asian-inspired island cuisine falls just short of the peerless scenery; lunch is the best value.

In **Hanalei**, the hippie-surfer vibe is palpable and, indeed, in magnificent **Hanalei Bay** the surfing is spectacular; it really swells in winter. Also popular are quiet, easy kayak trips up the **Hanalei River**; for rentals, try **Pedal & Paddle** (☎ 808-826-9069; www.pedalnpaddle.com; Ching Young Village; single/double kayaks per day $20/40).

For a stay that puts you in the right mood, book one of the unique studios at **Hanalei Surfboard House** (☎ 808-826-9825; www.hanaleisurfboard house.com; 5459 Weke Rd; r $150, cleaning fee $65; ☒ wi-fi); just look for the surfboard fence.

Hanalei has some great eats. For a fancy plate lunch (on paper plates) head for **Polynesia Café** (☎ 808-826-1999; Ching Young Village; mains $11-17; ☺ 8am-9pm). The urban-chic tapas bar **Bar Acuda** (☎ 808-826-7081; Hanalei Center; small plates $5-12; ☺ 6-9pm Tue-Sun) satisfies most gourmet cravings, as do meals at **Postcards Café** (☎ 808-826-1191; www.postcardscafe.com; 5-5075 Kuhio Hwy; mains $18-27; ☺ 6-9pm), where service can unfortunately be uneven.

Marking the western end of Hwy 56, at the little village of **Ha'ena**, are **Tunnels Beach** and lovely **Ke'e Beach**, both of which have excellent snorkeling. Camping is allowed (with a permit) at **Ha'ena Beach Park** (☎ 808-241-4463; www.kauai.gov; campsites per person $3), close to the Kalalau trailhead.

Hikers shouldn't miss the challenging but oh-so-rewarding 11-mile **Kalalau Trail**, which runs along the folded Na Pali cliffs and winds through a series of breathtakingly lush valleys in **Na Pali Coast State Park**. To hike past the first valley or for backcountry camping ($10 per site), you need a **permit** (☎ 808-274-3444; www.hawaii.gov/dlnr/dsp). Allow three days for the whole shebang.

Hardcore paddlers can admire the same scenery from the sea along the strenuous, 17-mile Na Pali Coast kayak. It takes all day (and feels longer) and is only possible from May to September. Two good outfitters are **Kayak Kaua'i** (☎ 808-826-9844, 800-437-3507; www .kayakkauai.com; Na Pali tours $185) and **Na Pali Kayak** (☎ 808-826-6900, 866-977-6900; www.napalikayak.com; Na Pali tours $180).

SOUTH SHORE

Sunny **Po'ipu**, Kaua'i's main resort area, fronts a fabulous run of sandy beaches. It's good for swimming and snorkeling year round and for surfing in summer. Tour five stunning gardens at the **National Tropical Botanical Garden** (NTBG; ☎ 808-742-2623; www.ntbg.org; 4425 Lawa'i Rd;

tours $10-35; 8:30am-5pm) and admire the windswept limestone cliffs of the Maha'ulepu Coast along the 2-mile **Maha'ulepu Heritage Trail** (www.hikemahaulepu.org).

Po'ipu is awash in condos and vacation rentals for all budgets; check the listings of **Po'ipu Beach Resort Association** (808-742-7444; www.poipubeach.org) and **Po'ipu Beach Vacation Rentals** (808-742-2850, 800-684-5133; www.pbvacationrentals.com). **Koloa Landing Cottages** (808-742-1470, 800-779-8773; www.koloa-landing.com; 2704B Ho'onani Rd; r $120-220) offers well-equipped, popular accommodations and plenty of aloha. A south-shore icon, **Beach House Restaurant** (808-742-1424; www.the-beach-house.com; 5022 Lawa'i Rd; dinner mains $20-32; 6-9:30pm) whips up delicious Hawaii Regional Cuisine focusing on fresh fish.

WEST SIDE

The top destinations here are **Waimea Canyon** – the 'Grand Canyon of the Pacific' with cascading waterfalls and spectacular gorges – and the adjacent **Koke'e State Park**. Both feature breathtaking views and a vast network of hiking trails; some, like Koke'e's Awa'awapuhi and Nu'alolo Trails, stroll the knife edge of precipitously eroded cliffs. Waimea Canyon Dr (Hwy 550) starts in the town of Waimea and is peppered with scenic lookouts along the way to the park. Pick up information on trails at the park's **Koke'e Museum** (808-335-9975; www.kokee.org; 3600 Koke'e Rd; donation $1; 10am-4pm).

Those with tents should aim for the comfortable Koke'e State Park campground; for permits, contact the **Division of State Parks** (808-274-3444; www.hawaii.gov/dlnr/dsp; campsites $5). The town of **Waimea** makes a good base for park explorations; in town, **Inn Waimea** (808-338-0031; www.innwaimea.com; 4469 Halepule Rd, Waimea; r from $110;) is a lovely old missionary home with four guest rooms and two-bedroom cottages.

Also worth exploring is **Hanapepe**, a quaint, historic town with false-fronted Old West buildings housing fun galleries and shops. Friday night is **Hanapepe Art Night** (6-9pm Fri), when galleries stay open late and the town comes alive. Near town, **Salt Pond Beach Park** is perfect for swimming and ideal for families. The best West-side meal is at the upscale **Hanapepe Café** (808-335-5011; 3830 Hanapepe Rd; lunch $6-10, dinner $18-25; 7am-3pm Mon-Thu, 6-9pm Fri); dinner Friday night includes live music, when reservations are advised.

MOLOKA'I

Sparsely populated by mostly Native Hawaiians and largely undeveloped for tourism, rural Moloka'i is ideal for those seeking the 'other' Hawaii: unpackaged, traditional, still wild and exuding genuine aloha. It is for travelers who willingly trade comfort for a taste of an untamed landscape – this one recalling Hawaii's awe-inspiring natural glory as it was half a century or more ago.

The quintessential Moloka'i experience is riding a mule (or hiking) down the steep, towering cliff face of the Kalaupapa Peninsula. Designated as the **Kalaupapa National Historical Park** (www.nps.gov/kala; Mon-Sat), the beautiful peninsula once served as a settlement for people with leprosy, and it is still home to an aging population of patients. Guided tours of the settlement are included in the cost of the **Moloka'i Mule Ride** (808-567-6088, 800-567-7550; www.muleride.com; tours $165).

From Moloka'i's main town, **Kaunakakai** (which has very simple hotels and eateries), a gorgeous 27-mile drive leads along the south coast past small towns and fishponds to the lush **Halawa Valley**, which shelters ancient heiau and waterfalls. Raw, nearly prehistoric forests are found in the **Moloka'i Forest Reserve** and the adjacent **Kamakou Preserve**, in central Moloka'i. Access is difficult (almost exclusively by 4WD and/or long hike), and it's worth joining the excellent monthly hike with the **Nature Conservancy** (808-553-5236; www.nature.org/hawaii; suggested donation $25), which provides transportation.

For cottages, houses and condos **Molokai Vacation Rental** (808-553-8334, 800-367-2984; www.molokai-vacation-rental.com) and **Moloka'i Resorts Vacation Rental Center** (808-553-3666, 800-600-4158; www.molokairesorts.com) have choices in all price ranges.

To reach Moloka'i, you can fly with **Island Air** (808-484-2222, 800-652-6541; www.islandair.com), which has seven daily flights between Honolulu and Moloka'i and two between Kahului, Maui, and Moloka'i. Or take a 90-minute passenger ferry from Lahaina, Maui, on the **Molokai Princess** (808-662-3355, 866-307-6524; www.molokaiferry.com; adult/child $40/20), which departs Maui at 5:30am and 4pm daily, and returns from Moloka'i at 7:15am and 6pm daily. It will also arrange ferry-car packages.

HAWAII

LANA'I

Once the world's largest pineapple plantation, Lana'i has been refashioned into a plaything for the wealthy, the sort of place Bill Gates rents out to get married. Home to a pair of Hawaii's most elite resorts, between them boasting more stars than the night sky, and two world-class golf courses, Lana'i can nevertheless make a satisfying visit or daytrip for mere-mortal travelers.

At its center is **Lana'i City**, a charming, well-preserved historic plantation town where the pace evokes a gentler, slower era. You can swim, snorkel and dive in the dolphin-rich waters off beautiful **Hulopo'e Beach**, and enjoy unparalleled views hiking along the ridgetop **Munro Trail**.

You can also **golf**, and sample the good life, at the resorts, which are run by **Four Seasons Resort Lana'i** (☎ 800-819-5053; www.fourseasons .com/lanai). Get your gourmet restaurants, spas and first-class lodgings at either **Manele Bay** (☎ 808-565-2000; r from $395; 🏊 🍴 💻) or **Lodge at Koele** (☎ 808-565-4000; r from $295; 🏊 🍴 💻). To spend the night without breaking the bank, the 1923 **Hotel Lanai** (☎ 808-565-7211, 877-665-2624; www.hotellanai.com; 828 Lana'i Ave; r $125-145) is a 10-room former plantation guesthouse that is a delightful throwback.

The recommended way to reach Lana'i is by ferry from Maui, since you often see whales and spinner dolphins en route. **Expeditions** (☎ 808-661-3756, 800-695-2624; www.go-lanai .com; adult/child $25/20) runs a passenger ferry five times daily. The first boat leaves Maui's Lahaina Harbor at 6:45am and the last boat departs Lana'i for the return to Maui at 6:45pm. Also, **Island Air** (☎ 800-484-222; www.island air.com) flies between Honolulu and Lana'i several times a day.

OTHER ISLANDS

KAHO'OLAWE

This uninhabited island, 7 miles southwest of Maui, was used exclusively by the US military as a bombing target from WWII until 1990. Despite a $400-million, 10-year cleanup by the military, the island remains littered with unexploded ordnance and is thus off-limits to tourists.

Considered sacred by Native Hawaiians, Kaho'olawe is currently managed by the **Kaho'olawe Island Reserve Commission** (www .kahoolawe.hawaii.gov). With the help of **Protect Kaho'olawe 'Ohana** (www.kahoolawe.org), it is rehabilitating the island's ecosystems and restoring cultural sites in the hopes of making the island livable once again. To learn more, or to volunteer to help during monthly visits, see the websites.

NI'IHAU

The smallest of the inhabited Hawaiian Islands and a Native Hawaiian preserve, Ni'ihau has long been closed to outsiders, earning it the nickname 'The Forbidden Island.' No other place in Hawaii has more successfully turned its back on change. The island's 160 residents still speak Hawaiian as a first language and Ni'ihau has no paved roads, no airport, no islandwide electricity and no telephones.

PAPAHANAUMOKUAKEA MARINE NATIONAL MONUMENT

On June 15, 2006, President Bush declared the Northwestern Hawaiian Islands the USA's first Marine National Monument. Encompassing around 140,000 sq miles and containing 33 islands and atolls, it is now the largest protected marine area in the world and is scattered across nearly 1400 miles of ocean northwest of Kaua'i.

The islands are home to the USA's largest and healthiest coral reef, and they support 7000 marine species and around 14 million seabirds. Governed by some form of protection since 1909, **Papahanaumokuakea Marine National Monument** (www.hawaiireef.noaa.gov) has only one island that can be visited by tourists, Midway Island, which was the site of a pivotal WWII battle between Japanese and American naval forces. Renewed in 2007 by the **US Fish & Wildlife Service** (www.fws.gov/midway), Midway visits are limited, costly (around $2400), and only allowed from November through July – to coincide with Midway's spectacular nesting season involving two million seabirds, particularly albatross.

Directory

CONTENTS

ACCOMMODATIONS

This guide includes recommendations for all budgets, but it emphasizes midrange accommodations. Unless otherwise noted, 'budget' is considered under $80, 'midrange' $80 to $200 and 'top end' over $200.

In the text, accommodation rates are based on standard double-occupancy in high season. These rates are a general guide only. Special events, busy weekends, conventions and holidays can drive prices higher; in some places, low-season rates can be significantly lower.

Note: *prices do not include hotel tax,* which can add 10% to 15%. When booking, always ask for the rate with tax.

Since nearly every US hotel has nonsmoking rooms, the nonsmoking icon (⊗) is used only when a hotel bans smoking entirely.

For all but the cheapest places and the slowest seasons, reservations are advised. In high-season tourist hot spots, hotels can book up months ahead. Walking in off the street without a reservation gets you a good deal only when things are really dead. In general, many hotels offer specials on their websites, but low-end chains sometimes give a moderately better rate over the phone. Chain hotels also increasingly have frequent flyer mileage deals; ask when booking.

Travel agency websites (p1133) are a good way to get discounted hotel rates. To make an environmentally friendly choice, check the national and state ecoguides listed in the Getting Started chapter (p27).

B&Bs

In the USA, most B&Bs are high-end romantic retreats in restored historic homes that include delicious breakfasts and are run by personable, independent innkeepers. These often take pains to evoke a theme – Victorian, rustic, Cape Cod and so on – and amenities range from merely comfortable to hopelessly indulgent. Rates normally top $100, and the best run $200 to $300+ a night; many have minimum night stay requirements, and some exclude young children.

Still, European-style B&Bs exist: these may be rooms in someone's home, with plainer furnishings, simpler breakfasts, shared baths and cheaper rates. These often welcome families.

B&Bs can close out of season and require reservations, which are essential for top-end places. To avoid surprises, always ask about kid policies and bathroom status (shared or private). Regional B&B agencies are sprinkled throughout this guide. National guides include *Bed & Breakfast USA* and the *Complete Guide to American Bed & Breakfasts*. Also check **Select Registry** (www.selectregistry.com), **BnB Finder** (www.bnbfinder.com) and **Bedandbreakfast.com** (www.bedandbreakfast.com).

Camping

Most federal lands and state parks offer camping (see Activities p1113 for agency websites).

'Primitive' campsites offer no facilities; these range from free to under $10 a night, first come, first served. 'Basic' sites usually provide toilets (flush or pit), drinking water, fire pits and picnic benches; they run $5 to $15 a night, and some or all may be reserved in advance. 'Developed' campsites, usually in national or state parks, have nicer facilities and more amenities: hot showers, BBQs, RV sites, coin laundry and so on. These run $12 to $30 a night, and most can be reserved in advance.

Camping on most federal lands – national parks, national forests, BLM land and so on – can be reserved through **Recreation.gov** (☎ 877-444-6777 in US, 518-885-3639 international; www.recreation .gov; no reservation fee). Camping is usually limited to 14 days, and can be reserved from six to eight months in advance. If the particular park

you're looking for isn't listed on Recreation .gov, check the agency website for details.

For state park campgrounds, make reservations with **ReserveAmerica** (www.reserveamerica.com). Its **Camping Club** (www.campingclub.com) has camping advice for families and kid stuff.

Private campgrounds tend to cater to RVs and families (tent sites may be few and lack character); facilities may include playgrounds, convenience stores, swimming pools and other activities and supplies. Many have camping cabins, ranging from canvas-sided wooden platforms to log-frame structures with real beds, heating and private baths.

KOA (Kampgrounds of America) is a national network of private campgrounds with a full range of facilities. You can order KOA's free annual **directory** (☎ 406-248-7444; http://koa .com; PO Box 30558, Billings, MT 59114; shipping fee $6).

Hostels

Hostels are clustered mainly in the northeast, the Northwest, California and the Rocky Mountains. Cities stock a handful, but across stretches of the Midwest it's hard to find even one.

Hostelling International USA (HI-USA; www.hiusa .org) runs over 100 hostels in the US. Most have gender-segregated dorms, a few private rooms, shared baths and a communal kitchen, provide linen (free or for a small fee; sleeping bags not allowed), prohibit alcohol and smoking, and organize social activities. In cities, hostels may be open 24 hours and forgo 'chores,' while others close in the afternoon (usually 10am to 5pm) and ask guests to do some cleaning. Dorm prices range from $15 to $25, and sometimes higher.

Reservations are accepted and advised during the high season, when there may be a maximum stay of three nights. Contact HI-USA for their handbook ($3). From the US, you can reserve most affiliated hostels through the central **booking service** (☎ 888-464-4872).

The USA has many independent hostels not affiliated with HI-USA. For online listings of these, check the **Hostel Handbook** (www .hostelhandbook.com; handbook $4) and **Hostels.com** (www.hostels.com).

Hotels

These days, every town's 'hotel corridor' seems an interchangeable row of bland, chain-owned choices. There's no escaping this, though what you lose in personality you gain in dependability. With chains, you have the (sometimes stifling) comfort of knowing what you'll get by looking at the sign. Sigh.

In this guide, we aim to highlight independently owned, family-run, quirky establishments – places designed to be remembered, not instantly forgotten. When these are too few to sustain the traveler, we also include the best choices among the chains. Some chains, as well, have made not-unwelcome stabs at individualism; it sounds oxymoronic, but chains occasionally offer unique stays.

What to expect? Hotels in all categories typically include phones, TVs (invariably with cable), alarm clocks, private baths and a simple continental breakfast. Many midrange properties also include minibars, microwaves, hairdryers, internet access, air-conditioning or heating (depending on region), pools and writing desks, while top-end hotels add fitness and business centers, concierge services, restaurants, bars and much more.

BUDGET

Days Inn (☎ 800-329-7466; www.daysinn.com)
Econo Lodge (☎ 877-424-6423; www.econolodge.com)
Motel 6 (☎ 800-466-8356; www.motel6.com)
Super 8 Motel (☎ 800-800-8000; www.super8.com)

MIDRANGE

Best Western (☎ 800-780-7234; www.bestwestern.com)
Clarion Hotel (☎ 877-424-6423; www.clarionhotel.com)
Comfort Inn (☎ 877-424-6423; www.comfortinn.com)
Fairfield Inn (☎ 888-236-2427; www.fairfieldinn.com)
Hampton Inn (☎ 800-445-8667; www.hamptoninn.com)
Holiday Inn (☎ 800-465-4329; www.holidayinn.com)
Howard Johnson (☎ 800-446-4656; www.hojo.com)
La Quinta (☎ 800-642-4271; www.lq.com)
Quality Inn (☎ 877-424-6423; www.qualityinn.com)
Red Roof Inn (☎ 800-733-7663; www.redroof.com)
Rodeway Inn (☎ 877-424-6423; www.rodewayinn.com)
Sleep Inn (☎ 877-424-6423; www.sleepinn.com)
Travelodge (☎ 800-578-7878; www.travelodge.com)

TOP END

Hilton (☎ 800-445-8667; www.hilton.com)
Hyatt (☎ 888-591-1234; www.hyatt.com)
Marriott (☎ 888-236-2427; www.marriott.com)
Radisson (☎ 888-201-1718; www.radisson.com)
Ramada (☎ 800-272-6232; www.ramada.com)
Sheraton (☎ 800-598-1753; www.starwoodhotels.com/sheraton)
Westin (☎ 800-937-8461; www.starwoodhotels.com/westin)

The downside to an independent hotel is that decor and cleanliness can vary greatly, even room to room. Don't like surprises? Ask to see your room before paying, particularly at cheaper places. In general, rooms will have one king-size bed or two double or queen-size beds, and rates will cover two adults, with small surcharges for a third or fourth person. Even if children 'sleep free,' cots or rollaway beds may cost extra. Also, always ask about the hotel's policy for telephone calls; all charge exorbitantly for long distance, but some also charge for local calls and toll-free numbers.

Motels

Motels were originally 'drive-up rooms' along the highway, where you parked your car outside your door. Today, many motels are equivalent to hotels, with one leftover distinguishing characteristic: motels have exterior room doors opening onto a parking lot, while most hotel rooms open into secured interior hallways.

Motels tend to cluster around interstate exits and along main routes into towns. Many remain smaller, less-expensive 'mom-and-pop' operations; breakfast is rarely included (unless you count burnt coffee and donuts); and amenities might top out at a phone and a TV (maybe with cable). However, motels often have a few rooms with simple kitchenettes.

Don't judge a motel solely on looks. Facades may be faded and tired, but not the proprietor, who keeps rooms spotlessly clean. Of course, the situation could be decidedly reversed. Always ask to see your room before you commit.

ACTIVITIES

For outdoor inspiration, see the Outdoors chapter (p121) and the special section on national parks (p105). Here, we've gathered practical details and contact information for national outdoors organizations. See destination chapters for specific regional and park descriptions, local groups and outfitters.

Perhaps the best all-around internet resource is the **Great Outdoor Recreation Pages** (GORP; http://gorp.away.com). A great general interest magazine is **Outside** (http://outside.away.com). If you just need gear, two national retailers are **REI** (www.rei.com) and the **Sports Authority** (www.thesportsauthority.com).

The USA has a wealth of public lands. Here are the main federal agencies and information sources:

Bureau of Land Management (www.blm.gov)
National Park Service (www.nps.gov)
Recreation.gov (www.recreation.gov) Links to all federal and state agencies.
US Fish & Wildlife Service (www.fws.gov)
US Forest Service (www.fs.fed.us)
Wilderness.net (www.wilderness.net) Provides a description and contact information for each national wilderness area.

Courses

For comprehensive instruction in a range of outdoor skills, contact the **National Outdoor Leadership School** (NOLS; ☎ 800-710-6657; www.nols .edu; 284 Lincoln St, Lander, WY 82520). **Outward Bound** (☎ 866-467-7651; www.outwardbound.org; 100 Mystery Point Rd, Garrison, NY 10524) is also famous for its courses emphasizing wilderness skills and personal growth.

Cycling & Mountain Biking

Bike rental companies are common; see destination chapters for local recommendations. See the Transportation chapter (p1139) for advice on touring the USA by bicycle and on transporting your own bicycle to the States. If you bring your own bike, bring a heavy-duty lock too; bicycle theft is big business.

Many parks have multi-use or dedicated bike trails, while bikes are typically banned from dedicated hiking trails. Bikes are also usually allowed on paved or dirt roads within parks; contact individual parks for details. Trail etiquette requires that cyclists yield to other users; otherwise, bicycles are subject to the same rules of the road as automobiles.

Useful bike resources:

Adventure Cycling Association (☎ 406-721-1776, 800-755-2453; www.adventurecycling.org; 150 E Pine St, PO Box 8308, Missoula, MT 59802) Organizes tours, sells bike routes (regional and cross-country) and publishes *Adventure Cyclist* magazine.

Backroads (☎ 510-527-1555, 800-462-2848; www .backroads.com; 801 Cedar St, Berkeley, CA 94710) Wide variety of tours nationwide, from cushy to strenuous.
Bicycling (www.bicycling.com)
Bike (www.bikemag.com)
Cycle America (☎ 800-245-3263; www.cycleamerica .com; PO Box 485, Cannon Falls, MN 55009) Specializes in supported cross-country rides.
League of American Bicyclists (LAB; ☎ 202-822-1333; www.bikeleague.org; 1612 K St NW, Ste 800, Washington, DC 20006) This national advocacy group publishes *American Bicyclist* magazine; its excellent website has links, touring advice and a database of local bike clubs and repair shops. Members get discounts and access to their annual *Almanac*.

Hiking & Backpacking

With very few exceptions, all of America's parks and preserves are open to hikers. The best-maintained trails are usually in national and state parks; these range from easy, paved, wheelchair-accessible paths to day- and week-long wilderness journeys.

At national and state parks, their free trail maps are usually adequate for day hikes. For backpacking and other lands, topographic maps may be useful and even necessary; see Maps (p1123). Before hiking, always ask at a ranger station or visitor center about current conditions. Overnight backpackers are usually required to get a permit or register with park rangers before departing. Whether free or costing a few dollars, backcountry permits are often limited; in popular national parks they can book up months ahead. In sensitive areas, backcountry use may have lots of restrictions.

For advice on low-impact camping and wilderness etiquette, see p102. The **Leave No Trace Center** (☎ 800-332-4100; www.lnt.org) is a great hikers' resource, while the nonprofit '**Tread Lightly' program** (☎ 800-966-9900; www.treadlightly .org) emphasizes vehicular etiquette.

Be prepared for a wilderness journey and know what to do if things go wrong. **Survive Outdoors** (www.surviveoutdoors.com) dispenses tons of safety and first-aid tips, plus helpful photos of dangerous critters. Need *real* wilderness survival? *How to Stay Alive in the Woods*, by Bradford Angier, covers every contingency.

Some useful national resources:

American Hiking Society (www.americanhiking.org) Lists local hiking clubs nationwide and organizes 'volunteer vacations' building trails.

Backpacker (www.backpacker.com)
Local Hikes (www.localhikes.com) Recommends good hikes near cities and towns.
Rails-to-Trails Conservancy (☎ 202-331-9696; www .railstotrails.org) Converts abandoned railroad corridors into public biking and hiking trails; sells a nationwide trail guide. Also lists and reviews trails at www.traillink.com.

The continental USA's three mountain systems are traversed by legendary, epic trails, which can be broken up into smaller segments. Contact the following:

Appalachian Trail Appalachian Trail Conservancy (☎ 304-535-6331; www.appalachiantrail.org; PO Box 807, Harpers Ferry, WV 25425)
Continental Divide Trail Continental Divide Trail Alliance (☎ 888-909-2382; www.cdtrail.org; PO Box 628, Pine, CO 80470); Continental Divide Trail Society (☎ 410-235-9610; www.cdtsociety.org; 3704 N Charles St, Suite 601, Baltimore, MD 21218)
Pacific Crest Trail Pacific Crest Trail Association (☎ 916-349-2109; www.pcta.org; 5325 Elkhorn Blvd, Suite 256, Sacramento, CA 95842)

Rafting, Kayaking & Canoeing

If a river or body of water is big enough to support watercraft, an outfitter or rental operation will invariably be found nearby. In national parks, rafting, kayaking and canoeing always requires a permit, and in some cases – such as whitewater rafting on the Colorado River – waitlists for individual permits are years long. In these cases, book in advance with an organized tour. The following websites are helpful resources:

American Canoe Association (ACA; ☎ 703-451-0141; www.americancanoe.org; 7432 Alban Station Blvd, Suite B-232, Springfield, VA 22150) ACA publishes a newsletter, has a water trails database and organizes courses.
American Whitewater (☎ 866-262-8429; www .americanwhitewater.org; PO Box 1540, Cullowhee, NC 28723) This nonprofit is dedicated to preserving America's remaining wild rivers.
Canoe & Kayak (www.canoekayak.com)
Kayak Online (www.kayakonline.com) Good resource for kayak gear; links to outfitters nationwide.
Paddler (www.paddlermagazine.com)

Rock Climbing & Canyoneering

For a general rock climbing resource, pick up *Climbing magazine* (www.climbing.com). Canyoneers should contact the **American Canyoneering Association** (☎ 435-590-8889; www .canyoneering.net), which has a canyons database and courses.

Skiing & Snowboarding

Most of the USA's ski resorts are all-inclusive experiences: they typically offer equipment rental, lessons, kids' programs, restaurants, lodging and day care. Ski season is normally mid-December to April, though some resorts have longer seasons. In summer many resorts are great places to mountain bike and hike. Ski packages (including airfare, hotel and lift tickets) are easy to find through resorts and travel agencies; they're a good deal if your main goal is to ski.

Charles Leocha's *Ski Snowboard America* has overviews of North America's main resorts. Virtually every ski resort has its own website. Here are more resources:

Powder (www.powdermag.com)
SkiNet (www.skinet.com) Online versions of *Ski* and *Skiing* magazines.
Ski Resorts Guide (www.skiresortsguide.com) Comprehensive guide to resorts, with downloadable slope maps, lodging info and more.
SnoCountry Mountain Reports (www.snocountry .com) Snow reports for all of North America, plus events and resort links.
Snowboard.com (http://snowboard.colonies.com) A community website for snowboarders; lots of unvarnished advice.

CROSS-COUNTRY SKIING

Cross-country (or Nordic) skiing is as popular as downhill. Most downhill ski resorts have cross-country trails, and in winter many hiking trails in national parks, national forests and city parks become cross-country ski trails. For more information, try:

Cross-Country Ski Areas Association (www.xcski.org) Comprehensive information for North America.
Cross Country Skier (www.crosscountryskier.com) Great links.

Surfing

Pick up a copy of **Surfer magazine** (☎ 949-661-5147; www.surfermag.com). *Surfer*'s travel reports cover just about every break in the USA; order copies by phone or on the web. *Stormrider Guide North America* is also recommended.

BUSINESS HOURS

Unless otherwise noted, standard business hours in this guide are as follows. Businesses are open from 9am to 5pm Monday to Friday. Banks are open 8:30am to 4:30pm Monday to Thursday, until 5:30pm Friday. Some post offices and banks are also open from 9am to noon or 1pm on Saturday.

Stores are open 10am to 6pm Monday to Saturday, noon to 5pm Sunday. In malls and downtown shopping areas, hours may be extended to 8pm or 9pm. Supermarkets are generally open from 8am to 8pm, and most cities have a few 24-hour supermarkets. Note that in some parts of the country, all businesses except a few restaurants may close on Sunday.

Restaurant hours vary so widely that they are impossible to generalize; they can fluctuate with seasonal demand and owner whim. We provide high-season restaurant hours for every listing, but if it's winter, and your heart's set, and/or you're making a special trip, call ahead to confirm.

Bars and pubs are usually open from 5pm to midnight daily, extending to 2am on Friday and Saturday. Nightclubs and dance clubs generally open at 9pm and close at 2am Wednesday to Saturday. Hours may be longer in larger cities.

CHILDREN

Traveling with kids is often like possessing a secret key that unlocks locals, who brighten and coo and embrace your family like long-lost cousins. From the city to the country, most facilities are ready to accommodate a child's needs, and there are boundless options for entertaining restless young minds.

Practicalities

Restaurants of all stripes have high chairs, and if a restaurant doesn't have a specific children's menu, it can make a kid-tailored meal. Many diners and family restaurants break out paper placemats and crayons for drawing. Many public toilets have a baby changing table (sometimes in men's toilets too), and gender-neutral 'family' facilities appear in airports.

Motels and hotels typically have rooms with two beds, which are ideal for families. They also have 'roll-away beds' or 'cots' that can be brought into the room for an extra charge. Some have 'kids stay free' programs, which range up to 12, and sometimes 18, years old. Some B&Bs, to preserve a romantic atmosphere, don't allow children; ask when reserving.

Every car rental agency should be able to provide an appropriate child seat or restraint, since these are required in every state, but you need to request it when booking. Airlines also sometimes offer 'kids fly free' promotions, and they usually offer steep discounts for traveling infants.

In addition, most tourist bureaus list local resources for children's programs, childcare facilities and so on.

Sights & Activities

In this guide, most large cities include a 'City for Children' section highlighting the area's best kids' activities and resources. The USA is full to bursting with hands-on science museums, playgrounds, theme parks and fun centers.

In addition, nearly every national and state park gears a certain number of exhibits, trails and programs (such as national park Junior Ranger kits) for kids and families. For more outdoor advice, read *Kids in the Wild: A Family Guide to Outdoor Recreation* by Cindy Ross and Todd Gladfelter, and *Parents' Guide to Hiking & Camping* by Alice Cary. For all-around information and advice, check out Lonely Planet's *Travel with Children*. Other useful resources include:

Family Travel Times (www.familytraveltimes.com)

Go City Kids (www.gocitykids.com) Excellent coverage of kid-centric play and resources in over 20 US cities.

Kids.gov (www.kids.gov) Eclectic, huge national resource; download songs and activities or link to the CIA kids home page!

CLIMATE CHARTS

For general advice on seasonal travel in the USA, see p25. Every chapter has a When to Go section with specific regional information. The climate charts provide a snapshot of the USA's weather patterns. The **National Weather Service** (www.nws.noaa.gov) has an addictive array of radar and satellite maps.

CUSTOMS

For a complete list of US customs regulations, visit the official portal for **US Customs and Border Protection** (www.cbp.gov); the downloadable 'Know Before You Go' brochure covers the basics.

US Customs allows each person to bring 1L of liquor (provided you are at least 21 years old), 100 cigars and 200 cigarettes duty-free into the USA. US citizens are allowed to import, duty-free, $800 worth of gifts and purchases from abroad, while non-US citizens are allowed to bring in $100 worth.

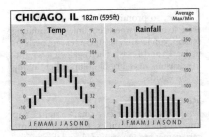

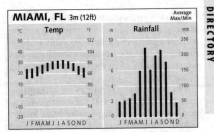

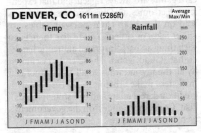

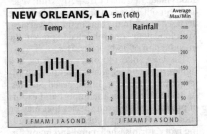

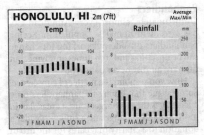

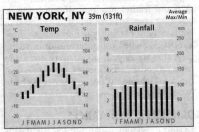

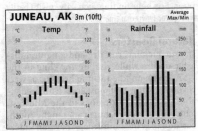

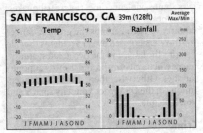

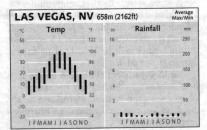

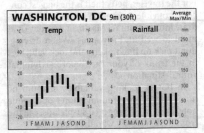

US law permits you to bring in, or take out, as much as $10,000 in US or foreign currency, traveler's checks or letters of credit without formality. There's no maximum limit, but larger amounts of money must be declared to customs.

There are heavy penalties for attempting to import illegal drugs. It's also forbidden to bring in to the US drug paraphernalia, lottery tickets, items with fake brand names, and goods made in Cuba or Iraq. Any fruit, vegetables, or other food or plant material must be declared or left in the bins in the arrival area. Most food items are prohibited to prevent the introduction of pests or diseases.

The USA, like 140 other countries, is a signatory to CITES, the Convention on International Trade in Endangered Species. As such, it prohibits the import and export of products made from species that may be endangered in any part of the world, including ivory, tortoiseshell, coral and many fur, skin and feather products. If you bring or buy a fur coat, snakeskin belt, alligator-skin boots or bone carving, you may have to show a certificate when you enter and/or leave the USA that states your goods were not made from an endangered species. For more, visit the US Fish and Wildlife Service website (www.fws.gov).

DANGERS & ANNOYANCES

Despite its seemingly Babylon-like list of dangers – guns, violent crime, riots, earthquakes, tornadoes – the USA is actually a very safe country to visit. Perhaps the greatest danger for travelers is posed by car accidents (buckle up – it's the law), and the two greatest annoyances will be city traffic and crowds at popular sites. Otherwise, there are a few dangers unique to the USA; pack your city smarts and you'll be fine.

Crime

For the traveler, petty theft is the biggest concern, not violent crime. When possible, withdraw money from ATMs during the day or at night in well-lit, busy areas. When driving, don't pick up hitchhikers, and lock valuables in the trunk of your car (before arriving at your destination).

In hotels, locking valuables in room or hotel safes is prudent, and don't open your hotel door to a stranger (if suspicious, call the front desk to verify who they are).

Guns, so prominent in the news, would seem to be everywhere, but unless it's hunting season, you'll rarely see them (except perhaps in Alaska and Texas). Then again, if it *is* hunting season, wear bright colors when hiking in the woods.

Scams

You did pack your city smarts, right? You know that, in big cities, three-card-monte card games are always rigged, and that expensive electronics, watches and designer items sold on the cheap from sidewalk tables are either fakes or stolen? You realize there is no such thing as 'bargain-priced authentic handicrafts?' Good, good. Those truly fascinated by all the myriad ways small-time American hucksters make a living today (usually with credit card, real estate and investment frauds), visit 'Consumer Guides' on the government's website, www.usa.gov.

Panhandlers

Unfortunately, almost every American city has a resident homeless population. Seeing panhandlers on sidewalks asking for change can be upsetting and sometimes annoying, but they are almost never dangerous.

How you respond is a matter of conscience. Some argue that giving to panhandlers only encourages them to target tourist areas. To do more than give change and a smile, consider a donation to a charity that cares for the urban poor. For help finding a charity, visit **Charity Navigator** (www.charitynavigator.org).

Natural Disasters

If your luck has run dry and a natural disaster occurs while you are traveling in the USA, you won't be turning here for advice. If you do, know that most areas with predictable troubles – tornadoes in the Midwest, tsunamis in Hawaii, hurricanes in the South, earthquakes in California – have an emergency siren system to alert communities to imminent danger. These sirens are tested periodically at noon, but if you hear one and suspect trouble, turn on a local TV or radio station, which will be broadcasting safety warnings and advice.

The **US Department of Health & Human Services** (www.dhhs.gov/disasters) has preparedness advice, news and general information on all the ways your vacation could go horribly, horribly wrong.

DISCOUNTS

Travelers will find a plethora of ways to shave costs of hotel rooms, meals, rental cars, museum admissions and just about anything else that can be had for a price. Persistence and ingenuity go a long way when it comes to finding deals in the USA.

Students and seniors (generally age 62 and up) are not issued separate discount cards, but they benefit from savings of all kinds. Simply carry proof of age or student status; international students should consider getting an **International Student Identity Card** (ISIC; www.isiccard.com), which provides its own discounts and should convince any dubious merchants of your student status. Then, as a matter of policy, ask about a discount every time you book a room, reserve a car, order a meal or pay an entrance fee. Most of the time this saves 10% or so, but sometimes as much as 50%. American seniors should seriously consider getting an America the Beautiful Senior Pass, which allows free access to all federal lands and 50% off use fees like camping.

Auto club membership (p1141) comes with a raft of discounts; AAA also has reciprocal agreements with several international auto associations. Other people whose status might lead to discounts are war veterans, the disabled, children, business travelers and foreign visitors. These discounts may not be advertised – it always pays to ask.

Discount coupons can be found at every tourist locale. Some are hardly worth reading, but scour tourist agencies and highway welcome centers for publications, brochures and flyers and you'll find a few good ones. Coupon flyers also accompany Sunday newspapers. Coupons always have restrictions and conditions; read the fine print.

Dedicated coupon clippers: don't neglect the internet! Two compendiums of retail, consumer electronics, car rental and other discounts are **eDealinfo** (www.edealinfo.com) and **Pricezilla** (www.pricezilla.com). For hotels, browse **Roomsaver.com** (www.roomsaver.com).

EMBASSIES & CONSULATES

International travelers needing to locate the US embassy in their home country should visit the **US Department of State website** (http://usembassy .state.gov), which has links to all of them.

International travelers who want to contact their home country's embassy while in the United States should visit www.embassy .org to get contact information for all foreign embassies in Washington, DC. Many countries also have consulates in other large cities. Look under 'Consulates' in the yellow pages, or call local information. Most countries have an embassy for the UN in New York City.

FESTIVALS & EVENTS

The festivals and events listed here are celebrated nationally, though with much more fanfare in some places. For more festival highlights, see 'Parties & Parades' under Getting Started (p28) and see 'Festivals & Events' sections in regional chapters; also see Holidays (p1121). Contact individual tourist offices for complete local calendars.

JANUARY

Chinese New Year Two weeks at the end of January. The first day is celebrated with parades, fireworks and lots of food. San Francisco's parade is notable.

FEBRUARY

Black History Month African American history is celebrated nationwide.
Valentine's Day The 14th. For some reason, St Valentine is associated with romance.
Mardi Gras In late February or early March, the day before Ash Wednesday. Parades, revelry and abandonment accompany the culmination of Carnival. New Orleans is legendary.

MARCH

St Patrick's Day The 17th. The patron saint of Ireland is honored. Huge celebrations occur in New York, Boston and Chicago. Wear green – if you don't, you could get pinched.
Easter In late March or April, the Sunday following Good Friday (which is not a public holiday). After morning

---

TRAVEL ADVISORIES

- **Australia** (☎ 1300-555-135; www.smart raveler.gov.au)
- **Canada** (☎ 800-267-6788; www.voyage.gc.ca)
- **Germany** (☎ 49-30-5000-2000; www .auswaertiges-amt.de)
- **New Zealand** (☎ 64-4-439-8000; www .safetravel.govt.nz)
- **UK** (☎ 020-7008-1500; www.fco.gov.uk)
- **USA** (☎ 888-407-4747; www.travel.state.gov)

church, kids hunt for chocolate eggs hidden by the mysterious Easter bunny.

MAY
Cinco de Mayo The 5th. The day the Mexicans wiped out the French Army in 1862. In the South and West, cities celebrate their Mexican heritage with parades.
Mother's Day The second Sunday. Children send cards and call Mom (or feel guilty for a *whole year*).

JUNE
Father's Day The third Sunday. Same idea, different parent, less guilt.
Gay Pride Month (www.interpride.org) In some cities, gay pride celebrations last a week, but in San Francisco, it's a month-long party. The last weekend in June culminates in parades.

JULY
Independence Day The 4th. American independence inspires parades and fireworks. Chicago pulls out the stops on the 3rd.

OCTOBER
Halloween The 31st. Kids dress in costumes and go door-to-door trick-or-treating for candy. Adults dress in costumes and act out alter egos at parties. New York and San Francisco are the wildest.

NOVEMBER
Day of the Dead The 2nd. Areas with Mexican communities honor deceased relatives; candy skulls and skeletons are popular.
Election Day The second Tuesday. Annual ritual in which Americans engage in participatory democracy.
Thanksgiving The fourth Thursday. A latter-day harvest festival; family and friends gather for daylong feasts, traditionally involving roasted turkey. New York City hosts a huge parade.

DECEMBER
Chanukkah Date determined by the Hebrew calendar, but usually begins before Christmas. This eight-day Jewish holiday (also called the Festival of Lights) commemorates the victory of the Maccabees over the armies of Syria.
Christmas The 25th. Christ's birth inspires church choir concerts, midnight church services, tree-lighting ceremonies, caroling in the streets and an unseemly consumer binge – culminating, of course, in a visit from Santa.
Kwanzaa (www.officialkwanzaawebsite.org) From the 26th to the 31st. This African American celebration is a time to give thanks and honor the seven principles.
New Year's Eve The 31st. Out with the old, in with the new. Millions get drunk, resolve to do better, and the next day nurse hangovers while watching college football.

FOOD
In this book, prices for restaurants usually refer to an average main dish at dinner; prices usually do not include drinks, appetizers, desserts, taxes or tips, and the same dish at lunch will usually be cheaper. When price categories are used in text, 'budget' means a meal under $12, 'midrange' means most dinner mains are $12 to $23, and 'top end' means most dinner mains are over $23. Remember that most US restaurants now ban or restrict smoking.

For the skinny on US cuisine, customs and table manners, see the Food & Drink chapter, p85.

GAY & LESBIAN TRAVELERS
Most major US cities have a visible and open gay community that is easy to connect with. For highlights, see the 'We're Here, We're Queer' Itinerary (p30); in this guide, most large cities include a boxed text or section dedicated to describing the city's best gay offerings.

The level of acceptance nationwide varies greatly. Gay and lesbian travelers should avoid hand-holding and outward displays of affection unless acceptance is obvious and unmistakable. In some places, there is absolutely no tolerance whatsoever, and in others tolerance and acceptance is predicated on gays and lesbians not 'flaunting' their sexual preference.

Damron (☎ 415-255-0404, 800-462-6654; www .damron.com) publishes several excellent travel guides, including *Men's Travel Guide, Women's Traveller* and *Damron Accommodations. The Queerest Places: A Guide to Gay and Lesbian Historic Sites* by Paula Martinac is full of juicy details and history, and covers the country.

Other useful national resources:
Advocate (www.advocate.com)
Gay.com (www.gay.com) Comprehensive resource; lots of travel information.
Gay & Lesbian National Hotline (☎ 888-843-4564; www.glnh.org) A national hotline for help, counseling, information and referrals; see website for hours.
Gay Yellow Network (☎ 800-697-2812; www .gay yellow.com) Yellow page listings for over 30 US cities.
National Gay and Lesbian Task Force (☎ 202-393-5177; www.thetaskforce.org) A national advocacy group; website has current news and lists of referrals.
Out Traveler (www.outtraveler.com)
Purple Roofs (www.purpleroofs.com) Lists queer accommodations, travel agencies and tours worldwide.

HOLIDAYS

On the following national public holidays, banks, schools and government offices (including post offices) are closed, and transportation, museums and other services operate on a Sunday schedule. Many stores, however, maintain regular business hours. Holidays falling on a weekend are usually observed the following Monday.

National public holidays:

New Year's Day January 1
Martin Luther King Jr Day Third Monday in January
Presidents' Day Third Monday in February
Memorial Day Last Monday in May
Independence Day (or the Fourth of July) July 4
Labor Day First Monday in September
Columbus Day Second Monday in October
Veterans' Day November 11
Thanksgiving Fourth Thursday in November
Christmas Day December 25

Special mention should be made of **Spring Break**, when university students get one week off from school so they can overrun beach towns with wild shenanigans. Be warned: colleges don't all choose the same week; spring breaks occur throughout March and April.

INSURANCE

No matter how long or short your trip, make sure you have adequate travel insurance, purchased before departure. At a minimum, you need coverage for medical emergencies and treatment, including hospital stays and an emergency flight home if necessary. Medical treatment in the USA is of the highest caliber, but the expense could kill you. See p1148 for complete information.

You should also consider coverage for luggage theft or loss and trip cancellation. If you already have a home-owner's policy, see what it will cover and consider getting supplemental insurance to cover the rest. If you have prepaid a large portion of your trip, cancellation insurance is a worthwhile expense.

A comprehensive travel insurance policy that covers all these things should cost about 5% to 7% of the total cost of your trip.

Finally, if you will be driving, it's also essential that you have liability insurance. Car rental agencies offer insurance that covers damage to the rental vehicle and separate liability insurance (which covers damage to people and other vehicles). See p1142 for details.

In addition to student travel agencies (p1135), here are some agencies offering comprehensive travel policies:

Access America (☎ 800-284-8300; www.access america.com)
Insure.com (☎ 800-487-4722; www.insure.com) An independent site that compares quotes among 200 insurance companies and gives advice about the different types of coverage. In the UK, they run Quoteline Direct, www.quotelinedirect.co.uk; in Canada, Kanetix, www.kanetix.ca.
Travelex (☎ 888-457-4602; www.travelex.com)
Travel Guard (☎ 800-826-4919; www.travelguard.com)

INTERNET ACCESS

Travelers will have few problems staying connected in the tech-savvy USA.

This guides uses an internet icon (🖳) when a place has an internet terminal for public use and the word 'wi-fi' when it offers wireless internet access. These days, most hotels (except the cheapest) have either inroom

---

LOOK MA, NO WIRES

The USA has nearly 10,000 wi-fi hotspots. That doesn't quite cover the continent, but 'wireless fidelity' is very common: most cities and college towns sponsor neighborhood hotspots, and even the smallest towns usually have at least one café or hotel with wi-fi. You can even connect in the woods: private campgrounds (like KOA) increasingly offer it, and so do some state parks (like in California and Michigan).

The following websites provide wi-fi hotspot lists (both free and for a fee) nationwide, and they provide lots of helpful advice and links to gear:

- www.hotspot-locations.com
- www.wi-fi.com Run by the nonprofit Wi-Fi Alliance.
- www.wififreespot.com
- www.wi-fihotspotlist.com

dial-up or high-speed access for connecting your own equipment, a public computer terminal or wi-fi (sometimes for free, sometimes a fee). Ask when reserving. For more on wi-fi hotspots, see boxed text 'Look Ma, No Wires,' p1121.

Most towns have at least one internet café or copy center (rates run $10 to $20 per hour) and cities have dozens; in this guide, city 'Internet Access' sections list convenient options. In addition to providing internet access, full-service internet cafés let you hook up your own peripherals to upload photos and/or burn them onto CDs (see also 'Photography,' p1124).

For quick internet surfing and email, other dependable bets are public libraries, which offer public terminals (though they have time limits). Occasionally out-of-state residents are charged a small fee ($1 to $2).

If you're not from the US, remember that you will need an AC adapter and a plug adapter for US sockets.

LEGAL MATTERS

In everyday matters, if you are stopped by the police, bear in mind that there is no system of paying traffic or other fines on the spot. Attempting to pay a fine to an officer is frowned upon at best and may result in a charge of bribery. For traffic offenses, the police officer or highway patroller will explain the options to you. There is usually a 30-day period to pay a fine, but the officer has the authority to take you directly to a magistrate to pay immediately.

If you are arrested for a more serious offense, you have a legal right to an attorney, and you are allowed to remain silent. There is no legal reason to speak to a police officer if you don't wish, but never walk away from an officer until given permission. All persons who are arrested are legally allowed the right to make one phone call. If you don't have a lawyer, friend or family member to help you, call your embassy. The police will give you the number upon request. As a matter of principle, the US legal system presumes a person innocent until proven guilty.

Each state has its own civil and criminal laws, and what is legal in one state may be illegal in others. Federal laws are applicable to the postal service, US government property and many interstate activities.

One wrinkle for foreign visitors is the USA Patriot Act, which was passed in the wake of September 11 to improve national security. Among other things, it expanded the federal government's ability to detain foreign visitors and immigrants they believe are linked to terrorism or terrorist organizations for an extended period of time without submitting charges or bringing them to trial. While this should be taken seriously, it is extremely unlikely to affect you. For more information and referrals for help, contact the **American Civil Liberties Union** (ACLU; www.aclu.org/safeandfree).

Driving

In all states, driving under the influence of alcohol or drugs is a serious offense, subject to stiff fines and even imprisonment. For more information on driving and road rules, see p1145.

Drinking

Bars and stores often ask for photo identification to prove you are of legal drinking age. Being 'carded' is standard practice; don't take it personally. The sale of liquor is subject to local government regulations, and some counties ban liquor sales on Sunday, after midnight or before breakfast. In 'dry' counties, liquor sales are banned altogether.

Drugs

Recreational drugs are prohibited by federal and state laws. Some states, such as California and Alaska, treat possession of small quantities of marijuana as a misdemeanor, though it is still punishable with fines and/or imprisonment.

Possession of any illicit drug, including cocaine, ecstasy, LSD, heroin, hashish or more than an ounce of pot, is a felony punishable by lengthy jail sentences, depending on the circumstances. For foreigners, conviction of any drug offense is grounds for deportation.

THE LEGAL AGE FOR...

- Drinking: 21
- Driving: 16
- Heterosexual consensual sex: 16–18 (varies by state)
- Homosexual consensual sex: where legal, 16–18 (varies by state)
- Voting: 18

MAPS

For a good road atlas, try **Rand McNally** (www
.randmcnally.com) and its Thomas Brothers city
guides; both can be found in most bookstores and some gas stations. If you are a
member of **AAA** (www.aaa.com) or one of its
international affiliates, you can get AAA's
high-quality free maps from any regional
office. Both Rand McNally's and AAA's
websites also provide driving directions and
free downloadable maps, as does **Google Maps**
(http://maps.google.com).

Hikers in need of a good topographical
(topo) map should turn to the **US Geological
Survey** (USGS; ☎ 888-275-8747; http://store.usgs.gov),
which produces a series of 1:24,000 scale
maps (or 7.5-minute maps) that cover the
entire country (and individual national parks)
and are ideal for backpackers. These can be
found at many national parks, ranger stations
and outdoor stores; the USGS website has a
comprehensive list of retailers. The USFS (US
Forest Service) publishes 1:126,720 scale (2
inches = 1 mile) topo maps of the national
forests, but they aren't quite as useful as the
USGS maps.

Cartophiles shouldn't miss the online map
library at the **University of Texas** (www.lib.utexas
.edu/maps/index.html): it has both current and historical maps of just about every place in the
US and the world.

Create custom, downloadable topo maps
for a fee at **Trails.com** (www.trails.com) and relatively small ones for free at **National Geographic**
(www.nationalgeographic.com), whose online store
has all the products you'd want, including
GPS maps. GPS gear and software can also
be purchased from **Magellan** (www.magellangps
.com) and **Garmin** (www.garmin.com).

MONEY
Cash
The stable US dollar – aka greenback, simo-
leon or buck – is the only currency generally accepted in the country, though a few
places near the Canadian border also accept
Canadian dollars.

The US dollar is divided into 100 cents (¢).
Coins come in denominations of 1¢ (penny),
5¢ (nickel), 10¢ (dime), 25¢ (quarter), the
seldom-seen 50¢ (half-dollar) and the $1
coin. Quarters are most commonly used in
vending machines and parking meters. Bills
come in $1, $2 (rare), $5, $10, $20, $50 and
$100 denominations.

ATMS
ATMs are available 24/7 at most banks,
and in shopping centers, airports, grocery
stores and casinos. Withdrawing cash from
an ATM using a credit card usually incurs a
fee ($1 to $3), but if your home bank account
is affiliated with one of the main worldwide
ATM networks (Plus, Cirrus, Exchange,
Accel), you can sometimes avoid the fee by
using your bank card. The exchange rate
on ATM transactions is usually as good as
you'll get anywhere.

Check with your bank or credit card company for exact information about using its
cards in stateside ATMs. If you will be relying
on ATMs (not a bad strategy), bring more
than one card and carry them separately.

Credit Cards
Major credit cards are almost universally accepted. In fact, it's almost impossible to rent
a car or make phone reservations without one
(though some airlines require your credit card
billing address to be in the USA – a hassle if
you're booking domestic flights once here).
It's highly recommended that you carry at
least one credit card; Visa and MasterCard
are the most widely accepted.

Carry copies of your credit card numbers
separately. If your credit cards are lost or sto-
len, contact the company immediately:
American Express (☎ 800-528-4800; www.american
express.com)
Diners Club (☎ 800-234-6377; www.dinersclub.com)
Discover (☎ 800-347-2683; www.discovercard.com)
MasterCard (☎ 800-622-7747; www.mastercard.com)
Visa (☎ 800-847-2911; www.visa.com)

Currency Exchange
Banks are the best places to exchange foreign currencies. Currency exchange counters
at the airport and in tourist centers typically have the worst rates. Most large city
banks offer currency exchange, but not always banks in rural areas. **Travelex** (☎ 888-
457-4602; www.travelex.com) is a major currency
exchange company.

For a list of exchange rates at the time
this guide went to press, see the inside front
cover.

Taxes
Sales tax varies by state and county; see each
state's Fast Facts boxed text for specifics.
Or, check out state sales taxes at **Sales Tax**

Clearinghouse (http://thestc.com/STRates.stm). Hotel taxes vary by city, and these are listed under city Sleeping sections.

Tipping

Tipping is standard practice across America. In city restaurants, tipping 15% of the bill is expected; less is OK in an informal diner, while top-end restaurants expect 20%. Bartenders expect $1 per drink. Taxi drivers and hairdressers expect 10% to 15%. Skycaps at airports and porters at nice hotels expect $1 a bag or so. It's polite to leave a few dollars for the hotel maid, especially if you spend several nights.

Traveler's Checks

Because of ATMs, traveler's checks are becoming obsolete except as a trustworthy backup. If you carry them, buy them in US dollars; local businesses may not cash ones in a foreign currency. Keep a separate record of their numbers in case they are lost or stolen. American Express traveler's checks are the most widely accepted.

PHOTOGRAPHY

Print film is ubiquitous; digital camera memory cards can be found in drugstores, chain retailers like Target or Circuit City and camera stores. For advice on picture-taking, see Lonely Planet's *Travel Photography*.

Drugstores and supermarkets will process print film cheaply – around $7 for a roll of 24 exposures. One-hour processing services are more expensive, usually around $12. Walgreens and Wal-Mart are two major chains where you can burn digital photos onto a CD (around $5).

About the only caution when it comes to photography concerns people. Always ask permission if you want to photograph someone close up. Some Native American reservations prohibit photography and video completely; when it's allowed, photo subjects expect a small tip (about $1).

POST

The US Postal Service (USPS) is the world's busiest postal service; it's also inexpensive and reliable. Still, for urgent and important documents, some people prefer the more expensive door-to-door services of **Federal Express** (FedEx; ☎ 800-463-3339; www.fedex.com) or **United Parcel Service** (UPS; ☎ 800-742-5877; www.ups.com).

Postal Rates

At the time of research, the postal rates for 1st-class mail within the USA were 41¢ for letters weighing up to one ounce (17¢ for each additional ounce) and 26¢ for postcards. First-class mail goes up to 13oz, and then priority-mail rates apply.

International airmail rates (except to Canada and Mexico) are 90¢ for both a 1oz letter and a postcard. To Canada and Mexico it's 69¢ for both a 1oz letter and a postcard. Aerograms are no longer offered, but they can be used if postage is increased to match first-class rates.

For 24-hour postal information, call ☎ 800-275-8777 or check www.usps.com. You can get zip (postal) codes for a given address, the rules about parcel sizes, and the location and hours of any post office.

Sending & Receiving Mail

If you have the correct postage, you can drop mail weighing less than 16oz into any blue mailbox. To send a package 16oz or heavier, go to a post office. There are branch post offices and post office centers in many supermarkets and drugstores.

General delivery mail (ie poste restante) can be sent to you c/o General Delivery at any post office that has its own zip code. Mail is usually held for 30 days before it's returned to the sender; you might request your correspondents to write 'Hold for Arrival' on their letters. You'll need photo identification to collect general delivery mail. In some big cities, general delivery mail is not held at the main post office but at a postal facility away from downtown.

SHOPPING

Most visitors won't want to leave before procuring a little brand-name American kitsch, and you'll find it's merely abundant when it isn't truly bizarre. Some tacky roadside souvenirs achieve the status of folk art, and if nothing else, they prove that Americans really do have a sense of humor about themselves.

Many regions are known for excellent local handicrafts or native artwork and goods. Traditional quilts, Pueblo jewelry, Navajo blankets, traditional or modern pottery, Gullah sweetgrass baskets and tooled leather cowboy boots are just a few of the things to look for. Good pieces will be expensive; if they are cheap, they are probably not authentic.

Another popular item is antiques. As with handicrafts, real antiques will be expensive; bargains are rare and sometimes suspect. The most popular types – anything colonial, Victorian, Amish, Shaker, art deco or '50s moderne – are guaranteed to have a hefty price tag.

For hip, unusual souvenirs, try modern art museum stores, which specialize in items that play off the museum's collection. They also often sell high-quality original designs by local artists.

Finally, bargain hunters should track down local factory outlets. These are usually malls near a freeway exit on the outskirts of a city where brand-name stores sell their damaged, left over or out-of-season stock at discounts ranging from modest to practically giveaway. Service will be minimal and choices limited, but the chance of half-price Levi's, Nike shoes or Polo shirts can be a siren song.

SOLO TRAVELERS

There are no particular problems traveling alone in the USA.

Hotels often offer lower rates for a single person, but single rooms tend to be small and badly located; for more comfort, reserve a double. To meet people, eat at the restaurant bar.

Hitchhiking is always risky and not recommended, *especially* hitchhiking alone. And don't pick up hitchhikers when driving alone.

When first meeting someone, don't advertise where you are staying, or even that you are traveling alone. Americans can be eager to help and even take in solo travelers, and this is one of the pluses of traveling this way. However, don't take all offers of help at face value. If someone who seems trustworthy invites you to his or her home, let someone know where you're going (even your hotel manager). This advice also applies if you go for a long hike by yourself. If something happens and you don't return as expected, you want to know that someone will notice and know where to begin looking for you.

TELEPHONE

The US phone system comprises numerous regional phone companies, plus competing long-distance carriers and lots of smaller mobile-phone and pay-phone companies. Overall, the system is very efficient, but it can be confusing and expensive. Avoid making long-distance calls on a hotel phone or on a pay phone. It's always cheaper to use a regular landline or cell phone.

Note that most telephone books are fantastic resources: in addition to complete calling information, they list community services, public transportation and things to see and do. Online, a good resource for phone numbers is www.yellowpages.com.

Cell Phones

In the USA cell phones use GSM 1900 or CDMA 800, operating on different frequencies from systems in other countries. The only foreign phones that will work in the USA are tri-band models, operating on GSM 1900 as well as other frequencies. If you have a GSM tri-band phone, check with your service provider about using it in the USA. Make sure to ask if roaming charges apply; these will turn even local US calls into pricey international calls.

You may be able to take the SIM card from your home phone, install it in a rented mobile phone that's compatible with the US systems, and use the rental phone as if it were your own phone – same number, same billing basis. Ask your mobile phone company about this. You can rent a phone for about $45 per week, but rates vary.

You can also rent a GSM 1900 compatible phone with a set amount of prepaid call time. **T-Mobile** (www.t-mobile.com) is one US company that provides this service, but it ain't cheap.

Finally, huge swaths of rural America don't pick up a signal. Check your provider's coverage.

Dialing Codes

If you're calling from abroad, the international country code for the USA is ☎ 1 (the same as Canada, but international rates apply between the two countries). To make an international call from the USA, dial ☎ 011, then the country code, followed by the area code (usually without the initial '0') and the phone number.

All phone numbers within the USA consist of a three-digit area code followed by a seven-digit local number. Typically, if you are calling a number within the same area code, you only have to dial the seven-digit number; however, some places now require you to dial the entire 10-digit number even for a local call. If dialing the seven-digit number doesn't work, try all 10.

If you are calling long distance, dial ☎ 1 plus the area code plus the phone number. If you're not sure whether the number is local or long distance (new area codes are added all the time, confusing even residents), try one way, and if it's wrong, usually a recorded voice will correct you.

For local directory assistance, dial ☎ 411. For directory assistance outside your area code, dial ☎ 1 plus the three-digit area code of the place you want to call plus 555-1212; this is charged as a long-distance call. For international assistance, dial ☎ 00.

The 800, 888, 877 and 866 prefixes are for toll-free numbers. Most can only be used within the USA, some only within the state, and some only outside the state. To find an organization's 800 number, call ☎ 800-555-1212.

The 550, 554, 900, 920, 940, 976 codes and some other prefixes are for calls charged at a premium rate – phone sex, horoscopes, jokes etc.

Pay Phones

Local calls at pay phones cost 35¢ to 50¢ for the first few minutes; talking longer costs more. Only put in the exact amount, since phones don't give change. Local-call charges only apply to a small area. If the number you're trying to call is beyond this area, a recorded voice will tell you to insert more money. Local calls from pay phones get expensive quickly, and long-distance calls are prohibitive. It's best to use a prepaid phone card, a phone credit card or the access line of a major carrier, such as AT&T (☎ 800-321-0288) or MCI (☎ 800-888-8000).

Phone Cards

Phone cards are now almost essential for travelers using the US phone system. There are two basic types.

A phone credit card bills calls to your home phone number. Some cards issued by foreign phone companies will work in the USA – inquire before you leave home.

A prepaid phone card is a good alternative for travelers and are widely available in big cities and major retailers. Be sure to always check the card's connection fees (see if it has a toll-free access number from pay phones) in addition to the rate. AT&T sells a reliable phone card that is available at many retailers.

TIME

America subscribes to daylight savings time (DST), and in 2007 the government extended how long it lasts: now, in early March, clocks are set one hour ahead ('spring ahead'). Then, in early November, clocks are turned back one hour ('fall back'). Just to keep you on your toes, Arizona, Hawaii and most of Indiana don't use DST.

Foreigners are sometimes confused by the US date system, which is written as month/day/year. Thus, 8 June 2008 becomes 6/8/08. Clear as mud?

See p1190-1 for a map of time zones.

TOURIST INFORMATION

There is no national office promoting US tourism. However, visit the federal government's official web portal (www.usa.gov), go to the 'Travel and Recreation' page, and you'll find links to all the nation's state travel bureaus, plus a wealth of links to other recreation information.

In this guide, state tourism bureaus are listed in each regional chapter's Information section, while city and county tourist bureaus are listed throughout.

Any tourist office worth contacting has a website and, on request, will send out a clutch of free promotional material. They also field phone calls; some local offices maintain daily lists of hotel room availability, but few offer reservation services. All tourist offices have self-service racks of brochures and discount coupons to local attractions. Some also sell maps and books.

State-run 'welcome centers,' usually placed along interstates, tend to have materials that cover wider territories, and offices are usually open longer hours, including weekends and holidays.

Many cities have an official convention and visitors bureau (CVB); these sometimes double as tourist bureaus, but since their main focus is drawing the convention trade, CVBs can be less useful for independent travelers.

Keep in mind that, in smaller towns, when the local chamber of commerce runs the tourist bureau, their lists of hotels, restaurants and services usually mention only chamber members; the town's cheapest options may be missing.

Similarly, in prime tourist destinations, some private 'tourist bureaus' are really agents who book hotel rooms and tours on commission. They may offer excellent service and deals, but you'll get what they're selling and nothing else.

TRAVELERS WITH DISABILITIES

The USA is a world leader in providing facilities for the disabled. The Americans with Disabilities Act (ADA) requires that all public buildings – including hotels, restaurants, theaters and museums – and public transit be wheelchair accessible. However, always call ahead to confirm what is available.

Telephone companies are required to provide relay operators – available via teletypewriter (TTY) numbers – for the hearing impaired. Most banks now provide ATM instructions in Braille. All major airlines, Greyhound buses and Amtrak trains assist disabled travelers; just describe your needs when making reservations, and they will help make the necessary arrangements.

Some car rental agencies – such as Budget and Hertz – offer hand-controlled vehicles and vans with wheelchair lifts at no extra charge, but you must reserve them well in advance.

A number of organizations specialize in serving disabled travelers:

Access-Able Travel Source (☎ 303-232-2979; www .access-able.com; PO Box 1796, Wheat Ridge, CO 80034) An excellent website with many links. They also run the Travelin' Talk Network (www.travelintalk.net), a global network of service providers.

Disabled Sports USA (☎ 301-217-0960; www.dsusa .org; 451 Hungerford Drv, Suite 100, Rockville, MD 20850) Nationwide organization that offers sports and recreation programs for the disabled, selects US athletes for Paralympic Games and publishes *Challenge* magazine.

Flying Wheels Travel (☎ 507-451-5005; www.flying wheelstravel.com; 143 W Bridge St, Owatonna, MN 55060) A full-service travel agency specializing in disabled travel.

Mobility International USA (☎ 541-343-1284; www .miusa.org; 132 E Broadway, Ste 343, Eugene, OR 97401) Advises disabled travelers on mobility issues and runs an educational exchange program.

Moss Rehabilitation Hospital's Travel Information Service (www.mossresourcenet.org/travel.htm) This hospital's website provides a concise list of useful contacts.

Society for Accessible Travel & Hospitality (SATH; ☎ 212-447-7284; www.sath.org; 347 Fifth Ave, Suite 605, New York, NY 10016) Lobbies for better facilities and publishes *Open World* magazine.

VISAS

US entry requirements continue to evolve as the USA fine-tunes its national security guidelines. All travelers should double-check current visa and passport regulations *before* coming to the USA.

The main portal for US visa information is www.unitedstatesvisas.gov, though you can also access visa information through www .usa.gov. Both of these link to the **US State Department** (www.travel.state.gov), which maintains the most comprehensive visa information, providing downloadable forms, lists of US consulates abroad and even visa wait times calculated by country. The website maintained by **US Citizenship and Immigration Services** (USCIS; http://uscis.gov) focuses on immigrants, not temporary visitors.

Visa Application

Apart from Canadians and those entering under the Visa Waiver Program (see p1128), foreign visitors need to obtain a visa from a US consulate or embassy. Most applicants must now schedule a personal interview, to which you must bring all your documentation and proof of fee payment. Wait times for interviews vary, but afterward, barring problems, visa issuance takes from a few days to a few weeks. The US consular office should also inform you if you must follow the National Security Entry/Exit Registration System (NSEERS) procedures upon arrival (p1129).

Your passport must be valid for at least six months longer than your intended stay in the USA. You'll need a recent photo (2in by 2in), and you must pay a $100 processing fee, plus in a few cases an additional visa issuance reciprocity fee (check the State Department website for details). In addition to the main nonimmigrant visa application form (DS-156), all men aged 16 to 45 must complete an additional form (DS-157) that details their travel plans.

Visa applicants are required to show documents of financial stability (or evidence that a US resident will provide financial support), a round-trip or onward ticket and 'binding obligations' that will ensure their return home, such as family ties, a home or a job.

Because of these requirements, those planning to travel through other countries before arriving in the USA are generally better off applying for a US visa while they are still in their home country, rather than while on the road.

The most common visa is a nonimmigrant visitor's visa, type B1 for business purposes,

B2 for tourism or visiting friends and relatives. A visitor's visa is good for multiple entries over one or five years, and specifically prohibits the visitor from taking paid employment in the USA. The validity period depends on what country you are from. The length of time you'll be allowed to stay in the USA is determined by US immigration at the port of entry (see opposite).

If you're coming to the USA to work or study, you will need a different type of visa, and the company or institution to which you are going should make the arrangements. Other categories of nonimmigrant visas include an F1 visa for students undertaking a recognized course; an H1, H2 or H3 visa for temporary employment; a J1 visa for exchange visitors in approved programs; a K1 visa for the fiancé or fiancée of an American citizen; and an L1 visa for intracompany transfers.

VISA WAIVER PROGRAM

Under the Visa Waiver Program, citizens of certain countries may enter the USA without a US visa for stays of 90 days or less; no extensions are allowed. Currently, 27 countries are included: Andorra, Australia, Austria, Belgium, Brunei, Denmark, Finland, France, Germany, Iceland, Ireland, Italy, Japan, Liechtenstein, Luxembourg, Monaco, the Netherlands, New Zealand, Norway, Portugal, San Marino, Singapore, Slovenia, Spain, Sweden, Switzerland and the UK.

Under this program, visitors must produce at the port of entry all the same evidence as for a nonimmigrant visa application: ie they must demonstrate that the trip is for a limited time, and that they have a round-trip or onward ticket, adequate funds to cover the trip and binding obligations abroad. You don't need a visa if: your passport was issued before October 26, 2005, but is 'machine readable' (with two lines of letters, numbers and <<< at the bottom); if it was issued between October 26, 2005, and October 25, 2006, and includes a digital photo as well as being machine readable; or if it was issued on or after October 26, 2006, and is an e-Passport containing a digital photo and an imbedded computer chip with 'biometric data.' Confirm with your passport issuing agency that your passport meets current US standards. You'll be turned back if it doesn't, even though you belong to a VWP country.

In addition, the same 'grounds for exclusion' apply (see following), except that you will have no opportunity to appeal the grounds or apply for an exemption. If you are denied under the Visa Waiver Program at a US point of entry, you will have to use your onward or return ticket on the next available flight.

GROUNDS FOR EXCLUSION & DEPORTATION

If on your visa application form you admit to being a subversive, smuggler, prostitute, junkie, terrorist or an ex-Nazi, you may be excluded. You can also be refused a visa or entry to the USA if you have a 'communicable disease of public health significance,' a criminal record or if you've ever made a false statement in connection with a US visa application. However, if these last three apply, you can request an exemption; many people are granted them and then given visas.

US immigration has a very broad definition of a criminal record. If you've ever been arrested or charged with an offense, that's a criminal record, even if you were acquitted or discharged without conviction. Don't attempt to enter through the Visa Waiver Program if you have a criminal record of any kind; assume US authorities will find out about it.

Communicable diseases include tuberculosis, the Ebola virus, SARS and most particularly HIV. US immigration doesn't test people for disease, but officials at the point of entry may question anyone about his or her health. They can exclude anyone whom they believe has a communicable disease, perhaps because they are carrying medical documents, prescriptions or AIDS/HIV medicine. Being gay is not a ground for exclusion; being an IV drug user is. Visitors may be deported if US immigration finds that they have HIV but did not declare it. Being HIV-positive is not a ground for deportation, but failing to provide accurate information on the visa application is.

Often USCIS will grant an exemption (a 'waiver of ineligibility') to a person who would normally be subject to exclusion, but this requires referral to a regional immigration office and can take some time (allow at least two months). If you're tempted to conceal something, remember that US immigration is strictest of all about false statements. It will often view favorably an applicant who admits to an old criminal charge or a communicable disease, but it is extremely harsh on anyone who has ever attempted to mislead it, even on minor points. After you're admitted to the USA, any evidence of a false statement to US immigration is grounds for deportation.

Prospective visitors to whom grounds of exclusion may apply should consider their options *before* applying for a visa.

Entering the USA

If you have a non-US passport, you must complete an arrival/departure record (form I-94) before you reach the immigration desk. It's usually handed out on the plane along with the customs declaration. For the question, 'Address While in the United States,' give the address where you will spend the first night (a hotel address is fine).

No matter what your visa says, US immigration officers have an absolute authority to refuse admission to the USA or to impose conditions on admission. They will ask about your plans and whether you have sufficient funds; it's a good idea to list an itinerary, produce an onward or round-trip ticket and have at least one major credit card. Showing that you have over $400 per week of your stay should be enough. Don't make too much of having friends, relatives or business contacts in the USA; the immigration official may decide that this will make you more likely to overstay. It also helps to be neatly dressed and polite. If they think you're OK, a six-month entry is usually approved.

REGISTRATION

The Department of Homeland Security's registration program – called **US-VISIT** (www.dhs.gov/us-visit) – is essentially phased in. It includes every port of entry and nearly every foreign visitor to the USA.

For most visitors (excluding, for now, most Canadian and Mexican citizens), registration consists of having a digital photo taken and electronic (inkless) fingerprints made of each index finger; the process takes less than a minute. As of June 2007, no second registration was required to exit the USA.

A 'special registration' called NSEERS (the National Security Entry/Exit Registration System) applies to citizens of certain countries that have been deemed particular risks; however, US officials can require this registration of any traveler. Currently, the countries included are Iran, Iraq, Libya, Sudan and Syria, but visit www.travel.state.gov for updates. Registration in these cases also includes a short interview in a separate room and computer verification of all personal information supplied on travel documents.

Visa Extensions

If you want, need or hope to stay in the USA longer than the date stamped on your passport, go to the local USCIS office (call ☎ 800-375-5283 or look in the local white pages telephone directory under 'US Government') to apply for an extension well *before* the stamped date. If the date has passed, your best chance will be to bring a US citizen with you to vouch for your character, and to produce lots of other verification that you are not trying to work illegally and have enough money to support yourself. However, if you've overstayed, the most likely scenario is that you will be deported.

Short-Term Departures & Reentry

It's quite easy to make trips across the border to Canada or Mexico, but upon return to the USA, non-Americans will be subject to the full immigration procedure. Always take your passport when you cross the border. If your immigration card still has plenty of time on it, you will probably be able to reenter using the same one, but if it has nearly expired, however, you will have to apply for a new card, and border control may want to see your onward air ticket, sufficient funds and so on.

Traditionally, a quick trip across the border has been a way to extend your stay in the USA without applying for an extension at a USCIS office. This can still be done, but don't assume it will work. First, make sure you hand in your old immigration card to the immigration authorities when you leave the USA, and when you return make sure you have all the necessary application documentation from when you first entered the country. US immigration will be very suspicious of anyone who leaves for a few days and returns immediately hoping for a new six-month stay; expect to be questioned closely.

Citizens of most Western countries will not need a visa for Canada, so it's really not a problem at all to cross to the Canadian side of Niagara Falls, detour up to Quebec or

DIRECTORY

pass through on the way to Alaska. Travelers entering the USA by bus from Canada can be closely scrutinized. A round-trip ticket that takes you back to Canada will most likely make US immigration feel less suspicious. Mexico has a visa-free zone along most of its border with the USA, including the Baja Peninsula and most of the border towns, such as Tijuana and Ciudad Juárez. You'll need a Mexican visa or tourist card only if you want to go beyond the border zone. For more, see 'Border Crossings,' p1137, and El Paso, p738.

VOLUNTEERING

Volunteer opportunities abound in the USA, and they can be a great way to break up a long trip. They can also provide some of your most memorable experiences: you will interact with Americans, society and the land in ways you never would just passing through.

Most programs charge a fee; this usually runs from $200 to $500, depending on the length of the program and the amenities. None cover travel to the USA.

In addition to the groups here, all of the trail alliances under 'Hiking' (p1115), use volunteers:

Global Volunteers (☎ 800-487-1074; www.global volunteers.org; 375 E Little Canada Rd, St Paul, MN 55117)

The Green Project (☎ 504-945-0240; www.the greenproject.org; 2831 Marais St, New Orleans, LA 70117) Working to rebuild New Orleans post-Katrina in sustainable, green ways.

Habitat for Humanity (☎ 229-924-6935, ext 2551; www.habitat.org; 121 Habitat St, Americus, GA 31709) Focuses on housing and homelessness.

Volunteers for Peace (VFP; ☎ 802-259-2759; www .vfp.org; 1034 Tiffany Rd, Belmont, VT 05730)

Wilderness Volunteers (☎ 928-556-0038; www .wildernessvolunteers.org; PO Box 22292, Flagstaff, AZ 86002) Weeklong trips helping maintain America's parks and wildlands.

WOMEN TRAVELERS

Women traveling by themselves or in a group should not encounter any particular problems in the USA. Indeed, there are a number of excellent resources that facilitate just this.

The community website www.journey woman.com helps women talk to each other, and it has links to other sites. As for guides, try the inspirational *A Journey of One's Own* (1992) by Thalia Zepatos; the pocketsize

expertise of *Gutsy Women: Travel Tips and Wisdom for the Road* (1996) by Marybeth Bond; or the irreverent, equally portable *The Bad Girl's Guide to the Open Road* (1999) by Cameron Tuttle.

These two national advocacy groups might also be helpful:

National Organization for Women (NOW; ☎ 202-628-8669; www.now.org; 1100 H St NW, 3rd fl, Washington, DC 20005)

Planned Parenthood (☎ 800-230-7526; www .plannedparenthood.org) Offers referrals to medical clinics throughout the country.

In terms of safety issues, single women need to exhibit the same street smarts as any solo traveler (p1125), but they are sometimes more often the target of unwanted attention or harassment. Some women like to carry a whistle, mace or cayenne-pepper spray in case of assault. If you purchase a spray, contact a police station to find out about local regulations. Laws regarding sprays vary from state to state; federal law prohibits them being carried on planes.

If you are assaulted, it may be better to call a rape crisis hotline before calling the **police** (☎ 911); telephone books have listings of local organizations, or contact the **Rape, Abuse & Incest National Network** (☎ 800-656-4673; www .rainn.org), a 24-hour hotline. Or, go straight to a hospital. Police can sometimes be insensitive with assault victims, whereas a rape crisis center or hospital will advocate on behalf of survivors and act as a link to other services, including the police.

WORK

If you are a foreigner in the USA with a standard nonimmigrant visitor's visa, you are expressly forbidden to take paid work in the USA and will be deported if you're caught working illegally. In addition, employers are required to establish the bona fides of their employees or face fines, making it much tougher for a foreigner to get work than it once was.

To work legally, foreigners need to apply for a work visa before leaving home. A J1 visa, for exchange visitors, is issued to young people (age limits vary) for study, student vacation employment, work in summer camps, and short-term traineeships with a specific employer. The following organizations will help arrange student exchanges, placements and J1 visas:

American Institute for Foreign Study (AIFS; ☎ 866-906-2437; www.aifs.com; River Plaza, 9 West Broad St, Stamford, CT 06902)

BUNAC (☎ 020-7251-3472; www.bunac.org; 16 Bowling Green Lane, London EC1R 0QH)

Camp America (☎ 020-7581-7373; www.camp america.co.uk; 37A Queens Gate, London SW7 5HR)

Council on International Educational Exchange (CIEE; ☎ 800-407-8839; www.ciee.org; 7 Custom House St, 3rd fl, Portland, ME 04101)

InterExchange (☎ 212-924-0446; www.interexchange .org; 161 Sixth Ave, NY, NY 10013) Camp and au pair programs.

International Exchange Programs (IEP) Australia (☎ 1300-300-912; www.iep.org.au; Level 3, 362 La Trobe St, Melbourne, VIC 3000; Level 3, 333 George St, Sydney, NSW 2000); New Zealand (☎ 0800-443-769; www.iep .co.nz; Level 10, 220 Queen St, Auckland 1010)

For nonstudent jobs, temporary or permanent, you need to be sponsored by a US employer who will have to arrange one of the various H-category visas. These are not easy to obtain, since the employer has to prove that no US citizen or permanent resident is available to do the job. Seasonal work is possible in national parks, tourist sites and especially ski areas. Contact park concessionaires, local chambers of commerce and ski-resort management. Lonely Planet's *Gap Year Book* is another good resource for ideas on how to combine work and travel.

Transportation

CONTENTS

GETTING THERE & AWAY

ENTERING THE USA

The USA is working hard to counter any lingering 'Fortress America' image post-September 11, and in fact, despite new security procedures, it's not really any more time-consuming to enter the country now than pre-September 11. That said, US officials are strict and vigilant: have all your papers in order; neatness and politeness count. For details on forms and current registration procedures, see Entering the USA, p1129.

If you are flying to America, the first airport that you land in is where you must go through immigration and customs, even if you are continuing on the flight to another destination.

Once you go through immigration, you collect your baggage and pass through customs. If you have nothing to declare, you'll probably clear customs without a baggage search, but don't assume this. For details on customs, see p1116. If you are continuing on the same plane or connecting to another one, it is your responsibility to get your bags to the right place. Normally, airline representatives are just outside the customs area to help you.

If you are a single parent, grandparent or guardian traveling with anyone under 18, carry proof of legal custody or a notarized letter from the nonaccompanying parent(s) authorizing the trip. This isn't required, but the USA is concerned with thwarting child abduction, and not having authorizing papers could cause delays or even result in being denied admittance to the country.

Passport

Very soon, every person entering the USA from abroad – meaning every foreign visitor and every US citizen – will need a passport. Currently, passports are required of everyone arriving by air. At land and sea checkpoints, the only exceptions are for US and Canadian citizens, who may enter with proof of citizenship, such as a citizenship card with photo identification. Unless foreign visitors qualify for the Visa Waiver Program (see p1128), visitors must also have a visa.

The US planned to implement its mandatory passport policy at all borders in 2008, but due to a backlog in passport applications, this may not become a reality until 2009.

AIR

Airports & Airlines

The USA has more than 400 domestic airports, and a baker's dozen are the main international gateways. Many other airports are called 'international' but most have only a few flights from other countries – typically Mexico or Canada. Even travel to an international gateway sometimes requires a connection

THINGS CHANGE...

The information in this chapter is particularly vulnerable to change. Check directly with the airline or a travel agent to make sure you understand how a fare (and ticket you may buy) works and be aware of the security requirements for international travel. Shop carefully. The details given in this chapter should be regarded as pointers and are not a substitute for your own careful, up-to-date research.

in another gateway city. For example, many of the London–Los Angeles flights involve a transfer connection in Chicago.

Airports in the USA:

Atlanta Hartsfield-Jackson International (ATL; ☎ 404-530-7300; www.atlanta-airport.com)

Boston Logan International (BOS; ☎ 800-235-6426; www.massport.com/logan)

Chicago O'Hare International (ORD; ☎ 773-686-2200; www.flychicago.com)

Dallas-Fort Worth (DFW; ☎ 972-574-8888; www.dfwairport.com)

Honolulu (HNL; ☎ 808-836-6413; www.honoluluairport.com)

Houston George Bush Intercontinental (IAH; ☎ 281-230-3000; www.worldairportguides.com/houston-iah)

Los Angeles (LAX; ☎ 310-646-5252; www.lawa.org/lax)

Miami (MIA; ☎ 305-876-7000; www.miami-airport.com)

New York John F Kennedy (JFK; ☎ 718-244-4444; www.panynj.gov)

Newark Liberty International (EWR; ☎ 973-961-6000; www.panynj.gov)

San Francisco (SFO; ☎ 650-821-8211; www.flysfo.com)

Seattle Seattle-Tacoma International (SEA; ☎ 206-433-5388; www.portseattle.org/seatac)

Washington, DC Dulles International (IAD; ☎ 703-572-2700; www.metwashairports.com/dulles)

The national airlines of most countries have flights to the USA, and the USA has several airlines serving the world. Here is a list of the main international carriers. Online, www.smilinjack.com has links to international airlines, and www.seatguru.com has extensive airline information, including seat-by-seat reviews for each aircraft.

Airlines flying to/from the USA:

Aer Lingus (EI; ☎ 800-474-7424; www.aerlingus.com; hub Dublin)

Aerolíneas Argentinas (AR; ☎ 800-333-0276; www.aerolineas.com.au; hub Buenos Aires)

Air Canada (AC; ☎ 888-247-2262; www.aircanada.com; hub Toronto)

Air France (AF; ☎ 800-237-2747; www.airfrance.com; hub Paris)

Air India (AI; ☎ 800-223-7776; www.airindia.com; hub Delhi)

Air New Zealand (NZ; ☎ 800-262-1234; www.airnewzealand.com; hub Auckland)

Alitalia (AZ; ☎ 800-223-5730; www.alitalia.com; hub Milan)

American Airlines (AA; ☎ 800-433-7300; www.aa.com; hub Dallas)

British Airways (BA; ☎ 800-247-9297; www.britishairways.com; hub London)

Cathay Pacific (CX; ☎ 800-233-2742; www.cathaypacific.com; hub Hong Kong)

Continental Airlines (CO; ☎ 800-231-0856; www.continental.com; hubs Houston, Cleveland, Newark)

Delta Air Lines (DL; ☎ 800-241-4141; www.delta.com; hub Atlanta)

El Al (LY; ☎ 800-223-6700; www.elal.com; hub Tel Aviv)

Garuda Indonesia (GA; ☎ 800-342-7832; www.garuda-indonesia.com; hub Jakarta)

Iberia (IB; ☎ 800-772-4642; www.iberia.com; hub Madrid)

Icelandair (FI; ☎ 800-223-5500; www.icelandair.com; hub Keflavik Airport, Iceland)

Japan Airlines (JL; ☎ 800-525-3663; www.jal.com; hub Tokyo)

KLM (KL; ☎ 800-225-2525; www.klm.com; hub Amsterdam)

Korean Air (KE; ☎ 800-438-5000; www.koreanair.com; hub Seoul)

Kuwait Airways (KU; ☎ 800-458-9248; www.kuwait-airways.com; hub Kuwait)

Lufthansa (LH; ☎ 800-399-5838; www.lufthansa.com; hub Frankfurt)

Northwest Airlines (NW; ☎ 800-225-2525; www.nwa.com; hubs Minneapolis/St Paul, Memphis, Detroit)

Polynesian Airlines (PH; www.polynesianairlines.com; hub Samoa)

Qantas (QF; ☎ 800-227-4500; www.qantas.com.au; hub Sydney)

Scandinavian Airlines (SAS; ☎ 800-221-2350; www.flysas.com; hubs Copenhagen, Helsinki, Oslo, Stockholm)

Singapore Airlines (SQ; ☎ 800-742-3333; www.singaporeair.com; hub Singapore)

South African Airways (SA; ☎ 800-722-9675; ww2.flysaa.com; hub Johannesburg)

Thai Airways International (TG; ☎ 800-426-5204; www.thaiair.com; hub Bangkok)

United Airlines (UA; ☎ 800-538-2929; www.united.com; hub Los Angeles)

US Airways (US; ☎ 800-622-1015; www.usairways.com; hubs Philadelphia, Charlotte)

Virgin Atlantic (VS; ☎ 800-821-5438; www.virgin-atlantic.com; hub London)

Tickets

Getting a cheap airline ticket is a matter of research, reserving early – at least three to four weeks in advance – and timing. Flying midweek and in the off-season (normally, fall to spring, excluding holiday periods) is always less expensive, but fare wars crop up anytime. The only way to ensure you've found the cheapest possible ticket for the flight you want is to check every angle: compare several online travel agencies with the airline's website, and

TRANSPORTATION

CLIMATE CHANGE & TRAVEL
Climate change is a serious threat to the ecosystems that humans rely upon, and air travel is the fastest-growing contributor to the problem. Lonely Planet regards travel, overall, as a global benefit, but believes we all have a responsibility to limit our personal impact on global warming.

Flying & Climate Change
Pretty much every form of motorized travel generates CO_2 (the main cause of human-induced climate change) but planes are far and away the worst offenders, not just because of the sheer distances they allow us to travel, but because they release greenhouse gases high into the atmosphere. The statistics are frightening: two people taking a return flight between Europe and the US will contribute as much to climate change as an average household's gas and electricity consumption over a whole year.

Carbon Offset Schemes
Climatecare.org and other websites use 'carbon calculators' that allow travelers to offset the level of greenhouse gases they are responsible for with financial contributions to sustainable travel schemes that reduce global warming – including projects in India, Honduras, Kazakhstan and Uganda.

Lonely Planet, together with Rough Guides and other concerned partners in the travel industry, support the carbon offset scheme run by climatecare.org. Lonely Planet offsets all of its staff and author travel.

For more information check out our website: www.lonelyplanet.com.

then call the airline directly. Engaging a living, breathing travel agent is best when your plans are long and/or complicated.

Keep in mind your entire US itinerary. Some deals for travel within the USA can only be purchased overseas in conjunction with an international air ticket, or you may get discounts for booking air and car rental together. Or, you may find domestic flights within the USA are less expensive when added on to your international airfare.

For a good overview of online ticket agencies, visit **Airinfo** (www.airinfo.aero), which also lists travel agents worldwide.

The big three agency websites are **Travelocity** (www.travelocity.com), **Orbitz** (www.orbitz.com) and **Expedia** (www.expedia.com). Similar and worth trying are **Cheap Tickets** (www.cheaptickets.com) and **Lowest Fare** (www.lowestfare.com). Typically, these sites don't include budget airlines such as Southwest.

Meta sites are good for price comparisons, as they gather from many sources (but don't provide direct booking): try **Kayak** (www.kayak.com), **Mobissimo** (www.mobissimo.com) and **Sidestep** (www.sidestep.com).

Bidding for travel can be very successful, but carefully read the fine print before bidding. Try **Hotwire** (www.hotwire.com), **Skyauction** (www.skyauction.com) and **Priceline** (www.priceline.com). See www.biddingfortravel.com for advice about Priceline, which can be great for car rentals.

Finally, peruse **Travelzoo** (www.travelzoo.com), which gathers and passes along the airlines' promotional deals; their email alerts might inspire a trip!

COURIER FLIGHTS
Some firms provide very cheap fares to travelers who will be couriers, hand-delivering documents or packages. Courier opportunities are not easy to come by; they are available mainly on principal international routes (they are nonexistent on domestic routes). The traveler is usually allowed only one piece of carry-on baggage, with the checked-baggage allowance being taken by the item to be delivered. Two agencies to try are the **International Association of Air Travel Couriers** (www.courier.org) and the **Air Courier Association** (www.aircourier.org); both require membership and don't guarantee you'll get a courier flight.

INTERCONTINENTAL (RTW) TICKETS
Round-the-world (RTW) tickets are great if you want to visit other regions besides the USA; otherwise, a simple round-trip ticket is usually cheaper. They're of most value for

trips that combine the USA with Europe, Asia and/or Australasia.

RTW tickets go by different names depending on their itineraries (such as Pacific Circle, and so on); they use the routes of an airline alliance, such as **Star Alliance** (www.star alliance.com) and **One World** (www.oneworld.com); and they are valid for a fixed period, usually a year. Most RTW fares restrict the number of stops within the USA and Canada. The cheapest fares permit only one stop; others allow two or more. Some airlines 'black out' a few heavily traveled routes (such as Honolulu to Tokyo). In most cases a 14-day advance purchase is required. After the ticket is purchased, dates can usually be changed without penalty, and tickets can be rewritten to add or delete stops for an extra charge.

For RTW tickets, try the following:
Air Brokers (www.airbrokers.com)
Air Treks (www.airtreks.com)
Circle the Planet (www.circletheplanet.com)
Just Fares (www.justfares.com)

Africa

A few cities in West and North Africa have direct flights to the USA – Abidjan (Côte d'Ivoire), Accra (Ghana), Cairo (Egypt), Casablanca (Morocco) and Dakar (Senegal). Apart from South African Airways flights from Johannesburg to New York, most flights from Africa to the USA go via a European hub, most commonly London.

Agents serving Africa:
Flight Centre South Africa (☎ 0860-400-727; www .flightcentre.co.za)
STA Travel South Africa (☎ 0861-781-781; www .statravel.co.za)

Asia

Bangkok, Singapore, Kuala Lumpur, Hong Kong, Seoul and Tokyo all have good connections to the US West Coast. Many flights to the USA go via Honolulu and allow a stopover. Bangkok is the discounted fare capital of the region, though its cheapest agents can be unreliable.

Agents serving Asia:
Concorde Travel Hong Kong (☎ 852-2526-3391; www .concorde-travel.com)
No 1 Travel Japan (☎ 03-3205-6073; www.no1-travel.com)
STA Travel Bangkok (☎ 662-236-0262; www.statravel .co.th); Japan (☎ 03-5391-2922; www.statravel.co.jp); Singapore (☎ 65-6737-7188; www.statravel.com.sg)

Traveller Services Hong Kong (☎ 852-2375-2222; www.taketraveller.com)

Australia

Some flights go from Sydney and Melbourne direct to Los Angeles and San Francisco. Flights to other US cities will usually involve a stop in Los Angeles, or possibly San Francisco or Honolulu. Qantas, Air New Zealand and United are the main airlines on the route. Fares from Melbourne, Sydney, Brisbane and sometimes Adelaide and Canberra are 'common rated' (the same for all cities). From Hobart and Perth, there'll be an add-on fare.

Low season is roughly February, March, October and November. High season is around mid-June to mid-July and mid-December to mid-January. The rest of the year is considered shoulder season. Discounted tickets have minimum- and maximum-stay provisions.

Agents serving Australia:
Flight Centre (☎ 1300-133-133; www.flightcentre .com.au)
STA Travel (☎ 1300-134-782; www.statravel.com.au)
Travel.com (☎ 1300-130-483; www.travel.com.au)
Zuji (☎ 1300-888-180; www.zuji.com.au)

Canada

Daily flights go from Vancouver, Toronto, and many smaller cities to all the big US centers. Commuter flights to cities such as New York and Chicago can be very expensive. Some of the best deals are charter and package fares to sunny destinations such as Florida, California and Hawaii, with higher prices in the winter peak season.

It may be much cheaper to travel by land to the nearest US city, then take a discounted domestic flight. For example, round-trip fares to New York are much cheaper from Seattle, WA, than from Vancouver, BC, only 130 miles away.

Agents serving Canada:
Travel Cuts (☎ 866-246-9762; www.travelcuts.com)
Travelocity (☎ 877-282-2925; www.travelocity.ca)

Continental Europe

There are nonstop flights to many US cities, but the discounted fares often involve indirect routes and changing planes. The main airlines between Europe and the USA are Air France, Alitalia, British Airways, KLM, Continental, United, American, Delta,

TRANSPORTATION

YOU MAY NOW BOARD YOUR FLIGHT

Got your refillable lighter, pocketknife and a jug of homemade lemonade? Great, you're ready to board your flight…in the 20th century.

By now, most everyone knows that airport security measures restrict many common household items from being carried on planes. These regulations change often, so get up-to-date information on current restrictions from the **Transportation Security Administration** (TSA; ☎ 866-289-9673; www.tsa.gov), which also provides average security wait times by airport (20 minutes is standard).

To get through airport security checkpoints, you need a boarding pass and photo ID. If you beep going through the metal detector, or x-rays of your carry-on bags look suspicious, you will undergo a second screening, involving hand wand and pat down checks and opening your bags. You can request a private room.

If you suspect you were stopped because your name appears on the TSA Watch List, afterward file a complaint with the Traveler Redress Inquiry Program (TRIP; see the TSA website); this doesn't remove your name from the list, but it establishes that you are not the 'John Doe' they want, expediting screening next time.

All checked luggage is screened for explosives; TSA may open your suitcase for visual confirmation, breaking the lock if necessary. Either leave your bags unlocked or use a TSA-approved lock; see **Travel Sentry** (www.travelsentry.org) or **Safe Skies** (www.safeskieslocks.com). Also, screening machines damage undeveloped film, so carry this on the plane.

As for that lemonade, you *can* bring it: just put it in a 3oz container and gather it with other gels and liquids in a quart-size zip-top bag. That's TSA's new 3-1-1 rule! For more information, see its website. Have a nice flight.

Scandinavian Airlines and Lufthansa. Sometimes an Asian or Middle Eastern carrier will have cheap deals on flights in transit to the USA, if you can get a seat. Also try Icelandair connections via London.

BELGIUM
Airstop (☎ 070-233-188; www.airstop.be)

FRANCE
Nouvelles Frontieres (☎ 0825-000-747; www.nouvelles-frontieres.fr)
Voyages Wasteels (☎ 01-55-82-32-33; www.wasteels.fr)
Voyageurs du Monde (☎ 0892-235-656; www.vdm.com)

GERMANY
Just Travel (☎ 089-747-3330; www.justtravel.de)
Reiseboerse.com (☎ 030-2800-2800; www.reiseboerse.com)
STA Travel (☎ 069-743-032-92; www.statravel.de)

ITALY
CTS Viaggi (☎ 199-50-11-50; www.cts.it) Student and youth travel.

NETHERLANDS
ISSTA (☎ 31-20-589-3000; www.issta.nl)

SCANDINAVIA
Kilroy Travels (www.kilroytravels.com); Denmark (☎ 70-15-40-15); Norway (☎ 026-33); Sweden (☎ 0771-545-769)

SPAIN
Barcelo Viajes (☎ 902-116-226; www.barceloviajes.com)

Latin America
The main gateway from Central and South America is Miami, but there are also many direct flights to Los Angeles and Houston. Check the national airlines of the countries you want to connect to as well as US airlines such as United and American. At times, it can be much cheaper to fly to a Mexican border town than to the adjacent town on the US side. A flight from Mexico City to Tijuana can cost quite a bit less than a flight to San Diego, just a few miles north on the US side.

Agents serving Latin America:
Mundo Joven Mexico (☎ 01800-000-0789; www.mundojoven.com)
OTEC Viajes (www.otecviajes.com); Costa Rica (☎ 256-0633); El Salvador (☎ 2264-0200); Honduras (☎ 552-3900); Nicaragua (☎ 278-3788)
Star Travel Argentina (☎ 54-11-5199-4445; www.startravel.com.ar)

Student Travel Bureau Brazil (☎ 11-3038-1555; www.stb.com.br)

Student Travel Center Colombia (☎ 1635-3827; www .travelstc.com)

Viajo.com (www.viajo.com); Argentina (☎ 0810-777-1010); Brazil (☎ 11-2244-7000); Chile (☎ 484-84-84); Mexico (☎ 55-1084-0450); Venezuela (☎ 0212-335-0115)

New Zealand

Air New Zealand has regular flights from Auckland direct to Los Angeles. Flights from Christchurch and Wellington require a plane change in Auckland or the Pacific Islands. You'll find that low, shoulder and peak seasons are roughly the same as for Australia.

Agents serving New Zealand:

Flight Centre (☎ 0800-24-35-44; www.flightcentre.co.nz)

STA Travel (☎ 0800-474-400; www.statravel.co.nz)

UK & Ireland

One of the busiest and most competitive air sectors in the world is from the UK to the USA, with hundreds of scheduled flights by British Airways, American Airlines, United, Delta, Northwest, Continental, Kuwait, Air India and discount specialist Virgin Atlantic.

Discount air travel is big business in London. Advertisements for many travel agencies appear in the travel pages of the weekend broadsheet newspapers, in *Time Out*, the *Evening Standard* and in the free magazine *TNT*. Discounted fares are highly variable and subject to restrictions. From UK regional airports, discounted flights may be routed via London, Paris or Amsterdam, and will probably not fly direct to smaller US cities such as Las Vegas or Denver.

Most British travel agents are registered with the Association of British Travel Agents (ABTA), which will guarantee a refund or an alternative if you've paid money to an agent who goes out of business. Using an unregistered agent is not recommended.

Agents serving the UK and Ireland:

Ebookers.com (☎ 0800-082-3000; www.ebookers.com)

Flight Centre (☎ 0870-499-0040; www.flightcentre.co.uk)

North-South Travel (☎ 01245-608-291; www.north southtravel.co.uk) Donates part of its profit to projects in the developing world.

STA Travel (☎ 0871-2300-040; www.statravel.co.uk) Discount and student travel specialist.

Trailfinders (☎ 0845-058-5858; www.trailfinders.com)

Travel Bag (☎ 0800-804-8911; www.travelbag.co.uk)

Travelocity (☎ 0870-273-3273; www.travelocity.co.uk)

LAND
Border Crossings

The USA shares long land borders with Canada in the north and Mexico in the south. It is relatively easy crossing from the USA into either country; it's crossing into the USA that can pose problems if you haven't brought all your documents; see Entering the Country, p1129. The **US Customs & Border Protection Agency** (http://apps.cbp.gov/bwt/) tracks current wait times at every border crossing. Some borders are open 24 hours, but most are not.

The USA has more than 20 official border crossings with Canada. Busy entry points include those at Detroit (MI)/Windsor, Buffalo (NY)/Fort Erie, Niagara Falls (NY) and Blaine (WA)/British Columbia. The downside to choosing a quiet border crossing is that officers have plenty of time to take apart your luggage. For border wait times returning to Canada, visit www.cbsa-asfc.gc.ca/general /times/menu-e.html.

The USA has more than 30 official entry points with Mexico. The main ones are San Diego (CA)/Tijuana, Nogales (AZ), El Paso (TX)/Ciudad Juárez and Brownsville (TX)/Matamoros. As always, have your papers in order, act polite and don't make jokes or casual conversation – officers take a dim view of friendliness.

Canada
BUS

Greyhound has direct connections between main cities in Canada and the northern USA, but you may have to transfer to a different bus at the border. Book through either **Greyhound US** (☎ US customer service 214-849-8966, international customer service 214-849-8100, reservations 800-231-2222; www .greyhound.com) or **Greyhound Canada** (☎ 800-661-8747; www.greyhound.ca). Greyhound's Discovery Pass (p1141) allows unrestricted travel in both the USA and Canada.

CAR & MOTORCYCLE

If you're driving into the USA from Canada, don't forget the vehicle's registration papers, liability insurance and your home driver's license. Canadian auto insurance is valid in the USA. Canadian driver's licenses are valid and an international driver's permit is a good supplement.

If your papers are in order, taking your own car across the US–Canadian border is usually quick and easy, but occasionally the

TRANSPORTATION

authorities of either country decide to search a car *thoroughly*. On weekends and holidays, especially in summer, traffic at the main border crossings can be heavy and waits long.

TRAIN

Amtrak (☎ 800-872-7245; www.amtrak.com) and Canada's **VIA Rail** (☎ 888-842-7245; www.viarail .ca) run daily services from Montreal to New York, Toronto to New York via Niagara Falls, Toronto to Chicago, and Vancouver to Seattle. See p1147 for information on Amtrak's North American Rail Pass, which includes Canadian travel. Customs inspections happen at the border, not on boarding.

Mexico

BUS

Greyhound US (☎ US customer service 214-849-8966, international customer service 214-849-8100, reservations 800-231-2222; www.greyhound.com) and **Greyhound Mexico** (☎ in US 800-229-9424, in Mexico 800-710-8819; www.greyhound.com.mx) have cooperative service, with direct buses between main towns in Mexico and the USA. Northbound buses can take some time to cross the US border, as sometimes US immigration insists on checking every person on board.

There are numerous domestic Mexican bus companies; **Ticketbus** (☎ in US 800-950-0287, in Mexico 800-702-8000; www.ticketbus.com.mx) is an alliance of several.

CAR & MOTORCYCLE

If you're driving into the USA from Mexico, don't forget the vehicle's registration papers, liability insurance and your home driver's license. Mexican driver's licenses are valid and an international driver's permit is a good supplement. Very few car-rental companies will let you take a car from the US into Mexico.

US auto insurance is not valid in Mexico, so even a short trip into Mexico's border region requires you to buy Mexican car insurance, available for under $20 per day at most border crossings, as well as from the **AAA** (☎ 800-874-7532; www.aaa.com). At some border towns, including Tijuana or Ciudad Juárez, there can be long lines of vehicles waiting to re-enter the USA. For a short visit, it's usually more convenient to leave your car in a lot on the US side and walk or bus across the border. For a longer driving trip into Mexico, beyond the border zone or Baja California, you'll need a Mexican *permiso de*

importación temporal de vehículos (temporary vehicle import permit). See Lonely Planet's *Mexico* guide for the tedious details, or call the Mexican tourist information number in the USA ☎ 800-446-3942).

TRAIN

Amtrak gets close to the Mexican border at San Diego, CA, and El Paso, TX, but there are currently no cross-border services. There are no Mexican train services to towns on the US border.

SEA

Cargo Ship/Freighter

You can travel to and from the USA on a freighter, though it will be much slower and less cushy than a cruise ship (below). Nevertheless, freighters aren't spartan (some advertise cruise-ship-level amenities), and they are much cheaper (sometimes by half). Trips range from a week to two months, and stops at interim ports are usually quick. Excellent sources of information are the **Cruise & Freighter Travel Association** (☎ 800-872-8584; www .travltips.com) and **Freighter World Cruises** (☎ 800-531-7774; www.freighterworld.com).

TOURS

Group travel can be an enjoyable way to get to and tour the USA. For more tours once you're in the country, see p1146.

If you're interested in taking a cruise ship to America – as well as to other interesting ports o' call – a good specialized travel agency is **Cruise Web** (☎ 800-377-9383; www .cruiseweb.com). Or just book a bunk ($1500 and up) on a luxury liner run by **Cunard** (☎ in US 800-728-6273, in UK 0845-071-0300; www.cunardline.com). The standard London–New York run is six days, but there are oodle more options.

Reputable tour companies:

American Holidays (☎ 01-673-3840; www.american holidays.com) This Ireland-based company specializes in tours to North America.

Elderhostel (☎ 800-454-5768; www.elderhostel .org) This venerable, nonprofit runs 'learning adventures' around the world for those 55-plus years young.

North America Travel Service (☎ 020-7569-6710; www.northamericatravelservice.co.uk) This UK-based tour operator specializes in US trips.

Trek America (☎ in US 800-221-0596, in UK 0870-444-8735; www.trekamerica.com) Specializes in active outdoor adventures; Trek America will book flights from the UK only. Group sizes are small.

GETTING AROUND

AIR

When time is tight, book a flight. The domestic air system is extensive and reliable, with dozens of competing airlines, hundreds of airports and thousands of flights daily. Flying is usually more expensive than traveling by bus, train or car, but it's the way to go when your destination *is* the destination. All the advice for buying an international airline ticket applies to domestic flights as well.

Main 'hub' airports include all of the international gateways (p1132) plus a number of other large cities. Most cities and towns have a local or county airport, but you usually have to travel via a hub airport to reach them.

If you need to park your car, www.parking access.com offers information, reservations and discounts on parking at most major airports.

Airlines in the USA

Domestic airlines have mostly rebounded since September 11, 2001. Delta, Northwest, United and US Airways have each entered and emerged from bankruptcy still flying, though mergers and downsizing have had an impact on traveler experiences. For instance, free meal service has often been replaced with for-purchase sandwiches, and thin staffs mean that any disruptions (say, from a storm) can strand flights for hours or even days.

Overall, air travel in the USA is very safe (much safer than America's highways); for comprehensive details by carrier, check out **Airsafe.com** (www.airsafe.com), which also has good advice on current airport security procedures (see boxed text, p1136).

The main domestic carriers:

AirTran (☎ 800-247-8726; www.airtranairways.com) Atlanta-based airline primarily serves Midwest and eastern US.

Alaska Airlines (☎ 800-252-7522; www.alaskaair .com) Serves Alaska and western US, with flights to East Coast cities.

American Airlines (☎ 800-433-7300; www.aa.com) Nationwide service.

ATA Airlines (☎ 800-435-9282; www.ata.com) Connects major US cities and Hawaii; shares routes with Southwest.

Continental Airlines (☎ 800-523-3273; www .continental.com) Nationwide service.

Delta Air Lines (☎ 800-221-1212; www.delta.com) Nationwide service.

Frontier Airlines (☎ 800-432-1359; www.frontier airlines.com) Denver-based airline with nationwide service, including Alaska and Mexico.

Hawaiian Airlines (☎ 800-367-5320; www.hawaiian air.com) Serves Hawaiian Islands and West Coast cities.

JetBlue (☎ 800-538-2583; www.jetblue.com) Nonstop connections between East and West Coast cities and the Caribbean.

Midwest Express (☎ 800-452-2022; www2.midwest express.com) Milwaukee-based carrier serves major US cities.

Northwest Airlines (☎ 800-225-2525; www.nwa .com) Nationwide service, including Alaska and Hawaii.

Southwest Airlines (☎ 800-435-9792; www.iflyswa .com) Service across continental USA.

Spirit Airlines (☎ 800-772-7117; www.spiritair.com) Serves eastern seaboard, Florida and Caribbean.

Ted (☎ 800-225-5833; www.flyted.com) United's low-cost service connects major cities nationwide, including Los Angeles, Chicago, Washington DC, Las Vegas and Miami.

United Airlines (☎ 800-864-8331; www.united.com) Nationwide service, including Alaska and Hawaii.

US Airways (☎ 800-428-4322; www.usairways.com) Primarily serves eastern United States, Midwest and the Caribbean.

Air Passes

International travelers who plan on doing a lot of flying in the USA might consider buying an air pass. Air passes are available only to non-US citizens, and they must be purchased in conjunction with an international ticket. Conditions and cost structures can be complicated, but all include a certain number of domestic flights (from three to 10) that must be used within 60 days. Sometimes you must plan your itinerary in advance, but sometimes dates (and even destinations) can be left open. Talk with a travel agent to determine if an air pass would save you money based on your plans.

Two of the biggest airline networks offering air passes are **Star Alliance** (www.staralliance.com) and **One World** (www.oneworld.com).

BICYCLE

Regional bicycle touring is very popular; it means coasting winding backroads (since bicycles are not permitted on freeways), and calculating progress in miles per day, not miles per hour. Cyclists must follow the same rules of the road as automobiles, but don't expect drivers to respect the right of way of cyclists. **Better World Club** (☎ 866-238-1137; www.betterworld club.com) offers a bicycle roadside assistance program.

For a list of bicycling associations, tour groups and magazines, see p1114, and turn to p122 for bicycling and mountain-biking highlights. For epic cross-country journeys, get the support of a tour operator; it's about two months of dedicated pedaling coast to coast.

For advice, and lists of local bike clubs and repair shops, check the website of the **League of American Bicyclists** (LAB; ☎ 202-822-1333; www.bikeleague.org; 1612 K St NW, Suite 800, Washington, DC 20006). If you're bringing your own bike to the USA, visit the **International Bicycle Fund** (www .ibike.org), which lists bike regulations by airline and has lots of advice. In the past, most international and domestic airlines have carried bikes as checked baggage without charge when they're in a box. However, recently, many have changed their regulations and imposed or increased fees (typically $50 to $100, but sometimes higher). Amtrak trains and Greyhound buses will transport bikes within the USA, sometimes charging extra.

Also, it's not hard to buy a bike once you're here and resell it before you leave. Every city and town has bike shops; if you prefer a cheaper, used bicycle, try flea markets, garage sales and the notice boards at hostels and colleges. These are also the best places to sell your bike, though stores selling used bikes may also buy from you. If you're relaxed about price, selling a bike is a snap.

Long-term bike rentals are also easy to find; recommended rental places are listed throughout this guide. Rates run from $100 per week and up, and a credit card authorization for several hundred dollars is usually necessary as a security deposit.

BOAT

There is no river or canal public transportation system in the USA, but there are many smaller, often state-run, coastal ferry services, which provide efficient, scenic links to the many islands off the US coasts. Most larger ferries will transport private cars, motorcycles and bicycles. For details, see the regional chapters. The most spectacular coastal ferry runs are on the south coast of Alaska and along the Inside Passage (p1059). The Great

Lakes have a number of islands that can be visited only by boat, such as Mackinac Island, MI (p609); the Apostle Islands, off Wisconsin (p622); and the remote Isle Royale National Park (p634), MN. Or check out **Majestic America Line** (☎ 800-434-1232; www.majesticamericaline .com): it offers week-long boat tours of the Mississippi and Ohio River systems, of the Columbia and Snake Rivers, and of Alaska's Inside Passage.

BUS

To save money, travel by bus, particularly between major towns and cities. Gotta-go middle-class Americans prefer to fly or drive, but buses let you see the countryside and meet folks along the way. As a rule, buses are reliable, clean and comfortable, with air-conditioning, reclining seats, onboard lavatories and no smoking permitted.

Greyhound (☎ for reservations 800-231-2222, for customer service 214-849-8966; www.greyhound.com) is the major long-distance bus company, with routes throughout the USA and Canada. To improve efficiency and profitability, Greyhound has recently stopped service to many small towns; routes generally trace major highways and stop at larger population centers. To reach country towns on rural roads, you may need to transfer to local or county bus systems; Greyhound usually has their contact information.

Competing with Greyhound are the 50-plus franchises of **Trailways** (☎ 703-691-3052; www.trailways.com). Trailways may not be as useful as Greyhound for long trips, but fares are competitive. A few regional Trailways bus companies:

Atlantic Coast Trailways (☎ 800-548-8584; www .atlanticcoasttrailways.com) On the Atlantic Coast.
Capitol Trailways (☎ 800-333-8444; www.capitoltrail ways.com) In the northeast.
Pacific Coachways Trailways (☎ 714-892-5000; www.pacificcoachways.com) On the Pacific Coast.

Most baggage has to be checked in; label it loudly and clearly to avoid it getting lost. Larger items, including skis and bicycles, can be transported, but there may be an extra charge. Call to check.

The frequency of bus services varies widely, depending entirely on the route. Despite the elimination of many tiny destinations, non-express Greyhound buses still stop every 50 to 100 miles to pick up passengers, and long-distance buses stop for meal breaks and driver changes.

Many bus stations are clean and safe, but some are in dodgy areas; if you arrive in the evening, spend the money on a taxi. Some towns have just a flag stop. If you are boarding at one of these, pay the driver with exact change.

Bus Passes

A Greyhound bus pass turns cross-country travel into a bargain. Greyhound's **North American Discovery Pass** (www.discoverypass.com; $285-645, purchase fee $4), which is available to both domestic and international travelers, allows unlimited, unrestricted travel for periods from seven to 60 consecutive days in both the USA and Canada (plus a few Mexican border towns). Besides the length of the pass, the only real decision to make is which country you want to start your travels in.

International travelers can buy the pass before arriving in the US through their home travel agent (Greyhound has a list) or on the internet three weeks in advance. Or, purchase one in person the day before departure.

Costs

Substantial ticket discounts can be had if you purchase seven days in advance, and special promotional fares are regularly offered. If you're traveling with a friend, ask about Greyhound's companion fares, where the second traveler gets 50% off with a three-day advance purchase.

As for other discounts: tickets for children ages two to 11 get 40% off; people over 62 can get a 5% discount; a companion for a disabled passenger gets 50% off; and students who purchase the Student Advantage Discount Card ($20) will get 15% off most routes.

Here are some samples of standard (non-seven-day-advance) Greyhound fares: New York to San Francisco ($185, three days); Los Angeles to San Francisco ($45, eight hours); Boston to Philadelphia ($55, eight hours); New York to Miami ($125, 32 hours).

Reservations

Tickets for some Trailways and other buses can only be purchased immediately prior to departure. Greyhound bus tickets can be bought over the phone or on the internet. If you purchase 10 days in advance with a major US credit card, tickets will be mailed to you.

International credit cards are accepted when buying in person at the terminal, or online in advance for Will Call tickets, where you pick the tickets up at the terminal (bring ID). Greyhound terminals also accept traveler's checks and cash.

On Greyhound, a prepurchased ticket does not reserve or guarantee a seat on a bus. All seating is first-come, first-served. Greyhound recommends arriving an hour before departure to get a seat.

CAR & MOTORCYCLE

The American love of the auto runs so deep it often verges on the pathological. And it will abide for at least one practical reason: the continent is too damn big. Public transportation can't cover it. For maximum flexibility and convenience, and to explore rural America and its wide-open spaces, you have to have a car. Independence costs you, though, as rental rates and gas prices can eat a good chunk of a travel budget. Only for stays in large cities can you easily dispense with an auto.

For recommended drives, see the boxed text (p29) and Scenic Drive boxed texts in destination chapters.

Automobile Associations

Until recently, the only US auto club was the **American Automobile Association** (AAA; ☎ 800-874-7532; www.aaa.com), which has reciprocal membership agreements with several international auto clubs (check with AAA and bring your membership card). However, an ecofriendly alternative has emerged: the **Better World Club** (☎ 866-238-1137; www.betterworldclub.com). In both organizations, the central member benefit is 24-hour emergency roadside assistance anywhere in the USA. Both clubs also offer trip planning and free maps, travel agency services, car insurance and a range of discounts (car rentals, hotels etc).

The differences are that Better World donates 1% of earnings to assist environmental cleanup, it offers ecologically sensitive choices for every service and it advocates politically for environmental causes. Better World also has a roadside assistance program for bicycles. AAA, on the other hand, offers travel insurance, its popular tour books, diagnostic centers for used-car buyers and a greater number of regional offices, and it advocates politically for the auto industry (which, naturally, frequently opposes environmental causes).

TRANSPORTATION

Bring Your Own Vehicle

For details on driving your own car over the border from Canada, see p1137, and from Mexico, see p1138. Unless you're moving to the USA, don't even think about freighting your car.

Drive-Away Cars

'Drive-away cars' refers to the business of driving cars across the country for people who are moving or otherwise can't transport their cars themselves. For flexible travelers, they can be a dream come true: you can cover the long distances between A and B for the price of gas. Timing and availability are key.

To be a driver you must be at least 23 years old with a valid driver's license (non-US citizens should have an International Driving Permit); you'll also need to provide a $300 to $400 cash deposit (which is refunded upon safe delivery of the car), sometimes a printout of your driving record, a major credit card and/or three forms of identification (or a passport). The auto transport company provides insurance; you pay for gas. The stipulation is that you must deliver the car to its destination within a specified time and mileage, which usually requires that you drive about six hours a day along the shortest route. Availability depends on demand. Coast-to-coast routes at holiday times are the easiest to arrange.

Two of the larger drive-away companies are **Auto Driveaway** (☎ 323-666-6100; www.autodrive awayla.com) and **Auto Driveaway Co** (☎ 800-346-2277; www.autodriveaway.com).

Driver's License

Visitors can legally drive in the USA for up to 12 months with their home driver's license. However, it is recommended that you also get an International Driving Permit (IDP); this will have more credibility with US traffic police, especially if your home license doesn't have a photo or is in a foreign language. Your automobile association at home can issue an IDP, valid for one year, for a small fee. You must carry your home license together with the IDP.

Insurance

Don't put the key into the ignition if you don't have insurance. You risk financial ruin if there's an accident and you don't have any. If you already have auto insurance (even over-seas), or if you buy travel insurance, make sure that the policy has adequate liability coverage for a rental car where you will be driving; it probably does, but most states specify a minimum level of coverage.

Rental car companies will provide liability insurance, but most charge extra. Always ask. Rental companies almost never include collision damage insurance for the vehicle. Instead, they offer an optional Collision Damage Waiver (CDW) or Loss Damage Waiver (LDW), usually with an initial deductible cost of $100 to $500. For an extra premium, you can usually get this deductible covered as well. However, most credit cards now offer collision damage coverage for rental cars if you rent for 15 days or less and charge the total rental to your card. This is a good way to avoid paying extra fees to the rental company, but note that if there's an accident, you sometimes must pay the rental car company first and then seek reimbursement from the credit card company. Check your credit card policy. Paying extra for some or all of this insurance increases the cost of a rental car by as much as $10 to $30 a day.

Purchase

Buying a car is usually much more hassle than it's worth, particularly for foreign visitors and trips under four months. Foreigners will have the easiest time arranging this if they have stateside friends or relatives who can provide a fixed address for registration, licensing and insurance, or by working with one of the companies below.

To find a new or used auto, check newspapers and visit dealers. To evaluate prices, check the **Kelley Blue Book** (www.kbb.com); also hire an independent auto mechanic to inspect the car before you buy. Once purchased, the car's transfer of ownership papers must be registered with the state's Department of Motor Vehicles (DMV) within 10 days; you'll need the bill of sale, the title (or 'pink slip') and proof of insurance. Some states also require a 'smog certificate.' This is the seller's responsibility; don't buy a car without a certificate. A dealer will submit the paperwork to the DMV for you.

For foreigners, getting independent liability insurance is the toughest part; it is difficult to virtually impossible to arrange without a US driver's license. A car dealer or AAA may be able to suggest an insurer who will do this.

TRANSPORTATION

DRIVING DISTANCES & TIMES

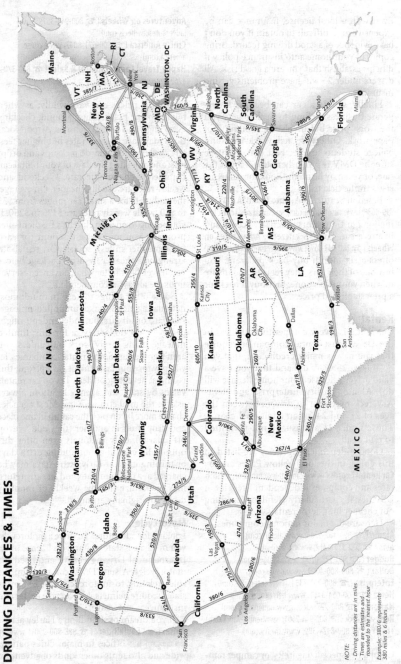

NOTE:
- Driving distances are in miles.
- Times are estimates and
  rounded to the nearest hour.

Example: 380/6 represents
380 miles & 6 hours

Even with a local license, insurance can be expensive and difficult to obtain if you don't have evidence of a good driving record. Bring copies of your home auto insurance policy if it helps establish that you are a good risk. All drivers under 25 will have problems getting insurance.

Finally, selling a car can become a desperate business. Selling to dealers gets you the worst price but involves a minimum of paperwork. Otherwise, fellow travelers and college students are the best bets – but be sure the DMV is properly notified about the sale, or you may be on the hook for someone else's traffic tickets.

Based in Seattle, WA, **Auto Tour USA** (☎ 206-999-4686; www.autotourusa.com) specializes in helping foreign US visitors purchase, license and insure a car. For US citizens, **Adventures on Wheels** (☎ 800-943-3579; www.adventuresonwheels.com) offers a six-month buy-back program: you buy one of their cars, they register and insure it; when your trip's done, they buy it back for a pre-established price.

Rental

Car rental is a very competitive business in the USA. Most rental companies require that you have a major credit card, that you be at least 25 years old and that you have a valid driver's license (your home license will do). Alamo, Thrifty, Enterprise and Rent-A-Wreck may rent to drivers between the ages of 21 and 24 for an additional charge. Those under 21 are usually not permitted to rent at all.

Good independent agencies are listed in this guide, in the local Yellow Pages and by **Car Rental Express** (www.carrentalexpress.com), which rates and compares independent agencies in US cities; it's particularly useful for searching out cheaper long-term rentals.

Here are the major national companies:

Alamo (☎ 800-462-5266; www.alamo.com)
Avis (☎ 800-331-1212; www.avis.com)
Budget (☎ 800-527-0700; www.budget.com)
Dollar (☎ 800-800-4000; www.dollar.com)
Enterprise (☎ 800-261-7331; www.enterprise.com)
Hertz (☎ 800-654-3131; www.hertz.com)
National (☎ 800-227-7368; www.nationalcar.com)
Rent-a-Wreck (☎ 800-944-7501; www.rent-a-wreck.com)
Thrifty (☎ 800-847-4389; www.thrifty.com)

Companies specializing in RV or camper rentals include:

Adventures on Wheels (☎ 800-943-3579; www.adventuresonwheels.com)
Cruise America (☎ 800-671-8042; www.cruiseamerica.com)
Happy Travel Camper Rental & Sales (☎ 800-370-1262; www.camperusa.com)

Car-rental prices can vary wildly; as when buying plane tickets, shop around, checking every angle and several websites. Airport locations may have cheaper rates but higher fees; city-center offices may do pick-ups and drop-offs; and adjusting the days of your rental can completely change the rate. Weekend and weekly rates are usually cheaper. On average, the daily rate for a small car ranges from $35 to $50, while weekly rates are $175 to $250. If you belong to an auto club or a frequent-flier program, you may get a discount (or earn frequent-flier miles), so ask. Or, see about arranging a cheaper fly-drive package before you travel. No matter what, advance reservations are always recommended.

Some other things to keep in mind: most national agencies make 'unlimited mileage' standard on all cars, but independents might charge a few dollars extra for this; limited mileage plans rarely work out unless you aren't going far. Some rental companies let you pay for your last tank of gas upfront; this is almost never a good deal. Tax on car rentals varies by state and agency location; always ask for the total cost *with tax*. Most agencies charge more if you pick the car up in one place and drop it off in another (they add a 'drop off' charge); only nationals even offer this option. Be careful about adding extra days or turning in a car early; extra days may be charged at a premium rate, and an early return may jeopardize the low weekly or monthly deal you originally arranged.

Motorcycle

Looking for adventure? To drive a motorcycle, you need a US state motorcycle license or an International Driving Permit endorsed for motorcycles. A state DMV can give you the rules relating to motorcycle use, but most states require helmets. Motorcycle rental and insurance is expensive.

If you dream of straddling a Harley across America, **EagleRider** (☎ 888-900-9901; www.eaglerider.com) has offices in major cities nationwide and also rents other kinds of adventure vehicles.

Road Conditions & Hazards

America's highways are legendary ribbons of unblemished asphalt, but not always. Road hazards include potholes, city commuter traffic, wandering wildlife and, of course, other enraged, cell-phone-wielding, kid-distracted drivers. Caution, foresight, courtesy and luck usually gets you past them. For nationwide traffic and road closure information, visit the website www.fhwa.dot.gov/trafficinfo/index .htm.

In places where winter driving is an issue, many cars are fitted with steel-studded snow tires; snow chains can sometimes be required in mountain areas. Driving off-road, or on dirt roads, is often forbidden by rental-car companies, and it can be very dangerous in wet weather.

In deserts and range country, livestock sometimes graze next to unfenced roads. These areas are signed as Open Range or with the silhouette of a steer. Where deer and other wild animals frequently appear roadside, you'll see signs with the silhouette of a leaping deer. Take these signs seriously, particularly at night.

Road Rules

In the USA, cars drive on the right side of the road (not the correct side, perhaps, but the opposite of left). The use of seat belts and child safety seats is required in every state.

The speed limit is generally 55mph or 65mph on highways, 25mph to 35mph in cities and towns and as low as 15mph in school zones (strictly enforced during school hours). On interstate highways, the speed limit is sometimes raised to 75mph. It's forbidden to pass a school bus when its lights are flashing.

Most states have laws against (and high fines for) littering along the highway. Sure, no one ever gets caught, but don't do it anyway.

Penalties are very severe for 'DUI' – driving under the influence of alcohol and/or drugs. Police can give roadside sobriety checks to assess if you've been drinking or using drugs. If you fail, they'll require you take a breath test, urine test or blood test to determine the level of alcohol or drugs in your body. Refusing to be tested is treated as if you'd taken the test and failed. The maximum legal blood-alcohol concentration is 0.08%.

In some states it is illegal to carry 'open containers' of alcohol in a vehicle, even if they are empty. Containers that are full and sealed may be carried, but if they have ever been opened, they must be carried in the trunk.

HITCHHIKING

Hitchhiking in the USA is potentially dangerous and definitely not recommended. Indeed, drivers have heard so many lurid reports they tend to be just as afraid of those with their thumbs out. Hitchhiking on freeways is prohibited. You'll see more people hitchhiking (and stopping) in rural areas and in Alaska, but these places aren't any safer than anywhere else, and with sparse traffic, you may well get stranded.

In and around national parks, hitching to and from trailheads is sometimes common, but a more reliable bet is to check ride-share boards at ranger stations and hostels.

LOCAL TRANSPORTATION

Except in large US cities, public transit is rarely the most convenient option for travelers, and coverage can be sparse to outlying towns and suburbs. However, it is usually cheap, safe and reliable. For regional details, see the Getting Around sections in the main cities. In addition, more than half the states in the nation have adopted ☎ 511 as the all-purpose local transit help phone line.

Airport Shuttles

Shuttle buses provide inexpensive and convenient transport to/from airports in most cities. Most are 12-seat vans; some have regular routes and stops (which include the main hotels) and some pick up and deliver passengers 'door to door' in their service area; costs are $12 to $18 per person.

Bicycle

Some cities are much more amenable to bicycles than others, but generally, bicycle rentals are everywhere (and listed throughout this guide), most towns have at least a few dedicated bike lanes and paths, and bikes can usually be carried on public transportation. See p1139 for more on bicycling in the USA.

Bus

Most cities and larger towns have dependable local bus systems, though they are often designed for commuters and provide limited service in the evening and on weekends. Costs range from free to $1 to $2 per ride.

TRANSPORTATION

Subway

Some cities have underground subways or elevated metropolitan rail systems, which provide the best local transport. The largest systems are in New York, Washington, DC, Chicago and the San Francisco Bay Area. Other cities have small, one- or two-line rail systems that mainly serve downtown.

Taxi

Taxis are metered, with charges from $1 or $2 to start, plus at least $1.20 per mile. They charge extra for handling baggage, and drivers expect a 10% to 15% tip. Taxis cruise the busiest areas in large cities, but if you're anywhere else, it's easiest to call and order one.

TOURS

Companies offer all kinds of tours in the USA; most focus on regions or cities. See Tours in the city sections for other recommendations, or p1140 for riverboat tours.

Recommended tour companies:

Backroads (☎ 510-527-1555, 800-462-2848; www .backroads.com; 801 Cedar St, Berkeley, CA 94710) Primarily emphasizing bicycle tours, Backroads also creates a range of active, multisport trips for all abilities and budgets.

Gray Line (☎ 800-826-0202; www.grayline.com) For those short on time, Gray Line offers a comprehensive range of standard tours.

Green Tortoise (☎ 800-867-8647; www.greentortoise .com) Offering budget adventures for independent travelers, Green Tortoise is famous for its sleeping-bunk buses and camaraderie. Most trips leave from San Francisco, traipsing through the West and across the country.

TRAIN

Amtrak (☎ 800-872-7245; www.amtrak.com) has an extensive rail system throughout the USA, with Amtrak Thruway buses providing convenient connections to and from the rail network to some smaller centers and national parks. Compared with other modes of travel, trains are rarely the quickest, cheapest or most convenient option, but they can be close on all counts, and they turn the journey into a relaxing, social and scenic experience.

Amtrak has several long-distance lines traversing the nation east to west, and even more running from north to south, and in total these connect all of America's biggest cities and many of its smaller ones. Long-distance services (on named trains) run daily on most routes, but some run only three to five days per week. See Amtrak's website for detailed route maps, as well as the Getting There & Around sections in this guide's regional chapters.

Amtrak's commuter trains provide fast and more frequent services on shorter routes, especially along the northeast corridor from Boston to Washington, DC. High-speed Acela trains on these routes are the fastest and most expensive. Other commuter rail lines serve the Lake Michigan shore near Chicago, the main cities on the California coast and the Miami area. Many are included in an Amtrak rail pass (see opposite).

Classes & Costs

Fares vary according to type of train and seating; on long-distance lines, you can travel in coach seats, business class, or 1st class, which includes all sleeping compartments. Sleeping cars include simple bunks (called 'Roomettes'), bedrooms with private facilities and suites sleeping four with two bathrooms. Sleeping car rates include meals in the dining car, which offers everyone sit-down meal service (pricey if not included). Commuter lines offer only business or 1st-class seating; food service, when it exists, consists of sandwich and snack bars. Bringing your own food is allowed, and recommended, on all trains.

Various one-way, round-trip and touring fares are available, with discounts of 15% for seniors age 62 and over and for students (with a 'Student Advantage' card, $20, or with an International Student Identity Card), and 50% discounts for children ages two to 15. Fares are generally lower on all tickets from early January to mid-June and from late August to mid-December. Web-only 'Weekly Specials' offer deep discounts on certain undersold routes. To get many standard discounts, you need to reserve three days ahead.

Generally, the earlier you book, the lower the price. If you want to take an Acela or Metroliner train, avoid peak commuter times and aim for weekends.

Service	Price	Duration
New York-Chicago	$130	19 hr
New York-Los Angeles	$240	62 hr
Los Angeles-San Antonio	$250	30 hr
Seattle-Oakland	$90	23 hr
Chicago-New Orleans	$105	20 hr
Washington, DC-Miami	$115	24 hr

ALL ABOARD!

Dozens of historic narrow-gauge railroads operate as attractions rather than as transport. Most only run in the warmer months, and they can be extremely popular – so book ahead. Who doesn't enjoy the steamy puff and whistle of a mighty locomotive as America's most glorious scenery streams by?

Here are some of the best:

Big Trees & Roaring Camp Railroad (www.roaringcamprr.com) Through the mountains around Santa Cruz, CA.

Cass Scenic Railroad Appalachian Mountains in West Virginia (p369).

Cumbres & Toltec Scenic Railroad Chama, NM, into Colorado's Rocky Mountains (p889).

Durango & Silverton Narrow Gauge Railroad Ends at Silverton mining town in Colorado's Rocky Mountains (p768).

Grand Canyon Railway Williams, AZ, to south rim of Grand Canyon (p833).

Great Smoky Mountains Railroad From Dillsboro to Bryson City, NC, through the Great Smoky Mountains (p389).

Mount Hood Railroad (www.mthoodrr.com) Through the Hood River Valley outside Portland, OR.

Skunk Train Fort Bragg north past California coast redwoods (p979).

White Pass & Yukon Railroad Skagway, AK, to Fraser, British Columbia, Canada (p1067).

Amtrak offers vacation packages that include rental cars, hotels, tours and attractions; call ☎ 800-268-7252 for details. Air-Rail packages offer train travel in one direction and a plane trip going the other way.

For some examples of the time and cost of Amtrak's long-distance services for a standard, one-way, coach-class fare, see the boxed table, left.

Reservations

Reservations can be made any time from 11 months in advance to the day of departure. Space on most trains is limited, and certain routes can be crowded, so it's a good idea to reserve as far in advance as you can. This also gives you the best chance of fare discounts.

Train Passes

A USA Rail Pass is available only to international travelers (not to US or Canadian residents). The pass offers unlimited coach-class travel within a specific region for either 15 or 30 days, with the price depending on region, number of days and season traveled (fares range from $300 to $600).

Present your pass at an Amtrak office to buy a ticket for each trip. Reservations should be made as far in advance as possible. You can get on and off the train as often as you like, but each sector of the journey must be booked. At some rural stations, trains will only stop if there's a reservation. Tickets are not for specific seats, but a conductor on board may allocate you a seat. First-class or sleeper accommodations cost extra and must be reserved separately.

A North America Rail Pass ($710 to $1000) is offered by Amtrak in conjunction with Canada's VIA Rail. It allows unlimited travel on US and Canadian railways for 30 consecutive days (but requires one trip in both countries), and it's available to American and Canadian residents as well as foreign visitors.

Health Dr David Goldberg

CONTENTS

The North American continent encompasses an extraordinary range of climates and terrains, from the freezing heights of the Rockies to tropical areas in southern Florida. Because of the high level of hygiene, infectious diseases will not be a significant concern for most travelers, who will experience nothing worse than a little diarrhea or a mild respiratory infection.

BEFORE YOU GO

INSURANCE

The USA offers possibly the finest health care in the world. The problem is that, unless you have good insurance, it can be prohibitively expensive. It's essential to purchase travel health insurance if your regular policy doesn't cover you when you're abroad.

Bring any medications you may need in their original containers, clearly labeled. A signed, dated letter from your physician that describes all medical conditions and medications, including generic names, is also a good idea.

If your health insurance does not cover you for medical expenses abroad, consider supplemental insurance. Check the Travel Links section of the **Lonely Planet website** (www .lonelyplanet.com) for more information. Find out in advance if your insurance plan will make payments directly to providers or reimburse you later for overseas health expenditures.

RECOMMENDED VACCINATIONS

No special vaccines are required or recommended for the USA. All travelers should be up-to-date on routine immunizations. See the boxed text below.

MEDICAL CHECKLIST

Recommended items for a medical kit:

- acetaminophen (Tylenol) or aspirin
- adhesive or paper tape
- antibacterial ointment (eg Bactroban) for cuts and abrasions
- antihistamines (for hay fever and allergic reactions)
- anti-inflammatory drugs (eg ibuprofen)
- bandages, gauze, gauze rolls
- DEET-containing insect repellent for the skin
- permethrin-containing insect spray for clothing, tents and bed nets
- pocket knife
- scissors, safety pins, tweezers
- steroid cream or cortisone (for poison ivy and other allergic rashes)
- sunblock
- thermometer

Vaccine	Recommended for	Dosage	Side effects
chicken pox	travelers who've never had chicken pox	two doses a month apart	fever; mild case of chicken pox
influenza	all travelers during flu season (Nov through Mar)	one dose	soreness at injection site; fever
measles	travelers born after 1956 who've had only one measles vaccination	one dose	fever; rash; joint pains; allergic reactions
tetanus-diphtheria	all travelers who haven't had a booster within 10 years	one dose lasts 10 years	soreness at injection site

INTERNET RESOURCES

There is a wealth of travel health advice on the internet. The World Health Organization publishes a superb book, called *International Travel and Health,* which is revised annually and is available online at no cost at www .who.int/ith/en. Another website of general interest is **MD Travel Health** (www.mdtravelhealth .com), which provides complete travel health recommendations for every country, updated daily, also at no cost.

It's usually a good idea to consult your government's travel health website before departure, if one is available:

Australia (www.smarttraveller.gov.au)
Canada (www.hc-sc.gc.ca; www.phac-aspc.gc.ca)
UK (www.dh.gov.uk/travellers)

IN THE USA

AVAILABILITY & COST OF HEALTH CARE

In general, if you have a medical emergency, the best bet is to find the nearest hospital and go to its emergency room. If the problem isn't urgent, you can call a nearby hospital and ask for a referral to a local physician, which is usually cheaper than a trip to the emergency room. You should avoid standalone, for-profit urgent care centers, which tend to perform large numbers of expensive tests, even for minor illnesses.

Pharmacies are abundantly supplied, but you may find that some medications that are available over-the-counter in your home country require a prescription in the USA, and, as always, if you don't have insurance to cover the cost of prescriptions, they can be shockingly expensive.

INFECTIOUS DISEASES

In addition to more common ailments, there are several infectious diseases that are unknown or uncommon outside North America. Most are acquired by mosquito or tick bites.

Giardiasis

This parasitic infection of the small intestine occurs throughout the world. Symptoms may include nausea, bloating, cramps and diarrhea, and may last for weeks. To protect yourself from Giardia, avoid drinking directly from lakes, ponds, streams and rivers, which may be contaminated by animal or human feces. The infection can also be transmitted from person-to-person if proper hand washing is not performed. Giardiasis is easily diagnosed by a stool test and readily treated with antibiotics.

HIV/AIDS

As with most parts of the world, HIV infection occurs throughout the USA. You should never assume, on the basis of someone's background or appearance, that they're free of this or any other sexually transmitted disease. Be sure to use a condom for all sexual encounters.

Lyme Disease

This disease has been reported from many states, but most documented cases occur in the northeastern part of the country, especially New York, New Jersey, Connecticut and Massachusetts. A smaller number of cases occur in the northern Midwest and in the northern Pacific coastal regions, including northern California. Lyme disease is transmitted by deer ticks, which are only 1mm to 2mm long. Most cases occur in the late spring and summer. The **Center for Disease Control** (CDC; www .cdc.gov/nci dod/dvbid/lyme) has an informative, if slightly scary, web page on Lyme disease.

The first symptom is usually an expanding red rash that is often pale in the center, known as a bull's-eye rash. However, in many cases, no rash is observed. Flu-like symptoms are common, including fever, headache, joint pains, body aches and malaise. When the infection is treated promptly with an appropriate antibiotic, usually doxycycline or amoxicillin, the cure rate is high. Luckily, since the tick must be attached for 36 hours or more to transmit Lyme disease, most cases can be prevented by performing a thorough tick check after you've been outdoors. For information, see Tick Bites (p1151).

Rabies

Rabies is a viral infection of the brain and spinal cord that is almost always fatal. The rabies virus is carried in the saliva of infected animals and is typically transmitted through an animal bite, though contamination of any break in the skin with infected saliva may result in rabies. In the USA, most cases of human rabies are related to exposure to bats. Rabies may also be contracted from raccoons, skunks, foxes, and unvaccinated cats and dogs.

If there is any possibility, however small, that you have been exposed to rabies, you should seek preventative treatment, which consists of rabies immune globulin and rabies vaccine, and is quite safe. In particular, any contact with a bat should be discussed with health authorities, because bats have small teeth and may not leave obvious bite marks. If you wake up to find a bat in your room, or discover a bat in a room with small children, rabies prophylaxis may be necessary.

West Nile Virus

These infections were unknown in the USA until a few years ago, but have now been reported in almost all 50 states. The virus is transmitted by culex mosquitoes, which are active in late summer and early fall, and generally bite after dusk. Most infections are mild or asymptomatic, but the virus may infect the central nervous system, leading to fever, headache, confusion, lethargy, coma and sometimes death. There is no treatment for West Nile virus. For the latest update on the areas affected by West Nile, go to the **US Geological Survey website** (http://diseasemaps.usgs.gov).

ENVIRONMENTAL HAZARDS
Bites & Stings

Common sense approaches to these concerns are the most effective: wear boots when hiking to protect from snakes, wear long sleeves and pants to protect from ticks and mosquitoes. If you're bitten, don't overreact. Stay calm and follow the recommended treatment.

ANIMAL BITES

Do not attempt to pet, handle or feed any animal, with the exception of domestic animals known to be free of any infectious disease. Most animal injuries are directly related to a person's attempt to touch or feed the animal.

Any bite or scratch by a mammal, including bats, should be promptly and thoroughly cleansed with large amounts of soap and water, followed by application of an antiseptic, such as iodine or alcohol. The local health authorities should be contacted immediately for possible postexposure rabies treatment, whether or not you've been immunized against rabies. It may also be advisable to start an antibiotic, since wounds caused by animal bites and scratches frequently become infected.

MOSQUITO BITES

When traveling in areas where West Nile or other mosquito-borne illnesses have been reported, keep yourself covered (wear long sleeves, long pants, hats and shoes rather than sandals) and apply a good insect repellent, preferably one containing DEET, to exposed skin and clothing. In general, adults and children over 12 should use preparations containing 25% to 35% DEET, which usually lasts about six hours. Children between two and 12 years of age should use preparations containing no more than 10% DEET, applied sparingly, which will usually last about three hours. Neurologic toxicity has been reported from DEET, especially in children, but appears to be extremely uncommon and generally related to overuse. DEET-containing compounds should not be used on children under age two.

Insect repellents containing certain botanical products, including oil of eucalyptus and soybean oil, are effective but last only 1½ to two hours. Products based on citronella are not effective.

Visit the **Center for Disease Control's website** (CDC; www.cdc.gov/ncidod/dvbid/westnile/prevention_info.htm) for prevention information.

SNAKE BITES

There are several varieties of venomous snakes in the USA, but unlike those in other countries they do not cause instantaneous death, and antivenins are available. First aid is to place a light constricting bandage over the bite, keep the wounded part below the level of the heart and move it as little as possible. Stay calm and get to a medical facility as soon as possible. Bring the dead snake for identification if you can, but don't risk being bitten again. Do not use the mythic 'cut an X and suck out the venom' trick; this causes more damage to snakebite victims than the bites themselves.

SPIDER & SCORPION BITES

Although there are many species of spider in the USA, the only ones that cause significant human illness are the black widow, brown recluse and hobo spiders. The black widow is black or brown in color, measuring about 15mm in body length, with a shiny top, fat body, and distinctive red or orange hourglass figure on its underside. It's found throughout the USA, usually in barns, woodpiles, sheds, harvested crops and bowls of outdoor toilets. The brown recluse spider is brown in color, usually 10mm in body length, with a dark violin-shaped mark on the top of the upper section of the body. It's usually found in the South and southern Midwest, but has spread to other parts of the country in recent years. The brown recluse is active mostly at night, lives in dark sheltered areas, such as under porches and in woodpiles, and typically bites when trapped. Hobo spiders are found chiefly in the northwestern USA and western Canada. The symptoms of a hobo spider bite are similar to those of a brown recluse, but milder.

If bitten by a black widow, you should apply ice or cold packs and go immediately to the nearest emergency room. Complications of a black widow bite may include muscle spasms, breathing difficulties and high blood pressure. The bite of a brown recluse or hobo spider typically causes a large, inflamed wound, sometimes associated with fever and chills. If bitten, apply ice and see a physician.

The only dangerous species of scorpion in the USA is the bark scorpion, which is found in the southwestern part of the country, chiefly Arizona. If stung, you should immediately apply ice or cold packs, immobilize the affected body part and go to the nearest emergency room. To prevent scorpion stings, be sure to inspect and shake out clothing, shoes and sleeping bags before use, and wear gloves and protective clothing when working around piles of wood or leaves.

TICK BITES

Ticks are parasitic arachnids that may be present in brush, forest and grasslands, where hikers often get them on their legs or in their boots. Adult ticks suck blood from hosts by burrowing into the skin and can carry infections such as Lyme disease.

Always check your body for ticks after walking through high grass or thickly forested area. If ticks are found unattached, they can simply be brushed off. If a tick is found attached, press down around the tick's head with tweezers, grab the head and gently pull upwards – do not twist it. (If no tweezers are available, use your fingers, but protect them from contamination with a piece of tissue or paper.) Do not rub oil, alcohol or petroleum jelly on it. If you get sick in the next couple of weeks, consult a doctor.

Glossary

The best primer in what has happened to the English language since its arrival on the continent is Bill Bryson's *Made in America* (1994), which tackles American slang and expressions (and good dollops of history) from the *Mayflower* onwards.

4WD – four-wheel-drive vehicle
9/11 – September 11, 2001; the date of the Al-Qaeda terrorist attacks, in which hijacked airplanes hit the Pentagon and destroyed New York's World Trade Center
24/7 – 24 hours a day, seven days a week

AAA – the American Automobile Association, also called Triple A
Acela – high-speed trains operating in the northeast
adobe – a traditional Spanish-Mexican building material of sun-baked bricks made with mud and straw; a structure built with this type of brick
aka – also known as
alien – official government term for a non-US citizen, visiting or resident in the USA (as in 'resident alien,' 'illegal alien' etc); impolite generally
Amtrak – national government-supported passenger railroad company
Angeleno/Angelena – a resident of Los Angeles
antebellum – of the period before the Civil War; pre-1861
antojito – an appetizer, snack or light meal (Spanish)
ANWR – Arctic National Wildlife Refuge; the 1.5-million-acre wilderness area that's the subject of controversial oil and gas drilling proposals
Arts and Crafts – an architecture and design movement popular at the turn of the 20th century; the style emphasizes simple craftsmanship and functional design; also called (American) craftsman
ATF – Bureau of Alcohol, Tobacco & Firearms, a federal law enforcement agency
ATM – automated teller machine
ATV – all-terrain vehicle, used for off-road transportation and recreation; see also *OHV*

back east – a West Coast reference to the East Coast
backpacker – one who hikes or camps out overnight; less commonly, a young, low-budget traveler
bling – hip-hop term for expensive jewelry and goods, the status symbols of success
BLM – Bureau of Land Management, an agency of the federal Department of the Interior that manages certain public land for resources and recreation
blog – short for web log; a personal diary available online

blue book – the *Kelley Blue Book*, a used-car pricing guide
bluegrass – a form of Appalachian folk music that evolved in the bluegrass country of Kentucky and Tennessee
bodega – especially in New York City, a small local store selling liquor, food and other basics
boomtown – as during the gold rush, a town that experiences rapid economic and population growth
booster – an avid promoter of a town or university; sometimes has parochial connotations
brick-and-mortar – a business' actual premises, as opposed to its internet presence
buffalo soldier – an African American soldier serving in the West after the Civil War
burro – a small donkey used as a pack animal
Bush, the – the greater part of Alaska, inaccessible by road or sea; to get there, charter a 'bush plane'
BYOB – bring your own booze; a staple of party invitations

Cajun – corruption of 'Acadia'; refers to Louisiana people who descended from 18th-century French-speaking Acadian exiles from eastern Canada
camper – pickup truck with a detachable roof or shell fitted out for camping
carded – to be asked to show your ID to buy liquor or cigarettes, or to enter a bar
carpetbaggers – exploitative Northerners who migrated to the South following the Civil War
CCC – Civilian Conservation Corps, a Depression-era federal program established in 1933 to employ unskilled young men
CDW – collision damage waiver; optional insurance against damaging a rental car
cell – cellular or mobile phone
chamber of commerce – COC; an association of local businesses that often provides tourist information
Chicano/Chicana – a Mexican-American man/woman
CNN – Cable News Network, a 24-hour cable TV news station
coach class – an economical class of travel on an airplane or train
coed – coeducational, open to both males and females; often used in noneducational contexts (eg hostel dorms)
conch (pronounced conk) – pink mollusk eaten as seafood; also a nickname for long-term Key West residents (new Key Westers are Freshwater Conchs)
conestoga – a big covered wagon drawn by horses or oxen, the vehicle of westward migration; also called a prairie schooner
Confederacy – the 11 Southern states that seceded from the USA in 1860-61

contiguous states – all states except Alaska and Hawaii; also called the lower 48

cot – camp bed (babies sleep in cribs)

country and western – an amalgam of folk music of the southern and western USA

coyote – a small wild dog; also a person who assists illegal immigrants to cross the Mexican border into the USA

cracker – in the South, a derogatory term for a poor white person

CVB – convention and visitors bureau, a city-run organization promoting tourism and assisting visitors

DEA – Drug Enforcement Agency, the federal body responsible for enforcing US drug laws

Deep South – in this book, the states of Louisiana, Mississippi and Alabama

Dixie – the South; the states south of the *Mason-Dixon Line*

DIY – do it yourself, as in DIY crafts or DIY magazines

DMV – Department of Motor Vehicles, the state agency that administers the registration of vehicles and the licensing of drivers

docent – a guide or attendant at a museum

dog, to ride the – to travel by Greyhound bus

downtown – the center of a city, central business district; in the direction of downtown (eg a downtown bus)

Dubya – George W Bush, the nation's 43rd president

DUI – driving under the influence of alcohol or drugs or both; sometimes called DWI (driving while intoxicated)

East – generally, the states east of the Mississippi River

efficiency – a small furnished apartment with a kitchen, often for short-term rental

Emancipation – refers to Abraham Lincoln's 1863 Emancipation Proclamation, which freed all slaves in the Confederate-controlled states (made official with the US Constitution's 13th Amendment)

entrée – the main course of a meal

express bus/train – bus/train that stops only at selected stations, and not at 'local' stations

express stop/station – stop/station served by express buses/trains as well as local ones

fanzine – a DIY magazine, often written by obsessive 'fanboys'

flag stop – a place where a bus stops only if you flag it down

foldaway – portable folding bed in a hotel

forty-niners – immigrants to California during the 1849 gold rush; also, San Francisco's pro-football team (49ers)

funnel cake – a specialty of the Pennsylvania Dutch, these deep-fried, spiral-shaped pastries are served dusted with powdered sugar, usually at outdoor fairs

gallery – a commercial establishment selling artwork; institutions that exhibit art collections are usually called museums

gated community – walled upscale residential area accessible only through security gates

general delivery – poste restante

Generation X – 1980s disaffected youth, replaced by Generations Y & Z

gimme cap – promotional baseball cap with company logo; often used pejoratively to refer to rural or lower-class white culture

GLBT – gay, lesbian, bisexual, transgender; *aka* inclusive of all nonheterosexuals

GOP – Grand Old Party, nickname of the Republican Party

graduate study – advanced-degree study, after completion of a bachelor's degree

green card – technically, a Registration Receipt Card, issued to holders of immigrant visas; it's actually pink, and it allows the holder to live and work legally in the USA

hip-hop – rap music; also black urban youth culture generally

Hispanic – of Latin American descent or culture (often used interchangeably with *Latino/Latina*)

HI-USA – Hostelling International USA; refers to US hostels affiliated with Hostelling International, a member group of International Youth Hostel Federation (IYHF)

hogan – a traditional Navajo home used for religious practices

hookup – at campgrounds, refers to *RV* connections for electricity, water and sewage; in social situations, refers to a romantic coupling

Imax – specialized, giant-screen theaters and movies

INS – Immigration & Naturalization Service; as of 2002 replaced by the *USCIS* and no longer operating

interstate – an interstate highway, part of the national, federally funded highway system

IRS – Internal Revenue Service, the branch of the US Treasury Department that oversees tax collection

Jim Crow laws – in the post–Civil War South, laws intended to limit the civil or voting rights of blacks; Jim Crow is an old pejorative term for a black person

Joshua tree – a tall, treelike type of yucca plant, common in the arid Southwest

kachina – Hopi sacred spirits; also refers to kachina dolls, a traditional Hopi carving

kiva – a round underground chamber built by Southwestern American Indian cultures for ceremonial and everyday purposes

KOA – Kampgrounds of America, a private chain of campgrounds throughout the USA

lagniappe – (lan-yap) a little something extra or a bene

Latino/Latina – a man/woman of Latin American descent (often used interchangeably with *Hispanic*)

LDS – from the Church of Jesus Christ of Latter-Day Saints, the formal name of the Mormon church

live oak – a hardwood, evergreen oak, native to the South; dead live oaks make excellent boat-building timber

local – a bus or train that stops at every bus stop or station; see also *express bus/train*

lower 48 – the 48 *contiguous states* of the continental USA; all states except Alaska and Hawaii

Mason-Dixon Line – the 1767 delineation between Pennsylvania and Maryland that was later regarded as the boundary between free and slave states in the period before the Civil War

MLB – Major League Baseball

MLS – Major League Soccer

mojito – sweet rum drink laden with mint

moonshine – illegal liquor, usually corn whiskey, associated with backwoods stills in the Appalachian Mountains

morteros – hollows in rocks used by American Indians for grinding seeds; also called mortar holes

Mother Road – nickname for Route 66, once the main route from Chicago to Los Angeles

NAACP – National Association for the Advancement of Colored People

National Guard – each state's federally supported military reserves, used most often in civil emergencies

National Recreation Area – National Park Service areas of scenic or ecological importance that are also reserved for recreation; they often incorporate public works, such as dams

National Register of Historic Places – the National Park Service list of historic sites; designation restricts modifications to help preserve the integrity of original buildings

NBA – National Basketball Association

NCAA – National Collegiate Athletic Association, the body that regulates intercollegiate sports

New Deal – wide-ranging domestic program of public works and regulations introduced by President Franklin D Roosevelt to counteract the effects of the Depression

NFL – National Football League

NHL – National Hockey League

NHS – National Historic Site

NM – National Monument

NOW – National Organization for Women, a political organization dedicated to promoting women's rights and issues

NPR – National Public Radio, a noncommercial, listener-supported national network of radio stations; notable for news and cultural programming

NPS – National Park Service, the division of the

Department of the Interior that administers US national parks and monuments

NRA – National Recreation Area; also National Rifle Association, an influential pro-gun lobby

NWR – National Wildlife Refuge

OHV/ORV – off-highway vehicle or off-road vehicle

out west – the opposite of *back east;* any place west of the Mississippi River

outfitter – business providing supplies, equipment, transport, guides etc for fishing, canoeing, rafting and hiking trips

panhandle – a narrow piece of land projecting from the main body of a state (eg the Florida panhandle); also, to beg from passersby

parking lot/garage – paved area/building for parking cars (the word 'car park' is not used)

PBS – Public Broadcasting System, a noncommercial TV network; the TV equivalent of *NPR*

PC – politically correct; also personal computer

petroglyph – a work of rock art in which the design is pecked, chipped or abraded into the surface of the rock

PGA – Professional Golfers' Association

pickup – small truck with an open bed

pictograph – work of rock art in which the design is painted on a rock surface

po'boy – a fat sandwich on a bread roll

powwow – gathering of Native American people

pueblo – Native American village of the Southwest, with adjoining dwellings of *adobe* or stone

ranchero – a Mexican rancher; a Mexican-American musical style blending German and Spanish influences

rancho – a small ranch (Mexican Spanish)

raw bar – a restaurant counter that serves raw shellfish

Reconstruction – a period after the Civil War, when secessionist states were placed under federal control before they were readmitted to the Union

redneck – derogatory term for an extremely conservative, working-class or rural person

ristra – chili tied on a string and hanging vertically

RV – recreational vehicle, also known as a motor home

scalawags – Southern whites with Northern sympathies who profited under *Reconstruction* after the Civil War

schlep – carry awkwardly or with difficulty (Yiddish)

schlock – cheap, trashy products (Yiddish)

shotgun shack – a small timber house with rooms in a line (as if you could fire a shotgun straight through from front to back); once-common dwellings for poor whites and blacks in the South

sierra – mountain range (Spanish)

snail mail – stamped letter, as opposed to email

snowbirds – term for wealthy retirees who travel to southern US vacation spots each winter

SoCal – Southern California

soul food – traditionally cuisine of Southern black Americans (such as chitterlings, ham hocks and collard greens)

sourdough – a 19th-century California miner; also old-time Alaskans who, it is said, are 'sour on the country but without enough dough to get out;' also, a 'yeasty' mixture used to make bread or pancakes

SSN – social security number, a nine-digit ID code required for employment

stick, stick shift – manually operated gearshift; a car with manual transmission ('Can you drive a stick?')

strip mall – any collection of businesses and stores arranged around a parking lot

SUV – sports utility vehicle

swag – free promotional items given away to function as advertisements

terroir – a French term used in California wine country to specify the region in which grapes are grown and in which wine is made

trailer – transportable dwelling; a trailer park is a collection that doesn't move and provides low-cost housing

TTY, TDD – telecommunications devices for the deaf

two-by-four – standard-size timber, 2in thick and 4in wide

Union, the – the United States; in a Civil War context, the Union refers to the northern states at war with the southern Confederate states

USAF – United States Air Force

USCIS – US Citizenship & Immigration Services, the agency within the Department of Homeland Security that oversees immigration, naturalization and visa processing

USFS – United States Forest Service, the division of the Department of Agriculture that manages federal forests for resources and recreation

USGS – United States Geological Survey, an agency of the Department of the Interior responsible for, among other things, creating detailed topographic maps of the country

USMC – United States Marine Corps

USN – United States Navy

wash – a watercourse in the desert, usually dry but subject to flash flooding

Wasp – White, Anglo-Saxon Protestant; often used to refer to white-bread middle-class values

well drinks – bar drinks with less-expensive, generic-brand hard liquor, as opposed to name-brand 'top-shelf' drinks

WNBA – Women's National Basketball Association

wonk – a person overly obsessed with minute details, usually pejorative; equivalent to political nerd or computer geek

WPA – Works Progress (later, Works Projects) Administration; a Depression-era, New Deal program to increase employment by funding public works projects

zip code – a five- or nine-digit postal code; refers to the Zone Improvement Program, which expedited delivery of US mail

The Authors

JEFF CAMPBELL
**Coordinating Author, Hawaii,
History, Arts, Environment**

Jeff's been other places, but his heart skips a beat in the American West, and in all, he's made contact with 41 of the 50 states. A writer and an editor for Lonely Planet for 15 years, he's been the coordinating author of *USA* since the third edition, which won the Society of American Travel Writers 2004 Silver Award for best guidebook. He's also been the coordinating author on *Southwest, Zion & Bryce Canyon National Parks* and *Hawaii*. He currently lives in New Jersey with his wife and two children.

ALEXIS AVERBUCK
The South

Alexis has lived in New Orleans for 10 years and written about all things New Orleans during that time. A resident of the Bywater neighborhood, she makes any excuse to travel throughout Louisiana and Arkansas, sample the food and dance to the music. She has lived in Antarctica for a year, crossed the Pacific by sailboat and written books on her journeys through Asia and the Americas. Also a painter, each trip inspires new work, both written and visual – see her paintings at www.alexisaverbuck.com.

SANDRA BAO
Pacific Northwest

After years of traveling to dozens of countries, Sandra finally got tired of not having a vegetable garden and settled down in Portland, Oregon with her husband. She finally has her heirloom tomatoes, but their health is constantly compromised by her continued trips. Researching Oregon has been a highlight of Sandra's Lonely Planet career, bringing the realization of how beautiful her home state is, how much there is to do and how friendly people are in all those tiny country towns.

LONELY PLANET AUTHORS

Why is our travel information the best in the world? It's simple: our authors are independent, dedicated travelers. They don't research using just the internet or phone, and they don't take freebies in exchange for positive coverage. They travel widely, to all the popular spots and off the beaten track. They personally visit thousands of hotels, restaurants, cafés, bars, galleries, palaces, museums and more – and they take pride in getting all the details right, and telling it how it is. Think you can do it? Find out how at lonelyplanet.com.

THE AUTHORS

TIM BEWER
Great Plains

Tim Bewer has lived on both edges of the Great Plains – previously in Denver and currently in Minneapolis – and has traveled through the region too many times to keep count, including twice along Route 66. When not hunkered down in front of his computer battling another deadline, he travels, hikes, canoes and reads as much as possible.

BECCA BLOND
Rocky Mountains

Becca migrated to Colorado from DC to attend university, and fell so madly in love she never left. Following reporting stints at the *Denver Post* and *Colorado Springs Gazette*, Becca traded breaking news and entertainment journalism for travel writing and has authored more than two dozen books for Lonely Planet, including the previous edition of this guide and the Rocky Mountain chapter of *USA & Canada on a Shoestring*. When not on the road, Becca lives in Boulder with her fiancé, Aaron (also a Lonely Planet author) and their bulldog Duke.

DOMINIQUE CHANNELL
California

Whisked around the globe every four years as a military brat, Dominique caught the travel bug early and has happily discovered that it has no cure. Past years have found her bartending in Ireland, getting stuck on a glacier in Tierra del Fuego, and crashing birthday parties in Malaysia. She is currently stopping for breath in the Bay Area, where she lives with her husband, works as a freelance editor, and might even stay awhile. If you're crazy like her and happen to be up at 5am, you might see her training with a competitive women's crew on Lake Merritt.

JIM DUFRESNE
Alaska

Jim DuFresne has lived, worked and wandered across Alaska and even cashed a Permanent Fund Dividend check. As the sports editor of the *Juneau Empire*, he was the first Alaskan sportswriter to win a national award from Associated Press. As a guide for Alaska Discovery he has witnessed Hubbard Glacier shed icebergs the size of pick-up trucks off its 8-mile-wide face. Jim now lives in Michigan but is constantly returning to the Far North to write books on Alaska including Lonely Planet's *Hiking In Alaska*.

LISA DUNFORD   Texas

Lisa might be considered a naturalized Texan since she moved there 12 years ago and married a native. During that time she's driven the breadth and width of her very large adopted state, always on the lookout for a dance hall concert or good BBQ. She was a features-department editor and restaurant reviewer at the *Corpus Christi Caller-Times* newspaper before turning freelance. No matter where this wanderer roams, she'll always return to the patch of riverfront that she, her husband and their dog call home.

NED FRIARY &   New England
GLENDA BENDURE

Ned grew up near Boston. Upon graduating from the University of Massachusetts, he bought a van and went on a yearlong journey across the USA, landing in Santa Cruz, California, where he met Glenda. After her university graduation they took to the road, through Europe and Asia, teaching English in Japan and eventually returning to the US. After years of travel, the place that caught their fancy was Cape Cod – and they've lived there ever since. Free time? Road trips around New England, natch.

BETH GREENFIELD   New York, New Jersey
                                         & Pennsylvania, Destination

Beth, a Jersey Shore native, is now a 16-year (and counting) New Yorker living on the Upper West Side with her partner. A writer and editor at *Time Out* New York magazine, she is also a freelance writer who covers travel and culture for publications including the *New York Times, Out* and *New York.* She's contributed to Lonely Planet guides including *New York City, Mexico* and *Miami & the Keys,* and previous editions of *USA.* When necessary, she can turn on a mean Jersey accent.

ADAM KARLIN   Washington, DC & the Capitol Region

Adam Karlin has filed from India, Sri Lanka, Vietnam, Thailand, Laos, Burma and Argentina, so it's only appropriate one of his first Lonely Planet assignments was covering home. Born in Washington, DC, and raised in Maryland, Adam used to cover crime and politics (and yes, those were different beats) for newspapers in his home state. His work has also appeared in the *Christian Science Monitor, USA Today,* the *Houston Chronicle* and the *Chicago Tribune,* among other publications. He is the recent recipient of an MA in International Studies and Diplomacy from the School of Oriental and African Studies in London.

BETH KOHN   Southwest

Though she usually navigates her San Francisco hometown by bicycle, during this trip Beth left her favorite wheels at home to gallivant through the sprawling Southwest. Her little red pickup truck did the trick on some tortuous unpaved roads, and she camped out in some of the most scenic red rock overlooks in the country. All the while, she kept an eye out for the best local swimming holes and the most far-fetched roadside kitsch. You can see more of her work at www.bethkohn.com.

MARIELLA KRAUSE   Florida

As a fan of amusement parks, kitschy tourist attractions and states with Panhandles, Mariella was thrilled to take to the highways of Florida to uncover its every eccentricity. Having spent her formative years in the middle states, she's delighted to call San Francisco home. She started her career as an advertising copywriter and now writes a little bit of everything, from books to newspaper articles to glossy brochures, all from her Victorian flat in Noe Valley, usually with a cat in her lap. Mariella can tell you the difference between an alligator and a crocodile, if you'd like.

NICK MARINO   The South

Nick Marino has spent almost half his life in the South. He has eaten ribs in Alabama, toured William Faulkner's house in Mississippi, climbed Stone Mountain in Georgia and currently lives in Atlanta. He's the managing editor of *Paste* magazine, and his writing has appeared in *Entertainment Weekly*, *Spin*, the *Boston Globe* and the *Atlanta Journal-Constitution*. He has taught critical writing at the University of Mississippi, and he currently coaches women's rowing for Georgia Tech.

EMILY MATCHAR   The South

A native North Carolinian, Emily has an inborn affection for BBQ and college basketball, though she sadly lacks a Southern drawl. After suffering several freezing years in New England she hightailed it back below the Mason-Dixon line and currently lives in Carrboro, NC (Paris of the Piedmont!), where she works as a newspaper reporter and freelance magazine writer. In her spare time she enjoys cooking, rock climbing and planning the next great escape.

THE AUTHORS

BRENDAN SAINSBURY
Pacific Northwest

An expat Brit, Brendan's first exposure to Pacific Northwest culture came via a well-used copy of *Nevermind* by Washington grunge merchants Nirvana purchased in London's Oxford Street in 1992. Moving to BC, Canada in 2004, he made his first sorties across the US–Canadian border to the Evergreen state in search of snow-capped volcanoes, enlightening music and a half-decent cup of coffee. Somewhere between Mount Baker and downtown Seattle he found all three.

ANDREA SCHULTE-PEEVERS
California

Andrea fell in love with California – its pizzazz, people and sunshine – almost the instant she landed in the Golden State. She grew up in Germany, lived in London and traveled the world before getting a degree from UCLA and embarking on a career in travel writing. Andrea has written or contributed to more than 30 Lonely Planet books, including earlier editions of this one and the *California* and *Los Angeles & Southern California* guides. She's explored nearly every nook and cranny of the state and still thinks it's a fabulous place to be.

KARLA ZIMMERMAN
Great Lakes, The Culture

Karla is a life-long Midwesterner, weaned on a diet of corndogs, cheese and fruit pies. During her Great Lakes travels, she got snowed on in Minnesota, stepped in pig doo in Indiana, watched sausage-racing in Wisconsin and drank an embarrassing number of milkshakes in Ohio. She lives in Chicago with husband Eric and writes travel features for newspapers, books, magazines and radio. She has authored or coauthored several of Lonely Planet's US and Canadian titles.

CONTRIBUTORS

Axel Alonso is the Executive Editor of Marvel Comics. An 11-year industry veteran, he was once anointed one of the '100 Hottest People in Entertainment' by *Vibe* magazine. He lives in Brooklyn with his wife, Kara, and 4-year-old son, Tito, who has so far exhibited no superpowers. Axel wrote the Campfire Tales (On Steroids) boxed text in the Arts chapter.

Andy Bender, a native New Englander, has lived in Southern California for 17 years. Yet another LP author with an MBA, he left the business world to do what every MBA secretly dreams: traveling the world and writing about it. His articles appear in the *Los Angeles Times*, *Forbes* and Singapore Airlines in-flight magazine, and at www.andrewbender.com. Andy covered San Diego and the California deserts for this book.

Sara Benson has an affinity for the USA's national parks, which she has traveled around, worked at and explored in depth for more than 15 years, ever since her parents took her to Yellowstone National Park during a cross-country road trip. Already the author of more than 20 travel and nonfiction books and an award-winning journalist, she also works as a seasonal ranger in Kings Canyon National Park in California. Sara wrote the National Parks chapter for this book.

Alison Bing has done everything you're supposed to do in San Francisco, and many things you're not, including falling in love on the 7 Haight bus and gorging on Mission burritos before Berlioz symphonies. Alison holds degrees in art history and international diplomacy – respectable diplomatic credentials she regularly undermines with opinionated culture commentary for radio, newspapers and books, including Lonely Planet's *San Francisco* and *San Francisco Encounter*. Alison covered San Francisco for this book.

Michael Grosberg was raised near Washington DC but spent many family vacations in New York City and driving throughout the region because of his father's unanalyzed fear of flight. After college, travel and jobs abroad, he turned up in graduate school in NYC. Ten years on he feels like a native, especially because of his frequent need for the great outdoors upstate. Michael covered New York State for this book.

Karen A Levine earned a Master's degree in Art History at San Francisco State University and currently serves as Managing Editor, Publications, at the San Francisco Museum of Modern Art. She has contributed essays, interviews and reviews to a number of art publications, including *Tema Celeste* and *Artweek*. Karen wrote the Painting & Sculpture section and the boxed text on Early American Photography in the Arts chapter.

John Mariani is the author of *The Encyclopedia of American Food & Drink* (1999), *America Eats Out: An Illustrated History of Restaurants, Taverns, Coffee Shops, Speakeasies, and Other Establishments That Have Fed Us for 350 Years* (1991) and, with his wife, Galina, *The Italian-American Cookbook* (2000). He is also food and travel correspondent for *Esquire* magazine, and writes the weekly 'Mariani's Virtual Gourmet Newsletter' (www.johnmariani.com). John wrote the Food & Drink chapter for this book.

Amy Marr has explored every US national park, hoofed and pedaled all over the world, and led more than 40 biking and hiking trips. Now a cookbook publisher and travel writer, she's rooted in Marin County, where she bikes and hikes on Mt Tam and cooks up Italian feasts. Amy wrote the USA Outdoors chapter for this book.

THE AUTHORS

Edward Nawotka is a widely published book critic and columnist for *Bloomberg News* and *Publishers Weekly*. Edward lives in Texas in a house with a small menagerie of animals and some 10,000 books. An archive of his work and his blog can be found at www.edwardn.com. Edward wrote the boxed text entitled The End is Nigh! in the Arts chapter.

Becky Ohlsen was originally drawn to the Pacific Northwest 12 years ago by a hopeless crush on Mudhoney singer Mark Arm. She's seen the Emerald City from the water, the gutter and the tops of numerous buildings, with wildly varying degrees of clarity. Sadly, she has yet to leave any impression whatsoever on Mark Arm. Becky authored Lonely Planet's *Seattle* city guide and covered Seattle for this book.

TophOne is a DJ, graffiti artist and music writer from San Francisco. He grew up skating and going to punkrock shows, but now rides his bike between bars and gigs across the West. As Senior Writer for *XLR8R* magazine, he pens the popular 'Lucky 13' column, is founder of the RedWine DJs and loves baseball. TophOne wrote the Hip-Hop section of the Arts chapter.

Behind the Scenes

THIS BOOK

For this fifth edition of *USA*, Jeff Campbell coordinated a stellar author team (see The Authors, p1156) – the largest yet for this title. Rawk! Contributions were also made by Emily K Wolman, Jay Cooke and Suki Gear. This guidebook was commissioned in Lonely Planet's Oakland, California, office and produced by the following:

Lead Commissioning Editor Emily K Wolman
Assisting Commissioning Editors Jay Cooke, Heather Dickson, Suki Gear
Coordinating Editor Trent Holden
Coordinating Cartographer Owen Eszeki
Coordinating Layout Designer Paul Iacono
Managing Editor Katie Lynch
Managing Cartographers Alison Lyall, Amanda Sierp
Layout Managers Adam McCrow, Celia Wood
Assisting Editors David Andrew, Sarah Bailey, Kate Evans, Penelope Goodes, Rosie Nicholson
Proofreaders Cathryn Game, Jocelyn Harewood
Assisting Cartographers Anna Clarkson, Mick Garrett, Tadhgh Knaggs, Sam Sayer
Assisting Layout Designer Jessica Rose
Cover Designer Pepi Bluck
Project Managers Glenn van der Knijff, Bronwyn Hicks
Talk2Us Coordinator Raphael Richards

Thanks to David Burnett, David Carroll, Sin Choo, David Connolly, Melanie Dankel, Justin Flynn, Jennye Garibaldi, Pablo Gastar, Mark Germanchis, Jim Hsu, Rachel Imeson, Laura Jane, Lisa Knights, Marina Kosmatos, Rebecca Lalor, Katherine Marsh, John Mazzocchi, Carolina A Miranda, Clara Monitto, Wibowo Rusli, Suzannah Shwer, Sarah Sloane, Cara Smith, Jeanette Wall

THANKS
Jeff Campbell

To the meticulous and unflappable Emily Wolman, I owe boundless thanks. To my coauthors, I owe a round – and you guys fill a bar! A humble shout out to Bruce Frubin, Eric Quinones, Bobby Camara and Terry Tempest Williams, who defines gracious: thank you. None of this would be possible without the patience and loving support of my wife, Deanna, and my kids, Jackson and Miranda. This one's for you, Susan Birkeland; write on.

Alexis Averbuck

Many thanks to Wayne Tabor for his invaluable insider's view on Memphis, Chef Paul Prudhomme, Patti Averbuck and David Averbuck for their assistance in New Orleans, and Tristan Thompson for his hospitality in Lafayette. Special thanks are also due to Jay Cooke and Emily Wolman for their excellent leadership and editorial wisdom.

THE LONELY PLANET STORY

Fresh from an epic journey across Europe, Asia and Australia in 1972, Tony and Maureen Wheeler sat at their kitchen table stapling together notes. The first Lonely Planet guidebook, *Across Asia on the Cheap*, was born.

Travelers snapped up the guides. Inspired by their success, the Wheelers began publishing books to Southeast Asia, India and beyond. Demand was prodigious, and the Wheelers expanded the business rapidly to keep up. Over the years, Lonely Planet extended its coverage to every country and into the virtual world via lonelyplanet.com and the Thorn Tree message board.

As Lonely Planet became a globally loved brand, Tony and Maureen received several offers for the company. But it wasn't until 2007 that they found a partner whom they trusted to remain true to the company's principles of traveling widely, treading lightly and giving sustainably. In October of that year, BBC Worldwide acquired a 75% share in the company, pledging to uphold Lonely Planet's commitment to independent travel, trustworthy advice and editorial independence.

Today, Lonely Planet has offices in Melbourne, London and Oakland, with over 500 staff members and 300 authors. Tony and Maureen are still actively involved with Lonely Planet. They're traveling more often than ever, and they're devoting their spare time to charitable projects. And the company is still driven by the philosophy of *Across Asia on the Cheap*: 'All you've got to do is decide to go and the hardest part is over. So go!'

Sandra Bao

My husband, Ben Greensfelder, deserves top honors for conceding to drive me everywhere around Oregon – though he really enjoyed the trips as well. My coauthors Becky, Brendan and John – along with expert authors Elle, Lucy and David – all helped me in some way or another, and I truly appreciate it. My CE, Heather Dickson, was ace as well. Friends (especially Stacey Henke and Todd Guren) showered me with tips and opinions. Thanks to you all.

Tim Bewer

An anonymous cast of thousands helped me during this project, so a big thank you goes out to all the people who answered my questions and offered advice during my travels. Thanks to Karla Zimmerman and Amy Waterman for the contacts and advice, and to Jeff Campbell and Emily Wolman for being pleasures to work with.

Becca Blond

Big thanks to Aaron and Duke for joining me on the road. To Doug Wall, thanks for everything in Silverton. In Boulder, thanks to Danielle for the great boxed text. To all my friends and family, thanks for your unwavering support. To my best friend, Natalie Swetye, who married her middle school sweetheart, Mike Pugh, on June 30, 2007 in Ward, Colorado: not only did your wedding count as research, it was perfect and I wish you both a future of blue drinks.

Dominique Channell

Special thanks to my husband, Joshua, for enduring as my chauffeur and valet during my trips through Yosemite and Sequoia! Thanks also to Suki Gear for including me on this project and showing me the Lonely Planet ropes, John Vlahides for his planning and hitting-the-road tips, and Emily Wolman for boosting my ego. Thanks also to my ever-supportive family – my parents, Dan and Gisele, and my little sis Nicole. Northern California – well, you rock.

Lisa Dunford

I'm much obliged to friends and family across Texas who suggested and shared adventures: Anna and Seth Sosolik, Tara and Doug Hrbacek, Lindsay and Jack Day, Daryn and Mark Polanco, David Lynch, Ashley Robison, Nancy Shropshire, Joe Kulbeth, Mary Kay and Jim Dunford, George and Carol Springs. Thanks to Emily, Suki and Jeff for their help on the LP end. Billy, I'm so glad you're traveling this road with me.

Ned Friary & Glenda Bendure

We'd like to thank everyone who pointed us in the right direction, from the farmer in Quechee who told us to drive 6 miles down that rutted dirt road (oops…wrong turn), to Patti Bangert, Rob Hunter, Bill O'Neill, Susan Milton and Bryan Lantz for sharing the scoop on their favorite haunts. And a special thanks to Emily Wolman, Jay Cooke and Jeff Campbell for their spot-on guidance.

Beth Greenfield

Many thanks to the wonderful folks at Lonely Planet – Emily Wolman, Jeff Campbell, Jay Cooke, Alison Lyall, Melanie Dankel and all the rest – for your support and professionalism. Thank you also to the folks who helped me unearth good stuff – Dan Eldridge, John Fleenor, Greg Wessner, Michael Grosberg, Lisa Neel – and my loving travel partner, Kiki Herold. And thank you always to Mom and Dad.

Adam Karlin

Thanks: Ben, Jessie, Alex, Dylan, Sarah, Rian, Vijay, Chris, Stef, Matt, Mark, Kelly, Brycen, Kate, Brian, Sean, Fliss, the Aung family, Uncle U Maung, Aunty Htwe, the entire CISD 2007-08 class, Phil, and everyone else who helped on the road. Jay Cooke, Emily Wolman, Nick Marino and Jeff Campbell for helping a new Lonely Planet writer find his legs (and figure out Felix). Thanks especially Mom and Dad for making home my favorite place to travel.

Beth Kohn

Thanks to Emily Wolman and Suki Gear for getting the road trip in gear. Echo and Mavis Gaffney shared excellent Arizona tips, as did the amazing Stephanie Heckathorne at the Phoenix CVB. Shari and Tim Wong helped beat the heat in Las Vegas, and Zack Zdinak and Robert in Flagstaff kept the chinchillas at bay. Shawn Stinson in Salt Lake City and Corinne Humphrey in Park City pitched in for Utah. Thanks to Jenny G for bringing me chocolate donuts, Pati Fuentes for holding down the home front, and Claude Moller for going nowhere, anytime.

Mariella Krause

A big thanks to Ben van Horn, not just for the use of his couch, but for being an excellent tour guide. Hats off to the fabulous Lonely Planet crew – Emily Wolman, Jay Cooke and Jeff Campbell – for your guidance and support. Thanks to Pete and Kay Bauer for making St Pete's so much fun, and to Tim Bauer, Jeff Fowler and Cara Burgoyne for the moral support, patience, proofreading and Red Bull.

Nick Marino

Thanks to every chef, musician, folk artist and writer in the great American South for making this part of the country so special. Thanks to Jeff Campbell, Jay

Cooke, Tasmin McNaughtan and Emily Wolman for your enthusiasm and, especially, your patience.

Emily Matchar

Thanks to Bobbi and David Matchar for hosting my all-night internet sessions and to everyone who spent time, whether a day or a week, in the passenger seat of my sea-green Honda Civic. Also thanks to all the Lonely Planet editors and authors who patiently answered my newbie questions.

Brendan Sainsbury

A hearty thanks to all the untold park rangers, taxi drivers, tourist info reps, ski bums and innocent bystanders who helped me during my research, particularly to Emily Wolman, my commissioning editor, and Heather Dickson, who opened up a few doors to get me in on the project. Special thanks also to Connie Ruffo for her invaluable tips on Northwest Washington, and to my wife and son for accompanying me for most of the research.

Andrea Schulte-Peevers

Many good folks deserve a big round of applause for sharing insights and giving me valuable help. They are (in alpha order): Shannon Turner Brooks, Kim Cooper, Koleen Hamblin, Michael Kidd, Bob Maguglin, Megan Rodriguez, Fred Sater and Richard Schave. Big thanks also to Lonely Planet's Emily Wolman and Suki Gear and coordinating author Jeff Campbell for cobbling it all together. Last but not least: big kisses to David for always being there.

Karla Zimmerman

Thanks to the following for sharing their considerable local knowledge: Ronald Aukerman, Tim Bewer, Carrie Biolo, Nate Cavalieri, Mary Decker, Roger Fatica, JoAnn Hornak, Mike Kirda, Kari Lydersen, Doug Seibold, Diana Slickman, Susan H Stephan, Ray Zielinksi, Don and Karen Zimmerman, and the helpful workers in the Midwest's visitors centers. Thanks to Lonely Planet's Jeff Campbell and Emily Wolman for patience and idea-slinging. Thanks most of all to Eric Markowitz, the world's best partner-for-life.

OUR READERS

Gerald Adams, Yoram Afek, Isabel Alonso, John Anderson, Kristy Anderson, Veronica & Calum Archibald, Jon Bailey, Russell Barnett, Kristin Basel, Harriet Bickley, Kathrin Bode, Jennifer Burgess, Maria Cestelli, Ni Cher, Norm Clerman, Douglas Cortinovis, Randall Cotten, Katie Coulson, Bob Culley, Jessie Curtis, Jean Czerlinski, Elizabeth Donat, Matt & Cal Edge, Delame Emy, Paul Ertelt, Kathie Etulain, Asdfsd Fdasdf, Albert L Fisher, Kym Fisher, Garry Fox, Manfred Gerrits, Patrice Glancy, Liwayway Gomez, Colin Griffiths, Klaus Hahn, Robert Hajek, Yana Hana, Allison Hauser, Mary Hext, Melanie Hindhead, Kirsten Hurley, Ruth E Imershein, William James, Phyllis Jarvis, Julia Johnson, Barry Johnston, Mark Jones, Betty Kane, Jamie Keller, Martin Kienl, David King, Susanne Krawinkel, Nick Kurlas, Jai Lusser, Byron Malcolm, Paul Martin, Trevor Mazzucchelli, Mary McCalman, Marianne McCarroll, Barry McGurk, Ruth Messenger, Chris Miller, Bob Moffatt, Heather Monell, Brian Mooney, Jim Morrison, Jaimie Navalli, Susan O'Neill, Brian Richard Peterson, Mark St Pierre, Steven & Elaine Prevost, Dawn Quiett, Brian Quinn, Brian & Cate Quinn, Bridget Ramsay, Nicholas Redding, Ross Rivas, Antje Rösch, Russell Shoebotham, Thomas Sickinger, Marco Snoeren, Jo Spangaro, L Stevens, Dave Stone, Diana Stuart, Luc Tardif, Darla Tishman, Chad Utterback, Tijmen van Dobbenburgh, Marieke van Geldermalsen, Kim van Hest, Bob van Koetsveld, Josine van Koetsveld, Erik van Rossum, Sila van Velten, Kaposi Viktor, Martine De Vries, Barrie Westley, Ken Westmoreland, Anne White, Gale Wrausmann, Calina Yee, Lisa Zimmerman

ACKNOWLEDGMENTS

Many thanks to the following for the use of their content: Globe on title page ©Mountain High Maps 1993 Digital Wisdom, Inc.

SEND US YOUR FEEDBACK

We love to hear from travelers – your comments keep us on our toes and help make our books better. Our well-traveled team reads every word on what you loved or loathed about this book. Although we cannot reply individually to postal submissions, we always guarantee that your feedback goes straight to the appropriate authors, in time for the next edition. Each person who sends us information is thanked in the next edition – and the most useful submissions are rewarded with a free book.

To send us your updates – and find out about Lonely Planet events, newsletters and travel news – visit our award-winning website: **www.lonelyplanet.com**.

Note: we may edit, reproduce and incorporate your comments in Lonely Planet products such as guidebooks, websites and digital products, so let us know if you don't want your comments reproduced or your name acknowledged. For a copy of our privacy policy visit www.lonelyplanet.com/privacy.

Index

ABBREVIATIONS

AK	Alaska	KY	Kentucky	NY	New York
AL	Alabama	LA	Louisiana	OH	Ohio
AR	Arkansas	MA	Massachusetts	OK	Oklahoma
AZ	Arizona	MD	Maryland	OR	Oregon
CA	California	ME	Maine	PA	Pennsylvania
CO	Colorado	MI	Michigan	RI	Rhode Island
CT	Connecticut	MN	Minnesota	SC	South Carolina
DC	District of Columbia	MO	Missouri	SD	South Dakota
DE	Delaware	MS	Mississippi	TN	Tennessee
FL	Florida	MT	Montana	TX	Texas
GA	Georgia	NC	North Carolina	UT	Utah
HI	Hawaii	ND	North Dakota	VA	Virginia
IA	Iowa	NE	Nebraska	VT	Vermont
ID	Idaho	NH	New Hampshire	WA	Washington
IL	Illinois	NJ	New Jersey	WI	Wisconsin
IN	Indiana	NM	New Mexico	WV	West Virginia
KS	Kansas	NV	Nevada	WY	Wyoming

INDEX

INDEX

INDEX

INDEX

INDEX

Manassas battlefield 347
manatees 98, 127
Manchester (NH) 282-3
Manchester (VT) 274-5
Mancos 776
Manhattan 140-44, **142-3**, **150-1**, **156-7**
Manhattan Project 874, 893
Manteo 377-8
Manzanar National Historic Site 995
maps 1123
Marathon 736
Mardi Gras 425, 440, 443, **10**
Marfa 735
margarita 710
Marin County 972-3
Marin Headlands 972
Marquette 612
Marshall Gold Discovery State Historic Park 983
Martha's Vineyard 255-7
Maryland 325-41, **304-5**
Mashomack Nature Preserve 181
Mass MoCA 260
Massachusetts 229-60, **226-7**
Maui 1103-7
Mauna Kea 1101
Maze 867
McCall 801-2
McCarthy 1079-80
McCloud 986
McKay, Claude 67
McKenzie River Valley 1042
Mead National Recreation Area 818
measures 1112
medical services 1149
Medicine Bow Mountains & Snowy Range 787
Medicine Wheel National Historic Landmark 779
Memphis 460-8, **462-3**
Mendenhall Glacier 1064
Mendocino 979
Menemsha 256
Merritt Island National Wildlife Refuge 521
Mesa 825
Mesa Verde National Park 776-7
Mesilla 890-1
Messud, Claire 67
Methow Valley 1023

000 Map pages
000 Photograph pages

metric conversions, *see inside front cover*
Metropolitan Museum of Art 155
Mexican Hat 868
Mexico 738, 932
Miami 492-504, **493**, **495**, **498**, **14**
accommodations 501
drinking 502-3
entertainment 502-3
festivals & events 500
food 501-2
internet access 494
itineraries 492
medical services 494
Miami Beach 494-6, **495**, **14**
shopping 503
tourist information 494
tours 500
travel to/from 503
travel within 504
walking tour 496, **496**
Miami Beach 494-6, **495**, **14**
Michigan 598-613, **544-5**
Middle Bass Island 590
Middlebury 277
Milan 589
Milford 223
Miller, Arthur 81
Miller, Henry 945
Milltown 583
Milwaukee 614-17
Minneapolis 623-9, **626-7**
Minnesota 623-36, **544-5**
Minnewaska State Park Preserve 182
Minot 663
Minuteman Missile National Historic Site 665
Miro, Joan 551
Mirror Lake Highway 863
Mission, the 960-1
Mission San Xavier del Bac 850
Mississippi 425-32, **372-3**
Mississippi Delta 427-30
Mississippi Palisades State Park 575
Mississippi River 32, 49, 95, 463-4, 620
Mississippi Valley 632
Missoula 792-3
Missouri 642-57, **638-9**
Misty Fjords National Monument 1060
Mitchell 665
Moab 865-6, **9**
Mobile 425
mobile phones 1125
modern dance 81-2

Modoc National Forest 987
Modoc National Wildlife Refuge 987
Mogollon peoples 806
Mojave National Preserve 938
Mokelumne Hill 984
Moline 575
Moloka'i 1109
Moloka'i Forest Reserve 1109
Monarch Sanctuary 947
money 25-6, 1123-4, *see also inside front cover*
ATMs 1123
credit cards 1123
traveler's checks 1124
Monhegan Island 295-6
Mono Lake 995
Monongahela National Forest 368
Monroe (LA) 454
Monroe (WI) 620
Monroe, James 46
Montana 788-97, **742-3**, **107**, **114**
Montaña de Oro State Park 944-943
Montauk 180-1
Montauk Point State Park 180
Monterey 946-8
Monterey State Historic Park 946
Montgomery 423-4
Monticello 360
Montpelier 277-8
Monument Rocks 679
Monument Valley 868, **16**
Monument Valley Navajo Tribal Park 843
moose 128, 284, 612, 783, 785
Moosehorn National Wildlife Refuge 299
Moran State Park 1022
Morehead City 380
Morgantown 369
mormons 852, 853, 854
Morro Bay 943
Morro Bay State Park 943
motels 1113
motor racing 522-3, 579, 730
motorcycle travel 1141-5, 1144
to/from the USA 1137-8
Mound City 593
Mt Adams (OH) 596
Mt Adams (WA) 1026
Mt Anderson 1018
Mt Bachelo 1044
Mt Baker 1022-3
Mt Hood 1043-4
Mt Pleasant 396-7
Mt Rainier National Park 1025-6, **119**

INDEX

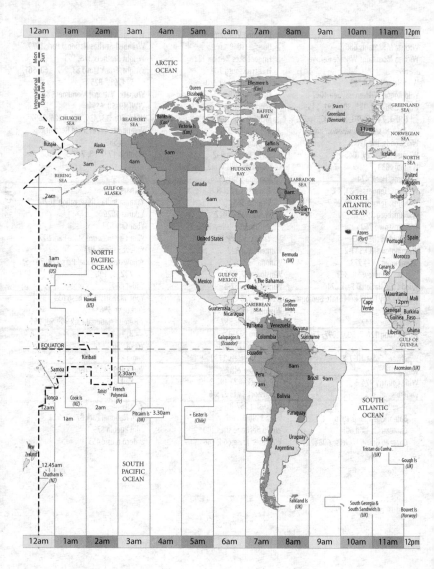